The Thomas Guide®

2003

San Bernardino County

AF731464

CONTENTS

RAND McNALLY

map legend symbols

- Freeway
- Interchange/Ramp
- Highway
- Primary Road
- Secondary Road
- Minor Road
- Restricted Road
- Alley
- Unpaved Road
- Tunnel
- Toll Road
- High Occupancy Veh. Lane
- Stacked Multiple Roadways
- Proposed Road
- Proposed Freeway
- Freeway Under Construction

- One-Way Road
- Two-Way Road
- Trail, Walkway
- Stairs
- Railroad
- Rapid Transit
- Rapid Transit, Underground
- Ferry
- City Boundary
- County Boundary
- State Boundary
- International Boundary
- Military Base, Indian Resv.
- Township, Range, Rancho
- River, Creek, Shoreline
- 98607 ZIP Code Boundary

- 5 Interstate
- 5 Interstate (Business)
- 3 U.S. Highway
- 1 4 8 9 State Highways
- Carpool Lane
- A Street List Marker
- Street Name Continuation
- Street Name Change
- Station (Train, Bus)
- Building (see List of Abbr. page)
- Building Footprint
- Public Elementary School
- Public High School
- Private Elementary School
- Private High School

- Shopping Center
- Fire Station
- Library
- Mission
- Winery
- Campground
- H Hospital
- Mountain
- Section Corner
- Boat Launch
- Gate, Locks, Barricades
- Lighthouse
- Dry Lake, Beach
- Dam
- Intermittent Lake, Marsh

PageFinder™ Map

PageFinder™ Map
U.S. Patent No. 5,419,586
Canadian Patent No. 2,116,425
Patente Mexicana No. 188186

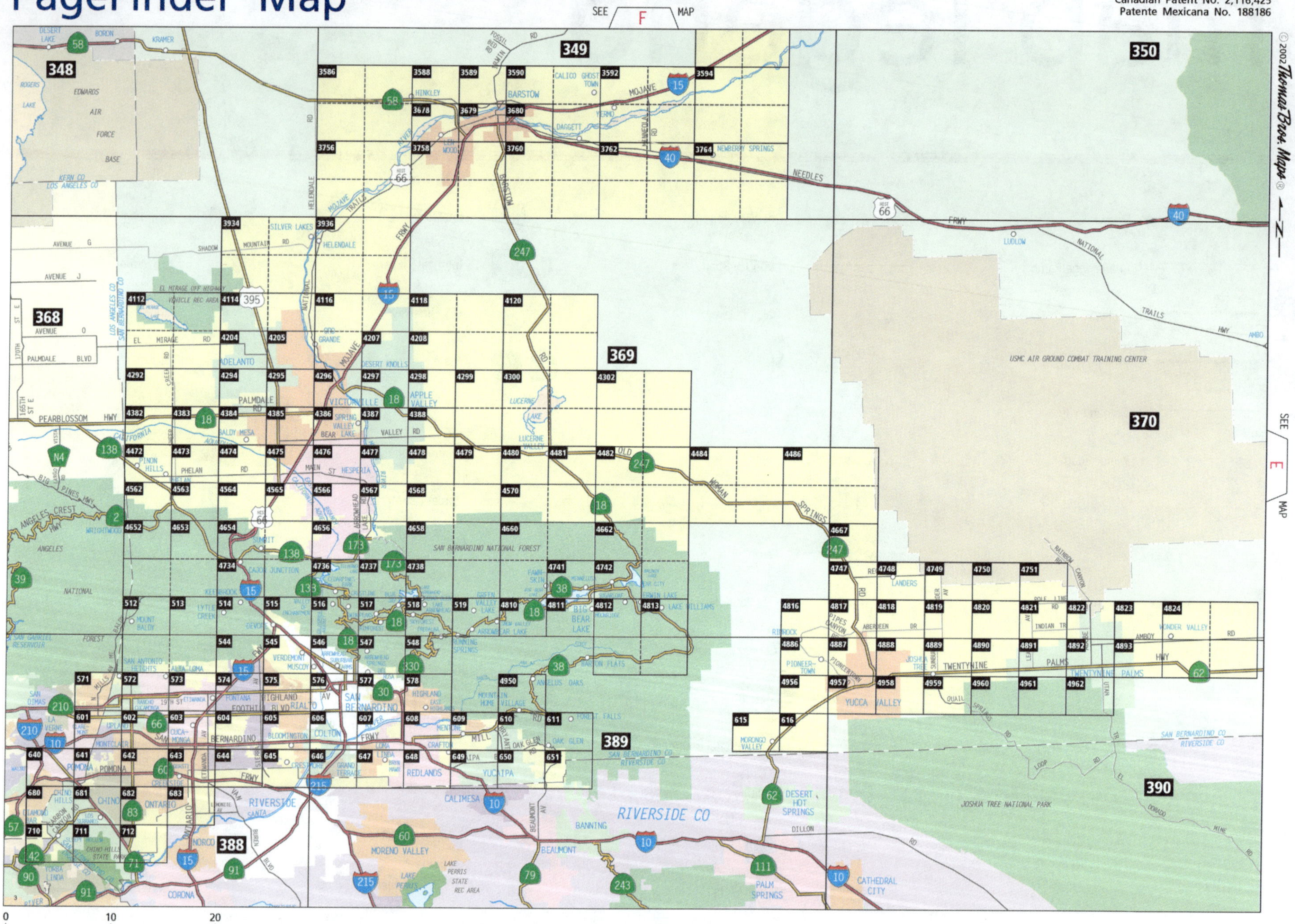

0 10 20 miles One inch equals 12.5 miles

PageFinder™ Map

PageFinder™ Map
U.S. Patent No. 5,419,586
Canadian Patent No. 2,116,425
Patente Mexicana No. 188186

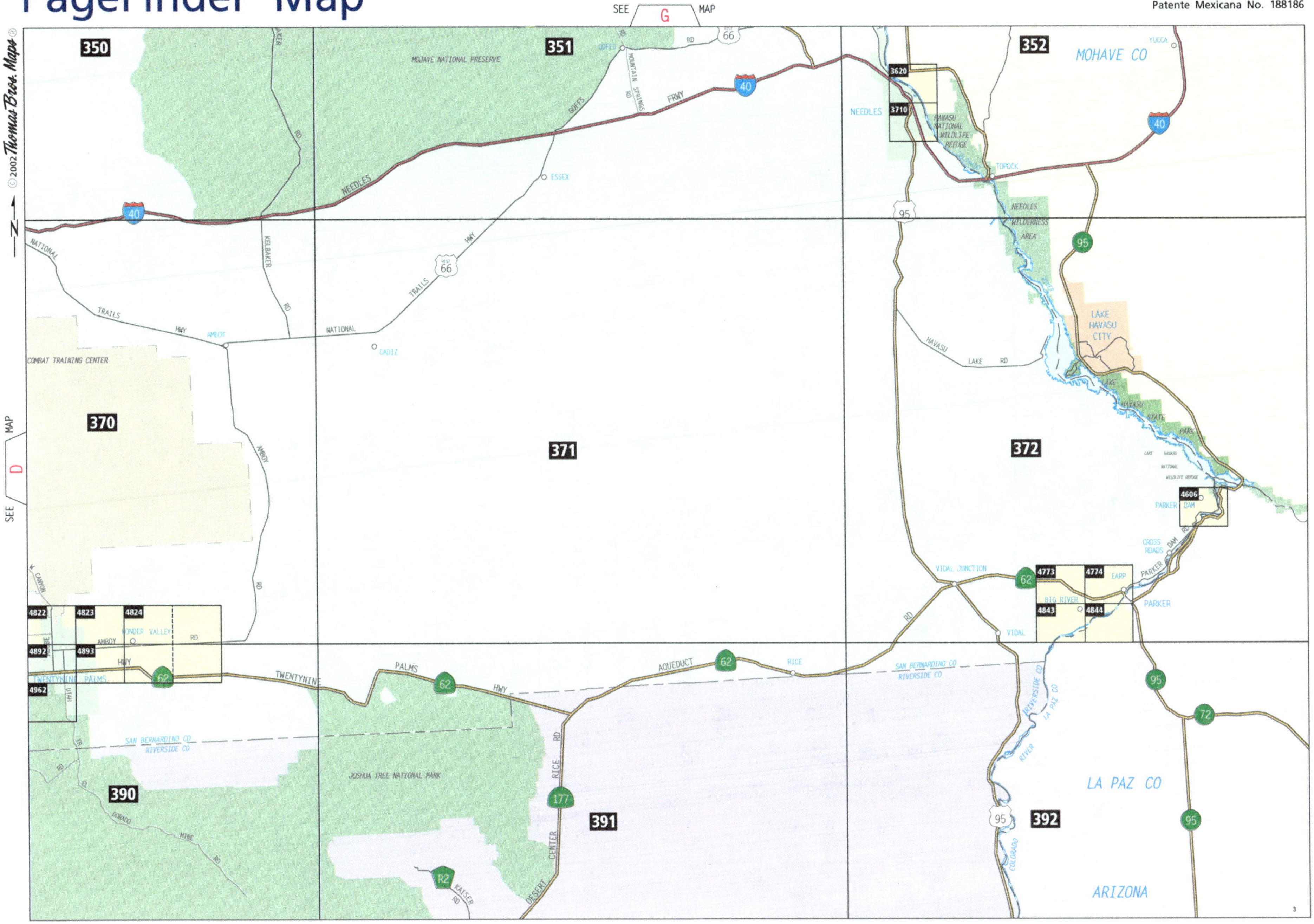

0 10 20 miles One inch equals 12.5 miles

PageFinder™ Map

PageFinder™ Map
U.S. Patent No. 5,419,586
Canadian Patent No. 2,116,425
Patente Mexicana No. 188186

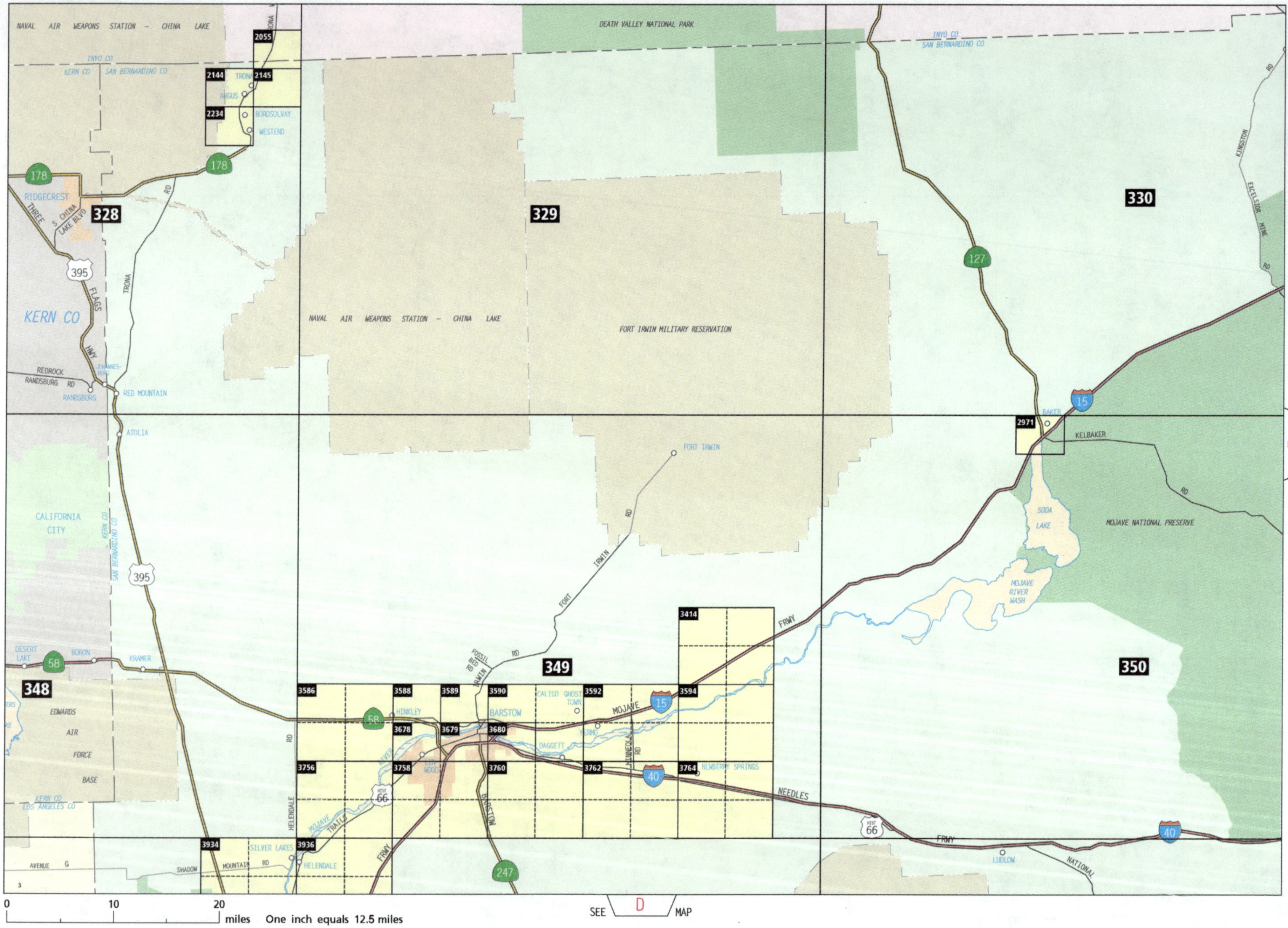

SEE G MAP

SEE D MAP

PageFinder™ Map

PageFinder™ Map
U.S. Patent No. 5,419,586
Canadian Patent No. 2,116,425
Patente Mexicana No. 188186

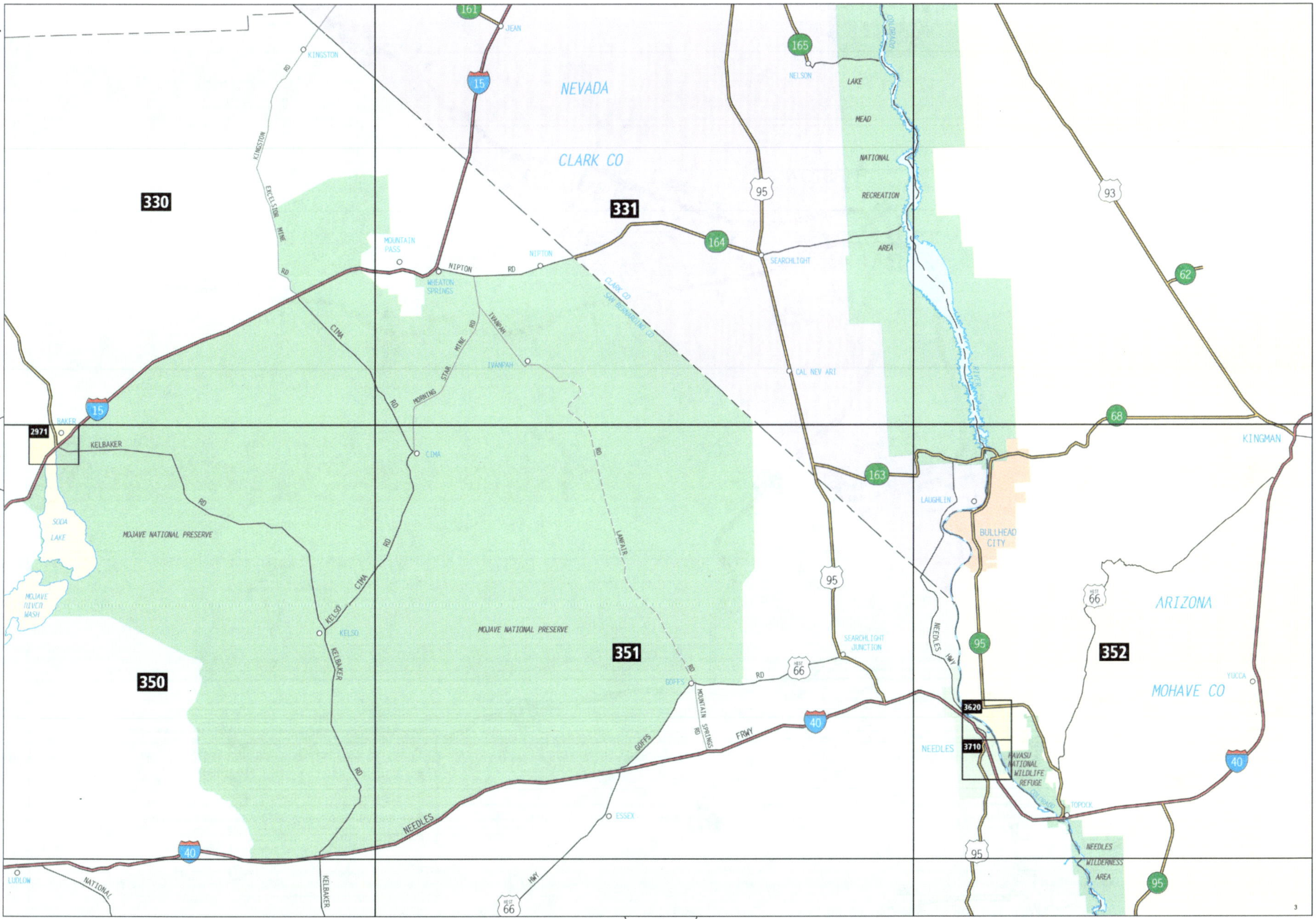

0 10 20 miles One inch equals 12.5 miles

SAN BERNARDINO COUNTY FREEWAY ACCESS MAP

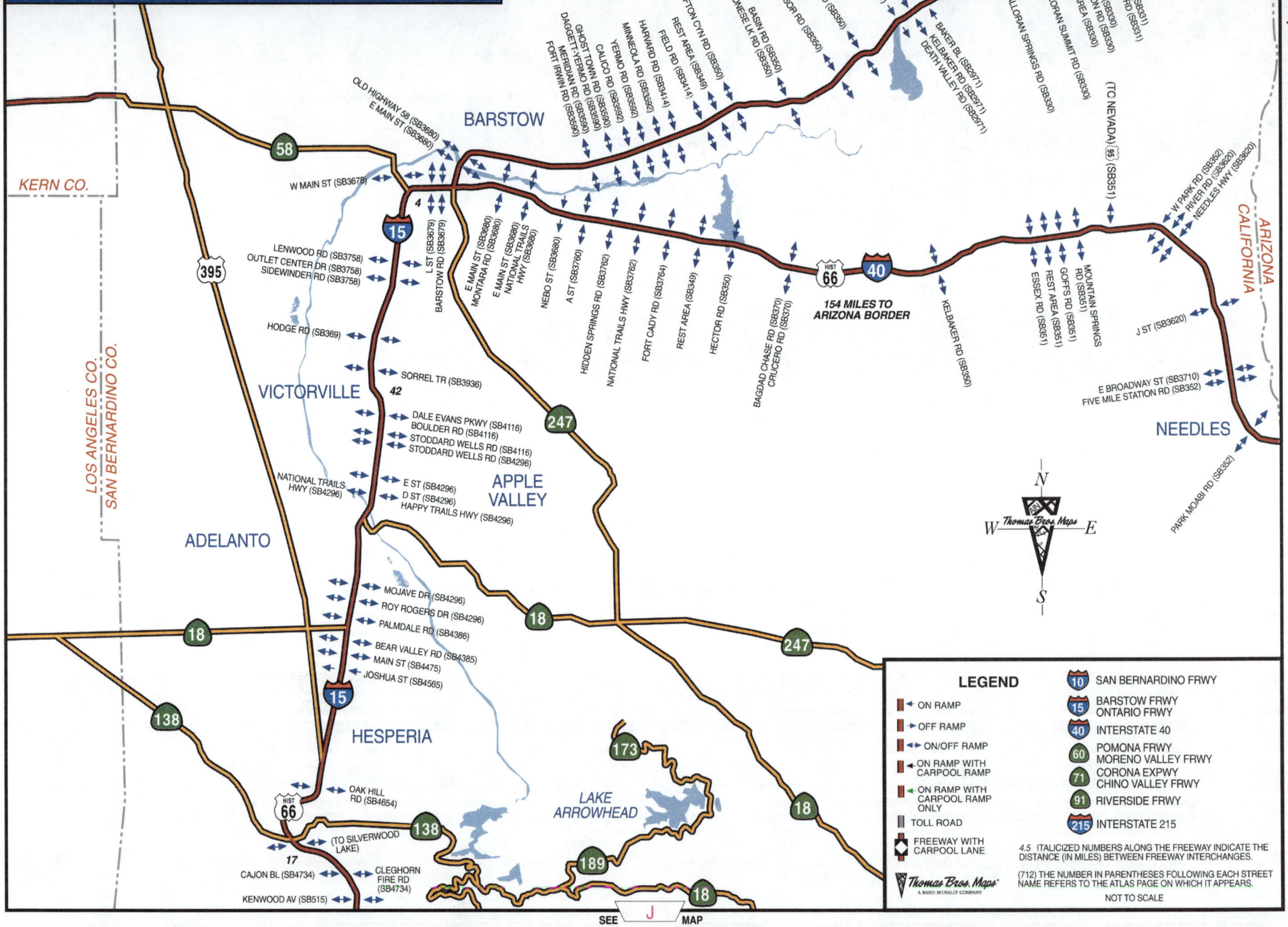

SEE J MAP

SEE H MAP

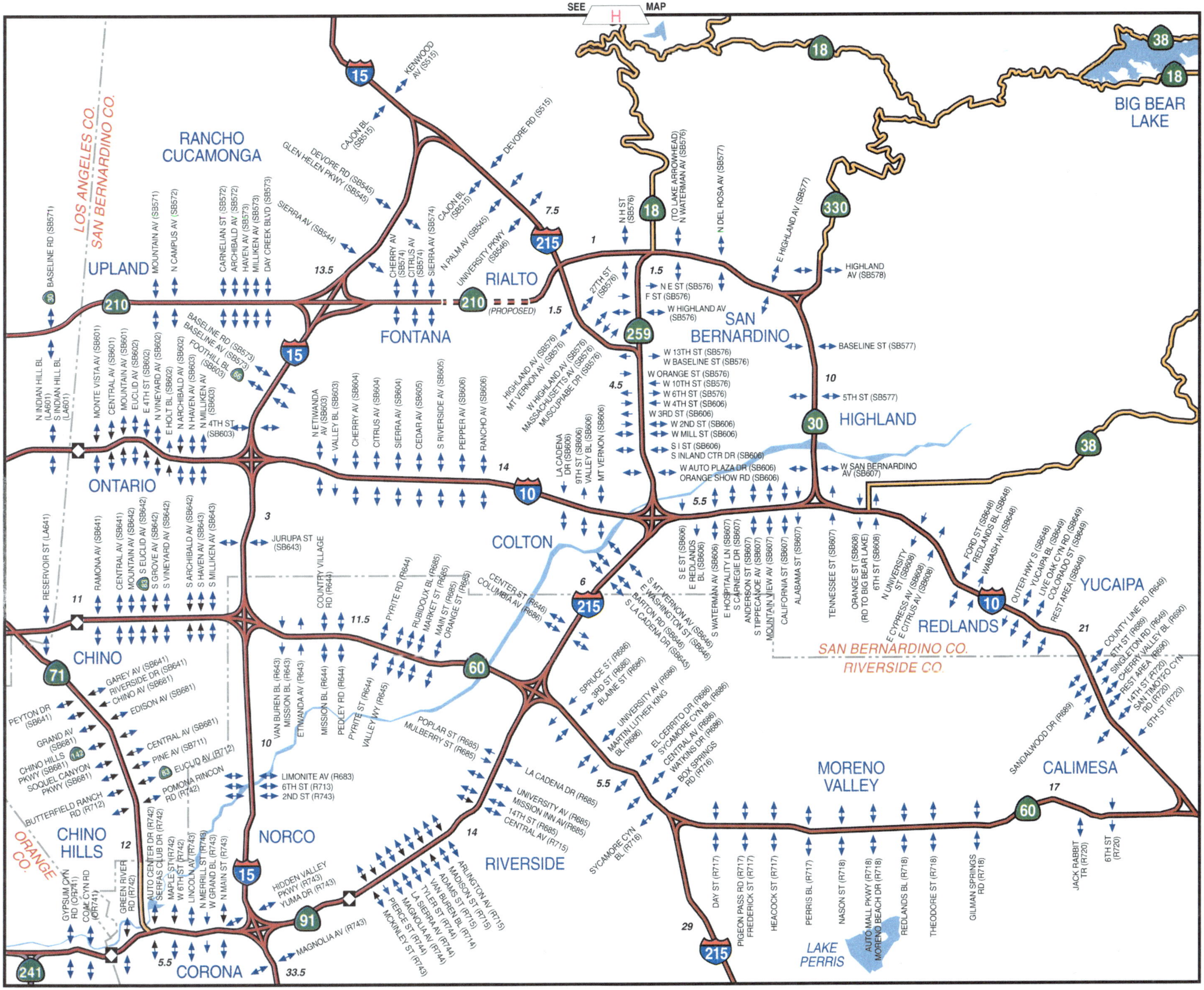
BIG BEAR LAKE
RANCHO CUCAMONGA
UPLAND
RIALTO
FONTANA
SAN BERNARDINO
HIGHLAND
ONTARIO
COLTON
REDLANDS
YUCAIPA
CHINO
CHINO HILLS
NORCO
RIVERSIDE
MORENO VALLEY
CALIMESA
CORONA
LAKE PERRIS
LOS ANGELES CO.
SAN BERNARDINO CO.
RIVERSIDE CO.
ORANGE CO.
(PROPOSED)
KENWOOD AV (S515)
CAJON BL (SB515)
DEVORE RD (SB515)
DEVORE RD (SB545)
GLEN HELEN PKWY (SB545)
SIERRA AV (SB544)
CHERRY AV (SB574)
CITRUS AV (SB574)
SIERRA AV (SB574)
CAJON BL (SB515)
N PALM AV (SB545)
UNIVERSITY PKWY (SB546)
N H ST (SB576)
(TO LAKE ARROWHEAD) N WATERMAN AV (SB576)
N DEL ROSA AV (SB577)
E HIGHLAND AV (SB577)
HIGHLAND AV (SB578)
BASELINE RD (SB571)
MOUNTAIN AV (SB571)
N CAMPUS AV (SB572)
CARNELIAN ST (SB572)
ARCHIBALD AV (SB572)
HAVEN AV (SB573)
MILLIKEN AV (SB573)
DAY CREEK BLVD (SB573)
BASELINE RD (SB573)
BASELINE AV (SB573)
FOOTHILL BL (SB603)
27TH ST (SB576)
N E ST (SB576)
F ST (SB576)
W HIGHLAND AV (SB576)
W 13TH ST (SB576)
W BASELINE ST (SB576)
BASELINE ST (SB577)
W ORANGE ST (SB576)
W 10TH ST (SB576)
W 6TH ST (SB576)
W 4TH ST (SB606)
W 3RD ST (SB606)
W 2ND ST (SB606)
W MILL ST (SB606)
S I ST (SB606)
S INLAND CTR DR (SB606)
W AUTO PLAZA DR (SB606)
ORANGE SHOW RD (SB606)
5TH ST (SB577)
W SAN BERNARDINO AV (SB607)
N INDIAN HILL BL (LA601)
S INDIAN HILL BL (LA601)
MONTE VISTA AV (SB601)
CENTRAL AV (SB601)
MOUNTAIN AV (SB601)
EUCLID AV (SB602)
E 4TH ST (SB602)
N VINEYARD AV (SB602)
E HOLT BL (SB602)
N ARCHIBALD AV (SB602)
N HAVEN AV (SB603)
N MILLIKEN AV (SB603)
4TH ST (SB603)
N ETIWANDA AV (SB603)
VALLEY BL (SB603)
CHERRY AV (SB604)
CITRUS AV (SB604)
SIERRA AV (SB604)
CEDAR AV (SB605)
S RIVERSIDE AV (SB605)
PEPPER AV (SB606)
RANCHO AV (SB606)
HIGHLAND AV (SB576)
MT VERNON AV (SB576)
W HIGHLAND AV (SB576)
MASSACHUSETTS AV (SB576)
MUSCUPIABE DR (SB576)
LA CADENA DR (SB606)
9TH ST (SB606)
VALLEY BL (SB606)
MT VERNON (SB606)
RESERVOIR ST (LA641)
RAMONA AV (SB641)
CENTRAL AV (SB641)
MOUNTAIN AV (SB642)
S EUCLID AV (SB642)
S GROVE AV (SB642)
S VINEYARD AV (SB642)
S ARCHIBALD AV (SB642)
S HAVEN AV (SB643)
S MILLIKEN AV (SB643)
JURUPA ST (SB643)
COUNTRY VILLAGE RD (R644)
PYRITE RD (R644)
RUBIDOUX BL (R685)
MARKET ST (R685)
MAIN ST (R685)
ORANGE ST (R685)
CENTER ST (R646)
COLUMBIA AV (R686)
S MT VERNON AV (SB646)
E WASHINGTON ST (SB646)
BARTON RD (SB646)
S LA CADENA DR (SB645)
S E ST (SB606)
E REDLANDS BL (SB606)
S WATERMAN AV (SB606)
E HOSPITALITY LN (SB607)
S CARNEGIE DR (SB607)
ANDERSON ST (SB607)
S TIPPECANOE AV (SB607)
MOUNTAIN VIEW AV (SB607)
CALIFORNIA ST (SB607)
ALABAMA ST (SB607)
TENNESSEE ST (SB607)
ORANGE ST (SB608) (RD TO BIG BEAR LAKE)
6TH ST (SB608)
N UNIVERSITY ST (SB608)
E CYPRESS AV (SB608)
E CITRUS AV (SB608)
FORD ST (SB648)
REDLANDS BL (SB648)
WABASH AV (SB648)
OUTER HWY S (SB648)
YUCAIPA BL (SB649)
LIVE OAK CYN RD (SB649)
COLORADO ST (SB649)
REST AREA (SB649)
COUNTY LINE RD (R689)
5TH ST (R689)
SINGLETON RD (R689)
CHERRY VALLEY BL (R690)
REST AREA (R690)
14TH ST (R720)
SAN TIMOTEO CYN RD (R720)
6TH ST (R720)
SANDALWOOD DR (R689)
GAREY AV (SB641)
RIVERSIDE DR (SB641)
CHINO AV (SB681)
EDISON AV (SB681)
PEYTON DR (SB641)
GRAND AV (SB681)
CHINO HILLS PKWY (SB681)
SOQUEL CANYON PKWY (SB681)
CENTRAL AV (SB681)
PINE AV (SB711)
EUCLID AV (R712)
POMONA RINCON RD (R742)
BUTTERFIELD RANCH RD (R712)
VAN BUREN BL (R643)
MISSION BL (R643)
ETIWANDA AV (R643)
MISSION BL (R644)
PEDLEY RD (R644)
PYRITE ST (R644)
VALLEY WY (R645)
POPLAR ST (R685)
MULBERRY ST (R685)
SPRUCE ST (R686)
3RD ST (R686)
BLAINE ST (R686)
UNIVERSITY AV (R686)
MARTIN LUTHER KING BL (R686)
EL CERRITO DR (R686)
SYCAMORE CYN BL (R686)
CENTRAL AV (R686)
WATKINS DR (R686)
BOX SPRINGS RD (R716)
LA CADENA DR (R685)
UNIVERSITY AV (R685)
MISSION INN AV (R685)
14TH ST (R685)
CENTRAL AV (R715)
SYCAMORE CYN BL (R716)
LIMONITE AV (R683)
6TH ST (R713)
2ND ST (R743)
HIDDEN VALLEY PKWY (R743)
YUMA DR (R743)
MAGNOLIA AV (R743)
AUTO CENTER DR (R742)
SERFAS CLUB DR (R742)
MAPLE ST (R742)
W 6TH ST (R742)
LINCOLN AV (R743)
N MERRILL ST (R743)
W GRAND BL (R743)
N MAIN ST (R743)
GYPSUM CYN RD (OR741)
COAL CYN RD (OR741)
GREEN RIVER RD (R742)
ARLINGTON AV (R715)
MADISON ST (R715)
ADAMS ST (R715)
VAN BUREN BL (R714)
TYLER ST (R744)
LA SIERRA AV (R744)
MAGNOLIA AV (R744)
PIERCE ST (R744)
MCKINLEY ST (R743)
DAY ST (R717)
PIGEON PASS RD (R717)
FREDERICK ST (R717)
HEACOCK ST (R717)
PERRIS BL (R717)
NASON ST (R718)
AUTO MALL PKWY (R718)
MORENO BEACH DR (R718)
REDLANDS BL (R718)
THEODORE ST (R718)
GILMAN SPRINGS RD (R718)
JACK RABBIT TR (R720)
6TH ST (R720)
15
215
210
10
60
91
71
241
18
38
30
330
259
7.5
13.5
1
1.5
4.5
10
14
5.5
3
6
11
11.5
21
17
12
29
33.5

For further information contact
County of San Bernardino Planning Department
385 N. Arrowhead Av. 3rd floor
San Bernardino, CA 92415-0182

SAN BERNARDINO COUNTY
Cities And Communities

	Community Name	City Abbr.	Miles To SBDO	ZIP Code	Est. Sq. Mi.	Map Page
❖	ADELANTO	ADEL	48.50	92301	50.80	4204
	ALTA LOMA		28.00	91737		572
	AMBOY			92304		370
	ANGELUS OAKS			92305		4950
❖	APPLE VALLEY	APLV	49.50	92307	72.90	4297
	ARGUS			93562		2144
	ARROWBEAR LAKE			92382		519
	ARROWHEAD SPRINGS			92404		547
	ARROWHEAD SUBURBAN FARMS			92407		546
	ATOLIA					348
	BAKER		140.00	92309		2971
	BALDY MESA			92371		4384
❖	BARSTOW	BARS	72.50	92311	23.70	3679
	BARTON FLATS			92305		389
	BIG BEAR CITY			92314		4742
❖	BIG BEAR LAKE	BBLK	35.00	92315	6.30	4811
	BIG RIVER			92242		4843
	BLOOMINGTON		9.00	92316		605
	BLUE JAY			92317		517
	BOROSOLVAY			93562		2234
	BRYN MAWR		6.00	92354		647
	CADIZ			92319		371
	CAJON JUNCTION			92358		4654
	CALICO GHOST TOWN					3591
	CEDAR GLEN			92321		518
	CEDARPINES PARK			92322		4736
❖	CHINO	CHNO	34.00	91710	18.10	641
❖	CHINO HILLS	CHLS	40.20	91709	44.90	681
	CIMA			92323		351
❖	COLTON	CLTN	5.00	92324	15.90	606
	CRAFTON			92374		608
	CREEKSIDE			91761		643
	CRESTLINE		15.00	92325		516
	CRESTMORE			92316		645
	CROSS ROADS			92238		372
	CUCAMONGA			91730		603
	DAGGETT		82.50	92327		3681
	DEL ROSA			92404		577
	DESERT KNOLLS			92307		4297
	DEVORE			92407		515
	EARP			92242		4774
	EAST HIGHLANDS			92346		578
	ERWIN LAKE			92314		4813
	ESSEX			92332		351
	ETIWANDA		19.00	91739		573
	FAWNSKIN			92333		4741
❖	FONTANA	FONT	13.50	92335	35.80	604
	FOREST FALLS			92339		611
	FORT IRWIN			92310		349
	FREDALBA			92382		548
	GOFFS			92332		351
❖	GRAND TERRACE	GTER	15.00	92313	3.50	646
	GREEN VALLEY LAKE			92341		519
	GUASTI		25.00	91761		603
	HELENDALE			92342		3936
❖	HESPERIA	HESP	36.50	92345	66.90	4476
❖	HIGHLAND	HIGH	6.00	92346	13.60	577
	HINKLEY		80.50	92347		3587
	IVANPAH			92364		331
	JOSHUA TREE		78.50	92252		4889
	KEENBROOK			92407		514
	KELSO			92309		350
	KINGSTON					330
	KRAMER			93516		348
	LAKE ARROWHEAD		30.00	92352		518
	LAKE WILLIAMS			92314		4813
	LANDERS			92285		4748
	LENWOOD		70.50	92311		3678
❖	LOMA LINDA	LMLN		92354	7.40	647
	LOS SERRANOS			91709		681
	LUCERNE VALLEY		63.00	92356		4480
	LUDLOW			92357		370
	LYTLE CREEK			92358		514
	MENTONE		14.00	92359		608
	MINNELUSA			92333		4741
❖	MONTCLAIR	MTCL	30.00	91763	5.10	601
	MOONRIDGE			92315		4811
	MORONGO VALLEY		61.00	92256		615
	MOUNTAIN HOME VILLAGE			92359		4950
	MOUNTAIN PASS			92366		331
	MOUNT BALDY			91759		368
	MUSCOY		5.50	92405		546
❖	NEEDLES	NDLS	233.50	92363	30.10	3620
	NEWBERRY SPRINGS		96.00	92365		3764
	NIPTON			92364		331
	OAK GLEN			92399		611
❖	ONTARIO	ONT	25.50	91761	36.80	642
	ORO GRANDE			92368		4206
	PARKER DAM		238.00	92267		4606
	PHELAN			92371		4472
	PINON HILLS			92372		4472
	PIONEERTOWN			92268		4886
❖	RANCHO CUCAMONGA	RCUC	23.00	91730	37.70	602
❖	REDLANDS	RDL	11.00	92374	36.00	608
	RED MOUNTAIN			93558		328
❖	RIALTO	RLTO	4.50	92376	21.80	605
	RICE			92280		391
	RIMFOREST			92378		517
	RIMROCK			92268		4816
	RUNNING SPRINGS		22.00	92382		519
	SAN ANTONIO HEIGHTS			91786		572
❖	SAN BERNARDINO	SBDO		92405	57.80	576
--	SAN BERNARDINO COUNTY	SBdC			19319	
	SEARCHLIGHT JUNCTION					351
	SILVER LAKES			92342		3935
	SKYFOREST			92385		518
	SLEEPY HOLLOW			91709		710
	SPRING VALLEY LAKE		41.00	92392		4387
	SUGAR LOAF			92386		4812
	SUMMIT					4654
	TRONA		137.50	93562		2144
❖	TWENTYNINE PALMS	TNP	93.50	92277	54.70	4892
	TWIN PEAKS			92391		517
❖	UPLAND	UPL	27.00	91786	15.00	602
	VALLEY OF ENCHANTMENT			92322		516
	VERDEMONT			92407		545
❖	VICTORVILLE	VCTV	41.00	92392	73.30	4386
	VIDAL			92280		372
	VIDAL JUNCTION			92280		372
	WESTEND			93562		2234
	WHEATON SPRINGS					331
	WRIGHTWOOD		33.00	92397		4652
	YERMO		87.00	92398		3682
❖	YUCAIPA	YCPA	12.00	92399	27.50	649
❖	YUCCA VALLEY	YUCA	71.70	92284	38.90	4957

❖ INDICATES INCORPORATED CITY

MILES ARE ESTIMATED FROM DOWNTOWN CIVIC CENTER

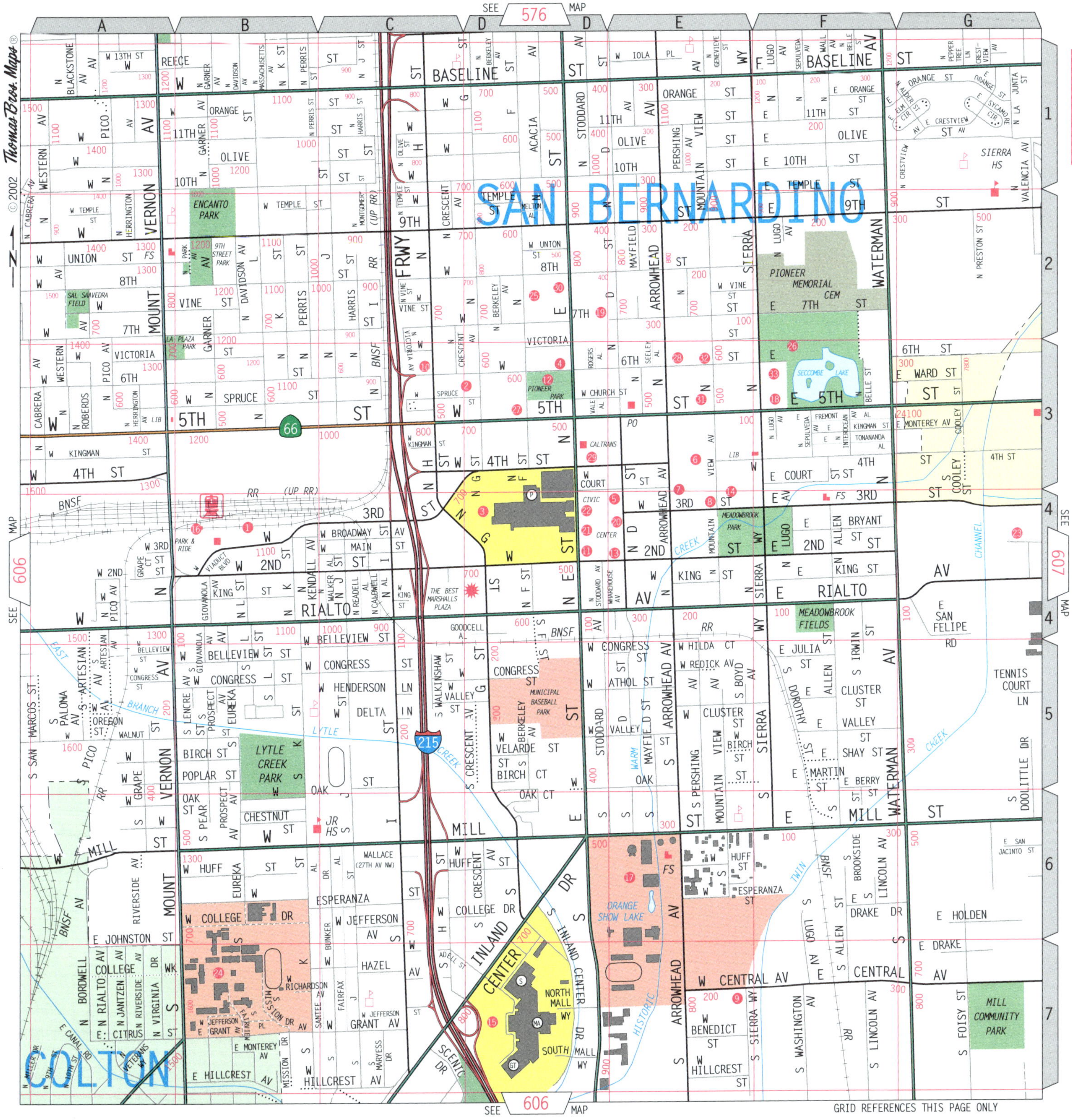

Downtown San Bernardino

Points of Interest

1	Amtrak Station	B4
2	Bus Station	D3
3	Carousel Mall	D4
4	Chamber of Commerce	D3
5	City Hall	E4
6	County Administration Building	E3
7	County Court House	E3
8	County Government Building	E4
9	Department of Motor Vehicles	E7
10	Econo Lodge	C3
11	Economic Development Agency	D4
12	Feldheym Central Library	D3
13	Franchise Tax Board	E4
14	Health Department	E4
15	Inland Center	D7
16	Metrolink Station	B4
17	National Orange Show Grounds	E6
18	Parks, Recreation, & Community Services	F3
19	Police Department	D2
20	Public Utilities Commission	E4
21	Radisson Hotel	D4
22	San Bernardino Convention & Visitors Bureau	D4
23	San Bernardino County Jail	G4
24	San Bernardino Valley College	B7
25	School Administration Building	D2
26	Seccombe Lake Recreation Area	F3
27	Senior Citizens Center	D3
28	Social Security Administration	E3
29	State Building	D3
30	Sturges Auditorium	D2
31	Unemployment Office	E3
32	YMCA	E3
33	YWCA	F3

Map Scale

Feet: 0, 660, 1320, 1980, 2640
Miles: 0, .125, .25, .375, .5

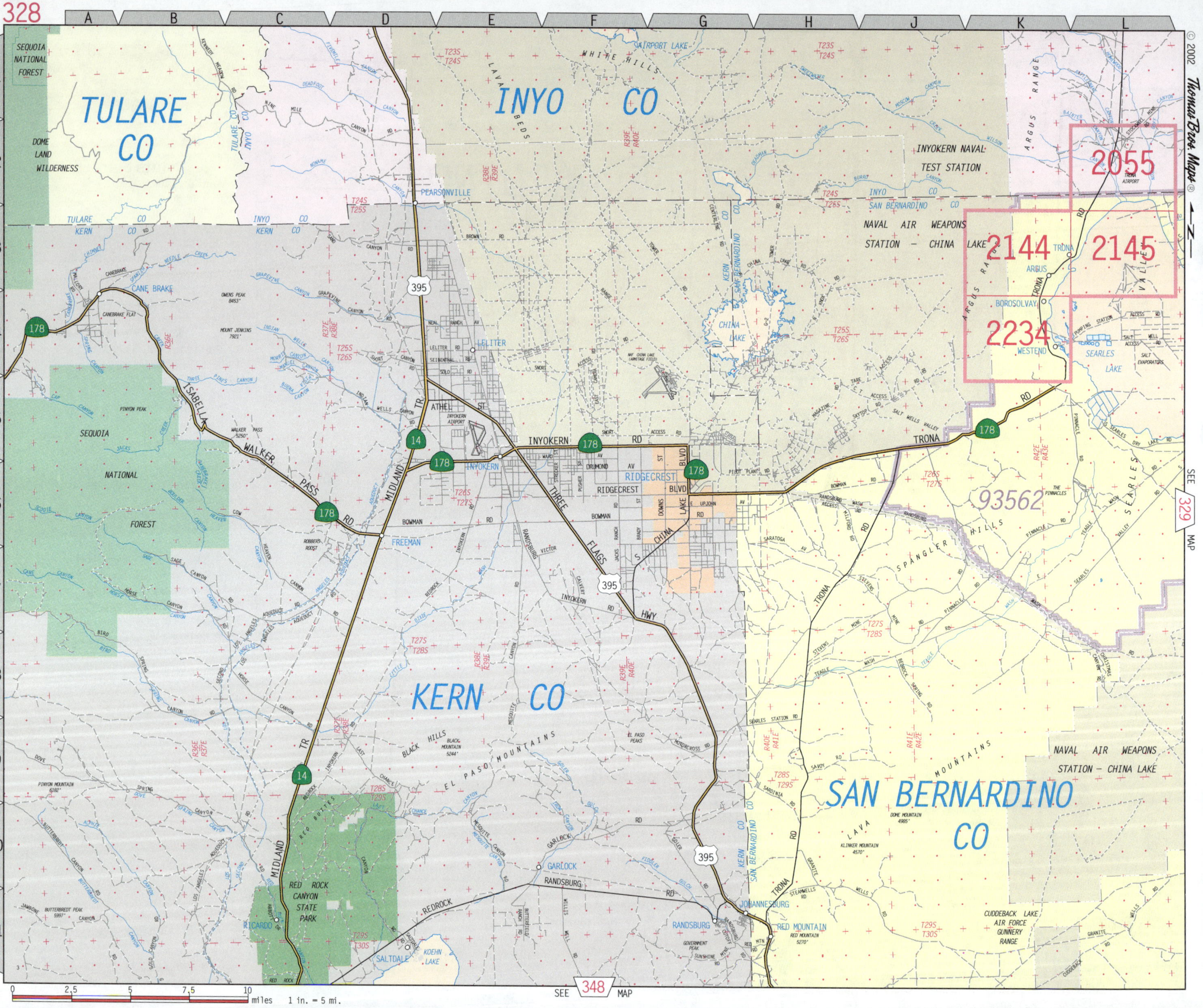
SAN BERNARDINO
TULARE CO
INYO CO
KERN CO
SAN BERNARDINO CO
SEQUOIA NATIONAL FOREST
DOME LAND WILDERNESS
INYOKERN NAVAL TEST STATION
NAVAL AIR WEAPONS STATION - CHINA LAKE
RED ROCK CANYON STATE PARK
CUDDEBACK LAKE AIR FORCE GUNNERY RANGE
PEARSONVILLE
CANE BRAKE
LELITER
INYOKERN
RIDGECREST
FREEMAN
GARLOCK
RANDSBURG
JOHANNESBURG
RED MOUNTAIN
RICARDO
SALTDALE
KOEHN LAKE
TRONA
ARGUS
BOROSOLVAY
WESTEND
SEARLES LAKE
CHINA LAKE
WHITE HILLS
LAVA BEDS
ARGUS RANGE
SPANGLER HILLS
EL PASO MOUNTAINS
LAVA MOUNTAINS
BLACK HILLS
WALKER PASS
ISABELLA WALKER PASS RD
MIDLAND TR
THREE FLAGS HWY
INYOKERN RD
TRONA RD
CHINA LAKE BLVD
RIDGECREST BLVD
93562
2055
2144
2145
2234
178
395
14
SEE 329 MAP
SEE 348 MAP
0 2.5 5 7.5 10 miles 1 in. = 5 mi.
© 2002 Thomas Bros. Maps®

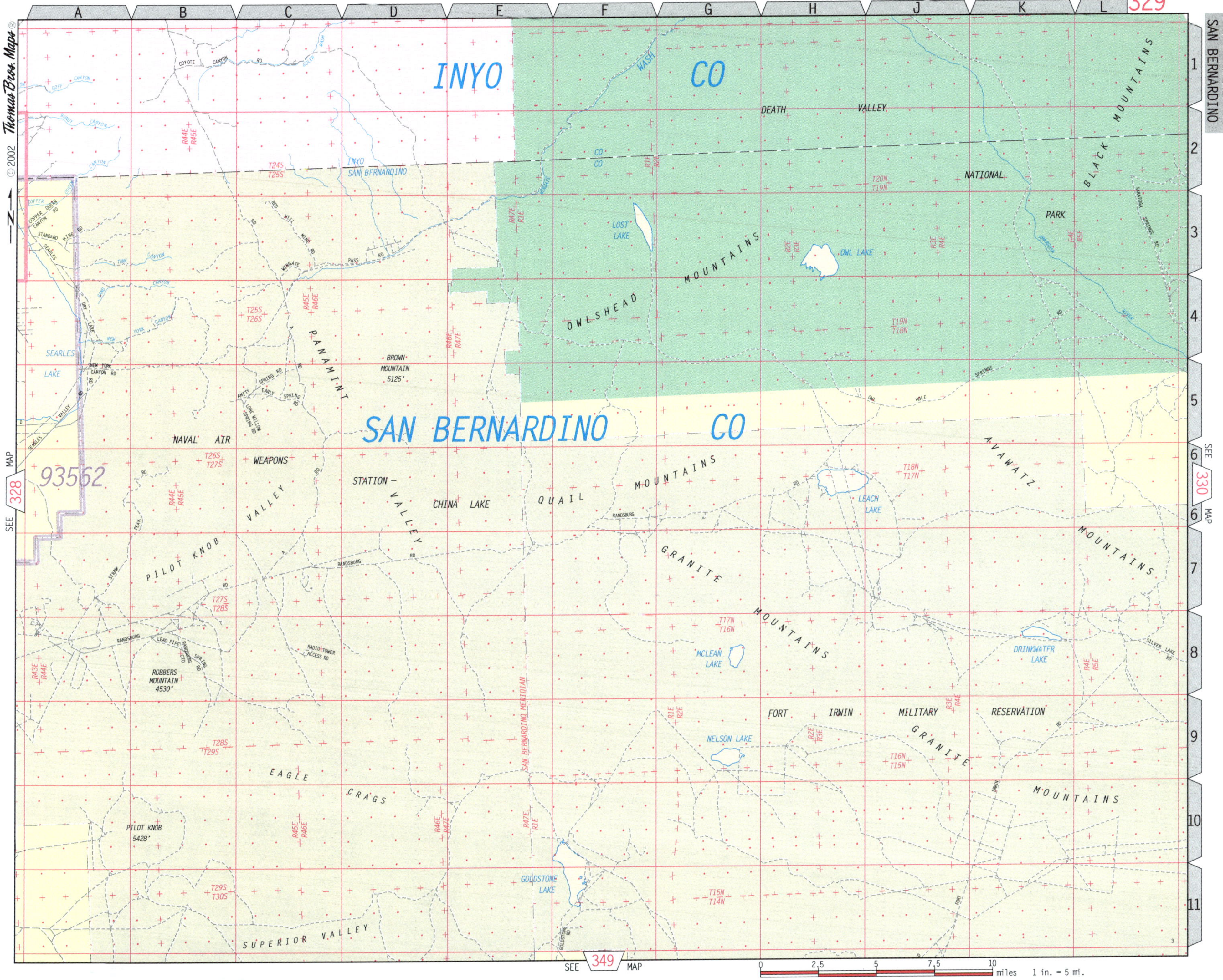

SAN BERNARDINO
INYO CO
CO
DEATH VALLEY NATIONAL PARK
BLACK MOUNTAINS
OWLSHEAD MOUNTAINS
LOST LAKE
OWL LAKE
SAN BERNARDINO CO
SEARLES LAKE
PANAMINT VALLEY
BROWN MOUNTAIN 5125'
NAVAL AIR WEAPONS STATION - CHINA LAKE
93562
QUAIL MOUNTAINS
AVAWATZ MOUNTAINS
LEACH LAKE
GRANITE MOUNTAINS
PILOT KNOB VALLEY
ROBBERS MOUNTAIN 4530'
MCLEAN LAKE
DRINKWATER LAKE
FORT IRWIN MILITARY RESERVATION
NELSON LAKE
GRANITE MOUNTAINS
EAGLE CRAGS
PILOT KNOB 5428'
GOLDSTONE LAKE
SUPERIOR VALLEY
SAN BERNARDINO MERIDIAN
SEE 328 MAP
SEE 330 MAP
SEE 349 MAP
0 2.5 5 7.5 10 miles 1 in. = 5 mi.

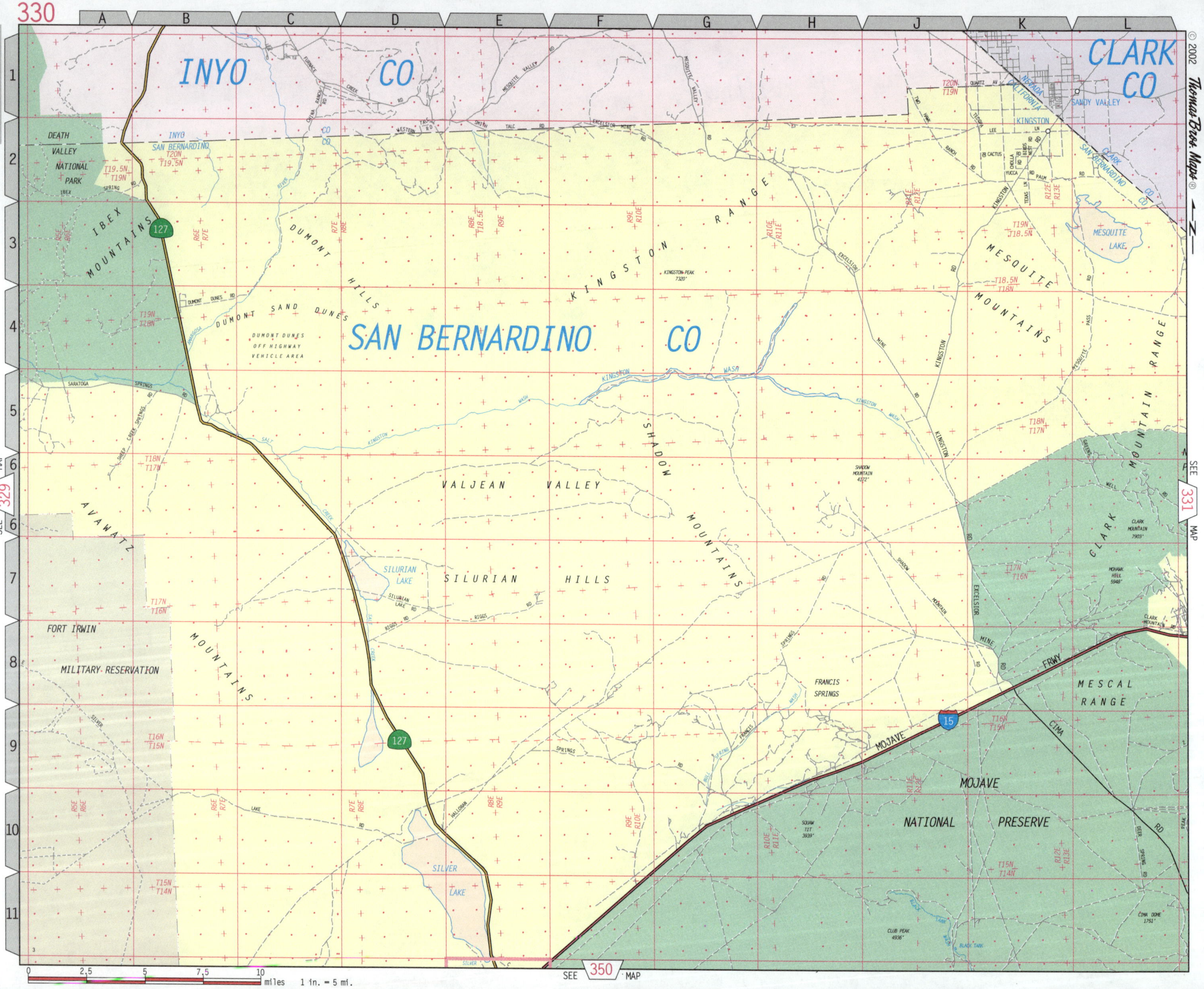
A B C D E F G H J K L
1 2 3 4 5 6 7 8 9 10 11
SAN BERNARDINO
INYO CO
CLARK CO
SANDY VALLEY
KINGSTON
NEVADA
CALIFORNIA
SAN BERNARDINO CO
DEATH VALLEY NATIONAL PARK
IBEX MOUNTAINS
DUMONT HILLS
DUMONT SAND DUNES
DUMONT DUNES OFF HIGHWAY VEHICLE AREA
KINGSTON RANGE
KINGSTON PEAK 7320'
MESQUITE MOUNTAINS
MESQUITE LAKE
CLARK MOUNTAIN RANGE
CLARK MOUNTAIN 7903'
MOHAWK HILL 5948'
SHADOW MOUNTAINS
SHADOW MOUNTAIN 4172'
VALJEAN VALLEY
SILURIAN HILLS
SILURIAN LAKE
AVAWATZ MOUNTAINS
FORT IRWIN MILITARY RESERVATION
FRANCIS SPRINGS
MESCAL RANGE
MOJAVE NATIONAL PRESERVE
SQUAW TIT 3939'
CLUB PEAK 4936'
CIMA DOME 5791'
SILVER LAKE
127
15
MOJAVE FRWY
KINGSTON WASH
SALT CREEK
CIMA RD
EXCELSIOR MINE RD
SEE 329 MAP
SEE 331 MAP
SEE 350 MAP
0 2.5 5 7.5 10 miles 1 in. = 5 mi.
© 2002 Thomas Bros. Maps®

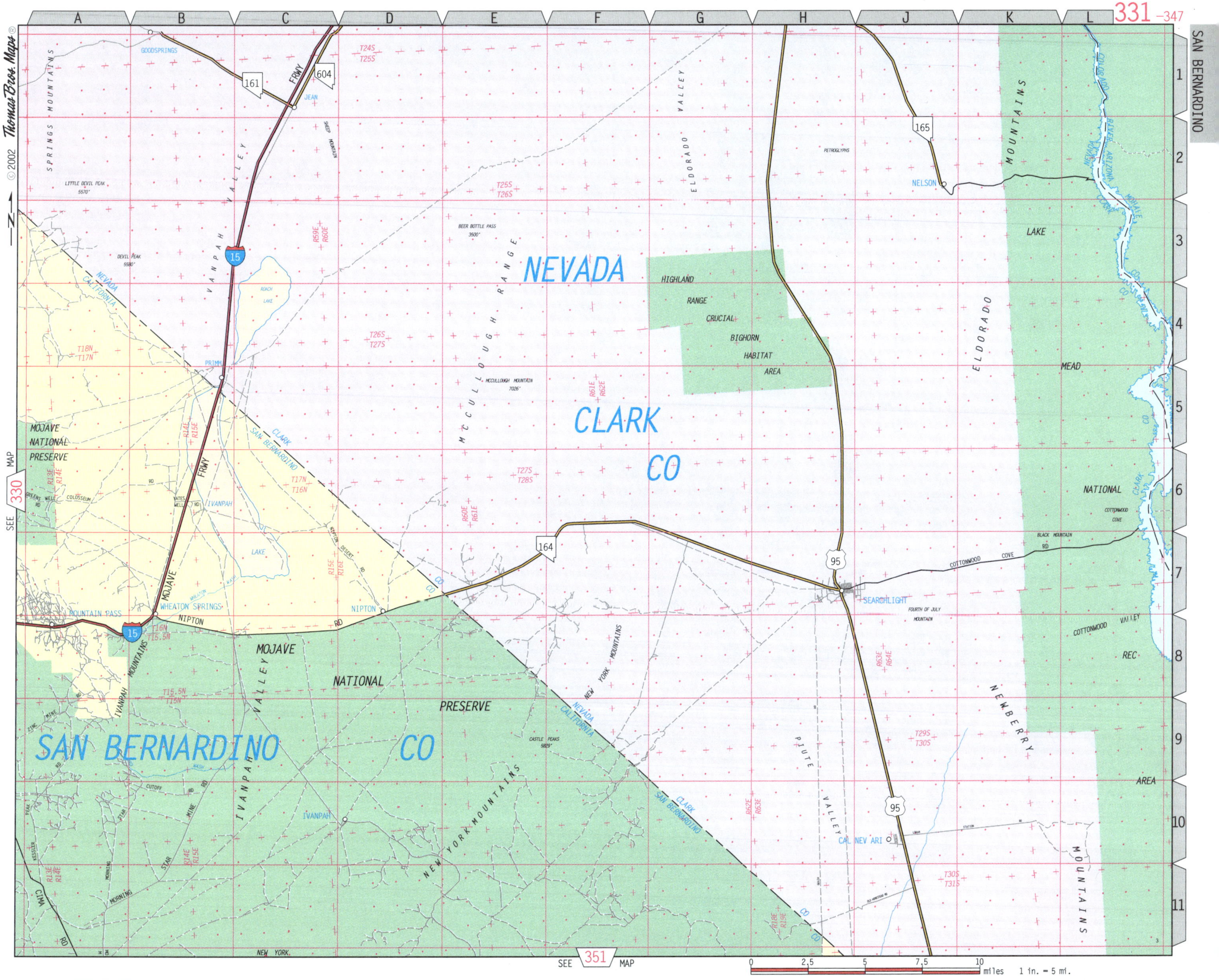
A
B
C
D
E
F
G
H
J
K
L
SAN BERNARDINO
Thomas Bros. Maps ®
© 2002
GOODSPRINGS
SPRINGS MOUNTAINS
LITTLE DEVIL PEAK 5570'
DEVIL PEAK 5580'
161
604
FRWY
JEAN
SHEEP MOUNTAIN
T24S T25S
T25S T26S
T26S T27S
T27S T28S
IVANPAH VALLEY
15
ROACH LAKE
PRIMM
ELDORADO VALLEY
BEER BOTTLE PASS 3500'
McCULLOUGH RANGE
McCULLOUGH MOUNTAIN 7026'
NEVADA
CLARK CO
HIGHLAND RANGE CRUCIAL BIGHORN HABITAT AREA
165
NELSON
PETROGLYPHS
ELDORADO MOUNTAINS
LAKE MEAD NATIONAL REC AREA
COLORADO RIVER
NEVADA ARIZONA
MOHAVE CO
CLARK CO
COTTONWOOD COVE
BLACK MOUNTAIN
COTTONWOOD COVE RD
COTTONWOOD VALLEY
MOJAVE NATIONAL PRESERVE
T18N T17N
T17N T16N
R14E R15E
R13E R14E
GREENS WELL RD
COLOSSEUM
YATES WELL RD
IVANPAH LAKE
NEVADA CALIFORNIA
CLARK CO
SAN BERNARDINO CO
NIPTON DESERT RD
R15E R16E
164
95
SEARCHLIGHT
FOURTH OF JULY MOUNTAIN
MOUNTAIN PASS
WHEATON SPRINGS
MOJAVE
NIPTON
NIPTON RD
T16N T15.5N
T15.5N T15N
IVANPAH MOUNTAINS
IVANPAH VALLEY
NEW YORK MOUNTAINS
CASTLE PEAKS 5829'
R59E R60E
R60E R61E
R61E R62E
R62E R63E
R63E R64E
R18E R19E
T29S T30S
T30S T31S
SAN BERNARDINO CO
ZINC MINE
CUTOFF RD
MINE RD
STAR
MORNING STAR
IVANPAH
KESSLER PEAK
CIMA RD
NEW YORK
PIUTE VALLEY
CAL NEV ARI
NEWBERRY MOUNTAINS
1
2
3
4
5
6
7
8
9
10
11
SEE 330 MAP
SEE 351 MAP
0 2.5 5 7.5 10 miles 1 in. = 5 mi.

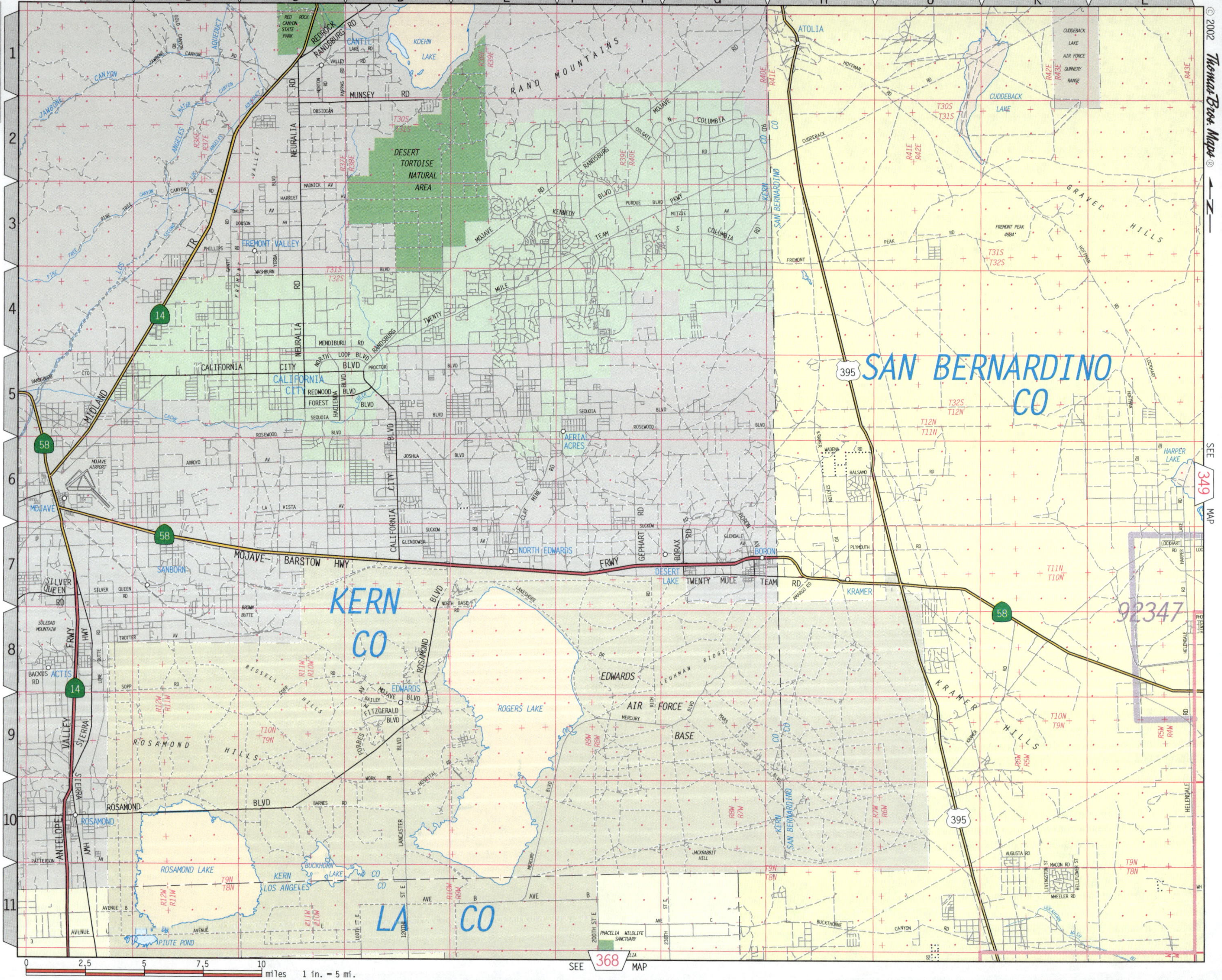
SEE 328 MAP
SEE 349 MAP
SEE 368 MAP
A B C D E F F G H J K L
SAN BERNARDINO
KERN CO
SAN BERNARDINO CO
LA CO
RAND MOUNTAINS
DESERT TORTOISE NATURAL AREA
RED ROCK CANYON STATE PARK
KOEHN LAKE
CANTIL
CUDDEBACK LAKE
CUDDEBACK LAKE AIR FORCE GUNNERY RANGE
ATOLIA
FREMONT VALLEY
CALIFORNIA CITY
MOJAVE
MOJAVE AIRPORT
SANBORN
AERIAL ACRES
NORTH EDWARDS
DESERT LAKE
BORON
KRAMER
HARPER LAKE
GRAVEL HILLS
FREMONT PEAK 4584'
KRAMER HILLS
EDWARDS AIR FORCE BASE
ROGERS LAKE
EDWARDS
ROSAMOND HILLS
BISSELL HILLS
ROSAMOND
ROSAMOND LAKE
BUCKHORN LAKE
ACTIS
SOLEDAD MOUNTAIN
PIUTE POND
JACKRABBIT HILL
PHACELIA WILDLIFE SANCTUARY
MOJAVE BARSTOW HWY
TWENTY MULE TEAM RD
CALIFORNIA CITY BLVD
NEURALIA RD
ROSAMOND BLVD
SIERRA HWY
ANTELOPE VALLEY FRWY
14
58
395
92347
0 2.5 5 7.5 10 miles 1 in. = 5 mi.

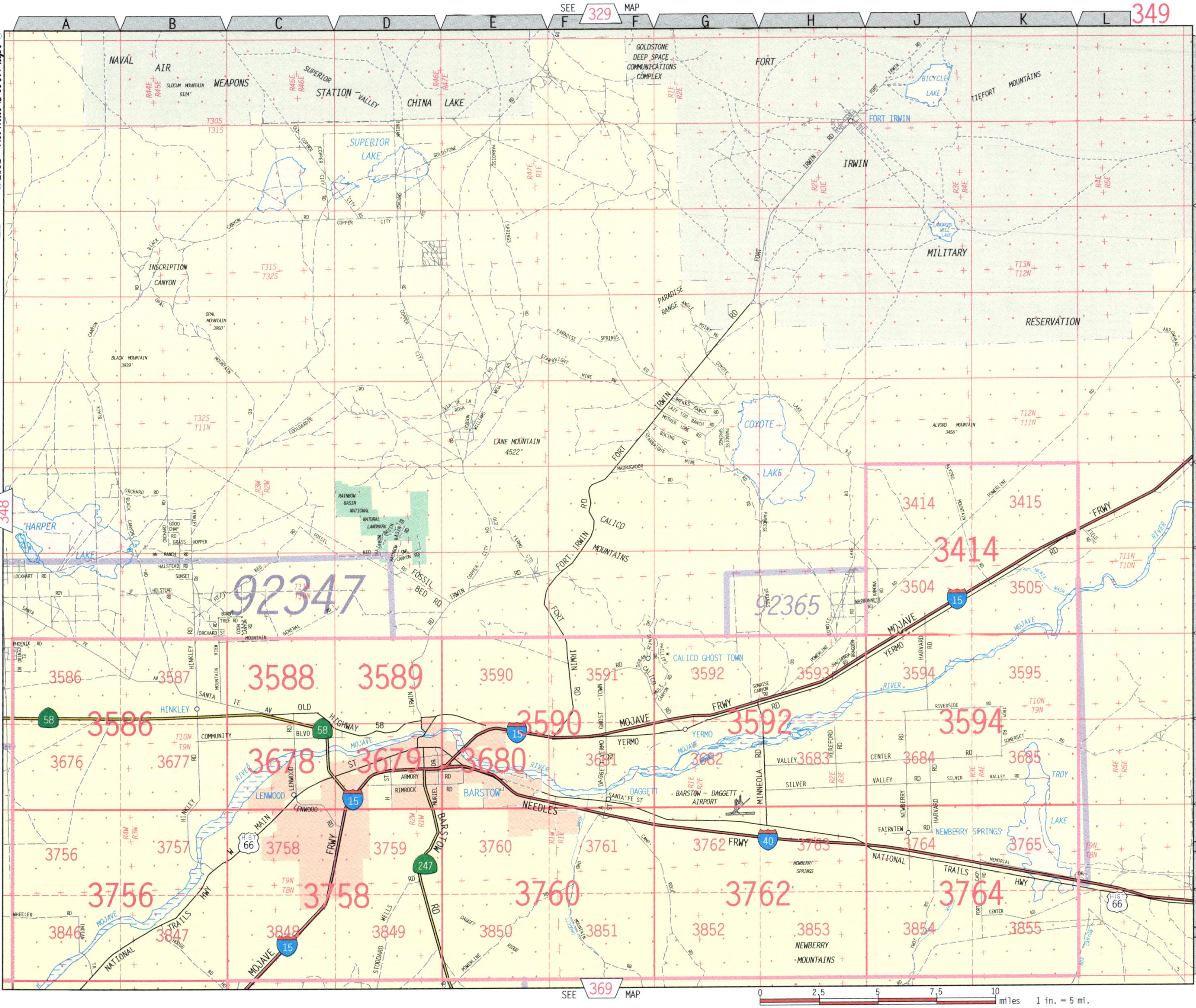
SEE 329 MAP
A B C D E F F G H J K L
1 2 3 4 5 6 6 7 8 9 10 11
NAVAL AIR WEAPONS STATION - CHINA LAKE
SUPERIOR VALLEY
SLOCUM MOUNTAIN 5124'
GOLDSTONE DEEP SPACE COMMUNICATIONS COMPLEX
FORT IRWIN MILITARY RESERVATION
BICYCLE LAKE
TIEFORT MOUNTAINS
FORT IRWIN
IRWIN
SUPERIOR LAKE
INSCRIPTION CANYON
OPAL MOUNTAIN 3950'
BLACK MOUNTAIN 3939'
LANE MOUNTAIN 4522'
PARADISE RANGE
COYOTE LAKE
ALVORD MOUNTAIN 3456'
CALICO MOUNTAINS
RAINBOW BASIN NATIONAL NATURAL LANDMARK
HARPER LAKE
SEE 348 MAP
SEE 350 MAP
92347
92365
CALICO GHOST TOWN
HINKLEY
LENWOOD
BARSTOW
YERMO
DAGGETT
BARSTOW - DAGGETT AIRPORT
NEWBERRY SPRINGS
NEWBERRY MOUNTAINS
MOJAVE RIVER
MOJAVE FRWY
NEEDLES FRWY
NATIONAL TRAILS HWY
15
40
58
247
66
3414 3415 3504 3505
3586 3587 3588 3589 3590 3591 3592 3593 3594 3595
3676 3677 3678 3679 3680 3681 3682 3683 3684 3685
3756 3757 3758 3759 3760 3761 3762 3763 3764 3765
3846 3847 3848 3849 3850 3851 3852 3853 3854 3855
SEE 369 MAP
0 2.5 5 7.5 10 miles 1 in. = 5 mi.

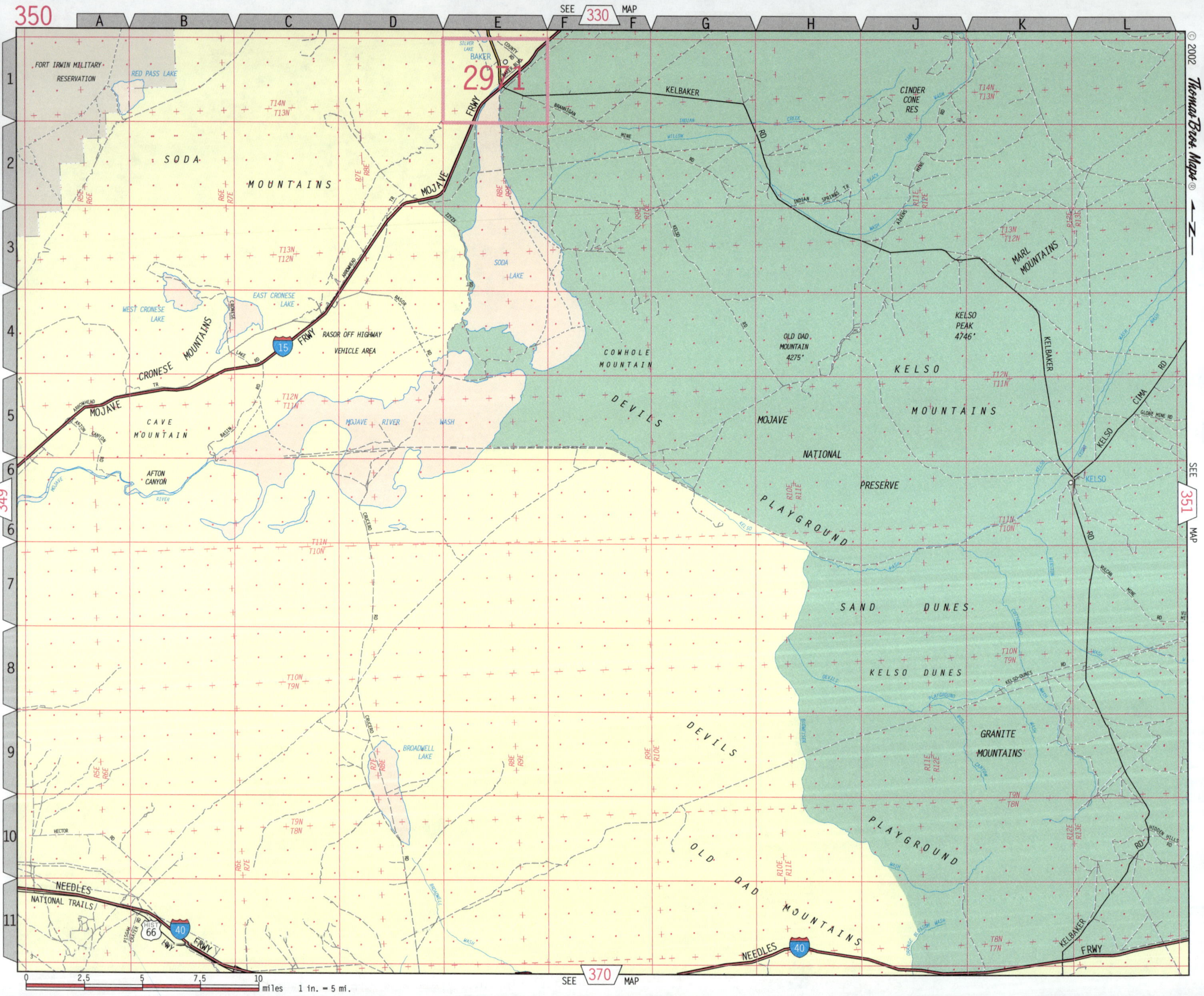
SEE 330 MAP
SAN BERNARDINO
FORT IRWIN MILITARY RESERVATION
RED PASS LAKE
SILVER LAKE
BAKER
297
KELBAKER
BRANNIGAN
MINE
INDIAN
WILLOW
CREEK
CINDER CONE RES
T14N
T13N
SODA
MOUNTAINS
MOJAVE
FRWY
INDIAN SPRINGS TR
AIKENS
MARL MOUNTAINS
T13N
T12N
SODA LAKE
EAST CRONESE LAKE
WEST CRONESE LAKE
CRONESE MOUNTAINS
RASOR OFF HIGHWAY VEHICLE AREA
15
KELSO PEAK 4746'
OLD DAD MOUNTAIN 4275'
COWHOLE MOUNTAIN
KELSO
MOUNTAINS
CIMA
RD
GLOBE MINE RD
ARROWHEAD
AFTON CANYON
CAVE MOUNTAIN
MOJAVE RIVER WASH
DEVILS
MOJAVE NATIONAL PRESERVE
KELSO
AFTON CANYON
SEE 349 MAP
SEE 351 MAP
PLAYGROUND
T11N
T10N
CRUCERO
SAND DUNES
KELSO DUNES
KELSO-DUNES
T10N
T9N
GRANITE MOUNTAINS
BROADWELL LAKE
DEVILS
HECTOR
T9N
T8N
PLAYGROUND
HIDDEN HILLS RD
OLD DAD MOUNTAINS
NEEDLES
NATIONAL TRAILS
HIST 66
40
FRWY
KELBAKER
T8N
T7N
SEE 370 MAP
0 2.5 5 7.5 10 miles 1 in. = 5 mi.
© 2002 Thomas Bros. Maps®

SEE 331 MAP

SEE 350 MAP

SEE 352 MAP

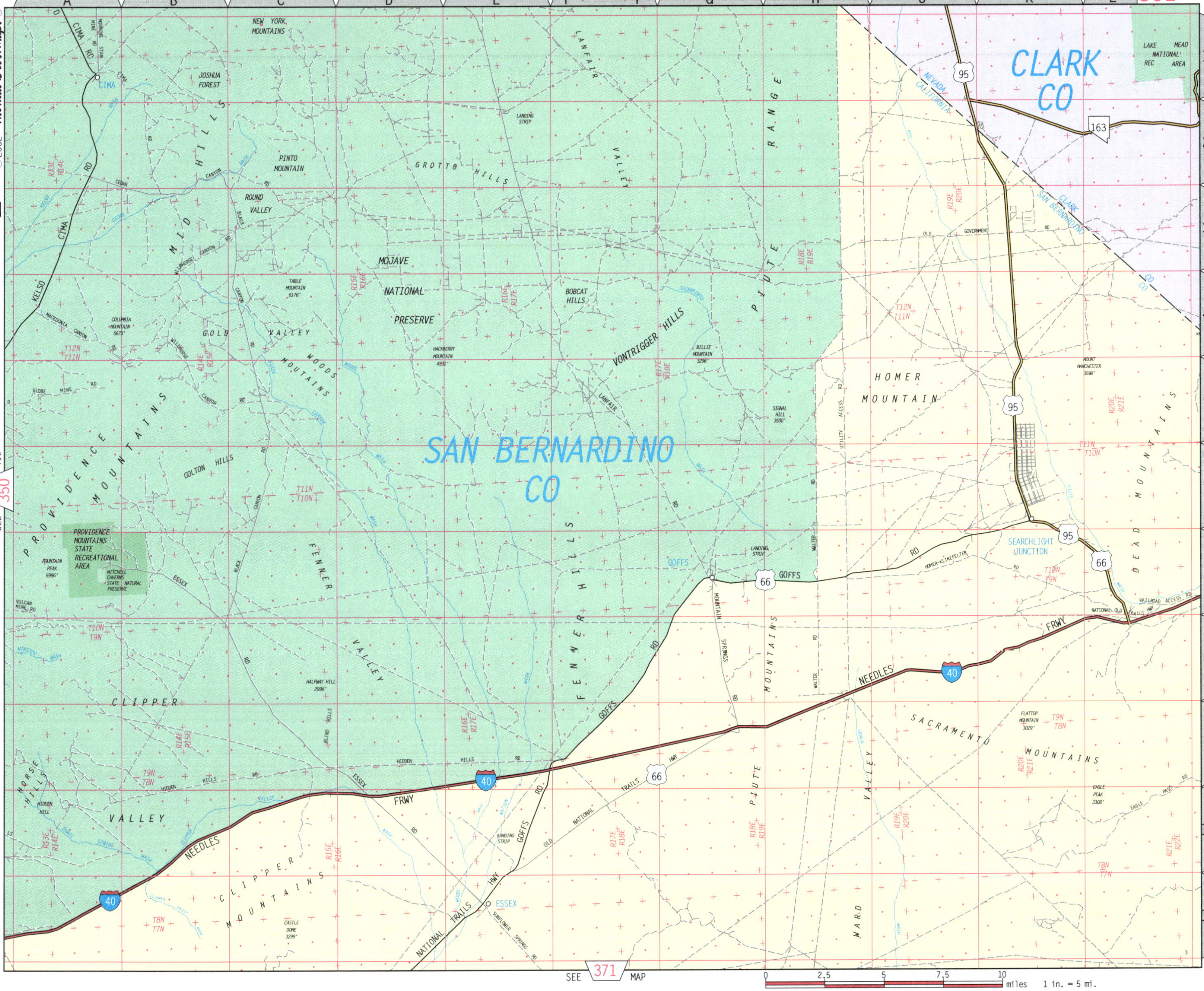

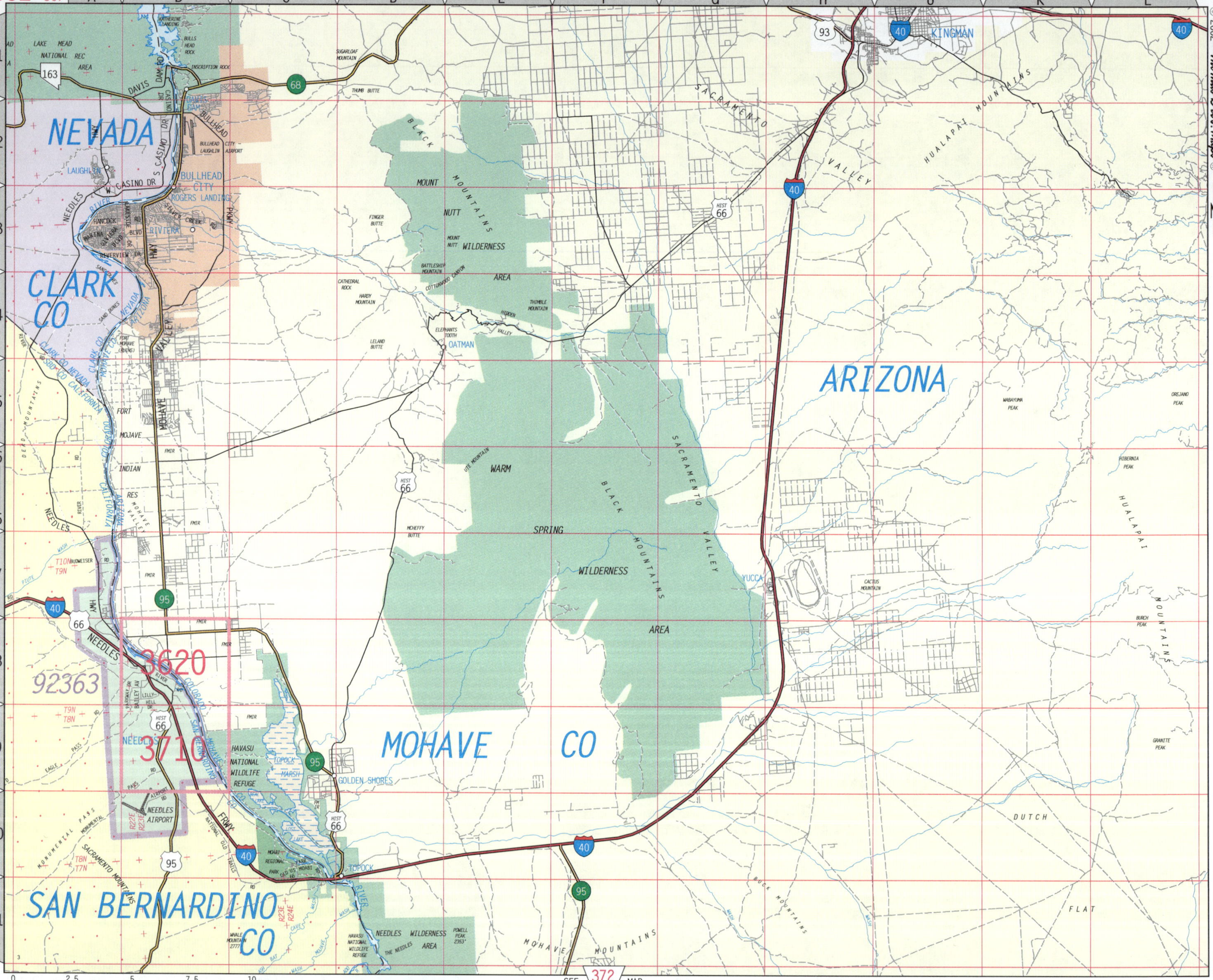

SEE 351 MAP
SEE 372 MAP

0 2.5 5 7.5 10 miles 1 in. = 5 mi.

SEE 348 MAP

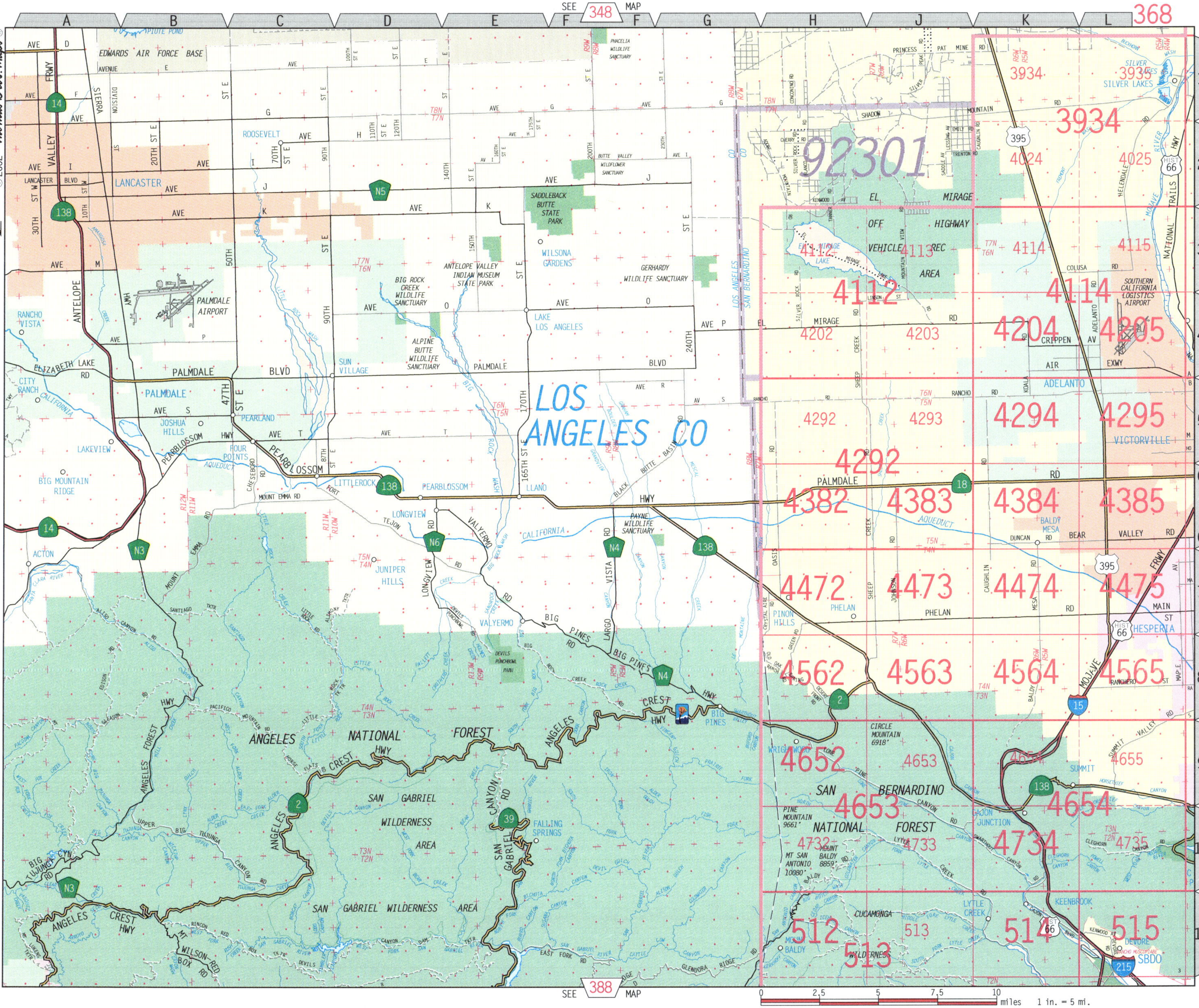

SEE 369 MAP

SEE 388 MAP

SEE 349 MAP

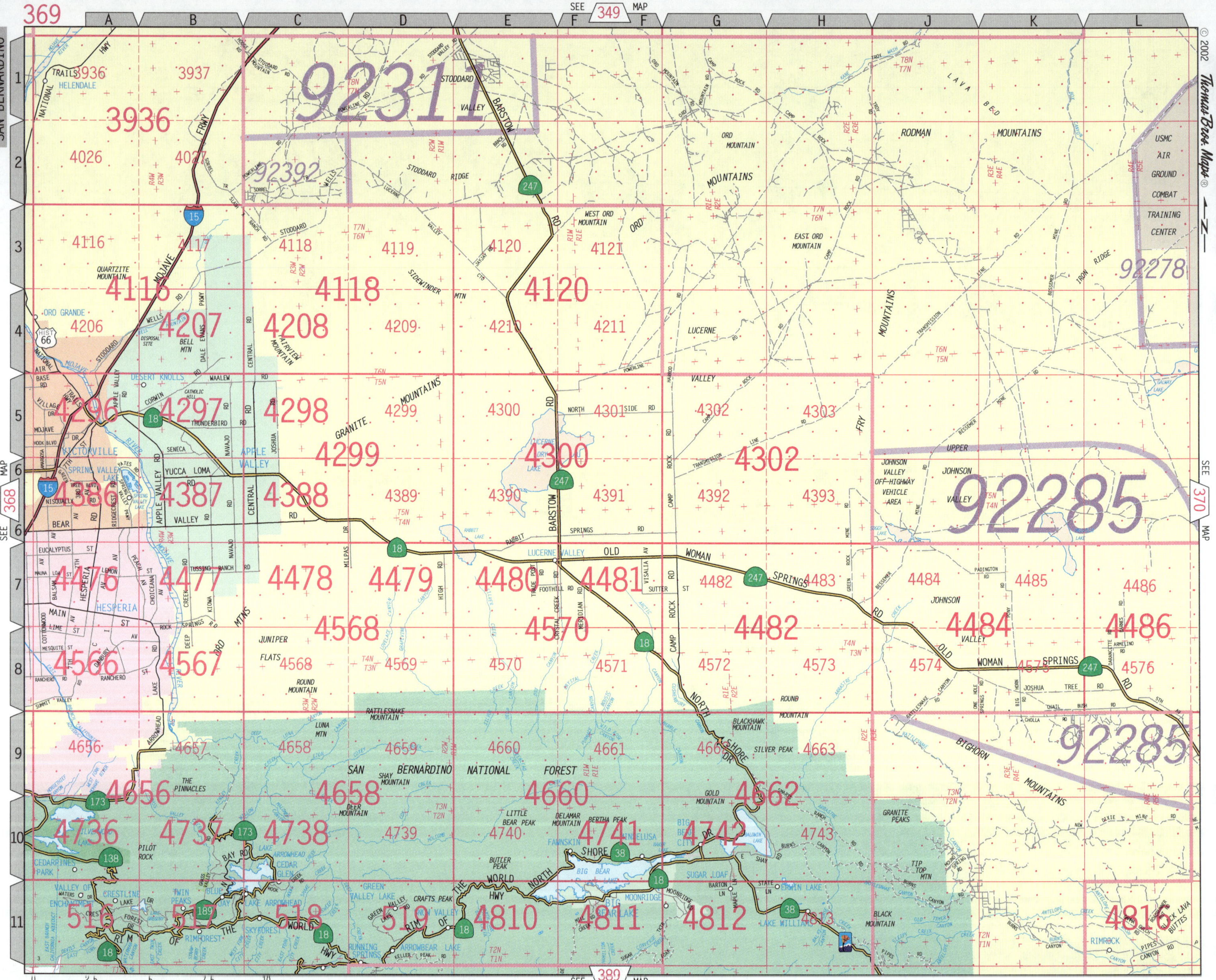

0 2.5 5 7.5 10 miles 1 in. = 5 mi.

SEE 350 MAP

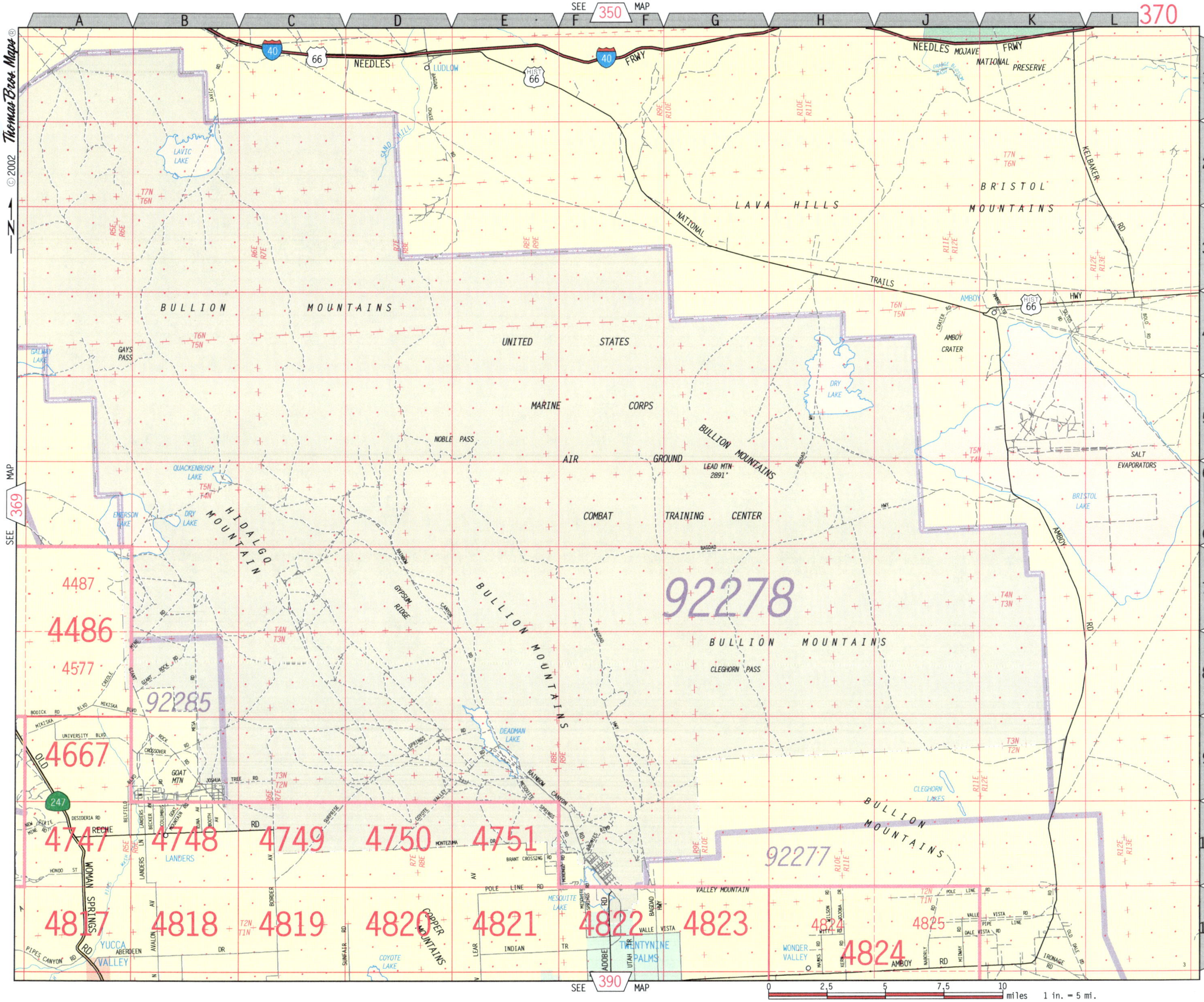

SEE 369 MAP

SEE 371 MAP

SEE 390 MAP

SEE 351 MAP

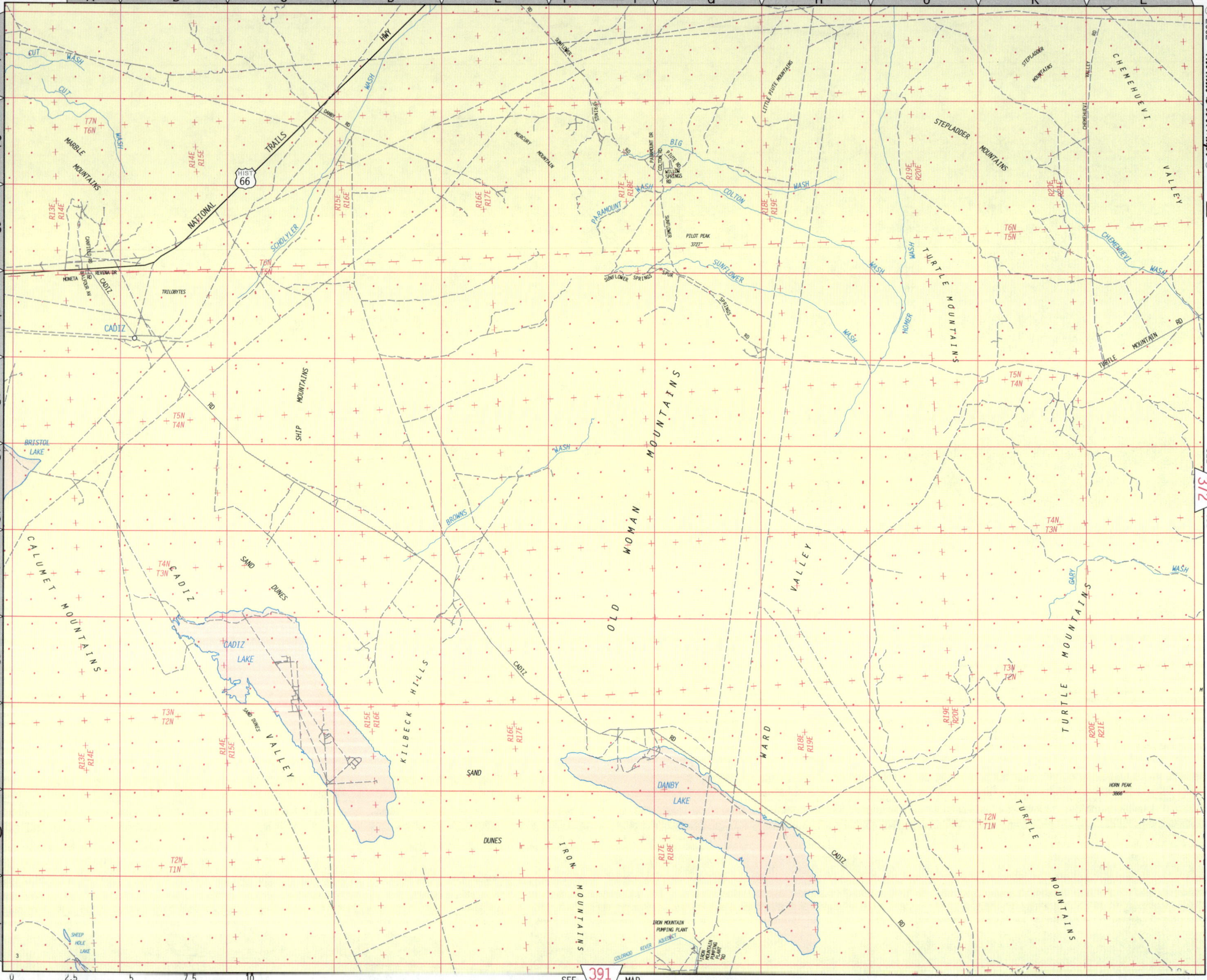

SEE 370 MAP
SEE 372 MAP
SEE 391 MAP

0 2.5 5 7.5 10 miles 1 in. = 5 mi.

SEE 352 MAP
A B C D E F F G H J K L

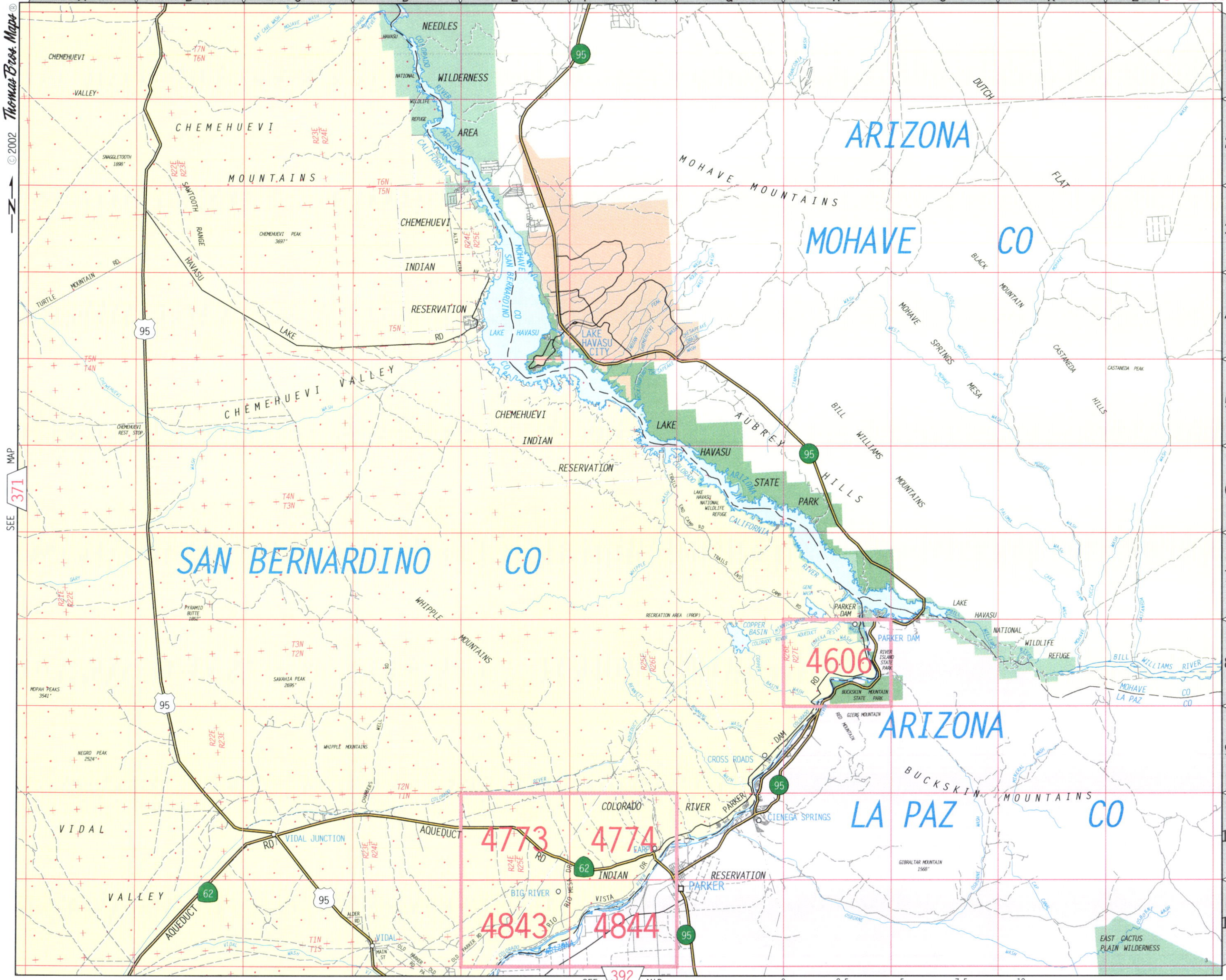

SEE 371 MAP
SEE 392 MAP

SEE 368 MAP

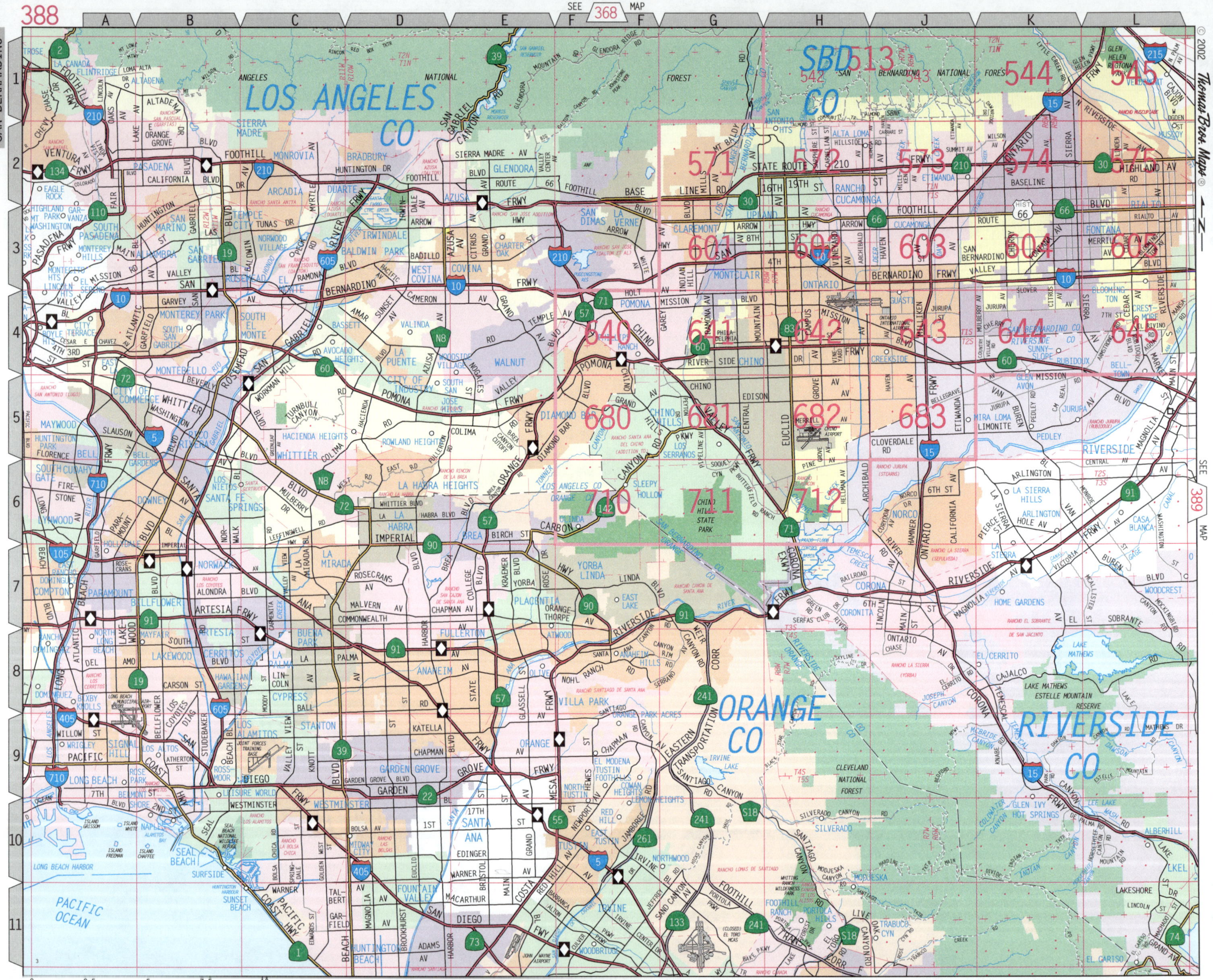

SEE 389 MAP

0 2.5 5 7.5 10 miles 1 in. = 5 mi.

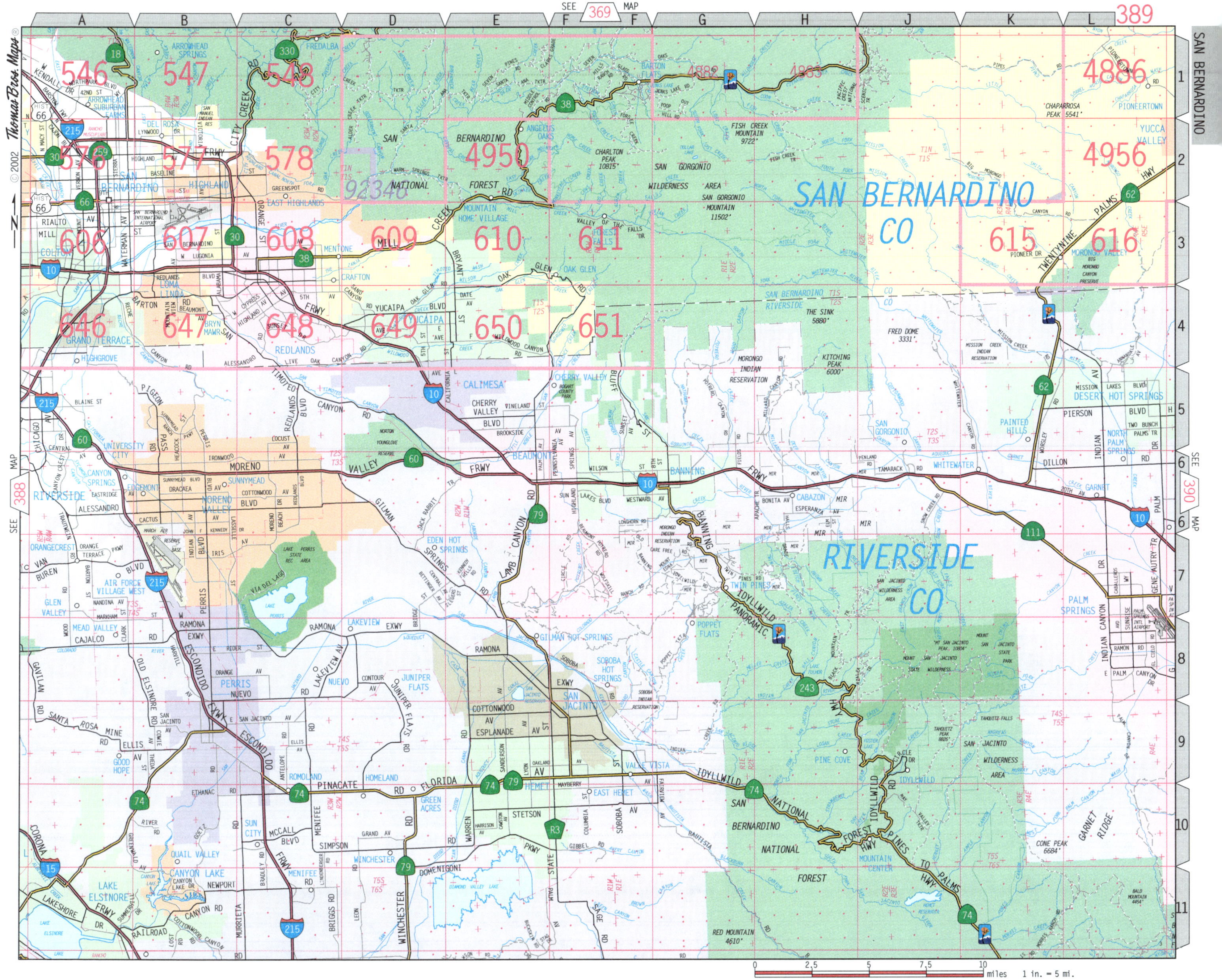

389
SAN BERNARDINO
SEE 369 MAP
SEE 388 MAP
SEE 390 MAP
Thomas Bros. Maps
© 2002
A B C D E F F G H J K L
1 2 3 4 5 6 7 8 9 10 11
546
547
548
4882
4883
4886
576
577
578
4950
4956
606
607
608
609
610
611
615
616
646
647
648
649
650
651
92346
SAN BERNARDINO CO
RIVERSIDE CO
SAN BERNARDINO RIVERSIDE
SAN BERNARDINO NATIONAL FOREST
SAN GORGONIO WILDERNESS AREA
SAN GORGONIO MOUNTAIN 11502'
FISH CREEK MOUNTAIN 9722'
CHARLTON PEAK 10815'
CHAPARROSA PEAK 5541'
ARROWHEAD SPRINGS
FREDALBA
BARTON FLATS
ANGELUS OAKS
PIONEERTOWN
YUCCA VALLEY
MORONGO VALLEY
DEL ROSA
HIGHLAND
EAST HIGHLANDS
SAN BERNARDINO
RIALTO
COLTON
LOMA LINDA
REDLANDS
MENTONE
CRAFTON
YUCAIPA
OAK GLEN
FOREST FALLS
MOUNTAIN HOME VILLAGE
GRAND TERRACE
HIGHGROVE
BRYN MAWR
CALIMESA
CHERRY VALLEY
BEAUMONT
BANNING
CABAZON
WHITEWATER
DESERT HOT SPRINGS
PAINTED HILLS
NORTH PALM SPRINGS
GARNET
PALM SPRINGS
MORONGO INDIAN RESERVATION
THE SINK 5880'
FRED DOME 3331'
KITCHING PEAK 6000'
UNIVERSITY CITY
RIVERSIDE
CANYON CREST
EDGEMONT
SUNNYMEAD
MORENO VALLEY
ORANGECREST
AIR FORCE VILLAGE WEST
GLEN VALLEY
MEAD VALLEY
LAKE PERRIS STATE REC AREA
PERRIS
NUEVO
LAKEVIEW
ROMOLAND
HOMELAND
GREEN ACRES
WINCHESTER
MENIFEE
SUN CITY
QUAIL VALLEY
CANYON LAKE
LAKE ELSINORE
GOOD HOPE
CORONA
EDEN HOT SPRINGS
GILMAN HOT SPRINGS
SOBOBA HOT SPRINGS
SAN JACINTO
HEMET
EAST HEMET
VALLE VISTA
TWIN PINES
POPPET FLATS
IDYLLWILD
PINE COVE
MOUNTAIN CENTER
SAN JACINTO WILDERNESS AREA
MT SAN JACINTO STATE PARK
CONE PEAK 6684'
GARNET RIDGE
RED MOUNTAIN 4610'
JUNIPER FLATS
DIAMOND VALLEY LAKE
PINES TO PALMS HWY
IDYLLWILD PANORAMIC HWY
TWENTYNINE PALMS HWY
MORENO VALLEY FRWY
ESCONDIDO FRWY
LAMB CANYON
0 2.5 5 7.5 10 miles 1 in. = 5 mi.

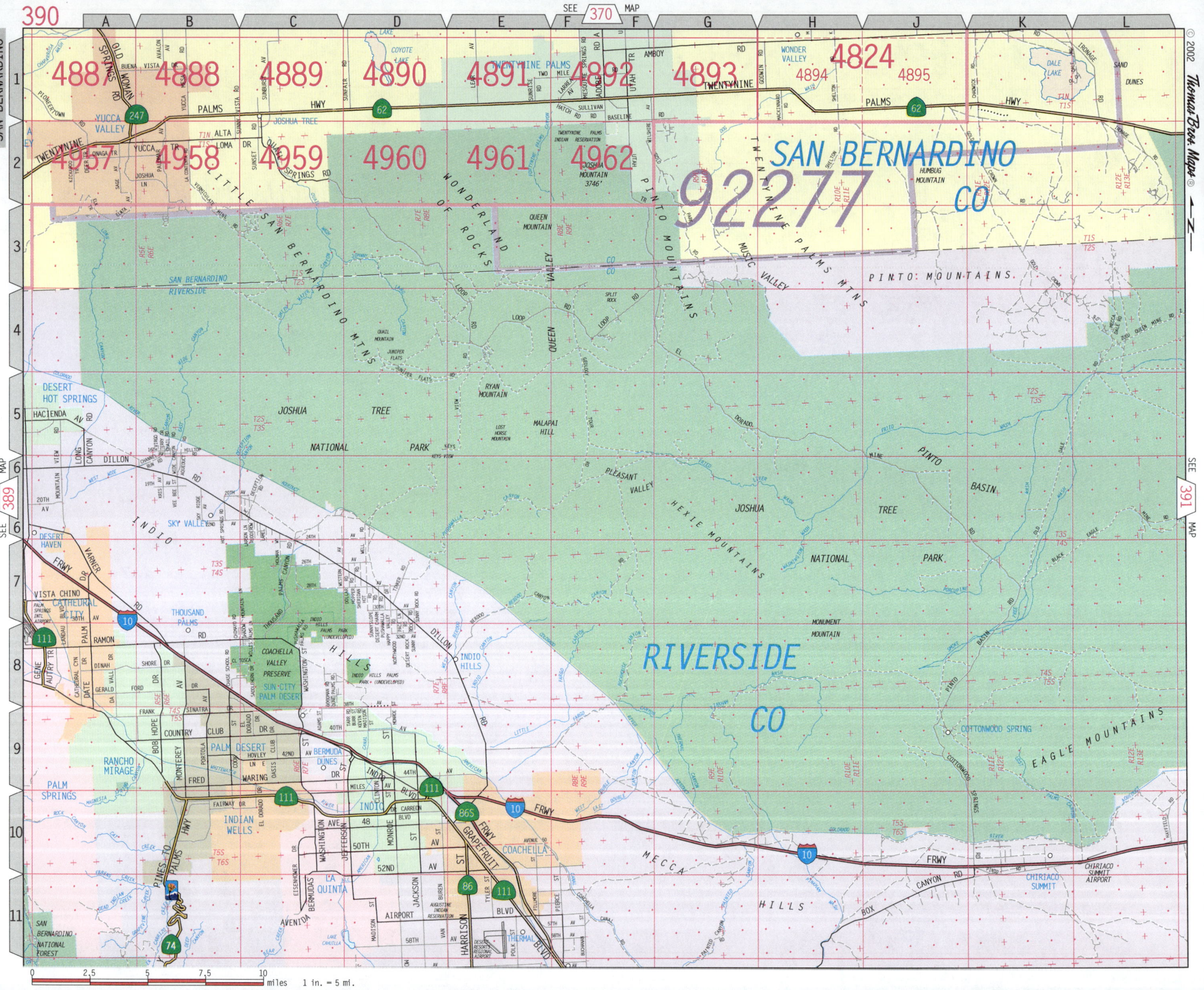
SAN BERNARDINO
SEE 370 MAP
SEE 389 MAP
SEE 391 MAP
© 2002 Thomas Bros. Maps ®
4887
4888
4889
4890
4891
4892
4893
4824
4894
4895
4957
4958
4959
4960
4961
4962
92277
SAN BERNARDINO CO
RIVERSIDE CO
YUCCA VALLEY
JOSHUA TREE
TWENTYNINE PALMS
WONDER VALLEY
TWENTYNINE PALMS HWY
AMBOY
DALE LAKE
SAND DUNES
COYOTE LAKE
TWENTYNINE PALMS INDIAN RESERVATION
JOSHUA MOUNTAIN 3746'
QUEEN MOUNTAIN
HUMBUG MOUNTAIN
LITTLE SAN BERNARDINO MTNS
WONDERLAND OF ROCKS
PINTO MOUNTAINS
TWENTYNINE PALMS MTNS
MUSIC VALLEY
QUEEN VALLEY
JOSHUA TREE NATIONAL PARK
RYAN MOUNTAIN
MALAPAI HILL
PLEASANT VALLEY
HEXIE MOUNTAINS
PINTO BASIN
MONUMENT MOUNTAIN
COTTONWOOD SPRING
EAGLE MOUNTAINS
MECCA HILLS
BOX CANYON RD
CHIRIACO SUMMIT
CHIRIACO SUMMIT AIRPORT
DESERT HOT SPRINGS
SKY VALLEY
INDIO HILLS
THOUSAND PALMS
COACHELLA VALLEY PRESERVE
SUN CITY PALM DESERT
CATHEDRAL CITY
RANCHO MIRAGE
PALM SPRINGS
PALM DESERT
INDIAN WELLS
BERMUDA DUNES
INDIO
LA QUINTA
COACHELLA
THERMAL
DESERT RESORTS REGIONAL AIRPORT
SAN BERNARDINO NATIONAL FOREST
INDIO FRWY
GRAPEFRUIT BLVD
PINES TO PALMS HWY
0 2.5 5 7.5 10 miles 1 in. = 5 mi.

SEE 371 MAP

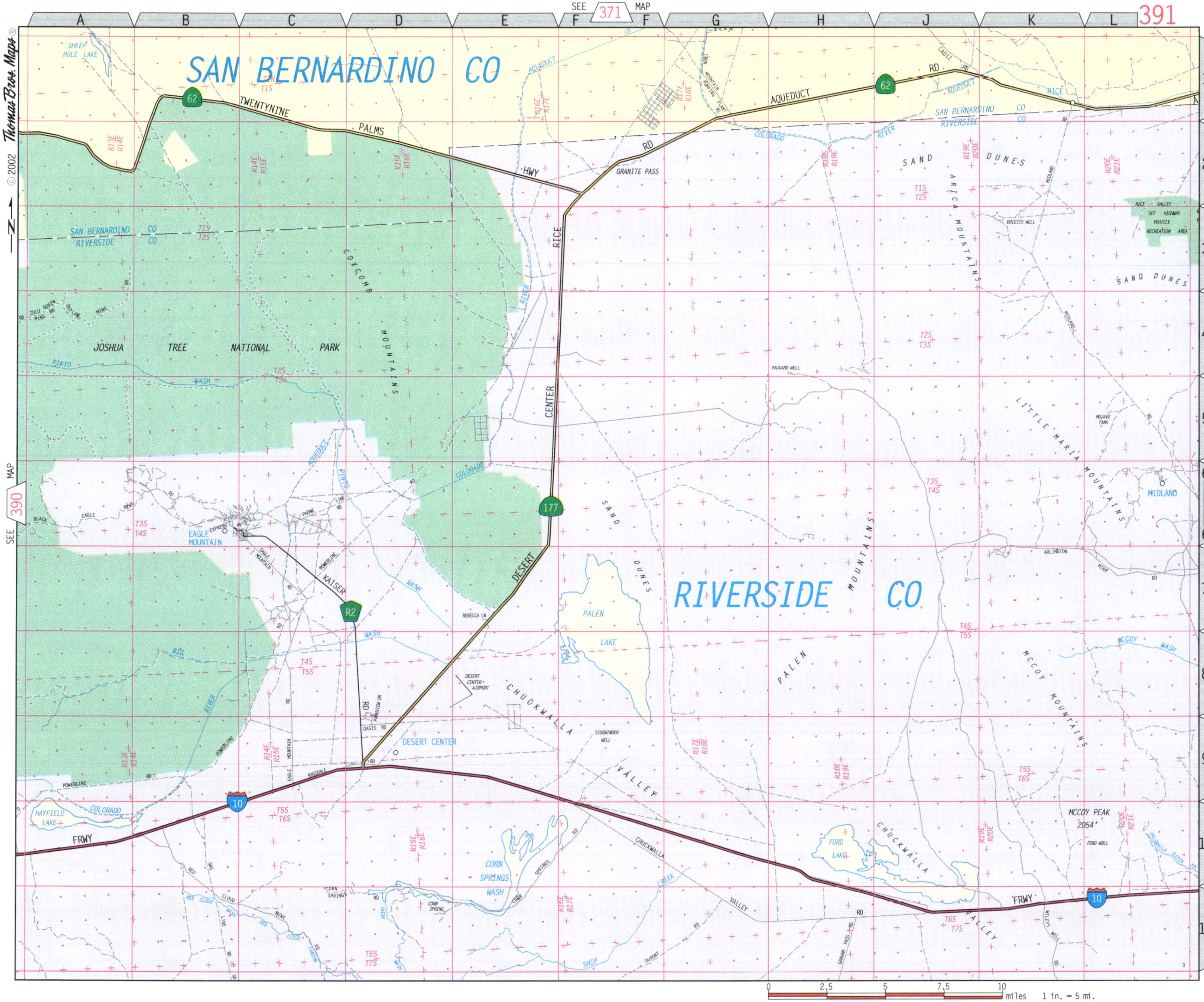

SEE 390 MAP

SEE 392 MAP

SEE 372 MAP
SEE 391 MAP

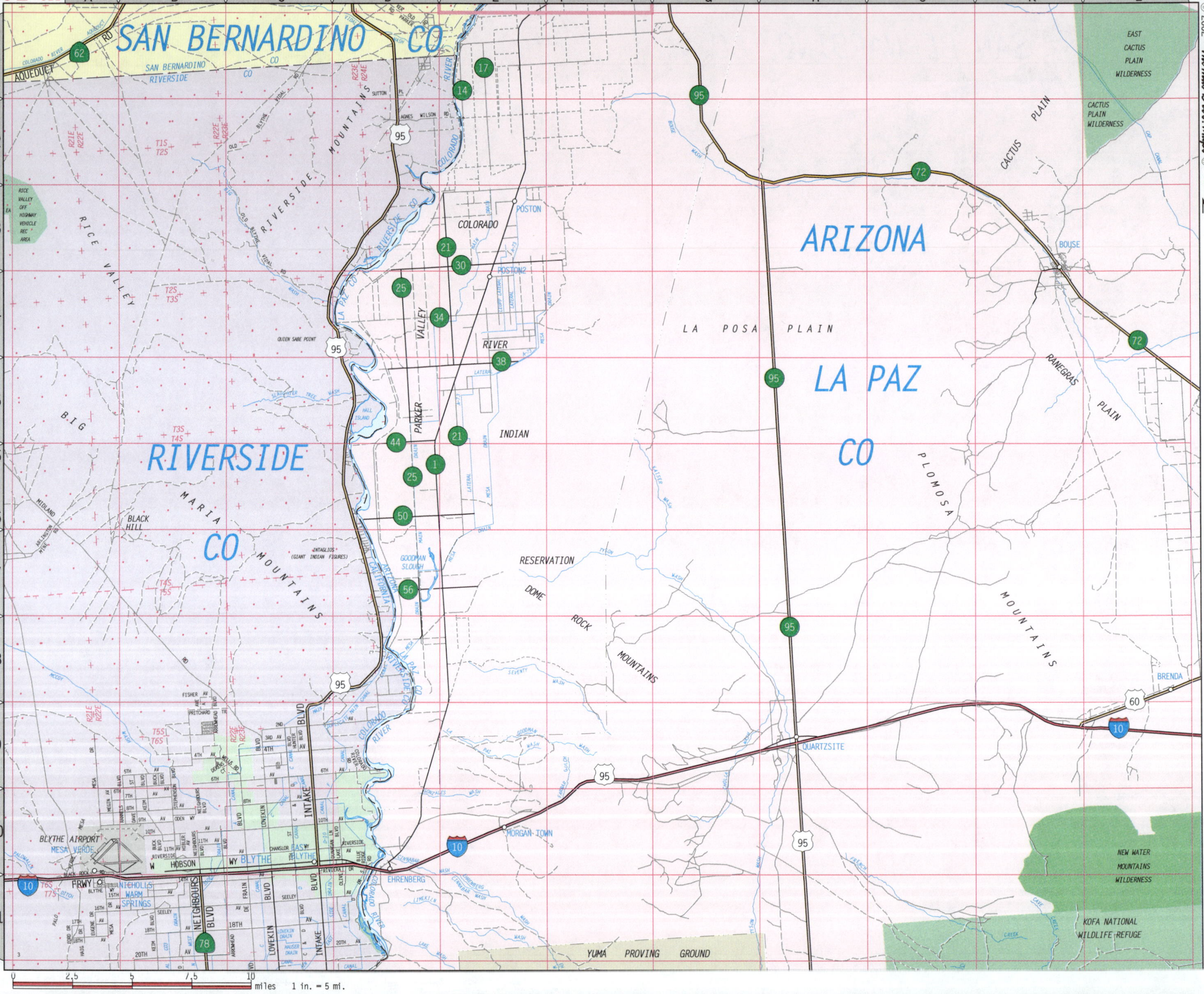

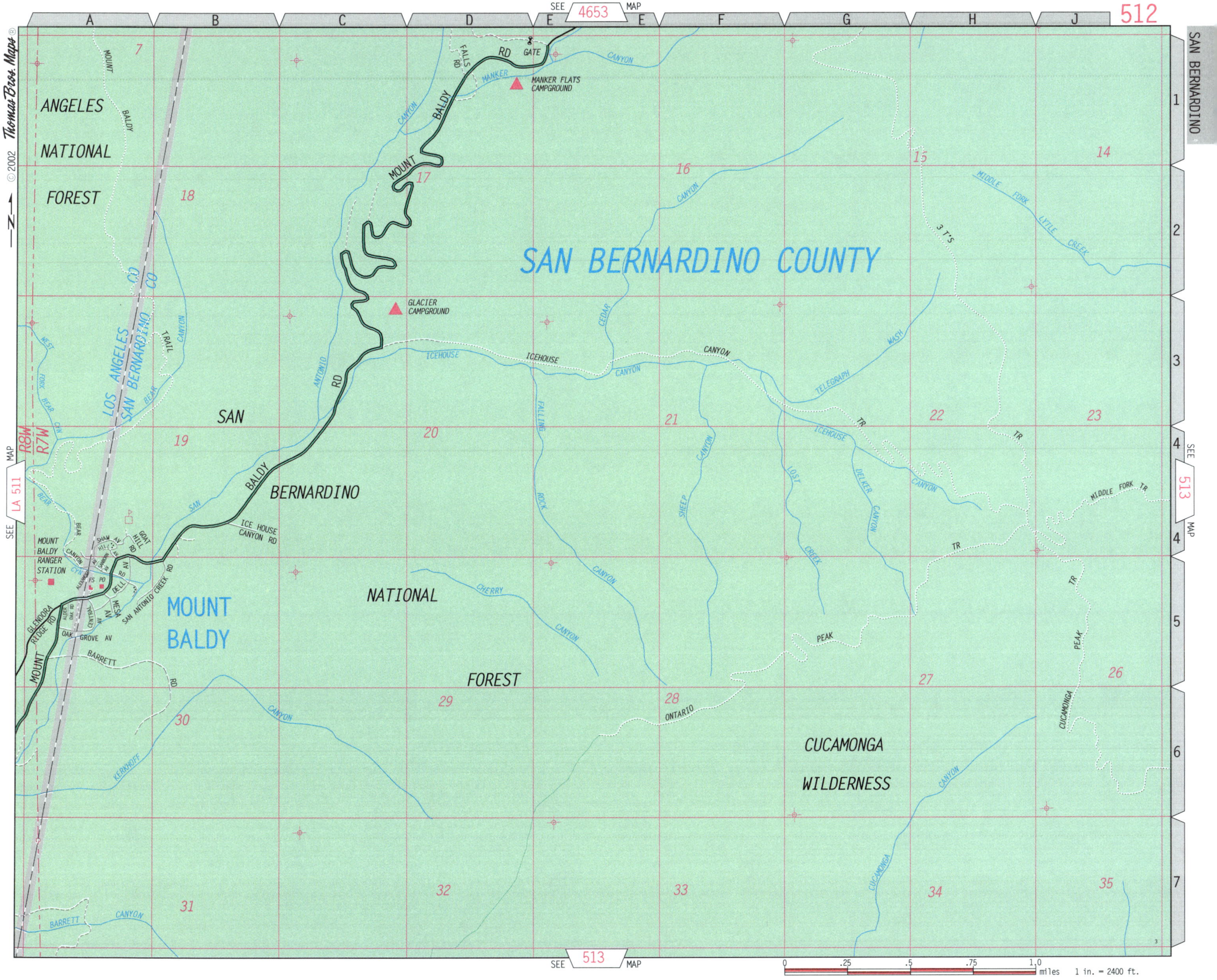
SEE 4653 MAP
SEE 513 MAP
SEE LA 511 MAP
SEE 513 MAP
SAN BERNARDINO
A
B
C
D
E
F
G
H
J
1
2
3
4
5
6
7
SAN BERNARDINO COUNTY
ANGELES NATIONAL FOREST
SAN BERNARDINO NATIONAL FOREST
CUCAMONGA WILDERNESS
MOUNT BALDY
LOS ANGELES CO
SAN BERNARDINO CO
R8W
R7W
MANKER FLATS CAMPGROUND
GLACIER CAMPGROUND
GATE
MOUNT BALDY RD
FALLS RD
MANKER CANYON
ICEHOUSE CANYON
TELEGRAPH WASH
CEDAR CANYON
FALLING ROCK CANYON
SHEEP CANYON
LOST CREEK
DELKER CANYON
MIDDLE FORK LYTLE CREEK
MIDDLE FORK TR
3 T'S TR
PEAK
ONTARIO PEAK
CUCAMONGA PEAK TR
CUCAMONGA CANYON
CHERRY CANYON
SAN ANTONIO CANYON
ICE HOUSE CANYON RD
SAN ANTONIO CREEK RD
MOUNT BALDY RANGER STATION
GLENDORA RIDGE RD
BEAR CANYON
WEST FORK BEAR CYN
BEAR CANYON TRAIL
MOUNT BALDY
BARRETT RD
BARRETT CANYON
KERKHOFF CANYON
OAK GROVE AV
MESA AV
DELL AV
SHAW AV
GOAT HILL RD
ALDER
FS
PO
7
18
17
16
15
14
19
20
21
22
23
30
29
28
27
26
31
32
33
34
35
0
.25
.5
.75
1.0
miles
1 in. = 2400 ft.

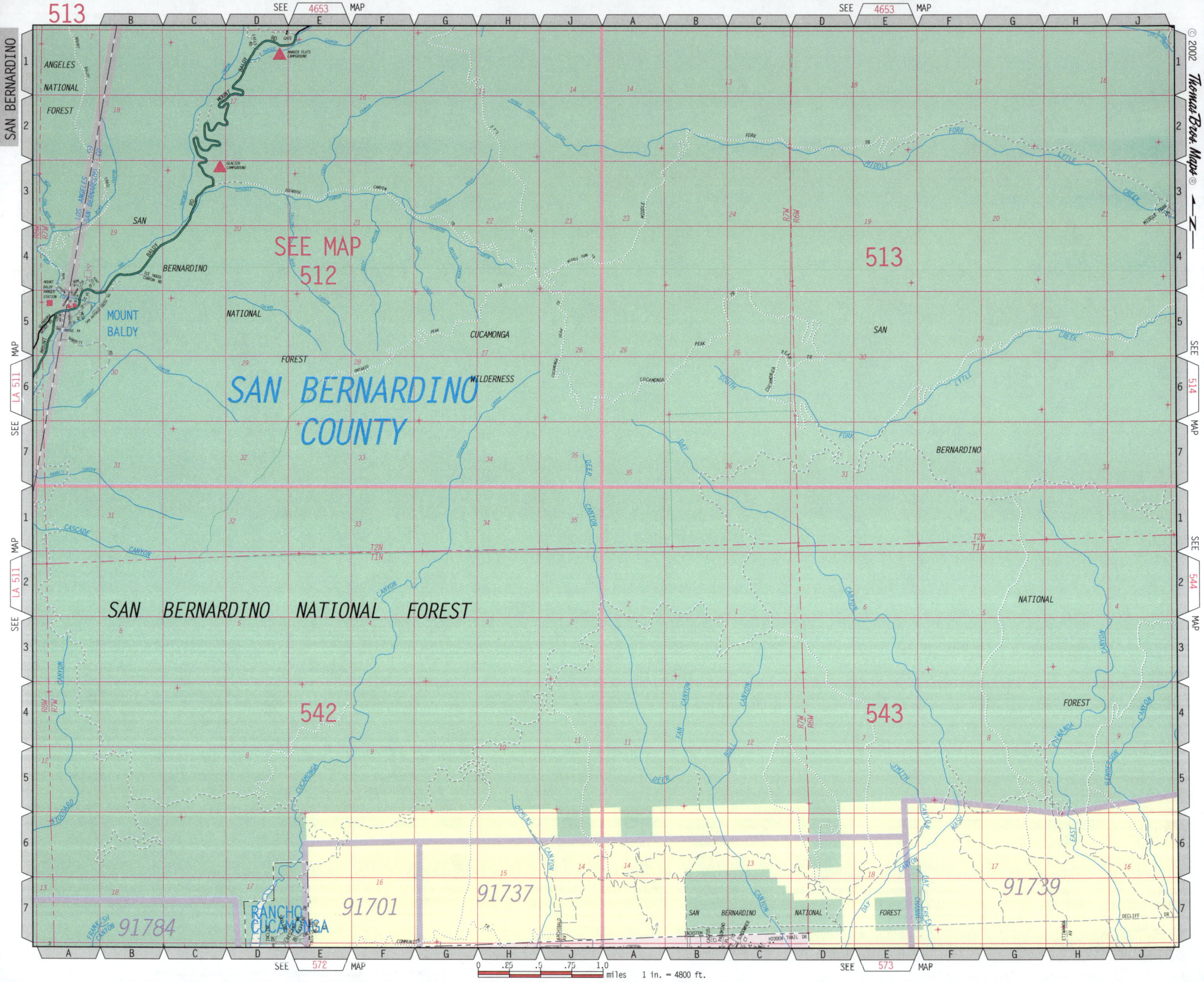
SAN BERNARDINO
SEE 4653 MAP
ANGELES NATIONAL FOREST
MANKER FLATS CAMPGROUND
GLACIER CAMPGROUND
MOUNT BALDY RD
SAN BERNARDINO NATIONAL FOREST
MOUNT BALDY
CUCAMONGA WILDERNESS
SEE MAP 512
513
SAN BERNARDINO COUNTY
MIDDLE FORK LYTLE CREEK
SOUTH FORK LYTLE CREEK
CUCAMONGA PEAK
DEER CANYON
DAY CANYON
CASCADE CANYON
T2N T1N
R7W R6W
SEE LA 511 MAP
SEE 514 MAP
SEE 544 MAP
SAN BERNARDINO NATIONAL FOREST
542
543
FAN CANYON
BULL CANYON
CUCAMONGA CANYON
DEMENS CANYON
ETIWANDA CANYON
HENDERSON CANYON
SMITH CANYON
EAST ETIWANDA CREEK
FRANKISH CANYON
STODDARD CANYON
RANCHO CUCAMONGA
91784
91701
91737
91739
HIDDEN TRAIL DR
DECLIFF DR
SEE 572 MAP
SEE 573 MAP
miles
1 in. = 4800 ft.

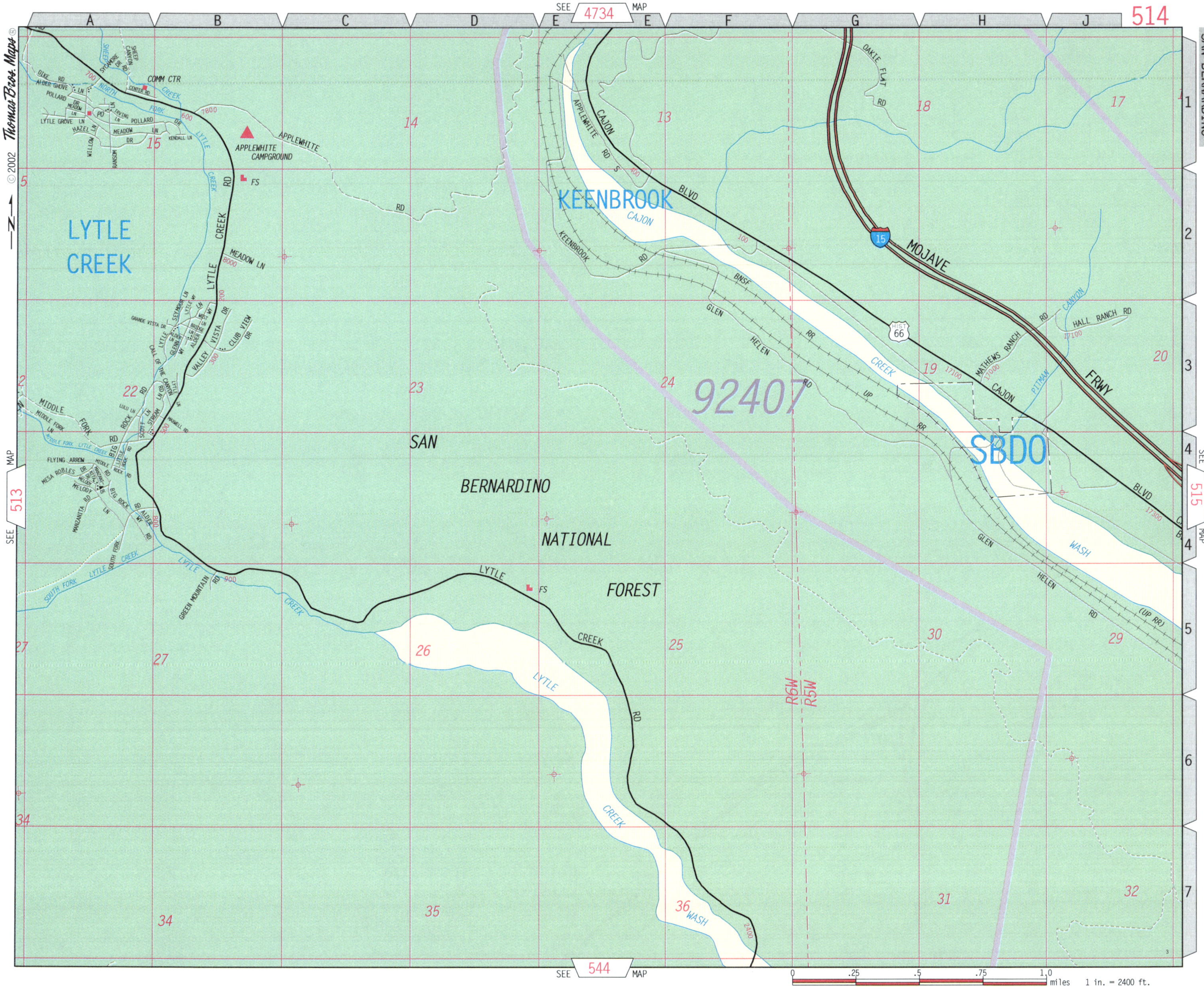
SEE 4734 MAP
SEE 544 MAP
SEE 513 MAP
SEE 515 MAP
SAN BERNARDINO
LYTLE CREEK
KEENBROOK
SBDO
92407
SAN BERNARDINO NATIONAL FOREST
APPLEWHITE CAMPGROUND
COMM CTR
FS
LYTLE CREEK RD
CAJON BLVD
MOJAVE FRWY
15
66
APPLEWHITE RD
CAJON WASH
LYTLE CREEK WASH
BNSF RR
UP RR
GLEN HELEN RD
MATHEWS RANCH RD
HALL RANCH RD
OAKIE FLAT RD
MEADOW LN
VALLEY VISTA DR
CLUB VIEW DR
MIDDLE FORK RD
BIG ROCK RD
GREEN MOUNTAIN RD
NORTH FORK LYTLE CREEK
SOUTH FORK LYTLE CREEK
MIDDLE FORK LYTLE CREEK
FLYING ARROW
MESA ROBLES DR
MELODY
MANZANITA
PITMAN CANYON
R6W R5W
0 .25 .5 .75 1.0 miles 1 in. = 2400 ft.

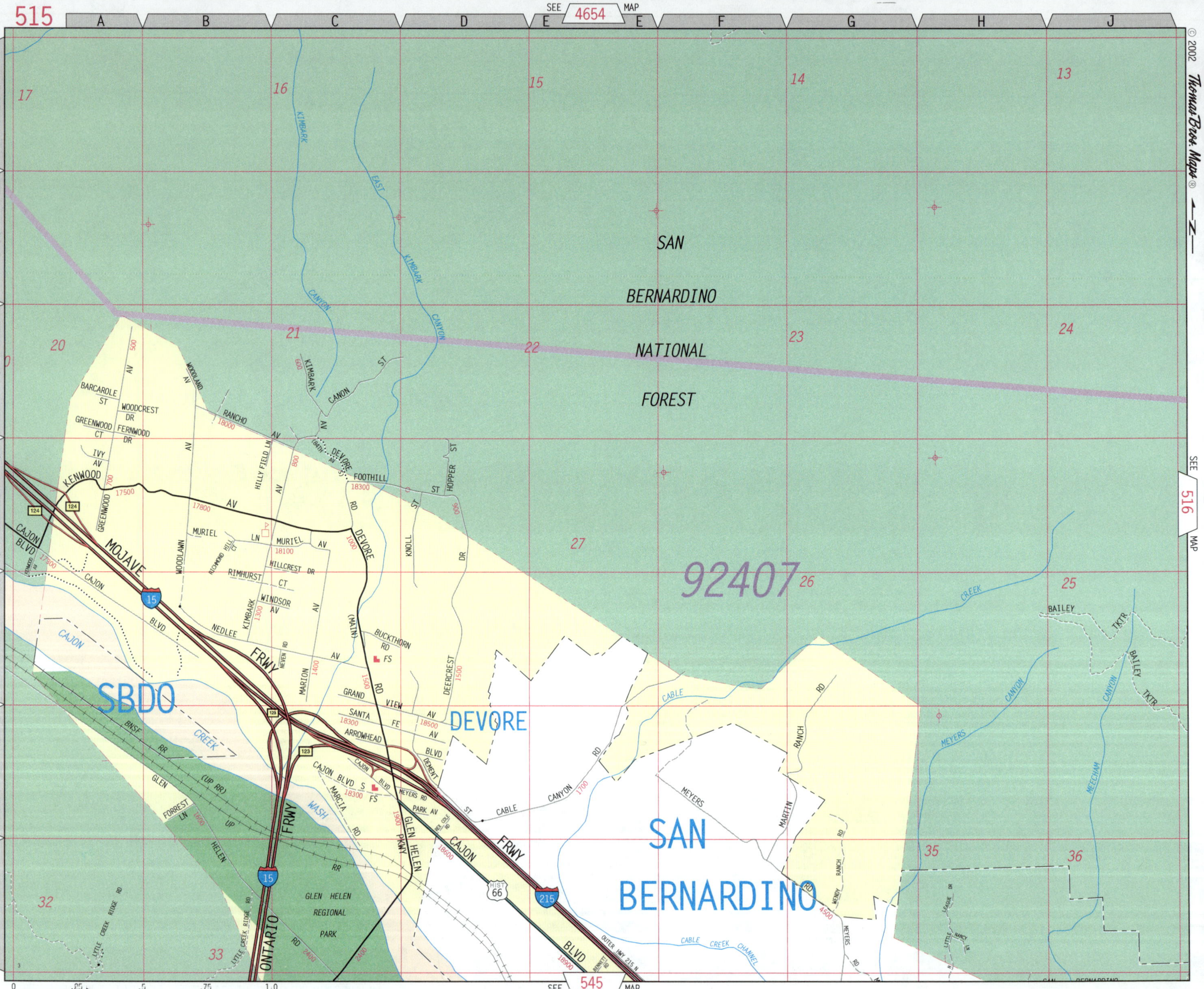

0 .25 .5 .75 1.0 miles 1 in. = 2400 ft.

SEE 4736 MAP

SEE 515 MAP

SEE 517 MAP

SEE 546 MAP

SEE 4737 MAP

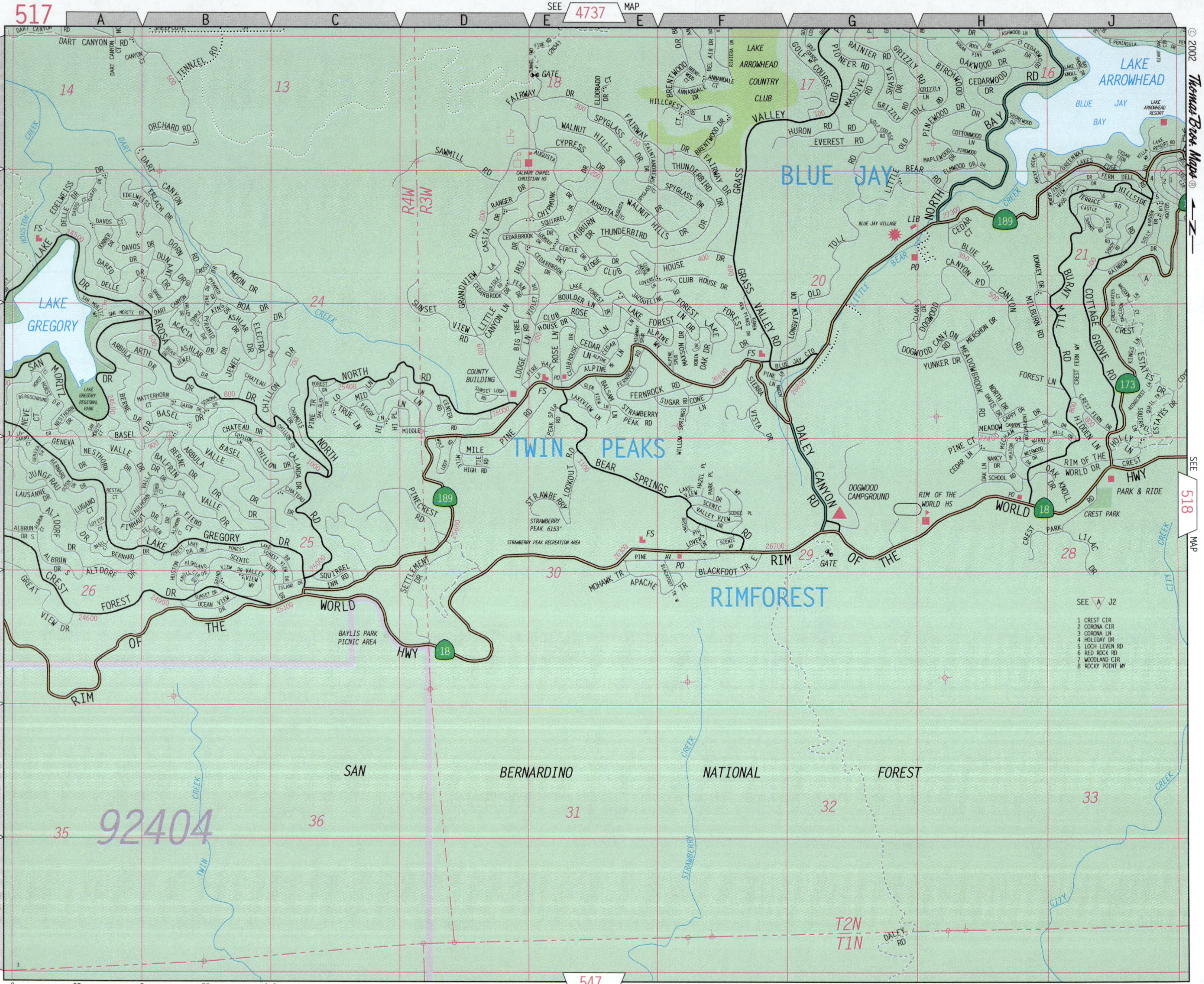

SEE 516 MAP
SEE 518 MAP
SEE 547 MAP

SEE 4738 MAP

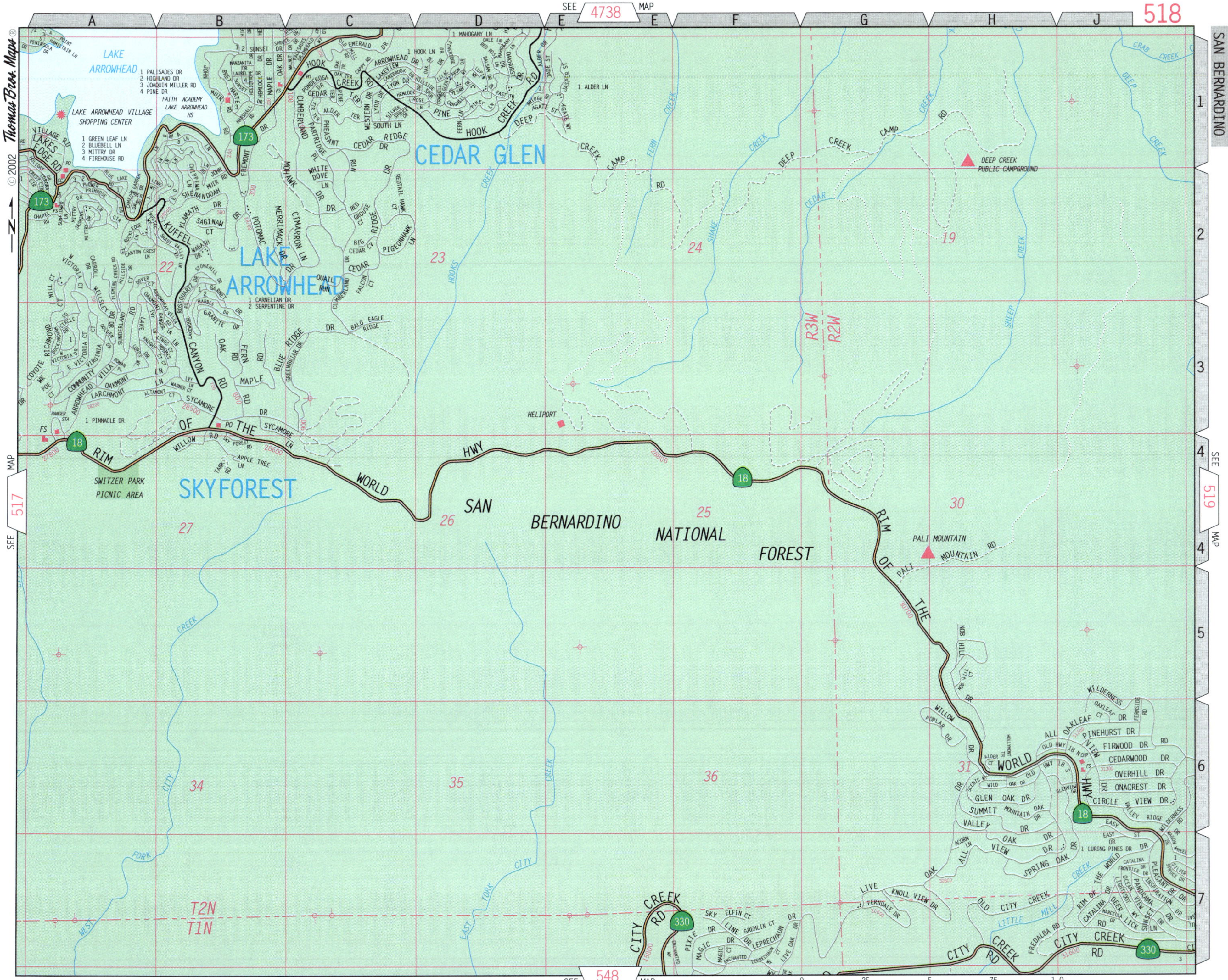

SEE 517 MAP

SEE 519 MAP

SEE 548 MAP

SEE 4658 MAP

SEE 518 MAP
SEE 4810 MAP
SEE 389 MAP

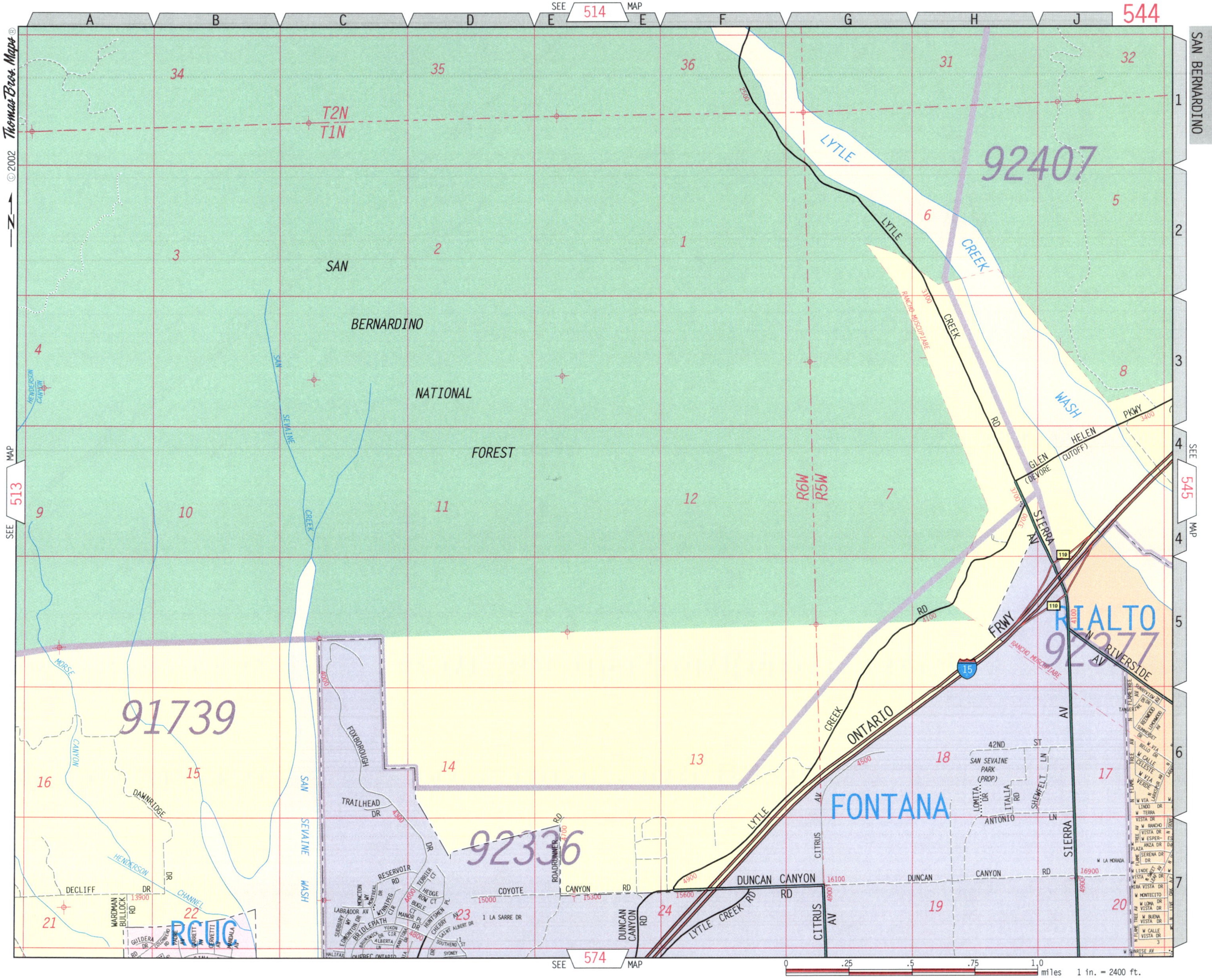
SEE 514 MAP
A
B
C
D
E
F
G
H
J
SAN BERNARDINO
SEE 545 MAP
SEE 513 MAP
SEE 574 MAP
Thomas Bros. Maps
© 2002
T2N
T1N
R6W
R5W
SAN
BERNARDINO
NATIONAL
FOREST
92407
91739
92336
92377
RIALTO
FONTANA
LYTLE
CREEK
WASH
SAN SEVAINE WASH
SAN SEVAINE CREEK
HENDERSON CANYON
MORSE CANYON
HENDERSON CHANNEL
LYTLE CREEK RD
GLEN HELEN PKWY
(DEVORE CUTOFF)
SIERRA AV
FRWY
ONTARIO
RANCHO MUSCUPIABE
N RIVERSIDE AV
42ND ST
SAN SEVAINE PARK (PROP)
LOMITA DR
ITALIA RD
SHEWFELT LN
ANTONIO LN
CITRUS AV
DUNCAN CANYON RD
COYOTE CANYON RD
ROADRUNNER RD
FOXBOROUGH DR
TRAILHEAD DR
RESERVOIR RD
DAWNRIDGE DR
DECLIFF DR
WARDMAN BULLOCK RD
LYTLE CREEK RD
1 LA SARRE DR
15

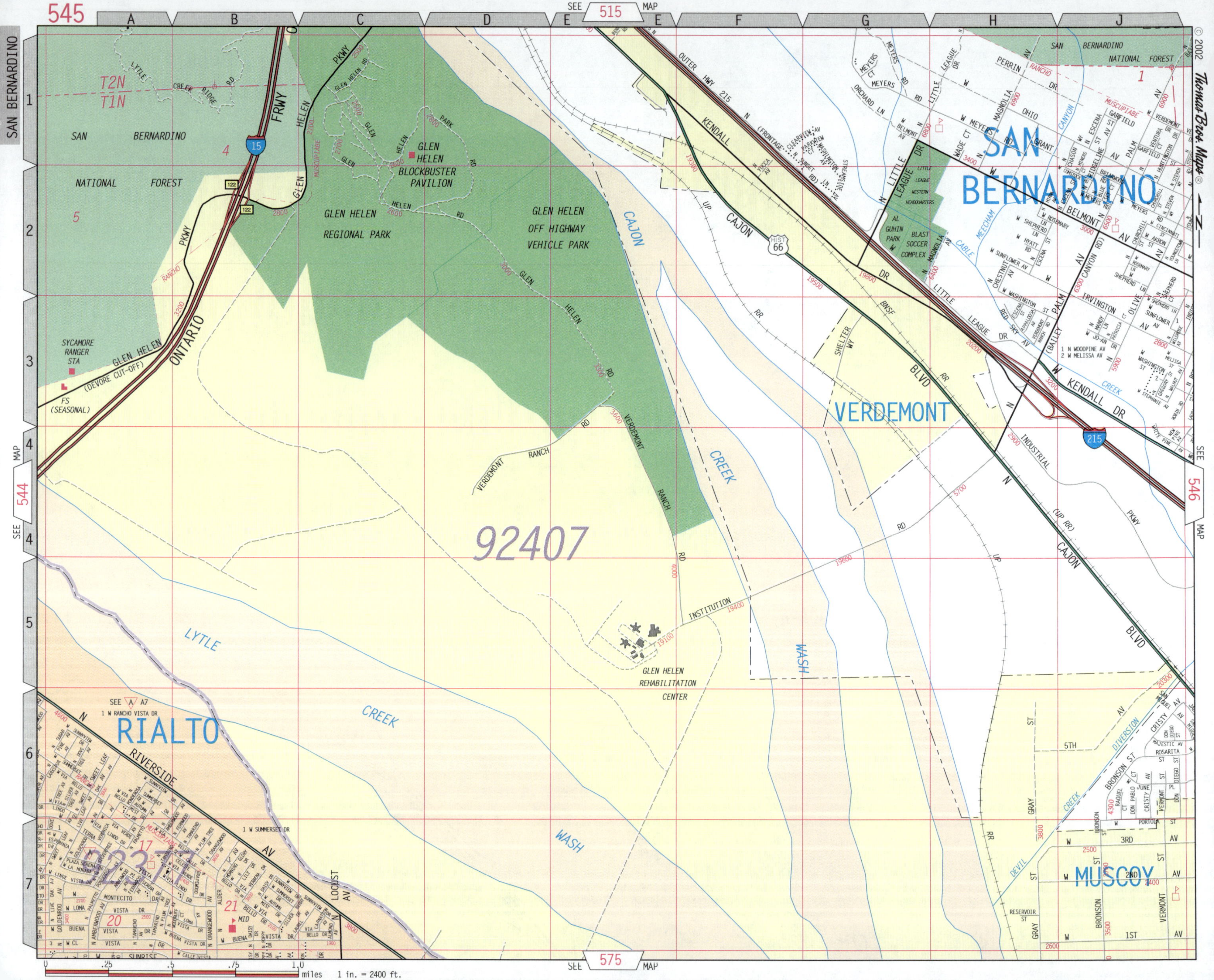

0 .25 .5 .75 1.0 miles 1 in. = 2400 ft.

SEE 516 MAP

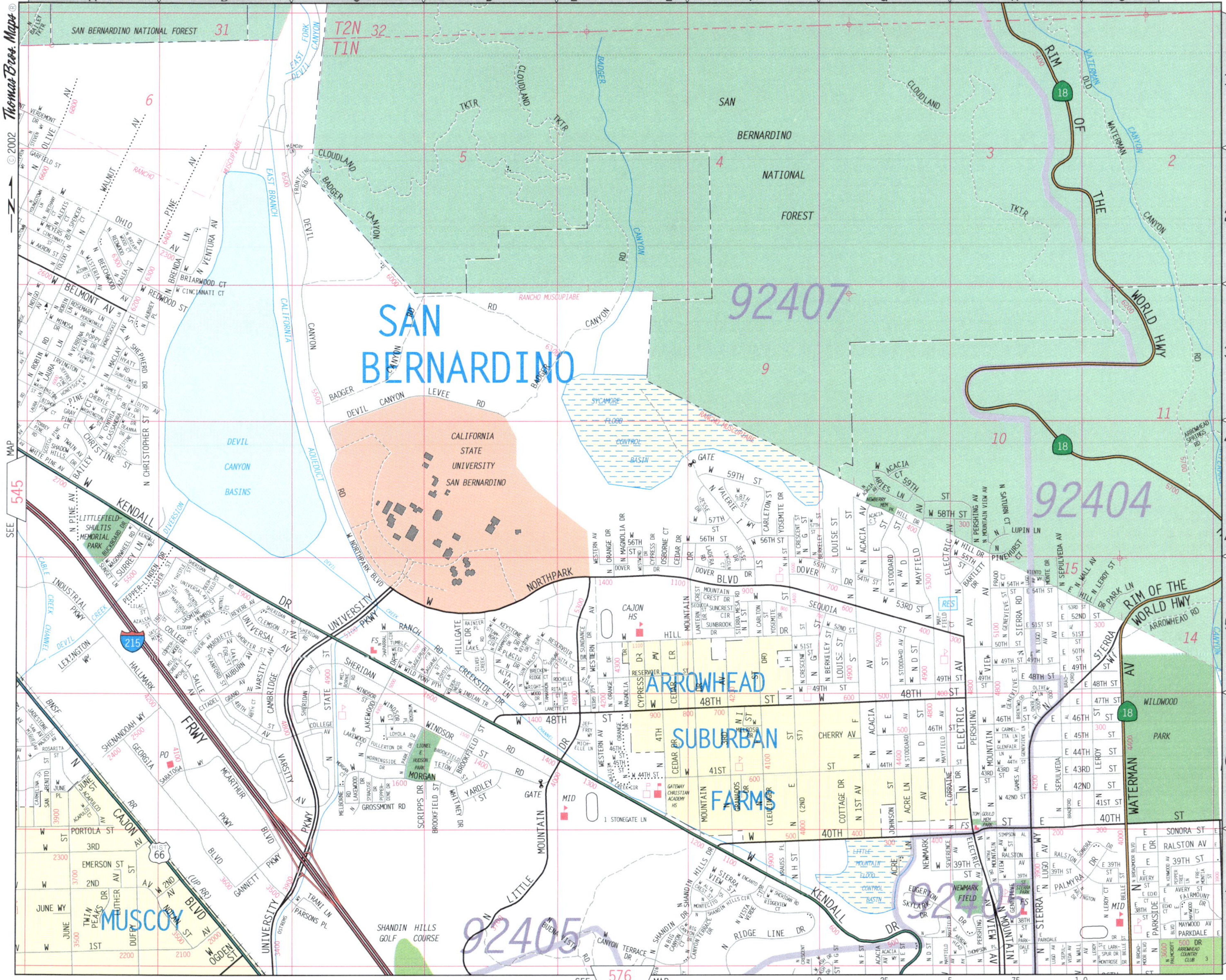

SEE 545 MAP

SEE 547 MAP

SEE 576 MAP

0 .25 .5 .75 1.0 miles 1 in. = 2400 ft.

SAN BERNARDINO

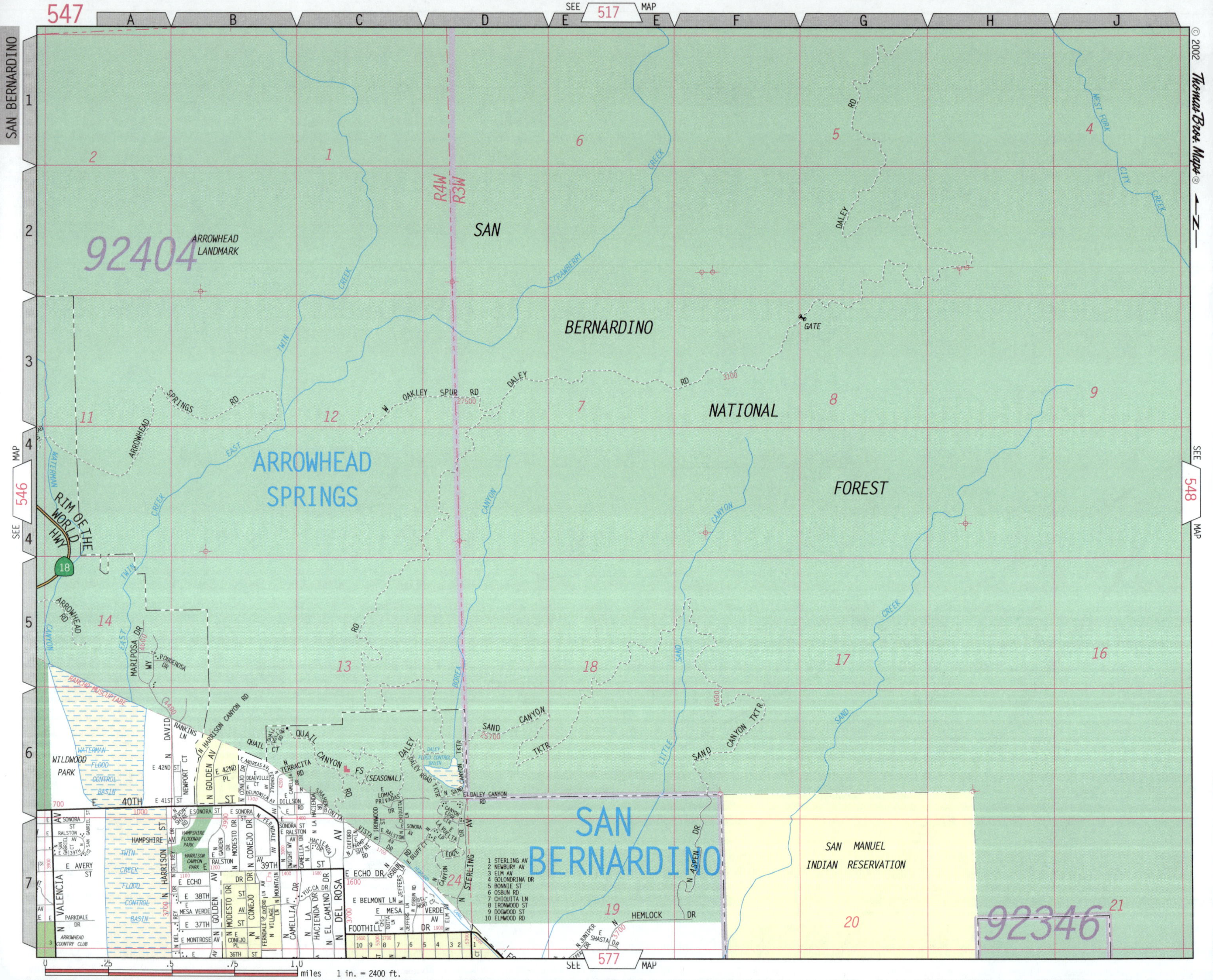
SEE 517 MAP
SEE 546 MAP
SEE 548 MAP
SEE 577 MAP
SAN BERNARDINO
92404
ARROWHEAD LANDMARK
SAN
BERNARDINO
NATIONAL
FOREST
R4W
R3W
ARROWHEAD SPRINGS
GATE
DALEY RD
W OAKLEY SPUR RD
SPRINGS RD
ARROWHEAD
TWIN CREEK
EAST TWIN
STRAWBERRY CREEK
EAST CREEK
WATERMAN CANYON
RIM OF THE WORLD HWY
18
CITY CREEK
WEST FORK
CANYON
LITTLE SAND CANYON
SAND CREEK
BOREA CANYON
SAND CANYON TKTR
ARROWHEAD RD
MARIPOSA DR
PONDEROSA DR
WY
RANKINS LN
HARRISON CANYON RD
DAVID
QUAIL CT
QUAIL CANYON RD
CANYON FS
(SEASONAL)
TERRACITA
WILDWOOD PARK
WATERMAN FLOOD CONTROL BASIN
RANCHO BUSCIPTARE
E 42ND ST
NEWPORT CT
GOLDEN AV
E 42ND PL
E 40TH ST
E 41ST ST
E SONORA ST
HAMPSHIRE AV
HARRISON ST
TWIN CREEK FLOOD CONTROL BASIN
HAMPSHIRE FLOODWAY PARK
HARRISON CANYON PARK
RALSTON
E ECHO
E 38TH ST
E 37TH ST
E MESA VERDE
E MONTROSE
36TH ST
MODESTO DR
CONEJO DR
CONEJO PL
DEL REY
VALENCIA AV
E AVERY ST
PARKDALE DR
ARROWHEAD COUNTRY CLUB
39TH
CAMELLIA DR
LA HACIENDA DR
EL CAMINO
DEL ROSA AV
E ECHO DR
E BELMONT LN
E MESA VERDE AV
FOOTHILL DR
OSBUN RD
JEFFERS
E DALEY CANYON RD
LAS VUELTA
STERLING AV
EDGE
24
SAN BERNARDINO
1 STERLING AV
2 NEWBURY AV
3 ELM AV
4 GOLONDRINA DR
5 BONNIE ST
6 OSBUN RD
7 CHIQUITA LN
8 IRONWOOD ST
9 DOGWOOD ST
10 ELMWOOD RD
HEMLOCK DR
N ASPEN DR
JUNIPER
SHASTA DR
SAN MANUEL INDIAN RESERVATION
92346
1 2 4 5 6 7 8 9 11 12 13 14 16 17 18 19 20 21
0 .25 .5 .75 1.0 miles 1 in. = 2400 ft.
© 2002 Thomas Bros. Maps ®

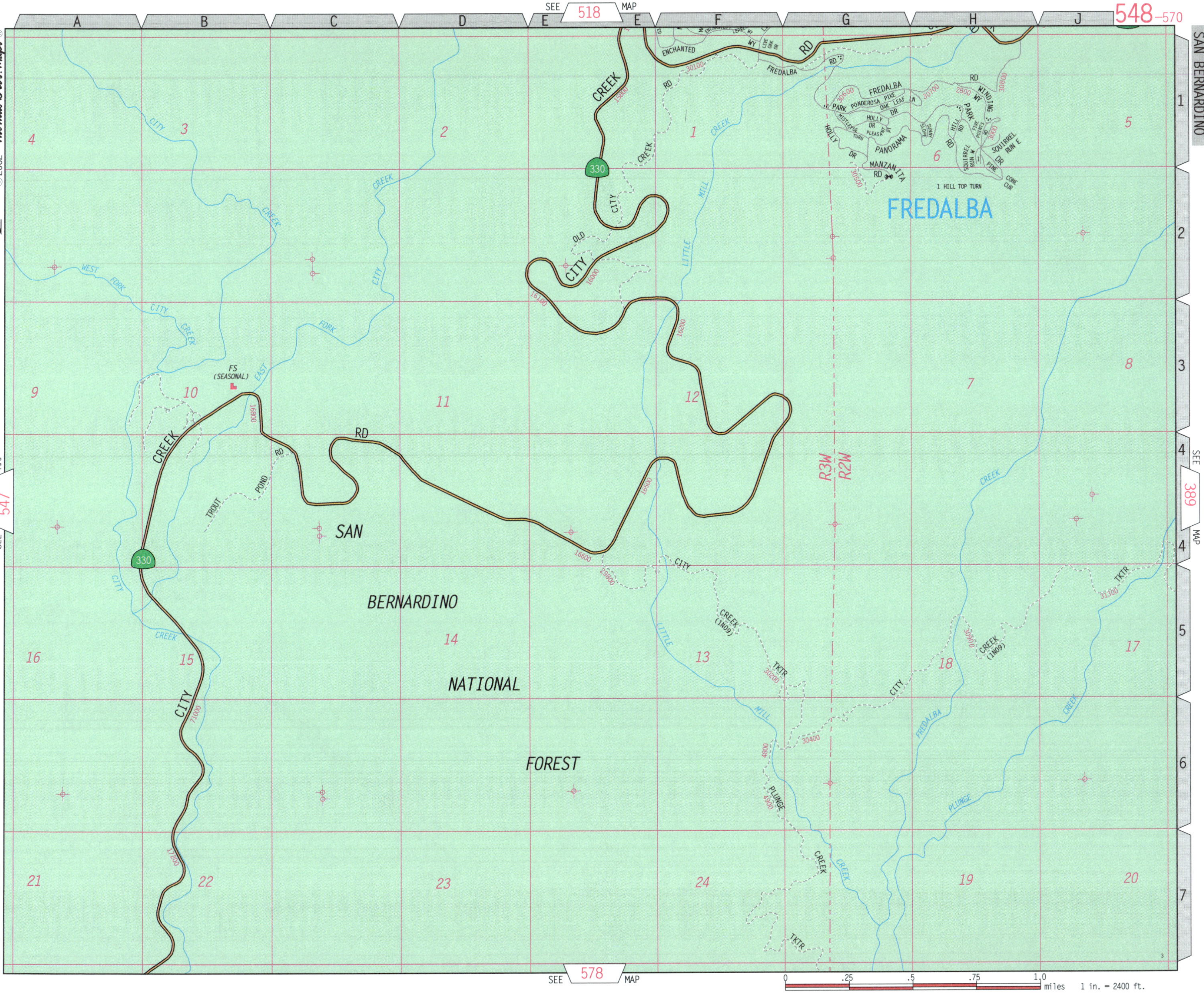
SEE 518 MAP
SEE 547 MAP
SEE 389 MAP
SEE 578 MAP
A
B
C
D
E
F
G
H
J
1
2
3
4
5
6
7
FREDALBA
SAN
BERNARDINO
NATIONAL
FOREST
330
CITY CREEK RD
OLD CITY CREEK RD
WEST FORK CITY CREEK
EAST FORK
LITTLE MILL CREEK
MILL CREEK
PLUNGE CREEK
FREDALBA CREEK
FS (SEASONAL)
TROUT POND RD
ENCHANTED
FREDALBA RD
PARK
PONDEROSA PIKE
OAK LEAF LN
HOLLY DR
PANORAMA
MANZANITA RD
WINDING WY
SQUIRREL RUN E
CONE CUR
1 HILL TOP TURN
CITY CREEK (1N09)
TKTR
R3W
R2W
0 .25 .5 .75 1.0 miles 1 in. = 2400 ft.

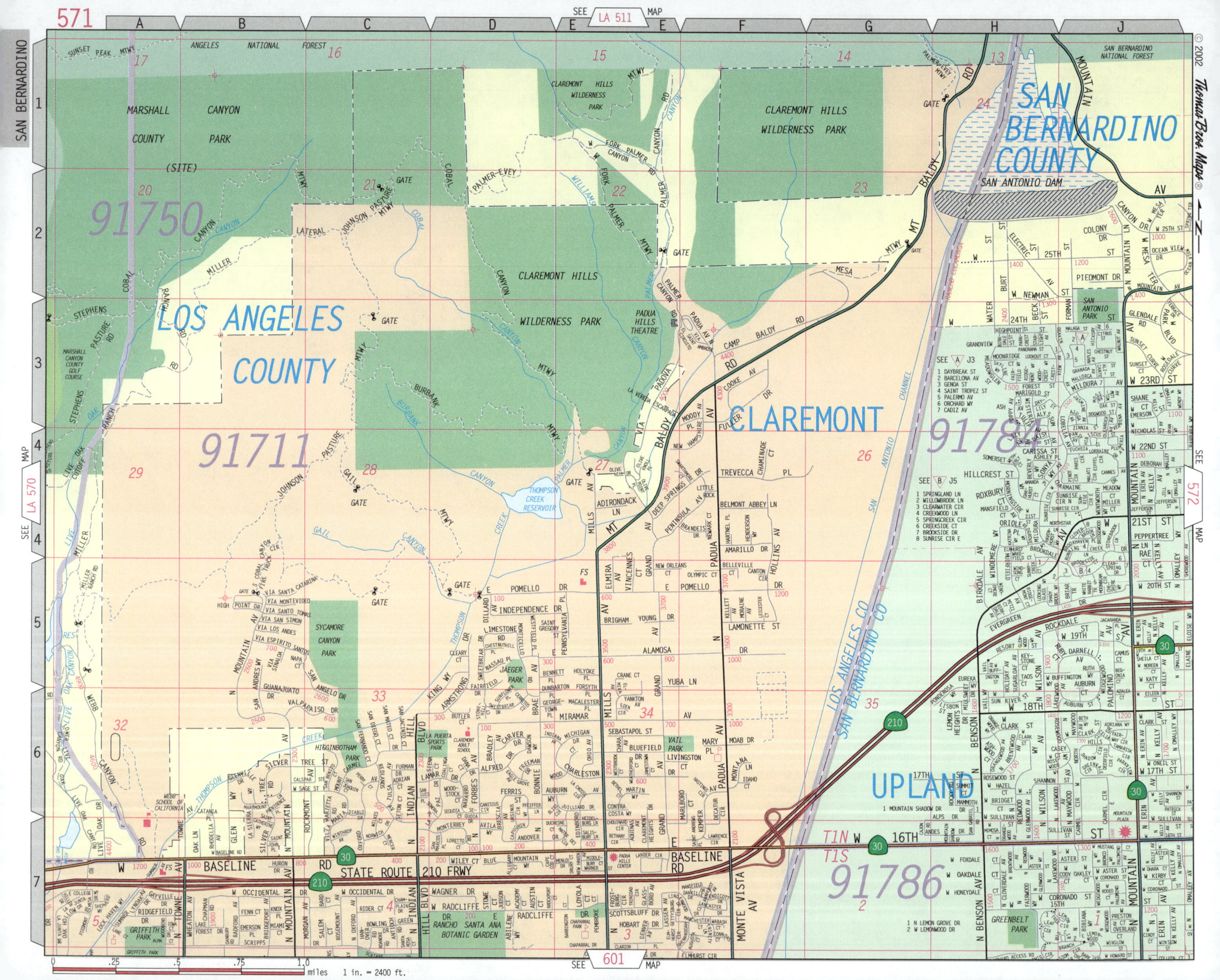
SEE LA 511 MAP
SEE LA 570 MAP
SEE 572 MAP
SEE 601 MAP
SAN BERNARDINO
© 2002 Thomas Bros. Maps ®
ANGELES NATIONAL FOREST
SAN BERNARDINO NATIONAL FOREST
MARSHALL CANYON COUNTY PARK (SITE)
MARSHALL CANYON COUNTY GOLF COURSE
CLAREMONT HILLS WILDERNESS PARK
LOS ANGELES COUNTY
SAN BERNARDINO COUNTY
CLAREMONT
UPLAND
SAN ANTONIO DAM
THOMPSON CREEK RESERVOIR
PADUA HILLS THEATRE
SYCAMORE CANYON PARK
JAEGER PARK
VAIL PARK
LA PUERTA SPORTS PARK
HIGGINBOTHAM PARK
WEBB SCHOOL OF CALIFORNIA
RANCHO SANTA ANA BOTANIC GARDEN
GRIFFITH PARK
GREENBELT PARK
PADUA HILLS CENTER
91750
91711
91786
LOS ANGELES CO
SAN BERNARDINO CO
SAN ANTONIO CHANNEL
BASELINE RD
STATE ROUTE 210 FRWY
MILLS AV
PADUA AV
MONTE VISTA AV
MOUNTAIN AV
TOWNE AV
INDIAN HILL BLVD
BENSON AV
CAMP BALDY RD
MT BALDY RD
FOOTHILL
W 16TH ST
W 19TH ST
W 18TH ST
W 17TH ST
W 20TH ST
W 21ST ST
W 22ND ST
W 23RD ST
24TH ST
25TH ST
POMELLO DR
INDEPENDENCE DR
ALAMOSA DR
MIRAMAR AV
SEE A J3
1 DAYBREAK ST
2 BARCELONA AV
3 GENOA ST
4 SAINT TROPEZ ST
5 PALERMO AV
6 ORCHARD WY
7 CADIZ AV
SEE B J5
1 SPRINGLAND LN
2 WILLOWBROOK LN
3 CLEARWATER CIR
4 CREEKWOOD LN
5 SPRINGCREEK CIR
6 CREEKSIDE CT
7 BROOKSIDE DR
8 SUNRISE CIR E
1 MOUNTAIN SHADOW DR
1 N LEMON GROVE DR
2 W LEMONWOOD DR
T1N
T1S
0 .25 .5 .75 1.0 miles 1 in. = 2400 ft.

SEE 513 MAP

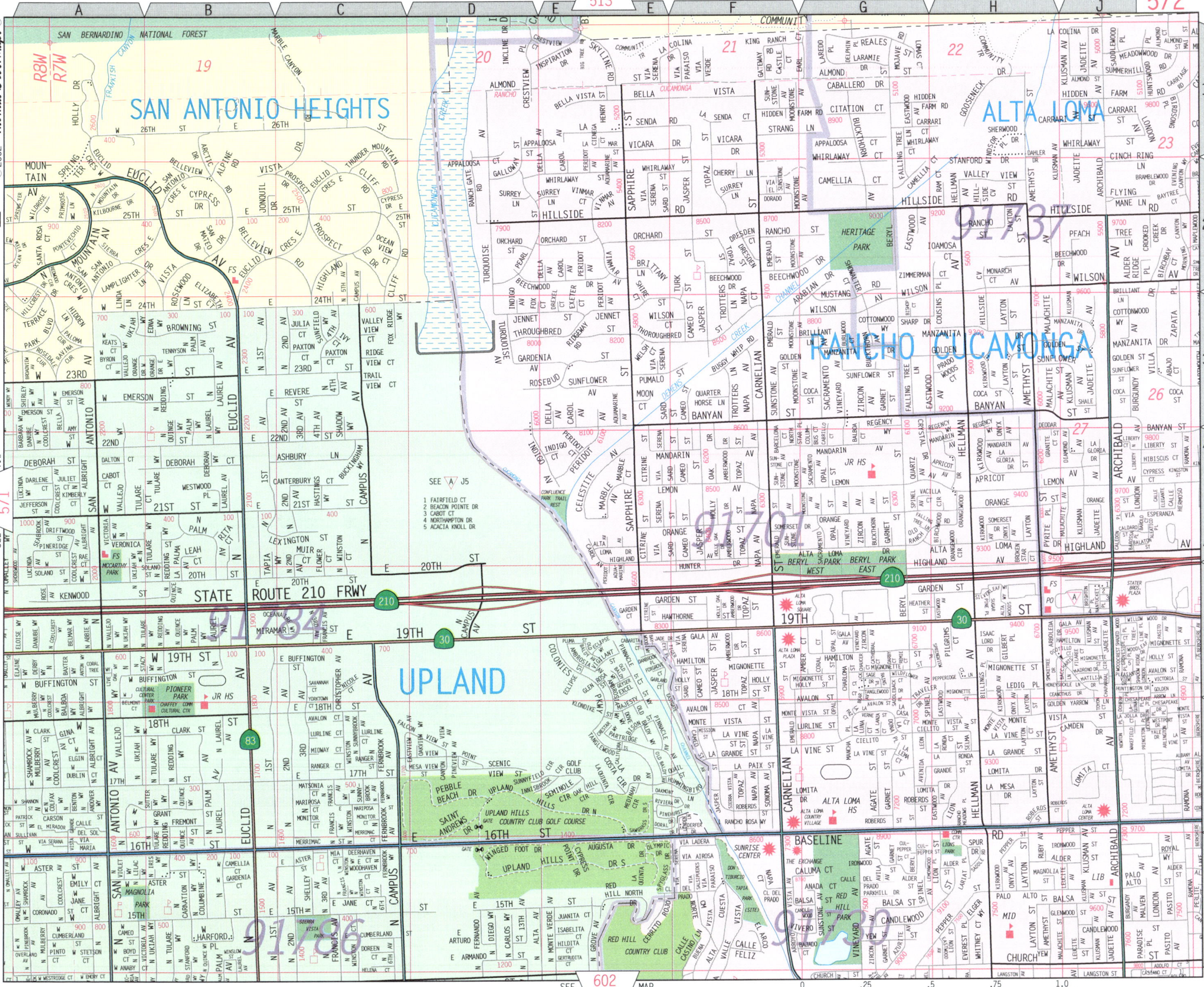

SEE 602 MAP

0 .25 .5 .75 1.0 miles 1 in. = 2400 ft.

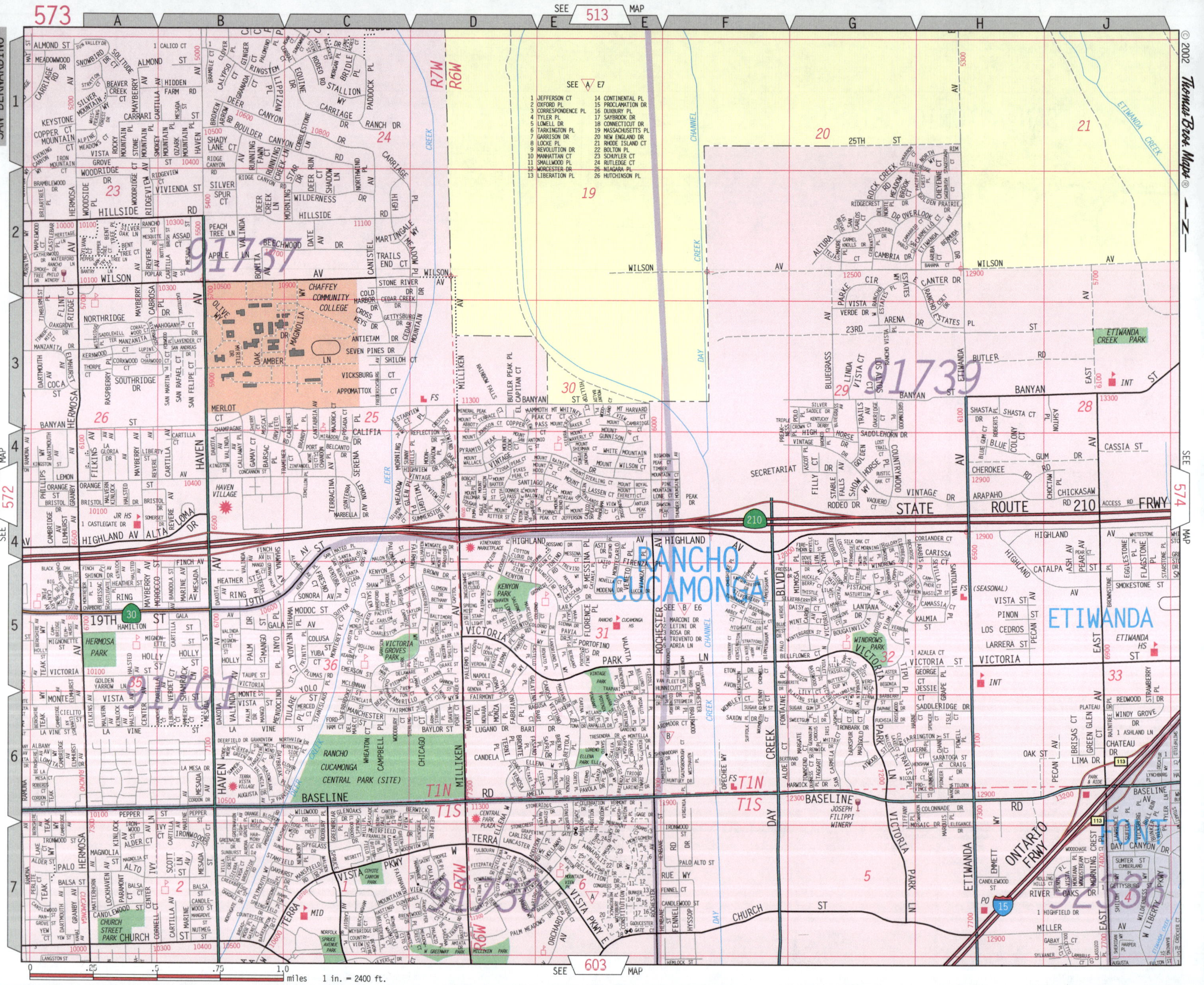
SEE 513 MAP
SEE 603 MAP
SEE 572 MAP
SEE 574 MAP
A
B
C
D
E
F
G
H
J
1
2
3
4
5
6
7
R7W
R6W
T1N
T1S
91737
91739
91701
91730
92336
RANCHO CUCAMONGA
ETIWANDA
FONTANA
CHAFFEY COMMUNITY COLLEGE
HAVEN VILLAGE
HERMOSA PARK
VICTORIA GROVES PARK
RANCHO CUCAMONGA CENTRAL PARK (SITE)
KENYON PARK
VINTAGE PARK
ELLENA PARK
WINDROWS PARK
CHURCH STREET PARK
COYOTE CANYON PARK
ETIWANDA CREEK PARK
JOSEPH FILIPPI WINERY
VINEYARDS MARKETPLACE
CENTRAL PARK PLAZA
RANCHO CUCAMONGA HS
ETIWANDA HS
STATE ROUTE 210 FRWY
ONTARIO FRWY
BASELINE RD
HIGHLAND AV
VICTORIA PARK LN
WILSON AV
BANYAN ST
CHURCH ST
19TH ST
HAVEN AV
MILLIKEN AV
ROCHESTER AV
DAY CREEK BLVD
ETIWANDA AV
EAST AV
HERMOSA AV
CARNELIAN ST
VISTA PKWY
TERRA VISTA PKWY
DEER CREEK
DAY CREEK CHANNEL
ETIWANDA CREEK
SEE A E7
1 JEFFERSON CT
2 OXFORD PL
3 CORRESPONDENCE PL
4 TYLER PL
5 LOWELL DR
6 TARKINGTON PL
7 GARRISON DR
8 LOCKE PL
9 REVOLUTION DR
10 MANHATTAN CT
11 SMALLWOOD PL
12 WORCESTER DR
13 LIBERATION PL
14 CONTINENTAL PL
15 PROCLAMATION DR
16 DUXBURY PL
17 SAYBROOK DR
18 CONNECTICUT DR
19 MASSACHUSETTS PL
20 NEW ENGLAND DR
21 RHODE ISLAND CT
22 BOLTON PL
23 SCHUYLER CT
24 RUTLEDGE CT
25 NIAGARA PL
26 HUTCHINSON PL
SEE B E6
1 MARCONI DR
2 LETINI DR
3 ROSA DR
4 TRIVENTO DR
5 ADRIA LN
0 .25 .5 .75 1.0 miles 1 in. = 2400 ft.

SEE 544 MAP

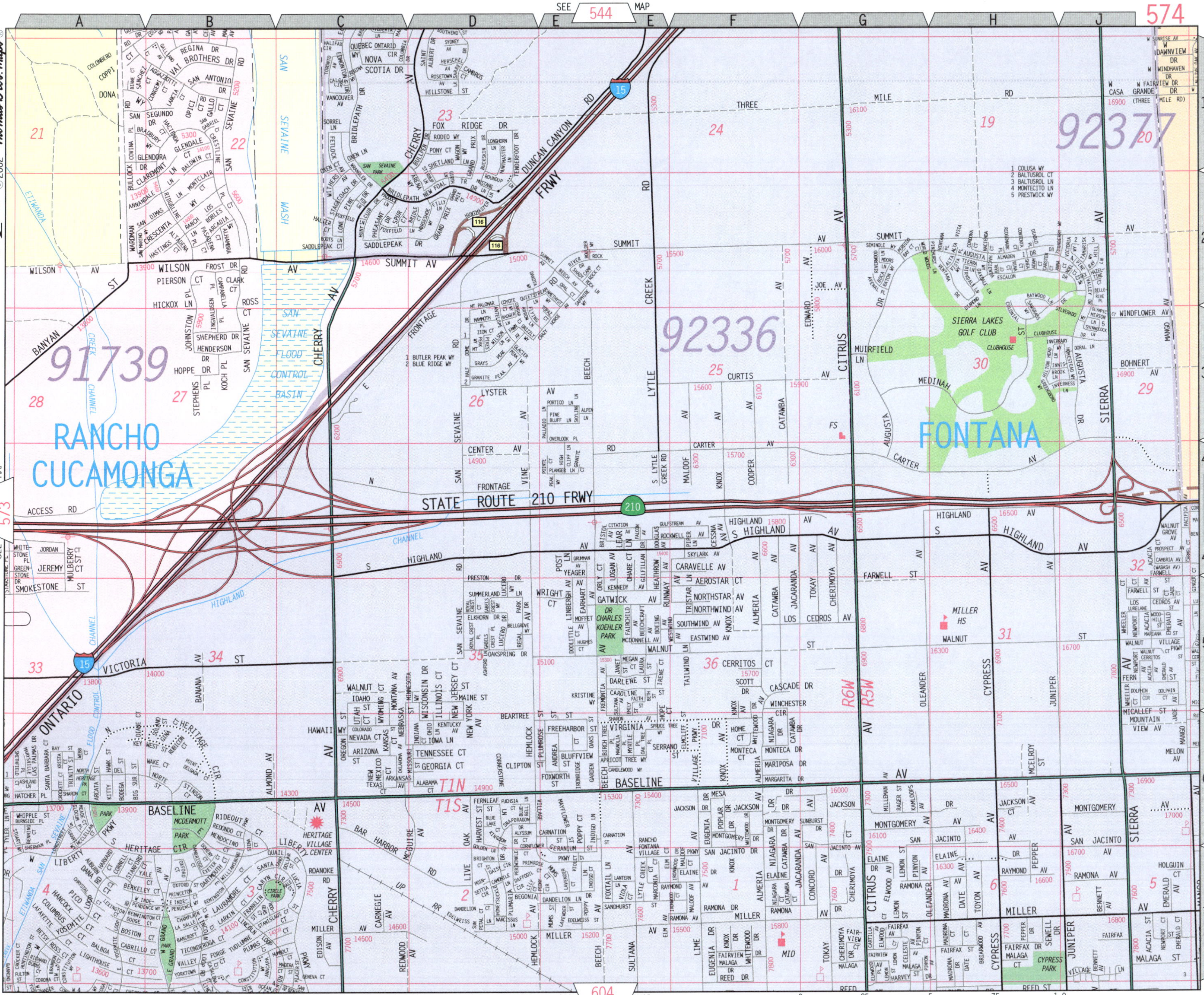

SEE 573 MAP
SEE 575 MAP
SEE 604 MAP

0 .25 .5 .75 1.0 miles 1 in. = 2400 ft.

SEE 545 MAP

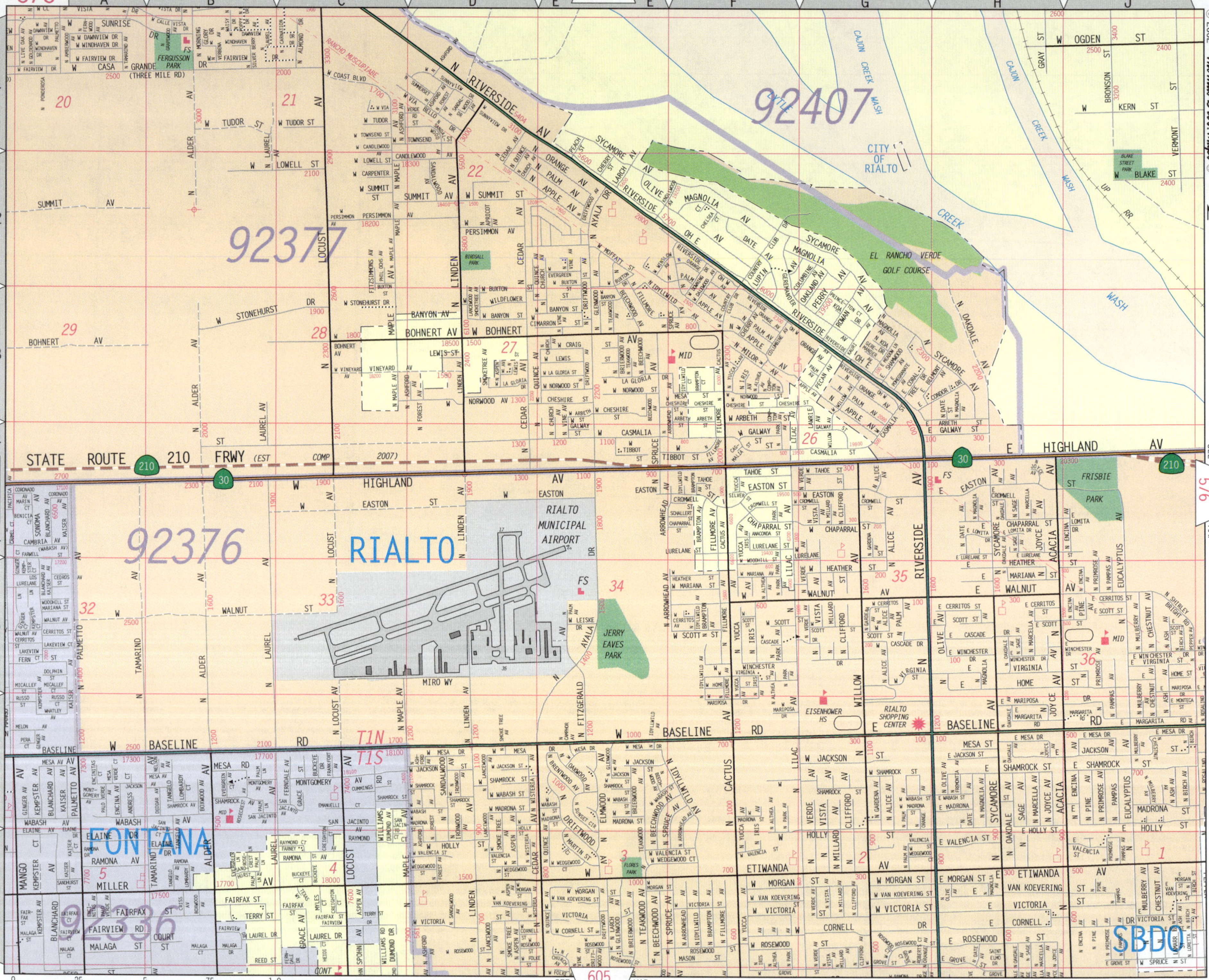

SEE 605 MAP

SEE 546 MAP

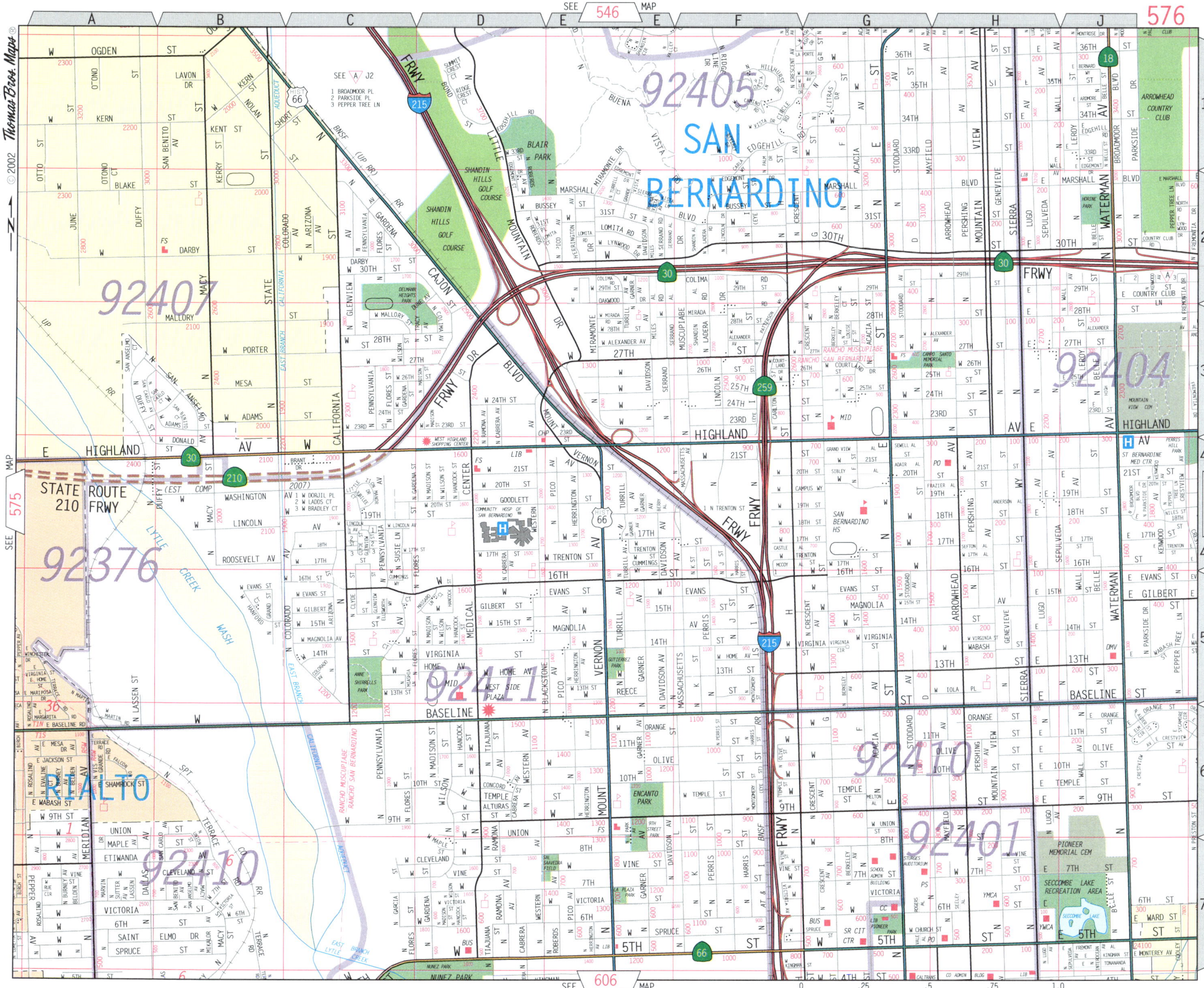

SEE 575 MAP
SEE 577 MAP
SEE 606 MAP

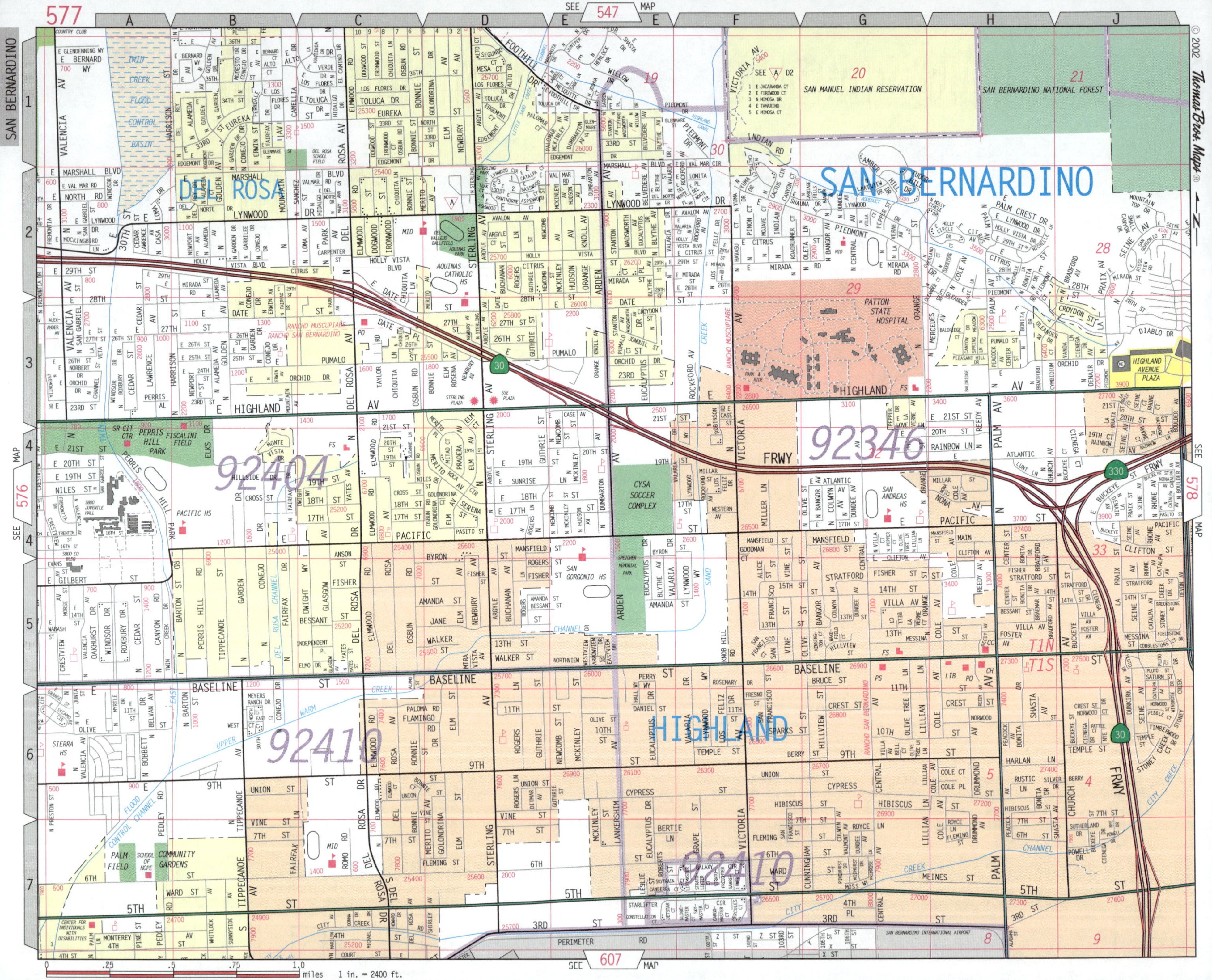
SAN BERNARDINO
SEE 547 MAP
SEE 576 MAP
SEE 578 MAP
SEE 607 MAP
A
B
C
D
E
F
G
H
J
1
2
3
4
5
6
7
DEL ROSA
SAN BERNARDINO
HIGHLAND
92404
92346
92410
SAN MANUEL INDIAN RESERVATION
SAN BERNARDINO NATIONAL FOREST
PATTON STATE HOSPITAL
HIGHLAND AVENUE PLAZA
PERRIS HILL PARK
FISCALINI FIELD
CYSA SOCCER COMPLEX
SAN GORGONIO HS
PACIFIC HS
SIERRA HS
SAN ANDREAS HS
AQUINAS CATHOLIC HS
PALM FIELD
COMMUNITY GARDENS
TWIN CREEK FLOOD CONTROL BASIN
SAN BERNARDINO INTERNATIONAL AIRPORT
FOOTHILL
HIGHLAND
BASELINE
PACIFIC
FRWY
PERIMETER RD
T1N
T1S
0 .25 .5 .75 1.0 miles 1 in. = 2400 ft.
© 2002 Thomas Bros. Maps®

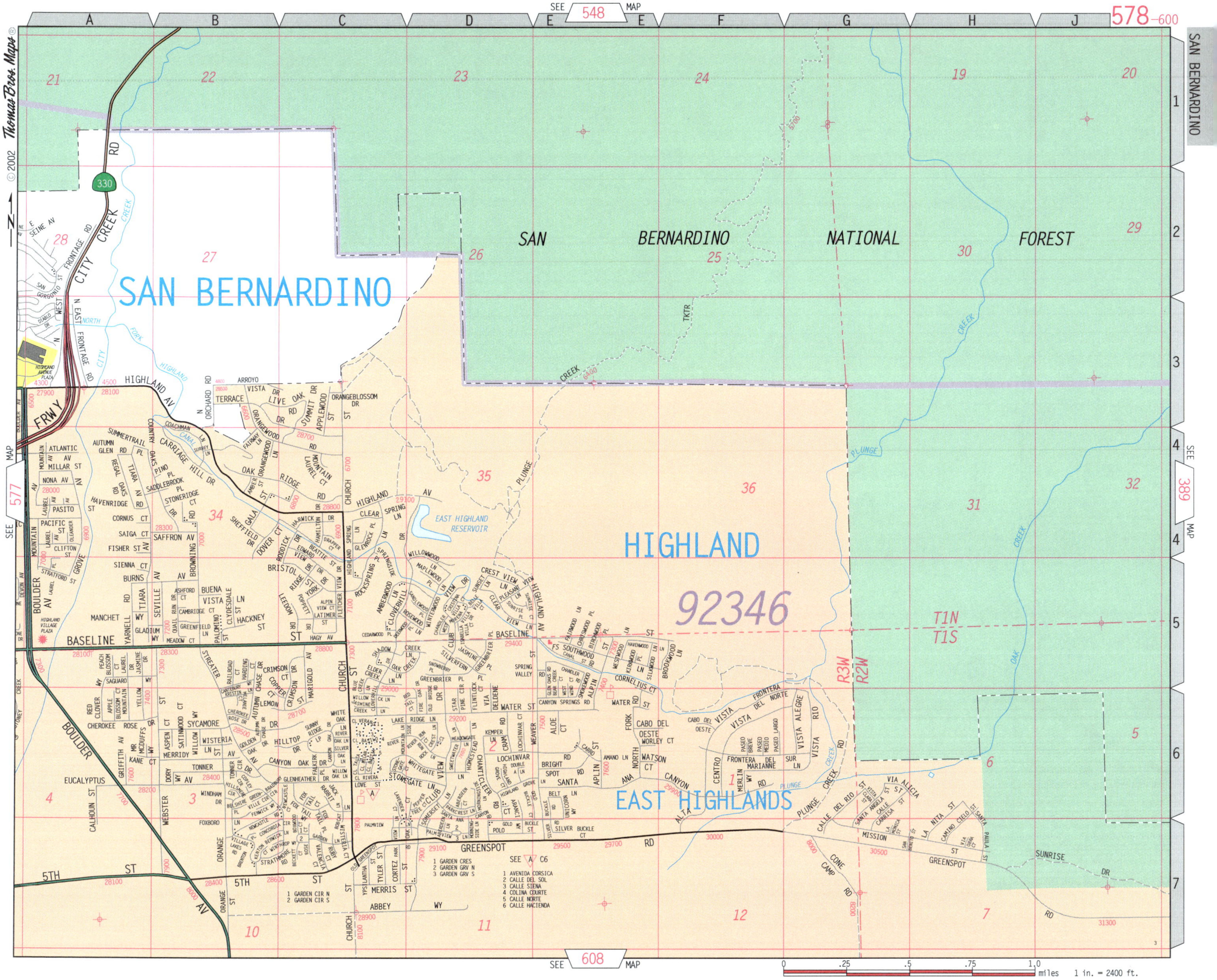
578-600
SAN BERNARDINO
SEE 548 MAP
SEE 608 MAP
SEE 577 MAP
SEE 389 MAP
Thomas Bros. Maps
© 2002
SAN BERNARDINO NATIONAL FOREST
SAN BERNARDINO
HIGHLAND
EAST HIGHLANDS
92346
EAST HIGHLAND RESERVOIR
CITY CREEK RD
330
HIGHLAND AV
BASELINE
5TH ST
GREENSPOT RD
BOULDER AV
CHURCH ST
PLUNGE CREEK
OAK CREEK
T1N
T1S
R3W
R2W
1 GARDEN CRES
2 GARDEN GRV N
3 GARDEN GRV S
1 GARDEN CIR N
2 GARDEN CIR S
1 AVENIDA CORSICA
2 CALLE DEL SOL
3 CALLE SIENA
4 COLINA COURTE
5 CALLE NORTE
6 CALLE HACIENDA
miles 1 in. = 2400 ft.

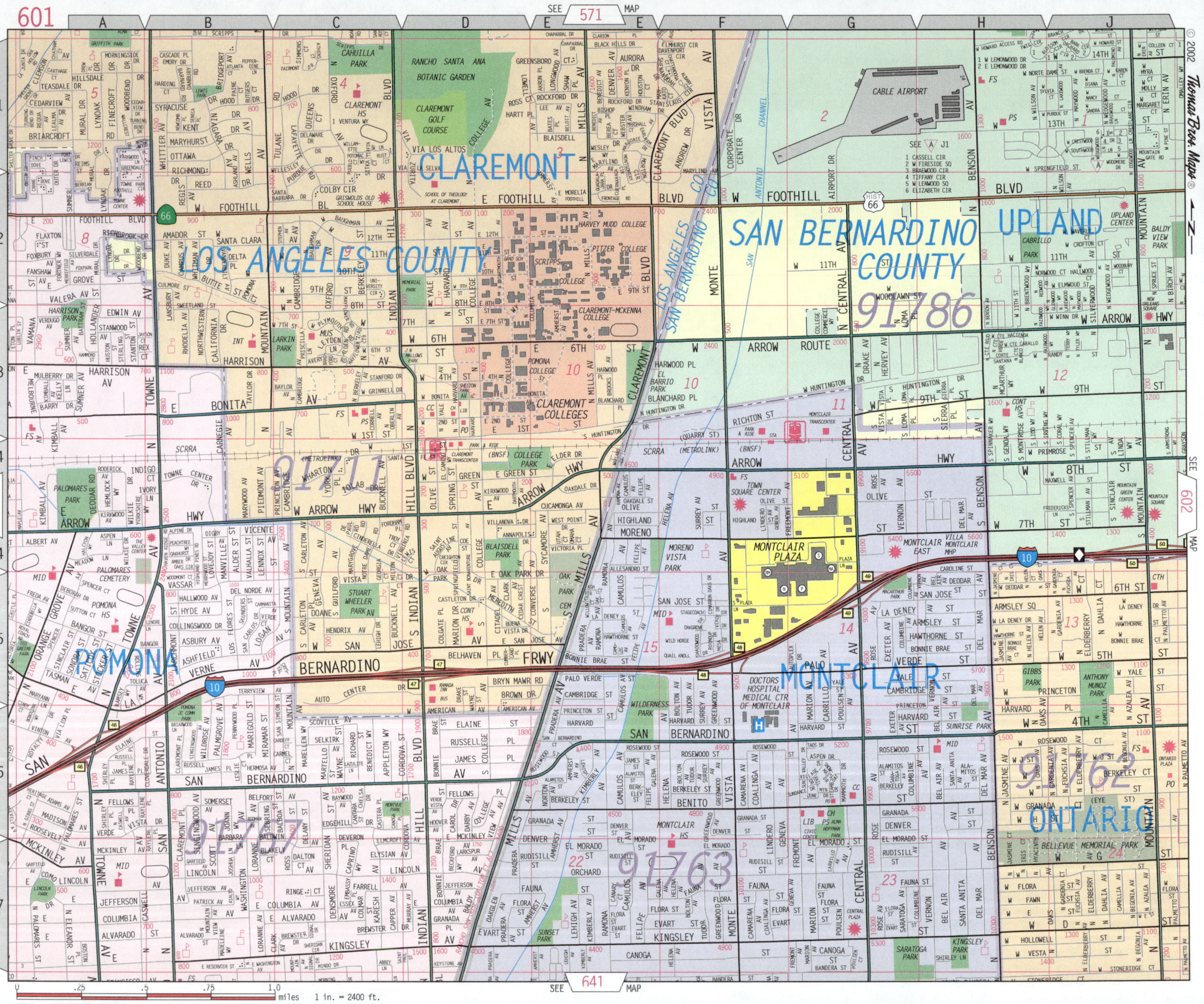
SAN BERNARDINO
SEE 571 MAP
SEE 641 MAP
SEE LA 600 MAP
SEE 602 MAP
CLAREMONT
LOS ANGELES COUNTY
SAN BERNARDINO COUNTY
UPLAND
POMONA
MONTCLAIR
ONTARIO
91711
91786
91767
91763
91762
RANCHO SANTA ANA BOTANIC GARDEN
CLAREMONT GOLF COURSE
CABLE AIRPORT
HARVEY MUDD COLLEGE
PITZER COLLEGE
SCRIPPS COLLEGE
CLAREMONT-MCKENNA COLLEGE
POMONA COLLEGE
CLAREMONT COLLEGES
MONTCLAIR PLAZA
PALOMARES CEMETERY
DOCTORS HOSPITAL MEDICAL CTR OF MONTCLAIR
MONTCLAIR HS
CLAREMONT HS
POMONA HS
WILDERNESS PARK
FOOTHILL BLVD
ARROW HWY
ARROW ROUTE
SAN BERNARDINO FRWY
SAN BERNARDINO AV
HOLT
TOWNE AV
INDIAN HILL BLVD
MILLS AV
MONTE VISTA
CENTRAL AV
BENSON AV
MOUNTAIN AV
LOS ANGELES CO
SAN BERNARDINO CO
SAN ANTONIO CHANNEL
0 .25 .5 .75 1.0 miles 1 in. = 2400 ft.
© 2002 Thomas Bros. Maps ®

SEE 572 MAP

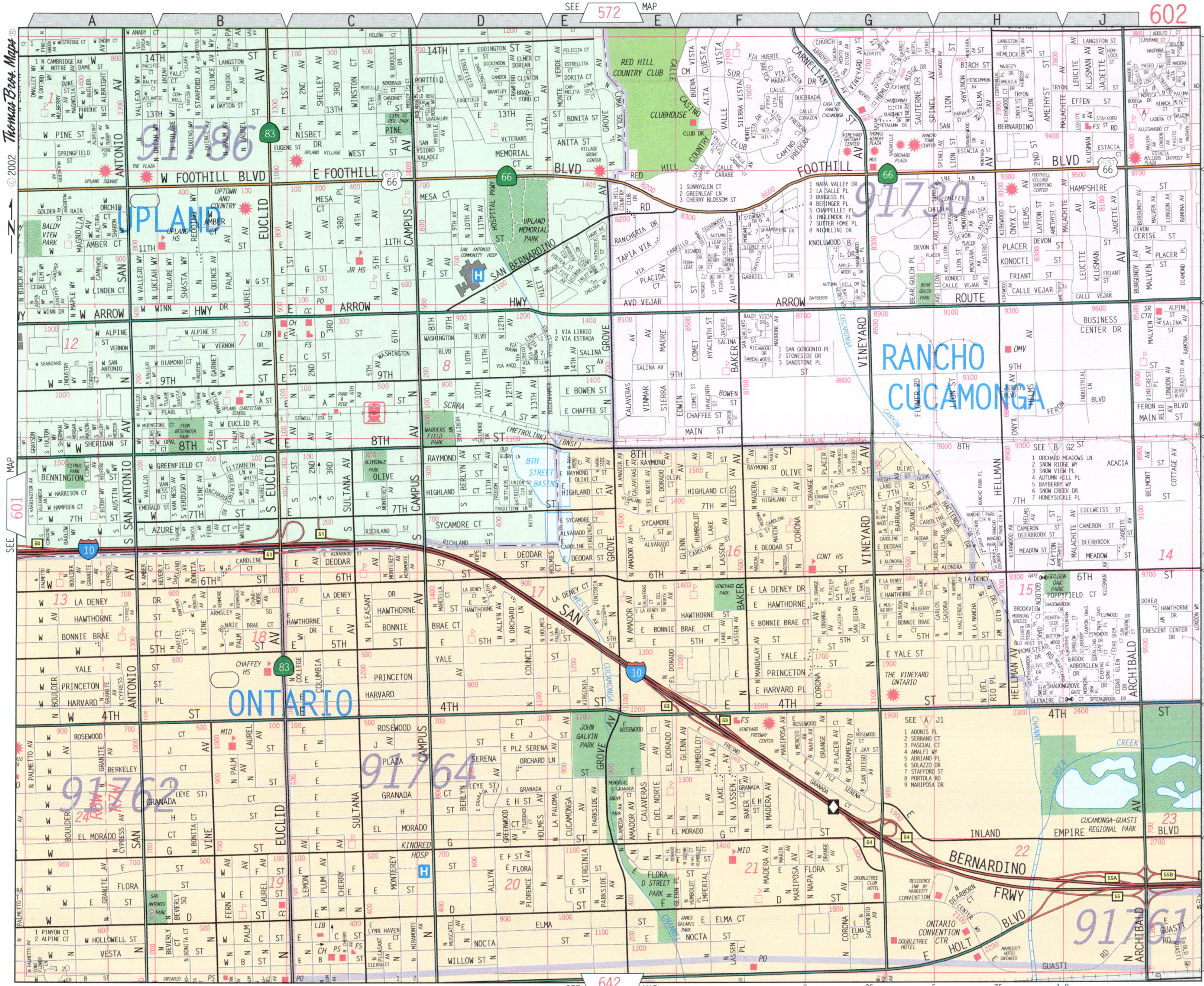

SEE 601 MAP
SEE 603 MAP
SEE 642 MAP

0 .25 .5 .75 1.0 miles 1 in. = 2400 ft.

SEE 573 MAP

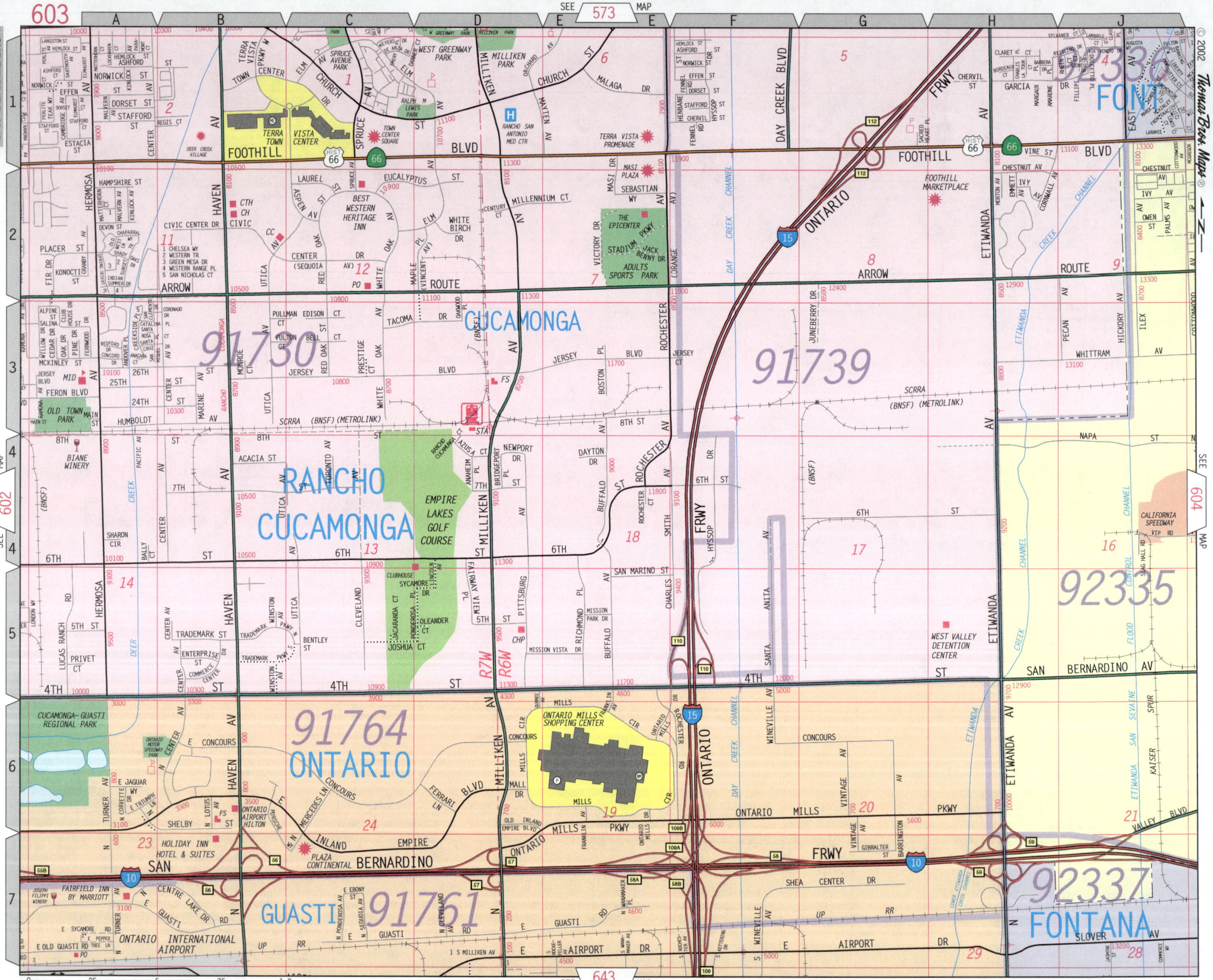

0 .25 .5 .75 1.0 miles 1 in. = 2400 ft.

SEE 643 MAP

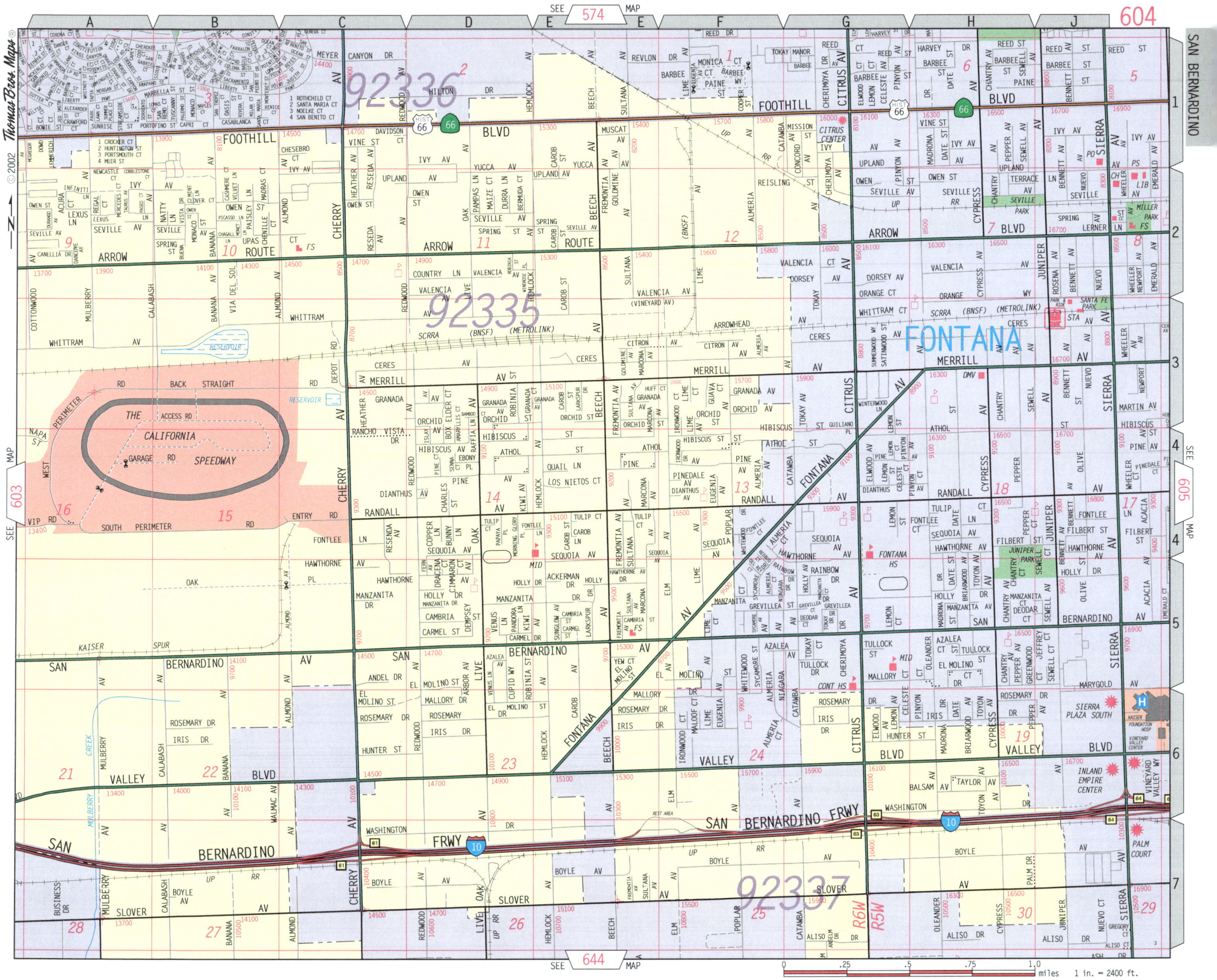
SEE 574 MAP
SEE 644 MAP
SEE 603 MAP
SEE 605 MAP
SAN BERNARDINO
FONTANA
92336
92335
92337
FOOTHILL BLVD
ARROW ROUTE
ARROW BLVD
MERRILL AV
RANDALL AV
SAN BERNARDINO AV
VALLEY BLVD
SAN BERNARDINO FRWY
SLOVER AV
THE CALIFORNIA SPEEDWAY
CHERRY AV
CITRUS AV
SIERRA AV
FONTANA AV
FONTANA HS
JUNIPER PARK
MILLER PARK
SEVILLE PARK
SANTA FE PARK
INLAND EMPIRE CENTER
SIERRA PLAZA SOUTH
PALM COURT
KAISER FOUNDATION HOSP
RESERVOIR
R6W
R5W
Thomas Bros. Maps
© 2002
0 .25 .5 .75 1.0 miles 1 in. = 2400 ft.

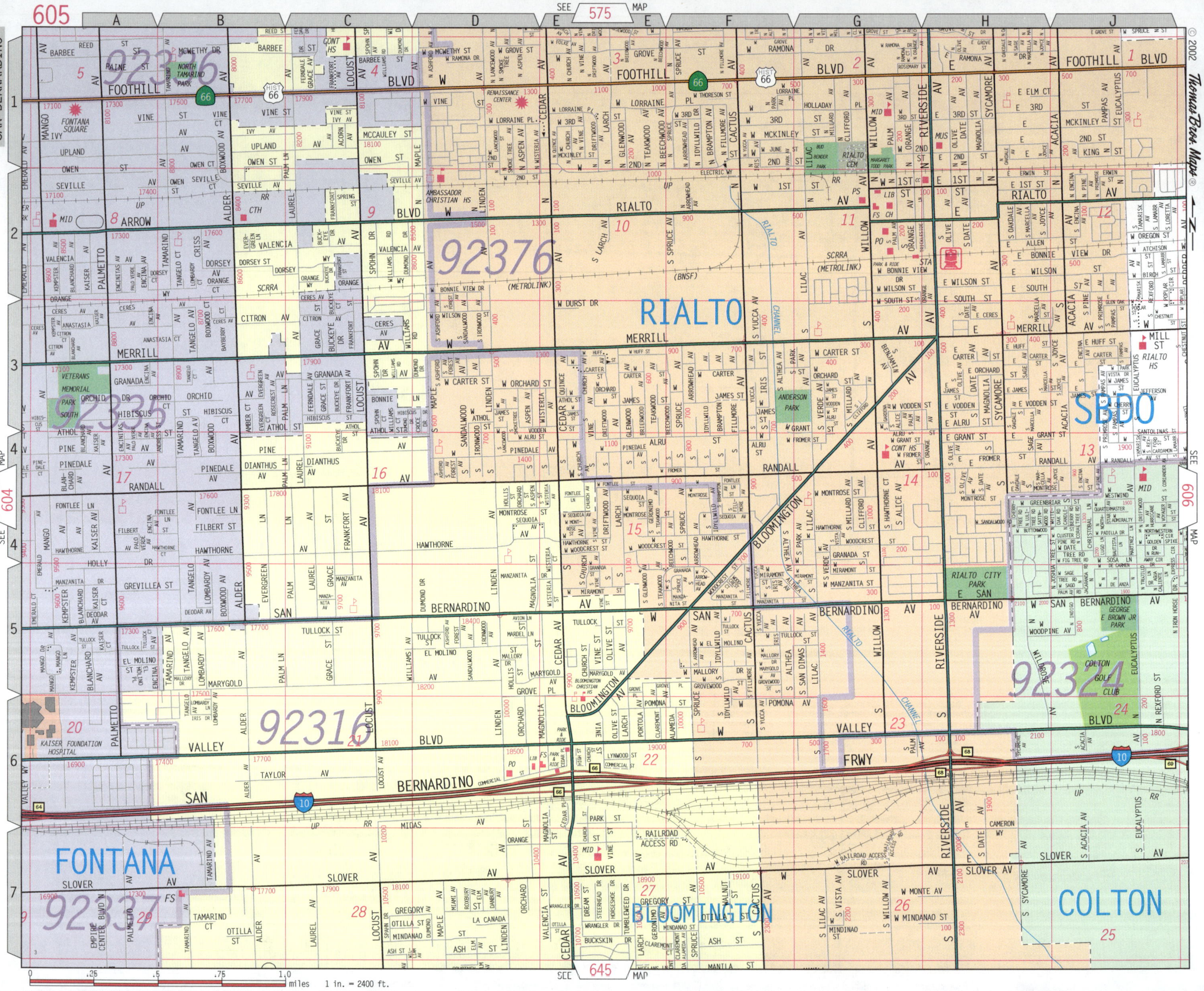
SAN BERNARDINO
SEE 575 MAP
SEE 604 MAP
SEE 606 MAP
SEE 645 MAP
A
B
C
D
E
F
G
H
J
1
2
3
4
5
6
7
RIALTO
FONTANA
BLOOMINGTON
COLTON
SBDO
92376
92335
92316
92324
92337
FOOTHILL BLVD
RIALTO AV
MERRILL AV
RANDALL AV
SAN BERNARDINO AV
VALLEY BLVD
SAN BERNARDINO FRWY
SLOVER AV
ARROW BLVD
BLOOMINGTON AV
CEDAR AV
RIVERSIDE AV
LOCUST AV
ALDER AV
LINDEN AV
WILLOW AV
ACACIA AV
EUCALYPTUS AV
PEPPER AV
RIALTO CHANNEL
RIALTO CITY PARK
ANDERSON PARK
RIALTO CEM
NORTH TAMARIND PARK
VETERANS MEMORIAL PARK
COLTON GOLF CLUB
GEORGE E BROWN JR PARK
KAISER FOUNDATION HOSPITAL
FONTANA SQUARE
RENAISSANCE CENTER
AMBASSADOR CHRISTIAN HS
RIALTO HS
(METROLINK)
(BNSF)
0 .25 .5 .75 1.0 miles 1 in. = 2400 ft.
© 2002 Thomas Bros. Maps ®

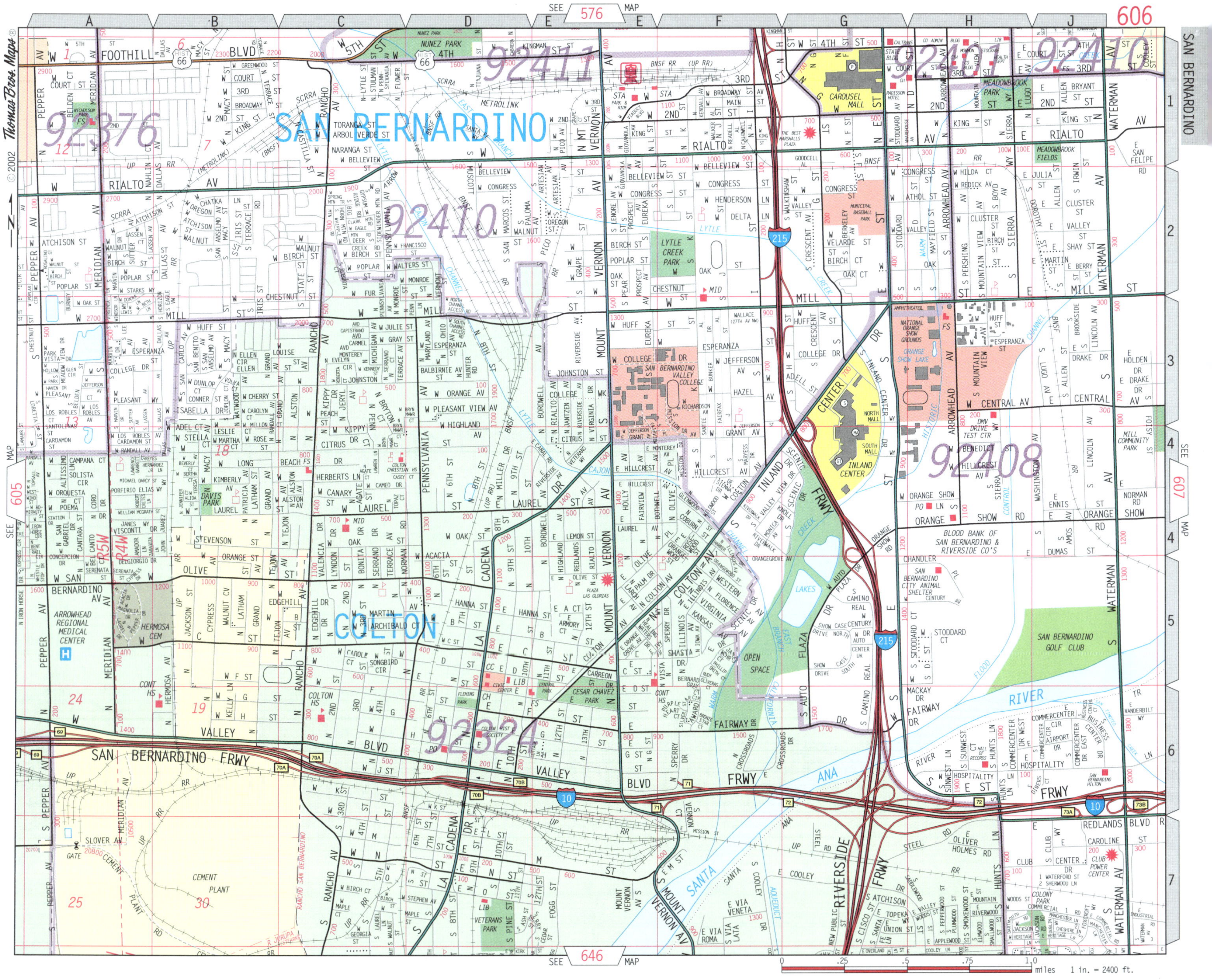
SEE 576 MAP
SEE 646 MAP
SEE 605 MAP
SEE 607 MAP
SAN BERNARDINO
COLTON
92376
92410
92411
92401
92408
92324
FOOTHILL BLVD
RIALTO AV
MILL ST
VALLEY BLVD
SAN BERNARDINO FRWY
INLAND CENTER DR
MOUNT VERNON AV
WATERMAN AV
PEPPER AV
MERIDIAN AV
RANCHO AV
CAROUSEL MALL
INLAND CENTER
SAN BERNARDINO VALLEY COLLEGE
NATIONAL ORANGE SHOW GROUNDS
ARROWHEAD REGIONAL MEDICAL CENTER
HERMOSA CEM
LYTLE CREEK PARK
CESAR CHAVEZ PARK
SAN BERNARDINO GOLF CLUB
OPEN SPACE
CEMENT PLANT
SANTA ANA RIVER
BLOOD BANK OF SAN BERNARDINO & RIVERSIDE CO'S
SAN BERNARDINO CITY ANIMAL SHELTER
miles
1 in. = 2400 ft.
© 2002 Thomas Bros. Maps

SEE 577 MAP

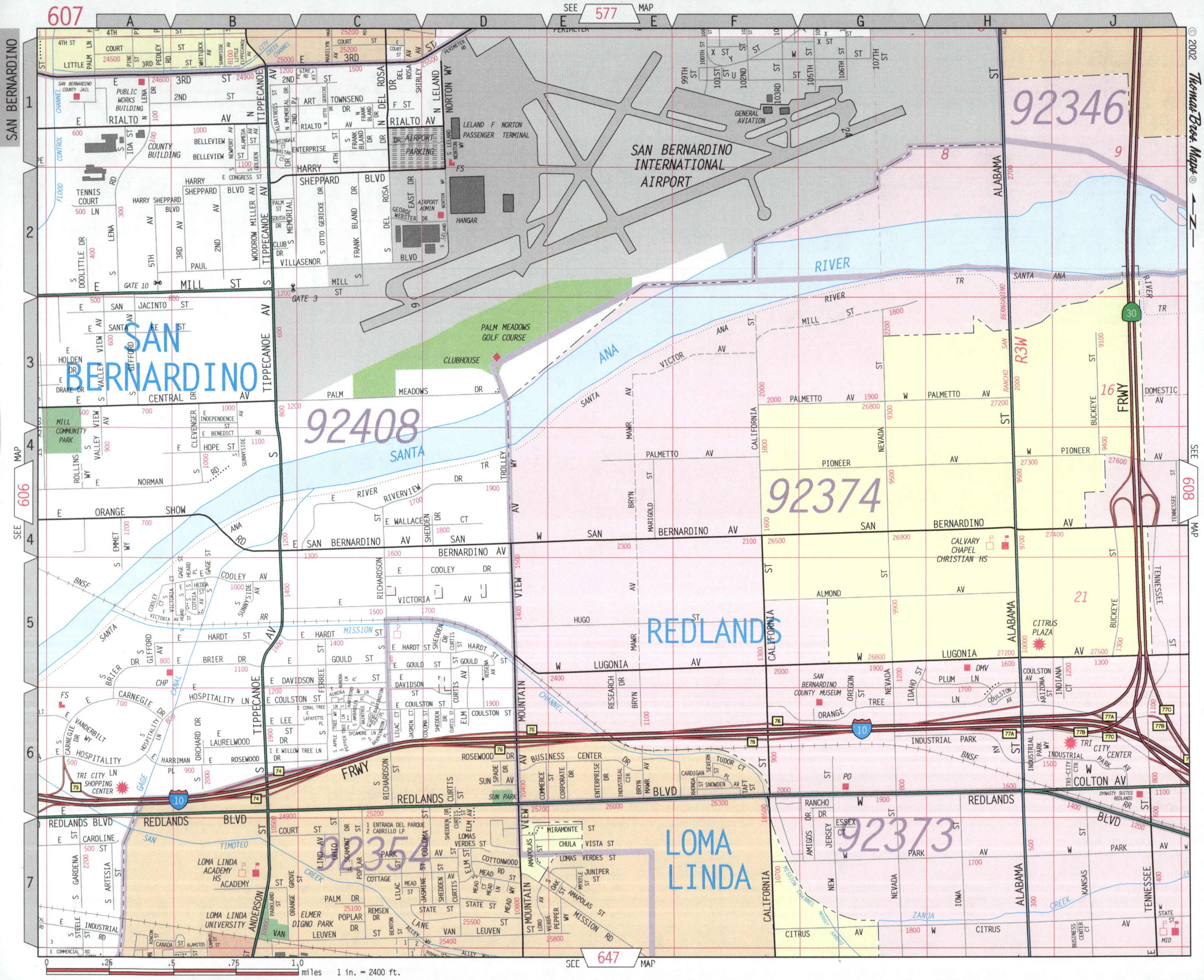

0 .25 .5 .75 1.0 miles 1 in. = 2400 ft.

SEE 647 MAP

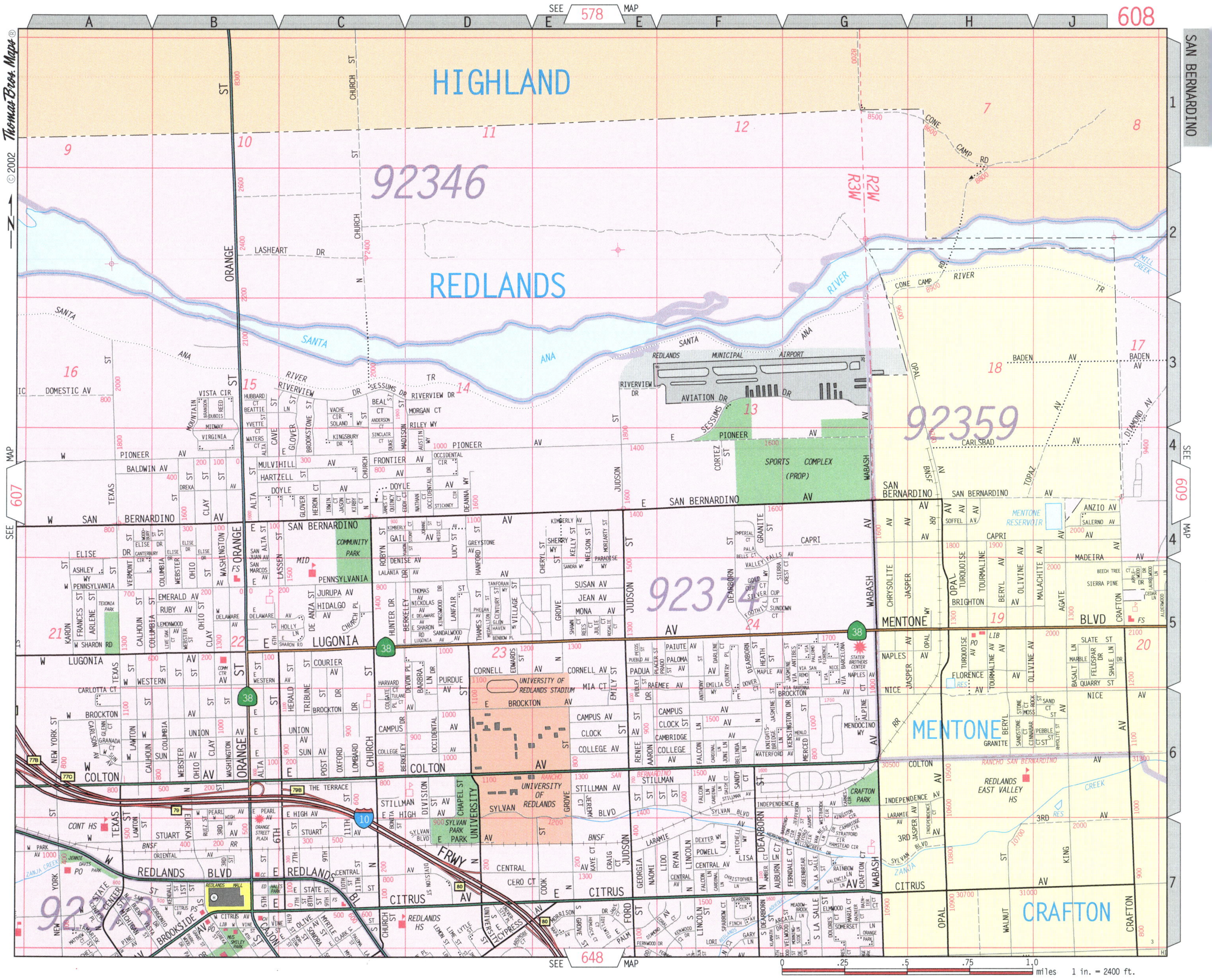
SEE 578 MAP
SEE 648 MAP
SEE 607 MAP
SEE 609 MAP
SAN BERNARDINO
HIGHLAND
REDLANDS
MENTONE
CRAFTON
92346
92359
92374
SANTA ANA RIVER
REDLANDS MUNICIPAL AIRPORT
SPORTS COMPLEX (PROP)
UNIVERSITY OF REDLANDS
UNIVERSITY OF REDLANDS STADIUM
REDLANDS EAST VALLEY HS
REDLANDS HS
SYLVAN PARK
COMMUNITY PARK
CRAFTON PARK
MENTONE RESERVOIR
ORANGE STREET PLAZA
REDLANDS MALL
STATER BROTHERS CENTER
RANCHO SAN BERNARDINO
ZANJA CREEK
MILL CREEK
R3W R2W
ORANGE ST
SAN BERNARDINO AV
LUGONIA AV
MENTONE BLVD
COLTON AV
REDLANDS BLVD
CITRUS AV
PIONEER AV
WABASH AV
JUDSON ST
CHURCH ST
UNIVERSITY ST
OPAL AV
CRAFTON AV
ALABAMA ST
DEARBORN ST
STILLMAN AV
BROCKTON AV
SYLVAN BLVD
FRWY
Thomas Bros. Maps ®
© 2002
0 .25 .5 .75 1.0 miles 1 in. = 2400 ft.

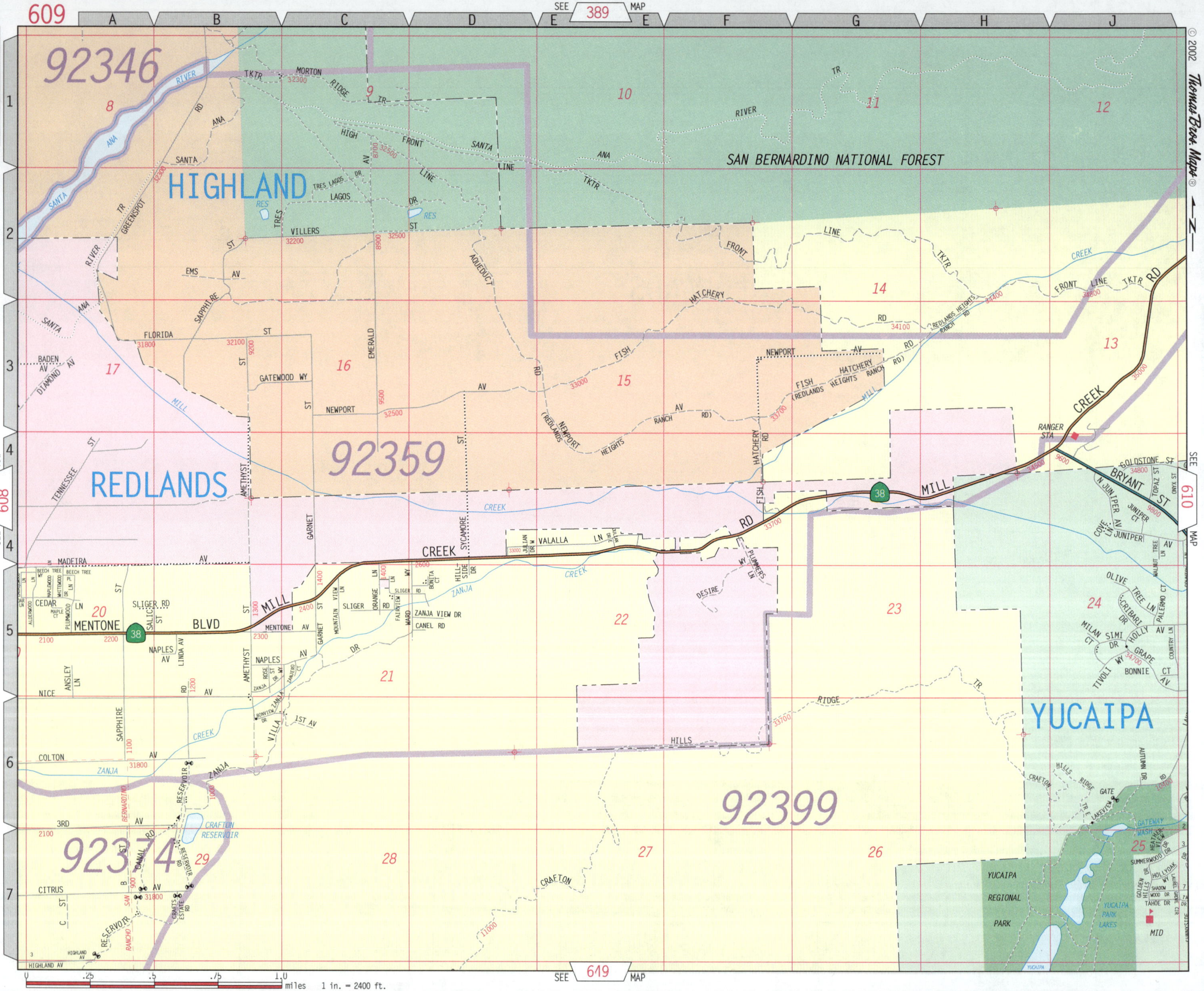

0 .25 .5 .75 1.0 miles 1 in. = 2400 ft.

SEE 4950 MAP

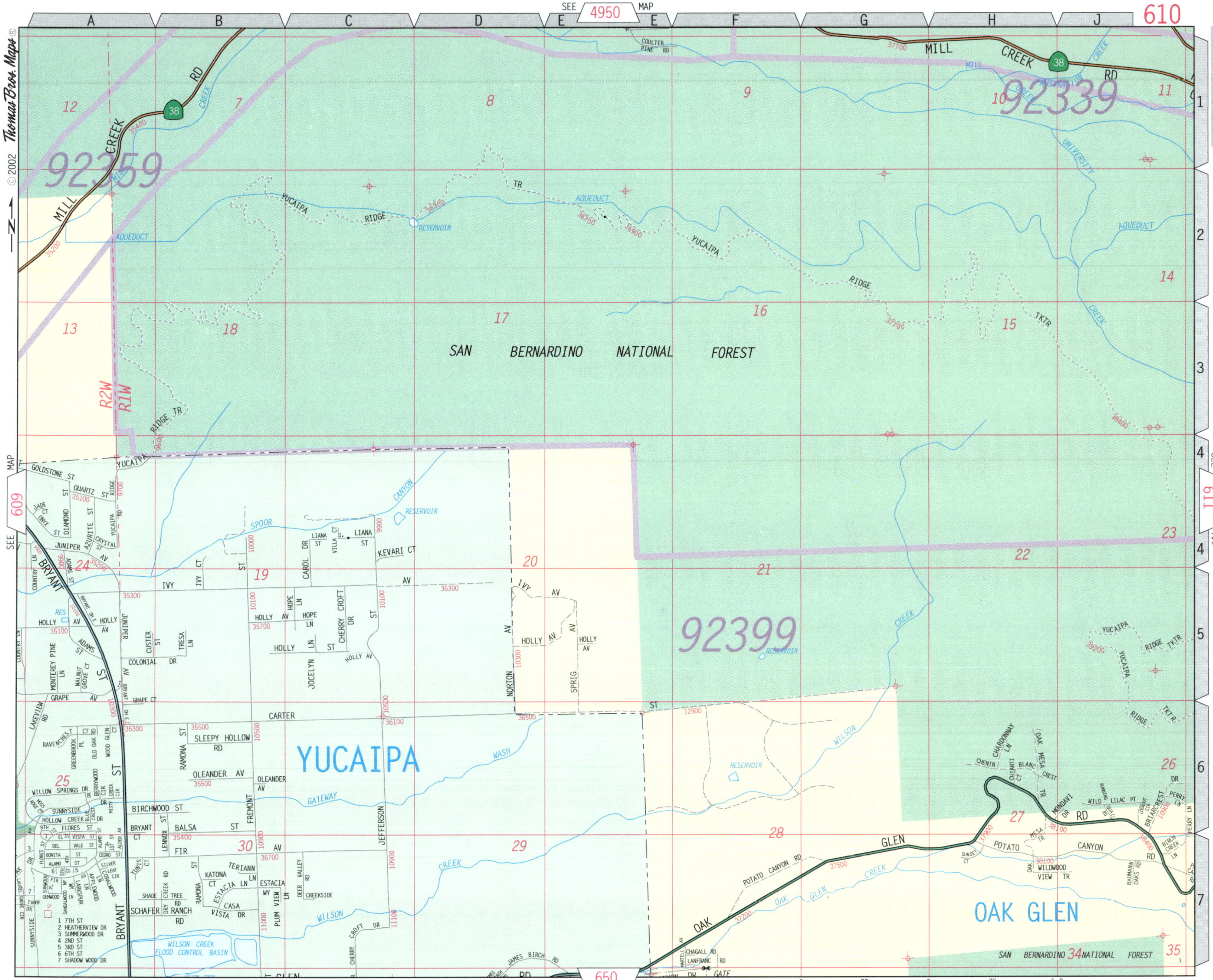

SEE 609 MAP
SEE 611 MAP
SEE 650 MAP

0 .25 .5 .75 1.0 miles 1 in. = 2400 ft.

SEE 389 MAP

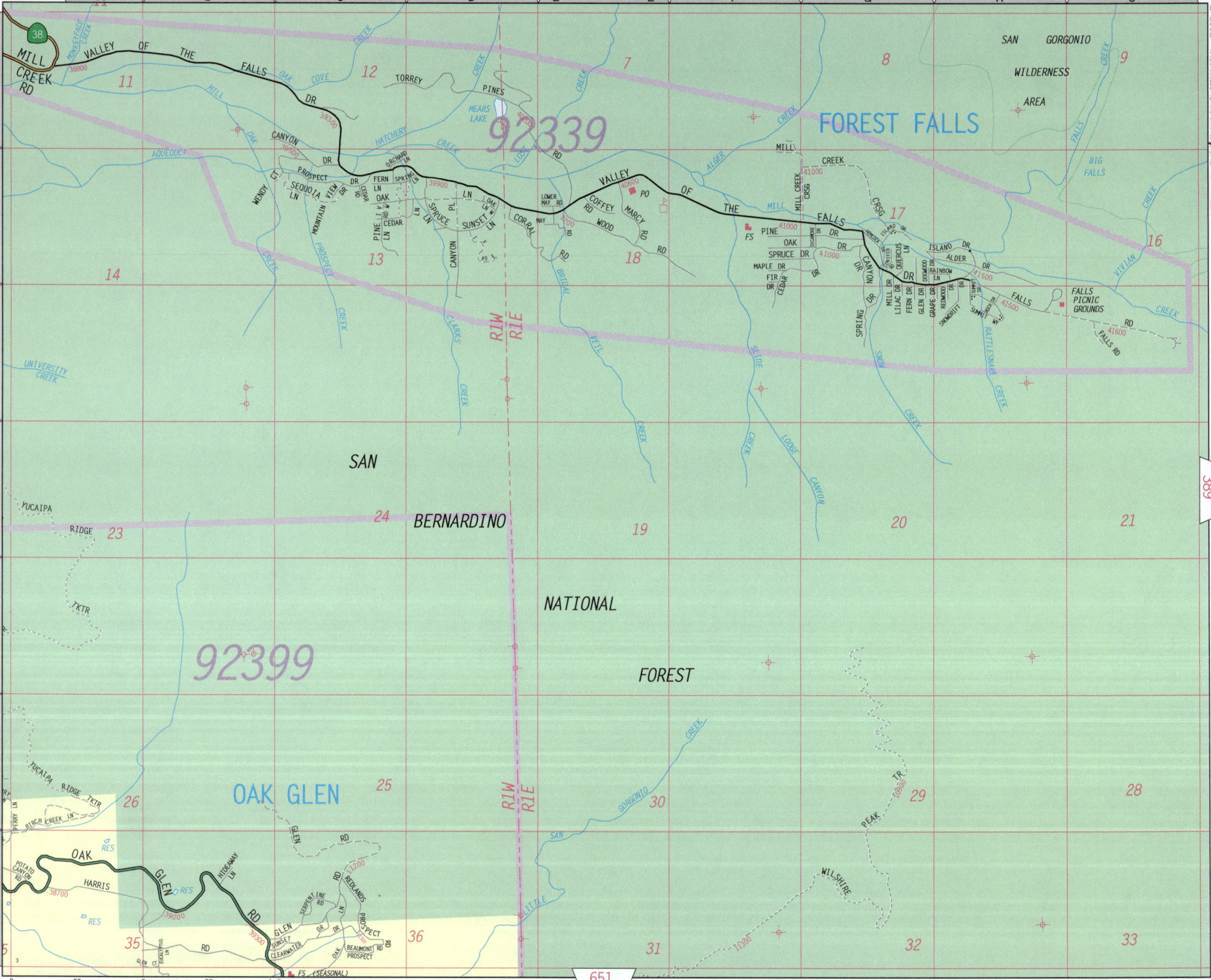

SEE 610 MAP
SEE 389 MAP
SEE 651 MAP

0 .25 .5 .75 1.0 miles 1 in. = 2400 ft.

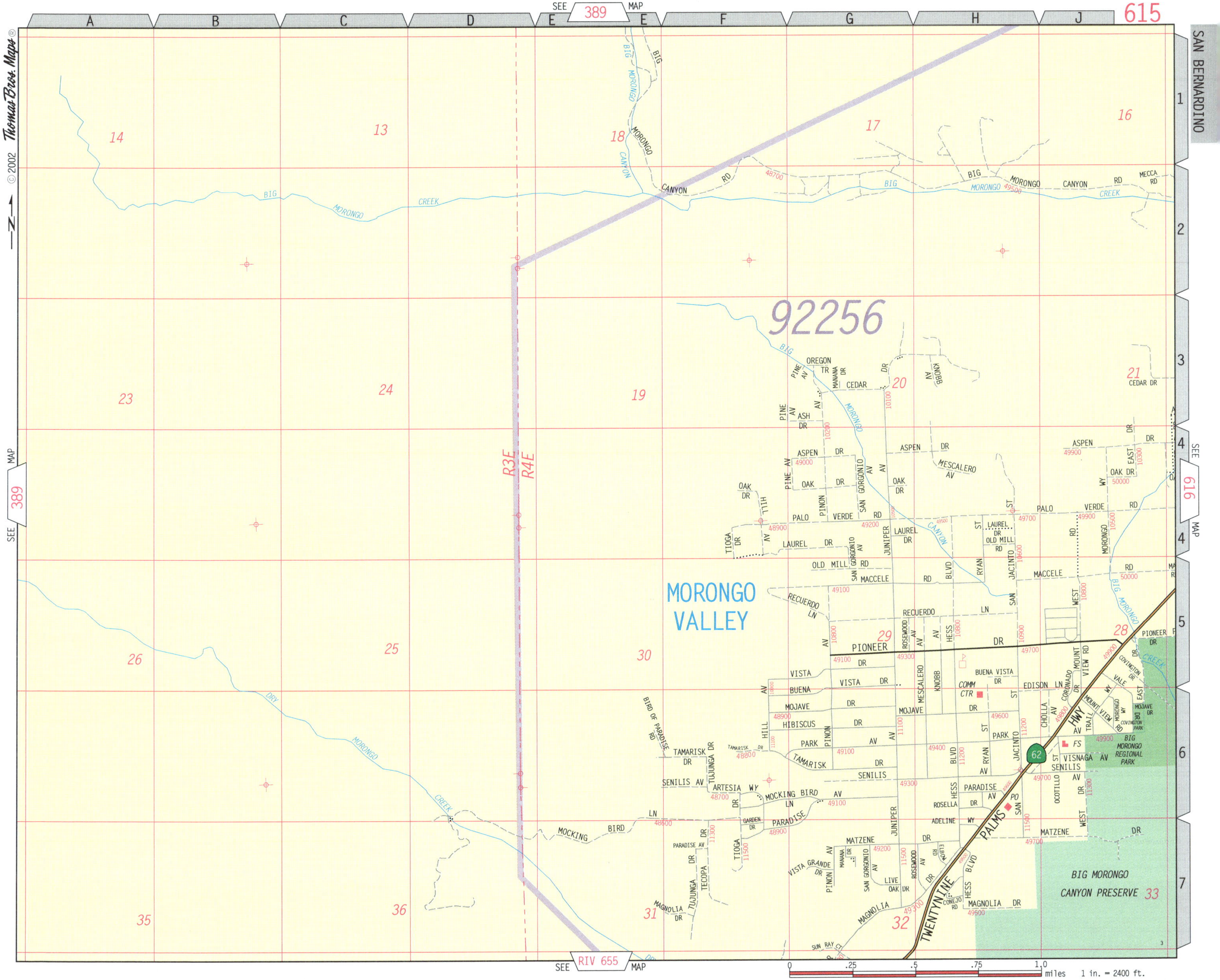

SEE 389 MAP
A
B
C
D
E
F
G
H
J
SAN BERNARDINO
1
2
3
4
5
6
7
SEE 389 MAP
SEE 616 MAP
SEE RIV 655 MAP
Thomas Bros. Maps
© 2002
R3E
R4E
92256
MORONGO VALLEY
BIG MORONGO CANYON RD
BIG MORONGO CREEK
DRY MORONGO CREEK
BIG MORONGO REGIONAL PARK
BIG MORONGO CANYON PRESERVE
TWENTYNINE PALMS HWY
62
PIONEER DR
PALO VERDE RD
MACCELE RD
OLD MILL RD
RECUERDO LN
VISTA DR
BUENA VISTA DR
EDISON LN
MOJAVE DR
HIBISCUS DR
PARK AV
TAMARISK DR
SENILIS AV
PARADISE AV
MOCKING BIRD LN
MATZENE DR
MAGNOLIA DR
ASPEN DR
OAK DR
LAUREL DR
CEDAR DR
OREGON TR
ASH DR
PINE AV
SAN GORGONIO AV
JUNIPER AV
MESCALERO AV
KNOBB AV
HESS BLVD
RYAN AV
SAN JACINTO ST
WEST ST
MOUNT VIEW RD
CHOLLA AV
CORONADO DR
OCOTILLO DR
COMM CTR
FS
PO
MECCA RD
13
14
16
17
18
19
20
21
23
24
25
26
28
29
30
31
32
33
35
36
0
.25
.5
.75
1.0
miles
1 in. = 2400 ft.

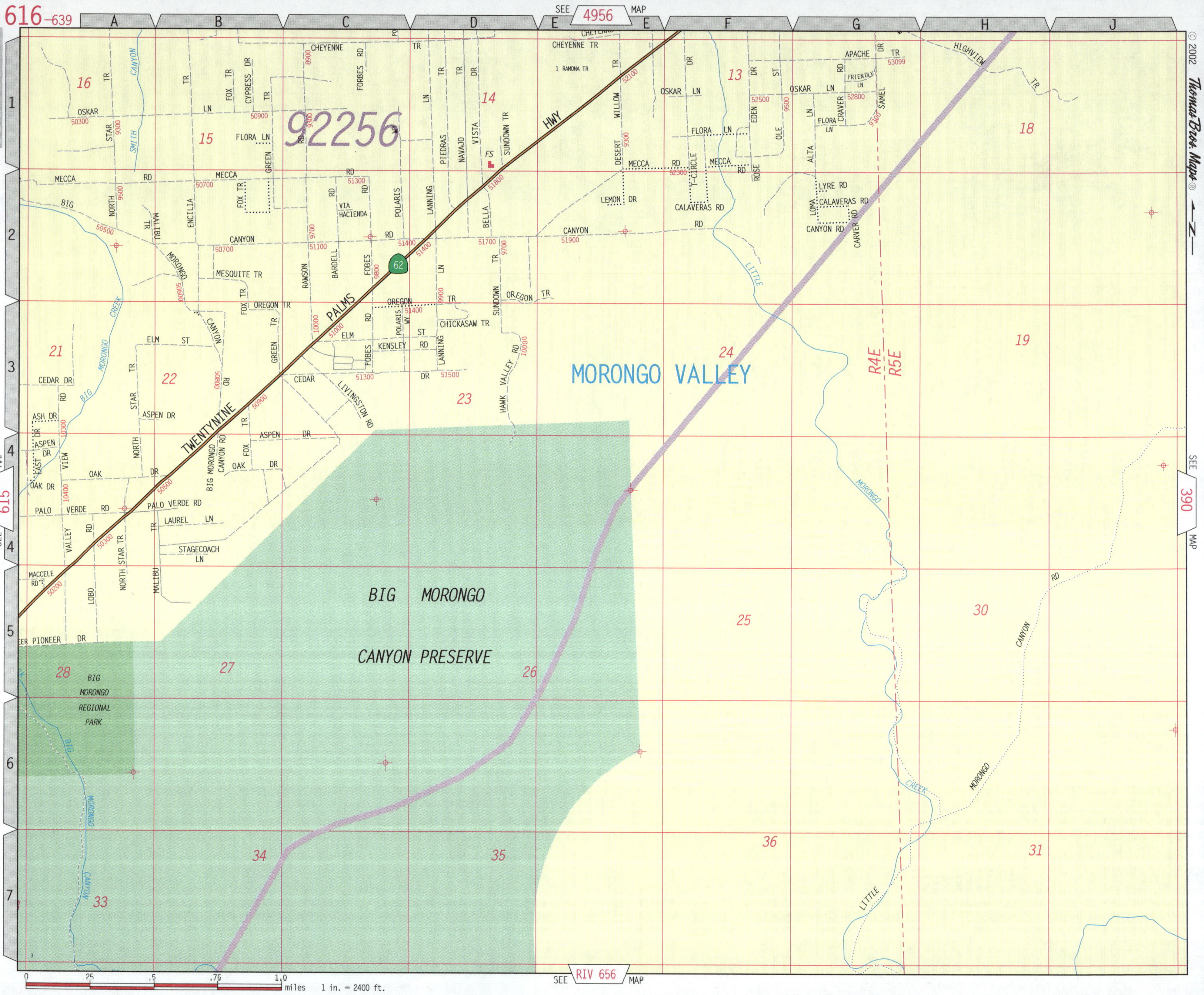

SEE 4956 MAP
SEE 615 MAP
SEE 390 MAP
SEE RIV 656 MAP
SAN BERNARDINO
A
B
C
D
E
F
G
H
J
1
2
3
4
5
6
7
92256
MORONGO VALLEY
BIG MORONGO CANYON PRESERVE
BIG MORONGO REGIONAL PARK
TWENTYNINE PALMS HWY
62
R4E
R5E
16
15
14
13
18
21
22
23
24
19
28
27
26
25
30
33
34
35
36
31
CHEYENNE TR
RAMONA TR
OSKAR LN
FLORA LN
MECCA RD
CANYON RD
MESQUITE TR
OREGON TR
ELM ST
CEDAR DR
ASPEN DR
ASH DR
OAK DR
PALO VERDE RD
LAUREL LN
STAGECOACH LN
MACCELE RD
PIONEER DR
KENSLEY RD
CHICKASAW TR
LIVINGSTON RD
HAWK VALLEY RD
SUNDOWN TR
BELLA TR
VISTA DR
NAVAJO TR
PIEDRAS TR
LANNING LN
POLARIS WY
FOBES RD
BARDELL RD
RAWSON RD
VIA HACIENDA
FORBES RD
GREEN TR
FOX TR
CYPRESS DR
ENCILIA
MALIBU TR
NORTH STAR TR
BIG MORONGO CANYON RD
MORONGO RD
LOBO
VALLEY VIEW RD
EAST DR
DESERT WILLOW TR
LEMON DR
CALAVERAS RD
T-CIRCLE
EDEN DR
ROSE ST
OLE
ALTA LN
LOMA
LYRE RD
CANYON RD
CARVER RD
CRAVER
FRIENDLY LN
APACHE TR
SAMEL DR
HIGHVIEW TR
SMITH CANYON
BIG MORONGO CREEK
LITTLE MORONGO CREEK
MORONGO CANYON RD
FS
0
.25
.5
.75
1.0
miles
1 in. = 2400 ft.

SEE LA 600 MAP

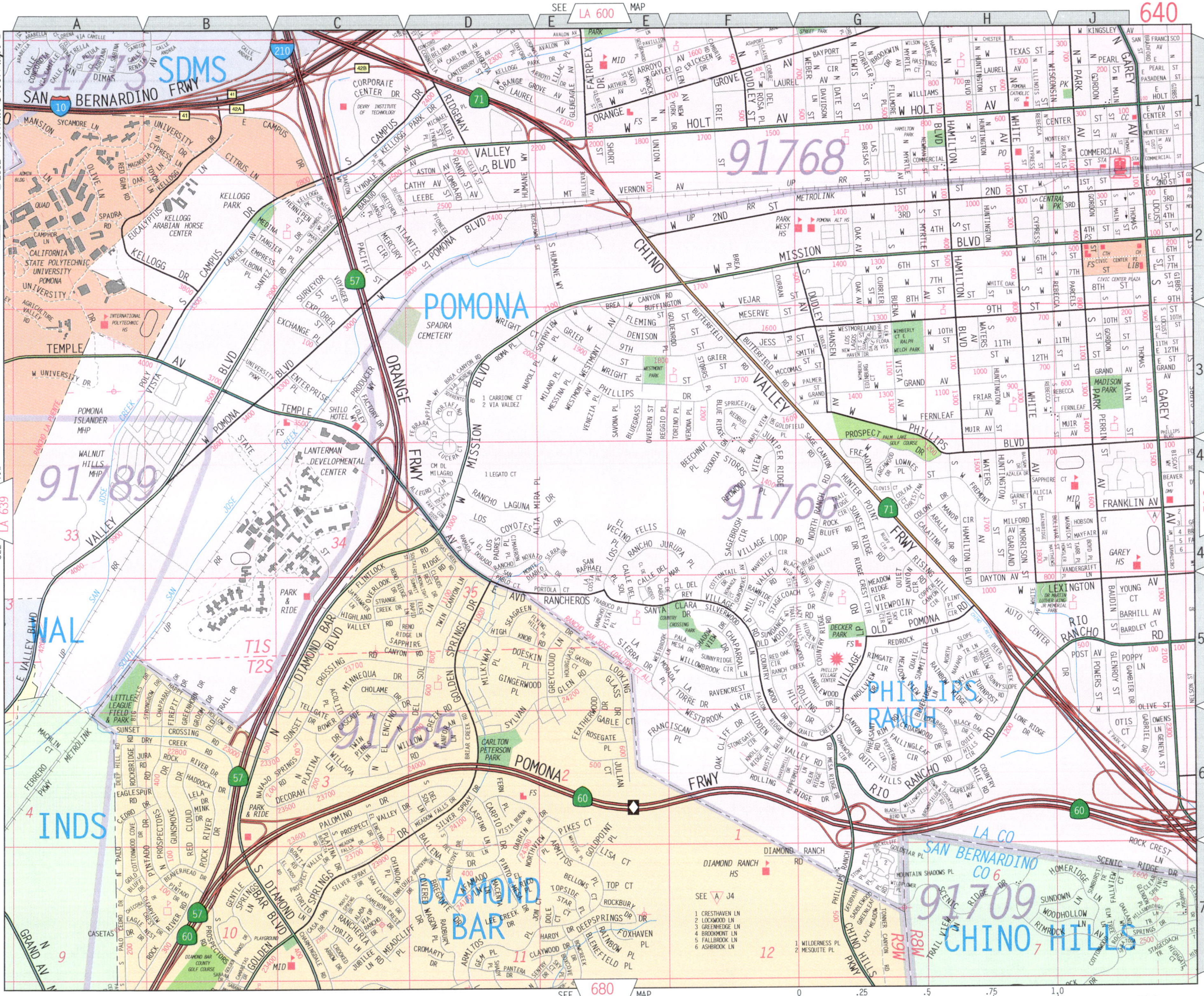

SEE 601 MAP

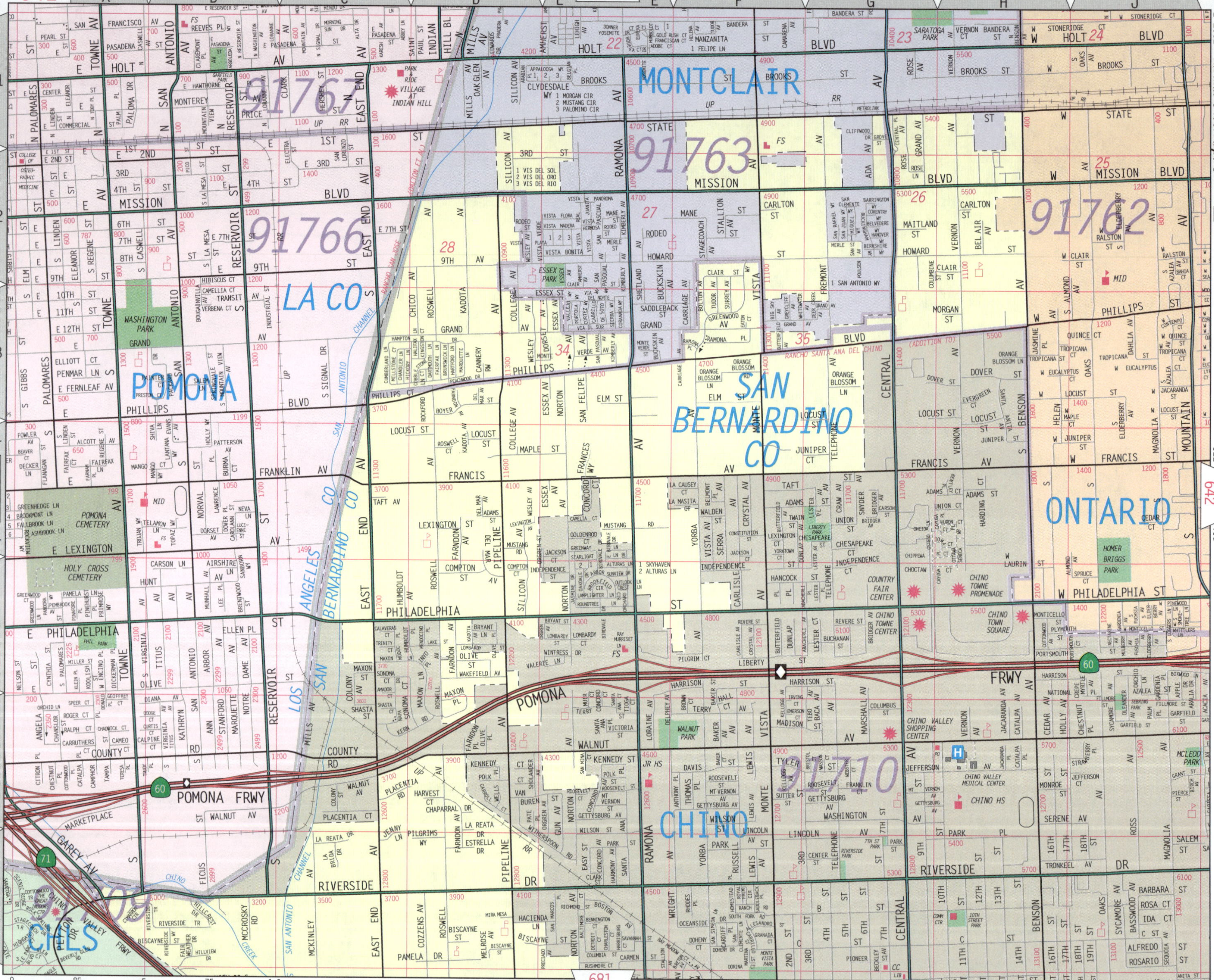

SEE 640 MAP

SEE 642 MAP

SEE 681 MAP

SEE 602 MAP

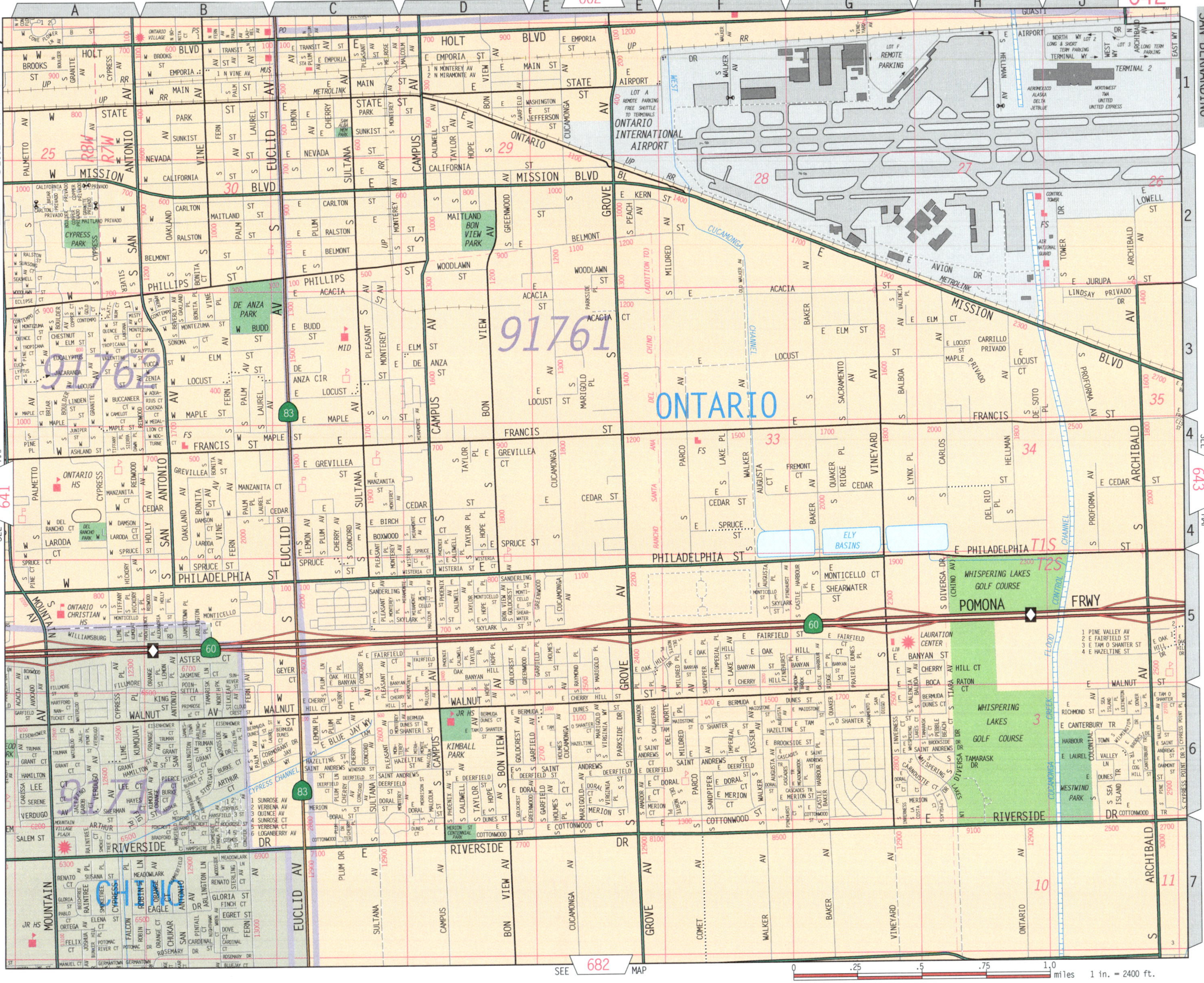

SEE 641 MAP
SEE 643 MAP
SEE 682 MAP

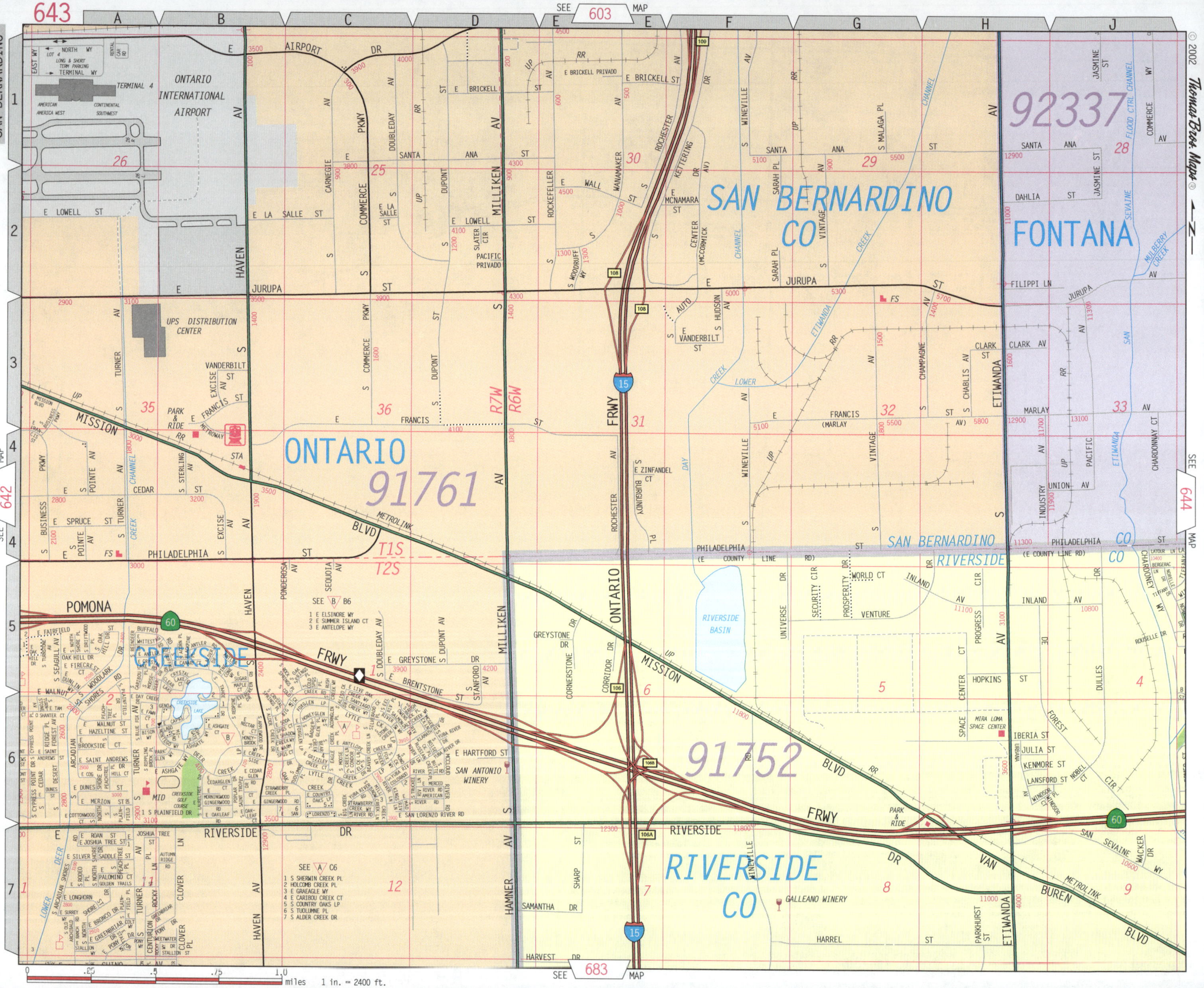
SEE 603 MAP
SAN BERNARDINO
ONTARIO INTERNATIONAL AIRPORT
TERMINAL 4
UPS DISTRIBUTION CENTER
ONTARIO
91761
SAN BERNARDINO CO
FONTANA
92337
RIVERSIDE CO
91752
CREEKSIDE
RIVERSIDE BASIN
CREEKSIDE LAKE
CREEKSIDE GOLF COURSE
SAN ANTONIO WINERY
GALLEANO WINERY
MIRA LOMA SPACE CENTER
PARK & RIDE
METROLINK STA
AIRPORT DR
JURUPA ST
FRANCIS ST
PHILADELPHIA ST
RIVERSIDE DR
MISSION BLVD
POMONA FRWY
ONTARIO FRWY
VAN BUREN BLVD
HAVEN AV
MILLIKEN AV
HAMNER AV
ETIWANDA AV
WINEVILLE AV
ROCHESTER AV
SANTA ANA ST
T1S T2S
R7W R6W
SEE 642 MAP
SEE 644 MAP
SEE 683 MAP
miles 1 in. = 2400 ft.

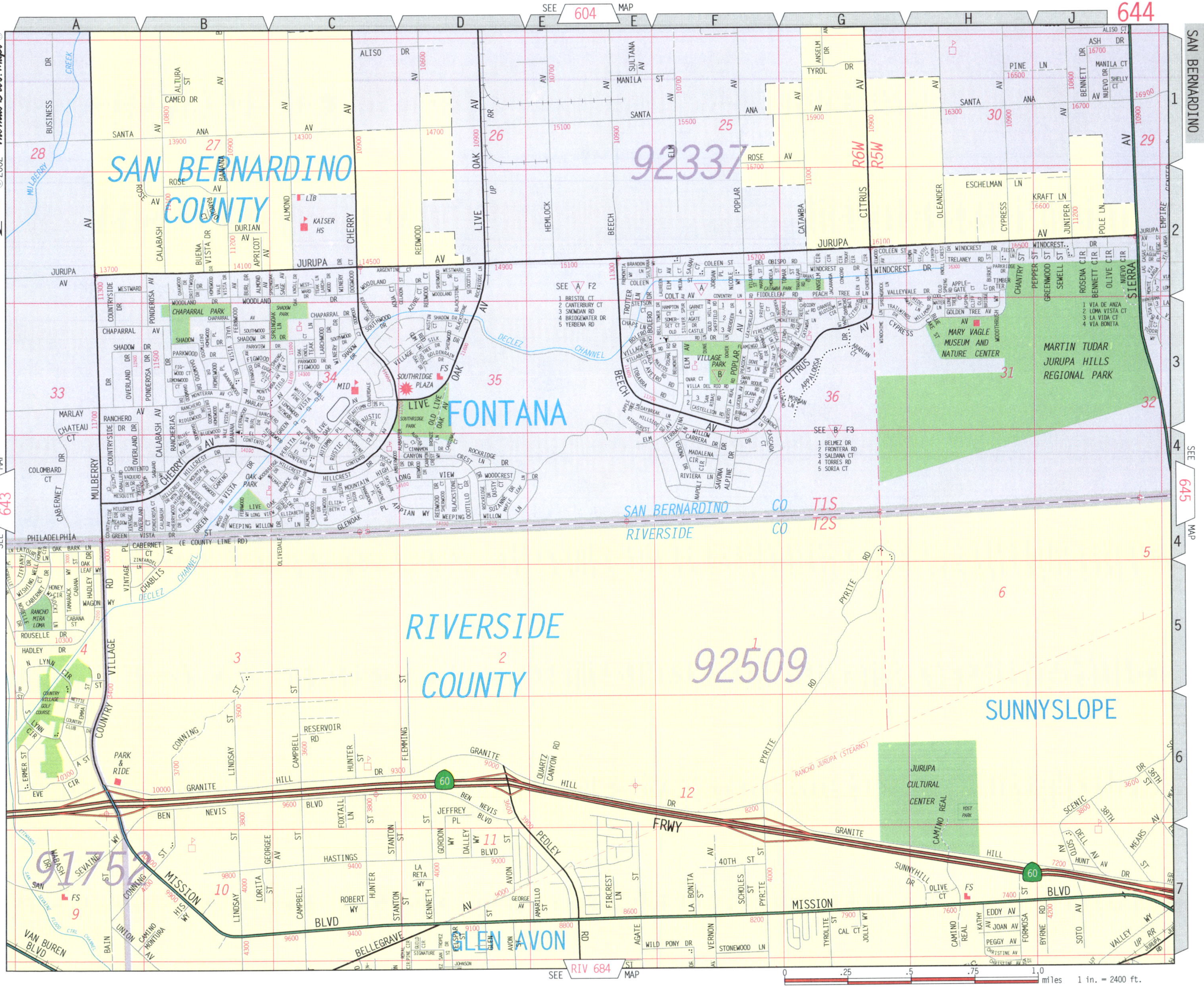
SEE 604 MAP
SAN BERNARDINO
SAN BERNARDINO COUNTY
FONTANA
92337
RIVERSIDE COUNTY
92509
SUNNYSLOPE
GLEN AVON
91752
SAN BERNARDINO CO
RIVERSIDE CO
T1S
T2S
R6W
R5W
MARTIN TUDAR JURUPA HILLS REGIONAL PARK
MARY VAGLE MUSEUM AND NATURE CENTER
JURUPA CULTURAL CENTER
SOUTHRIDGE PLAZA
KAISER HS
DECLEZ CHANNEL
JURUPA AV
SANTA ANA AV
CITRUS AV
LIVE OAK AV
MULBERRY AV
COUNTRY VILLAGE RD
MISSION BLVD
GRANITE HILL DR
PYRITE ST
PEDLEY RD
60
FRWY
SEE 643 MAP
SEE 645 MAP
SEE RIV 684 MAP
1 in. = 2400 ft.
miles
© 2002 Thomas Bros. Maps ®

SEE 605 MAP

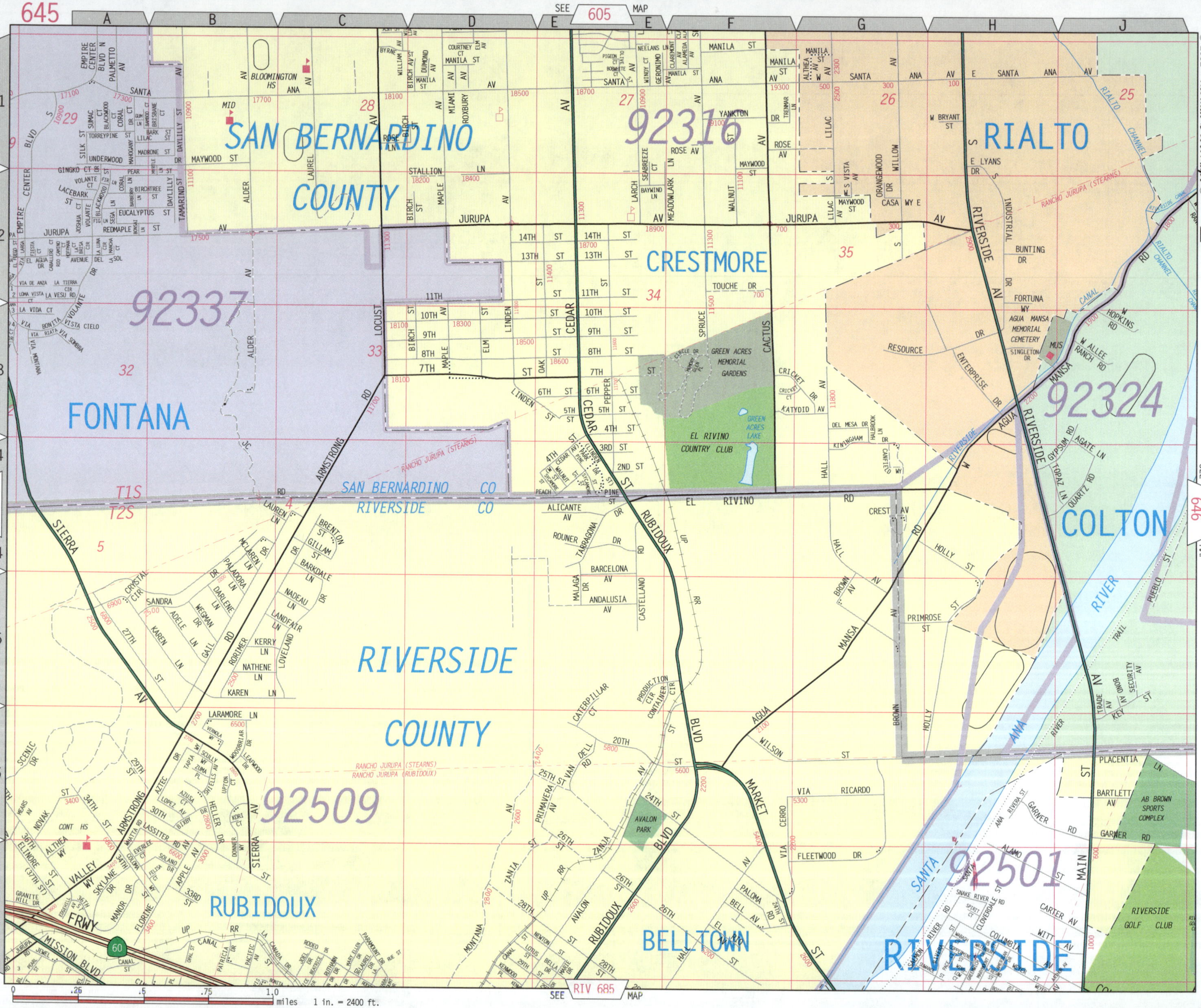

SEE RIV 685 MAP

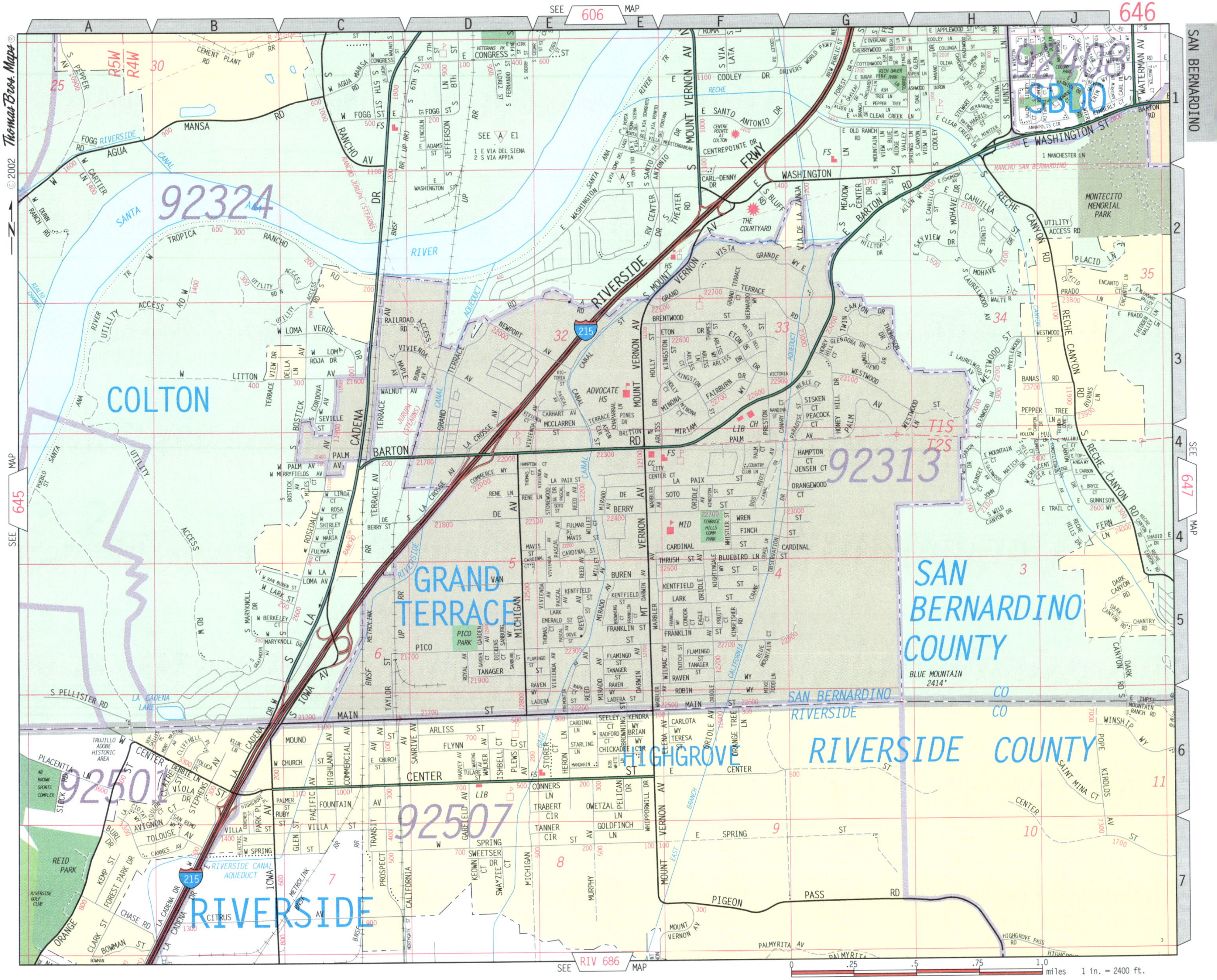

646
SEE 606 MAP
SEE 645 MAP
SEE 647 MAP
SEE RIV 686 MAP
SAN BERNARDINO
Thomas Bros. Maps
© 2002
COLTON
GRAND TERRACE
SAN BERNARDINO COUNTY
RIVERSIDE COUNTY
RIVERSIDE
HIGHGROVE
92324
92313
92408
92501
92507
SBDO
R5W R4W
T1S T2S
SAN BERNARDINO CO
RIVERSIDE CO
SANTA ANA RIVER
BLUE MOUNTAIN 2414'
MONTECITO MEMORIAL PARK
PICO PARK
REID PARK
LA CADENA LAKE
THE COURTYARD
CENTRE POINTE AT COLTON
RIVERSIDE CANAL AQUEDUCT
TRUJILLO ADOBE HISTORIC AREA
RIVERSIDE GOLF CLUB
ADVOCATE HS
RIVERSIDE FRWY
215
MAIN ST
BARTON RD
WASHINGTON ST
E WASHINGTON ST
MOUNT VERNON AV
IOWA AV
CENTER ST
PIGEON PASS RD
LA CADENA DR
RECHE CANYON RD
MICHIGAN AV
TERRACE AV
1 in. = 2400 ft.
miles
0 .25 .5 .75 1.0

SEE 607 MAP

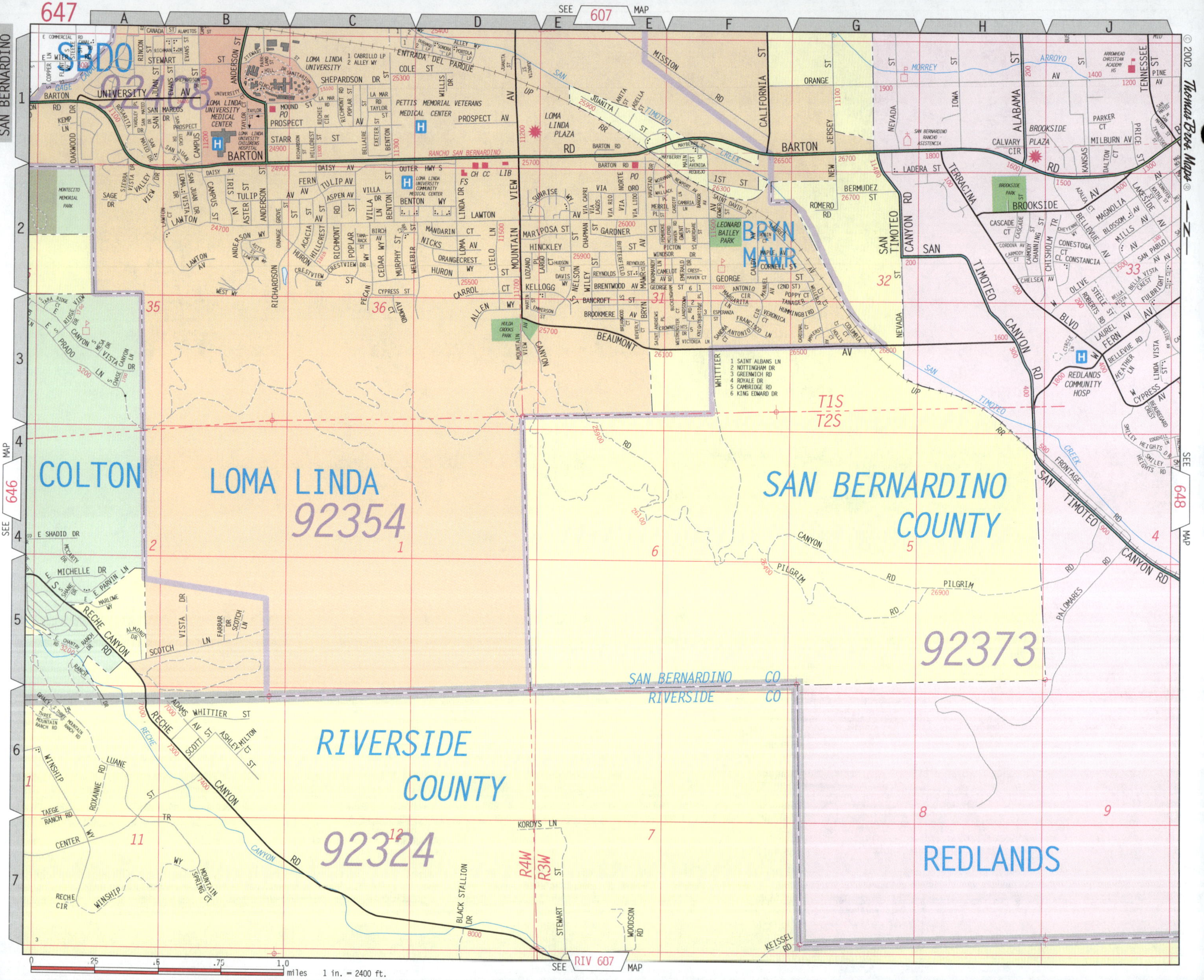
SAN BERNARDINO
SBDO
92408
LOMA LINDA
92354
COLTON
SAN BERNARDINO COUNTY
92373
BRYN MAWR
RIVERSIDE COUNTY
92324
REDLANDS
SAN BERNARDINO CO
RIVERSIDE CO
LOMA LINDA UNIVERSITY
LOMA LINDA UNIVERSITY MEDICAL CENTER
PETTIS MEMORIAL VETERANS MEDICAL CENTER
LOMA LINDA UNIVERSITY COMMUNITY MEDICAL CENTER
LOMA LINDA PLAZA
LEONARD BAILEY PARK
HULDA CROOKS PARK
MONTECITO MEMORIAL PARK
BROOKSIDE PARK
BROOKSIDE PLAZA
REDLANDS COMMUNITY HOSP
ARROWHEAD CHRISTIAN ACADEMY HS
SAN BERNARDINO RANCHO ASISTENCIA
RANCHO SAN BERNARDINO
BARTON RD
UNIVERSITY AV
MISSION RD
CALIFORNIA ST
SAN TIMOTEO CANYON RD
REDLANDS BLVD
BEAUMONT AV
MOUNTAIN VIEW AV
ANDERSON ST
RECHE CANYON RD
PILGRIM RD
CANYON
1 SAINT ALBANS LN
2 NOTTINGHAM DR
3 GREENWICH RD
4 ROYALE DR
5 CAMBRIDGE RD
6 KING EDWARD DR
T1S
T2S
R4W
R3W
SEE 646 MAP
SEE 648 MAP
SEE RIV 607 MAP
Thomas Bros. Maps ® © 2002
0 .25 .5 .75 1.0 miles 1 in. = 2400 ft.

SEE 608 MAP

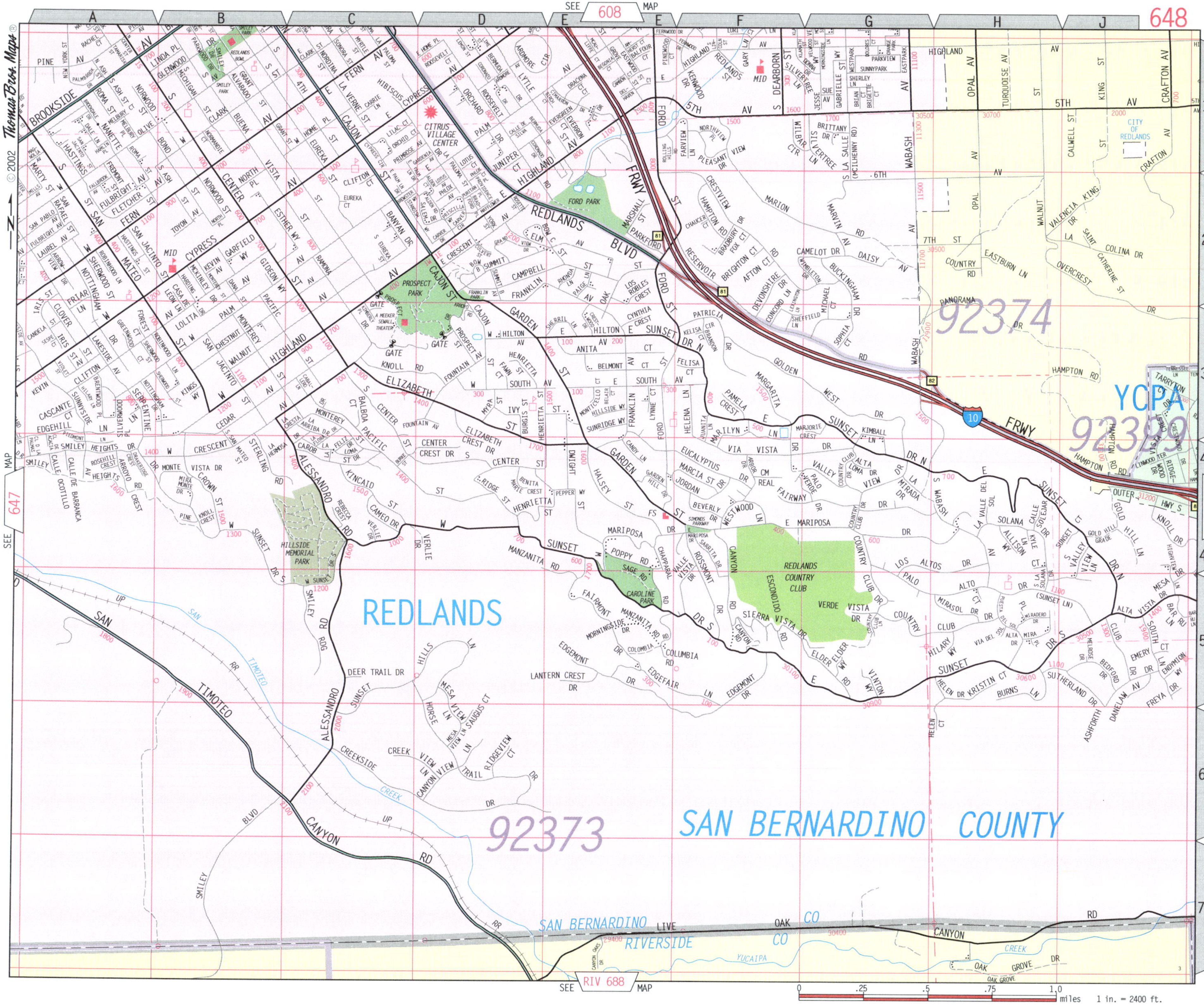

SEE 647 MAP

SEE 649 MAP

SEE RIV 688 MAP

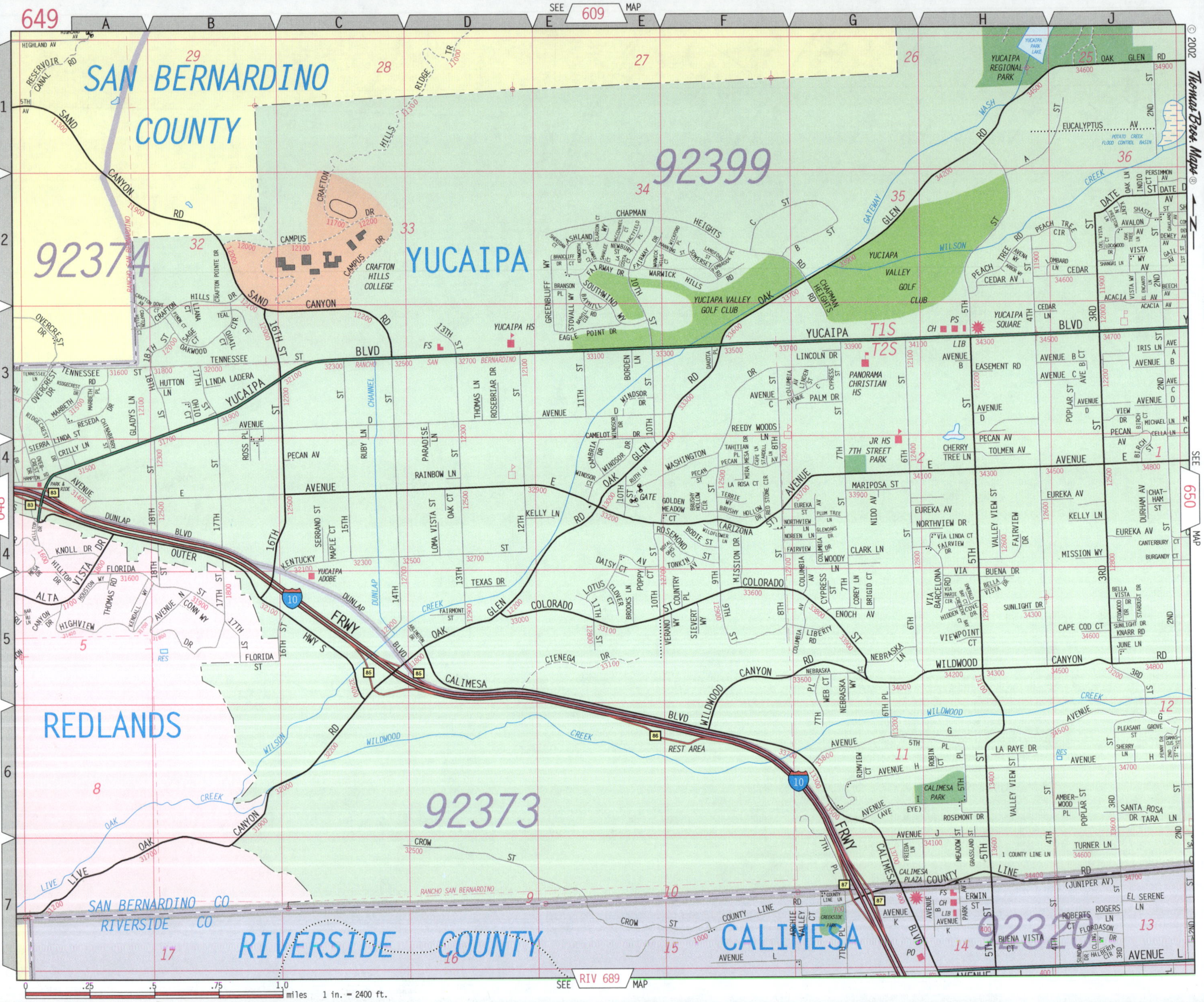
SEE 609 MAP
SEE 648 MAP
SEE 650 MAP
SEE RIV 689 MAP
SAN BERNARDINO
SAN BERNARDINO COUNTY
YUCAIPA
REDLANDS
CALIMESA
RIVERSIDE COUNTY
SAN BERNARDINO CO
RIVERSIDE CO
92399
92374
92373
92320
CRAFTON HILLS COLLEGE
YUCAIPA REGIONAL PARK
YUCAIPA VALLEY GOLF CLUB
YUCAIPA HS
PANORAMA CHRISTIAN HS
JR HS
7TH STREET PARK
CALIMESA PARK
YUCAIPA SQUARE
YUCAIPA ADOBE
REST AREA
YUCAIPA BLVD
OAK GLEN RD
SAND CANYON RD
CALIMESA BLVD
COUNTY LINE RD
WILDWOOD CANYON RD
T1S
T2S
0 .25 .5 .75 1.0 miles 1 in. = 2400 ft.
© 2002 Thomas Bros. Maps ®

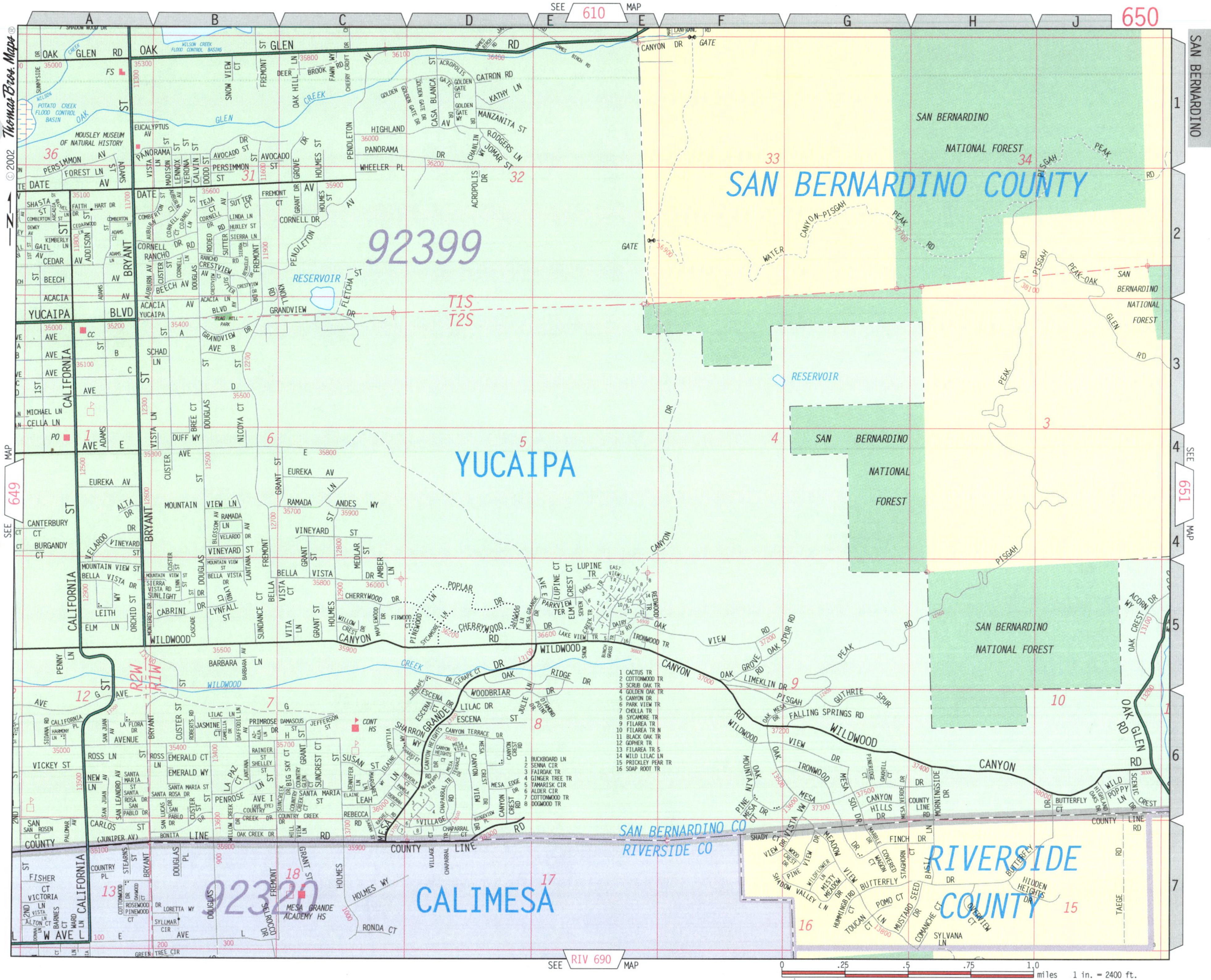
SEE 610 MAP
SEE 649 MAP
SEE 651 MAP
SEE RIV 690 MAP
SAN BERNARDINO
Thomas Bros. Maps
© 2002
A B C D E F G H J
1 2 3 4 5 6 7
92399
YUCAIPA
SAN BERNARDINO COUNTY
SAN BERNARDINO NATIONAL FOREST
92320
CALIMESA
RIVERSIDE COUNTY
SAN BERNARDINO CO
RIVERSIDE CO
T1S
T2S
R2W
R1W
OAK GLEN RD
WILDWOOD CANYON RD
YUCAIPA BLVD
CALIFORNIA ST
BRYANT ST
COUNTY LINE RD
MOUSLEY MUSEUM OF NATURAL HISTORY
WILSON CREEK FLOOD CONTROL BASINS
WILSON POTATO CREEK FLOOD CONTROL BASIN
RESERVOIR
MESA GRANDE ACADEMY HS
CONT HS
1 CACTUS TR
2 COTTONWOOD TR
3 SCRUB OAK TR
4 GOLDEN OAK TR
5 CANYON DR
6 PARK VIEW TR
7 CHOLLA TR
8 SYCAMORE TR
9 FILAREA TR
10 FILAREA TR N
11 BLACK OAK TR
12 GOPHER TR
13 FILAREA TR S
14 WILD LILAC LN
15 PRICKLEY PEAR TR
16 SOAP ROOT TR
1 BUCKBOARD LN
2 SENNA CIR
3 FAIROAK TR
4 GINGER TREE TR
5 TAMARISK CIR
6 ALDER CIR
7 COTTONWOOD TR
8 DOGWOOD TR
0 .25 .5 .75 1.0 miles
1 in. = 2400 ft.

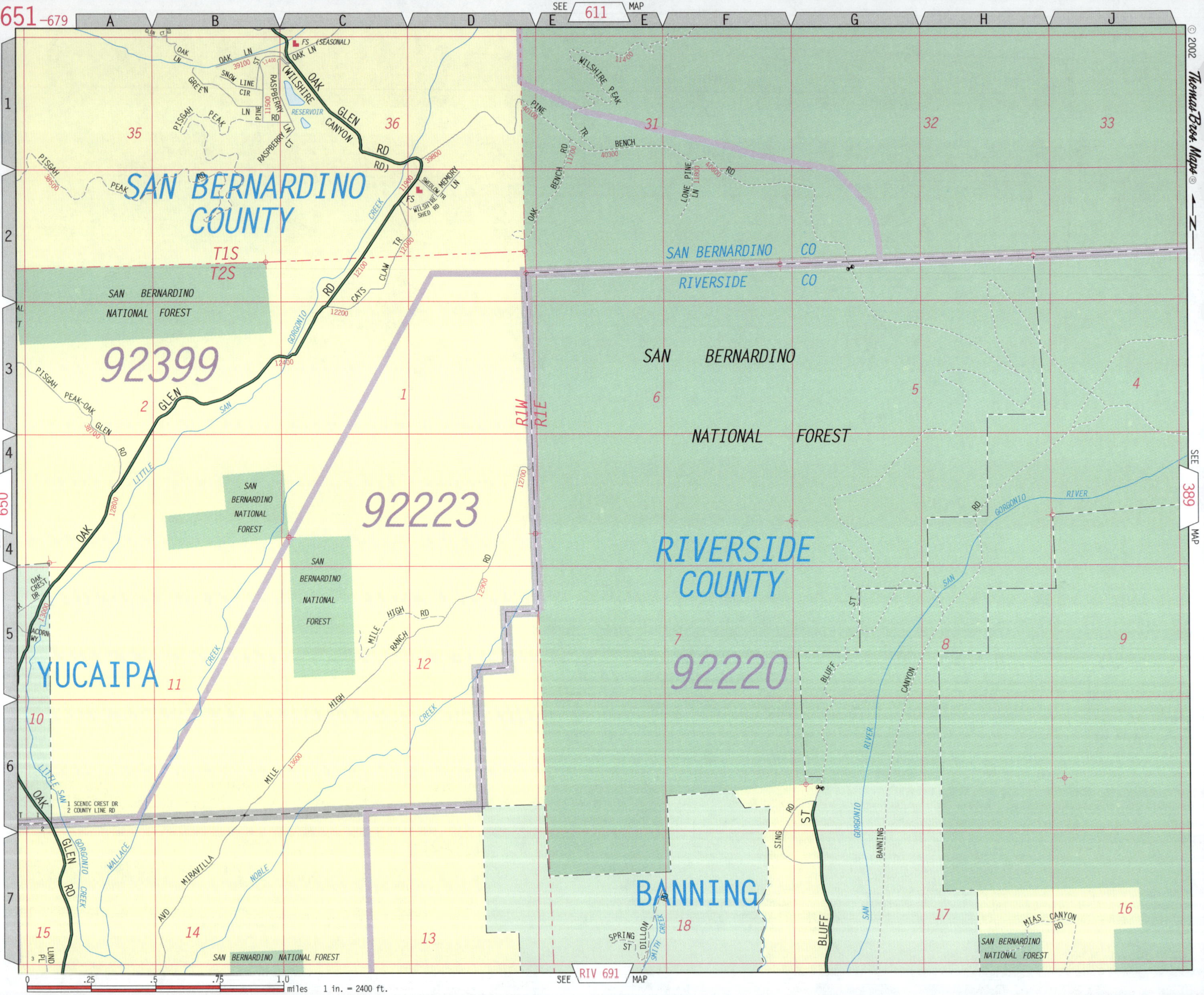
A B C D E F G H J
1 2 3 4 5 6 7
SEE 611 MAP
SEE 650 MAP
SEE 389 MAP
SEE RIV 691 MAP
SAN BERNARDINO
SAN BERNARDINO COUNTY
RIVERSIDE COUNTY
SAN BERNARDINO CO
RIVERSIDE CO
SAN BERNARDINO NATIONAL FOREST
92399
92223
92220
YUCAIPA
BANNING
T1S
T2S
R1W
R1E
OAK GLEN RD
OAK GLEN CANYON RD
WILSHIRE OAK LN
WILSHIRE PEAK
PISGAH PEAK RD
PISGAH PEAK-OAK GLEN RD
GREEN LN
SNOW LINE CIR
RASPBERRY ST
RASPBERRY LN
RASPBERRY CT
PINE RD
RESERVOIR
FS (SEASONAL)
FS
SWEDLOW MEMORY LN
WILSHIRE SHED RD
CATS CLAW TR
PINE BENCH TR
BENCH RD
OAK
LONE PINE LN
GORGONIO CREEK
LITTLE SAN GORGONIO CREEK
MILE HIGH RD
MILE HIGH RANCH RD
OAK CREST DR
ACORN WY
SCENIC CREST DR
COUNTY LINE RD
WALLACE CREEK
NOBLE CREEK
MIRAVILLA AVD
LUND PL
SAN GORGONIO RIVER
BLUFF ST
SING RD
CANYON
BANNING
SPRING ST
DILLON RD
SMITH CREEK
MIAS CANYON RD
35 36 31 32 33 2 1 6 5 4 11 12 7 8 9 10 15 14 13 18 17 16
0 .25 .5 .75 1.0 miles 1 in. = 2400 ft.
Thomas Bros. Maps

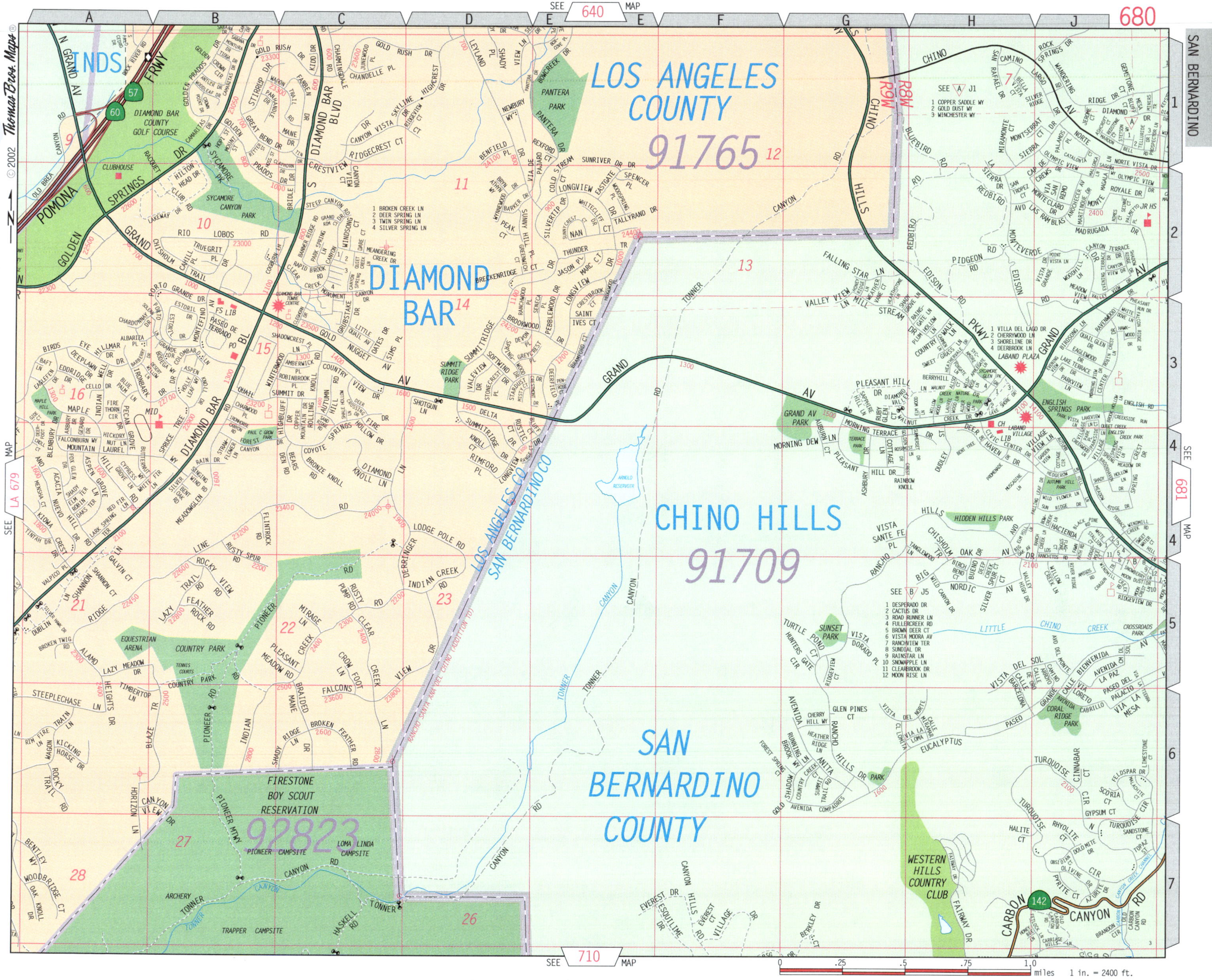
SEE 640 MAP
SAN BERNARDINO
Thomas Bros. Maps ® © 2002
LOS ANGELES COUNTY
91765
DIAMOND BAR
CHINO HILLS
91709
SAN BERNARDINO COUNTY
92823
LOS ANGELES CO
SAN BERNARDINO CO
POMONA FRWY
GRAND AV
DIAMOND BAR BLVD
GOLDEN SPRINGS DR
CHINO HILLS PKWY
CARBON CANYON RD
DIAMOND BAR COUNTY GOLF COURSE
SYCAMORE CANYON PARK
PANTERA PARK
SUMMIT RIDGE PARK
GRAND AV PARK
ENGLISH SPRINGS PARK
HIDDEN HILLS PARK
SUNSET PARK
CORAL RIDGE PARK
EQUESTRIAN ARENA
COUNTRY PARK
FIRESTONE BOY SCOUT RESERVATION
WESTERN HILLS COUNTRY CLUB
PIONEER CAMPSITE
LOMA LINDA CAMPSITE
ARCHERY
TRAPPER CAMPSITE
LITTLE CHINO CREEK
TONNER CANYON
SEE LA 679 MAP
SEE 681 MAP
SEE 710 MAP
0 .25 .5 .75 1.0 miles 1 in. = 2400 ft.

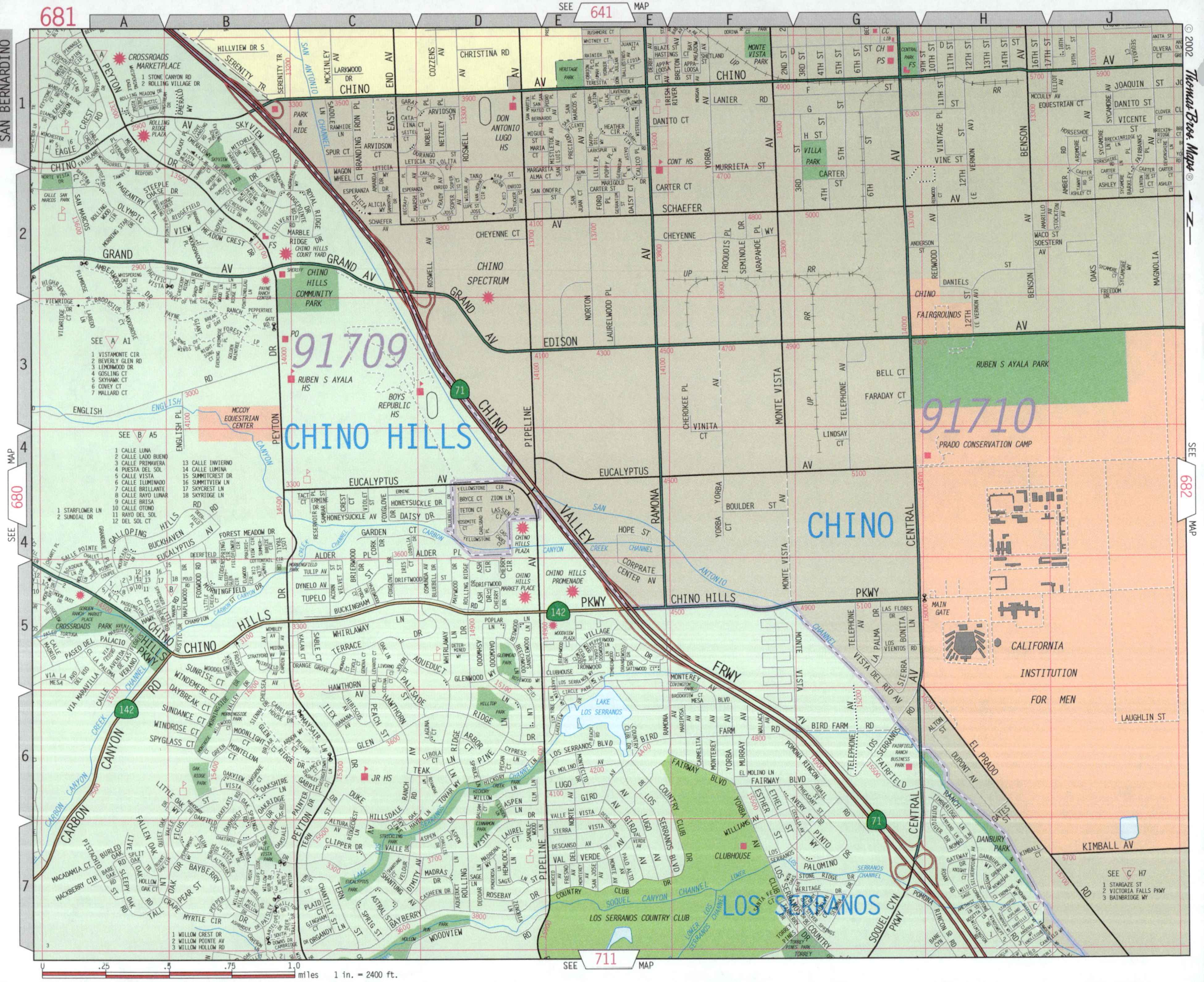
SEE 641 MAP
SEE 711 MAP
SEE 680 MAP
SEE 682 MAP
SAN BERNARDINO
CHINO HILLS
CHINO
LOS SERRANOS
91709
91710
CHINO VALLEY FRWY
CHINO HILLS PKWY
GRAND AV
EDISON AV
CHINO AV
SCHAEFER AV
EUCALYPTUS AV
PEYTON DR
PIPELINE AV
CENTRAL AV
RAMONA AV
MONTE VISTA AV
CARBON CANYON RD
SOQUEL CYN PKWY
EL PRADO RD
KIMBALL AV
BIRD FARM RD
CROSSROADS MARKETPLACE
CHINO SPECTRUM
CHINO HILLS COMMUNITY PARK
RUBEN S AYALA HS
BOYS REPUBLIC HS
MCCOY EQUESTRIAN CENTER
RUBEN S AYALA PARK
PRADO CONSERVATION CAMP
CALIFORNIA INSTITUTION FOR MEN
CHINO HILLS PROMENADE
CHINO HILLS MARKET PLACE
CHINO HILLS PLAZA
CHINO FAIRGROUNDS
DON ANTONIO LUGO HS
CONT HS
JR HS
LAKE LOS SERRANOS
LOS SERRANOS COUNTRY CLUB
CLUBHOUSE
VILLA PARK
MONTE VISTA PARK
SEE A A1
1 VISTAMONTE CIR
2 BEVERLY GLEN RD
3 LEMONWOOD DR
4 GOSLING CT
5 SKYHAWK CT
6 COVEY CT
7 MALLARD CT
SEE B A5
1 CALLE LUNA
2 CALLE LADO BUENO
3 CALLE PRIMAVERA
4 PUESTA DEL SOL
5 CALLE VISTA
6 CALLE ILUMINADO
7 CALLE BRILLANTE
8 CALLE RAYO LUNAR
9 CALLE BRISA
10 CALLE OTONO
11 RAYO DEL SOL
12 DEL SOL CT
13 CALLE INVIERNO
14 CALLE LUMINA
15 SUMMITCREST DR
16 SUMMITVIEW LN
17 SKYCREST LN
18 SKYRIDGE LN
1 STARFLOWER LN
2 SUNDIAL DR
1 STONE CANYON RD
2 ROLLING VILLAGE DR
1 WILLOW CREST DR
2 WILLOW POINTE AV
3 WILLOW HOLLOW RD
SEE C H7
1 STARGAZE ST
2 VICTORIA FALLS PKWY
3 BAINBRIDGE WY
0 .25 .5 .75 1.0 miles 1 in. = 2400 ft.
© 2002 Thomas Bros. Maps®

SEE 642 MAP

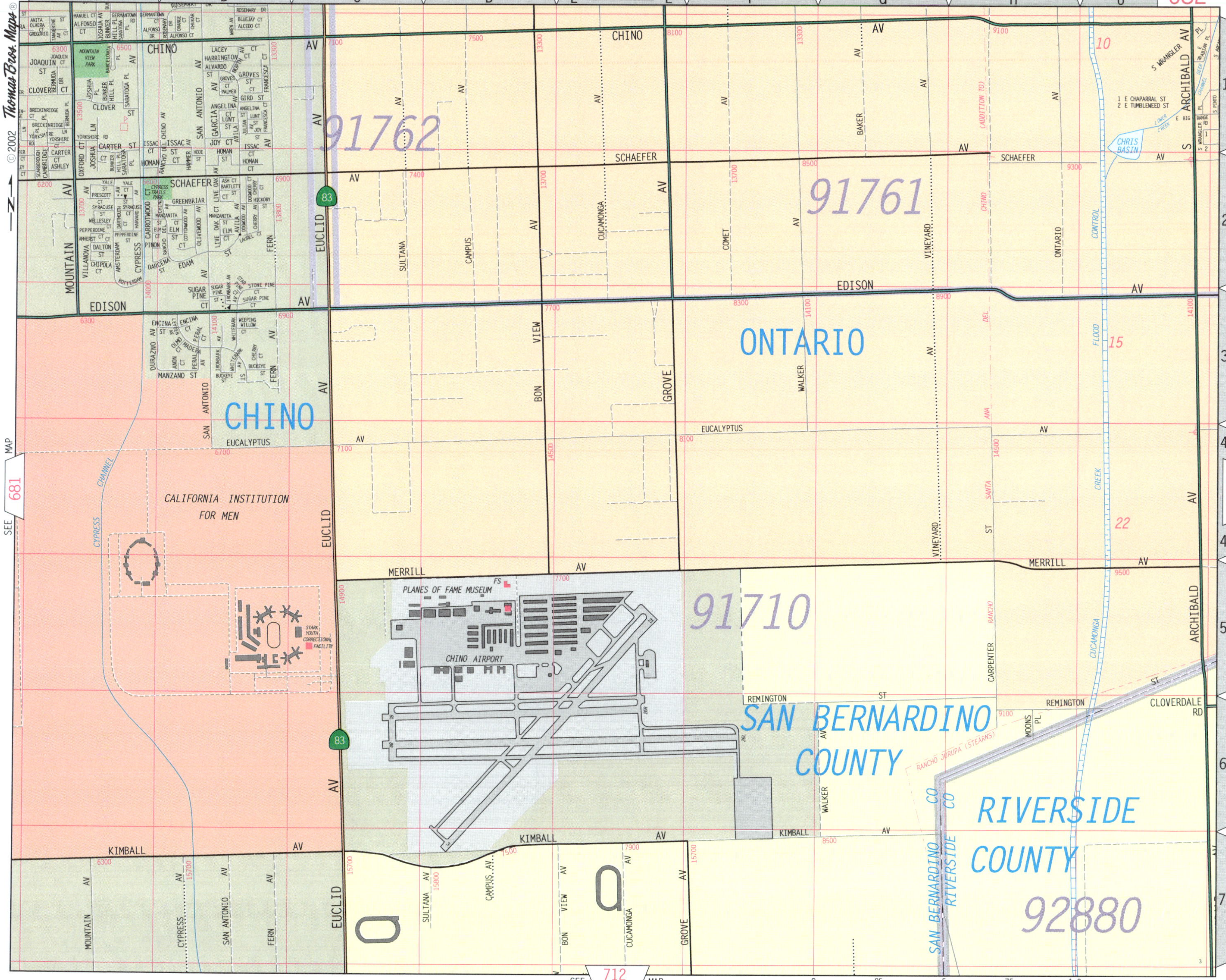

SEE 681 MAP
SEE 683 MAP
SEE 712 MAP

0 .25 .5 .75 1.0 miles 1 in. = 2400 ft.

SEE 643 MAP

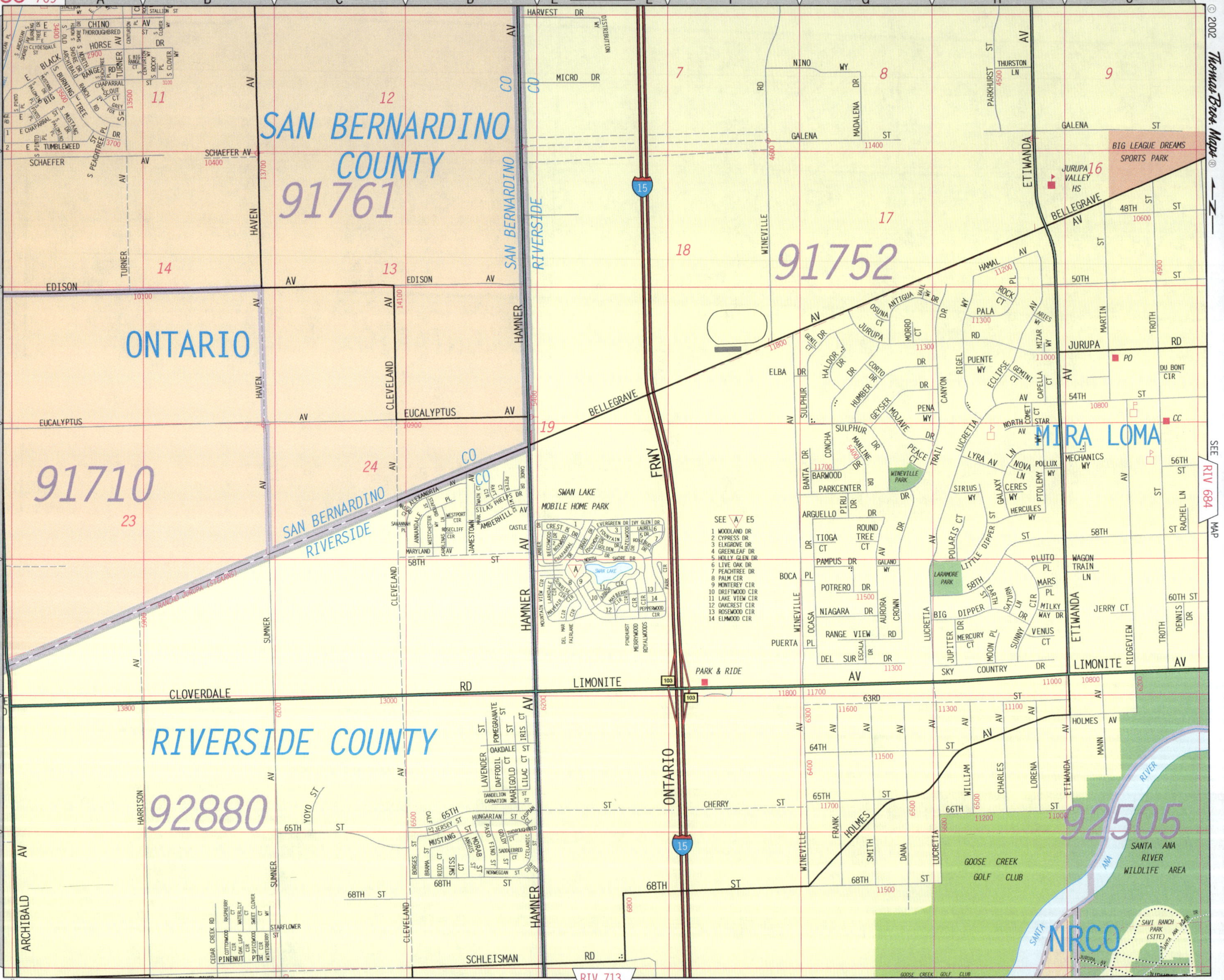

SEE 682 MAP

SEE RIV 684 MAP

SEE RIV 713 MAP

0 .25 .5 .75 1.0 miles 1 in. = 2400 ft.

SEE 680 MAP

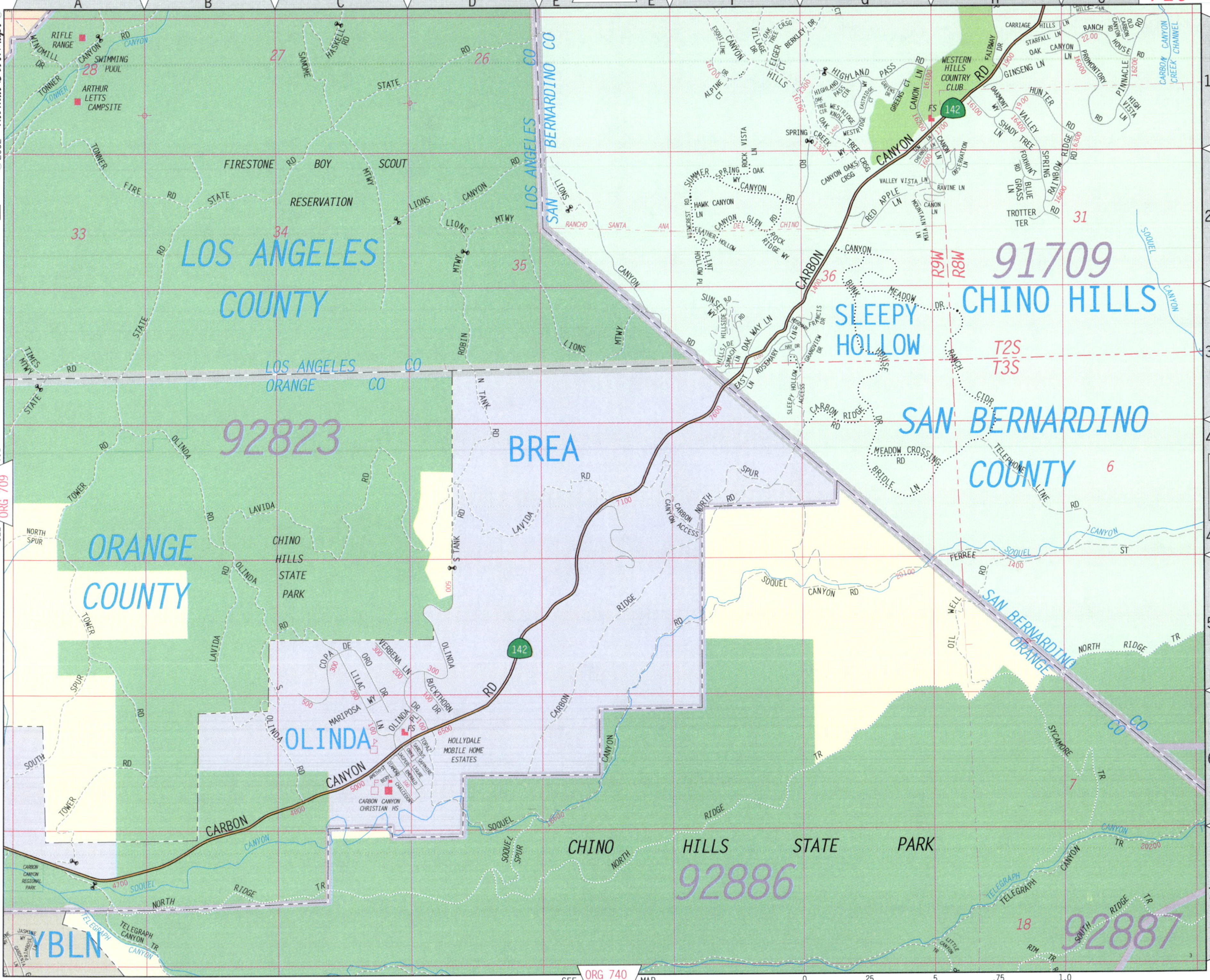

SEE ORG 740 MAP

0 .25 .5 .75 1.0 miles 1 in. = 2400 ft.

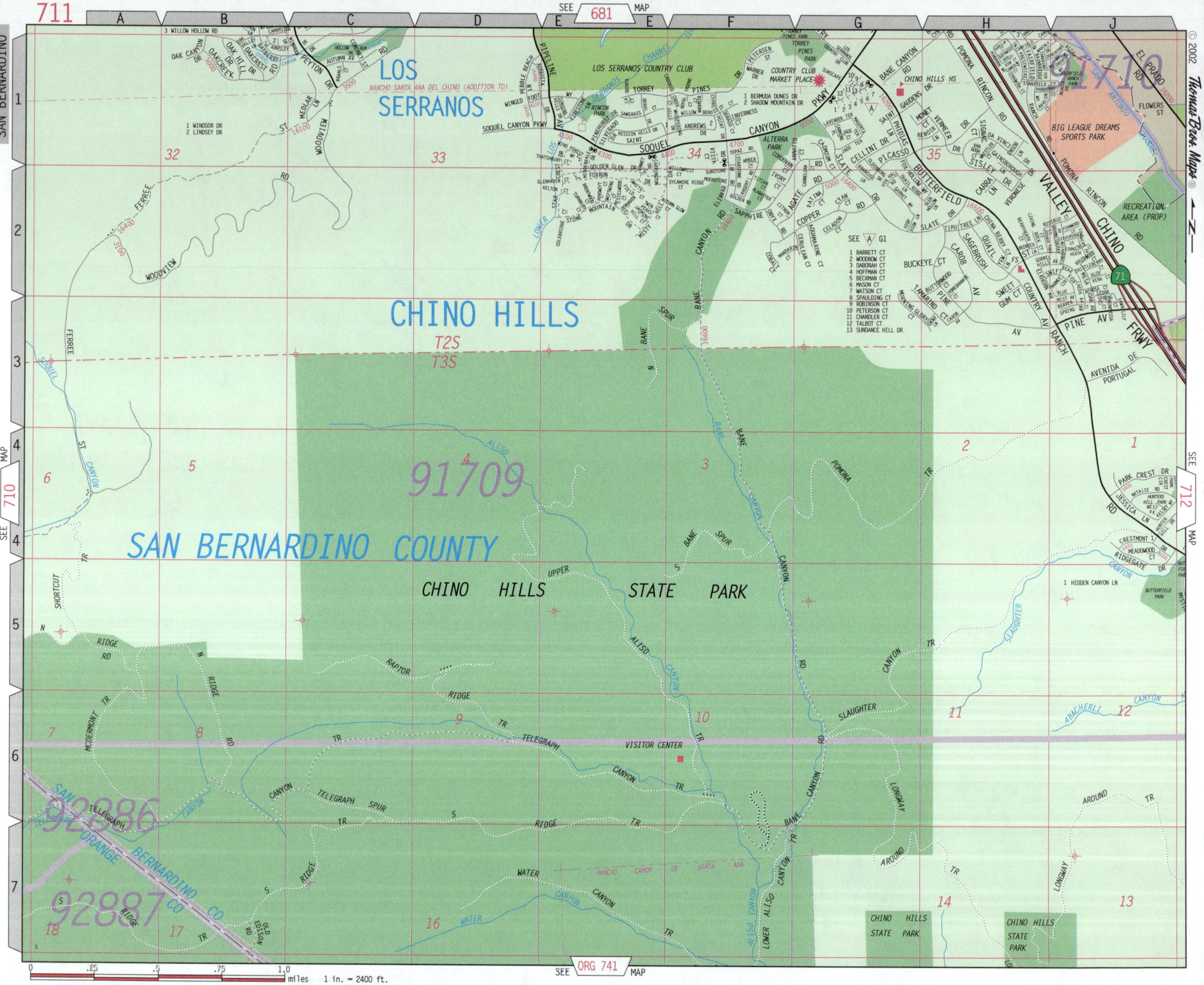
SEE 681 MAP
A
B
C
D
E
F
G
H
J
SAN BERNARDINO
LOS SERRANOS
LOS SERRANOS COUNTRY CLUB
RANCHO SANTA ANA DEL CHINO (ADDITION TO)
COUNTRY CLUB MARKET PLACE
CHINO HILLS HS
91710
BIG LEAGUE DREAMS SPORTS PARK
RECREATION AREA (PROP)
CHINO HILLS
T2S
T3S
CHINO VALLEY FRWY
71
91709
SAN BERNARDINO COUNTY
CHINO HILLS STATE PARK
VISITOR CENTER
92886
92887
ORANGE CO
SAN BERNARDINO CO
RANCHO CANON DE SANTA ANA
PEYTON DR
SOQUEL CANYON PKWY
PIPELINE AV
BUTTERFIELD RANCH RD
PINE AV
AVENIDA DE PORTUGAL
BANE CANYON RD
ALISO CANYON
SLAUGHTER CANYON RD
TELEGRAPH CANYON
WATER CANYON
ABACHERLI CANYON
ROCKRIDGE CANYON
FERREE ST
WOODVIEW
CHINO HILLS STATE PARK
CHINO HILLS STATE PARK
1 WINDSOR DR
2 LINDSEY DR
1 BERMUDA DUNES DR
2 SHADOW MOUNTAIN DR
SEE A G1
1 BARRETT CT
2 WOODROW CT
3 DABORAH CT
4 HOFFMAN CT
5 BECKMAN CT
6 MASON CT
7 WATSON CT
8 SPAULDING CT
9 ROBINSON CT
10 PETERSON CT
11 CHANDLER CT
12 TALBOT CT
13 SUNDANCE HILL DR
1 HIDDEN CANYON LN
SEE 710 MAP
SEE 712 MAP
SEE ORG 741 MAP
0 .25 .5 .75 1.0 miles 1 in. = 2400 ft.

SEE 682 MAP

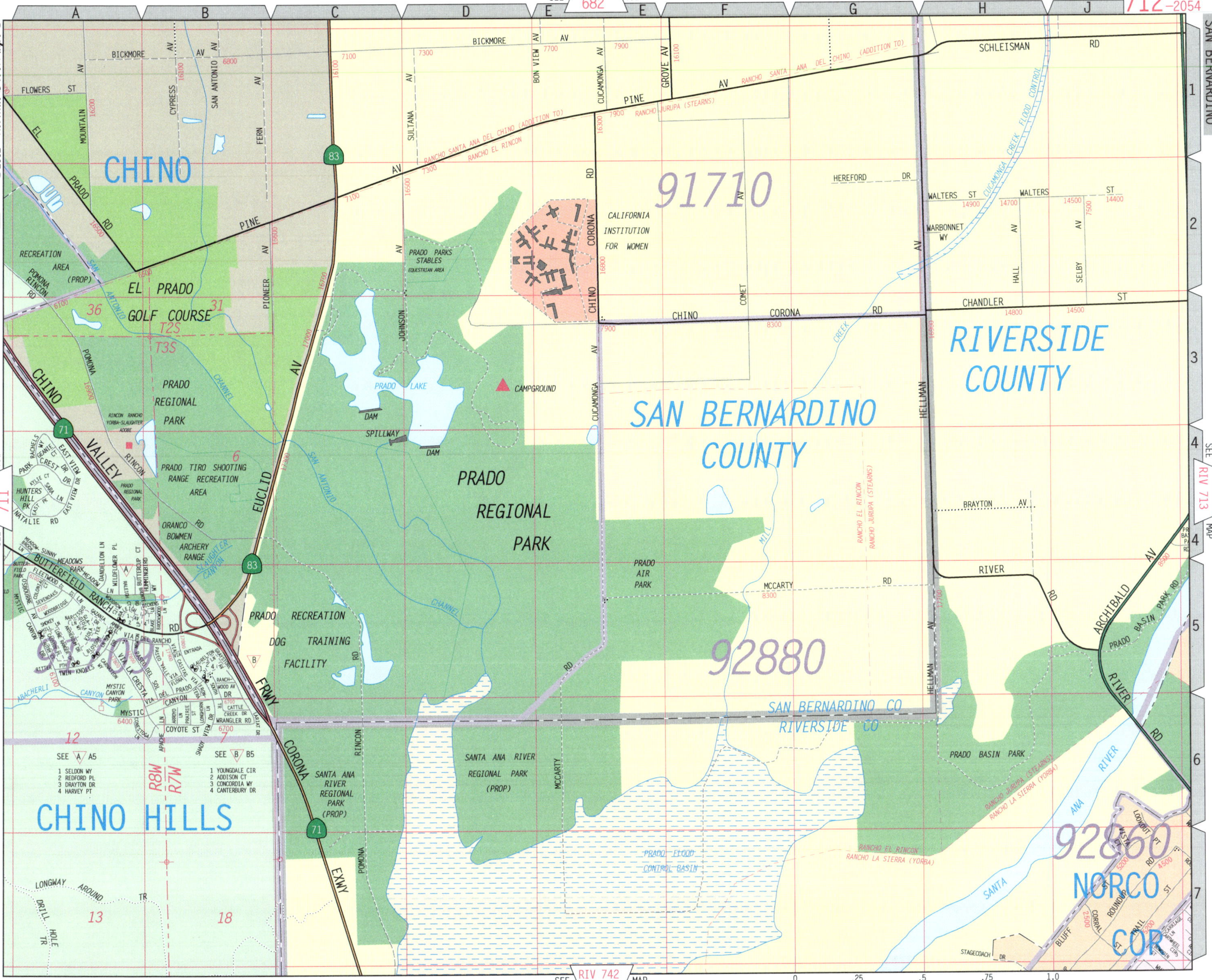

SEE RIV 742 MAP

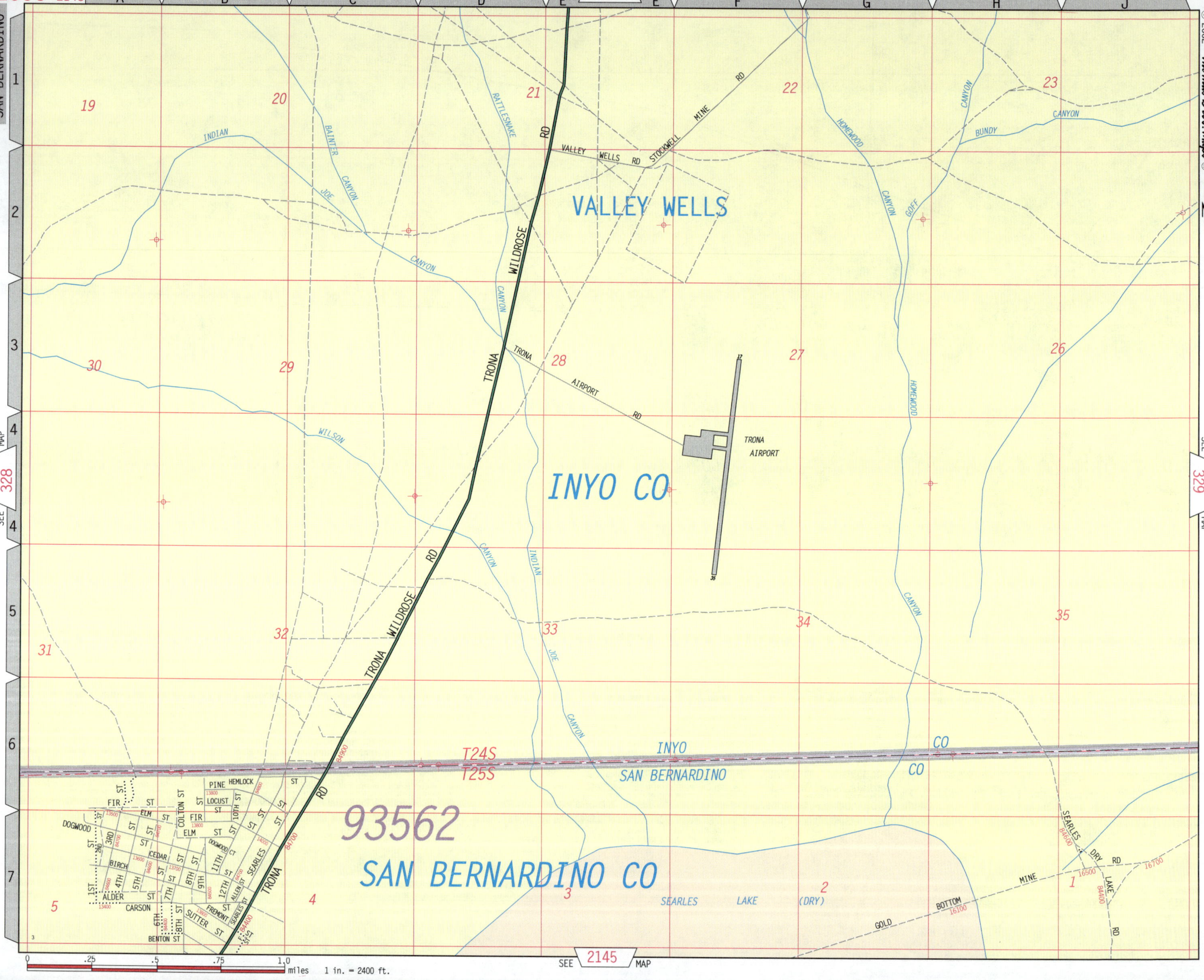

SEE 328 MAP
SEE 2145 MAP
SEE 329 MAP
SEE 328 MAP

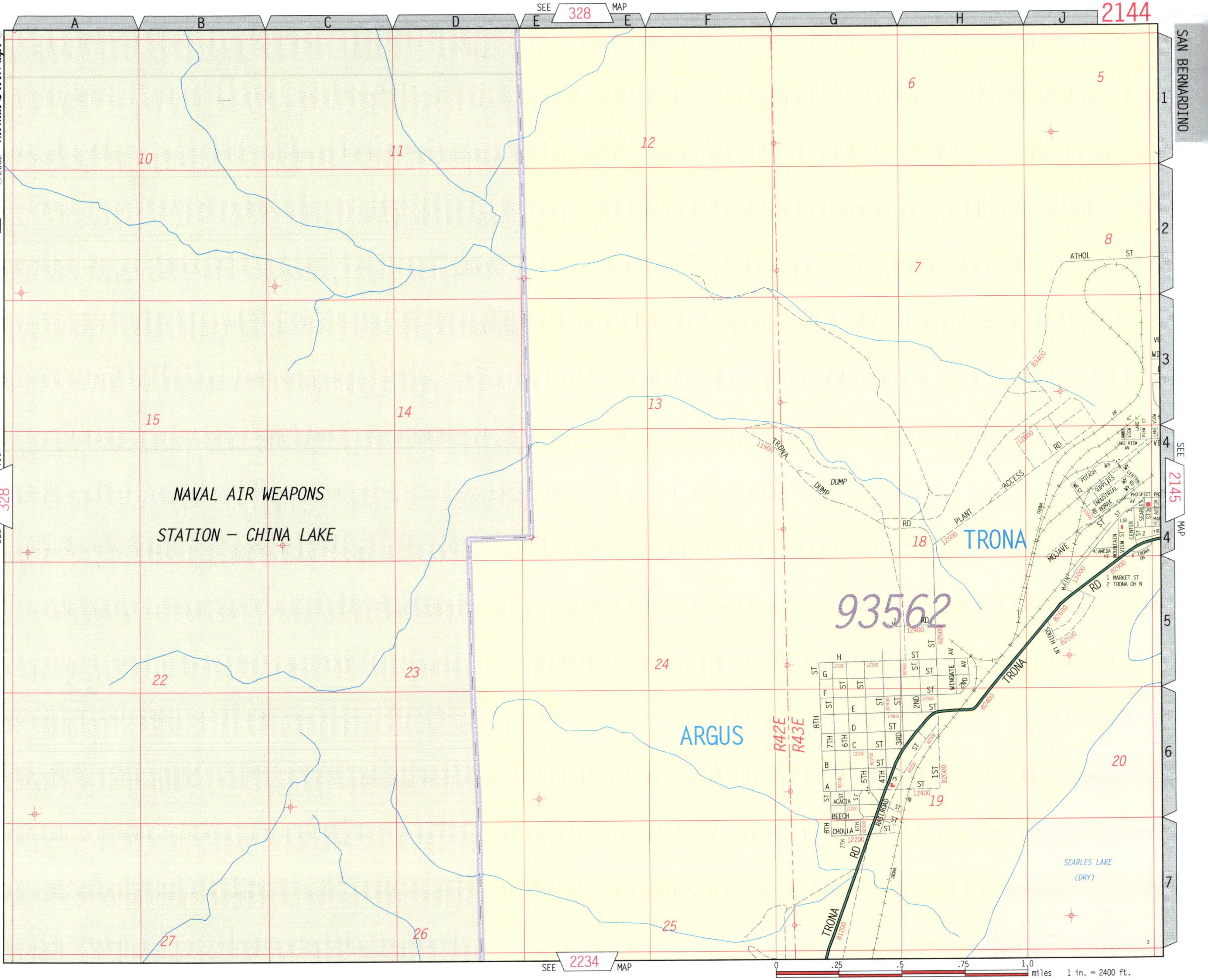
SEE 328 MAP
SEE 2145 MAP
SEE 2234 MAP
SAN BERNARDINO
A
B
C
D
E
F
G
H
J
1
2
3
4
5
6
7
NAVAL AIR WEAPONS
STATION - CHINA LAKE
TRONA
ARGUS
93562
R42E
R43E
TRONA RD
ATHOL ST
TRONA DUMP
DUMP
PLANT ACCESS RD
MOJAVE
MAIN
SOUTH MT
RAILROAD
WINGATE
ACACIA
BEECH
CHOLLA
8TH
7TH
6TH
5TH
4TH
3RD
2ND
1ST
POTASH
SUPPLIES
INDUSTRIAL
BORAX
CENTER
MOUNTAIN VIEW
LAKE VIEW
ALAMEDA
1 MARKET ST
2 TRONA OH N
SEARLES LAKE
(DRY)
miles
1 in. = 2400 ft.
0
.25
.5
.75
1.0

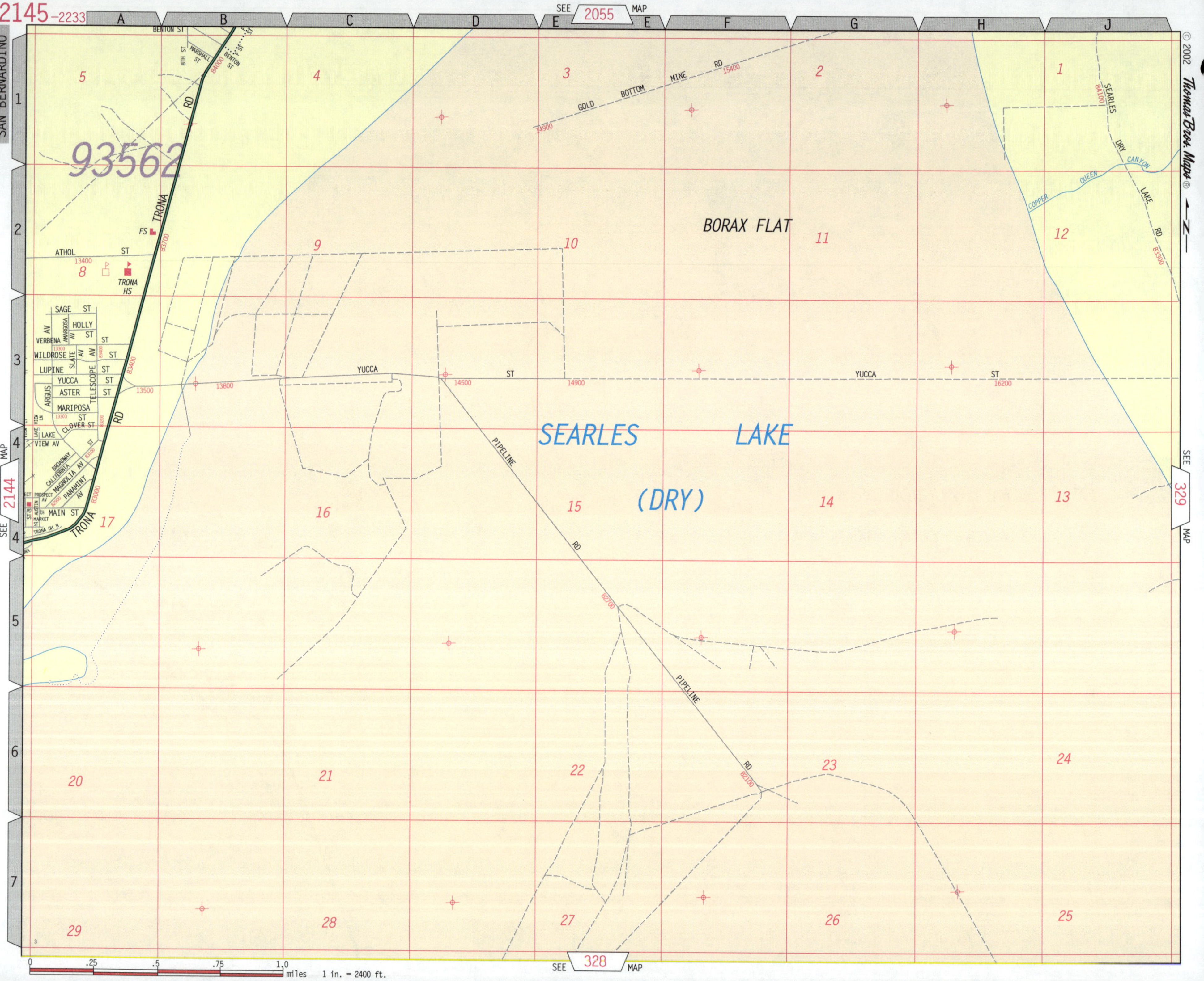
SEE 2055 MAP
SEE 2144 MAP
SEE 329 MAP
SEE 328 MAP
SAN BERNARDINO
© 2002 Thomas Bros. Maps®
A
B
C
D
E
F
G
H
J
1
2
3
4
5
6
7
93562
BORAX FLAT
SEARLES LAKE
(DRY)
GOLD BOTTOM MINE RD
14900
15400
SEARLES DRY LAKE RD
84100
83300
COPPER QUEEN CANYON
TRONA RD
84000
83700
83400
83000
BENTON ST
8TH ST
MARSHALL ST
FS
ATHOL ST
13400
TRONA HS
SAGE ST
HOLLY ST
VERBENA AV
AMARGOSA AV
WILDROSE ST
SLATE AV
LUPINE ST
YUCCA ST
TELESCOPE AV
ASTER ST
ARGUS AV
MARIPOSA ST
CLOVER ST
LAKE VIEW AV
BROADWAY
CALIFORNIA
MAGNOLIA AV
PANAMINT AV
MAIN ST
MARKET ST
13500
13800
YUCCA ST
14500
14900
16200
PIPELINE RD
82700
82100
1
2
3
4
5
8
9
10
11
12
13
14
15
16
17
20
21
22
23
24
25
26
27
28
29
0
.25
.5
.75
1.0
miles
1 in. = 2400 ft.

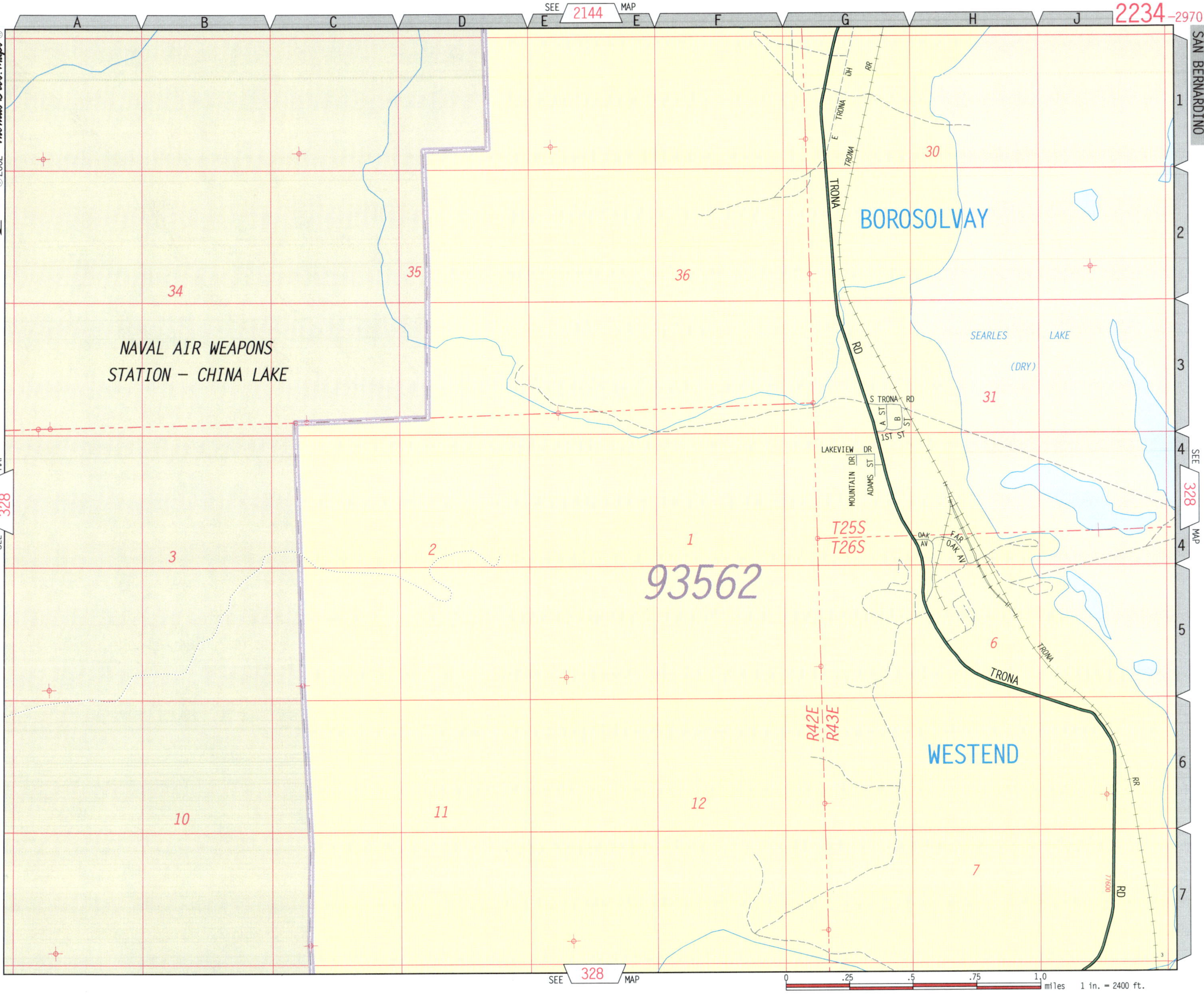
SEE 2144 MAP
A
B
C
D
E
F
G
H
J
1
2
3
4
5
6
7
NAVAL AIR WEAPONS
STATION - CHINA LAKE
BOROSOLVAY
WESTEND
SEARLES LAKE
(DRY)
93562
TRONA RD
E TRONA OH
RR
S TRONA RD
A ST
B ST
1ST ST
LAKEVIEW DR
MOUNTAIN DR
ADAMS ST
OAK AV
FAR OAK AV
T25S
T26S
R42E
R43E
34
35
36
30
31
3
2
1
6
10
11
12
7
SEE 328 MAP
SEE 328 MAP
SEE 328 MAP
0 .25 .5 .75 1.0 miles 1 in. = 2400 ft.

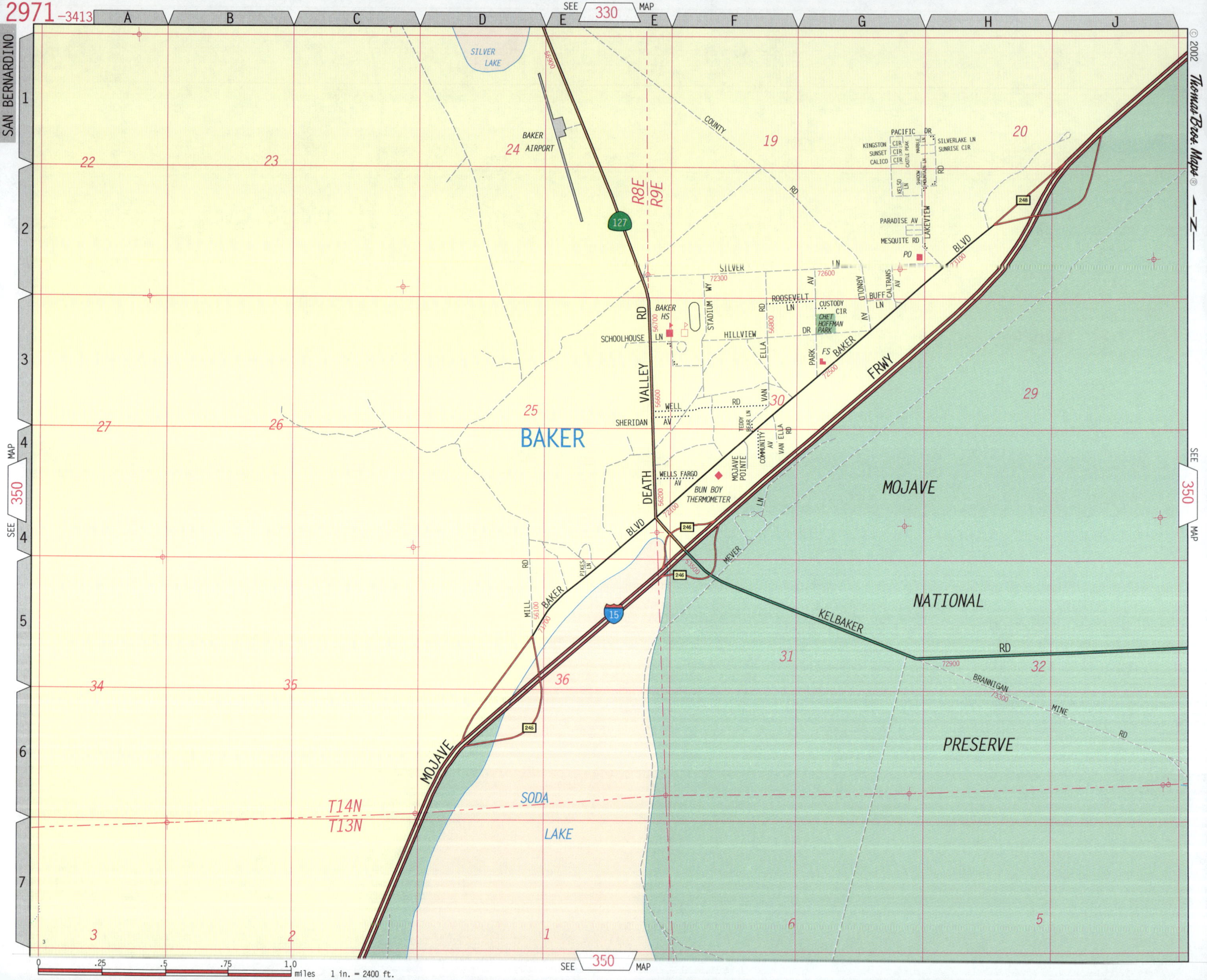

SAN BERNARDINO
SEE 330 MAP
SILVER LAKE
BAKER AIRPORT
COUNTY RD
R8E
R9E
127
PACIFIC DR
KINGSTON CIR
SUNSET CIR
CALICO CIR
SILVERLAKE LN
SUNRISE CIR
KELSO LN
LAKEVIEW RD
PARADISE AV
MESQUITE RD
PO
SILVER LN
ROOSEVELT LN
CUSTODY CIR
CHET HOFFMAN PARK
BUFF LN
ARNOLD AV
CALTRANS AV
STADIUM WY
BAKER HS
SCHOOLHOUSE LN
HILLVIEW DR
ELLA
PARK
FS
BAKER BLVD
FRWY
VALLEY RD
DEATH
WELL RD
SHERIDAN AV
VAN
TEDDY BEAR LN
COMMUNITY AV
VAN ELLA RD
MOJAVE POINTE
WELLS FARGO AV
BUN BOY THERMOMETER
BAKER
MOJAVE
NATIONAL
PRESERVE
248
246
245
15
MEYER LN
KELBAKER RD
BRANNIGAN MINE RD
MILL RD
PIKES LN
MOJAVE
SODA LAKE
T14N
T13N
22 23 24 19 20
27 26 25 30 29
34 35 36 31 32
3 2 1 6 5
SEE 350 MAP
0 .25 .5 .75 1.0 miles 1 in. = 2400 ft.

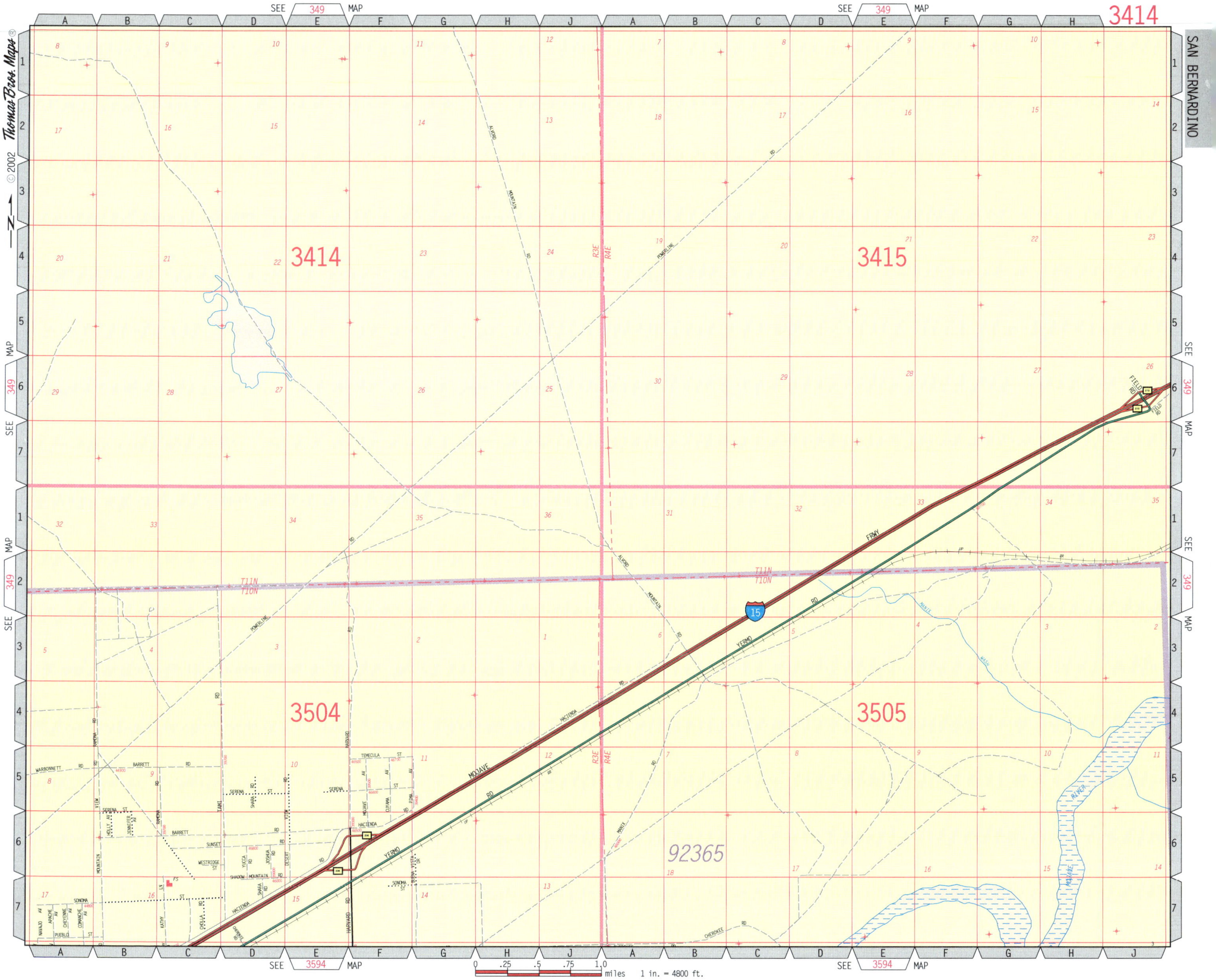
Thomas Bros. Maps
© 2002
SAN BERNARDINO
SEE 349 MAP
SEE 3594 MAP
3414
3415
3504
3505
R3E
R4E
T11N
T10N
MOJAVE FRWY
YERMO RD
POWERLINE RD
ALVORD MOUNTAIN RD
HACIENDA RD
HARVARD RD
FIELD RD
MANIX WASH
MOJAVE RIVER
CHEROKEE RD
92365
0 .25 .5 .75 1.0 miles
1 in. = 4800 ft.

SEE 349 MAP

SEE 349 MAP

SAN BERNARDINO

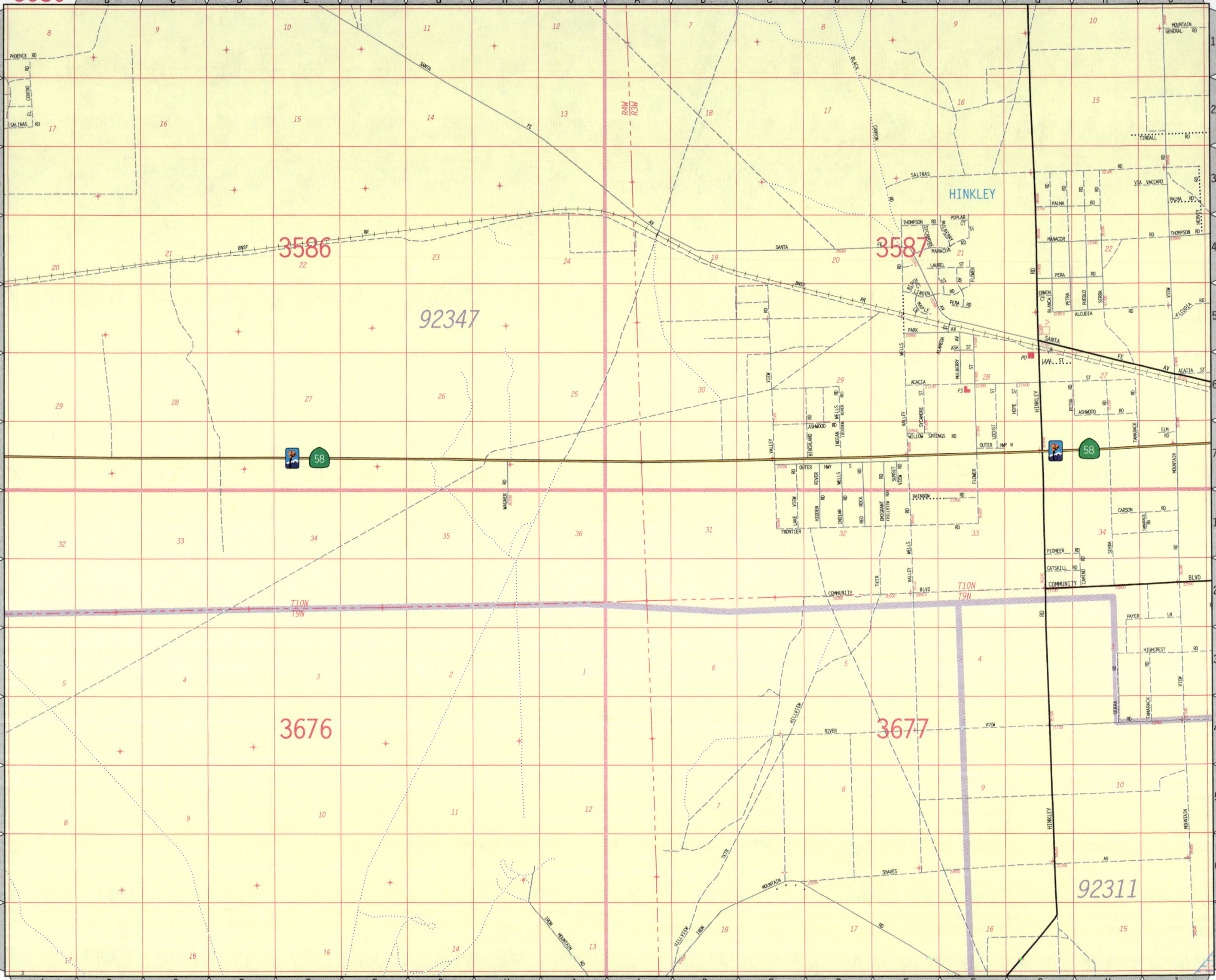

SEE 348 MAP

SEE 348 MAP

SEE 3588 MAP

SEE 3678 MAP

SEE 3756 MAP

SEE 3756 MAP

0 .25 .5 .75 1.0 miles 1 in. = 4800 ft.

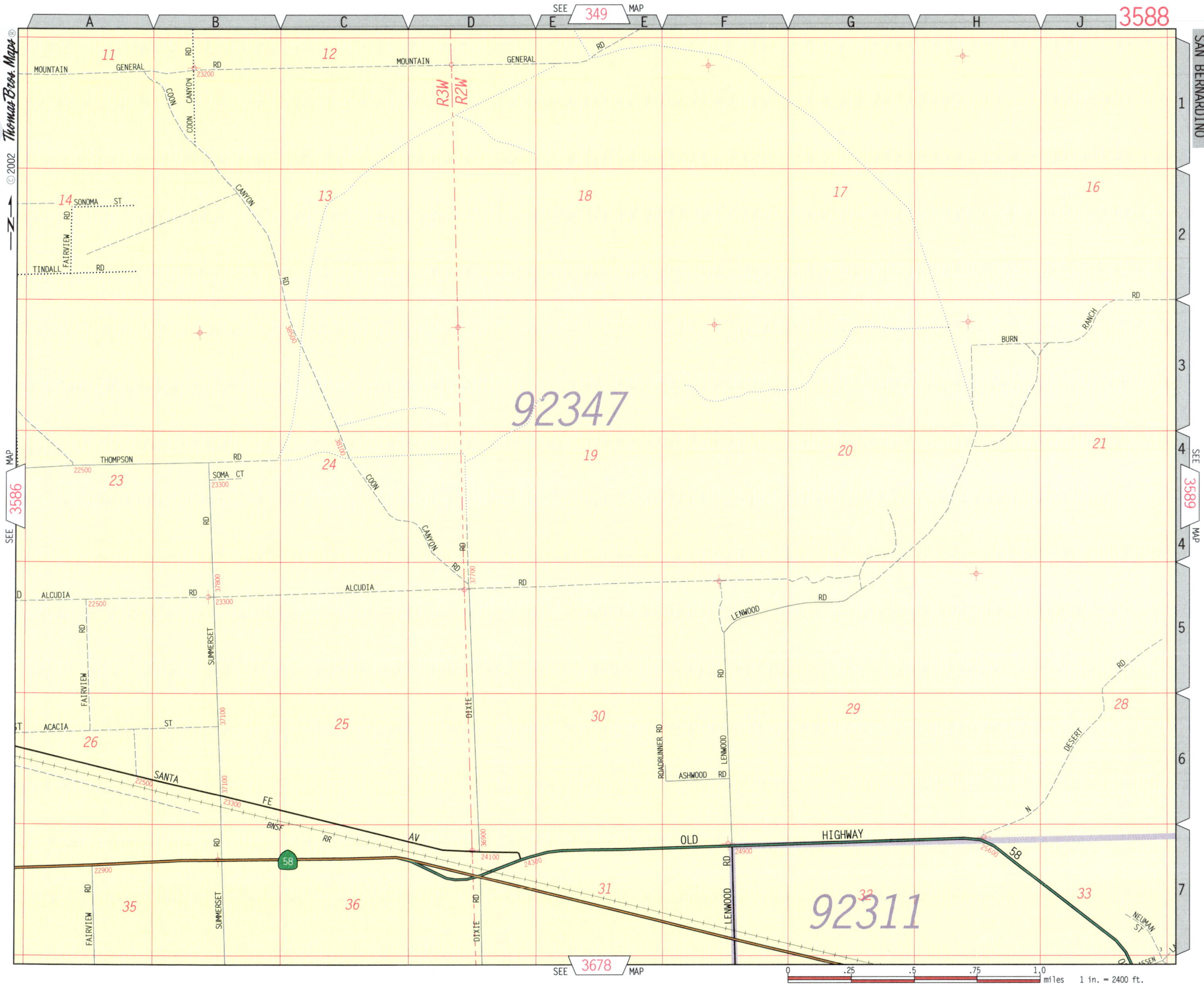
SEE 349 MAP
SEE 3586 MAP
SEE 3589 MAP
SEE 3678 MAP
SAN BERNARDINO
A B C D E F G H J
1 2 3 4 5 6 7
R3W
R2W
92347
92311
MOUNTAIN GENERAL RD
COON CANYON RD
SONOMA ST
FAIRVIEW RD
TINDALL RD
THOMPSON RD
SOMA CT
BURN RD
RANCH RD
ALCUDIA RD
LENWOOD RD
SUMMERSET RD
DIXIE RD
ACACIA ST
ROADRUNNER RD
ASHWOOD RD
DESERT N RD
SANTA FE AV
BNSF RR
OLD HIGHWAY 58
NEUMAN ST
11 12 13 14 16 17 18 19 20 21 23 24 25 26 28 29 30 31 32 33 35 36
23200 38500 38100 22500 23300 37800 37700 37100 22900 36900 24100 24300 24900 25600
0 .25 .5 .75 1.0 miles 1 in. = 2400 ft.

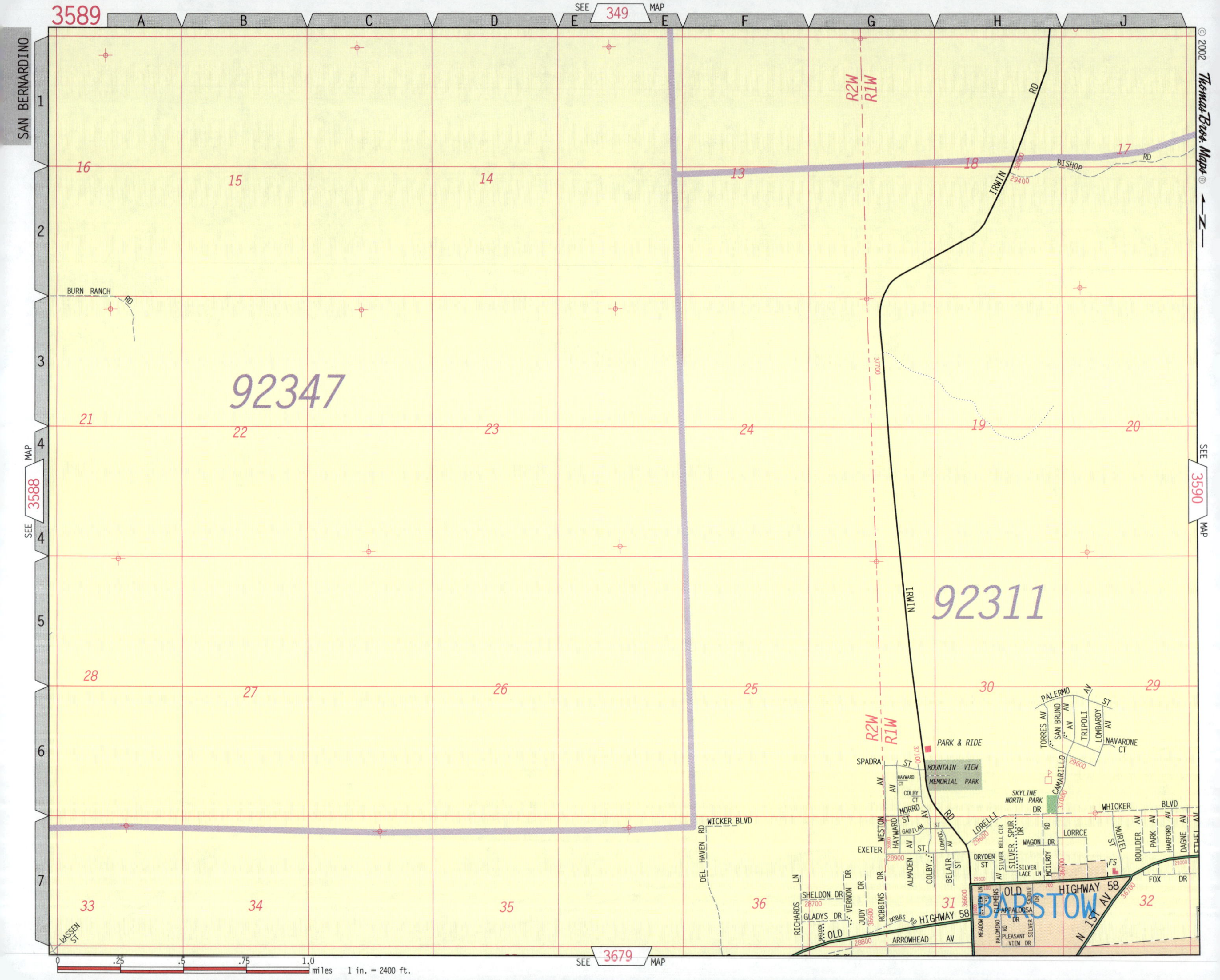
SEE 349 MAP
A
B
C
D
E
F
G
H
J
SAN BERNARDINO
1
2
3
4
5
6
7
SEE 3588 MAP
SEE 3590 MAP
SEE 3679 MAP
© 2002 Thomas Bros. Maps ®
N
R2W
R1W
16
15
14
13
18
17
IRWIN RD
BISHOP RD
29400
28900
BURN RANCH RD
92347
92311
21
22
23
24
19
20
37100
IRWIN
28
27
26
25
30
29
PALERMO AV
ST
TORRES AV
SAN BRUNO AV
AV
TRIPOLI
LOMBARDY AV
NAVARONE CT
PARK & RIDE
SPADRA
ST
37100
MOUNTAIN VIEW MEMORIAL PARK
HAYWARD CT
COLBY CT
CAMARILLO
29600
SKYLINE NORTH PARK
37000
DR
WHICKER BLVD
MORRO AV
ST
RD
LORELLI
29600
WICKER BLVD
DEL HAVEN RD
WESTON AV
HAYWARD AV
GABILAN ST
LOMPOC AV
SILVER BELL CIR
SILVER SPUR DR
WAGON DR
RD
LORRCE
MURIEL ST
BOULDER AV
PARK AV
HARFORD AV
DAGNE AV
ETHEL AV
EXETER
36800
AV
ST.
28900
ALMADEN
COLBY
BELAIR ST
DRYDEN ST
AV
SILVER LACE LN
MCILROY
36700
FS
29000
29300
FOX DR
RICHARDS LN
SHELDON DR
28700
VERNON DR
JUDY DR
36600
ROBBINS DR
GLADYS DR
SHELDON
OLD
DOBBS RD
HIGHWAY 58
28800
ARROWHEAD AV
36600
MEADOW VIEW LN
CLEMENS
OLD HIGHWAY 58
BARSTOW
SADDLE DR
APPALOOSA DR
PALOMINO RD
PLEASANT VIEW DR
SILVER
N 1ST AV
36700
31
32
33
34
35
36
LASSEN ST
0
.25
.5
.75
1.0
miles
1 in. = 2400 ft.

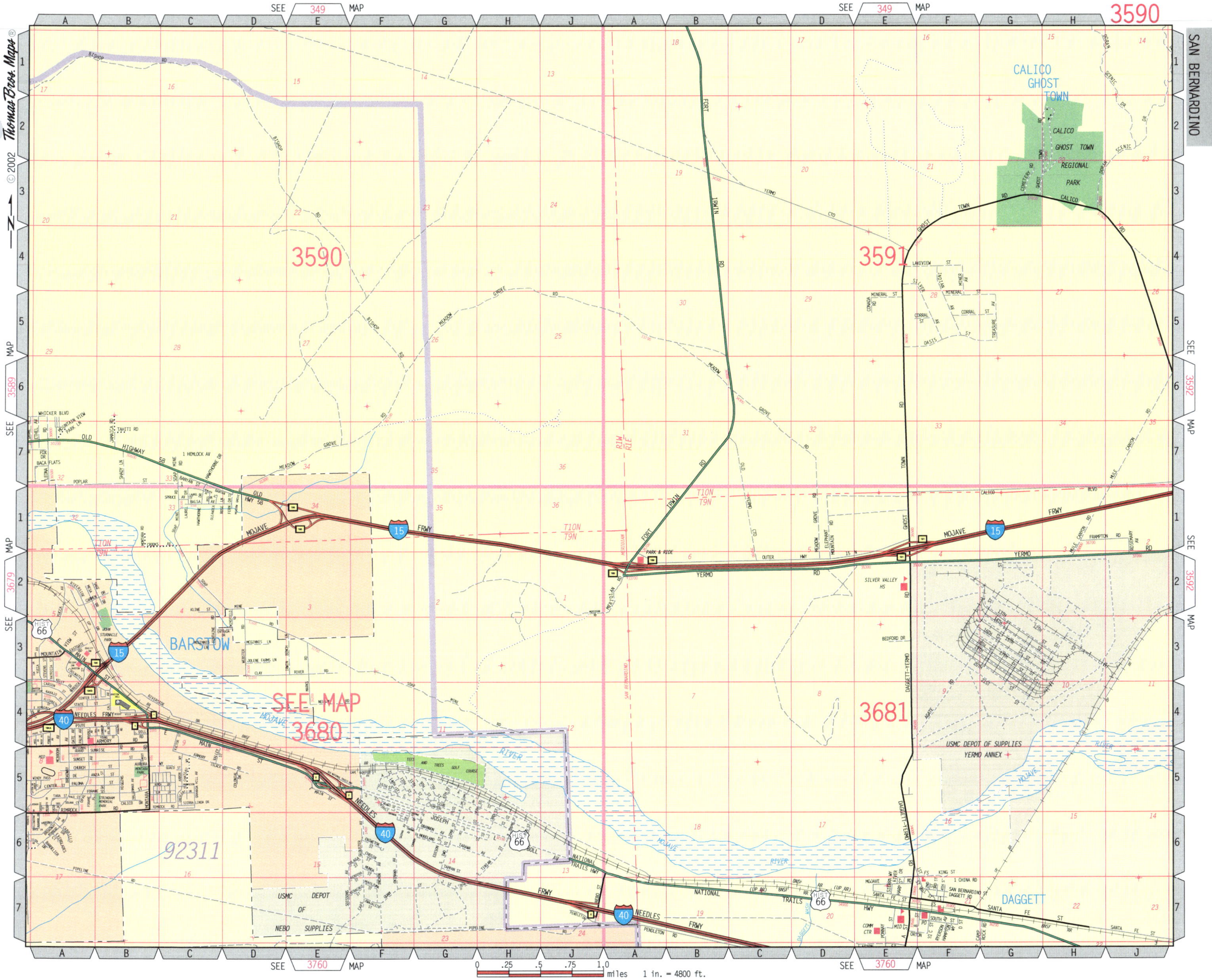
SEE 349 MAP
SEE 349 MAP
3590
3591
3681
SEE MAP 3680
SEE 3589 MAP
SEE 3679 MAP
SEE 3592 MAP
SEE 3592 MAP
SEE 3760 MAP
SEE 3760 MAP
CALICO GHOST TOWN
CALICO GHOST TOWN REGIONAL PARK
BARSTOW
DAGGETT
92311
USMC DEPOT OF SUPPLIES YERMO ANNEX
USMC DEPOT OF NEBO SUPPLIES
SILVER VALLEY HS
MOJAVE RIVER
MOJAVE FRWY
NEEDLES FRWY
NATIONAL TRAILS HWY
YERMO RD
FORT IRWIN RD
GHOST TOWN RD
DAGGETT-YERMO RD
OLD HIGHWAY 58
BISHOP RD
MEADOW GROVE RD
CALICO BLVD
MAIN ST
SANTA FE ST
T10N T9N
R1W R1E
Thomas Bros. Maps ©2002
0 .25 .5 .75 1.0 miles 1 in. = 4800 ft.

SEE 349 MAP
SEE 349 MAP

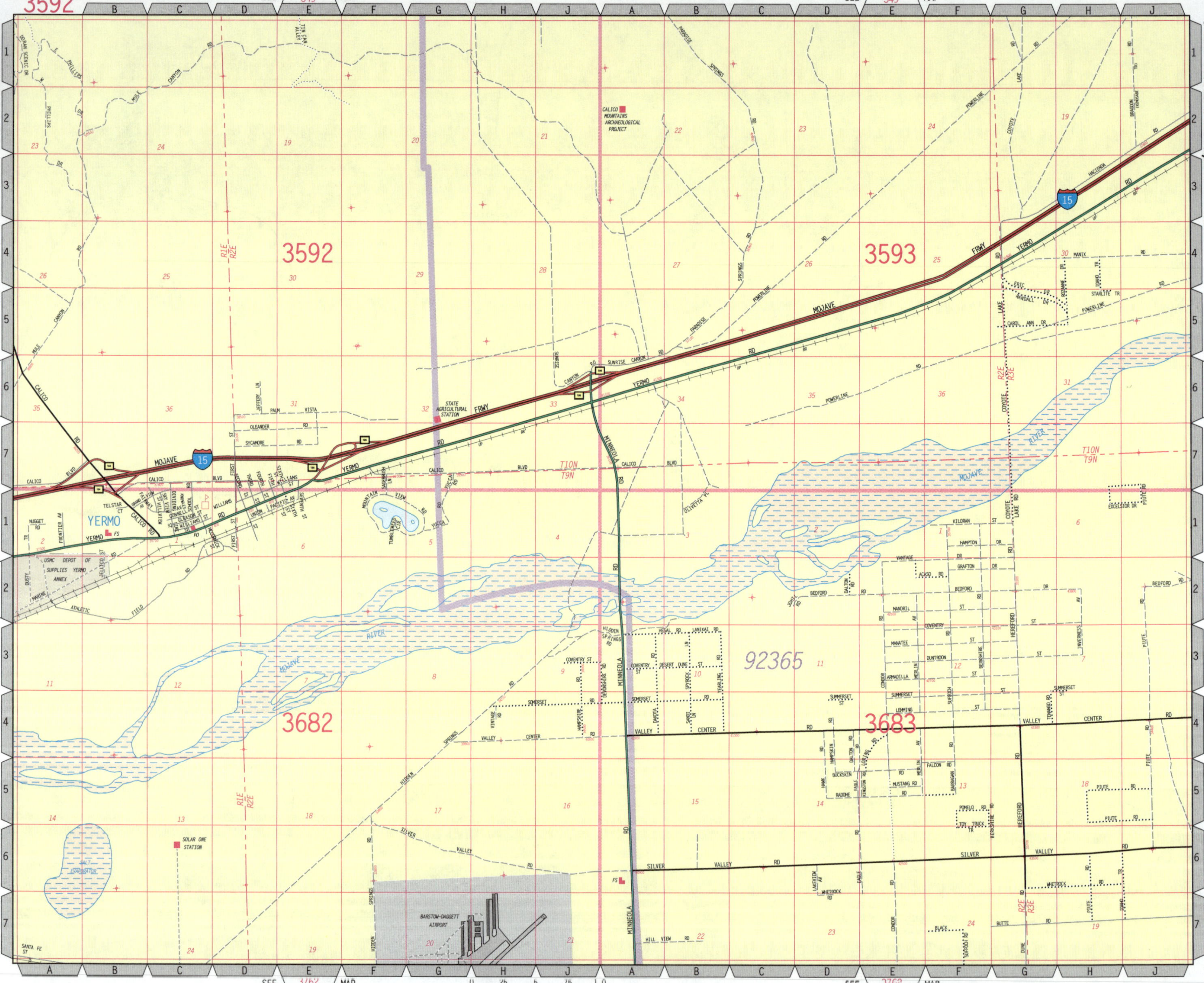

SEE 3762 MAP
SEE 3762 MAP

0 .25 .5 .75 1.0 miles 1 in. = 4800 ft.

SEE 3414 MAP

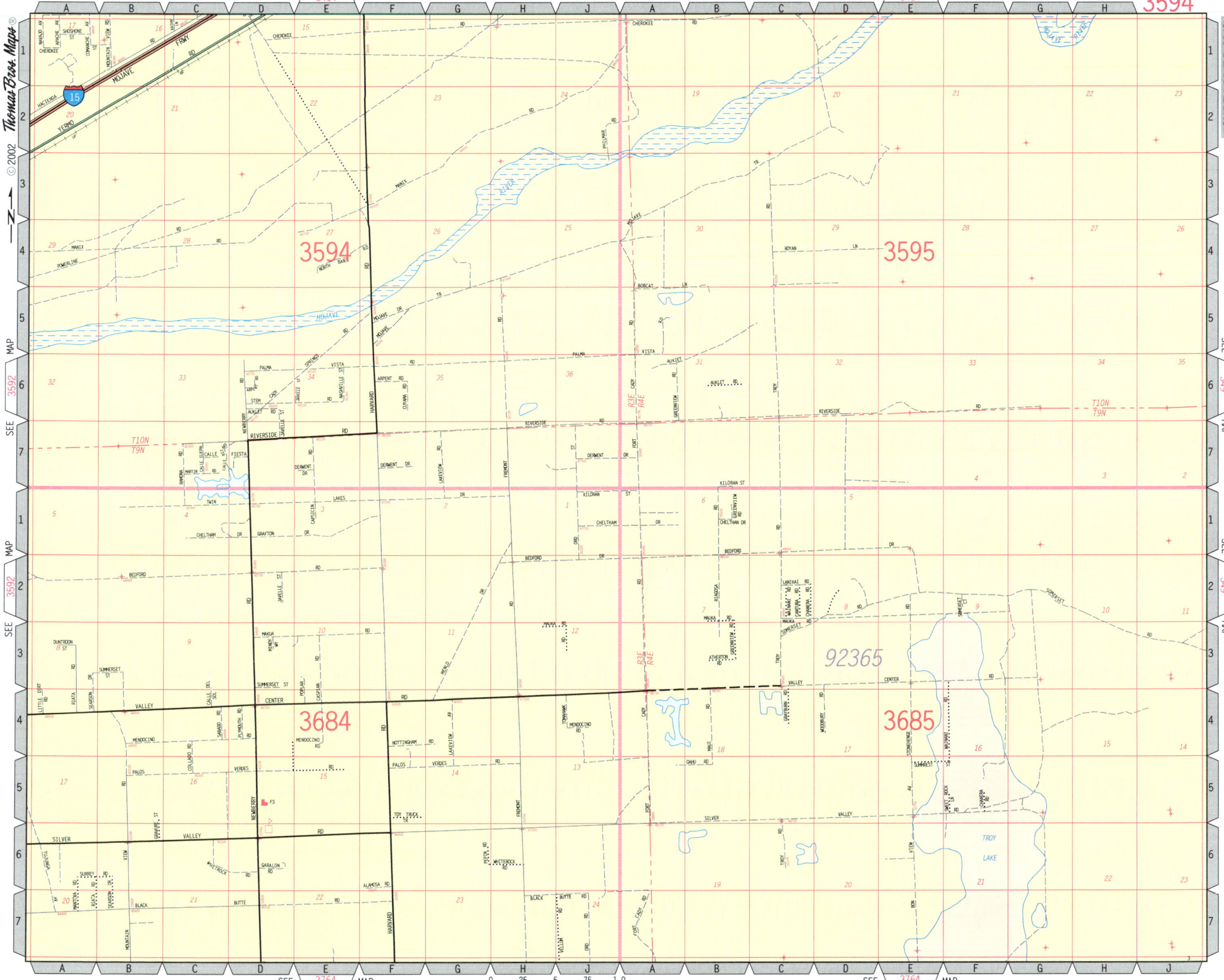

SEE 3592 MAP
SEE 3592 MAP
SEE 3595 MAP
SEE 3595 MAP
SEE 3764 MAP

0 .25 .5 .75 1.0 miles 1 in. = 4800 ft.

SEE 352 MAP

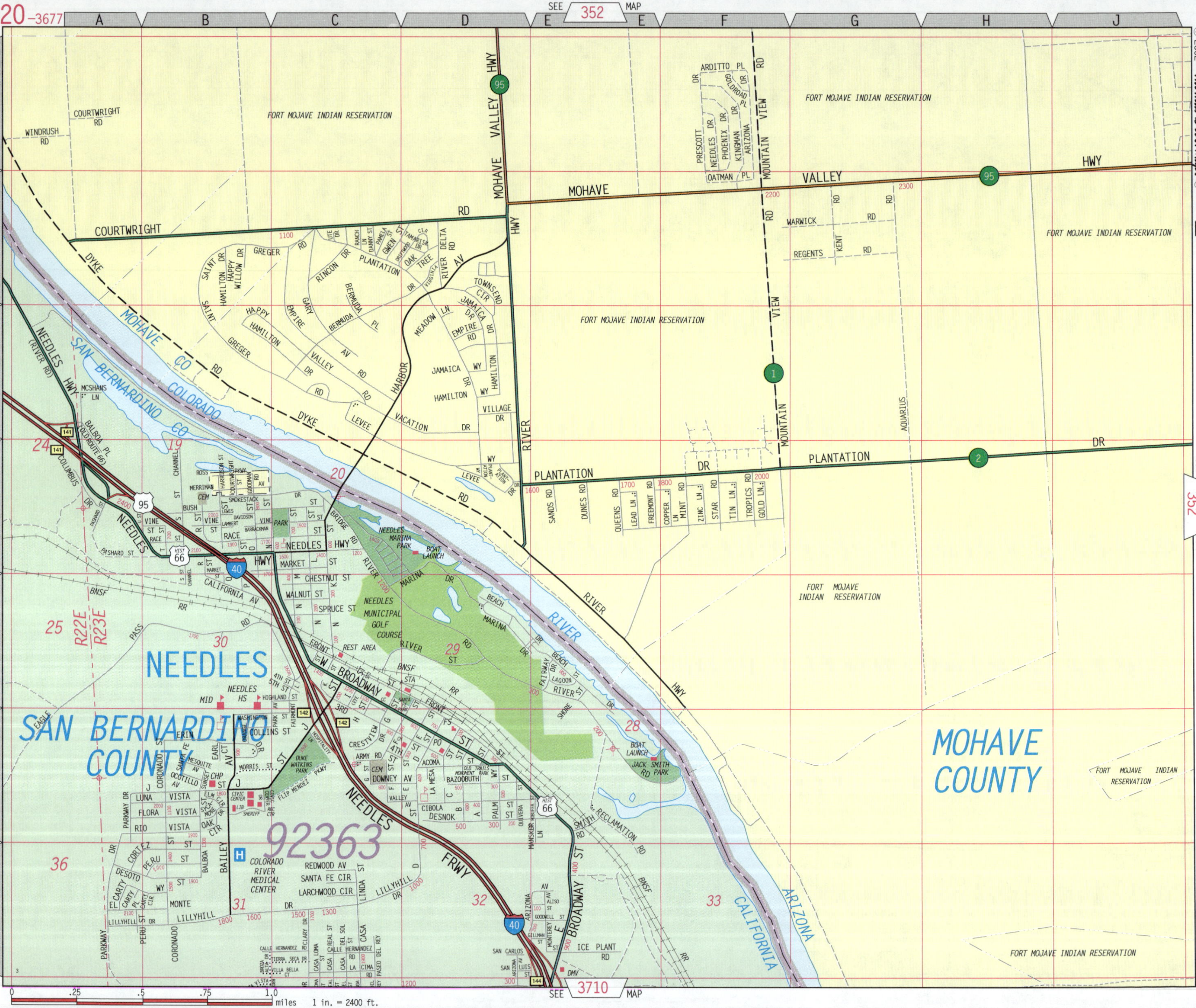

SEE 352 MAP
SEE 3710 MAP

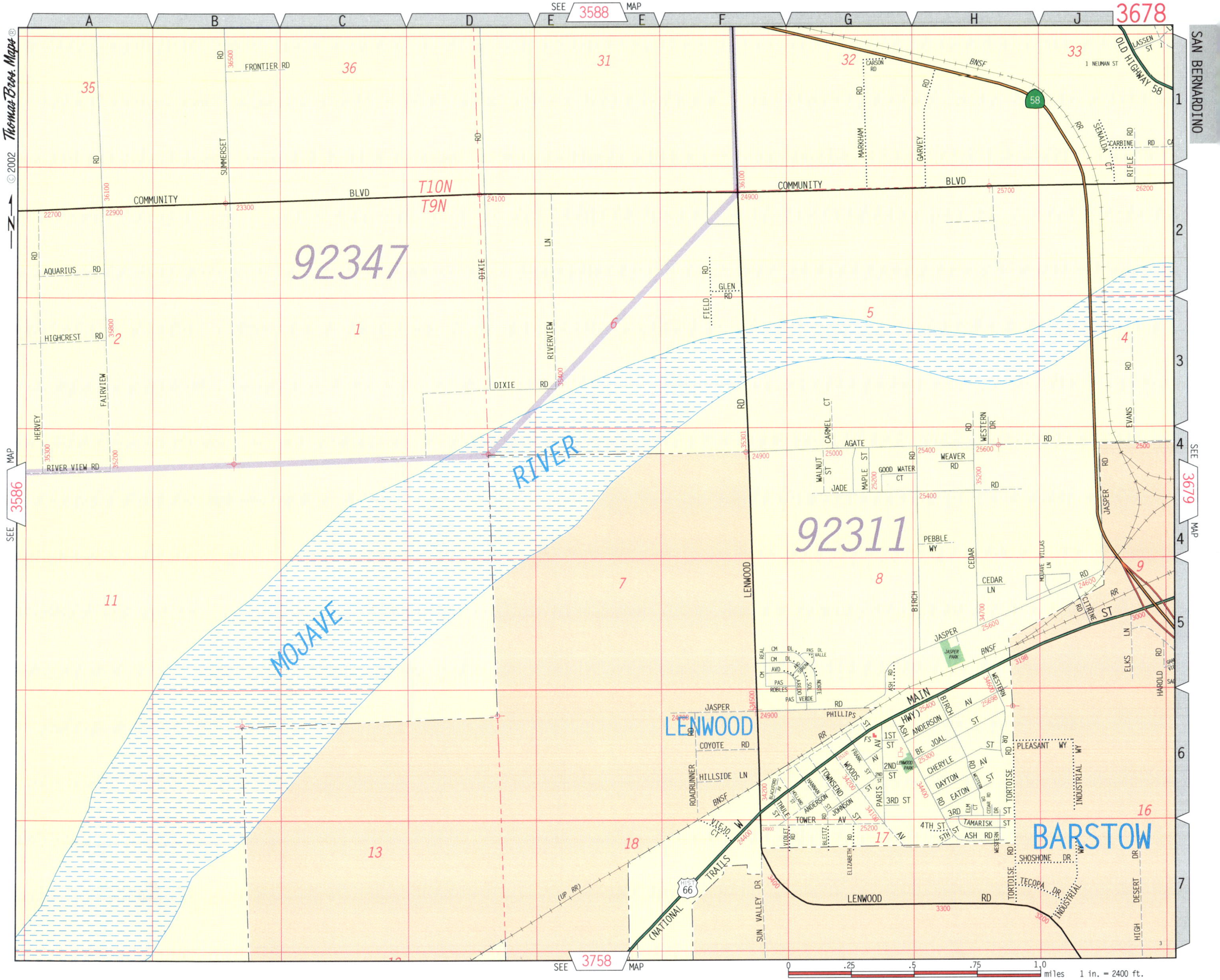
SEE 3588 MAP
A
B
C
D
E
F
G
H
J
SAN BERNARDINO
Thomas Bros. Maps
© 2002
SEE 3586 MAP
SEE 3679 MAP
SEE 3758 MAP
92347
92311
T10N
T9N
MOJAVE RIVER
LENWOOD
BARSTOW
COMMUNITY BLVD
FRONTIER RD
SUMMERSET RD
DIXIE RD
RIVERVIEW LN
AQUARIUS RD
HIGHCREST RD
FAIRVIEW
HERVEY RD
RIVER VIEW RD
FIELD RD
GLEN RD
LENWOOD RD
BNSF
OLD HIGHWAY 58
LASSEN ST
NEUMAN ST
CARSON RD
MARKHAM RD
GARVEY RD
SENALDA CT
CARBINE RD
RIFLE RD
EVANS RD
JASPER RD
AGATE
CARMEL CT
WALNUT ST
JADE
MAPLE ST
GOOD WATER CT
WEAVER RD
WESTERN DR
PEBBLE WY
CEDAR LN
BIRCH
MOJAVE VILLAS LN
CITRINE ST
JASPER PARK
MAIN ST
PHILLIPS
COYOTE RD
HILLSIDE LN
ROADRUNNER RD
VIEJO CT
NATIONAL TRAILS HWY
HIST 66
(UP RR)
SUN VALLEY DR
LENWOOD RD
TOWNSEND
ANDERSON
JOHNSON
TOWER
WOODS ST
PARIS ST
1ST ST
2ND ST
3RD ST
4TH ST
5TH ST
ASH RD
TAMARISK ST
CHERYLE
DAYTON
EATON
JOAL
PLEASANT WY
INDUSTRIAL WY
TORTOISE RD
SHOSHONE DR
TECOPA DR
DESERT
HIGH DR
ELKS LN
HAROLD RD
0 .25 .5 .75 1.0 miles 1 in. = 2400 ft.

SEE 3589 MAP

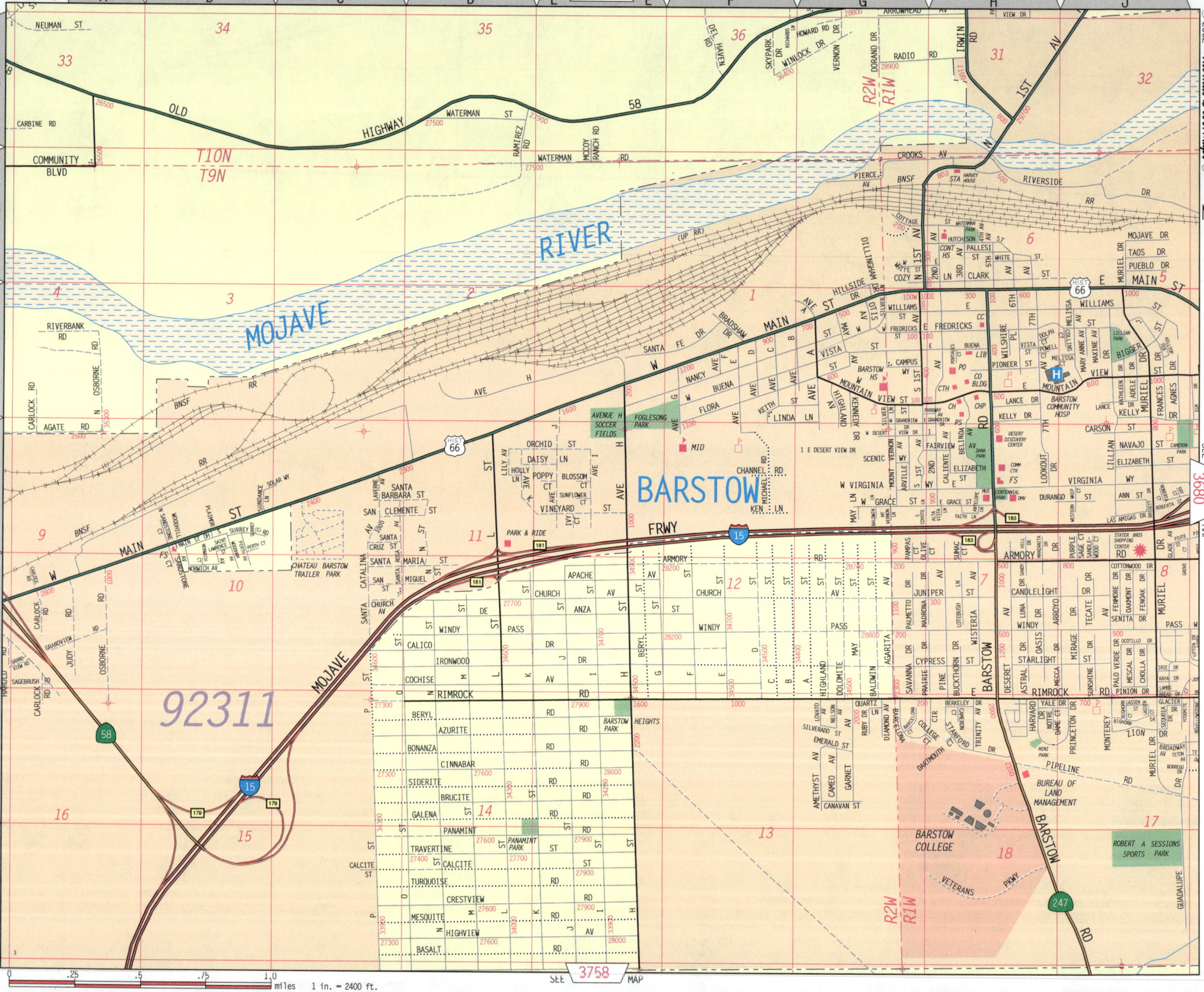

SEE 3678 MAP

SEE 3680 MAP

SEE 3758 MAP

SEE 3590 MAP
SEE 3679 MAP
SEE 3590 MAP
SEE 3760 MAP
A
B
C
D
E
F
G
H
J
1
2
3
4
5
6
7
BARSTOW
92311
MOJAVE RIVER
MOJAVE FRWY
NEEDLES FRWY
OLD HWY 58
T10N
T9N
JOHN STURNACLE PARK
MONTARA PARK
STRINGHAM PARK
BARSTOW MALL
TEES AND TREES GOLF COURSE
USMC DEPOT OF NEBO SUPPLIES
NATIONAL TRAILS HWY
E MAIN ST
BOLL AV
CLUB QUARTERS
NATIONAL GUARD ARMORY
BNSF
PIPELINE RD
SOAP MINE RD
RIVERSIDE DR
E MOUNTAIN VIEW ST
MCGINNIS LN
JOLENE FARMS LN
CLAY
RIVER RD
NELSON RD
KLINE ST
CROOKS AV
RIMROCK RD
ARMORY RD
SUNRISE
CHURCH
FORANE
MERIDIAN RD
PENDLETON RD
NEBO ST
32
33
34
35
36
5
4
3
2
1
8
9
10
11
12
17
16
15
14
13
23
24
0
.25
.5
.75
1.0
miles
1 in. = 2400 ft.

SEE 3620 MAP

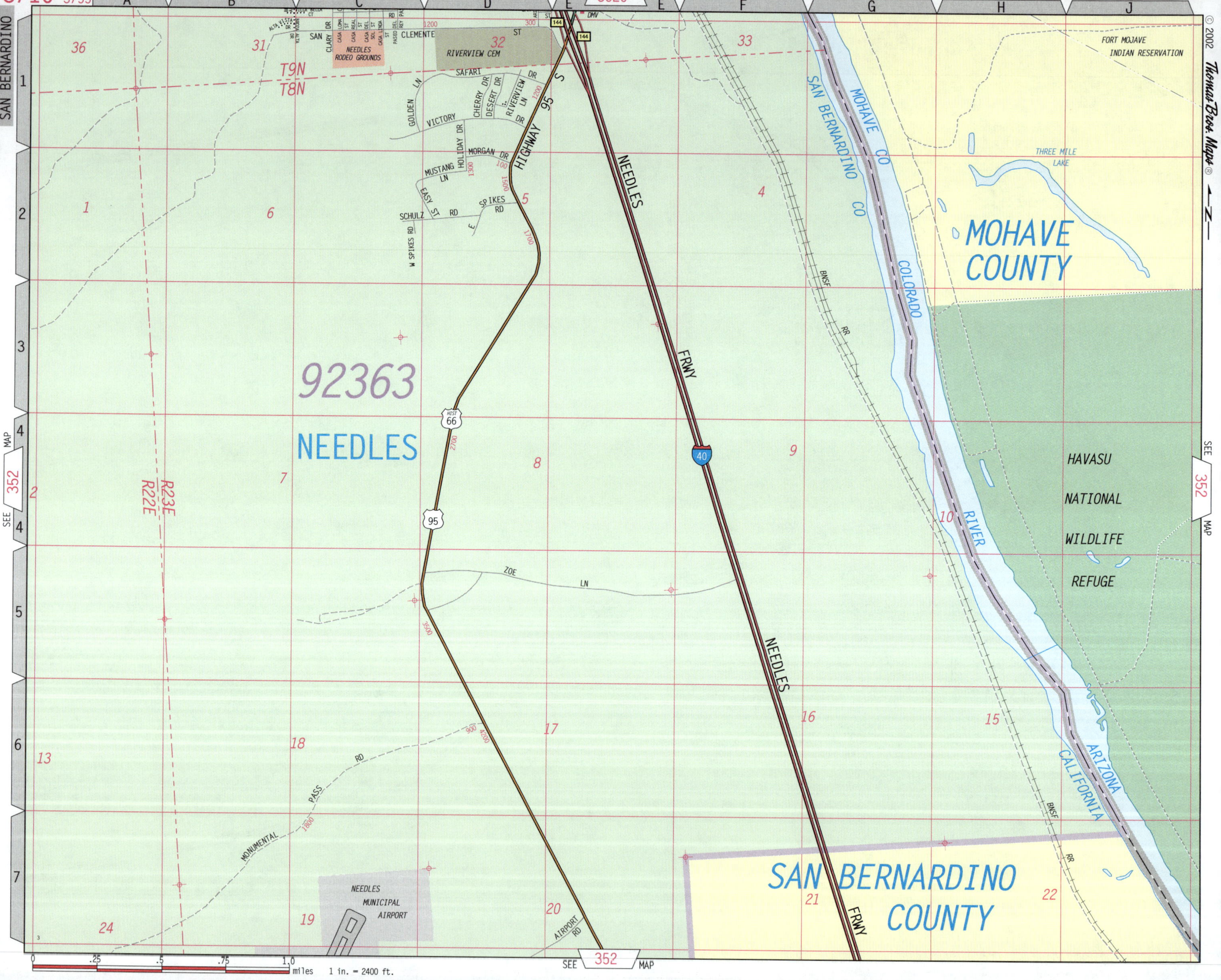

SEE 352 MAP

SEE 352 MAP

SEE 352 MAP

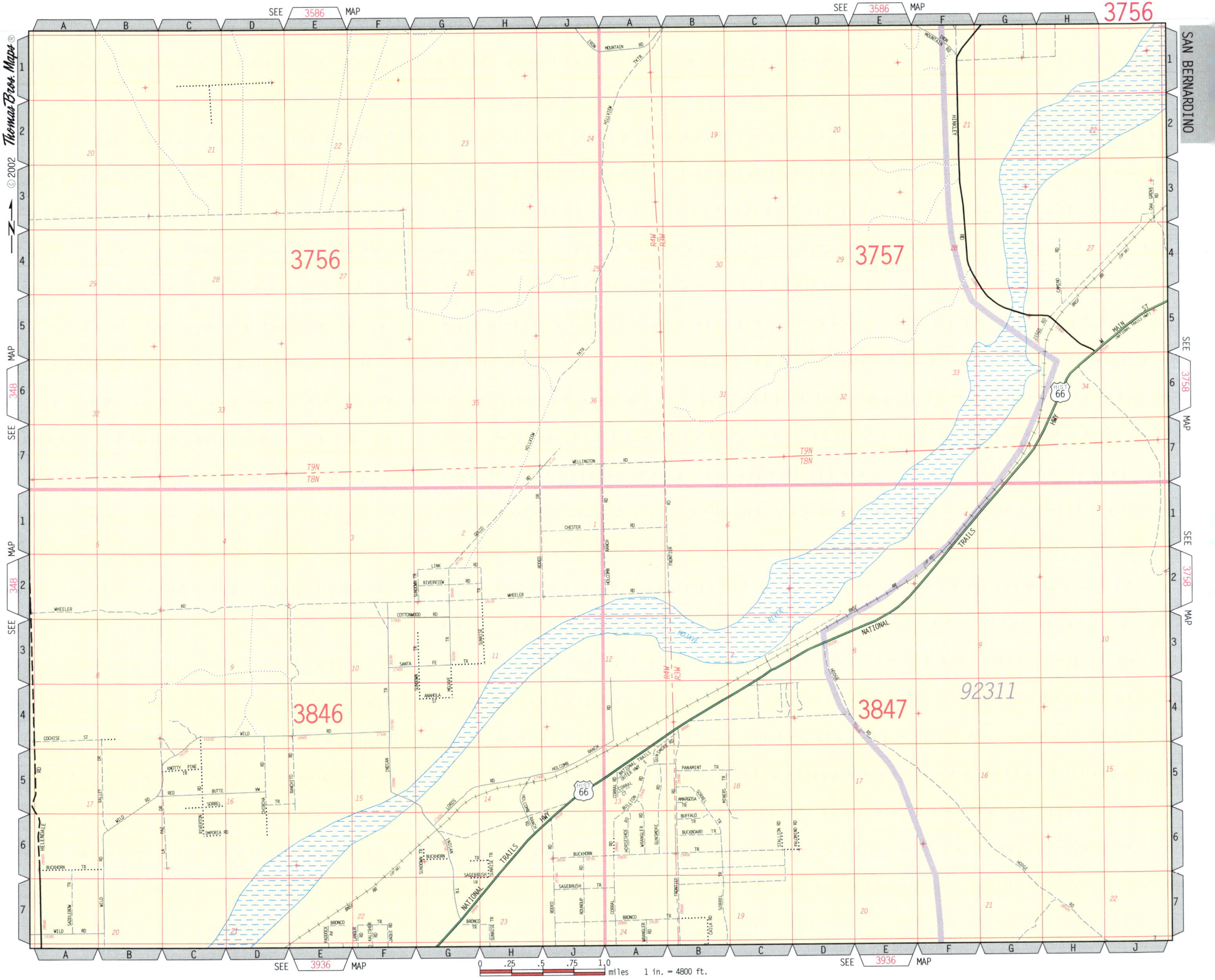
SAN BERNARDINO
3756
3757
3846
3847
92311
SEE 3586 MAP
SEE 3758 MAP
SEE 348 MAP
SEE 3936 MAP
T9N
T8N
R4W
R3W
MOJAVE
RIVER
NATIONAL TRAILS HWY
HIST 66
WHEELER RD
WELLINGTON RD
CHESTER RD
HOLCOMB RANCH RD
FRONTIER RD
HILLVIEW RD
HINKLEY RD
HODGE RD
IRON MOUNTAIN RD
RIVERVIEW RD
COTTONWOOD RD
SANTA FE TR
LINK RD
WILD RD
COCHISE ST
HELENDALE RD
BUCKHORN TR
SAGEBRUSH TR
BRONCO TR
PANAMINT TR
W MAIN ST
BNSF
miles 1 in. = 4800 ft.

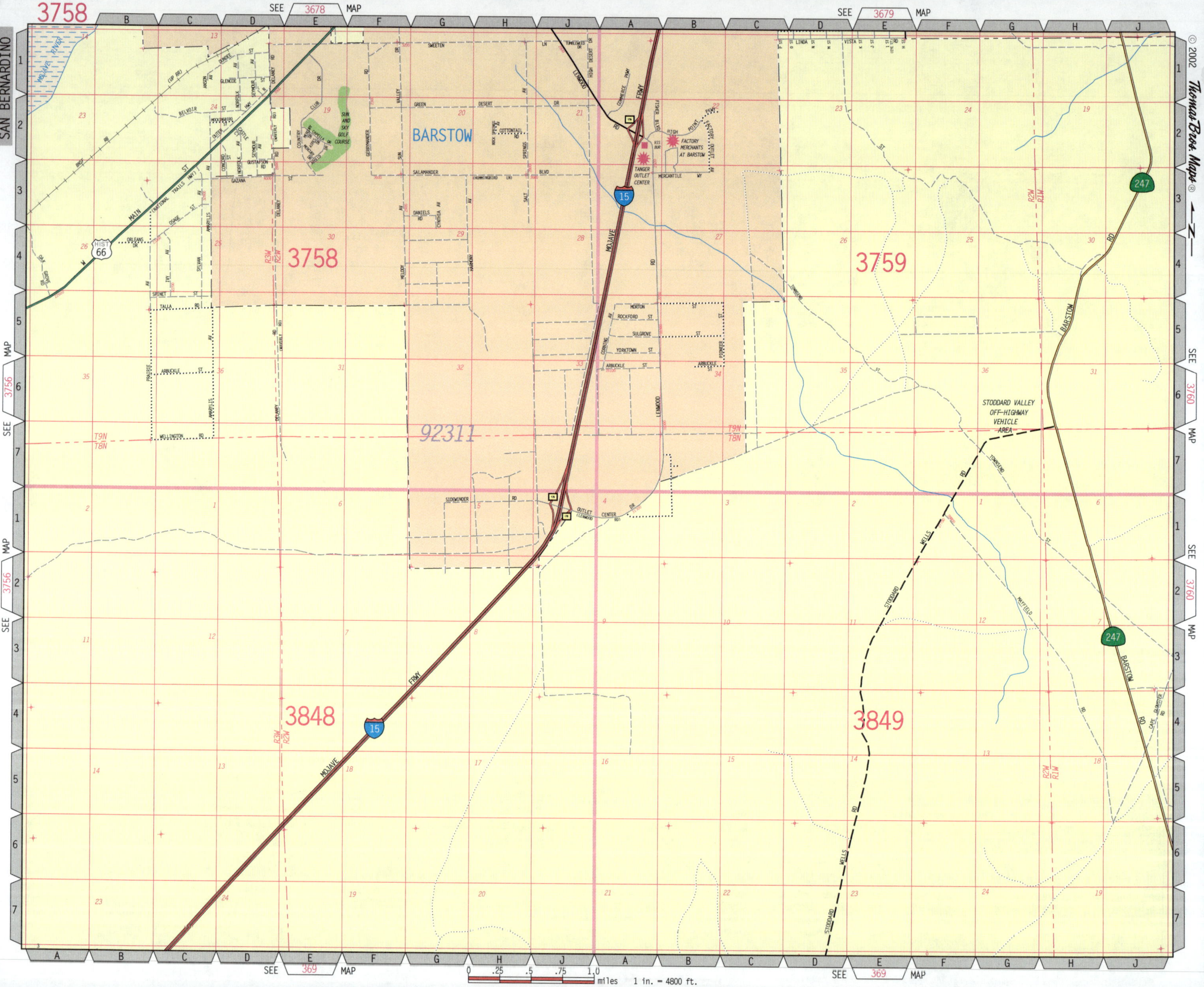
SEE 3678 MAP
SEE 3679 MAP
SEE 3756 MAP
SEE 3760 MAP
SEE 369 MAP
SAN BERNARDINO
BARSTOW
3758
3759
3848
3849
92311
MOJAVE FRWY
15
HIST 66
247
MOJAVE RIVER
MAIN ST
NATIONAL TRAILS HWY
SUN AND SKY GOLF COURSE
TANGER OUTLET CENTER
FACTORY MERCHANTS AT BARSTOW
MERCANTILE WY
LENWOOD RD
OUTLET CENTER DR
SALAMANDER BLVD
SWEETEN
GREEN
DESERT DR
COTTONTAIL
DANIELS RD
CYNTHIA AV
MORTON
ROCKFORD ST
SULGROVE
YORKTOWN ST
ARBUCKLE ST
PIONEER
SIDEWINDER RD
WELLINGTON RD
SPINET ST
TALLA RD
ORLEANS DR
OAK GROVE RD
BELVOIR
GAZANA
GUSTAFSON RD
DELANEY
STODDARD VALLEY OFF-HIGHWAY VEHICLE AREA
STODDARD WELLS RD
BARSTOW RD
TOWNSEND
MAYFIELD
T9N
T8N
R3W
R2W
R1W
0 .25 .5 .75 1.0 miles 1 in. = 4800 ft.
© 2002 Thomas Bros Maps ®

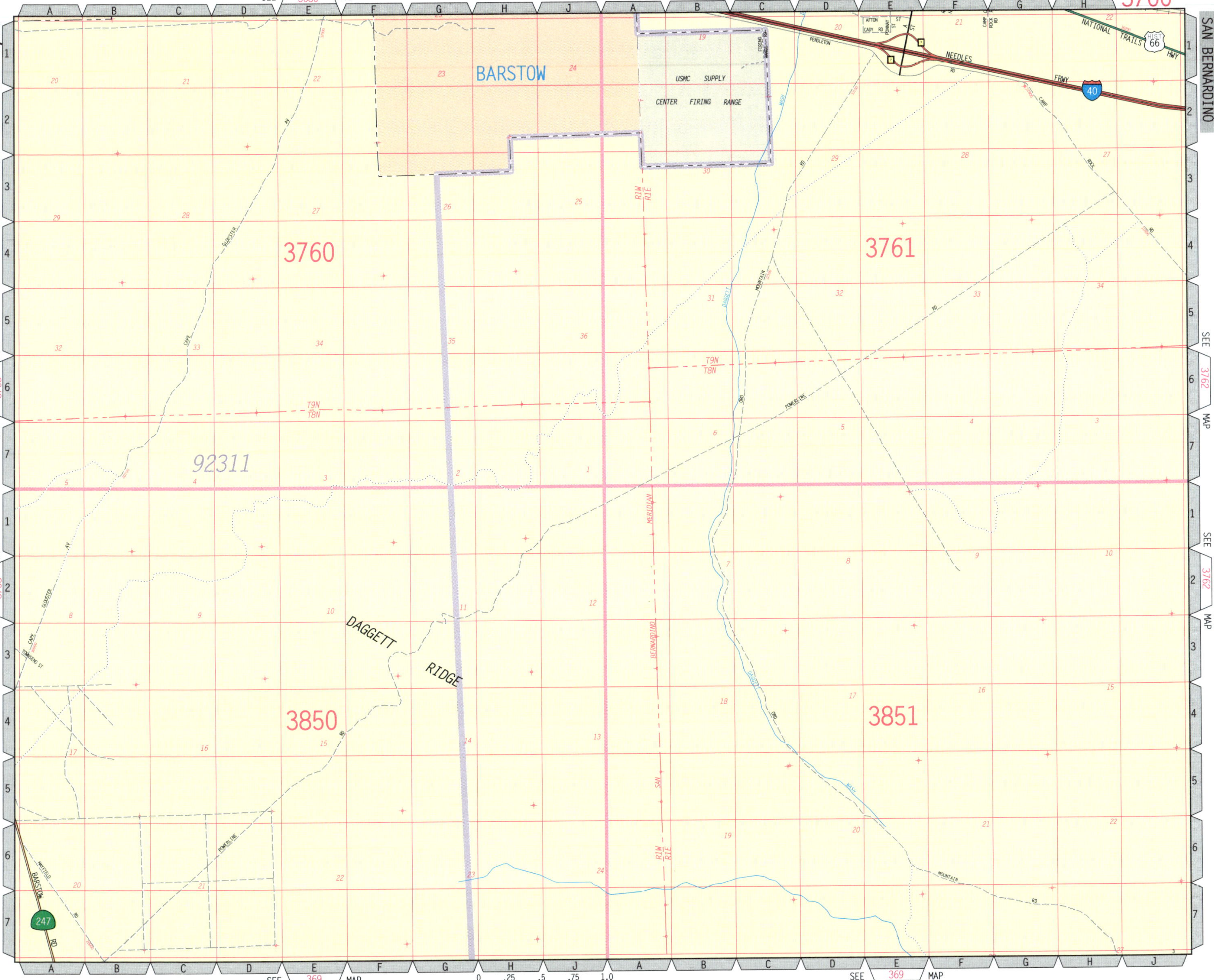
SEE 3680 MAP
SEE 3590 MAP
BARSTOW
USMC SUPPLY CENTER FIRING RANGE
NATIONAL TRAILS HWY
HIST 66
NEEDLES FRWY
40
PENDLETON
AFTON
CADY RD
PENNWAY ST
A ST
CAMP ROCK RD
CAMP ROCK RD
SAN BERNARDINO
3760
3761
3850
3851
92311
T9N T8N
R1W R1E
SAN BERNARDINO MERIDIAN
DAGGETT RIDGE
GLOUSTER AV
CAPE
TOWNSEND ST
POWERLINE
MOUNTAIN RD
DAGGETT
WASH
MAYFIELD
BARSTOW RD
247
SEE 3758 MAP
SEE 3762 MAP
SEE 369 MAP
0 .25 .5 .75 1.0 miles 1 in. = 4800 ft.

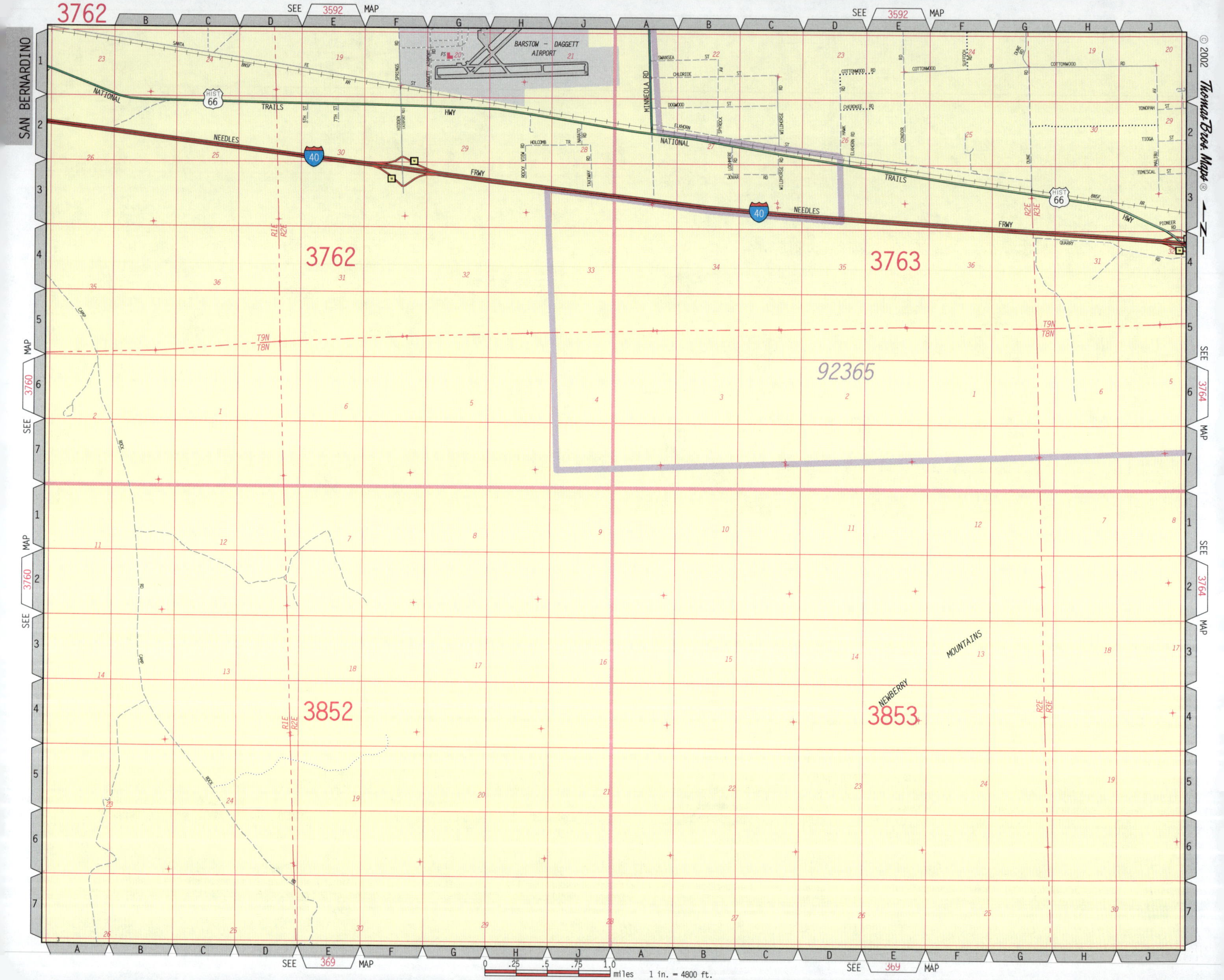
SEE 3592 MAP
SAN BERNARDINO
BARSTOW - DAGGETT AIRPORT
FS
SANTA FE RR
BNSF
NATIONAL TRAILS HWY
HIST 66
NEEDLES FRWY
40
5TH ST
7TH ST
HIDDEN SPRINGS RD
DAGGETT AIRPORT RD
HOLCOMB
ROCKY VIEW RD
TR
NARATO RD
TAXIWAY RD
MINNEOLA RD
SWANSEA ST
CHLORIDE
DOGWOOD
ELKHORN
AV
ST
SPYROCK
LOCHMERE RD
JOVAR RD
WILDHORSE RD
COTTONWOOD RD
CHEROKEE
HAWK
ELKHORN RD
CONDOR
SUFFOCK RD
DUNE RD
DUNE
COTTONWOOD
TONOPAH ST
TIOGA ST
MALIBU
TEMESCAL ST
PIONEER
QUARRY
R1E R2E
R2E R3E
T9N T8N
3762
3763
92365
3852
3853
SEE 3760 MAP
SEE 3764 MAP
CAMP ROCK RD
NEWBERRY MOUNTAINS
SEE 369 MAP
Thomas Bros Maps ®
© 2002
0 .25 .5 .75 1.0 miles 1 in. = 4800 ft.

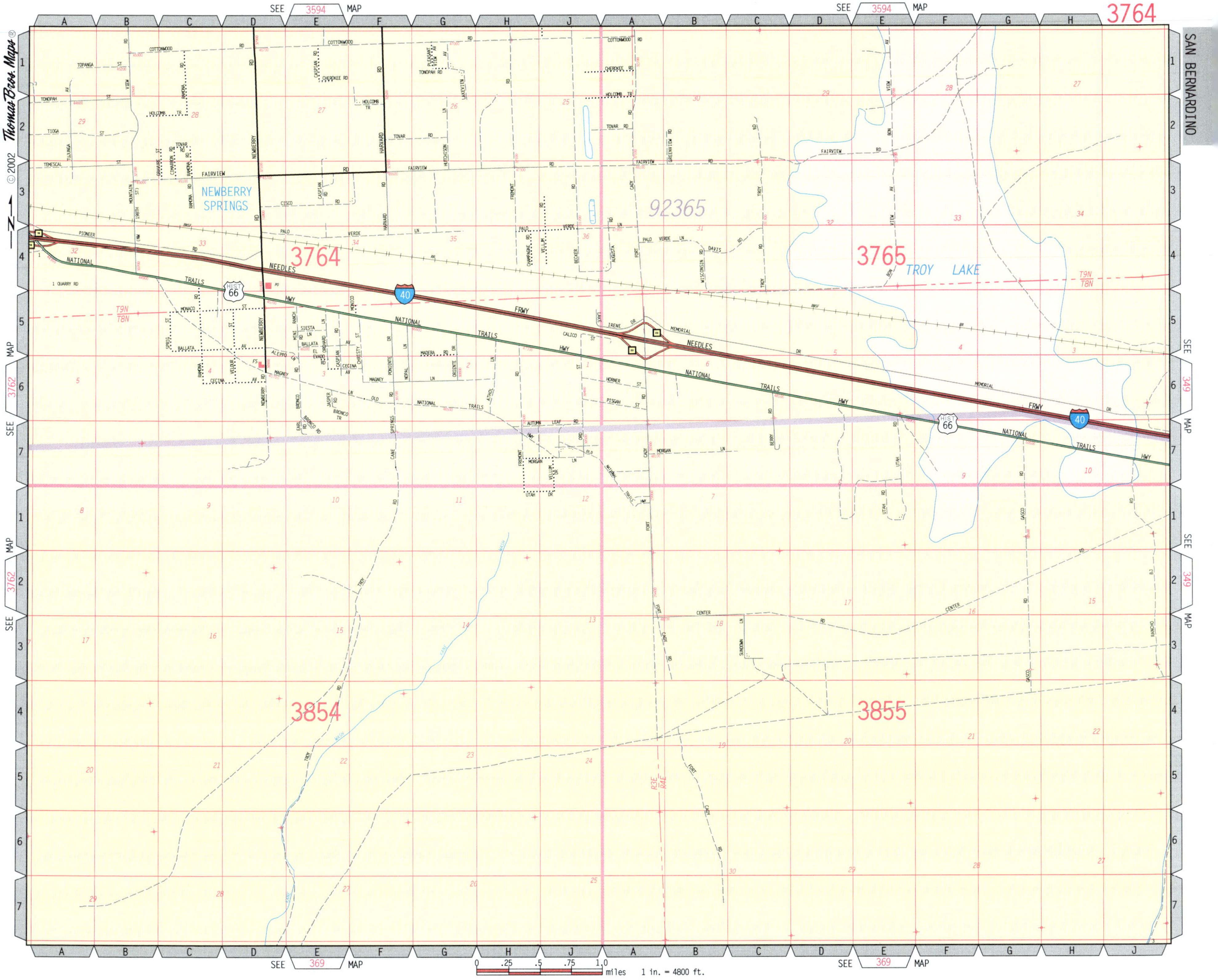
SEE 3594 MAP
SAN BERNARDINO
Thomas Bros. Maps
© 2002
NEWBERRY SPRINGS
92365
3764
3765
3854
3855
TROY LAKE
NEEDLES FRWY
NATIONAL TRAILS HWY
HIST 66
40
T9N
T8N
R3E
R4E
COTTONWOOD
TOPANGA ST
TONOPAH AV
TIOGA ST
TEMESCAL ST
FAIRVIEW
CHEROKEE RD
HOLCOMB TR
TOVAR RD
NEWBERRY RD
HARVARD RD
CISCO
PALO
VERDE
PIONEER
CALICO ST
IRENE DR
MEMORIAL DR
HORNER ST
PISGAH ST
MORGAN LN
FORT CADY RD
CENTER RD
TROY RD
SEE 3762 MAP
SEE 349 MAP
SEE 369 MAP
miles
1 in. = 4800 ft.

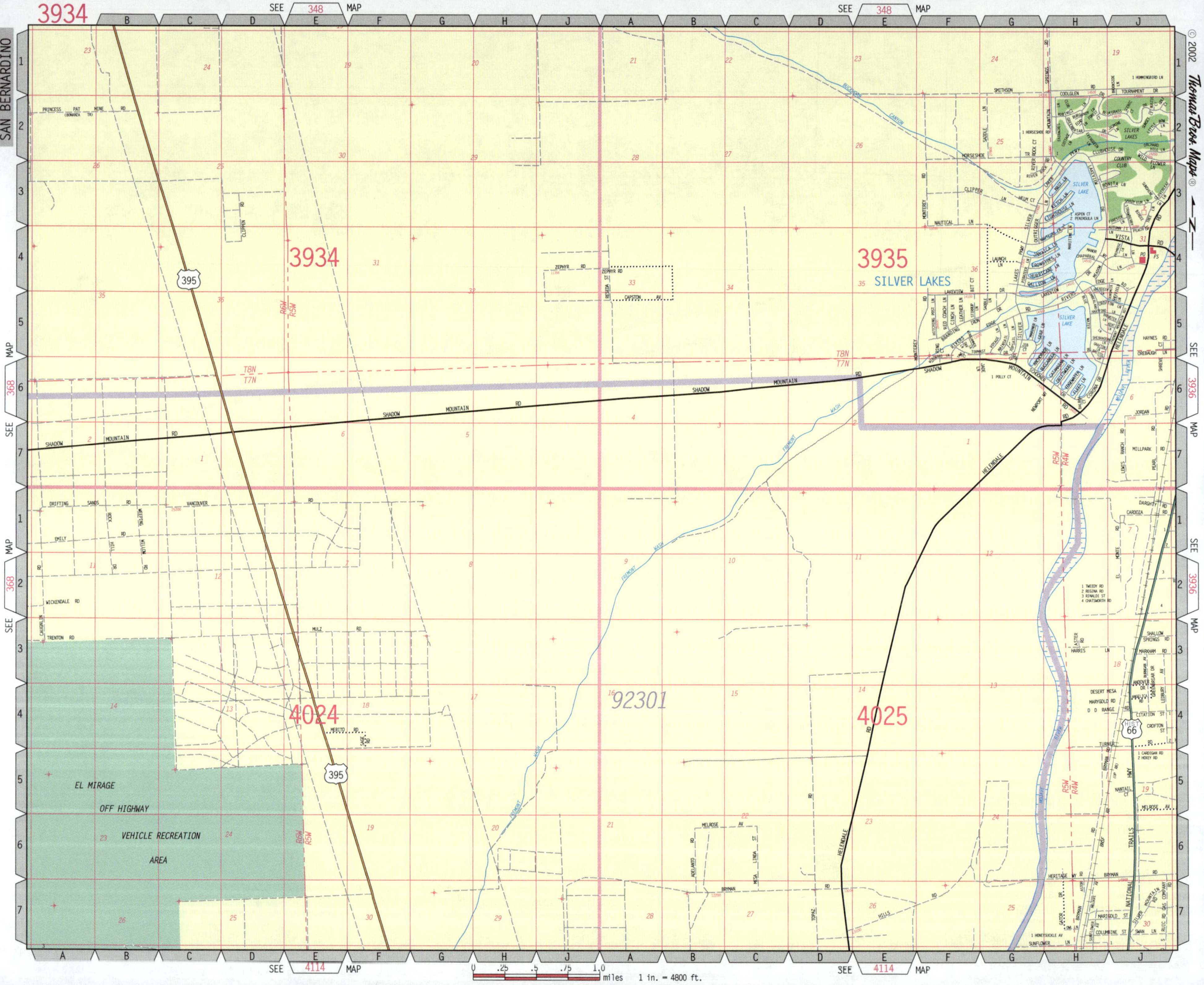

3934
SEE 348 MAP
SAN BERNARDINO
© 2002 Thomas Bros. Maps
3934
3935
SILVER LAKES
SILVER LAKE
COUNTRY CLUB
4024
4025
92301
395
HIST 66
SHADOW MOUNTAIN RD
HELENDALE RD
NATIONAL TRAILS HWY
FREMONT WASH
MOJAVE RIVER
BUCKTHORN CANYON
EL MIRAGE OFF HIGHWAY VEHICLE RECREATION AREA
T8N T7N
R6W R5W
R5W R4W
PRINCESS PAT MINE RD
CLIPPER RD
ZEPHYR RD
CAPSTON AV
SMITHSON
HORSESHOE
NAUTICAL LN
VISTA RD
DRIFTING SANDS RD
VANCOUVER
EMILY
WICKENDALE RD
TRENTON RD
MULZ RD
MERITO RD
MELROSE AV
BRYMAN RD
HARRIS LN
MILLPARK RD
JORDAN
HAYNES RD
DARGHTY RD
CARDOZA RD
SEE 368 MAP
SEE 3936 MAP
SEE 4114 MAP
0 .25 .5 .75 1.0 miles 1 in. = 4800 ft.

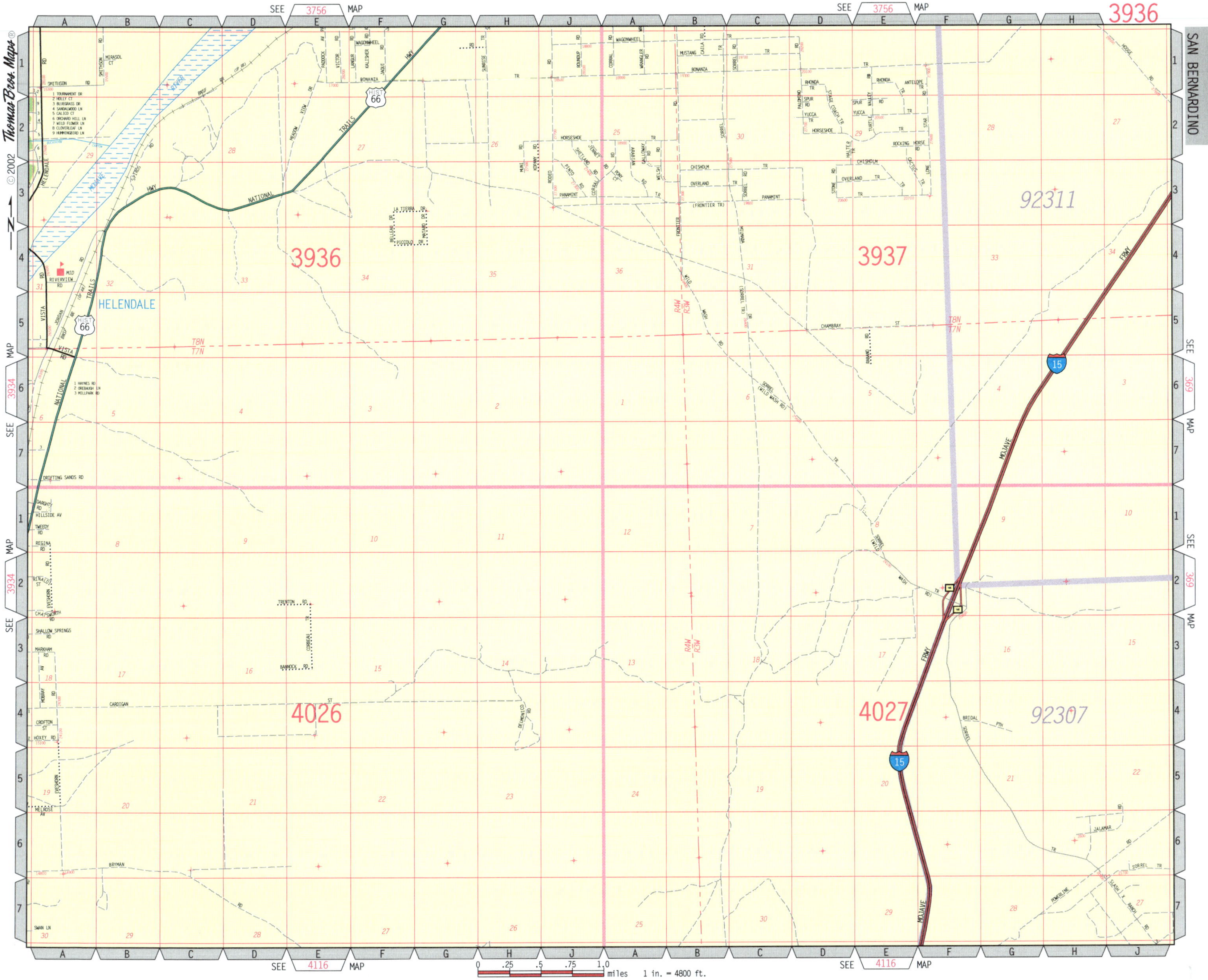
SEE 3756 MAP
SEE 3934 MAP
SEE 369 MAP
SEE 4116 MAP
Thomas Bros. Maps
© 2002
3936
3937
4026
4027
92311
92307
HELENDALE
MOJAVE RIVER
NATIONAL TRAILS HWY
HIST 66
15
MOJAVE FRWY
T8N
T7N
R4W
R3W
MID RIVERVIEW RD
VISTA RD
JORDAN
BNSF
SPRGS
HELENDALE RD
SMITHSON RD
MIRASOL CT
1 TOURNAMENT DR
2 HOLLY CT
3 BLUEGRASS DR
4 SANDALWOOD LN
5 CALICO CT
6 ORCHARD HILL LN
7 WILD FLOWER LN
8 CLOVERLEAF LN
9 HUMMINGBIRD LN
1 HAYNES RD
2 OREBAUGH LN
3 MILLPARK RD
MEADOW VIEW
PADDOCK AV
VICTOR
LANGUR
KALISHER
JACKOT
WAGONWHEEL
BONANZA
SUNRISE TR
LA TIERRA DR
BELLEAU DR
MATANO DR
PICCOLO DR
ROUNDUP RD
CORRAL RD
WRANGLER
MUSTANG
SORREL
HORSESHOE
SHETLAND
PINTO
PONY CT
ARABIAN
GALLOWAY RD
WELSH
RODEO RD
KIOWA
CHISHOLM
OVERLAND
PANAMINT
(FRONTIER TR)
FRONTIER
MILWANA
WILD WASH
SORREL TR
CHAMBRAY ST
RHONDA
PALOMINO RD
SPUR RD
YUCCA
STAGE COACH TR
TURTLE
VALLEY
ANTELOPE TR
ROCKING HORSE RD
HALTER
STONE RD
CACTUS
LONE TR
STAR
RABANO
SORREL (WILD WASH RD)
WILD WASH RD
DRIFTING SANDS RD
DARGHTY RD
HILLSIDE AV
TWEEDY RD
REGINA RD
RINALDI ST
CHATSWORTH
EVERGREEN
SHALLOW SPRINGS RD
MARKHAM RD
MOBRAY RD
CARDIGAN
CROFTON ST
HOXEY RD
MELROSE AV
BRYMAN
SWAN LN
TRENTON RD
CORBEAU TR
BANNOCK RD
DELMONICO RD
BRIDAL PTH
JALAMAR
SORREL TR
POWERLINE
SLASH X RANCH RD
0 .25 .5 .75 1.0 miles
1 in. = 4800 ft.

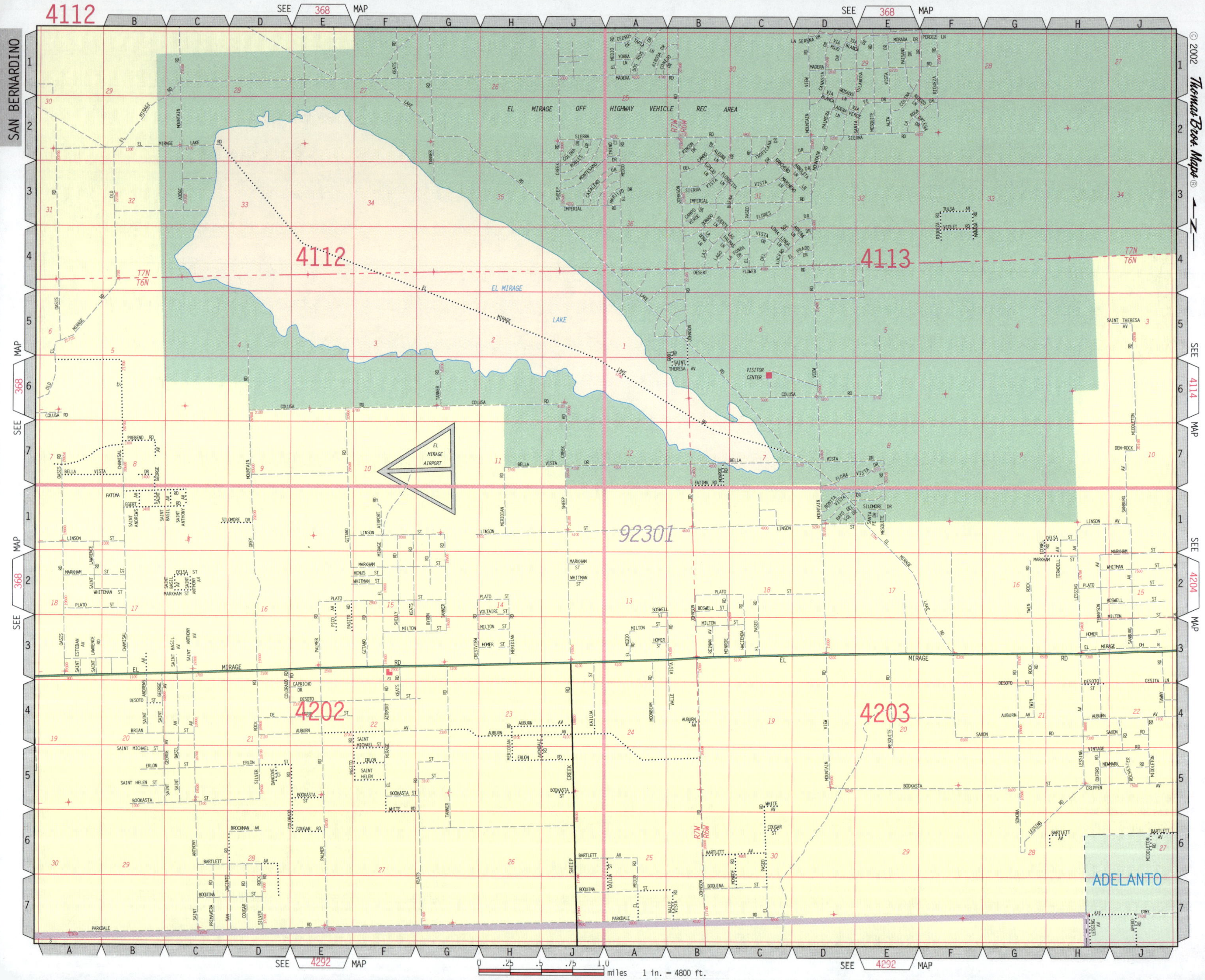

4112
SEE 368 MAP
SAN BERNARDINO
© 2002 Thomas Bros. Maps ®
EL MIRAGE OFF HIGHWAY VEHICLE REC AREA
EL MIRAGE LAKE
4112
4113
T7N
T6N
R7W
R6W
EL MIRAGE AIRPORT
VISITOR CENTER
92301
4202
4203
EL MIRAGE RD
ADELANTO
SEE 4114 MAP
SEE 4204 MAP
SEE 4292 MAP
0 .25 .5 .75 1.0 miles 1 in. = 4800 ft.

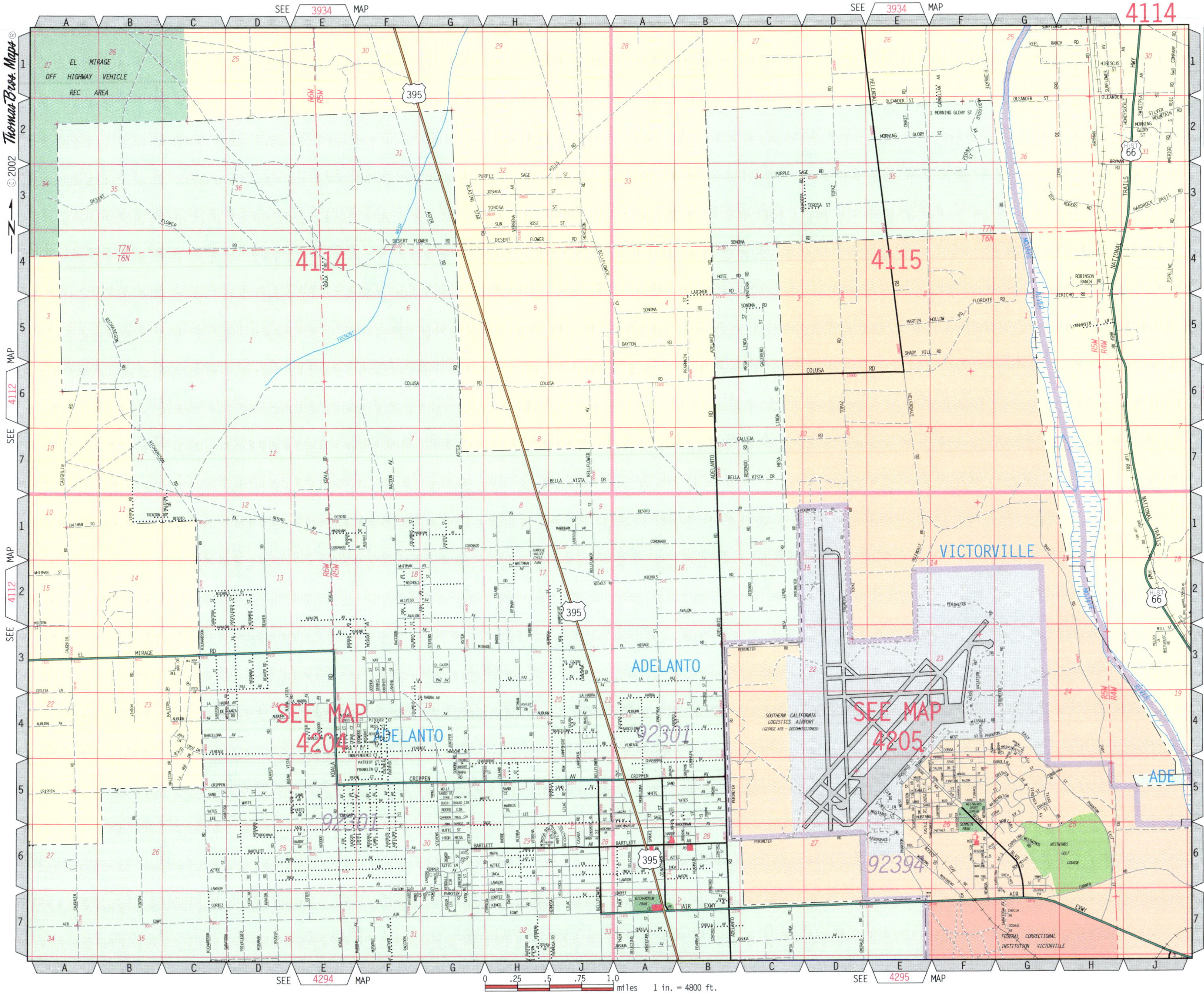
SEE 3934 MAP
SEE 3934 MAP
EL MIRAGE OFF HIGHWAY VEHICLE REC AREA
T7N
T6N
R6W
R5W
4114
4115
T7N
T6N
R5W
R4W
395
HIST 66
VICTORVILLE
ADELANTO
ADELANTO
SEE MAP 4204
SEE MAP 4205
SOUTHERN CALIFORNIA LOGISTICS AIRPORT (GEORGE AFB - DECOMMISSIONED)
92301
92301
92394
ADE
MOJAVE RIVER
NATIONAL TRAILS HWY
FEDERAL CORRECTIONAL INSTITUTION VICTORVILLE
WESTWINDS GOLF COURSE
COLUSA RD
BELLA VISTA DR
EL MIRAGE RD
CRIPPEN AV
AIR EXWY
SEE 4112 MAP
SEE 4112 MAP
SEE 4116 MAP
SEE 4116 MAP
SEE 4294 MAP
SEE 4295 MAP
0 .25 .5 .75 1.0 miles 1 in. = 4800 ft.

SEE 3936 MAP
SEE 3936 MAP
SAN BERNARDINO
© 2002 Thomas Bros. Maps ®
4116
4117
4206
SEE MAP 4207
APPLE VALLEY
APPLE VALLEY
ORO GRANDE
VICTORVILLE
92394
92307
MOJAVE FRWY
15
T7N
T6N
R4W
R3W
SILVER MOUNTAIN RD
HARDROCK
DAVIS
CANYON RD
ORO GRANDE
OLD QUARRY RD
VICTORVILLE
POWERLINE
STODDARD WELLS RD
NORTHERN
MINING
BELL MOUNTAIN WASH
DALE EVANS PKWY
WELLS
KIMSHEW
LANGLEY
MURIETA
CORDOVA
LABRADOR
DOBERMAN
SHEPHERD
JOHNSON
KENSINGTON
ALSTAIR
LAFAYETTE
CORBINA
BURBANK
LIVERMORE
LOS PADRES
ALTADENA
GUSTINE
GARNET
CORWIN
FALCHION
CHIPETA
HEMLOCK
PAPAGO
MALABI
APPLE VALLEY AIRPORT
NATIONAL TRAILS HWY
HIST 66
ROCKFIELD NATURE PARK
AIR EXWY
USAF
TURNER
SEALS
BRYMAN
1 WILDERNESS CT
SEE 4114 MAP
SEE 4205 MAP
SEE 4118 MAP
SEE 4208 MAP
SEE 4296 MAP
SEE 4297 MAP
miles 1 in. = 4800 ft.

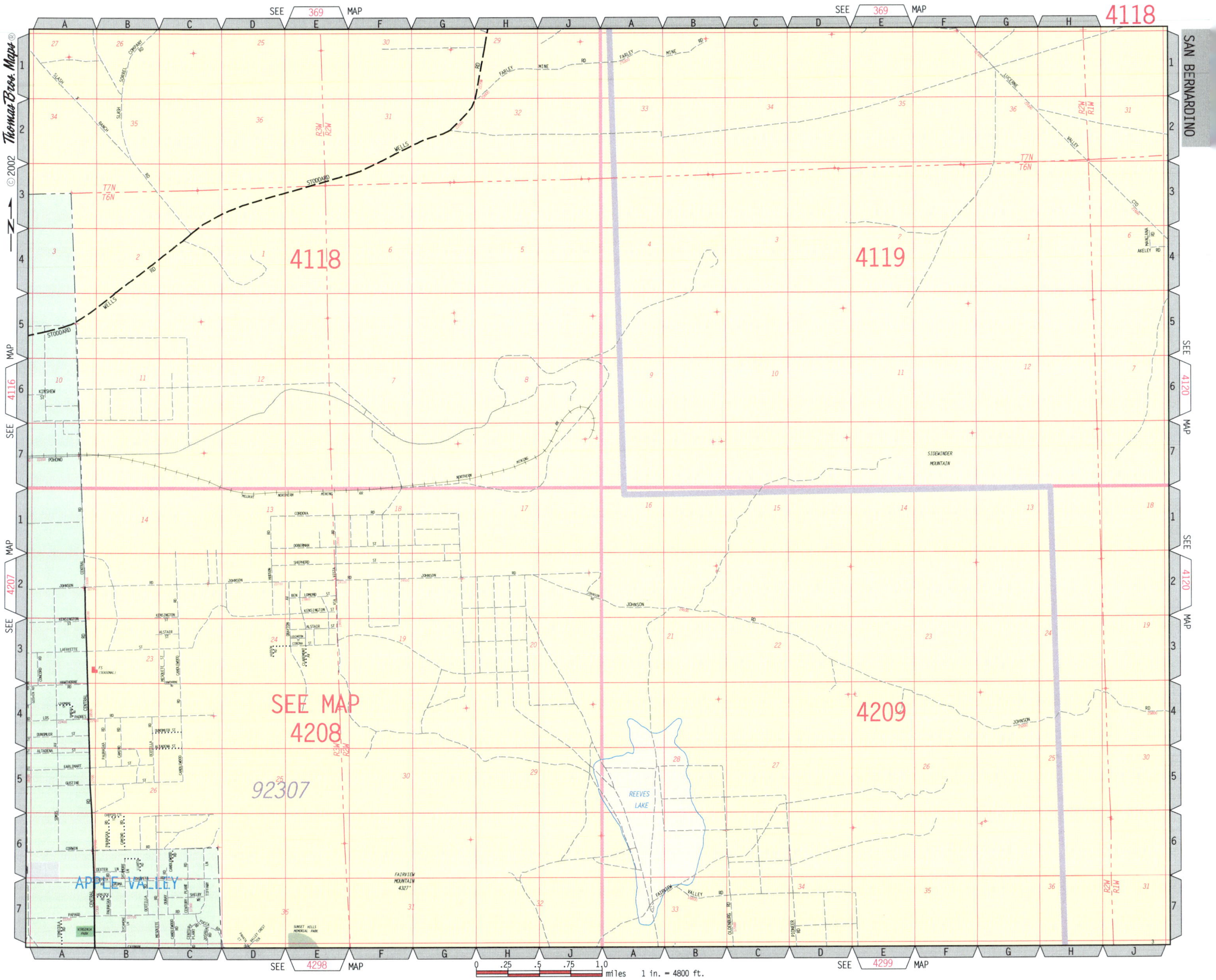
SEE 369 MAP
SAN BARNARDINO
Thomas Bros. Maps
©2002
4118
4119
4209
SEE MAP 4208
92307
APPLE VALLEY
STODDARD
WELLS
RD
FARLEY
MINE
LUCERNE
VALLEY
CTO
AKELEY RD
SIDEWINDER MOUNTAIN
NORTHERN
MINING
RR
KINSHEW ST
POHONO
CORDOVA
DOBERMAN
SHEPHERD
JOHNSON
KENSINGTON
ALSTAIR
LAFAYETTE
HAWTHORNE
DUNSMUIR
ALTADENA
EARLIMART
GUSTINE
CORWIN
DEXTER
PAPAGO
CAYMAN
CENTRAL
OCOTILLO
VIRGINIA PARK
REEVES LAKE
FAIRVIEW MOUNTAIN 4327'
FAIRVIEW
OLDENBURG RD
PIONEER RD
SUNSET HILLS MEMORIAL PARK
T7N
T6N
R3W
R2W
R1W
SEE 4116 MAP
SEE 4207 MAP
SEE 4120 MAP
SEE 4298 MAP
SEE 4299 MAP
0 .25 .5 .75 1.0 miles 1 in. = 4800 ft.

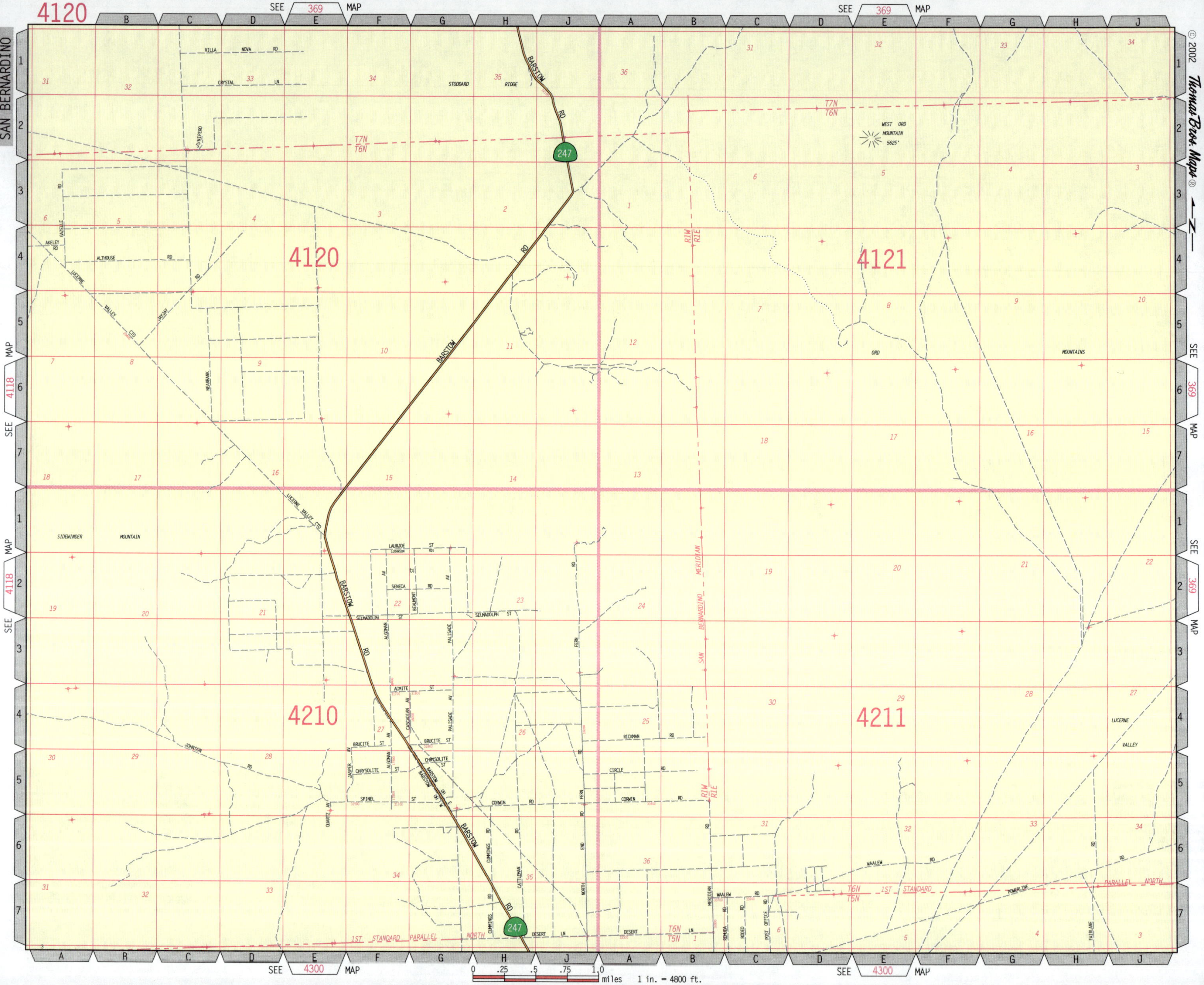
SAN BERNARDINO
SEE 369 MAP
SEE 4118 MAP
SEE 369 MAP
SEE 4300 MAP
4120
4121
4210
4211
VILLA NOVA RD
CRYSTAL LN
STODDARD RIDGE
BARSTOW RD
247
JUNIPERO
T7N
T6N
WEST ORD MOUNTAIN 5625'
R1W R1E
AKELEY RD
GAZELLE
ALTHOUSE RD
LUCERNE VALLEY CTO
JAGUAR RD
NEARBANK
ORD MOUNTAINS
SIDEWINDER MOUNTAIN
LUCERNE VALLEY CTO
LAUBJOE
STJOHNSON
SENECA RD
BEAUMONT
SELMADOLPH ST
ALGOMAN
PALISADE
FERN
SAN BERNARDINO MERIDIAN
ACMITE ST
CASCADIAN AV
BRUCITE ST
CHRYSOLITE ST
JASPER AV
SPINEL ST
QUARTZ AV
JOHNSON RD
RICKMAN RD
CIRCLE RD
CORWIN RD
BARSTOW OH
CUMMINGS RD
CATTLEMAN
END
NORTH
DESERT LN
T6N T5N
1ST STANDARD PARALLEL NORTH
MERIDIAN
WAALEW RD
POST OFFICE RD
RODEO
POWERLINE
LUCERNE VALLEY
FAIRLANE
0 .25 .5 .75 1.0 miles 1 in. = 4800 ft.

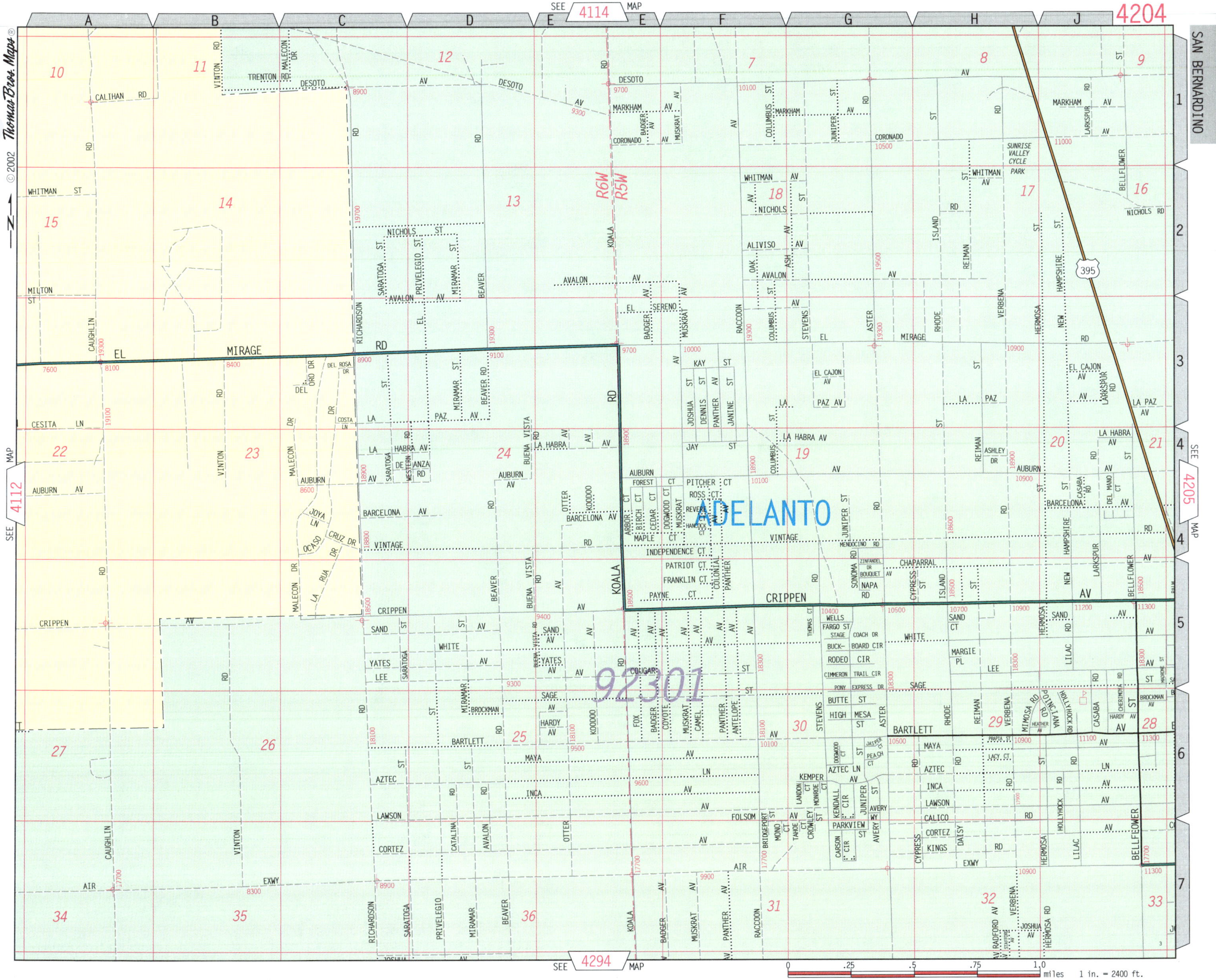
SEE 4114 MAP
SAN BERNARDINO
SEE 4112 MAP
SEE 4205 MAP
SEE 4294 MAP
A
B
C
D
E
F
G
H
J
1
2
3
4
5
6
7
ADELANTO
92301
R6W
R5W
395
EL MIRAGE RD
CRIPPEN AV
DESOTO AV
CALIHAN RD
TRENTON RD
VINTON RD
MALECON DR
WHITMAN ST
MILTON ST
CAUGHLIN RD
CESITA LN
AUBURN AV
AIR EXWY
RICHARDSON RD
NICHOLS ST
SARATOGA ST
PRIVELEGIO ST
MIRAMAR ST
BEAVER RD
AVALON AV
KOALA RD
MARKHAM AV
CORONADO AV
BADGER AV
MUSKRAT AV
EL SERENO AV
RACCOON AV
COLUMBUS ST
STEVENS ST
ASTER RD
ALIVISO AV
OAK ST
ASH ST
JUNIPER ST
ISLAND RD
REIMAN RD
RHODE RD
VERBENA RD
HERMOSA RD
NEW ST
HAMPSHIRE ST
BELLFLOWER ST
LARKSPUR RD
NICHOLS RD
SUNRISE VALLEY CYCLE PARK
LA PAZ AV
LA HABRA AV
EL CAJON AV
KAY ST
JAY ST
JOSHUA ST
DENNIS ST
PANTHER AV
JANINE ST
BARCELONA AV
VINTAGE RD
INDEPENDENCE CT
PATRIOT CT
FRANKLIN CT
PAYNE CT
COLONIAL
MAPLE CT
FOREST CT
ARBOR CT
BIRCH CT
CEDAR CT
DOGWOOD CT
PITCHER CT
ROSS CT
BUENA VISTA RD
OTTER ST
KOODOO
CHAPARRAL AV
MENDOCINO RD
SONOMA RD
NAPA RD
CYPRESS ST
ASHLEY DR
CASABA RD
DEL MANO CT
JOYA LN
OCASO
CRUZ DR
LA RUA DR
DEL ORO DR
DEL ROSA DR
COSTA LN
DE ANZA RD
WESTERN
SAND AV
WHITE AV
YATES AV
LEE AV
SAGE AV
HARDY AV
BROCKMAN AV
BARTLETT AV
MAYA AV
AZTEC LN
INCA AV
LAWSON AV
CORTEZ AV
CATALINA
FOLSOM AV
COUGAR
FOX
COYOTE
CAMEL
ANTELOPE
WELLS FARGO ST
STAGE COACH DR
BUCKBOARD CIR
RODEO CIR
CIMMERON TRAIL CIR
PONY EXPRESS DR
BUTTE ST
HIGH MESA ST
MARGIE PL
KEMPER AV
LANDON CT
MONROE CT
KENDALL CIR
PARKVIEW
AVERY WY
CARSON CIR
BRIDGEPORT ST
MONO CT
TAHOE CT
CROWLEY CT
CALICO
KINGS RD
DAISY
LILAC
HOLLYHOCK RD
MIMOSA RD
POINCIANA RD
HEATHER AV
CHERIMOYA
PAPAYA ST
LACY CT
RADFORD AV
JOSHUA AV
0 .25 .5 .75 1.0 miles
1 in. = 2400 ft.

SEE 4114 MAP

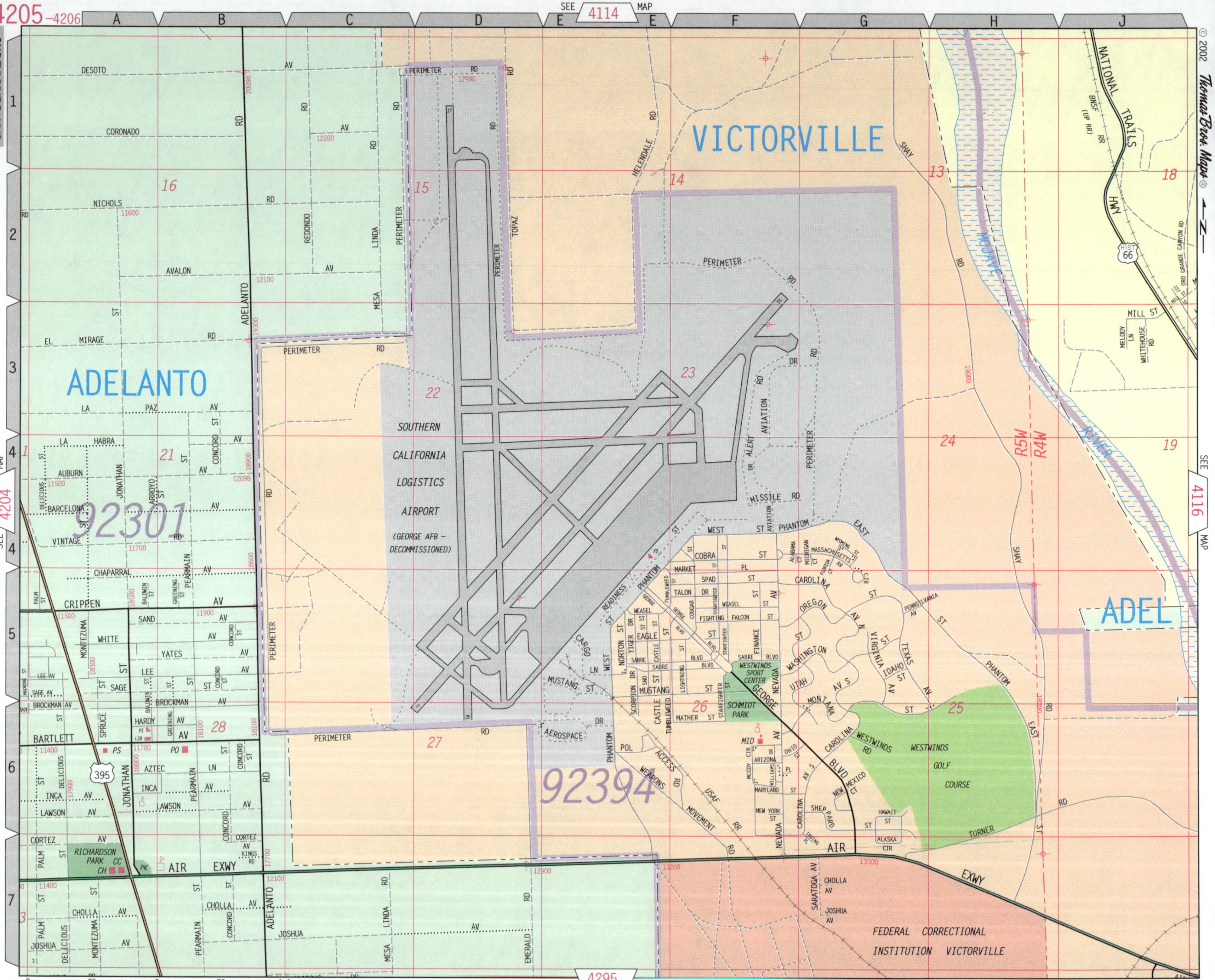

SEE 4204 MAP

SEE 4116 MAP

SEE 4295 MAP

0 .25 .5 .75 1.0 miles 1 in. = 2400 ft.

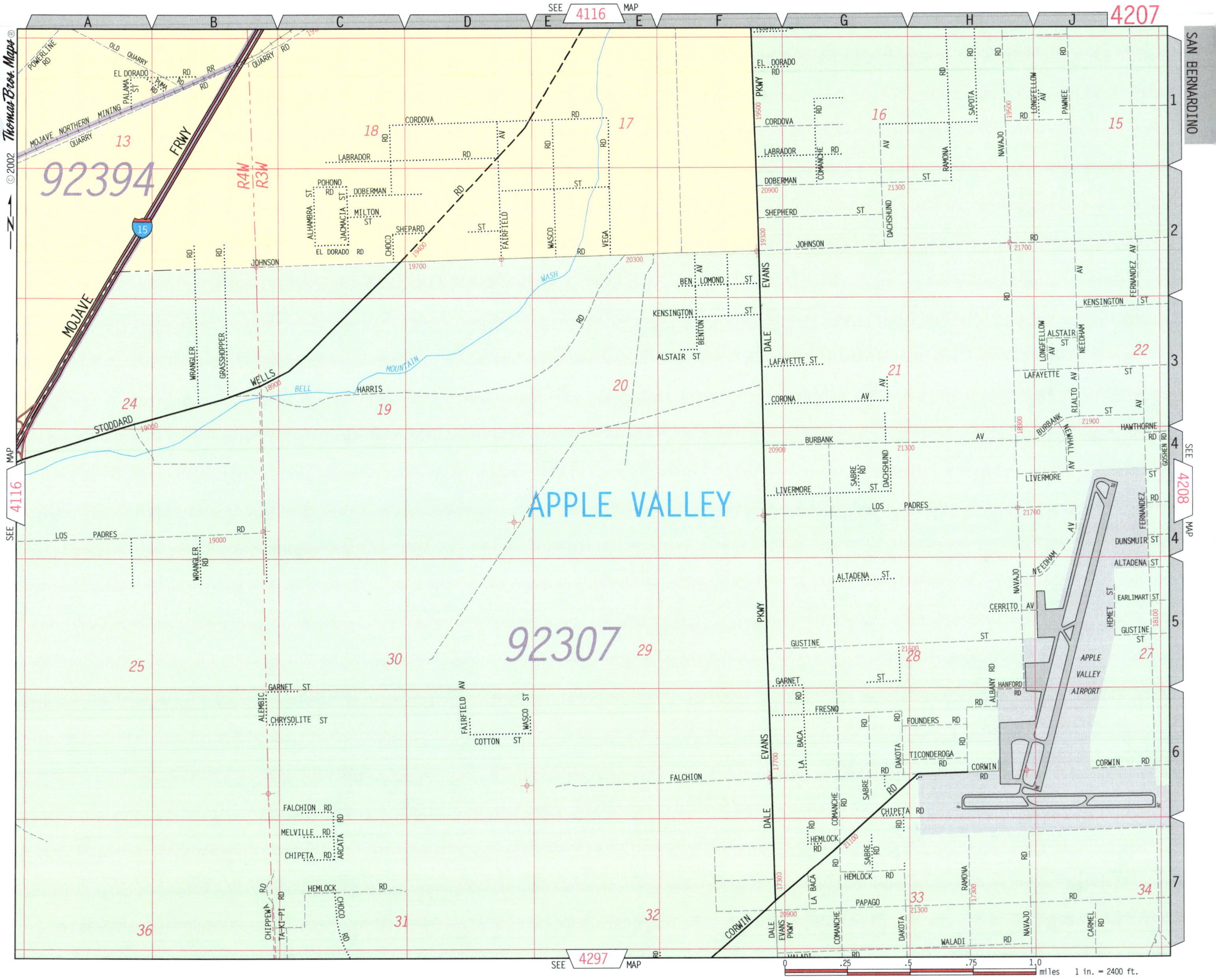
SEE 4116 MAP
SEE 4208 MAP
SEE 4297 MAP
SAN BERNARDINO
Thomas Bros. Maps ©2002
APPLE VALLEY
92394
92307
APPLE VALLEY AIRPORT
MOJAVE FRWY
15
R4W
R3W
MOJAVE NORTHERN MINING QUARRY
POWERLINE RD
OLD QUARRY RD
QUARRY RD
EL DORADO RD
PALAMA ST
PUMA RD
RR
CORDOVA RD
LABRADOR RD
POHONO RD
DOBERMAN
MILTON ST
ALHAMBRA ST
JACMACIA ST
SHEPARD
CHOCO
FAIRFIELD AV
WASCO RD
VEGA RD
JOHNSON
WELLS RD
STODDARD
WRANGLER RD
GRASSHOPPER RD
BELL MOUNTAIN WASH
HARRIS
BEN LOMOND ST
KENSINGTON ST
BENTON AV
ALSTAIR ST
DALE EVANS PKWY
LAFAYETTE ST
CORONA AV
BURBANK AV
LIVERMORE
LOS PADRES RD
ALTADENA ST
GUSTINE ST
GARNET ST
FRESNO
FOUNDERS RD
TICONDEROGA RD
FALCHION
CHIPETA RD
HEMLOCK RD
PAPAGO
WALADI RD
CORWIN RD
COMANCHE RD
SABRE RD
DACHSHUND RD
LA BACA RD
DAKOTA RD
RAMONA RD
NAVAJO RD
SAPOTA RD
LONGFELLOW AV
PAWNEE RD
SHEPHERD ST
NEEDHAM AV
RIALTO AV
NEWHALL AV
HAWTHORNE RD
GOSHEN RD
FERNANDEZ AV
DUNSMUIR ST
EARLIMART ST
HEMET ST
CERRITO AV
ALBANY RD
HANFORD RD
CARMEL RD
GARNET ST
ALEMBIC
CHRYSOLITE ST
COTTON ST
FALCHION RD
MELVILLE RD
ARCATA RD
CHIPPEWA RD
TA-KI-PI RD
13
15
16
17
18
19
20
21
22
24
25
27
28
29
30
31
32
33
34
36
19000
19400
19700
19900
20300
20900
21300
21700
21900
17300
17700
18100
18300
18900
19300
19500
0 .25 .5 .75 1.0 miles
1 in. = 2400 ft.

SEE 4118 MAP

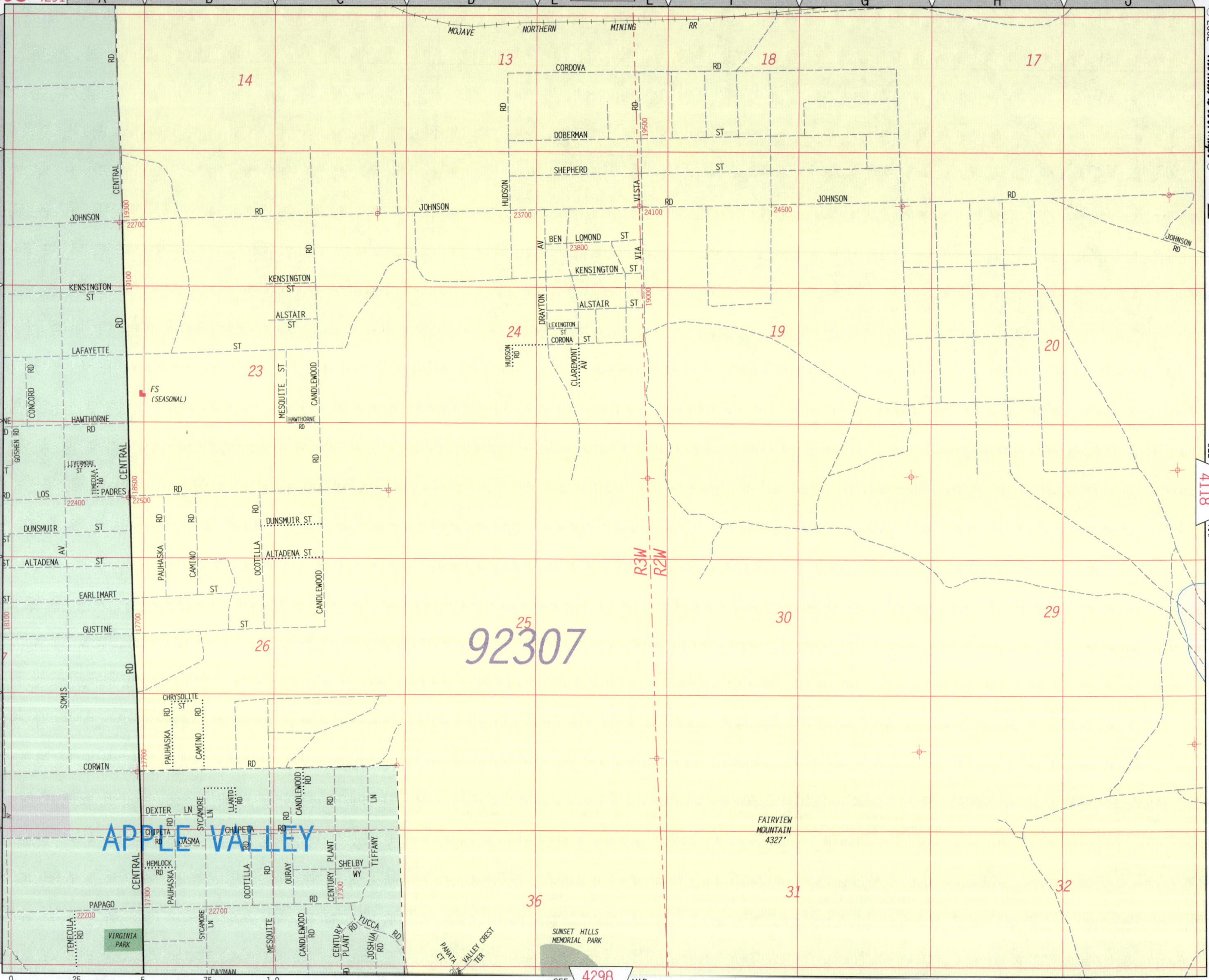

SEE 4207 MAP

SEE 4118 MAP

SEE 4298 MAP

0 .25 .5 .75 1.0 miles 1 in. = 2400 ft.

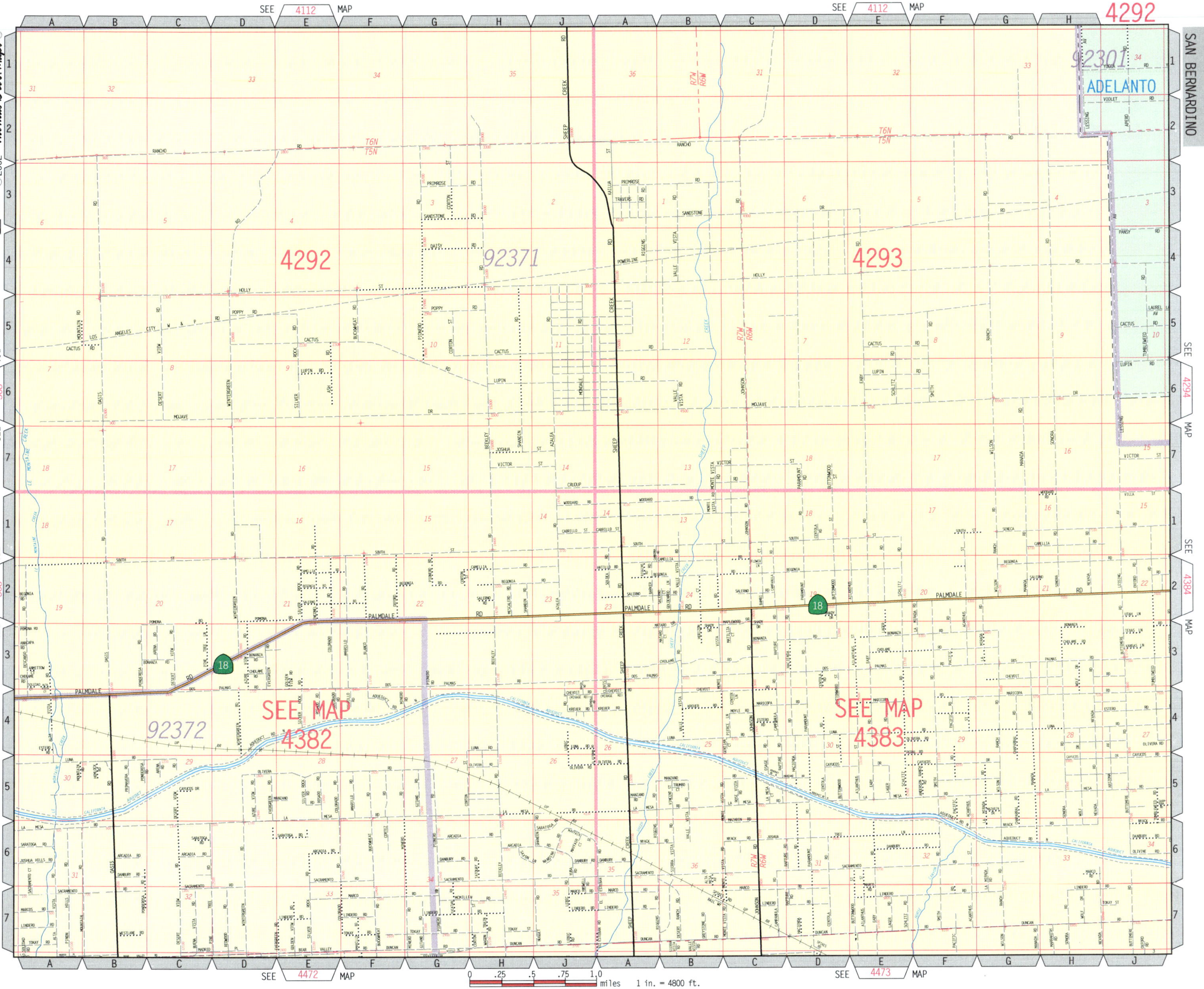
SEE 4112 MAP
SEE 4112 MAP
SEE 4472 MAP
SEE 4473 MAP
SEE 368 MAP
SEE 368 MAP
SEE 4294 MAP
SEE 4384 MAP
4292
4293
SEE MAP 4382
SEE MAP 4383
92371
92372
92301
ADELANTO
T6N
T5N
R7W
R6W
PALMDALE RD
SHEEP CREEK RD
CALIFORNIA AQUEDUCT
MONTAINE CREEK
LOS ANGELES CITY W & P
RANCHO RD
POWERLINE RD
HOLLY ST
POPPY RD
CACTUS RD
LUPIN RD
MOJAVE DR
VICTOR ST
SOUTH ST
OASIS RD
DESERT VIEW RD
WINTERGREEN
VALLE VISTA RD
JOHNSON RD
MONTE VISTA RD
LESSING AV
18
0 .25 .5 .75 1.0 miles 1 in. = 4800 ft.

SEE 4204 MAP

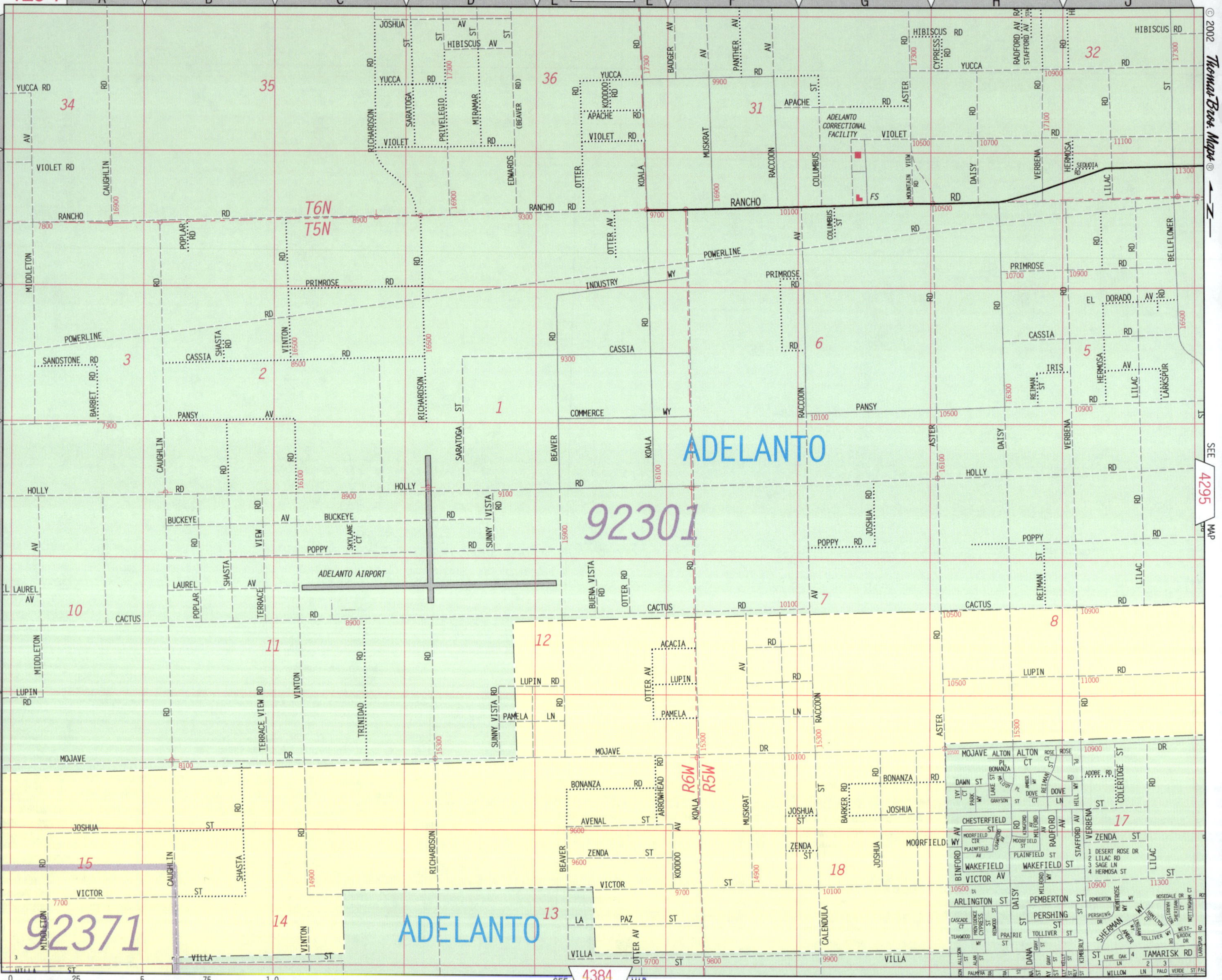

SEE 4292 MAP
SEE 4295 MAP
SEE 4384 MAP

0 .25 .5 .75 1.0 miles 1 in. = 2400 ft.

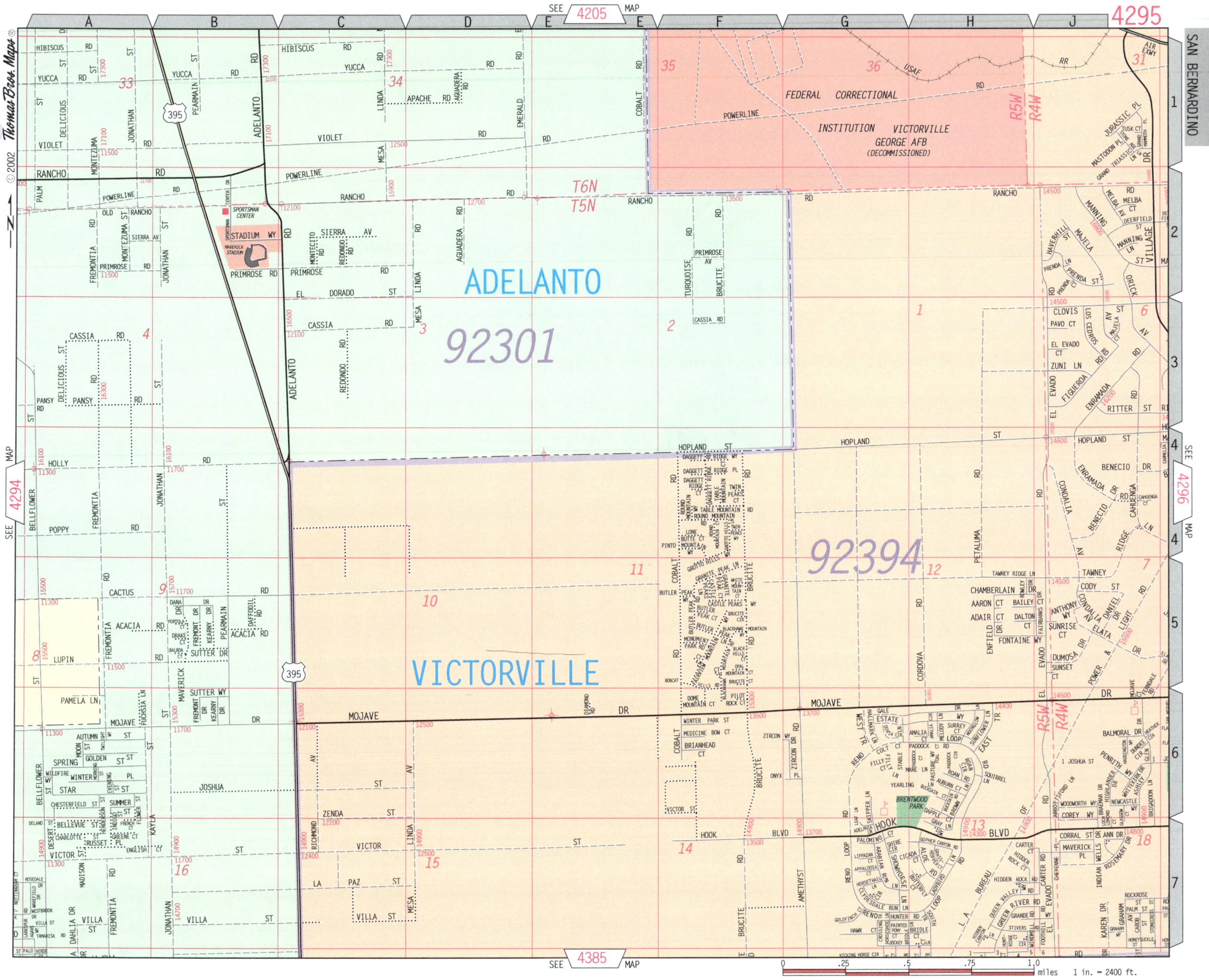
SEE 4205 MAP
SEE 4294 MAP
SEE 4296 MAP
SEE 4385 MAP
SAN BERNARDINO
Thomas Bros. Maps
© 2002
ADELANTO
92301
VICTORVILLE
92394
FEDERAL CORRECTIONAL INSTITUTION VICTORVILLE
GEORGE AFB
(DECOMMISSIONED)
USAF RR
AIR EXWY
T6N
T5N
R5W
R4W
SPORTSMAN CENTER
MAVERICK STADIUM
BRENTWOOD PARK
RANCHO RD
POWERLINE RD
MOJAVE DR
HOPLAND ST
HOOK BLVD
ADELANTO RD
HIBISCUS RD
YUCCA RD
VIOLET RD
PRIMROSE RD
CASSIA RD
CACTUS RD
ACACIA RD
JOSHUA ST
VICTOR ST
VILLA ST
LINDA RD
MESA RD
COBALT RD
BRUCITE RD
CORDOVA RD
PETALUMA RD
EL EVADO RD
BELLFLOWER ST
FREMONTIA RD
JONATHAN ST
MAVERICK ST
EMERALD RD
AGUADERA RD
TURQUOISE RD
ZENDA ST
LA PAZ ST
RICHMOND AV
AMETHYST ST
FORD
0 .25 .5 .75 1.0 miles 1 in. = 2400 ft.

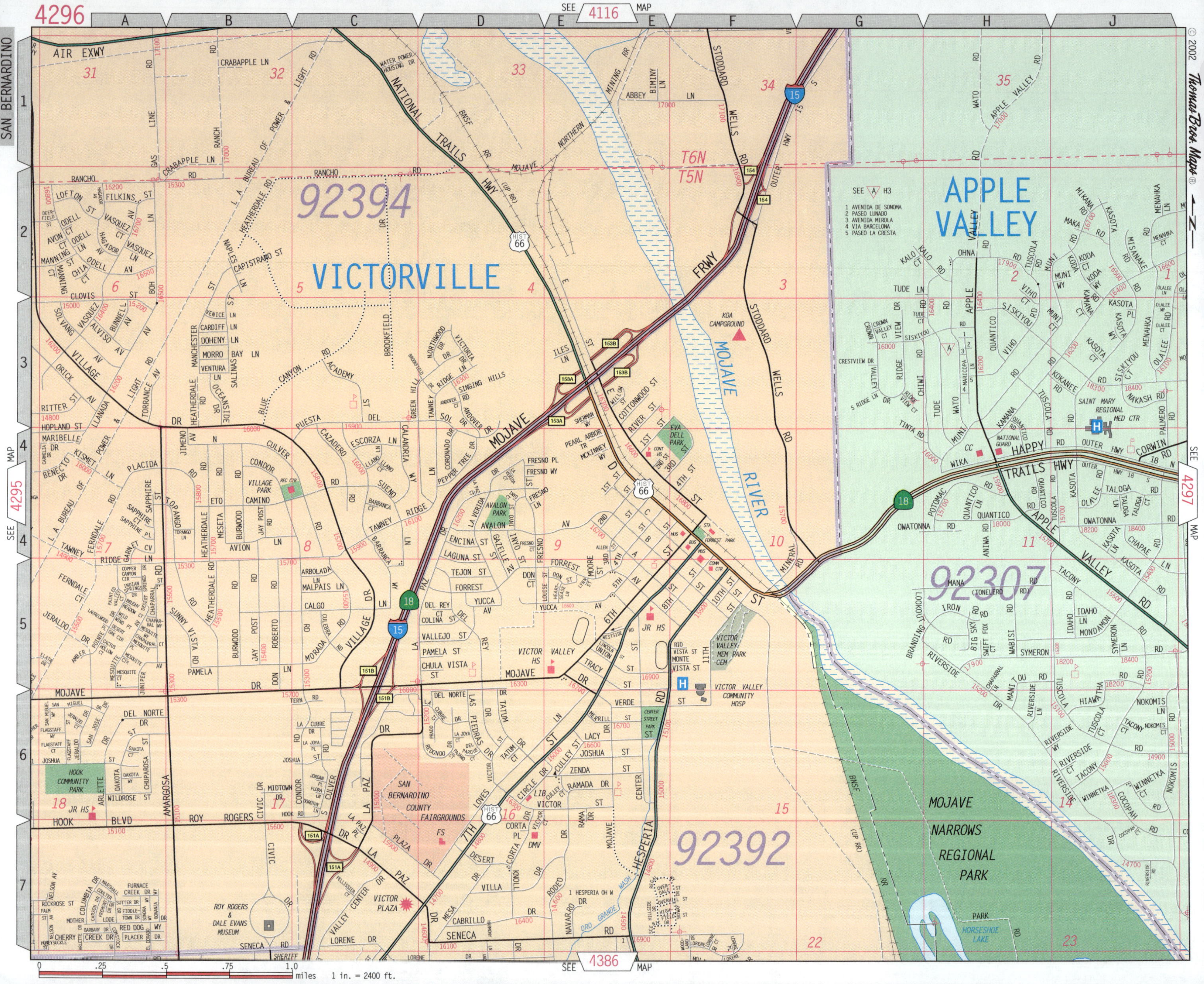
SEE 4116 MAP
SEE 4386 MAP
SEE 4295 MAP
SEE 4297 MAP
VICTORVILLE
APPLE VALLEY
92394
92307
92392
T6N
T5N
MOJAVE RIVER
MOJAVE NARROWS REGIONAL PARK
HORSESHOE LAKE
AIR EXWY
NATIONAL TRAILS HWY
MOJAVE FRWY
STODDARD WELLS RD
OUTER HWY
HAPPY TRAILS HWY
APPLE VALLEY RD
MOJAVE DR
HOOK BLVD
ROY ROGERS DR
LA PAZ DR
SENECA RD
7TH ST
HESPERIA RD
BNSF
L A BUREAU OF POWER & LIGHT RD
KOA CAMPGROUND
EVA DELL PARK
AVALON PARK
VILLAGE PARK
HOOK COMMUNITY PARK
CENTER STREET PARK
VICTOR VALLEY MEM PARK CEM
VICTOR VALLEY COMMUNITY HOSP
SAINT MARY REGIONAL MED CTR
SAN BERNARDINO COUNTY FAIRGROUNDS
ROY ROGERS & DALE EVANS MUSEUM
VICTOR PLAZA
VICTOR VALLEY HS
JR HS
NATIONAL GUARD
1 AVENIDA DE SONOMA
2 PASEO LUNADO
3 AVENIDA MIROLA
4 VIA BARCELONA
5 PASEO LA CRESTA
0 .25 .5 .75 1.0 miles 1 in. = 2400 ft.

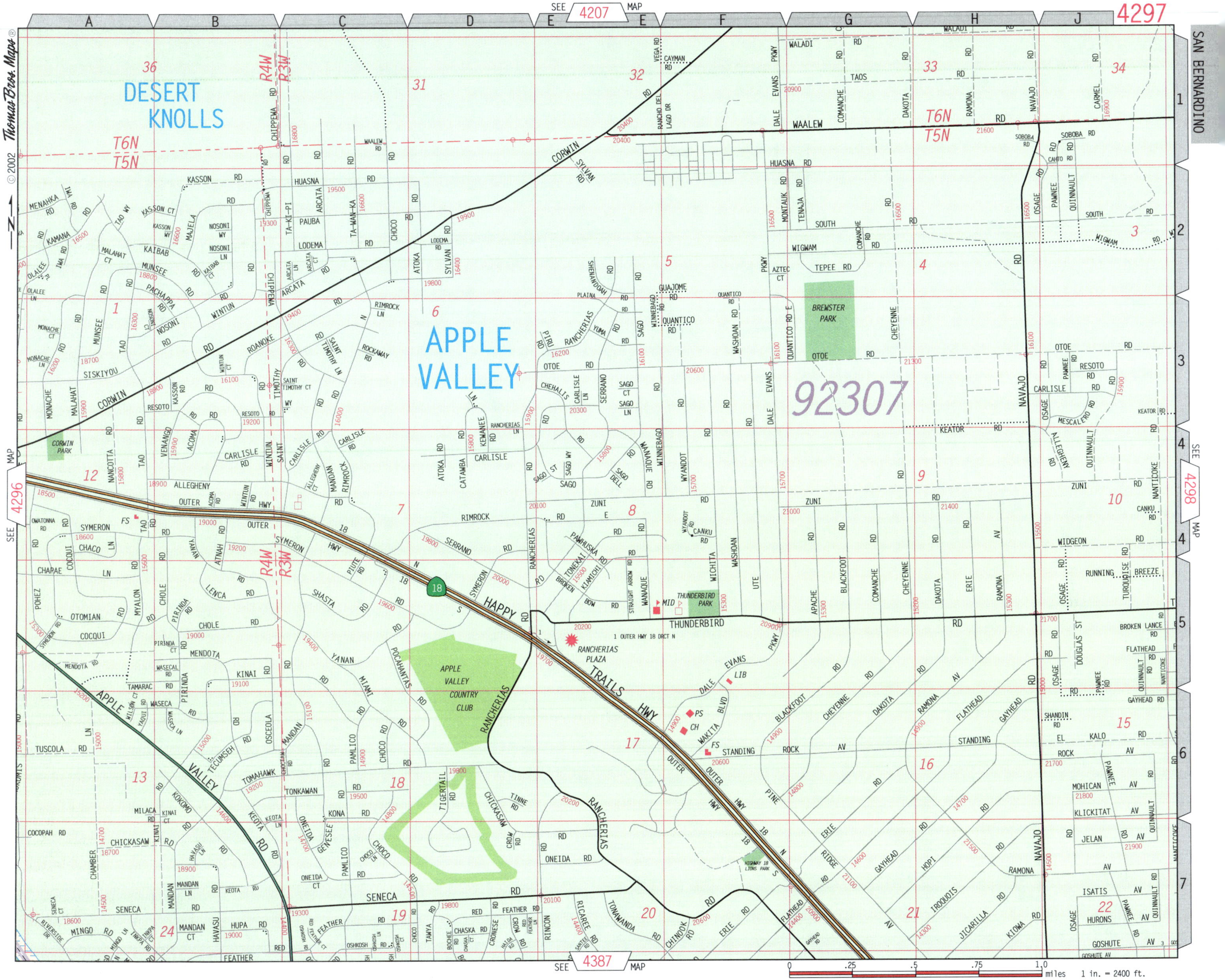
SEE 4207 MAP
SAN BERNARDINO
DESERT KNOLLS
APPLE VALLEY
92307
T6N
T5N
R4W
R3W
CORWIN RD
HAPPY TRAILS HWY
OUTER HWY 18
APPLE VALLEY RD
RANCHERIAS RD
THUNDERBIRD RD
NAVAJO RD
WAALEW RD
SENECA RD
STANDING ROCK AV
DALE EVANS PKWY
APPLE VALLEY COUNTRY CLUB
BREWSTER PARK
THUNDERBIRD PARK
CORWIN PARK
RANCHERIAS PLAZA
HIGHWAY 18 LIONS PARK
18
SEE 4296 MAP
SEE 4298 MAP
SEE 4387 MAP
0 .25 .5 .75 1.0 miles 1 in. = 2400 ft.
Thomas Bros. Maps
© 2002

SEE 4208 MAP

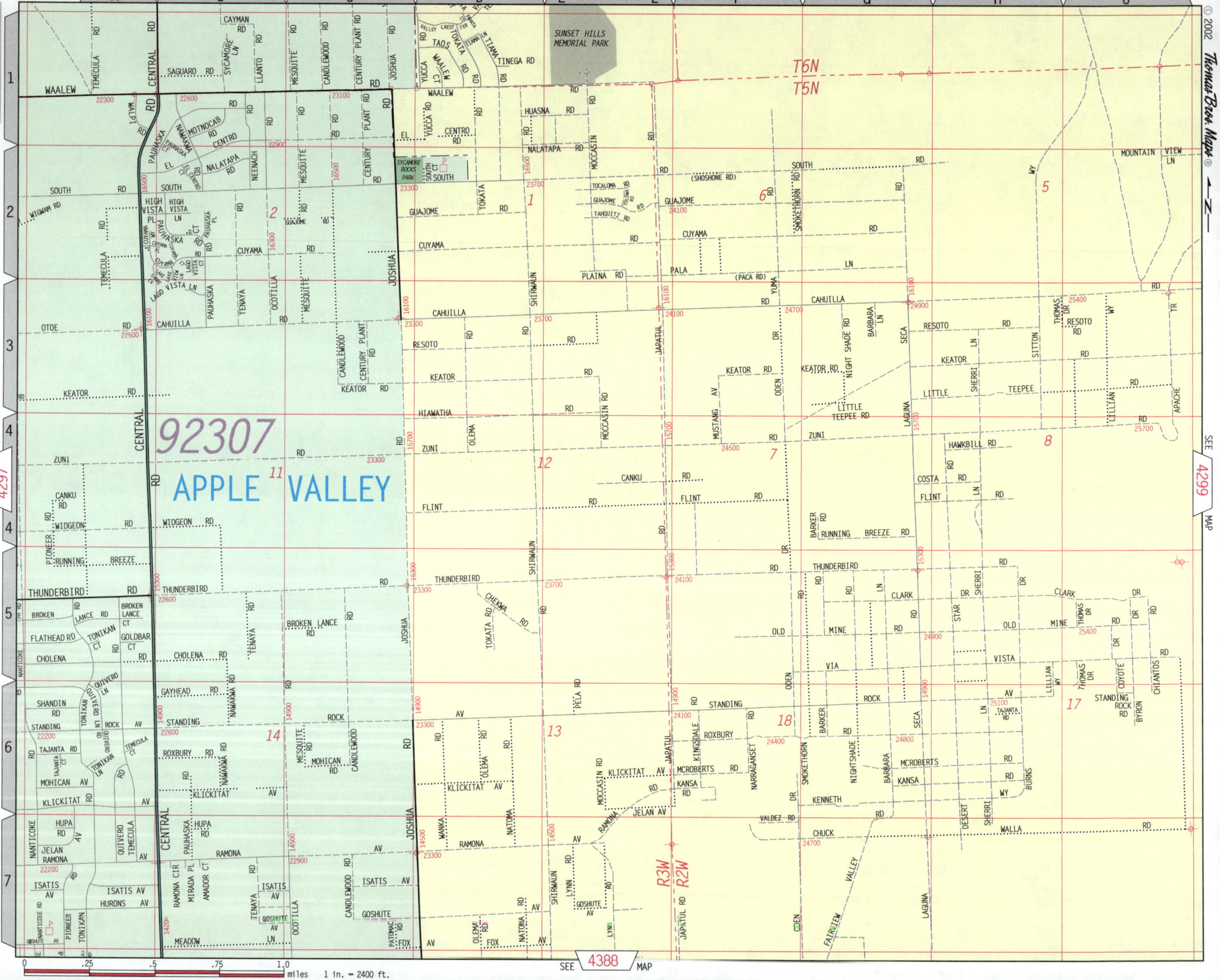

SEE 4297 MAP

SEE 4299 MAP

SEE 4388 MAP

SEE 4208 MAP
SEE 4118 MAP

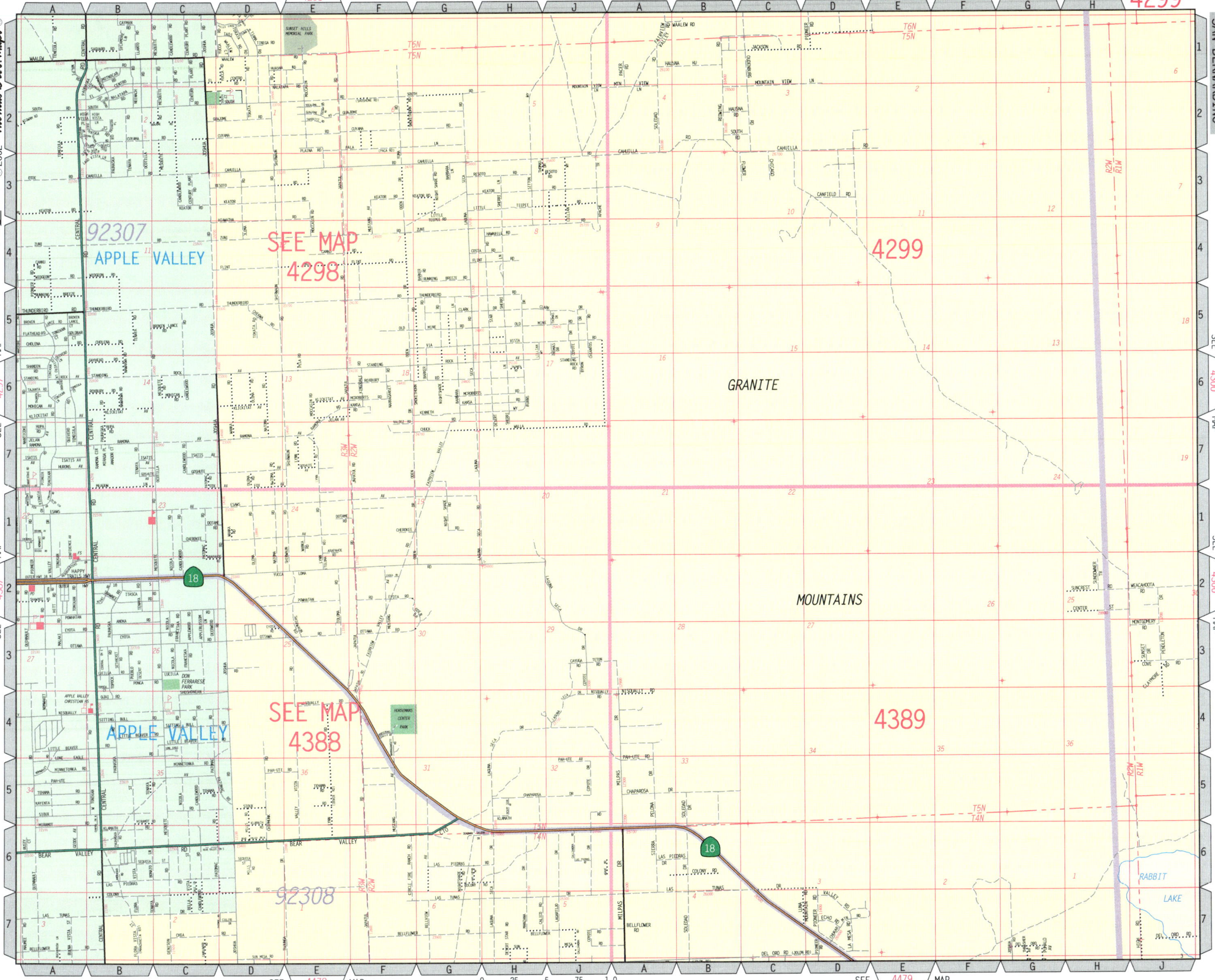

SEE 4478 MAP
SEE 4479 MAP

0 .25 .5 .75 1.0 miles 1 in. = 4800 ft.

SEE 4120 MAP

SEE 4120 MAP

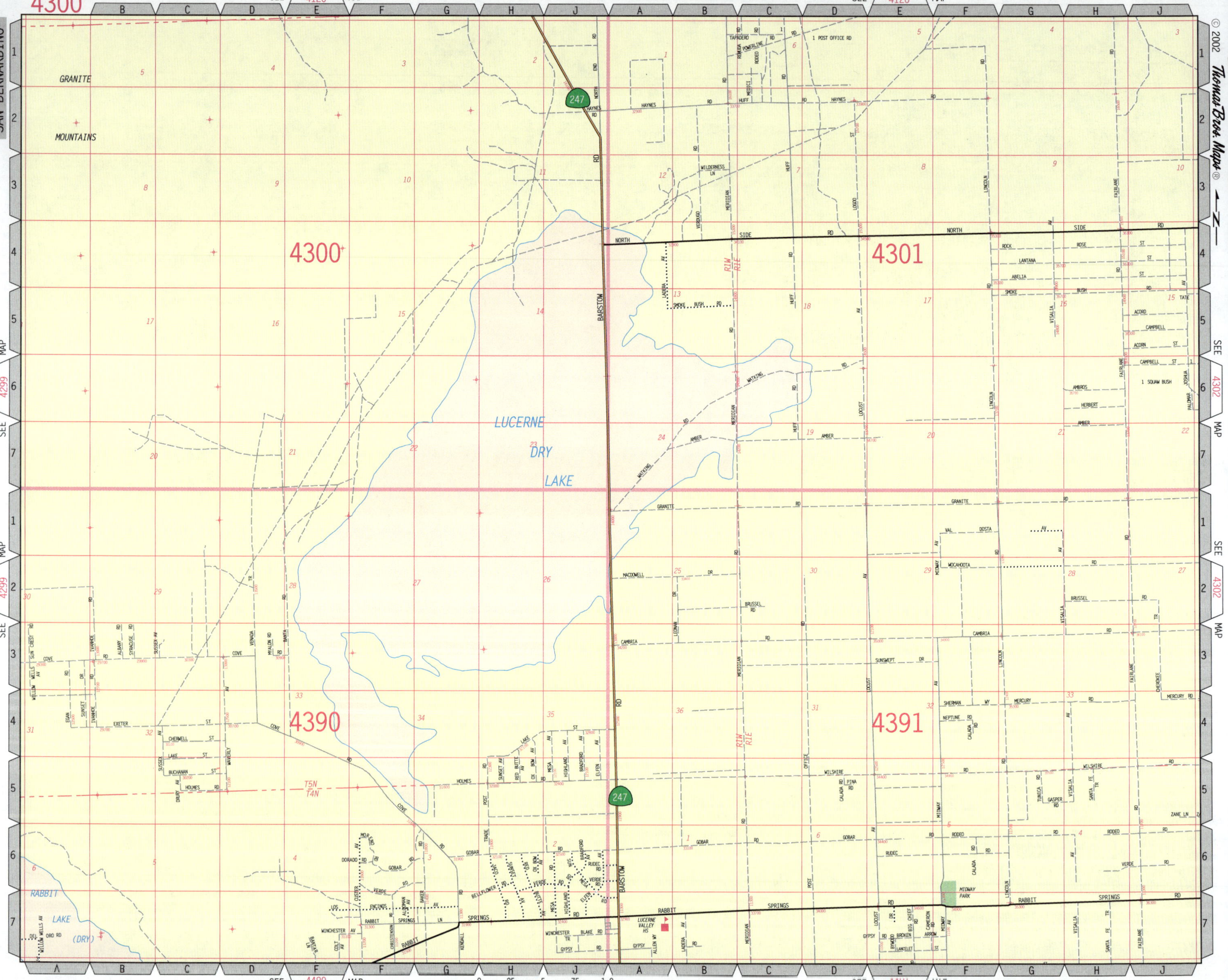

SEE 4299 MAP

SEE 4299 MAP

SEE 4302 MAP

SEE 4302 MAP

SEE 4480 MAP

SEE 4481 MAP

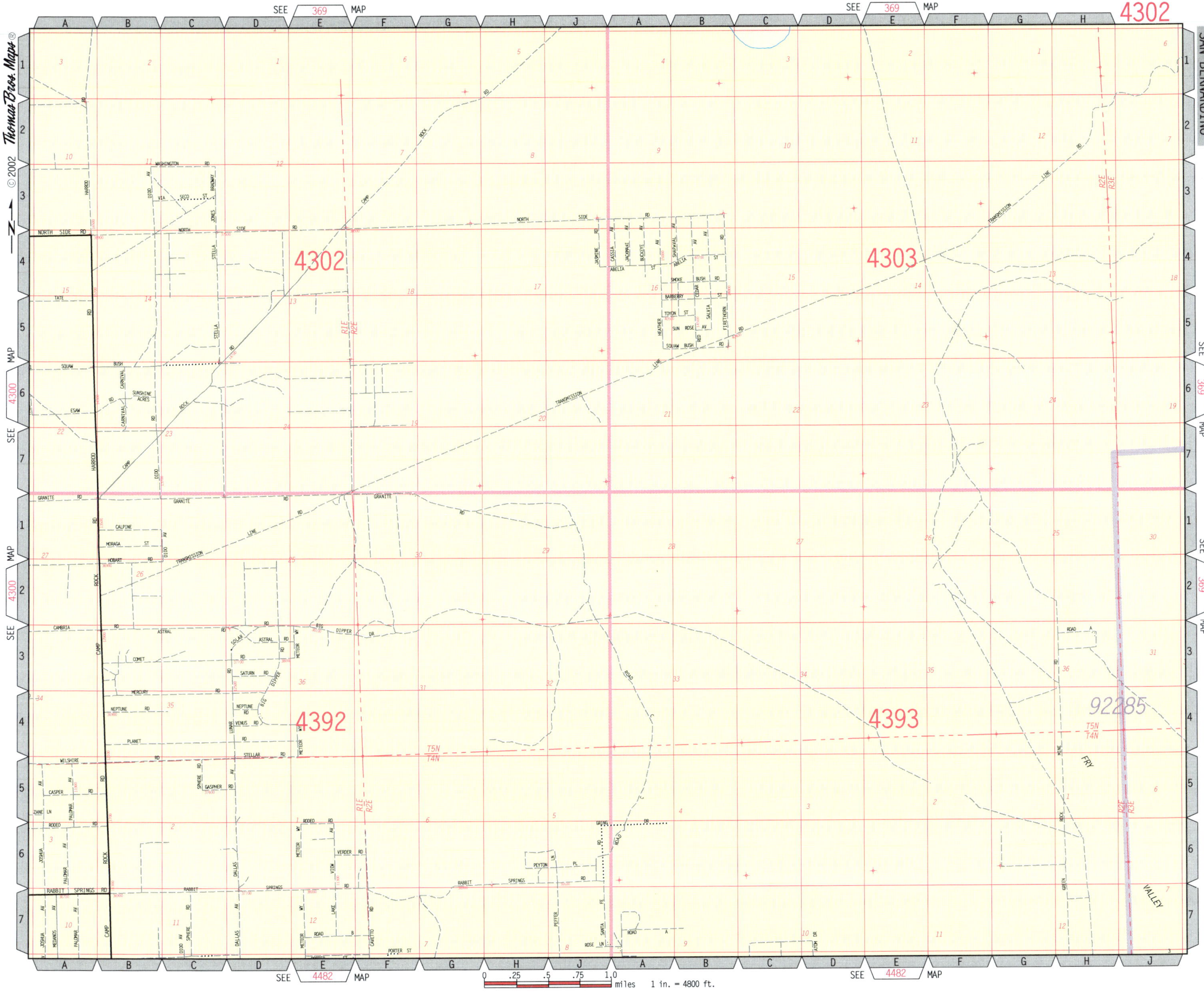
SEE 369 MAP
SEE 369 MAP
4302
4303
4392
4393
92285
NORTH SIDE RD
WASHINGTON RD
VIA SECO ST
BROADWAY
JONES
STELLA
DIDO AV
HARROD
TATE RD
SQUAW
BUSH
CARNIVAL
SUNSHINE ACRES
ESAW
ROCK RD
CAMP RD
JASMINE
CASSIA
JACKRABBIT
BUCKEYE
SHAPARRAL
ABELIA
SMOKE
BARBERRY
CEDAR
TOYON
SALVIA
FIRETHORN
HEATHER
SUN ROSE AV
SQUAW BUSH RD
TRANSMISSION LINE RD
GRANITE RD
CALPINE
MORAGA ST
HOBART RD
CAMBRIA
ASTRAL
COMET
MERCURY
NEPTUNE RD
PLANET
WILSHIRE
SOLAR
SATURN RD
BIG DIPPER DR
METEOR
LUNAR
VENUS RD
STELLAR RD
CASPER
ZANE LN
RODEO
PALOMAR
JOSHUA
SPHERE
GASPHER
DALLAS
VERDER RD
VIEW
RABBIT SPRINGS RD
MEDANOS
CAVETTO
PORTER ST
PEYTON LN
PL
PEFFER
SANTA FE
ROSE LN
ROAD A
ROAD B
ATOM DR
GREEN
MINE
FRY
VALLEY
R1E R2E
R2E R3E
T5N T4N
SEE 4300 MAP
SEE 4482 MAP
SEE 4482 MAP
0 .25 .5 .75 1.0 miles 1 in. = 4800 ft.

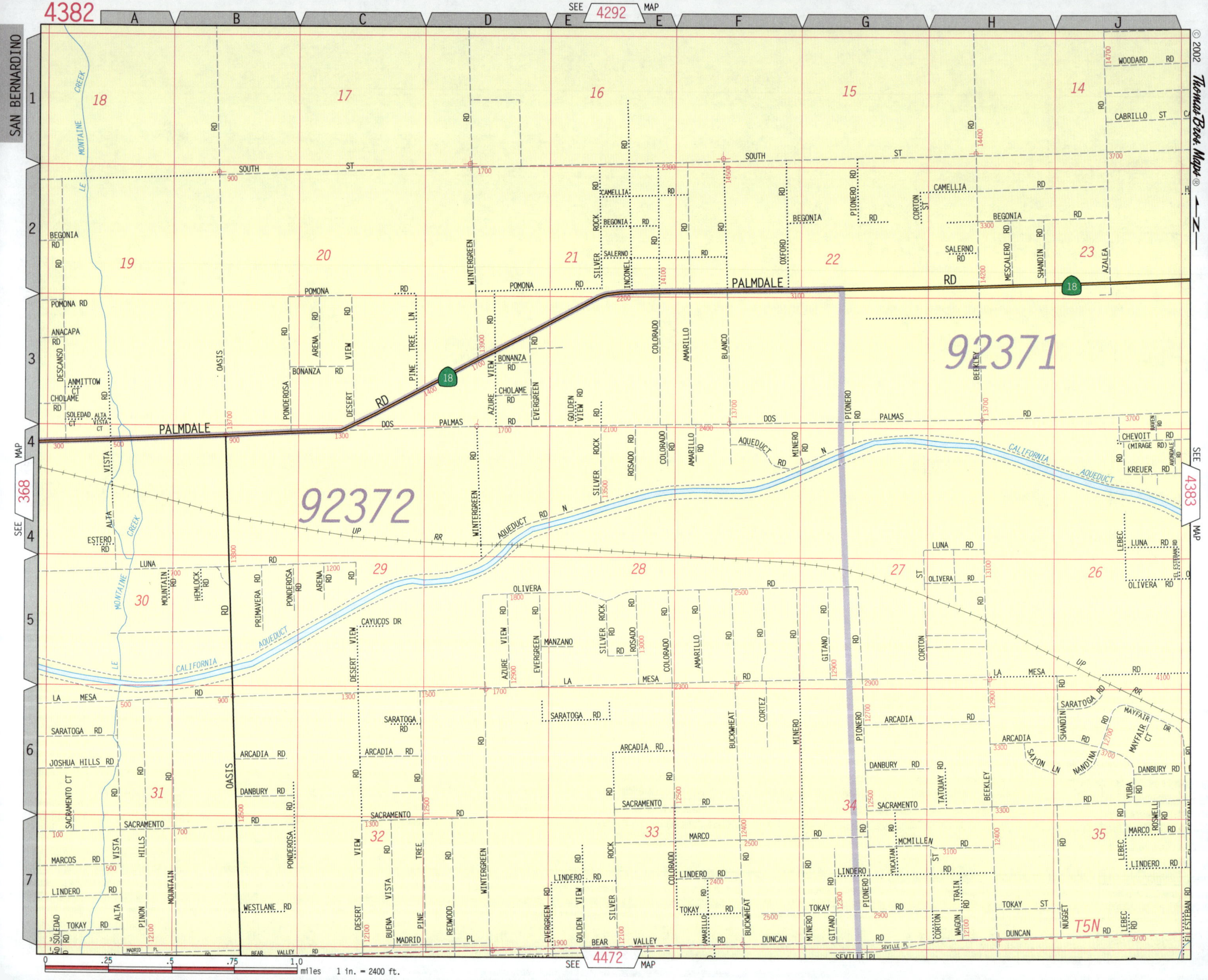
SEE 4292 MAP
SEE 4472 MAP
SEE 368 MAP
SEE 4383 MAP
SAN BERNARDINO
A
B
C
D
E
F
G
H
J
1
2
3
4
5
6
7
© 2002 Thomas Bros. Maps®
92371
92372
PALMDALE RD
SOUTH ST
DOS PALMAS RD
LE MONTAINE CREEK
CALIFORNIA AQUEDUCT
AQUEDUCT RD N
UP RR
OASIS RD
WINTERGREEN RD
POMONA RD
BONANZA RD
CHOLAME RD
BEGONIA RD
CAMELLIA RD
SALERNO RD
ANACAPA RD
DESCANSO
ANMITTOW CT
SOLEDAD CT
ALTA VISTA CT
VISTA
ESTERO RD
LUNA RD
OLIVERA RD
LA MESA RD
SARATOGA RD
JOSHUA HILLS RD
SACRAMENTO CT
SACRAMENTO RD
MARCOS RD
LINDERO RD
TOKAY RD
MADRID PL
BEAR VALLEY RD
SEVILLE PL
DUNCAN RD
ARCADIA RD
DANBURY RD
MARCO RD
WESTLANE RD
CAYUCOS DR
MANZANO
PONDEROSA RD
PRIMAVERA RD
ARENA RD
DESERT VIEW RD
PINE TREE LN
AZURE VIEW RD
EVERGREEN RD
GOLDEN VIEW RD
SILVER ROCK RD
ROSADO RD
COLORADO RD
AMARILLO RD
BLANCO RD
INCONEL RD
OXFORD RD
MINERO RD
PIONERO RD
GITANO RD
BUCKWHEAT RD
CORTEZ
CORTON ST
BEEKLEY RD
MESCALERO RD
SHANDIN RD
AZALEA
WOODARD RD
CABRILLO ST
CHEVOIT RD
MIRAGE RD
KREUER RD
LEBEC RD
EL ESTERAN RD
MAYFAIR DR
MAYFAIR CT
SAXON LN
NANDINA RD
YUBA RD
ROSWELL RD
MCMILLEN RD
YUCATAN
TATOUAY RD
TRAIN WAGON RD
NUGGET
MOUNTAIN RD
HEMLOCK RD
PINON RD
HILLS RD
BUENA VISTA RD
REDWOOD RD
T5N
18
14
15
16
17
19
20
21
22
23
26
27
28
29
30
31
32
33
34
35
0 .25 .5 .75 1.0 miles 1 in. = 2400 ft.

SEE 4292 MAP

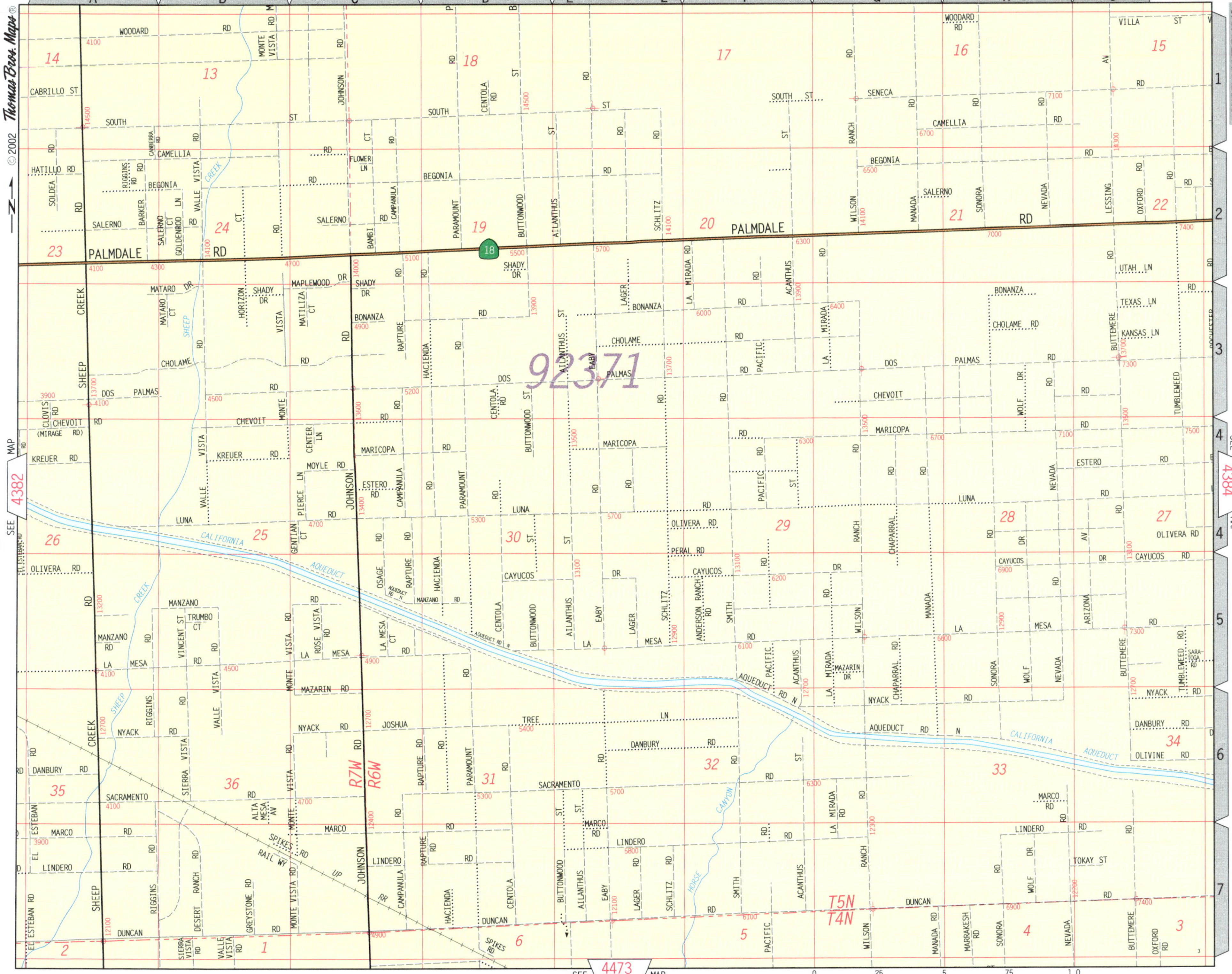

SEE 4473 MAP

0 .25 .5 .75 1.0 miles 1 in. = 2400 ft.

SEE 4294 MAP

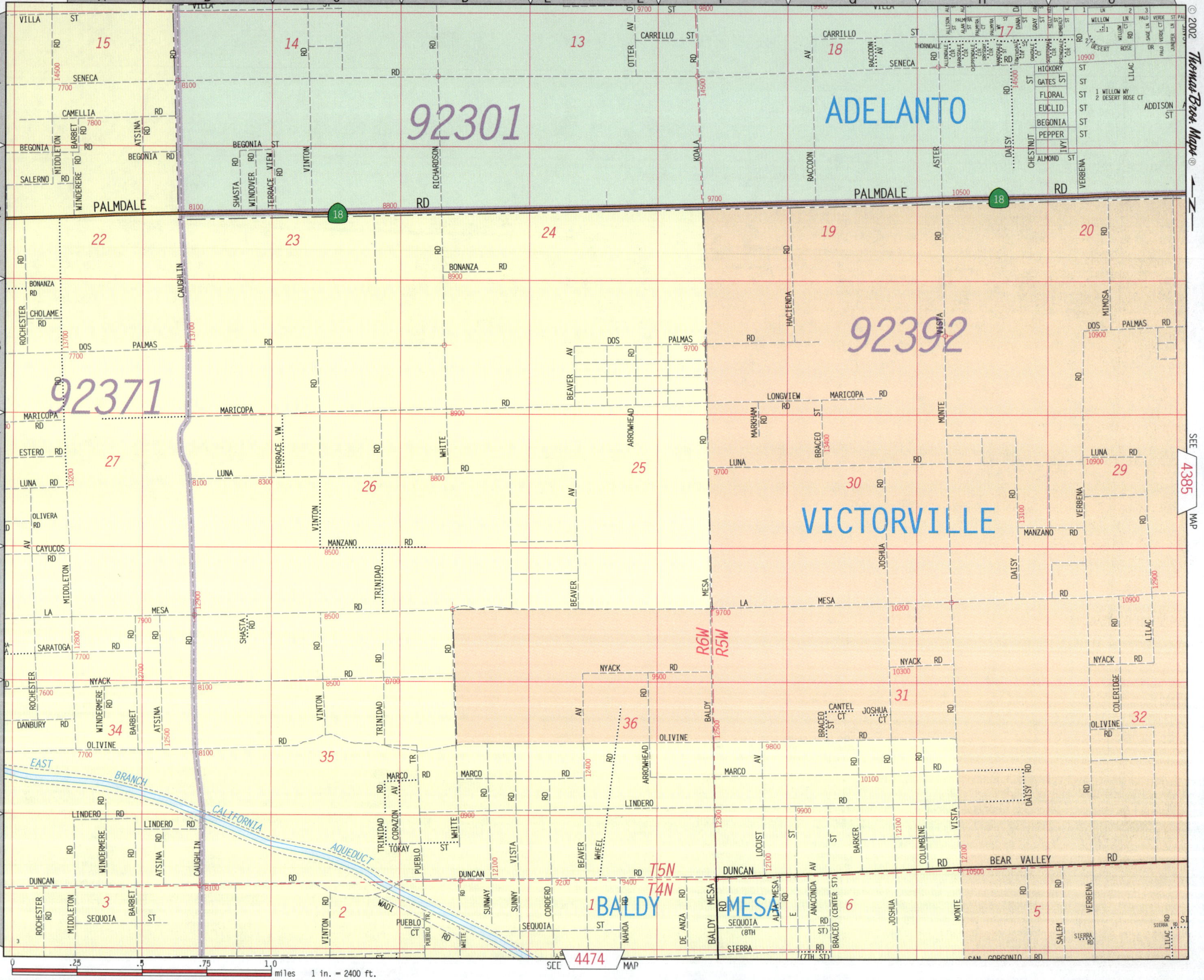

SEE 4383 MAP

SEE 4385 MAP

SEE 4474 MAP

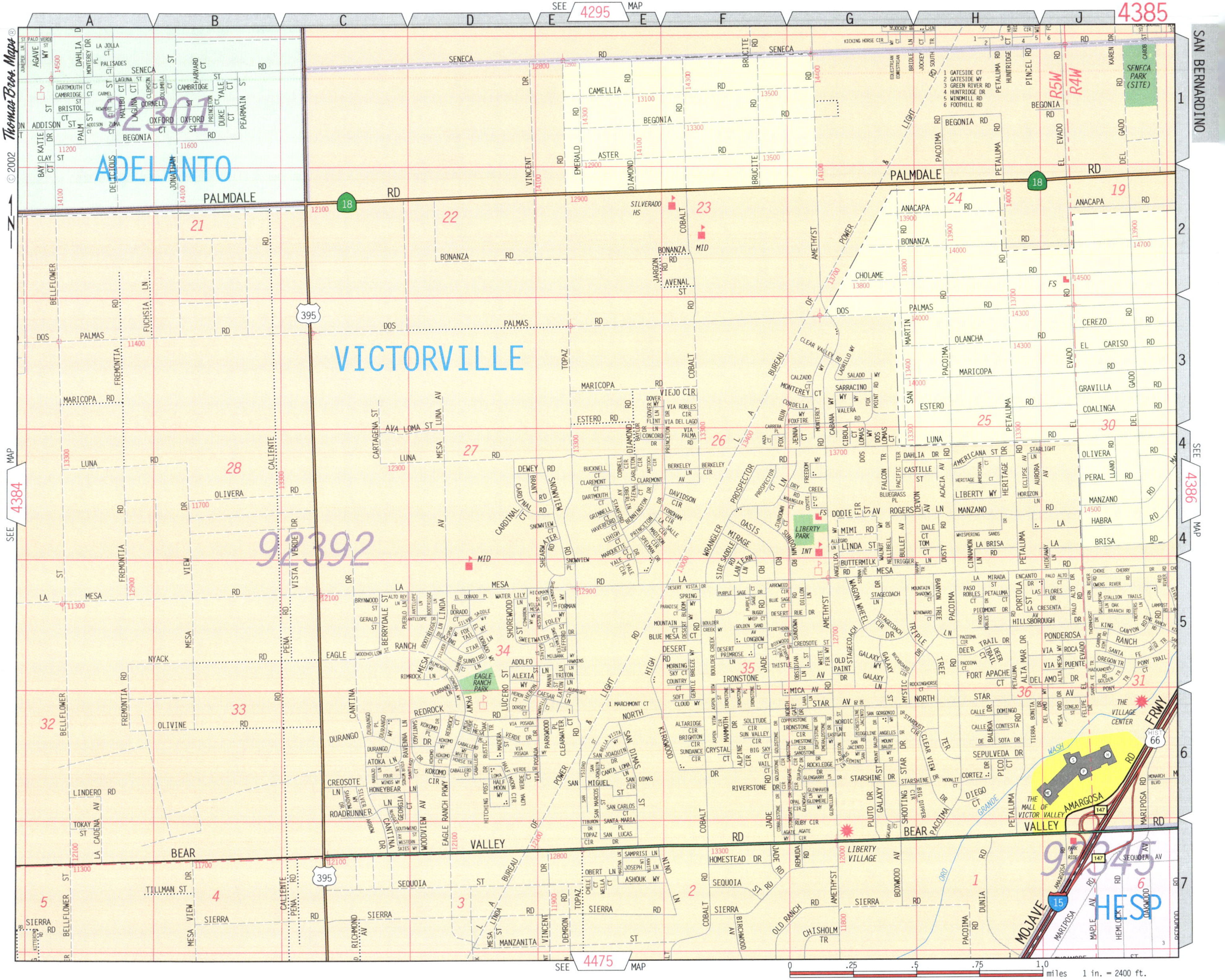
SEE 4295 MAP
SEE 4475 MAP
SEE 4384 MAP
SEE 4386 MAP
SAN BERNARDINO
Thomas Bros. Maps
© 2002
ADELANTO
VICTORVILLE
HESP
92301
92392
92345
SENECA
PALMDALE
RD
BONANZA
PALMAS
DOS
MARICOPA
LUNA
OLIVERA
MESA
NYACK
OLIVINE
BEAR
VALLEY
SEQUOIA
SIERRA
MANZANITA
TILLMAN ST
LINDERO RD
EAGLE RANCH PARK
LIBERTY PARK
LIBERTY VILLAGE
SENECA PARK (SITE)
THE MALL OF VICTOR VALLEY
THE VILLAGE CENTER
SILVERADO HS
MID
FS
INT
MOJAVE FRWY
AMARGOSA
CHOLAME
ANACAPA
BEGONIA
CAMELLIA
ASTER
ESTERO
NORTH
STAR
RIVERSTONE
IRONSTONE
CHISHOLM TR
OLD RANCH
BUREAU
BELLFLOWER
FREMONTIA
CANTINA
TOPAZ
COBALT
AMETHYST
PACOIMA
PETALUMA
EVADO
R5W
R4W
395
18
15
147
HIST 66
A B C D E F G H J
1 2 3 4 5 6 7
0 .25 .5 .75 1.0 miles 1 in. = 2400 ft.

SEE 4296 MAP

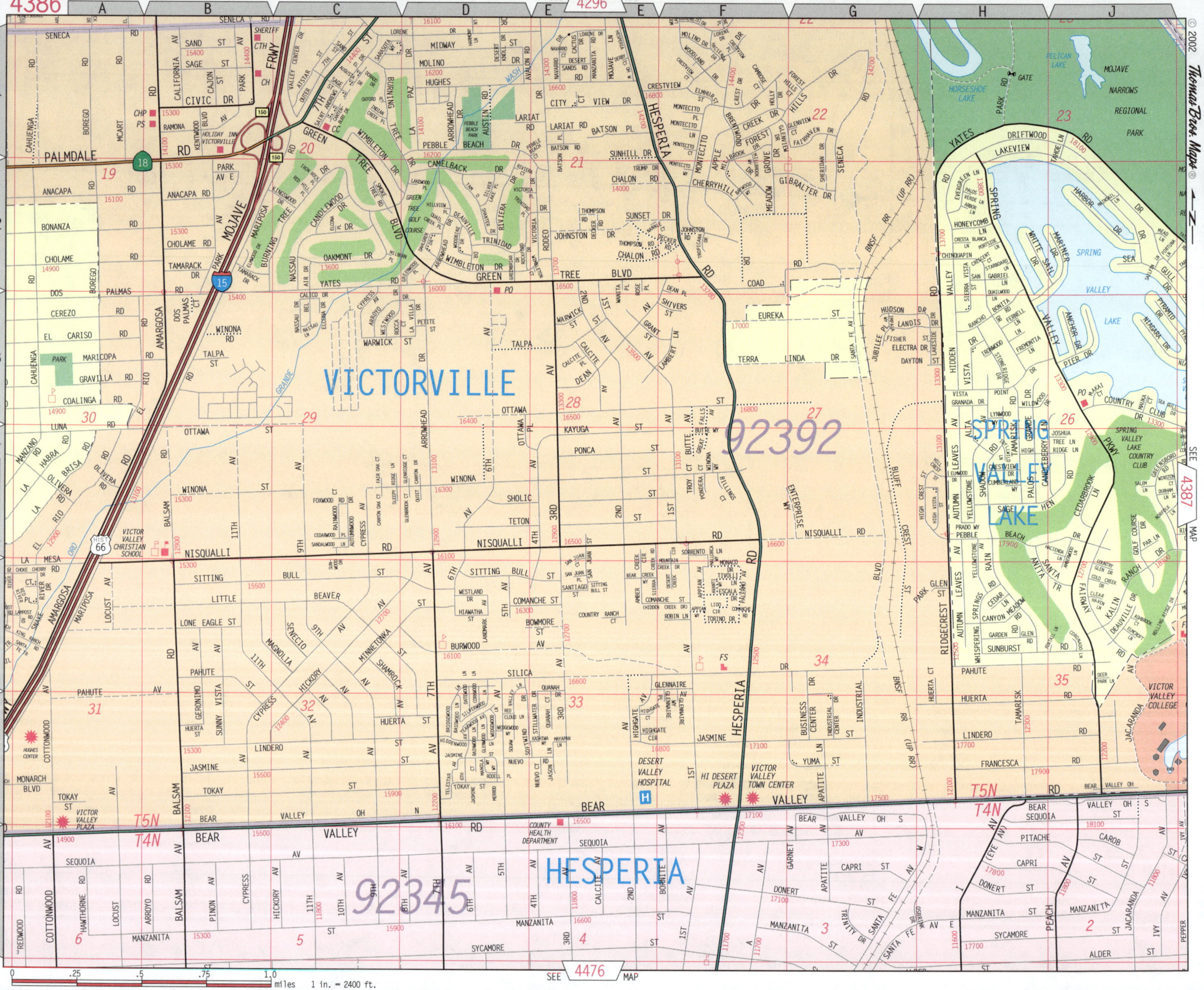

SEE 4385 MAP
SEE 4387 MAP
SEE 4476 MAP

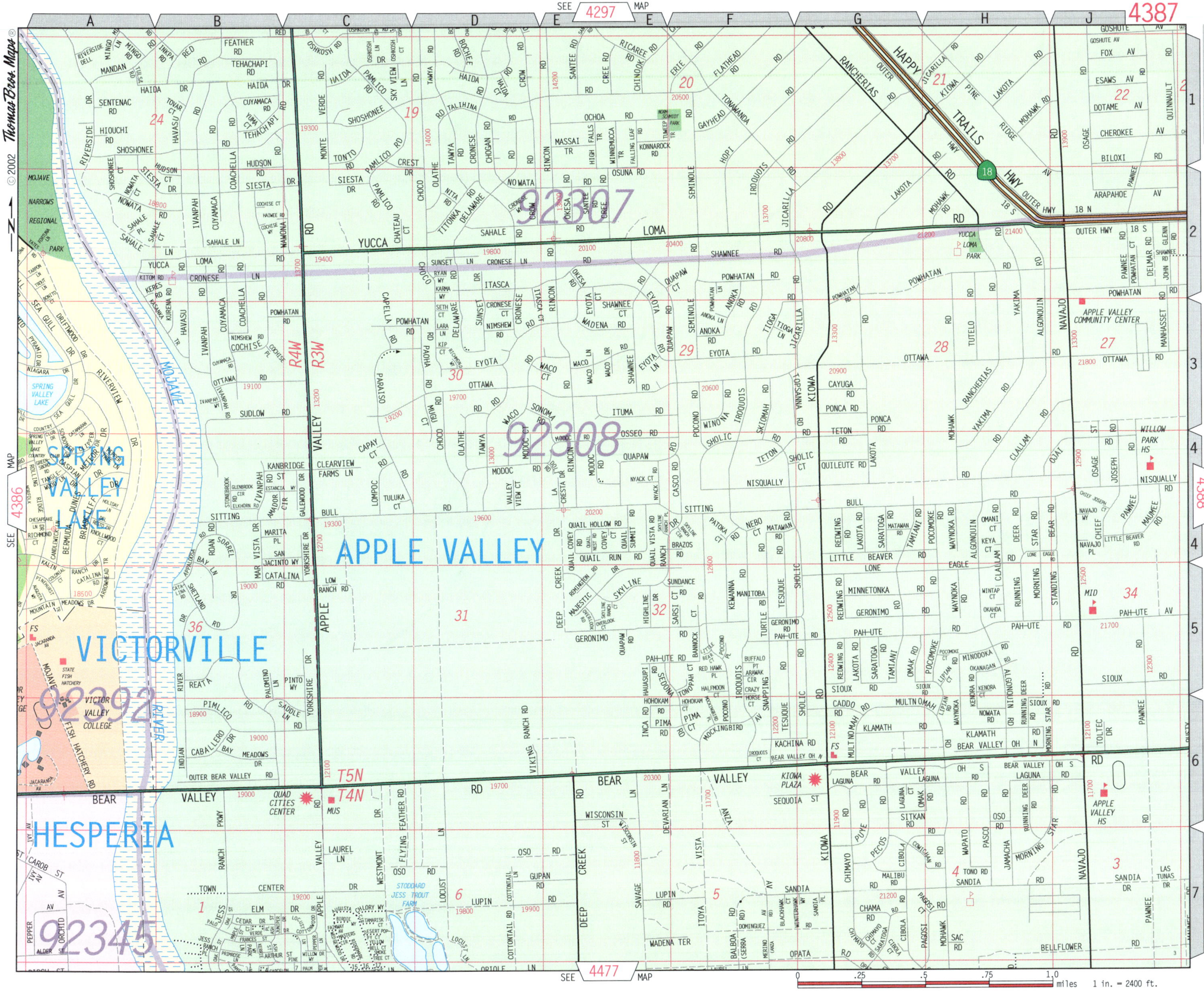
SEE 4297 MAP
SAN BERNARDINO
SEE 4388 MAP
SEE 4386 MAP
SEE 4477 MAP
APPLE VALLEY
VICTORVILLE
HESPERIA
SPRING VALLEY LAKE
92307
92308
92392
92345
MOJAVE RIVER
MOJAVE NARROWS REGIONAL PARK
HAPPY TRAILS HWY
18
YUCCA LOMA RD
BEAR VALLEY RD
APPLE VALLEY RD
NAVAJO RD
KIOWA RD
DEEP CREEK RD
APPLE VALLEY COMMUNITY CENTER
APPLE VALLEY HS
WILLOW PARK HS
VICTOR VALLEY COLLEGE
STATE FISH HATCHERY
QUAD CITIES CENTER
KIOWA PLAZA
STODDARD JESS TROUT FARM
YUCCA LOMA PARK
R4W
R3W
T5N
T4N
0 .25 .5 .75 1.0 miles 1 in. = 2400 ft.

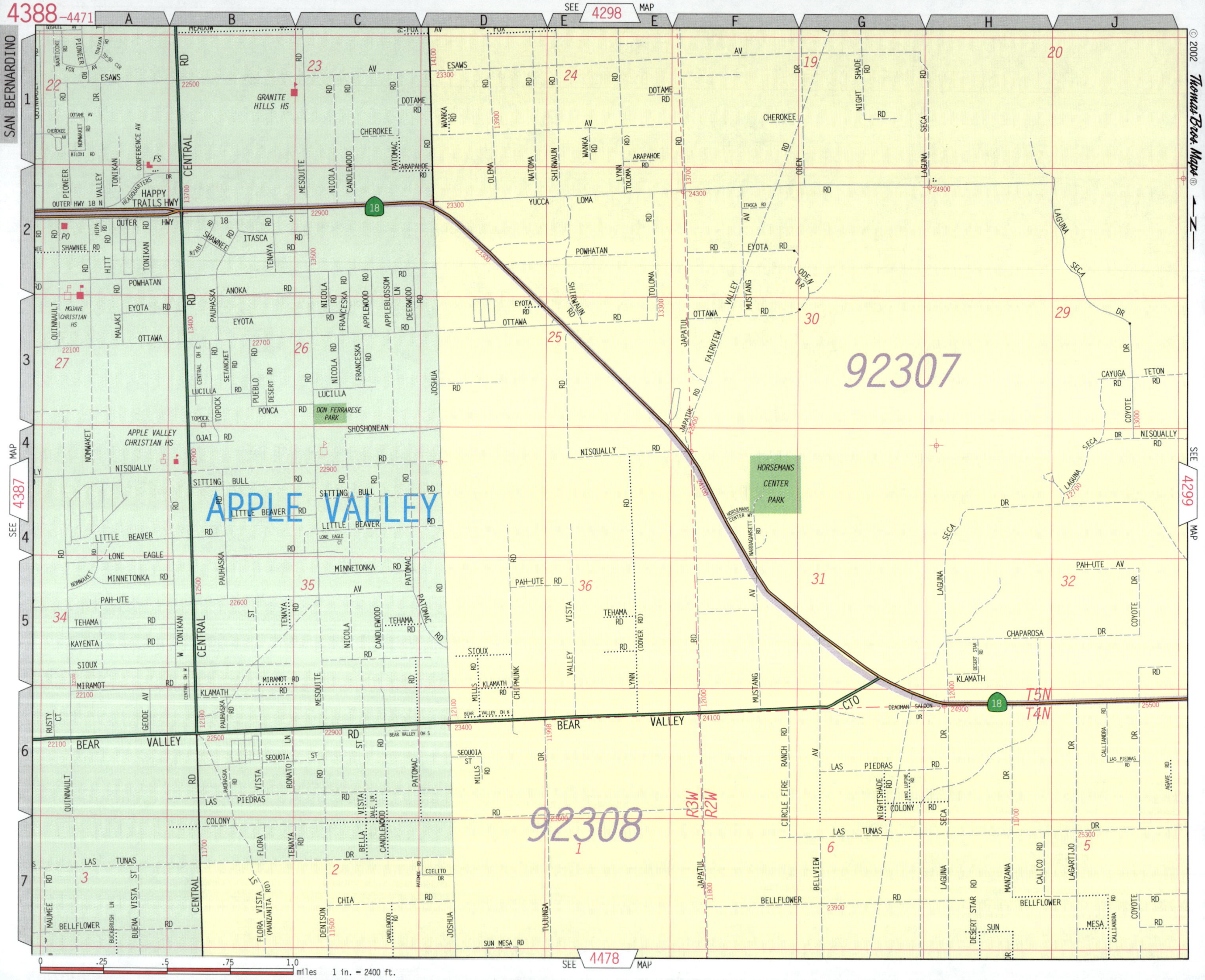
SEE 4298 MAP
SEE 4387 MAP
SEE 4299 MAP
SEE 4478 MAP
SAN BERNARDINO
APPLE VALLEY
92307
92308
GRANITE HILLS HS
MOJAVE CHRISTIAN HS
APPLE VALLEY CHRISTIAN HS
DON FERRARESE PARK
HORSEMANS CENTER PARK
HAPPY TRAILS HWY
OUTER HWY 18 N
CENTRAL RD
BEAR VALLEY RD
YUCCA LOMA RD
NISQUALLY RD
CHAPAROSA DR
JAPATUL RD
LAGUNA SECA DR
T5N
T4N
R3W
R2W
© 2002 Thomas Bros. Maps ®
0 .25 .5 .75 1.0 miles 1 in. = 2400 ft.

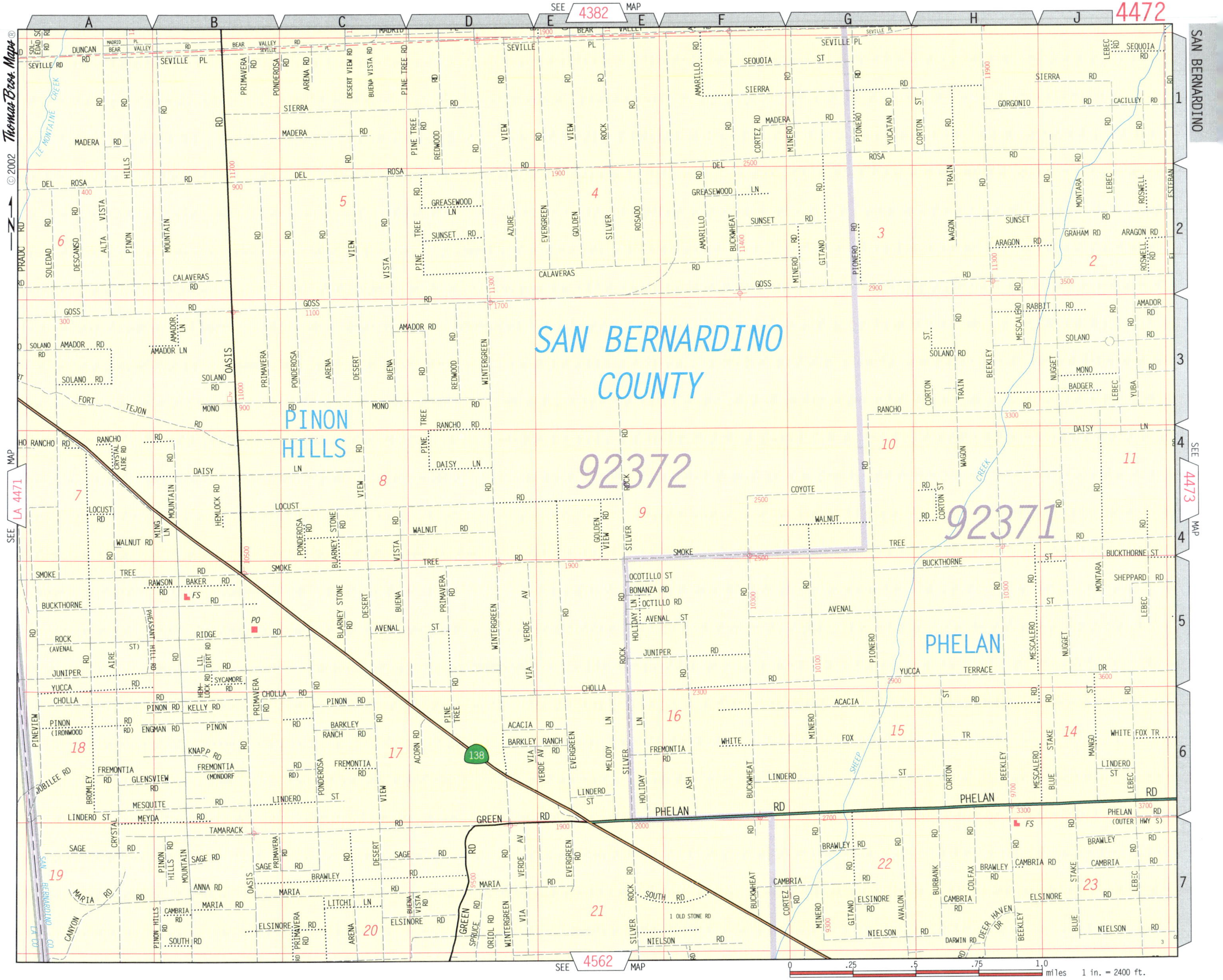
SEE 4382 MAP
A
B
C
D
E
F
G
H
J
SAN BERNARDINO
SAN BERNARDINO COUNTY
PINON HILLS
PHELAN
92372
92371
SEE LA 4471 MAP
SEE 4473 MAP
SEE 4562 MAP
138
SEVILLE PL
SEVILLE RD
SEQUOIA
SIERRA
MADERA
DEL ROSA
CALAVERAS
GOSS
AMADOR
SOLANO
FORT TEJON
RANCHO
DAISY
LOCUST
WALNUT
SMOKE TREE
BUCKTHORNE
OCOTILLO ST
JUNIPER
YUCCA
CHOLLA
PINON
ACACIA
FREMONTIA
LINDERO ST
PHELAN RD
SAGE
MARIA
ELSINORE
NIELSON
LE MONTAINE CREEK
SHEEP CREEK
OASIS
PRIMAVERA
PONDEROSA
WINTERGREEN
SILVER
BUCKWHEAT
PIONERO
BEEKLEY
NUGGET
GREEN RD
1 OLD STONE RD
0
.25
.5
.75
1.0
miles
1 in. = 2400 ft.

SEE 4383 MAP

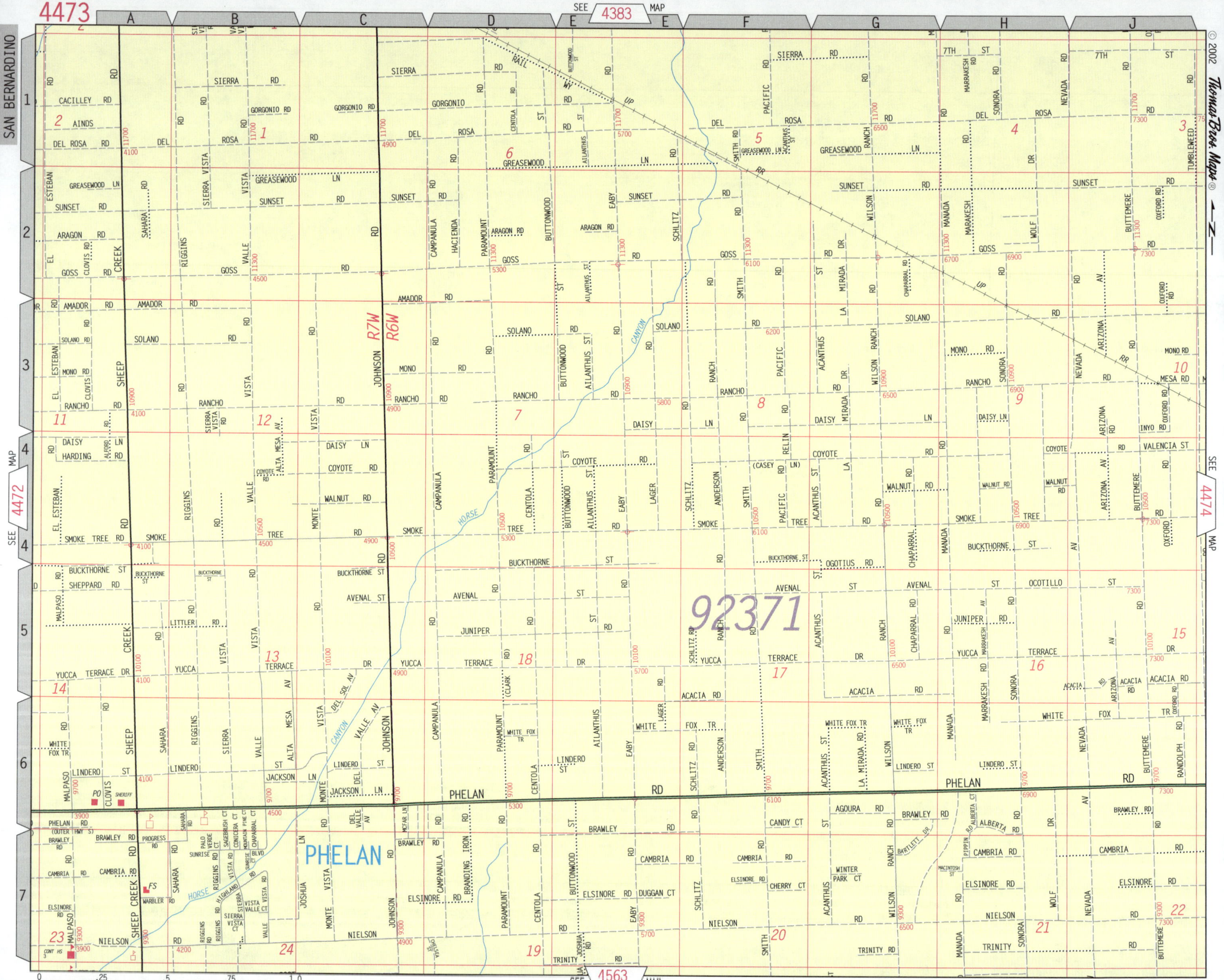

0 .25 .5 .75 1.0 miles 1 in. = 2400 ft.

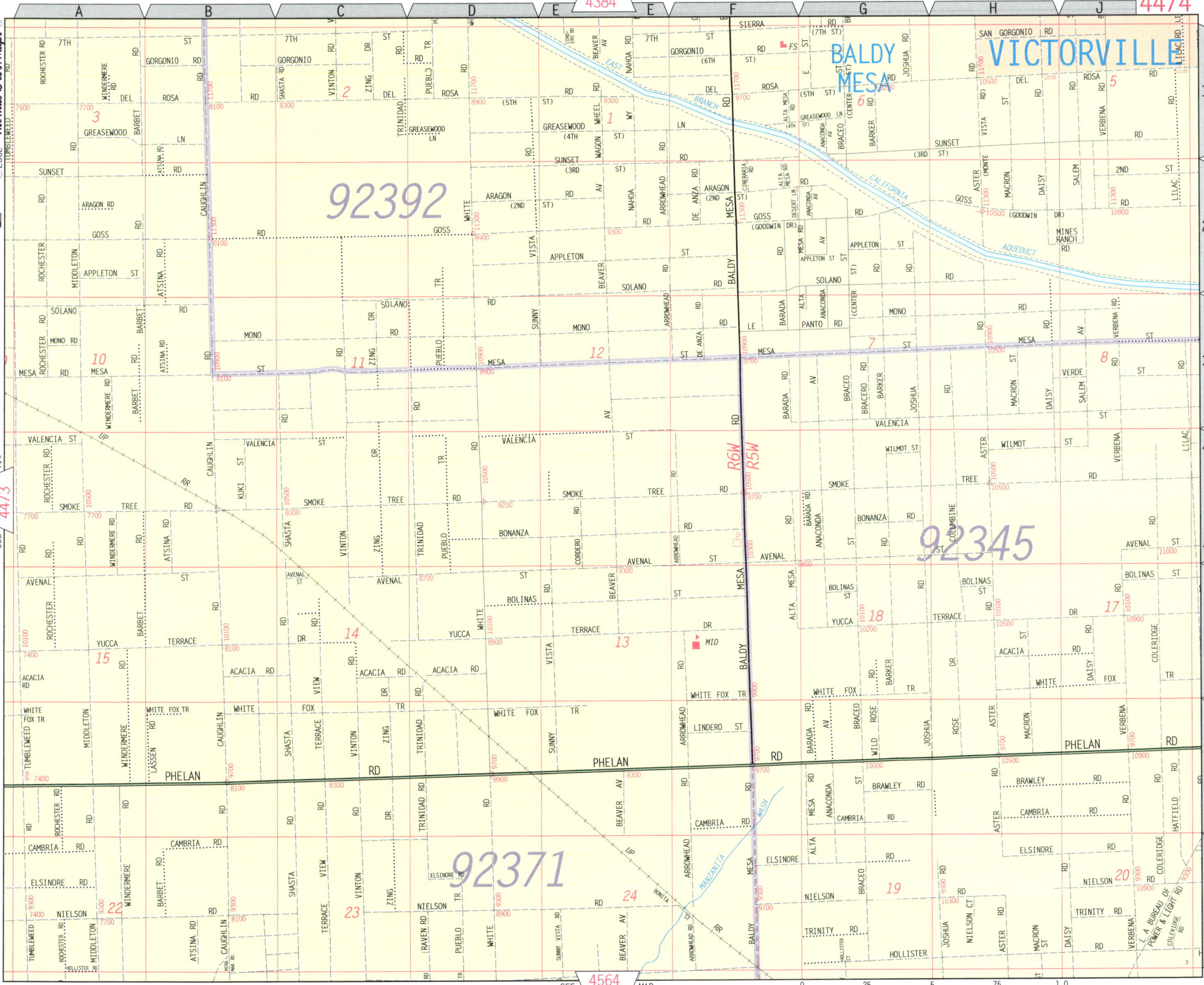

SEE 4384 MAP
SEE 4564 MAP
SEE 4473 MAP
SEE 4475 MAP
SAN BERNARDINO
VICTORVILLE
BALDY MESA
92392
92345
92371
R6W
R5W
CALIFORNIA AQUEDUCT
EAST BRANCH
MANZANITA WASH
UP RR
MID
FS
MINES RANCH
L A BUREAU OF POWER & LIGHT RD
PHELAN RD
MESA ST
BALDY MESA RD
CAUGHLIN RD
SAN GORGONIO RD
7TH ST
ROSA RD
DEL RD
GREASEWOOD LN
SUNSET RD
ARAGON RD
GOSS RD
APPLETON ST
SOLANO RD
MONO RD
VALENCIA ST
SMOKE TREE RD
BONANZA RD
AVENAL ST
BOLINAS ST
TERRACE DR
YUCCA RD
ACACIA RD
WHITE FOX TR
LINDERO ST
BRAWLEY RD
CAMBRIA RD
ELSINORE RD
NIELSON RD
TRINITY RD
HOLLISTER RD
WILMOT ST
ROCHESTER RD
TUMBLEWEED RD
MIDDLETON RD
WINDERMERE RD
BARBET RD
ATSINA RD
SHASTA RD
VINTON RD
ZING DR
TRINIDAD RD
PUEBLO TR
WHITE RD
VISTA RD
SUNNY VISTA RD
BEAVER AV
ARROWHEAD RD
DE ANZA RD
NAHOA RD
BARADA RD
ALTA MESA RD
ANACONDA AV
BRACEO RD
BARKER RD
JOSHUA RD
ASTER RD
MACRON RD
DAISY RD
SALEM RD
VERBENA RD
LILAC RD
COLERIDGE RD
HATFIELD RD
COLUMBINE ST
VERDE ST
MACRON ST
2ND ST
1 2 3 4 5 6 7 8 10 11 12 13 14 15 17 18 19 20 22 23 24
A B C D E F G H J
0 .25 .5 .75 1.0 miles 1 in. = 2400 ft.

SEE 4385 MAP

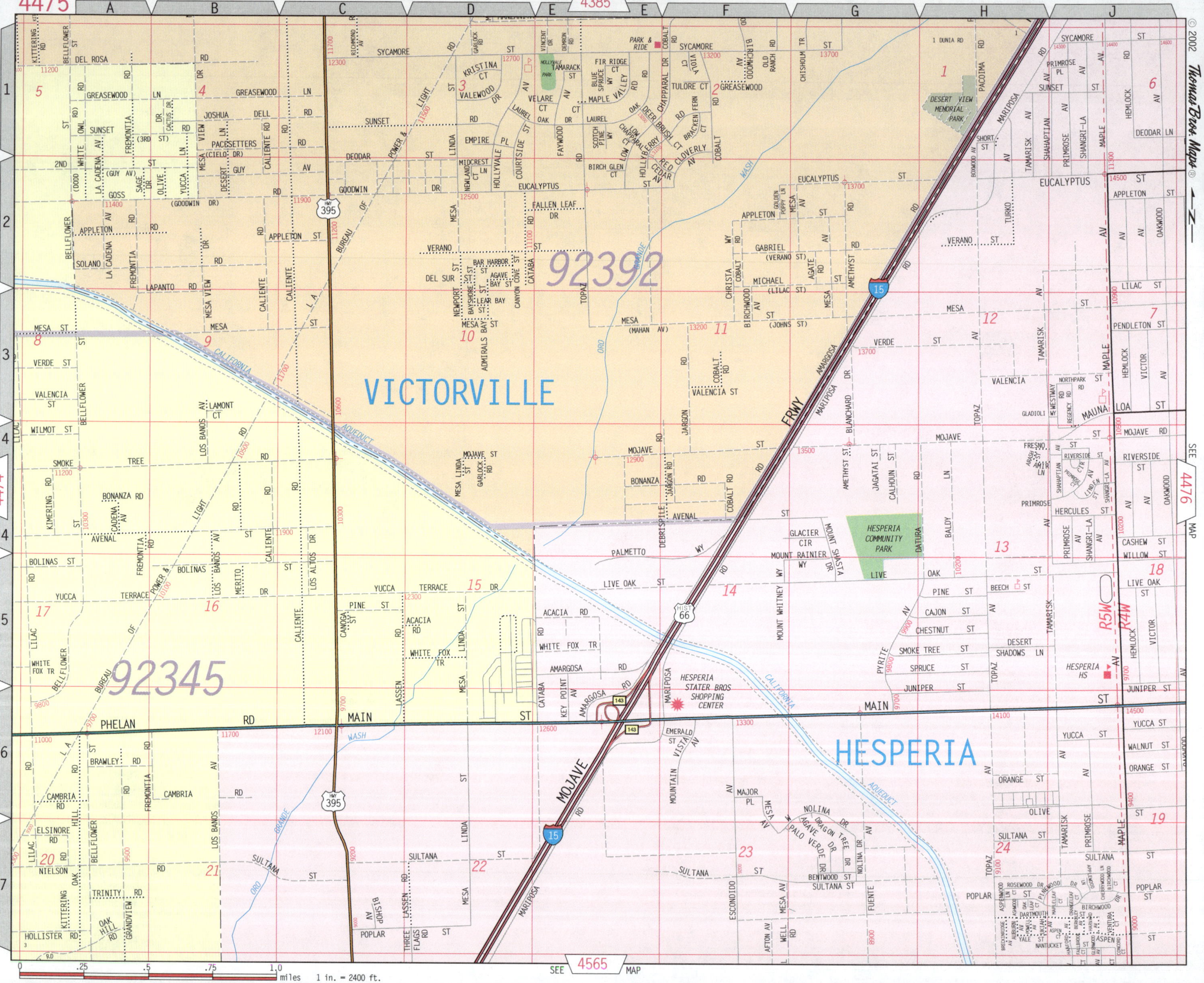

SEE 4474 MAP

SEE 4476 MAP

SEE 4565 MAP

SEE 4386 MAP

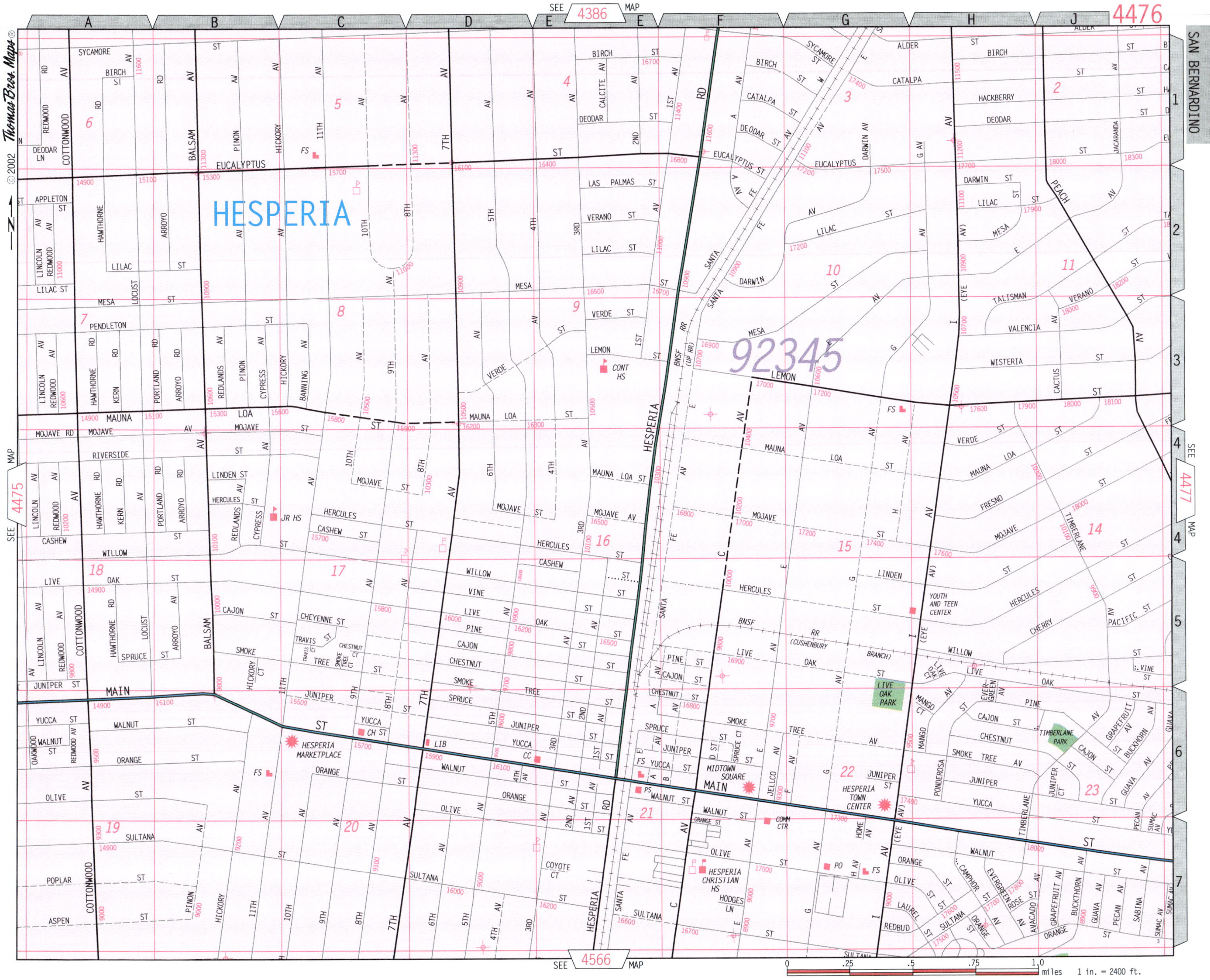

SEE 4475 MAP

SEE 4477 MAP

SEE 4566 MAP

SEE 4387 MAP

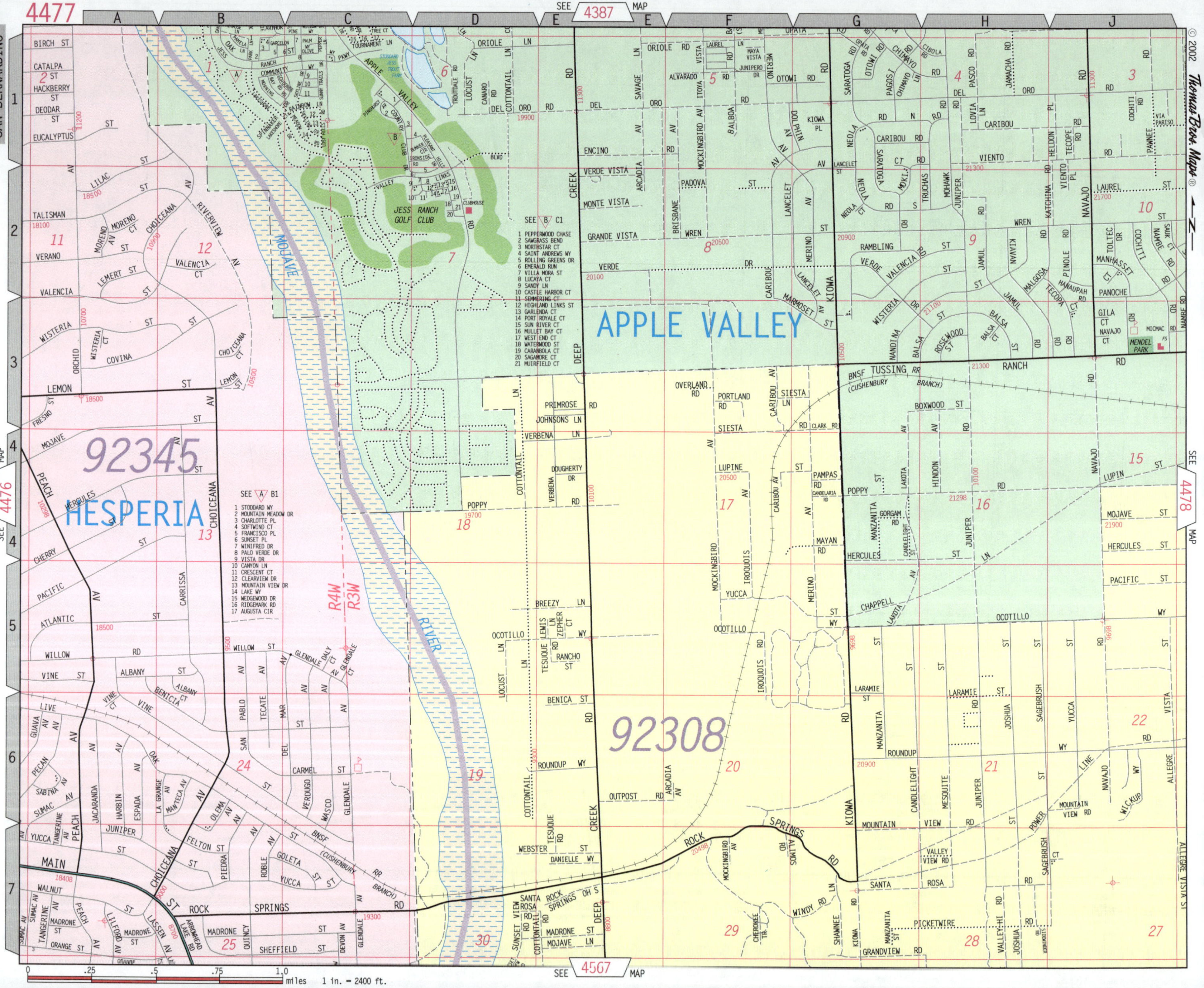

SEE 4567 MAP

SEE 4388 MAP

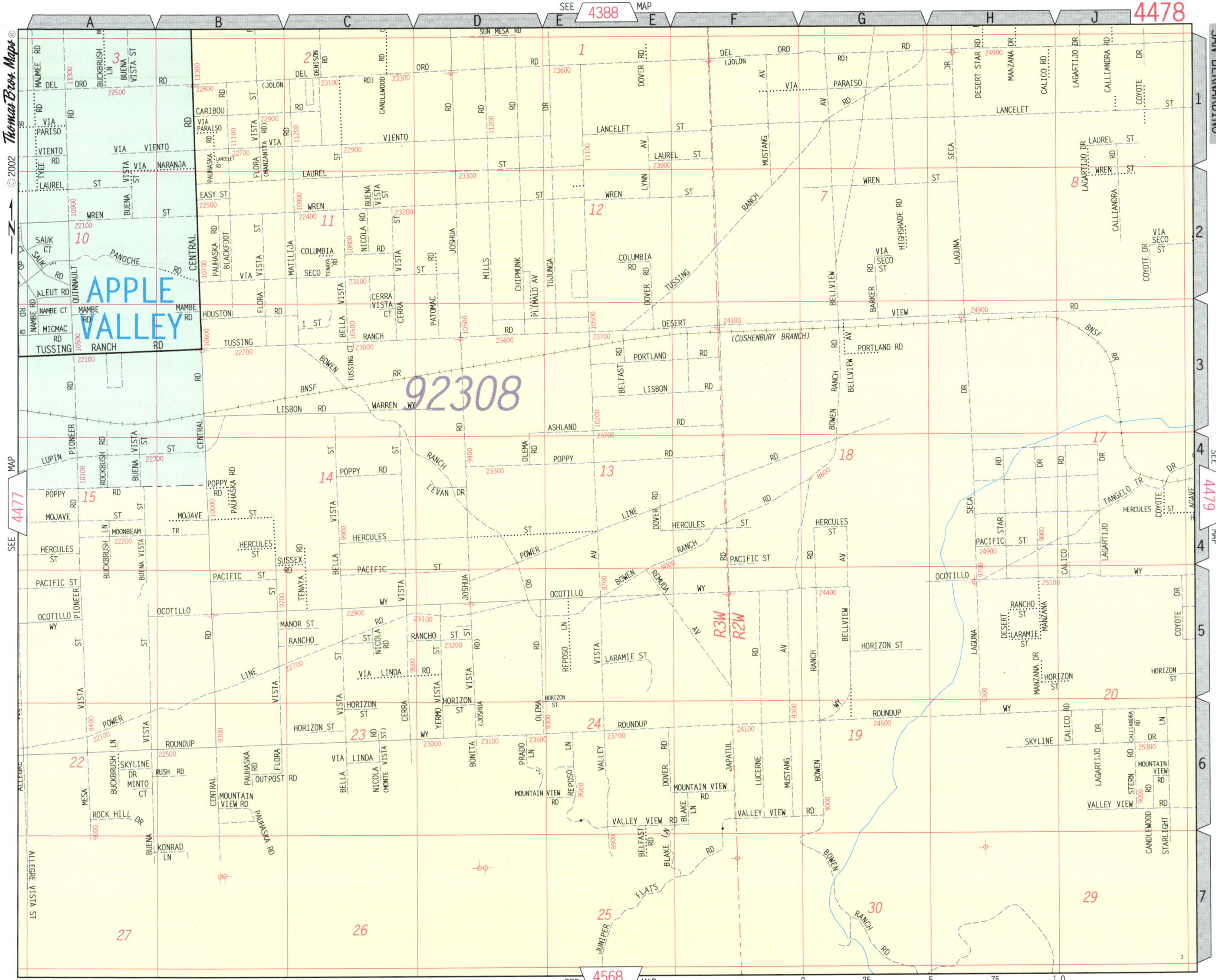

SEE 4568 MAP

0 .25 .5 .75 1.0 miles 1 in. = 2400 ft.

SEE 4299 MAP

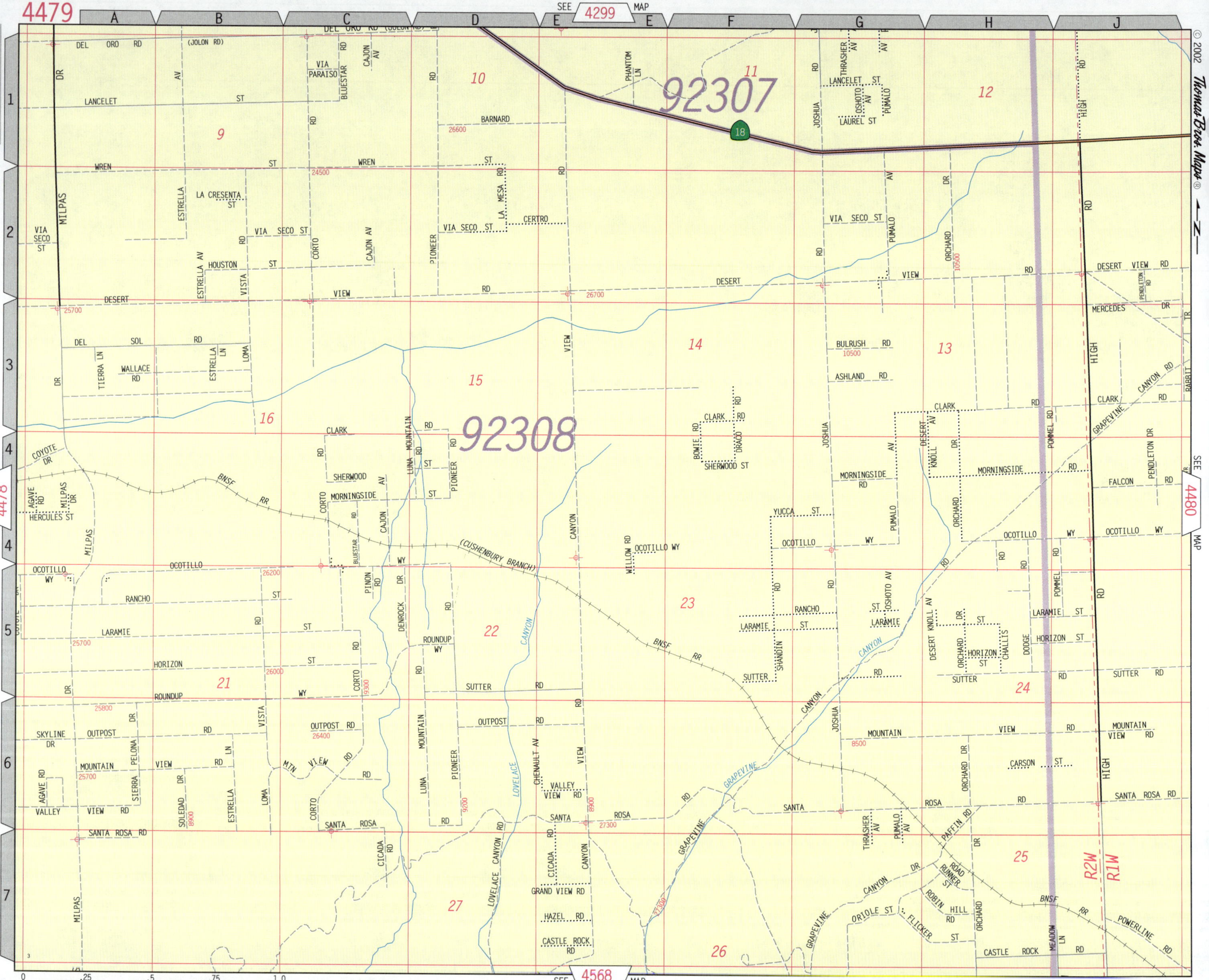

SEE 4478 MAP

SEE 4480 MAP

SEE 4568 MAP

0 .25 .5 .75 1.0 miles 1 in. = 2400 ft.

SEE 4300 MAP
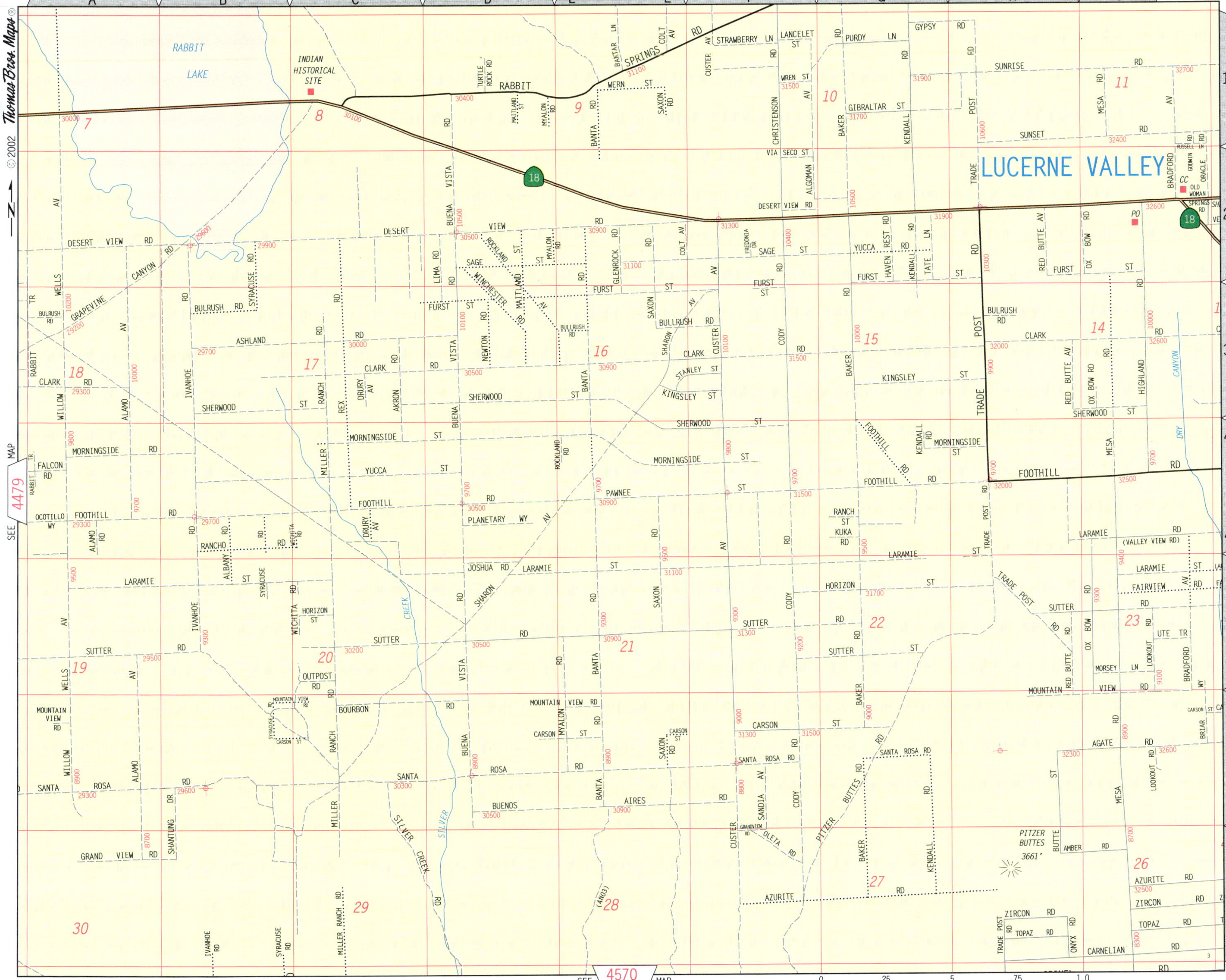

SEE 4479 MAP
SEE 4481 MAP
SEE 4570 MAP
0 .25 .5 .75 1.0 miles 1 in. = 2400 ft.

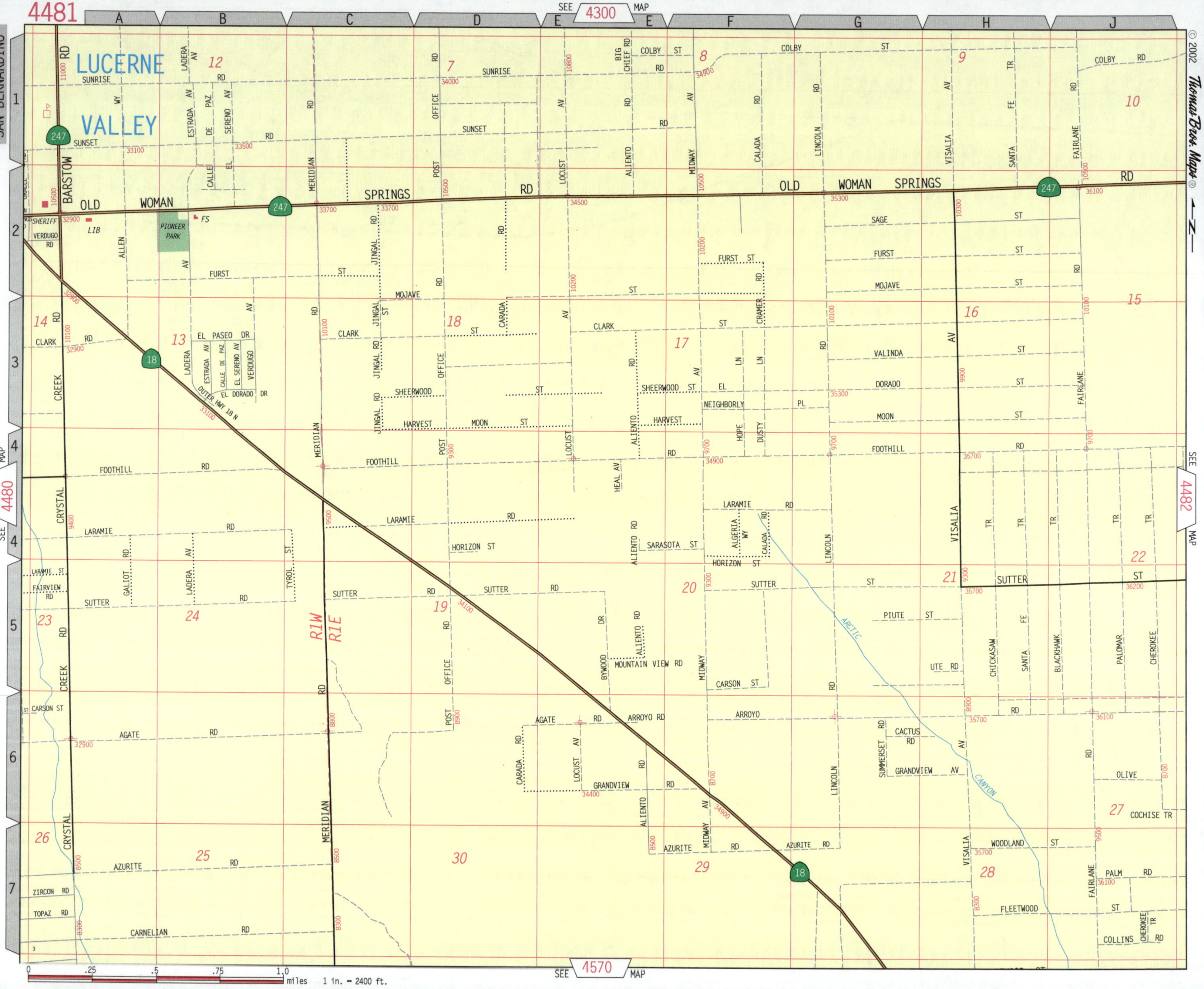
SEE 4300 MAP
A
B
C
D
E
F
G
H
J
1
2
3
4
5
6
7
SAN BERNARDINO
LUCERNE
VALLEY
SEE 4480 MAP
SEE 4482 MAP
SEE 4570 MAP
OLD WOMAN SPRINGS RD
BARSTOW RD
SUNRISE RD
SUNSET RD
COLBY ST
COLBY RD
BIG CHIEF RD
LADERA AV
ESTRADA AV
CALLE DE PAZ
EL SERENO AV
MERIDIAN RD
OFFICE RD
POST RD
LOCUST AV
ALIENTO RD
MIDWAY AV
CALADA RD
LINCOLN RD
VISALIA AV
SANTA FE TR
FAIRLANE RD
SHERIFF
VERDUGO RD
LIB
PIONEER PARK
FS
ALLEN AV
FURST ST
JINGAL RD
MOJAVE ST
CARADA RD
CLARK ST
CLARK RD
SAGE ST
FURST ST
MOJAVE ST
CRAMER RD
EL PASEO DR
EL DORADO DR
OUTER HWY 18 N
VALINDA ST
DORADO ST
MOON ST
SHEERWOOD ST
HARVEST MOON ST
HARVEST ST
EL NEIGHBORLY LN
HOPE LN
DUSTY LN
PL
FOOTHILL RD
HEAL AV
CREEK RD
CRYSTAL CREEK RD
LARAMIE RD
HORIZON ST
SARASOTA ST
ALGERIA WY
CALADA RD
LARAMIE ST
FAIRVIEW RD
GALIOT RD
LADERA AV
TYROL ST
SUTTER RD
SUTTER ST
PIUTE ST
ARCTIC CANYON
R1W
R1E
BYWOOD DR
ALIENTO RD
MOUNTAIN VIEW RD
CARSON ST
UTE RD
CHICKASAW
SANTA FE
BLACKHAWK
PALOMAR
CHEROKEE
TR
AGATE RD
ARROYO RD
CACTUS RD
SUMMERSET RD
GRANDVIEW AV
GRANDVIEW RD
OLIVE
COCHISE TR
AZURITE RD
WOODLAND ST
PALM RD
FLEETWOOD ST
ZIRCON RD
TOPAZ RD
CARNELIAN RD
COLLINS RD
CHEROKEE TR
247
18
7
8
9
10
12
13
14
15
16
17
18
19
20
21
22
23
24
25
26
27
28
29
30
11000
10500
32900
33100
33500
33700
34000
10800
34500
35300
36100
10200
10100
35700
9700
34900
9400
9500
34100
9300
36200
8900
8800
34400
8700
8500
8300
36100
0
.25
.5
.75
1.0
miles 1 in. = 2400 ft.

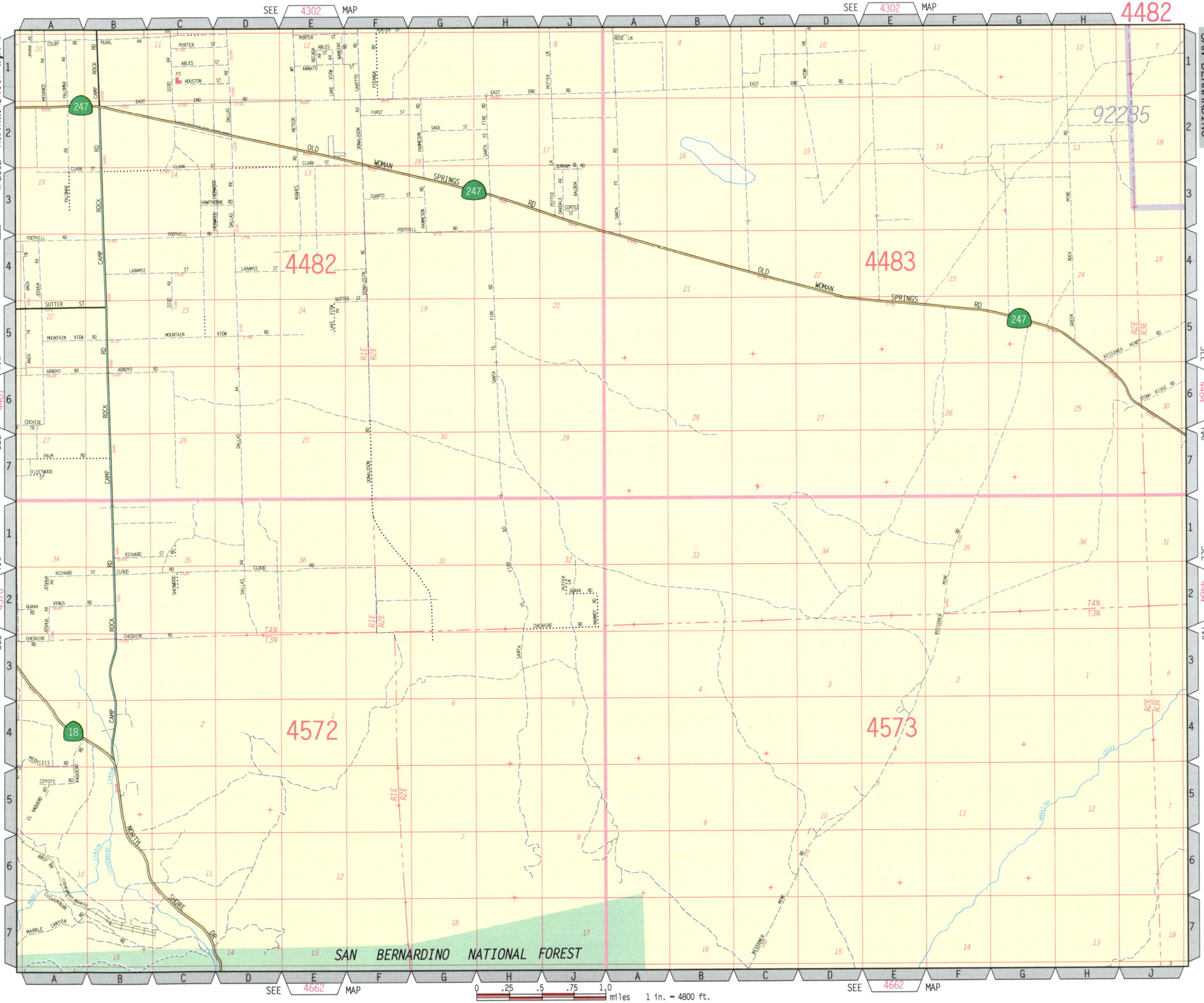
SEE 4302 MAP
SEE 4302 MAP
SEE 4481 MAP
SEE 4570 MAP
SEE 4484 MAP
SEE 4484 MAP
SEE 4662 MAP
SEE 4662 MAP
SAN BERNARDINO
Thomas Bros. Maps
© 2002
4482
4483
4572
4573
92285
OLD WOMAN SPRINGS RD
247
18
CAMP ROCK RD
NORTH SHORE DR
SAN BERNARDINO NATIONAL FOREST
FOOTHILL RD
LARAMIE ST
SUTTER ST
MOUNTAIN VIEW RD
ARROYO RD
CLARK ST
EAST END RD
PORTER ST
ABLES ST
HOUSTON ST
PEARL AV
COLBY RD
DALLAS AV
DONALDSON RD
SANTA FE FIRE RD
MINE RD
BESSEMER MINE RD
STONY RIDGE RD
ROCK RD
GREEN
RICHARD ST
CLOUD RD
CHESHIRE RD
GUAVA RD
COCHISE TR
PALM RD
FLEETWOOD ST
MEHLEIS RD
COYOTE RD
MARBLE CANYON
ARRASTRE CREEK
T4N
T3N
R1E
R2E
R3E
0 .25 .5 .75 1.0 miles 1 in. = 4800 ft.

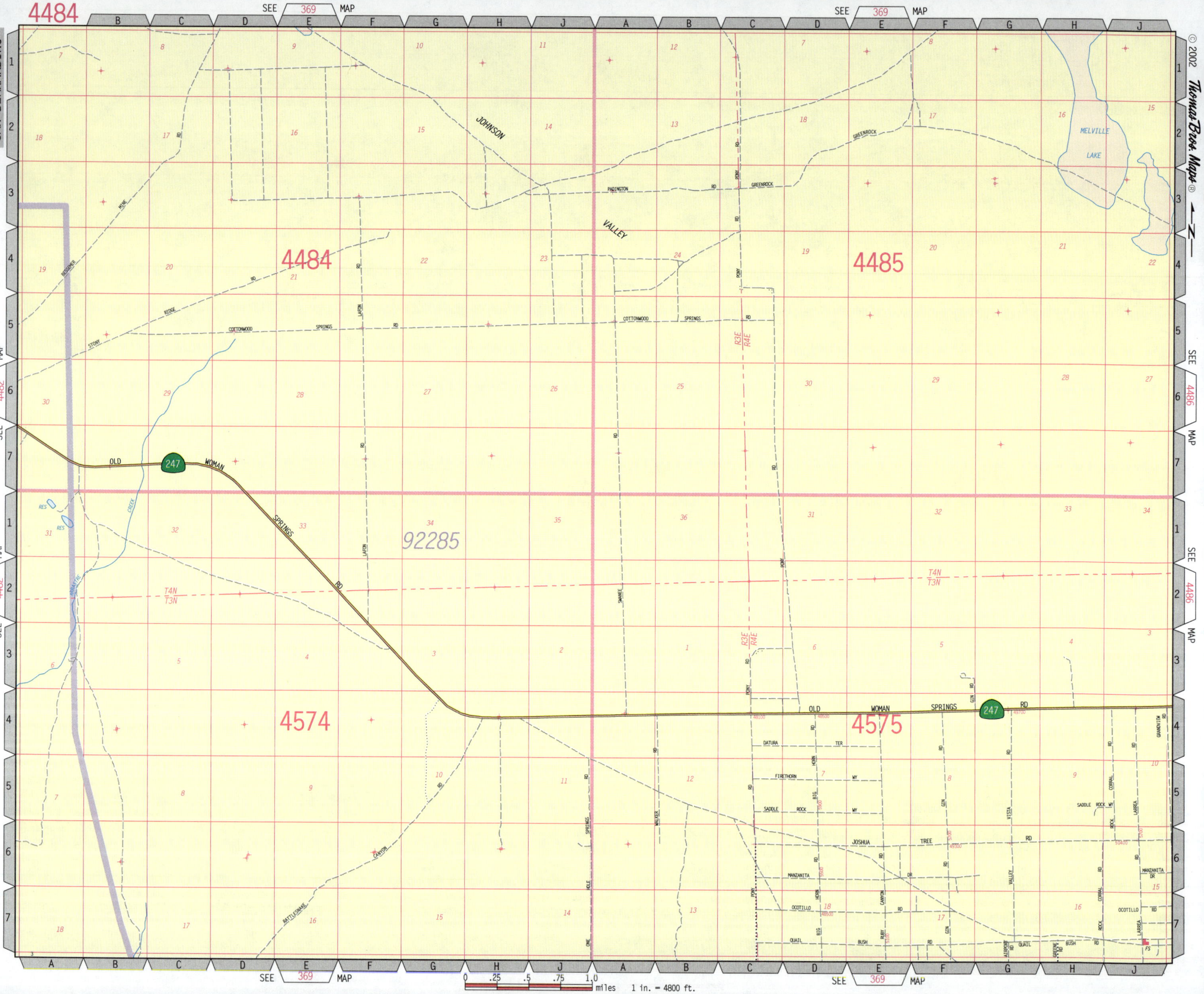

0 .25 .5 .75 1.0 miles 1 in. = 4800 ft.

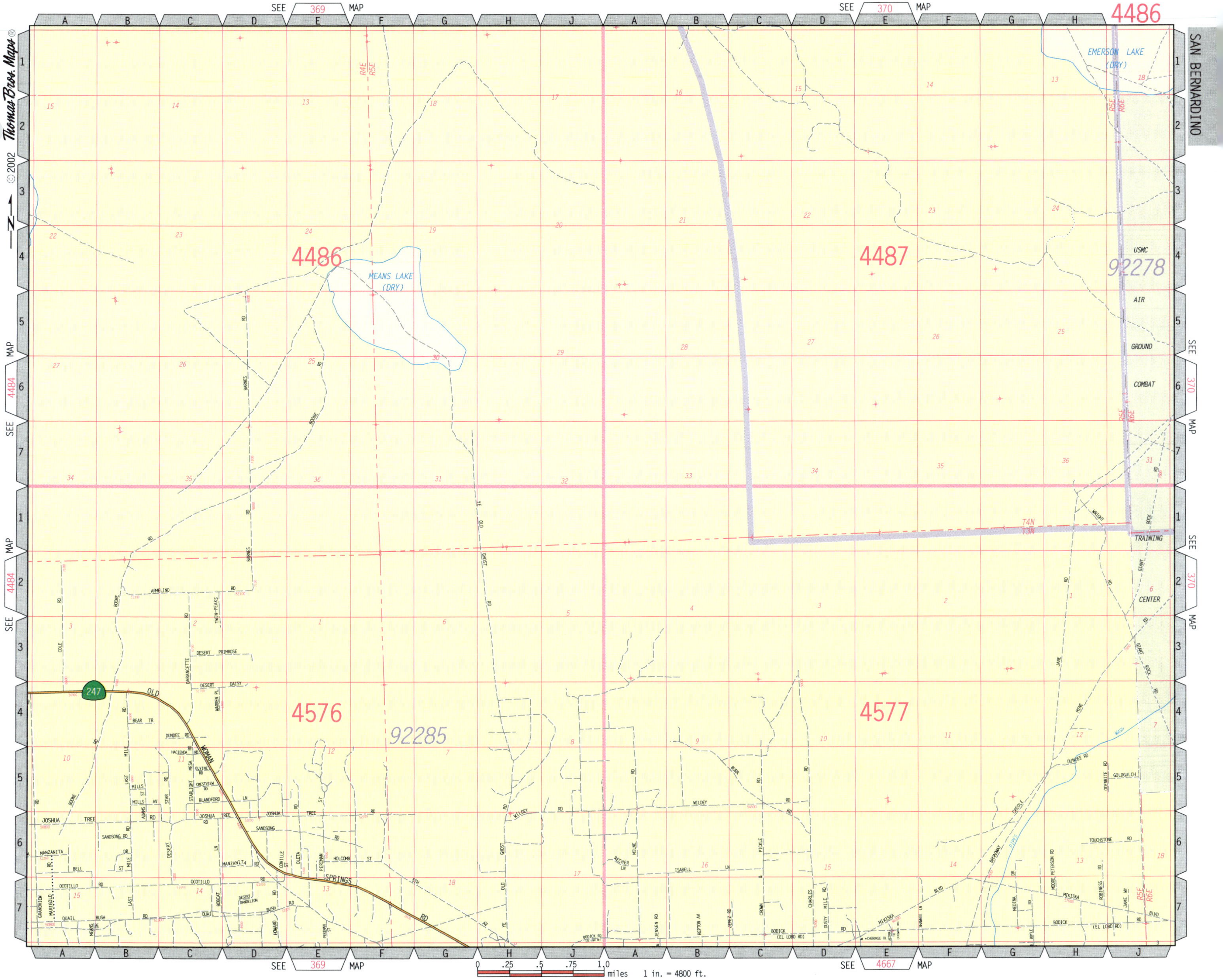
SEE 369 MAP
SEE 370 MAP
SEE 4484 MAP
SEE 370 MAP
SEE 369 MAP
SEE 4667 MAP
SAN BERNARDINO
EMERSON LAKE (DRY)
MEANS LAKE (DRY)
4486
4487
4576
4577
92278
92285
USMC
AIR
GROUND
COMBAT
TRAINING
CENTER
R4E R5E
R5E R6E
T4N T3N
247
OLD WOMAN SPRINGS RD
BARNES RD
BOONE RD
ARMELINO RD
TWIN PEAKS
DESERT PRIMROSE
DESERT DAISY
DARANCETTE
WARREN PL
BEAR TR
DUNDEE RD
HACIENDA
MESA
OLVINE
CRESTVIEW
BLANDFORD LN
STARLIGHT
JOSHUA TREE
SANDSONG
MANZANITA
BELL
OCOTILLO
QUAIL
BUSH
GRANDVIEW
MARIGOLD
COLE
MILLS
LAST MILE
ADAMS
DESERT
COVILLE
OLETA
PERIMAN
HOLCOMB ST
OLD GHOST RD
YE
WILDEY RD
RECHER LN
MILNE
JENSEN RD
REPTON AV
JEMEZ RD
CROWN
PICKLE
CHARLES
DUSTY MILE RD
ISABELL LN
BODICK RD (EL LOBO RD)
MIKISKA
SHAWNEE LN
CHEROKEE TR
BROADWAY
PIPES
CREOLE
MEDINA
DUNDEE RD
GOLDGULCH
OOCHRITE RD
TOUCHSTONE RD
MOORE PETERSON RD
ROBINESS
JAME WY
JANE
MINE
WRIGHT
ROCK
GIANT ROCK RD
WASH
miles 1 in. = 4800 ft.

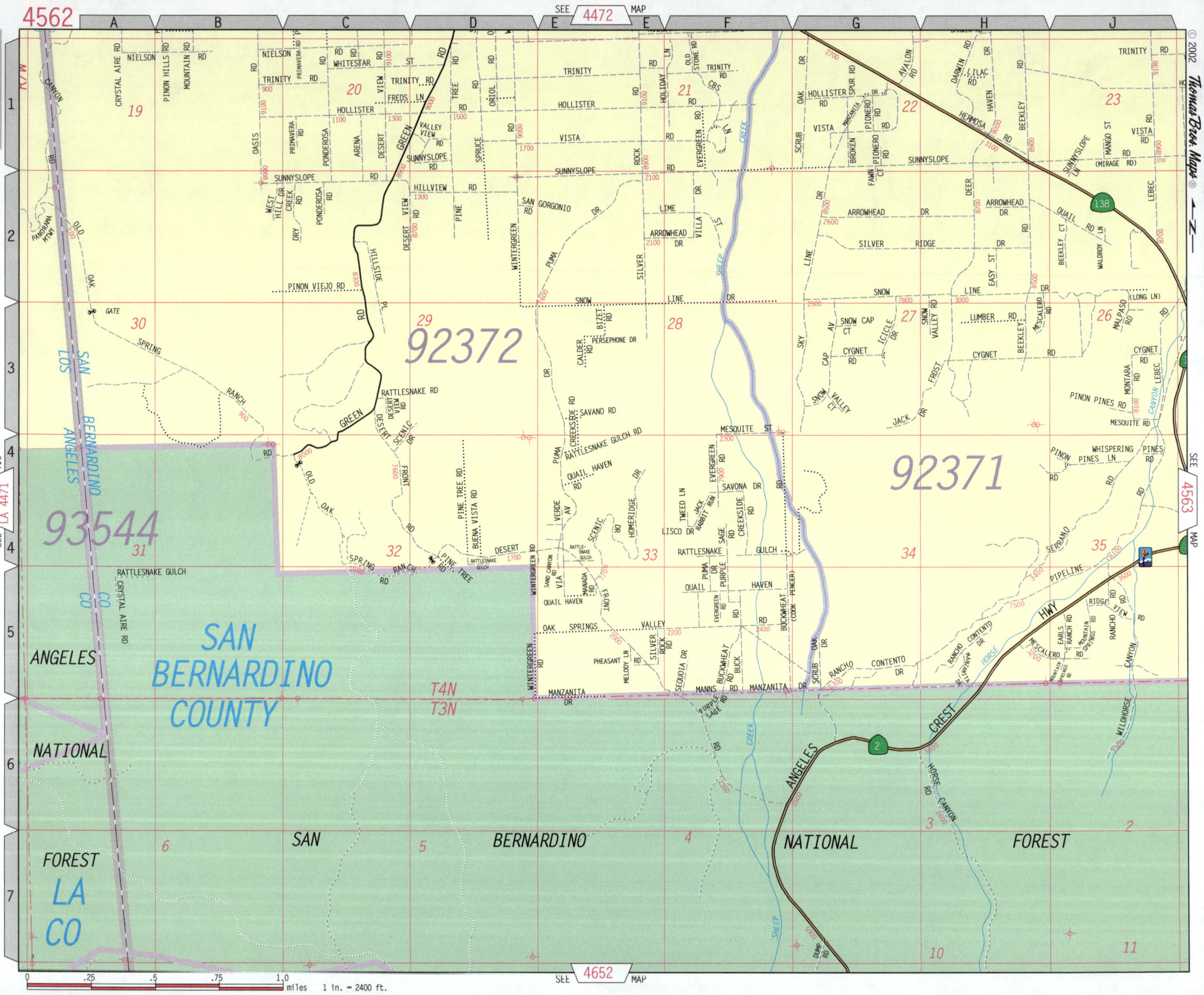
SAN BERNARDINO
SEE 4472 MAP
SEE 4652 MAP
SEE 4563 MAP
SEE LA 4471 MAP
92372
92371
93544
SAN BERNARDINO COUNTY
ANGELES NATIONAL FOREST
LA CO
SAN BERNARDINO NATIONAL FOREST
LOS ANGELES CO
SAN BERNARDINO CO
T4N
T3N
ANGELES CREST HWY
SHEEP CREEK
HORSE CANYON
TRINITY
HOLLISTER
VISTA
SUNNYSLOPE
SNOW LINE DR
ARROWHEAD
SILVER RIDGE DR
NIELSON
WHITESTAR
RATTLESNAKE RD
RATTLESNAKE GULCH RD
HILLSIDE PL
PINON VIEJO RD
SPRING RANCH
OLD OAK RD
GREEN RD
DESERT FRONT RD
WINTERGREEN
MESQUITE ST
CYGNET
PINON PINES RD
WHISPERING PINES LN
PIPELINE
RANCHO CONTENTO DR
MANZANITA DR
OAK SPRINGS VALLEY RD
MANNS RD
PURPLE SAGE RD
DUMP RD
1 in. = 2400 ft.
miles
Thomas Bros. Maps ®
© 2002

SEE 4473 MAP

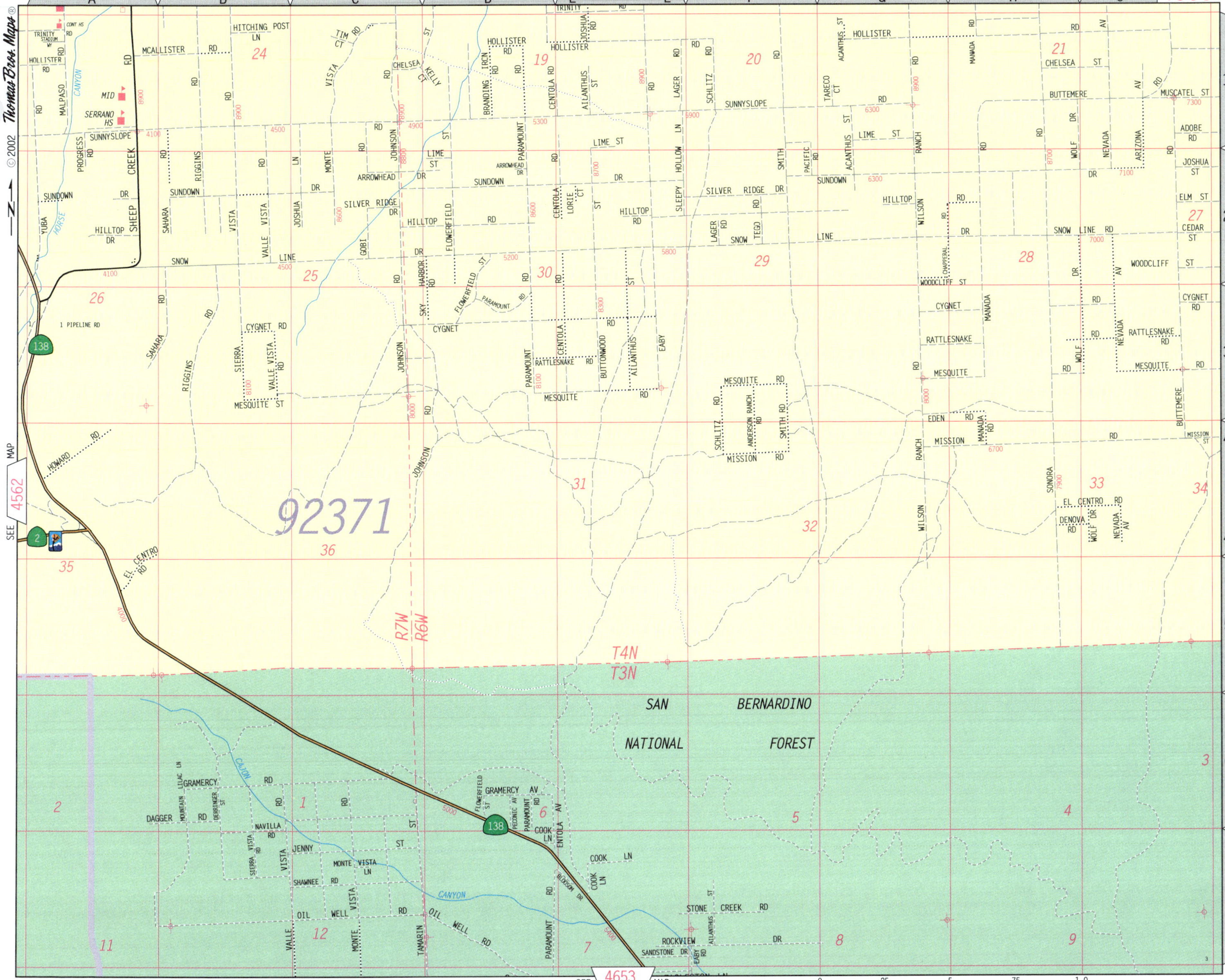

SEE 4562 MAP
SEE 4564 MAP
SEE 4653 MAP

0 .25 .5 .75 1.0 miles 1 in. = 2400 ft.

SEE 4474 MAP

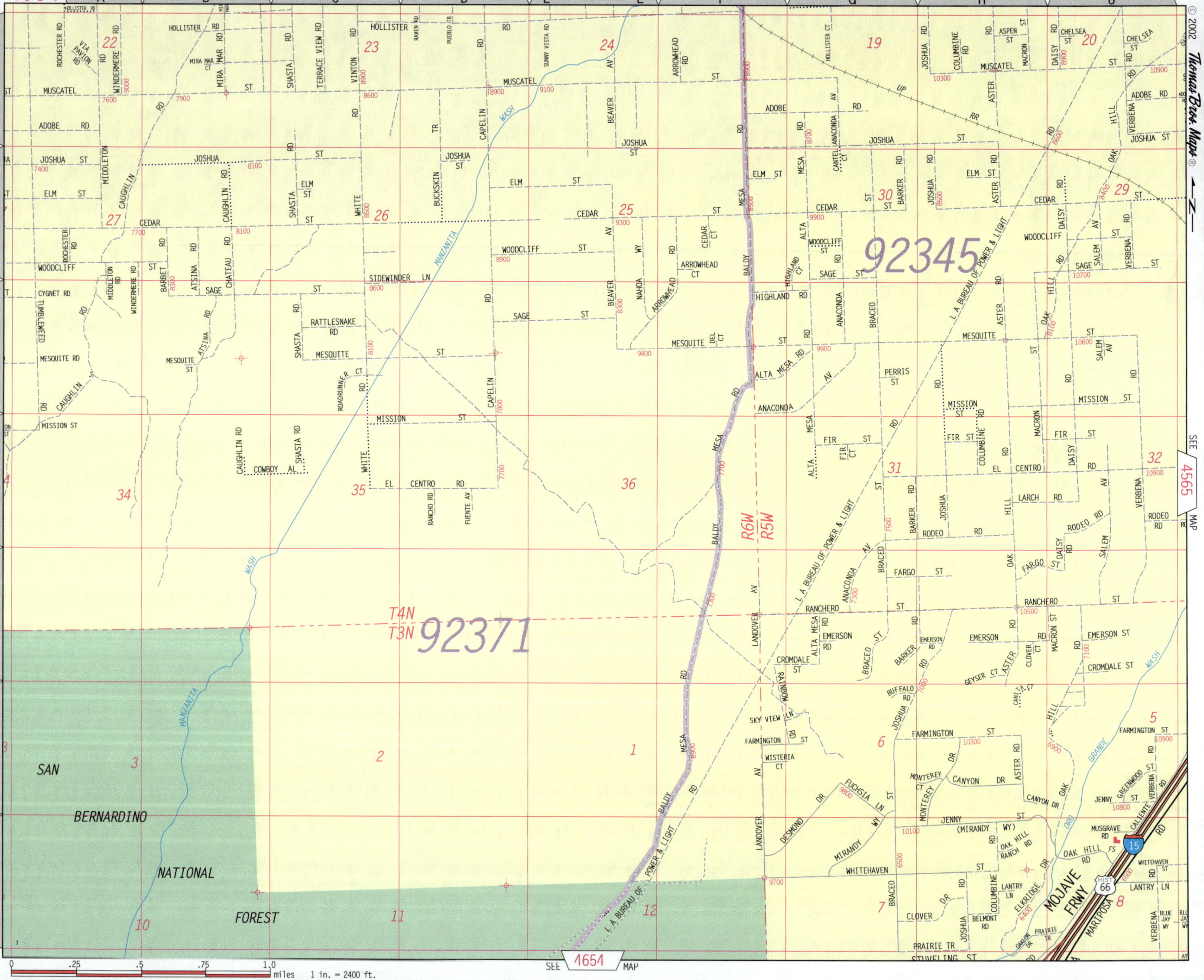

SEE 4563 MAP
SEE 4565 MAP
SEE 4654 MAP

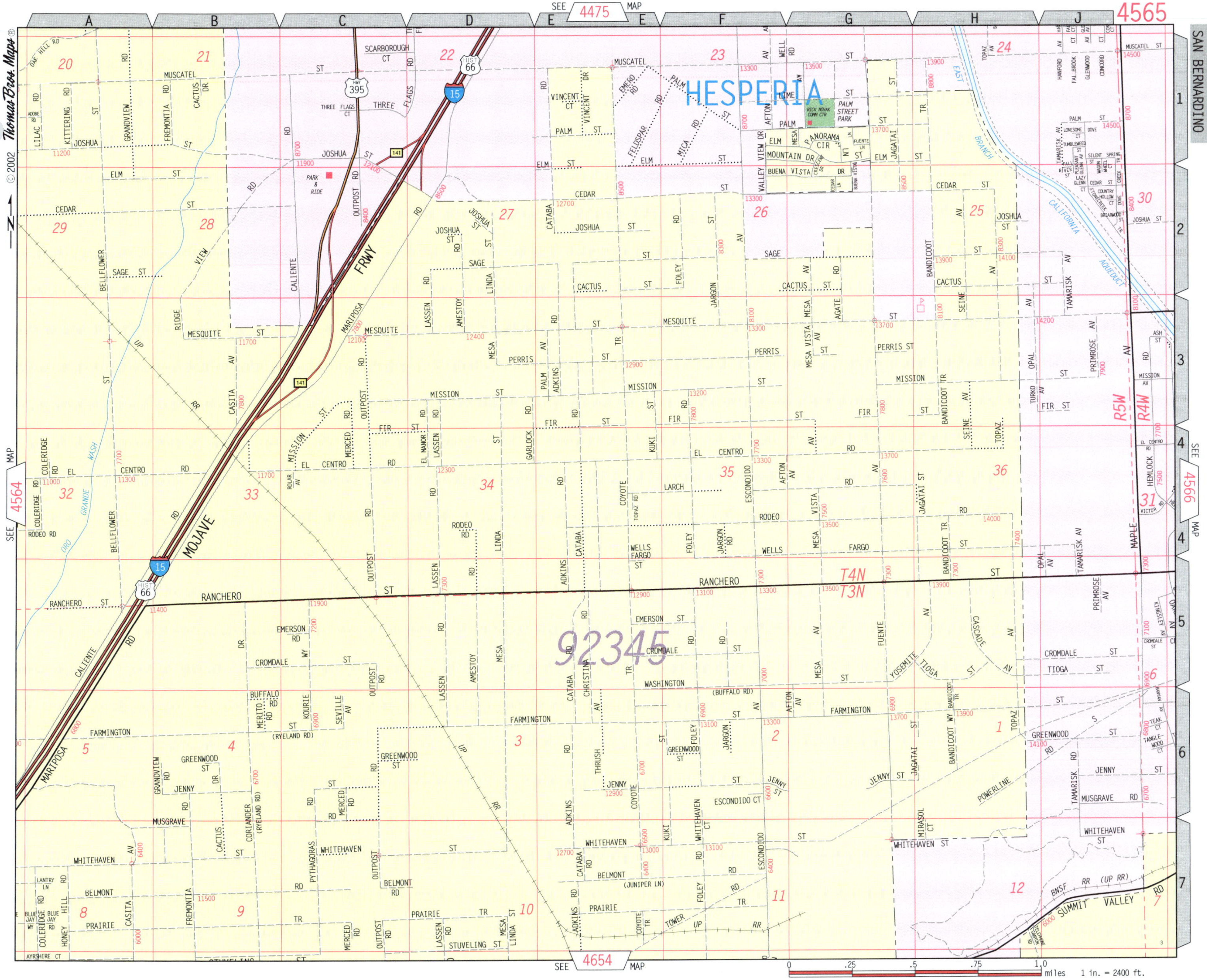
SEE 4475 MAP
SEE 4654 MAP
SEE 4564 MAP
SEE 4566 MAP
SAN BERNARDINO
HESPERIA
92345
Thomas Bros. Maps ® © 2002
A B C D E F G H J
1 2 3 4 5 6 7
T4N
T3N
R5W
R4W
MOJAVE FRWY
CALIFORNIA AQUEDUCT
EAST BRANCH
PARK & RIDE
RICK NOVAK COMM CTR
PALM STREET PARK
MUSCATEL ST
JOSHUA ST
ELM ST
CEDAR ST
SAGE ST
MESQUITE ST
PERRIS ST
MISSION ST
FIR ST
EL CENTRO RD
RANCHERO RD
EMERSON RD
CROMDALE ST
WASHINGTON ST
FARMINGTON ST
GREENWOOD ST
JENNY ST
MUSGRAVE RD
WHITEHAVEN ST
BELMONT RD
PRAIRIE TR
STUVELING ST
SUMMIT VALLEY RD
POWERLINE
BNSF RR (UP RR)
MARIPOSA RD
CALIENTE RD
OUTPOST RD
LASSEN RD
AMESTOY AV
LINDA ST
MESA ST
CATABA RD
ADKINS AV
COYOTE TR
FOLEY RD
JARGON RD
ESCONDIDO AV
AFTON AV
MESA VISTA AV
JAGATAI ST
BANDICOOT TR
SEINE AV
TOPAZ AV
TAMARISK AV
PRIMROSE AV
MAPLE AV
OPAL AV
FUENTE AV
CASCADE AV
TIOGA ST
YOSEMITE ST
WELLS FARGO ST
RODEO RD
KUKI ST
LARCH ST
THREE FLAGS
BELLFLOWER ST
CASITA AV
COLERIDGE RD
ORO GRANDE WASH
0 .25 .5 .75 1.0 miles 1 in. = 2400 ft.

SAN BERNARDINO

SEE 4476 MAP

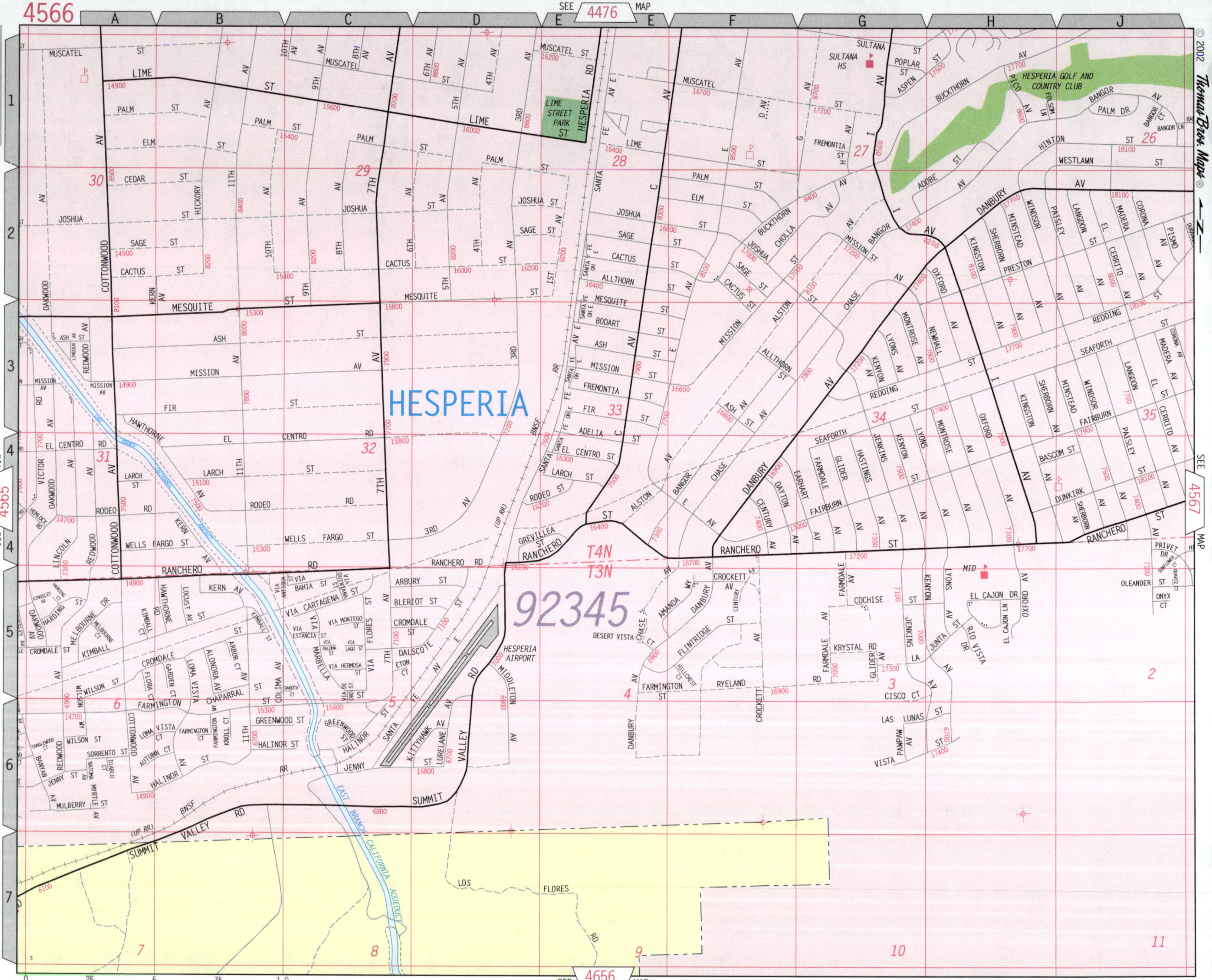

SEE 4565 MAP

SEE 4567 MAP

SEE 4656 MAP

0 .25 .5 .75 1.0 miles 1 in. = 2400 ft.

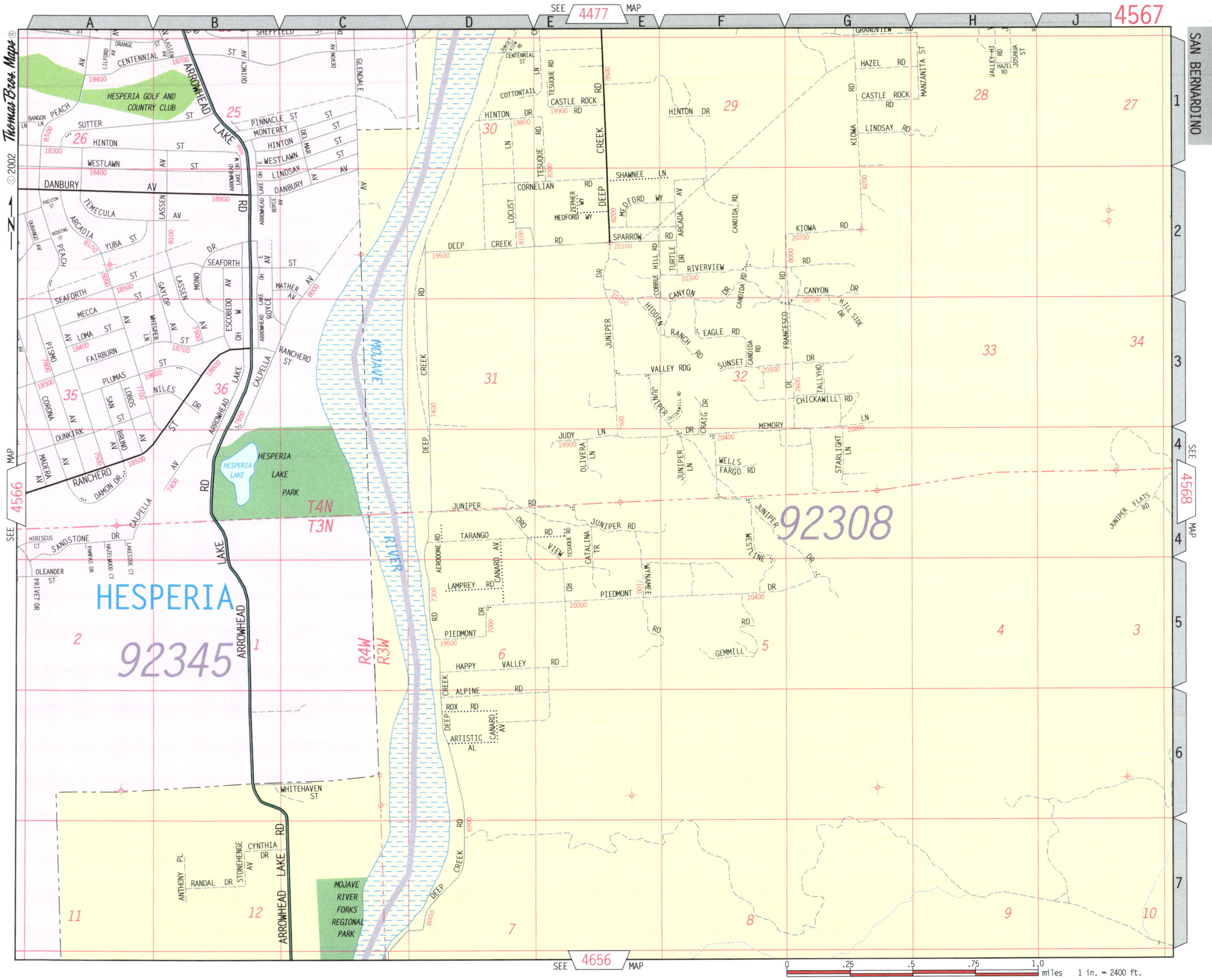

SEE 4477 MAP
SEE 4656 MAP
SEE 4566 MAP
SEE 4568 MAP
SAN BERNARDINO
HESPERIA
92345
92308
HESPERIA GOLF AND COUNTRY CLUB
HESPERIA LAKE
HESPERIA LAKE PARK
MOJAVE RIVER
MOJAVE RIVER FORKS REGIONAL PARK
T4N
T3N
R4W
R3W
ARROWHEAD LAKE RD
DEEP CREEK RD
DANBURY AV
RANCHERO ST
JUNIPER RD
PIEDMONT DR
HAPPY VALLEY RD
MEMORY LN
CENTENNIAL ST
SUTTER
HINTON ST
WESTLAWN ST
TEMECULA
SEAFORTH ST
MECCA
FAIRBURN
PLUMAS
NILES
DUNKIRK
CALPELLA
SANDSTONE DR
OLEANDER ST
WHITEHAVEN ST
CYNTHIA DR
RANDAL DR
STONEHENGE AV
ANTHONY PL
GLENDALE AV
MATHER AV
CORNELIAN RD
CASTLE ROCK RD
HINTON DR
SHAWNEE LN
MEDFORD WY
SPARROW RD
RIVERVIEW
CANYON DR
EAGLE RD
VALLEY RDG
SUNSET
CHICKAWILL RD
JUDY LN
WELLS FARGO RD
STARLIGHT LN
TARANGO
LAMPREY RD
ALPINE RD
ROX RD
ARTISTIC AL
GEMMILL
KIOWA RD
HAZEL RD
LINDSAY RD
GRANDVIEW RD
JUNIPER FLATS RD
0 .25 .5 .75 1.0 miles 1 in. = 2400 ft.

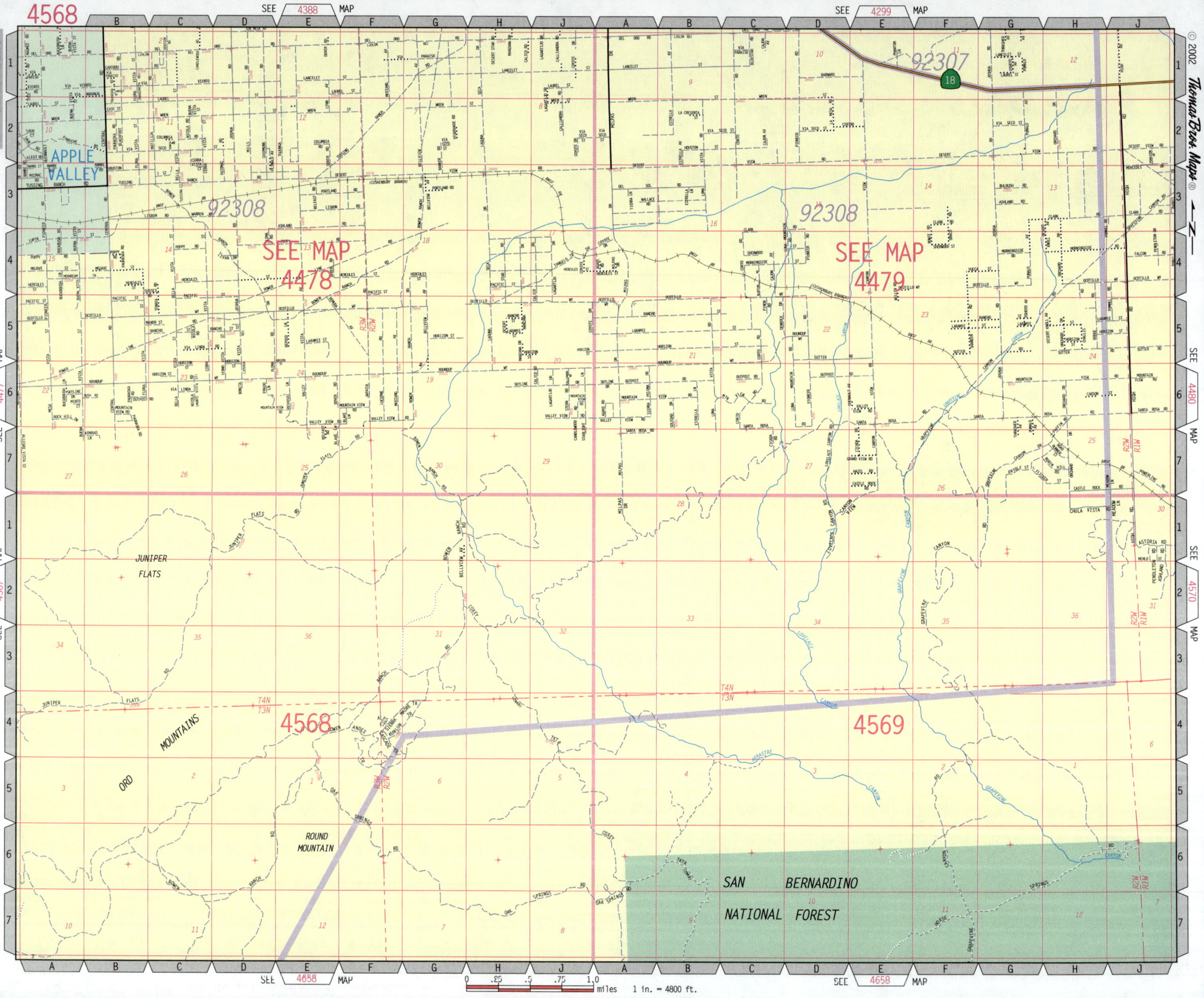
SAN BERNARDINO
APPLE VALLEY
92307
92308
SEE MAP 4478
SEE MAP 4479
SEE 4388 MAP
SEE 4299 MAP
SEE 4477 MAP
SEE 4480 MAP
SEE 4567 MAP
SEE 4570 MAP
SEE 4658 MAP
JUNIPER FLATS
ORD MOUNTAINS
ROUND MOUNTAIN
4568
4569
SAN BERNARDINO NATIONAL FOREST
T4N
T3N
R3W
R2W
R1W
© 2002 Thomas Bros. Maps ®
miles
1 in. = 4800 ft.

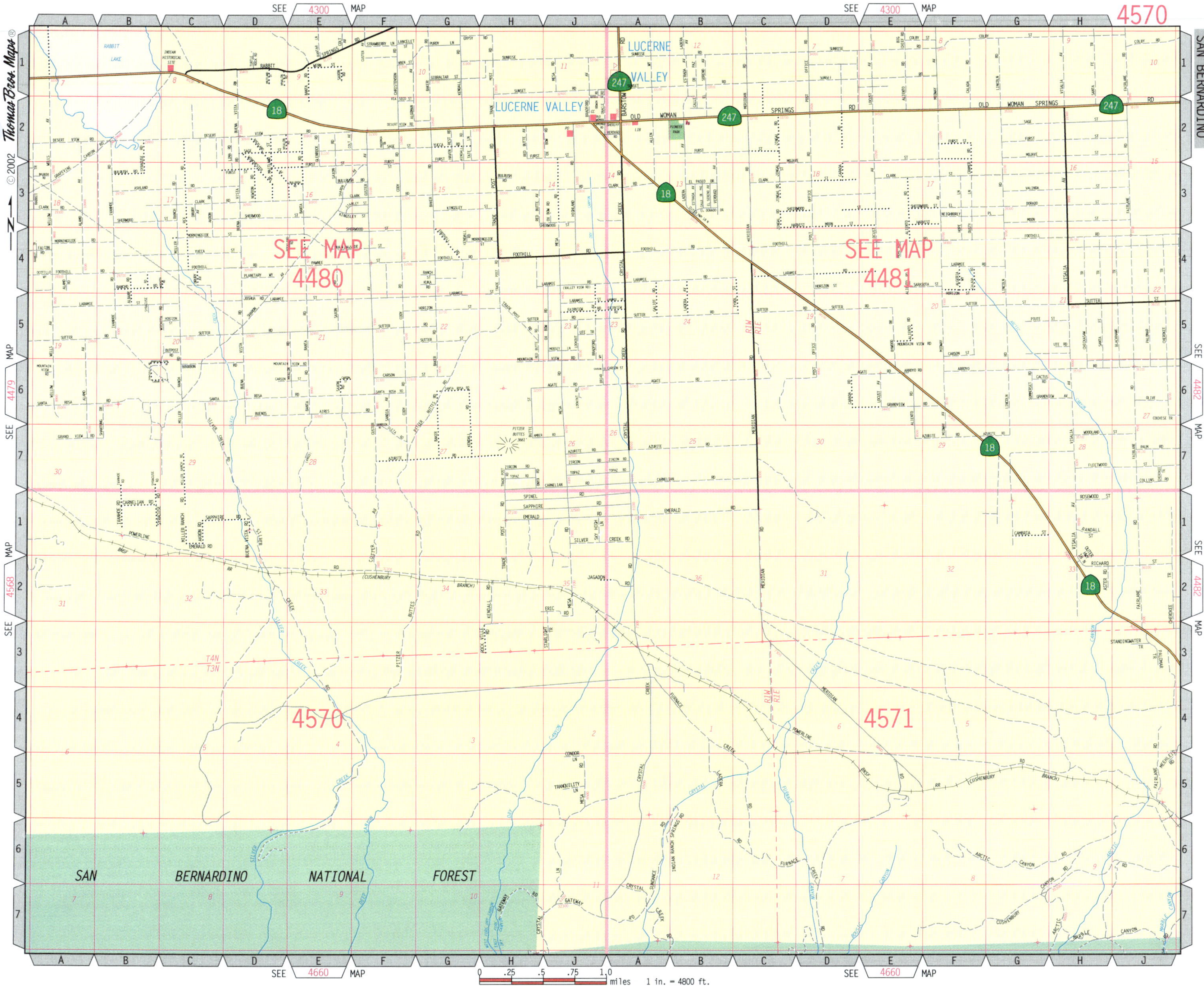
SEE 4300 MAP
SEE 4300 MAP
SAN BERNARDINO
Thomas Bros. Maps®
© 2002
LUCERNE VALLEY
LUCERNE
VALLEY
SEE MAP 4480
SEE MAP 4481
4570
4571
SEE MAP 4479
SEE MAP 4568
SEE MAP 4482
SEE MAP 4482
SAN BERNARDINO NATIONAL FOREST
OLD WOMAN SPRINGS RD
RABBIT LAKE
INDIAN HISTORICAL SITE
PITZER BUTTES 3661'
T4N
T3N
R1W R1E
BNSF
(CUSHENBURY BRANCH)
POWERLINE
ARCTIC CANYON RD
SEE 4660 MAP
SEE 4660 MAP
miles 1 in. = 4800 ft.

SEE 372 MAP

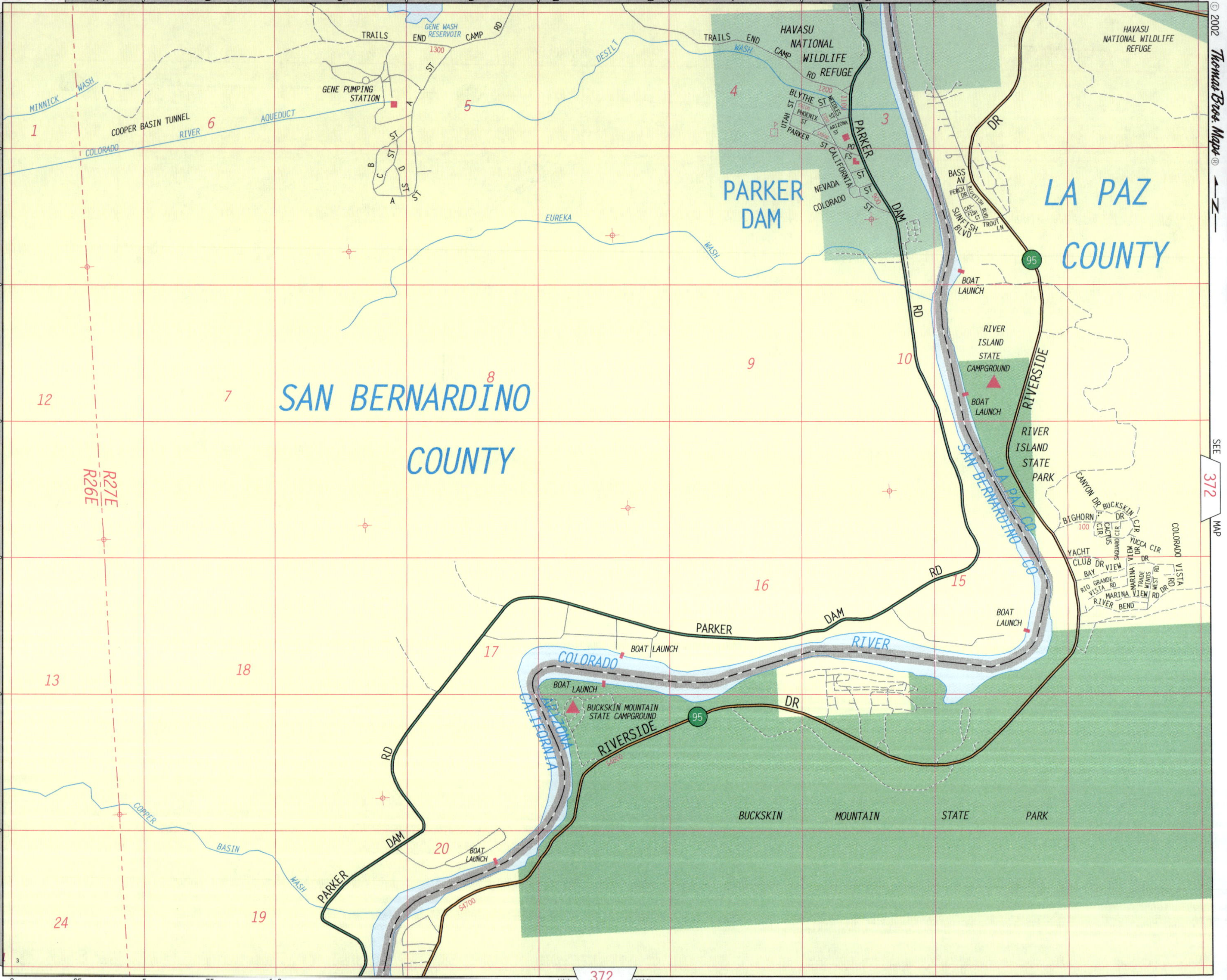

SEE 372 MAP
SEE 372 MAP
SEE 372 MAP

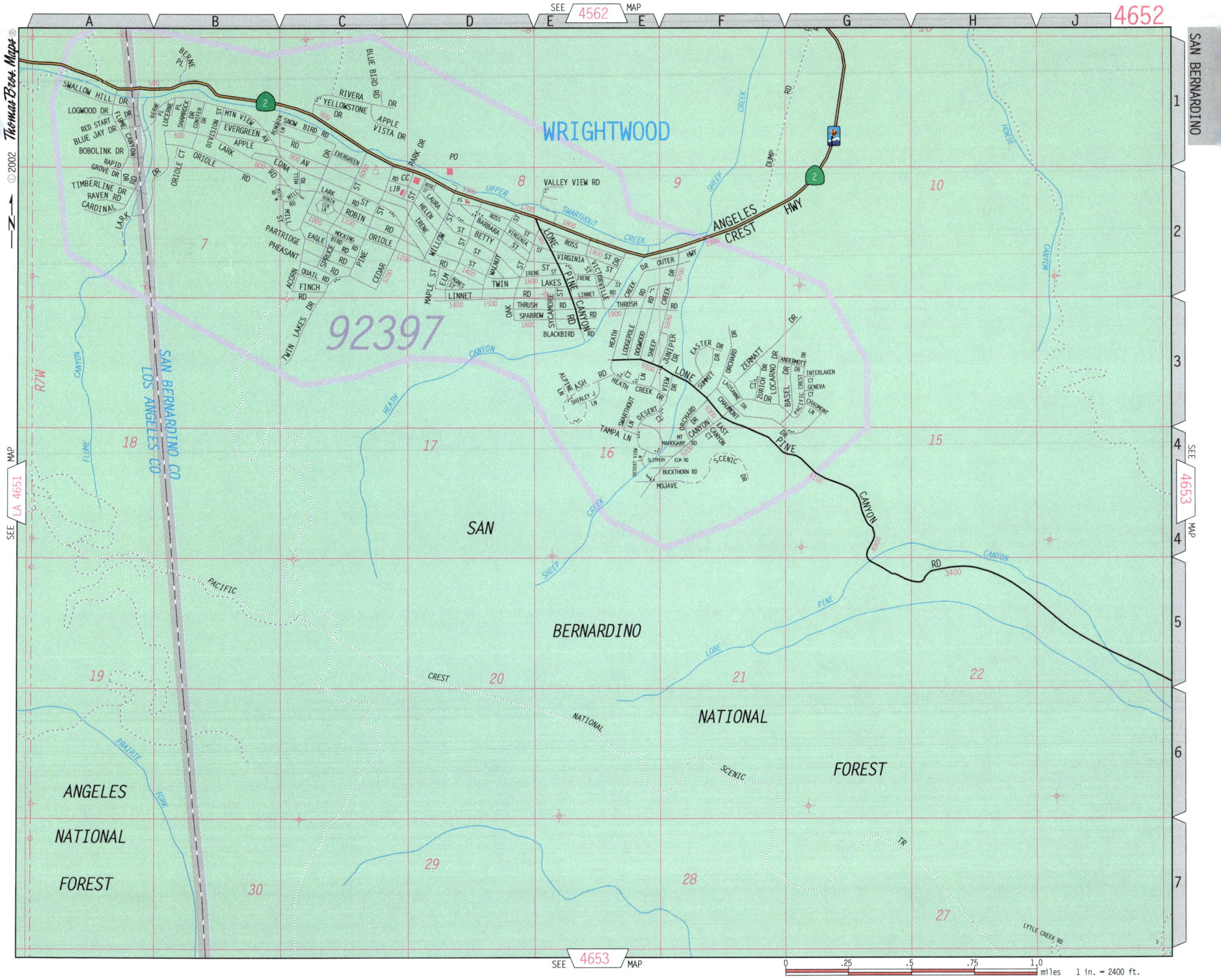
SEE 4562 MAP
A
B
C
D
E
F
G
H
J
1
2
3
4
5
6
7
SAN BERNARDINO
Thomas Bros. Maps ©2002
WRIGHTWOOD
92397
ANGELES CREST HWY
2
SWALLOW HILL DR
LOGWOOD DR
RED START
BLUE JAY DR
BOBOLINK DR
RAPID
GROVE DR
TIMBERLINE DR
RAVEN RD
CARDINAL
LARK
FLUME DR
CANYON
BERNE PL
LUCERNE PL
SHAMROCK DR
CONIFER DR
DIVISION ST
MTN VIEW
EVERGREEN AV
APPLE
LARK
ORIOLE CT
ORIOLE RD
EDNA RD
SNOW BIRD RD
EVERGREEN
RIVERA
YELLOWSTONE DR
BLUE BIRD RD
APPLE VISTA DR
PARK DR
PO
CC
LIB
VALLEY VIEW RD
UPPER
SWARTHOUT CREEK
MILL
PARTRIDGE
PHEASANT
EAGLE
MOCKING BIRD RD
ROBIN
ORIOLE
SPRUCE
PINE
CEDAR
QUAIL RD
ACORN
FINCH
TWIN LAKES DR
LAURA
HELEN
IRENE
WILLOW
MAPLE ST
ELM
LINNET
BARBARA
BETTY
VIRGINIA
WALNUT
TWIN
LAKES
THRUSH
SPARROW
OAK
SYCAMORE
BLACKBIRD
ROSS
LONE PINE CANYON RD
VICTORVILLE
OUTER HWY
CREEK DR
THRUSH
HEATH
LODGEPOLE
DOGWOOD
SHEEP
JUNIPER DR
EASTER DR
ORCHARD DR
ZERMATT
LOCARNO DR
ZURICH DR
BASEL DR
INTERLAKEN
GENEVA
CHAUMONT
LAUSANNE
SUMMIT
ALPINE LN
ASH
HEATH CREEK
VIEW DR
SWARTHOUT LN
DESERT CT
TAMPA LN
MAHOGANY
SLIPPERY ELM RD
BUCKTHORN RD
MOJAVE
SCENIC DR
ORCHARD CANYON DR
EAST CANYON CT
DUMP RD
SHEEP CREEK
HEATH CANYON
SHEEP CREEK
PINE CANYON RD
CANYON
PINE
LONE
HORSE CANYON
FLUME CANYON
PRAIRIE FORK
R7W
SAN BERNARDINO CO
LOS ANGELES CO
PACIFIC CREST NATIONAL SCENIC TR
SAN BERNARDINO NATIONAL FOREST
ANGELES NATIONAL FOREST
LYTLE CREEK RD
7
8
9
10
15
16
17
18
19
20
21
22
27
28
29
30
SEE LA 4651 MAP
SEE 4653 MAP
SEE 4653 MAP
0 .25 .5 .75 1.0 miles 1 in. = 2400 ft.

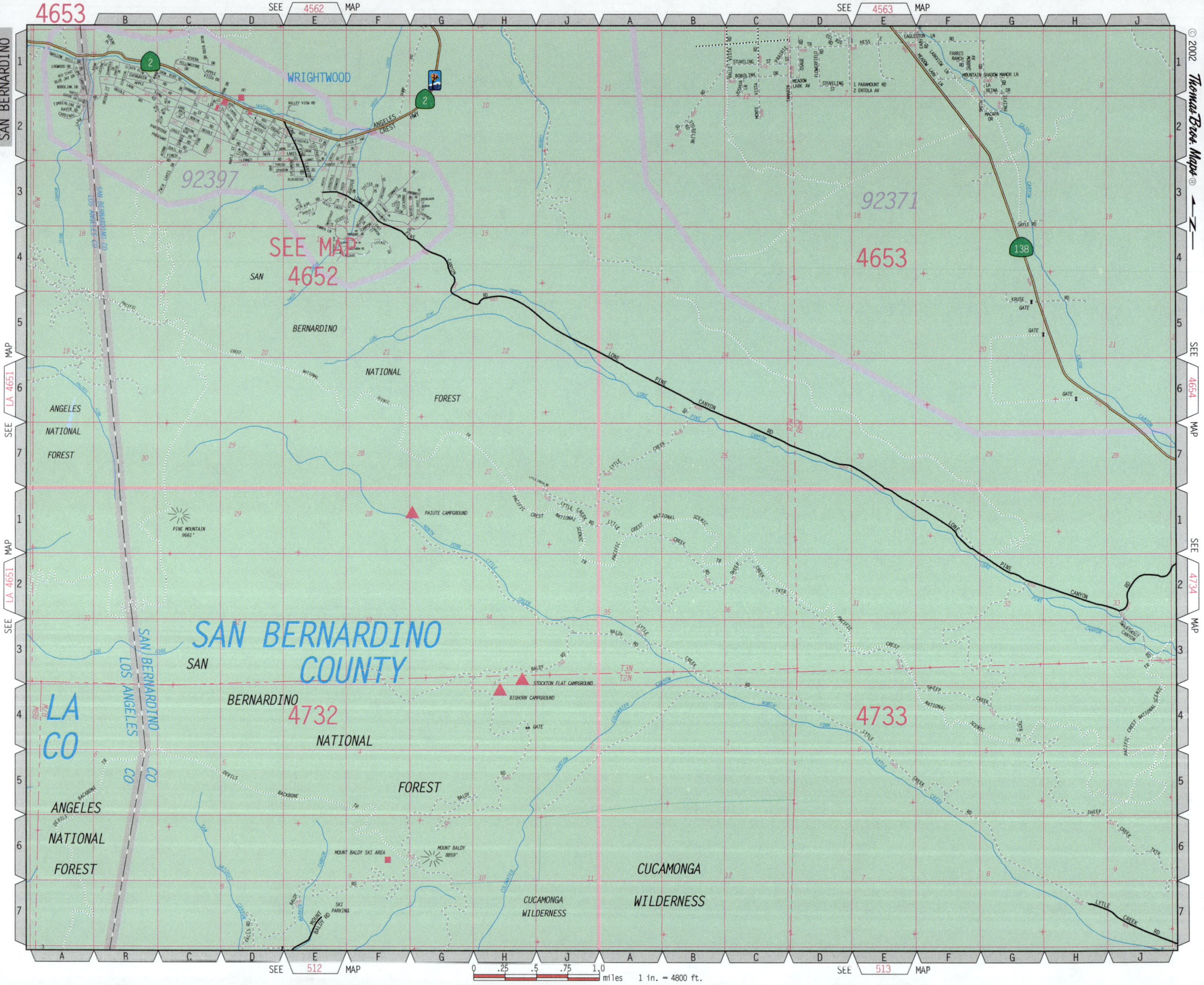
SEE 4562 MAP
SEE 4563 MAP
WRIGHTWOOD
92397
SEE MAP 4652
SAN
BERNARDINO
NATIONAL
FOREST
ANGELES CREST HWY
92371
4653
LONE PINE CANYON RD
138
2
ANGELES
NATIONAL
FOREST
SAN BERNARDINO CO
LOS ANGELES CO
PINE MOUNTAIN 9661'
PAIUTE CAMPGROUND
STOCKTON FLAT CAMPGROUND
BIGHORN CAMPGROUND
SAN BERNARDINO COUNTY
SAN
BERNARDINO
4732
NATIONAL
FOREST
4733
LA CO
ANGELES
NATIONAL
FOREST
MOUNT BALDY SKI AREA
MOUNT BALDY 8859'
CUCAMONGA WILDERNESS
CUCAMONGA
WILDERNESS
LYTLE CREEK RD
T3N
T2N
SEE LA 4651 MAP
SEE 4654 MAP
SEE 4734 MAP
SEE 512 MAP
SEE 513 MAP
miles 1 in. = 4800 ft.

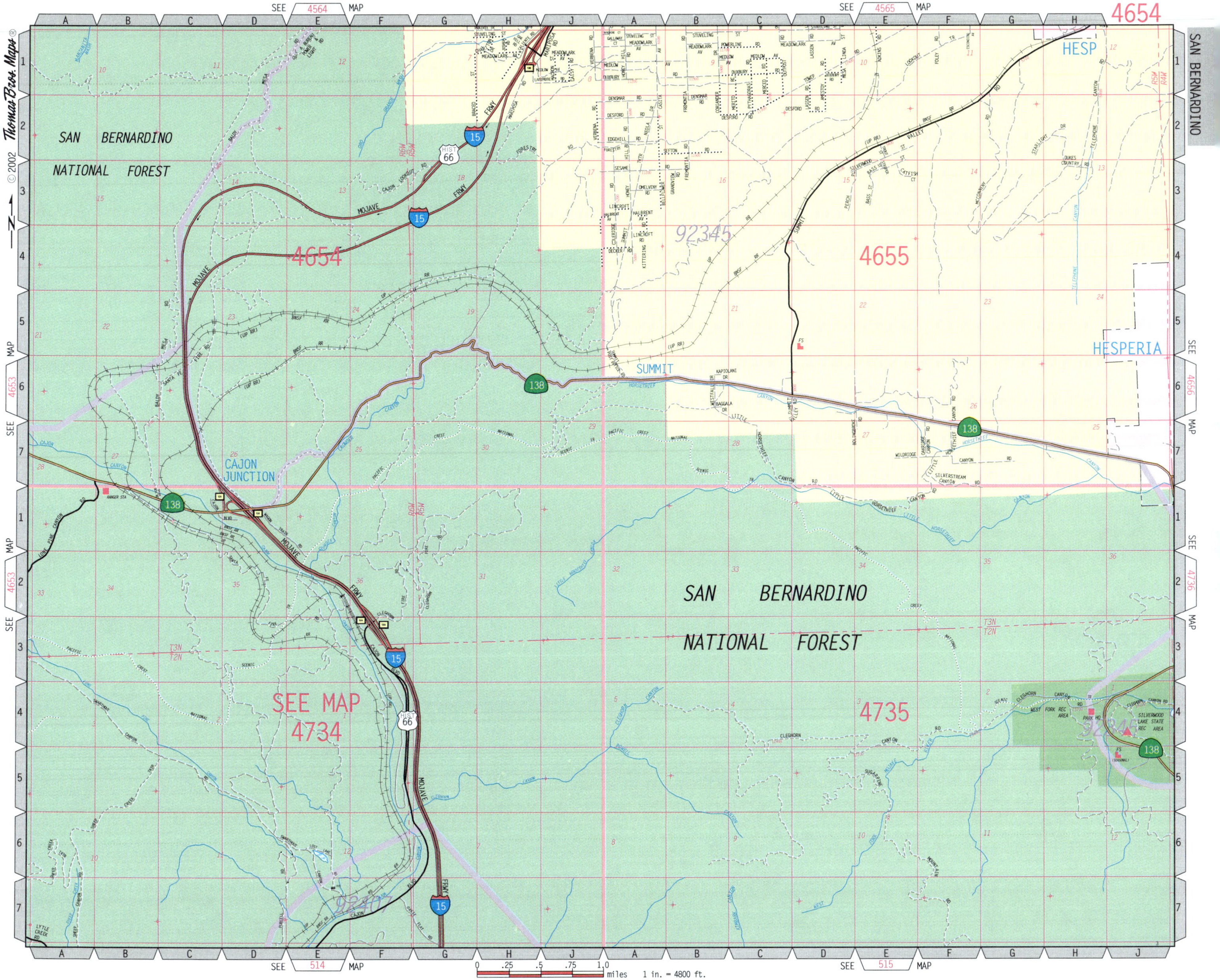
SEE 4564 MAP
SEE 4565 MAP
SAN BERNARDINO
Thomas Bros. Maps
© 2002
SAN BERNARDINO
NATIONAL FOREST
4654
4655
92345
HESP
HESPERIA
SUMMIT
CAJON
JUNCTION
SAN BERNARDINO
NATIONAL FOREST
SEE MAP
4734
4735
SEE 4653 MAP
SEE 4656 MAP
SEE 4736 MAP
MOJAVE
FRWY
SILVERWOOD
LAKE STATE
REC AREA
SEE 514 MAP
SEE 515 MAP
miles
1 in. = 4800 ft.

SEE 4566 MAP
SEE 4567 MAP

SAN BERNARDINO

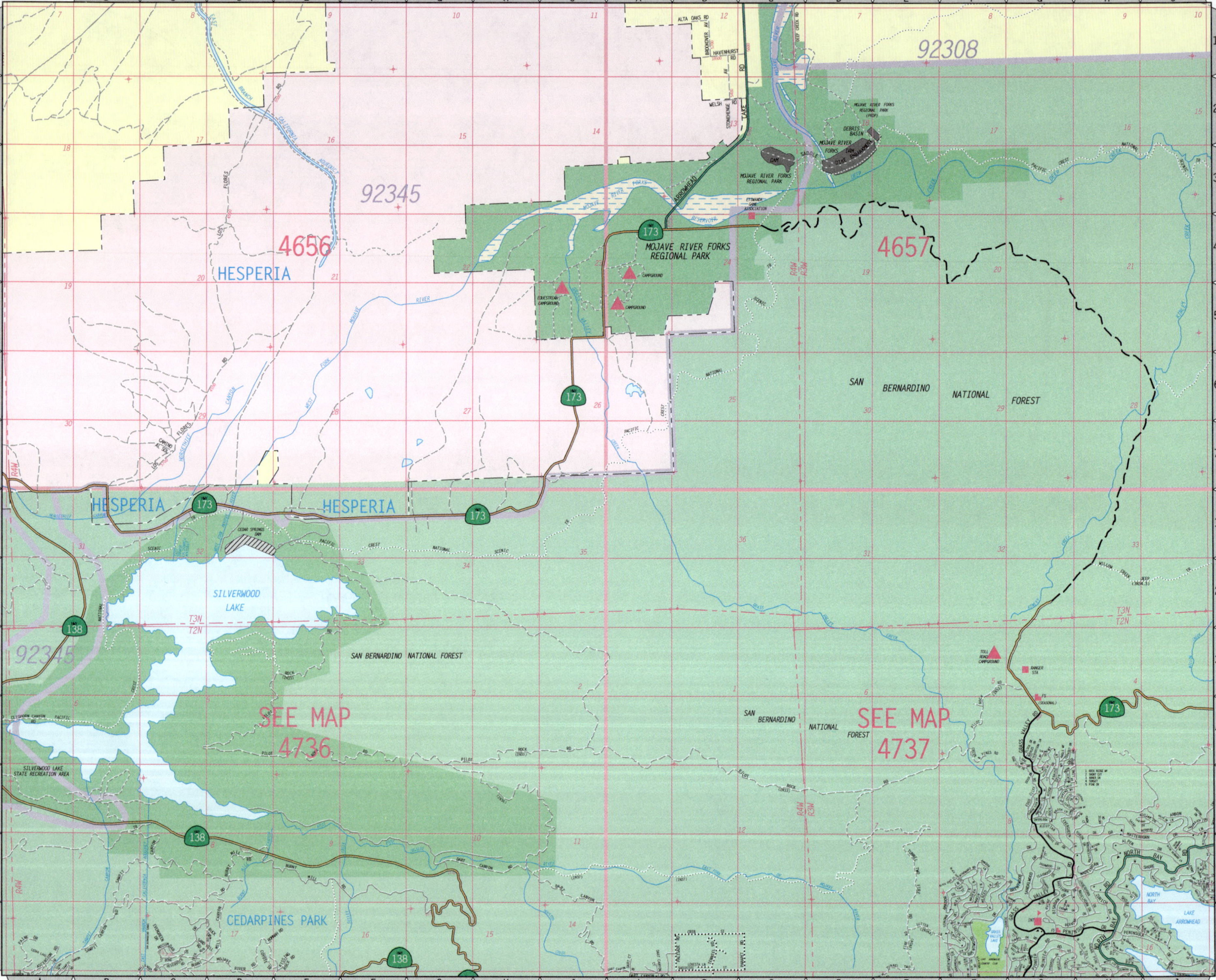

SEE 4654 MAP
SEE 4658 MAP
SEE 4738 MAP
SEE 516 MAP
SEE 517 MAP

0 .25 .5 .75 1.0 miles 1 in. = 4800 ft.

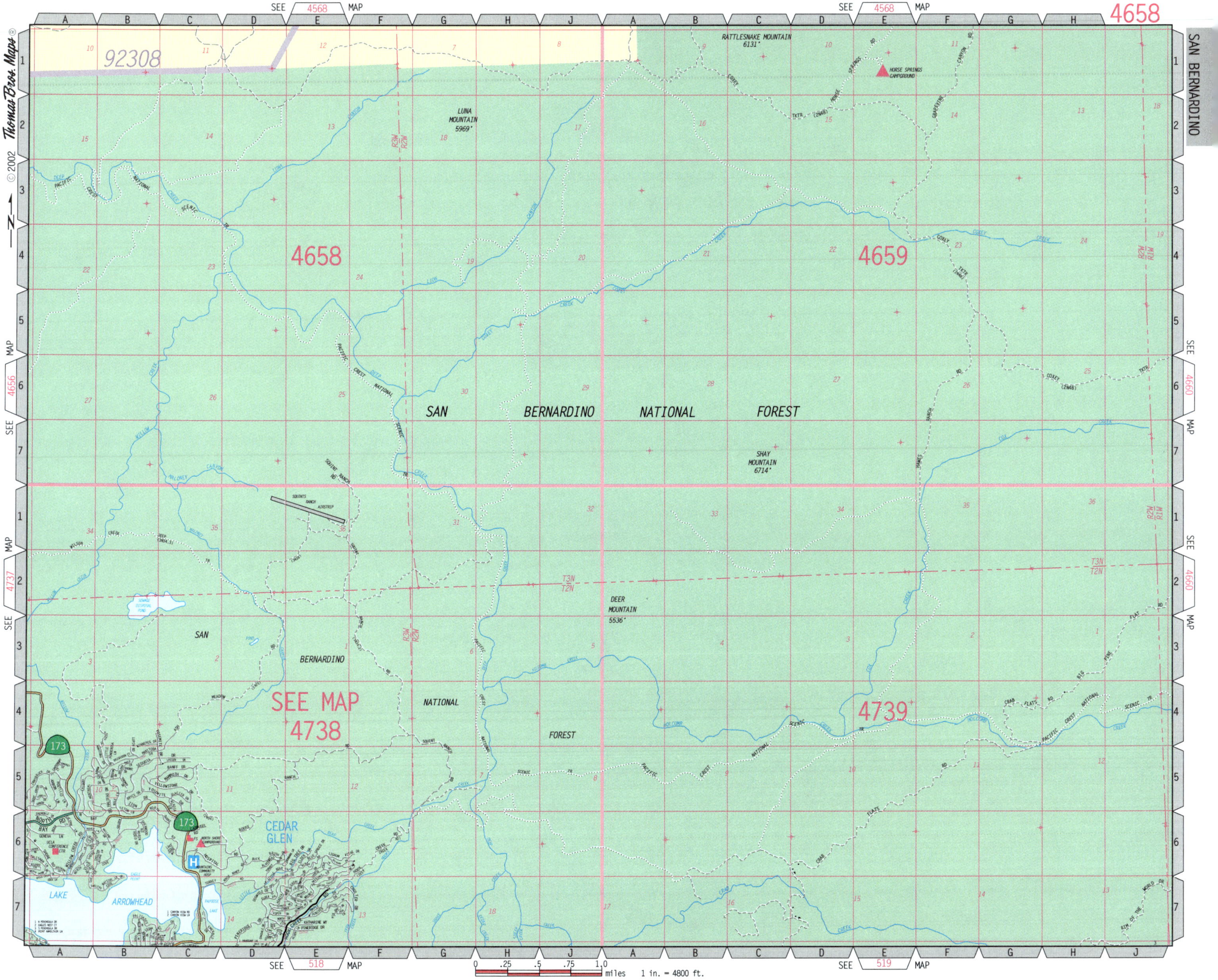
SEE 4568 MAP
SEE 4568 MAP
92308
RATTLESNAKE MOUNTAIN 6131'
HORSE SPRINGS CAMPGROUND
LUNA MOUNTAIN 5969'
4658
4659
SAN BERNARDINO NATIONAL FOREST
SHAY MOUNTAIN 6714'
SQUINTS RANCH AIRSTRIP
DEER MOUNTAIN 5536'
T3N
T2N
R2W
R1W
SAN BERNARDINO NATIONAL FOREST
SEE MAP 4738
4739
SEWAGE DISPOSAL POND
CEDAR GLEN
173
LAKE ARROWHEAD
NORTH SHORE CAMPGROUND
MOUNTAINS COMMUNITY HOSP
UCLA CONFERENCE CTR
PACIFIC CREST NATIONAL SCENIC TR
DEEP CREEK
HOLCOMB CREEK
CRAB CREEK
COXEY CREEK
SEE 4656 MAP
SEE 4737 MAP
SEE 4660 MAP
SEE 518 MAP
SEE 519 MAP
0 .25 .5 .75 1.0 miles
1 in. = 4800 ft.

SEE 4570 MAP

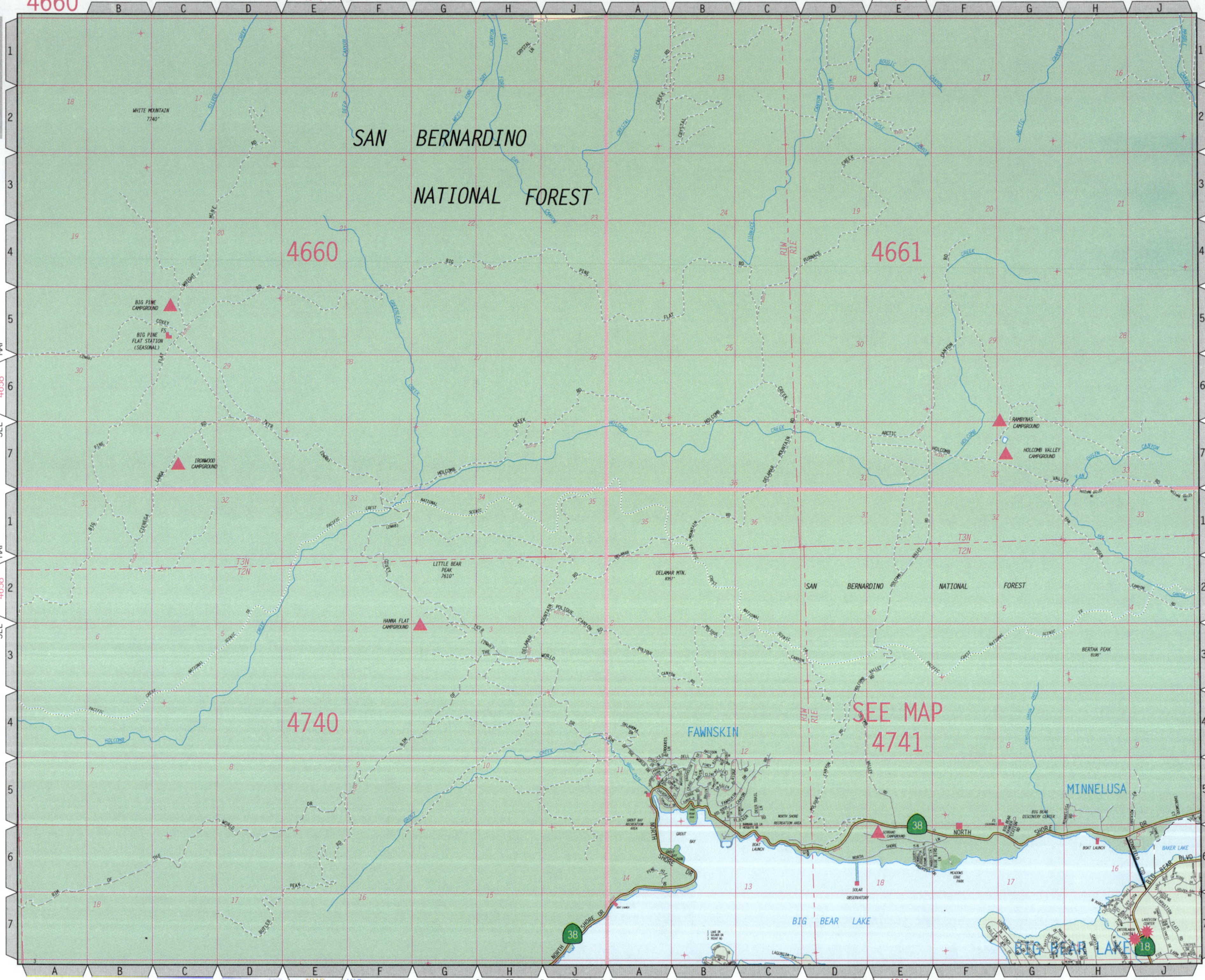

SEE 4810 MAP
SEE 4811 MAP

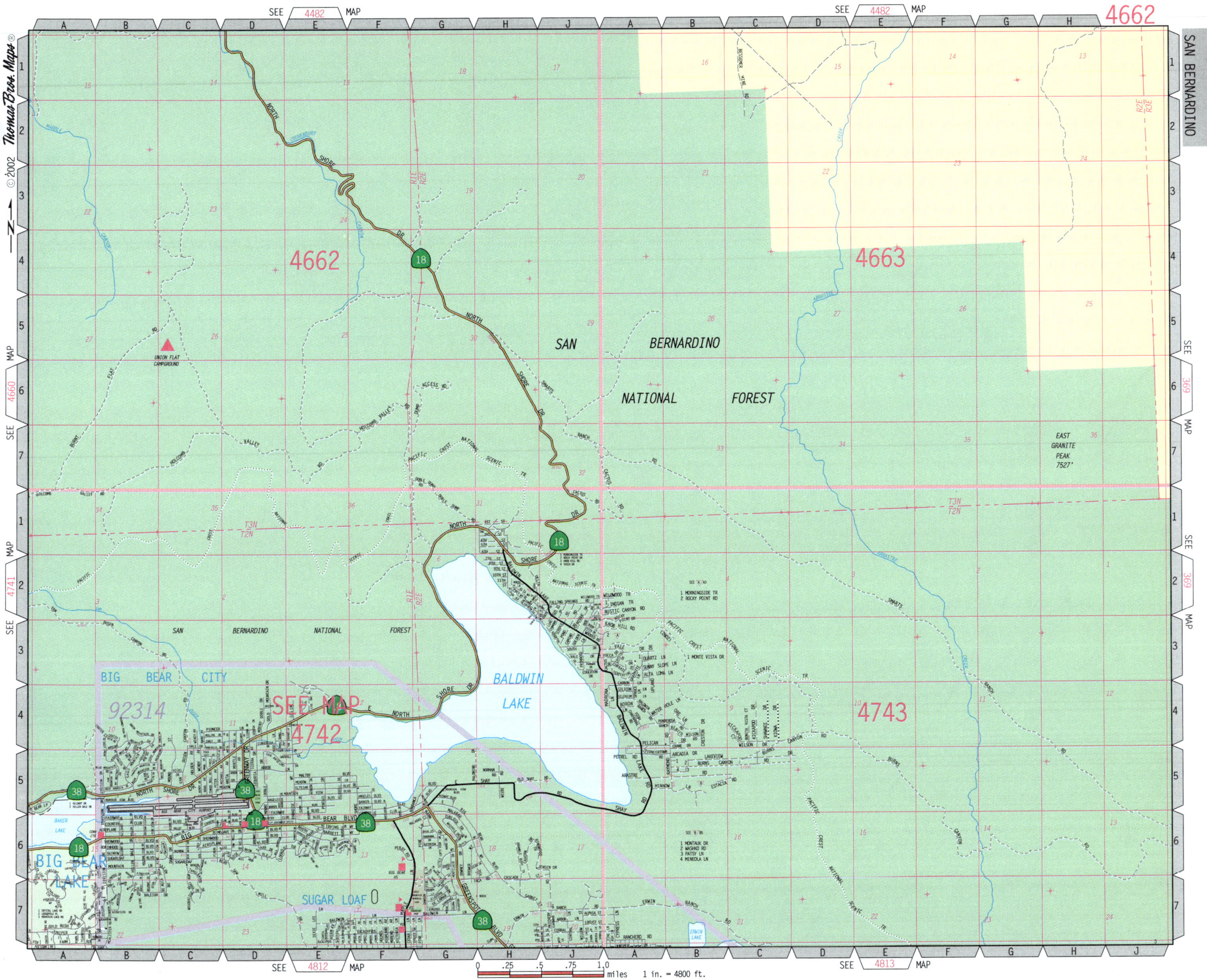
SEE 4482 MAP
SAN BERNARDINO
Thomas Bros. Maps
© 2002
4662
4663
4743
SEE MAP 4742
SAN BERNARDINO NATIONAL FOREST
SAN BERNARDINO NATIONAL FOREST
BALDWIN LAKE
BIG BEAR CITY
92314
BIG BEAR LAKE
BAKER LAKE
SUGAR LOAF
ERWIN LAKE
UNION FLAT CAMPGROUND
EAST GRANITE PEAK 7527'
NORTH SHORE DR
PACIFIC CREST NATIONAL SCENIC TR
HOLCOMB VALLEY RD
BURNT FLAT RD
SHAY RD
BALDWIN LAKE RD
GREENSPOT BLVD
BIG BEAR BLVD
T3N T2N
R1E R2E
SEE 4660 MAP
SEE 4741 MAP
SEE 369 MAP
SEE 4812 MAP
SEE 4813 MAP
1 in. = 4800 ft.
miles

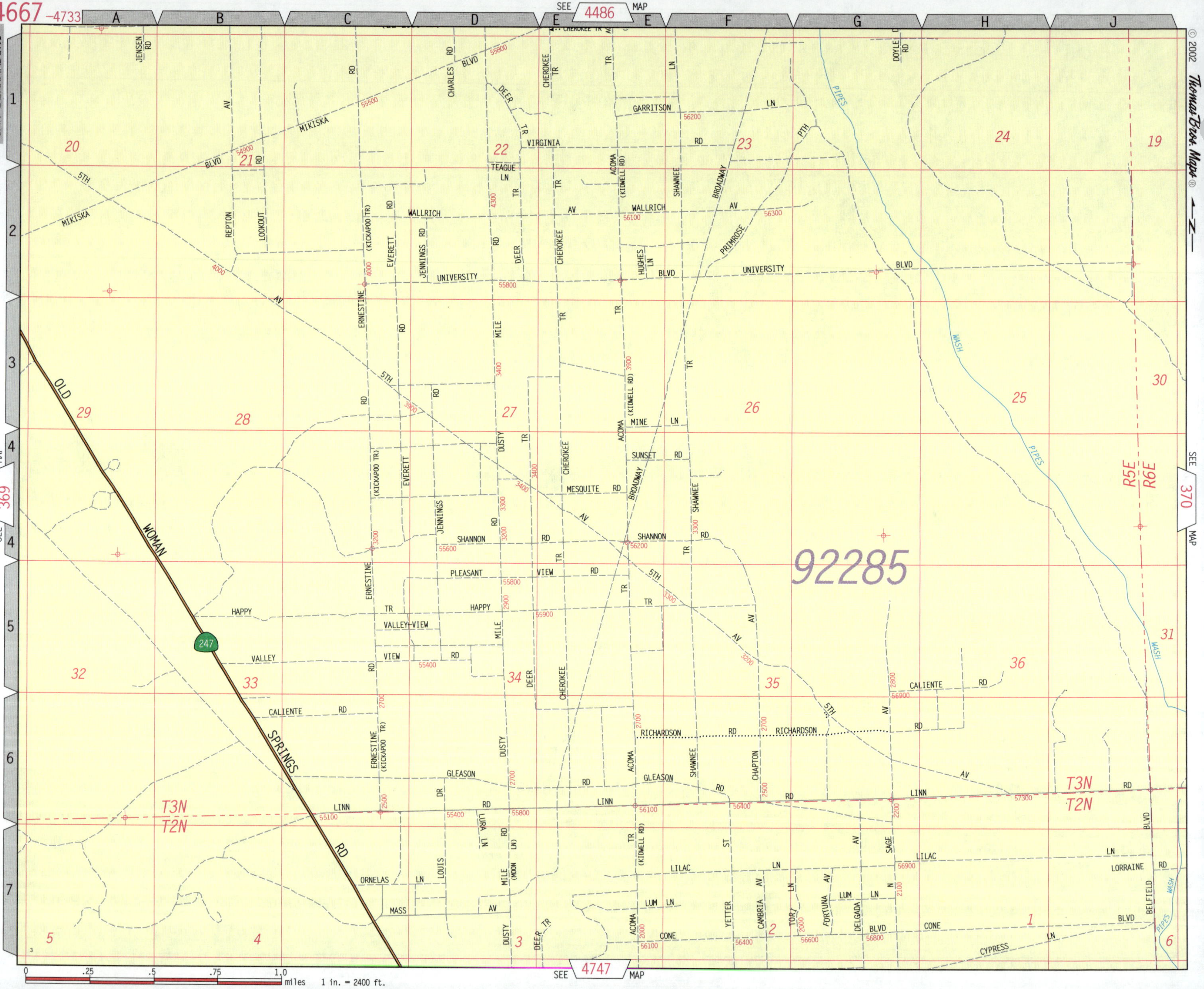
SEE 4486 MAP
A
B
C
D
E
F
G
H
J
1
2
3
4
5
6
7
SEE 369 MAP
SEE 370 MAP
SEE 4747 MAP
92285
JENSEN RD
CHARLES RD
CHEROKEE TR
DEER TR
DOYLE RD
PIPES
BLVD
MIKISKA
GARRITSON LN
VIRGINIA RD
TEAGUE LN
WALLRICH AV
REPTON
LOOKOUT
ERNESTINE (KICKAPOO TR)
EVERETT RD
JENNINGS RD
UNIVERSITY BLVD
HUGHES LN
ACOMA (KIDWELL RD)
SHAWNEE
BROADWAY
PRIMROSE
5TH AV
DUSTY MILE RD
MINE LN
SUNSET RD
MESQUITE RD
SHANNON RD
PLEASANT VIEW RD
HAPPY TR
VALLEY VIEW RD
OLD WOMAN SPRINGS RD
247
CALIENTE RD
RICHARDSON RD
GLEASON RD
CHAPTON
LINN RD
LURA LN
MOON LN
ORNELAS LN
LOUIS
MASS AV
LILAC LN
LUM LN
CONE BLVD
YETTER ST
CAMBRIA AV
TORI LN
FORTUNA AV
DELGADA
SAGE AV
LORRAINE RD
BELFIELD BLVD
CYPRESS LN
WASH
T3N
T2N
R5E
R6E
1
2
3
4
5
6
19
20
21
22
23
24
25
26
27
28
29
30
31
32
33
34
35
36
0
.25
.5
.75
1.0
miles
1 in. = 2400 ft.
© 2002 Thomas Bros. Maps

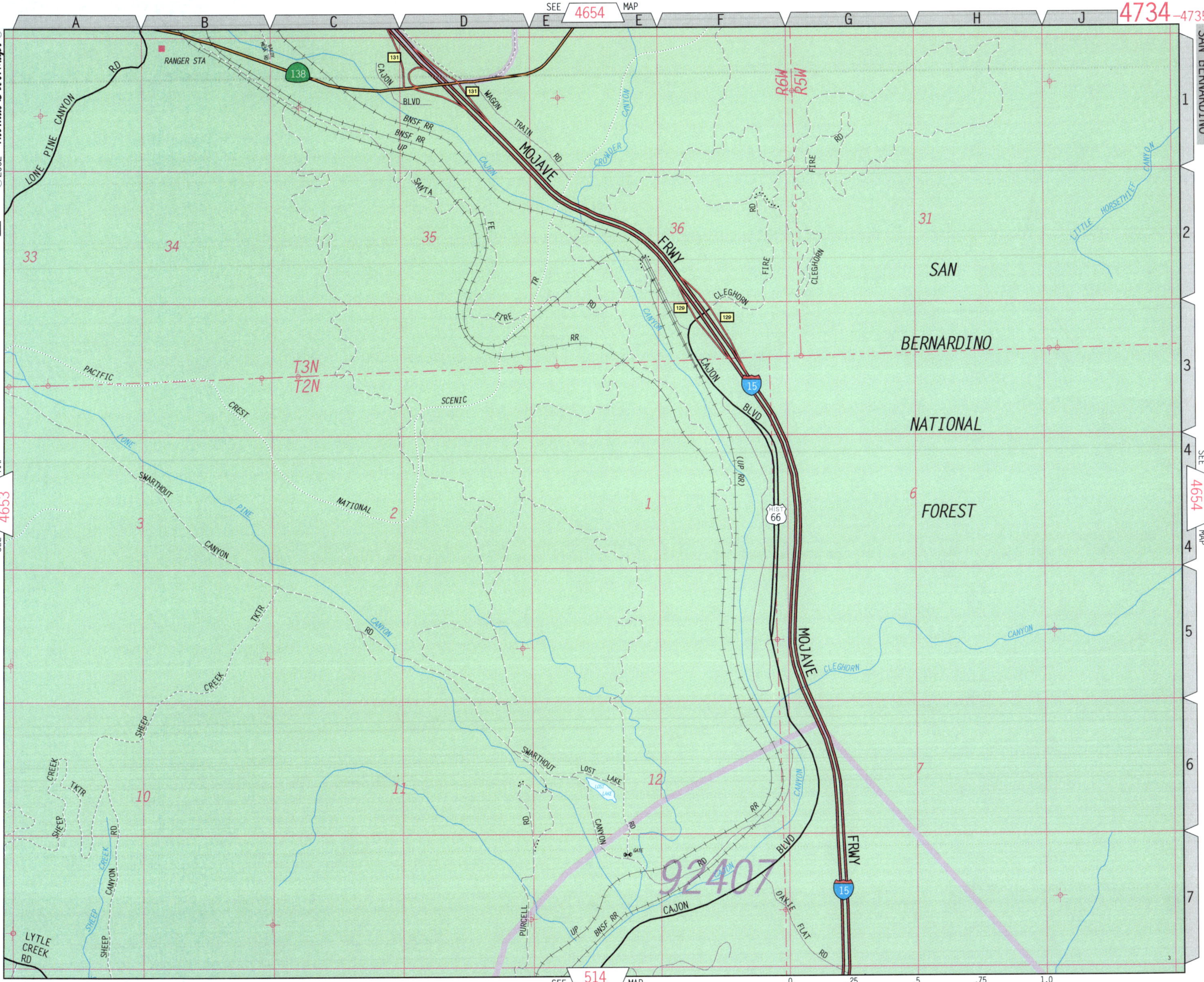
SEE 4654 MAP
A
B
C
D
E
F
G
H
J
1
2
3
4
5
6
7
SAN BERNARDINO
Thomas Bros. Maps®
© 2002
N
RANGER STA
LONE PINE CANYON RD
138
CAJON
BLVD
131
WAGON TRAIN RD
BNSF RR
BNSF RR
UP
SANTA FE
CAJON
MOJAVE FRWY
CROWDER CANYON
R6W
R5W
FIRE RD
FIRE
CLEGHORN
RD
36
31
33
34
35
LITTLE HORSETHIEF CANYON
SAN
BERNARDINO
NATIONAL
FOREST
TR
FIRE RD
RR
CLEGHORN
129
129
CANYON
CAJON BLVD
15
PACIFIC CREST
T3N
T2N
SCENIC
NATIONAL
2
1
6
(UP RR)
HIST 66
LONE PINE
SWARTHOUT CANYON RD
3
SEE 4653 MAP
SEE 4654 MAP
TKTR
CANYON
CREEK
SHEEP
MOJAVE
CLEGHORN
CANYON
SWARTHOUT
LOST LAKE
12
7
10
11
CREEK
TKTR
SHEEP
RD
SHEEP CREEK
CANYON
RD
CANYON
RD
GATE
92407
RR
CANYON
BLVD
FRWY
15
PURCELL
UP
BNSF RR
CAJON
RD
OAKIE FLAT RD
LYTLE CREEK RD
SHEEP
SEE 514 MAP
0 .25 .5 .75 1.0 miles
1 in. = 2400 ft.

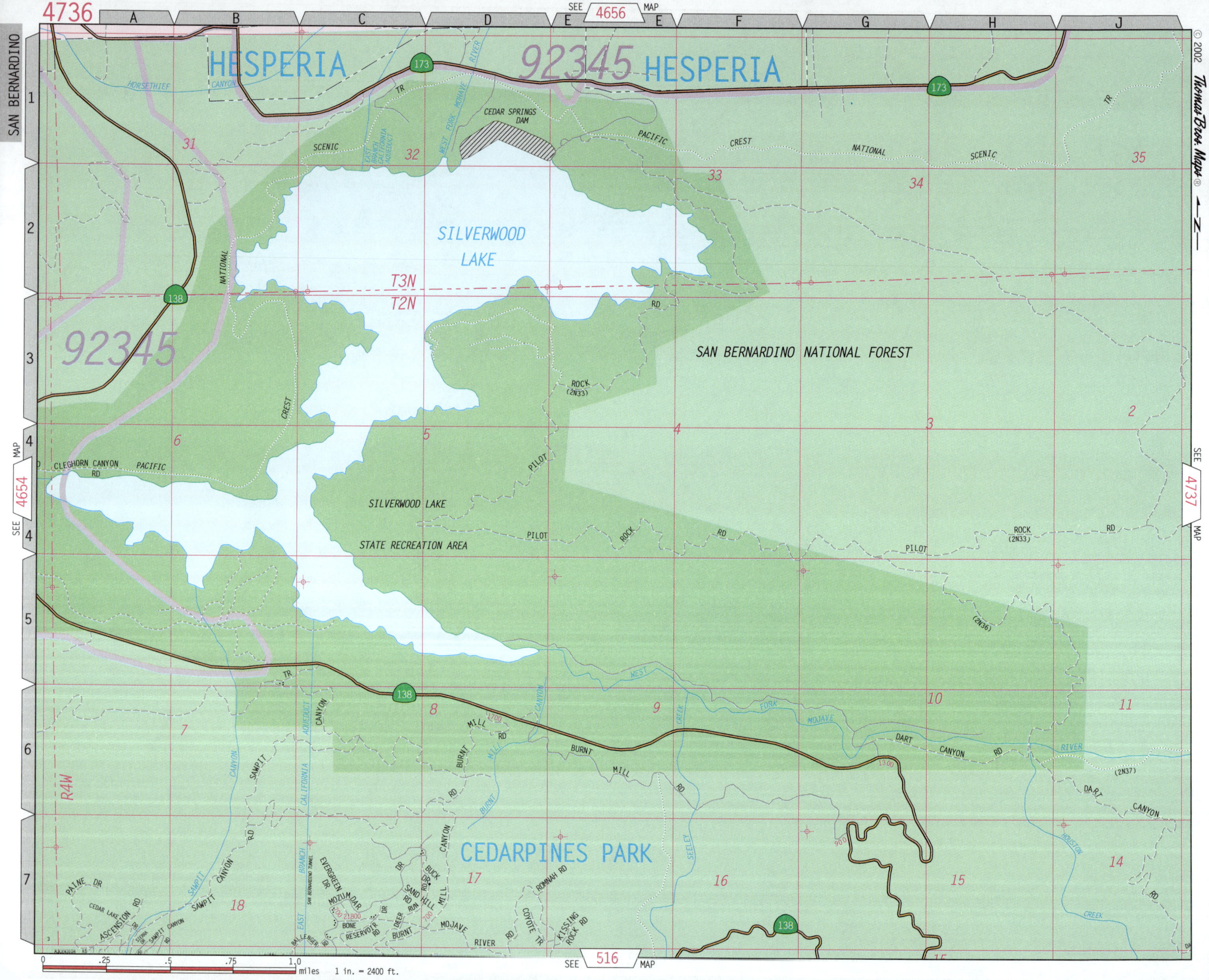
SEE 4656 MAP
SEE 4654 MAP
SEE 4737 MAP
SEE 516 MAP
SAN BERNARDINO
HESPERIA
92345
HESPERIA
92345
SILVERWOOD LAKE
T3N
T2N
SAN BERNARDINO NATIONAL FOREST
SILVERWOOD LAKE
STATE RECREATION AREA
CEDARPINES PARK
CEDAR SPRINGS DAM
PACIFIC CREST NATIONAL SCENIC TR
CLEGHORN CANYON RD
PILOT ROCK RD (2N33)
HORSETHIEF CANYON
WEST FORK MOJAVE RIVER
EAST BRANCH CALIFORNIA AQUEDUCT
BURNT MILL RD
DART CANYON RD
(2N37)
(2N36)
SAWPIT CANYON RD
SEELEY CREEK
HOUSTON CREEK
MOJAVE RIVER RD
KISSING ROCK RD
COYOTE TR
ROMNAH RD
EVERGREEN DR
MOZUMDAR DR
RESERVOIR RD
BUCK DR
SAND HILL DR
DEER RUN RD
PAINE DR
CEDAR LAKE RD
ASCENSION RD
BALLENGER RD
R4W
0 .25 .5 .75 1.0 miles 1 in. = 2400 ft.
© 2002 Thomas Bros. Maps®

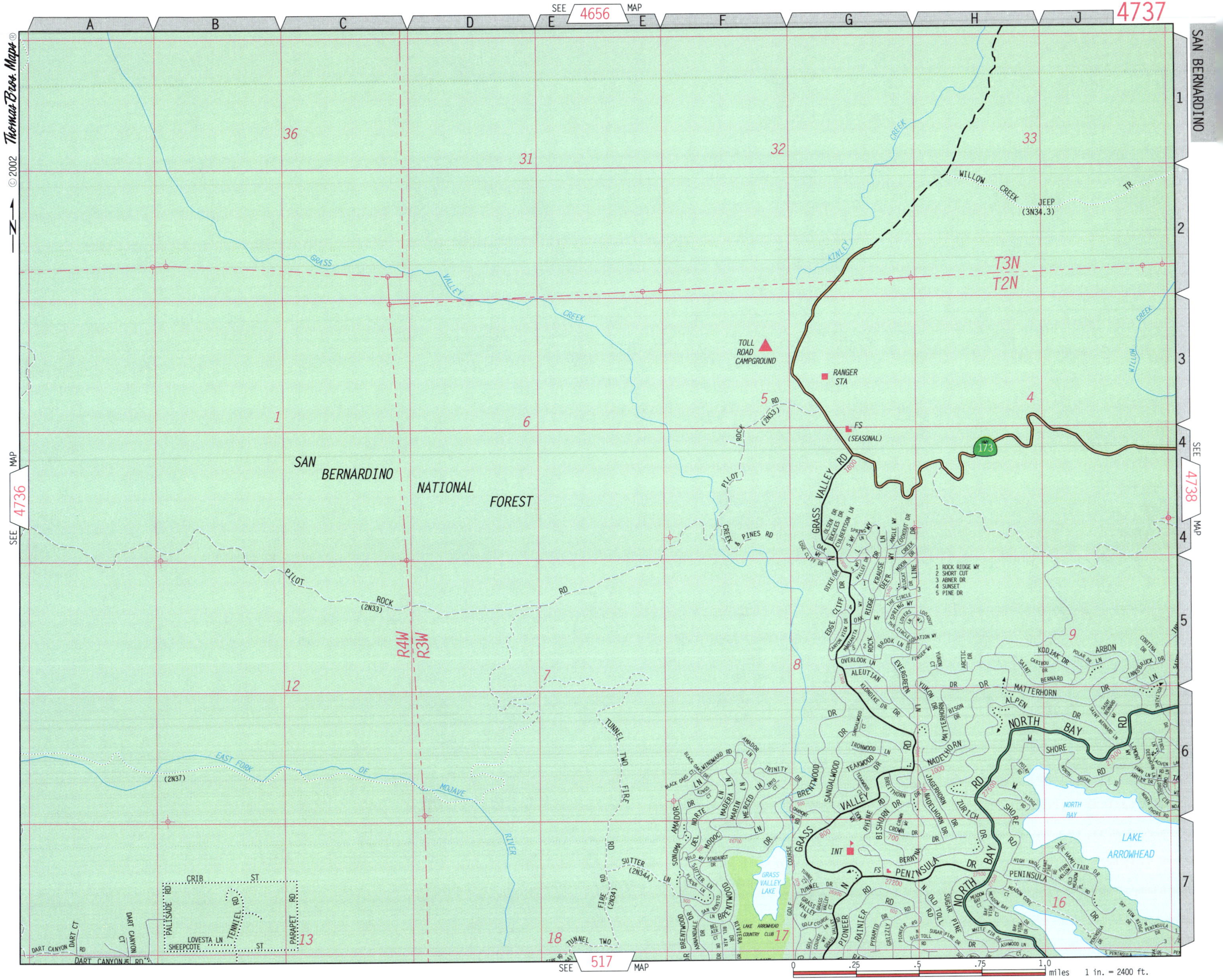
SEE 4656 MAP
A
B
C
D
E
F
G
H
J
1
2
3
4
5
6
7
SAN BERNARDINO
SEE 4736 MAP
SEE 4738 MAP
SEE 517 MAP
Thomas Bros. Maps
© 2002
N
36
31
32
33
1
6
5
4
12
7
8
9
13
18
17
16
T3N
T2N
R4W
R3W
SAN BERNARDINO NATIONAL FOREST
GRASS VALLEY CREEK
KINLEY CREEK
WILLOW CREEK
WILLOW CREEK JEEP TR (3N34.3)
TOLL ROAD CAMPGROUND
RANGER STA
FS (SEASONAL)
173
ROCK RD (2N33)
PILOT ROCK RD (2N33)
PILOT CREEK
PINES RD
GRASS VALLEY RD
EAST FORK OF MOJAVE RIVER
(2N37)
TUNNEL TWO FIRE RD
FIRE RD (2N34)
SUTTER (2N34A)
TUNNEL TWO
CRIB ST
PALISADE RD
LOVESTA LN
SHEEPCOTE ST
TENNIEL RD
PARAPET RD
DART CANYON RD
DART CT
DART CANYON CT
1 ROCK RIDGE WY
2 SHORT CUT
3 ABNER DR
4 SUNSET
5 PINE DR
NORTH BAY RD
NORTH SHORE RD
MATTERHORN DR
ALPEN DR
KODIAK DR
ARBON LN
CORTINA DR
INNSBRUCK DR
NADELHORN DR
JAGERHORN DR
ZURICH DR
PENINSULA DR
BERNINA DR
BISHORN DR
RHINE RD
BRENTWOOD DR
SANDALWOOD DR
TEAKWOOD DR
IRONWOOD LN
AMADOR DR
SONOMA DR
NORTE DR
MODOC LN
MADERA LN
MARIN LN
MERCED LN
TRINITY DR
ALEUTIAN DR
KLONDIKE DR
EVERGREEN DR
YUKON DR
OVERLOOK LN
EDGE CLIFF DR
RIDGE DR
KRAUSE DR
PIONEER RD
RAINIER RD
PYRAMID DR
GRIZZLY DR
OLD TOLL RD
SUGAR PINE DR
PENINSULA
INT
FS
GRASS VALLEY LAKE
LAKE ARROWHEAD COUNTRY CLUB
NORTH BAY
LAKE ARROWHEAD
0
.25
.5
.75
1.0
miles
1 in. = 2400 ft.

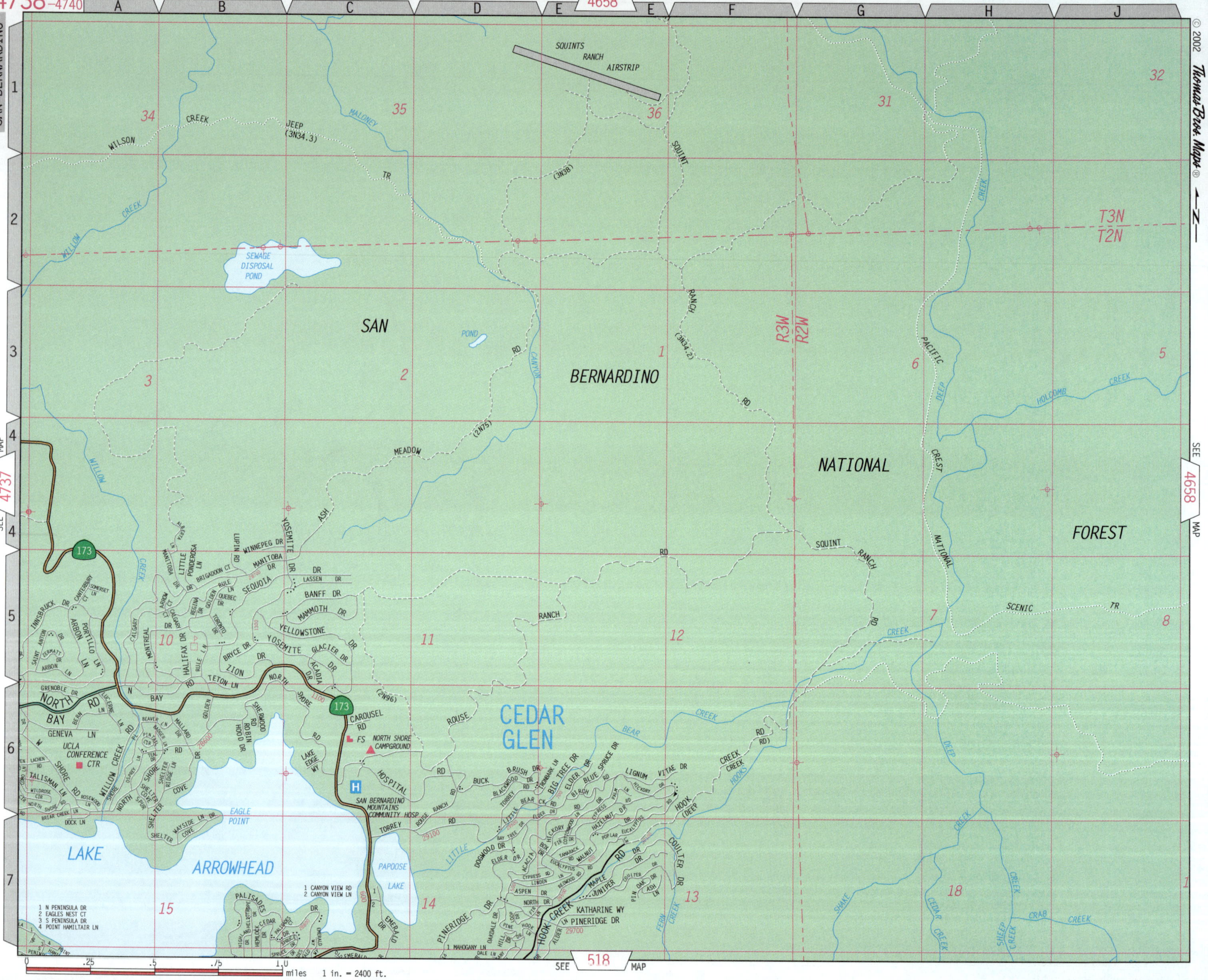
SEE 4658 MAP
SEE 4737 MAP
SEE 4658 MAP
SEE 518 MAP
SAN BERNARDINO
SAN
BERNARDINO
NATIONAL
FOREST
CEDAR
GLEN
LAKE
ARROWHEAD
SQUINTS
RANCH
AIRSTRIP
SEWAGE
DISPOSAL
POND
POND
T3N
T2N
R3W
R2W
WILSON
CREEK
JEEP
(3N34.3)
TR
MALONEY
WILLOW
CREEK
SQUINT
RANCH
(3N34.2)
RD
(3N38)
CANYON
MEADOW
(2N75)
ASH
PACIFIC
CREST
NATIONAL
SCENIC
TR
DEEP
CREEK
HOLCOMB
CREEK
BEAR
CREEK
HOOKS
SHAKE
CEDAR
CREEK
SHEEP
CREEK
CRAB
CREEK
LITTLE
BEAR
CREEK
FERN
CREEK
NORTH
BAY
RD
N
BAY
NORTH
SHORE
173
UCLA
CONFERENCE
CTR
FS
NORTH SHORE
CAMPGROUND
HOSPITAL
SAN BERNARDINO
MOUNTAINS
COMMUNITY HOSP
EAGLE
POINT
PAPOOSE
LAKE
PALISADES
1 CANYON VIEW RD
2 CANYON VIEW LN
1 N PENINSULA DR
2 EAGLES NEST CT
3 S PENINSULA DR
4 POINT HAMILTAIR LN
YOSEMITE
DR
LASSEN
BANFF
MAMMOTH
YELLOWSTONE
GLACIER
ACADIA
BRYCE
ZION
TETON
SEQUOIA
MANITOBA
WINNEPEG DR
LUPIN RD
LITTLE
PONDEROSA
LN
BRIGADOON CT
HALIFAX
MONTREAL
CALGARY
INNSBRUCK
ARBON
PORTILLO
CANTERBURY
GRENOBLE DR
GENEVA
LN
SHORE
RD
WILLOW CREEK
TALISMAN LN
DOCK LN
SHELTER
COVE
WAYSIDE LN
SHERWOOD
ROBIN
HOOD DR
CAROUSEL
RD
LAKE
EDGE
WY
(2N96)
ROUSE
RD
RANCH
TORREY
RD
BUCK
BRUSH
BLACKWOOD
BIG TREE DR
ELDER DR
BLUE SPRUCE DR
LIGNUM
VITAE DR
BIRCH
HICKORY
DOGWOOD DR
ELDER DR
HOOK
CREEK
RD
(DEEP
CREEK)
CREEK
RD
COULTER
DR
JUNIPER
MAPLE
KATHARINE WY
PINERIDGE DR
PINERIDGE
EMERALD
DR
1 MAHOGANY LN
29100
29700
34
35
36
31
32
3
2
1
6
5
10
11
12
7
8
15
14
13
18
0 .25 .5 .75 1.0 miles 1 in. = 2400 ft.

SEE 4660 MAP
A
B
C
D
E
F
G
H
J
SAN BERNARDINO
1
2
3
4
5
6
7
SEE 4742 MAP
SEE 4660 MAP
SEE 4811 MAP
T3N
T2N
R1W
R1E
SAN BERNARDINO NATIONAL FOREST
DELAMAR MTN. 8357'
DELAMAR
MOUNTAIN
PACIFIC
CREST
NATIONAL
SCENIC
TR
POLIQUE CANYON RD
HOLCOMB VALLEY RD
VAN DUSEN CANYON RD
HOLCOMB VALLEY RD
BERTHA PEAK 8198'
MINNELUSA CANYON CREEK
FAWNSKIN
MINNELUSA
GROUT CREEK
OKLAHOMA DR
RIM OF THE WORLD DR
IROQUOIS LN
CEDAR
CHOCTAW DR
DELL
RACCOON DR
PINEY
RIDGE
CLINE
MILLER PL
BROOKSIDE LN
CRAGS
BRUIN
LODGE RD
GLEN
FAWNSKIN
CANYON
DEER TRAIL LN
CHEROKEE
FLICKER RD
RED ROBIN
1 BARBARA LEE LN
2 MESQUITE DR
NORTH SHORE RECREATION AREA
GROUT BAY RECREATION AREA
DANA POINT PARK
GROUT BAY
GROUT BAY PARK
BOAT LAUNCH
NORTH SHORE DR
PINE HILL RD
SERRANO CAMPGROUND
38
BIG BEAR DISCOVERY CENTER
FS (SEASONAL)
BIG BEAR RANGER STATION RD
NORTH SHORE DR
MEADOWS EDGE PARK
LIBERTY LN
NEWELL DR
CROWN ROYAL PL
MARQUIS LN
BLUE BIRD LN
PREVOST DR
SOLAR OBSERVATORY
BIG BEAR LAKE
BAKER LAKE
STANFIELD CTO
BIG BEAR BLVD
LAKEVIEW LN
JAMES PL
DANESWOOD CT
BIG BEAR LAKEVIEW CENTER
INTERLAKEN CENTER
STARVATION FLATS RD
18
EUREKA
FINCH
CONDOR DR
BAYSIDE DR
MARINA POINT DR
PINECREST DR
GARSTIN DR
N SANDALWOOD DR
FOX FARM RD
JUNIPER DR
LAGUNITA LN
1 LAKE DR
2 GILNER DR
3 POINT RD
BIG BEAR LAKE
35
36
31
32
33
1
2
6
5
4
12
11
7
8
9
14
13
18
17
16
0 .25 .5 .75 1.0 miles 1 in. = 2400 ft.

SEE 4662 MAP

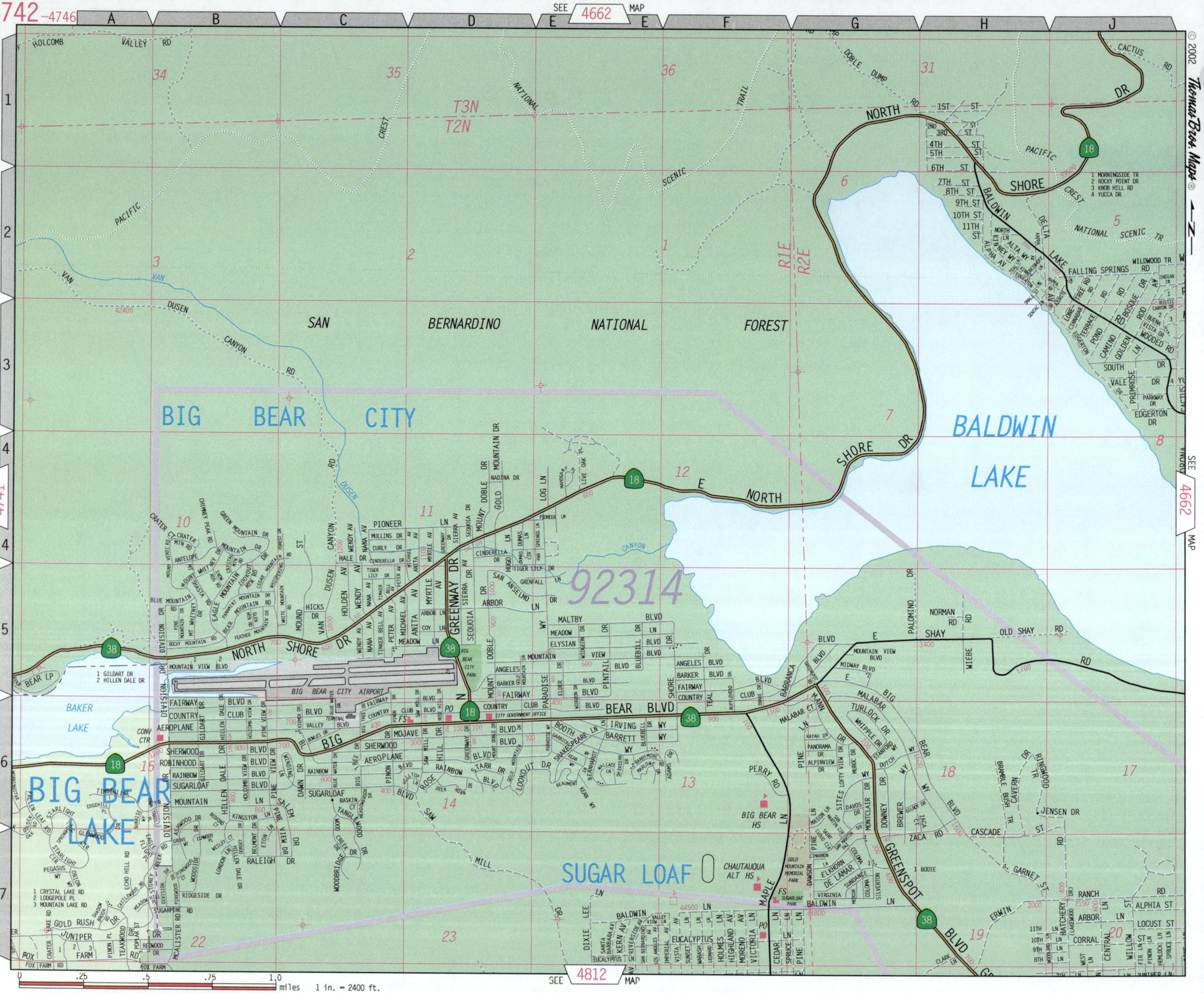

SEE 4741 MAP

SEE 4662 MAP

SEE 4812 MAP

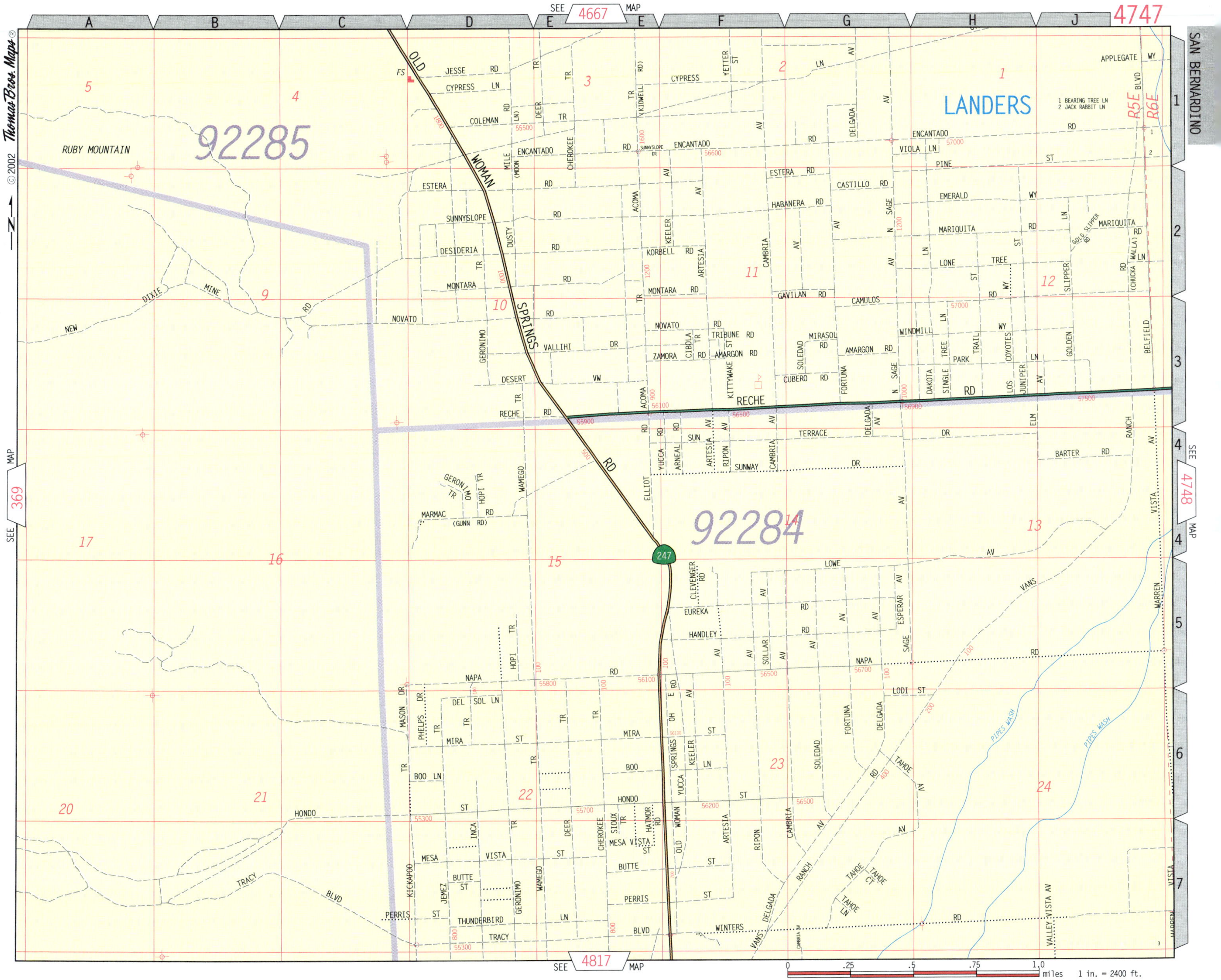
SEE 4667 MAP
A
B
C
D
E
F
G
H
J
1
2
3
4
5
6
7
SAN BERNARDINO
LANDERS
RUBY MOUNTAIN
92285
92284
R5E
R6E
OLD WOMAN SPRINGS RD
RECHE RD
JESSE RD
CYPRESS LN
COLEMAN
ENCANTADO RD
ESTERA RD
SUNNYSLOPE RD
DESIDERIA RD
MONTARA RD
NOVATO RD
VALLIHI DR
DESERT VW
DIXIE MINE RD
NEW
KORBELL RD
ACOMA AV
KEELER AV
ARTESIA AV
CAMBRIA AV
GAVILAN RD
CAMULOS
TRIBUNE RD
ZAMORA RD
AMARGON RD
MIRASOL RD
CUBERO RD
FORTUNA AV
DELGADA AV
SAGE AV
WINDMILL
DAKOTA
SINGLE TREE
PARK
TRAIL
COYOTES WY
LOS JUNIPER
GOLDEN
BELFIELD
VIOLA LN
PINE ST
EMERALD WY
MARIQUITA RD
LONE TREE
SLIPPER
GOLD SLIPPER RD
CASTILLO RD
HABANERA RD
APPLEGATE WY
1 BEARING TREE LN
2 JACK RABBIT LN
TERRACE DR
SUNWAY DR
BARTER RD
RANCH
VISTA AV
ELM
SUN
YUCCA
ARNEAL
RIPON
ELLIOT
GERONIMO TR
HOPI TR
MARMAC RD
(GUNN RD)
WAMEGO
247
LOWE
CLEVENGER RD
EUREKA
HANDLEY
NAPA RD
SOLLAR AV
ESPERAR AV
LODI ST
VANS AV
WARREN
MASON DR
PHELPS DR
DEL SOL LN
MIRA ST
BOO LN
HONDO ST
INCA
MESA VISTA
BUTTE ST
PERRIS ST
THUNDERBIRD
TRACY BLVD
KICKAPOO
JEMEZ
LN
WINTERS RD
VALLEY VISTA AV
TAHOE CT
TAHOE LN
PIPES WASH
DEER
CHEROKEE
SIOUX TR
HATHOR RD
ST
5
4
3
2
1
9
10
11
12
17
16
15
14
13
20
21
22
23
24
SEE 369 MAP
SEE 4748 MAP
SEE 4817 MAP
0 .25 .5 .75 1.0 miles
1 in. = 2400 ft.

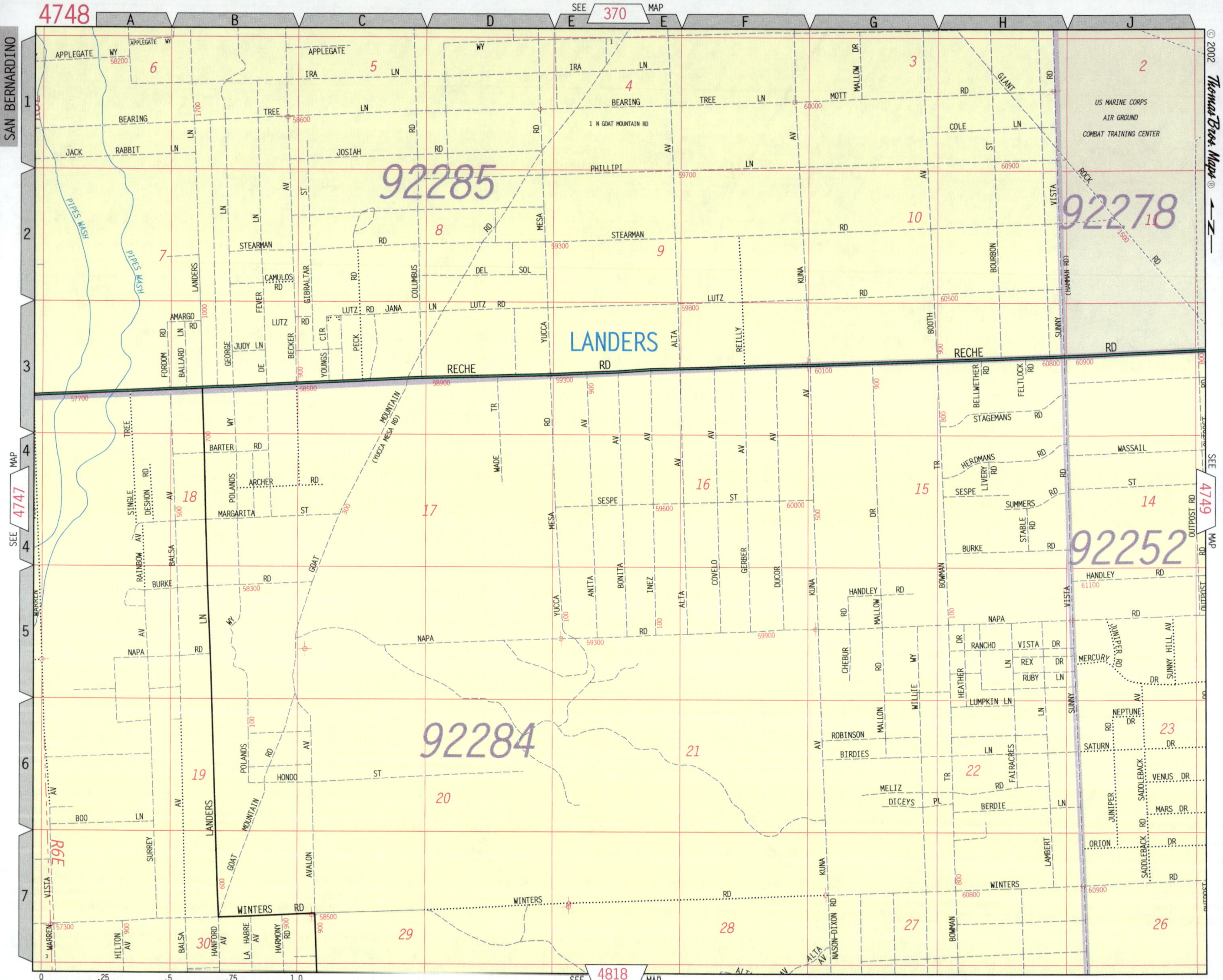

0 .25 .5 .75 1.0 miles 1 in. = 2400 ft.

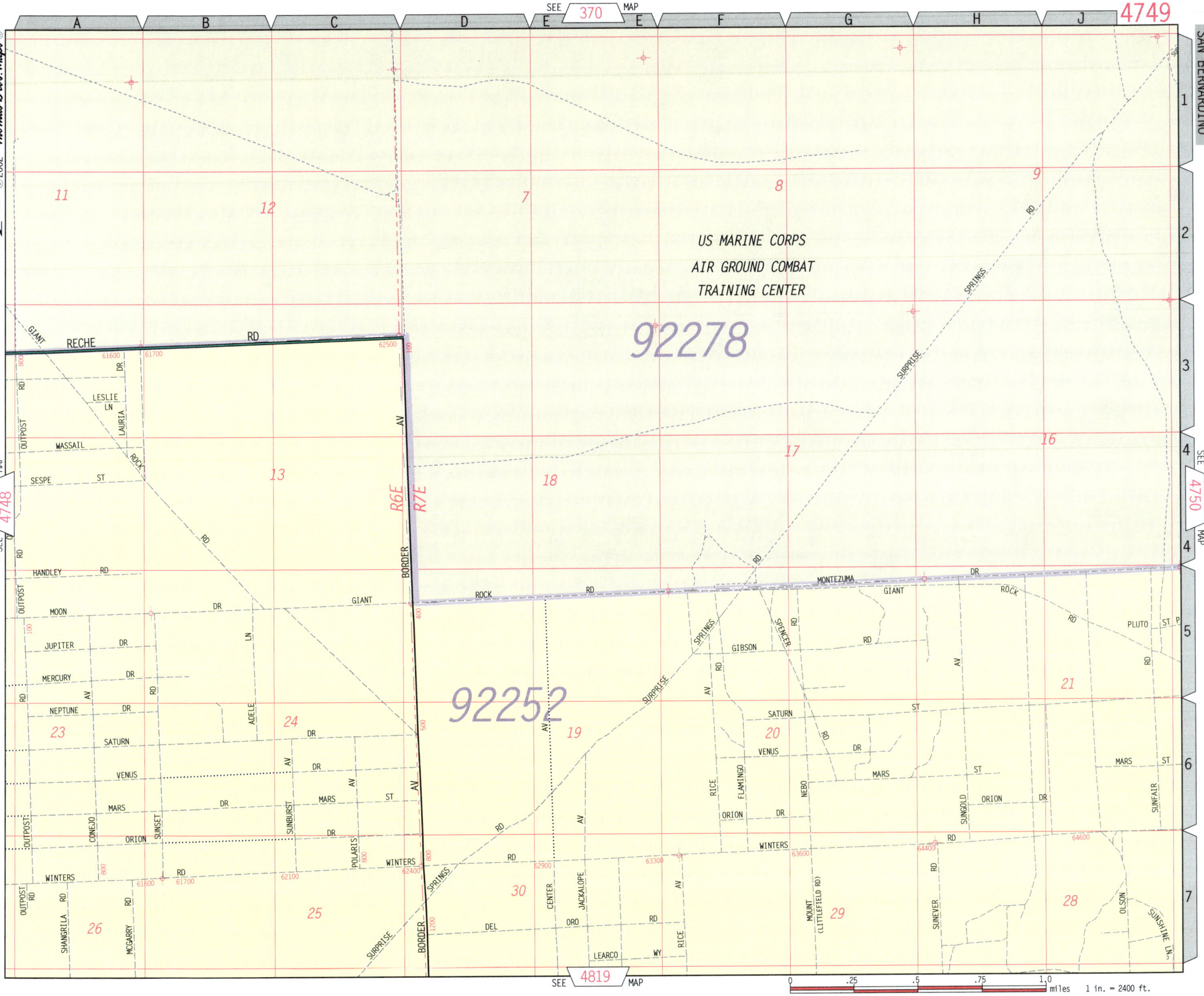
SEE 370 MAP
SEE 4748 MAP
SEE 4750 MAP
SEE 4819 MAP
SAN BERNARDINO
US MARINE CORPS
AIR GROUND COMBAT
TRAINING CENTER
92278
92252
R6E
R7E
RECHE RD
GIANT
LESLIE LN
LAURIA DR
OUTPOST RD
WASSAIL
SESPE ST
ROCK RD
HANDLEY RD
MOON DR
GIANT
JUPITER DR
MERCURY DR
NEPTUNE DR
SATURN
VENUS
MARS DR
ORION
WINTERS RD
CONEJO AV
SUNSET RD
ADELE
LN
SUNBURST AV
POLARIS AV
MARS ST
BORDER AV
SURPRISE SPRINGS RD
SHANGRILA RD
MCGARRY RD
ROCK RD
MONTEZUMA DR
GIANT ROCK RD
PLUTO ST
GIBSON RD
SPENCER RD
SATURN ST
VENUS DR
MARS ST
ORION DR
RICE AV
FLAMINGO
NEBO
SUNGOLD AV
SUNFAIR RD
MOUNT (LITTLEFIELD RD)
SUNEVER RD
OLSON
SUNSHINE LN
CENTER AV
JACKALOPE AV
DEL ORO RD
LEARCO WY
RICE AV
1 2 3 4 5 6 7
A B C D E F G H J
7 8 9 11 12 13 16 17 18 19 20 21 23 24 25 26 28 29 30
61600 61700 62100 62400 62500 62900 63300 63600 64400 64600
100 400 500 800 1200
0 .25 .5 .75 1.0 miles 1 in. = 2400 ft.

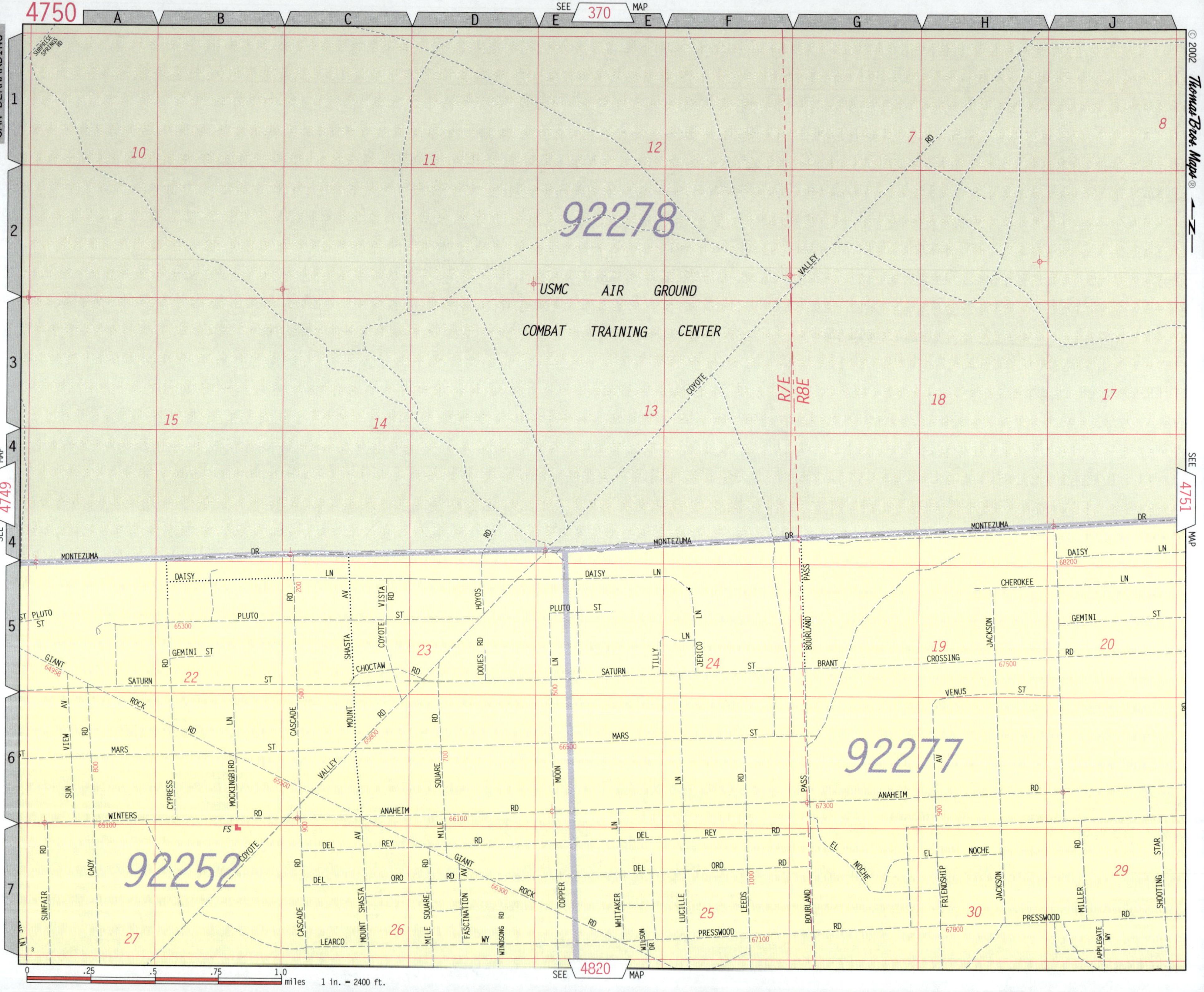
SEE 370 MAP
SAN BERNARDINO
A B C D E E F G H J
1 2 3 4 4 5 6 7
SEE 4749 MAP
SEE 4751 MAP
SEE 4820 MAP
© 2002 Thomas Bros. Maps ®
92278
USMC AIR GROUND
COMBAT TRAINING CENTER
92277
92252
R7E
R8E
SURPRISE SPRINGS RD
COYOTE VALLEY RD
MONTEZUMA DR
DAISY LN
PLUTO ST
GEMINI ST
SATURN ST
MARS ST
WINTERS RD
ANAHEIM RD
DEL REY RD
DEL ORO RD
LEARCO
PRESSWOOD RD
GIANT ROCK RD
CHEROKEE LN
CROSSING
BRANT
VENUS ST
EL NOCHE
BOURLAND
PASS
JACKSON
FRIENDSHIP
MILLER
SHOOTING STAR
APPLEGATE WY
SUNFAIR RD
CADY
SUN VIEW AV
CYPRESS
MOCKINGBIRD LN
CASCADE RD
MOUNT SHASTA AV
CHOCTAW RD
COYOTE VISTA RD
HOYOS
DOUES RD
MILE SQUARE RD
FASCINATION AV
WINDSONG RD
COPPER
MOON LN
WHITAKER
WILSON DR
LUCILLE LN
LEEDS RD
TILLY
JERICO LN
FS
10 11 12 7 8 15 14 13 18 17 22 23 24 19 20 27 26 25 30 29
0 .25 .5 .75 1.0 miles 1 in. = 2400 ft.

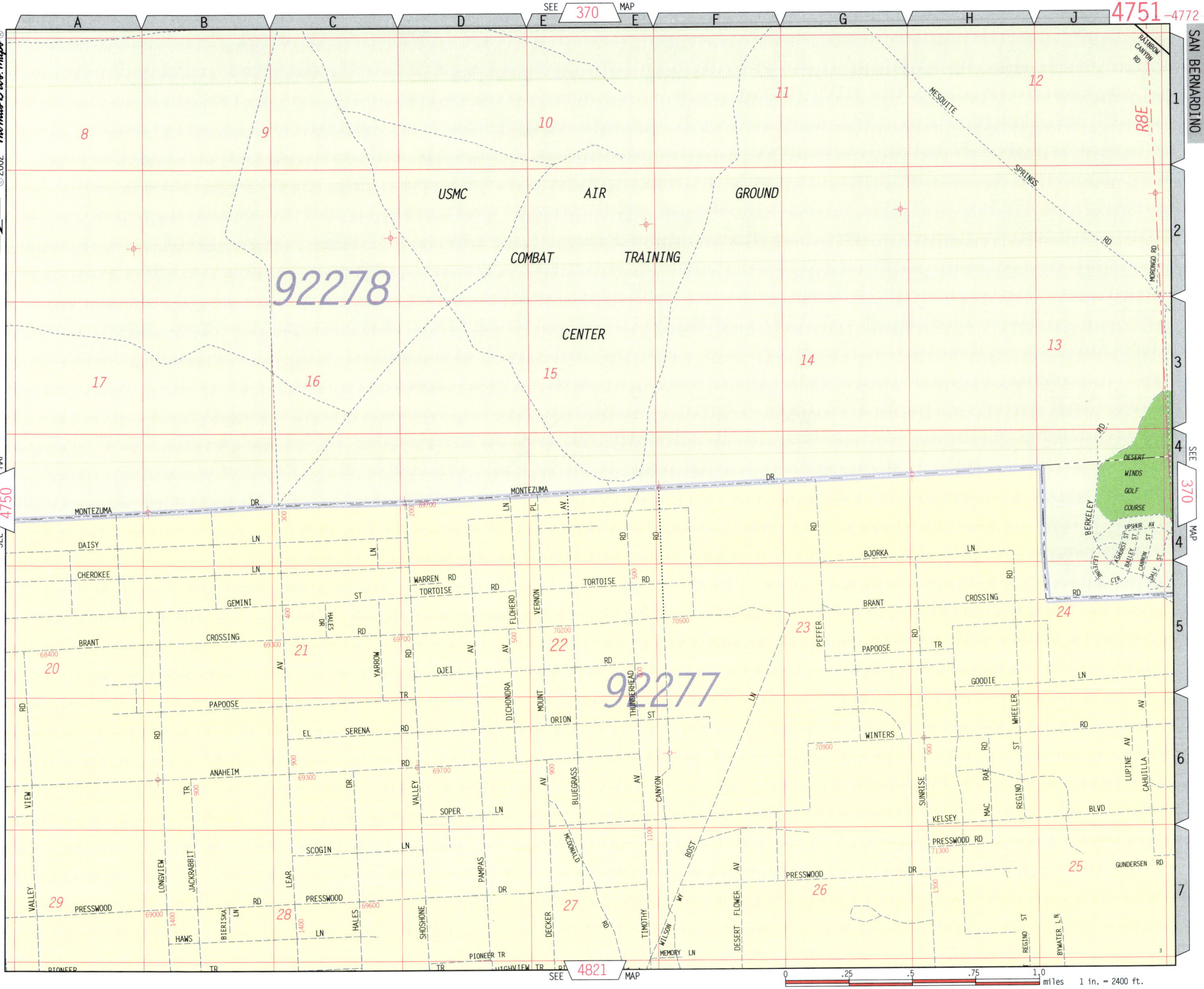
SEE 370 MAP
SAN BERNARDINO
USMC AIR GROUND
COMBAT TRAINING
CENTER
92278
92277
MONTEZUMA DR
MESQUITE SPRINGS RD
RAINBOW CANYON RD
MORONGO RD
R8E
DESERT WINDS GOLF COURSE
BERKELEY
DAISY LN
CHEROKEE LN
GEMINI ST
WARREN RD
TORTOISE RD
BJORKA LN
BRANT
CROSSING
PAPOOSE TR
GOODIE LN
WINTERS RD
SERENA RD
ANAHEIM RD
SOPER LN
SCOGIN LN
PRESSWOOD RD
PRESSWOOD DR
KELSEY
BLVD
GUNDERSEN RD
PIONEER TR
HIGHVIEW TR
MEMORY LN
HAWS
VIEW RD
VALLEY
LONGVIEW
JACKRABBIT TR
BIERISKA LN
LEAR
HALES
SHOSHONE
PAMPAS
DECKER
MCDONALD RD
TIMOTHY
WILSON WY
BOST
DESERT FLOWER AV
THUNDERHEAD AV
CANYON
BLUEGRASS
MOUNT
DICHONDRA
FLOHERO
VERNON
ORION ST
OJEI
YARROW
EL
PEFFER
SUNRISE
RAE
MAC
REGINO
WHEELER ST
LUPINE AV
CAHUILLA
BYWATER LN
SEE 4750 MAP
SEE 370 MAP
SEE 4821 MAP
0 .25 .5 .75 1.0 miles 1 in. = 2400 ft.

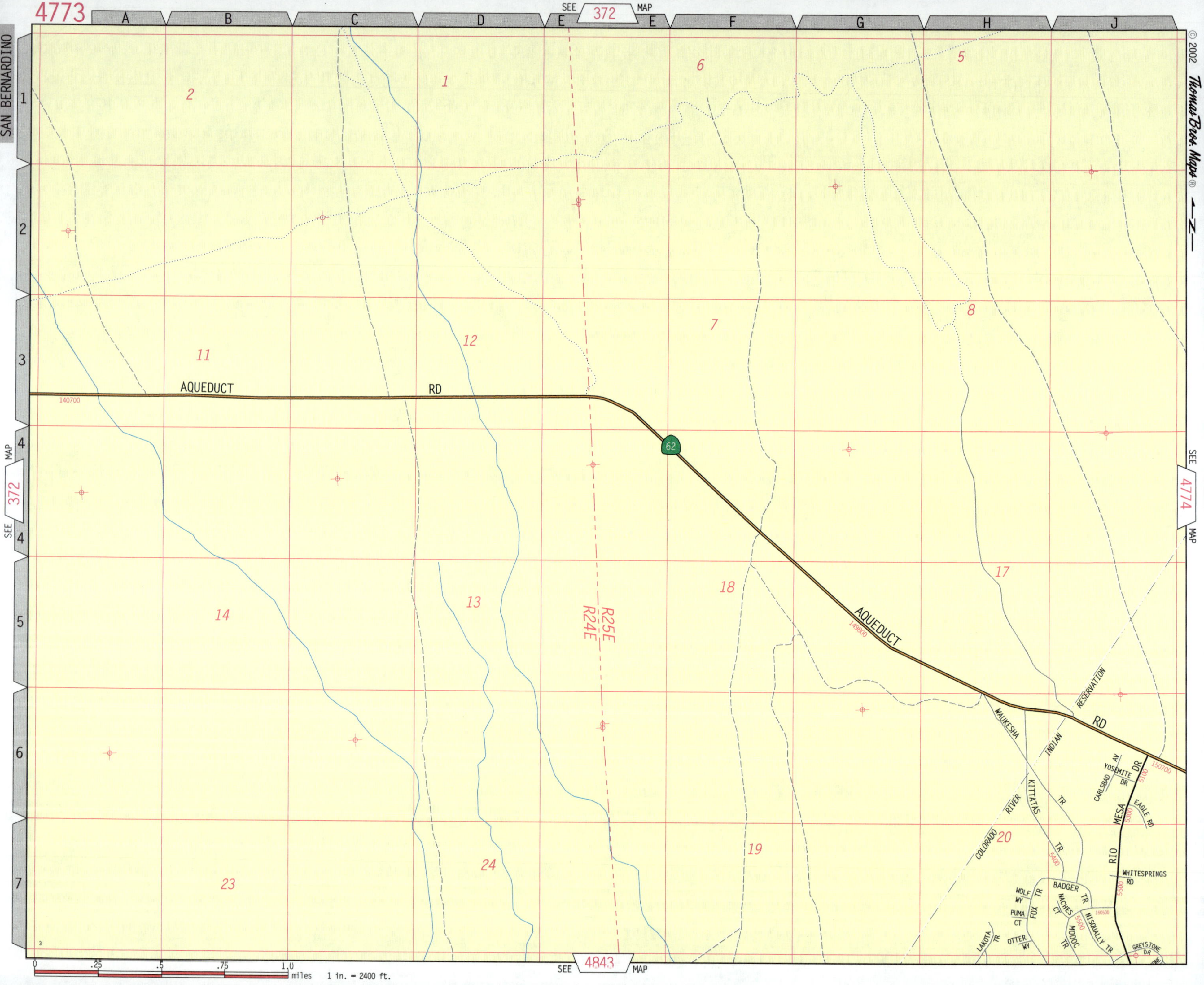
SAN BERNARDINO
SEE 372 MAP
SEE 372 MAP
SEE 4774 MAP
SEE 4843 MAP
AQUEDUCT RD
140700
62
AQUEDUCT RD
149800
R25E
R24E
1
2
5
6
7
8
11
12
13
14
17
18
19
20
23
24
RESERVATION
INDIAN
WAUKESHA
KITTATAS TR
COLORADO RIVER TR
5400
YOSEMITE DR
CARLSBAD AV
MESA DR
RIO
5100
150700
EAGLE RD
5300
WHITESPRINGS RD
5500
BADGER TR
WOLF WY
FOX TR
PUMA CT
NACHES CT
150500
5500
NISQUALLY TR
MODOC TR
OTTER WY
LAKOTA TR
GREYSTONE DR
0
.25
.5
.75
1.0
miles
1 in. = 2400 ft.
© 2002
Thomas Bros. Maps®

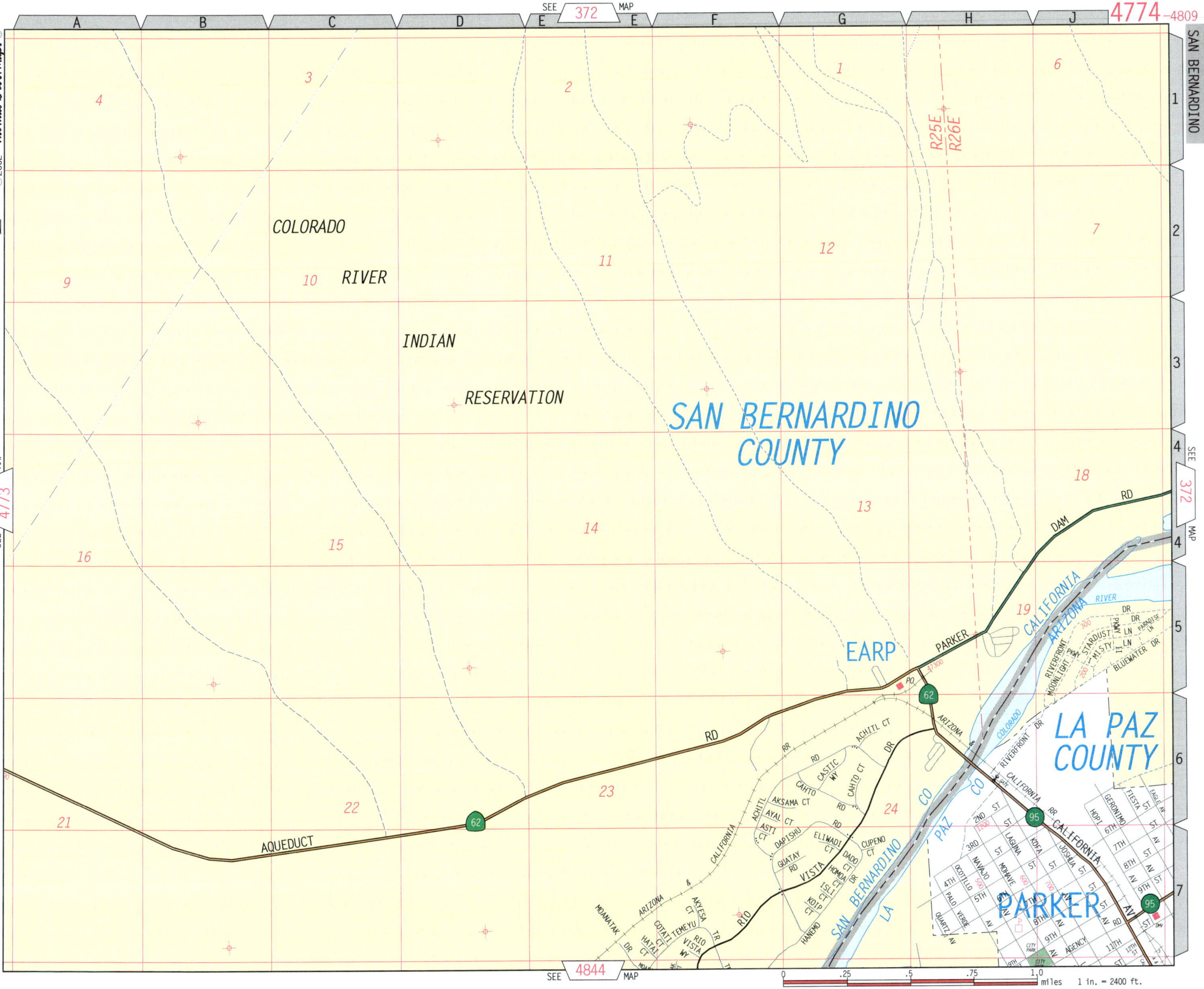

SEE 372 MAP
A B C D E E F G H J
1 2 3 4 5 6 7
SAN BERNARDINO
COLORADO
RIVER
INDIAN
RESERVATION
SAN BERNARDINO
COUNTY
LA PAZ
COUNTY
EARP
PARKER
R25E
R26E
PARKER
DAM
RD
AQUEDUCT
RD
62
95
CALIFORNIA
ARIZONA
RIVER
COLORADO
RIVERFRONT DR
MOONLIGHT
STARDUST
MISTY
BLUEWATER DR
PARADISE LN
ACHITL CT
CASTIC WY
CAHTO CT
CAHTO RD
AKSAMA CT
AYAL CT
ASTI CT
DAPISHU
GUATAY RD
ELIWADI CT
DADO CT
HOMDA DR
ISLI CT
KOIP CT
HANEMO
CUPENO CT
VISTA
RIO
MOANATAK DR
COTATI CT
HATAI CT
TEMEYU
AKYESA CT
RIO VISTA WY
LA PAZ CO
SAN BERNARDINO CO
2ND ST
3RD
4TH
5TH
6TH
7TH
8TH
9TH
11TH
12TH ST
OCOTILLO
PALO VERDE
QUARTZ
NAVAJO
MOHAVE
LAGUNA
KOFA
JOSHUA
HOPI
GERONIMO
FIESTA
EAGLE
AGENCY
CITY PARK
SEE 4773 MAP
SEE 372 MAP
SEE 4844 MAP
0 .25 .5 .75 1.0 miles
1 in. = 2400 ft.

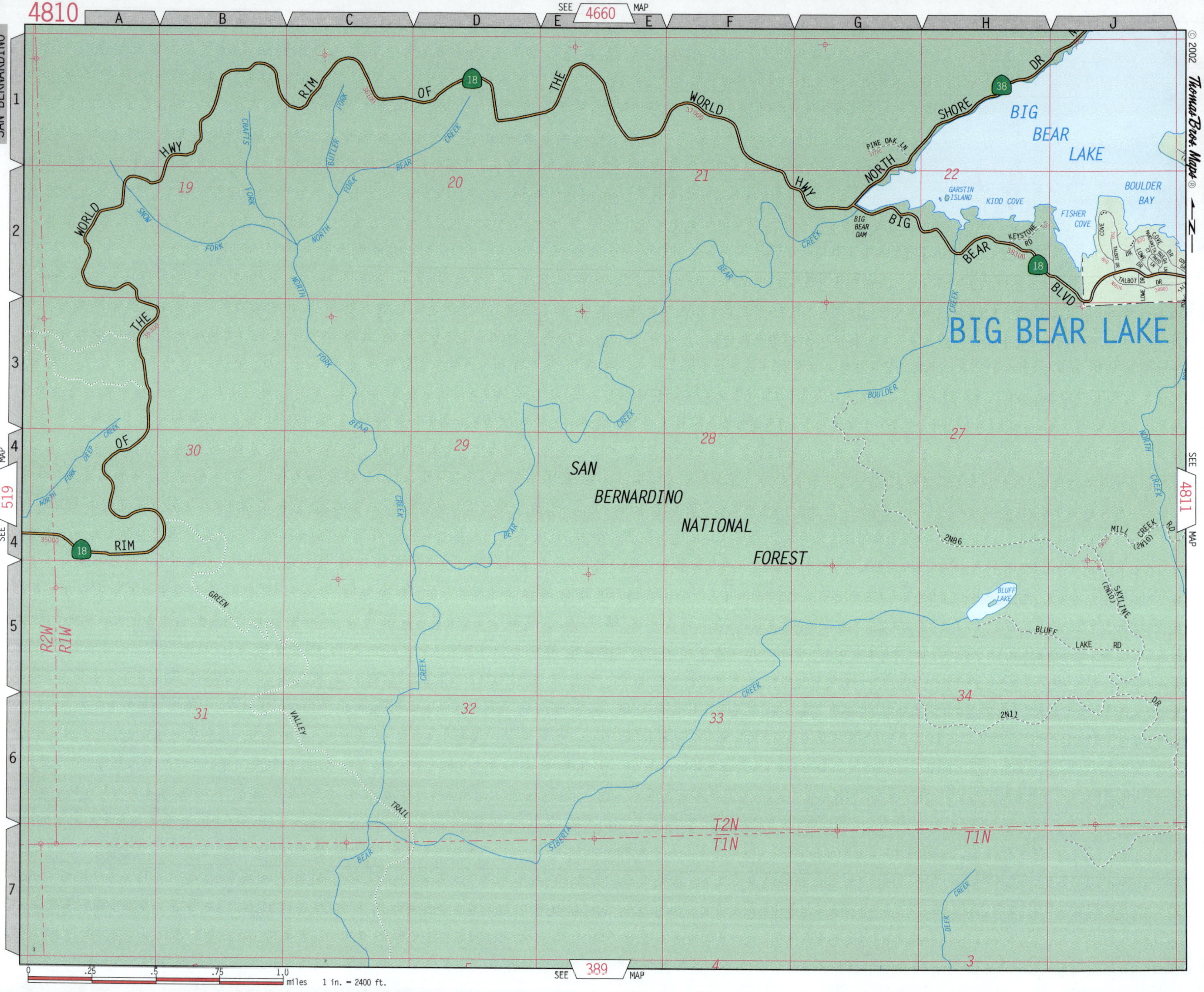
A
B
C
D
E
F
G
H
J
1
2
3
4
5
6
7
SEE 4660 MAP
SEE 519 MAP
SEE 4811 MAP
SEE 389 MAP
SAN BERNARDINO
RIM OF THE WORLD HWY
18
38
NORTH SHORE DR
PINE OAK LN
BIG BEAR LAKE
GARSTIN ISLAND
KIDD COVE
FISHER COVE
BOULDER BAY
BIG BEAR DAM
BIG BEAR BLVD
KEYSTONE RD
TALBOT DR
BIG BEAR LAKE
SNOW FORK
CRAFTS FORK
BUTLER FORK
NORTH FORK BEAR CREEK
BEAR CREEK
BOULDER CREEK
NORTH FORK DEEP CREEK
NORTH CREEK
SAN BERNARDINO NATIONAL FOREST
2N86
MILL CREEK RD (2N10)
SKYLINE (2N10)
BLUFF LAKE
BLUFF LAKE RD
2N11
DR
GREEN VALLEY TRAIL
SIBERIA CREEK
DEER CREEK
R2W R1W
T2N T1N
T1N
19
20
21
22
27
28
29
30
31
32
33
34
3
4
5
0 .25 .5 .75 1.0 miles 1 in. = 2400 ft.

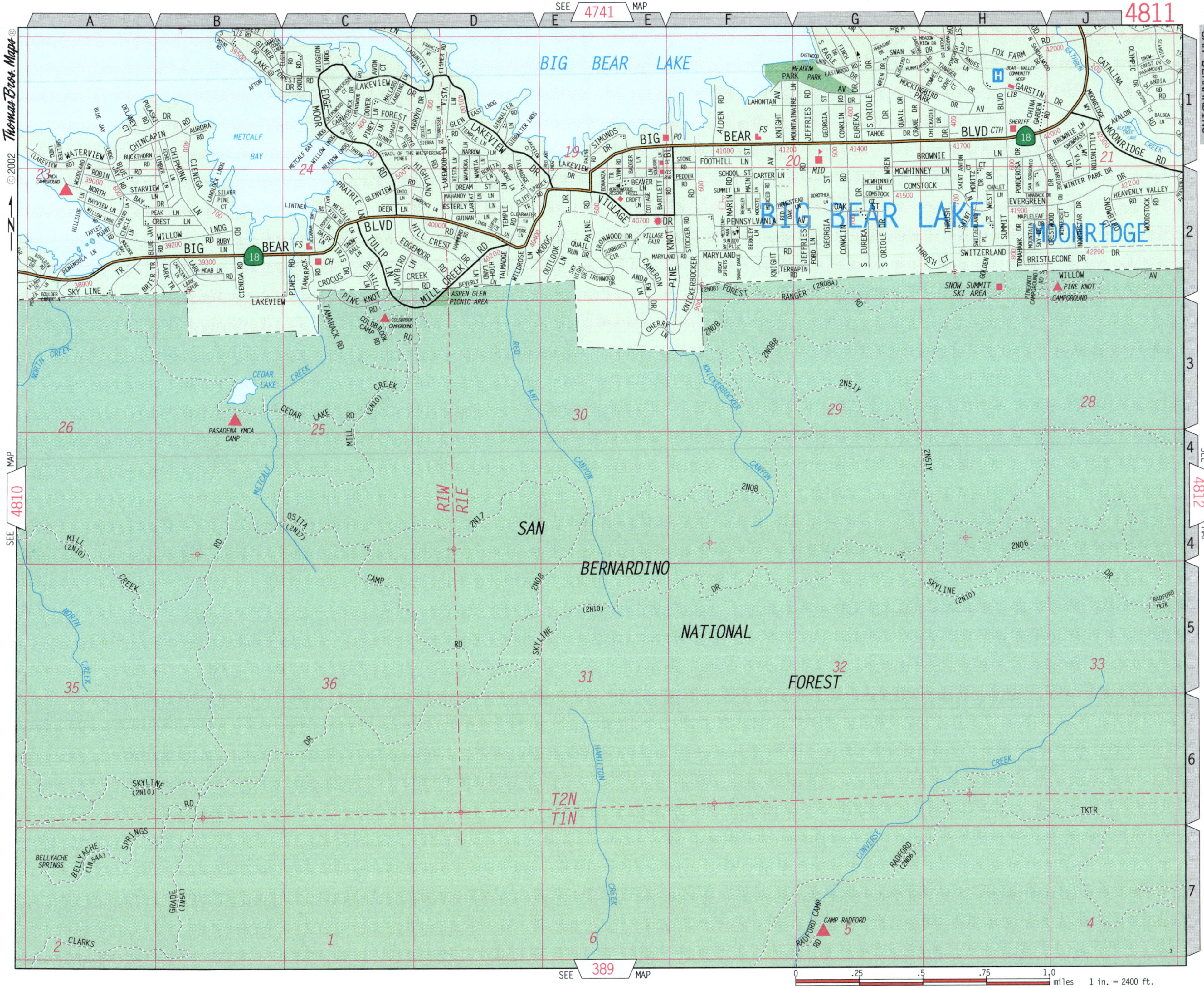
SEE 4741 MAP
BIG BEAR LAKE
METCALF BAY
BIG BEAR BLVD
BIG BEAR LAKE
MOONRIDGE
SAN BERNARDINO
SAN BERNARDINO NATIONAL FOREST
SNOW SUMMIT SKI AREA
PINE KNOT CAMPGROUND
ASPEN GLEN PICNIC AREA
COLDBROOK CAMPGROUND
PASADENA YMCA CAMP
YMCA CAMPGROUND
CEDAR LAKE
MEADOW PARK
FOX FARM
BEAR VALLEY COMMUNITY HOSP
CAMP RADFORD
BELLYACHE SPRINGS
NORTH CREEK
METCALF CREEK
RED ANT CANYON
KNICKERBOCKER CANYON
HAMILTON CREEK
CONVERSE CREEK
R1W R1E
T2N T1N
SEE 4810 MAP
SEE 4812 MAP
SEE 389 MAP
0 .25 .5 .75 1.0 miles 1 in. = 2400 ft.

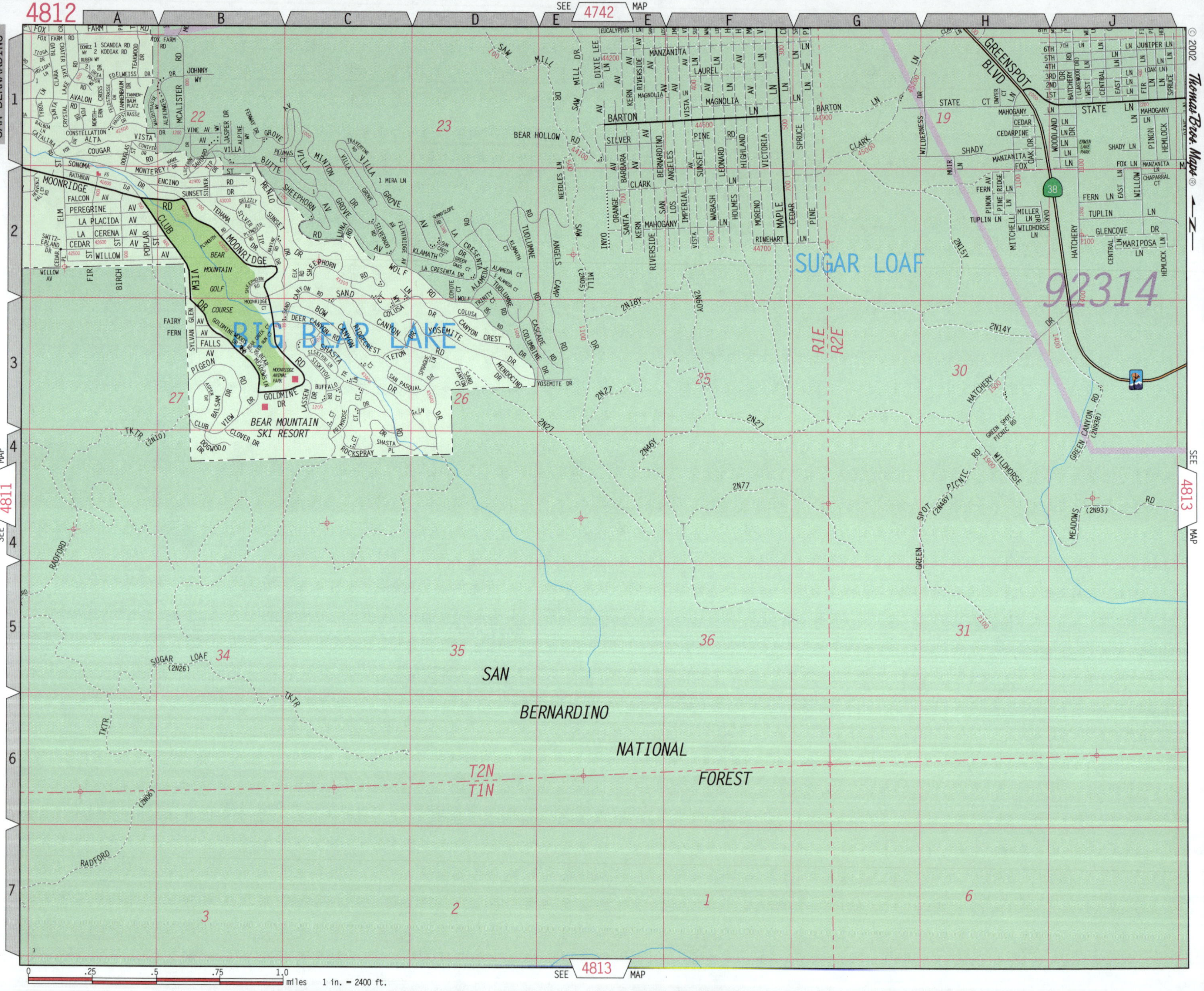
SEE 4742 MAP
SAN BERNARDINO
A
B
C
D
E
F
G
H
J
1
2
3
4
5
6
7
BIG BEAR LAKE
SUGAR LOAF
92314
BEAR MOUNTAIN GOLF COURSE
BEAR MOUNTAIN SKI RESORT
MOONRIDGE ANIMAL PARK
SAN BERNARDINO NATIONAL FOREST
GREENSPOT BLVD
MOONRIDGE
MOONRIDGE RD
CLUB VIEW DR
GOLDMINE DR
BEAR HOLLOW RD
BARTON
STATE
CLARK
MAPLE
SAW MILL DR
GREEN CANYON RD
HATCHERY
WILDHORSE
GREEN SPOT PICNIC RD
RADFORD
SUGAR LOAF (2N26)
2N27
2N77
2N18Y
2N14Y
R1E
R2E
T2N
T1N
22
23
19
27
26
25
30
34
35
36
31
3
2
1
6
38
SEE MAP 4811
SEE MAP 4813
SEE 4813 MAP
0 .25 .5 .75 1.0 miles 1 in. = 2400 ft.
© 2002 Thomas Bros. Maps ®

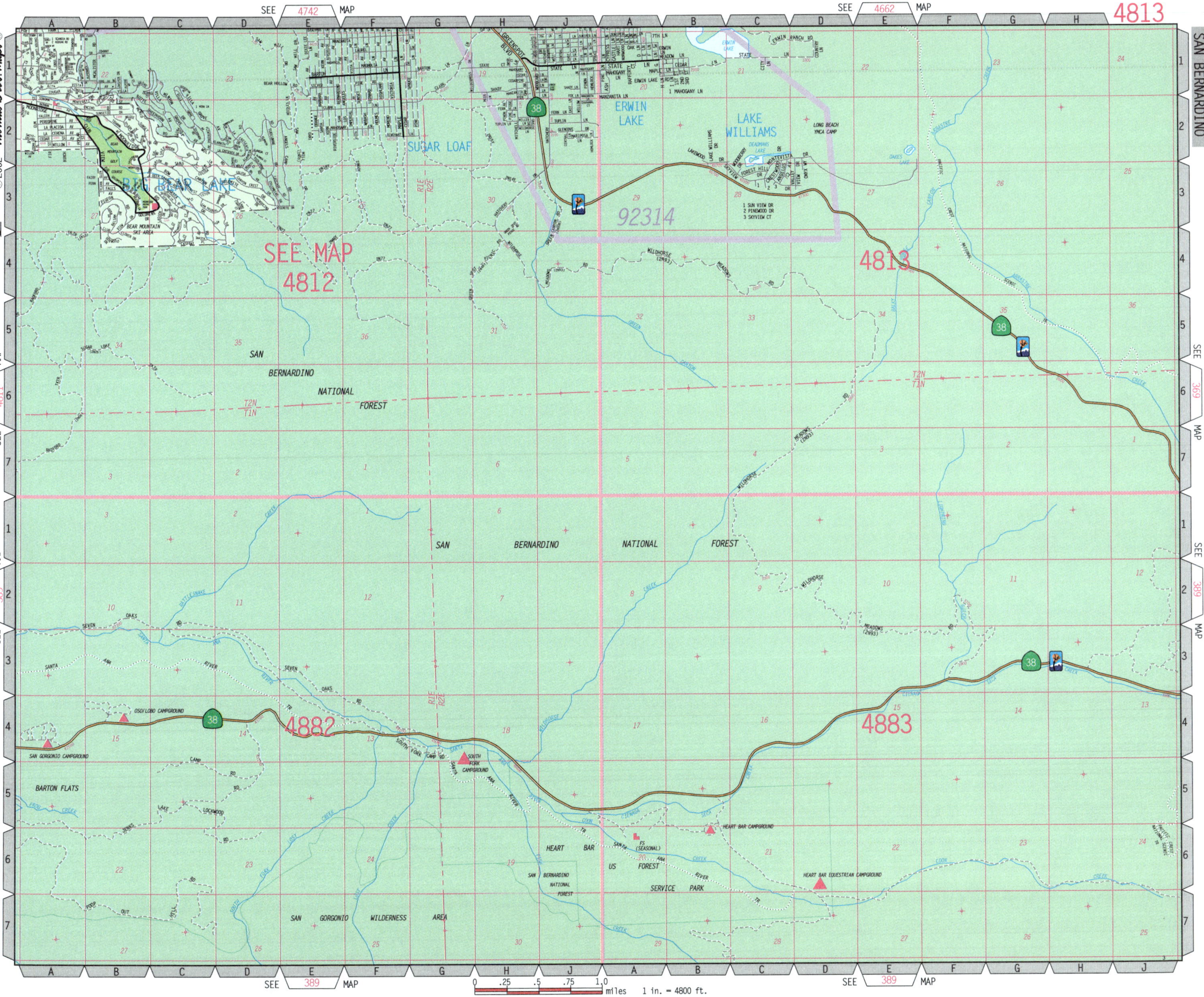
SEE 4742 MAP
SEE 4662 MAP
SEE 4811 MAP
SEE 369 MAP
SEE 389 MAP
SEE 389 MAP
SEE 389 MAP
SEE 389 MAP
BIG BEAR LAKE
BEAR MOUNTAIN SKI AREA
SUGAR LOAF
ERWIN LAKE
LAKE WILLIAMS
DEADMANS LAKE
LONG BEACH YMCA CAMP
GREENSPOT BLVD
ERWIN LAKE DR
STATE LN
92314
1 SUN VIEW DR
2 PINEWOOD DR
3 SKYVIEW CT
SEE MAP 4812
4813
SAN BERNARDINO NATIONAL FOREST
T2N T1N
R1E R2E
WILDHORSE MEADOWS
SEVEN OAKS RD
SANTA ANA RIVER
OSO/LOBO CAMPGROUND
SAN GORGONIO CAMPGROUND
4882
4883
SOUTH FORK CAMPGROUND
BARTON FLATS
HEART BAR CAMPGROUND
HEART BAR EQUESTRIAN CAMPGROUND
HEART BAR US FOREST SERVICE PARK
FS (SEASONAL)
SAN BERNARDINO NATIONAL FOREST
SAN GORGONIO WILDERNESS AREA
38
0 .25 .5 .75 1.0 miles 1 in. = 4800 ft.

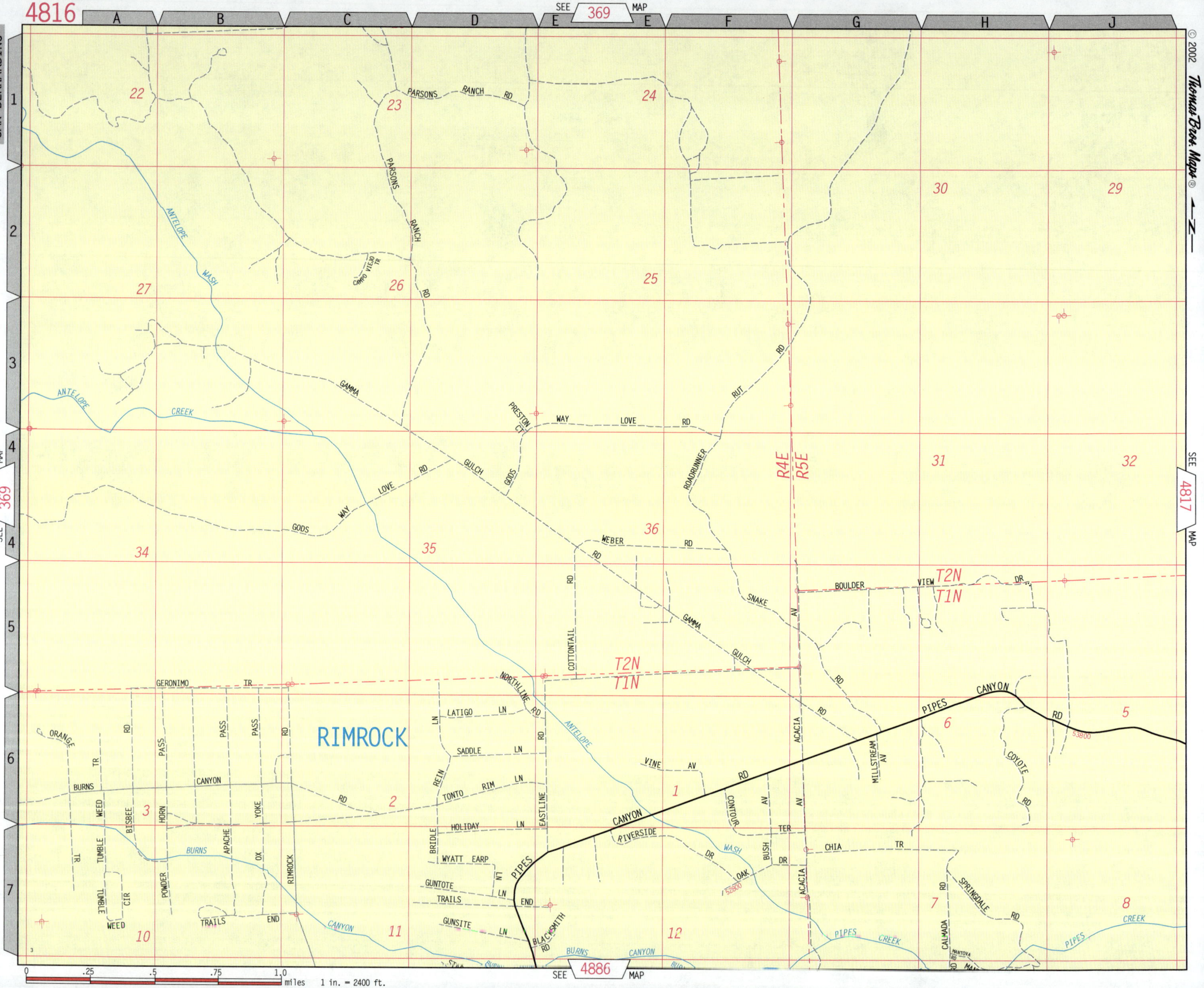

SEE 369 MAP
SAN BERNARDINO
A B C D E F G H J
1 2 3 4 5 6 7
PARSONS RANCH RD
PARSONS RANCH RD
CAMPO VIEJO TR
ANTELOPE WASH
ANTELOPE CREEK
GAMMA GULCH RD
GODS WAY LOVE RD
PRESTON CT
WAY LOVE RD
RUT RD
ROADRUNNER
WEBER RD
COTTONTAIL RD
SNAKE AV
BOULDER VIEW DR
R4E R5E
T2N T1N
GERONIMO TR
NORTHLINE RD
RIMROCK
ORANGE
BURNS TR
BURNS CANYON RD
WEED
TUMBLE TR
TUMBLE
CIR
WEED
BISBEE RD
HORN PASS
POWDER
APACHE PASS
YOKE PASS
OX
RIMROCK RD
TRAILS END
LATIGO LN
SADDLE LN
REIN LN
TONTO RIM LN
HOLIDAY LN
BRIDLE
WYATT EARP LN
GUNTOTE LN
TRAILS END
GUNSITE LN
BLACKSMITH RD
EASTLINE RD
PIPES CANYON RD
VINE AV
CONTOUR AV
RIVERSIDE DR
OAK
BUSH DR
TER
ACACIA AV
CHIA TR
MILLSTREAM AV
COYOTE RD
SPRINGDALE RD
CALMADA RD
MANTOVA RD
BURNS CANYON
PIPES CREEK
53800
52800
22 23 24 27 26 25 30 29 31 32 34 35 36 3 2 1 6 5 10 11 12 7 8
SEE 4817 MAP
SEE 369 MAP
SEE 4886 MAP
0 .25 .5 .75 1.0 miles 1 in. = 2400 ft.
Thomas Bros. Maps®
© 2002
N

SEE 4747 MAP

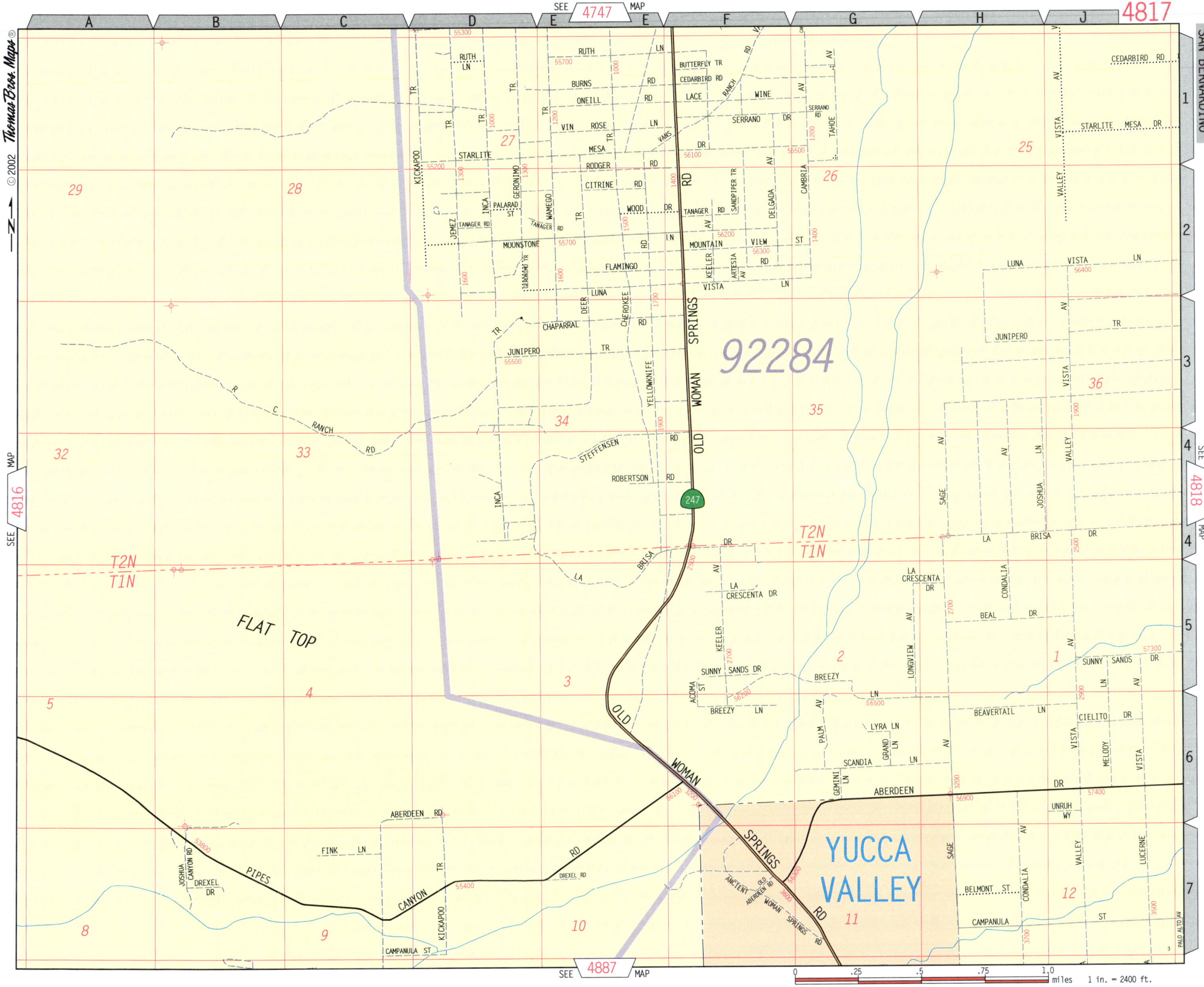

SEE 4816 MAP

SEE 4818 MAP

SEE 4887 MAP

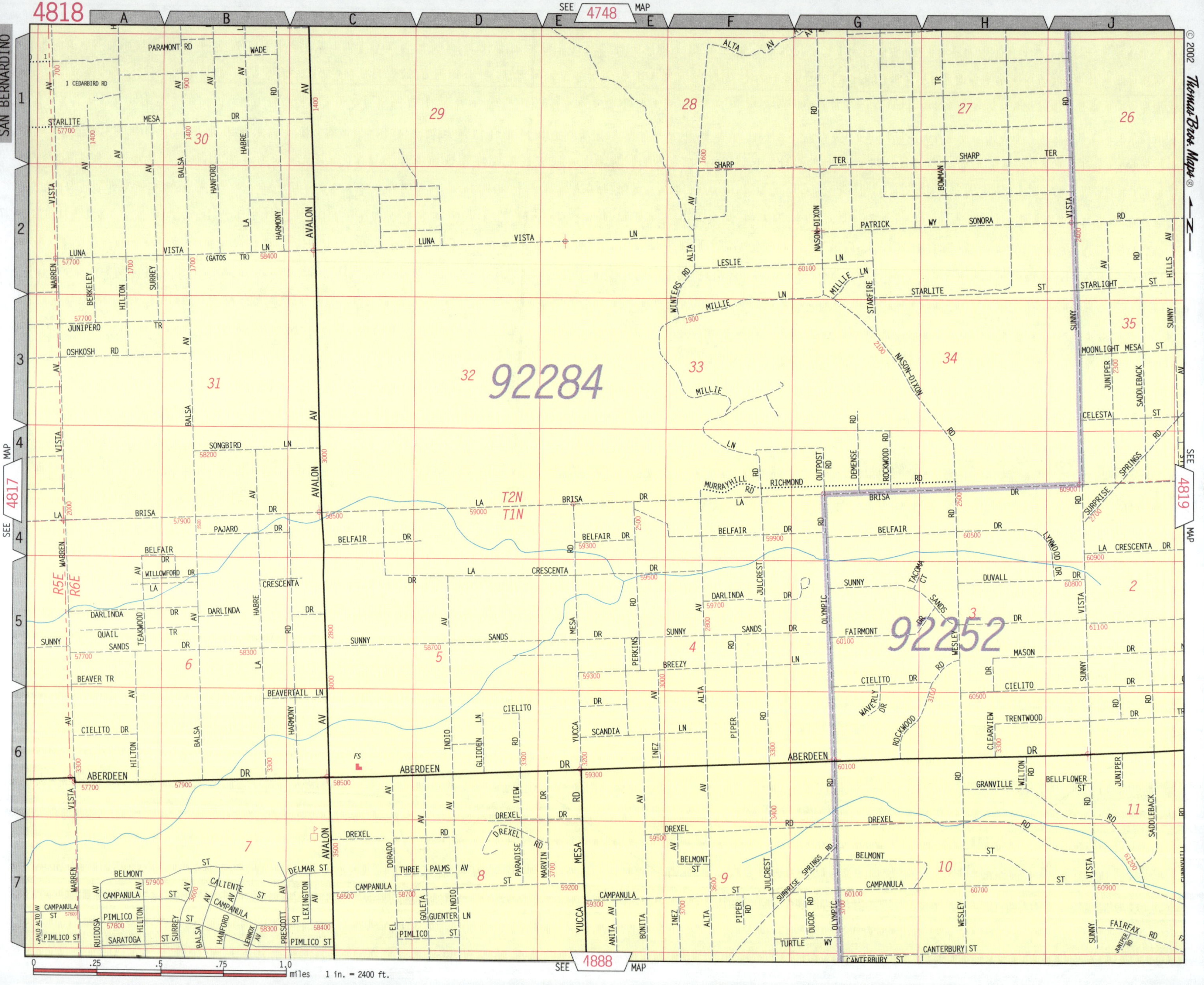
SEE 4748 MAP
SEE 1888 MAP
SEE 4817 MAP
SEE 4819 MAP
SAN BERNARDINO
© 2002 Thomas Bros. Maps®
92284
92252
T2N
T1N
R5E
R6E
PARAMONT RD
WADE
CEDARBIRD RD
STARLITE
MESA
DR
ALTA AV
SHARP
TER
PATRICK
WY
SONORA
RD
VISTA
LUNA
LN
(GATOS TR)
LESLIE
MILLIE
STARLITE
ST
STARLIGHT
WINTERS RD
NASON-DIXON
STARFIRE
BOWMAN
WARREN
BERKELEY
HILTON
SURREY
BALSA
HANFORD
HABRE
HARMONY
AVALON
JUNIPERO
OSHKOSH RD
SONGBIRD LN
BRISA
PAJARO
BELFAIR
WILLOWFORD
CRESCENTA
DARLINDA
QUAIL
SANDS
SUNNY
TEAKWOOD
BEAVER TR
BEAVERTAIL LN
CIELITO
ABERDEEN DR
MURRAYHILL RD
RICHMOND
OUTPOST RD
DEMENSE
ROCKWOOD RD
MOONLIGHT MESA
JUNIPER
SADDLEBACK
CELESTA
SPRINGS
SURPRISE
HILLS
OLYMPIC
JULCREST
PERKINS
BREEZY
PIPER
INEZ
YUCCA
SCANDIA
GLIDDEN LN
INDIO
TACOMA CT
DUVALL
LYNWOOD DR
FAIRMONT
MASON
WESLEY
WAVERLY DR
CLEARVIEW
TRENTWOOD
GRANVILLE
WILTON RD
BELLFLOWER ST
DREXEL
BELMONT
CAMPANULA
PIMLICO ST
SARATOGA
RUIDOSA
PALO ALTO AV
CALIENTE
LENNOX
PRESCOTT
LEXINGTON
DELMAR ST
DORADO
THREE PALMS AV
GOLETA
GUENTER LN
PARADISE ST
MARVIN
VIEW
ANITA AV
BONITA
DUCOR RD
TURTLE WY
CANTERBURY ST
FAIRFAX RD
FS
1 in. = 2400 ft.
0 .25 .5 .75 1.0 miles

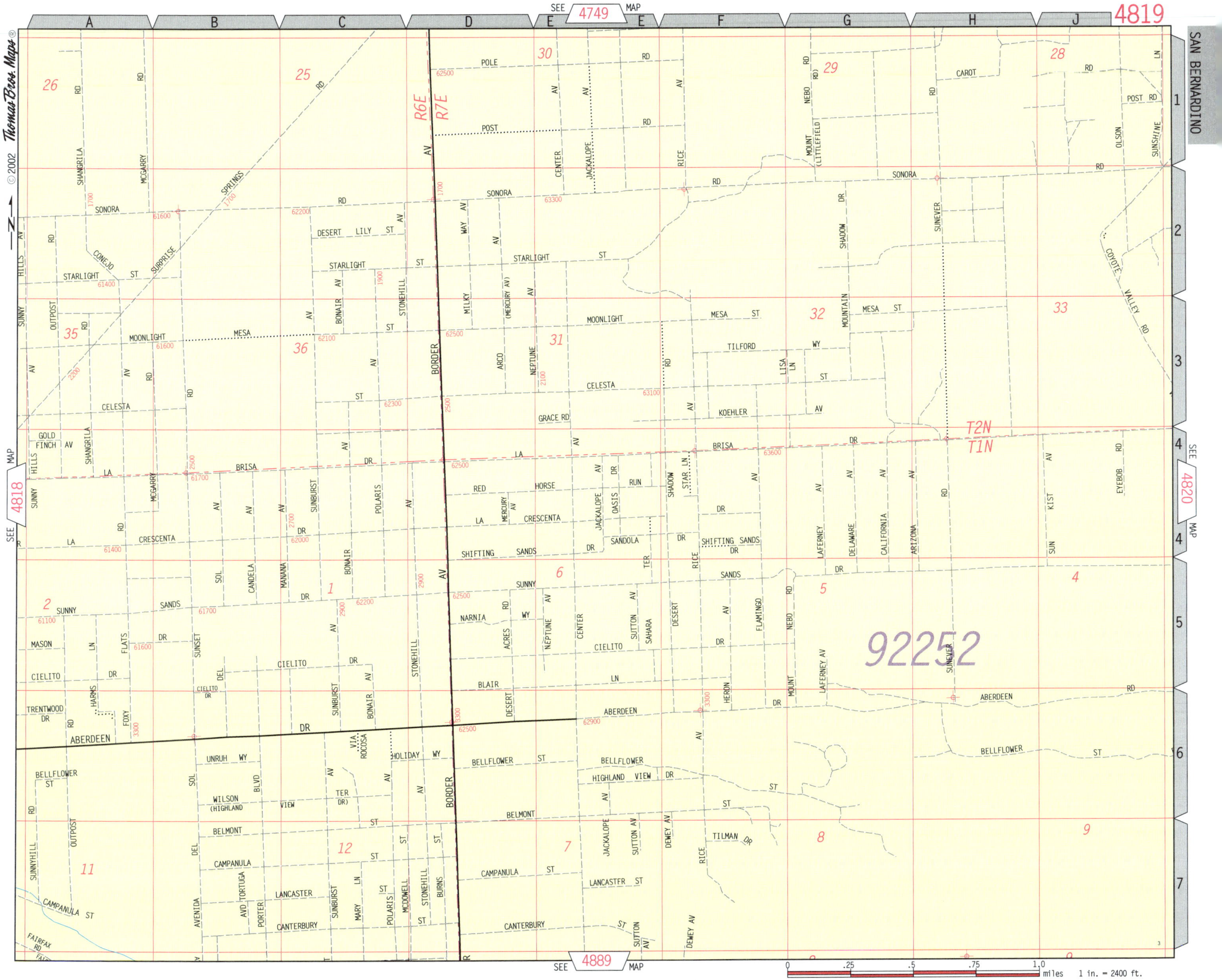
SEE 4749 MAP
SEE 4889 MAP
SEE 4818 MAP
SEE 4820 MAP
SAN BERNARDINO
Thomas Bros. Maps ©2002
R6E
R7E
T2N
T1N
92252
POLE RD
POST RD
SONORA RD
SPRINGS RD
SHANGRILA RD
MCGARRY RD
CONEJO
SURPRISE
STARLIGHT ST
DESERT LILY ST
BONAIR AV
STONEHILL AV
MILKY WAY AV
(MERCURY AV)
MOONLIGHT
MESA ST
CELESTA
GRACE RD
BRISA DR
ARCO
NEPTUNE AV
CENTER AV
JACKALOPE AV
RICE AV
MOUNT NEBO RD
MOUNT (LITTLEFIELD RD)
TILFORD WY
LISA LN
KOEHLER AV
SHADOW DR
MOUNTAIN AV
SUNEVER RD
CAROT RD
OLSON
SUNSHINE LN
COYOTE VALLEY RD
GOLD FINCH AV
SUNNY HILLS AV
OUTPOST RD
BORDER AV
RED HORSE RUN
OASIS DR
STAR LN
CRESCENTA LA
SHIFTING SANDS DR
SANDOLA
TER
SOL
CANDELA AV
MANANA AV
SUNBURST AV
POLARIS AV
LAFERNEY AV
DELAWARE AV
CALIFORNIA AV
ARIZONA AV
KIST AV
SUN
EYEBOB RD
SUNNY SANDS DR
NARNIA
ACRES RD
SUTTON AV
SAHARA
DESERT
FLAMINGO
MASON
FLATS DR
CIELITO DR
SUNSET
DEL
BLAIR LN
TRENTWOOD DR
HARMS
FOXY
ABERDEEN DR
ABERDEEN RD
HERON
UNRUH WY
HOLIDAY WY
VIA ROCOSA
BELLFLOWER ST
HIGHLAND VIEW DR
WILSON (HIGHLAND VIEW TER DR)
BLVD
BELMONT ST
CAMPANULA ST
TORTUGA AVD
LANCASTER ST
CANTERBURY ST
AVENIDA
PORTER
MARY LN
MCDOWELL
BURNS ST
DEWEY AV
TILMAN DR
SUNNYHILL
FAIRFAX RD
1 in. = 2400 ft.

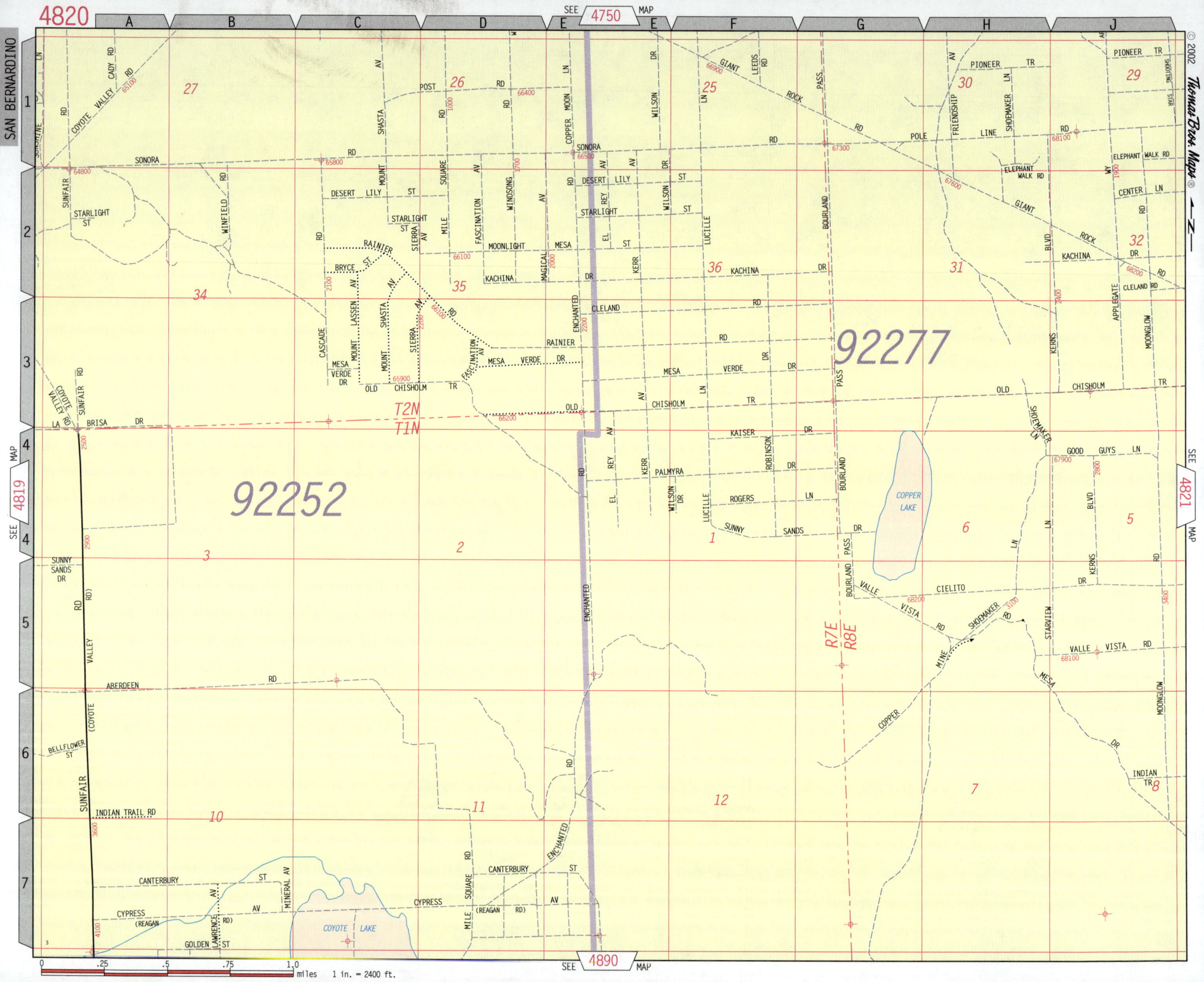

SEE 4750 MAP
SEE 4819 MAP
SEE 4821 MAP
SEE 4890 MAP
SAN BERNARDINO
A B C D E F G H J
1 2 3 4 5 6 7
92252
92277
T2N
T1N
R7E
R8E
COPPER LAKE
COYOTE LAKE
SONORA RD
GIANT ROCK RD
POLE LINE RD
COYOTE VALLEY RD
SUNFAIR RD
STARLIGHT ST
DESERT LILY ST
KACHINA DR
CLELAND RD
RAINIER RD
MESA VERDE DR
OLD CHISHOLM TR
BRISA DR
KAISER DR
PALMYRA DR
ROGERS LN
SUNNY SANDS DR
VALLE CIELITO DR
VALLE VISTA RD
SHOEMAKER MINE RD
COPPER MESA DR
ABERDEEN RD
BELLFLOWER ST
INDIAN TRAIL RD
INDIAN TR
CANTERBURY ST
CYPRESS AV
(REAGAN RD)
GOLDEN ST
ENCHANTED RD
BOURLAND PASS
PIONEER TR
GOOD GUYS LN
ELEPHANT WALK RD
CENTER LN
MOONGLOW RD
KERNS BLVD
STARVIEW
0 .25 .5 .75 1.0 miles 1 in. = 2400 ft.
© 2002 Thomas Bros. Maps®

SEE 4751 MAP

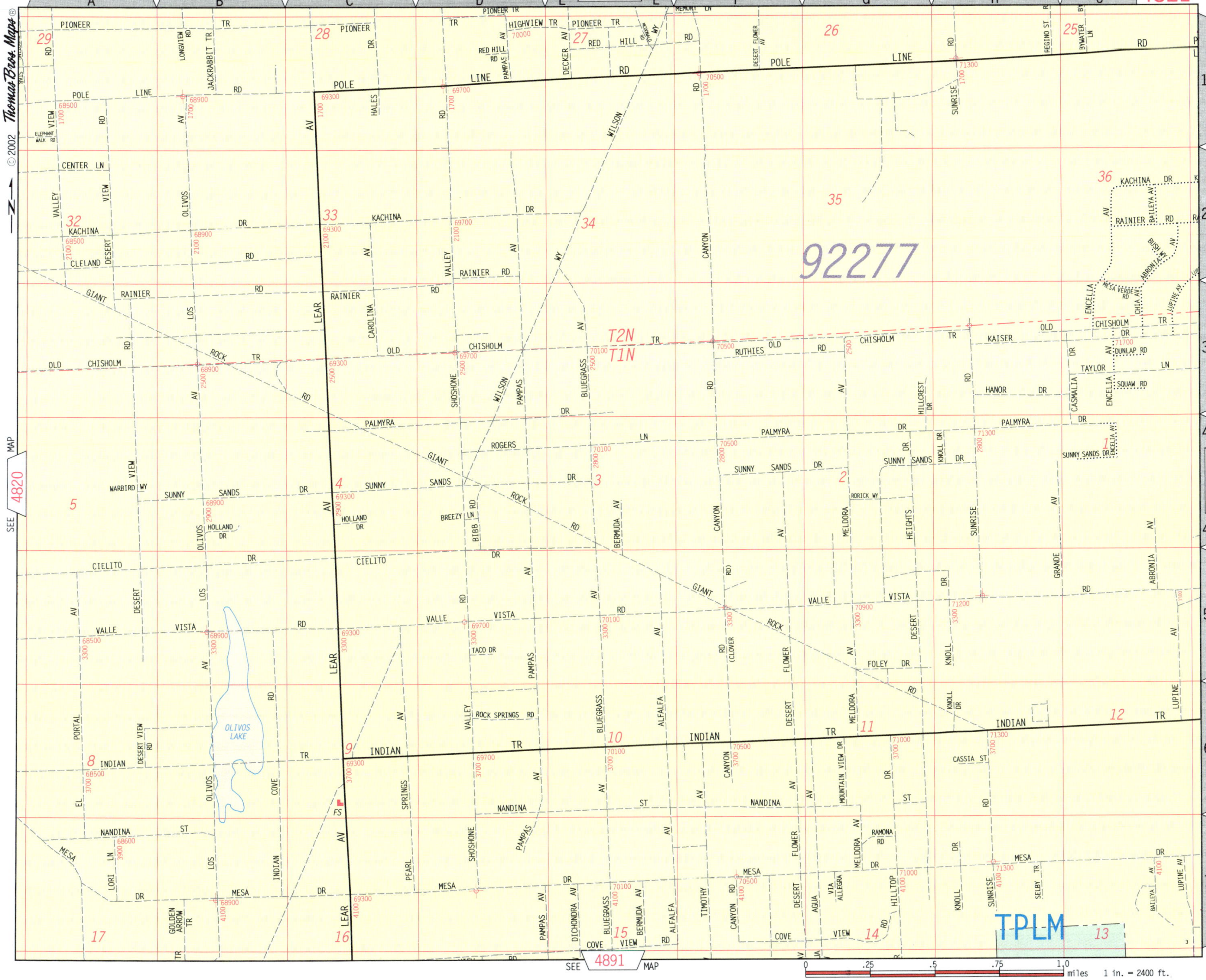

SEE 4820 MAP
SEE 4822 MAP
SEE 4891 MAP

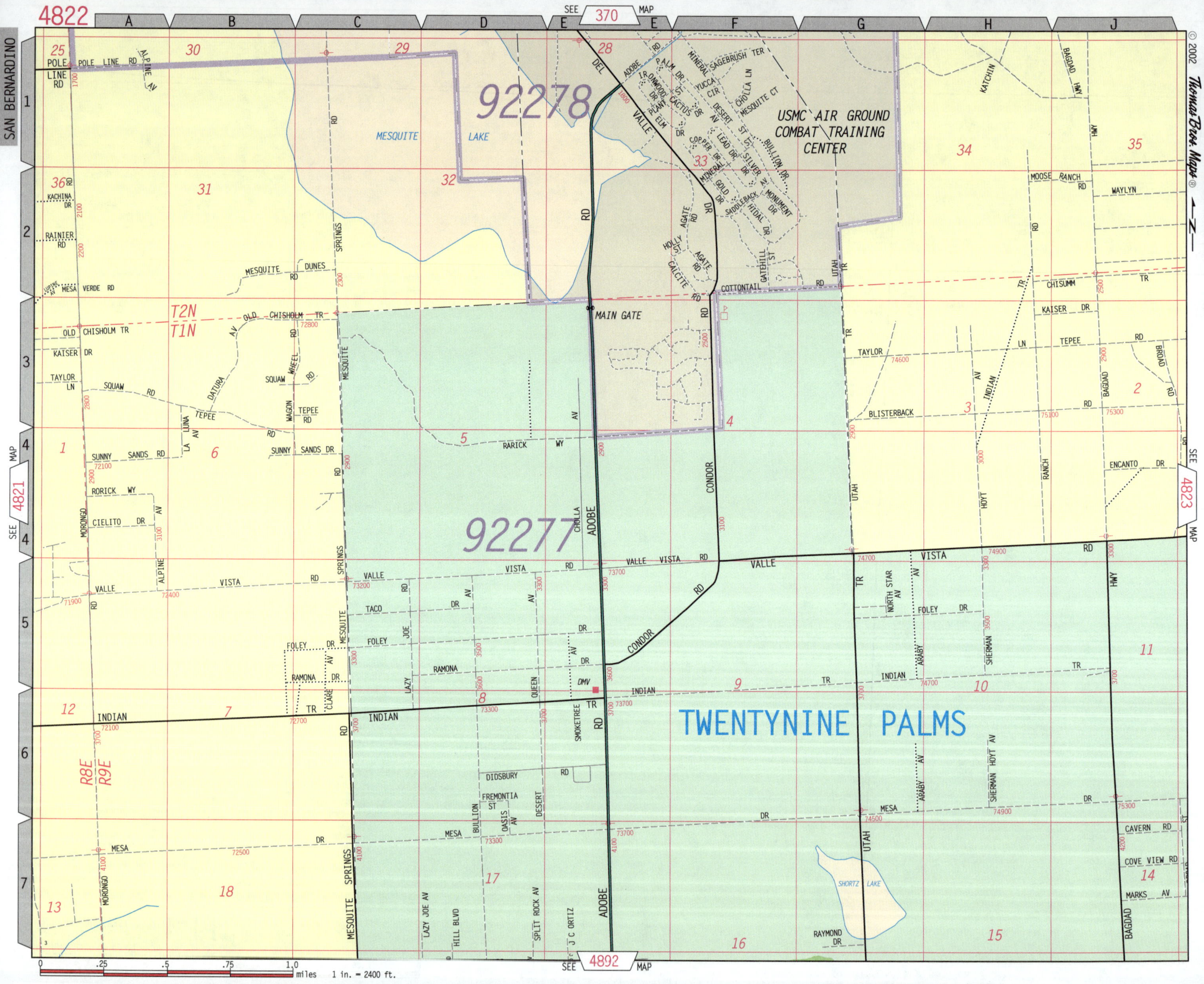
SEE 370 MAP
SEE 4892 MAP
SEE MAP 4821
SEE MAP 4823
SAN BERNARDINO
A
B
C
D
E
F
G
H
J
1
2
3
4
5
6
7
92278
92277
USMC AIR GROUND COMBAT TRAINING CENTER
MAIN GATE
TWENTYNINE PALMS
MESQUITE LAKE
SHORTZ LAKE
T2N
T1N
R8E
R9E
DMV
POLE LINE RD
ALPINE AV
DEL VALLE RD
ADOBE RD
MESQUITE SPRINGS RD
MESQUITE DUNES RD
MESA VERDE RD
LUPINE AV
KACHINA DR
RAINIER RD
OLD CHISHOLM TR
KAISER DR
TAYLOR LN
SQUAW RD
DATURA AV
WAGON WHEEL RD
SQUAW TEPEE RD
LA LUNA AV
SUNNY SANDS RD
SUNNY SANDS DR
RORICK WY
CIELITO DR
RARICK WY
CHOLLA AV
MORONGO RD
VALLE VISTA RD
TACO DR
FOLEY DR
RAMONA DR
CLARE AV
LAZY JOE AV
QUEEN AV
SMOKETREE AV
INDIAN TR
DIDSBURY RD
FREMONTIA ST
OASIS AV
BULLION AV
DESERT AV
MESA DR
HILL BLVD
SPLIT ROCK AV
J C ORTIZ
CONDOR RD
COTTONTAIL RD
GATEHILL ST
HOLLY ST
AGATE RD
CALCITE RD
IRONWOOD DR
PLANT DR
ELM DR
PALM DR
CACTUS DR
YUCCA CIR
MINERAL DR
SAGEBRUSH TER
CHOLLA LN
MESQUITE CT
DESERT AV
COPPER DR
LEAD DR
SILVER ST
BULLION DR
GOLD DR
SADDLEBACK AV
MONUMENT
HIDAL DR
UTAH TR
TAYLOR LN
BLISTERBACK RD
INDIAN AV
HOYT AV
RANCH RD
MOOSE RANCH RD
WAYLYN
KATCHIN
BAGDAD HWY
CHISUMM TR
KAISER DR
TEPEE RD
BROAD RD
ENCANTO DR
NORTH STAR AV
FOLEY DR
ARABY AV
SHERMAN AV
SHERMAN HOYT AV
MESA DR
CAVERN RD
COVE VIEW RD
MARKS AV
RAYMOND DR
0
.25
.5
.75
1.0
miles
1 in. = 2400 ft.
© 2002 Thomas Bros. Maps®

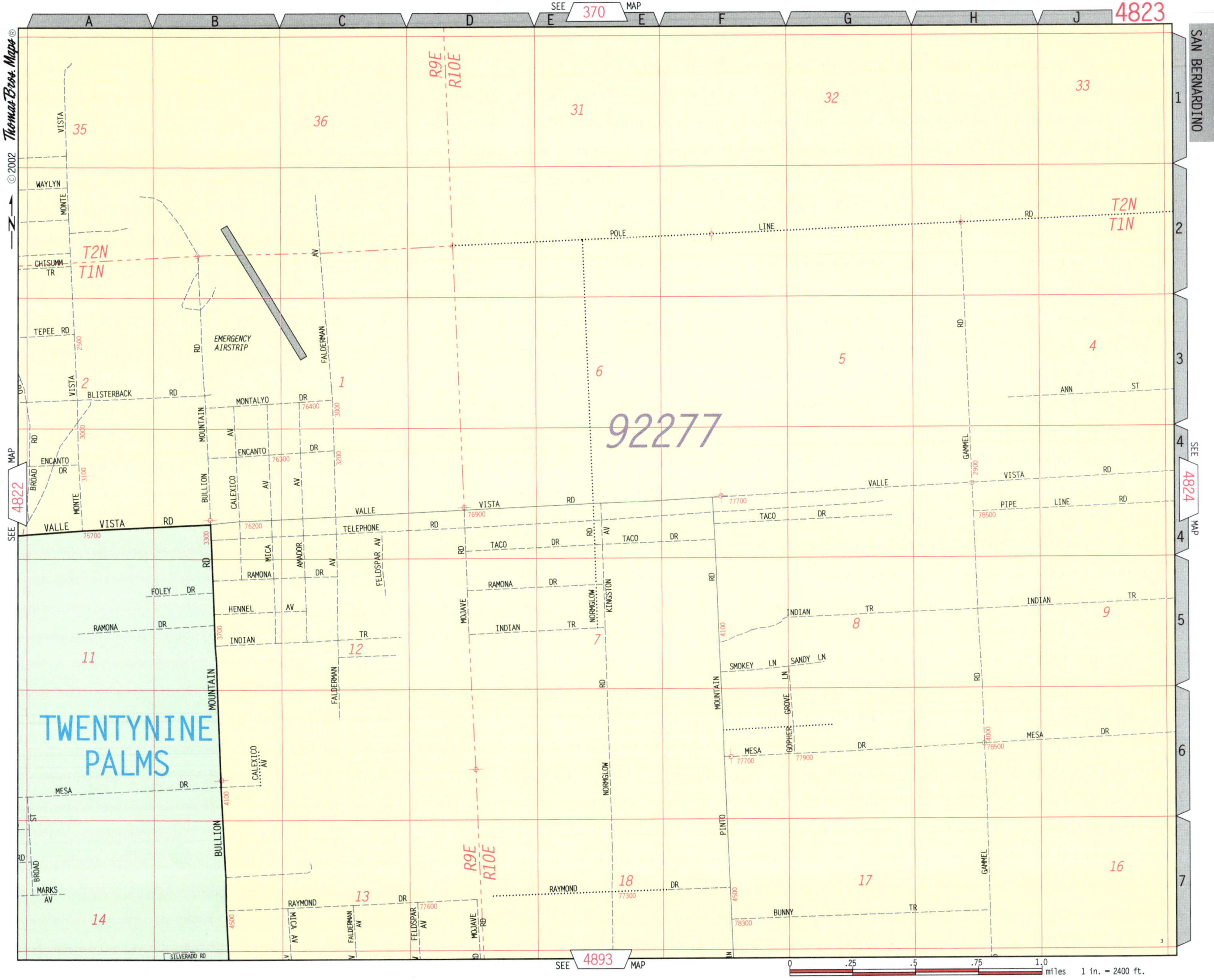
SEE 370 MAP
SEE 4824 MAP
SEE 4893 MAP
SEE 4822 MAP
SAN BERNARDINO
Thomas Bros. Maps
© 2002
TWENTYNINE PALMS
92277
EMERGENCY AIRSTRIP
R9E R10E
T2N T1N
VALLE VISTA RD
POLE LINE RD
TELEPHONE RD
BLISTERBACK RD
TEPEE RD
CHISUMM TR
WAYLYN
MONTALYO DR
ENCANTO DR
TACO DR
RAMONA DR
FOLEY DR
HENNEL AV
INDIAN TR
MESA DR
RAYMOND DR
BUNNY TR
SMOKEY LN
SANDY LN
ANN ST
PIPE LINE RD
MARKS AV
SILVERADO RD
VISTA
MONTE
BROAD RD
MOUNTAIN RD
BULLION RD
CALEXICO AV
MICA AV
AMADOR AV
FALDERMAN AV
FELDSPAR AV
MOJAVE RD
NORMGLOW RD
KINGSTON AV
PINTO MOUNTAIN RD
GROVE LN
GOPHER
GAMMEL RD
0 .25 .5 .75 1.0 miles
1 in. = 2400 ft.

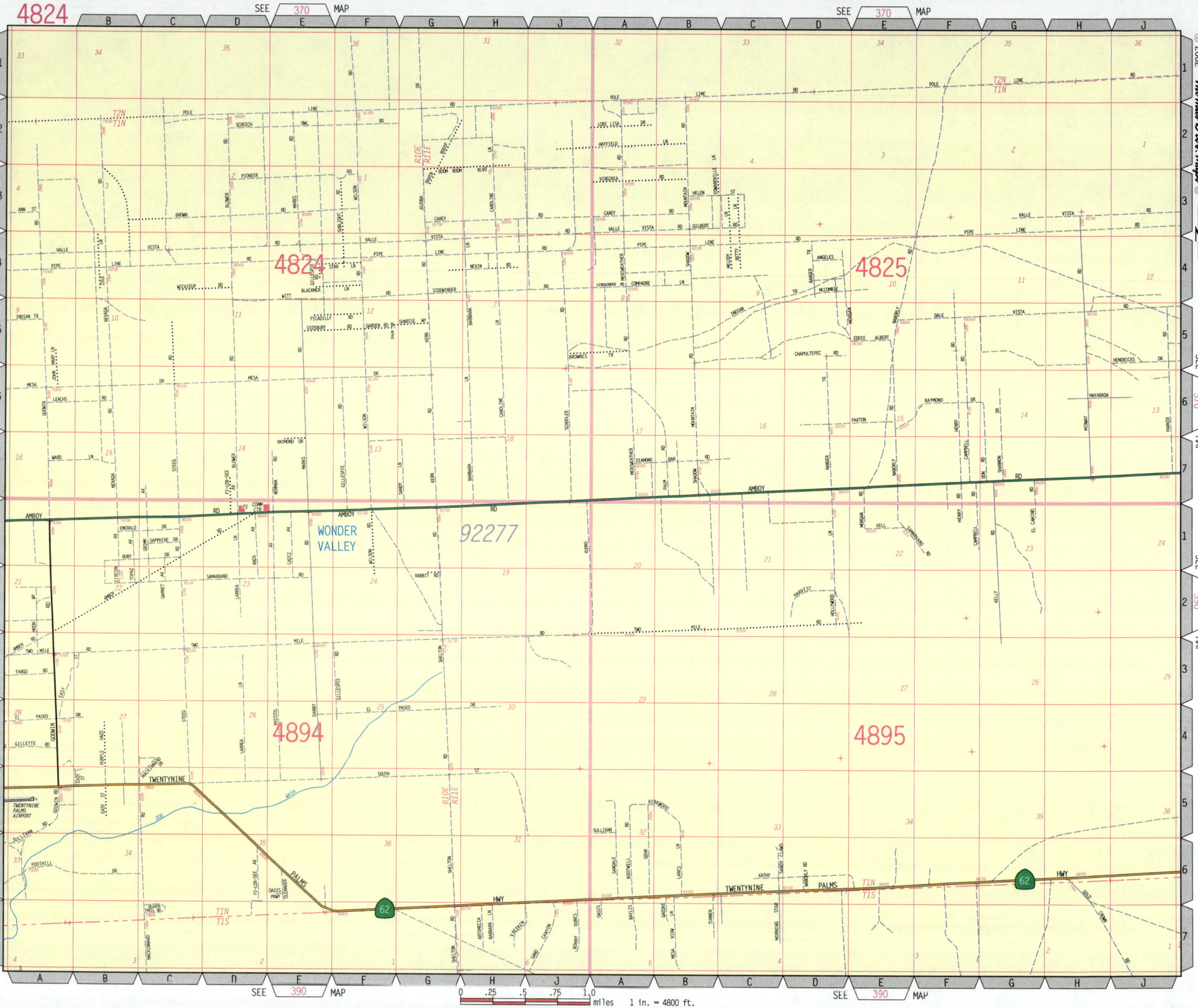
SEE 370 MAP
SEE 370 MAP
SAN BERNARDINO
Thomas Bros Maps
© 2002
4824
4825
4894
4895
WONDER VALLEY
92277
AMBOY RD
TWENTYNINE PALMS HWY
TWENTYNINE PALMS AIRPORT
POLE LINE RD
T2N
T1N
T1S
R10E
R11E
SEE 4823 MAP
SEE 4893 MAP
SEE 370 MAP
SEE 390 MAP
SEE 390 MAP
SEE 390 MAP
62
miles 1 in. = 4800 ft.

SEE 4773 MAP

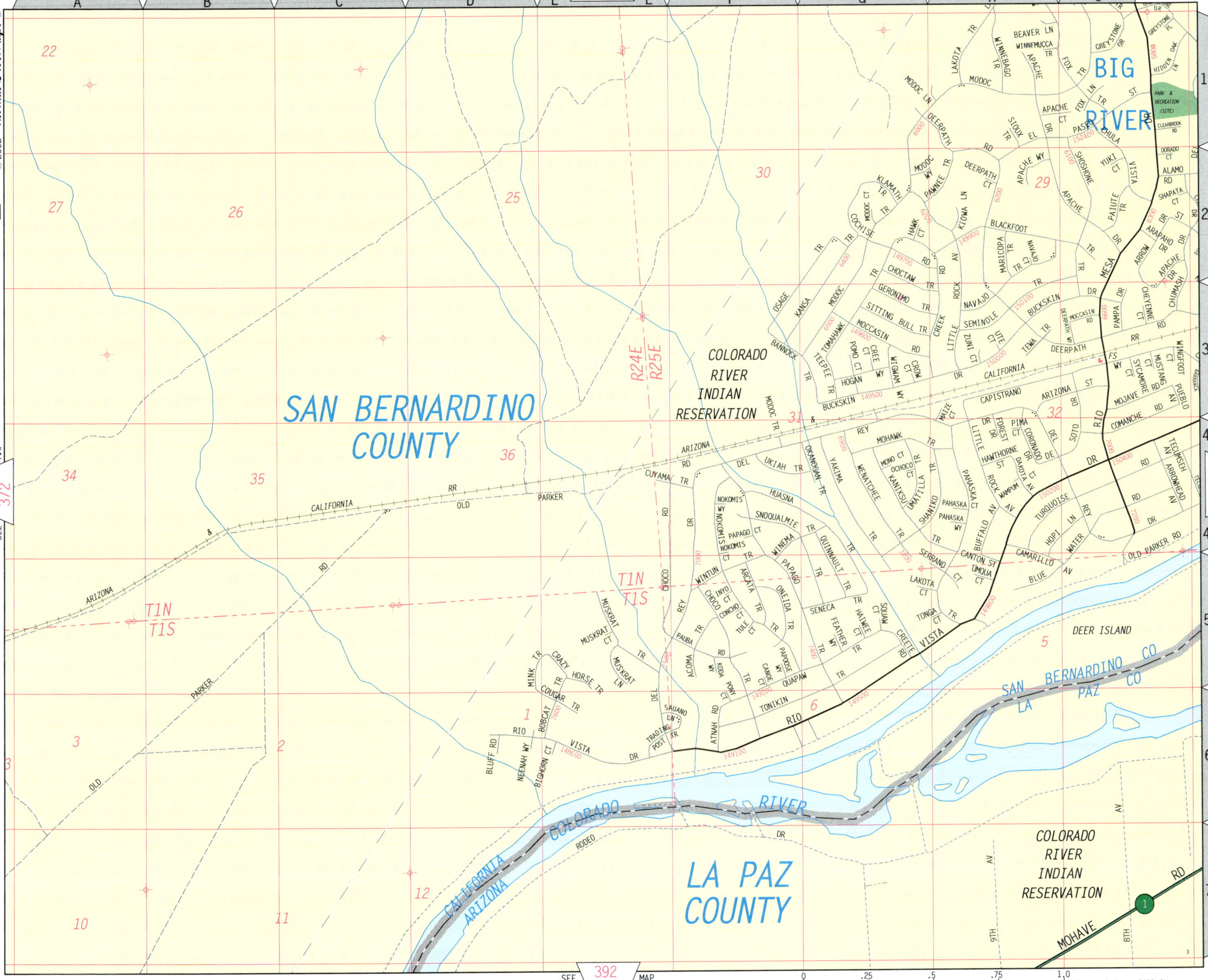

SEE 4844 MAP
SEE 372 MAP
SEE 392 MAP

SEE 4774 MAP

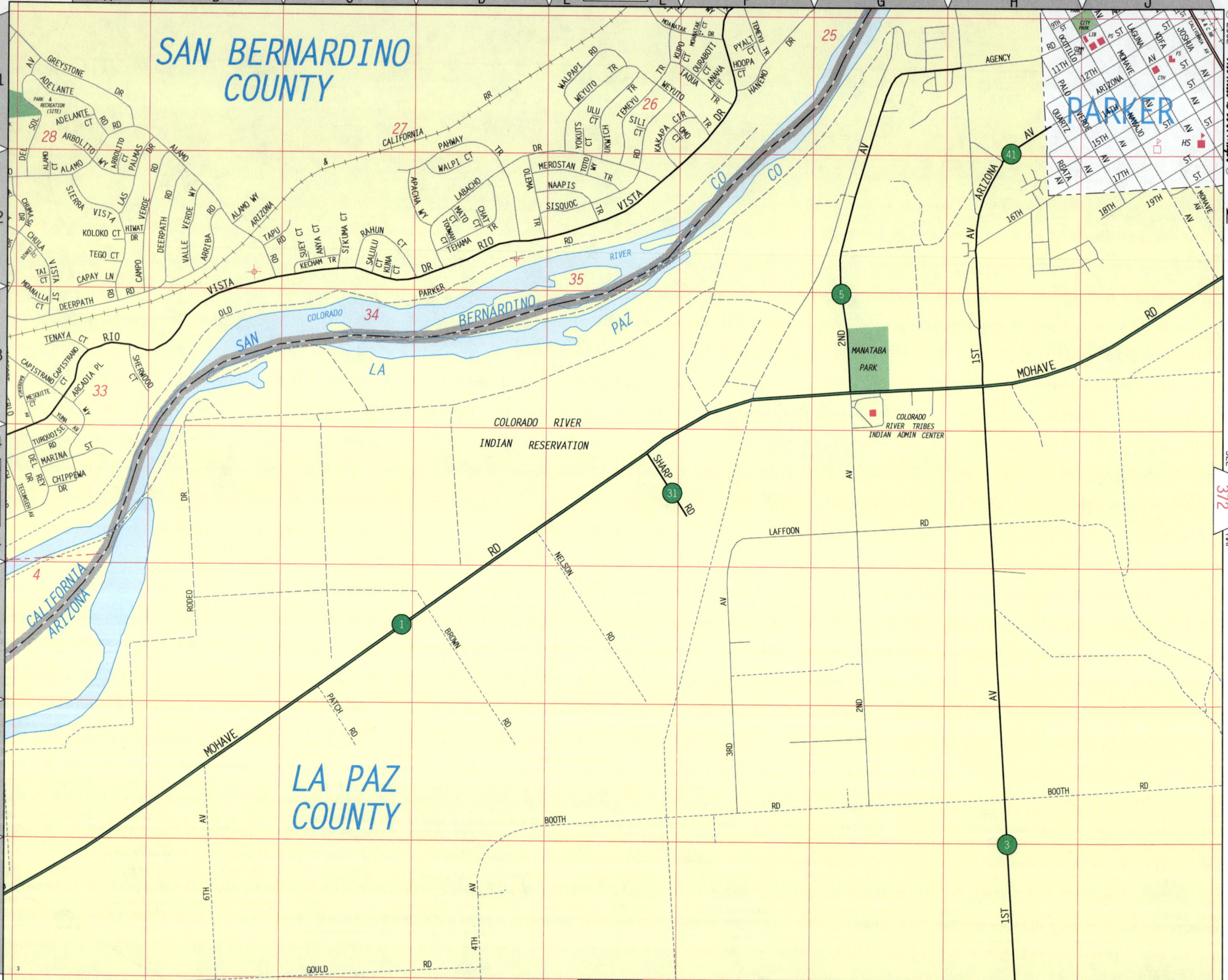

SEE 392 MAP

0 .25 .5 .75 1.0 miles 1 in. = 2400 ft.

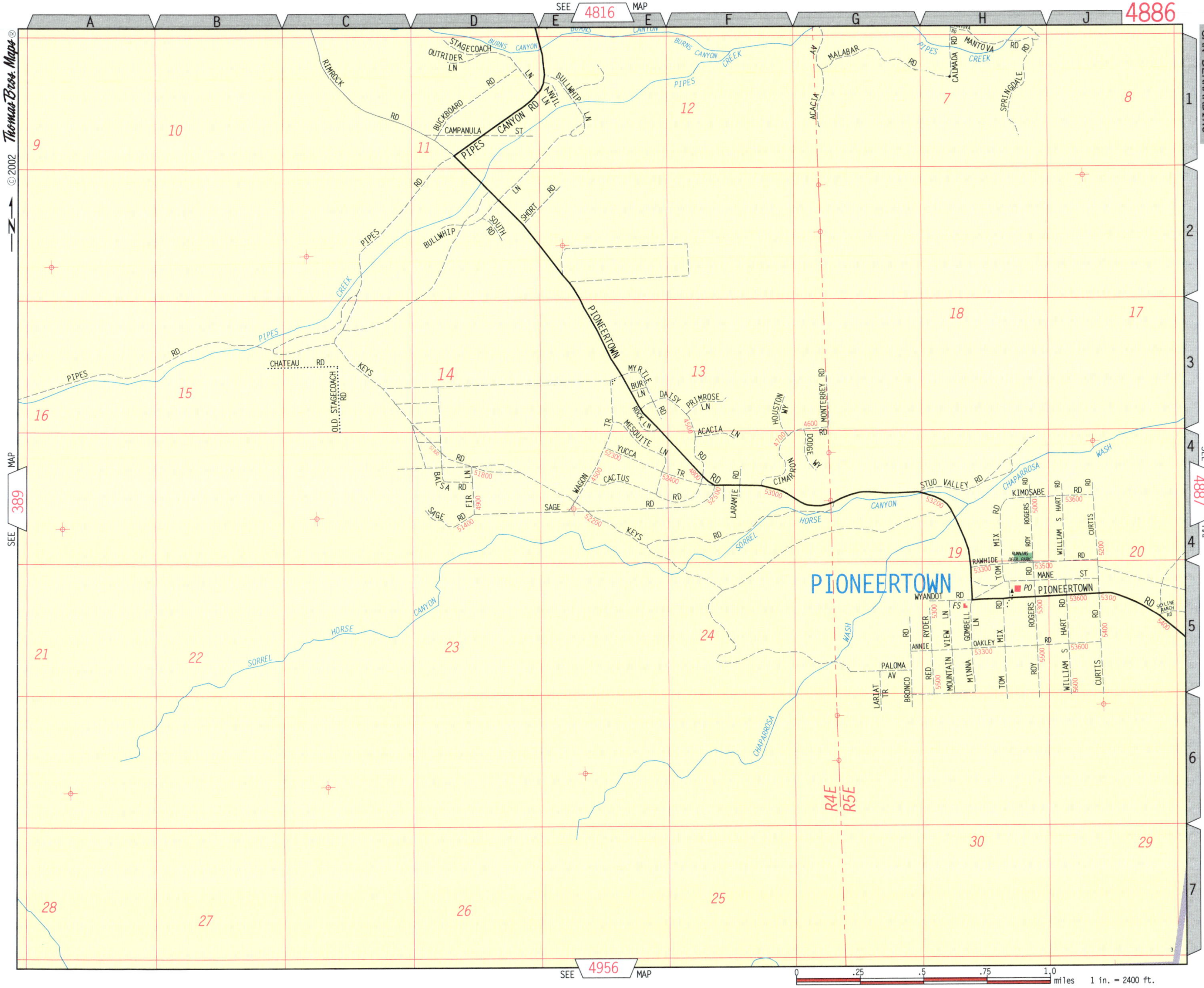

SEE 4816 MAP
SEE 4956 MAP
SEE 389 MAP
SEE 4887 MAP
SAN BERNARDINO
A
B
C
D
E
F
G
H
J
1
2
3
4
5
6
7
Thomas Bros. Maps
© 2002
PIONEERTOWN
PIONEERTOWN RD
PIPES CANYON RD
PIPES CREEK
BURNS CANYON
STAGECOACH
OUTRIDER LN
RIMROCK RD
BUCKBOARD RD
CAMPANULA ST
ANVIL LN
BULLWHIP LN
SHORT RD
SOUTH RD
BULLWHIP
PIPES RD
CHATEAU RD
OLD STAGECOACH RD
KEYS RD
MALABAR RD
ACACIA AV
CALMADA RD
MANTOVA RD
SPRINGDALE
MYRTLE
BUR LN
ROCK LN
DAISY RD
PRIMROSE LN
ACACIA LN
MESQUITE LN
YUCCA TR
CACTUS RD
WAGON
SAGE RD
BALSA RD
FIR LN
LARAMIE RD
HOUSTON WY
MONTERREY RD
39000 WY
CIMARRON
STUD VALLEY RD
CANYON
HORSE
SORREL
CHAPARROSA WASH
KIMOSABE
MIX RD
ROGERS RD
ROY
WILLIAM S HART RD
CURTIS RD
RAWHIDE
RUNNING DEER PARK
TOM
MANE ST
WYANDOT RD
PO
FS
RYDER RD
GOMBELL LN
VIEW LN
OAKLEY
ANNIE
PALOMA AV
LARIAT TR
BRONCO
RED
MOUNTAIN
MINNA
SKYLINE RANCH RD
R4E R5E
9
10
11
12
7
8
18
17
16
15
14
13
19
20
21
22
23
24
28
27
26
25
30
29
0 .25 .5 .75 1.0 miles
1 in. = 2400 ft.

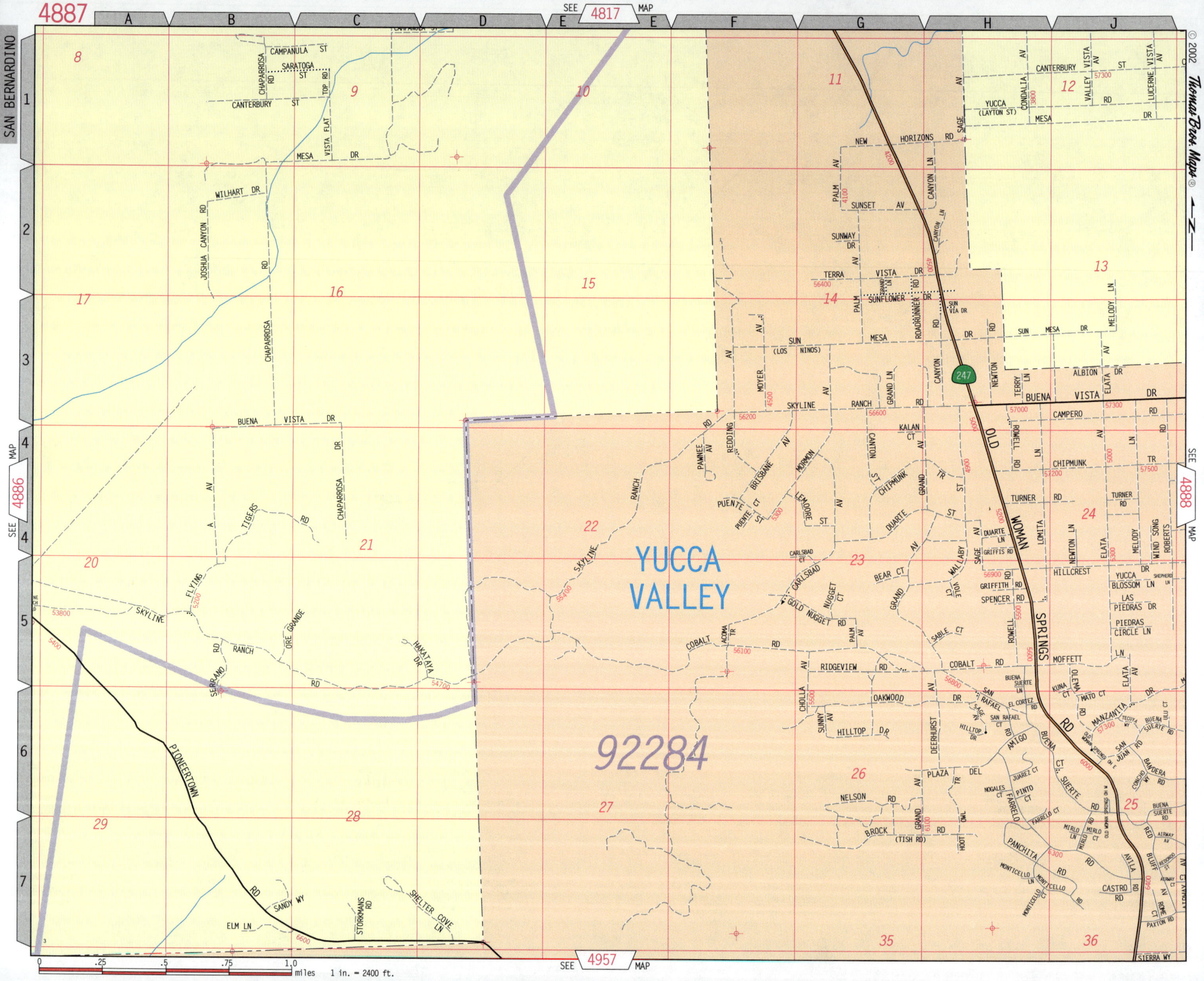
SAN BERNARDINO
SEE 4817 MAP
SEE 4886 MAP
SEE 4888 MAP
SEE 4957 MAP
YUCCA VALLEY
92284
247
CAMPANULA ST
SARATOGA ST
CHAPARROSA RD
TOP RD
CANTERBURY ST
VISTA FLAT
MESA DR
WILHART DR
JOSHUA CANYON RD
CHAPARROSA
BUENA VISTA DR
A AV
TIGERS RD
FLYING
SKYLINE
RANCH RD
ORE GRANDE
SERRANO RD
HAKATAYA DR
PIONEERTOWN RD
SANDY WY
ELM LN
STORKMANS RD
SHELTER COVE LN
NEW HORIZONS RD
SAGE
PALM AV
SUNSET AV
CANYON LN
SUNWAY DR
TERRA VISTA DR
GRAND LN
SUNFLOWER DR
ROADRUNNER RD
SUN VIA DR
SUN (LOS NINOS)
MESA DR
MOYER AV
SKYLINE RANCH RD
GRAND LN
CANYON RD
NEWTON
TERRY LN
ALBION DR
BUENA VISTA DR
ELATA AV
SUN MESA DR
MELODY LN
CANTERBURY ST
YUCCA (LAYTON ST)
CONDALIA
VALLEY VISTA AV
LUCERNE VISTA AV
MESA DR
PAWNEE AV
REDDING
BRISBANE AV
MORMON
PUENTE CT
LEMOORE ST
CANTON ST
KALAN CT
CHIPMUNK TR
DUARTE ST
OLD WOMAN SPRINGS RD
ROWELL RD
CAMPERO RD
CHIPMUNK TR
TURNER RD
LOMITA
NEWTON LN
ELATA
MELODY
WIND SONG
ROBERTS
HILLCREST DR
YUCCA BLOSSOM LN
SHEPHERD LN
LAS PIEDRAS DR
PIEDRAS CIRCLE LN
CARLSBAD CT
CARLSBAD
BEAR CT
WALLABY
VOLE CT
GRIFFITH RD
SPENCER RD
GOLD NUGGET RD
NUGGET CT
GRAND
SABLE CT
COBALT RD
ACOMA TR
PALM AV
RIDGEVIEW RD
MOFFETT LN
BUENA SUERTE LN
CHOLLA AV
OAKWOOD DR
SAN RAFAEL
EL CORTEZ RD
KUNA CT
OLEMA RD
MATO CT
MANZANITA DR
SUNNY AV
HILLTOP DR
DEERHURST
AMIGO
BUENA SUERTE RD
SAN JUAN RD
BANDERA RD
CONCHO WY
PLAZA DEL TR
NELSON RD
GRAND AV
BROCK RD
(TISH RD)
OWL
HOOT
JUAREZ CT
PINTO CT
NOGALES CT
FARRELO CT
MIRLO LN
MIRLO CT
PANCHITA RD
MONTICELLO LN
MONTICELLO CT
CASTRO RD
AVILA
RED BLUFF
AIRWAY AV
ROME AV
PAXTON RD
SIERRA WY
0 .25 .5 .75 1.0 miles 1 in. = 2400 ft.

SEE 4818 MAP

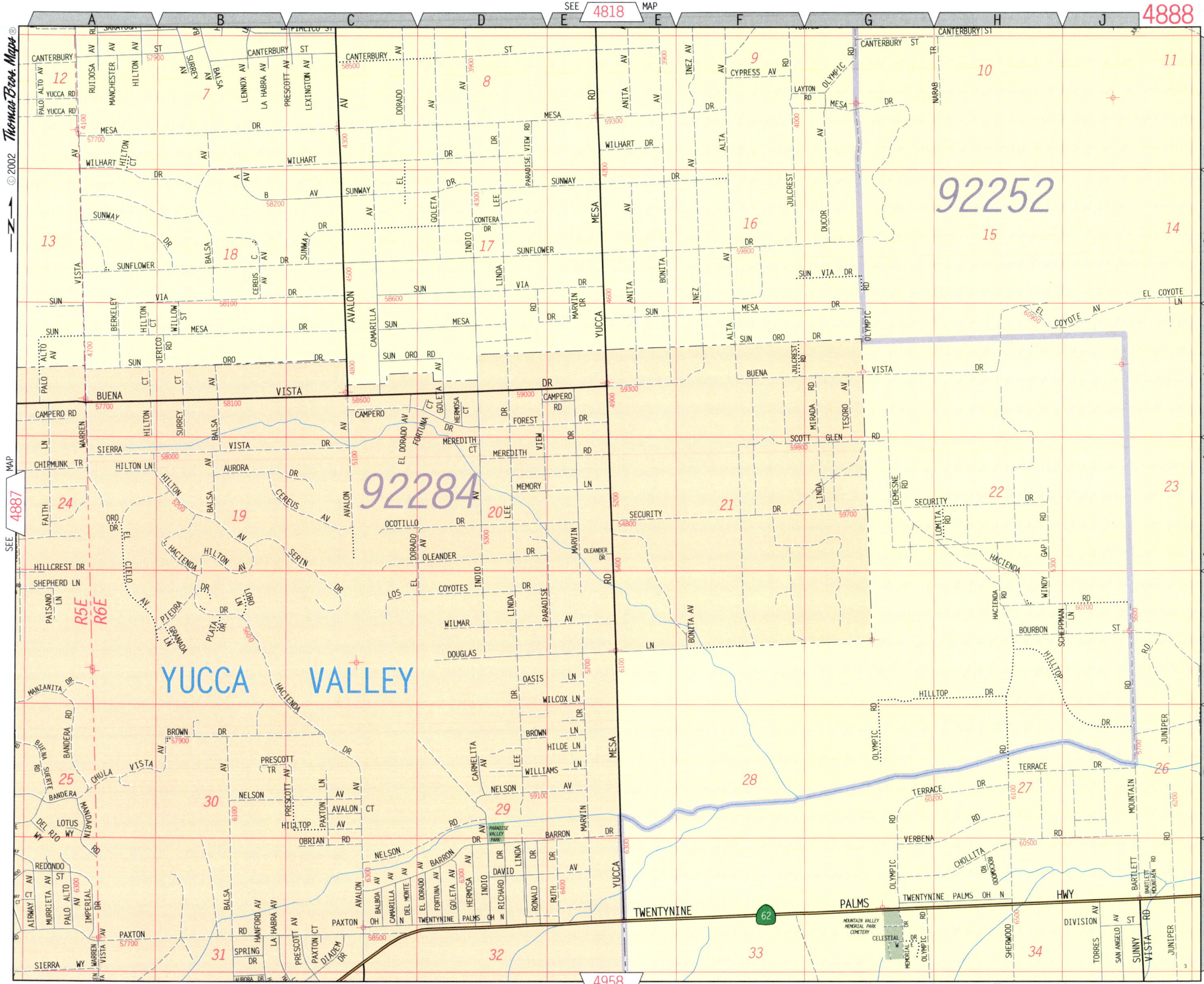

SEE 4887 MAP
SEE 4889 MAP
SEE 4958 MAP

0 .25 .5 .75 1.0 miles 1 in. = 2400 ft.

SEE 4819 MAP

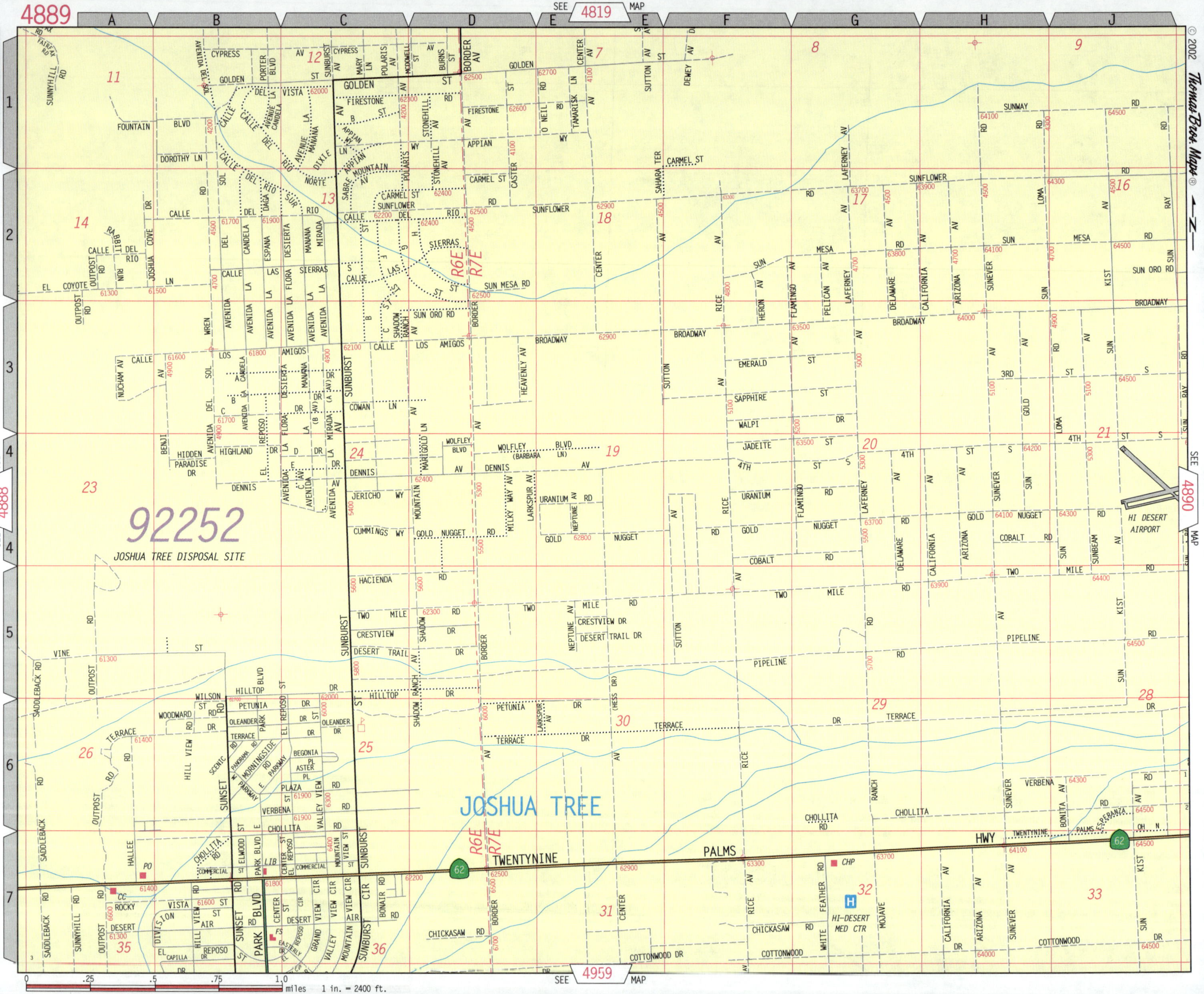

SEE 4888 MAP
SEE 4890 MAP
SEE 4959 MAP

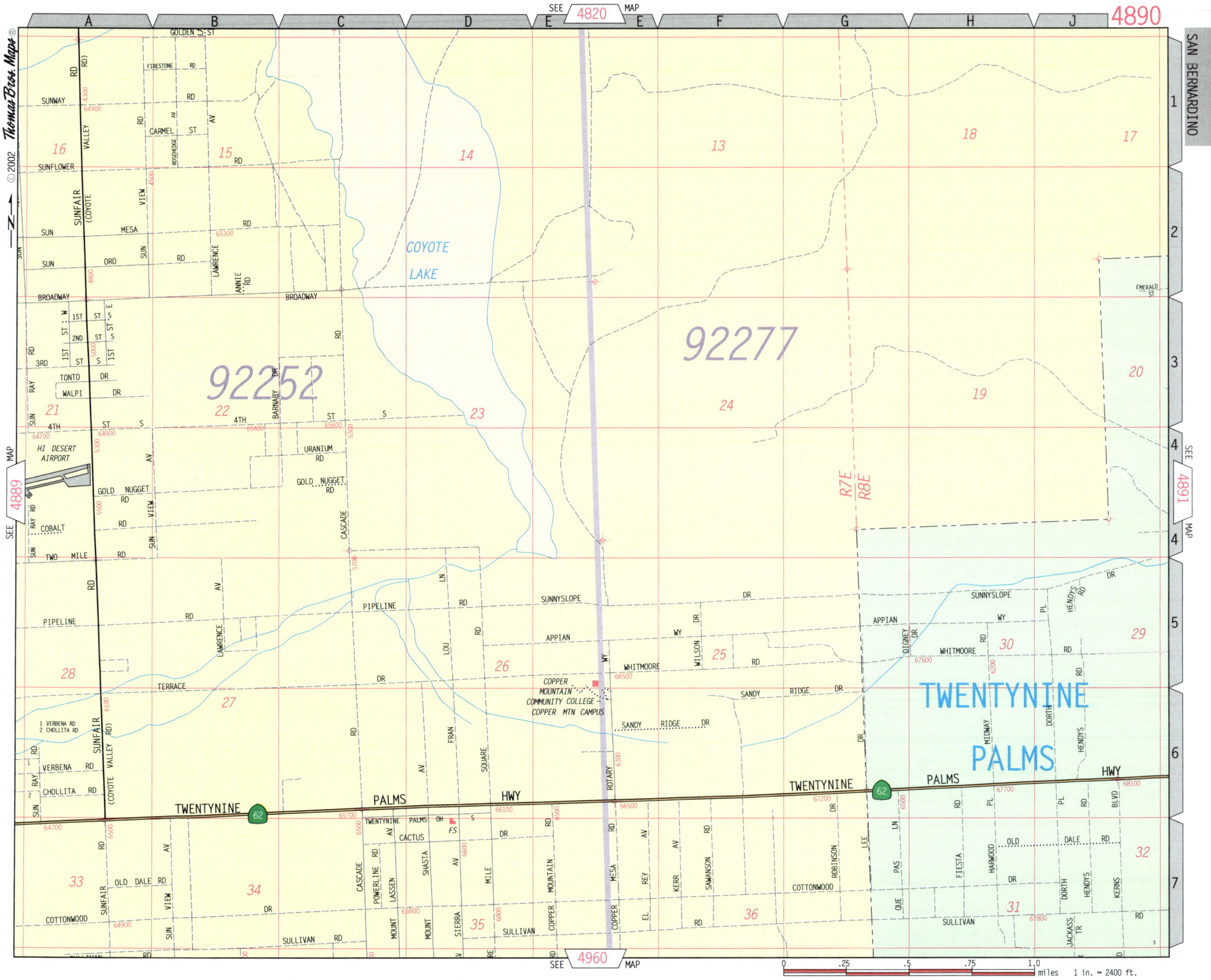

SEE 4820 MAP
SAN BERNARDINO
SEE 4891 MAP
SEE 4889 MAP
SEE 4960 MAP
92252
92277
TWENTYNINE PALMS
COYOTE LAKE
HI DESERT AIRPORT
COPPER MOUNTAIN COMMUNITY COLLEGE - COPPER MTN CAMPUS
TWENTYNINE PALMS HWY
62
R7E
R8E
GOLDEN SHORE ST
FIRESTONE RD
SUNWAY
SUNFLOWER
CARMEL ST
ROSEHEDGE RD
SUN MESA RD
SUN ORO RD
LAWRENCE
ANNIE RD
BROADWAY
1ST ST
2ND ST
3RD ST
TONTO DR
WALPI DR
4TH ST
BARNABY DR
URANIUM RD
GOLD NUGGET RD
COBALT
TWO MILE RD
PIPELINE RD
SUNFAIR (COYOTE VALLEY RD)
TERRACE DR
VERBENA RD
CHOLLITA RD
CASCADE RD
SUNNYSLOPE DR
APPIAN WY
WHITMOORE RD
SANDY RIDGE DR
WILSON DR
DIGNEY DR
HENDYS RD
MIDWAY
DORTH
ROTARY WY
LOU RD
FRAN SQUARE
OLD DALE RD
COTTONWOOD DR
SULLIVAN RD
POWERLINE RD
LASSEN
SHASTA AV
SIERRA
MOUNTAIN
COPPER MESA RD
EL REY AV
KERR AV
SAWANSON RD
ROBINSON DR
LEE
QUE PAS LN
FIESTA
HARWOOD PL
KERNS BLVD
JACKASS TR
CACTUS DR
FS
EMERALD ST
0 .25 .5 .75 1.0 miles 1 in. = 2400 ft.

SEE 4821 MAP

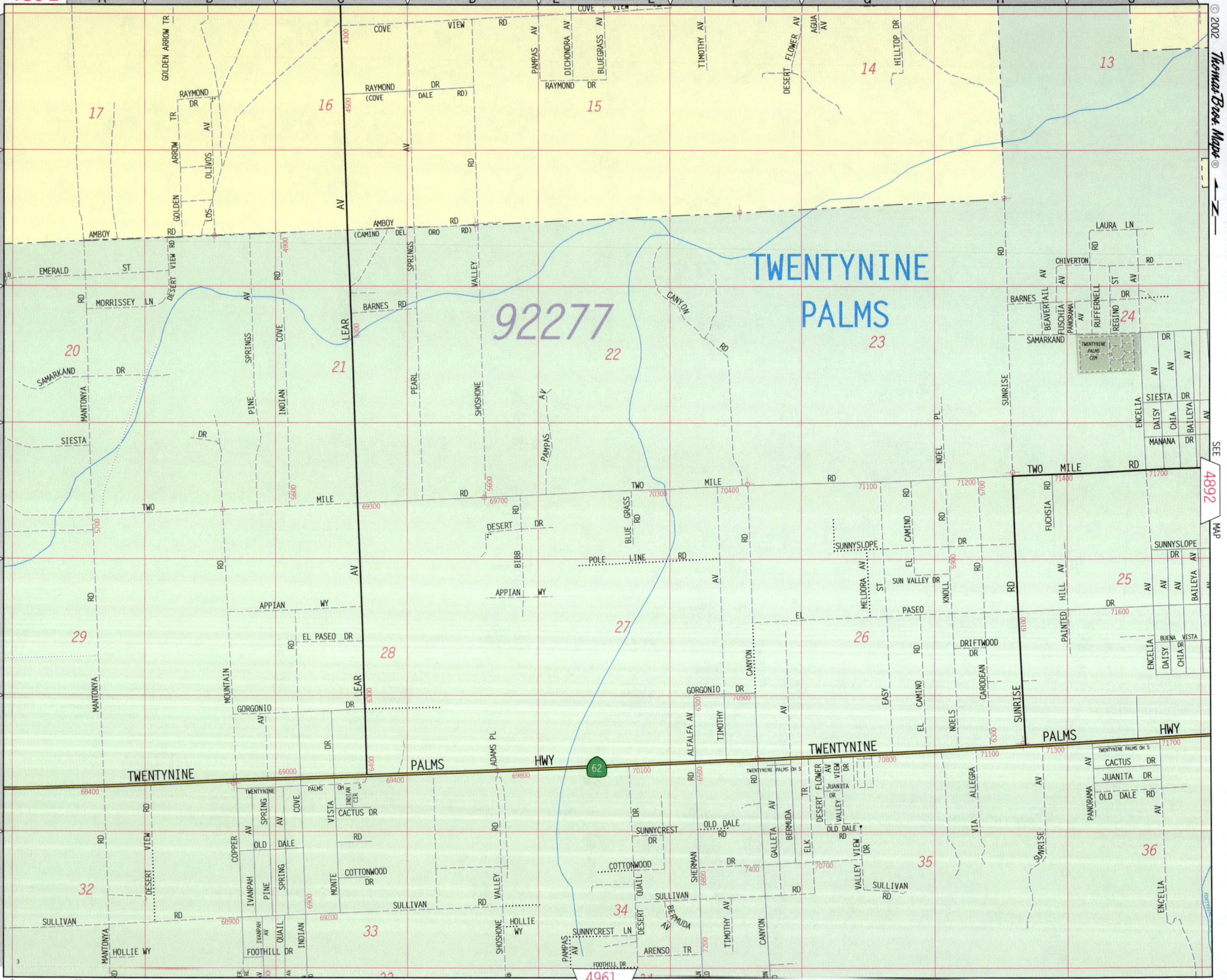

0 .25 .5 .75 1.0 miles 1 in. = 2400 ft.

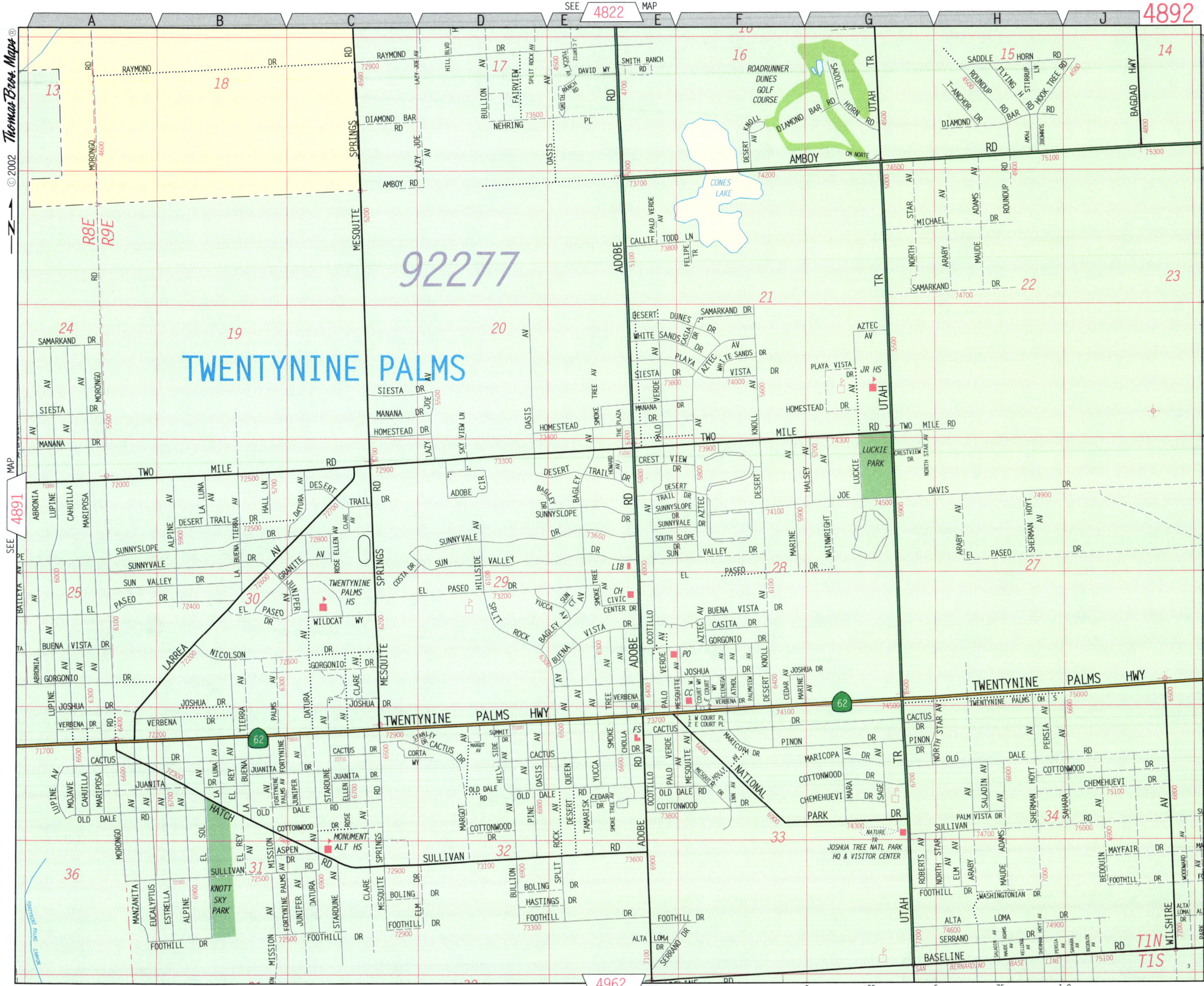
SEE 4822 MAP
SAN BERNARDINO
TWENTYNINE PALMS
92277
ROADRUNNER DUNES GOLF COURSE
CONES LAKE
LUCKIE PARK
KNOTT SKY PARK
TWENTYNINE PALMS HS
JR HS
MONUMENT ALT HS
CH CIVIC CENTER DR
LIB
PO
CC
FS
JOSHUA TREE NATL PARK HQ & VISITOR CENTER
NATURE TR
TWENTYNINE PALMS HWY
TWO MILE RD
AMBOY RD
RAYMOND DR
ADOBE RD
UTAH TR
MESQUITE SPRINGS RD
BAGDAD HWY
BASELINE RD
WILSHIRE
SAN BERNARDINO BASE LINE
R8E R9E
T1N T1S
SEE 4891 MAP
SEE 4893 MAP
SEE 4962 MAP
0 .25 .5 .75 1.0 miles 1 in. = 2400 ft.

SEE 4823 MAP

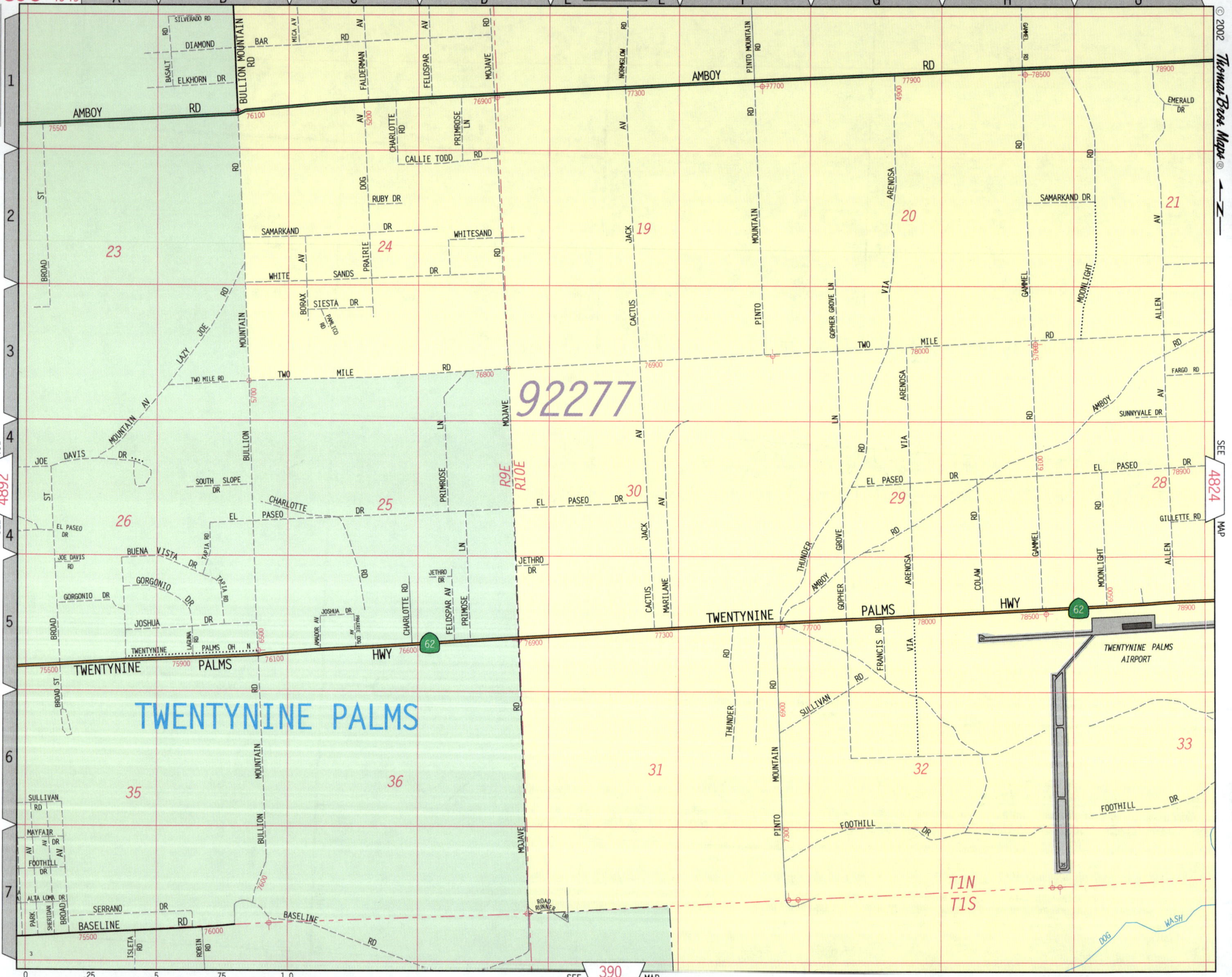

0 .25 .5 .75 1.0 miles 1 in. = 2400 ft.

SEE 390 MAP

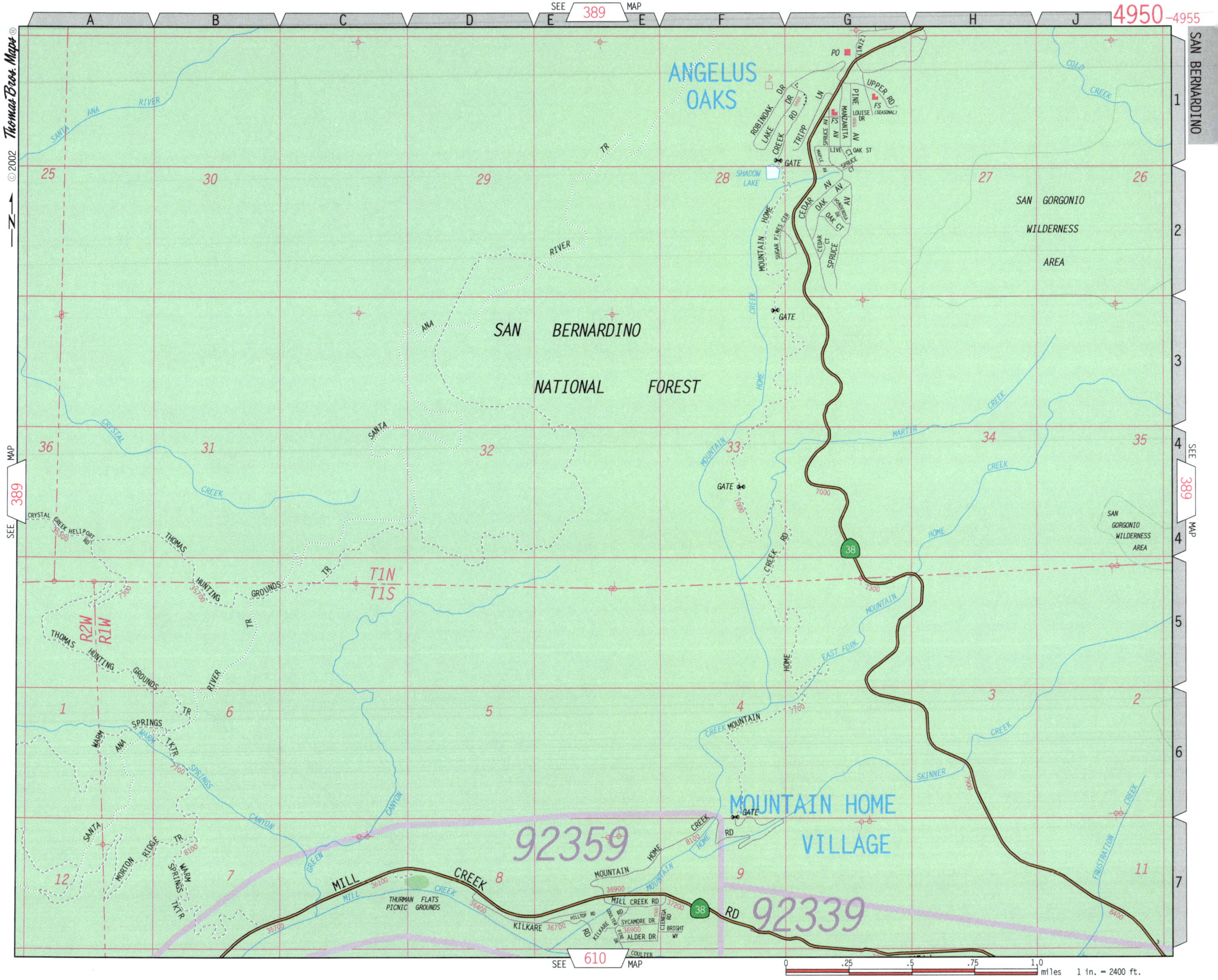
SEE 389 MAP
SEE 610 MAP
Thomas Bros. Maps © 2002
A
B
C
D
E
F
G
H
J
1
2
3
4
5
6
7
ANGELUS OAKS
SAN BERNARDINO NATIONAL FOREST
SAN GORGONIO WILDERNESS AREA
MOUNTAIN HOME VILLAGE
92359
92339
T1N
T1S
R2W
R1W
SANTA ANA RIVER
SANTA ANA RIVER TR
CRYSTAL CREEK
COLD CREEK
MARTIN CREEK
HOME CREEK
MOUNTAIN HOME CREEK
EAST FORK MOUNTAIN HOME CREEK
SKINNER CREEK
FRUSTRATION CREEK
WARM SPRINGS CANYON
GREEN CANYON
MILL CREEK
SHADOW LAKE
THOMAS HUNTING GROUNDS TR
THOMAS HUNTING GROUNDS RIVER TR
CRYSTAL CREEK HELIPORT RD
SANTA ANA WARM SPRINGS TKTR
MORTON RIDGE TR
WARM SPRINGS TKTR
MOUNTAIN HOME CREEK RD
MILL CREEK RD
THURMAN FLATS PICNIC GROUNDS
KILKARE RD
HILLTOP RD
SYCAMORE DR
ALDER DR
CIENEGA RD
BRIGHT WY
COULTER
ROBINOAK DR
LAKE CREEK RD
TRIPP LN
UPPER RD
PINE AV
MANZANITA AV
LOUISE DR
SPRUCE AV
LIVE OAK ST
CEDAR AV
OAK AV
SUGAR PINES CIR
PO
FS
FS (SEASONAL)
GATE
38
1
4
5
6
7
8
9
2
3
11
12
25
26
27
28
29
30
31
32
33
34
35
36
7000
7300
7700
7900
8100
8400
36100
36400
36700
36900
37200
35700
35500
0 .25 .5 .75 1.0 miles
1 in. = 2400 ft.

SEE 4886 MAP

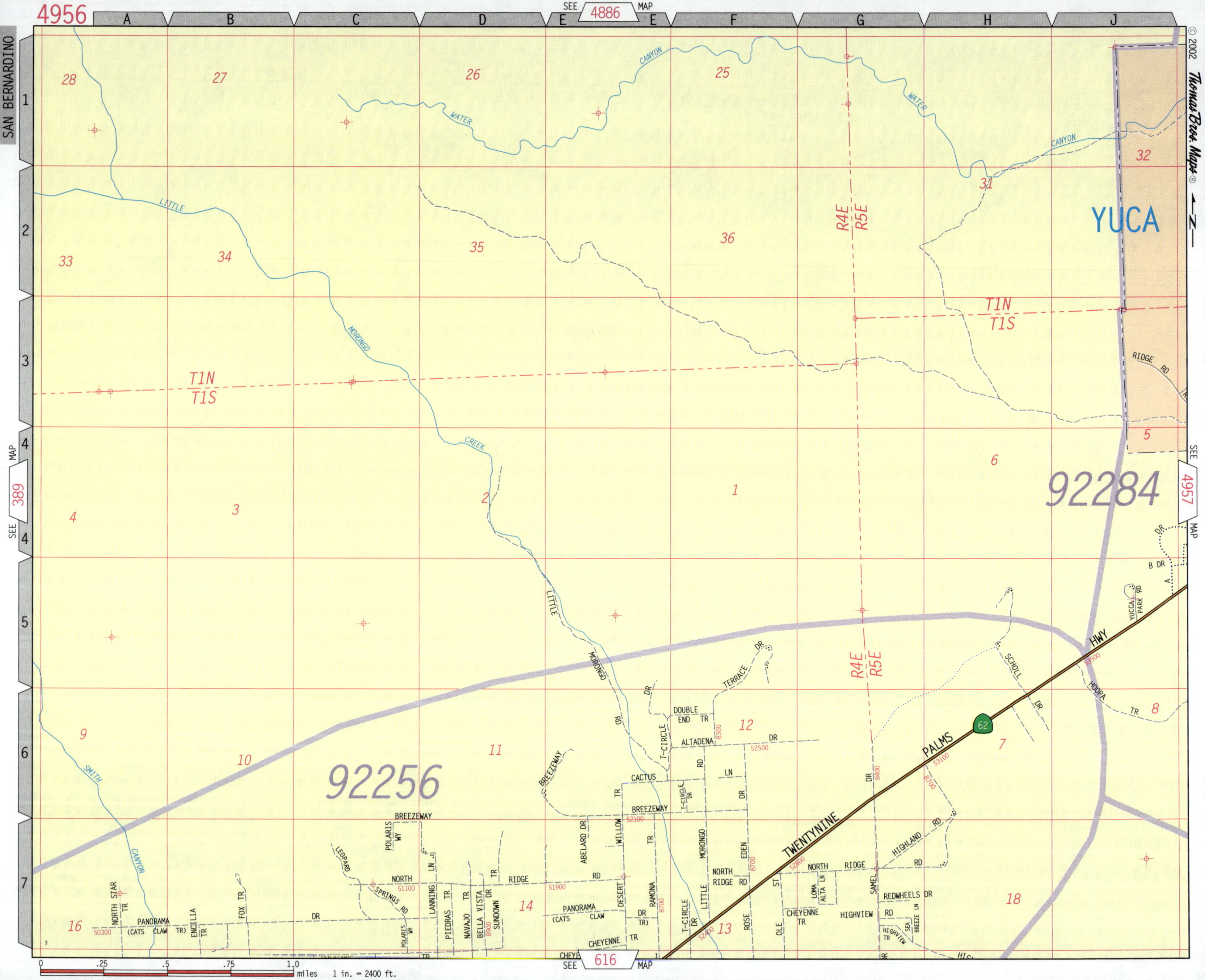

SEE 389 MAP

SEE 4957 MAP

SEE 616 MAP

SEE 4887 MAP

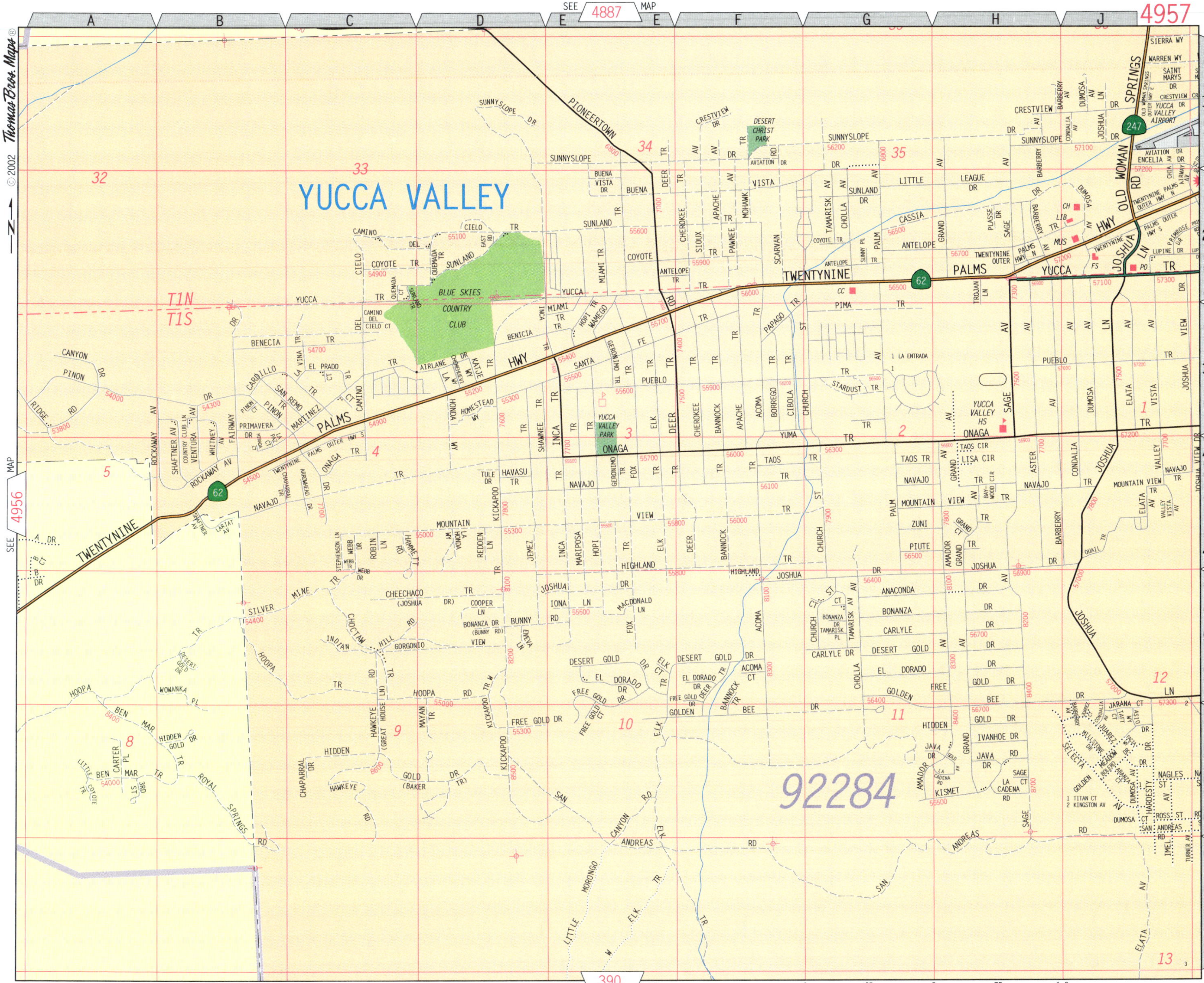

SEE 4956 MAP
SEE 4958 MAP
SEE 390 MAP

SEE 4888 MAP

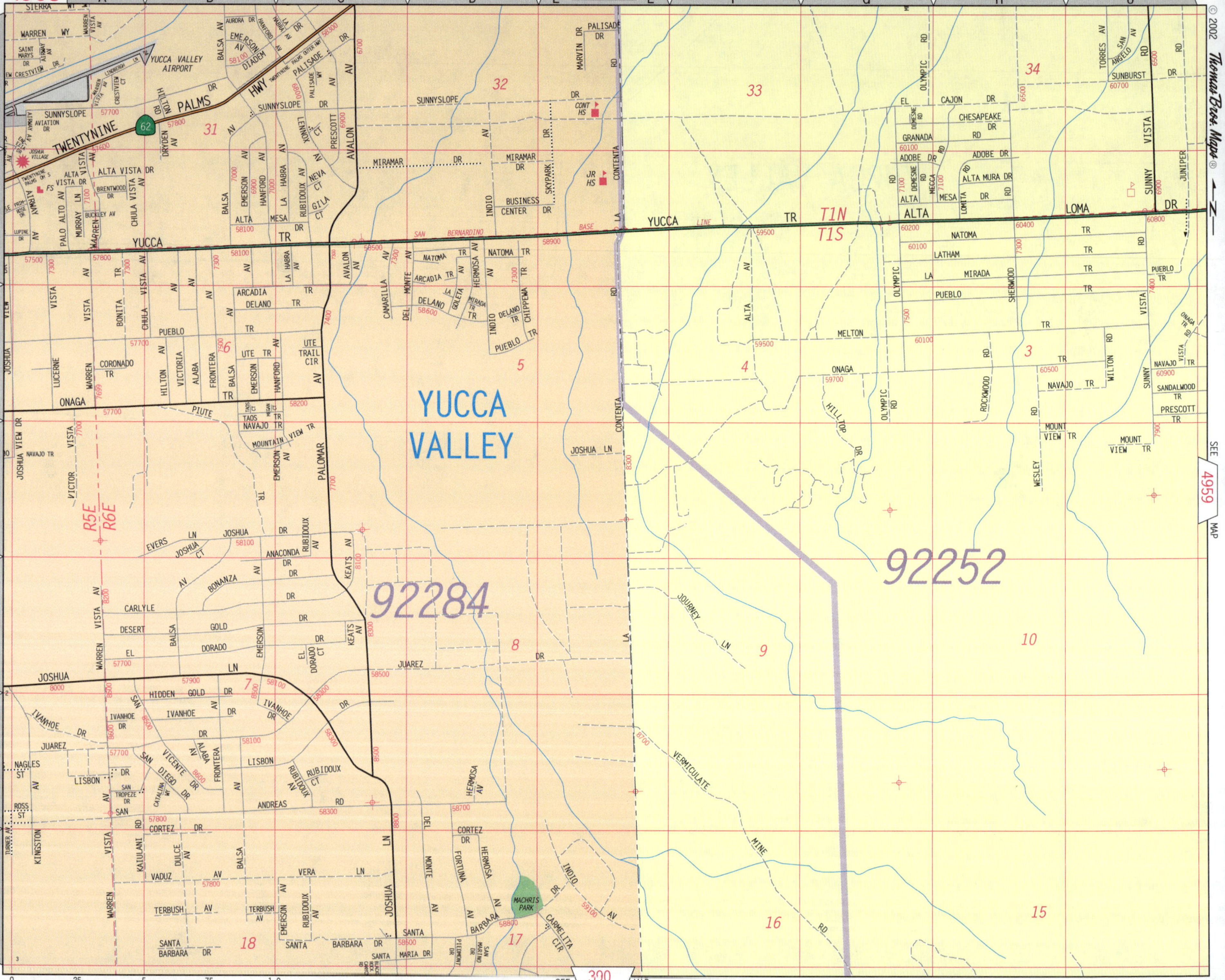

SEE 4957 MAP

SEE 4959 MAP

SEE 390 MAP

0 .25 .5 .75 1.0 miles 1 in. = 2400 ft.

SEE 4889 MAP

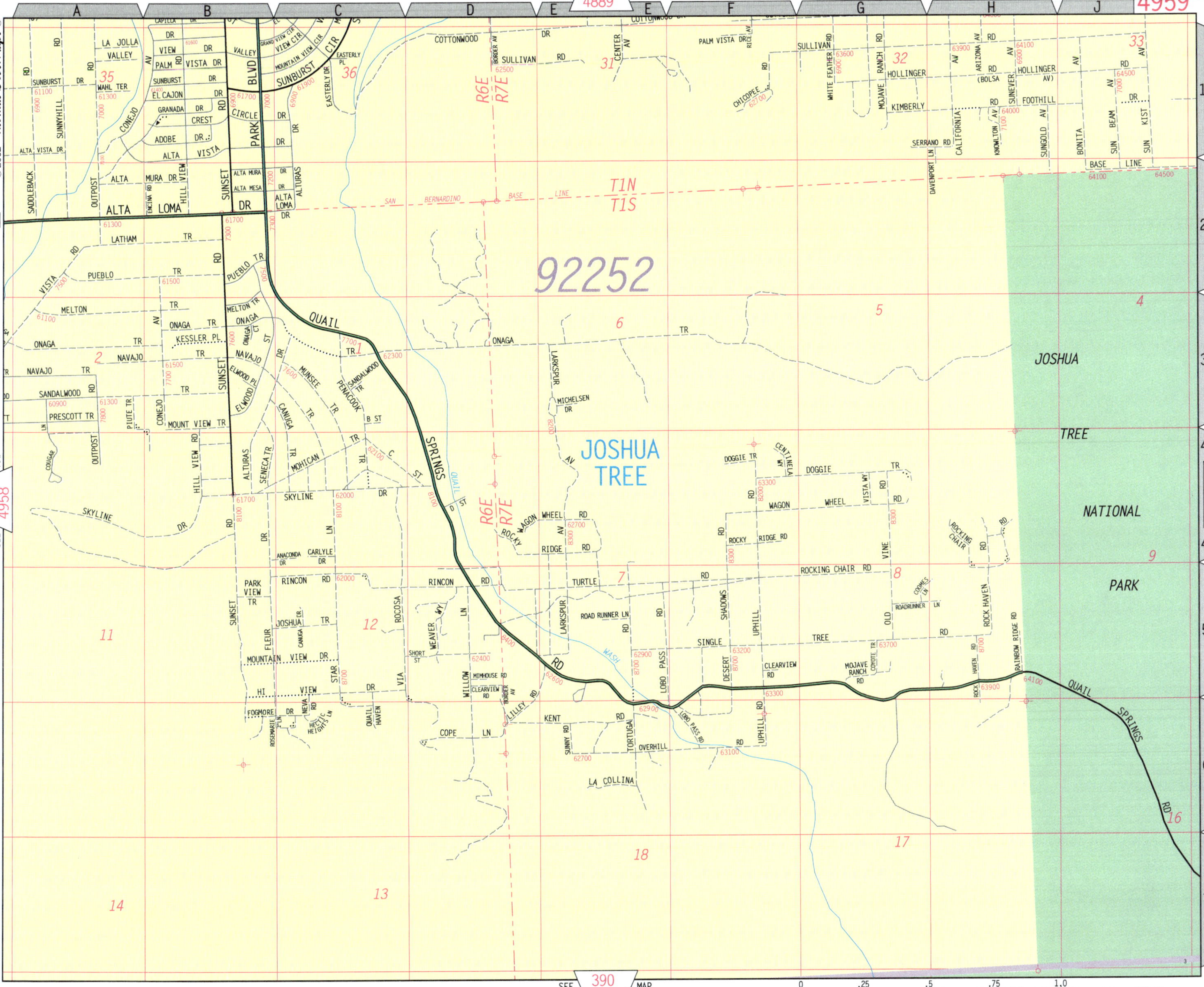

A
B
C
D
E
F
G
H
J
1
2
3
4
5
6
7
SAN BERNARDINO
92252
JOSHUA TREE
JOSHUA TREE NATIONAL PARK
T1N
T1S
R6E
R7E
SAN BERNARDINO BASE LINE
QUAIL SPRINGS RD
QUAIL WASH
ALTA LOMA DR
PARK BLVD
SUNSET RD
SUNBURST CIR
VALLEY VIEW CIR
MOUNTAIN VIEW CIR
EASTERLY DR
COTTONWOOD DR
SULLIVAN RD
CENTER AV
PALM VISTA DR
HOLLINGER RD
KIMBERLY
FOOTHILL
SERRANO RD
DAVENPORT LN
CALIFORNIA
SUNGOLD AV
BONITA
SUN BEAM
KIST
BASE LINE
LATHAM TR
PUEBLO TR
VISTA RD
MELTON TR
ONAGA TR
KESSLER PL
NAVAJO TR
SANDALWOOD RD
PRESCOTT TR
MOUNT VIEW TR
HILL VIEW RD
ALTURAS
SENECA TR
MOHICAN TR
SKYLINE DR
CANUGA
MUNSEE TR
PENACOOK TR
SANDALWOOD TR
B ST
C ST
D ST
LARKSPUR AV
MICHELSEN DR
DOGGIE TR
CENTINELA WY
VISTA WY
WAGON WHEEL RD
ROCKY RIDGE RD
VINE
ROCKING CHAIR RD
TURTLE RD
RINCON RD
PARK VIEW TR
JOSHUA TR
MOUNTAIN VIEW DR
HI VIEW DR
FOGMORE DR
ROCOSA
WEAVER
SHORT ST
WILLOW
ROAD RUNNER LN
SHADOWS
UPHILL
SINGLE TREE RD
DESERT
LOBO PASS
CLEARVIEW RD
MOJAVE RANCH RD
OLD
ROCK HAVEN
RAINBOW RIDGE RD
KENT RD
COPE LN
TORTUGA
OVERHILL RD
LA COLLINA
LILLEY RD
SUNNY RD
1
2
4
5
6
7
8
9
11
12
13
14
16
17
18
31
32
33
35
36
SEE 390 MAP
SEE 4958 MAP
SEE 4960 MAP
0
.25
.5
.75
1.0
miles
1 in. = 2400 ft.

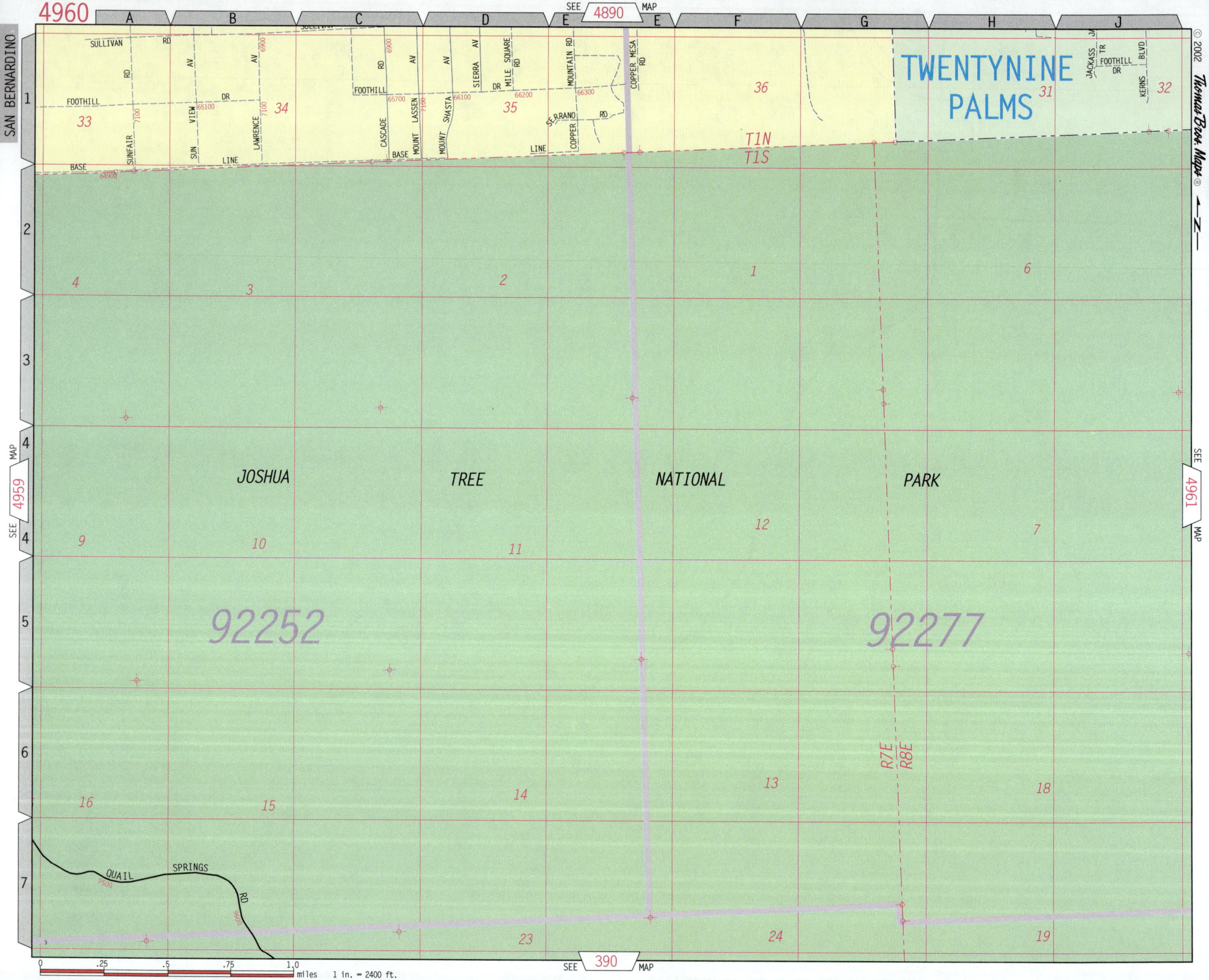
SAN BERNARDINO
SEE 4890 MAP
SEE 4959 MAP
SEE 4961 MAP
SEE 390 MAP
TWENTYNINE PALMS
JOSHUA TREE NATIONAL PARK
92252
92277
T1N
T1S
R7E
R8E
SULLIVAN RD
FOOTHILL DR
BASE LINE
SUNFAIR RD
SUN VIEW AV
LAWRENCE AV
CASCADE RD
MOUNT LASSEN AV
MOUNT SHASTA AV
SIERRA AV
MILE SQUARE RD
MOUNTAIN RD
COPPER MESA RD
SERRANO RD
COPPER
JACKASS TR
KERNS BLVD
QUAIL SPRINGS RD
0 .25 .5 .75 1.0 miles 1 in. = 2400 ft.
© 2002 Thomas Bros. Maps®

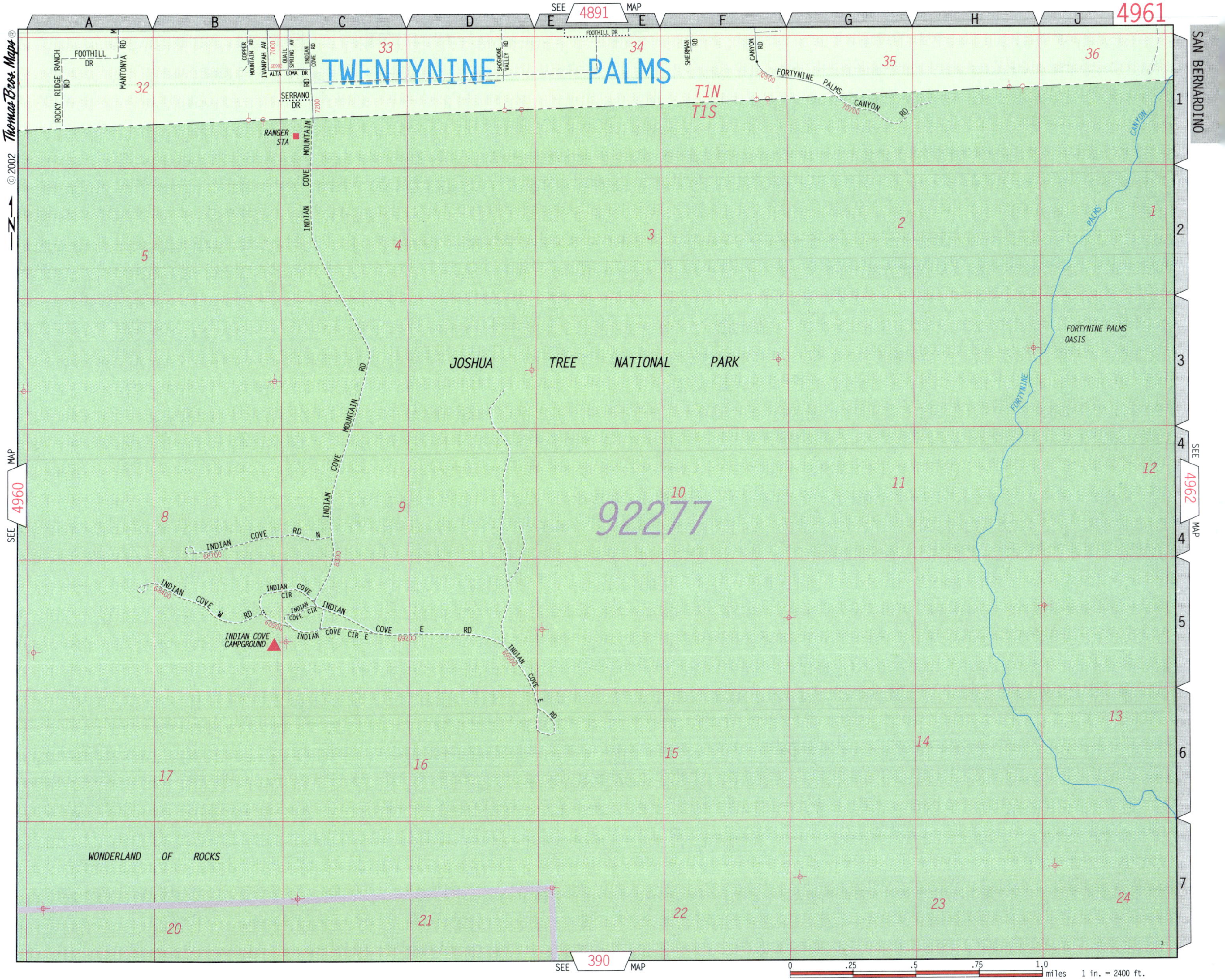
SEE 4891 MAP
SEE 4960 MAP
SEE 4962 MAP
SEE 390 MAP
A B C D E E F G H J
1 2 3 4 4 5 6 7
SAN BERNARDINO
Thomas Bros. Maps®
© 2002
TWENTYNINE PALMS
T1N
T1S
FOOTHILL DR
ROCKY RIDGE RANCH RD
MANTONYA RD
COPPER MOUNTAIN RD
IVANPAH AV
QUAIL SPRING AV
INDIAN COVE RD
ALTA LOMA DR
SERRANO DR
SHOSHONE VALLEY RD
SHERMAN RD
CANYON RD
FORTYNINE PALMS CANYON RD
RANGER STA
INDIAN COVE MOUNTAIN RD
JOSHUA TREE NATIONAL PARK
FORTYNINE PALMS OASIS
FORTYNINE PALMS CANYON
92277
INDIAN COVE RD N
INDIAN COVE W RD
INDIAN COVE CIR
INDIAN COVE E RD
INDIAN COVE CIR E
INDIAN COVE CAMPGROUND
WONDERLAND OF ROCKS
32 33 34 35 36
5 4 3 2 1
8 9 10 11 12
17 16 15 14 13
20 21 22 23 24
0 .25 .5 .75 1.0 miles 1 in. = 2400 ft.

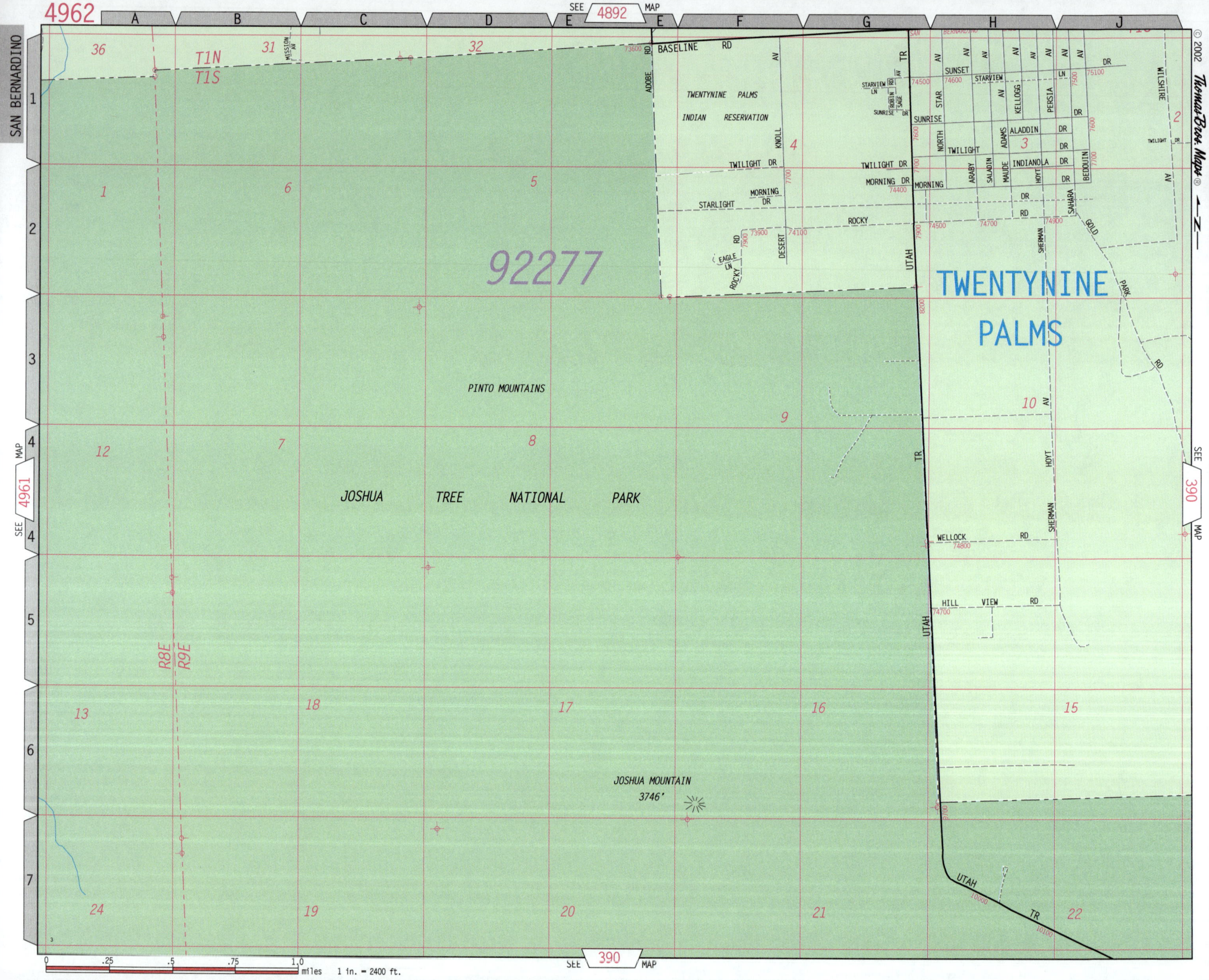
SAN BERNARDINO
SEE 4892 MAP
SEE 4961 MAP
SEE 390 MAP
SEE 390 MAP
92277
TWENTYNINE PALMS
TWENTYNINE PALMS INDIAN RESERVATION
PINTO MOUNTAINS
JOSHUA TREE NATIONAL PARK
JOSHUA MOUNTAIN
3746'
T1N
T1S
R8E
R9E
BASELINE RD
ADOBE RD
MISSION AV
UTAH TR
TWILIGHT DR
MORNING DR
STARLIGHT DR
ROCKY RD
EAGLE LN
DESERT
KNOLL
SUNSET
STARVIEW
SUNRISE
NORTH
STAR
KELLOGG
PERSIA
ALADDIN DR
ADAMS
INDIANOLA
ARABY
SALADIN
MAUDE
HOYT
BEDOUIN
SAHARA
GOLD PARK RD
SHERMAN
WILSHIRE AV
WELLOCK RD
HILL VIEW RD
ROBIN
SAGE
© 2002 Thomas Bros. Maps ®
0 .25 .5 .75 1.0 miles 1 in. = 2400 ft.

LIST OF ABBREVIATIONS

PREFIXES AND SUFFIXES

AL	ALLEY
ARC	ARCADE
AV, AVE	AVENUE
AVCT	AVENUE COURT
AVD	AVENIDA
AVD D LA	AVENIDA DE LA
AVD D LOS	AVENIDA DE LOS
AVD DE	AVENIDA DE
AVD DE LAS	AVENIDA DE LAS
AVD DEL	AVENIDA DEL
AVDR	AVENUE DRIVE
AVEX	AVENUE EXTENSION
AV OF	AVENUE OF
AV OF THE	AVENUE OF THE
AVPL	AVENUE PLACE
BAY	BAY
BEND	BEND
BL, BLVD	BOULEVARD
BLCT	BOULEVARD COURT
BLEX	BOULEVARD EXTENSION
BRCH	BRANCH
BRDG	BRIDGE
BYPS	BYPASS
BYWY	BYWAY
CIDR	CIRCLE DRIVE
CIR	CIRCLE
CL	CALLE
CL DE	CALLE DE
CL DL	CALLE DEL
CL D LA	CALLE DE LA
CL D LAS	CALLE DE LAS
CL D LOS	CALLE DE LOS
CL EL	CALLE EL
CLJ	CALLEJON
CL LA	CALLE LA
CL LAS	CALLE LAS
CL LOS	CALLE LOS
CLTR	CLUSTER
CM	CAMINO
CM D	CAMINO DE
CM DL	CAMINO DEL
CM D LA	CAMINO DE LA
CM D LAS	CAMINO DE LAS
CM D LOS	CAMINO DE LOS
CMTO	CAMINITO
CMTO DEL	CAMINITO DEL
CMTO D LA	CAMINITO DE LA
CMTO D LAS	CAMINITO DE LAS
CMTO D LOS	CAMINITO DE LOS
CNDR	CENTER DRIVE
COM	COMMON
COMS	COMMONS
CORR	CORRIDOR
CRES	CRESCENT
CRLO	CIRCULO
CRSG	CROSSING
CST	CIRCLE STREET
CSWY	CAUSEWAY
CT	COURT
CTAV	COURT AVENUE
CTE	CORTE
CTE D	CORTE DE
CTE DEL	CORTE DEL
CTE D LAS	CORTE DE LAS
CTO	CUT OFF
CTR	CENTER
CTST	COURT STREET
CUR	CURVE
CV	COVE
DE	DE
DIAG	DIAGONAL
DR	DRIVE
DRAV	DRIVE AVENUE
DRCT	DRIVE COURT
DRLP	DRIVE LOOP
DVDR	DIVISION DR
EXAV	EXTENSION AVENUE
EXBL	EXTENSION BOULEVARD
EXRD	EXTENSION ROAD
EXST	EXTENSION STREET
EXT	EXTENSION
EXWY	EXPRESSWAY
FOREST RT	FOREST ROUTE
FRWY	FREEWAY
FRY	FERRY
GDNS	GARDENS
GN, GLN	GLEN
GRN	GREEN
GRV	GROVE
HTS	HEIGHTS
HWY	HIGHWAY
ISL	ISLE
JCT	JUNCTION
LN	LANE
LNCR	LANE CIRCLE
LNDG	LANDING
LNDR	LANE DRIVE
LNLP	LANE LOOP
LP	LOOP
MNR	MANOR
MT	MOUNT
MTWY	MOTORWAY
MWCR	MEWS COURT
MWLN	MEWS LANE
NFD	NAT'L FOREST DEV
NK	NOOK
OH	OUTER HIGHWAY
OVL	OVAL
OVLK	OVERLOOK
OVPS	OVERPASS
PAS	PASEO
PAS DE	PASEO DE
PAS DE LA	PASEO DE LA
PAS DE LAS	PASEO DE LAS
PAS DE LOS	PASEO DE LOS
PAS DL	PASEO DEL
PASG	PASSAGE
PAS LA	PASEO LA
PAS LOS	PASEO LOS
PASS	PASS
PIKE	PIKE
PK	PARK
PKDR	PARK DRIVE
PKWY, PKY	PARKWAY
PL	PLACE
PLWY	PLACE WAY
PLZ, PZ	PLAZA
PT	POINT
PTAV	POINT AVENUE
PTH	PATH
PZ DE	PLAZA DE
PZ DEL	PLAZA DEL
PZ D LA	PLAZA DE LA
PZ D LAS	PLAZA DE LAS
PZWY	PLAZA WAY
RAMP	RAMP
RD	ROAD
RDAV	ROAD AVENUE
RDBP	ROAD BYPASS
RDCT	ROAD COURT
RDEX	ROAD EXTENSION
RDG	RIDGE
RDSP	ROAD SPUR
RDWY	ROAD WAY
RR	RAILROAD
RUE	RUE
RUE D	RUE DE
RW	ROW
RY	RAILWAY
SKWY	SKYWAY
SQ	SQUARE
ST	STREET
STAV	STREET AVENUE
STCT	STREET COURT
STDR	STREET DRIVE
STEX	STREET EXTENSION
STLN	STREET LANE
STLP	STREET LOOP
ST OF	STREET OF
ST OF THE	STREET OF THE
STOV	STREET OVERPASS
STPL	STREET PLACE
STPM	STREET PROMENADE
STWY	STREET WAY
STXP	STREET EXPRESSWAY
TER	TERRACE
TFWY	TRAFFICWAY
THWY	THROUGHWAY
TKTR	TRUCK TRAIL
TPKE	TURNPIKE
TRC	TRACE
TRCT	TERRACE COURT
TR, TRL	TRAIL
TRWY	TRAIL WAY
TTSP	TRUCK TRAIL SPUR
TUN	TUNNEL
UNPS	UNDERPASS
VIA D	VIA DE
VIA DL	VIA DEL
VIA D LA	VIA DE LA
VIA D LAS	VIA DE LAS
VIA D LOS	VIA DE LOS
VIA LA	VIA LA
VW	VIEW
VWY	VIEW WAY
VIS	VISTA
VIS D	VISTA DE
VIS D L	VISTA DE LA
VIS D LAS	VISTA DE LAS
VIS DEL	VISTA DEL
WK	WALK
WY	WAY
WYCR	WAY CIRCLE
WYDR	WAY DRIVE
WYLN	WAY LANE
WYPL	WAY PLACE

DIRECTIONS

E	EAST
KPN	KEY PENINSULA NORTH
KPS	KEY PENINSULA SOUTH
N	NORTH
NE	NORTHEAST
NW	NORTHWEST
S	SOUTH
SE	SOUTHEAST
SW	SOUTHWEST
W	WEST

DEPARTMENT STORES

BD	BLOOMINGDALES
BN	THE BON MARCHE
D	DIAMONDS
DL	DILLARDS
G	GOLDWATERS
GT	GOTTSCHALKS
H	HARRIS
IM	I MAGNIN
MA	MACY'S
ME	MERVYN'S
MF	MEIER & FRANK
N	NORDSTROM
NM	NEIMAN-MARCUS
P	J C PENNEY
RM	ROBINSONS MAY
S	SEARS
SF	SAKS FIFTH AVENUE

BUILDINGS

CC	CHAMBER OF COMMERCE
CH	CITY HALL
CHP	CALIFORNIA HIGHWAY PATROL
COMM CTR	COMMUNITY CENTER
CON CTR	CONVENTION CENTER
CONT HS	CONTINUATION HIGH SCHOOL
CTH	COURT HOUSE
DMV	DEPT OF MOTOR VEHICLES
FAA	FEDERAL AVIATION ADMIN
FS	FIRE STATION
HOSP	HOSPITAL
HS	HIGH SCHOOL
INT	INTERMEDIATE SCHOOL
LIB	LIBRARY
MID	MIDDLE SCHOOL
MUS	MUSEUM
PO	POST OFFICE
PS	POLICE STATION
SR CIT CTR	SENIOR CITIZENS CENTER
STA	STATION
THTR	THEATER
VIS BUR	VISITORS BUREAU

OTHER ABBREVIATIONS

BCH	BEACH
BLDG	BUILDING
CEM	CEMETERY
CK	CREEK
CO	COUNTY
COMM	COMMUNITY
CTR	CENTER
EST	ESTATE
HIST	HISTORIC
HTS	HEIGHTS
LK	LAKE
MDW	MEADOW
MED	MEDICAL
MEM	MEMORIAL
MHP	MOBILE HOME PARK
MT	MOUNT
MTN	MOUNTAIN
NATL	NATIONAL
PKG	PARKING
PLGD	PLAYGROUND
RCH	RANCH
RCHO	RANCHO
REC	RECREATION
RES	RESERVOIR
RIV	RIVER
RR	RAILROAD
SPG	SPRING
STA	SANTA
VLG	VILLAGE
VLY	VALLEY
VW	VIEW

STREET
Block City ZIP Pg-Grid

A

A AV
- SBdC - 4887-B4
4900 SBdC 92252 4889-C3
9400 HESP 92345 4476-F1
11500 HESP 92345 4386-F7
58200 SBdC 92284 4888-B2
E A CT
400 CLTN 92324 606-E5
A DR
- SBdC 92252 4889-B3
- SBdC 92284 4956-J5
- SBdC 92284 4957-A4
A LN
100 SBdC - 518-B1
800 SBdC 92314 (4743-A7
See Page 4662)
800 SBdC 92314 4813-A1
A RD
22000 CLTN 92313 646-E3
22000 CLTN 92324 646-E3
22000 GTER 92313 646-E3
22000 GTER 92324 646-E3
78100 SBdC - 329-C4
A ST
- BARS 92311 3680-F5
- SBdC - 4606-D1
- SBdC 92311 3679-G5
100 NDLS 92363 3620-D6
3600 RivC 91752 644-A6
12100 SBdC 93562 2144-G6
16600 VCTV 92392 4296-E4
32900 SBdC - (3761-E1
See Page 3760)
33300 SBdC - (3681-E7
See Page 3590)
34400 YCPA 92399 649-H1
80400 SBdC 93562 2234-G3
E A ST
- UPL 91786 602-C3
W A ST
200 UPL 91786 602-B3
AARON CT
14300 VCTV 92394 4295-H5
AARON DR
800 RDL 92374 608-E6
ABACHERLI AV
12100 CHNO 91710 641-G5
ABACHERLI PL
12000 CHNO 91710 641-G5
ABAJO CT
5900 RCUC 91737 572-J3
ABBEY CT
- RCUC 91739 573-F5
ABBEY LN
1400 POM 91767 601-C7
1400 POM 91767 641-C1
16900 VCTV 92394 4296-E1
ABBEY WY
28900 HIGH 92346 578-C7
N ABBIE WY
1900 UPL 91784 572-A5
ABBOTTSFORD LN
14900 VCTV 92394 4295-J6
ABELARD DR
8700 SBdC 92256 4956-E7
ABELIA ST
35300 SBdC - (4301-G4
See Page 4300)
40100 SBdC - 4302-J4
40100 SBdC - (4303-A4
See Page 4302)
ABERDARE ST
11500 LMLN 92354 647-F2
ABERDEEN CT
- RCUC 91739 573-F5
7700 HIGH 92346 578-D6
ABERDEEN DR
11400 FONT 92337 644-F3
56300 YUCA 92284 4817-G6
56600 SBdC 92284 4817-G6
57500 SBdC 92284 4818-A6
60100 SBdC 92252 4818-G6
61100 SBdC 92252 4819-A6
ABERDEEN LN
7800 HIGH 92346 578-D7
14700 SBdC - (3935-H4
See Page 3934)
ABERDEEN RD
- SBdC - 4817-C6
63300 SBdC 92252 4819-H6
63500 SBdC 92252 4820-A6
ABILENE WY
1800 CLAR 91711 571-D7
1800 CLAR 91711 601-D1
ABLES ST
37400 SBdC - 4482-C1
ABNER DR
27000 SBdC - 4737-H5
ABRONIA AV
2200 SBdC 92277 4821-J2
5300 TNP 92277 4892-A4
ACACIA AV
- VCTV 92392 4385-H4
500 SBDO 92405 546-G7
500 SBDO 92405 576-G1
3000 SBdC - 4816-G6
3100 SBdC - 4888-G1
6700 FONT 92336 574-J5
9000 FONT 92335 604-J4
12300 CHNO 91710 642-A6
34700 YCPA 92399 649-J3
34900 YCPA 92399 650-A3
N ACACIA AV
100 RLTO 92376 605-J1
400 RLTO 92376 575-H4
900 SBDO 92410 576-G6
1200 SBDO 92405 576-G1
1900 SBdC 92376 575-H4
1900 SBdC 92407 575-H4
4400 SBDO 92407 546-G4
S ACACIA AV
- CLTN 92316 605-J7
100 CLTN 92324 605-J6
100 RLTO 92376 605-J3
1100 CLTN 92376 605-J3
ACACIA CT
- ONT 91761 642-E3
500 SBDO 92407 546-G4
6600 FONT 92336 574-J4
ACACIA DR
500 SBdC - 517-B3
N ACACIA DR
700 CLTN 92324 606-A5
ACACIA LN
4500 SBdC - 4886-F4
35500 YCPA 92399 650-B3
ACACIA RD
500 SBdC - 4738-D7
1700 SBdC 92372 4472-D6
2400 SBdC 92371 4472-G6
5800 SBdC 92371 4473-F5
7400 SBdC 92371 4474-A5
9600 SBdC 92301 4294-E5
10500 SBdC 92345 4474-H5
11500 ADEL 92301 4295-A5
12300 SBdC 92345 4475-D5
12700 HESP 92345 4475-E5
ACACIA ST
- SBdC 92347 3588-A6
200 POM 91767 601-A4
7700 FONT 92336 574-J7
9700 RCUC 91730 602-J4
10500 RCUC 91730 603-B4
11400 LMLN 92354 647-C2
12200 SBdC 93562 2144-G6
20900 SBdC 92347 (3587-E6
See Page 3586)
E ACACIA ST
100 ONT 91761 642-C3
N ACACIA ST
2600 SBDO 92405 576-G3
W ACACIA ST
200 CLTN 92324 606-D5
ACACIA WY
500 SBDO 92405 546-G7
ACACIA HILL RD
1600 DBAR 91765 680-A4
ACACIA KNOLL DR
9700 RCUC 91701 572-D4
ACADEMY AV
2300 POM 91768 640-D1
18800 VCTV - (4206-A4
See Page 4116)
ACADEMY CT
1900 CLAR 91711 571-D7
ACADEMY ST
16200 VCTV 92394 4296-C3
24700 LMLN 92354 607-B7
ACADIA DR
- CHLS 91709 711-J1
1100 SBdC - 4738-C5
ACANTHUS ST
8600 SBdC 92371 4563-G1
9300 SBdC 92371 4473-F1
12100 SBdC 92371 4383-F3
ACAPULCO AV
3900 SBdC 92407 546-A6
4400 SBDO 92407 546-A6
W ACAPULCO CT
2200 SBdC 92407 546-A6
ACASO RD
- SBdC 92365 (3683-E2
See Page 3592)
ACCESS RD
- RCUC 91739 573-J4
- RCUC 91739 574-A4
- SBdC 92335 604-B3
ACER CT
8400 RCUC 91730 602-F2
ACHITL CT
- SBdC - 4774-G6
ACHITL RD
5100 SBdC - 4774-F6
ACKERMAN DR
15100 SBdC 92335 604-E5
ACMITE ST
31700 SBdC - (4210-F4
See Page 4120)
ACOLITO PL
600 DBAR 91765 640-C5
ACOMA CT
56000 YUCA 92284 4957-F5
ACOMA RD
15700 APLV 92307 4297-B4
ACOMA ST
- SBdC 92284 4017-F6
300 NDLS 92363 3620-D6
ACOMA TR
800 SBdC 92285 4747-E2
1900 SBdC 92285 4667-E2
4400 SBdC 92285 (4577-E7
See Page 4486)
5500 YUCA 92284 4887-F5
7300 YUCA 92284 4957-F3
7400 SBdC - 4843-F5
ACORD
36300 SBdC - (4301-J5
See Page 4300)
ACORN AV
8200 SBdC 92335 605-C1
N ACORN CIR
6300 SBDO 92407 546-A2
ACORN DR
5700 SBdC 92397 4652-C2
ACORN LN
700 SBdC - 517-F3
30800 SBdC - 518-H7
S ACORN PL
2400 ONT 91761 643-B5
ACORN RD
9900 SBdC 92372 4472-D6
ACORN ST
14700 CHLS 91709 681-C5
36100 SBdC - (4301-J5
See Page 4300)
ACORN WY
38300 YCPA 92399 650-J5
38300 YCPA 92399 651-A5
S ACORNGLEN PL
2600 ONT 91761 643-C6
ACRE LN
3900 SBDO 92405 546-G7
3900 SBDO 92407 546-G7
4000 SBdC 92407 546-G6
ACROPOLIS DR
11300 YCPA 92399 650-D1
ACURA CT
- SBdC 92335 604-A2
ADA AV
10700 MTCL 91763 641-G2
10700 SBdC 91763 641-G2
ADAIR AL
- SBDO 92405 576-G4
ADAIR CT
14300 VCTV 92394 4295-H5
ADAM CT
6500 FONT 92336 574-H2
ADAMS AV
300 POM 91767 601-A6
7000 RivC 92324 647-B6
ADAMS CT
- RCUC 91730 573-E7
5400 CHNO 91710 641-G4
11800 YCPA 92399 650-A2
S ADAMS DR
400 SBdC 92314 4742-F6
ADAMS LN
35200 YCPA 92399 650-A2
ADAMS PL
6500 TNP 92277 4891-D6
ADAMS ST
- SBdC 91710 641-D4
400 RDL 92374 608-G7
4900 CHNO 91710 641-F4
5700 SBdC 92285 (4576-B6
See Page 4486)
9900 YCPA 92399 610-A4
11600 YCPA 92399 650-A2
80200 SBdC 93562 2234-G4
E ADAMS ST
200 CLTN 92324 646-D1
W ADAMS ST
1900 SBdC 92407 576-B3
1900 SBDO 92407 576-B3
ADDISON CT
11400 ADEL 92301 4385-A1
17800 CHLS 91709 712-B6
ADDISON RD
7400 RCUC 91730 573-D7
ADDISON ST
11200 ADEL 92301 4384-J1
11200 ADEL 92301 4385-A1
11700 YCPA 92399 650-A2
W ADEL CT
1100 CLTN 92324 606-B4
ADELANTE CT
- SBdC - 4844-A1
ADELANTE RD
5800 SBdC - 4844-A1
ADELANTO RD
- SBdC 92301 (4025-B6
See Page 3934)
16000 ADEL 92301 4295-B1
16000 VCTV 92301 4295-C3
17300 ADEL 92301 4205-B3
20100 ADEL 92301 (4115-B7
See Page 4114)
20400 SBdC 92301 (4115-B5
See Page 4114)
ADELE DR
300 BARS 92311 3679-J3
ADELE LN
- SBdC 92252 4749-B6
6900 RivC 92509 645-B5
ADELIA ST
16200 HESP 92345 4566-E3
ADELINE WY
49500 SBdC 92256 615-H7
W ADELL ST
700 SBDO 92408 606-G3
700 SBDO 92410 606-G3
ADELLA ST
11100 SBdC 92354 647-E1
ADELPHIA LN
13800 VCTV 92394 4295-G7
ADIRONDACK LN
- CLAR 91711 571-E4
ADKINS RD
- SBdC 92345 (4655-E1
See Page 4654)
6300 SBdC 92345 4565-E3
ADMIRALS BAY ST
11000 VCTV 92392 4475-D3
W ADMIRALTY ST
1600 CLTN 92324 606-A4
1700 CLTN 92324 605-J4
ADOBE CIR
5700 TNP 92277 4892-D4
ADOBE CT
4500 MTCL 91763 641-E1
ADOBE DR
60100 SBdC 92252 4958-G2
61400 SBdC 92252 4959-B1
ADOBE RD
2600 TNP 92277 4822-E4
2600 TNP 92278 4822-E1
4100 TNP 92277 4892-E2
7000 TNP 92277 4962-E1
7300 SBdC 92371 4563-J1
7300 SBdC 92371 4564-A1
9700 SBdC 92345 4564-F1
10900 SBdC 92345 4565-A1
10900 ADEL 92301 4294-J6
ADOBE ST
17400 HESP 92345 4566-G2
ADOBE MOUNTAIN RD
22800 SBdC 92301 4112-C3
25000 SBdC 92301 368-H2
ADOLFO CT
9800 RCUC 91730 572-J7
9800 RCUC 91730 602-J1
ADOLFO LN
12700 VCTV 92392 4385-D5
ADONIS PL
7700 RCUC 91730 602-G6
ADRIA LN
12000 RCUC 91701 573-F5
ADRIAN CT
400 CLAR 91711 571-C6
ADRIANA WY
1700 UPL 91784 571-J6
ADRIANO PL
9700 RCUC 91730 602-G6
AERODONE RD
- SBdC 92308 4567-D5
E AEROPLANE BLVD
100 SBdC 92314 4742-D6
W AEROPLANE BLVD
100 SBdC 92314 4742-C6
AEROSPACE DR
12900 VCTV 92394 4205-E6
AEROSTAR CT
15500 FONT 92336 574-F5
AFAMADO LN
24100 DBAR 91765 640-D7
AFTON AV
6900 SBdC 92345 4565-F4
8700 HESP 92345 4565-F1
8900 HESP 92345 4475-F7
AFTON CT
700 RDL 92374 648-F2
AFTON RD
200 BBLK - 4811-B1
AFTON ST
35100 SBdC - (3761-E1
See Page 3760)
AFTON CANYON RD
57200 SBdC - 350-A5
AGARITA AV
900 BARS 92311 3679-G5
900 SBdC 92311 3679-G5
AGATE AV
1100 SBdC 92359 608-J5
1400 RDL 92359 608-J5
AGATE CIR
13600 VCTV 92392 4385-G7
N AGATE CT
1500 CLTN 92324 606-C4
AGATE DR
15500 FONT 92337 644-F3
AGATE LN
11900 CLTN 92324 645-J3
AGATE RD
- SBdC - (3681-F4
See Page 3590)
- TNP 92278 4822-F2
4900 CHLS 91709 711-G2
8100 SBdC 92345 4565-G3
11000 VCTV 92392 4475-G2
24500 SBdC 92311 3678-G4
24500 BARS 92311 3678-G4
25200 SBdC 92311 3679-A4
32300 SBdC - 4480-J6
32700 SBdC - 4481-A6
AGATE ST
- SBdC - 518-D1
4100 RivC 92509 644-E7
7000 RCUC 91701 572-G6
7300 RCUC 91730 572-G7
N AGATE ST
1400 CLTN 92324 606-C4
AGATE WY
100 SBdC - 518-E1
13600 VCTV 92392 4385-F7
AGAVE DR
9200 HESP 92345 4475-G6
AGAVE RD
- SBdC 92308 4388-J6
8700 SBdC 92308 4479-A4
AGAVE WY
14500 ADEL 92301 4385-A1
14500 ADEL 92301 4295-A7
AGAVE BAY ST
12500 VCTV 92392 4475-D2
AGENCY RD
- LPCo - 4844-H1
900 PRKR - 4774-J7
1200 PRKR - 4844-H1
AGGAZZOTTI RD
- RCUC 91739 574-B1
AGNES DR
500 BARS 92311 3679-J3
AGNES ST
1400 SBdC 92397 4652-D2
AGOURA RD
6300 SBdC 92371 4473-G6
AGRICULTURE VALLEY RD
- LACo 91768 640-A2
AGUA AV
3700 SBdC 92277 4821-G7
4300 SBdC 92277 4891-G1
N AGUA CALIENTE LN
1000 CLTN 92324 605-J5
AGUADERA RD
- ADEL 92301 (4115-D3
See Page 4114)
16600 ADEL 92301 4295-D1
AGUA MANSA RD
1300 RivC 92509 645-F6
19600 SBdC 92509 645-F6
19700 RLTO 92509 645-F6
W AGUA MANSA RD
400 CLTN 92324 646-A1
500 SBdC 92324 646-A1
1600 CLTN 92324 645-H3
1600 CLTN 92316 645-H3
1700 RLTO 92324 645-H3
1700 RLTO 92316 645-H3
2300 RLTO 92509 645-H3
AIKENS MINE RD
- SBdC - 350-J3
AILANTHUS RD
9700 SBdC 92371 4473-E6
AILANTHUS ST
6400 SBdC 92371 4563-E1
10300 SBdC 92371 4473-E1
12100 SBdC 92371 4383-E2
AINDS
3900 SBdC 92371 4473-A1
AIR EXWY
7200 ADEL 92301 (4203-H7
See Page 4112)
7400 ADEL 92301 4204-A7
11300 ADEL 92301 4205-B7
13200 VCTV 92301 4205-E7
13200 VCTV 92394 4205-G7
15200 VCTV 92394 4295-J1
15200 VCTV 92394 4296-A1
15600 VCTV 92394 (4206-B7
See Page 4116)
AIRES DR
2700 BARS 92311 3758-E2
AIRLANE DR
54900 YUCA 92284 4957-D3
AIROSA DR
4700 SBdC 92301 (4113-A1
See Page 4112)
AIRPORT DR
1000 UPL 91786 601-G2
E AIRPORT DR
100 SBDO 92408 606-J6
1300 ONT 91761 642-E1
2700 ONT 91761 643-C1
4100 ONT 91761 603-E7
AIRPORT RD
300 NDLS 92363 352-B10
300 NDLS 92363 3710-E7
4900 SBdC 92285 (4575-G7
See Page 4484)
32200 SBdC - 3762-F2
AIRSHIRE LN
1000 POM 91766 641-B5
AIRWAY AV
6200 YUCA 92284 4887-J7
6200 YUCA 92284 4888-A7
6700 YUCA 92284 4958-A1
6900 YUCA 92284 4957-J2
AIRWAY CT
57400 YUCA 92284 4887-J7
57400 YUCA 92284 4888-A7
AJUGA AV
1300 UPL 91784 571-J3
AKELEY RD
- SBdC - (4119-J4
See Page 4118)
- SBdC - 4120-A4
AKRON PL
1600 CLAR 91711 601-E1
AKRON RD
- SBdC - 4570-C1
9800 SBdC - 4480-C3
W AKRON ST
2600 SBDO 92407 545-J2
2600 SBDO 92407 546-A2
AKSAMA CT
- SBdC - 4774-F6
AKYESA CT
- SBdC - 4774-F7
ALABA AV
7300 YUCA 92284 4958-B3
ALABAMA CT
- VCTV 92394 4205-F4
14700 FONT 92336 574-D6
ALABAMA ST
- RDL 92373 647-H1
200 RDL 92373 607-H7
300 HIGH 92346 577-H7
300 SBDO 92408 577-H7
300 SBDO 92408 607-H2
800 RDL 92374 607-H2
2200 SBdC 92374 607-H5
2400 RDL - 607-H2
2700 HIGH 92346 607-H2
2700 RDL 92346 607-H2
ALABASTER CT
4800 CHLS 91709 711-F2
11800 FONT 92337 644-D4
ALADA DR
23600 DBAR 91765 640-C7
ALADDIN DR
74800 TNP 92277 4962-H1
ALAMEDA AV
100 SBDO 92408 607-B1
6500 RCUC 91737 573-C4
9700 RCUC 91701 573-C4
9900 SBdC 92316 605-F6
10600 SBdC 92316 645-F1
N ALAMEDA AV
700 ONT 91764 602-E6
1100 SBDO 92404 577-B2
3300 SBdC 92404 577-B1
ALAMEDA CT
1100 SBdC - 4812-D2
N ALAMEDA CT
3100 SBdC 92404 577-B2
S ALAMEDA CT
1100 SBdC - 4812-D2
ALAMEDA RD
1100 SBdC - 4812-D2
ALAMEDA ST
13000 SBdC 93562 2144-J4
37600 SBdC 92347 (3587-F5
See Page 3586)
ALAMITOS ST
4300 MTCL 91763 601-E6
24600 LMLN 92354 607-B7
24600 LMLN 92354 647-B1
ALAMO AV
8600 SBdC - 4480-A3
ALAMO CT
6100 SBdC - 4844-A2
ALAMO RD
- SBdC - 4843-J2
- SBdC - 4844-A2
9600 SBdC - 4480-A4
ALAMO ST
- YCPA 92399 610-A7
1100 HIGH 92404 577-C5
1100 HIGH 92410 577-C5
1100 SBDO 92410 577-C5
4300 RIV 92501 645-H7
ALAMO WY
50400 SBdC - 4844-B2
ALAMO HEIGHTS DR
2300 DBAR 91765 680-A5
E ALAMOSA DR
200 CLAR 91711 571-E5
ALAMOSA RD
46300 SBdC 92365 (3684-F6
See Page 3594)
ALAN ST
14500 ADEL 92301 4384-H1
14600 ADEL 92301 4294-H7
ALASKA CIR
- VCTV 92394 4205-G7
ALBANY AV
9900 RCUC 91701 572-J6
9900 RCUC 91701 573-A6
ALBANY CT
1500 CLAR 91711 601-F1
18700 HESP 92345 4477-B5
ALBANY RD
- SBdC - 4480-B5
13000 SBdC - (4390-B3
See Page 4300)
17900 APLV 92307 4207-H6
ALBANY ST
18500 HESP 92345 4477-A5
ALBARIZA PL
1200 DBAR 91765 680-A3
ALBATROSS ST
- SBDO 92408 607-B1
ALBERT AV
300 POM 91767 601-A4
ALBERTA CT
9500 SBdC 92371 4473-H6
ALBERTA LN
- FONT 92336 544-C7
- FONT 92336 574-C1
1600 SBdC - 4738-B4
ALBERTA PL
6600 RCUC 91701 573-C5
ALBERTA RD
6700 SBdC 92371 4473-H6
ALBION DR
57200 YUCA 92284 4887-J3
ALBONA PL
600 POM 91768 640-B2
N ALBRIGHT AV
1200 UPL 91786 602-A1
1400 UPL 91786 572-A7
1700 UPL 91784 572-A4
ALBRIGHT CT
12800 VCTV 92392 4385-E6
ALBRIGHT PL
6500 RCUC 91701 573-C5
ALBRIGHT WY
1800 UPL 91784 572-A6
ALBRUN CT
- SBdC - 517-A4
ALBRUN DR N
24200 SBdC - 516-J4
ALBRUN DR S
24200 SBdC - 516-J4
24200 SBdC - 517-A4
ALCALA CT
11600 FONT 92337 644-E3
ALCEA WY
- CHLS 91709 711-J1
ALCEDO CT
6800 CHNO 91710 682-B1
ALCOTT AV
600 POM 91766 641-A4
ALCUDIA RD
21800 SBdC 92347 (3587-H5
See Page 3586)
24000 SBdC 92347 3588-A5
ALDAMA AV
200 POM 91767 601-A3
ALDEN CT
- RDL 92373 648-D2
ALDEN RD
100 RDL 92373 648-D2
300 BBLK - 4811-F1
600 CLAR 91711 601-C3
ALDER AV
7300 FONT 92336 575-B7
7400 SBdC 92336 575-B7
7800 FONT 92336 605-B2
7800 SBdC 92336 605-B2
8100 FONT 92335 605-B2
8100 SBdC 92335 605-B2
9700 FONT 92316 605-B5
9700 SBdC 92316 605-B6
10600 SBdC 92316 645-B2
10800 YCPA 92399 610-A7
11200 FONT 92337 645-B3
N ALDER AV
1200 RLTO 92376 575-B5
2000 RLTO 92377 575-B2
3300 RLTO 92377 545-B7
ALDER CIR
36000 YCPA 92399 650-E6
ALDER CT
- SBdC - 518-H6
10200 RCUC 91730 573-A7
ALDER DR
200 SBdC - 518-D1
200 SBdC - 4738-E7
36900 SBdC 92359 4950-E7
41300 SBdC 92339 611-H2
S ALDER DR
2400 ONT 91761 643-B5
ALDER LN
100 SBdC - 518-E1
14100 SBdC - 514-B3
22800 SBdC - 516-E2
E ALDER LN
1700 CLTN 92324 646-G1
ALDER PL
3400 CHLS 91709 681-C4
ALDER RD
- SBdC - 372-C11
500 SBdC - 516-H3
ALDER ST
2400 POM 91767 601-B4
9000 RCUC 91730 572-G7
9900 RCUC 91730 573-A7
13400 SBdC 93562 2055-A7
17400 HESP 92345 4386-J7
17400 HESP 92345 4476-G1
18300 HESP 92345 4387-A7
N ALDER ST
1000 SBDO 92410 576-J6
ALDER TER
28900 SBdC - 518-C1
ALDER WY
200 SBdC - 514-B3
S ALDER CREEK DR
2600 ONT 91761 643-B6
ALDER CREEK RD
200 SBdC - 516-D2
ALDER CREEK TKTR
4500 SBdC - 389-D2
ALDER GROVE LN
13800 SBdC - 514-A1
ALDER OAK RD
- LACo - 512-A5
ALDER RIDGE PL
9800 RCUC 91737 572-J2
ALDERWOOD LN
1300 RDL 92359 609-A5
1300 SBdC 92359 609-A5
ALDER WOOD LN
14200 CHLS 91709 680-H3
ALDIS ST
500 POM 91768 640-D1
ALEATICO PL
6400 RCUC 91737 572-J4
ALEGRE LN
5000 SBdC 92301 (4113-B2
See Page 4112)
ALEMBIC
- APLV 92307 4207-B6
ALENCON DR
11100 RCUC 91730 573-D7
ALEPPO LN
45700 SBdC 92365 3764-D5
ALERT RD
- VCTV 92394 4205-F4
ALESSANDRO RD
1300 RDL 92373 648-C4
ALEUT RD
22000 APLV 92308 4478-A2
ALEUTIAN DR
1000 SBdC - 4737-G5
ALEXANDER AV
- SBdC - 512-A5
E ALEXANDER AV
100 SBDO 92404 576-J3
600 SBDO 92404 577-A3
S ALEXANDER AV
200 UPL 91786 602-A4
W ALEXANDER AV
300 SBDO 92405 576-E3
ALEXANDER CT
13600 FONT 92336 604-A1
ALEXANDRIA AV
- RivC 92880 683-D4
ALEXANDRIA PL
12200 CHNO 91710 642-B5
ALEXIA WY
12700 VCTV 92392 4385-D5
N ALEXIS CT
- SBDO 92407 546-A2
ALFALFA AV
3200 SBdC 92277 4821-E6
6300 TNP 92277 4891-F6
ALFONSO CT
6300 CHNO 91710 682-A1
ALFONSO DR
6500 CHNO 91710 682-A1
ALFORD RD
10700 SBdC 92371 4473-A4
ALFRED DR
100 CLAR 91711 571-D6
ALFREDO ST
5900 CHNO 91710 641-J7
ALGERIA WY
- SBdC - 4481-F4
ALGOMAN AV
- SBdC - (4390-F7
See Page 4300)
10500 SBdC - 4480-F2
17700 SBdC - (4210-F3
See Page 4120)
ALGONQUIN RD
12100 APLV 92308 4387-H3
ALHAMBRA CT
5600 RCUC 91739 574-B2
ALHAMBRA ST
- SBdC 92307 4207-C2
ALICANTE AV
2300 UPL 91784 571-J3
6000 RivC 92509 645-E4
N ALICE AV
100 RLTO 92376 575-G4
S ALICE AV
700 RLTO 92376 605-G3
ALICE ST
7000 HIGH 92346 577-F5
ALICIA CT
800 POM 91766 640-H4
13600 CHNO 91710 681-C2
ALICIA ST
3600 CHNO 91710 681-C2
ALICIA WY
3500 CHNO 91710 681-C2
W ALIDA ST
1100 CLTN 92324 606-B4
ALIENTO RD
8500 SBdC - 4481-E2
ALIMOS RD
8900 SBdC 92308 4477-F7
ALISO CT
14200 CHLS 91709 680-H3
16800 FONT 92337 604-J7
ALISO DR
14500 FONT 92337 644-C1
14500 SBdC 92337 644-C1
15900 SBdC 92337 604-G7
15900 FONT 92337 604-H7
ALISO ST
100 NDLS 92363 3620-E7
S ALISO CREEK DR
2500 ONT 91761 643-C6
ALIVISO AV
10100 ADEL 92301 4204-F2
W ALLEE RANCH RD
1800 CLTN 92324 645-J3
ALLEGANY CT
2000 CLAR 91711 571-D7
ALLEGHENY CT
15800 APLV 92307 4297-C4
ALLEGHENY RD
18900 APLV 92307 4297-B4
ALLEGRE VISTA ST
8900 SBdC 92308 4477-J6
8900 SBdC 92308 4478-A7
ALLEGRO LN
- POM 91766 640-D4
13700 VCTV 92392 4385-G4
ALLEN AV
4900 SBdC 92277 4893-J3
ALLEN ST
16600 VCTV 92392 4296-E4
84500 SBdC 93562 2055-B7
E ALLEN ST
300 RLTO 92376 605-H2
N ALLEN ST
100 SBDO 92408 606-J1
300 SBDO 92410 606-J1
S ALLEN ST
100 SBDO 92408 606-J2
ALLEN WY
10100 SBdC - 4481-A2
10700 SBdC - (4391-A7
See Page 4300)
25500 LMLN 92354 647-D3
S ALLEN WY
1200 CLTN 92324 646-G2
ALLENDALE CIR
14500 ADEL 92301 4384-H1
ALLESANDRO CT
9800 RCUC 91730 602-J1
ALLESANDRO ST
4500 MTCL 91763 601-E4
4800 CHNO 91710 641-F7
ALLEY WY
- LMLN 92354 607-C7
- LMLN 92354 647-C1
ALLISON ST
14500 ADEL 92301 4294-H7
14500 ADEL 92301 4384-H1
ALLISON WY
1700 RDL 92373 648-H4
ALLTHORN ST
16300 HESP 92345 4566-E2
ALL VIEW DR
30700 SBdC - 518-H6
N ALLYN AV
100 ONT 91761 602-D7
100 ONT 91761 642-D1
100 ONT 91764 602-D5
ALMA CT
1100 CLAR 91711 571-A7
13500 CHNO 91710 681-D2
ALMA LN
11500 FONT 92337 644-G3
ALMA ST
4200 CHNO 91710 681-E2
ALMADEN AV
36800 SBdC 92311 3589-G7
ALMADEN DR
- FONT 92336 574-H2
ALMENDRA WY
12400 VCTV 92392 4385-D5
ALMERIA AV
6500 FONT 92336 574-F5
7800 FONT 92336 604-F2
8100 FONT 92335 604-F6
8100 SBdC 92335 604-F2
ALMERIA CT
9400 FONT 92335 604-F4
ALMOND AV
- FONT 92336 574-B6
- RLTO 92377 545-C7
2000 SBdC 92374 607-G5
8100 FONT 92335 604-C2
8100 SBdC 92335 604-C2
10400 FONT 92337 604-C7
10500 SBdC 92337 604-C7
10500 SBdC 92337 644-C2
10900 FONT 92337 644-B2
26500 RDL 92374 607-G5
S ALMOND AV
1200 ONT 91762 641-J3
ALMOND CT
4900 RCUC 91737 (542-J7
See Page 513)
4900 RCUC 91737 572-J1
11700 LMLN 92354 647-C3
ALMOND DR
11900 FONT 92337 644-C4
12600 SBdC 92324 647-A5
N ALMOND DR
3200 RLTO 92377 575-C1
ALMOND ST
8100 RCUC 91701 572-D1
8800 RCUC 91737 572-G1
9900 RCUC 91737 573-A1
10700 ADEL 92301 4384-H2
ALOE CT
- RCUC 91739 573-F6
7500 HIGH 92346 578-E6
ALOE RD
14700 VCTV 92394 4295-H7
ALOE VERA CT
5900 CHLS 91709 711-J2
ALONDRA AV
6900 HESP 92345 4566-B5
E ALONDRA CT
1900 ONT 91764 602-G4
E ALONDRA ST
2000 ONT 91764 602-H4
2100 ONT 91730 602-H4
ALP CT
200 BBLK - 4811-H1
ALPEN DR
27300 SBdC - 4737-H6
ALPEN LN
- FONT 92336 574-E3
ALPENWEG DR
800 SBdC - 4812-B1
ALPHA AV
1900 SBdC - 4742-H2
ALPHIA ST
- SBdC 92314 4742-J7
- SBdC 92314 (4743-A7
See Page 4662)
ALPIN ST
7300 HIGH 92346 578-E6
ALPINE AV
1800 SBdC 92277 4822-A5
1800 SBdC 92278 4822-A1
5700 TNP 92277 4892-B4
ALPINE CIR
12300 VCTV 92392 4385-F6
ALPINE CT
100 ONT 91762 602-A7
100 ONT 91762 642-A1
900 RDL 92374 608-G6
1000 CHLS 91709 710-F1
ALPINE DR
800 POM 91767 601-B4
11800 FONT 92337 644-F4
24000 SBdC - 516-J3
ALPINE LN
- SBdC 92397 4652-E3
26100 SBdC - 517-E3
ALPINE RD
2500 SBdC 91784 572-B2
19500 SBdC 92308 4567-D6
ALPINE SPUR
600 SBdC - 517-F3
ALPINE ST
9800 RCUC 91730 602-J3
9900 RCUC 91730 603-A3
W ALPINE ST
200 UPL 91786 602-A3
ALPINE WY
900 SBdC - 4812-B1
26200 SBdC - 517-E3
ALPINE MEADOWS CT
5200 RCUC 91737 573-A1
ALPIN VIEW CT
28800 HIGH 92346 578-C5
E ALPINVIEW DR
1200 SBdC 92314 4742-G6
ALPS CT
24100 SBdC 92308 4568-F4
ALPS DR
- UPL 91784 571-H6
E ALRU ST
100 RLTO 92376 605-H3
W ALRU ST
100 RLTO 92376 605-G3
700 RLTO 92316 605-D4
ALSTAIR ST
21800 APLV 92307 4207-J3
22900 SBdC 92307 4208-C3
ALSTON AV
7400 HESP 92345 4566-F3
N ALSTON AV
1300 CLTN 92324 606-C3
W ALSTON AV
800 CLTN 92324 606-C4
ALTA AV
- SBdC 92252 4958-F3
100 SBdC 92284 4748-F5
400 SBdC 92285 4748-E3
1000 SBdC 92284 4818-F1
3700 SBdC 92284 4888-F1
4700 YUCA 92284 4888-F3
N ALTA AV
1000 UPL 91786 602-E1
1400 UPL 91786 572-D7
ALTA DR
600 POM 91767 641-C1
600 POM 91767 601-C7
35200 YCPA 92399 650-A4
N ALTA DR
4800 SBDO 92407 546-D5
ALTA ST
700 RDL 92374 608-B4
ALTA WY
2000 SBdC - 4742-H2
W ALTA CREST ST
900 SBDO 92407 546-F7
ALTA CUESTA
7300 RCUC 91730 572-F7
7600 RCUC 91730 602-F1

STREET
Block City ZIP Pg-Grid

ALTADENA CT
5600 RCUC 91739 574-B2
ALTADENA DR
52300 SBdC 92256 4956-F6
ALTADENA ST
21100 APLV 92307 4207-G5
22100 APLV 92307 4208-A5
23000 APLV 92307 4208-B4
ALTA LOMA DR
600 RDL 92373 648-G4
8100 RCUC 91701 572-E4
9500 RCUC 91737 572-H4
10300 RCUC 91737 573-A4
60100 SBdC 92252 4958-G2
61000 SBdC 92252 4959-A2
68900 TNP 92277 4961-B1
73500 TNP 92277 4892-E7
75300 TNP 92277 4893-A7
ALTA LOMA LN
46300 SBdC - (4743-A3 See Page 4662)
ALTA MAR DR
12600 VCTV 92392 4385-H5
ALTA MESA AV
9800 SBdC 92371 4473-B4
12400 SBdC 92371 4383-B6
ALTA MESA DR
7100 YUCA 92284 4958-B2
60100 SBdC 92252 4958-G2
61700 SBdC 92252 4959-B2
ALTA MESA RD
7200 SBdC 92345 4564-G2
8000 SBdC 92371 4564-F3
9400 SBdC 92345 4474-F5
11000 SBdC 92392 4474-F1
12000 SBdC 92392 4384-F7
ALTA MESA WY
12600 VCTV 92392 4385-J5
ALTA MIRA AV
46400 SBdC - 372-D3
ALTA MIRA DR
900 RDL 92373 648-H5
ALTAMIRA DR
15600 CHLS 91709 681-B7
ALTA MIRA PL
- POM 91766 640-E4
1900 RDL 92373 648-H5
ALTAMONT CT
28300 SBdC - 518-A3
ALTA MURA DR
60300 SBdC 92252 4958-H2
61200 SBdC 92252 4959-A2
ALTA OAKS RD
18700 SBdC 92345 (4657-B1 See Page 4656)
ALTARI PL
7200 RCUC 91701 573-D6
ALTARIDGE CIR
13200 VCTV 92392 4385-F6
ALTA VISTA
7500 HIGH 92346 578-F7
ALTA VISTA AV
1100 SBdC - 4812-A1
7000 BBLK - 4812-A1
ALTA VISTA CT
400 SBdC 92371 4382-A3
ALTA VISTA DR
- NDLS 92363 3710-B1
- YUCA 92284 4958-A2
13100 SBdC 92392 4386-H4
22500 SBdC 92301 (4113-E2 See Page 4112)
31100 RDL 92373 648-J5
31300 RDL 92373 649-A5
31500 YCPA 92373 649-A5
61000 SBdC 92252 4958-J2
61000 SBdC 92252 4959-A1
ALTA VISTA LN
1000 BARS 92311 3679-H4
ALTA VISTA PL
- FONT 92336 574-H2
ALTA VISTA RD
11300 SBdC 92372 4472-A2
12100 SBdC 92372 4382-A4
13700 SBdC 92371 4382-A4
ALTA VISTA WY
- FONT 92336 574-H2
ALTA WOODS WY
6500 RCUC 91701 572-H5
ALTDORF DR
23900 SBdC - 516-J4
24500 SBdC - 517-A4
ALTHEA AV
2300 RLTO 92316 645-G1
N ALTHEA AV
500 RLTO 92376 575-F5
500 RLTO 92376 605-F1
2200 RLTO 92377 575-F3
S ALTHEA AV
500 RLTO 92376 605-F3
1300 RLTO 92316 605-F5
ALTHEA WY
3500 RivC 92509 645-A7
ALTHORN CT
1100 SBdC - 517-B4
ALTHOUSE RD
- SBdC - 4120-B4
N ALTISSIMO LN
1300 CLTN 92324 606-A4

ALTO CT
5300 SBdC 92404 547-D7
5300 SBdC 92404 577-D1
E ALTO CT
1300 SBDO 92404 577-B1
ALTO DR
5400 SBdC 92404 577-D1
E ALTO DR
1400 SBDO 92404 577-B1
ALTON CT
100 CALI 92320 650-A7
10600 ADEL 92301 4294-H6
ALTON PL
10600 ADEL 92301 4294-H6
ALTON ST
5400 CHNO 91710 681-H6
ALTO REY LN
- VCTV 92392 4385-C5
ALTURA AV
3300 CHLS 91709 681-C7
ALTURA DR
12300 RCUC 91739 573-G2
ALTURA ST
10700 SBdC 92337 644-B1
N ALTURA WY
800 UPL 91786 602-A2
ALTURAS DR
6900 SBdC 92252 4959-C2
ALTURAS LN
4300 CHNO 91710 641-E5
W ALTURAS ST
1500 SBDO 92411 576-D6
E ALVARADO AV
1000 POM 91767 601-C7
E ALVARADO CT
1100 ONT 91764 602-E4
ALVARADO RD
20400 APLV 92308 4477-F1
ALVARADO ST
200 RDL 92373 648-B1
800 POM 91767 601-B7
E ALVARADO ST
300 ONT 91764 602-C4
300 POM 91767 601-A7
ALVARDO ST
6700 CHNO 91710 682-B1
ALVISO AV
16200 VCTV 92394 4296-A3
ALVORD MOUNTAIN RD
39300 SBdC 92365 (3505-A2 See Page 3414)
39600 SBdC - (3505-A2 See Page 3414)
40300 SBdC - (3504-J1 See Page 3414)
41200 SBdC - 3414-H2
ALYSSUM AV
2200 UPL 91784 571-H3
ALYSSUM CT
15000 FONT 92336 574-D6
AMADOR AV
3000 SBdC 92277 4823-C5
6400 TNP 92277 4893-C5
7700 YUCA 92284 4957-H4
N AMADOR AV
600 ONT 91764 602-E4
S AMADOR AV
2800 ONT 91761 642-E6
AMADOR CIR
- APLV 92308 4387-B4
AMADOR CT
3700 CHNO 91710 641-C5
14400 APLV 92307 4298-B7
AMADOR LN
600 SBdC 92372 4472-B3
1100 CLTN 92324 606-A4
26500 SBdC - 4737-F6
AMADOR PL
7700 RCUC 91730 602-J1
S AMADOR PL
2500 ONT 91761 642-E6
AMADOR RD
300 SBdC 92372 4472-A3
3700 SBdC 92371 4472-J3
3700 SBdC 92371 4473-A3
AMADOR ST
1100 CLAR 91711 601-B2
AMALFI WY
9800 RCUC 91730 602-G6
AMALIA CIR
15100 VCTV 92394 4295-H6
AMALIA CT
14000 VCTV 92394 4295-H6
AMANDA DR
13500 CHNO 91710 681-C2
AMANDA PL
2100 UPL 91784 571-H4
AMANDA ST
2100 SBDO 92404 577-D5
7900 FONT 92336 604-A1
25400 HIGH 92404 577-C5
26100 SBDO 92346 577-E5
AMANDA WY
7000 HESP 92345 4566-E5
AMAPOLAS ST
10500 SBdC 92373 607-D7
10600 SBdC 92354 607-D7
25800 LMLN 92354 607-E7
AMARGO RD
- SBdC - 348-H7

AMARGO RD
- SBdC 92285 4748-B3
AMARGON RD
56300 SBdC 92285 4747-F3
AMARGOSA AV
83400 SBdC 93562 2145-A3
AMARGOSA RD
9900 HESP 92345 4475-E5
10200 HESP 92392 4475-G3
10200 VCTV 92392 4475-G3
11700 VCTV 92392 4385-J6
12300 VCTV 92392 4386-B3
14500 VCTV 92394 4296-B6
14500 VCTV 92394 4386-B3
AMARGOSA TR
19300 SBdC - (3847-B5 See Page 3756)
AMARILLO AV
13700 CHNO 91710 681-H2
AMARILLO DR
1000 CLAR 91711 571-F4
AMARILLO RD
11500 SBdC 92372 4472-F1
11900 SBdC 92372 4382-F3
14100 SBdC 92371 4382-F3
AMARILLO ST
4100 RivC 92509 644-E7
11100 RCUC 91701 573-C6
AMARONE PL
- RCUC 91739 603-H1
AMARYLIS AV
32600 SBdC 92311 3758-C4
32700 BARS 92311 3758-C4
AMARYLLIS CT
9000 SBdC 92335 604-D4
AMBER
14100 SBdC - (4301-B7 See Page 4300)
AMBER CT
- RDL 92374 608-F7
4700 CHLS 91709 711-F1
6700 RCUC 91701 572-G5
9000 FONT 92335 605-B3
14600 ADEL 92301 4294-J7
N AMBER CT
1500 ONT 91762 602-A5
W AMBER CT
200 UPL 91786 602-A2
AMBER DR
- SBdC - 518-A2
600 RivC 91752 683-E4
AMBER LN
10400 RCUC 91737 573-B3
12800 YCPA 92399 650-C5
S AMBER PL
1300 ONT 91762 642-B3
AMBER RD
13500 CHNO 91710 681-J2
32300 SBdC - 4480-H7
AMBER ST
6800 HIGH 92346 578-B4
AMBER WY
15100 ADEL 92301 4294-H6
AMBER CREEK CIR
12700 VCTV 92392 4386-E5
AMBERHILL AV
- RivC 92880 683-D4
AMBER HILL DR
3000 SBDO 92346 577-G1
AMBER HILL WY
17700 CHLS 91709 712-A5
AMBER OAKS CIR
800 POM 91767 601-B4
AMBER POINTE DR
15400 VCTV 92394 4296-A5
AMBERWICK PL
1300 DBAR 91765 680-C3
N AMBERWOOD AV
3200 RLTO 92377 575-A1
3300 RLTO 92377 545-A7
AMBERWOOD DR
- CHLS 91709 681-A2
6100 RCUC 91701 572-F4
11900 FONT 92337 644-C4
AMBERWOOD LN
7100 HIGH 92346 578-C5
12700 VCTV 92392 4386-J5
AMBERWOOD PL
34500 YCPA 92399 649-J6
AMBOY CTO
15700 SBdC - 370-K4
AMBOY RD
6700 SBdC - 370-K6
26500 SBdC 92277 370-K6
26500 SBdC 92278 370-K6
68400 SBdC 92277 4891-A2
69500 TNP 92277 4891-C2
73000 TNP 92277 4892-F1
75300 TNP 92277 4893-A1
75700 SBdC 92277 4893-F1
78900 SBdC 92277 (4894-A1 See Page 4824)
81900 SBdC 92277 4824-J7
82500 SBdC 92277 (4825-C7 See Page 4824)
AMBROS
35700 SBdC - (4301-H6 See Page 4300)
AMBROSIA AV
- UPL 91784 572-E5

AMBROSIA RD
7300 RCUC 91730 573-B7
AMBROSIA WY
- UPL 91784 572-E5
S AMBROSIA WY
1800 SBDO 92408 607-C6
AMELIA DR
11400 RCUC 91701 573-D6
AMERICA DR
9300 RCUC 91730 602-H1
E AMERICAN AV
100 CLAR 91711 601-D6
1800 POM 91767 601-D6
1800 POM 91711 601-D6
W AMERICAN AV
100 CLAR 91711 601-D6
1600 POM 91767 601-D6
AMERICAN DR
1200 RIV 92501 645-H7
AMERICANA CT
13100 VCTV 92392 4385-H4
AMERICANA ST
14100 VCTV 92392 4385-H4
E AMERICAN RIVER RD
3800 ONT 91761 643-D6
AMERIGO RD
22000 SBdC - (4115-J2 See Page 4114)
AMERSHAM PL
- RCUC 91739 573-F5
AMESTOY RD
5900 SBdC 92345 (4655-D2 See Page 4654)
6900 SBdC 92345 4565-D3
AMETHYST
- BREA 92823 710-C6
AMETHYST AV
2000 BARS 92311 3679-G6
AMETHYST LN
- CHLS 91709 681-H7
AMETHYST RD
12100 VCTV 92392 4385-G2
12100 VCTV 92392 4475-G1
13600 SBdC 92392 4385-G2
14500 VCTV 92394 4295-G7
14500 VCTV 92394 4385-G2
AMETHYST ST
- HESP 92345 4475-G4
1100 SBdC 92359 609-B5
1200 RDL 92359 609-B4
5100 RCUC 91737 572-H2
6100 RCUC 91701 572-H6
7500 RCUC 91730 572-H7
7700 RCUC 91730 602-H1
9200 HIGH 92359 609-B4
10800 VCTV 92392 4475-G2
AMETHYST WY
- FONT 92336 574-E2
AMHERST AV
100 CLAR 91711 601-E2
9700 MTCL 91763 601-E6
10300 MTCL 91763 641-E1
AMHERST CT
- RCUC 91701 573-B6
1300 RDL 92374 608-E7
1300 RDL 92374 648-E1
6300 CHNO 91710 682-A2
26400 LMLN 92354 647-G3
AMIATA DR
11200 RCUC 91730 573-D7
AMIGOS DR
500 RDL 92373 607-G7
AMIGOS RD
14600 CHLS 91709 680-J5
AMIR LN
- HESP 92345 4475-H4
AMITY SPRING RD
24400 SBdC - 329-C5
S AMOS AV
1100 SBDO 92408 606-J4
AMSTERDAM AV
13700 CHNO 91710 682-A2
AMSTON CT
- CHLS 91709 681-H7
AMY ST
800 UPL 91784 572-A3
W ANABY CT
700 UPL 91786 572-A7
ANACAPA CT
8600 RCUC 91730 603-A3
14200 FONT 92336 574-B7
ANACAPA RD
100 SBdC 92371 4382-A3
13900 SBdC 92392 4385-G2
14200 VCTV 92392 4385-J2
14700 VCTV 92392 4386-A2
ANACONDA AV
7300 SBdC 92345 4564-G1
9400 SBdC 92345 4474-G4
11000 SBdC 92392 4474-G1
11900 SBdC 92392 4384-G7
ANACONDA DR
56400 YUCA 92284 4957-G5
58100 YUCA 92284 4958-B4
61800 SBdC 92252 4959-C4
ANACONDA RD
8100 SBdC 92345 4564-G3
ANACONDA ST
19300 SBdC 92376 575-F4

ANADA CT
8700 RCUC 91730 572-G7
ANAHA CT
- SBdC - 4844-F1
ANAHEIM PL
- RCUC 91730 603-D4
ANAHEIM RD
65900 SBdC 92252 4750-C6
66500 SBdC 92277 4750-G6
68400 SBdC 92277 4751-B6
ANAHOLA ST
- SBdC - (3846-G4 See Page 3756)
ANASTASIA AV
17100 FONT 92335 605-A3
ANASTASIA CT
17500 FONT 92335 605-A3
ANCHOR DR
13400 SBdC 92392 4386-J3
ANCHORAGE LN
26400 SBdC - (3935-G6 See Page 3934)
ANCIENT WOMAN SPRINGS RD
- YUCA 92284 4817-F7
ANDALUSIA AV
6000 RivC 92509 645-E5
ANDEL DR
14500 FONT 92335 604-C5
14500 SBdC 92335 604-C5
ANDERMOTT DR
- SBdC 92397 4652-F3
ANDERSON AL
- SBDO 92405 576-H4
ANDERSON AV
24900 SBdC 92311 3678-G6
ANDERSON CT
- BBLK - 4811-C1
800 RDL 92374 608-C3
ANDERSON ST
5300 CHNO 91710 681-G2
10400 LMLN 92354 607-B7
10900 LMLN 92354 647-B1
ANDERSON WY
11500 LMLN 92354 647-B2
ANDERSON RANCH RD
8000 SBdC 92371 4563-F4
9700 SBdC 92371 4473-F4
12900 SBdC 92371 4383-F5
ANDES DR
- UPL 91784 571-G7
ANDES LN
200 BBLK - 4811-H1
ANDES TR
23500 SBdC 92308 4568-F4
ANDES WY
35800 YCPA 92399 650-C4
ANDOVER CT
16200 VCTV 92394 4296-D3
ANDOVER DR
- SBdC - (4025-J3 See Page 3934)
100 CLAR 91711 571-D7
15900 VCTV 92394 4296-D3
ANDOVER PL
8600 RCUC 91730 603-A3
ANDOVER WY
- CHLS 91709 681-H7
N ANDOVER WY
1600 UPL 91784 572-A6
ANDREA ST
- FONT 92336 574-E6
E ANDREAS AV
1200 SBDO 92404 547-B6
ANDRESS CT
7300 FONT 92336 575-A6
ANDRESS ST
9100 FONT 92335 605-B4
ANDREW DR
1300 CLAR 91711 601-F1
ANDREW LN
- SBDO 92408 646-J1
800 BBLK - 4811-E2
ANGELA ST
2200 POM 91766 641-A6
ANGELES
- SBdC 92277 (4825-D4 See Page 4824)
E ANGELES BLVD
100 SBdC 92314 4742-D5
ANGELES DR
13700 VCTV 92392 4385-G6
33100 SBdC - 519-E3
ANGELES CREST HWY Rt#-2
- LACo - 4652-F2
- LACo 92397 4652-F2
3700 SBdC 92371 4563-A4
4100 SBdC 92371 4562-G6
7200 SBdC - 4562-G6
13700 SBdC - 4652-F2
17900 SBdC 92397 4652-F2
ANGELES CREST HWY Rt#-138
3900 SBdC 92371 4563-A4
ANGELICA RD
- SBdC - (4025-J4 See Page 3934)
ANGELICA WY
12900 VCTV 92392 4385-G5

ANGELINA CT
6700 CHNO 91710 682-B1
ANGELINA ST
- CHNO 91710 682-B1
ANGELS CAMP RD
1700 SBdC - 4812-E2
ANGELUS AV
1100 SBdC 92314 4813-C3
ANGELUS CT
47100 SBdC 92314 4813-C3
ANGLE WY
1600 SBdC - 4737-G4
ANGLE POINT RD
- SBdC - 349-G4
ANGUS ST
- RivC 92880 683-D7
ANITA AV
100 SBdC 92284 4748-E5
500 SBdC 92285 4748-E5
3700 SBdC 92284 4818-E7
3700 SBdC 92284 4888-E1
4700 YUCA 92284 4888-E2
N ANITA AV
900 SBdC 92314 4742-D5
ANITA CT
100 RDL 92373 648-E3
ANITA ST
1300 UPL 91786 602-E1
6100 CHNO 91710 681-J1
6100 CHNO 91710 682-A1
11100 SBdC 92354 647-E1
ANIWA RD
15700 APLV 92307 4296-H4
ANMITTOW CT
300 SBdC 92371 4382-A3
ANN DR
14600 VCTV 92394 4295-J7
ANN ST
900 BARS 92311 3679-J4
78600 SBdC 92277 4823-J3
78600 SBdC 92277 4824-A3
ANNA CT
- FONT 92336 574-H2
ANNA RD
700 SBdC 92372 4472-B7
ANNANDALE CT
26600 SBdC - 517-F1
ANNANDALE DR
300 SBdC - 517-F1
300 SBdC - 4737-F7
ANNANDALE LN
13900 RCUC 91739 574-A2
ANNANDALE PL
- RivC 92880 683-D4
ANNAPOLIS CIR
100 SBDO 92408 646-H1
ANNAPOLIS DR
- RCUC 91730 573-E7
100 CLAR 91711 601-D4
ANN ARBOR AV
2100 POM 91766 641-B6
ANNATO ST
38000 SBdC - 4482-E1
ANNATTO CT
16200 CHLS 91709 711-G1
ANNHURST AV
1800 CLAR 91711 571-F7
ANNIE RD
- SBdC 92252 4890-B2
ANNIE OAKLEY RD
51000 SBdC - 4886-G5
ANOCHECER AV
2200 CHLS 91709 680-J2
ANOKA LN
13400 APLV 92308 4387-F3
ANOKA RD
13500 APLV 92308 4387-F3
22600 APLV 92308 4388-B2
ANON CT
- CHNO 91710 682-B3
ANO NUEVO DR
1600 DBAR 91765 680-A4
ANSELM CIR
11300 FONT 92337 644-G2
ANSELM DR
10600 SBdC 92337 604-G7
10600 SBdC 92337 644-G1
ANSLEY LN
1200 SBdC 92359 609-A5
ANSON AV
36600 SBdC 92311 3758-C1
ANSON ST
25200 SBdC 92404 577-C4
ANTELOPE AV
18100 ADEL 92301 4204-F6
ANTELOPE DR
- VCTV 92392 4385-D5
15800 CHLS 91709 681-B7
ANTELOPE HWY Rt#-138
100 SBdC 92372 368-G7
200 SBdC 92372 4472-A3
ANTELOPE LN
- FONT 92336 574-D3
- VCTV 92392 4385-D5
1000 BARS 92311 3679-H4
ANTELOPE TR
20800 SBdC - (3937-E1 See Page 3936)
55800 YUCA 92284 4957-E2

E ANTELOPE WY
3100 ONT 91761 643-C5
E ANTELOPE CREEK DR
3700 ONT 91761 643-C6
W ANTELOPE MOUNTAIN DR
800 SBdC 92314 4742-B4
ANTHERIUM DR
17700 CHLS 91709 712-A5
ANTHONY PL
6000 SBdC 92345 4567-B7
12500 CHNO 91710 641-F6
ANTHONY ST
1100 RDL 92374 608-F6
ANTHONY WY
14500 VCTV 92394 4295-J5
ANTIETAM DR
10900 RCUC 91737 573-C3
ANTIGUA DR
11300 RivC 91752 683-G3
ANTIOCH CIR
13200 VCTV 92392 4385-E4
ANTIOCH RD
1800 CLAR 91711 571-C7
1800 CLAR 91711 601-C1
ANTLER DR
800 SBdC - 4737-J6
23200 DBAR 91765 680-B1
ANTLER RD
3200 ONT 91761 643-B5
E ANTLER RD
3100 ONT 91761 643-A5
ANTLER PEAK CT
11800 RCUC 91737 573-E4
ANTON WY
1800 UPL 91784 572-A5
ANTONIO CIR
- LMLN 92354 647-F2
ANTONIO LN
- FONT 92336 544-H7
ANVIL LN
3700 SBdC - 4886-E1
ANYA CT
6500 SBdC - 4844-C2
ANZA AV
4900 SBdC 92277 (4894-D1 See Page 4824)
ANZA CT
13300 VCTV 92392 4385-F4
ANZA RD
11300 APLV 92308 4387-F6
ANZA TR
8900 SBdC - 4482-A4
ANZIO AV
2000 SBdC 92359 608-J4
ANZIO CT
11400 RCUC 91701 573-D5
APACHA WY
- SBdC - 4844-C2
APACHE AV
6800 YUCA 92284 4957-F2
27700 SBdC 92311 3679-E5
38500 SBdC 92365 3594-A1
38600 SBdC 92365 (3504-A7 See Page 3414)
APACHE CT
- SBdC - 4843-H1
APACHE DR
6000 SBdC - 4843-H1
APACHE LN
18000 CHLS 91709 712-B6
APACHE PASS
2800 SBdC - 4816-B7
APACHE RD
9400 ADEL 92301 4294-E1
12400 ADEL 92301 4295-D1
15100 APLV 92307 4297-G5
APACHE TR
7200 YUCA 92284 4957-F3
9100 SBdC 92256 616-G1
15700 SBdC 92307 4298-J3
26300 SBdC - 517-E5
APACHE WY
- SBdC - 4843-H2
APATITE AV
11800 HESP 92345 4386-G7
APATITE LN
12200 VCTV 92345 4386-G6
12200 VCTV 92392 4386-G6
APERO RD
16900 ADEL 92301 (4293-J2 See Page 4292)
17200 ADEL 92301 (4203-J7 See Page 4112)
APLIN ST
7600 HIGH 92346 578-E6
APOLLO DR
2700 BARS 92311 3758-E3
APPALOOSA AV
- SBDO 92407 545-H3
APPALOOSA CT
4500 CHNO 91710 681-E1
7800 RCUC 91701 572-D2
8900 RCUC 91737 572-G1
13800 VCTV 92394 4295-G7
APPALOOSA DR
- BARS 92311 3589-H7
11500 FONT 92337 644-G3
APPALOOSA RD
18900 APLV 92308 4387-B5

APPALOOSA ST
4500 CHNO 91710 681-F1
7800 RCUC 91701 572-D1
APPALOOSA WY
15300 CHLS 91709 681-C5
- MTCL 91763 641-D1
APPIAN AV
- VCTV 92392 4386-F5
APPIAN WY
- SBdC 92252 4890-E5
- SBdC 92277 4890-E5
- TNP 92277 4891-B5
- VCTV 92392 4386-F5
- POM 91766 640-D3
14600 FONT 92337 644-C4
62100 SBdC 92252 4889-C1
67600 TNP 92277 4890-G5
APPLE AV
700 SBdC 92397 4652-B1
3000 RivC 92509 645-B7
6200 RLTO 92377 575-G3
6200 SBdC 92377 575-G3
N APPLE AV
2000 RLTO 92377 575-E2
2100 SBdC 92377 575-G3
APPLE DR
12300 CHNO 91710 641-J5
APPLE LN
10500 RCUC 91737 573-B2
APPLE BLOSSOM CT
7400 HIGH 92346 578-A6
APPLEBLOSSOM LN
13300 APLV 92308 4388-C3
APPLE CREEK DR
13800 VCTV 92392 4386-F2
APPLEGATE DR
16300 FONT 92337 644-H2
APPLEGATE LN
14100 CHLS 91709 680-H3
APPLEGATE WY
1400 SBdC 92277 4750-J7
1400 SBdC 92277 4820-J3
57600 SBdC 92285 4747-J1
57600 SBdC 92285 4748-A1
APPLETON RD
11300 SBdC 92392 4475-A2
11300 VCTV 92392 4475-A2
APPLETON ST
7700 SBdC 92371 4474-A2
8900 SBdC 92392 4474-E2
11900 VCTV 92392 4475-B2
14500 HESP 92345 4475-J2
14700 HESP 92345 4476-A2
APPLETON WY
1700 POM 91767 601-C6
APPLE TREE LN
- SBdC - 518-B4
11700 FONT 92337 644-E3
S APPLE TREE WY
1800 SBDO 92408 607-C6
APPLE VALLEY RD
10000 APLV 92308 4477-C1
10000 SBdC 92308 4477-C1
11300 APLV 92308 4387-C5
13500 APLV 92307 4387-C5
14200 APLV 92307 4297-A6
15300 APLV 92307 4296-H1
16900 APLV 92307 (4206-H7 See Page 4116)
APPLE VISTA DR
6200 SBdC 92397 4652-C1
APPLEWHITE RD
7700 SBdC - 514-C1
8100 SBdC 92407 514-C1
8100 SBdC 92407 4734-D7
APPLEWHITE RD S
300 SBdC 92407 514-E1
APPLEWOOD DR
8700 RCUC 91730 602-G2
9900 SBdC 92359 608-J5
S APPLEWOOD DR
2600 ONT 91761 643-B6
APPLEWOOD LN
9100 HESP 92345 4475-J7
10900 YCPA 92399 610-A7
APPLEWOOD RD
13300 APLV 92308 4388-C3
APPLEWOOD ST
6500 HIGH 92346 578-C3
E APPLEWOOD ST
2000 CLTN 92324 606-H7
APPOMATTOX CT
10900 RCUC 91737 573-C3
APRICOT AV
9100 RCUC 91701 572-H4
9500 RCUC 91737 572-H4
11200 SBdC 92337 644-B2
N APRICOT AV
2600 CHNO 91710 641-E5
APRICOT TREE WY
- FONT 92336 574-E6
AQUA CT
11300 FONT 92337 644-C3
AQUAMARINE AV
5300 RCUC 91701 572-E2
AQUAMARINE CT
16500 CHLS 91709 711-G2
W AQUARIUS CT
600 ONT 91762 642-B3
AQUARIUS RD
- MohC - 3620-G3

AQUARIUS RD
22700 SBdC 92347 3678-A2
AQUEDUCT LN
15300 CHLS 91709 681-C5
AQUEDUCT RD Rt#-62
- SBdC - 372-D10
- SBdC - 392-A1
- SBdC - 4773-B3
11700 SBdC - 391-H1
47300 SBdC - 4774-B7
AQUEDUCT RD N
1600 SBdC 92372 4382-D4
2700 SBdC 92371 4382-F4
5000 SBdC 92371 4383-C5
AQUINAS AV
2100 CLAR 91711 571-E7
ARABIAN CT
16000 FONT 92337 644-G3
ARABIAN DR
5700 RCUC 91701 572-F3
ARABIAN PL
- MTCL 91763 641-D1
E ARABIAN PL
- ONT 91761 682-J1
ARABIAN RD
27500 SBdC - (3937-A2 See Page 3936)
ARABIAN RUN LN
14000 VCTV 92394 4295-G7
ARABIS PL
6500 RCUC 91739 573-H4
ARABY AV
3500 TNP 92277 4822-G5
4900 TNP 92277 4892-H2
7300 TNP 92277 4962-H2
ARAGON RD
3300 SBdC 92371 4472-H2
3800 SBdC 92371 4473-A2
7700 SBdC 92371 4474-A2
8900 SBdC 92392 4474-D2
ARALIA DR
1700 POM 91766 640-H4
12300 CHNO 91710 641-J6
ARANCI WY
7700 HIGH 92346 578-D6
ARANZA CT
- YUCA 92284 4957-J6
ARAPAHO DR
6300 SBdC - 4843-J2
ARAPAHO RD
12900 RCUC 91739 573-H4
ARAPAHO ST
7800 FONT 92336 604-A1
ARAPAHOE AV
21700 APLV 92307 4387-J2
ARAPAHOE PL
13700 CHNO 91710 681-F2
ARAPAHOE RD
1200 SBdC - 4741-A5
23200 APLV 92307 4388-C2
23900 SBdC 92307 4388-E1
ARASH ST
- HESP 92345 4475-H4
ARASTRE RD
46700 SBdC - (4743-A5 See Page 4662)
ARAWAK CIR
20600 APLV 92308 4387-F5
ARBETH ST
19200 SBdC 92377 575-F3
E ARBETH ST
100 RLTO 92377 575-H3
W ARBETH ST
500 RLTO 92377 575-E3
800 SBdC 92377 575-F3
ARBOLADA LN
15700 VCTV 92394 4296-C5
ARBOLEDA DR
- RCUC 91701 572-H5
ARBOLEDA WY
500 POM 91767 641-B1
ARBOLITA LN
5500 SBdC 92301 (4113-D3 See Page 4112)
ARBOLITO CT
- SBdC - 4844-A2
ARBOLITO WY
- SBdC - 4844-A1
W ARBOL VERDE ST
2000 SBDO 92410 606-C1
ARBON LN
27900 SBdC - 4737-J5
28100 SBdC - 4738-A5
ARBOR AV
9800 SBdC 92335 604-D6
ARBOR CIR
200 RivC 91752 683-E5
12000 CHNO 91710 641-E5
ARBOR CT
3800 CHLS 91709 681-D6
7000 HESP 92345 4566-B5
18700 ADEL 92301 4204-E4
ARBOR DR
1600 RDL 92373 648-F4
ARBOR LN
100 SBdC 92314 4742-J7
17700 SBdC 92392 4386-H2
E ARBOR LN
100 SBdC 92314 4742-D5

W ARBOR LN
100 SBdC 92314 4742-D5
ARBOR WY
600 BARS 92311 3680-C5
34400 YCPA 92399 649-H2
ARBORGLEN DR
9500 RCUC 91730 602-J5
ARBUCKLE ST
- SBdC 92311 3758-C6
26000 BARS 92311 3758-C6
26000 BARS 92311 (3759-A6 See Page 3758)
ARBULA DR
500 SBdC - 517-A3
ARBURY DR
1500 DBAR 91765 680-A4
ARBURY ST
15700 HESP 92345 4566-C5
ARCADA AV
8100 SBdC 92308 4567-F2
ARCADIA AV
7500 HESP 92345 4567-A2
8100 SBdC 92308 4477-F6
11100 APLV 92308 4477-E2
ARCADIA DR
46500 SBdC - (4743-B5 See Page 4662)
ARCADIA PL
- SBdC - 4844-A3
ARCADIA RD
900 SBdC 92372 4382-B6
2900 SBdC 92371 4382-G6
ARCADIA ST
11700 YCPA 92399 650-A2
ARCADIA TR
58100 YUCA 92284 4958-D2
ARCADIA WY
1200 RCUC 91739 574-B2
S ARCADIAN SHORES AV
- ONT 91761 683-A1
S ARCADIAN SHORES RD
2500 ONT 91761 643-A6
ARCATA CT
16400 APLV 92307 4297-C2
ARCATA DR
1600 RDL 92374 608-F7
ARCATA LN
16400 APLV 92307 4297-C2
ARCATA RD
16500 APLV 92307 4297-C2
17300 APLV 92307 4207-C7
ARCATA ST
7100 FONT 92336 574-A6
ARCATA TR
7200 SBdC - 4843-F5
ARCHER RD
- SBdC 92284 4748-B4
ARCHIBALD AV
4800 RCUC 91737 (542-J7 See Page 513)
4800 RCUC 91737 572-J2
4800 SBdC 91737 (542-J7 See Page 513)
6100 RivC 92880 682-J5
6200 RivC 92880 683-A7
6700 RCUC 91701 572-J4
7100 RCUC 91730 572-J7
7700 RCUC 91730 602-J5
8200 RivC 92880 712-J5
13900 ONT 91761 682-J5
14100 ONT 91710 682-J5
N ARCHIBALD AV
- ONT 91761 642-J1
100 ONT 91761 602-J7
100 ONT 91764 602-J7
S ARCHIBALD AV
1100 ONT 91761 642-J2
3000 ONT 91761 682-J1
W ARCHIBALD AV
400 CLTN 92324 606-C5
ARCHIE VALLEY CT
900 CALI 92320 649-G7
ARCHWOOD DR
1300 POM 91766 640-G4
ARCO AV
1900 SBdC 92252 4819-D3
ARCTIC DR
1200 SBdC - 4737-H5
2500 SBdC 91784 572-B1
ARCTIC CANYON RD
3100 SBdC - (4661-E7 See Page 4660)
5700 SBdC - (4571-F6 See Page 4570)
ARDEN AV
1300 SBDO 92346 577-E5
1500 SBDO 92404 577-E5
2300 SBdC 92404 577-E2
2400 SBdC 92346 577-E2
ARDEN WY
- CHLS 91709 681-B6
ARDITTO PL
1800 MohC - 3620-F1
ARDMOOR CT
11900 RCUC 91701 573-F6
11900 RCUC 91739 573-F6
ARDMORE AV
700 RDL 92374 648-D1

STREET Block City ZIP Pg-Grid

ARDMORE CIR
800 RDL 92374 608-D7
800 RDL 92374 648-D1
ARDMORE CT
1000 RDL 92374 608-D7
ARDMORE PL
13500 CHNO 91710 681-J1
E ARDMORE ST
200 SBDO 92404 576-J1
ARENA DR
12600 RCUC 91739 573-G3
ARENA RD
8900 SBdC 92372 4562-C1
9300 SBdC 92372 4472-C1
13200 SBdC 92372 4382-C5
13900 SBdC 92371 4382-C3
ARENA WY
5300 FONT 92336 574-D2
ARENSO TR
70100 TNP 92277 4891-E7
ARGENT RD
16200 CHLS 91709 711-F2
ARGENTINE CT
14600 FONT 92337 644-C2
ARGONNE AV
- BARS 92311 3680-F6
ARGUELLO DR
11600 RivC 91752 683-G4
ARGUS AV
83000 SBdC 93562 2145-A3
ARGYLE AV
5500 SBdC 92404 577-D1
6900 HIGH 92404 577-D5
N ARGYLE AV
1700 SBDO 92404 577-D4
ARGYLE CT
25700 SBdC 92404 577-D2
ARIES LN
400 SBDO 92407 546-G4
ARIES WY
11000 RivC 91752 683-H3
ARIZONA AV
- SBdC 92252 4819-H4
100 NDLS 92363 3620-D7
900 PRKR - 4844-J1
1000 NDLS 92363 3710-D1
4500 SBdC 92252 4889-H2
6800 SBdC 92252 4959-H1
8700 SBdC 92371 4563-J2
9900 SBdC 92371 4473-J3
12900 SBdC 92371 4383-J5
ARIZONA AV Rt#-41
- LPCo - 4844-H2
- PRKR - 4844-H2
N ARIZONA AV
2800 SBdC 92407 576-C2
ARIZONA DR
- MohC - 3620-F1
ARIZONA PL
- VCTV 92394 4205-F6
ARIZONA ST
- FONT 92336 574-C6
- SBdC - 4843-H3
1100 RDL 92374 607-H6
55300 SBdC - 4606-G1
N ARIZONA ST
1200 SBDO 92411 576-C5
ARKANSAS AV
14600 FONT 92336 574-C6
ARLENE ST
1300 RDL 92374 608-A5
ARLETTE DR
14900 VCTV 92394 4296-A6
ARLINGTON DR
32500 YCPA 92399 649-D5
N ARLINGTON DR
3800 SBDO 92404 546-H7
ARLINGTON LN
12500 CHNO 91710 642-B6
ARLINGTON PL
6900 RCUC 91701 572-J6
12200 CHNO 91710 642-B5
ARLINGTON ST
10500 ADEL 92301 4294-H7
ARLISS CT
11800 GTER 92313 646-F3
ARLISS DR
11900 GTER 92313 646-F3
ARLISS LN
11800 GTER 92313 646-F3
ARLISS ST
600 RivC 92507 646-D6
ARLISS WY
11800 GTER 92313 646-F3
ARLISS DELL
11700 GTER 92313 646-F3
ARMADILLA ST
42500 SBdC 92365 (3683-E3 See Page 3592)
E ARMANDO ST
1100 UPL 91786 572-D7
ARMELINO RD
51200 SBdC 92285 (4576-B2 See Page 4486)
ARMITOS PL
300 DBAR 91765 640-D7
600 DBAR 91765 680-D1
E ARMORY CT
400 CLTN 92324 606-E5
ARMORY RD
200 BARS 92311 3679-H4
1100 BARS 92311 3680-B4
27900 SBdC 92311 3679-F5
ARMSLEY DR
3200 CHLS 91709 711-B1
ARMSLEY SQ
1300 ONT 91762 601-H5
W ARMSLEY SQ
100 ONT 91762 602-B5
ARMSLEY ST
5400 MTCL 91763 601-G5
ARMSTRONG DR
2400 CLAR 91711 571-D6
ARMSTRONG PL
7000 RCUC 91701 573-D6
ARMSTRONG RD
1100 FONT 92337 645-C4
2000 RivC 92509 645-A6
S ARMSTRONG WY
- UPL 91786 601-J4
ARMY RD
- NDLS 92363 3620-C6
ARNEAL RD
700 SBdC 92284 4747-F4
800 SBdC 92285 4747-F4
ARNOLD AV
56600 SBdC - 2971-G2
AROSA DR
500 SBdC - 517-B3
ARPENT RD
- SBdC 92365 3594-D6
ARRIBA LN
5500 SBdC 92301 (4113-D4 See Page 4112)
ARRIBA RD
6200 SBdC - 4844-B2
W ARROW
1800 SBDO 92410 606-C2
ARROW BLVD
16000 FONT 92335 604-G2
17000 FONT 92335 605-A2
17700 SBdC 92335 605-A2
ARROW CT
- SBdC - 4738-B5
ARROW DR
6300 SBdC - 4843-J2
ARROW HWY
4500 CLAR 91711 601-F4
4500 MTCL 91763 601-F4
E ARROW HWY
- UPL 91786 602-C3
100 CLAR 91711 601-D4
100 POM 91767 601-A4
1300 UPL 91730 602-C3
W ARROW HWY
- UPL 91786 602-A3
100 CLAR 91711 601-C4
900 POM 91767 601-C4
1000 UPL 91786 601-J3
ARROWBEAR DR
32800 SBdC - 519-D7
ARROWEED CIR
13500 VCTV 92392 4385-F5
ARROWHEAD AV
- FONT 92335 604-F3
- SBdC 92335 604-F3
1900 RLTO 92376 575-E4
6900 SBdC - 4843-J4
28800 SBdC 92311 3589-G7
N ARROWHEAD AV
100 RLTO 92376 605-F1
100 SBDO 92401 606-H1
100 SBDO 92408 606-H1
100 SBDO 92401 576-H5
600 RLTO 92376 575-F5
900 SBDO 92410 576-H5
1200 SBDO 92405 576-H2
2100 RLTO 92377 575-F4
3600 SBDO 92405 546-H7
3800 SBDO 92407 546-H7
S ARROWHEAD AV
100 SBDO 92401 606-H2
100 SBDO 92408 606-H4
500 RLTO 92376 605-F3
1000 RLTO 92316 605-F4
W ARROWHEAD AV
800 RLTO 92316 605-F5
ARROWHEAD BLVD
18300 SBdC 92407 515-C6
ARROWHEAD CT
9500 SBdC 92371 4564-F2
ARROWHEAD DR
300 SBdC - 518-C1
2100 SBdC 92372 4562-E2
2500 SBdC 92371 4562-F2
4800 SBdC 92371 4563-C2
7700 YUCA 92284 4957-C4
13000 VCTV 92392 4386-D1
ARROWHEAD RD
5100 SBDO 92404 546-J5
5100 SBDO 92404 547-A5
8100 SBdC 92371 4564-F1
9100 SBdC 92371 4474-F4
10900 SBdC 92392 4474-E2
12400 SBdC 92392 4384-E6
12500 VCTV 92392 4384-E4
15100 SBdC 92301 4294-E6
ARROWHEAD TR
18600 SBdC 92392 4387-A5
55100 SBdC - 349-L4
55100 SBdC - 350-D3
ARROWHEAD LAKE OH E
7800 HESP 92345 4567-B2
ARROWHEAD LAKE OH W
7500 HESP 92345 4567-B2
ARROWHEAD LAKE RD
4700 SBdC 92345 (4657-B3 See Page 4656)
5600 SBdC 92345 4567-C7
6400 HESP 92345 4567-B1
8800 HESP 92345 4477-B7
ARROWHEAD SPRINGS RD
- SBdC 92256 616-A3
5800 SBdC 92404 547-A4
5800 SBDO 92404 546-J4
5800 SBDO 92404 547-A4
ARROWHEAD VILLA RD
500 SBdC - 518-A2
ARROW ROUTE
8100 RCUC 91730 602-F3
9900 RCUC 91730 603-B2
11900 RCUC 91739 603-G2
13300 SBdC 91739 603-G2
13300 SBdC 92335 603-G2
13300 SBdC 92335 604-A2
15800 FONT 92335 604-D2
W ARROW ROUTE
1600 UPL 91786 601-F3
1600 SBdC 91786 601-F3
2400 CLAR 91711 601-F3
ARROWVIEW DR
- HIGH 92404 577-E5
300 RDL 92373 648-A2
ARROW WOOD DR
200 SBdC - 517-J2
ARROYO AV
1400 POM 91768 640-E1
9800 HESP 92345 4476-B5
N ARROYO AV
1400 ONT 91764 602-H5
ARROYO DR
200 BBLK - 4811-D1
900 BARS 92311 3679-J5
2100 POM 91768 640-D1
13500 VCTV 92392 4386-C3
ARROYO LN
18000 CHLS 91709 712-B6
ARROYO RD
100 RDL 92373 648-D3
10200 HESP 92345 4476-B2
11800 HESP 92345 4386-B7
34500 SBdC - 4481-E6
36300 SBdC - 4482-A6
ARROYO ST
18700 ADEL 92301 4205-A4
ARROYO CREST
1200 RDL 92373 648-A4
ARROYO VISTA AV
7400 RCUC 91730 572-F7
7700 RCUC 91730 602-G1
ARROYO VISTA DR
4800 SBDO 92346 578-B3
4900 HIGH 92346 578-B3
ARTEMECIA
7300 SBdC 92277 (4894-H7 See Page 4824)
ARTESIA AV
- SBdC 92284 4817-F2
100 SBdC 92284 4747-F4
800 SBdC 92285 4747-F2
S ARTESIA ST
2200 SBDO 92408 607-A7
ARTESIA WY
11300 SBdC 92256 615-F6
S ARTESIAN AV
100 SBDO 92410 606-E2
ARTH DR
600 SBdC - 517-A3
ARTHUR AV
700 POM 91768 640-E1
1200 RIV 92501 645-J7
ARTHUR CT
6600 CHNO 91710 642-B6
ARTHUR ST
6500 CHNO 91710 642-A7
19000 APLV 92308 4387-B7
ARTISTIC AL
- SBdC 92308 4567-D6
ART TOWNSEND DR
- SBDO 92408 607-C1
E ARTURO ST
1100 UPL 91786 572-D7
ARUBA CT
- RCUC 91739 573-H2
ARVIDSON CT
3600 CHNO 91710 681-C1
ARVIDSON ST
3700 CHNO 91710 681-D1
ARVILLE ST
500 BARS 92311 3679-G4
ASBURY AV
800 POM 91767 601-B5
ASCENSION CT
400 SBdC - 516-A1
ASCENSION RD
20900 SBdC - 516-A1
20900 SBdC - 4736-A7
ASCOT PL
6200 RCUC 91739 573-G4
ASH AV
2200 UPL 91784 571-H3
6500 RCUC 91739 573-J5
19400 ADEL 92301 4204-G2
N ASH AV
600 RLTO 92376 575-J5
ASH CIR
14700 CHLS 91709 681-D5
ASH CT
4400 MTCL 91763 601-E5
6700 CHNO 91710 682-B2
ASH DR
- SBdC 92256 616-A3
600 SBdC - 519-E2
14800 CHLS 91709 681-D5
16700 FONT 92337 644-J1
49000 SBdC 92256 615-G3
W ASH DR
700 SBDO 92405 546-G7
700 SBDO 92405 576-G1
ASH LN
- SBdC - 4738-E7
800 SBdC 92314 (4743-A7 See Page 4662)
800 SBdC 92314 4813-A1
ASH RD
1800 SBdC 92397 4652-E3
3400 SBdC 92371 3678-G5
9700 SBdC 92371 4472-F6
15400 SBdC 92371 4292-E6
ASH ST
11500 APLV 92308 4387-B7
14500 HESP 92345 4565-J3
14700 HESP 92345 4566-A3
18100 SBdC 92316 605-C7
20900 SBdC 92347 (3587-F5 See Page 3586)
N ASH ST
- RDL 92373 648-A1
S ASH ST
- RDL 92373 648-A1
600 CLTN 92324 606-D7
ASHBROOK CT
12500 SBdC 92392 4386-J5
ASHBROOK DR
3100 CHLS 91709 681-B7
ASHBROOK LN
- POM 91766 640-F7
- POM 91766 641-A4
ASHBURY DR
14300 CHLS 91709 680-G4
ASHBURY LN
200 UPL 91784 572-C4
ASHCROFT CT
13200 CHLS 91709 680-J1
ASHFIELD AV
1100 POM 91767 601-B5
ASHFORD AV
9700 SBdC 92316 605-D5
N ASHFORD AV
500 RLTO 92336 575-D7
500 RLTO 92336 605-D1
500 RLTO 92376 575-D6
500 RLTO 92376 605-D1
2200 RLTO 92377 575-C1
S ASHFORD AV
300 RLTO 92376 605-D3
500 RLTO 92316 605-D3
500 RLTO 92335 605-D3
ASHFORD CT
9900 RCUC 91730 603-A1
28300 HIGH 92346 578-B5
ASHFORD LN
- FONT 92336 574-D5
ASHFORD ST
10100 RCUC 91730 603-A1
11900 RCUC 91739 603-F1
ASHFORTH DR
1200 RDL 92373 648-J6
E ASHGATE CT
3200 ONT 91761 643-B6
ASHGATE PL
3200 ONT 91761 643-B6
ASHGATE WY
3200 ONT 91761 643-B6
E ASHGATE WY
2700 ONT 91761 643-B6
ASHLAND AV
1400 CLAR 91711 601-B2
ASHLAND CT
- CHLS 91709 681-H7
ASHLAND LN
- FONT 92336 573-J6
- FONT 92336 574-A6
ASHLAND RD
7800 SBdC - (4569-J2 See Page 4568)
10500 SBdC 92308 4479-G3
23600 SBdC 92308 4478-E3
29700 SBdC - 4480-B3
W ASHLAND ST
800 ONT 91762 642-A4
ASHLAND WY
- YCPA 92399 649-E2
ASHLAR DR
500 SBdC - 517-B3
ASHLEY CT
3200 CHLS 91709 681-C8
5800 CHNO 91710 681-J2
6100 CHNO 91710 682-A2
ASHLEY DR
10800 ADEL 92301 4204-H4
ASHLEY PL
2100 UPL 91784 571-H4
ASHLEY ST
7200 RivC 92324 647-B6
ASHLEY WY
800 RDL 92374 608-A5
ASHLEY GLEN DR
14900 VCTV 92394 4295-J6
ASH MEADOW RD
29600 SBdC - 4738-C4
ASHOUK WY
- VCTV 92392 4385-E7
ASHPORT ST
1300 POM 91768 640-F1
ASHTON PL
6100 RCUC 91739 573-J3
E ASH TREE LN
1800 CLTN 92324 646-G1
ASHURST ST
- TNP 92278 4751-J4
E ASHWOOD
2000 SBDO 92404 577-D2
ASHWOOD CT
1500 UPL 91784 571-H6
9100 HESP 92345 4475-H7
S ASHWOOD DR
400 SBdC 92314 4742-B7
ASHWOOD LN
14900 CHLS 91709 681-D5
27400 SBdC - 4737-H7
E ASHWOOD LN
1900 CLTN 92324 646-H1
ASHWOOD RD
22100 SBdC 92347 (3587-H6 See Page 3586)
24800 SBdC 92347 3588-F6
ASIO WY
8500 YUCA 92284 4957-J6
ASPEN AV
7700 FONT 92336 575-C7
8100 RCUC 91730 603-C2
25000 LMLN 92354 647-C2
N ASPEN AV
200 RLTO 92376 605-D1
500 RLTO 92376 575-D7
2300 RLTO 92377 575-D3
2300 SBdC 92377 575-D3
S ASPEN AV
600 RLTO 92316 605-D3
9300 SBdC 92316 605-D4
ASPEN CIR
11900 GTER 92313 646-E3
ASPEN CT
- HESP 92345 4475-J7
7500 HIGH 92346 578-B6
15500 CHLS 91709 681-D7
27200 SBdC - (3935-H3 See Page 3934)
ASPEN DR
1200 BBLK - 4812-B3
5100 MTCL 91763 601-G6
29500 SBdC - 4738-D7
49000 SBdC 92256 615-G4
50900 SBdC 92256 616-A3
72500 TNP 92277 4892-B7
N ASPEN DR
3700 SBDO 92404 547-F7
ASPEN LN
600 POM 91767 601-A4
3600 CHLS 91709 681-D6
E ASPEN LN
1900 CLTN 92324 646-H1
ASPEN ST
10500 SBdC 92345 4564-H1
14500 HESP 92345 4475-J7
14500 HESP 92345 4476-A7
17300 HESP 92345 4566-G1
N ASPEN WY
500 UPL 91786 602-A2
ASPENCLIFF CT
11500 FONT 92337 644-H3
ASPEN GROVE LN
1600 DBAR 91765 680-A4
ASPEN KNOLL DR
22900 DBAR 91765 680-B3
ASPEN VIEW CIR
12300 VCTV 92392 4385-F6
ASPEN VIEW ST
12500 VCTV 92392 4385-F6
E ASPENWOOD CT
2100 SBDO 92404 577-D2
ASPENWOOD LN
9100 HESP 92345 4475-H7
ASSAD CT
- RCUC 91737 573-B2
ASTER AV
7300 YUCA 92284 4957-H4
ASTER CT
6700 CHNO 91710 642-B5
12500 RCUC 91739 573-G5
ASTER PL
61900 SBdC 92252 4889-C6
ASTER RD
- SBdC - (4025-H3 See Page 3934)
6700 SBdC 92345 4564-H1
7600 SBdC - (4571-H2 See Page 4570)
8900 SBdC 92345 4474-H4
10900 SBdC 92392 4474-H2
12900 SBdC 92392 4385-E1
14100 ADEL 92301 4384-H2
14500 ADEL 92301 4294-G1
14800 SBdC 92301 4294-H6
17300 ADEL 92301 4204-G3
20100 ADEL 92301 4114-G3
20100 SBdC 92301 4114-G7
ASTER ST
2300 SBDO 92407 546-A5
11400 LMLN 92354 647-B2
13200 SBdC 93562 2145-A3
E ASTER ST
100 UPL 91786 572-C7
W ASTER ST
300 UPL 91786 572-B7
1000 UPL 91786 571-H7
ASTI CT
- SBdC - 4774-F7
ASTI DR
- RCUC 91701 573-E4
ASTON AV
2500 POM 91768 640-D2
ASTOR RD
25300 SBdC - (4025-H7 See Page 3934)
ASTORIA RD
29000 SBdC - (4569-J1 See Page 4568)
ASTRAL DR
1200 BARS 92311 3679-H5
ASTRAL RD
36900 SBdC - (4392-B3 See Page 4302)
ASTRAL ST
15700 CHLS 91709 681-C7
S ATCHISON ST
700 CLTN 92324 606-G7
800 CLTN 92324 646-H1
W ATCHISON ST
2300 SBDO 92410 606-A2
2900 SBDO 92376 606-A2
2900 SBDO 92376 605-J2
ATHENS CT
1700 CLAR 91711 601-C1
ATHERTON RD
- SBdC 92365 (3685-B3 See Page 3594)
ATHLETIC FIELD RD
37000 SBdC - (3682-A2 See Page 3592)
ATHOL AV
6300 TNP 92277 4892-F5
ATHOL LN
30500 SBdC 92365 3764-H6
ATHOL ST
13400 SBdC 93562 2144-J2
13400 SBdC 93562 2145-A2
14900 SBdC 92335 604-D4
15800 FONT 92335 604-F4
17100 FONT 92335 605-A4
17800 SBdC 92335 605-C3
W ATHOL ST
300 SBDO 92401 606-H2
1200 RLTO 92316 605-D3
ATLANTA CT
800 CLAR 91711 601-B1
ATLANTIC AV
3900 HIGH 92346 577-H4
27900 HIGH 92346 578-A4
E ATLANTIC AV
3000 SBDO 92346 577-G4
3400 HIGH 92346 577-G4
W ATLANTIC CT
600 UPL 91786 602-A1
ATLANTIC ST
100 POM 91768 640-C2
18200 HESP 92345 4477-A5
ATNAH RD
7600 SBdC - 4843-F6
15500 APLV 92307 4297-B4
ATOKA LN
12200 VCTV 92392 4385-C6
ATOKA RD
15800 APLV 92307 4297-D2
ATOM DR
10500 SBdC - (4483-D1 See Page 4482)
10700 SBdC - (4393-D7 See Page 4302)
ATSINA RD
8100 SBdC 92371 4564-B3
9100 SBdC 92371 4474-B2
12100 SBdC 92371 4384-A1
ATSTAR ST
14200 VCTV 92392 4386-C1
14400 VCTV 92392 4296-C7
ATWOOD ST
11700 RCUC 91739 573-G6
N AUBREY PL
6100 SBDO 92407 546-A3
AUBURN AV
- HESP 92345 4475-H7
2100 SBdC 92301 (4202-E4 See Page 4112)
5000 SBDO 92407 546-B5
6600 RCUC 91737 573-A5
6600 SBdC 92301 (4203-B4 See Page 4112)
7800 SBdC 92301 4204-A4
8700 ADEL 92301 4204-D4
11400 ADEL 92301 4205-A4
11700 YCPA 92399 650-A2
AUBURN CT
- RDL 92374 608-F7
1800 UPL 91784 571-J5
11700 YCPA 92399 650-B2
13400 FONT 92336 574-A7
14100 VCTV 92394 4295-H6
14300 CHLS 91709 680-G3
AUBURN DR
200 SBdC - 517-E2
AUBURN ST
1300 UPL 91784 571-J6
AUBURN WY
300 CLAR 91711 571-D6
S AUGUSTA AV
1500 ONT 91761 642-F6
AUGUSTA CIR
- APLV 92308 4387-C7
- APLV 92308 4477-B5
AUGUSTA CT
200 SBdC - 517-E2
1800 CLAR 91711 571-F7
1900 ONT 91761 642-F4
AUGUSTA DR
- FONT 92336 574-H2
- UPL 91784 572-E7
10600 RCUC 91701 573-B6
14200 VCTV 92392 4386-C1
16000 CHLS 91709 711-D1
26000 SBdC - 517-E1
S AUGUSTA PL
2200 ONT 91761 642-F5
AUGUSTA RD
- SBdC - 348-K10
31400 SBdC 92365 (3765-A4 See Page 3764)
31500 SBdC 92365 3764-J4
AUGUSTA ST
1100 POM 91768 640-D1
AUGUSTA WY
- FONT 92336 603-J1
12600 SBdC 92392 4387-A5
AUKIET
- SBdC 92365 (3595-A6 See Page 3594)
AUKLET RD
- SBdC 92365 3594-D6
- SBdC 92365 (3595-B6 See Page 3594)
AURORA AV
5700 RivC 91752 683-G5
13100 VCTV 92392 4385-H4
13200 SBdC 92392 4385-H4
AURORA CT
11800 FONT 92337 644-D4
AURORA DR
500 CLAR 91711 601-E1
58100 YUCA 92284 4888-B4
58100 YUCA 92284 4958-B1
E AURORA LN
1400 SBDO 92408 607-C6
S AURORA LN
1700 SBDO 92408 607-C5
AURORA PL
7400 RCUC 91730 573-B7
AURORA RD
39300 BBLK - 4811-B1
AURORA WY
1800 BARS 92311 3680-B5
AUSTIN CT
1900 CLAR 91711 571-D7
6600 RCUC 91701 573-C5
11400 FONT 92337 644-D3
AUSTIN RD
14200 VCTV 92392 4386-D1
AUSTIN ST
82900 SBdC 93562 2145-A4
AUSTIN WY
- RDL 92374 608-D4
S AUSTIN WY
200 UPL 91786 602-A4
AUTO CENTER DR
- POM 91766 640-H5
400 CLAR 91711 601-C5
S AUTO CENTER DR
700 ONT 91761 643-F3
W AUTO CENTER DR
600 SBDO 92408 606-G5
S AUTO PLAZA DR
800 SBDO 92408 606-G6
W AUTO PLAZA DR
500 SBDO 92408 606-G5
AUTOPLEX DR
9400 MTCL 91763 601-G5
AUTRY CT
17800 CHLS 91709 712-A5
AUTUMN AV
3400 CHLS 91709 711-C1
AUTUMN CT
14900 HESP 92345 4566-A6
AUTUMN DR
- YCPA 92399 609-J6
AUTUMN LN
14700 SBdC - (3935-J4 See Page 3934)
AUTUMN PL
11700 FONT 92337 644-C3
AUTUMN ST
11300 ADEL 92301 4295-A6
AUTUMN CHASE DR
7300 HIGH 92346 578-B6
AUTUMN GLEN CT
6500 RCUC 91701 573-D5
AUTUMN GLEN RD
28200 HIGH 92346 578-A4
AUTUMN GLOW CT
4400 CHLS 91709 711-E2
AUTUMN HILL DR
8800 RCUC 91730 602-G2
AUTUMN HILL LN
14300 CHLS 91709 680-J4
AUTUMN HILL PL
8800 RCUC 91730 602-H4
AUTUMN HILL RD
1500 DBAR 91765 680-C3
AUTUMN LEAF DR
8300 RCUC 91730 602-F2
AUTUMN LEAF RD
47300 SBdC 92365 3764-H7
AUTUMN LEAVES AV
12500 SBdC 92392 4386-H4
W AUTUMN MIST DR
2100 RLTO 92377 545-A6
AUTUMN RIDGE RD
3200 ONT 91761 643-B7
AUTUMNWOOD DR
12900 VCTV 92392 4386-C4
AVACADO AV
8800 HESP 92345 4476-H7
AVA LOMA ST
12300 VCTV 92392 4385-C4
AVALON AV
100 SBdC 92284 4748-C6
1000 SBdC 92284 4818-C1
2100 POM 91768 640-E1
3800 SBdC 92284 4888-C3
4700 YUCA 92284 4888-C7
6600 YUCA 92284 4958-C1
9000 ADEL 92301 4204-E2
11200 ADEL 92301 4205-B2
11700 YCPA 92399 649-J2
16100 VCTV 92392 4296-D4
25700 SBdC 92404 577-D2
E AVALON AV
2600 SBDO 92346 577-F2
AVALON CT
- CHLS 91709 711-H1
200 UPL 91784 572-C6
8400 RCUC 91701 572-F6
58300 YUCA 92284 4888-C6
AVALON RD
9100 SBdC 92371 4562-G1
9200 SBdC 92371 4472-G7
14300 VCTV 92392 4386-D1
17700 ADEL 92301 4204-D7
42300 BBLK - 4811-J1
42300 BBLK - 4812-A1
AVALON ST
1800 RivC 92509 645-E7
8700 RCUC 91701 572-J5
AVANTI WY
- VCTV 92392 4386-F5
AVEIRO RD
11600 FONT 92337 644-E3
AVENA WY
34400 YCPA 92399 649-H2
AVENAL PL
- FONT 92336 574-G2
AVENAL ST
- VCTV 92392 4385-F2
100 SBdC 92372 4472-A5
2100 SBdC 92371 4472-E5
4800 SBdC 92371 4473-C5
7500 SBdC 92371 4474-E4
9300 SBdC 92301 4294-E6
9700 SBdC 92345 4474-F4
11000 SBdC 92345 4475-A4
13000 HESP 92392 4475-F4
13000 HESP 92345 4475-F4
AVENIDA ANITA
15200 CHLS 91709 680-G6
AVENIDA CABRILLO
2300 CHLS 91709 680-J6
AVENIDA CAPISTRANO
- CLTN 92324 606-C3
AVENIDA CARMEL
- CLTN 92324 606-C3
AVENIDA CASTRO
8200 RCUC 91730 602-H2
AVENIDA COMPADRES
1300 CHLS 91709 680-G6
AVENIDA CORSICA
- HIGH 92346 578-D7
AVENIDA DE LAS FLORES
14900 CHLS 91709 681-A5
AVENIDA DEL MONTE
15000 CHLS 91709 680-J5
AVENIDA DEL RIO
15000 CHLS 91709 681-A5
AVENIDA DEL SOL
3300 SBdC 92252 4819-B6
3900 SBdC 92252 4889-B1
AVENIDA DE PORTUGAL
- CHLS 91709 711-J3
AVENIDA DE SONOMA
17800 APLV 92307 4296-G2
AVENIDA HACIENDA
2000 CHLS 91709 680-J4
AVENIDA LA CANDELA
4300 SBdC 92252 4889-B2
AVENIDA LA ESPANA DAGA
4300 SBdC 92252 4889-B2
AVENIDA LA FLORA DESIERTA
4400 SBdC 92252 4889-C2
AVENIDA LA MANANA
4500 SBdC 92252 4889-C2
AVENIDA LA MIRADA
4500 SBdC 92252 4889-C2
AVENIDA LA PAZ
2200 CHLS 91709 680-J5
AVENIDA LAREDO
24900 SBdC 92311 3678-G5
AVENIDA LAS RAMBLAS
2100 CHLS 91709 680-H2
AVENIDA LEON
7000 RCUC 91701 572-G6
8200 RCUC 91730 602-H2
AVENIDA MARGUERITE
2700 CHLS 91709 681-A5
AVENIDA MIRAVILLA
8500 RivC 92223 651-B7
AVENIDA MIROLA
17800 APLV 92307 4296-G2
AVENIDA MONTEREY
- CLTN 92324 606-C3
E AVENIDA RANCHEROS
- POM 91766 640-E5
24000 DBAR 91765 640-E5
AVENIDA REQUEJO
26200 SBdC 92354 647-F2
AVENIDA SERENA
34600 SBdC 92311 3678-G5
AVENIDA TORTUGA
3900 SBdC 92252 4819-B7
AVENIDA VEJAR
8100 RCUC 91730 602-E3
AVENUE A
100 BARS 92311 3679-G3
34900 YCPA 92399 649-J3
34900 YCPA 92399 650-B3
AVENUE B
100 BARS 92311 3679-F3
900 CALI 92320 649-H7
34200 YCPA 92399 649-H3
34900 YCPA 92399 650-A3
AVENUE B CT
34500 YCPA 92399 649-J3
AVENUE C
100 BARS 92311 3679-F3
33600 YCPA 92399 649-F3
34900 YCPA 92399 650-A3
AVENUE D
100 BARS 92311 3679-F3
31900 YCPA 92399 649-C3
34900 YCPA 92399 650-B3
AVENUE DEL SOL
17100 FONT 92337 645-A2
AVENUE E
100 BARS 92311 3679-F3
31300 YCPA 92399 649-B4
34900 YCPA 92399 650-A4
AVENUE EYE
33900 YCPA 92399 649-G6
35600 YCPA 92399 650-B6
AVENUE F
100 BARS 92311 3679-F3
AVENUE G
100 BARS 92311 3679-F3
33800 YCPA 92399 649-H6
34900 YCPA 92399 650-A6
AVENUE H
100 BARS 92311 3679-D3
33800 YCPA 92399 649-G6
34900 YCPA 92399 650-C6
AVENUE I
700 BARS 92311 3679-E4
33900 YCPA 92399 649-G6
35600 YCPA 92399 650-B6
AVENUE J
500 BARS 92311 3679-E4
33900 YCPA 92399 649-H7
AVENUE K
500 CALI 92320 649-G7
700 BARS 92311 3679-D4
AVENUE L
200 CALI 92320 649-B7
200 CALI 92320 650-A7
E AVENUE L
100 CALI 92320 650-B7
W AVENUE L
600 CALI 92320 650-A7
AVENUE LA CANDELA
4100 SBdC 92252 4889-B1
AVENUE LA MANANA
4100 SBdC 92252 4889-C1
AVENUE N
31700 RDL 92373 649-B5
AVENUE P
24600 SBdC 92301 368-G4
AVERY RD
600 CLAR 91711 601-C3
AVERY ST
15400 CHLS 91709 681-F6
17800 ADEL 92301 4204-G7
E AVERY ST
400 SBDO 92404 546-J7
600 SBDO 92404 547-A7
AVERY WY
10400 ADEL 92301 4204-G6
AVIAN WY
2300 SBdC - 519-A6
AVIATION DR
1400 RDL 92374 608-F3
19000 VCTV 92394 4205-F3
55100 YUCA 92284 4957-F1
57200 YUCA 92284 4958-A1
AVIGNON CT
400 RivC 92501 646-A7
AVILA AV
7400 RCUC 91730 572-G7
13400 CHNO 91710 682-B1
AVILA RD
6200 YUCA 92284 4887-J7
AVILA WY
100 CLAR 91711 571-D7
E AVION DR
- ONT 91761 642-H2
AVION LN
15500 VCTV 92394 4296-B4
18500 SBdC 92316 605-D5
AVOCADO AV
12300 CHNO 91710 642-A5
AVOCADO ST
35500 YCPA 92399 650-B1
AVON CT
- RCUC 91739 573-F5
200 BBLK - 4811-C1
14900 VCTV 92394 4296-A2
AVON ST
3800 RivC 92509 644-D7
AVONDALE RD
13500 SBdC 92371 4382-J4
18700 SBdC 92301 (4202-J5 See Page 4112)
AWARD DR
500 CLTN 92324 606-F6
AYAL CT
- SBdC - 4774-F6
N AYALA DR
1200 RLTO 92376 575-E5
2000 RLTO 92377 575-E2
2800 SBdC 92377 575-E2
AYRSHIRE CT
11000 SBdC 92345 (4655-A1 See Page 4654)
AZALEA AV
14900 SBdC 92335 604-D5
15800 FONT 92335 604-F5
N AZALEA AV
400 ONT 91762 601-J7
6200 SBDO 92407 546-A2
S AZALEA AV
1100 ONT 91762 641-J2
AZALEA CT
100 RDL 92373 647-J2
1200 UPL 91784 571-J6
6900 RCUC 91739 573-H5
16300 FONT 92335 604-H5
AZALEA DR
900 POM 91766 640-H4
AZALEA LN
13300 YCPA 92399 650-B6
AZALEA RD
14000 SBdC 92371 4382-J2
14700 SBdC 92371 4292-J7
AZALEA ST
5200 SBDO 92407 546-A5
6000 CHNO 91710 641-J5
AZALIA LN
300 SBdC - 516-E2
AZTEC AV
5500 TNP 92277 4892-F3
AZTEC CT
15800 APLV 92307 4297-F2
AZTEC DR
2800 RivC 92509 645-B6
AZTEC LN
8900 ADEL 92301 4204-C6
11700 ADEL 92301 4205-A6
AZURE CT
11300 FONT 92337 644-D3
W AZURE CT
200 UPL 91786 602-B4
AZURE VIEW RD
11400 SBdC 92372 4472-D2
12900 SBdC 92372 4382-D3
13900 SBdC 92371 4382-D3
AZURITE AV
8900 RCUC 91730 602-G1
8900 RCUC 91730 572-G7
AZURITE DR
1900 SBdC - 4742-J2
15600 CHLS 91709 680-J7
AZURITE RD
27300 SBdC 92311 3679-D6
31300 SBdC - 4480-F7
32500 SBdC - 4481-A7

STREET Block City ZIP Pg-Grid

AZURITE ST
9700 YCPA 92399 610-A4
AZUSA CT
6500 RivC 92509 645-B6
11200 RCUC 91730 603-D4

B

B AV
4900 SBdC 92252 4889-C3
9400 HESP 92345 4476-F6
58200 SBdC 92284 4888-B2
B CT
- SBdC 92284 4957-A4
B DR
- SBdC 92252 4889-B3
- SBdC 92284 4956-J5
- SBdC 92284 4957-A5
B LN
100 SBdC - 518-B1
800 SBdC 92314 (4743-A7 See Page 4662)
800 SBdC 92314 4813-A1
B ST
- BARS 92311 3680-G5
- SBdC - 4606-C2
100 NDLS 92363 3620-D6
900 SBdC 92374 609-A7
4500 SBdC 92252 4889-C1
4900 CHNO 91710 641-G7
10400 RivC 91752 644-A5
12100 SBdC 93562 2144-G6
16500 VCTV 92392 4296-E4
33300 SBdC - (3681-F7 See Page 3590)
33600 YCPA 92399 649-G2
34400 SBdC 92311 3679-F5
62000 SBdC 92252 4959-C3
80400 SBdC 93562 2234-G3
E B ST
100 CLTN 92324 606-E5
100 ONT 91764 602-C7
W B ST
100 CLTN 92324 606-D5
100 ONT 91762 602-B7
700 ONT 91762 642-A1
800 SBdC 92324 606-C5
BACA AV
12300 CHNO 91710 641-G6
BACA FLATS
36400 BARS 92311 3590-A7
36400 SBdC 92311 3590-A7
BACCHARIS LN
- RCUC 91701 572-J5
BACK STRAIGHT RD
14000 SBdC 92335 604-B3
BADEN AV
- RDL 92359 608-J3
- RDL 92359 609-A3
- SBdC 92359 608-H3
BADGER
3300 SBdC 92371 4472-J3
BADGER AV
17200 ADEL 92301 4204-E1
17200 ADEL 92301 4294-F1
BADGER LN
- FONT 92336 574-D3
500 BBLK - 4811-E2
1000 SBdC - 4738-A6
32700 SBdC - 519-C6
BADGER TR
- SBdC - 4773-J7
BADGER CANYON RD
5800 SBdC 92407 546-C2
5800 SBDO 92407 546-C3
S BADGERGLEN PL
2700 ONT 91761 643-C6
BAFT LN
1300 DBAR 91765 680-A3
BAGDAD HWY
100 SBdC 92278 370-F7
900 SBdC 92277 4822-J1
3300 TNP 92277 4822-J7
4500 TNP 92277 4892-J1
BAGDAD WY
- SBdC 92278 370-H6
BAGDAD CHASE RD
23500 SBdC - 370-D1
BAGGALA DR
- SBdC - (4655-B6 See Page 4654)
BAGLEY AV
5600 TNP 92277 4892-E4
BAGLEY DR
5800 TNP 92277 4892-D4
BAHAMA CT
- RCUC 91739 573-H2
BAHIA CT
1100 ONT 91762 641-J2
BAILEY AV
700 NDLS 92363 3620-B7
BAILEY CT
2600 SBDO 92407 546-A4
15500 VCTV 92394 4295-H5
BAILEY ST
- TNP 92278 4751-J5
BAILEY TKTR
- SBdC 92407 515-J5
- SBdC 92407 516-A6
- SBDO 92407 516-A6

N BAILEY TKTR
6700 SBdC 92407 516-A6
6700 SBDO 92407 516-A6
6700 SBDO 92407 545-J1
6700 SBDO 92407 546-A1
BAILEYA AV
2000 SBdC 92277 4821-J2
5300 TNP 92277 4891-J4
6100 TNP 92277 4892-A5
BAILEY CANYON RD
5800 SBdC 92407 545-H3
5900 SBDO 92407 545-H3
BAIN ST
3800 RivC 91752 644-A7
BAINBRIDGE ST
1700 POM 91766 640-H4
BAINBRIDGE WY
- CHLS 91709 681-J7
- CHLS 91709 711-H1
BAJADO CT
8700 RCUC 91730 572-G7
BAKER AV
8200 RCUC 91730 602-F3
12400 CHNO 91710 641-F6
12900 ONT 91761 642-G7
12900 ONT 91761 682-G1
N BAKER AV
700 ONT 91764 602-F5
S BAKER AV
1200 ONT 91761 642-G3
BAKER BLVD
71700 SBdC - 2971-G3
BAKER CT
12500 CHNO 91710 641-F6
BAKER RD
700 SBdC 92372 4472-B5
8500 SBdC - 4480-G1
11000 SBdC - (4390-G7 See Page 4300)
BAKER ST
12300 CHNO 91710 641-F6
BAKER TR
54800 YUCA 92284 4957-C6
BALATON ST
9700 RCUC 91737 572-J4
W BALBIRNIE AV
200 CLTN 92324 606-D3
BALBOA AV
6300 YUCA 92284 4888-C7
9700 SBdC - 4482-J3
N BALBOA AV
1300 ONT 91764 602-G5
S BALBOA AV
1400 ONT 91761 642-G3
BALBOA CT
800 RDL 92373 648-C3
6100 RCUC 91701 572-G4
11700 ADEL 92301 4295-B5
13600 FONT 92336 574-A7
26100 SBdC - (3935-H6 See Page 3934)
BALBOA DR
12300 VCTV 92392 4385-H6
BALBOA LN
42300 BBLK - 4811-J1
42300 BBLK - 4812-A1
BALBOA PL
100 NDLS 92363 3620-A3
BALBOA RD
11000 APLV 92308 4477-F1
11300 APLV 92308 4387-F7
BALBOA ST
1000 NDLS 92363 3620-B7
1400 POM 91767 601-C6
BALBOA WY
1800 UPL 91784 572-A6
BALD EAGLE RDG
- SBdC - 518-C3
BALDRIDGE CT
6300 SBdC 92346 577-H3
BALDRIDGE CANYON DR
6200 SBdC 92346 577-H3
BALDWIN AV
400 RDL 92374 608-A4
1000 POM 91767 601-B7
BALDWIN CT
14100 RCUC 91739 574-B1
BALDWIN LN
1000 BARS 92311 3679-G4
44300 SBdC - 4742-E7
44800 SBdC 92314 4742-G7
BALDWIN ST
18100 ADEL 92301 4205-A5
34500 SBdC 92311 3679-G5
BALDWIN LAKE RD
800 SBdC - (4743-A4 See Page 4662)
1000 SBdC - 4742-H2
BALDWIN RANCH RD
1200 SBdC - (4743-A4 See Page 4662)
BALDY LN
10100 HESP 92345 4475-H4
BALDY RD
900 SBdC - 512-D1
900 SBdC - (4732-H3 See Page 4653)
2500 SBdC - (4733-A3 See Page 4653)

BALDY MESA RD
3500 SBdC - 4734-B1
3500 SBdC - 4654-B6
4900 SBdC 92371 4654-D2
5400 SBdC 92345 4654-D2
6100 SBdC 92345 4564-F2
6100 SBdC 92371 4564-F2
9000 SBdC 92371 4474-F5
9000 SBdC 92345 4474-F2
10900 SBdC 92392 4474-F2
11800 SBdC 92392 4384-F7
12500 VCTV 92392 4384-F6
13600 ADEL 92301 4384-F6
13600 ADEL 92392 4384-F6
BALDY VIEW AV
900 POM 91767 601-D7
BALDY VIEW DR
33500 SBdC - 519-E3
BALDY VISTA DR
8500 RCUC 91730 602-F3
BALFOUR AV
16900 SBdC - 371-A4
BALFOUR CT
1300 RDL 92374 648-E1
BALFRIN DR
900 SBdC - 517-B4
BALLARD LN
- SBdC 92285 4748-B3
BALLATA AV
45700 SBdC 92365 3764-C5
BALLENA DR
200 DBAR 91765 640-D6
BALLENGER RD
- SBdC - 516-B1
- SBdC - 4736-C7
BALLESTROS AV
13100 CHNO 91710 641-E7
13100 CHNO 91710 681-E1
BALLY CT
9200 RCUC 91730 603-A4
BALMORAL DR
14700 VCTV 92394 4295-J6
BALSA AV
200 SBdC 92284 4748-B4
700 SBdC 92285 4748-B4
900 SBdC 92284 4818-B2
3700 SBdC 92284 4888-B1
4800 YUCA 92284 4888-B3
6500 YUCA 92284 4958-B1
30900 SBdC 92311 3680-C1
BALSA CT
10200 RCUC 91730 573-A7
10500 APLV 92308 4477-H3
BALSA RD
4800 SBdC - 4886-D4
BALSA ST
8700 RCUC 91730 572-F7
10000 RCUC 91730 573-A7
10500 APLV 92308 4477-G3
35400 YCPA 92399 610-B6
BALSAM AV
9700 HESP 92345 4476-B1
11700 HESP 92345 4386-B7
16300 SBdC 92335 604-H6
BALSAM CT
15400 CHLS 91709 681-D6
BALSAM DR
100 SBdC - 518-D1
1200 BBLK - 4812-B3
1500 POM 91766 640-H4
BALSAM LN
700 SBdC - 517-E3
23000 SBdC - 516-F3
BALSAM RD
12100 VCTV 92345 4386-B4
12100 VCTV 92392 4386-B4
BALSAMO RD
- SBdC - 348-H6
W BALTIC CT
600 UPL 91786 602-A1
BALTIMORE CT
6700 RCUC 91701 573-D5
12900 CHNO 91710 641-E7
BALTIMORE DR
11200 RCUC 91701 573-D5
BALTUSROL CT
- FONT 92336 574-H2
BALTUSROL LN
- FONT 92336 574-H2
BAMBI CT
14100 SBdC 92371 4383-C2
BAMBI TR
200 SBdC - 516-H2
BAMBOO CT
- FONT 92337 645-B1
14800 SBdC 92335 604-D3
BAMBOO PL
6500 RCUC 91739 573-G5
BANANA AV
- FONT 92336 604-B2
3300 CHLS 91709 681-C6
7100 FONT 92336 574-B5
8100 FONT 92335 604-B2
8100 SBdC 92335 604-B2
10300 SBdC 92337 604-B7
10500 SBdC 92337 604-B7
10500 SBdC 92337 644-B1
10500 SBdC 92337 644-B2
11200 FONT 92337 644-B4

BANANAWOOD CT
11600 FONT 92337 644-B3
BANAS RD
23700 SBdC 92324 646-H3
BANCROFT CT
14000 FONT 92336 574-B7
BANCROFT ST
25900 LMLN 92354 647-E3
BANDELIER DR
1200 BARS 92311 3680-A6
BANDERA RD
5700 YUCA 92284 4888-A6
57300 YUCA 92284 4887-J6
BANDERA ST
4200 MTCL 91763 641-F1
5000 MTCL 91763 601-G7
BANDICOOT TR
6900 SBdC 92345 4565-H3
8100 HESP 92345 4565-H2
BANDICOOT WY
6600 SBdC 92345 4565-H6
BANDINI RD
10700 SBdC - 4482-E1
BANDOLA ST
6500 RCUC 91737 573-B5
BANE CANYON RD
- CHLS - 711-F6
15900 CHLS 91709 681-H7
15900 CHLS 91709 711-G1
BANFF DR
28800 SBdC - 4738-C5
BANGOR AV
6900 HIGH 92346 577-G5
7300 HESP 92345 4566-J1
11400 LMLN 92354 647-F2
N BANGOR AV
1600 SBDO 92346 577-G2
BANGOR CT
18100 HESP 92345 4566-J1
BANGOR LN
500 SBdC - 518-B3
18200 HESP 92345 4566-J1
18200 HESP 92345 4567-A1
BANGOR ST
200 POM 91767 601-A5
BANNER RIDGE RD
900 DBAR 91765 680-C2
BANNING AV
10500 HESP 92345 4476-C3
BANNING ST
13400 FONT 92336 573-J7
13400 FONT 92336 603-J1
13400 FONT 92336 604-A1
BANNING CANYON RD
- BAN 92220 651-G7
- RivC 92220 651-G7
BANNOCK CT
12500 APLV 92308 4387-F5
BANNOCK RD
- SBdC - (4026-D3 See Page 3936)
BANNOCK TR
6500 SBdC - 4843-F3
7300 YUCA 92284 4957-F3
BANTA DR
5500 RivC 91752 683-G4
BANTA RD
8800 SBdC - 4480-E1
13000 SBdC - (4390-E3 See Page 4300)
BANTAR LN
11200 SBdC - (4390-E7 See Page 4300)
11200 SBdC - 4480-E1
BANTRY CT
- RCUC 91737 573-A2
BANTRY LN
- RCUC 91737 573-A2
BANYAN AV
6600 HESP 92345 4566-A6
6800 HESP 92345 4565-J6
E BANYAN CT
500 ONT 91761 642-C5
BANYAN DR
800 RDL 92373 648-C2
BANYAN ST
7900 RCUC 91701 572-F3
9100 RCUC 91737 572-H3
10000 RCUC 91737 573-A3
11300 SBdC 91737 573-D3
12500 RCUC 91739 573-G3
13200 RCUC 91739 574-A3
30900 SBdC 92311 3590-C7
31000 SBdC 92311 3680-C1
E BANYAN ST
200 ONT 91761 642-C5
BANYON AV
18300 SBdC 92377 575-D3
W BANYON ST
1000 RLTO 92377 575-D3
BANYON TREE LN
12700 VCTV 92392 4385-H5
BARADA RD
9700 SBdC 92345 4474-F3
11000 SBdC 92392 4474-F3
BARBARA AV
13100 YCPA 92399 650-B5
BARBARA LN
900 POM 91767 601-B7
3200 SBdC 92277 4824-H5

BARBARA LN
4500 SBdC 92277 (4894-H7 See Page 4824)
14500 SBdC 92307 4298-G3
35500 YCPA 92399 650-B5
62500 SBdC 92252 4889-D4
BARBARA ST
1400 SBdC 92397 4652-D2
6000 CHNO 91710 641-J7
BARBARA WY
2200 UPL 91784 572-A4
BARBARA LEE LN
39500 SBdC - 4741-C5
BARBARY DR
15000 VCTV 92394 4296-A7
BARBEE AV
16000 FONT 92336 604-G1
BARBEE CT
15600 FONT 92336 604-F1
BARBEE ST
16100 FONT 92336 604-G1
17100 FONT 92336 605-A1
17700 SBdC 92336 605-B1
BARBEE WY
15700 FONT 92336 604-F1
BARBERA DR
- RCUC 91739 603-H1
BARBERRY AV
6700 YUCA 92284 4957-H2
BARBERRY DR
1300 DBAR 91765 680-A3
BARBERRY LN
- FONT 92337 645-A2
BARBERRY ST
12500 RCUC 91739 573-G6
40500 SBdC - (4303-A5 See Page 4302)
BARBET RD
8300 SBdC 92371 4564-B3
9300 SBdC 92371 4474-A1
11900 SBdC 92371 4384-A1
16200 ADEL 92301 4294-A3
BARBRA LN
900 RDL 92374 608-D5
BARCAROLE ST
- SBdC 92407 515-A3
BARCELONA AV
2300 UPL 91784 571-H3
6000 RivC 92509 645-E4
8900 ADEL 92301 4204-C4
11400 ADEL 92301 4205-A4
BARCELONA CIR
2000 BARS 92311 3679-G6
BARCELONA CT
- BARS 92311 3679-G6
6100 RCUC 91701 572-F4
BARCELONIA PL
13300 CHNO 91710 682-A1
BARCLAY CT
- CHLS 91709 681-H7
- CHLS 91709 711-H1
BARD CT
1900 CLAR 91711 571-C7
BARDELL RD
9400 SBdC 92256 616-C2
BARDLEY CT
300 POM 91766 640-J5
BARE OAK RD
2600 CHLS 91709 681-A7
BAR HARBOR RD
14500 FONT 92336 574-C6
BAR HARBOR ST
12500 VCTV 92392 4475-D2
BARHILL AV
300 POM 91766 640-J5
BARI CT
7000 RCUC 91701 573-D6
BARI DR
11500 RCUC 91701 573-D6
BARJUD AV
100 POM 91768 640-C2
BARK CIR
1300 UPL 91786 601-J1
BARK ST
- FONT 92337 645-A1
BARKDALE LN
6600 RivC 92509 645-C4
E BARKER BLVD
100 SBdC 92314 4742-D5
BARKER DR
24200 DBAR 91765 680-D2
BARKER RD
7100 SBdC 92345 4564-G2
9900 SBdC 92345 4474-G3
10500 SBdC 92308 4478-G3
10900 SBdC 92392 4474-G1
12100 SBdC 92392 4384-G7
14100 SBdC 92371 4383-A2
14800 SBdC 92307 4298-G4
15100 SBdC 92301 4294-G6
BARKLEY PL
13500 CHNO 91710 681-J2
BARKLEY RANCH RD
1100 SBdC 92372 4472-C6
BARKSDALE CIR
14500 ADEL 92301 4384-H1
S BARLOW WY
400 UPL 91786 602-A4
BARNABY DR
- SBdC 92252 4890-B3

BARNARD
26600 SBdC 92308 4479-D1
BARNARD RD
1600 CLAR 91711 601-B1
BARNES CT
100 CALI 92320 650-A7
BARNES DR
71300 TNP 92277 4891-H3
BARNES RD
- TNP 92277 4891-C3
7100 SBdC 92285 4486-D6
7100 SBdC 92285 (4576-D2 See Page 4486)
BAROLO CT
6400 RCUC 91737 572-J4
BAROSSA PL
6400 RCUC 91737 572-J4
BARRACKMAN
1800 NDLS 92363 3620-B4
BARRAGAN RD
42800 SBdC 92365 (3683-F5 See Page 3592)
BARRANCA AV
6800 SBdC - 4844-A3
N BARRANCA AV
1400 ONT 91764 602-G4
1700 ONT 91730 602-G4
E BARRANCA BLVD
1100 SBdC 92314 4742-F5
BARRANCA CT
15800 VCTV 92394 4296-C4
BARRANCA WY
15500 VCTV 92394 4296-C4
BARRETT CT
- CHLS 91709 711-G2
BARRETT DR
11400 RCUC 91730 573-E7
BARRETT RD
- LACo - 512-A5
- SBdC - 512-A5
44900 SBdC 92365 (3504-B5 See Page 3414)
E BARRETT WY
400 SBdC 92314 4742-E6
BARRINGTON AV
500 ONT 91764 603-G7
BARRINGTON CIR
400 RDL 92374 608-G7
BARRINGTON CT
1900 CLAR 91711 571-E7
7600 RCUC 91730 573-B7
S BARRINGTON PL
1800 SBDO 92408 607-C6
BARRINGTON WY
5200 MTCL 91763 641-G2
BARRON DR
58500 YUCA 92284 4888-E6
BAR RU LN
1800 RDL 92373 648-J5
1800 RDL 92373 649-A5
BARRY DR
300 POM 91767 601-A3
E BARRYMORE RD
600 SBdC 92314 4742-E6
BARSAC PL
6200 RCUC 91737 573-B4
BARSTOW OH E
17600 SBdC - (4210-G5 See Page 4120)
BARSTOW OH W
- SBdC - (4210-G5 See Page 4120)
BARSTOW RD
100 BARS 92311 3679-H5
BARSTOW RD Rt#-247
900 BARS 92311 3679-H6
2100 BARS 92311 (3759-H5 See Page 3758)
2100 SBdC 92311 (3759-H5 See Page 3758)
10200 SBdC - 4481-A2
11000 SBdC - (4391-A6 See Page 4300)
14000 SBdC - 4300-J5
14000 SBdC - (4301-A7 See Page 4300)
16700 SBdC - (4210-E2 See Page 4120)
19600 SBdC - 4120-H1
22000 SBdC - 369-E1
23900 SBdC 92311 369-E1
28000 SBdC 92311 (3850-A6 See Page 3760)
28500 SBdC 92311 (3849-J3 See Page 3758)
BARTER RD
57500 SBdC 92284 4747-J4
58100 SBdC 92284 4748-B4
BARTLETT AV
1700 SBdC 92301 (4202-C6 See Page 4112)
3700 RivC 92501 645-J6
4100 SBdC 92301 (4203-B6 See Page 4112)
7600 ADEL 92301 (4203-J6 See Page 4112)
7600 ADEL 92301 4204-D6
11300 ADEL 92301 4205-A6
BARTLETT DR
5400 SBDO 92407 546-H5

BARTLETT DR
9500 SBdC 92371 4473-G7
BARTLETT RD
500 BBLK - 4811-E2
BARTLETT ST
- SBdC - (4206-A5 See Page 4116)
6700 CHNO 91710 682-B2
BARTLETT MOUNTAIN RD
5600 SBdC 92284 4888-J7
5600 SBdC 92252 4888-J7
BARTON CT
7900 FONT 92336 604-A1
BARTON LN
44200 SBdC - 4812-E1
BARTON RD
200 CLTN 92324 646-C4
200 GTER 92324 646-C4
200 GTER 92313 646-C4
1300 RDL 92373 647-F1
3100 LMLN 92354 646-C4
3100 LMLN 92354 647-A1
21500 SBdC 92324 646-C4
21600 CLTN 92313 646-C4
26100 SBdC 92354 647-E1
26400 LMLN 92373 647-F1
26600 SBdC 92373 647-F1
E BARTON RD
1600 CLTN 92324 646-J1
3100 CLTN 92354 646-J1
3100 CLTN 92408 646-J1
23300 CLTN 92313 646-G2
23300 GTER 92313 646-G2
N BARTON ST
1000 SBDO 92404 577-B5
1000 SBDO 92410 577-B6
1200 SBdC 92404 577-B5
BARWOOD DR
11600 RivC 91752 683-G4
BASALT LN
10100 SBdC 92359 608-J5
BASALT RD
- SBdC 92311 3679-D7
4600 TNP 92277 4893-B1
BASCOM ST
17700 HESP 92345 4566-H4
BASEL DR
5200 SBdC 92397 4652-G3
24700 SBdC - 517-B3
BASE LINE
7300 SBdC 92252 4960-C1
64100 SBdC 92252 4959-J2
BASELINE AV
13300 FONT 92336 573-J6
13500 FONT 92336 574-B6
17000 FONT 92336 575-A6
17000 RLTO 92376 575-A6
BASELINE RD
8100 RCUC 91784 572-F7
8100 UPL 91784 572-F7
8100 RCUC 91730 572-F7
8100 UPL 91730 572-F7
8100 UPL 91786 572-F7
8400 RCUC 91701 572-F7
9900 RCUC 91701 573-C6
9900 RCUC 91730 573-C6
11800 RCUC 91739 573-G6
73500 SBdC 92277 4962-E1
73500 TNP 92277 4962-E1
73800 TNP 92277 4892-G7
75300 TNP 92277 4893-A7
E BASELINE RD
100 RLTO 92376 575-H6
700 RLTO 92376 576-A6
1100 RLTO 92411 576-A6
1100 SBDO 92411 576-A6
1100 RLTO 92410 576-A6
1100 SBDO 92410 576-A6
E BASELINE RD Rt#-30
100 CLAR 91711 571-F7
W BASELINE RD
100 RLTO 92376 575-B6
1000 LACo 91711 571-B7
1500 FONT 92376 575-B6
1700 SBDO 92411 576-C6
4100 FONT 92336 575-B6
4100 RLTO 92336 575-B6
W BASELINE RD Rt#-30
100 CLAR 91711 571-B7
600 LACo 91711 571-B7
1300 LACo 91750 571-B7
BASELINE ST
1600 HIGH 92404 577-D5
1600 SBDO 92410 577-D5
25600 HIGH 92410 577-D5
26100 HIGH 92346 577-F5
26100 SBDO 92346 577-F5
27800 HIGH 92346 578-A5
E BASELINE ST
100 SBDO 92404 576-J5
100 SBDO 92410 576-J5
500 SBDO 92404 577-B6
500 SBDO 92410 577-B6
1100 SBdC 92404 577-B6
1500 HIGH 92404 577-B6
W BASELINE ST
100 SBDO 92405 576-D6

W BASELINE ST
100 SBDO 92410 576-D6
800 SBDO 92411 576 D6
BASIL CT
- SBdC - 517-A4
BASIL LN
- RivC 92399 650-H7
BASIL ST
12700 RCUC 91739 573-H5
BASILE CT
7800 FONT 92336 604-B1
BASILE ST
7900 FONT 92336 604-B1
BASIN RD
44200 SBdC - 350-B5
W BASKIN CT
500 SBdC 92314 4742-C6
BASS AV
- LPCo - 4606-H2
BASS ST
12500 SBdC 92345 (4655-E3 See Page 4654)
BASSETT DR
1200 BARS 92311 3679-J4
BASSWOOD AV
12900 CHNO 91710 641-J7
E BASSWOOD CT
2100 SBDO 92404 577-D2
BASSWOOD LN
12300 VCTV 92392 4386-D6
BASSWOOD PL
6800 RCUC 91739 573-G5
BASTIA CT
7700 RCUC 91730 573-D7
BASTIAN WY
- CHLS 91709 681-H7
BATES PL
1500 CLAR 91711 601-E1
BATSON PL
14100 VCTV 92392 4386-E1
BATSON RD
16500 VCTV 92392 4386-E1
BATTRAM ST
500 POM 91767 601-A3
BAUDIN ST
1900 POM 91766 640-J5
W BAUGHMAN AV
400 CLAR 91711 601-C2
N BAUGHMAN DR
1100 CLAR 91711 601-C2
BAUMANN OAKS RD
11000 SBdC 92399 610-J7
N BAUTISTA LN
1000 CLTN 92324 605-J4
BAXTER WY
1800 UPL 91784 572-A5
BAY CT
14100 ADEL 92301 4385-A2
BAY LN
12600 APLV 92308 4387-B4
BAY RD
11300 APLV 92308 4477-B1
N BAY RD
28300 SBdC - 4738-A6
BAY ST
7000 FONT 92336 574-A6
BAYBERRY CT
8700 FONT 92335 605-B3
BAYBERRY DR
3100 CHLS 91709 681-B7
3300 CHLS 91709 711-B1
8400 RCUC 91730 602-G2
BAYBERRY RD
8400 RCUC 91730 602-G2
BAYBERRY WY
8400 RCUC 91730 602-H4
BAYHILL CIR
- YCPA 92399 649-E3
BAY HILL LN
- FONT 92336 574-J2
BAYHILL RD
- YCPA 92399 649-E2
BAYLIS
7300 SBdC 92277 (4895-A7 See Page 4824)
BAYLOR AV
700 CLAR 91711 601-C3
BAYLOR DR
- VCTV 92392 4385-E4
BAYLOR ST
11200 RCUC 91701 573-D6
BAY MEADOW AV
13100 CHNO 91710 641-F7
13100 CHNO 91710 681-F1
BAY MEADOW CT
13100 CHNO 91710 641-E7
BAY MEADOWS DR
18900 APLV 92308 4387-B6
BAYPORT CIR
1200 POM 91768 640-G1
BAY SHORE DR
27400 SBdC - 517-J1
BAYSHORE ST
11000 VCTV 92392 4475-D3
BAYSIDE DR
100 BBLK - 4741-G7
BAYTREE CT
9800 RCUC 91737 572-J2
BAY TREE DR
600 SBdC - 4738-D7

BAY VIEW CT
27400 SBdC - 4737-H7
BAY VIEW DR
- LPCo - 4606-J5
400 SBdC - 4737-H7
BAYVIEW LN
38900 BBLK - 4811-A2
BAY VIEW RD
600 BBLK - 4811-C2
BAYWIND LN
- SBdC 92316 645-E2
BAYWOOD AV
1400 POM 91767 601-C6
BAYWOOD CIR
7800 YUCA 92284 4957-H4
BAYWOOD LN
- FONT 92336 574-H2
BAYWOOD WY
6700 RCUC 91701 572-E5
6700 RCUC 91784 572-E5
6700 UPL 91784 572-E5
10000 RCUC 91737 573-A5
1/100 VCTV 92392 4386-F2
BAZOOBUTH ST
100 NDLS 92363 3620-D6
BEACH DR
400 NDLS 92363 3620-D5
BEACH RD
15200 CHLS 91709 681-E6
BEACON POINTE DR
9600 RCUC 91737 572-D4
BEAL CT
800 RDL 92374 608-C3
7000 RCUC 91701 573-C6
BEAL DR
- SBdC 92284 4817-H5
BEAR CT
56500 YUCA 92284 4887-G5
BEAR DR
- SBdC - 519-E6
600 SBdC - 517-B3
BEAR LP
800 SBdC - 4741-J5
5100 SBdC - 4742-A5
BEAR TR
- SBdC 92285 (4576-B4 See Page 4486)
BEAR CANYON RD
6600 LACo - 512-A4
6600 SBdC - 512-A4
BEAR CREEK AV
6800 RCUC 91701 572-G6
16700 CHLS 91709 711-J2
BEAR CREEK CT
- BBLK - 4812-B3
7400 HIGH 92346 578-E6
S BEAR CREEK PL
2700 ONT 91761 643-C6
BEAR CREEK WY
16500 VCTV 92392 4386-E5
BEAR GULCH PL
8300 RCUC 91730 602-G2
BEAR HOLLOW RD
44100 SBdC - 4812-D1
BEARING TREE LN
- SBdC 92285 4747-J1
58200 SBdC 92285 4748-A1
BEAR MEADOWS LN
- BBLK - 4812-B3
W BEAR MOUNTAIN RD
700 SBdC 92314 4742-B5
BEARS DEN RD
1600 DBAR 91765 680-C4
BEAR SPRINGS RD
800 SBdC - 517-E4
BEARTREE ST
6900 FONT 92336 574-D6
BEAR VALLEY CTO
23000 SBdC 92308 4388-E6
23900 SBdC 92307 4388-E6
BEAR VALLEY OH
18000 VCTV 92392 4386-J6
BEAR VALLEY OH N
- SBdC 92308 4388-D6
15300 VCTV 92392 4386-B6
20700 APLV 92308 4387-F6
BEAR VALLEY OH S
17200 HESP 92345 4386-G6
20900 APLV 92308 4387-G6
21700 APLV 92308 4388-C6
BEAR VALLEY RD
- POM 91766 640-G4
500 SBdC 92372 4472-A1
1800 SBdC 92372 4382-E7
10500 SBdC 92392 4384-H7
10500 VCTV 92392 4384-H7
11000 VCTV 92392 4385-B7
14500 VCTV 92345 4385-G7
14600 HESP 92345 4385-G7
14600 VCTV 92345 4386-E6
14600 HESP 92345 4386-B7
18200 HESP 92392 4386-E6
18300 HESP 92392 4387-A6
18300 VCTV 92392 4387-A6
18700 VCTV 92308 4387-A6
18700 APLV 92308 4387-E6
21900 APLV 92308 4388-A6
BEATRICE DR
3300 RivC 92509 645-C7

BEATTIE LN
- RDL 92374 608-B3
BEATTIE ST
28700 HIGH 92346 578-C4
BEAUMONT AV
1600 RDL 92373 647-E3
25700 LMLN 92354 647-E3
26100 SBdC 92354 647-E3
26300 SBdC 92373 647-E3
E BEAUMONT LN
500 SBdC 92314 4742-E6
BEAUMONT ST
- SBdC - (4210-G2 See Page 4120)
BEAUMONT PROSPECT RD
11300 SBdC 92399 611-C7
BEAUREGARD CREST
600 RDL 92373 647-J3
BEAVER AV
8100 SBdC 92371 4564-E1
9100 SBdC 92371 4474-E5
10400 SBdC 92392 4474-E1
11800 SBdC 92392 4384-E3
12500 VCTV 92392 4384-E5
BEAVER CT
100 POM 91766 640-J4
200 POM 91766 641-A4
BEAVER LN
- SBdC - 4843-H1
1000 SBdC - 4738-A6
40600 BBLK - 4811-E2
BEAVER RD
14700 ADEL 92301 4294-D1
14900 SBdC 92301 4294-E7
17400 ADEL 92301 4204-D2
BEAVER ST
16900 ADEL 92301 4294-D1
BEAVER TR
- SBdC 92284 4818-A5
BEAVER CREEK CT
10200 RCUC 91737 573-A1
S BEAVER CREEK LN
2700 ONT 91761 643-C6
BEAVERHEAD DR
22600 DBAR 91765 640-B7
BEAVER SPRING CT
5800 CHLS 91709 711-J3
BEAVERTAIL AV
5200 TNP 92277 4891-H3
BEAVERTAIL LN
- SBdC 92284 4817-H6
58300 SBdC 92284 4818-B6
BEAVER TRAIL RD
79400 SBdC 92277 (4894-C7 See Page 4824)
BECK ST
2400 SBdC 91784 571-H3
BECKER AV
900 SBdC 92285 4748-B3
BECKER RD
31400 SBdC 92365 3764-J4
BECKETT CT
7800 HIGH 92346 578-C7
BECKFORD WY
1200 POM 91767 601-D7
BECKLEY AV
13100 CHNO 91710 641-G7
13100 CHNO 91710 681-G1
BECKMAN CT
- CHLS 91709 711-G2
BECRAFT PL
13500 CHNO 91710 681-C2
W BEDFORD CT
14900 SBdC 92314 4742-B6
BEDFORD DR
1100 RDL 92373 648-J5
10100 RCUC 91730 603-A3
35400 SBdC - (3681-E3 See Page 3590)
42000 SBdC 92365 (3683-F2 See Page 3592)
47200 SBdC 92365 (3684-H2 See Page 3594)
47700 SBdC 92365 (3685-B1 See Page 3594)
BEDFORD LN
2800 CHLS 91709 681-A2
BEDFORD RD
42100 SBdC 92365 (3683-D2 See Page 3592)
44100 SBdC 92365 (3684-B2 See Page 3594)
S BEDFORD WY
200 UPL 91786 602-A4
BEDOUIN AV
6700 TNP 92277 4892-J7
7300 TNP 92277 4962-J2
BEDROCK LN
- CHLS 91709 711-H2
BEDROCK SPRING RD
68500 SBdC - 328-J8
BEECH AV
- FONT 92336 574-E2
7700 FONT 92336 604-E1
8100 SBdC 92336 604-E1
8100 SBdC 92335 604-E2
10100 FONT 92335 604-E6
10400 SBdC 92337 604-E7
10500 FONT 92337 604-E7

STREET
Block City ZIP Pg-Grid

BEECH AV
10500 FONT 92337 644-E2
34900 YCPA 92399 649-J2
34900 YCPA 92399 650-A2
S BEECH LN
800 CLTN 92324 646-G1
BEECH ST
12200 SBdC 93562 2144-G6
14100 HESP 92345 4475-H5
BEECHCRAFT AV
6800 FONT 92336 574-E5
BEECHNUT DR
500 SBdC - 519-E2
BEECHNUT PL
1200 POM 91766 640-F4
BEECHTREE AV
12900 CHNO 91710 642-A7
BEECH TREE CT
31300 SBdC 92359 608-J5
BEECH TREE PL
2100 SBdC 92359 609-A5
BEECH TREE WY
31400 SBdC 92359 608-J5
31400 SBdC 92359 609-A5
N BEECHWOOD AV
200 RLTO 92376 605-E1
500 RLTO 92376 575-E6
2100 RLTO 92377 575-E3
6200 SBDO 92407 546-A2
S BEECHWOOD AV
500 RLTO 92376 605-F3
900 RLTO 92316 605-F4
BEECHWOOD DR
600 RivC 92509 683-E4
7900 RCUC 91701 572-D2
9500 RCUC 91737 572-H2
10600 RCUC 91737 573-B2
BEECHWOOD LN
14900 CHLS 91709 681-D5
BEEKLEY CT
8600 SBdC 92371 4562-J2
BEEKLEY RD
8200 SBdC 92371 4562-H1
9100 SBdC 92371 4472-H3
11900 SBdC 92371 4382-H3
14500 SBdC 92371 4292-H7
N BEGONIA AV
200 ONT 91762 601-J6
BEGONIA CT
1200 RDL 92374 648-E1
1200 UPL 91784 571-J5
12500 RCUC 91739 573-G5
BEGONIA DR
15000 FONT 92336 574-D7
BEGONIA PL
61900 SBdC 92252 4889-C6
BEGONIA RD
100 SBdC 92371 4382-A2
4100 SBdC 92371 4383-A2
7500 SBdC 92371 4384-A2
11300 ADEL 92301 4385-A1
12900 SBdC 92392 4385-E1
14400 VCTV 92392 4385-H1
BEGONIA ST
8200 ADEL 92301 4384-B2
10800 ADEL 92301 4384-H1
BEINHOFF LN
1900 SBdC - 4742-H2
BE JOAL ST
25300 SBdC 92311 3678-H6
BEL AIR AV
9200 MTCL 91763 601-H5
11000 SBdC 91762 641-H2
BELAIR CT
1500 RDL 92373 648-E3
BEL AIR CT
26500 SBdC - 4737-F7
BEL AIR DR
300 SBdC - 517-F1
300 SBdC - 4737-F7
13600 VCTV 92392 4386-C3
BELAIR ST
36700 SBdC 92311 3589-H7
BEL CANTO CT
1000 CLTN 92324 606-A5
BELCANTO DR
10900 RCUC 91737 573-C4
N BELDEN AV
500 SBDO 92376 576-A7
1000 RLTO 92376 576-A6
N BELDEN CT
300 SBDO 92376 606-A1
S BELDEN ST
600 SBDO 92376 606-A3
BELFAIR DR
58500 SBdC 92284 4818-A4
60100 SBdC 92252 4818-G4
BELFAST RD
10400 SBdC 92308 4478-E3
BELFIELD BLVD
1100 SBdC 92285 4747-J3
1800 SBdC 92285 4667-J7
BELFORT AV
1000 POM 91767 601-B6
BELGIAN PL
- MTCL 91763 641-E1
BELHAVEN CT
6500 RCUC 91701 573-D4
BELHAVEN PL
100 CLAR 91711 601-D5

BELINDA AV
600 BARS 92311 3679-H4
2200 POM 91768 640-D1
BELINDA LN
800 RDL 92374 608-F6
BELL AV
5100 RivC 92509 645-F7
BELL CT
5200 CHNO 91710 681-G3
7500 HIGH 92346 577-G5
10800 RCUC 91730 603-C3
BELL ST
50700 SBdC 92285 (4576-A6
See Page 4486)
BELLA AV
800 UPL 91784 572-A3
BELLA DR
5600 RivC 92509 645-E7
BELLAIRE ST
11000 LMLN 92354 647-C1
BELLA VISTA
8100 RCUC 91701 572-E1
BELLA VISTA CT
1500 RDL 92373 647-J2
12900 YCPA 92399 650-B5
13100 CHLS 91709 680-H1
BELLA VISTA DR
1400 SBdC 92301 4112-A7
2100 SBdC 92256 4956-D7
4100 SBdC 92301 (4113-C7
See Page 4112)
8900 SBdC 92256 616-D2
10900 ADEL 92301 4114-J7
11300 ADEL 92301 (4115-B7
See Page 4114)
34300 YCPA 92399 649-H5
35100 YCPA 92399 650-A5
BELLA VISTA ST
9000 SBdC 92308 4478-C3
11900 APLV 92308 4388-C7
BELLA VISTA WY
13000 VCTV 92392 4385-E6
BELLA VISTA CREST
1400 RDL 92373 647-J2
BELLE ST
200 SBDO 92404 546-J7
N BELLE ST
200 SBDO 92404 576-J1
500 SBDO 92410 576-J7
BELLEAU DR
- SBdC - 3936-F4
BELLEGRAVE AV
- RivC 92880 683-H2
9000 RivC 92509 644-C7
10400 RivC 91752 683-H2
12100 ONT 91761 683-H2
BELLERIVE PL
- FONT 92336 574-J2
BELLEVIEW RD
2400 SBdC 91784 572-B2
BELLEVIEW ST
1100 SBDO 92408 607-B1
W BELLEVIEW ST
900 SBDO 92410 606-C1
BELLE VILLA CT
29300 HIGH 92346 578-D5
BELLEVILLE CT
3700 CLAR 91711 571-F5
BELLEVUE AV
- RDL 92373 647-J2
100 POM 91768 640-E2
BELLEVUE RD
1500 RDL 92373 647-J3
BELLEVUE ST
- ADEL 92301 4295-A7
BELLFLOWER AV
20500 ADEL 92301 4114-J7
20500 SBdC 92301 4114-J7
BELLFLOWER CT
12200 RCUC 91739 573-F5
BELLFLOWER RD
- SBdC - (4390-G7
See Page 4300)
21300 APLV 92308 4387-H7
21900 APLV 92308 4388-A7
23600 SBdC 92308 4388-F7
25500 SBdC 92308 (4389-A7
See Page 4299)
BELLFLOWER ST
- SBdC - 348-K11
- SBdC 92252 4818-J6
- SBdC 92252 4820-A6
5000 SBdC 92345 (4655-A3
See Page 4654)
7600 SBdC 92345 4565-A2
8900 SBdC 92345 4475-A3
10800 SBdC 92392 4475-A2
11700 SBdC 92392 4385-A3
11700 VCTV 92392 4475-A1
13600 ADEL 92392 4385-A3
14100 ADEL 92301 4385-A3
14600 ADEL 92301 4295-A4
15300 SBdC 92301 4295-A4
16300 ADEL 92301 4294-J2
17300 ADEL 92301 4204-J2
20000 ADEL 92301 4114-J4
21300 ADEL 92301 4114-J4
21300 SBdC 92301 4114-J4
21300 SBdC 92301 (4115-A5
See Page 4114)
61100 SBdC 92252 4819-A6

BELLGROVE WY
- FONT 92336 574-D5
BELLOWS CT
500 DBAR 91765 640-E7
BELL TOWER DR
11400 FONT 92337 644-F3
BELLUNO PL
6900 RCUC 91701 573-E5
BELLVIEW AV
- SBdC 92308 4568-G2
9300 SBdC 92308 4478-G2
11000 SBdC 92308 4388-G7
BELLWETHER RD
800 SBdC 92284 4748-H3
BELLYACHE SPRINGS RD
38800 SBdC - 4811-A7
BELMAR WY
1900 UPL 91784 572-A5
BELMEZ DR
15500 FONT 92337 644-G4
BELMONT AV
8900 RCUC 91730 602-J4
E BELMONT AV
100 RLTO 92377 575-G3
W BELMONT AV
2300 SBDO 92407 546-A3
2600 SBDO 92407 545-G1
BELMONT CT
100 RDL 92373 648-E3
1800 SBDO 92404 547-C7
W BELMONT CT
600 UPL 91784 572-A6
S BELMONT DR
400 SBdC 92314 4742-B7
E BELMONT LN
1700 SBDO 92404 547-C7
BELMONT PL
4700 CHNO 91710 641-F4
BELMONT RD
10300 SBdC 92345 4564-H7
11200 SBdC 92345 4565-A7
BELMONT ST
- SBdC 92284 4817-H7
57800 SBdC 92284 4818-A7
60100 SBdC 92252 4818-G7
61700 SBdC 92252 4819-D6
E BELMONT ST
100 ONT 91761 642-C2
W BELMONT ST
100 ONT 91761 642-B2
100 ONT 91762 642-B2
BELMONT ABBEY LN
1000 CLAR 91711 571-F4
BELMONTE RD
11600 FONT 92337 644-F3
BELOIT AV
1500 CLAR 91711 601-E1
BELPINE PL
7300 RCUC 91730 573-D6
BELSHIRE PL
28500 HIGH 92346 578-B6
BELT LN
29500 HIGH 92346 578-E6
N BELVAN AV
1000 SBDO 92410 577-A6
1100 SBDO 92404 577-A6
BELVEDERE AV
3100 SBDO 92346 577-E2
5600 SBdC 92346 577-E1
BELVEDERE PL
7500 RCUC 91730 573-C7
BELVEDERE WY
5200 MTCL 91763 641-G2
BELVOIR ST
23700 SBdC 92311 3758-C2
BENBOW PL
1100 RDL 92374 608-D5
BENECIA TR
54500 YUCA 92284 4957-B3
BENECIO DR
15700 VCTV 92394 4295-J4
15800 VCTV 92394 4296-A4
BENEDICT AV
1500 CLAR 91711 601-E1
E BENEDICT RD
900 SBDO 92408 607-B4
W BENEDICT ST
200 SBDO 92408 606-H4
BENEDICT WY
1700 POM 91767 601-C6
BENEVENTO PL
6900 RCUC 91701 573-E5
BENFIELD PL
24100 DBAR 91765 680-D1
BENICA ST
20300 SBdC 92308 4477-E6
BENICIA CT
17100 FONT 92336 575-A4
BENICIA RD
200 DBAR 91765 640-C6
BENICIA ST
18600 HESP 92345 4477-B6
BENICIA TR
55400 YUCA 92284 4957-D3
BENITA MARIE CREST
1600 RDL 92373 648-D4
BENITO ST
4200 MTCL 91763 601-F6
5600 MTCL 91762 601-F6

BENITO-WILSON RD
46500 SBdC - (4743-B4
See Page 4662)
S BENJAMIN AV
500 RLTO 92376 605-G3
BENJI AV
4900 SBdC 92252 4889-B4
BEN LOMOND ST
- APLV 92307 4207-F2
23800 SBdC 92307 4208-E2
BEN MAR TR
8400 SBdC 92284 4957-A6
BENNETT AV
7600 FONT 92336 574-J7
7800 FONT 92336 604-J1
8200 FONT 92335 604-J2
BENNETT CIR
- FONT 92337 644-J3
BENNETT DR
10700 FONT 92337 644-J1
BENNETT PL
300 CLAR 91711 571-D5
BENNETT RD
- SBdC 92407 515-E7
- SBdC 92407 545-E1
BEN NEVIS BLVD
8900 RivC 92509 644-B6
BENNING CT
- FONT 92336 574-A6
BENNINGTON CT
4300 CHNO 91710 641-E7
13600 FONT 92336 574-A7
BENNINGTON DR
11900 VCTV 92392 4385-E4
W BENNINGTON ST
800 UPL 91786 602-A4
BENSON AV
12100 CHNO 91710 641-H7
13100 CHNO 91710 681-H1
N BENSON AV
- SBdC 91763 601-H2
- SBdC 91786 601-H2
- UPL 91786 601-H2
- UPL 91763 601-H2
100 ONT 91763 641-H1
100 MTCL 91762 601-H2
100 MTCL 91762 641-H1
200 ONT 91762 601-H2
1400 UPL 91786 571-H7
1600 UPL 91784 571-H6
9200 MTCL 91763 601-H7
10400 ONT 91762 641-H1
10400 MTCL 91763 641-H1
S BENSON AV
- MTCL 91763 601-H4
100 ONT 91763 641-H3
300 MTCL 91786 601-H4
400 ONT 91762 641-H3
2000 CHNO 91710 641-H3
2100 MTCL 91763 641-H3
8800 UPL 91763 601-H4
9000 UPL 91786 601-H4
10700 SBdC 91762 641-H3
BENTLEY PL
11700 CHNO 91710 641-H4
BENTLEY ST
- RCUC 91730 603-C5
BENTLEY WY
2800 DBAR 91765 680-A7
BENT OAK RD
23100 DBAR 91765 680-B4
BENTON AV
- APLV 92307 4207-F3
BENTON ST
10900 LMLN 92354 607-C7
10900 LMLN 92354 647-C1
13600 SBdC 93562 2055-A7
13700 SBdC 93562 2145-B1
BENTON WY
- LMLN 92354 647-C2
N BENTON WY
1600 UPL 91784 572-A6
N BENT RAIL CIR
1100 CLTN 92324 606-A4
BENT TREE CT
- RCUC 91737 573-A2
BENT TREE DR
14400 CHLS 91709 680-H4
BENT TREE PL
- RCUC 91737 573-A2
BENTWOOD ST
13500 HESP 92345 4475-G7
BERDIE LN
- SBdC 92284 4748-H6
BEREA CT
1500 CLAR 91711 601-E1
BERGANO PL
6800 RCUC 91701 573-E5
BERGERAC LN
10400 RivC 91752 643-J4
BERGSCHRUND DR
700 SBdC - 516-J4
700 SBdC - 517-A3
BERINGER PL
8200 RCUC 91730 602-G2
BERKELEY
4600 SBdC 92284 4888-A3
BERKELEY AV
- HESP 92345 4475-J7
1400 SBdC 92284 4818-A3

N BERKELEY AV
300 CLAR 91711 601-C2
700 SBDO 92410 576-G7
1200 SBDO 92405 576-G3
S BERKELEY AV
400 SBDO 92410 606-G2
BERKELEY CIR
13200 VCTV 92392 4385-F4
BERKELEY CT
13600 FONT 92336 574-A7
N BERKELEY CT
2800 SBDO 92405 576-G3
W BERKELEY CT
200 CLTN 92324 646-B5
500 ONT 91762 602-A6
1100 ONT 91762 601-J6
BERKELEY DR
400 BARS 92311 3679-H6
800 RDL 92374 608-D5
11900 YCPA 92399 650-B2
BERKELEY LN
13200 VCTV 92392 4385-F4
BERKELEY RD
- SBdC 92278 4751-J4
- TNP 92278 4751-J4
BERKELEY ST
4300 MTCL 91763 601-E6
N BERKELEY ST
4900 SBDO 92407 546-G4
BERKLEY CT
1300 CHLS 91709 680-G7
BERKLEY DR
1200 CHLS 91709 680-G7
1200 CHLS 91709 710-F1
BERKLEY LN
600 BBLK - 4811-F2
BERKSHIRE AV
6700 RCUC 91701 572-J5
6700 RCUC 91701 573-A5
7300 RCUC 91730 573-A7
BERKSHIRE RD
34600 SBdC 92365 (3683-F3
See Page 3592)
BERKSHIRE WY
5200 MTCL 91763 641-G2
N BERLYN AV
300 ONT 91764 602-D6
S BERLYN AV
200 UPL 91786 602-D4
BERMUDA AV
3100 SBdC 92277 4821-E4
6300 TNP 92277 4891-E7
BERMUDA CT
- RCUC 91739 573-H2
8300 SBdC 92335 604-D2
BERMUDA DR
600 RDL 92374 648-D1
10200 MohC - 3620-C3
13400 CHNO 91710 682-A1
BERMUDA PL
10100 MohC - 3620-C2
13500 CHNO 91710 682-A1
BERMUDA DUNES CT
- ONT 91761 642-D6
E BERMUDA DUNES CT
1900 ONT 91761 642-H6
W BERMUDA DUNES CT
100 ONT 91762 642-C6
BERMUDA DUNES DR
- CHLS 91709 711-F1
12700 SBdC 92392 4387-A4
BERMUDA DUNES ST
400 ONT 91761 642-D6
E BERMUDA DUNES ST
900 ONT 91761 642-D6
W BERMUDA DUNES ST
200 ONT 91762 642-B6
BERMUDEZ ST
26700 SBdC 92373 647-G2
BERN LN
28200 SBdC - 4738-A6
E BERNARD CT
1300 SBDO 92404 577-B1
BERNARD DR
24100 SBdC - 516-J3
24300 SBdC - 517-A4
E BERNARD WY
200 SBDO 92404 576-J1
700 SBDO 92404 577-A1
BERNARD GRAY CT
1000 CLTN 92324 606-F5
BERNARDO CT
4100 CHNO 91710 681-D1
BERNARDO WY
11600 GTER 92313 646-F3
BERNE DR
700 SBdC - 517-A3
BERNE PL
6200 SBdC 92397 4652-B1
BERNHARDT LN
500 SBdC 92314 4742-E6
E BERNHARDT LN
600 SBdC 92314 4742-E6
S BERNHARDT LN
100 SBdC 92314 4742-E6
BERNINA DR
27100 SBdC - 4737-G7
BERRA RD
11800 RCUC 91701 573-E6

BERRIAN ST
300 POM 91767 601-A2
1200 CLAR 91711 601-A2
BERRY AL
1900 SBDO 92411 576-E4
BERRY RD
30300 SBdC - (3765-C7
See Page 3764)
30300 SBdC 92365 (3765-C7
See Page 3764)
BERRY ST
26700 HIGH 92346 577-F6
E BERRY ST
200 SBDO 92408 606-J2
S BERRY ST
700 CLTN 92324 606-E7
700 CLTN 92324 646-D1
BERRYDALE ST
- VCTV 92392 4385-C5
BERRYESSA CT
16800 CHLS 91709 711-J2
BERRYHEATH CT
- CHLS 91709 711-H2
BERRYHILL DR
1800 CHLS 91709 680-H3
BERRYWOOD CIR
10600 YCPA 92399 610-A6
W BERTHA CT
1100 CLTN 92324 606-B4
BERTIE LN
26200 HIGH 92346 577-E7
BERTRAND DR
- RCUC 91739 573-F6
BERWICK DR
11000 RCUC 91730 573-D6
BERWICK LN
28600 HIGH 92346 578-B7
BERYL
100 BREA 92823 710-C6
BERYL AV
1300 SBdC 92359 608-H5
BERYL RD
27800 SBdC 92311 3679-D6
BERYL ST
- SBdC 92311 3679-E5
5000 RCUC 91737 572-G2
5500 RCUC 91701 572-G2
7300 RCUC 91730 572-G7
7700 RCUC 91730 602-G1
BESSANT ST
2100 SBDO 92404 577-D5
25100 SBdC 92404 577-C5
25100 HIGH 92404 577-C5
27300 HIGH 92346 577-H5
BESSEMER MINE RD
6000 SBdC - (4663-C1
See Page 4662)
6300 SBdC - (4573-F3
See Page 4482)
7300 SBdC - (4483-H5
See Page 4482)
7300 SBdC - 4484-A4
7300 SBdC 92285 4484-A4
9500 SBdC 92285 369-J5
14000 SBdC - 369-K4
W BETH LN
2500 SBDO 92410 606-A3
BETH ST
- FONT 92336 574-E5
BETH WY
1300 UPL 91784 571-J6
BETHANY CIR
600 CLAR 91711 571-E7
N BETHANY CT
- SBDO 92407 546-A2
BETHANY DR
11200 RCUC 91701 573-D5
BETHEL CT
2200 CLAR 91711 571-E6
BETSY ROSS CT
13400 FONT 92336 574-A7
BETSY ROSS RD
- UPL 91786 602-D4
BETTOLA PL
- RCUC 91701 573-E6
BETTY LN
- SBdC 92277 (4825-C4
See Page 4824)
BETTY ST
1300 SBdC 92397 4652-D2
BEVERLY AV
300 BARS 92311 3680-A4
S BEVERLY AV
1300 ONT 91762 642-B3
BEVERLY CT
11800 LMLN 92354 647-E3
13500 YCPA 92399 650-D6
N BEVERLY CT
300 ONT 91762 602-B5
W BEVERLY CT
1100 CLTN 92324 606-B4
BEVERLY DR
- SBDO 92408 646-J1
400 RDL 92373 648-F4
3300 SBDO 92405 576-F1
BEVERLY LN
40100 BBLK - 4811-D2
N BEVERLY SQ
400 ONT 91762 602-B7

BEVERLY WY
2100 UPL 91784 571-H4
BEVERLY GLEN RD
2600 CHLS 91709 681-A3
2600 CHLS 91709 641-A7
BIANCA CT
9800 RCUC 91730 602-J1
BIANE CT
5100 RCUC 91739 574-A1
BIARRITZ PL
7600 RCUC 91730 573-D7
BIBB RD
- SBdC 92277 4821-D4
- TNP 92277 4891-D5
N BIBIANA WY
1400 UPL 91786 571-J7
BICKMORE AV
6800 CHNO 91710 712-A1
7100 SBdC 91710 712-D1
BIERISKA LN
- SBdC 92277 4751-B7
BIG BEAR BLVD
RT#-18
200 BBLK - 4741-J6
200 BBLK - 4811-E1
500 BBLK - 4742-C6
1200 BBLK 92314 4742-C6
1200 SBdC 92314 4742-C6
37700 SBdC - 4810-G2
38400 BBLK - 4810-G2
38800 SBdC - 4811-B2
E BIG BEAR BLVD
1300 SBdC 92314 4742-G5
E BIG BEAR BLVD
RT#-38
100 SBdC 92314 4742-G5
W BIG BEAR BLVD
RT#-18
100 SBdC 92314 4742-D6
BIG BEAR LAKE RD
33100 SBdC - 519-E6
BIG BEAR RANGER STATION RD
700 SBdC - 4741-G6
N BIG CANYON CT
3700 SBDO 92407 546-E7
W BIG CANYON DR
900 SBDO 92407 546-F7
BIG CEDAR CV
29000 SBdC - 518-C2
BIG CHIEF RD
10900 SBdC - 4481-E1
10900 SBdC - (4391-E7
See Page 4300)
S BIG CREEK LN
2900 ONT 91761 643-C6
E BIG CREEK RD
3500 ONT 91761 643-C6
BIG DEER RD
200 SBdC - 516-C2
BIG DIPPER CIR
12100 VCTV 92392 4385-H6
BIG DIPPER DR
11100 RivC 91752 683-H5
12300 SBdC - (4392-E3
See Page 4302)
BIG FALLS DR
600 DBAR 91765 640-A6
BIGGER ST
900 BARS 92311 3679-J3
BIGHORN CT
2000 BARS 92311 3679-J6
7700 SBdC - 4843-D6
16100 CHLS 91709 711-F1
BIGHORN DR
- LPCo - 4606-J4
900 BARS 92311 3679-J6
BIG HORN RD
4900 SBdC 92285 (4575-D5
See Page 4484)
S BIG HORN MOUNTAIN RD
100 SBDO 92410 606-C2
BIGHORN PEAK CT
11900 RCUC 91737 573-E4
11900 RCUC 91739 573-E4
BIG MORONGO CANYON RD
- SBdC - 389-K2
48700 SBdC 92256 615-H2
48800 SBdC - 615-E1
49900 SBdC 92256 616-A2
BIG OAK AV
1700 CHLS 91709 680-H4
BIG OAK RD
700 SBdC - 516-C1
BIG PINE DR
10000 RCUC 91737 573-A5
BIG PINE FLAT RD
30400 SBdC - 4660-G4
31700 SBdC - (4661-B4
See Page 4660)
40000 SBdC - (4739-H3
See Page 4658)
40000 SBdC - (4740-B1
See Page 4660)
E BIG RANGE CT
3000 ONT 91761 683-A1
E BIG RANGE RD
2700 ONT 91761 682-J1

E BIG RANGE RD
2700 ONT 91761 683-A1
BIG ROCK RD
500 SBdC - 514-A4
BIG SKY AV
11200 MTCL 91763 641-F3
BIG SKY CT
13400 VCTV 92392 4385-F6
13500 YCPA 92399 650-C6
BIG SKY RD
- APLV 92307 4296-H5
BIG SUR ST
7000 FONT 92336 574-A6
BIG TREE DR
700 SBdC - 4738-E6
N BIG TREE DR
100 SBdC 92314 4742-C6
S BIG TREE DR
100 SBdC 92314 4742-C6
BIG TREE LN
1000 SBdC - 516-E3
BIG TREE RD
- RCUC 91701 (542-E7
See Page 513)
- RCUC 91701 572-E1
600 SBdC - 517-D3
BILLINGS CT
13000 VCTV 92392 4386-F4
BILLINGS PL
6800 RCUC 91701 572-H5
BILOXI RD
21700 APLV 92307 4387-J1
22100 APLV 92307 4388-A1
BIMINY LN
17100 VCTV 92394 4296-E1
BINFORD AV
19900 ADEL 92301 4294-H7
BIOLA PL
6900 RCUC 91701 573-D6
BIRCH AV
10800 SBdC 92316 645-D1
12600 CHNO 91710 641-J6
25200 LMLN 92354 647-C2
N BIRCH AV
500 UPL 91786 601-J2
600 RLTO 92376 575-J5
600 RLTO 92376 576-A7
600 SBDO 92376 575-J7
BIRCH CT
600 SBDO 92410 606-G2
800 RDL 92374 648-D1
12300 YCPA 92399 649-J3
18700 ADEL 92301 4204-E4
37800 SBdC 92347 (3587-E5
See Page 3586)
E BIRCH CT
500 ONT 91761 642-C4
W BIRCH CT
500 CLTN 92324 606-C7
BIRCH DR
2300 SBdC - 519-D6
BIRCH LN
- BARS 92311 3680-B5
BIRCH RD
29700 SBdC - 4738-E6
34300 SBdC 92311 3678-H5
BIRCH ST
600 BBLK - 4812-A2
9200 RCUC 91730 602-H1
11000 SBdC 92316 645-D1
11200 FONT 92337 645-D2
11200 SBdC 92337 645-D2
12400 YCPA 92399 649-J4
13400 SBdC 93562 2055-A7
15000 HESP 92345 4476-A1
18200 HESP 92345 4477-A1
N BIRCH ST
700 RLTO 92376 575-J7
W BIRCH ST
100 SBDO 92408 606-H2
300 CLTN 92324 606-C7
1200 SBDO 92410 606-A2
2800 SBDO 92376 606-A2
2900 SBDO 92376 605-J2
3000 RLTO 92376 605-J2
BIRCHBAY CT
5600 RCUC 91737 572-J2
BIRCH BEND CT
1900 CHLS 91709 680-H5
BIRCH CREEK LN
38400 SBdC 92399 610-J7
38500 SBdC 92399 611-A6
BIRCH GLEN CT
12900 VCTV 92392 4475-E2
BIRCHLAND RD
- SBdC 92347 (3587-D7
See Page 3586)
BIRCH TREE PL
- FONT 92336 574-E6
BIRCHTREE ST
- FONT 92337 645-A2
BIRCHWOOD AV
11700 VCTV 92392 4475-F1
11800 VCTV 92392 4385-F7
BIRCHWOOD CIR
6300 RCUC 91701 572-H4
BIRCHWOOD CT
9100 HESP 92345 4475-J7
BIRCHWOOD DR
100 SBdC - 517-H1

BIRCHWOOD DR
14300 HESP 92345 4475-J7
15000 CHLS 91709 681-E5
BIRCHWOOD PL
7300 HIGH 92346 578-E5
BIRCHWOOD ST
35300 YCPA 92399 610-A6
BIRD FARM RD
4300 CHLS 91709 681-E6
BIRDIE LN
15000 SBdC - (3935-J3
See Page 3934)
BIRDIE WY
- APLV 92308 4387-C7
BIRDIES LN
60200 SBdC 92284 4748-G6
BIRD OF PARADISE RD
48500 SBdC 92256 615-E6
BIRDS EYE DR
22100 DBAR 91765 680-A3
BIRDS NEST RD
- SBdC - 330-K2
BIRDSONG LN
14000 CHLS 91709 680-J3
BIRDSONG PL
5100 RCUC 91737 572-J1
BIRDVALE DR
11900 CHNO 91710 641-E5
E BIRDVALE DR
11900 CHNO 91710 641-E4
BIRKDALE AV
1900 UPL 91784 571-H5
BIRKDALE LN
- FONT 92336 574-H2
BIRKDALE PL
7300 RCUC 91730 573-C6
BIRKDALE ST
2300 UPL 91784 571-H3
BIRMINGHAM PL
- RCUC 91739 573-F5
BISBEE RD
- SBdC - 4816-A7
BISCAY WY
1500 POM 91766 640-J4
BISCAYNE ST
3000 SBdC 91710 641-D7
4200 CHNO 91710 641-D7
BISHOP AV
- HESP 92345 4475-C7
BISHOP CT
- RCUC 91737 572-G3
BISHOP DR
32900 SBdC - 519-D7
BISHOP PL
500 CLAR 91711 601-E1
BISHOP RD
29300 SBdC 92311 3589-H1
29300 SBdC 92311 3590-A1
30200 SBdC - 3590-D2
BISHOP PINE CT
- SBDO 92407 546-A3
BISHORN DR
600 SBdC - 4737-G7
BISON DR
27300 SBdC - 4737-H6
BISON ST
- UPL 91784 572-E6
E BISON WY
3100 ONT 91761 643-A6
BIT CT
26800 SBdC - (3935-F4
See Page 3934)
BIXBY DR
2800 RivC 92509 645-B6
S BIXBY WY
300 UPL 91786 602-A4
BIZET RD
8400 SBdC 92372 4562-E3
BJORKA LN
- SBdC 92277 4751-G4
BLACKBIRD LN
- POM 91766 640-G6
BLACKBIRD RD
1800 SBdC 92397 4652-E3
BLACK BUTTE RD
43100 SBdC 92365 (3683-F7
See Page 3592)
44100 SBdC 92365 (3684-B7
See Page 3594)
BLACK CANYON RD
24600 SBdC - 349-B3
37200 SBdC - 351-C3
BLACKFOOT RD
10600 SBdC 92308 4478-B2
14900 APLV 92307 4297-G5
BLACKFOOT TR
- SBdC - 4843-H2
BLACKFOOT TR E
26500 SBdC - 517-F5
BLACKFOOT TR W
1300 SBdC - 517-F4
BLACKFORD AV
34300 SBdC 92311 3678-F6
BLACKHAWK CT
11600 APLV 92308 4387-F7
BLACKHAWK TR
8900 SBdC - 4481-J5
BLACKHAWK MOUNTAIN CT
- VCTV 92394 4295-F5

BLACKHAWK MOUNTAIN RD
- VCTV 92394 4295-F6
BLACKHAWK MOUNTAIN WY
- VCTV 92394 4295-F5
BLACK HILLS CT
- VCTV 92394 4295-F5
BLACK HILLS DR
500 CLAR 91711 601-E1
E BLACK HORSE DR
2700 ONT 91761 682-J1
2700 ONT 91761 683-A1
BLACKMER LN
- SBdC 92277 4824-E4
BLACK OAK DR
- POM 91766 640-H6
BLACK OAK ST
10000 RCUC 91737 573-A5
BLACK OAK TR
36800 YCPA 92399 650-E6
BLACK OAKS CT
- SBdC - 4737-F6
BLACK OAKS DR
900 SBdC - 4737-F6
BLACKPINE PL
2400 ONT 91761 643-B5
BLACK PINE RD
2200 CHLS 91709 680-J4
BLACK ROCK CANYON RD
9100 YUCA 92284 4958-C7
BLACKSMITH CIR
- POM 91766 640-F4
BLACKSMITH RD
52100 SBdC - 4816-E7
BLACK STALLION DR
- RivC 92324 647-D7
N BLACKSTONE AV
1200 SBDO 92411 576-E5
BLACKSTONE CT
11300 FONT 92337 644-D3
BLACKWOOD CT
- FONT 92337 645-A1
BLACKWOOD DR
29500 SBdC - 4738-J6
BLACKWOOD ST
- FONT 92337 645-A2
BLAIR LN
62500 SBdC 92252 4819-D5
BLAISDELL DR
200 CLAR 91711 601-E1
BLAKE LN
- CHLS 91709 712-B5
8900 SBdC 92308 4478-F6
BLAKE RD
32700 SBdC - (4390-J7
See Page 4300)
32800 SBdC - (4391-A7
See Page 4300)
W BLAKE ST
2000 SBdC 92407 576-A2
2300 SBdC 92407 575-J2
BLAKELY CT
1000 POM 91767 601-B7
BLANCA RD
37700 SBdC 92347 (3587-G5
See Page 3586)
BLANCHARD AV
6500 FONT 92336 575-A4
7800 FONT 92336 605-A2
8500 FONT 92335 605-A2
BLANCHARD DR
10500 HESP 92345 4475-G4
BLANCHARD PL
500 CLAR 91711 601-E3
700 UPL 91786 601-E3
BLANCO RD
- SBdC 92301 368-H2
12900 SBdC 92372 4382-F3
14100 SBdC 92371 4382-F3
BLANDFORD LN
51600 SBdC 92285 (4576-C5
See Page 4486)
BLARNEY STONE RD
10200 SBdC 92372 4472-C5
BLAZE ST
4500 CHNO 91710 681-E1
BLAZE TR
2400 DBAR 91765 680-B6
BLAZEWOOD DR
11900 FONT 92337 644-C4
BLAZING STAR CT
12300 RCUC 91739 573-G5
BLAZING STAR LN
12500 VCTV 92392 4385-D5
BLAZING STAR RD
21700 SBdC 92301 4114-G3
BLEITZ RD
- BARS 92311 3678-G7
34100 SBdC 92311 3678-G7
BLENBURY DR
1400 DBAR 91765 680-A4
BLENEFIELD PL
600 DBAR 91765 640-E7
BLERIOT ST
15700 HESP 92345 4566-C5
BLISS CIR
2200 CLAR 91711 571-D6

STREET Block City ZIP Pg-Grid

BLISTERBACK RD
75100 SBdC 92277 4822-G3
75500 SBdC 92277 4823-A3
BLOOMINGTON AV
10 RLTO 92376 605-F4
700 RLTO 92316 605-F4
900 SBdC 92316 605-E6
BLOOSOM DR
- SBdC 92371 4563-E7
BLOSSOM AV
1300 RDL 92373 647-J2
12700 YCPA 92399 650-B4
BLOSSOM CIR
1400 UPL 91786 601-H1
BLOSSOM CT
1800 BARS 92311 3679-E4
BLOSSOM LN
6300 CHLS 91709 712-A5
BLOWER RD
2700 SBdC 92277 4824-D3
4300 SBdC 92277 (4894-D1 See Page 4824)
BLUEBELL DR
14500 CHLS 91709 681-D4
BLUEBELL LN
200 SBdC - 518-A1
7300 FONT 92336 574-D6
BLUEBERRY CT
8300 RCUC 91730 602-F2
N BLUEBILL DR
500 SBdC 92314 4742-E5
S BLUEBILL DR
100 SBdC 92314 4742-E6
BLUEBIRD CT
200 BBLK - 4811-G1
BLUEBIRD DR
33300 SBdC - 519-E2
BLUE BIRD LN
- SBdC - 4741-F6
BLUEBIRD LN
22700 GTER 92313 646-F5
33000 SBdC - 519-D7
BLUEBIRD RD
- CHLS 91709 680-G1
- DBAR 91765 680-G1
BLUE BIRD RD
6300 SBdC 92397 4652-C1
BLUE CANYON RD
- VCTV 92394 4296-B3
BLUE CREEK LN
7400 HIGH 92346 578-C5
BLUE CREST DR
10600 YCPA 92399 610-A6
BLUEFIELD DR
500 CLAR 91711 571-E6
BLUEFISH BLVD
- LPCo - 4606-H2
S BLUE FOX DR
2600 ONT 91761 643-A6
BLUEGRASS AV
300 SBdC 92277 4751-E6
2200 SBdC 92277 4821-E3
4300 SBdC 92277 4891-E1
6100 RCUC 91739 573-G3
BLUEGRASS DR
14700 SBdC - (3935-H2 See Page 3934)
15100 SBdC - 3936-A2
BLUE GRASS LN
16300 CHLS 91709 710-H2
BLUEGRASS PL
- VCTV 92392 4385-G4
900 POM 91766 640-E3
BLUE GRASS RD
- TNP 92277 4891-E4
BLUE GUM CT
6200 RCUC 91739 573-H4
BLUE GUM DR
12900 RCUC 91739 573-H4
BLUEJAY CT
6800 CHNO 91710 682-B1
BLUE JAY CTO
600 SBdC - 517-F3
BLUE JAY DR
- LACo 92397 4652-A1
- SBdC 92397 4652-A1
BLUE JAY LN
2200 SBdC - 519-D6
11600 FONT 92337 644-F3
BLUE JAY LNDG
400 BBLK - 4811-A1
BLUE JAY RD
- SBdC 92345 4565-A7
500 BBLK - 4811-A1
BLUE JAY WY
11000 SBdC 92345 4564-J7
11000 SBdC 92345 4565-A7
E BLUE JAY WY
200 ONT 91761 642-C6
W BLUE JAY WY
100 ONT 91762 642-B6
300 ONT 91710 642-B6
BLUE JAY CANYON RD
300 SBdC - 517-H2
BLUE LAKE CT
14900 FONT 92336 574-D6
BLUE LAKE RD
200 SBdC - 518-A2
BLUE LAKE ST
11500 FONT 92337 644-H3

BLUE MESA CT
13100 VCTV 92392 4385-E5
BLUE MIST AV
5800 CHLS 91709 711-J2
BLUE MIST DR
- RCUC 91739 573-F5
BLUE MOUNTAIN CT
12700 GTER 92313 646-F5
W BLUE MOUNTAIN RD
1000 SBdC 92314 4742-B5
BLUE MOUNTAIN WY
100 CLAR 91711 571-D7
BLUE PALM LN
22600 DBAR 91765 680-A3
BLUE RIDGE DR
700 SBdC - 518-B3
1100 POM 91766 640-F3
BLUERIDGE LN
- POM 91766 640-G6
S BLUE RIDGE LN
1100 CLTN 92324 646-G1
BLUE RIDGE PL
6600 RCUC 91701 573-C5
BLUE RIDGE WY
- FONT 92336 574-D3
BLUE SAGE CT
13500 VCTV 92392 4385-F5
N BLUE SKY CT
6600 SBDO 92407 545-J2
BLUE SPRUCE DR
700 SBdC - 4738-E6
BLUE SPRUCE WY
11600 VCTV 92392 4475-E1
BLUE STAKE RD
9200 SBdC 92371 4472-J6
BLUESTAR RD
9700 SBdC 92308 4479-C1
11100 SBdC 92308 (4389-C7 See Page 4299)
BLUEWATER DR
200 LPCo - 4774-J5
N BLUE WATER DR
200 SBdC 92314 4742-C6
S BLUE WATER DR
100 SBdC 92314 4742-C6
BLUE WATER RD
- SBdC - 4843-H5
26300 SBdC - (3935-H5 See Page 3934)
BLUEWOOD DR
13900 FONT 92337 644-B4
BLUFF CT
1500 DBAR 91765 680-D3
E BLUFF CT
1800 SBDO 92404 547-C7
BLUFF RD
7700 SBdC - 4843-D6
S BLUFF RD
1200 CLTN 92324 646-F2
BLUFF ST
4600 NRCO 92860 712-J7
8500 RivC 92220 651-G7
8700 BAN 92220 651-G5
BLUFF CREST ST
- VCTV 92392 4386-G4
BLUFF LAKE RD
38100 SBdC - 4810-H5
BLUFF POINT CIR
- POM 91766 640-G4
BLUFF SIDE CT
15700 CHLS 91709 681-B7
BLUFFVIEW ST
- FONT 92336 574-E6
BLYTHE AV
1300 SBDO 92346 577-E5
5600 SBdC 92346 577-E1
N BLYTHE AV
5900 SBdC 92346 577-E2
BLYTHE ST
55100 SBdC - 4606-F1
N BLYTHE ST
3100 SBDO 92346 577-E2
BN RANCH RD
- SBdC - 349-B7
BOA DR
25000 SBdC - 517-B3
N BOBBETT DR
900 SBDO 92410 577-A6
BOBCAT CT
- RCUC 91737 573-D4
BOBCAT LN
5300 SBdC 92285 (4576-C7 See Page 4486)
7700 HIGH 92346 578-C7
48100 SBdC 92365 (3595-A5 See Page 3594)
BOBCAT TR
7500 SBdC - 4843-E6
BOBCAT HILLS RD
- VCTV 92394 4295-F5
BOBOLINK DR
- LACo 92397 4652-A1
- SBdC 92397 4652-A1
4500 SBdC 92371 4653-C1
BOBOLINK WY
1900 POM 91767 601-A6
BOBWHITE CT
18800 SBdC 92316 645-E1
BOB WHITE LN
200 RivC 92507 646-E6

BOCA PL
11700 RivC 91752 683-F5
E BOCA RATON CT
1900 ONT 91761 642-H6
BOCA RATON WY
- FONT 92336 574-G2
BOCHEE RD
14200 APLV 92307 4297-D7
14200 APLV 92307 4387-D1
BODART ST
16300 HESP 92345 4566-E3
BODEGA CT
9700 RCUC 91730 602-J1
10400 MTCL 91763 641-E1
BODEGA ST
- SBdC 92307 (4117-D6 See Page 4116)
7100 FONT 92336 574-A6
BODEGA WY
1400 DBAR 91765 680-B3
N BODENHAMER ST
200 UPL 91786 602-E3
BODICK RD
54200 SBdC 92285 (4576-J7 See Page 4486)
54200 SBdC 92285 (4577-C7 See Page 4486)
S BODIE
400 SBdC 92314 4742-H7
BODIE ST
33300 YCPA 92399 649-F4
BOEING AV
6800 FONT 92336 574-E5
BOH LN
16500 VCTV 92394 4296-A2
BOHNERT AV
2700 RLTO 92377 574-J3
2700 RLTO 92377 575-A3
16900 FONT 92336 574-J3
16900 FONT 92377 574-J3
18200 SBdC 92377 575-D3
W BOHNERT AV
700 RLTO 92377 575-C3
1800 SBdC 92377 575-C3
S BOISE CREEK PL
2800 ONT 91761 643-D6
BOLERO DR
- YUCA 92284 4957-J6
9800 RCUC 91730 602-J1
11400 FONT 92337 644-E3
BOLINAS ST
8900 SBdC 92371 4474-D5
10000 SBdC 92345 4474-G5
11000 SBdC 92345 4475-A5
BOLING DR
72900 TNP 92277 4892-C7
BOLINGBROKE RD
- SBdC - (4655-E7 See Page 4654)
BOLIVAR ST
1700 POM 91766 640-H4
BOLO RD
15900 SBdC - 370-L4
BOLSA AV
63900 SBdC 92252 4959-H1
BOLSA CHICA
500 SBdC - 519-D2
BOLTON AV
9500 MTCL 91763 601-F6
11100 SBdC 91710 641-F3
BOLTON PL
- RCUC 91730 573-E1
BONAIR AV
1900 SBdC 92252 4819-C3
BONAIR RD
6500 SBdC 92252 4889-C7
BONANZA CT
- POM 91766 640-F5
BONANZA DR
55000 YUCA 92284 4957-D5
58000 YUCA 92284 4958-B5
BONANZA RD
1100 SBdC 92371 4382-B3
1800 SBdC 92372 4382-D3
2100 SBdC 92371 4472-E5
4900 SBdC 92371 4383-C3
7500 SBdC 92371 4384-A3
8800 SBdC 92371 4474-D4
8900 SBdC 92392 4384-D2
9300 SBdC 92301 4294-E6
10100 SBdC 92345 4474-G4
10600 ADEL 92301 4294-H6
11300 SBdC 92345 4475-A4
12500 VCTV 92392 4385-D2
13000 VCTV 92392 4475-E4
13800 SBdC 92392 4385-G2
14700 SBdC 92392 4386-A2
14900 VCTV 92392 4386-A2
27700 SBdC 92311 3679-D6
BONANZA TR
500 BBLK - 4811-E2
7200 SBdC - 368-J1
8000 SBdC - 3934-A2
17000 SBdC - 3936-F1
18600 SBdC - (3937-B1 See Page 3936)
BONANZA WY
14600 VCTV 92394 4296-A7
BONATO LN
11800 APLV 92308 4388-B6

BOND AV
12600 CLTN 92324 645-J5
BOND ST
200 RDL 92373 648-B1
3400 SBDO 92405 576-D1
BONE DR
21800 SBdC - 4736-C7
BONITA AV
100 SBdC 92284 4748-E5
500 SBdC 92285 4748-E5
3200 SBdC 92284 4818-E7
3700 SBdC 92284 4888-E2
4700 YUCA 92284 4888-F5
5600 RCUC 91737 573-B2
6300 SBdC 92252 4889-J6
6900 SBdC 92252 4959-J1
E BONITA AV
100 POM 91767 601-B3
400 CLAR 91711 601-D3
N BONITA AV
1400 ONT 91762 602-B5
S BONITA AV
1400 ONT 91762 642-B4
W BONITA AV
100 CLAR 91711 601-D3
BONITA CT
100 SBdC 92359 609-D5
N BONITA CT
100 ONT 91762 602-B5
100 ONT 91762 642-B1
S BONITA CT
1200 ONT 91762 642-B2
BONITA DR
6900 HIGH 92346 577-H5
35300 YCPA 92399 650-B7
N BONITA DR
1100 CLTN 92324 606-C5
2300 SBDO 92346 577-H2
BONITA LN
2400 SBdC - (3935-H3 See Page 3934)
40200 BBLK - 4811-D2
S BONITA PL
1300 ONT 91762 642-B3
BONITA ST
- YCPA 92399 610-A7
500 RDL 92374 608-C7
1300 UPL 91786 602-E1
9400 SBdC 92371 4474-E7
BONITA TR
7300 YUCA 92284 4958-A3
BONITA VISTA CT
- SBdC - (4743-C4 See Page 4662)
BONITA VISTA DR
5200 SBdC 92301 (4203-D1 See Page 4112)
5400 SBdC 92301 (4113-E7 See Page 4112)
E BONITA VISTA DR
1300 SBDO 92404 547-C6
BONITA VISTA ST
9200 SBdC 92308 4478-D6
BONITO CT
18400 SBdC 92392 4387-A2
BONNIE CT
7600 HIGH 92410 577-C6
34900 YCPA 92399 609-J5
BONNIE LN
18100 FONT 92335 605-C3
18100 RLTO 92335 605-C3
18100 SBdC 92335 605-C3
BONNIE ST
3200 SBdC 92404 577-C1
3200 SBDO 92404 577-D3
5300 SBdC 92404 547-D7
7400 HIGH 92410 577-C6
N BONNIE BRAE AV
200 CLAR 91711 571-D6
E BONNIE BRAE CT
300 ONT 91764 602-C5
W BONNIE BRAE CT
100 ONT 91762 602-A5
900 ONT 91762 601-H5
BONNIE BRAE ST
1000 POM 91767 601-D6
4400 MTCL 91763 601-E5
E BONNIE VIEW DR
300 RLTO 92376 605-H2
W BONNIE VIEW DR
100 RLTO 92376 605-D2
1600 RLTO 92335 605-D2
BONNY DUNES
7300 SBdC 92277 (4894-J7 See Page 4824)
BONSAI LN
- FONT 92337 645-A2
BON VIEW AV
12900 ONT 91761 642-D7
12900 ONT 91761 682-D3
14100 ONT 91710 682-D3
15700 SBdC 91710 682-E7
15700 SBdC 91710 712-E1
32700 SBdC 92365 (3765-E2 See Page 3764)
32700 SBdC 92365 (3685-E7 See Page 3594)
S BON VIEW AV
100 ONT 91761 642-D1

BONVIEW DR
1100 SBdC 92359 609-B6
BOO LN
- SBdC 92284 4748-A6
55200 SBdC 92284 4747-D6
BOOKASTA ST
1300 SBdC 92301 (4202-B5 See Page 4112)
5200 SBdC 92301 (4203-E5 See Page 4112)
BOOM BOOM BLVD
- SBdC 92277 4824-G3
BOONE RD
- SBdC 92285 4486-E7
6500 SBdC 92285 (4576-B2 See Page 4486)
BOONIES BLVD
- SBdC 92278 370-F10
- TNP 92278 370-F10
BOOTH AV
900 SBdC 92285 4748-G3
BOOTH RD
- LPCo - 4844-E6
E BOOTH WY
400 SBdC 92314 4742-E6
BOOTHE LN
400 SBdC - 516-E2
BOOTRIDGE LN
- VCTV 92392 4385-D5
BOOTS LN
14600 FONT 92336 574-C2
BOOTWELL RD
6700 SBdC 92277 (4895-A6 See Page 4824)
BOQUINA ST
1700 SBdC 92301 (4202-C7 See Page 4112)
4100 SBdC 92301 (4203-B7 See Page 4112)
BORAX AV
5300 SBdC 92277 4893-C3
BORAX WY
13000 SBdC 93562 2144-J4
BORDEAUX CT
- RCUC 91739 603-H1
- UPL 91786 602-C1
BORDEAUX LN
14700 CHLS 91709 681-A5
BORDEN LN
12100 YCPA 92399 649-E3
BORDER AV
100 SBdC 92252 4749-D5
1000 SBdC 92252 4819-D3
3900 SBdC 92252 4889-D1
6700 SBdC 92252 4959-D1
N BORDWELL AV
1100 CLTN 92324 606-E3
5000 SBDO 92410 606-E3
BORREGO RD
13400 VCTV 92392 4386-A1
13600 SBdC 92392 4386-A2
BORGES ST
- RivC 92880 683-D7
BORNITE AV
11800 HESP 92345 4386-F7
BORON LN
46100 SBdC - (4743-A4 See Page 4662)
BORREGO DR
1100 BARS 92311 3679-J6
1100 BARS 92311 3680-A6
BORREGO TR
7400 YUCA 92284 4957-F3
BOST LN
- SBdC 92277 4751-F7
S BOSTICK AV
200 CLTN 92324 646-C3
1700 CLTN 92313 646-C4
12000 GTER 92313 646-C3
12000 GTER 92324 646-C3
BOSTON AV
12900 CHNO 91710 641-E7
BOSTON CT
13600 FONT 92336 574-A7
BOSTON PL
800 POM 91767 601-A7
8500 RCUC 91730 603-E3
BOSWELL ST
4400 SBdC 92301 (4203-A2 See Page 4112)
N BOTHWELL AV
1200 CLTN 92324 606-F4
BOTTLE BRUSH ST
5500 RCUC 91737 573-B2
BOUGAINVILLA AV
- POM 91766 641-B3
BOUGAINVILLEA CT
6600 RCUC 91739 573-G5
BOUGAINVILLEA WY
12400 RCUC 91739 573-G5
BOULDER AV
6500 HIGH 92346 577-J4
6500 HIGH 92346 578-A6
6500 SBDO 92346 577-J4
6500 SBDO 92346 578-A6
36700 SBdC 92311 3589-J7
N BOULDER AV
100 ONT 91762 642-A1
100 ONT 91762 602-A5
1600 HIGH 92346 577-J4

N BOULDER AV
1600 HIGH 92346 578-A5
1600 SBDO 92346 577-J4
1600 SBDO 92346 578-A5
S BOULDER AV
1300 ONT 91762 642-A3
BOULDER LN
26100 SBdC - 517-E2
BOULDER RD
800 BBLK - 4811-A2
20000 SBdC - (4117-C2 See Page 4116)
BOULDER ST
- CHNO 91710 681-F4
BOULDER WY
- FONT 92336 574-E2
BOULDER BAY CT
700 BBLK - 4811-A2
BOULDER CANYON RD
10500 RCUC 91737 573-B1
BOULDER CREEK LN
38800 BBLK - 4811-A2
BOULDER CREEK RD
12600 VCTV 92392 4385-F5
BOULDER CREEK WY
13300 VCTV 92392 4385-F5
BOULDER PRIVADO
- ONT 91762 642-A2
BOULDER VIEW DR
- SBdC - 4816-G5
BOUQUET AV
10300 ADEL 92301 4204-G5
N BOUQUET DR
1300 UPL 91786 602-C1
BOURBON RD
30200 SBdC - 4480-C6
BOURBON ST
900 SBdC 92285 4748-H2
60500 SBdC 92284 4888-H5
60900 SBdC 92252 4888-H5
BOURLAND PASS
500 SBdC 92277 4750-G5
1300 SBdC 92277 4820-G2
BOW B
- RDL 92373 648-D2
BOW C
- RDL 92373 648-D2
BOW CANYON CT
1200 BBLK - 4812-C3
BOW CANYON DR
43200 BBLK - 4812-C3
BOW CANYON LN
43500 BBLK - 4812-D3
BOWCREEK DR
600 DBAR 91765 640-E7
600 DBAR 91765 680-E1
BOWCREEK LN
14500 CHLS 91709 680-J4
BOWDOIN ST
- COR 92880 712-J7
BOWEN ST
8400 RCUC 91730 602-F3
E BOWEN ST
1300 UPL 91730 602-E3
1300 UPL 91786 602-E3
BOWEN RANCH RD
5700 SBdC 92308 4568-G1
8500 SBdC 92308 4478-C3
BOWER CASCADE PL
23600 DBAR 91765 640-C6
BOWIE RD
- SBdC 92308 4479-F4
BOWIE ST
8000 FONT 92336 604-A1
13500 FONT 92336 603-J1
BOWL RD
23600 SBdC - 516-H3
W BOWLES DR
500 SBdC 92314 4742-C6
BOWLING GREEN DR
400 CLAR 91711 571-C7
BOWMAN RD
4600 SBdC - 328-H6
BOWMAN ST
3300 RivC 92501 646-A7
BOWMAN TR
100 SBdC 92284 4748-H5
1100 SBdC 92284 4818-H2
BOWMORE ST
16300 VCTV 92392 4386-E5
BOX DR
- SBdC - 4738-E7
BOXCOVE PL
600 DBAR 91765 640-E7
600 DBAR 91765 680-E1
BOX ELDER CT
8900 SBdC 92335 604-D4
BOXWOOD AV
7300 FONT 92336 575-B6
8200 FONT 92335 605-B1
9600 SBdC 92335 605-B5
11300 HESP 92345 4475-H2
12300 VCTV 92392 4385-G7
BOXWOOD CT
7800 HIGH 92346 578-C7
8700 FONT 92335 605-B3
E BOXWOOD CT
500 ONT 91761 642-C4
BOXWOOD DR
600 RivC 91752 683-E4

BOXWOOD LN
6100 CHNO 91710 641-J5
6100 CHNO 91710 642-A5
13500 VCTV 92392 4385-F5
BOXWOOD ST
21100 APLV 92308 4477-G3
S BOYD AV
200 SBDO 92408 606-H2
W BOYD CT
700 UPL 91786 572-A7
BOYD PL
1800 POM 91766 640-J4
BOYD TR
400 BBLK - 4811-C1
BOYER ST
3900 SBdC 91710 641-D3
BOYLE AV
10400 SBdC 92337 604-B7
15100 FONT 92337 604-E7
BOY SCOUT RD
10300 SBdC 92372 4472-A5
BRACEO ST
6300 SBdC 92345 4564-G3
6300 SBdC 92345 4654-G2
9100 SBdC 92345 4474-G3
10900 SBdC 92392 4474-G1
11900 SBdC 92392 4384-G7
13400 VCTV 92392 4384-G4
BRACERO RD
10700 SBdC 92345 4474-G3
BRACK RD
- SBdC - 369-E2
BRACKEN FERN CT
11400 VCTV 92392 4475-F1
BRADBURY CIR
28600 HIGH 92346 578-B6
BRADBURY DR
600 RDL 92374 648-F2
BRADBURY WY
13900 RCUC 91739 574-A1
BRADCLIFF CT
- YCPA 92399 649-E2
BRADCLIFF DR
- YCPA 92399 649-E2
BRADFORD AL
4200 SBDO 92404 546-H5
BRADFORD AV
6900 HIGH 92346 577-H5
9100 SBdC - 4480-J2
12100 SBdC - (4390-J5 See Page 4300)
N BRADFORD AV
2200 SBdC 92346 577-J2
2200 SBDO 92346 577-H3
BRADFORD CT
500 CLAR 91711 601-C3
1200 UPL 91786 602-D1
6500 RCUC 91701 573-D5
6700 CHNO 91710 642-B7
BRADFORD PL
1000 RDL 92373 648-D2
BRADFORD ST
700 POM 91767 640-J1
BRADLEY AV
2300 CLAR 91711 571-D6
W BRADLEY CT
1800 SBDO 92411 576-C4
BRADSHAW DR
100 BARS 92311 3679-F3
BRADY LN
1000 CALI 92320 649-J7
BRAEMAR AV
7100 HIGH 92346 577-H5
BRAEMAR DR
14900 VCTV 92394 4295-J6
BRAEWOOD CIR
1200 UPL 91786 601-G2
N BRAEWOOD LN
1200 UPL 91786 601-J1
BRAGA RD
15600 FONT 92337 644-F3
BRAGDON RD
37800 SBdC 92365 349-H7
37800 SBdC 92365 (3593-J2 See Page 3592)
BRAIDED MANE DR
2500 DBAR 91765 680-C6
BRAIRWOOD PL
7000 RCUC 91739 573-F6
BRAMA ST
- RivC 92880 683-D7
BRAMBLE CT
5000 RCUC 91737 573-B1
BRAMBLEBERRY CT
- CHLS 91709 711-J2
S BRAMBLE BUSH TR
2000 SBdC 92314 4742-H6
BRAMBLEWOOD DR
9900 RCUC 91737 572-J2
9900 RCUC 91737 573-A2
BRAMFORD CT
11000 DBAR 91765 680-E3
BRAMPTON AV
1900 RLTO 92376 575-F4
1900 SBdC 92376 575-F4
N BRAMPTON AV
200 RLTO 92376 605-F1
600 RLTO 92376 575-F5
1600 SBdC 92376 575-F5

S BRAMPTON AV
500 RLTO 92376 605-F3
BRAMPTON CT
6200 SBdC 92377 575-F3
BRANCH CIR
1300 UPL 91786 571-J7
S BRANCH DR
1000 CLTN 92324 646-G1
BRANCHWOOD PL
8300 RCUC 91730 602-G2
BRANCUSI LN
16300 CHLS 91709 711-G1
BRANDEIS DR
800 CLAR 91711 571-F4
BRANDING IRON DR
13700 SBdC - (3935-F5 See Page 3934)
BRANDING IRON PL
13300 CHNO 91710 681-C1
BRANDING IRON RD
8900 SBdC 92371 4563-D1
9400 SBdC 92371 4473-D7
15200 APLV 92307 4296-G5
BRANDON
1900 RDL 92374 608-B3
BRANDON CIR
2300 CHLS 91709 680-J7
BRANDON CT
- RDL 92373 648-F3
13500 FONT 92336 574-A7
13500 FONT 92336 604-A1
BRANDON LN
- FONT 92337 644-E2
BRANDY PL
6200 RCUC 91737 573-C4
13700 CHLS 91709 681-B2
BRANLE CT
16000 CHLS 91709 711-C1
BRANNIGAN MINE RD
72900 SBdC - 2971-H5
75100 SBdC - 350-F1
BRANSON PL
- YCPA 92399 649-E2
BRANT DR
20000 SBDO 92407 576-C4
BRANT RD
12700 VCTV 92392 4385-D4
BRANT CROSSING RD
3300 SBdC 92278 4751-G5
3400 SBdC 92277 4751-A5
67300 SBdC 92277 4750-G5
BRANTLEY CT
1100 UPL 91786 602-D1
BRAWLEY RD
900 SBdC 92372 4472-C7
2700 SBdC 92371 4472-G7
3600 SBdC 92371 4473-E6
9900 SBdC 92345 4474-G6
11300 SBdC 92345 4475-A6
BRAYTON AV
- RivC 92880 712-H4
BRAZOS RD
- APLV 92308 4387-F4
BREA PL
500 POM 91766 640-F2
BREA CANYON RD
- POM 91766 640-D3
W BREA CANYON RD
1800 POM 91766 640-E3
BREAK OF DAY CT
- CHLS 91709 681-B3
BRECKENRIDGE CT
24200 DBAR 91765 680-D2
W BRECKENRIDGE CT
1300 SBDO 92407 546-D5
BRECKENRIDGE RD
500 BBLK - 4811-J1
BRECKINRIDGE AV
- HESP 92345 4475-H7
BRECKINRIDGE CT
6100 CHNO 91710 681-J1
6100 CHNO 91710 682-A1
BRECKINRIDGE LN
5900 CHNO 91710 681-J1
6200 CHNO 91710 682-A1
BREE CT
12400 YCPA 92399 650-B3
BREEZEWAY
51100 SBdC 92256 4956-D6
BREEZY LN
20300 SBdC 92308 4477-E5
56100 SBdC 92284 4817-G5
59300 SBdC 92284 4818-F5
69700 SBdC 92277 4821-D4
BREGANTE DR
400 DBAR 91765 640-D7
BREITHORN DR
800 SBdC - 4737-G6
W BRENDA CT
1300 UPL 91786 601-J1
N BRENDA LN
6200 SBDO 92407 546-B2
BRENO PL
- RCUC 91701 573-E6
BRENTON PL
7900 HIGH 92346 578-B7
BRENTON ST
6600 RivC 92509 645-C4
E BRENTSTONE ST
3900 ONT 91761 643-C5

BRENTWOOD AV
25900 LMLN 92354 647-E2
N BRENTWOOD AV
1000 RLTO 92376 575-E6
1500 UPL 91786 571-H7
1700 UPL 91784 571-H6
BRENTWOOD CT
16400 CHLS 91709 711-E2
26500 SBdC - 517-F1
BRENTWOOD DR
- YUCA 92284 4958-A2
100 SBdC - 517-F1
300 SBdC - 4737-G6
7600 RCUC 91730 573-C7
13900 VCTV 92392 4386-F1
BRENTWOOD LN
4600 SBDO 92407 546-H6
BRENTWOOD PL
700 RDL 92373 648-A3
BRENTWOOD ST
2000 POM 91766 641-B5
22500 GTER 92313 646-E3
N BRENTWOOD WY
500 UPL 91786 601-H2
BRESCIA AV
2100 CLAR 91711 571-D7
BRET HARTE RD
100 SBdC - 518-B1
BRETON AV
13100 CHNO 91710 641-F7
13100 CHNO 91710 681-F1
S BREWER WY
200 SBdC 92314 4742-G6
BREWSTER DR
1000 POM 91767 601-C7
BREWSTER LN
14800 SBdC - (3935-H5 See Page 3934)
BREWSTER WY
- RDL 92373 648-C2
BRIAN CT
300 RDL 92374 648-G1
BRIAN ST
1300 SBdC 92301 (4202-B4 See Page 4112)
BRIAN WY
100 RivC 92507 646-E6
BRIANHEAD CT
13300 VCTV 92394 4295-F6
S BRIAR AV
1400 ONT 91762 642-A3
BRIAR CT
- CHLS 91709 681-B6
BRIAR LN
700 SBdC - 519-D2
BRIAR TR
1900 UPL 91784 571-J5
BRIAR WY
8900 SBdC - 4480-J6
BRIARCLIFF DR
12800 SBdC 92392 4387-A4
BRIAR CREEK LN
800 SBdC - 4738-A7
BRIAR CREEK RD
200 DBAR 91765 640-D6
BRIARCREST DR
10800 SBdC 92399 610-J6
BRIARCROFT RD
1100 CLAR 91711 601-A1
BRIAR PRIVADO
- ONT 91762 642-A2
BRIARTREE PL
5400 RCUC 91737 573-A2
BRIARWOOD AV
7700 FONT 92336 574-H7
9400 FONT 92335 604-H5
BRIARWOOD CT
11800 LMLN 92354 647-E3
N BRIARWOOD CT
6300 SBDO 92407 546-A2
W BRIARWOOD CT
2200 SBDO 92407 546-B2
BRIARWOOD LN
800 POM 91767 601-B6
22200 SBdC - 516-D2
BRIARWOOD RD
2900 SBDO 92407 545-J2
BRIARWOOD ST
14400 HESP 92345 4565-J2
E BRICKELL ST
4100 ONT 91761 643-D1
E BRICKELL PRIVADO
4500 ONT 91761 643-E1
BRIDAL PTH
- SBdC - 517-F4
- SBdC 92307 (4027-F4 See Page 3936)
BRIDGE LN
14000 SBdC - 514-B3
BRIDGE RD
100 SBdC - 518-D1
1400 NDLS 92363 3620-C4
E BRIDGE ST
2600 CLTN 92324 646-J4
BRIDGEPORT AV
1700 CLAR 91711 601-B1
1700 CLAR 91711 571-B7
BRIDGEPORT PL
9000 RCUC 91730 603-D4

BRIDGEPORT ST
17800 ADEL 92301 4204-F7
BRIDGER AV
12100 CHNO 91710 641-G4
W BRIDGET CT
1500 UPL 91784 571-H6
BRIDGEWATER DR
15600 FONT 92337 644-E3
BRIDGEWOOD LN
16100 VCTV 92392 4386-D6
BRIDGEWOOD WY
1300 UPL 91784 571-J4
BRIDLE CT
5500 FONT 92336 574-D2
14000 VCTV 92394 4295-H7
BRIDLE DR
800 DBAR 91765 680-C2
BRIDLE LN
- CHLS 91709 710-G4
14400 VCTV 92394 4295-G7
14400 VCTV 92394 4385-G1
BRIDLE PL
5000 RCUC 91737 573-C1
BRIDLEPATH DR
4800 FONT 92336 544-C7
4800 FONT 92336 574-C1
BRIDLE REIN LN
2500 SBdC - 4816-D7
BRIENZA PL
7200 RCUC 91701 573-E6
S BRIER DR
1600 SBDO 92408 607-A5
E BRIER ST
700 SBDO 92408 607-B5
BRIER TR
800 BBLK - 4811-A2
800 SBdC - 4811-A2
N BRIERWOOD AV
500 RLTO 92376 575-E6
500 RLTO 92376 605-E1
2200 RLTO 92377 575-E3
S BRIERWOOD AV
500 RLTO 92376 605-E3
BRIERWOOD DR
14700 CHLS 91709 681-C5
BRIGADOON CT
28600 SBdC - 4738-B5
BRIGADOON LN
14900 VCTV 92394 4295-J6
BRIGETTE CT
300 RDL 92374 648-G1
BRIGHAM YOUNG DR
600 CLAR 91711 571-E5
BRIGHT WY
- SBdC 92359 4950-F7
BRIGHTON AV
1800 SBdC 92359 608-H5
BRIGHTON CIR
13200 VCTV 92392 4385-F6
BRIGHTON CT
700 RDL 92374 648-F2
14900 FONT 92336 574-D7
BRIGHTON PL
- RCUC 91737 572-J5
BRIGHT SPOT RD
29500 HIGH 92346 578-E6
BRIGID CT
12800 YCPA 92399 649-G5
BRILLIANT LN
8700 RCUC 91701 572-G3
9700 RCUC 91737 572-J3
BRINDISI CT
11600 RCUC 91701 573-E5
BRINDISI WY
11600 RCUC 91701 573-E5
BRISAS CT
- RCUC 91739 573-J6
BRISBANE AV
4900 YUCA 92284 4887-F4
10900 APLV 92308 4477-F2
BRISBANE CT
- FONT 92337 645-B1
BRISSAC PL
6500 RCUC 91737 573-A5
BRISTLECONE DR
41900 BBLK - 4811-H2
BRISTOL AV
4900 SBdC 92277 (4894-E4 See Page 4824)
6500 FONT 92336 574-E4
BRISTOL CT
11300 ADEL 92301 4385-A1
12500 CHNO 91710 641-G6
15600 FONT 92337 644-E2
BRISTOL DR
10000 RCUC 91737 573-A4
BRISTOL LN
14700 SBdC - (3935-H5 See Page 3934)
BRISTOL ST
28700 HIGH 92346 578-B5
BRITTANY DR
400 RDL 92374 648-G1
BRITTANY LN
8300 RCUC 91701 572-E2
BRITTON WY
22400 GTER 92313 646-E4
BROAD AV
6900 TNP 92277 4893-A7

STREET
Block City ZIP Pg-Grid

C

STREET Block City ZIP Pg-Grid

CAJON AV
11100 SBdC 92308 (4389-C7
See Page 4299)
CAJON BLVD
- SBdC - 4734-C1
2600 SBdC - 4734-C1
13400 SBdC 92407 515-A5
CAJON BLVD U.S.-66 Hist
300 SBdC 92407 514-E1
400 SBdC 92407 4734-F7
1300 SBdC - 4734-F3
8100 SBDO 92407 514-H3
9000 SBdC - 4734-F3
11400 SBdC 92407 515-A4
18300 SBdC 92407 545-F2
18300 SBDO 92407 515-D7
18300 SBDO 92407 545-F2
N CAJON BLVD U.S.-66 Hist
2000 SBDO 92411 576-D2
2800 SBDO 92407 576-D2
3200 SBdC 92407 576-D2
3500 SBdC 92407 546 A6
4300 SBDO 92407 546-A6
4400 SBdC 92407 545-J4
4400 SBDO 92407 545-J4
CAJON BLVD S
18200 SBdC 92407 515-C6
CAJON RD
- UPL 91784 571-G7
CAJON ST
- RDL 92373 608-B7
100 RDL 92373 648-C1
13800 HESP 92345 4475-H5
14300 VCTV 92392 4386-B1
15300 HESP 92345 4476-B5
CAJON LOOKOUT RD
- SBdC 92345 4654-F3
CAL AV
100 BARS 92311 3680-B4
CAL CT
7800 RivC 92509 644-G7
CALABASH AV
8100 FONT 92335 604-B3
8100 SBdC 92335 604-B3
10400 SBdC 92337 604-B7
10500 SBdC 92337 644-B2
11100 FONT 92337 644-B4
CALADA RD
9400 SBdC - 4481-F1
11400 SBdC - (4391-F4
See Page 4300)
CALAIS CT
7500 RCUC 91730 573-D7
CALANDA DR
900 SBdC - 517-C4
CALANDRIA WY
15800 VCTV 92394 4296-C4
CALATINA DR
1600 POM 91766 640-G4
CALAVERAS AV
8500 RCUC 91730 602-E3
N CALAVERAS AV
600 ONT 91764 602-E4
CALAVERAS CT
3700 CHNO 91710 641-C5
N CALAVERAS CT
1400 ONT 91764 602-E5
S CALAVERAS PL
2400 ONT 91761 642-E6
CALAVERAS RD
- SBdC 92256 616-F2
200 SBdC 92372 4472-B2
CALCITE AV
11400 HESP 92345 4476-E1
11800 HESP 92345 4386-E7
13300 VCTV 92392 4386-E3
CALCITE PL
13400 VCTV 92392 4386-E3
CALCITE RD
- TNP 92278 4822-E2
CALCITE ST
27200 BARS 92311 3679-C7
27400 SBdC 92311 3679-D7
CALDARO ST
9700 RCUC 91737 572-J4
CALDER RD
8300 SBdC 92372 4562-E3
N CALDWELL AL
100 SBDO 92410 606-F1
S CALDWELL AV
400 ONT 91761 642-D1
S CALDWELL PL
2100 ONT 91761 642-D5
CALDY AV
11500 LMLN 92354 647-F2
CALEDON PL
6300 RCUC 91737 572-J4
CALENDULA ST
14700 ADEL 92301 4294-G7
14700 SBdC 92301 4294-G7
CALEXICO AV
3000 SBdC 92277 4823-B4
CALF ST
- RivC 92880 683-D6
CALGARY CIR
14500 FONT 92336 574-C1
CALGARY CT
1300 SBdC - 4738-B5

CALGARY DR
1100 SBdC - 4738-A5
CALGO LN
15500 VCTV 92394 4296-C5
CALHOUN ST
800 RDL 92374 608-A5
7700 HIGH 92346 578-A7
10300 HESP 92345 4475-G4
CALICO BLVD
100 SBdC - 3592-A7
35500 SBdC - (3681-G1
See Page 3590)
36800 SBdC - (3591-J7
See Page 3590)
37800 SBdC - (3682-B1
See Page 3592)
39300 SBdC 92365 3592-G7
39800 SBdC 92365 (3593-A7
See Page 3592)
CALICO CIR
- SBdC - 2971-G1
CALICO CT
4900 RCUC 91737 (543-B7
See Page 513)
4900 RCUC 91737 573-B1
27800 SBdC - 3936-A2
CALICO DR
1800 BARS 92311 3680-B5
15600 VCTV 92392 4386-C3
27300 BARS 92311 3679-D5
27300 SBdC 92311 3679-D5
CALICO PL
13500 CHNO 91710 681-E2
CALICO RD
9200 SBdC 92308 4478-H1
10500 ADEL 92301 4204-H7
11500 SBdC 92308 4388-H7
35700 SBdC - (3682-B1
See Page 3592)
36000 SBdC - 3592-A6
36600 SBdC - (3591-H3
See Page 3590)
CALICO ST
47700 SBdC 92365 3764-J5
47700 SBdC 92365 (3765-A5
See Page 3764)
CALICO PEAK PL
6400 RCUC 91737 573-E4
CALIENTE AV
700 BARS 92311 3679-H4
CALIENTE RD
6100 SBdC 92345 4654-H1
6100 SBdC 92345 4564-J7
6700 SBdC 92345 4565-A5
8100 HESP 92345 4565-C2
9700 SBdC 92345 4475-B5
10700 VCTV 92392 4475-B2
11500 VCTV 92392 4385-B4
13700 ADEL 92392 4385-B4
56900 SBdC 92285 4667-G5
CALIENTE ST
58100 SBdC 92284 4818-B7
CALIFIA DR
10900 RCUC 91737 573-C4
CALIFLORA ST
- UPL 91784 572-E6
CALIFORNIA AV
- GTER 92313 646-D7
- RivC 92507 646-D7
400 NDLS 92363 3620-B5
2400 SBdC 92252 4819-G4
4500 SBdC 92252 4889-H3
6700 SBdC 92252 4959-H1
14300 VCTV 92392 4386-B1
CALIFORNIA AV Rt#-95
- PRKR - 4844-J1
- SBdC - 4774-H6
600 PRKR - 4774-J7
CALIFORNIA DR
500 CLAR 91711 601-B3
CALIFORNIA PL
34900 YCPA 92399 650-A6
CALIFORNIA ST
800 RDL 92374 607-F4
900 SBdC - 4606-G2
900 YCPA 92399 650-A3
900 CALI 92320 650-A7
1400 SBdC 92374 607-F4
10500 LMLN 92373 607-F7
10500 RDL 92373 607-F5
10500 SBdC 92373 607-F5
10900 LMLN 92373 647-F1
10900 SBdC 92373 647-F1
26400 LMLN 92354 647-F1
83000 SBdC 93562 2145-A4
E CALIFORNIA ST
100 ONT 91761 642-D2
N CALIFORNIA ST
1200 SBDO 92411 576-C4
2100 SBDO 92407 576-C4
2800 SBdC 92407 576-C4
W CALIFORNIA ST
100 ONT 91761 642-B2
100 ONT 91762 642-B2
CALIFORNIA PRIVADO
- ONT 91762 642-A2
CALIHAN RD
8000 SBdC 92301 4204-A1

CALIMESA BLVD
11800 CALI 92320 649-G7
13300 YCPA 92399 649-D5
CALLAWAY CT
- YCPA 92399 649-E2
CALLAWAY PL
6100 RCUC 91737 573-B4
CALLE ADRIANA
2300 SDMS 91773 640-A1
CALLE ANDREA
100 SDMS 91773 640-B1
CALLE BARCELONA
15100 CHLS 91709 680-H5
CALLE BASILO
- HIGH 92346 578-C6
CALLE BASTIA
7600 HIGH 92346 578-C6
CALLE BELICIA
2200 SDMS 91773 640-A1
CALLE BIENVENIDA
2200 CHLS 91709 680-J5
CALLE BRESCA
7700 RCUC 91730 602-F1
CALLE BRILLANTE
14600 CHLS 91709 681-A4
CALLE BRISA
14600 CHLS 91709 681-A4
CALLE CANDIDA
100 SDMS 91773 640-A1
CALLE CARABE AV
8300 RCUC 91730 602-F2
CALLE CARABE CT
8400 RCUC 91730 602-F1
CALLE CARABE PL
8000 RCUC 91730 602-F2
CALLE CARRISA ST
- HIGH 92346 578-G7
CALLE CASINO
7700 RCUC 91730 602-F1
CALLE CASINO LN
7600 RCUC 91730 572-F7
7600 RCUC 91730 602-F1
W CALLE CELESTE
2300 RLTO 92377 545-B7
2800 RLTO 92377 544-J6
CALLE CLARIN
7700 RCUC 91730 602-F1
CALLE CONCORDIA
200 SDMS 91773 640-A1
CALLE CONSTANCIA
100 RDL 92373 647-J2
CALLE CONTESTA
14100 VCTV 92392 4385-H6
CALLE CORAZON
8700 RCUC 91730 602-F1
CALLE DE ACACIA
1000 RDL 92373 648-A4
CALLE DE BARRANCA
1200 RDL 92373 648-A4
CALLE DE CABOS
- POM 91766 640-E5
CALLE DE LA PALMAS
1000 RDL 92373 648-A4
CALLE DEL MAR
- POM 91766 640-F4
CALLE DEL PRADO
7400 RCUC 91730 572-F7
8200 UPL 91786 572-F7
8200 UPL 91730 572-F7
CALLE DEL REY
- POM 91766 640-F5
CALLE DEL RIO
61600 SBdC 92252 4889-A2
CALLE DEL RIO ST
- HIGH 92346 578-G6
CALLE DEL RIO NORTE
61800 SBdC 92252 4889-C1
CALLE DEL RIO SUR
- SBdC 92252 4889-B2
CALLE DEL SOL
- HIGH 92346 578-D7
- SBdC 92365 (3684-C4
See Page 3594)
- POM 91766 640-E5
800 UPL 91784 572-A6
CALLE DEL VISTA
61700 SBdC 92252 4889-C1
CALLE DE ORO
15100 CHLS 91709 680-H5
CALLE DE PAZ
10100 SBdC - 4481-B1
CALLE DE RODEO
- POM 91766 640-E5
CALLE DE SILVA
700 RDL 92374 648-D1
CALLE DOMINGO
14100 VCTV 92392 4385-H6
CALLE ELEGANTE
6300 RCUC 91737 572-J4
CALLE ELVIRA
35900 SBdC 92365 3594-C7
CALLE FELIZ
8500 RCUC 91730 572-F7
CALLE FIESTA
45400 SBdC 92365 3594-D7
CALLE HACIENDA
- HIGH 92346 578-D7
CALLE HERMOSO
6300 RCUC 91737 572-J4

CALLE HERNANDEZ RD
1300 NDLS 92363 3620-C7
CALLE ILUMINADO
2600 CHLS 91709 681-A4
CALLE INVIERNO
2900 CHLS 91709 681-B4
CALLEJA RD
12100 ADEL 92301 (4115-C7
See Page 4114)
12100 SBdC 92301 (4115-C7
See Page 4114)
12500 VCTV 92301 (4115-C7
See Page 4114)
CALLE LADO BUENO
14500 CHLS 91709 681-A4
CALLE LA PALOMA
15000 CHLS 91709 681-A5
CALLE LAS SIERRAS
62100 SBdC 92252 4889-D2
CALLE LAS SIERRAS S
61700 SBdC 92252 4889-C2
CALLE LOMITA
15200 CHLS 91709 680-G6
CALLE LORENA
100 SDMS 91773 640-A1
CALLE LOS AMIGOS
61400 SBdC 92252 4889-C3
CALLE LUMINA
2900 CHLS 91709 681-B4
CALLE LUNA
2600 CHLS 91709 681-A4
CALLE MADRID
14900 CHLS 91709 680-J5
14900 CHLS 91709 681-A5
CALLE MILAN
7600 HIGH 92346 578-C6
CALLE MIRAMAR
15200 CHLS 91709 680-H6
CALLE NORTE
- HIGH 92346 578-D7
CALLE OCOTILLO
1200 RDL 92373 648-A4
CALLE OTONO
14600 CHLS 91709 681-A4
CALLE PETULA
2300 SDMS 91773 640-A1
CALLE PRIMAVERA
14700 CHLS 91709 681-A4
CALLE QUEBRADA
8600 RCUC 91730 602-F1
CALLE RAYO LUNAR
14600 CHLS 91709 681-A4
CALLE RENATA
100 SDMS 91773 640-A1
CALLE RITARI
35900 SBdC 92365 3594-C7
CALLE RIVERA
28900 HIGH 92346 578-C6
CALLE SABINA
2300 SDMS 91773 640-A1
CALLE SAN MARCOS
13500 CHLS 91709 681-A2
CALLE SIENA
- HIGH 92346 578-D7
CALLE SOLEJAR
1700 RDL 92373 648-H4
CALLE TALIA
7600 HIGH 92346 578-C6
CALLE TRELLA
2300 SDMS 91773 640-A1
CALLE VEJAR
9100 RCUC 91730 602-H2
CALLE VERANO
- HIGH 92346 578-C6
15000 CHLS 91709 681-A5
CALLE VISTA
2600 CHLS 91709 681-A4
W CALLE VISTA DR
2300 RLTO 92377 575-B1
2300 RLTO 92377 545-A7
2800 RLTO 92377 544-J7
CALLIANDRA RD
9200 SBdC 92308 4478-J1
12000 SBdC 92308 4388-J6
CALLIE TODD LN
73700 TNP 92277 4892-E2
CALLIE TODD RD
- SBdC 92277 4893-C2
CALL OF THE CANYON RD
400 SBdC - 514-A3
CALMADA RD
- SBdC - 4816-H7
- SBdC - 4886-H1
CALPELLA AV
7300 HESP 92345 4567-B3
CALPINE
36900 SBdC - (4392-B1
See Page 4302)
CALPINE CT
800 POM 91766 641-A6
CALSPAR ST
700 LACo 91711 571-B6
CALTRANS AV
56600 SBdC - 2971-G2
CALUMA CT
8700 RCUC 91730 572-F7
CALVARY CIR
1600 RDL 92373 647-H1

CALVIN ST
11600 YCPA 92399 650-B2
CALWELL ST
31100 SBdC 92374 648-J1
CALYPSO CT
5000 RCUC 91737 573-B1
CALZADO CT
13600 VCTV 92392 4385-G3
CAMARENA AV
9700 MTCL 91763 601-F6
10400 MTCL 91763 641-F1
CAMARILLA AV
4200 SBdC 92284 4888-C3
4700 YUCA 92284 4888-C7
7300 YUCA 92284 4958-C3
CAMARILLO AV
- SBdC - 4843-H5
36700 BARS 92311 3589-H6
36700 SBdC 92311 3589-H6
CAMARITAS DR
400 DBAR 91765 640-B7
400 DBAR 91765 680-B1
CAMARRIO CT
5600 RCUC 91739 573-G2
CAMASSIA CT
12700 RCUC 91739 573-H5
CAMBON CT
1200 RDL 92374 648-E1
CAMBRIA AV
100 SBdC 92284 4747-F4
200 SBdC 92285 4747-F2
800 SBdC 92284 4817-G2
1700 SBdC 92285 4667-F7
17000 FONT 92336 574-J4
17100 FONT 92336 575-A4
CAMBRIA DR
12300 YCPA 92399 649-E4
12600 RCUC 91739 573-G2
CAMBRIA LN
26200 LMLN 92354 647-F2
CAMBRIA RD
500 SBdC 92372 4472-B7
2500 SBdC 92371 4472-F7
3600 SBdC 92371 4473-A7
7300 SBdC 92371 4474-F6
9800 SBdC 92345 4474-G6
11100 SBdC 92345 4475-A6
11700 HESP 92345 4475-B6
32900 SBdC - (4391-A3
See Page 4300)
36200 SBdC - (4392-A3
See Page 4302)
CAMBRIA ST
14700 SBdC 92335 604-D5
35300 SBdC - (4571-G1
See Page 4570)
CAMBRIDGE AV
1400 RDL 92374 608-F6
1800 SBDO 92407 546-B6
6400 RCUC 91737 573-A4
6700 RCUC 91701 573-A5
7300 RCUC 91730 573-A7
7900 RCUC 91730 603-A1
N CAMBRIDGE AV
100 CLAR 91711 601-C2
1000 UPL 91786 572-A7
1000 UPL 91786 602-A1
S CAMBRIDGE AV
100 CLAR 91711 601-C4
CAMBRIDGE CIR
1700 RDL 92374 608-G7
CAMBRIDGE CT
7400 FONT 92336 574-B6
11400 ADEL 92301 4385-A1
28300 HIGH 92346 578-B5
CAMBRIDGE DR
3200 CHLS 91709 711-B1
3200 CHLS 91709 681-B7
CAMBRIDGE PL
13500 CHNO 91710 682-A2
CAMBRIDGE RD
11800 LMLN 92354 647-F3
CAMBRIDGE ST
4300 MTCL 91763 601-E5
11300 ADEL 92301 4385-A1
CAMBRIN RD
1000 POM 91768 640-F1
CAMBROS CT
- FONT 92336 574-D1
CAMDEN AV
14900 CHLS 91709 681-B5
CAMDEN CT
1100 UPL 91786 602-D1
CAMDEN DR
9500 RCUC 91701 572-J6
CAMEL AV
18100 ADEL 92301 4204-F6
CAMELBACK DR
16000 VCTV 92392 4386-D2
CAMELIA CT
4300 CHNO 91710 641-E4
N CAMELIA AV
300 ONT 91762 601-J6
CAMELLIA CT
700 POM 91766 641-B3
8900 RCUC 91737 572-G2
W CAMELLIA CT
100 UPL 91786 572-B7
CAMELLIA DR
13300 YCPA 92399 650-B6

N CAMELLIA DR
3400 SBDO 92404 577-B1
3600 SBDO 92404 547-B6
CAMELLIA RD
2100 SBdC 92371 4382-E2
4100 SBdC 92371 4383-G1
7600 SBdC 92371 4384-A1
7900 ADEL 92301 4384-A1
7900 ADEL 92371 4384-A1
12900 SBdC 92392 4385-E1
CAMELOT AV
26100 LMLN 92354 647-E2
W CAMELOT CT
700 ONT 91762 642-A3
CAMELOT DR
1600 RDL 92374 648-F2
33100 YCPA 92399 649-E4
CAMEO AV
2100 BARS 92311 3679-G6
CAMEO CT
- CHLS 91709 711-H1
700 POM 91766 641-A6
CAMEO DR
200 SBdC - 518-A2
1500 RDL 92373 648-C4
13900 SBdC 92337 644-B1
W CAMEO DR
500 CLTN 92324 606-C4
CAMEO ST
5700 RCUC 91701 572-F3
W CAMEO ST
700 UPL 91786 572-A7
CAMERON CT
2000 BARS 92311 3679-H6
CAMERON DR
700 BBLK - 4811-E2
CAMERON LN
15800 CHLS 91709 681-B7
CAMERON RD
11000 SBdC - (4391-E7
See Page 4300)
CAMERON ST
900 CLTN 92324 646-H1
9300 RCUC 91730 602-H4
E CAMERON WY
100 RLTO 92316 605-H6
200 CLTN 92316 605-H6
CAMERON CREST DR
400 DBAR 91765 640-C7
CAMINO RD
17700 SBdC 92307 4208-B5
32400 SBdC 92311 (3757-H5
See Page 3756)
36100 SBdC 92347 (3677-H2
See Page 3586)
CAMINO AL SOL
- HESP 92345 4656-C7
CAMINO ARROYO
15100 CHLS 91709 680-J5
CAMINO BOSQUE DR
1700 SBdC - 4742-J3
CAMINO CIELO ST
- HIGH 92346 578-H7
CAMINO DEL CIELO
7100 YUCA 92284 4957-C2
CAMINO DEL CIELO CT
7300 YUCA 92284 4957-C3
CAMINO DEL MILAGRO
- POM 91766 640-D4
CAMINO DEL NORTE
24900 SBdC 92311 3678-G5
CAMINO DEL ORO RD
69300 SBdC 92277 4891-D2
69500 TNP 92277 4891-D2
CAMINO DEL SOL
15000 CHLS 91709 680-J5
25000 SBdC 92311 3678-G5
CAMINO LARGO DR
2300 CHLS 91709 680-H1
CAMINO MONTURA
4300 RivC 92509 644-B7
CAMINO NORTE
7400 RCUC 91730 572-F7
74400 TNP 92277 4892-G1
CAMINO PREDERA
7800 RCUC 91730 602-F1
CAMINO REAL
500 RDL 92373 648-F4
3900 RivC 92509 644-H6
34500 SBdC 92311 3678-F5
S CAMINO REAL
1300 SBDO 92408 606-G5
1500 CLTN 92324 606-G5
CAMINO SUR
8300 RCUC 91730 602-F1
CAMOLI CT
15100 CHLS 91709 681-C6
CAMOMILE LN
14900 FONT 92336 574-D7
CAMP RD
- SBdC - 519-F2
- SBdC - (4882-C4
See Page 4813)
W CAMPANA CT
1500 CLTN 92324 606-A4
CAMPANELLA PL
5700 RCUC 91739 574-B2
CAMPANULA RD
9300 SBdC 92371 4473-D2
12300 SBdC 92371 4383-C2

CAMPANULA ST
- SBdC - 4817-C7
- SBdC - 4886-D1
- SBdC - 4887-B1
56900 SBdC 92284 4817-H7
57400 SBdC 92284 4818-A7
60100 SBdC 92252 4818-G7
61000 SBdC 92252 4819-A7
CAMP BALDY RD
4300 CLAR 91711 571-F3
CAMPBELL
36300 SBdC - (4301-J5
See Page 4300)
CAMPBELL PL
7000 RCUC 91701 573-C6
CAMPBELL RD
4700 SBdC 92277 (4825-F7
See Page 4824)
4900 SBdC 92277 (4895-F1
See Page 4824)
CAMPBELL ST
- RDL 92373 648-D2
3400 RivC 92509 644-C6
36100 SBdC - (4301-J6
See Page 4300)
CAMP CEDAR CREST RD
- SBdC - 519-D5
CAMPERO DR
58500 YUCA 92284 4888-C3
CAMPERO RD
57000 YUCA 92284 4887-J3
59100 YUCA 92284 4888-A3
CAMPHOR AV
8800 HESP 92345 4476-H7
N CAMPHOR AV
1100 RLTO 92376 575-E6
CAMPHOR CT
12700 RCUC 91739 573-H5
CAMPHOR LN
- LACo 91768 640-A2
CAMPHOR PL
2300 POM 91766 641-A6
N CAMPHOR WY
600 UPL 91786 602-A2
CAMPO VERDE DR
- SBdC 92301 (4113-B3
See Page 4112)
CAMPO VERDE RD
6000 SBdC - 4844-A2
CAMPO VIEJO TR
- SBdC - 4816-C2
CAMP ROCK CT
- FONT 92336 574-E2
CAMP ROCK RD
- SBdC - (3681-F7
See Page 3590)
7100 SBdC - (4572-B4
See Page 4482)
8200 SBdC - 4482-B1
10800 SBdC - (4392-B3
See Page 4302)
13700 SBdC - 4302-F3
20800 SBdC - 369-G1
27800 SBdC - (3852-B3
See Page 3762)
30300 SBdC - 3762-A5
31100 SBdC - (3761-G2
See Page 3760)
CAMPUS AV
- CHNO 91710 682-D7
- SBdC 91710 682-D7
800 RDL 92374 608-C6
2400 SBdC 91784 572-C3
3300 CLAR 91711 601-B2
12900 ONT 91761 642-D7
12900 ONT 91761 682-D2
N CAMPUS AV
- UPL 91786 602-C2
100 ONT 91761 602-D6
100 ONT 91761 642-D1
100 ONT 91764 602-D6
1400 UPL 91786 572-C7
1600 UPL 91784 572-C4
S CAMPUS AV
- UPL 91786 602-D4
100 ONT 91761 642-D2
400 ONT 91764 602-D4
400 UPL 91764 602-D4
CAMPUS DR
2000 YCPA 92399 649-C2
E CAMPUS DR
- LACo 91768 640-B1
- POM 91768 640-B1
S CAMPUS DR
2400 POM 91768 640-C1
2800 LACo 91768 640-C1
CAMPUS ST
10800 LMLN 92354 607-B7
10900 LMLN 92354 647-B1
CAMPUS WY
100 BARS 92311 3679-G3
W CAMPUS WY
700 SBDO 92405 576-F4
CAMROSE CT
14400 VCTV 92392 4386-F1
CAMROSE PL
6600 RCUC 91701 573-C5
CAMULOS AV
8900 MTCL 91763 601-E4

CAMULOS RD
- SBdC 92285 4748-B2
56700 SBdC 92285 4747-G3
CAMUS CT
1200 UPL 91784 571-J5
CANADA ST
10900 LMLN 92354 607-A7
CANAL DR
12100 GTER 92313 646-F4
CANAL RD
- SBDO 92408 607-A7
- SBDO 92408 647-A1
E CANAL RD
300 CLTN 92324 606-E4
CANAL ST
2800 RivC 92509 645-A7
11600 GTER 92313 646-E3
29500 HIGH 92346 578-E5
CANARD AV
- SBdC 92308 4567-D5
CANARO RD
11300 APLV 92308 4477-D1
CANARY CT
4500 MTCL 91763 601-E7
11900 GTER 92313 646-F4
E CANARY CT
3200 ONT 91761 643-B5
CANARY DR
11600 FONT 92337 644-F3
W CANARY ST
700 CLTN 92324 606-C4
CANARY PINE AV
6700 RCUC 91737 573-A5
CANASTA DR
23000 SBdC 92301 (4113-D1
See Page 4112)
CANAVAN ST
300 BARS 92311 3679-G6
CANBERRA CT
26200 SBDO 92409 577-E7
CANBERRA RD
14400 SBdC 92371 4383-A2
CANDELA AV
2500 SBdC 92252 4819-B5
CANDELA DR
- RCUC 91701 573-D6
CANDELA ST
1300 RDL 92373 648-A3
CANDELARIA RD
20800 APLV 92308 4477-G4
20800 SBdC 92308 4477-G4
CANDIDA RD
7700 SBdC 92308 4567-F2
CANDLEBERRY LN
12900 SBdC 92392 4386-H4
N CANDLEBERRY RD
1300 CLTN 92324 605-J4
CANDLELIGHT DR
500 BARS 92311 3679-H5
CANDLELIGHT ST
- APLV 92308 4477-G4
9100 SBdC 92308 4477-G6
CANDLEWICK LN
12800 SBdC 92392 4387-A4
CANDLEWOOD AV
18300 RLTO 92377 575-C2
W CANDLEWOOD AV
1700 RLTO 92377 575-C1
CANDLEWOOD DR
15700 VCTV 92392 4386-C2
CANDLEWOOD RD
- SBdC 92308 4388-C7
9400 SBdC 92308 4478-C1
11900 APLV 92308 4388-C5
13700 APLV 92307 4388-C2
14300 APLV 92307 4298-C1
16900 APLV 92307 4208-C6
18100 SBdC 92307 4208-C3
CANDLEWOOD ST
8700 RCUC 91730 572-F7
9900 RCUC 91730 573-A7
11900 RCUC 91739 573-F7
CANDLEWOOD WY
- FONT 92336 574-E6
CANDY CT
6100 SBdC 92371 4473-F6
CANDY LN
200 RDL 92373 648-E4
CANEL RD
2600 SBdC 92359 609-D5
CANELLIA DR
13600 SBdC 92335 604-A2
CANE SPRINGS RD
30300 SBdC - 3764-F7
30300 SBdC 92365 3764-F7
CANFIELD RD
17100 SBdC - 371-A3
27000 SBdC 92307 4299-D3
CANFIELD WY
- CHLS 91709 681-H7
- CHLS 91709 711-H1
- CHNO 91709 681-H7
11900 SBdC 92316 645-G4
CANISIUS CIR
100 CLAR 91711 571-D6
CANISTEL AV
5100 RCUC 91737 573-C2
CANITA CT
- SBdC 92345 4564-H6

CANKU RD
20600 APLV 92307 4297-F4
22200 APLV 92307 4298-A4
23900 SBdC 92307 4298-E4
CANNERY RW
11300 SBdC 91766 641-D3
CANNES AV
1200 UPL 91784 571-J4
3100 RivC 92501 646-A7
CANNON ST
- BARS 92311 3680-F6
- TNP 92278 4751-J5
CANNON WY
2600 SBdC - 519-A7
CANOE CT
7500 SBdC - 4843-F5
CANOE DR
- RivC 92880 683-D4
CANOECOVE DR
300 DBAR 91765 640-D7
CANOGA PL
1500 POM 91767 601-C6
CANOGA ST
4500 MTCL 91763 601-E7
10000 SBdC 92345 4475-C5
CANON LN
16100 CHLS 91709 710-G1
CANON ST
18200 SBdC 92407 515-C3
CANOSA PL
6900 RCUC 91701 573-E5
CANTABRIA AV
6100 RCUC 91737 573-C4
CANTA LOMA LN
13000 VCTV 92392 4385-E6
CANTARA ST
1400 POM 91767 601-C6
N CANTARA ST
1000 CLTN 92324 606-A4
CANTEBURY WY
28500 HIGH 92346 578-B6
CANTEL CT
- VCTV 92392 4384-G6
8600 SBdC 92345 4564-G2
CANTER DR
- RCUC 91739 573-H2
CANTERBURY AV
2200 POM 91768 640-D1
CANTERBURY CIR
1500 RDL 92374 608-A4
CANTERBURY CT
200 UPL 91784 572-C4
1400 SBdC - 4738-A5
11000 RCUC 91730 573-C6
15600 FONT 92337 644-E3
34900 YCPA 92399 649-J4
34900 YCPA 92399 650-A4
CANTERBURY DR
6600 CHLS 91709 712-B6
14100 VCTV 92392 4386-C1
CANTERBURY ST
- SBdC - 4887-B1
- SBdC 92252 4820-A7
56900 SBdC 92284 4887-H1
57500 SBdC 92284 4888-A1
60100 SBdC 92252 4888-G1
60300 SBdC 92252 4818-H7
61700 SBdC 92252 4819-C7
E CANTERBURY TR
2600 ONT 91761 642-J6
S CANTERBURY TR
2600 ONT 91761 642-J6
CANTINA DR
12100 VCTV 92392 4385-C6
CANTON CIR
1100 CLAR 91711 571-F5
CANTON ST
- SBdC - 4843-H5
4900 YUCA 92284 4887-G4
CANTUBA RD
- SBdC 92365 (3685-C2
See Page 3594)
CANUGA DR
- SBdC 92252 4959-C5
CANUGA TR
7800 SBdC 92252 4959-C3
CANVASBACK DR
200 BBLK - 4811-C1
CANYON CT
- SBdC - 517-A1
CANYON DR
- LPCo - 4606-J4
1100 SBdC 91784 571-J2
1800 RDL 92373 649-A5
7300 YUCA 92284 4957-A3
9200 SBdC 92339 611-C1
10300 SBdC 92345 4564-H6
11300 SBdC 92399 650-E1
12100 YCPA 92399 650-E4
20100 SBdC 92308 4567-G2
27500 SBdC - 517-H3
32900 SBdC - 519-D3
E CANYON DR
2200 SBdC 92397 4652-F4
S CANYON DR
2100 SBdC 92324 646-H4
2100 CLTN 92324 646-J4
CANYON LN
- YUCA 92284 4887-H2
1700 SBdC 92404 516-G6

CANYON LN
19500 APLV 92308 4477-B5
CANYON PL
9100 SBdC 92339 611-D2
CANYON RD
- SBdC 92277 4751-F6
900 SBdC - 4741-C5
1700 RDL 92373 648-F4
2800 SBdC 92277 4821-F2
4600 YUCA 92284 4887-H3
5700 TNP 92277 4891-E3
7000 TNP 92277 4961-F1
9100 Llan 93544 4562-A1
9100 SBdC 92372 4472-A7
9100 SBdC 92372 4562-A1
25700 LMLN 92354 647-D3
25800 SBdC 92354 647-D3
25800 SBdC 92373 647-G4
50700 SBdC 92256 616-B2
N CANYON RD
1200 SBDO 92404 577-A5
CANYON COVE ST
11100 VCTV 92392 4475-D3
CANYON CREST DR
1700 BBLK - 4812-D3
1700 SBdC - 4812-D3
11900 FONT 92337 644-D4
12100 RivC 92509 644-D4
CANYON CREST LN
- SBdC - 518-A2
CANYON CREST RD
13300 YCPA 92399 650-D6
CANYON CREST WY
11900 FONT 92337 644-D4
CANYON EDGE CIR
1900 SBDO 92404 547-D6
N CANYON EDGE DR
3800 SBDO 92404 547-D7
CANYON GLEN RD
1000 CHLS 91709 710-F2
CANYON HEIGHTS CT
36200 YCPA 92399 650-D6
CANYON HEIGHTS DR
13300 YCPA 92399 650-D6
CANYON HILLS DR
37400 YCPA 92399 650-G6
CANYON HILLS RD
15600 CHLS 91709 680-F7
15700 CHLS 91709 710-F1
CANYON MEADOW DR
- CHLS 91709 710-G2
CANYON MEADOW RD
17700 SBdC 92392 4386-H5
CANYON OAK CT
13000 VCTV 92392 4386-C4
CANYON OAK DR
7500 HIGH 92346 578-B6
CANYON OAKS CRSG
16200 CHLS 91709 710-G2
CANYON OAKS CT
- RCUC 91730 602-J5
CANYON OAKS DR
- RivC 92373 648-E7
CANYON RIM RD
- POM 91766 640-G6
12500 VCTV 92392 4385-J5
CANYON SPRING LN
1000 DBAR 91765 680-C2
CANYON SPRINGS RD
29500 HIGH 92346 578-E6
CANYON TERRACE DR
2400 CHLS 91709 680-J2
36200 YCPA 92399 650-D6
N CANYON TERRACE DR
900 SBDO 92407 546-F7
W CANYON TERRACE DR
3600 SBDO 92407 546-E7
CANYON VIEW AV
1700 UPL 91784 572-D6
CANYON VIEW CT
- DBAR 91765 680-C2
CANYON VIEW DR
- DBAR 91765 680-A6
100 SBdC - 516-J1
1300 SBdC - 4737-G5
2400 CHLS 91709 680-J2
13400 YCPA 92399 650-D6
CANYON VIEW LN
- RDL 92373 648-D6
500 SBdC - 4738-C7
S CANYON VIEW LN
1100 CLTN 92324 646-H1
CANYON VIEW RD
- SBdC - 4738-C7
8400 SBdC 92308 4479-E4
8400 SBdC 92308 (4569-D1
See Page 4568)
CANYON VISTA
- SBdC - 516-C1
CANYON VISTA CT
- DBAR 91765 680-C1
E CANYON VISTA DR
3000 CLTN 92324 646-J3
3000 CLTN 92324 647-A3
CAPAY CT
19500 APLV 92308 4387-C4
CAPAY LN
- SBdC - 4844-A2

STREET
Block City ZIP Pg-Grid

CAPAZA RD
- ADEL - (4206-A5
See Page 4116)
- SBdC - (4206-A5
See Page 4116)
CAP DE CREWS
13400 CHLS 91709 680-H2
CAPE LN
- YCPA 92399 649-F4
CAPE COD CT
2000 CLAR 91711 571-D7
7800 FONT 92336 604-A1
34600 YCPA 92399 649-J5
CAPE GLOUSTER AV
1200 BARS 92311 3680-F5
30000 SBdC 92311 (3850-A3
See Page 3760)
30700 SBdC 92311 3760-C5
32900 SBdC 92311 3680-F7
CAPE GLOUSTER RD
29200 SBdC 92311 (3849-J4
See Page 3758)
29700 SBdC 92311 (3850-A3
See Page 3760)
CAPELIN RD
7700 SBdC 92371 4564-D1
CAPELLA CT
5300 RivC 91752 683-H3
CAPELLA DR
3800 BARS 92311 3758-E2
CAPELLA RD
- APLV 92308 4387-C2
CAPILLA DR
6700 SBdC 92252 4889-B7
6700 SBdC 92252 4959-B1
CAPISTRANO CT
6800 SBdC - 4844-A3
CAPISTRANO ST
16300 VCTV 92394 4296-B2
CAPISTRANO WY
- SBdC - 4844-A3
15000 SBdC - 4843-H3
CAPITOL PL
6600 RCUC 91701 573-D5
CAPPER AV
900 POM 91767 601-C7
CAPPY DR
27500 SBdC - 517-H3
CAPPY RD
300 SBdC - 518-C1
E CAPRI
3100 ONT 91761 643-B6
CAPRI AV
1600 RDL 92374 608-G4
1700 SBdC 92359 608-H4
2000 RDL 92359 608-H4
CAPRI CT
14100 FONT 92336 604-B1
CAPRI ST
17200 HESP 92345 4386-G7
CAPRICHO DR
2300 SBdC 92301 (4202-E4
See Page 4112)
CAPRINO WY
1200 POM 91767 601-C7
CAPSICIN RD
- SBdC 92365 3594-E7
- SBdC 92365 (3684-E1
See Page 3594)
CAPSTON AV
- SBdC - (3935-A5
See Page 3934)
CAPUCHIN WY
2100 CLAR 91711 571-D7
CARADA RD
8800 SBdC - 4481-D3
CARANBOLA CT
18900 APLV 92308 4477-D3
CARANO PL
- RCUC 91701 573-E6
CARAVELLE AV
15500 FONT 92336 574-F4
CARBINE RD
26200 SBdC 92311 3678-J1
26200 SBdC 92311 3679-A1
E CARBON CT
2500 CLTN 92324 646-J4
CARBON LN
46100 SBdC - (4743-A4
See Page 4662)
CARBON CANYON RD
Rt#-142
1000 BREA 92823 710-B7
1000 CHLS 91709 710-G2
1900 CHLS 91709 680-H7
2400 CHLS 91709 681-A7
CARBON CANYON ACCESS
- BREA 92823 710-F4
- BREA 92886 710-F4
- OrCo 92886 710-F4
CARBON RIDGE RD
- BREA 92823 710-E6
- BREA 92886 710-G3
- CHLS 91709 710-G3
- OrCo 92823 710-G3
- OrCo 92886 710-G3
CARDAMON ST
2600 SBDO 92410 606-A4

W CARDAMON ST
2900 SBDO 92376 605-J4
2900 SBDO 92376 606-A4
CARDIFF CT
1100 POM 91767 601-C6
CARDIFF LN
11400 LMLN 92354 647-F2
15400 VCTV 92394 4296-B3
CARDIFF PL
7600 RCUC 91730 573-C7
12900 CHNO 91710 641-F7
CARDIGAN PL
26300 LMLN 92374 607-F6
CARDIGAN ST
15100 SBdC - (4025-J5
See Page 3934)
15100 SBdC - (4026-B4
See Page 3936)
CARDILLO TR
7400 YUCA 92284 4957-B3
CARDINAL CT
6800 CHNO 91710 642-B7
11800 FONT 92337 644-D4
11800 LMLN 92354 647-G3
12700 VCTV 92392 4385-D4
22100 GTER 92313 646-D5
CARDINAL DR
200 BBLK - 4811-G1
CARDINAL LN
- RDL 92374 608-F6
200 RivC 92507 646-E6
CARDINAL RD
6000 LACo 92397 4652-A2
6000 SBdC 92397 4652-A2
12700 VCTV 92392 4385-D4
CARDINAL ST
6700 CHNO 91710 642-B7
22200 GTER 92313 646-E4
CARDOZA RD
- SBdC - (4026-A1
See Page 3936)
14900 SBdC - (4025-J1
See Page 3934)
CAREY RD
81700 SBdC 92277 4824-G3
82100 SBdC 92277 (4825-A3
See Page 4824)
CARGO LN
- VCTV 92394 4205-E5
CARGOMASTER CT
- SBDO 92346 577-F7
- SBDO 92409 577-F7
CARHART AV
22100 GTER 92313 646-E3
CARIBOU AV
10100 SBdC 92308 4477-F3
10500 APLV 92308 4477-F2
CARIBOU DR
27600 SBdC - 4737-H5
S CARIBOU PL
2500 ONT 91761 643-A5
CARIBOU RD
21000 APLV 92308 4477-G1
22500 SBdC 92308 4478-B1
E CARIBOU CREEK CT
3600 ONT 91761 643-C7
CARINA PL
7000 RCUC 91701 573-E6
CARISSA AV
12500 CHNO 91710 642-A6
CARISSA CT
12700 RCUC 91739 573-H4
CARISSA ST
1500 UPL 91784 571-H4
CARL PL
- SBDO 92408 646-J1
CARLA WY
900 SBDO 92405 576-F1
CARL-DENNY DR
1100 CLTN 92324 646-F2
S CARLETON AV
300 CLAR 91711 601-C4
CARLETON CIR
13200 VCTV 92392 4385-E4
S CARLETON PL
500 CLAR 91711 601-C5
CARLETON ST
5600 SBDO 92407 546-F4
CARLISLE AV
11700 CHNO 91710 641-F5
CARLISLE LN
16000 APLV 92307 4297-E3
CARLISLE PL
11500 RCUC 91730 573-D7
CARLISLE RD
19100 APLV 92307 4297-H3
CARLOCK RD
900 BARS 92311 3679-A5
35600 SBdC 92311 3679-A4
N CARLOS AV
1500 ONT 91764 602-H4
S CARLOS AV
1400 ONT 91761 642-H4
CARLOS CT
3700 CHNO 91710 681-D2
N CARLOS PL
1300 ONT 91764 602-H5
N CARLOS WY
1400 UPL 91786 572-D7

CARLOTA WY
100 RivC 92507 646-F6
CARLOTTA CT
800 RDL 92374 608-A6
CARLOW CT
11000 RCUC 91701 573-C5
CARLSBAD AV
- RDL 92359 608-H4
- SBdC 92359 608-H4
5000 YUCA 92284 4887-G5
5100 SBdC - 4773-J6
CARLSBAD CT
56100 YUCA 92284 4887-F4
CARLSBAD PL
14600 CHNO 91710 681-D4
CARLSON AV
900 RDL 92374 608-A6
CARLTON AV
2200 POM 91768 640-D1
CARLTON ST
4900 SBdC 91763 641-F2
5500 SBdC 91762 641-H2
E CARLTON ST
100 ONT 91761 642-C2
N CARLTON ST
2300 SBDO 92405 576-F3
5200 SBDO 92407 546-F5
W CARLTON ST
100 ONT 91761 642-B2
100 ONT 91762 642-B2
CARLTON PRIVADO
- ONT 91762 642-A2
CARLYLE DR
- SBdC 92252 4959-C4
56200 YUCA 92284 4957-G5
57700 YUCA 92284 4958-A5
CARMANITA AV
1100 POM 91767 601-B5
CARMEL CIR E
1600 UPL 91784 571-J6
CARMEL CIR W
1600 UPL 91784 571-J7
CARMEL CT
1100 POM 91767 601-C6
6600 FONT 92336 574-J4
11400 ADEL 92301 4385-A1
35300 SBdC 92311 3678-G4
CARMEL DR
14900 SBdC 92335 604-D5
CARMEL RD
16900 APLV 92307 4207-J7
16900 APLV 92307 4297-J1
CARMEL ST
14700 SBdC 92335 604-D5
19100 HESP 92345 4477-C6
62200 SBdC 92252 4889-F1
65100 SBdC 92252 4890-B1
CARMELIA DR
13600 VCTV 92394 4296-A4
CARMELINA ST
3900 SBdC 92407 546-A6
3900 SBDO 92407 546-A6
CARMELITA AV
5900 YUCA 92284 4888-D6
15200 CHLS 91709 681-F6
CARMELITA CIR
9100 YUCA 92284 4958-E7
CARMELITA CT
1300 UPL 91786 602-E1
W CARMELITA LN
100 SBDO 92407 546-H6
CARMEL KNOLLS DR
12500 RCUC 91739 573-G2
CARMELLO CT
5500 RCUC 91739 573-H2
CARMEN DR
1300 BARS 92311 3680-A2
CARMEN LN
1800 CHLS 91709 680-H3
CARMEN ST
4400 CHNO 91710 641-E7
CARMINE PL
- CHLS 91709 711-G1
CARMODY CT
100 RDL 92373 647-H2
CARMODY ST
100 RDL 92373 647-H2
N CARNATION
3300 RLTO 92377 545-C7
3300 RLTO 92377 575-C1
CARNATION AV
- RLTO 92377 545-C7
CARNATION PL
13300 CHNO 91710 681-E1
CARNATION ST
7400 FONT 92336 574-E6
12600 RivC 92880 683-D6
CARNATION WY
17800 CHLS 91709 712-A5
N CARNATION WY
1700 UPL 91786 572-B7
CARNEGIE AV
100 CLAR 91711 601-B4
2700 POM 91767 601-B4
7600 FONT 92336 574-C7
S CARNEGIE AV
300 ONT 91761 643-C2
E CARNEGIE DR
500 SBDO 92408 607-A6

S CARNEGIE DR
400 SBDO 92408 607-A6
CARNELIAN AV
- ADEL 92301 (4115-F2
See Page 4114)
- SBdC 92301 (4115-F2
See Page 4114)
CARNELIAN CT
16300 CHLS 91709 711-G2
CARNELIAN DR
- SBdC - 518-B2
CARNELIAN RD
- SBdC - 4570-B1
32100 SBdC - 4480-J7
32500 SBdC - 4481-A7
CARNELIAN ST
5100 RCUC 91701 572-F3
7300 RCUC 91730 572-F6
7600 RCUC 91730 602-F1
CARNES CIR
500 RDL 92374 608-G6
CARNIVAL
14200 SBdC - 4302-B6
S CARNOUSTIE CT
2800 ONT 91761 642-G6
CAROB AV
- CHLS 91709 711-H2
6600 RCUC 91739 573-G5
9700 SBdC 92335 604-E6
CAROB CT
12700 CHNO 91710 642-A6
CAROB LN
- SBdC 92335 604-E4
CAROB ST
900 RDL 92373 648-C4
8200 SBdC 92335 604-E1
14400 VCTV 92394 4295-J7
14400 VCTV 92394 4385-J1
18000 HESP 92345 4386-J7
18300 HESP 92345 4387-A7
CARODEAN RD
5700 TNP 92277 4891-H5
CAROL AV
5200 RCUC 91701 572-E2
CAROL DR
1400 POM 91767 601-D6
9900 YCPA 92399 610-C5
CAROL WY
- SBDO 92408 646-J1
CAROL ANN DR
- SBdC 92365 (3593-G5
See Page 3592)
CAROLANN ST
1800 POM 91766 641-B4
W CAROLE CT
600 CLTN 92324 606-C5
CAROLINA AV
2100 SBdC 92277 4821-C3
CAROLINA AV N
- VCTV 92394 4205-G5
CAROLINA AV S
- VCTV 92394 4205-G6
CAROLINAS LN
- RivC 92880 683-D4
E CAROLINE CT
1100 ONT 91764 602-E4
W CAROLINE CT
100 ONT 91762 602-B4
E CAROLINE DR
2000 ONT 91764 602-G4
CAROLINE LN
- SBdC 92277 (4894-H1
See Page 4824)
2500 SBdC 92277 4824-H3
CAROLINE ST
- FONT 92336 574-E5
5500 MTCL 91763 601-H4
E CAROLINE ST
100 SBDO 92408 606-J7
300 SBDO 92408 607-A7
1400 ONT 91764 602-F4
W CAROLYN CT
900 CLTN 92324 606-B3
CAROT RD
- SBdC 92252 4819-H1
CAROUSEL RD
1000 SBdC - 4738-C6
W CARPENTER
1700 RLTO 92377 575-C2
CARPENTER ST
14500 ONT 91710 682-H5
14800 SBdC 91710 682-H5
E CARPENTER ST
1500 SBdC 92404 577-C2
1500 SBDO 92404 577-C2
CARPIO DR
300 DBAR 91765 640-D6
CARRA LN
- CHLS 91709 711-H2
CARRARI CT
9100 RCUC 91737 572-G1
CARRARI ST
9500 RCUC 91737 572-J1
10200 RCUC 91737 573-A1
E CARREON DR
500 CLTN 92324 606-E5
CARRERA DR
15500 FONT 92337 644-F4
CARRERA PL
13300 VCTV 92392 4385-F4

CARRIAGE AV
11100 MTCL 91763 641-F3
11300 SBdC 91710 641-F3
11300 MTCL 91710 641-F3
CARRIAGE DR
10800 RCUC 91737 573-C1
CARRIAGE LN
1000 COR 92880 712-J7
CARRIAGE PL
5400 RCUC 91737 573-C1
CARRIAGE RD
4900 RCUC 91737 573-A1
5000 RCUC 91737 572-J1
CARRIAGE WY
- POM 91766 640-H6
CARRIAGE HILL DR
28300 HIGH 92346 578-B4
N CARRIAGE HILLS CT
3100 SBDO 92346 577-G2
CARRIAGE HILLS LN
2000 CHLS 91709 710-H1
2100 CHLS 91709 680-J7
CARRIAGE HOUSE DR
- CHLS 91709 681-B6
CARRIE LN
100 RDL 92373 648-C1
CARRILLO AV
9400 MTCL 91763 601-G6
CARRILLO ST
9500 ADEL 92301 4384-E1
13000 CHNO 91710 641-F7
CARRILLO PRIVADO
2100 ONT 91761 642-H3
CARRINGTON DR
16300 CHLS 91709 711-E1
CARRIONE CT
300 POM 91766 640-D3
CARRISSA AV
9400 HESP 92345 4477-B5
CARRO AMANO LN
29600 HIGH 92346 578-E6
CARROL CT
25500 LMLN 92354 647-D2
CARROLL CT
4000 CHNO 91710 641-D6
CARROLL DR
500 SBdC - 518-A2
CARROTWOOD CT
13800 CHNO 91710 682-A2
CARRUTHERS CT
500 POM 91766 641-A6
CARSON CIR
10300 ADEL 92301 4204-G7
CARSON DR
14600 VCTV 92394 4296-A7
CARSON LN
900 POM 91766 641-B5
CARSON RD
- SBdC 92311 3678-G1
- SBdC 92347 (3677-H1
See Page 3586)
CARSON ST
- CHNO 91710 641-G4
- SBdC - 4479-H6
- SBdC 92308 4479-H6
800 BARS 92311 3679-J4
1200 BARS 92311 3680-A4
13400 SBdC 93562 2055-A7
30700 SBdC - 4480-B6
32700 SBdC - 4481-F5
W CARSON ST
800 UPL 91784 572-A6
CARSTEN CT
- FONT 92336 574-H2
CARTAGENA ST
13300 VCTV 92392 4385-C4
CARTER AV
- FONT 92336 574-F4
3900 RIV 92501 645-H7
CARTER CT
4500 CHNO 91710 681-E2
6100 CHNO 91710 682-A2
14400 VCTV 92394 4295-H7
CARTER LN
41100 BBLK - 4811-F2
CARTER PL
8400 SBdC 92284 4957-A6
CARTER RD
14800 VCTV 92394 4295-J7
CARTER ST
4300 CHNO 91710 681-E2
6400 CHNO 91710 682-A2
12900 SBdC 92399 610-B6
35100 YCPA 92399 610-B6
E CARTER ST
200 RLTO 92376 605-H3
600 SBDO 92408 605-J3
W CARTER ST
400 RLTO 92376 605-E3
1100 RLTO 92316 605-D3
CARTERS CTO
300 SBdC - 516-E2
CARTHAGE CT
1300 CLAR 91711 601-A1
W CARTIER LN
1300 CLTN 92324 646-A2
CARTILLA AV
5000 RCUC 91737 573-B1
6700 RCUC 91701 573-B5
7300 RCUC 91730 573-B7

CARTILLA AV
7700 FONT 92336 574-G7
CARTILLA CT
10300 RCUC 91737 573-B4
CARTWHEEL CIR
- COR 92880 712-J7
CARTY CIR
2000 NDLS 92363 3620-B7
CARTY PL
2000 NDLS 92363 3620-B7
CARTY WY
2000 NDLS 92363 3620-A7
CARVER CIR
100 RDL 92373 648-D2
CARVER DR
- RDL 92373 648-D2
200 CLAR 91711 571-D6
CARVER RD
- SBdC 92256 616-G2
CARYN CIR
14200 FONT 92336 574-B7
CASA WY E
300 RLTO 92316 645-G2
CASABA RD
18100 ADEL 92301 4204-J4
CASABLANCA CT
14100 FONT 92336 604-B1
CASA BLANCA ST
11300 YCPA 92399 650-D1
CASA DE LEON LN
600 RDL 92373 648-B2
CASA DEL SOL ST
2100 NDLS 92363 3620-C7
2100 NDLS 92363 3710-C1
W CASA GRANDE DR
1900 RLTO 92377 575-A1
3800 FONT 92377 574-J1
3800 RLTO 92377 574-J1
10500 FONT 92336 574-J1
CASALERO DR
4300 SBdC 92301 4112-J3
4300 SBdC 92301 (4113-A3
See Page 4112)
CASA LINDA ST
1600 NDLS 92363 3620-C7
1900 NDLS 92363 3710-C1
CASA LOMA DR
23500 DBAR 91765 640-C7
N CASA LOMA DR
2900 SBDO 92404 577-A2
3100 SBdC 92404 577-A2
CASA LOMA ST
2100 NDLS 92363 3620-C7
2100 NDLS 92363 3710-C1
CASA REAL ST
2200 NDLS 92363 3620-C7
2200 NDLS 92363 3710-C1
CASA VISTA DR
35500 YCPA 92399 610-B7
CASCADA CT
11800 FONT 92337 644-F4
CASCADE AV
7000 SBdC 92345 4565-H5
CASCADE CT
1600 RDL 92373 647-H2
10500 ADEL 92301 4294-H7
CASCADE DR
- FONT 92336 574-F5
- UPL 91786 602-D2
E CASCADE DR
100 RLTO 92376 575-H5
W CASCADE DR
100 RLTO 92376 575-F5
CASCADE PL
1000 CLAR 91711 601-B1
7300 RCUC 91730 573-C6
CASCADE RD
100 SBdC 92252 4750-C6
1600 SBdC - 4819-H2
1700 SBdC 92252 4820-C3
4900 SBdC 92252 4890-C4
6900 SBdC 92252 4960-C1
CASCADE ST
- SBdC 92314 4742-H7
100 RDL 92373 647-H2
12900 YCPA 92399 650-B5
E CASCADE ST
2000 SBdC 92314 4742-H7
CASCADE TR
21400 SBdC 92308 4568-F4
24000 SBdC - 4568-F4
CASCADES CT
14600 CHNO 91710 681-D4
E CASCADES TR
1500 ONT 91761 642-F6
S CASCADES TR
1500 ONT 91761 642-F6
CASCADIAN AV
18100 SBdC - (4210-G4
See Page 4120)
CASCANTE CT
1500 RDL 92373 648-A3
CASCO RD
12900 APLV 92308 4387-F4
E CASE AV
2200 SBDO 92404 577-E3
E CASE ST
26400 HIGH 92346 577-F3
CASETAS DR
22700 DBAR 91765 640-A7

CASEY CT
- CLTN 92324 606-C4
1300 UPL 91784 571-H6
CASEY LN
5900 SBdC 92371 4473-F4
CASHEEN DR
3700 CHLS 91709 681-D7
CASHEW ST
14500 HESP 92345 4475-J4
14600 HESP 92345 4476-A4
CASHMERE CT
8300 SBdC 92335 604-B2
CASIA DR
5400 TNP 92277 4892-F3
CASIANO CT
9800 RCUC 91730 602-J1
CASITA AV
5600 SBdC 92345 (4655-A2
See Page 4654)
6200 SBdC 92345 4565-B3
CASITA DR
73900 TNP 92277 4892-F5
CASMALIA DR
2500 SBdC 92277 4821-J3
CASMALIA ST
19400 RLTO 92377 575-F4
19400 SBdC 92377 575-G4
W CASMALIA ST
100 RLTO 92377 575-E4
200 SBdC 92377 575-G4
CASPER RD
36500 SBdC - (4392-A5
See Page 4302)
CASPIAN CT
- RivC 92880 683-D6
CASPIAN DR
13000 SBdC 92392 4387-A4
CASPIAN RD
30900 SBdC 92365 3764-E1
34300 SBdC 92365 (3684-E4
See Page 3594)
N CASSANDRA DR
5800 SBDO 92407 546-A4
CASSELL CIR
- UPL 91786 601-G1
CASSIA AV
15000 SBdC - (4303-A4
See Page 4302)
CASSIA DR
56500 YUCA 92284 4957-G2
CASSIA RD
8000 ADEL 92301 4294-B3
11500 ADEL 92301 4295-A3
CASSIA ST
3800 SBdC 92277 4821-H6
13300 RCUC 91739 573-J4
CASSIDY PL
17800 CHLS 91709 712-A5
CASTELLA LN
300 BBLK - 4811-C1
CASTELLANO RD
1200 RivC 92509 645-E5
CASTELLION RD
15500 FONT 92337 644-F3
CASTELLO PL
6800 RCUC 91701 573-D5
CASTER ST
4100 SBdC 92252 4889-D2
CASTERA PL
1500 POM 91767 601-C6
CASTIC WY
5100 SBdC - 4774-G6
N CASTILLA ST
100 SBDO 92410 606-C1
CASTILLE ST
- VCTV 92392 4385-G4
CASTILLO RD
56700 SBdC 92285 4747-G2
CASTLE AL
800 SBDO 92405 576-F4
CASTLE CT
5000 RCUC 91701 572-F1
32100 SBdC 92311 3758-D2
CASTLE LN
800 SBdC 92314 (4743-A7
See Page 4662)
800 SBdC 92314 4813-A1
CASTLE ST
18200 VCTV 92394 4205-E5
CASTLEBAR PL
5500 RCUC 91737 573-A2
CASTLE CRAG RD
- BBLK - 4741-J7
CASTLE CREST DR
600 RivC 91752 683-D4
CASTLEGATE DR
10100 RCUC 91737 573-A4
CASTLEGATE PL
6600 RCUC 91737 573-A5
CASTLE GATE RD
300 SBdC - 517-J2
CASTLE HARBOR CT
19300 APLV 92308 4477-D2
S CASTLE HARBOUR AV
2400 ONT 91761 642-G6
S CASTLE HARBOUR PL
2200 ONT 91761 642-G5
CASTLE PEAK
- SBdC - 2971-G1

CASTLE PEAKS LN
15600 VCTV 92394 4295-F5
CASTLE PEAKS WY
13300 VCTV 92394 4295-F5
CASTLE ROCK RD
19900 SBdC 92308 4567-E1
28400 SBdC - 4479-H7
28400 SBdC 92308 4479-E7
CASTLETON DR
100 CLAR 91711 601-D5
CASTLEWOOD RD
- BBLK - 4742-A7
CASTRO RD
57200 YUCA 92284 4887-J7
N CASWELL AV
500 POM 91767 641-A1
700 POM 91767 601-A6
S CASWELL ST
200 POM 91766 641-A2
CATABA RD
6400 SBdC 92345 4565-E2
8500 HESP 92345 4565-E2
9700 HESP 92345 4475-E6
9700 SBdC 92345 4475-E6
11100 VCTV 92392 4475-D2
CATALINA CT
3700 CHNO 91710 681-C1
14000 FONT 92336 574-B7
14000 FONT 92336 604-B1
CATALINA DR
2500 SBdC - 518-J7
CATALINA PL
8500 RCUC 91730 603-A3
CATALINA RD
200 BBLK - 4811-J1
300 BBLK - 4812-A1
17700 ADEL 92301 4204-D7
18500 SBdC 92392 4387-A5
18800 APLV 92308 4387-B5
CATALINA TR
7000 SBdC 92308 4567-E5
CATALINA WY
8800 YUCA 92284 4958-B6
CATALONIA CT
13300 CHLS 91709 680-J1
CATALPA AV
1700 SBDO 92346 577-J4
7000 HIGH 92346 577-J5
12400 CHNO 91710 641-H6
N CATALPA AV
1600 SBDO 92346 577-J4
E CATALPA CT
2100 SBDO 92404 577-D2
CATALPA PL
2500 POM 91766 641-A6
12500 CHNO 91710 641-H6
CATALPA ST
13200 RCUC 91739 573-H5
17000 HESP 92345 4476-F1
18200 HESP 92345 4477-A1
CATAMARAN LN
18500 SBdC 92392 4387-A4
26300 SBdC - (3935-H6
See Page 3934)
CATANIA PL
- RCUC 91701 573-E5
800 LACo 91711 571-B6
CATAWBA AV
5700 FONT 92336 574-F3
8100 FONT 92335 604-G4
8100 SBdC 92335 604-G1
10300 SBdC 92337 604-G7
10400 FONT 92337 604-G7
10600 FONT 92337 644-G2
10600 SBdC 92337 644-G2
CATAWBA CT
7500 FONT 92336 574-F7
CATAWBA DR
7000 FONT 92336 574-F6
CATAWBA PL
11400 FONT 92337 644-G3
CATAWBA RD
15700 APLV 92307 4297-D4
CATBIRD LN
600 BBLK - 4811-A2
CATERPILLAR CT
2200 RivC 92509 645-E6
CATFISH CT
- LPCo - 4606-H2
5000 SBdC 92345 (4655-E3
See Page 4654)
CATHEDRAL CT
6800 RCUC 91701 572-G5
CATHEDRAL DR
21500 APLV 92307 (4117-H7
See Page 4116)
CATHERWOOD DR
9900 RCUC 91737 572-J2
9900 RCUC 91737 573-A2
CATHY AV
2500 POM 91768 640-D2
CATRON RD
36400 YCPA 92399 650-D1
CATS CLAW TR
11900 SBdC 92399 651-C2
50300 SBdC 92256 4956-A7
CATSKILL RD
21700 SBdC 92347 (3677-G2
See Page 3586)

CATTLE CREEK DR
6700 CHLS 91709 712-B6
CATTLEMAN RD
- SBdC - (4210-H7
See Page 4120)
CAUGHLIN RD
7300 SBdC 92371 4563-J4
7300 SBdC 92371 4564-A2
9100 SBdC 92371 4474-B2
10900 SBdC 92392 4474-B2
11900 SBdC 92371 4384-B3
11900 SBdC 92392 4384-B3
13700 ADEL 92371 4384-B3
13700 ADEL 92301 4384-B3
13700 ADEL 92392 4384-B3
14500 ADEL 92301 4294-A2
14600 SBdC 92301 4294-B7
16900 ADEL 92301 4204-A7
18000 SBdC 92301 4204-A3
20100 ADEL 92301 4114-A7
20100 SBdC 92301 4114-A7
CAUGHLIN RD
- SBdC 92301 (4024-A3
See Page 3934)
CAVALRY WY
11500 FONT 92337 644-E3
CAVE ST
1900 RDL 92374 608-B4
CAVERN DR
300 SBdC 92314 4742-H6
CAVERN RD
75300 TNP 92277 4822-J7
75300 TNP 92277 4823-A7
CAVETTO RD
10500 SBdC - 4482-F1
10800 SBdC - (4392-F7
See Page 4302)
CAYMAN RD
- APLV 92307 4297-F1
22700 APLV 92307 4298-B1
CAYUCOS DR
1300 SBdC 92372 4382-C5
5400 SBdC 92371 4383-D5
CAYUCOS RD
7300 SBdC 92371 4383-J5
7300 SBdC 92371 4384-A5
CAYUGA PL
- CHNO 91710 641-H4
CAYUGA RD
12300 SBdC 92307 4388-J3
20900 APLV 92308 4387-G3
CAZADERO RD
15800 VCTV 92394 4296-C4
CBS LN
2300 SBdC 92372 4562-F1
CEANOTHUS DR
- RCUC 91701 572-H5
CECELIA AV
15400 CHLS 91709 681-F6
CECINA AV
46400 SBdC 92365 3764-C6
CECINA CT
15100 CHLS 91709 681-C5
CEDAR AV
700 RDL 92373 648-B3
1200 RLTO 92316 605-E4
1200 SBdC 92316 605-E5
6100 SBdC - 4950-G2
6400 TNP 92277 4892-F5
10700 SBdC 92316 645-E3
12300 CHNO 91710 641-H6
34300 YCPA 92399 649-H2
34900 YCPA 92399 650-A2
42500 BBLK - 4812-A2
N CEDAR AV
100 RLTO 92376 605-E1
500 RLTO 92376 575-E7
2000 RLTO 92377 575-D2
2600 SBdC 92377 575-D3
S CEDAR AV
100 RLTO 92376 605-E3
500 RLTO 92316 605-E3
1100 SBdC 92316 605-E3
CEDAR CIDR
- SBdC - 517-J1
CEDAR CT
- SBdC - 517-H2
500 SBdC - 516-E3
1200 ONT 91762 641-J4
6300 SBdC - 4950-G2
8400 SBdC 92371 4564-F2
11600 APLV 92308 4387-B7
18700 ADEL 92301 4204-E4
W CEDAR CT
1000 UPL 91786 602-A2
1000 UPL 91786 601-J2
CEDAR DR
400 SBdC - 4738-B7
900 SBdC - 516-E4
4100 SBdC 92407 546-E6
5500 SBDO 92407 546-E5
8600 RCUC 91730 603-A3
9300 SBdC 92339 611-F3
10100 SBdC 92256 616-A3
19000 APLV 92308 4387-B7
33300 SBdC - 519-E6
49100 SBdC 92256 615-G3
73500 TNP 92277 4892-E6
CEDAR LN
- SBdC 92311 3678-H5

CEDAR LN
100 SBdC - 4742-F7
100 SBdC - 516-F2
200 SBdC - 4812-G2
500 SBdC - 517-E3
2000 SBdC 92314 4812-H1
2100 SBdC 92359 609-A5
2700 SBdC 92314 4813-B1
8500 HESP 92345 4565-G2
8500 SBdC 92345 4565-G2
12600 SBdC 92392 4386-H5
31400 SBdC 92359 608-J5
34500 YCPA 92399 649-H3
39800 SBdC 92339 611-C2
CEDAR PL
- SBdC - 516-F2
800 BBLK - 4812-A2
800 SBdC - 4812-A2
10200 SBdC 92316 605-E6
11600 APLV 92308 4387-B7
CEDAR RD
9000 SBdC 92339 611-C2
34200 SBdC 92311 3678-H5
CEDAR ST
1000 SBDO 92404 577-A2
5700 SBdC 92397 4652-C2
7300 SBdC 92371 4563-J2
7300 SBdC 92371 4564-B2
9700 SBdC 92345 4564-G2
10900 SBdC 92345 4565-A2
11300 HESP 92345 4565-J2
11700 SBdC 92316 645-E3
12000 RivC 92509 645-E3
13400 SBdC 93562 2055-A7
14900 HESP 92345 4566-A2
E CEDAR ST
100 ONT 91761 642-D4
100 ONT 91762 642-D4
2700 ONT 91761 643-A4
N CEDAR ST
1200 SBDO 92404 577-A5
S CEDAR ST
700 CLTN 92324 606-E7
700 CLTN 92324 646-E1
W CEDAR ST
100 ONT 91762 642-B4
CEDAR TER
28900 SBdC - 518-C1
CEDAR WY
200 SBdC - 516-F2
11500 LMLN 92354 647-C2
CEDARBIRD RD
- SBdC 92284 4818-A1
56000 SBdC 92284 4817-F1
CEDARBROOK DR
200 SBdC - 517-D2
CEDARBROOK LN
12900 SBdC 92392 4386-J4
CEDAR CANYON RD
98300 SBdC - 351-A2
CEDAR CREEK DR
11000 RCUC 91737 573-C3
CEDAR CREEK RD
- RivC 92880 683-B7
CEDAR CREST AV
400 CLAR 91711 601-D5
CEDAR DELL
39100 SBdC - 4741-A4
CEDAR GLEN CT
9500 RCUC 91730 602-J5
E CEDARGLEN CT
3300 ONT 91761 643-B6
CEDAR GLEN DR
9500 RCUC 91730 602-J5
E CEDAR GLEN RD
3400 ONT 91761 643-B6
CEDAR LAKE DR
100 SBdC - 4736-A7
CEDAR LAKE RD
39500 SBdC - 4811-C3
CEDAR LANE DR
100 SBdC - 516-H1
CEDAR MOUNTAIN DR
5800 RCUC 91737 573-C3
N CEDAR MOUNTAIN RD
1000 SBdC 92314 4742-B5
CEDAR OAK LN
33800 SBdC - 519-F2
CEDARPINE LN
2000 SBdC 92314 4812-H1
CEDAR PINES DR
21900 SBdC - 516-C1
CEDAR PINES LN
33700 SBdC - 519-F2
CEDAR RIDGE DR
200 SBdC - 518-C1
S CEDAR RIDGE PL
2600 ONT 91761 643-A6
CEDAR SPRING CT
5900 CHLS 91709 711-J2
CEDARVIEW DR
1100 CLAR 91711 601-A1
CEDARWOOD CT
15000 CHLS 91709 681-E5
CEDARWOOD DR
- POM 91766 640-G6
27400 SBdC - 517-H1
31200 SBdC - 518-J6
CEDARWOOD LN
8300 RCUC 91730 602-F2

STREET
Block City ZIP Pg-Grid

CHOLLA AV
16900 HESP 92345 4566-F2
CHOLLA DR
800 BARS 92311 3679-J5
CHOLLA LN
- TNP 92278 4822-F1
CHOLLA RD
- SBdC - 330-K2
- SBdC 92365 (3504-C7 See Page 3414)
100 SBdC 92372 4472-A6
2100 SBdC 92371 4472-E6
48500 SBdC 92285 369-K9
CHOLLA ST
12200 SBdC 93562 2144-G7
CHOLLA TR
13000 YCPA 92399 650-E6
CHOLLITA RD
60100 SBdC 92252 4888-H7
61500 SBdC 92252 4889-G6
64600 SBdC 92252 4890-A6
CHOSIN ST
1200 BARS 92311 3680-F6
CHOUINARD CIR
600 CLAR 91711 571-E7
CHRISTA WY
10800 VCTV 92392 4475-F3
CHRISTENSON RD
10500 SBdC - 4480-F1
11000 SBdC - (4390-F7 See Page 4300)
CHRISTINA CT
1200 POM 91766 640-G4
CHRISTINA RD
3900 SBdC 91710 681-D1
6900 SBdC 92345 4565-E6
CHRISTINE AV
7400 RivC 92509 644-H7
N CHRISTINE CT
5700 SBDO 92407 546-A4
W CHRISTINE ST
2400 SBDO 92407 546-A4
CHRISTMAS CANYON RD
68700 SBdC - 328-L8
CHRISTMAS TREE LN
31600 SBdC - 519-A7
N CHRISTOBAL LN
1000 CLTN 92324 605-J4
CHRISTOPHER AV
1800 UPL 91784 572-C6
CHRISTOPHER LN
1500 RDL 92374 608-F7
N CHRISTOPHER ST
5700 SBDO 92407 546-A4
CHRISTY ST
30800 SBdC 92365 3764-F6
CHRISWOOD PL
7300 HIGH 92346 578-E5
CHRYSOLITE AV
1200 SBdC 92359 608-G5
CHRYSOLITE ST
- APLV 92307 4207-B6
17900 SBdC - (4210-F5 See Page 4120)
22600 SBdC 92307 4208-B6
CHRYSTAL CT
13400 FONT 92336 574-A7
CHUCKA WALLA
900 SBdC 92285 4747-J2
CHUCK WALLA RD
24400 SBdC 92307 4298-G7
CHUKAR CT
12900 CHNO 91710 642-B7
13200 CHNO 91710 682-B1
CHUKAR MOUNTAIN RD
26900 SBdC 92307 (4389-D7 See Page 4299)
CHULA VISTA AV
7400 YUCA 92284 4958-A2
57600 YUCA 92284 4888-A6
CHULA VISTA CT
8500 RCUC 91730 602-F1
CHULA VISTA DR
7800 RCUC 91730 602-F1
CHULA VISTA RD
28400 SBdC - (4569-H1 See Page 4568)
28400 SBdC 92308 (4569-H1 See Page 4568)
CHULA VISTA ST
6100 SBdC - 4843-J1
6300 SBdC - 4844-A2
16100 VCTV 92392 4296-D5
25700 SBdC 92373 607-E7
E CHUMASH AV
2000 CLTN 92324 646-H2
CHUMASH DR
6200 SBdC - 4843-J3
6200 SBdC - 4844-A2
CHUPAROSA ST
15000 VCTV 92394 4296-A6
CHURCH AV
2300 BARS 92311 3679-C5
6900 HIGH 92346 577-J6
9300 RLTO 92316 605-E4
9300 SBdC 92316 605-E4
27400 SBdC 92311 3679-E5
N CHURCH AV
200 RLTO 92376 605-E1
500 RLTO 92376 575-E7

N CHURCH AV
1800 SBDO 92346 577-H4
2100 RLTO 92377 575-D2
S CHURCH AV
100 RLTO 92316 605-E4
500 RLTO 92376 605-E3
CHURCH CT
56200 YUCA 92284 4957-G5
CHURCH PL
500 RDL 92374 608-C5
CHURCH ST
- RDL 92374 608-C1
1400 BARS 92311 3680-A5
6500 HIGH 92346 578-C4
7300 YUCA 92284 4957-G3
8200 HIGH 92346 608-C1
8700 RCUC 91730 602-G1
9000 RCUC 91730 572-H7
9800 SBdC 92316 605-E5
9900 RCUC 91730 573-A7
10600 RCUC 91730 603-C1
11900 RCUC 91739 573-F7
21700 SBdC - 516-C1
N CHURCH ST
- RDL 92374 608-C4
2000 RDL - 608-C2
2100 RDL 92346 608-C2
2800 HIGH 92346 608-C2
S CHURCH ST
100 RDL 92374 608-C7
200 RDL 92374 648-C1
W CHURCH ST
400 SBDO 92401 576-G7
900 RivC 92507 646-C6
N CHURCHILL ST
6300 SBDO 92407 545-J2
CIBOLA CT
3700 CHLS 91709 681-D6
11500 APLV 92308 4387-G7
13300 VCTV 92392 4385-G4
CIBOLA RD
11400 APLV 92308 4477-H1
11400 APLV 92308 4387-G7
CIBOLA ST
100 NDLS 92363 3620-D6
CIBOLA TR
1000 SBdC 92285 4747-F3
7300 YUCA 92284 4957-F3
CICADA CT
14000 VCTV 92394 4295-G7
CICADA RD
8900 SBdC 92308 4479-C7
CIELITO DR
23200 SBdC 92308 4388-D7
57300 SBdC 92284 4817-J6
59000 SBdC 92284 4818-A6
60100 SBdC 92252 4818-G5
61100 SBdC 92252 4819-A5
67900 SBdC 92277 4820-H5
68500 SBdC 92277 4821-A5
72100 SBdC 92277 4822-A4
CIELITO ST
8800 RCUC 91701 572-G6
10000 RCUC 91701 573-A6
CIELO DR
11700 SBdC 92392 4475-B2
11700 VCTV 92392 4475-B2
CIELO LN
11500 LMLN 92354 647-D2
CIENEGA AV
6300 TNP 92277 4892-F5
CIENEGA CT
- RCUC 91701 572-E1
N CIENEGA CT
1800 SBDO 92346 577-J4
CIENEGA DR
6300 SBdC 92346 577-J3
6300 SBDO 92346 577-J3
7000 HIGH 92346 577-J5
32800 YCPA 92399 649-E5
CIENEGA RD
400 BBLK - 4811-B1
8300 SBdC 92359 4950-F7
CIENEGA LARGA RD
40500 SBdC - 4660-D6
40500 SBdC - (4740-B1 See Page 4660)
CIMA RD
54200 SBdC - 351-A1
56500 SBdC - 331-A11
59200 SBdC - 330-K9
E CIMARRON
- SBdC 92314 4742-G7
CIMARRON CIR
12900 SBdC 91710 641-A7
CIMARRON CT
900 RDL 92374 648-E1
5400 RCUC 91739 573-G1
CIMARRON DR
- RDL 92374 648-E1
CIMARRON LN
300 SBdC - 518-C2
CIMARRON PL
- POM 91766 640-D4
CIMARRON RD
- SBdC 92365 3764-C3
4600 SBdC - 4886-F4
W CIMARRON ST
1100 RLTO 92377 575-D3

CIMARRON WY
12700 VCTV 92392 4385-D5
CIMARRON OAKS DR
9300 MTCL 91763 601-F5
CIMMARON CT
9400 SBdC 92335 604-D5
CIMMERON TRAIL CIR
10300 ADEL 92301 4204-G5
CINCH LN
26700 SBdC - (3935-F5 See Page 3934)
CINCH RING LN
9700 RCUC 91737 572-J2
W CINCINNATI CT
2200 SBDO 92407 546-B3
W CINCINNATI ST
2600 SBDO 92407 545-J2
2600 SBDO 92407 546-A2
S CINDEE LN
1300 CLTN 92324 646-H2
CINDERELLA DR
400 CLAR 91711 601-C4
E CINDERELLA DR
100 SBdC 92314 4742-D4
W CINDERELLA DR
300 SBdC 92314 4742-C4
CINDERELLA WY
2100 POM 91767 601-A5
CINDY CT
300 POM 91767 601-A5
W CINDY CT
1100 UPL 91786 571-J7
CINERARIA RD
11400 SBdC 92392 4474-F2
CINNABAR CT
1100 SBdC 92359 608-J6
15200 CHLS 91709 680-J6
CINNABAR DR
6300 RivC 92509 645-B7
CINNABAR RD
1800 SBdC - 4742-J3
27300 SBdC 92311 3679-D6
CINNAMON DR
14600 FONT 92337 644-D4
CINNAMON LN
12900 VCTV 92392 4385-H5
CIRCLE DR
500 SBdC - 518-A3
14900 VCTV 92392 4296-D6
18900 SBdC 92316 645-F3
24800 LMLN 92354 647-B1
26100 SBdC - 517-E2
CIRCLE LN
700 BBLK - 4811-A2
1600 RDL 92373 647-J3
CIRCLE RD
3400 SBDO 92405 576-F1
33300 SBdC - (4210-J5 See Page 4120)
33300 SBdC - (4211-A5 See Page 4120)
CIRCLE FIRE RANCH RD
11100 SBdC 92308 4388-F7
CIRCLE PARK LN
4100 CHLS 91709 681-E6
CIRCLE VIEW DR
31200 SBdC - 518-J6
CISCO CT
17300 HESP 92345 4566-G5
CISCO RD
45900 SBdC 92365 3764-D3
S CISCO ST
700 CLTN 92324 606-G7
800 CLTN 92324 646-G1
CITADEL AV
100 CLAR 91711 601-D5
4900 SBDO 92407 546-B6
CITATION AV
15300 FONT 92336 574-E4
CITATION CT
8900 RCUC 91737 572-G1
CITATION ST
16100 SBdC - (4025-J4 See Page 3934)
CITRINE RD
100 BARS 92311 3678-J5
100 SBdC 92311 3678-J5
5500 SBdC 92284 4817-E2
CITRINE ST
6100 RCUC 91701 572-E4
CITRON AV
15400 SBdC 92335 604-E3
17100 FONT 92335 605-A3
17800 SBdC 92335 605-B3
CITRON CT
4900 CHLS 91709 711-F2
17100 FONT 92335 605-A3
CITRON PL
2500 POM 91766 641-A6
CITRUS AV
900 RivC 92507 646-B7
900 RIV 92507 646-B7
4500 FONT 92336 544-G7
4900 FONT 92336 574-G3
7800 FONT 92336 604-G1
8100 FONT 92335 604-G3
8200 SBdC 92335 604-G6
10200 SBdC 92337 604-G6
10400 FONT 92337 604-G6

CITRUS AV
10600 FONT 92337 644-G3
10700 SBdC 92337 644-G2
26500 SBdC 92373 607-F7
26700 RDL 92373 607-F7
30500 RDL 92374 608-G7
30500 SBdC 92374 608-G7
31300 SBdC 92374 609-A7
31900 SBdC 92399 609-A7
E CITRUS AV
- RDL 92373 608-C7
600 RDL 92374 608-C7
3400 SBDO 92346 577-H2
W CITRUS AV
- RDL 92373 608-B7
1200 RDL 92373 607-H7
CITRUS LN
800 LACo 91768 640-B1
800 POM 91768 640-B1
CITRUS PL
6500 RCUC 91739 573-G5
CITRUS ST
1200 UPL 91784 571-J3
2000 SBDO 92404 577-D2
2000 SBdC 92404 577-D2
26100 SBdC 92346 577-D2
E CITRUS ST
400 CLTN 92324 606-E4
600 SBdC 92410 606-E4
2600 SBdC 92346 577-F2
2600 SBDO 92346 577-F2
2900 SBDO 92404 577-B2
W CITRUS ST
100 CLTN 92324 606-C4
CITRUS GLEN LN
16000 FONT 92337 644-G3
CITY LN
- SBdC - 4813-C1
- SBdC 92314 4813-C1
CITY CENTER CT
22500 GTER 92313 646-E4
CITY CREEK RD
24900 HIGH 92410 577-C7
CITY CREEK RD Rt#-330
3800 SBdC - 548-E2
15700 SBdC - 518-E7
17100 SBdC - 578-A2
17100 SBdC 92346 578-A2
17100 SBDO 92346 578-A2
17100 SBDO - 578-A2
31100 SBdC - 519-A7
CITY CREEK TKTR
29800 SBdC - 548-F4
31500 SBdC - 389-D1
CITY VIEW CT
14200 VCTV 92392 4386-E1
CITY VIEW DR
16500 VCTV 92392 4386-E1
CIVIC DR
14300 VCTV 92392 4386-B1
14400 VCTV 92392 4296-B7
15100 VCTV 92394 4296-B6
CIVIC CENTER DR
- NDLS 92363 3620-B6
2000 CHLS 91709 680-H4
10300 RCUC 91730 603-B2
73600 TNP 92277 4892-E5
CIVIC CENTER PZ
100 POM 91766 640-J2
CLAIR ST
4300 MTCL 91763 641-E2
4700 SBdC 91710 641-F2
5400 SBdC 91762 641-H2
W CLAIR ST
1400 ONT 91762 641-J2
CLAIRE PL
900 POM 91768 640-F1
CLAIRE ST
300 RivC 92501 646-B6
CLALLAM RD
12500 APLV 92308 4387-H4
CLARE AV
- SBdC 92277 4822-C6
5800 TNP 92277 4892-C4
CLAREMONT AV
9900 SBdC 92316 605-E6
10600 SBdC 92316 645-F1
13000 VCTV 92392 4385-E4
18800 SBdC 92307 4208-E3
CLAREMONT BLVD
100 CLAR 91711 601-E3
CLAREMONT CT
12900 VCTV 92392 4385-E4
18900 SBdC 92316 605-E7
CLAREMONT LN
13900 RCUC 91739 574-A2
CLAREMONT PL
500 POM 91767 641-B1
800 POM 91767 601-B6
CLAREMONT HEIGHTS DR
2900 CLAR 91711 571-E7
CLARET CT
- RCUC 91739 603-H1
CLARIDGE DR
11400 RCUC 91730 573-D7
CLARIDGE PL
7500 RCUC 91730 573-E7

CLARION CT
- YCPA 92399 649-E2
CLARION PL
500 CLAR 91711 571-E7
CLARK AV
200 POM 91767 641-C1
500 CLAR 91711 601-D5
600 POM 91767 601-C7
12900 FONT 92337 643-H3
CLARK CT
14100 RCUC 91739 574-B2
CLARK DR
500 SBdC - 517-H3
24600 SBdC 92307 4298-G5
CLARK LN
33900 YCPA 92399 649-G4
44200 SBdC - 4812-G1
45100 SBdC 92314 4742-H7
45100 SBdC 92314 4812-G1
CLARK RD
9700 SBdC 92371 4473-D5
20800 APLV 92308 4477-G3
20800 SBdC 92308 4477-G3
26400 SBdC 92308 4479-F3
28600 SBdC - 4479-J3
29000 SBdC - 4480-A3
32600 SBdC - 4481-A3
CLARK ST
300 BARS 92311 3679-H2
900 RivC 92501 646-A7
4300 CHNO 91710 641-E7
5800 ONT 91761 643-H3
33700 SBdC - 4481-C3
36700 SBdC - 4482-E2
E CLARK ST
- RDL 92373 648-C1
200 RDL 92373 608-C7
600 RDL 92374 608-C7
W CLARK ST
- RDL 92373 648-B1
200 UPL 91784 572-A6
1100 UPL 91784 571-H6
CLARK MOUNTAIN RD
- SBdC - 330-L7
W CLARK MOUNTAIN RD
1900 SBDO 92410 606-C2
CLARKS GRADE
2400 SBdC - 4811-A7
2400 SBdC - 389-E1
CLARY DR
1800 NDLS 92363 3620-C7
1800 NDLS 92363 3710-C1
CLASSICO PL
- RCUC 91739 573-J7
- RCUC 91739 603-J1
CLAY ST
800 RDL 92374 608-B4
11200 ADEL 92301 4385-A1
CLAYHORN DR
23400 DBAR 91765 680-B1
CLAYMORE RD
- SBdC - (4389-J4 See Page 4299)
CLAY RIVER RD
31200 SBdC 92311 3680-D3
CLAYWOOD DR
24300 DBAR 91765 640-D7
CLEARBROOK DR
2300 CHLS 91709 680-G5
CLEARBROOK RD
- SBdC - 4843-J1
CLEAR CREEK LN
2400 DBAR 91765 680-C5
E CLEAR CREEK LN
1500 CLTN 92324 646-G1
CLEAR CREEK CANYON DR
700 DBAR 91765 680-C2
CLEAR HAVEN LN
18100 SBdC 92392 4386-J5
CLEAR LAKE CT
7100 RCUC 91739 573-G6
CLEAR LAKE RD
3100 ONT 91761 643-B5
CLEARSPRING DR
1200 UPL 91784 571-J5
CLEAR SPRING LN
28900 HIGH 92346 578-C4
CLEAR SPRINGS LN
11000 CHLS 91709 640-J7
CLEAR VALLEY RD
13700 VCTV 92392 4385-G3
CLEARVIEW AV
2500 SBDO 92407 545-F1
CLEARVIEW DR
- APLV 92308 4477-B5
3000 SBdC 92252 4818-H6
CLEAR VIEW DR
12100 VCTV 92392 4385-H6
CLEAR VIEW LN
29300 HIGH 92346 578-D5
CLEARVIEW RD
62400 SBdC 92252 4959-D5
CLEARVIEW CREST DR
100 DBAR 91765 640-A7
CLEARVIEW FARMS LN
19200 APLV 92308 4387-C4
CLEARWATER CIR
2000 UPL 91784 571-G4

CLEARWATER CT
12400 VCTV 92392 4385-E6
CLEARWATER DR
39300 SBdC 92399 611-B7
CLEARWATER TR
40300 BBLK - 4811-D2
CLEARY CT
200 CLAR 91711 571-D5
CLEGHORN DR
1200 DBAR 91765 680-C3
CLEGHORN CANYON RD
- SBdC - 4736-A4
10500 SBdC - (4735-C4 See Page 4654)
13700 SBdC 92345 (4735-J4 See Page 4654)
14200 SBdC 92345 4736-A4
CLEGHORN FIRE RD
9500 SBdC - 4734-F2
CLELAND RD
- SBdC 92252 4820-E3
68100 SBdC 92277 4820-J2
68100 SBdC 92277 4821-A2
CLEMENS AV
- BARS 92311 3589-H7
36700 SBdC 92311 3589-H7
CLEMSON AV
1300 CLAR 91711 601-A1
CLEMSON CT
14100 ADEL 92301 4385-A1
CLEMSON DR
11200 RCUC 91701 573-D5
CLEMSON ST
1800 SBDO 92407 546-B5
CLEVELAND AV
5400 ONT 91761 683-C3
5400 RivC 92880 683-C5
8900 RCUC 91730 603-C5
N CLEVELAND AV
200 ONT 91761 603-D7
W CLEVELAND AV
600 SBDO 92410 576-B7
W CLEVELAND ST
1500 SBDO 92411 576-D7
2200 SBDO 92410 576-D7
S CLEVENGER DR
800 SBDO 92408 607-B4
CLEVENGER RD
- SBdC 92284 4747-F5
CLIFF DR
100 SBdC - 516-B1
CLIFF RD
2400 SBdC 91784 572-C2
CLIFF TR
40300 BBLK - 4811-D2
CLIFFHILL PL
100 RivC 92501 646-B6
N CLIFFORD AV
200 RLTO 92376 605-G1
500 RLTO 92376 575-G6
S CLIFFORD AV
600 RLTO 92376 605-G3
N CLIFFORD ST
1400 RLTO 92376 575-G4
CLIFFWOOD DR
- MTCL 91763 641-G1
CLIFTON AV
600 RDL 92373 648-A3
27100 HIGH 92346 577-H4
E CLIFTON AV
3200 SBDO 92346 577-G5
3300 HIGH 92346 577-G5
CLIFTON CT
- RDL 92373 648-C2
CLIFTON ST
27700 HIGH 92346 577-J4
27700 SBDO 92346 577-J4
27900 HIGH 92346 578-A4
CLINE MILLER PL
39400 SBdC - 4741-B5
CLING WY
1000 CALI 92320 649-J7
CLINTON CT
1200 UPL 91786 602-D1
CLINTON DR
13600 CHNO 91710 681-J2
CLIPPEN RD
9500 SBdC - 3934-D4
CLIPPER DR
3300 CHLS 91709 681-C7
13100 SBdC 92392 4387-A4
CLIPPER LN
13700 SBdC - (3935-F3 See Page 3934)
CLIPTON ST
- FONT 92336 574-D6
CLOCK AV
1300 RDL 92374 608-E6
CLOUD RD
36900 SBdC - (4572-B2 See Page 4482)
CLOUD CREST ST
6800 CHNO 91710 642-B6
6800 CHNO 91710 642-B6
CLOUDLAND TKTR
300 SBdC 92407 546-D1
300 SBdC 92404 546-G1
300 SBDO 92407 546-G1
22200 SBdC 92407 516-D7

CLOUDS REST DR
1100 DBAR 91765 640-D4
CLOUDVIEW RD
23300 SBdC - 516-G3
CLOVER CT
6100 CHNO 91710 681-J1
6100 CHNO 91710 682-A1
7100 SBdC 92345 4564-H5
10700 RCUC 91701 573-C6
12800 YCPA 92399 649-E5
14000 SBdC 92335 604-B2
CLOVER DR
10100 SBdC 92345 4564-G7
43000 BBLK - 4812-B4
CLOVER LN
3000 ONT 91761 643-B7
CLOVER PL
3200 ONT 91761 643-B7
3300 ONT 91761 683-B1
4900 RCUC 91737 (543-B7 See Page 513)
4900 RCUC 91737 573-B1
CLOVER RD
2800 SBdC 92277 4821-F5
CLOVER ST
400 RDL 92373 648-A3
2600 SBdC 92373 648-A3
6300 CHNO 91710 682-A1
13300 SBdC 93562 2145-A4
S CLOVER WY
3500 ONT 91761 683-B1
CLOVERBROOK LN
1300 UPL 91784 571-J4
N CLOVERDALE AV
1500 UPL 91786 571-H7
CLOVERDALE CT
11000 RCUC 91730 573-C7
CLOVERDALE DR
700 POM 91767 601-B6
14400 FONT 92337 644-C3
CLOVERDALE RD
12700 RivC 92880 683-B6
13700 RivC 92880 682-J6
CLOVERDALE ST
1100 RIV 92501 645-H7
CLOVERHILL DR
6800 HIGH 92346 578-C5
CLOVERLEAF LN
27300 SBdC - (3935-J3 See Page 3934)
27400 SBdC - 3936-A2
CLOVERLY AV
13200 VCTV 92392 4475-F2
CLOVIS CT
1300 POM 91766 640-G4
CLOVIS RD
9700 SBdC 92371 4473-A2
13600 SBdC 92371 4383-A4
CLOVIS ST
14500 VCTV 92394 4295-J3
14900 VCTV 92394 4296-A3
CLUB CIR
- UPL 91786 602-E1
CLUB CT
27900 SBdC - (3935-H2 See Page 3934)
CLUB DR
1200 SBDO 92408 607-B2
1300 RDL 92373 648-J5
8300 RCUC 91730 602-F1
CLUB ST
- BARS 92311 3680-G5
S CLUB WY
2000 SBDO 92408 606-J7
CLUB CENTER DR
2000 SBDO 92408 606-H7
CLUB HOUSE CT
400 SBdC - 517-E2
CLUBHOUSE DR
- FONT 92336 574-H3
CLUB HOUSE DR
300 SBdC - 517-E2
8500 RCUC 91730 603-A3
CLUBHOUSE DR
14700 SBdC - (3935-H2 See Page 3934)
CLUBHOUSE WY
4100 CHLS 91709 681-E5
CLUB VIEW DR
100 SBdC - 514-B3
700 BBLK - 4812-B2
1400 SBdC - 4812-B3
7100 HIGH 92346 578-D5
E CLUSTER ST
100 SBDO 92408 606-J2
W CLUSTER ST
100 SBDO 92408 606-H2
W CLUSTER PINE RD
1900 CLTN 92324 605-J4
CLYDE ST
1700 SBDO 92411 576-C4
N CLYDE ST
1500 SBDO 92411 576-C5
CLYDESDALE CIR
14600 VCTV 92394 4295-G7
CLYDESDALE ST
7100 HIGH 92346 578-B5
E CLYDESDALE ST
- ONT 91761 683-A1
CLYDESDALE WY
- MTCL 91763 641-D1

CLYDESDALE RUN LN
13800 VCTV 92394 4295-G7
COACH LN
- SBdC - 4741-E6
COACHELLA RD
13400 APLV 92308 4387-B3
13600 APLV 92307 4387-B2
COACHMAN LN
28300 HIGH 92346 578-B3
COAD RD
13600 VCTV 92392 4386-F2
17000 SBdC 92392 4386-F2
COALINGA AV
9700 MTCL 91763 601-F6
COALINGA CT
2300 CLAR 91711 571-D6
COALINGA RD
14500 SBdC 92392 4385-J3
14600 SBdC 92392 4386-A3
14800 VCTV 92392 4386-A3
W COAST BLVD
1700 RLTO 92377 575-C1
COBAL CANYON MTWY
- CLAR 91711 571-D1
- LACo 91711 571-D1
- LACo 91750 571-A2
S COBAL CANYON FIRE TRUCK CIR
- CLAR 91711 571-B5
COBALT CT
16500 CHLS 91709 711-F2
COBALT RD
10300 HESP 92392 4475-F4
10300 VCTV 92392 4475-F1
11500 VCTV 92392 4385-F2
14100 SBdC 92392 4385-F2
15100 VCTV 92394 4295-F5
15800 ADEL 92301 4295-E1
15800 VCTV 92301 4295-F5
56000 YUCA 92284 4887-F5
63300 SBdC 92252 4889-F4
64900 SBdC 92252 4890-A4
COBBLE HILL RD
7800 SBdC 92308 4567-E2
COBBLESTONE CIR
12200 VCTV 92392 4385-F6
COBBLESTONE CT
3800 SBdC 91766 641-D3
13800 SBdC 92335 604-A2
27800 HIGH 92346 577-J5
COBBLESTONE DR
12100 VCTV 92392 4385-F7
COBBLESTONE LN
5100 RCUC 91737 573-C1
COBRA ST
13200 VCTV 92394 4205-F4
COBRE CT
800 POM 91768 640-F1
N COBURN ST
100 CLTN 92324 606-F4
COCA ST
5900 RCUC 91737 572-H3
8800 RCUC 91701 572-G3
9900 RCUC 91737 573-A3
COCHISE AV
27300 SBdC 92311 3679-D5
COCHISE CT
19100 APLV 92307 4387-B2
COCHISE PL
19100 APLV 92308 4387-B3
COCHISE RD
6200 SBdC - 4843-G2
13000 APLV 92308 4387-B3
13600 APLV 92307 4387-B3
COCHISE ST
- SBdC - (3846-A4 See Page 3756)
17100 HESP 92345 4566-G5
COCHISE TR
36300 SBdC - 4481-J6
36300 SBdC - 4482-A6
COCHISE WY
19100 APLV 92307 4387-B2
COCHITI RD
10500 APLV 92308 4477-J1
COCHRAN DR
21900 SBdC - 516-C2
COCOPAH CT
14700 APLV 92307 4296-J7
COCOPAH RD
18200 APLV 92307 4296-J6
18500 APLV 92307 4297-A7
COCQUI RD
18500 APLV 92307 4297-A5
W CODY CT
1300 UPL 91786 571-J7
CODY RD
8500 SBdC - 4480-F3
CODY ST
14600 VCTV 92394 4295-J5
COE ST
100 CLAR 91711 601-D4
COFFEY RD
9100 SBdC 92339 611-E2
COGBURN LN
900 DBAR 91765 680-B2
E COG HILL CT
2900 ONT 91761 643-A6
E COG HILL ST
2600 ONT 91761 642-J6

COLAW RD
6300 SBdC 92277 4893-H5
COLBY AV
36700 SBdC 92311 3589-G7
COLBY CIDR
400 CLAR 91711 601-C2
COLBY CT
36900 SBdC 92311 3589-G6
COLBY RD
36100 SBdC - 4481-J1
36100 SBdC - 4482-A1
COLBY ST
34700 SBdC - 4481-E1
COLDBROOK CAMP RD
900 SBdC - 4811-C3
COLD CREEK DR
18100 SBdC 92392 4386-J5
S COLD CREEK WY
2600 ONT 91761 643-B5
COLD HARBOR DR
10900 RCUC 91737 573-C2
COLD SPRING RD
21900 SBdC - 516-C1
S COLD SPRINGS PL
2500 ONT 91761 643-C5
COLD STREAM CT
800 DBAR 91765 680-E2
COLE AV
1400 SBDO 92346 577-H5
6700 HIGH 92346 577-H4
N COLE AV
2700 SBDO 92346 577-H2
COLE CT
27100 HIGH 92346 577-H6
COLE LN
60400 SBdC 92285 4748-H1
COLE PL
27100 HIGH 92346 577-H6
COLE RD
6500 SBdC 92285 (4576-A3 See Page 4486)
COLE ST
25300 LMLN 92354 647-C1
COLEBRIDGE CT
16400 CHLS 91709 711-E2
COLEEN ST
15400 FONT 92337 644-E2
COLEMAN TR
55500 SBdC 92285 4747-D1
COLERIDGE RD
5000 SBdC 92345 (4655-A4 See Page 4654)
5100 SBdC 92345 4474-J5
6200 SBdC 92345 4565-A4
12400 VCTV 92392 4384-J6
COLERIDGE ST
15100 ADEL 92301 4294-J6
COLFAX CT
1200 POM 91766 640-G4
COLFAX RD
9400 SBdC 92371 4472-H7
N COLFAX WY
1600 UPL 91784 572-A6
COLGATE PL
600 CLAR 91711 601-D5
1100 RDL 92374 608-C6
COLIMA AV
15300 HESP 92345 4566-B6
N COLIMA AV
2800 SBDO 92407 576-D3
COLIMA DR
4100 SBdC 92301 4112-J2
COLIMA RD
1200 SBDO 92405 576-E2
W COLIMA RD
800 SBDO 92405 576-F2
COLINA DR
6200 SBdC 92301 (4113-E2 See Page 4112)
COLINA ST
16100 VCTV 92392 4296-D5
COLINA COURTE
- HIGH 92346 578-D7
COLLADO RD
43100 SBdC 92365 (3684-C5 See Page 3594)
W COLLEEN CT
1100 UPL 91786 601-J1
COLLEGE AV
800 RDL 92374 608-C6
1400 POM 91767 601-D6
1900 SBDO 92407 546-B5
11100 MTCL 91763 641-D3
11100 SBdC 91766 641-D3
11600 SBdC 91710 641-D4
N COLLEGE AV
100 CLAR 91711 601-D1
S COLLEGE AV
100 CLAR 91711 601-D4
COLLEGE CT
100 BARS 92311 3679-G6
W COLLEGE DR
500 SBDO 92410 606-A3
2700 SBDO 92376 606-A3
COLLEGE WK
1500 CLTN 92324 606-E3
1700 SBDO 92410 606-E3
E COLLEGE WY
200 CLAR 91711 571-A7

N COLLEGE WY
300 CLAR 91711 601-D3
1200 ONT 91764 602-C5
COLLEGE COMMERCE WY
- UPL 91786 601-G3
COLLINGSWOOD DR
800 POM 91767 601-B5
COLLINS CT
300 BARS 92311 3679-J3
COLLINS RD
36100 SBdC - 4481-J7
COLLINS ST
1600 NDLS 92363 3620-B6
COLMAR ST
900 POM 91767 601-C7
S COLOMA
400 SBdC 92314 4742-G7
COLOMA AV
- APLV 92307 (4117-C7 See Page 4116)
20300 SBdC 92307 (4117-C7 See Page 4116)
COLOMA ST
- SBDO 92354 607-D6
10500 LMLN 92354 607-D7
14100 FONT 92336 604-B1
COLOMA WY
6500 RivC 92509 645-A7
COLOMBARD CT
13500 FONT 92337 644-A4
COLOMBARD LN
- DBAR 91765 680-B3
COLOMBIA RD
200 RDL 92373 648-E5
COLONBERO RD
- RCUC 91739 544-B7
- RCUC 91739 574-A1
COLONIAL AV
18500 ADEL 92301 4204-F5
S COLONIAL AV
2500 ONT 91761 642-J6
COLONIAL CT
17600 CHLS 91709 712-A5
18400 SBdC 92392 4387-A5
COLONIAL DR
- BARS 92311 3680-D5
- FONT 92336 574-H2
35300 YCPA 92399 610-A5
COLONIES PKWY
- UPL 91784 572-E5
COLONNADE DR
- RCUC 91739 573-H6
COLONY AV
12200 CHNO 91710 641-C6
COLONY CT
6200 RCUC 91739 573-H4
COLONY DR
1100 POM 91766 640-G4
1200 SBdC 91784 571-J2
COLONY RD
- SBdC 92308 (4389-B6 See Page 4299)
23000 APLV 92308 4388-B7
23500 SBdC 92308 4388-G6
COLONY ST
12600 CHNO 91710 641-C6
COLORADO AV
- SBdC 92407 576-C2
1300 SBDO 92411 576-C5
N COLORADO AV
1200 SBDO 92411 576-C5
COLORADO RD
12200 SBdC 92372 4382-E3
14100 SBdC 92371 4382-E3
18200 SBdC 92301 (4202-D4 See Page 4112)
COLORADO ST
- FONT 92336 574-C6
13000 YCPA 92399 649-F5
55800 SBdC - 4606-G2
COLORADO RIVER RD
3800 ONT 91761 643-C6
COLORADO VISTA RD
- LPCo - 4606-J4
COLORNO CT
6700 RCUC 91701 573-E5
COLORNO DR
11500 RCUC 91701 573-D5
COLOSSEUM RD
91800 SBdC - 331-A6
COLT AV
10300 SBdC - 4480-E1
11100 SBdC - (4390-E7 See Page 4300)
15400 FONT 92337 644-F2
COLT CT
13900 VCTV 92394 4295-G6
COLT DR
5800 RCUC 91739 573-H3
E COLT WY
2900 ONT 91761 643-A7
COLTON AV
600 CLTN 92324 606-E5
1700 RDL 92374 608-H6
3300 RDL 92359 608-H6
3300 SBdC 92359 608-H6
3300 SBdC 92374 608-H6
31300 SBdC 92359 609-A6
E COLTON AV
- RDL 92374 608-D6

STREET	Block	City	ZIP	Pg-Grid
N COLTON AV				
	400	CLTN	92324	606-E5
	1400	SBDO	92408	606-F5
W COLTON AV				
	-	RDL	92374	608-A6
	900	SBDO	92410	606-F4
	1000	RDL	92374	607-J6
COLTON RD				
	19000	SBdC	-	371-G2
COLTON ST				
	84700	SBdC	93562	2055-B7
COLUMBIA AV				
	3900	RIV	92501	645-H7
	12200	YCPA	92399	649-G4
E COLUMBIA AV				
	300	POM	91767	601-A7
N COLUMBIA AV				
	800	CLAR	91711	601-E3
	1000	ONT	91764	602-C5
COLUMBIA CT				
	11800	LMLN	92354	647-G3
	14100	ADEL	92301	4385-B1
COLUMBIA DR				
	-	FONT	92336	574-C1
	14600	VCTV	92394	4296-A7
COLUMBIA RD				
	1800	RDL	92373	648-E5
	22900	SBdC	92308	4478-C2
COLUMBIA ST				
	800	RDL	92374	608-B5
	4300	CHNO	91710	641-E7
COLUMBINE AV				
	9200	MTCL	91763	601-G5
	19500	SBdC	92377	575-F2
W COLUMBINE AV				
	100	RLTO	92377	575-F3
COLUMBINE CT				
	7000	RCUC	91739	573-G6
COLUMBINE DR				
	1500	SBdC	-	4812-D3
COLUMBINE RD				
	6400	SBdC	92345	4564-H1
	10100	SBdC	92345	4474-H4
	12100	SBdC	92392	4384-H7
COLUMBINE ST				
	11100	SBdC	91762	641-G2
	14500	SBdC	-	(4025-H7 See Page 3934)
COLUMBINE WY				
	12400	RCUC	91739	573-G6
N COLUMBINE WY				
	1500	UPL	91786	572-B7
COLUMBUS CT				
	6100	RCUC	91701	572-G4
	13400	FONT	92336	574-A7
COLUMBUS DR				
	-	NDLS	92363	3620-A4
COLUMBUS RD				
	1300	SBdC	92285	4748-C2
COLUMBUS ST				
	5200	CHNO	91710	641-G6
	16800	ADEL	92301	4294-G2
	18900	ADEL	92301	4204-F1
COLUNGA ST				
	2000	CLTN	92324	646-H1
COLUSA CT				
	43400	BBLK	-	4812-C3
COLUSA DR				
	1600	SBdC	-	4812-D3
	8300	BBLK	-	4812-C3
COLUSA LN				
	900	BBLK	-	4812-C2
COLUSA RD				
	400	SBdC	92301	4112-A6
	4800	SBdC	92301	(4113-C6 See Page 4112)
	9900	ADEL	92301	4114-F6
	10500	SBdC	92301	4114-H6
	11400	SBdC	92301	(4115-D6 See Page 4114)
	12100	ADEL	92301	(4115-D6 See Page 4114)
	12400	VCTV	92301	(4115-D6 See Page 4114)
	16400	SBdC	92307	(4117-E5 See Page 4116)
	18400	APLV	92307	(4117-E5 See Page 4116)
COLUSA ST				
	10800	RCUC	91701	573-C5
COLUSA WY				
	-	FONT	92336	574-H1
	1000	BBLK	-	4812-C3
COLWYN AV				
	7000	HIGH	92346	577-G5
N COLWYN AV				
	1600	SBDO	92346	577-G4
COMANCHE AV				
	38500	SBdC	92365	3594-A1
	38600	SBdC	92365	(3504-A7 See Page 3414)
COMANCHE CIR				
	-	POM	91766	640-G6
COMANCHE CT				
	-	RivC	92223	650-H7
	-	RivC	92399	650-H7
COMANCHE DR				
	1000	SBdC	-	4741-A5
COMANCHE RD				
	-	SBdC	-	4843-J4
	-	VCTV	92392	4386-F5
	15100	APLV	92307	4297-G1
	17100	APLV	92307	4207-G2
COMANCHE ST				
	16300	VCTV	92392	4386-D5
COMBERTON ST				
	34900	YCPA	92399	649-J2
	34900	YCPA	92399	650-A2
COMET AV				
	-	SBdC	91710	712-F3
	12900	ONT	91761	642-F7
	12900	ONT	91761	682-F2
	16900	SBdC	92880	712-F3
S COMET AV				
	200	UPL	91786	602-A4
COMET CT				
	5400	RivC	91752	683-H3
COMET RD				
	36900	SBdC	-	(4392-B3 See Page 4302)
COMET ST				
	8300	RCUC	91730	602-F3
COMISO WY				
	7200	RCUC	91701	573-E6
COMMERCE PKWY				
	2500	BARS	92311	(3759-A2 See Page 3758)
S COMMERCE PKWY				
	300	ONT	91761	643-C2
COMMERCE ST				
	10200	LMLN	92374	607-D6
COMMERCE WY				
	9300	ADEL	92301	4294-E3
	10500	FONT	92337	603-J7
	10500	FONT	92337	643-J1
	21900	GTER	92313	646-D4
COMMERCE CENTER DR				
	9500	RCUC	91730	603-B5
E COMMERCENTER CIR				
	100	SBDO	92408	606-J6
S COMMERCENTER CIR				
	1800	SBDO	92408	606-J6
S COMMERCENTER DR E				
	1800	SBDO	92408	606-J6
S COMMERCENTER DR W				
	1800	SBDO	92408	606-H6
COMMERCIAL AV				
	-	RivC	92507	646-C6
E COMMERCIAL RD				
	100	SBDO	92408	606-J7
	300	SBDO	92408	607-A7
	300	SBDO	92408	647-A1
W COMMERCIAL RD				
	100	SBDO	92408	606-H7
	100	CLTN	92324	606-H7
COMMERCIAL ST				
	10100	SBdC	92316	605-D6
	61500	SBdC	92252	4889-B7
E COMMERCIAL ST				
	100	POM	91767	640-J1
	300	POM	91767	641-A1
W COMMERCIAL ST				
	100	POM	91768	640-G1
COMMERCIAL WY				
	31900	SBdC	-	519-B6
COMMUNITY AV				
	-	SBdC	-	2971-F4
COMMUNITY BLVD				
	20200	SBdC	92347	(3677-D2 See Page 3586)
	22500	SBdC	92347	3678-A2
	24800	SBdC	92311	3678-F2
	26100	SBdC	92311	3679-A2
COMMUNITY DR				
	400	SBdC	-	518-A3
COMMUNITY WY				
	19500	APLV	92308	4477-B1
COMO DR				
	400	POM	91767	601-A7
COMO LN				
	900	SBdC	-	4737-J6
COMPADRE LN				
	83000	SBdC	92277	(4825-A4 See Page 4824)
COMPTON AV				
	2200	SBdC	92377	575-F3
N COMPTON AV				
	2200	RLTO	92377	575-F3
	2200	SBdC	92377	575-F3
COMPTON CT				
	4100	SBdC	91710	641-D5
COMPTON ST				
	3900	SBdC	91710	641-D5
COMSTOCK CT				
	41400	BBLK	-	4811-G2
COMSTOCK DR				
	14400	VCTV	92394	4296-A7
	14400	VCTV	92394	4386-A1
COMSTOCK LN				
	41500	BBLK	-	4811-G2
W COMSTOCK RD				
	3000	SBDO	92407	545-J2
CONADA RD				
	36800	SBdC	-	(3591-E5 See Page 3590)
CONCANNON ST				
	10600	RCUC	91737	573-B4
W CONCEPCION DR				
	1500	CLTN	92324	606-A5
CONCHA DR				
	5200	RivC	91752	683-G4
CONCHO CT				
	-	SBdC	-	4843-F5
CONCHO WY				
	6000	YUCA	92284	4887-J6
CONCONINO RD				
	-	SBdC	-	368-H1
CONCORD AV				
	-	ONT	91761	642-C6
	2300	POM	91768	640-D1
	7300	FONT	92336	574-G7
	8100	SBdC	92335	604-G2
	12500	CHNO	91710	641-E6
S CONCORD AV				
	2000	ONT	91761	642-C4
CONCORD CIR				
	11300	FONT	92337	644-G2
CONCORD CT				
	-	HESP	92345	4475-J7
	-	HESP	92345	4565-J1
	11700	CHNO	91710	641-E4
CONCORD DR				
	-	VCTV	92392	4385-E4
	10100	RCUC	91730	603-A3
CONCORD LN				
	700	RDL	92374	648-F3
S CONCORD PL				
	2400	ONT	91761	642-C5
CONCORD RD				
	18800	APLV	92307	4208-A3
CONCORD ST				
	17500	ADEL	92301	4205-B4
	32900	BARS	92311	3758-D3
	32900	SBdC	92311	3758-D3
W CONCORD ST				
	1500	SBDO	92411	576-D6
S CONCORD WY				
	400	UPL	91786	602-A4
CONCORDIA CIR				
	28600	HIGH	92346	578-B7
CONCORDIA WY				
	17800	CHLS	91709	712-B6
CONCOURS				
	5500	ONT	91764	603-C6
E CONCOURS				
	3300	ONT	91764	603-B6
CONDALIA AV				
	3300	SBdC	92284	4817-H5
	3700	SBdC	92284	4887-H1
	6800	YUCA	92284	4957-J1
	15600	VCTV	92394	4295-J4
CONDOR CT				
	12600	GTER	92313	646-F5
CONDOR DR				
	41300	BBLK	-	4741-G7
E CONDOR DR				
	100	RLTO	92377	575-H3
CONDOR LN				
	32100	SBdC	-	4570-J5
CONDOR RD				
	2500	TNP	92278	4822-F4
	3000	TNP	92277	4822-F4
	14900	VCTV	92394	4296-B4
	32900	SBdC	92365	(3683-E3 See Page 3592)
	32900	SBdC	92365	(3763-E2 See Page 3762)
S CONDOR CREEK LN				
	2700	ONT	91761	643-C6
CONE BLVD				
	56200	SBdC	92285	4667-F7
CONE CAMP RD				
	-	HIGH	-	608-H1
	-	RDL	-	608-H1
	-	SBdC	-	608-H1
	8000	HIGH	92346	578-G7
	8200	HIGH	92346	608-H1
	8500	RDL	92346	608-H1
	8900	SBdC	92359	608-G2
CONE FLOWER LN				
	900	ONT	91762	642-A1
	900	ONT	91762	602-A7
CONEJO AV				
	100	SBdC	92252	4749-A7
	2100	SBdC	92252	4819-A2
	6700	SBdC	92252	4959-A1
CONEJO DR				
	4800	SBdC	92301	(4113-A1 See Page 4112)
N CONEJO DR				
	1000	SBDO	92404	577-B1
	1000	SBDO	92410	577-B6
	1600	SBdC	92404	577-B1
	3600	SBdC	92404	547-B7
	3800	SBDO	92404	547-B6
E CONEJO PL				
	1200	SBdC	92404	547-B7
CONEJO RD				
	11600	SBdC	92256	615-H7
CONEJO ST				
	14000	VCTV	92392	4385-J6
CONESTOGA CT				
	1500	RDL	92373	647-J2
CONESTOGA LN				
	18000	CHLS	91709	712-A6
CONFERENCE AV				
	13800	APLV	92307	4388-A2
CONGEMI CT				
	-	RCUC	91739	574-B1
CONGRESS DR				
	-	RCUC	91730	573-E7
E CONGRESS ST				
	100	CLTN	92324	646-D1
	1100	SBDO	92408	607-B2
W CONGRESS ST				
	100	CLTN	92324	646-C1
	400	SBDO	92401	606-H2
	700	SBDO	92410	606-D2
CONICERA CT				
	9500	SBdC	92371	4473-B7
CONIFER AV				
	-	CHNO	91710	642-B7
CONIFER DR				
	6200	SBdC	92397	4652-B1
	9300	SBdC	92339	611-G2
	42700	BBLK	-	4812-A1
CONIFER LN				
	9100	RCUC	91730	602-H2
CONIFER CAMP RD				
	32700	SBdC	-	519-D7
CONKLIN RD				
	300	BBLK	-	4811-G1
CONN WY				
	2000	RDL	92373	649-B5
CONNECTICUT DR				
	-	RCUC	91730	573-E1
CONNELL ST				
	500	SBdC	-	(3682-C1 See Page 3592)
W CONNER ST				
	2300	SBDO	92324	606-B3
CONNERS LN				
	400	RivC	92507	646-D6
CONNING ST				
	3600	RivC	92509	644-B6
	4100	RivC	91752	644-A7
CONNORS CT				
	800	CLAR	91711	571-F7
CONSOLATION WY				
	1300	SBdC	-	4737-G5
CONSTELLATION CT				
	26100	SBDO	92346	577-E7
	26100	SBDO	92409	577-E7
CONSTELLATION DR				
	1200	SBdC	-	4812-A1
	42500	BBLK	-	4812-A1
CONSTITUTION ST				
	4800	CHNO	91710	641-F4
CONSTITUTION WY				
	-	RCUC	91730	573-E7
E CONSTITUTION WY				
	13800	FONT	92336	574-B7
	13800	FONT	92336	604-B1
W CONSTITUTION WY				
	13500	FONT	92336	574-A7
	13500	FONT	92336	604-A1
CONTAINER CIR				
	1900	RivC	92509	645-E6
CONTEMPO CT				
	1000	ONT	91762	641-J3
	1000	ONT	91762	642-A3
W CONTEMPO CT				
	500	ONT	91762	642-B3
	1100	ONT	91762	641-J3
W CONTEMPO ST				
	700	ONT	91762	642-A3
CONTENTA CT				
	-	FONT	92336	574-H2
CONTERA DR				
	58900	SBdC	92284	4888-D2
CONTINENTAL PL				
	-	RCUC	91730	573-E1
CONTOUR TER				
	52600	SBdC	-	4816-F6
CONTRA COSTA WY				
	500	CLAR	91711	571-E6
E CONVENTION CENTER WY				
	1900	ONT	91764	602-G7
CONVERSE AV				
	400	CLAR	91711	601-E5
CONWAY DR				
	33300	SBdC	-	519-E7
COOK LN				
	5200	SBdC	92371	4563-D7
COOK ST				
	-	RDL	92374	608-E7
COOKE AV				
	-	CLAR	91711	571-F3
COOK PENCER				
	7300	SBdC	-	4562-G5
	7300	SBdC	92372	4562-G5
N COOLCREST AV				
	1500	UPL	91786	572-A7
	1700	UPL	91784	572-A4
N COOLCREST WY				
	1800	UPL	91784	572-A4
E COOLEY AV				
	800	SBDO	92408	607-B5
COOLEY CT				
	1400	SBDO	92408	607-A5
E COOLEY DR				
	1000	CLTN	92324	646-F1
	1400	CLTN	92324	606-G7
	1600	RDL	92374	607-D5
	1600	RDL	92408	607-D5
	1600	SBDO	92408	607-D5
S COOLEY DR				
	600	CLTN	92324	606-F7
	700	CLTN	92324	646-F1
E COOLEY LN				
	1600	CLTN	92324	646-H1
COOLEY ST				
	7800	SBdC	92410	576-J7
	7900	SBdC	92410	606-J1
S COOLEY ST				
	8000	SBdC	92410	606-J1
COOLGARDIE RD				
	-	SBdC	-	349-C5
COOLGLEN DR				
	14500	SBdC	-	(3935-H1 See Page 3934)
COOLWATER LN				
	100	BARS	92311	3680-A3
	16200	FONT	92337	644-H3
COOMES LN				
	8600	SBdC	92252	4959-G5
COON CANYON RD				
	-	SBdC	92347	349-C7
	37900	SBdC	92347	3588-B1
COON HOLLOW				
	22100	SBdC	-	516-D3
COOPER AV				
	6100	FONT	92336	574-F4
COOPER LN				
	55000	YUCA	92284	4957-D5
COOPER ST				
	7900	FONT	92336	604-F1
COPA DE ORO				
	22300	SBdC	-	(4115-H3 See Page 4114)
COPA DE ORO DR				
	100	BREA	92823	710-C5
COPE LN				
	62300	SBdC	92252	4959-D6
COPLEY CIR				
	7700	HIGH	92346	578-B6
COPPER CT				
	28600	HIGH	92346	578-B5
S COPPER CT				
	1300	ONT	91762	642-A3
COPPER DR				
	-	TNP	92278	4822-F1
COPPER LN				
	-	MohC	-	3620-F4
	9300	SBdC	92335	604-D4
S COPPER LN				
	2600	SBDO	92408	647-A1
COPPER RD				
	4800	CHLS	91709	711-G2
COPPER CANYON CIR				
	-	POM	91766	640-G5
	15200	VCTV	92394	4296-A5
COPPER CITY RD				
	22000	SBdC	-	349-C2
COPPER MESA RD				
	6500	SBdC	92277	4890-E7
	6800	SBdC	92277	4960-E1
COPPER MINE RD				
	-	SBdC	92277	4820-G6
COPPERMINE ST				
	4500	RIV	92501	645-H7
COPPER MOON LN				
	300	SBdC	92252	4750-E7
	1300	SBdC	92252	4820-E1
COPPER MOUNTAIN CT				
	10000	RCUC	91737	573-A1
COPPER MOUNTAIN DR				
	1400	DBAR	91765	680-C4
COPPER MOUNTAIN RD				
	5400	TNP	92277	4891-B7
	6500	SBdC	92252	4890-E7
	7000	TNP	92277	4961-B1
	7000	SBdC	92252	4960-E1
COPPER PASS CT				
	11400	RCUC	91737	573-D3
COPPER PRIVADO				
	-	ONT	91762	642-A2
COPPER QUEEN CANYON RD				
	16900	SBdC	93562	329-A3
COPPER SADDLE WY				
	2400	CHLS	91709	680-H1
COPPERSTONE DR				
	13500	VCTV	92392	4385-F6
COPPERWOOD ST				
	5200	SBDO	92407	546-B5
COPPI CT				
	-	RCUC	91739	574-A1
CORAL CT				
	-	FONT	92337	645-A1
	-	RDL	92374	608-F7
	100	RDL	92374	648-F1
	6700	RCUC	91701	572-G5
CORAL LN				
	-	FONT	92337	645-A2
S CORAL WY				
	-	UPL	91786	601-J4
E CORAL TREE DR				
	100	RLTO	92377	575-G3
E CORAL TREE LN				
	1400	SBDO	92408	607-C6
CORAL TREE RD				
	12600	RCUC	91739	573-G5
N CORAL TREE RD				
	1200	CLTN	92324	605-J4
CORAL TREE WY				
	700	UPL	91784	572-A5
CORALWOOD CT				
	10200	RCUC	91737	573-A3
CORALWOOD DR				
	14900	CHLS	91709	681-E5
CORALWOOD LN				
	-	YCPA	92399	610-A7
CORANADA WY				
	11200	MTCL	91763	641-E3
CORAZON AV				
	12200	SBdC	92392	4384-C7
CORBEAU TR				
	-	SBdC	-	(4026-E3 See Page 3936)
CORDELIA WY				
	13600	VCTV	92392	4385-F3
CORDERO RD				
	10300	SBdC	92371	4474-E4
	11900	SBdC	92392	4384-E7
	11900	SBdC	92392	4474-E1
S CORDILLERA AV				
	2100	CLTN	92324	646-J4
CORDON CT				
	9900	RCUC	91701	573-A6
CORDON DR				
	10400	RCUC	91701	573-B6
CORDOVA AV				
	1600	RDL	92373	647-H2
S CORDOVA AV				
	200	CLTN	92324	646-C3
CORDOVA CT				
	-	FONT	92336	574-H2
CORDOVA RD				
	-	SBdC	92307	4207-D1
	15400	VCTV	92394	4295-H5
	20900	APLV	92307	4207-F1
	23700	SBdC	92307	4208-E1
CORDOVA ST				
	1300	POM	91767	601-D6
CORDOVAN CT				
	4800	CHLS	91709	711-F1
COREY LN				
	12800	YCPA	92399	649-G5
COREY WY				
	14500	VCTV	92394	4295-J6
S CORIANDER AV				
	800	SBDO	92376	605-J4
CORIANDER CT				
	12700	RCUC	91739	573-H4
CORIANDER DR				
	5600	SBdC	92345	(4655-B2 See Page 4654)
	6200	SBdC	92345	4565-B7
CORK DR				
	14700	CHLS	91709	681-C4
CORKWOOD CT				
	10200	RCUC	91737	573-A3
CORKWOOD LN				
	12400	VCTV	92392	4386-D6
W CORMORANT DR				
	100	ONT	91762	642-B6
CORNELIA ST				
	1100	POM	91768	640-D1
CORNELIAN RD				
	19700	SBdC	92308	4567-D2
CORNELIUS CT				
	-	HIGH	92346	578-E5
CORNELL AV				
	100	CLAR	91711	601-C3
	1100	RDL	92374	608-D5
CORNELL CIR				
	13200	VCTV	92392	4385-E4
CORNELL CT				
	7400	FONT	92336	574-A7
	7600	RCUC	91730	573-B7
	11800	YCPA	92399	650-B2
W CORNELL CT				
	400	UPL	91786	602-B1
CORNELL DR				
	35300	YCPA	92399	650-A2
E CORNELL DR				
	100	RLTO	92376	575-H7
W CORNELL DR				
	100	RLTO	92376	575-G7
CORNELL LN				
	11700	YCPA	92399	650-B2
CORNELL ST				
	11800	ADEL	92301	4385-A1
	26400	LMLN	92354	647-F2
W CORNELL ST				
	1100	RLTO	92376	575-D7
CORNERSTONE DR				
	-	RivC	91752	643-E5
CORNERSTONE LN				
	7300	FONT	92336	574-D6
CORNERSTONE ST				
	-	CHLS	91709	681-H7
CORNFLOWER CT				
	15000	FONT	92336	574-D7
CORNING AV				
	31700	BARS	92311	(3759-A5 See Page 3758)
CORNISH HEATH CT				
	5900	CHLS	91709	711-J2
CORNUS CT				
	28200	HIGH	92346	578-A4
CORNWALL AV				
	8100	RCUC	91739	603-H2
N CORO DR				
	1300	CLTN	92324	606-A4
CORONA AV				
	-	APLV	92307	4207-F3
	7400	HESP	92345	4567-A3
	7700	HESP	92345	4566-J2
N CORONA AV				
	100	ONT	91761	602-G7
	100	ONT	91764	602-F4
CORONA CIR				
	200	SBdC	-	518-A2
	200	SBdC	-	517-J5
CORONA CT				
	7600	FONT	92336	574-A7
CORONA DR				
	26100	SBdC	-	(3935-H6 See Page 3934)
CORONA EXWY Rt#-71				
	17900	CHLS	91709	712-C6
	17900	RivC	92880	712-C6
CORONA LN				
	100	SBdC	-	517-J5
	100	SBdC	-	518-A1
CORONA ST				
	23800	SBdC	92307	4208-E3
CORONADO AV				
	9700	ADEL	92301	4204-E1
	11300	ADEL	92301	4205-A1
	17100	FONT	92336	574-J4
	17100	FONT	92336	575-A4
CORONADO DR				
	600	RDL	92374	648-D1
	6800	SBdC	-	4843-H4
	10200	RCUC	91730	603-B3
	10900	SBdC	92256	615-J6
	15900	VCTV	92394	4296-D4
CORONADO LN				
	12500	SBdC	92392	4386-J5
CORONADO ST				
	700	NDLS	92363	3620-B6
W CORONADO ST				
	900	UPL	91786	572-A7
	1100	UPL	91786	571-H7
CORONADO TR				
	57700	YUCA	92284	4958-A3
CORONET ST				
	15900	CHLS	91709	711-C1
N CORPORATE CT				
	200	UPL	91786	602-A3
CORPORATE DR				
	10200	LMLN	92374	607-E6
CORPORATE CENTER DR				
	700	POM	91768	640-C1
	1000	UPL	91786	601-F1
CORPRATE CENTER AV				
	-	CHNO	91710	681-E5
CORRAL CT				
	5000	RCUC	91737	573-B1
	18900	SBdC	-	(3847-A5 See Page 3756)
CORRAL RD				
	-	SBdC	-	3936-J3
	9100	SBdC	92339	611-D2
	27500	SBdC	-	(3937-A1 See Page 3936)
	28300	SBdC	-	(3847-A5 See Page 3756)
CORRAL ST				
	-	SBdC	92314	4742-J7
	-	SBdC	92314	(4743-A7 See Page 4662)
	2000	NRCO	92860	712-J7
	14500	VCTV	92394	4295-J7
	35300	SBdC	-	(3591-F5 See Page 3590)
CORRESPONDENCE PL				
	-	RCUC	91730	573-E1
CORRIDOR DR				
	-	RivC	91752	643-E5
CORSICA CT				
	11100	RCUC	91730	573-D7
CORTA DR				
	16300	VCTV	92392	4296-D7
CORTA PL				
	16300	VCTV	92392	4296-D7
CORTA WY				
	6500	TNP	92277	4892-C6
CORTE PL				
	-	RCUC	91701	573-E6
N CORTE BLANCO				
	400	UPL	91786	601-H3
W CORTE CABALLO				
	1500	UPL	91786	601-H3
W CORTE HACIENDA				
	1500	UPL	91786	601-H3
N CORTE ROJO				
	300	UPL	91786	601-H3
CORTE SANTANA				
	1500	UPL	91786	601-H3
N CORTE VERDE				
	400	UPL	91786	601-H3
CORTEZ AV				
	8900	ADEL	92301	4204-C7
	11300	ADEL	92301	4205-A7
CORTEZ DR				
	12200	VCTV	92392	4385-H6
	57800	YUCA	92284	4958-B7
CORTEZ RD				
	9300	SBdC	92371	4472-F7
	11700	SBdC	92372	4472-F1
	12700	SBdC	92372	4382-F6
CORTEZ ST				
	-	RDL	92374	608-F4
	1400	NDLS	92363	3620-A7
	7900	HIGH	92346	578-C7
	39600	SBdC	-	4482-J3
CORTEZ WY				
	11200	MTCL	91763	641-E3
CORTINA DR				
	1200	SBdC	-	4737-J5
CORTLAND ST				
	11100	RCUC	91701	573-D5
CORTO DR				
	11500	RivC	91752	683-G3
CORTO RD				
	8900	SBdC	92308	4479-C2
	11300	SBdC	92308	(4389-C7 See Page 4299)
CORTON ST				
	9700	SBdC	92371	4472-H1
	12100	SBdC	92371	4382-G2
	15700	SBdC	92371	4292-G3
N CORVETTE DR				
	700	ONT	91764	603-A6
CORWIN RD				
	-	SBdC	-	(4210-H5 See Page 4120)
	-	SBdC	-	(4211-A5 See Page 4120)
	18300	APLV	92307	4296-J4
	18400	APLV	92307	4297-E1
	20600	APLV	92307	4207-H6
	22000	APLV	92307	4208-A6
	22500	SBdC	92307	4208-A6
CORYBUS ST				
	-	CHNO	91710	642-B6
COSENZA PL				
	-	RCUC	91701	573-E6
COSMOS ST				
	-	CHNO	91710	642-B7
COSTA DR				
	6500	TNP	92277	4892-C5
COSTA LN				
	8800	ADEL	92301	4204-C3
	8800	SBdC	92301	4204-C3
COSTA RD				
	24900	SBdC	92307	4298-G4
COTATI CT				
	-	SBdC	-	4774-E7
S COTRIA AV				
	1400	SBDO	92408	607-B5
COTTAGE AV				
	8900	RCUC	91730	602-J4
	25200	LMLN	92354	607-C7
COTTAGE CIR				
	14300	CHLS	91709	680-J4
COTTAGE DR				
	4000	SBdC	92407	546-G6
COTTAGE LN				
	-	CLTN	92324	606-E6
	500	BBLK	-	4811-E2
	14300	CHLS	91709	680-G4
	27800	SBdC	-	(3935-H2 See Page 3934)
COTTAGE ST				
	100	BARS	92311	3679-G2
COTTAGE GROVE RD				
	100	SBdC	-	517-J2
COTTON ST				
	-	APLV	92307	4207-D6
COTTON CLOUD DR				
	11400	RCUC	91701	573-D4
COTTONTAIL CIR				
	3200	CHLS	91709	681-B5
COTTONTAIL DR				
	-	POM	91766	640-F5
COTTONTAIL LN				
	8600	SBdC	92308	4567-D1
	8800	SBdC	92308	4477-D4
	11300	APLV	92308	4477-D1
	11700	APLV	92308	4387-D7
COTTONTAIL RD				
	-	TNP	92277	4822-F2
	-	TNP	92278	4822-F2
	2200	SBdC	-	4816-E5
	3200	BARS	92311	3758-H2
	8800	SBdC	92308	4477-E7
	11500	APLV	92308	4387-D7
	11500	APLV	92308	4477-E7
COTTONWOOD AV				
	6600	HESP	92345	4566-A2
	8100	FONT	92335	603-J1
	8100	SBdC	92335	603-J1
	8200	SBdC	92335	604-A3
	8900	HESP	92345	4476-A1
	11700	HESP	92345	4386-A7
	12100	VCTV	92345	4386-A7
	12100	VCTV	92392	4386-A6
	12100	CHNO	91710	641-H5
	13800	CHNO	91710	682-B2
COTTONWOOD CIR				
	-	RivC	92880	683-B7
E COTTONWOOD CT				
	1000	ONT	91761	642-E7
	2900	ONT	91761	643-A6
COTTONWOOD DR				
	-	CALI	92320	650-A7
	-	TNP	92277	4890-G7
	700	SBdC	-	516-F3
	900	BARS	92311	3679-J5
	7400	TNP	92277	4891-C7
	11600	APLV	92308	4387-C7
	62400	SBdC	92252	4959-D1
	62800	SBdC	92252	4889-E7
	64500	SBdC	92252	4890-A7
	66300	SBdC	92277	4890-G7
	72800	TNP	92277	4892-D6
E COTTONWOOD DR				
	1700	CLTN	92324	646-G1
COTTONWOOD LN				
	27300	SBdC	-	517-H1
	29700	SBdC	-	4738-E7
COTTONWOOD PL				
	2500	POM	91766	641-A6
COTTONWOOD RD				
	-	SBdC	92365	(3765-A1 See Page 3764)
	17400	SBdC	-	(3846-F2 See Page 3756)
	25500	LMLN	92354	607-D7
	25500	SBdC	92354	607-D7
	42500	SBdC	92365	(3763-D1 See Page 3762)
	44900	SBdC	92365	3764-B1
COTTONWOOD ST				
	15700	VCTV	92392	4296-E3
E COTTONWOOD ST				
	1200	ONT	91761	642-G6
COTTONWOOD TER				
	200	ONT	91761	642-C7
COTTONWOOD TR				
	2300	CHLS	91709	640-J7
	2600	CHLS	91709	641-A7
	13600	YCPA	92399	650-E5
E COTTONWOOD TR				
	2700	ONT	91761	642-J6
	2700	ONT	91761	643-A6
COTTONWOOD WY				
	8900	RCUC	91737	572-G3
COTTONWOOD COVE DR				
	100	DBAR	91765	640-A7
COTTONWOOD SPRINGS RD				
	-	SBdC	92285	4484-D5
	-	SBdC	92285	(4485-A5 See Page 4484)
COUGAR CT				
	-	RCUC	91737	573-D4
COUGAR LN				
	7900	SBdC	92252	4959-A4
	32700	SBdC	-	519-C7
COUGAR RD				
	1000	SBdC	-	4812-A1
	2300	SBdC	92301	(4202-E6 See Page 4112)
	11400	BBLK	-	4812-A1
COUGAR ST				
	8000	SBdC	92301	(4203-C6 See Page 4112)
	9600	ADEL	92301	4204-E5
	18600	VCTV	92394	4205-F5
COUGAR TR				
	-	SBdC	-	4843-E6
COUGAR WY				
	-	FONT	92336	574-D2
COUGAS CREEK RD				
	23900	DBAR	91765	640-D4
COULSTON AV				
	1500	RDL	92374	607-H5
E COULSTON ST				
	1200	SBDO	92408	607-B6
	1600	SBDO	92354	607-C6
	1900	RDL	92354	607-D6
COULTER DR				
	500	SBdC	-	4738-E7
	14600	VCTV	92394	4296-A7
COULTER PINE DR				
	900	SBdC	-	516-E4
	8300	SBdC	92359	4950-E7
	8400	SBdC	92359	610-E1
N COUNCIL AV				
	1100	ONT	91764	602-D5
COUNTRY CT				
	13100	VCTV	92392	4385-F5
COUNTRY LN				
	-	SBdC	-	4813-D1
	10000	YCPA	92399	610-A5
	10200	YCPA	92399	609-J5
	14700	SBdC	92335	604-D2
COUNTRY PL				
	100	CALI	92320	650-A7
	1100	RDL	92374	608-F5
	12800	YCPA	92399	649-F5
COUNTRY RD				
	30600	SBdC	92374	648-H2
E COUNTRY CLUB BLVD				
	100	SBdC	92314	4742-F5
W COUNTRY CLUB BLVD				
	100	SBdC	92314	4742-B6
COUNTRY CLUB DR				
	1400	RDL	92373	648-G4
	2500	BARS	92311	3758-E2
	10200	RivC	91752	644-A6
	11000	APLV	92308	4477-C1
	13200	SBdC	92392	4386-J3
	13200	SBdC	92392	4387-A3
	15200	CHLS	91709	681-E6
	19300	SBdC	92377	575-F2
	19400	RLTO	92377	575-F2
W COUNTRY CLUB DR				
	100	RLTO	92377	575-F3
	100	SBdC	92377	575-F3
COUNTRY CLUB LN				
	1900	RDL	92373	648-G5
	7500	YUCA	92284	4957-B4
	12100	GTER	92313	646-F4
E COUNTRY CLUB LN				
	300	SBDO	92404	576-J2
E COUNTRY CLUB RD				
	500	SBDO	92404	576-J2
COUNTRY CREEK CT				
	13500	YCPA	92399	650-C6
	15300	CHLS	91709	680-G6
COUNTRY CREEK DR				
	35700	YCPA	92399	650-B6
COUNTRY GLEN CT				
	13500	YCPA	92399	650-C6
COUNTRY GLEN DR				
	18100	SBdC	92392	4386-J5
COUNTRY HOLLOW CT				
	14400	HESP	92345	4565-J2
COUNTRY MILE RD				
	-	POM	91766	640-H6
COUNTRY OAKS DR				
	6700	HIGH	92346	578-A3
E COUNTRY OAKS LP				
	3600	ONT	91761	643-C6
S COUNTRY OAKS LP				
	2900	ONT	91761	643-C7
COUNTRY PARK RD				
	-	DBAR	91765	680-B6
COUNTRY RANCH CT				
	16700	VCTV	92392	4386-E5
COUNTRY RIDGE RD				
	-	POM	91766	640-G5
COUNTRYSIDE DR				
	10500	RCUC	91730	573-B7
	11300	FONT	92337	644-A3
COUNTRYVIEW DR				
	10900	RCUC	91730	573-C7
COUNTRY VIEW DR				
	23600	DBAR	91765	680-C3
COUNTRY VILLAGE RD				
	3000	FONT	92337	644-A6
	3000	RivC	91752	644-A6
	3000	RivC	92509	644-A6
COUNTRY WALK LN				
	14000	CHLS	91709	680-H3
COUNTRY WOOD DR				
	-	POM	91766	640-F5
COUNTRYWOOD PL				
	5700	RCUC	91739	573-G4
COUNTY RD				
	100	POM	91766	640-J6
	100	POM	91766	641-A6
	3400	CHNO	91710	641-C6
	56600	SBdC	-	2971-F1
COUNTY LINE LN				
	500	CALI	92320	649-G7
COUNTY LINE RD				
	100	CALI	92320	650-C7
	100	YCPA	92399	650-A7
	200	CALI	92320	649-F7
	33400	YCPA	92399	649-H7
	38600	RivC	92399	650-J7
	38700	RivC	92223	650-H6
	38700	RivC	92223	651-A6
E COUNTY LINE RD				
	4300	ONT	91761	643-H4
	4300	RivC	91752	643-H4
	11800	FONT	92337	643-H4
	11800	ONT	92337	643-H4
	13400	FONT	92337	644-A4
COURIER AV				
	400	RDL	92374	608-C5
E COURT PL				
	6400	TNP	92277	4892-F6
W COURT PL				
	6400	TNP	92277	4892-F6
COURT ST				
	17500	FONT	92336	575-B7
	24400	SBdC	92410	607-A1
	24900	LMLN	92354	607-B7
	25100	HIGH	92410	607-C1
E COURT ST				
	100	SBDO	92410	606-H1
	1600	HIGH	92410	607-C1
	1600	SBDO	92410	607-C1
W COURT ST				
	300	SBDO	92401	606-G1
	2200	SBDO	92410	606-B1
	2700	SBDO	92376	606-A1
E COURT WY				
	6400	TNP	92277	4892-F5
W COURT WY				
	6400	TNP	92277	4892-F5
W COURTLAND DR				
	500	SBDO	92405	576-F3
COURTNEY CT				
	18300	SBdC	92316	645-D1
COURTSIDE ST				
	11300	VCTV	92392	4475-D2
COURTWRIGHT RD				
	1100	MohC	-	3620-A1
COURTWRIGHT ST				
	-	NDLS	92363	3620-B4
	700	SBdC	92363	3620-B4
COUSINS PL				
	-	RCUC	91737	572-H3

STREET Block City ZIP Pg-Grid

COVE CIR
32100 SBdC - 519-B7
COVE DR
600 BBLK - 4810-J2
800 BBLK - 4811-A2
COVE LN
- YCPA 92399 609-J4
COVE RD
28900 SBdC - (4389-J3
See Page 4299)
29100 SBdC - (4390-A3
See Page 4300)
COVE DALE RD
69300 SBdC 92277 4891-C1
COVE LANDING RD
3100 CHLS 91709 681-B1
COVELO AV
100 SBdC 92284 4748-F5
500 SBdC 92285 4748-F5
COVENTRY CT
- RCUC 91739 573-F5
COVENTRY LN
15600 FONT 92337 644-F2
COVENTRY ST
- SBdC - (3683-A3
See Page 3592)
40500 SBdC - (3682-J3
See Page 3592)
42500 SBdC 92365 (3683-A3
See Page 3592)
COVENTRY WY
5200 MTCL 91763 641-G2
COVERED WAGON CT
- RivC 92399 650-G7
COVERED WAGON DR
300 DBAR 91765 640-D7
COVE VIEW RD
69300 SBdC 92277 4891-C1
69900 SBdC 92277 4821-E7
75300 TNP 92277 4822-J7
75300 TNP 92277 4823-A7
COVEY CT
12700 APLV 92308 4387-E4
13300 CHLS 91709 681-A3
COVILLE ST
5300 SBdC 92285 (4576-D6
See Page 4486)
COVINA PL
5300 RCUC 91739 574-A1
COVINA ST
18500 HESP 92345 4477-A3
COVINGTON DR
10900 SBdC 92256 615-J5
COVINGTON PL
- RCUC 91730 573-D7
COWAN LN
62100 SBdC 92252 4889-C3
COWBOY AL
- SBdC 92371 4564-B4
COWICHAN RD
21100 APLV 92308 4387-G7
COXEY TKTR
6000 SBdC - 4568-H2
6000 SBdC - (4569-A6
See Page 4568)
6800 SBdC 92308 4568-H2
30300 SBdC - 4660-C5
30500 SBdC - (4740-F2
See Page 4660)
37000 SBdC - (4659-C1
See Page 4658)
W COY LN
100 SBdC 92314 4742-D5
COYOTE AV
18100 ADEL 92301 4204-F6
COYOTE CT
- FONT 92336 574-D2
1500 SBdC - 4812-D2
13600 VCTV 92392 4385-G4
16200 HESP 92345 4476-F7
COYOTE DR
9600 SBdC 92308 4478-J1
11300 SBdC 92308 4388-J7
12200 SBdC 92307 4388-J3
14900 SBdC 92307 4298-J5
25500 SBdC 92308 4479-A4
N COYOTE LN
5000 SBDO 92407 546-D5
S COYOTE LN
1000 BARS 92311 3679-G4
COYOTE RD
- SBdC - 4816-H6
2500 SBdC 92371 4472-G4
2500 SBdC 92372 4472-G4
4500 SBdC 92371 4473-B4
24700 BARS 92311 3678-F6
36300 SBdC - (4572-A5
See Page 4482)
COYOTE ST
6400 CHLS 91709 712-B6
COYOTE TR
- SBdC - 4736-D7
6200 SBdC 92345 4565-E4
8500 HESP 92345 4565-E4
8700 SBdC 92252 4959-G5
54900 YUCA 92284 4957-C2
COYOTE WK
700 SBdC - 517-J3
700 SBdC - 518-A3

COYOTE CANYON RD
14900 FONT 92336 544-D7
15300 SBdC 92336 544-D7
COYOTE LAKE DR
37000 SBdC 92365 (3593-G6
See Page 3592)
COYOTE LAKE RD
- SBdC 92365 349-H7
- SBdC 92365 (3683-G1
See Page 3592)
37000 SBdC 92365 (3593-G2
See Page 3592)
47900 SBdC - 349-G4
COYOTE SPRINGS DR
23400 DBAR 91765 680-C4
COYOTE VALLEY RD
2100 SBdC 92252 4819-J2
2200 SBdC 92252 4820-A1
4100 SBdC 92252 4890-A2
65100 SBdC 92252 4750-B7
66600 SBdC 92278 370-E9
66600 SBdC 92278 4750-F3
COYOTE VISTA RD
100 SBdC 92252 4750-C5
COZY LN
100 BARS 92311 3679-G2
COZZENS AV
12900 SBdC 91710 641-D7
13100 SBdC 91710 681-D1
CRABAPPLE LN
15400 VCTV 92394 4296-B1
CRAB FLATS RD
- SBdC - (4739-G4
See Page 4658)
100 SBdC - 519-C1
CRAFTON AV
500 SBdC 92374 648-J1
800 SBdC 92374 608-J7
1000 SBdC 92359 608-J7
1300 RDL 92359 608-J5
11900 SBdC 92374 649-A2
11900 SBdC 92399 649-A2
11900 YCPA 92399 649-A2
CRAFTON CT
- RDL 92374 608-G7
CRAFTON HILLS CT
11900 YCPA 92399 649-A3
CRAFTON HILLS DR
31600 SBdC 92374 649-B3
31600 SBdC 92399 649-B3
31600 YCPA 92399 649-B3
CRAFTON HILLS RIDGE TR
2900 RDL 92359 609-E7
2900 SBdC 92359 609-E7
2900 SBdC 92399 609-E7
3000 RDL 92399 609-E7
10900 SBdC 92399 649-C2
11300 YCPA 92399 649-C2
CRAFTON HILLS RIDGE TR E
10600 SBdC 92399 609-H6
10600 YCPA 92399 609-H6
CRAFTON POINTE DR
11900 YCPA 92399 649-B2
CRAFTS ESTATE RD
800 SBdC 92374 609-B7
800 SBdC 92399 609-B7
CRAGHILL DR
200 SBdC - 518-D1
CRAGS LN
1000 SBdC - 4741-B5
CRAGUN TR
14700 CHLS 91709 680-J5
CRAIG CT
200 RDL 92374 608-E7
CRAIG DR
- SBdC 92308 4567-F4
12800 RCUC 91739 573-H6
W CRAIG ST
1000 RLTO 92377 575-E3
CRAM RD
7500 HIGH 92346 578-D6
CRAMER RD
- SBdC - 4481-F3
CRANE
200 POM 91767 601-A2
CRANE CT
600 CLAR 91711 571-E5
CRANE DR
300 BBLK - 4811-G1
46500 SBdC - (4743-B4
See Page 4662)
CRANE ST
12400 GTER 92313 646-F5
CRAPE MYRTLE CIR
2800 CHLS 91709 681-A7
N CRATER CT
1100 SBdC 92314 4742-A4
CRATER RD
- SBdC - 370-J4
CRATER LAKE RD
100 BBLK - 4742-A7
100 BBLK - 4812-A1
W CRATER MOUNTAIN RD
1100 SBdC 92314 4742-B4
CRAVER RD
9200 SBdC 92256 616-G1

CRAW AV
11700 CHNO 91710 641-G4
CRAWFORD AV
14900 ADEL 92301 4294-H7
N CRAWFORD AV
1300 UPL 91786 602-D1
CRAWFORD CT
13600 FONT 92336 604-A1
CRAZY HORSE AV
- FONT 92336 574-E3
CRAZY HORSE CT
20600 APLV 92308 4387-F5
CRAZY HORSE TR
- SBdC - 4843-E5
CREE CT
6700 SBdC - 4843-G3
CREE RD
13700 APLV 92307 4387-E1
CREEK DR
1600 SBdC - 4737-G4
CREEK RD
6300 SBdC - 4843-H3
39900 BBLK - 4811-D2
CREEK & PINES RD
- SBdC - 4737-F4
CREEKBRIDGE ST
10500 RCUC 91730 573-B7
CREEKSIDE
- YCPA 92399 610-C7
CREEKSIDE CT
1200 UPL 91784 571-G4
CREEKSIDE DR
- RDL 92373 648-C6
1400 SBDO 92407 546-D5
E CREEKSIDE DR
3400 ONT 91761 643-B6
CREEKSIDE PL
8500 RCUC 91730 603-A3
CREEKSIDE RD
7700 SBdC 92372 4562-E4
CREEKSIDE RUN
2300 CHLS 91709 680-J3
CREEK VIEW LN
- RDL 92373 648-C6
CREEKWOOD LN
2000 UPL 91784 571-G4
2200 CHLS 91709 680-J4
CREETE RD
- SBdC - 4843-G5
CREIGHTON CIR
200 CLAR 91711 601-D4
CREIGHTON CT
7700 SBdC 92336 575-C7
9500 FONT 92336 575-C7
CREMA PL
- RCUC 91701 573-E6
CREOLE MINE RD
- SBdC 92278 370-B7
- SBdC 92285 370-B8
5600 SBdC 92285 (4577-G6
See Page 4486)
CREOSOTE CT
900 BARS 92311 3680-A5
CREOSOTE LN
12200 VCTV 92392 4385-C6
CREOSOTE ST
13500 VCTV 92392 4385-G5
CREPE MYRTLE AV
12300 CHNO 91710 641-J5
E CRESCENT AV
- RDL 92373 648-D2
N CRESCENT AV
600 SBDO 92410 576-G6
1300 SBDO 92405 576-F1
3600 SBDO 92405 546-F7
S CRESCENT AV
200 SBDO 92410 606-G2
W CRESCENT AV
500 RDL 92373 648-B4
W CRESCENT CIR
2200 CLTN 92324 646-H4
CRESCENT CT
17800 SBdC 92392 4386-H2
19000 APLV 92308 4477-B5
CRESCENT DR
800 BARS 92311 3680-C5
2100 SBdC - 519-D6
8500 SBdC 92345 4565-G2
CRESCENT LN
800 BBLK - 4811-B2
N CRESCENT ST
4900 SBDO 92407 546-F4
CRESCENT WY
- RCUC - (542-D7
See Page 513)
CRESCENTA WY
13900 RCUC 91739 574-B2
CRESCENT BAY CT
- YCPA 92399 649-H5
CRESCENT CENTER DR
9700 RCUC 91730 602-J5
9800 RCUC 91730 603-A5
CRESCENT HILLS DR
13500 CHLS 91709 681-B2
CRESCENT RIDGE LN
13800 CHLS 91709 681-B2
CREST AV
12100 RivC 92509 645-G4
12100 SBdC 92509 645-G4

CREST CIR
200 SBdC - 517-J5
200 SBdC - 518-A2
CREST CT
14500 CHLS 91709 681-C4
CREST DR
- SBdC - 519-E7
14400 VCTV 92392 4386-F1
19500 APLV 92307 4387-C1
CREST LN
4400 CHNO 91710 641-E5
22200 SBdC - 516-D3
39100 BBLK - 4811-B2
CREST ST
26700 HIGH 92346 577-G6
CRESTA DR
23900 SBdC - 516-H4
CRESTA LN
24000 SBdC - 516-H3
CRESTA BLANCA LN
17700 SBdC 92392 4386-H2
CRESTAR WY
- UPL 91784 572-E6
CRESTBROOK CT
1100 DBAR 91765 680-E3
CREST CIRCLE DR
61400 SBdC 92252 4959-B1
CREST ESTATES CT
600 SBdC - 517-J3
CREST ESTATES DR
600 SBdC - 517-J4
CREST FERN DR
800 SBdC - 517-J3
CREST FERN WY
700 SBdC - 517-J3
CREST FOREST DR
900 SBdC - 516-C2
24200 SBdC - 517-A5
CRESTHAVEN CT
26200 LMLN 92354 647-F2
CRESTHAVEN LN
- POM 91766 640-F7
CRESTHAVEN WY
- POM 91766 640-J4
CRESTLANE CIR
1200 UPL 91786 601-J1
CRESTLINE CTO
800 SBdC - 516-F4
CRESTLINE PL
5300 RCUC 91739 574-B1
CRESTLINE RD
12400 VCTV 92392 4385-G6
23100 SBdC - 516-G4
CRESTMONT DR
1300 DBAR 91765 680-D3
5900 CHLS 91709 711-J4
CRESTON DR
1100 SBdC - (4743-B4
See Page 4662)
CREST PARK RD
27500 SBdC - 517-H4
CRESTRIDGE CT
11200 RCUC 91737 573-D3
CRESTVIEW AV
1100 SBDO 92410 577-A5
1200 SBDO 92404 577-A4
1400 UPL 91784 571-H3
1600 SBDO 92404 576-J4
35500 YCPA 92399 650-B2
E CRESTVIEW AV
400 SBDO 92410 576-J6
400 SBDO 92410 577-A6
N CRESTVIEW AV
1000 SBDO 92410 576-J6
CRESTVIEW CT
6700 YUCA 92284 4958-A1
8000 RCUC - 572-D1
8000 RCUC 91701 572-D1
11900 YCPA 92399 650-B2
14300 VCTV 92392 4386-F1
CRESTVIEW DR
- DBAR 91765 680-C2
- TNP 92277 4892-G4
- NDLS 92363 3620-C6
16800 VCTV 92392 4386-E1
17700 APLV 92307 4296-G3
17800 SBdC 92392 4386-H4
24900 LMLN 92354 647-C2
35600 YCPA 92399 650-B2
55700 YUCA 92284 4957-F1
57300 YUCA 92284 4958-A1
62100 SBdC 92252 4889-C5
CREST VIEW DR
73700 TNP 92277 4892-E4
CRESTVIEW LN
- SBdC - 516-G4
CREST VIEW LN
29300 HIGH 92346 578-D5
CRESTVIEW PL
5200 RCUC - (542-D7
See Page 513)
5200 RCUC - 572-D1
5200 RCUC 91701 572-D1
17000 VCTV 92392 4386-F1
CRESTVIEW RD
- SBdC 92285 (4576-C5
See Page 4486)
1300 RDL 92374 648-F2
19300 SBdC 92301 (4202-G3
See Page 4112)

CRESTVIEW RD
27300 SBdC 92311 3679-D7
CRESTWOOD DR
500 BBLK - 4811-J2
1100 SBdC 92314 4813-C3
1300 RDL 92373 648-E3
12300 YCPA 92399 648-J3
W CRESTWOOD DR
1200 UPL 91786 601-J1
CRIB ST
- SBdC - 4737-B7
CRIBARI DR
10000 YCPA 92399 609-J5
CRICKET CT
19300 SBdC 92316 645-F3
CRICKET DR
11700 SBdC 92316 645-F3
CRILLY LN
31400 YCPA 92399 649-A4
CRIMSON CT
28800 HIGH 92346 578-B5
CRIMSON DR
7300 HIGH 92346 578-C6
CRIPPEN AV
7200 SBdC 92301 (4203-H5
See Page 4112)
7600 SBdC 92301 4204-A5
8600 ADEL 92301 4204-C5
11300 ADEL 92301 4205-A5
CRISS AV
7700 FONT 92336 575-B7
8500 FONT 92335 605-B2
CRISTINA VILLA CT
7100 HIGH 92346 578-D5
CRISTY AV
4200 SBDO 92407 545-J6
CROCE DR
9000 FONT 92335 605-D3
CROCKER CT
13400 FONT 92336 574-A7
13400 FONT 92336 604-A1
CROCKETT AV
6900 HESP 92345 4566-F5
CROCKETT CT
13700 FONT 92336 574-A6
CROCUS CT
7000 RCUC 91739 573-G6
CROCUS DR
39700 BBLK - 4811-C2
CROFT LN
40600 BBLK - 4811-E2
W CROFTON CT
1300 UPL 91786 601-J2
CROFTON LN
14700 SBdC - (3935-H5
See Page 3934)
CROFTON ST
15100 SBdC - (4025-J4
See Page 3934)
15100 SBdC - (4026-A4
See Page 3936)
CROLL CT
22200 DBAR 91765 680-A4
CROMARTY DR
24100 DBAR 91765 640-D7
CROMDALE ST
9700 SBdC 92345 4564-F5
11700 SBdC 92345 4565-B5
14100 HESP 92345 4565-J5
14500 HESP 92345 4566-A5
CROMWELL CT
- RCUC 91739 573-F5
CROMWELL ST
- RLTO 92376 575-F4
1100 POM 91768 640-D1
19300 SBdC 92376 575-F4
E CROMWELL ST
300 RLTO 92376 575-H4
W CROMWELL ST
200 RLTO 92376 575-G4
CRONESE CT
19900 APLV 92308 4387-D3
CRONESE LN
18900 APLV 92308 4387-B2
19900 APLV 92307 4387-D2
CRONESE RD
13400 APLV 92308 4387-D3
13600 APLV 92307 4387-D1
14200 APLV 92307 4297-D7
CRONESE WY
13800 APLV 92307 4387-D2
CRONESE LAKE RD
57500 SBdC - 350-B4
CROOKED ARROW DR
500 DBAR 91765 640-C7
CROOKED CREEK CT
- CHLS 91709 711-E1
CROOKED CREEK DR
5500 RCUC 91737 572-J2
CROOKS AV
- SBdC 92311 3680-B1
100 BARS 92311 3679-G2
CROSS DR
400 SBdC - 517-B2
CROSS ST
1300 SBDO 92404 577-B4
25500 SBdC 92404 577-C4
CROSSING TR
14500 VCTV 92394 4295-G7

CROSS KEYS DR
10900 RCUC 91737 573-C3
CROSSOVER RD
- SBdC 92285 370-B9
E CROSSROADS DR
1500 CLTN 92324 606-G6
N CROSSROADS DR
300 CLTN 92324 606-F6
CROW CT
6700 SBdC - 4843-G3
CROW RD
13700 APLV 92307 4387-D1
14200 APLV 92307 4297-D7
CROW ST
800 CALI 92320 649-E7
32500 YCPA 92373 649-D7
CROW FOOT LN
2500 DBAR 91765 680-C5
CROWLEY ST
17700 ADEL 92301 4204-G7
CROWN DR
700 SBdC - 4737-G7
5900 RivC 91752 683-G5
CROWN ST
1200 RDL 92373 648-B4
CROWN WY
700 SBdC - 4737-G7
CROWN & PICKLE RD
4800 SBdC 92285 (4577-C7
See Page 4486)
CROWNE HEIGHTS DR
26100 LMLN 92354 647-E3
CROWN POINT DR
600 DBAR 91765 680-B1
CROWN ROYAL PL
- SBdC - 4741-E6
CROWN VALLEY CT
17600 APLV 92307 4296-G3
CROWN VALLEY DR
16100 APLV 92307 4296-G3
CROYDON ST
26200 SBdC 92346 577-E3
E CROYDON ST
3900 SBdC 92346 577-J3
3900 SBDO 92346 577-J3
CRUCERO RD
30000 SBdC - 350-D9
CRUCERO RD U.S.-66 Hist
25900 SBdC - 370-D1
CRUDUP RD
3700 SBdC 92371 4292-J7
3700 SBdC 92371 (4293-C7
See Page 4292)
CRUZ DR
8700 SBdC 92301 4204-C4
8800 ADEL 92301 4204-C4
CRYSTAL AV
11700 CHNO 91710 641-F4
CRYSTAL CIR
2500 RivC 92509 645-A5
CRYSTAL CT
400 BBLK - 4811-J1
13300 VCTV 92392 4385-F6
CRYSTAL DR
1600 SBdC - (4743-A3
See Page 4662)
6100 RCUC 91701 572-G3
CRYSTAL LN
- SBdC - 4120-C1
5700 SBdC - 4570-H7
5700 SBdC - 4660-H1
CRYSTAL PL
2100 POM 91767 601-C5
CRYSTAL ST
35100 YCPA 92399 610-A4
CRYSTAL AIRE RD
- SBdC - 4562-A5
9300 SBdC 92372 4472-A4
9300 SBdC 92372 4562-A1
CRYSTAL CREEK RD
4900 SBdC - (4661-B2
See Page 4660)
5400 SBdC - (4571-A5
See Page 4570)
8200 SBdC - 4481-A7
CRYSTAL CREEK HELIPORT RD
35100 SBdC - 4950-A4
CRYSTAL LAKE CT
3200 ONT 91761 643-B5
CRYSTAL LAKE RD
100 BBLK - 4742-A7
100 BBLK - 4812-A1
E CRYSTAL LAKE RD
3100 ONT 91761 643-A5
N CRYSTAL MOUNTAIN RD
1100 SBdC 92314 4742-B5
S CRYSTAL SPRINGS PL
2600 ONT 91761 643-B5
C T ACCESS RD
5300 SBdC - 328-H5
CUARTO ST
38300 SBdC - 4482-F3
CUBERO RD
56500 SBdC 92285 4747-G3
CUCAMONGA AV
200 CLAR 91711 601-E4

CUCAMONGA AV
12900 ONT 91761 642-E7
12900 ONT 91761 682-E2
15700 SBdC 91710 682-E7
15700 SBdC 91710 712-E1
17200 SBdC 92880 712-E3
N CUCAMONGA AV
400 ONT 91764 602-E6
S CUCAMONGA AV
100 ONT 91761 642-E1
CUDDEBACK RD
2500 SBdC - 348-H2
10900 SBdC - 328-K11
CUERNAVACA PL
600 CLAR 91711 601-E2
N CUESTA LN
3500 SBDO 92405 576-F1
CULBERTSON LN
1600 SBdC - 4737-G4
CULEBRA RD
15300 VCTV 92394 4296-C5
CULLEY CT
14900 VCTV 92392 4296-E6
CULLEY ST
14900 VCTV 92392 4296-E6
CULMORE ST
3100 CLAR 91711 601-B2
CULPEPPER CT
9000 RCUC 91730 572-G7
CULPEPPER ST
9100 RCUC 91730 572-G7
N CULVER RD
15700 VCTV 92394 4296-B4
S CULVER RD
14900 VCTV 92394 4296-C6
CULVERT ST
1100 RDL 92373 648-D2
CUMBERLAND CT
- RCUC 91739 573-F6
CUMBERLAND DR
100 SBdC - 518-C1
CUMBERLAND LN
11300 SBdC 91766 641-C3
26500 SBdC - (3935-H5
See Page 3934)
CUMBERLAND PL
- FONT 92336 573-J7
700 CLAR 91711 601-D5
E CUMBERLAND ST
400 UPL 91786 572-C7
W CUMBERLAND ST
800 UPL 91786 572-A7
CUMBERLAND WY
17800 SBdC 92392 4386-H4
CUMMINGS RD
17100 SBdC - (4210-H6
See Page 4120)
CUMMINGS ST
18100 FONT 92336 575-C6
CUMMINGS WY
62100 SBdC 92252 4889-C4
W CUMMINGS WY
1600 SBDO 92411 576-E4
CUNNINGHAM ST
7300 HIGH 92346 577-G7
CUPENO CT
- SBdC - 4774-G7
CUPID WY
9600 SBdC 92335 604-D6
W CURLY DR
300 SBdC 92314 4742-C4
CURRAN PL
500 POM 91766 640-F2
N CURRIER ST
500 POM 91768 640-G1
S CURRIER ST
600 POM 91766 640-G2
CURTIS AV
15500 FONT 92336 574-F3
CURTIS CT
800 POM 91766 641-B6
CURTIS RD
4900 SBdC - 4886-J4
CURTIS ST
1600 SBDO 92354 607-D5
10300 LMLN 92354 607-D6
CURVATE DR
46100 SBdC - (4743-A3
See Page 4662)
CUSHENBURY RD
- SBdC - (4572-A6
See Page 4482)
34500 SBdC - (4571-G7
See Page 4570)
CUSTER AV
7700 SBdC - 4570-F2
8200 SBdC - 4480-F1
11100 SBdC - (4390-F7
See Page 4300)
CUSTER ST
10100 YCPA 92399 610-A5
11900 YCPA 92399 650-B2
CUSTODY CIR
- SBdC - 2971-G3
CUYAMA AV
39300 SBdC 92365 (3504-F5
See Page 3414)
CUYAMA CT
22500 APLV 92307 4298-B2

CUYAMA PL
22500 APLV 92307 4298-A2
CUYAMA RD
- SBdC 92365 3594-F6
22500 APLV 92307 4298-B2
23300 SBdC 92307 4298-D2
CUYAMA TR
- SBdC - 4843-E4
CUYAMA WY
16300 APLV 92307 4298-A2
CUYAMACA RD
13100 APLV 92308 4387-B3
13600 APLV 92307 4387-B1
CYAN CT
16400 CHLS 91709 711-G2
CYGNET RD
2600 SBdC 92371 4562-G3
4400 SBdC 92371 4563-B3
7300 SBdC 92371 4564-A3
CYMBIDIUM CT
6300 SBdC 92346 577-H3
CYNTHIA AV
- BARS 92311 3758-G3
CYNTHIA DR
18800 SBdC 92345 4567-B7
CYNTHIA ST
400 POM 91766 641-A5
N CYNTHIA ST
5800 SBDO 92407 546-A4
CYNTHIA CREST
300 RDL 92373 648-E3
CYPRESS AV
- SBdC 92277 4820-D7
6500 FONT 92336 574-H5
7800 FONT 92336 604-H2
8100 FONT 92335 604-H2
9900 SBdC 92335 604-H6
10100 HESP 92345 4476-B3
10300 SBdC 92337 604-H7
10500 FONT 92337 604-H7
10500 FONT 92337 644-G3
10900 SBdC 92337 644-H2
11800 HESP 92345 4386-B7
12100 VCTV 92345 4386-B6
12100 VCTV 92392 4386-C3
12300 CHNO 91710 642-A6
13000 CHNO 91710 682-A2
16000 CHNO 91710 712-B1
59700 SBdC 92284 4888-F1
61700 SBdC 92252 4889-B1
65100 SBdC 92252 4820-A7
E CYPRESS AV
- RDL 92373 648-C1
600 RDL 92374 648-C1
800 RDL 92374 608-D7
N CYPRESS AV
100 SBdC 92324 606-B5
700 ONT 91762 602-A5
S CYPRESS AV
200 ONT 91762 642-A1
2200 CHNO 91710 642-A4
W CYPRESS AV
- RDL 92373 648-B2
1500 RDL 92373 647-J3
CYPRESS CIR
600 RDL 92373 648-C1
CYPRESS CT
9800 RCUC 91737 572-J4
CYPRESS DR
100 SBdC - 517-E1
600 RivC 91752 683-F4
800 SBdC 91784 572-B2
2900 SBdC 92256 616-B1
4200 SBdC 92407 546-E6
4200 SBDO 92407 546-E5
N CYPRESS DR
- CLTN 92324 606-A5
CYPRESS LN
- LACo 91768 640-B1
400 SBdC - 516-F3
600 SBdC 92314 (4743-A7
See Page 4662)
800 SBdC 92314 4813-A1
1900 SBdC 92285 4747-D1
3900 CHLS 91709 681-D6
57600 SBdC 92285 4667-H7
CYPRESS RD
200 SBdC 92252 4750-B6
500 SBdC - 4738-E6
17300 ADEL 92301 4294-H1
17700 ADEL 92301 4204-H7
CYPRESS ST
200 BARS 92311 3679-G5
12100 YCPA 92399 649-G3
14700 ADEL 92301 4294-H7
18500 ADEL 92301 4204-H5
25200 LMLN 92354 647-C2
26000 HIGH 92410 577-E6
26000 HIGH 92346 577-E6
N CYPRESS ST
100 POM 91768 640-H1
S CYPRESS ST
200 POM 91766 640-H2
CYPRESS GROVE LN
1600 DBAR 91765 680-A4
CYPRESS POINT DR
- CHLS 91709 711-F1
- UPL 91786 572-E7
S CYPRESS POINT DR
2800 ONT 91761 643-A6

S CYPRESS POINT PL
2600 ONT 91761 643-A6

D

D AV
- HESP 92345 4566-F1
D DR
61900 SBdC 92252 4889-C4
D LN
- SBdC - 518-B2
800 SBdC 92314 (4743-A7
See Page 4662)
800 SBdC 92314 4813-A1
D ST
- RivC 91752 644-A5
- SBdC - 4606-C2
100 NDLS 92363 3620-D6
4900 CHNO 91710 681-G1
9400 HESP 92345 4476-F6
12100 SBdC 93562 2144-G6
33500 SBdC - (3681-G3
See Page 3590)
34500 SBdC 92311 3679-F5
62200 SBdC 92252 4959-D4
D ST Rt#-18
- VCTV 92394 4296-E4
16300 VCTV 92392 4296-E4
D ST U.S.-66 Hist
- VCTV 92394 4296-E3
E D ST
- UPL 91786 602-C3
100 CLTN 92324 606-D5
100 ONT 91764 602-D7
N D ST
100 SBDO 92401 606-H1
400 SBDO 92401 576-G5
900 SBDO 92410 576-G5
1200 SBDO 92405 576-G2
3600 SBDO 92405 546-G7
4400 SBDO 92407 546-G5
S D ST
100 SBDO 92401 606-H2
1400 SBDO 92408 606-H5
W D ST
100 CLTN 92324 606-D5
100 ONT 91762 602-B7
100 ONT 91764 602-B7
900 ONT 91762 601-J7
DABORAH CT
- CHLS 91709 711-G2
DACHSHUND AV
19300 APLV 92307 4207-G2
19400 APLV 92307 (4117-G5
See Page 4116)
DADE DR
2600 SBdC - 519-B7
DADO CT
5600 SBdC - 4774-G7
DAFFODIL CIR
15000 FONT 92336 574-D7
DAFFODIL CT
6400 RivC 92880 683-D6
DAFFODIL LN
13300 YCPA 92399 650-B6
DAFFODIL RD
15500 ADEL 92301 4295-B5
DAFFODIL WY
13400 CHNO 91710 681-E1
DAGGER RD
- SBdC 92371 4563-A6
DAGGETT RD
35600 SBdC - (3681-F7
See Page 3590)
DAGGETT AIRPORT RD
- SBdC - 3762-G1
DAGGETT RIDGE CT
13300 VCTV 92394 4295-F4
DAGGETT RIDGE PL
13300 VCTV 92394 4295-F4
DAGGETT RIDGE RD
15900 VCTV 92394 4295-F4
15900 VCTV 92301 4295-F4
DAGGETT RIDGE WY
13300 VCTV 92394 4295-F4
DAGGETT-YERMO RD
33600 SBdC - (3681-E4
See Page 3590)
DAGNE AV
36700 SBdC 92311 3589-J7
DAHLER DR
9500 RCUC 91737 572-H1
DAHLGREN DR
13800 VCTV 92392 4386-D2
DAHLIA AV
1300 ONT 91762 641-J3
N DAHLIA AV
400 ONT 91762 601-J7
DAHLIA CT
6900 RCUC 91739 573-G5
N DAHLIA CT
1500 ONT 91762 601-J5
DAHLIA DR
- VCTV 92392 4385-G4
500 SBdC - 519-D2
14500 ADEL 92301 4295-A7
14500 ADEL 92301 4385-A1
DAHLIA RD
4400 CHNO 91710 681-E1

DAHLIA ST
5200 SBDO 92407 546-B5
12900 FONT 92337 643-H2
DAIRY RD
13000 YCPA 92399 650-E5
DAISY AV
1600 RDL 92374 648-G2
5300 TNP 92277 4891-J4
24700 LMLN 92354 647-B2
DAISY CIR
14900 FONT 92336 574-D7
DAISY CT
600 RDL 92374 608-F6
12200 RCUC 91739 573-G5
12800 YCPA 92399 649-E4
13600 CHNO 91710 681-E2
DAISY DR
3600 CHLS 91709 681-C4
N DAISY DR
3300 RLTO 92377 545-B7
3300 RLTO 92377 575-B1
DAISY LN
- BBLK - 4811-C2
500 SBdC 92372 4472-B4
2000 BARS 92311 3679-D4
3600 SBdC 92371 4472-J4
3700 SBdC 92371 4473-E3
13500 CHNO 91710 681-E1
65700 SBdC 92252 4750-B5
66500 SBdC 92277 4750-J4
68200 SBdC 92277 4751-A4
DAISY RD
2900 SBdC 92371 4292-G4
4700 SBdC - 4886-E3
5900 SBdC 92345 4654-J1
7400 SBdC 92345 4564-J1
8900 SBdC 92345 4474-H3
10900 SBdC 92392 4474-H2
11700 VCTV 92392 4474-H2
11800 VCTV 92392 4384-H5
14100 ADEL 92301 4384-H2
14700 ADEL 92301 4294-H2
15300 SBdC 92301 4294-H4
17700 ADEL 92301 4204-H7
DAISY ST
2200 UPL 91784 571-H4
DAKOTA AV
6100 RCUC 91737 573-B4
6700 RCUC 91701 573-B6
7000 SBdC - 4843-H4
DAKOTA CT
- HESP 92345 4566-C5
15100 VCTV 92394 4296-A6
DAKOTA LN
900 SBdC 92285 4747-H3
DAKOTA PL
12100 YCPA 92399 649-F3
DAKOTA RD
- SBdC 92365 (3683-A4
See Page 3592)
14700 APLV 92307 4297-G1
17000 APLV 92307 4207-G6
DAKOTA ST
15000 VCTV 92394 4296-A6
DAKOTA WY
- FONT 92336 574-D2
15100 VCTV 92394 4296-A6
DALE CT
13900 VCTV 92392 4385-H4
DALE LN
- APLV 92308 4388-C6
- SBdC - 518-D1
- RDL 92373 648-A1
1700 SBdC 92404 516-G6
DALE EVANS PKWY
14800 APLV 92307 4297-F1
17100 APLV 92307 4207-F3
19300 SBdC 92307 4207-F3
19500 SBdC 92307 (4117-E3
See Page 4116)
19500 APLV 92307 (4117-E3
See Page 4116)
21700 SBdC - (4117-E3
See Page 4116)
DALE VISTA RD
84500 SBdC 92277 (4825-F5
See Page 4824)
86100 SBdC 92277 370-K11
W DALEWOOD AV
100 RLTO 92377 575-F3
DALEY RD
- SBdC 92404 547-D3
- SBDO 92404 547-C6
3000 SBdC - 547-G2
3100 SBdC - 517-G7
DALEY CANYON RD
800 SBdC - 517-G3
E DALEY CANYON RD
2000 SBDO 92404 547-D6
DALEY ROAD TKTR
1700 SBDO 92404 547-C6
DALLAS AV
800 SBDO 92410 606-B3
7700 SBdC - (4572-D2
See Page 4482)
8100 SBdC - 4482-D2
10900 SBdC - (4392-D6
See Page 4302)
N DALLAS AV
100 SBDO 92410 606-B1

STREET	Block	City	ZIP	Pg-Grid
N DALLAS AV				
	400	SBDO	92410	576-A7
S DALLAS AV				
	100	SBDO	92410	606-B2
DALLEY WY				
	3900	RivC	92509	644-D7
DALSCOTE ST				
	7000	HESP	92345	4566-C5
DALTON CT				
	-	RDL	92373	647-J1
	700	UPL	91784	572-A4
	1100	POM	91767	601-C7
	15500	VCTV	92394	4295-H5
DALTON RD				
	-	SBdC	92365	(3683-D2 See Page 3592)
DALTON ST				
	6300	CHNO	91710	682-A2
DALY CT				
	19200	HESP	92345	4477-C5
DALY ST				
	-	TNP	92278	4751-J5
DAMASCUS ST				
	13300	YCPA	92399	649-J6
	35700	YCPA	92399	650-C6
DAMON DR				
	18300	HESP	92345	4567-A4
W DAMSON CT				
	400	ONT	91762	642-A4
DANA AV				
	6300	RivC	91752	683-G7
DANA CT				
	2300	CLAR	91711	571-D6
	13400	FONT	92336	574-A7
DANA DR				
	11600	ADEL	92301	4295-B5
DANA ST				
	700	RDL	92373	648-B2
	14500	ADEL	92301	4384-H1
	14600	ADEL	92301	4294-H7
DANBROOK PL				
	8300	UPL	91784	572-E5
DANBURY AV				
	6800	HESP	92345	4566-H2
	10500	SBdC	92316	605-D7
	18200	HESP	92345	4567-A2
	19100	SBdC	92345	4567-B2
DANBURY RD				
	900	SBdC	92372	4382-B6
	1600	CLAR	91711	601-B1
	1700	CLAR	91711	571-B7
	2900	SBdC	92371	4382-G6
	3900	SBdC	92371	4383-A6
	7500	SBdC	92371	4384-A6
DANBURY WY				
	-	CHLS	91709	681-H7
DANBY RD				
	-	SBdC	-	371-C2
	4900	SBdC	92277	(4894-E4 See Page 4824)
DANCOVE AV				
	8400	SBdC	92335	604-A2
DANCOVE CT				
	18600	SBdC	92301	(4202-D5 See Page 4112)
DANDELION CT				
	14900	FONT	92336	574-D7
DANDELION LN				
	15100	FONT	92336	574-E7
	17600	CHLS	91709	712-A5
DANDELION ST				
	12600	RivC	92880	683-D6
DANELAW AV				
	1300	RDL	92373	648-J6
DANESWOOD CT				
	900	SBdC	-	4741-J5
DANIEL DR				
	15500	VCTV	92394	4295-J5
DANIEL ST				
	26100	HIGH	92346	577-E6
DANIELLE WY				
	-	SBdC	92308	4477-E7
DANIELS RD				
	-	BARS	92311	3758-G3
DANIELS ST				
	-	CHNO	91710	681-H2
DANITO CT				
	4500	CHNO	91710	681-E1
DANITO ST				
	6000	CHNO	91710	681-J1
DANNER CT				
	7800	RCUC	91730	603-C1
DANNY ST				
	10000	MohC	-	3620-C2
DANSER CT				
	7700	FONT	92336	604-A1
DANTE RD				
	17800	APLV	92307	(4206-H7 See Page 4116)
DANTE ST				
	17100	VCTV	92394	(4206-F7 See Page 4116)
DANUBE WY				
	1900	UPL	91784	572-A4
DANVILLE CT				
	-	CHLS	91709	681-H7
DANVILLE DR				
	800	CLAR	91711	571-F7
DAPHNE DR				
	12500	RCUC	91739	573-G6
DAPISHU RD				
	5500	SBdC	-	4774-F7
DAPPLE CT				
	14000	VCTV	92394	4295-H6
DARANCETTE RD				
	6300	SBdC	92285	(4576-C3 See Page 4486)
DARBY AV				
	1400	POM	91767	601-D6
DARBY CT				
	6800	RCUC	91701	572-G5
W DARBY ST				
	1600	SBDO	92407	576-C2
	1800	SBdC	92407	576-B2
DARCENA ST				
	6500	CHNO	91710	682-A2
DARE CT				
	900	DBAR	91765	680-C2
DARFO CT				
	200	SBdC	-	517-A2
DARFO DR				
	100	SBdC	-	517-A2
DARGHTY RD				
	15100	SBdC	-	(4025-J1 See Page 3934)
	15100	SBdC	-	(4026-A1 See Page 3936)
DARK CANYON RD S				
	2800	CLTN	92324	646-J5
	2900	RivC	92324	646-J5
	12500	SBdC	92324	646-J5
DARLENE CT				
	800	UPL	91784	572-A4
	1200	RDL	92374	608-F5
DARLENE LN				
	6900	RivC	92509	645-B5
DARLENE ST				
	-	FONT	92336	574-E5
DARLINDA DR				
	58000	SBdC	92284	4818-A5
N DARLINGTON AV				
	1300	UPL	91786	602-D1
DARNELL AV				
	1200	UPL	91784	571-J5
N DARREN PL				
	3400	SBDO	92346	577-E1
DARRIN DR				
	24300	DBAR	91765	640-D7
DART CT				
	-	SBdC	-	517-A1
	-	SBdC	-	4737-A7
DART CANYON CT				
	-	SBdC	-	517-A1
	-	SBdC	-	4737-A7
DART CANYON RD				
	200	SBdC	-	517-A1
	600	SBdC	-	516-J1
	600	SBdC	-	4736-G6
	600	SBdC	-	4737-A7
DARTMOUTH AV				
	200	CLAR	91711	601-D4
	5900	RCUC	91737	573-A3
	7500	RCUC	91730	573-A7
	7800	RCUC	91730	603-A1
N DARTMOUTH AV				
	700	CLAR	91711	601-D2
DARTMOUTH CT				
	2000	BARS	92311	3679-G6
	11300	ADEL	92301	4385-A1
	12900	VCTV	92392	4385-E4
	13800	CHNO	91710	682-A2
	14100	FONT	92336	574-B7
DARTMOUTH LN				
	11300	SBdC	91766	641-D3
S DARTMOUTH RD				
	2300	SBDO	92408	606-H7
DARTMOUTH ST				
	-	HESP	92345	4475-H7
DARWIN AV				
	12500	GTER	92313	646-E5
	16900	HESP	92345	4476-G1
DARWIN RD				
	9100	SBdC	92371	4562-H1
	9100	SBdC	92371	4472-H7
DARWIN ST				
	17700	HESP	92345	4476-H2
DATE AV				
	300	BARS	92311	3680-A4
	5500	RCUC	91737	573-C2
	5700	SBdC	92377	575-F2
	7400	FONT	92336	574-H7
	34900	YCPA	92399	649-J2
	34900	YCPA	92399	650-A2
N DATE AV				
	100	RLTO	92376	605-H1
	500	RLTO	92376	575-H4
	2100	RLTO	92377	575-H3
S DATE AV				
	100	RLTO	92376	605-H2
	1900	RLTO	92316	605-H7
DATE CT				
	6100	SBdC	92404	577-D3
	7700	FONT	92336	574-H7
	7800	FONT	92336	604-H1
DATE PL				
	1600	SBDO	92404	577-C3
	25500	SBdC	92404	577-C3
DATE ST				
	7900	FONT	92336	604-H1
	8100	FONT	92335	604-H1
DATE ST				
	34700	YCPA	92399	649-J2
E DATE ST				
	1200	SBdC	92404	577-B3
	1200	SBDO	92404	577-C2
	2600	SBDO	92346	577-E3
	15400	SBdC	92346	577-E3
N DATE ST				
	500	POM	91768	640-G1
W DATE TREE RD				
	1900	CLTN	92324	605-J4
DATEWOOD LN				
	12400	VCTV	92392	4386-D6
DATURA AV				
	2500	SBdC	92277	4822-B3
	5700	TNP	92277	4892-C4
DATURA RD				
	10100	HESP	92345	4475-H4
DATURA TER				
	48100	SBdC	92285	(4575-C4 See Page 4484)
DAVENPORT CIR				
	700	CLAR	91711	601-F1
DAVENPORT CT				
	7000	RCUC	91701	573-D6
DAVENPORT LN				
	7200	SBdC	92252	4959-H2
DAVID AV				
	58900	YUCA	92284	4888-D7
DAVID WY				
	73500	TNP	92277	4892-E1
N DAVID WY				
	4000	SBDO	92404	547-A6
DAVIDSON				
	1800	NDLS	92363	3620-B4
N DAVIDSON AV				
	700	SBDO	92411	576-E5
	1200	SBDO	92405	576-E2
DAVIDSON CIR				
	13200	VCTV	92392	4385-F4
DAVIDSON CT				
	14600	SBdC	92335	604-C1
DAVIDSON LN				
	400	SBdC	-	516-E3
	500	POM	91768	640-G1
E DAVIDSON ST				
	1200	SBDO	92408	607-B5
	1600	RDL	92354	607-C5
	1600	SBDO	92354	607-C5
DA VINCI DR				
	16200	CHLS	91709	711-H1
DAVIS DR				
	900	SBdC	-	517-H3
DAVIS RD				
	48700	SBdC	92365	(3765-B4 See Page 3764)
DAVIS ST				
	4600	CHNO	91710	641-F6
DAVIS WY				
	25800	LMLN	92354	647-E2
DAVOS CT				
	200	SBdC	-	517-A2
DAVOS DR				
	200	SBdC	-	517-A2
E DAVOS DR				
	300	SBdC	92314	4742-G6
S DAWN DR				
	300	SBdC	92314	4742-C6
DAWN ST				
	10500	ADEL	92301	4294-H6
	10500	SBdC	92301	4294-H6
DAWNRIDGE DR				
	4300	SBdC	91739	544-A6
W DAWNVIEW DR				
	1900	RLTO	92377	575-A1
	2800	RLTO	92377	574-J1
S DAWSON				
	500	SBdC	92314	4742-G7
DAWSON WY				
	200	CLAR	91711	571-D6
DAWSON PEAK CT				
	-	RCUC	91737	573-E4
	-	RCUC	91739	573-E4
DAYBREAK CT				
	3000	CHLS	91709	681-B6
DAYBREAK LN				
	15300	FONT	92337	644-E3
DAYBREAK PL				
	7100	RCUC	91701	573-B6
DAYBREAK ST				
	1300	UPL	91784	571-H3
DAY CANYON DR				
	-	FONT	92336	573-J7
E DAY CREEK				
	3100	ONT	91761	643-A6
DAY CREEK BLVD				
	-	RCUC	91739	603-F1
	6500	RCUC	91739	573-F7
DAYLILLY ST				
	-	FONT	92337	645-B2
DAYLILY ST				
	1400	UPL	91784	571-H3
DAYTON AV				
	900	POM	91766	640-H5
	7300	HESP	92345	4566-F4
	25400	SBdC	92311	3678-H6
DAYTON DR				
	11600	RCUC	91730	603-E4
DAYTON RD				
	11500	SBdC	92301	4114-J5
DAYTON RD				
	11500	SBdC	92301	(4115-A5 See Page 4114)
DAYTON ST				
	17600	VCTV	92392	4386-G3
W DAYTON ST				
	100	UPL	91786	602-B1
D D RANGE RD				
	-	SBdC	-	(4025-H4 See Page 3934)
DEADMAN SALOON DR				
	24700	SBdC	92308	4388-G6
	24800	SBdC	92307	4388-G6
DEAKIN AV				
	2200	UPL	91784	571-H3
DEAN AV				
	13300	VCTV	92392	4386-E3
DEAN PL				
	13600	VCTV	92392	4386-F2
W DEANNA DR				
	2300	SBDO	92407	546-A4
DEANNA WY				
	1600	RDL	92374	608-D4
DE ANZA CIR				
	100	ONT	91761	642-C3
DE ANZA DR				
	10900	RCUC	91730	603-C1
W DE ANZA DR				
	1800	CLTN	92324	605-J5
DE ANZA RD				
	8900	ADEL	92301	4204-C4
	10900	SBdC	92392	4474-F2
	11900	SBdC	92392	4384-F7
DE ANZA ST				
	1400	BARS	92311	3680-A5
	1400	RDL	92374	608-C5
	27400	SBdC	92311	3679-D5
E DE ANZA ST				
	600	ONT	91761	642-D3
DEARBORN CIR				
	-	RDL	92374	608-F7
N DEARBORN CT				
	2100	ONT	91764	602-H7
DEARBORN ST				
	-	RDL	92374	608-F5
N DEARBORN ST				
	-	RDL	92374	608-F5
S DEARBORN ST				
	-	RDL	92374	608-F7
	-	RDL	92374	648-F1
DEATH VALLEY RD Rt#-127				
	56000	SBdC	-	2971-E4
E DEAUVILLE CT				
	1300	SBDO	92404	547-B6
DEAUVILLE DR				
	13700	VCTV	92392	4386-D2
	18100	SBdC	92392	4386-J5
DEBBIE LN				
	3200	RivC	92501	646-B6
DE BERRY ST				
	2100	SBdC	92301	(4202-D4 See Page 4112)
	21500	SBdC	92324	646-D4
	21700	GTER	92313	646-D4
E DE BERRY ST				
	300	CLTN	92324	646-C4
DEBORAH CT				
	-	UPL	91784	572-B4
	13500	YCPA	92399	650-C6
DEBORAH DR				
	300	POM	91767	601-A5
DEBORAH ST				
	800	UPL	91784	572-A4
	900	UPL	91784	571-J4
DEBORAH WY				
	2100	UPL	91784	572-B4
DEBRISPILE RD				
	11000	HESP	92392	4475-F4
	11000	VCTV	92392	4475-F4
W DE CARMEN DR				
	1800	CLTN	92324	605-J5
DECATUR CIR				
	900	CLAR	91711	571-F6
DECATUR WY				
	-	FONT	92336	573-J6
DECKER AV				
	400	SBdC	92277	4821-E1
	500	SBdC	92277	4751-E7
DECKER LN				
	300	POM	91766	641-A4
DECKER RD				
	-	SBdC	92345	4654-J4
	-	SBdC	92345	(4655-A4 See Page 4654)
	13800	VCTV	92392	4386-E2
DECLARATION DR				
	-	RCUC	91730	573-E7
DECLIFF DR				
	13700	SBdC	91739	(543-J7 See Page 513)
	13700	SBdC	91739	544-A7
DECORAH RD				
	23600	DBAR	91765	640-C6
DEEP CREEK CT				
	14600	CHLS	91709	680-H5
DEEP CREEK DR				
	2000	SBdC	-	519-A6
	12500	APLV	92308	4387-E5
DEEP CREEK RD				
	5700	SBdC	92308	(4657-C1 See Page 4656)
	5900	SBdC	92308	4567-D2
	8600	SBdC	92308	4477-E7
	10500	APLV	92308	4477-E3
	11500	APLV	92308	4387-E7
	29900	SBdC	-	4738-F6
DEEP CREEK CAMP RD				
	29400	SBdC	-	518-D1
DEEP HILL RD				
	400	DBAR	91765	640-A6
DEEPLAWN DR				
	1200	DBAR	91765	680-A3
DEEP SPRINGS DR				
	800	CLAR	91711	571-E4
DEEPSPRINGS DR				
	24400	DBAR	91765	640-E7
DEER LN				
	32800	SBdC	-	519-D6
	39900	BBLK	-	4811-C2
DEER TR				
	200	SBdC	92284	4747-E7
	700	SBdC	-	516-G4
	1300	SBdC	92284	4817-E3
	1600	SBdC	92285	4747-E1
	1700	SBdC	92285	4667-D1
	7300	YUCA	92284	4957-E2
DEER WY				
	1300	SBdC	-	4737-G5
DEERBROOK LN				
	14100	CHLS	91709	680-H3
DEER BROOK RD				
	35700	YCPA	92399	650-C1
DEERBROOK ST				
	9200	RCUC	91730	602-H4
DEER BRUSH CT				
	13200	VCTV	92392	4475-E1
DEER CANYON DR				
	10500	RCUC	91737	573-B1
DEER CANYON RD				
	43200	BBLK	-	4812-C3
DEER CREEK AV				
	11200	MTCL	91763	641-G3
DEER CREEK LN				
	5500	RCUC	91737	573-B2
DEER CREEK LP				
	-	ONT	91761	643-B6
DEER CREEK RD				
	-	POM	91766	640-H5
W DEER CREEK RD				
	1900	SBDO	92410	606-C2
DEERCREST DR				
	900	SBdC	92407	515-D5
DEER CROSSING DR				
	1500	DBAR	91765	680-C3
DEERFIELD CIR				
	1200	UPL	91784	571-J6
DEERFIELD CT				
	-	ONT	91761	642-C6
E DEERFIELD CT				
	1200	ONT	91761	642-E6
DEERFIELD DR				
	3000	CHLS	91709	681-B4
	10500	RCUC	91701	573-B6
DEERFIELD PL				
	1200	DBAR	91765	680-E3
	3000	CHLS	91709	681-B4
DEERFIELD ST				
	-	ONT	91761	642-C6
	5600	SBDO	92407	546-B5
	14700	VCTV	92394	4295-J2
	14900	VCTV	92394	4296-A2
E DEERFIELD ST				
	700	ONT	91761	642-D6
DEERFOOT DR				
	1400	DBAR	91765	680-A4
DEERHAVEN CT				
	600	UPL	91786	572-C7
DEER HAVEN DR				
	1900	CHLS	91709	680-H4
	8100	SBdC	92371	4562-H2
	9000	SBdC	92371	4472-H7
S DEER HORN DR				
	500	SBdC	92314	4742-D6
W DEER HORN DR				
	100	SBdC	92314	4742-D6
DEERHORN LN				
	900	SBdC	-	4737-J6
DEERHURST AV				
	5700	YUCA	92284	4887-H6
DEER LICK DR				
	32800	SBdC	-	519-D7
DEER LICK LN				
	31300	SBdC	-	518-J7
DEER PARK DR				
	42300	BBLK	-	4741-J7
DEER PARK LN				
	18100	SBdC	92392	4386-J5
DEERPATH CT				
	-	SBdC	-	4843-H2
DEERPATH PL				
	-	POM	91766	640-G7
DEERPATH RD				
	5900	SBdC	-	4843-H1
	6100	SBdC	-	4844-B2
DEERPATH WY				
	6600	SBdC	-	4843-J3
DEER RUN CT				
	-	BBLK	-	4812-B3
DEER RUN CT				
	5400	RCUC	91737	573-C2
DEER RUN RD				
	400	SBdC	-	516-C1
	400	SBdC	-	4736-C7
DEER SPRING LN				
	23500	DBAR	91765	680-C2
DEER SPRING RD				
	59800	SBdC	-	330-L10
DEER TRAIL CT				
	14100	VCTV	92392	4385-H5
DEER TRAIL DR				
	1600	RDL	92373	648-C5
	3200	CHLS	91709	681-B7
	14100	VCTV	92392	4385-H5
DEER TRAIL LN				
	900	SBdC	-	4741-C5
DEER VALLEY RD				
	-	YCPA	92399	610-C7
DEERWOOD PL				
	7200	HIGH	92346	578-C5
DEERWOOD RD				
	13300	APLV	92308	4388-C3
DE FEVER LN				
	900	SBdC	92285	4748-B3
DE FOREST CIR				
	3100	RivC	91752	643-H5
DE FRANCISCO RD				
	7600	SBdC	92308	4567-G3
DEL CT				
	8100	SBdC	92371	4564-F3
E DE LAMAR				
	1300	SBdC	92314	4742-G7
DELAMAR DR				
	600	BBLK	-	4811-C2
DELAMAR MOUNTAIN RD				
	1800	SBdC	-	(4740-H3 See Page 4660)
	32100	SBdC	-	(4661-C7 See Page 4660)
	32100	SBdC	-	4741-A2
DEL AMO DR				
	14300	VCTV	92392	4385-H5
DEL AMO WY				
	12400	VCTV	92392	4385-J6
DELANCEY CT				
	3200	CHLS	91709	681-C6
DELANEY CT				
	300	BBLK	-	4811-A1
DELANEY RD				
	2500	BARS	92311	3758-D1
	2500	SBdC	92311	3758-D6
DELANO ST				
	-	ADEL	92301	4295-A7
DELANO TR				
	57900	YUCA	92284	4958-B3
DELANY ST				
	1400	POM	91767	601-C7
DELAWARE AV				
	-	SBdC	92252	4819-G4
	4500	SBdC	92252	4889-G3
E DELAWARE AV				
	-	RDL	92374	608-B5
W DELAWARE AV				
	-	RDL	92374	608-B5
DELAWARE DR				
	600	CLAR	91711	601-C1
DELAWARE RD				
	13400	APLV	92308	4387-D3
	13600	APLV	92307	4387-D2
DELAWARE ST				
	11000	RCUC	91701	573-C5
DEL CAMRO DR				
	4900	SBdC	92301	(4113-B3 See Page 4112)
DELGADA AV				
	100	SBdC	92284	4747-G4
	1200	SBdC	92284	4817-F2
	1900	SBdC	92285	4667-G7
	1900	SBdC	92285	4747-G1
DEL GADO RD				
	12900	VCTV	92392	4385-J1
	12900	SBdC	92392	4385-J3
DELGIORGIO DR				
	1200	CLTN	92324	606-A5
DELHAVEN CT				
	1200	RDL	92374	648-E1
DEL HAVEN RD				
	-	SBdC	92311	3589-F7
	-	SBdC	92311	3679-F1
DELICIOUS ST				
	14100	ADEL	92301	4385-A2
	16300	ADEL	92301	4295-A1
	17300	ADEL	92301	4205-A4
DELL AV				
	800	SBdC	-	512-A5
	3900	RivC	92509	644-J7
DELLA AV				
	5200	RCUC	91701	572-E2
DELLA LN				
	11800	SBdC	92324	646-C3
DELLE DR				
	100	SBdC	-	517-A2
DEL MANO CT				
	18800	ADEL	92301	4204-J4
DEL MAR AV				
	300	BARS	92311	3680-B4
	8200	HESP	92345	4567-C1
	9000	MTCL	91763	601-H4
	9200	HESP	92345	4477-C6
DEL MAR AV				
	11400	SBdC	91710	641-D3
DEL MAR CIR				
	100	RivC	91752	683-E5
DEL MAR CT				
	7000	RCUC	91701	573-C6
DELMAR RD				
	13500	APLV	92308	4387-J2
DELMAR ST				
	58200	SBdC	92284	4818-C7
DEL MESA DR				
	19400	SBdC	92316	645-G3
E DELMONICA AV				
	1300	SBDO	92404	547-B6
DELMONICO RD				
	24000	SBdC	-	(4026-H4 See Page 3936)
DEL MONTE AV				
	6300	YUCA	92284	4888-C7
	7300	YUCA	92284	4958-D3
	15600	CHLS	91709	681-E7
DEL NORDE AV				
	1000	POM	91767	601-B5
DEL NORTE AV				
	15400	CHLS	91709	681-E7
N DEL NORTE AV				
	600	ONT	91764	602-E4
S DEL NORTE AV				
	2400	ONT	91761	642-F6
E DEL NORTE CIR				
	2700	SBDO	92346	577-F2
N DEL NORTE CT				
	1400	ONT	91764	602-E5
DEL NORTE DR				
	15100	VCTV	92392	4296-D6
	15100	VCTV	92394	4296-A6
E DEL NORTE DR				
	1500	SBDO	92404	577-C2
	2500	SBDO	92346	577-E2
N DEL NORTE DR				
	1100	SBdC	92404	577-B2
	1100	SBDO	92404	577-B2
DEL NORTE LN				
	700	SBdC	-	4737-F7
DEL NORTE PL				
	5500	RCUC	91739	573-G2
E DEL NORTE PL				
	2600	SBDO	92346	577-F2
S DEL NORTE PL				
	2400	ONT	91761	642-F5
DEL NORTE ST				
	13700	FONT	92336	574-A6
DEL OBISPO RD				
	15700	FONT	92337	644-F2
DEL ORO DR				
	8700	SBdC	92301	4204-C3
DEL ORO RD				
	-	SBdC	-	(4389-J7 See Page 4299)
	-	SBdC	-	(4390-A7 See Page 4300)
	-	SBdC	92307	(4389-G7 See Page 4299)
	800	SBdC	92252	4749-D7
	19500	APLV	92308	4477-D1
	21900	APLV	92308	4478-A1
	22800	SBdC	92308	4478-C1
	25200	SBdC	92308	4479-A1
	25500	SBdC	92308	(4389-C7 See Page 4299)
	65700	SBdC	92252	4750-C7
	66500	SBdC	92277	4750-E7
DEL PARQUE CT				
	16200	VCTV	92392	4296-D6
DELPHEY AV				
	12200	CHNO	91710	641-F6
DELPHIN PL				
	4900	RCUC	91737	572-G1
	4900	SBdC	91737	(542-G7 See Page 513)
	4900	SBdC	91737	572-G1
W DEL RANCHO CT				
	900	ONT	91762	642-A4
DEL RESTO DR				
	18500	SBdC	92392	4387-A4
DEL REY CT				
	15700	FONT	92335	604-F5
	16100	VCTV	92392	4296-D5
DEL REY DR				
	-	SBdC	-	4844-A4
	7000	SBdC	-	4843-F4
	15500	VCTV	92392	4296-D5
N DEL REY DR				
	1100	SBdC	92404	577-B1
	3100	SBDO	92404	577-B1
	3600	SBDO	92404	547-B7
DEL REY RD				
	900	SBdC	92252	4750-C7
	66500	SBdC	92277	4750-E7
DEL RIO PL				
	2000	ONT	91761	642-H4
N DEL RIO PL				
	1100	ONT	91764	602-H5
DEL RIO WY				
	6100	YUCA	92284	4888-A6
N DEL RIO WY				
	1300	ONT	91764	602-H5
DEL ROSA AV				
	300	HIGH	92410	607-C1
	300	SBDO	92410	607-C1
	4300	HIGH	92410	577-C6
	6700	SBdC	92404	577-C5
	6800	HIGH	92404	577-C5
	7200	SBDO	92410	577-C5
N DEL ROSA AV				
	1900	SBdC	92404	577-C2
	1900	SBDO	92404	577-C2
	3300	SBdC	92404	547-C7
	3500	SBDO	92404	547-C7
DEL ROSA DR				
	600	SBDO	92410	577-C7
	700	HIGH	92410	577-C5
	1100	HIGH	92404	577-C5
	6700	SBdC	92404	577-C5
	8800	ADEL	92301	4204-C3
	8800	SBdC	92301	4204-C3
N DEL ROSA DR				
	100	SBDO	92408	607-C1
S DEL ROSA DR				
	100	SBDO	92408	607-C2
	7800	HIGH	92410	577-C7
	7800	SBDO	92410	577-C7
	8000	HIGH	92410	607-C2
	8100	SBDO	92410	607-C2
DEL ROSA PL				
	600	POM	91768	640-F1
DEL ROSA RD				
	200	SBdC	92372	4472-A2
	2800	SBdC	92371	4472-F2
	3800	SBdC	92371	4473-A1
	7500	SBdC	92371	4474-A1
	8100	SBdC	92392	4474-C1
	10600	VCTV	92392	4474-H1
	11100	VCTV	92392	4475-A1
	11100	SBdC	92392	4475-A1
DELSA ST				
	-	SBdC	92301	(4202-C2 See Page 4112)
	3000	SBdC	92301	(4203-H1 See Page 4112)
DEL SOL				
	-	SBdC	92285	4748-D2
DEL SOL AV				
	2500	SBdC	92252	4819-B5
	5800	SBdC	-	4844-A2
	9900	SBdC	92371	4473-C6
DEL SOL CT				
	2600	CHLS	91709	681-A4
DEL SOL DR				
	5600	SBdC	92301	(4113-C4 See Page 4112)
DEL SOL LN				
	5500	SBdC	92284	4747-D6
N DEL SOL LN				
	200	DBAR	91765	640-D5
S DEL SOL LN				
	200	DBAR	91765	640-D6
DEL SOL RD				
	25700	SBdC	92308	4479-A3
DEL SUR DR				
	11500	RivC	91752	683-G5
DEL SUR ST				
	12500	VCTV	92392	4475-D2
DELTA AV				
	1900	SBdC	-	4742-H2
DELTA DR				
	24200	DBAR	91765	680-D3
W DELTA LN				
	800	SBDO	92410	606-F2
DELTA PL				
	800	CLAR	91711	601-B2
DEL VALE ST				
	100	YCPA	92399	610-A7
DEL VALLE AV				
	9600	SBdC	92371	4473-C6
DEL VALLE DR				
	1600	TNP	92278	4822-E1
DEL VISTA CT				
	11800	YCPA	92399	649-J2
DEMENSE RD				
	-	SBdC	92284	4818-G4
DEMENT ST				
	1600	SBdC	92407	515-D6
	1800	SBDO	92407	515-D6
DEMESNE RD				
	5100	SBdC	92284	4888-G4
	6900	SBdC	92252	4958-G1
DEMPSEY AV				
	9400	SBdC	92335	604-D5
DEMRON RD				
	11700	VCTV	92392	4385-E7
	11700	VCTV	92392	4475-E1
N DENAIR AV				
	1600	SBDO	92346	577-J3
	6300	SBdC	92346	577-J3
DENHAVEN CT				
	16400	CHLS	91709	711-E2
DENISE AV				
	800	RDL	92374	608-C5
DENISON RD				
	11500	SBdC	92308	4388-C7
	11500	SBdC	92308	4478-C1
	11600	APLV	92308	4388-C7
DENISON ST				
	1700	POM	91766	640-E3
DENNIS AV				
	61600	SBdC	92252	4889-B4
DENNIS DR				
	6000	RivC	91752	683-J5
DENNIS ST				
	19000	ADEL	92301	4204-F3
DENOVA RD				
	-	SBdC	92371	4563-H4
DEN-ROCK				
	-	SBdC	92301	(4113-J7 See Page 4112)
DENROCK DR				
	9400	SBdC	92308	4479-C5
DENSMAR RD				
	11000	SBdC	92345	4654-J2
	11000	SBdC	92345	(4655-A2 See Page 4654)
DENSMORE ST				
	900	POM	91767	601-C7
DENVER AV				
	1600	CLAR	91711	601-E1
	1700	CLAR	91711	571-E7
DENVER ST				
	4200	MTCL	91763	601-E6
DEODAR AV				
	7400	FONT	92336	575-B6
	17200	FONT	92335	605-A5
DEODAR CT				
	15700	FONT	92335	604-G5
DEODAR LN				
	3800	CHLS	91709	681-D7
	14600	HESP	92345	4475-J1
	14700	HESP	92345	4476-A1
DEODAR RD				
	2300	POM	91767	601-A4
DEODAR ST				
	5400	MTCL	91763	601-H5
	9500	RCUC	91737	572-H3
	12300	VCTV	92392	4475-C2
	16500	HESP	92345	4476-E1
	18200	HESP	92345	4477-A1
E DEODAR ST				
	100	ONT	91762	602-C4
	100	ONT	91764	602-C4
W DEODAR ST				
	1300	ONT	91762	601-H5
DE PAUL RD				
	300	CLAR	91711	601-C4
DEPOT RD				
	8700	SBdC	92335	604-C3
DERBY AV				
	13100	CHNO	91710	681-E1
DERBY CT				
	14300	VCTV	92392	4386-E1
DERBY PL				
	-	RCUC	91730	573-D7
DERBY WY				
	1800	UPL	91784	572-A5
DERFER DR				
	500	RCUC	91784	572-F6
DERRINGER LN				
	1500	DBAR	91765	680-D5
DERRINGER ST				
	-	SBdC	92371	4563-B6
DERWENT DR				
	46500	SBdC	92365	3594-E7
	47700	SBdC	92365	(3595-A7 See Page 3594)
DESCANSO AV				
	4100	CHLS	91709	681-E6
DESCANSO RD				
	11400	SBdC	92372	4472-A2
	13700	SBdC	92371	4382-A3
DESERET AV				
	900	BARS	92311	3679-H5
DESERT AV				
	-	TNP	92278	4822-F1
DESERT DR				
	-	TNP	92277	4891-D4
	1200	NDLS	92363	3710-D1
DESERT LN				
	11300	SBdC	92392	4474-F2
	11300	VCTV	92392	4475-B2
	32800	SBdC	-	(4210-H7 See Page 4120)
	33100	SBdC	-	(4211-A7 See Page 4120)
DESERT RD				
	13100	APLV	92308	4388-B3
N DESERT RD				
	-	SBdC	92347	3588-J6
DESERT ST				
	15000	ADEL	92301	4295-A7
DESERT VW				
	55200	SBdC	92285	4747-D3
DESERT ACRES RD				
	2900	SBdC	92252	4819-D6
DESERTAIR RD				
	61300	SBdC	92252	4889-A7
DESERT BLOOM WY				
	12700	VCTV	92392	4385-F5
DESERT CENTER RICE RD Rt#-62				
	-	SBdC	-	391-G2
DESERT CREEK CIR				
	12700	VCTV	92392	4386-F5
DESERT DAISY				
	51700	SBdC	92285	(4576-C4 See Page 4486)
DESERT DANDELION				
	4900	SBdC	92285	(4576-D7 See Page 4486)
DESERT DUNE ST				
	-	SBdC	92365	(3683-A3 See Page 3592)
DESERT DUNES DR				
	73700	TNP	92277	4892-E3
DESERT FLOWER AV				
	1100	SBdC	92277	4751-F7
	2800	SBdC	92277	4821-F1
	4300	SBdC	92277	4891-F1
	6500	TNP	92277	4891-G6
DESERT FLOWER RD				
	4500	SBdC	92301	(4113-B4 See Page 4112)
	8000	ADEL	92301	4114-A3
	8000	SBdC	92301	4114-H4
S DESERT FOREST AV				
	2600	ONT	91761	643-A6
DESERT FRONT RD				
	1700	SBdC	92372	4562-C3
	2100	SBdC	-	4562-D4
DESERT GOLD DR				
	8300	SBdC	92284	4957-B5
	55500	YUCA	92284	4957-E5
	57700	YUCA	92284	4958-A5
DESERT HEIGHTS DR				
	2800	SBdC	92277	4821-G5
DESERT KNOLL AV				
	-	SBdC	92308	4479-H4
	4700	TNP	92277	4892-F1
	7700	TNP	92277	4962-F2
DESERT KNOLL DR				
	14200	VCTV	92392	4386-D1
	14300	VCTV	92392	4296-D7
DESERT LILY ST				
	-	SBdC	92277	4820-E2
	62100	SBdC	92252	4819-C2
	65700	SBdC	92252	4820-C2
DESERT MESA				
	-	SBdC	-	(4025-H4 See Page 3934)
DESERT OAK CIR				
	15100	VCTV	92394	4296-A5
DESERT POPPY CT				
	-	APLV	92308	4387-C7
DESERT PRIMROSE				
	51700	SBdC	92285	(4576-C3 See Page 4486)
DESERT PRIMROSE LN				
	12600	VCTV	92392	4385-F5
DESERT QUAIL DR				
	6500	TNP	92277	4891-E7
DESERT QUEEN AV				
	3300	TNP	92277	4822-D6
	6300	TNP	92277	4892-E6
DESERT RANCH RD				
	12100	SBdC	92371	4383-B7
DESERT ROSE CT				
	10900	ADEL	92301	4384-J1
DESERT ROSE DR				
	11000	ADEL	92301	4384-J1
	13800	ADEL	92301	4294-J7
DESERT RUE DR				
	13500	VCTV	92392	4385-F5
DESERT SANDS RD				
	16500	VCTV	92392	4386-E1
DESERT SHADOW RD				
	2300	SBdC	92252	4819-F5
DESERT SHADOWS LN				
	14100	HESP	92345	4475-H5
DESERT SHADOWS RD				
	8300	SBdC	92252	4959-F5
DESERT SPRINGS DR				
	15500	VCTV	92394	4296-A5
DESERT STAR RD				
	-	SBdC	92308	4388-H7
	5300	SBdC	92285	(4576-C6 See Page 4486)
	9600	SBdC	92308	4478-H1
	12200	SBdC	92307	4388-H5
	14400	SBdC	92307	4298-H7
DESERT TRAIL DR				
	62100	SBdC	92252	4889-C5
	72300	TNP	92277	4892-B4
DESERT VIEW CT				
	5300	SBdC	92397	4652-E3
DESERT VIEW DR				
	5200	SBdC	92397	4652-E3
E DESERT VIEW DR				
	100	BARS	92311	3679-G4
W DESERT VIEW DR				
	100	BARS	92311	3679-G4
DESERT VIEW LN				
	-	SBdC	92397	4652-E4
DESERT VIEW RD				
	-	SBdC	92277	4891-B3
	2600	SBdC	92277	4821-A2
	6500	TNP	92277	4891-B3
	8300	SBdC	92372	4562-C1
	9300	SBdC	92372	4472-C1
	12100	SBdC	92372	4382-C5
	13700	SBdC	92371	4382-C3
	15300	SBdC	92371	4292-C6
	23700	SBdC	92308	4478-E3
	24500	SBdC	92308	4479-F2
	28500	SBdC	-	4479-J2
	28900	SBdC	-	4480-A2
	39000	SBdC	92365	(3504-E6 See Page 3414)
DESERT VILLA LN				
	-	BARS	92311	3680-B4

SAN BERNARDINO

STREET Block City ZIP Pg-Grid

EAGLE PASS RD
30800 SBdC - 351-L10
30800 SBdC - 352-A9
EAGLE PEAK PL
6400 RCUC 91737 573-D4
EAGLE POINT DR
- YCPA 92399 649-E3
EAGLE RANCH PKWY
12100 VCTV 92392 4385-D7
EAGLE RANCH RD
12600 VCTV 92392 4385-C5
EAGLE RIDGE DR
- BBLK - 4741-J6
- BBLK - 4742-A6
EAGLES NEST
42100 BBLK - 4741-H7
EAGLES NEST CT
300 SBdC - 4738-A7
EAGLESPUR RD
22700 DBAR 91765 640-A6
EAGLESTON LN
5600 SBdC 92371 4653-E1
EAGLE VIEW DR
41500 BBLK - 4741-G7
EAGLEWOOD DR
2300 CHLS 91709 680-J3
EARHART AV
6700 FONT 92336 574-E5
7300 HESP 92345 4566-F4
EARL CT
900 NDLS 92363 3620-B6
5000 RCUC 91701 572-G1
EARL RD
30500 SBdC 92365 3764-E7
EARLHAM DR
700 CLAR 91711 601-E1
EARLIMART ST
22100 APLV 92307 4207-J5
22100 APLV 92307 4208-A5
22500 SBdC 92307 4208-A5
EARLS RANCH RD
7300 SBdC 92371 4562-J5
EARLY SPRING RD
24300 SBdC - 329-C5
EARTH ST
6000 RivC 91752 683-H5
EASEMENT RD
34300 YCPA 92399 649-H3
EAST AV
5600 RCUC 91739 573-J3
7300 FONT 92336 573-J5
7700 RCUC 91739 603-J1
7700 FONT 92336 603-J1
EAST CT
900 SBDO 92410 577-B6
EAST DR
- SBdC 92256 616-A4
200 SBDO 92408 607-C2
2600 SBdC - 519-B7
10200 SBdC 92256 615-J4
EAST LN
800 SBdC 92314 4812-J1
16900 CHLS 91709 710-F3
EAST LNDG
40100 BBLK - 4811-D1
EAST PK
6000 CHLS 91709 712-A4
EAST RD
7000 YUCA 92284 4957-D2
EAST TR
- SBdC - 518-D1
15100 VCTV 92394 4295-H6
EAST WY
- ONT 91761 643-A1
EASTBURN LN
30700 SBdC 92374 648-H2
EAST CANYON CT
5300 SBdC 92397 4652-F4
EAST END AV
11300 SBdC 91710 641-C5
11300 SBdC 91766 641-C5
12100 CHNO 91710 641-C5
12900 SBdC 91710 681-C1
13300 CHNO 91710 681-C1
N EAST END AV
100 POM 91767 641-C1
600 POM 91767 601-C7
S EAST END AV
- POM 91767 641-C2
100 POM 91766 641-C2
1100 SBdC 91766 641-C2
EAST END RD
36900 SBdC - 4482-H1
39500 SBdC - (4483-C1 See Page 4482)
EASTER DR
5400 SBdC 92397 4652-F3
EASTERLY DR
6600 SBdC 92252 4889-B7
6700 SBdC 92252 4959-C1
EASTERLY PL
6600 SBdC 92252 4959-C1
N EAST FRONTAGE RD
- SBDO 92346 578-A3
EASTGATE AV
6700 UPL 91784 572-E5
EASTGATE DR
24400 DBAR 91765 680-E2
EASTGATE RD
100 BARS 92311 3680-A3

EASTGATE WY
13600 VCTV 92392 4385-G6
EASTLINE RD
2600 SBdC - 4816-E6
EASTON ST
700 RLTO 92376 575-E4
700 SBdC 92376 575-F4
E EASTON ST
100 RLTO 92376 575-H4
W EASTON ST
100 RLTO 92376 575-C4
EASTPARK
200 RDL 92374 648-G1
EASTRIDGE CT
16100 CHLS 91709 710-G1
EASTRIDGE PL
5800 RCUC 91737 573-B2
EASTVIEW AV
900 UPL 91784 572-D6
EAST VIEW DR
6100 CHLS 91709 712-A4
EASTVIEW DR
26000 HIGH 92404 577-E5
EAST VIEW TR
36700 YCPA 92399 650-E5
EASTWIND AV
15500 FONT 92336 574-F5
EASTWOOD AV
5100 RCUC 91737 572-G1
6600 RCUC 91701 572-H5
7600 RCUC 91730 572-H7
7700 RCUC 91730 602-H1
EASTWOOD LNDG
41200 BBLK - 4811-G1
EASTWOOD RD
41300 BBLK - 4811-G1
EASTWOOD ST
800 RDL 92374 648-E1
EASY DR
31300 SBdC - 518-J7
EASY ST
1400 NDLS 92363 3710-C2
5700 SBdC 92277 (4894-A3 See Page 4824)
6700 TNP 92277 4891-G6
8500 SBdC 92371 4562-H2
12700 CHNO 91710 641-E7
22500 SBdC 92308 4478-B2
31300 SBdC - 518-J6
EATON CT
4800 SBdC 91710 641-F3
W EATON CT
100 SBDO 92408 646-H1
EATON LN
12500 VCTV 92392 4385-E6
EATON ST
25400 SBdC 92311 3678-H6
EBONY LN
- CHLS 91709 711-H3
EBONY PL
14800 SBdC 92335 604-D4
E EBONY ST
3800 ONT 91761 603-C7
E ECHO CT
300 SBDO 92404 546-J7
E ECHO DR
1300 SBdC 92404 547-B7
1300 SBDO 92404 547-B7
ECHO LN
- BBLK - 4811-B1
14600 SBdC - (3935-H2 See Page 3934)
ECHO RD
26500 SBdC 92307 (4389-D7 See Page 4299)
ECHO HILL RD
- BBLK - 4742-A7
ECLIPSE AV
4900 RivC 91752 683-H3
13100 VCTV 92392 4385-H4
ECLIPSE CT
1000 ONT 91762 641-J3
1000 ONT 91762 642-A3
ECLIPSE ST
- UPL 91784 572-E5
ECLIPSE WY
- UPL 91784 572-E5
EDAM ST
6500 CHNO 91710 682-B2
EDDIE ALBERT
84300 SBdC 92277 (4825-E5 See Page 4824)
E EDDINGTON ST
900 UPL 91786 602-D1
EDDRIDGE DR
22500 DBAR 91765 680-A3
EDDY AV
7400 RivC 92509 644-H7
EDDY CT
1600 RDL 92374 608-D4
EDELWEISS DR
1200 BBLK - 4812-A1
1200 SBdC - 4812-A1
24500 SBdC - 517-A2
EDELWEISS LN
14900 FONT 92336 574-D7
EDELWEISS ST
9500 RCUC 91730 602-J4
15100 FONT 92336 574-E7

EDEN CIR
600 CLAR 91711 571-E6
EDEN RD
6500 SBdC 92371 4563-G4
EDGEBROOK DR
- POM 91766 640-G6
EDGE CLIFF DR
1300 SBdC - 4737-G4
EDGEFAIR LN
100 RDL 92373 648-E5
N EDGEFIELD AV
1300 UPL 91786 602-D1
EDGEFIELD ST
1300 UPL 91786 602-D1
EDGEHILL AV
3400 RivC 92509 645-A7
EDGEHILL CT
14200 FONT 92337 644-B3
EDGEHILL DR
1200 POM 91767 601-C6
N EDGEHILL DR
800 CLTN 92324 606-C5
EDGEHILL LN
1400 RDL 92373 648-A3
1500 RDL 92373 647-J4
EDGEHILL PL
- BBLK - 4742-A6
EDGEHILL RD
1400 SBDO 92405 576-D1
5500 SBdC 92345 (4655-A2 See Page 4654)
11000 SBdC 92345 4654-J2
E EDGEHILL RD
200 SBDO 92404 576-J1
W EDGEHILL RD
700 SBDO 92405 576-F1
EDGEMONT CT
3100 SBDO 92405 576-D1
3200 SBdC 92404 577-D1
EDGEMONT DR
- RDL 92373 648-E5
500 RivC 91752 683-E4
1400 SBDO 92405 576-D2
1800 SBdC 92404 577-C1
26100 SBdC 92346 577-E1
E EDGEMONT DR
1100 SBdC 92404 577-B1
3200 SBDO 92404 576-J1
W EDGEMONT DR
800 SBDO 92405 576-E1
EDGEMOOR RD
200 BBLK - 4811-C1
EDGERTON DR
200 SBDO 92405 546-G7
1500 SBdC - 4742-H2
EDGEWATER LN
26300 SBdC - (3935-H6 See Page 3934)
EDGEWOOD CT
10700 RCUC 91730 573-C7
N EDGEWOOD LN
1100 UPL 91786 601-J1
EDINBORO AV
2100 CLAR 91711 571-E7
EDINBURG CT
1200 POM 91766 640-G3
EDINBURGH PL
7000 RCUC 91701 573-F5
EDISON AV
3800 CHNO 91710 681-E3
6100 CHNO 91710 682-A3
6900 CHNO 91762 682-A3
7100 ONT 91761 682-G3
7100 ONT 91762 682-A3
7100 ONT 91710 682-A3
7700 FONT 92336 574-C7
9700 ONT 91761 683-D2
9700 ONT 91710 683-A3
EDISON CT
10800 RCUC 91730 603-C3
EDISON LN
49700 SBdC 92256 615-H6
EDISON RD
- CHLS 91709 680-H2
EDISON ST
- BARS 92311 3680-G6
EDISON WY
31900 SBdC - 519-B7
EDMONTON DR
- FONT 92336 544-C7
- FONT 92336 574-C1
EDNA ST
800 SBdC 92397 4652-B1
EDNA WY
2300 UPL 91784 572-B3
EDWARD AV
5700 FONT 92336 574-G3
EDWARDS DR
10400 MTCL 91763 641-D1
EDWARDS ST
1200 RDL 92374 608-D5
EDWARD VIEW DR
28700 HIGH 92346 578-C4
EDWARDVILLE LN
- SBdC 92277 (4825-B3 See Page 4824)
EDWIN AV
500 POM 91767 601-A3
EDWIN ST
8300 RCUC 91730 602-F3

S EEL RIVER PL
2600 ONT 91761 643-C6
EFFEN ST
9500 RCUC 91730 602-J1
10000 RCUC 91730 603-A1
11900 RCUC 91739 603-F1
EGAN RD
12500 SBdC - (4390-A4 See Page 4300)
EGERT RD
1300 SBdC 92301 (4202-B1 See Page 4112)
EGGLESTONE PL
- RCUC 91739 573-J5
EGRET ST
6800 CHNO 91710 642-B7
EIFFEL CIR
2100 UPL 91784 571-J4
EIGER CT
15900 CHLS 91709 710-F1
W EILEEN CT
1100 UPL 91784 571-J6
EISENHOWER CT
6200 CHNO 91710 642-A6
EL AGUA DR
16900 FONT 92337 644-J2
16900 FONT 92337 645-A2
ELAINE AV
17100 FONT 92336 575-A7
ELAINE DR
15500 FONT 92336 574-F7
17200 FONT 92336 575-A7
ELAINE ST
600 POM 91767 601-A6
ELAINE WY
1800 UPL 91784 572-A5
13300 YCPA 92399 650-C6
EL ARCO
7500 RCUC 91730 572-F7
ELATA AV
- SBdC - 390-A3
- SBdC 92284 390-A3
- YUCA 92284 390-A3
4700 SBdC 92284 4887-J3
4700 YUCA 92284 4887-J3
7300 YUCA 92284 4957-J3
ELATA DR
14800 VCTV 92394 4295-J5
14800 VCTV 92394 4296-A5
ELBA DR
11700 RivC 91752 683-F3
ELBOW RD
11500 SBdC 92256 615-H7
ELBURN CT
- RCUC 91701 573-B6
EL CAJON AV
10300 ADEL 92301 4204-G3
EL CAJON DR
7000 HESP 92345 4566-H5
60100 SBdC 92252 4958-G1
61400 SBdC 92252 4959-B1
EL CAJON LN
7000 HESP 92345 4566-H5
N EL CAMINO DR
3500 SBDO 92404 577-C1
3600 SBDO 92404 547-C7
EL CAMINO PL
11800 FONT 92337 644-B4
EL CAMINO RD
4900 SBdC 92277 (4825-G7 See Page 4824)
4900 SBdC 92277 (4895-G1 See Page 4824)
5700 TNP 92277 4891-G5
W EL CAMINO RD
800 SBDO 92405 576-F1
EL CAMINO WY
100 CLAR 91711 601-D4
EL CAPITAN CT
6100 RCUC 91737 573-D3
EL CARISO RD
14500 SBdC 92392 4385-J3
14700 SBdC 92392 4386-A3
14900 VCTV 92392 4386-A3
EL CENTRO CT
22600 APLV 92307 4298-B2
EL CENTRO RD
- SBdC 92371 4563-H4
8500 SBdC 92371 4564-C4
10100 SBdC 92345 4564-H4
10900 SBdC 92345 4565-A4
14500 HESP 92345 4565-J4
14500 HESP 92345 4566-A4
22500 APLV 92307 4298-B2
23200 SBdC 92307 4298-C1
38900 SBdC 92347 3586-A2
EL CENTRO ST
16200 HESP 92345 4566-E4
EL CERRITO AV
7400 HESP 92345 4566-J2
7400 HESP 92345 4567-A4
EL CIELO AV
5200 YUCA 92284 4888-A4
EL CIRCUITO
- CLAR 91711 571-F3
ELCONA DR
13600 VCTV 92392 4386-C3
ELCONA PL
15800 VCTV 92392 4386-C2

EL CONTENTO AV
13700 FONT 92337 644-A4
EL CORTEZ RD
57000 YUCA 92284 4887-H6
EL COYOTE AV
60900 SBdC 92252 4888-H3
EL COYOTE LN
60900 SBdC 92252 4888-J2
61000 SBdC 92252 4889-A2
ELDER DR
500 SBdC - 4738-E6
E ELDER DR
100 CLAR 91711 601-E4
N ELDER DR
300 SBdC 92314 4742-E5
ELDER RD
300 RDL 92373 648-G5
ELDER WY
500 RDL 92373 648-G5
ELDERBERRY AV
12200 CHNO 91710 641-J5
N ELDERBERRY AV
100 ONT 91762 601-J6
100 ONT 91762 641-J1
S ELDERBERRY AV
900 ONT 91762 641-J2
ELDERBERRY CT
6500 RCUC 91739 573-G4
N ELDERBERRY CT
1500 ONT 91762 601-J5
ELDER CREEK LN
28900 HIGH 92346 578-C5
ELDERWOOD DR
14400 FONT 92337 644-C3
EL DORADO AV
2500 SBdC 92284 4818-C7
3500 SBdC 92284 4888-C2
4900 YUCA 92284 4888-D7
11000 ADEL 92301 4294-J3
N EL DORADO AV
700 ONT 91764 602-E4
EL DORADO CT
- CHLS 91709 711-F1
- POM 91766 640-D4
ELDORADO CT
200 SBdC - 517-E1
EL DORADO CT
7300 RCUC 91730 573-C6
8300 YUCA 92284 4958-C5
12500 VCTV 92392 4385-D5
N EL DORADO CT
600 ONT 91764 602-E7
ELDORADO DR
200 SBdC - 517-E1
EL DORADO DR
14300 VCTV 92392 4386-C1
33300 SBdC - 4481-B3
55500 YUCA 92284 4957-E5
57700 YUCA 92284 4958-A5
EL DORADO PL
12500 VCTV 92392 4385-D5
EL DORADO RD
- SBdC - 4207-A1
- SBdC 92307 4207-C2
20900 APLV 92307 4207-F1
EL DORADO ST
7800 FONT 92336 604-B1
12100 ADEL 92301 4295-C2
34900 SBdC - 4481-F3
EL DORADO WY
12700 VCTV 92392 4385-D5
12700 VCTV 92394 4296-A7
12700 VCTV 92394 4386-A1
N ELEANOR ST
200 POM 91767 641-A1
800 POM 91767 601-A7
S ELEANOR ST
100 POM 91766 641-A2
ELECTRA DR
500 SBdC - 517-B3
17600 VCTV 92392 4386-G3
ELECTRA ST
100 POM 91766 641-C2
ELECTRIC AV
400 RivC 92507 646-B7
1400 SBdC 91784 571-H2
N ELECTRIC AV
200 SBDO 92407 546-H5
3800 SBDO 92405 546-H6
4000 SBdC 92407 546-H6
ELECTRIC WY
- RLTO 92376 605-F2
ELEGANCE DR
- RCUC 91739 573-H7
ELENA AV
- RivC 92507 646-F6
ELENA ST
6300 CHNO 91710 642-A7
EL ENCANTO LN
11900 YCPA 92399 649-J2
N EL ENCINO DR
200 DBAR 91765 640-C6
S EL ENCINO DR
200 DBAR 91765 640-C6
ELEPHANT MOUNTAIN RD
35700 SBdC - (3681-D1 See Page 3590)
ELEPHANT WALK RD
- SBdC 92277 4820-J1

ELEPHANT WALK RD
- SBdC 92277 4821-A1
EL ESTEBAN RD
10500 SBdC 92371 4473-A2
12000 SBdC 92371 4383-A7
13200 SBdC 92371 4382-J5
EL EVADO CT
14500 VCTV 92394 4295-J3
EL EVADO RD
- SBdC 92365 3764-E5
12500 VCTV 92392 4385-J1
12900 SBdC 92392 4385-J3
14400 VCTV 92394 4295-J3
14400 VCTV 92394 4385-J1
ELFEN AV
12100 SBdC - (4390-J5 See Page 4300)
ELFIN CT
30100 SBdC - 518-F7
EL FUEGO ST
11300 FONT 92337 644-J2
ELGER WY
9200 RCUC 91730 572-H7
W ELGIN CT
800 UPL 91784 572-A6
ELGIN RD
100 BBLK - 4811-C1
ELINORE ST
6800 RivC 92509 644-J6
6800 RivC 92509 645-A7
ELINVAR DR
16200 CHLS 91709 711-F2
ELISE DR
200 RDL 92374 608-A4
ELIWADI CT
- SBdC - 4774-G7
ELIZABETH CIR
1200 UPL 91786 601-G2
ELIZABETH CT
- SBdC 91784 572-B2
14200 FONT 92337 644-C4
W ELIZABETH LN
100 UPL 91786 602-B4
ELIZABETH RD
- BARS 92311 3678-G7
- SBdC 92311 3678-G7
ELIZABETH ST
200 BARS 92311 3679-H4
1000 BARS 92311 3680-A4
1300 RDL 92373 648-C3
ELIZABETH CREST DR
1400 RDL 92373 648-D3
ELK CT
8300 YUCA 92284 4957-E5
ELK RD
900 BBLK - 4812-C2
ELK TR
- YUCA 92284 390-A3
6500 TNP 92277 4891-G7
7300 YUCA 92284 4957-E3
EL KALO RD
21700 APLV 92307 4297-J6
21800 APLV 92307 4298-A6
E ELK CREEK DR
3700 ONT 91761 643-C6
ELKGROVE DR
500 RivC 91752 683-F4
E ELKHORN
1300 SBdC 92314 4742-G7
ELKHORN AV
16600 CHLS 91709 711-H2
ELKHORN DR
- FONT 92336 574-D5
75900 TNP 92277 4893-B1
ELKHORN RD
- APLV 92308 4387-B4
42100 SBdC 92365 (3763-D2 See Page 3762)
ELKHORN ST
40900 SBdC - (3763-A2 See Page 3762)
40900 SBdC 92365 (3763-A2 See Page 3762)
ELKO DR
2400 SBdC - 519-D7
ELKRIDGE DR
6400 SBdC 92345 4564-H7
6400 SBdC 92345 4654-H1
ELKS DR
2000 SBDO 92404 577-B4
ELKS LN
1100 BARS 92311 3678-J5
ELKS RAPID LN
1000 DBAR 91765 640-D5
ELKWOOD CIR
14700 CHLS 91709 681-B5
N ELLEN CIR
1800 CLTN 92324 606-B3
ELLEN PL
1100 POM 91766 641-B5
W ELLEN ST
800 CLTN 92324 606-B3
2300 SBDO 92324 606-B3
ELLENA E
11700 RCUC 91701 573-E6
11800 RCUC 91730 573-E6
ELLENA W
7200 RCUC 91701 573-D6
7300 RCUC 91730 573-D7

ELLIOT AV
13300 CHNO 91710 681-J1
ELLIOT RD
400 SBdC 92284 4747-E4
800 SBdC 92285 4747-E4
21900 SBdC - 516-D1
ELLIOTT CT
700 POM 91766 641-A3
EL LOBO RD
54200 SBdC 92285 (4576-J7 See Page 4486)
54200 SBdC 92285 (4577-C7 See Page 4486)
N ELLSWORTH WY
1500 SBDO 92411 576-C5
ELM AV
700 SBdC 92284 4747-H3
800 SBdC 92285 4747-H3
1800 SBDO 92354 607-D6
5300 SBdC 92404 547-D7
5300 SBdC 92404 577-D1
5300 SBDO 92404 547-D7
6800 HIGH 92404 577-D5
6900 TNP 92277 4892-H7
7600 FONT 92336 574-E7
8100 RCUC 91730 603-C1
8600 SBdC 92335 604-F5
10400 FONT 92337 604-F7
10400 SBdC 92337 604-F7
10500 FONT 92337 644-F1
10500 LMLN 92354 607-D7
10500 SBdC 92316 605-D7
10700 SBdC 92316 645-D1
N ELM AV
3700 SBDO 92404 547-D7
ELM CIR
100 NDLS 92363 3620-B6
E ELM CIR
300 SBDO 92410 576-J6
ELM CT
6500 SBdC 92404 577-D3
6500 CHNO 91710 682-A2
7500 FONT 92336 574-E7
34200 SBdC 92311 3678-H6
E ELM CT
400 RLTO 92376 605-H1
1900 ONT 91761 642-G3
ELM DR
- TNP 92278 4822-E1
200 SBdC - 516-E2
600 BARS 92311 3680-A3
6900 TNP 92277 4892-D7
18900 APLV 92308 4387-B7
S ELM DR
900 CLTN 92324 646-G1
ELM LN
- BARS 92311 3680-B5
- SBdC 92284 4887-B7
15400 CHLS 91709 681-D6
35100 YCPA 92399 650-A5
ELM RD
22100 SBdC 92347 (3587-J7 See Page 3586)
ELM ST
100 POM 91766 641-E3
500 BBLK - 4812-A2
1200 RDL 92373 648-D2
4400 SBdC 91710 641-E3
5600 SBdC 92397 4652-D2
6200 SBdC 92404 577-D3
6500 CHNO 91710 682-B2
7300 HIGH 92404 577-D6
7300 HIGH 92410 577-D6
7300 SBdC 92371 4563-J2
7300 SBdC 92371 4564-A2
9700 SBdC 92345 4564-F2
10600 LMLN 92354 607-D7
11300 SBdC 92345 4565-F1
11500 SBdC 92316 645-D3
12600 HESP 92345 4565-E1
13500 SBdC 93562 2055-A7
14900 HESP 92345 4566-A1
50500 SBdC 92256 616-A3
E ELM ST
600 ONT 91761 642-D3
S ELM ST
200 POM 91766 641-A2
W ELM ST
100 ONT 91761 642-B3
100 ONT 91762 642-A3
N ELM WY
600 UPL 91786 602-A2
E ELMA CT
1300 ONT 91764 602-F7
E ELMA ST
700 ONT 91764 602-D7
EL MANOR RD
7700 SBdC 92345 4565-D4
ELMCLIFF ST
7100 FONT 92336 574-F6
ELM CREST CT
12900 YCPA 92399 650-E5
ELMCROFT AV
1400 POM 91767 601-C7
ELMCROFT LN
12500 SBdC 92392 4386-J5
EL MEDIO RD
17700 SBdC 92301 (4203-A3 See Page 4112)

EL MEDIO RD
22600 SBdC 92301 (4113-A1 See Page 4112)
ELMER CT
1200 UPL 91786 602-D1
ELM HILL LN
14500 CHLS 91709 680-H4
ELMHURST AV
5800 RCUC 91737 573-A3
6700 RCUC 91701 573-A5
7700 RCUC 91730 603-A1
ELMHURST CIR
600 CLAR 91711 571-E7
700 CLAR 91711 601-F1
ELMHURST ST
16900 VCTV 92392 4386-F1
ELMHURST WY
1400 UPL 91784 571-H4
ELMIRA AV
3400 CLAR 91711 571-E5
EL MIRADOR
900 UPL 91784 572-A6
EL MIRAGE OH N
7600 SBdC 92301 (4203-H3 See Page 4112)
EL MIRAGE RD
300 SBdC 92301 368-G4
300 SBdC 92301 (4202-B3 See Page 4112)
4100 SBdC 92301 (4203-C3 See Page 4112)
7800 SBdC 92301 4204-A3
8800 ADEL 92301 4204-G3
11300 ADEL 92301 4205-A3
12100 ADEL 92394 4205-A3
EL MIRAGE AIRPORT RD
18400 SBdC 92301 (4202-F2 See Page 4112)
EL MIRAGE LAKE RD
1300 SBdC 92301 4112-B2
1700 SBdC 92301 (4113-A6 See Page 4112)
1700 SBdC 92301 (4203-E1 See Page 4112)
ELMO DR
25100 SBdC 92404 577-C5
EL MOLINO AV
4100 CHLS 91709 681-E6
EL MOLINO CT
16300 FONT 92335 604-H5
EL MOLINO LN
4700 CHLS 91709 681-F6
EL MOLINO PL
9800 FONT 92316 605-A5
EL MOLINO ST
9800 SBdC 92335 604-D5
15500 FONT 92335 604-F5
17300 FONT 92316 605-A5
18200 SBdC 92316 605-D5
W EL MOLINO ST
500 RLTO 92316 605-F5
EL MONTE
2000 NDLS 92363 3620-A7
EL MONTE RD
14900 SBdC - (4025-J2 See Page 3934)
E EL MORADO CT
100 ONT 91764 602-C6
W EL MORADO CT
500 ONT 91762 602-A7
800 ONT 91762 601-J7
EL MORADO ST
4300 MTCL 91763 601-E7
ELM TREE LN
12900 CHLS 91709 640-J7
15100 CHLS 91709 681-E6
N ELMWOOD AV
800 RLTO 92376 575-E6
ELMWOOD CIR
300 RivC 91752 683-F5
ELMWOOD CT
1700 RDL 92374 608-G7
7600 HIGH 92410 577-C6
ELMWOOD DR
- RCUC 91730 602-J5
15500 VCTV 92392 4386-B2
17700 SBdC 92392 4386-H4
27200 SBdC - 517-H2
ELM WOOD LN
14200 CHLS 91709 680-H3
ELMWOOD PL
7800 FONT 92336 574-G7
7800 FONT 92336 604-G1
W ELMWOOD PL
1100 SBdC 92314 4742-B7
ELMWOOD RD
2000 SBdC 92404 577-C1
2000 SBDO 92404 577-C4
5300 SBdC 92404 547-D7
6700 HIGH 92404 577-C5
7000 SBDO 92410 577-C5
7400 HIGH 92410 577-C6
N ELMWOOD RD
600 HIGH 92410 577-C6
600 SBDO 92410 577-C6
S ELMWOOD ST
800 CLTN 92324 606-H7
W ELMWOOD ST
1300 UPL 91786 601-J2

EL NOCHE
67500 SBdC 92277 4750-G7
ELODAM CT
2300 SBDO 92407 546-B5
ELOISE WY
1900 UPL 91784 572-A5
EL PASEO DR
9700 RCUC 91730 602-J1
33300 SBdC - 4481-B3
70500 TNP 92277 4891-C5
71800 TNP 92277 4892-H4
75300 TNP 92277 4893-A4
76800 SBdC 92277 4893-D4
78900 SBdC 92277 (4894-A4 See Page 4824)
EL PASEO RD
17700 SBdC 92301 (4203-C3 See Page 4112)
22300 SBdC 92301 (4113-C4 See Page 4112)
EL PASEO ST
5900 SBdC - 4843-H1
EL PORTAL AV
3200 SBdC 92277 4821-A6
EL PRADO CT
7400 YUCA 92284 4957-C3
EL PRADO DR
5500 SBdC 92301 (4113-C4 See Page 4112)
EL PRADO RD
15200 CHNO 91710 681-H6
15700 CHNO 91710 711-J1
16200 CHNO 91710 712-A1
EL PRADO TR
54700 YUCA 92284 4957-C3
EL PRIVELEGIO ST
18900 ADEL 92301 4204-D3
EL REPOSO
- SBdC 92252 4889-B4
EL REPOSO CIR
61800 SBdC 92252 4889-C7
EL REPOSO ST
5000 SBdC 92252 4889-C6
EL REY AV
- SBdC 92277 4820-E2
6200 TNP 92277 4892-B6
6800 SBdC 92277 4890-E7
EL RICO PL
24300 DBAR 91765 640-D7
EL RIO AV
5300 RivC 92509 645-F7
EL RIO RD
12900 VCTV 92392 4386-A4
EL RIVINO RD
18800 RivC 92509 645-F4
19400 SBdC 92316 645-F4
19400 SBdC 92509 645-F4
19500 RLTO 92509 645-F4
EL SERENA RD
- SBdC 92277 4751-C6
EL SERENE LN
200 CALI 92320 649-J7
EL SERENO AV
9700 ADEL 92301 4204-E3
10100 SBdC - 4481-B1
ELSINORE RD
800 SBdC 92372 4472-B7
2800 SBdC 92371 4472-G7
3600 SBdC 92371 4473-A7
7300 SBdC 92371 4474-A7
9700 SBdC 92345 4474-F7
11000 SBdC 92345 4475-A7
E ELSINORE WY
3300 ONT 91761 643-C5
EL SOL AV
6500 TNP 92277 4892-B7
EL VADO RD
200 DBAR 91765 640-C7
EL VALLE RD
21900 SBdC - 516-C1
EL VAQUERO RD
6600 SBdC - (4572-A5 See Page 4482)
EL VECINO PL
- POM 91766 640-E4
EL VISTA ST
- YCPA 92399 610-A7
ELWOOD AV
- FONT 92337 644-G2
7500 FONT 92336 574-G7
9100 FONT 92335 604-G4
9900 SBdC 92335 604-G6
ELWOOD CT
7700 FONT 92336 574-G7
7900 FONT 92336 604-G1
ELWOOD PL
61700 SBdC 92252 4959-B3
ELWOOD ST
6300 SBdC 92252 4889-B7
7400 SBdC 92252 4959-B3
ELYSIAN AV
1400 POM 91767 601-C7
E ELYSIAN BLVD
400 SBdC 92314 4742-E5
EMANUELLI CT
18100 FONT 92336 575-C6
EMBASSY PL
1000 POM 91767 601-C7
EMERALD
- BREA 92823 710-C6

EMERALD AV
300 RDL 92374 608-B5
6800 FONT 92336 574-J5
8200 FONT 92335 604-J2
8600 HIGH 92359 609-C3
9300 FONT 92335 605-A5
EMERALD CT
6700 FONT 92336 574-J7
9600 FONT 92335 605-A5
35300 YCPA 92399 650-B6
EMERALD DR
300 SBdC - 518-C1
300 SBdC - 4738-C7
11600 LMLN 92354 647-F2
78900 SBdC 92277 4893-J1
79800 SBdC 92277 (4894-B1 See Page 4824)
EMERALD RD
14100 SBdC 92392 4385-E2
14300 VCTV 92392 4385-E2
16900 ADEL 92301 4295-D1
17200 ADEL 92301 4205-D7
32100 SBdC - 4570-C1
32600 SBdC - (4571-A1 See Page 4570)
EMERALD RUN
11500 APLV 92308 4477-D2
EMERALD ST
400 BARS 92311 3679-G6
5600 RCUC 91701 572-F2
13000 HESP 92345 4475-F6
22100 GTER 92313 646-E5
63300 SBdC 92252 4889-F3
68300 TNP 92277 4890-J2
68300 TNP 92277 4891-A2
W EMERALD ST
600 UPL 91786 602-A4
EMERALD WY
300 SBdC - 518-C1
300 SBdC - 4738-C7
13300 CHLS 91709 681-B1
35300 YCPA 92399 650-B6
56900 SBdC 92285 4747-H2
EMERALD BAY CT
- YCPA 92399 649-H5
EMERALDSTONE DR
12300 VCTV 92392 4385-G6
EMERO RD
- HESP 92345 4565-E1
EMERSON AV
6900 YUCA 92284 4958-B1
EMERSON CT
4900 CHNO 91710 641-F6
EMERSON PL
900 CLAR 91711 571-B7
EMERSON RD
7100 SBdC 92345 4564-G5
11800 SBdC 92345 4565-C5
EMERSON ST
2200 SBdC 92407 546-A7
10700 SBdC 92345 4564-J5
10900 RCUC 91701 573-C5
12900 SBdC 92345 4565-E5
17100 VCTV 92394 (4206-F7 See Page 4116)
W EMERSON ST
100 UPL 91784 572-A3
1000 UPL 91784 571-J3
EMERY CT
1400 RDL 92373 648-J5
EMERY PL
7800 RCUC 91730 603-C1
EMIGRANT RD
36500 SBdC 92347 (3587-E7 See Page 3586)
36500 SBdC 92347 (3677-E1 See Page 3586)
EMILIA WY
1500 RDL 92374 608-F5
W EMILY CT
800 UPL 91786 572-A7
EMILY RD
- SBdC 92301 368-J2
- SBdC 92301 (4024-A1 See Page 3934)
EMILY ST
- FONT 92336 574-E5
1100 RDL 92374 608-E6
EMMA ST
3300 RivC 91752 644-A6
EMMERSON ST
25700 LMLN 92354 647-D3
S EMMET WY
1200 SBDO 92408 607-A4
EMMETT AV
8100 RCUC 91739 603-H2
EMMETT WY
- RCUC 91739 573-H7
W EMORY CT
800 UPL 91786 602-A1
EMORY DR
1600 CLAR 91711 601-B1
EMPIRE PL
12500 VCTV 92392 4475-D1
EMPIRE RD
1300 MohC - 3620-C3
EMPIRE CENTER BLVD N
10500 FONT 92337 605-A7
10500 FONT 92337 645-A1

STREET
Block City ZIP Pg-Grid

EMPIRE CENTER BLVD
S
- FONT 92337 645-A2
E EMPORIA ST
500 ONT 91761 642-C1
W EMPORIA ST
100 ONT 91762 642-B1
EMPRESS RD
500 POM 91768 640-B2
EMS AV
32000 HIGH 92359 609-B2
ENCANTADO RD
56100 SBdC 92285 4747-D1
ENCANTO CT
23900 SBdC 92324 646-J2
ENCANTO DR
12800 VCTV 92392 4385-H5
75300 SBdC 92277 4822-J4
75400 SBdC 92277 4823-A4
W ENCANTO DR
700 SBDO 92407 546-F7
ENCANTO LN
11600 SBdC 92324 646-J3
11600 CLTN 92324 646-J3
ENCELIA AV
2000 SBdC 92277 4821-J3
4800 TNP 92277 4891-J3
ENCELIA DR
57200 YUCA 92284 4957-J1
57400 YUCA 92284 4958-A1
ENCHANTED RD
- SBdC 92277 4820-E5
1700 SBdC 92252 4820-E3
ENCHANTED WY
30000 SBdC - 518-E7
30000 SBdC - 548-F1
ENCILIA TR
8900 SBdC 92256 616-B2
9100 SBdC 92256 4956-B7
ENCINA AV
7300 FONT 92336 575-A6
8600 FONT 92335 605-A2
9700 FONT 92316 605-A5
N ENCINA AV
100 RLTO 92376 605-J2
600 RLTO 92376 575-J4
S ENCINA AV
100 RLTO 92376 605-J2
ENCINA CT
- CHNO 91710 682-B3
ENCINA DR
32700 SBdC - 519-C7
ENCINA RD
7100 SBdC 92252 4959-B2
ENCINA ST
- CHNO 91710 682-A3
16100 VCTV 92392 4296-D4
ENCINA WY
31800 SBdC - 519-A7
ENCINITAS AV
7700 FONT 92336 575-A7
8600 FONT 92335 605-A2
ENCINITAS CT
7300 FONT 92336 575-A6
W ENCINO PL
2200 POM 91766 641-A5
ENCINO RD
20100 APLV 92308 4477-E1
42800 BBLK - 4812-B2
ENDICOTT DR
800 CLAR 91711 571-F7
ENDYMION WY
1500 RDL 92373 648-J5
ENEVA LN
8200 YUCA 92284 4957-D5
ENFIELD DR
15300 VCTV 92394 4295-H5
ENGLISH CT
- ADEL 92301 4295-A7
ENGLISH PL
14100 CHLS 91709 681-B4
ENGLISH RD
2500 CHLS 91709 680-J3
2500 CHLS 91709 681-A3
ENGMAN RD
500 SBdC 92372 4472-A6
ENIWETOK ST
1200 BARS 92311 3680-F6
E ENNIS ST
100 SBDO 92408 606-J4
ENOCH AV
33800 YCPA 92399 649-G5
ENRAMADA RD
15700 VCTV 92394 4295-J3
ENRICO ST
3800 CHNO 91710 681-D2
ENRIQUEZ DR
23800 DBAR 91765 640-C7
ENSOR LN
- CHLS 91709 711-H1
ENTERPRISE DR
- RLTO 92316 645-H3
- RLTO 92509 645-H3
1400 SBDO 92408 607-C1
10200 LMLN 92374 607-E6
ENTERPRISE PL
300 POM 91768 640-C3
ENTERPRISE ST
10300 RCUC 91730 603-B5

ENTERPRISE WY
- VCTV 92392 4386-F4
ENTOLA AV
- SBdC 92371 4653-E1
6900 SBdC 92371 4563-E7
ENTRADA DR
- BARS 92311 3680-C3
ENTRADA DEL PARQUE
- LMLN 92354 607-C7
- LMLN 92354 647-C1
ENTRY RD
14500 SBdC 92335 604-C4
EQUESTRIAN CT
5700 CHNO 91710 681-H1
14400 VCTV 92394 4295-G7
14400 VCTV 92394 4385-G1
EQUESTRIAN WY
14400 VCTV 92394 4295-G7
14400 VCTV 92394 4385-G1
EQUINE PL
5000 RCUC 91737 573-C1
ERIC DR
- SBdC 92365 (3593-G4
See Page 3592)
ERIC RD
32100 SBdC - 4570-J2
ERICA LN
11500 FONT 92337 644-F3
ERICKSEN DR
900 POM 91768 640-F1
ERIE RD
14100 APLV 92307 4387-F1
14200 APLV 92307 4297-H5
ERIE ST
100 POM 91768 640-F1
N ERIN AV
1300 UPL 91786 601-J1
1400 UPL 91786 571-J7
1600 UPL 91784 571-J4
ERIN DR
100 NDLS 92363 3620-B6
ERIN WY
- SBDO 92408 646-J1
ERLACH DR
100 SBdC - 517-B2
ERLON RD
3700 SBdC 92301 (4202-H5
See Page 4112)
ERLON ST
1300 SBdC 92301 (4202-B5
See Page 4112)
ERMER ST
3600 RivC 91752 644-A6
ERMINE DR
3400 CHLS 91709 681-C4
ERNESTINE RD
2500 SBdC 92285 4667-C3
4600 SBdC 92285 (4577-C7
See Page 4486)
ERVILLA ST
1100 POM 91767 601-A6
N ERWIN AV
2400 SBdC 92404 577-B3
ERWIN CT
21700 SBdC 92347 (3587-G5
See Page 3586)
ERWIN LN
2600 SBdC 92314 4813-A1
ERWIN ST
500 CALI 92320 649-H7
E ERWIN ST
300 RLTO 92376 605-H2
N ERWIN ST
3200 SBdC 92404 577-B1
3300 SBDO 92404 577-B1
ERWIN LAKE RD
2700 SBdC 92314 4813-A1
ERWIN RANCH RD
1900 SBdC 92314 4742-H7
1900 SBdC 92314 4812-H1
2200 SBdC 92314 (4743-A7
See Page 4662)
2800 SBdC - (4743-A7
See Page 4662)
2800 SBdC - 4813-C1
ESAW RD
36600 SBdC - (4301-J6
See Page 4300)
36600 SBdC - 4302-A6
ESAWS AV
21700 APLV 92307 4387-J1
22100 APLV 92307 4388-A1
23300 SBdC 92307 4388-D1
ESCALA DR
- VCTV 92392 4386-F5
6100 RivC 91752 683-G5
ESCALON DR
- FONT 92336 574-H2
ESCENA CT
13200 YCPA 92399 650-D6
ESCENA DR
36100 YCPA 92399 650-D6
ESCENA ST
- SBDO 92407 545-H3
36200 YCPA 92399 650-D6
N ESCENA ST
6300 SBDO 92407 545-J1
ESCHELMAN LN
16500 SBdC 92337 644-H2

ESCOBEDO AV
7800 HESP 92345 4567-B3
ESCONDIDO AV
6100 SBdC 92345 4565-F4
6100 SBdC 92345 (4655-F1
See Page 4654)
8100 HESP 92345 4565-F4
8900 HESP 92345 4475-F7
ESCONDIDO CT
12300 SBdC 92345 4565-F6
ESCONDIDO RD
100 RDL 92373 648-F5
ESCORZA LN
15900 VCTV 92394 4296-C4
ESPADA AV
9100 HESP 92345 4477-A6
ESPEJO LN
5000 SBdC 92301 (4113-B3
See Page 4112)
ESPERANZA
- SBdC 92252 4889-J6
ESPERANZA DR
3600 CHNO 91710 681-C2
W ESPERANZA DR
2800 RLTO 92377 544-J7
2800 RLTO 92377 545-A7
ESPERANZA ST
3700 CHNO 91710 681-C2
26200 LMLN 92354 647-F3
N ESPERANZA ST
200 SBDO 92408 606-H3
W ESPERANZA ST
200 CLTN 92324 606-D3
800 SBDO 92410 606-A3
2700 SBDO 92376 606-A3
ESPERAR AV
200 SBdC 92284 4747-G5
ESQUILIME DR
15700 CHLS 91709 680-F7
16000 CHLS 91709 710-F1
ESQUIMOUX DR
700 SBdC - 519-E3
ESSEX AV
1200 POM 91767 601-C7
11000 MTCL 91763 641-E2
11200 SBdC 91766 641-E3
11300 SBdC 91710 641-E3
ESSEX CT
- RDL 92373 607-G7
ESSEX PL
10600 RCUC 91730 573-B7
ESSEX RD
30400 SBdC - 351-B7
ESSEX ST
4200 MTCL 91763 641-D3
ESSEX WY
- FONT 92336 574-J2
ESTACIA CT
9600 RCUC 91730 602-J1
ESTACIA LN
11000 YCPA 92399 610-B7
ESTACIA RD
700 SBdC - (4743-B5
See Page 4662)
ESTACIA ST
9000 RCUC 91730 602-H1
10000 RCUC 91730 603-A1
ESTACIA WY
- YCPA 92399 610-B7
ESTANCIA WY
19100 APLV 92308 4387-B4
ESTATE WY
14100 VCTV 92394 4295-G6
ESTATES WY
5700 RCUC 91739 573-G2
ESTERA RD
55400 SBdC 92285 4747-D2
ESTERLY LN
40100 BBLK - 4811-D2
ESTERO RD
300 SBdC 92372 4382-A4
4900 SBdC 92371 4383-C4
7500 SBdC 92371 4384-A4
13700 SBdC 92392 4385-H3
13700 VCTV 92392 4385-E3
ESTHER ST
15400 CHLS 91709 681-F6
ESTHER WY
500 RDL 92373 648-B2
ESTORIL DR
22900 DBAR 91765 680-B3
ESTRADA AV
10100 SBdC - 4481-B1
ESTRELLA AV
6500 TNP 92277 4892-B7
10500 SBdC 92345 4479-B2
ESTRELLA DR
3900 SBdC 91710 641-D7
ESTRELLA LN
8900 SBdC 92308 4479-B2
ESTRELLITA CT
1300 UPL 91786 602-E1
ETHAN CT
- RCUC 91730 573-E7
ETHEL AV
36600 SBdC 92311 3590-A7
ETHEL ST
15400 CHLS 91709 681-F6
ETIWANDA AV
3000 RivC 91752 643-H7

ETIWANDA AV
4100 RivC 91752 683-H2
4800 SBdC 91739 573-H2
5200 SBdC 91739 (543-H7
See Page 513)
5200 RCUC 91739 573-H2
7700 RCUC 91739 603-H2
8800 SBdC 92335 603-H2
E ETIWANDA AV
100 RLTO 92376 575-H7
800 RLTO 92376 576-B7
800 SBDO 92376 576-B7
N ETIWANDA AV
100 ONT 91761 603-H6
200 ONT 91764 603-H6
500 ONT 91739 603-H6
9700 SBdC 92335 603-H6
10100 SBdC 92337 603-H6
10200 ONT 92337 603-H6
10200 FONT 92337 603-H6
S ETIWANDA AV
100 ONT 91761 603-H7
100 ONT 91761 643-H3
1500 FONT 92337 643-H3
1800 ONT 92337 643-H3
10500 FONT 92337 603-H7
W ETIWANDA AV
100 RLTO 92376 575-F7
2200 SBDO 92410 576-A7
2700 SBDO 92376 576-A7
ETO CAMINO RD
15300 VCTV 92394 4296-B4
ETON CT
6900 HESP 92345 4566-C5
ETON DR
- RCUC 91739 573-F5
22500 GTER 92313 646-F3
S ETON LN
400 SBdC 92314 4742-B7
EUCALYPTUS AV
- YCPA 92399 649-J1
1400 CHLS 91709 680-H6
2300 CHLS 91709 681-C4
3700 CHNO 91710 681-E4
6500 TNP 92277 4892-A7
6700 CHNO 91710 682-B4
7000 ONT 91710 682-F4
9700 ONT 91710 683-A4
10500 ONT 91761 683-C3
28100 HIGH 92346 578-A6
35300 YCPA 92399 650-A1
N EUCALYPTUS AV
100 RLTO 92376 605-J1
100 SBDO 92376 605-J1
200 CLTN 92324 605-J5
400 SBDO 92376 575-J6
500 RLTO 92376 575-J5
S EUCALYPTUS AV
- CLTN 92316 605-J7
100 CLTN 92324 605-J3
100 SBDO 92376 605-J3
100 RLTO 92376 605-J3
W EUCALYPTUS CT
1000 ONT 91762 641-H3
1000 ONT 91762 642-A3
EUCALYPTUS DR
200 RDL 92373 648-F4
1300 SBDO 92346 577-E3
5900 SBdC 92346 577-E2
7300 HIGH 92346 577-E6
EUCALYPTUS LN
- LACo 91768 640-A2
- POM 91768 640-A2
11300 SBdC 92399 611-B7
44300 SBdC - 4742-E7
EUCALYPTUS RD
500 SBdC - 4738-E7
EUCALYPTUS ST
- FONT 92337 645-A2
10900 RCUC 91730 603-C2
12500 VCTV 92392 4475-D2
14100 HESP 92345 4475-H2
14600 HESP 92345 4476-F1
18100 HESP 92345 4477-A1
W EUCALYPTUS ST
600 ONT 91762 642-A3
EUCLID AV
2400 SBdC 91784 572-A2
EUCLID AV Rt#-83
6500 CHLS 91709 712-B4
6500 CHLS 91710 712-B4
6500 CHNO 91710 712-B4
12900 CHNO 91762 642-C7
12900 CHNO 91762 682-C2
12900 ONT 91762 642-C7
12900 ONT 91762 682-C2
14000 CHNO 91710 682-C4
14000 ONT 91710 682-C2
15700 CHNO 91710 682-C7
15700 ONT 91710 682-C7
15700 SBdC 91710 712-B4
N EUCLID AV
1900 UPL 91784 572-B3
N EUCLID AV Rt#-83
- UPL 91786 602-B2
100 ONT 91762 602-B6
100 ONT 91762 642-C1
100 ONT 91764 602-B6
100 ONT 91764 642-C1
1400 UPL 91786 572-B7
1600 UPL 91784 572-B7

S EUCLID AV Rt#-83
- UPL 91786 602-B4
100 ONT 91762 642-C2
100 ONT 91761 642-C2
400 ONT 91762 602-B4
EUCLID CRES E
2400 SBdC 91784 572-B2
EUCLID CRES W
2500 SBdC 91784 572-A1
W EUCLID PL
- UPL 91786 602-B3
EUCLID ST
10700 ADEL 92301 4384-H1
EUGENE ST
- UPL 91786 602-B1
EUGENIA AV
7900 FONT 92336 604-F1
9100 SBdC 92335 604-F4
9800 FONT 92335 604-F6
EUGENIA DR
7300 FONT 92336 574-F6
EUREKA AV
34100 YCPA 92399 649-G4
35100 YCPA 92399 650-A4
S EUREKA AV
100 SBDO 92410 606-E2
EUREKA CT
- MTCL 91763 641-E1
700 RDL 92373 648-C2
EUREKA DR
100 BBLK - 4741-F7
S EUREKA DR
100 BBLK - 4741-G7
100 BBLK - 4811-G1
EUREKA RD
56100 SBdC 92284 4747-F5
EUREKA ST
1200 SBDO 92404 577-B1
1300 SBDO 92404 577-B1
17000 SBdC 92392 4386-F3
17000 VCTV 92392 4386-F3
33700 YCPA 92399 649-G4
N EUREKA ST
- RDL 92373 608-B6
200 RDL 92374 608-B6
S EUREKA ST
- RDL 92373 608-B7
- RDL 92373 648-C1
EUREKA WY
- UPL 91784 571-H5
N EVALINE CT
1000 RLTO 92376 576-A6
EVANS AV
1500 POM 91766 641-B4
EVANS DR
- SBdC - 519-E6
EVANS RD
35400 SBdC 92311 3678-J3
EVANS ST
10800 LMLN 92354 647-B1
E EVANS ST
300 SBDO 92404 576-J5
400 SBDO 92404 577-A5
W EVANS ST
500 SBDO 92405 576-G5
900 SBDO 92411 576-B5
EVART ST
4000 MTCL 91763 601-D7
EVE CIR
3600 RivC 91752 644-A6
N EVELYN CIR
1800 CLTN 92324 606-C3
EVENING ST
15000 ADEL 92301 4295-A6
EVENING CANYON WY
5200 RCUC 91737 572-J2
5200 RCUC 91737 573-A1
EVENING PRIMROSE PL
14000 CHLS 91709 681-B3
EVENING SONG PL
9600 RCUC 91730 602-J5
13300 CHLS 91709 681-B1
EVENING TERRACE DR
13700 CHLS 91709 680-J2
EVENING VIEW DR
2200 CHLS 91709 680-J3
EVEREST CT
900 CHLS 91709 680-F7
EVEREST DR
800 CHLS 91709 680-E7
EVEREST PL
7500 RCUC 91730 572-H7
EVEREST RD
26900 SBdC - 517-G1
EVERETT RD
3200 SBdC 92285 4667-C2
EVERGLADES CT
1200 BARS 92311 3680-A6
EVERGREEN AV
7300 FONT 92336 575-B6
8800 HESP 92345 4476-H6
17700 FONT 92335 605-B3
EVERGREEN CT
700 RDL 92374 648-E1
5500 CHNO 91710 641-H3
9000 FONT 92335 605-B3
EVERGREEN DR
500 RivC 91752 683-E4
600 SBdC - 4736-C7
1300 UPL 91784 571-H5

EVERGREEN DR
3400 ONT 91761 643-B6
10500 RCUC 91701 573-B6
41900 BBLK - 4811-H2
42200 BBLK - 4812-A2
EVERGREEN LN
1100 SBdC - 4737-G5
7600 SBdC 92336 575-B7
8500 SBdC 92335 605-B3
13800 SBdC 92392 4386-H2
27800 SBdC - (3935-H2
See Page 3934)
32700 SBdC - 519-D7
EVERGREEN RD
700 SBdC 92397 4652-B1
7500 SBdC 92372 4562-F1
9500 SBdC 92372 4472-E2
12000 SBdC 92372 4382-D3
W EVERGREEN ST
1100 RLTO 92377 575-E2
EVERLEE CT
3200 RivC 92509 645-A7
EVERRON CT
900 RDL 92374 648-E1
EVERS LN
57700 YUCA 92284 4958-B4
EVESHORN RD
24100 SBdC - (4026-A2
See Page 3936)
EXCEL CT
- UPL 91784 572-E5
EXCELSIOR DR
- SBdC 92365 (3683-H1
See Page 3592)
EXCELSIOR MINE RD
68100 SBdC - 330-H3
EXCHANGE PL
100 POM 91768 640-C3
EXCISE AV
- ONT 91761 643-B3
S EXCISE AV
2000 ONT 91761 643-B4
EXETER AV
9300 MTCL 91763 601-G5
EXETER CT
5700 RCUC 91701 572-E3
14100 FONT 92336 574-B7
EXETER ST
11200 LMLN 92354 647-C1
28900 SBdC 92311 3589-G7
29500 SBdC - (4390-B4
See Page 4300)
EXPLORER ST
100 POM 91768 640-C2
N EXPRESS CIR
1100 CLTN 92324 605-J5
1100 CLTN 92324 606-A4
EYE AV
8800 HESP 92345 4476-H3
11500 HESP 92345 4386-H7
EYE ST
100 NDLS 92363 3620-C5
100 ONT 91762 602-B6
100 ONT 91764 602-D6
500 SBDO 92411 576-F6
900 SBDO 92405 576-F2
1000 ONT 91762 601-J6
33700 SBdC 92311 3679-E7
33700 SBdC 92311 (3759-E1
See Page 3758)
EYEBOB RD
- SBdC 92252 4819-J4
EYOTA CT
20300 APLV 92308 4387-E3
EYOTA LN
20300 APLV 92308 4387-E3
EYOTA RD
- SBdC 92308 4388-D3
19700 APLV 92308 4387-E2
22300 APLV 92308 4388-A3
24300 SBdC 92307 4388-F2

F

F AV
9300 HESP 92345 4476-G6
F LN
800 SBdC 92314 4813-A1
F ST
- SBdC - (3681-G2
See Page 3590)
- SBdC 92252 4889-C2
- BARS 92311 3680-G6
100 NDLS 92363 3620-C6
1600 SBDO 92408 607-C1
4900 CHNO 91710 681-G1
12100 SBdC 93562 2144-G6
34500 SBdC 92311 3679-F5
84300 SBdC 93562 2055-B7
84300 SBdC 93562 2145-B1
E F ST
- UPL 91786 602-C2
100 CLTN 92324 606-D6
100 ONT 91764 602-C7
N F ST
100 SBDO 92410 606-G1
400 SBDO 92410 576-G6
400 SBDO 92401 576-G6
400 SBDO 92401 606-G1
1200 SBDO 92405 576-G1

N F ST
3600 SBDO 92405 546-G7
3900 SBDO 92407 546-G4
3900 SBdC 92407 546-F6
S F ST
- SBDO 92410 606-G2
W F ST
100 CLTN 92324 606-B5
100 ONT 91762 602-A7
900 ONT 91762 601-J7
900 SBdC 92324 606-B5
FABRIANO PL
6900 RCUC 91701 573-D6
FACIA WY
- YUCA 92284 4957-J6
FACTORY DR
500 POM 91768 640-C3
FACTORY OUTLET AV
- BARS 92311 (3759-B2
See Page 3758)
FAIRACRES LN
100 SBdC 92284 4748-H6
27800 SBdC - (3935-H2
See Page 3934)
FAIRBANKS DR
15300 VCTV 92394 4295-J5
FAIRBANKS PL
13500 CHNO 91710 681-J1
FAIRBURN DR
22600 GTER 92313 646-F3
FAIRBURN ST
16700 HESP 92345 4566-J3
18200 HESP 92345 4567-A3
FAIRCHILD AV
6800 FONT 92336 574-E5
FAIRFAX AL
- SBDO 92410 606-F3
FAIRFAX AV
16100 FONT 92336 574-G7
FAIRFAX CT
600 POM 91766 641-A4
17200 FONT 92336 575-A7
FAIRFAX DR
16500 FONT 92336 574-H7
N FAIRFAX DR
1300 SBdC 92404 577-B1
1700 SBDO 92404 577-B4
FAIRFAX LN
600 POM 91766 641-A4
600 HIGH 92410 577-B7
7500 SBDO 92410 577-B7
11300 SBdC 91766 641-D3
FAIRFAX RD
60900 SBdC 92252 4818-J7
61000 SBdC 92252 4819-A7
61000 SBdC 92252 4889-A1
FAIRFAX ST
16300 FONT 92336 574-H7
17000 FONT 92336 575-A7
17600 SBdC 92336 575-B7
FAIRFIELD AV
- APLV 92307 4207-D6
- SBdC 92307 4207-D2
19700 SBdC 92307 (4117-D7
See Page 4116)
FAIRFIELD CT
9600 RCUC 91737 572-D4
E FAIRFIELD CT
500 ONT 91761 642-C5
FAIRFIELD DR
100 CLAR 91711 571-D5
E FAIRFIELD ST
500 ONT 91761 642-D5
3000 ONT 91761 643-A5
FAIRFIELD WY
2300 UPL 91784 571-H3
FAIRFIELD RANCH RD
- CHLS 91709 711-H1
- CHLS 91709 681-G6
FAIRHAVEN DR
17100 VCTV 92392 4386-G1
FAIRHAVEN PL
7500 RCUC 91730 573-C7
FAIRLANE CIR
- RivC 91752 683-E5
FAIRLANE PL
2500 CHLS 91709 681-A1
FAIRLANE RD
6500 SBdC - (4571-J2
See Page 4570)
7800 SBdC - 4481-J1
10900 SBdC - (4391-J3
See Page 4300)
13300 SBdC - (4301-H3
See Page 4300)
15400 SBdC - (4211-H7
See Page 4120)
FAIRMONT AV
300 NDLS 92363 3620-C6
FAIRMONT DR
600 CLAR 91711 601-C1
1700 RDL 92373 648-E5
60100 SBdC 92252 4818-G5
60100 SBdC 92284 4818-G5
FAIRMONT ST
32500 YCPA 92399 649-D5
FAIRMONT WY
6500 RCUC 91701 573-D4
E FAIRMOUNT DR
400 SBDO 92404 546-J7

E FAIRMOUNT DR
500 SBDO 92404 547-A7
FAIR OAK CT
13100 VCTV 92392 4386-C4
FAIROAK TR
36100 YCPA 92399 650-E6
FAIRPLEX DR
500 POM 91768 640-E1
FAIRVIEW
4500 TNP 92277 4892-D1
FAIRVIEW AV
100 BARS 92311 3679-H4
16100 FONT 92336 574-G7
N FAIRVIEW AV
1000 CLTN 92324 606-E4
1400 SBDO 92410 606-E4
S FAIRVIEW AV
700 SBDO 92410 606-E3
FAIRVIEW CT
16000 FONT 92336 574-G7
17200 FONT 92336 575-A7
FAIRVIEW DR
- SBdC - 517-J2
15600 FONT 92336 574-F7
17600 FONT 92336 575-B7
17600 SBdC 92336 575-B7
33700 YCPA 92399 649-F4
W FAIRVIEW DR
1900 RLTO 92377 575-A1
2800 RLTO 92377 574-J1
FAIRVIEW LN
1300 SBdC 92359 609-C5
1300 RDL 92359 609-C5
FAIRVIEW RD
17300 FONT 92336 575-A7
32500 SBdC - 4480-J5
32700 SBdC - 4481-A5
35200 SBdC 92311 3678-A3
35200 SBdC 92347 3678-A3
36100 SBdC 92347 3588-A2
45000 SBdC 92365 3764-C3
47400 SBdC 92365 (3765-D2
See Page 3764)
FAIRVIEW MOUNTAIN CT
- VCTV 92394 4295-F5
FAIRVIEW MOUNTAIN WY
- VCTV 92394 4295-F5
FAIRVIEW VALLEY RD
12900 SBdC 92307 4388-F3
14100 SBdC 92307 4298-G7
16500 SBdC 92307 4299-A1
16800 SBdC 92307 (4209-A7
See Page 4118)
FAIRWAY AV
- APLV 92308 4387-C7
37900 SBdC - (3682-B1
See Page 3592)
FAIRWAY BLVD
4500 CHLS 91709 681-F6
E FAIRWAY BLVD
- SBdC 92314 4742-D5
W FAIRWAY BLVD
200 SBdC 92314 4742-B6
FAIRWAY CIR
1200 UPL 91784 571-J6
FAIRWAY DR
- YCPA 92399 649-E2
100 NDLS 92363 3620-E5
100 SBdC - 517-D1
500 RDL 92373 648-F4
1800 CHLS 91709 680-H7
1800 CHLS 91709 710-H1
7300 YUCA 92284 4957-B4
E FAIRWAY DR
800 CLTN 92324 606-F6
1600 CLTN 92408 606-F6
1600 SBDO 92408 606-F6
W FAIRWAY DR
500 SBDO 92408 606-H6
FAIRWAY LN
1900 HIGH 92346 578-B4
6600 SBDO 92346 578-B4
FAIRWAY RD
12400 SBdC 92392 4386-J5
FAIRWAY VIEW PL
- RCUC 91730 603-D4
FAIR WEATHER DR
13000 SBdC 91710 641-B7
FAIRWINDS CT
6700 RCUC 91701 573-D5
FAIRWOOD LN
7300 HIGH 92346 578-E5
N FAIRWOOD WY
400 UPL 91786 601-H3
1500 UPL 91786 571-H7
FAIRY AV
42900 BBLK - 4812-B3
FAITH DR
35100 YCPA 92399 650-A2
FAITH LN
200 BARS 92311 3679-H4
4900 YUCA 92284 4888-A4
FAITH ST
- FONT 92336 574-E5
FALCHION RD
17700 APLV 92307 (4206-H6
See Page 4116)
19400 APLV 92307 4207-C6

FALCON AV
6500 FONT 92336 574-E4
42500 BBLK - 4812-A2
FALCON CT
15800 FONT 92337 644-F3
29000 SBdC - 518-C2
E FALCON DR
1100 RLTO 92410 576-A6
FALCON LN
- RDL 92374 608-F6
33000 SBdC - 519-D7
FALCON PL
12900 CHNO 91710 642-A7
FALCON RD
- SBdC 92365 (3683-F5
See Page 3592)
29000 SBdC - 4479-J4
29100 SBdC - 4480-A4
FALCON TR
- VCTV 92392 4385-G4
FALCONBURN WY
22400 DBAR 91765 680-A4
FALCON RIDGE DR
- POM 91766 640-F5
13900 CHLS 91709 680-J3
FALCONS VIEW DR
23600 DBAR 91765 680-C6
FALCON VIEW ST
800 UPL 91784 572-C6
FALDERMAN AV
2500 SBdC 92277 4823-C3
4500 SBdC 92277 4893-C1
FALKIRK PL
7600 HIGH 92346 578-C6
FALLBROOK AV
1000 RDL 92373 648-A2
FALLBROOK CT
- HESP 92345 4475-J7
- HESP 92345 4565-J1
200 RDL 92373 648-A2
FALLBROOK LN
- POM 91766 640-F7
- POM 91766 641-A4
FALLEN LEAF DR
12600 VCTV 92392 4475-E2
FALLEN LEAF RD
- BBLK - 4742-A6
FALLEN OAK LN
15500 CHLS 91709 681-A7
FALLINGLEAF CIR
- POM 91766 640-G6
FALLING LEAF CT
9500 RCUC 91730 602-J5
FALLING LEAF DR
14400 CHLS 91709 680-J4
33300 SBdC - 519-E3
FALLING LEAF RD
13900 APLV 92307 4387-E1
FALLING SPRINGS RD
13300 YCPA 92399 650-G6
45700 SBdC - 4742-J2
FALLINGSTAR CT
11400 RCUC 91701 573-D5
FALLING STAR LN
1500 CHLS 91709 680-G2
FALLING TREE LN
5300 RCUC 91737 572-G2
6400 RCUC 91701 572-G4
FALL RIVER ST
14300 HESP 92345 4565-J2
FALLS AV
42900 BBLK - 4812-B3
FALLS RD
- SBdC - 512-D1
- SBdC - (4732-D7
See Page 4653)
9500 SBdC 92339 611-H3
FALLVIEW CT
- CHLS 91709 640-J7
FANO CT
6800 RCUC 91701 573-D5
FANSHAW AV
100 POM 91767 601-A2
FARADAY CT
5200 CHNO 91710 681-G3
FARBEN DR
600 DBAR 91765 680-C1
FARGO RD
78900 SBdC 92277 4893-J3
78900 SBdC 92277 (4894-A3
See Page 4824)
FARGO ST
10100 SBdC 92345 4564-G5
FARLEY MINE RD
25000 SBdC - (4119-A1
See Page 4118)
25000 SBdC 92307 4118-H1
25000 SBdC 92307 (4119-A1
See Page 4118)
FARMDALE AV
7000 HESP 92345 4566-G4
FARMINGTON CT
15100 HESP 92345 4566-B6
FARMINGTON ST
9700 SBdC 92345 4564-F6
10900 SBdC 92345 4565-A6
14100 HESP 92345 4565-G6
14500 HESP 92345 4566-E5
FARMINGTON WY
6700 HESP 92345 4566-B6

FARNAM PL
1600 POM 91766 641-A4
FARNDON AV
11400 SBdC 91710 641-D3
FARNDON PL
12400 CHNO 91710 641-D6
FARNEY AV
17900 SBdC 92336 575-C7
18000 FONT 92336 575-C7
FAR OAK AV
12300 SBdC 93562 2234-H4
FARRALON CT
14100 FONT 92336 604-B1
14200 FONT 92336 574-B7
FARRAR DR
12600 LMLN 92324 647-B5
FARRELL AV
1300 POM 91767 601-C7
FARRELO CT
57000 YUCA 92284 4887-H7
FARRELO RD
5900 YUCA 92284 4887-H6
FARRINGTON ST
12700 RCUC 91739 573-G6
FARRIS RANCH RD
- SBdC 92371 4653-F1
FARVIEW LN
1200 RDL 92374 648-F1
FARWELL ST
16100 FONT 92336 574-G5
17100 FONT 92336 575-A4
FASANO PL
- RCUC 91701 573-D6
FASCINATION AV
1000 SBdC 92252 4750-D7
1700 SBdC 92252 4820-D2
FATIMA RD
- SBdC 92301 (4113-B7
See Page 4112)
1300 SBdC 92301 (4202-B1
See Page 4112)
FAULHORN DR
24700 SBdC - 517-A4
FAUNA ST
4100 MTCL 91763 601-D7
FAVARA PL
7000 RCUC 91701 573-E6
FAWN CT
- FONT 92336 574-D3
1400 RDL 92373 648-D3
8800 SBdC 92371 4562-G2
E FAWN CT
3100 ONT 91761 643-A6
FAWN LN
900 SBdC - 4737-J6
W FAWN ST
1300 ONT 91762 601-H7
FAWN WY
11300 YCPA 92399 650-C1
FAWNGLEN CIR
14700 CHLS 91709 681-B5
FAWN LILY CT
16800 CHLS 91709 711-J2
FAWN PATH RD
2100 CHLS 91709 680-J4
FAWNSKIN DR
1000 SBdC - 4741-B5
FAWN TRAIL PL
- BBLK - 4742-A6
- BBLK 92314 4742-A6
FAYWOOD AV
11500 VCTV 92392 4475-E1
FEATHER WY
7400 SBdC - 4843-G5
FEATHER HOLLOW CT
1000 CHLS 91709 710-F2
N FEATHER MOUNTAIN DR
900 SBdC 92314 4742-B5
FEATHER ROCK RD
2200 DBAR 91765 680-B5
FEATHERWOOD DR
500 DBAR 91765 640-E6
FELDSPAR AV
4500 SBdC 92277 4823-C5
4500 SBdC 92277 4893-D1
6100 TNP 92277 4893-D5
FELDSPAR DR
10100 SBdC 92359 608-J5
15300 CHLS 91709 680-J6
15500 CHLS 91709 681-A7
FELDSPAR RD
- HESP 92345 4565-E1
FELDSTRASSE DR
300 BBLK - 4812-A1
FELICITA CT
1300 UPL 91786 602-E1
FELIPE AV
8900 MTCL 91763 601-E4
FELIPE DR
12400 VCTV 92392 4385-J6
FELIPE LN
10400 MTCL 91763 641-F1
FELIPE TR
5000 TNP 92277 4892-F2
FELISA CT
300 RDL 92373 648-F3
3200 RivC 92509 645-B7
FELIX CT
6300 CHNO 91710 642-A7

STREET
Block City ZIP Pg-Grid

FELLOWS PL
600 POM 91767 601-A6
FELSEN DR
24700 SBdC - 517-B4
FELSPAR ST
4200 RivC 92509 644-D7
FELTLOCK RD
- SBdC 92284 4748-H3
FELTON ST
18700 HESP 92345 4477-B7
FENMORE DR
400 BARS 92311 3679-J5
FENN CT
900 CLAR 91711 571-B7
FENNEL CT
11900 RCUC 91739 573-F7
FENNEL RD
7300 RCUC 91739 573-F7
7700 RCUC 91739 603-F1
FENOAK DR
400 BARS 92311 3679-J5
FENWAY DR
1000 SBdC - 4812-B1
FENWICK WY
28600 HIGH 92346 578-B6
FERMO PL
- RCUC 91701 573-E6
FERN AV
- ONT 91710 642-B7
- ONT 91762 642-B7
9400 SBdC 92335 604-D5
12900 CHNO 91710 642-B7
12900 CHNO 91762 642-B7
13100 CHNO 91710 682-B2
15700 CHNO 91710 712-B1
24900 LMLN 92354 647-C2
42900 BBLK - 4812-B3
E FERN AV
- RDL 92373 648-C1
N FERN AV
100 ONT 91762 602-B7
100 ONT 91762 642-B1
S FERN AV
100 ONT 91762 642-B1
100 UPL 91786 602-B4
2600 ONT 91710 642-B6
12300 CHNO 91762 642-B4
12500 CHNO 91710 642-B6
W FERN AV
- RDL 92373 648-A2
1300 RDL 92373 647-J3
FERN CT
800 SBdC - 516-G3
FERN DR
400 SBdC - 517-D2
700 SBdC - 516-G4
2600 SBdC - 519-E2
9400 SBdC 92339 611-G3
36200 SBdC 92311 3680-D1
FERN GN
24000 SBdC - 516-H1
FERN LN
100 SBdC - 518-D1
1900 SBdC 92314 4812-H2
23800 SBdC 92324 646-J4
23800 CLTN 92324 646-J4
39700 SBdC 92339 611-C2
FERN PL
300 DBAR 91765 640-D6
FERN RD
700 SBdC - 518-B3
3100 SBdC - (4210-J3 See Page 4120)
FERN ST
16900 FONT 92336 574-J5
17200 FONT 92336 575-A5
FERNANDEZ AV
18100 APLV 92307 4207-J3
N FERNANDO AV
1400 UPL 91786 572-D7
1400 UPL 91786 602-D1
S FERNANDO ST
900 CLTN 92324 646-D1
N FERNBROOK AV
1600 UPL 91784 572-C6
N FERNBROOK WY
1500 UPL 91786 572-C7
1600 UPL 91784 572-C6
FERN CANYON RD
21500 SBdC - 516-B1
FERNDALE AV
7300 FONT 92336 575-C6
8900 FONT 92335 605-C3
N FERNDALE AV
1300 SBDO 92404 547-B6
3400 SBDO 92404 577-B1
3500 SBdC 92404 547-B7
3500 SBdC 92404 577-B1
FERNDALE CT
- RDL 92374 608-G7
15200 VCTV 92394 4296-A5
FERNDALE DR
7900 FONT 92336 575-C7
7900 FONT 92336 605-C1
30500 SBdC - 518-G7
FERNDALE RD
15300 VCTV 92394 4295-J6
15300 VCTV 92394 4296-A4
FERN DELL RD
27700 SBdC - 517-J2
FERNELL LN
17800 SBdC 92392 4386-H3
FERN HILL DR
21800 SBdC - 516-D2
FERN HOLLOW
600 SBdC - 4737-J7
E FERNLEAF AV
500 POM 91766 641-A3
W FERNLEAF AV
500 POM 91766 640-G3
FERNLEAF DR
8300 RCUC 91730 602-F2
FERNLEAF ST
14900 FONT 92336 574-D6
FERNROCK RD
26200 SBdC - 517-E3
FERNSIDE RD
1900 SBdC - 518-J6
FERNWOOD AV
11300 FONT 92337 644-B3
N FERNWOOD AV
3300 RLTO 92377 575-A1
3500 RLTO 92377 545-A7
FERNWOOD CT
- CHLS 91709 711-J2
FERNWOOD DR
200 SBdC - 516-D2
1400 RDL 92374 608-E7
1400 RDL 92374 648-F1
8500 RCUC 91730 603-A3
17700 SBdC 92407 515-A3
FERNWOOD WY
12000 FONT 92337 644-B4
FERON BLVD
9300 RCUC 91730 602-H3
9800 RCUC 91730 603-A3
FERRARA CT
- POM 91766 640-D3
FERRARI LN
- ONT 91764 603-D6
FERREE ST
1400 CHLS 91709 710-H5
1400 OrCo 92886 710-H5
1600 CHLS 91709 711-A2
S FERREE ST
1600 SBDO 92408 607-C6
FERRERO PKWY
- INDS 91789 640-A6
FERRIS ST
100 CLAR 91711 571-D6
FETLOCK AV
5300 FONT 92336 574-C1
FETLOCK LN
15800 CHLS 91709 680-H7
15800 CHLS 91709 710-J1
FICUS CT
8400 RCUC 91730 602-F2
FICUS ST
2700 POM 91766 641-B7
2800 CHNO 91710 641-B7
2900 CHLS 91709 681-B7
FIDDLELEAF RD
15700 FONT 92337 644-F2
FIDDLETOWN DR
15100 VCTV 92394 4296-A7
FIDEN CT
1000 SBdC - 517-B4
FIELD RD
- SBdC 92311 3678-F3
41500 SBdC - 349-L6
41900 SBdC - (3415-J6 See Page 3414)
FIELDFLOWER CIR
14600 CHLS 91709 681-B5
FIELDSTONE DR
27800 HIGH 92346 577-J5
FIENO CT
24900 SBdC - 517-B4
FIESTA AV
600 PRKR - 4774-J6
FIESTA CT
11300 FONT 92337 645-A2
FIESTA LN
11300 FONT 92337 644-H2
FIESTA PL
7900 RCUC 91730 602-J1
FIESTA RD
6600 TNP 92277 4890-H7
FIFE AV
- UPL 91786 602-E2
FIFTH ST
100 SBdC - (3682-D1 See Page 3592)
200 SBdC - 3592-D7
FIG LN
- FONT 92337 645-A2
FIG PL
12800 CHNO 91710 642-A6
FIGHTING FALCON ST
- VCTV 92394 4205-F5
W FIG TREE RD
1900 CLTN 92324 605-J4
FIGUEROA RD
16000 VCTV 92394 4295-J3
FIGWOOD CT
13900 FONT 92337 644-B3
FIGWOOD DR
14100 FONT 92337 644-B3
FILAREA TR
13000 YCPA 92399 650-E6
FILAREA TR N
36800 YCPA 92399 650-E6
FILAREA TR S
36800 YCPA 92399 650-E6
FILAREE CT
- RCUC 91701 572-J5
FILBERT ST
16500 FONT 92335 604-H4
17000 FONT 92335 605-A4
FILIPPI LN
12900 FONT 92337 643-H2
FILKINS AV
6100 RCUC 91737 573-A4
6900 RCUC 91701 573-A6
FILKINS ST
15100 VCTV 92394 4296-A2
FILLIPI CT
- RCUC 91739 603-J1
FILLMORE AV
6300 SBdC 92377 575-F4
6300 RLTO 92377 575-F4
6600 SBdC 92376 575-F4
N FILLMORE AV
100 RLTO 92376 605-F1
500 RLTO 92376 575-F5
1600 SBdC 92376 575-F5
2000 RLTO 92377 575-E3
S FILLMORE AV
500 RLTO 92376 605-F3
1400 RLTO 92316 605-F5
N FILLMORE PL
500 POM 91768 640-G1
FILLMORE ST
5900 CHNO 91710 641-J6
6200 CHNO 91710 642-A5
FILLY CT
6200 RCUC 91739 573-G4
13900 VCTV 92394 4295-G6
FILLY LN
14800 FONT 92336 574-D2
15100 VCTV 92394 4295-G6
FI-LOX-SEE AV
- SBdC 92277 4824-D7
7100 SBdC 92277 (4894-D6 See Page 4824)
FINANCE ST
200 VCTV 92394 4205-F5
FINCH
200 POM 91767 601-A1
FINCH AV
1500 RDL 92374 608-F7
10100 RCUC 91737 573-B4
FINCH CT
6800 CHNO 91710 642-B7
11600 FONT 92337 644-G3
FINCH DR
- RivC 92399 650-G7
100 BBLK - 4741-G7
100 BBLK - 4811-G1
FINCH RD
900 SBdC 92397 4652-C2
FINCH ST
22700 GTER 92313 646-F4
FINECROFT DR
1500 CLAR 91711 601-A1
FINGER WY
1300 SBdC - 4737-G5
FINHAUT DR
24700 SBdC - 517-A4
FINK LN
54700 SBdC - 4817-C7
FIR AV
13600 YCPA 92399 610-A7
FIR CT
4000 CHLS 91709 681-D6
4400 MTCL 91763 601-E5
7700 SBdC 92345 4564-G4
FIR DR
500 SBdC - 519-E2
600 SBdC - 4738-E7
8300 RCUC 91730 603-A2
40900 SBdC 92339 611-F2
FIR LN
- FONT 92337 645-A2
400 SBdC - 4738-D7
800 SBdC 92314 4742-J7
800 SBdC 92314 4812-J1
4800 SBdC - 4886-D4
22700 SBdC - 516-E2
FIR ST
200 SBdC - 516-C2
600 BBLK - 4812-A2
9900 SBdC 92345 4564-G4
12700 SBdC 92345 4565-E3
13100 VCTV 92392 4385-G4
13400 SBdC 93562 2055-A6
14200 HESP 92345 4565-J3
14900 HESP 92345 4566-B3
FIR TER
100 SBdC - 518-C1
FIRCREST LN
4100 RivC 92509 644-E7
E FIRECREST CT
2900 ONT 91761 643-A5
FIRE HALL LP
600 SBdC - 517-E3
FIRE HOLLOW DR
1600 DBAR 91765 680-C3
FIREHOUSE RD
- SBdC - 518-A1
FIRENZA PL
- RCUC 91701 573-E5
FIRE OAK DR
7400 HIGH 92346 578-D6
FIREPIT DR
600 DBAR 91765 640-B6
FIRESIDE LN
14800 SBdC - (3935-J3 See Page 3934)
W FIRESIDE SQ
1200 UPL 91786 601-G1
FIRESTONE LN
16100 CHLS 91709 711-E1
FIRESTONE RD
- SBdC 92252 4890-A1
62100 SBdC 92252 4889-C1
FIRETHORN CIR
13500 VCTV 92392 4385-F5
FIRE THORN CIR
22600 DBAR 91765 680-A3
FIRETHORN RD
14500 SBdC - (4303-B5 See Page 4302)
15700 FONT 92337 644-F3
FIRETHORN ST
12300 RCUC 91739 573-G4
FIRETHORN WY
48100 SBdC 92285 (4575-C5 See Page 4484)
E FIREWOOD CT
2100 SBDO 92404 577-F1
FIRING RANGE RD
- BARS 92311 (3761-C1 See Page 3760)
- SBdC - (3761-C1 See Page 3760)
FIR RIDGE CT
12900 VCTV 92392 4475-E1
FIRST ST
100 SBdC - (3682-D1 See Page 3592)
300 SBdC - 3592-D7
FIRWOOD CT
36100 YCPA 92399 650-C5
FIRWOOD DR
31300 SBdC - 518-J6
FISH CREEK TR
- SBdC - 389-H2
FISHER BLVD
- BARS 92311 (3759-A2 See Page 3758)
FISHER CT
100 CALI 92320 650-A7
FISHER DR
13300 RCUC 91739 573-J4
13500 RCUC 91739 574-A4
FISHER RD
100 BBLK - 4811-D1
FISHER ST
3400 SBDO 92346 577-G5
5000 HIGH 92346 577-G5
17600 VCTV 92392 4386-G3
25200 HIGH 92404 577-D5
25200 SBdC 92404 577-C5
28200 HIGH 92346 578-A4
FISH HATCHERY RD
33000 HIGH - 609-E3
33000 HIGH 92359 609-E3
33000 SBdC - 609-G3
33700 SBdC 92359 609-G3
33900 RDL 92359 609-F4
FISK CT
6800 RCUC 91701 573-D5
N FITZGERALD AV
1200 RLTO 92376 575-E6
FITZPATRICK DR
- RCUC 91730 573-D7
FITZSIMMONS AV
- RLTO 92377 575-C3
FIVE POINTS RD
- SBdC - 548-H1
FLAGSTAFF CT
14900 VCTV 92394 4296-A6
FLAGSTAFF ST
15200 VCTV 92394 4296-A6
FLAGSTAFF WY
14900 VCTV 92394 4296-A6
FLAGSTONE CT
14500 CHLS 91709 680-J4
FLAGSTONE PL
6500 RCUC 91739 573-J5
N FLAME TREE AV
3300 RLTO 92377 544-J6
N FLAMETREE AV
4000 RLTO 92377 544-J6
FLAMINGO AV
2400 SBdC 92252 4819-F5
4700 SBdC 92252 4889-G3
FLAMINGO DR
15700 FONT 92337 644-F3
FLAMINGO RD
200 SBdC 92252 4749-F6
1800 SBdC 92284 4817-E2
25400 HIGH 92410 577-C6
FLAMINGO ST
22100 GTER 92313 646-D5
FLANAGAN ST
1500 POM 91766 641-A4
FLATHEAD RD
14100 APLV 92307 4297-J5
14100 APLV 92307 4387-F1
22100 APLV 92307 4298-A5
FLAXTON ST
300 POM 91767 601-A2
FLEET LN
26200 SBdC - (3935-H6 See Page 3934)
FLEETWOOD DR
2000 RivC 92509 645-G7
FLEETWOOD LN
6100 CHLS 91709 712-A5
FLEETWOOD ST
35700 SBdC - 4481-H7
36200 SBdC - 4482-A7
FLEMING ST
1700 POM 91766 640-E3
25400 HIGH 92410 577-D7
26600 HIGH 92346 577-F7
FLEMING CREEK RD
500 SBdC - 518-A2
FLEMMING ST
3600 RivC 92509 644-D6
FLETCHA ST
12000 YCPA 92399 650-C3
FLETCHER AV
900 RDL 92373 648-A2
FLETCHER VIEW DR
7100 HIGH 92346 578-C5
FLEUR DR
8100 SBdC 92252 4959-B5
FLICKER RD
39600 SBdC - 4741-C5
FLICKER ST
8500 SBdC 92308 4479-G7
FLINT LN
- VCTV 92392 4385-E3
FLINT RD
23300 SBdC 92307 4298-D4
S FLINT WY
2600 SBDO 92408 647-A1
FLINT HOLLOW PL
16600 CHLS 91709 710-F2
FLINTLOCK CT
7400 HIGH 92346 578-D6
FLINTLOCK RD
1000 DBAR 91765 640-C5
FLINT POINT CIR
- POM 91766 640-H5
FLINTRIDGE AV
1300 SBdC - 4812-C2
FLINT RIDGE CT
5800 RCUC 91737 573-A3
FLINTRIDGE ST
16500 HESP 92345 4566-F5
FLINTROCK RD
1900 DBAR 91765 680-B4
FLIP MENDEZ PKWY
1100 NDLS 92363 3620-C6
FLOHERO LN
200 SBdC 92277 4751-D5
200 SBdC 92278 4751-D5
FLORA CT
6900 HESP 92345 4566-A5
FLORA LN
14900 VCTV 92394 4296-C6
52200 SBdC 92256 616-B1
FLORA ST
600 BARS 92311 3679-F3
4200 MTCL 91763 601-D7
E FLORA ST
600 ONT 91764 602-D7
W FLORA ST
500 ONT 91762 602-A7
900 ONT 91762 601-H7
FLORAL ST
10700 ADEL 92301 4384-H1
FLORA VISTA
1300 POM 91766 640-G3
1900 NDLS 92363 3620-B6
FLORA VISTA DR
5200 SBdC 92301 (4113-D7 See Page 4112)
FLORA VISTA ST
9100 SBdC 92308 4478-B2
11300 SBdC 92308 4388-B7
11600 APLV 92308 4388-B7
FLORDASON DR
300 CALI 92320 649-J7
FLOREATE RD
21000 ADEL 92301 (4115-F1 See Page 4114)
21000 VCTV 92301 (4115-F5 See Page 4114)
21000 SBdC 92301 (4115-F1 See Page 4114)
FLORECITA LN
5100 SBdC 92301 (4113-B3 See Page 4112)
FLORENCE AV
1900 SBdC 92359 608-H5
N FLORENCE AV
400 ONT 91764 602-D7
900 CLTN 92324 606-F5
900 SBDO 92408 606-F5
N FLORENCE CT
700 ONT 91764 602-D6
FLORENCE LN
11800 FONT 92337 644-F3
FLORENCE PL
6700 RCUC 91701 573-E5
FLORES ST
- YCPA 92399 610-A6
N FLORES ST
500 SBDO 92411 576-D5
2300 SBDO 92407 576-C2
S FLOREZ ST
900 CLTN 92324 646-D1
FLORIDA CT
- VCTV 92394 4205-G5
FLORIDA ST
31500 RDL 92373 649-B5
31700 HIGH 92359 609-A3
31700 RDL 92359 609-A3
32000 YCPA 92373 649-B5
FLORINE AV
2900 RivC 92509 645-A7
FLOWER
16000 SBdC 92307 4299-C3
FLOWER CT
2000 UPL 91784 572-C5
FLOWER DR
- SBdC - 518-A2
FLOWER LN
4900 SBdC 92371 4383-C2
FLOWER RD
8700 RCUC 91730 602-G3
FLOWER ST
15000 ADEL 92301 4295-A7
36500 SBdC 92347 (3677-F1 See Page 3586)
36600 SBdC 92347 (3587-F4 See Page 3586)
N FLOWER ST
300 SBDO 92410 606-C1
FLOWERFIELD RD
- SBdC 92371 4653-D1
FLOWERFIELD ST
6900 SBdC 92371 4563-D2
FLOWERS ST
6000 CHNO 91710 711-J1
6000 CHNO 91710 712-A1
FLUME CANYON DR
23300 LACo 92397 4652-A1
FLYING ARROW LN
- FONT 92336 574-D2
FLYING ARROW RD
13900 SBdC - 514-A4
FLYING FEATHER RD
11800 APLV 92308 4387-C7
FLYING H RD
4500 TNP 92277 4892-H1
FLYING HILL PL
1100 DBAR 91765 640-D5
FLYING MANE LN
9700 RCUC 91737 572-J2
FLYING TIGERS RD
5200 SBdC - 4887-B5
FLYNN ST
100 RivC 92507 646-D6
FOAL CT
15100 VCTV 92394 4295-H6
FOBES RD
9500 SBdC 92256 616-C2
FOGG RD
- CLTN 92324 646-A1
FOGG ST
300 CLTN 92324 606-E7
300 CLTN 92324 646-E1
E FOGG ST
100 CLTN 92324 646-D1
W FOGG ST
400 CLTN 92324 646-C1
FOGMORE DR
- SBdC 92252 4959-B6
S FOISY ST
600 SBDO 92408 606-J3
FOLEY DR
- TNP 92277 4823-B5
70000 SBdC 92277 4821-G5
72900 SBdC 92277 4822-B5
72900 TNP 92277 4822-C5
FOLEY RD
6100 SBdC 92345 4565-F2
6100 SBdC 92345 (4655-F1 See Page 4654)
FOLEY ST
12700 VCTV 92392 4385-E5
FOLEY WY
500 POM 91768 640-C3
W FOLKE AV
1200 RLTO 92376 605-E1
W FOLKE ST
1300 RLTO 92376 575-D7
FOLSOM AV
10100 ADEL 92301 4204-F6
FOLSOM LN
17800 HESP 92345 4566-H1
FONTAINBLEAU LN
13800 CHLS 91709 681-B3
FONTAINE PL
- RCUC 91739 573-F6
FONTAINE RD
- BARS 92311 3680-C3
- SBdC 92311 3680-C3
FONTAINE WY
14300 VCTV 92394 4295-H5
FONTANA AV
8900 FONT 92335 604-G4
9500 SBdC 92335 604-E6
FONTLEE CT
15700 FONT 92335 604-F4
FONTLEE LN
14500 SBdC 92335 604-C4
16300 FONT 92335 604-J4
17100 FONT 92335 605-A4
18700 SBdC 92316 605-E4
W FONTLEE LN
700 RLTO 92376 605-F4
800 RLTO 92316 605-F4
W FONTLEE ST
1000 RLTO 92316 605-E4
1000 RLTO 92376 605-E4
FOOTHILL BLVD
Rt#-66
8100 RCUC 91730 602-G2
8100 UPL 91786 602-G2
9900 RCUC 91730 603-B1
11900 RCUC 91739 603-G1
13100 SBdC 91739 603-G1
13300 SBdC 92335 603-G1
13300 FONT 92336 603-G1
13300 FONT 92335 603-G1
13400 FONT 92336 604-F1
13400 FONT 92335 604-B1
13700 SBdC 92336 604-B1
13700 SBdC 92335 604-B1
16900 FONT 92336 605-A1
16900 FONT 92335 605-A1
17700 SBdC 92336 605-A1
17700 SBdC 92335 605-A1
FOOTHILL BLVD
U.S.-66 Hist
8100 RCUC 91730 602-G2
8100 UPL 91786 602-G2
9900 RCUC 91730 603-B1
11900 RCUC 91739 603-G1
13100 SBdC 91739 603-G1
13300 SBdC 92335 603-G1
13300 FONT 92336 603-G1
13300 FONT 92335 603-G1
13400 FONT 92336 604-F1
13400 FONT 92335 604-B1
13700 SBdC 92336 604-B1
13700 SBdC 92335 604-B1
16900 FONT 92336 605-A1
16900 FONT 92335 605-A1
17700 SBdC 92336 605-A1
17700 SBdC 92335 605-A1
E FOOTHILL BLVD
Rt#-66
- UPL 91786 602-C2
100 CLAR 91711 601-D2
100 RLTO 92376 605-J1
200 POM 91767 601-A2
700 RLTO 92376 606-A1
E FOOTHILL BLVD
U.S.-66 Hist
- UPL 91786 602-C2
100 RLTO 92376 605-J1
700 RLTO 92376 606-A1
W FOOTHILL BLVD
Rt#-66
- UPL 91786 602-B2
100 CLAR 91711 601-B2
100 RLTO 92376 605-E1
1000 UPL 91786 601-F2
1500 FONT 92336 605-E1
1500 RLTO 92335 605-E1
1500 FONT 92335 605-E1
1600 SBdC 91786 601-F2
2000 SBDO 92411 606-A1
2000 SBDO 92410 606-A1
2700 SBDO 92376 606-A1
2700 RLTO 92376 606-A1
W FOOTHILL BLVD
U.S.-66 Hist
- UPL 91786 602-B2
100 RLTO 92376 605-E1
1000 UPL 91786 601-F2
1500 FONT 92336 605-E1
1500 RLTO 92335 605-E1
1500 FONT 92335 605-E1
1600 SBdC 91786 601-F2
2000 SBDO 92411 606-A1
2000 SBDO 92410 606-A1
2700 SBDO 92376 606-A1
2700 RLTO 92376 606-A1
FOOTHILL DR
- TNP 92277 4960-J1
- TNP 92277 4961-A1
1600 SBdC 92404 547-C7
1600 SBDO 92404 547-C7
1900 SBdC 92404 577-D1
2000 SBDO 92404 577-D1
6900 TNP 92277 4892-A7
64000 SBdC 92252 4959-H1
64900 SBdC 92252 4960-A1
68900 TNP 92277 4891-B7
75300 TNP 92277 4893-A7
77700 SBdC 92277 4893-J6
77700 SBdC 92277 (4894-A6 See Page 4824)
E FOOTHILL DR
2200 SBDO 92404 577-E1
FOOTHILL LN
40900 BBLK - 4811-F1
FOOTHILL RD
14500 VCTV 92394 4295-J7
14500 VCTV 92394 4385-H1
29300 SBdC - 4480-A4
32700 SBdC - 4481-A4
36300 SBdC - 4482-F3
FOOTHILL ST
18300 SBdC 92407 515-C4
FOOTHILL WY
- RDL 92374 608-F5
FOOTHILL FRONTAGE RD
600 CLAR 91711 601-E2
FORANE PL
- BARS 92311 3680-A5
FORANE ST
1500 BARS 92311 3680-A5
N FORBES AV
2100 CLAR 91711 571-D6
FORBES RD
- SBdC 92256 616-C1
FORD LN
700 BBLK - 4811-G2
FORD PL
13600 CHNO 91710 681-E2
FORD ST
- RDL 92374 608-E7
100 RDL 92374 648-E1
1200 RDL 92373 648-E2
FORDHAM CIR
13200 VCTV 92392 4385-F4
FORDHAM CT
10900 RCUC 91701 573-C6
FORDHAM PL
400 CLAR 91711 601-C4
FORDOM RD
- SBdC 92285 4748-A3
FORENZA PL
- RCUC 91701 573-E6
FOREST AV
300 BARS 92311 3680-A4
9700 SBdC 92316 605-D5
N FOREST AV
800 RLTO 92376 575-D6
2200 RLTO 92377 575-D1
2200 SBdC 92377 575-D3
S FOREST AV
300 RLTO 92376 605-D3
500 RLTO 92316 605-D3
500 RLTO 92335 605-D3
FOREST CIR
200 SBdC - 516-E2
FOREST CT
600 RDL 92373 648-A3
9600 ADEL 92301 4204-E4
27900 SBdC - (3935-H2 See Page 3934)
FOREST DR
400 SBdC - 516-D3
2100 SBdC - 519-E6
6800 SBdC - 4843-H4
58900 YUCA 92284 4888-D3
S FOREST DR
900 CLTN 92324 646-G1
FOREST GN
25300 SBdC - 517-C3
FOREST LN
400 SBdC - 516-E2
700 SBdC - 517-F3
1700 SBdC 92404 516-G6
35100 YCPA 92399 650-A2
FOREST RD
39400 BBLK - 4741-B7
39400 BBLK - 4811-B1
FOREST ST
1300 UPL 91784 571-H3
FOREST CANYON DR
23200 DBAR 91765 680-B4
FOREST GROVE LN
8200 RCUC 91730 602-F2
FOREST HILL DR
46900 SBdC 92314 4813-C3
FOREST HILLS CT
17300 VCTV 92392 4386-G1
FOREST HILLS DR
17000 VCTV 92392 4386-F1
FOREST LAKE DR
24900 SBdC - 517-B4
FOREST MEADOW DR
3100 CHLS 91709 681-B4
FOREST PARK DR
600 RivC 92501 646-A7
FOREST RANGER RD
40900 BBLK - 4811-F2
40900 SBdC - 4811-F2
FORESTRY RD
5200 SBdC 92345 4654-H2
10800 SBdC 92345 (4655-A2 See Page 4654)
FOREST SHADE RD
500 SBdC - 516-H3
FOREST SPRING CT
15300 CHLS 91709 680-F6
FOREST VIEW DR
1200 SBdC - 517-B4
S FORK DR
- SBdC - 519-E6
W FORK PALMER MTWY
- CLAR 91711 571-E2
- LACo 91711 571-E2
W FORK PALMER CANYON RD
- LACo 91711 571-E1
FORLI DR
11700 RCUC 91701 573-E6
FORMAN ST
2400 UPL 91784 571-J3
2400 SBdC 91784 571-J3
FORMAN WY
12800 VCTV 92392 4385-E5
FORMOSA ST
4100 RivC 92509 644-H7
FORREST AV
16100 VCTV 92392 4296-D5
FORREST LN
17400 SBdC 92407 515-B6
FORSEE CREEK TR
- SBdC - 389-F1
FORSYTH PL
500 CLAR 91711 571-E5
FORT APACHE CT
14100 VCTV 92392 4385-H5
FORT CADY RD
26900 SBdC - (3855-A1 See Page 3764)
29900 SBdC - (3765-A4 See Page 3764)
30500 SBdC 92365 (3765-A4 See Page 3764)
33000 SBdC 92365 (3685-A5 See Page 3594)
35600 SBdC 92365 (3595-A7 See Page 3594)
FORT IRWIN RD
- SBdC - 329-J11
35500 SBdC - (3681-A1 See Page 3590)
35700 SBdC - (3591-B2 See Page 3590)
38000 SBdC - 349-J1
FORT LEWIS DR
400 POM 91767 601-A1
1200 CLAR 91711 601-A1
FORTNER WY
3200 POM 91767 601-A2
FORT ROSS CT
14000 FONT 92336 604-B1
FORT TEJON RD
200 SBdC 92372 4472-A3
FORTUNA AV
100 SBdC 92284 4747-G6
900 SBdC 92285 4747-G3
2000 SBdC 92285 4667-G7
6300 YUCA 92284 4888-D7
8800 YUCA 92284 4958-D7
FORTUNA CT
4900 YUCA 92284 4888-D4
FORTUNA LN
18400 SBdC 92392 4386-J2
18400 SBdC 92392 4387-A2
FORTUNA WY
- RLTO 92316 645-H2
FORTYNINE PALMS AV
6200 TNP 92277 4892-B6
FORTYNINE PALMS CANYON RD
70500 TNP 92277 4961-F1
70700 SBdC 92277 4961-F1
FOSSIL BED RD
22100 SBdC 92347 349-B7
26700 SBdC - 349-C6
FOSTER AV
27300 HIGH 92346 577-H5
FOSTER ST
- UPL 91786 602-E2
FOUNDERS RD
21300 APLV 92307 4207-H6
FOUNTAIN AV
100 RDL 92373 648-C3
900 RivC 92507 646-C6
FOUNTAIN BLVD
61400 SBdC 92252 4889-A1
FOUNTAIN DR
500 RivC 91752 683-E4
FOURTH ST
100 SBdC - (3682-D1 See Page 3592)
300 SBdC - 3592-D7
FOUR WINDS LN
12300 VCTV 92392 4385-C6
FOUR WINDS WY
12200 VCTV 92392 4385-C6
FOWLER AV
1500 POM 91766 640-J4
1500 POM 91766 641-A4
FOX AV
18100 ADEL 92301 4204-E6
21700 APLV 92307 4387-J1
22100 APLV 92307 4388-A1
23200 APLV 92307 4298-C7
23500 SBdC 92307 4298-D7
FOX CT
600 RDL 92374 648-F2
1000 CLTN 92324 646-H1
5700 RCUC 91701 572-D3
FOX DR
400 BBLK - 4812-A1
29800 SBdC 92311 3589-J7
30000 SBdC 92311 3590-A7
FOX LN
- SBdC - 4843-J1
1900 SBdC 92314 4812-J1
14600 FONT 92336 574-C2
32700 SBdC - 519-C6
FOX RUN
13300 VCTV 92392 4385-F4
FOX TR
4700 SBdC 92256 4956-B7
5400 SBdC - 4773-H7
5600 SBdC - 4843-J1
7300 YUCA 92284 4957-E4
9100 SBdC 92256 616-B1
12500 VCTV 92392 4385-J5
FOXBORO LN
28500 HIGH 92346 578-B7
FOXBOROUGH DR
4000 FONT 92336 544-C6
FOXBURY AV
300 POM 91767 601-A2
S FOX CREEK LN
2700 ONT 91761 643-C6
FOXCROFT CT
6600 CHNO 91710 642-B7
S FOXCROFT WY
2400 SBDO 92408 606-J7
W FOXDALE CT
1500 UPL 91786 571-H7
FOX FARM RD
1200 SBdC - 4812-A1
18400 BBLK - 4742-A7
18400 BBLK - 4812-A1
41800 BBLK - 4811-H1
42100 BBLK - 4741-J7
FOXFIELD LN
14600 FONT 92336 574-C2
FOXFIRE RD
13600 VCTV 92392 4385-F3
FOXGATE LN
1800 CHLS 91709 680-H3
FOX GLEN DR
1600 DBAR 91765 680-A4
FOXGLEN LP
3600 ONT 91761 643-C6
S FOXGLEN LP
2700 ONT 91761 643-C6
FOXGLOVE CT
12400 RCUC 91739 573-G5
FOXGLOVE DR
14500 CHLS 91709 681-C4
FOXGROVE CT
8200 UPL 91784 572-E5
FOX HALL RD
- CHLS 91709 711-G2
FOXHAVEN PL
600 DBAR 91765 640-E7
FOX HOLLOW WY
- CHLS 91709 711-G1
FOX HUNT RD
16300 CHLS 91709 710-H2
FOXPARK DR
400 POM 91767 601-A2
500 LACo 91711 601-A2
FOX POINT RD
13400 VCTV 92392 4385-G3
FOX RIDGE DR
14600 FONT 92336 574-D1
FOX RIDGE WY
2300 UPL 91784 572-C3
FOXRUN DR
4200 CHLS 91709 711-E2
FOX TAIL CT
7700 HIGH 92346 578-C6
FOXTAIL LN
3800 RivC 92509 644-C6
7500 FONT 92336 574-E7
12500 SBdC 92392 4386-J5
FOX TAIL PL
7800 HIGH 92346 578-C6
FOX TAIL WY
12500 VCTV 92392 4385-D5
28700 HIGH 92346 578-C6
FOXWOOD DR
12900 YCPA 92399 649-J5
FOXWOOD PL
5900 RCUC 91737 573-B3
FOXWOOD RD
14700 CHLS 91709 681-B5
15900 VCTV 92392 4386-C4
FOXWORTH ST
- FONT 92336 574-E6
FOXY FLATS RD
2500 SBdC 92252 4819-A6
FRADY AV
13500 CHNO 91710 681-D2
FRAMPTON RD
36600 SBdC - (3681-H1 See Page 3590)
FRANCES DR
300 BARS 92311 3679-J3
FRANCES ST
1300 RDL 92374 608-A5
19000 APLV 92308 4387-B7
FRANCES WY
11600 CHNO 91710 641-E4
11600 SBdC 91710 641-E4
FRANCESCA CT
13300 CHNO 91710 682-B1
FRANCESCA RD
17700 VCTV 92392 4386-H6

STREET Block City ZIP Pg-Grid

GINGKO CT
8400 RCUC 91730 602-F2
GINSENG LN
16000 CHLS 91709 710-H1
N GIOVANOLA AV
100 SBDO 92410 606-E1
S GIOVANOLA AV
100 SBDO 92410 606-E2
GIRD AV
4100 CHLS 91709 681-E6
GIRD ST
4100 CHNO 91710 682-B1
GIRTH LN
5300 FONT 92336 574-D2
GITA CT
- SBDO 92407 546-E5
GITANO RD
9300 SBdC 92371 4472-G7
11300 SBdC 92372 4472-G2
12100 SBdC 92372 4382-G5
19300 SBdC 92301 (4202-E1 See Page 4112)
20100 SBdC 92301 4112-E6
GLACIER CIR
13100 HESP 92345 4475-G4
GLACIER DR
1000 BARS 92311 3679-J6
1200 SBdC - 4738-C5
GLACIER PEAK WY
- FONT 92336 574-D3
GLADE AV
300 BARS 92311 3679-J4
GLADIOLA WY
6300 CHLS 91709 712-A5
GLADIOLI WY
14300 HESP 92345 4475-H3
GLADIUM WY
28200 HIGH 92346 578-A5
GLADYS DR
28700 SBdC 92311 3589-F7
GLADYS LN
12100 YCPA 92399 649-A3
GLASGOW AV
6700 SBdC 92404 577-C5
N GLASGOW AV
1200 SBdC 92404 577-C5
GLASGOW CT
14900 VCTV 92394 4295-J7
GLASS RD
4100 SBdC - 389-F1
GLASSBORO AV
1900 CLAR 91711 571-E7
GLEASON RD
- SBdC 92285 4667-D6
GLEASON ST
400 SBdC - (3682-C1 See Page 3592)
GLEN AV
900 POM 91768 640-F1
GLEN CT
13000 CHLS 91709 641-A7
38900 SBdC 92399 611-A7
38900 SBdC 92399 651-B1
GLEN DR
9400 SBdC 92339 611-G3
GLEN RD
- SBdC 92311 3678-F2
900 SBdC - 516-F4
10900 SBdC 92399 611-C7
40100 BBLK - 4811-D1
GLEN ST
400 RivC 92507 646-C7
4200 RivC 92509 644-D7
GLEN WY
4400 LACo 91711 571-B7
4400 CLAR 91711 571-B7
GLENAIRE CT
9400 RCUC 91730 602-H5
GLEN AVON DR
100 SBdC - 518-D1
GLENBROOK CIR
- APLV 92308 4387-B4
GLENBROOK CT
13000 VCTV 92392 4386-D4
GLENCOE ST
23700 SBdC 92311 3758-D1
24000 BARS 92311 3758-D1
GLENCOVE DR
2100 SBdC 92314 4812-J2
GLENDALE AV
8100 HESP 92345 4567-C1
8100 SBdC 92345 4567-C1
8700 HESP 92345 4477-C5
GLENDALE CT
14100 RCUC 91739 574-B1
19200 HESP 92345 4477-C5
GLENDALE RD
1100 SBdC 91784 571-J3
E GLENDENNING WY
700 SBDO 92404 577-A1
GLENDON PL
12900 CHLS 91709 640-J7
GLENDORA DR
13900 RCUC 91739 574-A1
23000 GTER 92313 646-G3
GLENDORA RIDGE RD
- LACo - 512-A5
GLENEAGLE AV
600 POM 91768 640-E1
GLENELLEN LN
12200 VCTV 92392 4385-G6
W GLENFAIR LN
100 SBDO 92407 546-H6
GLENGARRY DR
13600 VCTV 92392 4385-G6
GLEN HAVEN
900 POM 91766 640-G3
GLENHAVEN CT
4100 CHLS 91709 711-D2
GLEN HAVEN WY
1100 RDL 92374 608-D5
GLENHAVEN WY
12400 VCTV 92392 4385-G6
GLENHEATHER DR
11900 FONT 92337 644-B4
28600 HIGH 92346 578-C6
GLEN HELEN PKWY
1800 SBdC 92407 515-D6
2400 SBdC 92407 545-B2
2900 SBdC 92407 544-H4
3500 SBdC - 544-H4
GLEN HELEN RD
1500 SBdC 92407 515-B6
2000 SBdC 92407 514-F3
2100 SBdC 92407 545-C1
GLEN HELEN PARK RD
2400 SBdC 92407 545-C1
GLEN HOLLOW LN
- CHLS 91709 711-H2
GLENMARE ST
26000 SBdC 92404 577-E1
26200 SBdC 92346 577-E1
E GLENMARE ST
1300 SBdC 92404 577-B1
GLENMERE WY
12400 VCTV 92392 4385-G6
N GLEN MOUNTAIN RD
1000 SBdC 92314 4742-B5
N GLENN AV
700 ONT 91764 602-F4
GLENN CT
1000 RDL 92374 608-A6
N GLENN CT
600 ONT 91764 602-F7
N GLENN PL
400 ONT 91764 602-F7
GLENN WY
200 SBdC - 514-B3
GLENNAIRE AV
16700 VCTV 92392 4386-F5
GLENNAIRE PL
12400 VCTV 92392 4386-F5
GLENNAIRE WY
12400 VCTV 92392 4386-F6
GLEN OAK DR
30900 SBdC - 518-H6
GLENOAK PL
14300 FONT 92337 644-C4
E GLEN OAK ST
600 RLTO 92376 605-J3
GLENOAKS DR
- YCPA 92399 649-G4
10900 RCUC 91730 573-C6
GLENOAKS LN
12200 VCTV 92392 4385-G6
GLEN OAKS RD
7300 HIGH 92346 578-E6
GLEN PINES CT
1400 CHLS 91709 680-G6
GLENRIDGE CT
13100 VCTV 92392 4386-D4
GLEN RIDGE DR
3500 CHLS 91709 681-B6
GLEN RIDGE LN
- POM 91766 640-G6
GLENROCK PL
28900 HIGH 92346 578-C4
GLENROCK RD
10300 SBdC - 4480-E2
GLEN ROSA ST
- UPL 91784 572-E5
GLENROY CT
4300 RivC 92509 644-C7
GLENROY ST
2100 POM 91766 640-J5
GLENSVIEW RD
400 SBdC 92372 4472-A6
N GLENVIEW AV
2800 SBDO 92407 576-C3
GLENVIEW CT
14200 VCTV 92392 4386-G1
GLENVIEW DR
14300 VCTV 92392 4386-F1
31200 SBdC - 518-J6
GLEN VIEW LN
700 SBdC - 517-E3
GLENVIEW PL
7300 RCUC 91730 573-C7
GLENVIEW RD
39900 BBLK - 4811-C2
GLENVIEW ST
1600 SBDO 92411 576-C4
N GLENVIEW ST
1500 SBDO 92411 576-C5
GLENVILLE DR
900 CLAR 91711 571-B6
GLENWOOD AV
- HESP 92345 4475-J7
- HESP 92345 4565-J1
N GLENWOOD AV
200 RLTO 92376 605-E1
600 RLTO 92376 575-E6
1600 UPL 91784 571-H7
2400 RLTO 92377 575-E3
S GLENWOOD AV
600 RLTO 92376 605-E4
1100 RLTO 92316 605-E5
1900 CLTN 92324 646-H3
GLENWOOD DR
- BBLK - 4742-A7
400 RDL 92373 648-B1
22200 SBdC - 516-D2
GLENWOOD LN
12300 VCTV 92392 4386-D6
GLENWOOD ST
9500 RCUC 91730 572-H7
N GLENWOOD ST
100 CLTN 92324 606-F4
GLENWOOD WY
1900 UPL 91784 571-H5
3900 CHLS 91709 681-D5
N GLENWOOD WY
500 UPL 91786 601-J3
1500 UPL 91786 571-H7
GLIDDEN LN
- SBdC 92284 4818-D6
GLIDER AV
7000 HESP 92345 4566-G4
GLOBEMASTER CT
- SBDO 92346 577-F7
- SBDO 92409 577-F7
GLOBE MINE RD
- SBdC - 351-A5
46500 SBdC - 350-L5
GLORIA ST
6300 CHNO 91710 642-A7
GLOUCESTER CT
- RCUC 91730 573-E7
GLOVER ST
1600 RDL 92374 608-C4
GOAT HILL RD
6700 SBdC - 512-A4
GOAT MOUNTAIN RD
100 SBdC 92284 4748-C5
300 SBdC 92285 4748-C5
N GOAT MOUNTAIN RD
1700 SBdC 92285 4748-E1
GOBAR RD
31300 SBdC - (4390-F6 See Page 4300)
32800 SBdC - (4391-B6 See Page 4300)
GOBI RD
- SBdC 92301 (4113-B6 See Page 4112)
8500 SBdC 92371 4563-C2
GODS WAY LOVE RD
52100 SBdC - 4816-C4
GODWIN RD
2500 SBdC 92277 4824-A6
4600 SBdC 92277 (4894-A4 See Page 4824)
10600 SBdC - 4480-J2
GOFFS RD U.S.-66 Hist
27700 SBdC - 351-H7
GOLCO RD
30700 SBdC - (3846-H1 See Page 3756)
31000 SBdC - 3756-J7
GOLD AV
8600 YUCA 92284 4957-H6
S GOLD CT
1300 ONT 91762 642-A3
GOLD DR
- TNP 92278 4822-F2
GOLD LN
10500 MohC - 3620-F4
GOLDBAR CT
22400 APLV 92307 4298-A5
GOLD BLUFF DR
22700 DBAR 91765 640-A7
GOLD BOTTOM MINE RD
14800 SBdC 93562 2145-E1
15400 SBdC 93562 2055-G7
GOLD BUCKLE CT
7700 HIGH 92346 578-D6
GOLD BUCKLE RD
7800 HIGH 92346 578-D7
S GOLDCREST AV
2200 ONT 91761 642-D5
S GOLDCREST PL
2400 ONT 91761 642-D5
GOLD CROWN RD
7300 SBdC 92277 (4895-H6 See Page 4824)
GOLD CUP CT
- RDL 92374 608-F5
GOLD DUST WY
13200 CHLS 91709 680-H1
GOLDEN AV
100 SBDO 92408 607-B1
N GOLDEN AV
2200 SBDO 92404 577-B1
2700 SBdC 92404 577-B1
3600 SBdC 92404 547-B7
4000 SBdC 92404 547-B6
GOLDEN DR
500 RivC 91752 683-E4
600 SBdC - 518-A3
GOLDEN LN
300 SBdC - 517-J2
1200 NDLS 92363 3710-C1
14900 FONT 92336 574-D7
GOLDEN RD
4700 CHLS 91709 711-F2
GOLDEN ST
4000 SBdC 92252 4889-B1
8700 RCUC 91701 572-F3
9100 RCUC 91737 572-H3
11300 ADEL 92301 4295-A6
15100 SBdC - (4206-A3 See Page 4116)
65100 SBdC 92252 4820-B7
65100 SBdC 92252 4890-B1
GOLDEN TR
14500 VCTV 92392 4385-J5
GOLDEN ARROW LN
9800 RCUC 91701 572-J5
GOLDEN ARROW TR
- SBdC 92277 4821-B7
- SBdC 92277 4891-B1
GOLDEN BEE DR
55700 YUCA 92284 4957-G5
GOLDEN CREST DR
14300 CHLS 91709 680-G4
GOLDEN CROWN CIR
23200 DBAR 91765 680-B1
GOLDEN GATE CT
11400 YCPA 92399 650-D1
GOLDEN GATE DR
11300 YCPA 92399 650-C1
GOLDEN GATE WY
11400 YCPA 92399 650-D1
GOLDEN GLEN DR
4100 CHLS 91709 711-E2
GOLDEN HILLS DR
10900 YCPA 92399 609-J7
GOLDEN MEADOW CT
12500 YCPA 92399 649-F4
GOLDEN MEADOW DR
8600 YUCA 92284 4957-J6
GOLDEN OAK LN
28600 HIGH 92346 578-B6
GOLDEN OAK RD
- BBLK - 4741-J6
- BBLK - 4742-A7
9300 RCUC 91730 602-H5
GOLDEN OAK TR
36700 YCPA 92399 650-E6
GOLDEN POPPY LN
11200 VCTV 92392 4475-F2
GOLDEN PRADOS DR
400 DBAR 91765 640-B7
400 DBAR 91765 680-B1
GOLDEN PRAIRIE DR
12700 RCUC 91739 573-H2
GOLDENRAIN DR
- FONT 92337 644-D3
W GOLDEN RAIN ST
900 UPL 91786 602-A2
1000 UPL 91786 601-J2
GOLDENRAIN WY
6900 RCUC 91739 573-G5
GOLDEN RAINTREE LN
14000 CHLS 91709 681-B3
GOLDEN ROD AV
500 SBdC - 4742-J3
GOLDENROD AV
3600 RLTO 92377 545-A7
N GOLDENROD AV
3200 RLTO 92377 575-A1
3300 RLTO 92377 545-A7
GOLDENROD CT
4300 CHNO 91710 641-E4
GOLDENROD LN
14100 SBdC 92371 4383-B2
GOLDENROD PL
600 POM 91766 640-F3
1000 POM 91768 640-E1
GOLDEN RULE LN
1000 SBdC - 4738-B5
GOLDEN SAND AV
13400 VCTV 92392 4385-F5
GOLDEN SLIPPER LN
900 SBdC 92285 4747-J3
W GOLDEN SPIKE DR
1700 CLTN 92324 605-J4
1700 CLTN 92324 606-A4
GOLDEN SPRINGS DR
200 DBAR 91765 640-D5
22300 DBAR 91765 680-A2
GOLDEN TRAILS AV
6100 RCUC 91739 573-G4
E GOLDEN TRAILS ST
2800 ONT 91761 643-A7
GOLDEN TREE AV
16300 FONT 92337 644-H3
GOLDEN VIEW RD
10500 SBdC 92372 4472-E2
12000 SBdC 92372 4382-E3
GOLDEN WEST DR
500 BBLK - 4811-H2
600 RDL 92373 648-F3
GOLDEN WEST PL
41800 BBLK - 4811-H2
GOLDEN YARROW LN
- RCUC 91701 572-H6
10100 RCUC 91701 573-A5
GOLDFIELD PL
1600 POM 91766 640-F3
GOLD FINCH AV
- SBdC 92252 4819-A4
GOLDFINCH CT
13700 VCTV 92394 4295-G7
GOLDFINCH LN
100 RivC 92507 646-E7
GOLDGULCH
- SBdC 92285 (4577-J5 See Page 4486)
GOLD HILL AV
11400 FONT 92337 644-F3
GOLD HILL LN
12400 RDL 92373 648-J4
12400 SBdC 92373 648-J4
12400 YCPA 92373 648-J4
GOLD HILL GRADE
1700 RDL 92373 648-J4
GOLDMINE AV
8100 SBdC 92335 604-E2
GOLDMINE DR
43200 BBLK - 4812-B3
GOLDMINE WOODS DR
- BBLK - 4812-B3
N GOLD MOUNTAIN DR
100 SBdC 92314 4742-D4
S GOLD MOUNTAIN DR
100 SBdC 92314 4742-D6
GOLD NUGGET AV
23500 DBAR 91765 680-C3
GOLD NUGGET RD
56100 YUCA 92284 4887-F5
62600 SBdC 92252 4889-D4
64900 SBdC 92252 4890-A4
GOLD PARK RD
- SBdC 92277 390-G2
- TNP 92277 390-G2
- TNP 92277 4962-J2
GOLDPOINT PL
24400 DBAR 91765 640-E7
GOLDROAD PL
- MohC - 3620-F1
GOLD RUSH CT
4500 MTCL 91763 641-E1
GOLD RUSH DR
- BBLK - 4742-A7
23300 DBAR 91765 680-B1
GOLD SHADOW LN
15300 CHLS 91709 680-F6
GOLD SLIPPER RD
1200 SBdC 92285 4747-J2
GOLDSTAR PL
- POM 91766 640-G7
GOLDSTONE CIR
12300 VCTV 92392 4385-F6
GOLDSTONE DR
12300 VCTV 92392 4385-F6
GOLDSTONE RD
- SBdC - 329-F11
- SBdC - 349-D2
GOLDSTONE ST
34700 YCPA 92399 609-J4
34900 YCPA 92399 610-A4
GOLDY ST
- RivC 92880 683-D6
GOLETA AV
3300 SBdC 92284 4818-D7
3700 SBdC 92284 4888-D2
4900 YUCA 92284 4888-D3
7300 YUCA 92284 4958-D3
GOLETA ST
19000 HESP 92345 4477-B7
GOLF CT
27900 SBdC - (3935-J2 See Page 3934)
GOLF CLUB DR
1300 UPL 91784 572-E6
GOLF COURSE DR
12600 SBdC 92392 4386-J4
GOLF COURSE LN
26900 SBdC - 4737-G7
GOLF COURSE RD
100 SBdC - 517-G1
200 SBdC - 4737-F7
GOLF COURSE WY
400 SBdC - 517-G1
400 SBdC - 4737-G7
GOLONDRINA CT
6700 SBdC 92404 577-D4
GOLONDRINA DR
5300 SBdC 92404 547-D7
5300 SBdC 92404 577-D1
5700 SBDO 92404 577-D1
7300 HIGH 92404 577-D4
7300 HIGH 92410 577-D7
GOODCELL AL
- SBDO 92410 606-G1
GOOD CHAP RD
- SBdC - 349-B6
GOOD GUYS LN
67800 SBdC 92277 4820-J4
GOODIE LN
71700 SBdC 92277 4751-H5
W GOODLETT ST
1300 SBDO 92411 576-D4
GOODMAN CT
26500 HIGH 92346 577-F4
GOODMAN RD
600 NDLS 92363 3620-B4
600 SBdC 92363 3620-B4
GOOD WATER CT
- SBdC 92311 3678-G4
GOODWILL ST
100 NDLS 92363 3620-E7
GOODWIN DR
9700 SBdC 92392 4474-F2
11100 SBdC 92392 4475-B2
11300 VCTV 92392 4475-B2
GOOSENECK DR
9400 RCUC 91737 572-H1
GOPHER TR
13900 YCPA 92399 650-E6
GOPHER CANYON RD
14000 VCTV 92394 4295-H7
GOPHER GROVE LN
3900 SBdC 92277 4823-G6
6000 SBdC 92277 4893-G3
N GORDON ST
200 POM 91768 640-J1
S GORDON ST
100 POM 91766 640-J2
GORDON WY
3800 RivC 92509 644-D7
GORGAM RD
- APLV 92308 4477-G4
GORGONIO DR
6000 TNP 92277 4891-F5
7900 TNP 92277 4892-A5
75500 TNP 92277 4893-A5
GORGONIO RD
3300 SBdC 92371 4472-H1
4500 SBdC 92371 4473-B1
7900 SBdC 92371 4474-B1
8200 SBdC 92392 4474-C1
GORGONIO VW
55000 YUCA 92284 4957-C5
GOSHEN RD
18600 APLV 92307 4207-J4
18600 APLV 92307 4208-A4
GOSHUTE AV
21700 APLV 92307 4297-J7
21700 APLV 92307 4387-J1
22000 APLV 92307 4298-A7
23300 SBdC 92307 4298-E7
GOSLING CT
13300 CHLS 91709 681-A3
GOSS RD
200 SBdC 92372 4472-F2
2800 SBdC 92371 4472-F2
3800 SBdC 92371 4473-A2
7500 SBdC 92371 4474-A2
8100 SBdC 92392 4474-D2
11100 SBdC 92392 4475-A2
11300 VCTV 92392 4475-A2
GOULD RD
- LPCo - 4844-C7
E GOULD ST
1200 SBDO 92408 607-C5
1600 SBDO 92354 607-C5
GOWER ST
- LMLN 92354 647-F2
GRABLE CT
11500 FONT 92337 644-G3
GRACE AV
7700 SBdC 92336 575-C7
7900 FONT 92336 575-C7
7900 FONT 92336 605-C1
7900 SBdC 92336 605-C1
GRACE RD
63700 SBdC 92252 4819-E3
GRACE ST
7300 FONT 92336 575-C6
8700 FONT 92335 605-C3
9300 SBdC 92335 605-C5
9700 SBdC 92316 605-C5
E GRACE ST
100 BARS 92311 3679-H4
W GRACE ST
100 BARS 92311 3679-G4
E GRAEAGLE WY
3700 ONT 91761 643-C7
GRAFTON DR
42900 SBdC 92365 (3683-F2 See Page 3592)
45700 SBdC 92365 (3684-D1 See Page 3594)
GRAFTON LN
14700 SBdC - (3935-H5 See Page 3934)
GRAHAM AV
14400 VCTV 92394 4295-J7
GRAHAM DR
- SBdC - 519-A7
GRAHAM RD
3500 SBdC 92371 4472-J2
GRAHAM WY
14900 VCTV 92394 4295-J7
GRAMERCY AV
5000 SBdC 92371 4563-D6
GRAMERCY RD
- SBdC 92371 4563-B6
GRANADA AV
8900 FONT 92335 605-A3
14700 SBdC 92335 604-D3
18000 SBdC 92335 605-C3
GRANADA CT
800 RDL 92374 608-A6
4800 CHNO 91710 641-F7
5000 RCUC 91737 573-B1
8900 SBdC 92335 604-D3
E GRANADA CT
100 ONT 91764 602-C6
W GRANADA CT
100 ONT 91762 602-A6
900 ONT 91762 601-H6
GRANADA DR
7000 SBdC 92252 4959-B1
17700 SBdC 92392 4386-H3
GRANADA LN
5500 YUCA 92284 4888-B5
GRANADA PL
1600 POM 91767 601-D7
GRANADA RD
60100 SBdC 92252 4958-G1
GRANADA ST
1200 UPL 91784 571-J3
4200 MTCL 91763 601-E6
W GRANADA ST
300 RLTO 92376 605-G4
800 RLTO 92316 605-E5
GRANADA HILL AV
800 BARS 92311 3680-C5
GRANADOS DR
4000 SBdC 92407 546-F6
GRANBY AV
6100 RCUC 91737 573-A4
7500 RCUC 91730 573-A7
8200 RCUC 91730 603-A2
GRAND AV
- CHLS 91710 681-C2
- CHNO 91710 681-C2
100 DBAR 91789 680-A2
100 INDS 91789 680-A2
500 DBAR 91765 680-A2
1500 CHLS 91709 680-E3
2000 CLAR 91711 571-E5
2100 SBDO 92407 546-B6
2600 CHLS 91709 681-A2
3700 SBdC 91766 641-D3
4200 MTCL 91763 641-E3
4500 SBdC 91710 641-F3
4700 MTCL 91710 641-F3
4800 SBdC 91763 641-F3
4900 YUCA 92284 4887-H4
6800 YUCA 92284 4957-H2
10700 SBdC 91762 641-G1
E GRAND AV
100 POM 91766 640-J3
100 POM 91766 641-A3
1600 SBdC 91766 641-A3
7300 FONT 92336 574-B7
7800 FONT 92336 604-B1
N GRAND AV
100 INDS 91789 680-A7
100 INDS 91789 680-A1
100 SBdC 92324 606-B5
400 CLTN 92324 606-B3
W GRAND AV
100 POM 91766 640-G3
7300 FONT 92336 574-B7
7800 FONT 92336 604-B1
GRAND CT
56600 YUCA 92284 4957-H4
GRAND LN
- YUCA 92284 4887-G2
3100 SBdC 92284 4817-G6
N GRAND ST
1400 SBDO 92411 576-B5
GRANDE AV
2900 SBdC 92277 4821-H5
GRANDE WY
14400 VCTV 92394 4295-H7
GRANDE VISTA
20100 APLV 92308 4477-E2
GRANDE VISTA AV
3100 SBDO 92405 576-E2
GRANDE VISTA DR
200 SBdC - 514-A3
GRAND MAMMOTH PL
17000 VCTV 92394 4295-J1
GRAND PRIX
5300 FONT 92336 574-D2
GRAND PRIX CT
5500 FONT 92336 574-D2
GRAND RIM CT
1200 DBAR 91765 680-C2
GRANDRUE PL
14600 CHLS 91709 681-A4
GRAND TERRACE CT
11600 GTER 92313 646-F3
GRAND TERRACE RD
21800 GTER 92313 646-D3
22000 CLTN 92324 646-D3
22000 GTER 92324 646-D3
GRAND TRIASSIC LN
17100 VCTV 92394 4295-J2
GRAND VIEW AL
- SBDO 92405 576-G4
GRAND VIEW AV
18200 SBdC 92407 515-C5
GRANDVIEW AV
35400 SBdC - 4481-G6
GRAND VIEW AV
37800 SBdC - 3592-C7
37800 SBdC - (3682-B1 See Page 3592)
GRAND VIEW CIR
61800 SBdC 92252 4889-C7
61800 SBdC 92252 4959-B1
GRAND VIEW DR
200 RDL 92373 648-D2
GRANDVIEW DR
1200 CHLS 91709 710-G3
10600 RCUC 91701 573-B6
22600 SBdC - 516-E4
GRAND VIEW DR
25000 SBdC - 517-B5
GRANDVIEW DR
35500 YCPA 92399 650-B3
E GRANDVIEW DR
100 BARS 92311 3679-H3
W GRANDVIEW DR
100 BARS 92311 3679-G3
GRAND VIEW RD
- SBdC 92308 4479-D7
GRANDVIEW RD
100 SBdC - 517-D2
2800 BARS 92311 3679-A5
2900 BARS 92311 3678-J5
4800 SBdC 92285 (4576-A7 See Page 4486)
5200 SBdC 92345 (4655-B3 See Page 4654)
5700 SBdC 92285 (4575-J4 See Page 4484)
6700 SBdC 92345 4565-A1
8900 SBdC 92345 4475-A7
20900 SBdC 92308 4477-G7
GRAND VIEW RD
29300 SBdC - 4480-A7
GRANDVIEW RD
31300 SBdC - 4480-F6
34300 SBdC - 4481-E6
GRANDVIEW ST
1400 UPL 91784 571-H3
GRANITE AV
72500 TNP 92277 4892-B5
N GRANITE AV
400 ONT 91762 602-A5
S GRANITE AV
100 ONT 91762 642-A1
GRANITE CT
- FONT 92336 574-E4
6100 RCUC 91737 572-H4
GRANITE DR
600 SBdC - 518-B3
GRANITE RD
32900 SBdC - (4391-A1 See Page 4300)
36000 SBdC - (4392-A1 See Page 4302)
38400 SBdC - 4302-F7
GRANITE ST
1500 RDL 92374 608-F4
30900 SBdC 92359 608-H6
GRANITE HILL DR
6800 RivC 92509 644-B6
6800 RivC 92509 645-A7
GRANITE PEAK AV
- FONT 92336 574-D3
GRANITE PEAK CT
15600 VCTV 92394 4295-F5
GRANITE PEAK LN
13300 VCTV 92394 4295-F5
GRANITE PRIVADO
- ONT 91762 642-A2
GRANITE WELLS RD
8500 SBdC - 328-H10
GRANT
- SBDO 92407 545-H1
E GRANT AV
800 SBDO 92410 606-E4
1100 CLTN 92324 606-E4
1100 SBDO 92324 606-E4
W GRANT AV
900 SBDO 92410 606-F4
GRANT CT
6100 CHNO 91710 641-J6
6100 CHNO 91710 642-A6
GRANT DR
11700 YCPA 92399 650-C2
GRANT ST
- RDL 92373 608-B7
- RDL 92373 648-B1
900 CALI 92320 650-C7
6400 CHNO 91710 642-A6
12500 YCPA 92399 650-C4
16700 VCTV 92392 4386-E3
E GRANT ST
100 RLTO 92376 605-H4
W GRANT ST
100 RLTO 92376 605-G3
300 UPL 91784 572-B6
GRANT WY
- FONT 92336 574-A6
GRANVILLE RD
60500 SBdC 92252 4818-H6
GRAPE AV
34600 YCPA 92399 609-J5
34700 YCPA 92399 610-A5
GRAPE CT
200 SBDO 92410 606-E1
35100 YCPA 92399 610-A6
GRAPE DR
9400 SBdC 92339 611-H3
GRAPE PL
- RCUC 91739 573-H6
GRAPE ST
7700 HIGH 92346 577-F7
S GRAPE ST
200 SBDO 92410 606-E2
GRAPEFRUIT AV
8800 HESP 92345 4476-J6
GRAPEVINE DR
300 DBAR 91765 640-D7
GRAPEVINE ST
11500 RCUC 91730 573-D7
GRAPEVINE CANYON DR
27300 SBdC 92308 4479-G7
27300 SBdC 92308 (4569-G1 See Page 4568)
GRAPEVINE CANYON RD
100 SBdC - (4569-F7 See Page 4568)
300 SBdC - (4659-F2 See Page 4658)
6900 SBdC 92308 (4569-F2 See Page 4568)
27300 SBdC 92308 4479-F7
28500 SBdC - 4479-J3
29000 SBdC - 4480-A3
N GRAPEWOOD AV
3300 RLTO 92377 575-B1
3400 RLTO 92377 545-B7
GRAPHITE LN
1400 SBdC - (4743-A3 See Page 4662)
GRASS HOPPER
43500 SBdC - 349-B6
GRASSHOPPER CT
14800 VCTV 92394 4295-H7
GRASSHOPPER RD
- APLV 92307 4207-B3
- SBdC 92307 4207-B3
GRASSLAND ST
13500 YCPA 92399 649-H7
GRASS VALLEY CT
500 SBdC - 4737-G7
GRASS VALLEY LN
26900 SBdC - 4737-G7
GRASS VALLEY RD
100 SBdC - 517-F2
200 SBdC - 4737-G7
N GRASS VALLEY RD
500 SBdC - 4737-G4
GRAVILLA RD
14500 SBdC 92392 4385-J3
14700 SBdC 92392 4386-A3
15000 VCTV 92392 4386-A3
GRAVURE ST
- SBdC 92365 (3684-B6 See Page 3594)
- SBdC 92365 3764-C3
GRAY LN
14000 VCTV 92394 4295-H7
GRAY ST
3200 SBdC 92407 575-H1
3400 SBdC 92407 545-H6
14500 ADEL 92301 4294-H7
14500 ADEL 92301 4384-H1
W GRAY ST
400 CLTN 92324 606-C3
GRAY WY
14900 VCTV 92394 4295-H7
GRAYBURN RD
- SBdC 92365 (3685-C4 See Page 3594)
S GRAYMOOR AV
2700 CLTN 92324 646-B5
GRAY PINE CT
- SBDO 92407 546-A3
GRAYSON PL
6700 RCUC 91701 573-C5
GRAYSON ST
10600 ADEL 92301 4294-H6
S GRAYSON WY
100 UPL 91786 602-A4
GRAYS PEAK AV
- FONT 92336 574-D3
GRAYSTONE AV
17800 CHLS 91709 712-B5
GREASEWOOD LN
1500 SBdC 92372 4472-D2
3900 SBdC 92371 4473-D1
7700 SBdC 92371 4474-A1
8700 SBdC 92392 4474-D1
11300 SBdC 92392 4475-A1
11700 VCTV 92392 4475-B1
GREAT BEND DR
400 DBAR 91765 680-B1
GREAT FALLS AV
13100 VCTV 92392 4386-F4
GREAT HOUSE LN
8200 YUCA 92284 4957-C6
GREAT SPIRITS WY
700 BBLK - 4811-F2
GREAT VIEW DR
24200 SBdC - 516-J4
24200 SBdC - 517-A5
GREEN LN
11400 SBdC 92399 651-B1
GREEN RD
1600 SBdC 92372 4472-D7
8100 SBdC 92372 4562-C1
E GREEN ST
100 CLAR 91711 601-D4
W GREEN ST
100 CLAR 91711 601-D4
GREEN TR
9200 SBdC 92256 616-B1
GREENACRE DR
10500 RCUC 91730 573-B7
GREENACRE RD
3100 CHLS 91709 681-B2
GREENBLUFF WY
- YCPA 92399 649-E3
GREENBRIAR CT
- RDL 92374 608-G7
6500 CHNO 91710 682-B2
GREENBRIAR DR
- SBdC - (4025-J4 See Page 3934)
700 SBdC - 518-C3
3100 ONT 91761 643-A7
13700 VCTV 92392 4386-D2
14600 SBdC - (3935-H2 See Page 3934)
E GREENBRIAR DR
2900 ONT 91761 643-A7
GREENBRIAR PL
7300 RCUC 91730 573-C7
W GREENBRIAR ST
1900 CLTN 92324 605-H4
GREENBRIER PL
7300 HIGH 92346 578-D5
GREENBROOK PL
10500 YCPA 92399 610-A6
GREEN CANYON RD
1400 SBdC - 4812-J4
1400 SBdC 92314 4812-J4
GREENDALE LN
600 POM 91767 601-A1
GREEN DESERT DR
- BARS 92311 (3759-A2 See Page 3758)
3200 BARS 92311 3758-G2
GREENE CT
- ADEL 92301 4295-A7
GREENE RD
- SBdC 92285 (4575-H7 See Page 4484)
W GREENFIELD CT
400 UPL 91786 602-A4
GREENFIELD LN
28300 HIGH 92346 578-B5
GREEN GLEN CT
- RCUC 91739 573-J6
GREENHAVEN AV
7300 RCUC 91730 573-B7
GREENHEDGE LN
- POM 91766 640-F7
- POM 91766 641-A4
GREEN HILL DR
15800 VCTV 92394 4296-C3
GREENHORN DR
600 DBAR 91765 640-B6
GREENING ST
18100 ADEL 92301 4205-B5
GREENLEAF DR
400 RivC 91752 683-F4
GREEN LEAF LN
200 SBdC - 518-A1
GREENLEAF LN
8400 RCUC 91730 602-F2
GREENLEAF PL
- POM 91766 640-G7
GREEN MESA DR
10100 RCUC 91730 603-B2
N GREEN MOUNTAIN DR
1100 SBdC 92314 4742-B4
GREEN MOUNTAIN RD
1000 SBdC - 514-B5
GREEN OAKS CT
1400 SBdC - 4812-D2
GREEN RIVER RD
14500 VCTV 92394 4295-H7
14500 VCTV 92394 4385-H1
GREENROCK
- SBdC 92285 (4485-E2 See Page 4484)
GREEN ROCK MINE RD
9100 SBdC - (4483-H5 See Page 4482)
10500 SBdC - (4393-H7 See Page 4302)
GREENS CT
16100 CHLS 91709 710-G1
GREENS DR
1500 CHLS 91709 710-G1
GREENSBORO CT
400 CLAR 91711 601-D1
GREENSBORO RD
12800 SBdC 92392 4386-J4
13000 SBdC 92392 4387-A4
GREENSBORO WY
- FONT 92336 574-H3
GREENSPOT BLVD
Rt#-38
700 SBdC 92314 4742-G7
700 SBdC 92314 4812-H1

STREET
Block City ZIP Pg-Grid

S GREENSPOT BLVD
Rt#-38
100 SBdC 92314 4742-G5
GREENSPOT RD
7800 HIGH 92346 578-D7
32000 HIGH 92346 609-A2
32000 HIGH 92359 609-A2
32000 HIGH - 609-A2
32500 RDL 92359 609-A2
N GREENSPOT RD
100 SBdC 92314 4742-G5
GREEN SPOT PICNIC RD
1300 SBdC - 4812-H4
GREENSTONE DR
13500 RCUC 91739 573-J4
13500 RCUC 91739 574-A4
GREENS WELL RD
91800 SBdC - 330-L5
96800 SBdC - 331-A6
GREEN TREE BLVD
13900 VCTV 92392 4386-C1
GREEN TREE CT
13200 CHLS 91709 681-A1
GREENTREE LN
22200 SBdC - 516-D3
S GREENTREE RD
200 UPL 91786 602-B4
GREENVALE CIR
1200 UPL 91784 571-J6
GREEN VALLEY DR
15200 CHLS 91709 681-B6
GREEN VALLEY LN
33600 SBdC - 519-F2
GREEN VALLEY LAKE RD
3700 SBdC - 519-F2
GREENVIEW RD
- SBdC 92365 (3595-A6
See Page 3594)
32100 SBdC 92365 (3765-B3
See Page 3764)
35600 SBdC 92365 (3685-B1
See Page 3594)
GREENVILLE CIR
28600 HIGH 92346 578-B6
GREEN VISTA DR
13700 FONT 92337 644-C3
GREENWAY DR
27700 SBdC - 517-J1
N GREENWAY DR
1100 SBdC 92314 4742-D4
N GREENWAY DR
Rt#-38
100 SBdC 92314 4742-D5
S GREENWAY DR
100 SBdC 92314 4742-D6
GREENWAY LN
4300 CHNO 91710 641-E4
GREENWICH CT
1000 DBAR 91765 680-D2
GREENWICH DR
1300 RIV 92501 645-H7
GREENWICH PL
7400 RCUC 91730 573-C7
GREENWICH RD
26200 LMLN 92354 647-F3
S GREENWOOD
2200 ONT 91761 642-E5
GREENWOOD AV
- ONT 91761 642-D6
400 SBdC 92407 515-A4
9600 MTCL 91763 601-F6
N GREENWOOD AV
700 ONT 91764 602-D6
S GREENWOOD AV
800 ONT 91761 642-D2
GREENWOOD CT
300 POM 91766 641-A5
600 RDL 92373 648-A3
9800 FONT 92335 604-H5
17500 SBdC 92407 515-A3
GREENWOOD LN
2000 POM 91766 641-A5
GREENWOOD PL
5700 RCUC 91739 573-G3
13700 VCTV 92392 4386-D2
S GREENWOOD PL
2400 ONT 91761 642-D5
GREENWOOD ST
- FONT 92337 644-J3
10800 SBdC 92345 4564-J6
11500 SBdC 92345 4565-B6
14100 HESP 92345 4565-H6
15300 HESP 92345 4566-B6
W GREENWOOD ST
2200 SBDO 92410 606-B1
GREENWOOD WY
4700 SBdC 91710 641-F3
GREGORIO CT
6200 CHNO 91710 682-A1
GREGORY CT
16800 FONT 92337 604-J7
GREGORY PL
24000 SBdC - 516-J3
GREGORY ST
18100 SBdC 92316 605-C7
N GREGORY ST
5900 SBDO 92407 545-J3

GREMLIN CT
30200 SBdC - 518-F7
E GRENFALL LN
300 SBdC 92314 4742-D5
GRENOBLE DR
28100 SBdC - 4738-A6
GRENVIEW WY
- CHLS 91709 681-H7
GRETCHEN PL
400 POM 91768 640-C2
GREVILLEA CT
15900 FONT 92335 604-G5
E GREVILLEA CT
900 ONT 91761 642-D4
GREVILLEA DR
15900 FONT 92335 604-G5
GREVILLEA ST
15700 FONT 92335 604-F5
16100 HESP 92345 4566-D4
17300 FONT 92335 605-A5
E GREVILLEA ST
100 ONT 91761 642-C4
100 ONT 91762 642-C4
W GREVILLEA ST
400 ONT 91762 642-B4
E GREVILLIA ST
200 POM 91767 601-A4
GREY BACK TR
900 SBdC - 4741-B5
GREYCLIFF AV
11200 MTCL 91763 641-F3
GREYCLOUD LN
800 DBAR 91765 640-E5
GREYCREST PL
1200 DBAR 91765 680-D3
GREY FOX LN
2800 ONT 91761 683-A1
GREY MOUNTAIN RD
19300 SBdC 92301 (4202-D1
See Page 4112)
20200 SBdC 92301 4112-D5
GREYSTONE AV
1100 RDL 92374 608-D4
GREYSTONE DR
- RivC 91752 643-E5
5700 SBdC - 4773-J7
5700 SBdC - 4843-J1
5800 SBdC - 4844-A1
E GREYSTONE DR
3900 ONT 91761 643-C5
GREYSTONE PL
5700 SBdC - 4843-J1
GREYSTONE RD
12100 SBdC 92371 4383-B7
GRIDLEY ST
18300 APLV 92307 (4206-J5
See Page 4116)
GRIER ST
1700 POM 91766 640-E3
GRIFFIS RD
- YUCA 92284 4887-H4
GRIFFITH AV
7500 HIGH 92346 578-A6
GRIFFITH RD
56900 YUCA 92284 4887-H5
GRIMALDI RD
11600 RCUC 91701 573-D5
GRIMM AV
4700 SBdC 92277 4824-C7
4700 SBdC 92277 (4894-C1
See Page 4824)
GRING DR
- SBdC - (4392-J6
See Page 4302)
- SBdC - (4393-A6
See Page 4302)
GRINNELL CT
12900 VCTV 92392 4385-E4
W GRINNELL DR
400 CLAR 91711 601-C3
E GRIZZLEY CREEK CT
3600 ONT 91761 643-C6
GRIZZLY LN
27200 SBdC - 517-H1
GRIZZLY RD
100 SBdC - 517-G1
300 SBdC - 4737-G7
43000 BBLK - 4812-B2
GRIZZLY WY
- FONT 92336 574-D3
GROOM DR
600 DBAR 91765 640-B6
GROSSMONT RD
1500 SBDO 92407 546-C6
GROTTO HILLS LN
15700 VCTV 92394 4295-F4
GROTTO HILLS WY
13300 VCTV 92394 4295-F5
GROVE AV
6700 HIGH 92346 578-A5
12900 ONT 91761 642-E7
12900 ONT 91761 682-E3
14100 ONT 91710 682-E3
15700 SBdC 91710 682-F7
15700 SBdC 91710 712-F1
N GROVE AV
- UPL 91730 602-E1
- UPL 91786 602-E1
100 ONT 91761 602-E6
100 ONT 91761 642-E1

N GROVE AV
700 ONT 91764 602-E4
500 RCUC 91730 602-E1
700 RCUC 91786 602-E1
1400 UPL 91786 572-E7
S GROVE AV
100 ONT 91761 642-E2
GROVE CT
300 BARS 92311 3679-J5
N GROVE CT
200 RLTO 92376 575-G7
GROVE DR
- BARS 92311 3758-D3
- SBdC 92311 3758-D3
11500 YCPA 92399 650-C2
GROVE PL
18500 SBdC 92316 605-D5
19000 RLTO 92316 605-E5
GROVE ST
5200 SBdC 91762 641-G1
5200 SBdC 91763 641-G1
E GROVE ST
100 RLTO 92376 575-H7
100 POM 91767 601-A2
200 RLTO 92376 605-H1
500 LACo 91711 601-A2
600 SBDO 92376 575-J7
N GROVE ST
- RDL 92374 608-E5
S GROVE ST
600 RDL 92374 608-E7
700 RDL 92374 648-E1
W GROVE ST
100 RLTO 92376 575-G7
300 RLTO 92376 605-D1
W GROVE WY
1100 SBdC 92314 4742-B7
GROVES CT
6700 CHNO 91710 682-B1
GROVES ST
6800 CHNO 91710 682-B1
GROVESIDE PL
6700 RCUC 91701 572-J5
W GROVEWOOD ST
600 RLTO 92316 605-F5
GRUBSTAKE DR
1200 DBAR 91765 680-C3
GRUMMAN AV
15200 FONT 92336 574-E4
GUACO ST
2000 BARS 92311 3680-C5
GUADALAJARA PL
1400 CLAR 91711 601-E2
GUADALUPE DR
1100 BARS 92311 3679-J7
E GUADALUPE DR
700 UPL 91786 602-D1
GUAJOME RD
20500 APLV 92307 4297-F2
22900 APLV 92307 4298-C2
23300 SBdC 92307 4298-C2
GUAM ST
- BARS 92311 3680-F7
GUANAJUATO DR
800 CLAR 91711 571-B6
E GUASTI RD
2200 ONT 91761 602-H7
2200 ONT 91764 602-H7
2800 ONT 91761 603-B7
GUATAY RD
- SBdC - 4774-G7
GUAVA AV
8800 HESP 92345 4476-J6
9200 HESP 92345 4477-A6
GUAVA CT
- SBdC 92335 604-F3
GUAVA RD
36300 SBdC - (4571-J2
See Page 4570)
36300 SBdC - (4572-A2
See Page 4482)
GUENTER LN
- SBdC 92284 4818-D7
GUIDERA DR
- RCUC 91739 544-A7
GUILD CIR
4300 RivC 92509 644-D7
S GUILFORD AV
5300 RCUC 91739 574-B1
GUILIANO PL
16000 FONT 92335 604-G3
GUINAN LN
40100 BBLK - 4811-D2
GULFSTREAM AV
15500 FONT 92336 574-E4
GUM LN
- FONT 92337 645-A1
GUN AV
12600 CHNO 91710 641-E6
GUNDERSEN RD
- SBdC 92277 4751-J7
GUNN RD
55300 SBdC 92284 4747-D4
E GUNNISON WY
2500 CLTN 92324 646-J4
GUNSITE LN
51700 SBdC - 4816-D7
GUNSMOKE AV
- POM 91766 640-F5
GUNSMOKE DR
100 DBAR 91765 640-B6

GUNSMOKE RD
28900 SBdC - (3847-A5
See Page 3756)
GUNTOTE LN
51600 SBdC - 4816-D7
GUPAN RD
19900 APLV 92308 4387-D7
GURNEE AV
1000 ONT 91764 603-D6
GUSTAFSON RD
- BARS 92311 3758-J3
- SBdC 92311 3758-J3
GUSTINE ST
20900 APLV 92307 4207-G5
22100 APLV 92307 4208-A5
22500 SBdC 92307 4208-A5
GUTHRIE SPUR
37400 YCPA 92399 650-G6
GUTHRIE ST
5900 SBdC 92404 577-D2
6100 SBDO 92404 577-D3
7300 HIGH 92410 577-D6
N GUTHRIE ST
1600 SBDO 92404 577-D4
GUY AV
11300 SBdC 92392 4475-A2
11700 VCTV 92392 4475-B2
GWEN ST
10000 MohC - 3620-C2
GWENT ST
11500 LMLN 92354 647-F2
GYPSUM CT
2200 CHLS 91709 680-J6
GYPSUM RD
2100 CLTN 92324 645-H4
S GYPSUM RIDGE RD
100 SBDO 92410 606-C2
GYPSY RD
31900 SBdC - 4480-G1
32400 SBdC - (4390-J7
See Page 4300)
32500 SBdC - (4391-A7
See Page 4300)

H

H AV
8400 HESP 92345 4566-G1
9100 HESP 92345 4476-G4
H LN
1000 SBdC 92314 4813-B1
H ST
- BARS 92311 3680-G6
- SBdC 92252 4889-D2
100 NDLS 92363 3620-C6
2000 BARS 92311 3679-E5
3500 BARS 92311 (3759-E1
See Page 3758)
3500 SBdC 92311 (3759-E1
See Page 3758)
5000 CHNO 91710 681-G1
12100 SBdC 93562 2144-G5
33700 SBdC 92311 3679-E5
E H ST
100 CLTN 92324 606-E6
100 ONT 91764 602-C6
N H ST
300 SBDO 92410 606-G1
400 SBDO 92410 576-F5
1200 SBDO 92405 576-F2
3900 SBDO 92407 546-F7
4200 SBdC 92407 546-F5
S H ST
500 SBDO 92410 606-G3
700 SBDO 92408 606-G3
W H ST
100 CLTN 92324 606-D6
100 ONT 91762 602-B6
100 ONT 91761 602-B6
800 SBdC 92324 606-B6
900 ONT 91762 601-H6
HABANERA RD
56500 SBdC 92285 4747-F2
HACIENDA CT
- FONT 92336 574-H2
5300 RCUC 91739 574-B1
HACIENDA DR
5200 YUCA 92284 4888-B4
14300 VCTV 92392 4386-F1
N HACIENDA DR
1300 ONT 91764 602-H4
HACIENDA LN
4100 CHNO 91710 641-D7
4100 SBdC 91710 641-D7
18000 SBdC 92392 4386-H4
HACIENDA RD
11300 SBdC 92371 4473-D2
12000 SBdC 92371 4383-D3
13600 ADEL 92392 4384-G3
13600 VCTV 92392 4384-G3
19300 SBdC 92301 (4203-C3
See Page 4112)
37500 SBdC 92365 (3593-H3
See Page 3592)
37800 SBdC 92365 3594-A2
38500 SBdC 92365 (3504-J4
See Page 3414)
47500 SBdC 92365 (3505-B3
See Page 3414)

HACIENDA RD
51700 SBdC 92285 (4576-C5
See Page 4486)
59800 SBdC 92284 4888-H4
62100 SBdC 92252 4889-C5
HACIENDA WY
- FONT 92336 574-H2
HACKAMORE RD
14500 VCTV 92392 4385-J5
HACKBERRY CIR
2600 CHLS 91709 681-A7
HACKBERRY ST
17700 HESP 92345 4476-H1
18200 HESP 92345 4477-A1
HACKNEY ST
28500 HIGH 92346 578-B5
HADDINGTON WY
15100 VCTV 92394 4295-J6
HADDOCK DR
23000 DBAR 91765 640-B6
HADLEY DR
3000 RivC 91752 644-A5
HAGADOR AV
16600 VCTV 92394 4296-A2
HAGY AV
28800 HIGH 92346 578-C5
HAIDA CT
14100 APLV 92307 4387-D1
HAIDA DR
18900 APLV 92307 4387-A1
HAIDA RD
18800 APLV 92307 4387-H2
19900 APLV 92307 4297-D7
HAIWEE CT
7400 SBdC - 4843-G5
HAIWEE RD
19200 APLV 92307 4387-B2
HAKATAYA DR
- SBdC - 4887-C5
HALBERTA CIR
300 CALI 92320 649-J7
HALBRENT AV
- SBdC 92345 4654-J3
- SBdC 92345 (4655-A3
See Page 4654)
HALBROOK LN
11900 SBdC 92316 645-G3
HALCYON WY
2200 POM 91767 601-A4
HALDOR DR
5200 RivC 91752 683-G3
W HALE DR
400 SBdC 92314 4742-C4
HALE ST
14200 FONT 92336 574-C7
HALES DR
1100 SBdC 92277 4751-C5
1300 SBdC 92277 4821-C1
HALF DOME DR
- FONT 92336 574-D3
HALF MOON CIR
12200 VCTV 92392 4385-D6
HALFMOON CT
20400 APLV 92308 4387-F5
HALF MOON WY
12600 VCTV 92392 4385-D6
HALIFAX CIR
- FONT 92336 574-C1
HALIFAX DR
1200 SBdC - 4738-B5
HALIFAX LN
11300 SBdC 91766 641-D3
HALINOR ST
14900 HESP 92345 4566-B6
HALITE CT
2000 CHLS 91709 680-H7
HALL AV
2300 RivC 92509 645-G4
7700 RivC 92880 712-H2
11700 SBdC 92316 645-G4
HALL CT
4700 CHNO 91710 641-F6
HALL LN
5700 TNP 92277 4892-B4
HALL WY
7300 HIGH 92346 577-E6
HALLEE RD
6000 SBdC 92252 4889-A7
HALLENMAR AV
700 BARS 92311 3680-B5
HALLMARK LN
15100 VCTV 92394 4295-G6
HALLMARK PKWY
3500 SBDO 92407 546-A5
HALLORAN SPRINGS RD
68700 SBdC - 330-E9
HALL RANCH RD
17100 SBdC 92407 514-J3
HALLWOOD AV
800 POM 91767 601-B5
W HALLWOOD CT
1300 UPL 91786 601-J2
HALSEY AV
5700 TNP 92277 4892-G4
HALSEY ST
1600 RDL 92373 648-E4
HALSTEAD RD
21200 SBdC 92347 349-B7
HALSTED AV
6100 RCUC 91737 573-A4

HALSTED RD
6800 RCUC 91701 573-A5
HALTER CT
14500 FONT 92336 574-C2
HALTER TR
27500 SBdC - (3937-D2
See Page 3936)
HAMAL AV
11000 RivC 91752 683-H2
HAMILTAIR DR
27600 SBdC - 4737-J7
N HAMILTON BLVD
100 POM 91768 640-H1
1000 POM 91766 640-H1
S HAMILTON BLVD
100 POM 91766 640-H2
HAMILTON CT
6200 CHNO 91710 642-A6
14700 ADEL 92301 4294-J7
HAMILTON DR
6900 HIGH 92346 578-C4
10100 MohC - 3620-B2
HAMILTON ST
6500 CHNO 91710 642-A6
8300 RCUC 91701 572-F5
10100 RCUC 91701 573-A5
HAMILTON WY
- MohC - 3620-D3
HAMLIN PL
1000 RDL 92373 648-A1
HAMMAN RD
100 SBdC 92278 4748-J2
100 SBdC 92285 4748-J2
HAMMER AV
13600 CHNO 91710 682-B2
HAMMETT RD
8000 YUCA 92284 4957-C4
HAMMOND RD
700 BBLK - 4811-D2
HAMMOND ST
500 POM 91767 601-A3
HAMNER AV
3800 ONT 91761 643-D7
3800 ONT 91761 683-D3
3800 SBdC 91761 643-D7
3800 SBdC 91761 683-D3
5200 RivC 91752 683-D3
5200 RivC 92880 683-D5
W HAMPDEN CT
1000 UPL 91786 602-A4
HAMPSHIRE AV
1100 SBDO 92404 547-A7
HAMPSHIRE CT
700 POM 91768 640-H1
HAMPSHIRE PL
6700 CHNO 91710 642-B7
HAMPSHIRE RD
34500 SBdC - (3682-J4
See Page 3592)
E HAMPSHIRE RD
1600 SBDO 92404 547-C7
HAMPSHIRE ST
9400 RCUC 91730 602-J2
10100 RCUC 91730 603-A2
HAMPSKIN RD
34500 SBdC 92365 (3683-D5
See Page 3592)
HAMPTON CT
6700 CHNO 91710 642-B7
15400 FONT 92337 644-F3
22100 GTER 92313 646-D4
HAMPTON DR
3700 SBdC 91766 641-C3
42900 SBdC 92365 (3683-F1
See Page 3592)
HAMPTON PL
10600 RCUC 91730 573-B7
HAMPTON RD
1400 RDL 92374 648-E2
31000 YCPA 92374 648-J4
31100 SBdC 92374 648-H3
31100 YCPA 92399 648-J4
31300 YCPA 92399 649-A4
HAMPTON WY
33400 SBdC - (3681-F7
See Page 3590)
HAMSTEAD CIR
1700 RDL 92374 608-G7
HANAUPAH RD
21600 APLV 92308 4477-J2
HANCOCK CT
9900 ADEL 92301 4204-F4
13400 FONT 92336 574-A7
HANCOCK ST
4900 CHNO 91710 641-F5
N HANCOCK ST
600 SBDO 92411 576-D4
HANDLEY RD
56100 SBdC 92284 4747-F5
60200 SBdC 92284 4748-G5
61100 SBdC 92252 4748-J5
61100 SBdC 92252 4749-A5
HANDSDALE ST
14500 ADEL 92301 4384-H1
HANEMO DR
- SBdC - 4774-G7
- SBdC - 4844-F1
HANFORD AV
- HESP 92345 4475-J7
- HESP 92345 4565-J1

HANFORD LN
900 SBdC 92284 4748-B7
900 SBdC 92284 4818-B2
6500 YUCA 92284 4888-B7
6500 YUCA 92284 4958-B1
W HANFORD CT
2100 SBDO 92411 576-B5
HANFORD RD
21600 APLV 92307 4207-H5
HANFORD ST
1500 RDL 92374 608-D5
W HANFORD ST
2000 SBDO 92411 576-B5
E HANNA ST
100 CLTN 92324 606-D5
W HANNA ST
100 CLTN 92324 606-D5
HANNAN ST
34100 SBdC 92311 3678-G6
HANOR DR
- SBdC 92277 4821-H3
HANOVER CT
- RCUC 91701 573-B6
HANOVER RD
1800 CLAR 91711 571-C7
1800 CLAR 91711 601-C1
HANOVER WY
- CHLS 91709 681-H7
5200 MTCL 91763 641-G2
HANSEN AV
900 POM 91766 640-G3
HANSFIELD CT
6700 CHNO 91710 642-B6
HANSON CIR E
100 SBdC - 516-C2
HANSON CIR W
- SBdC - 516-C2
HAPPY TR
2700 SBdC 92285 4667-B5
12900 VCTV 92392 4385-H5
HAPPY HOLLOW RD
22700 DBAR 91765 640-B5
HAPPY TRAILS HWY
Rt#-18
13700 APLV 92308 4388-A2
15500 APLV 92307 4388-A2
15600 APLV 92307 4387-G1
17900 APLV 92307 4296-H4
18400 APLV 92307 4297-D5
21300 APLV 92308 4387-G1
HAPPY VALLEY RD
10100 MohC - 3620-B3
19400 SBdC 92307 4567-D5
HAPPY WILLOW DR
- MohC - 3620-B2
N HARBER DR
1000 CLTN 92324 606-F4
HARBIN AV
9100 HESP 92345 4477-A6
HARBOR AV
- MohC - 3620-C3
HARBOR DR
18000 SBdC 92392 4386-J2
HARBOUR TOWN TR
2500 ONT 91761 642-J6
HARDESTY DR
8500 YUCA 92284 4957-J6
HARDFORD CT
6500 RCUC 91701 573-C5
HARDING CT
1000 CLAR 91711 601-B1
7300 HIGH 92346 578-B5
11700 CHNO 91710 641-H4
14600 HESP 92345 4566-A5
HARDING DR
600 RDL 92373 648-B2
HARDING RD
3900 SBdC 92371 4473-A4
HARDING ST
14600 HESP 92345 4566-A5
HARDROCK DAVIS RD
- SBdC - (4115-J3
See Page 4114)
15600 SBdC - 4116-A3
E HARDT DR
800 SBDO 92408 607-B5
HARDT ST
1800 SBDO 92354 607-D5
E HARDT ST
1200 SBDO 92408 607-C5
1600 SBDO 92354 607-C5
HARDY AV
9400 ADEL 92301 4204-E6
11700 ADEL 92301 4205-A6
HARDY DR
24300 DBAR 91765 640-E7
HARDY WY
- SBdC - 519-E7
7500 RCUC 91730 573-D7
HARFORD AV
36700 SBdC 92311 3589-J7
W HARFORD PL
100 UPL 91786 572-B7
HARLAN LN
27300 HIGH 92346 577-H6
HARMONY AV
- BARS 92311 3758-H4
12700 CHNO 91710 641-E7
HARMONY DR
10600 RCUC 91730 573-D7

HARMONY LN
14400 VCTV 92392 4296-D7
14400 VCTV 92392 4386-D1
34900 YCPA 92399 650-A6
HARMONY RD
900 SBdC 92284 4748-B7
900 SBdC 92284 4818-B2
HARMS LN
- SBdC 92252 4819-A6
HARNE CT
- RCUC 91739 573-G6
HAROLD RD
1000 BARS 92311 3678-J6
HARP ST
33700 SBdC - (3681-E7
See Page 3590)
HARPER PL
- FONT 92336 573-J7
HARPER LAKE RD
40700 SBdC 92347 348-L7
HARREL ST
11000 RivC 91752 643-G7
HARRIET CT
36100 YCPA 92399 650-D6
E HARRIMAN PL
700 SBDO 92408 607-A6
S HARRINGTON AV
200 UPL 91786 602-A4
HARRINGTON CT
6700 CHNO 91710 682-B1
HARRIS LN
14500 SBdC - (4025-H3
See Page 3934)
HARRIS RD
11200 SBdC 92399 611-A7
18900 APLV 92307 4207-C3
HARRIS ST
2100 CLTN 92324 646-H1
N HARRIS ST
600 SBDO 92411 576-F5
HARRISBURG CT
13000 CHNO 91710 641-E7
HARRISON AV
100 CLAR 91711 601-B3
800 POM 91767 601-B3
6000 RivC 92880 683-A6
E HARRISON AV
100 POM 91767 601-A3
W HARRISON CT
1000 UPL 91786 602-A4
HARRISON DR
14700 ADEL 92301 4294-J7
HARRISON ST
600 NDLS 92363 3620-B4
600 SBdC 92363 3620-B4
4500 CHNO 91710 641-F5
N HARRISON ST
2200 SBDO 92404 577-B1
3100 SBdC 92404 577-B1
3600 SBDO 92404 547-A7
N HARRISON CANYON RD
4000 SBdC 92404 547-B6
4000 SBDO 92404 547-B6
HARROD RD
13300 SBdC - 4302-A3
13300 SBdC - (4392-B1
See Page 4302)
HARRY SHEPPARD BLVD
900 SBDO 92408 607-A2
HART AV
- UPL 91786 602-E2
HART DR
35100 YCPA 92399 650-A2
HART LN
800 SBdC 92314 (4743-A7
See Page 4662)
800 SBdC 92314 4813-A1
HARTFORD CIR
400 RDL 92374 608-G7
HARTFORD CT
6300 CHNO 91710 642-A6
HARTFORD LN
11300 SBdC 91766 641-D3
14700 SBdC - (3935-H5
See Page 3934)
HARTFORD PL
900 POM 91768 640-G1
S HARTFORD PL
1800 SBDO 92408 607-C6
E HARTFORD ST
4200 ONT 91761 643-D6
HARTMAN CIR
300 SBdC - 516-C1
HARTNEL PL
3700 CLAR 91711 571-F4
HARTT PL
200 CLAR 91711 601-D1
HARTZELL AV
100 RDL 92374 608-B4
HARVARD AV
- HESP 92345 4475-J7
13700 CHNO 91710 682-A2
N HARVARD AV
100 CLAR 91711 601-D2
HARVARD CT
800 RDL 92374 608-C5
13400 FONT 92336 574-A7
14100 ADEL 92301 4385-B1

HARVARD DR
2000 BARS 92311 3679-H6
HARVARD PL
100 CLAR 91711 601-D3
E HARVARD PL
100 ONT 91764 602-C5
W HARVARD PL
600 ONT 91762 602-A6
1300 ONT 91762 601-H6
HARVARD RD
- SBdC - (3504-F4
See Page 3414)
31700 SBdC 92365 3764-F2
32700 SBdC 92365 (3684-F7
See Page 3594)
35700 SBdC 92365 3594-F6
38500 SBdC 92365 (3504-F4
See Page 3414)
HARVARD ST
4300 MTCL 91763 601-E6
9100 RCUC 91730 602-H1
HARVEST
83800 SBdC 92277 (4895-D2
See Page 4824)
HARVEST CT
3800 SBdC 91710 641-D6
HARVEST DR
- RivC 91752 683-D1
- SBdC 91761 683-D1
HARVEST ST
7300 FONT 92336 574-D6
HARVEST MOON ST
33800 SBdC - 4481-C3
HARVEY AV
200 RivC 92507 646-D6
HARVEY DR
16100 FONT 92336 604-H1
16100 FONT 92336 574-G7
HARVEY PT
- CHLS 91709 712-A6
HARWICK DR
- RCUC 91739 573-G6
28700 HIGH 92346 578-C4
E HARWICK DR
100 SBDO 92408 646-J1
W HARWICK DR
100 SBDO 92408 646-H1
100 CLTN 92324 646-H1
HARWOOD PL
500 CLAR 91711 601-E3
700 UPL 91786 601-F3
6500 TNP 92277 4890-H7
HASKELL RD
- LACo 92823 680-C7
- LACo 92823 710-C1
HASTINGS AV
7300 HESP 92345 4566-G4
HASTINGS BLVD
9000 RivC 92509 644-C7
HASTINGS CIR
2200 CLAR 91711 571-F6
HASTINGS CT
800 POM 91768 640-G1
4500 CHNO 91710 681-E1
11000 RCUC 91730 573-C7
HASTINGS DR
73300 TNP 92277 4892-D7
HASTINGS ST
- RDL 92373 648-A2
HASTINGS WY
2100 UPL 91784 572-C4
HASTINGS RANCH LN
13900 RCUC 91739 574-B2
HATAI CT
- SBdC - 4774-E7
HATCH RD
72100 TNP 92277 4892-B6
HATCHER PL
- FONT 92336 574-A6
HATCHERY DR
1000 SBdC 92314 4812-J2
1400 SBdC 92314 4812-H3
HATCHERY RD
300 SBdC 92314 4742-J7
400 SBdC 92314 4812-J1
HATFIELD RD
9300 SBdC 92345 4474-J6
HATHCOCK ST
- UPL 91786 602-E2
HATILLO RD
3900 SBdC 92371 4383-A2
HATMOR RD
- SBdC 92284 4747-E7
HAUASUPI RD
12300 APLV 92308 4387-E5
HAUPSTRASSE DR
42600 BBLK - 4812-A1
HAUSNA RD
26100 SBdC 92307 4299-A1
N HAVASU CT
2800 SBDO 92346 577-F2
HAVASU LN
14600 APLV 92307 4297-B7
HAVASU RD
13000 APLV 92308 4387-B3
13600 APLV 92307 4387-B3
14300 APLV 92307 4297-B7
HAVASU TR
55300 YUCA 92284 4957-D4

HAVASU LAKE RD
14700 SBdC - 372-B3
HAVEN AV
- SBdC 91737 (543-B7
See Page 513)
4900 RCUC 91737 (543-B7
See Page 513)
4900 RCUC 91737 573-B1
6700 RCUC 91701 573-B6
7300 RCUC 91730 573-B6
7700 RCUC 91730 603-B2
12900 ONT 91761 643-B7
12900 ONT 91761 683-B2
14100 ONT 91710 683-B3
N HAVEN AV
100 ONT 91761 603-B6
100 ONT 91761 643-B2
400 ONT 91764 603-B6
S HAVEN AV
100 ONT 91761 643-B5
HAVENHURST RD
18500 SBdC 92345 (4657-B1
See Page 4656)
HAVENHURST WY
2000 UPL 91784 571-H4
HAVEN REST RD
10200 SBdC - 4480-G2
HAVEN RIDGE RD
2400 POM 91767 601-B4
HAVENRIDGE RD
28200 HIGH 92346 578-A4
HAVENWOOD LN
29700 HIGH 92346 578-E5
HAVERFORD CT
12900 VCTV 92392 4385-E4
HAVERHILL ST
16600 VCTV 92394 4295-J2
HAVSTAD DR
11300 LMLN 92354 647-E2
HAWAII ST
- VCTV 92394 4205-G6
HAWAII WY
- FONT 92336 574-C6
HAWES RANCH RD
- SBdC - (4659-F7
See Page 4658)
HAWK CT
- SBdC - 4843-G2
13700 VCTV 92394 4295-G7
HAWK DR
42800 BBLK - 4812-B1
HAWK RD
- SBdC 92365 (3763-D2
See Page 3762)
2800 CHLS 91709 681-A5
34100 SBdC 92365 (3683-D5
See Page 3592)
HAWKBILL RD
25000 SBdC 92307 4298-H4
HAWK CANYON LN
1000 CHLS 91709 710-F2
HAWKEYE RD
8200 YUCA 92284 4957-C6
HAWKINS LN
12800 VCTV 92392 4385-E5
HAWK VALLEY RD
10000 SBdC 92256 616-D3
HAWKWOOD DR
2400 CHLS 91709 680-J3
HAWS LN
69500 SBdC 92277 4751-B7
HAWTHORN AV
15000 CHLS 91709 681-C6
E HAWTHORNE
2100 SBDO 92404 577-D2
HAWTHORNE AV
7500 HESP 92345 4566-A3
9400 SBdC 92335 604-C5
15700 FONT 92335 604-F4
17100 FONT 92335 605-A4
17500 SBdC 92335 605-B4
18100 SBdC 92316 605-D4
HAWTHORNE CT
17400 FONT 92335 605-A4
E HAWTHORNE CT
1900 ONT 91764 602-G5
S HAWTHORNE CT
200 RLTO 92376 605-G4
HAWTHORNE DR
9700 RCUC 91730 602-J5
9700 RCUC 91730 603-A5
36300 SBdC 92311 3680-C1
36400 SBdC 92311 3590-C7
E HAWTHORNE DR
100 ONT 91762 602-C5
100 ONT 91764 602-C5
E HAWTHORNE PL
700 POM 91767 641-B1
HAWTHORNE RD
7100 HESP 92345 4566-B5
9800 HESP 92345 4476-A2
11700 HESP 92345 4386-A7
21100 APLV 92307 4207-J4
21300 APLV 92307 4208-A4
22900 SBdC 92307 4208-C3
37600 SBdC - 4482-C3
HAWTHORNE ST
- SBdC - 4843-H4
4500 MTCL 91763 601-E5
8300 RCUC 91701 572-E5

STREET Block City ZIP Pg-Grid

E HAWTHORNE ST
300 ONT 91764 602-C5
W HAWTHORNE ST
200 RLTO 92376 605-G4
600 ONT 91762 602-A5
700 RLTO 92376 605-E4
900 ONT 91762 601-H5
HAY DR
16800 CHLS 91709 710-F3
HAYES CT
6500 CHNO 91710 642-A6
HAYFIELD LN
- SBdC 92277 4824-J2
- SBdC 92277 (4825-A2
See Page 4824)
HAYNES RD
- SBdC - (3935-J5
See Page 3934)
- SBdC - 3936-A6
32900 SBdC - 4300-J2
32900 SBdC - (4301-A2
See Page 4300)
HAYWARD AV
36800 SBdC 92311 3589-G7
HAYWARD CT
28900 SBdC 92311 3589-G6
W HAZEL AV
800 SBDO 92410 606-F3
W HAZEL CT
1500 UPL 91784 571-H6
HAZEL DR
13700 SBdC - 514-A1
HAZEL PL
- SBdC - 517-F4
HAZEL RD
- SBdC 92308 4479-E7
8700 SBdC 92308 4567-G1
HAZELNUT DR
700 SBdC - 4738-E7
HAZELNUT WY
6500 RCUC 91739 573-G4
HAZELTINE CT
- FONT 92336 574-J2
E HAZELTINE CT
1000 ONT 91761 642-E6
HAZELTINE ST
- ONT 91762 642-C6
400 ONT 91761 642-C6
E HAZELTINE ST
2700 ONT 91761 642-F6
2900 ONT 91761 643-A6
HAZELWOOD CT
7000 HESP 92345 4567-A4
HAZELWOOD DR
400 RivC 91752 683-E4
14800 CHLS 91709 681-C5
HEADQUARTERS DR
22200 APLV 92307 4388-A2
HEAL AV
9600 SBdC - 4481-E4
N HEALING WATERS DR
800 CLTN 92324 606-E5
S HEARD PL
1400 SBDO 92408 607-B5
S HEARD ST
1500 SBDO 92408 607-B5
HEARTHSIDE CT
9400 RCUC 91730 602-H5
HEARTHSTONE LN
13800 CHLS 91709 680-G3
HEARTLAND PL
9600 RCUC 91730 602-H5
HEARTSEASE LN
15500 VCTV 92392 4296-E5
HEATH ST
1200 RDL 92374 608-F5
HEATH CREEK CT
5400 SBdC 92397 4652-E3
HEATH CREEK DR
5400 SBdC 92397 4652-E3
HEATH CREEK LN
5400 SBdC 92397 4652-E3
HEATHER AV
8100 SBdC 92335 604-C2
10900 ADEL 92301 4204-H6
14500 SBdC - (4303-A5
See Page 4302)
HEATHER CIR
4300 CHNO 91710 681-E1
15100 VCTV 92394 4295-J6
HEATHER DR
100 SBdC 92284 4748-H5
HEATHER LN
1600 RDL 92373 647-J3
HEATHER ST
9100 RCUC 91701 572-G5
10200 RCUC 91737 573-A5
E HEATHER ST
200 RLTO 92376 575-H5
W HEATHER ST
200 RLTO 92376 575-F5
HEATHERBROOK PL
9500 RCUC 91730 602-H5
HEATHERDALE RD
15500 VCTV 92394 4296-B2
HEATHERLEY LN
600 SBdC - 516-H3
HEATHER RIDGE LN
1400 CHLS 91709 680-G6

HEATHERVALE DR
14100 CHLS 91709 680-H3
HEATHERVIEW DR
34900 YCPA 92399 609-J7
34900 YCPA 92399 610-A7
HEATHROW AV
6600 FONT 92336 574-E5
HEATON DR
900 SBdC - 517-H4
HEAVENLY AV
4900 SBdC 92252 4889-D3
HEAVENLY VALLEY RD
42200 BBLK - 4811-J2
42300 BBLK - 4812-A2
HECTIC HEIGHTS LN
- SBdC 92252 4959-C6
HECTOR RD
41500 SBdC - 350-A10
E HEDDA ST
800 SBDO 92408 607-B5
HEDGE ROW CT
- FONT 92336 544-D7
HEDGEROW LN
2100 CHLS 91709 680-J4
HEDGEWOOD PL
1100 DBAR 91765 680-E3
HEIDELBURG LN
400 CLAR 91711 571-E7
HEIDI CT
1500 RDL 92374 608-D4
7800 SBdC 92336 575-C7
HELDON PL
11100 APLV 92308 4477-J1
N HELEN AV
1300 ONT 91762 601-H5
S HELEN AV
1300 ONT 91762 641-H3
HELEN CT
1900 RDL 92373 648-H6
N HELEN CT
1500 ONT 91762 601-H5
HELEN DR
13000 RDL 92373 648-H5
HELEN ST
1300 SBdC 92397 4652-D2
83300 SBdC 92277 (4825-B3
See Page 4824)
HELENA AV
8900 MTCL 91763 601-F4
10300 MTCL 91763 641-F1
HELENA CT
500 UPL 91786 572-C7
HELENA LN
1500 RDL 92373 648-F3
HELENA ST
900 CLTN 92324 646-H1
HELENDALE RD
19300 VCTV 92301 4205-E2
20000 VCTV 92301 (4115-E6
See Page 4114)
21300 ADEL 92301 (4115-E1
See Page 4114)
22200 SBdC 92301 (4115-E1
See Page 4114)
22600 SBdC 92301 (4025-D6
See Page 3934)
24400 SBdC - (3935-J5
See Page 3934)
24400 SBdC 92301 (3935-G7
See Page 3934)
27300 SBdC - 3936-A3
28100 SBdC - (3846-A6
See Page 3756)
33900 SBdC - 348-L10
38100 SBdC 92347 348-L8
HELIOTROPE DR
100 SBdC - 518-B1
300 SBdC - 4738-B7
HELLER DR
2700 RivC 92509 645-B6
HELLMAN AV
5400 RCUC 91737 572-H2
6100 RCUC 91701 572-H4
7300 RCUC 91730 572-H6
7700 RCUC 91730 602-H4
16300 SBdC 91710 712-H3
16800 RivC 92880 712-H3
16800 SBdC 92880 712-H3
N HELLMAN AV
1100 ONT 91730 602-H5
1100 ONT 91764 602-H5
1500 RCUC 91730 602-H5
S HELLMAN AV
1400 ONT 91761 642-H1
HELM CT
14400 SBdC - (3935-G3
See Page 3934)
HELMS AV
8100 RCUC 91730 602-H2
HEMET ST
18000 APLV 92307 4207-J5
HEMINGWAY DR
- COR 92880 712-J7
HEMLOCK AV
6500 FONT 92336 574-D6
7800 FONT 92336 604-D1
7900 SBdC 92336 604-D1
8100 SBdC 92335 604-E2
9700 HESP 92345 4475-J3
9900 FONT 92335 604-E6

HEMLOCK AV
10300 SBdC 92337 604-E7
10400 FONT 92337 604-E7
10500 FONT 92337 644-E2
30900 SBdC 92311 3590-C7
30900 SBdC 92311 3680-C1
HEMLOCK CT
700 RDL 92374 608-E7
HEMLOCK DR
100 SBdC - 518-B1
300 SBdC - 4738-B7
500 SBdC - 519-F2
9200 SBdC 92339 611-G2
N HEMLOCK DR
3600 SBDO 92404 547-E7
3600 SBDO 92404 577-E1
HEMLOCK LN
800 SBdC 92314 4742-J7
800 SBdC 92314 4812-J1
15500 CHLS 91709 681-D7
23000 SBdC - 516-F2
HEMLOCK RD
7400 HESP 92345 4565-J4
7400 HESP 92345 4566-A4
10100 SBdC 92372 4472-B4
11400 HESP 92345 4475-J1
11700 HESP 92345 4385-J7
13200 SBdC 92372 4382-B5
19400 APLV 92307 4207-C7
22500 APLV 92307 4208-B7
HEMLOCK ST
8800 RCUC 91730 602-G1
9900 RCUC 91730 603-A1
11900 RCUC 91739 603-F1
13900 SBdC 93562 2055-B6
HEMLOCK WY
2400 POM 91767 601-A4
HENBANE ST
7300 RCUC 91739 573-F7
7700 RCUC 91739 603-F1
HENDERSON DR
14000 RCUC 91739 574-B3
W HENDERSON LN
800 SBDO 92410 606-F2
HENDERSON ST
- ADEL 92301 4295-A7
HENDERSON WY
3700 CLAR 91711 571-F4
HENDRICKS DR
85800 SBdC 92277 (4825-J5
See Page 4824)
HENDRIX AV
500 CLAR 91711 601-C5
HENDYS RD
5700 TNP 92277 4890-J5
HENNEL AV
76500 SBdC 92277 4823-B5
HENNIPEN ST
500 POM 91768 640-C2
HENRIETTA ST
1400 RDL 92373 648-D3
HENRY RD
4900 SBdC 92277 (4825-F6
See Page 4824)
84900 SBdC 92277 (4895-F1
See Page 4824)
HENRY ST
5100 RCUC 91701 572-E1
HENSHAW CT
12700 RCUC 91739 573-G6
HERALD ST
800 RDL 92374 608-C6
HERBERT
14100 SBdC - (4301-H6
See Page 4300)
W HERBERTS LN
700 CLTN 92324 606-C4
HERCULES CT
- SBDO 92409 577-F7
HERCULES ST
- SBdC 92308 4479-A4
14300 HESP 92345 4475-J4
15300 HESP 92345 4476-B4
18000 HESP 92345 4477-A4
21000 APLV 92308 4477-G4
21600 SBdC 92308 4477-J4
21600 SBdC 92308 4478-A4
HERCULES WY
11000 RivC 91752 683-H4
HERDMANS RD
60400 SBdC 92284 4748-H6
HEREFORD DR
8600 SBdC 91710 712-G2
HEREFORD RD
33700 SBdC 92365 (3683-G3
See Page 3592)
N HERITAGE CIR
6900 FONT 92336 574-B6
S HERITAGE CIR
7300 FONT 92336 574-A7
HERITAGE CT
200 POM 91767 601-A6
14100 VCTV 92392 4385-H4
HERITAGE DR
- CHLS 91709 681-G7
13100 VCTV 92392 4385-H4
HERITAGE LN
10000 RCUC 91737 573-A2
E HERITAGE LN
100 SBDO 92408 606-J7

S HERITAGE LN
2400 SBDO 92408 606-J7
2400 SBDO 92408 646-J1
W HERITAGE LN
100 SBDO 92408 606-H7
100 CLTN 92324 606-H7
HERITAGE WY
100 UPL 91786 602-D3
14300 SBdC - (4025-H6
See Page 3934)
14300 SBdC 92301 (4025-H6
See Page 3934)
HERMOSA AV
1000 POM 91767 601-B6
4900 RCUC 91737 573-A2
6200 YUCA 92284 4888-D7
6700 RCUC 91701 573-A3
7200 RCUC 91730 573-A7
7300 YUCA 92284 4958-D2
7700 RCUC 91730 603-A2
N HERMOSA AV
600 CLTN 92324 606-B6
1100 SBdC 92324 606-B6
HERMOSA CT
4900 YUCA 92284 4888-D3
HERMOSA RD
3000 SBdC 92371 4562-H1
16200 ADEL 92301 4294-J2
17300 ADEL 92301 4204-J7
HERMOSA ST
14600 ADEL 92301 4294-J7
17700 ADEL 92301 4204-J3
HERNANDEZ CT
2100 CLTN 92324 646-H1
HERON AV
2900 SBdC 92252 4819-F6
4700 SBdC 92252 4889-F3
HERON CT
1600 RDL 92374 608-C4
12700 VCTV 92392 4385-D6
HERON LN
100 RivC 92507 646-E6
HERON ST
12500 VCTV 92392 4385-D6
N HERRINGTON AV
500 SBDO 92411 576-E4
2800 SBDO 92405 576-E2
HERRINGTON DR
1600 RDL 92374 608-F7
HERSCHEL AV
- FONT 92336 574-D1
HERSHEY ST
200 POM 91767 641-C1
S HERT ST
900 CLTN 92324 646-C1
N HERVEY AV
300 UPL 91786 601-G3
HERVEY RD
- SBdC 92347 (3587-J4
See Page 3586)
35200 SBdC 92311 3678-A4
35200 SBdC 92347 3678-A4
HESAL RD
- SBdC - (3683-A3
See Page 3592)
- SBdC 92365 (3683-A3
See Page 3592)
HESPERIA OH W
14300 VCTV 92392 4386-E1
14300 VCTV 92392 4296-E7
HESPERIA RD
8500 HESP 92345 4566-E1
8800 HESP 92345 4476-E4
11200 HESP 92345 4386-F6
12100 HESP 92345 4386-F6
12100 VCTV 92392 4386-E1
13400 SBdC 92392 4386-E1
14200 VCTV 92392 4296-E7
HESS BLVD
10300 SBdC 92256 615-H5
HESS DR
5700 SBdC 92252 4889-E6
HESS RD
- SBdC 92371 4653-E1
HESTON ST
12700 VCTV 92392 4385-E5
HI LN
25400 SBdC - 517-C3
HI PL
25500 SBdC - 517-C3
HIAWATHA RD
18100 APLV 92307 4296-J6
HIAWATHA ST
16100 VCTV 92392 4386-D5
HIBISCUS AV
3400 CHLS 91709 681-C6
9100 ADEL 92301 4294-D1
14700 SBdC 92335 604-D4
HIBISCUS CT
800 POM 91766 641-B2
9800 RCUC 91737 572-J4
17600 FONT 92335 605-B3
18000 HESP 92345 4566-J4
18000 HESP 92345 4567-A4
HIBISCUS DR
500 RDL 92373 648-C1
18200 FONT 92335 605-C3
48900 SBdC 92256 615-F6
HIBISCUS RD
10500 ADEL 92301 4294-G1

HIBISCUS RD
11300 ADEL 92301 4295-A1
HIBISCUS ST
1200 UPL 91784 571-J4
14600 SBdC - (4115-H1
See Page 4114)
14900 SBdC 92335 604-D4
15900 FONT 92335 604-J3
17000 FONT 92335 605-A3
26600 HIGH 92346 577-F6
HICKMAN RD
12700 VCTV 92392 4385-D5
HICKORY AV
2300 UPL 91784 571-J3
8200 HESP 92345 4566-B2
8500 RCUC 91739 603-J3
8500 SBdC 91739 603-J3
8900 HESP 92345 4476-C1
11800 HESP 92345 4386-C7
12400 VCTV 92392 4386-C5
S HICKORY AV
2100 ONT 91762 642-A5
HICKORY CIR
7800 RCUC 91730 602-G1
HICKORY CT
9700 HESP 92345 4476-B5
HICKORY DR
29600 SBdC - 4738-E6
HICKORY LN
3800 CHLS 91709 681-D6
11300 SBdC 91766 641-D3
S HICKORY PL
2200 ONT 91762 642-A5
HICKORY ST
6800 CHNO 91710 682-B2
10700 ADEL 92301 4384-H1
HICKORY NUT LN
22600 DBAR 91765 680-A4
HICKOX LN
14000 RCUC 91739 574-B3
W HICKS DR
600 SBdC 92314 4742-C5
HIDAL DR
- TNP 92278 4822-F2
HIDALGO AV
400 RDL 92374 608-C5
N HIDALGO DR
3100 SBDO 92404 577-C1
HIDDEN LN
800 SBdC - 517-J3
2300 SBdC 91784 572-A3
HIDDEN CANYON LN
5900 CHLS 91709 711-J5
14500 VCTV 92394 4295-H7
HIDDEN COVE CT
2000 CLTN 92324 646-J4
2000 SBdC 92324 646-J4
HIDDEN COVE DR
- YCPA 92399 649-H5
HIDDEN CREEK DR
16300 VCTV 92392 4386-E5
HIDDEN FARM RD
8700 RCUC 91701 572-F1
8800 RCUC 91737 572-G1
10300 RCUC 91737 573-B1
HIDDEN GOLD DR
54300 SBdC 92284 4957-B6
54600 YUCA 92284 4957-C6
57800 YUCA 92284 4958-B6
HIDDEN HEIGHTS DR
- RivC 92399 650-H7
HIDDEN HILLS CIR
- POM 91766 640-G5
HIDDEN HILLS RD
93600 SBdC - 350-L10
99800 SBdC - 351-B9
HIDDEN OAK LN
5700 SBdC - 4843-J1
HIDDEN PARADISE DR
61500 SBdC 92252 4889-B4
HIDDEN RANCH RD
20100 SBdC 92308 4567-E3
HIDDEN RIVER RD
36500 SBdC 92347 (3587-D7
See Page 3586)
36500 SBdC 92347 (3677-D1
See Page 3586)
HIDDEN ROCK CT
14800 VCTV 92394 4295-H7
HIDDEN ROCK RD
14400 VCTV 92394 4295-H7
HIDDEN ROCK WY
14700 VCTV 92394 4295-H7
HIDDENSPRING CIR
14600 CHLS 91709 681-B5
HIDDEN SPRINGS RD
32200 SBdC - 3762-F2
33200 SBdC - (3682-F5
See Page 3592)
35200 SBdC - (3683-A3
See Page 3592)
HIDDEN TRAIL DR
- RCUC 91737 (543-C7
See Page 513)
E HIDDEN VALLEY LN
3000 CLTN 92324 646-J3
HIDDEN VALLEY RD
- POM 91766 640-F6
13300 SBdC 92392 4386-H3

HIDDENWOOD LN
16100 VCTV 92392 4386-D6
HIDEAWAY LN
11500 FONT 92337 644-H3
12900 VCTV 92392 4385-J5
39200 SBdC 92399 611-B7
HIGGINS RD
300 BARS 92311 3680-B4
HIGH AL
- SBDO 92404 576-J3
E HIGH AV
200 RDL 92374 608-C6
W HIGH AV
100 RDL 92374 608-B7
HIGH RD
700 SBdC - 516-G3
7300 SBdC - (4569-J1
See Page 4568)
7700 SBdC - 4479-J1
10600 SBdC - (4389-J7
See Page 4299)
HIGH ST
600 BARS 92311 3680-B5
18700 SBdC 92316 605-E6
HIGHBLUFF DR
1500 DBAR 91765 680-C4
HIGH CHAPARRAL RD
1200 SBdC - (4743-A4
See Page 4662)
HIGH CLIFF LN
- FONT 92336 574-E4
HIGHCREST DR
23700 DBAR 91765 680-D1
HIGHCREST RD
22100 SBdC 92347 (3677-J3
See Page 3586)
22500 SBdC 92347 3678-A3
HIGH CREST ST
12900 VCTV 92392 4386-H4
HIGH DESERT DR
1100 BARS 92311 3678-J7
1100 BARS 92311 3758-J1
HIGH DESERT RD
12500 VCTV 92392 4385-E5
HIGH FALLS TR
13900 APLV 92307 4387-E1
HIGHFIELD DR
- RCUC 91739 573-J7
HIGHFIELD ST
- VCTV 92392 4296-E7
HIGHGATE AV
12300 VCTV 92392 4386-E6
HIGHGATE CIR
16700 VCTV 92392 4386-E6
HIGHGATE CT
2500 CHLS 91709 640-J7
2500 CHLS 91709 641-A7
16700 VCTV 92392 4386-E6
HIGHGATE DR
- RCUC 91739 573-F5
HIGHGROVE PL
1300 RivC 92507 646-B6
7300 RCUC 91730 573-B7
HIGHGROVE PASS RD
1200 RivC 92324 646-H7
HIGH HORSE DR
12300 RCUC 91739 573-G4
HIGH KNOB RD
24000 DBAR 91765 640-D5
HIGH KNOLL DR
15600 CHLS 91709 681-B7
HIGH KNOLL RD
27500 SBdC - 4737-H7
HIGHLAND
55700 YUCA 92284 4957-F5
HIGHLAND AV
- RivC 92507 646-C6
100 SBdC - 4742-F7
200 SBdC - 4812-F1
400 BARS 92311 3679-G3
1800 RDL 92374 648-G1
1800 SBdC 92374 648-G1
4200 SBDO 92346 577-J3
4200 SBDO 92346 578-A3
4300 HIGH 92346 578-C4
8200 RCUC 91701 572-E4
9500 RCUC 91737 572-J4
9800 RCUC 91737 573-A4
11400 RCUC 91701 573-D4
11900 RCUC 91739 573-E4
12100 SBdC - (4390-J5
See Page 4299)
15600 FONT 92336 574-F4
32200 SBdC 92374 609-A7
32200 SBdC 92374 649-A1
36000 YCPA 92399 650-C1
HIGHLAND AV Rt#-30
17000 FONT 92336 574-J4
17000 RLTO 92336 574-J4
E HIGHLAND AV
- RDL 92373 648-D2
100 SBDO 92404 576-J3
600 RDL 92374 648-F1
600 SBDO 92404 577-A3
1800 SBdC 92404 577-B3
2400 SBDO 92346 577-D3
2600 HIGH 92346 577-G3
3300 SBdC 92346 577-G3

E HIGHLAND AV Rt#-30
100 RLTO 92377 575-H4
100 RLTO 92376 575-H4
400 SBdC 92407 575-H4
700 RLTO 92376 576-A4
700 SBdC 92407 576-A4
2100 SBDO 92407 576-A4
N HIGHLAND AV
1200 CLTN 92324 606-E5
S HIGHLAND AV
15000 FONT 92336 574-C4
W HIGHLAND AV
100 CLTN 92324 606-D4
100 SBDO 92405 576-H3
300 RDL 92373 648-B3
1200 SBDO 92411 576-E4
W HIGHLAND AV Rt#-30
100 RLTO 92377 575-C4
100 RLTO 92376 575-C4
500 SBdC 92377 575-C4
500 SBdC 92376 575-C4
1700 SBDO 92411 576-F4
1700 SBDO 92407 576-F4
1900 SBdC 92407 576-F4
2400 FONT 92377 575-C4
2400 FONT 92336 575-C4
2400 RLTO 92336 575-C4
2600 FONT 92336 574-J4
9800 RLTO 92377 574-J4
HIGHLAND CT
8300 SBdC 92345 4564-G2
E HIGHLAND CT
400 UPL 91786 602-D4
1100 ONT 91764 602-E4
HIGHLAND DR
300 SBdC - 518-A1
300 SBdC - 4738-B7
2700 SBdC - 519-B7
24900 SBdC - 517-B4
61600 SBdC 92252 4889-B4
HIGHLAND LN
800 BBLK - 4811-D2
HIGHLAND RD
- SBdC - (4390-J7
See Page 4300)
500 BBLK - 4811-D2
2400 SBdC 91784 572-C2
4300 SBdC 92371 4473-B7
8600 SBdC 92256 4956-G7
9700 SBdC - 4480-J3
9700 SBdC 92345 4564-F3
HIGHLAND ST
1400 NDLS 92363 3620-B5
4500 MTCL 91763 601-E4
34500 SBdC 92311 3679-G5
HIGHLAND TR
55400 YUCA 92284 4957-E4
HIGHLANDER DR
14900 VCTV 92394 4295-J6
HIGHLAND GROVE CT
7600 HIGH 92346 578-D6
HIGHLAND GROVE LN
29300 HIGH 92346 578-D6
HIGHLAND LINKS ST
10800 APLV 92308 4477-D3
HIGHLAND OAKS DR
13500 YCPA 92399 650-J6
13600 RivC 92399 650-J6
HIGHLAND PASS CIR
16100 CHLS 91709 710-G1
HIGHLAND PASS RD
1200 CHLS 91709 710-G1
HIGHLAND PINES RD
2400 POM 91767 601-B5
HIGHLAND SPRING LN
6900 HIGH 92346 578-C5
HIGHLAND VALLEY RD
23500 POM 91765 640-C5
23600 DBAR 91765 640-C5
HIGHLAND VIEW DR
61700 SBdC 92252 4819-B6
HIGHLINE DR
- APLV 92308 4387-E5
HIGH LINE AQUEDUCT RD
8700 HIGH 92359 609-C1
HIGH MEADOW PL
5400 RCUC 91737 573-C2
HIGH MESA ST
10300 ADEL 92301 4204-G6
HIGH POINT DR
800 CLAR 91711 571-B5
HIGH POINT PKWY
- BARS 92311 (3759-B2
See Page 3758)
HIGHPOINT ST
1400 UPL 91784 571-H3
HIGHRIDGE DR
2500 CHLS 91709 680-J2
2500 CHLS 91709 681-A2
HIGH RIDGE LN
17900 SBdC 92392 4386-H4
HIGHSHADE RD
- SBdC 92308 4478-G2
HIGHVIEW AV
27300 SBdC 92311 3679-D7
HIGHVIEW DR
11100 RCUC 91737 573-C4

HIGHVIEW DR
12700 RDL 92373 649-A5
HIGH VIEW LN
- CHLS 91709 711-G2
HIGHVIEW LN
1700 RDL 92373 648-J4
HIGHVIEW RD
52900 SBdC 92256 4956-G7
HIGHVIEW TR
- SBdC - 616-H1
- SBdC 92256 616-H1
52900 SBdC 92256 4956-G7
70000 SBdC 92277 4821-D1
HIGH VISTA LN
16100 CHLS 91709 710-J1
22600 APLV 92307 4298-B2
HIGH VISTA PL
22500 APLV 92307 4298-A2
HIGH VISTA ST
12900 VCTV 92392 4386-H4
HIGHWAY Rt#-18
- APLV 92307 4296-H4
- APLV 92392 4296-G4
- SBdC 92392 4296-F5
- VCTV 92307 4296-G4
- VCTV 92392 4296-G4
22500 APLV 92308 4388-C2
22900 APLV 92307 4388-C2
23300 SBdC 92307 4388-D2
24900 SBdC 92308 4388-D2
25500 SBdC 92307 (4389-A6
See Page 4299)
25500 SBdC 92308 (4389-A6
See Page 4299)
26900 SBdC 92307 4479-D1
26900 SBdC 92308 4479-D1
28100 SBdC - 4479-J1
28900 SBdC - 4480-C1
32700 SBdC - 4481-A2
35100 SBdC - (4571-G1
See Page 4570)
36400 SBdC - (4572-A3
See Page 4482)
HIGHWAY Rt#-38
900 SBdC 92314 4812-H1
2500 SBdC - 4813-D3
2500 SBdC - 369-J11
2600 SBdC - 389-J1
3300 SBdC - (4883-H3
See Page 4813)
7000 SBdC - 4950-G1
8300 SBdC 92339 610-J1
8300 SBdC 92339 611-A1
8300 SBdC 92339 4950-J7
42100 SBdC - (4882-D4
See Page 4813)
46000 SBdC 92314 4813-B2
HIGHWAY Rt#-58
- BARS 92311 3678-J4
- BARS 92311 3679-A5
- SBdC 92311 3588-F7
- SBdC 92311 3678-G1
1700 SBdC - 348-H7
15300 SBdC 92347 348-L8
15300 SBdC 92347 3586-A7
18500 SBdC 92347 (3587-J7
See Page 3586)
22500 SBdC 92347 3588-C7
HIGHWAY Rt#-62
- SBdC - 4774-H5
11500 SBdC - 391-G1
HIGHWAY Rt#-127
56900 SBdC - 330-A2
56900 SBdC - 2971-E1
HIGHWAY Rt#-138
100 SBdC - 516-F1
200 SBdC 92372 4472-A3
500 SBdC - 4736-C5
800 SBdC 92404 516-G4
2000 SBdC 92345 (4735-J3
See Page 4654)
2000 SBdC 92345 4736-A1
2500 SBdC 92371 4472-F7
2600 SBdC 92371 4562-G1
3300 HESP 92345 4656-A7
3300 HESP 92345 4736-A1
3300 HESP 92345 (4655-J7
See Page 4654)
3400 HESP - (4655-J7
See Page 4654)
3400 SBdC - (4655-B6
See Page 4654)
3400 SBdC 92345 (4655-B6
See Page 4654)
3900 SBdC 92371 4563-A2
5400 SBdC 92371 4653-E1
7300 SBdC - 4653-J7
7300 SBdC - 4654-A7
7700 SBdC - 4734-B1
8500 SBdC - 4734-E1
8600 SBdC 92345 4734-D1
9100 SBdC - 4654-G5
9100 SBdC 92345 4654-G5
HIGHWAY Rt#-173
- HESP - 4656-B7
- HESP - 4736-B1
- SBdC - (4657-C4
See Page 4656)
- SBdC - 4736-B1

HIGHWAY Rt#-173
- SBdC 92345 (4657-B4
See Page 4656)
100 SBdC - 518-C1
300 SBdC - 4738-A4
300 SBdC - 517-J2
1300 SBdC - 4737-G2
14800 HESP 92345 4736-A1
14800 SBdC 92345 4736-B1
17300 HESP 92345 4656-J5
17300 SBdC 92345 4656-J4
HIGHWAY Rt#-178
1700 SBdC - 328-J5
HIGHWAY Rt#-189
25200 SBdC - 517-J2
HIGHWAY U.S.-66 Hist
2700 NDLS 92363 3710-D3
4100 NDLS 92363 352-B10
34300 SBdC - 351-K7
HIGHWAY U.S.-95
100 SBdC - 372-B1
2700 NDLS 92363 3710-D3
4100 NDLS 92363 352-B10
7500 SBdC - 392-D1
23000 SBdC - 352-B10
34300 SBdC - 351-J2
HIGHWAY U.S.-395
- SBdC - 3934-B1
- SBdC 92301 3934-D6
- SBdC 92301 (4024-D1
See Page 3934)
8500 HESP 92345 4565-C1
8600 HESP 92345 4475-C6
9700 SBdC 92345 4475-C4
10500 VCTV 92345 4475-C4
10500 VCTV 92392 4475-C1
11700 VCTV 92392 4385-C6
14100 VCTV 92301 4385-C1
14100 VCTV 92394 4295-C4
14100 VCTV 92394 4385-C1
14900 VCTV 92301 4295-C4
15300 ADEL 92301 4295-B1
16900 ADEL 92301 4205-A4
18700 ADEL 92301 4204-H1
20100 ADEL 92301 4114-G2
20500 SBdC 92301 4114-F1
41700 SBdC - 348-H1
59300 SBdC - 328-G11
HIGHWAY SPUR
600 SBdC - 517-E3
HILARY LN
700 RDL 92373 648-A3
HILARY WY
900 RDL 92373 648-H5
W HILDA CT
200 SBDO 92408 606-H2
HILDE LN
59100 YUCA 92284 4888-E6
HILDITA CT
1300 UPL 91786 572-E7
HILL
84300 SBdC 92277 (4895-E1
See Page 4824)
HILL AV
6700 SBdC - 512-A4
10300 SBdC 92256 615-F4
HILL BLVD
4400 TNP 92277 4822-D7
4400 TNP 92277 4892-D1
S HILL CT
2100 CLTN 92324 646-H4
HILL DR
- SBdC - 4738-D7
11000 LMLN 92354 647-B1
E HILL DR
200 SBDO 92404 546-J5
W HILL DR
200 SBDO 92407 546-G4
1000 SBDO 92407 546-E5
HILL LN
800 BBLK - 4811-C2
HILL RD
- SBdC - 548-H1
HILL ST
15000 SBdC - (4206-A3
See Page 4116)
HILL WY
15100 ADEL 92301 4294-J6
E HILLCREST AV
800 CLTN 92324 606-E4
W HILLCREST AV
200 SBDO 92408 606-H4
900 SBDO 92410 606-F4
HILLCREST CT
100 SBdC - 517-F1
7000 HESP 92345 4566-F5
10800 RCUC 91730 573-C7
HILLCREST DR
- SBdC - 519-D6
- YUCA 92284 4888-A4
200 SBdC - 517-F1
900 SBdC 91784 571-J2
900 SBdC 91784 572-A3
2600 SBdC 92277 4821-G3
11900 FONT 92337 644-A4
12900 SBdC 91710 641-B7
18000 SBdC 92407 515-C4
HILL CREST DR
39900 BBLK - 4811-D2

HILLCREST DR
56900 YUCA 92284 4887-J5
HILLCREST LN
26400 SBdC - 517-E1
HILLCREST RD
900 SBdC - 516-E4
HILLCREST ST
1500 UPL 91784 571-H4
11200 LMLN 92354 647-C1
HILLEN DR
4300 CLAR 91711 571-A7
N HILLEN DALE DR
100 SBdC 92314 4742-B6
S HILLEN DALE DR
100 SBdC 92314 4742-B6
HILLGATE DR
- SBDO 92407 546-D5
HILLHURST CT
7000 RCUC 91739 573-F5
N HILLHURST DR
3400 SBDO 92405 576-F1
HILLMAR DR
1200 DBAR 91765 680-A3
HILLS RD
13100 SBdC 92301 (4025-E7
See Page 3934)
22100 SBdC 92301 4114-J3
HILLSBOROUGH DR
14100 VCTV 92392 4385-H5
HILLSBOROUGH LN
2500 CHLS 91709 640-J7
HILLSDALE DR
1100 CLAR 91711 601-A1
HILLSDALE RANCH RD
3500 CHLS 91709 681-C6
HILLSIDE AV
5900 TNP 92277 4892-D5
HILL SIDE AV
6500 TNP 92277 4892-D6
HILLSIDE AV
15200 SBdC - (4026-A1
See Page 3936)
HILLSIDE CV
5400 RCUC 91737 572-H2
HILLSIDE DR
- VCTV 92392 4296-E7
200 BARS 92311 3679-G3
500 SBdC - 518-A2
1300 SBdC 92359 609-D5
1700 SBDO 92404 577-B4
11800 FONT 92337 644-E3
HILL SIDE DR
20700 SBdC 92308 4567-G3
HILLSIDE DR
23500 SBdC - 516-H3
HILLSIDE LN
600 BBLK - 4811-A2
24700 BARS 92311 3678-F6
HILLSIDE PL
8500 SBdC 92372 4562-C2
HILLSIDE RD
200 SBdC - 517-J2
2000 CHLS 91709 710-F3
7800 RCUC 91701 572-E2
8800 RCUC 91737 572-G2
9900 RCUC 91737 573-A2
HILLSIDE SPUR
- SBdC - 518-D1
HILLSIDE WY
100 RDL 92373 648-E3
HILLSMERE CIR
7700 HIGH 92346 578-B6
HILLS RANCH RD
- SBdC - 389-F1
HILLSTONE ST
- FONT 92336 574-D1
HILLTOP AV
58300 YUCA 92284 4888-C6
HILLTOP BLVD
32000 SBdC - 519-B6
HILLTOP BLVD Rt#-18
31600 SBdC - 519-E6
32200 SBdC - 389-D1
HILLTOP CT
6100 RCUC 91737 573-E3
HILLTOP DR
- SBdC 92284 4888-G5
1700 RDL 92373 649-A4
2900 SBdC 92277 4821-G7
3200 CHLS 91709 681-B7
3800 SBdC 92371 4563-A2
4100 SBdC 92277 4891-G1
5800 YUCA 92284 4887-G6
28600 HIGH 92346 578-C6
59700 SBdC 92252 4958-G3
61700 SBdC 92252 4889-B5
E HILLTOP DR
1600 CLTN 92324 646-G2
HILLTOP LN
21500 SBdC - 516-B1
W HILLTOP LN
300 SBdC 92314 4742-D6
HILLTOP RD
- SBdC 92359 4950-E7
4900 SBdC 92371 4563-C2
HILLTOP TER
400 BARS 92311 3679-J3
HILL TOP TURN
3000 SBdC - 548-H2

SAN BERNARDINO

STREET Block City ZIP Pg-Grid

HILLVIEW
- SBdC - 3592-C7
35900 SBdC - (3682-C1 See Page 3592)
HILLVIEW DR
3100 SBdC 91710 641-B7
3100 SBdC 91710 681-B1
72300 SBdC - 2971-F3
HILLVIEW DR S
- SBdC 91710 681-B1
HILL VIEW LN
13600 YCPA 92399 650-C7
HILLVIEW LP
6300 RCUC 91737 573-D4
HILLVIEW PL
13900 VCTV 92392 4386-D2
HILL VIEW RD
- SBdC - (3683-A7 See Page 3592)
- SBdC 92365 (3683-A7 See Page 3592)
HILLVIEW RD
1300 SBdC 92372 4562-D2
HILL VIEW RD
5100 SBdC 92252 4889-B6
6700 SBdC 92252 4959-B2
HILLVIEW RD
23600 SBdC 92404 516-G6
36500 SBdC 92347 (3587-E7 See Page 3586)
36500 SBdC 92347 (3677-E1 See Page 3586)
HILL VIEW RD
74600 TNP 92277 4962-H5
HILLVIEW ST
7300 HIGH 92346 577-G5
HILLVIEW TKTR
32000 SBdC - (3677-C4 See Page 3586)
32000 SBdC - 3756-J4
32000 SBdC - (3757-A2 See Page 3756)
35400 SBdC 92347 (3677-C4 See Page 3586)
HILLY FIELD LN
- SBdC 92407 515-B4
HILTON AV
900 SBdC 92284 4748-A7
900 SBdC 92284 4818-A3
3600 SBdC 92284 4888-A1
5000 YUCA 92284 4888-B4
7500 YUCA 92284 4958-B3
E HILTON AV
100 RDL 92373 648-E3
W HILTON AV
- RDL 92373 648-D3
HILTON CT
4600 SBdC 92284 4888-A1
4800 YUCA 92284 4888-A3
HILTON DR
14700 FONT 92336 604-D1
HILTON LN
57800 YUCA 92284 4888-A4
HILTON RD
6800 YUCA 92284 4958-B1
HILTON HEAD DR
22800 DBAR 91765 680-B2
HILTON HEAD LN
- FONT 92336 574-H3
HINCKLEY ST
25700 LMLN 92354 647-D2
HINDON AV
10100 APLV 92308 4477-H4
HINKLEY RD
21700 SBdC 92311 (3757-F2 See Page 3756)
25400 SBdC 92311 (3677-G5 See Page 3586)
28600 SBdC 92347 (3677-G5 See Page 3586)
30400 SBdC 92347 (3587-G6 See Page 3586)
36500 SBdC 92347 349-B6
43200 SBdC - 349-B6
HINSDALE PL
7300 RCUC 91730 573-D7
HINTON CT
- RCUC 91730 573-D7
HINTON DR
19700 SBdC 92308 4567-D1
HINTON ST
17700 HESP 92345 4566-H1
18200 HESP 92345 4567-A1
HIOUCHI RD
18600 APLV 92307 4387-A1
HIPA RD
13500 APLV 92308 4388-A2
HIPPARD PL
7000 RCUC 91739 573-F5
HIS WY
4200 RivC 92509 644-B7
HITCHING POST DR
12200 VCTV 92392 4385-D6
HITCHING POST LN
4400 SBdC 92371 4563-B1
26600 SBdC - (3935-F5 See Page 3934)
HITT RD
13500 APLV 92308 4388-A2

HI VIEW DR
61900 SBdC 92252 4959-B5
HIWAT DR
- SBdC - 4844-A2
HOADLEY CT
7800 FONT 92336 603-J1
HOBART DR
600 CLAR 91711 571-E7
HOBART RD
36900 SBdC - (4392-B2 See Page 4302)
HOBSON CT
600 POM 91766 640-J4
HODE ST
6600 CHNO 91710 682-B2
HODGE RD
21500 SBdC - (3847-D3 See Page 3756)
21500 SBdC 92311 (3847-D3 See Page 3756)
26000 SBdC 92311 369-C1
26000 SBdC 92311 (3937-J1 See Page 3936)
HODGES LN
16800 HESP 92345 4476-F7
HOFFMAN CT
- CHLS 91709 711-G2
11300 FONT 92337 645-A2
HOFFMAN RD
16000 SBdC - 348-H1
HOGAN WY
- SBdC - 4843-G3
HOHOKAM CT
20300 APLV 92308 4387-F6
HOHOKAM RD
- APLV 92308 4387-E6
HOLCOMB ST
52600 SBdC 92285 (4576-E6 See Page 4486)
HOLCOMB TR
- SBdC - 3762-H2
- SBdC 92365 (3765-A2 See Page 3764)
46300 SBdC 92365 3764-B2
HOLCOMB CREEK DR
33100 SBdC - 519-D2
HOLCOMB CREEK PL
200 ONT 91761 643-C7
HOLCOMB CREEK RD
- SBdC - (4740-F1 See Page 4660)
32000 SBdC - 4660-G7
32200 SBdC - (4661-B7 See Page 4660)
HOLCOMB RANCH RD
- SBdC - (3757-A7 See Page 3756)
17800 SBdC - (3846-H5 See Page 3756)
17900 SBdC - (3847-A2 See Page 3756)
HOLCOMB VALLEY RD
900 SBdC - 4741-H1
2300 SBdC - (4661-F7 See Page 4660)
35700 SBdC - 4742-A1
36200 SBdC - 4662-C7
N HOLCOMB VIEW DR
100 SBdC 92314 4742-B6
S HOLCOMB VIEW DR
100 SBdC 92314 4742-B6
N HOLDEN AV
1000 SBdC 92314 4742-C5
E HOLDEN DR
300 SBDO 92408 606-J3
400 SBDO 92408 607-A3
HOLGUIN CT
17000 FONT 92336 574-J7
17000 FONT 92336 575-A7
HOLIDAY AV
1800 UPL 91784 571-H5
HOLIDAY DR
100 SBdC - 517-J5
100 SBdC - 518-A1
1300 NDLS 92363 3710-D2
HOLIDAY LN
9000 SBdC 92372 4562-F1
9100 SBdC 92372 4472-E6
9700 SBdC 92371 4472-E5
18600 SBdC 92392 4387-A4
42400 BBLK - 4812-A1
51900 SBdC - 4816-D7
HOLIDAY WY
62300 SBdC 92252 4819-C6
W HOLLADAY PL
300 RLTO 92376 605-G1
HOLLAND DR
69300 SBdC 92277 4821-B4
HOLLAND ST
34100 SBdC 92311 3678-G6
HOLLANDER ST
2900 POM 91767 601-A3
HOLLAWAY RD
7400 RCUC 91730 573-E7
HOLLIE WY
68500 TNP 92277 4891-A7
HOLLINGER RD
63900 SBdC 92252 4959-G1
HOLLINS AV
3600 CLAR 91711 571-F5

HOLLIS CT
11800 LMLN 92354 647-G3
HOLLIS ST
9300 SBdC 92316 605-D4
HOLLISTER CT
9000 SBdC 92345 4474-G7
9000 SBdC 92345 4564-G1
HOLLISTER RD
900 SBdC 92372 4562-C1
2300 SBdC 92371 4562-G1
3700 SBdC 92371 4563-A1
7600 SBdC 92371 4474-A7
8000 SBdC 92371 4564-B1
9800 SBdC 92345 4474-G7
11000 SBdC 92345 4475-A7
HOLLOW WY
31800 SBdC - 519-A7
HOLLOW CREEK DR
35000 YCPA 92399 610-A6
W HOLLOWELL ST
700 ONT 91762 602-A7
900 ONT 91762 601-H7
W HOLLOW GLEN CIR
2800 SBDO 92376 606-A3
HOLLOW HILL LN
23700 SBdC 92324 646-H4
HOLLOW OAK CT
2800 CHLS 91709 681-A7
HOLLY AV
- SBdC 92365 (3504-B6 See Page 3414)
12300 CHNO 91710 641-H6
15900 FONT 92335 604-G5
34600 YCPA 92399 609-J5
34800 YCPA 92399 610-A5
36500 SBdC 92399 610-D5
73900 TNP 92277 4892-F6
N HOLLY AV
1200 SBDO 92410 606-E4
1200 CLTN 92324 606-E4
S HOLLY AV
1800 ONT 91762 642-B4
HOLLY CT
11900 GTER 92313 646-F3
28000 SBdC - 3936-A2
HOLLY DR
- SBdC - 548-G1
800 SBdC - 519-E3
2600 SBdC 91784 572-A1
14400 VCTV 92392 4386-F1
14700 SBdC 92335 604-D5
16300 FONT 92335 604-H5
17100 FONT 92335 605-A5
HOLLY LN
200 RDL 92374 608-C5
2000 BARS 92311 3679-D4
27800 SBdC - 517-J4
S HOLLY PL
2200 ONT 91762 642-B5
HOLLY RD
3900 SBdC 92371 4292-J4
3900 SBdC 92371 (4293-C4 See Page 4292)
6900 ADEL 92371 (4293-C4 See Page 4292)
7300 ADEL 92301 (4293-C4 See Page 4292)
7500 ADEL 92301 4294-A4
11100 ADEL 92301 4295-A4
HOLLY ST
- TNP 92278 4822-E2
900 SBdC 92371 4292-D4
6800 RCUC 91701 573-A5
8300 RCUC 91701 572-F5
11700 GTER 92313 646-E3
12200 SBdC 92509 645-H4
12600 RivC 92509 645-H6
13300 SBdC 93562 2145-A3
35800 YCPA 92399 610-B5
E HOLLY ST
100 RLTO 92376 575-J6
700 RLTO 92376 576-A6
W HOLLY ST
100 RLTO 92376 575-D6
HOLLY WY
1500 POM 91766 641-B4
HOLLYBERRY RD
13100 VCTV 92392 4475-E2
E HOLLY CIRCLE DR
3400 SBDO 92346 577-H2
N HOLLY CIRCLE DR
3000 SBDO 92346 577-H2
HOLLY GLEN DR
400 RivC 91752 683-F5
HOLLYHOCK RD
17700 ADEL 92301 4204-J6
HOLLY LEAF WY
1300 DBAR 91765 680-B3
HOLLYMONT TR
2100 SBdC - 518-H6
HOLLY OAK DR
- FONT 92337 644-D3
6100 RCUC 91701 572-F4
HOLLYOAK WY
34900 YCPA 92399 609-J7
HOLLYVALE AV
11300 VCTV 92392 4475-D2
HOLLY VISTA BLVD
2600 SBDO 92346 577-F2
25300 SBdC 92404 577-D2

HOLLY VISTA BLVD
26100 SBdC 92346 577-F2
E HOLLY VISTA BLVD
1100 SBDO 92404 577-B2
HOLLY VISTA DR
3600 SBDO 92346 577-H2
HOLLYWOOD LN
4900 SBdC 92277 (4825-D7 See Page 4824)
4900 SBdC 92277 (4895-D2 See Page 4824)
HOLMES AV
10700 RivC 91752 683-J6
N HOLMES AV
400 ONT 91764 602-D6
S HOLMES AV
2600 ONT 91761 642-E6
HOLMES CT
700 SBdC - 518-B3
N HOLMES CT
1500 ONT 91764 602-D5
HOLMES LN
100 SBdC - 4742-F7
200 SBdC - 4812-F2
S HOLMES PL
2400 ONT 91761 642-E5
HOLMES RD
30000 SBdC - (4390-C5 See Page 4300)
32800 SBdC - (4391-A5 See Page 4300)
HOLMES ST
1000 CALI 92320 650-C7
11600 YCPA 92399 650-C2
HOLMES WY
900 CALI 92320 650-C7
HOLSTEAD RD
20300 SBdC 92347 349-B7
E HOLT AV
100 POM 91767 640-J1
200 POM 91767 641-A1
1600 MTCL 91763 641-A1
W HOLT AV
100 POM 91768 640-F1
HOLT BLVD
4000 MTCL 91763 641-E1
E HOLT BLVD
100 ONT 91761 642-D1
100 ONT 91762 642-D1
1600 ONT 91761 602-H7
1900 ONT 91764 602-H7
W HOLT BLVD
100 ONT 91762 642-A1
900 ONT 91762 641-H1
1300 ONT 91763 641-H1
HOLYOKE PL
500 CLAR 91711 571-E5
HOMAN CT
6500 CHNO 91710 682-A2
HOMAN ST
- CHNO 91710 682-B2
HOME AV
9200 HESP 92345 4476-G7
E HOME AV
900 RLTO 92376 576-A5
W HOME AV
900 SBDO 92411 576-D5
900 SBDO 92411 576-F5
1800 SBDO 92411 576-C5
HOME CT
- FONT 92336 574-F6
E HOME PL
- RDL 92373 648-D1
600 RDL 92374 648-D1
W HOME PL
- RDL 92373 648-C1
E HOME ST
100 RLTO 92376 575-H5
W HOME ST
600 RLTO 92376 575-F5
HOMER CIR
3000 RivC 91752 644-A4
HOMER ST
3500 SBdC 92301 (4202-H3 See Page 4112)
4400 SBdC 92301 (4203-A3 See Page 4112)
HOMERIDGE DR
7700 SBdC 92372 4562-E4
HOMERIDGE LN
12800 CHLS 91709 640-H7
HOMER-KLINEFELTER RD
- SBdC - 351-J7
HOMESTEAD DR
9400 RCUC 91730 602-H5
13200 VCTV 92392 4385-F7
72900 TNP 92277 4892-C3
HOMESTEAD LN
7500 HIGH 92346 578-D6
41100 BBLK - 4811-F2
HOMESTEAD PL
12900 CHNO 91710 641-F7
HOMESTEAD WY
- FONT 92336 574-J3
55100 YUCA 92284 4957-D3
HOMEWOOD DR
11300 FONT 92337 644-B2
HOMEWOOD PL
11400 FONT 92337 644-B3

HOMOA CT
5700 SBdC - 4774-G7
HONDO ST
- SBdC 92284 4748-B6
54800 SBdC - 4747-C6
54800 SBdC 92284 4747-E6
HONEY CIR
10300 RivC 91752 644-A5
HONEYBEAR LN
12200 VCTV 92392 4385-C6
HONEY BEE LN
15800 CHLS 91709 680-H7
E HONEYBROOK WY
3400 ONT 91761 643-B6
HONEYCOMB LN
17700 SBdC 92392 4386-H2
W HONEYDALE CT
1500 UPL 91786 571-H7
E HONEYGLEN WY
3600 ONT 91761 643-C6
HONEY HILL CT
11800 GTER 92313 646-G3
HONEY HILL DR
11800 GTER 92313 646-G4
HONEY HILL RD
5000 SBdC 92345 (4655-A1 See Page 4654)
6200 SBdC 92345 4565-A7
HONEY RIDGE LN
13800 CHLS 91709 680-G2
HONEYSUCKLE AV
3400 CHLS 91709 681-C4
22500 SBdC - (4115-J2 See Page 4114)
22700 SBdC - (4025-G7 See Page 3934)
HONEYSUCKLE DR
3600 CHLS 91709 681-C4
HONEYSUCKLE LN
- RCUC 91701 572-H5
- SBDO 92407 546-A3
N HONEYSUCKLE LN
6000 SBDO 92407 546-A3
HONEYSUCKLE PL
8700 RCUC 91730 602-H4
HONEYSUCKLE ST
- VCTV 92394 4296-A7
7400 FONT 92336 574-D7
14900 VCTV 92394 4295-J7
HOOD DR
600 CLAR 91711 601-B1
HOOK BLVD
13100 VCTV 92394 4295-F7
15100 VCTV 92394 4296-A7
HOOK LN
100 SBdC - 518-D1
29500 SBdC - 4738-D7
HOOK RD
14800 VCTV 92394 4296-B6
HOOK CREEK RD
28700 SBdC - 518-C1
29500 SBdC - 4738-F6
HOOK TREE RD
4500 TNP 92277 4892-H1
HOOPA CT
- SBdC - 4844-F1
HOOPA RD
54900 YUCA 92284 4957-D5
HOOPA TR
53400 SBdC 92256 4956-J5
53400 SBdC 92284 4956-J5
53400 SBdC 92284 4957-A5
54400 YUCA 92284 4957-B5
HOOT OWL TR
6100 YUCA 92284 4887-H7
HOOVER AV
1600 POM 91767 601-D6
N HOPE AV
1400 ONT 91764 602-D4
1500 UPL 91764 602-D4
S HOPE AV
400 ONT 91761 642-D1
HOPE CT
- FONT 92336 574-E6
HOPE LN
9700 SBdC - 4481-F4
10100 YCPA 92399 610-C5
S HOPE PL
2000 ONT 91761 642-D4
HOPE ST
- CHNO 91710 681-E4
36400 SBdC 92347 (3587-G6 See Page 3586)
E HOPE ST
800 SBDO 92408 607-B4
HOPI AV
900 PRKR - 4774-J6
HOPI LN
- SBdC - 4843-H4
1200 SBdC - 4741-A5
HOPI RD
13700 APLV 92307 4387-F1
14400 APLV 92307 4297-H7
HOPI ST
600 DBAR 91765 680-B1
HOPI TR
100 SBdC 92284 4747-D4
7300 YUCA 92284 4957-E3
W HOPKINS RD
1700 CLTN 92324 645-J3

HOPKINS ST
10900 RivC 91752 643-H5
HOPLAND ST
13300 ADEL 92301 4295-F4
13300 VCTV 92301 4295-F4
14500 VCTV 92394 4295-G4
14800 VCTV 92394 4296-A4
HOPPE DR
14000 RCUC 91739 574-B3
HOPPER ST
700 SBdC 92407 515-D4
HORIZON CT
13900 SBdC 92371 4383-B3
HORIZON LN
- DBAR 91765 680-A6
- LACo 92823 680-A6
14300 VCTV 92392 4385-H4
S HORIZON LN
400 SBDO 92410 606-B3
HORIZON PL
6600 RCUC 91701 573-D5
HORIZON RD
8600 SBdC 92301 4114-J4
HORIZON ST
22800 SBdC 92308 4478-G5
25600 SBdC 92308 4479-B5
28700 SBdC - 4479-H5
30100 SBdC - 4480-C5
34100 SBdC - 4481-D4
HORNER ST
47800 SBdC 92365 3764-J6
47800 SBdC 92365 (3765-A6 See Page 3764)
HORSE CANYON RD
2600 SBdC - 4562-H6
HORSEMANS CENTER WY
24100 SBdC 92307 4388-F4
HORSESHOE CT
5700 CHNO 91710 681-J1
HORSESHOE DR
- SBdC 92316 605-E7
HORSESHOE LN
14500 VCTV 92394 4295-G7
HORSESHOE RD
- SBdC - (3935-G2 See Page 3934)
28900 SBdC - (3847-A6 See Page 3756)
HORSESHOE TR
13700 SBdC - (3935-F2 See Page 3934)
18500 SBdC - 3936-J2
18700 SBdC - (3937-D2 See Page 3936)
HORSESHOE WY
5500 FONT 92336 574-D2
HORSE SPRINGS RD
38500 SBdC - (4569-F7 See Page 4568)
HORSE TRAIL DR
- RDL 92373 648-D6
HORSETRAIL LN
13800 VCTV 92394 4295-G7
HORST CT
24500 SBdC - 517-A3
HORST DR
24100 SBdC - 516-J3
24100 SBdC - 517-A3
HOSPITAL PKWY
700 UPL 91786 602-D2
HOSPITAL RD
800 SBdC - 4738-C6
HOSPITALITY LN
1200 NDLS 92363 3620-C6
E HOSPITALITY LN
100 SBDO 92408 606-H6
300 SBDO 92408 607-A6
S HOSPITALITY LN
700 SBDO 92408 607-A6
W HOSPITALITY LN
100 SBDO 92408 606-H6
HOSS ST
600 DBAR 91765 680-B2
HOTE RD
12100 ADEL 92301 (4115-B4 See Page 4114)
HOURGLASS PL
1000 DBAR 91765 640-E5
HOUSTON CT
1600 CLAR 91711 601-E1
HOUSTON RD
22000 SBdC 92308 4478-B3
HOUSTON ST
26100 SBdC 92308 4479-B2
37500 SBdC - 4482-C1
HOUSTON WY
4500 SBdC - 4886-F3
31600 RDL 92373 649-A5
HOWARD AV
5700 TNP 92277 4892-E4
HOWARD DR
7900 HIGH 92410 577-C7
HOWARD RD
- SBdC 92371 4563-A4
4900 SBdC 92285 (4576-D7 See Page 4486)
28500 SBdC 92311 3679-G1
HOWARD ST
4300 MTCL 91763 641-E2
4500 SBdC 91710 641-G2

HOWARD ST
4700 MTCL 91710 641-G2
4900 SBdC 91763 641-G2
5300 SBdC 91762 641-G2
W HOWARD ST
1200 UPL 91786 601-J1
W HOWARD ACCESS RD
1500 UPL 91786 601-H1
HOWSLER PL
1800 POM 91766 640-J4
HOXEY RD
15100 SBdC - (4025-J5 See Page 3934)
15100 SBdC - (4026-A4 See Page 3936)
HOYOS RD
100 SBdC 92252 4750-D5
100 SBdC 92278 4750-D5
HUASNA RD
19300 APLV 92307 4297-C2
23700 SBdC 92307 4298-D1
HUASNA TR
- SBdC - 4843-F4
HUBBARD CT
- RDL 92374 608-B3
HUCKLEBERRY CT
12300 RCUC 91739 573-G5
HUDSON AV
3100 SBdC 92404 577-E2
3100 SBDO 92404 577-E2
N HUDSON AV
1600 SBDO 92404 577-E4
S HUDSON AV
1400 ONT 91761 643-F3
HUDSON CT
6800 RCUC 91701 573-D5
13900 APLV 92307 4387-B1
25800 LMLN 92354 647-E2
HUDSON DR
17600 VCTV 92392 4386-G3
HUDSON RD
19100 APLV 92307 4387-B1
19300 SBdC 92307 4208-D2
HUERTA CT
12400 VCTV 92392 4386-H6
HUERTA RD
21300 VCTV 92392 4386-H6
21300 SBdC 92392 4386-H6
HUERTA ST
15300 VCTV 92392 4386-B6
HUFF CT
15400 SBdC 92335 604-E3
HUFF RD
13700 SBdC - (4301-C2 See Page 4300)
E HUFF ST
300 RLTO 92376 605-H3
W HUFF ST
200 SBDO 92408 606-H3
600 SBDO 92410 606-E3
900 RLTO 92376 605-E3
1100 RLTO 92316 605-E3
2200 SBDO 92324 606-B3
HUGHES CT
15200 FONT 92336 574-E5
HUGHES LN
4200 SBdC 92285 4667-E2
HUGHES RD
9700 SBdC - 4482-E3
16100 VCTV 92392 4386-D1
N HUGO LN
1000 SBdC 92314 4742-D5
HUGO ST
2100 RDL 92374 607-E5
N HUMANE WY
100 POM 91768 640-D2
S HUMANE WY
100 POM 91768 640-E2
200 POM 91766 640-E2
HUMBER DR
11300 RivC 91752 683-G3
HUMBOLDT AV
10100 RCUC 91730 603-A3
12000 SBdC 91710 641-C5
N HUMBOLDT AV
700 ONT 91764 602-F4
HUMBOLDT CT
4500 MTCL 91763 641-E1
N HUMBOLDT CT
600 ONT 91764 602-F7
HUMBOLDT PL
12100 CHNO 91710 641-D5
N HUMBOLDT PL
400 ONT 91764 602-F7
HUMBOLT AV
5100 SBDO 92407 546-B5
HUMBOLT CT
14200 FONT 92336 574-B7
HUMBOLT WY
2700 POM 91768 640-C2
HUMMINGBIRD CT
- RivC 92399 650-G7
26400 LMLN 92354 647-F3
HUMMINGBIRD LN
1500 UPL 91784 572-E6
3000 BARS 92311 3758-G3
27700 SBdC - (3935-J1 See Page 3934)
27700 SBdC - 3936-A2
41600 BBLK - 4811-G1

HUMMINGBIRD WY
17600 CHLS 91709 712-B5
HUNGARIAN ST
- RivC 92880 683-D6
HUNNICUTT DR
11900 RCUC 91701 573-E5
11900 RCUC 91739 573-E5
HUNSAKER DR
2400 SBdC - 519-B7
HUNSAKER WY
2700 SBdC - 519-B7
HUNT AV
800 POM 91766 641-A5
7000 RivC 92509 644-J7
HUNT LN
300 SBdC - 516-E2
HUNT CLUB DR
5500 FONT 92336 574-C2
HUNTER DR
1300 RDL 92374 608-C5
8300 RCUC 91701 572-F5
HUNTER RD
1900 CHLS 91709 710-H1
13900 VCTV 92394 4295-G7
N HUNTER RD
1900 CLTN 92324 606-D3
HUNTER ST
3700 RivC 92509 644-C6
14500 SBdC 92335 604-C6
HUNTER HILL DR
6000 CHLS 91709 711-J4
6000 CHLS 91709 712-A4
HUNTER POINT RD
- POM 91766 640-G4
HUNTERS GATE CIR
15000 CHLS 91709 680-G5
N HUNTINGTON BLVD
500 POM 91768 640-H1
HUNTINGTON DR
9700 RCUC 91701 572-J5
N HUNTINGTON DR
600 CLAR 91711 601-E3
600 UPL 91786 601-E3
6600 SBDO 92407 545-J2
S HUNTINGTON DR
100 CLAR 91711 601-E3
4600 MTCL 91763 601-E3
W HUNTINGTON DR
1600 UPL 91786 601-G3
HUNTINGTON ST
13400 FONT 92336 574-A7
13400 FONT 92336 604-A1
N HUNTINGTON ST
100 POM 91768 640-H1
S HUNTINGTON ST
100 POM 91766 640-H2
HUNTLEY DR
- RCUC 91739 573-F6
HUNTMASTER LN
5200 FONT 92336 574-D1
HUNTRIDGE CT
14500 VCTV 92394 4385-H1
14500 VCTV 92394 4295-H7
HUNTRIDGE DR
14300 VCTV 92394 4385-H1
S HUNTS LN
300 SBDO 92408 606-H6
700 CLTN 92324 606-H7
800 CLTN 92324 646-H1
1100 CLTN 92408 646-H1
HUNTSMEN PL
- FONT 92336 544-D7
HUNTSWOOD PL
4900 RCUC 91737 572-J1
HUPA RD
19000 APLV 92307 4297-B7
22100 APLV 92307 4298-A7
HURON CT
- CHNO 91710 641-H4
HURON DR
800 CLAR 91711 571-B7
HURON RD
26800 SBdC - 517-G1
HURON ST
24900 LMLN 92354 647-C2
HURONS AV
21700 APLV 92307 4297-J7
22100 APLV 92307 4298-A7
N HURRICANE AV
1300 CLTN 92324 605-J4
HURRICANE LN
14300 SBdC - (3935-G4 See Page 3934)
HUSTON DR
24800 SBdC - 517-B5
HUSTON ST
2900 POM 91767 601-A3
HUTCHINSON PL
- RCUC 91730 573-E2
HUTCHISON LN
32100 SBdC 92365 3764-G3
HUTCHISON ST
100 BARS 92311 3679-H2
HUTTON LN
31700 YCPA 92399 649-B3
HUXLEY ST
- YCPA 92399 650-B2
N HYACINTH CT
600 ONT 91762 601-H7

HYACINTH ST
2300 SBDO 92407 546-B5
8500 RCUC 91730 602-F3
W HYATT RD
2300 SBDO 92407 546-A3
3100 SBDO 92407 545-H2
HYDE AV
800 POM 91767 601-B5
HYSSOP DR
7300 RCUC 91739 573-F7
7700 RCUC 91739 603-F1
9000 RCUC 91730 603-F1

I

I AV
7300 HESP 92345 4566-G1
8800 HESP 92345 4476-H3
11500 HESP 92345 4386-H7
I LN
1000 SBdC 92314 4813-B1
I ST
100 NDLS 92363 3620-C5
22900 SBdC 92308 4478-C3
33700 SBdC 92311 3679-E5
33700 SBdC 92311 (3759-E1 See Page 3758)
E I ST
100 ONT 91764 602-D6
N I ST
100 SBDO 92410 606-F1
500 SBDO 92411 576-F5
900 SBDO 92405 576-F2
4100 SBdC 92407 546-F6
5200 SBDO 92407 546-F4
S I ST
100 SBDO 92410 606-F2
800 SBDO 92408 606-F2
W I ST
100 ONT 91762 602-B6
100 ONT 91764 602-B6
1000 ONT 91762 601-J6
IAQUA TR
- SBdC - 4844-F1
IBERIA ST
10900 RivC 91752 643-H6
IBEX SPRING RD
- SBdC - 330-A2
ICE HOUSE CANYON RD
- SBdC - 512-B4
ICELANDIC ST
- RivC 92880 683-D7
ICE PLANT RD
- NDLS 92363 3620-E7
ICICLE DR
8200 SBdC 92371 4562-G3
ICONEL RD
- SBdC 92301 (4203-G1 See Page 4112)
IDA CT
6000 CHNO 91710 641-J7
S IDA ST
100 SBDO 92408 607-A1
IDAHO CT
1000 CLAR 91711 571-F6
IDAHO LN
15400 APLV 92307 4296-J5
IDAHO RD
15400 APLV 92307 4296-J5
IDAHO ST
- FONT 92336 574-C5
- VCTV 92394 4205-G5
1100 RDL 92374 607-G6
IDAHO TR
- SBdC 92365 (3593-H4 See Page 3592)
- SBdC 92365 (3683-J7 See Page 3592)
IDLE LN
- SBdC 92277 4824-B4
IDYLLWILD AV
1900 RLTO 92376 575-F4
N IDYLLWILD AV
600 RLTO 92376 575-F5
2400 RLTO 92377 575-E3
S IDYLLWILD AV
500 RLTO 92376 605-F3
800 RLTO 92316 605-F4
IDYLLWILD CT
700 RDL 92374 608-E7
6200 SBdC 92377 575-F3
IDYLLWILD DR
2500 SBdC - 519-B7
N IDYLLWILD DR
200 RLTO 92376 605-F1
IDYLLWILD LN
17800 SBdC 92392 4386-H4
ILES LN
15600 VCTV 92394 4296-E3
ILEX AV
8100 SBdC 92335 603-J3
ILEX DR
15000 CHLS 91709 681-C6
ILLINI DR
1100 SBdC - 4741-B5
ILLINOIS AV
1200 CLTN 92324 606-F4
E ILLINOIS AV
1000 CLTN 92324 606-F5

N ILLINOIS AV
800 CLTN 92324 606-F5
ILLINOIS CT
- FONT 92336 574-D6
N ILLINOIS ST
500 POM 91768 640-H1
IMEL AV
- YUCA 92284 4957-J7
IMPALA WY
13500 VCTV 92392 4386-G3
IMPERIAL AV
100 SBdC - 4742-F7
100 SBdC - 4812-F2
N IMPERIAL AV
100 ONT 91761 602-F7
100 ONT 91761 642-F1
100 ONT 91764 602-F7
IMPERIAL CT
- RDL 92374 608-F4
IMPERIAL DR
6300 YUCA 92284 4888-A7
S IMPERIAL PL
2400 ONT 91761 642-F5
IMPERIAL RD
4100 SBdC 92301 4112-J3
4200 SBdC 92301 (4113-B3 See Page 4112)
IMPORIA RD
- SBdC - (3846-C6 See Page 3756)
INADALE CT
32200 SBdC - 519-B7
INCA AV
9300 ADEL 92301 4204-D6
11300 ADEL 92301 4205-A6
INCA RD
- APLV 92308 4387-E6
INCA TR
200 SBdC 92284 4747-D7
900 SBdC 92284 4817-D2
7300 YUCA 92284 4957-D3
INCHON AV
- BARS 92311 3680-F7
INCLINE CT
5200 RCUC - (542-E7 See Page 513)
INCLINE DR
- RCUC - (542-D7 See Page 513)
- RCUC - 572-D1
INCONEL RD
14100 SBdC 92371 4382-E2
INDEPENDENCE AV
1600 RDL 92374 608-F6
30500 SBdC 92374 608-G6
INDEPENDENCE CT
5100 CHNO 91710 641-G5
9900 ADEL 92301 4204-E4
10600 SBdC 92374 608-H7
INDEPENDENCE DR
100 CLAR 91711 571-D5
INDEPENDENCE LN
2300 SBdC - 519-D7
INDEPENDENCE ST
4200 CHNO 91710 641-F5
E INDEPENDENCE ST
900 SBDO 92408 607-B3
E INDEPENDENCE WY
13800 FONT 92336 574-B7
W INDEPENDENCE WY
13800 FONT 92336 574-A7
INDEPENDENT PL
25100 SBdC 92404 577-C5
INDIAN AV
37100 SBdC - (3591-F4 See Page 3590)
INDIAN CIR
6500 TNP 92277 4891-C6
INDIAN RD
26500 SBdC 92346 577-F1
INDIAN TR
1400 SBDO 92407 546-D6
3600 SBdC 92277 4823-B5
28700 SBdC - (3846-F5 See Page 3756)
46000 SBdC - 4742-J2
46000 SBdC - (4743-A2 See Page 4662)
68700 SBdC 92277 4820-J6
68800 SBdC 92277 4821-A6
71900 SBdC 92277 4822-H3
72700 TNP 92277 4822-G5
78800 SBdC 92277 4824-A5
83300 SBdC 92277 (4825-C5 See Page 4824)
INDIANA AV
300 CLAR 91711 571-D6
INDIANA CT
- FONT 92336 574-D6
1200 RDL 92374 607-J6
N INDIAN CANYON CT
2800 SBDO 92346 577-F2
INDIAN COVE CIR
68900 SBdC 92277 4961-B5
INDIAN COVE CIR E
68900 SBdC 92277 4961-C5
INDIAN COVE RD
3300 SBdC 92277 4821-B7
4900 SBdC 92277 4891-C3
4900 TNP 92277 4891-C3

STREET Block City ZIP Pg-Grid

INDIAN COVE RD
6900 TNP 92277 4961-C1
INDIAN COVE RD N
68700 SBdC 92277 4961-B4
INDIAN COVE E RD
68900 SBdC 92277 4961-C5
INDIAN COVE MOUNTAIN RD
7100 TNP 92277 4961-C2
7200 SBdC 92277 4961-C2
INDIAN COVE W RD
68400 SBdC 92277 4961-B5
INDIAN CREEK PL
14100 VCTV 92392 4386-C1
INDIAN CREEK RD
2100 DBAR 91765 680-D5
INDIAN HILL BLVD
500 POM 91767 601-D7
500 POM 91767 641-D1
N INDIAN HILL BLVD
100 CLAR 91711 601-C3
1800 CLAR 91711 571-C6
S INDIAN HILL BLVD
100 CLAR 91711 601-D5
INDIAN HILL RD
8200 YUCA 92284 4957-C5
INDIANOLA DR
74800 TNP 92277 4962-H1
INDIAN RANCH SPRINGS RD
6300 SBdC - (4571-B6 See Page 4570)
INDIAN RIVER DR
12100 APLV 92308 4387-B6
INDIAN SPRINGS DR
15100 VCTV 92394 4296-A5
INDIAN SPRINGS RD
47000 SBdC - 349-D1
INDIAN SPRINGS TR
81300 SBdC - 350-H2
INDIAN SUMMER DR
10100 RCUC 91730 603-A2
INDIAN TRAIL RD
- SBdC 92252 4820-A6
INDIAN WELL DR
1300 DBAR 91765 680-A3
INDIAN WELLS DR
14800 VCTV 92394 4295-J7
INDIAN WELLS RD
36500 SBdC 92347 (3587-D7 See Page 3586)
36500 SBdC 92347 (3677-D1 See Page 3586)
INDIGO AV
5700 RCUC 91701 572-D3
N INDIGO AV
800 CLTN 92324 605-J5
6100 SBDO 92407 545-J3
6100 SBDO 92407 546-A3
INDIGO CT
700 POM 91767 601-A4
7500 FONT 92336 574-E7
8000 RCUC 91701 572-E4
INDIGO LN
7400 FONT 92336 574-E6
INDIGO ST
- ADEL 92301 4295-A7
INDIO AV
2700 SBdC 92284 4818-D6
3700 SBdC 92284 4888-D2
4700 YUCA 92284 4888-D5
6800 YUCA 92284 4958-D2
INDIO CT
11600 YCPA 92399 649-J2
INDUSTRIAL BLVD
12100 VCTV 92392 4386-G6
12100 VCTV 92345 4386-G6
INDUSTRIAL CIR
10200 LMLN 92374 607-E6
S INDUSTRIAL DR
2800 RLTO 92316 645-H2
INDUSTRIAL LN
8700 RCUC 91730 602-J3
INDUSTRIAL PKWY
2900 SBdC 92407 545-H4
2900 SBDO 92407 545-H4
2900 SBDO 92407 546-A5
E INDUSTRIAL RD
300 SBDO 92408 606-J7
300 SBDO 92408 607-A7
INDUSTRIAL ST
1000 POM 91766 641-B3
INDUSTRIAL WY
- BARS 92311 3678-J6
12900 SBdC 93562 2144-J4
INDUSTRIAL CENTER DR
12400 VCTV 92392 4386-G6
INDUSTRIAL PARK AV
1300 RDL 92374 607-G6
INDUSTRIAL PARK WY
- RDL 92374 607-H6
INDUSTRY AV
11700 FONT 92337 643-H4
INDUSTRY WY
9300 ADEL 92301 4294-E3
N INDUSTRY WY
200 UPL 91786 602-A3
INEZ AV
100 SBdC 92284 4748-E5

INEZ AV
400 SBdC 92285 4748-E5
3000 SBdC 92284 4818-E6
3700 SBdC 92284 4888-F1
4700 YUCA 92284 4888-F2
INFINITI LN
- SBdC 92335 604-A2
INGLENOOK PL
8200 RCUC 91730 602-G2
INGRAM WY
14600 ADEL 92301 4294-J7
INGVALDSEN PL
5900 RCUC 91739 574-B3
INKPA CT
14400 APLV 92307 4297-A7
INKPA RD
14300 APLV 92307 4387-B1
14300 APLV 92307 4297-A7
INLAND AV
10800 RivC 91752 643-G5
S INLAND CENTER DR
500 SBDO 92408 606-G3
E INLAND EMPIRE BLVD
1900 ONT 91764 602-H6
2700 ONT 91764 603-C7
INLET ST
- UPL 91786 602-E2
INN AV
6700 TNP 92277 4892-F6
INNISBROOK CIR
1300 UPL 91784 572-D6
INNISBROOK LN
- FONT 92336 574-H3
INNSBRUCK DR
1200 SBdC - 4737-J5
1200 SBdC - 4738-A5
INSPIRATION DR
900 SBdC - 517-H3
8100 RCUC - 572-E1
8100 RCUC 91701 572-E1
31400 SBdC - 518-J7
31500 SBdC - 519-A7
INSPIRATION RD
23700 SBdC - 516-H4
INSTITUTION RD
5800 SBDO 92407 545-F5
19100 SBdC 92407 545-F5
INTERLAKEN CT
- SBdC 92397 4652-G3
N INTEROCEAN AV
400 SBDO 92410 576-J7
400 SBDO 92410 606-J1
INVERNESS AV
35000 SBdC 92365 (3683-H3 See Page 3592)
INVERNESS CT
- CHLS 91709 711-F1
S INVERNESS CT
2700 ONT 91761 642-G6
INVERNESS LN
- FONT 92336 574-H3
INVERRARY WY
- FONT 92336 574-H3
INYO AV
400 SBdC - 4812-E2
INYO CT
- SBdC - 4843-F5
15900 VCTV 92392 4296-D4
26800 SBdC - 4737-F6
INYO PL
3800 CHNO 91710 641-D5
6700 RCUC 91701 573-B5
INYO RD
7300 SBdC 92371 4473-J3
INYO ST
15600 VCTV 92392 4296-D4
INYO LUPINE RD
- SBdC 92308 4388-G6
IOAMOSA CT
- RCUC 91737 572-G2
W IOLA PL
200 SBDO 92405 576-H5
IOLAB DR
500 CLAR 91711 601-C4
IONA LN
55400 YUCA 92284 4957-E5
IOWA AV
- RivC 92501 646-B7
- RivC 92507 646-B7
600 RIV 92507 646-B7
N IOWA AV
900 CLTN 92324 606-F5
S IOWA AV
2400 CLTN 92324 646-C6
2700 RivC 92507 646-C6
2700 RivC 92501 646-C6
IOWA CT
- CHNO 91710 641-H4
1100 CLAR 91711 571-A7
IOWA LN
- FONT 92336 574-D6
IOWA ST
- RDL 92373 647-H1
200 RDL 92373 607-H7
IRA LN
58600 SBdC 92285 4748-C1
IRENE CT
- FONT 92336 574-E5

IRENE ST
1200 SBdC 92397 4652-D2
IRIE DR
1300 BARS 92311 3679-J5
IRIS AV
6600 SBdC 92376 575-F4
10700 ADEL 92301 4294-H3
11300 LMLN 92354 647-B2
N IRIS AV
200 RLTO 92376 605-F1
500 RLTO 92376 575-F5
2200 RLTO 92377 575-F3
S IRIS AV
1200 RLTO 92376 605-F5
1300 RLTO 92316 605-F5
IRIS CT
6300 RivC 92880 683-D6
14700 CHLS 91709 681-C5
N IRIS CT
600 ONT 91762 601-H5
IRIS DR
- SBdC 92316 605-B6
300 SBdC - 517-D2
700 BBLK - 4811-C2
13900 SBdC 92335 604-B6
15500 FONT 92335 604-H6
33200 SBdC - 519-E2
36300 SBdC 92311 3680-C1
IRIS LN
34800 YCPA 92399 649-J3
IRIS PL
7000 RCUC 91739 573-G6
IRIS ST
400 RDL 92373 648-A3
5000 SBDO 92407 546-A5
S IRIS ST
- CLTN 92410 606-B3
200 SBDO 92410 606-B2
500 RLTO 92376 605-F3
N IRIS WY
1500 UPL 91786 572-B7
IRISH RIVER AV
13200 CHNO 91710 681-F1
IRONAGE RD
6200 SBdC 92277 390-L1
8300 SBdC - 390-L2
88100 SBdC 92277 370-K11
IRONBARK AV
14000 CHNO 91710 682-B3
IRONBARK CT
- CHNO 91710 682-B3
IRONBARK DR
12400 RCUC 91739 573-G6
22500 DBAR 91765 680-A3
IRONBARK LN
800 SBdC - 4738-E6
W IRON HORSE CIR
1200 CLTN 92324 606-A4
N IRON HORSE DR
1000 CLTN 92324 605-J5
1000 CLTN 92324 606-A4
IRONHORSE CANYON RD
23200 DBAR 91765 680-B3
IRON MOUNTAIN CT
10000 RCUC 91737 573-A1
IRON MOUNTAIN RD
18500 SBdC - (3676-J7 See Page 3586)
18500 SBdC - 3756-J1
18800 SBdC - (3677-B7 See Page 3586)
18800 SBdC - (3757-F1 See Page 3756)
20100 SBdC 92311 (3757-F1 See Page 3756)
IRON MOUNTAIN PUMPING PLANT RD
- SBdC - 371-G11
- SBdC - 391-G1
IRONRIDGE CT
- FONT 92336 574-E6
IRON ROCK PL
13800 VCTV 92392 4386-C2
IRONSIDE RD
11200 APLV 92308 4477-D1
IRONSIDES LN
14300 SBdC - (3935-G4 See Page 3934)
IRONSTONE AV
13300 VCTV 92392 4385-F5
IRONSTONE CIR
13500 VCTV 92392 4385-F6
IRONSTONE CT
12500 VCTV 92392 4385-F6
IRONSTONE PL
12500 VCTV 92392 4385-F6
IRONSTONE WY
12500 VCTV 92392 4385-F6
IRONWOOD
9700 SBdC - 4482-D3
IRONWOOD AV
9700 SBdC 92316 605-D5
N IRONWOOD AV
900 RLTO 92376 575-D6
S IRONWOOD AV
500 RLTO 92316 605-D4
500 RLTO 92335 605-D3
1500 RLTO 92376 605-D3
IRONWOOD CT
5600 SBdC 92404 577-C1

IRONWOOD CT
7600 FONT 92336 574-F7
9000 SBdC 92335 604-F4
9900 FONT 92335 604-F6
IRONWOOD DR
- RivC 92399 650-G6
- TNP 92278 4822-E1
4100 CHLS 91709 681-E5
7500 FONT 92336 574-F7
9100 SBdC 92335 604-F4
27300 SBdC 92311 3679-D5
37200 YCPA 92399 650-G6
40500 BBLK - 4811-E2
IRONWOOD LN
17800 SBdC 92392 4386-H3
27000 SBdC - 4737-G6
IRONWOOD RD
100 SBdC 92372 4472-A6
IRONWOOD ST
2900 SBdC 92404 577-C1
5300 SBdC 92404 547-D7
8900 RCUC 91730 572-G7
9900 RCUC 91730 573-A7
11900 RCUC 91739 573-F7
N IRONWOOD ST
3900 SBdC 92404 547-C7
IRONWOOD TR
13100 YCPA 92399 650-E5
IROQUOIS AV
9800 SBdC 92308 4477-F5
IROQUOIS CT
20600 APLV 92308 4387-F6
IROQUOIS LN
1200 SBdC - 4741-A4
IROQUOIS PL
13700 CHNO 91710 681-F2
IROQUOIS RD
9300 SBdC 92308 4477-F5
12000 APLV 92308 4387-F3
13600 APLV 92307 4387-F2
14300 APLV 92307 4297-H7
IROQUOIS ST
7800 FONT 92336 604-A1
IRVING CT
4900 CHNO 91710 641-F6
IRVING LN
13900 SBdC - 514-A1
IRVING PL
- VCTV 92394 4205-G7
E IRVING WY
500 SBdC 92314 4742-E6
S IRVING WY
- UPL 91786 601-J4
W IRVINGTON AV
2200 SBDO 92407 546-A3
2700 SBDO 92407 545-J3
IRWIN CT
1600 RDL 92374 608-C4
IRWIN RD
800 BARS 92311 3679-H1
1200 BARS 92311 3589-G5
36400 SBdC 92311 3589-H2
36400 SBdC 92311 3679-H1
38900 SBdC - 3589-H2
39200 SBdC - 349-E7
S IRWIN ST
100 SBDO 92408 606-J2
IRWIN BENCH LN
- BARS 92311 3680-E3
- SBdC 92311 3680-E3
IRWINDALE CIR
14500 ADEL 92301 4384-H1
ISAAC LORD DR
9300 RCUC 91701 572-H5
ISABELITA CT
1300 UPL 91786 572-E7
ISABELL LN
- SBdC 92285 (4577-B6 See Page 4486)
W ISABELLA DR
2200 SBDO 92324 606-B3
ISABELLA VILLA CT
7200 HIGH 92346 578-D5
N ISADORA WY
1500 ONT 91764 602-H4
ISATIS AV
21700 APLV 92307 4297-J7
22100 APLV 92307 4298-A7
ISHBELL CT
200 RivC 92507 646-D6
ISLAND DR
25000 SBdC - 517-C5
41200 SBdC 92339 611-G2
ISLAY AV
8900 SBdC 92335 604-D4
ISLE CT
- RCUC 91739 573-H6
ISLETA RD
6200 TNP 92277 4893-A7
ISLI CT
5700 SBdC - 4774-G7
ISSAC CT
6500 CHNO 91710 682-A1
ISSAC ST
6500 CHNO 91710 682-B1
ITALIA RD
- FONT 92336 544-H6
ITASCA CT
13500 APLV 92308 4387-D2

ITASCA RD
19600 APLV 92308 4387-D2
20100 APLV 92307 4387-D2
22600 APLV 92308 4388-B2
24300 SBdC 92307 4388-F2
ITOYA VISTA
11000 APLV 92308 4477-F1
11200 APLV 92308 4387-F7
ITUMA RD
20100 APLV 92308 4387-E3
I V RD E
9200 SBdC 92339 611-D2
I V RD W
9100 SBdC 92339 611-C2
IVANHOE DR
56500 YUCA 92284 4958-A6
56700 YUCA 92284 4957-H6
IVANHOE RD
- SBdC - 4570-B1
9300 SBdC - 4480-B3
12500 SBdC - (4390-B3 See Page 4300)
IVANPAH AV
6500 TNP 92277 4891-B7
7000 TNP 92277 4961-B1
IVANPAH RD
12800 APLV 92308 4387-B3
13600 APLV 92307 4387-B2
IVANPAH WY
18900 APLV 92308 4387-B3
IVORY CT
4800 CHLS 91709 711-F2
IVORY LN
2300 POM 91767 601-A4
IVY AV
- SBdC 92407 515-A4
11600 HESP 92345 4386-J7
11600 HESP 92345 4387-A7
12900 RCUC 91739 603-H2
13300 SBdC 92335 603-J2
13400 SBdC 92335 604-D1
16000 FONT 92335 604-H1
17000 FONT 92335 605-A1
17700 SBdC 92335 605-B1
32100 SBdC 92311 3758-C4
35100 YCPA 92399 610-B5
36500 SBdC 92399 610-D5
E IVY AV
800 CLTN 92324 606-F5
IVY CT
- YCPA 92399 610-B5
1000 BARS 92311 3679-E4
2300 UPL 91784 572-C3
10300 RCUC 91730 573-B7
15100 ADEL 92301 4294-H6
IVY LN
500 SBdC - 518-A3
7300 RCUC 91730 573-A7
IVY ST
- RDL 92373 648-D3
14200 ADEL 92301 4384-J1
IVY GLEN DR
300 RivC 91752 683-E4
IWA RD
16300 APLV 92307 4297-A2
N IWO JIMA AV
- BARS 92311 3680-G5
S IWO JIMA ST
- BARS 92311 3680-G6

J

J RD
12300 SBdC 93562 2144-G5
J ST
- BARS 92311 3680-G7
100 NDLS 92363 3620-B6
33700 SBdC 92311 3679-E5
33700 SBdC 92311 (3759-E1 See Page 3758)
E J ST
100 ONT 91764 602-C6
N J ST
100 SBDO 92410 606-F1
500 SBDO 92411 576-F4
S J ST
100 SBDO 92410 606-F2
W J ST
100 ONT 91762 602-B6
100 ONT 91764 602-B6
400 CLTN 92324 606-C6
900 ONT 91762 601-H6
JACARANDA AV
- VCTV 92392 4387-A5
6500 FONT 92336 574-F5
9100 HESP 92345 4477-A6
11200 HESP 92345 4476-J1
11500 HESP 92345 4386-J7
12000 HESP 92392 4386-J6
12100 VCTV 92392 4386-J6
12400 CHNO 91710 641-H6
JACARANDA CIR
11300 FONT 92337 644-G2
JACARANDA CT
- RCUC 91730 603-C5
E JACARANDA CT
2100 SBDO 92404 577-F1
JACARANDA PL
1200 UPL 91784 571-J5
12500 CHNO 91710 641-H6

N JACARANDA RD
1000 CLTN 92324 605-J5
W JACARANDA ST
800 ONT 91762 642-A3
1000 ONT 91762 641-J3
JACKALOPE AV
700 SBdC 92252 4749-E7
1200 SBdC 92252 4819-E2
JACKASS TR
- TNP 92277 4890-J7
- TNP 92277 4960-J1
JACK BENNY DR
- RCUC 91730 603-E2
JACK FROST DR
8100 SBdC 92371 4562-G3
JACKMANI AV
15000 SBdC - (4303-A4 See Page 4302)
JACK RABBIT LN
- SBdC 92285 4747-J1
- SBdC 92285 4748-A1
7700 HIGH 92346 578-C6
JACK RABBIT RUN
7500 SBdC 92372 4562-F4
JACKRABBIT TR
500 SBdC 92277 4751-B7
500 SBdC 92277 4821-B1
JACKSON
- SBdC 92277 4750-H5
JACKSON AV
17300 FONT 92336 575-A6
JACKSON CT
4200 CHNO 91710 641-E4
16500 FONT 92336 574-H6
JACKSON DR
15600 FONT 92336 574-F6
JACKSON LN
4500 SBdC 92371 4473-B6
JACKSON RD
26500 SBdC 92307 4299-C1
S JACKSON RD
2400 SBDO 92408 606-J7
W JACKSON RD
100 SBDO 92408 606-H7
E JACKSON ST
100 RLTO 92376 575-H6
900 RLTO 92376 576-A6
N JACKSON ST
400 SBdC 92324 606-B5
W JACKSON ST
200 RLTO 92376 575-D6
JACMACIA ST
- SBdC 92307 4207-C2
JACO RD
- SBdC - (4390-H6 See Page 4300)
JACOBS ST
900 CLTN 92324 646-H1
JACQUELINE RD
400 SBdC - 517-E2
JADE AV
7100 FONT 92336 574-J6
JADE CT
- CHLS 91709 711-G1
- RDL 92374 608-E7
6700 FONT 92336 574-J5
34900 YCPA 92399 610-A4
JADE DR
- RCUC 91701 572-E5
JADE LN
26400 SBdC - (3935-G6 See Page 3934)
JADE RD
12000 VCTV 92392 4385-F5
25200 SBdC 92311 3678-G4
JADE ST
100 SBdC - 518-E1
JADE TER
- CHLS 91709 711-G1
JADEITE AV
5000 RCUC 91737 572-J1
6700 RCUC 91701 572-J5
7500 RCUC 91730 572-J7
7700 RCUC 91730 602-J1
JADEITE ST
63300 SBdC 92252 4889-F4
JADESTONE AV
4700 SBDO 92407 545-J6
4700 SBDO 92407 546-A6
JAGADON RD
- SBdC - 4570-J2
32700 SBdC - (4571-A2 See Page 4570)
JAGATAI ST
6600 SBdC 92345 4565-G1
8700 HESP 92345 4565-G1
10400 HESP 92345 4475-G4
JAGERHORN DR
700 SBdC - 4737-H6
E JAGUAR WY
700 ONT 91764 603-A6
JALAMAR RD
2600 SBdC 92307 (4027-H6 See Page 3936)
JALEPENO AV
12500 CHNO 91710 642-A6
JALEPENO PL
12500 CHNO 91710 642-A6
JAMACHA RD
11300 APLV 92308 4387-H7

JAMACHA RD
11300 APLV 92308 4477-H1
JAMAICA DR
10200 MohC - 3620-D2
JAMAICA LN
14300 SBdC - (3935-G4 See Page 3934)
JAMAICA RD
36700 SBdC 92311 3590-B7
JAMAICA WY
1300 MohC - 3620-D3
JAME WY
- SBdC 92285 (4577-J7 See Page 4486)
JAMES CT
1600 RDL 92374 608-C4
JAMES PL
600 POM 91767 601-A6
700 SBdC - 4741-J6
W JAMES PL
2400 SBDO 92407 546-A3
JAMES ST
4500 MTCL 91763 601-E6
E JAMES ST
100 RLTO 92376 605-H3
W JAMES ST
400 RLTO 92376 605-E3
1200 RLTO 92316 605-D3
3100 SBDO 92376 605-J3
JAMES BIRCH RD
36400 YCPA 92399 650-D1
36400 YCPA 92399 610-D7
JAMESTOWN AV
- RivC 92880 683-D4
JAMESTOWN CT
2300 CLAR 91711 571-E6
JAMESTOWN PL
12200 CHNO 91710 642-B5
JAMES WEHR CT
1000 CLTN 92324 606-F5
JAMUL RD
10500 APLV 92308 4477-H2
JANA LN
58800 SBdC 92285 4748-C3
E JANE CT
300 UPL 91786 572-C7
W JANE CT
800 UPL 91786 572-A7
JANE RD
- SBdC - (4577-H3 See Page 4486)
- SBdC 92285 (4577-H3 See Page 4486)
JANE ST
2100 SBDO 92404 577-D5
25500 HIGH 92404 577-D5
JANES WY
- CLTN 92324 606-A4
JANET ST
- FONT 92336 574-E5
JANINE ST
19000 ADEL 92301 4204-F3
JANSU PL
400 POM 91768 640-C2
N JANTZEN AV
1500 CLTN 92324 606-E3
1700 SBDO 92410 606-E3
JAPATUL RD
8900 SBdC 92308 4478-F6
11000 SBdC 92308 4388-F7
12400 SBdC 92307 4388-F3
14100 SBdC 92307 4298-E3
JAQUI RD
- SBdC - (3846-F7 See Page 3756)
- SBdC - 3936-F1
JARANA CT
57200 YUCA 92284 4957-J6
JARGON RD
- VCTV 92392 4385-E2
6800 SBdC 92345 4565-F4
11000 VCTV 92392 4475-F4
JARGON ST
8100 SBdC 92345 4565-F3
JARROW AV
- SBdC 92371 4653-F1
JASMA
22600 APLV 92307 4208-B7
JASMIN CT
- SBDO 92354 607-C6
JASMINE AV
2200 UPL 91784 571-J3
N JASMINE AV
800 ONT 91762 601-H5
JASMINE CT
6700 CHNO 91710 642-B5
7000 RCUC 91739 573-G6
12200 VCTV 92392 4386-D6
35500 YCPA 92399 650-B6
N JASMINE CT
600 ONT 91762 601-H5
JASMINE DR
11900 CHNO 91710 641-E5
JASMINE LN
- SBdC - 518-A2
27800 SBdC - (3935-J2 See Page 3934)
JASMINE PL
1300 ONT 91762 641-H3
11800 FONT 92337 644-C4

JASMINE PL
29200 HIGH 92346 578-D5
JASMINE RD
15000 SBdC - 4302-J4
JASMINE ST
900 FONT 92337 643-J1
1000 RDL 92374 608-G5
5100 SBDO 92407 546-A5
10500 FONT 92337 603-J7
10700 LMLN 92354 607-D7
15300 VCTV 92392 4386-B6
JASMINE WY
- YBLN 92886 710-A7
JASMINE CREEK LN
28900 HIGH 92346 578-C6
JASMINE HILL CT
4300 CHLS 91709 711-E2
JASON CT
1600 RDL 92374 608-C4
JASON LN
12200 VCTV 92392 4386-E6
JASON PL
1000 DBAR 91765 680-E2
JASPER
- BREA 92823 710-C6
JASPER AV
1100 SBdC 92359 608-H5
10600 SBdC 92374 608-H7
17800 SBdC - (4210-F5 See Page 4120)
JASPER CT
10400 ADEL 92301 4204-G6
JASPER DR
900 SBdC - 4812-B1
JASPER RD
24600 BARS 92311 3678-J4
24600 SBdC 92311 3678-H5
30600 SBdC 92365 3764-E6
JASPER ST
100 SBdC - 518-E1
5200 RCUC 91701 572-F2
8500 RCUC 91730 602-F3
JAVA DR
56500 YUCA 92284 4957-G6
JAVELLE ST
- SBdC 92365 (3684-D2 See Page 3594)
36100 SBdC 92365 3594-E6
JAY ST
9900 ADEL 92301 4204-F4
E JAY ST
1800 ONT 91764 602-G6
JAYBIRD LN
800 BBLK - 4811-C2
800 SBdC - 4811-C2
JAYHAWKER LN
23700 DBAR 91765 640-C5
JAYJAY RD
- SBdC - 4120-C5
JAY POST RD
15300 VCTV 92394 4296-B4
JAYSON CT
700 POM 91767 601-A3
J BOCING RD
45500 SBdC - 349-G5
JC RD
11600 FONT 92337 645-B4
J C ORTIZ
- TNP 92277 4822-E7
- TNP 92277 4892-E1
JEAN AV
1300 RDL 92374 608-E5
JED SMITH ST
8000 FONT 92336 604-A1
N JEFFERS LN
3700 SBdC 92404 547-C7
3700 SBDO 92404 547-C7
JEFFERSON AV
5300 CHNO 91710 641-G6
E JEFFERSON AV
300 POM 91767 601-A7
W JEFFERSON AV
900 SBDO 92410 606-F3
2700 SBDO 92376 606-A3
3000 SBDO 92376 605-J3
JEFFERSON CT
- RCUC 91730 573-E1
5800 CHNO 91710 641-J6
S JEFFERSON LN
900 CLTN 92324 646-D1
W JEFFERSON PL
1100 SBDO 92410 606-E4
JEFFERSON ST
400 RDL 92374 608-G7
800 UPL 91784 572-A4
900 UPL 91784 571-J4
9900 YCPA 92399 610-C7
13200 YCPA 92399 650-C6
E JEFFERSON ST
1000 ONT 91761 642-E1
W JEFFERSON ST
800 SBDO 92410 606-F4
JEFFERY LN
- SBdC - 3592-D6
JEFFERY CT
9600 FONT 92335 604-J5
JEFFREY PL
2500 RivC 92509 644-D6

JEFFREY WY
1300 SBDO 92407 546-E6
JEFFREY PINE CT
- SBDO 92407 546-A3
JEFFRIES RD
300 BBLK - 4811-G1
JELAN AV
14500 APLV 92307 4298-A7
21700 APLV 92307 4297-J7
23900 SBdC 92307 4298-E6
JELLCO AV
9300 HESP 92345 4476-F6
JELLICO ST
- SBdC - (3682-B2 See Page 3592)
JEMEZ RD
5300 SBdC 92285 (4577-C7 See Page 4486)
JEMEZ TR
200 SBdC 92284 4747-D7
900 SBdC 92284 4817-D2
7500 YUCA 92284 4957-D4
JENKINS AV
6700 HESP 92345 4566-G4
JENKS LAKE RD
- SBdC - 389-F1
43100 SBdC - (4882-B6 See Page 4813)
JENNA CT
13300 VCTV 92392 4385-G4
JENNET RD
27500 SBdC - 3936-J2
27500 SBdC - (3937-A2 See Page 3936)
JENNET ST
7900 RCUC 91701 572-D3
JENNIFER AV
- SBdC 92365 (3504-B6 See Page 3414)
N JENNIFER CT
1400 CLTN 92324 606-B4
JENNIFER LN
- YCPA 92399 650-C6
JENNIFER ST
- RDL 92373 647-J2
- RDL 92373 648-A2
JENNINGS RD
3300 SBdC 92285 4667-D2
JENNY LN
3700 SBdC 91710 641-C7
JENNY ST
- SBdC 92371 4563-C7
10100 SBdC 92345 4564-J6
11400 SBdC 92345 4565-B6
14300 HESP 92345 4565-J6
14500 HESP 92345 4566-A6
JENSEN CT
22900 GTER 92313 646-G4
JENSEN DR
2000 SBdC 92314 4742-H6
JENSEN RD
4700 SBdC 92285 (4577-A7 See Page 4486)
4700 SBdC 92285 4667-A1
JERALDO CT
15000 VCTV 92394 4296-A6
JERALDO DR
15000 VCTV 92394 4296-A5
JEREMY CT
- RCUC 91739 574-A4
600 RDL 92374 608-E6
JERICHO RD
21200 SBdC - (4115-H5 See Page 4114)
JERICHO WY
62000 SBdC 92252 4889-C4
JERICO LN
200 SBdC 92277 4750-F5
JERICO RD
- SBdC 92284 4888-B3
JEROME CT
13200 CHLS 91709 680-J1
JERRY CT
10700 RivC 91752 683-J5
JERSEY BLVD
9300 RCUC 91730 602-H3
9800 RCUC 91730 603-A3
JERSEY CT
11600 RCUC 91730 603-F3
11700 RCUC 91739 603-F3
JERSEY ST
- RivC 92880 683-D6
N JERYL AV
1600 CLTN 92324 606-C3
JESS ST
1500 POM 91766 640-F3
JESSE DR
1000 SBDO 92407 546-F4
JESSE RD
55500 SBdC 92285 4747-D1
JESSE WY
200 RDL 92374 648-G1
JESSICA LN
17300 CHLS 91709 711-J4
JESSIE CT
- RCUC 91739 573-G5
JESS RANCH PKWY
17400 APLV 92308 4387-B7
18300 APLV 92308 4477-B1

JESS RANCH PL
19200 APLV 92308 4387-B7
JETHRO DR
- SBdC 92277 4893-D5
- TNP 92277 4893-D5
JETSTAR CT
- SBDO 92409 577-E7
JEWEL DR
24900 SBdC - 517-B3
JEWEL ST
6500 RivC 92509 645-A7
JG RD
5900 SBdC 92371 4653-B2
JIB CT
14200 SBdC - (3935-G5 See Page 3934)
JICARILLA RD
13300 APLV 92308 4387-G3
13600 APLV 92307 4387-F2
14200 APLV 92307 4297-H7
JICARILLA RD S
14100 APLV 92307 4387-H1
JIGGS RD
32000 SBdC 92311 (3757-G5 See Page 3756)
JILL WY
1000 UPL 91784 571-J4
JIMENO AV
16000 VCTV 92394 4296-B4
JINGAL RD
9900 SBdC - 4481-C2
JINGAL ST
10000 SBdC - 4481-C3
JOAN AV
7400 RivC 92509 644-H7
W JO-AN DR
2900 SBDO 92407 545-J3
JOANN WY
1400 POM 91767 601-B6
JOANNE ST
1500 RDL 92374 608-D4
JOAQUIN CT
- CHNO 91710 682-A1
JOAQUIN ST
5900 CHNO 91710 681-J1
6100 CHNO 91710 682-A1
JOAQUIN MILLER RD
100 SBdC - 518-A1
JOBS PEAK RD
21600 SBdC - 516-B1
JOCELYN LN
10100 YCPA 92399 610-C5
JOCKEY CT
14400 VCTV 92394 4295-H7
14400 VCTV 92394 4385-H1
JOCKEY LN
13900 VCTV 92394 4295-G7
JOE AV
16000 FONT 92336 574-G2
JOE DAVIS DR
74100 TNP 92277 4892-G4
75300 TNP 92277 4893-A4
JOE DAVIS RD
75500 TNP 92277 4893-A5
JOEL DR
3200 RivC 92509 645-C7
JOHIL RD
35000 SBdC 92365 (3683-C2 See Page 3592)
JOHN GLENN RD
13800 APLV 92308 4387-J2
JOHN JUAREZ WY
1100 CLTN 92324 606-B4
JOHN MARY LN
- SBdC 92277 4824-A6
E JOHN MATICH DR
2100 CLTN 92324 646-H4
JOHN MUIR RD
100 SBdC - 518-B1
JOHNNY WY
1100 SBdC - 4812-B1
JOHNS ST
13600 VCTV 92392 4475-F3
JOHNSON AV
16400 SBdC 91710 712-D3
JOHNSON RD
7800 SBdC 92371 4563-C2
9100 SBdC 92371 4473-C3
11900 SBdC 92371 4473-B3
14700 SBdC 92371 (4293-C6 See Page 4292)
17700 SBdC 92301 (4203-B3 See Page 4112)
19800 SBdC 92307 4207-B2
19800 APLV 92307 4207-G2
20100 SBdC 92301 (4113-B3 See Page 4112)
22000 APLV 92307 4208-A2
22500 SBdC 92307 4208-D2
24600 SBdC 92307 (4209-A2 See Page 4118)
24900 SBdC - (4209-G4 See Page 4118)
25800 SBdC - (4210-F1 See Page 4120)
JOHNSON ST
4000 SBdC 92407 546-G7
4000 SBDO 92407 546-G7
25000 SBdC 92311 3678-G6

STREET
Block City ZIP Pg-Grid

JOHNSON PASTURE MTWY
- CLAR 91711 571-C2
JOHNSONS LN
10200 SBdC 92308 4477-E3
JOHNSTON DR
16400 VCTV 92392 4386-E2
JOHNSTON PL
5700 RCUC 91739 574-B3
JOHNSTON RD
- VCTV 92392 4386-F2
E JOHNSTON ST
400 CLTN 92324 606-E3
500 SBDO 92410 606-E3
W JOHNSTON ST
100 CLTN 92324 606-C3
JOJOBA DR
3000 SBdC 92277 4824-G3
JOLENE FARMS LN
- SBdC 92311 3680-D3
JOLLY WY
4200 RivC 92509 644-G7
JOLON RD
22800 SBdC 92308 4478-B1
25200 SBdC 92308 4479-B1
25500 SBdC 92308 (4389-C7 See Page 4299)
JOLON ST
15100 CHLS 91709 681-C5
JOMAR ST
11600 YCPA 92399 650-D1
JON CT
500 DBAR 91765 640-D7
JONATHAN ST
14100 ADEL 92301 4385-B2
14500 ADEL 92301 4295-A1
17200 ADEL 92301 4205-A4
JONES BRADWAY
15600 SBdC - 4302-C3
JONI LN
800 RDL 92374 608-F6
JONQUIL DR
2500 SBdC 91784 572-B2
JONQUIL ST
26100 SBdC 92346 577-E3
S JOPLON CT
700 CLTN 92324 606-B3
700 SBDO 92324 606-B3
JORDAN CT
- RCUC 91739 574-A4
JORDAN DR
300 RDL 92373 648-F4
JORDAN PL
11300 FONT 92337 644-F2
14900 VCTV 92394 4296-C6
JORDAN RD
14600 SBdC - (3935-J6 See Page 3934)
19400 SBdC - 3936-A5
JOSE CT
3900 CHNO 91710 681-D2
JOSE ST
3800 CHNO 91710 681-D2
JOSEPH LN
- VCTV 92392 4385-E7
JOSEPH L BOLL AV
U.S.-66 Hist
32000 BARS 92311 3680-G6
JOSHUA AV
- VCTV 92394 4205-G7
600 PRKR - 4774-J7
1500 PRKR - 4844-J1
7600 SBdC - (4572-A2 See Page 4482)
8700 SBdC - 4482-A1
8900 ADEL 92301 4294-C1
10900 ADEL 92301 4204-H7
10900 SBdC - (4392-A6 See Page 4302)
11300 ADEL 92301 4205-A7
13100 CHNO 91710 642-A7
13100 CHNO 91710 682-A1
14300 SBdC - (4301-J6 See Page 4300)
JOSHUA CT
- FONT 92337 645-A2
- RCUC 91730 603-C5
- VCTV 92392 4384-G6
8100 YUCA 92284 4958-B4
N JOSHUA CT
3400 SBDO 92404 577-E1
JOSHUA DR
55100 YUCA 92284 4957-H4
55500 TNP 92277 4892-B5
58000 YUCA 92284 4958-B4
75700 TNP 92277 4893-A5
JOSHUA LN
- SBdC 92284 4817-H4
1200 POM 91767 601-B7
5900 SBdC 92371 4653-C1
6700 YUCA 92284 4957-J1
8600 SBdC 92371 4563-C2
8700 YUCA 92284 4958-E4
9300 SBdC 92371 4473-C7
13400 CHNO 91710 682-A2
59200 SBdC 92284 4958-E4
JOSHUA PL
13300 CHNO 91710 682-A1
JOSHUA RD
- SBdC 92345 4654-H1
6300 SBdC 92345 4564-H1
8900 SBdC 92345 4474-G3
9000 SBdC 92308 4479-G4
9100 SBdC 92308 4478-D2
9100 SBdC 92371 4473-E7
9100 SBdC 92371 4563-E1
10500 SBdC 92307 4479-G1
10800 SBdC 92307 (4389-G7 See Page 4299)
10900 SBdC 92392 4474-G1
11400 SBdC 92308 4388-D7
11700 SBdC 92392 4384-G7
11800 APLV 92308 4388-D3
12400 VCTV 92392 4384-G5
13500 APLV 92307 4388-D3
13500 SBdC 92307 4388-D3
14100 APLV 92307 4298-C1
14100 SBdC 92307 4298-C1
14900 SBdC 92301 4294-G7
15800 ADEL 92301 4294-G4
16900 APLV 92307 4208-C7
30500 SBdC - 4480-D5
39000 SBdC 92365 (3504-D6 See Page 3414)
JOSHUA ST
3300 SBdC 92371 4292-H7
7300 SBdC 92371 4563-J2
7300 SBdC 92371 4564-E1
7700 SBdC 92301 4294-F6
8700 SBdC 92308 4477-H6
8700 SBdC 92308 4567-H1
8700 SBdC 92345 4565-A1
9500 APLV 92308 4477-H6
9700 SBdC 92345 4564-G1
10500 ADEL 92301 4294-G6
10800 SBdC 92301 4114-H3
11600 HESP 92345 4565-C1
11700 ADEL 92301 4295-B6
11700 VCTV 92301 4295-B6
12100 VCTV 92394 4295-J6
14500 HESP 92345 4566-A2
15100 VCTV 92394 4296-A6
16500 VCTV 92392 4296-E6
19000 ADEL 92301 4204-F3
JOSHUA TR
61800 SBdC 92252 4959-C5
JOSHUA CANYON RD
- SBdC - 4817-B7
- SBdC - 4887-B2
JOSHUA COVE DR
4400 SBdC 92252 4889-B2
JOSHUA DELL RD
11700 SBdC 92392 4475-B1
11700 VCTV 92392 4475-B1
JOSHUA HILLS RD
100 SBdC 92372 4382-A6
JOSHUA TREE CT
- CHLS 91709 711-H2
JOSHUA TREE DR
1200 BARS 92311 3680-A5
JOSHUA TREE LN
4900 SBdC 92371 4383-C6
18000 SBdC 92392 4386-J4
JOSHUA TREE RD
- SBdC 92278 370-B9
2000 SBdC 92285 (4575-E6 See Page 4484)
50600 SBdC 92285 (4576-A6 See Page 4486)
JOSHUA TREE ST
- ONT 91761 643-A7
E JOSHUA TREE ST
2800 ONT 91761 643-A7
N JOSHUA TREE ST
1000 CLTN 92324 605-J5
JOSHUA VIEW DR
7300 YUCA 92284 4957-J3
7500 YUCA 92284 4958-A4
JOSIAH RD
58500 SBdC 92285 4748-C1
JOURNEY LN
59300 SBdC 92284 4958-F5
JOVAR RD
- SBdC - (3763-B3 See Page 3762)
JOY CT
6700 CHNO 91710 682-B1
JOY ST
- CHNO 91710 682-B1
JOYA LN
8600 SBdC 92301 4204-C4
N JOYCE AV
100 RLTO 92376 605-H1
400 RLTO 92376 575-H4
S JOYCE AV
100 RLTO 92376 605-H2
JUANITA CT
1300 UPL 91786 572-E7
4400 CHNO 91710 681-E1
JUANITA DR
70700 TNP 92277 4891-G6
72000 TNP 92277 4892-A6
JUANITA LN
1500 RDL 92373 648-F3
JUANITA ST
11000 LMLN 92354 647-D1
25900 SBdC 92354 647-E1
JUAREZ CT
- YUCA 92284 4957-J6
6000 YUCA 92284 4887-H6
JUAREZ DR
- YUCA 92284 4957-J6
57500 YUCA 92284 4958-C5
59100 SBdC 92284 4958-C5
JUBILEE CT
2000 SBDO 92411 576-C4
JUBILEE LN
23500 DBAR 91765 640-C7
JUBILEE PL
13400 VCTV 92392 4386-G3
JUBILEE RD
100 Llan 93544 4472-A6
100 SBdC 92372 4472-A6
JUDSON CT
1900 CLAR 91711 571-D7
JUDSON ST
- RDL 92374 608-E4
JUDY DR
36500 SBdC 92311 3589-G7
JUDY LN
7500 SBdC 92308 4567-E4
58300 SBdC 92285 4748-B3
JUDY RD
1000 BARS 92311 3679-A5
JUILLIARD DR
300 CLAR 91711 571-E6
JULCREST RD
- YUCA 92284 4888-F3
2000 SBdC 92284 4818-F5
3700 SBdC 92284 4888-F2
JULIA CT
200 UPL 91784 572-C3
JULIA ST
10900 RivC 91752 643-H6
E JULIA ST
100 SBDO 92408 606-J2
JULIAN AV
- CHNO 91710 682-B1
JULIAN CT
500 DBAR 91765 640-E6
JULIAN DR E
9800 SBdC 92359 609-E4
JULIAN DR W
9800 SBdC 92359 609-D4
JULIE CT
1300 RDL 92374 608-E5
JULIE LN
13300 YCPA 92399 650-D6
W JULIE ST
400 CLTN 92324 606-C3
JULIET CT
800 UPL 91784 572-A4
JUNE LN
- UPL 91786 602-E2
34700 YCPA 92399 649-J5
W JUNE PL
2200 SBdC 92407 546-A6
2200 SBDO 92407 546-A6
2600 SBDO 92407 545-J6
JUNE ST
2600 SBdC 92407 576-A2
3400 SBdC 92407 546-A6
W JUNE ST
500 RLTO 92376 605-F1
JUNE WY
2300 SBdC 92407 546-A7
JUNEBERRY DR
8500 RCUC 91739 603-G5
JUNE MOUNTAIN DR
5100 MTCL 91763 601-G6
JUNEWOOD PL
600 DBAR 91765 680-C1
JUNGFRAU DR
900 SBdC - 517-A4
JUNIPER AV
2100 SBdC 92252 4818-J3
6000 TNP 92277 4892-C5
6500 FONT 92336 574-H5
7800 FONT 92336 604-J2
8100 FONT 92335 604-J2
10000 YCPA 92399 610-A4
10100 SBdC 92256 615-G4
10300 FONT 92337 604-J7
10500 SBdC 92337 604-J7
10600 FONT 92337 644-J2
10900 SBdC 92337 644-J2
15200 VCTV 92394 4296-A6
34600 YCPA 92399 609-J4
N JUNIPER AV
500 UPL 91786 602-A2
9800 YCPA 92399 609-J4
JUNIPER CT
600 RDL 92374 648-D1
5000 SBDO 91710 641-F4
9800 YCPA 92399 609-J4
17800 HESP 92345 4476-J6
JUNIPER DR
1200 BBLK - 4742-A7
1200 SBdC - 4742-A7
1200 SBdC 92314 4742-A7
5400 SBdC 92397 4652-F3
7000 SBdC 92308 4567-E3
11500 APLV 92308 4387-F7
29700 SBdC - 4738-E7
42300 BBLK - 4741-J7
N JUNIPER DR
3600 SBDO 92404 547-E7
3600 SBDO 92404 577-E1
JUNIPER LN
1000 SBdC - 516-H4
2200 SBdC 92314 4812-J1
2200 SBdC 92314 4813-A1
7400 SBdC 92345 4567-F4
12600 SBdC 92345 4565-E7
14500 ADEL 92301 4384-J1
32800 SBdC - 519-D2
JUNIPER PL
22800 SBdC - 516-E3
JUNIPER RD
100 SBdC 92252 4748-J5
100 SBdC 92372 4472-A5
2100 SBdC 92371 4472-E5
3300 SBdC 92252 4818-J6
5100 SBdC 92371 4473-D5
5700 SBdC 92252 4888-J6
6500 SBdC 92252 4958-J2
9000 SBdC 92308 4477-H6
9300 APLV 92308 4477-H2
19400 SBdC 92308 4567-D4
JUNIPER RDG
1600 POM 91766 640-F3
JUNIPER ST
200 BARS 92311 3679-G5
900 SBdC 92285 4747-H3
5600 CHNO 91710 641-H4
8900 SBdC 92308 4477-A6
13800 HESP 92345 4475-G6
14600 HESP 92345 4476-A5
17800 ADEL 92301 4204-G1
18600 HESP 92345 4477-A7
25700 LMLN 92354 607-E7
W JUNIPER ST
800 ONT 91762 642-A4
1400 ONT 91762 641-J4
N JUNIPER WY
500 UPL 91786 602-A2
JUNIPER FLATS RD
21600 SBdC 92308 4567-J4
21700 SBdC 92308 4568-D1
22300 SBdC 92308 4478-E7
JUNIPERO
- SBdC - 4120-C2
JUNIPERO DR
20500 APLV 92308 4477-F1
JUNIPERO TR
55500 SBdC 92284 4817-D3
57300 SBdC 92284 4818-A3
JUPITER AV
17300 VCTV 92394 (4206-F7 See Page 4116)
JUPITER DR
6000 RivC 91752 683-H5
61300 SBdC 92252 4749-A5
JUPITER WY
1100 SBdC - 516-H4
JURA RD
22700 DBAR 91765 640-A6
JURASSIC PL
17100 VCTV 92394 4295-J1
JURUPA AV
100 RLTO 92316 645-F2
100 SBdC 92316 645-D2
400 RDL 92374 608-C5
10800 NRCO 92860 683-J7
10800 RivC 92505 683-J7
12900 FONT 92337 643-J2
13100 FONT 92337 644-A2
13700 SBdC 92337 644-G2
16900 FONT 92337 645-A2
17200 FONT 92316 645-A2
17200 SBdC 92337 645-A2
JURUPA RD
6800 RivC 92509 645-A4
6900 RivC 92509 644-J7
8900 RivC 91752 683-G3
E JURUPA ST
2400 ONT 91761 642-J3
2700 ONT 91761 643-B2

K

K ST
33700 SBdC 92311 3679-D5
33700 SBdC 92311 (3759-E1 See Page 3758)
E K ST
100 CLTN 92324 606-D6
N K ST
100 SBDO 92410 606-F1
100 NDLS 92363 3620-C5
600 SBDO 92411 576-F5
900 MohC - 3620-C5
S K ST
100 SBDO 92410 606-F2
W K ST
100 CLTN 92324 606-C6
KACHINA DR
66200 SBdC 92252 4820-D2
67900 SBdC 92277 4820-F2
68300 SBdC 92277 4821-A2
71900 SBdC 92277 4822-A2
KACHINA RD
20600 APLV 92308 4387-F6
KADOTA AV
10700 MTCL 91763 641-D3
10900 SBdC 91763 641-D3
11500 SBdC 91710 641-D4
12100 CHNO 91710 641-D5
KAHAI AV
7600 RCUC 91730 573-A7
KAIBAB CT
19100 APLV 92307 4297-B2
KAIBAB RD
18900 APLV 92307 4297-A2
KAILUA ST
16400 SBdC 92371 (4293-A3 See Page 4292)
17800 SBdC 92301 (4203-A7 See Page 4112)
18900 SBdC 92301 (4202-J4 See Page 4112)
KAISER AV
6500 FONT 92336 575-A4
8500 FONT 92335 605-A2
KAISER CT
7500 FONT 92336 575-A7
9700 FONT 92335 605-A5
KAISER DR
- SBdC 92277 4820-F4
71200 SBdC 92277 4821-H3
71900 SBdC 92277 4822-A3
KAIULANI RD
8800 YUCA 92284 4958-A7
KAKAPA CIR
- SBdC - 4844-E1
KALAN CT
14900 CHLS 91709 681-C5
56600 YUCA 92284 4887-G4
KALIN RANCH DR
18100 SBdC 92392 4386-J5
18300 SBdC 92392 4387-A4
KALISHER RD
- SBdC - (3846-F7 See Page 3756)
- SBdC - 3936-F1
KALMIA ST
12700 RCUC 91739 573-H5
KALO CT
16500 APLV 92307 4296-G2
KALO RD
16400 APLV 92307 4296-G2
KAMANA CT
16300 APLV 92307 4296-J2
KAMANA RD
15900 APLV 92307 4296-H3
16400 APLV 92307 4297-A2
KAMLOOPS AV
7300 FONT 92336 574-G6
KANBRIDGE ST
19100 APLV 92308 4387-B4
KANE CT
28200 HIGH 92346 578-A6
KANIKSU TR
6900 SBdC - 4843-G4
KANSA RD
24100 SBdC 92307 4298-F6
KANSA TR
6300 SBdC - 4843-G3
N KANSAS AV
900 CLTN 92324 606-F5
KANSAS CT
- FONT 92336 574-C6
KANSAS LN
7300 SBdC 92371 4383-J3
KANSAS ST
- RDL 92373 647-J1
100 RDL 92373 607-J7
KAPIOLANI DR
11700 SBdC 92345 (4655-B6 See Page 4654)
KAPPA AV
1900 SBdC - 4742-H2
KAREN CT
600 BARS 92311 3680-A5
W KAREN CT
1200 UPL 91786 601-J1
KAREN DR
14400 VCTV 92394 4295-J7
14400 VCTV 92394 4385-J1
KAREN LN
6200 RivC 92509 645-B5
KAREN KEN PINES DR
500 SBdC - 517-F3
KARESH AV
600 POM 91767 601-C7
600 POM 91767 641-C1
KARL CT
- FONT 92336 574-H2
KARMA WY
19700 APLV 92308 4387-D2
KARON ST
1300 RDL 92374 608-A5
KASANKA TR
- APLV 92307 4387-A2
- APLV 92308 4387-A2
KASHIWA WY
16300 VCTV 92392 4386-E6
KASOTA CT
16200 APLV 92307 4296-J3
KASOTA LN
15600 APLV 92307 4296-J4
KASOTA PL
18300 APLV 92307 4296-J3
KASOTA RD
15400 APLV 92307 4296-J2
KASOTA WY
16200 APLV 92307 4296-J3
KASSON CT
16300 APLV 92307 4297-A2
KASSON RD
16000 APLV 92307 4297-B2
KASSON WY
18900 APLV 92307 4297-B2
KATCHIN
- SBdC 92277 4822-H1
KATCHINA RD
10900 APLV 92308 4477-J2
KATHARINE WY
400 SBdC - 4738-E7
KATHI ST
- RDL 92373 647-J2
KATHLEEN DR
500 BARS 92311 3679-J3
KATHRYN AV
2000 POM 91766 641-B6
KATHY
83600 SBdC 92277 (4895-C6 See Page 4824)
KATHY AV
4100 RivC 92509 644-H7
KATHY LN
36400 YCPA 92399 650-D1
38500 SBdC 92365 (3504-C7 See Page 3414)
38500 SBdC 92365 3594-C1
KATIE DR
14200 ADEL 92301 4385-A1
KATJE WY
7400 YUCA 92284 4957-D3
KATONA CT
35500 YCPA 92399 610-B7
KATRINA WY
2000 UPL 91784 571-H4
W KATY CT
1100 UPL 91784 571-J5
KATYDID AV
19300 SBdC 92316 645-F3
KAURI AV
19600 SBdC 92377 575-G3
KAVITA LN
- VCTV 92392 4385-E7
KAY CT
- BARS 92311 3679-J4
KAY RD
23300 SBdC - 516-G3
KAY ST
9900 ADEL 92301 4204-F3
KAYA DR
- BARS 92311 3679-J5
E KAYAH DR
1200 SBdC 92314 4742-G6
KAYE CT
200 RDL 92374 608-E7
KAYENTA RD
22000 APLV 92308 4388-A5
KAYLA ST
14900 ADEL 92301 4295-B7
KAYUGA ST
16400 VCTV 92392 4386-E4
E KEAN WY
400 SBdC 92314 4742-E6
S KEAN WY
600 SBdC 92314 4742-E6
KEARNEY CT
10900 RCUC 91701 573-C5
KEARNY DR
15300 ADEL 92301 4295-B5
KEATER DR
2200 SBdC - 519-D6
KEATOR RD
21300 APLV 92307 4297-J3
22100 APLV 92307 4298-A3
23300 SBdC 92307 4298-D3
KEATS AV
8100 YUCA 92284 4958-C5
W KEATS CT
600 UPL 91784 572-A3
KEATS RD
- SBdC 92301 4112-F1
17700 SBdC 92301 (4202-F2 See Page 4112)
KECHAM TR
- SBdC - 4844-C2
KEELER AV
100 SBdC 92284 4747-F6
1300 SBdC 92285 4747-F2
1400 SBdC 92284 4817-F2
KEEL RANCH RD
- SBdC - (4115-G1 See Page 4114)
KEENBROOK RD
300 SBdC 92407 514-E2
KEISSEL RD
8100 RivC 92324 647-F7
KEITH ST
700 BARS 92311 3679-F3
KELBAKER RD
16200 SBdC - 370-K2
25500 SBdC - 350-G1
53500 SBdC - 2971-G5
KELISA CIR
- RDL 92373 648-F3
KELLER DR
33000 SBdC - 519-D7
KELLER PEAK RD
2600 SBdC - 519-E7
KELLETT AV
3600 CLAR 91711 571-F5
KELLOGG AV
7300 TNP 92277 4892-H7
7300 TNP 92277 4962-H1
12300 CHNO 91710 641-F6
KELLOGG DR
- LACo 91768 640-B2
- SDMS 91773 640-B2
3800 POM 91768 640-A2
KELLOGG ST
11700 LMLN 92354 647-D2
KELLOGG PARK DR
2100 POM 91768 640-C1
N KELLY AV
1000 UPL 91784 571-J3
1400 UPL 91786 571-J7
KELLY CT
9000 SBdC 92371 4563-D1
KELLY DR
500 BARS 92311 3679-H3
1100 BARS 92311 3680-A3
KELLY LN
300 SBdC 92324 606-B6
2800 POM 91767 601-A3
32900 YCPA 92399 649-D4
KELLY RD
700 SBdC 92372 4472-B6
4900 SBdC 92277 (4825-G7 See Page 4824)
4900 SBdC 92277 (4895-G2 See Page 4824)
KELLY ST
1500 RDL 92374 608-E4
14500 ADEL 92301 4294-J7
14500 ADEL 92301 4384-J1
KELSEY BLVD
71300 SBdC 92277 4751-H6
KELSEY WY
17400 CHLS 91709 711-J4
17400 CHLS 91709 712-A4
KELSO LN
- SBdC - 2971-G2
KELSO RD
48200 SBdC - 350-G3
KELSO CIMA RD
42500 SBdC - 350-L5
45600 SBdC - 351-A4
KELSO-DUNES RD
- SBdC - 350-K8
KELTON CT
4100 CHLS 91709 711-E2
KELTY CT
14700 CHLS 91709 681-A5
KEMOSABE TR
37800 SBdC 92365 349-H7
37800 SBdC 92365 (3593-J2 See Page 3592)
KEMP LN
24300 LMLN 92354 647-A1
KEMP ST
600 RivC 92501 646-A7
KEMPER AV
2100 CLAR 91711 571-F7
10300 ADEL 92301 4204-G6
KEMPER LN
29300 HIGH 92346 578-D6
KEMPSTER AV
7100 FONT 92336 575-A6
7800 FONT 92336 605-A2
8500 FONT 92335 605-A2
KEMPSTER CT
6700 FONT 92336 575-A5
KEMPSTER LN
6800 FONT 92336 575-A5
KEN LN
- BARS 92311 3679-F4
N KENDALL AV
200 SBDO 92410 606-F1
KENDALL CIR
10300 ADEL 92301 4204-G6
KENDALL DR
19200 SBDO 92407 545-F1
19400 SBDO 92407 545-F1
W KENDALL DR
400 SBDO 92405 546-F7
400 SBDO 92405 576-G1
900 SBDO 92407 546-A4
2600 SBDO 92407 545-J3
KENDALL LN
14100 SBdC - 514-B1
KENDALL RD
7500 SBdC - 4570-H2
9700 SBdC - 4480-G1
11000 SBdC - (4390-G7 See Page 4300)
KENDALL ST
- RDL 92373 608-B7
KENDALL WY
12700 RDL 92373 649-A5
W KENDALL WY
2400 SBDO 92407 546-A4
KENDRA WY
100 RivC 92507 646-E6
N KENMORE AV
1400 ONT 91762 602-B5
KENMORE ST
10900 RivC 91752 643-H6
KENNEDY AV
15300 FONT 92336 574-E5
KENNEDY CT
4000 CHNO 91710 641-D6
KENNEDY DR
400 BARS 92311 3679-G3
KENNEDY ST
- CHNO 91710 641-E6
W KENNEDY ST
500 CLTN 92324 606-C3
KENNETH ST
3800 RivC 92509 644-D7
KENNETH WY
24500 SBdC 92307 4298-G6
KENORA CT
21300 APLV 92308 4387-H5
KENORA RD
12200 APLV 92308 4387-H6
KENSINGTON CT
7200 HIGH 92346 577-G5
KENSINGTON DR
800 RDL 92374 608-G6
KENSINGTON PL
- RCUC 91739 573-F5
KENSINGTON ST
21900 APLV 92307 4207-J3
22000 APLV 92307 4208-A3
22900 SBdC 92307 4208-B2
KENSLEY RD
51300 SBdC 92256 616-C3
KENT DR
800 CLAR 91711 601-B1
KENT LN
11700 YCPA 92399 649-J2
14700 SBdC - (3935-J5 See Page 3934)
KENT RD
10000 MohC - 3620-G2
62500 SBdC 92252 4959-E6
KENT ST
2000 SBdC 92407 576-B1
KENTFIELD ST
22200 GTER 92313 646-E5
KENTON CT
8000 HIGH 92346 578-B7
KENTUCKY AV
- FONT 92336 574-D6
KENTUCKY ST
32100 YCPA 92399 649-C4
KENTUCKY DERBY CT
12400 RCUC 91739 573-G3
KENTWOOD BLVD
14100 VCTV 92392 4386-B1
KENWOOD AV
- SBdC 92301 368-H2
17300 SBdC 92407 515-A4
N KENWOOD AV
1500 SBDO 92404 576-J2
3800 SBDO 92404 546-J7
KENWOOD DR
100 RDL 92374 608-F7
200 RDL 92374 648-F1
11900 FONT 92337 644-C4
KENWOOD PL
5700 RivC 92509 645-D7
KENWOOD ST
300 UPL 91784 572-A5
KENWORTH CT
- YCPA 92399 649-E2
KENWORTH WY
- CHLS 91709 681-H7
- CHLS 91709 711-J1
- CHNO 91709 681-H7
- CHNO 91709 711-J1
KENYON AV
6700 HESP 92345 4566-G3
KENYON PL
1600 CLAR 91711 601-E1
KENYON WY
6600 RCUC 91701 573-C5
KEOTA LN
14700 APLV 92307 4297-B6
KEOTA RD
14500 APLV 92307 4297-B6
KEOWN CT
500 RivC 92507 646-D7
KERES RD
- APLV 92308 4387-A2
KERN AV
100 SBdC - 4742-E7
200 SBdC - 4812-E1
7200 HESP 92345 4566-B4
KERN PL
6500 RCUC 91701 573-C5
KERN RD
3200 SBdC 92277 4824-G5
3700 CHNO 91710 641-C6
4100 SBdC 92277 (4894-G1 See Page 4824)
10200 HESP 92345 4476-A3
E KERN ST
1200 ONT 91761 642-E2
W KERN ST
1900 SBdC 92407 576-A1
2300 SBdC 92407 575-J1
KERN RIVER RD
12700 VCTV 92392 4385-J5
KERNS BLVD
- TNP 92277 4960-J1
2800 SBdC 92277 4820-J3
6800 TNP 92277 4890-J7
KERNWOOD CT
10200 RCUC 91737 573-A3
KERR AV
- SBdC 92277 4820-E2
6900 SBdC 92277 4890-F7
KERRIE WY
11600 APLV 92308 4387-B7
KERRY LN
6600 RivC 92509 645-B5
KERRY ST
3000 SBdC 92407 576-B2
KERTE LN
16000 FONT 92337 644-G3
KESSLER PL
- SBdC 92252 4959-B3
KESSLER PEAK RD
58900 SBdC - 331-A10
KETCH LN
14400 SBdC - (3935-H3 See Page 3934)
S KETTERING DR
100 ONT 91761 603-F7
100 ONT 91761 643-F2
KETTLE PEAK PL
6300 RCUC 91737 573-D4
KEVARI CT
16100 YCPA 92399 610-C4
KEVIN AV
900 RDL 92373 648-B2
KEWANEE LN
15800 APLV 92307 4297-D3
KEWANEE RD
15700 APLV 92307 4297-D4
KEWANNA RD
12500 APLV 92308 4387-F5
KEY ST
20300 CLTN 92324 645-J6
KEYA CT
12700 APLV 92308 4387-H4
KEY POINT AV
- HESP 92345 4475-E6
KEYS RD
51300 SBdC - 4886-C3
KEYSTONE AV
1600 POM 91767 601-D7
KEYSTONE CT
1400 UPL 91784 571-H5
10000 RCUC 91737 573-A1
13200 CHLS 91709 681-A1
N KEYSTONE DR
5000 SBDO 92407 546-D5
W KEYSTONE DR
1300 SBDO 92407 546-D5
KEYSTONE RD
600 SBdC - 4810-H2
KEY WEST ST
- FONT 92336 574-A6
KIAMICHI RD
15300 APLV 92307 4297-E5
KIAVAN RD
10500 APLV 92308 4477-H2
KICKAPOO CT
- SBdC - (4743-C4 See Page 4662)
KICKAPOO DR
- SBdC - (4743-C4 See Page 4662)
KICKAPOO TR
- SBdC - 4817-D7
400 SBdC 92284 4747-D7
900 SBdC 92284 4817-D2
2500 SBdC 92285 4667-C2
4600 SBdC 92285 (4577-C7 See Page 4486)
7300 YUCA 92284 4957-D4
KICKAPOO TR W
8300 YUCA 92284 4957-D6
KICKING HORSE CIR
13800 VCTV 92394 4385-G1
KICKING HORSE DR
22300 DBAR 91765 680-A6
KIDD DR
23400 DBAR 91765 680-C1
KIDWELL RD
1600 SBdC 92285 4747-E1
1900 SBdC 92285 4667-E2
4400 SBdC 92285 (4577-E7 See Page 4486)
N KIEMER DR
200 SBdC 92314 4742-C6
KILBOURNE DR
700 SBdC 91784 572-A2
KILKARE RD
36400 SBdC 92359 4950-D7
KILLINGTON WY
400 BBLK - 4811-J1
KILORAN ST
42700 SBdC 92365 (3683-F1 See Page 3592)
47700 SBdC 92365 (3684-J1 See Page 3594)
47700 SBdC 92365 (3685-A1 See Page 3594)
48500 SBdC 92365 (3595-B7 See Page 3594)
KIMBALL AV
2300 POM 91767 601-A3
5700 CHNO 91710 681-J7
5700 CHNO 91710 682-A1
7100 SBdC 91710 682-D7
KIMBALL CT
5600 CHNO 91710 681-H7
7100 HESP 92345 4566-A5
KIMBALL LN
600 RDL 92373 648-G3
KIMBALL ST
7100 HESP 92345 4566-A5
KIMBARK AV
600 SBdC 92407 515-C3
KIMBERLY AV
800 RDL 92374 608-C4
9700 MTCL 91763 601-E6
10300 MTCL 91763 641-E2
11300 SBdC 91766 641-E3
W KIMBERLY AV
1000 CLTN 92324 606-B4
KIMBERLY CT
- SBDO 92408 646-J1
800 UPL 91784 572-A4
KIMBERLY LN
35000 YCPA 92399 650-A2
KIMBERLY PL
1100 RDL 92373 648-C3
KIMBERLY RD
63900 SBdC 92252 4959-G1
KIMBERLY ST
14500 ADEL 92301 4294-J7
14500 ADEL 92301 4384-J1
KIMERING RD
10300 SBdC 92345 4475-A4
KIMOSABE RD
53500 SBdC - 4886-H4
KIMSHEW ST
19800 SBdC 92307 (4117-D6 See Page 4116)
19900 APLV 92307 (4117-G6 See Page 4116)
KINAI CT
18900 APLV 92307 4297-B6
KINAI RD
14700 APLV 92307 4297-B5
KINCAID ST
1400 RDL 92373 648-C4
KING DR
600 SBdC - 517-B3
KING ST
600 SBdC 92374 648-J1
800 SBdC 92374 608-J7
1000 SBdC 92359 608-J7
6500 CHNO 91710 642-B6
33500 SBdC - (3681-F6 See Page 3590)
E KING ST
100 SBDO 92408 606-J1
300 RLTO 92376 605-J1
W KING ST
200 SBDO 92408 606-H1
800 SBDO 92410 606-B1
KING WY
2500 CLAR 91711 571-D6
KING CANYON RD
12700 VCTV 92392 4385-J5
KINGDOM CT
14900 FONT 92336 574-D6
KING EDWARD DR
26200 LMLN 92354 647-F3
KINGFISHER RD
12600 GTER 92313 646-F5
KINGFORD AV
15000 ADEL 92301 4294-H7
KINGMAN DR
- MohC - 3620-F1
E KINGMAN ST
200 SBDO 92410 576-J7
W KINGMAN ST
800 SBDO 92410 576-F7
1300 SBDO 92411 606-D1
KING RANCH RD
8700 RCUC 91701 572-F1
14600 VCTV 92392 4385-J5
14700 VCTV 92392 4386-A5
KINGS CT
500 SBdC - 518-B3
26500 SBdC - 4737-F6
KINGS LN
27900 SBdC - 517-J3
KINGS RD
10500 ADEL 92301 4204-H7
11900 ADEL 92301 4205-B7
KINGS WY
1200 RDL 92373 648-B3
KINGSBURY DR
1800 RDL 92374 608-C4
KINGS CANYON CT
13600 FONT 92336 604-A1
KINGSDALE RD
14600 SBdC 92307 4298-F6
KINGSLEY AV
7100 HESP 92345 4565-J5
7100 HESP 92345 4566-A5
E KINGSLEY AV
300 POM 91767 601-C7
KINGSLEY ST
4000 MTCL 91763 601-E7
5600 MTCL 91762 601-E7
31000 SBdC - 4480-E3
S KINGS RIVER LN
2800 ONT 91761 643-C6
KINGSTON AV
3300 SBdC 92277 4823-E5

STREET
Block City ZIP Pg-Grid

KINGSTON AV
7300 HESP 92345 4566-H2
8500 YUCA 92284 4957-J6
8500 YUCA 92284 4958-A7
KINGSTON CIR
- SBdC - 2971-G1
1700 RDL 92374 608-G7
KINGSTON CT
3800 SBdC 91766 641-D3
W KINGSTON LN
800 SBdC 92314 4742-B6
KINGSTON RD
- SBdC 92365 (3683-E5 See Page 3592)
72000 SBdC - 330-K3
KINGSTON ST
9900 RCUC 91737 572-J4
9900 RCUC 91737 573-A4
11700 GTER 92313 646-F3
KINGSWOOD DR
1300 RDL 92374 608-D5
15600 VCTV 92392 4386-C2
KININGHAM DR
19400 SBdC 92316 645-G4
19500 SBdC 92509 645-G4
KINLOCK AV
6100 RCUC 91737 573-A4
7000 RCUC 91701 573-A6
7400 RCUC 91730 573-A7
7700 RCUC 91730 603-A1
KINNEY WY
1900 SBdC - 4742-H2
KINSHEW ST
21500 APLV 92307 (4117-J6 See Page 4116)
21500 APLV 92307 4118-A6
KIOWA DR
- SBdC - (4743-C4 See Page 4662)
KIOWA LN
6200 SBdC - 4843-H2
KIOWA PL
11200 APLV 92308 4477-G1
KIOWA RD
7900 SBdC 92308 4567-G1
8500 SBdC 92308 4477-G6
9500 APLV 92308 4477-G2
11300 APLV 92308 4387-G3
13500 APLV 92307 4387-H1
14100 APLV 92307 4297-H7
KIOWA CREST DR
1600 DBAR 91765 680-A4
KIP CT
19700 APLV 92308 4387-D3
N KIPPY DR
1600 CLTN 92324 606-C3
W KIPPY DR
600 CLTN 92324 606-C4
KIRBY CT
1600 RDL 92374 608-C4
W KIRBY CT
1100 UPL 91786 571-J7
E KIRK ST
400 CLTN 92324 646-D1
KIRKWOOD
82800 SBdC 92277 (4895-A5 See Page 4824)
KIRKWOOD AV
100 CLAR 91711 601-D4
500 POM 91767 601-A4
5900 RCUC 91737 572-H3
6100 RCUC 91701 572-H4
7300 RCUC 91730 572-H7
8400 RCUC 91730 602-H2
KIRKWOOD CT
7800 RCUC 91730 602-H1
KIRKWOOD DR
12300 VCTV 92392 4385-E6
KIRKWOOD PL
7300 HIGH 92346 578-E5
KISMET LN
16000 VCTV 92394 4296-A4
KISMET RD
56500 YUCA 92284 4957-H6
KISSING ROCK RD
500 SBdC - 4736-E7
KITOM RD
- APLV 92307 4387-A2
KITTATAS TR
5300 SBdC - 4773-H6
KITTERING RD
- SBdC 92345 (4655-A4 See Page 4654)
8700 SBdC 92345 4565-A1
9100 SBdC 92345 4475-A7
11700 VCTV 92392 4385-A7
11700 VCTV 92392 4475-A1
KITTYHAWK AV
6700 HESP 92345 4566-D6
KITTY HAWK ST
7000 FONT 92336 574-A6
KITTYWAKE ST
- SBdC 92285 4747-F3
KIWI AV
9200 SBdC 92335 604-D4
KLAMATH CT
- SBdC - 4812-D2
7900 FONT 92336 604-A1
KLAMATH DR
300 SBdC - 518-B2
KLAMATH RD
- SBdC 92308 4388-D5
1300 SBdC - 4812-D2
20900 APLV 92308 4387-G6
22600 APLV 92308 4388-B6
24900 SBdC 92307 4388-H5
KLAMATH ST
100 RDL 92374 608-F7
100 RDL 92374 648-F1
KLAMATH TR
6100 SBdC - 4843-G2
KLAMATH RIVER DR
3900 ONT 91761 643-D6
KLEIN PL
2200 POM 91766 641-A5
KLICKITAT AV
21700 APLV 92307 4297-J6
22000 APLV 92307 4298-A6
23300 SBdC 92307 4298-D6
KLINE ST
- BARS 92311 3680-C2
KLONDIKE DR
1100 SBdC - 4737-G5
KLONDIKE ST
- UPL 91784 572-E6
KLUK LN
3200 RivC 92501 646-B6
KLUSMAN AV
4900 RCUC 91737 572-J1
6700 RCUC 91701 572-J5
7300 RCUC 91730 572-J7
7800 RCUC 91730 602-J1
KNAPP RD
700 SBdC 92372 4472-B6
KNAPPS CTO
23300 SBdC - 516-G3
KNARR RD
34700 YCPA 92399 649-J5
KNICKERBOCKER RD
400 BBLK - 4811-F3
KNIGHT AV
300 BBLK - 4811-F1
KNIGHT CT
- CHLS 91709 681-H7
700 SBdC - 518-A3
KNIGHTSBRIDGE DR
- RCUC 91739 573-F5
KNIGHTSBRIDGE LN
900 RDL 92374 608-F6
KNIGHTSBRIDGE PL
11700 LMLN 92354 647-F3
KNOBB AV
10800 SBdC 92256 615-H3
KNOB HILL RD
7200 HIGH 92346 577-F5
7200 SBDO 92346 577-F5
46000 SBdC - 4742-J2
46000 SBdC - (4743-A3 See Page 4662)
KNOLL CT
6700 HESP 92345 4566-B6
24300 DBAR 91765 680-D4
KNOLL DR
600 SBdC - 516-G3
900 SBDO 92408 606-F4
1400 RDL 92373 648-J4
1400 YCPA 92373 648-J4
1500 RDL 92373 649-A4
2800 SBdC 92277 4821-H4
KNOLL RD
100 BBLK - 4811-C1
1300 RDL 92373 648-C3
35700 YCPA 92399 650-C2
KNOLL ST
900 SBdC 92407 515-D4
KNOLL CIRCLE DR
24900 SBdC - 517-B5
KNOLL CREST DR
11100 FONT 92337 644-H2
KNOLL RIDGE DR
- POM 91766 640-F6
KNOLLSIDE WY
- CHLS 91709 681-H7
- CHNO 91709 681-H7
KNOLLVIEW DR
- POM 91766 640-G5
KNOLL VIEW DR
30600 SBdC - 518-G7
KNOLLWOOD AV
19000 SBdC 92377 575-E2
KNOLLWOOD CT
18600 SBdC 92392 4387-A4
KNOLLWOOD DR
8700 RCUC 91730 602-G2
KNOTTY PINE TR
- SBdC - (3846-C5 See Page 3756)
KNOWLES ST
200 SBdC - (3682-C1 See Page 3592)
KNOWLTON AV
- SBdC 92252 4959-H1
KNOX AV
6100 FONT 92336 574-F4
S KNOX CT
2500 SBDO 92408 646-H1
KNOX DR
7300 FONT 92336 574-F7
KNOX PL
800 CLAR 91711 571-B7
N KNOX RD
80800 SBdC - 328-H4
KNUTZFORD RD
21900 SBdC - 516-C1
KOA DR
5900 SBdC 92377 575-G3
N KOA DR
2400 RLTO 92377 575-G3
KOALA RD
14100 ADEL 92301 4384-F2
14600 ADEL 92301 4294-E2
14700 SBdC 92301 4294-F6
17400 ADEL 92301 4204-E2
20100 ADEL 92301 4114-E4
KOCH PL
- RCUC 91739 574-B3
KODA CT
18200 APLV 92307 4296-J2
KODA RD
16300 APLV 92307 4296-J2
KODA WY
7500 SBdC - 4843-F5
16400 APLV 92307 4296-J2
KODIAK DR
1200 SBdC - 4737-H5
KODIAK RD
300 BBLK - 4812-A1
KOEHLER AV
63300 SBdC 92252 4819-F3
KOFA AV
200 PRKR - 4774-H7
1300 PRKR - 4844-J1
KOIP CT
5800 SBdC - 4774-G7
KOKANEE RD
16100 APLV 92307 4296-J3
KOKOMO CIR
12300 VCTV 92392 4385-D6
KOKOMO CT
12400 VCTV 92392 4385-D6
KOKOMO DR
12300 VCTV 92392 4385-D6
KOKOMO PL
12400 VCTV 92392 4385-D6
KOKOMO RD
14500 APLV 92307 4297-B6
KOKOMO WY
12400 VCTV 92392 4385-D6
KOLOKO CT
- SBdC - 4844-A2
KONA RD
19400 APLV 92307 4297-C6
KONNAROCK RD
20300 APLV 92307 4387-E1
KONOCTI ST
9100 RCUC 91730 602-H2
9900 RCUC 91730 603-A2
KONRAD LN
22400 SBdC 92308 4478-B7
KOODOO AV
14900 SBdC 92301 4294-F7
18100 ADEL 92301 4204-E4
KOODOO RD
17200 ADEL 92301 4294-E1
KOOLISH ST
2200 POM 91766 641-A5
KOPANY RD
- SBdC - 3936-H3
KORBELL RD
56100 SBdC 92285 4747-E2
KORDYS LN
24100 RivC 92324 647-D7
KORI CT
6300 RivC 92509 645-B6
KOURIE WY
6900 SBdC 92345 4565-C6
KRAFT LN
10200 SBdC 92337 644-J2
KRAMER RD
- SBdC - 348-J9
KRAMER STATION RD
- SBdC - 348-H5
KRAUSE LN
1400 SBdC - 4737-G5
KRAUSS PL
3900 SBDO 92407 546-F7
KREUER RD
3700 SBdC 92371 4382-J4
3800 SBdC 92371 4383-A4
KRISTA CT
7000 FONT 92336 574-A6
KRISTIN CT
30600 RDL 92373 648-H5
KRISTIN LN
- HIGH 92346 578-B6
KRISTINA CT
12500 VCTV 92392 4475-D1
KRISTINE WY
- FONT 92336 574-E5
KRUSE RD
- SBdC 92371 4653-G5
KRYSTAL RD
17100 HESP 92345 4566-G5
KUFFEL CANYON RD
200 SBdC - 518-B2
KUHNS
4900 SBdC 92277 4824-J7
4900 SBdC 92277 (4894-J1 See Page 4824)
KUHNS
4900 SBdC 92277 (4895-A2 See Page 4824)
KUKA RD
31600 SBdC - 4480-G4
KUKI ST
6500 SBdC 92345 4565-E4
10500 SBdC 92371 4474-B4
KUMQUAT AV
12600 CHNO 91710 642-B6
KUMQUAT PL
12300 CHNO 91710 642-A5
KUNA AV
100 SBdC 92284 4748-G5
900 SBdC 92285 4748-F2
KUNA CT
6500 SBdC - 4844-C2
57000 YUCA 92284 4887-J5
KUNLUN TR
7200 SBdC 92308 4568-F4
KUPO CT
- SBdC - 4844-E1
KURENA RD
- APLV 92308 4387-B3
KWAJALEIN ST
1200 BARS 92311 3680-F7
KYLE LN
1700 RDL 92373 648-H4
KYLIE CT
6000 CHLS 91709 712-A4

L

L ST
- BARS 92311 3679-D4
100 NDLS 92363 3620-C5
33500 SBdC 92311 (3759-D2 See Page 3758)
33900 SBdC 92311 3679-D5
E L ST
100 CLTN 92324 606-D7
N L ST
100 NDLS 92363 3620-C4
100 SBDO 92410 606-E1
500 SBDO 92411 576-F6
S L ST
100 SBDO 92410 606-F2
W L ST
100 CLTN 92324 606-C7
L WY
1600 SBdC - 4737-G4
LA ARRIBA DR
1300 RDL 92373 648-C3
LA BACA RD
17300 APLV 92307 4207-G6
LABACHO DR
6500 SBdC - 4844-D2
LA BONITA RD
200 DBAR 91765 640-C7
LA BONITA ST
4000 RivC 92509 644-F7
LABRADOR AV
- FONT 92336 544-C7
LABRADOR RD
- SBdC 92307 4207-C1
20900 APLV 92307 4207-F1
LA BRIDA DR
12700 SBdC 91710 641-C7
LA BRISA CIR
11300 FONT 92337 645-A2
LA BRISA DR
- SBdC 92252 4820-A3
56100 SBdC 92284 4817-H4
57300 SBdC 92284 4818-A4
60100 SBdC 92252 4818-F4
61300 SBdC 92252 4819-A4
LA BRISA RD
14100 VCTV 92392 4385-H4
14400 SBdC 92392 4385-J4
14700 SBdC 92392 4386-A4
14700 VCTV 92392 4386-A4
LA BUENA TIERRA AV
5700 TNP 92277 4892-B5
L A BUREAU OF POWER & LIGHT RD
6100 SBdC 92345 4564-H3
6100 SBdC 92345 4654-E1
6100 SBdC 92371 4654-E1
9000 SBdC 92345 4474-J7
9300 SBdC 92345 4475-A6
10900 VCTV 92392 4475-C3
12000 VCTV 92392 4385-F4
14500 VCTV 92394 4295-H7
14500 VCTV 92394 4385-F4
15400 VCTV 92394 4296-B2
17100 VCTV 92394 (4206-C7 See Page 4116)
LA CADENA AV
11100 VCTV 92392 4475-A2
11300 SBdC 92392 4475-A2
12100 VCTV 92392 4385-A7
N LA CADENA DR
100 CLTN 92324 606-D5
S LA CADENA DR
100 CLTN 92324 606-D7
600 CLTN 92324 646-C5
1300 SBdC 92324 646-C5
11600 GTER 92313 646-C5
11600 GTER 92324 646-C5
11900 SBdC 92313 646-C5
LA CADENA DR E
100 RivC 92507 646-B7
100 RivC 92501 646-B7
400 RIV 92507 646-B7
400 RIV 92501 646-B7
LA CADENA DR W
100 RivC 92501 646-B6
700 RIV 92501 646-B7
2800 CLTN 92324 646-B6
LA CADENA RD
56600 YUCA 92284 4957-H6
LA CANADA
18400 SBdC 92316 605-D7
LA CANADA DR
6000 RivC 92509 645-B7
LA CASA CT
9000 RCUC 91701 572-G6
LA CASITA DR
200 SBdC - 517-D2
LA CAUSEY CT
4600 CHNO 91710 641-F4
LACEBARK ST
- FONT 92337 645-A2
LA CERENA AV
42500 BBLK - 4812-A2
LACE WINE
900 SBdC 92284 4817-F1
LACEY CT
6700 CHNO 91710 682-B1
LACHEN RD
28000 SBdC - 4737-J6
28000 SBdC - 4738-A6
LA CIMA RD
1300 NDLS 92363 3620-C7
LA CIOTAT WY
3500 RivC 92501 646-A6
LA COLINA DR
200 SBdC 92374 648-J2
8300 RCUC 91701 572-E1
9600 RCUC 91737 572-H1
LA COLLINA
9100 SBdC 92252 4959-E6
LA CONTENTA RD
- YUCA 92252 4888-E7
- YUCA 92284 4888-E7
6700 YUCA 92284 4958-E2
6700 YUCA 92252 4958-E2
7000 SBdC 92252 4958-E2
7900 SBdC 92284 4958-E2
LA COSTA CIR
1500 UPL 91784 572-E6
LA COSTA CT
- YCPA 92399 649-E2
S LA COSTA CT
2800 ONT 91761 642-G6
LA COSTA PL
- POM 91766 640-E5
LA CRESCENTA DR
56200 SBdC 92284 4817-F5
57700 SBdC 92284 4818-A5
60900 SBdC 92252 4818-J4
60900 SBdC 92252 4819-A4
LA CRESENTA AV
14300 VCTV 92392 4385-H5
LA CRESENTA DR
1300 SBdC - 4812-D2
LA CRESENTA ST
- SBdC 92308 4479-B2
LA CRESTA DR
1000 RDL 92373 648-C3
12900 APLV 92308 4387-E4
LA CROSSE AV
11900 GTER 92313 646-D4
12100 CLTN 92313 646-D4
12100 CLTN 92324 646-D4
LA CROSSE CIR
2200 CLAR 91711 571-E6
LA CUBRE DR
15700 VCTV 92392 4296-D6
15700 VCTV 92394 4296-C6
LACY CT
10800 ADEL 92301 4204-H6
LACY ST
16300 VCTV 92392 4296-E6
W LADDS CT
1800 SBDO 92411 576-C4
LA DENEY CT
800 ONT 91764 602-D5
E LA DENEY CT
1900 ONT 91764 602-G5
E LA DENEY DR
100 ONT 91764 602-C5
W LA DENEY DR
600 ONT 91762 602-A5
900 ONT 91762 601-H5
LA DENEY ST
4400 MTCL 91763 601-E5
E LA DENEY WY
2100 ONT 91764 602-H5
2100 ONT 91730 602-H5
LADERA AV
- SBdC - (4301-A5 See Page 4300)
9300 SBdC - 4481-B1
11000 SBdC - (4391-B7 See Page 4300)
LADERA CT
9800 RCUC 91730 602-J1
LADERA LN
5800 SBdC 92301 (4113-D2 See Page 4112)
LADERA RD
5500 SBDO 92407 546-F4
6200 SBdC - (4571-B5 See Page 4570)
N LADERA RD
2700 SBDO 92405 576-F2
LADERA ST
- RDL 92373 647-G1
22100 GTER 92313 646-D6
LADERA VISTA DR
15600 CHLS 91709 681-B7
LA DONA LN
5000 SBdC 92301 (4113-B4 See Page 4112)
LA DONA PL
6900 RCUC 91701 572-G6
LADRILLO WY
13500 VCTV 92392 4385-G3
LADYBIRD LN
14600 VCTV 92394 4295-H7
LA ENTRADA
- YUCA 92284 4957-G3
LAFAYETTE CT
13400 FONT 92336 574-A7
E LAFAYETTE PL
1400 SBDO 92408 607-C6
LAFAYETTE RD
1300 CLAR 91711 601-C1
LAFAYETTE ST
20900 APLV 92307 4207-F3
22100 APLV 92307 4208-A3
22500 SBdC 92307 4208-A3
LA FELIZ DR
900 RDL 92373 648-C4
LAFERNEY AV
4500 SBdC 92252 4889-G2
62500 SBdC 92252 4819-G4
LAFFOON RD
- LPCo - 4844-F4
LA FLORA DR
900 RDL 92373 648-C4
35200 YCPA 92399 650-A6
LAFON RD
- SBdC 92285 4484-F5
- SBdC 92285 (4574-F1 See Page 4484)
LA FONDA DR
5200 SBdC 92301 (4113-C4 See Page 4112)
LAGARTIJO DR
9200 SBdC 92308 4478-J1
11200 SBdC 92308 4388-J7
LAGER RD
8500 SBdC 92371 4563-E1
9900 SBdC 92371 4473-E4
12100 SBdC 92371 4383-E3
LA GLORIA DR
9300 RCUC 91701 572-H4
9600 RCUC 91737 572-J4
10100 RCUC 91737 573-A4
W LA GLORIA DR
800 RLTO 92377 575-D3
W LA GLORIA ST
1100 RLTO 92377 575-E3
LAGO
3200 ONT 91761 643-B6
LAGOON ST
600 NDLS 92363 3620-E5
LAGO VISTA CT
16200 APLV 92307 4298-B2
LAGO VISTA DR
5100 SBdC 92301 (4113-B4 See Page 4112)
LAGO VISTA LN
22600 APLV 92307 4298-A3
LA GRANDE ST
8400 RCUC 91701 572-F6
LA GRANGE AV
9100 HESP 92345 4477-B6
LAGUNA AV
300 PRKR - 4774-H7
1000 PRKR - 4844-J1
LAGUNA CT
14100 ADEL 92301 4385-A1
15200 CHLS 91709 681-D6
21100 APLV 92308 4387-G6
LAGUNA PL
6900 RCUC 91701 572-J6
LAGUNA RD
20900 APLV 92308 4387-G6
76000 TNP 92277 4893-B5
LAGUNA ST
11500 ADEL 92301 4385-A1
16100 VCTV 92392 4296-D4
LAGUNA SECA DR
9300 SBdC 92308 4478-H2
11400 SBdC 92308 4388-H7
11900 SBdC 92307 4388-J2
LAGUNA SECA RD
13700 SBdC 92307 4388-H2
14100 SBdC 92307 4298-G4
LAGUNITA LN
100 BBLK - 4741-C7
100 BBLK - 4811-C1
LA HABRA AV
3800 SBdC 92284 4888-B1
6500 YUCA 92284 4888-B7
LA HABRA AV
6500 YUCA 92284 4958-C1
8900 ADEL 92301 4204-C4
11500 ADEL 92301 4205-A4
LA HABRA RD
14100 SBdC 92392 4385-J4
14100 VCTV 92392 4385-J4
14700 SBdC 92392 4386-A4
LA HABRE AV
900 SBdC 92284 4748-B7
900 SBdC 92284 4818-B2
N LA HACIENDA
4000 SBDO 92404 547-C7
N LA HACIENDA DR
3600 SBDO 92404 547-C7
3600 SBDO 92404 577-C1
LA HERMOSA
1000 RDL 92373 648-B4
LA HONDA WY
7400 YUCA 92284 4957-D3
LAHONTAN DR
41100 BBLK - 4811-F1
LA JOLLA CT
11400 ADEL 92301 4385-A1
LA JOLLA DR
9700 RCUC 91701 572-J6
61300 SBdC 92252 4959-A1
LA JOYA CT
16200 VCTV 92392 4296-D6
LA JOYA PL
15700 VCTV 92394 4296-C6
LA JUNTA DR
4000 CLAR 91711 601-A1
4000 CLAR 91711 571-A7
LA JUNTA ST
17200 HESP 92345 4566-G5
N LA JUNTA ST
1000 SBDO 92410 577-A6
N LAKE AV
700 ONT 91764 602-F4
S LAKE AV
1400 ONT 91761 642-F5
LAKE CT
7400 RCUC 91730 573-A7
LAKE DR
100 BBLK - 4741-B7
500 SBdC - 518-A3
5800 SBdC - 4950-F1
23400 SBdC - 516-H3
24300 SBdC - 517-A2
39400 BBLK - 4811-B1
S LAKE PL
1800 ONT 91761 642-F4
LAKE RD
- SBdC 92301 4112-F2
- SBdC 92301 (4113-A5 See Page 4112)
LAKE ST
3800 CHNO 91710 641-D5
15100 ADEL 92301 4294-H6
30100 SBdC - (4390-H4 See Page 4300)
32800 SBdC - (4391-A4 See Page 4300)
LAKE WY
- APLV 92308 4477-B5
LAKEBROOK DR
29100 SBdC - 518-C1
LAKE EDGE WY
900 SBdC - 4738-C6
LAKE FOREST CT
2200 SBDO 92407 546-B5
LAKE FOREST DR
1000 CLAR 91711 571-B7
26100 SBdC - 517-E2
LAKE GREGORY DR
24000 SBdC - 516-J3
24100 SBdC - 517-B4
LAKE IRENE DR
47800 SBdC 92365 3764-J5
47800 SBdC 92365 (3765-A5 See Page 3764)
LAKE KNOLL DR
27400 SBdC - 517-J1
LAKELAND VW
21600 SBdC - 516-B1
W LAKE PLACID DR
1400 SBDO 92407 546-D5
LAKE RESORT RD
100 SBdC - 517-J1
LAKE RIDGE LN
29000 HIGH 92346 578-C6
LAKES EDGE RD Rt#-189
27600 SBdC - 517-J1
27900 SBdC - 518-A1
LAKESHORE CT
- APLV 92308 4477-B1
LAKE SHORE CV
16200 APLV 92307 4298-B2
LAKE SHORE DR
2000 CHLS 91709 680-H3
LAKESHORE DR
19700 APLV 92308 4477-B1
LAKESIDE AV
- RDL 92373 647-J2
200 RDL 92373 648-A3
LAKESIDE CT
7000 HESP 92345 4567-A4
LAKESIDE DR
13400 VCTV 92392 4386-H3
33000 SBdC - 519-E3
LAKE TERRACE DR
2300 CHLS 91709 680-J3
LAKE VIEW AV
10500 SBdC - 4482-E1
11000 SBdC - (4392-E7 See Page 4302)
13000 SBdC 93562 2144-J4
13200 SBdC 93562 2145-A4
LAKEVIEW AV
32700 SBdC 92365 3764-G2
33500 SBdC 92365 (3683-D6 See Page 3592)
34100 SBdC 92365 (3684-G4 See Page 3594)
LAKE VIEW CIR
200 RivC 91752 683-F5
LAKEVIEW CT
17100 FONT 92336 575-A5
40300 BBLK - 4811-D1
LAKE VIEW CT
83100 SBdC 93562 2144-J4
LAKEVIEW DR
- SBdC - (4743-B5 See Page 4662)
4100 CHLS 91709 681-E6
12100 SBdC 93562 2234-G4
17500 SBdC 92392 4386-H1
23600 SBdC - 516-H3
26500 SBdC - 517-F4
26500 SBdC - (3935-H3 See Page 3934)
29100 SBdC - 518-C1
LAKE VIEW DR
33200 SBdC - 519-E6
LAKEVIEW DR
39700 BBLK - 4811-C1
N LAKEVIEW DR
3200 SBDO 92346 577-G2
LAKEVIEW LN
600 SBdC - 4741-J5
800 SBdC - 517-E3
2200 CHLS 91709 680-J3
LAKE VIEW LN
16200 APLV 92307 4298-B2
83100 SBdC 93562 2145-A4
LAKE VIEW PL
83100 SBdC 93562 2144-J4
LAKEVIEW RD
10400 YCPA 92399 609-J6
10400 YCPA 92399 610-A6
35700 SBdC 92365 3594-G7
35700 SBdC 92365 (3684-G1 See Page 3594)
38700 BBLK - 4811-A1
56900 SBdC - 2971-H2
LAKE VIEW RD
36500 SBdC 92347 (3587-C7 See Page 3586)
36500 SBdC 92347 (3677-C1 See Page 3586)
LAKEVIEW ST
35500 SBdC - (3591-E4 See Page 3590)
LAKE VIEW TR
36700 YCPA 92399 650-E5
LAKEVIEW WY
15100 CHLS 91709 681-E5
LAKEVIEW PINES RD
39500 BBLK - 4811-B3
LAKEWAY DR
22700 DBAR 91765 680-B2
LAKE WILLIAMS DR
1100 SBdC 92314 4813-B2
LAKEWOOD AV
1800 UPL 91784 571-H6
N LAKEWOOD AV
1300 UPL 91786 601-J1
1600 UPL 91784 571-J6
N LAKEWOOD CT
4600 SBDO 92407 546-C6
LAKEWOOD DR
300 SBdC 92314 4742-J7
400 SBdC 92314 4812-J1
46300 SBdC 92314 4813-B2
N LAKEWOOD DR
4100 SBDO 92407 546-C6
LAKEWOOD LN
400 BBLK - 4811-D2
LAKEWOOD PL
16000 VCTV 92392 4386-D2
LAKEWOOD RD
600 SBdC - 518-B3
N LAKEWOOD WY
500 UPL 91786 601-J3
1500 UPL 91786 571-H7
LAKOTA AV
9600 APLV 92308 4477-G4
9600 SBdC 92308 4477-G5
LAKOTA CT
- SBdC - 4843-G5
LAKOTA RD
12300 APLV 92308 4387-G4
13600 APLV 92307 4387-H1
LAKOTA TR
- SBdC - 4773-H7
- SBdC - 4843-H1
LALANIA AV
800 RDL 92374 608-C5
LA LANZA CT
6900 RCUC 91701 572-G6
LA LEMA CT
9000 RCUC 91701 572-G6
W LA LOMA AV
100 CLTN 92324 646-C5
100 SBdC 92324 646-C5
LA LOMA DR
1300 RDL 92373 648-C4
LA LUNA AV
2700 SBdC 92277 4822-B4
5700 TNP 92277 4892-B4
LA LUNA CIR
11300 FONT 92337 645-A2
LA LUNA CT
6900 RCUC 91701 572-G6
LA MANCHA CT
11300 FONT 92337 645-A2
N LA MANCHA WY
1300 ONT 91764 602-H5
LAMANDA ST
18200 APLV 92307 (4206-J5 See Page 4116)
LAMAR CT
6900 RCUC 91701 573-D5
LAMAR DR
200 CLAR 91711 571-C6
LA MAR RD
25000 LMLN 92354 647-C1
LA MAR ST
- RCUC 91701 572-E1
S LAMARR AV
100 SBDO 92376 605-J2
N LAMARR ST
500 SBDO 92376 575-J7
S LAMARR ST
200 SBDO 92376 605-J2
LA MASITA CT
4600 CHNO 91710 641-F4
LAMBERT
1900 NDLS 92363 3620-B4
LAMBERT LN
300 SBdC 92284 4748-H7
16700 VCTV 92392 4386-F3
LAMBRUSCO CT
- RCUC 91739 603-J1
LAMBS BREAD DR
- BARS 92311 3679-J5
LA MESA
400 NDLS 92363 3620-D6
LA MESA CT
9900 RCUC 91701 573-A6
12900 SBdC 92371 4383-C5
LA MESA DR
9300 RCUC 91701 572-H6
10400 RCUC 91701 573-B6
LA MESA RD
- SBdC 92308 4479-D2
100 SBdC 92372 4382-E5
2800 SBdC 92371 4382-H5
3600 SBdC 92371 4383-A5
7500 SBdC 92371 4384-A5
8100 SBdC 92392 4384-A5
8900 VCTV 92392 4384-F5
11000 VCTV 92392 4385-A5
11400 SBdC 92307 (4389-D7 See Page 4299)
14600 VCTV 92392 4386-A5
S LA MESA ST
200 POM 91766 641-B2
LA MIRADA DR
600 RDL 92373 648-G4
10500 SBdC 92371 4473-G3
LA MIRADA RD
9700 SBdC 92371 4473-G6
12300 SBdC 92371 4383-F3
LA MIRADA ST
14100 VCTV 92392 4385-H5
LA MIRADA TR
58700 YUCA 92284 4958-D3
60100 SBdC 92252 4958-G2
LAMONETTE ST
1000 CLAR 91711 571-F5
LA MONICA DR
9700 RCUC 91730 602-J1
LA MONICA ST
- HIGH 92346 578-G7
LAMONT CT
11700 SBdC 92345 4475-B3
W LA MORADA DR
2600 RLTO 92377 545-A7
2800 RLTO 92377 544-J7
LA MORADA PL
- POM 91766 640-F5
LAMPLIGHTER LN
600 SBdC 91784 572-A2
4300 CHNO 91710 641-E5
LAMPOST RD
14700 VCTV 92392 4385-J5
14700 VCTV 92392 4386-A5
LAMPREY RD
- SBdC 92308 4567-D5
LANCASTER CT
800 CLAR 91711 571-F7
LANCASTER DR
800 CLAR 91711 571-F7
LANCASTER ST
61800 SBdC 92252 4819-B7
LANCASTER WY
11500 RCUC 91730 573-D7
LANCE DR
500 BARS 92311 3679-H3
LANCELET AV
10600 APLV 92308 4477-F2
LANCELET RD
- SBdC 92308 4478-B1
LANCELET ST
- SBdC 92307 4479-G1
20900 APLV 92308 4477-G1
23700 SBdC 92308 4478-E1
25200 SBdC 92308 4479-A1
31500 SBdC - 4480-F1
34400 SBdC - (4391-E7 See Page 4300)
LANCER AV
2800 POM 91768 640-B2
LANCEWOOD AV
2400 RLTO 92377 575-D3
N LANCEWOOD AV
500 RLTO 92376 575-D6
500 RLTO 92376 605-D1
S LANCEWOOD AV
600 RLTO 92316 605-D4
N LANCEWOOD ST
200 RLTO 92376 605-D1
LANCIA CT
- RCUC 91739 574-B1
LANDER CIR
500 CLAR 91711 571-E7
LANDERS LN
100 SBdC 92284 4748-B6
700 SBdC 92285 4748-B2
LANDFAIR LN
6600 RivC 92509 645-B5
LANDFORD ST
- YCPA 92399 649-F2
LANDIS DR
17600 VCTV 92392 4386-G3
LANDLOCK LNDG
500 BBLK - 4811-B2
LANDMARK AV
12700 VCTV 92392 4386-D5
LANDON CT
17900 ADEL 92301 4204-G6
LANDOVER AV
6500 SBdC 92345 4564-F5
LANDRIANO PL
6700 RCUC 91701 573-E5
LANDSDOWN RD
11700 LMLN 92354 647-F3
LANDS END TR
500 SBdC - 516-G3
LANE CT
1200 CLAR 91711 571-A7
7800 FONT 92336 604-A1
LANE ST
25300 LMLN 92354 607-C7
LANES LN
6600 SBdC 92277 (4895-B6 See Page 4824)
LANETTE CT
1200 SBDO 92407 546-D6
LANFAIR RD
38800 SBdC - 351-F5
LANFAIR ST
1300 RDL 92374 608-D5
LANFRANC RD
37000 SBdC 92399 610-F7
LANGDON AV
7300 HESP 92345 4566-J2
LANGHAM PL
7400 RCUC 91730 573-C7
LANGLEY ST
20200 SBdC 92307 (4117-D7 See Page 4116)
LANGSTON ST
9300 RCUC 91730 602-H1
9900 RCUC 91730 603-A1
W LANGSTON ST
100 UPL 91786 602-B1
LANGUR RD
- SBdC - (3846-F7 See Page 3756)
- SBdC - 3936-F1
LANIER RD
4800 CHNO 91710 681-F1
LANIKAI RD
- SBdC 92365 (3683-B3 See Page 3592)
48700 SBdC 92365 (3685-C2 See Page 3594)
LA NITA ST
- HIGH 92346 578-H7
LANKERSHIM AV
300 HIGH 92410 577-E7
300 SBDO 92410 577-E7
300 HIGH 92346 577-E7
300 SBDO 92346 577-E7
LANNING LN
8700 SBdC 92256 4956-D7
9000 SBdC 92256 616-D2
LANSBURY AV
3000 CLAR 91711 601-B3
LANSFORD ST
10800 RivC 91752 643-H6
LANTANA AV
12700 YCPA 92399 650-B5

STREET
Block City ZIP Pg-Grid

S LANTANA AV
1300 ONT 91762 642-A3
LANTANA DR
12500 RCUC 91739 573-G5
LANTANA ST
35300 SBdC - (4301-G4
See Page 4300)
LANTANA WY
1600 POM 91766 641-B4
LANTERN LN
12900 VCTV 92392 4385-F5
15300 FONT 92336 574-E7
LANTERN CREST DR
- SBDO 92407 546-F5
400 RDL 92373 648-D5
LANTRY LN
- SBdC 92345 4565-A7
10400 SBdC 92345 4564-H7
LANYARD LN
- CHLS 91709 681-H6
LA PAIX ST
8500 RCUC 91701 572-F6
22200 GTER 92313 646-E4
LA PALMA AV
2000 UPL 91784 572-B5
LA PALMA DR
14900 CHNO 91710 681-G5
N LA PALOMA AV
700 ONT 91764 602-E6
N LA PALOMA CT
1300 ONT 91764 602-E5
LA PALOMA ST
300 RDL 92373 608-C7
300 RDL 92373 648-C1
LAPANTO RD
11500 VCTV 92392 4475-A3
E LA PAZ
1300 SBdC 92314 4742-G7
LA PAZ AV
8900 ADEL 92301 4204-C3
11300 ADEL 92301 4205-A3
N LA PAZ AV
1600 ONT 91764 602-G4
LA PAZ CT
6900 RCUC 91701 572-G6
7600 YUCA 92284 4957-B3
13400 YCPA 92399 650-B6
15800 VCTV 92392 4296-D4
LA PAZ DR
- SBdC - (3846-C6
See Page 3756)
2200 CLAR 91711 571-D7
14100 VCTV 92392 4386-D1
14100 VCTV 92392 4296-C6
LA PAZ PL
15800 VCTV 92392 4296-C6
LA PAZ ST
9300 ADEL 92301 4294-E7
9300 SBdC 92301 4294-E7
11700 ADEL 92301 4295-C7
11700 VCTV 92301 4295-C7
11700 VCTV 92394 4295-C7
LA PLACIDA AV
42500 BBLK - 4812-A2
W LA PORTE AV
700 SBDO 92405 576-F1
N LA PRAIX AV
2500 SBdC 92346 577-J3
2500 SBDO 92346 577-J3
LA PRAIX CT
6500 HIGH 92346 577-J3
LA PRAIX ST
1500 SBDO 92346 577-J4
6500 HIGH 92346 577-J3
LA QUINTA CIR
1500 UPL 91784 572-E6
LA QUINTA CT
- CHLS 91709 711-E1
LA QUINTA DR
- UPL 91786 572-E7
LARA LN
19700 APLV 92308 4387-D3
LA RAMADA PL
- POM 91766 640-D4
LARAMIE AV
1400 RDL 92374 608-E7
30500 SBdC 92374 608-G6
LARAMIE CT
13500 FONT 92336 603-J1
LARAMIE DR
8900 RCUC 91737 572-G1
LARAMIE RD
4700 SBdC - 4886-F4
32400 SBdC - 4480-J4
32700 SBdC - 4481-A4
LARAMIE ST
- SBdC 92308 4477-G5
23700 SBdC 92308 4478-E5
25600 SBdC 92308 4479-A5
28700 SBdC - 4479-H5
29300 SBdC - 4480-A5
32700 SBdC - 4481-A5
37000 SBdC - 4482-B4
LARAMORE LN
2600 RivC 92509 645-B6
LA RAYE DR
34300 YCPA 92399 649-H6
LARCH AV
5500 SBdC 92377 575-E2
9700 SBdC 92316 605-E6

LARCH AV
9900 RLTO 92316 605-E6
10600 SBdC 92316 645-E2
N LARCH AV
200 RLTO 92376 605-E1
500 RLTO 92376 575-E7
1000 CLTN 92324 606-E5
S LARCH AV
100 RLTO 92376 605-E2
900 RLTO 92316 605-E4
1100 SBdC 92316 605-E4
LARCH RD
- SBdC 92345 4564-H4
12900 SBdC 92345 4565-F4
LARCH ST
14900 HESP 92345 4566-A4
LARCHMONT LN
28200 SBdC - 518-A3
LARCHMONT ST
2100 POM 91767 601-B5
LARCHWOOD CIR
1300 NDLS 92363 3620-C7
LARCHWOOD DR
11300 FONT 92337 644-C2
LA REATA DR
3500 SBdC 91710 641-D6
LAREDO LN
- CHLS 91709 681-A3
LAREDO PL
5000 RCUC 91737 572-G1
LA REINA DR
5800 SBdC 92371 4653-G1
LA RETA WY
9200 RivC 92509 644-D7
LARGO CT
11600 LMLN 92354 647-E2
LARIAT AV
- SBdC 92284 4957-B4
LARIAT DR
17900 CHLS 91709 712-B6
LARIAT LN
600 BBLK - 4811-D2
LARIAT PL
7300 RCUC 91730 572-H7
LARIAT RD
16400 VCTV 92392 4386-D1
LARIAT TR
5600 SBdC - 4886-G6
LARIMER RD
- SBdC 92301 (4115-B4
See Page 4114)
12100 ADEL 92301 (4115-B4
See Page 4114)
LARIMORE RD
10500 SBdC 92345 4654-H1
LARINO DR
11700 RCUC 91701 573-E6
LARK CT
11600 FONT 92337 644-F3
LARK DR
- LACo 92397 4652-A2
400 SBdC 92397 4652-A2
11600 RCUC 91701 573-E5
LARK RD
500 SBdC 92397 4652-B1
39200 BBLK - 4811-B2
LARK SPUR
39300 BBLK - 4811-B2
LARK ST
22100 GTER 92313 646-E5
W LARK ST
200 CLTN 92324 646-B5
LARK TR
800 BBLK - 4811-B2
800 SBdC - 4811-B2
LARKDALE CIR
- RivC 91752 683-E5
LARKIN CT
14100 FONT 92336 574-B7
LARK SPRING TER
22500 DBAR 91765 680-A4
LARKSPUR AV
1200 POM 91767 601-D7
6000 SBdC 92252 4889-D4
7700 SBdC 92252 4959-E3
N LARKSPUR AV
3800 RLTO 92377 544-J6
3800 RLTO 92377 545-A6
LARKSPUR DR
8900 SBdC 92335 604-E5
E LARKSPUR DR
200 SBDO 92404 546-J7
LARKSPUR LN
4300 CHNO 91710 681-E1
LARKSPUR PL
7000 RCUC 91739 573-G6
LARKSPUR RD
14600 ADEL 92301 4295-A7
16200 ADEL 92301 4294-J3
18100 ADEL 92301 4204-J1
LARKSPUR WY
10900 YCPA 92399 610-A7
LARKVIEW LN
- SBdC 92371 4653-F1
LARKWOOD DR
3500 SBdC 91710 681-C1
W LARODA CT
400 ONT 91762 642-A4
LA RONDA CT
7000 RCUC 91701 572-H6

LA RONDA ST
9100 RCUC 91701 572-H6
LA ROSA CT
33500 YCPA 92399 649-F4
LA ROSA DR
23000 SBdC 92301 (4113-E2
See Page 4112)
LARREA AV
6400 TNP 92277 4892-B5
LARREA LN
6200 SBdC 92277 (4894-D2
See Page 4824)
LARREA RD
4900 SBdC 92285 (4575-J5
See Page 4484)
LARRERA ST
13000 RCUC 91739 573-H5
LARRYS CAMP RD
- SBdC - 519-C4
LA RUA DR
18500 ADEL 92301 4204-C5
18500 SBdC 92301 4204-C5
LA RUE ST
3100 RivC 92509 645-C7
LA SALLE AV
2200 SBDO 92407 546-B5
LA SALLE CIR
13200 VCTV 92392 4385-E4
LA SALLE CT
14000 FONT 92336 574-B7
LA SALLE PL
8200 RCUC 91730 602-G2
E LA SALLE ST
3500 ONT 91761 643-B2
N LA SALLE ST
- RDL 92374 608-G7
S LA SALLE ST
- RDL 92374 608-G7
- RDL 92374 648-G1
LA SALLE POINTE
2400 CHLS 91709 681-A5
LAS AMIGAS DR
800 BARS 92311 3679-J4
LA SARRE DR
- FONT 92336 544-D7
- FONT 92336 574-D1
LAS BRISAS CIR
100 POM 91768 640-G1
LAS BRISAS CT
- RCUC 91739 573-G2
LAS CASAS CT
11300 FONT 92337 644-J2
LA SENDA CT
8500 RCUC 91701 572-F1
LA SENDA RD
8100 RCUC 91701 572-E1
LA SERENA DR
23100 SBdC 92301 (4113-D1
See Page 4112)
LAS FLORES DR
5200 SBdC 92301 (4113-B4
See Page 4112)
14300 VCTV 92392 4385-H5
15100 CHNO 91710 681-G5
LASHEART DR
- RDL 92346 608-B2
LA SIERRA DR
- POM 91766 640-E5
13400 CHLS 91709 680-H1
LA SIERRA WY
2100 CLAR 91711 571-B7
LAS LUNAS ST
17300 HESP 92345 4566-G6
LA SOLANA CT
1000 RDL 92373 648-H4
LA SOLANA DR
800 RDL 92373 648-H4
LAS PALMAS DR
- FONT 92336 574-A6
6200 SBdC - 4844-A2
LAS PALMAS LN
5100 SBdC 92301 (4113-B4
See Page 4112)
LAS PALMAS ST
16500 HESP 92345 4476-E2
LAS PIEDRAS DR
15000 VCTV 92392 4296-D6
25900 SBdC 92308 (4389-A6
See Page 4299)
57300 YUCA 92284 4887-J5
LAS PIEDRAS RD
22400 APLV 92308 4388-B6
24500 SBdC 92308 4388-G6
LASPINO LN
200 DBAR 91765 640-D6
LASSEN AV
1800 CLAR 91711 571-E7
7800 HESP 92345 4567-B1
8700 HESP 92345 4477-A7
N LASSEN AV
600 SBDO 92410 576-A7
700 ONT 91764 602-F4
S LASSEN AV
100 SBDO 92410 606-A2
1400 ONT 91761 642-F6
LASSEN CT
1300 BBLK - 4812-C3
2000 BARS 92311 3679-J6
3900 CHNO 91710 681-D4

W LASSEN CT
2500 SBDO 92410 606-A2
LASSEN DR
1200 BBLK - 4812-C3
28800 SBdC - 4738-C5
N LASSEN PL
100 ONT 91764 602-F7
LASSEN RD
6100 SBdC 92345 4565-D3
6100 SBdC 92345 (4655-D1
See Page 4654)
9100 HESP 92345 4475-D7
9700 SBdC 92371 4474-B6
9700 SBdC 92345 4475-C6
LASSEN ST
- SBdC 92311 3589-A7
- SBdC 92311 3679-J6
900 BARS 92311 3679-J6
1500 RDL 92374 608-C5
13500 FONT 92336 604-A1
26100 SBdC 92311 3678-J1
N LASSEN ST
1200 SBDO 92411 576-A6
LASSITER RD
6600 RivC 92509 645-B6
LAST MILE RD
5100 SBdC 92285 (4576-B5
See Page 4486)
LAS TUNAS DR
- SBdC 92307 (4389-A7
See Page 4299)
21800 APLV 92308 4387-J7
21800 APLV 92308 4388-A7
22100 SBdC 92308 4388-G7
25600 SBdC 92308 (4389-A7
See Page 4299)
N LATHAM ST
800 SBdC 92324 606-B5
1300 CLTN 92324 606-B4
LATHAM TR
60100 SBdC 92252 4958-H2
61300 SBdC 92252 4959-A2
LA TIERRA CIR
17100 FONT 92337 645-A2
LA TIERRA DR
- SBdC - 3936-F3
LATIGO LN
51800 SBdC - 4816-D6
LATIMER ST
28700 HIGH 92346 578-C5
LA TORRE DR
- POM 91766 640-F5
LA TOUR CT
- RCUC 91739 603-H1
LATOUR LN
10400 RivC 91752 644-A4
10400 RivC 91752 643-J4
LAUGHLIN ST
- CHNO 91710 681-J6
LAUNCH LN
14100 SBdC - (3935-G4
See Page 3934)
LAURA LN
- SBDO 92407 546-A3
71500 TNP 92277 4891-J2
N LAURA LN
5900 SBDO 92407 546-A3
LAURA ST
- FONT 92336 574-E5
1300 SBdC 92397 4652-D2
LAURAMORE CT
14100 FONT 92336 574-B7
LAUREEN CT
11300 FONT 92337 644-F2
LAUREL AV
- RLTO 92377 545-B7
- RLTO 92377 575-B4
1200 RDL 92373 648-A2
1400 UPL 91786 572-B7
1400 UPL 91786 602-B1
1400 POM 91768 640-D1
1500 RDL 92373 647-J3
6800 HIGH 92346 578-A4
7300 FONT 92336 575-C7
7500 SBdC 92336 575-C7
7500 ADEL 92301 (4293-J5
See Page 4292)
7500 ADEL 92301 4294-A5
7900 FONT 92336 605-C2
7900 SBdC 92336 605-C2
8100 FONT 92335 605-C2
8100 SBdC 92335 605-C4
10500 SBdC 92316 605-C7
10500 SBdC 92316 645-C2
11500 LMLN 92354 647-F2
E LAUREL AV
800 CLTN 92324 606-E4
N LAUREL AV
100 ONT 91762 602-B6
100 ONT 91762 642-B1
100 UPL 91784 572-B3
200 UPL 91786 602-B1
1400 FONT 92376 575-B5
1400 RLTO 92376 575-B5
1500 UPL 91786 572-B6
1800 RLTO 92377 575-B1
S LAUREL AV
100 ONT 91762 642-B1
100 UPL 91786 602-B4

W LAUREL AV
500 POM 91768 640-F1
LAUREL CT
3900 CHLS 91709 681-D7
6800 CHNO 91710 682-B2
30900 SBdC 92311 3680-C1
N LAUREL CT
3500 SBDO 92404 577-E1
LAUREL DR
400 RivC 91752 683-E4
3000 RivC 92509 645-C7
17700 FONT 92336 575-B7
17700 SBdC 92336 575-B7
28600 SBdC - 518-B1
36300 SBdC 92311 3680-C1
49000 SBdC 92256 615-F4
N LAUREL DR
700 CLTN 92324 606-A5
LAUREL LN
400 SBdC - 4812-F1
5700 SBdC 92256 616-B4
19300 APLV 92308 4387-C7
20600 APLV 92308 4477-F1
22700 SBdC - 516-E2
S LAUREL LN
600 CLTN 92324 606-C7
LAUREL PL
7000 HIGH 92346 578-A5
S LAUREL PL
1900 ONT 91762 642-B4
LAUREL ST
- APLV 92308 4477-J2
- SBdC 92307 4479-G1
10600 RCUC 91730 603-C2
17300 HESP 92345 4476-G7
20900 SBdC 92347 (3587-E4
See Page 3586)
22100 APLV 92308 4478-A2
22600 SBdC 92308 4478-E1
E LAUREL ST
100 CLTN 92324 606-D4
S LAUREL ST
2600 ONT 91762 642-B6
W LAUREL ST
100 CLTN 92324 606-B4
900 SBdC 92324 606-B4
LAUREL GROVE CIR
- YCPA 92399 610-A7
10900 YCPA 92399 609-J7
LAUREL OAK DR
11500 VCTV 92392 4475-D1
LAUREL OAK RD
12500 VCTV 92392 4475-E1
LAURELTON LN
6600 CHLS 91709 712-B5
S LAURELTREE DR
2800 ONT 91761 643-B6
E LAUREL VALLEY LN
2500 ONT 91761 642-J6
S LAURELWOOD AV
1500 CLTN 92324 646-H2
E LAURELWOOD DR
900 SBDO 92408 607-B6
LAURELWOOD LN
9900 SBdC 92359 608-J5
LAUREL WOOD LN
14200 CHLS 91709 680-H3
LAURELWOOD PL
14000 CHNO 91710 681-E3
15100 VCTV 92394 4296-A5
LAUREN LN
6800 RivC 92509 645-B4
LAURIA DR
700 SBdC 92252 4749-A3
W LAURIN ST
1500 ONT 91762 641-H5
LAURJOE ST
32400 SBdC - (4210-F1
See Page 4120)
LAUSANNE DR
800 SBdC - 516-J4
800 SBdC - 517-A4
2200 SBdC 92397 4652-F3
LAVA LN
12500 VCTV 92392 4385-G6
LAVA ST
- SBdC 92347 (3587-G6
See Page 3586)
LAVENDER CT
4300 CHNO 91710 681-E1
7500 FONT 92336 574-E7
7700 HIGH 92346 578-C6
10300 RCUC 91737 573-B3
LAVENDER ST
6300 RivC 92880 683-D6
7600 FONT 92336 574-E7
LAVENDER TER
- CHLS 91709 711-G1
LA VEREDA ESCARPADA
1100 RCUC 91711 571-E3
LA VERIDA CT
15900 VCTV 92392 4296-D4
LA VERIDA DR
15500 VCTV 92392 4296-D4
LAVERNE AV
700 BARS 92311 3679-C4
LA VERNE AV
600 SBdC 92346 577-G3
E LA VERNE AV
200 POM 91767 601-A6

N LA VERNE AV
2800 SBdC 92346 577-G2
LA VERNE CT
7100 HIGH 92346 577-G5
LA VERNE ST
400 RDL 92373 648-C1
8900 RCUC 91701 572-G6
LA VESU RD
17100 FONT 92337 645-A2
LA VETA ST
700 SBDO 92404 577-A3
LAVIC RD
24200 SBdC - 370-B1
LA VIDA CT
17000 FONT 92337 644-J3
17000 FONT 92337 645-A3
LAVIDA RD
- BREA 92823 710-D4
- OrCo 92823 710-B4
LA VILLA DR
13500 VCTV 92392 4386-D3
LA VINA TR
7300 YUCA 92284 4957-C3
LA VINE ST
8500 RCUC 91701 572-F6
9900 RCUC 91701 573-A6
LAVON DR
2100 SBDO 92407 576-B1
E LA VUELTA LP
1800 SBDO 92404 547-D7
N LA VUELTA LP
3900 SBDO 92404 547-D7
LAWREN LN
- CLTN 92324 606-C4
LAWRENCE AV
2200 SBDO 92404 577-A2
4200 SBdC 92252 4820-B7
4200 SBdC 92252 4890-B2
6900 SBdC 92252 4960-B1
LAWRENCE CIR
900 CLAR 91711 571-F7
LAWRENCE LN
40000 BBLK - 4811-D2
LAWRENCE PL
- FONT 92336 573-J7
1600 POM 91766 641-B4
LAWRENCE GARRETT ST
1500 CLTN 92324 606-A4
LAWRIE AV
6300 SBdC 92377 575-G3
LAWSON AV
8900 ADEL 92301 4204-C6
11300 ADEL 92301 4205-A6
LAWTON AV
24300 LMLN 92354 647-B2
LAWTON CT
11400 LMLN 92354 647-B2
LAWTON ST
500 RDL 92374 608-A6
LAWTON WY
24800 LMLN 92354 647-B2
LAYTON CT
7000 RCUC 91701 572-H6
LAYTON RD
59900 SBdC 92284 4888-F1
LAYTON ST
5500 RCUC 91737 572-H2
6100 RCUC 91701 572-H4
7300 RCUC 91730 572-H7
7700 RCUC 91730 602-H1
56900 SBdC 92284 4887-H1
LAZIO CT
- RCUC 91701 573-E5
LAZULITE LN
1300 POM 91767 601-C6
LAZY GLENN CT
14300 HESP 92345 4565-J2
LAZY JOE AV
4400 TNP 92277 4822-D7
4400 TNP 92277 4892-D1
LAZY JOE RD
3400 TNP 92277 4822-C5
5400 TNP 92277 4893-B3
LAZY MEADOW DR
22500 DBAR 91765 680-A5
LAZY MEADOW RD
- POM 91766 640-G7
LAZY TOO RANCH RD
39600 SBdC - 349-G5
LAZY TRAIL LN
- POM 91766 640-G5
LAZY TRAIL RD
22800 DBAR 91765 680-B5
LEACHS RD
4100 SBdC 92277 4824-A6
LEAD DR
- TNP 92278 4822-F1
LEAD LN
1200 MohC - 3620-E4
LEAD PIPE SPRING RD
20600 SBdC - 329-B8
LEAF CIR
1400 UPL 91786 571-H7
LEAF LN
14900 VCTV 92394 4295-G7
LEAFWOOD DR
6400 RivC 92509 645-B6
LEAFY LN
500 SBdC - 516-H3

LEAH CT
200 UPL 91784 572-B4
LEAH LN
35900 YCPA 92399 650-C6
LEALMA AV
3900 CLAR 91711 601-A1
LEAR AV
200 SBdC 92277 4751-C7
200 SBdC 92278 4751-C7
1300 SBdC 92277 4821-C3
4100 SBdC 92277 4891-C3
4900 TNP 92277 4891-C3
LEAR LN
6500 FONT 92336 574-E4
LEAR BAY ST
12500 VCTV 92392 4475-D3
LEARCO WY
62900 SBdC 92252 4749-E7
65700 SBdC 92252 4750-C7
LEATHER LN
26600 SBdC - (3935-F5
See Page 3934)
LEATHERLEAF RD
11500 FONT 92337 644-F3
LEBEC RD
8200 SBdC 92371 4562-J2
8300 SBdC 92371 4563-A2
9200 SBdC 92371 4472-J1
12100 SBdC 92371 4382-J4
LEDBURY AV
24100 SBdC - (4025-J4
See Page 3934)
LEDIG PL
9300 RCUC 91701 572-H5
LEE AV
300 CLAR 91711 601-E1
8900 ADEL 92301 4204-C5
11300 ADEL 92301 4205-A5
LEE CT
6200 CHNO 91710 642-A6
LEE DR
6200 TNP 92277 4890-G7
W LEE DR
3500 SBDO 92405 576-F1
LEE LN
- SBdC - 330-K2
LEE PL
2000 POM 91766 641-B5
E LEE ST
1200 SBDO 92408 607-B6
S LEE WY
400 SBDO 92410 606-A3
LEEBE AV
2400 POM 91768 640-D2
LEEBERT WY
600 SBdC - 516-H3
LEE CREEK DR
500 DBAR 91765 640-D7
LEEDOM DR
7100 HIGH 92346 578-C5
N LEEDS AV
1700 ONT 91764 602-F4
LEEDS RD
700 SBdC 92277 4750-F7
1300 SBdC 92277 4820-F1
LEGACY PL
- RCUC 91730 573-E6
LEGATO CT
- POM 91766 640-D4
LEHIGH AV
9700 MTCL 91763 601-E6
10300 MTCL 91763 641-E1
LEHIGH CT
12900 VCTV 92392 4385-E4
LEHIGH DR
600 CLAR 91711 601-C5
LEICESTER CT
3600 CLAR 91711 571-F5
W LEISKE DR
1100 RLTO 92376 575-E5
LEITH WY
12900 YCPA 92399 650-A5
LEJEUNE CIR
- TNP 92278 4751-J4
LELA DR
23000 DBAR 91765 640-B6
N LELAND NORTON WY
100 SBDO 92408 607-D1
S LELAND NORTON WY
100 SBDO 92408 607-D1
LEMERT ST
18500 HESP 92345 4477-A2
LEMMERICH CT
8000 FONT 92336 604-A1
LEMMING ST
42500 SBdC 92365 (3683-E4
See Page 3592)
LEMON AV
- FONT 92337 644-H2
6300 RCUC 91737 573-A4
8300 RCUC 91701 572-E4
9500 RCUC 91737 572-H4
9900 FONT 92335 604-G6
9900 SBdC 92335 604-G6
N LEMON AV
100 ONT 91761 642-C1
100 ONT 91764 602-C7
100 ONT 91764 642-C1
S LEMON AV
100 ONT 91761 642-C1

LEMON CT
7700 FONT 92336 574-G7
7900 FONT 92336 604-G1
9100 FONT 92335 604-G4
LEMON DR
- SBdC 92256 616-E2
LEMON PL
- ONT 91761 642-B5
12300 CHNO 91710 642-B5
S LEMON PL
2600 ONT 91761 642-C6
LEMON ST
500 RDL 92374 608-D7
500 RDL 92374 648-D1
7400 FONT 92336 574-G7
7800 FONT 92336 604-G1
9000 FONT 92335 604-G4
16500 HESP 92345 4476-E3
18200 HESP 92345 4477-A3
20200 SBdC 92308 4477-B3
28600 HIGH 92346 578-B6
E LEMON ST
400 CLTN 92324 606-E4
LEMON GROVE DR
8400 RCUC 91730 602-F2
N LEMON GROVE DR
1400 UPL 91786 571-G7
LEMON HEIGHTS DR
- UPL 91784 571-H6
LEMONT WY
900 SBdC - 4737-J6
LEMON TREE CIR
1300 UPL 91786 571-J7
LEMONWOOD AV
400 RDL 92374 608-B5
4000 RLTO 92377 544-J6
4000 RLTO 92377 545-A6
LEMONWOOD CT
11600 FONT 92337 644-B3
LEMONWOOD DR
13200 CHLS 91709 681-A3
E LEMONWOOD DR
100 UPL 91786 601-H1
1300 UPL 91786 571-J7
W LEMONWOOD DR
1300 UPL 91786 571-G7
1300 UPL 91786 601-H1
LEMONWOOD PL
9100 RCUC 91730 572-G7
LEMOORE ST
5200 YUCA 92284 4887-G4
N LENA DR
100 SBDO 92408 607-A1
200 SBdC 92408 607-A1
S LENA RD
100 SBDO 92408 607-A2
LENCA RD
15400 APLV 92307 4297-B5
LENNOX AV
3700 SBdC 92284 4818-B7
3700 SBdC 92284 4888-B1
6800 YUCA 92284 4958-C1
LENNOX CT
6900 YUCA 92284 4958-C1
LENNOX ST
2400 POM 91767 601-B4
10300 YCPA 92399 610-B7
11600 YCPA 92399 650-B2
S LENORE AV
200 SBDO 92410 606-E2
LENORE LN
700 POM 91767 601-B5
LENWOOD RD
2200 BARS 92311 (3759-A6
See Page 3758)
2800 BARS 92311 3758-J1
3200 BARS 92311 3678-F5
15300 SBdC 92311 3678-F5
25700 BARS 92311 (3848-J1
See Page 3758)
25900 BARS 92311 (3849-A1
See Page 3758)
25900 SBdC 92311 (3848-J1
See Page 3758)
25900 SBdC 92311 (3849-A1
See Page 3758)
31300 SBdC 92311 (3759-A6
See Page 3758)
36100 SBdC 92311 3588-F7
36600 SBdC 92347 3588-F5
W LENWOOD SQ
1200 UPL 91786 601-G2
LEONA RD
36400 BARS 92311 3590-A7
36400 SBdC 92311 3590-A7
LEONAN DR
13100 SBdC - (4391-B3
See Page 4300)
LEONARD LN
100 SBdC - 4742-F7
200 SBdC - 4812-F2
LEOPARD SPRINGS RD
- SBdC 92256 4956-C7
LE PANTO RD
9700 SBdC 92392 4474-F3
LE PARC BLVD
13000 CHLS 91709 641-A7
13000 CHLS 91709 681-A1
LEPRECHAUN CT
30200 SBdC - 518-F7

LEPRECHAUN DR
30200 SBdC - 518-F7
LERNER LN
16900 FONT 92335 604-J2
N LEROY CT
3800 SBDO 92404 546-J7
N LEROY ST
2200 SBDO 92404 576-J1
3600 SBDO 92404 546-J5
LESINA PL
7200 RCUC 91701 573-E6
LESLIE CT
1700 POM 91767 601-B6
W LESLIE CT
1000 CLTN 92324 606-B4
LESLIE LN
59500 SBdC 92284 4818-F2
61400 SBdC 92252 4749-A3
LESLIE ST
7900 HIGH 92346 577-E7
7900 SBDO 92346 577-E7
LESSING AV
14100 SBdC 92371 4383-J2
14700 SBdC 92371 (4293-J7
See Page 4292)
14900 ADEL 92371 (4293-H2
See Page 4292)
14900 SBdC 92301 (4293-J7
See Page 4292)
16600 ADEL 92371 (4293-H2
See Page 4292)
17200 ADEL 92371 (4203-H7
See Page 4112)
18500 SBdC 92301 (4203-H2
See Page 4112)
25100 SBdC 92301 368-J2
LESSING RD
18000 SBdC 92301 (4203-G6
See Page 4112)
LESTER AV
11700 CHNO 91710 641-G5
LESTER CT
12100 CHNO 91710 641-G5
LESTER PL
11800 CHNO 91710 641-G4
W LETA DR
2300 SBDO 92407 546-A3
LETICIA ST
3700 CHNO 91710 681-C1
LETICIA WY
3600 CHNO 91710 681-C2
LETINI DR
11800 RCUC 91701 573-F5
LEUCITE AV
7400 RCUC 91730 572-J7
7700 RCUC 91730 602-J1
LEUZINGER DR
3900 SBdC 92407 546-F6
3900 SBDO 92407 546-F6
LEVAN DR
23000 SBdC 92308 4478-D4
LEVANTO CT
15100 CHLS 91709 681-C5
LEVEE DR
1300 MohC - 3620-D4
LEVEE WY
1200 MohC - 3620-C3
LEWIS
1900 NDLS 92363 3620-B4
LEWIS AV
12300 CHNO 91710 641-F6
LEWIS CT
400 CLAR 91711 601-D4
13500 FONT 92336 603-J1
LEWIS LN
9600 SBdC 92308 4477-E5
LEWIS ST
18400 RLTO 92377 575-D3
18400 SBdC 92377 575-D3
N LEWIS ST
500 POM 91768 640-G1
2300 RLTO 92377 575-D3
W LEWIS ST
1000 RLTO 92377 575-E3
W LEWIS WY
2400 SBDO 92410 606-A3
LEWIS RANCH RD
- SBdC - (3935-J7
See Page 3934)
LEXINGTON AV
3500 SBdC 92284 4818-C7
3700 SBdC 92284 4888-C1
4200 SBdC 91710 641-D4
E LEXINGTON AV
100 POM 91766 640-J5
100 POM 91766 641-A4
W LEXINGTON AV
100 POM 91766 640-H5
LEXINGTON CT
4900 CHNO 91710 641-F4
13600 FONT 92336 574-A7
LEXINGTON LN
800 RDL 92374 648-F3
LEXINGTON PL
6900 RCUC 91701 572-J6
S LEXINGTON PL
2600 ONT 91761 642-J6
LEXINGTON ST
- UPL 91784 572-B4
3900 SBdC 91710 641-D4

LEXINGTON ST
23800 SBdC 92307 4208-E3
LEXINGTON WY
3300 SBDO 92407 546-A5
LEXUS LN
- SBdC 92335 604-A2
LEYDEN AV
- CHNO 91710 682-B3
LEYDEN LN
600 CLAR 91711 601-C3
LEYLAND DR
700 DBAR 91765 680-D1
LIANA CT
11900 YCPA 92399 649-B3
LIANA ST
35900 YCPA 92399 610-C4
LIBERATION PL
- RCUC 91730 573-E2
LIBERTY N
- RCUC 91737 572-J4
LIBERTY CT
- RCUC 91737 572-J4
2500 SBDO 92408 646-H1
LIBERTY LN
- SBdC - 4741-E6
E LIBERTY PKWY
7500 FONT 92336 574-C6
7700 FONT 92336 604-B1
W LIBERTY PKWY
7500 FONT 92336 573-J7
7500 FONT 92336 574-A7
9400 FONT 92336 603-J1
13500 FONT 92336 604-A1
LIBERTY RD
33700 YCPA 92399 649-G5
LIBERTY ST
4800 CHNO 91710 641-F5
9800 RCUC 91737 572-J4
10300 RCUC 91737 573-A4
LIBERTY WY
14100 VCTV 92392 4385-H4
LIDIA CT
4400 CHNO 91710 681-E1
LIDO CIR
- VCTV 92392 4386-F5
LIDO ST
- RDL 92374 608-F7
S LIDO WY
- UPL 91786 601-H4
LIFTMASTER CT
- SBDO 92409 577-F7
LIGHTFOOT WY
31300 SBdC - 518-J7
LIGHTHOUSE CT
13600 FONT 92336 574-A7
LIGHTHOUSE LN
14400 SBdC - (3935-H3
See Page 3934)
LIGHTNING ST
18200 VCTV 92394 4205-F5
LIGNUM VITAE DR
29900 SBdC - 4738-E6
LIGURE
100 BREA 92823 710-D6
LILAC AV
6300 SBdC 92377 575-F4
11200 SBdC 92316 645-G2
N LILAC AV
100 RLTO 92376 605-G1
500 RLTO 92376 575-F6
1700 SBdC 92376 575-F5
2000 RLTO 92377 575-F5
S LILAC AV
100 RLTO 92376 605-G2
1300 RLTO 92316 605-G5
2200 RLTO 92316 645-G1
2700 SBdC 92316 645-G1
LILAC CT
- SBDO 92354 607-C6
200 RDL 92373 648-C1
6400 RivC 92880 683-D6
12400 RCUC 91739 573-G5
LILAC DR
9400 SBdC 92339 611-G3
27800 SBdC - 517-J4
36200 YCPA 92399 650-D6
LILAC LN
100 BREA 92823 710-C5
22400 SBdC - 516-E2
35500 YCPA 92399 650-B6
55800 SBdC 92285 4667-F7
LILAC PL
900 POM 91768 640-E1
LILAC RD
3000 SBdC 92371 4562-H1
8700 SBdC 92345 4565-A1
9300 SBdC 92345 4475-A5
10500 SBdC 92345 4474-J4
11300 SBdC 92392 4474-J2
11700 VCTV 92392 4384-J5
11700 SBdC 92392 4474-J1
14500 ADEL 92301 4384-J1
14500 ADEL 92301 4294-J2
17700 ADEL 92301 4204-J5
LILAC ST
- FONT 92337 645-A1
5200 SBDO 92407 546-A5
10600 LMLN 92354 607-C7
13300 CHNO 91710 681-E1
13300 VCTV 92392 4475-F3

STREET
Block City ZIP Pg-Grid

LILAC ST
14500 HESP 92345 4475-J2
14700 HESP 92345 4476-A2
18500 HESP 92345 4477-A2
LILAC WY
200 SBdC - 518-D1
N LILAC WY
1500 UPL 91786 572-A7
LIL DIRT RD
10200 SBdC 92372 4472-B5
LILFORD AV
8700 HESP 92345 4567-A1
8800 HESP 92345 4477-A7
LILLEY RD
8600 SBdC 92252 4959-D6
LILLIAN DR
200 BARS 92311 3679-J4
LILLIAN LN
7300 HIGH 92346 577-G6
N LILLIAN LN
1500 SBDO 92346 577-G4
LILLIAN WY
14900 SBdC 92307 4298-J4
LILLYHILL DR
1000 NDLS 92363 3620-A7
LILY AV
700 BARS 92311 3679-D4
2200 UPL 91784 571-H4
LILY CT
7500 FONT 92336 574-D7
12300 RCUC 91739 573-G5
N LILY DR
3500 RLTO 92377 545-B7
LILY PL
13500 CHNO 91710 681-E2
LIMA DR
- RCUC 91739 573-J6
LIMA RD
10300 SBdC - 4480-D2
LIME AV
7300 FONT 92336 574-F7
7700 FONT 92336 604-F1
7900 SBdC 92336 604-F1
8100 SBdC 92335 604-F2
9700 FONT 92335 604-F6
LIME CT
8900 SBdC 92335 604-F3
9600 FONT 92335 604-F5
LIME PL
12200 CHNO 91710 642-A5
LIME ST
500 RDL 92374 608-D7
500 RDL 92374 648-D1
2100 SBdC 92372 4562-E2
5500 SBdC 92371 4563-E1
13300 HESP 92345 4565-F1
13600 SBdC 92345 4565-F1
14900 HESP 92345 4566-A1
LIMEKLIN DR
37200 YCPA 92399 650-F5
LIME ORCHARD LN
11400 FONT 92337 644-G3
LIMESTONE CIR
13500 VCTV 92392 4385-G6
LIMESTONE CT
15300 CHLS 91709 680-J6
LIMESTONE RD
2700 CLAR 91711 571-D5
LIMONITE AV
10200 RivC 91752 683-E5
LINARO RD
11200 RCUC 91730 573-D7
LINBERGH AV
6700 FONT 92336 574-E5
LINCOLN AV
- RCUC 91730 603-D5
800 POM 91767 601-B7
4800 CHNO 91710 641-F7
7300 HESP 92345 4566-A3
9700 HESP 92345 4476-A2
E LINCOLN AV
300 POM 91767 601-A7
S LINCOLN AV
700 SBDO 92408 606-J3
W LINCOLN AV
1700 SBDO 92411 576-B4
LINCOLN CT
5500 SBDO 92407 546-F4
LINCOLN DR
33800 YCPA 92399 649-G3
N LINCOLN DR
1800 SBDO 92405 576-F2
LINCOLN RD
8500 SBdC - 4481-G1
11300 SBdC - (4391-G3
See Page 4300)
13600 SBdC - (4301-F3
See Page 4300)
LINCOLN ST
16600 VCTV 92392 4296-E5
N LINCOLN ST
- RDL 92374 608-F7
S LINCOLN ST
- RDL 92374 608-F7
100 RDL 92374 648-F1
1100 CLTN 92324 646-D1
E LINCOLN LOOP RD
7300 FONT 92336 574-B7
7800 FONT 92336 604-B1

W LINCOLN LOOP RD
7300 FONT 92336 574-B7
14000 FONT 92336 604-B1
LINCROFT
- SBdC 92345 (4655-A3
See Page 4654)
LINCROFT RD
- SBdC 92345 (4655-A4
See Page 4654)
LIND AV
10500 LMLN 92354 607-C7
LINDA AV
1200 SBdC 92359 609-B5
W LINDA CT
100 CLTN 92324 646-C4
LINDA LN
700 BARS 92311 3679-F3
2400 SBdC 91784 572-A3
35600 YCPA 92399 650-B2
40200 BBLK - 4811-D2
LINDA PL
500 RDL 92373 648-A1
LINDA ST
13800 VCTV 92392 4385-G4
S LINDA WY
- UPL 91786 601-J4
LINDA LADERA
31900 YCPA 92399 649-B3
LINDA LEE DR
4200 SBdC 92284 4888-D2
4700 YUCA 92284 4888-D5
LINDA MIRADA RD
- YUCA 92284 4888-G4
LINDA VISTA CT
5700 RCUC 91739 573-G3
LINDA VISTA RD
27300 SBdC 92311 (3759-D1
See Page 3758)
LINDA VISTA ST
1500 RDL 92373 647-J3
1500 RDL 92373 648-A3
LINDBERGH LN
57700 YUCA 92284 4958-A1
LINDEN AV
9300 SBdC 92316 605-D5
9300 RLTO 92316 605-D5
10700 SBdC 92316 645-D3
N LINDEN AV
100 RLTO 92376 605-D2
500 RLTO 92376 575-D4
2000 RLTO 92377 575-D2
2300 SBdC 92377 575-D3
S LINDEN AV
100 RLTO 92376 605-D3
500 RLTO 92316 605-D3
W LINDEN CT
800 UPL 91786 602-A2
LINDEN LN
7200 RCUC 91784 572-F6
15400 CHLS 91709 681-D6
29500 SBdC - 4738-D7
LINDEN RD
20900 SBdC 92347 (3587-E5
See Page 3586)
LINDEN ST
11700 SBdC 92316 645-D3
12100 YCPA 92399 649-G3
14300 HESP 92345 4475-J4
15300 HESP 92345 4476-B4
N LINDEN ST
200 POM 91767 641-A1
S LINDEN ST
100 POM 91766 641-A2
W LINDEN ST
800 ONT 91762 642-A3
LINDEN WY
21800 SBdC - 516-C2
LINDENWOOD DR
700 CLAR 91711 571-E7
LINDERO AV
9000 MTCL 91763 601-F4
LINDERO RD
100 SBdC 92372 4382-A7
2800 SBdC 92371 4382-J7
3700 SBdC 92371 4383-A7
7700 SBdC 92371 4384-A7
8000 SBdC 92392 4384-E6
10500 VCTV 92392 4384-E6
11300 VCTV 92392 4385-A6
17600 VCTV 92392 4386-H6
LINDERO ST
300 SBdC 92372 4472-A6
2500 SBdC 92371 4472-F6
3900 SBdC 92371 4473-A6
9500 SBdC 92371 4474-F6
15300 VCTV 92392 4386-B6
W LINDE VISTA DR
2700 RLTO 92377 545-A7
2800 RLTO 92377 544-J7
LINDSAY CT
5000 CHNO 91710 681-G4
LINDSAY RD
20800 SBdC 92308 4567-G1
LINDSAY ST
3500 RivC 92509 644-B6
18900 HESP 92345 4567-B2
19000 SBdC 92345 4567-B2
LINDSAY PRIVADO DR
2500 ONT 91761 642-J3

LINDSEY DR
15900 CHLS 91709 711-B1
LINE DR
1500 SBdC - 4737-H5
LINK RD
17600 SBdC - (3846-G2
See Page 3756)
LINK WY
- SBdC - 518-A2
LINN RD
55100 SBdC 92285 4667-C6
LINN ST
12800 YCPA 92399 650-B5
LINNET RD
1200 SBdC 92397 4652-E2
LINSON AV
7300 SBdC 92301 (4203-H1
See Page 4112)
LINSON ST
100 SBdC 92301 (4202-A1
See Page 4112)
4100 SBdC 92301 (4203-C1
See Page 4112)
LINTNER RD
600 BBLK - 4811-C2
LINWOOD TER
31200 YCPA 92399 648-J4
31200 YCPA 92399 649-A4
LINX DR
23900 SBdC - 516-H3
LION ST
7000 RCUC 91701 572-H6
7300 RCUC 91730 572-H7
7700 RCUC 91730 602-H1
LIONS MTWY
- CHLS 91709 710-E3
- LACo 92823 710-D2
LIONS CANYON RD
- BREA 92823 710-E2
- CHLS 91709 710-E2
- LACo 92823 710-D2
LIPIAN CT
21200 APLV 92308 4387-H5
LIPIAN RD
21200 APLV 92308 4387-H6
LIPPAZAN CT
13800 VCTV 92394 4295-G7
LIPPIZAN PL
5000 RCUC 91737 573-B1
LISA CIR
- YUCA 92284 4957-H4
LISA CT
500 DBAR 91765 640-E7
LISA LN
1500 RDL 92374 608-F7
2100 SBdC 92252 4819-G3
LISBON DR
57600 YUCA 92284 4958-A6
LISBON RD
22500 SBdC 92308 4478-B3
LISBON ST
- UPL 91784 571-H6
LISCO DR
2200 SBdC 92372 4562-F4
LITA CTE
7800 RCUC 91730 602-F1
LITCHI LN
1100 SBdC 92372 4472-C7
N LITRAS DR
3400 SBDO 92405 576-G1
LITTLE 3RD ST
24400 SBdC 92410 607-A1
LITTLE BEAR CT
20400 APLV 92308 4387-F5
LITTLE BEAR RD
27100 SBdC - 517-G2
LITTLE BEAR CREEK
RD
29500 SBdC - 4738-D7
LITTLE BEAVER RD
20900 APLV 92308 4387-G4
22000 APLV 92308 4388-A4
LITTLE BEAVER ST
15300 VCTV 92392 4386-B5
LITTLE BEND RD
14800 CHLS 91709 681-A5
LITTLE BOW LN
15100 SBdC - (3935-J2
See Page 3934)
LITTLE CANYON LN
- SBdC - 517-D3
LITTLE COYOTE TR
8600 SBdC 92284 4957-A6
LITTLE CREEK CT
14800 CHLS 91709 681-B5
LITTLE DIPPER ST
11000 RivC 91752 683-H5
LITTLE DIRT RD
34500 SBdC 92365 (3684-A4
See Page 3594)
LITTLEFIELD RD
900 SBdC 92252 4749-G7
900 SBdC 92252 4819-G1
LITTLE HORSETHIEF
CANYON RD
- SBdC - (4735-D1
See Page 4654)
- SBdC 92345 (4655-F7
See Page 4654)

LITTLE HORSETHIEF
CANYON RD
13000 SBdC - (4655-C6
See Page 4654)
LITTLE LEAGUE DR
56500 YUCA 92284 4957-G2
N LITTLE LEAGUE DR
6500 SBDO 92407 545-H1
7000 SBDO 92407 515-H7
19400 SBdC 92407 545-G2
W LITTLE LEAGUE DR
3200 SBDO 92407 545-H2
LITTLE MORONGO RD
7500 SBdC - 4956-E5
7600 SBdC 92256 4956-F7
LITTLE MORONGO
CANYON RD
- YUCA 92284 4957-E7
LITTLE MOUNTAIN DR
3400 SBDO 92405 576-D1
3400 SBDO 92407 546-D7
3400 SBDO 92407 576-D1
N LITTLE MOUNTAIN
DR
2900 SBDO 92405 576-D1
3700 SBDO 92407 546-D7
LITTLE OAK PL
200 SBdC - 516-D1
LITTLE OAK WY
2900 CHLS 91709 681-A6
LITTLE PONDEROSA LN
1600 SBdC - 4738-B5
LITTLE QUAIL AV
1400 DBAR 91765 680-C3
LITTLER RD
4100 SBdC 92371 4473-B5
LITTLE ROCK
900 CLAR 91711 571-F4
LITTLE ROCK AV
6200 SBdC - 4843-H3
LITTLE ROCK RD
600 SBdC - 514-A4
LITTLE TEEPEE RD
23300 SBdC 92307 4298-G3
LITTLE TIPPECANOE
AV
8100 SBdC 92410 607-B1
LITTLE ZION MANOR
DR
1800 SBDO 92411 576-C4
W LITTON AV
100 CLTN 92313 646-B3
100 CLTN 92324 646-B3
100 GTER 92313 646-B3
200 SBdC 92324 646-B3
LIVE OAK AV
7300 FONT 92336 574-D7
8100 SBdC 92335 604-D2
10300 SBdC 92337 604-D7
10500 FONT 92337 604-D7
10500 FONT 92337 644-D2
13700 CHNO 91710 682-B2
N LIVE OAK AV
3200 RLTO 92377 575-A1
3400 RLTO 92377 545-A7
LIVE OAK CT
1300 RDL 92374 608-B5
13800 CHNO 91710 682-B2
17500 HESP 92345 4476-H5
LIVE OAK DR
400 LACo 91750 571-A7
400 RivC 91752 683-F5
9400 RCUC 91730 602-H5
30200 SBdC - 548-F1
30300 SBdC - 518-F7
49200 SBdC 92256 615-G7
LIVE OAK LN
10900 ADEL 92301 4294-J7
LIVE OAK PL
1100 SBdC 92314 4742-E4
LIVE OAK RD
15500 CHLS 91709 681-A7
28600 HIGH 92346 578-B3
LIVE OAK ST
13000 HESP 92345 4475-E5
14600 HESP 92345 4476-A5
18100 HESP 92345 4477-A6
37500 SBdC - 4950-G1
LIVE OAK WY
1800 UPL 91784 572-A5
LIVE OAK CANYON RD
- CLAR 91711 571-A6
1100 RivC 92373 648-E7
1100 RDL 92373 648-E7
4100 LACo 91750 571-A6
31100 RDL 92373 649-A7
31700 YCPA 92373 649-A7
E LIVE OAK CREEK WY
3700 ONT 91761 643-C5
LIVE OAK CUTOFF
- LACo 91711 571-A4
- LACo 91750 571-A4
LIVERMORE ST
- APLV 92307 4208-A4
20900 APLV 92307 4207-F4
LIVERY RD
- SBdC 92284 4748-H4
LIVING ROCK CT
- CHLS 91709 711-H2

LIVINGSTON CT
- CLAR 91711 571-E6
LIVINGSTON RD
51000 SBdC 92256 616-C3
LIVINGSTON ST
- SBdC - 348-K11
LIVORNO CT
3600 CHLS 91709 681-C5
LLANADA AV
16000 VCTV 92394 4296-A3
LLANO CT
15900 VCTV 92394 4296-C4
LLANO LN
15900 VCTV 92394 4296-C4
LLANO RD
13200 SBdC 92392 4385-J4
LLANTO RD
16900 APLV 92307 4298-B1
17600 APLV 92307 4208-B6
LO LN
25300 SBdC - 517-C3
LOBELIA AV
1300 UPL 91784 571-J3
LOBELIA DR
14700 CHLS 91709 681-C4
LOBO LN
5500 YUCA 92284 4888-B5
LOBO RD
10500 SBdC 92256 616-A5
LOBO PASS RD
8500 SBdC 92252 4959-E5
LOBOS AV
7500 HESP 92345 4567-A3
LOCARNO CT
900 SBdC - 517-A3
LOCARNO DR
- SBdC 92397 4652-F3
LOCHINVAR CT
7500 HIGH 92346 578-D6
LOCHINVAR RD
29300 HIGH 92346 578-D6
LOCH LEVEN RD
200 SBdC - 517-J5
200 SBdC - 518-A2
LOCH LOMOND CT
14900 VCTV 92394 4295-J7
LOCHMERE RD
- SBdC - (3763-B3
See Page 3762)
LOCKE PL
- RCUC 91730 573-E1
LOCKHART RD
13700 SBdC - 348-L5
33300 SBdC 92347 349-A7
38100 SBdC 92347 348-L7
LOCKHAVEN AV
7500 RCUC 91730 573-A7
LOCKHAVEN CT
7700 RCUC 91730 573-A7
7700 RCUC 91730 603-A1
LOCK HAVEN WY
1800 CLAR 91711 571-A7
LOCKWOOD DR
34700 YCPA 92399 649-J2
LOCKWOOD LN
- POM 91766 640-F7
LOCKWOOD RD
- SBdC - (4882-C5
See Page 4813)
E LOCUST
2000 SBDO 92404 577-D2
LOCUST AV
6500 RCUC 91739 573-G4
7100 HESP 92345 4566-B5
7300 FONT 92336 575-C7
7300 RLTO 92336 575-C7
7600 SBdC 92336 575-C7
7800 SBdC 92336 605-C1
8000 FONT 92336 605-C1
8100 FONT 92335 605-C3
8100 SBdC 92335 605-C1
8800 SBdC - 4481-E2
9700 HESP 92345 4476-A3
9700 SBdC 92316 605-C6
10700 SBdC 92316 645-C3
10800 SBdC - (4391-E3
See Page 4300)
11300 FONT 92337 645-C3
11700 HESP 92345 4386-A7
12100 SBdC 92392 4384-F7
12100 VCTV 92345 4386-A7
12100 VCTV 92392 4386-A5
13700 SBdC - (4301-D6
See Page 4300)
N LOCUST AV
1200 RLTO 92376 575-C4
2000 RLTO 92377 575-C2
3300 RLTO 92377 545-C7
E LOCUST CT
2300 ONT 91761 642-H3
LOCUST LN
8100 SBdC 92308 4567-D2
9700 SBdC 92308 4477-D5
11400 APLV 92308 4477-D1
11500 APLV 92308 4387-C7
LOCUST RD
300 SBdC 92372 4472-A4
LOCUST ST
- SBdC 92314 4742-J7

LOCUST ST
- SBdC 92314 (4743-A7
See Page 4662)
3800 SBdC 91710 641-G3
5400 CHNO 91710 641-G3
13800 SBdC 93562 2055-B6
36900 SBdC 92347 (3587-F7
See Page 3586)
E LOCUST ST
100 ONT 91761 642-C3
N LOCUST ST
200 POM 91767 640-J1
S LOCUST ST
100 POM 91766 640-J2
W LOCUST ST
100 ONT 91761 642-B3
100 ONT 91762 642-A3
1100 ONT 91762 641-J3
LODEMA RD
19300 APLV 92307 4297-C2
LODGE LN
600 SBdC - 517-D3
LODGE RD
39300 SBdC - 4741-B5
LODGEPOLE CT
14600 CHLS 91709 680-J4
LODGEPOLE PL
100 BBLK - 4742-A7
LODGEPOLE RD
5500 SBdC 92397 4652-E3
LODGE POLE RD
24000 DBAR 91765 680-D4
LODI ST
56800 SBdC 92284 4747-G6
LOFTON ST
15000 VCTV 92394 4296-A2
S LOFTY VIEW DR
200 SBdC 92314 4742-G6
LOG LN
300 SBdC - 516-F2
1100 SBdC 92314 4742-E4
LOGAN AV
6700 FONT 92336 574-E5
LOGAN ST
2200 POM 91767 601-B5
LOGANBERRY AV
- CHNO 91710 642-B7
S LOGGERS LN
2200 ONT 91762 641-J5
LOGOO ST
15300 SBdC - (4301-D3
See Page 4300)
LOGWOOD DR
26600 LACo 92397 4652-A1
LOLITA AV
900 RDL 92373 648-B3
LOLITA CT
3800 CHNO 91710 681-D1
N LOMA AV
2900 SBDO 92404 577-C2
LOMA DR
2600 SBdC - 519-A7
LOMA PL
- SBdC 91763 601-G3
- SBdC 91786 601-G3
N LOMA PL
- SBdC 91786 601-G3
- UPL 91786 601-G3
LOMA ST
18300 HESP 92345 4567-A3
LOMA ALTA
32900 SBdC - 519-D2
LOMA ALTA LN
- SBdC 92256 4956-G7
9400 SBdC 92256 616-G2
LOMA LINDA DR
11300 LMLN 92354 647-D2
LOMA LINDA LN
21700 SBdC 92301 (4113-C4
See Page 4112)
W LOMA ROJA DR
100 CLTN 92324 646-C3
LOMAS CT
4900 RCUC 91737 572-G1
8000 FONT 92336 604-A1
N LOMA SOLA AV
1100 UPL 91786 602-E1
LOMA SOLA CT
1400 UPL 91786 602-E1
E LOMAS PRIVADAS DR
1700 SBDO 92404 547-C6
LOMAS VERDES ST
25500 LMLN 92354 607-D7
25700 SBdC 92373 607-D7
25800 LMLN 92373 607-E7
LOMA VERDE CT
12300 VCTV 92392 4385-D6
LOMA VERDE DR
12500 VCTV 92392 4385-D6
W LOMA VERDE DR
100 CLTN 92324 646-C3
LOMA VISTA AV
6700 HESP 92345 4566-B5
LOMA VISTA CT
14900 HESP 92345 4566-A6
17000 FONT 92337 644-J3
17000 FONT 92337 645-A2
LOMA VISTA DR
11300 LMLN 92354 647-B2

W LOMA VISTA DR
2300 RLTO 92377 545-A7
2800 RLTO 92377 544-J7
LOMA VISTA RD
8700 SBdC 92308 4479-B3
LOMA VISTA ST
12600 YCPA 92399 649-D4
LOMBARD DR
800 RDL 92374 608-C6
LOMBARD LN
11800 YCPA 92399 649-J2
LOMBARD ST
200 POM 91768 640-D2
LOMBARDY AV
7600 FONT 92336 575-B7
9500 FONT 92335 605-B5
9600 SBdC 92335 605-B5
9700 SBdC 92316 605-B5
37000 SBdC 92311 3589-J6
LOMBARDY CT
4300 CHNO 91710 641-E5
7300 FONT 92336 575-B6
8600 FONT 92335 605-B2
LOMBARDY DR
- SBdC - 516-G2
LOMBARDY LN
- SBdC 92316 605-B6
LOMBARDY ST
3900 SBdC 91710 641-D5
4000 CHNO 91710 641-E5
LOMELLO WY
11400 RCUC 91701 573-D5
LOMITA CT
1400 SBDO 92405 576-E2
9600 RCUC 91701 572-J6
LOMITA DR
- FONT 92336 544-H6
8400 RCUC 91701 572-F6
9900 RCUC 91701 573-A6
E LOMITA DR
200 RLTO 92376 575-H4
LOMITA LN
4900 YUCA 92284 4887-H4
E LOMITA PL
2700 SBDO 92346 577-F2
LOMITA RD
- SBdC 92284 4888-H4
1200 SBDO 92405 576-E2
7100 SBdC 92252 4958-H2
LOMPOC AV
36800 SBdC 92311 3589-H7
LOMPOC RD
12800 APLV 92308 4387-C4
LONDON AV
5200 RCUC 91737 572-J1
6700 RCUC 91701 572-J5
7300 RCUC 91730 572-J7
7900 RCUC 91730 602-J1
W LONDON LN
1000 SBdC 92314 4742-B7
LONDON WY
9400 RCUC 91730 603-A5
LONDONDERRY CT
7000 RCUC 91701 573-F5
LONE ACRES
- RCUC 91737 (543-C7
See Page 513)
- RCUC 91737 573-C1
LONE BUTTE CT
13300 VCTV 92394 4295-F4
LONE EAGLE CT
22900 APLV 92308 4388-C4
LONE EAGLE RD
20800 APLV 92308 4387-H4
22100 APLV 92308 4388-A5
LONE EAGLE ST
15300 VCTV 92392 4386-B5
LONE PEAK DR
11900 RCUC 91737 573-E4
11900 RCUC 91739 573-E4
LONE PINE DR
5400 FONT 92336 574-C2
32800 SBdC - 519-D7
LONE PINE LN
600 SBdC - 519-F2
11800 SBdC 92399 651-F2
LONE PINE CANYON RD
4800 SBdC - 4652-F3
5100 SBdC 92397 4652-E2
5200 SBdC - 4653-A5
6100 SBdC - (4733-F1
See Page 4653)
6800 SBdC - 4734-A2
7100 SBdC - 4654-A7
LONE RANGER TR
17800 CHLS 91709 712-A5
LONE RIDGE RD
- POM 91766 640-H6
LONESOME DOVE CT
14300 HESP 92345 4565-J1
LONE STAR RD
27400 SBdC - (3937-F3
See Page 3936)
LONE TREE CT
11500 FONT 92337 644-H3
LONE TREE LN
- SBdC 92285 4748-A2
56900 SBdC 92285 4747-H2
LONETREE RD
1800 SBdC - 4742-J3

LONE WILLOW SPRING
RD
77100 SBdC - 329-C5
LONG LN
3600 SBdC 92371 4562-J2
LONGACRE AV
16600 CHLS 91709 711-J2
LONG BEACH AV
500 SBdC - 516-D2
W LONG BEACH DR
700 CLTN 92324 606-B4
LONGBOW CT
13300 VCTV 92392 4385-F5
LONGFELLOW AV
- APLV 92307 (4117-H6
See Page 4116)
18900 APLV 92307 4207-J1
LONGHORN LN
6600 CHLS 91709 712-B6
14900 FONT 92336 574-D1
E LONGHORN ST
2800 ONT 91761 643-A7
LONGSTREET LN
- FONT 92336 574-A7
LONGVIEW AV
2800 SBdC 92284 4817-G5
LONGVIEW DR
500 SBdC - 517-G3
900 DBAR 91765 680-E2
LONG VIEW DR
14000 FONT 92337 644-B4
LONGVIEW RD
1100 SBdC 92277 4751-B7
1400 SBdC 92277 4821-B1
9800 VCTV 92392 4384-F3
LONGWOOD AV
1600 CLAR 91711 601-E1
LOOKING GLASS DR
500 DBAR 91765 640-E5
LOOKING GLASS WY
1900 UPL 91784 571-H5
LOOKOUT CIR
- CHLS 91709 681-A1
10900 SBdC 92399 610-J6
LOOKOUT CT
1300 UPL 91784 571-H3
LOOKOUT DR
- SBdC - 517-E2
800 BARS 92311 3679-H4
1600 SBdC - 4737-G4
2300 SBdC - 519-D6
E LOOKOUT DR
300 SBdC 92314 4742-D6
LOOKOUT LN
300 SBdC - 516-C1
LOOKOUT PT
2500 NRCO 92860 712-J6
LOOKOUT RD
- APLV 92307 4296-G5
4400 SBdC 92285 4667-B2
8800 SBdC - 4480-J5
LOOKOUT RDG
200 SBdC - 516-G2
LOOKOUT TR
12900 SBdC 92345 (4655-E1
See Page 4654)
LOOKOUT WY
1300 SBdC - 4737-H5
N LOOKOUT MOUNTAIN
RD
1000 SBdC 92314 4742-B5
LOOP DR
29500 SBdC - 4738-D7
LOPEZ AV
6700 RivC 92509 645-B6
LORAINE AV
12300 CHNO 91710 641-E6
LORANNE AV
700 POM 91767 641-B1
800 POM 91767 601-B7
N LORANNE AV
100 POM 91767 641-B1
LORDS RD
17500 SBdC - (3846-G5
See Page 3756)
LORDS WY
700 SBdC - 518-A3
LORELLI DR
29500 SBdC 92311 3589-H7
LORENA AV
6300 RivC 91752 683-H6
LORENE CT
16900 VCTV 92392 4296-F7
LORENE DR
15700 VCTV 92392 4296-C7
15900 VCTV 92392 4386-C1
LORENE PL
17000 VCTV 92392 4296-F7
17000 VCTV 92392 4386-F1
LORENO DR
- RCUC 91701 573-E6
S LORETTA AV
100 SBDO 92376 605-J2
N LORETTA ST
500 SBDO 92376 575-J7
S LORETTA ST
200 SBDO 92376 606-A3
LORETTA WY
200 CALI 92320 650-B7

LORETTO CT
100 CLAR 91711 571-D7
LORI CT
1500 RDL 92374 608-F7
1500 RDL 92374 648-F1
LORI LN
3900 SBdC 92277 4821-A7
LORIE CT
8600 SBdC 92371 4563-E2
LORI LISA DR
- SBdC 92277 4824-J2
- SBdC 92277 (4825-A2
See Page 4824)
LORING RD
- SBdC 92365 (3683-E5
See Page 3592)
LORITA ST
4000 RivC 92509 644-B7
LORO VERDE AV
10700 LMLN 92354 607-D7
LORRAINE DR
1200 UPL 91784 571-J4
N LORRAINE DR
4000 SBDO 92407 546-H6
4000 SBdC 92407 546-H6
W LORRAINE PL
500 RLTO 92376 605-D1
LORRAINE RD
57700 SBdC 92285 4667-J7
LORRCE
29600 SBdC 92311 3589-J7
LOS ALTOS CT
5700 RCUC 91739 573-G3
LOS ALTOS DR
600 RDL 92373 648-G4
10100 SBdC 92345 4475-C5
LOS ANGELES AV
100 SBdC - 4742-E7
200 SBdC - 4812-F2
LOS ANGELES CITY W
& P RD
800 SBdC 92371 4292-B5
3300 SBdC 92371 (4293-A4
See Page 4292)
LOS BANOS AV
9200 SBdC 92345 4475-B4
9200 HESP 92345 4475-B5
LOS CEDROS
13000 RCUC 91739 573-H5
LOS CEDROS AV
16900 FONT 92336 574-F5
17100 FONT 92336 575-A5
LOS CEDROS RD
16300 VCTV 92394 4295-J3
LOS COYOTES DR
- POM 91766 640-D4
58600 YUCA 92284 4888-C5
LOS COYOTES WY
900 SBdC 92285 4747-H3
LOS ENCINOS AV
- SBdC - (4390-E7
See Page 4300)
LOS FELIS DR
- POM 91766 640-E4
LOS FELIZ DR
6700 HIGH 92346 577-F4
N LOS FELIZ DR
2800 SBDO 92346 577-F2
LOS FLORES DR
25300 SBdC 92404 577-C1
E LOS FLORES DR
1300 SBDO 92404 577-B1
1500 SBdC 92404 577-C1
LOS FLORES RD
3500 HESP 92345 4656-D4
5500 SBdC 92345 4656-D4
5800 HESP 92345 4566-D7
5800 SBdC 92345 4566-D7
LOS FLORES ST
2100 POM 91767 601-B5
LOS LAGOS
900 POM 91766 640-G3
LOS NIETOS CT
15100 SBdC 92335 604-E4
LOS NINOS
56400 YUCA 92284 4887-F3
LOS OLIVOS AV
2000 SBdC 92277 4821-B3
4100 SBdC 92277 4891-B2
LOS OSOS WY
6500 RCUC 91701 573-C4
LOS PADRES PL
- POM 91766 640-D4
LOS PADRES RD
18500 APLV 92307 (4206-J4
See Page 4116)
18500 APLV 92307 4207-A4
21100 APLV 92307 4208-A4
22500 SBdC 92307 4208-A4
LOS RANCHITOS RD
2100 CHLS 91709 680-J4
W LOS ROBLES AV
2500 SBDO 92410 606-A4
2700 SBDO 92376 606-A3
LOS ROBLES CT
14100 RCUC 91739 574-B2
W LOS ROBLES CT
2800 SBDO 92376 606-A3
LOS ROBLES CREST
300 RDL 92373 648-E2

LOS SERRANOS BLVD
4100 CHLS 91709 681-E6
LOS SERRANOS RD
4800 CHLS 91709 681-G6
5000 CHNO 91710 681-G6
LOS SERRANOS WY
4100 CHLS 91709 681-E5
LOS SERRANOS
COUNTRY CLUB DR
15600 CHLS 91709 681-F7
15600 CHLS 91709 711-G1
LOST HILLS RD
- APLV 92308 4477-C1
LOST LAKE RD
800 SBdC - 4734-E6
1100 SBdC 92407 4734-E6
LOST TRAIL CT
12600 RCUC 91739 573-G4
LOST TRAIL DR
14600 CHLS 91709 681-B4
LOS VIENTOS RD
5200 CHNO 91710 681-G5
LOTEBUSH LN
1000 BARS 92311 3679-H5
LOTITO CT
24600 SBdC - 517-A4
LOTUS AV
200 RDL 92373 648-D2
33100 YCPA 92399 649-E5
N LOTUS AV
700 ONT 91764 603-B6
LOTUS CT
400 RDL 92373 648-D1
6700 RCUC 91739 573-G5
LOTUS ST
5700 RivC 92509 645-D7
LOTUS WY
57600 YUCA 92284 4888-A6
LOUIS DR
- SBdC 92285 4667-D7
LOUISE DR
37600 SBdC - 4950-G1
LOUISE ST
4900 SBDO 92407 546-G4
15500 VCTV 92392 4296-E5
N LOUISE ST
2700 SBDO 92405 576-G3
W LOUISE ST
800 CLTN 92324 606-B3
LOUISE WY
9700 RCUC 91730 602-J1
LOVATO AV
2000 BARS 92311 3679-G6
E LOVE LN
3300 SBdC 92346 577-G3
3300 SBDO 92346 577-G3
LOVE ST
28900 HIGH 92346 578-C6
LOVEJOY ST
2200 POM 91767 601-B5
LOVELACE CANYON RD
8000 SBdC 92308 (4569-D1
See Page 4568)
8300 SBdC 92308 4479-D7
LOVELAND DR
2100 RivC 92509 645-C5
LOVERS LN
300 SBdC - 516-C3
500 SBdC 92407 516-C3
1200 SBdC - 517-E2
1300 SBdC - 4737-G5
LOVES LN
14800 VCTV 92392 4296-D6
LOVESTA LN
- SBdC - 4737-B7
LOVIA LN
11200 APLV 92308 4477-H1
LOW LN
1600 CHLS 91709 710-G1
LOW CHAPPARAL CT
11400 VCTV 92392 4475-E1
LOW CHAPPARAL DR
11300 VCTV 92392 4475-E1
LOWE AV
56400 SBdC 92284 4747-G5
LOWE DR
700 BBLK - 4810-J2
LOWELL AV
1500 CLAR 91711 601-D1
LOWELL DR
- RCUC 91730 573-E1
E LOWELL ST
2700 ONT 91761 642-J2
2700 ONT 91761 643-A2
W LOWELL ST
1700 RLTO 92377 575-C2
LOWER BOULDER RD
32800 SBdC - 519-D6
LOWER LIVE OAK
CANYON RD
- LACo 91711 571-A6
- LACo 91750 571-A6
LOWER MAY RD
9100 SBdC 92339 611-E2
LOWNES PL
1200 POM 91766 640-G4
LOW RANCH RD
12400 APLV 92308 4387-C5
LOYOLA CT
1900 CLAR 91711 571-E7

STREET Block City ZIP Pg-Grid

LOYOLA CT
10900 RCUC 91701 573-C5
W LOYOLA DR
1500 SBDO 92407 546-C6
LOZANO PL
11600 LMLN 92354 647-D2
LUANE TR
7100 RivC 92324 647-A6
LUBLIN ST
200 POM 91767 601-A3
LUCAS RANCH RD
9300 RCUC 91730 603-A5
LUCAYA CT
10800 APLV 92308 4477-D2
LUCCA DR
- RCUC 91701 573-E5
LUCENA AV
11700 FONT 92337 644-F3
LUCERA CT
- POM 91766 640-D4
LUCERA DR
11600 RCUC 91701 573-E6
LUCERNE CT
12700 RCUC 91739 573-G6
LUCERNE DR
500 SBdC - 4812-B2
500 BBLK - 4812-B2
LUCERNE LN
900 SBdC - 4738-A6
LUCERNE PL
6200 SBdC 92397 4652-B1
LUCERNE RD
8900 SBdC 92308 4478-F6
N LUCERNE WY
100 UPL 91786 602-B3
LUCERNE VALLEY CTO
19400 SBdC - (4210-E1 See Page 4120)
19400 SBdC - 4120-A4
21600 SBdC - (4119-G1 See Page 4118)
23200 SBdC - 369-D2
LUCERNE VISTA
7300 YUCA 92284 4958-A3
LUCERNE VISTA AV
2900 SBdC 92284 4817-J7
3700 SBdC 92284 4887-J1
LUCERO DR
- FONT 92336 574-D5
5600 SBdC 92301 (4113-C4 See Page 4112)
LUCERO ST
12500 VCTV 92392 4385-D6
LUCERO WY
- FONT 92336 574-D5
LUCIENNE ST
1100 POM 91766 641-B4
LUCILLA RD
22500 APLV 92308 4388-B3
23300 SBdC 92308 4388-C3
LUCILLE LN
500 SBdC 92277 4750-F7
1300 SBdC 92277 4820-F2
LUCINDA AV
2000 UPL 91784 572-A5
LUCINDA DR
1400 UPL 91786 602-E2
LUCINDA WY
2100 UPL 91784 572-A4
LUCKIE AV
5400 TNP 92277 4892-G4
LUCRETIA AV
5200 RivC 91752 683-H4
LUCY ST
1500 RDL 92374 608-D4
LUGANO CT
1100 SBdC - 517-A4
LUGANO DR
11300 RCUC 91701 573-D6
LUGO AV
4100 CHLS 91709 681-E6
N LUGO AV
100 SBDO 92404 546-H5
200 SBDO 92408 606-H1
400 SBDO 92410 576-H6
1200 SBDO 92404 576-H2
5400 SBDO 92407 546-H5
S LUGO AV
700 SBDO 92408 606-J3
N LUGO LN
1000 CLTN 92324 605-J4
E LUGONIA AV
800 RDL 92374 608-D5
E LUGONIA AV Rt#-38
- SBdC 92359 608-C5
- RDL 92374 608-C5
W LUGONIA AV
- RDL 92374 608-A5
900 RDL 92374 607-E5
1100 SBdC 92374 607-H5
N LULITREE RD
1300 CLTN 92324 605-H4
LULU LN
14000 SBdC - 514-A3
LUM LN
56100 SBdC 92285 4667-E7
LUMBER RD
3200 SBdC 92371 4562-H3
LUMPKIN LN
60500 SBdC 92284 4748-H6

LUNA DR
1000 BARS 92311 3679-H5
LUNA RD
100 SBdC 92372 4382-A5
800 BBLK - 4812-C2
800 SBdC - 4812-C2
3100 SBdC 92371 4382-H4
4100 SBdC 92371 4383-B4
7500 SBdC 92371 4384-A4
8100 SBdC 92392 4384-B4
9700 VCTV 92392 4384-F4
11300 VCTV 92392 4385-A4
14000 SBdC 92392 4385-H4
14700 SBdC 92392 4386-A4
15000 VCTV 92392 4386-A4
LUNA MOUNTAIN RD
- SBdC 92307 (4389-C7 See Page 4299)
9200 SBdC 92308 4479-D4
LUNAR RD
12100 SBdC - (4392-D4 See Page 4302)
LUNA VISTA
1900 NDLS 92363 3620-A6
LUNA VISTA LN
55800 SBdC 92284 4817-E2
56700 SBdC 92284 4818-A2
LUND PL
39900 RivC 92223 651-A7
LUNT LN
- SBDO 92346 577-H4
LUNT ST
6700 CHNO 91710 682-B1
LUPE CT
3700 CHNO 91710 681-D2
LUPE ST
3900 CHNO 91710 681-D2
LUPIN AV
19400 SBdC 92377 575-F2
LUPIN DR
33300 SBdC - 519-E2
LUPIN LN
300 SBdC - 516-F2
600 BBLK - 4811-D2
32700 SBdC - 519-C7
N LUPIN LN
100 SBDO 92407 546-H4
LUPIN RD
1500 SBdC - 4738-B4
2100 SBdC 92371 4292-E6
3900 SBdC 92371 (4293-E6 See Page 4292)
7300 ADEL 92301 (4293-J6 See Page 4292)
7300 ADEL 92371 (4293-J6 See Page 4292)
7500 ADEL 92301 4294-A6
9100 SBdC 92301 4294-D5
11000 SBdC 92301 4295-A5
11300 ADEL 92301 4295-A5
19700 APLV 92308 4387-D7
LUPIN ST
22000 APLV 92308 4477-J4
22000 APLV 92308 4478-A4
LUPIN WY
200 SBdC - 518-D1
LUPINE AV
- SBdC 92277 4751-J6
2300 SBdC 92277 4821-J3
2300 SBdC 92277 4822-A2
4300 SBdC 92277 4892-A4
5300 TNP 92277 4892-A4
LUPINE CT
10200 RCUC 91737 573-A3
12900 YCPA 92399 650-E5
LUPINE DR
57300 YUCA 92284 4957-J2
57400 YUCA 92284 4958-A2
LUPINE ST
13200 SBdC 93562 2145-A3
20500 SBdC 92308 4477-F4
LUPINE TR
36700 YCPA 92399 650-E5
LURA LN
- SBdC 92285 4667-D6
LURELANE AV
6700 HESP 92345 4566-D6
LURELANE ST
16900 FONT 92336 574-J5
17100 FONT 92336 575-A5
19200 SBdC 92376 575-F4
E LURELANE ST
200 RLTO 92376 575-H4
W LURELANE ST
200 RLTO 92376 575-F4
LURING PINES CIR
31700 SBdC - 519-A7
LURING PINES DR
31500 SBdC - 518-J7
31500 SBdC - 519-A7
LURLINE CT
300 UPL 91784 572-C6
LURLINE ST
8700 RCUC 91701 572-G6
LUTHER AV
3700 SBdC 92407 546-A7
LUTZ RD
58500 SBdC 92285 4748-F2
E LYANS DR
100 RLTO 92316 645-H1

LYNCHBURG PL
- FONT 92336 573-J6
LYND CT
12900 YCPA 92399 650-B5
LYNDALE AV
2400 POM 91768 640-C2
N LYNDON DR
1100 CLTN 92324 606-C5
LYNFALL ST
35500 YCPA 92399 650-B5
LYNN AV
10900 SBdC 92308 4478-E2
N LYNN CIR
10300 RivC 91752 644-A5
S LYNN CIR
10300 RivC 91752 644-A6
LYNN RD
- SBdC 92308 4388-E5
500 BBLK - 4811-E2
13700 SBdC 92307 4388-E2
14100 SBdC 92307 4298-E7
LYNN ST
16600 VCTV 92392 4296-E5
LYNNE CT
1500 RDL 92373 648-E3
E LYNN HAVEN CT
500 ONT 91764 602-C7
LYNNHAVEN LN
- SBdC - (4115-H5 See Page 4114)
LYNOAK DR
600 CLAR 91711 571-A7
1700 CLAR 91711 601-A1
3200 LACo 91711 601-A2
3300 POM 91767 601-A2
LYNVUE PL
500 POM 91768 640-D1
N LYNWOOD CIR
2100 SBDO 92404 577-D2
LYNWOOD DR
2600 SBdC 92252 4818-H4
E LYNWOOD DR
600 SBDO 92404 576-J2
600 SBDO 92404 577-A2
1100 SBdC 92404 577-B2
2500 SBdC 92346 577-E2
2500 SBDO 92346 577-G2
W LYNWOOD DR
1200 SBDO 92405 576-E2
LYNWOOD ST
18800 SBdC 92316 605-E6
LYNWOOD WY
1300 SBDO 92346 577-F5
6500 HIGH 92346 577-F4
17800 SBdC 92392 4386-H3
S LYNX PL
1900 ONT 91761 642-G4
LYON DR
- SBdC - 518-C1
LYONS AV
7000 HESP 92345 4566-G3
LYRA AV
11200 RivC 91752 683-H4
LYRA LN
3100 SBdC 92284 4817-G6
LYRE RD
- SBdC 92256 616-G2
LYSTER AV
- FONT 92336 574-D3
LYTLE LN
200 SBdC - 514-B3
LYTLE ST
500 RDL 92374 608-D7
500 RDL 92374 648-D1
N LYTLE ST
300 SBDO 92410 606-C1
LYTLE WY
200 SBdC - 514-B3
LYTLE CREEK CT
7500 FONT 92336 574-E7
LYTLE CREEK LP
100 ONT 91761 643-C6
LYTLE CREEK RD
200 SBdC - 514-B2
700 SBdC - (4733-A1 See Page 4653)
700 SBdC - 4734-A7
2300 SBdC - 544-G2
3000 SBdC - (4732-J1 See Page 4653)
3400 SBdC - 4652-H7
3600 SBdC - 4653-A7
3600 SBdC 92336 544-F7
4900 FONT 92336 544-F7
4900 FONT 92336 574-E3
S LYTLE CREEK RD
6300 FONT 92336 574-E4
LYTLE CREEK RIDGE RD
- SBdC 92407 515-A7
- SBdC 92407 545-A1
LYTLE GROVE LN
13800 SBdC - 514-A1

M

M ST
33700 SBdC 92311 3679-D5
33700 SBdC 92311 (3759-D1 See Page 3750)

E M ST
100 CLTN 92324 606-E7
N M ST
100 NDLS 92363 3620-C4
W M ST
100 CLTN 92324 606-C7
MACADAMIA CT
2600 CHLS 91709 681-A7
MACALESTER PL
500 CLAR 91711 571-E6
MACAPA DR
5800 SBdC 92371 4653-G2
MACCELE RD
49100 SBdC 92256 615-G5
50000 SBdC 92256 616-A5
MACDONALD LN
55600 YUCA 92284 4957-E5
MACDOWELL DR
33200 SBdC - (4391-A2 See Page 4300)
MACEDONIA CANYON RD
- SBdC - 351-A4
MACENTA LN
500 DBAR 91765 640-D7
MACHLIN CT
- INDS 91789 640-A6
MACINTOSH ST
6600 SBdC 92371 4473-H7
W MACKAY DR
400 SBDO 92408 606-H6
MACKINNARD DR
- SBdC 92277 (4894-C5 See Page 4824)
MACKINNARD RD
6400 SBdC 92277 (4894-C7 See Page 4824)
N MACLAY ST
6000 SBDO 92407 546-A3
MACON RD
- SBdC - 348-K11
MAC RAE RD
71300 SBdC 92277 4751-H6
MACRON ST
5900 SBdC 92345 4654-J1
7200 SBdC 92345 4564-H1
9000 SBdC 92345 4474-H3
11300 SBdC 92392 4474-H2
N MACY AV
1500 CLTN 92324 606-B4
N MACY ST
100 SBDO 92410 606-B1
400 SBDO 92410 576-B7
1900 SBDO 92411 576-B4
2100 SBDO 92407 576-B2
2300 SBdC 92407 576-B2
S MACY ST
100 SBDO 92410 606-B2
500 SBDO 92324 606-B3
800 CLTN 92324 606-B3
MADALENA CIR
15500 FONT 92337 644-F4
MADALENA DR
4500 RivC 91752 683-G1
MADEIRA AV
1900 SBdC 92359 608-J5
2100 RDL 92359 608-J5
2100 RDL 92359 609-A5
2100 SBdC 92359 609-A5
MADELEINE WY
800 POM 91767 601-B7
MADELYN CT
- CHLS 91709 681-G7
MADERA AV
7400 HESP 92345 4567-A4
7500 HESP 92345 4566-J2
N MADERA AV
600 ONT 91764 602-F4
MADERA CT
9800 RCUC 91730 602-J1
14200 FONT 92336 574-C7
MADERA LN
700 SBdC - 4737-F6
MADERA RD
- SBdC 92365 3764-G5
500 SBdC 92372 4472-A1
2800 SBdC 92371 4472-F1
4400 SBdC 92301 (4113-A1 See Page 4112)
MADERA ST
- CHNO 91710 682-B3
12300 VCTV 92392 4385-D6
14200 FONT 92336 574-C7
MADISON AV
300 POM 91767 601-A6
MADISON CIR
13200 VCTV 92392 4385-E4
MADISON PL
- RCUC 91730 573-E7
MADISON ST
- ADEL 92301 4295-A7
- RDL 92374 608-D4
4900 CHNO 91710 641-F6
11600 YCPA 92399 650-B2
N MADISON ST
600 SBDO 92411 576-D3
2500 SBDO 92407 576-D3
MADONNA CT
9800 RCUC 91730 602-J1
MADRAS CT
0300 SBdC 92335 604 B2

MADRAS DR
3700 CHLS 91709 681-D7
MADRE PL
5600 RCUC 91739 573-G2
MADRID PL
500 SBdC 92372 4472-A1
1300 SBdC 92372 4382-C7
S MAD RIVER LN
2900 ONT 91761 643-C6
MADRONA AV
7500 FONT 92336 574-H7
MADRONA CT
7700 FONT 92336 574-H7
MADRONA DR
1000 BARS 92311 3679-H5
7800 FONT 92336 574-H7
7800 FONT 92336 604-H1
8100 FONT 92335 604-H1
MADRONA LN
1300 SBdC - (4743-A4 See Page 4662)
E MADRONA ST
100 RLTO 92376 575-H6
800 RLTO 92376 576-A6
W MADRONA ST
100 RLTO 92376 575-D6
MADRONA WY
3800 CHLS 91709 681-D7
MADRONE AV
8500 RCUC 91730 602-F3
MADRONE ST
- FONT 92337 645-A1
18100 ADEL 92301 4205-A5
18200 ADEL 92301 4204-J5
18300 HESP 92345 4477-A7
19800 SBdC 92308 4477-E7
MADRONO DR
- RCUC 91701 572-J5
MADRUGADA DR
2300 CHLS 91709 680-J2
MADRUGADOR RD
- SBdC - 349-F6
MAGALA LN
13300 CHLS 91709 680-J2
MAGAZINE RD
77100 SBdC - 328-H5
MAGENTA TER
- CHLS 91709 711-G1
MAGIC CT
13100 SBdC - 518-F7
MAGIC DR
30000 SBdC - 518-F7
MAGICAL AV
1700 SBdC 92252 4820-E2
MAGNEY LN
45700 SBdC 92365 3764-D6
MAGNOLIA AV
1200 RDL 92373 647-J2
1200 RDL 92373 648-A1
5600 SBdC 92377 575-F2
12300 CHNO 91710 641-J7
12300 VCTV 92392 4386-B5
13100 CHNO 91710 681-J2
82900 SBdC 93562 2145-A4
N MAGNOLIA AV
100 RLTO 92376 605-H1
600 UPL 91786 602-A1
700 RLTO 92376 575-H4
2100 RLTO 92377 575-G3
2400 SBdC 92377 575-G3
6300 SBDO 92407 545-H1
6800 SBDO 92407 515-H7
S MAGNOLIA AV
200 RLTO 92376 605-H3
400 ONT 91762 641-J4
2200 CHNO 91710 641-J4
2200 CHNO 91762 641-J4
W MAGNOLIA AV
100 SBDO 92405 576-G5
900 SBDO 92411 576-C5
MAGNOLIA CT
5700 SBdC 92377 575-F2
10200 RCUC 91730 573-A7
W MAGNOLIA CT
1400 SBDO 92411 576-C5
MAGNOLIA DR
49100 SBdC 92256 615-G7
N MAGNOLIA DR
4200 SBdC 92407 546-E4
4200 SBDO 92407 546-E4
W MAGNOLIA DR
1300 CLTN 92324 606-A5
MAGNOLIA LN
- LACo 91768 640-A1
44400 SBdC - 4812-E1
MAGNOLIA PL
- FONT 92336 574-E6
MAGNOLIA ST
7400 RCUC 91730 572-H7
9500 SBdC 92316 605-D5
10100 RCUC 91730 573-A7
E MAGNOLIA ST
100 POM 91767 601-A4
MAGNOLIA WY
5700 RCUC 91737 573-C3
MAHAN AV
14500 VCTV 92392 4475-E3
MAHANOY LN
40100 BBLK - 4811-D2

MAHOGANY CT
10300 RCUC 91737 573-B3
MAHOGANY DR
- FONT 92337 645-A1
2900 CHLS 91709 681-B6
MAHOGANY LN
2000 SBdC 92314 4812-H1
2200 SBdC 92314 4813-A1
25900 SBdC - 518-D1
25900 SBdC - 4738-D7
44500 SBdC - 4812-H1
N MAHOGANY PL
1100 SBdC 92314 4742-E4
MAHOGANY RD
44200 SBdC - 4812-E2
MAI ST
4900 RCUC 91737 (542-J7 See Page 513)
4900 RCUC 91737 572-J1
MAIDENHAIR CT
6600 RCUC 91739 573-G5
E MAIDSTONE ST
1300 ONT 91761 642-F6
MAIN
1000 SBdC 92407 515-C5
MAIN ST
- SBdC 92345 4475-C6
100 RivC 92507 646-C6
200 RivC 92501 645-J7
300 GTER 92313 646-C6
300 RIV 92501 645-J7
500 BBLK - 4811-F2
8300 RCUC 91730 602-F3
9800 RCUC 91730 603-A3
11300 SBdC 92354 647-F1
12700 HESP 92345 4475-G6
13000 SBdC 93562 2144-J5
13300 SBdC 93562 2145-A4
14400 HESP 92345 4476-A6
18200 HESP 92345 4477-A7
27100 HIGH 92346 577-H4
38900 SBdC - 372-D11
E MAIN ST
300 ONT 91761 642-C1
1600 BARS 92311 3680-E5
E MAIN ST U.S.-66 Hist
100 BARS 92311 3679-J2
200 BARS 92311 3680-A3
N MAIN ST
- POM 91766 640-J1
100 POM 91768 640-J1
S MAIN ST
100 POM 91766 640-J2
W MAIN ST
100 ONT 91762 642-B1
800 SBDO 92410 606-F1
W MAIN ST U.S.-66 Hist
100 BARS 92311 3679-F3
2900 BARS 92311 3678-H6
3100 SBdC 92311 3678-H6
3800 BARS 92311 3758-B3
6100 SBdC 92311 3758-B3
18200 SBdC 92311 (3757-J5 See Page 3756)
MAINE ST
- FONT 92336 574-D5
MAINSAIL LN
18200 SBdC 92392 4386-J2
26400 SBdC - (3935-G5 See Page 3934)
MAIN ST OH S
26500 SBdC 92311 3679-B4
MAITLAND ST
- SBdC - 4480-D1
5300 SBdC 91762 641-G2
E MAITLAND ST
100 ONT 91761 642-D2
W MAITLAND ST
100 ONT 91761 642-B2
100 ONT 91762 642-B2
MAITLAND PRIVADO
- ONT 91762 642-A2
MAIZE CT
- SBdC - 4843-H3
8300 SBdC 92335 604-D2
MAJELA AV
16300 VCTV 92394 4295-J2
MAJELA CT
16400 VCTV 92394 4295-J3
MAJELA RD
19000 APLV 92307 4297-B2
MAJESTIC AV
2500 SBDO 92407 546-A6
2600 SBDO 92407 545-J6
MAJESTIC DR
- APLV 92308 4387-E5
MAJESTY DR
9300 RCUC 91730 602-H1
MAJESTY ST
- UPL 91784 572-E6
MAJOR PL
13300 HESP 92345 4475-F6
MAJORCA CT
- RCUC 91737 573-C3
MAKA RD
16300 APLV 92307 4296-J2
MAKAI CT
13200 SBdC 92392 4386-J3

MAKUA RD
45700 SBdC 92365 (3684-D3 See Page 3594)
E MALABAR CT
1200 SBdC 92314 4742-F6
MALABAR RD
- SBdC - 4886-G1
S MALABAR WY
1300 SBdC 92314 4742-G5
MALACHITE AV
1300 SBdC 92359 608-J5
5500 RCUC 91737 572-H3
7700 RCUC 91730 602-J1
MALACHITE CT
15300 CHLS 91709 680-J6
MALACHITE ST
7500 RCUC 91730 572-H7
MALAGA AV
16000 FONT 92336 574-G7
MALAGA CT
16500 FONT 92336 574-H7
17200 FONT 92336 575-A7
MALAGA DR
- RCUC 91730 603-E1
1200 RivC 92509 645-E5
15600 FONT 92336 574-F7
17700 FONT 92336 575-B7
S MALAGA PL
600 ONT 91761 643-G1
MALAGA ST
1200 UPL 91784 571-J3
16200 FONT 92336 574-G7
16900 FONT 92336 575-A7
MALAGON DR
11700 FONT 92337 644-F3
MALAHAT CT
16500 APLV 92307 4297-A2
MALAHAT RD
15800 APLV 92307 4297-A3
MALAKI RD
11300 APLV 92308 4388-A3
MALATI CIR
2100 UPL 91784 571-J4
MALCOLM AV
2600 ONT 91761 642-D6
S MALCOLM AV
100 ONT 91761 642-D1
S MALCOLM ST
12700 ONT 91761 642-D6
MALECON DR
18500 ADEL 92301 4204-C1
18500 SBdC 92301 4204-C4
20100 ADEL 92301 4114-C7
MALGOSA RD
10700 APLV 92308 4477-H2
MALIBU AV
32100 SBdC 92365 (3763-J2 See Page 3762)
MALIBU CT
14100 ADEL 92301 4385-A1
E MALIBU CT
2500 CLTN 92324 646-J4
MALIBU RD
21000 APLV 92308 4387-G7
MALIBU TR
9600 SBdC 92256 616-A2
MALL DR
- ONT 91764 603-D6
MALLARD CT
13300 CHLS 91709 681-A3
MALLARD DR
1000 SBdC - 4738-B6
MALLARD LANDING LN
200 BBLK - 4811-C1
MALLON RD
- SBdC 92284 4748-G6
MALLORCA LN
13300 CHLS 91709 680-J2
MALLORCA ST
1200 UPL 91784 571-J3
MALLORCA WY
12800 VCTV 92392 4386-F5
MALLORY DR
14700 SBdC 92335 604-D6
15500 FONT 92335 604-G5
17400 SBdC 92316 605-B5
W MALLORY DR
600 RLTO 92316 605-F5
MALLORY ST
1900 SBdC 92407 576-B3
1900 SBDO 92407 576-B3
W MALLORY ST
1700 SBDO 92407 576-C3
MALLOW DR
100 SBdC 92284 4748-G5
1800 SBdC 92285 4748-G1
MALONE ST
11000 RCUC 91701 573-C4
MALOOF AV
6100 FONT 92336 574-F7
MALOOF CT
7500 FONT 92336 574-F7
9900 FONT 92335 604-F6
MALPAIS LN
15700 VCTV 92394 4296-C5
MALPASO RD
8300 SBdC 92371 4562-J3
8900 SBdC 92371 4563-A1
9200 SBdC 92371 4473-A5

E MALTBY BLVD
400 SBdC 92314 4742-E5
MALVEN AV
7400 RCUC 91730 572-J7
7900 RCUC 91730 602-J1
MALVERN AV
6100 RCUC 91737 573-A4
7000 RCUC 91701 573-A6
7900 RCUC 91730 603-A1
MAMBE RD
22500 APLV 92308 4478-A3
MAMMOTH DR
- UPL 91784 571-H6
9700 MTCL 91763 601-G6
12300 VCTV 92392 4385-F6
28800 SBdC - 4738-C5
N MAMMOTH DR
5000 SBDO 92407 546-D5
MAMMOTH PL
- FONT 92336 574-D3
MAMMOTH PEAK CT
11500 RCUC 91737 573-D3
MANA RD
17500 APLV 92307 4296-H5
MANACOR RD
20900 SBdC 92347 (3587-E4 See Page 3586)
MANADA RD
- SBdC 92301 (4113-F4 See Page 4112)
- SBdC 92371 4653-H1
7500 SBdC 92372 4562-E5
8100 SBdC 92371 4563-H1
9100 SBdC 92371 4473-H2
11900 SBdC 92371 4383-G2
14500 SBdC 92371 (4293-G7 See Page 4292)
MANANA AV
2500 SBdC 92252 4819-C5
MANANA DR
10000 SBdC 92256 615-G3
71700 TNP 92277 4891-J4
71800 TNP 92277 4892-C3
MANATEE ST
42500 SBdC 92365 (3683-E3 See Page 3592)
MANCHA PL
6900 RCUC 91701 572-G6
MANCHESTER AV
3800 SBdC 92284 4888-A1
MANCHESTER CT
700 CLAR 91711 571-F7
MANCHESTER LN
- SBDO 92408 646-J1
100 SBDO 92408 606-J7
MANCHESTER ST
10800 RCUC 91701 573-C6
16200 VCTV 92394 4296-B3
MANCHET WY
28200 HIGH 92346 578-A5
MANDALA AV
- RCUC 91739 544-B7
- RCUC 91739 574-B1
N MANDALAY AV
1200 ONT 91764 602-F5
MANDAN CT
14400 APLV 92307 4297-B7
MANDAN LN
14500 APLV 92307 4297-B7
MANDAN RD
14200 APLV 92307 4387-A1
14500 APLV 92307 4297-C4
MANDARIN AV
8300 RCUC 91701 572-E4
MANDARIN CT
4900 CHLS 91709 711-F2
25400 LMLN 92354 647-D2
MANDARIN RD
6000 YUCA 92284 4888-A6
MANDARIN WY
- RivC 92507 646-E6
MANDRIL ST
42500 SBdC 92365 (3683-E2 See Page 3592)
N MANDY LN
6100 SBDO 92407 545-J3
MANE DR
23400 DBAR 91765 680-C1
MANE ST
4400 MTCL 91763 641-E2
53500 SBdC - 4886-H5
MANGO AV
5800 FONT 92336 574-J3
7300 FONT 92336 575-A7
7800 FONT 92336 605-A1
8100 FONT 92335 605-A1
9400 HESP 92345 4476-H6
MANGO CT
800 POM 91766 641-A4
9500 HESP 92345 4476-H6
10600 RCUC 91737 573-B5
MANGO DR
9700 FONT 92335 605-A5
MANGO LN
9700 FONT 92335 605-A5
MANGO ST
6500 RCUC 91737 573-B5
6700 RCUC 91701 573-B5
8900 SBdC 92371 4562-J1
9700 SBdC 92371 4472-J6

MANGO WY
1600 POM 91766 641-B4
MANGROVE CT
11900 FONT 92337 644-C4
MANGROVE ST
9900 RCUC 91730 572-J7
9900 RCUC 91730 573-A7
MANHASSET CT
10700 APLV 92308 4477-J2
MANHASSET RD
1300 APLV 92308 4387-J3
10500 APLV 92308 4477-J3
MANHATTAN CT
- RCUC 91730 573-E1
MANILA CT
16800 FONT 92337 644-J1
MANILA ST
500 RLTO 92316 645-G1
15300 FONT 92337 644-E1
18200 SBdC 92316 645-D1
MANITOBA DR
- FONT 92336 544-C7
- FONT 92336 574-C1
28500 SBdC - 4738-B5
MANITOBA RD
20600 APLV 92308 4387-F5
MANITOU RD
17900 APLV 92307 4296-H6
MANIX RD
43300 SBdC 92365 3594-F3
43500 SBdC 92365 (3593-H4 See Page 3592)
48000 SBdC 92365 (3595-A1 See Page 3594)
48000 SBdC 92365 (3505-A6 See Page 3414)
MANKATO CT
1500 CLAR 91711 601-F1
MANLINE DR
5400 RivC 91752 683-G4
MANN AV
6200 RivC 91752 683-J6
S MANN DR
100 SBdC 92314 4742-G5
MANN ST
12500 VCTV 92392 4385-E5
MANNING CT
15500 VCTV 92394 4296-A2
MANNING LN
14800 VCTV 92394 4295-J2
MANNING ST
- YCPA 92399 649-E2
14900 VCTV 92394 4295-J2
14900 VCTV 92394 4296-A2
MANNS RD
2300 SBdC - 4562-F5
MANOLA WY
12200 VCTV 92392 4386-D6
MANOR CIR
1600 POM 91766 640-H4
MANOR CT
14800 CHLS 91709 681-B5
MANOR DR
3500 RivC 92509 645-A7
MANOR PL
- FONT 92336 544-C7
MANOR ST
22700 SBdC 92308 4478-B5
MANOR WY
- SBdC - (3935-H4 See Page 3934)
MANSFIELD CT
1500 UPL 91784 571-H4
MANSFIELD DR
800 CLAR 91711 571-F7
MANSFIELD PL
6700 CHNO 91710 642-B7
MANSFIELD RD
7300 RCUC 91730 573-C7
MANSFIELD ST
3100 HIGH 92346 577-F4
3100 SBDO 92346 577-G4
25800 HIGH 92404 577-D4
MANSION LN
- LACo 91724 640-A1
- LACo 91768 640-A1
MANSKER LN
- NDLS 92363 3620-E7
MANTECA AV
9200 HESP 92345 4477-B6
MANTONYA RD
5000 TNP 92277 4891-A3
5000 SBdC 92277 4891-A3
6900 TNP 92277 4961-A1
MANTOVA PL
6900 RCUC 91701 573-D6
MANTOVA RD
- SBdC - 4816-H7
- SBdC - 4886-H1
- SBdC 92365 (3684-A7 See Page 3594)
MANUEL AV
- LMLN 92354 647-F2
MANUEL CT
6300 CHNO 91710 682-A1
MANVILLE ST
2400 POM 91767 601-B5
MANZANA DR
9700 SBdC 92308 4478-H1
11500 SBdC 92308 4388-H7

MANZANA RD
- SBdC - (4119-J4 See Page 4118)
MANZANITA AV
5800 SBdC - 4950-G1
6500 TNP 92277 4892-A7
9500 SBdC 92335 605-C5
16300 FONT 92335 604-H5
MANZANITA CT
- ONT 91762 642-B4
700 BBLK - 4810-J2
6000 SBdC - 4950-G1
6500 CHNO 91710 682-B2
9500 FONT 92335 604-G5
W MANZANITA CT
700 ONT 91762 642-A4
MANZANITA DR
200 SBdC - 518-B1
900 BARS 92311 3679-H4
1700 SBdC 92372 4562-E5
2400 SBdC - 4562-F5
2500 SBdC 92371 4562-G1
5800 YUCA 92284 4887-J6
8800 RCUC 91701 572-G3
8900 RCUC 91737 572-G3
9900 RCUC 91737 573-A3
13900 SBdC - 514-A4
14500 SBdC 92335 604-C5
15700 FONT 92335 604-D5
17000 FONT 92335 605-A5
18600 SBdC 92316 605-D5
23500 SBdC - 516-G3
33400 SBdC - 519-E3
48100 SBdC 92285 (4575-D6 See Page 4484)
50600 SBdC 92285 (4576-A6 See Page 4486)
57400 YUCA 92284 4888-A5
N MANZANITA DR
3400 SBDO 92404 577-D1
MANZANITA LN
2000 SBdC 92314 4812-H1
2200 SBdC 92314 4813-A2
44200 SBdC - 4812-E1
MANZANITA RD
500 RDL 92373 648-D4
5400 SBdC 92285 (4576-D6 See Page 4486)
11000 SBdC 92308 4478-B2
11300 SBdC 92308 4388-B7
13800 SBdC - 514-A4
14300 VCTV 92392 4386-E1
30500 SBdC - 548-G1
MANZANITA ST
- APLV 92308 4477-G4
4700 MTCL 91763 641-F1
6500 CHNO 91710 682-A2
8600 SBdC 92308 4477-G6
8600 SBdC 92308 4567-H1
12600 VCTV 92392 4385-D7
15000 HESP 92345 4386-A7
17000 HESP 92345 4476-G1
18200 HESP 92392 4386-J7
36400 YCPA 92399 650-D1
E MANZANITA ST
500 ONT 91761 642-C4
W MANZANITA ST
300 RLTO 92376 605-F5
900 RLTO 92316 605-F5
MANZANITA WY
1300 SBdC - 4737-G5
MANZANO RD
1900 SBdC 92372 4382-D5
4100 SBdC 92371 4383-A5
8500 SBdC 92392 4384-C4
10700 VCTV 92392 4384-H4
14100 VCTV 92392 4385-H4
14500 SBdC 92392 4385-J4
14700 SBdC 92392 4386-A4
MANZANO ST
- CHNO 91710 682-B3
MAPLE AV
1600 RDL 92374 608-F5
2200 POM 91767 601-A4
2400 RLTO 92377 575-C2
2400 SBdC 92377 575-C3
6000 SBdC - 4950-G1
6600 HESP 92345 4565-J4
8900 HESP 92345 4475-J1
10500 SBdC 92316 605-D7
10700 SBdC 92316 645-D2
11100 SBdC 92337 645-D2
11700 HESP 92345 4385-J7
11800 CLTN 92324 646-C3
11800 GTER 92313 646-C3
26400 LMLN 92354 647-F2
N MAPLE AV
100 RLTO 92335 605-D1
100 SBdC 92335 605-D1
300 FONT 92335 605-D1
400 FONT 92336 605-D1
400 RLTO 92376 605-D1
500 SBdC 92336 605-D1
500 SBdC 92336 575-D7
500 SBdC 92376 575-D7
600 RLTO 92376 575-C6
1000 FONT 92336 575-C6
1000 RLTO 92336 575-C6
1000 FONT 92376 575-C6
2200 RLTO 92377 575-C2

STREET
Block City ZIP Pg-Grid

N MAPLE AV
2200 SBdC 92377 575-C3
S MAPLE AV
100 SBdC 92335 605-D3
200 RLTO 92335 605-D3
500 RLTO 92316 605-D3
600 RLTO 92316 605-D3
600 FONT 92316 605-D3
600 SBdC 92316 605-D3
9000 FONT 92335 605-D3
MAPLE CT
- SBdC 92359 609-A5
9600 ADEL 92301 4204-E4
12600 YCPA 92399 649-C4
W MAPLE CT
400 CLTN 92324 606-C7
1000 ONT 91762 642-A3
1400 ONT 91762 641-H3
MAPLE DR
100 SBdC - 518-B1
300 SBdC - 4738-E7
40900 SBdC 92339 611-F2
MAPLE LN
100 SBdC - 4742-F7
100 SBdC 92314 4742-F7
200 SBdC - 4812-F2
300 SBdC - 516-F2
2700 SBdC 92314 4813-A1
32900 SBdC - 519-D2
37600 SBdC 92347 (3587-E5
See Page 3586)
MAPLE PL
8300 RCUC 91730 603-D2
MAPLE RD
700 SBdC - 518-B3
MAPLE ST
4000 SBdC 91710 641-D4
5700 SBdC 92397 4652-D3
18200 APLV 92308 4387-B7
25200 SBdC 92311 3678-G4
E MAPLE ST
100 ONT 91761 642-C3
W MAPLE ST
100 ONT 91761 642-B4
100 ONT 91762 642-A3
200 CLTN 92324 606-D7
1700 SBDO 92411 576-D7
2200 SBDO 92410 576-A7
2700 SBDO 92376 576-A7
N MAPLE WY
500 UPL 91786 602-A3
MAPLE HILL RD
1300 DBAR 91765 680-A3
MAPLELEAF CT
9100 HESP 92345 4475-J7
MAPLELEAF DR
41900 BBLK - 4811-H2
MAPLE LEAF LN
11900 FONT 92337 644-D4
MAPLE PRIVADO
2100 ONT 91761 642-H3
MAPLE RIDGE LN
13800 CHLS 91709 681-B2
MAPLE SPRING DR
23600 DBAR 91765 640-C7
MAPLE VALLEY CT
12800 VCTV 92392 4475-E1
MAPLE VALLEY RD
11500 VCTV 92392 4475-E1
MAPLE VIEW DR
1100 POM 91766 640-F4
MAPLEWOOD CT
5500 RCUC 91737 573-A2
MAPLEWOOD DR
- YCPA 92399 650-C5
4700 SBdC 92371 4383-C3
14700 CHLS 91709 681-B5
27300 SBdC - 517-H1
MAPLEWOOD LN
1300 SBdC 92359 609-A5
MAPLEWOOD PL
29100 HIGH 92346 578-D5
MARA AV
6600 TNP 92277 4892-G6
MARAKESH RD
11300 SBdC 92371 4473-H2
MARBELLA DR
10900 RCUC 91737 573-C4
MARBELLA ST
13800 FONT 92336 604-A1
MARBETH PL
12100 YCPA 92399 649-A3
MARBETH RD
31400 YCPA 92399 649-A3
MARBLE AV
6300 RCUC 91701 572-E4
MARBLE CT
6200 RCUC 91701 572-E4
MARBLE DR
- RivC 92399 650-G7
- SBdC - 518-B3
31100 SBdC 92359 608-J5
MARBLE LN
- SBdC - 2971-G1
MARBLE CANYON RD
- SBdC 91784 572-B1
35400 SBdC - (4571-H7
See Page 4570)
36100 SBdC - (4572-A7
See Page 4482)

MARBLE RIDGE DR
3300 CHLS 91709 681-C2
MARC CT
1000 DBAR 91765 680-E2
N MARCELLA AV
400 RLTO 92376 575-H4
400 RLTO 92376 605-H1
S MARCELLA AV
100 RLTO 92376 605-H2
N MARCELLA CT
1400 ONT 91764 602-D5
MARCELLA DR
31300 SBdC - 518-J7
MARCELLO WY
11500 RCUC 91701 573-D5
MARCHMONT CT
12500 VCTV 92392 4385-E6
MARCIA RD
18200 SBdC 92407 515-C6
MARCIA ST
300 RDL 92373 648-F4
MARCO RD
2100 SBdC 92372 4382-F7
2700 SBdC 92371 4382-J7
3800 SBdC 92371 4383-H6
8600 SBdC 92392 4384-C6
10500 VCTV 92392 4384-F6
MARCONA AV
8800 SBdC 92335 604-E3
MARCONI DR
- RCUC 91701 573-F5
MARCONIA CT
7500 FONT 92336 574-E7
MARCOS RD
200 SBdC 92372 4382-A7
MARCY RD
9000 SBdC 92339 611-E2
MARDEL LN
- SBdC 92316 605-D5
MARE LN
14100 VCTV 92394 4295-H6
MAREK CT
7800 FONT 92336 603-J1
MARELLEN WY
1900 POM 91767 601-C6
MARFA ST
11300 FONT 92337 644-F2
W MARGARET CT
1100 UPL 91786 601-J1
MARGARET LN
- YCPA 92399 650-C6
MARGARITA DR
1500 RDL 92373 648-F3
15800 FONT 92336 574-F6
MARGARITA LN
- LMLN 92354 647-F2
E MARGARITA RD
300 RLTO 92376 575-H6
900 RLTO 92376 576-A6
MARGARITA ST
4100 CHNO 91710 681-D2
58000 SBdC 92284 4748-B4
MARGATE CT
- RCUC 91739 573-G6
MARGAUX PL
- RCUC 91739 603-H1
MARGIE PL
10600 ADEL 92301 4204-H5
MARGOT AV
6500 TNP 92277 4892-D6
MARGUERITE DR
- RCUC 91739 573-F5
MARIA CT
- RDL 92374 608-G7
4100 CHNO 91710 681-D1
W MARIA CT
100 CLTN 92324 646-C4
100 SBdC 92324 646-C4
MARIA RD
100 SBdC 92372 4472-A7
W MARIANA AV
500 RLTO 92376 575-F5
MARIANA ST
17000 FONT 92336 574-J5
17200 FONT 92336 575-A5
E MARIANA ST
200 RLTO 92376 575-H5
W MARIANA ST
700 RLTO 92376 575-F5
MARIANNE LN
- HIGH 92346 578-F6
MARIBELLE DR
15000 VCTV 92394 4296-A4
MARICOPA DR
6500 TNP 92277 4892-F6
MARICOPA LN
16100 APLV 92307 4296-H3
MARICOPA RD
4900 SBdC 92371 4383-C4
7500 SBdC 92371 4384-A4
8100 SBdC 92392 4384-B3
9600 VCTV 92392 4384-G3
11200 VCTV 92392 4385-A3
14000 SBdC 92392 4385-J3
14700 SBdC 92392 4386-A3
15000 VCTV 92392 4386-A3
MARICOPA TR
3600 SBdC - 4843-H2
MARIE DR
2800 RivC 92509 645-E7

MARIETTA RD
2200 CLAR 91711 571-C7
MARIGOLD AV
7300 HIGH 92346 578-C6
21700 ADEL 92301 (4115-F2
See Page 4114)
22000 SBdC 92301 (4115-F2
See Page 4114)
S MARIGOLD AV
1100 ONT 91761 642-E6
MARIGOLD CT
7000 RCUC 91739 573-G6
MARIGOLD DR
4300 CHNO 91710 681-E2
MARIGOLD LN
- SBdC 92252 4889-D4
S MARIGOLD PL
1600 ONT 91761 642-E3
MARIGOLD RD
- SBdC 92285 (4576-A7
See Page 4486)
MARIGOLD ST
- RDL 92374 607-E4
1400 UPL 91784 571-H3
1900 POM 91767 601-B6
2300 SBDO 92407 546-B5
6300 RivC 92880 683-D6
14600 SBdC - (4025-H7
See Page 3934)
MARILANE AV
5900 SBdC 92277 4893-E5
MARILLO DR
4400 SBdC 92301 (4113-A3
See Page 4112)
MARILYN AV
7900 HIGH 92410 577-C7
8100 HIGH 92410 607-C1
MARILYN LN
400 RDL 92373 648-F4
N MARIN AV
600 ONT 91764 602-F4
MARIN CT
17100 FONT 92336 575-A4
MARIN LN
800 SBdC - 4737-F6
MARIN RD
600 BBLK - 4811-F2
MARIN ST
18100 APLV 92307 (4206-J5
See Page 4116)
N MARINA CT
300 BBLK - 4741-H7
MARINA DR
100 NDLS 92363 3620-D5
MARINA LN
- VCTV 92392 4385-E7
MARINA ST
- SBdC - 4844-A4
MARINA POINT DR
100 BBLK - 4741-G7
200 BBLK - 4811-H1
MARINA VIEW DR
100 LPCo - 4606-J5
MARINA VIEW RD
- LPCo - 4606-J5
MARINE AV
5700 TNP 92277 4892-F4
6500 RCUC 91737 573-B5
7100 RCUC 91701 573-B5
7300 RCUC 91730 573-B7
8700 RCUC 91730 603-B3
MARINE RD
37300 SBdC - (3682-A2
See Page 3592)
MARINER DR
17900 SBdC 92392 4386-J2
MARINER LN
26500 SBdC - (3935-G5
See Page 3934)
MARINERO LN
5400 SBdC 92301 (4113-C3
See Page 4112)
MARINO PL
7000 RCUC 91701 573-E6
MARION AV
1100 SBdC 92407 515-C5
9500 MTCL 91763 601-G6
MARION DR
100 SBdC - 516-A1
600 CLAR 91711 601-D5
MARION RD
1500 RDL 92374 648-F2
MARIPOSA AV
5300 TNP 92277 4892-A4
15200 CHLS 91709 681-F6
N MARIPOSA AV
600 ONT 91764 602-F5
MARIPOSA CT
300 UPL 91784 572-C6
MARIPOSA DR
4500 SBDO 92404 547-A5
9800 RCUC 91730 602-G6
15800 FONT 92336 574-F6
E MARIPOSA DR
- RDL 92373 648-F4
300 RLTO 92376 575-J5
900 RLTO 92376 576-A5
W MARIPOSA DR
100 RDL 92373 648-E4
500 RLTO 92376 575-F6

MARIPOSA LN
2100 SBdC 92314 4812-J2
MARIPOSA RD
5500 SBdC 92345 4654-J1
6000 SBdC 92345 4564-J7
6500 HESP 92345 4565-C3
8500 HESP 92345 4565-C3
8900 HESP 92345 4475-H1
13400 HESP 92345 4385-J7
13500 VCTV 92345 4385-J7
13500 VCTV 92392 4385-J7
13500 VCTV 92392 4386-B2
MARIPOSA ST
13100 SBdC 93562 2145-A3
25700 LMLN 92354 647-D2
33900 YCPA 92399 649-G4
E MARIPOSA ST
400 UPL 91784 572-C6
MARIPOSA TR
7500 YUCA 92284 4957-E4
MARIPOSA WY
100 BREA 92823 710-C6
MARIQUITA RD
56700 SBdC 92285 4747-H2
MARITA PL
19100 APLV 92308 4387-B4
MARITIME LN
27200 SBdC - (3935-H4
See Page 3934)
MARJORIE AV
1400 CLAR 91711 601-E1
MARJORIE CREST
1600 RDL 92373 648-F3
MARKET PL
- VCTV 92394 4205-F5
MARKET ST
100 NDLS 92363 3620-B4
1800 RivC 92509 645-F6
1900 RivC 92501 645-F6
13100 SBdC 93562 2144-J5
13100 SBdC 93562 2145-A4
MARKETPLACE
- POM 91766 641-A7
MARKHAM AV
9700 ADEL 92301 4204-E1
MARKHAM RD
13400 VCTV 92392 4384-F4
14900 SBdC - (4025-J3
See Page 3934)
15100 SBdC - (4026-A3
See Page 3936)
36100 SBdC 92311 3678-G1
MARKHAM ST
900 SBdC 92301 (4202-A2
See Page 4112)
3000 SBdC 92301 (4203-G2
See Page 4112)
MARKS AV
75300 TNP 92277 4822-J7
75300 TNP 92277 4823-A7
MARKS RD
2800 SBdC 92277 4824-E3
4600 SBdC 92277 (4894-E1
See Page 4824)
35200 SBdC 92311 3680-E4
MARK TWAIN CT
- RivC 92880 683-D4
MARLAY AV
5100 ONT 91761 643-G3
11500 FONT 92337 644-A3
12900 FONT 92337 643-H3
MARLBORO CT
700 CLAR 91711 571-F6
S MARLOWE DR
400 SBdC 92314 4742-E6
E MARLOWE WY
3300 CLTN 92324 647-A5
3300 SBdC 92324 647-A5
MARMAC RD
55300 SBdC 92284 4747-D4
MARMANDE PL
7500 RCUC 91730 573-D7
MARMOSET ST
20700 APLV 92308 4477-F3
MARMOT CIR
5800 CHLS 91709 711-J2
MARMOT RD
- SBdC - (4572-J2
See Page 4482)
MAROON BELL RD
2400 CHLS 91709 680-J1
MARQUETTE AV
2100 POM 91766 641-B6
5100 SBDO 92407 546-B5
MARQUETTE CT
12900 VCTV 92392 4385-E4
MARQUETTE LN
11300 SBdC 91766 641-D3
MARQUIS LN
- SBdC - 4741-E6
MARQUIS PL
- RCUC 91739 573-H7
MARRAKESH AV
10100 SBdC 92371 4473-H5
MARRAKESH RD
9900 SBdC 92371 4473-H1
11900 SBdC 92371 4383-H7
MARS AV
17200 VCTV 92394 (4206-F7
See Page 4116)

MARS DR
- SBdC 92252 4748-J6
61300 SBdC 92252 4749-A6
MARS PL
11000 RivC 91752 683-H5
MARS ST
62100 SBdC 92252 4749-C6
64900 SBdC 92252 4750-A6
66500 SBdC 92277 4750-E6
MARS WY
1000 SBdC - 516-H4
MARSALA PL
6700 RCUC 91701 573-E5
MARSH AV
13500 CHNO 91710 681-D2
MARSHALL AV
12300 CHNO 91710 641-G6
E MARSHALL BLVD
100 SBDO 92404 576-J2
600 SBDO 92404 577-A2
1100 SBdC 92404 577-B2
2400 SBdC 92346 577-E2
2400 SBDO 92346 577-E2
W MARSHALL BLVD
100 SBDO 92405 576-E2
MARSHALL CT
600 CLAR 91711 601-E1
MARSHALL DR
14600 VCTV 92394 4296-A7
MARSHALL RD
100 SBdC - 518-B1
MARSHALL ST
1400 RDL 92374 648-E2
13700 SBdC 93562 2145-B1
MARTANO PL
6900 RCUC 91701 573-E5
MARTELL AV
1400 SBdC 92399 610-F7
MARTELLO ST
1700 POM 91767 601-C6
W MARTHA CT
1000 CLTN 92324 606-B4
MARTIN AV
16900 FONT 92335 604-J3
W MARTIN AV
400 CLTN 92324 606-C5
N MARTIN CT
800 RLTO 92376 575-E7
MARTIN RD
45300 SBdC 92365 3594-C7
N MARTIN RD
1200 RLTO 92376 576-A5
1200 SBDO 92411 576-A5
W MARTIN RD
1200 SBDO 92411 576-A6
MARTIN ST
4700 RivC 91752 683-J3
11700 LMLN 92354 647-D3
E MARTIN ST
100 SBDO 92408 606-J2
N MARTIN ST
800 RLTO 92376 575-E7
MARTIN WY
500 CLAR 91711 571-E6
MARTINA ST
13100 CHNO 91710 641-F7
MARTINEZ CT
7500 YUCA 92284 4957-C3
N MARTINEZ LN
1000 CLTN 92324 605-J4
MARTINEZ TR
54500 YUCA 92284 4957-C3
MARTINGALE WY
11100 RCUC 91737 573-C2
MARTIN HOLLOW RD
13300 VCTV 92301 (4115-E5
See Page 4114)
MARTINIQUE DR
13600 CHLS 91709 680-J2
MARTIN RANCH RD
1400 SBdC 92407 515-F6
1400 SBDO 92407 515-F6
MARTOS RD
11600 FONT 92337 644-F3
MARTY ST
- RDL 92373 648-A2
MARVIN AV
1600 RDL 92374 648-G2
MARVIN DR
3300 SBdC 92284 4818-E7
5000 YUCA 92284 4888-E4
6300 SBdC 92284 4888-E3
6700 YUCA 92284 4958-E1
N MARVIN DR
500 SBDO 92410 576-A7
S MARVIN DR
200 SBDO 92410 606-A2
MAR VISTA DR
12600 APLV 92308 4387-B5
MARY LN
3700 SBdC 92252 4819-C7
3900 SBdC 92252 4889-C1
MARY PL
900 CLAR 91711 571-F6
MARYANN LN
300 POM 91767 601-A5
N MARY ANN LN
3100 SBDO 92404 577-C2
MARY ANNE AV
300 BARS 92311 3679-J3

MARY ELLEN DR
2900 RivC 92509 645-C7
S MARYESS DR
800 SBDO 92410 606-F4
MARYGOLD AV
16700 FONT 92335 604-J5
16900 FONT 92335 605-B5
17200 FONT 92316 605-B5
17400 SBdC 92316 605-B5
W MARYGOLD AV
600 RLTO 92316 605-F5
MARYGOLD RD
- SBdC - (4025-H4
See Page 3934)
MARYGROVE RD
300 CLAR 91711 601-C4
MARYHURST DR
200 CLAR 91711 601-B1
W MARYKNOLL DR
100 CLTN 92324 646-B5
MARYLAND AV
- RivC 92880 683-C4
N MARYLAND AV
2000 CLTN 92324 606-D3
MARYLAND RD
40800 BBLK - 4811-F2
MARYLAND ST
- VCTV 92394 4205-F6
MARYLIND AV
- CLAR 91711 601-F2
- UPL 91786 601-F2
E MARYLIND AV
600 CLAR 91711 601-E1
MARYMOUNT LN
800 CLAR 91711 571-B6
MARYMOUNT ST
1200 RIV 92501 645-H7
MARYSVILLE PL
- FONT 92336 574-A6
MARYWOOD AV
200 CLAR 91711 601-B4
MASI DR
8100 RCUC 91730 603-E2
MASON CT
- CHLS 91709 711-G2
MASON DR
100 SBdC 92284 4747-C6
60600 SBdC 92252 4818-H5
61100 SBdC 92252 4819-A5
E MASON LN
- SBdC 92314 4742-G6
MASON PL
- RCUC 91730 573-E7
W MASON ST
700 RLTO 92376 575-F7
S MASON WY
- UPL 91786 602-A3
MASS AV
55300 SBdC 92285 4667-C7
MASSACHUSETTS AV
- VCTV 92394 4205-G4
1900 SBDO 92411 576-F5
N MASSACHUSETTS AV
1200 SBDO 92411 576-F4
1900 SBDO 92405 576-F4
MASSACHUSETTS CIR
- VCTV 92394 4205-G5
MASSACHUSETTS PL
- RCUC 91730 573-E1
MASSAI TR
20100 APLV 92307 4387-E1
MASSARO CT
1500 SBDO 92411 576-D5
N MASSARO LN
1500 SBDO 92411 576-D5
MASSIVE RD
100 SBdC - 517-G1
MAST LN
14400 SBdC - (3935-H3
See Page 3934)
MASTERS CIR
19300 APLV 92308 4387-C7
MASTODON PL
17100 VCTV 92394 4295-J1
MATARO CT
13900 SBdC 92371 4383-B3
MATARO DR
- SBdC - 3936-G4
4300 SBdC 92371 4383-A3
MATAWAN RD
20700 APLV 92308 4387-F4
MATERA PL
6600 RCUC 91701 573-E5
MATER DEI CIR
300 CLAR 91711 571-E7
MATHER AV
19000 HESP 92345 4567-C2
MATHER ST
- VCTV 92394 4205-F6
MATHEWS LN
17000 VCTV 92394 (4206-A7
See Page 4116)
MATHEWS RANCH RD
17000 SBdC 92407 514-H3
MATILIJA DR
- RCUC 91701 572-J5
MATILIJA RD
10400 SBdC 92308 4478-C2
MATILIZA CT
13900 SBdC 92371 4383-C3

MATO CT
6300 SBdC - 4844-D2
57100 YUCA 92284 4887-J6
MATSONIA CT
300 UPL 91784 572-C6
MATTERHORN AV
7400 RCUC 91730 573-A7
MATTERHORN CT
7700 RCUC 91730 573-A7
7700 RCUC 91730 603-A1
24800 SBdC - 517-A3
MATTERHORN DR
27200 SBdC - 4737-H6
MATTHEW CT
800 RDL 92373 608-A7
MATTHEWS PL
1800 POM 91766 640-H4
MATZENE DR
49100 SBdC 92256 615-G7
MAUDE ADAMS AV
4900 TNP 92277 4892-H2
7300 TNP 92277 4962-H2
MAUI RD
34300 SBdC 92365 (3685-B4
See Page 3594)
MAUKA CT
13200 SBdC 92392 4386-J3
MAUKA RD
- SBdC 92365 (3684-H3
See Page 3594)
48700 SBdC 92365 (3685-B2
See Page 3594)
MAUMEE RD
11300 APLV 92308 4388-A7
11300 APLV 92308 4478-A1
21900 APLV 92308 4387-J4
MAUNA LOA ST
14200 HESP 92345 4475-J3
14500 HESP 92345 4476-A3
MAVERICK CIR
- POM 91766 640-F4
MAVERICK DR
15500 ADEL 92301 4295-B6
MAVERICK PL
14400 VCTV 92394 4295-J7
MAVIS ST
22100 GTER 92313 646-D4
MAXINE AV
300 BARS 92311 3679-J3
MAXON LN
3700 CHNO 91710 641-C5
3800 SBdC 91710 641-D6
MAXON PL
12300 SBdC 91710 641-D6
MAXON ST
3600 CHNO 91710 641-C5
MAXSON DR
600 SBdC - 517-F3
MAXWELL RD
14000 SBdC - 514-B3
W MAXWELL ST
1300 UPL 91786 601-J4
MAY AV
100 BARS 92311 3679-G3
MAY LN
1000 BARS 92311 3679-G4
MAY RD
9100 SBdC 92339 611-E2
MAY ST
34500 SBdC 92311 3679-G5
MAYA AV
9300 ADEL 92301 4204-D6
MAYAN RD
20800 APLV 92308 4477-G4
20800 SBdC 92308 4477-G4
MAYAN TR
8400 YUCA 92284 4957-D6
MAYAPAN LN
16400 VCTV 92392 4386-E6
MAYARADA
85700 SBdC 92277 (4825-H6
See Page 4824)
MAYA VISTA
19900 APLV 92308 4477-F1
MAYBERRY AV
5000 RCUC 91737 573-A1
MAYBERRY CIR
200 RivC 91752 683-E5
MAYBERRY ST
26100 SBdC 92354 647-E1
26100 LMLN 92354 647-F1
MAYFAIR AV
500 POM 91766 640-J4
MAYFAIR CIR
- RivC 91752 683-E5
MAYFAIR CT
12700 SBdC 92371 4382-J6
MAYFAIR DR
3700 SBdC 92371 4382-J6
3800 SBdC 92371 4383-A6
75100 TNP 92277 4892-J7
75300 TNP 92277 4893-A7
N MAYFIELD AV
300 SBDO 92405 546-G7
300 SBDO 92405 576-H1
300 SBDO 92407 546-G5
500 SBDO 92401 576-H6
900 SBDO 92410 576-H6
MAYFIELD CT
5200 SBDO 92407 546-G5

N MAYFIELD PL
3700 SBDO 92405 546-H7
MAYFIELD RD
27800 SBdC 92311 (3850-A6
See Page 3760)
28800 SBdC 92311 (3849-G2
See Page 3758)
S MAYFIELD ST
300 SBDO 92401 606-H2
MAYFLOWER
200 RDL 92373 648-D2
MAYFLOWER CIR
600 CLAR 91711 601-C3
MAYFLOWER RD
500 CLAR 91711 601-C3
MAYFLOWER ST
7400 FONT 92336 574-E6
MAYSAIR LN
- CHLS 91709 681-C6
MAYTEN AV
- RCUC 91730 603-D1
MAYWOOD AV
1700 UPL 91784 571-J6
E MAYWOOD AV
400 SBDO 92404 546-J7
600 SBDO 92404 547-A7
N MAYWOOD AV
1300 UPL 91786 601-J1
1500 UPL 91786 571-J6
1600 UPL 91784 571-J6
N MAYWOOD CT
3700 SBDO 92404 546-J7
MAYWOOD DR
14700 CHLS 91709 681-D5
MAYWOOD ST
17500 SBdC 92316 645-B1
W MAYWOOD ST
400 SBdC 92316 645-G2
N MAYWOOD WY
500 UPL 91786 601-J3
MAZARIN DR
6400 SBdC 92371 4383-G5
MAZARIN RD
4700 SBdC 92371 4383-C6
MCALISTER RD
600 SBdC - 4742-B7
600 SBdC - 4812-B1
600 SBdC 92314 4742-B7
S MCALISTER RD
500 SBdC 92314 4742-B7
MCALLISTER RD
4100 SBdC 92371 4563-A1
MCART RD
14100 VCTV 92392 4386-A1
MCARTHUR BLVD
3500 SBDO 92407 546-B6
N MCARTHUR WY
200 UPL 91786 601-H3
MCAULIFFE CT
700 RDL 92374 608-E7
700 RDL 92374 648-E1
MCBROOM AV
300 BARS 92311 3680-A5
MCCARTY DR
2500 CLTN 92324 647-A4
MCCARTY RD
- SBdC 91710 712-F5
8300 RivC 92880 712-E6
8300 SBdC 92880 712-F5
MCCAULEY ST
18100 RLTO 92335 605-C1
18100 SBdC 92335 605-C1
MCCLARREN ST
22100 GTER 92313 646-E3
MCCLELLAN CT
- FONT 92336 574-A6
S MCCLOUD RIVER RD
2800 ONT 91761 643-D6
MC COMAS ST
1500 POM 91766 640-G3
MCCOMBIE
- SBdC 92277 (4825-D4
See Page 4824)
MCCONNEL CT
- YCPA 92399 649-E2
MCCONNENY RD
5000 SBdC 92345 (4655-F3
See Page 4654)
MCCORMICK AV
700 ONT 91761 643-F2
MCCORMICK ST
200 SBdC - (3682-C1
See Page 3592)
MCCOY AL
700 SBDO 92405 576-F4
MCCOY CIR
- VCTV 92394 4205-F6
MCCOY RANCH RD
- SBdC 92311 3679-E2
MCCROSKY RD
12900 SBdC 91710 641-B7
MCCULLY AV
5700 CHNO 91710 681-H1
MCDONALD RD
- SBdC 92277 4751-E7
- SBdC 92277 4821-E1
MCDONNELL AV
15400 FONT 92336 574-E5
MCDOWELL ST
3600 SBdC 92252 4819-C7

MCDOWELL ST
3900 SBdC 92252 4889-D1
MCELROY ST
7200 FONT 92336 574-H6
MCFAR LN
9600 SBdC 92371 4473-C6
MCGARRY RD
900 SBdC 92252 4749-A7
900 SBdC 92252 4819-A2
MCGEE CREEK LN
3900 ONT 91761 643-D6
MCGINNIS LN
- BARS 92311 3680-C3
- SBdC 92311 3680-D3
MCGREGOR CT
8000 FONT 92336 604-A1
MCGUIRE AV
7400 FONT 92336 574-C7
MCILROY RD
36700 SBdC 92311 3589-H7
MCKINLEY AV
200 POM 91767 601-A7
3400 SBdC 92404 577-E1
3400 SBDO 92404 577-E1
12700 SBdC 91710 641-C7
12900 SBdC 91710 681-C1
E MCKINLEY AV
1600 POM 91767 601-D6
MCKINLEY CT
7700 FONT 92336 604-A1
MCKINLEY DR
600 RDL 92373 648-B2
7800 FONT 92336 603-J1
7800 FONT 92336 604-A1
MCKINLEY ST
7300 HIGH 92410 577-E6
8600 RCUC 91730 603-A3
9800 RCUC 91730 602-J3
26000 HIGH 92346 577-E7
E MCKINLEY ST
300 RLTO 92376 605-J1
N MCKINLEY ST
1600 SBDO 92404 577-E4
W MCKINLEY ST
400 RLTO 92376 605-E1
MCKINNEY WY
16600 VCTV 92392 4296-E4
MCLAREN LN
6800 RivC 92509 645-B4
MCLENNAN ST
10800 RCUC 91701 573-C5
MCMILLEN RD
2900 SBdC 92371 4382-G7
E MCNAMARA ST
4800 ONT 91761 643-F2
MCROBERTS RD
24100 SBdC 92307 4298-F6
MCSHANS LN
1000 NDLS 92363 3620-A3
MCWETHY DR
17600 FONT 92336 605-B1
W MCWETHY ST
1600 RLTO 92336 605-D1
1600 SBdC 92336 605-D1
MCWHINNEY LN
41400 BBLK - 4811-G2
MEAD CT
10700 LMLN 92354 607-D7
MEAD LN
10700 LMLN 92354 607-D7
18300 SBdC 92392 4386-J2
MEAD ST
25300 LMLN 92354 607-C7
MEAD WY
10700 LMLN 92354 607-D7
MEADCLIFF PL
23600 DBAR 91765 640-C7
MEADE CT
- FONT 92336 574-A6
MEADOW CIR
42000 BBLK - 4741-H7
MEADOW CIR N
200 BBLK - 4741-H7
MEADOW CIR S
300 BBLK - 4741-H7
MEADOW CT
1200 UPL 91784 571-J4
13700 FONT 92337 644-A4
28300 HIGH 92346 578-B5
MEADOW DR
27400 SBdC - 517-H3
MEADOW LN
100 SBdC - 516-F2
500 POM 91767 601-A4
2700 SBdC 92314 4813-B1
7700 SBdC - 4479-J7
7700 SBdC - (4569-J1
See Page 4568)
8000 SBdC - 514-A1
10200 MohC - 3620-D3
14700 SBdC - (3935-H4
See Page 3934)
22500 APLV 92307 4298-B7
33700 SBdC - 519-F2
E MEADOW LN
100 SBdC 92314 4742-E5
100 RLTO 92377 575-G3
S MEADOW LN
1000 CLTN 92324 646-G2

W MEADOW LN
100 SBdC 92314 4742-C5
MEADOW LNDG
400 BBLK - 4811-C1
MEADOW ST
9300 RCUC 91730 602-H4
13500 YCPA 92399 649-H7
MEADOW BAY CT
27400 SBdC - 4737-H7
MEADOW BAY DR
400 SBdC - 4737-H7
S MEADOWBROOK AV
2500 ONT 91761 642-G6
MEADOW BROOK CT
- RCUC 91739 573-G2
S MEADOWBROOK DR
400 SBdC 92314 4742-C6
MEADOWBROOK LN
- RDL 92374 608-G7
6000 CHLS 91709 712-A4
S MEADOWBROOK PL
2800 ONT 91761 642-G6
MEADOWBROOK RD
600 SBdC - 517-H3
MEADOW COVE CT
27500 SBdC - 4737-H7
MEADOWCREST CT
7600 RCUC 91730 573-D7
MEADOW CREST DR
3000 CHLS 91709 681-B2
MEADOW CROSSING RD
- CHLS 91709 710-G4
MEADOW FALLS DR
23700 DBAR 91765 640-D6
MEADOWGATE LN
29200 HIGH 92346 578-D6
MEADOW GLEN PL
6300 RCUC 91737 573-C4
MEADOWGLEN RD
1400 DBAR 91765 680-B4
MEADOWGLEN ST
1500 UPL 91784 571-H3
MEADOW GROVE DR
14200 VCTV 92394 4386-F2
MEADOW GROVE RD
31300 BARS 92311 3590-D7
31300 BARS 92311 3680-D1
31300 SBdC 92311 3590-D7
31300 SBdC 92311 3680-D1
32500 SBdC - 3590-G5
32500 SBdC - (3591-B6
See Page 3590)
34300 SBdC - (3681-D1
See Page 3590)
MEADOW HILL PL
- BBLK - 4742-A7
MEADOW LARK AV
4900 SBdC 92371 4653-D1
MEADOWLARK AV
10200 SBdC 92345 4654-H1
11000 SBdC 92345 (4655-A1
See Page 4654)
MEADOWLARK LN
- SBdC 92316 645-F2
6500 CHNO 91710 642-A7
MEADOW LARK LN
- SBdC 92371 4653-F1
MEADOWLARK PL
7100 RCUC 91701 573-B6
MEADOWOOD CT
5900 CHLS 91709 711-J4
MEADOW RIDGE CIR
- POM 91766 640-G5
MEADOW RIDGE DR
2300 CHLS 91709 680-J4
MEADOW VIEW DR
- SBdC - 3936-E2
- POM 91766 640-G5
100 BBLK - 4741-G7
100 BBLK - 4811-H1
S MEADOW VIEW DR
600 SBDO 92376 606-A3
MEADOW VIEW LN
- RivC 92223 650-G7
2400 CHLS 91709 680-J2
13700 RivC 92399 650-G7
36600 BARS 92311 3589-H7
MEADOWWOOD DR
9700 RCUC 91737 572-J1
9900 RCUC 91737 573-A1
MEANDERING CREEK DR
23500 DBAR 91765 680-C2
MEANS DR
- SBdC 92285 (4576-A7
See Page 4486)
MEARS AV
3600 RivC 92509 644-J7
3600 RivC 92509 645-A6
MECCA DR
1200 BARS 92311 3679-J5
MECCA RD
7000 SBdC 92252 4958-H2
50300 SBdC 92256 615-J2
50300 SBdC 92256 616-E1
MECCA ST
18300 HESP 92345 4567-A3
MECHAM DR
900 SBdC - 517-H3
MECHANICS WY
10900 RivC 91752 683-H4

STREET Block City ZIP Pg-Grid

STREET
Block City ZIP Pg-Grid

MORNING GLORY CT
- CHLS 91709 711-G2
MORNING GLORY DR
12400 RCUC 91739 573-G4
N MORNING GLORY DR
3300 RLTO 92377 575-B1
3500 RLTO 92377 545-B7
MORNING GLORY PL
9300 SBdC 92335 604-D4
MORNING GLORY ST
12900 ADEL 92301 (4115-E2
See Page 4114)
14700 SBdC - (4115-J2
See Page 4114)
MORNING MEADOW RD
11300 APLV 92308 4477-B1
MORNING MIST WY
13500 CHLS 91709 681-C2
MORNINGSIDE AV
1400 UPL 91784 571-H4
MORNINGSIDE CT
10700 RCUC 91701 573-C6
MORNINGSIDE DR
- RDL 92373 648-E5
- RivC 92399 650-H6
1100 CLAR 91711 601-A1
1500 SBDO 92407 546-C6
3100 CHLS 91709 681-B6
13500 YCPA 92399 650-H6
MORNINGSIDE LN
100 RDL 92374 608-G7
100 RDL 92374 648-G1
7700 HIGH 92346 578-D6
MORNINGSIDE RD
- SBdC - 4479-H4
27200 SBdC 92308 4479-G4
29300 SBdC - 4480-A4
61700 SBdC 92252 4889-B6
MORNINGSIDE ST
24500 SBdC 92308 4479-C4
30100 SBdC - 4480-C4
MORNINGSIDE TR
1800 SBdC - 4742-J2
17700 SBdC - (4743-B2
See Page 4662)
MORNING SKY CT
13100 VCTV 92392 4385-F5
MORNING STAR
7400 SBdC 92277 (4895-C7
See Page 4824)
MORNING STAR DR
2600 CHLS 91709 681-A2
5300 RCUC 91737 573-C2
MORNINGSTAR PL
- BBLK - 4741-J6
MORNING STAR RD
11800 APLV 92308 4387-H5
MORNING STAR CUTOFF RD
57900 SBdC - 331-A11
MORNING STAR MINE RD
54800 SBdC - 351-A1
57900 SBdC - 331-A11
MORNING SUN DR
1100 POM 91767 641-C1
MORNING TERRACE DR
1500 CHLS 91709 680-G3
MORNING VIEW DR
14100 CHLS 91709 680-J3
E MORNINGWOOD CT
3300 ONT 91761 643-B6
MOROCCO ST
6500 RCUC 91737 573-B5
MORONGO RD
- SBdC 92278 4751-J2
1400 SBdC 92277 370-F10
1400 SBdC 92277 4822-A4
4300 SBdC 92277 4892-A1
4600 TNP 92277 4892-A3
MORONGO WY
10300 SBdC 92256 615-J4
MORRIS ST
- NDLS 92363 3620-B6
MORRISON DR
1200 RDL 92374 608-E7
MORRISON ST
1700 POM 91766 640-H4
S MORRISON ST
12700 ONT 91761 642-D6
MORRISSEY LN
- TNP 92277 4891-A3
MORRO CT
5100 RivC 91752 683-G3
MORRO RD
21200 APLV 92307 (4117-F4
See Page 4116)
21200 SBdC 92307 (4117-F4
See Page 4116)
MORRO ST
28900 SBdC 92311 3589-G6
MORRO BAY LN
15400 VCTV 92394 4296-B3
MORSE ST
1400 SBDO 92404 577-A5
MORSE CANYON DR
7800 FONT 92336 604-A1
MORSEY LN
32400 SBdC - 4480-J5

MORTON AV
8100 RCUC 91739 603-H2
MORTON CIR
1300 CLAR 91711 601-E1
MORTON ST
2700 BARS 92311 (3759-A5
See Page 3758)
MORTON RIDGE TR
32200 HIGH 92359 609-C1
32400 SBdC 92359 609-C1
34800 SBdC - 4950-A7
MORUS CT
8400 RCUC 91730 602-F2
MOSAIC DR
- RCUC 91739 573-G7
MOSS AV
300 BARS 92311 3680-A4
1200 UPL 91784 571-J3
MOSS ST
30900 SBdC 92359 608-H6
MOSS WY
26700 HIGH 92346 577-G7
MOSS ROSE CT
10700 YCPA 92399 610-A6
MOTHER LODE DR
15000 VCTV 92394 4296-A7
MOTHER LODE RD
39600 SBdC - 349-G5
MOTNOCAB RD
22600 APLV 92307 4298-B1
MOTT RD
60000 SBdC 92285 4748-G1
MOUND ST
900 RivC 92507 646-C6
24900 LMLN 92354 647-B1
N MOUND ST
1000 SBdC 92314 4742-C5
MOUND SPRING RD
- SBdC - 369-J10
MOUNT ST
600 DBAR 91765 680-B1
MOUNT ABBOTT CT
11300 RCUC 91737 573-D3
MOUNTAIN AV
600 POM 91767 601-C6
600 POM 91767 641-C1
1900 CLAR 91711 601-C6
2500 SBdC 91784 571-J1
2500 SBdC 91784 572-A2
2700 SBdC 91784 388-G1
2800 SBdC - 388-G1
2900 CLAR 91711 571-J1
5700 TNP 92277 4893-A4
6600 HIGH 92346 578-A4
12200 CHNO 91710 642-A7
12200 ONT 91710 642-A7
13100 CHNO 91710 682-A3
15700 CHNO 91710 712-A1
N MOUNTAIN AV
- UPL 91786 601-J2
100 CLAR 91711 601-B3
100 ONT 91762 601-J7
100 ONT 91762 641-J1
1400 UPL 91786 571-J4
1700 CLAR 91711 571-B5
1900 UPL 91784 571-J4
2200 SBdC 92404 577-B2
2200 SBDO 92404 577-B3
2300 SBdC 91784 571-J2
2300 LACo 91711 571-B7
2400 SBdC 92404 572-A2
3500 SBdC 92404 547-B7
3500 SBDO 92404 547-B7
N MOUNTAIN AV Rt#-30
1600 UPL 91784 571-J7
S MOUNTAIN AV
- UPL 91786 601-J4
100 ONT 91762 641-J4
300 POM 91767 601-C5
400 ONT 91762 601-J4
400 ONT 91786 601-J4
2100 CLAR 91711 601-C5
2100 ONT 91762 642-A5
2200 CHNO 91710 642-A5
2200 CHNO 91762 642-A5
2200 ONT 91710 642-A5
MOUNTAIN CT
13200 VCTV 92392 4385-E5
E MOUNTAIN CT
2200 CLTN 92324 646-H4
MOUNTAIN DR
4000 SBdC 92407 546-F6
4000 SBDO 92407 546-F5
13300 HESP 92345 4565-F1
13300 SBdC 92345 4565-F1
80300 SBdC 93562 2234-G4
N MOUNTAIN DR
2500 SBdC 91784 572-A2
N MOUNTAIN LN
2400 SBdC 91784 571-J2
2400 UPL 91784 571-J2
W MOUNTAIN LN
800 SBdC 92314 4742-B6
MOUNTAIN RD
9300 SBdC 92372 4472-B2
9300 SBdC 92372 4562-B1
12100 SBdC 92372 4382-A5
15800 SBdC 92371 4292-A5

MOUNTAIN RD
22600 SBdC 92301 (4113-D3
See Page 4112)
MOUNTAINAIRE LN
300 BBLK - 4811-G1
MOUNTAIN CREEK DR
16700 VCTV 92392 4386-F5
MOUNTAIN CREST DR
- SBDO 92407 546-F5
MOUNTAIN GATE RD
1100 UPL 91786 601-J1
MOUNTAIN GENERAL RD
- SBdC 92347 349-D7
22500 SBdC 92347 (3587-J1
See Page 3586)
22500 SBdC 92347 3588-A1
MOUNTAIN HIGH DR
13900 FONT 92337 644-B4
MOUNTAIN HILLS LN
2800 CHLS 91709 681-A5
MOUNTAIN HOME CREEK RD
5800 SBdC - 4950-F2
8100 SBdC 92359 4950-E7
MOUNTAIN LAKE RD
100 BBLK - 4742-A7
MOUNTAIN LAUREL CT
6700 HIGH 92346 578-C4
MOUNTAIN LAUREL DR
7300 HIGH 92346 578-A6
MOUNTAIN LAUREL WY
22300 DBAR 91765 680-A4
MOUNTAIN LILAC LN
- SBdC 92371 4563-B6
MOUNTAIN MEADOW DR
11500 APLV 92308 4477-B4
11600 APLV 92308 4387-B7
MOUNTAIN MEADOWS DR
18400 SBdC 92392 4386-J5
18400 SBdC 92392 4387-A5
MOUNTAIN OAK DR
31000 SBdC - 518-H6
MOUNTAIN PINE CT
9500 SBdC 92371 4473-B7
MOUNTAIN SHADOW DR
- UPL 91784 571-G6
1700 SBdC 92252 4819-G3
MOUNTAIN SHADOW RD
- UPL 91784 571-H7
MOUNTAIN SHADOW MANOR LN
5800 SBdC 92371 4653-F1
MOUNTAIN SHADOWS CT
12800 VCTV 92392 4385-G5
MOUNTAIN SHADOWS PL
- POM 91766 640-G7
9400 RCUC 91730 602-J5
MOUNTAIN SIDE LN
7500 HIGH 92346 578-C6
MOUNTAIN SKY DR
700 BBLK - 4811-H2
MOUNTAIN SPRING CT
7900 RivC 92324 647-B7
MOUNTAIN SPRINGS RD
7300 SBdC 92371 4562-J5
27800 SBdC - (3935-H2
See Page 3934)
MOUNTAIN SPGS RD U.S.-66 Hist
31300 SBdC - 351-G9
N MOUNTAIN TOP DR
3000 SBDO 92346 577-J2
MOUNTAIN VIEW AV
200 POM 91767 641-B1
500 SBdC 92397 4652-B1
1100 LMLN 92354 607-D7
1100 RDL 92354 607-D6
1100 SBDO 92408 607-D6
1200 RDL 92408 607-D6
1300 RDL 92374 607-D6
1800 LMLN 92374 607-D6
10500 SBdC 92373 607-D7
10500 LMLN 92373 607-D6
10600 SBdC 92354 607-D7
10900 LMLN 92354 647-D2
16900 FONT 92336 574-J6
N MOUNTAIN VIEW AV
100 SBDO 92408 606-H1
200 SBDO 92401 606-H1
400 SBDO 92401 576-H6
900 SBDO 92410 576-H6
1000 POM 91767 601-B7
1200 SBDO 92405 576-H2
3600 SBDO 92405 546-H7
4000 SBDO 92407 546-H4
S MOUNTAIN VIEW AV
200 SBDO 92408 606-H2
1300 POM 91766 641-B3
E MOUNTAIN VIEW BLVD
100 SBdC 92314 4742-D5
W MOUNTAIN VIEW BLVD
900 SBdC 92314 4742-B5
MOUNTAIN VIEW CIR
- RivC 91752 683-E5
61800 SBdC 92252 4959-C1
61900 SBdC 92252 4889-C7
MOUNTAIN VIEW DR
- APLV 92308 4477-B3

MOUNTAIN VIEW DR
- SBdC 92252 4959-B5
2700 SBdC - 519-B7
3700 SBdC 92277 4821-G6
7300 RCUC 91730 573-C7
9000 SBdC 92339 611-C2
MOUNTAIN VIEW LN
1300 SBdC 92359 609-C5
1600 CHLS 91709 710-G2
5300 SBdC - 4886-H5
25700 SBdC 92307 4298-J2
25700 SBdC 92307 4299-C2
35500 YCPA 92399 650-B4
S MOUNTAIN VIEW LN
1100 CLTN 92324 646-G1
MOUNTAIN VIEW RD
- SBdC - 4481-E5
8500 SBdC 92308 4479-A6
16900 ADEL 92301 4294-G2
18500 SBdC - 4479-J6
19200 SBdC 92301 (4203-D1
See Page 4112)
20800 SBdC 92301 (4113-D2
See Page 4112)
20900 SBdC 92308 4477-J6
22200 SBdC 92308 4478-B6
29200 SBdC - 4480-A6
30700 SBdC 92365 3764-B3
32900 SBdC 92365 (3684-B7
See Page 3594)
34000 SBdC 92311 (3677-J5
See Page 3586)
35000 SBdC 92347 (3677-J5
See Page 3586)
36500 SBdC - 4482-A5
36500 SBdC 92347 (3587-J7
See Page 3586)
38300 SBdC 92365 3594-B1
38500 SBdC 92365 (3504-B6
See Page 3414)
39400 SBdC 92347 349-B7
39800 SBdC - (3682-F1
See Page 3592)
MOUNTAIN VIEW RD Rt#-1
- MohC - 3620-F2
MOUNTAIN VIEW ST
6300 SBdC 92252 4889-C7
35100 YCPA 92399 650-A5
56100 SBdC 92284 4817-F2
82700 SBdC 93562 2144-J4
E MOUNTAIN VIEW ST
100 BARS 92311 3679-H3
1000 BARS 92311 3680-A3
W MOUNTAIN VIEW ST
100 BARS 92311 3679-G3
MOUNTAIN VIEW TR
- YUCA 92284 4958-B4
54700 YUCA 92284 4957-D4
MOUNTAIN VIEW PARK LN
- SBdC 92311 3590-A7
MOUNTAIN VISTA AV
9400 HESP 92345 4475-F6
MOUNTAIN VISTA CIR
- RDL 92374 608-B3
E MOUNTAIN WOODS ST
2200 CLTN 92324 606-H7
MOUNT BAKER CT
11500 RCUC 91737 573-E3
MOUNT BALDWIN CT
11500 RCUC 91737 573-D4
MOUNT BALDY DR
12300 VCTV 92392 4385-G6
MOUNT BALDY PL
6100 RCUC 91737 573-E3
MOUNT BALDY RD
800 SBdC - 512-D1
900 LACo - 512-B4
900 SBdC - (4732-E7
See Page 4653)
3800 CLAR 91711 571-G2
3900 LACo 91711 571-G2
MOUNT BALDY WY
13700 VCTV 92392 4385-G6
MOUNT BAXTER CT
11400 RCUC 91737 573-D4
MOUNT BEND PL
6400 RCUC 91737 573-E4
MOUNT CAMBRIDGE CT
11700 RCUC 91737 573-E3
MOUNT CARMEL DR
400 CLAR 91711 571-C6
MOUNT COOK CT
6200 RCUC 91737 573-D4
N MOUNT DOBLE DR
100 SBdC 92314 4742-D4
S MOUNT DOBLE DR
100 SBdC 92314 4742-D6
MOUNT EVERETT CT
11700 RCUC 91737 573-E4
MOUNT GUNNISON CT
11700 RCUC 91737 573-E4
MOUNT HARVARD CT
11800 RCUC 91737 573-E3
MOUNT HOOD CT
11500 RCUC 91737 573-D4
MOUNT JEFFERSON DR
11600 RCUC 91737 573-E4

MOUNT JOHNSON CT
11300 RCUC 91737 573-D4
MOUNT LASSEN AV
2000 SBdC 92252 4820-C3
6500 SBdC 92252 4890-C7
6700 SBdC 92252 4960-C1
MOUNT LASSEN CT
11600 RCUC 91737 573-E4
MOUNT MAHOGANY RD
2000 SBdC 92397 4652-F4
MOUNT MIRIAH DR
11600 RCUC 91737 573-E4
MOUNT NEBO RD
200 SBdC 92252 4749-G6
900 SBdC 92252 4819-G1
MOUNT PALOMAR LN
- FONT 92336 574-D2
MOUNT PALOMAR ST
11400 RCUC 91737 573-D4
MOUNT PINOS CT
6200 RCUC 91737 573-E4
MOUNT RAINIER CT
11500 RCUC 91737 573-E4
MOUNT RAINIER WY
13100 HESP 92345 4475-F5
MOUNT RITTER ST
11400 RCUC 91737 573-D4
MOUNT ROYAL CT
11800 RCUC 91737 573-E4
MOUNT RUSHMORE PL
6400 RCUC 91737 573-D4
MOUNT SAN ANTONIO ST
11400 RCUC 91737 573-D4
MOUNT SHASTA AV
500 SBdC 92252 4750-C5
1300 SBdC 92252 4820-C1
6200 SBdC 92252 4890-D7
6900 SBdC 92252 4960-D1
MOUNT SHASTA DR
10100 HESP 92345 4475-G4
N MOUNT SHASTA RD
1000 SBdC 92314 4742-B5
MOUNT SHERMAN CT
11600 RCUC 91737 573-E4
MOUNT STERLING CT
11600 RCUC 91737 573-E4
N MOUNT VERDI RD
1000 SBdC 92314 4742-B4
MOUNT VERNON AV
- RivC 92507 646-F7
500 BARS 92311 3679-G4
700 RIV 92507 646-F7
1500 POM 91768 640-E2
4700 CHNO 91710 641-F6
11600 GTER 92313 646-E3
N MOUNT VERNON AV
100 CLTN 92324 606-E5
100 SBDO 92410 606-E1
400 SBDO 92411 606-E1
400 SBDO 92411 576-E4
2500 SBDO 92405 576-E4
N MOUNT VERNON AV U.S.-66 Hist
500 SBDO 92411 576-E5
S MOUNT VERNON AV
100 CLTN 92324 606-E7
100 SBDO 92410 606-E2
700 CLTN 92324 646-F1
1400 GTER 92313 646-F2
1400 GTER 92324 646-F2
MOUNT VERNON AV S
300 CLTN 92324 606-E7
MOUNT VERNON LN
1000 BARS 92311 3679-G4
MOUNT VERNON PL
- SBdC 92278 4751-E5
100 SBdC 92277 4751-E5
MOUNT VERNON ST
4300 CHNO 91710 641-E6
MOUNT VIEW RD
10900 SBdC 92256 615-J5
MOUNT VIEW TR
60500 SBdC 92252 4958-H4
61600 SBdC 92252 4959-B3
MOUNT WALLACE CT
11300 RCUC 91737 573-D4
MOUNT WAVERLY CT
11600 RCUC 91737 573-E4
MOUNT WELLINGTON CT
6300 RCUC 91737 573-D4
MOUNT WHITNEY CT
11600 RCUC 91737 573-E3
N MOUNT WHITNEY DR
1000 SBdC 92314 4742-B5
MOUNT WHITNEY WY
10100 HESP 92345 4475-F5
MOUNT WILSON CT
11700 RCUC 91737 573-E4
MOUNT WILSON LN
- FONT 92336 574-D3
MOYER AV
4500 YUCA 92284 4887-F3
MOYLE RD
4700 SBdC 92371 4383-C4
MOZUMDAR DR
300 SBdC - 516-C1
300 SBdC - 4736-C7
MR MCDUFFS WY
7500 HIGH 92346 578-A6

MUELLER CT
- RCUC 91739 573-H4
MUGU CT
13000 APLV 92308 4387-D3
MUIR AV
300 BARS 92311 3680-A4
500 POM 91766 640-H3
MUIR CT
200 UPL 91784 572-C4
12300 CHNO 91710 641-E6
MUIR LN
- SBdC - 4812-H2
- SBdC 92314 4812-H2
MUIR ST
7800 FONT 92336 604-A1
MUIRFIELD AV
1900 UPL 91784 571-H4
3200 CHLS 91709 681-B5
MUIRFIELD CT
18900 APLV 92308 4477-D3
MUIRFIELD DR
11000 RCUC 91730 573-C7
MUIRFIELD LN
- FONT 92336 574-G3
MULBERRY AV
8000 FONT 92336 604-A3
8100 FONT 92335 604-A3
8100 SBdC 92335 604-A3
10300 FONT 92337 604-A7
10500 FONT 92337 644-A4
10500 SBdC 92337 644-A4
12200 CHNO 91710 641-J5
37300 SBdC 92347 (3587-F4
See Page 3586)
N MULBERRY AV
500 SBDO 92376 575-J7
600 RLTO 92376 575-J5
900 UPL 91786 602-A1
1400 UPL 91786 572-A7
1600 UPL 91784 572-A6
MULBERRY CIR
13500 YCPA 92399 650-D6
E MULBERRY CT
2000 ONT 91764 602-G5
MULBERRY DR
300 POM 91767 601-A3
MULBERRY ST
6500 RCUC 91739 574-A4
14600 HESP 92345 4566-A6
E MULBERRY ST
1900 ONT 91764 602-G5
N MULBERRY WY
1800 UPL 91784 572-A6
MULE CANYON RD
35800 SBdC - (3681-H1
See Page 3590)
36100 SBdC - (3591-J7
See Page 3590)
36100 SBdC - 3592-B2
MULLET BAY CT
18900 APLV 92308 4477-D3
W MULLINS DR
300 SBdC 92314 4742-C4
MULTNOMAH RD
20900 APLV 92308 4387-G6
MULVIHILL AV
100 RDL 92374 608-B4
MULZ RD
- SBdC 92301 (4024-E3
See Page 3934)
MUMS CT
7500 FONT 92336 574-E7
MUMS ST
7600 FONT 92336 574-E7
MUNDA ST
1200 BARS 92311 3680-F6
MUNHALL AV
1900 POM 91766 641-B5
MUNI CT
16300 APLV 92307 4296-H3
MUNI RD
15800 APLV 92307 4296-H4
17500 APLV 92307 (4206-J7
See Page 4116)
27500 SBdC - 3936-H3
MUNI WY
18100 APLV 92307 4296-J2
MUNSEE RD
18700 APLV 92307 4297-A2
MUNSEE TR
7700 SBdC 92252 4959-C3
MURAL DR
1400 CLAR 91711 601-A2
3100 POM 91767 601-A2
MURIEL AV
18000 SBdC 92407 515-C4
MURIEL DR
100 BARS 92311 3679-J2
MURIEL LN
17900 SBdC 92407 515-B4
MURIEL ST
36700 SBdC 92311 3589-J7
MURIETA ST
20100 SBdC 92307 (4117-D7
See Page 4116)
20200 APLV 92307 (4117-H7
See Page 4116)
S MUROC DR
200 SBdC 92314 4742-G6

MURPHY AV
300 RivC 92507 646-E7
MURPHY ST
11500 LMLN 92354 647-C2
MURRAY AV
900 POM 91767 601-D7
15200 CHLS 91709 681-F6
MURRAY LN
7100 YUCA 92284 4958-A2
MURRAYHILL RD
- SBdC 92284 4818-F4
MURRIETA AV
6200 YUCA 92284 4888-A7
MURRIETA ST
4700 CHNO 91710 681-F2
MUSCADINE LN
14400 CHLS 91709 680-H4
MUSCAT AV
15300 SBdC 92335 604-E1
MUSCAT PL
6000 RCUC 91737 573-B4
N MUSCATEL AV
300 ONT 91764 602-D7
MUSCATEL ST
7200 SBdC 92371 4563-J1
7400 SBdC 92371 4564-A1
9700 SBdC 92345 4564-H1
10900 SBdC 92345 4565-B1
11600 HESP 92345 4565-E1
14500 HESP 92345 4566-A1
S MUSCOTT ST
100 SBDO 92410 606-D2
N MUSCUPIABE DR
2000 SBDO 92405 576-F3
MUSGRAVE RD
10800 SBdC 92345 4564-J7
11400 SBdC 92345 4565-B7
14300 HESP 92345 4565-J6
MUSIC CAMP RD
2100 SBdC - 519-E6
MUSKRAT AV
14900 SBdC 92301 4294-F6
15600 ADEL 92301 4294-F1
17200 ADEL 92301 4204-F1
MUSKRAT CT
- SBdC - 4843-E5
MUSKRAT LN
7400 SBdC - 4843-E5
MUSKRAT TR
7300 SBdC - 4843-E5
MUSTANG AV
8900 SBdC 92308 4478-F1
12000 SBdC 92308 4388-F6
12000 SBdC 92307 4388-F3
15700 SBdC 92307 4298-F4
MUSTANG CIR
- MTCL 91763 641-E1
MUSTANG CT
6700 SBdC - 4843-J3
W MUSTANG CT
1200 UPL 91786 571-J7
S MUSTANG DR
3500 ONT 91761 683-A1
MUSTANG LN
200 NDLS 92363 3710-D2
5200 FONT 92336 574-D2
MUSTANG RD
- RCUC 91737 572-G3
- SBdC 92365 (3683-E5
See Page 3592)
4100 SBdC 91710 641-D4
8800 RCUC 91701 572-G3
MUSTANG ST
- RivC 92880 683-D7
12900 VCTV 92394 4205-E5
MUSTANG TR
19300 SBdC - (3937-B1
See Page 3936)
MUSTARD SEED DR
- RivC 92399 650-G7
MYALON RD
8900 SBdC - 4480-D1
13000 SBdC - (4390-D3
See Page 4300)
15200 APLV 92307 4297-A5
MYLES CT
7700 SBdC 92336 575-C7
W MYRA CT
1100 UPL 91786 601-J1
MYRA ST
1500 RDL 92373 648-D3
MYRTLE AV
1200 UPL 91786 602-D1
6500 HESP 92345 4566-A6
N MYRTLE AV
100 POM 91768 640-G1
900 SBdC 92314 4742-D4
S MYRTLE AV
100 POM 91766 640-G2
MYRTLE CT
6500 RCUC 91739 573-G4
MYRTLE DR
- RCUC 91737 573-B3
N MYRTLE DR
1000 SBDO 92410 577-A6
MYRTLE LN
- FONT 92337 645-B2
MYRTLE PL
- FONT 92336 574-E6

MYRTLE RD
4100 SBdC - 4886-E3
MYRTLE ST
200 RDL 92373 608-C7
300 RDL 92373 648-C1
10700 LMLN 92354 607-E7
S MYRTLEWOOD AV
1800 CLTN 92324 646-H3
MYSTIC DR
12500 VCTV 92392 4385-G6
MYSTIC CANYON DR
6100 CHLS 91709 712-A5

N

N ST
600 NDLS 92363 3620-C4
800 BARS 92311 3679-D4
33700 SBdC 92311 3679-D5
33700 SBdC 92311 (3759-D1
See Page 3758)
E N ST
100 CLTN 92324 606-D7
W N ST
100 CLTN 92324 606-C7
NAAPIS TR
6300 SBdC - 4844-E2
NABORLY RD
- SBdC 92277 (4895-D6
See Page 4824)
3800 SBdC 92277 (4825-E5
See Page 4824)
NACHES CT
5500 SBdC - 4773-J7
NADEAU LN
6600 RivC 92509 645-C5
NADELHORN DR
700 SBdC - 4737-H6
E NADINA DR
1100 SBdC 92314 4742-D4
NAGLES ST
- YUCA 92284 4957-J6
- YUCA 92284 4958-A6
N NAHLIN CT
- SBDO 92410 606-A2
NAHOA RD
11700 SBdC 92392 4474-E1
11900 SBdC 92392 4384-E7
NAHOA WY
8200 SBdC 92371 4564-E3
11300 SBdC 92392 4474-E2
NAKASH RD
18300 APLV 92307 4296-J3
NALATAPA RD
22600 APLV 92307 4298-B2
23700 SBdC 92307 4298-D2
NAMBE CT
22000 APLV 92308 4478-A3
NAMBE RD
10500 APLV 92308 4478-A3
10600 APLV 92308 4477-J2
NAN CT
24300 DBAR 91765 680-E2
N NANA AV
900 SBdC 92314 4742-C4
NANCOTTA RD
15800 APLV 92307 4297-A4
W NANCY CT
1200 UPL 91786 601-J1
NANCY DR
27400 SBdC - 517-H4
NANCY LN
- SBDO 92407 515-H7
NANCY ST
600 BARS 92311 3679-F3
NANDINA RD
12600 SBdC 92371 4382-J6
NANDINA ST
21000 APLV 92308 4477-G3
22900 GTER 92313 646-F3
69700 SBdC 92277 4821-D6
NANETTE ST
100 RDL 92373 648-A1
NANNLE CT
- VCTV 92392 4386-E2
NANTAIL CT
- SBdC - (4025-J5
See Page 3934)
NANTICOKE RD
14100 APLV 92307 4298-A7
14100 APLV 92307 4388-A1
14900 APLV 92307 4297-J4
NANTUCKET CT
6300 CHNO 91710 642-A6
NANTUCKET PL
6600 RCUC 91737 572-J5
NANTUCKET ST
- HESP 92345 4475-H7
NAOMI ST
- RDL 92374 608-E7
NAPA AV
1100 RDL 92374 608-E7
5900 RCUC 91701 572-F3
N NAPA AV
600 ONT 91764 602-G6
NAPA CT
700 CLAR 91711 571-B5
5700 RCUC 91701 572-F3
8600 RCUC 91730 572-F7
22200 GTER 92313 646-E5

NAPA DR
3700 CHNO 91710 641-C6
NAPA RD
10300 ADEL 92301 4204-G5
55200 SBdC 92284 4747-D5
57700 SBdC 92284 4748-A5
60800 SBdC 92252 4748-H5
61300 SBdC 92252 4749-A5
NAPA ST
12900 SBdC 92335 603-J4
13300 SBdC 92335 604-A4
NAPA VALLEY DR
8500 RCUC 91730 602-G2
NAPLES AV
1700 RDL 92374 608-G5
1700 SBdC 92359 608-G5
2200 SBdC 92359 609-B5
2300 UPL 91784 571-J3
NAPLES CT
14100 FONT 92336 604-B1
NAPLES LN
16500 VCTV 92394 4296-B2
NAPOLI CIR
11900 FONT 92337 644-F4
NAPOLI DR
11300 RCUC 91701 573-D5
NAPOLI PL
1200 POM 91766 640-D3
NARAB TR
- SBdC 92252 4888-H1
W NARANGA ST
2000 SBDO 92410 606-C1
NARATO RD
- SBdC - 3762-J2
NARCISSUS LN
6200 CHLS 91709 712-A5
14900 FONT 92336 574-D7
NARDI LN
100 SBdC - 516-C2
NARNIA WY
62500 SBdC 92252 4819-D5
NARRAGANSET RD
14700 SBdC 92307 4298-F6
NARRAGANSETT RD
12100 SBdC 92307 4388-F4
NARROW LN
40100 BBLK - 4811-D1
NASH ST
3500 RIV 92501 646-A7
NASHVILLE ST
36300 SBdC 92365 3594-E6
NASON-DIXON RD
900 SBdC 92284 4748-G7
1100 SBdC 92284 4818-G2
NASSAU CT
- RivC 92880 683-C4
NASSAU DR
13500 VCTV 92392 4386-C2
NASSAU LN
15600 VCTV 92392 4386-C3
NASSAU PL
100 CLAR 91711 571-D5
NASTURTIUM DR
12500 RCUC 91739 573-G5
NATALIE RD
5900 CHLS 91709 711-J4
5900 CHLS 91709 712-A4
NATHAN CT
1600 RDL 92374 608-D4
NATHENE LN
6600 RivC 92509 645-B5
NATIONAL PL
5800 CHNO 91710 641-H5
NATIONAL OLD TRAILS HWY
- SBdC - 351-L7
NATIONAL OLD TRAILS RD
26100 SBdC - 352-B10
NATIONAL PARK DR
6500 TNP 92277 4892-F6
NATIONAL TRLS HWY U.S.-66 Hist
- SBdC - 351-D11
3800 BARS 92311 3758-B3
5000 BARS 92311 3678-E7
5000 SBdC 92311 3678-E7
6100 SBdC 92311 3758-B3
16200 VCTV 92394 4296-C1
16300 VCTV 92394 (4206-A4
See Page 4116)
16800 SBdC - (4206-A4
See Page 4116)
16800 SBdC 92394 (4206-A4
See Page 4116)
16900 VCTV - (4206-A4
See Page 4116)
18100 SBdC - 4205-J1
18200 SBdC 92311 (3757-J5
See Page 3756)
19000 SBdC - (4115-H4
See Page 4114)
21000 SBdC - (4025-J7
See Page 3934)
23400 SBdC - (4026-A1
See Page 3936)
23500 SBdC - 3936-D3
26800 SBdC - (3846-G7
See Page 3756)

NATIONAL TRLS HWY U.S.-66 Hist
28100 SBdC - (3847-E3
See Page 3756)
29700 SBdC 92311 (3847-E3
See Page 3756)
31900 BARS 92311 3680-J6
33300 SBdC - 3680-J6
33300 SBdC - (3681-B7
See Page 3590)
36200 SBdC - (3761-H1
See Page 3760)
36200 SBdC - 3762-A1
40000 SBdC - (3763-A2
See Page 3762)
41300 SBdC 92365 (3763-A2
See Page 3762)
44100 SBdC 92365 3764-A4
47700 SBdC 92365 (3765-B6
See Page 3764)
49700 SBdC - (3765-G7
See Page 3764)
51100 SBdC - 349-L10
54400 SBdC - 350-A11
60200 SBdC - 370-G3
92900 SBdC - 371-B3
NATIONAL TRAILS OH S
18900 SBdC - (3847-A5
See Page 3756)
NATOMA AV
6600 HESP 92345 4566-A6
NATOMA RD
13700 SBdC 92307 4388-D2
14100 SBdC 92307 4298-D7
NATOMA TR
58600 YUCA 92284 4958-D2
60100 SBdC 92252 4958-H2
NATTY LN
8300 SBdC 92335 604-B2
NAUTICAL LN
13700 SBdC - (3935-F3
See Page 3934)
NAVAHO TRAIL LN
- POM 91766 640-H5
NAVAJO AV
300 PRKR - 4774-H7
800 PRKR - 4844-J1
1800 LPCo - 4844-J1
38500 SBdC 92365 (3504-A7
See Page 3414)
38500 SBdC 92365 3594-A1
NAVAJO CT
- SBdC - 4843-H2
10500 APLV 92308 4477-J3
NAVAJO LN
12300 VCTV 92392 4385-C6
NAVAJO PL
12700 APLV 92308 4387-J4
NAVAJO RD
9200 SBdC 92308 4477-J6
10000 APLV 92308 4477-J2
11300 APLV 92308 4387-J3
13600 APLV 92307 4387-J3
14100 APLV 92307 4297-H1
16800 APLV 92307 4207-H1
19600 APLV 92307 (4117-H6
See Page 4116)
NAVAJO ST
900 BARS 92311 3679-J4
1000 BARS 92311 3680-A4
1100 SBdC - 4741-A5
NAVAJO TR
6300 SBdC - 4843-H3
7800 SBdC 92252 4959-A3
8900 SBdC 92256 616-D1
8900 SBdC 92256 4956-D7
54500 YUCA 92284 4957-B4
57300 YUCA 92284 4958-A4
60500 SBdC 92252 4958-H3
NAVAJO WY
12700 APLV 92308 4387-J4
NAVAJO SPRINGS RD
23600 DBAR 91765 640-B6
NAVANO ST
900 CLTN 92324 646-H1
NAVARONE CT
29700 SBdC 92311 3589-J6
NAVARRO CT
14300 VCTV 92392 4386-E1
NAVARRO DR
2200 CLAR 91711 571-D6
13800 VCTV 92392 4386-E1
14600 VCTV 92392 4296-E7
NAVILLA RD
- SBdC 92371 4563-B6
NAWAKWA RD
14700 APLV 92307 4298-B1
NEARBANK
20500 SBdC - 4120-C6
NEBO CT
12700 APLV 92308 4387-F4
NEBO ST
33400 SBdC - 3680-J7
33500 SBdC - (3681-A6
See Page 3590)
NEBRASKA LN
33900 YCPA 92399 649-G5
NEBRASKA ST
- FONT 92336 574-C6

STREET Block	City	ZIP	Pg-Grid
NEBRASKA ST			
33500	YCPA	92399	649-G5
NEBRASKA WY			
13100	YCPA	92399	649-G6
E NECTAR CT			
3400	ONT	91761	643-B6
NECTARINE AV			
12200	CHNO	91710	641-J5
NEDLEE AV			
1300	SBdC	92407	515-B5
NEEDHAM AV			
18300	APLV	92307	4207-J3
NEEDLES DR			
-	MohC	-	3620-F1
NEEDLES FRWY I-40			
-	BARS	-	3679-J4
-	BARS	-	3680-A4
-	NDLS	-	352-A8
-	NDLS	-	3620-C6
-	NDLS	-	3710-E2
-	SBdC	-	349-L10
-	SBdC	-	350-A11
-	SBdC	-	351-H8
-	SBdC	-	352-A8
-	SBdC	-	370-D1
-	SBdC	-	3680-F5
-	SBdC	-	(3681-A7 See Page 3590)
-	SBdC	-	3710-F5
-	SBdC	-	(3761-F1 See Page 3760)
-	SBdC	-	3762-C2
-	SBdC	-	(3763-C3 See Page 3762)
-	SBdC	-	3764-D4
-	SBdC	-	(3765-B5 See Page 3764)
NEEDLES FRWY U.S.-66 Hist			
-	SBdC	-	352-B10
NEEDLES HWY			
1200	NDLS	92363	3620-C4
2200	NDLS	92363	352-A6
23100	SBdC	-	352-A6
NEEDLES HWY U.S.-66 Hist			
1100	NDLS	92363	3620-A3
NEEDLES LN			
-	SBdC	-	4812-E2
NEEDLES ST			
1000	SBdC	-	4606-G1
NEEDLES HY RIV RD U.S.-66 Hist			
-	NDLS	92363	3620-A4
NEELANS LN			
18900	SBdC	92316	645-E1
NEENACH RD			
16500	APLV	92307	4298-B2
NEENAH WY			
7700	SBdC	-	4843-D6
NEHRING PL			
73300	TNP	92277	4892-D1
NEIGHBORLY PL			
34900	SBdC	-	4481-F3
NELLIBELL DR			
12900	VCTV	92392	4385-G5
NELSON AV			
-	VCTV	92394	4296-A7
2000	BARS	92311	3679-G6
7300	FONT	92336	575-B6
58100	YUCA	92284	4888-B6
NELSON RD			
-	LPCo	-	4844-E4
31700	SBdC	92311	3680-E4
56300	YUCA	92284	4887-G6
58600	YUCA	92284	4888-C7
NELSON ST			
1500	RDL	92374	608-E4
2200	POM	91766	641-A5
11500	LMLN	92354	647-E2
NEOLA CT			
10900	APLV	92308	4477-G2
NEOLA DR			
5500	SBdC	92345	(4655-A2 See Page 4654)
NEOLA RD N			
11100	APLV	92308	4477-G1
NEOLA RD S			
10700	APLV	92308	4477-G2
NEPTUNE AV			
1900	SBdC	92252	4819-E3
5700	SBdC	92252	4889-E4
17200	VCTV	92394	(4206-F7 See Page 4116)
NEPTUNE DR			
61000	SBdC	92252	4748-J6
63100	SBdC	92252	4749-A6
NEPTUNE RD			
34900	SBdC	-	(4391-F4 See Page 4300)
36900	SBdC	-	(4392-B4 See Page 4302)
NEPTUNE WY			
1100	SBdC	-	516-H4
NESBITT DR			
11000	RCUC	91730	573-C7
NESSELWOOD CT			
16400	CHLS	91709	711-E2
NESTAL CT			
24700	SBdC	-	517-A4
NESTHORN DR			
1000	SBdC	-	517-A3
NETHERLANDS VIEW LP			
6300	RCUC	91737	573-E4
NETTIE ST			
10200	RivC	91752	644-A6
NETZLEY PL			
13300	CHNO	91710	681-D1
NEUMAN ST			
26000	SBdC	92311	3588-J7
26000	SBdC	92311	3678-J1
26200	SBdC	92311	3679-A1
NEVA CT			
58300	YUCA	92284	4958-C2
NEVA LN			
1100	POM	91766	641-B4
NEVA RD			
-	SBdC	92252	4959-C6
NEVADA AV			
-	VCTV	92394	4205-F5
7000	SBdC	92371	4473-J6
8100	SBdC	92371	4563-J2
NEVADA CT			
-	FONT	92336	574-C6
6700	RCUC	91701	573-C5
NEVADA RD			
-	SBdC	92277	(4894-B1 See Page 4824)
3200	SBdC	92277	4824-B5
10700	SBdC	92371	4473-H1
11900	SBdC	92371	4383-H2
NEVADA ST			
-	RDL	92373	647-G1
100	RDL	92373	607-G7
800	RDL	92374	607-G6
1200	SBdC	92374	607-G4
55700	SBdC	-	4606-G2
E NEVADA ST			
100	ONT	91761	642-C1
W NEVADA ST			
100	ONT	91761	642-B2
100	ONT	91762	642-B2
NEVE CT			
800	SBdC	-	517-A3
NEVEN RD			
1300	SBdC	92407	515-C5
NEVIN RD			
81900	SBdC	92277	4824-H4
NEW LN			
35100	YCPA	92399	650-A6
NEWARK CT			
3800	CLAR	91711	571-F4
NEWBERRY RD			
30700	SBdC	92365	3764-D2
32900	SBdC	92365	(3684-D5 See Page 3594)
35700	SBdC	92365	3594-D7
NEWBRIAR WY			
-	CHLS	91709	681-H7
NEWBURY AV			
1900	SBdC	92404	577-D1
1900	SBDO	92404	577-D1
5300	SBdC	92404	547-D7
5300	SBDO	92404	547-D7
6900	HIGH	92404	577-D5
NEWBURY CT			
12700	CHNO	91710	642-B6
NEWBURY PL			
7300	RCUC	91730	573-C7
NEWBURY ST			
-	YCPA	92399	649-E2
NEWBURY WY			
700	DBAR	91765	680-D1
NEWCASTLE CT			
7700	HIGH	92346	578-C6
13700	SBdC	92335	604-A2
NEWCASTLE RD			
28500	HIGH	92346	578-B7
NEWCASTLE WY			
14700	VCTV	92394	4295-J6
NEWCOMB PL			
1500	CLAR	91711	601-B1
NEWCOMB ST			
3100	SBdC	92404	577-D2
3100	SBDO	92404	577-D2
7400	HIGH	92410	577-E6
N NEWCOMB ST			
1600	SBdC	92404	577-E4
NEW DIXIE MINE RD			
-	SBdC	-	369-L10
55300	SBdC	-	4747-A3
55300	SBdC	92285	4747-A3
NEWELL DR			
-	SBdC	-	4741-E6
NEW ENGLAND DR			
-	RCUC	91730	573-E1
NEW FOAL TR			
14600	FONT	92336	574-D2
NEWHALL AV			
7300	HESP	92345	4566-H3
18600	APLV	92307	4207-J4
NEW HAMPSHIRE AV			
-	CLAR	91711	571-E4
NEW HAMPSHIRE ST			
18500	ADEL	92301	4204-J3
NEW HAVEN AV			
2000	CLAR	91711	571-E7
NEW HAVEN DR			
1300	POM	91766	640-G3
NEW HORIZONS RD			
56500	YUCA	92284	4887-G1
NEW JERSEY CT			
-	FONT	92336	574-D6
NEW JERSEY ST			
-	RDL	92374	607-G7
400	RDL	92373	607-G7
2700	SBdC	92373	607-G7
3500	SBdC	92373	647-G2
6100	LMLN	92373	647-G2
NEWLAND CT			
11300	VCTV	92392	4475-D2
NEWMAN ST			
100	POM	91768	640-G1
W NEWMAN ST			
1300	SBdC	91784	571-H2
NEWMARK AV			
3900	SBDO	92405	546-G7
4000	SBdC	92407	546-G7
4000	SBDO	92407	546-G7
NEWMARK RD			
7400	SBdC	92301	(4203-H5 See Page 4112)
NEW MEXICO CT			
-	FONT	92336	574-C6
-	VCTV	92394	4205-G6
NEW ORLEANS CT			
800	CLAR	91711	571-E5
NEW PINE AV			
5800	SBDO	92407	545-J4
5800	SBDO	92407	546-A4
NEWPORT AV			
100	SBDO	92408	607-B1
2900	SBdC	92404	577-B2
2900	SBDO	92404	577-B2
7000	FONT	92336	574-J5
8500	FONT	92335	604-J2
20000	GTER	92313	646-D3
26100	LMLN	92354	647-F2
32300	HIGH	92359	609-C3
NEWPORT CT			
1100	SBDO	92404	547-B6
6700	FONT	92336	574-J5
11400	ADEL	92301	4385-A1
NEWPORT DR			
11300	RCUC	91730	603-D4
NEWPORT ST			
1100	SBDO	92404	577-B3
11000	VCTV	92392	4475-D3
NEWPORT WY			
26200	SBdC	-	(3935-G6 See Page 3934)
NEW PUBLIC ST			
-	CLTN	92324	606-G7
-	CLTN	92324	646-G1
NEWTON LN			
-	YUCA	92284	4887-J4
NEWTON LP			
-	CHLS	91709	712-A5
NEWTON PL			
7000	RCUC	91701	572-J6
NEWTON RD			
-	SBdC	-	4480-D3
4800	YUCA	92284	4887-H3
NEWTON ST			
5600	RivC	92509	645-E7
NEW YORK AV			
-	FONT	92336	574-D6
NEW YORK DR			
500	POM	91768	640-F1
NEW YORK ST			
-	VCTV	92394	4205-F6
-	RDL	92373	648-A1
100	RDL	92373	608-A7
500	RDL	92374	608-A6
NEW YORK CANYON RD			
18800	SBdC	-	329-A5
NIABI RD			
13500	APLV	92308	4388-B2
NIAGARA AV			
1400	CLAR	91711	601-B1
9600	FONT	92335	604-G6
NIAGARA CT			
7500	FONT	92336	574-F7
NIAGARA DR			
7100	FONT	92336	574-F6
9500	FONT	92335	604-F5
11500	RivC	91752	683-G5
13400	SBdC	92392	4386-J3
13400	SBdC	92392	4387-A3
NIAGARA PL			
-	RCUC	91730	573-E2
NICE AV			
1700	RDL	92374	608-G6
1700	SBdC	92359	608-G6
2100	SBdC	92359	609-A5
NICHELINI DR			
8500	RCUC	91730	602-G2
W NICHOLAS ST			
1000	UPL	91784	571-J4
1000	UPL	91784	572-A4
NICHOLET ST			
2700	POM	91768	640-C2
NICHOLS RD			
10100	ADEL	92301	4204-F2
11300	ADEL	92301	4205-A2
NICHOLS ST			
9000	ADEL	92301	4204-C2
NICKOLAS AV			
900	RDL	92374	608-D5
NICKS AV			
25400	LMLN	92354	647-D2
NICOLA RD			
9100	SBdC	92308	4478-C2
12300	APLV	92308	4388-C3
13700	APLV	92307	4388-C2
NICOLE CT			
400	UPL	91784	572-C5
NICOLE WY			
11300	FONT	92337	644-F2
NICOLET CT			
12700	RCUC	91739	573-G6
NICOLSON DR			
72300	TNP	92277	4892-B5
NICOYA CT			
12400	YCPA	92399	650-B4
NIDO AV			
12400	YCPA	92399	649-G4
NIELSON CT			
-	SBdC	92345	4474-H7
NIELSON RD			
400	SBdC	92372	4562-A1
1700	SBdC	92372	4472-E7
2700	SBdC	92371	4472-G7
3600	SBdC	92371	4473-A7
7400	SBdC	92371	4474-A7
9700	SBdC	92345	4474-G7
11000	SBdC	92345	4475-A7
NIGHTHAWK CT			
13100	CHNO	91710	642-B7
NIGHTINGALE CT			
-	SBDO	92408	607-B1
NIGHTINGALE WY			
12400	GTER	92313	646-F5
NIGHTSHADE RD			
-	SBdC	92308	4388-G6
14800	SBdC	92307	4298-G6
NIGHT SHADE RD			
13900	SBdC	92307	4388-G1
15700	SBdC	92307	4298-G3
NIGHT SONG CT			
14100	CHLS	91709	681-B3
NILES DR			
18600	HESP	92345	4567-B3
NILES ST			
400	SBDO	92404	576-J4
500	SBDO	92404	577-A4
25500	SBdC	92404	577-C4
NIMES CT			
13600	CHLS	91709	680-J2
NIMSHEW RD			
19000	APLV	92308	4387-B3
NINO LN			
-	VCTV	92392	4385-E7
NINO WY			
11600	RivC	91752	683-F1
NIPTON RD			
-	SBdC	-	331-B8
NIPTON DESERT RD			
67600	SBdC	-	331-C6
E NISBET DR			
100	UPL	91786	602-C1
NISQUALLI RD			
15100	VCTV	92392	4386-B4
NISQUALLY RD			
20500	APLV	92308	4387-F4
21900	APLV	92308	4388-A4
23500	SBdC	92308	4388-E4
23600	SBdC	92307	4388-E3
25500	SBdC	92307	(4389-A4 See Page 4299)
NISQUALLY TR			
5500	SBdC	-	4773-J7
5500	SBdC	-	4843-J1
NITA RD			
19700	APLV	92307	4387-D2
NOB PL			
100	SBdC	-	516-E2
NOBEL CT			
3500	RivC	91752	643-J6
NOB HILL CT			
-	SBdC	-	518-H5
NOB HILL DR			
1700	SBdC	-	518-H5
NOBLE PL			
13300	CHNO	91710	681-D1
E NOCTA ST			
500	ONT	91764	602-D7
W NOCTURNE CT			
600	ONT	91762	642-B4
NOEL CT			
-	FONT	92336	574-J2
NOEL PL			
5400	TNP	92277	4891-H4
NOELKE CT			
7800	FONT	92336	604-C1
NOELKE ST			
7900	FONT	92336	604-B1
NOELS KNOLL RD			
5700	TNP	92277	4891-H6
NOGALES CT			
56900	YUCA	92284	4887-H6
NOKOMIS CT			
-	SBdC	-	4843-F4
18400	APLV	92307	4296-J6
NOKOMIS LN			
18400	APLV	92307	4296-J6
NOKOMIS RD			
14600	APLV	92307	4296-J6
NOKOMIS TR			
7000	SBdC	-	4843-F4
NOKOMIS WY			
-	SBdC	-	4843-F4
NOLAN ST			
1900	SBdC	92407	576-B1
3500	SBdC	92407	546-B7
NOLINA DR			
9200	HESP	92345	4475-G7
W NOLINA DR			
9300	HESP	92345	4475-G6
NOMAD LN			
-	CHLS	91709	681-H7
NOMWAKET RD			
13600	APLV	92308	4388-A4
13800	APLV	92307	4388-A1
NONA AV			
4100	SBDO	92346	577-J4
27100	HIGH	92346	577-H4
27900	HIGH	92346	578-A4
NONA CT			
27100	HIGH	92346	577-H4
NOPAL LN			
30800	SBdC	92365	3764-F6
NOPAL PL			
11800	FONT	92337	644-B4
E NORBERT DR			
2400	SBDO	92404	577-A3
NORCO ST			
18100	APLV	92307	(4206-J5 See Page 4116)
NORDIC AV			
1800	CHLS	91709	680-H5
NORDIC DR			
32300	SBdC	-	519-B7
NORDIC LN			
13600	VCTV	92392	4385-G6
NORDINA ST			
200	RDL	92373	608-C7
200	RDL	92373	648-C1
W NOREEN CT			
1100	UPL	91784	571-J5
NOREEN LN			
33700	YCPA	92399	649-F4
NORELLE DR			
3000	RivC	91752	643-J5
3100	RivC	91752	644-A5
NORFOLK AV			
-	BARS	92311	3758-D3
33300	SBdC	92311	3758-D2
NORFOLK DR			
9400	RCUC	91730	573-C7
NORFOLK LN			
12900	SBdC	92392	4386-J4
12900	SBdC	92392	4387-A4
NORMAN RD			
-	SBdC	92277	4824-E7
-	SBdC	92277	(4894-E1 See Page 4824)
1400	SBdC	92314	4742-H5
E NORMAN RD			
300	SBDO	92408	606-J4
400	SBDO	92408	607-A4
N NORMAN RD			
1100	CLTN	92324	606-D5
NORMANDIE CT			
300	RDL	92373	648-B1
NORMANDY LN			
11600	LMLN	92354	647-E2
NORMGLOW RD			
3300	SBdC	92277	4823-E5
4600	SBdC	92277	4893-E1
W NORTE DAME ST			
1300	UPL	91786	601-H1
NORTE VISTA DR			
2400	CHLS	91709	680-J1
2400	CHLS	91709	681-A2
NORTH AV			
13300	CHNO	91710	682-B1
NORTH CT			
-	SBDO	92410	577-B6
NORTH DR			
900	SBdC	-	517-H3
29500	SBdC	-	4738-D7
NORTH LN			
2100	SBdC	-	4742-H2
NORTH PK			
12400	CHNO	91710	642-B6
NORTH PL			
500	RDL	92373	648-B2
NORTH RD			
25100	SBdC	-	517-C3
E NORTH RD			
500	SBDO	92404	576-J2
500	SBDO	92404	577-A2
NORTH SPUR			
-	BREA	92823	710-F4
-	BREA	92886	710-F4
-	OrCo	92823	710-A4
-	OrCo	92886	710-F4
NORTH ST			
25500	SBdC	92404	577-D1
NORTH WY			
-	ONT	91761	642-J1
-	ONT	91761	643-A1
NORTHAMPTON DR			
9600	RCUC	91737	572-D4
NORTH BANK RD			
46000	SBdC	92365	3594-E4
NORTH BAY DR			
600	BBLK	-	4811-A2
NORTH BAY RD			
27200	SBdC	-	517-H2
27400	SBdC	-	4737-H6
28000	SBdC	-	4738-A6
W NORTH CHANNEL ACCESS RD			
1600	SBDO	92410	606-D3
NORTHCROFT RD			
4300	RivC	92509	644-C7
NORTH END RD			
3100	SBdC	-	(4210-J7 See Page 4120)
5500	SBdC	-	4300-J2
NORTHERN CROSS DR			
300	BBLK	-	4812-A1
NORTH FORK RD			
-	HIGH	92346	578-E6
NORTH GATE DR			
12300	VCTV	92392	4385-G6
NORTHGATE PL			
7500	RCUC	91730	573-B7
NORTHGATE ST			
700	RIV	92507	646-C7
NORTH HILLS DR			
1200	UPL	91784	571-J6
NORTHLINE RD			
51800	SBdC	-	4816-D5
NORTH MALL WY			
500	SBDO	92408	606-G3
W NORTHPARK BLVD			
300	SBDO	92407	546-C4
NORTHPARK RD			
14300	HESP	92345	4475-J3
NORTH RANCH RD			
-	POM	91766	640-G4
NORTHRIDGE DR			
10100	RCUC	91737	573-A3
NORTH RIDGE RD			
50800	SBdC	92256	4956-C7
NORTH RIDGE TR			
-	BREA	92823	710-B7
NORTH RIM WY			
12700	RCUC	91739	573-H1
NORTH SHORE DR			
300	RivC	91752	683-E5
NORTH SHORE DR Rt#-18			
3800	SBdC	-	4662-G5
36600	SBdC	-	(4572-B5 See Page 4482)
39400	SBdC	-	4742-G1
NORTH SHORE DR Rt#-38			
37700	SBdC	-	4810-G2
38100	SBdC	-	(4740-J7 See Page 4660)
38500	SBdC	-	4741-A6
42400	SBdC	-	4742-B5
42800	SBdC	92314	4742-B5
E NORTH SHORE DR Rt#-18			
100	SBdC	92314	4742-F4
44300	SBdC	-	4742-F4
S NORTH SHORE DR			
2800	ONT	91761	643-A6
3500	ONT	91761	683-A1
W NORTH SHORE DR Rt#-38			
100	SBdC	92314	4742-D4
NORTH SHORE LN			
40200	SBdC	-	4741-D6
S NORTH SHORE PL			
2400	ONT	91761	643-A5
NORTH SHORE RD			
27900	SBdC	-	4737-J6
28100	SBdC	-	4738-B5
NORTH SHORE RD Rt#-18			
37300	SBdC	-	4662-D2
NORTH SIDE RD			
32900	SBdC	-	4300-J4
32900	SBdC	-	(4301-A4 See Page 4300)
36700	SBdC	-	4302-H3
40100	SBdC	-	(4303-B3 See Page 4302)
NORTH SLOPE LN			
-	POM	91766	640-H5
NORTH STAR AV			
3300	TNP	92277	4822-G5
4900	TNP	92277	4892-G2
7300	TNP	92277	4962-H1
11000	RivC	91752	683-H4
13000	VCTV	92392	4385-E6
NORTHSTAR AV			
15500	FONT	92336	574-F5
N NORTHSTAR AV			
1300	CLTN	92324	605-J4
NORTHSTAR CT			
19300	APLV	92308	4477-D2
NORTHSTAR DR			
700	BBLK	-	4811-J2
NORTHSTAR LN			
1300	UPL	91784	571-H4
NORTH STAR PL			
6100	RCUC	91701	572-F4
NORTH STAR TR			
8900	SBdC	92256	4956-A7
NORTH STAR TR			
8900	SBdC	92256	616-A2
NORTHVIEW DR			
	HIGH	92404	577-E5
10700	RCUC	91701	573-B6
34100	YCPA	92399	649-G4
NORTHVIEW LN			
33600	YCPA	92399	649-F4
NORTHVIEW PL			
1400	RDL	92374	648-F1
24300	DBAR	91765	640-D7
N NORTHWESTERN CIR			
1200	CLTN	92324	605-J4
NORTHWESTERN DR			
500	CLAR	91711	601-B3
NORTHWIND AV			
15500	FONT	92336	574-F5
NORTHWIND PL			
5400	RCUC	91737	573-C2
NORTHWOOD DR			
16200	VCTV	92394	4296-D3
NORTHWOOD PL			
700	POM	91767	601-B1
NORTON AV			
9800	MTCL	91763	601-E6
10100	SBdC	92399	610-D5
10100	YCPA	92399	610-D5
11300	SBdC	91766	641-E3
11400	SBdC	91710	641-E3
11700	CHNO	91710	641-E6
13100	SBdC	91710	681-E3
13100	CHNO	91710	681-E3
NORTON ST			
-	VCTV	92394	4205-E5
NORVAL ST			
1600	POM	91766	641-B4
NORWEGIAN ST			
-	RivC	92880	683-D7
NORWICH AV			
2600	SBdC	92311	3679-B5
NORWICH CT			
34900	SBdC	92311	3679-B4
NORWICH DR			
400	CLAR	91711	571-C7
NORWICK ST			
9900	RCUC	91730	602-J1
9900	RCUC	91730	603-A1
11900	RCUC	91730	603-F1
W NORWOOD AV			
1300	RLTO	92377	575-D3
NORWOOD CT			
27600	HIGH	92346	577-J6
W NORWOOD CT			
1400	UPL	91786	601-H2
NORWOOD LN			
800	SBdC	92314	(4743-A7 See Page 4662)
800	SBdC	92314	4813-A1
NORWOOD ST			
-	RDL	92373	648-A1
27100	HIGH	92346	577-H6
W NORWOOD ST			
500	RLTO	92377	575-E3
800	SBdC	92377	575-F3
NOSONI CT			
16200	APLV	92307	4297-A3
NOSONI LN			
16500	APLV	92307	4297-B2
NOSONI RD			
16200	APLV	92307	4297-B3
NOSONI WY			
16500	APLV	92307	4297-B2
NOTNIL CT			
5200	SBDO	92407	546-B5
NOTRE DAME AV			
2100	POM	91766	641-B6
NOTRE DAME CT			
2000	BARS	92311	3679-H6
NOTRE DAME RD			
300	CLAR	91711	601-C5
W NOTRE DAME ST			
800	UPL	91786	602-A1
NOTTINGHAM CT			
14700	ADEL	92301	4294-J7
NOTTINGHAM DR			
300	RDL	92373	648-A2
26200	LMLN	92354	647-F3
NOTTINGHAM RD			
-	SBdC	92365	(3684-F4 See Page 3594)
NOVA CT			
6900	RCUC	91701	573-D6
NOVA LN			
11000	RivC	91752	683-H4
NOVAK ST			
3400	RivC	92509	645-A6
NOVARA PL			
6900	RCUC	91701	573-D6
NOVA SCOTIA DR			
-	FONT	92336	574-C1
NOVATO RD			
55200	SBdC	92285	4747-C3
NOVELLA CT			
-	RCUC	91701	573-E5
NOWATA CT			
13800	APLV	92307	4387-A2
NOWATA RD			
18700	APLV	92307	4387-A2
21300	APLV	92308	4387-H6
NUCHAM AV			
4900	SBdC	92252	4889-E3
NUEVO AV			
8200	FONT	92335	604-J2
NUEVO CIR			
-	FONT	92337	644-J2
NUEVO CT			
10600	FONT	92337	604-J7
12200	VCTV	92392	4386-E6
NUEVO DR			
10700	FONT	92337	644-J1
NUEVO RD			
16300	VCTV	92392	4386-D6
NUGGET AV			
12100	VCTV	92392	4385-C6
NUGGET CT			
5400	YUCA	92284	4887-G5
NUGGET RD			
-	SBdC	-	(3682-A1 See Page 3592)
10100	SBdC	92371	4472-J3
12100	SBdC	92371	4382-J7
NUTMEG ST			
10400	RCUC	91730	573-B7
NUTWOOD CT			
11700	FONT	92337	644-C3
NYACK CT			
20300	APLV	92308	4387-E4
NYACK RD			
4100	SBdC	92371	4383-A6
7500	SBdC	92371	4384-A6
8100	SBdC	92392	4384-E5
9300	VCTV	92392	4384-E5
11500	VCTV	92392	4385-A5
12900	APLV	92308	4387-E4
NYE DR			
7300	HIGH	92346	577-J6
O			
O ST			
400	NDLS	92363	3620-B4
33700	SBdC	92311	3679-C5
33700	SBdC	92311	(3759-D1 See Page 3758)
E O ST			
100	CLTN	92324	606-D7
W O ST			
100	CLTN	92324	606-C7
OAHU RD			
48200	SBdC	92365	(3685-B5 See Page 3594)
OAK AV			
100	POM	91766	640-G2
6100	SBdC	-	4950-G2
12300	SBdC	93562	2234-H4
19300	ADEL	92301	4204-F2
OAK CT			
200	NDLS	92363	3620-B6
600	SBDO	92410	606-G2
6200	SBdC	-	4950-G2
7700	HIGH	92346	578-D7
9200	MTCL	91763	601-E5
12500	YCPA	92399	649-D4
OAK DR			
-	RCUC	91737	573-B3
200	SBdC	-	518-B1
300	SBdC	-	4738-B7
600	SBdC	-	517-F3
900	SBdC	-	516-E4
1000	SBdC	92314	4812-H1
2300	SBdC	-	519-D6
8600	RCUC	91730	603-A3
10300	SBdC	92256	615-F4
40900	SBdC	92339	611-F2
50800	SBdC	92256	616-A4
52700	SBdC	-	4816-F7
OAK LN			
-	LACo	91768	640-A2
500	SBdC	-	519-E2
800	SBdC	92314	4813-A1
4400	LACo	91711	571-B7
11200	SBdC	92399	611-C7
11600	YCPA	92399	649-J2
15000	CHLS	91709	681-C5
22900	SBdC	-	516-F2
27400	SBdC	-	517-H4
39000	SBdC	92399	651-B1
39700	SBdC	92339	611-C2
OAK LN W			
39900	SBdC	92339	611-D2
OAK PL			
-	SBdC	92335	604-B5
OAK PT			
700	SBdC	-	4737-J7
OAK RD			
700	SBdC	-	518-B3
OAK ST			
-	RCUC	91739	573-H6
1200	UPL	91784	571-J3
1300	RDL	92373	648-E2
5500	SBdC	92397	4652-D3
11300	SBdC	92316	645-E3
11500	APLV	92308	4387-B7
11700	APLV	92308	4477-B1
41300	BBLK	-	4811-G2
S OAK ST			
10700	LMLN	92354	607-E7
W OAK ST			
100	CLTN	92324	606-C4
W OAK ST			
100	SBDO	92408	606-H2
300	SBDO	92401	606-H2
500	SBDO	92410	606-E2
2700	SBDO	92376	606-A3
OAK TER			
28900	SBdC	-	518-C1
OAK TR			
200	SBdC	-	518-C1
OAK WY			
1300	SBdC	-	4737-G4
OAK BARK LN			
10200	RivC	91752	644-A4
OAK BENCH RD			
11700	SBdC	92399	651-D2
OAK BRANCH RD			
14500	VCTV	92392	4385-J5
OAKBROOK CT			
11200	RCUC	91737	573-D4
OAK CANYON DR			
15900	CHLS	91709	711-B1
OAK CANYON LN			
2000	CHLS	91709	710-H1
OAK CLIFF DR			
-	POM	91766	640-F6
OAK CREEK DR			
-	YCPA	92399	650-B7
3500	ONT	91761	643-C6
OAK CREEK LN			
28900	HIGH	92346	578-C5
OAKCREEK RD			
3000	CHLS	91709	711-B1
OAKCREST CIR			
100	RivC	91752	683-F5
OAKCREST DR			
3000	CHLS	91709	711-B1
OAK CREST DR			
12900	YCPA	92399	651-A5
12900	YCPA	92399	650-J5
OAKDALE AV			
9700	SBdC	-	4482-J3
N OAKDALE AV			
100	RLTO	92376	605-H1
400	RLTO	92376	575-H4
2000	RLTO	92377	575-H3
S OAKDALE AV			
100	RLTO	92376	605-H2
OAKDALE CT			
14500	ADEL	92301	4384-H1
W OAKDALE CT			
1500	UPL	91786	571-H7
OAKDALE DR			
300	CLAR	91711	601-E4
4300	CHNO	91710	641-E5
10500	RCUC	91730	573-B7
29300	SBdC	-	4738-D7
OAKDALE LN			
-	FONT	92336	574-H2
OAKDALE RD			
15400	CHLS	91709	681-B7
OAKDALE ST			
4500	CLAR	91711	601-E4
4500	MTCL	91763	601-E4
12600	RivC	92880	683-D6
OAKFIELD CT			
3000	CHLS	91709	681-B6
OAKFLATS RD			
15400	CHLS	91709	681-B6
OAKGLEN AV			
10100	MTCL	91763	601-D7
OAK GLEN AV			
10500	MTCL	91763	641-D1
S OAK GLEN LN			
900	CLTN	92324	646-H1
OAK GLEN RD			
8300	RivC	92223	651-A6
11400	SBdC	92399	651-C1
11800	YCPA	92399	649-J1
12900	YCPA	92399	651-A6
13100	YCPA	92399	650-A1
32400	YCPA	92373	649-D5
36800	SBdC	92399	610-F7
36800	YCPA	92399	610-F7
38500	SBdC	92399	611-A7
OAKGLEN RD			
39500	SBdC	-	4741-B5
OAK GLEN TR			
700	SBdC	-	517-C3
OAK GROVE AV			
1100	LACo	-	512-A5
OAKGROVE CT			
15400	CHLS	91709	681-B6
OAK GROVE DR			
-	RivC	92373	648-H7
OAKGROVE DR			
4800	MTCL	91763	601-F5
10000	RCUC	91737	573-A3
OAK GROVE RD			
32100	SBdC	92311	(3757-J3 See Page 3756)
32100	SBdC	92311	3758-A4
37000	YCPA	92399	650-F5
OAK HAVEN LN			
15500	CHLS	91709	681-C6
OAK HILL CIR			
1400	UPL	91784	572-E6
OAKHILL CT			
13500	YCPA	92399	650-G6
E OAK HILL CT			
1400	ONT	91761	642-F5
OAK HILL DR			
15900	CHLS	91709	711-B1
E OAK HILL DR			
1200	ONT	91761	642-E5
2800	ONT	91761	643-A5
S OAK HILL DR			
2400	ONT	91761	643-A5
OAK HILL LN			
11300	YCPA	92399	650-C1
OAK HILL RD			
5900	SBdC	92345	4654-H1
7200	SBdC	92345	4564-J2
8900	SBdC	92345	4475-A7
8900	SBdC	92345	4565-A1
E OAK HILL ST			
200	ONT	91761	642-C5
OAK HILL RANCH RD			
10300	SBdC	92345	4564-H7
OAK HOLLOW RD			
4100	CLAR	91711	571-A7
4100	CLAR	91711	601-A1
OAKHURST CT			
2100	UPL	91784	571-H4
OAKHURST DR			
800	POM	91767	601-B4
1300	SBDO	92404	577-A5
10700	RCUC	91730	573-B7
29500	SBdC	-	518-D1
OAKHURST ST			
15500	CHLS	91709	681-B7
OAKIE FLAT RD			
-	SBdC	92407	514-G1
-	SBdC	92407	4734-F7
OAK KNOLL CIR			
500	SBdC	-	519-E2
OAK KNOLL CT			
11500	FONT	92337	644-C3
OAK KNOLL DR			
500	SBdC	-	519-E2
2800	DBAR	91765	680-A7
11300	FONT	92337	644-C3
27500	SBdC	-	517-J4
OAKLAND AV			
11700	YCPA	92399	649-J2
19500	SBdC	92377	575-G3
N OAKLAND AV			
500	ONT	91762	602-B5
S OAKLAND AV			
400	ONT	91762	642-B2
S OAKLAND PL			
1300	ONT	91762	642-B3
OAKLAND WY			
12900	CHLS	91709	640-J7
OAK LEAF CIR			
-	RivC	92880	683-B7
OAKLEAF CT			
1900	SBdC	-	518-J6
3200	CHLS	91709	681-B7
OAK LEAF CT			
9100	HESP	92345	4475-H7
E OAKLEAF CT			
3400	ONT	91761	643-B6
OAKLEAF DR			
31200	SBdC	-	518-J6
S OAKLEAF DR			
900	CLTN	92324	646-G1
OAK LEAF LN			
30600	SBdC	-	548-G1
E OAKLEAF RD			
3300	ONT	91761	643-B6
OAK LEAF WY			
10200	RivC	91752	644-A4
W OAKLEY CT			
1300	UPL	91786	571-J7
W OAKLEY SPUR RD			
27100	SBdC	-	547-C3
27100	SBdC	92404	547-C3
OAKLON DR			
10400	SBdC	92345	4564-H7
10400	SBdC	92345	4654-H1
OAK MESA DR			
13300	YCPA	92399	650-F6
OAK MESA TR			
10600	SBdC	92399	610-H6
OAKMONT DR			
400	BARS	92311	3679-J5
800	SBdC	-	4737-G6
1600	UPL	91784	572-E6
13500	VCTV	92392	4386-C2
OAKMONT LN			
500	SBdC	-	518-A2
E OAKMONT ST			
2800	ONT	91761	642-J6
2800	ONT	91761	643-A6
OAKMONT WY			
16100	CHLS	91709	710-H1
OAK MOUNTAIN DR			
13400	YCPA	92399	650-F6
E OAK PARK DR			
100	CLAR	91711	601-D5
W OAK PARK DR			
100	CLAR	91711	601-D4
OAKRIDGE CT			
5700	RCUC	91739	573-G3
N OAKRIDGE CT			
2800	SBDO	92346	577-H2
OAKRIDGE DR			
3100	CHLS	91709	681-B6
OAK RIDGE DR			
36300	YCPA	92399	650-D5

STREET
Block City ZIP Pg-Grid

OAK RIDGE RD
28500 HIGH 92346 578-B4
OAKRIDGE CANYON RD
- SBdC - (4655-F7 See Page 4654)
OAKS AV
12200 CHNO 91710 641-J7
12200 CHNO 91762 641-J7
12200 ONT 91762 641-J7
13100 CHNO 91710 681-J2
N OAKS AV
200 ONT 91762 601-H6
S OAKS AV
100 ONT 91762 641-J1
N OAKS CT
1500 ONT 91762 601-H5
OAKSHIRE LN
3100 CHLS 91709 681-B6
OAKSPRING DR
- FONT 92336 574-D5
S OAK SPRINGS PL
2500 ONT 91761 643-C5
OAK SPRINGS RD
15400 CHLS 91709 681-B6
23700 SBdC - 4568-H7
23700 SBdC 92308 4568-E5
24900 SBdC - (4569-A7 See Page 4568)
OAK SPRINGS VALLEY RD
1700 SBdC 92372 4562-E5
OAK SPUR RD
37100 YCPA 92399 650-F5
OAKTON WY
2500 POM 91768 640-C2
OAKTRAIL RD
3000 CHLS 91709 681-B7
OAK TREE
10000 MohC - 3620-D2
OAK TREE CIR
1300 CHLS 91709 710-G1
OAK TREE CRSG
1100 CHLS 91709 710-F1
OAK TREE LN
11700 YCPA 92399 649-J2
OAK TREE PL
- FONT 92336 574-E6
OAK VALLEY LN
3100 CHLS 91709 711-B1
OAKVIEW LN
3000 CHLS 91709 681-B6
OAK VIEW RD
36800 YCPA 92399 650-F5
OAKVIEW WY
1700 UPL 91784 572-D6
OAKVILLE PL
8200 RCUC 91730 602-F2
OAK WAY LN
16700 CHLS 91709 710-F3
OAKWOOD AV
7100 HESP 92345 4566-A3
9500 HESP 92345 4476-A6
9700 HESP 92345 4475-J2
11700 HESP 92345 4385-J7
N OAKWOOD AV
1000 RLTO 92376 575-E6
OAKWOOD CIR
31800 YCPA 92399 649-B3
OAKWOOD CT
900 CALI 92320 650-A7
OAKWOOD DR
11100 LMLN 92354 647-A1
11100 CLTN 92324 647-A1
11300 FONT 92337 644-B2
27300 SBdC - 517-H1
56300 YUCA 92284 4887-G6
W OAKWOOD DR
1200 SBDO 92405 576-E2
OAKWOOD LN
14900 CHLS 91709 681-D5
OAKWOOD PL
11300 RCUC 91730 603-D3
OAR LN
26500 SBdC - (3935-F5 See Page 3934)
OASIS
7300 SBdC 92277 (4895-A7 See Page 4824)
OASIS AV
4000 TNP 92277 4822-D7
4500 TNP 92277 4892-E1
OASIS DR
1000 BARS 92311 3679-H5
2500 SBdC 92252 4819-E4
OASIS LN
59000 YUCA 92284 4888-D5
OASIS PKWY
- SBdC 92277 (4894-E6 See Page 4824)
OASIS RD
8900 SBdC 92372 4562-B1
9300 SBdC 92372 4472-B3
12100 SBdC 92372 4382-B6
12900 VCTV 92392 4385-F4
13700 SBdC 92371 4382-B3
14800 SBdC 92371 4292-B6
19300 SBdC 92301 (4202-A3 See Page 4112)
19900 SBdC 92301 4112-A5

OASIS ST
8000 FONT 92336 604-B1
35400 SBdC - (3591-F5 See Page 3590)
OATES DR
1200 DBAR 91765 680-C3
OATMAN PL
- MohC - 3620-F2
OBANNON AV
- BARS 92311 3680-F6
OBERLIN AV
13000 VCTV 92392 4385-E4
N OBERLIN AV
100 CLAR 91711 601-C3
OBERT LN
- VCTV 92392 4385-E7
OBRIAN RD
58300 YUCA 92284 4888-C7
OBRION PL
13200 CHNO 91710 681-E1
OBRIT RD
21700 ADEL 92301 (4115-E2 See Page 4114)
22600 SBdC 92301 (4115-E2 See Page 4114)
OBSERVATION DR
12100 GTER 92313 646-F5
OBSERVATION LN
16200 CHLS 91709 710-H2
OBSIDIAN CT
2200 CHLS 91709 680-J7
OBSIDIAN LN
12500 VCTV 92392 4385-G5
OCANA CT
15700 FONT 92337 644-F3
OCASA DR
5600 RivC 91752 683-G5
OCASO DR
18700 SBdC 92301 4204-C4
OCCIDENTAL CIR
1000 RDL 92374 608-D4
OCCIDENTAL DR
800 RDL 92374 608-D4
W OCCIDENTAL DR
500 CLAR 91711 571-B7
OCEAN CT
7800 FONT 92336 604-B1
OCEAN ST
7900 FONT 92336 604-C1
OCEANAIRE WY
1900 UPL 91784 572-B5
OCEANSIDE DR
4600 CHNO 91710 641-F7
16100 VCTV 92394 4296-B3
OCEAN VIEW CT
600 SBdC 91784 572-C2
OCEAN VIEW DR
2400 SBdC 91784 571-J2
2400 SBdC 91784 572-A2
24900 SBdC - 517-B5
31400 SBdC - 518-J7
OCHOA RD
20100 APLV 92307 4387-E1
OCHOCO CT
- SBdC - 4843-G4
OCOTILLA RD
14200 APLV 92307 4298-B3
17300 APLV 92307 4208-B7
17700 SBdC 92307 4208-B5
OCOTILLO AV
300 PRKR - 4774-H7
600 LPCo - 4774-H7
800 PRKR - 4844-H1
1700 LPCo - 4844-H1
1800 NDLS 92363 3620-B6
5700 TNP 92277 4892-E5
OCOTILLO CT
- RCUC 91701 572-H5
OCOTILLO DR
900 BARS 92311 3679-J5
11300 FONT 92337 644-D2
58600 YUCA 92284 4888-C4
OCOTILLO RD
48100 SBdC 92285 (4575-D7 See Page 4484)
50600 SBdC 92285 (4576-A7 See Page 4486)
OCOTILLO ST
2100 SBdC 92371 4472-E5
6900 SBdC 92371 4473-H5
11200 SBdC 92256 615-J6
OCOTILLO WY
20100 SBdC 92308 4477-D5
21200 APLV 92308 4477-H5
21800 SBdC 92308 4478-A5
25600 SBdC 92308 4479-E4
27700 SBdC - 4479-J4
28800 SBdC - 4480-A4
OCTILLO RD
2100 SBdC 92371 4472-E5
ODELL AV
16500 VCTV 92394 4296-A2
ODELL CT
15000 VCTV 92394 4296-A2
ODELL LN
15000 VCTV 92394 4296-A2
ODEN DR
13100 SBdC 92307 4388-G2
14100 SBdC 92307 4298-F3

ODENRITE RD
- SBdC 92285 (4577-J5 See Page 4486)
W OGDEN ST
2000 SBdC 92407 546-B7
2000 SBdC 92407 576-A1
2300 SBdC 92407 575-J1
OGOTIUS RD
6300 SBdC 92371 4473-G4
W OHARA CT
1100 UPL 91786 571-J7
OHARE CT
6600 FONT 92336 574-E5
OHIO AV
3100 CLAR 91711 571-E6
N OHIO AV
1900 CLTN 92324 606-D3
2000 SBDO 92410 606-D3
W OHIO AV
2300 SBDO 92407 546-A2
2700 SBDO 92407 545-H1
OHIO CT
12200 YCPA 92399 649-B3
OHIO LN
- FONT 92336 574-D6
39900 BBLK - 4811-C2
OHIO ST
- VCTV 92394 4205-F6
800 RDL 92374 608-B5
10500 LMLN 92354 607-C7
OHNA RD
17800 APLV 92307 4296-H2
OIL RIG RD
5100 SBdC 92371 4653-D1
OIL WELL RD
- CHLS 91709 710-H5
- OrCo 92886 710-H5
4900 SBdC 92371 4563-C7
5000 SBdC 92371 4653-D1
OJAI RD
12900 APLV 92308 4387-J4
22400 APLV 92308 4388-B4
OJEI RD
- SBdC 92277 4751-D5
OKAHDA CT
12500 APLV 92308 4387-H5
OKANAGAN RD
21300 APLV 92308 4387-H5
OKANOGAN TR
6900 SBdC - 4843-G4
OKESA RD
13500 APLV 92308 4387-E2
13700 APLV 92307 4387-E2
OKINAWA AV
- BARS 92311 3680-F7
OKLAHOMA AV
- FONT 92336 574-C6
OKLAHOMA DR
- SBdC - 4741-A4
OLALEE CT
18500 APLV 92307 4296-J3
OLALEE LN
18500 APLV 92307 4296-J2
18500 APLV 92307 4297-A2
OLALEE PL
16400 APLV 92307 4297-A2
OLALEE RD
15700 APLV 92307 4296-J3
16400 APLV 92307 4297-A2
OLALEE WY
18500 APLV 92307 4296-J3
OLANCHA RD
14000 SBdC 92392 4385-H3
OLATHE RD
13000 APLV 92308 4387-D4
13800 APLV 92307 4387-D2
OLD ABERDEEN RD
- YUCA 92284 4817-F7
S OLD ARCHIBALD RANCH RD
3200 ONT 91761 643-A7
3300 ONT 91761 683-A1
OLD BALDY AV
- UPL 91784 572-E5
OLD BALDY WY
- UPL 91784 572-E5
OLD BELL MOUNTAIN RD
19300 SBdC 92307 (4117-F4 See Page 4116)
19800 APLV 92307 (4117-F4 See Page 4116)
OLD BREA CANYON RD
22300 DBAR 91789 680-A2
22300 INDS 91789 680-A2
OLD BRIDGE CT
11500 FONT 92337 644-H3
OLD BRIDGE RD
7400 HIGH 92346 578-D6
OLD CARBON CANYON RD
2000 CHLS 91709 680-J7
2100 CHLS 91709 710-J1
OLD CASTLE RD
15400 FONT 92337 644-F3
OLD CHISHOLM TR
65800 SBdC 92252 4820-C3
66800 SBdC 92277 4820-H3
68400 SBdC 92277 4821-A3
71700 SBdC 92277 4822-A3

OLD CHISHOLM TR
72700 TNP 92277 4822-B3
OLD CITY CREEK RD
- SBdC - 548-E2
30900 SBdC - 518-H7
31600 SBdC - 519-A7
OLD COPPER CITY RD
52300 SBdC - 349-C2
OLD DALE RD
- SBdC 92252 4890-A7
- TNP 92277 4890-H7
3900 SBdC 92277 370-K11
5800 SBdC 92277 390-L1
68900 TNP 92277 4891-F6
71900 TNP 92277 4892-A6
OLD EDISON RD
- CHLS - 711-B7
- OrCo 92887 711-B7
OLD EL MIRAGE RD
100 SBdC 92301 4112-B3
OLDENBURG DR
16300 CHLS 91709 711-G1
OLDENBURG RD
16100 SBdC 92307 4299-C1
16600 SBdC 92307 (4209-C7 See Page 4118)
OLD FIELD AV
11500 FONT 92337 644-B3
OLD GLORY LN
1000 UPL 91786 602-D4
OLD GOVERNMENT RD
- SBdC - 351-J3
OLD GREENSPOT RD
28900 HIGH 92346 578-C7
E OLD GUASTI RD
2800 ONT 91761 602-J7
2800 ONT 91761 603-A7
OLD HICKORY LN
- CHLS 91709 681-G7
OLD HIGHWAY 58
100 BARS 92311 3589-H7
700 SBdC 92311 3589-G7
23800 SBdC 92347 3588-F7
25600 SBdC 92311 3588-H7
25700 SBdC 92311 3678-J1
26100 SBdC 92311 3679-B1
30000 SBdC 92311 3590-A7
31100 SBdC 92311 3680-D1
31300 BARS 92311 3680-D1
OLD HWY 18 N
- SBdC - 518-H6
OLD HWY 18 S
30900 SBdC - 518-H6
OLD INLAND EMPIRE BLVD
- ONT 91764 603-D6
OLD LIVE OAK AV
11600 FONT 92337 644-D3
OLD MEADOW PL
500 SBdC - 4737-J7
OLD MILL RD
200 SBdC - 516-G1
300 SBdC - 518-C1
49000 SBdC 92256 615-H4
OLD MINE RD
24400 SBdC 92307 4298-F5
OLD NATIONAL TRAILS HWY
- BARS 92311 3680-E5
- SBdC - 351-F10
46100 SBdC 92365 3764-F6
47100 SBdC - 3764-J7
47700 SBdC - (3765-A7 See Page 3764)
47800 SBdC - (3855-A1 See Page 3764)
OLD NATIONAL TRAILS HWY Bus-66
- SBdC - 351-E10
OLD NATIONAL TRAILS HWY U.S.-6
- SBdC - 351-F10
OLD OAK RD
10500 YCPA 92399 610-A6
OLD OAK SPRING RANCH RD
100 SBdC 92372 4562-A2
1000 SBdC - 4562-C4
OLD PAINT DR
13700 VCTV 92392 4385-G5
OLD PARKER RD
- SBdC - 4844-B3
39300 SBdC - 372-D11
40100 SBdC - 392-D1
41800 SBdC - 4843-D4
OLD POMONA RD
- POM 91766 640-G5
OLD POST DR
9300 RCUC 91730 602-H5
OLD QUARRY RD
18100 SBdC - 4116-J7
19000 SBdC 92394 4207-A1
19000 SBdC - 4207-A1
19100 SBdC - (4117-A7 See Page 4116)
OLD RANCH RD
9100 RCUC 91701 572-G4
11700 VCTV 92392 4385-F7
11700 VCTV 92392 4475-F1

E OLD RANCH RD
1500 CLTN 92324 646-G1
OLD RANCHO
11400 ADEL 92301 4295-A2
E OLD SHAY RD
1500 SBdC - 4742-H5
1500 SBdC 92314 4742-H5
OLD SPRING RD
11500 FONT 92337 644-H2
OLD STAGECOACH RD
- SBdC - 4886-C3
OLD STONE RD
9200 SBdC 92372 4472-F7
9200 SBdC 92372 4562-F1
OLD TOLL RD
100 SBdC - 517-G1
100 SBdC - 4737-G7
N OLD TOLL RD
400 SBdC - 4737-G7
OLD TRAIL DR
600 DBAR 91765 640-B6
OLD US 66
- SBdC - 352-C10
OLD VINE RD
8200 SBdC 92252 4959-G5
OLD WALKER AV
- ONT 91761 642-F3
OLD WATERMAN CANYON RD
1700 SBdC 92404 516-G6
1700 SBdC 92404 546-J1
1700 SBDO 92404 546-J1
OLD WEST LN
10200 RCUC 91730 603-A2
OLD WOMAN SPRINGS OH E
200 SBdC 92284 4747-F7
5800 YUCA 92284 4887-J6
6800 YUCA 92284 4957-J1
OLD WOMAN SPRINGS OH W
6100 YUCA 92284 4887-J7
OLD WOMAN SPRINGS RD Rt#-247
100 SBdC 92284 4747-D1
400 SBdC 92285 4747-D1
900 SBdC 92284 4817-F4
1800 SBdC 92285 4667-A3
1900 SBdC 92285 (4576-B4 See Page 4486)
1900 SBdC 92285 369-L9
3100 SBdC - 4817-E6
3400 YUCA - 4817-E6
3400 YUCA 92284 4817-E6
3600 YUCA 92284 4887-H4
6500 YUCA 92284 4957-J2
32600 SBdC - 4480-J2
32700 SBdC - 4481-A2
36100 SBdC - 4482-E2
39700 SBdC - (4483-C4 See Page 4482)
43200 SBdC - 4484-B7
43300 SBdC 92285 4484-B7
44300 SBdC 92285 (4574-D1 See Page 4484)
47000 SBdC 92285 (4575-D4 See Page 4484)
OLD WOOD RD
- POM 91766 640-F5
OLD YERMO CTO
35700 SBdC - (3591-C7 See Page 3590)
35700 SBdC - (3681-C1 See Page 3590)
41200 SBdC - 349-E6
OLE ST
8900 SBdC 92256 4956-F7
9000 SBdC 92256 616-F1
OLEANDER
7100 SBdC 92277 (4894-E6 See Page 4824)
OLEANDER AV
1200 UPL 91784 571-J4
6500 FONT 92336 574-G5
6800 HIGH 92346 578-A4
7800 FONT 92336 604-H5
8100 FONT 92335 604-H5
9900 SBdC 92335 604-H5
10300 SBdC 92337 604-H7
10400 FONT 92337 604-H7
10500 FONT 92337 644-H2
10900 SBdC 92337 644-H2
12300 CHNO 91710 641-J6
35500 YCPA 92399 610-B6
OLEANDER CT
- RCUC 91730 603-D5
N OLEANDER CT
2700 SBDO 92346 577-H3
OLEANDER DR
58600 YUCA 92284 4888-D4
61700 SBdC 92252 4889-B6
E OLEANDER DR
3400 SBDO 92346 577-H3
3700 SBdC 92346 577-H3
OLEANDER PL
36300 SBdC 92311 3680-C1
OLEANDER RD
38500 SBdC - 3592-D7

OLEANDER ST
13000 ADEL 92301 (4115-E2 See Page 4114)
14600 SBdC - (4115-G2 See Page 4114)
18100 HESP 92345 4566-J5
18100 HESP 92345 4567-A5
OLEMA AV
9100 HESP 92345 4477-B6
OLEMA RD
5700 YUCA 92284 4887-J5
9500 SBdC 92308 4478-D4
13700 SBdC 92307 4388-D2
14100 SBdC 92307 4298-D4
OLEMA TR
6200 SBdC - 4844-D2
N OLETA LN
2800 SBDO 92346 577-G2
OLETA RD
5300 SBdC 92285 (4576-E6 See Page 4486)
31300 SBdC - 4480-F7
OLINDA DR
100 BREA 92823 710-D5
200 OrCo 92823 710-D5
OLINDA PL
100 BREA 92823 710-C6
OLINDA RD
- BREA 92823 710-B5
- OrCo 92823 710-B4
S OLINDA RD
- BREA 92823 710-B6
- OrCo 92823 710-B6
OLIVA CT
2000 CLTN 92324 646-H1
OLIVE
36100 SBdC - 4481-J6
OLIVE AV
5600 SBdC 92377 575-E2
E OLIVE AV
- RDL 92373 608-C7
- RDL 92373 648-B1
N OLIVE AV
100 RLTO 92376 605-H1
700 RLTO 92376 575-H5
5900 SBDO 92407 545-J3
6500 SBDO 92407 546-A1
S OLIVE AV
100 RLTO 92376 605-H2
W OLIVE AV
- RDL 92373 648-A1
1200 RDL 92373 647-J2
OLIVE CIR
- FONT 92337 644-J2
OLIVE CT
900 BARS 92311 3679-G4
7600 RivC 92509 644-H7
E OLIVE CT
1100 ONT 91764 602-E4
2000 ONT 91730 602-G4
OLIVE DR
11300 SBdC 92392 4475-B2
OLIVE LN
2500 LACo 91768 640-A1
OLIVE PL
12100 CHNO 91710 641-D6
E OLIVE PL
900 CLTN 92324 606-E5
N OLIVE PL
1100 CLTN 92324 606-F4
OLIVE ST
100 CLAR 91711 601-D4
3900 SBdC 91710 641-D5
4500 MTCL 91763 601-E4
6900 HIGH 92346 577-G5
8900 FONT 92335 604-J4
9400 HESP 92345 4475-H6
9700 SBdC 92316 605-E5
10800 SBdC 92316 645-E1
14500 HESP 92345 4476-A6
15000 SBdC - (4206-A3 See Page 4116)
26000 HIGH 92410 577-E6
E OLIVE ST
- UPL 91786 602-C4
100 CLTN 92324 606-E5
100 POM 91766 640-J6
100 POM 91766 641-B5
100 SBDO 92410 576-J6
300 SBDO 92410 577-A6
1400 ONT 91764 602-F4
1700 ONT 91730 602-G4
N OLIVE ST
800 SBDO 92410 576-F6
1600 SBDO 92346 577-G4
W OLIVE ST
100 CLTN 92324 606-B5
100 POM 91766 640-J6
100 SBDO 92410 576-H6
800 SBdC 92324 606-B5
900 SBDO 92411 576-E6
OLIVE WY
- RCUC 91737 573-B3
19200 APLV 92308 4477-C1
OLIVEDALE DR
12000 FONT 92337 644-C4
OLIVE HILL DR
4000 LACo 91711 571-E4
OLIVE KNOLL PL
4000 LACo 91711 571-E4

OLIVE POINT PL
4000 LACo 91711 571-E4
OLIVERA LN
7500 SBdC 92308 4567-E4
OLIVERA RD
1700 SBdC 92372 4382-D5
2800 SBdC 92371 4382-H5
3900 SBdC 92371 4383-E4
7500 SBdC 92371 4384-A4
11700 VCTV 92392 4385-B4
14500 SBdC 92392 4385-J4
14700 SBdC 92392 4386-A4
15000 VCTV 92392 4386-A4
E OLIVER HOLMES RD
2000 CLTN 92324 606-H7
2000 SBDO 92408 606-H7
OLIVE TREE LN
7300 HIGH 92346 577-G6
34800 YCPA 92399 609-J5
N OLIVE TREE LN
1500 SBDO 92346 577-G4
OLIVETTA PL
- SBdC 92365 (3593-B7 See Page 3592)
- SBdC 92365 (3683-B1 See Page 3592)
OLIVEWOOD AV
13800 CHNO 91710 682-B2
OLIVEWOOD LN
4700 SBDO 92407 546-H5
OLIVINE AV
1100 SBdC 92359 608-H5
OLIVINE DR
15600 CHLS 91709 680-J7
OLIVINE RD
7300 SBdC 92371 4383-J6
7400 SBdC 92371 4384-A6
8100 SBdC 92392 4384-A6
8900 VCTV 92392 4384-F6
11400 VCTV 92392 4385-B6
OLMO CT
- CHNO 91710 682-B3
OLSEN DR
1600 SBdC - 4737-G4
OLSON
- SBdC 92252 4749-J7
- SBdC 92252 4819-J1
OLTEN DR
1000 SBdC - 517-A4
OLVERA CT
6100 CHNO 91710 681-J1
6100 CHNO 91710 682-A1
OLVINE RD
51700 SBdC 92285 (4576-C5 See Page 4486)
OLYMPIC CT
- CLAR 91711 571-F5
- FONT 92336 574-J3
OLYMPIC DR
- UPL 91786 572-E7
100 BBLK - 4741-J7
200 BBLK - 4811-J1
OLYMPIC RD
2500 SBdC 92284 4818-G5
2500 SBdC 92252 4818-G5
3800 SBdC 92284 4888-G1
3800 SBdC 92252 4888-G7
6500 SBdC 92252 4958-G1
OLYMPIC VIEW DR
2400 CHLS 91709 680-J1
2500 CHLS 91709 681-A2
OMAHA CT
300 CLAR 91711 601-E4
OMAK RD
11900 APLV 92308 4387-G5
N OMALLEY AV
1000 UPL 91784 571-J3
1400 UPL 91786 571-J7
1400 UPL 91786 572-A7
OMALLEY WY
- UPL 91786 602-A1
N OMALLEY WY
1700 UPL 91784 571-J5
OMANI CT
12700 APLV 92308 4387-H4
OMAR ST
500 POM 91768 640-C2
OMELVENY RD
11200 SBdC 92345 (4655-A3 See Page 4654)
OMO CT
6100 SBdC - 4844-F1
ONACREST DR
31300 SBdC - 518-J6
ONAGA CT
7600 SBdC 92252 4959-B3
ONAGA TR
54700 YUCA 92284 4957-C4
57300 YUCA 92284 4958-A3
59700 SBdC 92252 4958-G3
61000 SBdC 92252 4959-A3
ONAKNOLL CT
2500 SBdC - 519-B7
ONE HOLE SPRINGS RD
- SBdC 92285 369-J9
- SBdC 92285 (4574-J7 See Page 4484)
ONEIDA CT
- CHNO 91710 641-G4
19400 APLV 92307 4297-C7

ONEIDA RD
14700 APLV 92307 4297-C7
ONEIDA TR
7300 SBdC - 4843-F5
O NEIL RD
4200 SBdC 92252 4889-E1
W ONEIL ST
1100 UPL 91784 571-J6
ONEILL RD
55700 SBdC 92284 4817-E1
ONTARIO AV
12900 ONT 91761 642-H7
12900 ONT 91761 682-H2
E ONTARIO BLVD
700 ONT 91761 642-D1
ONTARIO CIR
- FONT 92336 574-C1
ONTARIO FRWY I-15
- FONT - 544-G6
- FONT - 573-H7
- FONT - 574-A6
- ONT - 603-F6
- ONT - 643-E5
- RCUC - 573-H7
- RCUC - 574-A6
- RCUC - 603-G2
- RivC - 643-E5
- RivC - 683-F6
- SBdC - 515-B7
- SBdC - 544-G6
- SBdC - 545-B3
ONTARIO MILLS DR
700 ONT 91764 603-E6
ONTARIO MILLS PKWY
4300 ONT 91764 603-F6
5600 ONT 91739 603-F6
ONYX
- BREA 92823 710-C6
ONYX AV
6100 RCUC 91701 572-H4
7300 RCUC 91730 572-H7
7700 RCUC 91730 602-H1
ONYX CT
8200 RCUC 91730 602-H2
18100 HESP 92345 4566-J5
ONYX PL
13600 VCTV 92394 4295-F6
ONYX RD
8300 SBdC - 4480-H7
16400 CHLS 91709 711-F2
ONYX ST
7900 RCUC 91730 602-H1
9700 YCPA 92399 609-J4
9700 YCPA 92399 610-A4
ONYX WY
1100 SBdC 92314 4813-D3
OPAL AV
400 BARS 92311 3680-A5
700 SBdC 92359 608-H3
7300 HESP 92345 4565-J5
10500 SBdC 92374 608-H7
10900 SBdC 92374 648-H1
OPAL CIR
13600 VCTV 92392 4385-G6
OPAL CT
- FONT 92336 574-E2
W OPAL CT
600 UPL 91786 602-B4
OPAL ST
3400 RivC 92509 645-B7
6200 RCUC 91701 572-G4
OPAL WY
1200 SBdC 92359 608-H5
OPAL MOUNTAIN CT
- VCTV 92394 4295-F5
OPAL MOUNTAIN RD
45600 SBdC - 349-B4
OPATA RD
20900 APLV 92308 4387-F7
20900 APLV 92308 4477-G1
OPECHEE WY
- RCUC 91739 573-F6
OPICI CT
- RCUC 91739 574-B1
ORACLE RD
10300 SBdC - 4480-J2
ORANGE
200 NDLS 92363 3620-B6
ORANGE AV
400 SBdC - 4812-E2
1200 RDL 92373 647-G1
6200 SBdC 92377 575-G3
8100 RCUC 91730 603-E1
12500 CHNO 91710 642-B6
26400 LMLN 92373 647-G1
26400 SBdC 92373 647-G1
N ORANGE AV
100 RLTO 92376 605-G1
400 RLTO 92376 575-G6
600 ONT 91764 602-G4
2000 RLTO 92377 575-E2
S ORANGE AV
100 RLTO 92376 605-G2
W ORANGE AV
100 CLTN 92324 606-D3
ORANGE CT
13200 CHNO 91710 642-B7
13200 CHNO 91710 682-B1
16100 FONT 92335 604-G2
17600 FONT 92335 605-B2

ORANGE CT
17600 SBdC 92335 605-B2
E ORANGE CT
1800 ONT 91764 602-G4
N ORANGE DR
4200 SBDO 92407 546-E5
ORANGE DR E
2300 UPL 91784 572-B3
ORANGE DR W
2300 UPL 91784 572-A3
ORANGE FRWY Rt#-57
- DBAR - 640-C3
- POM - 640-C3
ORANGE FRWY Rt#-60
- DBAR - 640-B7
- DBAR - 680-B1
ORANGE LN
1300 SBdC 92359 609-C5
1300 RDL 92359 609-C5
ORANGE PK
100 RDL 92374 608-G7
100 RDL 92374 648-G1
ORANGE PL
12300 CHNO 91710 642-B5
N ORANGE PL
1400 ONT 91764 602-G5
ORANGE ST
- RDL 92373 608-B4
- RIV 92501 646-A7
- RivC 92501 646-A7
200 RDL 92374 608-B4
2100 RDL - 608-B2
2200 RDL 92346 608-B2
2600 HIGH 92346 608-B2
4300 HIGH 92346 578-B7
8300 RCUC 91701 572-E4
8800 HESP 92345 4476-A6
8800 HESP 92345 4566-H1
9500 RCUC 91737 572-J4
10000 RCUC 91737 573-A4
14100 HESP 92345 4475-H6
18200 HESP 92345 4477-A7
18400 HESP 92345 4567-A1
18500 SBdC 92316 605-D7
ORANGE ST Rt#-38
600 RDL 92374 608-B6
E ORANGE ST
200 SBDO 92410 576-J6
300 SBDO 92410 577-A6
N ORANGE ST
1800 HIGH 92346 577-G4
1800 SBDO 92346 577-G3
W ORANGE ST
100 SBDO 92410 576-H6
900 SBDO 92411 576-E6
1000 SBdC 92324 606-B5
ORANGE TR
2700 SBdC - 4816-A6
ORANGE WY
16300 FONT 92335 604-H3
17000 FONT 92335 605-C2
17900 SBdC 92335 605-C2
18200 RLTO 92335 605-C2
ORANGE BLOSSOM CIR
16000 FONT 92337 644-G3
ORANGE BLOSSOM DR
10600 RCUC 91730 573-B6
ORANGEBLOSSOM DR
28800 HIGH 92346 578-C3
ORANGE BLOSSOM LN
4700 SBdC 91710 641-F3
5600 CHNO 91710 641-H3
ORANGE BLOSSOM RD
4800 SBdC 91710 641-F3
ORANGECREST WY
25400 LMLN 92354 647-D2
ORANGEGROVE AV
1200 CLTN 92324 606-F5
ORANGE GROVE AV
3300 CHLS 91709 681-C5
E ORANGE GROVE AV
800 CLTN 92324 606-E5
N ORANGE GROVE AV
2000 POM 91767 601-A5
W ORANGE GROVE AV
1000 POM 91768 640-D1
ORANGE GROVE ST
10700 LMLN 92354 607-B7
11400 LMLN 92354 647-B2
ORANGE KNOLL AV
5900 SBdC 92404 577-E2
ORANGELEAF CT
9100 HESP 92345 4475-J7
W ORANGE SHOW LN
300 SBDO 92408 606-H4
ORANGE SHOW RD
200 SBDO 92408 606-G4
E ORANGE SHOW RD
300 SBDO 92408 606-J4
300 SBDO 92408 607-A4
ORANGE TREE LN
- RivC 92507 646-F6
1600 RDL 92374 607-G6
ORANGEWOOD AV
1700 UPL 91784 571-H6
N ORANGEWOOD AV
1600 UPL 91784 571-H7
3300 RLTO 92377 545-B7
3300 RLTO 92377 575-B1

ORANGEWOOD CIR
6400 RCUC 91701 572-H4
ORANGEWOOD CT
22900 GTER 92313 646-G4
ORANGEWOOD DR
2800 RLTO 92316 645-G2
6100 RCUC 91701 572-H4
8000 RCUC 91730 602-H1
14900 CHLS 91709 681-E5
ORANGEWOOD LN
6600 HIGH 92346 578-B4
ORANGEWOOD RD
6500 HIGH 92346 578-B3
ORANGEWOOD ST
900 CLTN 92324 606-F5
E ORANGEWOOD ST
100 CLTN 92324 606-F4
ORANGEWOOD WY
1700 UPL 91784 571-H6
ORCHARD AV
- RCUC 91730 573-E7
- RCUC 91730 603-D1
ORCHARD CIR
1300 UPL 91786 601-J1
ORCHARD DR
600 RDL 92374 648-D1
5200 SBdC 92397 4652-F3
8300 SBdC 92308 4479-H2
8300 SBdC 92308 (4569-H1 See Page 4568)
11900 CHNO 91710 641-E5
S ORCHARD DR
1800 SBDO 92408 607-B6
ORCHARD LN
- SBDO 92407 545-G1
900 ONT 91764 602-D6
30900 SBdC 92365 3764-E5
39800 SBdC 92339 611-C2
N ORCHARD LN
1300 ONT 91764 602-D5
S ORCHARD LN
900 CLTN 92324 646-G1
W ORCHARD LN
100 UPL 91786 602-B4
ORCHARD RD
- SBdC - 517-B1
43300 SBdC - 349-B6
N ORCHARD RD
2000 HIGH 92346 578-B3
2000 SBDO 92346 578-B3
ORCHARD ST
4100 MTCL 91763 601-E7
5600 MTCL 91762 601-E7
7900 RCUC 91701 572-D2
9300 SBdC 92316 605-D4
22500 SBdC 92347 349-B7
E ORCHARD ST
200 RLTO 92376 605-H3
W ORCHARD ST
300 RLTO 92376 605-E3
1300 RLTO 92316 605-D3
ORCHARD WY
2300 UPL 91784 571-H3
ORCHARD HILL LN
15000 SBdC - (3935-J2 See Page 3934)
15000 SBdC - 3936-A2
ORCHARD MEADOWS LN
8800 RCUC 91730 602-H4
ORCHID AV
10500 HESP 92345 4477-A3
11500 HESP 92345 4387-A7
14700 SBdC 92335 604-D3
17500 FONT 92335 605-B3
ORCHID CT
200 RDL 92373 648-C1
6500 RCUC 91739 573-G5
17400 FONT 92335 605-A3
W ORCHID CT
800 UPL 91786 602-A2
ORCHID DR
17200 FONT 92335 605-A3
26100 SBdC 92346 577-E3
E ORCHID DR
700 SBDO 92404 577-A3
1200 SBdC 92404 577-B3
3600 SBdC 92346 577-J3
3600 SBDO 92346 577-J3
ORCHID LN
300 POM 91766 641-A6
12300 CHNO 91710 641-J5
ORCHID ST
1800 BARS 92311 3679-D4
13000 YCPA 92399 650-A5
14900 SBdC 92335 604-D3
ORD RD
- SBdC 92365 (3684-J7 See Page 3594)
- SBdC 92365 3764-J1
ORD ST
30300 SBdC 92365 3764-J7
30400 SBdC - 3764-J7
35300 SBdC 92365 (3684-J1 See Page 3594)
35700 SBdC 92365 3594-J7
ORD MOUNTAIN RD
- SBdC - 369-F1
- SBdC - (3851-C4 See Page 3760)

STREET
Block City ZIP Pg-Grid

ORD MOUNTAIN RD
30900 SBdC - (3761-C6 See Page 3760)
ORE LN
1200 SBdC - (4743-B4 See Page 4662)
OREBAUGH LN
15100 SBdC - (3935-J5 See Page 3934)
15100 SBdC - 3936-A6
OREGON ST
- FONT 92336 574-C6
- RDL 92374 607-G6
- VCTV 92394 4205-G5
W OREGON ST
1400 SBDO 92410 606-B2
2900 SBDO 92376 605-J2
OREGON TR
12300 VCTV 92392 4385-J5
49000 SBdC 92256 615-G3
50900 SBdC 92256 616-D2
ORE GRANDE
- SBdC - 4887-B5
ORGANDY LN
3400 CHLS 91709 681-C7
ORGREN AV
12600 CHNO 91710 641-E5
ORGREN ST
11900 CHNO 91710 641-E4
ORICK AV
16100 VCTV 92394 4296-A3
16200 VCTV 92394 4295-J2
ORIENTAL AV
200 RDL 92374 608-B7
ORIENTE DR
30800 SBdC 92365 3764-G6
ORIOL RD
9100 SBdC 92372 4562-D1
9200 SBdC 92372 4472-D7
ORIOLE AV
12200 GTER 92313 646-F4
12800 RivC 92507 646-F6
ORIOLE CT
500 SBdC 92397 4652-B2
ORIOLE DR
400 SBdC - 517-D2
S ORIOLE DR
100 BBLK - 4741-G7
100 BBLK - 4811-G1
ORIOLE LN
800 SBdC - 4741-B5
19800 APLV 92308 4477-D1
ORIOLE PL
1500 UPL 91784 571-H4
ORIOLE RD
500 SBdC 92397 4652-B1
19700 APLV 92308 4477-E1
ORIOLE ST
8500 SBdC 92308 4479-G7
ORION DR
60900 SBdC 92252 4748-J7
61300 SBdC 92252 4749-F6
ORION ST
12300 VCTV 92392 4385-G6
70300 SBdC 92277 4751-E6
ORION WY
- BBLK - 4742-A7
ORLEANS DR
- SBdC 92311 3758-B4
ORLY CT
6700 FONT 92336 574-E5
ORNELAS LN
55500 SBdC 92285 4667-C7
ORO DR
57700 YUCA 92284 4888-A4
ORO GRANDE CANYON RD
- SBdC - 4205-J2
14900 SBdC - 4116-F7
14900 SBdC - (4206-A1 See Page 4116)
ORO VIEW RD
6900 SBdC 92308 4567-D4
W ORQUESTA CT
1500 CLTN 92324 606-A4
ORTEGA CT
6300 CHNO 91710 642-A7
ORTEGA DR
22500 SBdC 92301 (4113-F2 See Page 4112)
ORTON ST
35500 SBdC - (3681-E7 See Page 3590)
ORVIETO CT
6000 RCUC 91737 573-B4
OSAGE RD
6100 SBdC 92371 4653-D1
13100 SBdC 92371 4383-C5
13800 APLV 92307 4387-J1
14200 APLV 92307 4297-J2
OSAGE ST
12900 APLV 92308 4387-J4
23300 SBdC 92311 3758-C3
OSAGE TR
6300 SBdC - 4843-F3
OSBORNE CT
5500 SBDO 92407 546-E5
OSBORNE RD
1000 BARS 92311 3679-A5
17900 SBdC 92394 (4206-H4 See Page 4116)
17900 VCTV 92394 (4206-H4 See Page 4116)
N OSBORNE RD
35300 SBdC 92311 3679-A3
OSBOURNE AV
17600 CHLS 91709 712-A5
OSBRINK DR
11700 HESP 92345 4386-G7
OSBUN RD
2200 SBDO 92404 577-C3
5300 SBdC 92404 547-D7
5300 SBdC 92404 577-C1
6900 HIGH 92404 577-C5
N OSBUN RD
3700 SBdC 92404 547-C7
3700 SBDO 92404 547-C7
OSCEOLA RD
14900 APLV 92307 4297-B6
OSHKOSH CT
19600 APLV 92307 4297-C7
19600 APLV 92307 4387-C1
OSHKOSH LN
19500 APLV 92307 4297-C7
19500 APLV 92307 4387-C1
OSHKOSH RD
19300 APLV 92307 4297-C7
19300 APLV 92307 4387-C1
57700 SBdC 92284 4818-A3
OSHOTO AV
- SBdC 92307 4479-G1
11200 SBdC 92308 4479-G5
OSITA CAMP RD
1800 SBdC - 4811-C4
OSKAR LN
9300 SBdC 92256 616-A1
OSMUNDA AV
14700 CHLS 91709 681-D5
OSO RD
19700 APLV 92308 4387-H6
OSPREY LN
800 SBdC - 4738-A6
OSSEO RD
20100 APLV 92308 4387-E4
OSTEGO LN
- CHNO 91710 641-G4
OSTREMS WY
3600 SBDO 92407 546-B7
OSUMA RD
11600 FONT 92337 644-F3
OSUNA CT
5100 RivC 91752 683-G3
OSUNA RD
20200 APLV 92307 4387-E2
OTILLA ST
17600 SBdC 92316 605-B7
OTIS AV
100 BARS 92311 3679-G3
OTIS CT
300 POM 91766 640-J6
OTOE RD
20100 APLV 92307 4297-E3
22100 APLV 92307 4298-A3
OTOMIAN RD
18400 APLV 92307 4297-A5
OTONO CT
3000 SBdC 92407 576-A1
OTOWI RD
11300 APLV 92308 4477-F1
OTTAWA DR
800 CLAR 91711 601-B1
OTTAWA PL
- CHNO 91710 641-H4
13100 VCTV 92392 4386-D4
OTTAWA RD
19000 APLV 92308 4387-B3
21900 APLV 92308 4388-A3
23300 SBdC 92308 4388-D3
23400 SBdC 92307 4388-F3
OTTAWA ST
15300 VCTV 92392 4386-D3
OTTER AV
14500 ADEL 92301 4384-E1
14600 ADEL 92301 4294-E2
15400 SBdC 92301 4294-E6
17700 ADEL 92301 4204-E4
OTTER RD
15700 ADEL 92301 4294-E2
OTTER WY
- SBdC - 4773-H7
OTTO ST
3000 SBdC 92407 576-A2
N OTTO GERICKE DR
100 SBDO 92408 607-C1
S OTTO GERICKE DR
100 SBDO 92408 607-C2
OURABOTI CT
- SBdC - 4844-F1
OURAY RD
17300 APLV 92307 4208-C7
OUTER DR
3700 POM 91767 601-A2
3700 LACo 91711 601-A2
OUTER HWY
1900 SBdC 92397 4652-E2
OUTER HWY N
21300 SBdC 92347 (3587-F7 See Page 3586)
23800 SBdC 92311 3758-C2
24000 BARS 92311 3758-C2
OUTER HWY S
20200 SBdC 92347 (3587-C7 See Page 3586)
25300 LMLN 92354 647-C2
31100 SBdC 92373 648-J4
31100 YCPA 92373 648-J4
31100 YCPA 92373 649-B4
31200 RDL 92373 649-B4
OUTER 7TH ST
14200 VCTV 92392 4386-C1
14400 VCTV 92392 4296-C7
OUTER BEAR VALLEY RD
18800 APLV 92308 4387-B6
OUTER HWY 15 N
33800 SBdC - (3681-C2 See Page 3590)
OUTER HWY 15 S
16700 VCTV 92392 4296-F2
17100 APLV 92307 (4206-G7 See Page 4116)
17100 VCTV 92307 (4206-G7 See Page 4116)
17100 VCTV 92392 (4206-G7 See Page 4116)
OUTER HWY 18 N
10000 SBdC - 4481-B3
18100 APLV 92307 4296-J4
18400 APLV 92307 4297-B4
20900 APLV 92307 4387-H2
22100 APLV 92307 4388-A2
35700 SBdC - (4571-H1 See Page 4570)
OUTER HWY 18 S
13700 APLV 92307 4387-G1
13700 APLV 92308 4387-J2
17700 APLV 92307 4296-J4
18500 APLV 92307 4297-B4
21700 APLV 92308 4388-A2
OUTER HWY 18 DRCT N
19700 APLV 92307 4297-E5
OUTER HWY 215 N
3700 SBDO 92407 545-F1
9300 SBDO 92407 515-E7
OUTER HWY S
3700 SBdC 92371 4472-J7
3700 SBdC 92371 4473-A7
OUTLET CENTER DR
25700 BARS 92311 (3848-J1 See Page 3758)
25900 BARS 92311 (3849-A1 See Page 3758)
25900 SBdC 92311 (3848-J1 See Page 3758)
25900 SBdC 92311 (3849-A1 See Page 3758)
OUTLOOK LN
700 BBLK - 4811-E2
4400 CHNO 91710 641-E5
23300 SBdC - 516-G3
OUTPOST RD
- SBdC 92284 4818-G4
100 SBdC 92252 4749-A4
2900 SBdC 92252 4819-A3
4500 SBdC 92252 4889-A2
5700 SBdC 92345 (4655-C1 See Page 4654)
6200 SBdC 92345 4565-C3
6600 SBdC 92252 4959-A2
8400 HESP 92345 4565-C2
19600 SBdC 92308 4477-E6
22000 SBdC 92308 4479-A6
22600 SBdC 92308 4478-B6
30100 SBdC - 4480-C5
30600 SBdC 92252 4748-J4
OUTRIDER LN
51500 SBdC - 4886-D1
OUTRIGGER DR
- CHLS 91709 681-H6
OUTRIGGER LN
27100 SBdC - (3935-G4 See Page 3934)
OVAR CT
15400 FONT 92337 644-F3
OVERCREST DR
11600 SBdC 92374 648-H2
12100 YCPA 92399 649-A3
12200 YCPA 92399 648-H2
31100 SBdC 92374 649-A3
OVERDALE ST
- VCTV 92392 4296-E7
OVERDEN ST
1200 POM 91766 640-E3
OVERHILL DR
31300 SBdC - 518-J6
OVERHILL RD
62700 SBdC 92252 4959-E6
OVERHILL ST
- VCTV 92392 4296-E7
W OVERLAND AV
1000 UPL 91786 572-A7
OVERLAND CT
1200 UPL 91786 571-J7
12000 FONT 92337 644-B4
N OVERLAND CT
2800 SBDO 92346 577-G2
OVERLAND DR
11500 FONT 92337 644-A3
OVERLAND RD
- SBdC 92308 4477-F3
E OVERLAND ST
1700 CLTN 92324 646-G1
OVERLAND TR
19300 SBdC - (3937-B3 See Page 3936)
OVERLOOK CT
- APLV 92308 4387-E5
OVERLOOK DR
5500 RCUC 91739 573-G2
OVERLOOK LN
1300 SBdC - 4737-G5
OVERLOOK PL
- FONT 92336 574-E3
OVERLOOK RD
- APLV 92308 4387-E5
OVERLOOK RIDGE RD
1000 DBAR 91765 640-C5
OVERVIEW CT
- RivC 92399 650-H7
OWATONNA RD
17500 APLV 92307 4296-G4
18400 APLV 92307 4297-A4
OWEN CT
17600 FONT 92335 605-B1
OWEN ST
8300 SBdC 92335 603-J2
14000 SBdC 92335 604-A2
16100 FONT 92335 604-G2
17100 FONT 92335 605-A2
17700 SBdC 92335 605-B1
OWENS LN
100 POM 91766 640-J6
S OWENS RIVER LN
2600 ONT 91761 643-C6
OWENS RIVER RD
14500 VCTV 92392 4385-J5
OWETZAL LN
100 RivC 92507 646-E6
OWING WY
600 SBdC - 516-H3
OWL DR
41200 BBLK - 4741-G7
OWL LN
- SBdC - (4025-H7 See Page 3934)
OWL CANYON RD
- SBdC - 349-D7
OWL HOLE SPRINGS RD
37400 SBdC - 329-J5
OX BOW AV
12100 SBdC - (4390-H5 See Page 4300)
OX BOW RD
9100 SBdC - 4480-J2
OXEN CT
14500 FONT 92336 574-C1
OXEN LN
- FONT 92336 574-C1
OXFORD AV
800 CLAR 91711 601-C2
2100 CLAR 91711 571-C7
7000 HESP 92345 4566-H2
N OXFORD AV
1300 CLAR 91711 601-C1
1700 CLAR 91711 571-C7
OXFORD CT
7400 FONT 92336 574-B7
11600 ADEL 92301 4385-B1
13600 CHNO 91710 682-A2
OXFORD DR
800 RDL 92374 608-C6
N OXFORD LN
3700 SBdC 92404 547-B7
3900 SBDO 92404 547-C7
OXFORD PL
- RCUC 91730 573-E1
1100 POM 91768 640-D1
14200 VCTV 92392 4386-C1
OXFORD RD
9900 SBdC 92371 4473-J2
11900 SBdC 92371 4383-J2
14100 SBdC 92371 4382-F2
18500 SBdC 92301 (4203-H5 See Page 4112)
OXFORD ST
11700 ADEL 92301 4385-B1
14000 FONT 92336 574-B7
N OXFORD WY
1300 UPL 91786 602-A1
OX YOKE PASS
2500 SBdC - 4816-B7
OZARK MOUNTAIN PL
5200 RCUC 91737 573-B1

P

P ST
300 NDLS 92363 3620-B5
1200 BARS 92311 3679-C6
2000 BARS 92311 (3759-C1 See Page 3758)
33700 SBdC 92311 3679-C6
33700 SBdC 92311 (3759-C1 See Page 3758)
PABLO CT
6300 CHNO 91710 642-A7
PACA RD
24100 SBdC 92307 4298-F2
PACE CT
1400 RIV 92501 645-H7
PACER RD
16500 SBdC 92307 4299-A1
PACESETTERS RD
11700 SBdC 92392 4475-B1
11700 VCTV 92392 4475-B1
PACHAPPA RD
18900 APLV 92307 4297-A2
PACIFIC AV
- RCUC 91730 603-A4
100 RivC 92507 646-C6
3400 RivC 92509 645-B7
11300 FONT 92337 643-J4
W PACIFIC CT
600 UPL 91786 602-A1
PACIFIC DR
- SBdC - 2971-G1
PACIFIC RD
5700 SBdC 92371 4653-G2
8700 SBdC 92371 4563-F2
10500 SBdC 92371 4473-F1
11900 SBdC 92371 4383-F3
PACIFIC ST
100 POM 91768 640-C2
800 RDL 92373 648-B2
11000 RCUC 91701 573-C5
18100 HESP 92345 4476-J5
18100 HESP 92345 4477-A5
21600 SBdC 92308 4477-J5
21600 SBdC 92308 4478-F4
27900 HIGH 92346 578-A4
27900 SBDO 92346 578-A4
E PACIFIC ST
1000 SBdC 92404 577-C4
1000 SBDO 92404 577-C4
2100 HIGH 92404 577-C4
2400 SBDO 92346 577-C4
3600 HIGH 92346 577-H4
4100 SBDO 92346 578-A4
27800 HIGH 92346 578-A4
PACIFIC TER
- VCTV 92392 4385-G4
PACIFICA AV
6500 FONT 92336 574-J4
6500 FONT 92336 575-A4
PACIFIC CREST DR
2400 SBdC 92397 4652-G3
PACIFIC CREST PL
5500 RCUC 91739 573-H2
PACIFIC PRIVADO
- ONT 91761 643-D2
PACIFIC VISTA
13800 CHLS 91709 681-A2
PACKARD DR
900 POM 91766 641-B3
PACOIMA CIR
14100 VCTV 92392 4385-H5
PACOIMA CT
- VCTV 92392 4385-H5
PACOIMA RD
11500 VCTV 92392 4385-H1
11500 VCTV 92392 4475-H1
13200 SBdC 92392 4385-H3
PACTFIELD PL
- YCPA 92399 649-E2
PADDINGTON CIR
14700 CHLS 91709 681-A5
PADDOCK AV
28200 SBdC - (3846-E7 See Page 3756)
28200 SBdC - 3936-E1
PADDOCK CIR
15100 VCTV 92394 4295-H6
PADDOCK CT
15100 VCTV 92394 4295-H6
PADDOCK LN
14600 FONT 92336 574-C2
PADDOCK PL
- RCUC 91737 (543-C7 See Page 513)
4900 RCUC 91737 573-C1
PADDOCK RD
14100 VCTV 92394 4295-H6
W PADILLA DR
1900 CLTN 92324 605-J4
PADINGTON RD
47300 SBdC 92285 4484-J3
47300 SBdC 92285 (4485-A3 See Page 4484)
PADOVA CT
6800 RCUC 91701 573-D5
PADOVA DR
11300 RCUC 91701 573-D5
PADOVA ST
20400 APLV 92308 4477-F2
PADRE AV
- RCUC 91739 544-B7
- RCUC 91739 574-B1
PADUA AV
1400 RDL 92374 608-E5
2100 CLAR 91711 571-F6
N PADUA AV
700 CLAR 91711 571-F5
PADUA AV N
4400 CLAR 91711 571-F3
PAFFIN RD
8700 SBdC 92308 4479-H7
PAGEANTRY PL
13500 CHLS 91709 681-A2
PAGOSI CT
11600 APLV 92308 4387 G7
PAGOSI RD
11200 APLV 92308 4477-G1
11400 APLV 92308 4387-H7
PAHASKA CT
- SBdC - 4843-H4
PAHASKA TR
6900 SBdC - 4843-H4
PAHASKA WY
- SBdC - 4843-H4
PAHATA CT
17100 SBdC 92307 4208-D7
17100 SBdC 92307 4298-D1
PAHUTE AV
15400 VCTV 92392 4386-A6
PAH-UTE AV
21700 APLV 92308 4387-J5
21900 APLV 92308 4388-A5
25200 SBdC 92307 4388-J5
PAHUTE RD
17700 SBdC 92392 4386-H5
17700 VCTV 92392 4386-H5
PAH-UTE RD
20200 APLV 92308 4387-E5
23200 SBdC 92308 4388-D5
25700 SBdC 92307 (4389-A5 See Page 4299)
PAHUTE ST
15300 VCTV 92392 4386-B5
PAHWAY TR
- SBdC - 4844-D1
PAIGE LN
1300 RDL 92373 648-E2
PAINE CT
1600 CLAR 91711 601-B1
PAINE DR
- SBdC - 4736-A7
PAINE RD
400 BBLK - 4811-E1
PAINE ST
15600 FONT 92336 604-F1
17300 FONT 92336 605-A1
PAINT BRUSH LN
21900 DBAR 91765 680-A5
PAINTED HILL AV
5900 TNP 92277 4891-H5
PAINTED PONY CT
13900 VCTV 92394 4295-G7
PAINTED VALLEY CT
15500 VCTV 92394 4296-A5
PAINTER CT
900 POM 91766 641-A3
PAINTER DR
3000 CHLS 91709 681-C6
PAISANO DR
22800 SBdC 92301 (4113-E1 See Page 4112)
PAISANO LN
5500 YUCA 92284 4888-A5
PAISLEY AV
7000 HESP 92345 4566-H2
PAISLEY LN
8300 SBdC 92335 604-B2
PAISLEY ST
3300 CHLS 91709 681-B7
PAIUTE AV
1400 RDL 92374 608-F5
PAIUTE TR
6200 SBdC - 4843-J2
PAJARO CT
15000 VCTV 92392 4296-D6
PAJARO DR
57800 SBdC 92284 4818-B4
PALA LN
24100 SBdC 92307 4298-F2
PALA PL
11000 RivC 91752 683-H3
PALA BELLS CT
- RDL 92374 608-F4
PALACIO CT
7700 RCUC 91730 573-D7
PALADORA LN
6900 RivC 92509 645-B4
PALAMA ST
- SBdC - 4207-A1
PALA MESA DR
- POM 91766 640-F5
PALAMOS PL
13200 CHLS 91709 680-J1
PALARAD ST
- SBdC 92284 4817-D2
PALERMO AV
- VCTV 92392 4386-F5
2300 UPL 91784 571-H3
PALERMO CT
10100 YCPA 92399 609-J5
PALERMO PL
6800 RCUC 91701 573-D5
PALERMO ST
7900 FONT 92336 604-B1
29500 SBdC 92311 3589-H6
PALI MOUNTAIN RD
- SBdC - 518-G5
PALISADE AV
17900 SBdC - (4210-G3 See Page 4120)
PALISADE DR
58200 YUCA 92284 4958-C1
PALISADE RD
- SBdC - 4737-B7
PALISADE ST
3400 CHLS 91709 681-C5
PALISADE WY
6700 YUCA 92284 4958-C1
PALISADES CT
400 SBdC - 4738-B7
11400 ADEL 92301 4385-A1
PALISADES DR
28700 SBdC - 518-C1
28700 SBdC - 4738-B7
PALLADIO LN
- FONT 92336 574-E3
PALLESI ST
300 BARS 92311 3679-H2
PALM AV
300 BARS 92311 3680-A4
1300 HIGH 92346 577-H7
1300 SBDO 92346 577-H7
1400 UPL 91786 572-B7
1400 UPL 91786 602-B1
3100 SBdC 92284 4817-G6
4100 YUCA 92284 4887-G2
6200 SBdC 92377 575-G3
6800 YUCA 92284 4957-G2
7900 SBdC 92345 4565-E3
21500 GTER 92313 646-C4
21500 SBdC 92313 646-C4
21500 SBdC 92324 646-C4
E PALM AV
- RDL 92373 648-D1
600 RDL 92374 648-D1
1300 RDL 92374 608-E7
N PALM AV
100 ONT 91762 602-B5
100 ONT 91762 642-B1
100 RLTO 92376 605-G1
200 UPL 91786 602-B1
800 RLTO 92376 575-E5
1600 UPL 91784 572-B3
1600 HIGH 92346 577-H4
1600 SBDO 92346 577-H2
2000 RLTO 92377 575-E2
2200 SBdC 92346 577-H3
5800 SBdC 92407 545-J3
5900 SBDO 92407 545-J1
S PALM AV
100 ONT 91762 642-B1
100 RLTO 92376 605-G2
100 UPL 91786 602-B4
1700 RLTO 92316 605-G6
W PALM AV
- RDL 92373 648-B3
200 CLTN 92313 646-C4
200 CLTN 92324 646-C4
200 GTER 92313 646-C4
PALM CIR
- RivC 91752 683-F5
PALM CT
12100 GTER 92313 646-F4
12400 CHNO 91710 641-J6
PALM DR
- SBdC 92277 4824-F5
- SBdC 92337 604-H7
- TNP 92278 4822-E1
6600 RCUC 91737 573-B5
6700 RCUC 91701 573-B5
18000 HESP 92345 4566-J1
25000 LMLN 92354 607-C7
33700 YCPA 92399 649-G3
E PALM DR
800 CLTN 92324 606-E5
N PALM DR
3200 SBDO 92405 576-F1
3900 SBDO 92405 546-H7
PALM LN
700 SBdC - 4738-E6
7300 FONT 92336 575-B6
7600 SBdC 92336 575-B7
7900 SBdC 92410 577-A7
7900 SBdC 92410 607-A1
8900 FONT 92335 605-C3
9300 SBdC 92335 605-C4
9800 SBdC 92316 605-B5
PALM PL
200 POM 91767 641-A1
S PALM PL
1900 ONT 91762 642-B4
PALM RD
4500 SBdC 92277 (4825-B7 See Page 4824)
36100 SBdC - 4481-J7
36200 SBdC - 4482-A7
88700 SBdC - 330-K2
PALM ST
- VCTV 92394 4295-J7
- VCTV 92394 4296-A7
1200 SBDO 92408 607-B2
12600 HESP 92345 4565-F1
12700 SBdC 92345 4565-E1
14200 ADEL 92301 4385-A1
14900 HESP 92345 4566-A1
16900 ADEL 92301 4295-A2
17300 ADEL 92301 4205-A5
PALM WY
400 NDLS 92363 3620-D6
1900 UPL 91784 572-B3
19200 APLV 92308 4477-C1
PALMA RD
21700 SBdC 92347 (3587-G3 See Page 3586)
PALMA VISTA RD
45700 SBdC 92365 3594-D6
47900 SBdC 92365 (3595-A5 See Page 3594)
PALMBROOK DR
900 RDL 92373 648-A1
E PALM CREST DR
3600 SBDO 92346 577-H2
N PALMCROFT BLVD
3700 SBDO 92404 546-J7
PALMDALE RD Rt#-18
100 SBdC 92371 368-G6
100 SBdC 92371 4382-F2
100 SBdC 92372 368-G6
100 SBdC 92372 4382-F2
3700 SBdC 92371 4383-A2
7500 SBdC 92371 4384-A2
7800 ADEL 92371 4384-A2
8100 ADEL 92301 4384-G2
8400 ADEL 92392 4384-A2
10900 VCTV 92301 4385-B2
10900 VCTV 92392 4385-G2
11100 ADEL 92301 4385-B2
11100 ADEL 92392 4385-B2
11900 SBdC 92392 4385-G2
14300 VCTV 92392 4386-B1
PALMDALE RD U.S.-66 Hist
15300 VCTV 92392 4386-A2
PALMER CT
6700 CHNO 91710 682-B1
PALMER RD
17700 SBdC 92301 (4202-E3 See Page 4112)
PALMER ST
1200 RivC 92507 646-B6
W PALMER ST
1500 POM 91766 640-G3
PALMERA DR
22800 SBdC 92301 (4113-D2 See Page 4112)
PALMER CANYON RD
4500 CLAR 91711 571-E2
4600 LACo 91711 571-E2
PALMER-EVEY MTWY
- CLAR 91711 571-G1
- LACo 91711 571-G1
PALMERO RD
16000 APLV 92307 4296-J4
PALMETTO AV
1900 SBdC 92374 607-F3
7300 FONT 92336 575-A6
7300 RLTO 92376 575-A6
7800 FONT 92336 605-A2
8100 FONT 92335 605-A2
9700 FONT 92316 605-A6
9800 SBdC 92316 605-A6
10300 FONT 92337 605-A7
10500 FONT 92337 645-A1
26500 RDL 92374 607-F3
N PALMETTO AV
100 ONT 91762 602-A5
100 ONT 91762 642-A1
400 ONT 91762 601-J5
1200 RLTO 92336 575-A5
1200 RLTO 92376 575-A5
3100 RLTO 92377 575-A1
3300 RLTO 92377 545-A7
4200 FONT 92336 575-A5
S PALMETTO AV
400 ONT 91762 642-A2
W PALMETTO AV
26900 SBdC 92374 607-H3
PALMETTO DR
1000 BARS 92311 3679-G5
PALMETTO PL
13600 CHLS 91709 680-J2
PALMETTO WY
13000 HESP 92345 4475-E5
PALMGROVE AV
1700 POM 91767 601-B6
PALMI DR
11800 RCUC 91701 573-E6
E PALM LANE DR
700 RDL 92373 648-C2
PALM MEADOWS DR
1200 SBDO 92408 607-C3
11500 RCUC 91730 573-D7
PALMS AV
8300 SBdC 92335 603-J2
PALMVIEW AV
6300 TNP 92277 4892-F5
PALMVIEW LN
7800 HIGH 92346 578-C7
PALM VIEW LN
29100 HIGH 92346 578-D7
PALM VISTA
38500 SBdC - 3592-D6
PALM VISTA DR
61400 SBdC 92252 4959-B1
74700 TNP 92277 4892-H6
PALMYRA CT
14500 ADEL 92301 4384-H1
PALMYRA DR
- SBdC 92277 4820-E4
69400 SBdC 92277 4821-C4
E PALMYRA DR
100 SBDO 92404 546-H7
PALMYRA ST
10600 ADEL 92301 4384-H1
PALMYRA WY
14500 ADEL 92301 4384-H1
PALMYRITA AV
- RivC 92507 646-F7
PALO CT
1500 BARS 92311 3680-A5
PALO ALTO AV
3700 SBdC 92284 4818-A7
3900 SBdC 92284 4888-A1
6200 YUCA 92284 4888-A3
7100 YUCA 92284 4958-A2
15600 CHLS 91709 681-E7
PALO ALTO CT
800 RDL 92373 648-H5
14400 VCTV 92392 4385-J5
PALO ALTO DR
600 RDL 92373 648-G5
12700 VCTV 92392 4385-J5
PALO ALTO ST
9300 RCUC 91730 572-H7
9900 RCUC 91730 573-A7
11900 RCUC 91739 573-F7
PALO ALTO WY
2300 SBdC - 519-A7
N PALO CEDRO DR
100 DBAR 91765 640-A7
S PALO CEDRO DR
100 DBAR 91765 640-A7
200 DBAR 91765 680-A1
PALOMA AV
1400 RDL 92374 608-F5
5500 SBdC - 4886-G5
S PALOMA AV
200 SBDO 92410 606-D2
PALOMA CT
9800 RCUC 91730 602-J1
PALOMA CUR
2300 SBdC 91784 572-A3
PALOMA DR
200 POM 91767 641-A1
PALOMA RD
5200 RivC 92509 645-F7
25300 HIGH 92410 577-C6
PALOMA ST
1500 BARS 92311 3680-A5
PALOMAR
14400 SBdC - (4301-J6 See Page 4300)
PALOMAR AV
3400 SBDO 92404 577-E1
5600 SBdC 92404 577-E1
7300 YUCA 92284 4958-C4
9900 SBdC - 4482-A1
10900 SBdC - (4392-A5 See Page 4302)
13600 YCPA 92399 650-A7
PALOMAR CT
6500 RCUC 91701 573-C4
25900 SBdC 92404 577-D1
PALOMAR TR
6900 SBdC - (4571-J3 See Page 4570)
8900 SBdC - 4481-J5
PALOMARES RD
1500 RDL 92373 647-J5
N PALOMARES ST
100 POM 91767 641-A1
800 POM 91767 601-A6
S PALOMARES ST
100 POM 91766 641-A3
PALOMINO AV
1700 UPL 91784 571-J6
N PALOMINO AV
1300 UPL 91786 601-J1
1400 UPL 91786 571-J7
PALOMINO CIR
- MTCL 91763 641-E1
PALOMINO CT
13800 VCTV 92394 4295-G7
E PALOMINO CT
2900 ONT 91761 643-A7
PALOMINO DR
100 SBdC 92314 4742-G5
15600 CHLS 91709 681-G7
23400 DBAR 91765 640-C6
PALOMINO LN
11700 FONT 92337 644-F3
12300 APLV 92308 4387-B5
PALOMINO PL
5000 RCUC 91737 (543-B7 See Page 513)
5000 RCUC 91737 573-B1
S PALOMINO PL
3600 ONT 91761 683-A1
PALOMINO RD
- BARS 92311 3589-H7
- SBdC - (3847-D6 See Page 3756)
27700 SBdC - (3937-D2 See Page 3936)
PALOMINO ST
7200 HIGH 92346 578-B5
PALOS GRANDE DR
12900 SBdC 92392 4386-H4
PALOS VERDE LN
17800 SBdC 92392 4386-H2
PALOS VERDES RD
44900 SBdC 92365 (3684-B5 See Page 3594)
PALO VERDE
300 PRKR - 4774-H7
PALO VERDE AV
1000 PRKR - 4844-H1
1700 LPCo - 4844-H1
4900 TNP 92277 4892-E2
7300 FONT 92336 575-A6
8600 FONT 92335 605-A2
PALO VERDE CT
9500 SBdC 92371 4473-B7
14500 ADEL 92301 4384-J1
PALO VERDE DR
800 BARS 92311 3679-J5
1500 RDL 92373 648-G4
9200 HESP 92345 4475-G7
19200 APLV 92308 4387-B7
19700 APLV 92308 4477-B4
PALO VERDE LN
46100 SBdC 92365 3764-D4
47700 SBdC 92365 (3765-A4 See Page 3764)
PALO VERDE PL
- RCUC 91739 573-F5
PALO VERDE RD
48800 SBdC 92256 615-G4
50000 SBdC 92256 616-A4
PALO VERDE ST
4300 MTCL 91763 601-E5
5600 MTCL 91762 601-G5
11100 ADEL 92301 4384-J1
11200 ADEL 92301 4385-A1
PAMELA CT
13500 YCPA 92399 650-C6
PAMELA DR
3800 SBdC 91710 641-C7
PAMELA LN
500 POM 91766 641-A5
9100 ADEL 92301 4294-D6
9100 SBdC 92301 4294-E6
11300 ADEL 92301 4295-A6
11300 SBdC 92301 4295-A6
11700 APLV 92308 4387-B7
11700 APLV 92308 4477-B1
15300 VCTV 92394 4296-B5
PAMELA ST
10000 MohC - 3620-C2
16100 VCTV 92392 4296-D5
PAMELA CREST
1500 RDL 92373 648-F3
PAMLICO RD
- SBdC 92277 4893-C3
13800 APLV 92307 4387-C1
14200 APLV 92307 4297-C6
PAMPA DR
6500 SBdC - 4843-J3
PAMPAS AV
- TNP 92277 4891-E4
- TNP 92277 4961-E1
1500 SBdC 92277 4751-D7
1500 SBdC 92277 4821-D1
4100 SBdC 92277 4891-D1
N PAMPAS AV
100 RLTO 92376 605-J1
500 RLTO 92376 575-J5
S PAMPAS AV
300 RLTO 92376 605-J3
600 SBDO 92376 605-J3
PAMPAS CT
900 BARS 92311 3679-G4
PAMPAS DR
7000 HESP 92345 4567-A4
PAMPAS LN
8300 SBdC 92335 604-D2
PAMPAS RD
20800 APLV 92308 4477-G4
20800 SBdC 92308 4477-G4
PAMPUS DR
11600 RivC 91752 683-G5
PANAMINT AV
82900 SBdC 93562 2145-A4
PANAMINT RD
27300 SBdC 92311 3679-D7
PANAMINT TR
- SBdC - 3936-J3
19100 SBdC - (3937-C3 See Page 3936)
19300 SBdC - (3847-B5 See Page 3756)
W PANAMINT MOUNTAIN DR
700 SBdC 92314 4742-B5
PANCHITA RD
56900 YUCA 92284 4887-H7
PANDINO CT
6800 RCUC 91701 573-D5
PANDORA LN
9600 SBdC 92335 604-D5
PANDORA WY
2000 POM 91766 641-A5
PANHANDLE DR
700 DBAR 91765 680-B1
PANOCHE RD
21600 APLV 92308 4477-J2
21800 APLV 92308 4478-A2

STREET Block City ZIP Pg-Grid

PANORAMA AV
5400 TNP 92277 4891-J3
PANORAMA CIR
13400 SBdC 92345 4565-G1
PANORAMA CT
6400 RCUC 91737 573-E4
PANORAMA DR
- SBdC 92374 648-H2
16900 FONT 92337 644-J3
31400 SBdC - 518-J7
31400 SBdC - 519-A7
35300 YCPA 92399 650-A1
50300 SBdC 92256 4956-A7
E PANORAMA DR
1200 SBdC 92314 4742-G6
PANORAMA MTWY
- Llan 93544 4562-A2
PANORAMA RD
6000 SBdC 92252 4889-B6
30600 SBdC - 548-G1
PANORAMA ST
1300 UPL 91784 571-H3
N PAN SPRINGS LN
1000 SBdC 92314 4742-E4
PANSY AV
1300 UPL 91784 571-J4
8000 ADEL 92301 4294-B3
PANSY RD
7300 ADEL 92301 (4293-J4 See Page 4292)
7300 ADEL 92301 4294-G3
7300 ADEL 92371 (4293-J4 See Page 4292)
11100 ADEL 92301 4295-A3
PANTERA DR
600 DBAR 91765 640-D7
600 DBAR 91765 680-D1
PANTHER AV
17200 ADEL 92301 4204-F3
17200 ADEL 92301 4294-F1
PAOHA RD
- APLV 92308 4387-D3
PAPAGO CT
- SBdC - 4843-F4
PAPAGO RD
20800 APLV 92307 4207-G7
22300 APLV 92307 4208-A7
PAPAGO TR
2300 SBdC - 4843-F5
56100 YUCA 92284 4957-F3
PAPAYA PL
9300 SBdC 92335 604-D4
PAPOOSE TR
69300 SBdC 92277 4751-G5
PAPOOSE WY
7500 SBdC - 4843-F5
PAR LN
18300 SBdC 92392 4386-J4
PARADISE AV
48800 SBdC 92256 615-H6
72900 SBdC - 2971-G2
PARADISE CT
13200 VCTV 92392 4385-F5
PARADISE LN
400 LPCo - 4774-J5
12300 YCPA 92399 649-D4
PARADISE PL
- RCUC 91730 572-J7
PARADISE ST
11900 GTER 92313 646-G4
PARADISE WY
1000 SBdC 92314 4742-E5
1300 RDL 92374 608-E5
N PARADISE WY
100 SBdC 92314 4742-E6
S PARADISE WY
100 SBdC 92314 4742-E6
PARADISE SPRINGS RD
300 SBdC - 349-E2
36900 SBdC 92365 (3593-B1 See Page 3592)
PARADISE VIEW RD
3100 SBdC 92284 4818-D7
4000 SBdC 92284 4888-D2
4900 YUCA 92284 4888-E5
PARAISO RD
12800 APLV 92308 4387-C3
PARAMONT CT
7500 RCUC 91730 573-A7
7700 RCUC 91730 603-A1
PARAMONT RD
58300 SBdC 92284 4818-A1
PARAMOUNT DR
3000 RivC 92509 645-C7
18800 SBdC - 371-F2
PARAMOUNT RD
- SBdC 92371 4653-E1
5100 SBdC 92371 4563-D2
9300 SBdC 92371 4473-D2
12500 SBdC 92371 4383-D2
14500 SBdC 92371 (4293-D7 See Page 4292)
42300 BBLK - 4811-J1
PARAPET RD
- SBdC - 4737-C7
N PARCELS ST
200 POM 91768 640-J1
S PARCELS ST
100 POM 91766 640-J2

S PARCO AV
1600 ONT 91761 642-F4
PARIS AV
34100 SBdC 92311 3678-G6
PARIS CIR
2100 UPL 91784 571-J4
PARK AV
100 NDLS 92363 3620-C6
900 CALI 92320 649-H7
1600 SBdC 92407 515-D6
6600 SBdC 92376 575-F4
6800 RLTO 92376 575-F5
6900 TNP 92277 4893-A7
13700 VCTV 92392 4386-B1
14400 VCTV 92392 4296-B7
20900 SBdC 92347 (3587-E5 See Page 3586)
25200 LMLN 92354 607-C7
36700 SBdC 92311 3589-J7
41100 BBLK - 4811-F1
48900 SBdC 92256 615-G6
56500 SBdC - 2971-G3
E PARK AV
1000 RDL 92374 608-D7
N PARK AV
- POM 91766 640-J1
100 POM 91768 640-J1
200 RLTO 92376 605-F1
500 RLTO 92376 575-F5
800 SBDO 92411 576-E6
2000 RLTO 92377 575-F4
2700 SBdC 92404 577-C3
2800 SBDO 92404 577-C2
S PARK AV
100 POM 91766 640-J3
500 RLTO 92376 605-G3
W PARK AV
900 RDL 92373 608-A7
1000 RDL 92373 607-G7
2000 SBdC 92373 607-G7
PARK AV E
15500 VCTV 92392 4386-B2
PARK BLVD
2300 SBdC 91784 572-A3
5900 SBdC 92252 4889-B6
6700 SBdC 92252 4959-B1
W PARK BLVD
2300 SBdC 91784 572-A3
2300 SBdC 91784 571-J3
PARK CIR
300 RivC 91752 683-F5
PARK DR
6000 SBdC 92397 4652-D1
11900 SBdC 92316 645-E4
30400 SBdC - 548-G1
N PARK DR
4500 SBDO 92407 546-C6
PARK LN
5300 SBDO 92404 546-J5
11600 APLV 92308 4387-B7
19700 APLV 92308 4477-B1
23800 SBdC - 516-H3
56900 SBdC 92285 4747-H3
PARK PL
400 RivC 92507 646-B7
1100 SBdC - 517-F4
5300 CHNO 91710 641-H7
PARK RD
- SBdC 92392 4296-H7
- SBdC 92392 4386-H1
PARK ST
4300 CHNO 91710 641-E7
18700 SBdC 92316 605-E6
E PARK ST
100 ONT 91761 642-C1
W PARK ST
100 ONT 91761 642-B1
100 ONT 91762 642-B1
PARK WY
15100 ADEL 92301 4294-H6
PARKCENTER DR
11500 RivC 91752 683-G4
PARK CREST CIR
17300 CHLS 91709 711-J4
PARK CREST DR
5800 CHLS 91709 711-J4
6000 CHLS 91709 712-A4
PARKCREST LN
29200 HIGH 92346 578-D6
PARKCREST ST
1400 UPL 91784 571-H3
E PARKDALE DR
100 SBDO 92404 546-H7
500 SBDO 92404 547-A7
PARKDALE RD
1000 SBdC 92301 (4202-A7 See Page 4112)
3500 SBdC 92301 (4203-A7 See Page 4112)
W PARKDALE ST
100 SBDO 92405 546-H7
PARKE CIR
12500 RCUC 91739 573-G2
PARKER CT
1300 RDL 92373 647-J1
PARKER RD
3900 SBdC 92277 (4825-J6 See Page 4824)
PARKER ST
55400 SBdC - 4606-F1

PARKER DAM RD
800 SBdC - 4606-G1
1300 SBdC - 372-G10
47200 SBdC - 4774-H5
PARKFORD
900 RDL 92374 648-E2
PARK GLEN ST
- VCTV 92392 4386-H5
PARKGLEN WY
3100 ONT 91761 643-B6
W PARK HAVEN DR
2800 SBDO 92376 606-A3
PARKHILL DR
8900 RCUC 91730 572-G7
PARKHURST CT
- CHLS 91709 711-H1
PARKHURST ST
4400 RivC 91752 643-H7
4400 RivC 91752 683-H1
PARKLAND DR
1900 SBdC 92404 516-G6
32200 SBdC - 519-B7
PARKLAND ST
10700 LMLN 92354 607-B7
10900 LMLN 92354 647-B1
PARK LAWN CT
8000 FONT 92336 604-A1
PARK MOABI RD
25600 SBdC - 352-C10
PARKRIDGE DR
11300 FONT 92337 644-H2
N PARKSIDE AV
400 ONT 91764 602-E4
PARKSIDE CT
14200 CHLS 91709 680-J4
N PARKSIDE DR
1300 SBDO 92404 576-J1
3600 SBDO 92404 546-J7
S PARKSIDE DR
2600 ONT 91761 642-E6
PARKSIDE PL
1300 ONT 91761 642-E3
2900 SBDO 92404 576-C1
7100 RCUC 91701 573-B6
PARK SPRING LN
900 DBAR 91765 680-C2
PARKVIEW
200 RDL 92374 648-G1
PARKVIEW CIR
1200 UPL 91784 571-J6
PARKVIEW CT
6200 SBDO 92407 545-G1
PARKVIEW DR
14100 FONT 92337 644-B3
PARKVIEW LN
2200 CHLS 91709 680-J3
PARK VIEW LN
7700 HIGH 92346 578-C7
PARKVIEW ST
10300 ADEL 92301 4204-G7
PARKVIEW TER
3100 CHLS 91709 681-B1
12900 YCPA 92399 650-E5
PARK VIEW TR
61600 SBdC 92252 4959-B5
W PARK VISTA DR
2800 SBDO 92376 606-A3
3100 SBDO 92376 605-J3
PARK VISTA LN
2200 CHLS 91709 680-J3
E PARKWAY
6100 SBdC 92252 4889-B6
W PARKWAY
6100 SBdC 92252 4889-B6
PARKWAY AV
100 BARS 92311 3679-H3
PARKWAY DR
1000 NDLS 92363 3620-A6
3100 NDLS 92363 3710-A1
45900 SBdC - 4742-J3
PARKWOOD DR
- RDL 92373 608-B7
- RDL 92373 648-B1
13900 FONT 92337 644-B3
PARKWOOD LN
600 POM 91767 601-A1
PARKWOOD PL
12400 VCTV 92392 4385-E6
PARLIAMENT DR
- RCUC 91730 573-E7
PARMA PL
6800 RCUC 91701 573-D5
PARMESON RD
9700 SBdC - 4482-G2
PARSONS PL
4000 SBDO 92407 546-C7
PARSONS RANCH RD
- SBdC - 4816-C1
PARTRIDGE AV
- UPL 91784 572-E6
PARTRIDGE LN
21800 SBdC - 516-C2
PARTRIDGE PL
28900 SBdC - 518-C1
PARTRIDGE RD
900 SBdC 92397 4652-B2
E PARVIN LN
3000 CLTN 92324 647-A5
PASADENA CT
5600 RCUC 91739 574-B2

E PASADENA ST
100 POM 91767 640-J1
200 POM 91767 641-A1
PASCAL AV
11800 GTER 92313 646-E3
PASCO RD
11300 APLV 92308 4387-H7
11300 APLV 92308 4477-H1
PASCUAL CT
9800 RCUC 91730 602-G6
PASEO CT
- SBdC 92335 604-A2
PASEO BREVE
7600 HIGH 92346 578-F6
PASEO DEL PALACIO
2200 CHLS 91709 680-J6
2300 CHLS 91709 681-A5
PASEO DEL REY
2000 NDLS 92363 3620-C7
2100 NDLS 92363 3710-C1
PASEO DEL SOL
17800 CHLS 91709 712-B5
PASEO DEL VALLE
34600 SBdC 92311 3678-G5
PASEO DE TERRADO
23000 DBAR 91765 680-B3
PASEO GRANDE
2000 CHLS 91709 680-J6
PASEO LA CRESTA
17800 APLV 92307 4296-G2
PASEO LARGO
7600 HIGH 92346 578-F6
PASEO LUNADO
17800 APLV 92307 4296-G2
PASEO MEDIO
7600 HIGH 92346 578-F6
PASEO ROBLES
24900 SBdC 92311 3678-F6
PASEO TORTUGA
2500 CHLS 91709 680-J5
2500 CHLS 91709 681-A5
PASEO VALLE
17800 CHLS 91709 712-B5
PASEO VERDE
25000 SBdC 92311 3678-G6
PASHARD ST
- NDLS 92363 3620-A4
PASITO AV
6700 RCUC 91701 572-J5
7300 RCUC 91730 572-J7
7700 RCUC 91730 602-J1
PASITO RD
18600 SBdC 92301 (4202-E3 See Page 4112)
PASITO ST
25500 SBdC 92404 577-D4
27900 HIGH 92346 578-A4
E PASITO ST
4100 SBDO 92346 577-J4
PASO FINO ST
- RivC 92880 683-D6
PASO ROBLES CT
14100 VCTV 92392 4385-H5
PASO ROBLES DR
12700 VCTV 92392 4385-H5
PASTURE WY
15100 VCTV 92394 4295-H6
PASTY LN
46500 SBdC - (4743-B6 See Page 4662)
PATCH RD
- LPCo - 4844-C5
PATE PL
12600 CHNO 91710 641-D6
PATINA CT
16400 CHLS 91709 711-G2
PATOKA CT
12700 APLV 92308 4387-F4
PATOMAC RD
10800 SBdC 92308 4478-D3
11900 APLV 92308 4388-C5
13800 APLV 92307 4388-C2
14200 APLV 92307 4298-C7
PATOMOC RD
11700 APLV 92308 4388-D7
11700 SBdC 92308 4388-D7
N PATRICIA AV
1500 CLTN 92324 606-B4
N PATRICIA CT
6100 SBDO 92407 545-J3
PATRICIA DR
- RDL 92373 648-F3
6100 RivC 92509 645-B7
PATRICIA ST
600 BARS 92311 3680-A3
PATRICK AV
800 POM 91767 601-B7
PATRICK ST
1600 UPL 91784 571-J6
1600 UPL 91784 572-A6
PATRICK WY
60100 SBdC 92284 4818-G2
PATRIOT CIR
- UPL 91786 602-D4
PATRIOT CT
9900 ADEL 92301 4204-F5
PATRIOT PL
7800 RCUC 91730 602-H1
PATTEE CT
27600 HIGH 92346 577-J6

PATTERSON AV
1000 POM 91766 641-B4
N PATTERSON WY
2700 SBDO 92405 576-F3
PAUBA RD
- SBdC - 4843-F5
19200 APLV 92307 4297-C2
PAUHASKA CT
16300 APLV 92307 4298-B1
PAUHASKA PL
16300 APLV 92307 4298-B2
PAUHASKA RD
8900 SBdC 92308 4478-B2
11800 APLV 92308 4388-B3
14500 APLV 92307 4298-A2
17300 APLV 92307 4208-B7
17700 SBdC 92307 4208-B5
PAUL VILLASENOR BLVD
900 SBDO 92408 607-B2
PAVIA DR
11600 RCUC 91701 573-E5
PAVILLION DR
1700 POM 91768 640-E1
PAVO CT
14500 VCTV 92394 4295-J3
PAVOLA DR
- RCUC 91701 573-E6
PAWHUSKA RD
20200 APLV 92307 4297-E4
PAWNEE AV
- YUCA 92284 4887-F4
6900 YUCA 92284 4957-F2
PAWNEE RD
11800 APLV 92308 4387-J2
11800 APLV 92308 4477-J1
13700 APLV 92307 4387-J2
14100 APLV 92307 4297-J2
19500 APLV 92307 (4117-J6 See Page 4116)
19500 APLV 92307 4207-J1
PAWNEE ST
30800 SBdC - 4480-E4
PAWNEE TR
6100 SBdC - 4843-H2
PAWPAW AV
6600 HESP 92345 4566-G6
PAXTON
- SBdC 92277 (4825-E6 See Page 4824)
PAXTON CT
200 UPL 91784 572-C3
6500 YUCA 92284 4888-C7
PAXTON LN
58300 YUCA 92284 4888-C6
PAXTON OH N
58500 YUCA 92284 4888-C7
PAXTON RD
57300 YUCA 92284 4887-J7
57400 YUCA 92284 4888-A7
PAYER LN
22100 SBdC 92347 (3677-H2 See Page 3586)
PAYNE CT
9700 ADEL 92301 4204-E5
PAYNE RANCH RD
2900 CHLS 91709 681-B3
PEACE CT
11400 RivC 91752 683-G4
PEACH AV
7500 HESP 92345 4567-A1
8700 HESP 92345 4477-A4
10100 HESP 92345 4476-J2
11400 HESP 92345 4386-J7
S PEACH AV
1000 ONT 91761 642-E2
PEACH CT
10400 ADEL 92301 4204-G6
PEACH PL
6600 RCUC 91739 573-G5
PEACH ST
5500 SBdC 92377 575-E1
15000 CHLS 91709 681-C6
18500 SBdC 92316 645-E4
W PEACH ST
700 CLTN 92324 606-C3
PEACH BLOSSOM CT
7400 HIGH 92346 578-A5
PEACH TREE CIR
11700 YCPA 92399 649-H2
PEACHTREE DR
400 RivC 91752 683-F5
PEACH TREE LN
9600 RCUC 91737 572-J2
10500 RCUC 91737 573-B2
15900 FONT 92337 644-G2
27200 SBdC - (3935-J4 See Page 3934)
S PEACHTREE PL
2600 ONT 91761 643-A6
3500 ONT 91761 683-A1
PEACH TREE RD
11900 YCPA 92399 649-H2
PEACHTREE WY
800 POM 91767 601-B4
PEACHWOOD DR
3700 SBdC 91766 641-D3
S PEACHWOOD ST
800 CLTN 92324 606-H7
800 CLTN 92324 646-H1

PEACOCK AV
6300 SBdC 92346 577-H3
7500 HIGH 92346 577-H6
PEACOCK CT
23000 GTER 92313 646-G3
PEACOCK LN
11600 FONT 92337 644-F3
N PEAK CIR
21400 SBdC - 516-B1
S PEAK CIR
21400 SBdC - 516-C1
PEAK CT
24200 DBAR 91765 680-D2
PEAK LN
39100 BBLK - 4811-A2
PEAK WY
- FONT 92336 574-E4
PEAK SPUR RD
800 SBdC - 517-E3
PEAR AV
6500 RCUC 91739 573-J5
PEAR CT
13200 RCUC 91739 573-J4
PEAR ST
- FONT 92337 645-A2
15700 CHLS 91709 681-B7
S PEAR ST
200 SBDO 92410 606-E2
PEARL AV
37000 SBdC - 4482-B1
E PEARL AV
- RDL 92374 608-B6
W PEARL AV
- RDL 92374 608-B6
PEARL RD
25700 SBdC - (3935-J7 See Page 3934)
PEARL ST
5300 RCUC 91701 572-D2
6800 RivC 92509 645-A7
E PEARL ST
100 POM 91767 640-J1
200 POM 91767 641-A1
W PEARL ST
100 POM 91768 640-J1
400 UPL 91786 602-B3
PEARL ARBOR TR
16600 VCTV 92392 4296-E4
PEARL SPRINGS AV
3300 SBdC 92277 4821-C7
4300 SBdC 92277 4891-D3
4700 TNP 92277 4891-D3
PEARMAIN ST
14300 ADEL 92301 4385-B1
15300 ADEL 92301 4295-B1
17300 ADEL 92301 4205-B5
20900 SBdC 92301 (4115-B6 See Page 4114)
PEBBLE CT
27700 HIGH 92346 577-J6
PEBBLE ST
31000 SBdC 92359 608-J6
PEBBLE WY
25400 SBdC 92311 3678-H4
PEBBLE BEACH CT
16700 VCTV 92392 4386-D1
S PEBBLE BEACH CT
2700 ONT 91761 642-H6
PEBBLE BEACH DR
- UPL 91784 572-D6
16000 VCTV 92392 4386-D1
17700 SBdC 92392 4386-H4
PEBBLE BEACH LN
16000 CHLS 91709 711-D1
PEBBLEWOOD DR
1100 DBAR 91765 680-E3
PECAN AV
6700 RCUC 91739 573-H5
8500 RCUC 91739 603-J3
8800 HESP 92345 4476-J7
9100 HESP 92345 4477-A6
19500 SBdC 92377 575-G3
32100 YCPA 92399 649-C4
PECAN CT
3900 CHLS 91709 681-D6
8900 RCUC 91730 602-G1
PECAN ST
33400 YCPA 92399 649-F4
PECAN WY
11500 LMLN 92354 647-C3
PECAN GROVE DR
1300 DBAR 91765 680-A3
PECK RD
- SBdC 92285 4748-C3
PECONIC AV
6900 SBdC 92371 4563-D6
PECOS RD
11700 APLV 92308 4387-G7
PECOS ST
1200 RDL 92374 608-E5
PEDDER RD
40800 BBLK - 4811-F2
PEDLEY RD
- SBDO 92410 577-A7
3700 RivC 92509 644-E7
7800 SBdC 92410 577-A7
8000 SBdC 92410 607-A1
PEDLEY ST
1100 RDL 92374 608-E6

PEFFER LN
7900 SBdC - (4572-J2 See Page 4482)
9700 SBdC - 4482-J1
10500 SBdC - (4392-J7 See Page 4302)
PEFFER RD
- SBdC 92277 4751-G5
PEGASUS WY
200 BBLK - 4742-A7
PEGGY AV
7400 RivC 92509 644-H7
PEGGY LN
25400 SBdC - 517-C3
PELA RD
14900 SBdC 92307 4298-E6
PELHAM CT
- CHLS 91709 681-C6
PELICAN AV
4700 SBdC 92252 4889-G3
PELICAN DR
300 RivC 92507 646-E6
46200 SBdC - (4743-A4 See Page 4662)
S PELLISIER RD
- RivC 92501 646-A6
2100 CLTN 92501 646-A6
2800 CLTN 92324 646-A6
12800 RIV 92501 646-A6
PELLISSIER CT
- VCTV 92392 4296-C7
PEMBERTON ST
10700 ADEL 92301 4294-H7
PEMBERTON WY
10700 ADEL 92301 4294-J7
PEMBROKE CT
- RCUC 91739 573-F5
1900 CLAR 91711 571-E7
PEMBROKE ST
11400 LMLN 92354 647-E2
PEMBROOK AV
300 POM 91766 641-A5
PEMBROOK PL
- YCPA 92399 649-F2
PEMBROOK WY
- CHLS 91709 711-H1
PENA RD
11800 VCTV 92392 4385-C5
PENA WY
11300 RivC 91752 683-G3
PENACOOK TR
7600 SBdC 92252 4959-C3
PENDLETON AV
11300 YCPA 92399 650-C1
PENDLETON DR
9700 SBdC - 4479-J4
12800 SBdC - (4389-J3 See Page 4299)
PENDLETON RD
7800 SBdC - (4569-J2 See Page 4568)
10400 SBdC - 4479-J2
32800 SBdC - 3680-J7
33000 BARS 92311 (3681-A7 See Page 3590)
33000 SBdC - (3681-A7 See Page 3590)
33400 SBdC - (3761-D1 See Page 3760)
PENDLETON ST
14500 HESP 92345 4475-J3
14600 HESP 92345 4476-A3
PENGUIN LN
6200 SBdC 92397 4652-B1
PENINSULA AV
800 CLAR 91711 571-E4
PENINSULA DR
27100 SBdC - 4737-G7
N PENINSULA DR
27800 SBdC - 4737-J7
27800 SBdC - 4738-A7
S PENINSULA DR
27800 SBdC - 517-J1
27800 SBdC - 518-A1
27800 SBdC - 4738-A7
27800 SBdC - 4737-J7
PENINSULA LN
800 BBLK - 4811-A2
14600 SBdC - (3935-H3 See Page 3934)
PENMAR LN
600 POM 91766 641-A3
N PENN CT
1600 CLTN 92324 606-C3
N PENN LN
2100 CLTN 92324 606-D3
PENNSYLVANIA AV
- VCTV 92394 4205-G5
40900 BBLK - 4811-F2
E PENNSYLVANIA AV
- RDL 92374 608-C5
N PENNSYLVANIA AV
100 CLTN 92324 606-C3
300 SBDO 92410 606-C1
900 SBDO 92411 576-C4
2300 SBDO 92407 576-C2
S PENNSYLVANIA AV
100 SBDO 92410 606-C2
300 CLTN 92324 606-C2

W PENNSYLVANIA AV
- RDL 92374 608-A5
N PENNSYLVANIA CT
1500 SBDO 92411 576-C5
PENNSYLVANIA PL
3600 CLAR 91711 571-E5
PENNY CT
- RCUC 91739 573-F6
PENNY DR
13300 YCPA 92399 649-J6
PENNY LN
13100 YCPA 92399 650-A5
PENNYWOOD PL
2000 POM 91767 601-B6
PENRITH WY
14700 VCTV 92394 4295-J6
PENROSE CT
24400 DBAR 91765 680-E3
PENROSE LN
35500 YCPA 92399 650-B6
PENSWIFT CT
16400 CHLS 91709 711-E2
PEONY CIR
7500 FONT 92336 574-E7
PEONY ST
13100 ADEL 92301 (4115-F2 See Page 4114)
PEPIN RD
- SBdC 92365 (3684-G6 See Page 3594)
PEPPER AV
7400 FONT 92336 574-H7
8100 FONT 92335 604-H1
11600 HESP 92345 4387-A7
N PEPPER AV
100 SBDO 92376 606-A1
200 CLTN 92324 606-A5
200 RLTO 92376 606-A1
400 SBDO 92376 576-A7
600 RLTO 92376 576-A7
1200 RLTO 92376 575-J5
S PEPPER AV
100 CLTN 92316 606-A6
100 CLTN 92324 606-A2
100 SBDO 92376 606-A2
100 SBdC 92324 606-A7
200 SBdC 92316 606-A7
10500 SBdC 92324 646-A1
10900 CLTN 92324 646-A1
PEPPER CT
9400 FONT 92335 604-H4
N PEPPER CT
1500 SBDO 92346 577-G4
PEPPER DR
6500 SBdC 92346 577-G3
7700 FONT 92336 574-H7
N PEPPER DR
700 CLTN 92324 606-A5
PEPPER LN
11600 APLV 92308 4387-C7
19700 APLV 92308 4477-C1
PEPPER ST
- FONT 92337 644-J2
7300 RCUC 91730 572-H7
10200 RCUC 91730 573-A6
10700 ADEL 92301 4384-H1
11300 SBdC 92316 645-E3
15700 CHLS 91709 681-B7
N PEPPER ST
2800 SBDO 92346 577-G2
PEPPER WY
1700 RDL 92373 648-E4
10800 LMLN 92354 607-E7
PEPPERDINE CT
6300 CHNO 91710 682-A2
PEPPERDINE DR
1500 SBDO 92407 546-C6
PEPPERDINE LN
800 CLAR 91711 601-B1
PEPPERDINE ST
6300 CHNO 91710 682-A2
PEPPERIDGE CT
6800 RCUC 91701 572-H5
PEPPERIDGE LN
9200 RCUC 91701 572-H5
PEPPER-LINDEN DR
- SBDO 92407 546-A5
PEPPERMILL LN
- POM 91766 640-F6
PEPPERMINT WY
15500 CHLS 91709 681-B7
PEPPER TREE CT
- RCUC 91737 573-A2
29000 HIGH 92346 578-D6
PEPPER TREE DR
16200 VCTV 92394 4296-D4
PEPPERTREE LN
1000 UPL 91784 571-J4
PEPPER TREE LN
- RCUC 91737 573-A2
1400 SBDO 92404 576-J4
1700 CLTN 92324 646-G1
3800 SBDO 92404 546-J7
18600 SBdC 92392 4387-A4
23700 SBdC 92324 646-H3
E PEPPER TREE LN
3000 ONT 91761 603-A7
N PEPPER TREE LN
1200 SBDO 92404 576-J2

S PEPPER TREE LN
1800 SBDO 92408 607-C6
PEPPERTREE PT
- CHLS 91709 681-B3
PEPPERWOOD CIR
- POM 91766 640-G6
200 RivC 91752 683-E5
PEPPERWOOD LN
4200 CHLS 91709 681-E5
S PEPPERWOOD ST
700 CLTN 92324 606-H7
PEPPERWOOD CHASE
19400 APLV 92308 4477-D2
PERA CT
17100 FONT 92336 575-A6
PERA RD
21700 SBdC 92347 (3587-G4 See Page 3586)
PERAL AV
- CHNO 91710 682-B3
PERAL CT
- CHNO 91710 682-B3
PERAL RD
5900 SBdC 92371 4383-E5
14500 SBdC 92392 4385-J4
PERALTA RD
7800 RCUC 91730 602-J1
PERCH DR
- LPCo - 4606-H2
PERCH PL
5000 SBdC 92345 (4655-D3 See Page 4654)
PERDIDO BAY CT
- FONT 92336 574-G2
PERDIZ LN
6400 SBdC 92301 (4113-F1 See Page 4112)
PEREGRINE AV
42500 BBLK - 4812-A2
PERIDOT AV
5300 RCUC 91701 572-E2
PERIDOT CT
8100 RCUC 91701 572-E4
PERIMAN ST
4900 SBdC 92285 (4576-E6 See Page 4486)
PERIMETER RD
- ADEL 92394 4205-C3
- SBDO 92408 577-E7
200 SBDO 92408 607-C1
12100 ADEL 92301 4205-C2
12100 VCTV 92301 4205-C6
12900 VCTV 92394 4205-C1
PERIWINKLE DR
7400 FONT 92336 574-D7
W PERIWINKLE DR
2500 SBDO 92407 546-A3
PERKINS RD
2500 SBdC 92284 4818-E5
PERLITA PL
11800 FONT 92337 644-C4
PERLITE AV
7700 RCUC 91730 603-A1
PERLITE CT
7500 RCUC 91730 573-A7
7800 RCUC 91730 603-A1
PERRIN DR
- SBDO 92407 545-H1
PERRIN ST
1500 POM 91766 640-J3
PERRIS AL
2300 SBDO 92404 577-A3
PERRIS ST
- SBdC - 4747-C7
10100 SBdC 92345 4564-G3
12500 SBdC 92345 4565-D3
55200 SBdC 92284 4747-E7
N PERRIS ST
600 SBDO 92411 576-F5
PERRIS HILL RD
6900 SBdC 92404 577-B5
6900 SBDO 92404 577-B5
PERRIS HILL PARK RD
1600 SBDO 92404 577-A4
PERRY AV
19500 SBdC 92377 575-G3
PERRY CT
2300 CLAR 91711 571-C6
PERRY LN
10900 SBdC 92399 610-J6
10900 SBdC 92399 611-A6
PERRY RD
- SBdC 92314 4742-F6
PERRY WY
26100 HIGH 92346 577-E5
PERSEPHONE DR
1700 SBdC 92372 4562-E3
N PERSHING AV
200 SBDO 92407 546-H4
700 SBDO 92401 576-H6
1000 SBDO 92410 576-H6
1500 SBDO 92405 576-H2
3400 SBDO 92405 546-H7
S PERSHING AV
100 SBDO 92408 606-H2
PERSHING DR
10900 ADEL 92301 4294-J7
PERSHING ST
10700 ADEL 92301 4294-H7

PERSIA AV
6500 TNP 92277 4892-H6
7300 TNP 92277 4962-H1
PERSIMMON AV
9200 RCUC 91730 602-H1
18200 RLTO 92377 575-C2
34900 YCPA 92399 649-J2
34900 YCPA 92399 650-A2
W PERSIMMON AV
1300 RLTO 92377 575-C2
PERSIMMON ST
35500 YCPA 92399 650-B2
PERTH AV
34900 SBdC 92311 3679-B4
PERTH CT
26900 SBdC 92311 3679-B4
PERU ST
1800 NDLS 92363 3620-B7
PESCARA RD
11600 RCUC 91701 573-E5
PETALUMA CT
14200 VCTV 92392 4385-H5
PETALUMA DR
- RCUC 91730 602-G1
PETALUMA RD
- VCTV 92394 4295-H5
12100 VCTV 92392 4385-H1
13200 SBdC 92392 4385-H4
N PETER AV
900 SBdC 92314 4742-C5
PETERS ST
7800 FONT 92336 604-B1
PETERSEN ST
- CHLS 91709 711-F1
PETERSON CT
- CHLS 91709 711-G3
PETER WILKS CT
- RivC 92880 683-D4
PETITE ST
13600 VCTV 92392 4386-D3
PETRA RD
37100 SBdC 92347 (3587-G5 See Page 3586)
PETREL RD
46200 SBdC - (4743-A5 See Page 4662)
PETUNIA DR
61700 SBdC 92252 4889-B6
PEYTON DR
12800 CHLS 91709 641-A7
12800 SBdC 91710 641-A7
13100 CHLS 91709 681-A1
14200 CHLS 91709 711-C1
PEYTON PL
39400 SBdC - (4392-H6 See Page 4302)
PFEIFFER LN
200 CLAR 91711 571-D6
PHANTOM LN
11000 SBdC 92307 4479-E1
PHANTOM EAST ST
- VCTV 92394 4205-F4
PHANTOM WEST ST
- ADEL 92301 4205-E6
- ADEL 92394 4205-E6
- VCTV 92394 4205-E5
PHEASANT DR
5500 FONT 92336 574-C2
41400 BBLK - 4811-G1
PHEASANT RD
- POM 91766 640-G6
900 SBdC 92397 4652-B2
2100 SBdC 92372 4562-E5
PHEASANT RUN
100 SBdC - 518-C1
PHEASANT ST
15400 CHLS 91709 681-G6
PHEASANT HILL RD
10200 SBdC 92372 4472-A5
PHEASANT RUN DR
2400 CHLS 91709 680-J3
PHELAN AV
1100 RDL 92374 608-D5
PHELAN RD
1900 SBdC 92372 4472-E6
2000 SBdC 92371 4472-E6
3600 SBdC 92371 4473-A6
7400 SBdC 92371 4474-B6
9700 SBdC 92345 4474-J6
11000 SBdC 92345 4475-A6
11700 HESP 92345 4475-A6
PHELPS DR
- SBdC 92284 4747-D6
PHIDIAS LN
- CHLS 91709 711-G1
PHILADELPHIA ST
3500 POM 91766 641-C5
3500 SBdC 91710 641-C5
3500 CHNO 91710 641-C5
4300 ONT 91761 643-F4
4300 RivC 91752 643-F4
5600 ONT 91710 641-C5
9500 RivC 92509 644-A4
10000 FONT 92337 644-A4
11800 FONT 92337 643-J4
11800 ONT 92337 643-J4
E PHILADELPHIA ST
100 ONT 91761 642-E5
100 ONT 91762 642-E5
100 POM 91766 640-J5

STREET Block City ZIP Pg-Grid

E PHILADELPHIA ST
100 POM 91766 641-A5
2700 ONT 91761 643-A4
W PHILADELPHIA ST
100 ONT 91762 642-B5
1000 ONT 91762 641-J5
1400 CHNO 91710 641-J5
PHILLIPI LN
59000 SBdC 92285 4748-E2
60600 SBdC 92278 4748-E2
PHILLIPS BLVD
3700 SBdC 91710 641-D3
3900 SBdC 91766 641-D3
4500 MTCL 91710 641-D3
4600 MTCL 91763 641-D3
4600 SBdC 91763 641-D3
5200 CHNO 91710 641-D3
5300 SBdC 91762 641-D3
5300 CHNO 91762 641-D3
5600 ONT 91762 641-D3
E PHILLIPS BLVD
100 POM 91766 640-J3
100 POM 91766 641-A3
1400 SBdC 91710 641-A3
W PHILLIPS BLVD
100 POM 91766 640-G3
PHILLIPS CT
3700 SBdC 91766 641-C3
E PHILLIPS DR
37800 SBdC - 3592-A1
W PHILLIPS DR
1600 POM 91766 640-E3
37500 SBdC - 3592-A2
PHILLIPS ST
34400 SBdC 92311 3678-G6
E PHILLIPS ST
100 ONT 91761 642-C2
W PHILLIPS ST
100 ONT 91761 642-B2
100 ONT 91762 642-B2
1000 ONT 91762 641-J3
PHILLIPS WY
6100 RCUC 91737 573-A4
PHILLIP SMITH CT
1000 CLTN 92324 606-F5
PHILLIPS RANCH RD
- POM 91766 640-G7
PHILMAR RD
46900 SBdC 92365 3594-J2
46900 SBdC 92365 (3595-A1
See Page 3594)
PHIL OCHS AV
- RLTO 92377 575-C2
PHLOX AV
200 RDL 92373 648-D2
PHLOX CT
400 RDL 92373 648-D2
S PHOENIX AV
2200 ONT 91761 642-D5
PHOENIX DR
- MohC - 3620-F1
S PHOENIX PL
2100 ONT 91761 642-D4
PHOENIX RD
15500 SBdC 92347 3586-A1
PHOENIX ST
55000 SBdC - 4606-F1
PICADILLY RD
- SBdC 92277 4824-E5
PICASSO DR
5000 CHLS 91709 711-G1
PICASSO LN
- SBdC 92335 604-B2
PICCADILLY CT
- RCUC 91739 573-F5
PICCOLO DR
- SBdC - 3936-F4
PICKETWIRE RD
- SBdC 92308 4477-G7
PICO AV
8500 HESP 92345 4566-H1
19500 SBdC 92301 (4202-E3
See Page 4112)
N PICO AV
100 SBDO 92410 606-E1
500 SBDO 92411 576-E4
2900 SBDO 92405 576-E2
S PICO AV
100 SBDO 92410 606-E2
PICO CT
12200 VCTV 92392 4385-H6
13400 FONT 92336 574-A7
PICO ST
100 POM 91766 641-B2
21700 GTER 92313 646-D5
PICTON ST
26100 LMLN 92354 647-F2
PIDGEON RD
- CHLS 91709 680-H2
PIEDMONT AV
100 CLAR 91711 601-B4
2200 SBDO 92346 577-J3
N PIEDMONT CT
2600 SBDO 92346 577-H2
PIEDMONT DR
- SBDO 92346 577-F1
1200 SBdC 91784 571-J2
14100 VCTV 92392 4385-H5
19500 SBdC 92308 4567-D5
58500 YUCA 92284 4958-D7

E PIEDMONT DR
2400 SBDO 92346 577-G2
2400 SBdC 92346 577-E1
PIEDMONT LN
1400 RDL 92373 648-A4
PIEDMONT ST
10900 RCUC 91701 573-C5
PIEDMONT MESA DR
4200 CLAR 91711 571-A7
PIEDRA AV
9000 HESP 92345 4477-B7
PIEDRA DR
57300 YUCA 92284 4888-B5
PIEDRAS TR
- SBdC 92256 4956-D7
8900 SBdC 92256 616-D1
PIEDRAS CIRCLE LN
57300 YUCA 92284 4887-J5
PIEDRAS GRANDE
32900 SBdC - 519-D2
PIER DR
18000 SBdC 92392 4386-J3
PIERCE AV
100 BARS 92311 3679-G2
PIERCE CT
6600 CHNO 91710 642-B6
PIERCE LN
13300 SBdC 92371 4383-C4
PIERCE ST
6100 CHNO 91710 641-J6
PIERSON CT
14000 RCUC 91739 574-B2
PIGEON CT
18800 SBdC 92316 645-E1
PIGEON RD
1200 BBLK - 4812-B3
PIGEONHAWK LN
29100 SBdC - 518-C2
PIGEON PASS RD
100 RivC 92507 646-F7
500 RivC 92324 646-F7
PIKES CT
24400 DBAR 91765 640-E6
PIKES LN
- SBdC - 2971-E5
PIKES PEAK CT
11400 RCUC 91737 573-D4
PIKES PEAK WY
- FONT 92336 574-D3
PILGRIM CT
4600 CHNO 91710 641-F5
PILGRIM RD
1500 RDL 92373 647-H5
1500 SBdC 92373 647-F5
PILGRIMS CT
6700 RCUC 91701 572-H5
PILGRIMS WY
3700 SBdC 91710 641-D7
PILOT PLANT RD
1700 SBdC - 328-G6
PILOT ROCK CT
- VCTV 92394 4295-F6
PILOT ROCK RD
- SBdC - 4736-D4
- SBdC - 4737-F4
PIMA AV
39400 SBdC 92365 (3504-G5
See Page 3414)
PIMA CT
- SBdC - 4843-H4
12200 APLV 92308 4387-F6
PIMA RD
- APLV 92308 4387-E6
PIMA TR
56300 YUCA 92284 4957-G3
PIMLICO RD
18800 APLV 92308 4387-B6
PIMLICO ST
57700 SBdC 92284 4818-A7
PINA RD
34300 SBdC - (4391-D5
See Page 4300)
PINAFORE PL
2000 POM 91766 641-A5
PINCEL RD
14300 VCTV 92392 4385-H1
PINE AV
- RivC 92880 712-E1
600 RDL 92373 608-A7
600 RDL 92373 648-A1
900 BARS 92311 3679-H5
1100 RDL 92373 647-J1
5800 CHLS 91709 711-H2
5800 SBdC - 4950-G1
5800 SBDO 92407 546-A3
6100 CHLS 91709 712-B2
6100 CHNO 91710 712-B2
6500 TNP 92277 4892-D6
6700 CHLS 91709 712-E1
10100 SBdC 92256 615-F3
14700 SBdC 92335 604-D4
16100 FONT 92335 604-G4
17000 FONT 92335 605-A4
17700 SBdC 92335 605-B4
18100 RLTO 92335 605-B4
26300 SBdC - 517-E4
N PINE AV
100 RLTO 92376 605-J2
600 RLTO 92376 575-J5
6000 SBDO 92407 546-B2

S PINE AV
300 RLTO 92376 605-J3
1100 ONT 91762 642-A3
PINE CT
900 SBdC - 517-H4
9100 SBdC 92335 604-D4
S PINE CT
2100 ONT 91762 642-A5
PINE DR
100 SBdC - 518-D1
100 SBdC - 4738-D7
400 SBdC - 517-B2
1300 SBdC - 4737-H5
2300 SBdC - 519-E7
8600 RCUC 91730 603-A3
22100 SBdC - 516-D3
40900 SBdC 92339 611-F2
PINE LN
100 SBdC - 4742-G7
200 SBdC - 4812-G2
200 SBdC 92314 4742-G6
500 SBdC - 519-E2
800 SBdC 92314 (4743-A7
See Page 4662)
800 SBdC 92314 4813-A1
9100 SBdC 92339 611-C2
15200 CHLS 91709 681-D6
16500 FONT 92337 644-H1
22900 SBdC - 516-F2
26700 SBdC - 517-F3
S PINE LN
300 SBdC 92314 4742-G7
S PINE PL
1700 ONT 91762 642-A4
PINE RDG
200 SBdC - 516-H1
PINE ST
500 UPL 91786 602-C1
5700 SBdC 92397 4652-C2
7900 SBdC 92410 577-A7
8000 SBdC 92410 607-A1
11400 SBdC 92399 651-B1
11900 SBdC 92316 645-E4
12000 RivC 92509 645-E4
12100 SBdC 92345 4475-C5
13800 SBdC 93562 2055-B6
13900 HESP 92345 4475-H5
15900 HESP 92345 4476-D5
57300 SBdC 92285 4747-H2
S PINE ST
500 CLTN 92324 606-D7
700 CLTN 92324 646-D1
W PINE ST
800 UPL 91786 602-A1
1000 UPL 91786 601-J1
PINE TER
100 SBdC - 518-C1
PINE TR
700 SBdC - 517-C3
PINE WY
12100 APLV 92308 4387-C7
12100 APLV 92308 4477-C1
PINE BENCH RD
39700 SBdC 92399 651-D1
PINE BLUFF LN
- FONT 92336 574-E3
N PINEBROOK AV
1000 UPL 91786 572-A7
1400 UPL 91786 602-A1
PINE CONE CUR
- SBdC - 548-H1
PINE CONE DR
32000 SBdC - 519-B6
S PINECONE WY
2500 ONT 91761 643-B5
PINECREST DR
100 BBLK - 4741-H7
100 BBLK - 4811-H1
PINECREST PL
8700 RCUC 91730 602-J3
PINECREST RD
- SBdC - 517-D4
PINEDALE AV
15500 SBdC 92335 604-F4
17100 FONT 92335 605-A4
W PINEDALE AV
1000 RLTO 92376 605-E4
1300 RLTO 92316 605-D4
PINEDALE CT
17000 FONT 92335 604-J4
17000 FONT 92335 605-A4
PINE HILL RD
38800 SBdC - 4741-A6
PINEHURST AV
19300 APLV 92308 4477-C1
S PINEHURST AV
2200 ONT 91761 642-F5
PINEHURST CIR
200 RivC 91752 683-E5
N PINEHURST CT
100 SBDO 92407 546-H5
S PINEHURST CT
2900 ONT 91761 642-F7
PINEHURST DR
- CHLS 91709 711-E1
1600 UPL 91784 572-E6
7900 HIGH 92346 577-G7
26500 SBdC - 4737-F7
31200 SBdC - 518-J6

PINEHURST LN
- FONT 92336 574-H2
PINEHURST PL
2000 POM 91766 641-A5
S PINEHURST PL
1500 ONT 91761 642-F5
PINEHURST TR
12600 SBdC 92392 4387-A5
PINE KNOLL CREST
1400 RDL 92373 648-B4
PINE KNOT BLVD
400 BBLK - 4811-F2
PINE KNOT RD
39700 SBdC - 4811-C2
PINEKNOT CAMPGROUND RD S
42000 SBdC - 4811-H2
PINE MESA CT
13600 YCPA 92399 650-F6
PINE MOUNTAIN CT
- RCUC 91737 573-F4
- RCUC 91739 573-F4
N PINE MOUNTAIN DR
1000 SBdC 92314 4742-B5
PINENUT PTH
- RivC 92880 683-B7
PINE OAK LN
37700 SBdC - 4810-G1
PINE RIDGE AV
20700 APLV 92307 4297-F6
21200 APLV 92307 4387-H1
PINERIDGE CT
13500 YCPA 92399 650-G6
PINERIDGE DR
29300 SBdC - 518-D1
29300 SBdC - 4738-D7
PINE RIDGE LN
1100 SBdC 92314 4812-H2
PINERIDGE CT
800 UPL 91784 572-A4
PINE SPRING AV
6500 TNP 92277 4891-B7
PINE SPRINGS AV
- SBdC 92277 4891-B3
- TNP 92277 4891-B3
PINE SUMMIT DR
15600 CHLS 91709 681-B7
PINE TREE LN
13800 SBdC 92371 4382-C3
PINE TREE RD
7500 SBdC - 4562-D4
7500 SBdC 92372 4562-D2
9900 SBdC 92372 4472-D1
12100 SBdC 92372 4382-D7
PINE VALLEY AV
- ONT 91761 642-J5
S PINE VALLEY AV
2700 ONT 91761 642-J6
PINE VALLEY DR
- FONT 92336 574-J2
PINEVIEW AV
1700 UPL 91784 572-D6
PINE VIEW DR
400 SBdC 92314 4742-B6
13700 RivC 92399 650-G7
13700 YCPA 92399 650-G7
N PINE VIEW DR
100 SBdC 92314 4742-B6
S PINE VIEW DR
100 SBdC 92314 4742-B6
PINEVIEW RD
9800 SBdC 92372 4472-A6
PINEWOOD CT
- CALI 92320 650-A7
100 RDL 92374 648-E1
W PINEWOOD CT
500 SBdC 92314 4742-B7
PINEWOOD DR
- RCUC 91730 602-J5
200 BBLK - 4811-C1
1200 SBdC 92314 4813-C3
14200 HESP 92345 4475-H7
27300 SBdC - 517-H1
S PINEWOOD DR
500 SBdC 92314 4742-B7
PINEWOOD LN
12900 YCPA 92399 650-D5
W PINEWOOD LN
1200 ONT 91762 641-J5
PINEY LN
300 BBLK - 4811-C1
29300 SBdC - 518-D1
PINEY RIDGE PL
1200 SBdC - 4741-B5
PINION DR
900 BARS 92311 3679-J5
PINNACLE AV
- UPL 91784 572-E6
PINNACLE CT
13100 CHLS 91709 681-A1
PINNACLE DR
600 SBdC - 518-A3
PINNACLE RD
- CHLS 91709 680-J7
8700 SBdC - 328-J7
11000 SBdC 93562 328-L5
16000 CHLS 91709 710-J1
PINNACLE ST
18900 HESP 92345 4567-B1

PINNACLE WY
- UPL 91784 572-E5
PINNACLE PEAK CT
11500 RCUC 91737 573-E4
PINO PL
28300 HIGH 92346 578-B4
PIN OAK DR
- SBdC - 4738-E7
PINOLE RD
10700 APLV 92308 4477-J2
PINON AV
1100 SBdC 92314 4812-H2
9000 HESP 92345 4476-B1
9800 SBdC 92256 615-G4
11800 HESP 92345 4386-B7
PINON CT
6500 CHNO 91710 682-A2
11900 YCPA 92399 649-B3
54500 YUCA 92284 4957-B3
N PINON CT
2800 SBDO 92346 577-F2
PINON DR
7500 YUCA 92284 4957-A3
74000 TNP 92277 4892-F6
N PINON DR
100 SBdC 92314 4742-C6
S PINON DR
100 SBdC 92314 4742-C6
PINON LN
800 SBdC 92314 4742-J7
800 SBdC 92314 4812-J1
PINON PL
100 BBLK - 4742-A7
PINON RD
100 SBdC 92372 4472-A6
9500 SBdC 92308 4479-C5
PINON ST
13000 RCUC 91739 573-H5
PINON HILLS RD
9300 SBdC 92372 4472-A2
9300 SBdC 92372 4562-B1
12100 SBdC 92372 4382-A7
PINON PINES LN
3300 SBdC 92371 4562-J4
PINON PINES RD
3300 SBdC 92371 4562-J3
PINON VIEJO RD
- SBdC 92372 4562-C2
PINOT CIR
2100 UPL 91784 571-J4
PINOT PL
- RCUC 91739 573-J7
PINTADO DR
100 DBAR 91765 640-B7
S PINTADO DR
100 DBAR 91765 640-B7
PINTAIL CIR
1000 SBdC - 4738-A6
PINTAIL CT
13100 CHNO 91710 642-B7
N PINTAIL DR
300 SBdC 92314 4742-E5
PINTO CT
56900 YUCA 92284 4887-H6
N PINTO CT
200 BBLK - 4741-H7
W PINTO CT
900 UPL 91786 572-A7
S PINTO PL
3600 ONT 91761 683-A1
PINTO RD
27300 SBdC - 3936-J3
PINTO WY
15600 CHLS 91709 681-G7
19200 APLV 92308 4387-C5
PINTO MESA DR
500 DBAR 91765 640-D7
PINTO MOUNTAIN RD
3300 SBdC 92277 4823-F7
4500 SBdC 92277 4893-F1
PINTO MOUNTAIN WY
13300 VCTV 92394 4295-F4
PINYON AV
7500 FONT 92336 574-G7
7800 FONT 92336 604-G1
8200 FONT 92335 604-G2
PINYON CT
- FONT 92337 644-H2
900 ONT 91762 602-A7
7700 FONT 92336 574-G7
9200 FONT 92335 604-H4
PINYON PL
- SBdC - 516-C2
PINYON PINE CT
12600 VCTV 92392 4385-F5
PINZANO PL
7000 RCUC 91701 573-E6
PIONEER AV
16600 CHNO 91710 712-B3
26500 SBdC 92374 607-G4
E PIONEER AV
- RDL 92374 608-D4
W PIONEER AV
- RDL 92374 608-A4
800 RDL 92374 607-J4
27500 SBdC 92374 607-J4
PIONEER DR
49100 SBdC 92256 615-G5
50000 SBdC 92256 616-A5

E PIONEER LN
100 SBdC 92314 4742-E4
W PIONEER LN
100 SBdC 92314 4742-C4
PIONEER MTWY
- DBAR 91765 680-B6
- LACo 92823 680-B6
PIONEER PL
100 POM 91768 640-D2
7200 RCUC 91739 573-H6
PIONEER RD
- DBAR 91765 680-B5
200 SBdC - 517-G1
300 SBdC - 4737-G7
9000 SBdC 92308 (4389-D7
See Page 4299)
9000 SBdC 92308 4479-D2
9700 SBdC 92308 4478-A5
10100 APLV 92308 4478-A4
11400 SBdC 92307 (4389-D7
See Page 4299)
13700 APLV 92307 4388-A1
14100 APLV 92307 4298-A5
16600 SBdC 92307 4299-D1
16600 SBdC 92307 (4209-D7
See Page 4118)
21800 SBdC 92347 (3677-G1
See Page 3586)
44100 SBdC 92365 (3763-J3
See Page 3762)
44100 SBdC 92365 3764-A4
80500 SBdC 92277 4824-D3
PIONEER ST
- BARS 92311 (3759-B5
See Page 3758)
300 BARS 92311 3679-H3
5100 CHNO 91710 641-G7
PIONEER TR
- SBdC 92277 4751-D7
67700 SBdC 92277 4820-H1
68300 SBdC 92277 4821-A1
PIONEER CAMP RD
23800 SBdC - 516-H3
PIONEERTOWN RD
1000 SBdC - (4743-A5
See Page 4662)
3700 SBdC - 4886-E3
5400 SBdC - 4887-B6
5400 SBdC 92284 4887-B6
6700 YUCA 92284 4887-B6
6700 YUCA 92284 4957-E1
PIONERO RD
8900 SBdC 92371 4562-G1
9700 SBdC 92371 4472-G1
12000 SBdC 92371 4382-G3
15600 SBdC 92371 4292-G5
PIPELINE AV
10900 SBdC 91766 641-D5
11100 MTCL 91763 641-D5
11400 SBdC 91710 641-D5
12100 CHNO 91710 641-D5
13000 CHNO 91710 681-D4
13000 SBdC 91710 681-D4
14500 CHLS 91709 681-E7
15800 CHLS 91709 711-D1
PIPELINE RD
- BARS 92311 3679-H6
- BARS 92311 3680-A6
- SBdC - 3680-G7
- SBdC - (4115-J4
See Page 4114)
- SBdC 92252 4890-A5
- SBdC 92311 3680-A6
2800 SBdC 92371 4562-J5
8300 SBdC 92371 4563-A3
63700 SBdC 92252 4889-F5
82000 SBdC 93562 2145-D4
PIPE LINE RD
- SBdC 92277 370-K11
78500 SBdC 92277 4823-H4
78900 SBdC 92277 4824-A4
82500 SBdC 92277 (4825-F3
See Page 4824)
PIPER LN
6500 FONT 92336 574-F4
PIPER RD
2900 SBdC 92284 4818-F6
PIPES RD
- SBdC - 369-J11
- SBdC - 389-K1
51300 SBdC - 4886-C2
PIPES CANYON RD
51700 SBdC - 4886-D1
51900 SBdC - 4816-H6
53700 SBdC - 4817-B7
55700 SBdC 92284 4817-B7
PIPPIN RD
9500 SBdC 92371 4473-H7
PIRATEER LN
26900 SBdC - (3935-G4
See Page 3934)
PIRINDA CT
15300 APLV 92307 4297-B5
PIRINDA RD
15100 APLV 92307 4297-B5
PIRU DR
5600 RivC 91752 683-G4
PIRU RD
16100 APLV 92307 4297-E3

PISA PL
6800 RCUC 91701 573-E5
PISGAH ST
47700 SBdC 92365 3764-J6
47700 SBdC 92365 (3765-A6
See Page 3764)
PISGAH CRATER RD
27700 SBdC - 350-A11
PISGAH PEAK RD
11600 SBdC 92399 650-J2
12400 YCPA 92399 650-F6
28800 SBdC 92399 651-A1
PISGAH PEAK-OAK GLEN RD
38000 SBdC 92399 650-J2
38200 SBdC 92399 651-A3
PISMO AV
7400 HESP 92345 4567-A3
8100 HESP 92345 4566-J2
PISTACHE ST
12500 RCUC 91739 573-G5
PISTACHIO ST
15600 CHLS 91709 681-A7
PITACHE ST
17800 HESP 92345 4386-H7
PITANGA RD
- SBdC - (4392-F7
See Page 4302)
- SBdC - 4482-F1
PITCHER CT
9900 ADEL 92301 4204-F4
PITTSBURG AV
9000 RCUC 91730 603-D5
PITZER BUTTES RD
7000 SBdC - 4570-F3
7700 SBdC - 4480-G7
PIUTE RD
- SBdC 92365 (3593-J7
See Page 3592)
15500 APLV 92307 4297-C5
19000 SBdC - 371-G2
33700 SBdC 92365 (3683-J1
See Page 3592)
PIUTE ST
1100 BARS 92311 3679-J4
1100 BARS 92311 3680-A4
35400 SBdC - 4481-G5
PIUTE TR
56500 YUCA 92284 4957-G4
58100 YUCA 92284 4958-B3
61400 SBdC 92252 4959-A3
PIXIE DR
30000 SBdC - 518-F7
30000 SBdC - 548-F1
PIZZOLI PL
6900 RCUC 91701 573-E5
PKWY I
- LPCo - 4774-J5
PKWY II
- LPCo - 4774-J5
PLACENTIA CT
3500 CHNO 91710 641-C6
PLACENTIA LN
3600 RIV 92501 646-A6
3700 RivC 92501 645-J6
3700 RIV 92501 645-J6
PLACENTIA RD
3700 SBdC 91710 641-C6
N PLACER AV
900 ONT 91764 602-G4
E PLACER CT
1800 ONT 91764 602-G4
PLACER DR
15100 VCTV 92394 4296-A7
PLACER LN
26500 SBdC - 4737-F7
N PLACER PL
1400 ONT 91764 602-G5
PLACER ST
1200 RDL 92374 608-F5
7800 FONT 92336 574-C7
7800 FONT 92336 604-C1
9100 RCUC 91730 602-H2
9900 RCUC 91730 603-A2
PLACID CT
11500 SBdC 92324 646-J2
PLACID LN
23800 SBdC 92324 646-J2
23800 CLTN 92324 646-J2
PLACIDA CT
8200 RCUC 91730 602-E2
PLACIDA RD
15600 VCTV 92394 4296-A4
PLAID CT
3300 CHLS 91709 681-C7
PLAIMOR AV
34900 SBdC 92311 3679-B4
34900 BARS 92311 3679-B4
PLAINA RD
20300 APLV 92307 4297-E2
23800 SBdC 92307 4298-E2
PLAINFIELD AV
10500 ADEL 92301 4294-H7
S PLAINFIELD DR
2600 ONT 91761 643-A5
S PLAINFIELD PL
3200 ONT 91761 643-A7
PLAINFIELD ST
10600 ADEL 92301 4294-H7

PLANET RD
36900 SBdC - (4392-B4
See Page 4302)
PLANETARY WY
30500 SBdC - 4480-D4
PLANE TREE RD
11500 FONT 92337 644-G3
PLANGER LN
- FONT 92336 574-E4
PLANT ST
- TNP 92278 4822-E1
PLANT ACCESS RD
12400 SBdC 93562 2144-H4
PLANTATION DR
- MohC - 3620-C2
PLANTATION DR Rt#-2
1500 MohC - 3620-E4
PLANTATION WY
- MohC - 3620-D4
PLASSE DR
7000 YUCA 92284 4957-H2
PLATA DR
5600 YUCA 92284 4888-B5
PLATEAU DR
- RCUC 91739 573-J6
N PLATINA DR
200 DBAR 91765 640-C6
S PLATINA DR
200 DBAR 91765 640-C6
S PLATINUM CT
1300 ONT 91762 642-A3
PLATO ST
900 SBdC 92301 (4202-A2
See Page 4112)
4900 SBdC 92301 (4203-B2
See Page 4112)
PLAYA VISTA DR
73700 TNP 92277 4892-F3
PLAYGROUND DR
800 SBdC - 516-D4
800 SBdC 92407 516-D4
PLAZA DR
15900 VCTV 92392 4296-C7
PLAZA LN
5200 MTCL 91763 601-G4
S PLAZA LN
4900 MTCL 91763 601-F5
PLAZA RD
61800 SBdC 92252 4889-C6
PLAZA DEL AMIGO
56600 YUCA 92284 4887-H6
E PLAZA SERENA
100 ONT 91764 602-D6
W PLAZA SERENA DR
2500 RLTO 92377 545-A7
2800 RLTO 92377 544-J7
PLEASANT AV
2600 ONT 91761 642-C6
N PLEASANT AV
100 ONT 91761 642-C1
100 ONT 91764 602-C5
100 ONT 91764 642-C1
S PLEASANT AV
100 ONT 91761 642-C1
W PLEASANT CT
2700 SBDO 92376 606-A3
PLEASANT DR
31400 SBdC - 518-J7
31500 SBdC - 519-A6
S PLEASANT PL
2100 ONT 91761 642-C4
PLEASANT PT
- SBdC - 548-G1
PLEASANT WY
- BARS 92311 3678-H6
- SBdC 92311 3678-H6
W PLEASANT WY
2500 SBDO 92410 606-A3
PLEASANT GLENN AV
8500 HESP 92345 4565-J2
PLEASANT GROVE ST
34700 YCPA 92399 649-J6
PLEASANT HILL DR
1500 CHLS 91709 680-G3
27100 SBdC 92346 577-H3
PLEASANT HILLS DR
10900 APLV 92308 4477-D1
PLEASANT MEADOW RD
23400 DBAR 91765 680-B5
E PLEASANT VALLEY CT
3000 CLTN 92324 646-J2
PLEASANT VIEW AV
- SBdC 92365 3764-G1
W PLEASANT VIEW AV
100 CLTN 92324 606-D3
PLEASANT VIEW DR
- BARS 92311 3589-H7
1400 RDL 92374 648-F1
9700 RCUC 91701 572-J5
PLEASANT VIEW LN
7100 HIGH 92346 578-D5
PLEASANT VIEW RD
55400 SBdC 92285 4667-D5
PLEWS CT
200 RivC 92507 646-D6
PLIMALO AV
10800 SBdC 92308 4478-D3
N PLUM AV
100 ONT 91761 642-C1

N PLUM AV
100 ONT 91764 602-C7
100 ONT 91764 642-C1
S PLUM AV
100 ONT 91761 642-C1
PLUM DR
200 ONT 91761 642-C7
PLUM LN
- ONT 91761 642-C6
1600 RDL 92374 607-H5
S PLUM LN
2400 ONT 91761 642-C5
S PLUM PL
2600 ONT 91761 642-C6
PLUM ST
3000 CHLS 91709 681-B7
PLUM WY
6600 RCUC 91739 573-G5
PLUMA ST
- UPL 91784 572-E5
PLUMARIA DR
7400 FONT 92336 574-D7
PLUMAS CT
800 SBdC - 4812-B1
14100 FONT 92336 574-B7
PLUMAS RD
10800 RCUC 91701 573-C5
PLUMAS ST
18400 HESP 92345 4567-A3
PLUMERIA AV
1200 UPL 91784 571-J4
PLUM HOLLOW LN
14000 CHLS 91709 680-H3
PLUMMERS LN
1300 RDL 92359 609-F4
1300 SBdC 92359 609-F4
PLUMROSE PL
- CHLS 91709 681-A2
PLUMROSE ST
- FONT 92336 574-E6
N PLUM TREE AV
3400 RLTO 92377 545-A7
PLUM TREE LN
33800 YCPA 92399 649-G4
PLUM VIEW LN
- YCPA 92399 610-B7
PLUMWOOD LN
1300 SBdC 92359 609-A5
S PLUMWOOD ST
700 CLTN 92324 606-H7
PLUNGE RD
200 SBdC - 516-C2
PLUNGE CREEK RD
30200 HIGH 92346 578-G6
PLUNGE CREEK TKTR
4700 SBdC - 548-F6
4900 SBdC - 578-D4
6400 HIGH 92346 578-D4
PLUTO CT
7300 HIGH 92346 577-J5
PLUTO DR
12100 VCTV 92392 4385-G7
27700 HIGH 92346 577-J5
PLUTO PL
11000 RivC 91752 683-H5
PLUTO ST
27700 HIGH 92346 577-J5
64900 SBdC 92252 4749-J5
64900 SBdC 92252 4750-A5
66500 SBdC 92277 4750-E5
PLYMOUTH RD
4500 SBdC - 348-H7
43000 BBLK - 4812-B2
43300 SBdC 92365 (3684-D4
See Page 3594)
W PLYMOUTH RD
600 CLAR 91711 601-C3
PLYMOUTH ST
5700 CHNO 91710 641-H5
PLYMOUTH WY
100 SBDO 92408 646-J1
7400 RCUC 91730 573-B7
POCAHANTAS RD
15000 APLV 92307 4297-C5
POCOMOKE CT
21200 APLV 92308 4387-H5
POCOMOKE RD
12300 APLV 92308 4387-H4
POCONO PL
12400 APLV 92308 4387-F5
POCONO RD
12200 APLV 92308 4387-F3
POE CT
- SBdC - 518-A3
W POEMA DR
1100 CLTN 92324 606-A4
POHEZ RD
15300 APLV 92307 4297-A5
POHONO RD
- SBdC 92307 4207-C2
20900 APLV 92307 (4117-G7
See Page 4116)
22200 APLV 92307 4118-A7
POINCIANA RD
18100 ADEL 92301 4204-J6
POINSETTIA CIR
14900 FONT 92336 574-D7
POINSETTIA CT
6700 CHNO 91710 642-B5

POINT RD
900 SBdC - 4737-H6
39400 SBdC - 4741-B7
39400 BBLK - 4811-B1
POINT DELGADA CT
- FONT 92336 574-B6
S POINTE AV
1700 ONT 91761 643-A4
POINTE CT
- FONT 92336 574-E4
POINTE COUPEE
2400 CHLS 91709 681-A5
POINT HAMILTAIR LN
28000 SBdC - 518-A1
28000 SBdC - 4738-A7
POINT JUDITH ST
14200 FONT 92336 604-B1
POINT LOMA ST
14200 FONT 92336 604-B1
POINT REYES ST
14200 FONT 92336 604-B1
POINT VISTA LN
2400 CHLS 91709 680-J2
POL ACCESS RD
13100 VCTV 92394 4205-E6
POLANDS WY
100 SBdC 92284 4748-B4
700 SBdC 92285 4748-B4
POLAR DR
27700 SBdC - 4737-J5
POLARIS AV
500 SBdC 92252 4749-C7
1900 SBdC 92252 4819-C4
3900 SBdC 92252 4889-C1
POLARIS CT
5700 RivC 91752 683-H4
POLARIS WY
8800 SBdC 92256 616-C2
8800 SBdC 92256 4956-C7
POLE LN
- FONT 92337 644-J2
- SBdC 92337 644-J2
POLE RD
62500 SBdC 92252 4819-D1
POLE LINE RD
- SBdC 92277 370-K11
- SBdC 92277 4823-E2
- SBdC 92278 4822-A1
- TNP 92277 4891-E5
67300 SBdC 92277 4820-G1
68400 SBdC 92277 4821-A1
71300 SBdC 92277 4822-A1
80500 SBdC 92277 4824-C2
82000 SBdC 92277 (4825-A1
See Page 4824)
POLIQUE CANYON RD
40100 SBdC - (4740-J2
See Page 4660)
40100 SBdC - 4741-A3
POLK CT
4000 CHNO 91710 641-D6
POLK ST
4400 CHNO 91710 641-E6
POLLARD DR
13800 SBdC - 514-A1
POLLUX WY
11000 RivC 91752 683-H4
POLLY CT
14100 SBdC - (3935-G6
See Page 3934)
POLO CT
14500 VCTV 92394 4295-H7
POLO PL
6100 RCUC 91739 573-G3
POLO RD
2800 CHLS 91709 681-B5
14500 VCTV 92394 4295-H7
POLO ST
29300 HIGH 92346 578-D7
POLY VISTA
3400 POM 91768 640-B3
E POMEGRANATE AV
100 RLTO 92377 575-G3
POMEGRANATE CT
- CHLS 91709 711-H2
POMEGRANATE ST
6300 RivC 92880 683-D6
E POMELLO DR
100 CLAR 91711 571-D5
POMELO RD
- SBdC 92365 (3683-F5
See Page 3592)
POMMEL RD
9400 SBdC - 4479-J4
POMO CT
- RivC 92399 650-G7
6600 SBdC - 4843-G3
W POMONA AV
500 RLTO 92316 605-F6
W POMONA BLVD
2200 POM 91768 640-D2
3500 POM 91789 640-B3
POMONA CT
900 CLAR 91711 601-B2
POMONA FRWY Rt#-57
- DBAR - 680-B1
POMONA FRWY Rt#-60
- CHLS - 640-D6
- CHNO - 641-D6
- CHNO - 642-H5

STREET
Block City ZIP Pg-Grid

RACOON AV
19600 ADEL 92301 4204-F1
20100 ADEL 92301 4114-F7
RACQUET CLUB RD
700 DBAR 91765 680-A1
RADBURY PL
600 DBAR 91765 640-D7
600 DBAR 91765 680-D1
E RADCLIFFE DR
100 CLAR 91711 571-D7
W RADCLIFFE DR
100 CLAR 91711 571-D7
RADFORD AV
1800 CLAR 91711 571-B7
15000 ADEL 92301 4294-H1
17300 ADEL 92301 4204-H7
RADFORD CT
100 RivC 92507 646-E6
RADFORD TKTR
1300 BBLK - 4812-A5
1300 SBdC - 4812-A5
1600 SBdC - 4811-J5
RADFORD CAMP RD
- SBdC - 4811-G7
RADIO RD
28900 SBdC 92311 3679-G1
28900 BARS 92311 3679-G1
RADIO TOWER ACCESS RD
25800 SBdC - 329-C8
RADOME RD
42100 SBdC 92365 (3683-D5 See Page 3592)
RAE CT
800 UPL 91784 572-A4
1100 UPL 91784 571-J4
RAEMEE AV
1400 RDL 92374 608-E5
RAFFERTY CT
1000 SBdC 92314 4813-A1
RAFFIA LN
9000 SBdC 92335 604-D4
RAFT CIR
- RivC 92880 683-D4
RAGER ST
7300 FONT 92336 574-G6
RAGUSA DR
11500 RCUC 91701 573-D6
RAHUN CT
- SBdC - 4844-C2
RAIL WY
4600 SBdC 92371 4383-B7
5300 SBdC 92371 4473-D1
RAILROAD CT
7300 HIGH 92346 578-B5
RAILROAD ST
82000 SBdC 93562 2144-G7
RAILROAD ACCESS RD
- SBdC - 351-L7
10300 SBdC 92316 605-E7
21600 GTER 92313 646-C3
S RAILROAD ACCESS RD
1900 RLTO 92316 605-G7
W RAILROAD ACCESS RD
300 RLTO 92316 605-G7
RAINBOW AV
- SBdC 92284 4748-A5
E RAINBOW BLVD
100 SBdC 92314 4742-D6
W RAINBOW BLVD
100 SBdC 92314 4742-B6
RAINBOW CT
27600 HIGH 92346 577-J4
RAINBOW DR
15800 FONT 92335 604-F5
27800 SBdC - 517-J2
RAINBOW LN
- APLV 92308 4477-C1
1700 RDL 92374 608-G7
6500 HIGH 92346 577-J4
32600 YCPA 92399 649-D4
41300 SBdC 92339 611-G2
E RAINBOW LN
3300 SBDO 92346 577-H4
RAINBOW PL
600 DBAR 91765 640-E7
6600 HIGH 92346 577-J3
RAINBOW RD
6900 SBdC 92345 4564-F5
21100 SBdC 92347 (3677-E1 See Page 3586)
RAINBOW BASIN RD
- SBdC - 349-D6
RAINBOW CANYON RD
1800 SBdC 92278 370-D7
1800 SBdC 92278 4751-J1
RAINBOW FALLS CT
6100 RCUC 91737 573-D3
RAINBOW KNOLL
14400 CHLS 91709 680-G4
RAINBOW RIDGE RD
- SBdC 92252 4959-H5
- POM 91766 640-H5
16200 CHLS 91709 710-H2
RAINIER CT
- RDL 92374 608-G7
4300 CHNO 91710 681-E1
RAINIER PL
- SBDO 92407 546-D5
RAINIER RD
- SBdC 92277 4820-E3
300 SBdC - 517-G1
300 SBdC - 4737-G7
65700 SBdC 92252 4820-C2
68500 SBdC 92277 4821-D2
71900 SBdC 92277 4822-A2
RAINIER ST
35600 YCPA 92399 650-B6
RAINS PL
6800 RCUC 91701 572-G5
RAINSGATE LN
13900 CHLS 91709 680-H3
RAIN SHADOW RD
12500 SBdC 92392 4386-H5
RAINSTAR LN
2400 CHLS 91709 680-G5
RAINTREE CT
12800 CHNO 91710 642-A7
RAINTREE PL
- RCUC 91739 573-J6
12900 CHNO 91710 642-A7
S RAINTREE PL
1800 SBDO 92408 607-C6
RAINWOOD CT
12900 VCTV 92392 4386-C4
RAINWOOD LN
12300 VCTV 92392 4386-D6
RALEIGH AV
- CHLS 91709 712-A5
RALEIGH CT
- CHLS 91709 712-A5
W RALEIGH DR
700 SBdC 92314 4742-B7
RALPH CT
500 POM 91766 641-A6
E RALSTON AV
100 SBDO 92404 546-H7
400 SBDO 92404 547-A7
W RALSTON AV
100 SBDO 92405 546-H7
E RALSTON ST
100 ONT 91761 642-C2
W RALSTON ST
100 ONT 91762 642-A2
1000 ONT 91762 641-J2
RAM CT
5400 RCUC 91737 572-H2
RAMA DR
14800 VCTV 92392 4296-E7
RAMADA DR
16500 VCTV 92392 4296-E6
RAMADA LN
35500 YCPA 92399 650-B4
RAMBLING RD
10400 APLV 92308 4477-G2
RAMIREZ RD
36000 SBdC 92311 3679-D2
RAMONA AV
6100 RCUC 91737 572-J4
6600 RCUC 91701 572-J5
7300 RCUC 91730 572-J7
7700 RCUC 91730 602-J1
8700 RCUC 91730 603-A3
8900 MTCL 91763 601-E4
10300 MTCL 91763 641-E2
11300 MTCL 91763 641-E2
11300 SBdC 91766 641-E2
11400 SBdC 91710 641-E2
11800 CHNO 91710 641-E7
13100 CHNO 91710 681-E4
14900 CHLS 91709 681-E6
15100 APLV 92307 4297-H5
15300 VCTV 92392 4386-B1
15500 FONT 92336 574-F7
17300 FONT 92336 575-A7
17900 SBdC 92336 575-C7
18900 APLV 92307 4298-A7
22300 SBdC 92307 4298-D7
N RAMONA AV
500 SBDO 92411 576-D4
RAMONA CIR
14400 APLV 92307 4298-B7
N RAMONA CT
100 RLTO 92376 605-G1
RAMONA DR
- SBdC 92277 4822-C5
800 RDL 92373 648-C2
15600 FONT 92336 574-F7
17200 FONT 92336 575-A7
73100 TNP 92277 4822-D5
76200 TNP 92277 4823-A5
76200 SBdC 92277 4823-B5
E RAMONA DR
100 RLTO 92376 605-H1
W RAMONA DR
100 RLTO 92376 605-D1
RAMONA PL
4600 SBdC 91710 641-F3
RAMONA RD
16900 APLV 92307 4297-H1
17000 APLV 92307 4207-H2
19500 APLV 92307 (4117-H7 See Page 4116)
23800 SBdC 92307 4298-E7
31800 SBdC 92365 3764-C1
35700 SBdC 92365 3594-C7
RAMONA RD
35700 SBdC 92365 (3684-C1 See Page 3594)
39700 SBdC 92365 (3504-B4 See Page 3414)
70700 SBdC 92277 4821-G7
RAMONA ST
10500 YCPA 92399 610-B6
RAMONA TR
8700 SBdC 92256 4956-E7
9000 SBdC 92256 616-E1
RAMSEY WY
2000 POM 91767 601-A5
RANCH CIDR
- CHLS 91709 710-H3
RANCH DR
300 CLTN 92324 647-A5
2900 RivC 92324 647-A5
10800 RCUC 91737 573-C1
RANCH LN
10000 MohC - 3620-C2
RANCH RD
2700 SBdC 92277 4822-H4
4700 CHNO 91710 641-F7
17000 VCTV 92394 (4206-B7 See Page 4116)
17100 VCTV 92394 4296-B1
W RANCH RD
1500 SBDO 92407 546-C5
RANCH ST
31600 SBdC - 4480-G4
RANCH CREEK CT
- POM 91766 640-F5
RANCH CREEK LN
14500 CHLS 91709 680-J4
RANCHERIA DR
8100 RCUC 91730 602-E2
RANCHERIA RD
400 DBAR 91765 640-C7
RANCHERIAS DR
11300 FONT 92337 644-B4
RANCHERIAS LN
20000 APLV 92307 4297-D3
RANCHERIAS RD
13000 APLV 92308 4387-H3
15200 APLV 92307 4297-E3
19200 APLV 92307 4387-G1
RANCHERO DR
13700 FONT 92337 644-A3
RANCHERO LN
5400 SBdC 92301 (4113-C2 See Page 4112)
RANCHERO RD
800 SBdC 92314 (4743-A7 See Page 4662)
14900 HESP 92345 4566-D4
RANCHERO ST
9700 SBdC 92345 4564-G5
10700 SBdC 92345 4565-A5
14000 HESP 92345 4565-F5
14500 HESP 92345 4566-D4
18100 HESP 92345 4567-A4
RANCH GATE RD
5200 RCUC 91701 572-D2
RANCH HOUSE RD
2100 CHLS 91709 710-J1
RANCHITO RD
29100 SBdC - (3846-E5 See Page 3756)
RANCHO AV
600 SBdC 92407 515-B3
N RANCHO AV
100 CLTN 92324 606-C3
100 SBDO 92410 606-C1
S RANCHO AV
100 CLTN 92324 606-C7
100 SBdC 92324 606-C7
100 SBDO 92410 606-C7
600 CLTN 92324 646-C1
RANCHO CT
14000 SBdC 92337 644-B2
RANCHO DR
2000 RDL 92373 607-G6
RANCHO RD
- SBdC - 4480-B4
200 SBdC 92372 4472-D3
400 SBdC 92371 4292-C2
2900 SBdC 92371 4472-G3
3700 SBdC 92371 4473-A3
3800 SBdC 92371 (4293-B2 See Page 4292)
6900 ADEL 92301 (4293-B2 See Page 4292)
6900 ADEL 92301 (4293-B2 See Page 4292)
7400 SBdC 92371 4562-J5
7400 ADEL 92301 4294-A2
7600 SBdC 92371 4564-D4
11300 ADEL 92301 4295-A2
13600 ADFI 92394 4295-H2
13600 VCTV 92394 4295-H2
15100 VCTV 92394 4296-A2
35300 YCPA 92399 650-A2
RANCHO ST
8700 RCUC 91701 572-F2
9300 RCUC 91737 572-H2
10300 RCUC 91737 573-A2
20400 SBdC 92308 4477-E5
22700 SBdC 92308 4478-C5
25600 SBdC 92308 4479-A5
RANCHO BJ RD
- SBdC - (3765-J7 See Page 3764)
- SBdC - (3855-J3 See Page 3764)
RANCHO BONITA RD
17700 SBdC 92392 4386-H3
RANCHO CONTENTO DR
2600 SBdC 92371 4562-G5
RANCHO CUCAMUNGA CT
- RCUC 91730 603-D4
RANCHO DEL CHINO AV
13500 CHNO 91710 682-B2
RANCHO DEL LAGO DR
- APLV 92307 4297-F1
E RANCHO ESTATES PL
12700 RCUC 91739 573-H2
W RANCHO ESTATES PL
12600 RCUC 91739 573-G3
RANCHO FONTANA VILLAGE PKWY
15400 FONT 92336 574-E6
RANCHO HILLS DR
1400 CHLS 91709 680-G5
RANCHO JURUPA PL
- POM 91766 640-E4
RANCHO LAGUNA DR
- POM 91766 640-D4
RANCHO MEADOWS PL
7300 RCUC 91730 572-H6
RANCHO NOVATO DR
- POM 91766 640-D4
RANCHO PARK CIR E
9100 RCUC 91730 602-H4
RANCHO PARK CIR N
9100 RCUC 91730 602-H4
RANCHO PARK CIR W
9100 RCUC 91730 602-H4
RANCHO PARK DR
9200 RCUC 91730 602-H4
RANCHO PARK PL
9100 RCUC 91730 602-H4
RANCHO ROSA WY
600 RCUC 91784 572-F6
RANCHO VISTA DR
- SBdC 92335 604-C4
100 SBdC 92284 4748-H5
W RANCHO VISTA DR
2800 RLTO 92377 545-A6
2800 RLTO 92377 544-J7
RANCHO VISTA PL
- POM 91766 640-E5
5900 RCUC 91739 573-G3
RANCHVIEW TER
14600 CHLS 91709 680-G5
RANCHWOOD AV
17900 CHLS 91709 712-B5
RANCHWOOD PL
11100 DBAR 91765 680-D3
RANDAL DR
18500 SBdC 92345 4567-B7
RANDALL AV
14500 SBdC 92335 604-C4
15700 FONT 92335 604-H4
17000 FONT 92335 605-A4
17700 SBdC 92335 605-A4
18100 RLTO 92335 605-A4
18100 SBdC 92316 605-A4
E RANDALL AV
100 RLTO 92376 605-H4
500 CLTN 92324 605-H4
N RANDALL AV
1600 CLTN 92324 606-B4
W RANDALL AV
- SBDO 92376 606-A4
100 RLTO 92376 605-F4
1100 RLTO 92316 605-F4
1300 CLTN 92324 606-A4
1300 SBDO 92410 606-A4
1500 SBdC 92316 605-F4
1700 CLTN 92324 605-J4
1700 SBDO 92376 605-J4
RANDALL DR
- SBdC 92365 (3593-G5 See Page 3592)
RANDALL ST
35700 SBdC - (4571-H1 See Page 4570)
RANDOLPH RD
9700 SBdC 92371 4473-J6
RANDSBURG CTO
68800 SBdC - 329-B8
RANDSBURG RD
19300 SBdC - 329-C7
RANDSBURG WASH RD
6000 SBdC - 328-J6
RANDSBURG WASH ACCESS RD
3600 SBdC - 328-H6
RANDY ST
200 POM 91768 640-D1
W RANDY ST
1300 UPL 91786 601-J3
RANGE CT
1600 DBAR 91765 680-D4
RANGER CT
300 UPL 91784 572-C6
RANGER DR
200 SBdC - 517-D2
RANGER ST
1700 UPL 91784 572-C6
RANGER TR
4700 SBdC 92277 (4825-D4 See Page 4824)
RANGERS RD
- SBdC - 516-G4
RANGE VIEW RD
11500 RivC 91752 683-G5
RANKINS LN
1100 SBDO 92404 547-B6
RANSOM LN
400 SBdC - 514-A1
RAPALLO DR
11700 RCUC 91701 573-E6
RAPID BROOK RD
1200 DBAR 91765 680-C2
RAPID GROVE DR
26600 LACo 92397 4652-A1
RAPTURE RD
12100 SBdC 92371 4383-C3
RAQUEL CT
4200 SBDO 92407 545-J6
RARICK WY
- TNP 92277 4822-D4
RASOR RD
67800 SBdC - 350-D4
RASPBERRY CT
- RivC 92880 683-B7
11600 SBdC 92399 651-B1
RASPBERRY LN
11400 SBdC 92399 651-B1
RASPBERRY PL
5900 RCUC 91737 573-A3
RATE DR
300 SBdC - 516-C2
RATE RD
300 SBdC - 516-C2
RATHBUN DR
42500 BBLK - 4812-A2
RATTLESNAKE RD
1200 SBdC 92372 4562-C3
5300 SBdC 92371 4563-D3
8300 SBdC 92371 4564-C3
RATTLESNAKE CANYON RD
- SBdC - 369-J9
- SBdC 92285 369-J9
- SBdC 92285 (4574-E7 See Page 4484)
RATTLESNAKE GULCH
- SBdC - 4562-A5
1700 SBdC 92372 4562-D4
RATTLESNAKE GULCH RD
2300 SBdC 92372 4562-E4
RAVEN RD
9100 SBdC 92371 4474-D7
9100 SBdC 92371 4564-D1
13600 SBdC 92371 4382-J3
26700 LACo 92397 4652-A2
RAVEN WY
22100 GTER 92313 646-D5
RAVENCREST CIR
- POM 91766 640-F5
RAVENCREST CT
35100 YCPA 92399 610-A6
RAVENHILL DR
- POM 91766 640-F6
RAVENNA CT
13500 CHLS 91709 681-A2
RAVENNA LN
12400 VCTV 92392 4385-C6
RAVEN ROOST
- SBdC 92277 4824-G3
RAVENWOOD DR
13900 CHLS 91709 680-J3
RAVINA CUR
2300 SBdC 91784 572-A3
RAVINE LN
1600 CHLS 91709 710-H2
RAVINE RD
800 BBLK - 4812-B2
RAWHIDE LN
3500 CHNO 91710 681-C1
RAWHIDE RD
53300 SBdC - 4886-H5
RAWHIDE ST
- POM 91766 640-F5
RAWSON RD
500 SBdC 92372 4472-A5
8900 SBdC 92256 616-C2
RAY CT
11500 LMLN 92354 647-C2
RAYLENE PL
1300 POM 91767 601-A6
RAYMOND AV
15400 FONT 92336 574-E7
RAYMOND CT
17900 SBdC 92336 575-C7
18100 FONT 92336 575-C7
N RAYMOND CT
1800 ONT 91764 602-E4
RAYMOND DR
- SBdC 92277 4824-E7
- SBdC 92277 4892-A1
- TNP 92277 4822-G7
69300 SBdC 92277 4891-B1
72900 TNP 92277 4892-C1
76300 SBdC 92277 4823-C7
RAYMOND DR
84500 SBdC 92277 (4825-F6 See Page 4824)
S RAYMOND PL
2400 ONT 91761 642-E5
RAYMOND RD
800 SBdC - (4743-B5 See Page 4662)
E RAYMOND ST
500 UPL 91786 602-D4
1100 ONT 91764 602-E4
RAY MURRISET LN
- CHNO 91710 641-E5
RAYNOR ST
1100 CLTN 92324 646-H1
RAYO LN
- BBLK - 4810-J2
RAYO DEL SOL
14600 CHLS 91709 681-A4
RAYO DEL SOL DR
5300 SBdC 92301 (4203-D1 See Page 4112)
R C RANCH RD
- SBdC - 4817-B3
- SBdC 92284 4817-B3
N READELL AL
100 SBDO 92410 606-F1
READINESS ST
- VCTV 92394 4205-E5
REAGAN RD
- SBdC 92277 4820-D7
65100 SBdC 92252 4820-A7
REALES ST
8900 RCUC 91737 572-G1
REATA AV
1400 PRKR - 4844-H2
REATA RD
12000 APLV 92308 4387-B5
REBECCA CT
- POM 91766 640-J3
REBECCA RD
35900 YCPA 92399 650-C6
N REBECCA ST
100 POM 91768 640-H1
S REBECCA ST
100 POM 91766 640-H2
REBECCA CREST
800 RDL 92373 648-C4
REBOZO LN
6300 SBdC 92301 (4113-E1 See Page 4112)
RECADA AV
10700 SBdC - 4482-E1
RECHE CIR
22200 RivC 92324 647-A7
RECHE RD
55500 SBdC 92285 4747-D3
57300 SBdC 92285 4748-D3
60000 SBdC 92284 4748-H3
60200 SBdC 92278 4748-H3
60900 SBdC 92252 4748-H3
60900 SBdC 92252 4749-A3
RECHE CANYON RD
7000 LMLN 92324 647-A6
7000 RivC 92324 647-A6
7000 SBdC 92324 647-A6
11600 SBdC 92324 646-J3
S RECHE CANYON RD
1100 CLTN 92324 646-H2
1400 SBdC 92324 646-H2
2500 CLTN 92324 647-A5
2700 SBdC 92324 647-A5
RECHE HILLS DR
2300 CLTN 92324 646-J4
RECHER LN
- SBdC 92285 (4576-J6 See Page 4486)
- SBdC 92285 (4577-A6 See Page 4486)
RECLAMATION RD
100 NDLS 92363 3620-E6
RECUERDO LN
10700 SBdC 92256 615-G5
RED ANT LNDG
500 BBLK - 4811-E1
RED APPLE LN
1400 CHLS 91709 710-G2
REDBIRD RD
- CHLS 91709 680-H2
RED BLUFF AV
6100 YUCA 92284 4887-J7
REDBUD CT
15700 FONT 92335 604-F4
REDBUD PL
1700 POM 91766 640-F3
6500 RCUC 91739 573-G4
REDBUD ST
17300 HESP 92345 4476-G7
RED BUTTE AV
9900 SBdC - 4480-H2
12100 SBdC - (4390-H5 See Page 4300)
RED BUTTE RD
9100 SBdC - 4480-H5
RED BUTTE VW
- SBdC - (3846-C5 See Page 3756)
RED CEDAR AV
13100 VCTV 92392 4475-F2
RED CEDAR AV
14500 SBdC - (4303-B5 See Page 4302)
RED CLOUD DR
100 DBAR 91765 640-B7
RED CLOUD LN
16300 VCTV 92392 4386-D6
RED CLOVER WY
7300 HIGH 92346 578-A6
RED COACH LN
26600 SBdC - (3935-F5 See Page 3934)
REDDEN LN
8000 YUCA 92284 4957-D4
REDDING AV
4500 YUCA 92284 4887-F4
REDDING ST
17100 HESP 92345 4566-G3
18200 HESP 92345 4567-A2
N REDDING WY
500 UPL 91786 602-B1
1500 UPL 91786 572-B7
1600 UPL 91784 572-B3
RED DOG WY
15100 VCTV 92394 4296-A7
RED FEATHER CT
19300 APLV 92307 4297-C7
RED FEATHER LN
20000 APLV 92307 4297-D7
RED FEATHER RD
18900 APLV 92307 4387-B1
19000 APLV 92307 4297-B7
RED FIR LN
22600 DBAR 91765 680-A4
REDFORD PL
- CHLS 91709 712-A6
RED GROUSE CT
29000 SBdC - 518-C2
REDGROVE WY
1500 UPL 91784 571-H4
RED GUM LN
- FONT 92337 644-D3
RED GUM RD
- LACo 91768 640-A1
RED HAWK PL
20400 APLV 92308 4387-F5
RED HILL DR
1400 RCUC 91730 602-F1
RED HILL PL
13900 VCTV 92392 4386-C2
RED HILL RD
69800 SBdC 92277 4821-D1
RED HILL COUNTRY CLUB DR
8100 RCUC 91730 602-E2
RED HILL MINE RD
81600 SBdC - 329-C3
RED HILL NORTH DR
1400 UPL 91786 572-E7
1400 RCUC 91730 572-E7
1400 UPL 91730 572-E7
RED HORSE RUN
62500 SBdC 92252 4819-D4
W REDICK AV
200 SBDO 92408 606-H2
REDLANDS AV
400 CLAR 91711 571-C6
10100 HESP 92345 4476-B3
N REDLANDS AV
1200 CLTN 92324 606-E5
REDLANDS BLVD
500 LMLN 92354 607-C6
500 SBDO 92408 607-A7
700 RDL 92373 648-D2
800 RDL 92374 648-D2
25700 LMLN 92374 607-C6
25700 LMLN 92373 607-C6
26400 RDL 92374 607-C6
26400 RDL 92373 607-C6
E REDLANDS BLVD
- RDL 92374 608-C7
- RDL 92373 608-C7
100 SBDO 92408 606-J7
300 SBDO 92408 607-A7
600 RDL 92373 648-C1
600 RDL 92374 648-C1
W REDLANDS BLVD
- RDL 92373 608-A7
- RDL 92374 608-A7
1000 RDL 92374 607-H6
1000 RDL 92373 607-H6
REDLANDS ST
300 RDL 92374 648-F1
REDLANDS HEIGHTS RANCH RD
32900 HIGH 92359 609-F3
33700 SBdC 92359 609-H3
34100 SBdC - 609-H3
REDLANDS PROSPECT RD
11100 SBdC 92399 611-C7
RED LEAF DR
3100 CHLS 91709 681-B7
REDMAPLE ST
- FONT 92337 645-A2
RED MOUNTAIN RD
600 SBdC - 328-G11
RED OAK
600 BBLK - 4811-F2
RED OAK CIR
- POM 91766 640-F5
RED OAK ST
8100 RCUC 91730 603-C2
REDONDO CT
14100 FONT 92336 574-B6
REDONDO DR
15100 VCTV 92392 4296-D6
REDONDO RD
16700 ADEL 92301 4295-C2
19300 ADEL 92301 4205-C2
20000 ADEL 92301 (4115-C7 See Page 4114)
REDONDO ST
57400 YUCA 92284 4887-J7
57400 YUCA 92284 4888-A7
S REDPINE PL
2600 ONT 91761 643-B6
RED RIVER RD
12700 VCTV 92392 4385-J5
12700 VCTV 92392 4386-A5
RED ROBIN DR
39500 SBdC - 4741-B5
REDROCK CT
11900 FONT 92337 644-C4
12400 VCTV 92392 4385-D6
REDROCK LN
- POM 91766 640-G5
RED ROCK DR
200 SBdC - 517-J5
REDROCK RD
12300 VCTV 92392 4385-D6
RED ROCK RD
36500 SBdC 92347 (3587-D7 See Page 3586)
36500 SBdC 92347 (3677-D1 See Page 3586)
RED ROSE LN
- SBdC - 518-D1
RED ROSE PL
- UPL 91786 602-D1
RED RYDER
5300 SBdC - 4886-H5
RED SKY AV
- SBDO 92407 545-H3
RED START DR
26700 SBdC 92397 4652-A1
26700 LACo 92397 4652-A1
RED STONE CIR
12500 YCPA 92399 649-F4
REDSTONE CT
13200 CHLS 91709 680-J1
RED TAIL CT
29000 HIGH 92346 578-D6
REDTAIL HAWK CT
300 SBdC - 518-C2
REDWHEELS DR
53100 SBdC 92256 4956-G7
REDWING RD
12300 APLV 92308 4387-G4
16100 SBdC 92307 4299-B2
REDWOOD AV
1100 NDLS 92363 3620-C7
4100 RLTO 92377 544-J6
6600 HESP 92345 4566-A3
7500 FONT 92336 574-C7
7700 FONT 92336 604-C1
8000 SBdC 92336 604-C1
8100 SBdC 92335 604-D3
9500 HESP 92345 4476-A2
10300 SBdC 92337 604-D7
10500 FONT 92337 604-D7
10500 FONT 92337 644-D2
10600 SBdC 92337 644-D2
13700 CHNO 91710 681-H2
N REDWOOD AV
600 UPL 91786 601-H2
S REDWOOD AV
1500 ONT 91762 642-A4
REDWOOD CIR
- SBdC 91784 572-A2
REDWOOD CT
- CHNO 91710 681-H2
11300 FONT 92337 644-D3
REDWOOD DR
- RCUC 91739 573-J6
300 SBdC - 516-F2
1200 BBLK - 4742-B7
1200 SBdC - 4742-B7
1200 SBdC 92314 4742-B7
9500 SBdC 92339 611-H3
11900 FONT 92337 644-D4
W REDWOOD DR
1200 BBLK - 4742-A7
REDWOOD LN
12900 YCPA 92399 650-D5
14900 CHLS 91709 681-D5
REDWOOD RD
400 SBdC - 4738-E7
11000 SBdC 92372 4472-D1
11400 HESP 92345 4476-A1
11700 HESP 92345 4386-A7
12100 SBdC 92372 4382-D7
REDWOOD ST
14700 ADEL 92301 4294-H7
N REDWOOD ST
6300 SBDO 92407 546-A2
W REDWOOD ST
2300 SBDO 92407 546-A3
REDWOOD TR
12900 YCPA 92399 650-E5
REDWOOD WY
22900 SBdC - 516-F2
N REDWOOD WY
1500 UPL 91786 571-H7
1600 UPL 91784 571-H6
REDWOOD VIEW DR
1200 POM 91766 640-F4
W REECE ST
900 SBDO 92411 576-E5
REED
1900 RDL 92374 608-B3
REED AV
12200 GTER 92313 646-E4
REED CT
16000 FONT 92336 604-G1
REED DR
800 CLAR 91711 601-B2
15600 FONT 92336 574-F7
15600 FONT 92336 604-F1
REED ST
16200 FONT 92336 604-G1
17100 FONT 92336 605-A1
17800 FONT 92336 575-B7
17800 SBdC 92336 575-B7
REEDY AV
1400 HIGH 92346 577-H5
1400 SBDO 92346 577-H5
N REEDY AV
1900 SBDO 92346 577-H3
REEDY WOODS LN
33600 YCPA 92399 649-F3
REES CT
1300 RDL 92374 608-E5
REEVES CT
8900 RCUC 91730 602-G1
REEVES PL
700 POM 91767 641-B1
REFLECTION DR
11200 RCUC 91737 573-D4
REGAL CT
- SBdC 92335 604-A2
REGAL WY
- VCTV 92392 4296-E7
REGAL OAKS RD
6700 HIGH 92346 578-A4
REGAL PARK DR
- FONT 92336 574-D5
REGENCY RD
10600 HESP 92345 4475-J3
REGENCY WY
8900 RCUC 91701 572-G3
REGENE ST
1500 POM 91766 641-A4
S REGENE ST
500 POM 91766 641-A2
REGENT DR
- RCUC 91730 573-D7
REGENTS RD
2000 MohC - 3620-G2
REGGIO PL
1200 POM 91766 640-E3
REGINA DR
1300 SBdC - 4738-B5
14000 RCUC 91739 574-B1
REGINA RD
- SBdC - (4025-H2 See Page 3934)
- SBdC - (4026-A1 See Page 3936)
REGINA WY
- FONT 92336 574-C1
REGINO ST
- SBdC 92277 4751-H6
- SBdC 92277 4821-H1
5100 TNP 92277 4891-J3
REGIS AV
1000 CLAR 91711 601-B2
REGIS CT
10300 RCUC 91730 603-A1
REID AV
8800 RCUC 91730 602-J3
REILLY
- SBdC 92285 4748-F3
REIMAN ST
15100 ADEL 92301 4294-H3
17700 ADEL 92301 4204-H2
REIMS ST
400 POM 91767 601-A1
1200 CLAR 91711 601-A1
REINAN AV
19300 SBdC 92301 (4203-B3 See Page 4112)
S REINDEER LN
2400 ONT 91761 643-A5
REISLING DR
- RCUC 91739 603-H1
REISLING ST
15900 SBdC 92335 604-F2
RELIN RD
10700 SBdC 92371 4473-F4
REMIE CT
6800 RCUC 91701 572-G5
REMINGTON CT
14100 FONT 92336 574-B7
REMINGTON RD
- APLV 92308 4387-E5
REMINGTON ST
8100 SBdC 91710 682-F6
REMINGTON ST
8800 CHNO 91710 682-F6
9100 ONT 91710 682-H6
9400 RivC 92880 682-H6
REMSEN DR
25200 LMLN 92354 607-C7
REMUDA AV
9700 SBdC 92308 4478-E5
REMUDA RD
12000 VCTV 92392 4385-G7
16500 SBdC - (4211-C7 See Page 4120)
16500 SBdC - (4301-C1 See Page 4300)
RENATO CT
6300 CHNO 91710 642-A7
RENDOVA ST
1000 BARS 92311 3680-F7
RENE LN
22000 GTER 92313 646-D4
RENEE ST
800 RDL 92374 608-E6
RENOIR LN
5200 CHLS 91709 711-G1
RENO LOOP RD
14000 VCTV 92394 4295-G6
RENO RIDGE DR
1100 DBAR 91765 640-C4
RENO RIDGE LN
900 DBAR 91765 640-C5
RENTAL CAR RD
10500 ONT 91761 643-A1
RENWICK DR
- RCUC 91739 573-G6
REPOSO LN
8900 SBdC 92308 4478-E5
REPTON AV
4300 SBdC 92285 4667-B2
4500 SBdC 92285 (4577-B7 See Page 4486)
REQUA AV
3900 CLAR 91711 601-A1
RESEARCH DR
1100 RDL 92374 607-E6
RESEDA AV
8100 SBdC 92335 604-C2
RESEDA DR
12100 YCPA 92399 649-A3
RESEDA ST
- SBdC - (3935-A5 See Page 3934)
RESENDA AV
9300 SBdC 92335 604-C4
W RESERVOIR DR
1300 SBDO 92407 546-D5
RESERVOIR PL
14500 CHLS 91709 681-C4
RESERVOIR RD
- FONT 92336 544-C7
300 SBdC - 516-C1
300 SBdC - 4736-C7
900 SBdC 92374 609-B6
900 SBdC 92399 609-B6
1000 SBdC 92359 609-B6
1400 RDL 92374 648-F2
1500 RDL 92373 648-F2
9400 RivC 92509 644-C6
RESERVOIR ST
2600 SBdC 92407 545-H7
N RESERVOIR ST
200 POM 91767 641-B1
500 POM 91767 601-B7
S RESERVOIR ST
100 POM 91766 641-B2
100 POM 91767 641-B2
12800 CHNO 91710 641-C6
W RESERVOIR ST
600 SBdC 92407 546-E5
700 SBDO 92407 546-E5
RESERVOIR CANAL RD
700 SBdC 92374 609-A7
700 SBdC 92374 649-A1
RESORT ST
1400 UPL 91784 571-H5
RESOTO RD
18900 APLV 92307 4297-A3
23300 SBdC 92307 4298-D3
RESOURCE DR
- RLTO 92316 645-G3
REVENA DR
97000 SBdC - 371-A4
REVERE AV
5100 SBDO 92407 546-B5
5600 RCUC 91737 573-A2
REVERE CT
9900 ADEL 92301 4204-F4
REVERE ST
4800 CHNO 91710 641-F5
E REVERE ST
100 UPL 91784 572-C3
REVLON DR
- FONT 92336 604-E1
REVOLUTION DR
- RCUC 91730 573-E1
REX CT
700 POM 91767 601-A3
REX DR
60600 SBdC 92284 4748-H5
REX RD
- SBdC - 4480-C3

STREET
Block City ZIP Pg-Grid

REX COLE RD
1900 SBdC 92407 515-D6
REXFORD CT
800 DBAR 91765 680-E1
N REXFORD ST
200 CLTN 92324 605-J6
S REXFORD ST
200 SBDO 92376 605-J2
REYES AV
20300 SBdC 92307 (4117-D7 See Page 4116)
REYES HERNANDEZ JR LN
1200 CLTN 92324 606-A4
REYNOLDS ST
25900 LMLN 92354 647-E2
RHEIN CT
- RCUC 91739 603-J1
RHINE RD
600 SBdC - 4737-G7
RHODE ISLAND CT
- RCUC 91730 573-E1
RHODE ISLAND ST
18100 ADEL 92301 4204-H3
RHODELIA AV
500 CLAR 91711 601-B3
4400 LACo 91711 571-B7
RHODES PL
12900 CHNO 91710 641-F7
RHONDA LN
1300 RDL 92373 648-E2
RHONDA ST
10400 LMLN 92374 607-F6
RHONDA TR
20100 SBdC - (3937-D1 See Page 3936)
RHONE AV
6900 HIGH 92346 577-J4
N RHONE AV
1600 SBDO 92346 577-J4
RHONE CT
6500 HIGH 92346 577-J3
RHYOLITE CT
2200 CHLS 91709 680-J7
RHYOLITE ST
1200 SBdC 92359 608-J6
RIAGOSA RD
35300 SBdC 92365 (3685-B2 See Page 3594)
35500 SBdC 92365 (3595-B7 See Page 3594)
RIALTO AV
- SBDO 92408 607-C1
18700 APLV 92307 4207-J3
E RIALTO AV
- RLTO 92376 605-H2
100 SBDO 92408 606-E3
300 SBDO 92408 607-A1
600 SBDO 92376 605-H2
2000 SBDO 92410 606-J1
N RIALTO AV
1200 CLTN 92324 606-E3
W RIALTO AV
- RLTO 92376 605-E2
100 SBDO 92408 606-F1
300 SBDO 92401 606-F1
500 SBDO 92410 606-F1
1600 RLTO 92335 605-E2
1600 SBdC 92335 605-E2
2600 SBDO 92376 606-A2
2800 SBDO 92376 605-E2
RIALTO WY
900 POM 91767 601-B7
RIATA RD
- SBdC 92365 (3684-A4 See Page 3594)
RICARDO DR
8300 RCUC 91730 602-F2
RICAREE RD
14200 APLV 92307 4387-E1
14300 APLV 92307 4297-E7
RICE AV
200 SBdC 92252 4749-F6
1100 SBdC 92252 4819-F1
1300 SBdC 92252 4889-F3
6900 SBdC 92252 4959-F1
RICHARD DR
6200 YUCA 92284 4888-D7
RICHARD ST
1700 POM 91767 601-C6
35800 SBdC - (4571-H2 See Page 4570)
36500 SBdC - (4572-B1 See Page 4482)
RICHARD BURNS CT
7600 FONT 92336 574-A7
RICHARDS LN
36600 SBdC 92311 3589-F7
36600 SBdC 92311 3679-F1
W RICHARDSON AV
1100 SBDO 92410 606-F3
RICHARDSON RD
7400 ADEL 92392 4384-D2
7400 SBdC 92392 4384-D2
14100 ADEL 92301 4384-D2
14500 ADEL 92301 4294-C1
14500 SBdC 92301 4294-D7
17400 ADEL 92301 4204-C3
20100 ADEL 92301 4114-B5
20500 SBdC 92301 4114-B5
RICHARDSON RD
56100 SBdC 92285 4667-E6
RICHARDSON ST
11200 LMLN 92354 647-C1
S RICHARDSON ST
1100 SBDO 92408 607-C5
1400 RDL 92408 607-C5
1500 SBDO 92354 607-C5
10300 LMLN 92354 607-C6
RICHBROOK DR
600 LACo 91711 601-A2
600 POM 91767 601-A2
RICHELE CT
3200 CHLS 91709 681-B2
RICHIE CIR
11100 LMLN 92354 647-C1
RICHLAND ST
400 UPL 91786 602-C4
700 UPL 91764 602-D4
700 ONT 91764 602-D4
RICHMAN DR
10900 LMLN 92354 647-A1
RICHMOND AV
- VCTV 92392 4385-C7
- VCTV 92392 4475-C1
14900 VCTV 92394 4295-C7
RICHMOND CT
500 SBdC - 518-A3
18400 SBdC 92392 4386-J4
18400 SBdC 92392 4387-A4
S RICHMOND CT
2600 SBDO 92408 646-J1
RICHMOND DR
900 CLAR 91711 601-B2
32600 SBdC - 519-C6
RICHMOND PL
9300 RCUC 91730 603-E5
RICHMOND RD
- SBdC 92284 4818-F4
RICHMOND ST
4300 CHNO 91710 641-E7
E RICHMOND ST
2500 ONT 91761 642-J6
RICHMOND WY
13300 APLV 92308 4387-D3
RICHMOND HILL CT
1000 SBdC 92407 515-B5
RICHMONT RD
11000 LMLN 92354 647-C1
RICHTON ST
4900 MTCL 91763 601-F3
RICHWOOD DR
8500 RCUC 91730 602-F3
RICKMAN RD
- SBdC - (4210-J4 See Page 4120)
- SBdC - (4211-A4 See Page 4120)
RICO CT
- RivC 92880 683-D7
RIDEOUT CT
14100 FONT 92336 574-B6
RIDER CT
500 CLAR 91711 571-C7
RIDGE DR
2300 SBdC - 519-D7
7000 HIGH 92346 578-C5
21000 SBdC - 516-C2
21000 SBdC 92407 516-C2
S RIDGE LN
17500 APLV 92307 4296-G3
RIDGE PL
500 SBdC - 516-G3
RIDGE RD
800 SBdC - 4737-H6
1100 SBdC - 4741-B4
33000 SBdC - 519-D7
53700 YUCA 92284 4956-J3
53700 YUCA 92284 4957-A3
RIDGE SPUR
33000 SBdC - 519-D7
RIDGE ST
1500 RDL 92373 648-D4
RIDGE WY
600 SBdC - 519-E2
RIDGE CANYON RD
10500 RCUC 91737 573-B1
RIDGECREST BLVD Rt#-178
1700 SBdC - 328-G6
RIDGE CREST CIR
1200 POM 91766 640-G4
RIDGECREST CIR
2900 CHLS 91709 681-A2
RIDGECREST CT
- DBAR 91765 680-C1
RIDGE CREST CT
1500 SBDO 92405 576-D1
RIDGECREST DR
12100 YCPA 92399 649-A3
12600 RCUC 91739 573-G2
15300 FONT 92337 644-E3
43300 BBLK - 4812-C3
43700 SBdC - 4812-C3
RIDGECREST LN
3000 CHLS 91709 681-C7
27900 SBdC - 517-J3
RIDGECREST RD
12100 HESP 92345 4386-H5
12100 VCTV 92345 4386-H5
12100 VCTV 92392 4386-H5
13400 SBdC 92392 4386-H5
RIDGEFIELD DR
500 CLAR 91711 571-A7
2900 CHLS 91709 681-B2
RIDGEGATE DR
5800 CHLS 91709 711-J4
N RIDGELINE AV
6600 SBDO 92407 545-J2
N RIDGE LINE DR
3700 SBDO 92405 576-F1
3700 SBDO 92407 546-F7
3700 SBDO 92407 576-F1
RIDGELINE PL
5300 RCUC 91739 574-B2
RIDGELINE RD
13600 VCTV 92392 4385-G6
RIDGE LINE RD
22400 DBAR 91765 680-A5
RIDGEMARK PL
- FONT 92336 574-H2
RIDGEMARK RD
- APLV 92308 4387-C7
- APLV 92308 4477-B5
RIDGEMONT CT
2000 UPL 91784 571-H5
RIDGEMONT WY
2300 UPL 91784 571-H3
RIDGEPOINTE RD
3300 CHLS 91709 681-B2
W RIDGESIDE DR
500 SBdC 92314 4742-B7
RIDGEVIEW AV
5300 RCUC 91737 573-A2
5400 RivC 91752 683-J5
RIDGEVIEW CT
- DBAR 91765 680-D1
- RDL 92373 648-D6
10300 RCUC 91737 573-A2
15000 CHLS 91709 680-G5
RIDGE VIEW CT
600 UPL 91784 572-C3
17600 APLV 92307 4296-G3
W RIDGEVIEW CT
700 SBDO 92407 546-F7
RIDGEVIEW DR
2400 CHLS 91709 681-A5
14500 CHLS 91709 680-J5
RIDGE VIEW DR
16100 APLV 92307 4296-G3
S RIDGE VIEW DR
1700 CLTN 92324 647-A3
RIDGEVIEW PL
36300 YCPA 92399 650-D7
RIDGE VIEW RD
3400 SBdC 92371 4562-J5
8100 SBdC 92345 4565-B3
8200 HESP 92345 4565-B3
RIDGEVIEW RD
56300 YUCA 92284 4887-G5
E RIDGE VIEW RD
2800 SBDO 92346 577-J2
RIDGEWAY RD
8100 RCUC 91701 572-E3
RIDGEWAY ST
100 POM 91768 640-D1
RIDGEWOOD CT
- POM 91766 640-F5
14200 FONT 92337 644-B3
RIDGEWOOD DR
11400 FONT 92337 644-B3
12300 YCPA 92399 648-J4
RIDLEY CT
- SBdC 92371 4653-F3
RIFLE RD
26000 SBdC 92311 3678-J2
RIGEL WY
4800 RivC 91752 683-H3
RIGGINS RD
8200 SBdC 92371 4563-B2
9200 SBdC 92371 4473-B2
11800 SBdC 92371 4383-A2
16100 SBdC 92371 (4293-A4 See Page 4292)
RIGGS RD
67800 SBdC - 330-E7
RILEY WY
- RDL 92374 608-D3
RIM FIRE LN
22100 DBAR 91765 680-A6
RIMFORD PL
24300 DBAR 91765 680-D4
RIMGATE CIR
- POM 91766 640-G5
RIMHURST CT
17900 SBdC 92407 515-B5
RIM OF THE WORLD DR
2300 SBdC - 518-J7
3700 SBdC - 519-F2
3700 SBdC - (4739-J7 See Page 4658)
3700 SBdC - (4740-F4 See Page 4660)
27500 SBdC - 517-J4
38900 SBdC - 4741-A4
RIM OF THE WORLD HWY Rt#-18
- SBDO 92404 546-J5
- SBDO 92404 547-A4
1100 SBdC 92404 516-F5
2100 SBdC - 518-A4
2400 SBdC 92404 546-H1
5700 SBDO 92407 546-H1
23500 SBdC - 516-H5
23500 SBdC - 517-F4
24400 SBdC 92404 517-A5
31500 SBdC - 519-F5
35000 SBdC - 4810-C1
RIMROCK AV
12800 CHLS 91709 640-H7
RIMROCK LN
12400 VCTV 92392 4385-C5
19600 APLV 92307 4297-C3
RIMROCK RD
200 SBdC 92311 3679-D6
1200 BARS 92311 3680-B5
2500 SBdC - 4816-C7
3000 SBdC - 4886-C1
28100 BARS 92311 3679-D6
E RIMROCK RD
200 BARS 92311 3679-H6
1000 SBdC 92311 3680-A6
14600 SBdC 92311 3679-H6
RIMROCK RD E
19600 APLV 92307 4297-D4
RIMROCK RD N
15600 APLV 92307 4297-C4
RIMVIEW CT
12300 YCPA 92399 649-G6
RINA CT
- FONT 92336 574-H2
RINALDI ST
- SBdC - (4025-H2 See Page 3934)
- SBdC - (4026-A2 See Page 3936)
RINCON DR
10000 MohC - 3620-C2
22400 SBdC 92301 (4113-B2 See Page 4112)
RINCON RD
12900 APLV 92308 4387-E3
13600 APLV 92307 4387-E1
14100 APLV 92307 4297-E7
61800 SBdC 92252 4959-C5
RINCON ST
10900 LMLN 92354 607-A7
10900 LMLN 92354 647-A1
RINEHART LN
44600 SBdC - 4812-F2
RING AV
10200 RCUC 91737 573-A5
RING CT
26400 SBdC - (3935-F5 See Page 3934)
RINGE CT
1100 POM 91767 601-C7
RINGSTEM DR
10500 RCUC 91737 573-B1
RINGWOOD TR
300 SBdC 92314 4742-H6
RIO CAMINO CT
11300 FONT 92337 645-A2
RIO GRANDE VISTA RD
- LPCo - 4606-J5
RIO LOBOS RD
22800 DBAR 91765 680-B2
RIO MESA DR
5100 SBdC - 4773-J7
5700 SBdC - 4843-J4
RIO RANCHO RD
100 POM 91766 640-J5
RIO VISTA
1900 NDLS 92363 3620-A6
RIO VISTA DR
5300 SBdC - 4774-F7
6900 HESP 92345 4566-H5
6900 SBdC - 4844-D2
7800 SBdC - 4843-D6
RIO VISTA ST
16900 VCTV 92392 4296-F5
RIO VISTA WY
- SBdC - 4774-F7
RIPON AV
100 SBdC 92284 4747-F4
800 SBdC 92285 4747-F4
S RIPPLING BROOK PL
2700 ONT 91761 643-A6
RIQUEZA RD
22700 SBdC 92301 (4113-F1 See Page 4112)
RISING HILL RD
- POM 91766 640-G4
RITA CT
100 UPL 91784 572-B4
1200 SBDO 92407 546-D5
RITTER PTH
6100 CHLS 91709 712-A5
RITTER ST
500 DBAR 91765 680-B1
14700 VCTV 92394 4295-J3
14800 VCTV 92394 4296-A3
RIVA PL
- RCUC 91701 573-E6
RIVER DR
33700 SBdC - (3681-E7 See Page 3590)
RIVER HWY
- MohC - 3620-E4
RIVER RD
100 NDLS 92363 3620-C4
1900 NDLS 92363 352-A6
2700 NRCO 92880 712-J5
2700 NRCO 92860 712-J5
9000 RivC 92880 712-H5
23100 SBdC - 352-A4
RIVER RD U.S.-66 Hist
1100 NDLS 92363 3620-A3
1500 NDLS 92363 352-A8
RIVER ST
100 NDLS 92363 3620-D5
15700 VCTV 92392 4296-E4
RIVERA CT
8000 FONT 92336 604-B1
RIVERA DR
1000 SBdC 92397 4652-C1
RIVERA ST
500 RIV 92501 645-H6
RIVERBANK RD
- SBdC 92311 3679-A3
RIVER BEND DR
- LPCo - 4606-J5
RIVER DELTA RD
10000 MohC - 3620-D2
RIVERFRONT DR
- PRKR - 4774-H6
200 LPCo - 4774-J5
RIVER OAK LN
28800 HIGH 92346 578-C6
RIVER OAKS DR
- RCUC 91739 573-H7
RIVER RIDGE CT
14600 CHLS 91709 680-J5
RIVER ROCK CT
27600 SBdC - (3935-G3 See Page 3934)
RIVER ROCK DR
- FONT 92336 574-E2
RIVER ROCK RD
27500 SBdC - (3935-G3 See Page 3934)
RIVER RUN CT
7500 HIGH 92346 578-D6
RIVER RUN LN
29000 HIGH 92346 578-C6
RIVERS EDGE RD
13800 SBdC - (3935-F5 See Page 3934)
RIVERSIDE AV
- SBDO 92410 606-E3
100 SBdC - 4742-E7
200 SBdC - 4812-E1
6200 RLTO 92377 575-G3
6200 SBdC 92377 575-G3
11900 CLTN 92324 645-H3
11900 CLTN 92501 645-H3
11900 RLTO 92316 645-H3
11900 RLTO 92324 645-H3
11900 RLTO 92501 645-H3
12800 RivC 92501 645-H3
E RIVERSIDE AV
400 CLTN 92324 606-E4
N RIVERSIDE AV
100 RLTO 92376 605-H1
400 RLTO 92316 575-G5
1500 CLTN 92324 606-E3
1700 SBDO 92410 606-E3
2000 RLTO 92377 575-D1
2100 SBdC 92377 575-D1
3300 RLTO 92377 545-A6
4000 RLTO 92377 544-J5
4100 FONT 92336 544-J5
S RIVERSIDE AV
100 RLTO 92376 605-H5
1700 RLTO 92316 605-H7
2300 RLTO 92316 645-H3
RIVERSIDE CIR
14300 HESP 92345 4475-J4
RIVERSIDE CT
14900 APLV 92307 4296-J6
RIVERSIDE DR
500 BARS 92311 3679-H2
500 BARS 92311 3680-A2
2800 SBdC 91710 641-C7
2900 POM 91766 641-C7
3100 CHNO 91710 641-G7
3100 ONT 91761 643-F7
6100 CHNO 91710 642-A7
6900 CHNO 91710 642-A7
6900 ONT 91762 642-A7
11300 RivC 91752 643-F7
13700 APLV 92307 4387-A1
14300 APLV 92307 4297-A7
14500 APLV 92307 4296-H5
52300 SBdC - 4816-E7
RIVERSIDE DR Rt#-95
- PRKR - 4774-J7
54700 LPCo - 4606-H3
E RIVERSIDE DR
100 ONT 91761 642-D7
100 ONT 91762 642-D7
2700 ONT 91761 643-B7
RIVERSIDE FRWY I-215
- CLTN - 606-G7
- CLTN - 646-E3
- GTER - 646-E3
- RIV - 646-E3
- RivC - 646-E3
- SBDO - 606-G7
RIVERSIDE LN
15000 APLV 92307 4296-H6
RIVERSIDE OH E
2100 RLTO 92377 575-F3
2400 SBdC 92377 575-E2
RIVERSIDE OH W
2000 RLTO 92377 575-F2
2100 SBdC 92377 575-G3
RIVERSIDE RD
14600 APLV 92307 4296-J7
45300 SBdC 92365 3594-D7
47300 SBdC 92365 (3595-D6 See Page 3594)
RIVERSIDE ST
14300 HESP 92345 4475-J4
14600 HESP 92345 4476-A4
RIVERSIDE TR
2900 SBdC 91710 641-B7
RIVERSIDE WY
13000 SBdC 91710 641-B7
15000 APLV 92307 4296-H6
RIVERSIDE DELL
14300 APLV 92307 4387-A1
RIVERSTONE DR
13600 VCTV 92392 4385-F6
RIVERTON RD
- SBdC - (3846-C6 See Page 3756)
RIVERVIEW AV
10500 HESP 92345 4477-B2
RIVERVIEW DR
200 RDL 92374 608-C3
12800 SBdC 92392 4387-A3
E RIVERVIEW DR
1200 SBDO 92408 607-C4
RIVERVIEW LN
1100 NDLS 92363 3710-D1
35400 SBdC 92311 3678-E3
35400 SBdC 92347 3678-E3
RIVERVIEW RD
15300 SBdC - 3936-A4
17700 SBdC - (3846-G2 See Page 3756)
20100 SBdC 92308 4567-F2
RIVER VIEW RD
20700 SBdC - (3677-D4 See Page 3586)
20800 SBdC 92311 (3677-D4 See Page 3586)
21700 SBdC 92347 (3677-D4 See Page 3586)
22500 SBdC 92311 3678-A4
RIVERWALK DR
- SBDO 92408 606-F4
RIVERWOOD DR
- FONT 92336 574-G2
RIVERWOOD PL
5800 RCUC 91737 573-A3
E RIVERWOOD ST
2200 CLTN 92324 606-H7
RIVIERA CT
14100 VCTV 92392 4386-D2
RIVIERA DR
200 SBdC - 517-F1
300 SBdC - 4737-F7
1600 UPL 91784 572-E6
13700 VCTV 92392 4386-D2
RIVIERA LN
15500 FONT 92337 644-F4
ROAD A
40000 SBdC - (4393-H3 See Page 4302)
ROAD B
38000 SBdC - (4392-E7 See Page 4302)
ROAD C
11400 SBdC - (4392-J2 See Page 4302)
11400 SBdC - (4393-A4 See Page 4302)
ROADRUNNER CT
8400 SBdC 92371 4564-C3
N ROADRUNNER CT
2800 SBDO 92346 577-F2
ROAD RUNNER DR
7200 SBdC 92277 4893-D7
7200 TNP 92277 4893-D7
ROADRUNNER LN
12200 VCTV 92392 4385-C6
63800 SBdC 92252 4959-G5
ROAD RUNNER LN
14600 CHLS 91709 680-G5
62800 SBdC 92252 4959-E5
ROADRUNNER RD
- SBdC 92347 3588-F6
- YUCA 92284 4887-G3
4700 FONT 92336 544-E7
4700 SBDO 92336 544-E7
34100 BARS 92311 3678-F6
ROAD RUNNER ST
28300 SBdC 92308 4479-H7
ROADRUNNER RUT RD
- SBdC - 4816-F4
ROAN CIR
15000 VCTV 92394 4295-H6
ROAN CT
5000 RCUC 91737 (543-C7 See Page 513)
5000 RCUC 91737 573-C1
ROAN RD
- CHLS 91709 681-H7
12800 APLV 92308 4387-B4
14100 VCTV 92394 4295-H6
E ROAN ST
2800 ONT 91761 643-A7
ROANOAK WY
15300 CHLS 91709 681-D6
ROANOKE RD
1800 CLAR 91711 571-C7
1800 CLAR 91711 601-C1
14300 FONT 92336 574-C7
19200 APLV 92307 4297-B3
ROBBINS DR
36600 SBdC 92311 3589-G7
N ROBERDS AV
500 SBDO 92411 576-E7
3000 SBDO 92405 576-D2
ROBERDS CT
9500 RCUC 91701 572-H6
9900 RCUC 91701 573-A6
ROBERDS ST
7200 RCUC 91701 572-F6
ROBERT WY
9400 RivC 92509 644-C7
ROBERTA CT
- BARS 92311 3679-J4
S ROBERTA CT
300 SBDO 92410 606-C2
W ROBERTA CT
700 CLTN 92324 606-C3
ROBERTA ST
- BARS 92311 3679-J4
1100 BARS 92311 3680-A4
ROBERT CRITES LN
1400 CLTN 92324 606-A4
ROBERTS AV
6900 TNP 92277 4892-G7
ROBERTS CT
300 CALI 92320 649-J7
N ROBERTS CT
- RLTO 92376 575-G7
ROBERTS PL
6100 RCUC 91739 573-H4
ROBERTS RD
200 RDL 92373 647-J2
4900 YUCA 92284 4887-J4
13300 YCPA 92399 650-B6
ROBERTS ST
7900 HIGH 92346 577-E7
7900 SBDO 92409 577-E7
ROBERTSON RD
55900 SBdC 92284 4817-E4
ROBIN CT
13100 CHNO 91710 642-A7
13100 CHNO 91710 682-A1
13300 YCPA 92399 649-H6
26400 LMLN 92354 647-F2
ROBIN DR
600 SBdC - 517-F3
11600 FONT 92337 644-F3
33300 SBdC - 519-E3
ROBIN LN
8000 YUCA 92284 4957-C4
12900 CHNO 91710 642-A7
14500 SBdC - (3935-H2 See Page 3934)
16800 VCTV 92392 4386-F5
33000 SBdC - 519-D6
N ROBIN LN
6200 SBDO 92407 546-A3
ROBIN MTWY
- BREA 92823 710-D3
- LACo 92823 710-D3
ROBIN RD
- SBDO 92407 545-J3
- SBDO 92407 546-A3
1000 SBdC 92397 4652-C2
7300 TNP 92277 4893-B7
7300 TNP 92277 4962-G1
38900 BBLK - 4811-A2
N ROBIN RD
5900 SBDO 92407 546-A3
ROBIN WY
22500 GTER 92313 646-F6
ROBINBROOK PL
23400 DBAR 91765 680-C3
ROBIN CIRCLE LN
1000 SBdC 92397 4652-C2
ROBIN CREST LN
14000 CHLS 91709 680-J3
ROBINESS RD
- SBdC 92285 (4577-H7 See Page 4486)
ROBIN HILL RD
28300 SBdC 92308 4479-H7
W ROBINHOOD BLVD
800 SBdC 92314 4742-B6
ROBIN HOOD DR
1000 SBdC - 4738-B6
ROBINHOOD LN
400 RDL 92373 648-A2
ROBINIA ST
8900 SBdC 92335 604-D2
ROBINOAK DR
5800 SBdC - 4950-F1
ROBIN OAKS TER
22400 DBAR 91765 680-A4
ROBINSON
- SBdC 92284 4748-G6
ROBINSON CT
- CHLS 91709 711-G3
ROBINSON DR
- SBdC 92277 4820-F4
- SBdC 92277 4890-G7
N ROBINSON RD
6500 HIGH 92346 577-F4
ROBINSON RANCH RD
14400 SBdC - (4115-H4 See Page 4114)
ROBLE AV
9000 HESP 92345 4477-B7
ROBLES DR
4100 SBdC 92301 4112-J3
ROBUFFA ST
100 NDLS 92363 3620-E6
ROBYN ST
1500 RDL 92374 608-C5
ROCA CIR
- SBdC 92404 577-D4
ROCCA CT
13500 VCTV 92392 4386-C3
ROCHELLE CT
- SBDO 92407 546-D5
ROCHESTER AV
- ONT 91761 643-E4
6000 RCUC 91737 573-F5
6300 RCUC 91701 573-F5
7300 RCUC 91739 573-E7
7400 RCUC 91739 573-E7
7600 RCUC 91730 603-E3
7600 RCUC 91739 603-E3
12600 SBdC 92371 4384-A6
S ROCHESTER AV
100 ONT 91761 603-F7
100 ONT 91761 643-E1
ROCHESTER CT
9100 RCUC 91730 603-E4
ROCHESTER RD
700 ONT 91764 603-F6
8400 SBdC 92371 4564-A1
9000 SBdC 92371 4474-A1
11900 SBdC 92371 4384-A3
18500 SBdC 92301 (4203-J5 See Page 4112)
ROCK CT
4900 RivC 91752 683-H3
ROCK DR
9400 SBdC 92339 611-H3
ROCK LN
52100 SBdC - 4886-E3
ROCK ST
10300 SBdC 92359 608-J6
ROCKAWAY AV
7500 YUCA 92284 4957-B4
ROCKAWAY RD
19500 APLV 92307 4297-C3
ROCK BLUFF RD
- POM 91766 640-G4
ROCKBRIDGE RD
400 DBAR 91765 640-A6
ROCKBURY DR
24400 DBAR 91765 640-E7
ROCKBUSH RD
10300 APLV 92308 4478-A4
ROCKCLIFF PL
- POM 91766 640-G7
ROCK CORRAL RD
4900 SBdC 92285 (4575-J5 See Page 4484)
ROCK CREEK RD
5400 RCUC 91737 573-G2
ROCK CREST CT
29100 HIGH 92346 578-D6
ROCK CREST LN
- POM 91766 640-J7
7500 HIGH 92346 578-D6
12800 CHLS 91709 640-J7
ROCKDALE ST
1200 UPL 91784 571-H5
S ROCKEFELLER AV
100 ONT 91761 603-E7
100 ONT 91761 643-E2
ROCKFORD AV
2200 SBDO 92346 577-F3
6700 HIGH 92346 577-F4
N ROCKFORD AV
2900 SBDO 92346 577-F2
ROCKFORD DR
300 CLAR 91711 601-E1
13700 VCTV 92392 4386-D2
ROCKFORD LN
11300 SBdC 91766 641-D3
ROCKFORD ST
26100 BARS 92311 (3759-A5 See Page 3758)
ROCK HAVEN RD
8300 SBdC 92252 4959-H5
ROCK HILL DR
- SBdC 92301 (4024-B1 See Page 3934)
22100 SBdC 92308 4478-A6
ROCKING CHAIR RD
63300 SBdC 92252 4959-H4
ROCKINGHORSE CT
12500 VCTV 92392 4385-G5
ROCKING HORSE RD
20600 SBdC - (3937-E2 See Page 3936)
ROCK KNOLL CT
- SBdC - 517-H1
ROCKLAND AV
- SBdC - 4480-D2
ROCKLAND RD
9800 SBdC - 4480-E4
ROCKLEDGE DR
13600 VCTV 92392 4385-G6
ROCKLEDGE LN
- SBdC - 518-A2
ROCKMONT AV
700 LACo 91711 571-C7
ROCK RIDGE DR
1300 SBdC - 4737-G5
ROCKRIDGE DR
11900 FONT 92337 644-D4
ROCKRIDGE LN
11300 FONT 92337 644-D2
14800 FONT 92337 644-D4
ROCK RIDGE RD
100 SBdC 92372 4472-A5
ROCK RIDGE WY
1500 SBdC - 4737-H5
16600 CHLS 91709 710-F2
ROCK RIVER DR
100 DBAR 91765 640-B6
ROCK RIVER RD
200 DBAR 91765 640-B7
400 DBAR 91765 680-A1
ROCKROSE AV
6500 RCUC 91739 573-G4
ROCKROSE ST
- CHNO 91710 642-B7
- VCTV 92394 4295-J7
- VCTV 92394 4296-A7
ROCK ROSE ST
35300 SBdC - (4301-G4 See Page 4300)
ROCKSPRAY CT
1400 BBLK - 4812-C4
ROCKSPRAY DR
1400 BBLK - 4812-C4
ROCKSPRING LN
6800 HIGH 92346 578-C5
ROCK SPRINGS AV
- BARS 92311 3758-H2
ROCK SPRINGS DR
2300 CHLS 91709 640-J7
2300 CHLS 91709 680-J1
2500 CHLS 91709 641-A7
ROCK SPRINGS OH S
19800 SBdC 92308 4477-E7
S ROCK SPRINGS PL
2500 ONT 91761 643-B5
ROCK SPRINGS RD
- SBdC 92277 4821-D6
18700 HESP 92345 4477-B7
19500 SBdC 92345 4477-E7
19600 SBdC 92308 4477-F7
ROCKVIEW DR
5600 SBdC 92371 4563-E7
24100 SBdC - 516-J4
ROCKVIEW WY
- POM 91766 641-A4
ROCK VILLE RD
- SBdC - 4570-H3
ROCK VISTA LN
16200 CHLS 91709 710-F2
ROCKWELL AV
15300 FONT 92336 574-E4
ROCKWELL RD
22300 SBdC - 516-D3
ROCKWOOD RD
- SBdC 92284 4818-G4
2900 SBdC 92252 4818-G6
6400 SBdC 92252 4888-H7
7600 SBdC 92252 4958-H3
ROCKY LN
3200 ONT 91761 643-B7
ROCKY LP
600 SBdC - 516-J3
S ROCKY PL
3500 ONT 91761 683-B1
ROCKY RD
- UPL 91784 571-H6
7900 TNP 92277 4962-F2
ROCKY WY
3200 ONT 91761 643-B7
ROCKY DELL RD
23600 SBdC - 516-H3
ROCKY MOUNTAIN PL
5200 RCUC 91737 573-A1
W ROCKY MOUNTAIN RD
1000 SBdC 92314 4742-B5
ROCKY POINT DR
46000 SBdC - (4743-A3 See Page 4662)
46000 SBdC - 4742-J2
ROCKY POINT RD
100 SBdC - 517-H2
46000 SBdC - (4743-B2 See Page 4662)
ROCKY POINT WY
100 SBdC - 517-J5
ROCKY RIDGE RD
62500 SBdC 92252 4959-D4
ROCKY RIDGE RANCH RD
- TNP 92277 4961-A1
ROCKY TRAIL RD
2600 DBAR 91765 680-A6
ROCKY VIEW RD
- SBdC - 3762-H3
2000 DBAR 91765 680-B5
ROCKY VISTA ST
61300 SBdC 92252 4889-A7
RODDICK DR
6900 HIGH 92346 578-C5
RODELL PL
16200 VCTV 92392 4386-D6
RODEO CIR
10300 ADEL 92301 4204-G5
W RODEO CT
1200 UPL 91786 571-J7
RODEO DR
- LPCo - 4843-E7
- LPCo - 4844-B5
- SBdC - 3756-J7
- SBdC - (3846-J2 See Page 3756)
5800 RivC 92509 645-C7
12500 RCUC 91739 573-G4
13700 VCTV 92392 4386-E2
14400 VCTV 92392 4296-E7
S RODEO PL
3100 ONT 91761 643-A7
RODEO RD
- RCUC 91737 573-C1
10100 SBdC 92345 4564-H4
10900 SBdC 92345 4565-A4
14700 HESP 92345 4566-A4
16600 SBdC - (4211-C7 See Page 4120)
16600 SBdC - (4301-C1 See Page 4300)
27300 SBdC - 3936-J3
28200 SBdC - (3846-J7 See Page 3756)
34900 SBdC - (4391-F6 See Page 4300)
35500 YCPA 92399 650-B2
35900 SBdC - (4392-A6 See Page 4302)
RODEO ST
4200 MTCL 91763 641-E2
4200 SBdC 91766 641-D2
16100 HESP 92345 4566-D4
RODEO WY
14700 FONT 92336 574-D1
RODERICK AV
500 POM 91767 601-A4
RODGER RD
55700 SBdC 92284 4817-E2
RODGERS CT
7600 FONT 92336 574-B7
RODGERS LN
36400 YCPA 92399 650-D1
RODMAN AV
1000 POM 91767 601-B6
ROGER CT
500 POM 91766 641-A6
ROGERS AL
600 SBDO 92401 576-G7
ROGERS LN
- SBdC 92277 4820-F4
300 CALI 92320 649-J7
1300 SBDO 92404 577-D5
5900 SBdC 92404 577-D2
6900 HIGH 92404 577-D5
7300 HIGH 92410 577-D6
13900 VCTV 92392 4385-G4
69700 SBdC 92277 4821-D4
N ROGERS LN
1600 SBDO 92404 577-D4
ROGERS ST
25800 HIGH 92404 577-D5
ROLAR AV
7600 SBdC 92345 4565-C4
ROLLING GREENS DR
11500 APLV 92308 4477-D2
ROLLING HILLS CT
- RCUC 91739 573-H7
ROLLING HILLS DR
- POM 91766 640-G5
ROLLING HILLS RD
1300 RDL 92374 648-E1
ROLLING KNOLL RD
1300 DBAR 91765 680-C3
ROLLING MEADOW DR
2800 CHLS 91709 681-A1
ROLLING RIDGE DR
- POM 91766 640-F6
12600 SBdC 92392 4386-J5
12600 SBdC 92392 4387-A4
14700 CHLS 91709 681-D5
ROLLING VILLAGE DR
2800 CHLS 91709 681-A1
ROLLING WOOD CIR
2600 CHLS 91709 681-A2
ROLLINS CT
10900 RCUC 91701 573-C5
ROLLINS WY
800 SBDO 92408 607-A4
2100 POM 91767 601-A5

STREET
Block City ZIP Pg-Grid

ROMA PL
1200 POM 91766 640-D3
6900 RCUC 91701 573-D5
ROMA ST
- RDL 92373 648-A1
ROMAN PL
700 SBdC - 518-A3
ROME CT
6400 YUCA 92284 4887-J7
ROMERO RD
26600 SBdC 92373 647-G2
ROMERO RANCH RD
- SBdC 92311 3590-A7
- SBdC 92311 3680-A1
ROMNAH RD
- SBdC - 4736-D7
ROMO RD
600 SBDO 92410 577-C7
RONALD DR
6200 YUCA 92284 4888-D7
RONDA CT
500 CALI 92320 650-C7
ROOSEVELT AV
200 POM 91767 601-A6
2100 SBDO 92411 576-B4
ROOSEVELT CT
600 RDL 92374 648-D1
4300 CHNO 91710 641-E6
ROOSEVELT LN
- SBdC - 2971-F3
ROOSEVELT RD
500 RDL 92374 648-D1
ROOSEVELT ST
4300 CHNO 91710 641-E6
RORICK WY
70900 SBdC 92277 4821-G4
72100 SBdC 92277 4822-A4
RORIMER DR
2000 RivC 92509 645-B5
ROSA CT
6000 CHNO 91710 641-J7
W ROSA CT
100 CLTN 92324 646-C4
100 SBdC 92324 646-C4
ROSA DR
- RCUC 91701 573-F5
ROSADO LN
- SBdC 92301 (4113-D1
See Page 4112)
ROSADO RD
11400 SBdC 92372 4472-E2
12000 SBdC 92372 4382-E4
ROSALIE AV
11300 APLV 92308 4477-F1
ROSALIE CT
1300 RDL 92374 608-E5
N ROSALIND AV
500 SBDO 92376 576-A7
1000 RLTO 92376 576-A6
S ROSALIND ST
300 SBDO 92376 606-A2
ROSARIO ST
5900 CHNO 91710 641-J7
ROSARITA DR
11100 LMLN 92354 647-A1
W ROSARITA ST
2500 SBDO 92407 546-A6
2600 SBDO 92407 545-J6
ROSE AV
1900 UPL 91784 572-A5
8900 MTCL 91763 601-G4
10500 MTCL 91763 641-G1
10700 SBdC 91762 641-G2
13800 SBdC 92337 644-F1
19000 SBdC 92316 645-F1
19300 RLTO 92316 645-F1
ROSE CT
- FONT 92337 644-J2
7800 HIGH 92346 578-C7
10700 ADEL 92301 4294-H6
ROSE DR
9700 SBdC 92345 4474-H6
ROSE LN
- SBdC - 518-C1
500 SBdC - 517-E3
10700 SBdC 91762 641-G2
18100 SBdC 92316 645-C1
36300 SBdC 92311 3680-D1
39700 SBdC - (4392-J7
See Page 4302)
40100 SBdC - (4483-A1
See Page 4482)
ROSE PL
10800 ADEL 92301 4294-J6
13600 VCTV 92392 4386-E2
ROSE ST
1200 SBdC 92359 609-B5
1300 SBdC 92397 4652-D2
17700 HESP 92345 4476-H7
W ROSE ST
900 CLTN 92324 606-B4
ROSEBAY ST
3800 CHLS 91709 681-D7
ROSEBRIAR DR
12200 YCPA 92399 649-D3
ROSEBUD CT
- CHLS 91709 711-H2
ROSEBUD DR
400 RivC 91752 683-E4
ROSEBUD ST
7900 RCUC 91701 572-D3

ROSECLIFF CIR
- RivC 92880 683-D4
ROSECREST AV
7300 FONT 92336 575-B6
8900 FONT 92335 605-B3
ROSECREST LN
7600 SBdC 92336 575-B7
S ROSEDALE AV
1800 CLTN 92313 646-C4
1800 CLTN 92324 646-C4
1800 GTER 92313 646-C4
2100 GTER 92324 646-C4
2100 SBdC 92324 646-C4
ROSEDALE CUR
2300 SBdC 91784 572-A3
W ROSEDALE CUR
2300 SBdC 91784 571-J3
2300 SBdC 91784 572-A3
ROSEDALE DR
11100 ADEL 92301 4294-J7
11200 ADEL 92301 4295-A7
ROSE EDEN DR
8500 SBdC 92256 4956-F7
8900 SBdC 92256 616-F2
ROSE ELLEN AV
5900 TNP 92277 4892-C4
ROSEGATE PL
24400 DBAR 91765 640-E6
ROSEHEDGE AV
4300 SBdC 92252 4890-B1
ROSE HILL DR
600 SBdC - 516-G3
11900 FONT 92337 644-C4
N ROSE HILL DR
100 SBdC 92314 4742-D6
S ROSE HILL DR
100 SBdC 92314 4742-D6
ROSEHILL CREST
1400 RDL 92373 648-A4
ROSELAWN ST
100 POM 91768 640-D2
ROSELLA DR
49500 SBdC 92256 615-H6
ROSEMARIE LN
61800 SBdC 92252 4959-B6
ROSEMARY AV
35800 SBdC - (3681-J1
See Page 3590)
ROSEMARY CT
6600 RCUC 91739 573-G5
ROSEMARY DR
6700 CHNO 91710 642-B7
13200 CHNO 91710 682-B1
13900 SBdC 92335 604-B6
14700 VCTV 92394 4295-J7
16100 FONT 92335 604-H6
26400 HIGH 92346 577-F5
ROSEMARY LN
16700 CHLS 91709 710-F3
W ROSEMARY LN
100 RLTO 92376 605-G1
2400 SBDO 92407 546-A3
2600 SBDO 92407 545-H2
ROSEMIST LN
1600 CHLS 91709 680-G4
ROSEMOND ST
33300 YCPA 92399 649-E4
ROSEMONT DR
34200 YCPA 92399 649-H6
ROSEMOUNT AV
1800 CLAR 91711 571-C7
ROSENA AV
1800 SBDO 92354 607-D5
6300 SBdC 92404 577-D3
8500 FONT 92335 604-J2
ROSENA CIR
- FONT 92337 644-J2
ROSEQUARTZ DR
500 SBdC - 518-B3
ROSETOWN AV
- FONT 92336 574-D1
ROSETTA LN
- CHLS 91709 681-H7
ROSETTE ST
1100 RDL 92373 648-D2
ROSE VISTA RD
12900 SBdC 92371 4383-C5
ROSEWOOD AV
10800 SBdC 92256 615-G5
ROSEWOOD CIR
300 RivC 91752 683-F5
E ROSEWOOD CT
100 ONT 91764 602-C6
W ROSEWOOD CT
200 RLTO 92376 575-G7
500 ONT 91762 602-A6
1200 ONT 91762 601-H6
ROSEWOOD DR
100 CALI 92320 650-A7
14100 HESP 92345 4475-H7
25600 LMLN 92354 607-D6
E ROSEWOOD DR
900 SBDO 92408 607-B6
ROSEWOOD LN
2400 SBdC 91784 572-B3
28300 SBdC - 4738-A6
29000 HIGH 92346 578-C5
ROSEWOOD PL
6900 RCUC 91739 573-G6

ROSEWOOD ST
1500 UPL 91784 571-H6
4300 MTCL 91763 601-E6
21100 APLV 92308 4477-H3
35700 SBdC - (4571-H1
See Page 4570)
E ROSEWOOD ST
100 RLTO 92376 575-H7
1300 CLTN 92324 606-F4
W ROSEWOOD ST
100 RLTO 92376 575-D7
ROSEWOOD WY
4000 CHLS 91709 681-D5
N ROSEWOOD WY
1700 UPL 91784 571-H6
W ROSEWOOD WY
1300 UPL 91784 571-H6
ROSS AV
12400 CHNO 91710 641-J6
ROSS CT
200 CLAR 91711 601-D1
9900 ADEL 92301 4204-F4
14200 RCUC 91739 574-B2
ROSS LN
35100 YCPA 92399 650-A6
ROSS PKWY
1800 SBdC 92363 3620-B4
ROSS PL
12300 YCPA 92399 649-B4
ROSS ST
- YUCA 92284 4957-J6
- YUCA 92284 4958-A6
1200 POM 91767 601-C7
1400 SBdC 92397 4652-E2
ROSSANO DR
11600 RCUC 91701 573-E4
ROSSMONT DR
1600 RDL 92373 648-F4
ROSWELL AV
10900 SBdC 91766 641-D3
11400 SBdC 91710 641-D5
12100 CHNO 91710 641-D6
13100 SBdC 91710 681-D1
13300 CHNO 91710 681-D1
ROSWELL CT
3900 SBdC 91710 641-D4
ROSWELL RD
11300 SBdC 92371 4472-J2
12400 SBdC 92371 4382-J7
ROTARY WY
6100 SBdC 92277 4890-E6
ROTHCHILD CT
14000 FONT 92336 604-C1
ROTHCHILD ST
14000 FONT 92336 604-B1
ROTTERDAM
13900 CHNO 91710 682-A2
ROUND DR
100 BBLK - 4741-B7
100 BBLK - 4811-B1
ROUND MOUNTAIN CT
15800 VCTV 92394 4295-F4
ROUND MOUNTAIN RD
13300 VCTV 92394 4295-F4
ROUND MOUNTAIN WY
15800 VCTV 92394 4295-F4
ROUND TREE CT
11500 RivC 91752 683-G4
ROUNDTREE LN
4300 CHNO 91710 641-E5
ROUND-UP CT
14600 VCTV 92394 4295-H7
ROUNDUP DR
9300 MTCL 91763 601-F5
ROUNDUP LN
5200 FONT 92336 574-D2
ROUNDUP RD
2400 NRCO 92860 712-J7
4400 TNP 92277 4892-H1
28100 SBdC - 3936-J1
28300 SBdC - (3846-J7
See Page 3756)
ROUND-UP RD
14300 VCTV 92394 4295-H7
ROUNDUP WY
19900 SBdC 92308 4477-E6
21900 SBdC 92308 4478-B6
25500 SBdC 92308 4479-D5
ROUNER DR
6000 RivC 92509 645-E4
ROUSELLE DR
10200 RivC 91752 644-A5
10500 RivC 91752 643-J5
ROUSE RANCH RD
29200 SBdC - 4738-D6
ROUTE 210 FRWY
- POM - 640-C1
- SDMS - 640-C1
ROVATO PL
6800 RCUC 91701 573-E5
ROWAN AV
19600 SBdC 92377 575-G3
ROWELL RD
4900 YUCA 92284 4887-H3
ROWLEY DR
15400 VCTV 92394 4295-H5
ROX RD
- SBdC 92308 4567-D6

ROXANNE RD
22300 RivC 92324 647-A6
ROXBURY AV
10500 SBdC 92316 605-D7
10800 SBdC 92316 645-D1
ROXBURY CT
1500 UPL 91784 571-H4
ROXBURY DR
700 SBDO 92404 577-A5
N ROXBURY DR
2200 SBDO 92404 577-A3
ROXBURY PL
7300 RCUC 91730 573-C7
ROXBURY RD
22500 APLV 92307 4298-B6
24100 SBdC 92307 4298-F6
ROY ST
300 SBdC 92347 349-A7
ROYAL AV
12700 GTER 92313 646-D5
ROYAL CT
3100 CHLS 91709 681-B2
ROYAL WY
9800 RCUC 91730 572-J7
ROYAL COACH AV
200 POM 91767 601-A5
ROYAL CREST CT
- FONT 92336 574-D5
ROYAL CREST PL
- FONT 92336 574-D5
ROYALE DR
26200 LMLN 92354 647-F3
ROYAL OAKS CT
33300 YCPA 92399 649-F4
ROYAL PALM CIR
12900 CHNO 91710 641-F7
ROYAL PINE CIR
4300 RivC 92509 644-D7
ROYAL RIDGE DR
3100 CHLS 91709 681-C2
ROYAL SPRINGS RD
8600 SBdC 92284 4957-B6
8600 YUCA 92284 4957-B6
ROYAL TROONE CT
- CHLS 91709 711-F1
ROYALTY DR
1900 POM 91767 601-A6
ROYALWOODS CIR
300 RivC 91752 683-E5
ROYAN LN
48900 SBdC 92365 (3595-C4
See Page 3594)
ROYCE AV
7900 HESP 92345 4567-B2
ROYCE LN
26800 HIGH 92346 577-G7
ROY ROGERS DR
14900 VCTV 92394 4296-B7
15700 VCTV 92392 4296-B3
ROY ROGERS RD
- SBdC - (4115-G3
See Page 4114)
4900 SBdC - 4886-H4
ROZANNE DR
- SBdC 92365 (3593-H5
See Page 3592)
RUBEN WY
42500 BBLK - 4812-A1
RUBICON CT
- FONT 92336 574-B6
RUBICON ST
21200 APLV 92307 (4117-G4
See Page 4116)
RUBIDOUX AV
7000 YUCA 92284 4958-C2
RUBIDOUX BLVD
1000 RivC 92509 645-E4
RUBIDOUX CT
58300 YUCA 92284 4958-C6
RUBY AV
300 RDL 92374 608-B5
7300 RCUC 91730 572-H7
RUBY CIR
13600 VCTV 92392 4385-G7
RUBY CT
1300 UPL 91784 571-H5
7800 HIGH 92346 578-C7
RUBY DR
- SBdC 92277 4893-C2
2000 BARS 92311 3679-G6
79700 SBdC 92277 (4894-B1
See Page 4824)
RUBY LN
12300 YCPA 92399 649-C4
39400 BBLK - 4811-B2
60600 SBdC 92284 4748-H5
RUBY ST
1200 RivC 92507 646-B6
RUBY CANYON RD
4900 SBdC 92285 (4575-E7
See Page 4484)
RUBY GLEN CT
13000 CHLS 91709 680-G3
RUDEC RD
- SBdC - (4390-J6
See Page 4300)
34400 SBdC - (4391-E6
See Page 4300)
RUDISILL ST
4100 MTCL 91763 601-D7

RUDY OLIVERAS CT
1000 CLTN 92324 606-F5
W RUE CIR
2800 SBDO 92376 576-A7
RUE WY
11900 RCUC 91739 573-F7
RUEDA LN
700 BBLK - 4810-J2
RUFFERNELL RD
5000 TNP 92277 4891-J3
RUFINO PL
- RCUC 91701 573-E4
N RUGBY WY
1200 UPL 91786 602-A1
S RUIC RD GAS
COMPANY RD
- SBdC - (4025-J7
See Page 3934)
- SBdC - (4115-J2
See Page 4114)
RUIDOSA AV
3500 SBdC 92284 4818-A7
3700 SBdC 92284 4888-A1
RUIZ ST
500 RDL 92374 608-B7
N RUNAWAY CIR
1100 CLTN 92324 605-J4
RUNNING BREEZE
21800 APLV 92307 4297-J5
22200 APLV 92307 4298-A5
RUNNING BREEZE RD
24600 SBdC 92307 4298-G4
RUNNING BROOK WY
15200 CHLS 91709 680-G6
RUNNING CREEK LN
1200 UPL 91784 571-J4
5200 RCUC 91737 573-B2
RUNNING DEER RD
11800 APLV 92308 4387-H5
RUNNING FAWN CT
5200 RCUC 91737 573-B1
RUNNING QUAIL RD
10900 SBdC 92399 610-J6
RUNNING SPRINGS DR
13500 CHLS 91709 681-A2
RUNNING SPRINGS LN
100 SBdC - 516-C2
RUNNING SPRINGS
ACCESS RD
- SBdC - 519-B6
RUNWAY AV
6600 FONT 92336 574-E5
W RUSH AV
3500 SBDO 92405 576-G1
RUSH RD
22500 SBdC 92308 4478-B6
S RUSH CREEK WY
2500 ONT 91761 643-C5
RUSHMORE CT
4300 CHNO 91710 641-E7
RUSHMORE DR
2000 BARS 92311 3680-A6
RUSSELL AV
12300 CHNO 91710 641-F7
RUSSELL LN
32600 SBdC - 4480-J2
RUSSELL PL
600 POM 91767 601-A6
RUSSET PL
- ADEL 92301 4295-A7
RUSSIAN RIVER LN
2800 ONT 91761 643-D6
RUSSO CT
17200 FONT 92336 575-A6
RUSSO ST
17100 FONT 92336 574-J6
17100 FONT 92336 575-A6
RUST CT
1400 CLAR 91711 601-C1
RUSTIC BRDG
2900 CHLS 91709 681-A1
RUSTIC CT
1500 DBAR 91765 680-D3
27900 SBdC - (3935-J2
See Page 3934)
RUSTIC DR
11900 FONT 92337 644-C4
14700 CHLS 91709 681-B5
RUSTIC LN
27300 HIGH 92346 577-H6
RUSTIC PL
11700 FONT 92337 644-C3
RUSTIC WY
- SBdC - 518-A2
RUSTIC CANYON RD
46000 SBdC - 4742-J2
46000 SBdC - (4743-A2
See Page 4662)
RUSTIC GLEN DR
- POM 91766 640-F6
RUSTIC OAK CT
12600 RCUC 91739 573-G4
RUSTIC OAK TR
13000 VCTV 92392 4385-D6
RUSTY CT
12100 APLV 92308 4388-A6
RUSTY PUMP RD
23500 DBAR 91765 680-C5
RUSTY SPUR RD
2000 DBAR 91765 680-B4

RUTGERS CT
1600 CLAR 91711 601-B1
RUTH DR
6200 YUCA 92284 4888-E7
RUTH LN
1000 SBdC 92284 4817-D1
12400 YCPA 92399 649-E4
RUTH WY
1200 UPL 91784 571-J5
RUTHANN DR
3300 RivC 92509 645-C7
RUTHIES RD
- SBdC 92277 4821-F3
RUTLEDGE CT
- RCUC 91730 573-E1
RV CENTER DR
1200 CLTN 92324 646-E2
RYAN ST
- RDL 92374 608-F7
10500 SBdC 92256 615-H5
RYAN WY
2200 UPL 91784 571-J3
19700 APLV 92308 4387-D2
RYELAND RD
6500 SBdC 92345 4565-B6
16700 HESP 92345 4566-F5
RYERSON AV
33400 SBdC - (3681-F7
See Page 3590)

S

S WY
1500 SBdC - 4737-G4
SABADO RD
44400 SBdC 92365 (3684-C4
See Page 3594)
SABANA DR
23200 DBAR 91765 640-B7
23200 DBAR 91765 680-B1
SABINA AV
8800 HESP 92345 4476-J7
9300 HESP 92345 4477-A6
SABLE CT
14900 CHLS 91709 681-C5
56700 YUCA 92284 4887-H5
SABRE BLVD
200 VCTV 92394 4205-E5
SABRE RD
17400 APLV 92307 4207-G4
SABRELINER CT
- SBDO 92409 577-F7
SABRE MOUNTAIN AV
62100 SBdC 92252 4889-C2
SAC RD
21200 APLV 92308 4387-H7
SACRAMENTO AV
5800 RCUC 91701 572-G3
7700 RCUC 91730 602-G1
N SACRAMENTO AV
800 ONT 91764 602-G4
S SACRAMENTO AV
1600 ONT 91761 642-G3
SACRAMENTO CT
12500 SBdC 92372 4382-A7
N SACRAMENTO PL
1400 ONT 91764 602-G5
S SACRAMENTO PL
2600 ONT 91761 642-G6
SACRAMENTO RD
200 SBdC 92372 4382-E6
2900 SBdC 92371 4382-G6
3800 SBdC 92371 4383-A6
SACRAMENTO ST
14100 FONT 92336 604-B1
SACRED HEART PL
- RCUC 91739 603-G1
SADDLE AV
25200 SBdC 92301 368-J2
SADDLE LN
13300 CHNO 91710 681-C1
19100 APLV 92308 4387-B6
26800 SBdC - (3935-G2
See Page 3934)
51700 SBdC - 4816-D6
SADDLE RD
7300 RCUC 91730 572-H7
SADDLEBACK AV
- TNP 92278 4822-F2
300 SBdC 92252 4748-J6
SADDLEBACK PL
6800 RCUC 91701 572-G6
12900 CHNO 91710 641-F7
SADDLEBACK RD
700 SBdC 92252 4748-J7
2100 SBdC 92252 4818-J3
5700 SBdC 92252 4889-A6
6500 SBdC 92252 4959-A2
SADDLEBACK ST
4500 MTCL 91763 641-E3
SADDLEBOW TR
28500 SBdC - (3846-A7
See Page 3756)
SADDLEBRED CT
- RivC 92880 683-D7
SADDLEBROOK PL
28300 HIGH 92346 578-A4

SADDLE DIKE
EMBANKMENT
19000 SBdC - (4657-C3
See Page 4656)
19000 SBdC 92345 (4657-C3
See Page 4656)
SADDLEHILL TER
10100 RCUC 91737 573-A3
SADDLEHORN DR
12600 RCUC 91739 573-G4
SADDLE HORN RD
74300 TNP 92277 4892-G1
SADDLEPEAK CT
14600 FONT 92336 574-C2
SADDLEPEAK DR
14500 FONT 92336 574-C2
SADDLERIDGE DR
- RCUC 91739 573-H6
SADDLE ROCK WY
48100 SBdC 92285 (4575-C5
See Page 4484)
SADDLEWOOD PL
- POM 91766 640-G7
4900 RCUC 91737 572-J1
S SADDLEWOOD ST
700 CLTN 92324 606-H7
SAED ST
700 POM 91768 640-E1
SAFARI DR
100 NDLS 92363 3710-D1
SAFFRON AV
28300 HIGH 92346 578-B4
SAFFRON CT
12600 RCUC 91739 573-G5
SAFIRO CT
11800 FONT 92337 644-C4
SAGAMORE CT
18800 APLV 92308 4477-D3
SAGE AV
100 SBdC 92284 4747-G5
700 SBdC 92285 4747-G2
1900 SBdC 92285 4667-G7
2200 SBdC 92284 4817-H4
3800 SBdC 92284 4887-H1
4100 YUCA 92284 4887-H1
6600 TNP 92277 4892-G6
7100 YUCA 92284 4957-H2
7500 TNP 92277 4962-G1
11300 FONT 92337 644-C2
11300 ADEL 92301 4205-A5
N SAGE AV
400 RLTO 92376 575-H4
400 RLTO 92376 605-H1
1200 SBdC 92285 4747-G3
S SAGE AV
400 RLTO 92376 605-H3
SAGE CT
8800 RCUC 91701 572-G5
12000 YCPA 92399 649-B3
56800 YUCA 92284 4957-H6
SAGE DR
1300 BARS 92311 3680-A2
8900 RCUC 91701 572-G5
11100 LMLN 92354 647-A2
11300 SBdC 92392 4475-A2
SAGE LN
3800 CHLS 91709 681-D7
14500 ADEL 92301 4384-J1
14500 ADEL 92301 4294-J7
N SAGE LN
3500 SBDO 92404 577-E1
SAGE RD
- SBdC 92301 (4024-F4
See Page 3934)
100 SBdC 92372 4472-A7
200 RDL 92373 648-E4
51400 SBdC - 4886-D4
SAGE ST
7900 SBdC 92371 4564-B3
9300 ADEL 92301 4204-H5
9900 SBdC 92345 4564-G2
11300 SBdC 92345 4565-A2
11600 ADEL 92301 4205-A5
13200 SBdC 93562 2145-A3
13300 HESP 92345 4565-F2
14200 VCTV 92392 4386-B1
14900 HESP 92345 4566-A2
31100 SBdC - 4480-D2
35300 SBdC - 4481-G2
38700 SBdC - 4482-G2
W SAGE ST
600 CLAR 91711 571-B6
600 LACo 91711 571-B6
SAGEBRUSH CIR
- POM 91766 640-F4
SAGEBRUSH CT
5500 RCUC 91739 573-H2
9500 SBdC 92371 4473-B7
21500 SBdC 92308 4477-J7
SAGEBRUSH LN
35800 SBdC - 3592-F7
35800 SBdC - (3682-F1
See Page 3592)
SAGEBRUSH RD
2800 BARS 92311 3679-A5
SAGEBRUSH ST
5800 CHLS 91709 711-H2
8700 SBdC 92308 4477-H6
9300 APLV 92308 4477-H6

SAGEBRUSH TER
- TNP 92278 4822-F1
N SAGEBRUSH TER
5100 SBDO 92407 546-C5
SAGEBRUSH TR
18500 SBdC - (3846-J7
See Page 3756)
18700 SBdC - (3847-A7
See Page 3756)
SAGE CANYON RD
- POM 91766 640-G3
SAGE HEN RD
12900 SBdC 92392 4386-H4
W SAGE TREE RD
1900 CLTN 92324 605-J5
SAGINAW CT
28500 SBdC - 518-B2
SAGO CT
7300 RCUC 91730 573-B7
20400 APLV 92307 4297-E3
SAGO LN
20400 APLV 92307 4297-E3
SAGO RD
- SBdC 92307 (4117-E6
See Page 4116)
15700 APLV 92307 4297-E3
SAGO ST
15700 APLV 92307 4297-E4
SAGO WY
15700 APLV 92307 4297-E4
SAGO DELL
15700 APLV 92307 4297-E4
W SAGO PALM RD
1900 CLTN 92324 605-J5
SAGORA WY
2400 CHLS 91709 680-J1
SAGUARO CIR
- LPCo - 4606-J4
SAGUARO RD
22500 APLV 92307 4298-B1
N SAGUARO ST
5000 SBDO 92407 546-D5
SAGUARO WY
11900 FONT 92337 644-B4
28100 HIGH 92346 578-A5
SAHALE CT
13700 APLV 92307 4387-A2
SAHALE LN
18700 APLV 92307 4387-A2
SAHALE PL
13700 APLV 92307 4387-A2
SAHALE RD
19800 APLV 92307 4387-D2
SAHALEE CT
- YCPA 92399 649-E2
SAHARA AV
6500 TNP 92277 4892-J6
7300 TNP 92277 4962-J2
SAHARA RD
8200 SBdC 92371 4563-B2
9400 SBdC 92371 4473-A2
SAHARA TER
- SBdC 92252 4889-E2
2700 SBdC 92252 4819-E5
SAHUARO WY
500 BBLK - 4812-B2
500 SBdC - 4812-B2
SAIGA CT
28200 HIGH 92346 578-A4
SAILFIN LN
18300 SBdC 92392 4386-J2
SAINT ALBANS LN
11700 LMLN 92354 647-F3
SAINT ALBERT DR
- FONT 92336 544-D7
- FONT 92336 574-D1
SAINT ANDREWS AV
19000 SBdC 92301 (4202-B1
See Page 4112)
E SAINT ANDREWS CT
1200 ONT 91761 642-E6
SAINT ANDREWS DR
- CHLS 91709 711-E1
- UPL 91784 572-D6
100 SBdC - 517-E1
14200 VCTV 92392 4386-C1
E SAINT ANDREWS DR
1900 ONT 91761 642-G6
2900 ONT 91761 643-A6
SAINT ANDREWS PL
2100 CLAR 91711 571-F7
11800 LMLN 92354 647-E3
SAINT ANDREWS ST
- ONT 91762 642-C6
400 ONT 91761 642-C6
E SAINT ANDREWS ST
900 ONT 91761 642-E6
2700 ONT 91761 643-A6
SAINT ANDREWS WY
11200 APLV 92308 4477-D2
SAINT ANTHONY AV
17700 SBdC 92301 (4202-C1
See Page 4112)
SAINT ANTON CT
500 BBLK - 4811-H2
SAINT ANTON DR
1200 SBdC - 4738-A5
SAINT AUGUSTINE AV
400 CLAR 91711 601-D4

SAINT BASIL AV
18500 SBdC 92301 (4202-C2
See Page 4112)
SAINT BERNARD LN
27400 SBdC - 4737-H5
SAINT BERNARD WY
1100 SBdC - 4737-J6
SAINT BONAVENTURE
AV
300 CLAR 91711 601-D5
SAINT CATHERINE ST
200 SBdC 92374 648-J2
SAINT CATHERINE WY
900 CLAR 91711 571-B6
S SAINT CLOUD CIR
400 SBdC 92314 4742-G6
SAINT DAVID ST
- LMLN 92354 647-F2
SAINT ELMO DR
200 RLTO 92376 575-H7
W SAINT ELMO DR
7300 SBDO 92410 576-A7
2700 SBDO 92376 576-A7
2900 SBDO 92376 575-J7
SAINT ESTEBAN AV
19300 SBdC 92301 (4202-A3
See Page 4112)
SAINT GAUDENS DR
- CHLS 91709 711-G1
SAINT GEORGE AV
19100 SBdC 92301 (4202-B1
See Page 4112)
20400 SBdC 92301 4112-B7
SAINT GREGER RD
- MohC - 3620-B2
SAINT GREGORY ST
300 CLAR 91711 571-D5
SAINT HELEN ST
1300 SBdC 92301 (4202-B5
See Page 4112)
SAINT HELENA CT
7800 FONT 92336 604-B1
SAINT HELENA ST
7900 FONT 92336 604-B1
SAINT IVES CT
24400 DBAR 91765 680-E3
SAINT JOHN PL
800 CLAR 91711 571-B7
SAINT LAWRENCE RD
19300 SBdC 92301 (4202-A2
See Page 4112)
SAINT LAWRENCE ST
26900 SBdC 92311 3679-B4
SAINT MARYS DR
57300 YUCA 92284 4957-J1
57300 YUCA 92284 4958-A1
SAINT MICHAEL ST
1300 SBdC 92301 (4202-B5
See Page 4112)
SAINT MINA CT
1500 RivC 92324 646-J6
SAINT MORITZ CT
41800 BBLK - 4811-H2
SAINT MORITZ DR
500 BBLK - 4811-H2
SAINT PAUL ST
500 POM 91767 601-C7
500 POM 91767 641-D1
SAINT THERESA AV
7500 SBdC 92301 (4113-J5
See Page 4112)
SAINT TIMOTHY CT
19300 APLV 92307 4297-C3
SAINT TIMOTHY LN
19400 APLV 92307 4297-C3
SAINT TIMOTHY RD
15700 APLV 92307 4297-C4
SAINT TIMOTHY WY
15900 APLV 92307 4297-C3
SAINT TROPEZ DR
11100 RCUC 91730 573-D7
S SAINT TROPEZ DR
2800 ONT 91761 643-B6
SAINT TROPEZ ST
2300 UPL 91784 571-H3
SAIPAN AV
- BARS 92311 3680-B6
SALADIN AV
6700 TNP 92277 4892-H6
7300 TNP 92277 4962-H2
SALADO WY
13800 VCTV 92392 4385-G3
SALAMANDER BLVD
3000 BARS 92311 3758-G3
SALANO RD
18100 APLV 92307 (4206-J4
See Page 4116)
SALDANA CT
15500 FONT 92337 644-G4
SALEM AV
7300 SBdC 92345 4564-J2
10600 SBdC 92345 4474-J3
10900 SBdC 92392 4474-J3
SALEM CT
1800 CLAR 91711 571-C7
6500 RCUC 91701 573-C5
S SALEM CT
2600 SBDO 92408 646-H1
SALEM DR
800 RDL 92373 648-D2

S SALEM DR
400 SBdC 92314 4742-C6
SALEM LN
1000 POM 91766 641-B3
18300 SBdC 92392 4386-J4
SALEM RD
11300 SBdC 92392 4474-J2
11700 VCTV 92392 4474-J2
11800 VCTV 92392 4384-J7
SALEM ST
6100 CHNO 91710 641-J7
6100 CHNO 91710 642-A7
SALERNO AV
2000 SBdC 92359 608-J4
SALERNO CT
14200 SBdC 92371 4383-B2
SALERNO PL
6700 RCUC 91701 573-D5
SALERNO RD
2100 SBdC 92371 4382-E2
3900 SBdC 92371 4383-C2
7500 SBdC 92371 4384-A2
SALIC ST
10000 SBdC 92359 609-A5
SALINA AV
1400 UPL 91784 602-E3
1400 UPL 91786 602-E3
8100 RCUC 91730 602-E3
SALINA ST
8400 RCUC 91730 602-F3
9900 RCUC 91730 603-A3
SALINAS RD
15300 SBdC 92347 3586-A2
21700 SBdC 92347 (3587-E3
See Page 3586)
SALINAS ST
16200 VCTV 92394 4296-B3
SALISBURY LN
400 CLAR 91711 571-E7
SALMON RIVER RD
1100 RIV 92501 645-G7
SALMON RIVER WY
3800 ONT 91761 643-C6
SALT CREEK WY
3900 ONT 91761 643-C6
SALT SPRINGS AV
2300 BARS 92311 3758-H3
SALTUS RD
15900 SBdC - 370-K4
SALT WELL ACCESS RD
13300 SBdC 93562 328-L4
SALULU CT
6500 SBdC - 4844-C2
SALVIA AV
14500 SBdC - (4303-B5
See Page 4302)
SAMANTHA DR
- ONT 91761 643-D7
- RivC 91752 643-D7
- SBdC 91761 643-D7
13600 CHNO 91710 681-C2
SAMARITAN CT
- SBDO 92408 607-B1
SAMARKAND DR
68000 TNP 92277 4891-A3
71800 TNP 92277 4892-G2
76100 SBdC 92277 4893-B2
SAMARKAND RD
5100 SBdC 92277 (4895-E1
See Page 4824)
79700 SBdC 92277 (4894-D2
See Page 4824)
SAMBAR ST
14500 CHLS 91709 681-C4
SAMEL DR
8400 SBdC 92256 4956-G7
9100 SBdC 92256 616-G1
SAMPRISI LN
- VCTV 92392 4385-E7
SAN ANDREAS DR
10400 RCUC 91737 573-B3
SAN ANDREAS RD
56300 YUCA 92284 4957-E6
57500 YUCA 92284 4958-A6
SAN ANDRES WY
2500 CLAR 91711 571-B6
SAN ANGELO AV
6500 SBdC 92252 4888-J7
6500 SBdC 92252 4958-J1
SAN ANGELO DR
2600 CLAR 91711 571-C5
N SAN ANSELMO AV
600 SBDO 92410 576-B7
2300 SBDO 92407 576-B3
S SAN ANSELMO AV
100 SBDO 92410 606-B2
500 SBDO 92324 606-B3
N SAN ANSELMO CT
2700 SBDO 92407 576-A3
E SAN ANSELMO DR
200 SBdC 92314 4742-D5
SAN ANTONIO AV
12200 CHNO 91710 642-B6
13200 CHNO 91710 682-B1
15700 CHNO 91710 712-B1
N SAN ANTONIO AV
- UPL 91786 602-A2
100 ONT 91762 642-A1
100 POM 91767 641-B1
100 ONT 91762 602-A7

SAN BERNARDINO

STREET Block City ZIP Pg-Grid

N SAN ANTONIO AV
700 POM 91767 601-B7
1400 UPL 91786 572-A7
1500 ONT 91786 602-A2
1600 UPL 91784 572-A4
2300 SBdC 91784 572-A4
S SAN ANTONIO AV
- UPL 91786 602-A4
100 ONT 91762 642-A2
100 POM 91766 641-B3
2200 CHNO 91710 642-B5
SAN ANTONIO CRES E
2400 SBdC 91784 572-A2
SAN ANTONIO CRES W
2400 SBdC 91784 572-A2
SAN ANTONIO DR
- RCUC 91739 574-B1
33400 SBdC - 519-E3
W SAN ANTONIO PL
800 UPL 91786 602-A3
SAN ANTONIO WY
5300 MTCL 91763 641-G2
SAN ANTONIO CREEK RD
100 NDLS 92363 3620-A3
7600 SBdC - 512-A5
SAN BENITO AV
3100 SBdC 92407 576-B1
6500 RCUC 91701 573-C5
N SAN BENITO AV
600 SBDO 92410 576-B7
S SAN BENITO AV
500 SBDO 92324 606-B3
SAN BENITO CT
2300 CLAR 91711 571-C6
2400 SBDO 92407 576-B3
14200 FONT 92336 574-C7
14200 FONT 92336 604-C1
SAN BENITO LN
500 SBdC - 4737-F7
SAN BENITO ST
- HIGH 92346 578-G7
3900 SBdC 92407 546-A6
3900 SBDO 92407 546-A6
14200 FONT 92336 604-C1
SAN BERNARDINO AV
100 SBdC - 4742-E7
200 SBdC - 4812-E2
300 POM 91767 601-B6
1700 RDL 92374 608-G4
1700 SBdC 92359 608-G4
1700 SBdC 92374 608-G4
2100 RDL 92373 607-G4
12900 SBdC 92335 603-H5
13300 SBdC 92335 604-A5
15500 FONT 92335 604-H5
17000 FONT 92335 605-B5
17300 FONT 92316 605-B5
17400 SBdC 92335 605-B5
17400 SBdC 92316 605-B5
26500 SBdC 92374 607-G4
E SAN BERNARDINO AV
- RDL 92374 608-C4
100 RLTO 92376 605-H5
1200 SBDO 92408 607-C4
1700 RDL 92408 607-D4
W SAN BERNARDINO AV
- RDL 92374 608-A4
100 RLTO 92376 605-F5
300 RLTO 92316 605-F5
800 RDL 92374 607-E4
900 SBdC 92316 605-F5
1400 CLTN 92324 606-A5
1600 CLTN 92324 605-J5
2000 RLTO 92324 605-J5
27600 SBdC 92374 607-E4
SAN BERNARDINO CT
4200 MTCL 91763 601-E6
SAN BERNARDINO FRWY I-10
- CLAR - 601-A6
- CLTN - 605-B6
- CLTN - 606-A6
- FONT - 603-A7
- FONT - 604-A7
- FONT - 605-B6
- LACo - 640-A1
- MTCL - 601-A6
- ONT - 602-E5
- ONT - 603-A7
- POM - 601-A6
- POM - 640-A1
- RLTO - 605-B6
- SBdC - 603-A7
- SBdC - 604-A7
- SBdC - 605-B6
- SBdC - 606-A6
- SDMS - 640-A1
- UPL - 601-A6
- UPL - 602-E5
SAN BERNARDINO RD
800 UPL 91786 602-D2
8000 RCUC 91730 602-H1
8100 RCUC 91786 602-D2
SAN BERNARDINO ST
4200 MTCL 91763 601-E6
5500 MTCL 91762 601-E6
33600 SBdC - (3681-F7 See Page 3590)

SANBORN AV
- SBdC - 512-A5
SANBORN WY
1900 POM 91766 641-B5
SAN BRUNO AV
7500 HESP 92345 4567-A3
37000 SBdC 92311 3589-H6
SANBURG AV
19300 SBdC 92301 (4203-J1 See Page 4112)
20100 SBdC 92301 (4113-J7 See Page 4112)
SANBURG CT
12700 GTER 92313 646-D5
SANBURG WY
12600 GTER 92313 646-D5
N SAN CARLO AV
600 SBDO 92410 576-B7
2300 SBDO 92407 576-A3
S SAN CARLO AV
500 SBDO 92324 606-B3
SAN CARLO CT
2300 SBDO 92407 576-A3
SAN CARLOS CT
- RCUC 91739 573-G2
13000 VCTV 92392 4385-E6
SAN CARLOS DR
2200 POM 91767 601-B5
SAN CARLOS ST
100 NDLS 92363 3620-D7
34900 YCPA 92399 649-J7
34900 YCPA 92399 650-A7
SAN CARMELA CT
- RCUC 91739 573-G6
SANCHEZ CT
- RCUC 91739 574-A1
N SANCHEZ ST
3100 SBDO 92404 577-C2
SAN CLEMENTE DR
8500 RCUC 91730 603-A3
SAN CLEMENTE LN
13000 CHNO 91710 641-F7
SAN CLEMENTE ST
100 NDLS 92363 3710-C1
2300 BARS 92311 3679-C4
SAN CLEMENTE WY
5100 MTCL 91763 641-G2
SAND AV
8900 ADEL 92301 4204-C5
11700 ADEL 92301 4205-A5
SAND CT
10600 ADEL 92301 4204-H5
31000 SBdC 92359 608-J6
SAND ST
15400 VCTV 92392 4386-B1
SANDALE
6500 SBdC 92277 (4895-A6 See Page 4824)
SANDALWOOD AV
1000 RDL 92374 608-D5
5500 RLTO 92377 575-D2
9700 SBdC 92316 605-D5
N SANDALWOOD AV
600 RLTO 92376 575-D6
1100 RLTO 92377 575-D1
S SANDALWOOD AV
300 RLTO 92376 605-D3
300 RLTO 92316 605-D4
500 RLTO 92335 605-D3
SANDALWOOD CT
900 SBdC - 4737-G6
8500 RCUC 91730 602-F3
SANDALWOOD DR
800 SBdC - 4737-G6
N SANDALWOOD DR
100 BBLK - 4741-H7
100 BBLK - 4811-H1
SANDALWOOD LN
15200 SBdC - 3936-A2
15700 VCTV 92392 4386-C4
W SANDALWOOD RD
2000 CLTN 92324 605-H4
2000 RLTO 92324 605-H4
2000 RLTO 92376 605-H4
SANDALWOOD TR
60900 SBdC 92252 4959-A3
60900 SBdC 92252 4958-J3
SANDALWOOD WY
10900 YCPA 92399 610-A7
SAND CANYON
7300 SBdC 92277 (4894-J7 See Page 4824)
SAND CANYON CT
1200 BBLK - 4812-D3
SAND CANYON RD
7500 SBdC 92372 4562-E5
11200 SBdC 92374 649-A1
11300 SBdC 92399 649-A1
12000 YCPA 92399 649-B2
43100 BBLK - 4812-C2
43700 SBdC - 4812-C3
SAND CANYON TKTR
4200 SBdC - 547-D6
4700 SBDO 92404 547-F6
N SAND CANYON TKTR
4100 SBdC - 547-D6
4100 SBDO 92404 547-D6
SAND DOLLAR ST
7400 FONT 92336 574-C7

SANDEFUR RD
- SBdC 92371 4653-E2
E SANDERLING ST
500 ONT 91761 642-C5
SAND HILL RD
700 SBdC - 4736-C7
SANDHURST AV
17700 SBdC 92336 575-B7
SANDHURST ST
15300 FONT 92336 574-E7
17200 FONT 92336 575-A7
SANDI LN
- SBdC 92365 (3683-B4 See Page 3592)
SANDIA AV
8700 SBdC - 4480-F6
SANDIA PL
11600 APLV 92308 4387-G7
SANDIA RD
20600 APLV 92308 4387-F7
SAN DIEGO AV
7700 RCUC 91730 602-G1
N SAN DIEGO AV
800 ONT 91764 602-G4
SAN DIEGO CT
2400 CLAR 91711 571-C6
SAN DIEGO DR
8600 YUCA 92284 4958-A6
N SAN DIEGO PL
1400 ONT 91764 602-G5
S SAN DIEGO PL
2600 ONT 91761 642-G6
SAN DIMAS AV
100 SDMS 91773 640-A1
S SAN DIMAS AV
1300 RLTO 92316 605-G5
SAN DIMAS CIR
13000 VCTV 92392 4385-E6
SAN DIMAS LN
13900 RCUC 91739 574-A2
SAN DIMAS ST
12100 VCTV 92392 4385-E6
SANDLEWOOD CT
900 BARS 92311 3679-J4
SANDLEWOOD LN
14900 CHLS 91709 681-D5
SANDLEWOOD PL
29100 HIGH 92346 578-D5
SANDOLA DR
63000 SBdC 92252 4819-E4
S SANDPIPER AV
2600 ONT 91761 642-F6
SANDPIPER CT
7600 RCUC 91730 573-D7
S SANDPIPER PL
2400 ONT 91761 642-F6
SANDPIPER TR
- SBdC 92284 4817-F2
SANDRA CT
- LMLN 92354 647-F3
W SANDRA CT
1200 UPL 91786 601-J1
SANDRA DR
2100 RivC 92509 645-B5
SANDRA WY
1300 RDL 92374 608-E5
SAND RIDGE RD
23400 DBAR 91765 680-C3
SANDS RD
10500 MohC - 3620-E4
SANDSONG RD
50700 SBdC 92285 (4576-B6 See Page 4486)
SANDSTONE CIR
12300 VCTV 92392 4385-G6
SANDSTONE CT
- BARS 92311 3679-B5
2400 CHLS 91709 680-J7
10400 SBdC 92359 608-H6
N SANDSTONE CT
- BARS 92311 3679-B4
SANDSTONE DR
4100 SBdC 92371 (4293-B3 See Page 4292)
5600 SBdC 92371 4563-E7
13500 VCTV 92392 4385-G6
18200 HESP 92345 4567-A4
SANDSTONE PL
8500 RCUC 91730 602-F3
SANDSTONE RD
2900 SBdC 92371 4292-G3
7700 ADEL 92301 4294-A3
SANDY CT
600 RDL 92374 608-F6
SANDY LN
- SBdC 92277 4823-G5
4400 SBdC 92277 4824-G7
4400 SBdC 92277 (4894-G1 See Page 4824)
10700 APLV 92308 4477-D2
SANDY WY
54600 SBdC 92284 4887-B7
SANDY CLAWS
- SBdC 92277 (4895-D6 See Page 4824)
SANDY HILL DR
900 BARS 92311 3679-H5
SANDY RIDGE DR
- SBdC 92277 4890-F6
- TNP 92277 4890-F6

SAN FELIPE AV
11300 SBdC 91766 641-E3
11300 SBdC 91710 641-E3
SAN FELIPE CT
5900 RCUC 91737 573-B3
E SAN FELIPE RD
100 SBDO 92408 606-J1
SAN FELIPE ST
200 POM 91767 601-A5
SAN FERNANDO CT
2400 CLAR 91711 571-C6
SAN FRANCISCO AV
200 POM 91767 640-J1
300 POM 91767 641-A1
SAN FRANCISCO CT
26500 HIGH 92346 577-F5
SAN FRANCISCO ST
6900 HIGH 92346 577-F5
SAN GABRIEL CT
5200 RCUC 91739 574-B1
13700 FONT 92336 604-A1
N SAN GABRIEL CT
3900 SBDO 92404 547-A7
N SAN GABRIEL DR
1200 CLTN 92324 606-A4
SAN GABRIEL LN
17800 SBdC 92392 4386-H2
SAN GABRIEL RD
- UPL 91784 571-H7
N SAN GABRIEL ST
700 SBDO 92404 547-A7
700 SBDO 92404 577-A2
SAN GIOVESE DR
- RCUC 91739 603-J1
SAN GORGONIO AV
10300 SBdC 92256 615-G4
SAN GORGONIO DR
- RDL 92373 608-A7
600 BBLK - 4811-H2
13800 VCTV 92392 4385-G6
SAN GORGONIO PL
8500 RCUC 91730 602-F3
SAN GORGONIO RD
1700 SBdC 92372 4562-D2
10500 SBdC 92392 4474-H1
10500 VCTV 92392 4474-H1
SAN GORGONIO ST
- SBDO 92346 577-J2
- SBDO 92346 578-A2
7900 FONT 92336 604-A1
SAN GORGONIO WY
12400 VCTV 92392 4385-G6
SANITARIUM DR
24800 LMLN 92354 647-B1
SAN JACINTO AV
15900 FONT 92336 574-G6
17800 FONT 92336 575-B6
SAN JACINTO CT
2400 CLAR 91711 571-C6
8500 RCUC 91730 602-F3
17500 FONT 92336 575-B6
18200 SBdC 92336 575-C6
SAN JACINTO DR
12300 VCTV 92392 4385-G6
15600 FONT 92336 574-F7
SAN JACINTO RD
17700 SBdC 92301 (4202-D7 See Page 4112)
SAN JACINTO ST
100 RDL 92373 648-A1
10200 SBdC 92256 615-H5
E SAN JACINTO ST
400 SBDO 92408 607-A3
SAN JACINTO WY
13600 VCTV 92392 4385-G6
19100 APLV 92308 4387-B4
SAN JOAQUIN CT
2300 CLAR 91711 571-C6
12300 VCTV 92392 4385-E6
SAN JOAQUIN DR
12900 VCTV 92392 4385-E6
SAN JOSE AV
15600 CHLS 91709 681-E7
E SAN JOSE AV
100 CLAR 91711 601-D5
W SAN JOSE AV
100 CLAR 91711 601-C5
SAN JOSE DR
15100 VCTV 92394 4296-A6
SAN JOSE ST
4400 MTCL 91763 601-F5
5600 MTCL 91762 601-H5
SAN JUAN AV
100 RDL 92374 608-B4
13300 YCPA 92399 650-A6
SAN JUAN CT
13600 CHNO 91710 681-E2
16500 VCTV 92392 4386-E5
SAN JUAN DR
11300 LMLN 92354 647-B2
SAN JUAN PL
16500 VCTV 92392 4386-E5
SAN JUAN RD
57200 YUCA 92284 4887-J6
SAN JUAN ST
11000 LMLN 92354 647-A1
12700 VCTV 92392 4386-E5
SAN JUAN WY
11000 MTCL 91763 641-G2

SAN LEANDRO AV
13500 YCPA 92399 650-A6
SAN LEANDRO DR
300 DBAR 91765 640-C7
SAN LORENZO ST
100 POM 91766 641-C2
SAN LORENZO RIVER RD
3600 ONT 91761 643-C6
E SAN LORENZO RIVER RD
3500 ONT 91761 643-C6
SAN LUCAS DR
1100 LMLN 92354 647-B1
12900 VCTV 92392 4385-E7
13400 YCPA 92399 650-B7
SAN LUIS AV
13400 CHNO 91710 681-E2
SAN LUIS PL
200 CLAR 91711 571-C6
SAN LUIS ST
100 NDLS 92363 3620-D7
SAN MARCOS AV
100 RDL 92374 608-B5
SAN MARCOS DR
24500 LMLN 92354 647-A1
SAN MARCOS PL
2100 CLAR 91711 571-D7
12900 CHNO 91710 641-E7
13300 CHNO 91710 681-E1
SAN MARCOS ST
12100 VCTV 92392 4385-E6
S SAN MARCOS ST
200 SBDO 92410 606-D2
SAN MARINO DR
58500 YUCA 92284 4958-D7
SAN MARINO ST
11700 RCUC 91730 603-E5
SAN MARINO WY
5600 RCUC 91739 574-A2
S SAN MARTIN CIR
300 SBdC 92314 4742-G6
SAN MARTIN CT
5900 RCUC 91737 573-B3
E SAN MARTIN DR
300 SBdC 92314 4742-G7
SAN MARTIN PL
13300 CHNO 91710 681-D1
SAN MARTIN RD
13300 SBdC 92392 4385-G3
14000 VCTV 92392 4385-G3
SAN MATEO
- RDL 92373 647-J1
SAN MATEO CT
2400 CLAR 91711 571-C6
4100 CHNO 91710 681-D1
SAN MATEO DR
2400 SBdC 91784 572-B2
11100 LMLN 92354 647-A1
SAN MATEO PL
10800 RCUC 91701 573-C4
N SAN MATEO ST
- RDL 92373 647-J1
- RDL 92373 648-A1
S SAN MATEO ST
- RDL 92373 648-A2
SAN MIGUEL AV
4700 SBDO 92407 545-J6
4700 SBDO 92407 546-A6
SAN MIGUEL DR
14900 VCTV 92394 4296-A6
SAN MIGUEL PL
8600 RCUC 91730 603-A3
SAN MIGUEL ST
2300 BARS 92311 3679-C5
12900 VCTV 92392 4385-E6
SAN MIGUEL WY
11000 MTCL 91763 641-G2
14900 VCTV 92394 4296-A6
SAN MINA CT
- CHNO 91710 641-E6
SAN MORITZ CT
800 SBdC - 517-A3
SAN MORITZ DR
24000 SBdC - 516-J3
24400 SBdC - 517-A3
SAN MORITZ WY
400 SBdC - 517-A2
SAN NICHOLAS CT
10200 RCUC 91730 603-B2
SANOME MTWY
- LACo 92823 710-C1
SAN ONOFRE ST
4100 CHNO 91710 681-D2
SAN PABLO AV
1200 RDL 92373 647-J2
1200 RDL 92373 648-A2
9300 HESP 92345 4477-B6
SAN PABLO CT
- POM 91766 640-D4
12600 RCUC 91739 573-G2
SAN PABLO DR
35200 YCPA 92399 650-A6
SAN PASCUAL AV
10900 MTCL 91763 641-E2
SAN PASQUAL AV
11000 MTCL 91763 641-E2
11300 SBdC 91766 641-E3
SAN PASQUAL DR
1200 BBLK - 4812-C3

SAN PEDRO PL
13300 CHNO 91710 681-E1
SAN PEDRO ST
7900 FONT 92336 604-B1
SAN RAFAEL CT
5900 RCUC 91737 573-B3
56800 YUCA 92284 4887-H6
SAN RAFAEL DR
13100 CHLS 91709 680-H1
SAN RAFAEL RD
5700 YUCA 92284 4887-H6
SAN RAFAEL ST
200 RDL 92373 648-A2
SAN RAFAEL WY
11000 MTCL 91763 641-G2
SAN RAPHAEL PL
- POM 91766 640-E4
SAN REMO CT
8000 FONT 92336 604-B1
SAN REMO TR
7400 YUCA 92284 4957-B3
SAN REMO WY
3200 RivC 92501 646-B6
SAN RIBAS RD
11700 FONT 92337 644-F3
SANRIVE AV
- GTER 92313 646-D6
- RivC 92507 646-D6
SAN ROQUE RD
15600 FONT 92337 644-F3
SAN ROSEN CT
34900 YCPA 92399 649-J7
34900 YCPA 92399 650-A7
SAN SEGUNDO DR
13000 RCUC 91739 574-A1
SAN SEVAINE RD
5200 RCUC 91739 574-B1
5800 FONT 92336 574-D4
SAN SEVAINE WY
4000 RivC 91752 644-A7
6600 RivC 91752 643-J7
SAN SIMEON LN
13000 CHNO 91710 641-F7
SAN SIMEON ST
1700 POM 91767 601-C6
SANTA ANA AV
12900 FONT 92337 643-H1
13300 FONT 92337 644-E1
13700 SBdC 92337 644-A1
16900 FONT 92337 645-A1
17300 FONT 92316 645-A1
17500 SBdC 92316 645-E1
E SANTA ANA AV
100 RLTO 92316 645-H1
W SANTA ANA AV
100 RLTO 92316 645-G1
500 SBdC 92316 645-G1
SANTA ANA CT
12300 CHNO 91710 641-E6
SANTA ANA PL
12400 CHNO 91710 641-E6
SANTA ANA ST
5100 ONT 91761 643-F1
E SANTA ANA ST
3800 ONT 91761 643-C1
SANTA ANA TKTR
- SBdC - 389-E1
8300 HIGH 92346 609-B1
8400 HIGH 92359 609-B1
SANTA ANA CANYON RD
29100 HIGH 92346 578-D6
SANTA ANGELA ST
- HIGH 92346 578-G7
SANTA ANITA AV
9300 RCUC 91730 603-F5
9300 RCUC 91739 603-F5
9800 MTCL 91763 601-H6
11400 CHNO 91710 641-H3
SANTA ANITA TR
12700 SBdC 92386 4386-H5
SANTA BARBARA AV
100 SBdC - 4742-E7
200 SBdC - 4812-E2
SANTA BARBARA CT
7000 FONT 92336 574-A6
SANTA BARBARA DR
700 CLAR 91711 601-C2
9000 YUCA 92284 4958-B7
SANTA BARBARA PL
10900 RCUC 91730 573-C4
SANTA BARBARA ST
2300 BARS 92311 3679-C4
SANTA CATALINA AV
900 BARS 92311 3679-C5
W SANTA CLARA AV
700 CLAR 91711 601-B2
SANTA CLARA BLVD
200 BBLK - 4812-A1
SANTA CLARA CT
10900 RCUC 91701 573-C5
SANTA CLARA DR
- POM 91766 640-E5
SANTA CRUZ DR
10200 RCUC 91730 603-A3
SANTA CRUZ ST
2300 BARS 92311 3679-C4
SANTA FE
900 NDLS 92363 3620-B6
SANTA FE AV
- SBdC 92347 349-A7

SANTA FE AV
13400 SBdC 92392 4386-G3
18200 SBdC 92407 515-C6
18500 SBdC 92392 3586-G1
18500 SBdC 92347 (3587-C4 See Page 3586)
22500 SBdC 92347 3588-B6
SANTA FE AV E
6700 HESP 92345 4566-E2
8700 HESP 92345 4476-F3
11500 HESP 92345 4386-G7
SANTA FE AV W
10700 HESP 92345 4476-F2
11500 HESP 92345 4386-G7
SANTA FE CIR
1300 NDLS 92363 3620-C7
SANTA FE CT
- CHLS 91709 681-F7
SANTA FE DR
1100 BARS 92311 3679-E3
20100 SBdC 92301 (4203-E1 See Page 4112)
23000 SBdC 92301 (4113-E2 See Page 4112)
S SANTA FE LN
700 CLTN 92324 606-G7
800 CLTN 92324 646-G1
SANTA FE OH E
7600 HESP 92345 4566-E2
SANTA FE RD
9700 SBdC - (4483-A3 See Page 4482)
10800 SBdC - (4393-A7 See Page 4302)
10800 SBdC - (4392-J7 See Page 4302)
SANTA FE ST
100 CLAR 91711 601-C4
7800 FONT 92336 604-B1
35300 SBdC - (3681-E7 See Page 3590)
36200 SBdC - (3682-A7 See Page 3592)
36200 SBdC - 3762-B1
E SANTA FE ST
500 SBDO 92408 607-A3
SANTA FE TR
8900 SBdC - 4481-H1
10900 SBdC - (4391-H5 See Page 4300)
12500 VCTV 92392 4385-J5
14700 VCTV 92392 4386-A5
17400 SBdC - (3846-F3 See Page 3756)
55300 YUCA 92284 4957-E3
SANTA FE WY
1600 SBDO 92410 606-D1
SANTA FE FIRE RD
- SBdC - 4654-C6
6500 SBdC - (4572-H3 See Page 4482)
7200 SBdC - 4482-H2
8000 SBdC - 4734-D2
8100 SBdC 92345 4654-C6
SANTA LUCIA ST
7500 FONT 92336 574-B7
SANTA MARIA CT
7800 FONT 92336 604-C1
SANTA MARIA DR
7900 FONT 92336 604-B1
58500 YUCA 92284 4958-C7
SANTA MARIA PL
13000 VCTV 92392 4385-E7
SANTA MARIA ST
2300 BARS 92311 3679-C5
35200 YCPA 92399 650-A6
SANTA PAULA ST
- HIGH 92346 578-H6
SANTA ROSA AV
900 BARS 92311 3679-C5
SANTA ROSA CT
1800 CLAR 91711 571-C7
1800 CLAR 91711 601-C1
2400 SBdC 91784 572-A2
10200 RCUC 91730 603-A3
SANTA ROSA DR
34700 YCPA 92399 649-J6
35200 YCPA 92399 650-A6
SANTA ROSA RD
19800 SBdC 92308 4477-D7
21900 SBdC 92308 4479-C6
28700 SBdC - 4479-J6
28800 SBdC - 4480-A6
SANTEE AL
- SBDO 92410 606-F4
SANTEE RD
13800 APLV 92307 4387-E1
14100 APLV 92307 4297-E7
SANTEZ DR
2800 POM 91768 640-B2
SANTIAGO CT
12300 VCTV 92392 4385-D6
SANTIAGO DR
12300 VCTV 92392 4385-D6
SANTIAGO ST
16500 VCTV 92392 4386-E5
E SANTIAGO CREEK WY
3700 ONT 91761 643-C6
SANTIAGO PEAK CT
11300 RCUC 91737 573-D4

SAN TIMOTEO CANYON RD
- RivC 92373 648-A5
- RDL 92373 647-H2
- SBdC 92373 647-G2
1000 RDL 92373 648-A5
SANTO PL
7100 RCUC 91701 573-E6
E SANTO ANTONIO DR
1100 CLTN 92324 646-F1
S SANTO ANTONIO DR
1000 CLTN 92324 646-E2
SANTOLINA PL
6600 RCUC 91739 573-H5
W SANTOLINAS ST
1900 SBDO 92376 605-J4
2900 SBDO 92376 606-A4
SAN TROPEZ CT
8000 FONT 92336 604-B1
13500 CHLS 91709 680-H2
SAN TROPEZ DR
4300 RivC 92509 644-D7
SAN TROPEZE DR
57700 YUCA 92284 4958-A6
SAN VICENTE DR
8500 YUCA 92284 4958-A6
SAN VICENTE ST
4200 CHNO 91710 681-E1
SAN YSIDRO ST
700 UPL 91786 602-D1
12200 VCTV 92392 4385-E6
SANZA PL
- RCUC 91701 573-E6
SAPOTA RD
19500 APLV 92307 (4117-H7 See Page 4116)
19500 APLV 92307 4207-H1
SAPPADA DR
- RCUC 91701 573-E6
SAPPHIRE
- BREA 92823 710-D6
SAPPHIRE CT
800 POM 91766 640-H4
15200 VCTV 92394 4296-A4
SAPPHIRE DR
79900 SBdC 92277 (4894-C1 See Page 4824)
SAPPHIRE PL
15200 VCTV 92394 4296-A4
SAPPHIRE RD
4700 CHLS 91709 711-F2
32100 SBdC - 4570-C1
32500 SBdC - (4571-A1 See Page 4570)
SAPPHIRE ST
1100 SBdC 92359 609-A6
1300 RDL 92359 609-A6
5100 RCUC 91701 572-E2
8900 HIGH 92359 609-B3
15600 VCTV 92394 4296-A4
63300 SBdC 92252 4889-F3
SAPPHIRE WY
- FONT 92336 574-E2
SAPPHIRE CANYON RD
23800 DBAR 91765 640-C5
SAPPHIRE HILL LN
14000 CHLS 91709 680-G3
SAPRI PL
- RCUC 91701 573-E6
SARA LN
17300 CHLS 91709 712-A4
SARAH CT
11300 FONT 92337 644-F2
SARAH PL
1300 ONT 91761 643-F2
SARAH ST
13600 YCPA 92399 650-C7
SARASOTA ST
34700 SBdC - 4481-E4
SARASOTA WY
14300 VCTV 92392 4386-C1
SARATOGA AV
- VCTV 92394 4205-G7
2500 SBdC - 328-H6
9800 MTCL 91763 601-G6
SARATOGA LN
- CHLS 91709 640-J7
SARATOGA PL
2600 CHLS 91709 640-J7
13200 CHNO 91710 682-A1
SARATOGA RD
100 SBdC 92372 4382-A6
3500 SBdC 92371 4382-J6
7500 SBdC 92371 4383-J5
7500 SBdC 92371 4384-A5
10800 APLV 92308 4477-G1
11400 APLV 92308 4387-G4
SARATOGA ST
- SBdC - 4887-B1
12700 RCUC 91739 573-H6
16000 ADEL 92301 4294-D1
17400 ADEL 92301 4204-C2
57800 SBdC 92284 4818-A7
SARATOGA WY
3200 SBDO 92407 546-B6
SARATOGA SPRINGS RD
- SBdC - 329-L2
70700 SBdC - 330-A5
SARD ST
5400 RCUC 91701 573-E2

SARDINIA RD
- SBdC - 328-H9
SARDIUS
- BREA 92823 710-D6
SARRACINO WY
13700 VCTV 92392 4385-G3
SARRITA DR
1700 RDL 92373 648-F4
SARSI CT
12500 APLV 92308 4387-F5
SARZANA PL
7700 RCUC 91730 573-D7
SATICOY ST
2100 POM 91767 601-A5
SATINWOOD CT
4400 CHLS 91709 681-E5
7500 HIGH 92346 578-B6
N SATINWOOD RD
1300 CLTN 92324 605-H4
SATINWOOD ST
8900 FONT 92335 604-G3
N SATURN CT
5700 SBDO 92407 546-H4
SATURN DR
60900 SBdC 92252 4748-J6
61300 SBdC 92252 4749-A6
SATURN LN
6000 RivC 91752 683-H5
SATURN RD
37700 SBdC - (4392-D3 See Page 4302)
SATURN ST
27700 HIGH 92346 577-J5
54700 SBdC 92252 4749-F6
64900 SBdC 92252 4750-A5
66500 SBdC 92277 4750-E5
SATURN WY
1100 SBdC - 516-H4
SAUANO LN
- SBdC - 4843-E6
SAUGUS CT
- RDL 92373 648-D6
SAUGUS RD
18300 APLV 92307 (4206-J4 See Page 4116)
SAUK CT
10800 APLV 92308 4477-J2
10800 APLV 92308 4478-A2
SAUK RD
10700 APLV 92308 4478-A2
10700 APLV 92308 4477-J2
SAUNDERS ST
2200 POM 91767 601-B5
SAUTERNE DR
7800 RCUC 91730 602-G1
SAVAGE LN
11300 APLV 92308 4477-E1
11500 APLV 92308 4387-E7
SAVANNA DR
1200 BARS 92311 3679-G5
SAVANNAH CT
300 UPL 91784 572-C5
SAVANNAH PL
- RivC 92880 683-C4
SAVANNAH ST
4400 CHNO 91710 641-E7
SAVANO RD
- SBdC 92372 4562-E3
SAVONA DR
2200 SBdC 92372 4562-F4
11800 FONT 92337 644-F4
SAVONA PL
1200 POM 91766 640-E3
SAVOY RD
- SBdC - 328-H9
SAWANSON RD
6500 SBdC 92277 4890-F7
SAWGRASS BEND
11000 APLV 92308 4477-D2
SAWGRASS CT
4300 CHLS 91709 711-E1
SAWGRASS DR S
- UPL 91784 572-E6
SAWGRASS WY
- FONT 92336 574-H2
SAW MILL DR
100 SBdC - 4742-D6
100 SBdC - 4812-D1
100 SBdC 92314 4742-D6
N SAW MILL DR
100 SBdC 92314 4742-D6
S SAW MILL DR
100 SBdC 92314 4742-D6
SAWMILL RD
25900 SBdC - 517-D1
SAWMILL COVE LNDG
39500 BBLK - 4811-B1
SAWPIT CANYON RD
300 SBdC - 4736-A7
400 SBdC - 516-A1
SAWPIT CANYON TR
- SBdC - 4736-B6
SAWPIT CREEK RD
200 SBdC - 516-A1
SAWPIT CREEK SPUR
100 SBdC - 516-B1
SAXON DR
- RCUC 91739 573-F6
600 SBdC - 517-B3

SAXON LN
12600 SBdC 92371 4382-H6
SAXON RD
6500 SBdC 92301 (4203-F4 See Page 4112)
9300 SBdC - 4480-E1
SAYBROOK DR
- RCUC 91730 573-E1
SAYLE RD
- SBdC 92371 4653-G3
SCALEA DR
- RCUC 91701 573-E6
SCANDIA DR
32300 SBdC - 519-B7
SCANDIA LN
56300 SBdC 92284 4817-G6
59300 SBdC 92284 4818-E6
SCANDIA RD
100 BBLK - 4741-J7
100 BBLK - 4811-J1
200 BBLK - 4812-A1
SCARBOROUGH PL
13500 CHNO 91710 682-A2
SCARVAN RD
6800 YUCA 92284 4957-F2
SCENIC CT
27900 SBdC - (3935-J2 See Page 3934)
SCENIC DR
- VCTV 92392 4296-E7
100 SBdC - 516-A1
900 SBDO 92408 606-G4
3500 RivC 92509 644-J6
3500 RivC 92509 645-A6
7700 SBdC 92372 4562-C4
E SCENIC DR
900 CLTN 92324 606-F5
1000 SBDO 92408 606-F5
S SCENIC DR
900 SBDO 92408 606-G4
SCENIC PL
1100 SBdC - 517-F4
SCENIC RD
6000 SBdC 92252 4889-B6
SCENIC WY
- SBdC - 518-H6
100 BARS 92311 3679-G4
1000 SBdC - 517-F4
SCENIC CREST DR
13500 YCPA 92399 650-J6
13500 YCPA 92399 651-A6
SCENIC RIDGE DR
- CHLS 91709 640-H7
- POM 91766 640-J7
2600 CHLS 91709 641-A7
SCENIC VIEW DR
24900 SBdC - 517-B4
SCENIC VIEW ST
1000 UPL 91784 572-D6
SCHAD LN
35300 YCPA 92399 650-A3
SCHAEFER AV
3500 CHNO 91710 681-C2
6100 CHNO 91710 682-B2
6800 CHNO 92762 682-B2
7100 ONT 91761 682-E2
7100 ONT 91761 682-B2
9500 ONT 91761 683-A2
SCHAFER RANCH RD
35300 YCPA 92399 610-A7
SCHALLERT ST
- RLTO 92376 575-F4
SCHEPPMAN LN
60800 SBdC 92284 4888-J5
SCHLEISMAN RD
- SBdC 91710 712-H1
12500 RivC 91752 683-D7
12600 RivC 92880 683-D7
14100 RivC 92880 712-H1
SCHLITZ RD
8000 SBdC 92371 4563-F1
9300 SBdC 92371 4473-E2
12100 SBdC 92371 4383-E2
15300 SBdC 92371 (4293-E6 See Page 4292)
SCHOLES ST
4000 RivC 92509 644-F7
SCHOLL DR
53200 SBdC - 4956-H5
53200 SBdC 92256 4956-H5
SCHOOL RD
- SBdC - 3592-C7
- SBdC - (3682-C1 See Page 3592)
27400 SBdC - 517-H4
SCHOOL ST
41000 BBLK - 4811-F2
SCHOOLER RD
3300 SBdC 92277 4824-J6
SCHOOLHOUSE LN
71900 SBdC - 2971-E3
SCHOONER DR
13200 SBdC 92392 4387-A3
14200 SBdC - (3935-G6 See Page 3934)
SCHOONER RD
11300 APLV 92308 4477-B1
SCHULZ RD
200 NDLS 92363 3710-C2

STREET Block City ZIP Pg-Grid

STREET
Block City ZIP Pg-Grid

SHORT AV
20500 SBdC 92307 (4117-F5
See Page 4116)
SHORT LN
- BBLK - 4811-D2
SHORT RD
- SBdC - 4886-D2
SHORT ST
300 POM 91768 640-E1
1900 SBdC 92407 576-B1
14100 HESP 92345 4475-H1
62200 SBdC 92252 4959-D5
SHORT WY
23400 SBdC - 516-G3
SHORT CUT
- SBdC - 4737-H5
SHORTER ST
1900 SBDO 92407 546-B5
SHOSHONE DR
- BARS 92311 3678-H7
SHOSHONE RD
23900 SBdC 92307 4298-F2
SHOSHONE ST
44600 SBdC 92365 3594-A1
SHOSHONE TR
6000 SBdC - 4843-J2
SHOSHONEAN
22900 APLV 92308 4388-C4
SHOSHONEE CT
13900 APLV 92307 4387-A2
SHOSHONEE RD
18600 APLV 92307 4387-A1
SHOSHONE VALLEY RD
100 SBdC 92277 4751-D7
100 SBdC 92278 4751-D7
1300 SBdC 92277 4821-D3
4300 SBdC 92277 4891-D3
4900 TNP 92277 4891-D3
6900 TNP 92277 4961-D1
SHOTGUN LN
1500 DBAR 91765 680-D3
SHOWALTER CT
- RCUC 91701 572-G2
- RCUC 91737 572-G2
SHOW CASE DR N
600 SBDO 92408 606-G5
SHOW CASE DR S
1500 SBDO 92408 606-G5
SHOWHORSE LN
14600 VCTV 92394 4295-G7
SHOW HORSE WY
6300 RCUC 91739 573-G4
SHRAMSBERG DR
8500 RCUC 91730 602-F2
SHREVE CT
26500 SBdC - (3935-J6
See Page 3934)
SHRINE CT
- SBDO 92407 546-D5
SIBLEY AL
500 SBDO 92405 576-G4
SIDANA RD
13300 YCPA 92399 650-A6
SIDERITE RD
27900 SBdC 92311 3679-D6
SIDE SADDLE RD
12900 VCTV 92392 4385-F5
SIDEWINDER LN
8500 SBdC 92371 4564-C3
SIDEWINDER RD
8700 SBdC 92308 4477-H7
25700 BARS 92311 (3848-G1
See Page 3758)
81700 SBdC 92277 4824-G4
82400 SBdC 92277 (4825-A4
See Page 4824)
S SIDEWINDER MOUNTAIN RD
100 SBDO 92410 606-C2
SIECK RD
500 RIV 92501 646-A6
SIENA CT
2300 CLAR 91711 571-D6
7300 FONT 92336 574-B6
13100 VCTV 92392 4385-E4
SIENNA CT
28200 HIGH 92346 578-A5
SIENNA DR
- CHLS 91709 681-B6
11600 RCUC 91701 573-E5
SIENNA PTH
12900 VCTV 92392 4385-G5
SIERRA AV
2200 SBdC 92252 4820-C2
2400 RivC 92509 645-A4
3700 FONT 92336 544-J7
3700 SBdC 92336 544-H4
4000 RLTO 92377 544-H4
4700 FONT 92336 574-J3
6500 SBdC 92252 4890-D7
6800 SBdC 92252 4960-D1
7800 FONT 92336 604-J1
8100 FONT 92335 604-J1
10200 FONT 92337 604-J7
10700 FONT 92337 644-J3
10900 SBdC 92337 644-J3
11500 FONT 92337 645-A4
11600 ADEL 92301 4295-A2
N SIERRA AV
900 SBdC 92314 4742-D4

SIERRA CT
500 ONT 91764 602-C7
35600 YCPA 92399 650-B2
SIERRA DR
400 SBdC - 516-A1
400 SBdC - 4736-A7
2400 SBdC 91784 572-A2
SIERRA LN
35600 YCPA 92399 650-B2
N SIERRA PL
100 SBdC 91786 601-H3
100 UPL 91786 601-H3
S SIERRA PL
- SBdC 91786 601-H3
100 SBdC 91763 601-H3
SIERRA RD
900 SBdC 92372 4472-C1
2700 SBdC 92371 4472-J1
4100 SBdC 92301 4112-J2
4200 SBdC 92301 (4113-D2
See Page 4112)
4300 SBdC 92371 4473-B1
9700 SBdC 92392 4474-F1
10800 VCTV 92392 4384-J7
11100 VCTV 92392 4385-A7
N SIERRA RD
4900 SBDO 92407 546-H5
SIERRA TR
40000 BBLK - 4811-D1
SIERRA WY
11200 MTCL 91763 641-E3
33600 SBdC - (3681-E7
See Page 3590)
57300 YUCA 92284 4887-J7
57300 YUCA 92284 4888-A7
57300 YUCA 92284 4957-J1
N SIERRA WY
100 SBDO 92408 606-H1
200 SBDO 92401 606-H1
300 SBDO 92410 606-H1
400 SBDO 92401 576-H5
400 SBDO 92410 576-H5
1200 SBDO 92405 576-H2
1200 SBDO 92404 576-H2
3600 SBDO 92405 546-H7
3600 SBDO 92404 546-J5
3900 SBDO 92407 546-H7
S SIERRA WY
100 SBDO 92408 606-H2
SIERRA BONITA LN
14900 CHNO 91710 681-G5
SIERRA CREEK RD
12700 VCTV 92392 4386-E5
SIERRA CREST CT
- RDL 92374 608-F5
SIERRA CREST VIEW LP
6100 RCUC 91737 573-E4
S SIERRA DAWN PL
1700 ONT 91762 642-A4
SIERRA LINDA CT
7400 RCUC 91730 573-B7
SIERRA LINDA DR
2000 BARS 92311 3680-C5
SIERRA LINDA ST
31300 YCPA 92399 649-A4
SIERRA MADRE AV
8300 RCUC 91730 602-E3
SIERRA MADRE TR
7200 SBdC 92308 4568-F4
SIERRA MESA RD
- SBDO 92407 546-F5
SIERRA PELONA DR
8900 SBdC 92308 4479-A6
11800 SBdC 92308 (4389-A6
See Page 4299)
12100 SBdC 92307 (4389-A6
See Page 4299)
SIERRA PINE DR
31300 SBdC 92359 608-J5
SIERRA VIEW DR
33300 SBdC - 519-E6
W SIERRA VIEW ST
900 SBDO 92407 546-F7
SIERRA VISTA
7700 RCUC 91730 602-F1
SIERRA VISTA AV
7100 RCUC 91701 572-F6
SIERRA VISTA CT
4300 SBdC 92371 4473-B7
SIERRA VISTA DR
- RDL 92373 648-F5
600 SBdC - 518-E3
4100 CHLS 91709 681-E7
4900 SBdC 92301 (4113-B3
See Page 4112)
11200 LMLN 92354 647-A2
57700 YUCA 92284 4888-A4
SIERRA VISTA LN
1100 SBDO 92405 576-E2
SIERRA VISTA RD
6100 SBdC - 4844-A2
8100 SBdC 92371 4563-B3
9100 SBdC 92371 4473-B2
11900 SBdC 92371 4383-B6
35300 YCPA 92399 650-A5
SIERRA VISTA ST
13700 SBdC 92392 4386-H3
SIESTA DR
18800 APLV 92307 4387-A2

SIESTA DR
71700 TNP 92277 4891-J3
71800 TNP 92277 4892-A3
76300 SBdC 92277 4893-C3
SIESTA LN
20300 SBdC 92308 4477-F3
45900 SBdC 92365 3764-E5
SIESTA RD
20400 SBdC 92308 4477-F3
SIEVERT WY
12900 YCPA 92399 649-F5
SIGNAC CT
5400 CHLS 91709 711-H1
SIGNAL DR
1000 POM 91767 601-C7
N SIGNAL DR
600 POM 91767 641-C1
600 POM 91767 601-C7
S SIGNAL DR
1300 POM 91766 641-C3
SIGNATURE ST
9200 RivC 92509 644-D7
SIKUMA CT
6500 SBdC - 4844-C2
SILAS PHELPS DR
- RivC 92880 683-D4
SILENT SPRING ST
14400 HESP 92345 4565-J1
SILI CT
6100 SBdC - 4844-E1
SILICA DR
16300 VCTV 92392 4386-D5
SILICON AV
10500 MTCL 91763 641-D1
10700 SBdC 91763 641-D2
10800 SBdC 91766 641-D2
11800 SBdC 91710 641-D5
SILICON LN
46100 SBdC - (4743-A4
See Page 4662)
SILK ST
- FONT 92337 645-A1
SILKBERRY CT
9500 RCUC 91730 602-J5
SILKLEAF AV
12400 CHNO 91710 642-B6
SILK OAK CT
12400 RCUC 91739 573-G4
SILKTASSEL DR
12400 RCUC 91739 573-G5
SILK TREE DR
- FONT 92337 644-D3
SILKWOOD LN
7300 HIGH 92346 578-E5
SILOMORE DR
- SBdC 92301 (4202-C1
See Page 4112)
5300 SBdC 92301 (4203-E1
See Page 4112)
SILURIAN LAKE RD
67300 SBdC - 330-D7
SILVER AV
37000 SBdC - (3591-E4
See Page 3590)
S SILVER CT
1300 ONT 91762 642-A2
SILVER DR
- TNP 92278 4822-F1
SILVER LN
100 BARS 92311 3679-G3
71700 SBdC - 2971-F2
SILVER ST
19300 SBdC 92376 575-F4
SILVERADO DR
- CHLS 91709 711-E1
SILVERADO RD
1300 SBdC - 4812-C2
76000 TNP 92277 4893-B1
SILVERADO ST
400 BARS 92311 3679-G6
SILVERADO WY
- FONT 92336 574-H3
S SILVERADO CREEK PL
2600 ONT 91761 643-C6
SILVER ARROW WY
12200 VCTV 92392 4385-C6
SILVER BELL CIR
36700 SBdC 92311 3589-H7
N SILVER BERRY AV
3200 RLTO 92377 575-B1
SILVER BERRY DR
27400 HIGH 92346 577-H6
N SILVER BERRY DR
3400 RLTO 92377 545-B7
SILVERBERRY ST
12200 RCUC 91739 573-F5
SILVER BUCKLE CT
29500 HIGH 92346 578-E7
SILVER BUCKLE RD
7700 HIGH 92346 578-E7
SILVER CREEK RD
- SBDO 92407 546-D5
6500 SBdC - 4570-D1
7700 SBdC - 4480-C6
32600 SBdC - (4571-A1
See Page 4570)
SILVER CUP CT
- RDL 92374 608-F5

SILVERDALE DR
600 LACo 91711 601-A2
3200 POM 91767 601-A2
SILVER FERN PL
9400 RCUC 91730 602-H5
SILVERFERN PL
29200 HIGH 92346 578-D5
SILVER HAWK DR
1900 DBAR 91765 680-A5
SILVERIDGE RD
12700 RCUC 91739 573-G1
SILVER LACE LN
29400 SBdC 92311 3589-H7
SILVERLAKE LN
- SBdC - 2971-H1
SILVER LAKE PL
13900 VCTV 92392 4386-D2
SILVER LAKE RD
- SBdC - 329-L8
- SBdC - 330-A9
SILVER LAKES PKWY
26400 SBdC - (3935-G3
See Page 3934)
SILVER LEAF CIR
35200 YCPA 92399 610-A7
SILVERLEAF WY
9300 RCUC 91701 572-H5
SILVER MINE TR
8000 YUCA 92284 4957-B5
54400 SBdC 92284 4957-B5
SILVER MOUNTAIN RD
- SBdC - (4025-J7
See Page 3934)
- SBdC - (4115-J2
See Page 4114)
14800 SBdC - 4116-A2
SILVER MOUNTAIN WY
5000 RCUC 91737 573-A1
SILVER OAK LN
- RCUC 91737 573-A2
28800 HIGH 92346 578-C6
SILVER PEAK RD
26900 SBdC - 368-J1
SILVER PICK RD
100 BBLK - 4741-J7
SILVER PINE CT
39400 BBLK - 4811-B2
SILVER PINE RD
500 SBdC - 4812-E1
SILVERPOINTE AV
- CHLS 91709 681-H7
SILVER RAIN DR
1500 DBAR 91765 680-B4
SILVER RIDGE DR
2500 SBdC 92371 4562-G2
4800 SBdC 92371 4563-C2
SILVER RIDGE RD
13200 CHLS 91709 680-H1
SILVER ROCK RD
- SBdC 92301 368-H2
7400 SBdC 92372 4562-E2
9200 SBdC 92372 4472-E2
9700 SBdC 92371 4472-E4
12000 SBdC 92371 4382-E4
14100 SBdC 92372 4382-E2
15300 SBdC 92365 4292-E6
17700 SBdC 92301 (4202-D5
See Page 4112)
SILVER SADDLE DR
- BARS 92311 3589-H7
12300 RCUC 91739 573-G3
E SILVER SADDLE ST
2800 ONT 91761 643-A7
SILVER SADDLE WY
12500 VCTV 92392 4385-D5
SILVERSAGE CT
5900 CHLS 91709 711-J2
SILVER SPRAY DR
23700 DBAR 91765 640-D6
SILVER SPRING LN
23500 DBAR 91765 680-C2
SILVER SPRINGS DR
- CHLS 91709 681-G7
SILVER SPRUCE DR
100 SBdC - 518-C1
31500 SBdC - 519-A7
SILVER SPUR AV
11400 FONT 92337 644-F3
SILVER SPUR CT
10500 RCUC 91737 573-B2
14700 CHLS 91709 680-H5
SILVER SPUR DR
36700 SBdC 92311 3589-H7
SILVER SPUR WY
12700 VCTV 92392 4385-D5
SILVER STAR CIR
500 CLTN 92324 606-F6
SILVERSTREAM CANYON RD
- SBdC - (4655-F7
See Page 4654)
- SBdC - (4735-F1
See Page 4654)
SILVERSUN CT
11100 RCUC 91737 573-C4
SILVER TIP DR
500 BBLK - 4812-B2
500 SBdC - 4812-B2
SILVERTIP RD
900 DBAR 91765 680-E2

SILVERTIP RD
3200 CHLS 91709 681-B2
S SILVERTON
400 SBdC 92314 4742-G7
SILVERTREE
3600 RLTO 92377 545-A7
N SILVER TREE AV
3800 RLTO 92377 545-A6
SILVERTREE LN
200 RDL 92374 648-F1
SILVER TREE RD
2100 CLAR 91711 571-B7
SILVER TREE ST
600 CLAR 91711 571-B6
600 LACo 91711 571-B6
SILVER VALLEY RD
40500 SBdC - (3682-F6
See Page 3592)
40500 SBdC - (3683-A6
See Page 3592)
40900 SBdC 92365 (3683-A6
See Page 3592)
44100 SBdC 92365 (3684-A6
See Page 3594)
47500 SBdC 92365 (3685-B5
See Page 3594)
N SILVERWOOD AV
400 UPL 91786 601-J3
SILVERWOOD LN
- POM 91766 640-F5
12400 VCTV 92392 4386-D6
SILVER WOOD LN
13800 CHLS 91709 681-B2
SILVERWOOD PL
700 RDL 92373 648-A3
6300 RCUC 91737 573-D4
SILVERWOOD ST
12500 SBdC 92345 (4655-D3
See Page 4654)
SIMI DR
34600 YCPA 92399 609-J5
SIMMONS CT
1700 CLAR 91711 571-C7
1700 CLAR 91711 601-C1
SIMONDS DR
40500 BBLK - 4811-E1
SIMPSON AL
- SBDO 92405 546-H7
SIMS PL
1200 DBAR 91765 680-C3
S SINCLAIR AV
- UPL 91786 601-J4
SINCLAIR CT
800 RDL 92374 608-C4
SINCLAIR ST
2100 POM 91767 601-A5
10800 RCUC 91701 573-C6
SING RD
- RivC 92220 651-F7
SINGING HILLS DR
16100 CHLS 91709 711-E1
SINGING HILLS RD
16200 VCTV 92394 4296-D3
SINGING WIND RD
23100 DBAR 91765 680-B4
SINGINGWOOD AV
1300 POM 91767 601-B7
SINGLETON DR
- RLTO 92316 645-H3
SINGLE TREE
- SBdC 92284 4748-A4
- SBdC 92285 4748-A4
SINGLE TREE LN
900 SBdC 92285 4747-H3
SINGLE TREE RD
62900 SBdC 92252 4959-F5
SIOUX AV
6800 YUCA 92284 4957-F2
SIOUX DR
39100 SBdC - 4741-A5
SIOUX RD
- SBdC 92308 4388-D5
20900 APLV 92308 4387-G5
21900 APLV 92308 4388-A5
SIOUX ST
7800 FONT 92336 604-B1
SIOUX TR
500 SBdC 92284 4747-E7
6000 SBdC - 4843-H1
SIRAH CT
1300 UPL 91786 602-C1
SIRIUS WY
11200 RivC 91752 683-H4
SISKEN CT
23000 GTER 92313 646-G3
SISKIYOU CT
16100 APLV 92307 4296-J3
SISKIYOU DR
1100 BBLK - 4812-C3
SISKIYOU LN
1100 BBLK - 4812-C3
SISKIYOU RD
16000 APLV 92307 4296-G3
18500 APLV 92307 4297-A3
SISLEY DR
16300 CHLS 91709 711-H1
SISQUOC RD
- SBdC - 4844-E2
S SITES WY
200 SBdC 92314 4742-G6

SITKA CT
1400 CLAR 91711 601-C1
SITKAN RD
21100 APLV 92308 4387-G6
SITTING BULL RD
19000 APLV 92308 4387-B4
22500 APLV 92308 4388-B4
SITTING BULL ST
15300 VCTV 92392 4386-B5
SITTING BULL TR
- SBdC - 4843-G3
SITTON WY
15700 SBdC 92307 4298-H3
SIXTH ST
200 SBdC - 3592-E7
200 SBdC - (3682-E1
See Page 3592)
SKIOMAH RD
13000 APLV 92308 4387-F3
SKIPPER LN
14900 VCTV 92394 4295-G7
SKY CT
600 DBAR 91765 640-E7
SKY DR
2400 SBdC - 519-D7
SKY COUNTRY DR
11000 RivC 91752 683-H5
SKYCREST LN
- CHLS 91709 681-B4
SKY FOREST RD
28500 SBdC - 518-B4
SKY HARBOR RD
8300 SBdC 92371 4563-D3
SKYHAVEN
4300 CHNO 91710 641-E5
SKYHAWK CT
13300 CHLS 91709 681-A3
SKY HIGH DR
800 BBLK - 4811-E2
SKY HIGH LN
8000 SBdC - 4570-J1
SKYLAND DR
23700 SBdC - 516-H4
SKYLANE CT
15900 ADEL 92301 4294-C4
SKYLANE DR
3400 RivC 92509 645-A7
SKYLARK AV
15500 FONT 92336 574-F4
SKYLARK DR
400 SBDO 92405 546-G7
11900 FONT 92337 644-C4
E SKYLARK ST
500 ONT 91761 642-C5
SKYLINE CT
15500 CHLS 91709 681-C7
SKYLINE DR
- DBAR 91765 680-C1
- RCUC - (542-E7
See Page 513)
100 SBdC - 516-B1
1700 SBdC - 4810-J5
11300 APLV 92308 4477-C1
22300 SBdC 92308 4478-A6
25400 SBdC 92308 4479-A6
38500 SBdC - 4811-D5
61500 SBdC 92252 4959-A4
SKY LINE DR
8100 SBdC 92371 4562-G3
30100 SBdC - 518-F7
SKYLINE LN
- FONT 92336 574-E3
- POM 91766 640-H5
SKYLINE RD
5200 RCUC - (542-D7
See Page 513)
5200 RCUC - 572-E1
5200 RCUC 91701 572-E1
5200 SBdC 91701 572-E1
SKY LINE TR
38800 BBLK - 4811-A2
SKYLINE WY
2300 UPL 91784 571-H3
SKYLINE RANCH CIR
- APLV 92308 4387-F4
SKYLINE RANCH CT
- APLV 92308 4387-E5
SKYLINE RANCH DR
- APLV 92308 4387-E5
SKYLINE RANCH PL
- APLV 92308 4387-E4
SKYLINE RANCH RD
53800 SBdC - 4886-J5
53800 SBdC - 4887-A5
55200 YUCA 92284 4887-F3
SKYMASTER CT
- SBDO 92409 577-F7
SKYPARK DR
- SBdC 92311 3679-F1
6900 YUCA 92284 4958-E2
SKY RIDGE DR
26100 SBdC - 517-E2
SKYRIDGE LN
- CHLS 91709 681-B4
SKYTOP RD
5400 SBdC - 328-H5
SKYTRAIN CT
- SBDO 92409 577-E7
SKY VIEW CIR
- POM 91766 640-G5

SKYVIEW CT
- SBdC - 516-E2
1200 SBdC 92314 4813-C3
SKYVIEW DR
46800 SBdC 92314 4813-B3
E SKYVIEW DR
1800 CLTN 92324 646-H2
SKYVIEW LN
- SBdC - 516-E2
11200 RCUC 91737 573-D4
SKY VIEW LN
5600 TNP 92277 4892-D4
9800 SBdC 92345 4564-F6
14200 APLV 92307 4387-C1
SKYVIEW RDG
3100 CHLS 91709 681-B1
SKY VIEW RDG
42000 BBLK - 4741-H7
SKY VIEW ST
36000 SBdC - (3682-C1
See Page 3592)
SKY VIEW RIDGE DR
400 SBdC - 4737-J7
SKYWAY DR
- VCTV 92392 4296-F7
SLACK RD
2300 BARS 92311 3680-C5
SLAG HALL RD
9200 SBdC 92335 603-J5
SLASH SORREL COMPANY RD
- SBdC 92307 4118-B2
SLASH X RANCH RD
- SBdC 92307 (4027-J7
See Page 3936)
- SBdC 92307 (4117-J1
See Page 4116)
- SBdC 92307 4118-A1
SLATE AV
83300 SBdC 93562 2145-A3
SLATE DR
16000 CHLS 91709 711-G1
SLATE ST
31100 SBdC 92359 608-J5
SLATER CIR
- ONT 91761 643-D2
SLEEPYGLEN CIR
14700 CHLS 91709 681-B5
SLEEPY HOLLOW LN
8600 SBdC 92371 4563-E2
SLEEPY HOLLOW RD
35500 YCPA 92399 610-B6
SLEEPY HOLLOW ACCESS
1200 CHLS 91709 710-F3
SLEEPY OAK RD
15600 CHLS 91709 681-A7
SLEEPY RIDGE LN
13000 VCTV 92392 4386-C4
SLIGER RD
2400 SBdC 92359 609-A5
SLIPPERY ELM RD
2000 SBdC 92397 4652-E4
SLOCUM PL
- FONT 92336 574-A6
SLOVER AV
1700 CLTN 92316 605-H7
1700 CLTN 92316 606-A7
1700 SBdC 92316 606-A7
12900 FONT 92337 603-J7
13200 FONT 92337 604-A7
13700 SBdC 92337 604-A7
16700 FONT 92337 605-A7
17600 SBdC 92316 605-C7
17600 SBdC 92337 605-C7
19200 RLTO 92316 605-E7
20700 SBdC 92324 606-A7
E SLOVER AV
100 RLTO 92316 605-H7
200 CLTN 92316 605-H7
W SLOVER AV
100 RLTO 92316 605-G7
SMALL ST
1900 SBdC - 4742-H2
N SMALL CANYON DR
3000 SBDO 92346 577-J2
SMALLWOOD PL
- RCUC 91730 573-E1
S SMALLWOOD ST
800 CLTN 92324 606-H7
SMARTS RANCH RD
41700 SBdC - (4743-E2
See Page 4662)
45400 SBdC - 4662-J6
46000 SBdC - (4663-A7
See Page 4662)
SMILEY BLVD
- RivC 92324 648-B7
2000 RDL 92373 648-B7
SMILEY DR
- RDL 92373 648-B1
SMILEY RDG
- RDL 92373 648-C5
SMILEY HEIGHTS DR
1300 RDL 92373 648-A4
1500 RDL 92373 647-J3
SMILEY HEIGHTS RD
900 RDL 92373 648-A4
1100 RDL 92373 647-J4

SMITH AV
6300 RivC 91752 683-G7
SMITH RD
900 NDLS 92363 3620-E6
5800 SBdC 92371 4653-G2
8000 SBdC 92371 4563-F2
8900 SBdC 92371 4473-F1
12100 SBdC 92371 4383-F5
15300 SBdC 92371 (4293-F6
See Page 4292)
W SMITH ST
1500 POM 91766 640-G3
SMITHFIELD CT
- FONT 92336 574-A6
SMITH RANCH RD
- TNP 92277 4892-E1
SMITHSON RD
14300 SBdC - (3935-G1
See Page 3934)
14900 SBdC - 3936-A1
15400 SBdC - (3846-B7
See Page 3756)
SMITH TALC RD
72300 SBdC - 330-E2
SMOKE BUSH RD
35300 SBdC - (4301-B5
See Page 4300)
40500 SBdC - (4303-B4
See Page 4302)
SMOKESTACK DR
100 NDLS 92363 3620-B4
SMOKESTONE ST
13300 RCUC 91739 573-J5
13500 RCUC 91739 574-A5
SMOKETHORN RD
14800 SBdC 92307 4298-F2
SMOKETREE AV
- TNP 92277 4822-E6
2200 RLTO 92377 575-D3
2200 SBdC 92377 575-D3
SMOKE TREE AV
5600 TNP 92277 4892-E3
16600 HESP 92345 4476-F6
N SMOKE TREE AV
200 RLTO 92376 605-D1
500 RLTO 92376 575-D6
S SMOKETREE AV
600 RLTO 92316 605-D3
SMOKETREE CT
12800 CHNO 91710 642-A7
SMOKE TREE CT
9700 HESP 92345 4476-C5
19500 APLV 92308 4387-C7
SMOKETREE DR
- RCUC 91701 572-H5
9900 RCUC 91737 572-H5
9900 RCUC 91737 573-A2
SMOKETREE LN
15700 FONT 92337 644-F3
S SMOKETREE LN
2200 ONT 91762 641-J5
SMOKETREE PL
12900 CHNO 91710 642-A7
SMOKE TREE RD
100 SBdC 92372 4472-F4
2100 SBdC 92372 4472-F4
3600 SBdC 92371 4473-A4
7400 SBdC 92371 4474-A4
9700 SBdC 92345 4474-G4
11100 SBdC 92345 4475-A4
13800 VCTV 92392 4386-C2
SMOKE TREE ST
13800 HESP 92345 4475-G5
15300 HESP 92345 4476-B5
SMOKEWOOD RD
7400 HIGH 92346 578-E6
S SMOKEWOOD ST
800 CLTN 92324 606-H7
SMOKEY LN
3800 SBdC 92277 4823-F5
SMOKEY WY
- SBdC - 519-C5
SMOKEY HILL LN
6100 CHLS 91709 712-A5
SMOKEY MOUNTAIN PL
5200 RCUC 91737 573-B1
SNAKE RD
- SBdC - 4816-F5
SNAKE DANCE PL
700 BBLK - 4811-F2
SNAKE RIVER CT
14800 VCTV 92392 4386-A5
SNAKE RIVER DR
12700 VCTV 92392 4386-A5
SNAKE RIVER PL
14800 VCTV 92392 4386-A5
SNAKE RIVER RD
4500 RIV 92501 645-H7
SNAPDRAGON DR
7400 FONT 92336 574-D6
SNAPDRAGON ST
12300 RCUC 91739 573-F5
SNAPPING TURTLE RD
12000 APLV 92308 4387-F6
SNO ST
400 VCTV 92394 4205-E5
SNOQUALMIE TR
- SBdC - 4843-F4
SNOWAPPLE LN
14700 CHLS 91709 680-G5

SNOWBALL LN
39800 BBLK - 4811-C2
SNOWBERRY LN
2400 CHLS 91709 680-J5
SNOWBERRY PL
29100 HIGH 92346 578-D5
SNOWBIRD CT
600 BBLK - 4811-J2
SNOWBIRD DR
10100 RCUC 91737 573-A1
SNOW BIRD RD
800 SBdC 92397 4652-C1
SNOW CAP AV
8100 SBdC 92371 4562-G3
SNOW CAP CT
2600 SBdC 92371 4562-G3
SNOW CREEK DR
8300 RCUC 91730 602-H4
S SNOW CREEK LN
2900 ONT 91761 643-C6
SNOW CREEK TR
13000 YCPA 92399 650-E5
SNOWCREST DR
42300 BBLK - 4811-J1
SNOWDAN RD
15600 FONT 92337 644-E3
SNOWDEN AV
26200 LMLN 92374 607-F6
SNOWDRIFT DR
9500 SBdC 92339 611-H3
SNOWFLOWER DR
2700 SBdC - 519-A7
SNOW LINE CIR
39100 SBdC 92399 651-B1
SNOW LINE DR
1700 SBdC 92372 4562-E3
2000 SBdC 92371 4562-G2
4100 SBdC 92371 4563-B2
SNOW LINE RD
6800 SBdC 92371 4563-H2
SNOWMASS DR
9700 MTCL 91763 601-G6
SNOWMASS LN
42100 BBLK - 4811-J1
N SNOW RIDGE RD
1000 SBdC 92314 4742-B5
SNOW RIDGE WY
8800 RCUC 91730 602-H4
SNOW VALLEY RD
8300 SBdC 92371 4562-H3
SNOW VIEW CT
11300 YCPA 92399 650-B1
SNOWVIEW CT
12700 VCTV 92392 4385-D4
SNOW VIEW PL
8400 RCUC 91730 602-H4
SNOWVIEW PL
12800 VCTV 92392 4385-E5
SNOWVIEW RD
12900 VCTV 92392 4385-E4
SNYDER AV
11700 CHNO 91710 641-G4
SOAP MINE RD
30900 SBdC 92311 3590-C7
30900 SBdC 92311 3680-C1
31300 BARS 92311 3680-C2
31800 SBdC - 3680-F4
SOAP ROOT TR
13000 YCPA 92399 650-E6
SOBOBA RD
21700 APLV 92307 4297-H1
SOCORRO DR
12600 RCUC 91739 573-G2
E SODA SPRINGS CT
3500 ONT 91761 643-C6
SOESTERN AV
5700 CHNO 91710 681-H2
SOFFEL AV
1800 SBdC 92359 608-H4
SOFT CLOUD WY
13100 VCTV 92392 4385-F6
SOFTWIND CT
11500 APLV 92308 4477-B4
SOFTWIND DR
12300 VCTV 92392 4386-E6
13500 CHLS 91709 681-B2
24200 DBAR 91765 680-D3
SOFTWIND PL
6100 RCUC 91737 573-D3
SOISSONS AV
- BARS 92311 3680-E7
SOLANA CT
1500 BARS 92311 3680-A5
N SOLANO AV
1500 ONT 91764 602-G4
1700 ONT 91730 602-G4
SOLANO DR
6600 RivC 92509 645-B7
N SOLANO PL
1400 ONT 91764 602-G5
SOLANO RD
100 SBdC 92372 4472-A3
3100 SBdC 92371 4472-H3
3700 SBdC 92371 4473-A3
7400 SBdC 92371 4474-A3
8500 SBdC 92392 4474-E2
11300 SBdC 92392 4475-A2
11300 VCTV 92392 4475-A2
SOLANO ST
- FONT 92336 574-B6

W SOLANO ST
400 UPL 91784 572-A5
SOLANO WY
500 RDL 92374 608-C3
SOLAR RD
37700 SBdC - (4392-D3
See Page 4302)
SOLAR WY
2500 BARS 92311 3679-B4
SOLAZZO DR
9800 RCUC 91730 602-G6
SOLDEA RD
14200 SBdC 92371 4383-A2
SOLEDAD AV
100 SBdC 92284 4747-G6
1000 SBdC 92285 4747-G3
SOLEDAD CT
300 SBdC 92371 4382-A3
SOLEDAD DR
8900 SBdC 92308 4479-B6
11300 SBdC 92308 (4389-B7
See Page 4299)
12000 SBdC 92307 (4389-B5
See Page 4299)
SOLEDAD RD
11100 SBdC 92372 4472-A1
12100 SBdC 92372 4382-A7
16100 SBdC 92307 4299-A2
SOLERA LN
- DBAR 91765 680-A3
W SOLISTA CIR
1500 CLTN 92324 606-A4
SOLITUDE CIR
13400 VCTV 92392 4385-F6
SOLITUDE CT
5000 RCUC 91737 573-A1
SOLLAR AV
100 SBdC 92284 4747-F5
SOLTAIRE ST
23900 DBAR 91765 640-D4
SOLVANG AV
16200 VCTV 92394 4296-A3
SOMA CT
23300 SBdC 92347 3588-B4
SOMBRE ST
20600 SBdC 92307 (4117-E5
See Page 4116)
SOMERSET AV
800 POM 91767 601-B6
SOMERSET CT
- SBdC 92365 (3685-F2
See Page 3594)
15400 FONT 92337 644-F3
SOMERSET DR
8700 RCUC 91701 572-F4
10300 RCUC 91737 573-A4
SOMERSET LN
1700 RDL 92374 608-G7
7700 HIGH 92346 578-D7
28200 SBdC - 4738-A5
SOMERSET PL
6700 CHNO 91710 642-B7
SOMERSET RD
- SBdC - (3682-H4
See Page 3592)
- SBdC - (3683-A4
See Page 3592)
- SBdC 92365 (3683-A4
See Page 3592)
- SBdC 92365 (3685-G2
See Page 3594)
- YCPA 92399 649-F2
SOMERSET WY
2100 UPL 91784 571-H4
SOMIS AV
18100 APLV 92307 4208-A6
W SONGBIRD CIR
500 CLTN 92324 606-C5
SONGBIRD LN
58200 SBdC 92284 4818-B4
SONG OF THE WINDS DR
14000 CHLS 91709 681-B3
SONNET PL
16300 CHLS 91709 711-E2
SONOMA AV
6500 FONT 92336 575-A4
7100 RCUC 91701 572-F6
SONOMA CT
3700 CHNO 91710 641-C5
W SONOMA CT
400 ONT 91762 642-B3
SONOMA DR
500 SBdC - 4737-F7
25000 SBdC - 517-B3
42500 BBLK - 4812-A2
SONOMA RD
11400 SBdC 92301 (4115-A5
See Page 4114)
11900 ADEL 92301 (4115-B4
See Page 4114)
18500 ADEL 92301 4204-G5
19900 APLV 92308 4387-D3
SONOMA ST
- SBdC 92347 3588-A2
44500 SBdC 92365 (3504-A7
See Page 3414)
SONORA AV
10700 RCUC 91701 573-C5

STREET
Block City ZIP Pg-Grid

E SONORA AV
1700 SBDO 92404 547-C7
E SONORA DR
200 SBDO 92404 546-J7
SONORA LP
- LMLN 92354 647-D1
SONORA PL
200 CLAR 91711 571-C6
SONORA RD
- SBdC 92252 4818-H2
- SBdC 92284 4818-H2
7500 SBdC 92371 4563-H4
9100 SBdC 92371 4473-H1
11900 SBdC 92371 4383-H2
14700 SBdC 92371 (4293-H7 See Page 4292)
18100 SBdC 92301 (4203-G6 See Page 4112)
61300 SBdC 92252 4819-A2
64700 SBdC 92252 4820-A1
66500 SBdC 92277 4820-E1
SONORA ST
200 RDL 92373 608-C7
200 RDL 92373 648-C1
2100 POM 91767 601-A5
E SONORA ST
300 SBDO 92404 546-J7
400 SBDO 92404 547-B6
SONORA WY
12500 VCTV 92392 4385-D5
14600 VCTV 92394 4296-A7
SONRISA DR
13200 CHLS 91709 681-A1
SONTERRA CT
6300 RCUC 91737 573-C4
SONYA WY
2100 UPL 91784 571-H4
SOPER AV
13600 CHNO 91710 681-D2
SOPER CT
13500 CHNO 91710 681-D2
SOPER LN
1000 SBdC 92277 4751-D6
SOPHIA CT
800 RDL 92374 648-G3
SOQUEL CANYON PKWY
- CHLS 91709 681-G7
3400 CHLS 91709 711-D1
SOQUEL CANYON RD
1400 OrCo 92886 710-F5
18600 BREA 92823 710-F5
SORIA CT
15700 FONT 92337 644-G4
SORREL DR
12600 APLV 92308 4387-B4
SORREL LN
14500 FONT 92336 574-C1
SORREL RD
27300 SBdC - (3937-C1 See Page 3936)
SORREL TR
- SBdC 92307 369-C2
16600 SBdC - (3846-C5 See Page 3756)
20700 SBdC 92307 (4027-F4 See Page 3936)
20700 SBdC - (4027-E1 See Page 3936)
24100 SBdC - (3937-B2 See Page 3936)
28300 SBdC - (3847-B5 See Page 3756)
SORREL HILLS AV
5800 CHLS 91709 711-H2
SORRENTO LN
16900 VCTV 92392 4386-F4
SORRENTO RD
- POM 91766 640-D3
6700 RCUC 91701 573-D5
SORRENTO ST
8000 FONT 92336 604-A1
14800 HESP 92345 4566-A6
W SOSA LN
1900 CLTN 92324 605-J4
SOTO AV
4000 RivC 92509 644-J7
SOUTAR DR
2600 SBdC - 519-B7
E SOUTH AV
100 RDL 92373 648-E3
W SOUTH AV
- RDL 92373 648-D3
SOUTH CT
- SBDO 92410 577-B6
16500 APLV 92307 4298-D2
SOUTH DR
1200 SBDO 92408 607-B2
45900 SBdC - 4742-J3
46000 SBdC - (4743-A3 See Page 4662)
SOUTH LN
100 SBdC - 518-C1
1800 RDL 92373 648-J5
12800 SBdC 93562 2144-J5
SOUTH RD
500 SBdC 92372 4472-B7
4000 SBdC - 4886-D2
21000 APLV 92307 4297-G2
21900 APLV 92307 4298-A2
23300 SBdC 92307 4298-F2

SOUTH RD
26500 SBdC 92307 4299-B2
SOUTH SPUR
- BREA 92823 710-A6
- OrCo 92823 710-A6
SOUTH ST
100 SBdC 92371 4382-F1
3700 SBdC 92371 4383-A1
35500 SBdC - (3681-F7 See Page 3590)
80500 SBdC 92277 (4894-F5 See Page 4824)
E SOUTH ST
100 RLTO 92376 605-H2
W SOUTH ST
100 RLTO 92376 605-G3
SOUTH TR
14400 VCTV 92394 4295-H7
14400 VCTV 92394 4385-H1
17900 CHLS 91709 712-B5
SOUTHAMPTON CT
- RCUC 91730 573-D7
W SOUTH CHANNEL ACCESS RD
100 CLTN 92324 606-D3
100 SBDO 92410 606-D3
SOUTH DOWNS DR
3200 CHLS 91709 681-B7
SOUTHEND ST
- FONT 92336 544-D7
SOUTH FORK RD
800 SBdC - 514-A5
4700 CHNO 91710 641-F7
SOUTH FORK CAMP RD
17000 SBdC - (4882-F4 See Page 4813)
SOUTH MALL WY
500 SBDO 92408 606-G4
SOUTH PERIMETER RD
13900 SBdC 92335 604-A4
SOUTHRIDGE DR
10200 RCUC 91737 573-A3
SOUTHRIDGE LN
11800 FONT 92337 644-A4
SOUTH SLOPE DR
73700 TNP 92277 4892-E4
75900 TNP 92277 4893-B4
SOUTHVIEW PL
900 POM 91766 640-E3
SOUTHWIND AV
15500 FONT 92336 574-F5
SOUTHWIND ST
12300 VCTV 92392 4385-C7
SOUTHWIND WY
- YCPA 92399 649-E2
SOUTHWOOD DR
14100 FONT 92337 644-B3
SOUTHWOOD LN
29500 HIGH 92346 578-E5
W SOUTHWOOD LN
1200 UPL 91786 601-J1
SPACE CENTER CT
3200 RivC 91752 643-H6
SPADE ST
- VCTV 92394 4205-F5
SPADE DR
10300 LMLN 92354 607-D6
SPADRA RD
- LACo 91768 640-A2
SPADRA ST
28900 SBdC 92311 3589-G6
SPAHN DR
10600 SBdC 92316 605-C7
SPAR LN
26500 SBdC - (3935-G5 See Page 3934)
SPARKS ST
26500 HIGH 92346 577-F6
SPARROW CT
- RDL 92374 608-F7
SPARROW DR
11600 FONT 92337 644-G3
SPARROW RD
1600 SBdC 92397 4652-D3
20000 SBdC 92308 4567-E2
SPAULDING CT
- CHLS 91709 711-G2
SPEER CT
500 POM 91766 641-A6
SPELMAN DR
13100 VCTV 92392 4385-E4
SPENCER AV
2100 POM 91767 601-A5
S SPENCER AV
- UPL 91786 601-J4
SPENCER CT
- RCUC 91739 573-H6
300 POM 91767 601-A5
N SPENCER CT
- SBDO 92407 546-A2
SPENCER PL
900 DBAR 91765 680-E2
SPENCER RD
100 SBdC 92252 4749-F5
17500 VCTV 92394 (4206-B7 See Page 4116)
56900 YUCA 92284 4887-H5
N SPERRY DR
200 CLTN 92324 606-F5

SPHERE RD
10900 SBdC - (4392-C5 See Page 4302)
10900 SBdC - 4482-C1
SPICEWOOD CIR
- RivC 92880 683-B7
SPIKES RD
4600 SBdC 92371 4383-B7
E SPIKES RD
100 NDLS 92363 3710-D2
W SPIKES RD
400 NDLS 92363 3710-C2
SPINEL AV
6300 RCUC 91701 572-G4
7400 RCUC 91730 572-G7
7700 RCUC 91730 602-G1
SPINEL RD
32100 SBdC - 4570-H1
32400 SBdC - (4571-A1 See Page 4570)
SPINEL ST
31200 SBdC - (4210-F5 See Page 4120)
SPINET ST
23300 SBdC 92311 3758-B5
23600 BARS 92311 3758-B5
SPINNAKER DR
11300 APLV 92308 4477-B1
S SPINNAKER WY
- UPL 91786 601-H4
SPIRE CIR
13100 CHLS 91709 681-A1
SPIRIT CT
4500 RIV 92501 645-H7
SPIROS RD
- SBdC - 3936-B3
SPLIT OAK TR
15600 CHLS 91709 681-A7
SPLIT ROCK AV
- TNP 92277 4822-D7
6100 TNP 92277 4892-D1
SPOHN AV
7800 FONT 92336 575-C7
7800 SBdC 92336 575-C7
7800 SBdC 92336 605-C1
SPOHN CT
9000 FONT 92335 605-C3
SPOHN DR
8500 FONT 92335 605-C2
8500 SBdC 92335 605-C2
SPORTSMAN CENTER DR
- ADEL 92301 4295-B2
SPRAGUE LN
1200 BBLK - 4812-D3
SPRIG AV
10100 SBdC 92399 610-E5
SPRIG ST
- SBdC 92365 3764-C5
15500 CHLS 91709 681-C7
SPRING DR
500 SBdC - 516-D3
2400 SBdC - 519-A7
9300 SBdC 92339 611-G3
58100 YUCA 92284 4888-B7
SPRING LN
500 SBdC - 519-E2
1600 SBdC - 4737-G4
39800 SBdC 92339 611-C2
SPRING ST
- BAN 92220 651-E7
100 CLAR 91711 601-D4
11300 ADEL 92301 4295-A6
13900 SBdC 92335 604-B2
16700 FONT 92335 604-J2
18000 FONT 92335 605-C2
18000 SBdC 92335 605-C2
E SPRING ST
200 RivC 92507 646-F7
W SPRING ST
100 RivC 92507 646-B7
1100 RIV 92507 646-B7
SPRING TER
2500 SBdC 91784 572-A2
SPRING WY
1300 SBdC - 4737-G5
13200 VCTV 92392 4385-F5
SPRINGBROOK CT
9500 RCUC 91730 602-J5
SPRINGBROOK DR
9600 RCUC 91730 602-J5
SPRINGCREEK CIR
2000 UPL 91784 571-G4
SPRING CREEK WY
1300 CHLS 91709 710-F1
SPRING CREST DR
14200 CHLS 91709 680-J4
SPRINGDALE CIR
14500 ADEL 92301 4384-J1
SPRINGDALE RD
- SBdC - 4816-H7
- SBdC - 4886-H1
SPRING DESERT PL
8300 RCUC 91730 603-A2
SPRINGER CIR
14700 CHLS 91709 681-A5
SPRINGFIELD DR
10600 RCUC 91730 573-B7
SPRINGFIELD ST
300 CLAR 91711 601-D5

W SPRINGFIELD ST
900 UPL 91786 602-A1
1000 UPL 91786 601-H1
SPRINGHILL PL
- BBLK - 4742-A7
SPRINGLAND LN
2000 UPL 91784 571-G4
SPRING MEADOW DR
2300 CHLS 91709 680-J4
SPRING MEADOW LN
6200 SBdC 92346 577-H3
SPRINGMILL PL
7300 RCUC 91730 573-C7
SPRING MIST DR
11300 RCUC 91701 573-D5
W SPRING MOUNTAIN TR
1900 SBDO 92410 606-C2
SPRINGOAK CT
11500 FONT 92337 644-C3
SPRING OAK DR
2100 SBdC - 518-H7
SPRINGOAK LN
11300 FONT 92337 644-C2
SPRING OAK WY
1100 CHLS 91709 710-F2
SPRINGROCK LN
11500 FONT 92337 644-G3
SPRINGSIDE PL
29000 HIGH 92346 578-C4
SPRINGVALE ST
1300 POM 91766 641-B3
SPRING VALLEY PKWY
12100 HESP 92345 4386-H2
12100 HESP 92392 4386-H2
12100 VCTV 92392 4386-H2
12300 SBdC 92392 4386-H2
SPRING VALLEY RD
29500 HIGH 92346 578-D5
SPRINGVIEW PL
6800 RCUC 91701 572-H5
SPRING VISTA LN
14200 CHLS 91709 680-J4
SPRINGWATER RD
23700 SBdC - 516-H3
SPRINGWOOD DR
24200 DBAR 91765 680-D3
SPRINGY PTH
500 SBdC - 516-H2
SPRUCE AV
5800 SBdC - 4950-G1
7300 RCUC 91730 573-C7
7800 RCUC 91730 603-C1
10500 SBdC 92316 605-F7
10700 SBdC 92316 645-F3
30900 SBdC 92311 3680-C1
N SPRUCE AV
200 RLTO 92376 605-F1
500 RLTO 92376 575-F7
2000 RLTO 92377 575-E4
S SPRUCE AV
100 RLTO 92376 605-F2
900 RLTO 92376 605-F4
1700 SBdC 92316 605-F6
SPRUCE CT
9400 HESP 92345 4476-F6
37600 SBdC - 4950-G2
W SPRUCE CT
1400 ONT 91762 641-J5
2100 ONT 91762 642-A5
SPRUCE DR
200 SBdC - 516-F2
300 SBdC - 4738-C7
2300 SBdC - 519-D3
12900 SBdC - 518-B1
40900 SBdC 92339 611-F2
SPRUCE LN
100 SBdC - 4742-G7
200 SBdC - 4812-G1
800 SBdC 92314 4742-J7
800 SBdC 92314 4812-J1
15300 CHLS 91709 681-D6
39800 SBdC 92339 611-D2
SPRUCE RD
500 BBLK - 4811-D2
8800 SBdC 92372 4562-D1
9200 SBdC 92372 4472-D7
SPRUCE ST
100 NDLS 92363 3620-C5
5700 SBdC 92397 4652-C2
13800 HESP 92345 4475-G5
15000 HESP 92345 4476-A5
18100 ADEL 92301 4205-A6
E SPRUCE ST
100 ONT 91761 642-D4
2800 ONT 91761 643-A4
N SPRUCE ST
600 UPL 91786 601-J2
W SPRUCE ST
400 ONT 91762 642-A4
500 SBDO 92410 576-A7
900 SBDO 92411 576-E7
2700 SBDO 92376 576-A7
2900 SBDO 92376 575-J7
SPRUCE TREE DR
1300 DBAR 91765 680-B4
SPRUCE TREE WY
- FONT 92336 574-E6
SPRUCEVIEW
1700 POM 91766 640-F3

SPUR CT
3500 CHNO 91710 681-C1
5500 FONT 92336 574-C2
SPUR DR
9200 RCUC 91730 572-H7
SPUR LN
- SBdC - 519-D6
SPUR RD
20100 SBdC - (3937-D2 See Page 3936)
SPYGLASS CT
3000 CHLS 91709 681-A6
26300 SBdC - 517-E2
S SPYGLASS CT
2900 ONT 91761 642-H6
SPYGLASS DR
- UPL 91786 572-E7
10700 RCUC 91730 573-C7
26200 SBdC - 517-E1
SPYROCK AV
32500 SBdC 92365 (3763-B2 See Page 3762)
SPYROCK LN
- SBdC 92365 (3683-B3 See Page 3592)
SQUAW CT
7400 SBdC - 4843-G5
SQUAW RD
- SBdC 92277 4821-J3
72100 SBdC 92277 4822-A3
SQUAW BUSH
36600 SBdC - (4301-J6 See Page 4300)
36600 SBdC - 4302-A6
SQUAW BUSH RD
40500 SBdC - (4303-A5 See Page 4302)
SQUAW VALLEY LN
12400 VCTV 92392 4386-D6
SQUINT RANCH RD
900 SBdC - 4738-F1
2800 SBdC - 4658-E7
SQUIRREL DR
200 SBdC - 517-E2
33300 SBdC - 519-E2
SQUIRREL LN
500 BBLK - 4811-E2
14200 VCTV 92394 4295-H6
27800 SBdC - 517-J3
32800 SBdC - 519-D6
SQUIRREL RUN E
- SBdC - 548-H1
SQUIRREL RUN W
- SBdC - 548-H1
SQUIRREL INN RD
1200 SBdC - 517-C5
S ST CHANNEL
800 NDLS 92363 3620-B4
STABLE LN
15100 VCTV 92394 4295-G6
STABLE RD
- SBdC 92284 4748-H4
STABLE FALLS AV
6200 RCUC 91739 573-G4
N STACY WY
1800 UPL 91784 572-A5
STADIUM PKWY
- RCUC 91730 603-E2
STADIUM WY
- SBdC 92371 4563-A1
11900 ADEL 92301 4295-B2
56700 SBdC - 2971-F3
STAFFORD AV
15000 ADEL 92301 4294-H1
17300 ADEL 92301 4204-H7
STAFFORD CT
- CHLS 91709 681-H7
10000 RCUC 91730 603-A1
STAFFORD ST
- RivC 92880 683-D4
7800 RCUC 91730 603-A1
9500 RCUC 91730 602-J1
11900 RCUC 91739 603-F1
STAFFORD WY
7800 RCUC 91730 602-J1
STAGECOACH AV
10900 MTCL 91763 641-F2
STAGECOACH CIR
13800 VCTV 92392 4385-G5
STAGECOACH CT
5400 RCUC 91739 573-H2
STAGECOACH DR
- POM 91766 640-F5
1900 NRCO 92880 712-H7
1900 RivC 92880 712-H7
4800 MTCL 91763 601-F5
5400 FONT 92336 574-C2
STAGE COACH DR
10300 ADEL 92301 4204-G5
STAGECOACH DR
12500 VCTV 92392 4385-G5
STAGECOACH LN
10600 SBdC 92256 616-B4
13800 VCTV 92392 4385-G5
51500 SBdC - 4886-D1
STAGECOACH TR
2500 CHLS 91709 640-J7
2500 CHLS 91709 641-A7

STAGE COACH TR
27700 SBdC - (3937-D1 See Page 3936)
STAGEMANS RD
60400 SBdC 92284 4748-H3
STAGHORN CT
- RivC 92399 650-G7
STALLION AV
11000 MTCL 91763 641-F2
13100 CHNO 91710 641-E7
13100 CHNO 91710 681-E1
STALLION LN
18200 SBdC 92316 645-D2
STALLION RD
- SBdC - (3847-C6 See Page 3756)
STALLION ST
3100 ONT 91761 643-B7
STALLION WY
10800 RCUC 91737 573-C1
E STALLION WY
2800 ONT 91761 643-A7
STALLION TRAILS
14500 VCTV 92392 4385-J5
STAMFIELD DR
7500 RCUC 91730 573-B7
STANDARD MINE RD
17000 SBdC 93562 329-A3
STANDING BEAR RD
12500 APLV 92308 4387-J5
STANDING ROCK AV
20600 APLV 92307 4297-F6
22100 APLV 92307 4298-A6
23300 SBdC 92307 4298-F6
STANDING ROCK RD
25400 SBdC 92307 4298-J6
STANDINGWATER TR
36200 SBdC - (4571-J3 See Page 4570)
STANDISH WY
800 RDL 92373 648-C2
STANFIELD CT
- CHLS 91709 711-H1
STANFIELD CTO
500 BBLK - 4741-H6
500 SBdC - 4741-H6
STANFORD AV
2100 POM 91766 641-B6
N STANFORD AV
1300 UPL 91786 602-B1
S STANFORD AV
2500 ONT 91761 643-D5
STANFORD CT
7400 FONT 92336 574-A7
STANFORD DR
- RCUC 91737 572-H2
300 CLAR 91711 601-C3
400 BARS 92311 3679-H6
12900 VCTV 92392 4385-E4
STANFORD ST
2200 SBDO 92407 546-B5
N STANFORD WY
1400 UPL 91786 572-B7
1400 UPL 91786 602-B1
S STANFORD WY
200 SBdC 92314 4742-G6
STANISLAUS CIR
600 CLAR 91711 601-E1
STANISLAUS CT
14100 FONT 92336 574-B7
STANISLAUS PL
6800 RCUC 91701 573-C6
STANLEY DR
73000 TNP 92277 4892-C6
STANLEY ST
31100 SBdC - 4480-E3
STANTON AV
5600 SBdC 92346 577-E1
STANTON ST
2900 POM 91767 601-A3
3800 RivC 92509 644-C7
STANWOOD AV
600 POM 91767 601-A3
STAR CT
24400 DBAR 91765 640-E7
STAR LN
- SBdC 92252 4819-F4
- SBdC 92277 4824-E4
8100 SBdC 92252 4959-C5
STAR RD
10500 MohC - 3620-F4
STAR ST
11300 ADEL 92301 4295-A6
STARBOARD LN
17800 SBdC 92392 4386-H2
STARBRIGHT MINE RD
44300 SBdC - 349-E4
STAR CREST DR
16200 CHLS 91709 711-E2
STARDELL LN
- YCPA 92399 649-F4
STARDUNE AV
6400 TNP 92277 4892-C6
STARDUST CIR
12400 VCTV 92392 4385-G6
STARDUST DR
1300 DBAR 91765 680-D3
12900 YCPA 92399 649-J5
STARDUST LN
200 LPCo - 4774-J5

STARDUST TR
56200 YUCA 92284 4957-G3
STARFALL LN
2000 CHLS 91709 710-H1
STARFIGHTER ST
- VCTV 92394 4205-F4
STARFIRE
1700 SBdC 92284 4818-G3
STARFLOWER LN
14600 CHLS 91709 681-A4
STARFLOWER ST
- RivC 92880 683-B7
STARGAZE ST
- CHLS 91709 681-J7
W STARKS WY
2400 SBDO 92410 606-A2
STARLIFTER CIR
- SBDO 92409 577-E7
- SBDO 92346 577-E7
STARLIGHT AV
2300 UPL 91784 571-H3
STARLIGHT CIR
- BBLK - 4742-A6
STARLIGHT DR
5000 SBdC 92345 (4655-G2 See Page 4654)
11300 RCUC 91701 573-D5
73800 TNP 92277 4962-F2
STARLIGHT LN
4300 CHNO 91710 641-E4
7300 SBdC 92308 4567-G4
9200 SBdC 92285 4478-J7
14300 VCTV 92392 4385-H4
STARLIGHT ST
- SBdC 92277 4820-F2
500 BARS 92311 3679-H5
60900 SBdC 92252 4818-J2
60900 SBdC 92252 4819-A2
64900 SBdC 92252 4820-A2
STARLIGHT TR
7400 SBdC - 4570-J3
STARLIGHT MESA RD
5700 SBdC 92285 (4576-C5 See Page 4486)
STARLING LN
200 RivC 92507 646-E6
STARLITE ST
- SBdC 92284 4818-G2
STARLITE TR
- SBdC 92365 (3593-H5 See Page 3592)
STARLITE MESA DR
55200 SBdC 92284 4817-D1
57700 SBdC 92284 4818-A1
STAR PINE CIR
7400 HIGH 92346 578-D6
STAR PINE CT
14000 CHNO 91710 682-B2
E STARR DR
200 SBdC 92314 4742-D6
STARR ST
24900 LMLN 92354 647-B1
STARSHINE DR
13700 VCTV 92392 4385-G6
STARSTONE PL
6500 RCUC 91739 573-J5
STARSTONE RD
16300 CHLS 91709 711-F1
STARVATION FLATS RD
100 BBLK - 4741-J7
STARVIEW CT
6100 RCUC 91737 573-C3
STARVIEW LN
- SBdC 92277 4820-J5
39100 BBLK - 4811-A2
74300 TNP 92277 4962-G1
STARVIEW PL
6100 RCUC 91737 573-C3
STATE CT
- SBdC - 4812-H1
1800 SBdC 92314 4812-H1
STATE LN
2000 SBdC 92314 4812-J1
2300 SBdC 92314 4813-A1
2900 SBdC - 4813-C1
STATE RD
- CHLS 91709 710-C1
- LACo 92823 710-C1
- OrCo 92823 710-A3
STATE ST
1500 BARS 92311 3680-A4
3000 POM 91765 640-C4
3000 POM 91768 640-B3
4000 MTCL 91763 641-E1
4000 SBdC 91763 641-E1
5200 MTCL 91762 641-H1
5200 SBdC 91762 641-H1
15100 SBdC - (4206-A3 See Page 4116)
25300 LMLN 92354 607-D7
E STATE ST
- RDL 92373 608-C7
100 ONT 91761 642-C1
500 RDL 92374 608-C7
N STATE ST
1500 SBDO 92411 576-B2
2100 SBDO 92407 576-B1
2200 SBDO 92407 576-B1
4200 SBDO 92407 546-C5

S STATE ST
200 SBDO 92410 606-C2
W STATE ST
100 ONT 91761 642-B1
100 ONT 91762 642-A1
300 RDL 92373 608-A7
1000 RDL 92373 607-J7
1000 ONT 91762 641-J1
STATE ROUTE 210 FRWY Rt#-210
- CLAR - 571-C7
- FONT - 574-D4
- RCUC - 572-B5
- RCUC - 573-G4
- RCUC - 574-D4
- RLTO - 574-D4
- RLTO - 575-A4
- RLTO - 576-A4
- SBdC - 575-A4
- SBDO - 576-A4
- UPL - 571-C7
- UPL - 572-B5
W STATION DR
1600 CLTN 92324 606-A4
W STEAMBOAT CIR
1500 SBDO 92407 546-D5
STEAMBOAT DR
9700 MTCL 91763 601-G6
STEAMWELLS RD
2700 SBdC - 328-H11
STEARMAN RD
58300 SBdC 92285 4748-B2
60600 SBdC 92278 4748-E2
STEARNS ST
900 YCPA 92399 650-A7
900 CALI 92320 650-A7
STEEG RD
4500 SBdC 92277 4824-C7
4500 SBdC 92277 (4894-C4 See Page 4824)
STEEL RD
1600 CLTN 92324 606-G7
1800 SBDO 92408 606-H7
STEELE ST
200 RDL 92373 647-J2
S STEELE ST
2400 SBDO 92408 607-A7
2400 SBDO 92408 647-A1
STEEP CANYON RD
1200 DBAR 91765 680-C2
STEEPLE CHASE DR
2800 CHLS 91709 681-A2
STEEPLECHASE LN
22100 DBAR 91765 680-A6
STEEPLECHASE RD
14800 VCTV 92394 4295-H7
STEERHEAD DR
- SBdC 92316 605-E7
STEFFENSEN RD
55800 SBdC 92284 4817-E4
STEGMEIR DR
11900 RCUC 91701 573-F6
11900 RCUC 91739 573-F6
STELLA
14500 SBdC - 4302-C4
W STELLA CT
1100 CLTN 92324 606-B4
STELLAR RD
37700 SBdC - (4392-D4 See Page 4302)
STEM RD
45700 SBdC 92365 3594-D6
W STEPHANIE AV
2700 SBDO 92407 545-J3
STEPHEN AV
1100 CLAR 91711 601-C2
W STEPHEN AV
200 CLTN 92324 606-C7
STEPHENS AV
200 RivC 92501 646-B6
STEPHENS PL
6000 RCUC 91739 574-B3
STEPHENSON LN
7900 YUCA 92284 4957-C4
STEPHENS PASTURE RD
- LACo 91750 571-A3
STEPHENS RANCH RD
- LACo 91711 571-A3
- LACo 91750 571-A3
STERLING AV
1600 SBdC 92404 577-D2
2200 SBDO 92404 577-D2
5300 SBdC 92404 547-D7
6700 CHNO 91710 642-B7
6900 HIGH 92404 577-D4
7300 HIGH 92410 577-D7
7800 SBDO 92410 577-D7
N STERLING AV
3100 SBdC 92404 577-D3
3100 SBDO 92404 577-D2
3700 SBdC 92404 547-D7
3700 SBDO 92404 547-D7
S STERLING AV
1800 ONT 91761 643-B4
STERLING CT
7000 RCUC 91701 573-D6
STERLING PL
12500 CHNO 91710 642-B6
STERLING RD
1300 RDL 92373 648-B4

STERLING ST
2900 POM 91767 601-A3
STERN RD
9000 SBdC 92308 4478-J6
STETSON CT
15300 FONT 92337 644-E3
W STETSON CT
800 UPL 91786 572-A7
STETSON WY
13200 CHLS 91709 680-J1
N STEVEN WY
6500 SBDO 92407 545-J2
6700 SBDO 92407 546-A1
STEVENS RD
17700 ADEL 92301 4204-G6
STEVENS ST
600 BARS 92311 3680-A3
19100 ADEL 92301 4204-G2
STEVENS MINE RD
5200 SBdC - 328-J7
W STEVENSON ST
800 CLTN 92324 606-B4
800 SBdC 92324 606-B4
STEWART RD
7800 RivC 92324 647-E7
STEWART ST
2100 CLTN 92324 646-H1
24500 LMLN 92354 647-A1
STICKNEY CIR
800 RDL 92374 608-D4
STILLMAN AV
800 RDL 92374 608-C6
S STILLMAN AV
300 UPL 91786 601-J4
S STILLMAN WY
1300 UPL 91786 601-J4
STILLWATER DR
12300 VCTV 92392 4386-E6
STINSON CT
7000 FONT 92336 574-B6
STIRRUP DR
23300 DBAR 91765 680-B1
STIRRUP LN
4600 TNP 92277 4892-H1
5300 FONT 92336 574-D1
26700 SBdC - (3935-F5 See Page 3934)
STIVERS RD
14400 VCTV 92394 4295-H7
STOCKER RD
700 BBLK - 4811-F2
STOCKER ST
2100 POM 91767 601-A5
STOCKTON AV
13700 CHNO 91710 681-J2
STOCKWELL MINE RD
- InCo 93545 2055-E2
N STODDARD AV
100 SBDO 92401 606-G1
1000 SBDO 92410 576-G6
1200 SBDO 92405 576-G1
4400 SBDO 92407 546-G5
S STODDARD AV
100 SBDO 92401 606-G2
S STODDARD CT
1500 SBDO 92408 606-H5
W STODDARD CT
400 SBDO 92408 606-H5
STODDARD WY
19000 APLV 92308 4387-B7
19000 APLV 92308 4477-B4
STODDARD MOUNTAIN RD
- SBdC 92311 369-C1
STODDARD VALLEY RD
- SBdC 92311 369-D1
STODDARD WELLS RD
15500 VCTV 92392 4296-F3
16700 VCTV 92394 4296-F1
17100 VCTV 92394 (4206-G6 See Page 4116)
18200 SBdC 92394 (4206-G6 See Page 4116)
18500 APLV 92394 (4206-G6 See Page 4116)
18500 APLV 92307 (4206-G6 See Page 4116)
18500 APLV 92307 4207-A4
19400 SBdC 92307 4207-A4
19900 SBdC 92307 (4117-F6 See Page 4116)
20900 APLV 92307 (4117-F6 See Page 4116)
21200 APLV 92307 4118-A5
21400 SBdC 92307 4118-E3
23200 SBdC 92307 369-C2
25500 SBdC 92311 369-D1
27500 SBdC 92311 (3849-E2 See Page 3758)
30800 SBdC 92311 (3759-H6 See Page 3758)
STONE CT
10300 SBdC 92359 608-H6
STONE DR
33100 SBdC - 519-D6
STONE RD
27300 SBdC - (3937-D3 See Page 3936)
40800 BBLK - 4811-F1

STONE AGE LN
17000 VCTV 92394 4295-J1
STONE BASIN RD
- SBdC 92371 4653-E2
STONE BRIDGE CIR
100 BBLK - 4741-G7
STONE BRIDGE RD
41400 BBLK - 4741-G7
STONEBROOK LN
2000 UPL 91784 571-J4
STONEBROOK PL
7300 RCUC 91730 573-E6
STONEBROOK RD
- APLV 92308 4387-B4
STONE CANYON RD
2800 CHLS 91709 681-A1
STONECREEK PL
- CHLS 91709 681-A3
STONE CREEK RD
5700 SBdC 92345 4563-F7
STONECREEK TR
8300 HESP 92345 4565-J2
S STONE CREEK WY
2600 ONT 91761 643-C6
STONECRESS ST
- VCTV 92394 4295-J7
STONECREST DR
11500 RCUC 91730 573-D7
STONECREST PL
1400 DBAR 91765 680-D3
STONECROSS ST
- VCTV 92394 4295-J7
STONEGATE CIR
- POM 91766 640-F6
12200 VCTV 92392 4385-G6
STONEGATE CT
29000 HIGH 92346 578-C6
STONEGATE DR
6700 CHNO 91710 642-B6
6800 CHNO 91762 642-B6
8500 RCUC 91730 602-F2
12100 VCTV 92392 4385-G7
STONEGATE LN
1300 SBDO 92407 546-E6
29000 HIGH 92346 578-C6
STONEHAVEN PL
7300 RCUC 91730 573-E6
STONEHENGE AV
5400 HESP 92345 (4657-B2 See Page 4656)
5400 SBdC 92345 (4657-B2 See Page 4656)
5800 SBdC 92345 4567-B7
STONEHENGE RD
32700 SBdC 92365 (3685-E4 See Page 3594)
STONEHILL AV
1700 SBdC 92252 4819-D5
4100 SBdC 92252 4889-D1
STONEHILL CT
2500 CLAR 91711 571-D6
STONEHILL DR
500 SBdC - 518-B2
W STONEHURST DR
1900 RLTO 92377 575-B3
STONE MOUNTAIN DR
4100 CHLS 91709 711-E2
STONE MOUNTAIN PL
5200 RCUC 91737 573-A1
STONE PINE CT
6800 CHNO 91710 682-B3
STONERIDGE CT
28300 HIGH 92346 578-B4
W STONERIDGE CT
1100 ONT 91762 601-J7
1100 ONT 91762 641-H1
STONE RIDGE DR
- CHLS 91709 681-G7
STONERIDGE DR
11500 RCUC 91730 573-D6
13300 SBdC 92392 4386-H3
STONE RIVER DR
10900 RCUC 91737 573-C2
STONESIDE DR
8500 RCUC 91730 602-F3
STONEWOOD DR
12200 GTER 92313 646-E4
STONEWOOD LN
8300 RivC 92509 644-F7
STONEY CREEK CT
7600 HIGH 92346 577-J6
STONEY CREEK DR
7100 HIGH 92346 577-J5
STONEY CREEK RD
100 BBLK - 4742-B7
300 BBLK 92314 4742-B7
300 SBdC 92314 4742-B7
STONEY HILL DR
8500 RCUC 91730 602-F2
STONY CT
1500 RDL 92374 608-D4
STONYBROOK PL
12700 CHNO 91710 642-B6
STONY POINT PL
- POM 91766 640-G7
STONY RIDGE RD
43200 SBdC - (4483-J6 See Page 4482)
43200 SBdC - 4484-B5
43200 SBdC 92285 4484-B5

STREET	Block	City	ZIP	Pg-Grid
STORELINE RD				
	-	SBdC	92371	4653-B2
STORER CT				
	100	RivC	92507	646-E6
STORKMANS RD				
	-	SBdC	92284	4887-C7
STORRS PL				
	900	POM	91766	640-F3
STOVALL WY				
	-	YCPA	92399	649-E3
STOWE CT				
	1900	CLAR	91711	571-D7
E STOWELL ST				
	-	UPL	91786	602-C3
STRAIGHT WY				
	23700	SBdC	-	516-H3
STRAIGHT ARROW RD				
	15300	APLV	92307	4297-E5
STRANG LN				
	8700	RCUC	91701	572-F1
STRANGE CREEK DR				
	23800	DBAR	91765	640-C5
STRATFORD AV				
	3200	CHLS	91709	681-B5
STRATFORD CIR				
	1700	RDL	92374	608-G7
STRATFORD DR				
	-	RCUC	91739	573-F5
STRATFORD ST				
	3400	HIGH	92346	577-G5
	3400	SBDO	92346	577-H5
	27900	HIGH	92346	578-A5
STRATHMORE RD				
	7700	HIGH	92346	578-B7
STRATOFREIGHTER CT				
	-	SBDO	92409	577-F7
STRATOLIFTER CT				
	-	SBDO	92409	577-F7
STRATTON CT				
	10100	RCUC	91737	573-A1
STRAWBERRY LN				
	27000	SBdC	-	(3935-J3 See Page 3934)
	31300	SBdC	-	4480-F1
STRAWBERRY PL				
	-	RCUC	91739	573-J6
	5800	CHNO	91710	641-J6
STRAWBERRY ST				
	4100	RIV	92501	645-H7
STRAWBERRY CREEK PL				
	3500	ONT	91761	643-B6
STRAWBERRY CREEK WY				
	3700	ONT	91761	643-C6
STRAWBERRY LOOKOUT RD				
	900	SBdC	-	517-E4
STRAWBERRY PEAK RD				
	800	SBdC	-	517-E3
STRAWFLOWER LN				
	1500	DBAR	91765	680-B4
STRAW PEAK RD				
	70500	SBdC	-	329-A7
STREAM LN				
	400	SBdC	-	514-A3
STREAMSIDE AV				
	6200	SBDO	92407	545-G1
STREAMSIDE CT				
	8000	FONT	92336	604-A1
STREATER AV				
	7300	HIGH	92346	578-B5
STREET OF THE CHIMES				
	13900	CHLS	91709	681-B2
STRIPER ST				
	5200	SBdC	92345	(4655-E3 See Page 4654)
STRONGBOW DR				
	600	DBAR	91765	640-B6
E STUART AV				
	200	RDL	92374	608-C7
W STUART AV				
	-	RDL	92374	608-B7
STUART WY				
	-	FONT	92336	574-A6
STUD VALLEY RD				
	52500	SBdC	-	4886-H4
N STULMAN ST				
	300	SBDO	92410	606-C1
STUVELING ST				
	4500	SBdC	92371	4653-C1
	10100	SBdC	92345	4654-H1
	11200	SBdC	92345	(4655-A1 See Page 4654)
	12100	SBdC	92345	4565-D7
SUDBURY WY				
	-	FONT	92336	544-C7
SUDLOW RD				
	19000	APLV	92308	4387-B3
SUE AV				
	1600	RDL	92374	648-G1
SUENO CT				
	11600	FONT	92337	644-J3
	11600	FONT	92337	645-A3
SUENO LN				
	15600	VCTV	92394	4296-C4
SUEY CT				
	6500	SBdC	-	4844-C2
SUFFOCH RD				
	-	SBdC	92365	(3763-F1 See Page 3762)
SUFFOCH RD				
	34500	SBdC	92365	(3683-F4 See Page 3592)
SUFFOLK PL				
	-	FONT	92336	573-J7
	-	RCUC	91739	573-F6
SUGAR CONE LN				
	26400	SBdC	-	517-F3
SUGAR GUM ST				
	12300	RCUC	91739	573-F6
SUGARLOAF AV				
	1800	UPL	91784	571-H5
W SUGARLOAF BLVD				
	200	SBdC	92314	4742-B6
SUGAR LOAF TKTR				
	42500	SBdC	-	4812-A5
E SUGAR MAPLE CT				
	3400	ONT	91761	643-B5
N SUGAR PINE AV				
	2700	RLTO	92377	545-A6
SUGAR PINE CT				
	6600	CHNO	91710	682-B3
SUGAR PINE DR				
	27400	SBdC	-	4737-H7
	32100	SBdC	-	517-H1
E SUGAR PINE LN				
	1700	CLTN	92324	646-G1
SUGAR PINE PL				
	6600	RCUC	91701	572-H5
W SUGARPINE RD				
	1100	SBdC	92314	4742-B7
	12000	BBLK	-	4742-B7
SUGAR PINE ST				
	6700	CHNO	91710	682-B3
SUGARPINE MOUNTAIN RD				
	600	SBdC	-	515-F1
	600	SBdC	-	(4735-E5 See Page 4654)
SUGAR PINES CIR				
	6300	SBdC	-	4950-F2
SULGROVE ST				
	26100	BARS	92311	(3759-A5 See Page 3758)
SULLIVAN				
	82300	SBdC	92277	(4895-A5 See Page 4824)
SULLIVAN RD				
	62500	SBdC	92252	4959-D1
	64700	SBdC	92252	4960-A1
	65100	SBdC	92252	4890-C7
	66300	SBdC	92277	4890-D7
	66300	TNP	92277	4890-H7
	68200	TNP	92277	4891-A7
	72100	TNP	92277	4892-H6
	75300	TNP	92277	4893-A6
	77700	SBdC	92277	4893-F6
	77900	SBdC	92277	(4894-A6 See Page 4824)
W SULLIVAN ST				
	1100	UPL	91784	571-H6
	1100	UPL	91784	572-A6
SULPHUR DR				
	4900	RivC	91752	683-G3
SULTANA AV				
	7300	FONT	92336	574-E6
	7700	FONT	92336	604-E1
	7900	SBdC	92336	604-E1
	8100	SBdC	92335	604-E2
	10400	FONT	92337	604-E7
	10400	SBdC	92337	604-E7
	10600	FONT	92337	644-E1
	12900	ONT	91761	642-C7
	13700	ONT	91761	682-C2
	14000	ONT	91710	682-C2
	15800	SBdC	91710	682-D7
	16100	SBdC	91710	712-D1
N SULTANA AV				
	100	ONT	91761	642-C1
	100	ONT	91764	602-C6
	100	ONT	91764	642-C1
	1500	ONT	91786	602-C6
	1500	UPL	91786	602-C6
S SULTANA AV				
	-	UPL	91786	602-C4
	100	ONT	91761	642-C2
SULTANA ST				
	11700	HESP	92345	4475-B7
	14500	HESP	92345	4476-A7
	17100	HESP	92345	4566-G1
SULTANA WY				
	-	FONT	92337	644-E2
SUMAC AV				
	8800	HESP	92345	4476-J7
	8800	HESP	92345	4477-A6
SUMAC CT				
	-	FONT	92337	645-A1
	900	BARS	92311	3679-H4
SUMACH LN				
	16800	CHLS	91709	710-F3
SUMMER ST				
	11400	ADEL	92301	4295-A6
SUMMERBREEZE CIR				
	14600	CHLS	91709	681-B4
SUMMER CANYON RD				
	1000	CHLS	91709	710-F2
SUMMERDALE DR				
	1300	POM	91766	640-G3
SUMMERFIELD CT				
	12700	CHNO	91710	642-B7
SUMMERFIELD PL				
	7100	RCUC	91701	573-B6
SUMMERHILL RD				
	9700	RCUC	91737	572-J1
E SUMMER ISLAND CT				
	3200	ONT	91761	643-C5
SUMMERLAND LN				
	-	FONT	92336	574-D5
SUMMER PLACE CT				
	8000	FONT	92336	604-A1
SUMMERS RD				
	-	SBdC	92284	4748-H4
SUMMERSET DR				
	2900	RLTO	92377	544-J6
	14300	CHLS	91709	680-H4
N SUMMERSET DR				
	1500	RLTO	92377	575-D1
W SUMMERSET DR				
	2100	RLTO	92377	545-A6
SUMMERSET RD				
	8700	SBdC	-	4481-G6
	23300	SBdC	92347	3588-B5
	36100	SBdC	92347	3678-B2
SUMMERSET ST				
	42500	SBdC	92365	(3683-G3 See Page 3592)
	45700	SBdC	92365	(3684-B3 See Page 3594)
SUMMERSIDE DR				
	11100	RCUC	91737	573-D4
SUMMERSTONE CT				
	6700	RCUC	91701	573-D5
SUMMERTRAIL PL				
	28200	HIGH	92346	578-A4
SUMMERWOOD DR				
	34800	YCPA	92399	609-J7
	34800	YCPA	92399	610-A7
SUMMERWOOD WY				
	8900	FONT	92335	604-G3
SUMMIT AV				
	-	RLTO	92377	574-G2
	-	RDL	92373	648-D2
	14600	FONT	92336	574-E2
	14600	RCUC	91739	574-E2
	18300	RLTO	92377	575-A2
SUMMIT BLVD				
	300	BBLK	-	4811-H2
	800	SBdC	-	4811-H2
SUMMIT CT				
	-	UPL	91784	571-H6
S SUMMIT CT				
	2100	CLTN	92324	646-H4
SUMMIT DR				
	900	SBdC	-	516-E4
	5400	SBdC	92397	4652-F3
	6500	HIGH	92346	578-C3
	9500	SBdC	92339	611-H3
	30800	SBdC	-	518-H6
	73200	TNP	92277	4892-D6
SUMMIT LN				
	41000	BBLK	-	4811-F2
SUMMIT RD				
	300	SBdC	-	517-J2
W SUMMIT ST				
	1200	RLTO	92377	575-C2
SUMMIT TKTR				
	4300	SBdC	92345	(4655-A4 See Page 4654)
SUMMIT WY				
	9500	SBdC	92339	611-H3
SUMMIT B AV				
	1300	RDL	92373	648-D2
SUMMIT CREST CT				
	1500	SBDO	92405	576-D1
SUMMITCREST DR				
	-	CHLS	91709	681-B4
SUMMIT POST OFFICE RD				
	4000	SBdC	92345	(4655-A5 See Page 4654)
SUMMITRIDGE DR				
	900	DBAR	91765	680-D3
SUMMIT TRAIL RD				
	15300	CHLS	91709	680-G6
SUMMIT VALLEY RD				
	3800	SBdC	-	(4655-D6 See Page 4654)
	3800	SBdC	92345	(4655-D4 See Page 4654)
	5700	HESP	92345	4565-J7
	5700	HESP	92345	(4655-D4 See Page 4654)
	5900	SBdC	92345	4565-J7
	6000	SBdC	92345	4566-A7
	6200	HESP	92345	4566-D6
SUMMITVIEW LN				
	-	CHLS	91709	681-B4
SUMMREST ST				
	-	SBdC	92365	(3685-E5 See Page 3594)
SUMNER AV				
	1400	CLAR	91711	601-A2
	1800	CLAR	91711	571-A7
	2800	POM	91767	601-A2
	5800	RivC	92880	683-B5
	14400	ONT	91710	683-B5
	14400	ONT	91761	683-B5
SUMTER ST				
	-	FONT	92336	573-J7
SUN AV				
	25600	LMLN	92354	607-D6
E SUN AV				
	-	RDL	92374	608-C6
W SUN AV				
	-	RDL	92374	608-A6
SUN CT				
	6100	TNP	92277	4892-E5
SUNBEAM AV				
	4900	SBdC	92252	4889-J4
SUN BEAM AV				
	7100	SBdC	92252	4959-J1
SUNBIRD CT				
	12600	VCTV	92392	4385-D5
SUNBIRD LN				
	12400	VCTV	92392	4385-D5
SUNBROOK DR				
	1000	SBDO	92407	546-F5
SUNBURST AV				
	500	SBdC	92252	4749-C6
	1700	SBdC	92252	4819-C4
	3800	SBdC	92252	4889-C1
SUNBURST CIR				
	40500	BBLK	-	4811-E2
	61700	SBdC	92252	4959-C1
	61900	SBdC	92252	4889-C7
SUNBURST DR				
	10500	RCUC	91730	573-B7
	15900	FONT	92336	574-G6
	60700	SBdC	92252	4958-J1
	61000	SBdC	92252	4959-A1
SUNBURST RD				
	17700	SBdC	92392	4386-H5
SUNBURST ST				
	5800	SBdC	92252	4889-C7
SUNBURST TR				
	-	CHLS	91709	640-J7
SUNCREEK DR				
	13500	YCPA	92399	650-C6
SUNCREST CIR				
	-	SBDO	92407	546-F5
SUN CREST CT				
	400	SBdC	-	4812-D2
SUNCREST CT				
	13500	YCPA	92399	650-C6
SUN CREST RD				
	13500	SBdC	-	(4390-A3 See Page 4300)
SUNCREST RD				
	28700	SBdC	-	(4389-H2 See Page 4299)
	28700	SBdC	92307	(4389-H2 See Page 4299)
E SUNDANCE				
	1300	SBdC	92314	4742-G7
SUNDANCE CIR				
	13200	VCTV	92392	4385-F6
SUNDANCE CT				
	3000	CHLS	91709	681-A6
	35600	YCPA	92399	650-B5
SUNDANCE DR				
	-	POM	91766	640-F5
	5100	MTCL	91763	601-G6
	10700	RCUC	91730	573-B7
N SUNDANCE DR				
	5000	SBDO	92407	546-E5
SUNDANCE LN				
	100	BARS	92311	3679-B4
SUNDANCE RD				
	-	APLV	92308	4387-F5
	5900	SBdC	-	(4571-A7 See Page 4570)
SUNDANCE HILL DR				
	5100	CHLS	91709	711-G3
SUNDAR DR				
	1000	CALI	92320	649-J7
SUNDERLAND CT				
	500	SBdC	-	518-A3
SUNDIAL DR				
	2400	CHLS	91709	680-G5
	2400	CHLS	91709	681-A4
SUNDOWN CT				
	-	RDL	92374	608-F5
	13100	VCTV	92392	4385-F4
SUNDOWN DR				
	3700	SBdC	92371	4563-A2
SUNDOWN LN				
	-	SBdC	-	(3855-C3 See Page 3764)
	12800	CHLS	91709	640-H7
SUNDOWN RD				
	12600	VCTV	92392	4385-F4
SUNDOWN TR				
	8700	SBdC	92256	4956-D7
	8900	SBdC	92256	616-D1
	30500	SBdC	-	(3846-G2 See Page 3756)
SUNDOWNER CT				
	4900	RCUC	91737	(543-C7 See Page 513)
	4900	RCUC	91737	573-C1
SUNDOWNER TR				
	13600	SBdC	92307	(4389-H2 See Page 4299)
SUNEVER AV				
	4300	SBdC	92252	4889-H4
	6900	SBdC	92252	4959-H1
SUNEVER RD				
	-	SBdC	92252	4749-H7
	1700	SBdC	92252	4819-H2
SUNEVER RD				
	4300	SBdC	92252	4889-H2
SUNFAIR RD				
	-	SBdC	92252	4750-A7
	200	SBdC	92252	4749-J6
	200	SBdC	92278	4749-J6
	1600	SBdC	92252	4820-A2
	4100	SBdC	92252	4890-A2
	6800	SBdC	92252	4960-A1
SUNFIELD WY				
	2300	UPL	91784	572-C3
SUNFISH BLVD				
	-	LPCo	-	4606-H2
SUNFLOWER AV				
	8000	RCUC	91701	572-E3
	22700	SBdC	-	(4115-H1 See Page 4114)
	22800	SBdC	-	(4025-H7 See Page 3934)
W SUNFLOWER AV				
	2300	SBDO	92407	546-A3
	2700	SBDO	92407	545-H2
SUNFLOWER CT				
	1800	BARS	92311	3679-E4
	18000	HESP	92345	4566-J5
SUNFLOWER DR				
	-	YUCA	92284	4887-G3
	57700	SBdC	92284	4888-A2
SUNFLOWER LN				
	-	SBdC	-	518-A2
	-	SBdC	-	(4025-G7 See Page 3934)
	-	SBdC	-	(4115-G1 See Page 4114)
	15100	VCTV	92394	4295-H6
SUNFLOWER PL				
	100	CLAR	91711	571-D6
SUNFLOWER RD				
	62100	SBdC	92252	4889-C2
	64600	SBdC	92252	4890-A2
SUNFLOWER ST				
	8900	RCUC	91701	572-G3
	9500	RCUC	91737	572-H3
SUNFLOWER WY				
	4400	CHNO	91710	681-E1
SUNFLOWER SPRINGS RD				
	16100	SBdC	-	371-F1
	22400	SBdC	-	351-E11
SUNFLOWER SPRINGS SPUR				
	-	SBdC	-	371-F4
SUNGLOW AV				
	9600	SBdC	92335	604-E5
SUNGLOW CT				
	9500	RCUC	91730	602-J5
SUN GOD PL				
	700	BBLK	-	4811-F2
SUNGOLD AV				
	-	SBdC	92252	4959-H1
	-	SBdC	92278	4749-H6
	400	SBdC	92252	4749-H6
SUN GOLD AV				
	4900	SBdC	92252	4889-H4
SUNHILL DR				
	-	VCTV	92392	4386-E1
SUN KIST AV				
	-	SBdC	92252	4819-J4
	4300	SBdC	92252	4889-J3
	6800	SBdC	92252	4959-J1
E SUNKIST ST				
	100	ONT	91761	642-C1
W SUNKIST ST				
	100	ONT	91762	642-B1
SUNLAND DR				
	56300	YUCA	92284	4957-G2
SUNLAND TR				
	54900	YUCA	92284	4957-C2
SUNLIGHT DR				
	34300	YCPA	92399	649-H5
	35300	YCPA	92399	650-B5
SUNLIGHT RD				
	-	SBdC	92277	4824-F3
SUN LOMA RD				
	4300	SBdC	92252	4889-H2
SUN MEADOW CT				
	-	RCUC	91730	602-J5
SUN MESA DR				
	56400	YUCA	92284	4887-F3
	57100	SBdC	92284	4887-H3
	57700	SBdC	92284	4888-A3
	59800	SBdC	92252	4888-E3
SUN MESA RD				
	-	SBdC	-	(4390-J6 See Page 4300)
	-	SBdC	-	(4391-A7 See Page 4300)
	23300	SBdC	92308	4388-D7
	23300	SBdC	92308	4478-D1
	25500	SBdC	92308	(4389-A7 See Page 4299)
	62500	SBdC	92252	4889-D2
	64700	SBdC	92252	4890-A2
SUNMORE PKWY				
	4700	TNP	92277	4892-H1
SUNNY AV				
	5800	YUCA	92284	4887-G6
SUNNY CIR				
	5800	RivC	91752	683-H5
SUNNY LN				
	400	BBLK	-	4811-C1
SUNNY PL				
	7100	YUCA	92284	4957-G2
SUNNY RD				
	8800	SBdC	92252	4959-E6
N SUNNYBROOK AV				
	1600	UPL	91784	572-C6
SUNNY BROOK LN				
	2900	CHLS	91709	681-B2
SUNNYCREEK CT				
	2000	UPL	91784	571-H5
SUNNYCREST CT				
	24300	DBAR	91765	680-E2
SUNNYCREST DR				
	-	TNP	92277	4891-E7
SUNNYCREST LN				
	69900	TNP	92277	4891-E7
SUNNYFIELD CIR				
	1300	UPL	91784	572-D6
SUNNYGLEN CT				
	3000	CHLS	91709	681-B2
	8300	RCUC	91730	602-F2
SUNNY HILL AV				
	-	SBdC	92252	4748-J5
SUNNYHILL DR				
	4000	RivC	92509	644-G7
SUNNY HILL PL				
	900	DBAR	91765	680-D2
SUNNYHILL RD				
	3300	SBdC	92252	4819-A7
	4000	SBdC	92252	4889-A1
	6500	SBdC	92252	4959-A1
SUNNY HILLS AV				
	-	SBdC	92252	4819-A4
	1800	SBdC	92252	4818-J3
SUNNY HILLS PL				
	6200	RCUC	91737	573-C4
SUNNY MEADOW LN				
	6000	CHLS	91709	712-A4
SUNNYPARK				
	1700	RDL	92374	648-G1
SUNNYRIDGE CIR				
	-	POM	91766	640-F5
SUNNY RIDGE LP				
	7500	HIGH	92346	578-C6
SUNNY SANDS DR				
	-	SBdC	92252	4820-A5
	57300	SBdC	92284	4817-F5
	57400	SBdC	92284	4818-A5
	60100	SBdC	92252	4818-G5
	61100	SBdC	92252	4819-A5
	67300	SBdC	92277	4820-F4
	68900	SBdC	92277	4821-B4
	72600	SBdC	92277	4822-B4
SUNNY SANDS RD				
	-	TNP	92277	4822-A4
	-	TNP	92278	4822-A4
	72100	SBdC	92277	4822-A4
SUNNYSIDE AV				
	400	RDL	92373	647-J3
	400	RDL	92373	648-A3
	7800	SBdC	92410	577-B7
	8100	SBdC	92410	607-B1
S SUNNYSIDE AV				
	800	SBDO	92408	607-B4
SUNNYSIDE DR				
	10700	YCPA	92399	610-A6
	11000	YCPA	92399	650-A1
SUNNY SLOPE				
	-	SBdC	-	548-H1
SUNNYSLOPE DR				
	5600	YUCA	92284	4957-D1
	13200	CHLS	91709	681-A1
	56100	SBdC	92285	4747-E1
	57500	YUCA	92284	4958-A1
	66300	SBdC	92252	4890-E5
	66300	SBdC	92277	4890-E5
	66700	TNP	92277	4890-H5
	70900	TNP	92277	4891-G4
	71800	TNP	92277	4892-A4
SUNNYSLOPE LN				
	8800	SBdC	92371	4562-J1
SUNNY SLOPE LN				
	46300	SBdC	-	(4743-A3 See Page 4662)
SUNNYSLOPE RD				
	-	SBdC	-	4812-D2
	-	POM	91766	640-H5
	900	SBdC	92372	4562-D1
	2200	SBdC	92371	4562-G1
	3600	SBdC	92371	4563-A1
	55400	SBdC	92285	4747-D2
SUNNY TRAILS DR				
	11300	APLV	92308	4477-C1
SUNNYVALE DR				
	-	SBdC	92277	4893-J3
	72100	TNP	92277	4892-A4
SUNNYVIEW DR				
	2800	RLTO	92377	544-J6
	2800	RLTO	92377	545-C7
W SUNNYVIEW DR				
	1500	RLTO	92377	575-D1
	2100	RLTO	92377	545-A6
SUNNY VISTA AV				
	12300	VCTV	92392	4386-B6
SUNNY VISTA RD				
	100	SBdC	92284	4748-J6
	100	SBdC	92252	4748-H3
	100	SBdC	92285	4748-H3
SUNNY VISTA RD				
	100	SBdC	92278	4748-H3
	1000	SBdC	92284	4818-J3
	1000	SBdC	92252	4818-J5
	6500	SBdC	92252	4888-J7
	6500	SBdC	92252	4958-J2
	9100	SBdC	92371	4474-E6
	9100	SBdC	92371	4564-E1
	10900	SBdC	92392	4474-D3
	11900	SBdC	92392	4384-D7
	15300	ADEL	92301	4294-D4
	15300	VCTV	92394	4296-B5
SUN ORO DR				
	4700	SBdC	92284	4888-A3
	33600	YUCA	92284	4888-A3
SUN ORO RD				
	58600	SBdC	92284	4888-C3
	64700	SBdC	92252	4889-J2
	64700	SBdC	92252	4890-A2
SUN PETAL CT				
	7600	FONT	92336	574-D7
SUN RAY CT				
	11900	SBdC	92256	615-G7
SUN RAY RD				
	4300	SBdC	92252	4889-J2
	4900	SBdC	92252	4890-A3
SUNRIDGE CT				
	6400	RCUC	91737	573-E4
SUN RIDGE DR				
	2100	CHLS	91709	680-J4
SUNRIDGE WY				
	100	RDL	92373	648-E3
SUNRISE AV				
	-	TNP	92277	4891-H7
W SUNRISE AV				
	2800	RLTO	92377	574-J1
	2800	RLTO	92377	575-A1
SUNRISE BLVD				
	4300	SBdC	92371	4473-B7
SUNRISE CIR				
	-	SBdC	-	2971-H1
	-	RivC	91752	683-E5
SUNRISE CIR E				
	1300	UPL	91784	571-G4
SUNRISE CIR N				
	1300	UPL	91784	571-J4
SUNRISE CIR S				
	1300	UPL	91784	571-H4
SUNRISE CIR W				
	1400	UPL	91784	571-H4
SUNRISE CT				
	3000	CHLS	91709	681-B5
	7100	HIGH	92346	578-D5
	9500	SBdC	92371	4473-B7
	11300	RCUC	91701	573-D5
	14400	VCTV	92394	4295-J5
SUNRISE DR				
	30900	HIGH	92346	578-J7
	74400	TNP	92277	4962-G1
W SUNRISE DR				
	2300	RLTO	92377	575-A1
E SUNRISE LN				
	2000	SBdC	92404	577-D4
	2000	SBDO	92404	577-D4
SUNRISE PL				
	29300	HIGH	92346	578-D5
SUNRISE RD				
	900	SBdC	92277	4751-H6
	1300	SBdC	92277	4821-H1
	1500	BARS	92311	3680-A5
	4600	SBdC	92277	4891-H3
	4600	TNP	92277	4891-H3
	31900	SBdC	-	4480-H1
	32700	SBdC	-	4481-A1
SUNRISE ST				
	8000	FONT	92336	604-A1
SUNRISE TR				
	-	SBdC	-	3936-H1
	30500	SBdC	-	(3846-H3 See Page 3756)
SUNRISE WY				
	-	BBLK	-	4742-A6
	-	SBdC	92277	4824-G5
	25700	LMLN	92354	647-D2
SUNRISE CANYON RD				
	36500	SBdC	92365	3592-J5
	36500	SBdC	92365	(3593-A6 See Page 3592)
SUN RIVER CT				
	10700	APLV	92308	4477-D3
SUNRIVER DR				
	800	DBAR	91765	680-E1
SUNRIVER ST				
	6800	CHNO	91710	642-B5
	6800	CHNO	91762	642-B5
W SUN RIVER ST				
	1400	UPL	91784	571-H6
SUNROSE AV				
	-	CHNO	91710	642-B6
SUN ROSE AV				
	14500	SBdC	-	(4303-B5 See Page 4302)
SUNROSE CT				
	-	CHNO	91710	642-B6
SUN ROSE ST				
	10600	SBdC	92301	4114-H3
SUNSCAPE CT				
	16100	CHLS	91709	711-G1
SUNSET				
	900	NDLS	92363	3620-B6
SUNSET				
	1300	SBdC	-	4737-H5
	21600	SBdC	92347	349-B7
SUNSET AV				
	12100	SBdC	-	(4390-H5 See Page 4300)
	56500	YUCA	92284	4887-G2
SUNSET CIR				
	-	SBdC	-	2971-G1
N SUNSET CIR				
	900	RLTO	92376	575-E6
SUNSET CT				
	1100	SBdC	91784	571-J3
	1700	RDL	92373	648-J4
	1800	BARS	92311	3680-B5
	15500	VCTV	92394	4295-J5
	27900	SBdC	-	(3935-J2 See Page 3934)
	37800	SBdC	92399	610-H7
E SUNSET CT				
	2100	CLTN	92324	646-H4
SUNSET CUR				
	2300	SBdC	91784	571-J3
SUNSET DR				
	100	SBdC	-	518-B1
	11200	SBdC	92399	611-C7
	12500	SBdC	-	(4390-A4 See Page 4300)
	13000	SBdC	-	(4389-J3 See Page 4299)
	13400	APLV	92308	4387-D3
	16700	VCTV	92392	4386-E2
	20300	SBdC	92308	4567-F3
	24900	SBdC	-	517-B5
	42900	BBLK	-	4812-B2
	74500	TNP	92277	4962-H1
E SUNSET DR N				
	200	RDL	92373	648-E3
E SUNSET DR S				
	30100	RDL	92373	648-H5
W SUNSET DR S				
	-	RDL	92373	648-B4
SUNSET LN				
	100	SBdC	-	4742-F7
	200	SBdC	-	4812-F2
	500	SBdC	-	516-G2
	7100	HIGH	92346	578-D5
	19700	APLV	92307	4387-D2
	39900	SBdC	92339	611-D2
N SUNSET LN				
	3700	SBDO	92407	545-F1
W SUNSET LN				
	2500	SBDO	92407	546-A5
SUNSET PL				
	11500	APLV	92308	4477-B4
SUNSET RD				
	-	SBdC	92285	4667-E4
	100	SBdC	92252	4749-B6
	1500	SBdC	92372	4472-D2
	1900	SBdC	92252	4819-B5
	3200	SBdC	92371	4472-H2
	3800	SBdC	92371	4473-A2
	5700	SBdC	92252	4889-B6
	6700	SBdC	92252	4959-B2
	7500	SBdC	92371	4474-A2
	8900	SBdC	92392	4474-H1
	11300	SBdC	92392	4475-A1
	12600	VCTV	92392	4475-C1
	32100	SBdC	-	4480-H1
	32700	SBdC	-	4481-A1
	45700	SBdC	92365	(3504-C6 See Page 3414)
SUNSET ST				
	1400	BARS	92311	3680-A5
	14200	HESP	92345	4475-H1
SUNSET TR				
	8300	RCUC	91730	603-A2
SUNSET WY				
	16700	CHLS	91709	710-F3
SUNSET CROSSING RD				
	22600	DBAR	91765	640-A6
	22600	INDS	91789	640-A6
SUNSET HILLS LN				
	1000	RDL	92373	648-C6
SUNSET LOOP RD				
	25800	SBdC	-	517-D3
SUNSET PEAK MTWY				
	-	LACo	91711	571-A1
	-	LACo	91750	571-A1
SUNSET RIDGE DR				
	-	POM	91766	640-G4
SUNSET VIEW RD				
	600	SBdC	-	517-D3
	8800	SBdC	92308	4477-D7
	8800	SBdC	92308	4567-D1
	36500	SBdC	92347	(3587-E7 See Page 3586)
SUNSET VISTA CT				
	3100	CHLS	91709	681-B2
SUNSHINE DR				
	1200	BARS	92311	3679-J5
SUNSHINE LN				
	-	SBdC	92252	4749-J7
	-	SBdC	92252	4819-J1
	-	SBdC	92252	4820-A2
	15100	SBdC	-	(3935-J3 See Page 3934)
SUNSHINE ACRES				
	37100	SBdC	-	4302-B6
W SUNSONG CT				
	1000	ONT	91762	641-J2
	1000	ONT	91762	642-A2
SUNSTONE AV				
	5100	RCUC	91701	572-F1
	7400	RCUC	91730	572-G7
SUNSTONE CT				
	8700	RCUC	91701	572-F4
SUNSTONE RD				
	4700	CHLS	91709	711-F2
SUNSTREAM DR				
	13200	CHLS	91709	681-A1
SUNSWEPT DR				
	34400	SBdC	-	(4391-E3 See Page 4300)
SUN TERRACE DR				
	56100	SBdC	92284	4747-F4
SUN VALLEY CIR				
	13400	VCTV	92392	4385-F6
SUN VALLEY DR				
	100	BARS	92311	3678-F7
	100	BARS	92311	3758-F2
	100	SBdC	92311	3678-F7
	9700	MTCL	91763	601-G6
	10100	RCUC	91737	573-A1
	71000	TNP	92277	4891-G5
	72100	TNP	92277	4892-D4
N SUN VALLEY DR				
	4800	SBDO	92407	546-D5
SUN VIA DR				
	-	YUCA	92284	4887-H3
	57900	SBdC	92284	4888-D2
SUN VIEW AV				
	4700	SBdC	92252	4890-B4
	6800	SBdC	92252	4960-B1
	65000	SBdC	92252	4750-A6
SUN VIEW DR				
	1200	SBdC	92314	4813-C3
SUNVIEW DR				
	4400	CHNO	91710	641-E5
SUN VIEW RD				
	4300	SBdC	92252	4890-A2
SUNWAY DR				
	-	YUCA	92284	4887-G2
	56100	SBdC	92284	4747-F4
	57700	SBdC	92284	4888-A2
SUNWAY RD				
	12000	SBdC	92392	4384-D7
	64100	SBdC	92252	4889-H1
	64600	SBdC	92252	4890-A1
S SUNWEST CT				
	1900	SBDO	92408	606-H6
S SUNWEST LN				
	1900	SBDO	92408	606-H6
SUNWOOD DR				
	12900	VCTV	92392	4386-C5
SUNWOOD PL				
	10900	YCPA	92399	610-A7
SUPPLIES WY				
	12900	SBdC	93562	2144-J4
SURPRISE SPRINGS RD				
	-	SBdC	92284	4818-F7
	100	SBdC	92252	4749-E6
	900	SBdC	92252	4819-B2
	2200	SBdC	92252	4818-J4
	63500	SBdC	92278	4749-G3
	63500	SBdC	92278	4750-A1
	66000	SBdC	92278	370-D9
SURREY AV				
	100	SBdC	92284	4748-A7
	1400	SBdC	92284	4818-A2
	3700	SBdC	92284	4888-B1
	9000	MTCL	91763	601-F4
	11100	SBdC	91710	641-F3
SURREY CT				
	4800	YUCA	92284	4888-B3
	14100	VCTV	92394	4295-H6
	35000	SBdC	92311	3679-B4
SURREY LN				
	5500	SBDO	92407	546-A5
	7900	RCUC	91701	572-D2
	28400	HIGH	92346	578-B4
SURREY RD				
	-	SBdC	92365	(3684-A6 See Page 3594)
	26800	SBdC	92311	3679-B4
E SURREY WY				
	2800	ONT	91761	643-A7
SURVEYOR ST				
	3000	POM	91768	640-C2
SUSAN AV				
	1300	RDL	92374	608-E5
SUSAN ST				
	-	YCPA	92399	650-C6
SUSANA ST				
	6300	CHNO	91710	642-A7
N SUSIE LN				
	1700	SBDO	92411	576-C4
SUSSEX AV				
	12200	SBdC	-	(4390-C3 See Page 4300)
SUSSEX RD				
	22700	SBdC	92308	4478-B4
SUTHERLAND DR				
	1000	RDL	92373	648-H5
	27500	HIGH	92346	577-J7
SUTTER AV				
	11700	YCPA	92399	650-B2
N SUTTER AV				
	600	SBDO	92410	576-A7
S SUTTER AV				
	100	SBDO	92410	606-A2
SUTTER CT				
	10900	RCUC	91701	573-C5
	13500	FONT	92336	603-J1
	13500	FONT	92336	604-A1
	35600	YCPA	92399	650-B2
SUTTER DR				
	11600	ADEL	92301	4295-B5
	15100	VCTV	92394	4296-A7
SUTTER LN				
	500	SBdC	-	4737-E7
SUTTER RD				
	21900	SBdC	92308	4479-D5
	28500	SBdC	-	4479-J5
	28900	SBdC	-	4480-A5
	32700	SBdC	-	4481-A5
SUTTER ST				
	4900	CHNO	91710	641-F6
	13700	SBdC	93562	2055-B7
	18300	HESP	92345	4567-A1
	31500	SBdC	-	4480-G5
	34900	SBdC	-	4481-F5
	36300	SBdC	-	4482-A5
SUTTER WY				
	11800	ADEL	92301	4295-B6
N SUTTER WY				
	1600	UPL	91784	572-B6
SUTTER HOME PL				
	8200	RCUC	91730	602-G2
SUTTON AV				
	3900	SBdC	92252	4819-E5
	3900	SBdC	92252	4889-E1
SUTTON CT				
	300	POM	91767	601-A5
SUWANEE ST				
	4500	RIV	92501	645-G7
SUZANNE DR				
	11900	FONT	92337	644-D4
SUZANNE LN				
	6600	SBDO	92404	577-C4
SWALLOW DR				
	41100	BBLK	-	4741-F7
SWALLOW HILL DR				
	-	SBdC	92397	4652-A1
	26600	LACo	92397	4652-A1
SWAN DR				
	41400	BBLK	-	4811-G1
SWAN LN				
	-	SBdC	-	(4026-A7 See Page 3936)
	14900	SBdC	-	(4025-J7 See Page 3934)
SWAN RD				
	15700	FONT	92337	644-F3
SWANEE RD				
	-	SBdC	92285	(4485-A5 See Page 4484)
	-	SBdC	92285	(4575-A2 See Page 4484)
SWANSEA ST				
	-	SBdC	-	(3763-A1 See Page 3762)
	-	SBdC	92365	(3763-A1 See Page 3762)
SWANSON PL				
	7200	RCUC	91739	573-H6
SWARTHMORE CT				
	-	CLAR	91711	571-E4
SWARTHOUT LN				
	-	SBdC	92397	4652-E3
SWARTHOUT CANYON RD				
	6100	SBdC	-	(4733-J3 See Page 4653)
	6300	SBdC	-	4734-B4
	9100	SBdC	92407	4734-D6
SWAYZEE CT				
	500	RivC	92507	646-D7
SWEDLOW TR				
	39700	SBdC	92399	651-D2
SWEETBRIAR DR				
	100	CLAR	91711	571-D5
SWEET CLOVER CT				
	-	RivC	92880	683-B7
SWEETEN LN				
	3100	BARS	92311	3758-G1
SWEET GRASS LN				
	14000	CHLS	91709	680-H3
SWEET GUM CT				
	-	CHLS	91709	711-H2
SWEETGUM DR				
	12300	RCUC	91739	573-G6
SWEETLAND ST				
	800	CLAR	91711	601-B3
N SWEET LEAF AV				
	3700	RLTO	92377	544-J7
	3700	RLTO	92377	545-A6
SWEETPEA AV				
	22300	SBdC	-	(4115-J2 See Page 4114)
SWEET RAIN PL				
	9600	RCUC	91730	602-H5
SWEET ROCK LN				
	-	SBdC	92365	(3685-F5 See Page 3594)
SWEETSER DR				
	600	RivC	92507	646-D7
SWEET WATER CT				
	2400	CHLS	91709	680-J4

STREET	Block	City	ZIP	Pg-Grid
SWEETWATER CT				
	12700	VCTV	92392	4385-E5
SWEETWATER DR				
	3200	ONT	91761	643-B7
	12700	VCTV	92392	4385-D5
SWEETWATER LN				
	7500	HIGH	92346	578-D6
SWIFT FOX AV				
	16700	CHLS	91709	711-H2
SWIFT FOX CT				
	-	APLV	92307	4296-H5
SWIFTWING CT				
	16400	CHLS	91709	711-E2
SWISS CT				
	-	RivC	92880	683-D7
SWITZERLAND DR				
	41700	BBLK	-	4811-H2
	42000	BBLK	-	4812-A2
SWITZERLAND PL				
	800	BBLK	-	4811-H2
SYCAMORE AV				
	5400	SBdC	92377	575-E1
	9600	FONT	92335	604-F5
	12300	CHNO	91710	641-J6
	13400	CHNO	91710	681-J1
N SYCAMORE AV				
	100	RLTO	92376	605-H1
	500	RLTO	92376	575-H4
	2100	RLTO	92377	575-H3
	2300	SBdC	92377	575-H3
S SYCAMORE AV				
	-	RLTO	92316	605-H6
	100	RLTO	92376	605-H3
	300	CLAR	91711	601-E4
	1700	RLTO	92324	605-H6
	1900	CLTN	92316	605-H7
E SYCAMORE CIR				
	500	SBDO	92410	576-J6
	500	SBDO	92410	577-A6
SYCAMORE CT				
	700	UPL	91786	602-D4
	5900	CHNO	91710	681-J2
	6700	SBdC	-	4843-J3
E SYCAMORE CT				
	1100	ONT	91764	602-E4
SYCAMORE DR				
	-	RCUC	91730	603-C5
	500	SBdC	-	514-A1
	900	NDLS	92363	3620-B6
	9200	SBdC	92339	611-G2
	9400	FONT	92335	604-F5
	28300	HIGH	92346	578-B6
	28500	SBdC	-	518-B3
	36900	SBdC	92359	4950-E7
SYCAMORE GN				
	1800	CHLS	91709	680-H3
SYCAMORE LN				
	-	LACo	91768	640-A1
	12900	YCPA	92399	650-D5
	13300	CHNO	91710	681-J1
	16900	APLV	92307	4298-B1
	17000	APLV	92307	4208-B6
	23000	SBdC	-	516-F2
	28700	SBdC	-	518-B3
E SYCAMORE LN				
	1400	SBDO	92408	607-C6
SYCAMORE PK				
	-	DBAR	91765	680-B1
SYCAMORE RD				
	700	SBdC	92372	4472-B5
	38500	SBdC	-	3592-D7
E SYCAMORE RD				
	3000	ONT	91761	603-A7
SYCAMORE ST				
	-	HIGH	92359	609-D4
	-	RDL	92359	609-D4
	5300	SBdC	92397	4652-E3
	9700	FONT	92335	604-F5
	12000	SBdC	92316	645-E4
	12200	VCTV	92392	4475-C1
	14300	HESP	92345	4475-J1
	14600	HESP	92345	4476-A1
	15500	HESP	92345	4386-D7
	37000	SBdC	92347	(3587-E4 See Page 3586)
E SYCAMORE ST				
	1300	ONT	91764	602-E4
SYCAMORE TR				
	12900	YCPA	92399	650-E6
SYCAMORE WY				
	13900	CHNO	91710	681-J2
SYCAMORE RIDGE CT				
	4400	CHLS	91709	711-F2
SYDNEY AV				
	-	FONT	92336	574-D1
SYLLMAR CIR				
	200	CALI	92320	650-B7
SYLVAN AV				
	32100	SBdC	92311	3758-C4
SYLVAN BLVD				
	800	RDL	92374	608-D6
	1700	SBdC	92374	608-G7
SYLVAN CT				
	-	RCUC	91737	573-A2
SYLVAN GN				
	1000	BBLK	-	4812-B3
SYLVAN RD				
	16400	APLV	92307	4297-E1
SYLVANA LN				
	8500	RivC	92223	650-H7
SYLVANER CT				
	-	RCUC	91739	573-J7
	-	RCUC	91739	603-H1
SYLVAN GLEN RD				
	24100	DBAR	91765	640-D6
W SYLVIA CT				
	1400	UPL	91786	601-H1
SYMERON LN				
	15300	APLV	92307	4296-J5
SYMERON RD				
	17700	APLV	92307	4296-H5
	18300	APLV	92307	4297-A4
SYRACUSE CT				
	6400	CHNO	91710	682-A2
SYRACUSE DR				
	800	CLAR	91711	601-B1
	4300	SBDO	92407	546-C6
SYRACUSE RD				
	-	SBdC	-	4570-C1
	9400	SBdC	-	4480-B3
	13000	SBdC	-	(4390-B3 See Page 4300)
SYRACUSE ST				
	6300	CHNO	91710	682-A2
T				
T ST				
	600	NDLS	92363	3620-B4
TABLE MOUNTAIN CT				
	15900	VCTV	92394	4295-F4
TABLE MOUNTAIN RD				
	13300	VCTV	92394	4295-F4
TACKSTEM ST				
	10500	RCUC	91737	(543-B7 See Page 513)
	10700	RCUC	91737	573-C1
TACO DR				
	3300	SBdC	92277	4823-D4
	69700	SBdC	92277	4821-D5
	72900	SBdC	92277	4822-C5
	72900	TNP	92277	4822-C5
TACOMA CT				
	2800	SBdC	92252	4818-G5
TACOMA DR				
	11000	RCUC	91730	603-C3
TACONY CT				
	18300	APLV	92307	4296-J6
TACONY RD				
	14900	APLV	92307	4296-J5
TACT CT				
	3300	CHLS	91709	681-C4
TAEGE RD				
	-	RivC	92399	650-J7
TAEGE RANCH RD				
	7200	RivC	92324	647-A6
TAFT AV				
	3700	SBdC	91710	641-C4
TAFT CT				
	8500	YUCA	92284	4957-J6
TAFT ST				
	4900	CHNO	91710	641-F4
	25400	LMLN	92374	607-F6
TAGGART PL				
	-	RCUC	91739	573-G6
TAHITI RD				
	-	SBdC	92311	3590-B7
TAHITIAN PL				
	33500	YCPA	92399	649-F4
TAHOE AV				
	300	SBdC	92284	4747-G6
	900	SBdC	92284	4817-G1
TAHOE CT				
	800	SBdC	92284	4747-G7
	17700	ADEL	92301	4204-G7
TAHOE DR				
	-	YCPA	92399	609-J7
	-	YCPA	92399	610-A7
	41400	BBLK	-	4811-G1
S TAHOE DR				
	2500	ONT	91761	643-B5
TAHOE LN				
	800	SBdC	92284	4747-G7
	14000	SBdC	92392	4386-J1
TAHOE ST				
	700	RLTO	92376	575-F4
	19300	SBdC	92376	575-F4
W TAHOE ST				
	300	RLTO	92376	575-G4
TAHQUITZ RD				
	23800	SBdC	92307	4298-E2
TAI CT				
	-	SBdC	-	4844-A2
TAILWIND LN				
	6800	FONT	92336	574-F5
TAJANTA CT				
	14800	APLV	92307	4298-A6
TAJANTA RD				
	22100	APLV	92307	4298-A6
	25100	SBdC	92307	4298-H6
TA-KI-PI RD				
	16500	APLV	92307	4297-C2
	16800	APLV	92307	4207-C7
TALBOT CT				
	-	CHLS	91709	711-G3
TALBOT DR				
	38500	BBLK	-	4810-J2
	38700	BBLK	-	4811-A2
TALIHINA RD				
	19800	APLV	92307	4387-D1
TALISMAN LN				
	800	SBdC	-	4737-J6
	800	SBdC	-	4738-A6
TALISMAN ST				
	17700	HESP	92345	4476-H3
	18100	HESP	92345	4477-A2
TALLA RD				
	-	SBdC	92311	3758-C5
TALL OAK DR				
	2800	CHLS	91709	681-A7
TALLYHO				
	-	SBdC	92308	4567-G3
TALLYRAND DR				
	24400	DBAR	91765	680-E2
TALMADGE RD				
	500	BBLK	-	4811-D1
TALOGA CT				
	15700	APLV	92307	4296-J4
TALOGA LN				
	15700	APLV	92307	4296-J4
TALOGA RD				
	18300	APLV	92307	4296-J4
TALON DR				
	-	VCTV	92394	4205-F5
TALPA ST				
	15300	VCTV	92392	4386-B3
TAMARAC RD				
	18800	APLV	92307	4297-A5
TAMARACK DR				
	15300	VCTV	92392	4386-B2
	41900	BBLK	-	4811-H2
TAMARACK RD				
	-	SBdC	-	4738-E7
	400	SBdC	92372	4472-B7
	800	BBLK	-	4811-C2
	900	SBdC	-	4811-C3
	35300	SBdC	92311	(3677-J4 See Page 3586)
	35300	SBdC	92347	(3677-J1 See Page 3586)
	37100	SBdC	92347	(3587-H7 See Page 3586)
TAMARACK ST				
	12800	VCTV	92392	4475-E1
	25100	LMLN	92354	647-C2
TAMARACK WY				
	3000	RivC	91752	644-A5
S TAMARASK CT				
	2700	ONT	91761	642-H6
S TAMARASK DR				
	2700	ONT	91761	642-H6
TAMARIN ST				
	6000	SBdC	92371	4653-D2
	6300	SBdC	92371	4563-C7
E TAMARIND				
	2000	SBDO	92404	577-F1
TAMARIND AV				
	7300	FONT	92336	575-B7
	7800	FONT	92336	605-B1
	8100	FONT	92335	605-B2
	9600	SBdC	92335	605-B5
	9700	SBdC	92316	605-B5
	10500	FONT	92316	605-B7
	10500	FONT	92337	605-B7
	10600	FONT	92316	645-B2
	10600	SBdC	92316	645-B2
N TAMARIND AV				
	1200	FONT	92376	575-A5
	1200	RLTO	92376	575-A5
	3200	RLTO	92377	575-A1
	3300	RLTO	92377	545-A7
TAMARIND CT				
	-	CHLS	91709	711-G2
	17500	FONT	92316	605-B7
	17500	SBdC	92316	605-B7
TAMARIND TER				
	-	CHLS	91709	711-H1
TAMARISK AV				
	6200	TNP	92277	4892-E6
	6900	YUCA	92284	4957-G2
	7300	HESP	92345	4565-J1
	9100	HESP	92345	4475-H2
S TAMARISK AV				
	42700	BBLK	-	4812-A1
TAMARISK CIR				
	1200	UPL	91784	571-J6
	36100	YCPA	92399	650-E6
TAMARISK CT				
	-	APLV	92308	4387-C7
	56200	YUCA	92284	4957-G5
TAMARISK DR				
	1300	MohC	-	3620-D2
	12400	RCUC	91739	573-G5
	48600	SBdC	92256	615-F6
TAMARISK LN				
	4100	SBdC	92252	4889-E1
	12300	CHNO	91710	642-B6
TAMARISK PL				
	56200	YUCA	92284	4957-G5
TAMARISK RD				
	6600	HESP	92345	4565-J6
	11000	ADEL	92301	4294-J7
	11100	ADEL	92301	4295-A7
	12100	HESP	92345	4386-H6
	12100	HESP	92392	4386-H6
	12100	VCTV	92392	4386-H6
	12500	SBdC	92392	4386-H4
TAMARISK ST				
	100	RDL	92373	648-A1
	100	RDL	92373	608-A7
	25400	SBdC	92311	3678-H7
TAMARISK WY				
	-	FONT	92336	574-J2
N TAMARRON CT				
	4800	SBDO	92407	546-D6
TAMI RD				
	-	SBdC	-	(3504-D5 See Page 3414)
	38700	SBdC	92365	(3504-D5 See Page 3414)
TAMIANI RD				
	12300	APLV	92308	4387-G4
E TAM O SHANTER CT				
	1000	ONT	91761	642-E6
	2700	ONT	91761	643-A6
TAM O SHANTER DR				
	13800	VCTV	92392	4386-D2
E TAM O SHANTER ST				
	400	ONT	91761	642-C6
TAMPA LN				
	-	SBdC	92397	4652-E4
TAMPA ST				
	2400	POM	91766	641-A6
TANAGER CT				
	26400	LMLN	92354	647-F3
TANAGER DR				
	41600	BBLK	-	4811-H1
TANAGER RD				
	55400	SBdC	92284	4817-D2
TANAGER ST				
	21900	GTER	92313	646-D5
TANBERRY DR				
	-	CHLS	91709	681-F7
T-ANCHOR DR				
	74600	TNP	92277	4892-H1
N TANFORAN LN				
	200	DBAR	91765	640-D6
TANFORAN WY				
	1100	RDL	92374	608-D5
TANGELO AV				
	7300	FONT	92336	575-B6
	8700	FONT	92335	605-B3
	9700	SBdC	92316	605-B5
TANGELO CT				
	8600	FONT	92335	605-B2
TANGELO TR				
	25300	SBdC	92308	4478-J4
TANGERINE AV				
	8800	HESP	92345	4477-A7
	13200	CHNO	91710	682-A1
TANGERINE DR				
	-	RLTO	92377	544-J6
TANGERINE PL				
	7100	RCUC	91701	573-B6
TANGIER PL				
	600	POM	91768	640-B2
TANGLEWOOD AV				
	-	UPL	91786	572-E6
	1600	UPL	91784	572-E6
TANGLEWOOD CT				
	8900	RCUC	91701	572-G5
	14500	HESP	92345	4565-J6
	14500	HESP	92345	4566-A6
TANGLEWOOD DR				
	-	POM	91766	640-G5
	8900	RCUC	91701	572-G5
S TANGLEWOOD DR				
	300	SBdC	92314	4742-C6
TANGLEWOOD LN				
	14600	CHLS	91709	680-H4
	18400	SBdC	92392	4387-A4
TANK RD				
	-	SBdC	-	518-B4
N TANK RD				
	-	BREA	92823	710-D3
S TANK RD				
	-	BREA	92823	710-D4
	-	OrCo	92823	710-D4
TANNENBAUM DR				
	300	BBLK	-	4812-A1
TANNENBAUM PLATZ				
	42700	BBLK	-	4812-A1
TANNER CIR				
	400	RivC	92507	646-E7
TANNER RD				
	18300	SBdC	92301	(4202-G2 See Page 4112)
	20900	SBdC	92301	4112-G2
TANO ST				
	3900	CHNO	91710	681-D2
TAO RD				
	15600	APLV	92307	4297-A3
TAO WY				
	18800	APLV	92307	4297-A2
TAOS CIR				
	-	YUCA	92284	4957-H4
TAOS CT				
	1400	UPL	91784	571-H5
	7700	YUCA	92284	4958-B3
TAOS DR				
	1000	BARS	92311	3679-J2
	5100	MTCL	91763	601-G6
TAOS RD				
	20900	APLV	92307	4297-G1
	23300	SBdC	92307	4298-D1
TAOS TR				
	56100	YUCA	92284	4957-F4
	58100	YUCA	92284	4958-B3
TAPADERO RD				
	33700	SBdC	-	(4301-B1 See Page 4300)
TAPIA CT				
	7800	FONT	92336	604-A1
TAPIA LN				
	4500	SBdC	92301	(4113-A1 See Page 4112)
TAPIA RD				
	6100	TNP	92277	4893-B5
TAPIA ST				
	7900	FONT	92336	604-A1
TAPIA VIA				
	8100	RCUC	91730	602-E2
TAPIA WY				
	2000	UPL	91784	572-B5
	2700	RivC	92509	645-B6
TAPPAN ST				
	-	BARS	92311	3680-G6
TAPU RD				
	-	SBdC	-	4844-B2
TARA LN				
	34700	YCPA	92399	649-J6
TARA ST				
	1200	BARS	92311	3680-A5
TARANGO RD				
	19500	SBdC	92308	4567-D4
S TARA RIDGE CT				
	1700	CLTN	92324	647-A3
TARAWA AV				
	-	BARS	92311	3680-F6
TARE ACCESS RD				
	5300	SBdC	-	328-H5
TARECO CT				
	8900	SBdC	92371	4563-G1
TARKINGTON PL				
	-	RCUC	91730	573-E1
TARPON LN				
	18400	SBdC	92392	4386-J2
	18400	SBdC	92392	4387-A2
TARR PL				
	1800	POM	91766	640-J4
TARRAGONA DR				
	6000	RivC	92509	645-E4
TARRYTON CT				
	31200	YCPA	92399	648-J3
	31200	YCPA	92399	649-A3
TASMAN AV				
	300	POM	91767	601-A5
TATE				
	36700	SBdC	-	(4301-J5 See Page 4300)
	36700	SBdC	-	4302-A5
TATE LN				
	10200	SBdC	-	4480-G2
TATQUAY RD				
	12500	SBdC	92371	4382-H6
TATUM CT				
	15000	VCTV	92392	4296-D6
TATUM DR				
	15000	VCTV	92392	4296-D6
TAUPE ST				
	10600	RCUC	91701	573-B5
TAURUS AV				
	-	SBdC	92335	604-A2
TAURUS LN				
	13600	VCTV	92392	4385-G6
TAVERN LN				
	100	BBLK	-	4811-C1
TA-WAN-KA RD				
	16500	APLV	92307	4297-C2
TAWNEY RIDGE LN				
	14800	VCTV	92394	4295-H5
	15000	VCTV	92394	4296-D3
TAWNY LN				
	13500	CHLS	91709	681-A2
TAWNY RD				
	13600	CHNO	91710	681-J2
	18900	SBdC	92301	(4203-J4 See Page 4112)
TAWYA RD				
	12900	APLV	92308	4387-D4
	13900	APLV	92307	4387-D1
	14200	APLV	92307	4297-D7
TAXIWAY RD				
	-	SBdC	-	3762-J3
TAYLES POINT RD				
	700	BBLK	-	4811-A2
TAYLOR AV				
	16300	SBdC	92335	604-H6
	16400	FONT	92335	604-H6
	17500	SBdC	92316	605-B6
S TAYLOR AV				
	400	ONT	91761	642-D1
TAYLOR CT				
	11100	LMLN	92354	647-B1
	11100	RCUC	91701	573-C5
TAYLOR DR				
	300	CLAR	91711	601-B3
TAYLOR LN				
	36400	SBdC	92311	3590-B7
	71600	SBdC	92277	4821-J3
	71700	SBdC	92277	4822-A3
S TAYLOR PL				
	1800	ONT	91761	642-D4
TAYLOR RD				
	2500	SBDO	92404	577-C3
	2600	SBdC	92404	577-C3
TAYLOR ST				
	12700	GTER	92313	646-C6
	24800	LMLN	92354	647-B1
N TAYLOR WY				
	1300	UPL	91786	602-B1
T-CIRCLE DR				
	8900	SBdC	92256	4956-E6
	9100	SBdC	92256	616-F2
TEAGLE WASH RD				
	5100	SBdC	-	328-H8
E TEAGLE WASH RD				
	11300	SBdC	-	328-L6
TEAGUE LN				
	-	SBdC	92285	4667-D2
TEAK CT				
	14500	HESP	92345	4565-J6
E TEAK CT				
	2000	SBDO	92404	577-D2
TEAK LN				
	3700	CHLS	91709	681-C6
	11300	FONT	92337	644-C2
TEAK WY				
	6700	RCUC	91701	573-A5
	7200	RCUC	91730	573-A7
	7800	RCUC	91730	603-A1
TEAKWOOD AV				
	2700	SBdC	92284	4818-A5
	12400	VCTV	92392	4386-D6
N TEAKWOOD AV				
	200	RLTO	92376	605-E1
	500	RLTO	92376	575-E5
	2200	RLTO	92377	575-E3
S TEAKWOOD AV				
	600	RLTO	92376	605-E3
	900	RLTO	92316	605-E4
TEAKWOOD CT				
	-	SBdC	-	4737-G6
TEAKWOOD DR				
	100	BBLK	-	4742-A7
	200	BBLK	-	4812-A1
	900	SBdC	-	4737-G6
TEAKWOOD WY				
	10500	ADEL	92301	4294-H7
TEAL CT				
	32000	YCPA	92399	649-B3
TEAL DR				
	28300	SBdC	-	4738-A6
N TEAL DR				
	100	SBdC	92314	4742-F6
TEAL LN				
	1900	SBdC	-	4742-H2
TEASDALE DR				
	1200	CLAR	91711	601-A1
TEBO AV				
	12300	CHNO	91710	641-G6
TECATE AV				
	9400	HESP	92345	4477-B6
TECATE DR				
	1000	BARS	92311	3679-J5
TECAYA RD				
	20900	APLV	92307	(4117-F7 See Page 4116)
TECOPA CT				
	10600	APLV	92308	4477-H2
TECOPA DR				
	-	BARS	92311	3678-H7
	11300	SBdC	92256	615-F7
TECOPA RD				
	10500	APLV	92308	4477-J3
	82500	SBdC	-	330-K1
TECOPE RD				
	11200	APLV	92308	4477-J1
TECUMSEH AV				
	7000	SBdC	-	4843-J4
	7000	SBdC	-	4844-A4
TECUMSEH RD				
	19000	APLV	92307	4297-B6
TECUYA WY				
	5800	YUCA	92284	4887-J6
TEDDY BEAR LN				
	-	SBdC	-	2971-F3
TEEPEE TR				
	6600	SBdC	-	4843-G3
TEGO CT				
	-	SBdC	-	4844-A2
TEGO RD				
	8500	SBdC	92371	4563-F2
TEHACHAPI RD				
	14000	APLV	92307	4387-B1
TEHAMA DR				
	700	BBLK	-	4812-B2
TEHAMA PL				
	6700	RCUC	91701	573-C5
TEHAMA RD				
	-	SBdC	92308	4388-E5
	22000	APLV	92308	4388-A5
TEHAMA TR				
	-	SBdC	-	4844-D2
TEJA CT				
	35500	YCPA	92399	650-B2
TEJAS CT				
	12400	RCUC	91739	573-G2
N TEJON AV				
	700	SBdC	92324	606-C5
	800	CLTN	92324	606-C4
TEJON ST				
	16100	VCTV	92392	4296-D5
TELAMON LN				
	800	POM	91766	641-B4
TELEGRAPH CANYON TR				
	-	BREA	92823	710-A7
	-	CHLS	-	711-A6
	-	CHLS	91709	711-A6
	17600	OrCo	92886	710-A7
	17600	OrCo	92886	711-A6
TELEPHONE AV				
	11300	SBdC	91710	641-G4
	11700	CHNO	91710	641-G5
	14100	CHNO	91710	681-G3
	15200	CHLS	91709	681-G6
TELEPHONE RD				
	-	SBdC	92277	4823-C4
TELEPHONE CANYON RD				
	4800	SBdC	92345	(4655-H2 See Page 4654)
	5600	SBdC	92345	4565-H7
	5900	HESP	92345	4565-H7
TELEPHONE LINE RD				
	-	CHLS	91709	710-H4
TELESCOPE AV				
	83100	SBdC	93562	2145-A3
TELESTAR AV				
	12200	VCTV	92392	4386-D6
TELLGATE DR				
	23600	DBAR	91765	640-C5
TELLURIDE DR				
	13200	CHLS	91709	680-J1
TELSTAR CT				
	-	SBdC	-	(3682-B1 See Page 3592)
TEMECULA AV				
	8300	HESP	92345	4567-A2
TEMECULA CT				
	14800	APLV	92307	4298-A6
TEMECULA RD				
	14500	APLV	92307	4298-A1
	17000	APLV	92307	4208-A4
TEMECULA ST				
	46500	SBdC	92365	(3504-F5 See Page 3414)
TEMESCAL ST				
	44100	SBdC	92365	(3763-J3 See Page 3762)
	44100	SBdC	92365	3764-A3
TEMEYU TR				
	-	SBdC	-	4774-F7
	-	SBdC	-	4844-E1
TEMPLE AV				
	3000	POM	91765	640-C3
	3200	POM	91766	640-C3
	3200	POM	91768	640-C3
	21900	LACo	91768	640-A3
	23900	DBAR	91765	640-C3
TEMPLE CT				
	500	SBdC	-	517-B3
TEMPLE LN				
	400	BBLK	-	4811-D1
TEMPLE ST				
	26300	HIGH	92346	577-F6
E TEMPLE ST				
	100	SBDO	92410	576-J6
N TEMPLE ST				
	900	SBDO	92410	576-F6
W TEMPLE ST				
	600	SBDO	92410	576-G6
	900	SBDO	92411	576-F6
TENAJA RD				
	16500	APLV	92307	4297-G2
TENANGO RD				
	-	SBdC	92365	(3683-G4 See Page 3592)
TENAYA CT				
	6600	SBdC	-	4844-A3
TENAYA RD				
	-	SBdC	92308	4478-C2
	11800	APLV	92308	4388-B2
	14300	APLV	92307	4298-B3
TENDERFOOT DR				
	5300	FONT	92336	574-D2
TENNESSEE CT				
	-	FONT	92336	574-D6
TENNESSEE LN				
	400	BBLK	-	4811-D1
	31200	YCPA	92399	648-J3
	31200	YCPA	92399	649-A3
TENNESSEE ST				
	-	RDL	92359	608-J4
	-	RDL	92359	609-A4
	-	SBdC	92359	608-J5
	-	RDL	92373	647-J1
	200	RDL	92373	607-J7
	500	RDL	92374	607-J4
	31400	SBdC	92374	649-A3
	31400	YCPA	92399	649-A3
TENNIEL RD				
	-	SBdC	-	517-B1
	-	SBdC	-	4737-B7
TENNIS COURT LN				
	500	SBDO	92408	607-A2
TENNYSON AV				
	19400	SBdC	92301	(4203-H3 See Page 4112)
TENNYSON ST				
	100	UPL	91784	572-B3
TEPEE RD				
	-	SBdC	92277	4823-A3
	21000	APLV	92307	4297-G2
	72400	SBdC	92277	4822-B3
TERADELL AV				
	19700	SBdC	92301	(4203-H2 See Page 4112)
TERBUSH AV				
	8900	YUCA	92284	4958-B7
N TERESA AV				
	1300	CLTN	92324	606-B4
TERESA PL				
	2500	POM	91766	641-A6
TERESA ST				
	100	RivC	92507	646-F6
TERESITA CT				
	4300	CHNO	91710	681-E1
TERIANN LN				
	35600	YCPA	92399	610-B7
TERMINAL WY				
	-	ONT	91761	642-J1
	-	ONT	91761	643-A1
TERN CT				
	3300	CHLS	91709	681-C7
TERN RD				
	15700	VCTV	92394	4296-C6
TERN ST				
	15400	CHLS	91709	681-C7
TERNI PL				
	-	RCUC	91701	573-D6
TERRACE AV				
	2000	CLTN	92324	646-C3
	11600	GTER	92313	646-C3
	11700	GTER	92324	646-C3
	11700	SBdC	92324	646-C3
	11800	CLTN	92313	646-C3
N TERRACE AV				
	800	CLTN	92324	606-C3
TERRACE DR				
	-	SBdC	92252	4890-B6
	900	SBdC	91784	571-J3
	900	SBdC	91784	572-A3
	3400	CHLS	91709	681-C5
	4800	HIGH	92346	578-B3
	4800	SBDO	92346	578-B3
	6000	SBdC	92252	4889-A6
	8200	SBdC	92256	4956-F5
	60100	SBdC	92252	4888-G6
TERRACE LN				
	16600	FONT	92335	604-H2
TERRACE RD				
	200	SBdC	-	517-J2
	1800	SBdC	-	4742-J3
E TERRACE RD				
	1100	RLTO	92410	576-A6
N TERRACE RD				
	400	SBDO	92410	576-B6
	400	SBDO	92410	606-B1
	800	RLTO	92410	576-A5
	900	RLTO	92376	576-A5
S TERRACE RD				
	100	SBDO	92410	606-B2
N TERRACE ST				
	200	SBDO	92410	606-B1
TERRACE VW				
	13300	SBdC	92392	4384-C4
TERRACE HILL LN				
	2300	CHLS	91709	680-J4
TERRACE PINES DR				
	22400	GTER	92313	646-E3
TERRACE VIEW DR				
	11700	SBdC	92324	646-B3
TERRACE VIEW LP				
	6100	RCUC	91737	573-D3
TERRACE VIEW RD				
	8900	SBdC	92371	4474-C6
	8900	SBdC	92371	4564-C1
	14100	ADEL	92301	4384-C2
	15300	ADEL	92301	4294-B5
TERRACINA AV				
	6200	RCUC	91737	573-C4
TERRACINA BLVD				
	900	RDL	92373	647-H1
TERRACINA LN				
	15400	FONT	92337	644-F4
N TERRACITA RD				
	1400	SBDO	92404	547-B6
	3800	SBdC	92404	547-B6
TERRA LINDA DR				
	17100	SBdC	92392	4386-F3
	17100	VCTV	92392	4386-F3
TERRANO LN				
	12400	VCTV	92392	4385-D6
TERRAPIN RD				
	41100	BBLK	-	4811-F2
TERRA VISTA DR				
	56400	YUCA	92284	4887-G2
W TERRA VISTA DR				
	2300	RLTO	92377	545-A7
	2800	RLTO	92377	544-J6
TERRA VISTA PKWY E				
	-	RCUC	91730	573-D7
TERRA VISTA PKWY W				
	10500	RCUC	91730	573-C7
	10500	RCUC	91730	603-B1
TERRIE WY				
	33500	YCPA	92399	649-F4
TERRIER CT				
	-	FONT	92336	544-D7
TERRY AV				
	4600	CHNO	91710	641-F6
TERRY LN				
	4200	SBDO	92407	546-E6
	4800	YUCA	92284	4887-H3
TERRY ST				
	4300	CHNO	91710	641-E6
	7700	FONT	92336	575-C7
	7700	SBdC	92336	575-B7
N TERRY WY				
	400	UPL	91786	601-J3
TERRYVIEW AV				
	800	POM	91767	601-B5
TESORO AV				
	-	YUCA	92284	4888-G3
TESUQUE RD				
	8300	SBdC	92308	4567-E1
	9000	SBdC	92308	4477-E5
	12100	APLV	92308	4387-F5
TETLEY LN				
	300	SBdC	-	516-E3
TETON CT				
	3800	CHNO	91710	681-D4
TETON DR				
	1000	BARS	92311	3679-J6
	1000	BARS	92311	3680-A6
	1000	BBLK	-	4812-C3
TETON LN				
	28600	SBdC	-	4738-B5
TETON RD				
	20600	APLV	92308	4387-F4
	25500	SBdC	92307	4388-J3
	25500	SBdC	92307	(4389-A3 See Page 4299)
TETON ST				
	1400	SBDO	92407	546-D6
	16100	VCTV	92392	4386-D4
TETON PEAK CT				
	6400	RCUC	91737	573-D4
TEWA TR				
	6600	SBdC	-	4843-H3
TEXAS AV				
	-	VCTV	92394	4205-G5
TEXAS CT				
	-	FONT	92336	574-C6
TEXAS DR				
	32700	YCPA	92399	649-D5
TEXAS LN				
	7300	SBdC	92371	4383-J3
	82000	SBdC	-	330-K2
TEXAS ST				
	200	RDL	92373	608-A7
	300	RDL	92374	608-A4
W TEXAS ST				
	400	POM	91768	640-H1
TEXAS WY				
	18000	SBdC	92336	575-C7
THAMES ST				
	1300	RDL	92374	608-D5
	11700	GTER	92313	646-F3
THATCHBURY CT				
	4100	CHLS	91709	711-D1
S THEATER RD				
	1200	CLTN	92324	646-F2
THE BLIND TR				
	500	SBdC	-	516-G3
THE CIRCLE				
	1300	SBdC	-	4737-G5
THE PLAZA				
	5600	TNP	92277	4892-E3
THE TERRACE				
	100	RDL	92374	608-C6
THIRD ST				
	100	SBdC	-	(3682-D1 See Page 3592)
	300	SBdC	-	3592-D7
THISTLE DR				
	12300	RCUC	91739	573-G5
THISTLE ST				
	5500	SBDO	92407	546-B5
	13400	VCTV	92392	4385-F5
THISTLEBERRY CT				
	5900	CHLS	91709	711-J2
THOMAS AV				
	900	RDL	92374	608-D5
THOMAS CT				
	12100	GTER	92313	646-D4
	18300	ADEL	92301	4204-G5
THOMAS DR				
	14900	SBdC	92307	4298-H3
THOMAS LN				
	12200	YCPA	92399	649-D3
THOMAS PL				
	12500	CHNO	91710	641-F6
THOMAS RD				
	-	SBdC	-	516-B2
	12700	RDL	92373	649-A5
N THOMAS ST				
	200	POM	91768	640-J1
S THOMAS ST				
	200	POM	91766	640-J2
THOMAS HUNTING GROUNDS TR				
	7100	SBdC	-	4950-B4
THOMPSON DR				
	23200	GTER	92313	646-G3
W THOMPSON PL				
	200	SBDO	92405	546-H7
THOMPSON RD				
	16600	VCTV	92392	4386-E2
	20900	SBdC	92347	(3587-E4 See Page 3586)
	22500	SBdC	92347	3588-A4
THOR WY				
	32500	SBdC	-	519-C7
W THORESON ST				
	-	RLTO	92376	605-F1
THORNDALE ST				
	10500	ADEL	92301	4384-H1
THORNE PL				
	-	SBdC	-	516-C2
THORNHURST DR				
	14500	VCTV	92392	4385-J5
THOROUGHBRED CT				
	-	RivC	92880	683-D7
THOROUGHBRED ST				
	8300	RCUC	91701	572-E3
E THOROUGHBRED ST				
	-	ONT	91761	683-A1
THORPE CT				
	-	RCUC	91737	573-A3
THOUSAND PINES RD				
	100	SBdC	-	516-H1
S THOUSAND PINES RD				
	300	SBdC	-	516-H3
THRASHER AV				
	-	SBdC	92307	(4389-G7 See Page 4299)
	-	SBdC	92307	4479-G1
	-	SBdC	92308	4479-G7
THREE FLAGS CT				
	9800	HESP	92345	4565-C1
THREE MILE RD				
	1900	RLTO	92377	575-A1
	3800	FONT	92377	574-J1
	3800	RLTO	92377	574-J1
	10500	FONT	92336	574-F1
E THREE MOUNTAIN RANCH RD				
	2900	CLTN	92324	646-J6
	2900	RivC	92324	646-J6
	2900	RivC	92324	647-A6
S THREE MOUNTAIN RANCH RD				
	2900	CLTN	92324	647-A6
	2900	RivC	92324	647-A6
THREE PALMS AV				
	58700	SBdC	92284	4818-C7
THROUGHBRED ST				
	7200	RCUC	91701	572-D3
THRUSH AV				
	6700	SBdC	92345	4565-E6
THRUSH CT				
	41600	BBLK	-	4811-G2
THRUSH DR				
	400	BBLK	-	4811-H2
THRUSH RD				
	1600	SBdC	92397	4652-D3
THRUSH ST				
	22500	GTER	92313	646-F5
THULE LN				
	2600	SBdC	-	519-C7
THULE ST				
	34100	SBdC	92311	3678-F6
THUNDER RD				
	6100	SBdC	92277	4893-F5
THUNDER TR				
	24300	DBAR	91765	680-E2
THUNDERBIRD DR				
	26200	SBdC	-	517-F1
THUNDERBIRD LN				
	55300	SBdC	92284	4747-D7
THUNDERBIRD RD				
	20100	APLV	92307	4297-F5
	22100	APLV	92307	4298-A5
	23300	SBdC	92307	4298-D5
THUNDERHEAD RD				
	100	SBdC	92277	4751-E6
THUNDER MOUNTAIN AV				
	6200	RCUC	91739	573-F4
THUNDER MOUNTAIN RD				
	2500	SBdC	91784	572-C2
THURSTON LN				
	11100	RivC	91752	683-H1
N TIAJUANA ST				
	400	SBDO	92411	606-D1
	400	SBDO	92411	576-D6
TIAMA LN				
	2600	SBdC	92307	4298-D1
TIAMA RD				
	16900	SBdC	92307	4298-D1
TIARA AV				
	6700	HIGH	92346	578-A4
S TIARA AV				
	2000	ONT	91761	642-H6
W TIBBOT ST				
	700	RLTO	92377	575-E4
TIBURON DR				
	12900	VCTV	92392	4385-E7
TICONDEROGA CT				
	14000	FONT	92336	574-B7
TICONDEROGA RD				
	21300	APLV	92307	4207-H6
TIE RD				
	1000	SBdC	-	517-D4
TIERRA LN				
	-	FONT	92336	574-H2
	10300	SBdC	92308	4479-A3
TIERRA BONITA DR				
	12400	VCTV	92392	4385-H6
TIERRA SECA DR				
	-	NDLS	92363	3620-B7
N TIFFANI PL				
	3400	SBDO	92346	577-E1

STREET Block City ZIP Pg-Grid

STREET	Block	City	ZIP	Pg-Grid
TWENTY MULE TEAM RD Rt#-58				
	2400	SBdC	-	348-H7
TWENTYNINE PALMS HWY Rt#-62				
	49100	SBdC	92256	389-K4
	49300	SBdC	92256	615-H7
	50000	SBdC	92256	616-B4
	52200	SBdC	92256	4956-F7
	53400	SBdC	-	4956-F7
	53400	SBdC	92284	4956-F7
	53700	SBdC	92284	4957-A4
	53700	YUCA	92284	4957-F2
	57300	YUCA	92284	4958-A2
	58300	YUCA	92284	4888-E7
	59200	SBdC	92252	4888-E7
	61000	SBdC	92252	4889-D7
	64500	SBdC	92252	4890-B6
	66300	SBdC	92277	4890-G6
	67200	TNP	92277	4890-G6
	68200	TNP	92277	4891-A6
	71600	TNP	92277	4892-H5
	75300	TNP	92277	4893-A5
	76900	SBdC	92277	4893-F5
	78900	SBdC	92277	(4894-C5 See Page 4824)
	82400	SBdC	92277	(4895-C6 See Page 4824)
	86400	SBdC	92277	390-K1
	90600	SBdC	-	390-L2
	90600	SBdC	-	391-C1
TWENTYNINE PALMS OH N				
	-	SBdC	92252	4889-H7
	-	TNP	92277	4893-A5
	56900	YUCA	92284	4957-H2
	57300	YUCA	92284	4958-A2
	58600	YUCA	92284	4888-D7
	60100	SBdC	92252	4888-G7
TWENTYNINE PALMS OH S				
	54600	YUCA	92284	4957-J2
	57300	YUCA	92284	4958-A2
	65700	SBdC	92252	4890-C7
	68900	TNP	92277	4891-B6
	74800	TNP	92277	4892-H6
TWENTYNINE PALMS OUTER HWY				
	58200	YUCA	92284	4958-B1
TWIG CIR				
	1400	UPL	91786	601-H1
TWILIGHT DR				
	73900	TNP	92277	4962-H1
TWILIGHT PL				
	6300	RCUC	91737	573-D4
TWILIGHT WY				
	15200	ADEL	92301	4295-A6
TWIN CANYON DR				
	23200	GTER	92313	646-G3
TWIN CANYON LN				
	1000	DBAR	91765	640-D5
TWIN CREEK DR				
	7000	SBDO	92404	577-A5
TWIN KNOLLS DR				
	6100	CHLS	91709	712-A5
TWIN LAKES DR				
	1000	SBdC	92397	4652-D2
	44500	SBdC	92365	(3684-C1 See Page 3594)
TWIN OAKS LN				
	-	CHLS	91709	681-F7
TWIN OAKS PL				
	-	RCUC	91730	602-J5
TWIN-PEAKS				
	6900	SBdC	92285	(4576-C3 See Page 4486)
TWIN PEAKS CT				
	4400	CHLS	91709	711-E2
	13400	VCTV	92394	4295-F4
TWIN PEAKS DR				
	3500	SBdC	92407	546-A7
TWIN PEAKS WY				
	13400	VCTV	92394	4295-F4
TWIN PINES LN				
	23800	DBAR	91765	640-C6
TWIN ROCK RD				
	18900	SBdC	92301	(4203-G2 See Page 4112)
TWIN SPRING LN				
	23500	DBAR	91765	680-C2
TWINSPUR PL				
	6500	RCUC	91739	573-G5
TWO HAWK RANCH RD				
	-	SBdC	-	330-J1
TWO MILE RD				
	7100	TNP	92277	4892-G3
	62100	SBdC	92252	4889-C5
	64500	SBdC	92252	4890-A5
	66200	TNP	92277	4891-B4
	75900	TNP	92277	4893-B3
	76100	SBdC	92277	4893-B3
	78900	SBdC	92277	(4894-A3 See Page 4824)
	82500	SBdC	92277	(4895-A2 See Page 4824)
TYEE RD				
	11000	APLV	92308	4478-A2
TYLER LN				
	-	FONT	92336	573-J6
	-	FONT	92336	574-A6
TYLER PL				
	-	RCUC	91730	573-E1
TYLER ST				
	4900	CHNO	91710	641-F6
	7900	HIGH	92346	578-C7
N TYLER WY				
	400	UPL	91786	601-J3
TYROL CT				
	700	SBdC	-	516-J3
	14800	CHLS	91709	681-C5
TYROL DR				
	600	SBdC	-	516-J3
	15900	SBdC	92337	644-G1
	15900	FONT	92337	644-G1
TYROL LN				
	300	BBLK	-	4812-A1
TYROL ST				
	9300	SBdC	-	4481-C5
TYROLITE ST				
	4200	RivC	92509	644-G7
U				
U ST				
	800	NDLS	92363	3620-A4
	2700	SBDO	92408	607-F1
UKIAH AV				
	-	HESP	92345	4475-H7
UKIAH PL				
	-	RCUC	91730	602-G1
UKIAH TR				
	-	SBdC	-	4843-F4
N UKIAH WY				
	500	UPL	91786	602-B1
	1400	UPL	91786	572-B7
	1700	UPL	91784	572-A3
S UKIAH WY				
	100	UPL	91786	602-A4
UKWICH TR				
	-	SBdC	-	4844-E1
ULU CT				
	-	YUCA	92284	4887-J6
	6000	SBdC	-	4844-E1
UMAH PL				
	6000	CHNO	91710	681-E1
UMATILLA TR				
	6900	SBdC	-	4843-G4
UMQUA CT				
	-	SBdC	-	4843-H5
UNDERWOOD DR				
	-	FONT	92316	645-A1
	-	FONT	92337	645-A1
UNICORN WY				
	7700	HIGH	92346	578-E6
UNION AV				
	9800	RivC	91752	644-A7
	9800	RivC	92509	644-A7
	13000	FONT	92337	643-J4
E UNION AV				
	-	RDL	92374	608-C6
N UNION AV				
	100	POM	91768	640-E1
W UNION AV				
	-	RDL	92374	608-B6
UNION CT				
	5400	CHNO	91710	641-H4
UNION ST				
	-	UPL	91786	602-D4
	5100	CHNO	91710	641-G4
	16600	VCTV	92392	4296-E5
	24900	HIGH	92410	577-B6
	26500	HIGH	92346	577-F6
E UNION ST				
	1800	CLTN	92324	606-G7
N UNION ST				
	800	SBDO	92410	576-B6
W UNION ST				
	500	SBDO	92410	576-A6
	1200	SBDO	92411	576-D6
	2700	SBDO	92376	576-A6
UNION PACIFIC AV				
	100	SBdC	-	(3682-D1 See Page 3592)
UNIVERSAL AV				
	1800	SBDO	92407	546-B5
UNIVERSE DR				
	3200	RivC	91752	643-F5
UNIVERSITY AV				
	24300	LMLN	92354	647-A1
UNIVERSITY BLVD				
	55400	SBdC	92285	4667-D2
UNIVERSITY CIR				
	400	CLAR	91711	601-C2
UNIVERSITY CT				
	24700	LMLN	92354	647-B1
UNIVERSITY DR				
	-	LACo	91768	640-B1
	-	POM	91768	640-A2
W UNIVERSITY DR				
	-	LACo	91768	640-A3
	-	POM	91768	640-A3
UNIVERSITY PKWY				
	400	POM	91768	640-B3
	3300	SBDO	92407	546-C5
	3300	SBDO	92407	576-B1
UNIVERSITY PL				
	500	RDL	92374	608-D7
N UNIVERSITY ST				
	-	RDL	92374	608-D7
S UNIVERSITY ST				
	500	RDL	92374	608-D7
UNRUH WY				
	57200	SBdC	92284	4817-J6
	61700	SBdC	92252	4819-B6
UPAS CT				
	14300	SBdC	92335	604-B2
UPHILL RD				
	8100	SBdC	92252	4959-F5
E UPJOHN AV				
	1700	SBdC	-	328-G6
UPLAND AV				
	14700	SBdC	92335	604-C2
	16100	FONT	92335	604-G1
	17000	FONT	92335	605-A1
	17700	SBdC	92335	605-B1
UPLAND DR				
	1500	SBdC	-	(4743-A4 See Page 4662)
UPLAND HILLS DR N				
	-	UPL	91784	572-D6
UPLAND HILLS DR S				
	-	UPL	91786	572-D7
UPPER RD				
	37600	SBdC	-	4950-G1
UPPER BOULDER RD				
	32800	SBdC	-	519-D6
UPSHUR AV				
	-	TNP	92278	4751-J4
UPTON CT				
	2700	RivC	92509	645-B6
UPTON DR				
	600	BARS	92311	3680-A5
URANIUM RD				
	-	SBdC	92252	4890-C4
	63300	SBdC	92252	4889-E4
URBANA AV				
	3500	RivC	91752	643-H6
URSA MAJOR WY				
	42500	BBLK	-	4812-A1
URSINUS CIR				
	2200	CLAR	91711	571-D6
UTAH CT				
	-	FONT	92336	574-C6
	300	CLAR	91711	601-E4
UTAH DR				
	-	SBdC	-	(3854-H1 See Page 3764)
UTAH LN				
	7300	SBdC	92371	4383-J2
UTAH RD				
	-	SBdC	-	(3765-E7 See Page 3764)
	-	SBdC	-	(3855-E1 See Page 3764)
	-	SBdC	92365	(3765-E7 See Page 3764)
UTAH ST				
	-	VCTV	92394	4205-F5
	1000	SBdC	-	4606-F1
UTAH TR				
	2300	TNP	92278	4822-G2
	2500	SBdC	92277	4822-G4
	3300	TNP	92277	4822-G7
	3900	TNP	92277	4892-G1
	7300	TNP	92277	4962-G2
	9500	SBdC	92277	4962-H7
UTE CT				
	9900	SBdC	-	4843-H3
UTE DR				
	10000	MohC	-	3620-C2
UTE RD				
	300	BARS	92311	3680-B4
	15300	APLV	92307	4297-F5
	35600	SBdC	-	4481-H5
UTE TR				
	32600	SBdC	-	4480-J5
	58100	YUCA	92284	4958-B3
UTE TRAIL CIR				
	58300	YUCA	92284	4958-C3
UTICA AV				
	8300	RCUC	91730	603-B2
UTILITY ACCESS RD				
	2500	CLTN	92324	646-J2
	40900	SBdC	-	351-H6
UTILITY ACCESS RD N				
	200	CLTN	92324	646-B2
UTILITY ACCESS RD S				
	100	CLTN	92324	646-B3
UTILITY ACCESS RD W				
	1400	CLTN	92324	646-A3
	1700	CLTN	92501	646-A4
UVA PL				
	4300	CHNO	91710	681-E1
V				
VACATION DR				
	-	MohC	-	3620-C3
VACAVILLE CT				
	-	RCUC	91730	602-G1
VACHE CIR				
	500	RDL	92374	608-C3
VACILLA CT				
	9100	RCUC	91701	572-G4
VADUZ AV				
	57700	YUCA	92284	4958-B7
VAI BROTHERS DR				
	14000	RCUC	91739	574-B1
VAIL AV				
	1500	UPL	91784	571-H5
VAIL CT				
	13400	VCTV	92392	4385-F6
VAIL DR				
	9800	MTCL	91763	601-G6
VAIL LN				
	500	BBLK	-	4811-J1
N VAIL LN				
	4900	SBDO	92407	546-D5
VAIL WY				
	1800	UPL	91784	571-H6
	5000	RivC	91752	683-G3
VALADEZ ST				
	700	UPL	91786	602-D1
VALALLA LN				
	32900	SBdC	92359	609-E4
E VALARIA CT				
	2600	SBDO	92346	577-F2
VALARIA DR				
	1300	SBDO	92346	577-E5
	6500	HIGH	92346	577-F4
N VALARIA DR				
	2100	HIGH	92346	577-E2
	2100	SBDO	92346	577-E2
VALATTA PL				
	6900	RCUC	91701	573-E5
VALDEZ RD				
	24400	SBdC	92307	4298-F7
VAL DOSTA AV				
	34900	SBdC	-	(4391-F1 See Page 4300)
VALE AL				
	500	SBDO	92401	576-G7
VALE DR				
	11000	SBdC	92256	615-J5
	45800	SBdC	-	4742-J3
	46000	SBdC	-	(4743-A3 See Page 4662)
VALENCIA AV				
	7300	RCUC	91730	573-B6
	7700	RCUC	91701	573-B6
	14700	SBdC	92335	604-D2
	16300	FONT	92335	604-H2
	17000	FONT	92335	605-A2
	17700	SBdC	92335	605-B2
N VALENCIA AV				
	900	SBDO	92410	577-A6
	1200	SBDO	92404	577-A1
	3600	SBDO	92404	547-A7
S VALENCIA AV				
	2500	ONT	91761	642-G6
VALENCIA CT				
	7800	HIGH	92346	578-C7
	16000	FONT	92335	604-G2
	18700	HESP	92345	4477-B2
VALENCIA DR				
	11500	SBdC	92374	648-H2
N VALENCIA DR				
	800	CLTN	92324	606-C5
VALENCIA LN				
	-	RDL	92374	608-G7
S VALENCIA PL				
	1900	ONT	91761	642-G3
VALENCIA ST				
	-	HESP	92345	4475-H3
	-	VCTV	92392	4475-F3
	200	RLTO	92376	575-G7
	7300	SBdC	92371	4473-J4
	7300	SBdC	92371	4474-A4
	9900	SBdC	92345	4474-G3
	10500	SBdC	92316	605-E7
	11100	SBdC	92345	4475-A3
	17700	HESP	92345	4476-H3
	18200	HESP	92345	4477-A2
	20900	APLV	92308	4477-G2
E VALENCIA ST				
	100	RLTO	92376	575-H7
W VALENCIA ST				
	100	RLTO	92376	575-D7
W VALENTINE CT				
	700	ONT	91762	642-A3
VALERA AV				
	300	POM	91767	601-A2
VALERA WY				
	13700	VCTV	92392	4385-G3
VALERIE LN				
	4200	CHNO	91710	641-D5
VALERIE WY				
	5800	SBDO	92407	546-F4
VALEVIEW DR				
	1400	DBAR	91765	680-D3
VALE VISTA DR				
	11300	FONT	92337	644-B2
VALEWOOD DR				
	11600	VCTV	92392	4475-D1
VALHALLA DR				
	2500	SBdC	-	519-C7
VALHALLA ST				
	2400	POM	91767	601-B5
VALINDA AV				
	5200	RCUC	91737	573-B2
	6700	RCUC	91701	573-B6
VALINDA CT				
	10500	RCUC	91701	573-B5
VALINDA ST				
	35300	SBdC	-	4481-G3
VALKYRIE DR				
	2500	SBdC	-	519-C7
VALLE DR				
	24600	SBdC	-	517-A4
VALLE DEL SOL				
	1700	RDL	92373	648-H4
VALLEJO ST				
	16100	VCTV	92392	4296-D5
VALLEJO WY				
	11200	MTCL	91763	641-E3
N VALLEJO WY				
	200	UPL	91786	602-A1
	600	UPL	91784	572-A3
S VALLEJO WY				
	100	UPL	91786	602-A4
VALLE VERDE WY				
	6200	SBdC	-	4844-B2
VALLE VISTA				
	7400	RCUC	91730	572-F7
	7600	RCUC	91730	602-F1
VALLE VISTA AV				
	4100	CHLS	91709	681-E6
VALLE VISTA CT				
	4400	SBdC	92371	4473-B7
VALLE VISTA DR				
	1800	RDL	92373	648-F4
	3200	CHLS	91709	681-B7
VALLE VISTA PL				
	8400	RCUC	91730	602-F1
VALLE VISTA RD				
	-	SBdC	92277	370-K11
	4700	SBdC	92371	4653-C1
	8100	SBdC	92371	4563-B2
	9300	SBdC	92371	4473-B2
	11900	SBdC	92371	4383-B2
	15300	SBdC	92371	(4293-B4 See Page 4292)
	17700	SBdC	92301	(4203-B4 See Page 4112)
	68100	SBdC	92277	4820-G5
	68100	SBdC	92277	4821-A5
	71900	SBdC	92277	4822-A5
	72800	TNP	92277	4822-C5
	75500	SBdC	92277	4823-A4
	75500	TNP	92277	4823-A4
	78600	SBdC	92277	4824-A4
	82400	SBdC	92277	(4825-A3 See Page 4824)
VALLEY AV				
	700	NDLS	92363	3620-C6
VALLEY BLVD				
	2100	POM	91768	640-D1
	3500	POM	91789	640-A4
	13100	SBdC	92335	603-J6
	13400	SBdC	92335	604-A6
	13900	FONT	92335	604-F6
	16900	FONT	92335	605-B6
	17400	SBdC	92316	605-B6
	19000	RLTO	92316	605-B6
E VALLEY BLVD				
	100	CLTN	92324	606-E6
	4100	LACo	91789	640-A5
	4100	POM	91789	640-A5
	4100	WAL	91789	640-A5
W VALLEY BLVD				
	100	CLTN	92324	606-B6
	100	RLTO	92316	605-G6
	100	RLTO	92324	605-G6
	100	RLTO	92376	605-G6
	100	CLTN	92324	605-G6
	500	SBdC	92314	4742-C6
	800	SBdC	92324	606-B6
VALLEY CT				
	400	SBdC	-	516-F2
	8100	SBdC	92371	4562-G3
N VALLEY CT				
	3600	SBDO	92407	546-E7
	3600	SBDO	92407	576-E1
VALLEY DR				
	-	SBdC	-	(3846-B5 See Page 3756)
	500	SBdC	-	517-B3
	1500	SBdC	-	4737-G5
	13700	APLV	92307	4388-A2
VALLEY RD				
	400	SBdC	-	516-G2
	11500	SBdC	92307	(4389-D7 See Page 4299)
VALLEY RDG				
	20200	SBdC	92308	4567-E3
VALLEY ST				
	-	BARS	92311	3680-C5
E VALLEY ST				
	100	SBDO	92408	606-J2
W VALLEY ST				
	300	SBDO	92401	606-H2
	700	SBDO	92410	606-G2
VALLEY WY				
	3400	RivC	92509	645-A7
	5400	RivC	92509	644-J7
VALLEY CENTER DR				
	14200	VCTV	92392	4296-C7
	14400	VCTV	92392	4386-C1
VALLEY CENTER RD				
	34400	SBdC	-	(3682-H4 See Page 3592)
	40600	SBdC	-	(3683-A4 See Page 3592)
	40900	SBdC	92365	(3683-A4 See Page 3592)
	44100	SBdC	92365	(3684-B4 See Page 3594)
	47700	SBdC	92365	(3685-C3 See Page 3594)
VALLEY CREST TER				
	23400	SBdC	92307	4298-D1
	24000	SBdC	92307	4208-D7
VALLEY FALLS AV				
	-	RDL	92374	608-F5
VALLEY FORGE CT				
	14000	FONT	92336	574-B7
VALLEY-HI RD				
	8700	SBdC	92308	4477-H7
	8900	SBdC	92308	4567-H1
VALLEY HIGH DR				
	14600	CHLS	91709	680-H5
VALLEY LINKS BLVD				
	19000	APLV	92308	4477-C2
VALLEY OAK DR				
	30800	SBdC	-	518-H6
VALLEY OF THE FALLS DR				
	38700	SBdC	92339	611-A1
VALLEY RIDGE DR				
	31300	SBdC	-	518-J6
VALLEY SPRING RD				
	2000	CHLS	91709	710-H1
S VALLEY SPRINGS LN				
	1100	CLTN	92324	646-G1
VALLEYVALE DR				
	16100	FONT	92337	644-G2
VALLEY-VIEW				
	55400	SBdC	92285	4667-C5
S VALLEY VIEW AV				
	500	SBDO	92408	607-A3
VALLEY VIEW CIR				
	61700	SBdC	92252	4959-B1
	61900	SBdC	92252	4889-C7
VALLEY VIEW CT				
	600	UPL	91784	572-C3
	12900	APLV	92308	4387-D4
VALLEY VIEW DR				
	-	SBdC	-	517-F4
	600	RDL	92373	648-G4
	1100	SBdC	92314	4813-D3
	2400	CHLS	91709	680-J3
	6500	TNP	92277	4891-G6
	8500	HESP	92345	4565-F2
	8500	SBdC	92345	4565-F2
	22600	SBdC	-	516-E4
	24400	LMLN	92354	647-A2
	31600	SBdC	-	519-A7
	61300	SBdC	92252	4959-A1
S VALLEY VIEW DR				
	800	SBDO	92408	606-F4
VALLEY VIEW LN				
	12600	RDL	92373	648-J4
	13900	CHLS	91709	680-G3
	44400	SBdC	-	4742-E7
VALLEY VIEW RD				
	-	SBdC	92308	4477-H7
	1200	SBdC	92277	4751-A7
	1300	SBdC	92372	4562-D1
	1300	SBdC	92277	4821-A2
	5900	SBdC	92397	4652-E2
	10100	SBdC	92256	616-A4
	22100	SBdC	92308	4479-A6
	22400	SBdC	92308	4478-E6
	36500	SBdC	92347	(3587-C7 See Page 3586)
	36500	SBdC	92347	(3677-C1 See Page 3586)
	54800	SBdC	92285	4667-B5
VALLEY VIEW ST				
	5900	SBdC	92252	4889-C6
	9300	RCUC	91737	572-H2
	12600	YCPA	92399	649-H4
VALLEY VIEW WY				
	1300	SBdC	-	517-B5
VALLEY VISTA AV				
	-	SBdC	92284	4747-J7
	1700	SBdC	92284	4817-J2
	3700	SBdC	92284	4887-J1
	7300	YUCA	92284	4957-J4
	8800	SBdC	92308	4478-E6
VALLEY VISTA DR				
	200	SBdC	-	514-B3
VALLEY VISTA LN				
	1600	CHLS	91709	710-G2
VALLEY VISTA RD				
	5200	SBdC	92285	(4575-G6 See Page 4484)
	12900	SBdC	92307	4388-E5
	12900	SBdC	92308	4388-E5
VALLEY WELLS RD				
	-	InCo	93545	2055-E2
	36100	SBdC	92347	(3677-E2 See Page 3586)
	36500	SBdC	92347	(3587-E7 See Page 3586)
E VALLEY WOODS ST				
	2000	CLTN	92324	606-H7
VALLIHI DR				
	55200	SBdC	92285	4747-E3
E VAL MAR CIR				
	2700	SBDO	92346	577-F1
VALMAR RD				
	2700	SBDO	92404	577-C2
E VAL MAR RD				
	700	SBDO	92404	577-A2
VALMONT AV				
	7800	HIGH	92346	577-G7
VALPARAISO DR				
	600	CLAR	91711	571-B6
VALPICO PL				
	22300	DBAR	91765	680-A5
VAL VERDE AV				
	4100	CHLS	91709	681-E7
VAMANA ST				
	2900	POM	91767	601-A3
VAN BUREN BLVD				
	4400	RivC	91752	643-H7
	4400	RivC	91752	644-A7
VAN BUREN ST				
	4100	CHNO	91710	641-D6
	21900	GTER	92313	646-D5
W VAN BUREN ST				
	200	CLTN	92324	646-B5
VANCOUVER AV				
	-	FONT	92336	574-C1
VANCOUVER RD				
	25300	SBdC	92301	(4024-C1 See Page 3934)
VANDA LN				
	6300	SBdC	92346	577-J3
	6300	SBDO	92346	577-J3
VAN DELL RD				
	2100	RivC	92509	645-E6
VANDERBILT AV				
	900	CLAR	91711	601-B2
VANDERBILT PL				
	6600	RCUC	91701	573-D5
VANDERBILT ST				
	-	ONT	91761	643-B3
E VANDERBILT ST				
	4800	ONT	91761	643-F3
E VANDERBILT WY				
	300	SBDO	92408	606-J6
	300	SBDO	92408	607-A6
VANDERGRIFT LN				
	500	POM	91766	640-J4
VAN DUSEN CANYON RD				
	-	SBdC	-	(4661-G7 See Page 4660)
	41700	SBdC	-	4741-H1
	41700	SBdC	-	4742-A2
	42400	SBdC	92314	4742-A2
N VAN DUSEN CANYON RD				
	1000	SBdC	92314	4742-C5
VAN ELLA RD				
	56500	SBdC	-	2971-F3
VAN FLEET DR				
	11900	RCUC	91701	573-E5
	11900	RCUC	91739	573-E5
VAN GOGH CT				
	-	CHLS	91709	711-H1
VAN HORN CIR E				
	13500	CHNO	91710	681-D2
VAN HORN CIR W				
	13500	CHNO	91710	681-D2
E VAN KOEVERING ST				
	100	RLTO	92376	575-H7
	800	RLTO	92376	576-A7
	800	SBDO	92376	576-A7
W VAN KOEVERING ST				
	100	RLTO	92376	575-D7
VAN LEUVEN ST				
	10800	LMLN	92354	607-B7
S VAN NESS AV				
	200	UPL	91786	602-B4
W VAN NESS CT				
	600	UPL	91786	602-B4
VAN NESS LN				
	400	RDL	92374	608-G7
VANS RANCH RD				
	100	SBdC	92284	4747-H5
	700	SBdC	92285	4747-H5
	800	SBdC	92284	4817-E1
VANTAGE DR				
	42500	SBdC	92365	(3683-E2 See Page 3592)
VAQUERO CT				
	12600	RCUC	91739	573-G4
VAQUERO DR				
	13800	FONT	92337	644-A4
VAQUERO RD				
	6700	SBdC	-	(4572-A5 See Page 4482)
VARSITY AV				
	4300	SBDO	92407	546-B5
VASQUEZ AV				
	16200	VCTV	92394	4296-A3
VASQUEZ CT				
	15100	VCTV	92394	4296-A2
VASQUEZ LN				
	15200	VCTV	92394	4296-A2
VASSAR ST				
	700	CLAR	91711	601-B5
	800	POM	91767	601-B5
VAYA CON DIOS				
	-	POM	91766	640-D4
VEGA RD				
	-	APLV	92307	4297-E1
	-	SBdC	92307	4207-E2
W VEJAR ST				
	1400	POM	91766	640-F2
W VELARDE ST				
	600	SBDO	92410	606-G2
VELARDO DR				
	35100	YCPA	92399	650-A4
VELARE CT				
	12700	VCTV	92392	4475-D1
VELLUM DR				
	-	SBdC	-	3764-J7
	-	SBdC	-	(3854-J1 See Page 3764)
VELLUM RD				
	-	SBdC	92365	(3684-J7 See Page 3594)
	-	SBdC	92365	3764-J4
VELOUR DR				
	15600	CHLS	91709	681-C7
VELOUR ST				
	-	SBdC	92365	3764-D6
VELVET LN				
	8300	SBdC	92335	604-B2
VELVET ST				
	14700	CHLS	91709	681-C5
VELWOOD ST				
	100	RDL	92374	608-G7
	100	RDL	92374	648-G1
VENADA TR				
	13000	SBdC	-	(4390-D3 See Page 4300)
VENANGO RD				
	15800	APLV	92307	4297-B4
VENETO PL				
	-	RCUC	91701	573-E5
VENEZIA PL				
	1200	POM	91766	640-E3
VENICE CT				
	14200	FONT	92336	604-B1
VENICE LN				
	15400	VCTV	92394	4296-B3
VENICE PL				
	6800	RCUC	91701	573-D5
VENOSA PL				
	7200	RCUC	91701	573-D6
VENTANA DR				
	-	FONT	92336	574-H2
VENTANA PL				
	-	FONT	92336	574-H2
VENTURA AV				
	7500	YUCA	92284	4957-B4
N VENTURA AV				
	2200	SBDO	92407	546-B2
VENTURA CT				
	-	HESP	92345	4475-J7
N VENTURA CT				
	6600	SBDO	92407	545-J1
VENTURA LN				
	15400	VCTV	92394	4296-B3
VENTURA PL				
	6500	RCUC	91701	573-C5
VENTURA RD				
	-	ADEL	92301	(4115-C5 See Page 4114)
VENTURA WY				
	400	CLAR	91711	601-C1
VENTURE DR				
	11000	RivC	91752	643-G5
VENUS AV				
	17200	VCTV	92394	(4206-F7 See Page 4116)
VENUS CT				
	11000	RivC	91752	683-H5
VENUS DR				
	-	SBdC	92252	4748-J6
	61300	SBdC	92252	4749-A6
VENUS LN				
	9600	SBdC	92335	604-D5
VENUS RD				
	36500	SBdC	-	(4572-A2 See Page 4482)
	37700	SBdC	-	(4392-D4 See Page 4302)
VENUS ST				
	2700	SBdC	92301	(4202-F2 See Page 4112)
	67700	SBdC	92277	4750-H5
VENUS WY				
	900	SBdC	-	516-H4
VERA LN				
	58300	YUCA	92284	4958-C7
VERACRUZ ST				
	1000	BARS	92311	3680-F7
VERANDA CV				
	13500	CHLS	91709	681-A1
VERANO ST				
	12400	VCTV	92392	4475-D2
	13800	HESP	92345	4475-H2
	16500	HESP	92345	4476-E2
	18100	HESP	92345	4477-A2
VERANO WY				
	12900	YCPA	92399	649-F5
VERBENA				
	10000	SBdC	92308	4477-E4
VERBENA AV				
	-	CHNO	91710	642-B6
	1700	UPL	91784	571-J3
	21700	SBdC	92301	4114-H3
N VERBENA AV				
	3200	RLTO	92377	575-B1
VERBENA CT				
	-	CHNO	91710	642-B7
	-	POM	91766	641-B3
	12600	RCUC	91739	573-G5
VERBENA DR				
	72100	TNP	92277	4892-E5
N VERBENA DR				
	3400	RLTO	92377	545-B7
VERBENA LN				
	200	BREA	92823	710-C5
	10200	SBdC	92308	4477-D4
N VERBENA LN				
	6000	SBDO	92407	546-A3
VERBENA RD				
	5000	SBdC	92345	4654-J1
	6100	SBdC	92345	4564-J1
	8900	SBdC	92345	4474-J4
	11000	SBdC	92392	4474-J1
	11700	VCTV	92392	4474-J1
	11800	VCTV	92392	4384-J4
	14100	ADEL	92301	4384-J2
	14500	ADEL	92301	4294-H2
	15200	SBdC	92301	4294-J4
	17300	ADEL	92301	4204-H3
	60100	SBdC	92252	4888-G7
	61800	SBdC	92252	4889-B6
	64700	SBdC	92252	4890-A6
VERBENA ST				
	13200	SBdC	93562	2145-A3
N VERDE AV				
	500	RLTO	92376	575-G4
	500	RLTO	92376	605-G1
S VERDE AV				
	600	RLTO	92376	605-G3
VERDE CT				
	1100	POM	91767	601-B5
VERDE DR				
	20100	APLV	92308	4477-E2
E VERDE DR				
	1400	SBDO	92404	577-C1
VERDE RD				
	31300	SBdC	-	(4390-H6 See Page 4300)
	35700	SBdC	-	(4391-H6 See Page 4300)
VERDE ST				
	10700	SBdC	92345	4474-J3
	11100	SBdC	92345	4475-A3
	13700	HESP	92345	4475-G3
	16100	HESP	92345	4476-D3
	16700	VCTV	92392	4296-E6
W VERDEMONT DR				
	2600	SBDO	92407	545-J1
	2600	SBDO	92407	546-A1
VERDEMONT RANCH RD				
	-	SBDO	92407	545-H3
	3500	SBdC	92407	545-E3
VERDER RD				
	38200	SBdC	-	(4392-E6 See Page 4302)
VERDET CT				
	6800	RCUC	91701	573-B6
VERDE VISTA				
	11000	APLV	92308	4477-E2
VERDE VISTA AV				
	1600	POM	91767	601-D6
VERDE VISTA DR				
	600	POM	91767	601-A6
	1900	RDL	92373	648-G5
VERDUGO AV				
	300	POM	91767	601-A3
	6200	CHNO	91710	642-A6
	9200	HESP	92345	4477-C6
	10000	SBdC	-	4481-B3
VERDUGO RD				
	15300	SBdC	-	(4301-B4 See Page 4300)
	32800	SBdC	-	4480-J2
	32800	SBdC	-	4481-A2
S VERDUGO WY				
	200	UPL	91786	602-B4
VERLIE DR				
	-	RDL	92373	648-C4
VERMEER DR				
	16200	CHLS	91709	711-H1
VERMICULATE MINE RD				
	8700	SBdC	92284	4958-F6
	9100	SBdC	92252	4958-F6
VERMICULITE MINE RD				
	-	SBdC	-	390-B3
VERMONT DR				
	-	RCUC	91730	573-E6
VERMONT ST				
	1400	RDL	92374	608-A5
	2900	SBdC	92407	575-J1
	3400	SBdC	92407	545-J6
	3900	SBDO	92407	545-J6
N VERMONT ST				
	2100	CLTN	92324	606-D3
VERNOLA WY				
	2600	RivC	92509	645-B6
VERNON AV				
	3900	RivC	92509	644-F7
	8900	MTCL	91763	601-G4
	10300	MTCL	91763	641-H1
	10700	SBdC	91762	641-H2
	11300	CHNO	91710	641-H4
	11300	CHNO	91762	641-H2
E VERNON AV				
	13300	CHNO	91710	681-H3
VERNON CT				
	5500	MTCL	91763	641-H1
VERNON DR				
	700	UPL	91786	602-A3
	36400	SBdC	92311	3589-G7
	36400	SBdC	92311	3679-G1
W VERNON DR				
	-	UPL	91786	602-B3
VERONA DR				
	11300	RCUC	91701	573-D5
	11800	FONT	92337	644-F4
VERONA PL				
	1200	POM	91766	640-F3
VERONA ST				
	11600	YCPA	92399	650-B2
VERONESE DR				
	-	CHLS	91709	711-H2
VERONICA AV				
	3700	RLTO	92377	545-A7
VERONICA CT				
	-	LMLN	92354	647-F3
	12400	RCUC	91739	573-G5
W VERONICA ST				
	300	UPL	91784	572-A4
VERSAILLES PL				
	200	RivC	92501	646-A6
W VESTA ST				
	500	ONT	91762	602-A7
	1000	ONT	91762	601-H7
VETERANS CT				
	1200	UPL	91786	602-D1
VETERANS PKWY				
	-	BARS	92311	3679-H7
N VETERANS WY				
	1400	CLTN	92324	606-E4
VETTUNO CT				
	7000	RCUC	91701	573-E6
VIA AIROSA				
	8300	RCUC	91730	572-F7
VIA ALICIA ST				
	-	HIGH	92346	578-G6
VIA ALLEGRA				
	4100	SBdC	92277	4821-G7
	6500	TNP	92277	4891-H6
VIA ANTIBES				
	1100	RDL	92374	608-G5
VIA ANTIQUA ST				
	7200	HESP	92345	4566-C5
S VIA APPIA				
	1000	CLTN	92324	646-D1
VIA ARABELLA				
	200	SDMS	91773	640-A1
VIA ARCO				
	-	UPL	91786	602-D3
VIA ARENOSA				
	4900	SBdC	92277	4893-G2
VIA BAHIA ST				
	15400	HESP	92345	4566-C5
VIA BARCELONA				
	1200	RDL	92374	608-G5
	17800	APLV	92307	4296-G2
VIA BARCELONA RD				
	12700	YCPA	92399	649-H5
VIA BELLO DR				
	-	RLTO	92377	545-C7
W VIA BELLO DR				
	1500	RLTO	92377	575-D1
	2100	RLTO	92377	545-A6
	2800	RLTO	92377	544-J6
VIA BLANCA				
	5800	SBdC	92301	(4113-D1 See Page 4112)
VIA BONITA				
	16900	FONT	92337	644-J3
	16900	FONT	92337	645-A3
VIA BUENA				
	-	UPL	91786	602-D3
VIA BUENA DR				
	34200	YCPA	92399	649-H5
VIA CAMILLE				
	2300	SDMS	91773	640-A1
VIA CAPRI				
	11400	LMLN	92354	647-E2
VIA CARRILLO				
	8100	RCUC	91730	602-E2
VIA CARTAGENA ST				
	15400	HESP	92345	4566-C5
VIA CASITAS				
	17800	CHLS	91709	712-B5
VIA CERRO				
	2200	RivC	92509	645-F6
VIA CHICO				
	-	UPL	91786	602-D3
S VIA COMO DEL LAGO				
	1000	CLTN	92324	646-E2
VIA CORONA				
	-	UPL	91786	602-D3
VIA DE ANZA				
	17000	FONT	92337	644-J3
	17000	FONT	92337	645-A2
VIA DE LA ROSA				
	-	SBdC	-	349-E5
VIA DE LA ZANJA				
	1200	CLTN	92324	646-G2
	1200	SBdC	92313	646-G2
VIA DELDENE				
	7400	HIGH	92346	578-D6
S VIA DEL FONTANA				
	1000	CLTN	92324	646-F1
VIA DEL LAGO				
	13300	VCTV	92392	4385-F3
S VIA DEL LAGO				
	1000	CLTN	92324	646-E1

STREET
Block City ZIP Pg-Grid

WALLCREST DR
1400 CLAR 91711 601-A1
1400 POM 91767 601-A1
WALLRICH AV
55300 SBdC 92285 4667-D2
WALMAC AV
10100 SBdC 92335 604-B6
WALMAC PL
14200 FONT 92337 644-B4
WALNUT AV
100 RDL 92373 648-B3
1000 POM 91766 641-B6
2300 UPL 91784 571-J3
3400 CHNO 91710 641-C6
3700 SBdC 91710 641-C6
6100 CHNO 91710 642-A6
6800 CHNO 91762 642-A6
17100 FONT 92336 574-J5
17100 FONT 92336 575-A5
21600 CLTN 92324 646-C3
21600 GTER 92313 646-C3
21700 CLTN 92313 646-C3
E WALNUT AV
100 RLTO 92376 575-H5
N WALNUT AV
5900 SBDO 92407 545-J3
6000 SBDO 92407 546-A2
W WALNUT AV
100 RLTO 92376 575-F5
WALNUT CT
16900 FONT 92336 574-J5
WALNUT CV
700 SBdC 92324 606-B5
WALNUT DR
200 SBdC - 518-C1
600 SBdC - 4738-E7
WALNUT RD
400 SBdC 92372 4472-A4
2700 SBdC 92371 4472-G4
4600 SBdC 92371 4473-C4
WALNUT ST
100 NDLS 92363 3620-C5
5600 SBdC 92397 4652-D2
10600 SBdC 92316 605-F7
10700 SBdC 92374 608-H7
10900 SBdC 92374 648-H2
11000 SBdC 92316 645-F2
14500 HESP 92345 4475-J6
14500 HESP 92345 4476-A6
15100 FONT 92336 574-C5
18300 HESP 92345 4477-A7
35100 SBdC 92311 3678-G4
E WALNUT ST
100 ONT 91761 642-D6
100 ONT 91762 642-D6
2700 ONT 91761 643-A6
S WALNUT ST
600 CLTN 92324 606-C7
600 CLTN 92324 646-C1
W WALNUT ST
100 ONT 91762 642-B6
1200 SBDO 92410 606-A4
1900 RLTO 92376 575-A5
2500 RLTO 92336 575-A5
2800 SBDO 92376 606-A2
WALNUT WY
12900 VCTV 92392 4385-G4
WALNUT CREEK DR
1600 CHLS 91709 680-G3
WALNUT GROVE AV
17100 FONT 92336 574-J4
WALNUT GROVE CT
10300 YCPA 92399 610-A5
WALNUT HILLS DR
26000 SBdC - 517-E1
WALNUT TREE LN
- YCPA 92399 609-J5
WALNUT VILLAGE PKWY
16900 FONT 92336 574-J5
WALPAPI RD
- SBdC - 4844-E1
WALPI CT
- SBdC - 4844-D2
WALPI DR
64800 SBdC 92252 4890-A3
WALPI RD
16700 APLV 92307 4298-A1
WALPI ST
63300 SBdC 92252 4889-F3
S WALTER CT
1600 CLTN 92324 646-H3
WALTER RD
- SBdC - 351-H8
WALTERS ST
14600 RivC 92880 712-H2
14800 SBdC 91710 712-H2
W WALTERS ST
300 CLTN 92324 606-C2
300 SBDO 92410 606-C2
WALTON DR
10400 VCTV - (4206-A3 See Page 4116)
WAMEGO TR
100 SBdC 92284 4747-D4
500 SBdC 92285 4747-D4
900 SBdC 92284 4817-E2
6800 YUCA 92284 4957-E3
WAMPUM CT
- SBdC - 4843-H4

S WANAMAKER AV
100 ONT 91761 603-E7
100 ONT 91761 643-E2
N WANAMAKER PL
200 ONT 91761 603-E7
WANAQUE RD
15300 APLV 92307 4297-E4
WANDERING RIDGE DR
2400 CHLS 91709 680-J1
2500 CHLS 91709 681-A1
WANDERING RIDGE WY
13400 CHLS 91709 681-B1
WANITA LN
500 BBLK - 4811-D2
WANITA PL
13600 VCTV 92392 4386-E3
WANKA RD
13800 SBdC 92307 4388-D1
14500 SBdC 92307 4298-D7
WANONA PL
7200 RCUC 91739 573-H6
WAPATO RD
11700 APLV 92308 4387-H7
WARBIRD WY
- SBdC 92277 4821-A4
WARBLER AV
12200 GTER 92313 646-E4
WARBLER RD
4100 SBdC 92371 4473-A7
WARBONNET WY
7600 RivC 92880 712-H2
7600 SBdC 91710 712-H2
WARBONNETT RD
44100 SBdC 92365 349-H7
44100 SBdC 92365 (3504-A5 See Page 3414)
WARD LN
100 CALI 92320 650-A7
79300 SBdC 92277 4824-A7
WARD ST
24600 SBdC 92410 577-A7
26300 HIGH 92346 577-F7
E WARD ST
300 SBdC 92410 576-J7
WARD WY
1300 SBdC 92359 609-D5
1300 RDL 92359 609-D5
WARDER CIR
- UPL 91786 602-E2
WARDMAN BULLOCK RD
4400 RCUC 91739 544-A7
4400 RCUC 91739 574-A2
4400 SBdC 91739 544-A7
WARING AV
200 RivC 92507 646-D6
E WARM SPRINGS CT
3500 ONT 91761 643-C6
WARM SPRINGS TKTR
7700 SBdC - 4950-A6
8100 SBdC 92359 4950-B7
33100 SBdC - 389-D2
WARNER CT
- SBdC - 518-B3
WARNER DR
- CHLS 91709 711-F1
WARNER ST
- CLAR 91711 571-E7
WARREN PL
6400 SBdC 92285 (4576-C4 See Page 4486)
WARREN RD
69800 SBdC 92277 4751-D5
WARREN WY
23000 SBdC 92308 4478-C3
57300 YUCA 92284 4957-J1
57300 YUCA 92284 4958-A1
WARREN VISTA AV
- SBdC 92284 4747-J5
- SBdC 92285 4747-J5
600 SBdC 92284 4748-A7
600 SBdC 92284 4818-A2
3800 SBdC 92284 4888-A4
4700 YUCA 92284 4888-A4
6800 YUCA 92284 4958-A1
WARWICK CT
7700 RCUC 91730 573-C7
WARWICK RD
2000 MohC - 3620-G2
WARWICK ST
1700 POM 91766 640-J4
13600 VCTV 92392 4386-C3
WARWICK HILLS CT
- YCPA 92399 649-E2
WARWICK HILLS RD
- YCPA 92399 649-E2
WASCO AV
9100 HESP 92345 4477-C6
WASCO RD
- SBdC 92307 4207-E2
WASCO ST
- APLV 92307 4207-D6
WASECA LN
15000 APLV 92307 4297-B6
WASECA RD
18800 APLV 92307 4297-B6
WASECAL RD
18900 APLV 92307 4297-B5
WASHINGTON AV
800 POM 91767 601-B7
900 POM 91767 641-B1

WASHINGTON AV
3700 SBDO 92407 545-G1
5000 CHNO 91710 641-G6
S WASHINGTON AV
800 SBDO 92408 606-J4
W WASHINGTON AV
1900 SBDO 92411 576-B4
WASHINGTON BLVD
500 UPL 91786 602-C3
WASHINGTON DR
14500 SBdC 92335 604-G6
15100 FONT 92335 604-G6
33200 YCPA 92399 649-F4
WASHINGTON PL
- RCUC 91730 573-E6
WASHINGTON RD
- SBdC - 4302-B3
WASHINGTON ST
- VCTV 92394 4205-F5
800 RDL 92374 608-B5
1500 NDLS 92363 3620-B6
12900 SBdC 92345 4565-E5
E WASHINGTON ST
200 CLTN 92324 646-D2
900 ONT 91761 642-D1
2200 CLTN 92408 646-J1
W WASHINGTON ST
2500 SBDO 92407 546-A3
2700 SBDO 92407 545-H2
WASHINGTONIAN DR
74700 TNP 92277 4892-H7
WASHKO RD
- SBdC - (4743-B6 See Page 4662)
WASHOAN RD
15300 APLV 92307 4297-F3
WASSAIL
- SBdC 92252 4748-J4
- SBdC 92252 4749-A4
WASSON CT
12500 CHNO 91710 641-G6
WATER ST
- SBdC 91784 571-H3
- UPL 91784 571-H3
28900 HIGH 92346 578-D6
WATERBURY CT
4300 RIV 92501 645-H7
WATERBURY PL
- RCUC 91730 573-E7
WATER CANYON-PISGAH PEAK
36900 SBdC 92399 650-F2
WATERFORD AV
1600 RDL 92374 608-F6
WATERFORD CT
2400 SBDO 92408 646-J1
WATERFORD LN
10000 RCUC 91737 573-A2
WATERFORD ST
2400 SBDO 92408 606-J7
WATER HOLE LN
40000 SBdC - (4743-A4 See Page 4662)
WATERLILY CT
- RivC 92880 683-B7
WATER LILY LN
12700 VCTV 92392 4385-D5
WATERLOO DR
6900 CHNO 91710 642-A6
N WATERMAN AV
100 SBDO 92408 606-J1
300 SBdC 92410 606-J1
300 SBDO 92410 606-J1
400 SBDO 92410 576-J5
500 SBdC 92410 576-J5
1200 SBDO 92404 576-J5
N WATERMAN AV Rt#-18
2900 SBDO 92404 576-J2
3600 SBDO 92404 546-J6
S WATERMAN AV
100 SBDO 92408 606-J2
2500 SBDO 92408 646-J1
2600 CLTN 92408 646-J1
11000 CLTN 92324 646-J1
WATERMAN RD
27800 SBdC 92311 3679-E2
WATERMAN ST
27500 SBdC 92311 3679-D1
WATERMAN CANYON RD
900 SBdC - 516-F4
WATER POWER HOUSING DR
15400 VCTV 92394 4296-C1
WATERS AV
1500 POM 91766 640-H4
S WATERS AV
900 POM 91766 640-H3
WATERS CT
- RDL 92374 608-B4
WATERS DR
21800 SBdC - 516-D2
WATERVIEW DR
38700 BBLK - 4811-A1
WATERWOOD ST
10800 APLV 92308 4477-D3
WATKING RD
13600 SBdC - (4301-C6 See Page 4300)

WATKING RD
13600 SBdC - (4391-A1 See Page 4300)
WATO RD
16100 APLV 92307 4296-H1
17000 APLV 92307 (4206-H7 See Page 4116)
WATSON CT
- CHLS 91709 711-G2
- HIGH 92346 578-E6
N WATWOOD AV
1600 CLTN 92324 606-B3
WAUKESHA TR
5200 SBdC - 4773-H6
WAVERLY AV
12100 SBdC - (4390-D5 See Page 4300)
W WAVERLY CT
1300 UPL 91786 601-J2
WAVERLY DR
- CHLS 91709 711-H1
3000 SBdC 92252 4818-G6
WAVERLY RD
2500 BARS 92311 3758-D2
2500 SBdC 92311 3758-D2
WAWONA RD
13700 APLV 92307 4387-C2
WAYLAND CT
500 CLAR 91711 601-E4
500 MTCL 91763 601-E4
WAYLYN
- SBdC 92277 4822-J2
- SBdC 92277 4823-A2
WAYMOUTH CT
- RCUC 91739 573-F6
WAYNE ST
800 CLAR 91711 601-C6
1700 POM 91767 601-C6
WAYNOKA LN
500 BBLK - 4811-D2
WAYNOKA RD
12100 APLV 92308 4387-H4
WAYSIDE LN
700 SBdC - 4738-B7
WAYSIDE PL
400 DBAR 91765 640-E6
WEACAHOOTA RD
28900 SBdC - (4389-J2 See Page 4299)
WEAPONS MOVEMENT RD
- VCTV 92394 4205-E6
WEASEL ST
- VCTV 92394 4205-E5
WEATHERFORD CT
2300 CLAR 91711 571-E6
WEATHERLY PL
7300 RCUC 91730 573-B7
WEATHER VANE CT
13800 CHLS 91709 680-G3
WEAVER RD
25500 SBdC 92311 3678-H4
WEAVER ST
7200 HIGH 92346 578-E6
WEAVER WY
8500 SBdC 92252 4959-D5
WEB CT
13100 YCPA 92399 649-G5
WEBB CT
7100 FONT 92336 574-A6
WEBB DR
54700 YUCA 92284 4957-C4
WEBB TR
54700 YUCA 92284 4957-C4
WEBB CANYON RD
4400 CLAR 91711 571-A6
4400 LACo 91750 571-A6
4700 LACo 91711 571-A6
WEBER RD
- SBdC - 4816-E4
N WEBER ST
500 POM 91768 640-G1
WEBSTER AV
1400 CLAR 91711 601-E1
WEBSTER CT
12600 CHNO 91710 641-G6
WEBSTER RD
35300 BARS 92311 3680-D3
35300 SBdC 92311 3680-D3
WEBSTER ST
800 RDL 92374 608-B5
7300 HIGH 92346 578-B7
19800 SBdC 92308 4477-D7
WEDGEWOOD AV
1800 UPL 91784 571-J5
N WEDGEWOOD AV
600 UPL 91786 601-J1
1400 UPL 91786 571-J7
W WEDGEWOOD CT
100 RLTO 92376 575-E7
WEDGEWOOD DR
- APLV 92308 4387-C7
- APLV 92308 4477-B5
WEDGEWOOD LN
12300 VCTV 92392 4386-D6
N WEDGEWOOD LN
1100 UPL 91786 601-J1
W WEDGEWOOD ST
1300 RLTO 92376 575-D7
WEDGEWOOD WY
16300 VCTV 92392 4386-D6

N WEDGEWOOD WY
1500 UPL 91786 571-J7
WEEPING WILLOW CT
- CHNO 91710 682-B3
WEEPING WILLOW DR
33300 SBdC - 519-E2
WEEPING WILLOW LN
11900 FONT 92337 644-B4
WEEPING WILLOW RD
- SBdC 92301 (4024-B1 See Page 3934)
WEGMAN DR
6900 RivC 92509 645-B5
WEIMAR AV
19400 APLV 92307 (4117-G5 See Page 4116)
WEIRWOOD DR
27500 SBdC - 517-H4
WEISSHORN DR
200 SBdC - 516-J2
WELEBIR ST
11500 LMLN 92354 647-D2
WELL RD
- SBdC - 2971-E3
8900 HESP 92345 4475-F7
8900 HESP 92345 4565-F1
WELLA CT
- VCTV 92392 4385-E7
WELLESLEY AV
11700 LMLN 92354 647-G2
11800 SBdC 92373 647-G2
WELLESLEY CT
6300 CHNO 91710 682-A2
WELLESLEY DR
600 CLAR 91711 601-C2
WELLINGTON PL
- RCUC 91730 573-D7
WELLINGTON RD
- SBdC - 3756-J7
- SBdC - (3757-B7 See Page 3756)
- SBdC 92311 3758-C7
WELLOCK RD
74800 TNP 92277 4962-H4
WELLS AV
1400 CLAR 91711 601-B1
WELLS PL
12500 CHNO 91710 641-D6
WELLS FARGO AV
- SBdC - 2971-E4
WELLS FARGO RD
20400 SBdC 92308 4567-F4
WELLS FARGO ST
10300 ADEL 92301 4204-G5
12900 SBdC 92345 4565-F4
14100 HESP 92345 4565-F4
14900 HESP 92345 4566-A4
WELLSLEY DR
500 SBdC - 518-A2
WELSH CT
5800 RCUC 91701 572-E3
WELSH RD
18700 HESP 92345 (4657-B2 See Page 4656)
18700 SBdC 92345 (4657-B2 See Page 4656)
27400 SBdC - (3937-A3 See Page 3936)
WEMBLEY AV
3200 CHLS 91709 681-B5
WEMBLEY CT
- RCUC 91739 573-F6
WENATCHEE TR
6900 SBdC - 4843-G4
N WENDY AV
900 SBdC 92314 4742-C4
WENDY CT
9000 SBdC 92339 611 B2
WENDY WY
2200 UPL 91784 571-J3
WENDY RANCH RD
1900 SBdC 92407 515-G7
WENTWORTH WY
1200 UPL 91784 571-J4
WERN ST
- SBdC - 4480-E1
WESLEY AV
- SBdC 91710 641-D4
10900 MTCL 91763 641-D2
11200 SBdC 91766 641-D3
W WESLEY CT
400 SBdC 92314 4742-B7
WESLEY RD
2500 SBdC 92252 4818-H5
7700 SBdC 92252 4958-H4
WESLEY WY
500 CLAR 91711 601-E1
WEST CT
- SBDO 92410 577-B6
WEST DR
11300 SBdC 92256 615-J7
32100 SBdC - 519-B7
WEST LN
- SBdC 92314 4742-J7
200 SBdC - 514-B3
800 SBdC 92314 4812-J1
WEST PK
6000 CHLS 91709 711-J4
WEST RD
10500 SBdC 92256 615-J5

WEST RD
82900 SBdC 93562 2144-J4
WEST ST
400 UPL 91786 602-C1
WEST TR
15100 VCTV 92394 4295-G6
WEST WY
- ONT 91761 642-J1
24700 LMLN 92354 647-B2
WESTBROOK CIR
400 RDL 92374 608-G7
WESTBROOK CT
2300 CLAR 91711 571-E6
WESTBROOK DR
11100 ADEL 92301 4294-J7
11100 ADEL 92301 4295-A7
WESTBROOK LN
- POM 91766 640-E5
WESTCHESTER WY
- RivC 92880 683-D4
WEST END CT
18800 APLV 92308 4477-D3
WESTERN AV
4000 SBDO 92407 546-E5
26400 HIGH 92346 577-F4
E WESTERN AV
- RDL 92374 608-B5
N WESTERN AV
500 SBDO 92411 576-D4
800 CLTN 92324 606-F5
W WESTERN AV
- RDL 92374 608-A5
WESTERN DR
100 SBdC - 518-C1
34100 SBdC 92311 3678-H4
WESTERN RD
18900 ADEL 92301 4204-D4
WESTERN TR
8300 RCUC 91730 603-B2
WESTERN CREEK CIR
- SBDO 92407 546-E6
WESTERN RANGE PL
8400 RCUC 91730 603-B2
WESTERN SKIES WY
12300 VCTV 92392 4385-C7
WESTERN TALC RD
- SBdC - 330-D2
WESTERN WHIP CT
900 BARS 92311 3679-J4
WESTFALL DR
- SBdC - (4655-B6 See Page 4654)
3900 SBdC 92345 (4655-B6 See Page 4654)
WESTFIELD PL
2700 CLAR 91711 571-D5
N WEST FRONTAGE RD
2200 SBDO 92346 578-A3
WESTHAVEN PL
- RCUC 91739 573-F6
WEST HILL DR
8800 SBdC 92372 4562-B2
WESTLAND DR
16100 VCTV 92392 4386-D5
WESTLANE RD
900 SBdC 92372 4382-B7
WESTLAWN ST
17800 HESP 92345 4566-J1
18000 HESP 92345 4567-A1
19000 SBdC 92345 4567-B1
WESTLINE
7100 SBdC 92308 4567-F4
WESTMINSTER CT
11800 LMLN 92354 647-F3
WESTMONT AV
500 POM 91766 640-E3
6500 RCUC 91701 573-D5
WESTMONT DR
12000 APLV 92308 4387-C7
WESTMORELAND ST
1300 POM 91766 640-G3
WESTON AV
36800 SBdC 92311 3589-G7
WESTON PL
11500 RCUC 91730 573-E7
WESTPARK
200 RDL 92374 648-G1
WEST PERIMETER RD
8900 SBdC 92335 604-A4
WEST POINT DR
300 CLAR 91711 601-E4
WESTPORT CIR
- RivC 92880 683-D4
WESTPORT DR
9800 RCUC 91701 572-J6
W WESTRIDGE CT
900 UPL 91786 602-A1
WESTRIDGE PL
5800 RCUC 91737 573-A3
WESTRIDGE ST
- SBdC 92365 (3504-C6 See Page 3414)
WESTRIDGE WY
1400 CHLS 91709 710-G1
WESTRIDGE KNOLL
16100 CHLS 91709 710-G1
WESTSIDE RD
15300 VCTV 92392 4296-E5
WESTVIEW DR
- HIGH 92404 577-E5

WESTWARD DR
13700 FONT 92337 644-A2
WESTWAY RD
10600 HESP 92345 4475-J3
WESTWIND AV
6800 FONT 92336 574-F5
WEST WIND CT
7400 HIGH 92346 578-E6
WESTWIND DR
5500 SBDO 92407 546-E5
10600 RCUC 91701 573-B6
W WESTWIND ST
1600 CLTN 92324 605-J4
1600 CLTN 92324 606-A4
WESTWINDS RD
13300 VCTV 92394 4205-G6
WESTWOOD DR
13500 VCTV 92392 4386-C3
WESTWOOD LN
- RDL 92373 648-F4
7300 HIGH 92346 578-E5
12000 GTER 92313 646-G3
WESTWOOD PL
100 UPL 91784 572-B4
WESTWOOD ST
23100 GTER 92313 646-G3
23400 CLTN 92324 646-J3
23700 SBdC 92324 646-J3
E WESTWOOD ST
2100 CLTN 92324 646-H3
2200 SBdC 92324 646-H3
WETHERLY CT
2200 UPL 91784 571-H4
WEYBRIDGE DR
10900 RCUC 91730 573-C7
WEYER ST
4000 RIV 92501 645-H7
WEYUTO TR
- SBdC - 4844-E1
WHAREHOUSE AV
- SBDO 92401 606-H1
WHARTON DR
500 CLAR 91711 601-C4
WHATLEY AV
17200 FONT 92336 575-A6
WHATTA RD
3000 RivC 92509 645-A7
WHEATON AV
1800 CLAR 91711 571-B7
WHEEL RD
12100 SBdC 92392 4384-E7
12500 VCTV 92392 4384-E7
WHEELER AV
8100 FONT 92335 604-J2
WHEELER CT
6700 FONT 92336 574-J5
9200 FONT 92335 604-J4
WHEELER PL
36000 YCPA 92399 650-C2
WHEELER RD
- SBdC - 348-K11
- SBdC - (3847-B2 See Page 3756)
200 SBdC 92277 4751-H6
16500 SBdC - (3846-A2 See Page 3756)
WHETROCK RD
42100 SBdC 92365 (3683-G6 See Page 3592)
45400 SBdC 92365 (3684-C6 See Page 3594)
WHICKER BLVD
29800 SBdC 92311 3589-J6
30000 SBdC 92311 3590-A6
S WHIPPLE DR
200 SBdC 92314 4742-G6
WHIPPLE ST
- FONT 92336 573-J6
- FONT 92336 574-A6
S WHIPPLE MOUNTAIN RD
100 SBDO 92410 606-C2
WHIPPORWILL DR
300 RivC 92507 646-E7
WHIRLAWAY CT
8900 RCUC 91737 572-G1
WHIRLAWAY LN
3300 CHLS 91709 681-C5
WHIRLAWAY ST
8000 RCUC 91701 572-E2
9500 RCUC 91737 572-J1
WHISPER LN
7800 HESP 92345 4567-A3
WHISPERING CREEK
13200 CHLS 91709 681-A1
WHISPERING FOREST DR
10100 RCUC 91737 573-A1
N WHISPERING FOREST DR
1000 SBdC 92314 4742-B5
WHISPERING HILLS DR
- CHLS 91709 711-F1
S WHISPERING LAKES CT
2700 ONT 91761 642-G6
S WHISPERING LAKES LN
2800 ONT 91761 642-G6

WHISPERING OAK CT
- CHLS 91709 681-A2
WHISPERING PINES DR
100 SBdC - 516-C2
2300 SBdC - 519-A7
WHISPERING PINES RD
3600 SBdC 92371 4562-J4
WHISPERING SANDS DR
14100 VCTV 92392 4385-H4
WHISPERING SPRINGS RD
12500 SBdC 92392 4386-H5
WHISPERING WILLOW DR
13500 CHLS 91709 681-B2
WHISTLER CT
- CHLS 91709 711-H1
WHISTLER ST
12300 GTER 92313 646-F4
N WHISTLE STOP DR
1000 CLTN 92324 606-A5
WHITAKER LN
200 SBdC 92277 4750-E7
WHITBY DR
- RCUC 91739 573-G6
WHITE AV
- SBdC 92301 (4203-C5 See Page 4112)
8900 ADEL 92301 4204-D5
11300 ADEL 92301 4205-A5
N WHITE AV
- POM 91766 640-H1
100 POM 91768 640-H1
S WHITE AV
100 POM 91766 640-H3
200 UPL 91786 602-B4
W WHITE CT
100 UPL 91786 602-B4
WHITE RD
2900 SBdC 92301 (4202-F5 See Page 4112)
7700 SBdC 92371 4564-C2
9100 SBdC 92371 4474-D5
10300 SBdC 92392 4474-D2
11700 SBdC 92392 4384-D4
E WHITE ST
100 BARS 92311 3679-H2
W WHITE ST
100 BARS 92311 3679-G2
WHITEBARK AV
14000 CHNO 91710 682-B3
WHITE BIRCH DR
11100 RCUC 91730 603-D2
WHITECLIFF DR
900 DBAR 91765 680-E2
WHITE CLOUD CT
3200 CHLS 91709 681-B2
11300 RCUC 91701 573-D5
WHITE DOVE LN
2300 CHLS 91709 680-J3
28900 SBdC - 518-C2
WHITE FEATHER RD
6500 SBdC 92252 4889-G7
6900 SBdC 92252 4959-G1
WHITEFIELD CT
16300 CHLS 91709 711-E2
WHITE FIR DR
- SBdC - 517-H1
27400 SBdC - 4737-H7
WHITE FIR LN
1600 DBAR 91765 680-A4
WHITE FIR WY
13500 VCTV 92392 4385-G5
WHITE FOX TR
2300 SBdC 92371 4472-F6
3700 SBdC 92371 4473-A6
7400 SBdC 92371 4474-F5
9900 SBdC 92345 4474-G5
11000 SBdC 92345 4475-A5
12700 HESP 92345 4475-E5
WHITEGATE LN
29000 HIGH 92346 578-D6
WHITEHAVEN CT
6500 SBdC 92345 4565-F7
WHITEHAVEN ST
- SBdC 92345 4567-C6
9700 SBdC 92345 4564-G7
11000 SBdC 92345 4565-A7
13700 HESP 92345 4565-G7
WHITE HORSE TR
12500 VCTV 92392 4385-D6
WHITEHOUSE RD
19200 SBdC - 4205-J3
WHITEKIRK DR
15000 VCTV 92394 4295-J6
WHITEMAN ST
1000 SBdC 92301 (4202-A2 See Page 4112)
WHITE MOUNTAIN CT
11700 RCUC 91737 573-E4
13400 VCTV 92394 4295-F5
N WHITE MOUNTAIN RD
1000 SBdC 92314 4742-C5
WHITE OAK AV
8400 RCUC 91730 603-C2
WHITE OAK LN
100 POM 91766 640-H2
28800 HIGH 92346 578-C6
N WHITEOAK RD
1500 CLTN 92324 605-J4

WHITE OWL RD
11300 SBdC 92392 4475-A2
WHITE PINE AV
2600 SBDO 92407 545-J4
2600 SBDO 92407 546-A4
WHITE PINE CT
11600 FONT 92337 644-C3
WHITE RABBIT TR
1900 UPL 91784 571-J5
WHITEROCK RD
- SBdC 92365 (3684-H6 See Page 3594)
WHITE SAIL DR
13600 SBdC 92392 4386-H2
WHITESAND
49300 SBdC 92277 4893-D2
WHITE SANDS DR
73700 TNP 92277 4892-E3
76100 SBdC 92277 4893-B2
WHITESPRINGS RD
- SBdC - 4773-J7
E WHITESTAG RD
3100 ONT 91761 643-A5
WHITE STALLION CT
14500 CHLS 91709 680-J4
WHITESTAR ST
1100 SBdC 92372 4562-C1
WHITESTONE PL
13300 RCUC 91739 573-J4
13500 RCUC 91739 574-A4
WHITEWATER AV
11200 MTCL 91763 641-F3
WHITEWOOD CT
9500 FONT 92335 604-F5
WHITEWOOD DR
- RDL 92359 609-A5
1300 SBdC 92359 609-A5
7000 FONT 92336 574-F6
9300 FONT 92335 604-F4
9300 SBdC 92335 604-F4
WHITLOCK AV
7800 SBdC 92410 577-B7
8000 SBdC 92410 607-B1
WHITMAN AV
1000 CLAR 91711 601-B2
10100 ADEL 92301 4204-F2
WHITMAN ST
2700 SBdC 92301 (4202-F2 See Page 4112)
7300 SBdC 92301 (4203-J2 See Page 4112)
7500 SBdC 92301 4204-A2
WHITMAN WY
- COR 92880 712-J7
WHITMOORE RD
66500 SBdC 92277 4890-E5
67300 TNP 92277 4890-H5
WHITNEY AV
7600 YUCA 92284 4957-B4
WHITNEY CT
4300 CHNO 91710 681-E1
7600 RCUC 91730 572-H7
7800 FONT 92336 604-A1
WHITNEY DR
3800 SBDO 92407 546-D6
WHITNEY ST
7900 FONT 92336 604-A1
WHITTIER AV
1400 CLAR 91711 601-B1
11300 LMLN 92354 647-F3
11300 SBdC 92354 647-F3
11800 LMLN 92373 647-F3
11900 SBdC 92373 647-F3
WHITTIER ST
22600 RivC 92324 647-B6
W WHITTLERS LN
1000 ONT 91762 641-J5
1100 ONT 91762 642-A5
WHITTRAM AV
12900 RCUC 91739 603-J3
13300 SBdC 91739 603-J3
13300 SBdC 92335 603-J3
13300 SBdC 92335 604-A3
WHITTRAM CT
16100 FONT 92335 604-G3
WICHITA RD
9300 SBdC - 4480-C4
15300 APLV 92307 4297-F5
WICKENDALE RD
- SBdC 92301 (4024-A2 See Page 3934)
WICKER BLVD
- SBdC 92311 3589-F7
WICKFORD PL
- YCPA 92399 649-F2
WICKIEUP RD
- SBdC 92277 4824-C4
WICKUP WY
9100 SBdC 92308 4477-J6
N WIDGEON DR
200 SBdC 92314 4742-E5
WIDGEON LNDG
- BBLK - 4811-C1
WIDGEON RD
21700 APLV 92307 4297-J4
22100 APLV 92307 4298-A4
WIEBE RD
- SBdC 92314 4742-H5
E WIER RD
200 SBDO 92408 646-J1

E WIER RD
300 SBDO 92408 647-A1
S WIER RD
2600 CLTN 92408 646-J1
2600 SBDO 92408 646-J1
WIGWAM RD
21000 APLV 92307 4297-G2
21800 APLV 92307 4298-A2
WIGWAM WY
6600 SBdC - 4843-G3
WIKA RD
17700 APLV 92307 4296-H4
WILBAR CIR
400 RDL 92374 648-F1
WILBUR AV
13500 CHNO 91710 681-D2
WILCOX LN
59000 YUCA 92284 4888-E5
WILD RD
15100 SBdC - (3846-D4 See Page 3756)
WILD CANYON DR
14700 CHLS 91709 680-H5
S WILD CANYON DR
2100 CLTN 92324 646-H4
WILDCAT DR
1500 SBdC - 4737-G5
WILDCAT WY
72700 TNP 92277 4892-C5
WILD CHERRY DR
33100 SBdC - 519-D2
WILDERNESS CT
- SBdC - (4206-B5 See Page 4116)
- SBdC 92394 (4206-B5 See Page 4116)
WILDERNESS DR
- SBdC - 4812-H1
- SBdC 92314 4812-H1
10700 RCUC 91737 573-C2
WILDERNESS LN
33300 SBdC - (4301-B3 See Page 4300)
WILDERNESS PL
- POM 91766 640-G7
WILDERNESS RD
1900 SBdC - 518-J5
2100 SBdC - 519-A6
WILDERNESS WY
- FONT 92336 573-J7
4900 SBDO 92407 546-D5
WILDEY RD
53900 SBdC 92285 (4576-H6 See Page 4486)
54000 SBdC 92285 (4577-B5 See Page 4486)
WILDFIRE WY
11300 ADEL 92301 4295-A6
WILDFLOWER CT
9000 RCUC 91701 572-G5
WILD FLOWER LN
2100 CHLS 91709 680-J4
15000 SBdC - (3935-J2 See Page 3934)
15000 SBdC - 3936-A2
WILDFLOWER LN
33300 YCPA 92399 649-F4
38500 RivC 92399 650-G7
WILDFLOWER PL
- POM 91766 640-G7
17600 CHLS 91709 712-A5
W WILDFLOWER ST
1100 RLTO 92377 575-D3
WILD HORSE DR
4800 MTCL 91763 601-F5
WILDHORSE LN
2000 SBdC 92314 4812-H2
WILDHORSE RD
- SBdC - (3763-C3 See Page 3762)
32400 SBdC 92365 (3763-C2 See Page 3762)
WILDHORSE CANYON RD
- SBdC - 351-B3
7100 SBdC - 4562-J6
7200 SBdC 92371 4562-J6
WILDHORSE MEADOWS RD
1900 SBdC - 4812-H4
2200 SBdC - 4813-A4
2800 SBdC - (4883-D2 See Page 4813)
WILD LILAC LN
12900 YCPA 92399 650-E6
WILD LILAC PT
38300 SBdC 92399 610-J6
WILD OAK DR
30900 SBdC - 518-H6
WILD PONY DR
8400 RivC 92509 644-E7
W WILD PONY PTH
1500 SBDO 92407 546-C5
WILD POPPY LN
38300 YCPA 92399 650-J6
WILDRIDGE CANYON RD
12900 SBdC - (4655-E7 See Page 4654)
WILDROSE AV
1800 POM 91767 601-B6

STREET Block City ZIP Pg-Grid

N WILDROSE AV
200 CLTN 92324 605-H5
6100 SBDO 92407 545-J3
WILDROSE CIR
900 SBdC - 4737-J6
900 SBdC - 4738-A6
WILDROSE DR
10600 RCUC 91730 573-B6
WILD ROSE DR
33000 SBdC - 519-D2
WILD ROSE LN
- UPL 91786 602-C1
WILDROSE LN
500 SBdC - 516-H3
800 BBLK - 4811-D2
2500 SBdC 91784 572-A2
14100 CHLS 91709 680-H3
WILD ROSE RD
9700 SBdC 92345 4474-G6
WILDROSE ST
13200 SBdC 93562 2145-A3
15100 VCTV 92394 4296-A6
WILD SAGE PL
- CHLS 91709 681-H7
WILD WASH RD
18400 SBdC - (3937-B4 See Page 3936)
20700 SBdC 92307 (4027-E1 See Page 3936)
20700 SBdC - (4027-E1 See Page 3936)
WILD WEST CIR
- POM 91766 640-F4
WILD WIND PT
15100 VCTV 92394 4296-A5
WILDWOOD CT
3100 CHLS 91709 681-B6
WILDWOOD DR
10700 RCUC 91730 573-C6
17900 SBdC 92392 4386-H3
WILDWOOD LN
23700 SBdC - 516-H3
N WILDWOOD ST
1400 CLTN 92324 606-F4
WILDWOOD TR
46000 SBdC - 4742-J2
46000 SBdC - (4743-A2 See Page 4662)
WILDWOOD CANYON RD
33400 YCPA 92399 649-H5
34900 YCPA 92399 650-A5
WILDWOOD VIEW DR
37200 YCPA 92399 650-F6
WILDWOOD VIEW TR
38100 SBdC 92399 610-H7
WILEY CT
200 CLAR 91711 571-D7
WILEY ST
11600 LMLN 92354 647-E2
WILHART DR
- SBdC - 4887-B2
57700 SBdC 92284 4888-A1
WILKES CT
2100 CLAR 91711 571-C7
WILKIE DR
2200 POM 91767 601-A4
WILLAPA LN
300 DBAR 91765 640-C6
WILLET AV
12300 GTER 92313 646-E5
WILLET CT
12300 GTER 92313 646-E4
WILLIAM AV
6300 RivC 91752 683-H6
10700 SBdC 92316 645-C1
10700 SBdC 92316 645-C1
WILLIAMETTE LN
400 CLAR 91711 601-C1
WILLIAM MCGRATH ST
1200 CLTN 92324 606-A4
WILLIAMS AV
4700 CHLS 91709 681-F7
9700 SBdC 92316 605-C5
WILLIAMS CT
9000 FONT 92335 605-C3
WILLIAMS DR
- VCTV 92394 4205-F6
WILLIAMS LN
59000 YUCA 92284 4888-D6
WILLIAMS RD
7300 FONT 92336 575-C7
7500 SBdC 92336 575-C7
7800 SBdC 92336 605-C1
8500 FONT 92335 605-C2
8500 SBdC 92335 605-C2
WILLIAMS ST
100 SBdC - (3682-C1 See Page 3592)
400 SBdC - 3592-E7
500 POM 91768 640-G1
E WILLIAMS ST
100 BARS 92311 3679-J3
W WILLIAMS ST
100 BARS 92311 3679-G3
WILLIAMSBURG PKWY
7300 FONT 92336 574-B7
WILLIAMSBURG RD
2200 CHNO 91710 642-A5
WILLIAM S HART RD
4900 SBdC - 4886-J4

WILLIAMS WELL RD
46200 SBdC - 349-E5
WILLIE WY
60200 SBdC 92284 4748-G6
WILLIS CT
1000 CLTN 92324 646-H1
WILLIS DR
11000 LMLN 92354 647-D1
WILLOW AV
2200 UPL 91784 571-J3
6300 RLTO 92377 575-G4
6300 SBdC 92377 575-G4
41800 SBdC - 4811-J2
42000 BBLK - 4811-J2
42400 SBdC - 4812-A2
42500 BBLK - 4812-A2
N WILLOW AV
100 RLTO 92376 605-G1
400 RLTO 92376 575-G6
S WILLOW AV
- SBdC 92316 645-G1
100 RLTO 92316 605-G2
1700 RLTO 92316 605-G7
2300 RLTO 92316 645-G1
W WILLOW AV
100 RLTO 92377 575-G3
WILLOW CT
9200 MTCL 91763 601-E5
14500 ADEL 92301 4384-J1
WILLOW DR
1900 SBdC - 518-H6
8500 RCUC 91730 603-A3
15500 FONT 92337 644-F4
19200 APLV 92308 4387-C7
E WILLOW DR
2200 SBDO 92404 577-E1
2300 SBDO 92346 577-E1
N WILLOW DR
3400 SBDO 92346 577-E1
WILLOW LN
500 SBdC - 514-A1
600 SBdC 92314 4742-J7
700 SBdC 92314 4812-J2
3800 CHLS 91709 681-D6
8600 SBdC 92252 4959-D5
10900 ADEL 92301 4384-J1
32700 SBdC - 519-D7
WILLOW LNDG
400 BBLK - 4811-C1
WILLOW RD
9600 SBdC 92308 4479-E5
18900 HESP 92345 4477-B5
28500 SBdC - 518-B4
WILLOW ST
700 ONT 91764 602-D7
4600 SBdC 92284 4888-B3
5800 SBdC 92397 4652-D2
11400 HESP 92345 4475-J5
14400 HESP 92345 4476-A4
15700 VCTV 92392 4296-E3
18200 HESP 92345 4477-B5
WILLOW WY
7500 HIGH 92346 578-B6
14500 ADEL 92301 4384-J1
WILLOW BEND CT
4500 CHLS 91709 711-F1
WILLOWBROOK LN
- POM 91766 640-F5
1300 UPL 91784 571-G4
WILLOW CREEK DR
- YCPA 92399 650-B7
WILLOWCREEK DR
400 RDL 92374 608-G7
WILLOW CREEK LN
14600 CHLS 91709 680-J5
28900 HIGH 92346 578-C6
WILLOW CREEK RD
800 SBdC - 4738-A6
24000 DBAR 91765 640-C6
WILLOW CREST DR
- CHLS 91709 681-B7
- YCPA 92399 650-C5
WILLOWCREST LN
- POM 91766 640-G6
WILLOWFORD DR
- SBdC 92284 4818-A5
WILLOW GLEN DR
- CHLS 91709 681-B7
WILLOW HILL DR
15800 CHLS 91709 681-B7
WILLOW HOLLOW RD
- CHLS 91709 681-B7
WILLOW LANDING RD
38900 BBLK - 4811-A2
WILLOWMIST CT
16300 CHLS 91709 711-F2
WILLOW OAK LN
28800 HIGH 92346 578-C6
WILLOW POINTE AV
- CHLS 91709 681-B7
WILLOW RUN DR
- CHLS 91709 681-B7
WILLOW SPRINGS AV
20600 APLV 92307 (4117-E6 See Page 4116)
20600 SBdC 92307 (4117-E6 See Page 4116)
WILLOW SPRINGS DR
34900 YCPA 92399 610-A6

WILLOW SPRINGS RD
900 SBdC - 517-F4
16100 SBdC - 371-G2
20900 SBdC 92347 (3587-E7 See Page 3586)
E WILLOW TREE LN
1400 SBDO 92408 607-B6
WILLOW WELLS AV
8900 SBdC - 4480-A3
10900 SBdC - (4390-A4 See Page 4300)
WILLOW WITCH RD
300 SBdC - 516-C2
WILLOW WOOD DR
9700 RCUC 91701 572-J5
WILLOW WOOD LN
14200 CHLS 91709 680-H3
WILLOWWOOD LN
29100 HIGH 92346 578-D4
WILMAC AV
12700 GTER 92313 646-F5
WILMAR AV
58800 YUCA 92284 4888-D5
S WILMINGTON DR
2600 ONT 91761 642-J6
WILMINGTON RD
- CHLS 91709 681-H7
WILMOT ST
10200 SBdC 92345 4474-G4
11100 SBdC 92345 4475-A4
WILSHIRE AV
- TNP 92277 4962-J1
6500 TNP 92277 4892-J7
WILSHIRE PL
300 BARS 92311 3679-H3
WILSHIRE RD
34100 SBdC - (4391-D5 See Page 4300)
36000 SBdC - (4392-A5 See Page 4302)
WILSHIRE PEAK TR
10500 SBdC - 611-G7
11300 SBdC - 651-E1
11300 SBdC 92399 651-E1
WILSHIRE SHED RD
- SBdC 92399 651-D2
WILSON AV
- SBdC 91737 573-E2
8700 RCUC 91701 572-G3
8800 RCUC 91737 572-J2
9900 RCUC 91737 573-A2
12500 RCUC 91739 573-E2
12900 RCUC 91739 573-H2
13400 RCUC 91739 574-A2
13400 SBdC 91739 574-A2
14200 FONT 92336 574-B2
14200 SBdC 92336 574-B2
N WILSON AV
1000 UPL 91786 601-H1
1600 UPL 91784 571-H5
WILSON CT
8300 RCUC 91701 572-E3
15000 APLV 92307 4297-A6
WILSON DR
- SBdC 92277 4820-E1
1300 SBdC 92277 4750-E7
5800 SBdC 92277 4890-F5
46700 SBdC - (4743-C4 See Page 4662)
WILSON RD
2600 SBdC 92277 4824-F3
4400 SBdC 92277 (4894-F1 See Page 4824)
WILSON ST
600 POM 91768 640-G1
4300 CHNO 91710 641-E6
5200 RivC 92509 645-F6
5900 SBdC 92252 4889-B6
14700 HESP 92345 4566-A5
E WILSON ST
100 RLTO 92376 605-H2
N WILSON ST
600 SBDO 92411 576-D4
2700 SBDO 92407 576-C3
W WILSON ST
300 RLTO 92376 605-G2
1600 RLTO 92335 605-D3
WILSON TER
61700 SBdC 92252 4819-B6
WILSON WY
- SBdC 92277 4751-F7
- SBdC 92277 4821-E1
6800 HESP 92345 4566-A5
WILSON RANCH RD
7600 SBdC 92371 4563-G2
9000 SBdC 92371 4473-G2
11900 SBdC 92371 4383-G2
14500 SBdC 92371 (4293-G7 See Page 4292)
WILTON RD
3300 SBdC 92252 4818-H6
7600 SBdC 92252 4958-J3
WILTSE CT
7900 FONT 92336 603-J1
7900 FONT 92336 604-A1
WIMBERLY CT E
1300 POM 91766 640-G3
WIMBERLY CT S
1000 POM 91766 640-G3

WIMBLETON CT
7600 RCUC 91730 573-C7
13700 VCTV 92392 4386-E2
WIMBLETON DR
700 RDL 92374 648-F2
13900 VCTV 92392 4386-C1
WINBROOK DR
15900 CHLS 91709 681-B7
15900 CHLS 91709 711-C1
WINCHESTER AV
31100 SBdC - (4390-E7 See Page 4300)
WINCHESTER CIR
15800 FONT 92336 574-F5
E WINCHESTER DR
100 RLTO 92376 575-H5
900 RLTO 92376 576-A5
W WINCHESTER DR
300 RLTO 92376 575-F5
WINCHESTER RD
- SBdC - 4480-D2
WINCHESTER TR
32600 SBdC - (4390-J7 See Page 4300)
WINCHESTER WY
2500 CHLS 91709 680-H1
2500 CHLS 91709 681-A1
WINDCHIME LN
11500 FONT 92337 644-G3
WINDCREST DR
15900 FONT 92337 644-G2
WINDEMERE CT
2000 UPL 91784 571-H5
3000 CHLS 91709 681-B5
WINDEMERE PL
7100 RCUC 91701 573-B6
WINDEMERE WY
1500 UPL 91784 571-H5
WINDERERE RD
14100 SBdC 92371 4384-A2
WINDERMERE RD
8300 SBdC 92371 4564-A1
8900 SBdC 92371 4474-A1
12100 SBdC 92371 4384-A6
WINDFIELD RD
31200 BARS 92311 3680-D3
31200 SBdC 92311 3680-D3
WINDFLOWER AV
16900 FONT 92336 574-J3
WIND FOREST WY
16200 CHLS 91709 711-E1
WINDHAM DR
600 CLAR 91711 601-E1
28500 HIGH 92346 578-B6
WINDHAVEN CT
11400 RCUC 91701 573-D5
W WINDHAVEN DR
1900 RLTO 92377 575-A1
2800 RLTO 92377 574-J1
S WINDING LN E
100 SBdC 92314 4742-C6
S WINDING LN W
100 SBdC 92314 4742-C6
WINDING WY
2800 SBdC - 548-H1
WINDJAMMER LN
26500 SBdC - (3935-F5 See Page 3934)
WINDMILL CIR
14400 VCTV 92394 4295-H7
WINDMILL DR
3000 DBAR 91765 710-A1
3000 LACo 92823 710-A1
WINDMILL RD
14400 VCTV 92394 4295-H7
14400 VCTV 92394 4385-H1
WINDMILL WY
56900 SBdC 92285 4747-G3
WINDMILL CREEK RD
2400 CHLS 91709 680-J4
WINDOVER RD
14100 ADEL 92301 4384-B2
WINDROSE CT
3000 CHLS 91709 681-A6
WINDROSE DR
7400 HIGH 92346 577-J6
WINDROSE PL
- SBdC 92335 604-D2
WINDRUSH RD
2400 MohC - 3620-A1
WIND SONG
5200 YUCA 92284 4887-J4
WINDSONG CT
900 DBAR 91765 680-C2
3100 CHLS 91709 681-B5
WINDSONG PL
- BBLK - 4741-J6
7500 RCUC 91730 573-B7
WINDSONG RD
1400 SBdC 92252 4750-D7
1400 SBdC 92252 4820-D2
WINDSOR AV
7300 HESP 92345 4566-H2
17800 SBdC 92407 515-B5
WINDSOR CT
3700 RivC 91752 643-J6
4700 SBDO 92407 546-C6
33000 YCPA 92399 649-E4
WINDSOR DR
700 SBDO 92404 577-A2

WINDSOR DR
3200 CHLS 91709 711-B1
12200 YCPA 92399 649-E3
26100 LMLN 92354 647-E2
S WINDSOR LN
400 SBDO 92410 606-A3
WINDSOR PL
- RCUC 91737 572-H2
10800 RivC 91752 643-H6
W WINDSOR PL
1500 SBDO 92407 546-C6
WINDSOR ST
- ONT 91761 642-C6
1600 SBDO 92407 546-C5
W WINDSOR ST
1400 SBDO 92407 546-C6
WINDSWEPT RD
- CHLS 91709 681-H7
WINDWARD CT
12700 VCTV 92392 4385-H5
WINDWARD LN
13700 SBdC - (3935-F6 See Page 3934)
WINDWARD RD
26600 SBdC - 4737-F6
WINDY CT
10700 SBdC 92316 645-E1
WINDY PASS
200 BARS 92311 3679-H5
1000 BARS 92311 3680-A5
27300 SBdC 92311 3679-D5
WINDY RD
8800 SBdC 92308 4477-G7
WINDY GAP RD
5300 SBdC 92284 4888-H5
WINDY GROVE DR
- RCUC 91739 573-J6
WINE CT
6300 RCUC 91737 573-C4
WINEMA TR
- SBdC - 4843-F4
WINERY DR
11300 FONT 92337 644-C2
WINERY RIDGE DR
7800 RCUC 91730 602-G1
WINEVILLE AV
1000 ONT 91764 603-F6
5100 RivC 91752 683-G7
S WINEVILLE AV
- ONT 91764 603-F7
100 ONT 91761 603-F7
100 ONT 91761 643-F1
WINEVILLE RD
3500 RivC 91752 643-F7
4100 RivC 91752 683-F2
WINFIELD RD
1700 SBdC 92252 4820-B2
WINGATE AV
82300 SBdC 93562 2144-H5
WINGATE DR
11200 RCUC 91701 573-D4
WINGATE PASS RD
25400 SBdC - 329-C3
WINGED FOOT DR
- UPL 91786 572-D7
WINGED FOOT WY
4000 CHLS 91709 711-D1
WINGFOOT CT
6700 SBdC - 4843-J3
WINGSONG CT
1400 UPL 91784 571-H5
WINIFRED DR
11500 APLV 92308 4387-C7
11500 APLV 92308 4477-B4
WINLOCK DR
36400 SBdC 92311 3679-F1
W WINN DR
200 UPL 91786 602-A3
1000 UPL 91786 601-J3
WINNEBAGO RD
15700 APLV 92307 4297-E3
WINNEBAGO TR
- SBdC - 4773-H7
- SBdC - 4843-H1
WINNEMUCCA TR
- SBdC - 4843-H1
13900 APLV 92307 4387-E1
WINNEPEG DR
28700 SBdC - 4738-B5
WINNETKA CT
18300 APLV 92307 4296-J6
WINNETKA RD
18100 APLV 92307 4296-J6
WINNIPEG CIR
- FONT 92336 544-C7
WINONA RD
- VCTV 92392 4386-B3
13100 APLV 92308 4387-F3
WINONA ST
15300 VCTV 92392 4386-B4
WINONA WY
13100 VCTV 92392 4386-F4
WINSHIP WY
7500 RivC 92324 646-J6
7500 RivC 92324 647-A6
W WINSLOW AV
100 RLTO 92377 575-E2
WINSLOW CT
4400 RIV 92501 645-H7

WINSLOW ST
100 UPL 91786 572-B7
1400 UPL 91786 571-J7
WINSTON AV
1700 UPL 91784 572-C6
9300 RCUC 91730 603-B5
WINSTON CT
18300 SBdC 92392 4386-J4
N WINSTON CT
1100 UPL 91786 602-C1
1400 UPL 91786 572-C7
2000 UPL 91784 572-C4
S WINSTON CT
2500 SBDO 92408 646-H1
N WINSTON WY
1500 UPL 91786 572-C7
1600 UPL 91784 572-C6
WINTAP CT
12600 APLV 92308 4387-H5
WINTER PL
11300 ADEL 92301 4295-A6
WINTERBERRY WY
- RivC 92880 683-B7
WINTERGREEN RD
7700 SBdC 92372 4562-D2
9300 SBdC 92372 4472-D3
12100 SBdC 92372 4382-D4
13900 SBdC 92371 4382-D2
14600 SBdC 92371 4292-D6
WINTERGREEN ST
12200 RCUC 91739 573-G5
WINTERHAWK WY
11600 APLV 92308 4387-G7
WINTER PARK CT
6300 SBdC 92371 4473-G7
WINTER PARK DR
42000 BBLK - 4811-J2
WINTER PARK ST
13300 VCTV 92394 4295-F6
WINTERS RD
57300 SBdC 92284 4747-F7
57500 SBdC 92284 4748-B7
59400 SBdC 92284 4818-F3
60800 SBdC 92252 4748-H7
61100 SBdC 92252 4749-A6
64900 SBdC 92252 4750-A6
70900 SBdC 92277 4751-G6
WINTERSET CT
700 BBLK - 4811-J2
WINTERWOOD LN
1300 DBAR 91765 680-B3
7100 HIGH 92346 578-D5
16100 FONT 92335 604-G3
WINTHROP AV
600 CLAR 91711 571-C7
WINTHROP WY
28600 HIGH 92346 578-B7
WINTRESS DR
4200 CHNO 91710 641-E5
WINTUN CT
16100 APLV 92307 4297-B3
WINTUN RD
15700 APLV 92307 4297-B3
WINTUN TR
- SBdC - 4843-F5
WISCONSIN DR
- FONT 92336 574-D6
WISCONSIN RD
31500 SBdC 92365 (3765-B4 See Page 3764)
WISCONSIN ST
20000 APLV 92308 4387-E6
N WISCONSIN ST
500 POM 91768 640-H1
S WISEMAN WY
100 UPL 91786 602-B3
WISHING WELL CT
3000 RivC 91752 643-J5
3000 RivC 91752 644-A5
WISTERIA AV
1000 BARS 92311 3679-H5
2200 UPL 91784 571-H3
6600 RCUC 91737 573-B5
N WISTERIA AV
200 RLTO 92376 605-D1
700 RLTO 92376 575-D6
6200 SBDO 92407 546-A2
S WISTERIA AV
600 RLTO 92316 605-E3
9300 RLTO 92316 605-E4
WISTERIA CT
7800 HIGH 92346 578-C7
9500 SBdC 92316 605-E5
9700 SBdC 92316 605-E6
18500 HESP 92345 4477-A3
E WISTERIA CT
800 ONT 91761 642-D5
S WISTERIA CT
2100 ONT 91761 642-D5
WISTERIA LN
28400 HIGH 92346 578-B6
WISTERIA PL
13300 CHNO 91710 681-E1
WISTERIA ST
9600 SBdC 92316 605-E5
17600 HESP 92345 4476-H3
18200 HESP 92345 4477-A3
21000 APLV 92308 4477-G3
E WISTERIA ST
700 ONT 91761 642-D5

WITHERS AV
5400 FONT 92336 574-C2
WITHERSPOON RD
12600 CHNO 91710 641-D6
WITT AV
4000 RIV 92501 645-H7
WITT RD
80500 SBdC 92277 4824-E4
WOCAHOOTA RD
34900 SBdC - (4391-F2 See Page 4300)
WOFLEY BLVD
- SBdC 92252 4889-E4
WOLF DR
8100 SBdC 92371 4563-H2
9300 SBdC 92371 4473-H2
12100 SBdC 92371 4383-H3
WOLF RD
1400 BBLK - 4812-C2
1400 SBdC - 4812-D3
WOLF WY
- SBdC - 4773-H7
WOLFLEY BLVD
62400 SBdC 92252 4889-D4
WOLF LOOP RD
25600 SBdC - 517-D4
WOOD CT
300 CLAR 91711 571-D6
WOOD DR
- SBdC 92284 4817-E2
WOOD RD
9100 SBdC 92339 611-E2
WOODARD RD
3700 SBdC 92371 4382-J1
3700 SBdC 92371 4383-A1
WOODBEND DR
1500 CLAR 91711 601-A1
1700 CLAR 91711 571-A7
3200 LACo 91711 601-A2
WOODBEND LN
4600 SBDO 92407 546-H6
WOODBERRY DR
1200 SBdC 92314 4813-C3
WOODBINE DR
13700 VCTV 92392 4386-D2
WOODBRIAR DR
2600 RivC 92509 645-B6
36300 YCPA 92399 650-D6
WOODBRIDGE CT
2800 DBAR 91765 680-A7
WOODBRIDGE DR
11900 FONT 92337 644-B4
WOOD BRIDGE DR
12000 FONT 92337 644-B4
W WOODBRIDGE DR
500 SBdC 92314 4742-C7
WOODBRIDGE ST
6100 CHLS 91709 712-A5
WOODBURY CT
7000 RCUC 91701 573-C6
W WOODBURY CT
1200 UPL 91786 601-J2
WOODBURY RD
- SBdC 92365 (3685-D4 See Page 3594)
WOODBURY ST
1500 RDL 92374 608-A4
WOODCHASE CT
- RCUC 91739 573-J7
WOODCLIFF ST
6500 SBdC 92371 4563-J2
7300 SBdC 92371 4564-A2
9900 SBdC 92345 4564-G2
S WOOD CREEK DR
400 SBdC 92314 4742-C6
WOODCREST CT
- RLTO 92316 605-F5
WOOD CREST DR
- RivC 92399 650-G7
WOODCREST DR
14800 FONT 92337 644-D4
17600 SBdC 92407 515-A3
WOODCREST PL
6800 RCUC 91701 572-J5
WOODCREST ST
1200 RLTO 92316 605-F5
W WOODCREST ST
200 RLTO 92316 605-G4
900 RLTO 92316 605-E4
WOODCREST WY
2300 UPL 91784 571-H3
WOODED RD
45900 SBdC - 4742-J3
45900 SBdC - (4743-A3 See Page 4662)
WOOD GLEN CT
10500 YCPA 92399 610-A6
WOODGLEN DR
15200 CHLS 91709 681-B5
WOODHAM AV
34900 SBdC 92311 3679-B4
E WOODHAVEN CT
600 UPL 91786 572-C7
WOODHILL AV
34900 SBdC 92311 3679-B4
WOODHILL LN
13700 CHLS 91709 680-J2
WOODHILL ST
17000 FONT 92336 574-J5
17200 FONT 92336 575-A5

W WOODHILL ST
500 RLTO 92376 575-F5
500 SBdC 92376 575-F5
WOODHOLLOW LN
12700 CHLS 91709 640-H7
WOODHOLLOW ST
- VCTV 92392 4385-C5
WOODLAND AV
600 SBdC 92407 515-B3
WOODLAND CIR
200 SBdC - 517-J5
WOODLAND CT
6100 RCUC 91737 573-E3
WOODLAND DR
500 RivC 91752 683-F4
700 SBdC 92314 4742-J7
700 SBdC 92314 4812-J1
13900 FONT 92337 644-C2
14200 VCTV 92392 4386-F1
14400 VCTV 92392 4296-F7
WOODLAND LN
700 SBdC 92314 4742-J7
WOODLAND RD
700 SBdC - 516-G3
WOODLAND ST
35700 SBdC - 4481-H7
WOODLAND WY
400 BBLK - 4811-A2
S WOODLARK DR
2400 ONT 91761 643-A5
WOODLAWN AV
500 SBdC 92407 515-B4
WOODLAWN ST
700 ONT 91761 642-D2
W WOODLAWN ST
1000 ONT 91762 642-A2
1700 SBdC 91786 601-G2
WOODLEAF DR
9700 RCUC 91701 572-J5
23200 DBAR 91765 680-B1
W WOODMERE DR
1200 UPL 91786 601-J1
WOODMONT CT
800 POM 91767 601-B5
N WOODPINE AV
6200 SBDO 92407 545-J3
6200 SBDO 92407 546-A2
W WOODPINE AV
800 CLTN 92324 605-H5
WOODRIDGE CT
10100 RCUC 91737 573-A2
WOODRIDGE DR
10100 RCUC 91737 573-A2
WOODROSE CT
- CHLS 91709 681-A3
WOODROW CT
- CHLS 91709 711-G2
- CHLS 91709 712-A5
WOODROW MILLER AV
200 SBDO 92408 607-B2
N WOODRUFF CT
3400 RLTO 92377 545-B7
WOODRUFF PL
6500 RCUC 91701 573-D5
S WOODRUFF WY
1300 ONT 91761 643-E2
WOODS AV
- BARS 92311 3678-G6
34100 SBdC 92311 3678-G6
WOODSEY RD
400 SBdC - 516-G3
S WOODSIDE DR
400 SBdC 92314 4742-B7
WOODSIDE PL
5400 RCUC 91737 573-A2
WOODSIDE WY
12500 CHNO 91710 642-B6
WOODSON RD
24100 RivC 92324 647-E7
WOODSORREL DR
13500 CHLS 91709 681-A1
WOODSPRING PL
900 DBAR 91765 680-E2
WOODSTOCK CT
100 CLAR 91711 571-D6
WOODSTOCK RD
600 BBLK - 4811-J2
WOODSTREAM CT
- RCUC 91739 573-J7
WOODTHRUSH WY
11500 FONT 92337 644-H3
WOODVIEW AV
12200 VCTV 92392 4385-D7
WOODVIEW DR
11000 RCUC 91730 573-C7
WOODVIEW RD
3000 CHLS 91709 711-C1
3500 CHLS 91709 681-D7
WOODWARD AV
6900 TNP 92277 4892-J7
WOODWARD RD
61500 SBdC 92252 4889-B6
WOODWORTH WY
14500 VCTV 92394 4295-J6
WOODY LN
33800 YCPA 92399 649-G4
WORCESTER DR
- RCUC 91730 573-E2
WORKMAN PL
28100 LMLN 92354 647-E2

WORLD CT
11400 RivC 91752 643-G5
WORLD WOODS CT
- FONT 92336 574-G2
WORLEY CT
- HIGH 92346 578-E6
WOWANKA PL
8300 SBdC 92284 4957-B5
WRANGLER CT
13500 VCTV 92392 4385-F4
WRANGLER DR
5300 FONT 92336 574-C1
10500 SBdC 92316 605-E7
WRANGLER LN
12900 VCTV 92392 4385-F4
S WRANGLER PL
3400 ONT 91761 682-J1
WRANGLER RD
- SBdC 92307 4207-B3
6600 CHLS 91709 712-B6
18900 APLV 92307 4207-B3
28100 SBdC - (3937-A1 See Page 3936)
28300 SBdC - (3847-A6 See Page 3756)
WREN AV
12900 CHNO 91710 642-B7
13100 CHNO 91710 682-B1
WREN DR
200 BBLK - 4811-G1
WREN RD
4200 SBdC 92252 4889-B3
WREN ST
20400 APLV 92308 4477-F2
21900 APLV 92308 4478-A2
22100 SBdC 92308 4478-C2
22700 GTER 92313 646-F4
24500 SBdC 92308 4479-C1
31500 SBdC - 4480-F1
WRIGHT AV
12700 CHNO 91710 641-F7
WRIGHT CT
2000 POM 91766 640-D3
15100 FONT 92336 574-E5
WRIGHT RD
- SBdC - (4487-H7 See Page 4486)
- SBdC - (4577-H1 See Page 4486)
- SBdC 92285 (4577-H1 See Page 4486)
WRIGHT ST
1700 POM 91766 640-E3
WRIGHT MINE RD
- SBdC - 4660-C4
W WRIGHTWOOD DR
1300 SBDO 92407 546-D5
WYANDOT RD
- SBdC - 4886-G5
15500 APLV 92307 4297-F4
WYATT EARP LN
51600 SBdC - 4816-D7
WYCHE CT
5000 SBDO 92407 546-B5
WYLERHORN DR
100 SBdC - 516-J2
WYNAMEE RD
6700 SBdC 92308 4567-E5
WYNDHAM WY
- CHLS 91709 681-H7
WYNNEWOOD DR
900 DBAR 91765 680-D2
WYOMING CT
- FONT 92336 574-C6
WYOMING ST
- VCTV 92394 4205-G4
WYSOCKI LN
3200 RivC 91752 644-A5

X

X ST
- SBDO 92408 577-G7
- SBDO 92408 607-F1

Y

Y ST
- SBDO 92408 577-G7
- SBDO 92408 607-F1
YACHT CLUB DR
- LPCo - 4606-J4
YAKIMA RD
13000 APLV 92308 4387-H3
YAKIMA TR
6900 SBdC - 4843-G4
N YALE AV
100 CLAR 91711 601-D2
YALE CIR
12900 VCTV 92392 4385-E5
YALE CT
6400 CHNO 91710 682-A2
12900 VCTV 92392 4385-E5
13700 FONT 92336 574-A7
14100 ADEL 92301 4385-B1
W YALE CT
500 UPL 91786 602-B1
YALE DR
700 BARS 92311 3679-H6
9800 RCUC 91701 572-J6

YALE ST
- HESP 92345 4475-H7
5200 MTCL 91763 601-G5
6300 CHNO 91710 682-A2
E YALE ST
300 ONT 91764 602-D5
W YALE ST
600 ONT 91762 602-A5
900 ONT 91762 601-J5
YANAN RD
19000 APLV 92307 4297-B4
YANKTON AV
3300 CLAR 91711 571-E6
YANKTON DR
19100 SBdC 92316 645-F1
YAQUI RD
15000 APLV 92307 4297-A6
YARDLEY PL
11100 LMLN 92354 647-A1
YARDLEY ST
4300 SBDO 92407 546-D6
YARNELL RD
7100 HIGH 92346 578-A5
YARRON CT
11500 FONT 92337 644-F3
YARROW LN
68500 SBdC 92277 4751-C5
YATES AV
6700 SBdC 92404 577-C4
8900 ADEL 92301 4204-C5
11700 ADEL 92301 4205-B5
YATES RD
15400 VCTV 92392 4386-C2
17700 SBdC 92392 4386-H1
18200 SBdC 92392 4387-A2
YATES ST
7200 SBdC 92404 577-C5
7200 SBDO 92404 577-C5
N YATES ST
1200 SBDO 92404 577-C5
7200 SBdC 92404 577-C5
YATES WELL RD
- SBdC - 331-B6
YAWL CT
26400 SBdC - (3935-F5 See Page 3934)
YEAGER AV
15200 FONT 92336 574-E4
YEARLING LN
14000 VCTV 92394 4295-G6
YEARLING RD
- SBdC 92365 (3683-B3 See Page 3592)
YELLOW BELL CT
- APLV 92308 4387-C7
YELLOW JASMINE DR
7300 HIGH 92346 578-A6
YELLOWKNIFE RD
1300 SBdC 92284 4817-E3
YELLOW ROSE WY
- UPL 91786 602-D1
YELLOWSTONE AV
12700 SBdC 92392 4386-H4
YELLOWSTONE CIR
3800 CHNO 91710 681-D4
YELLOWSTONE DR
1000 SBdC 92397 4652-C1
1100 SBdC - 4738-B5
2000 BARS 92311 3680-A6
YE OLD GHOST RD
- SBdC 92285 4486-G7
- SBdC 92285 (4576-H1 See Page 4486)
YERBENA RD
15700 FONT 92337 644-E3
YERMO CTO
34300 SBdC - (3591-C3 See Page 3590)
YERMO RD
100 SBdC - (3682-B1 See Page 3592)
600 SBdC - 3592-F7
33700 SBdC - (3681-B2 See Page 3590)
39400 SBdC 92365 3592-F7
41100 SBdC 92365 (3593-G4 See Page 3592)
43500 SBdC 92365 3594-A2
45800 SBdC 92365 (3504-F6 See Page 3414)
46500 SBdC 92365 (3505-C3 See Page 3414)
50000 SBdC - (3505-C3 See Page 3414)
50700 SBdC - (3415-J6 See Page 3414)
YERMO VISTA ST
9100 SBdC 92308 4478-D6
YETTER ST
2000 SBdC 92285 4667-F7
2000 SBdC 92285 4747-F1
YEW CT
9900 RCUC 91730 573-A7
15300 SBdC 92335 604-E5
YEW LN
- CHLS 91709 711-H2
YEW ST
8900 RCUC 91730 572-G7
10000 RCUC 91730 573-A7

STREET Block City ZIP Pg-Grid

YOKUTS CT
6100 SBdC - 4844-E1
YOLO ST
10800 RCUC 91701 573-C5
YOLO WY
26500 SBdC - 4737-F7
YORBA AV
11300 SBdC 91710 641-F4
11600 CHNO 91710 641-F7
13000 CHNO 91710 681-F1
15200 CHLS 91709 681-F6
YORBA CT
- CHNO 91710 681-F4
YORBA LN
4500 SBdC 92301 (4113-A1 See Page 4112)
S YORK CT
2400 SBDO 92408 606-H7
2400 SBDO 92408 646-H1
YORK DR
7100 HIGH 92346 578-C5
YORK LN
40300 BBLK - 4811-D2
YORK PL
100 CLAR 91711 601-C4
6800 RCUC 91701 573-C5
YORK ST
1100 RDL 92373 648-D2
YORKER PL
- CHNO 91710 681-E1
YORKSHIRE DR
12300 APLV 92308 4387-C5
YORKSHIRE RD
5900 CHNO 91710 681-J1
6100 CHNO 91710 682-A1
YORKSHIRE WY
2300 POM 91767 601-A4
YORKTOWN CT
300 UPL 91784 572-C5
4900 CHNO 91710 641-F4
14000 FONT 92336 574-B7
YORKTOWN ST
26100 BARS 92311 (3759-A5 See Page 3758)
YORSHIRE CT
6200 CHNO 91710 682-A1
YOSEMITE AV
7000 SBdC 92345 4565-G5
YOSEMITE CT
900 BARS 92311 3679-J6
900 BARS 92311 3680-A5
3800 CHNO 91710 681-D4
YOSEMITE DR
- SBdC - 4773-J6
100 SBdC - 4812-E3
1100 SBdC - 4738-B4
4500 MTCL 91763 641-E1
5200 SBDO 92407 546-F4
18400 BBLK - 4812-D3
E YOSEMITE LOOP RD
7500 FONT 92336 574-A7
7600 FONT 92336 604-A1
W YOSEMITE LOOP RD
7500 FONT 92336 574-A7
7700 FONT 92336 604-A1
YOUNG CT
- SBDO 92408 646-J1
300 POM 91766 640-J5
YOUNG ST
1600 BARS 92311 3680-B4
YOUNGDALE CIR
17800 CHLS 91709 712-B6
YOUNGS CIR
900 SBdC 92285 4748-C3
N YOUNGSTOWN LN
- SBDO 92407 546-A2
6400 SBDO 92407 545-J2
YOYO ST
- RivC 92880 683-C6
YPSILANTHA ST
7900 HIGH 92346 578-C7
YUBA CT
10800 RCUC 91701 573-C5
YUBA LN
800 CLAR 91711 571-E5
YUBA RD
8500 SBdC 92371 4563-A2
10900 SBdC 92371 4472-J3
12500 SBdC 92371 4382-J6
YUBA ST
18400 HESP 92345 4567-A2
YUBA RIVER DR
3800 ONT 91761 643-C6
YUBA RIVER RD
3700 ONT 91761 643-C6
YUCAIPA BLVD
31200 RDL 92373 649-B3
31200 YCPA 92373 649-B3
31300 YCPA 92399 649-B3
34900 YCPA 92399 650-A3
YUCAIPA RIDGE RD
9700 YCPA 92399 610-A4
YUCAIPA RIDGE TKTR
36800 SBdC - 610-F2
38500 SBdC - 611-A4
38500 SBdC 92399 611-A6
39000 SBdC 92399 610-J5
YUCAIPA RIDGE TR
9000 SBdC - 610-B2
9600 SBdC 92399 610-A4
YUCAIPA RIDGE TR
9600 YCPA 92399 610-A4
YUCATAN RD
11700 SBdC 92371 4472-G1
12300 SBdC 92371 4382-G7
YUCCA AV
100 BARS 92311 3680-A2
6100 TNP 92277 4892-E1
6500 SBdC 92376 575-F4
14800 SBdC 92335 604-D2
16200 VCTV 92392 4296-D5
N YUCCA AV
200 RLTO 92376 605-F1
500 RLTO 92376 575-F5
1600 SBdC 92376 575-F5
2200 RLTO 92377 575-F3
2800 SBdC 92407 545-F2
S YUCCA AV
100 RLTO 92376 605-F3
1100 RLTO 92316 605-F5
YUCCA CIR
- LPCo - 4606-J4
- TNP 92278 4822-F1
YUCCA DR
11800 FONT 92337 644-C4
46000 SBdC - 4742-J2
46000 SBdC - (4743-A3 See Page 4662)
E YUCCA DR
1300 SBdC 92404 547-C7
1400 SBDO 92404 547-C7
YUCCA LN
11300 SBdC 92392 4475-B2
YUCCA RD
- SBdC - 330-K2
- SBdC - 4480-G2
100 SBdC 92284 4747-F4
100 SBdC 92372 4472-A5
800 SBdC 92285 4747-F4
3900 SBdC 92284 4887-H1
7200 ADEL 92301 (4293-J1 See Page 4292)
7400 ADEL 92301 4294-A1
11300 ADEL 92301 4295-A1
16700 SBdC 92307 4298-D1
17100 APLV 92307 4208-C7
17100 SBdC 92307 4208-C7
35700 SBdC - (3682-G1 See Page 3592)
35700 SBdC 92365 3592-G7
35700 SBdC 92365 (3682-G1 See Page 3592)
39000 SBdC 92365 (3504-D6 See Page 3414)
57500 SBdC 92284 4888-A1
YUCCA ST
- SBdC 92308 4479-F4
9200 SBdC 92308 4477-F5
13200 SBdC 92345 2145-A3
14300 HESP 92345 4475-J6
14500 HESP 92345 4476-A6
18200 HESP 92345 4477-A7
30100 SBdC - 4480-C4
W YUCCA ST
600 ONT 91762 642-B3
YUCCA TR
20100 SBdC - (3937-D2 See Page 3936)
52300 SBdC - 4886-E4
54900 YUCA 92284 4957-C2
57300 YUCA 92284 4958-A2
59100 SBdC 92284 4958-E2
59200 SBdC 92252 4958-E2
YUCCA BLOSSOM LN
57300 YUCA 92284 4887-J5
YUCCA LOMA RD
18600 APLV 92307 4387-A2
21400 APLV 92308 4387-C2
23300 SBdC 92307 4388-D2
YUCCA MESA RD
100 SBdC 92284 4748-C4
300 SBdC 92285 4748-D3
2500 SBdC 92284 4818-E6
3700 SBdC 92284 4888-E3
4800 YUCA 92284 4888-E7
6200 SBdC 92252 4888-E7
YUCCA PARK RD
9900 SBdC 92284 4956-J5
YUCCA TERRACE DR
2900 SBdC 92371 4472-G5
3600 SBdC 92371 4473-A5
7300 SBdC 92371 4474-A5
9900 SBdC 92345 4474-G5
11000 SBdC 92345 4475-A5
YUKI CT
- SBdC - 4843-J2
YUKON CIR
- FONT 92336 544-C7
YUKON CT
1200 SBdC - 4737-H5
YUKON DR
500 SBdC - 519-E2
1100 SBdC - 4737-H5
YUKON ST
1500 RDL 92374 608-D4
YUMA AV
6900 SBdC - 4844-A3
YUMA CT
14100 APLV 92307 4387-B1
N YUMA DR
3100 SBDO 92346 577-F2
YUMA RD
16100 SBdC 92307 4298-F3
20300 APLV 92307 4297-E3
YUMA ST
17000 VCTV 92392 4386-G6
YUMA TR
56100 YUCA 92284 4957-F4
YUNIS CT
10900 YCPA 92399 610-A7
YUNKER DR
- SBdC - 517-H3
YVETTE CT
- RDL 92374 608-B3

Z

Z ST
- SBDO 92408 577-F7
S ZACA CT
300 SBdC 92314 4742-H6
S ZACA RD
100 SBdC 92314 4742-G7
ZAMORA RD
56100 SBdC 92285 4747-E3
ZANE LN
36400 SBdC - (4391-J5 See Page 4300)
36400 SBdC - (4392-A5 See Page 4302)
ZANIA ST
2600 RivC 92509 645-D7
ZANJA AV
2100 RivC 92509 645-E7
ZANJA DR
2300 SBdC 92359 609-B5
ZANJA WY
2300 SBdC 92359 609-B6
ZANJA VIEW DR
2600 SBdC 92359 609-D5
ZANJA VILLA DR
1000 SBdC 92374 609-B6
1000 SBdC 92399 609-B6
1000 SBdC 92359 609-B6
ZANJERO CT
1200 SBdC 92359 609-C5
ZAPATA PL
5800 RCUC 91737 572-J3
ZARAGOZA LN
1100 CLTN 92324 606-B4
ZELL CT
24100 SBdC - 516-J2
ZENDA ST
9300 SBdC 92301 4294-E7
10800 ADEL 92301 4294-J7
12200 VCTV 92394 4295-C6
16500 VCTV 92392 4296-E6
W ZENIA CT
600 ONT 91762 642-B3
ZENOBIA LN
15700 CHLS 91709 681-D7
ZEPHER CT
9700 SBdC 92308 4477-E5
ZEPHER WY
- SBdC 92308 4567-E2
ZEPHYR RD
11300 SBdC - 3934-J4
11300 SBdC - (3935-A4 See Page 3934)
ZEPHYR ST
7800 FONT 92336 604-A1
ZERMATT DR
100 SBdC - 516-J2
100 SBdC - 517-A2
5400 SBdC 92397 4652-F3
28100 SBdC - 4738-A5
E ZERMATT DR
24100 SBdC - 516-J2
24300 SBdC - 517-A2
ZIMMERMAN CT
- RCUC 91737 572-G2
ZINC LN
10500 MohC - 3620-F4
ZINC MINE RD
62100 SBdC - 331-A9
E ZINFANDEL CT
4700 ONT 91761 643-E4
ZINFANDEL DR
10300 ADEL 92301 4204-G5
ZINFANDEL LN
10100 RivC 92509 644-A4
ZINFANDEL ST
10700 RCUC 91737 573-C4
ZING DR
9300 SBdC 92371 4474-C4
10900 SBdC 92392 4474-C1
ZINNA CT
12400 RCUC 91739 573-G6
ZINNEA AV
- CHNO 91710 642-B7
ZINNIA ST
1200 UPL 91784 571-J3
ZION CT
- FONT 92336 574-D3
ZION DR
900 BARS 92311 3679-J6
28600 SBdC - 4738-B5
ZION LN
3900 CHNO 91710 681-D4
ZIRCON AV
4900 SBdC 92277 (4894-B2 See Page 4824)
6000 RCUC 91701 572-G3
7500 RCUC 91730 572-G7
7600 RCUC 91730 602-G1
ZIRCON DR
15000 VCTV 92394 4295-G6
ZIRCON RD
32100 SBdC - 4480-H7
32500 SBdC - 4481-A7
ZIRCON WY
13600 VCTV 92394 4295-F6
ZOE LN
- NDLS 92363 3710-D5
ZUGER CT
400 SBdC - 516-H3
ZUGER DR
23700 SBdC - 516-H2
ZUGER LN
23800 SBdC - 516-H3
ZUMA CT
11400 ADEL 92301 4385-A1
ZUMA PL
6600 RivC 92509 645-B6
ZUNI CT
9900 SBdC - 4843-H3
ZUNI LN
14500 VCTV 92394 4295-J3
ZUNI RD
20100 APLV 92307 4297-E4
22100 APLV 92307 4298-A4
23300 SBdC 92307 4298-D4
ZUNI TR
56100 YUCA 92284 4957-G4
ZURICH CT
2300 SBdC 92397 4652-F3
23900 SBdC - 516-H2
ZURICH DR
600 SBdC - 4737-H6
5300 SBdC 92397 4652-F3
23700 SBdC - 516-H2
ZZYZX RD
49500 SBdC - 350-E3

#

1N09
- SBdC - 389-E1
29800 SBdC - 548-F5
1N54
2400 SBdC - 4811-B7
2400 SBdC - 389-F1
1N54A
38800 SBdC - 4811-A7
1N64
- SBdC - 389-E1
1N86
- SBdC - 389-F1
1ST AV
- LPCo - 4844-H3
2300 SBdC 92359 609-C6
8100 HESP 92345 4566-E2
9200 HESP 92345 4476-F1
11600 HESP 92345 4386-F7
12200 HESP 92345 4386-F6
12200 VCTV 92345 4386-F6
12200 VCTV 92392 4386-E3
1ST AV Rt#-3
- LPCo - 4844-H7
N 1ST AV
- UPL 91786 602-C1
100 BARS 92311 3679-H1
1400 UPL 91786 572-B7
1600 UPL 91784 572-B3
4000 SBdC 92407 546-G6
4000 SBDO 92407 546-G6
29600 BARS 92311 3589-J7
29600 SBdC 92311 3589-J7
S 1ST AV
100 BARS 92311 3679-G3
100 UPL 91786 602-C4
W 1ST AV
2000 SBdC 92407 546-A7
2300 SBdC 92407 545-J7
1ST LN
2000 SBdC 92314 4812-H1
1ST ST
- BARS 92311 3680-H6
- RDL 92373 608-B7
200 YCPA 92399 610-A7
1000 SBdC 92314 4813-B1
11800 YCPA 92399 650-A2
12200 SBdC 93562 2234-G4
13400 SBdC 93562 2055-A7
15500 VCTV 92392 4296-E4
18900 VCTV - (4206-A3 See Page 4116)
19000 SBdC - (4206-A3 See Page 4116)
19300 SBdC - 4205-J2
25200 SBdC 92311 3678-G6
26300 LMLN 92354 647-F2
26300 SBdC 92354 647-F2
33600 SBdC - (3681-F6 See Page 3590)
45300 SBdC - 4742-H1
82000 SBdC 93562 2144-H6
E 1ST ST
- RLTO 92376 605-H2
100 CLAR 91711 601-D3
100 POM 91766 640-J2
300 POM 91766 641-C1
4000 MTCL 91763 641-C1
W 1ST ST
- RLTO 92376 605-F2
100 CLAR 91711 601-C3
100 POM 91766 640-G2
1ST ST E
4900 SBdC 92252 4890-A3
1ST ST S
64800 SBdC 92252 4890-A3
1ST ST W
4900 SBdC 92252 4890-A3
2N05
500 SBdC - 4812-E2
2N06
42300 SBdC - 4811-H4
42300 SBdC - 4812-A6
2N08
900 SBdC - 4811-F2
40900 BBLK - 4811-F2
2N08A
41100 SBdC - 4811-G2
2N08B
41000 SBdC - 4811-F3
2N10
1300 SBdC - 4812-A4
1600 SBdC - 4811-C3
1700 SBdC - 4810-J4
2N11
37800 SBdC - 4810-H6
2N14Y
44900 SBdC - 4812-H3
2N15Y
- SBdC - 4812-H2
2N17
- SBdC - 4811-C4
2N18Y
44200 SBdC - 4812-E3
2N26
42500 SBdC - 4812-B5
2N27
43900 SBdC - 4812-E3
2N33
- SBdC - 4736-E3
- SBdC - 4737-F3
2N34
- SBdC - 517-E1
- SBdC - 4737-E7
2N34A
- SBdC - 4737-E7
2N36
- SBdC - 4736-H5
2N46Y
- SBdC - 4812-E4
2N48
6000 SBdC - 4568-H4
6000 SBdC - (4569-B6 See Page 4568)
6800 SBdC 92308 4568-H4
30300 SBdC - 4660-A6
30500 SBdC - (4740-F1 See Page 4660)
37000 SBdC - (4659-D2 See Page 4658)
2N48Y
1500 SBdC - 4812-H4
2N51Y
41200 SBdC - 4811-G3
2N60Y
900 SBdC - 4812-F2
2N75
29600 SBdC - 4738-D4
2N77
- SBdC - 4812-F4
2N86
37700 SBdC - 4810-H4
2N93
1900 SBdC - 4812-J4
2200 SBdC - 4813-A4
2800 SBdC - (4883-E3 See Page 4813)
2N93B
1400 SBdC - 4812-J4
1400 SBdC 92314 4812-J4
2N96
- SBdC - 4738-C6
2ND AV
- LPCo - 4844-G6
100 BARS 92311 3679-H2
300 SBDO 92408 607-B2
2200 UPL 91784 572-C4
9300 HESP 92345 4476-E1
11600 HESP 92345 4386-E7
12200 VCTV 92345 4386-E7
12200 VCTV 92392 4386-E3
82400 SBdC 93562 2144-H5
2ND AV Rt#-5
- LPCo - 4844-G3
N 2ND AV
- UPL 91786 602-C1
1400 UPL 91786 572-C7
1500 UPL 91784 572-C3
S 2ND AV
100 UPL 91786 602-C4
W 2ND AV
2100 SBdC 92407 546-A7
2300 SBdC 92407 545-J7
2ND LN
2000 SBdC 92314 4812-H1
2ND PL
100 SBDO 92408 607-C1
1000 CALI 92320 649-J7
2ND ST
200 YCPA 92399 610-A7
900 CALI 92320 650-A7
1000 SBdC 92314 4813-B1
1200 SBDO 92408 607-B1
1200 PRKR - 4774-H6
4000 SBdC 92407 546-F6
4000 SBDO 92407 546-F6
8000 RCUC 91730 602-H1
8900 SBdC 92392 4474-D2
11100 SBdC 92392 4475-A2
11300 YCPA 92399 649-J1
13000 CHNO 91710 641-F7
13100 CHNO 91710 681-F1
13600 CALI 92320 649-J7
15500 VCTV 92392 4296-E4
18800 SBdC 92316 645-E4
19200 SBdC - (4206-A3 See Page 4116)
25200 SBdC 92311 3678-G6
33600 SBdC - (3681-F7 See Page 3590)
45300 SBdC - 4742-H1
82300 SBdC 93562 2144-H6
84600 SBdC 93562 2055-A7
E 2ND ST
- CLAR 91711 601-D3
100 POM 91766 640-J2
100 RLTO 92376 605-H1
100 SBDO 92408 606-J1
300 POM 91766 641-A2
N 2ND ST
100 CLTN 92324 606-C5
W 2ND ST
- RLTO 92376 605-D1
100 CLAR 91711 601-D3
100 POM 91766 640-F2
100 SBDO 92408 606-H1
100 SBDO 92410 606-A1
300 SBDO 92401 606-H1
2700 SBDO 92376 606-A1
2ND ST S
64800 SBdC 92252 4890-A3
3N34.2
1700 SBdC - 4738-F3
3N38
30100 SBdC - 4738-E2
3RD AV
- LPCo - 4844-F6
100 BARS 92311 3679-H2
200 SBDO 92408 607-B2
2200 SBdC 92374 609-A6
2200 UPL 91784 572-C4
7100 SBdC 92374 608-J7
7300 HESP 92345 4566-D1
8700 HESP 92345 4476-E2
11600 HESP 92345 4386-E7
12200 VCTV 92392 4386-E4
N 3RD AV
- UPL 91786 602-C1
1500 UPL 91786 572-C7
1600 UPL 91784 572-C5
3900 SBDO 92407 546-F6
3900 SBdC 92407 546-F6
S 3RD AV
100 UPL 91786 602-C4
W 3RD AV
2100 SBdC 92407 546-A7
2300 SBdC 92407 545-J7
3RD LN
2000 SBdC 92314 4812-H1
N 3RD PL
800 UPL 91786 602-C2
3RD ST
- BARS 92311 3680-H6
- YCPA 92399 610-A7
200 POM 91766 641-D2
200 RDL 92374 608-B7
600 NDLS 92363 3620-C6
900 CALI 92320 649-J7
1000 SBdC 92314 4813-B1
1100 PRKR - 4774-H7
1600 HIGH 92408 607-B1
1600 HIGH 92410 607-B1
1600 SBDO 92408 607-B1
2400 HIGH 92346 577-G7
2400 SBDO 92346 577-D7
2400 SBDO 92408 577-D7
4100 SBdC 91763 641-D2
4200 MTCL 91763 641-D2
8600 SBdC 92284 4957-A6
8900 SBdC 92392 4474-E2
11300 SBdC 92392 4475-A1
11700 YCPA 92399 649-J3
12500 CHNO 91710 641-G7
13100 CHNO 91710 681-G1
15400 VCTV 92392 4296-F4
18700 SBdC 92316 645-E4
19100 SBdC - (4206-A2 See Page 4116)
24600 SBdC 92410 607-B1
24600 SBdC 92408 607-B1
25200 SBdC 92311 3678-G6
25400 SBdC 92410 607-B1
25400 SBDO 92410 577-D7
3RD ST
33600 SBdC - (3681-F7 See Page 3590)
45300 SBdC - 4742-H1
82200 SBdC 93562 2144-H6
84500 SBdC 93562 2055-A7
E 3RD ST
100 POM 91766 640-J2
100 RLTO 92376 605-H1
100 SBDO 92410 606-J1
100 SBDO 92408 606-J1
300 POM 91766 641-A2
300 SBdC 92408 606-J1
300 SBdC 92408 607-C1
300 SBDO 92408 607-C1
1200 HIGH 92408 607-C1
1600 SBDO 92410 607-C1
10000 SBdC 92410 606-J1
10000 SBdC 92410 607-C1
24900 HIGH 92410 607-C1
N 3RD ST
100 CLTN 92324 606-C5
S 3RD ST
100 CLTN 92324 606-C6
W 3RD ST
- RLTO 92376 605-E1
100 POM 91766 640-G2
100 SBDO 92401 606-H1
700 SBDO 92410 606-B1
3RD ST S
64100 SBdC 92252 4889-H3
64500 SBdC 92252 4890-A3
4N03
- SBdC - 4480-E7
- SBdC - 4570-E1
4TH AV
- LPCo - 4844-D7
400 BARS 92311 3679-H2
2200 UPL 91784 572-C4
8200 HESP 92345 4566-D1
8700 HESP 92345 4476-E2
11300 HESP 92345 4386-E7
12700 VCTV 92392 4386-E4
N 4TH AV
- UPL 91786 602-C2
2200 UPL 91784 572-C3
4000 SBdC 92407 546-E6
4000 SBDO 92407 546-E6
4TH LN
2000 SBdC 92314 4812-H1
2300 SBdC 92314 4813-A1
4TH PL
26800 HIGH 92346 577-G7
4TH ST
- BARS 92311 3680-H5
- LPCo - 4774-H7
- SBdC 92311 3678-H7
- YCPA 92399 610-A7
800 CALI 92320 649-J7
800 NDLS 92363 3620-C5
800 YCPA 92399 649-H3
1000 PRKR - 4774-H7
2300 ONT 91730 602-H6
2300 ONT 91764 602-H6
2300 RCUC 91730 602-H6
2700 ONT 91764 603-A5
5300 ONT 91739 603-F5
8900 SBdC 92392 4474-E1
9700 RCUC 91730 603-A5
12100 RCUC 91739 603-F5
12900 CHNO 91710 641-G7
13100 CHNO 91710 681-G1
15400 VCTV 92392 4296-F4
18600 SBdC 92316 645-E3
19100 SBdC - (4206-A3 See Page 4116)
24300 SBdC 92410 606-J1
24300 SBdC 92410 607-A1
24400 SBdC 92410 577-A7
24800 HIGH 92410 577-C7
33600 SBdC - (3681-F7 See Page 3590)
45300 SBdC - 4742-H1
82100 SBdC 93562 2144-G6
84500 SBdC 93562 2055-A7
E 4TH ST
- CLAR 91711 601-D3
100 ONT 91764 602-D6
100 POM 91766 640-J2
100 SBdC 92410 606-J1
200 SBdC 92410 606-J1
300 POM 91766 641-A2
N 4TH ST
100 CLTN 92324 606-C6
S 4TH ST
- RDL 92373 608-B7
100 CLTN 92324 606-C7
100 RDL 92373 648-C1
W 4TH ST
100 CLAR 91711 601-D3
100 ONT 91762 602-A6
100 ONT 91764 602-A6
100 POM 91766 640-H2
100 SBDO 92401 606-G1
600 SBDO 92410 606-G1
1000 ONT 91762 601-J6
W 4TH ST Rt#-66
1300 SBDO 92410 606-D1
1300 SBDO 92410 606-D1
W 4TH ST U.S.-66 Hist
1300 SBDO 92411 606-D1
1300 SBDO 92410 606-D1
4TH ST S
63300 SBdC 92252 4889-F4
64500 SBdC 92252 4890-B3
5TH AV
- SBdC 92285 (4576-G7 See Page 4486)
100 BARS 92311 3679-H2
200 SBDO 92408 607-A2
1300 RDL 92374 648-F1
1800 SBdC 92374 648-H1
2100 SBdC 92374 649-A1
2400 SBdC 92285 4667-A2
8100 HESP 92345 4566-D1
8700 HESP 92345 4476-D2
11300 HESP 92345 4386-D7
12100 VCTV 92345 4386-D5
12100 VCTV 92392 4386-E4
20300 SBdC 92407 545-J6
N 5TH AV
- SBdC 91784 572-C2
- UPL 91786 602-C1
5TH LN
2000 SBdC 92314 4812-H1
5TH PL
13200 YCPA 92399 649-G6
5TH ST
- SBdC - 3762-E2
- RDL 92373 608-B7
- YCPA 92399 610-A7
200 RDL 92374 608-B7
700 CALI 92320 649-H7
1100 PRKR - 4774-H7
1400 NDLS 92363 3620-C5
1900 SBDO 92410 577-A7
1900 HIGH 92410 577-A7
2400 HIGH 92346 577-A7
2400 SBDO 92346 577-E7
2500 SBDO 92409 577-E7
9300 SBdC 92392 4474-D1
10000 RCUC 91730 603-A5
11700 YCPA 92399 649-H3
12900 CHNO 91710 641-G7
13100 CHNO 91710 681-G1
15400 VCTV 92392 4296-E5
18600 SBdC 92316 645-E3
24200 SBdC 92410 577-J7
24200 SBdC 92410 577-A7
27700 HIGH 92346 577-G7
34100 BARS 92311 3678-H7
34100 SBdC 92311 3678-H7
45300 SBdC - 4742-H1
82000 SBdC 93562 2144-G6
84500 SBdC 93562 2055-A7
E 5TH ST
100 ONT 91764 602-C5
100 SBDO 92410 576-J7
2200 ONT 91730 602-G5
7000 SBdC 92410 576-J7
S 5TH ST
100 CLTN 92324 606-C7
700 CLTN 92324 646-C1
W 5TH ST
100 ONT 91762 602-B5
100 SBDO 92401 576-G7
600 SBDO 92410 576-G7
900 ONT 91762 601-J5
2600 SBDO 92410 606-A1
2700 SBDO 92376 606-A1
W 5TH ST Rt#-66
800 SBDO 92410 576-E7
800 SBDO 92411 576-E7
1700 SBDO 92411 606-C1
W 5TH ST U.S.-66 Hist
1300 SBDO 92411 576-E7
1700 SBDO 92411 606-C1
6TH AV
- LPCo - 4844-B7
100 BARS 92311 3679-H3
1600 RDL 92374 648-G2
1800 SBdC 92374 648-G2
8200 HESP 92345 4566-D1
8700 HESP 92345 4476-D4
11800 HESP 92345 4386-D7
12200 VCTV 92392 4386-D4
N 6TH AV
- UPL 91786 602-C3
1400 UPL 91786 572-C7
6TH LN
2000 SBdC 92314 4812-H1
6TH PL
13100 YCPA 92399 649-G6
6TH ST
- BARS 92311 3680-G5
- LPCo - 4774-H7
- YCPA 92399 610-A7
- RDL 92373 608-C7
300 RDL 92374 608-B5
400 PRKR - 4774-H7
500 SBdC 92410 576-J7
500 SBdC 92410 577-A7
1400 HIGH 92410 577-A7
1400 SBDO 92410 577-D7
9200 RCUC 91730 602-J5
9400 SBdC 92392 4474-F1
9700 RCUC 91730 603-A4
6TH ST
12000 RCUC 91739 603-G4
12100 YCPA 92399 649-G4
12900 CHNO 91710 641-G7
13100 CHNO 91710 681-G1
15200 VCTV 92392 4296-E5
18500 SBdC 92316 645-E3
26000 HIGH 92346 577-F7
26200 SBDO 92409 577-F7
45300 SBdC - 4742-H1
81900 SBdC 93562 2144-G6
84400 SBdC 93562 2055-B7
E 6TH ST
100 CLAR 91711 601-E3
100 ONT 91762 602-C5
100 ONT 91764 602-C5
100 POM 91766 640-J2
100 SBDO 92410 576-H7
300 POM 91766 641-A2
300 SBdC 92410 576-J7
2100 ONT 91730 602-E5
2900 SBDO 92376 575-J7
2900 SBDO 92376 576-A7
N 6TH ST
300 CLTN 92324 606-D4
S 6TH ST
100 CLTN 92324 606-D7
900 CLTN 92324 646-D1
W 6TH ST
100 CLAR 91711 601-C3
100 ONT 91762 602-B5
100 SBDO 92401 576-H7
500 POM 91766 640-G2
500 SBDO 92376 576-A7
600 SBDO 92410 576-A7
900 SBDO 92376 576-E7
900 ONT 91762 601-J5
7TH AV
100 BARS 92311 3679-H3
6900 HESP 92345 4566-C2
8700 HESP 92345 4476-D1
11300 HESP 92345 4386-D7
12100 VCTV 92392 4386-D5
12100 VCTV 92345 4386-D5
7TH LN
800 SBdC 92314 4813-A1
2000 SBdC 92314 4812-J1
7TH PL
900 CALI 92320 649-G7
13100 YCPA 92399 649-G6
13600 YCPA 92373 649-G7
7TH ST
- BARS 92311 3680-G5
- SBdC - 3762-E2
- RDL 92373 608-C7
- YCPA 92399 610-A7
200 RDL 92374 608-C7
1000 PRKR - 4774-H7
1400 LPCo - 4774-H7
1700 RDL 92374 648-G2
6700 SBdC 92371 4473-H1
7500 SBdC 92371 4474-A1
8100 SBdC 92392 4474-C1
9100 RCUC 91730 602-H4
10300 RCUC 91730 603-B4
12100 YCPA 92399 649-G4
12700 CHNO 91710 641-G6
13100 CHNO 91710 681-G1
18100 FONT 92337 645-D3
18100 SBdC 92316 645-D3
24900 HIGH 92410 577-B7
25300 SBDO 92410 577-C7
26500 HIGH 92346 577-J6
30500 SBdC 92374 648-G2
45300 SBdC - 4742-H2
81900 SBdC 93562 2144-G6
84400 SBdC 93562 2055-B7
7TH ST U.S.-66 Hist
14200 VCTV 92392 4386-C1
14400 VCTV 92392 4296-D7
E 7TH ST
- UPL 91786 602-C4
100 CLAR 91711 601-D3
100 POM 91766 640-J2
100 SBDO 92410 576-J7
200 SBdC 92410 576-J7
300 POM 91766 641-A2
1000 ONT 91764 602-F4
1600 SBdC 91766 641-C2
N 7TH ST
200 CLTN 92324 606-D5
S 7TH ST
100 CLTN 92324 606-D7
700 CLTN 92324 646-D1
W 7TH ST
- UPL 91786 602-A4
100 CLAR 91711 601-C3
100 POM 91766 640-H2
100 SBDO 92401 576-H7
100 SBDO 92411 576-E7
1200 UPL 91786 601-H4
2700 SBDO 92376 576-B7
8TH AV
- LPCo - 4843-J7
8200 HESP 92345 4566-C1
8800 HESP 92345 4476-D2
11300 HESP 92345 4386-D7
N 8TH AV
- UPL 91786 602-D3
8TH LN
2000 SBdC 92314 4742-H7
8TH ST
- RDL 92373 608-C7
- YCPA 92399 610-A6
500 PRKR - 4774-J7
1300 RCUC 91730 602-H4
1300 ONT 91764 602-E4
1900 ONT 91730 602-H4
8900 RCUC 91730 603-E3
9700 SBdC 92392 4384-F7
12200 YCPA 92399 649-F4
15400 VCTV 92392 4296-E5
18100 SBdC 92316 645-D3
45300 SBdC - 4742-H2
81900 SBdC 93562 2144-G6
84300 SBdC 93562 2145-B1
84300 SBdC 93562 2055-B7
E 8TH ST
- UPL 91786 602-C4
100 CLAR 91711 601-D2
300 POM 91766 640-J2
300 POM 91766 641-A2
1000 ONT 91764 602-C4
1100 UPL 91764 602-C4
N 8TH ST
1200 CLTN 92324 606-D3
S 8TH ST
500 CLTN 92324 606-D7
500 CLTN 92324 646-D1
W 8TH ST
- UPL 91786 602-B4
100 CLAR 91711 601-C3
100 SBDO 92401 576-G7
200 POM 91766 640-G2
200 UPL 91786 601-J4
500 SBDO 92410 576-G7
900 SBDO 92411 576-E7
1500 UPL 91763 601-J4
9TH AV
- LPCo - 4843-H7
1600 SBdC 91766 641-D2
4100 MTCL 91763 641-D2
8100 HESP 92345 4566-C1
8800 HESP 92345 4476-C3
11800 HESP 92345 4386-C7
12100 VCTV 92345 4386-C5
12100 VCTV 92392 4386-C4
N 9TH AV
- UPL 91786 602-D2
9TH LN
2000 SBdC 92314 4742-H7
9TH ST
- BARS 92311 3680-G5
- RDL 92373 608-C7
100 RDL 92374 608-C7
1000 PRKR - 4774-J7
1300 PRKR - 4844-H1
8100 RCUC 91730 602-E3
12400 YCPA 92399 649-F5
12600 CHNO 91710 641-G7
13100 CHNO 91710 681-H1
18100 SBdC 92316 645-D3
25300 HIGH 92410 577-D6
26000 HIGH 92346 577-G6
45400 SBdC - 4742-H2
84500 SBdC 93562 2055-B7
E 9TH ST
- UPL 91786 602-C3
100 POM 91766 640-J2
100 SBDO 92410 576-J6
300 CLAR 91711 601-E2
300 POM 91766 641-A2
300 SBdC 92410 577-B6
900 HIGH 92410 577-B6
1400 UPL 91730 602-C3
N 9TH ST
100 CLTN 92324 606-D4
W 9TH ST
- UPL 91786 602-B3
100 CLAR 91711 601-C2
100 POM 91766 640-E3
100 SBDO 92410 576-F6
100 SBDO 92401 576-F6
800 SBDO 92411 576-C6
1000 UPL 91786 601-J3
1600 SBdC 91763 601-H3
1900 SBdC 91763 601-H3
2700 RLTO 92376 576-A6
2700 SBDO 92376 576-A6
10TH AV
8200 HESP 92345 4566-C1
8800 HESP 92345 4476-C2
11300 HESP 92345 4386-C7
N 10TH AV
- UPL 91786 602-D2
E 10TH LN
2000 SBdC 92314 4742-H7
10TH ST
100 RDL 92374 608-C7
12100 YCPA 92399 649-E2
12500 CHNO 91710 641-H7
13100 CHNO 91710 681-H1
15500 VCTV 92392 4296-F5
18100 SBdC 92316 645-D3
26000 HIGH 92346 577-G6
26000 HIGH 92410 577-E6
45400 SBdC - 4742-H2
84700 SBdC 93562 2055-B7

STREET Block City ZIP Pg-Grid

E 10TH ST
100 CLAR 91711 601-D2
100 POM 91766 640-J3
100 SBDO 92410 576-H6
200 POM 91766 641-A3
N 10TH ST
200 CLTN 92324 606-D4
S 10TH ST
100 CLTN 92324 606-D7
W 10TH ST
100 CLAR 91711 601-C2
100 POM 91766 640-H3
100 SBDO 92410 576-H6
900 SBDO 92411 576-C6
11TH AV
6700 HESP 92345 4566-B2
8700 HESP 92345 4476-C1
11300 HESP 92345 4386-C7
12200 VCTV 92345 4386-C7
12200 VCTV 92392 4386-B4
N 11TH AV
200 UPL 91786 602-D2
S 11TH AV
200 UPL 91786 602-D4
800 ONT 91764 602-D4
800 UPL 91764 602-D4
11TH LN
2000 SBdC 92314 4742-H7
11TH ST
- BARS 92311 3680-F5
100 RDL 92374 608-C7
900 PRKR - 4774-J7
1200 PRKR - 4844-H1
12100 YCPA 92399 649-E3
12900 CHNO 91710 641-H7
13100 CHNO 91710 681-H1
15200 VCTV 92392 4296-F5
18100 SBdC 92316 645-E2
25700 HIGH 92410 577-D6
26400 HIGH 92346 577-F6
45400 SBdC - 4742-H2
84500 SBdC 93562 2055-B7
E 11TH ST
- UPL 91786 602-C2
100 CLAR 91711 601-D2
100 POM 91766 640-J3
100 SBDO 92410 576-J6
200 POM 91766 641-A3
800 SBDO 92410 577-A6
N 11TH ST
600 CLTN 92324 606-E5
S 11TH ST
300 CLTN 92324 606-D7
W 11TH ST
- UPL 91786 602-A2
100 CLAR 91711 601-C2
100 POM 91766 640-H3
100 SBDO 92410 576-G6
900 UPL 91786 601-J2
900 SBDO 92411 576-E6
5000 SBdC 91786 601-G2
N 12TH AV
- UPL 91786 602-D3
12TH ST
- PRKR - 4774-J7
- SBdC - (3681-G3
See Page 3590)
1200 PRKR - 4844-J1
12100 YCPA 92399 649-D4
12700 CHNO 91710 641-H7
13100 CHNO 91710 681-H1
84500 SBdC 93562 2055-B7
E 12TH ST
100 CLAR 91711 601-D2
100 POM 91766 640-J3
100 POM 91766 641-A3
N 12TH ST
200 CLTN 92324 606-E5
S 12TH ST
400 CLTN 92324 606-E7
W 12TH ST
100 CLAR 91711 601-C2
100 POM 91766 640-H3
N 13TH AV
- UPL 91786 602-D1
1400 UPL 91786 572-D7
13TH ST
- BARS 92311 3680-F5
- SBdC - (3681-G2
See Page 3590)
12000 YCPA 92399 649-D3
12700 CHNO 91710 641-H7
13100 CHNO 91710 681-H1
18400 SBdC 92316 645-D2
25700 HIGH 92404 577-D5
26500 HIGH 92346 577-F5
E 13TH ST
- UPL 91786 602-C1
100 SBDO 92404 576-J5
N 13TH ST
200 CLTN 92324 606-E6
W 13TH ST
- UPL 91786 602-A1
100 SBDO 92405 576-H5
900 SBDO 92411 576-C5
1000 UPL 91786 601-J1
N 14TH AV
200 UPL 91786 602-E3
14TH ST
- BARS 92311 3680-F5

14TH ST
- SBdC - (3681-G3
See Page 3590)
1000 PRKR - 4844-J1
12100 YCPA 92399 649-C5
12900 CHNO 91710 641-H7
13100 CHNO 91710 681-H1
18500 SBdC 92316 645-D2
26400 HIGH 92346 577-F5
26400 SBDO 92346 577-F5
E 14TH ST
- UPL 91786 602-D1
100 SBDO 92404 576-J5
600 SBDO 92404 577-A5
W 14TH ST
- UPL 91786 602-A1
200 SBDO 92405 576-G5
900 SBDO 92411 576-C5
1100 UPL 91786 601-J1
15TH ST
- BARS 92311 3680-F5
- LPCo - 4844-J1
- SBdC - (3681-G3
See Page 3590)
1200 PRKR - 4844-J1
12100 YCPA 92399 649-C4
26500 HIGH 92346 577-F5
E 15TH ST
- UPL 91786 572-C7
100 SBDO 92404 576-H5
W 15TH ST
- UPL 91786 572-A7
400 SBDO 92405 576-G5
900 SBDO 92411 576-C5
1000 UPL 91786 571-H7
16TH ST
- SBdC - (3681-G3
See Page 3590)
- SBDO 92404 577-A4
1400 PRKR - 4844-H2
1800 LPCo - 4844-H2
1900 RDL 92373 649-B4
1900 YCPA 92373 649-C5
12000 YCPA 92399 649-B3
12600 CHNO 91710 641-H7
13100 CHNO 91710 681-H1
E 16TH ST
- UPL 91786 572-D7
- UPL 91786 572-D7
100 SBDO 92404 576-J4
400 SBDO 92404 577-A4
W 16TH ST
- UPL 91784 572-A7
- UPL 91786 572-A7
100 SBDO 92405 576-F4
800 UPL 91786 571-J7
800 UPL 91784 571-J7
900 SBDO 92411 576-C5
W 16TH ST Rt#-30
1200 UPL 91786 571-G7
1200 UPL 91784 571-G7
1600 CLAR 91711 571-G7
W 17TH AL
200 SBDO 92405 576-H4
17TH ST
- SBdC - (3681-G3
See Page 3590)
1400 PRKR - 4844-J2
1600 UPL 91784 571-G6
1800 RDL 92373 649-B5
1800 YCPA 92373 649-B4
12100 YCPA 92399 649-B3
12500 CHNO 91710 641-J7
13100 CHNO 91710 681-J1
25100 SBdC 92404 577-C4
25100 SBDO 92404 577-C4
26300 HIGH 92346 577-F4
26300 SBDO 92346 577-F4
E 17TH ST
- UPL 91784 572-C6
200 SBDO 92404 576-J4
2000 SBDO 92404 577-D4
3000 SBDO 92346 577-G4
W 17TH ST
- UPL 91784 572-A6
100 SBDO 92405 576-F4
900 UPL 91784 571-J6
1000 SBDO 92411 576-C4
18TH ST
- SBdC - (3681-F3
See Page 3590)
1300 PRKR - 4844-J2
1400 LPCo - 4844-J2
1700 RDL 92373 649-B5
8400 RCUC 91701 572-F5
10500 YCPA 92373 649-B4
12000 YCPA 92399 649-B3
12700 CHNO 91710 641-J7
13100 CHNO 91710 681-J1
25100 SBdC 92404 577-C4
E 18TH ST
- UPL 91784 572-C6
100 SBDO 92404 576-J4
1800 SBDO 92411 576-C4
2000 SBDO 92404 577-D4
2000 SBDO 92404 577-D4
W 18TH ST
- UPL 91784 572-B6
100 SBDO 92405 576-F4
1000 UPL 91784 571-H6

W 18TH ST
1900 SBDO 92411 576-F4
19TH CT
1100 SBDO 92404 577-B3
27600 HIGH 92346 577-J4
19TH ST
- LPCo - 4844-J2
- SBdC - (3681-F3
See Page 3590)
1100 PRKR - 4844-J2
6600 SBdC 92404 577-C4
10500 RCUC 91737 573-B5
10500 RCUC 91701 573-B5
13100 CHNO 91710 641-J7
13100 CHNO 91710 681-J1
25400 SBDO 92404 577-C4
26300 HIGH 92346 577-E4
19TH ST Rt#-30
- UPL 91784 572-F5
1600 RCUC 91701 572-F5
1600 RCUC 91784 572-F5
8200 UPL 91701 572-F5
9500 RCUC 91737 572-F5
9800 RCUC 91737 573-A5
9800 RCUC 91701 573-A5
E 19TH ST
100 SBDO 92404 576-J4
500 SBDO 92404 577-A4
E 19TH ST Rt#-30
- UPL 91784 572-C5
W 19TH ST
300 SBDO 92405 576-F4
1100 SBDO 92411 576-C4
1200 UPL 91784 571-J5
W 19TH ST Rt#-30
- UPL 91784 572-B5
1000 UPL 91784 571-J5
20TH ST
- SBdC - (3681-F3
See Page 3590)
5600 RivC 92509 645-E6
25300 SBdC 92404 577-C4
25300 SBDO 92404 577-C4
27600 HIGH 92346 577-J3
E 20TH ST
- UPL 91784 572-C5
300 SBDO 92404 576-J4
500 SBDO 92404 577-A4
3300 SBDO 92346 577-H4
W 20TH ST
- UPL 91784 572-B5
200 SBDO 92405 576-F4
1000 UPL 91784 571-J5
1500 SBDO 92411 576-D4
21ST ST
- SBdC - (3681-G4
See Page 3590)
1600 SBDO 92404 577-C4
26300 HIGH 92346 577-J3
E 21ST ST
100 SBDO 92404 576-J4
500 SBDO 92404 577-A4
3400 SBDO 92346 577-H3
W 21ST ST
- UPL 91784 572-B4
100 SBDO 92405 576-F4
1000 UPL 91784 571-J4
1200 SBDO 92411 576-D4
E 22ND ST
- UPL 91784 572-B4
W 22ND ST
- UPL 91784 572-A4
1000 UPL 91784 571-J4
23RD ST
12900 RCUC 91739 573-G3
26100 SBdC 92346 577-E3
E 23RD ST
- UPL 91784 572-C3
200 SBDO 92404 576-J3
600 SBDO 92404 577-A3
W 23RD ST
- UPL 91784 572-A3
200 SBDO 92405 576-F3
800 SBdC 91784 572-A3
1000 UPL 91784 571-J3
1000 SBdC 91784 571-J3
1400 SBDO 92411 576-D3
1800 SBDO 92407 576-C3
24TH ST
5200 RivC 92509 645-E6
10100 RCUC 91730 603-A3
E 24TH ST
- SBdC 91784 572-C3
- UPL 91784 572-C3
1100 SBDO 92404 577-B3
W 24TH ST
- SBdC 91784 572-A3
- UPL 91784 572-A3
200 SBDO 92405 576-F3
1200 UPL 91784 571-H3
1300 SBdC 91784 571-H3
1500 SBDO 92411 576-D3
2300 SBDO 92407 576-C3
25TH ST
- RCUC 91739 573-G1
- SBdC 91739 573-G1
6000 RivC 92509 645-E6
10100 RCUC 91730 603-A3
E 25TH ST
- SBdC 91784 572-C2

E 25TH ST
200 SBDO 92404 576-J3
1100 SBDO 92404 577-B3
W 25TH ST
- SBdC 91784 572-A2
100 SBDO 92405 576-F3
1000 SBdC 91784 571-H2
26TH ST
5200 RivC 92509 645-E6
10100 RCUC 91730 603-A3
25400 SBdC 92404 577-C3
E 26TH ST
- SBdC 91784 572-C1
600 SBDO 92404 576-J3
600 SBDO 92404 577-A3
W 26TH ST
- SBdC 91784 572-B1
200 SBDO 92405 576-F3
1600 SBDO 92407 576-C3
27TH AV NW
- SBDO 92410 606-F3
27TH ST
6900 RivC 92509 645-A5
25600 SBdC 92404 577-D3
E 27TH ST
100 SBDO 92404 576-J3
700 SBDO 92404 577-A3
W 27TH ST
100 SBDO 92405 576-E3
1600 SBDO 92411 576-E3
1600 SBDO 92407 576-C3
28TH ST
5500 RivC 92509 645-D7
25800 SBdC 92404 577-D3
26200 SBdC 92346 577-E2
E 28TH ST
100 SBDO 92404 576-J3
600 SBDO 92404 577-A3
1100 SBdC 92404 577-A3
2600 SBDO 92346 577-F3
3900 SBdC 92346 577-H2
W 28TH ST
100 SBDO 92405 576-E3
1600 SBDO 92407 576-C3
29TH ST
2700 SBdC 92404 577-B2
5600 RivC 92509 645-A6
26200 SBdC 92346 577-E2
E 29TH ST
100 SBDO 92404 576-J2
600 SBDO 92404 577-A2
2600 SBdC 92346 577-F2
2600 SBDO 92346 577-F2
W 29TH ST
100 SBDO 92405 576-E2
30TH ST
6100 RivC 92509 645-B6
E 30TH ST
100 SBDO 92404 576-J2
600 SBDO 92404 577-A2
W 30TH ST
500 SBDO 92405 576-G2
1000 SBDO 92405 576-E2
1700 SBDO 92407 576-C2
W 31ST PL
1400 SBDO 92405 576-D2
W 31ST ST
100 SBDO 92405 576-E2
33RD ST
6400 RivC 92509 645-B7
25400 SBdC 92404 577-C1
26100 SBdC 92346 577-E1
E 33RD ST
200 SBDO 92404 576-J1
1100 SBdC 92404 577-B1
W 33RD ST
100 SBDO 92405 576-D1
34TH ST
6500 RivC 92509 645-A6
E 34TH ST
100 SBDO 92404 576-J1
1100 SBdC 92404 577-B1
W 34TH ST
100 SBDO 92405 576-G1
35TH ST
25300 SBdC 92404 577-C1
E 35TH ST
100 SBDO 92404 576-H1
1100 SBDO 92404 577-B1
1200 SBdC 92404 577-B1
W 35TH ST
100 SBDO 92405 576-G1
36TH ST
6600 RivC 92509 645-A6
7000 RivC 92509 644-J6
E 36TH ST
100 SBDO 92404 576-J1
1100 SBDO 92404 577-B1
1200 SBdC 92404 577-B1
W 36TH ST
100 SBDO 92405 576-G1
E 37TH ST
1100 SBDO 92404 547-B7
1200 SBdC 92404 547-B7
38TH ST
6900 RivC 92509 644-J6
E 38TH ST
300 SBDO 92404 546-J7
1100 SBDO 92404 547-B7
1200 SBdC 92404 547-B7

W 38TH ST
100 SBDO 92405 546-H7
E 39TH ST
100 SBDO 92404 546-H7
700 SBDO 92404 547-A7
W 39TH ST
100 SBDO 92405 546-H7
40TH ST
8200 RivC 92509 644-F7
E 40TH ST
100 SBDO 92404 546-J6
100 SBDO 92407 546-J6
100 SBDO 92405 546-J6
400 SBDO 92404 547-A6
W 40TH ST
100 SBDO 92405 546-G7
100 SBDO 92407 546-G7
300 SBdC 92407 546-G7
E 41ST ST
200 SBDO 92404 546-J6
1100 SBDO 92404 547-A6
W 41ST ST
300 SBdC 92407 546-F6
E 42ND PL
1200 SBdC 92404 547-B6
42ND ST
- FONT 92336 544-H6
E 42ND ST
100 SBDO 92404 546-H6
100 SBDO 92407 546-H6
4100 SBDO 92404 547-A6
W 42ND ST
100 SBDO 92407 546-H6
E 43RD ST
200 SBDO 92404 546-H6
W 43RD ST
100 SBDO 92407 546-H6
E 44TH ST
100 SBDO 92404 546-H6
100 SBDO 92407 546-H6
W 44TH ST
100 SBDO 92407 546-E6
500 SBdC 92407 546-G6
E 45TH ST
100 SBDO 92404 546-H6
100 SBDO 92407 546-H6
W 45TH ST
- SBDO 92407 546-E6
E 46TH ST
100 SBDO 92407 546-H6
100 SBDO 92404 546-H6
W 46TH ST
100 SBDO 92407 546-E6
E 47TH ST
200 SBDO 92404 546-J6
48TH CT
2100 SBDO 92407 546-B6
48TH ST
700 SBdC 92407 546-F6
700 SBDO 92407 546-B6
10500 RivC 91752 683-J2
E 48TH ST
100 SBDO 92407 546-H5
200 SBDO 92404 546-J5
W 48TH ST
200 SBDO 92407 546-D6
1200 SBdC 92407 546-D6
E 49TH ST
100 SBDO 92404 546-H5
100 SBDO 92407 546-H5
W 49TH ST
100 SBDO 92407 546-F5
700 SBdC 92407 546-F5
50TH ST
10400 RivC 91752 683-J2
E 50TH ST
200 SBDO 92404 546-H5
W 50TH ST
100 SBDO 92407 546-H5
E 51ST ST
100 SBDO 92404 546-H5
100 SBDO 92407 546-H5
W 51ST ST
4900 SBDO 92407 546-F5
E 52ND ST
200 SBDO 92404 546-H5
W 52ND ST
600 SBDO 92407 546-G5
E 53RD ST
200 SBDO 92404 546-H5
W 53RD ST
400 SBDO 92407 546-G5
54TH ST
10500 RivC 91752 683-J3
E 54TH ST
100 SBDO 92407 546-H5
100 SBDO 92404 546-H5
W 54TH ST
100 SBDO 92407 546-G5
W 55TH ST
600 SBDO 92407 546-F5
56TH ST
10500 RivC 91752 683-J4
W 56TH ST
800 SBDO 92407 546-E4
W 57TH ST
600 SBDO 92407 546-F4
58TH ST
- RivC 92880 683-D5
10400 RivC 91752 683-J4

W 58TH ST
200 SBDO 92407 546-F4
W 59TH ST
200 SBDO 92407 546-F4
60TH ST
10500 RivC 91752 683-J5
63RD ST
11000 RivC 91752 683-G6
64TH ST
11300 RivC 91752 683-G6
65TH ST
11500 RivC 91752 683-G6
12900 RivC 92880 683-D6
66TH ST
11000 RivC 91752 683-H6
68TH ST
- RivC 92880 683-C7
11400 RivC 91752 683-E7
84TH AV S
800 SBdC 92407 515-C4
HIGHWAY 95 S U.S.-66 Hist
1000 NDLS 92363 3710-D1
HIGHWAY 95 S U.S.-95
1000 NDLS 92363 3710-D1
99TH ST
- SBDO 92408 607-F1
100TH ST
- SBDO 92408 577-F7
- SBDO 92408 607-F1
101 MILE DR
3800 SBdC - 519-E2
101ST ST
- SBDO 92408 607-F1
102ND ST
- SBDO 92408 577-F7
- SBDO 92408 607-F1
103RD ST
- SBDO 92408 577-F7
- SBDO 92408 607-F1
105TH ST
- HIGH 92346 577-G7
- SBDO 92408 577-G7
- SBDO 92408 607-G1
106TH ST
- SBDO 92408 577-G7
- SBDO 92408 607-G1
107TH ST
- SBDO 92408 577-G7
- SBDO 92408 607-G1
NW 198TH ST
30700 SBdC 92365 3764-B3
I-10 FRWY
- CALI - 649-G7
- CLTN - 606-C6
- LMLN - 607-C6
- RDL - 607-H6
- RDL - 608-A6
- RDL - 648-E2
- SBdC - 648-J4
- SBDO - 606-J6
- SBDO - 607-C6
- YCPA - 648-J4
- YCPA - 649-A4
I-10 SAN BERNARDINO FRWY
- CLAR - 601-A6
- CLTN - 605-B6
- CLTN - 606-A6
- FONT - 603-A7
- FONT - 604-A7
- FONT - 605-B6
- LACo - 640-A1
- MTCL - 601-A6
- ONT - 602-E5
- ONT - 603-A7
- POM - 601-A6
- POM - 640-A1
- RLTO - 605-B6
- SBdC - 603-A7
- SBdC - 604-A7
- SBdC - 605-B6
- SBdC - 606-A6
- SDMS - 640-A1
- UPL - 601-A6
- UPL - 602-E5
I-15 FRWY
- BARS - 3680-B3
I-15 MOJAVE FRWY
- APLV - (4117-D5
See Page 4116)
- APLV - (4206-G7
See Page 4116)
- APLV - 4207-A3
- BARS - 3679-C5
- BARS - 3680-D1
- BARS - 3758-J5
- BARS - (3759-A4
See Page 3758)
- BARS - (3848-E5
See Page 3758)
- HESP - 4385-H7
- HESP - 4475-E6
- HESP - 4565-B4
- SBdC - 330-L8
- SBdC - 331-B5
- SBdC - 349-L6
- SBdC - 350-D2
- SBdC - 369-C1

I-15 MOJAVE FRWY
- SBdC - 514-G2
- SBdC - 515-A4
- SBdC - 2971-D6
- SBdC - (3415-J6
See Page 3414)
- SBdC - (3504-G5
See Page 3414)
- SBdC - (3505-E1
See Page 3414)
- SBdC - 3592-C7
- SBdC - (3593-D5
See Page 3592)
- SBdC - 3594-B1
- SBdC - 3679-C5
- SBdC - 3680-D1
- SBdC - (3681-F1
See Page 3590)
- SBdC - (3682-A1
See Page 3592)
- SBdC - (3848-E5
See Page 3758)
- SBdC - (3937-G7
See Page 3936)
- SBdC - (4027-F7
See Page 3936)
- SBdC - (4117-D5
See Page 4116)
- SBdC - (4206-G7
See Page 4116)
- SBdC - 4207-A3
- SBdC - 4564-J7
- SBdC - 4565-B4
- SBdC - 4654-C4
- SBdC - 4734-D1
- VCTV - (4206-G7
See Page 4116)
- VCTV - 4296-D4
- VCTV - 4385-H7
- VCTV - 4386-B2
- VCTV - 4475-E6
I-15 ONTARIO FRWY
- FONT - 544-G6
- FONT - 573-H7
- FONT - 574-A6
- ONT - 603-F6
- ONT - 643-E5
- RCUC - 573-H7
- RCUC - 574-A6
- RCUC - 603-G2
- RivC - 643-E5
- RivC - 683-F6
- SBdC - 515-B7
- SBdC - 544-G6
- SBdC - 545-B3
I-40 NEEDLES FRWY
- BARS - 3679-J4
- BARS - 3680-A4
- NDLS - 352-A8
- NDLS - 3620-C6
- NDLS - 3710-E2
- SBdC - 349-L10
- SBdC - 350-A11
- SBdC - 351-H8
- SBdC - 352-A8
- SBdC - 370-D1
- SBdC - 3680-F5
- SBdC - (3681-A7
See Page 3590)
- SBdC - 3710-E5
- SBdC - (3761-F1
See Page 3760)
- SBdC - 3762-C2
- SBdC - (3763-C3
See Page 3762)
- SBdC - 3764-D4
- SBdC - (3765-B5
See Page 3764)
I-210 ROUTE 210 FRWY
- POM - 640-C1
- SDMS - 640-C1
I-215 FRWY
- SBdC - 515-C6
- SBdC - 545-E1
- SBDO - 515-D6
- SBDO - 545-E1
- SBDO - 576-F6
- SBDO - 606-G4
I-215 RIVERSIDE FRWY
- CLTN - 606-G7
- CLTN - 646-E3
- GTER - 646-E3
- RIV - 646-E3
- RivC - 646-E3
- SBDO - 606-G7
Rt#-1 MOHAVE RD
- LPCo - 4843-J7
- LPCo - 4844-H3
Rt#-1 MOUNTAIN VIEW RD
- MohC - 3620-F2
Rt#-2 ANGELES CREST HWY
- LACo - 4652-F2
- LACo 92397 4652-F2
3700 SBdC 92371 4563-A4
4100 SBdC 92371 4562-G6

Rt#-2 ANGELES CREST HWY
- SBdC - 4562-G6
13700 SBdC - 4652-F2
17900 SBdC 92397 4652-F2
Rt#-2 PLANTATION DR
1500 MohC - 3620-E4
Rt#-3 1ST AV
- LPCo - 4844-H7
Rt#-5 2ND AV
- LPCo - 4844-G3
Rt#-18 BIG BEAR BLVD
200 BBLK - 4741-J6
200 BBLK - 4811-E1
500 BBLK - 4742-C6
1200 BBLK 92314 4742-C6
1200 SBdC 92314 4742-C6
37700 SBdC - 4810-G2
38400 BBLK - 4810-G2
38800 SBdC - 4811-B2
Rt#-18 W BIG BEAR BLVD
100 SBdC 92314 4742-D6
Rt#-18 D ST
- VCTV 92394 4296-E4
16300 VCTV 92392 4296-E4
Rt#-18 HAPPY TRAILS HWY
13700 APLV 92308 4388-A2
15500 APLV 92307 4388-A2
15600 APLV 92307 4387-G1
17900 APLV 92307 4296-H4
18400 APLV 92307 4297-D5
21300 APLV 92308 4387-G1
Rt#-18 HIGHWAY
- APLV 92307 4296-H4
- APLV 92392 4296-G4
- SBdC 92392 4296-F5
- VCTV 92307 4296-G4
- VCTV 92392 4296-G4
22500 APLV 92308 4388-C2
22900 APLV 92307 4388-C2
23300 SBdC 92307 4388-D2
24900 SBdC 92308 4388-D2
25500 SBdC 92307 (4389-A6
See Page 4299)
25500 SBdC 92308 (4389-A6
See Page 4299)
26900 SBdC 92307 4479-D1
26900 SBdC 92308 4479-D1
28100 SBdC - 4479-J1
28900 SBdC - 4480-C1
32700 SBdC - 4481-A2
35100 SBdC - (4571-G1
See Page 4570)
36400 SBdC - (4572-A3
See Page 4482)
Rt#-18 HILLTOP BLVD
31600 SBdC - 519-E6
32200 SBdC - 389-D1
Rt#-18 NORTH SHORE DR
3800 SBdC - 4662-G5
36600 SBdC - (4572-B5
See Page 4482)
39400 SBdC - 4742-G1
Rt#-18 E NORTH SHORE DR
100 SBdC 92314 4742-F4
44300 SBdC - 4742-F4
Rt#-18 NORTH SHORE RD
37300 SBdC - 4662-D2
Rt#-18 PALMDALE RD
100 SBdC 92371 368-G6
100 SBdC 92371 4382-F2
100 SBdC 92372 368-G6
100 SBdC 92372 4382-F2
3700 SBdC 92371 4383-A2
7500 SBdC 92371 4384-A2
7800 ADEL 92371 4384-A2
8100 ADEL 92301 4384-G2
8400 ADEL 92392 4384-A2
10900 VCTV 92301 4385-B2
10900 VCTV 92392 4385-G2
11100 ADEL 92301 4385-B2
11100 ADEL 92392 4385-B2
11900 SBdC 92392 4385-G2
14300 VCTV 92392 4386-B1
Rt#-18 RIM OF THE WORLD HWY
- SBDO 92404 546-J5
- SBDO 92404 547-A4
1100 SBdC 92404 516-F5
2100 SBdC - 518-A4
2400 SBdC 92404 546-H1
5700 SBDO 92407 546-H1
23500 SBdC - 516-H5
23500 SBdC - 517-F4
24400 SBdC 92404 517-A5
31500 SBdC - 519-F5
35000 SBdC - 4810-C1
Rt#-18 N WATERMAN AV
2900 SBDO 92404 576-J2
3600 SBDO 92404 546-J6
Rt#-30 W 16TH ST
1200 UPL 91786 571-G7
1200 UPL 91784 571-G7

Rt#-30 W 16TH ST
1600 CLAR 91711 571-G7
Rt#-30 19TH ST
1400 UPL 91784 572-F5
1600 RCUC 91701 572-F5
1600 RCUC 91784 572-F5
8200 UPL 91701 572-F5
9500 RCUC 91737 572-F5
9800 RCUC 91737 573-A5
9800 RCUC 91701 573-A5
Rt#-30 E 19TH ST
- UPL 91784 572-C5
Rt#-30 W 19TH ST
- UPL 91784 572-B5
1000 UPL 91784 571-J5
Rt#-30 E BASELINE RD
100 CLAR 91711 571-F7
Rt#-30 W BASELINE RD
100 CLAR 91711 571-B7
600 LACo 91711 571-B7
1300 LACo 91750 571-B7
Rt#-30 FRWY
- HIGH - 577-E4
- HIGH - 607-J1
- RDL - 607-J3
- RDL - 608-A6
- SBdC - 577-B2
- SBdC - 607-J2
- SBDO - 576-H2
- SBDO - 577-D3
Rt#-30 HIGHLAND AV
17000 FONT 92336 574-J4
17000 RLTO 92336 574-J4
Rt#-30 E HIGHLAND AV
100 RLTO 92377 575-H4
100 RLTO 92376 575-H4
400 SBdC 92407 575-H4
700 RLTO 92376 576-A4
700 SBdC 92407 576-A4
2100 SBDO 92407 576-A4
Rt#-30 W HIGHLAND AV
100 RLTO 92377 575-C4
100 RLTO 92376 575-C4
500 SBdC 92377 575-C4
500 SBdC 92376 575-C4
1700 SBDO 92411 576-F4
1700 SBDO 92407 576-F4
1900 SBdC 92407 576-F4
2400 FONT 92377 575-C4
2400 FONT 92336 575-C4
2400 RLTO 92336 575-C4
2600 FONT 92336 574-J4
2600 RLTO 92377 574-J4
Rt#-30 N MOUNTAIN AV
1600 UPL 91784 571-J7
Rt#-31 SHARP RD
- LPCo - 4844-E4
Rt#-38 E BIG BEAR BLVD
100 SBdC 92314 4742-G5
Rt#-38 GREENSPOT BLVD
700 SBdC 92314 4742-G7
700 SBdC 92314 4812-H1
Rt#-38 S GREENSPOT BLVD
100 SBdC 92314 4742-G5
Rt#-38 N GREENWAY DR
100 SBdC 92314 4742-D5
Rt#-38 HIGHWAY
900 SBdC 92314 4812-H1
2500 SBdC - 4813-D3
2500 SBdC - 369-J11
2600 SBdC - 389-J1
3300 SBdC - (4883-H3
See Page 4813)
7000 SBdC - 4950-G1
8300 SBdC 92339 610-J1
8300 SBdC 92339 611-A1
8300 SBdC 92339 4950-J7
42100 SBdC - (4882-D4
See Page 4813)
46000 SBdC 92314 4813-B2
Rt#-38 E LUGONIA AV
- SBdC 92359 608-C5
- RDL 92374 608-C5
Rt#-38 MENTONE BLVD
1700 SBdC 92359 608-G5
2100 SBdC 92359 609-A5
Rt#-38 MILL CREEK RD
2300 SBdC 92359 609-H4
2300 RDL 92359 609-H4
34200 YCPA 92359 609-H4
34400 SBdC 92399 609-H4
35000 SBdC 92359 610-A2
35300 SBdC 92359 4950-C7
37200 SBdC 92339 610-H1
37200 SBdC 92339 4950-C7
38300 SBdC 92359 611-A1
Rt#-38 NORTH SHORE DR
37700 SBdC - 4810-G2

Rt#-38 NORTH SHORE DR
38100 SBdC - (4740-J7
See Page 4660)
38500 SBdC - 4741-A6
42400 SBdC - 4742-B5
42800 SBdC 92314 4742-B5
Rt#-38 W NORTH SHORE DR
100 SBdC 92314 4742-D4
Rt#-38 ORANGE ST
600 RDL 92374 608-B6
Rt#-41 ARIZONA AV
- LPCo - 4844-H2
- PRKR - 4844-H2
Rt#-57 ORANGE FRWY
- DBAR - 640-C3
- POM - 640-C3
Rt#-57 POMONA FRWY
- DBAR - 680-B1
Rt#-58 FRWY
- SBdC - 348-H7
Rt#-58 HIGHWAY
- BARS 92311 3678-J4
- BARS 92311 3679-A5
- SBdC 92311 3588-F7
- SBdC 92311 3678-G1
1700 SBdC - 348-H7
15300 SBdC 92347 348-L8
15300 SBdC 92347 3586-A7
18500 SBdC 92347 (3587-J7
See Page 3586)
22500 SBdC 92347 3588-C7
Rt#-58 TWENTY MULE TEAM RD
2400 SBdC - 348-H7
Rt#-60 FRWY
- RivC - 643-D6
- RivC - 644-D6
- RivC - 645-A7
Rt#-60 ORANGE FRWY
- DBAR - 640-B7
- DBAR - 680-B1
Rt#-60 POMONA FRWY
- CHLS - 640-D6
- CHNO - 641-D6
- CHNO - 642-H5
- DBAR - 640-D6
- DBAR - 680-A2
- ONT - 641-D6
- ONT - 642-H5
- ONT - 643-A5
- POM - 640-D6
- POM - 641-B6
- RivC - 643-A5
- SBdC - 641-D6
Rt#-62 AQUEDUCT RD
- SBdC - 372-D10
- SBdC - 392-A1
- SBdC - 4773-B3
11700 SBdC - 391-H1
47300 SBdC - 4774-B7
Rt#-62 DESERT CENTER RICE RD
- SBdC - 391-G2
Rt#-62 HIGHWAY
- SBdC - 4774-H5
11500 SBdC - 391-G1
Rt#-62 TWENTYNINE PALMS HWY
49100 SBdC 92256 389-K4
49300 SBdC 92256 615-H7
50000 SBdC 92256 616-B4
52200 SBdC 92256 4956-F7
53400 SBdC - 4956-F7
53400 SBdC 92284 4956-F7
53700 SBdC 92284 4957-A4
53700 YUCA 92284 4957-F2
57300 YUCA 92284 4958-A2
58300 YUCA 92284 4888-E7
59200 SBdC 92252 4888-E7
61000 SBdC 92252 4889-D7
64500 SBdC 92252 4890-B6
66300 SBdC 92277 4890-G6
67200 TNP 92277 4890-G6
68200 TNP 92277 4891-A6
71600 TNP 92277 4892-H5
75300 TNP 92277 4893-A5
76900 SBdC 92277 4893-F5
78900 SBdC 92277 (4894-C5
See Page 4824)
82400 SBdC 92277 (4895-C6
See Page 4824)
86400 SBdC 92277 390-K1
90600 SBdC - 390-L2
90600 SBdC - 391-C1
Rt#-66 W 4TH ST
1300 SBDO 92410 606-D1
1300 SBDO 92410 606-D1
Rt#-66 W 5TH ST
800 SBDO 92410 576-E7
800 SBDO 92411 576-E7
1700 SBDO 92411 606-C1
Rt#-66 FOOTHILL BLVD
8100 RCUC 91730 602-G2
8100 UPL 91786 602-G2
9900 RCUC 91730 603-B1
11900 RCUC 91739 603-G1
13100 SBdC 91739 603-G1

AIRPORTS

FEATURE NAME	Address City, ZIP Code	PAGE-GRID
ADELANTO	CACTUS RD & VINTON RD, ADEL, 92301	4294 - C5
APPLE VALLEY	21600 CORWIN RD, APLV, 92307	4207 - J5
BAKER	56900 HWY 127, SBdC	2971 - D1
BARSTOW - DAGGETT	35900 NATIONAL TRAILS HWY, SBdC	3762 - H1
BIG BEAR CITY	501 W VALLEY BLVD, SBdC, 92314	4742 - C5
CABLE	1749 W 13TH ST, UPL, 91786	601 - G1
CHINO	7000 MERRILL AV, CHNO, 91710	682 - D5
EL MIRAGE	EL MIRAGE AIRPORT RD, SBdC, 92301	4112 - G7
EMERGENCY AIRSTRIP	FALDERMAN AV & MONTALYO DR, SBdC, 92277	4823 - B3
HESPERIA	7070 SUMMIT VALLEY RD, HESP, 92345	4566 - D5
HI DESERT	5500 SUNFAIR RD, SBdC, 92252	4890 - A4
NEEDLES MUNICIPAL	AIRPORT RD & HWY 95, NDLS, 92363	3710 - C7
ONTARIO INTL	2900 E AIRPORT DR, ONT, 91761	642 - E1
REDLANDS MUNICIPAL	1755 SESSUMS DR, RDL, 92374	608 - E3
RIALTO MUNICIPAL	1554 N LINDEN AV, RLTO, 92376	575 - E4
SAN BERNARDINO INTL	2885 E U ST, SBDO, 92408	607 - E1
SOUTHERN CALIF LOGISTICS	18374 READINESS ST, VCTV, 92394	4205 - C3
SQUINTS RANCH AIRSTRIP	SQUINT RANCH RD, SBdC	4738 - E1
TRONA	TRONA AIRPORT RD, InCo, 93545	2055 - F4
TWENTYNINE PALMS	78569 TWENTYNINE PALMS HWY, SBdC, 92277	4893 - J5
YUCCA VALLEY	AIRWAY & TWENTYNINE PALMS, YUCA, 92284	4958 - B1

BEACHES, HARBORS & WATER REC

FEATURE NAME	Address City, ZIP Code	PAGE-GRID
LAKE ARROWHEAD	HWY 173, SBdC	4738 - A7

BUILDINGS

FEATURE NAME	Address City, ZIP Code	PAGE-GRID
FOR DOWNTOWN BLDGS SEE PAGE L		-
CTR FOR INDIVIDUALS WITH-DISABILITIES	5TH ST & COOLEY ST, SBdC, 92410	577 - A7
MIRA LOMA SPACE CTR	3401 ETIWANDA AV, RivC, 91752	643 - H6
SCHOOL OF HOPE	796 6TH ST, SBDO, 92410	577 - A7
SOLAR ONE STA (SEE PAGE 3592)	SANTA FE ST, SBdC	3682 - C6
UPS DISTRIBUTION CTR	3480 E JURUPA ST, ONT, 91761	643 - B3

BUILDINGS - GOVERNMENTAL

FEATURE NAME	Address City, ZIP Code	PAGE-GRID
ADELANTO CORRECTIONAL FACILITY	10400 RANCHO RD, ADEL, 92301	4294 - G1
BLOOD BANK OF SAN BERN &-RIVERSIDE	384 W ORANGE SHOW RD, SBDO, 92408	606 - H4
CALIFORNIA INSTITUTION FOR MEN	14901 CENTRAL AV, CHNO, 91710	681 - H5
CALIFORNIA INSTITUTION FOR-WOMEN	16756 CHINO CORONA RD, SBdC, 91710	712 - E2
CALTRANS, DEPT OF-TRANSPORTATION	464 W 4TH ST, SBDO, 92401	576 - G7
CITY GOVERNMENT OFFICE	BIG BEAR BLVD & MOUNT DOBLE DR, SBdC, 92314	4742 - D6
COLORADO INDIAN TRIBES INDIAN-ADMIN	MOHAVE RD & 2ND AV, LPCo	4844 - G3
COUNTY ADMIN BLDG	157 W 5TH ST, SBDO, 92401	576 - H7
COUNTY ADMIN BLDG	385 N ARROWHEAD AV, SBDO, 92401	606 - H1
COUNTY BLDG	175 S LENA RD, SBDO, 92408	607 - A1
COUNTY BLDG	W 3RD ST & N MOUNTAIN VIEW AV, SBDO, 92401	606 - H1
COUNTY HEALTH DEPT	16453 BEAR VALLEY RD, HESP, 92345	4386 - E7
COUNTY OF SAN BERNARDINO-COURTHOUSE	235 E MOUNTAIN VIEW ST, BARS, 92311	3679 - H3
COUNTY OF SAN BERNARDINO-OFFICES	301 E MOUNTAIN VIEW ST, BARS, 92311	3679 - H3
COURTHOUSE	477 SUMMIT BLVD, BBLK	4811 - H1
COURTHOUSE	MOUNTAIN AV & 6TH ST, ONT, 91762	601 - J5
FEDERAL CORRECTIONAL INST-VICTORVILLE	AIR EXWY & GEORGE BLVD, VCTV, 92394	4205 - G7
FONTANA COURTHOUSE	17780 ARROW BLVD, FONT, 92335	605 - B2
GLEN HELEN REHABILITATION CTR	18000 INSTITUTION RD, SBdC, 92407	545 - E5
LA PAZ COUNTY COURTHOUSE	1107 ARIZONA AV, PRKR	4844 - J1
POMONA MUNICIPAL COURT	350 W MISSION BLVD, POM, 91766	640 - J2
PUBLIC WORKS BLDG	N LENA DR & E 3RD ST, SBDO, 92408	607 - A1
SAN BERNARDINO CITY ANIMAL-SHELTER	333 CHANDLER PL, SBDO, 92408	606 - H5
SAN BERNARDINO COUNTY BLDG	EVANS ST & CRESTVIEW AV, SBDO, 92404	577 - A5
SAN BERNARDINO COUNTY-COURTHOUSE	351 N ARROWHEAD AV, SBDO, 92401	606 - H1
SAN BERNARDINO CO HALL OF-RECORDS	222 W HOSPITALITY LN, SBDO, 92408	606 - H6
SAN BERNARDINO COUNTY HEALTH-DEPT	351 N MOUNTAIN VIEW AV, SBDO, 92401	606 - H1
SAN BERNARDINO COUNTY JAIL	E RIALTO AV & N WATERMAN AV, SBDO, 92408	607 - A1
SAN BERNARDINO COURTHOUSE	8303 HAVEN AV, RCUC, 91730	603 - B2
SAN BERNARDINO JUVENILE HALL	900 E GILBERT ST, SBDO, 92404	577 - A4
SCHOOL ADMIN BLDG	N F ST & W 8TH ST, SBDO, 92410	576 - G7
STARK YOUTH CORRECTIONAL-FACILITY	15180 EUCLID AV, CHNO, 91710	682 - C5
STATE AGRICULTURAL STA	I-15, SBdC, 92365	3592 - G6
STATE BLDG	464 W 4TH ST, SBDO, 92401	606 - G1
VICTORVILLE COURTHOUSE	14455 CIVIC DR, VCTV, 92392	4386 - B1
WEST VALLEY DETENTION CTR	9500 ETIWANDA AV, RCUC, 91739	603 - H5

CEMETERIES

FEATURE NAME	Address City, ZIP Code	PAGE-GRID
AGUA MANSA MEM CEM	2001 W AGUA MANSA RD, CLTN, 92316	645 - H3
BELLEVUE MEM PK	1240 W G ST, ONT, 91762	601 - H7
DESERT VIEW MEM PK	11500 AMARGOSA RD, VCTV, 92392	4475 - H1
GOLD MTN MEM PK	370 MAPLE LN, SBdC, 92314	4742 - G7
GREEN ACRES MEM GARDENS	11715 CEDAR AV, SBdC, 92316	645 - F3
HERMOSA CEM	900 N MERIDIAN AV, CLTN, 92324	606 - A5
HILLSIDE MEM PK	1540 ALESSANDRO RD, RDL, 92373	648 - C4
HOLY CROSS CEM	444 E LEXINGTON AV, POM, 91766	641 - A5
MONTECITO MEM PK	24145 BARTON RD, CLTN, 92324	646 - J2
MTN VALLEY MEM PK CEM	60121 TWENTYNINE PALMS HWY, SBdC, 92252	4888 - G7
MTN VIEW CEM	570 E HIGHLAND AV, SBDO, 92404	576 - J3
MTN VIEW MEM PK	SPADRA ST, SBdC, 92311	3589 - G6
OAK PK CEM	410 S SYCAMORE AV, CLAR, 91711	601 - E5
PALOMARES CEM	N TOWNE AV, POM, 91767	601 - A5
PIONEER MEM CEM	211 E 9TH ST, SBDO, 92410	576 - J7
POMONA CEM	502 E FRANKLIN AV, POM, 91766	641 - A4
RIALTO CEM	200 N WILLOW AV, RLTO, 92376	605 - G1
RIVERVIEW CEM	1705 HIGHWAY 95 S, NDLS, 92363	3710 - D1
SPADRA CEM	W POMONA BLVD, POM, 91766	640 - D3
SUNSET HILLS MEM PK	24000 WAALEW RD, SBdC, 92307	4298 - E1
TWENTYNINE PALMS CEM	5350 ENCELIA AV, TNP, 92277	4891 - J3
VICTOR VALLEY MEM PK	17150 C ST, VCTV, 92392	4296 - F5

CHAMBERS OF COMMERCE

FEATURE NAME	Address City, ZIP Code	PAGE-GRID
ADELANTO	11600 AIR EXWY, ADEL, 92301	4205 - A7
APPLE VALLEY	17874 HWY 18, APLV, 92307	4296 - H4
BARSTOW	409 E FREDRICKS ST, BARS, 92311	3679 - H3
BIG BEAR LAKE	630 BARTLETT RD, BBLK	4811 - E1
CALIFORNIA WELCOME CTR-(SEE PAGE 3758)	MOJAVE FRWY & LENWOOD RD, BARS, 92311	3759 - A2
CHINO VALLEY	13150 7TH ST, CHNO, 91710	641 - G7
CLAREMONT	205 N YALE AV, CLAR, 91711	601 - D3
COLTON	620 N LA CADENA DR, CLTN, 92324	606 - D5
CRESTLINE	23846 LAKE DR, SBdC	516 - H3
FONTANA	8435 SIERRA AV, FONT, 92335	604 - J2
GRAND TERRACE	12139 MOUNT VERNON AV, GTER, 92313	646 - E4
HESPERIA	16367 MAIN ST, HESP, 92345	4476 - E6
HIGHLAND	27268 BASELINE ST, HIGH, 92346	577 - H5
JOSHUA TREE	61325 TWENTYNINE PALMS HWY, SBdC, 92252	4889 - A7
LAKE ARROWHEAD	28200 HWY 189, SBdC	518 - A2
LOMA LINDA	25541 BARTON RD, LMLN, 92354	647 - D1
LUCERNE VALLEY	32750 OLD WOMAN SPRINGS RD, SBdC	4480 - J2
MIRA LOMA	5506 TROTH ST, RivC, 91752	683 - J3
MONTCLAIR	5220 BENITO ST, MTCL, 91763	601 - G6
NEEDLES	100 G ST, NDLS, 92363	3620 - C5
ONTARIO	421 N EUCLID AV, ONT, 91762	602 - B7
ONTARIO VISITOR & CONV BUREAU	2000 CONVENTION CENTER WY, ONT, 91764	602 - H7
POMONA	485 N GAREY AV, POM, 91768	640 - J1
RANCHO CUCAMONGA	8280 UTICA AV, RCUC, 91730	603 - B2
REDLANDS	1 E REDLANDS BLVD, RDL, 92374	608 - B7
RIALTO	120 N RIVERSIDE AV, RLTO, 92376	605 - H2
RUNNING SPRINGS	31944 HILLTOP BLVD, SBdC	519 - A7
SAN BERNARDINO	546 W 6TH ST, SBDO, 92401	576 - G7
TWENTYNINE PALMS	6455 MESQUITE AV, TNP, 92277	4892 - F5
UPLAND	433 N 2ND AV, UPL, 91786	602 - C3
VICTORVILLE	14174 GREEN TREE BLVD, VCTV, 92392	4386 - C1
VISITOR CTR (SEE PAGE 4112)	73 COLUSA RD, SBdC, 92301	4113 - C6
VISITORS BUREAU	BARTLETT RD & BEAVER LN, BBLK	4811 - F2
WRIGHTWOOD	6063 PARK DR, SBdC, 92397	4652 - D2
YUCAIPA VALLEY	35139 YUCAIPA BLVD, YCPA, 92399	650 - A3
YUCCA VALLEY	55569 TWENTYNINE PALMS HWY, YUCA, 92284	4957 - G2

CITY HALLS

FEATURE NAME	Address City, ZIP Code	PAGE-GRID
ADELANTO	11600 AIR EXWY, ADEL, 92301	4205 - A7
APPLE VALLEY	20440 HWY 18, APLV, 92307	4297 - F6
BARSTOW	220 E MOUNTAIN VIEW ST, BARS, 92311	3679 - H3
BIG BEAR LAKE	39707 BIG BEAR BLVD, BBLK	4811 - C2
CALIMESA	908 PARK AV, CALI, 92320	649 - H7
CHINO	13220 CENTRAL AV, CHNO, 91710	681 - G1
CHINO HILLS	2001 GRAND AV, CHLS, 91709	680 - H3
CLAREMONT	207 N HARVARD AV, CLAR, 91711	601 - D3
COLTON	650 N LA CADENA DR, CLTN, 92324	606 - D5
FONTANA	8353 SIERRA AV, FONT, 92335	604 - J2
GRAND TERRACE	22795 BARTON RD, GTER, 92313	646 - F3
HESPERIA	15776 MAIN ST, HESP, 92345	4476 - C6
HIGHLAND	27215 BASELINE ST, HIGH, 92346	577 - H5
LOMA LINDA	25541 BARTON RD, LMLN, 92354	647 - D1
MONTCLAIR	5111 BENITO ST, MTCL, 91763	601 - G6
NEEDLES	817 THIRD ST, NDLS, 92363	3620 - D6
ONTARIO	303 E B ST, ONT, 91764	602 - C7
POMONA	505 S GAREY AV, POM, 91766	640 - J2
RANCHO CUCAMONGA	10500 CIVIC CENTER DR, RCUC, 91730	603 - B2
REDLANDS	35 CAJON ST, RDL, 92373	608 - B7
RIALTO	150 S PALM AV, RLTO, 92376	605 - G2
SAN BERNARDINO	300 N D ST, SBDO, 92401	606 - H1
TWENTYNINE PALMS	6136 ADOBE RD, TNP, 92277	4892 - E5
UPLAND	460 N EUCLID AV, UPL, 91786	602 - B3
VICTORVILLE	14343 CIVIC DR, VCTV, 92392	4386 - B1
YUCAIPA	34272 YUCAIPA BLVD, YCPA, 92399	649 - H3
YUCCA VALLEY	57090 TWENTYNINE PALMS HWY, YUCA, 92284	4957 - J2

COLLEGES & UNIVERSITIES

FEATURE NAME	Address City, ZIP Code	PAGE-GRID
BARSTOW COLLEGE	2700 BARSTOW RD, BARS, 92311	3679 - G7
CALIF STATE POLY UNIV POMONA	3801 TEMPLE AV, POM, 91768	640 - A2
CALIF STATE UNIV SAN BERNARDINO	5500 UNIVERSITY PKWY, SBDO, 92407	546 - D4
CHAFFEY COMM COLLEGE	5885 HAVEN AV, RCUC, 91737	573 - C2
CLAREMONT COLLEGES	747 N DARTMOUTH AV, CLAR, 91711	601 - E3
CLAREMONT-MCKENNA COLLEGE	500 E 9TH ST, CLAR, 91711	601 - E3
COLLEGE OF OSTEOPATHIC MEDICINE	309 E 2ND ST, POM, 91766	641 - A2
COPPER MTN COMM COLLEGE	6162 ROTARY WY, SBdC, 92252	4890 - E5
CRAFTON HILLS COLLEGE	11711 SAND CANYON RD, YCPA, 92399	649 - C2
DEVRY INSTITUTE OF TECHNOLOGY	901 CORPORATE CENTER DR, POM, 91768	640 - C1
HARVEY MUDD COLLEGE	301 E 12TH ST, CLAR, 91711	601 - E2
LOMA LINDA UNIV	ANDERSON ST & BARTON RD, LMLN, 92354	647 - C1
PITZER COLLEGE	1050 N MILLS AV, CLAR, 91711	601 - E2
POMONA COLLEGE	550 N COLLEGE AV, CLAR, 91711	601 - E3
SAN BERNARDINO VALLEY COLLEGE	701 S MOUNT VERNON AV, SBDO, 92410	606 - E3
SCH OF THEOLOGY AT CLAREMONT	1325 N COLLEGE AV, CLAR, 91711	601 - D2
SCRIPPS COLLEGE	1030 N COLUMBIA AV, CLAR, 91711	601 - E2
UNIV OF REDLANDS	1200 E COLTON AV, RDL, 92374	608 - D6
VICTOR VALLEY COMM COLLEGE	18422 BEAR VALLEY RD, VCTV, 92392	4387 - A6

DEPARTMENT OF MOTOR VEHICLES

FEATURE NAME	Address City, ZIP Code	PAGE-GRID
BARSTOW	528 E VIRGINIA WY, BARS, 92311	3679 - H4
DMV COMMERCIAL DRIVING TEST CTR	110 W CENTRAL AV, SBDO, 92408	606 - H3
FONTANA	16499 MERRILL AV, FONT, 92335	604 - H3
MOTOR VEHICLE DIVISION	701 W 11TH ST, PRKR	4774 - J7
NEEDLES	1040 E BROADWAY ST, NDLS, 92363	3620 - E7
POMONA	1600 S GAREY AV, POM, 91766	640 - J4
RANCHO CUCAMONGA	8629 HELLMAN AV, RCUC, 91730	602 - H3
REDLANDS	1659 W LUGONIA AV, RDL, 92374	607 - H5
SAN BERNARDINO	1310 N WATERMAN AV, SBDO, 92404	576 - J5
TWENTYNINE PALMS	3668 ADOBE RD, TNP, 92277	4822 - E5
VICTORVILLE	14855 CORTA DR, VCTV, 92392	4296 - D7

ENTERTAINMENT & SPORTS

FEATURE NAME	Address City, ZIP Code	PAGE-GRID
BIG BEAR LAKE CONV CTR	42900 BIG BEAR BLVD, BBLK, 92314	4742 - B6
BIG LEAGUE DREAMS SPORTS PK	POMONA RINCON & FAIRFIELD RNCH, CHLS, 91709	711 - J1
CALIFORNIA SPEEDWAY, THE	CHERRY AV & RANDALL AV, SBdC, 92335	604 - A3
CHINO FAIRGROUNDS	EDISON AV & CENTRAL AV, CHNO, 91710	681 - G3
EPICENTER, THE	8408 ROCHESTER AV, RCUC, 91730	603 - E2
FISCALINI FIELD	1103 E HIGHLAND AV, SBDO, 92404	577 - A4
MAVERICK STADIUM	12000 STADIUM WY, ADEL, 92301	4295 - B2
MCCOY EQUESTRIAN CTR	PEYTON DR, CHLS, 91709	681 - B3
MUNICIPAL BASEBALL PK	S G ST, SBDO, 92410	606 - G2
NATL ORANGE SHOW GROUNDS	689 S E ST, SBDO, 92408	606 - G3
NEEDLES RODEO GROUNDS	SAN CLEMENTE ST & CLARY DR, NDLS, 92363	3710 - C1
ONTARIO CONV CTR	2000 CONVENTION CENTER WY, ONT, 91764	602 - G7
SAN BERNARDINO CO FAIRGROUNDS	14800 7TH ST, VCTV, 92392	4296 - C6

GOLF COURSES

FEATURE NAME	Address City, ZIP Code	PAGE-GRID
APPLE VALLEY CC	15200 RANCHERIAS RD, APLV, 92307	4297 - D5
ARROWHEAD CC	3433 N PARKSIDE DR, SBDO, 92404	576 - J1
BEAR MTN GC	43101 GOLDMINE DR, BBLK	4812 - B2
BLUE SKIES CC	55100 MARTINEZ TR, YUCA, 92284	4957 - D2
CLAREMONT GC	1550 N INDIAN HILL BLVD, CLAR, 91711	601 - D1
COLTON GC	1901 W VALLEY BLVD, CLTN, 92324	605 - J5
COUNTRY VILLAGE GC	10301 COUNTRY CLUB DR, RivC, 91752	644 - A5
CREEKSIDE GC	3151 E RIVERSIDE DR, ONT, 91761	643 - B6
DESERT WINDS GC	BERKELEY RD, TNP, 92278	4751 - J4
DIAMOND BAR COUNTY GC	22751 GOLDEN SPRINGS DR, DBAR, 91765	680 - A1
EL PRADO GC	6555 PINE AV, CHNO, 91710	712 - A2
EL RANCHO VERDE GC	19494 COUNTRY CLUB DR, RLTO, 92407	575 - G2
EL RIVINO CC	5530 EL RIVINO RD, SBdC, 92316	645 - F4
EMPIRE LAKES GC	11015 6TH ST, RCUC, 91730	603 - D4
GOOSE CREEK GC	11418 68TH ST, RivC, 91752	683 - H7
GREEN TREE GC	14144 GREEN TREE BLVD, VCTV, 92392	4386 - D2
HESPERIA GOLF AND CC	17970 BANGOR AV, HESP, 92345	4566 - H1
JESS RANCH GC	10885 APPLE VALLEY RD, APLV, 92308	4477 - C2
LAKE ARROWHEAD CC	250 GOLF COURSE RD, SBdC	517 - F1
LOS SERRANOS CC	15656 YORBA AV, CHLS, 91709	681 - E7
MARSHALL CANYON COUNTY GC	6100 N STEPHENS RANCH RD, LACo, 91750	571 - A3
NEEDLES MUNICIPAL GC	144 MARINA DR, NDLS, 92363	3620 - C5
PALM LAKE GC	1300 W PHILLIPS BLVD, POM, 91766	640 - G4
PALM MEADOWS GC	1964 E PALM MEADOWS DR, SBDO, 92408	607 - D3
RED HILL CC	8358 RED HILL COUNTRY CLUB DR, RCUC, 91730	572 - E7
REDLANDS CC	E MARIPOSA DR, RDL, 92373	648 - F4
RIVERSIDE GC	1011 ORANGE ST, RIV, 92501	645 - J7
ROADRUNNER DUNES GC	4733 DESERT KNOLL AV, TNP, 92277	4892 - F1
SAN BERNARDINO GC	1494 S WATERMAN AV, SBDO, 92408	606 - J5
SHANDIN HILLS GC	3380 N LITTLE MOUNTAIN DR, SBDO, 92405	576 - D2
SIERRA LAKES GC	16600 CLUBHOUSE DR, FONT, 92336	574 - H3
SILVER LAKES CC (SEE PAGE 3934)	14814 CLUBHOUSE DR, SBdC	3935 - J2
SPRING VALLEY LAKE CC	13229 SPRING VALLEY PKWY, SBdC, 92392	4386 - J4
SUN AND SKY GC	2781 COUNTRY CLUB DR, BARS, 92311	3758 - E2
TEES AND TREES GC	CAPE GLOUSTER AV, BARS, 92311	3680 - F5
UPLAND HILLS CC GC	1231 E 16TH ST, UPL, 91784	572 - D6
WESTERN HILLS CC	1800 CARBON CANYON RD, CHLS, 91709	710 - H1
WESTWINDS GC	TURNER RD & PHANTOM E ST, VCTV, 92394	4205 - G6
WHISPERING LAKES GC	2525 E RIVERSIDE DR, ONT, 91761	642 - H5
YUCIAPA VALLEY GC	33725 CHAPMAN HEIGHTS RD, YCPA, 92399	649 - G2

HOSPITALS

FEATURE NAME	Address City, ZIP Code	PAGE-GRID
ARROWHEAD REGL MED CTR	400 N PEPPER AV, CLTN, 92324	606 - A5
BARSTOW COMM HOSP	555 S 7TH AV, BARS, 92311	3679 - H3
BEAR VALLEY COMM HOSP	41870 GARSTIN DR, BBLK	4811 - H1
CHINO VALLEY MED CTR	5451 WALNUT AV, CHNO, 91710	641 - H6
COLORADO RIVER MED CTR	1401 BAILEY AV, NDLS, 92363	3620 - B7
COMM HOSP OF SAN BERNARDINO	1805 N MEDICAL CENTER DR, SBDO, 92411	576 - D4
DESERT VALLEY HOSP	16850 BEAR VALLEY RD, VCTV, 92392	4386 - E6
DOCTORS HOSP MED CTR OF-MONTCLAIR	5000 SAN BERNARDINO ST, MTCL, 91763	601 - F5
HI-DESERT MED CTR	6601 WHITE FEATHER RD, SBdC, 92252	4889 - G7
KAISER FOUNDATION HOSP	9961 SIERRA AV, FONT, 92335	604 - J6
KINDRED HOSP	550 N MONTEREY AV, ONT, 91764	602 - C7
LANTERMAN DEVELOPMENTAL CTR	3530 W POMONA BLVD, POM, 91768	640 - C4
LOMA LINDA UNIV CHILDRENS HOSP	11234 ANDERSON ST, LMLN, 92354	647 - B1
LOMA LINDA UNIV COMM MED	25333 BARTON RD, LMLN, 92354	647 - D2
LOMA LINDA UNIV MED CTR	11234 ANDERSON ST, LMLN, 92354	647 - B1
PATTON STATE HOSP	3102 E HIGHLAND AV, SBDO, 92346	577 - G3
PETTIS MEM VETERANS MED CTR	11201 BENTON ST, LMLN, 92354	647 - C1
RANCHO SAN ANTONIO MED CTR	MILLIKEN AV, RCUC, 91730	603 - D1
REDLANDS COMM HOSP	350 TERRACINA BLVD, RDL, 92373	647 - J3
ST BERNARDINE MED CTR	2101 N WATERMAN AV, SBDO, 92404	576 - J4
SAINT MARY REGL MED CTR	18300 HWY 18, APLV, 92307	4296 - J3
SAN ANTONIO COMM HOSP	999 SAN BERNARDINO RD, UPL, 91786	602 - D2
SAN BERNARDINO MTNS COMM HOSP	29101 HOSPITAL RD, SBdC	4738 - C6
VICTOR VALLEY COMM HOSP	15248 11TH ST, VCTV, 92392	4296 - F5

HOTELS

FEATURE NAME	Address City, ZIP Code	PAGE-GRID
BEST WESTERN EMPIRE INN	475 W VALLEY BLVD, RLTO, 92376	605 - G6
BEST WESTERN GARDENS MOTEL	71487 TWENTYNINE PALMS HWY, TNP, 92277	4891 - J6
BEST WESTERN HOTEL-DIAMOND BAR	259 GENTLE SPRINGS LN, DBAR, 91765	640 - B7
BEST WESTERN PINE TREE MOTEL	12018 CENTRAL AV, CHNO, 91710	641 - G5
BEST WESTERN SANDMAN MOTEL	1120 W COLTON AV, RDL, 92374	607 - J6
COUNTRY SUITES BY AYRES	1945 E HOLT AV, ONT, 91764	602 - G7
DOUBLETREE CLUB HOTEL	429 N VINEYARD AV, ONT, 91764	602 - G7
DOUBLETREE HOTEL	222 N VINEYARD AV, ONT, 91764	602 - G7
DYNASTY SUITES REDLANDS	1235 W COLTON AV, RDL, 92374	607 - J6
FAIRFIELD INN BY MARRIOTT	3201 N CENTRE LAKE DR, ONT, 91761	603 - A7
GOOD NITE INN	1801 E G ST, ONT, 91764	602 - G6
GRISWOLDS INN	555 W FOOTHILL BLVD, CLAR, 91711	601 - C2
HOLIDAY INN BARSTOW	1511 E MAIN ST, BARS, 92311	3680 - A3
HOLIDAY INN HOTEL & SUITES	3400 SHELBY ST, ONT, 91764	603 - B7
HOLIDAY INN VICTORVILLE	15494 PALMDALE RD, VCTV, 92392	4386 - B1
LAKE ARROWHEAD RESORT	27984 HWY 189, SBdC	517 - J1

HOTELS

FEATURE NAME Address City, ZIP Code	PAGE-GRID
MARRIOTT HOTEL ONTARIO 2200 E HOLT BLVD, ONT, 91764	602 - H7
NORTHWOODS RESORT HOTEL 40650 VILLAGE DR, BBLK	4811 - E2
ONTARIO HILTON 700 N HAVEN AV, ONT, 91764	603 - B6
QUALITY INN 1520 E MAIN ST, BARS, 92311	3680 - A3
RADISSON HOTEL 295 N E ST, SBDO, 92401	606 - G1
RAMADA INN 840 S INDIAN HILL BLVD, CLAR, 91711	601 - D5
RED ROOF INN 1818 E HOLT BLVD, ONT, 91764	602 - H7
RESIDENCE INN BY MARRIOTT 2025 CONVENTION CENTER WY, ONT, 91764	602 - G7
SAN BERNARDINO HILTON 285 E HOSPITALITY LN, SBDO, 92408	606 - J6
SHILO HOTEL 3200 TEMPLE AV, POM, 91768	640 - C3
TRAVELERS INN 1195 3RD ST, NDLS, 92363	3620 - C6

LIBRARIES

FEATURE NAME Address City, ZIP Code	PAGE-GRID
ADELANTO BRANCH 11744 BARTLETT AV, ADEL, 92301	4205 - A6
APPLE VALLEY BRANCH 15001 WAKITA BLVD, APLV, 92307	4297 - F5
BARSTOW BRANCH 304 E BUENA VISTA ST, BARS, 92311	3679 - H3
BIG BEAR LAKE BRANCH 41930 GARSTIN DR, BBLK	4811 - H1
BLOOMINGTON BRANCH 10145 ORCHARD ST, SBdC, 92316	605 - D6
CALIMESA BRANCH 908 PARK AV, CALI, 92320	649 - H7
CHINO BRANCH 13180 CENTRAL AV, CHNO, 91710	681 - G1
CHINO HILLS BRANCH 2003 GRAND AV, CHLS, 91709	680 - H4
CLAREMONT 208 N HARVARD AV, CLAR, 91711	601 - D3
COLTON 656 N 9TH ST, CLTN, 92324	606 - D5
CRESTLINE BRANCH 23555 KNAPPS CTO, SBdC	516 - G3
DIAMOND BAR 1061 S GRAND AV, DBAR, 91765	680 - B3
FELDHEYM CENTRAL 555 W 6TH ST, SBDO, 92401	576 - G7
FONTANA BRANCH 8334 EMERALD AV, FONT, 92335	604 - J2
GRAND TERRACE BRANCH 22795 BARTON RD, GTER, 92313	646 - F3
HESPERIA BRANCH 9565 7TH AV, HESP, 92345	4476 - D6
HIGHGROVE BRANCH 690 CENTER ST, RivC, 92507	646 - D6
HIGHLAND BRANCH 27167 BASELINE ST, HIGH, 92346	577 - H5
INGHRAM BRANCH 1505 W HIGHLAND AV, SBDO, 92411	576 - D4
JOSHUA TREE BRANCH 6465 PARK BLVD E, SBdC, 92252	4889 - B7
KAISER BRANCH 11155 ALMOND AV, FONT, 92337	644 - C2
LAKE ARROWHEAD BRANCH 27235 HWY 189, SBdC	517 - G2
LOMA LINDA BRANCH 25581 BARTON RD, LMLN, 92354	647 - D1
LUCERNE VALLEY BRANCH 33103 OLD WOMAN SPRINGS RD, SBdC	4481 - A2
LUQUE BRANCH 294 E O ST, CLTN, 92324	606 - D7
MENTONE BRANCH 1870 MENTONE BLVD, SBdC, 92359	608 - H5
MONTCLAIR BRANCH 9955 FREMONT AV, MTCL, 91763	601 - G6
NEEDLES BRANCH 1111 BAILEY AV, NDLS, 92363	3620 - B6
ONTARIO 215 E C ST, ONT, 91764	602 - C7
PARKER 1001 NAVAJO AV, PRKR	4844 - J1
POMONA 625 S GAREY AV, POM, 91766	640 - J2
RANCHO CUCAMONGA 7368 ARCHIBALD AV, RCUC, 91730	572 - J7
RIALTO BRANCH 251 W 1ST ST, RLTO, 92376	605 - G2
ROWE BRANCH 108 E MARSHALL BLVD, SBDO, 92404	576 - H2
RUNNING SPRINGS BRANCH 31976 HILLTOP BLVD, SBdC	519 - B7
SAN BERNARDINO COUNTY 104 W 4TH ST, SBDO, 92401	606 - H1
SMILEY, A K 125 W VINE ST, RDL, 92373	608 - B7
SOUTH ONTARIO BRANCH 2403 S VINEYARD AV, ONT, 91761	642 - G5
TRONA BRANCH 82805 MOUNTAIN VIEW ST, SBdC, 93562	2144 - J4
TWENTYNINE PALMS BRANCH 6078 ADOBE RD, TNP, 92277	4892 - E4
UPLAND 450 N EUCLID AV, UPL, 91786	602 - B3
VICTORVILLE BRANCH 15011 CIRCLE DR, VCTV, 92392	4296 - D6
VILLASENOR BRANCH 525 N MOUNT VERNON AV, SBDO, 92411	576 - E7
WRIGHTWOOD BRANCH 6014 PARK DR, SBdC, 92397	4652 - C2
YUCAIPA BRANCH 12040 5TH ST, YCPA, 92399	649 - H3
YUCCA VALLEY BRANCH 57098 TWENTYNINE PALMS HWY, YUCA, 92284	4957 - J2

MILITARY INSTALLATIONS

FEATURE NAME Address City, ZIP Code	PAGE-GRID
AIR NATL GUARD E AVION DR, ONT, 91761	642 - H2
CALIFORNIA ARMY NATL GUARD 17988 HAPPY TRAILS HWY, APLV, 92307	4296 - H4
CUDDEBACK LAKE AIRFORCE-GUNNERY RANGE SBdC	348 - K1
EDWARDS AIR FORCE BASE ROSAMOND BLVD OFF HWY 58, KeCo, 93523	348 - F8
FORT IRWIN MILITARY RESV SBdC	349 - H1
MARCH AIR RESERVE BASE RIVERSIDE DR & CACTUS AV, RivC, 92518	389 - B6
NATL GUARD ARMORY ARMORY RD & OPAL AV, BARS, 92311	3680 - A5
NAVAL AIR WEAPONS STA - CHINA-LAKE SBdC	2144 - B4
USMC AIR GROUND COMBAT-TRAINING CTR TNP, 92278	4822 - F1
USMC DEPOT OF NEBO SUPPLIES JOSEPH L BOLL AV & S IWO JIMA, BARS, 92311	3680 - D7
USMC DEPOT OF SUPPLIES YERMO-ANNEX (SEE PAGE 3590) DAGGETT-YERMO RD, SBdC	3681 - F4
USMC SUPPLY CTR FIRING RANGE-(SEE PAGE 3760) FIRING RANGE RD & PENDLETON RD, BARS, 92311	3761 - B1

MUSEUMS

FEATURE NAME Address City, ZIP Code	PAGE-GRID
AGUA MANSA CEM MUS 2001 W AGUA MANSA RD, CLTN, 92316	645 - H3
CALIFORNIA ROUTE 66 MUS 16849 D ST, VCTV, 92392	4296 - F4
FIRE MUS D ST & 8TH ST, VCTV, 92392	4296 - F4
HI-DESERT NATURE MUS 57116 TWENTYNINE PALMS HWY, YUCA, 92284	4957 - J2
LINCOLN MEM SHRINE 125 W VINE ST, RDL, 92373	608 - B7
MOJAVE RIVER VALLEY MUS 270 E VIRGINIA WY, BARS, 92311	3679 - H4
MOUSLEY MUS OF NATURAL HIST 35308 PANORAMA DR, YCPA, 92399	650 - A1
MUS OF HIST AND ART, ONTARIO 225 S EUCLID AV, ONT, 91762	642 - B1
PETTERSON MUS 730 W PLYMOUTH RD, CLAR, 91711	601 - C3
PLANES OF FAME MUS 7000 MERRILL AV, CHNO, 91710	682 - C5
RIALTO HIST SOCIETY MUS 205 N RIVERSIDE AV, RLTO, 92376	605 - H1
ROUTE 66 VISITOR CTR & MUS 7965 VINEYARD AV, RCUC, 91730	602 - G1
ROY ROGERS & DALE EVANS MUS 15650 SENECA RD, VCTV, 92394	4296 - B7
SAN BERNARDINO COUNTY MUS 2024 ORANGE TREE LN, RDL, 92374	607 - G5
VAGLE, MARY MUS AND NATURE CTR 11501 CYPRESS AV, FONT, 92337	644 - H3
VICTOR VALLEY MUS & ART GALLERY 11873 APPLE VALLEY RD, APLV, 92308	4387 - C6

OPEN SPACE PRESERVES

FEATURE NAME Address City, ZIP Code	PAGE-GRID
BIG MORONGO CANYON PRESERVE TWENTYNINE PALMS HWY, SBdC, 92256	616 - B7
BIG ROCK CREEK WILDLIFE-SANCTUARY 120TH ST E & AVENUE O, PMDL, 93591	368 - D3
CLAREMONT HILLS WILDERNESS PK PALMER CANYON RD, CLAR, 91711	571 - F1
CUCAMONGA WILDERNESS LYTLE CREEK RD, SBdC	512 - G6
HAVASU NATL WILDLIFE REFUGE STATE HWY 95, SBdC	4606 - G1
MITCHELL CAVERNS STATE NATURAL-PRESERVE ESSEX RD, SBdC	351 - A7
MOJAVE NATL PRESERVE MOJAVE FWY & KELBAKER RD, SBdC	2971 - G4
OPEN SPACE S AUTO PLAZA DR, SBDO, 92408	606 - F5
RAINBOW BASIN NATL NATURAL-LANDMARK SBdC	349 - D6
SAN GORGONIO WILDERNESS AREA-(SEE PAGE 4813) SBdC	4882 - E7
SANTA ANA RIVER WILDLIFE AREA 5500 RIVERVIEW DR, RivC, 92505	683 - J7

PARK & RIDE

FEATURE NAME Address City, ZIP Code	PAGE-GRID
BASELINE RD AT I-15 13231 BASELINE RD, RCUC, 91739	573 - J6
BEAR VALLEY 12000 AMARGOSA RD, VCTV, 92392	4385 - J7
BLOOMINGTON 10175 CEDAR AV, SBdC, 92316	605 - E6
BLOOMINGTON 18645 COMMERCIAL ST, SBdC, 92316	605 - E6
CHINO 3321 CHINO AV, CHNO, 91710	681 - B1
CLAREMONT METROLINK W 1ST ST & S COLLEGE AV, CLAR, 91711	601 - D4
COUNTRY VILLAGE 10180 GRANITE HILL DR, RivC, 92509	644 - A6
DIAMOND BAR WEST DIAMOND BAR BL & ROUTE 60, DBAR, 91765	640 - B6
INDIAN HILL MARKETPLACE E HOLT AV & N EAST END AV, POM, 91767	641 - C1
LAKE ARROWHEAD 27801 HWY 18, SBdC	517 - J4
LANTERMAN STATE ST & ORANGE FRWY, POM, 91768	640 - C5
MERIDIAN ROAD (SEE PAGE 3590) 33800 OUTER HWY 15 N, SBdC	3681 - A2
METROLINK EAST ONTARIO STA 3330 E FRANCIS ST, ONT, 91761	643 - B4
METROLINK FONTANA STA 16777 ORANGE WY, FONT, 92335	604 - J3
METROLINK RIALTO STA 261 S PALM AV, RLTO, 92376	605 - G2
METROLINK SAN BERNARDINO STA 1204 W 3RD ST, SBDO, 92410	606 - E1
METROLINK UPLAND 300 E A ST, UPL, 91786	602 - C3
MIRA LOMA 12105 LIMONITE AV, RivC, 91752	683 - F5
MIRA LOMA MISSION BLVD & 60 FRWY, RivC, 91752	643 - H6
MONTCLAIR TRANSCENTER 5091 RICHTON ST, MTCL, 91763	601 - F3
PARK & RIDE E HIGHLAND AV & N VICTORIA AV, SBDO, 92346	577 - F3
PARK & RIDE IRWIN RD, SBdC, 92311	3589 - H6
PARK & RIDE JOSHUA ST & HWY 395, HESP, 92345	4565 - C2
PARK & RIDE L ST & 15 FRWY, BARS, 92311	3679 - D4
RUNNING SPRINGS 31960 COMMERCIAL WY, SBdC	519 - A7
VICTOR VALLEY CRCH OF CHRIST 13150 SYCAMORE ST, VCTV, 92392	4475 - E1
YUCAIPA 31341 HAMPTON RD, YCPA, 92399	649 - A4

PARKS & RECREATION

FEATURE NAME Address City, ZIP Code	PAGE-GRID
7TH STREET PK, YCPA	649 - G4
7TH STREET PK, CHNO	641 - G7
9TH STREET PK, SBDO	576 - E6
10TH STREET PK, CHNO	641 - H7
13TH STREET RESERVOIR PK, UPL	602 - C1
ADULTS SPORTS PK, RCUC	603 - E2
ALAMITOS PK, LBCH	388 - B10
ALTERRA PK, CHLS	711 - F1
ANDERSON PK, RLTO	605 - F3
ANGELES NATL FOREST, LACo	512 - A2
ANTELOPE VLY IND MUS STATE PK,-LACo	368 - E3
AQUINAS PK, SBDO	577 - D2
ASPEN GLEN PICNIC AREA, SBdC	4811 - D2
AUTUMN HILL PK, CHLS	680 - J4
AVALON PK, VCTV	4296 - D4
AVALON PK, RivC	645 - E6
AVENUE H SOCCER FIELDS, BARS	3679 - E3
AYALA, RUBEN S PK, CHNO	681 - H3
BAILEY, LEONARD PK, LMLN	647 - F2
BALDY VIEW PK, UPL	601 - J2
BARSTOW HEIGHTS PK, SBdC	3679 - E6
BAYLIS PK PICNIC AREA, SBdC	517 - C5
BEAR GULCH PK, RCUC	602 - G2
BEAR MTN SKI RESORT, BBLK	4812 - B3
BENDER, BUD PK, RLTO	605 - G1
BERYL PK EAST, RCUC	572 - G4
BERYL PK WEST, RCUC	572 - F5
BIG BEAR CITY PK, SBdC	4742 - D5
BIG MORONGO REGL PK, SBdC	615 - J6
BIRDSALL PK, RLTO	575 - D2
BLAIR PK, SBDO	576 - D1
BLAISDELL PK, CLAR	601 - D4
BLAKE STREET PK, SBdC	575 - J2
BLAST SOCCER COMPLEX, SBDO	545 - G2
BOGART COUNTY PK, RivC	389 - F5
BON VIEW PK, ONT	642 - D2
BRENTWOOD PK, VCTV	4295 - G6
BREWSTER PK, APLV	4297 - G3
BRIGGS, HOMER PK, ONT	641 - J4
BROOKSIDE PK, RDL	647 - H2
BROWN, AB SPORTS COMPLEX, RIV	645 - J6
BROWN, GEORGE E JR PK, CLTN	605 - J5
BUCKSKIN MTN STATE PK, LPCo	4606 - F6
BUTTERFIELD PK, CHLS	711 - J5
CABRILLO PK, UPL	601 - H2
CAHUILLA PK, CLAR	601 - C1
CALICO GHOST TOWN REGL PK, -SBdC (SEE PAGE 3590)	3591 - H2
CALIMESA PK, YCPA	649 - H6
CALLE SAN MARCOS PK, CHLS	681 - A2
CAMERON PK, BARS	3679 - J4
CAMPO SANTO MEM PK, SBDO	576 - G3
CARBON CANYON REGL PK, BREA	710 - A7
CAROLINE PK, RDL	648 - E5
CATAWBA PK, FONT	644 - F2
CENTENNIAL PK, BARS	3679 - H4
CENTENNIAL PK, ONT	642 - D7
CTR STREET PK, VCTV	4296 - E6
CENTRAL PK, CHNO	681 - G1
CENTRAL PK, CLTN	606 - E5
CENTRAL PK, POM	640 - H2
CHAPARRAL PK, CLAR	571 - E7
CHAPARRAL PK, FONT	644 - B3
CHAVEZ, CESAR PK, CLTN	606 - E6
CHET HOFFMAN PK, SBdC	2971 - G3
CHINO HILLS COMM PK, CHLS	681 - C2
CHINO HILLS STATE PK, CHLS	711 - D5
CHURCH STREET PK, RCUC	573 - A7
CINNAMON PK, CHLS	681 - D7
CIRCLE PK, FONT	574 - B7
CITRUS PK, UPL	602 - A4
CITY PK, PRKR	4774 - H7
CITY PK, PRKR	4844 - J1
COLLEGE PK, CLAR	601 - D4
COLONY PK, SBDO	646 - J1
COMM GARDENS, SBDO	577 - A7
COMM PK, RDL	608 - C4
CONFLUENCE PK TRAIL REST, -RCUC	572 - E4
CORAL RIDGE PK, CHLS	680 - J6
CORWIN PK, APLV	4297 - A4
COUNTRY CROSSING PK, POM	640 - E5
COUNTRY PK, DBAR	680 - B5
COVINGTON PK, CHLS	681 - F5
COVINGTON PK, SBdC	615 - J6
COYOTE CANYON PK, RCUC	573 - C7
CRAFTON PK, RDL	608 - G6
CREEKSIDE PK, CALI	649 - G7
CRESTLINE PK, SBdC	516 - J3
CREST PK, SBdC	517 - J4
CROOKS, HULDA PK, LMLN	647 - D3
CROSSROADS PK, CHLS	681 - A5
CUCAMONGA-GUASTI REGL PK, ONT	602 - J6
CULTURAL CTR PK, UPL	572 - A5
CYPRESS PK, FONT	574 - H7
CYPRESS PK, ONT	642 - A2
CYPRESS TRAILS PK, CHNO	682 - A2
CYSA SOCCER COMPLEX, SBDO	577 - E4
DANA PK, BARS	3679 - H4
DANA POINT PK, SBdC	4741 - B5
DANBURY PK, CHLS	681 - H7
DAUER, RICH PK, CLTN	646 - G1
DAVIS, JENNIE PK, RDL	608 - A7
DAVIS PK, CLTN	606 - B4
DE ANZA PK, ONT	642 - B3
DEATH VALLEY NATL PK, SBdC	329 - K2
DECKER PK, POM	640 - G5
DELL, EVA PK, VCTV	4296 - F4
DELMANN HEIGHTS PK, SBDO	576 - C2
DEL RANCHO PK, ONT	642 - A4
DEL ROSA FIELD, SBDO	577 - C1
DEL VALLEJO BALLFIELD, SBDO	577 - D2
DESERT CHRIST PK, YUCA	4957 - F1
DEVILS PUNCHBOWL COUNTY PK, -LACo	368 - E8
DIGNO, ELMER PK, LMLN	607 - B7
D STREET PK, ONT	602 - E7
EAGLE RANCH PK, VCTV	4385 - D5
EAVES, JERRY PK, RLTO	575 - E5
EL BARRIO PK, CLAR	601 - F3
ELLENA PK, RCUC	573 - E6
EL MIRAGE OFF HWY VHCL REC-AREA, SBdC	4112 - H2
ENCANTO PK, SBDO	576 - E6
ENGLISH CREEK PK, CHLS	680 - J4
ENGLISH SPRINGS PK, CHLS	680 - J3
ERWIN LAKE PK, SBdC	4812 - J1
ESSEX PK, MTCL	641 - E2
ETIWANDA CREEK PK, RCUC	573 - J3
EUCALYPTUS PK, CHLS	681 - C7
FAIRFIELD RANCH PK, CHLS	711 - J1
FERGUSSON PK, RLTO	575 - B1
FERN RESERVOIR PK, UPL	602 - B3
FERRARESE, DON PK, APLV	4388 - C3
FIRESTONE BOY SCOUT RESV, -LACo	680 - B6
FLAG HILL PK, YCPA	650 - B3
FLEMING PK, CLTN	606 - D6
FLORES PK, RLTO	575 - E7
FOGLESONG PK, BARS	3679 - E3
FORD PK, RDL	648 - E2
FORREST PK, VCTV	4296 - F4
FRANKLIN PK, RDL	648 - D2
FRISBIE PK, RLTO	575 - J4
GALANIS, JAMES PK, ONT	602 - F7
GALVIN, JOHN PK, ONT	602 - E6
GARFIELD PK, POM	641 - B1
GIBBS PK, ONT	601 - H5
GLEN HELEN OFF HIGHWAY VEHICLE-PK, SBdC	545 - D2
GLEN HELEN REGL PK, SBdC	545 - C2
GLENMEAD PK, CHLS	681 - D5
GOLDEN OAK PK, RCUC	602 - H5
GOULD,TOM MEM PK, SBDO	546 - H6
GRAND AVENUE PK, CHLS	680 - G3
GREENBELT PK, UPL	571 - H7
GREENE, TED PK, POM	601 - A5
GRIFFITH PK, CLAR	571 - A7
GROUT BAY PK, SBdC	4741 - A6
GROW, PAUL C PK, DBAR	680 - B4
GUHIN, AL PK, SBDO	545 - G2
GUTIERREZ PK, SBDO	576 - E5
HALES, ED PK, RDL	608 - B7
HAMILTON PK, POM	640 - G1
HAMPSHIRE FLOODWAY PK, SBDO	547 - B7
HARRISON CANYON PK, SBDO	547 - B7
HARRISON PK, POM	601 - A3
HEART BAR US FOREST SERVICE-PK, SBdC (SEE PAGE 4813)	4882 - J6
HELLMAN WILDERNESS PK, WHIT	388 - C5
HERITAGE PK, CHNO	681 - E1
HERITAGE PK, RCUC	572 - G2
HERMOSA PK, RCUC	573 - A5
HESPERIA COMM PK, HESP	4475 - G4
HESPERIA LAKE PK, HESP	4567 - B4
HICKORY CREEK PK, CHLS	681 - D6
HIDDEN HILLS PK, CHLS	680 - H4
HIGGINBOTHAM PK, CLAR	571 - C6
HIGHWAY 18 LIONS PK, APLV	4297 - F7
HILLTOP PK, CHLS	681 - D6
HOFFMAN, ALMA PK, MTCL	601 - G6
HOLLOW RUN PK, CHLS	711 - C1
HOLLYVALE PK, VCTV	4475 - E1
HOOK COMM PK, VCTV	4296 - A6
HORINE PK, SBDO	576 - J2
HORSEMANS CTR PK, SBdC	4388 - F4
HUDSON, LIONEL E PK, SBDO	546 - C6
HUMBER PK, RivC	389 - J9
HUNTERS HILL PK, CHLS	712 - A4
IDYLLWILD PARK AND NATURE CTR,-RivC	389 - J9
INDIO HILLS PALMS PK-(UNDEVELOPED), RivC	390 - C7
JACK SMITH PK, NDLS	3620 - F6
JAEGER PK, CLAR	571 - D5
JASPER PK, SBdC	3678 - H5
JOSHUA TREE NATL PK, SBdC	4962 - C4
JUNIPER PK, FONT	604 - H4
JURUPA CULTURAL CTR, RivC	644 - H6
KELLOGG PK, POM	640 - B2
KENNEDY PK, POM	640 - E1
KENYON PK, RCUC	573 - D5
KIMBALL PK, ONT	642 - D6
KINGSLEY PK, MTCL	601 - H7
KNOTT SKY PK, TNP	4892 - B7
KOEHLER, DR CHARLES PK, FONT	574 - E5
LAKE GREGORY REGL PK, SBdC	516 - J3
LA PLAZA PK, SBDO	576 - E7
LA PUERTA SPORTS PK, CLAR	571 - D6
LARAMORE PK, RivC	683 - H5
LARKIN PK, CLAR	601 - C3
LAUREL PK, CYP	388 - C9
LENWOOD PK, SBdC	3678 - G6
LEWIS PK, CLAR	601 - B1
LEWIS, RALPH M PK, RCUC	603 - C1
LIBERTY PK, VCTV	4385 - G4
LIBERTY PK, CHNO	641 - G4
LILLIAN PK, BARS	3679 - J3
LIME STREET PK, HESP	4566 - E1
LINCOLN PK, POM	601 - A7
LIONS PK, RCUC	572 - H7
LITTLEFIELD-SHULTIS MEM PK, -SBDO	546 - A4
LITTLE LEAGUE FIELD & PK, -DBAR	640 - A5
LITTLE LEAGUE WESTERN-HEADQUARTERS, SBDO	545 - G2
LIVE OAK PK, HESP	4476 - G6
LONGDEN PK, LACo	388 - C3
LUCKIE PK, TNP	4892 - G4
LYTLE CREEK PK, SBDO	606 - F2
MACARTHUR PK, MTCL	601 - G5
MACHRIS PK, YUCA	4958 - D7
MADISON PK, POM	640 - J3
MAGNOLIA PK, UPL	572 - A7
MALLOWS, J N PK, CLAR	601 - D3
MANATABA PK, LPCo	4844 - G3
MAPLE HILL PK, DBAR	680 - A3
MLK JR MEM PARK, DR, POM	640 - H5
MCCALL MEM PK, RivC	389 - J10
MCCARTHY PK, UPL	572 - A5
MCDERMOTT PK, FONT	574 - B6
MCLEOD PK, CHNO	641 - J6
MEADOWBROOK FIELDS, SBDO	606 - J1
MEADOWBROOK PK, SBDO	606 - H1
MEADOW PK, BBLK	4811 - G1
MEADOWS EDGE PK, SBdC	4741 - F6
MEADOWS PK, CHLS	712 - A4
MEM GROVE PK, ONT	602 - E6
MEM PK, CLAR	601 - D2
MENDEL PK, APLV	4477 - J3
MIDWAY PK, SBdC-(SEE PAGE 4300)	4391 - F6
MILL COMM PK, SBDO	607 - A3
MILLER PK, FONT	604 - J2
MILLIKEN PK, RCUC	573 - D7
MINI PK, BARS	3679 - H6
MOABI REGL PK, SBdC	352 - C10
MOJAVE NARROWS REGL PK, SBdC	4386 - J1
MOJAVE RIVER FORKS REGL PK, -SBdC (SEE PAGE 4656)	4657 - A4
MONTARA PK, BARS	3680 - B5
MONTE VISTA PK, CHNO	681 - F1
MONTVUE PK, POM	601 - C6
MORENO VISTA PK, MTCL	601 - F4
MORNINGFIELD PK, CHLS	681 - B5
MORNINGSIDE PK, CHLS	681 - B6
MTN VIEW PK, CHNO	682 - A1
MTN VIEW PK, RCUC	573 - E7
MOUNT BALDY SKI AREA, SBdC-(SEE PAGE 4653)	4732 - E6
MOUNT SAN JACINTO STATE PK, -RivC	389 - K8
MUNOZ, ANTHONY PK, ONT	601 - J5
MYSTIC CANYON PK, CHLS	712 - A5
NAPLES PLAZA PK, LBCH	388 - B10
NEEDLES MARINA PK, NDLS	3620 - C4
NEWBERRY MEM PK, SBDO	546 - G4
NEWMARK FIELD, SBDO	546 - H7
NICHOLSON PK, SBDO	606 - A1
NORTH HERITAGE PK, FONT	574 - A6
NORTH TAMARIND PK, FONT	605 - B1
NUNEZ PK, SBDO	606 - D1
OAK PK, FONT	644 - B4
OAK RIDGE PK, CHLS	681 - B6
OLD TOWN PK, RCUC	603 - A3
OLD TRAILS MONUMENT PK, NDLS	3620 - D6
OLIVEDALE PK, UPL	602 - C4
ONTARIO MOTOR SPEEDWAY PK, -ONT	603 - A6
ORANCO BOWMEN ARCHERY RANGE, -CHNO	712 - B4
OWENS, LEE PK, WHIT	388 - C6
PALM FIELD, SBDO	577 - A7
PALM STREET PK, HESP	4565 - G1
PALOMARES PK, POM	601 - A4
PANAMINT PK, SBdC	3679 - D7
PANTERA PK, DBAR	680 - E1
PARADISE VALLEY PK, YUCA	4888 - D6
PEBBLE BEACH PK, VCTV	4386 - D1
PERRIS HILL PK, SBDO	577 - A4
PETERSON, CARLTON PK, DBAR	640 - D6
PHIL PK, POM	641 - A5
PICO PK, GTER	646 - D5
PIONEER PK, SBDO	576 - G7
PIONEER PK, SBdC	4481 - B2
PIONEER PK, UPL	572 - B5
POMONA JC COMM PK, POM	601 - B6
PRADO AIR PK, SBdC	712 - E5
PRADO BASIN PK, RivC	712 - H6
PRADO PARKS STABLES, SBdC	712 - D2
PRADO RECREATION DOG TRAINING-FACILITY, SBdC	712 - B5
PRADO REGL PK, CHNO	712 - B3
PRADO TIRO SHOOTING RANGE REC-AREA, CHNO	712 - B4
PROSPECT PK, RDL	648 - C2
PROVIDENCE MTNS STATE REC-AREA, SBdC	351 - A7
RANCHO MIRA LOMA, RivC	644 - A5
RANCHO SANTA ANA BOTANIC-GARDEN, CLAR	571 - D7

FEATURE NAME Address City, ZIP Code	PAGE-GRID
RED HILL PK, RCUC	572 - G7
REID PK, RIV	646 - A7
RIALTO CITY PK, RLTO	605 - H5
RICHARDSON PK, ADEL	4205 - A7
RINCON PK, CHLS	711 - E1
RIVER ISLAND STATE PK, LPCo	4606 - H4
RIVERSIDE PK, CHNO	641 - G7
ROCKFIELD NATURE PK, VCTV- (SEE PAGE 4116)	4206 - B7
RUNNING DEER PK, SBdC	4886 - H4
SAAVEDRA, SAL FIELD, SBDO	576 - E7
SADDLEBACK BUTTE STATE PK, - LACo	368 - E2
SAM ALBA MEM PK, ONT	642 - C1
SAN ANTONIO PK, ONT	602 - A7
SAN ANTONIO PK, UPL	571 - J3
SAN BERNARDINO NATL FOREST, - SBdC	512 - B3
SAN SEVAINE PK, FONT	574 - C1
SANTA FE DAM REC AREA, IRW	388 - D2
SANTA FE PK, NDLS	3620 - C5
SANTA FE PK, FONT	604 - J3
SARATOGA PK, MTCL	601 - G7
SCHMIDT, NORM PK, APLV	4387 - E1
SCHMIDT PK, VCTV	4205 - F6
SEBRING PK, CHNO	641 - J6
SECCOMBE LAKE REC AREA, SBDO	576 - H7
SESSIONS, ROBERT A SPORTS PK, - BARS	3679 - J7
SEVILLE PK, FONT	604 - H2
SHADOW PK, FONT	644 - C3
SHELTON PK, CLAR	601 - D3
SHIRRELLS, ANNE PK, SBDO	576 - C5
SIERRA PK, SBDO	546 - H7
SIERRA VISTA PK, UPL	572 - C7
SIERRA VISTA PK, SMAD	388 - C2
SILVERWOOD LAKE STATE REC- AREA, SBdC	4736 - C4
SIMONDS PARKWAY, RDL	648 - F4
SKYLINE NORTH PK, SBdC	3589 - H6
SKYVIEW PK, CHLS	681 - B1
SMILEY PK, RDL	608 - B7
SNOW SUMMIT SKI AREA, SBdC	4811 - H2
SNOW VALLEY SKI AREA, SBdC	519 - J5
SOUTHRIDGE PK, FONT	644 - D3
SPEICHER MEM PK, SBDO	577 - E5
SPRUCE AVENUE PK, RCUC	573 - C7
STERLING PK, SBDO	577 - D2
STRICKLING PK, CHLS	681 - C7
STRINGHAM PK, BARS	3680 - B5
STURNACLE, JOHN PK, BARS	3680 - B3
SUGARLOAF PK, SBdC	4742 - F7
SUMMIT RIDGE PK, DBAR	680 - D3
SUN PK, LMLN	607 - D6
SUNRISE PK, MTCL	601 - H6
SUNSET PK, MTCL	601 - E7
SUNSET PK, CHLS	680 - G5
SWITZER PK PICNIC AREA, SBdC	518 - A4
SYCAMORE CANYON PK, DBAR	680 - B2
SYCAMORE CANYON PK, CLAR	571 - C5
SYCAMORE GLEN PK, CHLS	680 - H3
SYCAMORE ROCKS PK, APLV	4298 - C2
SYLVAN PK, RDL	608 - D7
TERRACE HILLS COMM PK, GTER	646 - F4
TERRACE PK, CHLS	680 - G4
TEXONIA PK, RDL	608 - A5
THUNDERBIRD PK, APLV	4297 - F5
THURMAN FLATS PICNIC GROUNDS, - SBdC	4950 - C7
TIMBERLANE PK, HESP	4476 - J6
TODD, MARGARET PK, RLTO	605 - G1
TORREY PINES PK, CHLS	711 - F1
TUDAR, MARTIN JURUPA HILLS- REGL PK, FONT	644 - J3
UPLAND MEM PK, UPL	602 - D2
VAIL PK, CLAR	571 - E6
VALLE VISTA PK, CHLS	681 - B7
VETERANS MEM PK SOUTH, FONT	605 - A3
VETERANS PK, CLTN	606 - D7
VICTORIA GROVES PK, RCUC	573 - C5
VILLAGE PK, VCTV	4296 - B4
VILLAGE PK, FONT	644 - F3
VILLA PK, CHNO	681 - G1
VINEYARD PK, ONT	602 - F5
VINTAGE PK, RCUC	573 - E5
VIRGINIA PK, APLV	4208 - A7
WALNUT CREEK NATURE PK, CHLS	680 - H3
WALNUT PK, CHNO	641 - F6
WARDERS FIELD PK, UPL	602 - D3
WASHINGTON PK, POM	641 - A3
WATERMAN PK, BARS	3679 - H2
WATKINS, DUKE PK, NDLS	3620 - C6
WELCH, RALPH PK, POM	640 - G3
WEST FORK REC AREA, SBdC- (SEE PAGE 4654)	4735 - H4
WEST GREENWAY PK, RCUC	573 - D7
WESTMONT PK, POM	640 - E3
WESTWIND PK, ONT	642 - J6
WESTWINDS SPORT CTR, VCTV	4205 - F5
WHEELER, STUART PK, CLAR	601 - C5
WHITTIER, JG PK, WHIT	388 - C5
WILDERNESS PK, MTCL	601 - E6
WILDWOOD PK, SBDO	546 - J6
WINDROWS PK, RCUC	573 - G5
WINEVILLE PK, RivC	683 - G4
YOST PK, RivC	644 - H6
YUCAIPA REGL PK, YCPA	649 - H1
YUCCA LOMA PK, APLV	4387 - H2
YUCCA VALLEY PK, YUCA	4957 - E3

PERFORMING ARTS

FEATURE NAME Address City, ZIP Code	PAGE-GRID
CHAFFEY COMMUNITIES CULTURAL- CTR 525 W 18TH ST, UPL, 91784	572 - B6
GLEN HELEN BLOCKBUSTER PAVILION 2575 GLEN HELEN PKWY, SBdC, 92407	545 - C1
NATL ORANGE SHOW AMPHITHEATER 689 S E ST, SBDO, 92401	606 - H3
PADUA HILLS THEATRE 4467 VIA PADOVA, CLAR, 91711	571 - E3
REDLANDS BOWL OLIVE AV & EUREKA ST, RDL, 92373	648 - B1
SEWALL, A MEEKER THEATER CAJON ST & HIGHLAND AV, RDL, 92373	648 - C3
STURGES AUDITORIUM 780 N E ST, SBDO, 92410	576 - G7

POINTS OF INTEREST

FEATURE NAME Address City, ZIP Code	PAGE-GRID
ARTHUR LETTS CAMPSITE FIRESTONE BOY SCOUT RES, LACo, 92823	710 - A1
BIG BEAR DISCOVERY CENTER NORTH SHORE DR, SBdC	4741 - G5
BIG LEAGUE DREAMS SPORTS PK 10550 GALENA ST, RivC, 91752	683 - J1
BUN BOY THERMOMETER BAKER BLVD, SBdC	2971 - F4
BUREAU OF LAND MANAGEMENT 2601 BARSTOW RD, BARS, 92311	3679 - H6
CALICO MTNS ARCHAEOLOGICAL- PROJECT (SEE PAGE 3592) PARADISE SPRINGS RD, SBdC, 92365	3593 - A2
DESERT DISCOVERY CTR 831 BARSTOW RD, BARS, 92311	3679 - H4
ETIWANDA GAME ASSOCIATION- (SEE PAGE 4656) HWY 173, SBdC	4657 - C3
FALLS PICNIC GROUNDS FALLS RD, SBdC, 92339	611 - J3
JOSHUA TREE NATL PK HQ & VIS 74485 NATL PARK DR, TNP, 92277	4892 - G7
KELLOGG ARABIAN HORSE CTR KELLOGG DR, POM, 91768	640 - B2
MOONRIDGE ANIMAL PK MOONRIDGE RD & GOLDMINE DR, BBLK	4812 - B3
PANORAMA POINT RIM OF THE WORLD HWY, SBdC, 92404	516 - E5
PRADO CONSERVATION CAMP 14467 CENTRAL AV, CHNO, 91710	681 - H4
PRADO TIRO SHOOTING RANGE 17501 POMONA RINCON RD, CHNO, 91710	712 - B4
RIFLE RANGE FIRESTONE BOY SCOUT RES, LACo, 92823	710 - A1
RIM OF THE WORLD HIGHWAY HWY 18, SBdC	4810 - B4
SOLAR OBSERVATORY NORTH SHORE LN, SBdC	4741 - D6
STATE FISH HATCHERY MOJAVE FISH HATCHERY RD, VCTV, 92392	4387 - A5
UCLA CONFERENCE CTR WEST SHORE RD & ROSEWOOD LN, SBdC	4738 - A6

POINTS OF INTEREST - HISTORIC

FEATURE NAME Address City, ZIP Code	PAGE-GRID
CALICO GHOST TOWN- (SEE PAGE 3590) CALICO RD, SBdC	3591 - H3
CASA DE RANCHO CUCAMONGA 8810 HEMLOCK ST, RCUC, 91730	602 - G1
COLTON HIST SOCIETY PO BOX 233, CLTN, 92324	606 - D6
INDIAN HIST SITE HWY 18 & RABBIT SPRINGS RD, SBdC	4480 - C1
INDIAN RELIC ARCHAEOLOGICAL- SITE PINE CREST AV, RivC	389 - J9
MORMON STOCKADE COURT ST, SBDO, 92401	606 - H1
RINCON RANCHO YORBA-SLAUGHTER- ADOBE 17127 POMONA RINCON RD, CHNO, 91710	712 - A3
SAN BERNARDINO RANCHO- ASISTENCIA 26930 BARTON RD, RDL, 92373	647 - G1
TRUJILLO ADOBE HIST AREA S PELLISIER RD, RivC, 92501	646 - A6
YUCAIPA ADOBE 32183 KENTUCKY ST, YCPA, 92399	649 - C5

SCHOOLS - PRIVATE ELEMENTARY

FEATURE NAME Address City, ZIP Code	PAGE-GRID
ALTA LOMA CHRISTIAN 9974 19TH ST, RCUC, 91737	573 - A5
AMBASSADOR CHRISTIAN 8405 N MAPLE AV, RLTO, 92376	605 - D2
APPLE VALLEY CHRISTIAN 22434 NISQUALLY RD, APLV, 92308	4388 - A4
AZURE HILLS ADVENTIST 22577 CITY CENTER CT, GTER, 92313	646 - F4
BANNER 2626 E PACIFIC ST, SBDO, 92346	577 - F4
BARTSOW CHRISTIAN 800 YUCCA AV, BARS, 92311	3680 - A4
BLESSED SACRAMENT 6755 SAGE AV, TNP, 92277	4892 - G6
BLOOMINGTON CHRISTIAN 9904 BLOOMINGTON AV, SBdC, 92316	605 - E6
CALVARY CHAPEL CHRISTIAN 101 GRANDVIEW RD, SBdC	517 - D1
CALVARY CHAPEL CHRISTIAN 9700 ALABAMA ST, SBdC, 92374	607 - H4
CALVARY CHRISTIAN 1430 N GROVE AV, ONT, 91764	602 - E5
CARBON CANYON CHRISTIAN 5600 CARBON CANYON RD, BREA, 92823	710 - C6
CARDEN ARBOR VIEW 1530 N SAN ANTONIO AV, UPL, 91786	572 - A7
CENTRAL CHRISTIAN 395 SAN BERNARDINO AV, POM, 91767	601 - A6
CHINO VALLEY CHRISTIAN 12410 NORTON AV, CHNO, 91710	641 - E6
CHRISTIAN CTR ACADEMY 1401 S MOUNT VERNON AV, CLTN, 92324	646 - F2
COLTON CHRISTIAN 450 W CITRUS ST, CLTN, 92324	606 - C4
CONGREGATION EMANU EL CLARE- CHERRY 3512 N E ST, SBDO, 92405	576 - G1
CORNERSTONE CHRISTIAN 13000 PIPELINE AV, SBdC, 91710	641 - D7
DEL ROSA CHRISTIAN 1333 E 39TH ST, SBDO, 92404	547 - B7
ECHOS OF FAITH CHRISTIAN 11255 CENTRAL AV, SBdC, 91762	641 - G3
FAITH CHRISTIAN 11616 HESPERIA RD, HESP, 92345	4386 - F7
FIRST LUTHERAN CHRISTIAN DAY 9315 CITRUS AV, FONT, 92335	604 - G4
FONTANA CHRISTIAN 17777 MERRILL AV, FONT, 92335	605 - B3
FOOTHILL COUNTRY DAY 1035 HARRISON AV, CLAR, 91711	601 - B3
GATEWAY CHRISTIAN ACADEMY 4380 N 4TH AV, SBDO, 92407	546 - E6
HESPERIA CHRISTIAN 16775 OLIVE ST, HESP, 92345	4476 - F7
HOLY ROSARY 2620 ARROWHEAD AV, SBDO, 92405	576 - H3
IMMANUEL BAPTIST 45 MICHIGAN AV, RivC, 92507	646 - D6
LIFE CTR CHRISTIAN 305 E ARROW HWY, POM, 91767	601 - A4
LOMA LINDA ACADEMY 10656 ANDERSON ST, LMLN, 92354	607 - B7
MESA GRANDE ACADEMY 975 FREMONT ST, CALI, 92320	650 - C7
MOJAVE CHRISTIAN 22275 POWHATAN RD, APLV, 92308	4388 - A2
MONTESSORI IN REDLANDS 1890 ORANGE AV, RDL, 92373	647 - G1
MTN AVENUE CHRISTIAN 1951 S MOUNTAIN AV, ONT, 91762	642 - A4
MTNSIDE CHRISTIAN 2050 E PACIFIC ST, SBDO, 92404	577 - D4
MOUNT CALVARY LUTHERAN 23300 GOLDEN SPRINGS DR, DBAR, 91765	680 - B1
MOUNT SAINT JOSEPHS 555 E MOUNTAIN VIEW AV, BARS, 92311	3679 - H3
NEW HOPE CHRISTIAN 13333 RAMONA AV, CHNO, 91710	681 - E1
NEW LIFE CHRISTIAN 15975 HERCULES ST, HESP, 92345	4476 - D4
ONTARIO CHRISTIAN 1907 S EUCLID AV, ONT, 91761	642 - C4
OUR LADY OF LOURDES 5303 ORCHARD ST, MTCL, 91763	601 - G7
OUR LADY OF THE ASSUMPTION 611 W BONITA AV, CLAR, 91711	601 - C3
OUR LADY OF THE ASSUMPTION 796 W 48TH ST, SBDO, 92407	546 - F6
OUR LADY OF VICTORY 601 E PALMER ST, COMP, 90221	388 - A7
POMONA ADVENTIST JR ACADEMY 850 E GRAND AV, POM, 91766	641 - A3
REDEEMER LUTHERAN 920 W 6TH ST, ONT, 91762	602 - A5
REDLANDS CHRISTIAN 1145 N CHURCH ST, RDL, 92374	608 - C6
REDLANDS JUNIOR ACADEMY 130 TENNESSEE ST, RDL, 92373	607 - J7
RESURRECTION ACADEMY 17434 MILLER AV, FONT, 92336	575 - A7
RITA BLAIR 1250 GRAND AV, DBAR, 91765	680 - C3
SACRED HEART 12676 FOOTHILL BLVD, RCUC, 91739	603 - G1
SACRED HEART 215 S EUREKA ST, RDL, 92373	648 - B1
SAINT ADELAIDE 27487 E BASELINE ST, HIGH, 92346	577 - H5
SAINT ANNES 6886 DEL ROSA AV, SBdC, 92404	577 - C4
SAINT ANTHONY 1510 W 16TH ST, SBDO, 92411	576 - D5
SAINT CATHERINE OF SIENA 335 N SYCAMORE AV, RLTO, 92376	605 - H1
SAINT GEORGE 322 W D ST, ONT, 91762	602 - B7
SAINT JOSEPH ACADEMY 8460 MANGO AV, FONT, 92335	605 - A2
SAINT JOSEPH 1200 W HOLT AV, POM, 91768	640 - G1
SAINT JOSEPH 905 N CAMPUS AV, CLAR, 91711	601 - B2
SAINT JOSEPH 905 N CAMPUS AV, UPL, 91786	602 - C2
SAINT MADELEINE 935 E KINGSLEY AV, POM, 91767	601 - B7
SAINT MARGARET MARY 12664 CENTRAL AV, CHNO, 91710	641 - G6
SAINT MARKS EPISCOPAL 330 E 16TH ST, UPL, 91786	572 - C7
SAINT MARYS REGL 18350 HIGHWAY 18, APLV, 92307	4296 - J4
SAINT PETERS EPISCOPAL DAY 1648 W 9TH ST, UPL, 91786	601 - H3
SAINT TIMOTHYS EPISCOPAL 15757 SAINT TIMOTHY RD, APLV, 92307	4297 - C4
SAN BERNARDINO CHRISTIAN 2898 N G ST, SBDO, 92405	576 - G2
SON SHINE CHRISTIAN 5430 RIDGEVIEW AV, RivC, 91752	683 - J3
SUNRISE CHRISTIAN 2759 N AYALA DR, RLTO, 92377	575 - E2
UPLAND CHRISTIAN 100 W 9TH ST, UPL, 91786	602 - B3
VALLEY CHRISTIAN 1671 N SIERRA WY, SBDO, 92405	576 - H4
VALLEY PREP 1605 FORD ST, RDL, 92373	648 - E3
VICTOR VALLEY CHRISTIAN 15260 NISQUALLI RD, VCTV, 92392	4386 - B4
WESTERN CHRISTIAN 3105 PADUA AV, CLAR, 91711	571 - F6
YUCAIPA CHRISTIAN 34784 YUCAIPA BLVD, YCPA, 92399	649 - J3

SCHOOLS - PRIVATE HIGH

FEATURE NAME Address City, ZIP Code	PAGE-GRID
ADVOCATE 11980 MOUNT VERNON AV, GTER, 92313	646 - E3
AMBASSADOR CHRISTIAN 8405 N MAPLE AV, RLTO, 92376	605 - D2
APPLE VALLEY CHRISTIAN 22434 NISQUALLY RD, APLV, 92308	4388 - A4
AQUINAS CATHOLIC 2772 N STERLING AV, SBDO, 92404	577 - D2
ARROWHEAD CHRISTIAN ACADEMY 105 TENNESSEE ST, RDL, 92373	647 - J1
BLOOMINGTON CHRISTIAN 9904 BLOOMINGTON AV, SBdC, 92316	605 - E5
CALVARY CHAPEL CHRISTIAN 101 GRANDVIEW RD, SBdC	517 - D2
CALVARY CHAPEL CHRISTIAN 9700 ALABAMA ST, SBdC, 92374	607 - H4
CARBON CANYON CHRISTIAN 5600 CARBON CANYON RD, BREA, 92823	710 - C6
CHRISTIAN CTR ACADEMY 1401 S MOUNT VERNON AV, CLTN, 92324	646 - F2
COLTON CHRISTIAN 450 W CITRUS ST, CLTN, 92324	606 - C4
FAITH ACADEMY LAKE ARROWHEAD 232 BRET HARTE RD, SBdC	518 - B1
GATEWAY CHRISTIAN ACADEMY 4380 N 4TH AV, SBDO, 92407	546 - E6
HESPERIA CHRISTIAN 16775 OLIVE ST, HESP, 92345	4476 - F7
LOMA LINDA ACADEMY 10656 ANDERSON ST, LMLN, 92354	607 - B7
MESA GRANDE ACADEMY 975 FREMONT ST, CALI, 92320	650 - C7
MOJAVE CHRISTIAN 22275 POWHATAN RD, APLV, 92308	4388 - A3
ONTARIO CHRISTIAN 931 W PHILADELPHIA ST, ONT, 91762	642 - A5
PANORAMA CHRISTIAN 33981 YUCAIPA BLVD, YCPA, 92399	649 - G3
POMONA CATHOLIC 533 W HOLT AV, POM, 91768	640 - H1
UPLAND CHRISTIAN 100 W 9TH ST, UPL, 91786	602 - B3
VICTOR VALLEY CHRISTIAN 15260 NISQUALLI RD, VCTV, 92392	4386 - A4
WEBB OF CALIFORNIA 1175 W BASELINE RD, CLAR, 91711	571 - A6

SCHOOLS - PRIVATE MIDDLE

FEATURE NAME Address City, ZIP Code	PAGE-GRID
REDLANDS JUNIOR ACADEMY 130 TENNESSEE ST, RDL, 92373	607 - J7

SCHOOLS - PUBLIC ELEMENTARY

FEATURE NAME Address City, ZIP Code	PAGE-GRID
ADELANTO 17931 JONATHAN RD, ADEL, 92301	4205 - A6
ALCOTT 1600 S TOWNE AV, POM, 91766	641 - A4
ALLISON 1011 RUSSELL PL, POM, 91767	601 - B6
ALTA LOMA 7085 AMETHYST ST, RCUC, 91701	572 - J6
ARMSTRONG 22750 BEAVERHEAD DR, DBAR, 91765	640 - B7
ARROWHEAD 3825 MOUNTAIN VIEW AV, SBDO, 92405	546 - H7
ARROYO 1605 ARROYO AV, POM, 91768	640 - F1
ARROYO 1700 E 7TH ST, ONT, 91764	602 - F4
ARROYO VERDE 7701 CHURCH ST, HIGH, 92346	578 - C6
BAKER SCHOOLHOUSE LN & DEATH VALLEY, SBdC	2971 - F3
BALDWIN LAKE 44500 BALDWIN LN, SBdC	4742 - F7
BALDY MESA 10376 BALDY MESA RD, SBdC, 92371	4474 - F4
BALDY VIEW 979 W 11TH ST, UPL, 91786	602 - A2
BANYAN 10900 MIRADOR DR, RCUC, 91737	573 - C3
BARFIELD 2181 N SAN ANTONIO AV, POM, 91767	601 - B5
BARTON 2214 PUMALO ST, SBDO, 92404	577 - D3
BEAR GULCH 8355 BEAR GULCH PL, RCUC, 91730	602 - G2
BELVEDERE 2501 E MARSHALL BLVD, SBDO, 92346	577 - E2
BEMIS, LEVI 774 E ETIWANDA AV, RLTO, 92376	575 - J7
BERLYN 1320 N BERLYN AV, ONT, 91764	602 - D5
BIG BEAR 40940 PENNSYLVANIA AV, BBLK	4811 - F2
BIRNEY, ALICE 1050 E OLIVE PL, CLTN, 92324	606 - F5
BLAKE 701 S NAVAJO AV, PRKR	4774 - H7
BON VIEW 2121 S BON VIEW AV, ONT, 91761	642 - D4
BORBA, ANNA FUNDAMENTAL 12970 3RD ST, CHNO, 91710	641 - F7
BOYD, CALVIN J 310 E MERRILL ST, RLTO, 92376	605 - H3
BRADACH, DONALD F 11824 AIR EXWY, ADEL, 92301	4205 - B7
BRADLEY 1300 VALENCIA AV, SBDO, 92404	577 - A5
BRENTWOOD 13962 HOOK BLVD, VCTV, 92394	4295 - G6
BRIGGS, LYLE S. FUNDAMENTAL 11800 ROSWELL AV, SBdC, 91710	641 - D4
BRYN MAWR 11680 WHITTIER AV, LMLN, 92354	647 - F2
BUENA VISTA ARTS-INTERGRATED 5685 SAN BERNARDINO ST, MTCL, 91763	601 - H6
BURBANK 198 W MILL ST, SBDO, 92408	606 - H2
BUTTERFIELD RANCH 6350 MYSTIC CANYON DR, CHLS, 91709	712 - A6
CABRILLO 1562 W 11TH ST, UPL, 91786	601 - H2
CALIFORNIA 2699 N CALIFORNIA ST, SBDO, 92407	576 - C3
CALIMESA 13523 2ND ST, YCPA, 92399	650 - A6
CAMERON 801 MURIEL DR, BARS, 92311	3679 - J4
CANYON CREST 11851 CHERRY AV, FONT, 92337	644 - C4
CARMEL 9321 GLENDALE AV, HESP, 92345	4477 - C6
CARNELIAN 7105 CARNELIAN ST, RCUC, 91701	572 - F6
CARYN 6290 SIERRA CREST VIEW LP, RCUC, 91737	573 - E4
CASEY, MERLE S 219 N EUCALYPTUS, RLTO, 92376	605 - J1
CATTLE 13590 CYPRESS AV, CHNO, 91710	682 - A1
CENTRAL 415 E G ST, ONT, 91764	602 - C7
CENTRAL 7955 ARCHIBALD AV, RCUC, 91730	602 - J1
CHAPARRAL 451 CHAPARRAL DR, CLAR, 91711	571 - E7
CITRUS 16041 RANDALL AV, FONT, 92335	604 - G4
CITRUS 925 W 7TH ST, UPL, 91786	602 - A4
COLE 1331 COLE AV, SBDO, 92346	577 - H5
CONDIT 1750 N MOUNTAIN AV, CLAR, 91711	601 - C1
CONDOR 2551 CONDOR RD, TNP, 92277	4822 - F3
COOLEY RANCH 1000 S COOLEY DR, CLTN, 92324	646 - H1
CORONA 1140 N CORONA AV, ONT, 91764	602 - G5
CORTEZ, ALICE E. 12750 CARISSA AV, CHNO, 91710	641 - J6
COTTONWOOD 8850 COTTONWOOD AV, HESP, 92345	4566 - A1
COUNTRY SPRINGS 14145 VILLAGE CENTER DR, CHLS, 91709	680 - J3
COYOTE CANYON 7889 ELM AV, RCUC, 91730	603 - D1
CRAFTON 311 N WABASH AV, RDL, 92374	608 - G7
CRAM 29700 WATER ST, HIGH, 92346	578 - E6
CREEK VIEW 3742 LYTLE CREEK LP, ONT, 91761	643 - C6
CRESTLINE 2020 MONTEREY AV, BARS, 92311	3679 - J6
CRESTMORE 18870 JURUPA AV, SBdC, 92316	645 - E2
CUCAMONGA 8677 ARCHIBALD AV, RCUC, 91730	602 - J3
CURTIS, SAMUEL 451 S LILAC AV, RLTO, 92376	605 - G3
CYPRESS 26825 CYPRESS ST, HIGH, 92346	577 - G6
CYPRESS 9751 CYPRESS AV, FONT, 92335	604 - H5
DANBURY 1745 LYNOAK DR, CLAR, 91711	601 - A1
DARCY, MICHAEL 11645 ELM AV, FONT, 92337	644 - F3
DATE 9011 OLEANDER AV, FONT, 92335	604 - H3
DAVIDSON 2844 N DAVIDSON AV, SBDO, 92405	576 - E3
DECKER 20 VILLAGE LOOP RD, POM, 91766	640 - G5
DEER CANYON 10225 HAMILTON ST, RCUC, 91701	573 - A5
DEL NORTE 850 N DEL NORTE AV, ONT, 91764	602 - E6
DEL REY 15332 DEL REY DR, VCTV, 92392	4296 - D5
DEL ROSA 3395 MOUNTAIN AV, SBDO, 92404	577 - B1
DESERT KNOLLS 18213 SYMERON RD, APLV, 92307	4296 - J5
DESERT TRAILS 14350 BELLFLOWER ST, ADEL, 92301	4385 - A1
DIAMOND POINT 24150 SUNSET CROSSING RD, DBAR, 91765	640 - D5
DICKEY, LEVI H 2840 PARCO AV, ONT, 91761	642 - F6
DICKSON 3930 PAMELA DR, SBdC, 91710	641 - D7
DOLLAHAN, HELEN L 1060 W ETIWANDA AV, RLTO, 92376	575 - E7
DONA MERCED 10333 PALO ALTO ST, RCUC, 91730	573 - B7
DUNLAP 32870 AVE E, YCPA, 92399	649 - D4
DUNN, GEORGE H 830 N LILAC AV, RLTO, 92376	575 - F7
EAGLE CANYON 13435 EAGLE CANYON DR, CHLS, 91709	681 - A1
EAGLE RANCH 12545 EAGLE RANCH PKWY, VCTV, 92392	4385 - D6
EAGLE SUMMIT ACADEMY 4367 PHELAN RD, SBdC, 92371	4473 - B6
EAST HERITAGE 14250 E CONSTITUTION WY, FONT, 92336	574 - B7
EDISON 515 E 6TH ST, ONT, 91764	602 - C4
EL CAMINO 1525 W 5TH ST, ONT, 91762	601 - H5

SCHOOLS - PUBLIC ELEMENTARY

FEATURE NAME	Address City, ZIP Code	PAGE-GRID
ELDERBERRY	950 N ELDERBERRY AV, ONT, 91762	601 - J6
EL RANCHO	5862 C ST, CHINO, 91710	641 - J7
EMMERTON	1888 N ARDEN AV, SBDO, 92404	577 - E4
EUCALYPTUS	11224 10TH AV, HESP, 92345	4476 - C2
EUCLID	1120 S EUCLID AV, ONT, 91762	642 - B2
FAIRFAX	1362 PACIFIC ST, SBDO, 92404	577 - B4
FALLSVALE	40600 VALLEY OF THE FALLS DR, SBdC, 92339	611 - E2
FITZGERALD	2568 W TERRA VISTA DR, RLTO, 92377	545 - A7
FOOTHILL KNOLLS	1245 VETERANS CT, UPL, 91786	602 - D1
FRANKLIN	850 E COLTON AV, RDL, 92374	608 - D6
FRIENDLY HILLS	7252 SUNNY VISTA RD, SBdC, 92252	4958 - J2
GARCIA, ERNEST	1390 W RANDAL AV, CLTN, 92324	606 - A4
GEORGE, HAROLD H VISUAL ARTS-PERF ARTS	17738 NEVADA AV, VCTV, 92394	4205 - F6
GIRD	4980 RIVERSIDE DR, CHNO, 91710	641 - F7
GLENMEADE	15000 WHIRLAWAY LN, CHLS, 91709	681 - D5
GOLDEN SPRINGS	245 BALLENA DR, DBAR, 91765	640 - C6
GRACE HENDERSON	N ST & NEEDLES HWY, NDLS, 92363	3620 - C4
GRAND TERRACE	12066 VIVIENDA AV, GTER, 92313	646 - D4
GRANDVIEW	180 GRANDVIEW RD, SBdC	517 - D1
GRANITE HILL	9371 GRANITE HILL DR, RivC, 92509	644 - C6
GRANT, ULYSSES	550 W OLIVE ST, CLTN, 92324	606 - C5
GREEN TREE EAST	17246 GIBRALTER DR, VCTV, 92392	4386 - G2
GRIMES, RUTH	10009 SPRUCE AV, RLTO, 92316	605 - F6
HARRISON	425 E HARRISON AV, POM, 91767	601 - A3
HAWTHORNE	705 W HAWTHORNE ST, ONT, 91762	602 - A5
HAYNES, RICHARD E	715 W FRANCIS ST, ONT, 91762	642 - A4
HELENDALE (SEE PAGE 3934)	27274 PEACH TREE LN, SBdC	3935 - J3
HEMLOCK	15080 MILLER AV, FONT, 92336	574 - D7
HENDERSON	400 S AVE E, BARS, 92311	3679 - F4
HENRY	470 E ETIWANDA AV, RLTO, 92376	575 - H7
HERITAGE	9298 SHEEP CREEK RD, SBdC, 92371	4473 - A7
HERMOSA	10133 WILSON AV, RCUC, 91737	573 - A3
HIDDEN TRAILS	2550 RIDGEVIEW DR, CHLS, 91709	680 - J5
HIGHGROVE	690 CENTER ST, RivC, 92507	646 - D6
HIGHLAND PACIFIC	3340 E PACIFIC ST, SBDO, 92346	577 - G4
HILLSIDE	4975 N MAYFIELD AV, SBDO, 92407	546 - G5
HINKLEY (SEE PAGE 3586)	37600 HINKLEY RD, SBDO, 92347	3587 - G5
HOHSTADT, KATIE	D ST & CIBOLA ST, NDLS, 92363	3620 - D6
HOLLYVALE	11645 HOLLYVALE AV, VCTV, 92392	4475 - D1
HOWARD	4650 HOWARD ST, MTCL, 91763	641 - F2
HUGHBANKS, ELIZABETH T	2241 N APPLE AV, RLTO, 92377	575 - F3
HUNT	1342 E PUMALO ST, SBDO, 92404	577 - B3
INGHRAM, HOWARD	1695 W 19TH ST, SBDO, 92411	576 - D4
IRWIN	14907 MOJAVE DR, VCTV, 92392	4296 - E6
JASPER	6881 JASPER ST, RCUC, 91701	572 - F5
JOSHUA CIRCLE	10140 8TH AV, HESP, 92345	4476 - C4
JOSHUA TREE	6051 SUNBURST ST, SBdC, 92252	4889 - C6
JUNIPER	7655 JUNIPER AV, FONT, 92336	574 - J7
JUNIPER	9400 I AV, HESP, 92345	4476 - G6
JURUPA HILLS	10755 OLEANDER AV, FONT, 92337	644 - H1
JURUPA VISTA	15920 VILLAGE DR E, FONT, 92337	644 - G3
KELLEY	380 S MERIDIAN AV, SBDO, 92376	606 - A2
KELLOGG POLYTECHNIC	610 MEDINA ST, POM, 91768	640 - C2
KENDALL	4951 STATE ST, SBDO, 92407	546 - C6
KIMBARK	18021 KENWOOD AV, SBdC, 92407	515 - B4
KIMBERLY	301 W SOUTH AV, RDL, 92373	648 - D3
KINGSBURY	600 CAJON ST, RDL, 92373	648 - C1
KINGSLEY	1170 WASHINGTON AV, POM, 91767	601 - B7
KINGSLEY	5625 KINGSLEY ST, MTCL, 91763	601 - H7
KINGSTON	7473 KINGSTON AV, HESP, 92345	4566 - J4
LAKE ARROWHEAD	13000 GOLDEN RULE LN, SBdC	4738 - B5
LAKE GREGORY	24683 SAN MORITZ WY, SBdC	517 - A3
LANDERS	56450 RECHE RD, SBdC, 92285	4747 - F3
LANKERSHIM	7499 LANKERSHIM AV, HIGH, 92346	577 - E6
LEHIGH	10200 LEHIGH AV, MTCL, 91763	601 - E7
LENWOOD	34374 ASH RD, SBdC, 92311	3678 - G6
LEWIS, MARY	18040 SAN BERNARDINO AV, SBdC, 92335	605 - C5
LEXINGTON	550 W LEXINGTON AV, POM, 91766	640 - J5
LIBERTY PRIMARY	12900 AMETHYST RD, VCTV, 92392	4385 - G5
LIGHTFOOT, CARLETON P	6989 KENYON WY, RCUC, 91701	573 - E5
LIME STREET	16852 LIME ST, HESP, 92345	4566 - F1
LINCOLN, ABRAHAM	255 W 13TH ST, SBDO, 92405	576 - H5
LINCOLN, ABRAHAM	444 E OLIVE ST, CLTN, 92324	606 - E5
LITEL, GERALD F	3425 EUCALYPTUS AV, CHLS, 91709	681 - C4
LIVE OAK	9522 LIVE OAK AV, SBdC, 92335	604 - D5
LOCUST	7420 LOCUST AV, FONT, 92336	575 - C6
LOMA VISTA	1556 S SULTANA AV, ONT, 91761	642 - C3
LOMITAS	12571 1ST AV, VCTV, 92392	4386 - F5
LOS AMIGOS	8498 9TH ST, RCUC, 91730	602 - F3
LOS SERRANOS	15650 PIPELINE AV, CHLS, 91709	681 - D7
LUCERNE VALLEY	10788 BARSTOW RD, SBdC	4481 - A1
LUGONIA	202 E PENNSYLVANIA AV, RDL, 92374	608 - B5
LYTLE CREEK	275 S K ST, SBDO, 92410	606 - F2
MADISON	351 W PHILLIPS BLVD, POM, 91766	640 - J3
MAGNOLIA	465 W 15TH ST, UPL, 91786	572 - B7
MANGO	7450 MANGO AV, FONT, 92336	574 - J6
MAPLE	10616 MAPLE AV, HESP, 92345	4475 - J3
MAPLE	751 S MAPLE AV, RLTO, 92316	605 - D4
MAPLE HILL	1350 MAPLE HILL RD, DBAR, 91765	680 - A3
MARIANA	10601 MANHASSET RD, APLV, 92308	4477 - J3
MARIPOSA	1605 E D ST, ONT, 91764	602 - F7
MARIPOSA	30800 PALO ALTO DR, RDL, 92373	648 - H5
MARSHALL	12045 TELEPHONE AV, CHNO, 91710	641 - G5
MARSHALL	3288 G ST, SBDO, 92405	576 - G2
MARTIN, GLEN	MOUNTAIN HOME CREEK RD, SBdC	4950 - F1
MCKINLEY	645 W OLIVE AV, RDL, 92373	648 - B1
MCKINLEY, WILLIAM	600 W JOHNSON ST, CLTN, 92324	606 - C3
MENDOZA	851 S HAMILTON BLVD, POM, 91766	640 - H3
MENTONE	1320 CRAFTON AV, SBdC, 92359	608 - J5
MESA GRANDE	9172 3RD AV, HESP, 92345	4476 - E7
MESQUITE	12951 MESQUITE RD, APLV, 92308	4388 - C4
MESQUITE TRAILS	13884 MESQUITE ST, HESP, 92345	4565 - H3
MISSION BELL	4020 CONNING ST, RivC, 92509	644 - B7
MISSION	5555 HOWARD ST, SBdC, 91762	641 - H2
MOJAVE MESA	15552 WICHITA RD, APLV, 92307	4297 - F5
MOJAVE VISTA	16100 BURWOOD AV, VCTV, 92392	4386 - D5
MONTARA	700 MONTARA RD, BARS, 92311	3680 - B5
MONTEREY	794 MONTEREY AV, SBDO, 92410	577 - A7
MONTE VISTA	4900 ORCHARD ST, MTCL, 91763	601 - F7
MONTVUE	1440 SAN BERNARDINO AV, POM, 91767	601 - C6
MORENO	4825 MORENO ST, MTCL, 91763	601 - F4
MORGAN, A H	1571 N SYCAMORE AV, RLTO, 92376	575 - H5
MORONGO VALLEY	10951 HESS BLVD, SBdC, 92256	615 - H5
MORRIS, GEORGE F	1900 W RANDALL AV, CLTN, 92324	605 - J4
MTN VIEW	2825 WALNUT ST, ONT, 91761	642 - J5
MTN VIEW	851 SANTA CLARA AV, CLAR, 91711	601 - B2
MOUNT BALDY JOINT	1 MOUNT BALDY RD, SBdC	512 - A4
MOUNT VERNON	1271 W 10TH ST, SBDO, 92411	576 - E6
MUSCOY	2119 W BLAKE ST, SBdC, 92407	576 - B2
MYERS, W A	975 N MERIDIAN AV, RLTO, 92410	576 - A6
NEWBERRY SPRINGS- (SEE PAGE 3594)	33713 NEWBERRY RD, SBdC, 92365	3684 - D6
NEWMAN	4150 WALNUT AV, CHNO, 91710	641 - D6
NEWMARK	4121 N 3RD AV, SBdC, 92407	546 - F6
NORTH PK	5378 N H ST, SBDO, 92407	546 - F5
NORTH SHORE	765 N STANFIELD CTO, SBdC	4741 - J6
NORTH TAMARIND	7961 TAMARIND AV, FONT, 92336	605 - B1
NORTH VERDEMONT	3555 MEYERS RD, SBDO, 92407	545 - H1
OAKMONT	120 W GREEN ST, CLAR, 91711	601 - D4
OAK PK	14200 LIVE OAK AV, FONT, 92337	644 - B4
OAK RIDGE	15452 VALLE VISTA DR, CHLS, 91709	681 - B6
OASIS	73175 EL PASEO DR, TNP, 92277	4892 - D5
OEHL	2525 N PALM AV, SBDO, 92346	577 - H3
OLEANDER	8650 OLEANDER AV, FONT, 92335	604 - H3
OLINDA	109 LILAC LN, BREA, 92823	710 - C6
ONTARIO CTR	835 N CENTER AV, ONT, 91764	603 - A6
ORO GRANDE (SEE PAGE 4116)	19175 3RD ST, SBdC	4206 - A3
PALM AVENUE	6565 PALM AV, SBDO, 92407	545 - J2
PALMETTO	9325 PALMETTO AV, FONT, 92335	605 - A4
PALM VISTA	74350 BASELINE RD, TNP, 92277	4892 - G7
PARKER DAM	UTAH ST & PARKER ST, SBdC	4606 - F1
PARKSIDE	3775 WATERMAN AV, SBDO, 92404	546 - J7
PK VIEW	13427 CAHUENGA RD, SBdC, 92392	4386 - A3
PEPPER TREE	1045 W 18TH ST, UPL, 91784	571 - J6
PHELAN	4167 PHELAN RD, SBdC, 92371	4473 - A6
PHILADELPHIA	600 PHILADELPHIA ST, POM, 91766	641 - A5
PINON HILLS	878 MONO RD, SBdC, 92372	4472 - B3
POPLAR	9937 POPLAR AV, FONT, 92335	604 - F6
PRESTON, LENA M	1750 N WILLOW AV, RLTO, 92376	575 - G4
PRIMROSE, VIRGINIA	751 N MAPLE AV, RLTO, 92376	575 - D7
PUEBLO	1460 E HOLT AV, POM, 91767	641 - D1
PUESTA DEL SOL	15887 ACADEMY ST, VCTV, 92394	4296 - C3
QUAIL SUMMIT	23330 QUAIL SUMMIT DR, DBAR, 91765	680 - B3
RAMONA-ALESSANDRO	670 N RAMONA AV, SBDO, 92411	576 - D7
RAMONA	4225 HOWARD ST, MTCL, 91763	641 - D2
RANCH HILLS	2 TRABUCO PL, POM, 91766	640 - E5
RANCHO VERDE	14334 PIONEER RD, APLV, 92307	4298 - A7
RANCH VIEW	3300 OLD ARCHIBALD RD, ONT, 91761	643 - A7
RANDALL PEPPER	16613 RANDALL AV, FONT, 92335	604 - J4
RECHE CANYON	3101 E CANYON VISTA DR, CLTN, 92324	647 - A3
REDWOOD	8570 REDWOOD AV, SBdC, 92335	604 - C2
RIDGEVIEW	11021 SUNNYSIDE DR, YCPA, 92399	610 - A7
RILEY	1266 N G ST, SBDO, 92405	576 - G5
RIO VISTA	13590 HAVASU RD, APLV, 92308	4387 - B2
RIO VISTA	1451 N CALIFORNIA ST, SBDO, 92411	576 - C5
ROBERTS, E NEAL	494 E NINTH ST, SBDO, 92410	576 - J6
ROGERS, PAUL	955 W LAUREL ST, CLTN, 92324	606 - B4
ROLLING RIDGE	13677 CL SAN MARCOS, CHLS, 91709	681 - A2
ROOSEVELT	1554 N GARNER AV, SBDO, 92411	576 - E5
ROOSEVELT	701 N HUNTINGTON BLVD, POM, 91768	640 - H1
SAN ANTONIO	855 E KINGSLEY AV, POM, 91767	601 - B7
SANDIA	21331 SANDIA RD, APLV, 92308	4387 - H7
SHADOW HILLS	14300 SHADOW DR, FONT, 92337	644 - C3
SIERRA VISTA	253 E 14TH ST, UPL, 91786	572 - C7
SIMPSON, SAMUEL W	1050 S LILAC AV, RLTO, 92376	605 - G4
SKY COUNTY	5520 LUCRETIA AV, RivC, 91752	683 - H4
SKYLINE NORTH	36968 CAMARILLO AV, SBdC, 92311	3589 - H6
SMILEY	1210 W CYPRESS AV, RDL, 92373	648 - A2
SMITH, GERALD A	9551 LINDEN AV, SBdC, 92316	605 - D4
SOUTH TAMARIND	8561 TAMARIND AV, FONT, 92335	605 - B2
STORK	5646 JASPER ST, RCUC, 91701	572 - F2
SULTANA	1845 S SULTANA AV, ONT, 91761	642 - C4
SUMNER	1770 SUMNER AV, CLAR, 91711	571 - A7
SUNNYSLOPE	7050 38TH ST, RivC, 92509	644 - J7
SYCAMORE	1075 W 13TH ST, UPL, 91786	602 - A1
SYCAMORE	225 W 8TH ST, CLAR, 91711	601 - D2
SYCAMORE ROCKS	23450 SOUTH RD, APLV, 92307	4298 - D2
TERRACE VIEW	22731 GRAND TERRACE RD, GTER, 92313	646 - F3
TERRA VISTA	7497 MOUNTAIN VIEW DR, RCUC, 91730	573 - E7
THOMPSON	7401 CHURCH AV, HIGH, 92346	577 - J5
THOMSON	310 W MOUNTAIN VIEW ST, BARS, 92311	3679 - G3
TOKAY	7846 TOKAY AV, FONT, 92336	574 - G7
TOPAZ	14110 BEECH ST, HESP, 92345	4475 - H5
TRAPP, W J C	2720 N RIVERSIDE AV, RLTO, 92377	575 - E2
TRONA	83600 TRONA RD, SBdC, 93562	2145 - A2
TROTH STREET	5565 TROTH ST, RivC, 91752	683 - J4
TWENTYNINE PALMS	74350 PLAYA VISTA DR, TNP, 92277	4892 - G3
UPLAND	601 N 5TH AV, UPL, 91786	602 - C2
URBITA	771 S J ST, SBDO, 92410	606 - F3
VALENCIA	541 W 22ND ST, UPL, 91784	572 - B4
VALLE VISTA	7727 VALLE VISTA DR, RCUC, 91730	602 - F1
VALLEY	12333 8TH ST, YCPA, 92399	649 - F3
VALLEY OF ENCHANTMENT	22836 FIR LN, SBdC	516 - E2
VEJAR	950 W GRAND AV, POM, 91766	640 - H3
VERMONT	3695 VERMONT ST, SBdC, 92407	545 - J7
VICTORIA	1505 RICHARDSON ST, SBDO, 92354	607 - C5
VICTORIA GROVES	10950 EMERSON ST, RCUC, 91701	573 - C5
VICTOR PRIMARY	15478 6TH ST, VCTV, 92392	4296 - E5
VILLAGE	14711 MOJAVE DR, VCTV, 92394	4295 - J6
VINEYARD	1500 E 6TH ST, ONT, 91764	602 - F5
VISTA COLORADO	WASHINGTON ST & BAILEY AV, NDLS, 92363	3620 - B6
VISTA	550 VISTA DR, CLAR, 91711	601 - C5
WALLACE	1201 11TH ST, PRKR	4844 - J1
WALNUT AVENUE	5550 WALNUT AV, CHNO, 91710	641 - H6
WARM SPRINGS	7497 STERLING AV, HIGH, 92410	577 - D6
WASHINGTON	975 E 9TH ST, POM, 91766	641 - B2
WEST HERITAGE	13690 W CONSTITUTION WY, FONT, 92336	574 - A7
WESTMONT	1780 W 9TH ST, POM, 91766	640 - F3
WEST RANDALL	15620 RANDALL AV, SBdC, 92335	604 - F4
WESTSIDE PK	18270 CASABA RD, ADEL, 92301	4204 - J6
WICKMAN, MICHAEL G	SOQUEL CANYON PKWY & PINEHURST, CHLS, 91709	711 - E1
WILDWOOD	35972 SUSAN ST, YCPA, 92399	650 - C6
WILSON	2894 BELLE ST, SBDO, 92404	576 - J2
WILSON, WOODROW	750 S 8TH ST, CLTN, 92324	646 - D1
WINDROWS	6855 VICTORIA PARK LN, RCUC, 91739	573 - G5
WRIGHTWOOD	1175 STATE HWY 2, SBdC, 92397	4652 - C2
YERMO (SEE PAGE 3592)	38280 GLEASON ST, SBdC	3682 - C1
YUCAIPA	12375 CALIFORNIA ST, YCPA, 92399	650 - A3
YUCCA LOMA	21351 YUCCA LOMA RD, APLV, 92308	4387 - H2
YUCCA MESA	3380 AVALON AV, SBdC, 92284	4818 - C7
YUCCA VALLEY	7601 HOPI TR, YUCA, 92284	4957 - E3
ZIMMERMAN, WALTER	11050 LINDEN ST, SBdC, 92316	645 - D1

SCHOOLS - PUBLIC HIGH

FEATURE NAME	Address City, ZIP Code	PAGE-GRID
ALTA LOMA	8880 BASELINE RD, RCUC, 91701	572 - G6
APPLE VALLEY	11837 NAVAJO RD, APLV, 92308	4387 - J6
AYALA, RUBEN S	14255 PEYTON AV, CHLS, 91709	681 - C3
BAKER	SCHOOLHOUSE LN & DEATH VALLEY, SBdC	2971 - E3
BARSTOW	430 S 1ST AV, BARS, 92311	3679 - G3
BIG BEAR	351 MAPLE LN, SBdC, 92314	4742 - F6
BIRCH, ERIC	7930 LOCUST AV, SBdC, 92336	605 - C1
BLOOMINGTON	10750 LAUREL AV, SBdC, 92316	645 - B1
BOYS REPUB	3493 GRAND AV, CHLS, 91709	681 - C3
BUENA VISTA	13509 RAMONA AV, CHNO, 91710	681 - E2
CAJON	1200 W HILL DR, SBDO, 92407	546 - E5
CENTRAL HIGH (CONT)	405 N 2ND AV, BARS, 92311	3679 - H2
CHAFFEY	1245 N EUCLID AV, ONT, 91762	602 - B5
CHAPARRAL	9258 MALPASO RD, SBdC, 92371	4473 - A7
CHAUTAUQUA ALTERNATIVE	525 N MAPLE LN, SBdC, 92314	4742 - F7
CHINO	5472 PARK PL, CHNO, 91710	641 - H6
CHINO HILLS	BUTTERFIELD RANCH & ST GAUDENS, CHLS, 91709	711 - G1
CITRUS	9820 CITRUS AV, FONT, 92335	604 - G5
CLAREMONT	1601 N INDIAN HILL BLVD, CLAR, 91711	601 - C1
COLTON	777 W VALLEY BLVD, CLTN, 92324	606 - C6
DIAMOND RANCH	100 DIAMOND RANCH RD, DBAR, 91765	640 - F7
DON ANTONIO LUGO	13400 PIPELINE AV, CHNO, 91710	681 - D1
EAGLE SUMMIT ACADEMY	3850 TRINITY RD, SBdC, 92371	4563 - A1
EISENHOWER	1321 N LILAC AV, RLTO, 92376	575 - G6
ETIWANDA	13500 VICTORIA ST, RCUC, 91739	573 - J5
FONTANA	9453 CITRUS AV, FONT, 92335	604 - G4
GAREY	321 W LEXINGTON AV, POM, 91766	640 - J4
GOODWILL	15733 1ST ST, VCTV, 92392	4296 - E4
GRANITE HILLS	22900 ESAWS RD, APLV, 92307	4388 - B1
GREEN VALLEY	35912 AVE H, YCPA, 92399	650 - C6
HESPERIA	9898 MAPLE AV, HESP, 92345	4475 - J5
HILLSIDE	1558 W 9TH ST, UPL, 91786	601 - H3
INTL POLYTECHNIC	3801 TEMPLE AV, LACo, 91768	640 - A3
JURUPA VALLEY	10551 BELLEGRAVE AV, RivC, 91752	683 - J2
KAISER	11155 ALMOND AV, FONT, 92337	644 - C2
LUCERNE VALLEY (SEE PAGE 4300)	33233 RABBIT SPRINGS RD, SBdC	4391 - A7
MILLER	6821 OLEANDER AV, FONT, 92336	574 - H5
MILOR	266 W RANDALL AV, RLTO, 92376	605 - G4
MOJAVE	16633 LEMON ST, HESP, 92345	4476 - E3
MONTCLAIR	4725 BENITO ST, MTCL, 91763	601 - F6
MONUMENT ALTERNATIVE	72700 HATCH RD, TNP, 92277	4892 - C6
MTN	23332 CRESTLINE RD, SBdC	516 - G3
NEEDLES	1600 WASHINGTON ST, NDLS, 92363	3620 - B5
NUEVA VISTA	6836 34TH ST, RivC, 92509	645 - A7
ONTARIO	901 W FRANCIS ST, ONT, 91762	642 - A4
ORANGEWOOD	515 TEXAS ST, RDL, 92374	608 - A7
PACIFIC	1020 E PACIFIC ST, SBDO, 92404	577 - B4
PARKER	1600 S KOFA AV, PRKR	4844 - J1
PK WEST	1540 W 2ND ST, POM, 91766	640 - F2
POMONA ALTERNATIVE	1530 W 2ND ST, POM, 91766	640 - G2
POMONA	475 BANGOR ST, POM, 91767	601 - A5
RANCHO CUCAMONGA	11801 LARK DR, RCUC, 91701	573 - E5
REDLANDS EAST VALLEY	31000 COLTON AV, SBdC, 92374	608 - H6
REDLANDS	840 E CITRUS AV, RDL, 92374	608 - D7
RIALTO	595 S EUCALYPTUS AV, SBDO, 92376	605 - J3
RIM OF THE WORLD	27400 HWY 18, SBdC	517 - H4
SAN ANDREAS	3232 E PACIFIC ST, SBDO, 92346	577 - G4
SAN ANTONIO	125 W SAN JOSE AV, CLAR, 91711	601 - D5
SAN BERNARDINO	1850 N E ST, SBDO, 92405	576 - G4
SAN GORGONIO	2299 E PACIFIC ST, SBDO, 92404	577 - F5
SERRANO	9292 SHEEP CREEK RD, SBdC, 92371	4563 - A1
SIERRA	570 E 9TH ST, SBDO, 92410	577 - A6
SILVERADO	14048 COBALT RD, VCTV, 92392	4385 - E2
SILVER VALLEY (SEE PAGE 3590)	35484 DAGGETT-YERMO RD, SBdC	3681 - E2
SKY CONT	59273 SUNNYSLOPE DR, YUCA, 92284	4958 - E1

FEATURE NAME Address City, ZIP Code	PAGE-GRID
SLOVER MTN 325 HERMOSA ST, CLTN, 92324	606 - B6
SULTANA 17311 SULTANA ST, HESP, 92345	4566 - G1
TRONA 83600 TRONA RD, SBdC, 93562	2145 - A2
TWENTYNINE PALMS 72750 WILDCAT WY, TNP, 92277	4892 - C5
UPLAND 565 W 11TH ST, UPL, 91786	602 - B2
VALLEY VIEW 1801 E 6TH ST, ONT, 91764	602 - G4
VICTOR VALLEY 16500 MOJAVE DR, VCTV, 92392	4296 - D5
WASHINGTON 900 E C ST, CLTN, 92324	606 - E5
WILLOW PK 21950 NISQUALLY RD, APLV, 92308	4387 - J4
YUCAIPA 33000 YUCAIPA BLVD, YCPA, 92399	649 - D3
YUCCA VALLEY 7600 SAGE AV, YUCA, 92284	4957 - H3

SCHOOLS - PUBLIC INTERMEDIATE

FEATURE NAME Address City, ZIP Code	PAGE-GRID
EL ROBLE 665 N MOUNTAIN AV, CLAR, 91711	601 - B3
ETIWANDA 6925 ETIWANDA AV, RCUC, 91739	573 - H5
HENCK, MARY P 730 RHINE RD, SBdC	4737 - G7
LIBERTY 12900 AMETHYST RD, VCTV, 92392	4385 - G4
SILVER VALLEY (SEE PAGE 3590) 33525 PONNAY ST, SBdC	3681 - E7
SUMMIT 5959 EAST AV, RCUC, 91739	573 - J3

SCHOOLS - PUBLIC JUNIOR HIGH

FEATURE NAME Address City, ZIP Code	PAGE-GRID
ALTA LOMA 9000 LEMON AV, RCUC, 91701	572 - G4
CANYON HILLS 2500 MADRUGADA DR, CHLS, 91709	680 - J2
HESPERIA 10275 CYPRESS AV, HESP, 92345	4476 - B4
HOOK, IMOGENE G 15000 HOOK BLVD, VCTV, 92394	4296 - A6
LA CONTENTA 7050 LA CONTENTA RD, YUCA, 92284	4958 - E2
MAGNOLIA 13150 MOUNTAIN AV, CHNO, 91710	642 - A7
PIONEER 245 W 18TH ST, UPL, 91784	572 - B5
RAMONA 4575 WALNUT AV, CHNO, 91710	641 - E6
TOWNSEND 15359 ILEX DR, CHLS, 91709	681 - C6
TWENTYNINE PALMS 5798 UTAH TR, TNP, 92277	4892 - G3
UPLAND 444 E 11TH ST, UPL, 91786	602 - C2
VICTOR VALLEY 16925 FORREST AV, VCTV, 92392	4296 - E5
VINEYARD 6440 MAYBERRY AV, RCUC, 91737	573 - A4
WOODCREST 2725 S CAMPUS AV, ONT, 91761	642 - D6
YUCAIPA 12358 6TH ST, YCPA, 92399	649 - G4

SCHOOLS - PUBLIC MIDDLE

FEATURE NAME Address City, ZIP Code	PAGE-GRID
ALDER 7555 ALDER AV, FONT, 92336	575 - B6
ALMERIA 7723 ALMERIA AV, FONT, 92336	574 - F7
APPLE VALLEY 12555 NAVAJO RD, APLV, 92308	4387 - J5
ARROWVIEW 2299 N G ST, SBDO, 92405	576 - G3
BARSTOW 500 S AVE G, BARS, 92311	3679 - F4
BIG BEAR 41275 BIG BEAR BLVD, BBLK	4811 - G1
BLOOMINGTON 18829 ORANGE ST, SBdC, 92316	605 - E7
CHAPARRAL 1405 SPRUCE TREE DR, DBAR, 91765	680 - B3
CLEMENT 501 E PENNSYLVANIA AV, RDL, 92374	608 - C5
COBALT 13801 COBALT RD, VCTV, 92392	4385 - F2
COLE 3126 E AVE I, LAN, 93535	368 - B2
COLTON 670 W LAUREL ST, CLTN, 92324	606 - C4
COPE 1000 W CYPRESS AV, RDL, 92373	648 - B2
CUCAMONGA 7611 HELLMAN AV, RCUC, 91730	572 - H7
CURTIS 1472 E 6TH ST, SBDO, 92410	577 - C7
DE ANZA 1450 S SULTANA AV, ONT, 91761	642 - C3
DEL VALLEJO 1855 E LYNWOOD DR, SBDO, 92404	577 - D2
EMERSON 635 LINCOLN AV, POM, 91767	601 - A7
FONTANA 8425 MANGO AV, FONT, 92335	605 - A2
FREMONT 725 W FRANKLIN AV, POM, 91766	640 - J4
FRISBIE 1442 N EUCALYPTUS, RLTO, 92376	575 - J5
GOLDEN VALLEY 3800 WATERMAN AV, SBDO, 92404	546 - J7
HARRIS, RUTH 11150 ALDER AV, SBdC, 92316	645 - B1
JEHUE, WILLIAM 1500 EUCALYPTUS AV, CLTN, 92324	605 - J4
KENNEDY 1000 ARMORY RD, BARS, 92311	3680 - A5
KING JR, MARTIN LUTHER 1250 N MEDICAL CENTER DR, SBDO, 92411	576 - D5
KOLB, BEN F 2351 N SPRUCE AV, RLTO, 92377	575 - F3
KUCERA, ETHEL 2140 W BUENA VISTA DR, RLTO, 92377	545 - B7
LORBEER 501 S DIAMOND BAR BLVD, DBAR, 91765	640 - C7
MARSHALL, JOHN 1921 ARROYO AV, POM, 91768	640 - E1
MESA LINDA 13001 MESA LINDA AV, VCTV, 92392	4385 - D5
MOORE 1550 E HIGHLAND AV, RDL, 92374	648 - F1
MUSSER, RUTH 10789 TERRA VISTA PKWY, RCUC, 91730	573 - C7
NEEDLES 1600 WASHINGTON ST, NDLS, 92363	3620 - B5
OAKS 1221 S OAKS AV, ONT, 91762	641 - J2
PALOMARES 2211 N ORANGE GROVE AV, POM, 91767	601 - A5
PK VIEW 34875 TAHOE DR, YCPA, 92399	609 - J7
PINON MESA 9298 SHEEP CREEK RD, SBdC, 92371	4563 - A1
QUAIL VALLEY 10050 ARROWHEAD RD, SBdC, 92371	4474 - F5
RANCHERO 17607 RANCHERO ST, HESP, 92345	4566 - H5
RANCHO CUCAMONGA 10022 FERON BLVD, RCUC, 91730	603 - A3
RIALTO 324 N PALM AV, RLTO, 92376	605 - G1
RICHARDSON PREP 455 S K ST, SBDO, 92410	606 - F2
RIVERVIEW 15350 RIVERVIEW RD, SBdC	3936 - A4
SEQUOIA 9452 HEMLOCK AV, SBdC, 92335	604 - E4
SERRANO 3131 PIEDMONT DR, SBDO, 92346	577 - G2
SERRANO 4725 SAN JOSE ST, MTCL, 91763	601 - F5
SHANDIN HILLS 4301 LITTLE MOUNTAIN DR, SBDO, 92407	546 - E6
SHEPPARD, HARRY R 18000 MCCOY CIR, VCTV, 92394	4205 - F6
SIMONS 900 E FRANKLIN AV, POM, 91766	641 - A4
SOUTHRIDGE 14500 LIVE OAK AV, FONT, 92337	644 - C3
TERRACE HILLS 22579 DE BERRY ST, GTER, 92313	646 - F4
TRUMAN, HARRY S 16200 MALLORY DR, FONT, 92335	604 - G5
VERNON 9775 VERNON AV, MTCL, 91763	601 - H6
VINA DANKS 1020 N VINE ST, ONT, 91762	602 - B6
VISTA CAMPANA 20700 THUNDERBIRD RD, APLV, 92307	4297 - E5
WILTSEY, RAY 1450 E G ST, ONT, 91764	602 - F7
YOKLEY, GRACE 2947 S TURNER AV, ONT, 91761	643 - A6

SHOPPING - COMMUNITY

FEATURE NAME Address City, ZIP Code	PAGE-GRID
ALTA LOMA CTR BASELINE RD & ARCHIBALD AV, RCUC, 91701	572 - J6
ALTA LOMA COUNTRY VILLAGE BASELINE RD & CARNELIAN ST, RCUC, 91701	572 - G6
ALTA LOMA PLAZA 19TH ST & CARNELIAN ST, RCUC, 91701	572 - F5
ALTA LOMA SQUARE 19TH ST & CARNELIAN ST, RCUC, 91701	572 - F5
BEST MARSHALLS PLAZA, THE W 2ND ST & N G ST, SBDO, 92410	606 - G1
BIG BEAR LAKEVIEW CTR BIG BEAR BLVD & FOX FARM RD, BBLK	4741 - J7
BLUE JAY VILLAGE 27264 HWY 189, SBdC	517 - G2
BROOKSIDE PLAZA ALABAMA ST & BARTON RD, RDL, 92373	647 - H1
CALIMESA PLAZA COUNTY LINE RD & CALIMESA BL, CALI, 92320	649 - G7
CC MARKET PLACE SOQUEL CYN & BUTTERFIELD RANCH, CHLS, 91709	711 - F1
CENTRAL PK PLAZA BASELINE RD & MILLIKEN AV, RCUC, 91730	573 - D6
CENTRAL PLAZA 10254 CENTRAL AV, MTCL, 91763	601 - G7
CENTRE POINTE AT COLTON E SANTO ANTONIO & S MT VERNON, CLTN, 92324	646 - F1
CHINO HILLS COURT YARD GRAND AV & PEYTON DR, CHLS, 91709	681 - C2
CHINO HILLS MARKET PLACE CHINO HILLS PKWY & PIPELINE AV, CHLS, 91709	681 - D5
CHINO HILLS PLAZA PIPELINE AV, CHLS, 91709	681 - D4
CHINO HILLS PROMENADE 4200 CHINO HILLS PKWY, CHLS, 91709	681 - E5
CHINO SPECTRUM 71 FRWY & GRAND AV, CHNO, 91710	681 - D2
CHINO TOWNE CTR POMONA FRWY & CENTRAL AV, CHNO, 91710	641 - G5
CHINO TOWNE PROMENADE PHILADELPHIA ST & VERNON AV, CHNO, 91710	641 - H5
CHINO TOWN SQUARE PHILADELPHIA ST & BENSON AV, CHNO, 91710	641 - H5
CHINO VALLEY SHOPPING CTR CENTRAL AV & WALNUT AV, CHNO, 91710	641 - G6
CITRUS CTR CITRUS AV & FOOTHILL BL, FONT, 92335	604 - G1
CITRUS PLAZA ALABAMA ST & LUGONIA AV, SBdC, 92374	607 - H5
CITRUS VILLAGE CTR REDLANDS BLVD & CYPRESS AV, RDL, 92373	648 - D1
CLUB POWER CTR 295 E CAROLINE ST, SBDO, 92408	606 - J7
COUNTRY FAIR CTR CENTRAL AV & PHILADELPHIA ST, CHNO, 91710	641 - G5
COURTYARD, THE E WASHINGTON ST & I-215, CLTN, 92324	646 - F2
CROSSROADS MARKETPLACE PEYTON DR & CHINO VALLEY FRWY, CHLS, 91709	681 - A1
DEER CREEK VILLAGE FOOTHILL BL & HAVEN AV, RCUC, 91730	603 - B1
DIAMOND BAR TOWNE CENTRE 1128 S DIAMOND BAR BLVD, DBAR, 91765	680 - C3
EXCHANGE, THE 8770 BASELINE AV, RCUC, 91730	572 - F7
FACTORY MERCHANTS AT BARSTOW- (SEE PAGE 3758) 2552 MERCANTILE WY, BARS, 92311	3759 - B2
FONTANA SQUARE FOOTHILL BL & MANGO BL, FONT, 92335	605 - A1
FOOTHILL & TOWNE CTR E FOOTHILL BLVD & N TOWNE AV, POM, 91767	601 - A2
FOOTHILL MARKETPLACE FOOTHILL BL & ONTARIO FRWY, RCUC, 91739	603 - H2
FOOTHILL VILLAGE SHOPPING CTR 9309 FOOTHILL BLVD, RCUC, 91730	602 - H2
GORDEN RANCH MARKET PLACE 2587 CHINO HILLS PKWY, CHLS, 91709	681 - A5
GREAT INDOORS CENTER, THE HWY 71 & PEYTON DR, CHLS, 91709	641 - A7
GRISWOLDS OLD HOUSE 555 W FOOTHILL BLVD, CLAR, 91711	601 - C2
HAVEN VILLAGE HAVEN AV & LEMON AV, RCUC, 91737	573 - B4
HERITAGE VILLAGE CTR BASELINE RD & CHERRY AV, FONT, 92336	574 - C6
HESPERIA MARKETPLACE 15555 MAIN ST, HESP, 92345	4476 - C6
HESPERIA STATER BROS SHOPPING-CTR MAIN ST & MARIPOSA RD, HESP, 92345	4475 - F5
HESPERIA TOWN CTR MAIN ST & I AV, HESP, 92345	4476 - G6
HI DESERT PLAZA HESPERIA RD & BEAR VALLEY RD, VCTV, 92392	4386 - F6
HIGHLAND VILLAGE PLAZA BOULDER AV & BASELINE ST, HIGH, 92346	578 - A5
HUGHES CTR MARIPOSA RD & COTTONWOOD AV, VCTV, 92392	4386 - A6
INLAND EMPIRE CTR I-10 & SIERRA AV, FONT, 92335	604 - J6
INTERLAKEN CTR BIG BEAR BLVD & FOX FARM RD, BBLK	4741 - H7
JOSHUA VILLAGE 57500 TWENTYNINE PALMS HWY, YUCA, 92284	4958 - A2
KIOWA PLAZA BEAR VALLEY RD & KIOWA RD, APLV, 92308	4387 - F6
LABAND PLAZA GRAND AV & CHINO HILLS PKWY, CHLS, 91709	680 - H3
LABAND VILLAGE GRAND AV & CHINO HILLS PKWY, CHLS, 91709	680 - H4
LAKE ARROWHEAD VILLAGE-SHOPPING CTR 28200 HWY 189, SBdC	518 - A1
LAURATION CTR 2401 S VINEYARD AV, ONT, 91761	642 - H5
LIBERTY VILLAGE BEAR VALLEY RD & AMETHYST RD, VCTV, 92392	4385 - G7
LOMA LINDA PLAZA MOUNTAIN VIEW AV & BARTON RD, LMLN, 92354	647 - E1
MASI PLAZA FOOTHILL BL & ROCHESTER AV, RCUC, 91730	603 - E2
MIDTOWN SQUARE MAIN ST & C AV, HESP, 92345	4476 - F6
MILLERS OUTPOST PLAZA FOOTHILL BL & ARCHIBALD AV, RCUC, 91730	602 - J1
MONTCLAIR EAST CENTRAL AV & MORENO ST, MTCL, 91763	601 - G4
MTN GREEN CTR 1255 W 7TH ST, UPL, 91786	601 - J4
MTN PLAZA W 16TH ST & N MOUNTAIN AV, UPL, 91784	571 - J6
MTN SQUARE 250 S MOUNTAIN AV, UPL, 91786	601 - J4
MTN VILLAGE PLAZA RIVERSIDE DR & MOUNTAIN AV, CHNO, 91710	642 - A6
NEW ORLEANS SQUARE N MOUNTAIN AV & W ARROW HWY, UPL, 91786	601 - J2
ONTARIO PLAZA N MOUNTAIN AV & W 4TH ST, ONT, 91762	601 - J6
ONTARIO VILLAGE SAN ANTONIO AV & W HOLT BLVD, ONT, 91762	642 - B1
ORANGE STREET PLAZA I-10 & ORANGE ST, RDL, 92374	608 - B7
ORCHARD PLAZA SAB BERNARDINO & VINEYARD, RCUC, 91730	602 - G1
PADUA HILLS CTR BASELINE RD & MILLS AV, CLAR, 91711	571 - E7
PALM COURT I-10 & SIERRA AV, FONT, 92337	604 - J7
PAYNE RANCH CTR GRAND AV & PEYTON DR, CHLS, 91709	681 - B2
PHILLIP VILLAGE CTR VILLAGE LP RD & TANGLEWOOD DR, POM, 91766	640 - G5
PLAZA CONTINENTAL INLAND EMPIRE BL & MERCEDES LN, ONT, 91764	603 - C7
PLAZA LAS GLORIAS MOUNT VERNON AV & E OLIVE ST, CLTN, 92324	606 - E5
PLAZA, THE FOOTHILL BL & SAN ANTONIO AV, UPL, 91786	602 - A1
QUAD CITIES CTR BEAR VALLEY RD & APPLE VALLEY, APLV, 92308	4387 - B6
RANCHERIAS PLAZA RANCHERIAS RD & HWY 18, APLV, 92307	4297 - E5
RANCHO TOWN CTR 9080 FOOTHILL BLVD, RCUC, 91730	602 - G1
RENAISSANCE CTR CEDAR AV & FOOTHILL BLVD, RLTO, 92376	605 - D1
RIALTO SHOPPING CTR BASELINE RD & RIVERSIDE AV, RLTO, 92376	575 - G6
ROLLING RIDGE PLAZA 2959 CHINO AV, CHLS, 91709	681 - A1
SIERRA PLAZA SOUTH 10048 S SIERRA AV, FONT, 92335	604 - J6
SOUTHRIDGE PLAZA CHERRY AV & LIVE OAK AV, FONT, 92337	644 - D3
SSE PLAZA E HIGHLAND AV & N STERLING AV, SBDO, 92404	577 - D3
STATER BROS SHOPPING CTR ARMORY RD & MURIEL DR, BARS, 92311	3679 - J4
STATER BROTHERS CTR WABASH AV & E LUGONIA AV, RDL, 92374	608 - G5
STATER BROTHERS PLAZA ARCHIBALD AV & 19TH ST, RCUC, 91737	572 - J5
STERLING PLAZA E HIGHLAND AV & N STERLING AV, SBDO, 92404	577 - D3
SUNRISE CTR BASELINE RD & CARNELIAN ST, RCUC, 91730	572 - F7
TANGER OUTLET CTR- (SEE PAGE 3758) LENWOOD RD & MOJAVE FRWY, BARS, 92311	3759 - A3
TERRA VISTA PROMENADE FOOTHILL BL & ROCHESTER AV, RCUC, 91730	603 - E1
TERRA VISTA VILLAGE BASELINE RD & HAVEN AV, RCUC, 91701	573 - B6
THOMAS WINERY PLAZA VINEYARD AV & FOOTHILL BLVD, RCUC, 91730	602 - G1
TOWN CTR SQUARE FOOTHILL BL & SPRUCE AV, RCUC, 91730	603 - C1
TOWN SQUARE CTR MONTE VISTA AV & MORENO ST, MTCL, 91763	601 - F4
TRI CITY CTR INDUSTRIAL PARK AV & ALABAMA, RDL, 92374	607 - J6
TRI CITY SHOPPING CTR S WATERMAN AV & HOSPITALITY LN, SBDO, 92408	607 - A6
UPLAND CTR FOOTHILL BLVD & N MOUNTAIN AV, UPL, 91786	601 - J2
UPLAND SQUARE FOOTHILL BL & SAN ANTONIO AV, UPL, 91786	602 - A2
UPLAND VILLAGE FOOTHILL BL & EUCLID AV, UPL, 91786	602 - C1
UPTOWN AND CC FOOTHILL BL & EUCLID AV, UPL, 91786	602 - B2
VALLEY CENTER, THE E ARROW HWY & N TOWNE AV, POM, 91767	601 - A4
VICTOR PLAZA LA PAZ DR & 7TH ST, VCTV, 92392	4296 - C7
VICTOR VALLEY PLAZA COTTONWOOD AV & BEAR VALLEY RD, VCTV, 92392	4386 - A6
VICTOR VALLEY TOWN CTR HESPERIA RD & BEAR VALLEY RD, VCTV, 92392	4386 - F6
VILLAGE AT INDIAN HILL N EAST END AV & E HOLT AV, POM, 91767	641 - C1
VILLAGE CENTER, THE BEAR VALLEY RD & AMARGOSA RD, VCTV, 92392	4385 - J6
VILLAGE FAIR 40794 VILLAGE DR, BBLK	4811 - E2
VILLAGE GROVE CTR FOOTHILL BL & GROVE AV, UPL, 91786	602 - E1
VINEYARD FREEWAY CTR N BAKER AV & E 4TH ST, ONT, 91764	602 - F6
VINEYARD GATEWAY CTR FOOTHILL BLVD & VINEYARD AV, RCUC, 91730	602 - G1
VINEYARD ONTARIO, THE N VINEYARD AV & E 4TH ST, ONT, 91764	602 - G5
VINEYARDS MARKETPLACE MILLIKEN AV & KENYON WY, RCUC, 91701	573 - D4
VINEYARD VALLEY CTR SIERRA AV & VALLEY BLVD, FONT, 92335	604 - J6
WEST HIGHLAND SHOPPING CTR W HIGHLAND AV & 30 FRWY, SBDO, 92411	576 - D4
WEST SIDE PLAZA W BASELINE ST & N MED CTR DR, SBDO, 92411	576 - D5
WOODVIEW PLAZA 4191 CHINO HILLS PKWY, CHLS, 91709	681 - E5
YUCAIPA SQUARE YUCAIPA BL & 5TH ST, YCPA, 92399	649 - H3

SHOPPING - REGIONAL

FEATURE NAME Address City, ZIP Code	PAGE-GRID
BARSTOW MALL CAL AV & E MAIN ST, BARS, 92311	3680 - B4
CAROUSEL MALL N E ST & W 2ND ST, SBDO, 92401	606 - G1
COVINA TOWN SQUARE N AZUSA AV & W ARROW HWY, COV, 91722	388 - D3
HIGHLAND AVENUE PLAZA E HIGHLAND AV & BOULDER AV, SBDO, 92346	577 - J3
HIGHLAND AVENUE PLAZA E HIGHLAND AV & BOULDER AV, SBDO, 92346	578 - A3
INLAND CTR 460 S INLAND CENTER DR, SBDO, 92408	606 - G4
MALL OF VICTOR VALLEY, THE 14400 BEAR VALLEY RD, VCTV, 92392	4385 - H6
MONTCLAIR PLAZA 5060 PLAZA LN, MTCL, 91763	601 - F4
ONTARIO MILLS SHOPPING CTR 4TH ST & MILLIKEN AV, ONT, 91764	603 - E6
REDLANDS MALL 100 ORANGE ST, RDL, 92373	608 - B7
TERRA VISTA TOWN CTR FOOTHILL BLVD & HAVEN AV, RCUC, 91730	603 - B1

TRANSPORTATION

FEATURE NAME Address City, ZIP Code	PAGE-GRID
AMTRAK & GREYHOUND BUS STA-BARSTOW 681 N 1ST AV, BARS, 92311	3679 - H2
AMTRAK NEEDLES STA 900 FRONT ST, NDLS, 92363	3620 - D5
AMTRAK ONTARIO STA 228 S PLUM AV, ONT, 91761	642 - C1
AMTRAK POMONA STA S MAIN ST & W 1ST ST, POM, 91768	640 - J1
AMTRAK SAN BERNARDINO STA 1170 W 3RD ST, SBDO, 92410	606 - E1
AMTRAK VICTORVILLE STA 16858 E ST, VCTV, 92392	4296 - F4
CLAREMONT TRANSCENTER 200 W 1ST ST, CLAR, 91711	601 - D4
GREYHOUND BUS STA 16886 C ST, VCTV, 92392	4296 - F4
GREYHOUND BUS STA 888 S INDIAN HILL BLVD, CLAR, 91711	601 - D5
GREYHOUND BUS STA SAN-BERNARDINO 596 N G ST, SBDO, 92410	576 - G7
METROLINK CLAREMONT 200 W 1ST ST, CLAR, 91711	601 - D4
METROLINK DOWNTOWN POMONA 101 W 1ST ST, POM, 91768	640 - J1
METROLINK EAST ONTARIO STA 3330 E FRANCIS ST, ONT, 91761	643 - B4
METROLINK FONTANA STA 16777 ORANGE WY, FONT, 92335	604 - J3
METROLINK MONTCLAIR STA 5091 RICHTON ST, MTCL, 91763	601 - F4
METROLINK RCHO CUCAMONGA STA 11208 AZUSA CT, RCUC, 91730	603 - D3
METROLINK RIALTO STA 261 S PALM AV, RLTO, 92376	605 - G2
METROLINK SAN BERNARDINO STA 1204 W 3RD ST, SBDO, 92410	606 - E1
METROLINK UPLAND STA 300 E A ST, UPL, 91786	602 - C3
MONTCLAIR TRANSCENTER 5091 RICHTON ST, MTCL, 91763	601 - G3
OMNITRANS 1700 W 5TH ST, SBDO, 92411	576 - D7

WINERIES

FEATURE NAME Address City, ZIP Code	PAGE-GRID
BIANE 10013 8TH ST, RCUC, 91730	603 - A4
FILIPPI, JOSEPH 12467 BASELINE RD, RCUC, 91739	573 - G6
FILIPPI, JOSEPH 2803 E GUASTI RD, ONT, 91761	603 - A7
GALLEANO 4231 WINEVILLE RD, RivC, 91752	643 - G7
RANCHO DE PHILO 10050 WILSON AV, RCUC, 91737	573 - A2
SAN ANTONIO 2802 S MILLIKEN AV, ONT, 91761	643 - D6

RAND McNALLY

Thank you for purchasing The Thomas Guide®! Our goal is to provide you with the information you need.

Please complete the information below so we will be able to serve you better in the future. We value your comments and suggestions for improvements, and feedback on corrections. This information can also be e-mailed to: **consumeraffairs@randmcnally.com**. *(This information is for internal use ONLY and will not be distributed or sold to any external third party.)*

The Thomas Guide® Title:

ISBN# **Edition Year:**

2ND FOLD LINE

Today's Date: ____________

1. Your Name: ____________ Title: ____________
2. Address ☐ Business ☐ Personal: ____________
3. City/State/Zip: ____________
4. Phone Number: ____________ E-mail address: ____________
5. Age Group: ☐ 18 – 24 ☐ 25-31 ☐ 32-40 ☐ 41- 50 ☐ 51+
6. Company name: ____________
7. Type of business: ____________
8. Where did you purchase this Thomas Guide? (store name & location) ____________
9. How often do you purchase an updated Thomas Guide? ☐ Annually ☐ Every 2 Years ☐ Other ____________
10. How often do you use it? ☐ Daily ☐ Weekly ☐ Monthly ☐ Other ____________
11. What do you use your Thomas Guide for?
    ☐ Find Address ☐ Find Unincorporated Areas ☐ Navigation ☐ Identifying Routes ☐ Other ____________
12. Do you use it for: ☐ Business ☐ Personal ☐ Both

1st FOLD LINE

13. If you have used the Digital Edition software:
    What features do you use? ____________
    How often do you use it? ☐ Daily ☐ Weekly ☐ Monthly ☐ Other ____________
14. What information would you add/correct in this Thomas Guide to better meet your needs?
    Map Page # ____________ Grid # ____________ Index Page # ____________
    ☐ Street Name Missing ☐ Street Name Misspelled ☐ Street Information Incorrect
    ☐ Incorrect Location for Point of Interest ☐ Index Error ☐ Other
    ____
    ____
15. Please provide any additional comments and suggestions you have: ____________
    ____
    ____
16. Would you like to receive information about updated editions and special offers from Rand McNally? ☐ Yes ☐ No

CUT ALONG DOTTED LINE

CUT ALONG DOTTED LINE

TG-LTri

2nd FOLD LINE

NO POSTAGE
NECESSARY
IF MAILED
IN THE
UNITED STATES

BUSINESS REPLY MAIL

FIRST-CLASS MAIL PERMIT NO. 388 CHICAGO IL

POSTAGE WILL BE PAID BY ADDRESSEE

CONSUMER AFFAIRS
RAND MCNALLY
PO BOX 7600
CHICAGO IL 60680-9915

1st FOLD LINE

CUT ALONG DOTTED LINE

CUT ALONG DOTTED LINE

The Thomas Guide®

2003

Riverside County

CONTENTS

intro

maps

index

RAND MCNALLY

using your thomas guide

the PageFinder™ Map

- Turn to the PageFinder™ Map
- Find your general area of interest
- Note page number in black box
- Turn to that page in the book

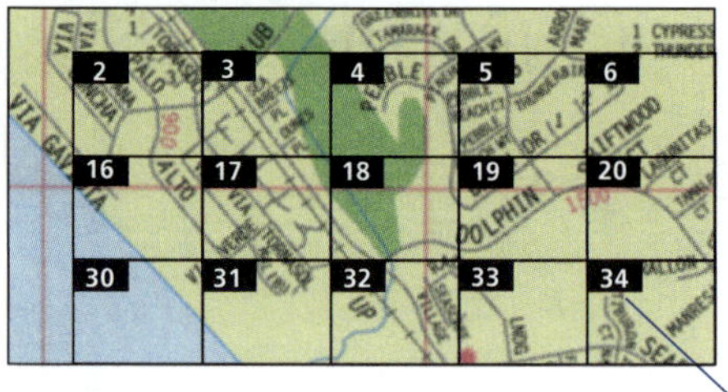

page number

▸ important!

Please note that map pages in this book are numbered according to the PageFinder™ Map, not according to traditional page numbers. For this reason, your book may look as though it is missing pages. It is not. One page may be numbered 15, but the next page could be numbered 25.

the index

- Listings include streets, schools, parks, cemeteries, golf courses, and more
- Street listings are separate from points of interest
- In the street listings, read across for block range, city, ZIP code, page numbers, and grid reference

STREET Block	City	ZIP	Pg-Grid
BROADWAY DR			
4400	SCH	60646	533-B6
6200	PLA	61644	532-D2
7800	WCH	60656	532-A3

- The grid reference, a letter-number combination (533-B6), tells where on the map to find a listing

the maps

- The grid is created by combining letters running along the top of the map with numbers running along the side
- To use a grid reference, follow the numbered row until it crosses the lettered column
- To find an adjacent map, turn to the page indicated on the map edges
- The legend on page C explains symbols and colors

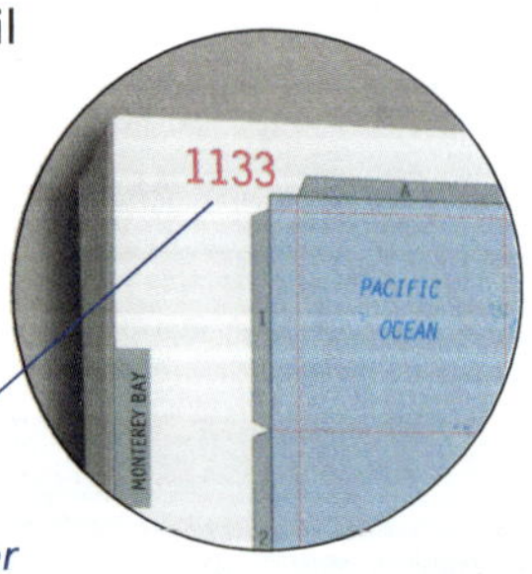

page number

the software

- Use The Thomas Guide® ***Digital****Edition*® mapping software to locate addresses, create maps for presentations, place individualized markers, and more
- Find The Thomas Guide® ***Digital****Edition*® software sold separately or included inside designated versions of The Thomas Guide®

map legend symbols

Freeway

Interchange/Ramp

Highway

Primary Road

Secondary Road

Minor Road

Restricted Road

Alley

Unpaved Road

Tunnel

Toll Road

High Occupancy Veh. Lane

Stacked Multiple Roadways

Proposed Road

Proposed Freeway

Freeway Under Construction

One-Way Road

Two-Way Road

Trail, Walkway

Stairs

Railroad

Rapid Transit

Rapid Transit, Underground

Ferry

City Boundary

County Boundary

State Boundary

International Boundary

Military Base, Indian Resv.

Township, Range, Rancho

River, Creek, Shoreline

98607 ZIP Code Boundary

5 Interstate

5 Interstate (Business)

3 U.S. Highway

1 4 8 9 State Highways

Carpool Lane

A Street List Marker

Street Name Continuation

Street Name Change

Station (Train, Bus)

Building (see List of Abbr. page)

Building Footprint

Public Elementary School

Public High School

Private Elementary School

Private High School

Shopping Center

Fire Station

Library

Mission

Winery

Campground

H Hospital

Mountain

Section Corner

Boat Launch

Gate, Locks, Barricades

Lighthouse

Dry Lake, Beach

Dam

Intermittent Lake, Marsh

PageFinder™ Map

PageFinder™ Map
U.S. Patent No. 5,419,586
Canadian Patent No. 2,116,425
Patente Mexicana No. 188186

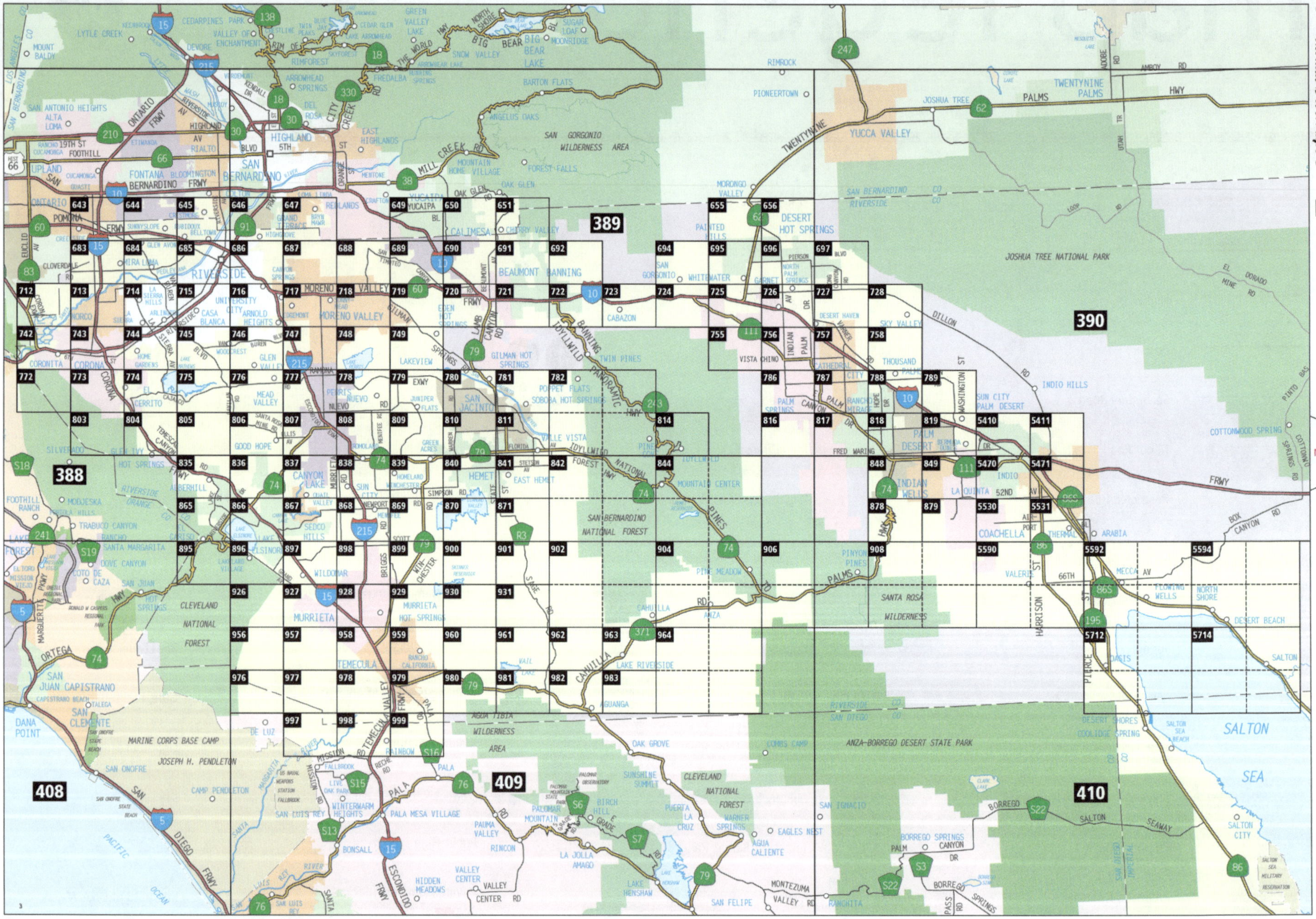

0 10 20 miles One inch equals 11 miles

PageFinder™ Map

PageFinder™ Map
U.S. Patent No. 5,419,586
Canadian Patent No. 2,116,425
Patente Mexicana No. 188186

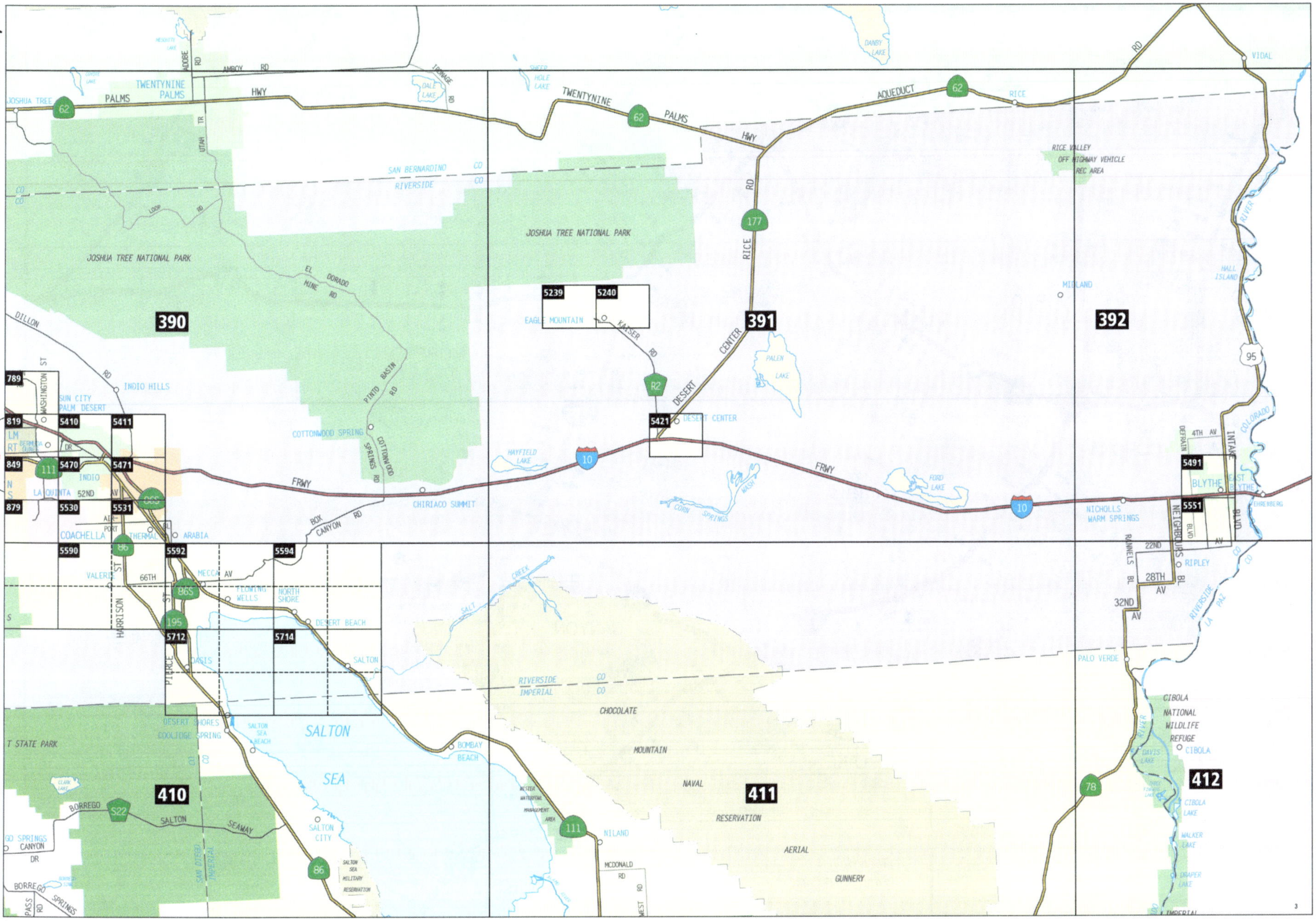

0 10 20 miles One inch equals 11 miles

RIVERSIDE COUNTY FREEWAY ACCESS MAP

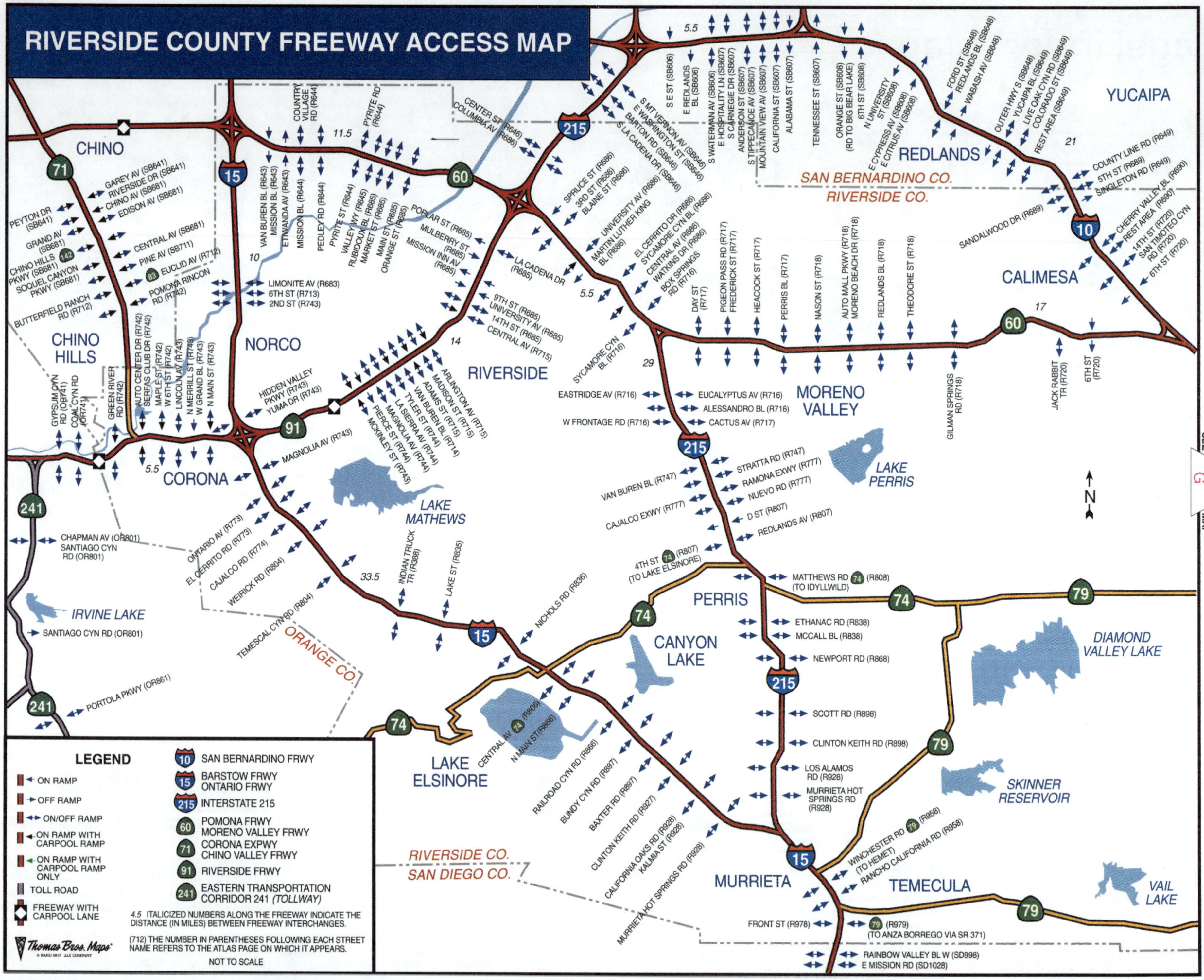

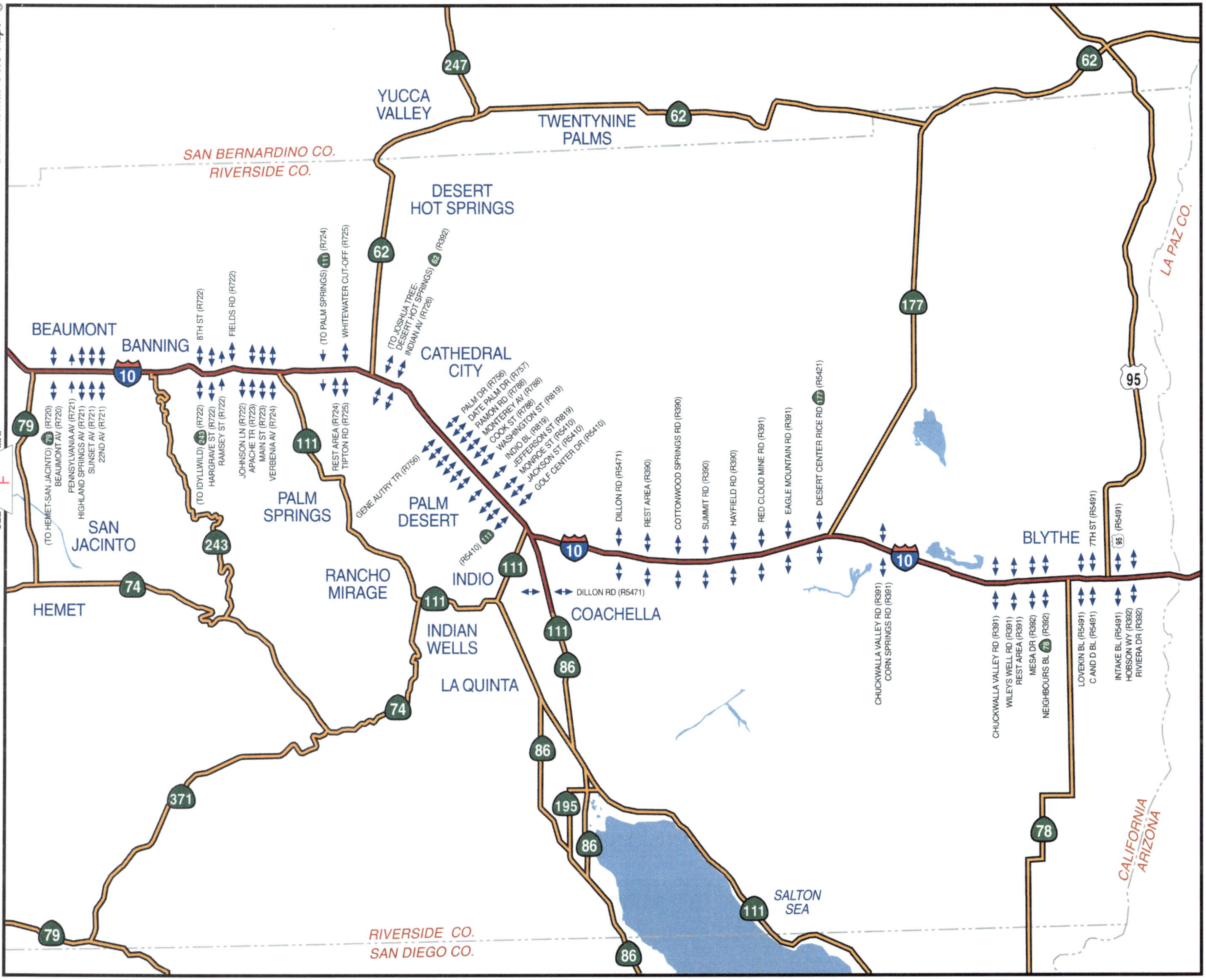
YUCCA VALLEY
TWENTYNINE PALMS
SAN BERNARDINO CO.
RIVERSIDE CO.
DESERT HOT SPRINGS
LA PAZ CO.
BEAUMONT
BANNING
CATHEDRAL CITY
PALM SPRINGS
PALM DESERT
SAN JACINTO
HEMET
RANCHO MIRAGE
INDIO
INDIAN WELLS
LA QUINTA
COACHELLA
BLYTHE
SALTON SEA
CALIFORNIA
ARIZONA
RIVERSIDE CO.
SAN DIEGO CO.
SEE F MAP
8TH ST (R722)
FIELDS RD (R722)
(TO PALM SPRINGS) 111 (R724)
WHITEWATER CUT-OFF (R725)
(TO JOSHUA TREE-DESERT HOT SPRINGS) 62 (R392)
INDIAN AV (R726)
(TO HEMET-SAN JACINTO) 79 (R720)
BEAUMONT AV (R720)
PENNSYLVANIA AV (R721)
HIGHLAND SPRINGS AV (R721)
SUNSET AV (R721)
22ND AV (R721)
(TO IDYLLWILD) 243 (R722)
HARGRAVE ST (R722)
RAMSEY ST (R722)
JOHNSON LN (R722)
APACHE TR (R723)
MAIN ST (R723)
VERBENIA AV (R724)
REST AREA (R724)
TIPTON RD (R725)
GENE AUTRY TR (R756)
PALM DR (R756)
DATE PALM DR (R757)
RAMON RD (R788)
MONTEREY AV (R788)
COOK ST (R788)
WASHINGTON ST (R819)
INDIO BL (R819)
JEFFERSON ST (R819)
MONROE ST (R5410)
JACKSON ST (R5410)
GOLF CENTER DR (R5410)
(R5410) 111
DILLON RD (R5471)
REST AREA (R390)
COTTONWOOD SPRINGS RD (R390)
SUMMIT RD (R390)
HAYFIELD RD (R390)
RED CLOUD MINE RD (R391)
EAGLE MOUNTAIN RD (R391)
DESERT CENTER RICE RD 177 (R5421)
CHUCKWALLA VALLEY RD (R391)
CORN SPRINGS RD (R391)
CHUCKWALLA VALLEY RD (R391)
WILEYS WELL RD (R391)
REST AREA (R391)
MESA DR (R392)
NEIGHBOURS BL 78 (R392)
LOVEKIN BL (R5491)
C AND D BL (R5491)
7TH ST (R5491)
95 (R5491)
INTAKE BL (R5491)
HOBSON WY (R392)
RIVIERA DR (R392)
10
62
247
177
95
79
111
243
74
371
86
195
78

For further information contact
Riverside County Planning Department
4080 Lemon St.
Riverside, CA 92501
(909) 955-3200

RIVERSIDE COUNTY
Cities And Communities

Community Name	City Abbr.	Miles To Riv	ZIP Code	Est. Sq. Mi.	Map Page
AGUANGA		59.00	92536		982
AIR FORCE VILLAGE WEST			92518		746
ALBERHILL		29.00	92530		835
ANZA		68.00	92539		904
ARABIA			92274		5592
ARLINGTON		6.00	92503		714
ARLINGTON HEIGHTS			92504		745
❖ BANNING	BAN	31.00	92220	18.70	722
❖ BEAUMONT	BEAU	25.00	92223	7.00	720
BELLTOWN			92509		645
BERMUDA DUNES		70.00	92201		819
❖ BLYTHE	BLY	171.00	92225	2.84	5491
CABAZON		37.00	92230		723
CAHUILLA		58.00	92539		902
❖ CALIMESA	CALI	30.00	92320	14.70	690
❖ CANYON LAKE	CYNL	31.00	92587	4.60	867
CANYON SPRINGS			92507		716
CASA BLANCA			92504		715
❖ CATHEDRAL CITY	CTHC	72.00	92234	16.50	787
CHERRY VALLEY			92223		690
CHIRIACO SUMMIT					390
❖ COACHELLA	COAC	80.00	92236	12.00	5471
❖ CORONA	COR	14.80	92882	27.65	743
CORONITA			92882		742
COTTONWOOD SPRING					390
DESERT BEACH					5654
DESERT CENTER			92239		5421
DESERT HAVEN			92241		726
❖ DESERT HOT SPRINGS	DHSP	53.00	92240	10.00	696
EAGLE MOUNTAIN					5240
EAST BLYTHE			92225		5491
EAST HEMET			92544		811
EDEN HOT SPRINGS			92223		749
EDGEMONT			92553		717
EL CARISO			92530		865
EL CERRITO			92881		774
FLOWING WELLS			92254		5653
GARDENLAND					906
GARNET		52.00	92258		726
GILMAN HOT SPRINGS		28.00	92583		780
GLEN AVON		9.00	92509		684
GLEN IVY HOT SPRINGS		23.00	92883		804
GLEN VALLEY			92570		746
GOOD HOPE			92570		806
GREEN ACRES			92545		839
❖ HEMET	HEMT	34.50	92543	15.50	811
HIGHGROVE		3.00	92507		646
HOME GARDENS		13.50	92503		744
HOMELAND		25.50	92548		839
IDYLLWILD		52.00	92549		814
❖ INDIAN WELLS	INDW	72.00	92210	12.00	849
❖ INDIO	INDO	76.00	92201	16.55	5410
INDIO HILLS			92236		390
JUNIPER FLATS			92567		779
JURUPA			92509		684
❖ LAKE ELSINORE	LKEL	31.00	92530	26.00	866
LAKELAND VILLAGE			92530		896
LAKE RIVERSIDE			92536		963
LAKEVIEW		22.00	92567		779

Community Name	City Abbr.	Miles To Riv	ZIP Code	Est. Sq. Mi.	Map Page
❖ LA QUINTA	LQNT	75.00	92253	22.70	849
LA SIERRA		10.00	92505		714
LA SIERRA HILLS		9.00	92505		714
MARCH AIR RESERVE BASE			92508		747
MEAD VALLEY			92570		776
MECCA		90.00	92254		5592
MENIFEE			92584		868
MESA VERDE					392
MIDLAND		200.00	92255		391
MIRA LOMA		9.00	91752		683
❖ MORENO VALLEY	MORV	12.50	92553	46.00	717
MOUNTAIN CENTER		52.50	92561		844
❖ MURRIETA	MURR	36.00	92563	27.00	928
MURRIETA HOT SPRINGS		35.50	92563		928
NICHOLLS WARM SPRINGS					392
❖ NORCO	NRCO	14.00	92880	14.00	713
NORTH PALM SPRINGS		56.00	92258		726
NORTH SHORE					5654
NUEVO		21.00	92567		778
OASIS		97.00	92274		5712
ORANGECREST			92508		746
PAINTED HILLS			92282		695
❖ PALM DESERT	PDST	69.50	92260	17.00	818
❖ PALM SPRINGS	PMSP	55.00	92264	76.00	786
PEDLEY		7.00	92509		684
❖ PERRIS	PER	20.00	92570	23.00	777
PINE COVE			92549		814
PINE MEADOW			92561		905
PINYON PINES			92561		907
POPPET FLATS			92220		782
QUAIL VALLEY		31.00	92587		837
RANCHO CALIFORNIA		45.00	92592		959
❖ RANCHO MIRAGE	RMIR	67.00	92270	21.50	818
RIPLEY		181.00	92272		412
❖ RIVERSIDE	RIV		92501	76.50	685
-- RIVERSIDE COUNTY	RivC				
ROMOLAND		22.50	92585		838
RUBIDOUX		2.00	92509		645
SALTON					5715
SAN GORGONIO		42.00	92282		724
❖ SAN JACINTO	SJCT	30.50	92583	7.00	811
SEDCO HILLS			92532		897
SKY VALLEY			92240		728
SOBOBA HOT SPRINGS			92583		781
SUN CITY		24.50	92584		838
SUN CITY PALM DESERT			92211		819
SUNNYMEAD			92553		717
SUNNYSLOPE			92509		644
❖ TEMECULA	TEM	40.50	92590	26.00	959
THERMAL		83.00	92274		5531
THOUSAND PALMS		64.00	92276		788
TWIN PINES			92220		389
UNIVERSITY CITY			92507		716
VALERIE			92274		5590
VALLE VISTA		28.50	92544		811
WHITEWATER			92282		725
WILDOMAR		32.00	92595		897
WINCHESTER		36.00	92596		839
WOODCREST			92508		746

❖ INDICATES INCORPORATED CITY

MILES ARE ESTIMATED FROM DOWNTOWN CIVIC CENTER

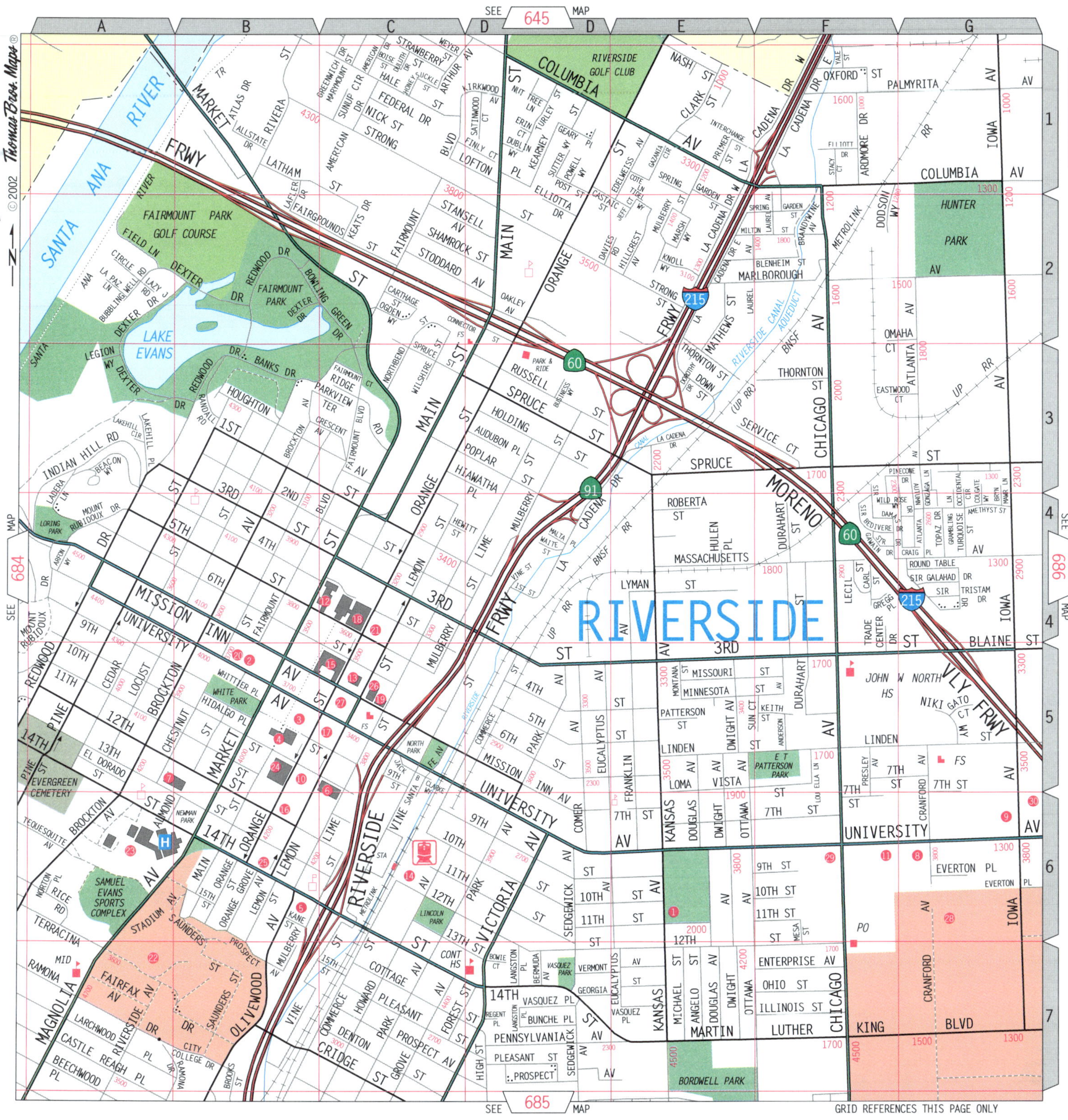

Downtown Riverside

Points of Interest

1	Bobby Bonds Park & Sports Complex	E6
2	Bus Station	B5
3	California Museum of Photography	B5
4	City Hall	B5
5	City School Administration	B6
6	County Administration	C5
7	County School Administration	A5
8	Courtyard by Marriott	G6
9	Dynasty Suites	G6
10	Federal Building	B5
11	Hampton Inn	F6
12	Holiday Inn	C4
13	Main Library	C5
14	Metrolink, Riverside Station	C6
15	Mission Inn Hotel & Museum	C5
16	Police Station	B6
17	Post Office, Downtown Station	C5
18	Raincross Square, Riverside Convention Center	C4
19	Riverside Art Museum	C5
20	Riverside Chamber of Commerce	B5
21	Riverside Convention & Visitors Bureau	C4
22	Riverside Community College	A7
23	Riverside Community Hospital	A6
24	Riverside County Courthouse	B5
25	Riverside County Economic Development Agency	B6
26	Riverside Municipal Auditorium	C5
27	Riverside Municipal Museum	C5
28	University of California, Riverside	G6
29	Town Square Shopping Center	F6
30	University Town Center	G6

Map Scale

0 660 1320 1980 2640 Feet

0 .125 .25 .375 .5 Miles

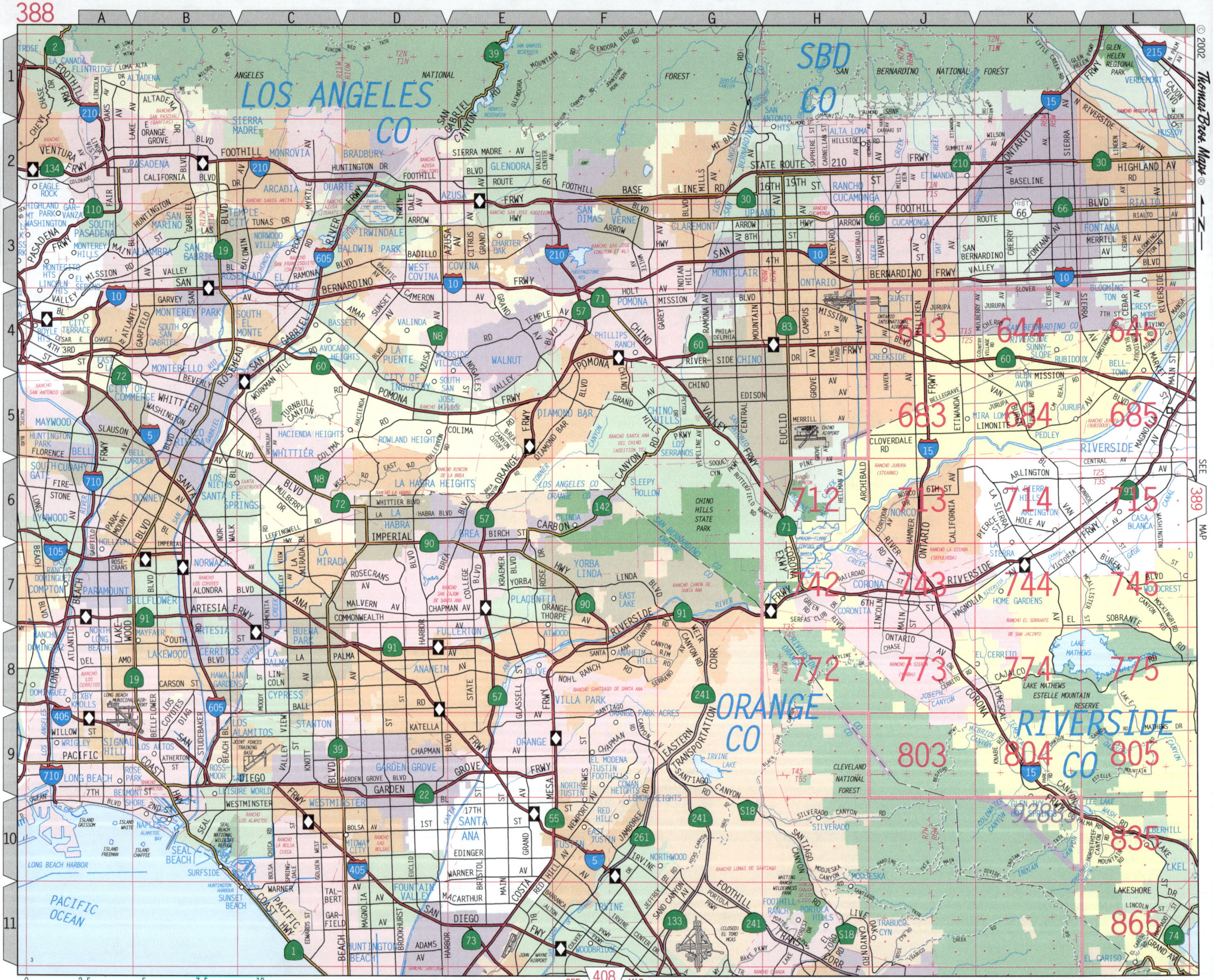

RIVERSIDE CO.

0 2.5 5 7.5 10 miles 1 in. = 5 mi.

SEE 408 MAP

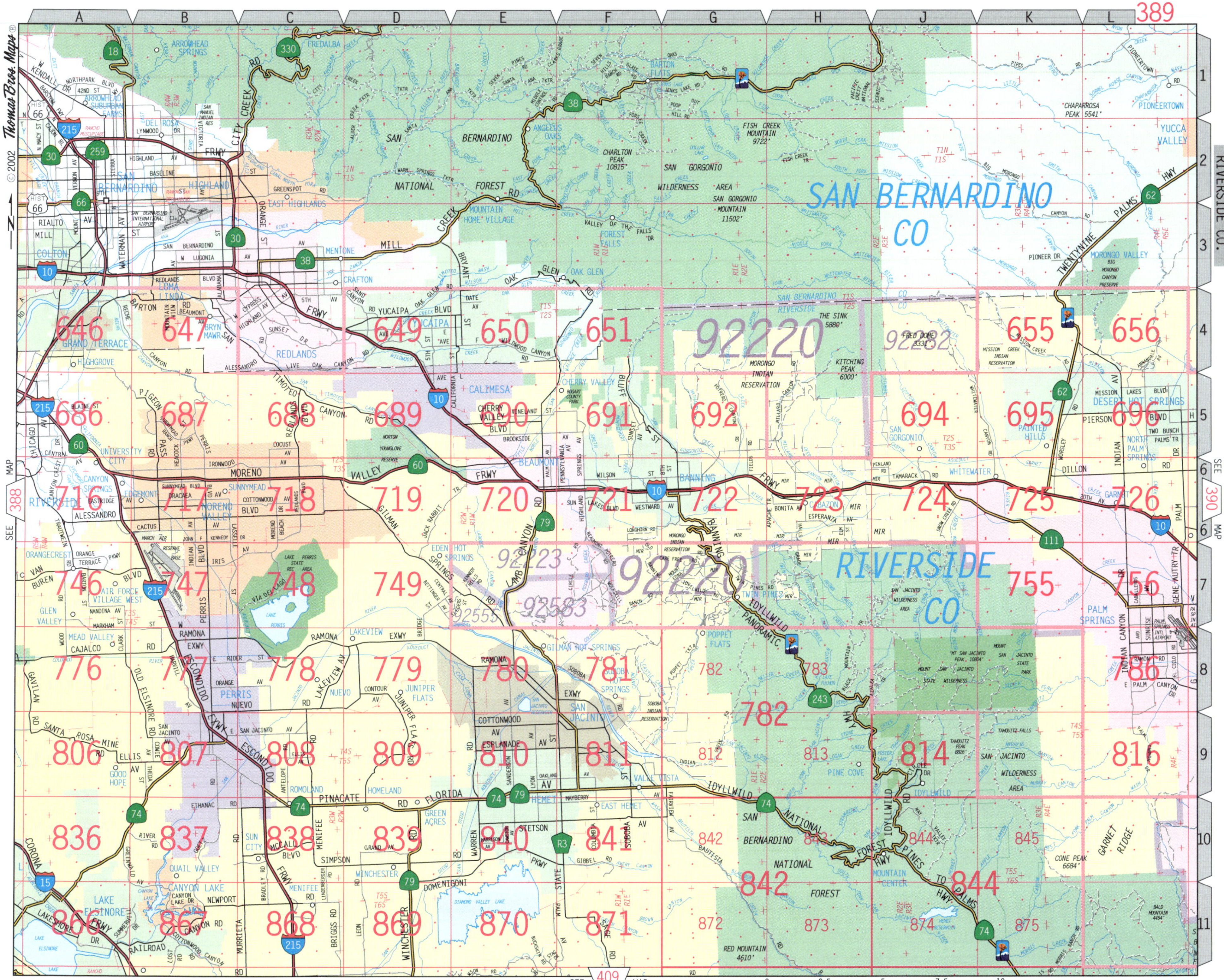

SEE 409 MAP

0 2.5 5 7.5 10 miles 1 in. = 5 mi.

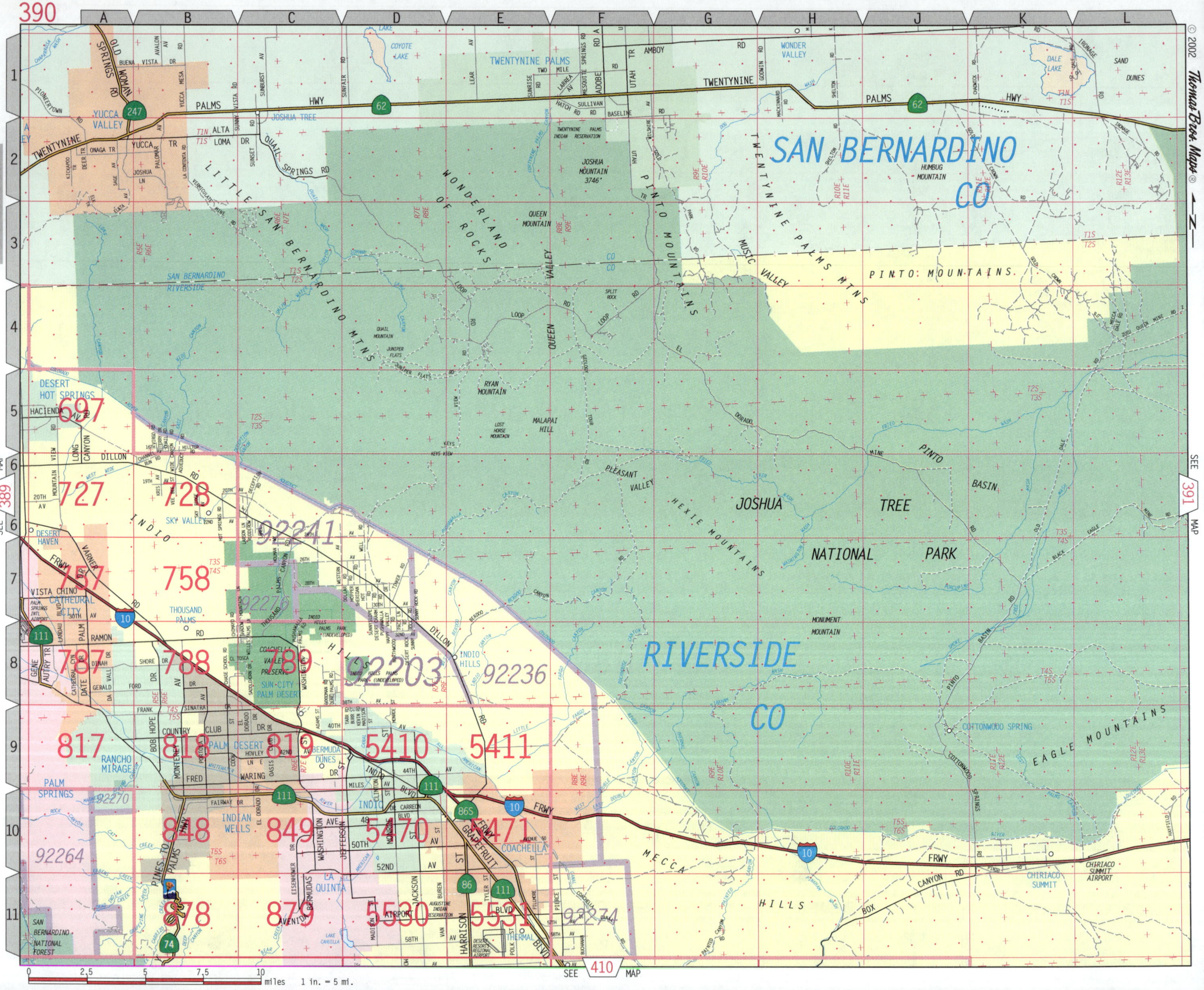
SAN BERNARDINO CO
RIVERSIDE CO
JOSHUA TREE NATIONAL PARK
TWENTYNINE PALMS
YUCCA VALLEY
JOSHUA TREE
LITTLE SAN BERNARDINO MTNS
WONDERLAND OF ROCKS
PINTO MOUNTAINS
TWENTYNINE PALMS MTNS
HEXIE MOUNTAINS
PINTO BASIN
EAGLE MOUNTAINS
MECCA HILLS
INDIO HILLS
DESERT HOT SPRINGS
SKY VALLEY
THOUSAND PALMS
CATHEDRAL CITY
PALM SPRINGS
RANCHO MIRAGE
PALM DESERT
INDIAN WELLS
LA QUINTA
INDIO
COACHELLA
BERMUDA DUNES
THERMAL
CHIRIACO SUMMIT
COTTONWOOD SPRING
QUEEN MOUNTAIN
RYAN MOUNTAIN
MALAPAI HILL
MONUMENT MOUNTAIN
HUMBUG MOUNTAIN
JOSHUA MOUNTAIN 3746'
COYOTE LAKE
DALE LAKE
WONDER VALLEY
PLEASANT VALLEY
QUEEN VALLEY
MUSIC VALLEY
SAN BERNARDINO NATIONAL FOREST
92241
92276
92203
92236
92270
92264
92274
697
727
728
757
758
787
788
789
817
818
819
5410
5411
848
849
5470
5471
878
879
5530
5531
SEE 389 MAP
SEE 391 MAP
SEE 410 MAP
0 2.5 5 7.5 10 miles 1 in. = 5 mi.

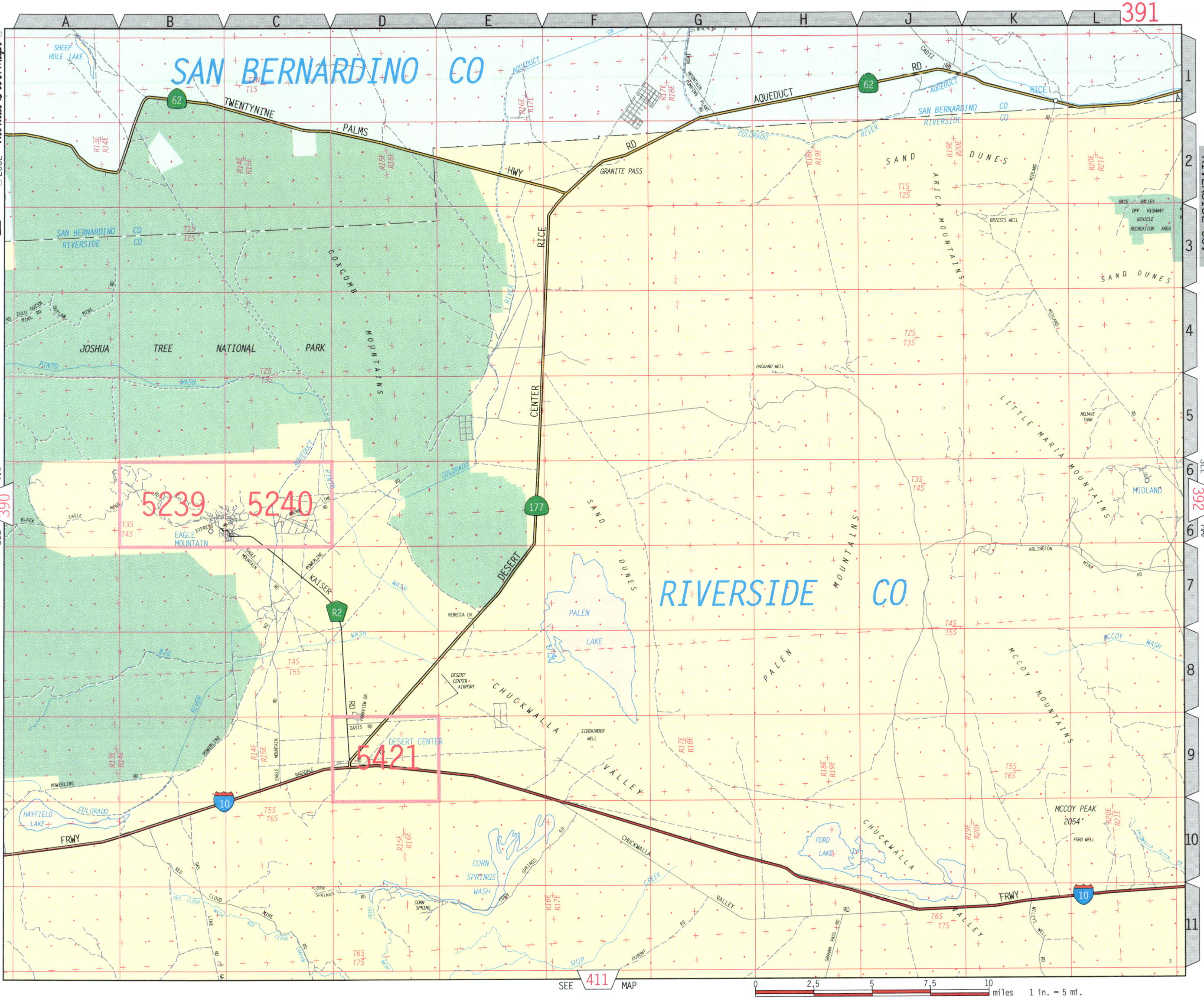
SAN BERNARDINO CO
RIVERSIDE CO
RIVERSIDE CO.
JOSHUA TREE NATIONAL PARK
COXCOMB MOUNTAINS
SHEEP HOLE LAKE
TWENTYNINE PALMS HWY
AQUEDUCT RD
GRANITE PASS
RICE
CENTER
DESERT
SAND DUNES
ARICA MOUNTAINS
LITTLE MARIA MOUNTAINS
MIDLAND
PALEN LAKE
PALEN MOUNTAINS
MCCOY MOUNTAINS
MCCOY PEAK 2054'
CHUCKWALLA VALLEY
EAGLE MOUNTAIN
KAISER
DESERT CENTER
DESERT CENTER AIRPORT
CORN SPRINGS WASH
HAYFIELD LAKE
FORD LAKE
FRWY
5239
5240
5421
SEE 390 MAP
SEE 392 MAP
SEE 411 MAP
miles 1 in. = 5 mi.

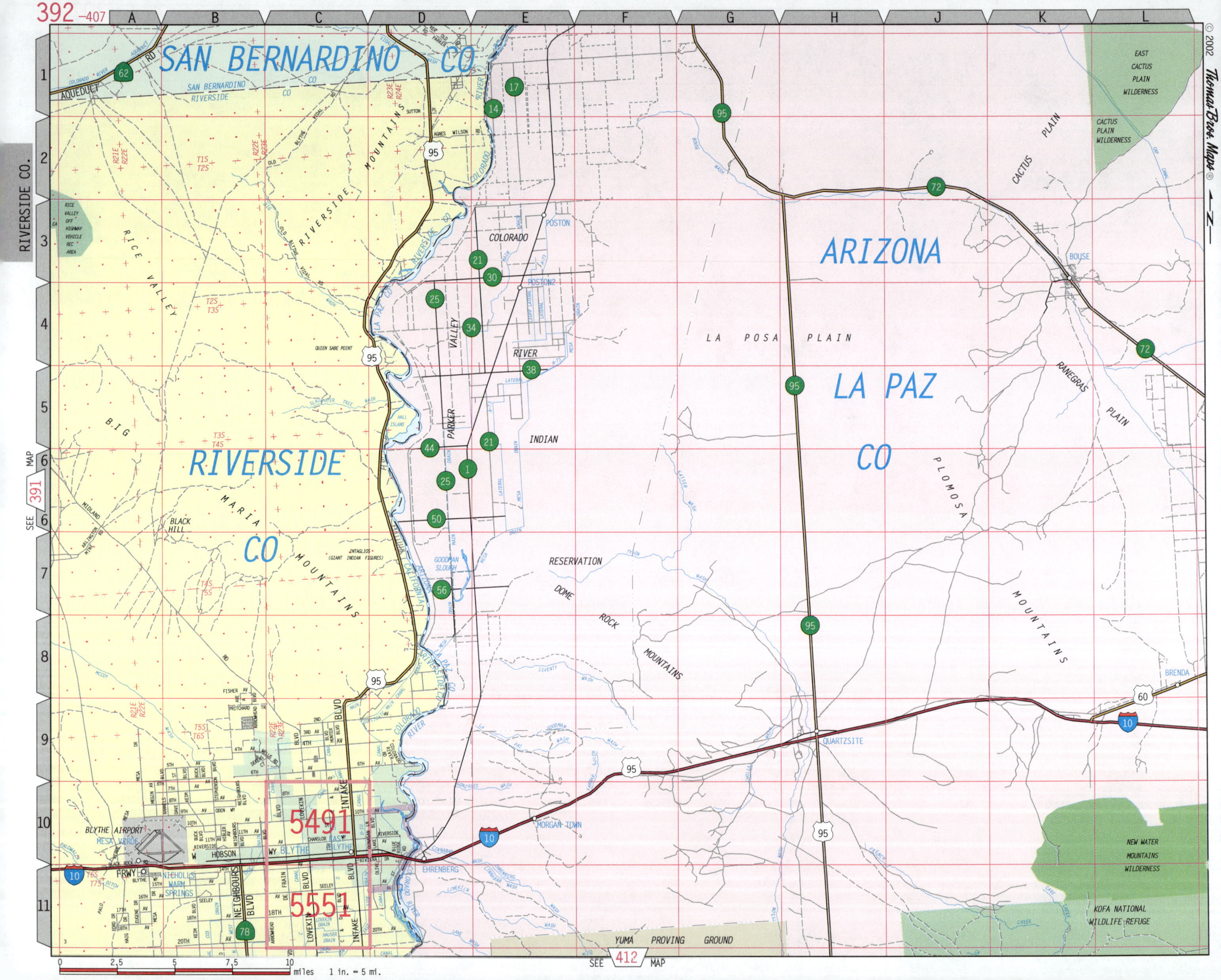
SAN BERNARDINO CO
SAN BERNARDINO
RIVERSIDE
RIVERSIDE CO.
RIVERSIDE CO
ARIZONA
LA PAZ CO
RICE VALLEY OFF HIGHWAY VEHICLE REC AREA
RICE VALLEY
RIVERSIDE MOUNTAINS
BIG MARIA MOUNTAINS
BLACK HILL
QUIEN SABE POINT
INTAGLIOS (GIANT INDIAN FIGURES)
COLORADO RIVER INDIAN RESERVATION
PARKER VALLEY
POSTON
POSTON2
HALL ISLAND
GOODMAN SLOUGH
LA POSA PLAIN
CACTUS PLAIN
EAST CACTUS PLAIN WILDERNESS
CACTUS PLAIN WILDERNESS
BOUSE
RANEGRAS PLAIN
PLOMOSA MOUNTAINS
DOME ROCK MOUNTAINS
BRENDA
QUARTZSITE
MORGAN TOWN
EHRENBERG
NEW WATER MOUNTAINS WILDERNESS
KOFA NATIONAL WILDLIFE REFUGE
YUMA PROVING GROUND
BLYTHE AIRPORT
MESA VERDE
BLYTHE
EAST BLYTHE
NICHOLLS WARM SPRINGS
HOBSON WY
NEIGHBOURS BLVD
INTAKE BLVD
LOVEKIN BLVD
5491
5551
SEE 391 MAP
SEE 412 MAP
© 2002 Thomas Bros. Maps®
0 2.5 5 7.5 10 miles 1 in. = 5 mi.

SEE 388 MAP

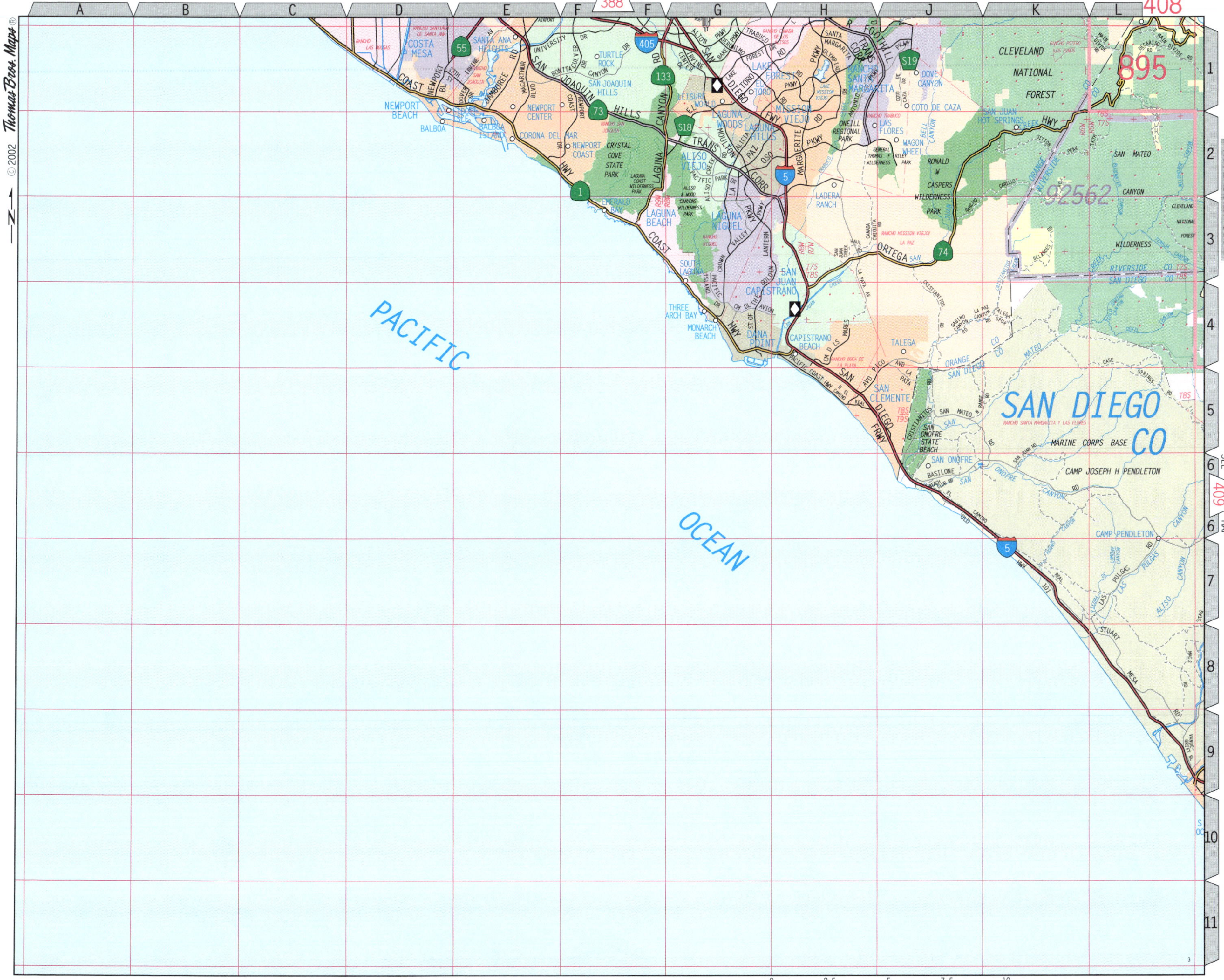

SEE 409 MAP

0 2.5 5 7.5 10 miles 1 in. = 5 mi.

SEE 389 MAP

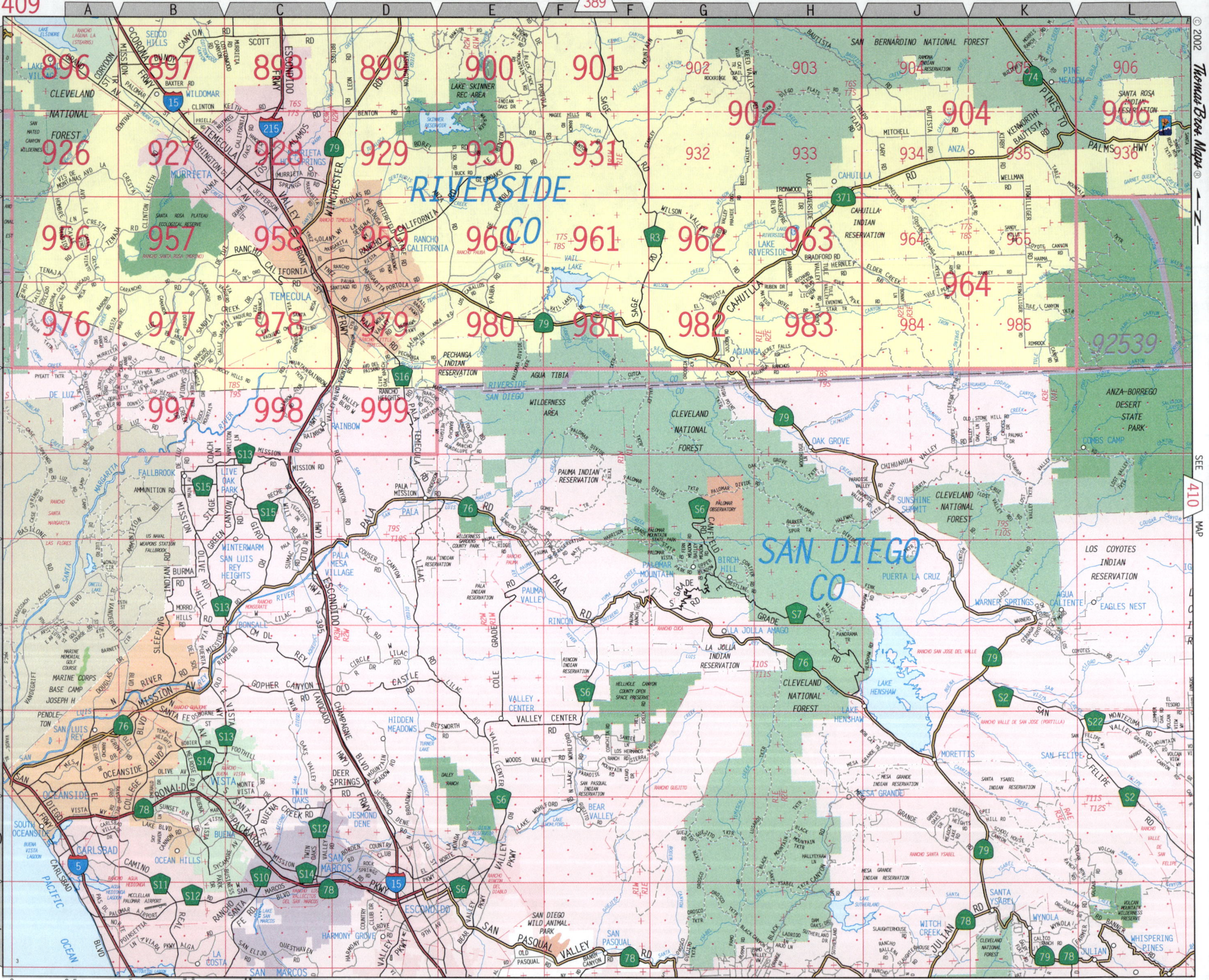

SEE 408 MAP

SEE 410 MAP

0 2.5 5 7.5 10 miles 1 in. = 5 mi.

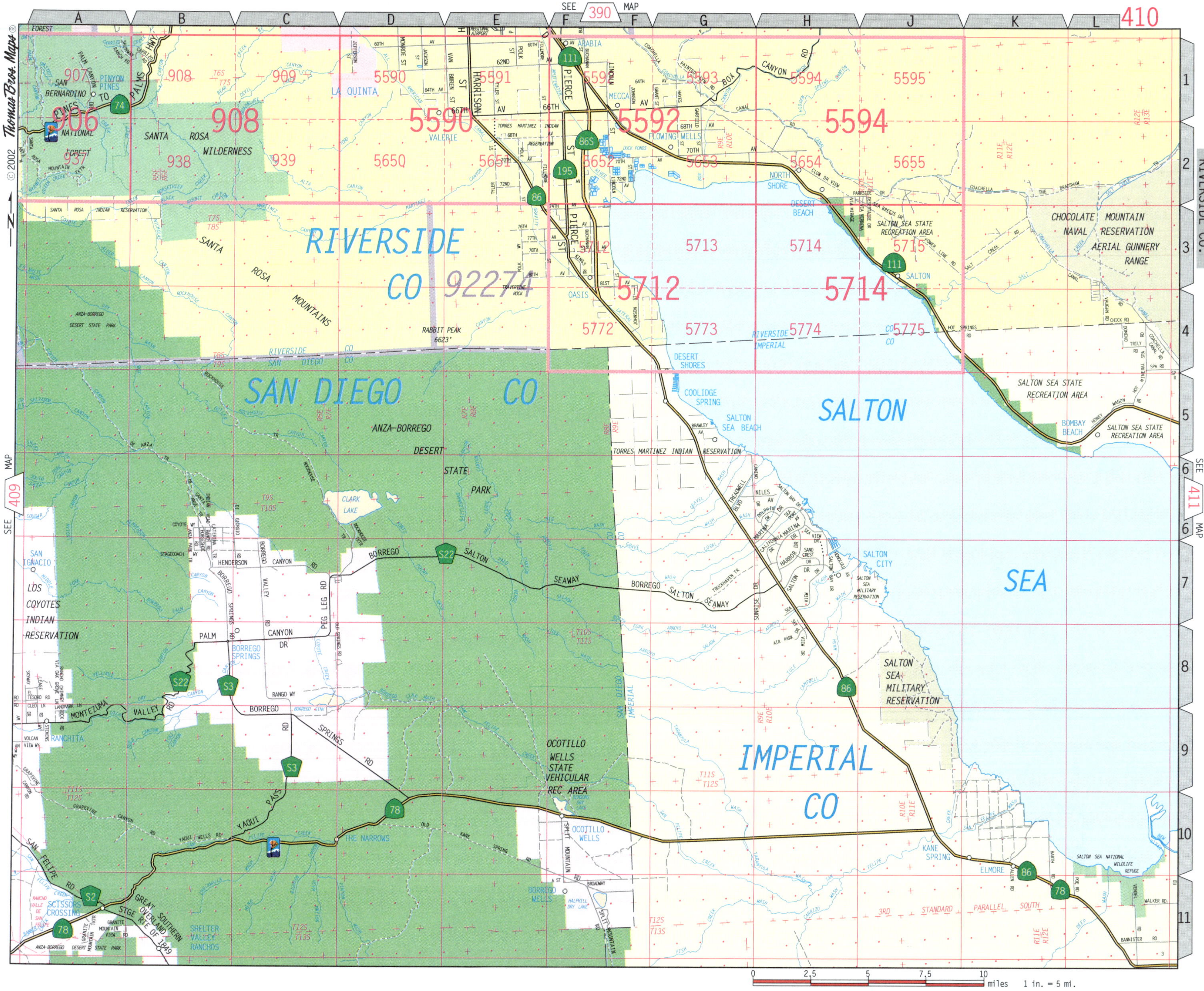
SEE 390 MAP
SEE 409 MAP
SEE 411 MAP
RIVERSIDE CO.
RIVERSIDE CO 92274
SAN DIEGO CO
IMPERIAL CO
SALTON SEA
LA QUINTA
VALERIE
MECCA
ARABIA
FLOWING WELLS
NORTH SHORE
DESERT BEACH
SALTON
OASIS
DESERT SHORES
COOLIDGE SPRING
SALTON SEA BEACH
SALTON CITY
SALTON SEA STATE RECREATION AREA
BOMBAY BEACH
CHOCOLATE MOUNTAIN NAVAL RESERVATION AERIAL GUNNERY RANGE
TORRES MARTINEZ INDIAN RESERVATION
SANTA ROSA INDIAN RESERVATION
SANTA ROSA WILDERNESS
SANTA ROSA MOUNTAINS
SAN BERNARDINO NATIONAL FOREST
PINYON PINES
ANZA-BORREGO DESERT STATE PARK
RABBIT PEAK 6623'
CLARK LAKE
BORREGO SPRINGS
SAN IGNACIO
LOS COYOTES INDIAN RESERVATION
RANCHITA
OCOTILLO WELLS STATE VEHICULAR REC AREA
OCOTILLO WELLS
BORREGO WELLS
THE NARROWS
SCISSORS CROSSING
SHELTER VALLEY RANCHOS
GREAT SOUTHERN OVERLAND STGE RTE OF 1849
SALTON SEA MILITARY RESERVATION
KANE SPRING
ELMORE
SALTON SEA NATIONAL WILDLIFE REFUGE
BORREGO SALTON SEAWAY
MONTEZUMA VALLEY RD
YAQUI PASS
PALM CANYON DR
PEG LEG RD
HARRISON ST
PIERCE ST
5590 5591 5592 5593 5594 5595
5650 5651 5652 5653 5654 5655
5712 5713 5714 5715
5772 5773 5774 5775
906 907 908 909 937 938 939
0 2.5 5 7.5 10 miles 1 in. = 5 mi.

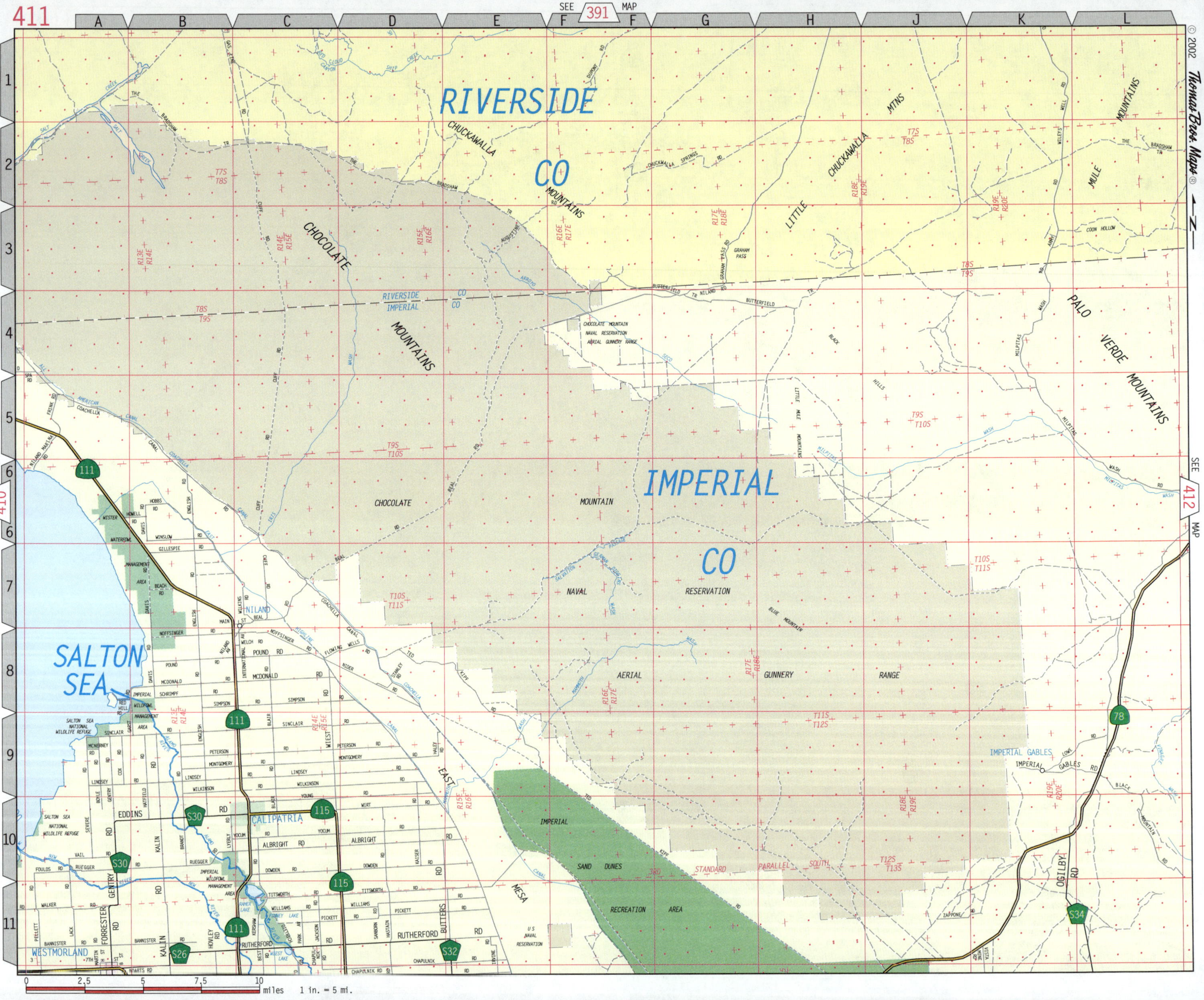
RIVERSIDE CO
IMPERIAL CO
RIVERSIDE CO.
SEE 391 MAP
SEE 410 MAP
SEE 412 MAP
CHUCKAWALLA MOUNTAINS
LITTLE CHUCKAWALLA MTNS
MULE MOUNTAINS
CHOCOLATE MOUNTAINS
PALO VERDE MOUNTAINS
CHOCOLATE MOUNTAIN NAVAL RESERVATION
CHOCOLATE MOUNTAIN AERIAL GUNNERY RANGE
NAVAL RESERVATION
AERIAL GUNNERY RANGE
IMPERIAL SAND DUNES RECREATION AREA
SALTON SEA
SALTON SEA NATIONAL WILDLIFE REFUGE
IMPERIAL WILDFOWL MANAGEMENT AREA
NILAND
CALIPATRIA
WESTMORLAND
IMPERIAL GABLES
EDDINS
GRAHAM PASS
COON HOLLOW
THE BRADSHAW TR
BUTTERFIELD TR
COACHELLA CANAL
EAST HIGHLINE CANAL
OGILBY RD
111
115
78
S30
S26
S32
S34
© 2002 Thomas Bros. Maps
0 2.5 5 7.5 10 miles 1 in. = 5 mi.

SEE 392 MAP

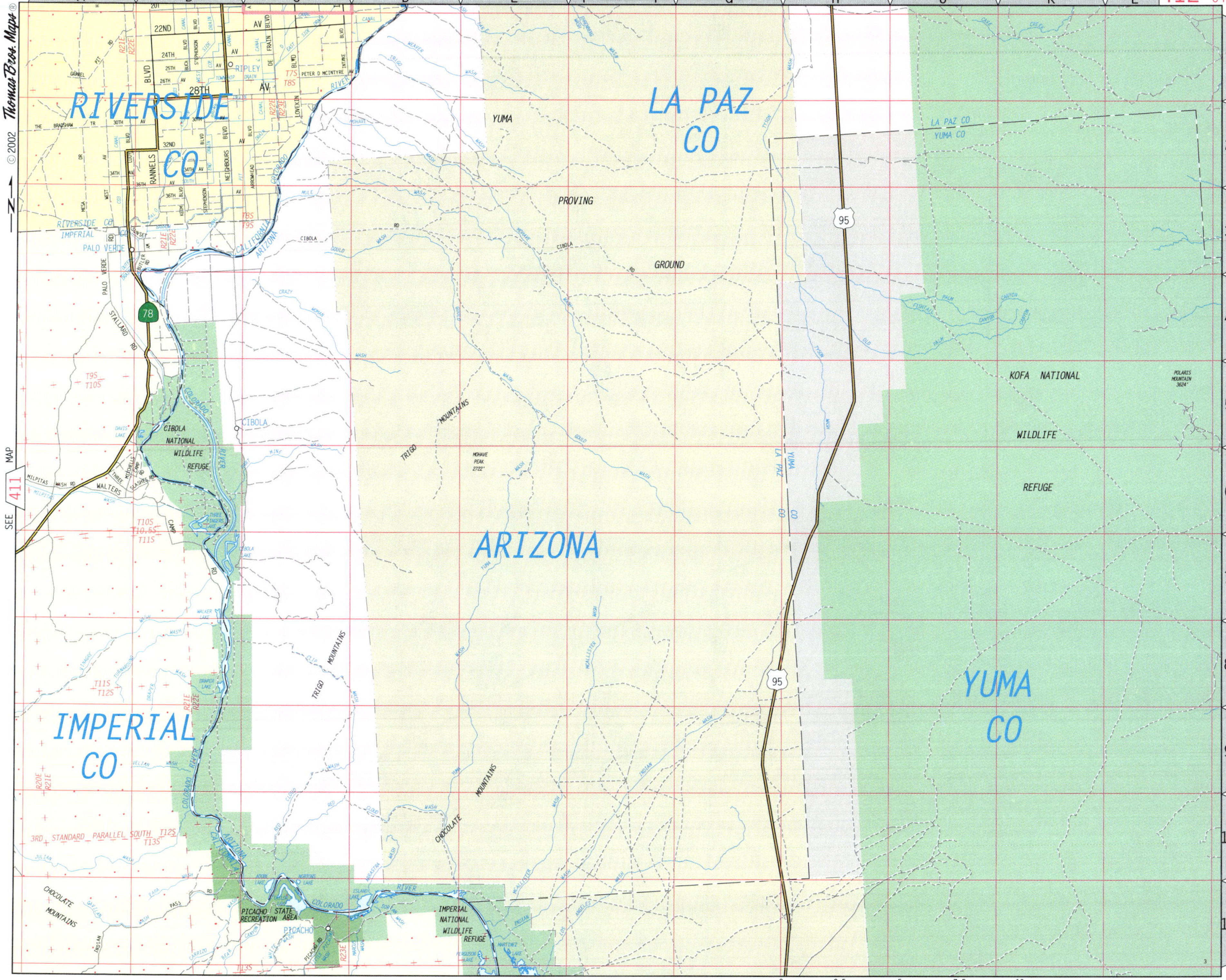

SEE 411 MAP

0 2.5 5 7.5 10 miles 1 in. = 5 mi.

SEE SBD 603 MAP

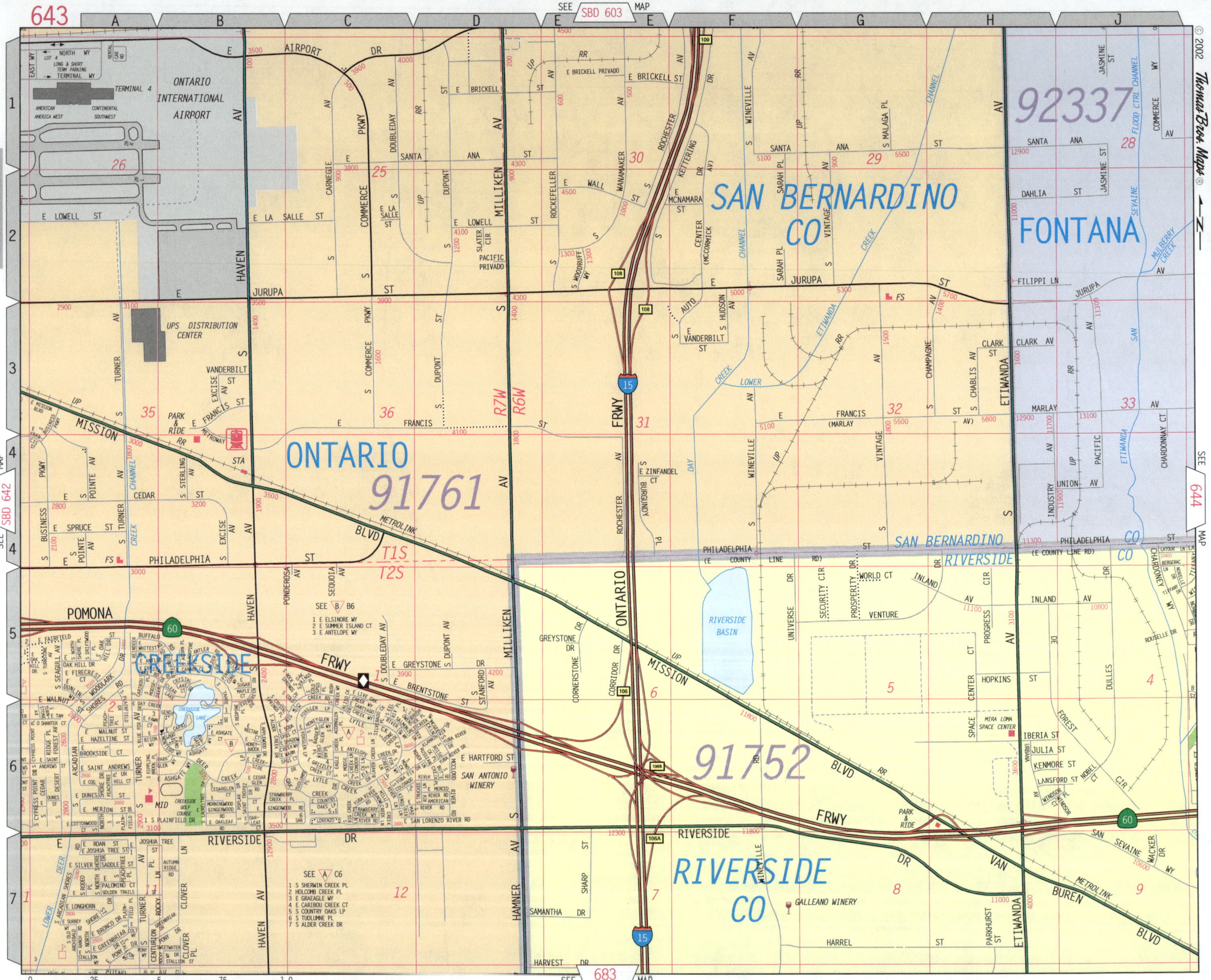

SEE SBD 642 MAP

SEE 644 MAP

SEE 683 MAP

RIVERSIDE CO.

0 .25 .5 .75 1.0 miles 1 in. = 2400 ft.

SEE SBD 604 MAP

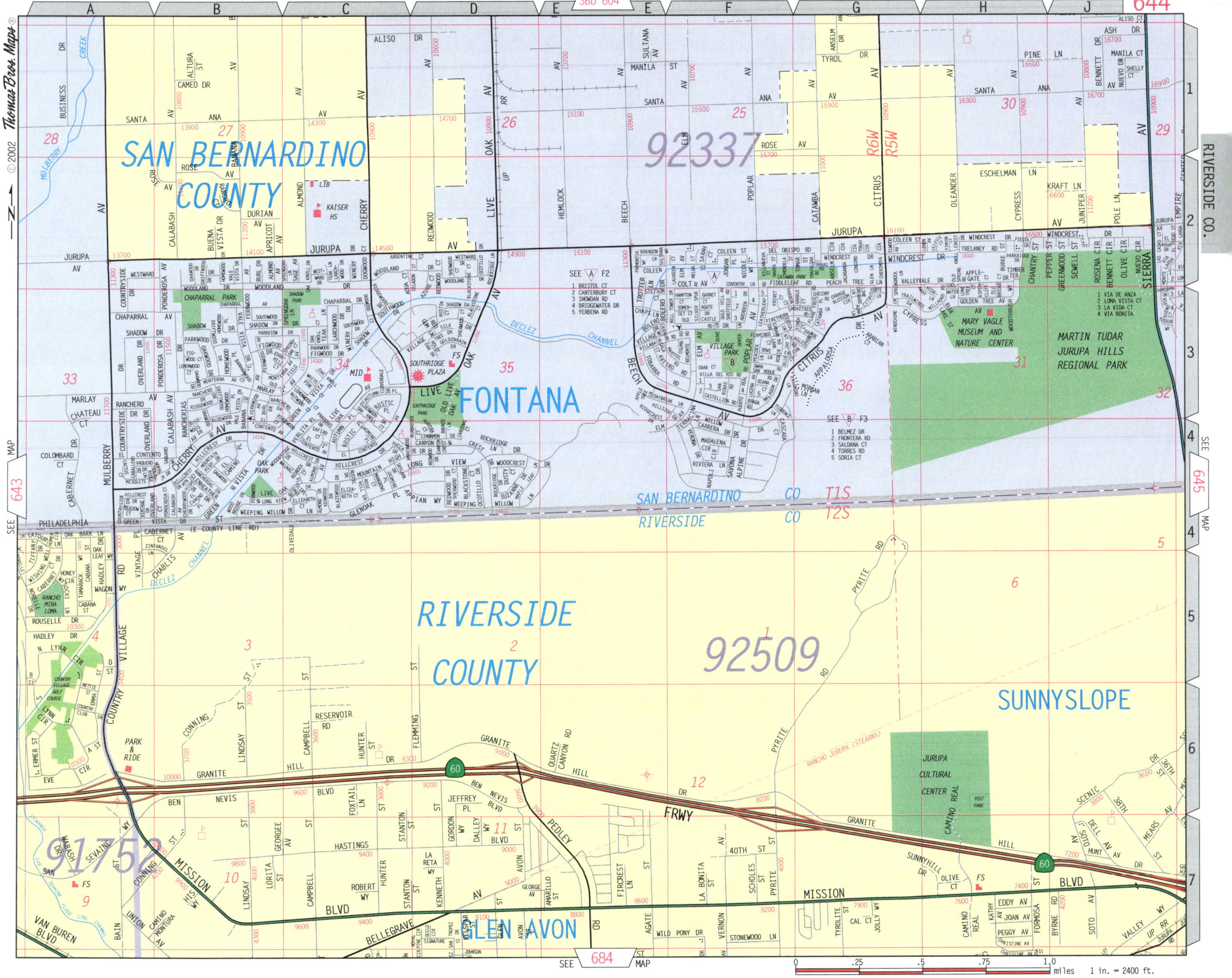

SEE 643 MAP
SEE 645 MAP
SEE 684 MAP

SEE SBD 605 MAP

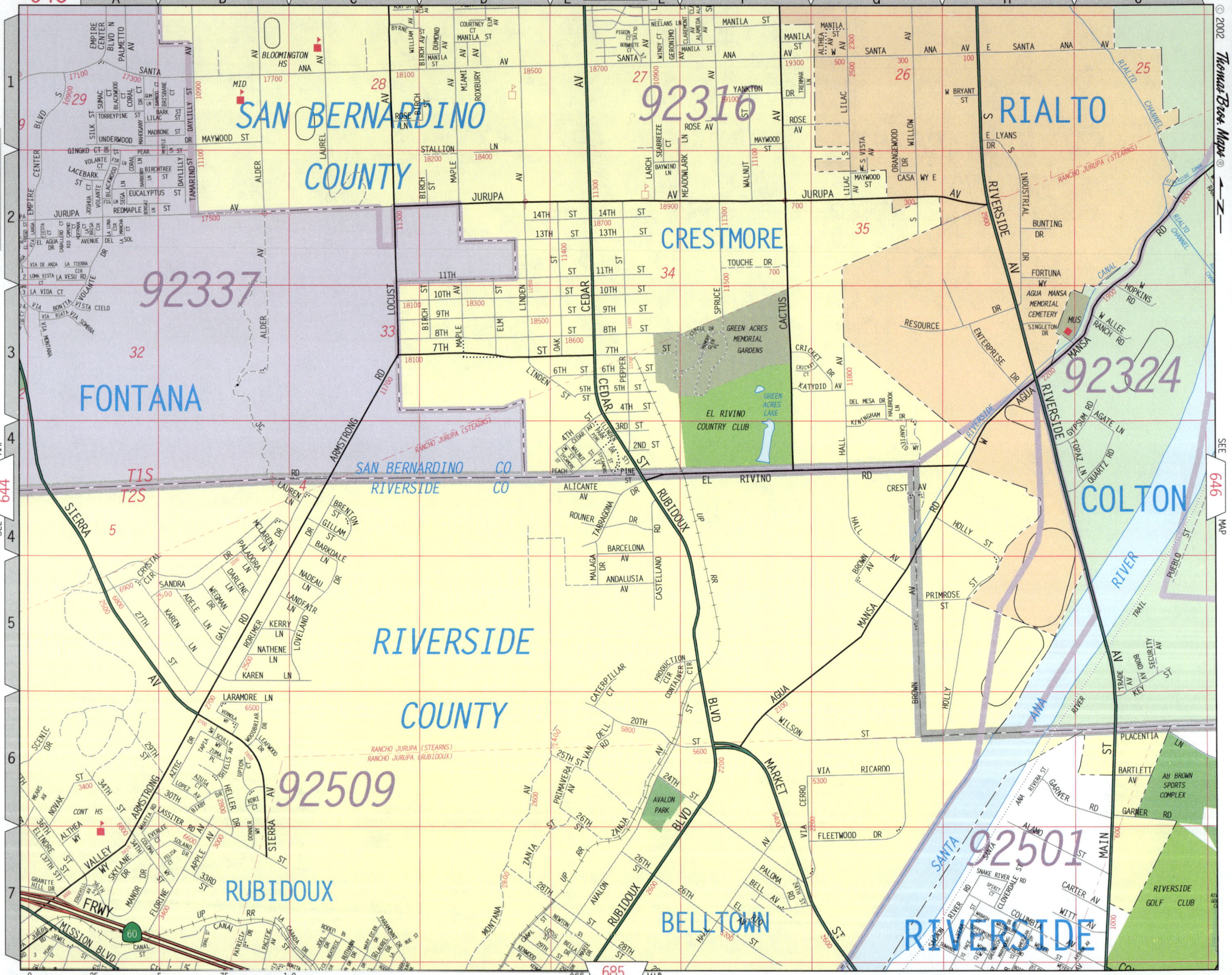

SEE 644 MAP

SEE 646 MAP

SEE 685 MAP

0 .25 .5 .75 1.0 miles 1 in. = 2400 ft.

SEE SBD 606 MAP

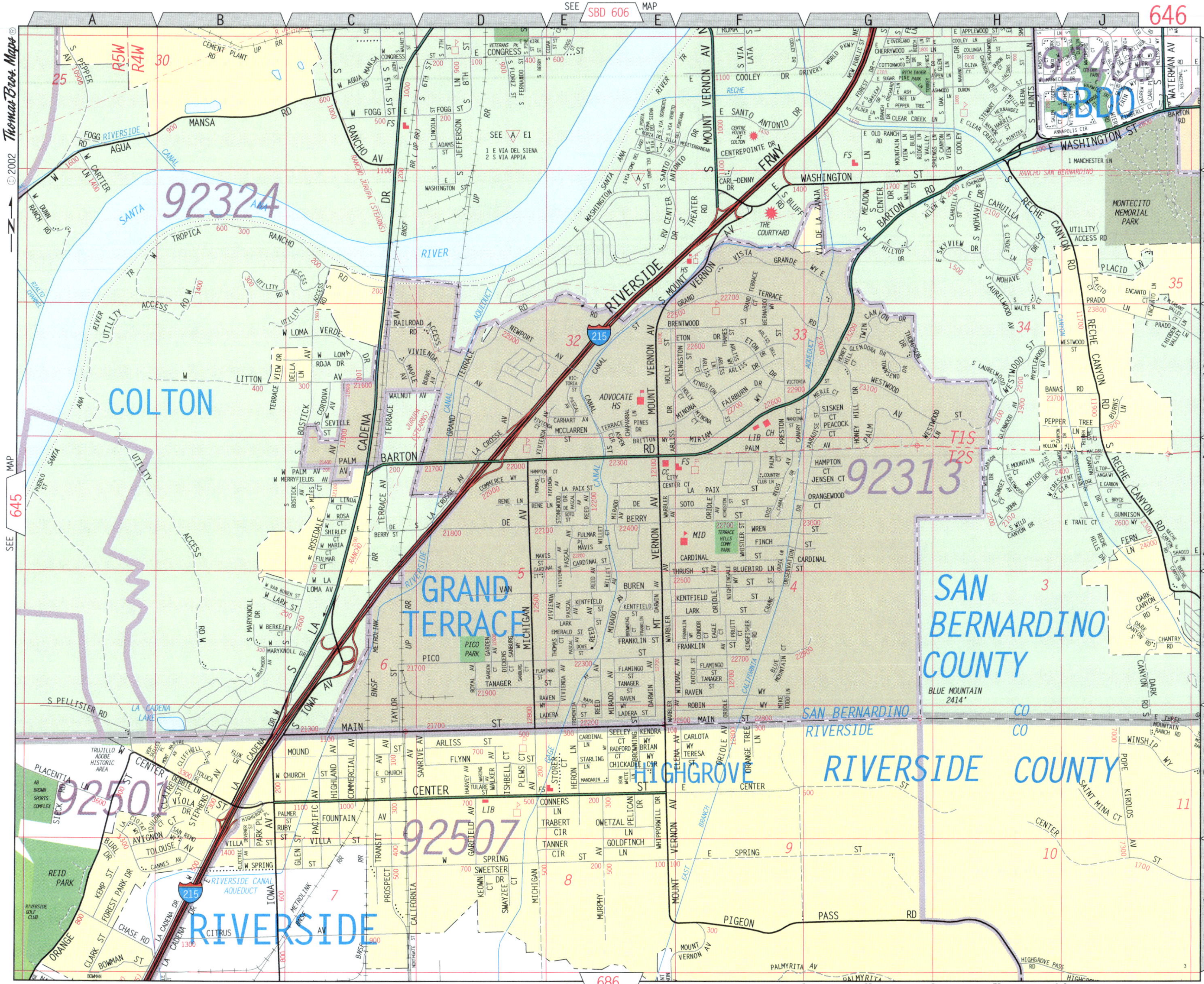

SEE 645 MAP

SEE 647 MAP

RIVERSIDE CO.

SEE 686 MAP

0 .25 .5 .75 1.0 miles 1 in. = 2400 ft.

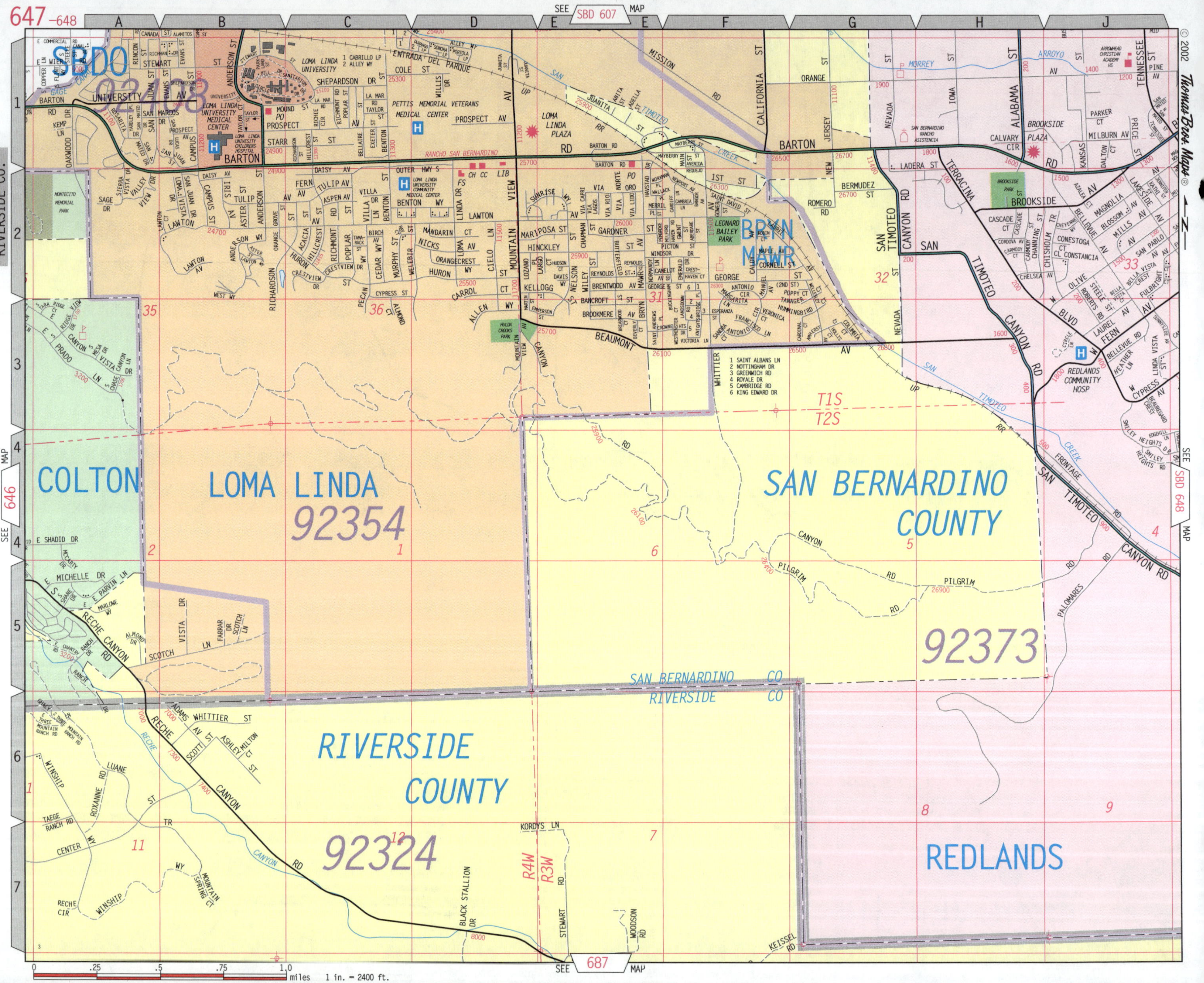
SEE SBD 607 MAP
SEE SBD 648 MAP
SEE 646 MAP
SEE 687 MAP
A B C D E F G H J
1 2 3 4 5 6 7
RIVERSIDE CO.
SBDO
92408
COLTON
LOMA LINDA
92354
SAN BERNARDINO COUNTY
92373
RIVERSIDE COUNTY
92324
REDLANDS
BRYN MAWR
SAN BERNARDINO CO
RIVERSIDE CO
LOMA LINDA UNIVERSITY
LOMA LINDA UNIVERSITY MEDICAL CENTER
PETTIS MEMORIAL VETERANS MEDICAL CENTER
LOMA LINDA PLAZA
BROOKSIDE PLAZA
REDLANDS COMMUNITY HOSP
LEONARD BAILEY PARK
HULDA CROOKS PARK
MONTECITO MEMORIAL PARK
BARTON RD
BARTON
UNIVERSITY AV
REDLANDS BLVD
MISSION RD
CALIFORNIA ST
MOUNTAIN VIEW AV
ANDERSON ST
BEAUMONT AV
SAN TIMOTEO CANYON RD
SAN TIMOTEO CREEK
RECHE CANYON RD
PILGRIM RD
CANYON RD
PALOMARES RD
KEISSEL RD
T1S
T2S
R4W
R3W
1 SAINT ALBANS LN
2 NOTTINGHAM DR
3 GREENWICH RD
4 ROYALE DR
5 CAMBRIDGE RD
6 KING EDWARD DR
0 .25 .5 .75 1.0 miles 1 in. = 2400 ft.
© 2002 Thomas Bros. Maps®

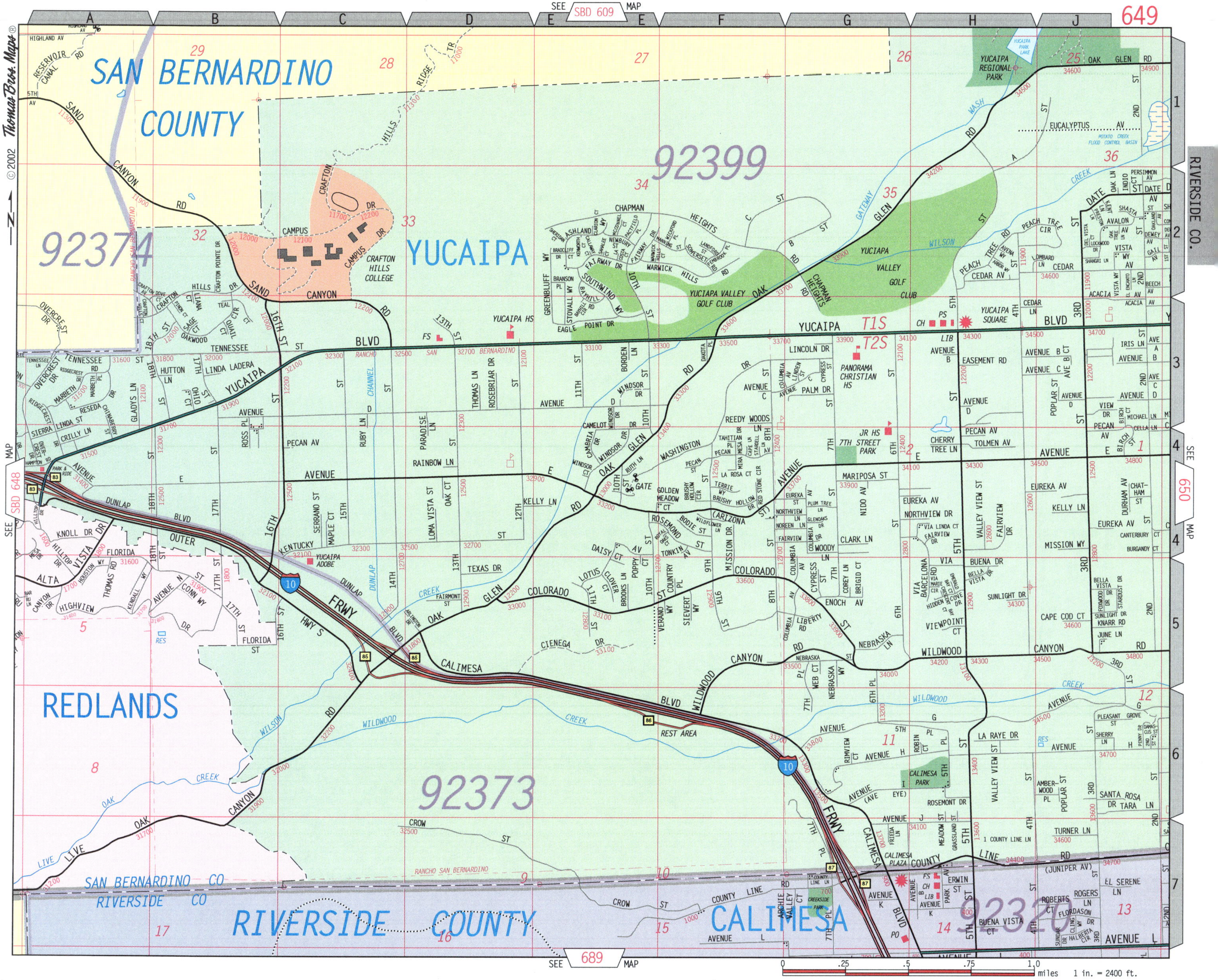
SEE SBD 609 MAP
SAN BERNARDINO COUNTY
YUCAIPA
REDLANDS
CALIMESA
RIVERSIDE COUNTY
SAN BERNARDINO CO
RIVERSIDE CO
RIVERSIDE CO.
92374
92399
92373
92320
CRAFTON HILLS COLLEGE
YUCAIPA REGIONAL PARK
YUCAIPA VALLEY GOLF CLUB
YUCAIPA VALLEY GOLF COURSE
YUCAIPA HS
PANORAMA CHRISTIAN HS
JR HS
7TH STREET PARK
CALIMESA PARK
YUCAIPA SQUARE
YUCAIPA ADOBE
REST AREA
YUCAIPA BLVD
OAK GLEN RD
SAND CANYON RD
CALIMESA BLVD
COUNTY LINE RD
WILDWOOD CANYON RD
DUNLAP BLVD
OUTER HWY S
FRWY
COLORADO
T1S
T2S
SEE SBD 648 MAP
SEE 650 MAP
SEE 689 MAP
Thomas Bros. Maps ©2002
miles 1 in. = 2400 ft.

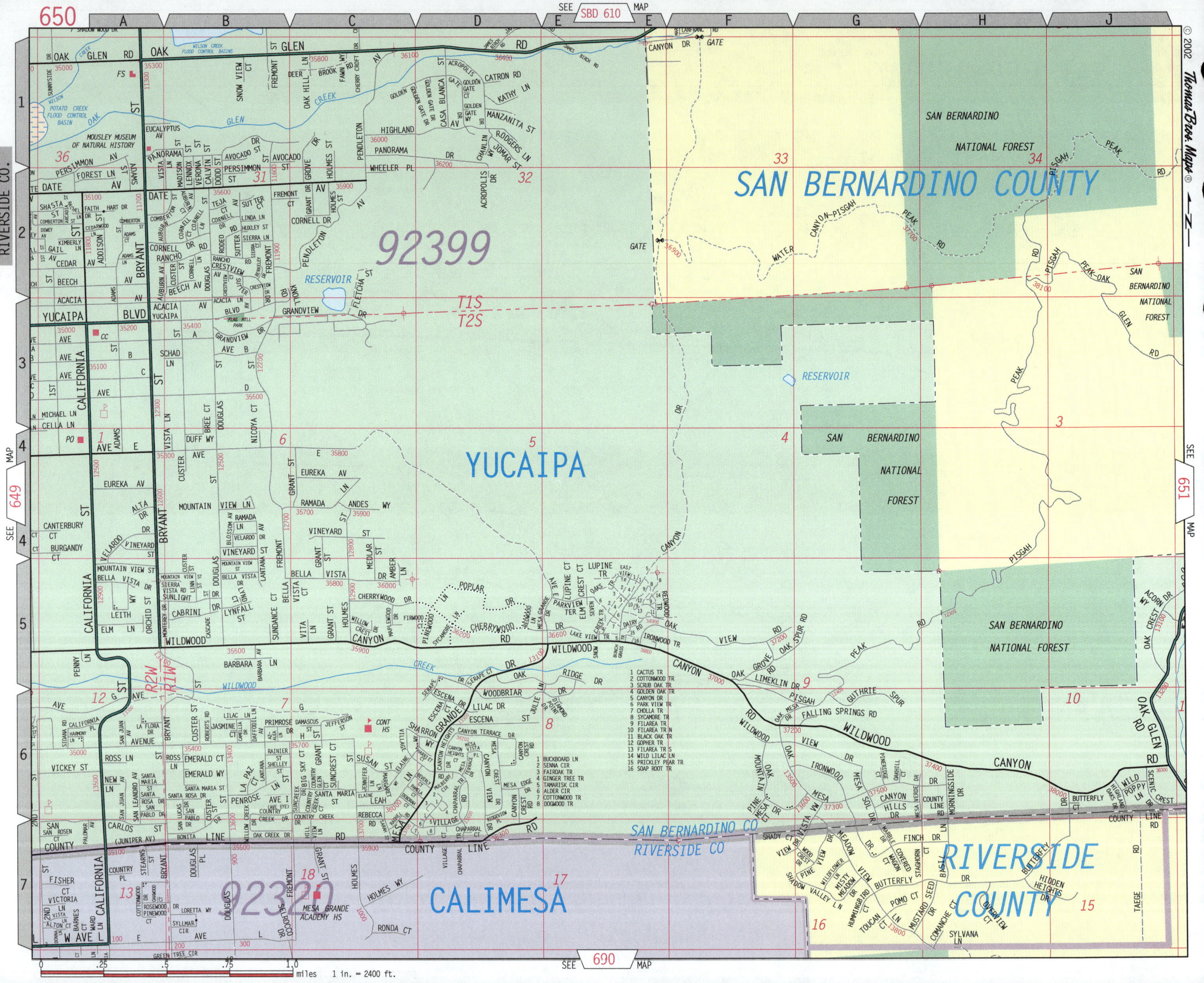
SEE SBD 610 MAP
SAN BERNARDINO COUNTY
SAN BERNARDINO NATIONAL FOREST
YUCAIPA
92399
CALIMESA
92320
RIVERSIDE COUNTY
RIVERSIDE CO.
SAN BERNARDINO CO
RIVERSIDE CO
OAK GLEN RD
YUCAIPA BLVD
WILDWOOD CANYON RD
COUNTY LINE RD
BRYANT ST
CALIFORNIA ST
PISGAH PEAK RD
CANYON-PISGAH
RESERVOIR
WILSON CREEK FLOOD CONTROL BASINS
POTATO CREEK FLOOD CONTROL BASIN
MOUSLEY MUSEUM OF NATURAL HISTORY
MESA GRANDE ACADEMY HS
CONT HS
T1S
T2S
R2W
R1W
SEE 649 MAP
SEE 651 MAP
SEE 690 MAP
miles 1 in. = 2400 ft.
© 2002 Thomas Bros. Maps ®

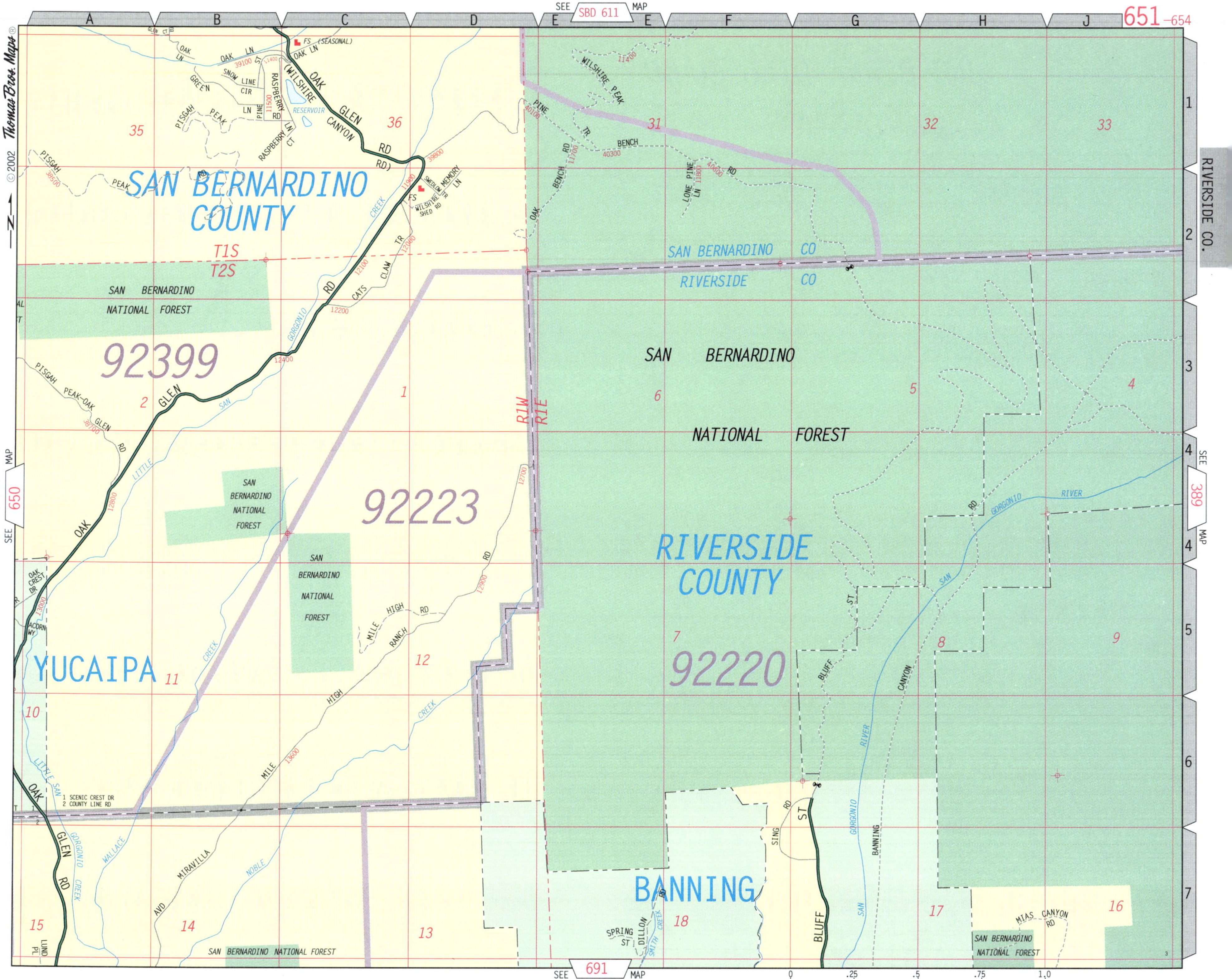

SEE SBD 611 MAP
SEE 650 MAP
SEE 389 MAP
SEE 691 MAP
RIVERSIDE CO.
Thomas Bros. Maps
© 2002
SAN BERNARDINO COUNTY
RIVERSIDE COUNTY
SAN BERNARDINO CO
RIVERSIDE CO
SAN BERNARDINO NATIONAL FOREST
YUCAIPA
BANNING
92399
92223
92220
T1S
T2S
R1W
R1E
OAK GLEN RD
OAK GLEN CANYON RD
(WILSHIRE OAK LN)
FS (SEASONAL)
OAK LN
GLEN CT
SNOW LINE CIR
GREEN LN
PISGAH PEAK LN
PINE RD
RASPBERRY ST
RASPBERRY LN CT
RESERVOIR
PISGAH PEAK RD
PISGAH PEAK-OAK GLEN RD
SWEDLOW TR
MEMORY LN
WILSHIRE SHED RD
CATS CLAW TR
GORGONIO CREEK
LITTLE SAN GORGONIO CREEK
WILSHIRE PEAK
PINE BENCH RD
BENCH RD
OAK TR
LONE PINE LN
OAK CREST DR
ACORN WY
HIGH RANCH RD
MILE HIGH RD
MILE HIGH RANCH RD
WALLACE CREEK
MIRAVILLA AVD
NOBLE CREEK
LUND PL
1 SCENIC CREST DR
2 COUNTY LINE RD
SAN GORGONIO RIVER
BLUFF ST
SING RD
CANYON RD
BANNING CANYON RD
SPRING ST
DILLON RD
SMITH CREEK
MIAS CANYON RD

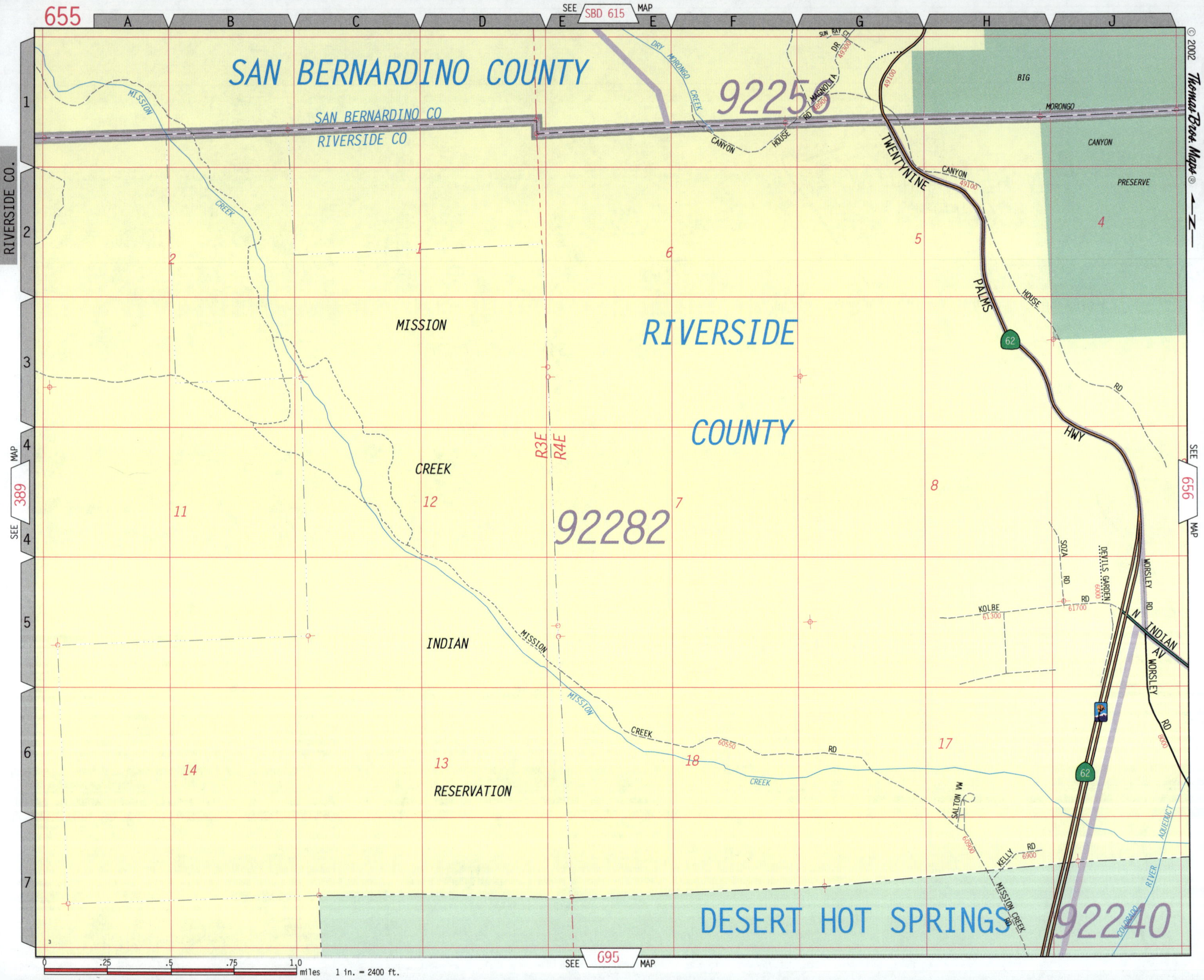
SEE SBD 615 MAP
A
B
C
D
E
F
G
H
J
1
2
3
4
5
6
7
SAN BERNARDINO COUNTY
SAN BERNARDINO CO
RIVERSIDE CO
RIVERSIDE CO.
92256
92282
92240
RIVERSIDE
COUNTY
MISSION
CREEK
INDIAN
RESERVATION
DRY MORONGO CREEK
MISSION CREEK
MAGNOLIA RD
SUN RAY CT
DR
CANYON HOUSE RD
TWENTYNINE PALMS HWY
62
49100
49300
49100
BIG MORONGO CANYON PRESERVE
CANYON HOUSE RD
R3E
R4E
SOZA RD
DEVILS GARDEN RD
WORSLEY RD
N INDIAN AV
KOLBE
61300
61700
6900
6800
MISSION CREEK RD
60550
SALTON VW
60900
KELLY RD
6900
MISSION CREEK RD
COLORADO RIVER AQUEDUCT
DESERT HOT SPRINGS
1
2
4
5
6
7
8
11
12
13
14
17
18
SEE 389 MAP
SEE 656 MAP
SEE 695 MAP
0 .25 .5 .75 1.0 miles 1 in. = 2400 ft.
© 2002 Thomas Bros. Maps ®
N

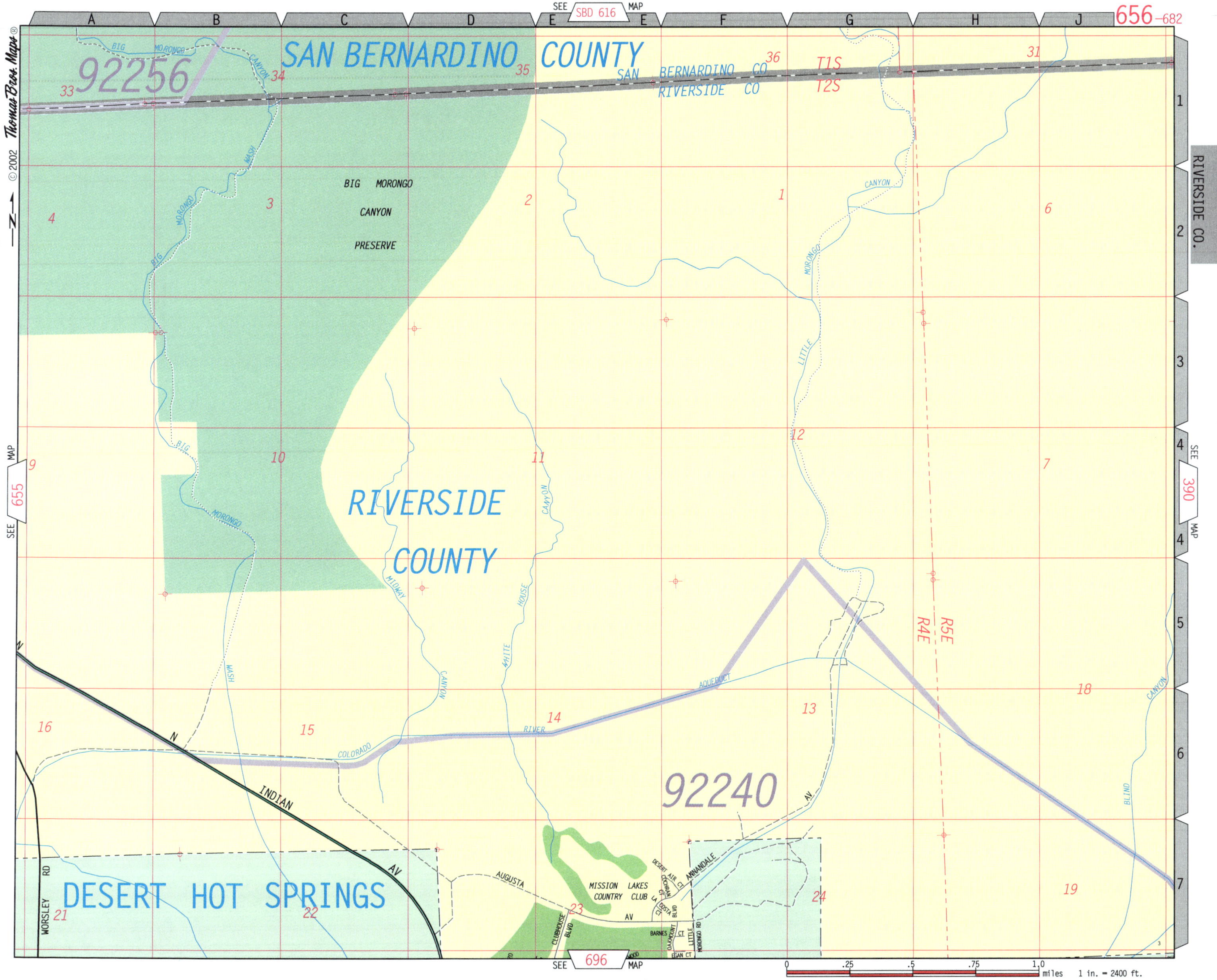
SEE SBD 616 MAP
A
B
C
D
E
F
G
H
J
SAN BERNARDINO COUNTY
SAN BERNARDINO CO
RIVERSIDE CO
T1S
T2S
92256
BIG MORONGO CANYON WASH
BIG MORONGO CANYON PRESERVE
RIVERSIDE COUNTY
MIDWAY
CANYON
HOUSE
WHITE
LITTLE MORONGO CANYON
R4E
R5E
COLORADO RIVER AQUEDUCT
N INDIAN AV
92240
DESERT HOT SPRINGS
WORSLEY RD
AUGUSTA AV
MISSION LAKES COUNTRY CLUB
CLUBHOUSE BLVD
DESERT AIR CT
COCHRAN CT
LA COSTA BLVD
ANNANDALE AV
BARNES CT
OAKMONT
LITTLE MORONGO RD
EGAN CT
BLIND CANYON
RIVERSIDE CO.
SEE 655 MAP
SEE 390 MAP
SEE 696 MAP
33
34
35
36
31
1
2
3
4
6
7
9
10
11
12
13
14
15
16
18
19
21
22
23
24
0 .25 .5 .75 1.0 miles
1 in. = 2400 ft.

SEE 643 MAP

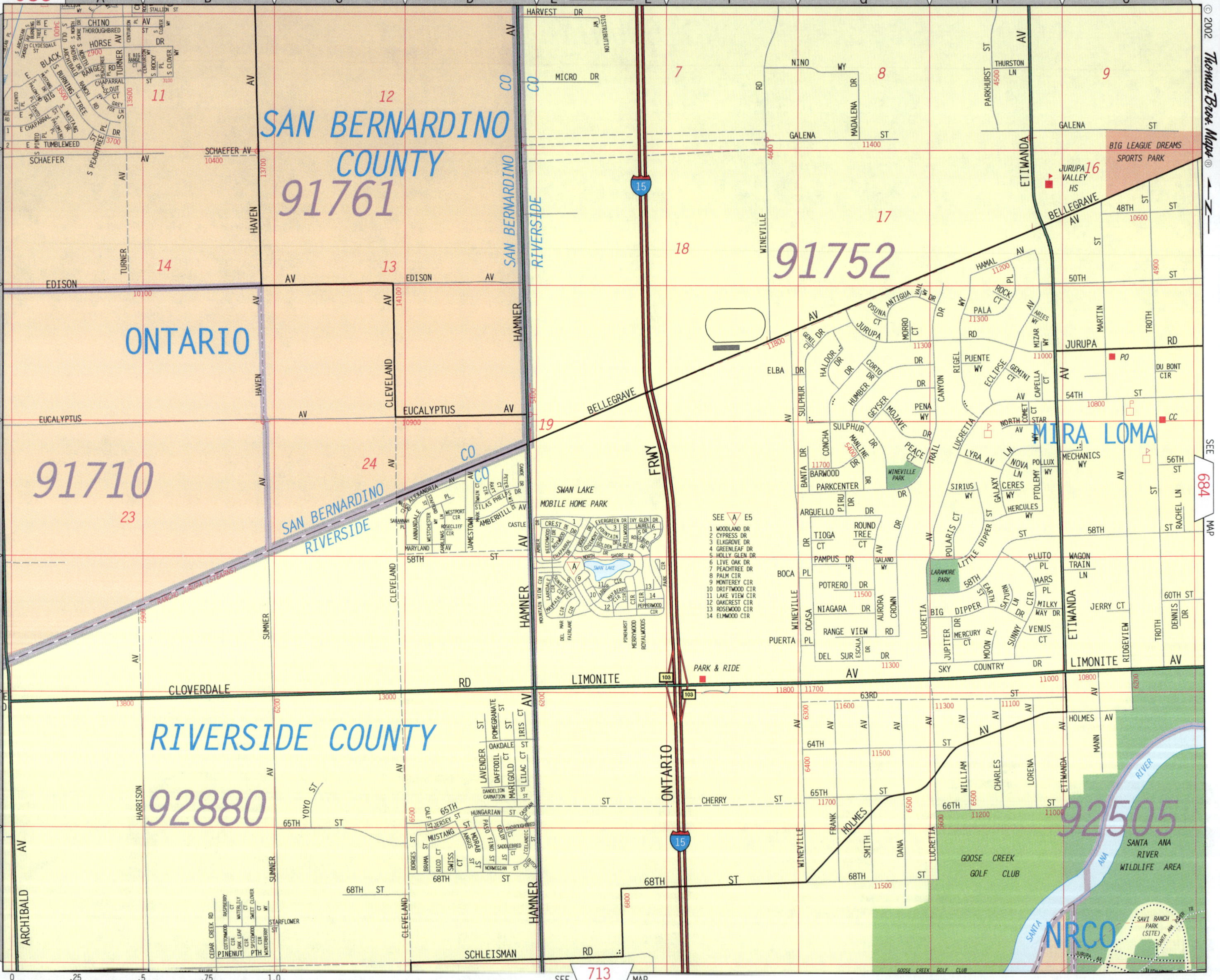
SAN BERNARDINO COUNTY
91761
ONTARIO
91710
RIVERSIDE COUNTY
92880
91752
MIRA LOMA
92505
NRCO
RIVERSIDE CO.
SAN BERNARDINO CO
RIVERSIDE CO
SWAN LAKE MOBILE HOME PARK
BIG LEAGUE DREAMS SPORTS PARK
JURUPA VALLEY HS
WINEVILLE PARK
LARAMORE PARK
GOOSE CREEK GOLF CLUB
SANTA ANA RIVER WILDLIFE AREA
SANTA ANA RIVER
PARK & RIDE
ONTARIO FRWY
HAMNER AV
ARCHIBALD AV
HAVEN AV
CLEVELAND AV
SUMNER AV
HARRISON AV
WINEVILLE RD
ETIWANDA AV
EDISON AV
EUCALYPTUS AV
SCHAEFER AV
BELLEGRAVE AV
JURUPA RD
LIMONITE AV
CLOVERDALE RD
68TH ST
SCHLEISMAN RD
GALENA ST
CHERRY ST
RANCHO JURUPA (STEARNS)
SEE A E5
1 WOODLAND DR
2 CYPRESS DR
3 ELKGROVE DR
4 GREENLEAF DR
5 HOLLY GLEN DR
6 LIVE OAK DR
7 PEACHTREE DR
8 PALM CIR
9 MONTEREY CIR
10 DRIFTWOOD CIR
11 LAKE VIEW CIR
12 OAKCREST CIR
13 ROSEWOOD CIR
14 ELMWOOD CIR
SEE SBD 682 MAP
SEE 684 MAP
SEE 713 MAP
0 .25 .5 .75 1.0 miles 1 in. = 2400 ft.
Thomas Bros. Maps
© 2002

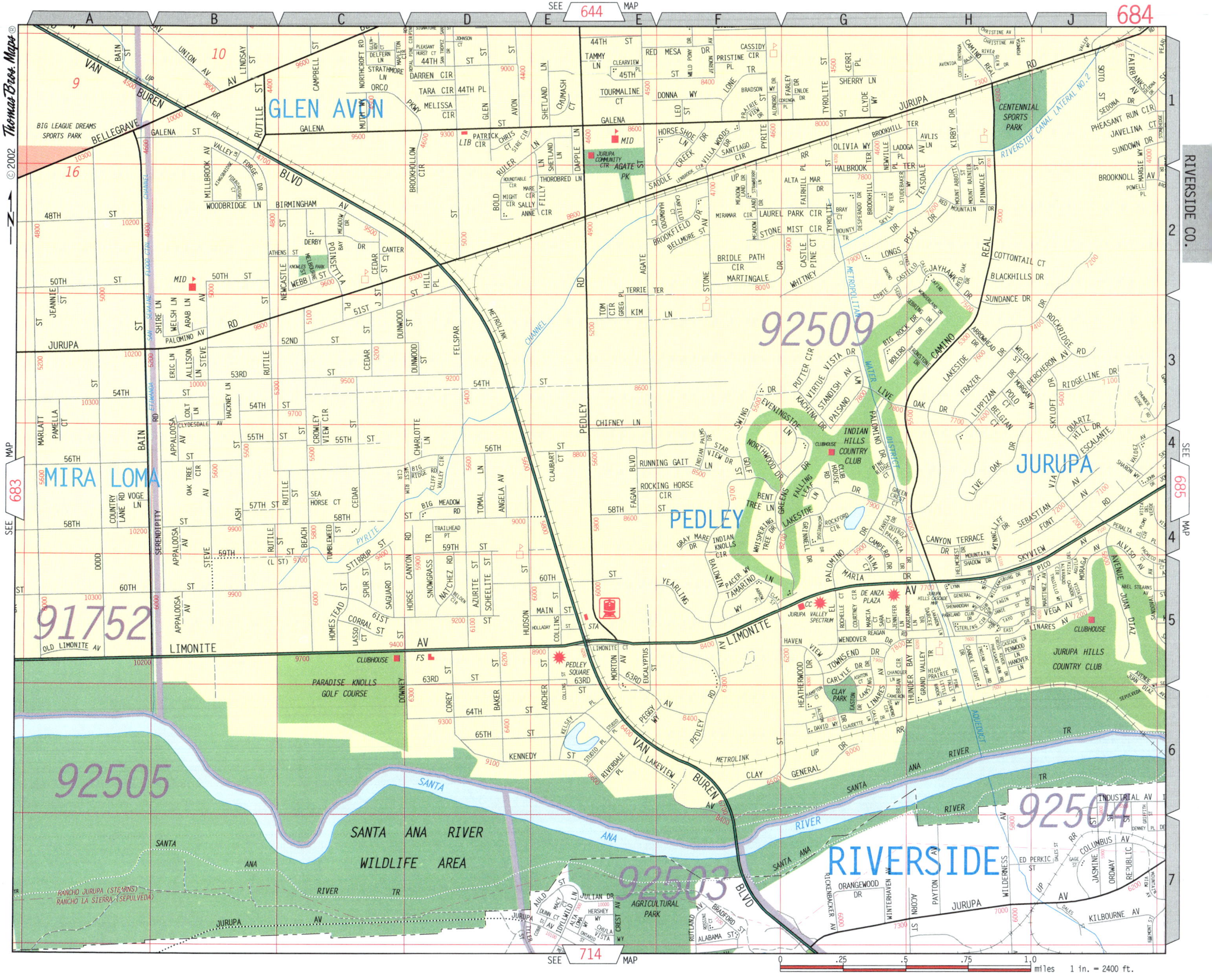
SEE 644 MAP
SEE 683 MAP
SEE 685 MAP
SEE 714 MAP
RIVERSIDE CO.
GLEN AVON
MIRA LOMA
PEDLEY
JURUPA
RIVERSIDE
91752
92509
92505
92504
92503
BIG LEAGUE DREAMS SPORTS PARK
CENTENNIAL SPORTS PARK
JURUPA COMMUNITY CTR
AGATE PK
INDIAN HILLS COUNTRY CLUB
PARADISE KNOLLS GOLF COURSE
JURUPA HILLS COUNTRY CLUB
DE ANZA PLAZA
PEDLEY SQUARE
JURUPA VALLEY SPECTRUM
CLAY PARK
AGRICULTURAL PARK
SANTA ANA RIVER WILDLIFE AREA
SANTA ANA RIVER
RANCHO JURUPA (STEARNS)
RANCHO LA SIERRA (SEPULVEDA)
VAN BUREN BLVD
LIMONITE AV
JURUPA RD
JURUPA AV
PEDLEY RD
METROLINK
RIVERSIDE CANAL LATERAL NO. 2
METROPOLITAN WATER DISTRICT
AQUEDUCT
CHANNEL
0 .25 .5 .75 1.0 miles 1 in. = 2400 ft.

SEE 645 MAP

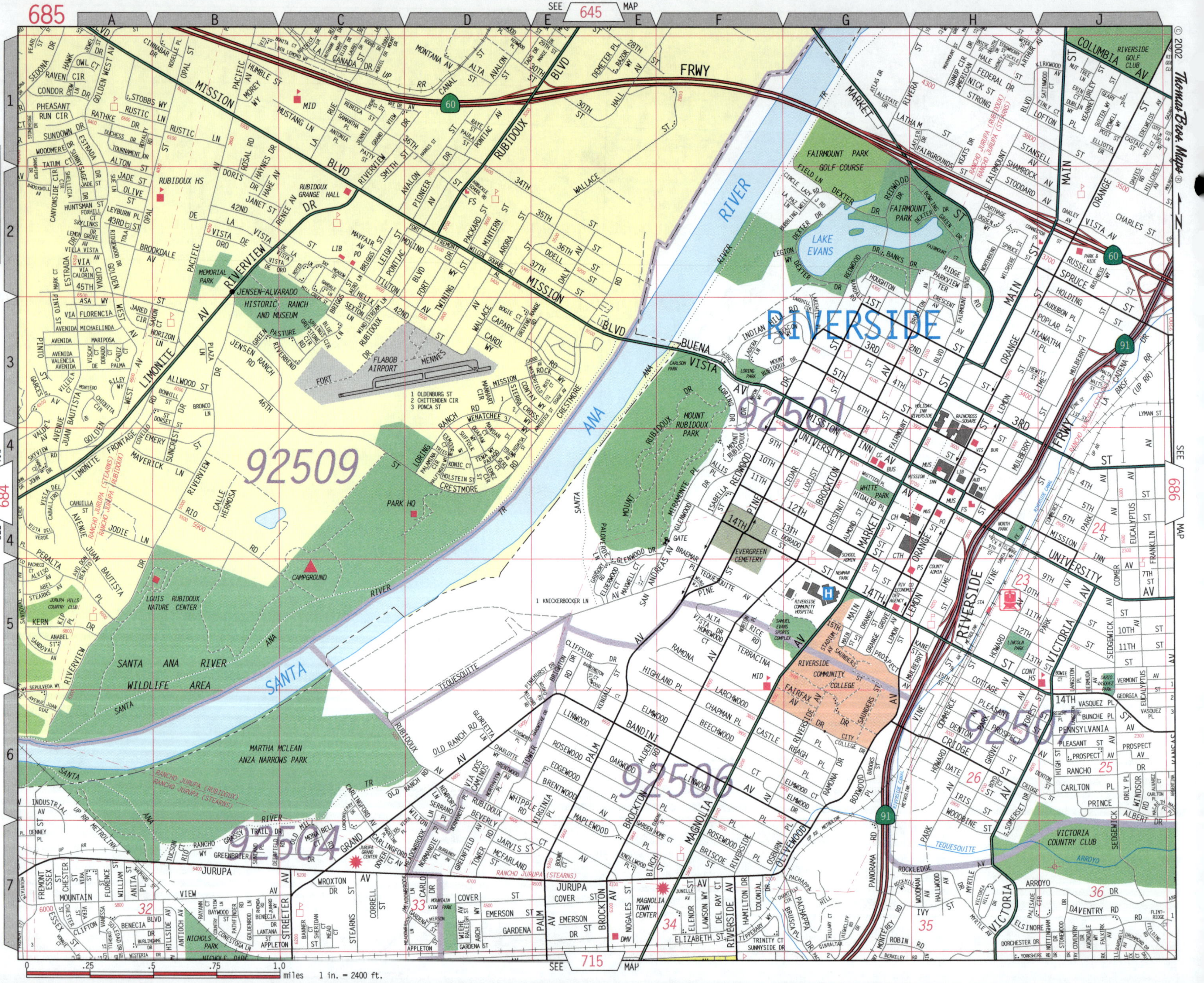

SEE 684 MAP

SEE 686 MAP

SEE 715 MAP

SEE 646 MAP

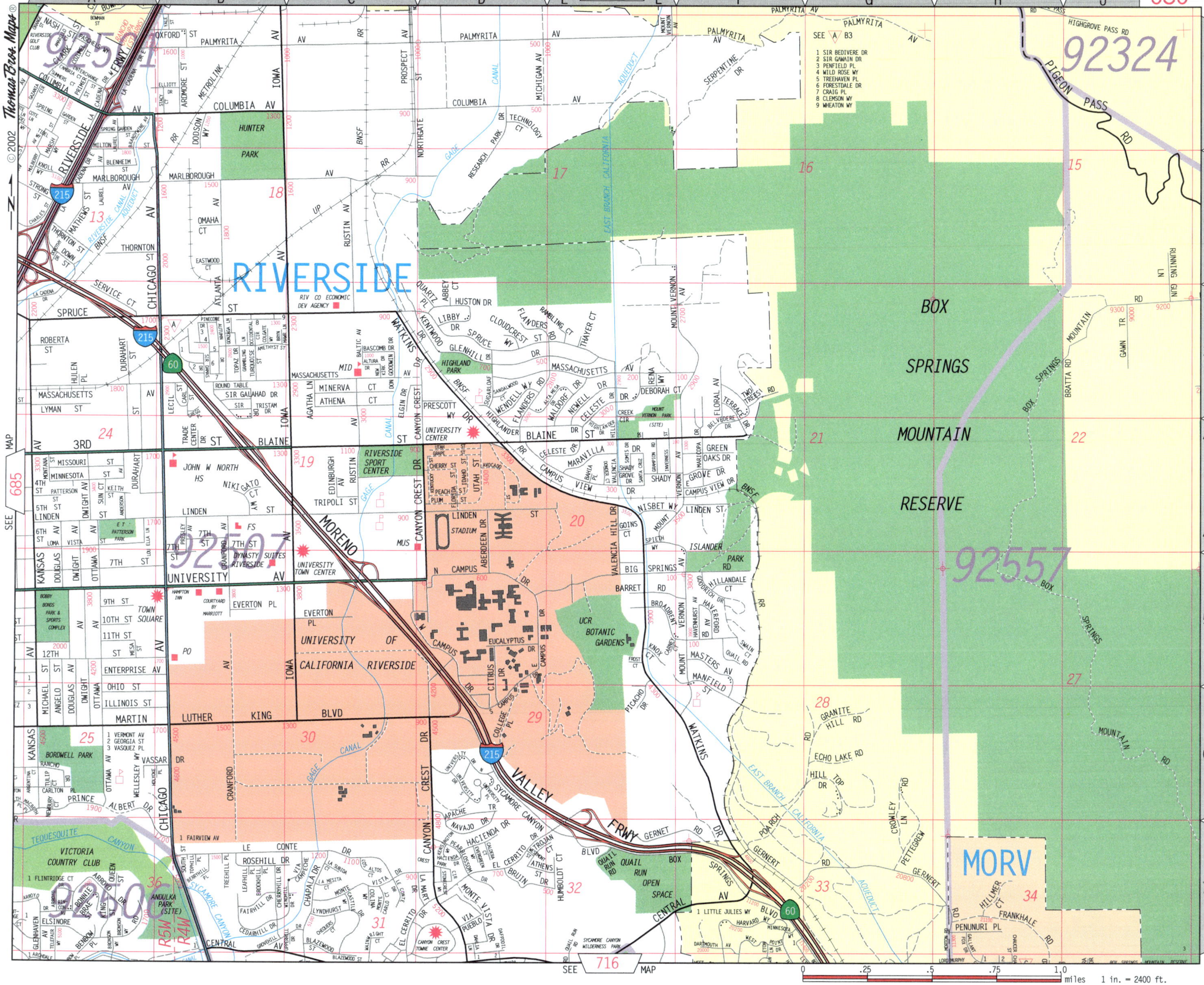

SEE 685 MAP
SEE 687 MAP
SEE 716 MAP

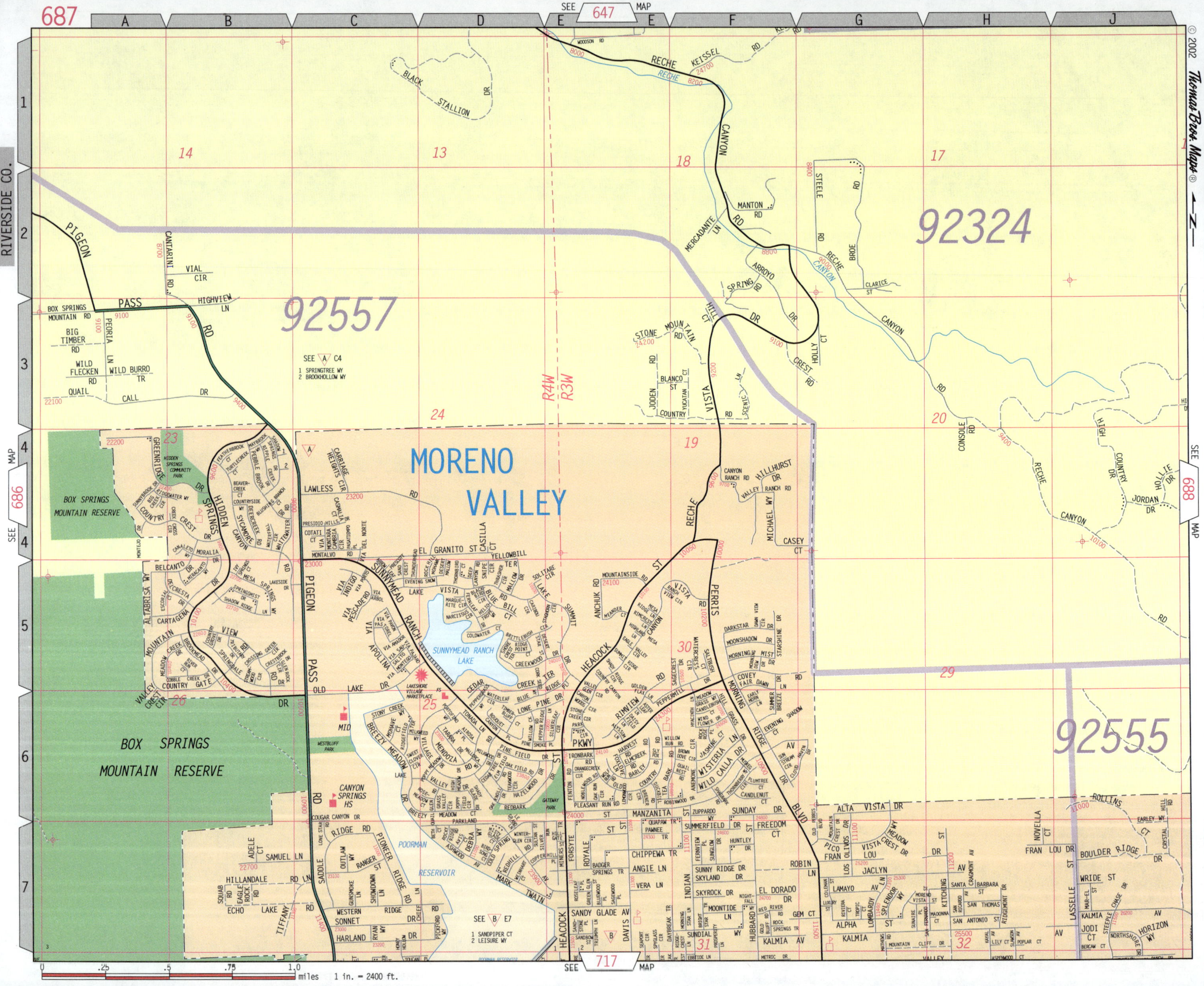
SEE 647 MAP
SEE 686 MAP
SEE 688 MAP
SEE 717 MAP
RIVERSIDE CO.
MORENO VALLEY
92557
92324
92555
BOX SPRINGS MOUNTAIN RESERVE
SUNNYMEAD RANCH LAKE
POORMAN RESERVOIR
CANYON SPRINGS HS
MID
WESTBLUFF PARK
GATEWAY PARK
LAKESHORE VILLAGE MARKETPLACE
HIDDEN SPRINGS COMMUNITY PARK
R4W R3W
PIGEON PASS RD
RECHE CANYON RD
HEACOCK ST
PERRIS BLVD
SUNNYMEAD RANCH PKWY
KEISSEL RD
BLACK STALLION DR
HIGHVIEW LN
VIAL CIR
CANTARINI RD
BOX SPRINGS MOUNTAIN RD
QUAIL CALL DR
LAWLESS RD
EL GRANITO ST
CASEY CT
ALTA VISTA DR
ROLLINS
BOULDER RIDGE
MANZANITA ST
SUNDAY DR
KALMIA AV
ALPHA ST
JACLYN AV
SEE A C4
1 SPRINGTREE WY
2 BROOKHOLLOW WY
SEE B E7
1 SANDPIPER CT
2 LEISURE WY
0 .25 .5 .75 1.0 miles 1 in. = 2400 ft.
Thomas Bros. Maps®

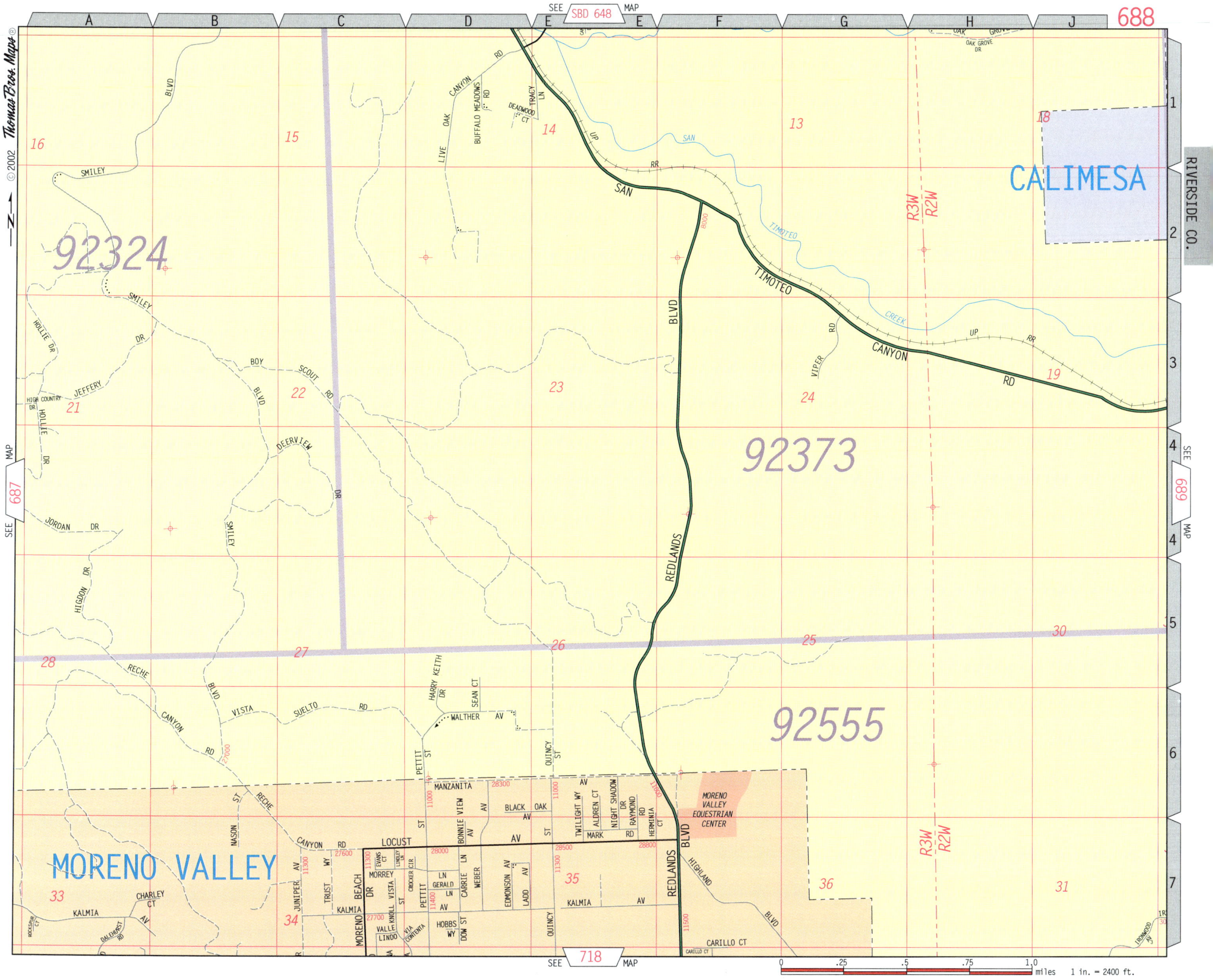
SEE SBD 648 MAP
SEE 687 MAP
SEE 689 MAP
SEE 718 MAP
A
B
C
D
E
F
G
H
J
1
2
3
4
5
6
7
RIVERSIDE CO.
CALIMESA
MORENO VALLEY
92324
92373
92555
SMILEY BLVD
SMILEY
HOLLIE DR
HIGH COUNTRY DR
JEFFERY DR
BOY SCOUT RD
DEERVIEW
JORDAN DR
HIGDON DR
REDLANDS BLVD
SAN TIMOTEO CANYON RD
UP RR
SAN TIMOTEO CREEK
VIPER RD
LIVE OAK CANYON RD
BUFFALO MEADOWS RD
DEADWOOD CT
TRACY LN
OAK GROVE DR
R3W
R2W
RECHE CANYON RD
RECHE VISTA DR
VISTA SUELTO RD
HARRY KEITH DR
SEAN CT
WALTHER AV
PETTIT ST
QUINCY ST
MANZANITA AV
BONNIE VIEW AV
BLACK OAK AV
TWILIGHT WY
ALDREN CT
NIGHT SHADOW DR
RAYMOND RD
HERMINIA CT
MARK RD
LOCUST AV
NASON ST
JUNIPER AV
TRUST WY
MORENO BEACH DR
KALMIA
MORREY
KNOLL VISTA ST
CROCKER CIR
GERALD LN
CARRIE LN
WEBER
EDMONSON AV
LADD AV
HOBBS WY
DOW ST
VALLE LINDO
VIA CENTENTA
CHARLEY CT
DALEHURST RD
HIGHLAND BLVD
CARILLO CT
IRONWOOD AV
MORENO VALLEY EQUESTRIAN CENTER
27000
27600
27700
28000
28300
28500
28800
8000
11000
11300
11400
11500
11600
13
14
15
16
18
19
21
22
23
24
25
26
27
28
30
31
33
34
35
36
0 .25 .5 .75 1.0 miles
1 in. = 2400 ft.

SEE 649 MAP
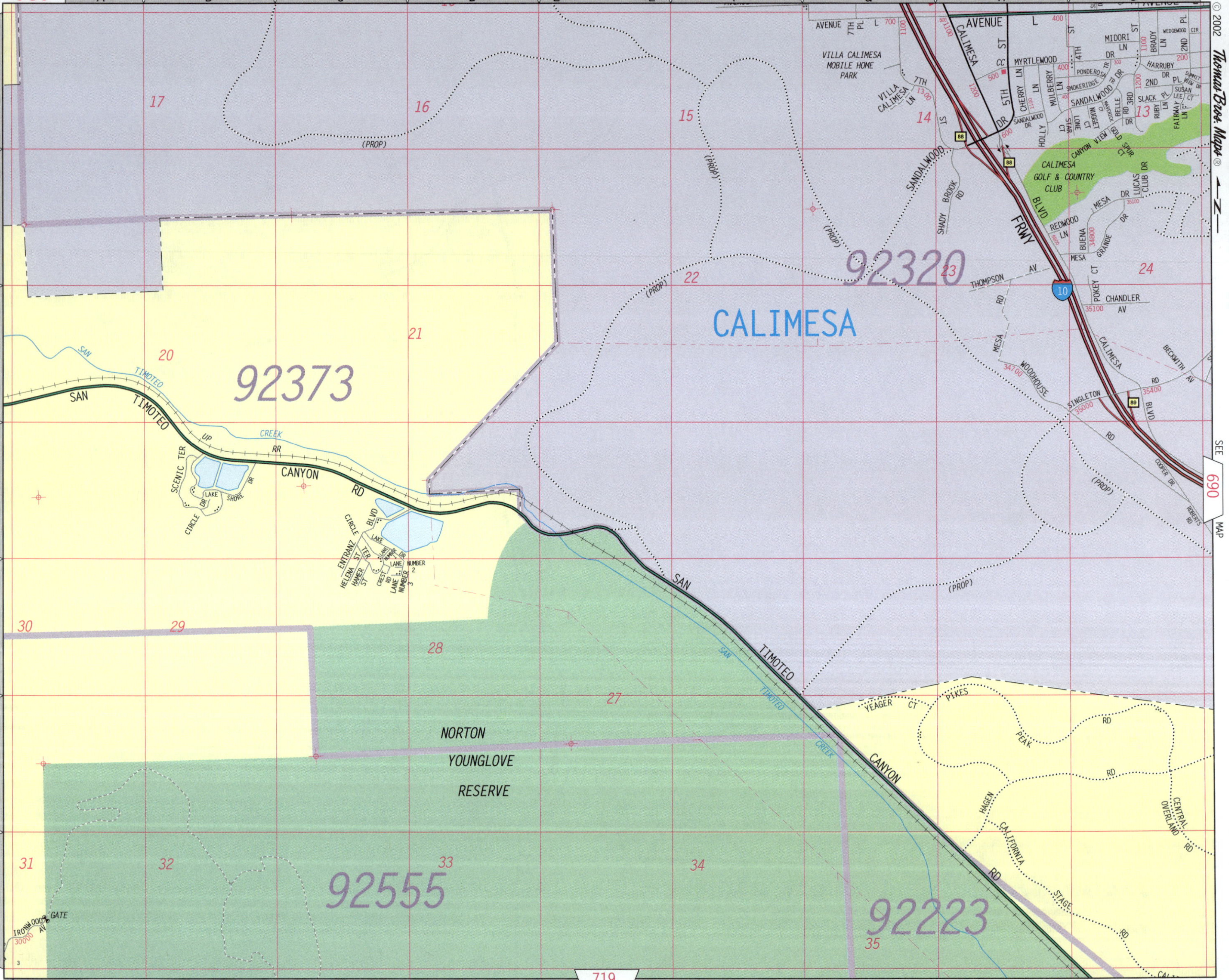

SEE 688 MAP
SEE 690 MAP
SEE 719 MAP
0 .25 .5 .75 1.0 miles 1 in. = 2400 ft.

SEE 650 MAP

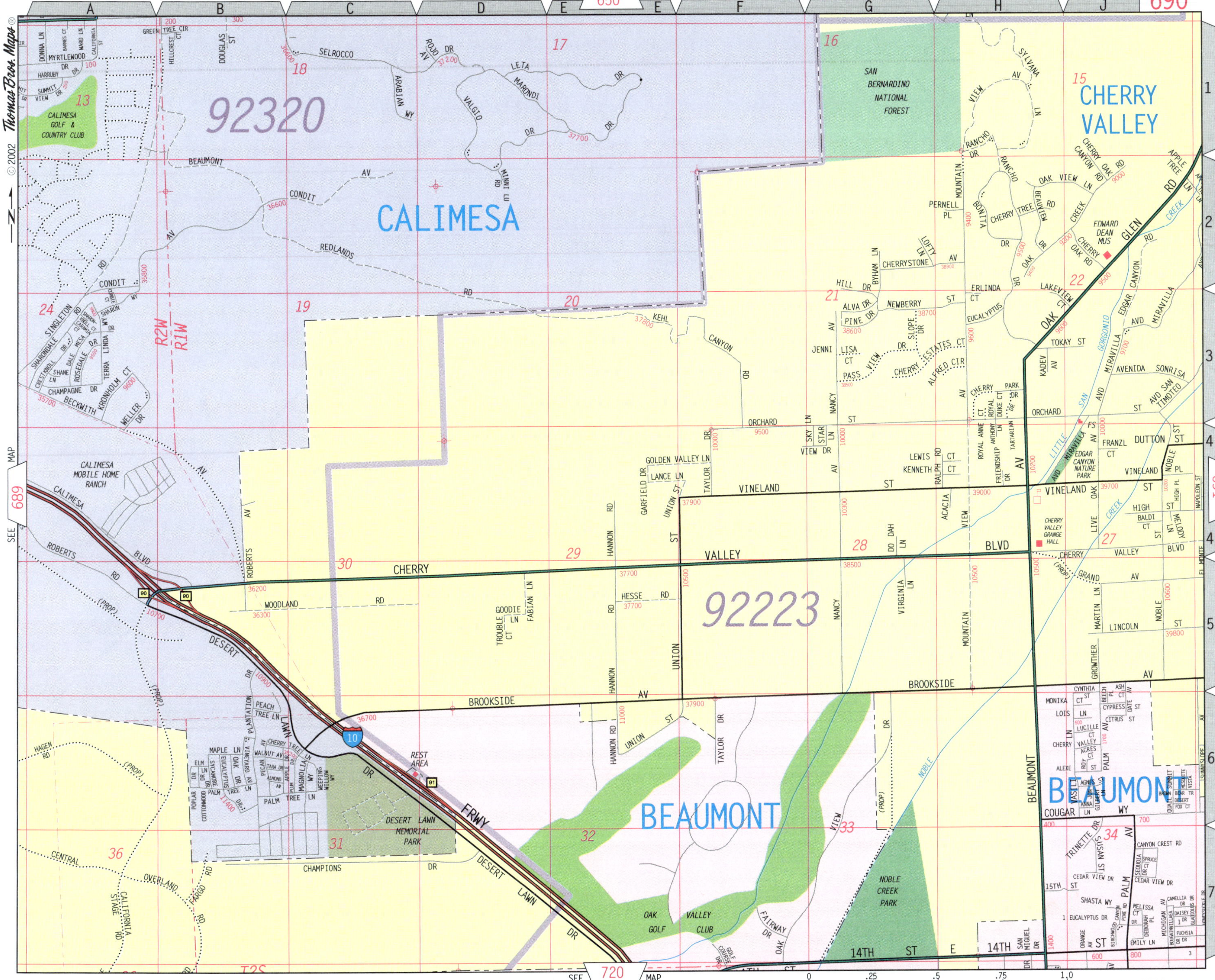

SEE 689 MAP
SEE 691 MAP
SEE 720 MAP

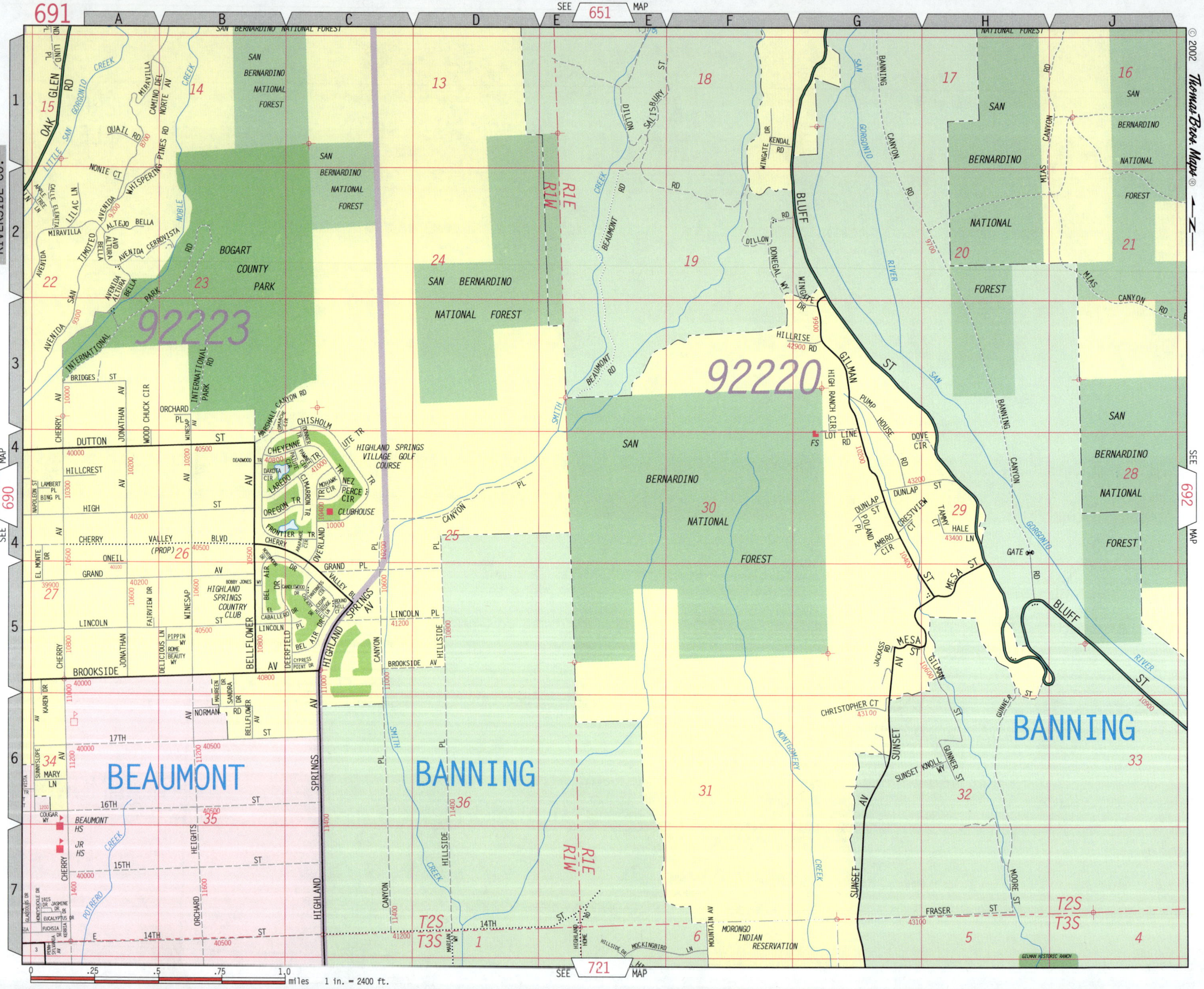
SEE 651 MAP
SEE 690 MAP
SEE 692 MAP
SEE 721 MAP
RIVERSIDE CO.
92223
92220
BEAUMONT
BANNING
SAN BERNARDINO NATIONAL FOREST
BOGART COUNTY PARK
HIGHLAND SPRINGS VILLAGE GOLF COURSE
HIGHLAND SPRINGS COUNTRY CLUB
CLUBHOUSE
BEAUMONT HS
JR HS
MORONGO INDIAN RESERVATION
GILMAN HISTORIC RANCH
OAK GLEN RD
BLUFF ST
GILMAN ST
MESA ST
SUNSET AV
HIGHLAND SPRINGS AV
BELLFLOWER AV
BROOKSIDE AV
LINCOLN
CHERRY VALLEY BLVD
DUTTON ST
HILLCREST
14TH ST
15TH ST
16TH ST
17TH ST
FRASER ST
T2S
T3S
R1E
R1W
miles 1 in. = 2400 ft.

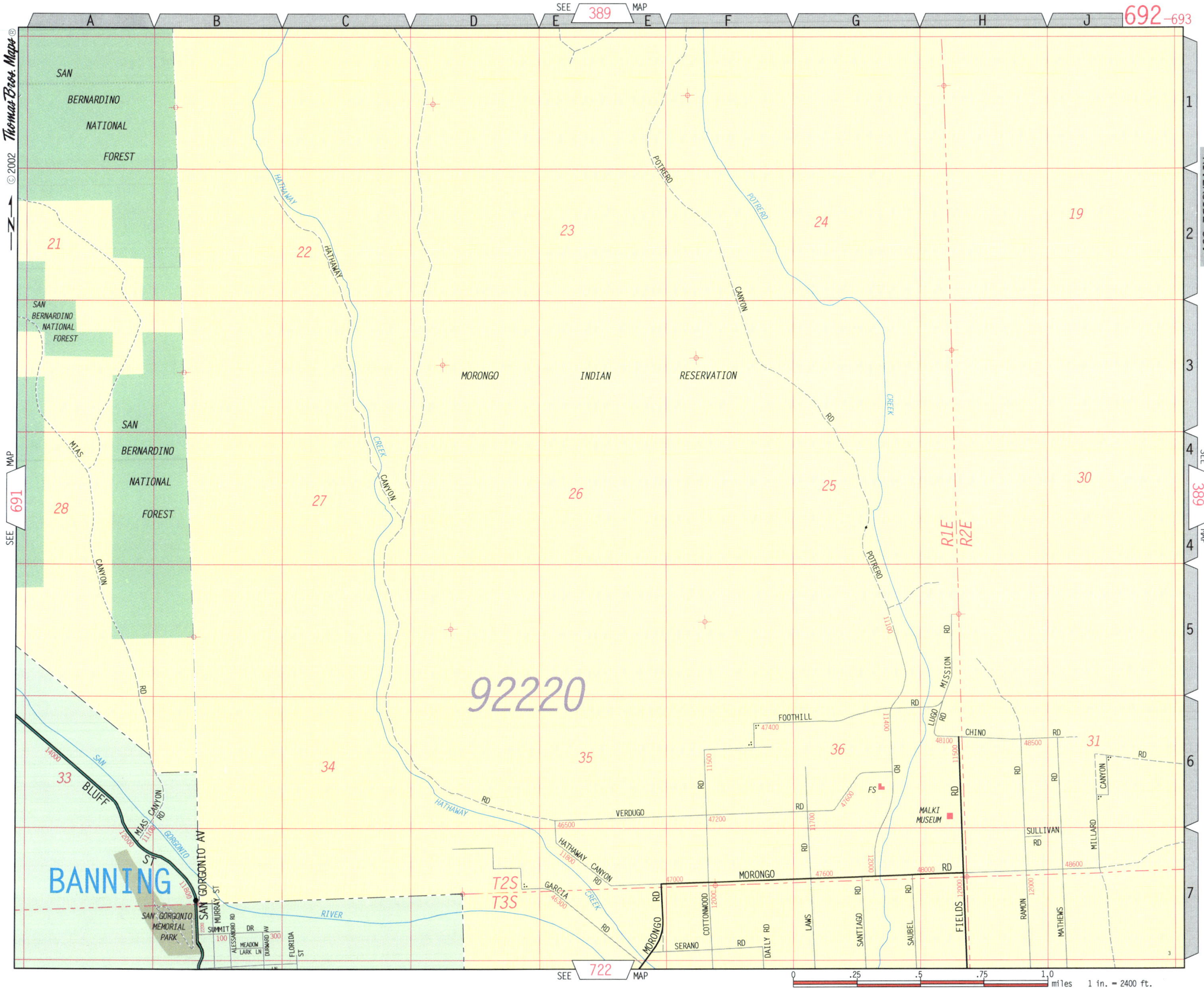
SEE 389 MAP
SEE 691 MAP
SEE 389 MAP
SEE 722 MAP
A
B
C
D
E
F
G
H
J
1
2
3
4
5
6
7
RIVERSIDE CO.
SAN BERNARDINO NATIONAL FOREST
MORONGO INDIAN RESERVATION
92220
BANNING
SAN GORGONIO MEMORIAL PARK
MALKI MUSEUM
FS
R1E
R2E
T2S
T3S
HATHAWAY CREEK
HATHAWAY CANYON
POTRERO CREEK
POTRERO CANYON RD
MIAS CANYON RD
SAN GORGONIO RIVER
BLUFF ST
SAN GORGONIO AV
MURRAY ST
SUMMIT DR
ALESSANDRO RD
MEADOW LARK LN
DURWARD AV
FLORIDA ST
HATHAWAY CANYON RD
GARCIA RD
MORONGO RD
VERDUGO RD
FOOTHILL RD
MISSION RD
LUGO RD
CHINO RD
SULLIVAN RD
MILLARD
CANYON RD
SERANO RD
COTTONWOOD RD
DAILY RD
LAWS RD
SANTIAGO RD
SAUBEL RD
FIELDS RD
RAMON RD
MATHEWS RD
21
22
23
24
19
28
27
26
25
30
33
34
35
36
31
14000
12000
11100
11800
2200
100
300
46500
46300
11800
47000
47200
47400
47600
47600
11500
11700
12000
12000
11400
11100
48000
48100
48500
48600
11500
12000
12000
0
.25
.5
.75
1.0
miles
1 in. = 2400 ft.

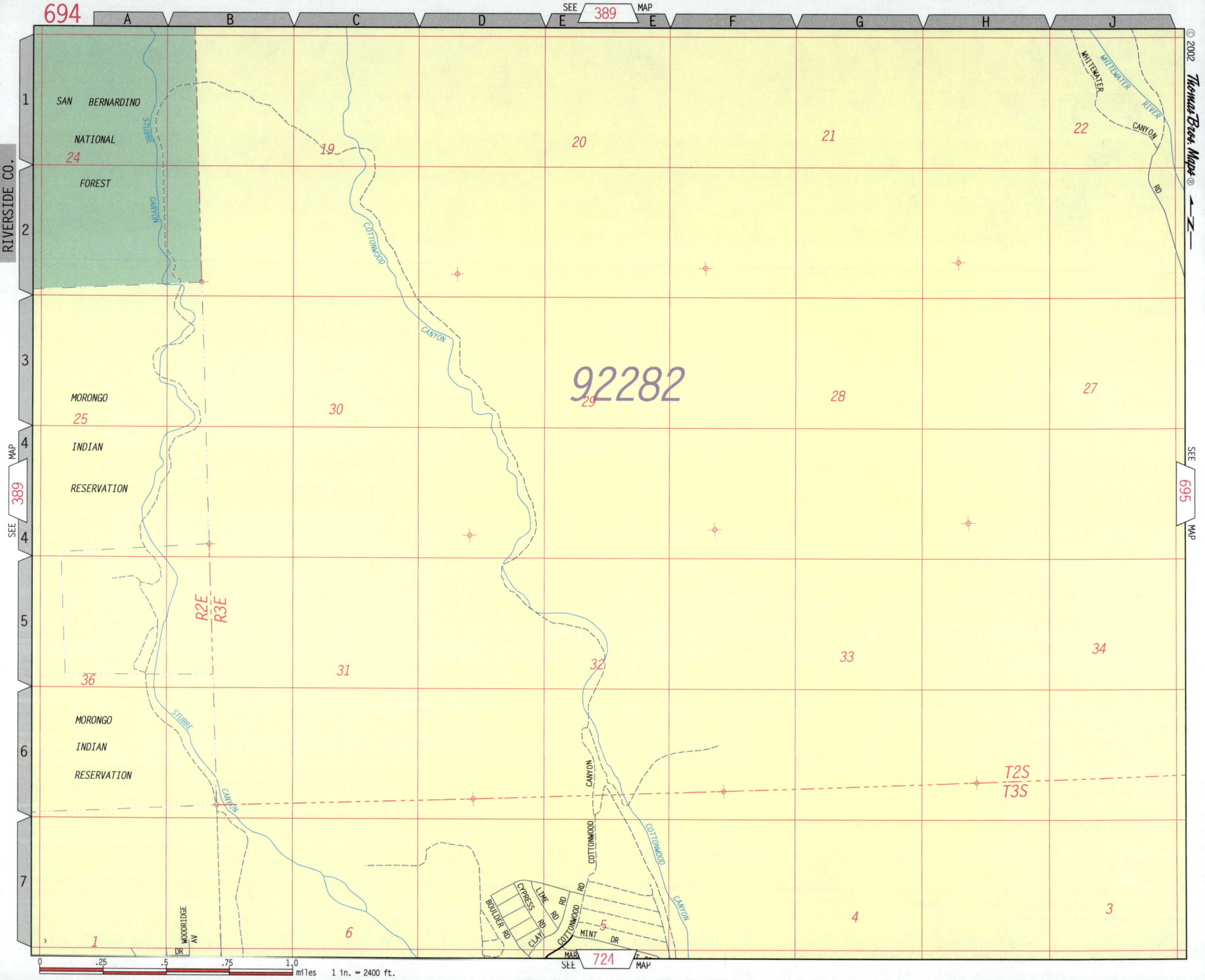
SEE 389 MAP
A
B
C
D
E
F
G
H
J
1
2
3
4
5
6
7
RIVERSIDE CO.
SAN BERNARDINO
NATIONAL
FOREST
24
STUBBE
CANYON
19
20
21
22
WHITEWATER
WHITEWATER
RIVER
CANYON
RD
COTTONWOOD
CANYON
92282
29
30
28
27
MORONGO
INDIAN
RESERVATION
25
SEE MAP 389
SEE MAP 695
R2E
R3E
31
32
33
34
36
MORONGO
INDIAN
RESERVATION
STUBBE
CANYON
T2S
T3S
CANYON
COTTONWOOD
RD
COTTONWOOD
CANYON
CYPRESS
LIME
RD
BOULDER
RD
CLAY
COTTONWOOD
RD
MINT
DR
5
4
3
6
1
WOODRIDGE
AV
DR
SEE 724 MAP
0
.25
.5
.75
1.0
miles
1 in. = 2400 ft.
© 2002
Thomas Bros. Maps®
N

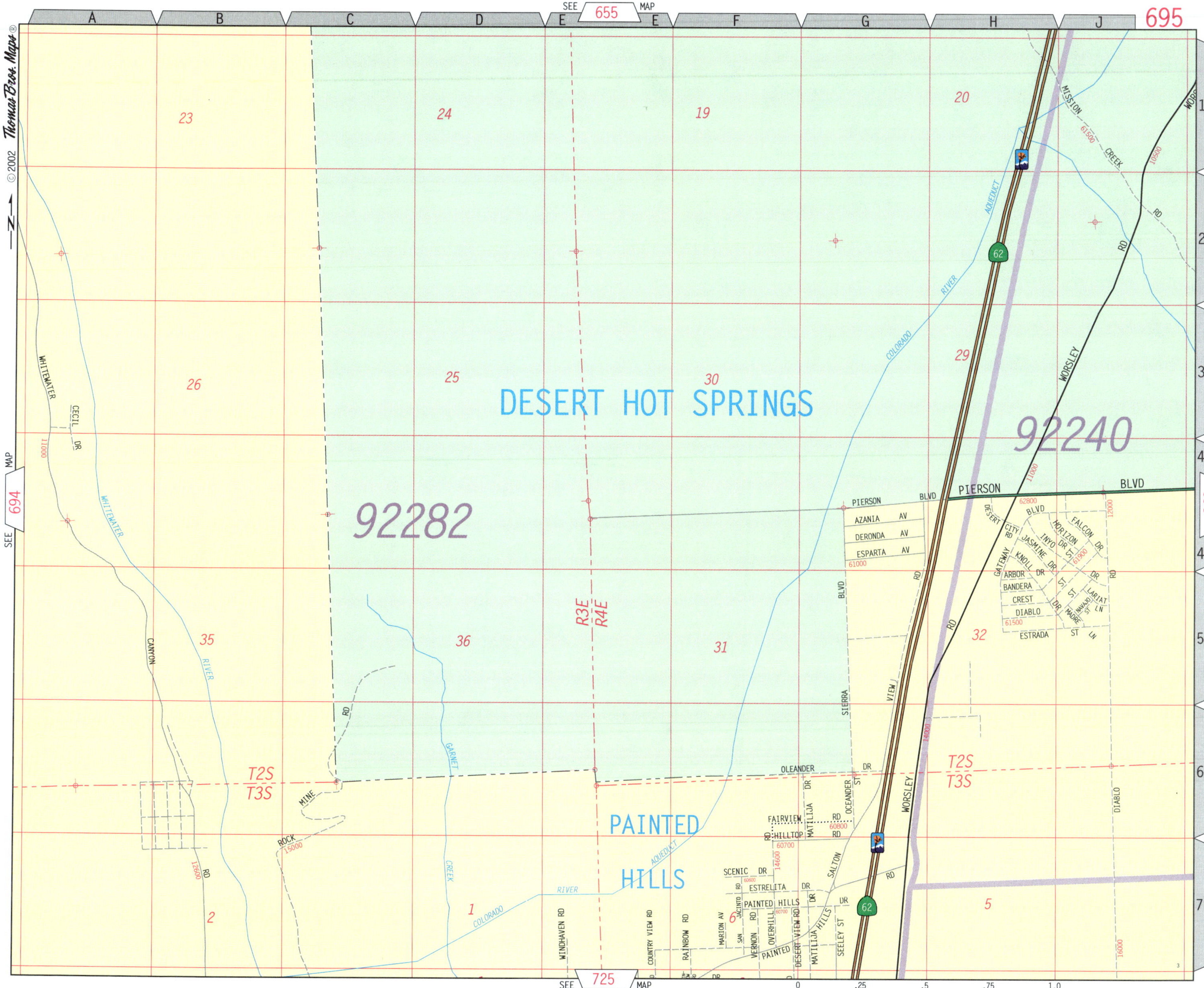
SEE 655 MAP
SEE 725 MAP
SEE 694 MAP
SEE 696 MAP
RIVERSIDE CO.
DESERT HOT SPRINGS
PAINTED HILLS
92282
92240
PIERSON BLVD
AZANIA AV
DERONDA AV
ESPARTA AV
OLEANDER DR
FAIRVIEW RD
HILLTOP RD
SCENIC DR
ESTRELITA DR
PAINTED HILLS DR
WORSLEY RD
WHITEWATER RIVER
COLORADO RIVER AQUEDUCT
GARNET CREEK
MISSION CREEK RD
WHITEWATER CANYON RD
CECIL DR
MINE RD
ROCK RD
SIERRA BLVD
VIEW RD
SALTON
WINDHAVEN RD
COUNTRY VIEW RD
RAINBOW RD
MARION AV
SAN JACINTO RD
VERNON
OVERHILL
DESERT VIEW RD
MATILIJA HILLS
SEELEY ST
OCEANDER ST
MATILIJA DR
DIABLO
DESERT CITY RD
GATEWAY
JASMINE DR
INYO DR
HORIZON ST
FALCON DR
KNOLL
ARBOR DR
BANDERA ST
CREST
DIABLO DR
ESTRADA ST
LARIAT LN
NAVAJO ST
MADRE
LN
R3E R4E
T2S T3S
miles 1 in. = 2400 ft.
0 .25 .5 .75 1.0

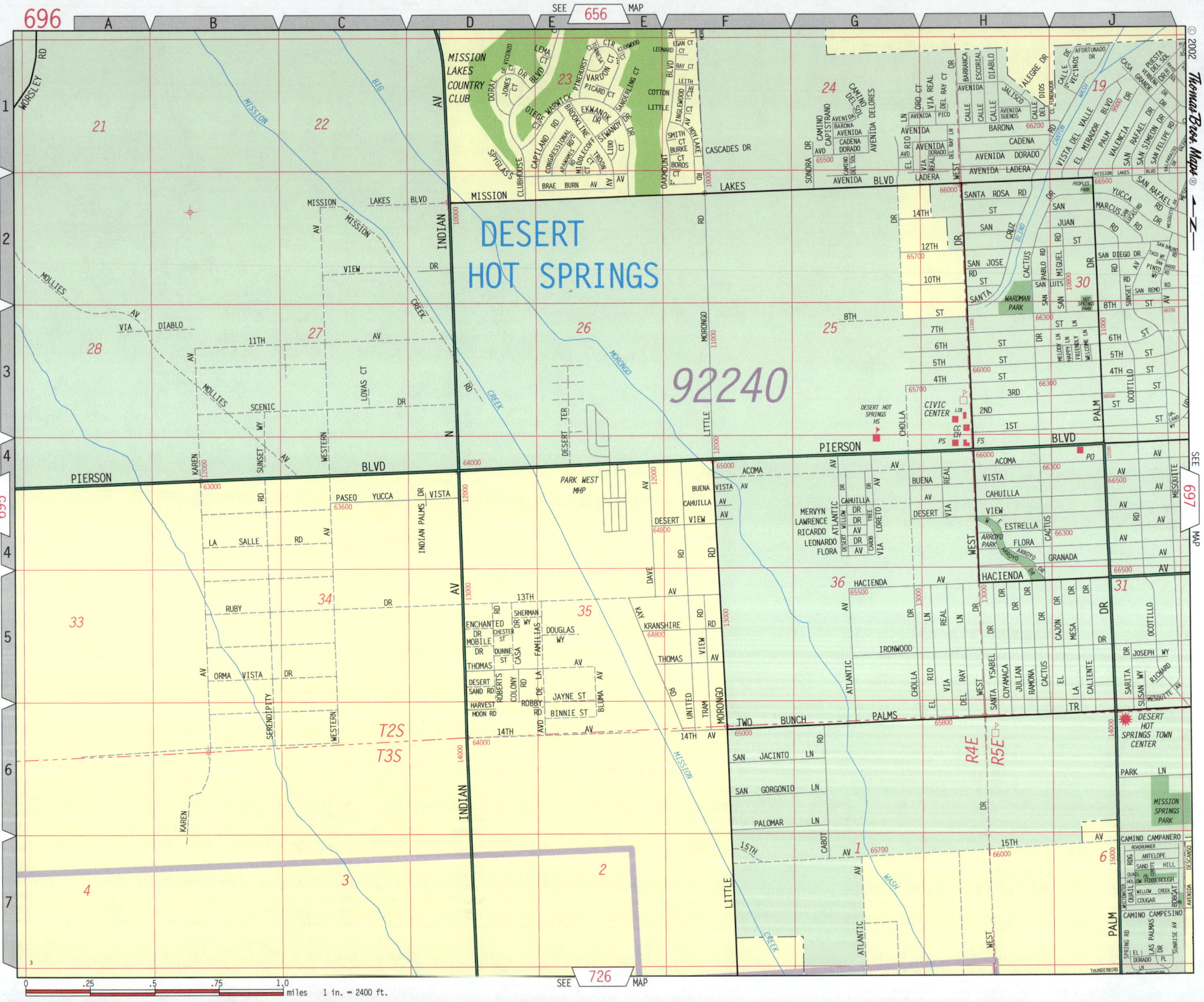
SEE 656 MAP
A
B
C
D
E
F
G
H
J
RIVERSIDE CO.
MISSION LAKES COUNTRY CLUB
DESERT HOT SPRINGS
92240
DESERT HOT SPRINGS HS
CIVIC CENTER
WARDMAN PARK
ARROYO PARK
PARK WEST MHP
MISSION SPRINGS PARK
DESERT HOT SPRINGS TOWN CENTER
MISSION LAKES BLVD
PIERSON BLVD
INDIAN AV
LITTLE MORONGO RD
PALM DR
WEST DR
HACIENDA AV
TWO BUNCH PALMS
MISSION CREEK
BIG MORONGO CREEK
T2S
T3S
R4E
R5E
SEE 695 MAP
SEE 697 MAP
SEE 726 MAP
0 .25 .5 .75 1.0 miles 1 in. = 2400 ft.
© 2002 Thomas Bros. Maps ®

SEE 390 MAP

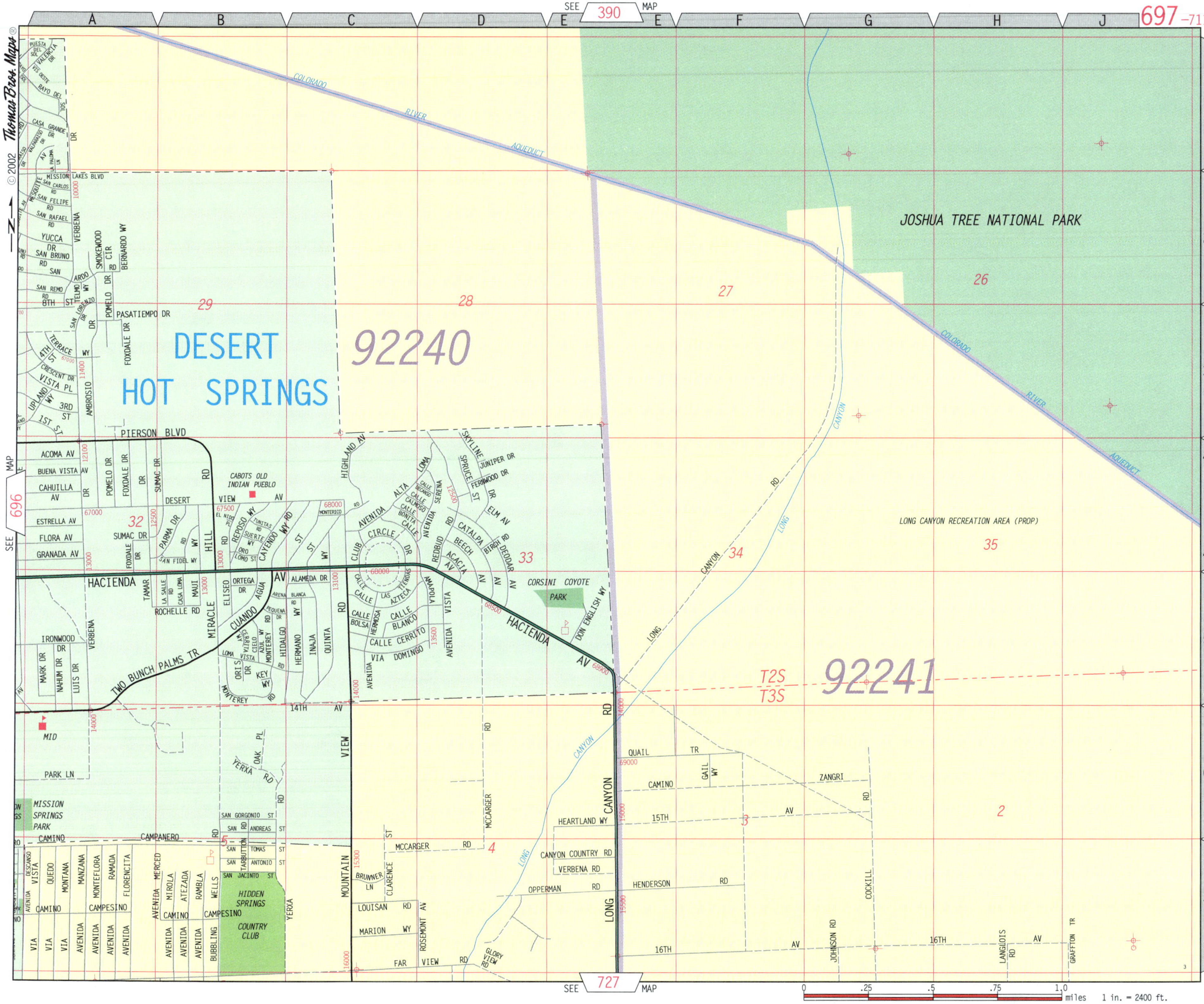

SEE 696 MAP

SEE 390 MAP

SEE 727 MAP

SEE SBD 682 MAP

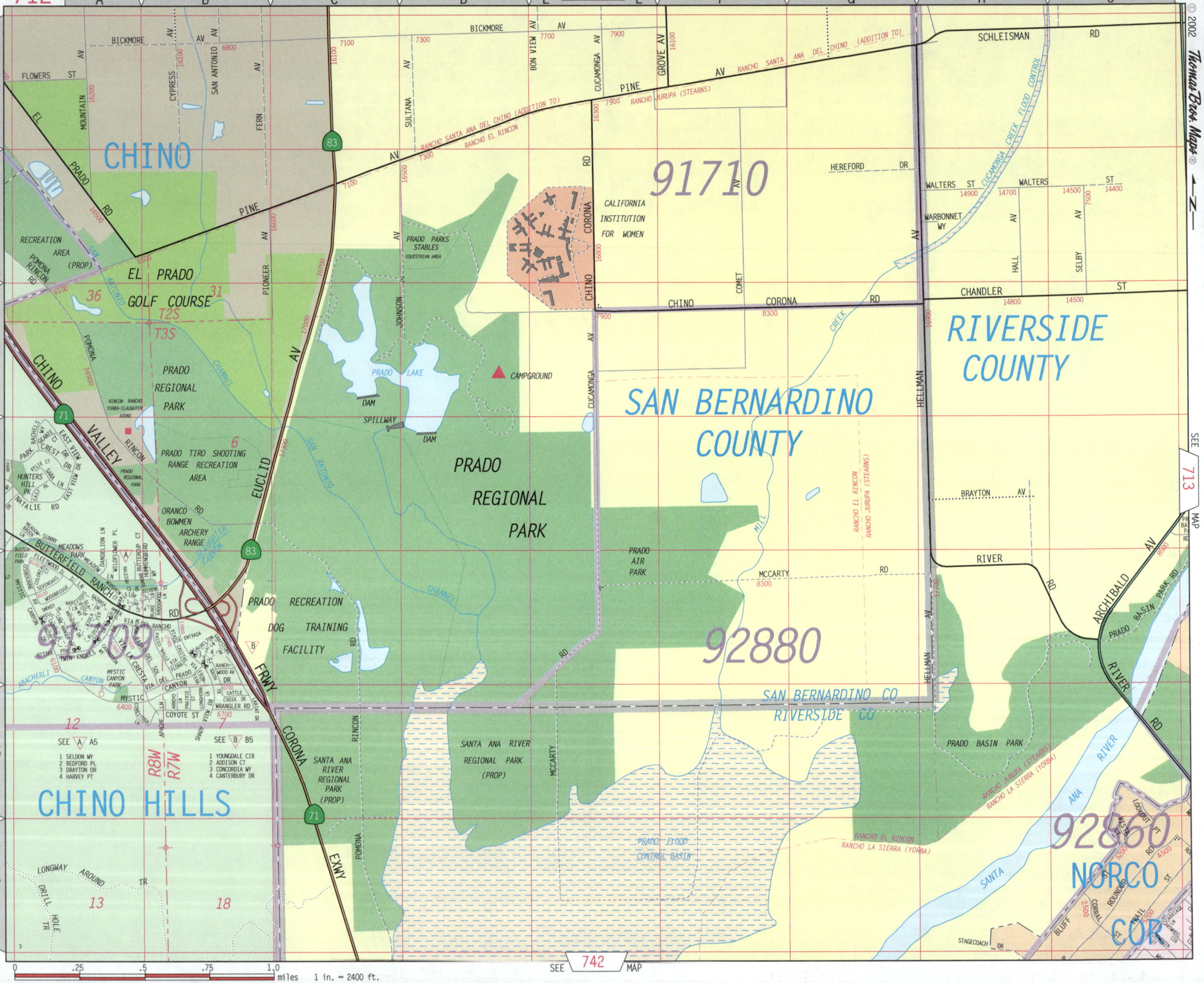

SEE 742 MAP

SEE 683 MAP

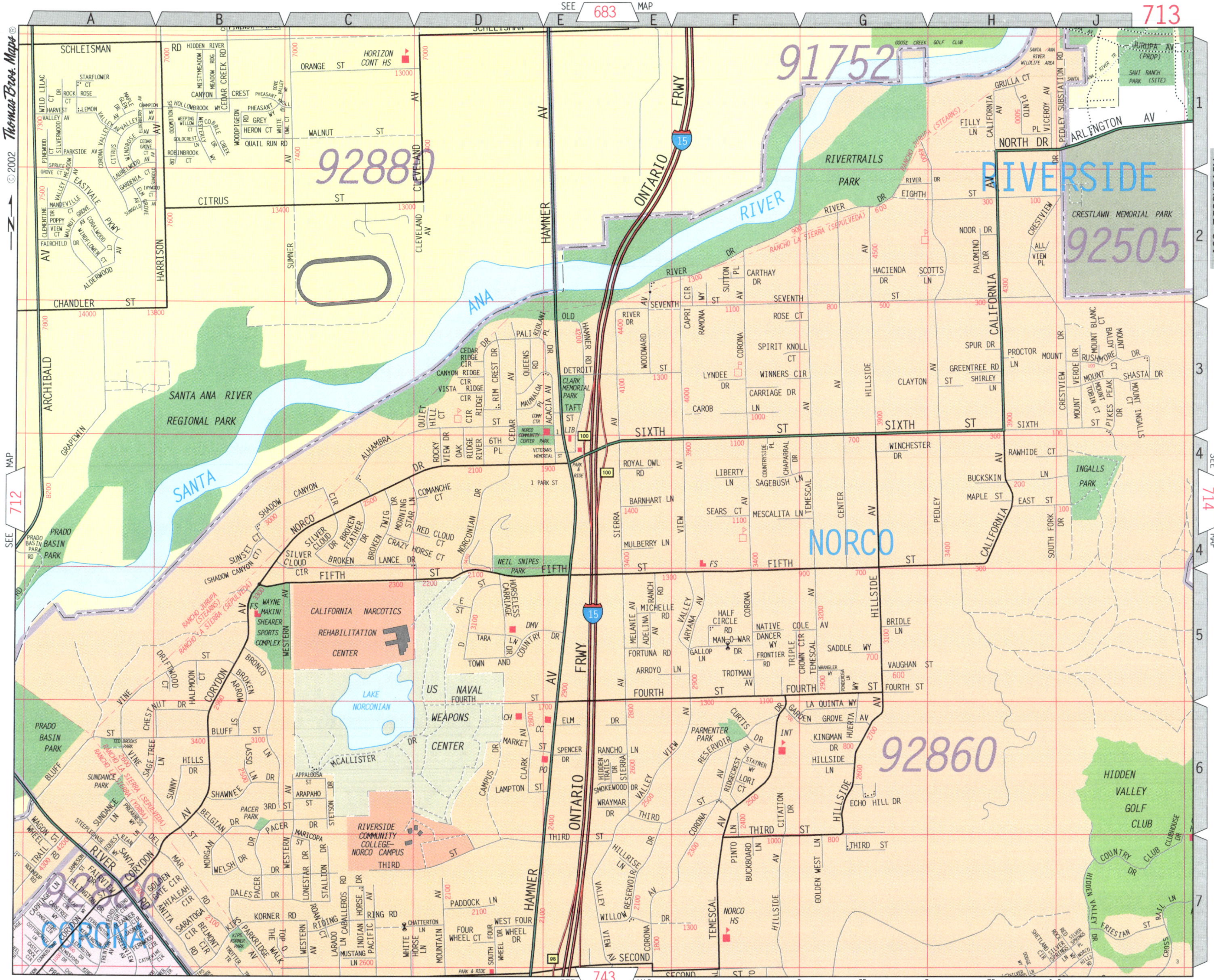

SEE 743 MAP

SEE 712 MAP

SEE 714 MAP

0 .25 .5 .75 1.0 miles 1 in. = 2400 ft.

SEE 684 MAP

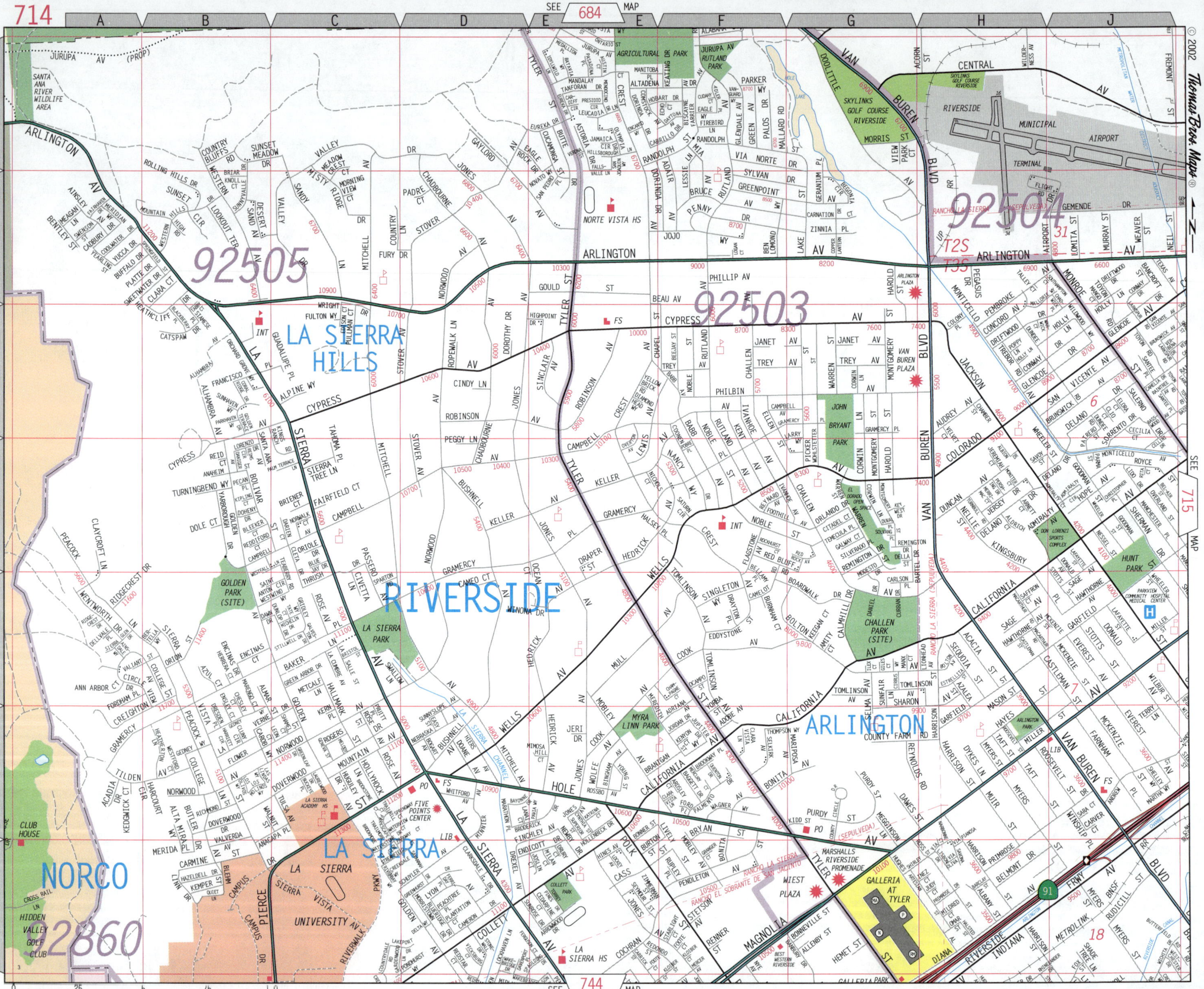

SEE 713 MAP

SEE 715 MAP

SEE 744 MAP

0 .25 .5 .75 1.0 miles 1 in. = 2400 ft.

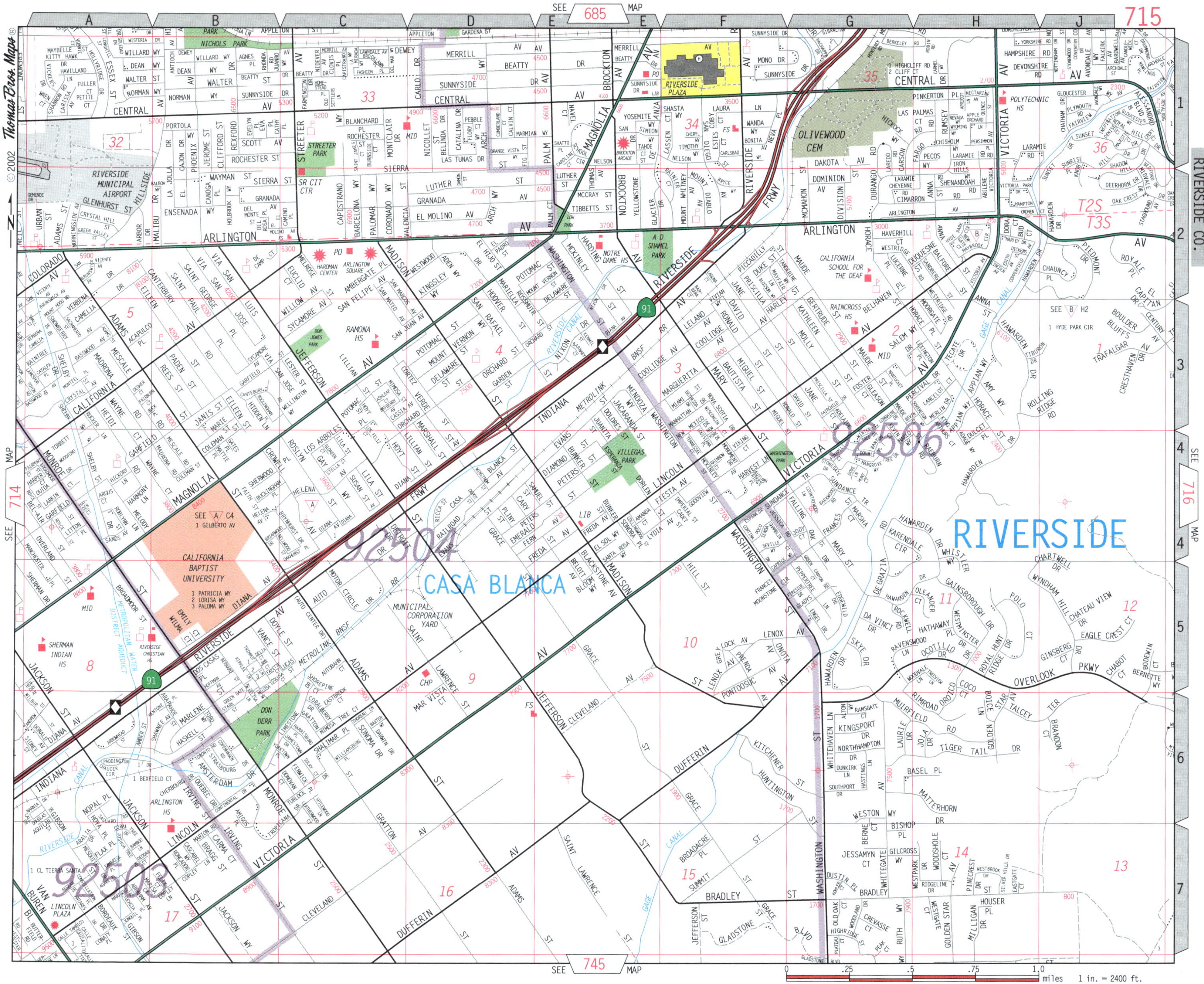
SEE 685 MAP
SEE 745 MAP
SEE 714 MAP
SEE 716 MAP
RIVERSIDE
RIVERSIDE CO.
CASA BLANCA
92504
92506
92503
Thomas Bros. Maps
© 2002
RIVERSIDE MUNICIPAL AIRPORT
CALIFORNIA BAPTIST UNIVERSITY
OLIVEWOOD CEM
RIVERSIDE PLAZA
NICHOLS PARK
STREETER PARK
VILLEGAS PARK
DON DERR PARK
A D SHAMEL PARK
WASHINGTON PARK
RAMONA HS
NOTRE DAME HS
POLYTECHNIC HS
SHERMAN INDIAN HS
ARLINGTON HS
CALIFORNIA SCHOOL FOR THE DEAF
RAINCROSS HS
HARDMAN CENTER
ARLINGTON SQUARE
LINCOLN PLAZA
MUNICIPAL CORPORATION YARD
METROPOLITAN WATER DISTRICT AQUEDUCT
RIVERSIDE CANAL
GAGE CANAL
ARLINGTON AV
CENTRAL AV
VICTORIA AV
MAGNOLIA AV
RIVERSIDE FRWY
INDIANA AV
WASHINGTON ST
MADISON ST
JEFFERSON ST
ADAMS ST
LINCOLN AV
OVERLOOK PKWY
DUFFERIN AV
CLEVELAND AV
BRADLEY ST
T2S
T3S
0 .25 .5 .75 1.0 miles
1 in. = 2400 ft.

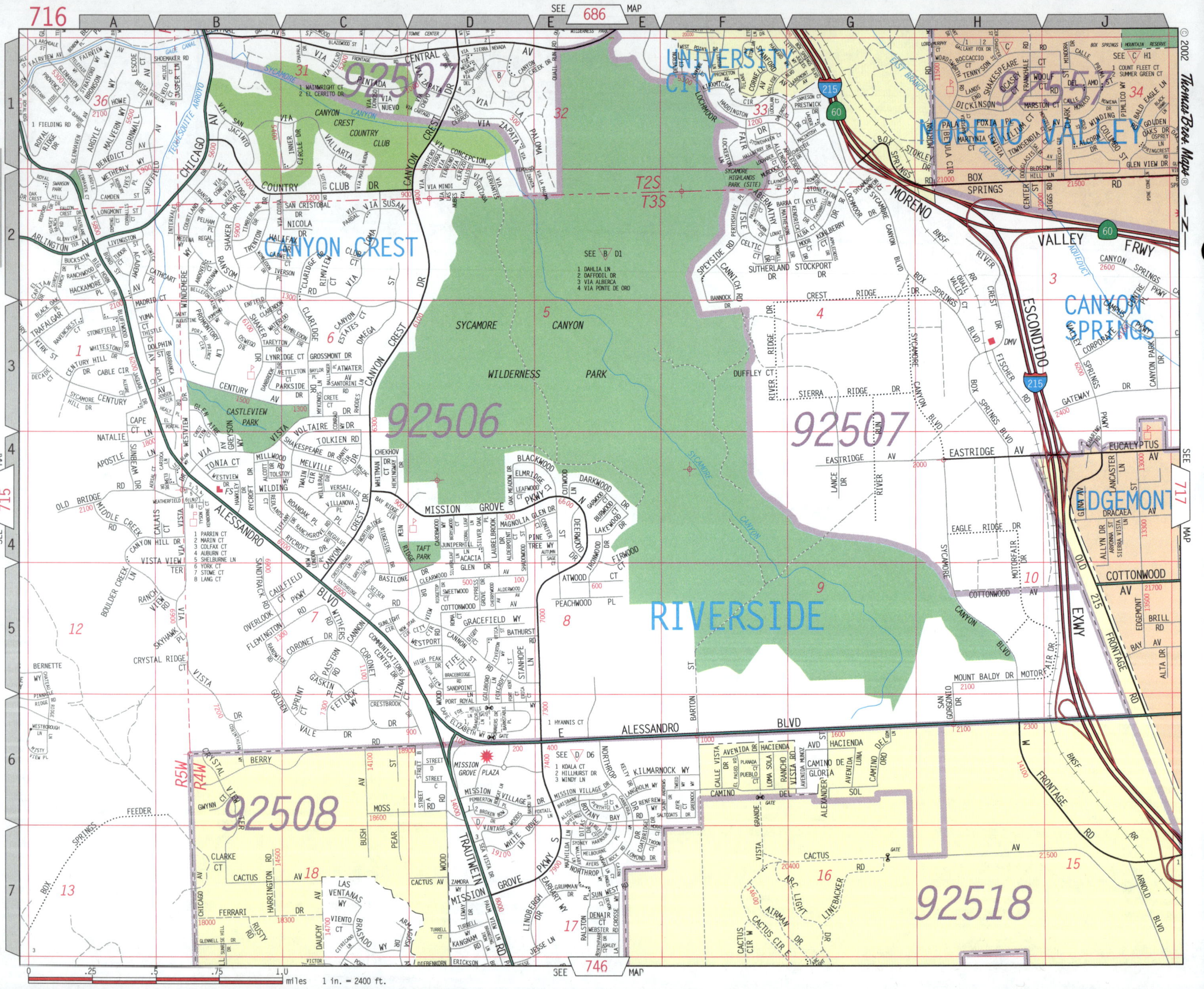
SEE 686 MAP
A
B
C
D
E
F
G
H
J
1
2
3
4
5
6
7
RIVERSIDE CO.
UNIVERSITY CITY
MORENO VALLEY
CANYON CREST
CANYON SPRINGS
EDGEMONT
RIVERSIDE
92507
92557
92506
92508
92518
SYCAMORE CANYON WILDERNESS PARK
CANYON CREST COUNTRY CLUB
CASTLEVIEW PARK
TAFT PARK
MISSION GROVE PLAZA
T2S
T3S
R5W
R4W
SEE 715 MAP
SEE 717 MAP
SEE 746 MAP
CHICAGO AV
CENTRAL AV
CANYON CREST DR
ALESSANDRO BLVD
MISSION GROVE PKWY
TRAUTWEIN RD
VALLEY FRWY
MORENO VALLEY FRWY
ESCONDIDO EXWY
BOX SPRINGS RD
EASTRIDGE AV
CACTUS AV
SYCAMORE CANYON BLVD
EUCALYPTUS AV
COTTONWOOD AV
0 .25 .5 .75 1.0 miles 1 in. = 2400 ft.
© 2002 Thomas Bros. Maps ®

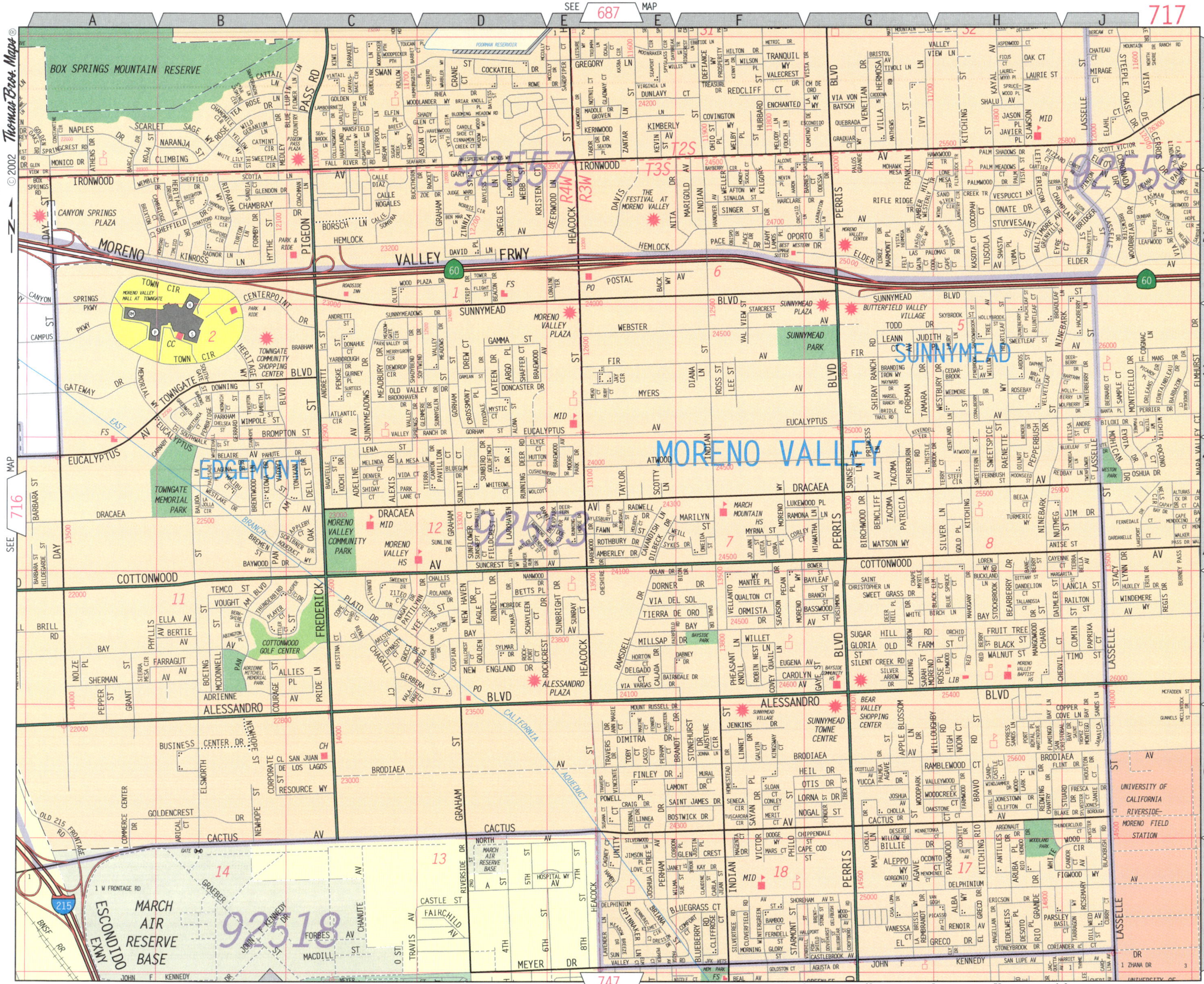

0 .25 .5 .75 1.0 miles 1 in. = 2400 ft.

SEE 688 MAP

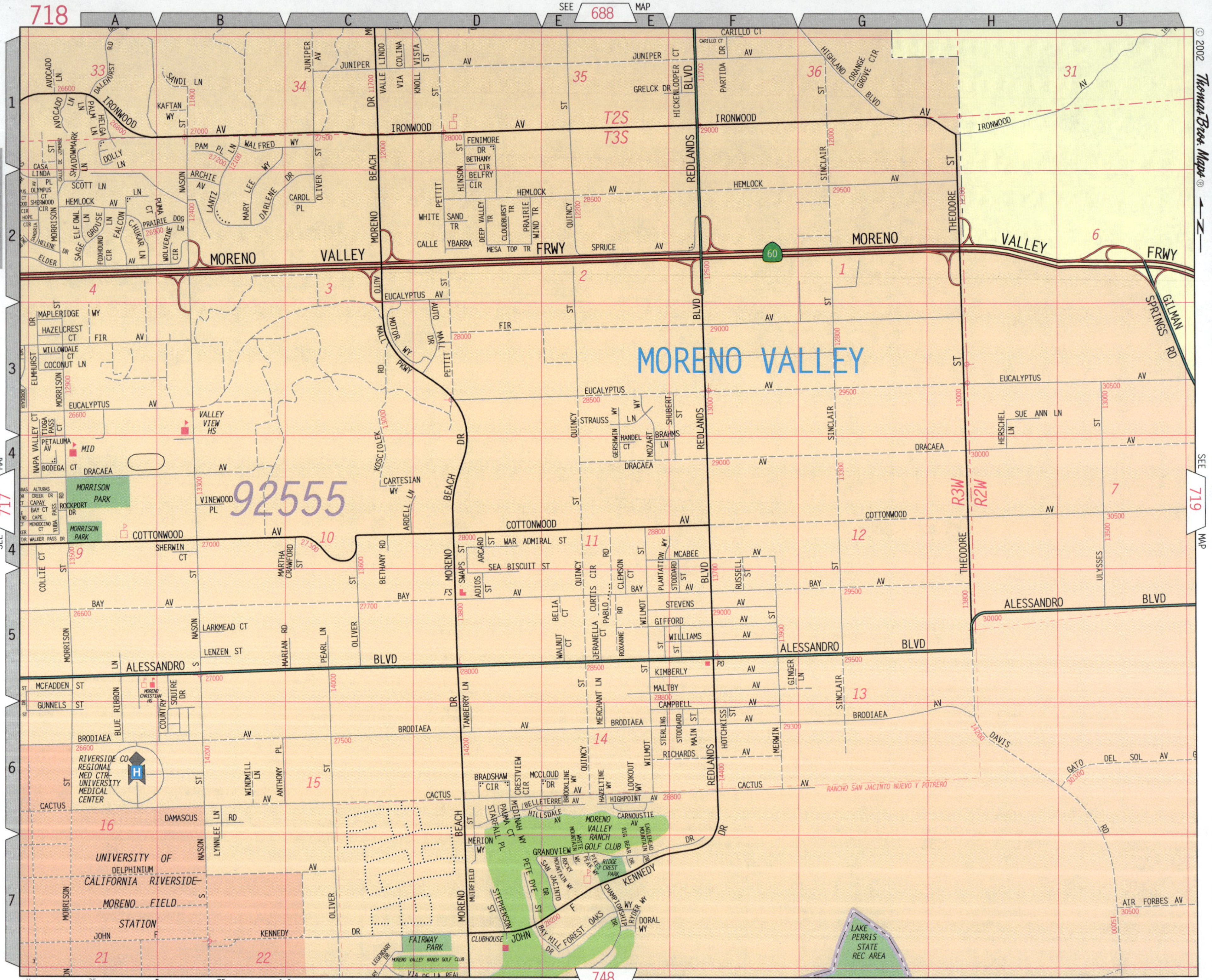

SEE 717 MAP

SEE 719 MAP

SEE 748 MAP

0 .25 .5 .75 1.0 miles 1 in. = 2400 ft.

SEE 689 MAP

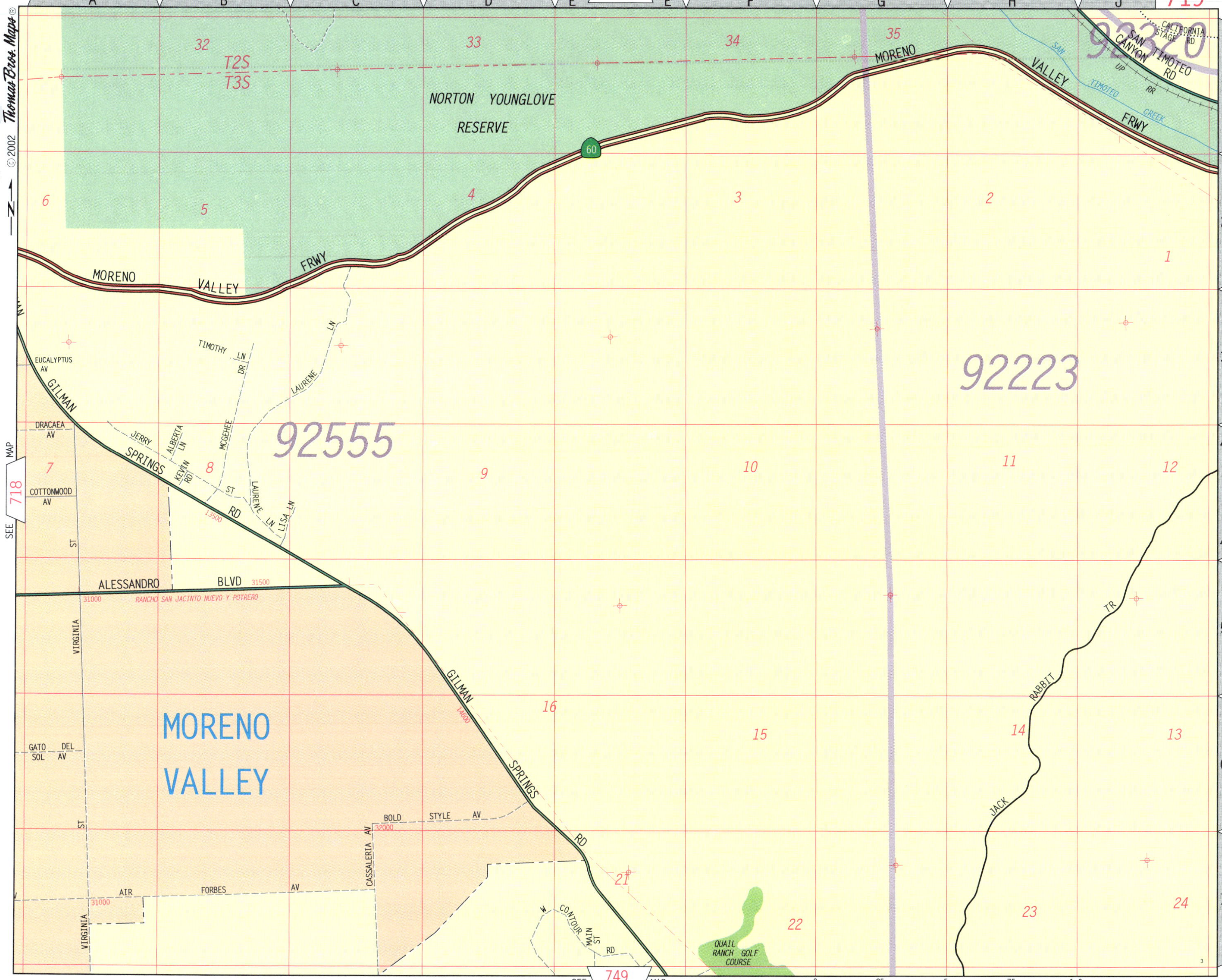

SEE 718 MAP
SEE 720 MAP
SEE 749 MAP

0 .25 .5 .75 1.0 miles 1 in. = 2400 ft.

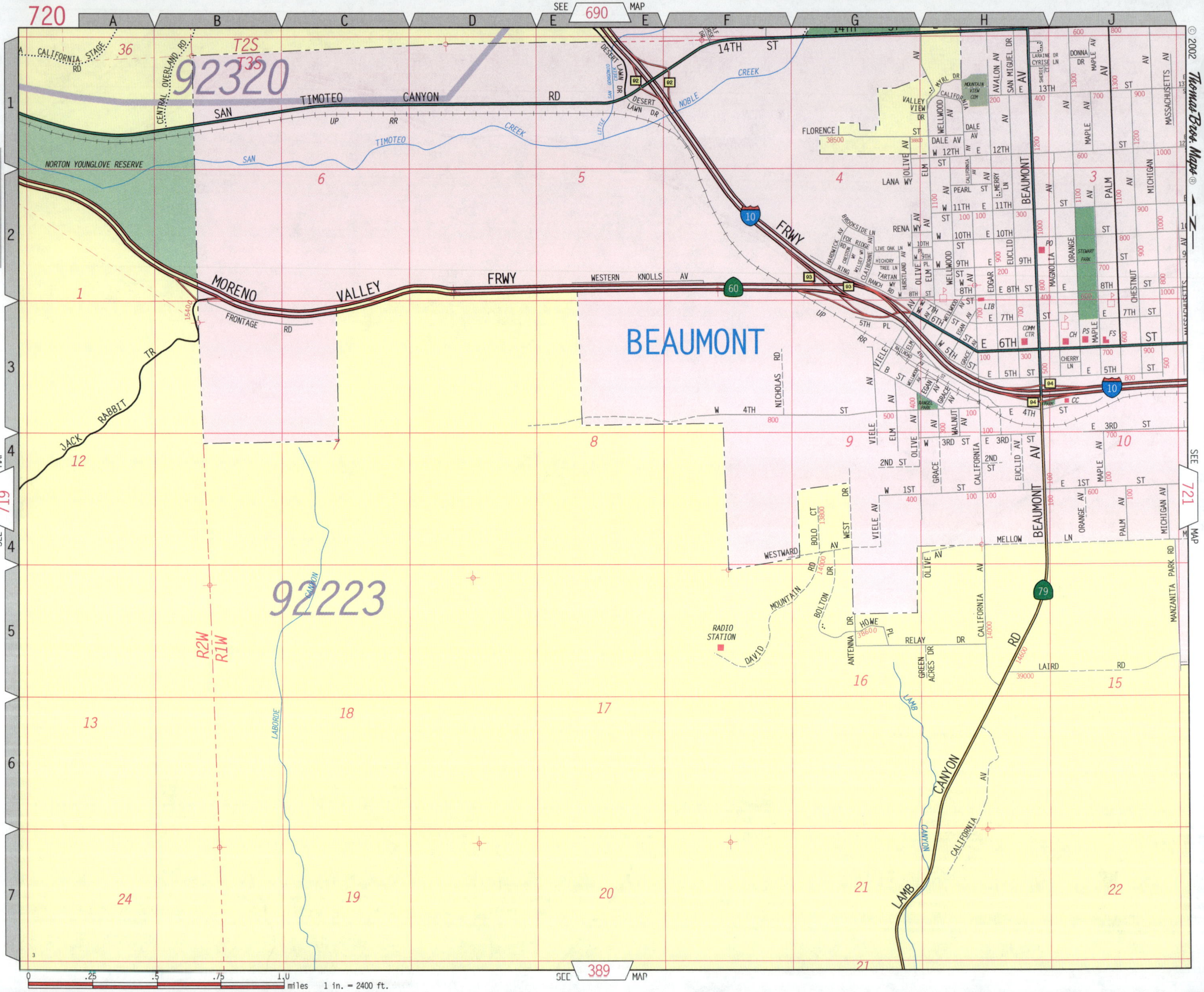

SEE 690 MAP
SEE 719 MAP
SEE 721 MAP
SEE 389 MAP
RIVERSIDE CO.
92320
92223
BEAUMONT
T2S
T3S
R2W
R1W
CALIFORNIA STAGE RD
CENTRAL OVERLAND RD
SAN TIMOTEO CANYON RD
UP RR
SAN TIMOTEO CREEK
NOBLE CREEK
LITTLE SAN GORGONIO CREEK
NORTON YOUNGLOVE RESERVE
MORENO VALLEY FRWY
FRONTAGE RD
JACK RABBIT TR
WESTERN KNOLLS AV
DESERT LAWN DR
14TH ST
13TH
12TH
11TH
10TH
9TH
8TH ST
7TH ST
6TH ST
5TH ST
W 4TH ST
E 3RD ST
2ND ST
1ST ST
MELLOW LN
FLORENCE ST
VALLEY VIEW DR
MOUNTAIN VIEW CEM
CALIFORNIA AV
WELLWOOD AV
DALE AV
OLIVE AV
ELM ST
LANA WY
PEARL ST
MERRY LN
RENA WY
BROOKSIDE LN
FOX RIDGE
HARDWICK AV
CRESTON
WILSEY WY
CLAIBORNE
LIVE OAK LN
HICKORY
TREE LN
TARTAN
HURSTLAND AV
RING RANCH RD
BEAUMONT AV
EDGAR AV
EUCLID AV
MAGNOLIA AV
ORANGE AV
STEWART PARK
PALM AV
CHESTNUT AV
MICHIGAN AV
MASSACHUSETTS AV
AVALON AV
SAN MIGUEL DR
LARAINE DR
CYRISE LN
SHERIE CT
DONNA DR
MAPLE AV
CHERRY LN
I-10 FRWY
60
92
93
94
79
10
LIB
PO
CH
PS
FS
CC
COMM CTR
RANGEL PARK
VIELE AV
NICHOLAS RD
GRACE AV
WALNUT AV
EGAN AV
WESTWARD AV
BOLO CT
WEST DR
MOUNTAIN RD
BOLTON DR
DAVID
RADIO STATION
ANTENNA DR
HOWE PL
RELAY DR
GREEN ACRES DR
LAIRD RD
MANZANITA PARK RD
BEAUMONT AV
LAMB CANYON RD
LAMB CANYON
CALIFORNIA AV
LABORDE CANYON
1 2 3 4 5 6 7
A B C D E F G H J
0 .25 .5 .75 1.0 miles 1 in. = 2400 ft.

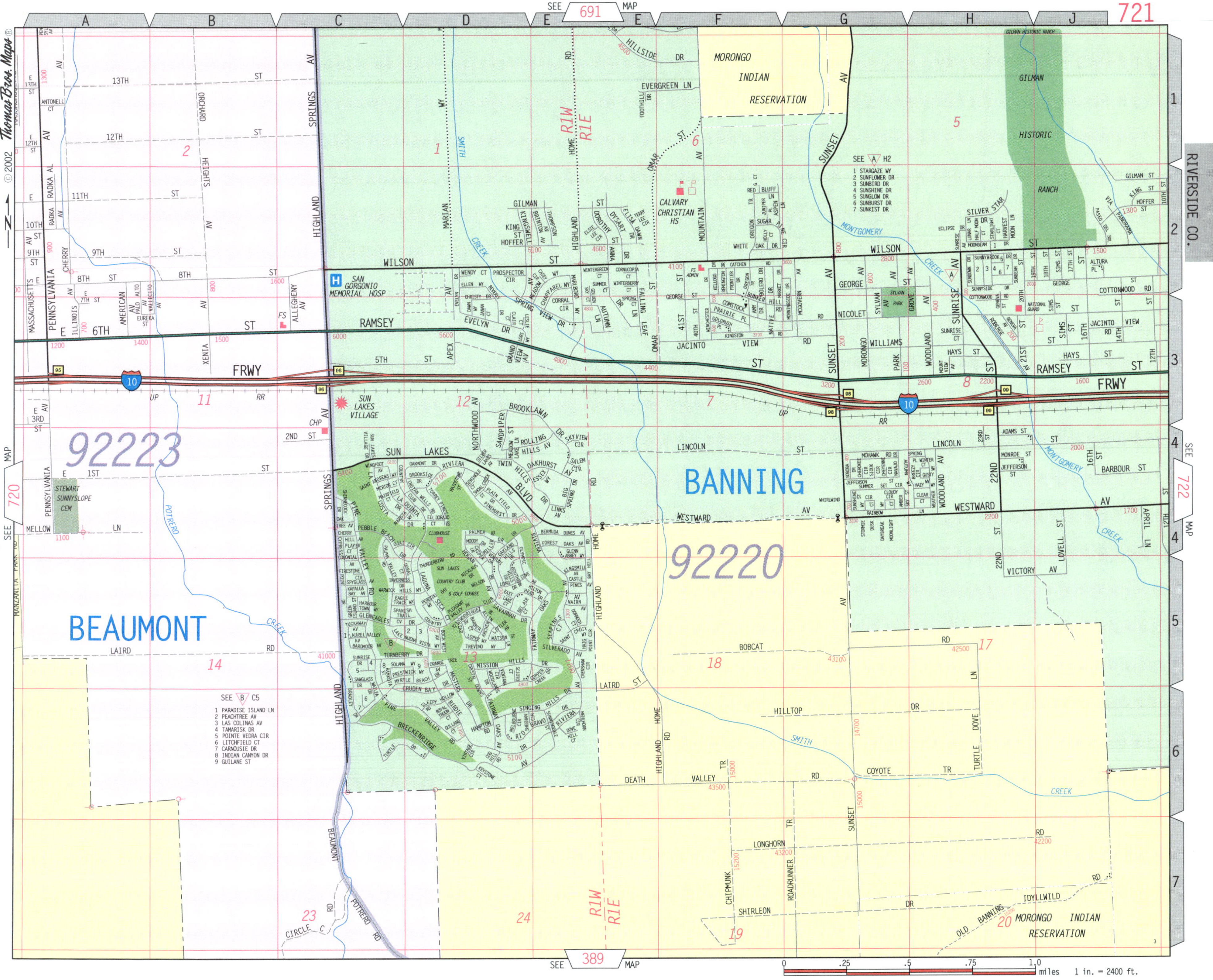
SEE 691 MAP
A
B
C
D
E
F
G
H
J
1
2
3
4
5
6
7
RIVERSIDE CO.
SEE 722 MAP
SEE 720 MAP
SEE 389 MAP
BANNING
BEAUMONT
92223
92220
MORONGO INDIAN RESERVATION
GILMAN HISTORIC RANCH
CALVARY CHRISTIAN HS
SAN GORGONIO MEMORIAL HOSP
SUN LAKES VILLAGE
SUN LAKES COUNTRY CLUB & GOLF COURSE
STEWART SUNNYSLOPE CEM
RAMSEY ST
WILSON ST
LINCOLN ST
WESTWARD AV
HIGHLAND SPRINGS AV
SUNSET AV
SUN LAKES BLVD
FRWY
DEATH VALLEY RD
COYOTE TR
HILLTOP DR
BOBCAT RD
LAIRD RD
SMITH CREEK
POTRERO CREEK
MONTGOMERY CREEK
R1W R1E
SEE A H2
1 STARGAZE WY
2 SUNFLOWER DR
3 SUNBIRD DR
4 SUNSHINE DR
5 SUNGLOW DR
6 SUNBURST DR
7 SUNKIST DR
SEE B C5
1 PARADISE ISLAND LN
2 PEACHTREE AV
3 LAS COLINAS AV
4 TAMARISK DR
5 POINTE VEDRA CIR
6 LITCHFIELD CT
7 CARNOUSTIE DR
8 INDIAN CANYON DR
9 GUILANE ST
0 .25 .5 .75 1.0 miles
1 in. = 2400 ft.
© 2002 Thomas Bros. Maps ®

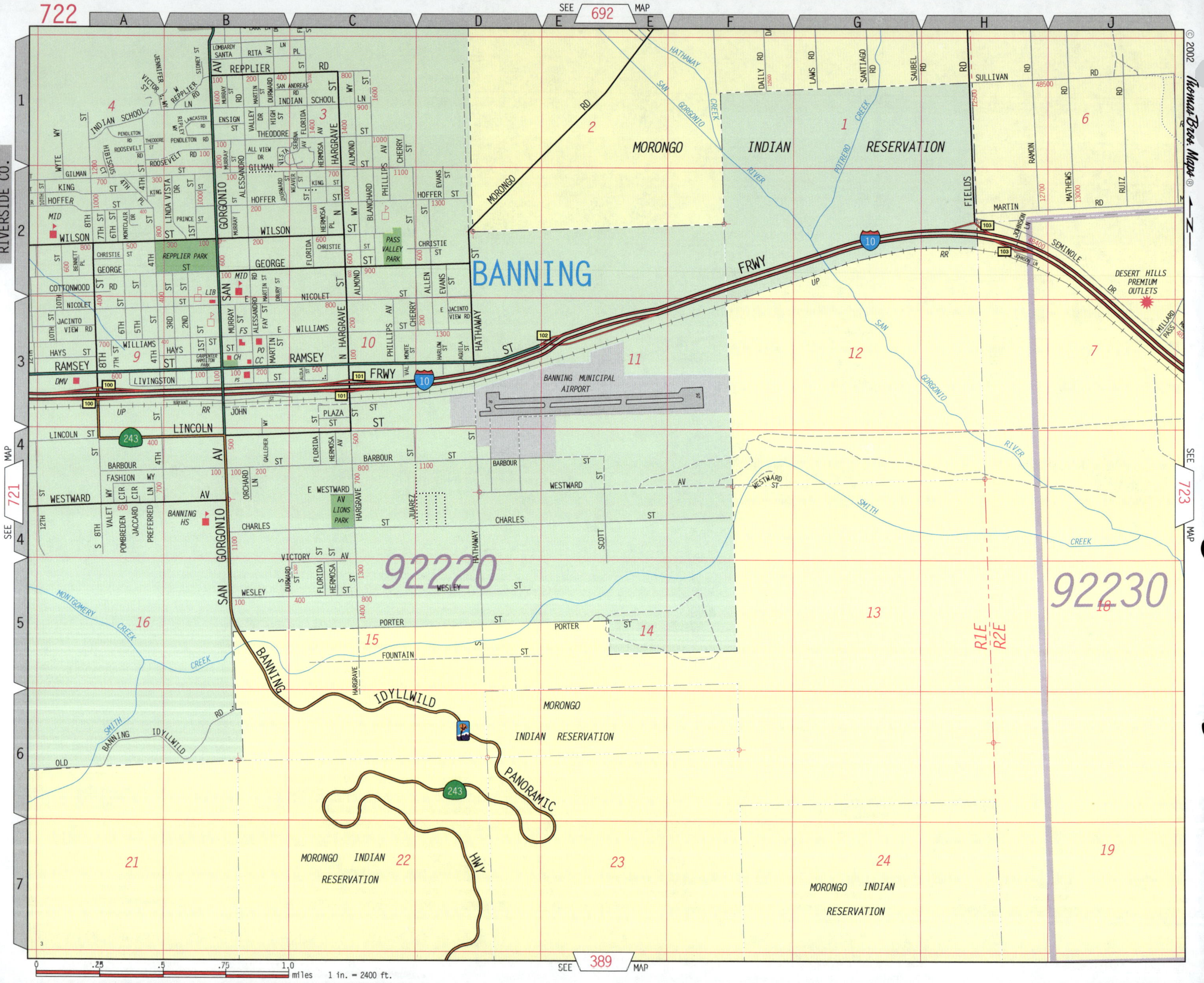

SEE 692 MAP
A B C D E F G H J
1 2 3 4 5 6 7
RIVERSIDE CO.
BANNING
MORONGO INDIAN RESERVATION
BANNING MUNICIPAL AIRPORT
DESERT HILLS PREMIUM OUTLETS
92220
92230
FRWY
SAN GORGONIO AV
SAN GORGONIO RIVER
SMITH CREEK
MONTGOMERY CREEK
POTRERO CREEK
HATHAWAY CREEK
REPPLIER PARK
PASS VALLEY PARK
LIONS PARK
BANNING HS
RAMSEY ST
LINCOLN ST
WILSON ST
GEORGE ST
NICOLET ST
WILLIAMS ST
HOFFER ST
GILMAN ST
BARBOUR ST
WESTWARD AV
CHARLES ST
WESLEY ST
PORTER ST
FOUNTAIN ST
VICTORY AV
HARGRAVE ST
HATHAWAY ST
SUNSET AV
MORONGO RD
FIELDS RD
MARTIN RD
SULLIVAN RD
SEMINOLE DR
BANNING IDYLLWILD PANORAMIC HWY
R1E R2E
SEE 721 MAP
SEE 723 MAP
SEE 389 MAP
0 .25 .5 .75 1.0 miles 1 in. = 2400 ft.
© 2002 Thomas Bros. Maps®

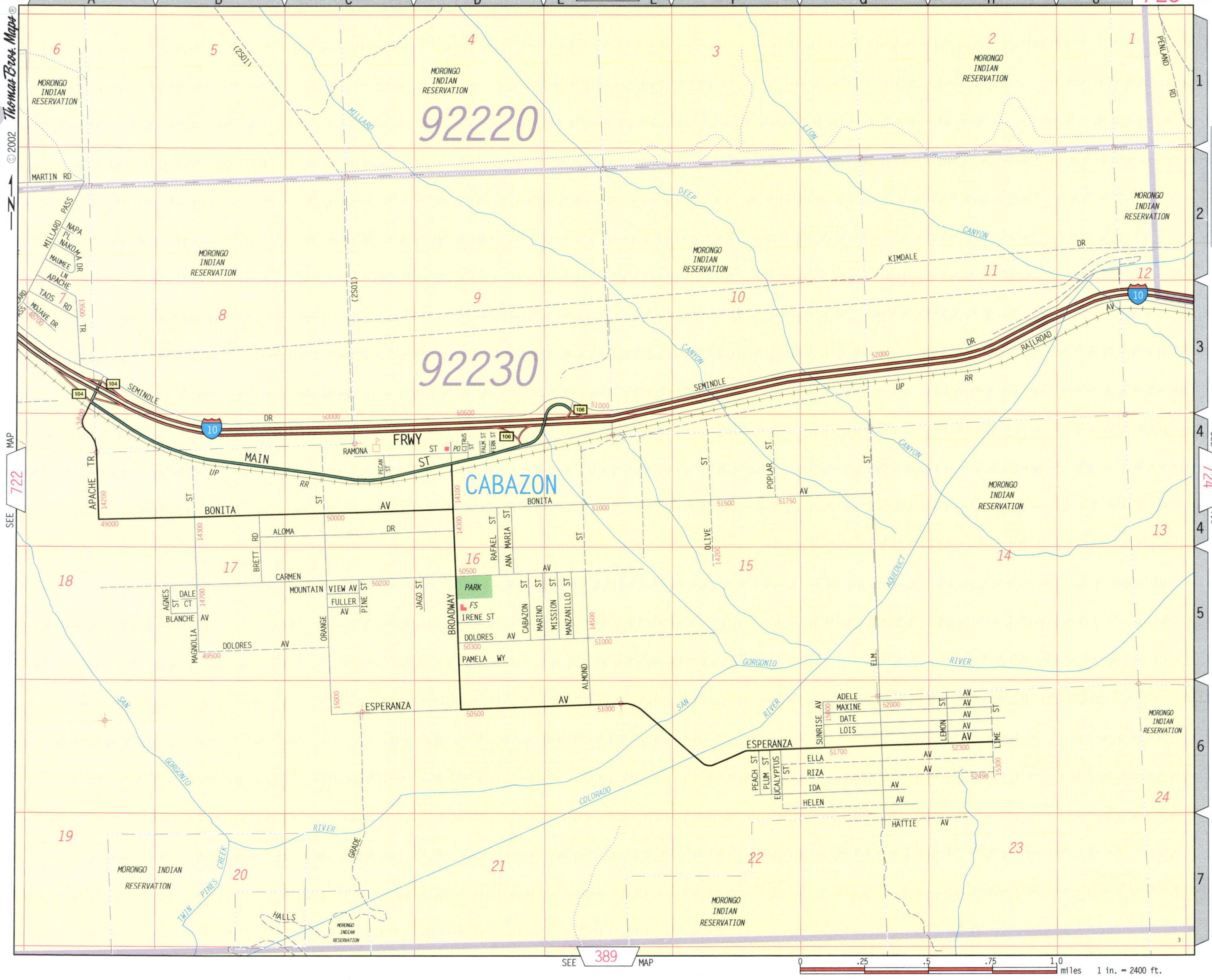
SEE 389 MAP
A B C D E F G H J
MORONGO INDIAN RESERVATION
92220
92230
CABAZON
MARTIN RD
SEMINOLE DR
FRWY
MAIN ST
BONITA AV
ALOMA DR
CARMEN
MOUNTAIN VIEW AV
FULLER AV
BLANCHE AV
DOLORES AV
ESPERANZA AV
PAMELA WY
IRENE ST
BROADWAY
APACHE TR
KIMDALE DR
RAILROAD AV
DEEP CANYON
MILLARD CANYON
LION
SAN GORGONIO RIVER
COLORADO AQUEDUCT
TWIN PINES CREEK
HALLS GRADE
ADELE AV
MAXINE AV
DATE AV
LOIS AV
ELLA AV
RIZA AV
IDA AV
HELEN AV
HATTIE AV
SUNRISE AV
LEMON ST
LIME ST
PEACH ST
PLUM ST
EUCALYPTUS ST
PENLAND RD
RIVERSIDE CO.
SEE 722 MAP
SEE 724 MAP
SEE 389 MAP
0 .25 .5 .75 1.0 miles 1 in. = 2400 ft.

SEE 694 MAP

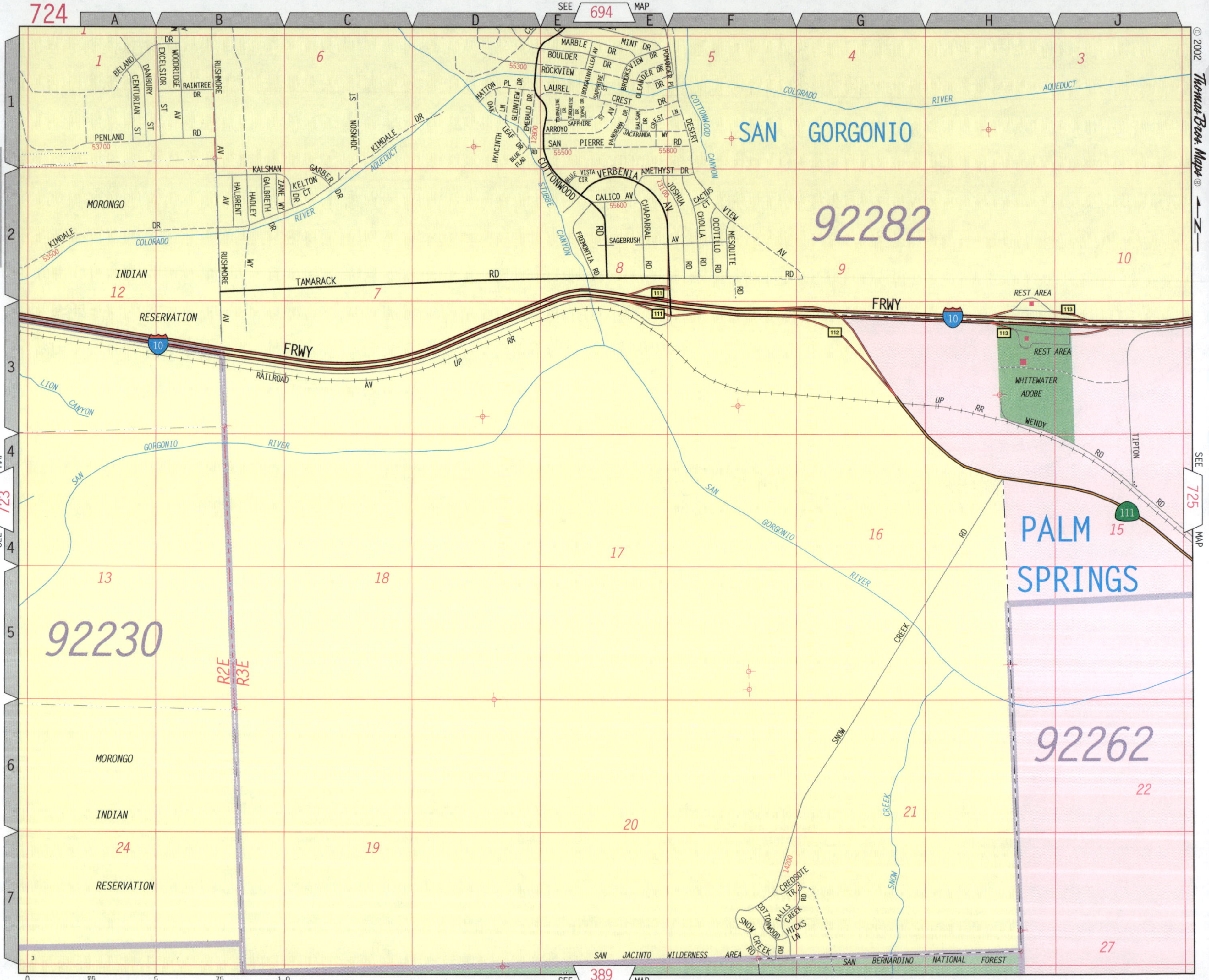

SEE 389 MAP

0 .25 .5 .75 1.0 miles 1 in. = 2400 ft.

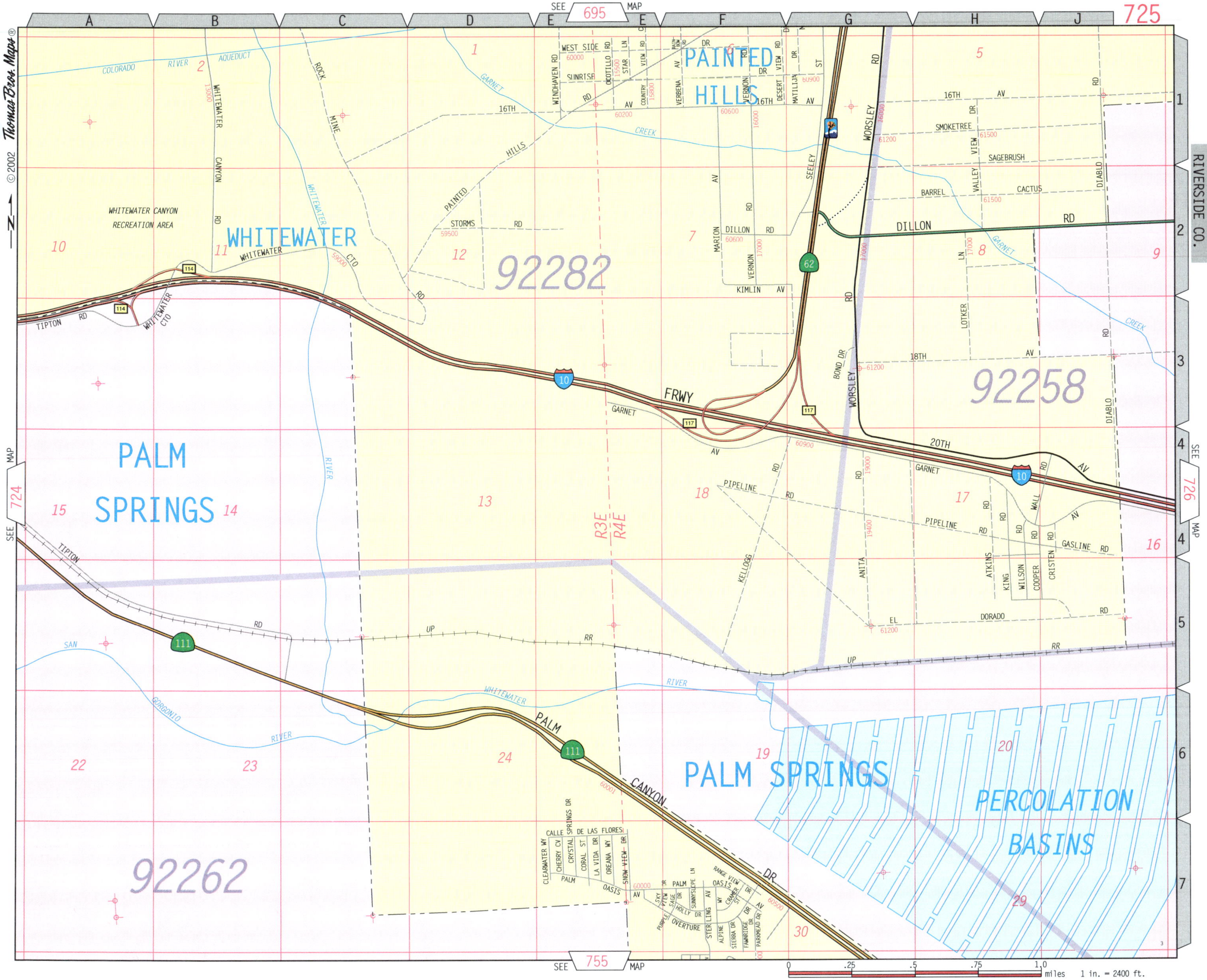
SEE 695 MAP
SEE 755 MAP
SEE 724 MAP
SEE 726 MAP
RIVERSIDE CO.
A
B
C
D
E
F
G
H
J
1
2
3
4
5
6
7
WHITEWATER
PAINTED HILLS
PALM SPRINGS
PALM SPRINGS
PERCOLATION BASINS
WHITEWATER CANYON RECREATION AREA
92282
92258
92262
R3E
R4E
COLORADO RIVER AQUEDUCT
GARNET CREEK
WHITEWATER RIVER
SAN GORGONIO RIVER
FRWY
PALM CANYON DR
UP RR
TIPTON RD
WHITEWATER CTO
WHITEWATER CANYON RD
ROCK MINE
HILLS
PAINTED
STORMS RD
16TH
WEST SIDE RD
SUNRISE RD
OCOTILLO LN
STAR RD
COUNTRY VIEW
VERBENA AV
VERNON RD
DESERT VIEW RD
MATILIJA DR
ST
SEELEY
MARION AV
DILLON RD
VERNON
KIMLIN AV
WORSLEY RD
BOND DR
16TH AV
SMOKETREE DR
VIEW
SAGEBRUSH
BARREL
VALLEY
CACTUS
DILLON RD
DIABLO RD
LN
LOTKER
18TH AV
20TH AV
GARNET AV
GARNET
PIPELINE RD
KELLOGG
ANITA
RD
GASLINE RD
WALL
ATKINS
KING
WILSON
COOPER
CRISTEN
EL DORADO RD
CALLE DE LAS FLORES
CLEARWATER WY
CHERRY CV
CRYSTAL SPRINGS DR
CORAL ST
LA VIDA DR
OREANA WY
SNOW VIEW DR
PALM
OASIS AV
SKY VIEW
SAGE DR
HOLLY DR
PURPLE
OVERTURE
SUNNYSLOPE LN
STERLING AV
ALPINE WY
SIERRA DR
RANGE VIEW
FAWNRIDGE DR
PARKMEAD DR
CRAMER ST
10
62
111
114
117
0 .25 .5 .75 1.0 miles
1 in. = 2400 ft.

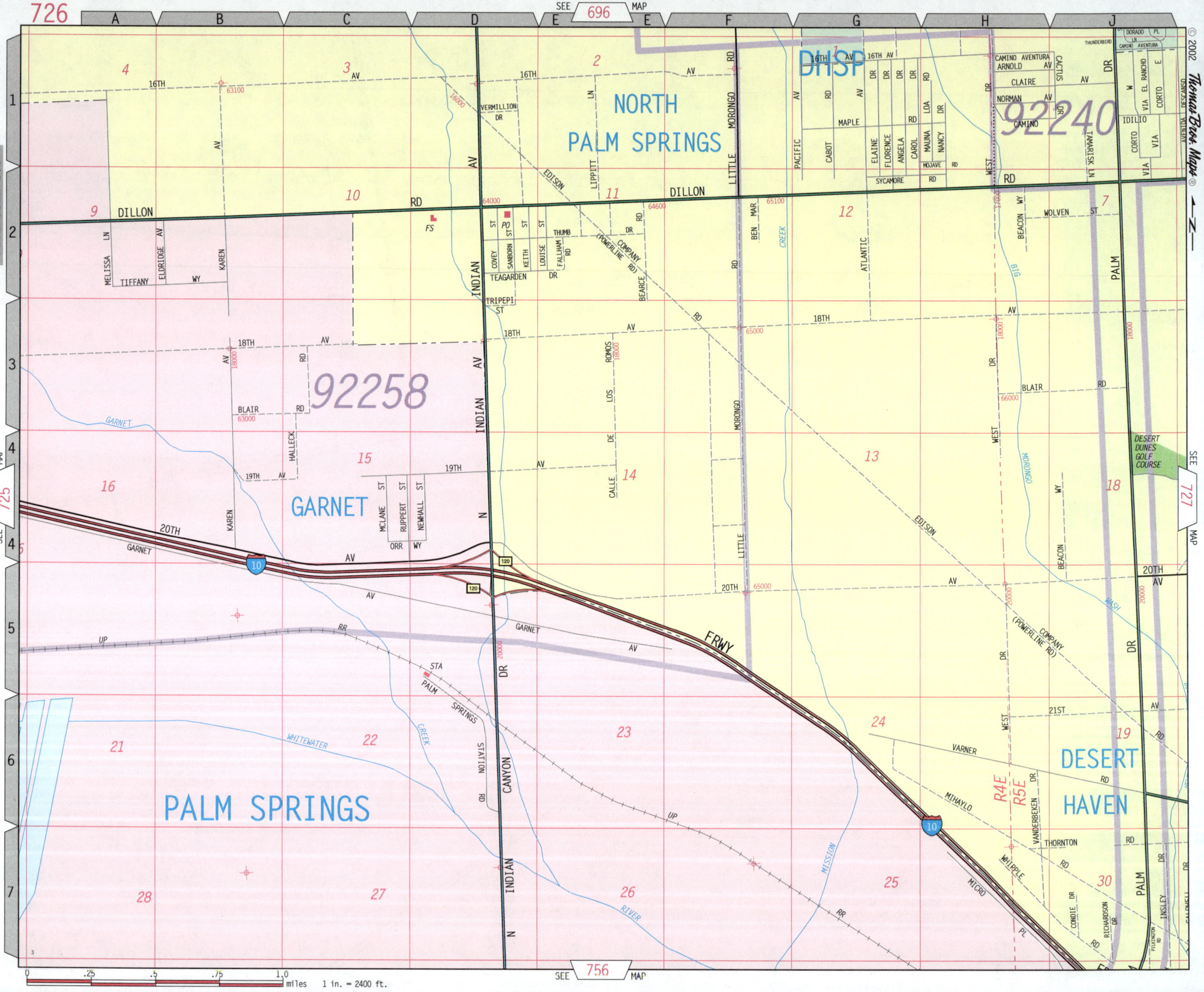
SEE 696 MAP
SEE 725 MAP
SEE 727 MAP
SEE 756 MAP
RIVERSIDE CO.
NORTH PALM SPRINGS
DHSP
92240
92258
GARNET
PALM SPRINGS
DESERT HAVEN
DESERT DUNES GOLF COURSE
DILLON RD
16TH AV
18TH AV
19TH AV
20TH AV
21ST AV
INDIAN AV
N INDIAN CANYON DR
LITTLE MORONGO RD
WEST DR
PALM DR
GARNET AV
EDISON COMPANY (POWERLINE RD)
FRWY
UP RR
PALM SPRINGS STA
STATION RD
WHITEWATER RIVER
MISSION CREEK
BIG MORONGO WASH
R4E R5E
1 in. = 2400 ft.
0 .25 .5 .75 1.0 miles

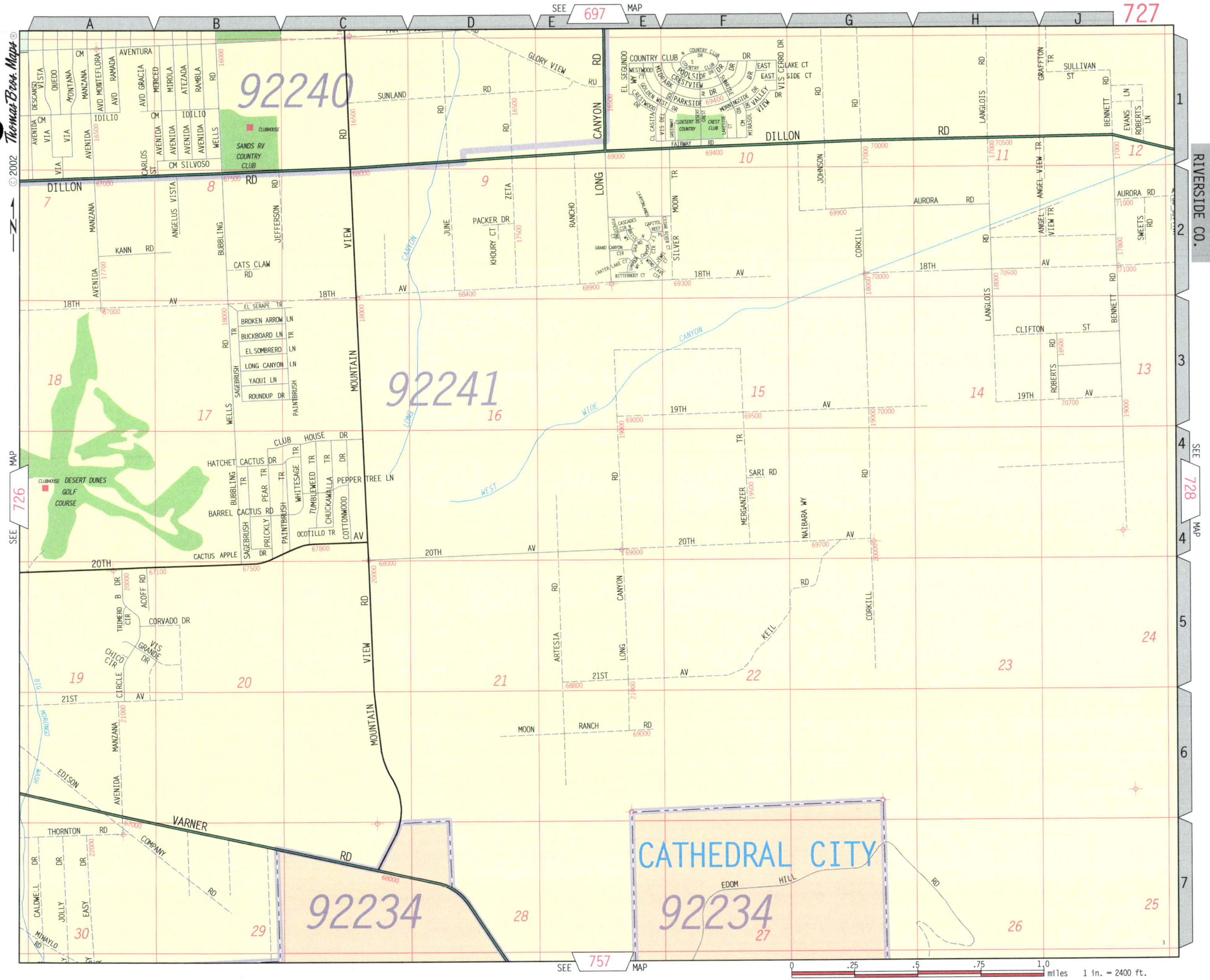
SEE 697 MAP
A
B
C
D
E
F
G
H
J
1
2
3
4
5
6
7
SEE 726 MAP
SEE 728 MAP
SEE 757 MAP
RIVERSIDE CO.
92240
92241
92234
CATHEDRAL CITY
DILLON RD
SANDS RV COUNTRY CLUB
CLUBHOUSE
DESERT DUNES GOLF COURSE
DESERT CREST COUNTRY CLUB
MOUNTAIN VIEW RD
LONG CANYON RD
VARNER RD
18TH AV
19TH AV
20TH AV
21ST AV
CORKILL RD
LANGLOIS RD
BENNETT RD
AURORA RD
CLIFTON ST
SULLIVAN ST
GLORY VIEW RD
SUNLAND RD
PACKER DR
KHOURY CT
ZETA RD
JUNE RD
RANCHO RD
SILVER MOON TR
JOHNSON RD
ANGEL VIEW TR
SWEETS RD
ROBERTS RD
EVANS LN
GRAFFTON TR
MERGANZER RD
SARI RD
NAIBARA WY
KEIL RD
ARTESIA RD
MOON RANCH RD
EDOM HILL RD
EDISON COMPANY RD
THORNTON RD
CALDWELL DR
JOLLY DR
EASY DR
MIHAYLO RD
AVENIDA MANZANA
CORVADO DR
VIS GRANDE DR
CHICO CIR
CIRCLE
TRIMERO CIR
ACOFF RD
CACTUS APPLE DR
BARREL CACTUS RD
HATCHET CACTUS DR
PEPPER TREE LN
CLUB HOUSE DR
OCOTILLO TR
BUBBLING WELLS RD
SAGEBRUSH TR
PAINTBRUSH TR
JEFFERSON RD
CATS CLAW RD
KANN RD
ANGELUS VISTA
CM SILVOSO
AVENTURA
IDILIO
WEST WIDE CANYON
LONG CANYON
BIG MORONGO WASH
0 .25 .5 .75 1.0 miles 1 in. = 2400 ft.
© 2002 Thomas Bros. Maps®

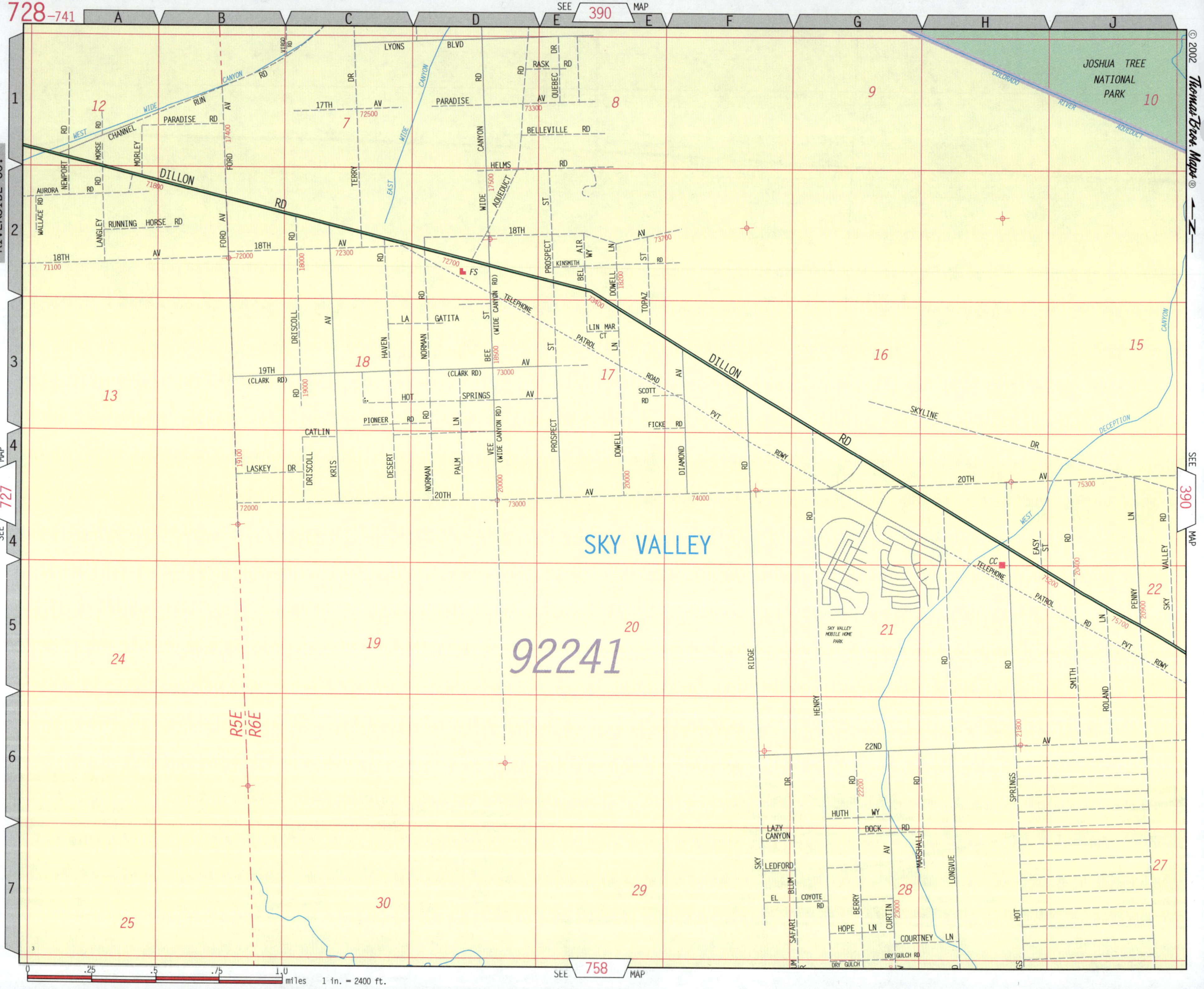
SEE 390 MAP
JOSHUA TREE NATIONAL PARK
COLORADO RIVER AQUEDUCT
RIVERSIDE CO.
DILLON RD
SKY VALLEY
92241
SKY VALLEY MOBILE HOME PARK
WEST WIDE CANYON
EAST WIDE CANYON
DECEPTION CANYON
LYONS BLVD
RASK RD
QUEBEC DR
17TH AV
PARADISE AV
PARADISE RD
BELLEVILLE RD
HELMS RD
18TH AV
19TH (CLARK RD)
20TH AV
22ND AV
SKYLINE DR
TELEPHONE PATROL ROAD PVT RDWY
AURORA RD
WALLACE RD
NEWPORT RD
MORSE RD
MORLEY RD
LANGLEY RD
RUNNING HORSE RD
FORD AV
TERRY DR
DRISCOLL AV
HAVEN RD
LA GATITA
NORMAN RD
BEE ST
WIDE CANYON RD
VEE ST
PALM LN
HOT SPRINGS AV
PIONEER RD
CATLIN
LASKEY DR
KRIS
DESERT
PROSPECT ST
KINSMITH
BEL AIR WY
DOWELL LN
TOPAZ ST
LIN MAR CT
SCOTT RD
FICKE RD
DIAMOND AV
RIDGE RD
HENRY RD
CC
FS
EASY ST
SMITH RD
ROLAND
PENNY LN
SKY VALLEY RD
HOT SPRINGS RD
LONGVUE RD
MARSHALL RD
HUTH WY
DOCK RD
LAZY CANYON DR
SKY LEDFORD
EL BLUM
SAFARI
COYOTE RD
BERRY RD
CURTIN AV
HOPE LN
COURTNEY LN
DRY GULCH RD
R5E R6E
SEE 727 MAP
SEE 758 MAP
© 2002 Thomas Bros. Maps®
miles 1 in. = 2400 ft.

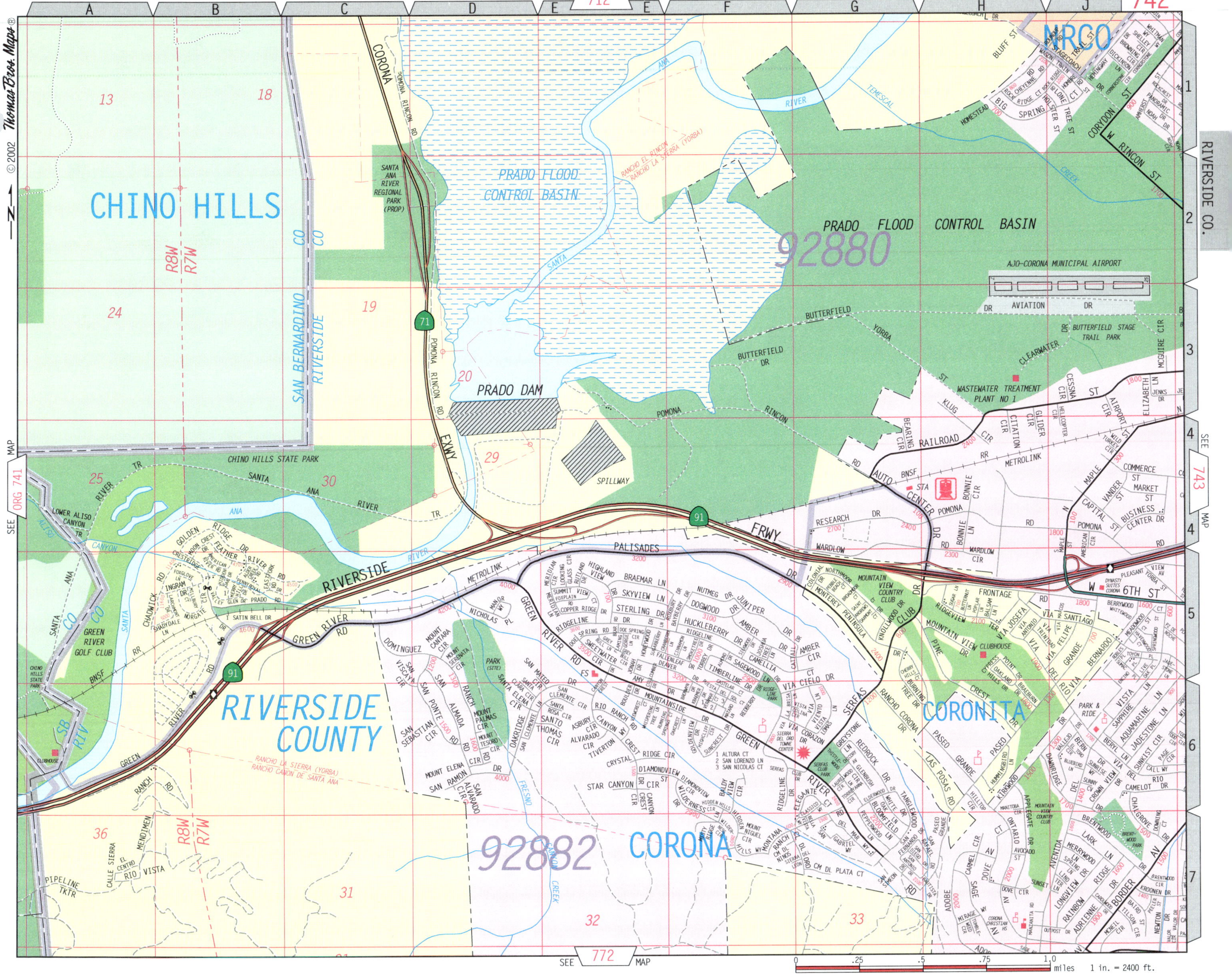
SEE 712 MAP
A
B
C
D
E
F
G
H
J
Thomas Bros. Maps ®
© 2002
CHINO HILLS
NRCO
PRADO FLOOD CONTROL BASIN
SANTA ANA RIVER REGIONAL PARK (PROP)
92880
AJO-CORONA MUNICIPAL AIRPORT
AVIATION DR
BUTTERFIELD STAGE TRAIL PARK
WASTEWATER TREATMENT PLANT NO 1
PRADO DAM
SPILLWAY
CHINO HILLS STATE PARK
SANTA ANA RIVER
SAN BERNARDINO CO
RIVERSIDE CO
R8W
R7W
CORONA RINCON RD
POMONA RINCON RD
CORONA EXWY
RIVERSIDE FRWY
GREEN RIVER RD
PALISADES
METROLINK
LOWER ALISO CANYON TR
GREEN RIVER GOLF CLUB
RIVERSIDE COUNTY
RANCHO LA SIERRA (YORBA)
RANCHO CANON DE SANTA ANA
RANCHO EL RINCON
MOUNTAIN VIEW COUNTRY CLUB
CORONITA
CORONA
92882
W 6TH ST
RESEARCH DR
WARDLOW
AUTO CENTER DR
SERFAS CLUB DR
PIPELINE TKTR
FRESNO CANYON
RIVERSIDE CO.
SEE 743 MAP
SEE ORG 741 MAP
13
18
24
19
20
25
29
30
31
32
33
36
1
2
3
4
5
6
7
SEE 772 MAP
0 .25 .5 .75 1.0 miles 1 in. = 2400 ft.

SEE 713 MAP
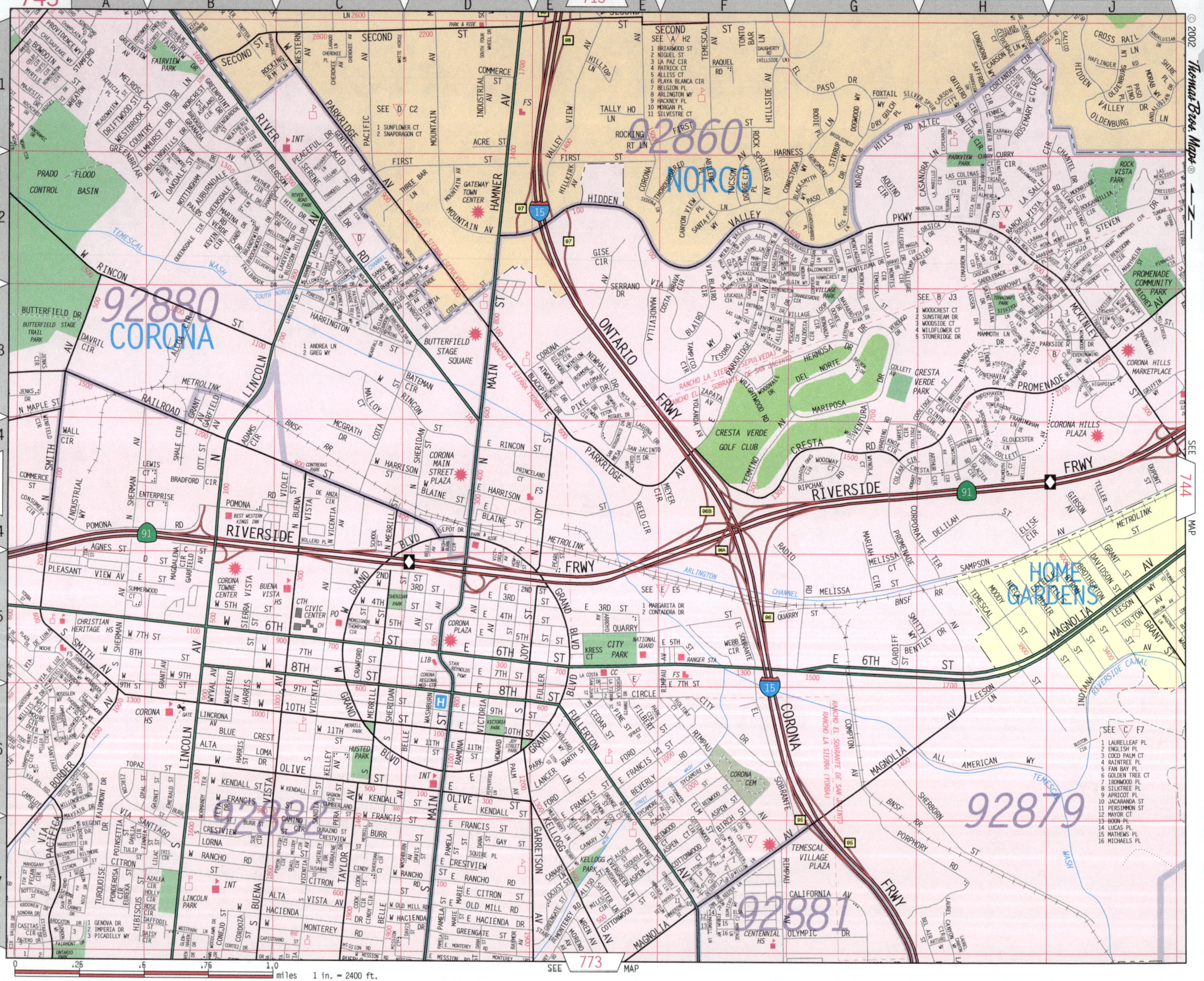

SEE 773 MAP

SEE 714 MAP

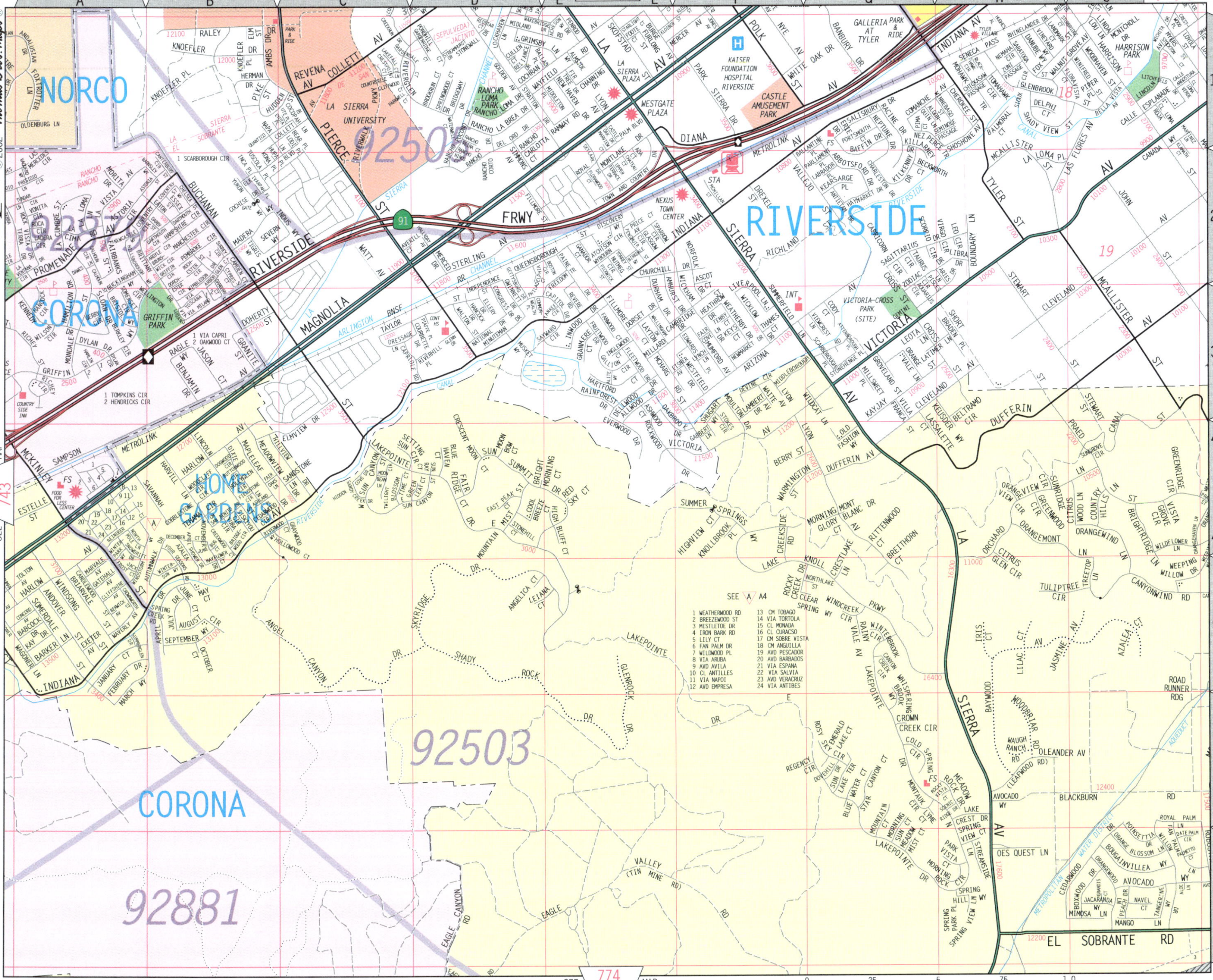

SEE 743 MAP

SEE 745 MAP

SEE 774 MAP

SEE 715 MAP

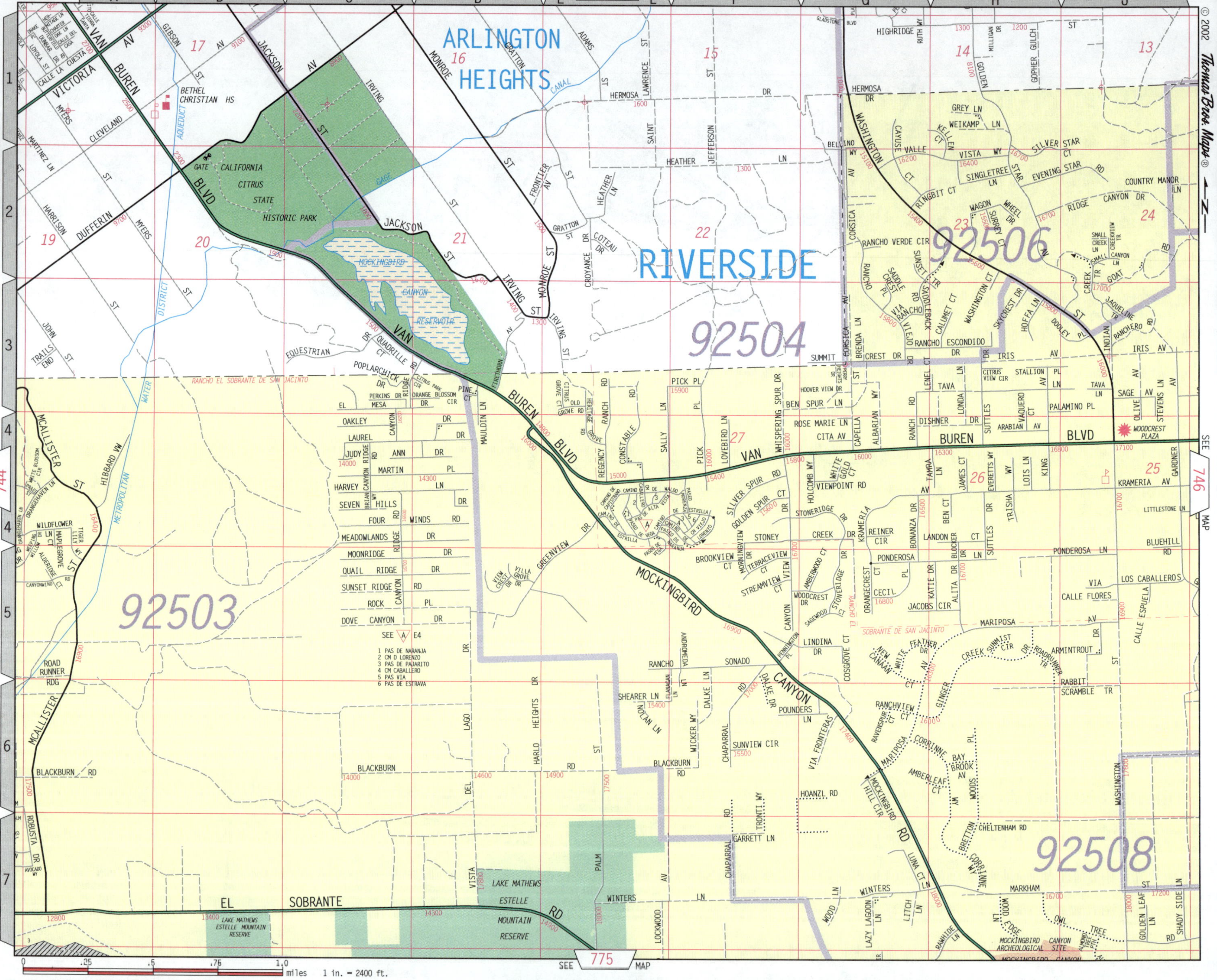

SEE 744 MAP
SEE 746 MAP
SEE 775 MAP

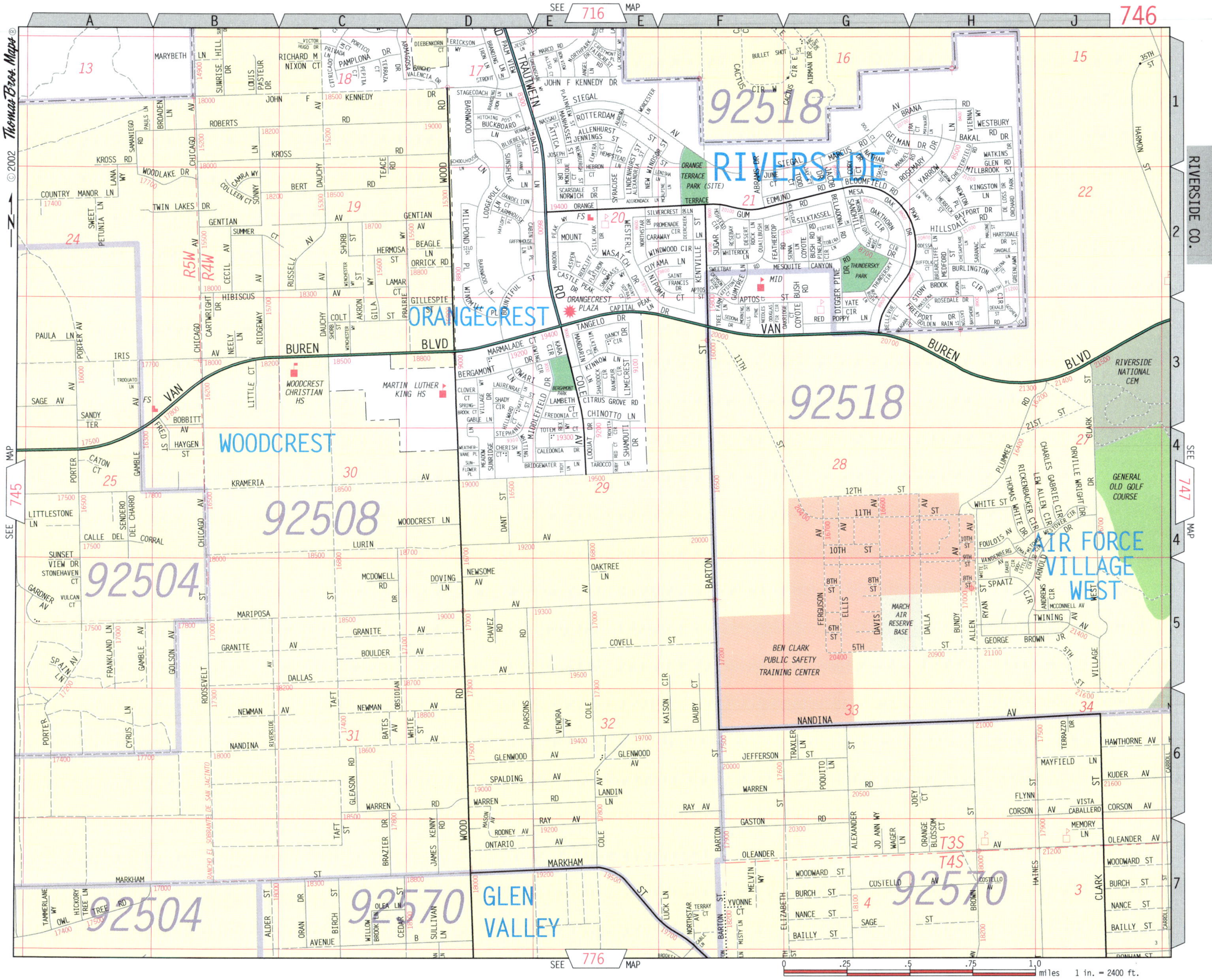
SEE 716 MAP
SEE 745 MAP
SEE 747 MAP
SEE 776 MAP
RIVERSIDE CO.
RIVERSIDE
ORANGECREST
WOODCREST
GLEN VALLEY
AIR FORCE VILLAGE WEST
92518
92508
92504
92570
ORANGE TERRACE PARK (SITE)
THUNDERSKY PARK
WOODCREST CHRISTIAN HS
MARTIN LUTHER KING HS
ORANGECREST PLAZA
BERGAMONT PARK
MARCH AIR RESERVE BASE
BEN CLARK PUBLIC SAFETY TRAINING CENTER
RIVERSIDE NATIONAL CEM
GENERAL OLD GOLF COURSE
VAN BUREN BLVD
TRAUTWEIN RD
BARTON ST
WOOD RD
ORANGE TERRACE
MARKHAM ST
NANDINA AV
MARIPOSA AV
KRAMERIA AV
LURIN AV
CHICAGO AV
ROOSEVELT
ALEXANDER
CLARK ST
R5W
R4W
T3S
T4S
miles
1 in. = 2400 ft.

SEE 717 MAP

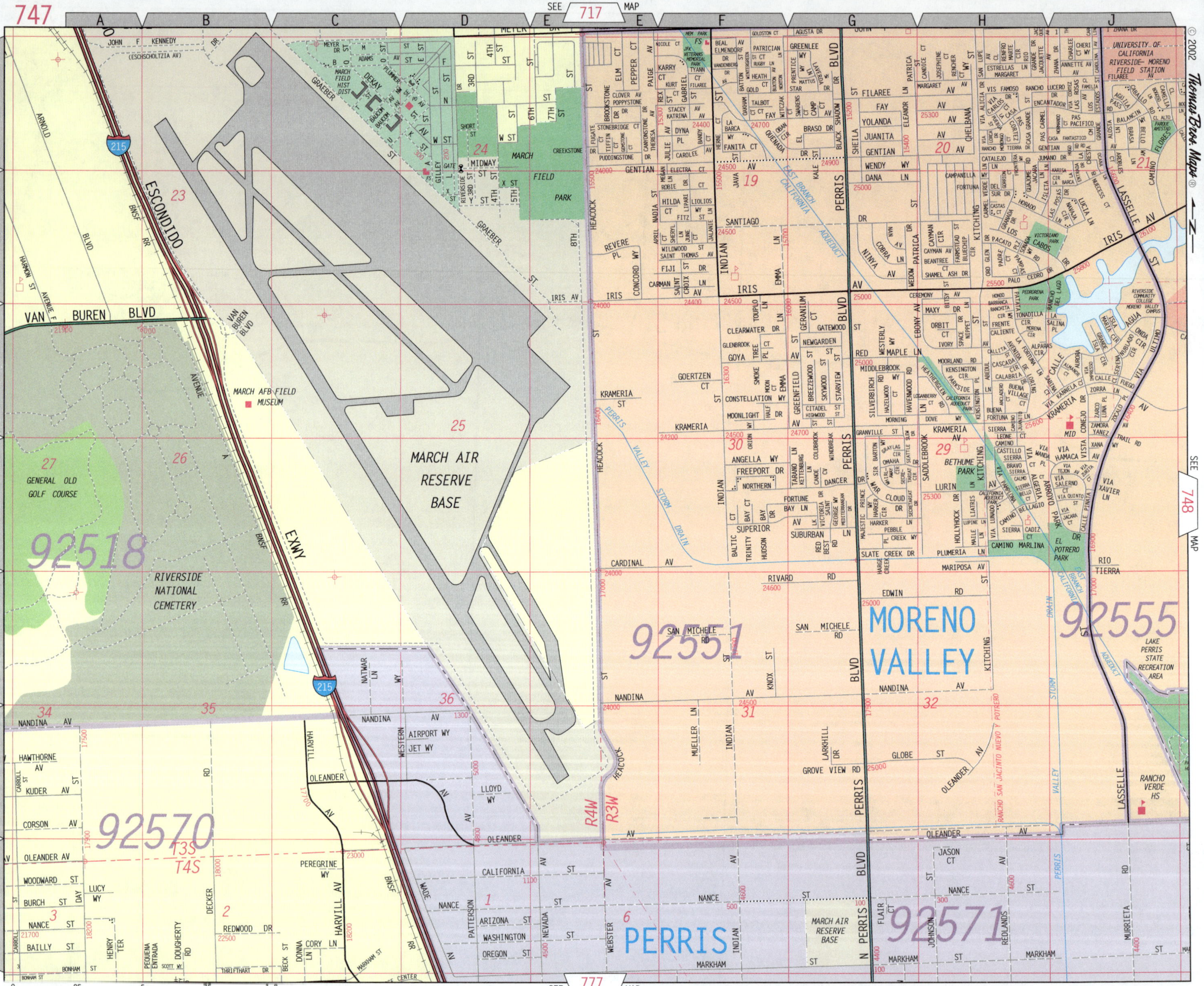

SEE 746 MAP

SEE 748 MAP

SEE 777 MAP

0 .25 .5 .75 1.0 miles 1 in. = 2400 ft.

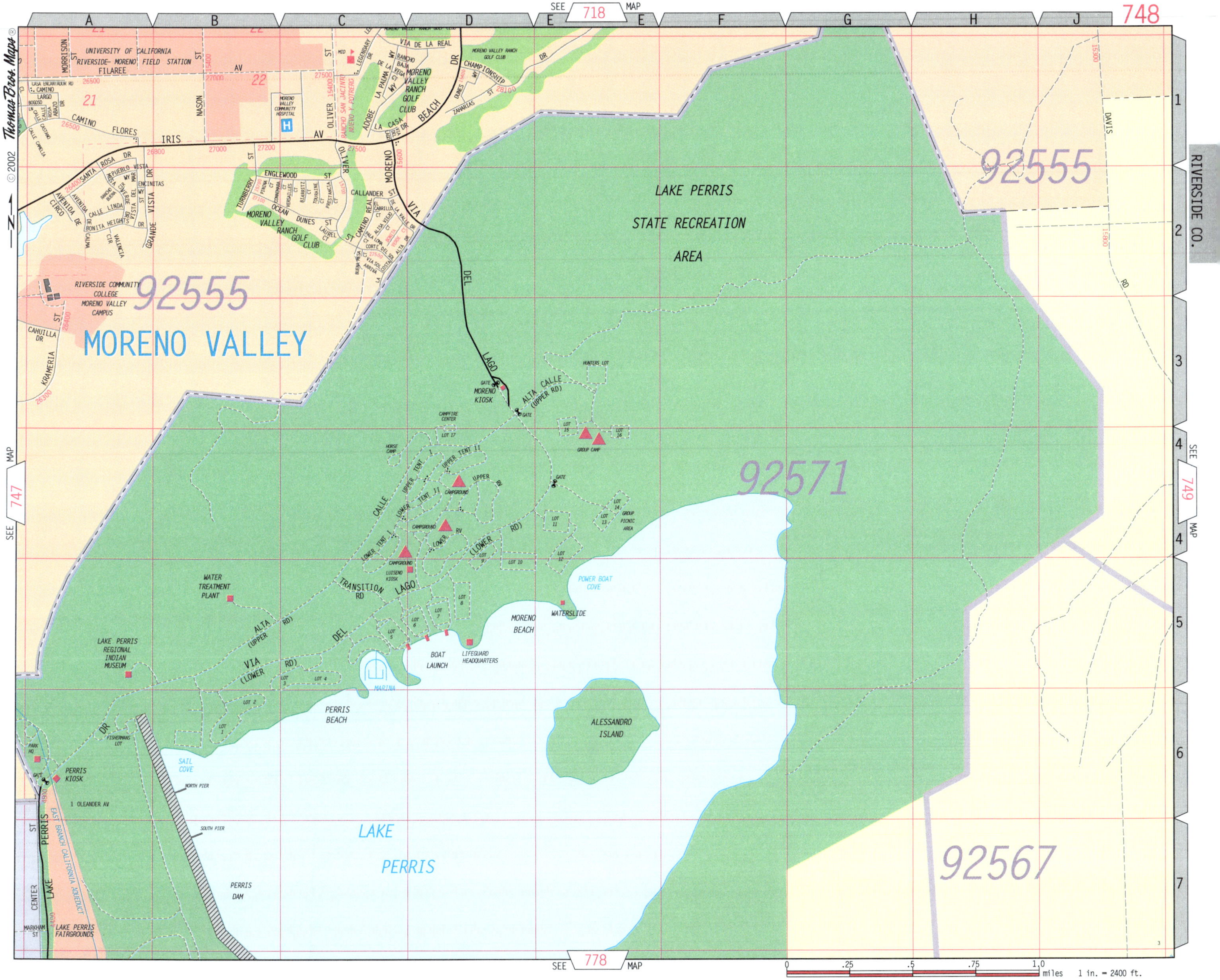

SEE 718 MAP
A B C D E E F G H J
1 2 3 4 4 5 6 7
Thomas Bros. Maps © 2002
UNIVERSITY OF CALIFORNIA RIVERSIDE- MORENO FIELD STATION
FILAREE
MORRISON ST
NASON ST
IRIS AV
CAMINO FLORES
OLIVER ST
MORENO VALLEY COMMUNITY HOSPITAL
VIA DE LA REAL
MORENO VALLEY RANCH GOLF CLUB
CHAMPIONSHIP DR
MORENO DR
ENGLEWOOD ST
CALLANDER ST
MORENO VALLEY RANCH GOLF CLUB
OCEAN DUNES ST
VIA DEL LAGO
RIVERSIDE COMMUNITY COLLEGE MORENO VALLEY CAMPUS
92555
MORENO VALLEY
CAHUILLA DR
KRAMERIA
LAKE PERRIS
STATE RECREATION
AREA
92555
DAVIS RD
RIVERSIDE CO.
MORENO KIOSK
ALTA CALLE (UPPER RD)
HUNTERS LOT
GROUP CAMP
CAMPFIRE CENTER
HORSE CAMP
UPPER TENT I
UPPER TENT II
UPPER RV
LOWER TENT I
LOWER TENT II
LOWER RV
CAMPGROUND
LUISENO KIOSK
92571
GROUP PICNIC AREA
POWER BOAT COVE
WATERSLIDE
MORENO BEACH
WATER TREATMENT PLANT
TRANSITION RD
ALTA (UPPER RD)
VIA (LOWER RD)
LAKE PERRIS REGIONAL INDIAN MUSEUM
BOAT LAUNCH
LIFEGUARD HEADQUARTERS
MARINA
PERRIS BEACH
ALESSANDRO ISLAND
FISHERMANS LOT
PARK HQ
PERRIS KIOSK
1 OLEANDER AV
SAIL COVE
NORTH PIER
SOUTH PIER
LAKE PERRIS
PERRIS DAM
EAST BRANCH CALIFORNIA AQUEDUCT
PERRIS ST
LAKE
CENTER ST
MARKHAM ST
LAKE PERRIS FAIRGROUNDS
92567
SEE 747 MAP
SEE 749 MAP
SEE 778 MAP
0 .25 .5 .75 1.0 miles 1 in. = 2400 ft.

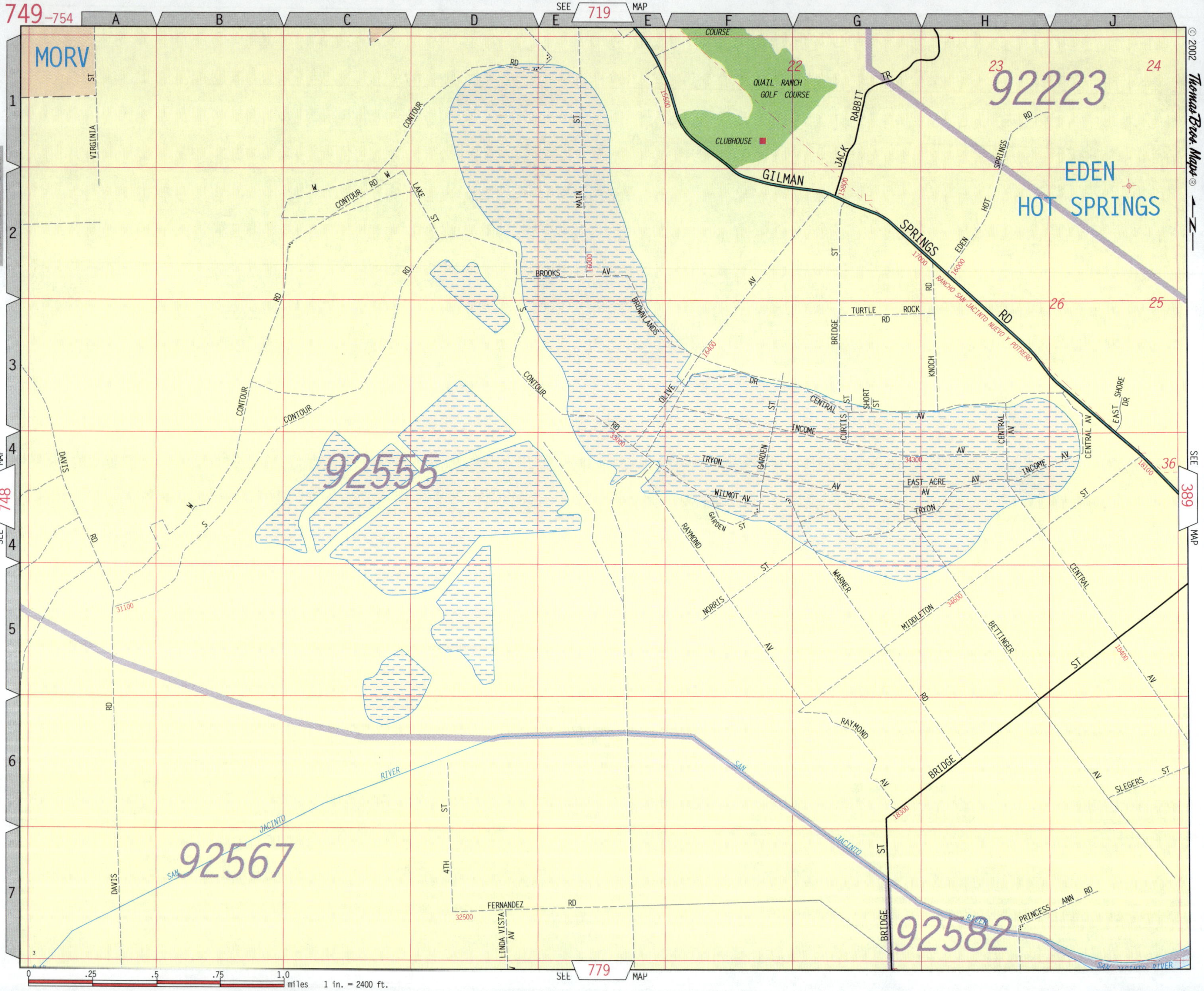
A
B
C
D
E
F
G
H
J
1
2
3
4
5
6
7
SEE 719 MAP
SEE 748 MAP
SEE 389 MAP
SEE 779 MAP
RIVERSIDE CO.
MORV
EDEN
HOT SPRINGS
92223
92555
92567
92582
QUAIL RANCH
GOLF COURSE
CLUBHOUSE
COURSE
GILMAN SPRINGS RD
JACK RABBIT TR
HOT SPRINGS RD
EDEN RD
TURTLE ROCK RD
BRIDGE ST
KNOCH RD
SHORT ST
CURTIS ST
CENTRAL AV
INCOME AV
EAST ACRE AV
TRYON AV
WILMOT AV
GARDEN ST
OLIVE DR
BROWNLANDS RD
BROOKS AV
MAIN ST
CONTOUR RD
W CONTOUR RD
LAKE ST
VIRGINIA ST
DAVIS RD
RAYMOND AV
NORRIS ST
WARNER RD
MIDDLETON ST
BETTINGER AV
SLEGERS ST
EAST SHORE DR
PRINCESS ANN RD
FERNANDEZ RD
LINDA VISTA AV
4TH ST
SAN JACINTO RIVER
RANCHO SAN JACINTO NUEVO Y POTRERO
22
23
24
25
26
36
15500
15600
16000
16400
17000
18100
18300
16400
31100
32500
33000
34300
34600
0 .25 .5 .75 1.0 miles 1 in. = 2400 ft.
Thomas Bros. Maps

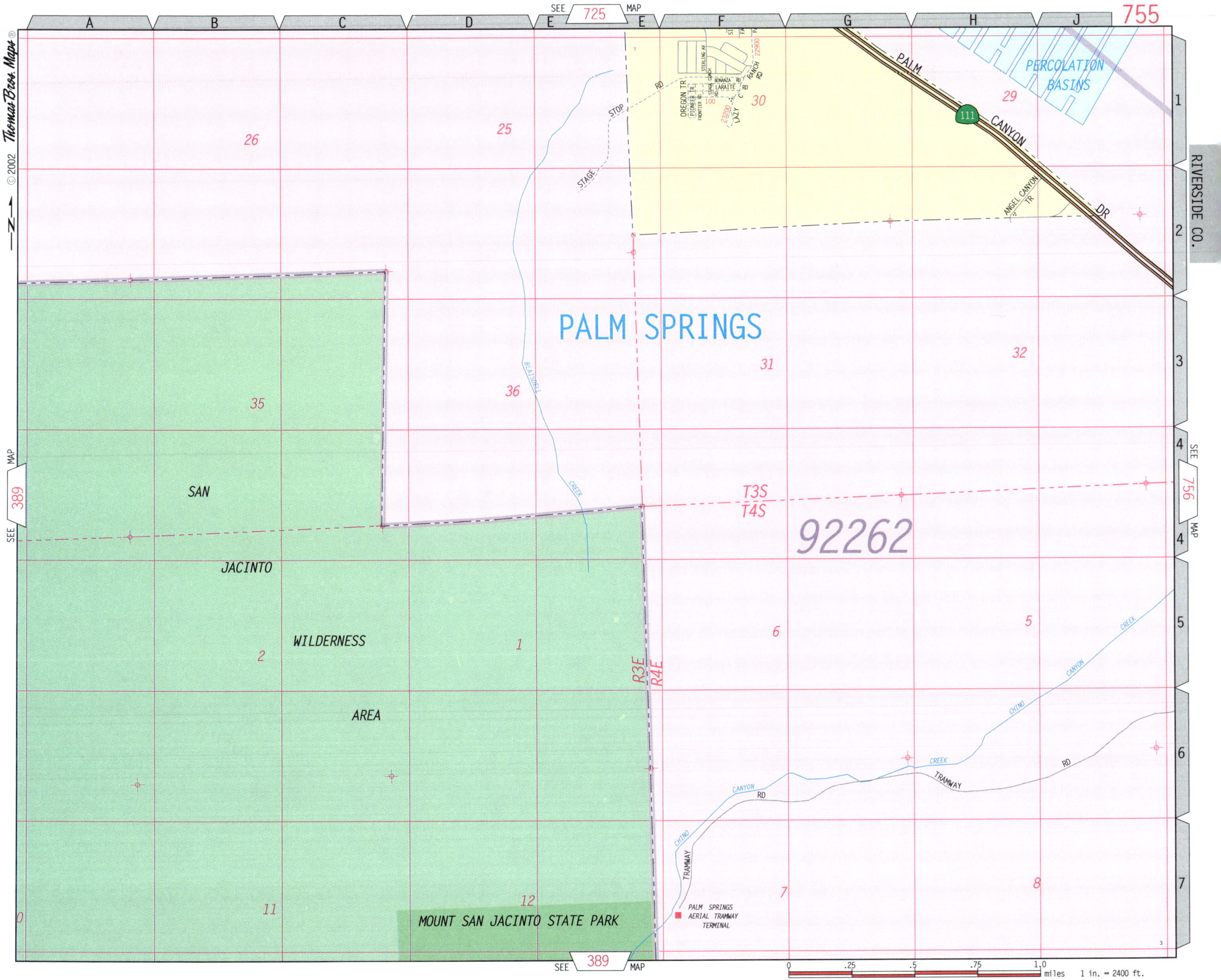
SEE 725 MAP
SEE 389 MAP
SEE 756 MAP
RIVERSIDE CO.
PALM SPRINGS
92262
PALM CANYON DR
111
PERCOLATION BASINS
STAGE STOP RD
OREGON TR
PIONEER TR
FRONTIER RD
STERLING AV
STAGE COACH RD
BONANZA RD
LARAITE RD
LAZY C RANCH RD
22900
23200
100
ANGEL CANYON TR
BLAISDELL CREEK
T3S
T4S
R3E
R4E
SAN JACINTO WILDERNESS AREA
MOUNT SAN JACINTO STATE PARK
CHINO CANYON CREEK
TRAMWAY RD
PALM SPRINGS AERIAL TRAMWAY TERMINAL
26
25
30
29
35
36
31
32
2
1
6
5
11
12
7
8
0 .25 .5 .75 1.0 miles
1 in. = 2400 ft.

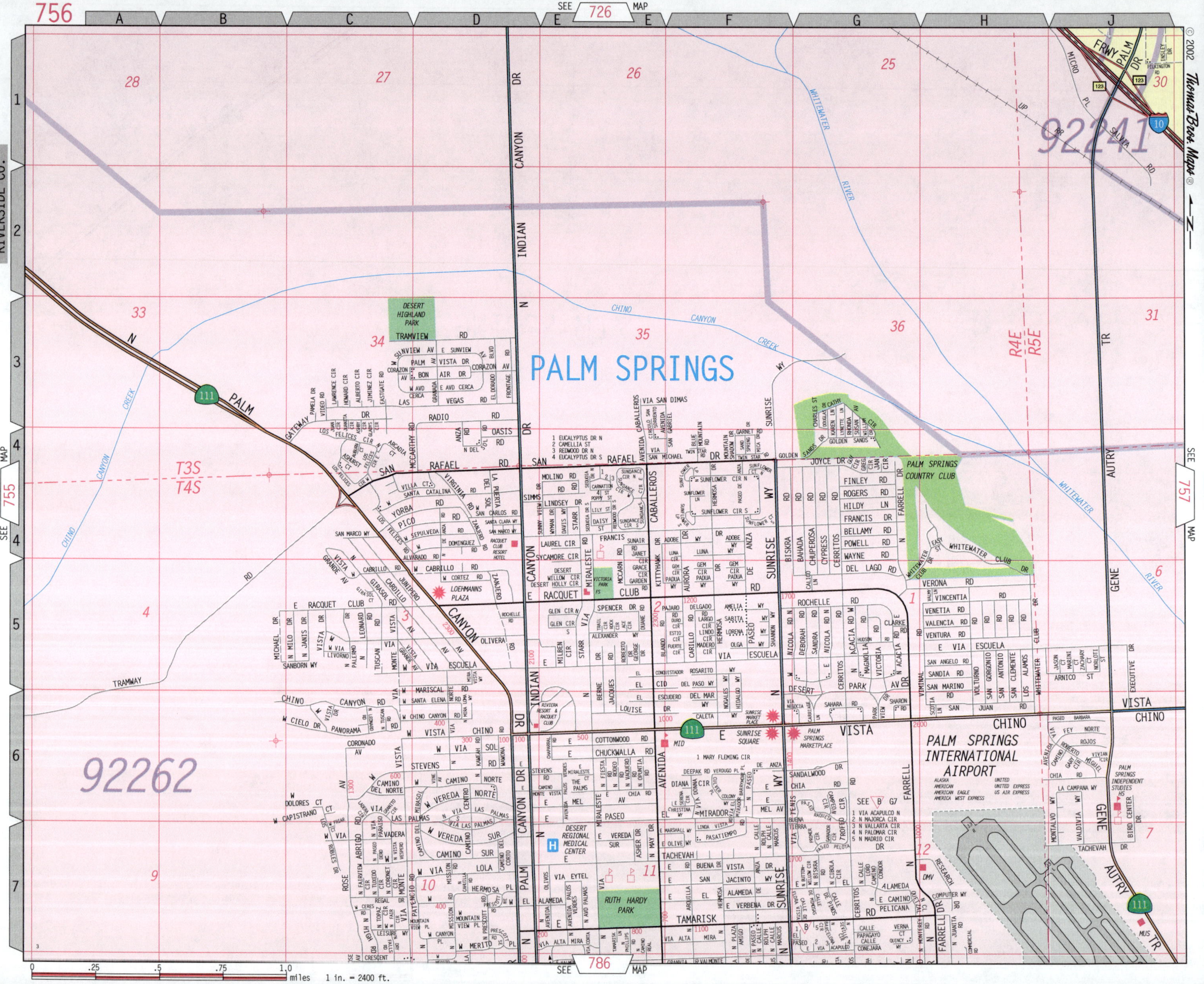
SEE 726 MAP
SEE 786 MAP
SEE 755 MAP
SEE 757 MAP
RIVERSIDE CO.
PALM SPRINGS
92262
92241
PALM SPRINGS INTERNATIONAL AIRPORT
PALM SPRINGS COUNTRY CLUB
DESERT HIGHLAND PARK
RUTH HARDY PARK
DESERT REGIONAL MEDICAL CENTER
LOEHMANNS PLAZA
SUNRISE SQUARE
PALM SPRINGS MARKETPLACE
RIVIERA RESORT & RACQUET CLUB
RACQUET CLUB RESORT HOTEL
VICTORIA PARK
PALM SPRINGS INDEPENDENT STUDIES
DMV
MUS
N INDIAN CANYON DR
N PALM CANYON DR
GENE AUTRY TR
E VISTA CHINO
SAN RAFAEL RD
RACQUET CLUB RD
TRAMWAY RD
CHINO CANYON CREEK
WHITEWATER RIVER
SUNRISE WY
AVENIDA CABALLEROS
FARRELL DR
TAHQUITZ
TAMARISK RD
ALEJO RD
T3S
T4S
R4E
R5E
FRWY
PALM DR
0 .25 .5 .75 1.0 miles 1 in. = 2400 ft.

SEE 727 MAP

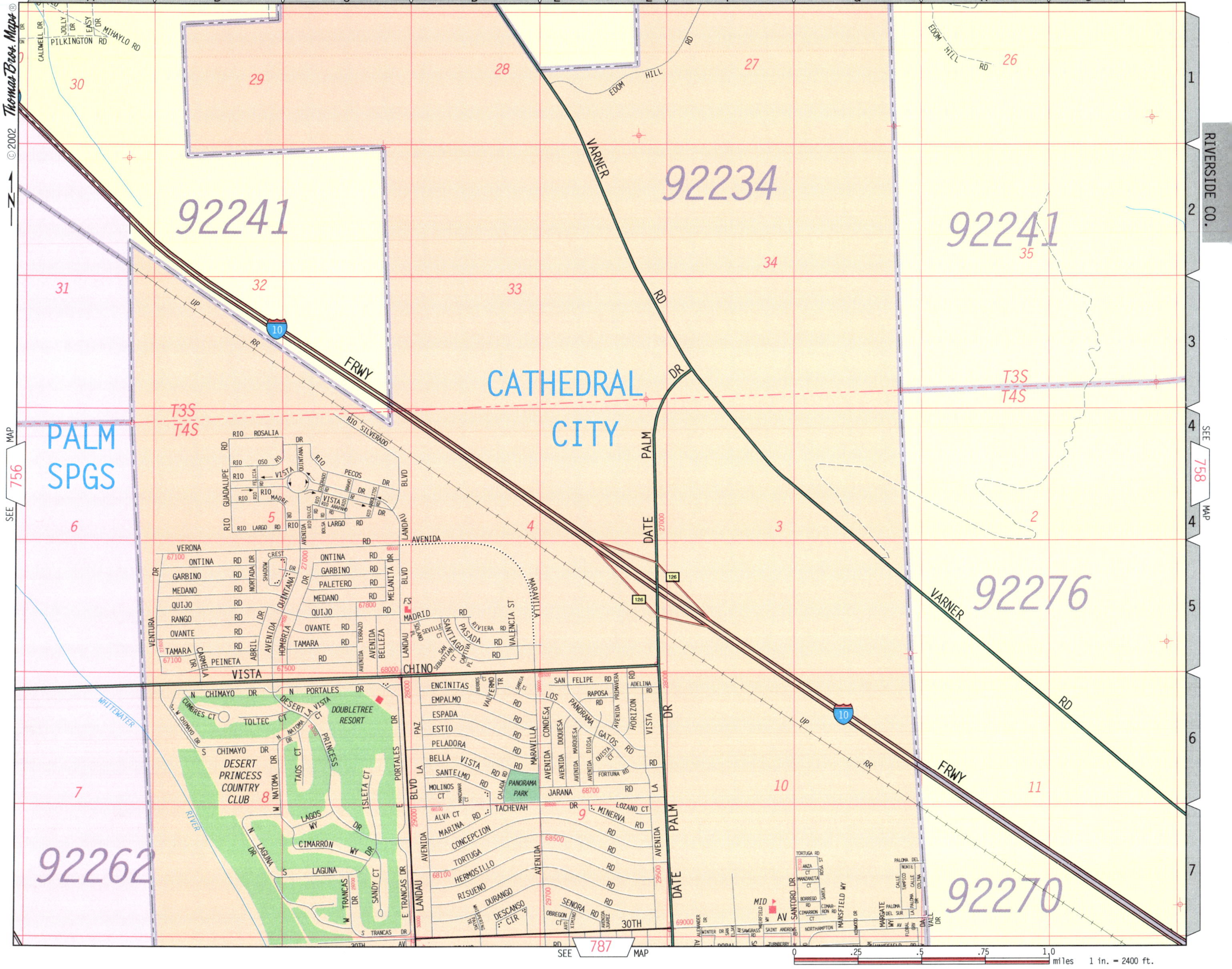

SEE 756 MAP
SEE 758 MAP
SEE 787 MAP

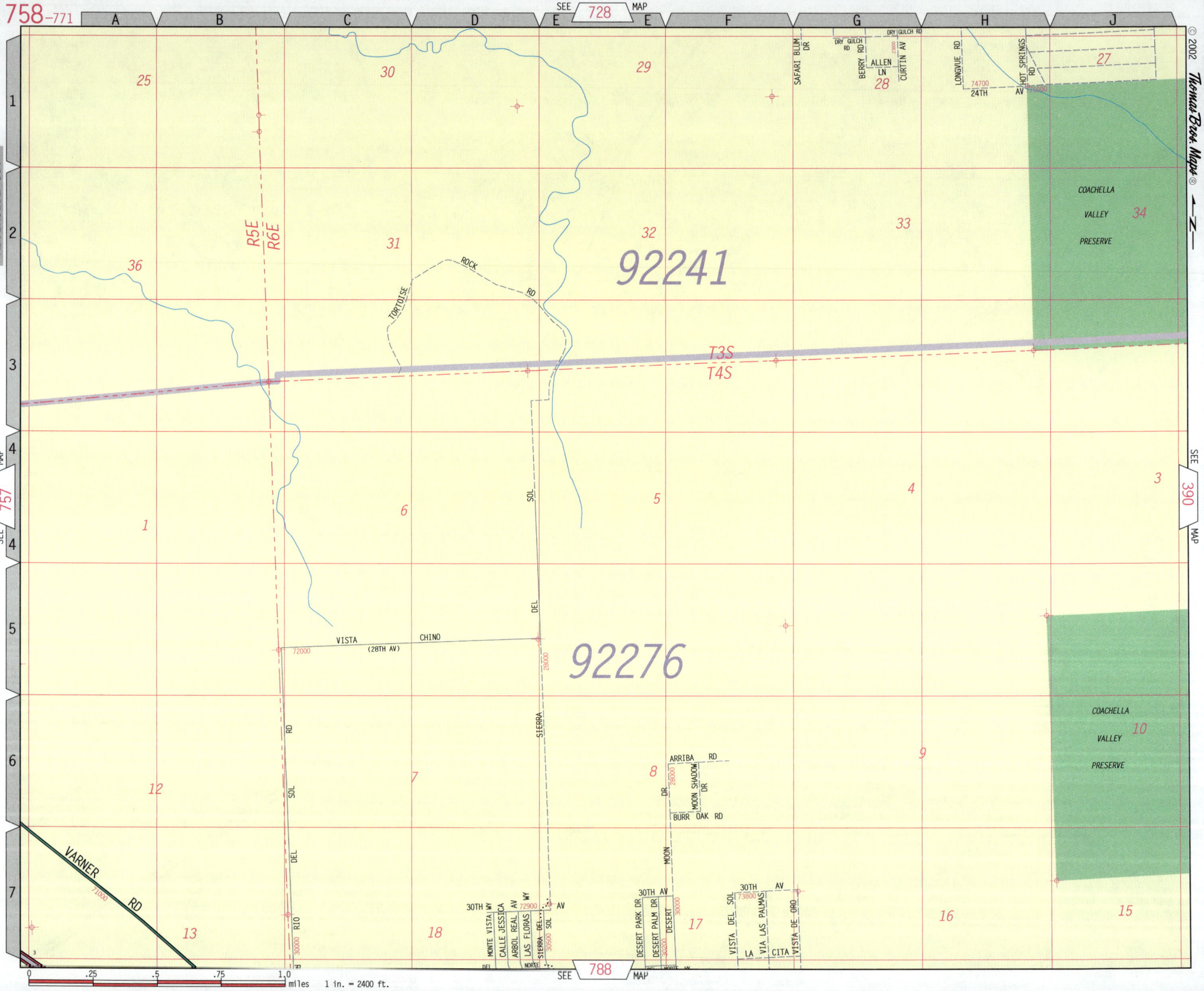
SEE 728 MAP
A
B
C
D
E
F
G
H
J
1
2
3
4
5
6
7
RIVERSIDE CO.
SEE 757 MAP
SEE 390 MAP
25
30
29
28
27
36
31
32
33
34
1
6
5
4
3
12
7
8
9
10
13
18
17
16
15
R5E
R6E
T3S
T4S
92241
92276
COACHELLA VALLEY PRESERVE
COACHELLA VALLEY PRESERVE
SAFARI BLUM DR
DRY GULCH RD
DRY GULCH RD
BERRY RD
ALLEN LN
CURTIN AV
2300
LONGVUE RD
HOT SPRINGS RD
74700
24TH AV
TORTOISE
ROCK RD
SOL DEL SIERRA
28000
VISTA CHINO
(28TH AV)
72000
RIO DEL SOL RD
30000
VARNER RD
71000
30TH AV
MONTE VISTA WY
CALLE JESSICA
ARBOL REAL AV
LAS FLORAS WY
SIERRA DEL SOL
72900
30500
DEL NORTE
30TH AV
DESERT PARK DR
DESERT PALM DR
DESERT MOON DR
30200
30000
ARRIBA RD
MOON SHADOW DR
BURR OAK RD
28000
30TH AV
73800
VISTA DEL SOL
VIA LAS PALMAS
VISTA DE ORO
LA CITA
SEE 788 MAP
0 .25 .5 .75 1.0 miles 1 in. = 2400 ft.
Thomas Bros. Maps®
N

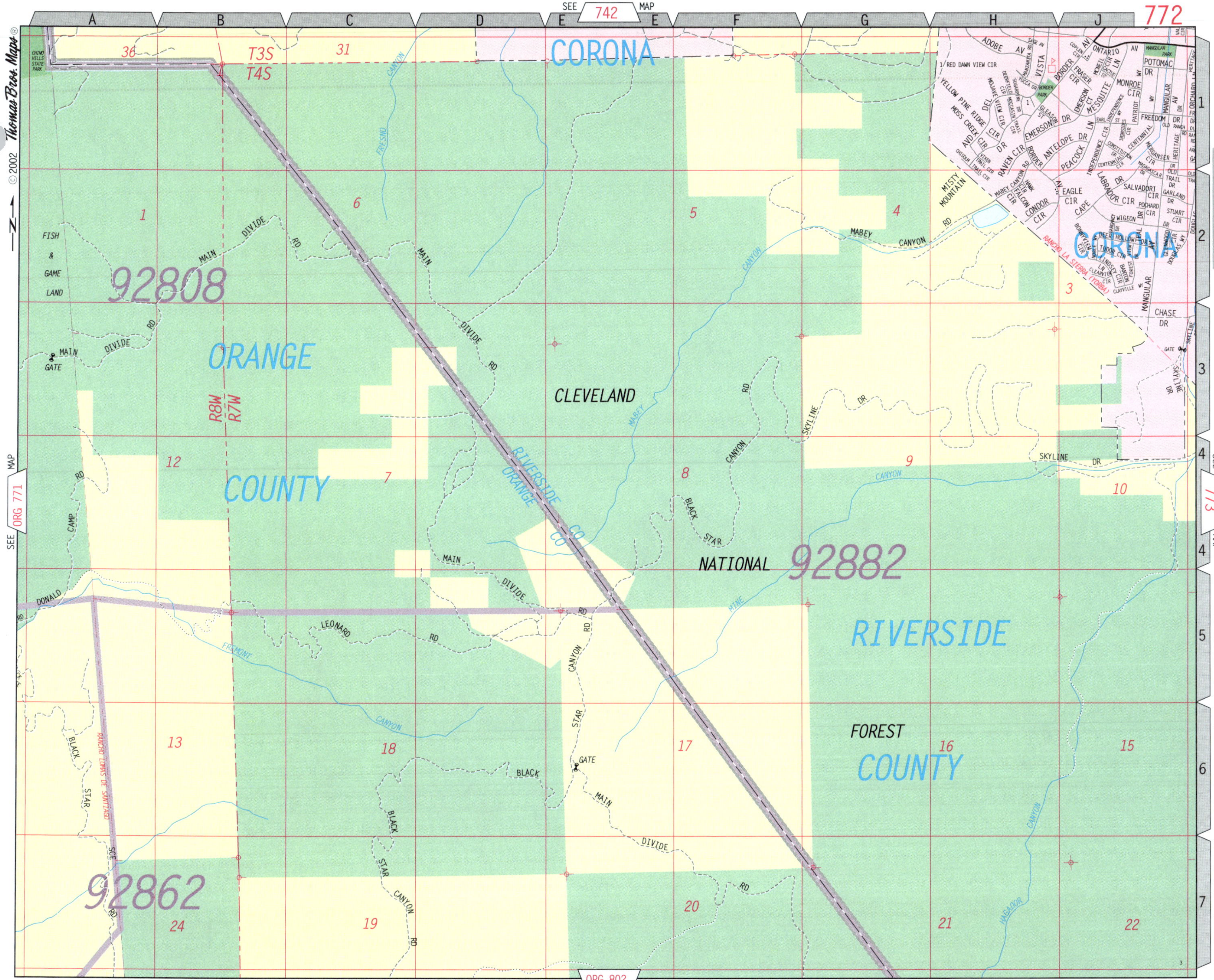

0 .25 .5 .75 1.0 miles 1 in. = 2400 ft.

SEE 743 MAP

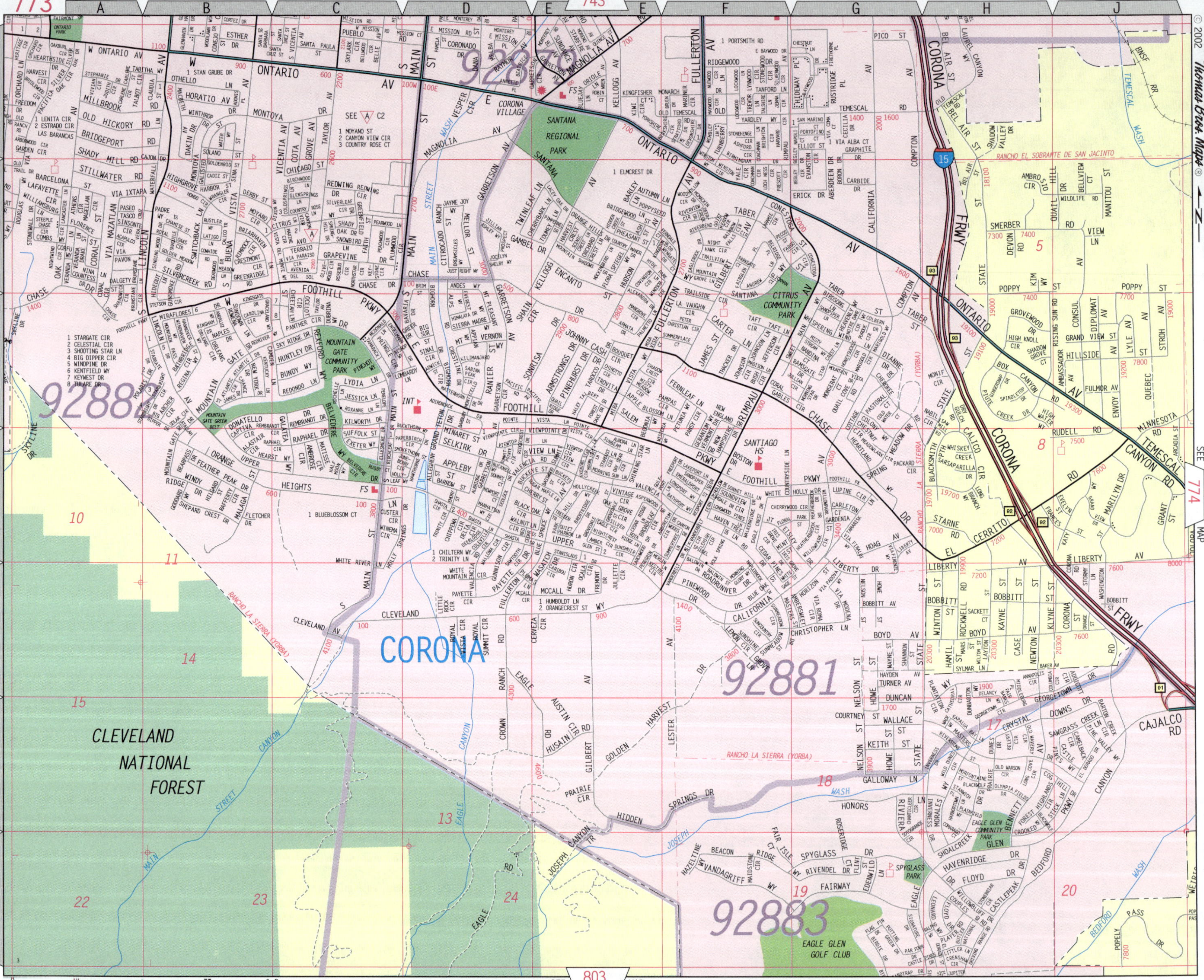

SEE 772 MAP
SEE 774 MAP
SEE 803 MAP

0 .25 .5 .75 1.0 miles 1 in. = 2400 ft.

SEE 744 MAP

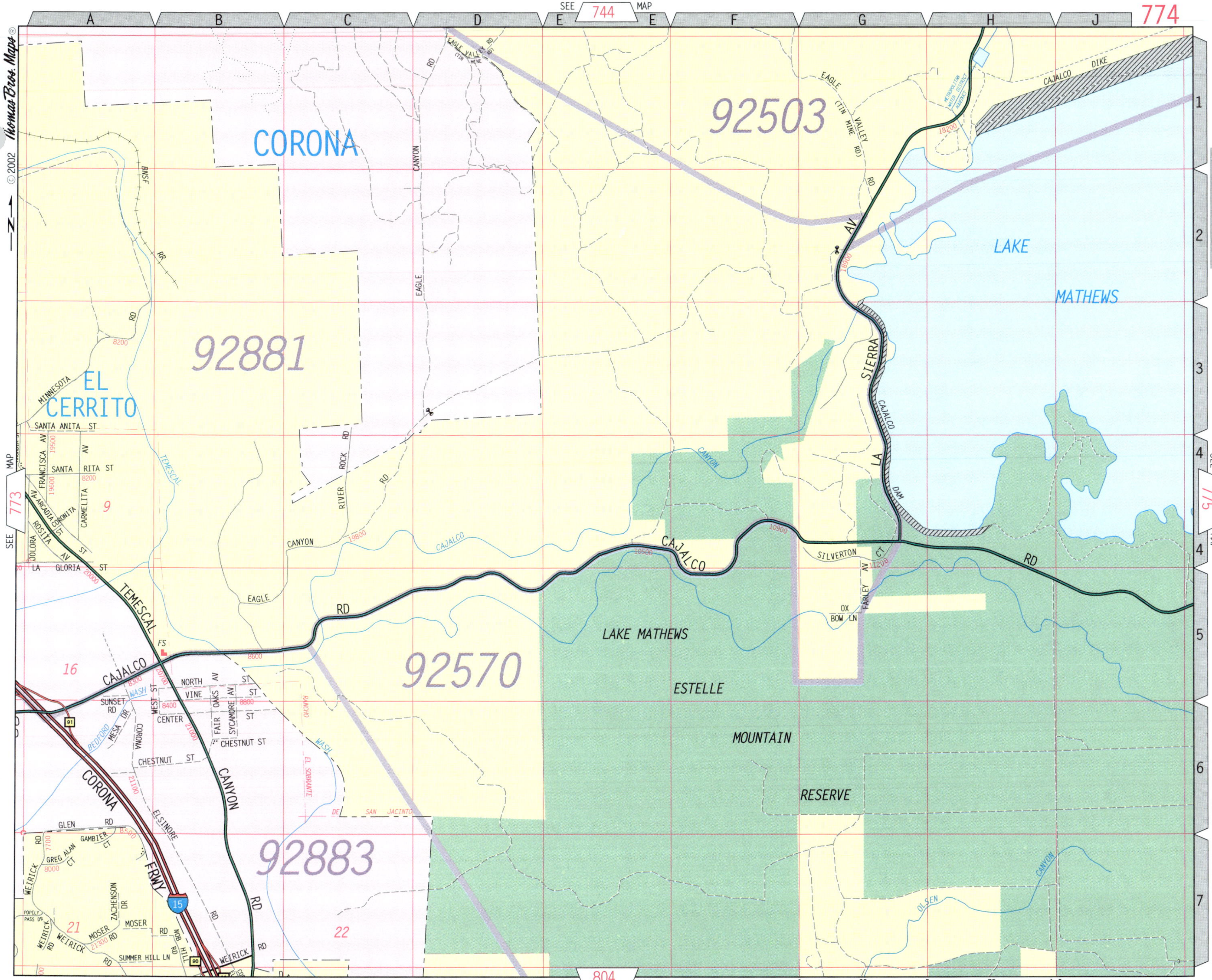

SEE 773 MAP

SEE 775 MAP

SEE 804 MAP

0 .25 .5 .75 1.0 miles 1 in. = 2400 ft.

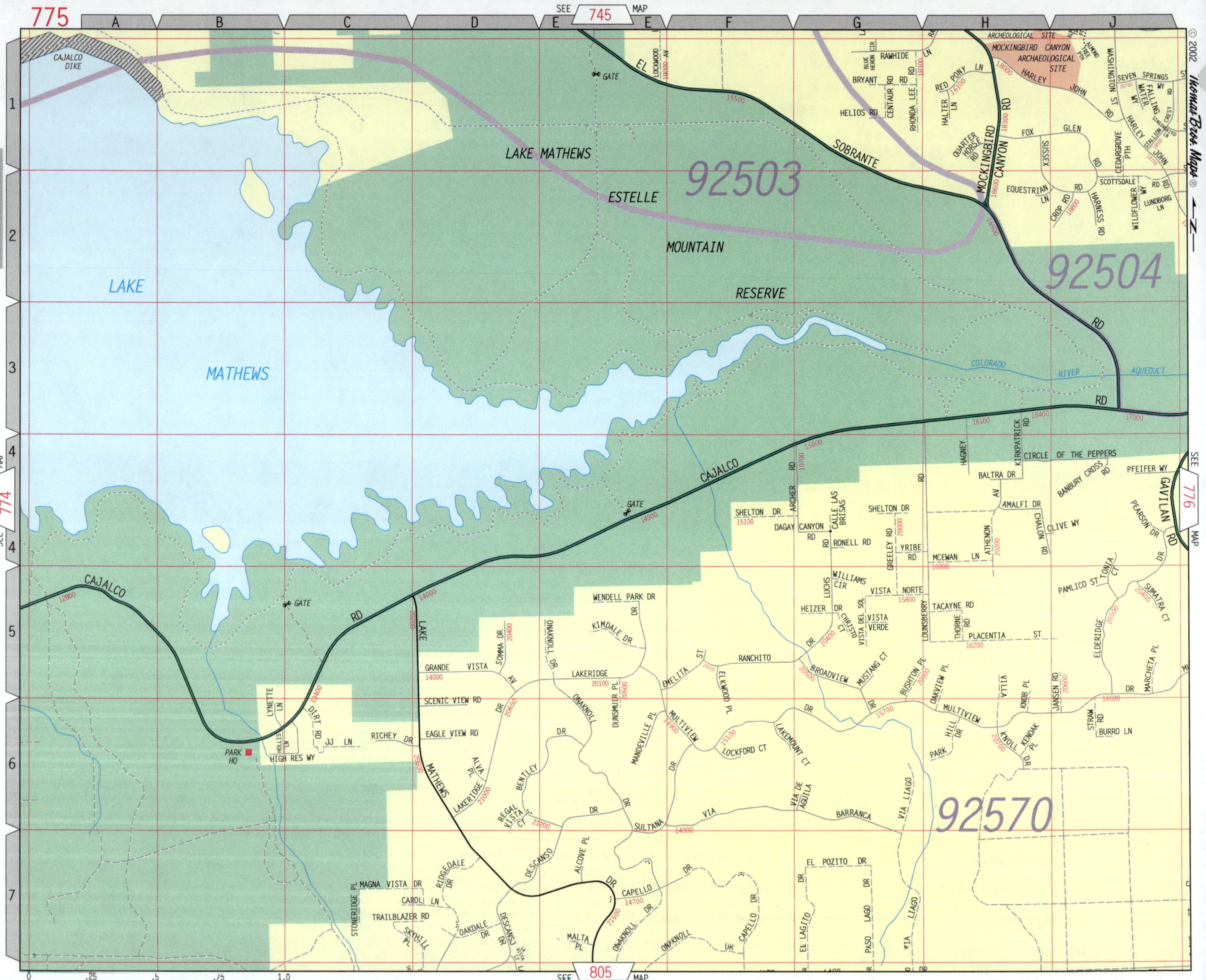

0 .25 .5 .75 1.0 miles 1 in. = 2400 ft.

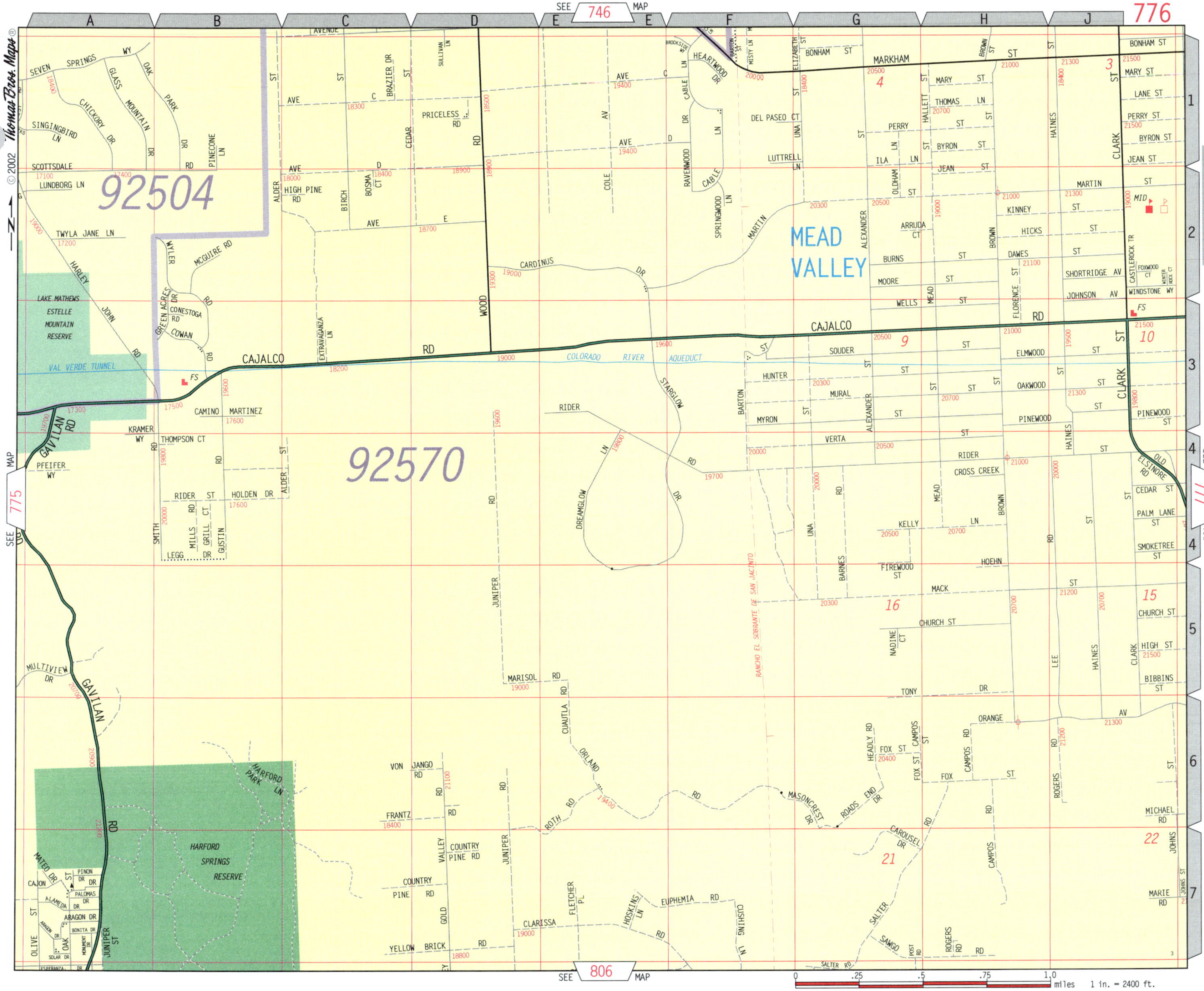

0 .25 .5 .75 1.0 miles 1 in. = 2400 ft.

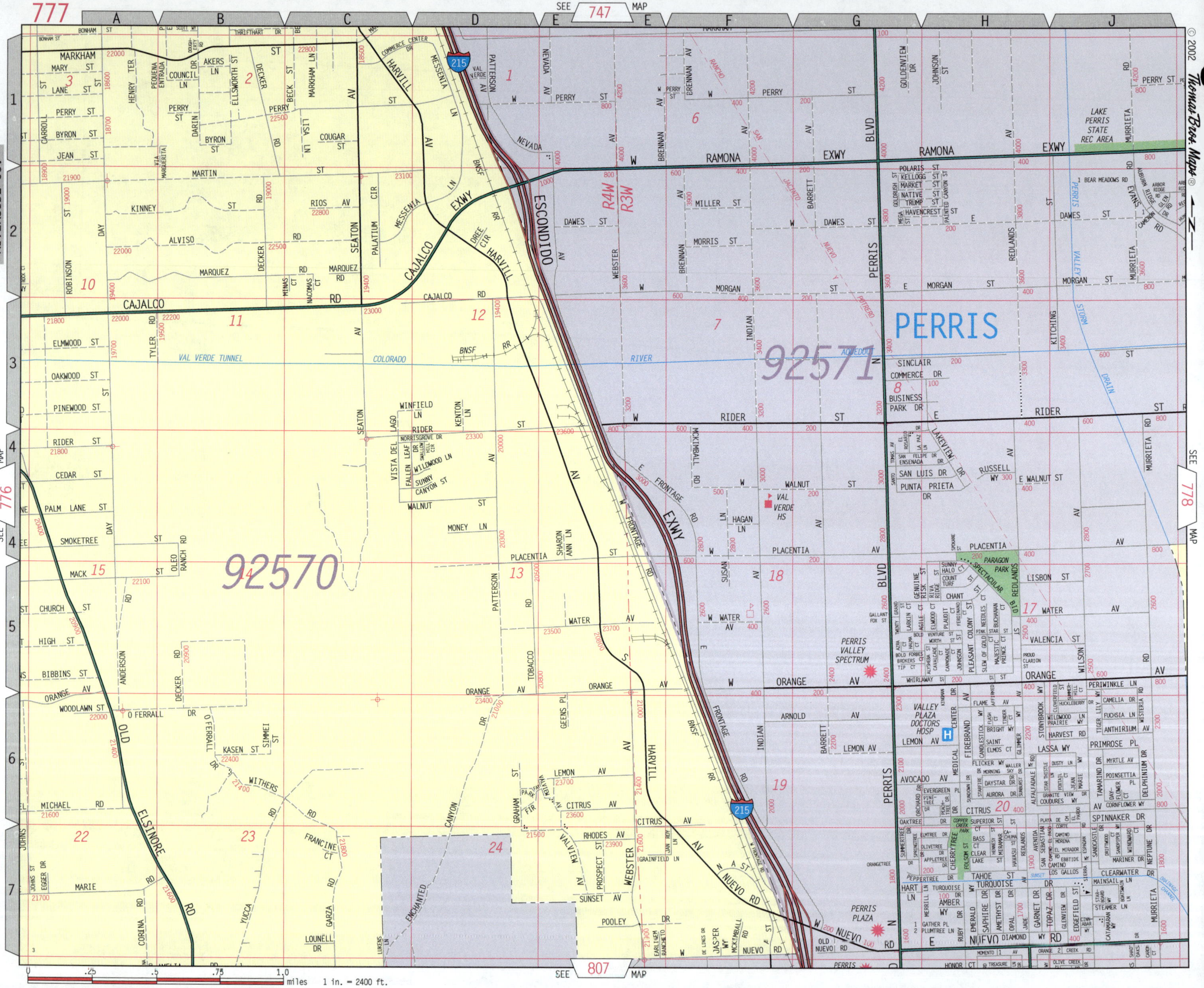
SEE 747 MAP
SEE 807 MAP
SEE 776 MAP
SEE 778 MAP
RIVERSIDE CO.
PERRIS
92570
92571
R4W R3W
MARKHAM ST
CAJALCO RD
CAJALCO EXWY
RAMONA EXWY
RIDER ST
PLACENTIA AV
ORANGE AV
NUEVO RD
PERRIS BLVD
ESCONDIDO EXWY
HARVILL AV
OLD ELSINORE RD
PATTERSON AV
WEBSTER AV
INDIAN AV
REDLANDS AV
MURRIETA RD
VAL VERDE TUNNEL
COLORADO RIVER AQUEDUCT
LAKE PERRIS STATE REC AREA
VAL VERDE HS
PERRIS VALLEY SPECTRUM
VALLEY PLAZA DOCTORS HOSP
PERRIS PLAZA
PARAGON PARK
PERRIS VALLEY STORM DRAIN
215
miles 1 in. = 2400 ft.
© 2002 Thomas Bros. Maps®

SEE 748 MAP

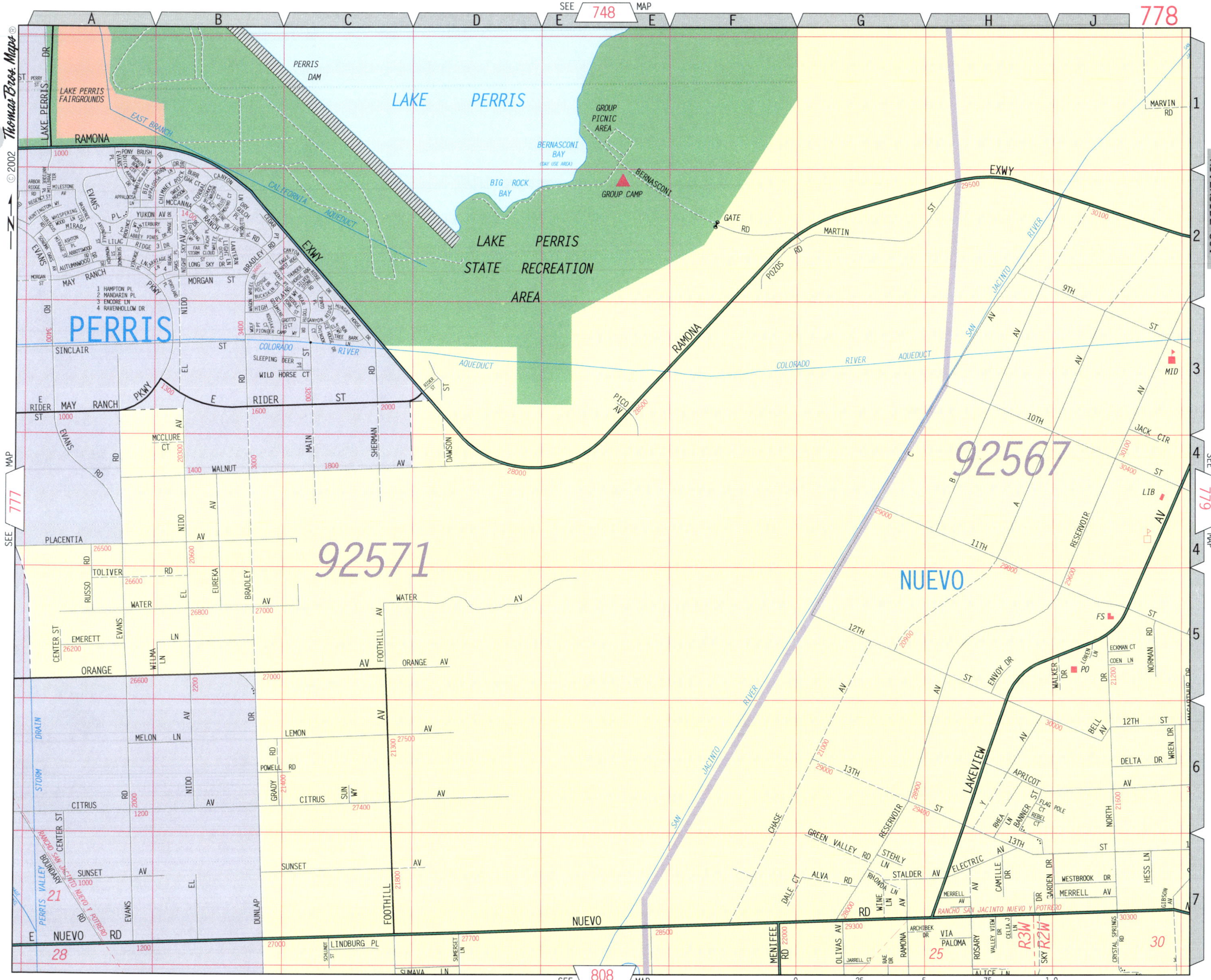

SEE 777 MAP

SEE 779 MAP

SEE 808 MAP

0 .25 .5 .75 1.0 miles 1 in. = 2400 ft.

SEE 749 MAP

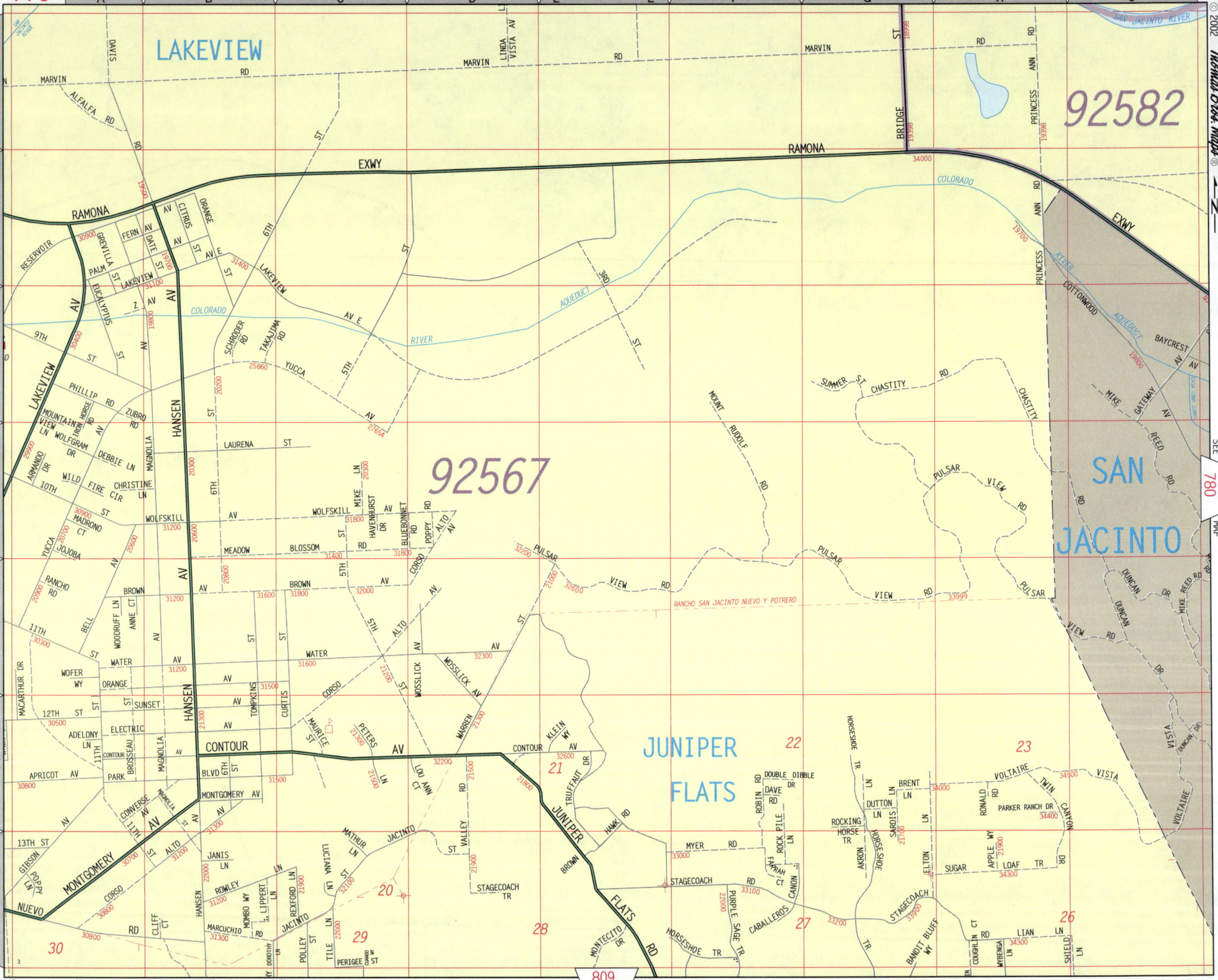

0 .25 .5 .75 1.0 miles 1 in. = 2400 ft.

SEE 778 MAP

SEE 780 MAP

SEE 809 MAP

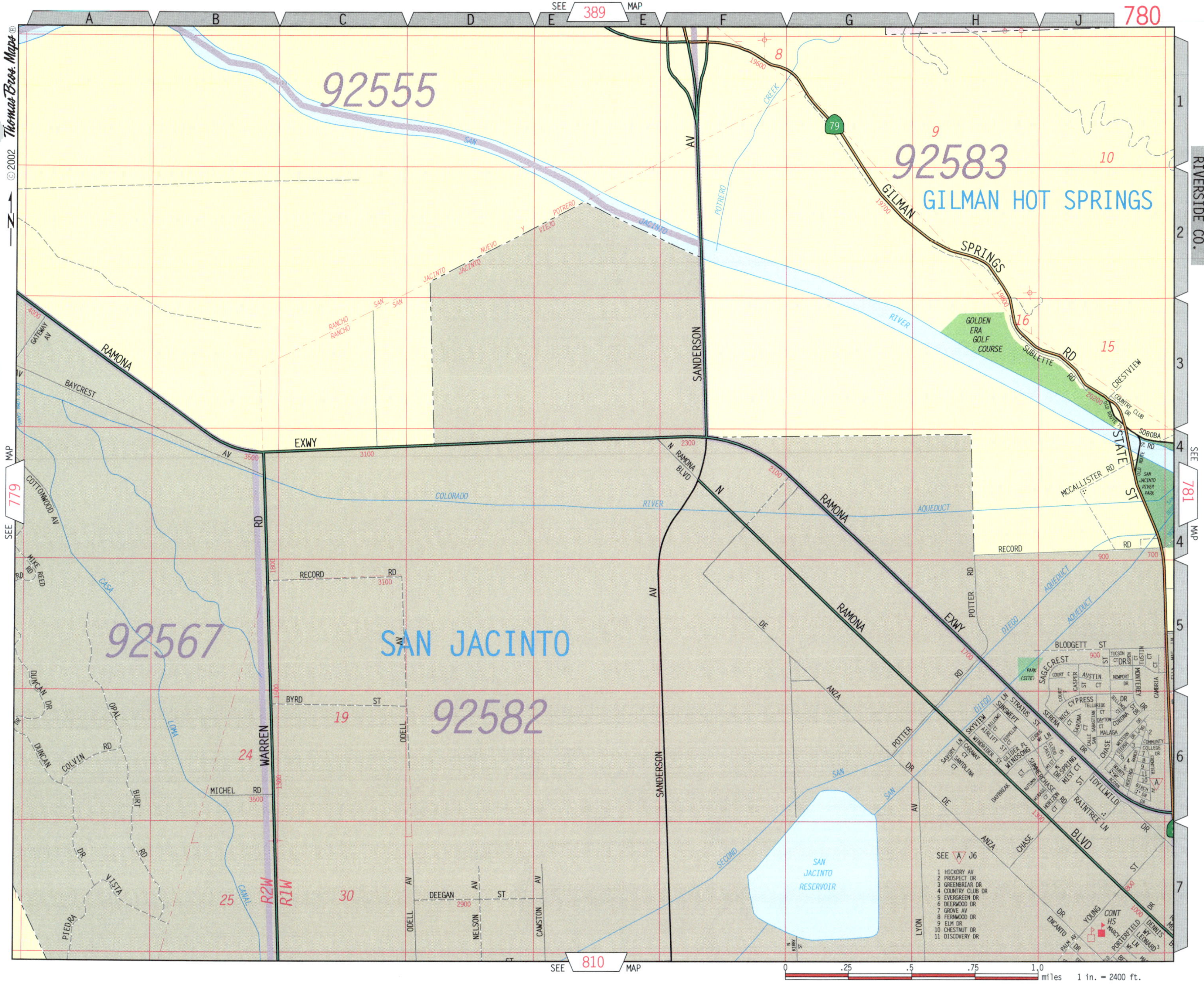
SEE 389 MAP
SEE 779 MAP
SEE 781 MAP
SEE 810 MAP
A
B
C
D
E
F
G
H
J
1
2
3
4
5
6
7
92555
92583
92567
92582
GILMAN HOT SPRINGS
SAN JACINTO
RIVERSIDE CO.
GILMAN SPRINGS RD
79
SAN JACINTO RIVER
POTRERO CREEK
GOLDEN ERA GOLF COURSE
SUBLETTE RD
CRESTVIEW
COUNTRY CLUB DR
OLD ROUTE 79
SOBOBA RD
STATE ST
MCCALLISTER RD
SAN JACINTO RIVER PARK
SANDERSON AV
RAMONA EXWY
N RAMONA BLVD
RAMONA BLVD
GATEWAY AV
BAYCREST AV
COTTONWOOD AV
MIKE REED RD
COLORADO RIVER AQUEDUCT
RECORD RD
WARREN RD
BYRD ST
ODELL AV
MICHEL RD
DEEGAN ST
NELSON AV
CAWSTON AV
CASA LOMA CANAL
DUNCAN DR
OPAL DR
COLVIN RD
BURT RD
VISTA DR
PIEDRA
DE ANZA DR
POTTER RD
LYON AV
SAN DIEGO AQUEDUCT
SECOND SAN DIEGO AQUEDUCT
SAN JACINTO RESERVOIR
BLODGETT ST
SAGECREST
AUSTIN CT
CYPRESS DR
PARK (SITE)
IDYLLWILD DR
RAINTREE LN
CHASE ST
YOUNG
ENCANTO DR
PORTERFIELD WY
CONT HS
R2W
R1W
8
9
10
15
16
19
24
25
30
SEE A J6
1 HICKORY AV
2 PROSPECT DR
3 GREENBRIAR DR
4 COUNTRY CLUB DR
5 EVERGREEN DR
6 DEERWOOD DR
7 GROVE AV
8 FERNWOOD DR
9 ELM DR
10 CHESTNUT DR
11 DISCOVERY DR
0 .25 .5 .75 1.0 miles
1 in. = 2400 ft.

SEE 389 MAP

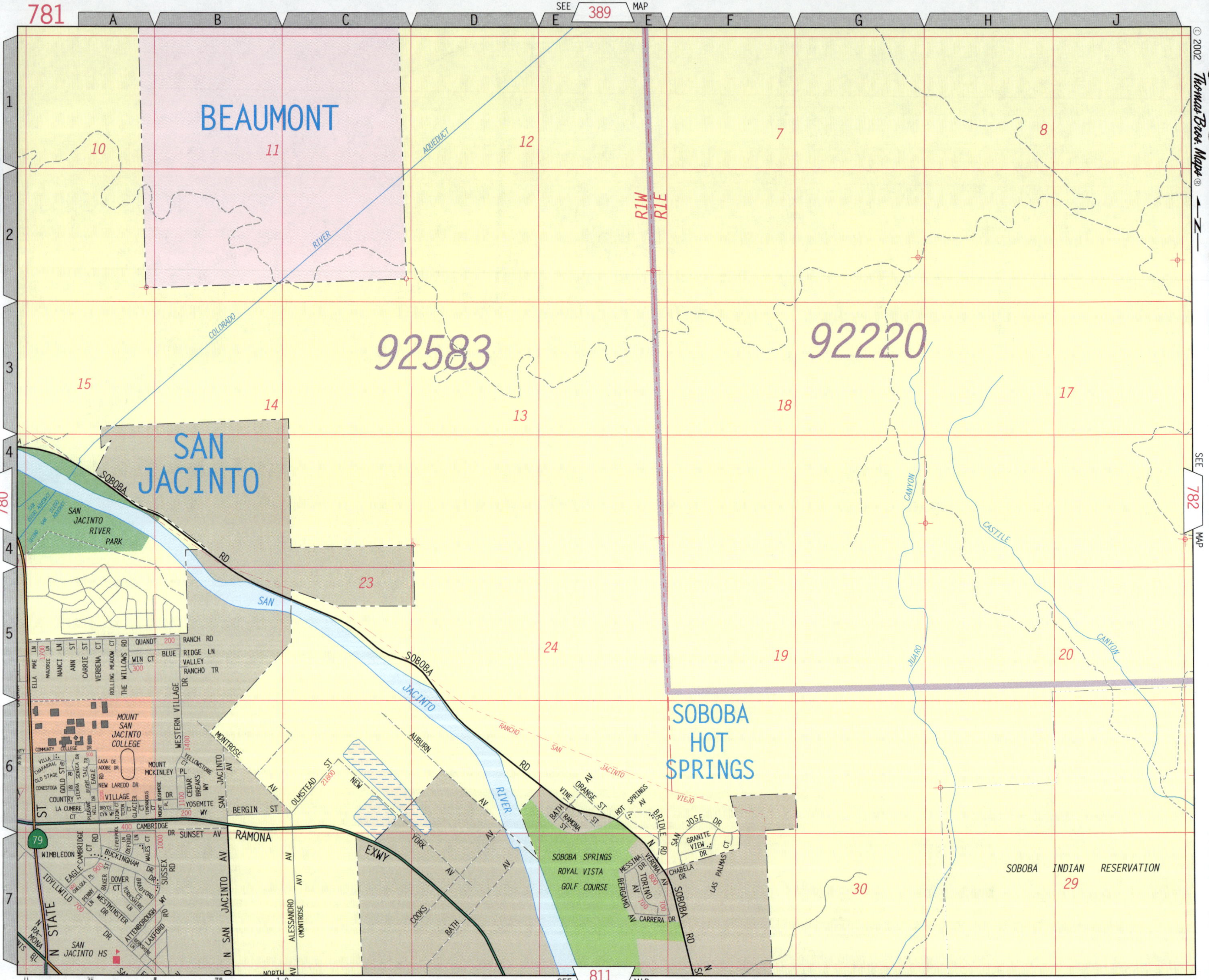

SEE 811 MAP

0 .25 .5 .75 1.0 miles 1 in. = 2400 ft.

SEE 389 MAP

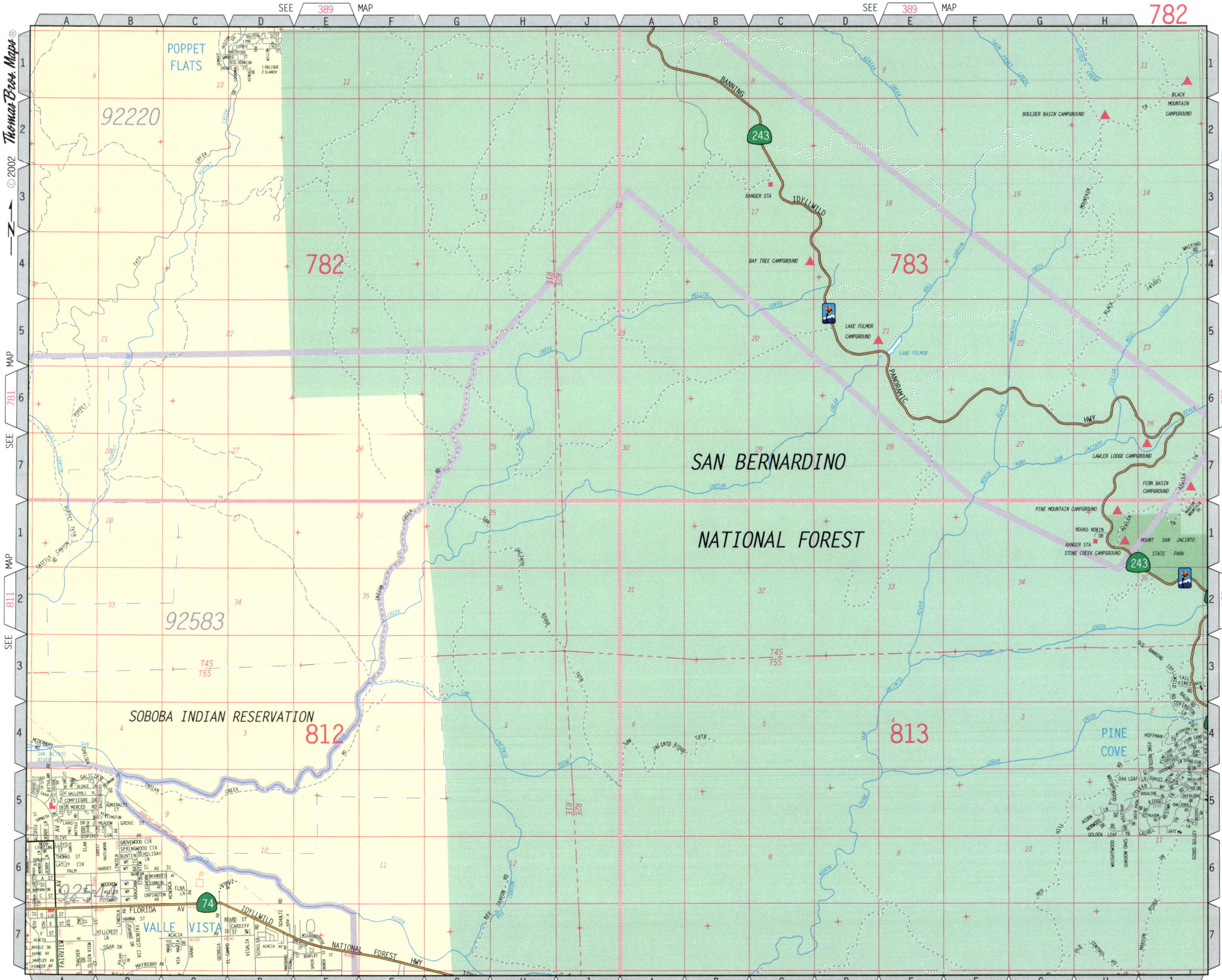

Thomas Bros. Maps® © 2002

0 .25 .5 .75 1.0 miles 1 in. = 4800 ft.

SEE 756 MAP

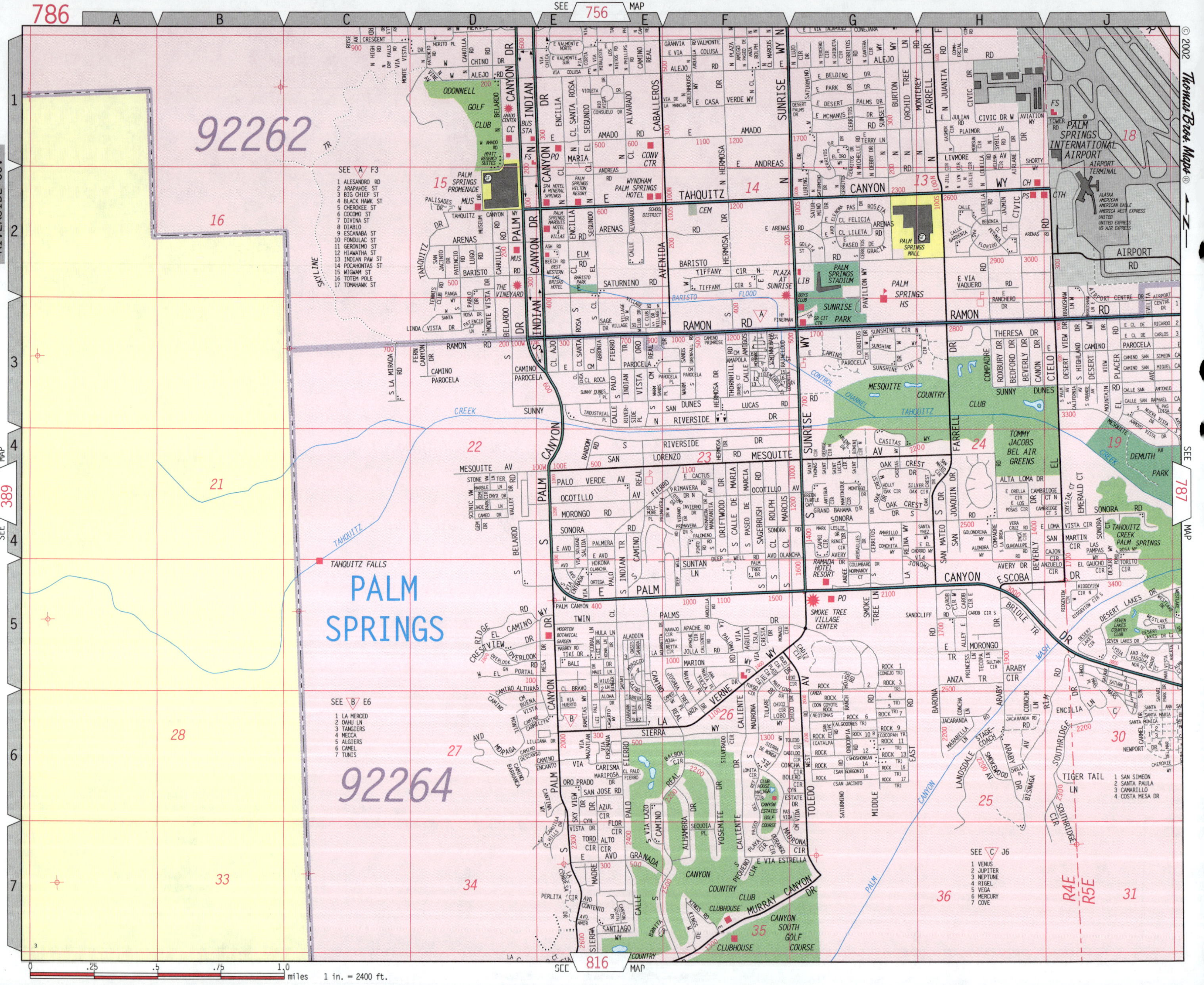

SEE 389 MAP

SEE 787 MAP

SEE 816 MAP

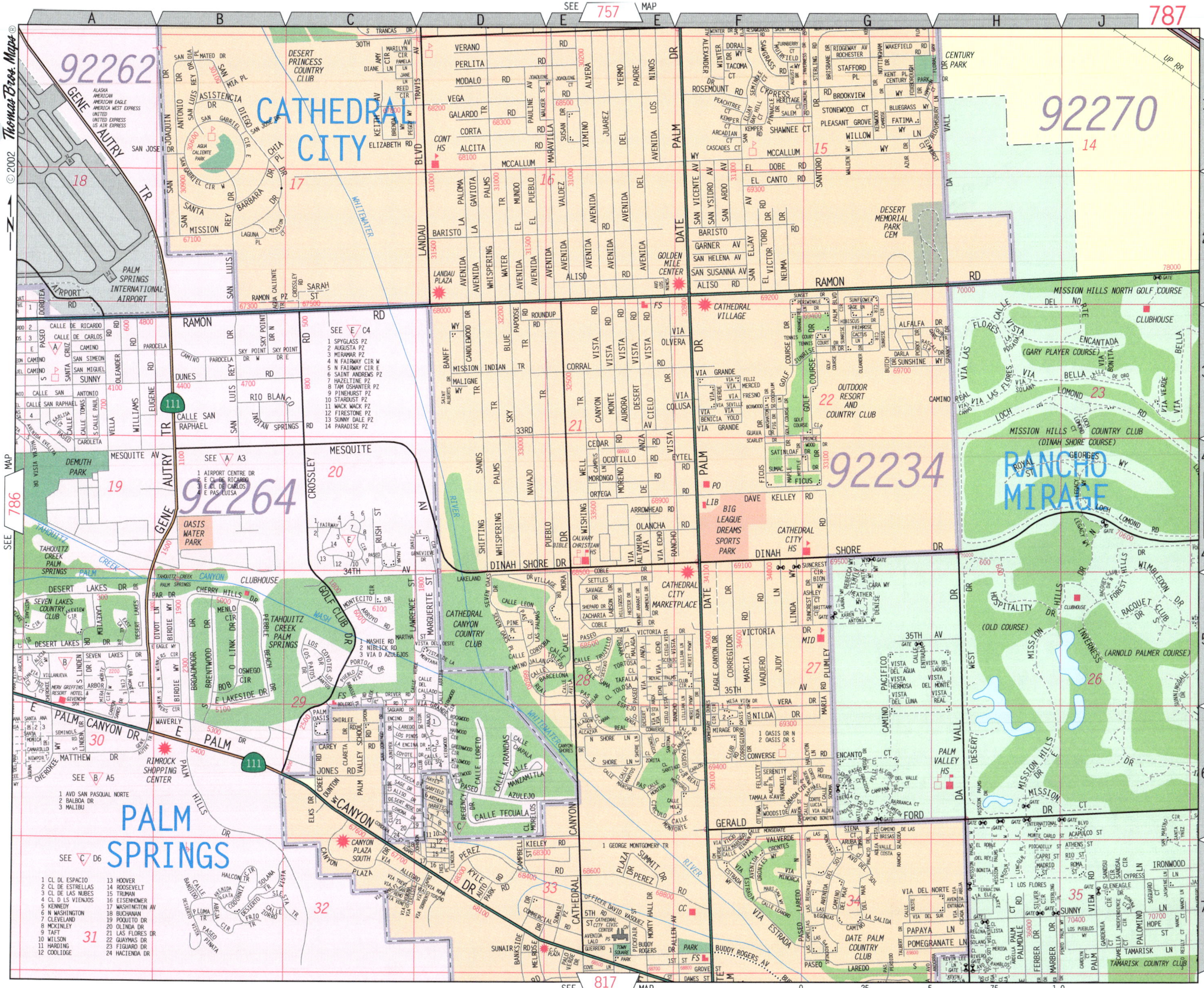

SEE 757 MAP
SEE 817 MAP
SEE 786 MAP
SEE 788 MAP
RIVERSIDE CO.
Thomas Bros. Maps ®
© 2002
92262
92270
92264
92234
CATHEDRAL CITY
RANCHO MIRAGE
PALM SPRINGS
PALM SPRINGS INTERNATIONAL AIRPORT
DESERT PRINCESS COUNTRY CLUB
CENTURY PARK
DESERT MEMORIAL PARK CEM
GOLDEN MILE CENTER
CATHEDRAL VILLAGE
MISSION HILLS NORTH GOLF COURSE
(GARY PLAYER COURSE)
MISSION HILLS COUNTRY CLUB
(DINAH SHORE COURSE)
(OLD COURSE)
(ARNOLD PALMER COURSE)
OUTDOOR RESORT AND COUNTRY CLUB
BIG LEAGUE DREAMS SPORTS PARK
CATHEDRAL CITY MARKETPLACE
CATHEDRAL CANYON COUNTRY CLUB
DEMUTH PARK
OASIS WATER PARK
TAHQUITZ CREEK PALM SPRINGS
SEVEN LAKES COUNTRY CLUB
TAHQUITZ CREEK PALM SPRINGS
RIMROCK SHOPPING CENTER
CANYON PLAZA SOUTH
DATE PALM COUNTRY CLUB
TAMARISK COUNTRY CLUB
PALM VALLEY HS
CATHEDRAL CITY HS
RAMON RD
DINAH SHORE DR
GERALD FORD DR
E PALM CANYON DR
DATE PALM DR
GENE AUTRY TR
LANDAU BLVD
CROSSLEY RD
111
WHITEWATER RIVER
0 .25 .5 .75 1.0 miles 1 in. = 2400 ft.

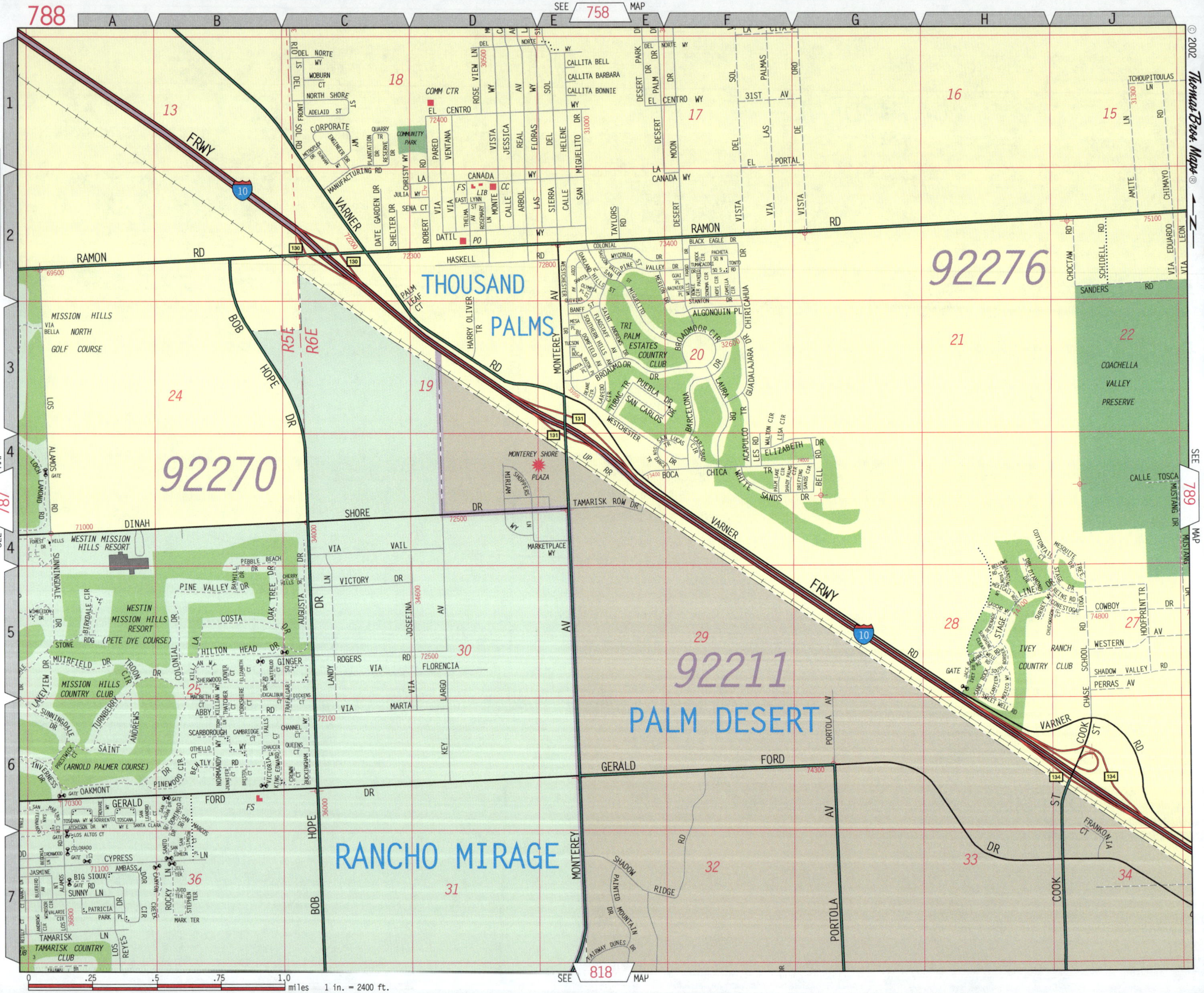

0 .25 .5 .75 1.0 miles 1 in. = 2400 ft.

SEE 390 MAP
A
B
C
D
E
F
G
H
J
1
2
3
4
5
6
7
Thomas Bros. Maps
© 2002
SEE 788 MAP
SEE 390 MAP
SEE 819 MAP
RIVERSIDE CO.
92203
92276
92211
COACHELLA VALLEY PRESERVE
PALM DESERT
INDIO
SUN CITY PALM DESERT
INDIO HILLS PALMS PARK (UNDEVELOPED)
GOLF COURSE (PROPOSED)
MOUNTAIN VISTA GOLF COURSE
REC CTR
R6E
R7E
RAMON RD
WASHINGTON ST
THOUSAND PALMS CANYON RD
PALMS RD
PUSHAWALLA
CHUCKWALLA RD
CONCHITA RD
OAKADO LN
PARADISE RD
SHADOW MOUNTAIN LN
WILLIS PALMS LN
CALLE TOSCA
SADDLEHORN DR
MUSTANG DR
COWBOY DR
WESTERN AV
PEGASUS CT
VARNER RD
FRWY
10
AVENUE 37
AVENUE 38
GOODMAN RD
DUNE PALMS RD
ADAMS
SUNRISE
CANYON
MOUNTAIN VW
WEBB
HOLLISTER DR
KENSINGTON
SILVERLEAF
IVERNESS
ROYAL
SAGE
13
14
15
17
18
19
20
22
23
24
25
26
27
29
30
31
32
34
35
36
0
.25
.5
.75
1.0
miles
1 in. = 2400 ft.

SEE 773 MAP

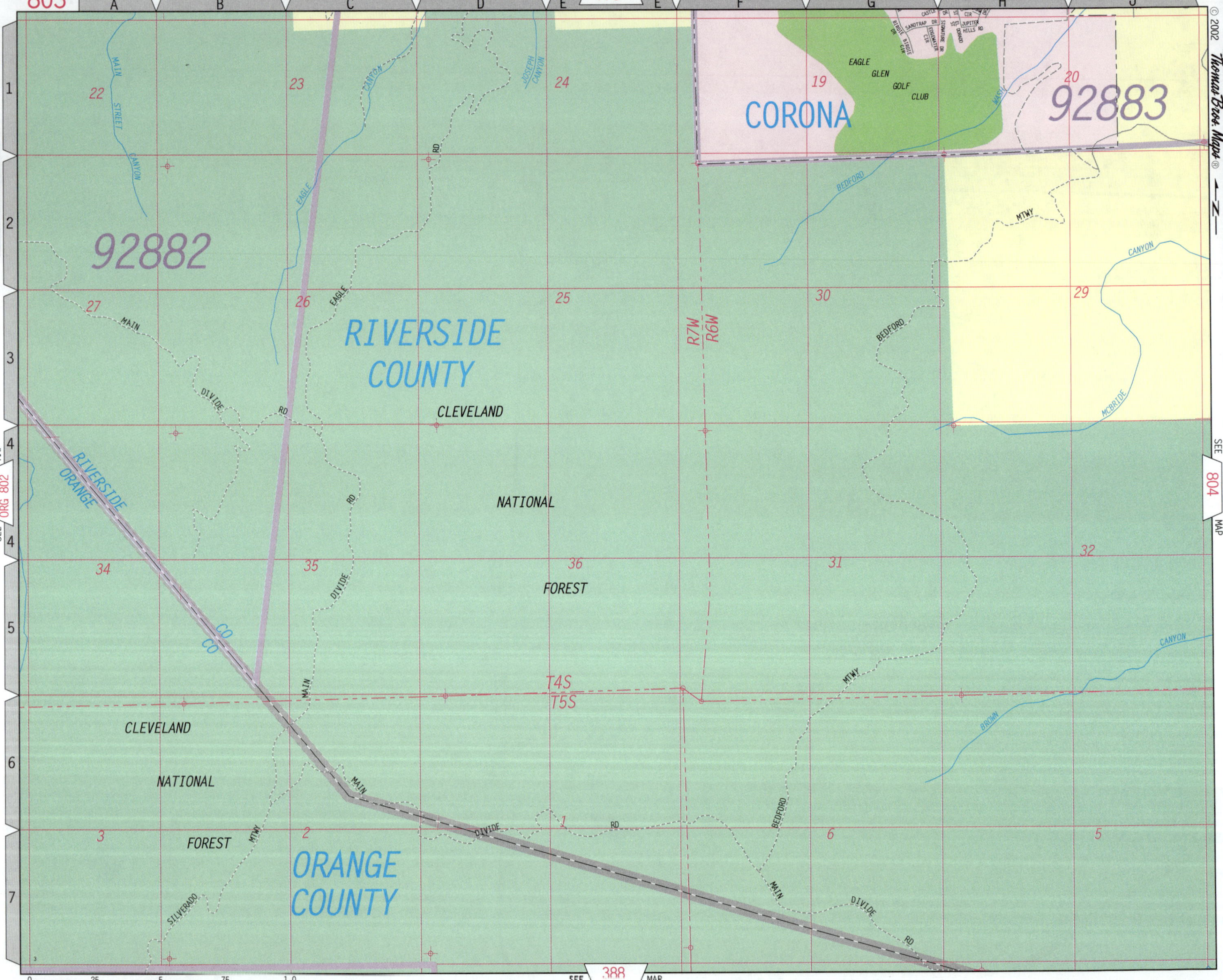

SEE ORG 802 MAP

SEE 804 MAP

SEE 388 MAP

0 .25 .5 .75 1.0 miles 1 in. = 2400 ft.

SEE 774 MAP

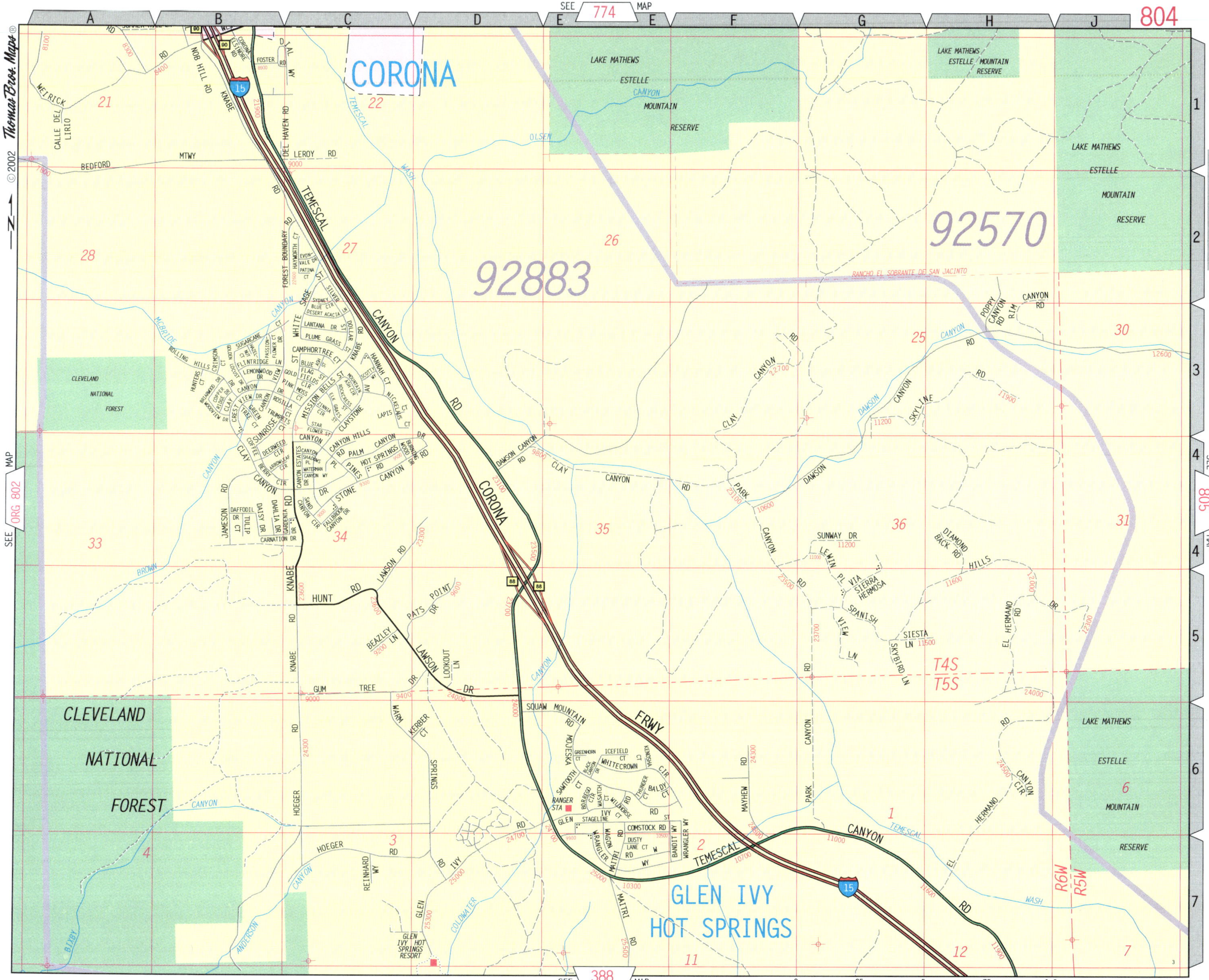

SEE ORG 802 MAP
SEE 805 MAP
SEE 388 MAP

0 .25 .5 .75 1.0 miles 1 in. = 2400 ft.

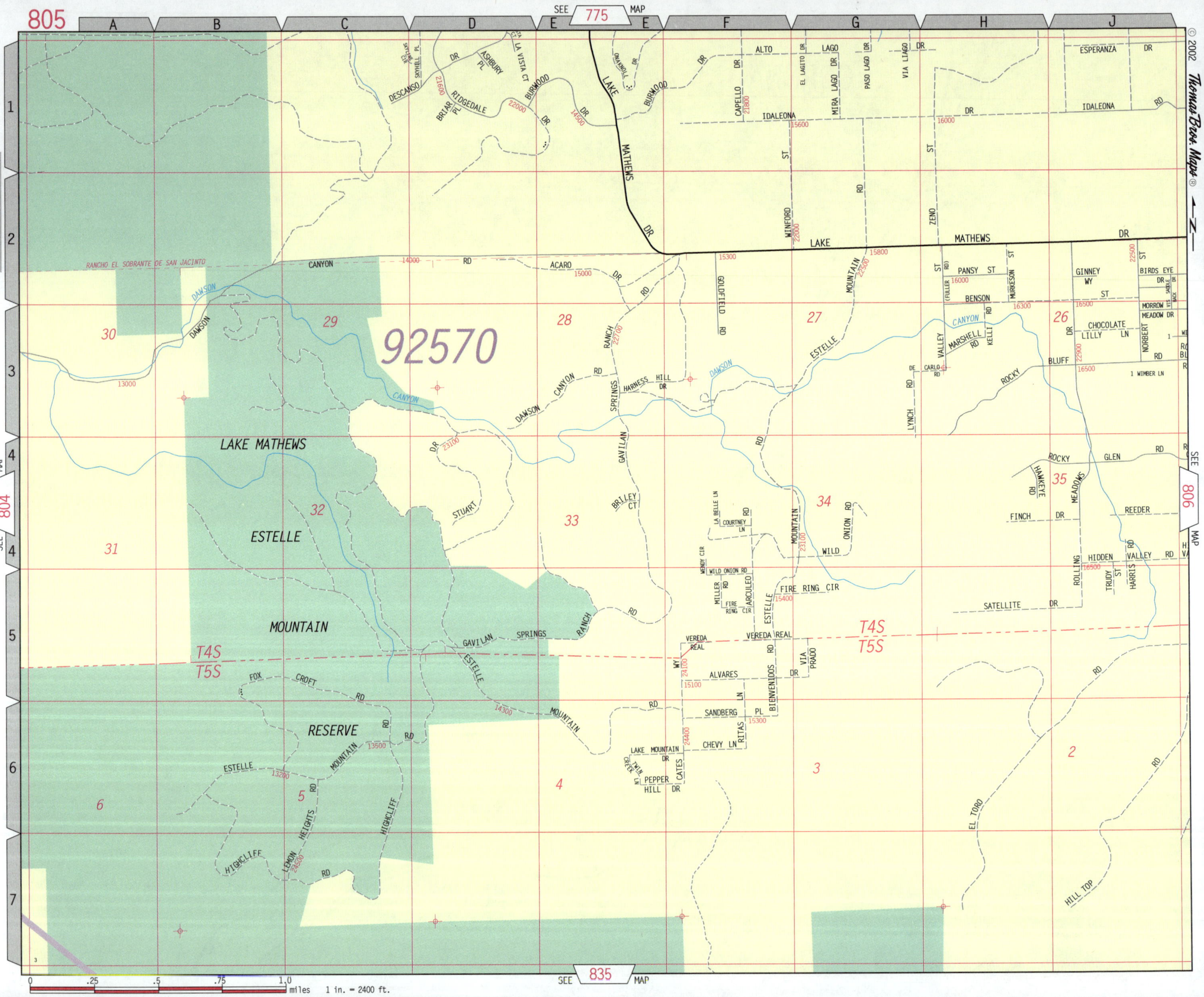
SEE 775 MAP
SEE 835 MAP
SEE 804 MAP
SEE 806 MAP
RIVERSIDE CO.
A
B
C
D
E
F
G
H
J
1
2
3
4
5
6
7
92570
LAKE MATHEWS
ESTELLE
MOUNTAIN
RESERVE
RANCHO EL SOBRANTE DE SAN JACINTO
T4S
T5S
LAKE MATHEWS DR
CANYON RD
ACARO DR
DAWSON CANYON
DAWSON
RANCH RD
SPRINGS
GAVILAN
HARNESS HILL DR
BRILEY CT
STUART
GOLDFIELD RD
MOUNTAIN
ESTELLE
WINFORD ST
ZENO ST
IDALEONA DR
IDALEONA RD
ESPERANZA DR
ALTO DR
LAGO DR
EL LAGITO DR
MIRA LAGO DR
PASO LAGO DR
VIA LAGO DR
CAPELLO DR
BURWOOD DR
DESCANSO DR
ASHBURY PL
LA VISTA CT
RIDGEDALE
BRIAR PL
SKYHILL PL
PANSY ST
BENSON
MURKESON ST
MARSHELL RD
KELLI
VALLEY
DE CARLO RD
LYNCH RD
ROCKY BLUFF
GINNEY WY
BIRDS EYE DR
MORROW
MEADOW DR
CHOCOLATE LILLY LN
NORBERT
WIMBER LN
ROCKY GLEN RD
HAWKEYE RD
MEADOWS
FINCH DR
REEDER
ROLLING HIDDEN VALLEY RD
TRUDY ST
HARRIS RD
SATELLITE DR
ONION RD
WILD
LA BELLE LN
COURTNEY LN
WENDY CIR
WILD ONION RD
MILLER RD
FIRE RING CIR
ARCULEO
VEREDA REAL
VIA PRADO
ALVARES DR
BIENVENIDOS RD
SANDBERG PL
RITAS LN
CHEVY LN
LAKE MOUNTAIN DR
TWIN CREEK LN
PEPPER HILL DR
CATES
FOX CROFT RD
GAVILAN SPRINGS RANCH RD
MOUNTAIN RD
ESTELLE MOUNTAIN RD
HIGHCLIFF RD
LEMON HEIGHTS RD
EL TORO RD
HILL TOP RD
28
29
30
31
32
33
34
35
26
27
2
3
4
5
6
0 .25 .5 .75 1.0 miles 1 in. = 2400 ft.

SEE 776 MAP

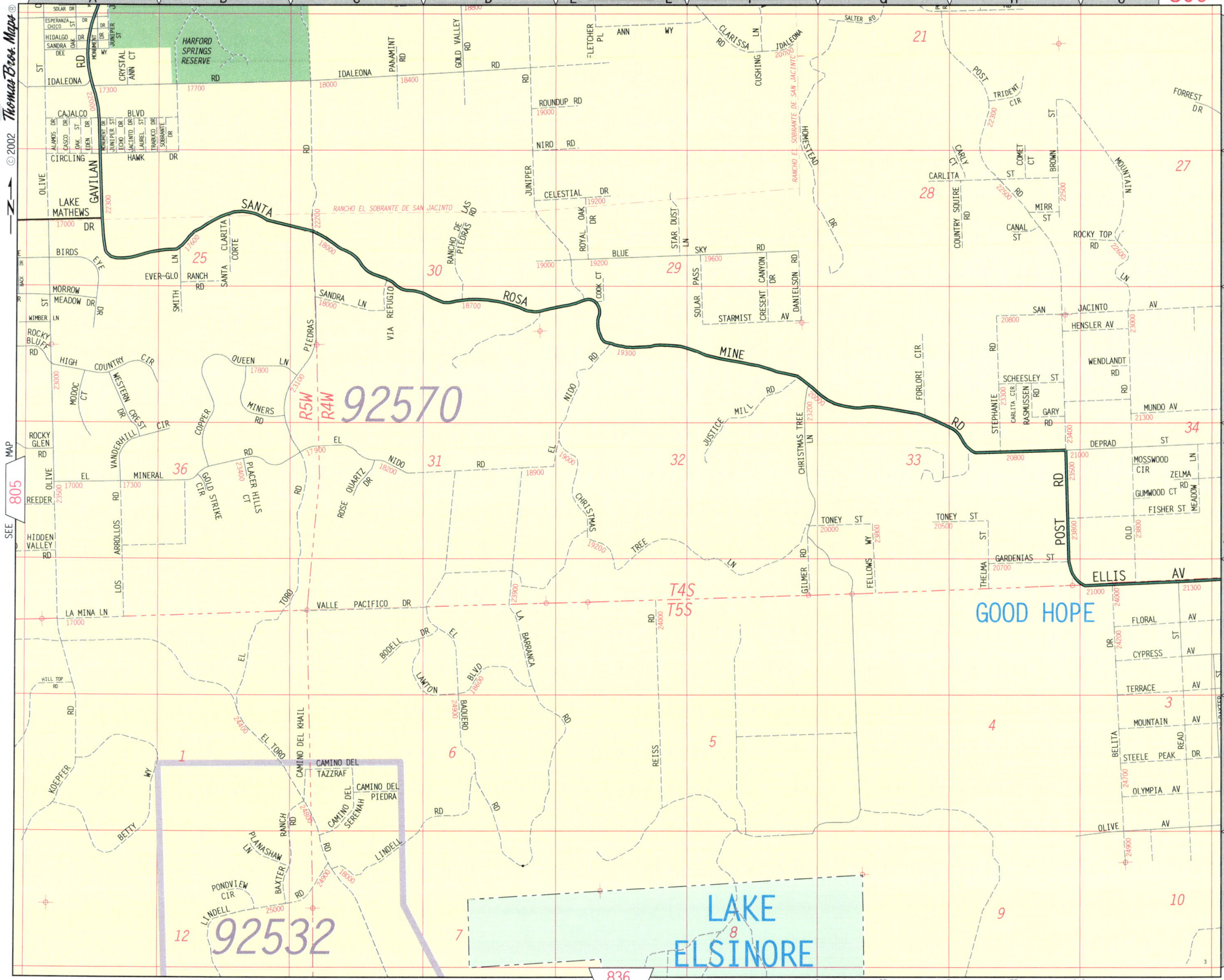

SEE 805 MAP

SEE 807 MAP

SEE 836 MAP

SEE 777 MAP

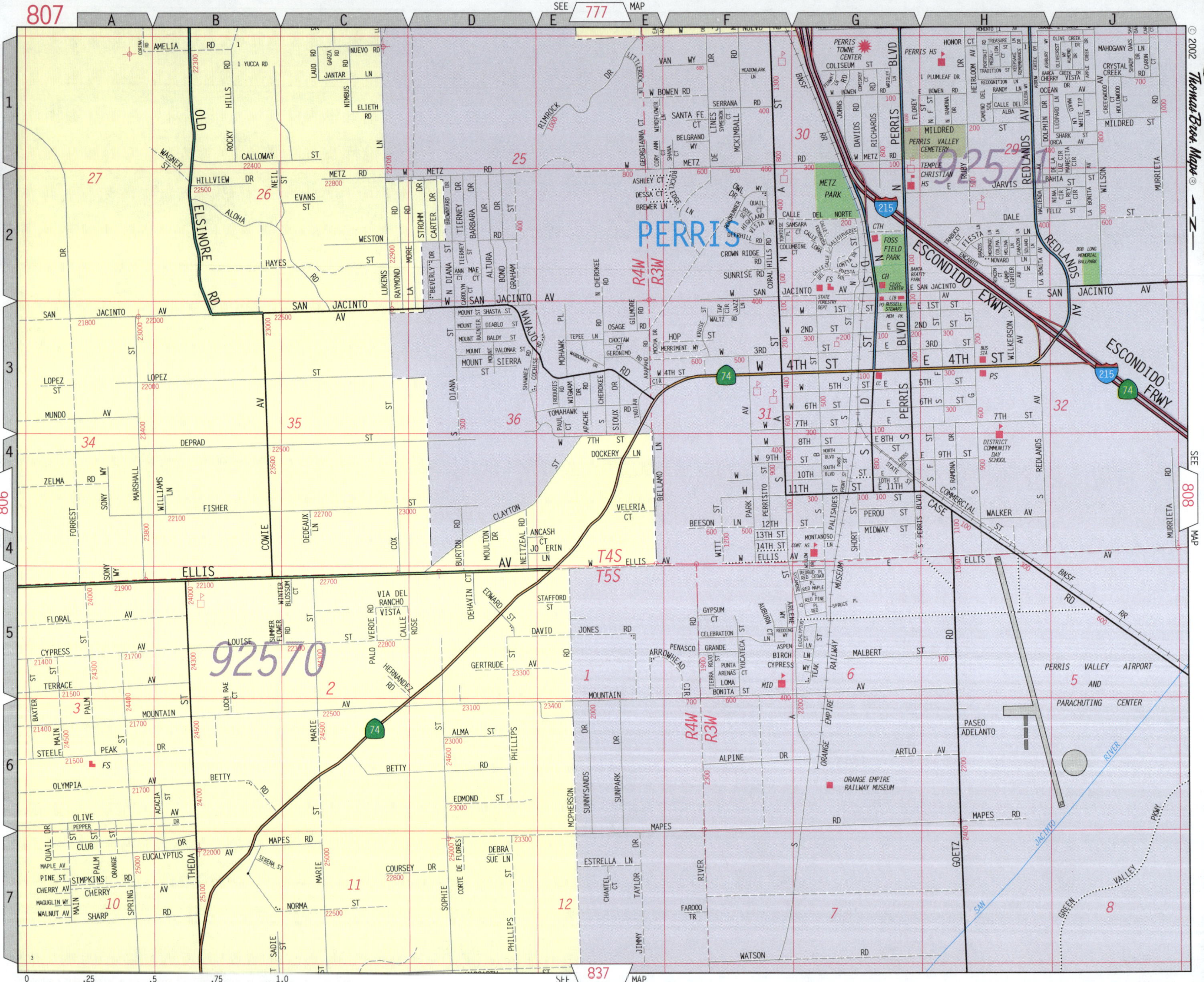

SEE 806 MAP

SEE 808 MAP

SEE 837 MAP

0 .25 .5 .75 1.0 miles 1 in. = 2400 ft.

SEE 778 MAP

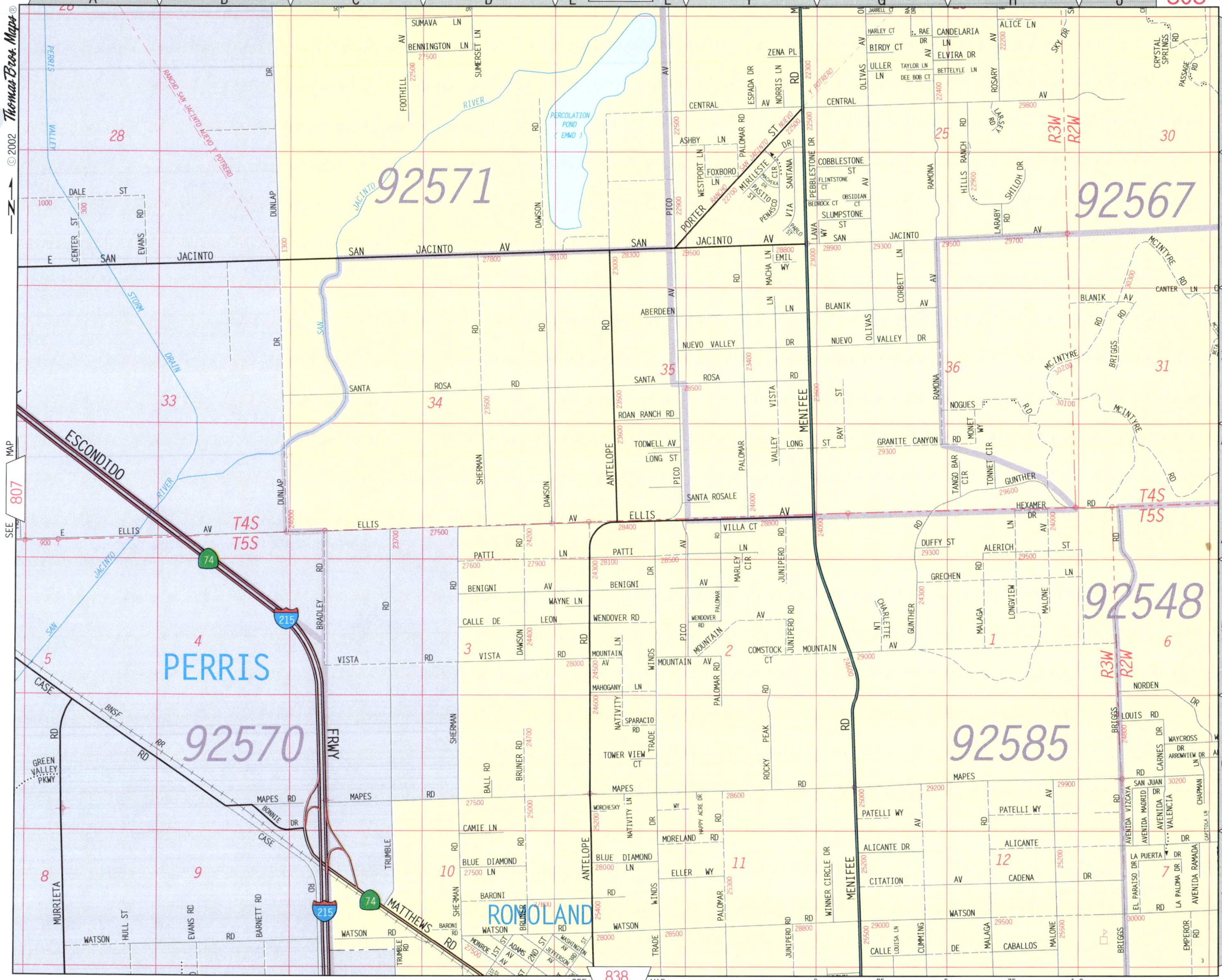

SEE 807 MAP

SEE 809 MAP

SEE 838 MAP

0 .25 .5 .75 1.0 miles 1 in. = 2400 ft.

SEE 779 MAP

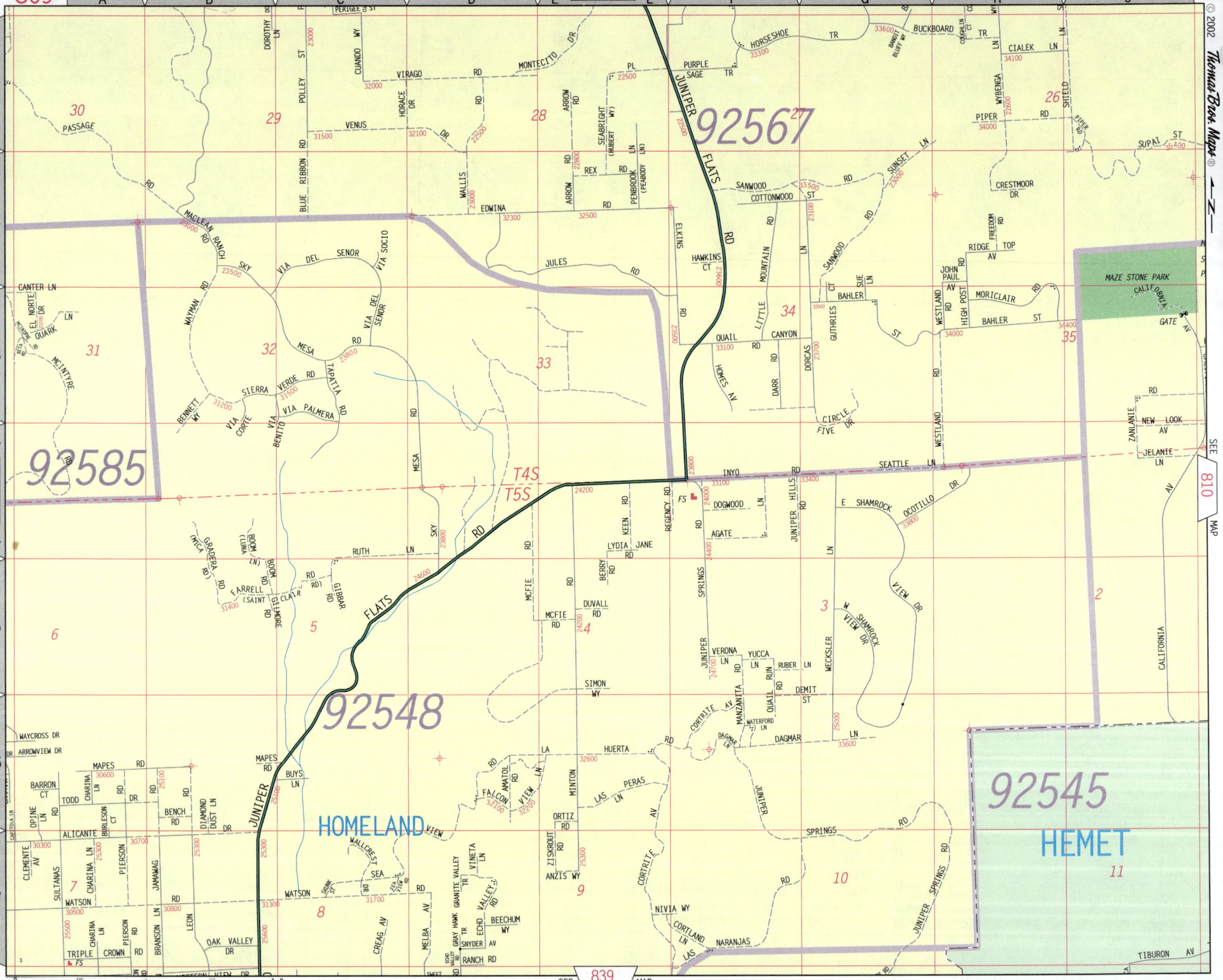

SEE 839 MAP

0 .25 .5 .75 1.0 miles 1 in. = 2400 ft.

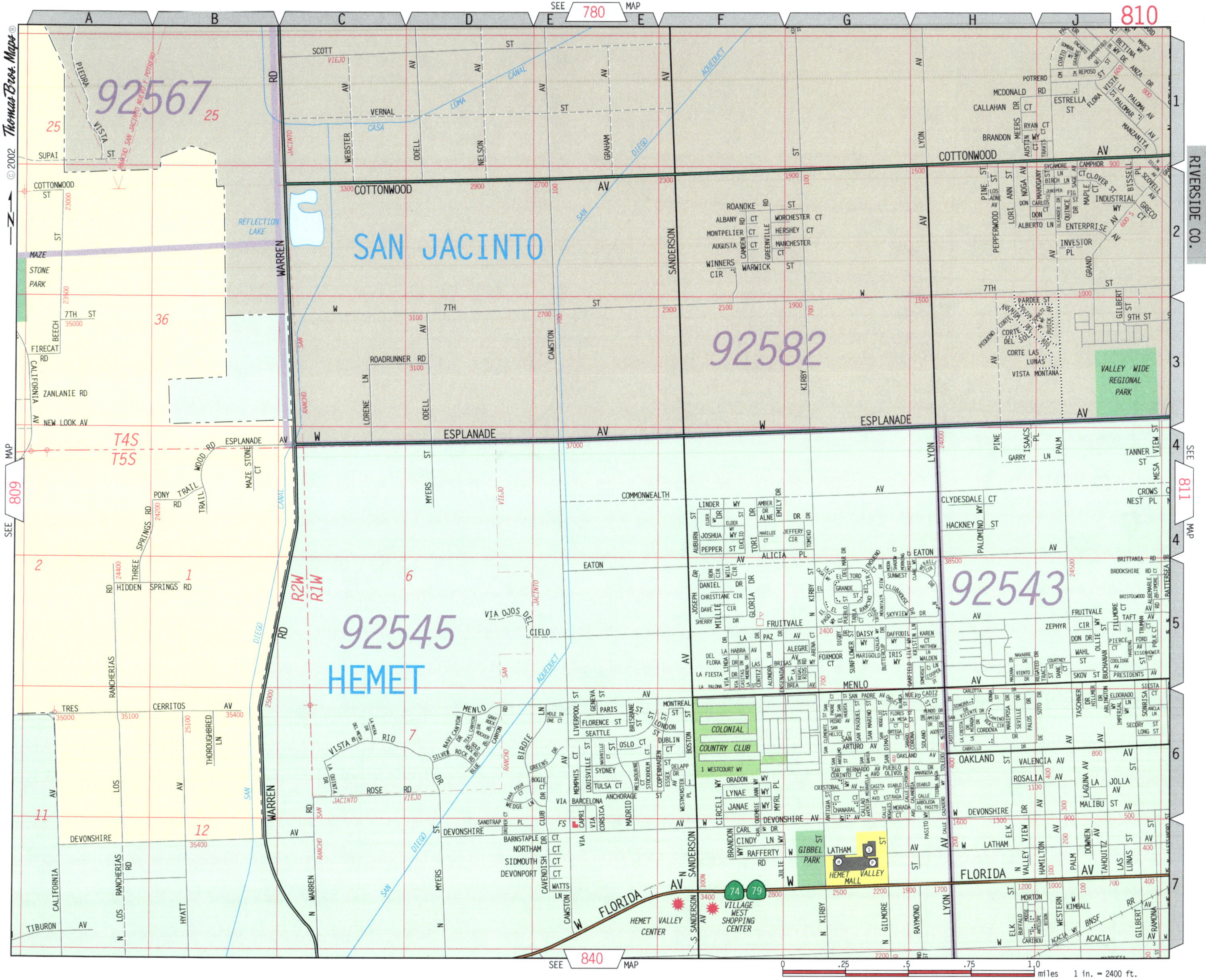
SEE 780 MAP
SEE 809 MAP
SEE 811 MAP
SEE 840 MAP
RIVERSIDE CO.
SAN JACINTO
HEMET
92567
92582
92545
92543
COTTONWOOD AV
ESPLANADE AV
FLORIDA AV
DEVONSHIRE AV
MENLO AV
WARREN RD
SANDERSON AV
LYON AV
KIRBY ST
STATE ST
7TH ST
EATON AV
COMMONWEALTH AV
REFLECTION LAKE
MAZE STONE PARK
COLONIAL COUNTRY CLUB
GIBBEL PARK
HEMET VALLEY MALL
VILLAGE WEST SHOPPING CENTER
HEMET VALLEY CENTER
VALLEY WIDE REGIONAL PARK
SAN DIEGO AQUEDUCT
SAN DIEGO CANAL
T4S
T5S
R2W
R1W
1 in. = 2400 ft.
miles

RIVERSIDE CO.

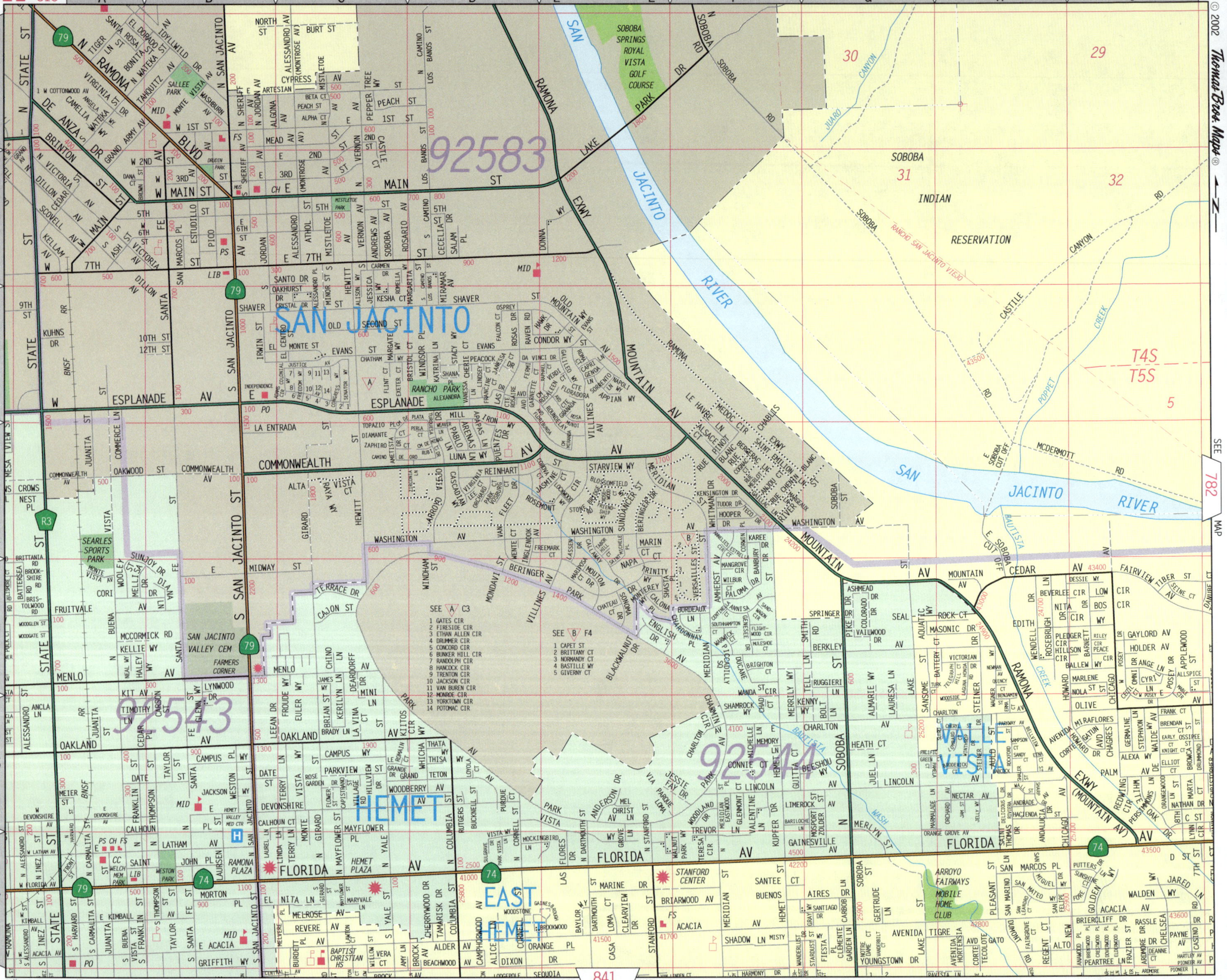

© 2002 Thomas Bros. Maps ®

0 .25 .5 .75 1.0 miles 1 in. = 2400 ft.

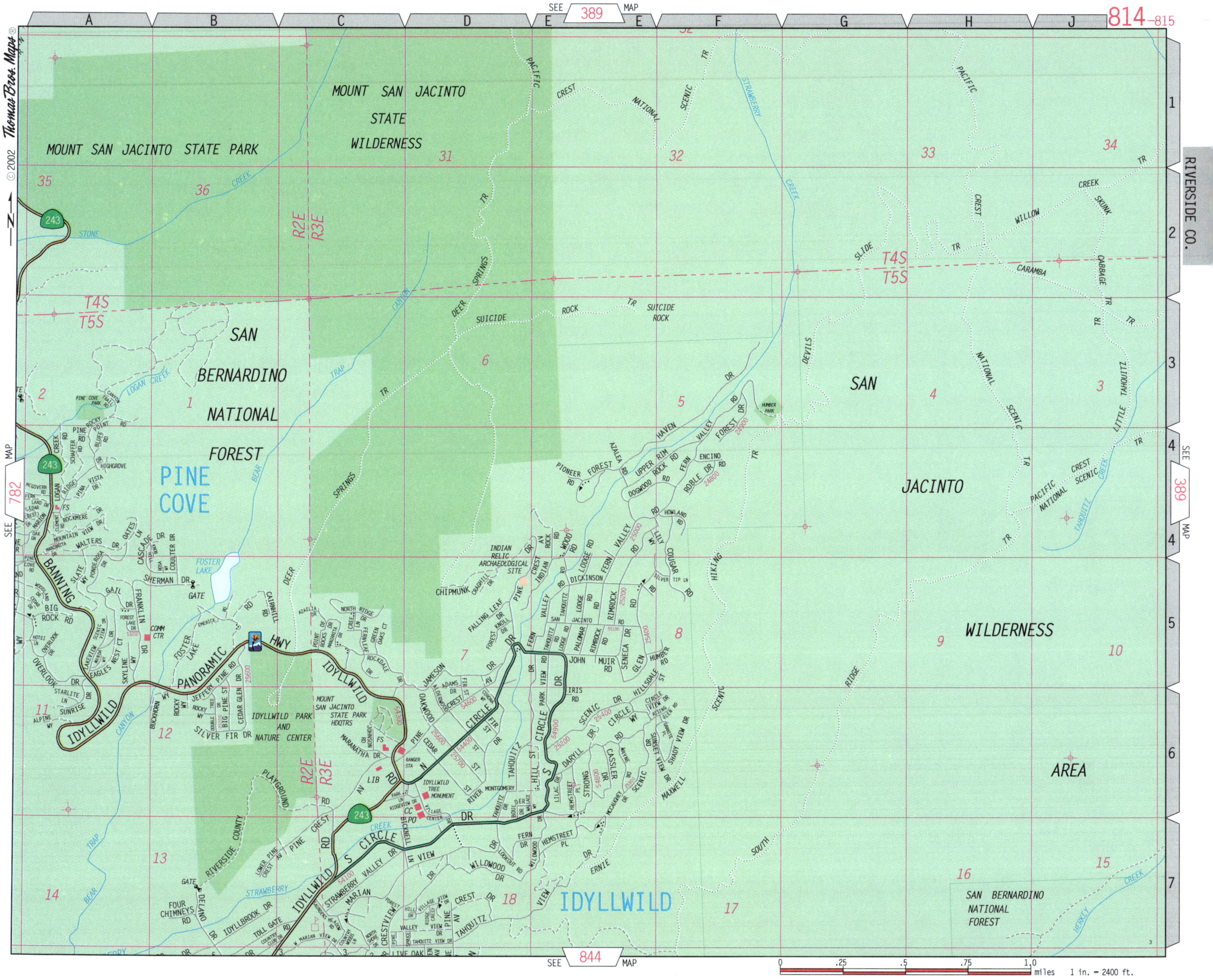
SEE 389 MAP
SEE 844 MAP
SEE 782 MAP
SEE 389 MAP
RIVERSIDE CO.
Thomas Bros. Maps ©
© 2002
MOUNT SAN JACINTO STATE PARK
MOUNT SAN JACINTO STATE WILDERNESS
SAN BERNARDINO NATIONAL FOREST
PINE COVE
SAN JACINTO WILDERNESS AREA
IDYLLWILD
SAN BERNARDINO NATIONAL FOREST
T4S
T5S
R2E
R3E
243
IDYLLWILD PARK AND NATURE CENTER
MOUNT SAN JACINTO STATE PARK HDQTRS
INDIAN RELIC ARCHAEOLOGICAL SITE
IDYLLWILD TREE MONUMENT
FOSTER LAKE
SUICIDE ROCK
HUMBER PARK
PACIFIC CREST NATIONAL SCENIC TR
STRAWBERRY CREEK
DEVILS SLIDE TR
DEER SPRINGS TR
SUICIDE ROCK TR
WILLOW CREEK TR
CARAMBA TR
SKUNK CABBAGE TR
LITTLE TAHQUITZ CREEK
SOUTH RIDGE HIKING TR
BANNING IDYLLWILD PANORAMIC HWY
CIRCLE DR
RIVERSIDE COUNTY PLAYGROUND
0 .25 .5 .75 1.0 miles 1 in. = 2400 ft.

SEE 786 MAP

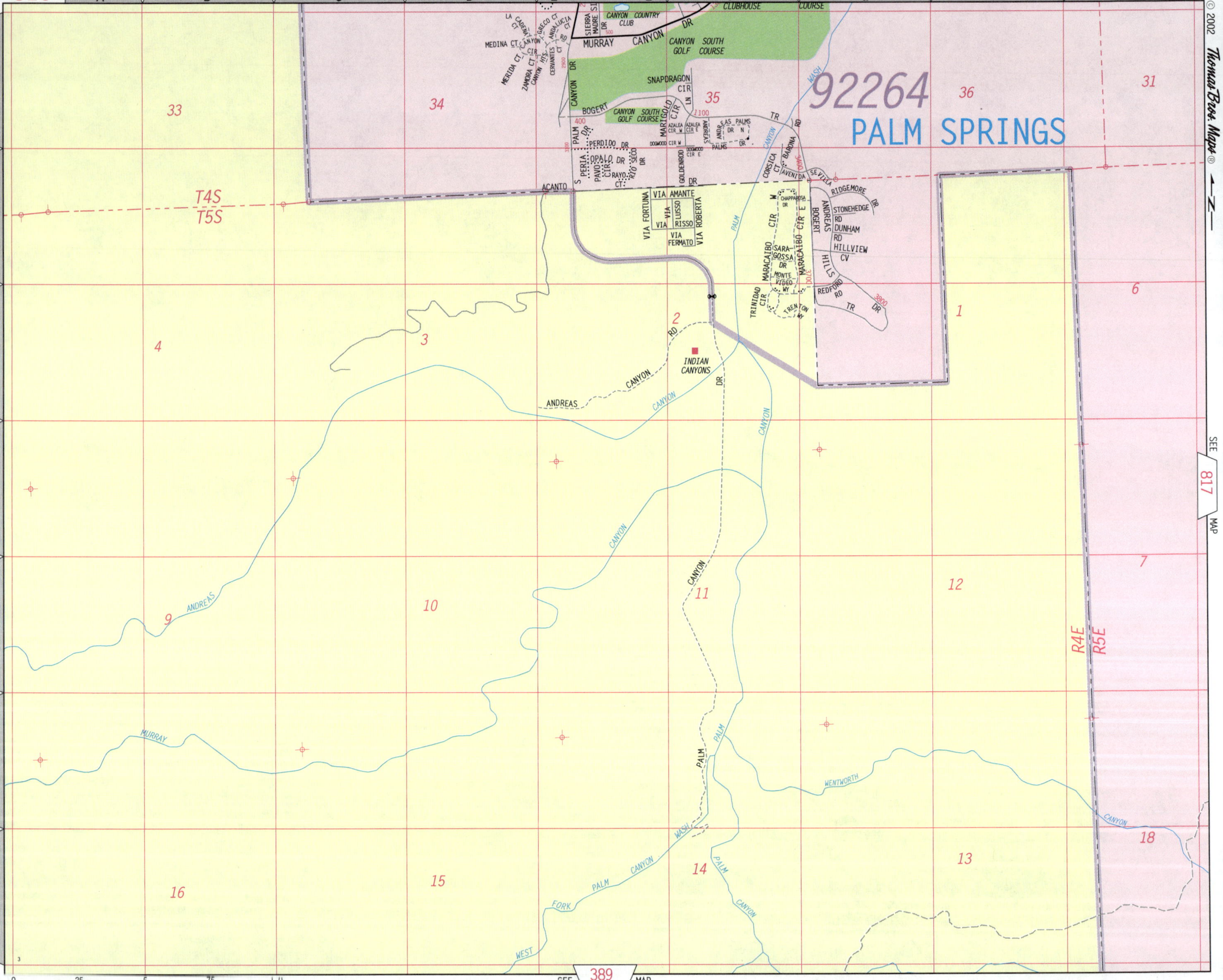

SEE 389 MAP

SEE 817 MAP

SEE 389 MAP

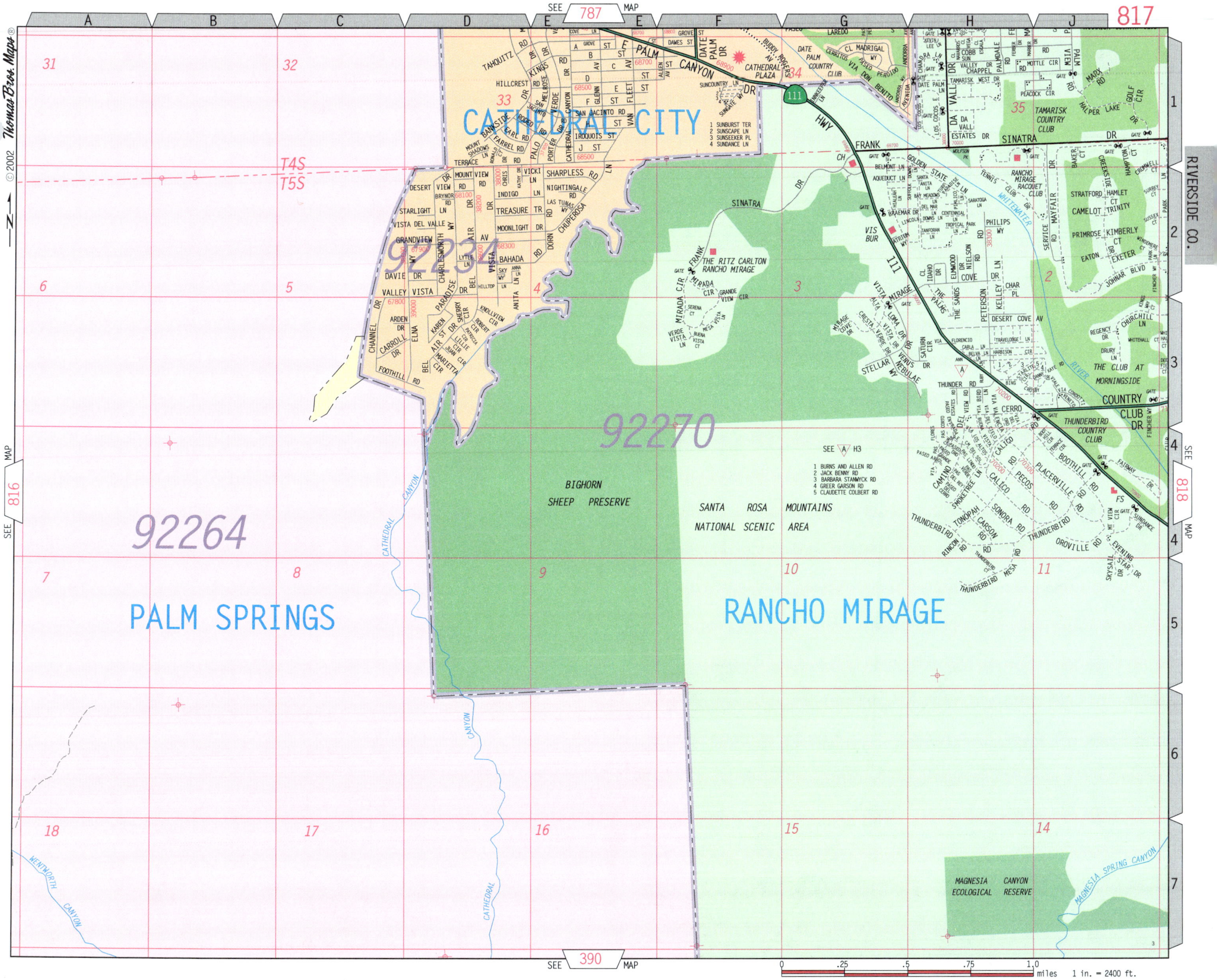
SEE 787 MAP
A
B
C
D
E
F
G
H
J
CATHEDRAL CITY
PALM SPRINGS
RANCHO MIRAGE
92264
92234
92270
T4S
T5S
BIGHORN
SHEEP PRESERVE
SANTA ROSA MOUNTAINS
NATIONAL SCENIC AREA
MAGNESIA CANYON
ECOLOGICAL RESERVE
TAMARISK
COUNTRY
CLUB
RANCHO
MIRAGE
RACQUET
CLUB
THUNDERBIRD
COUNTRY
CLUB
THE RITZ CARLTON
RANCHO MIRAGE
CATHEDRAL
PLAZA
DATE
PALM
COUNTRY
CLUB
THE CLUB AT
MORNINGSIDE
E PALM CANYON DR
HWY 111
FRANK SINATRA DR
COUNTRY CLUB DR
CATHEDRAL CANYON
WENTWORTH CANYON
MAGNESIA SPRING CANYON
WHITEWATER RIVER
1 SUNBURST TER
2 SUNSCAPE LN
3 SUNSEEKER PL
4 SUNDANCE LN
SEE A H3
1 BURNS AND ALLEN RD
2 JACK BENNY RD
3 BARBARA STANWYCK RD
4 GREER GARSON RD
5 CLAUDETTE COLBERT RD
RIVERSIDE CO.
SEE 816 MAP
SEE 818 MAP
SEE 390 MAP
0 .25 .5 .75 1.0 miles 1 in. = 2400 ft.

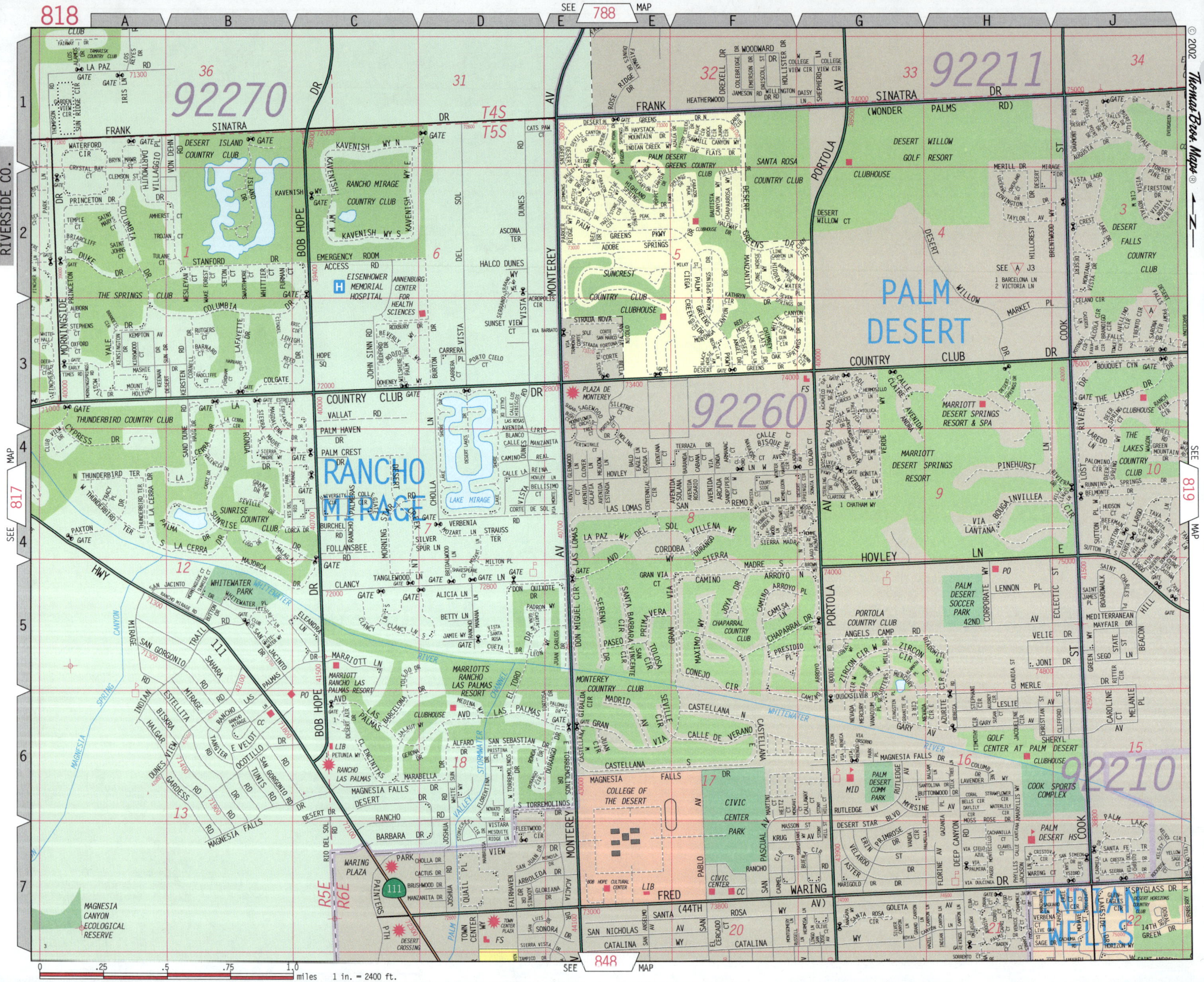
SEE 788 MAP
A
B
C
D
E
F
G
H
J
1
2
3
4
5
6
7
RIVERSIDE CO.
92270
92211
92260
92210
RANCHO MIRAGE
PALM DESERT
INDIAN WELLS
FRANK SINATRA DR
COUNTRY CLUB DR
HOVLEY LN
BOB HOPE DR
MONTEREY AV
PORTOLA AV
COOK ST
DESERT ISLAND COUNTRY CLUB
RANCHO MIRAGE COUNTRY CLUB
THE SPRINGS CLUB
EISENHOWER MEMORIAL HOSPITAL
ANNENBURG CENTER FOR HEALTH SCIENCES
THUNDERBIRD COUNTRY CLUB
SUNRISE COUNTRY CLUB
WHITEWATER PARK
LAKE MIRAGE
PALM DESERT GREENS COUNTRY CLUB
SANTA ROSA COUNTRY CLUB
SUNCREST COUNTRY CLUB
DESERT WILLOW GOLF RESORT
MARRIOTT DESERT SPRINGS RESORT & SPA
MARRIOTT DESERT SPRINGS RESORT
THE LAKES COUNTRY CLUB
CHAPARRAL COUNTRY CLUB
MONTEREY COUNTRY CLUB
PORTOLA COUNTRY CLUB
PALM DESERT SOCCER PARK
MARRIOTT RANCHO LAS PALMAS RESORT
MARRIOTTS RANCHO LAS PALMAS RESORT
COLLEGE OF THE DESERT
CIVIC CENTER PARK
GOLF CENTER AT PALM DESERT
COOK SPORTS COMPLEX
PALM DESERT COMM PARK
WARING PLAZA
MAGNESIA CANYON ECOLOGICAL RESERVE
WHITEWATER RIVER
HWY 111
SEE 817 MAP
SEE 819 MAP
SEE 848 MAP
0 .25 .5 .75 1.0 miles 1 in. = 2400 ft.
© 2002 Thomas Bros. Maps ®

SEE 789 MAP

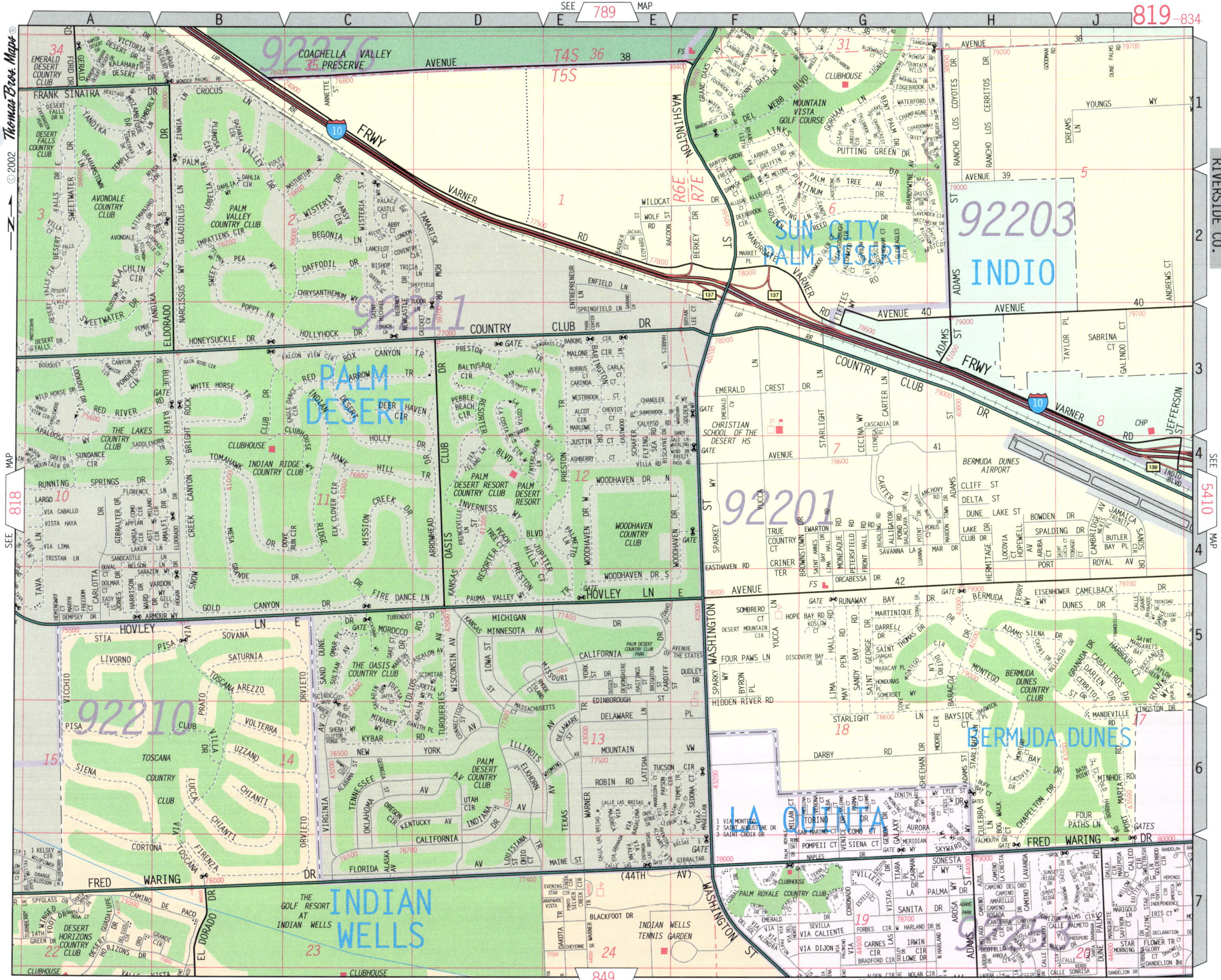

SEE 849 MAP

0 .25 .5 .75 1.0 miles 1 in. = 2400 ft.

SEE 805 MAP

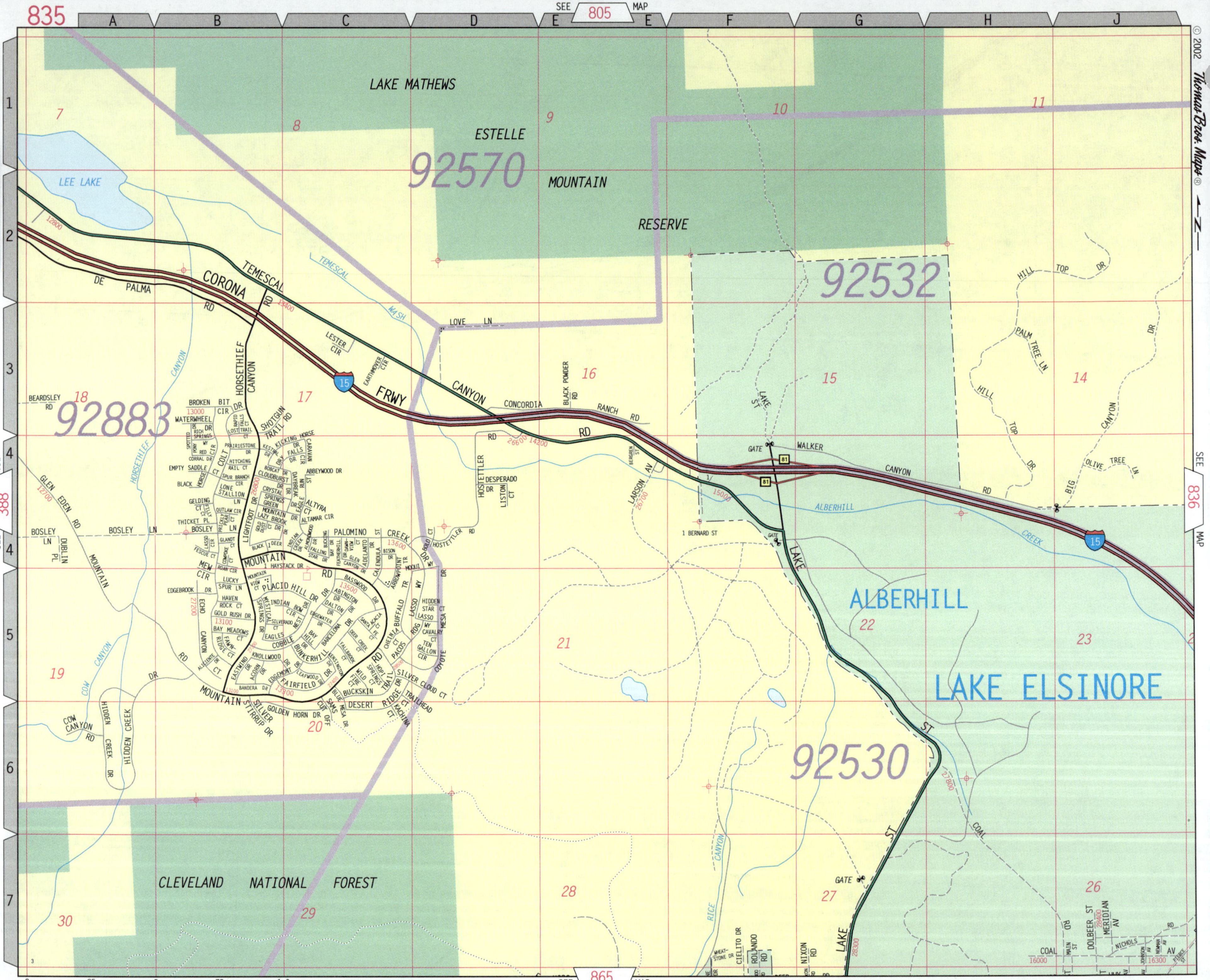

SEE 388 MAP

SEE 836 MAP

SEE 865 MAP

0 .25 .5 .75 1.0 miles 1 in. = 2400 ft.

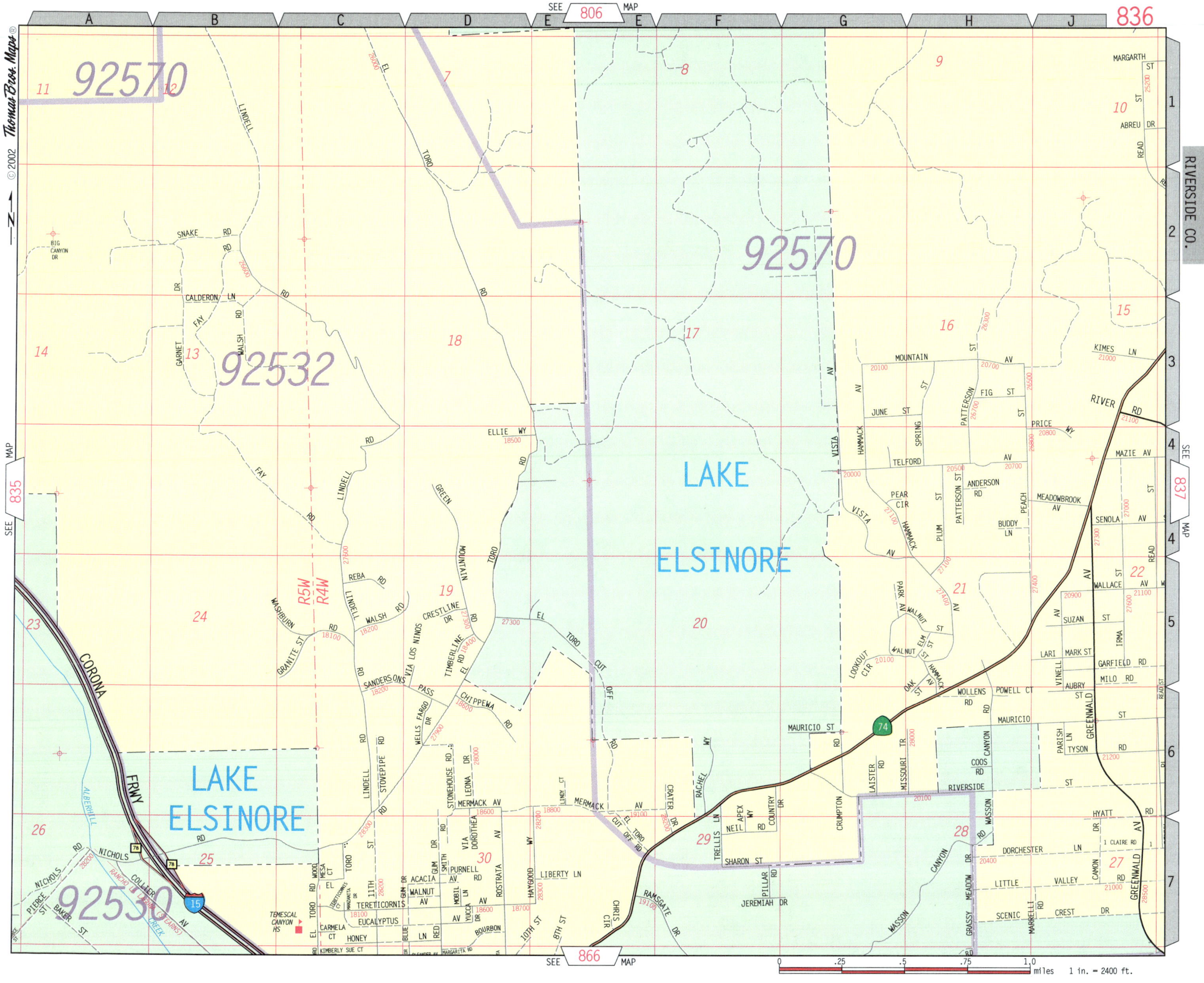
SEE 806 MAP
SEE 866 MAP
SEE MAP 835
SEE 837 MAP
A B C D E E F G H J
1 2 3 4 4 5 6 7
RIVERSIDE CO.
Thomas Bros. Maps ® © 2002
92570
92570
92532
92530
LAKE ELSINORE
LAKE ELSINORE
R5W R4W
CORONA FRWY
15
74
78
MARGARTH ST
ABREU DR
READ RD
SNAKE RD
BIG CANYON DR
CALDERON LN
GARNET DR
FAY RD
WALSH RD
LINDELL RD
EL TORO RD
ELLIE WY
GREEN MOUNTAIN RD
MOUNTAIN ST
MOUNTAIN AV
FIG ST
JUNE ST
SPRING ST
PATTERSON ST
PRICE WY
RIVER RD
KIMES LN
MAZIE AV
TELFORD AV
HAMMACK AV
VISTA AV
PEAR CIR
ANDERSON RD
PLUM ST
MEADOWBROOK AV
BUDDY LN
PEACH ST
SENOLA AV
WALLACE AV
SUZAN ST
MARK ST
LARI
IRMA
GARFIELD RD
MILO RD
AUBRY ST
VINELL AV
GREENWALD AV
PARK AV
WALNUT ST
ELM ST
LOOKOUT CIR
OAK ST
WOLLENS RD
POWELL CT
MAURICIO ST
MAURICIO ST
PARISH LN
TYSON RD
COOS RD
CANYON
RIVERSIDE ST
HYATT RD
CLAIRE RD
DORCHESTER LN
CAMON
LITTLE VALLEY RD
SCENIC CREST DR
MARRELLI RD
GRASSY MEADOW DR
WASSON CANYON RD
LAISTER RD
MISSOURI TR
CRUMPTON
SHARON ST
PILLAR RD
JEREMIAH DR
TRELLIS LN
APEX WY
NEIL RD
COUNTRY DR
RACHEL WY
CRATER DR
EL TORO CUT OFF RD
MERMACK AV
RAMSGATE DR
CHRIS CIR
8TH ST
10TH ST
LIBERTY LN
HAYGOOD WY
ROSTRATA AV
BOURBON
PURNELL RD
VIA DOROTHEA
LEONA DR
STONEHOUSE RD
STOVEPIPE RD
WELLS FARGO DR
CHIPPEWA RD
SANDERSONS PASS
TIMBERLINE RD
CRESTLINE DR
VIA LOS NINOS
REBA RD
WASHBURN RD
GRANITE ST
ACACIA AV
WALNUT AV
GUM DR
SMITH DR
MOBIL LN
YUCCA DR
TERETICORNIS
EUCALYPTUS
CARMELA CT
HONEY
BLUE GUM
RED LN
11TH ST
KIMBERLY SUE CT
TEMESCAL CANYON HS
NICHOLS RD
PIERCE ST
BAKER ST
COLLIER AV
RANCHO LA LAGUNA (STEARNS)
ALBERHILL CREEK
0 .25 .5 .75 1.0 miles 1 in. = 2400 ft.

SEE 807 MAP

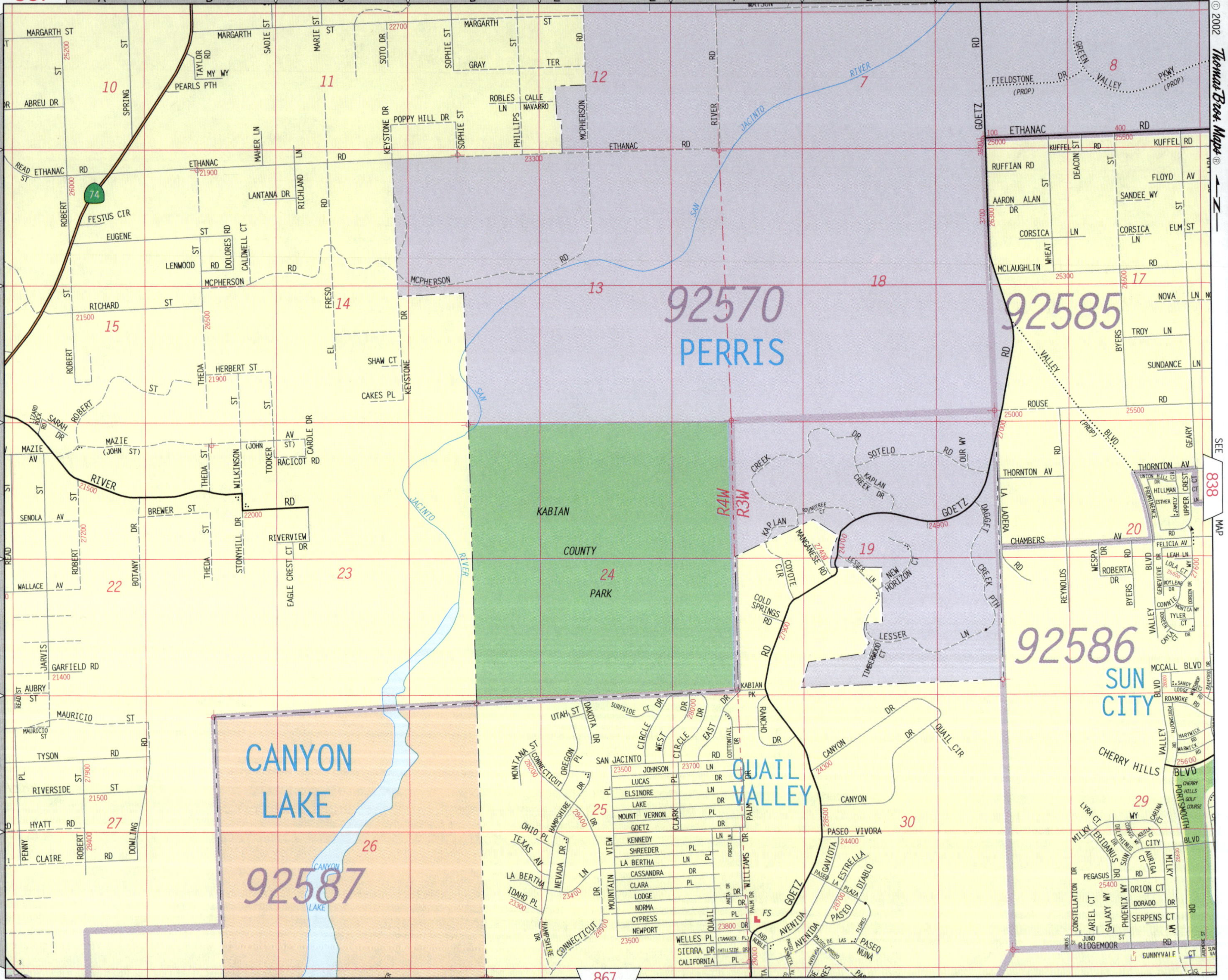

SEE 836 MAP

SEE 838 MAP

SEE 867 MAP

0 .25 .5 .75 1.0 miles 1 in. = 2400 ft.

SEE 808 MAP

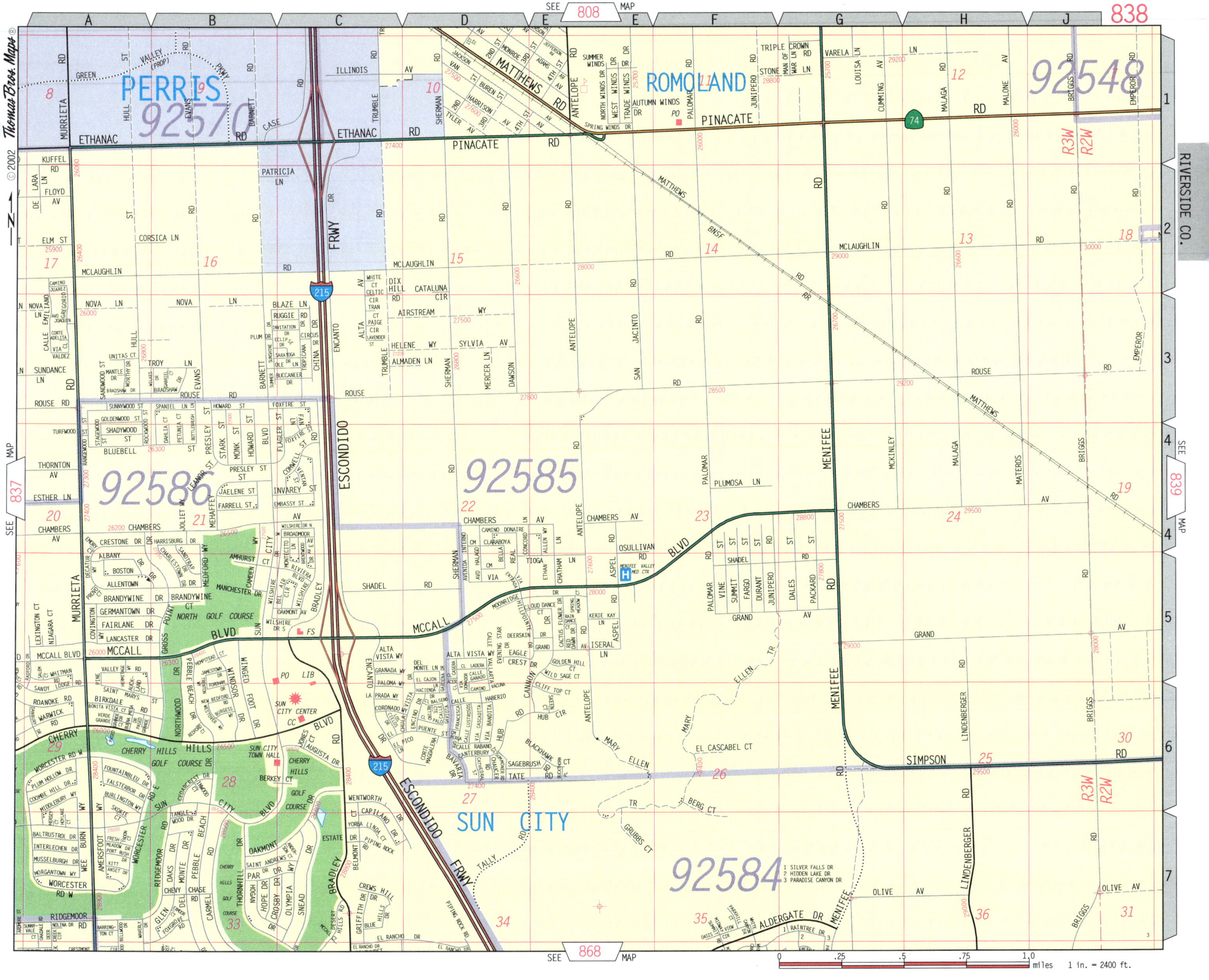

SEE 868 MAP

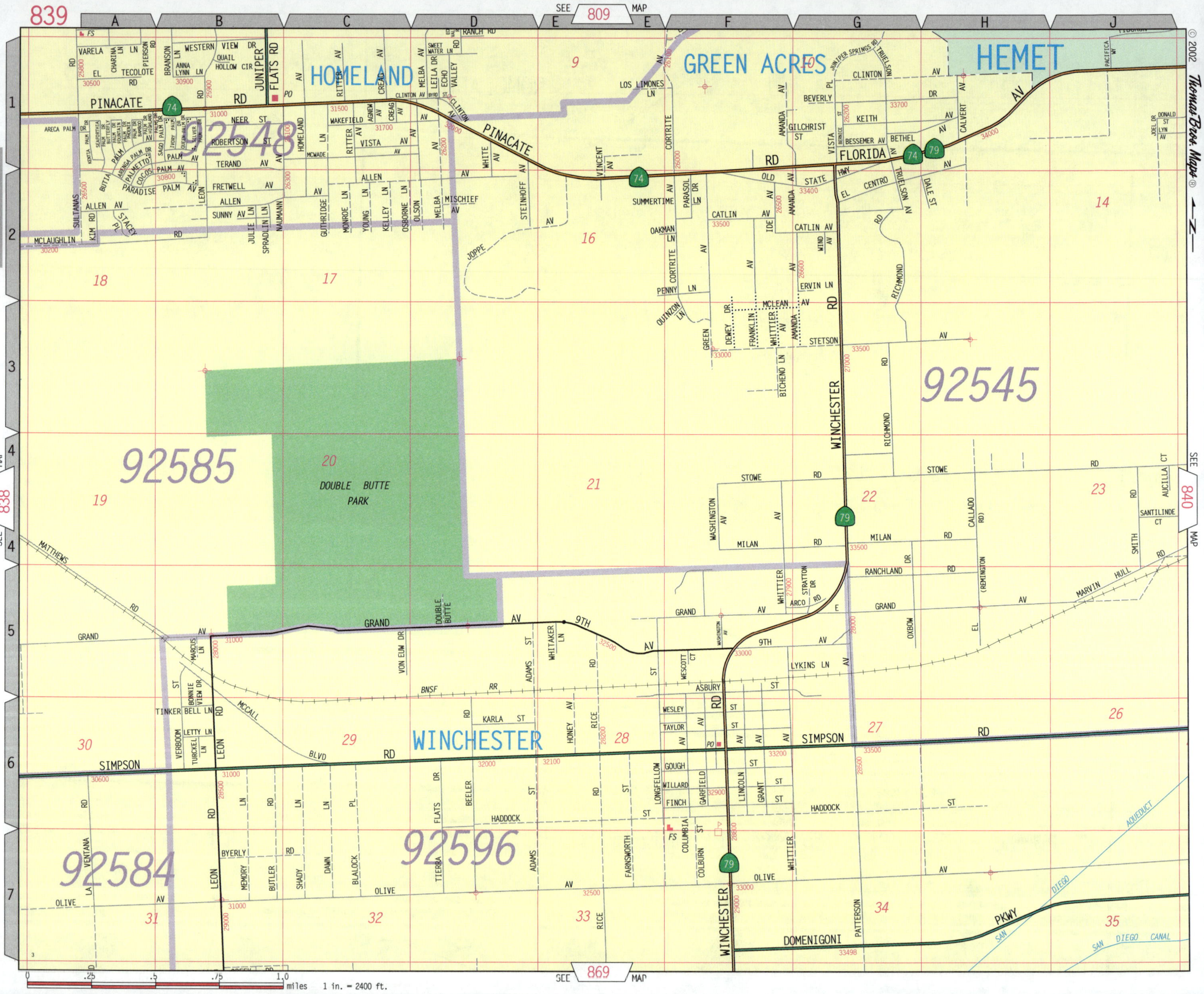
SEE 809 MAP
A
B
C
D
E
F
G
H
J
HOMELAND
GREEN ACRES
HEMET
WINCHESTER
92548
92545
92585
92584
92596
DOUBLE BUTTE PARK
RIVERSIDE CO.
PINACATE RD
FLORIDA AV
WINCHESTER RD
SIMPSON RD
DOMENIGONI PKWY
GRAND AV
9TH AV
OLIVE AV
STOWE RD
MILAN RD
RANCHLAND RD
MARVIN HULL RD
MATTHEWS RD
MCCALL BLVD
LEON RD
JUNIPER FLATS RD
HADDOCK ST
BNSF RR
SAN DIEGO AQUEDUCT
SAN DIEGO CANAL
MCLAUGHLIN RD
LOS LIMONES LN
CLINTON AV
OLD STATE HWY
EL CENTRO RD
CATLIN AV
STETSON AV
LYKINS LN
ASBURY ST
74
79
9
14
16
17
18
19
20
21
22
23
26
27
28
29
30
31
32
33
34
35
SEE 838 MAP
SEE 840 MAP
SEE 869 MAP
0 .25 .5 .75 1.0 miles 1 in. = 2400 ft.
© 2002 Thomas Bros. Maps ®

SEE 810 MAP

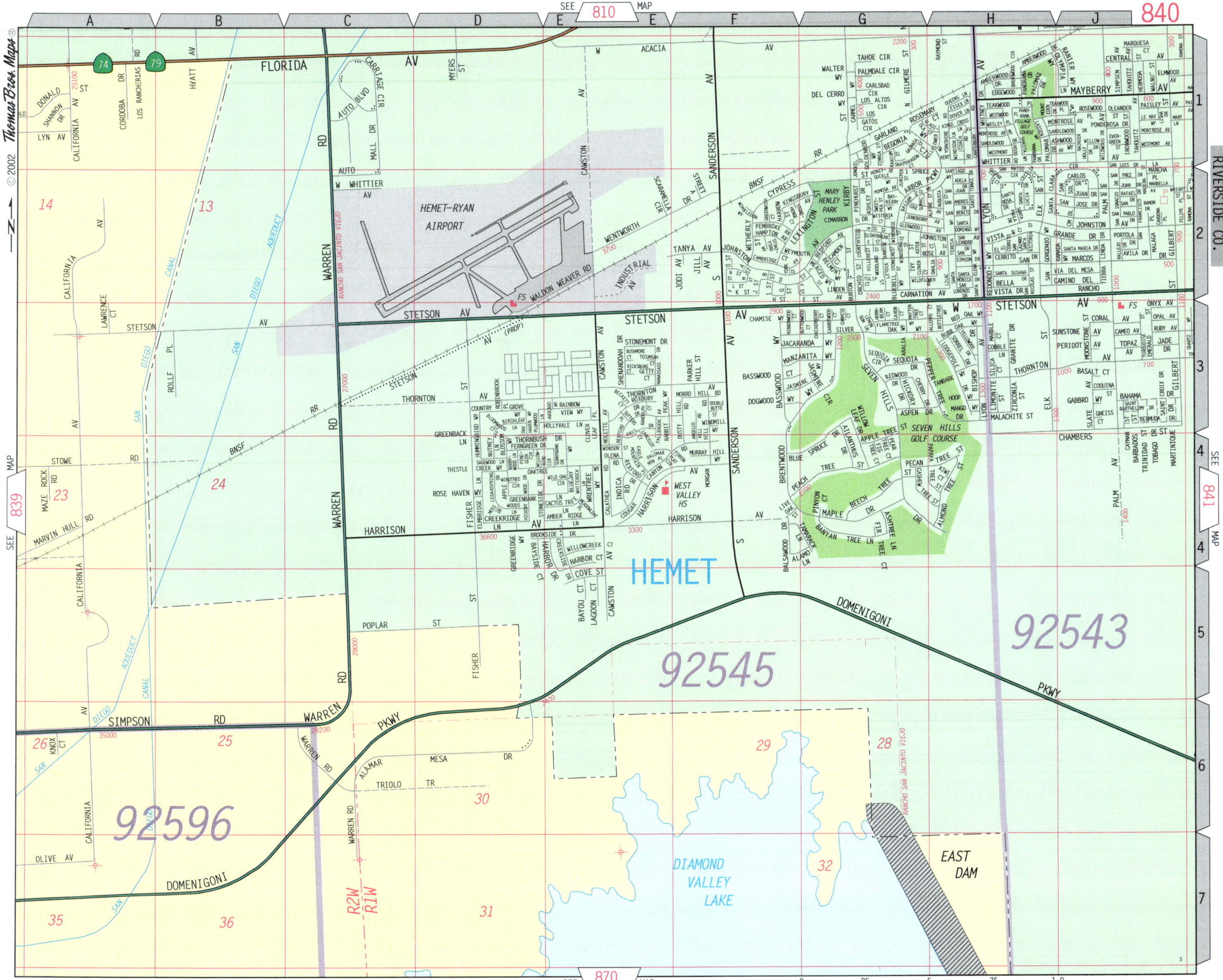

SEE 839 MAP

SEE 841 MAP

SEE 870 MAP

0 .25 .5 .75 1.0 miles 1 in. = 2400 ft.

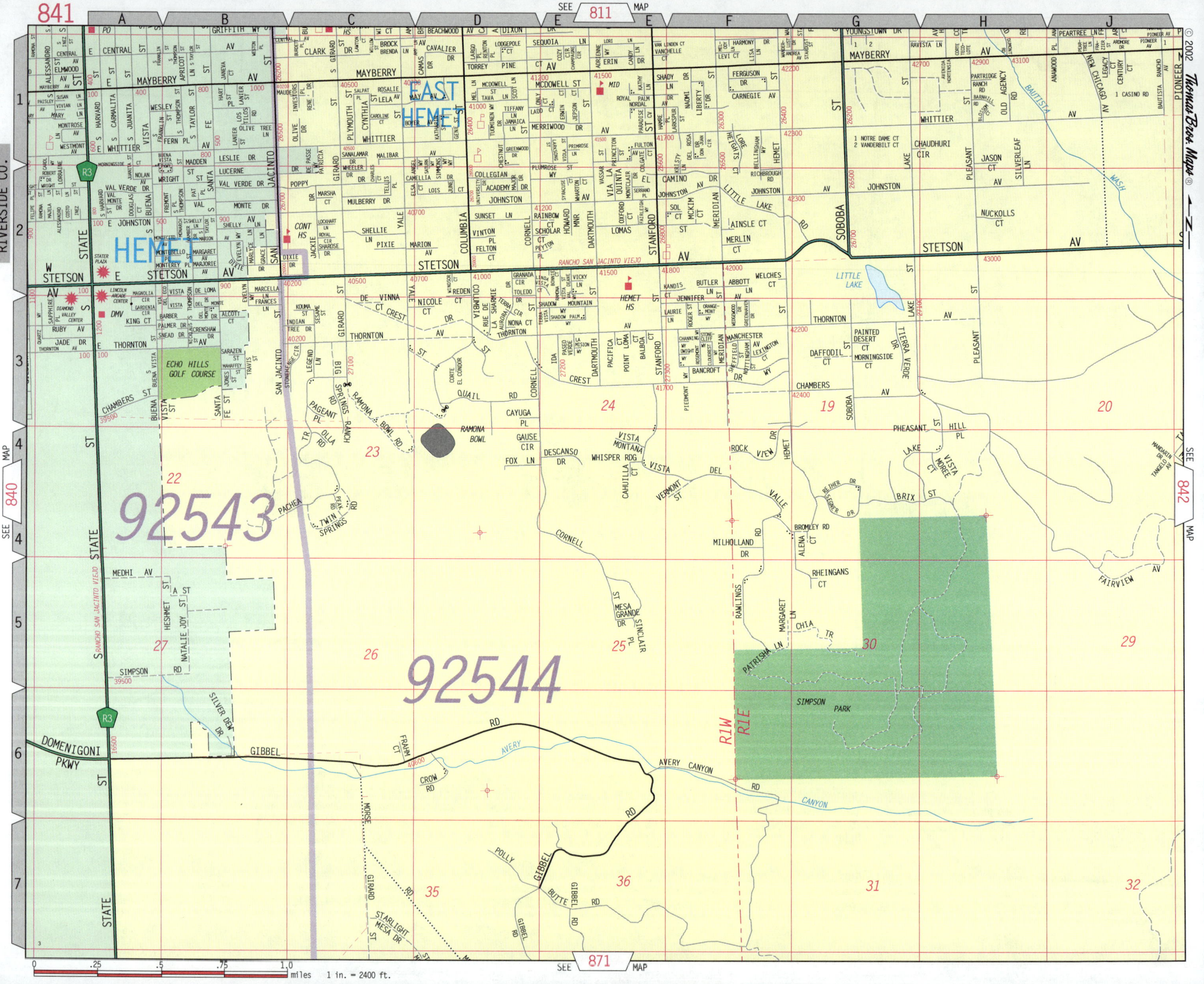
SEE 811 MAP
SEE 840 MAP
SEE 842 MAP
SEE 871 MAP
A
B
C
D
E
F
G
H
J
1
2
3
4
5
6
7
RIVERSIDE CO.
HEMET
EAST HEMET
92543
92544
MAYBERRY AV
WHITTIER
JOHNSTON
STETSON AV
E STETSON
W STETSON
THORNTON
CHAMBERS
STATE ST
SAN JACINTO
COLUMBIA
CORNELL
STANFORD
SOBOBA
LAKE
PLEASANT
BAUTISTA WASH
LITTLE LAKE
ECHO HILLS GOLF COURSE
RAMONA BOWL
QUAIL RD
CAYUGA PL
GAUSE CIR
DESCANSO DR
FOX LN
WHISPER RDG
VISTA MONTANA
VISTA DEL VALLE
ROCK VIEW DR
PHEASANT HILL PL
BRIX ST
BROMLEY RD
MILHOLLAND DR
RHEINGANS CT
FAIRVIEW AV
MEDHI AV
HESHMET
NATALIE JOY ST
SIMPSON RD
SILVER DEW DR
DOMENIGONI PKWY
GIBBEL RD
AVERY CANYON RD
CROW RD
FRAHM CT
MORSE
POLLY
BUTTE
STARLIGHT MESA DR
GIRARD
TWIN SPRINGS
PACHEA
PEAK RD
SIMPSON PARK
R1W
R1E
R3
RANCHO SAN JACINTO VIEJO
HEMET HS
CONT HS
DMV
STATER PLAZA
LINCOLN ARCADE CENTER
DIAMOND VALLEY CENTER
22
23
24
19
20
27
26
25
30
29
35
36
31
32
© 2002 Thomas Bros. Maps ®
0 .25 .5 .75 1.0 miles 1 in. = 2400 ft.

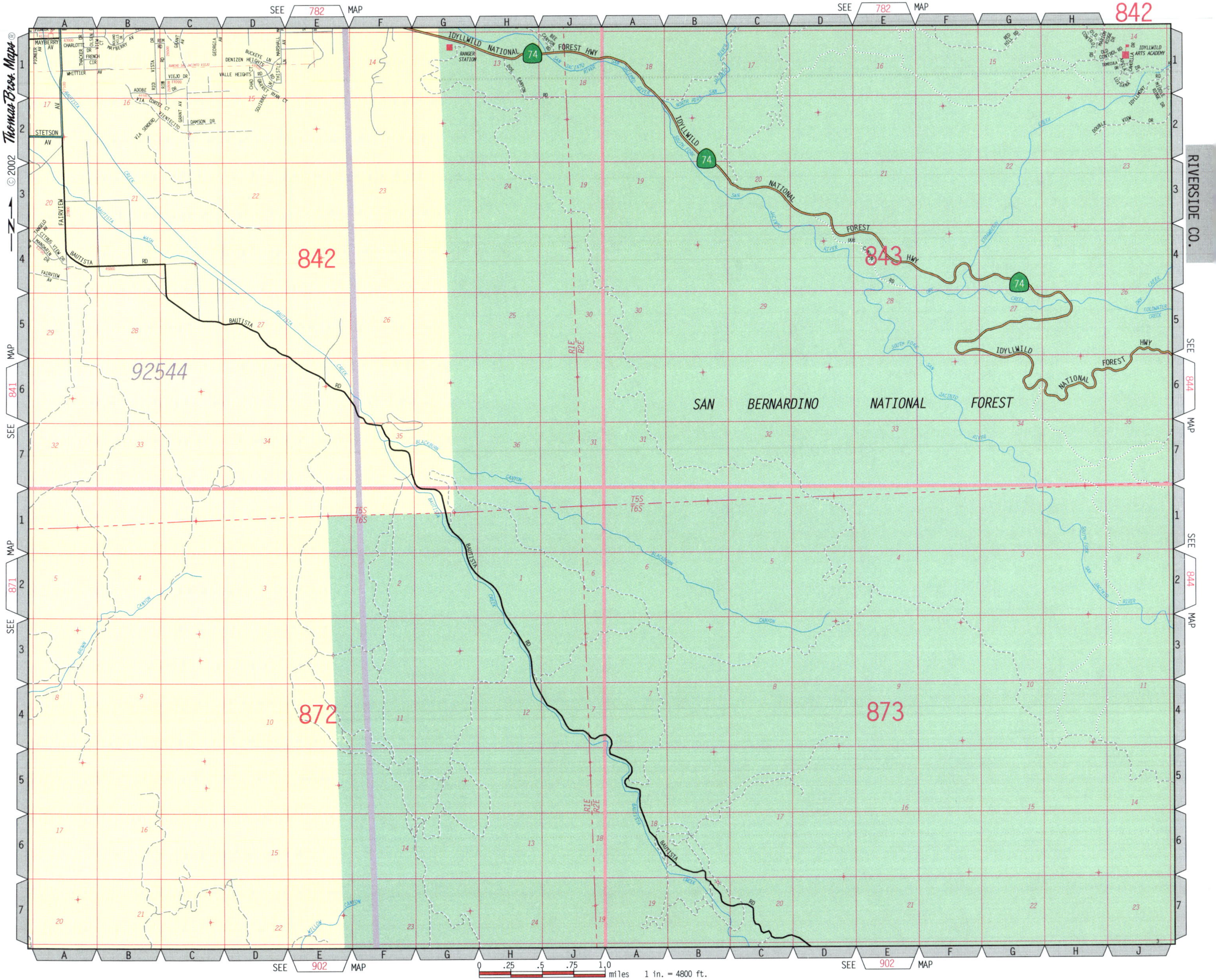
SEE 782 MAP
SEE 782 MAP
SEE 844 MAP
SEE 844 MAP
SEE 841 MAP
SEE 871 MAP
SEE 902 MAP
SEE 902 MAP
RIVERSIDE CO.
842
843
872
873
92544
SAN BERNARDINO NATIONAL FOREST
IDYLLWILD NATIONAL FOREST HWY
74
RANGER STATION
IDYLLWILD ARTS ACADEMY
BAUTISTA RD
BAUTISTA CREEK
BAUTISTA CANYON RD
BLACKBURN CANYON
SOUTH FORK SAN JACINTO RIVER
NORTH FORK SAN JACINTO RIVER
STRAWBERRY CREEK
FAIRVIEW AV
STETSON AV
MAYBERRY AV
WHITTIER AV
DENIZEN HEIGHTS
VALLE HEIGHTS
DAMSON DR
T5S
T6S
R1E
R2E
Thomas Bros. Maps®
© 2002
0 .25 .5 .75 1.0 miles 1 in. = 4800 ft.

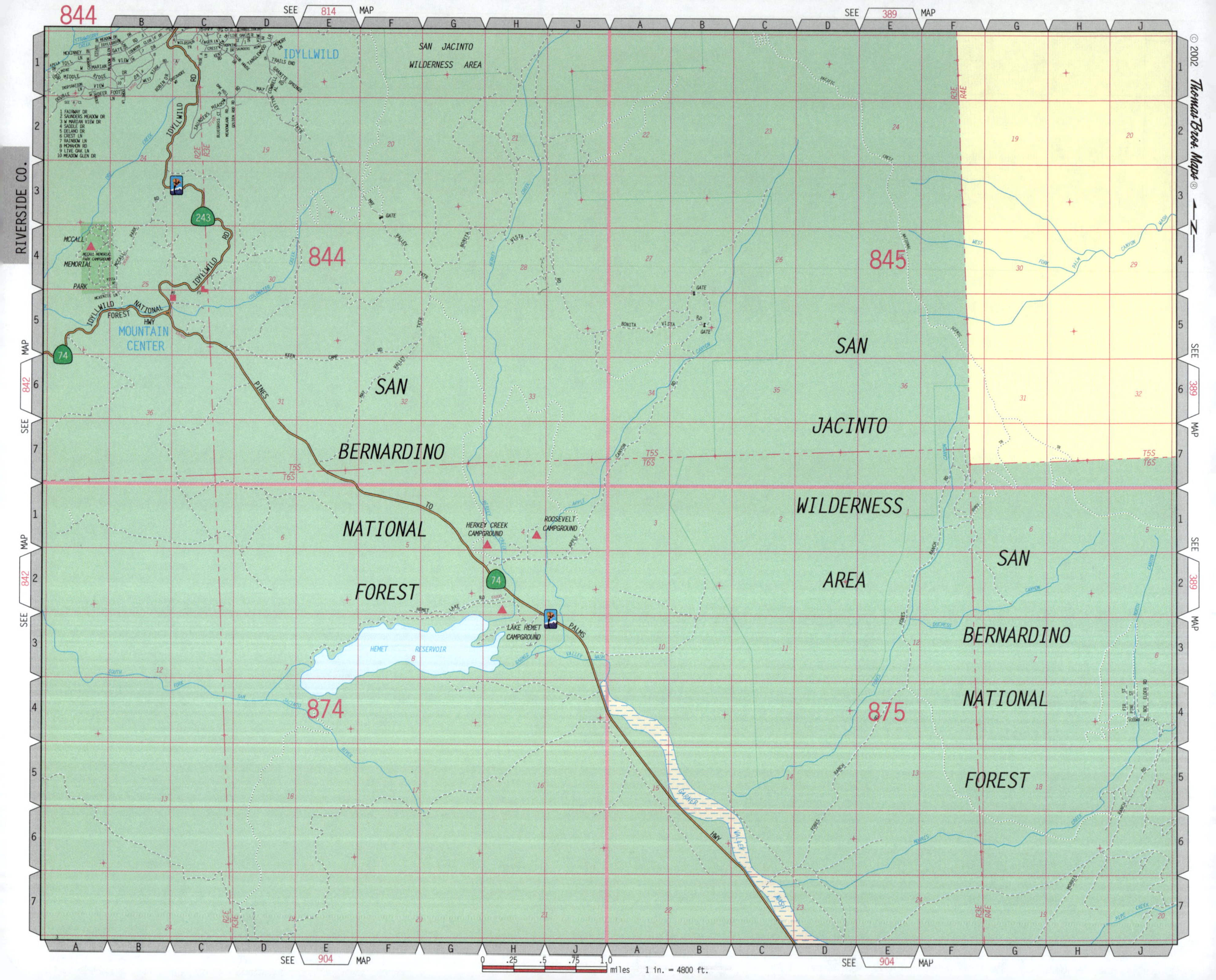
SEE 814 MAP
SEE 389 MAP
IDYLLWILD
SAN JACINTO WILDERNESS AREA
MCCALL MEMORIAL PARK
MOUNTAIN CENTER
IDYLLWILD FOREST NATIONAL HWY
PINES TO PALMS HWY
844
845
874
875
SAN BERNARDINO NATIONAL FOREST
SAN JACINTO WILDERNESS AREA
SAN BERNARDINO NATIONAL FOREST
HERKEY CREEK CAMPGROUND
ROOSEVELT CAMPGROUND
LAKE HEMET CAMPGROUND
HEMET RESERVOIR
RIVERSIDE CO.
SEE 842 MAP
SEE 904 MAP
1 FAIRWAY DR
2 SAUNDERS MEADOW DR
3 W MARIAN VIEW DR
4 SADDLE DR
5 DELANO DR
6 CREST LN
7 RAINBOW LN
8 MCMAHON RD
9 LIVE OAK LN
10 MEADOW GLEN DR
T5S T6S
R2E R3E
R3E R4E
miles 1 in. = 4800 ft.

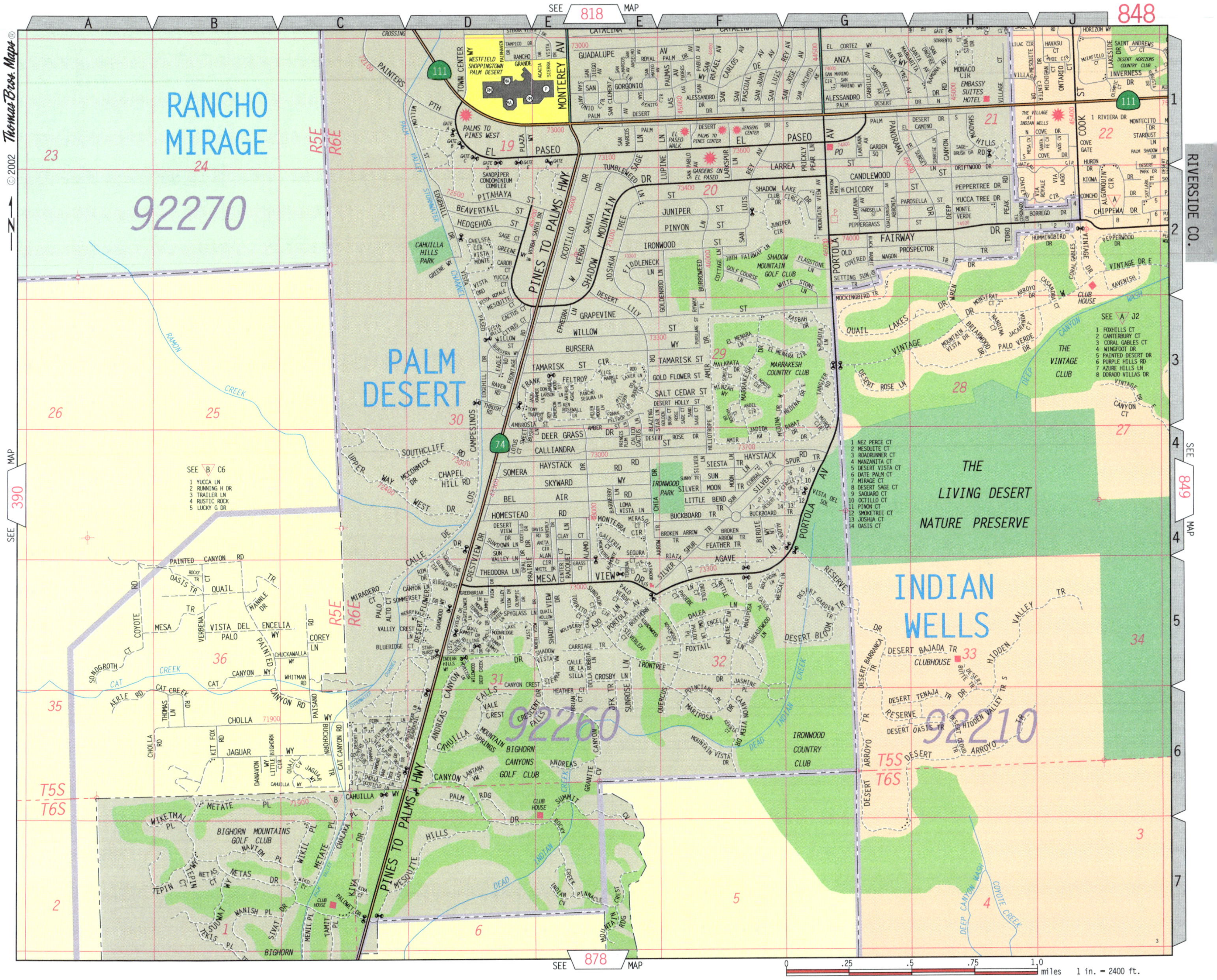
SEE 818 MAP
RANCHO MIRAGE
92270
PALM DESERT
92260
INDIAN WELLS
92210
THE LIVING DESERT NATURE PRESERVE
RIVERSIDE CO.
WESTFIELD SHOPPINGTOWN PALM DESERT
SHADOW MOUNTAIN GOLF CLUB
MARRAKESH COUNTRY CLUB
THE VINTAGE CLUB
IRONWOOD COUNTRY CLUB
BIGHORN CANYONS GOLF CLUB
BIGHORN MOUNTAINS GOLF CLUB
CAHUILLA HILLS PARK
IRONWOOD PARK
PINES TO PALMS HWY
EL PASEO
MONTEREY AV
PORTOLA AV
FAIRWAY DR
HAYSTACK RD
MESA VIEW DR
PALM DESERT
EMBASSY SUITES HOTEL
CLUBHOUSE
SEE 390 MAP
SEE 849 MAP
SEE 878 MAP
© 2002 Thomas Bros. Maps
1 in. = 2400 ft.
miles

SEE 819 MAP

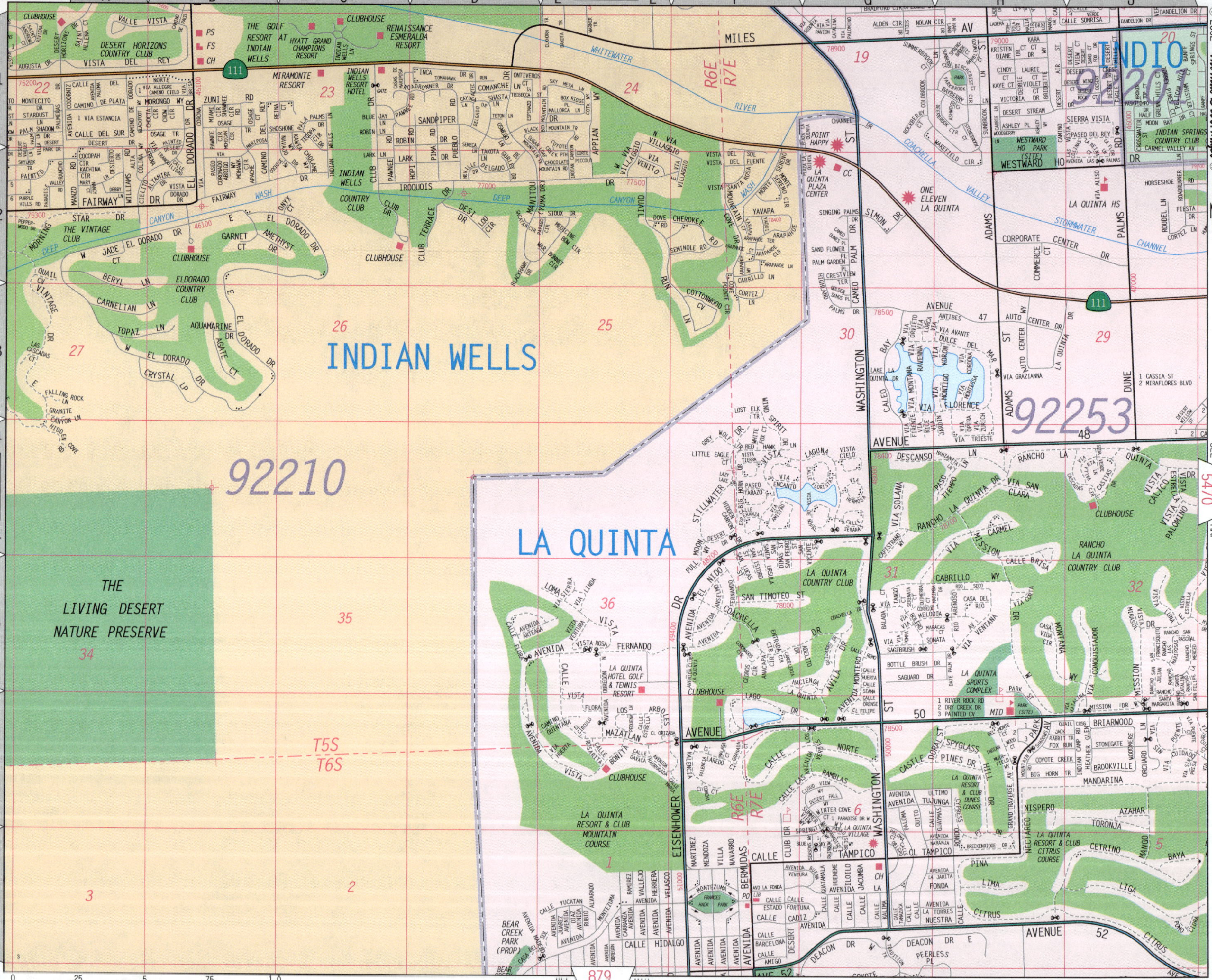

SEE 848 MAP
SEE 5470 MAP
SEE 879 MAP

0 .25 .5 .75 1.0 miles 1 in. = 2400 ft.

SEE 835 MAP

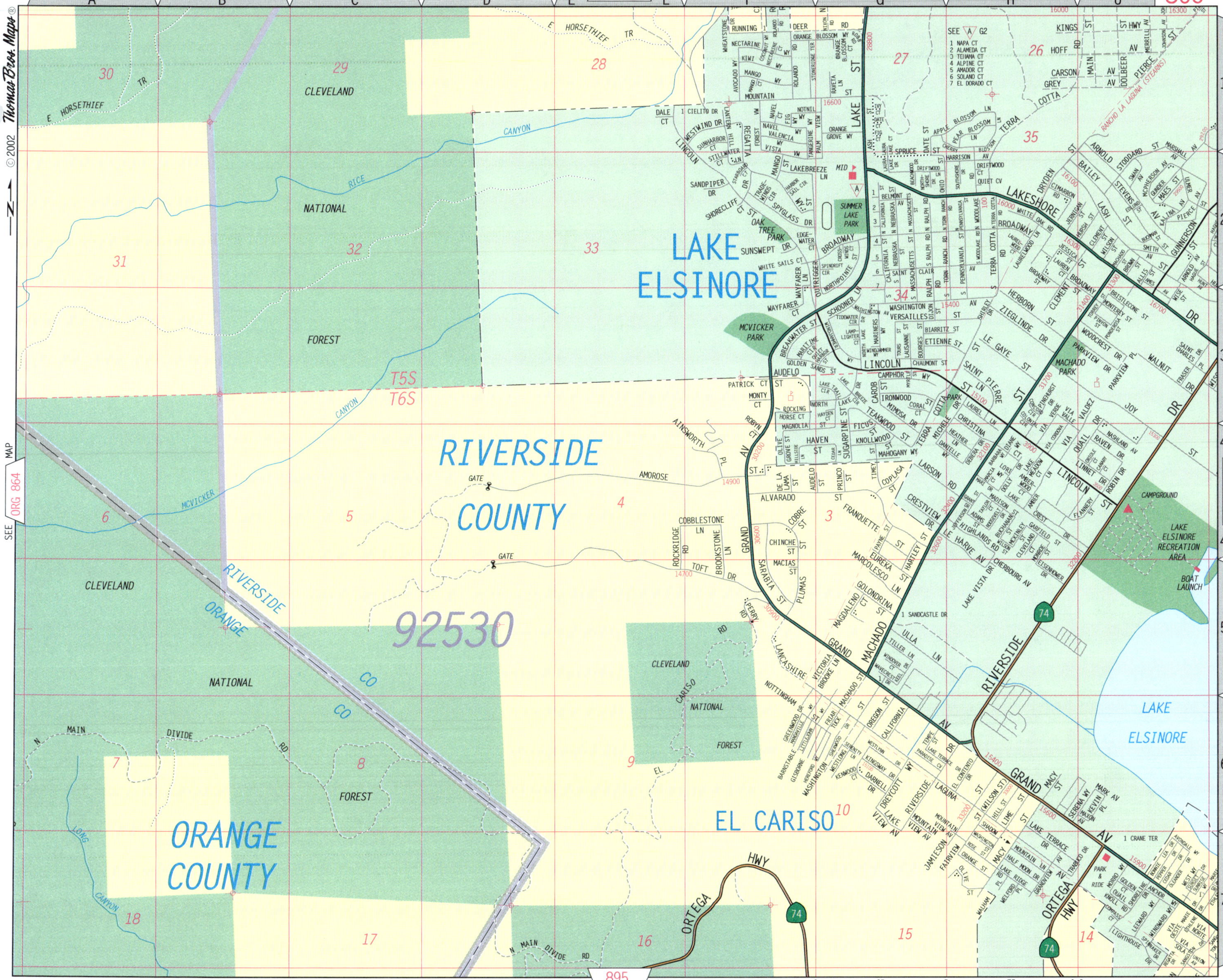

SEE ORG 864 MAP
SEE 866 MAP
SEE 895 MAP

0 .25 .5 .75 1.0 miles 1 in. = 2400 ft.

SEE 836 MAP

SEE 865 MAP

SEE 867 MAP

SEE 896 MAP

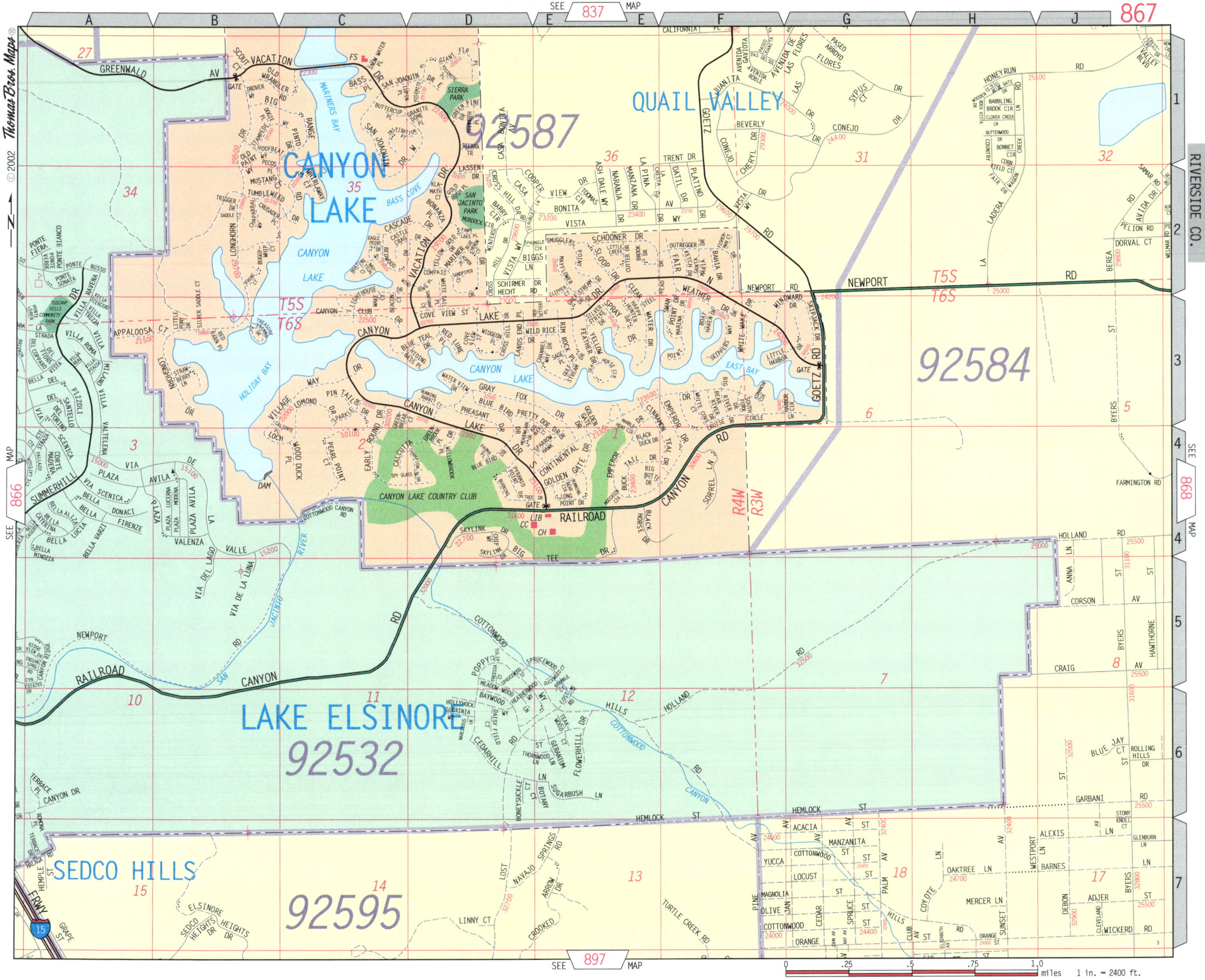
SEE 837 MAP
A
B
C
D
E
F
G
H
J
1
2
3
4
5
6
7
RIVERSIDE CO.
Thomas Bros. Maps
© 2002
CANYON LAKE
QUAIL VALLEY
92587
92584
LAKE ELSINORE
92532
SEDCO HILLS
92595
CANYON LAKE COUNTRY CLUB
HOLIDAY BAY
EAST BAY
BASS COVE
MARINERS BAY
SIERRA PARK
SAN JACINTO PARK
T5S
T6S
R4W
R3W
NEWPORT RD
RAILROAD CANYON RD
GOETZ RD
GREENWALD AV
HOLLAND RD
HEMLOCK ST
CORSON AV
CRAIG AV
GARBANI RD
SAN JACINTO RIVER
COTTONWOOD CANYON
15
SEE 866 MAP
SEE 868 MAP
SEE 897 MAP
0
.25
.5
.75
1.0
miles
1 in. = 2400 ft.

SEE 838 MAP

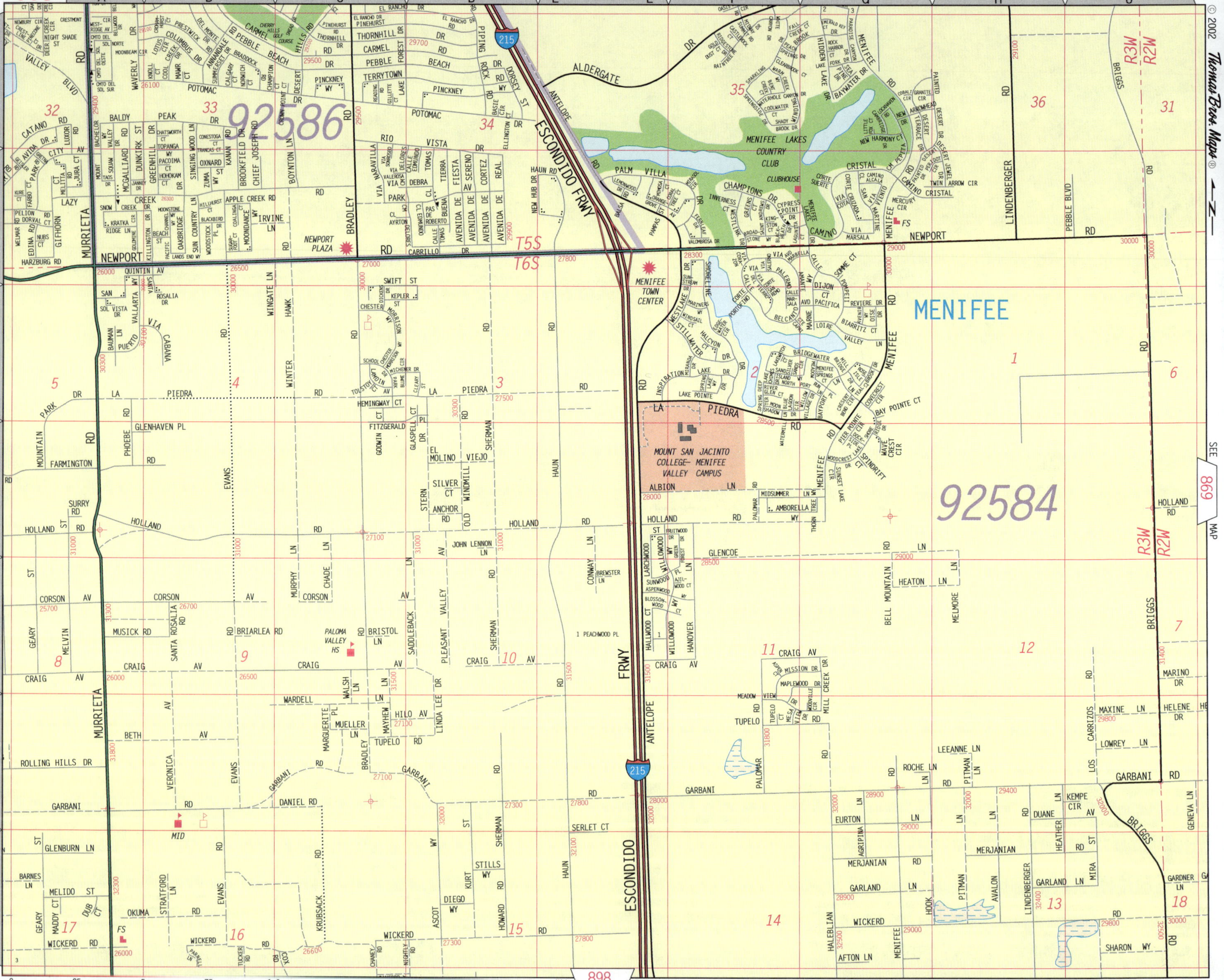

SEE 867 MAP

SEE 869 MAP

SEE 898 MAP

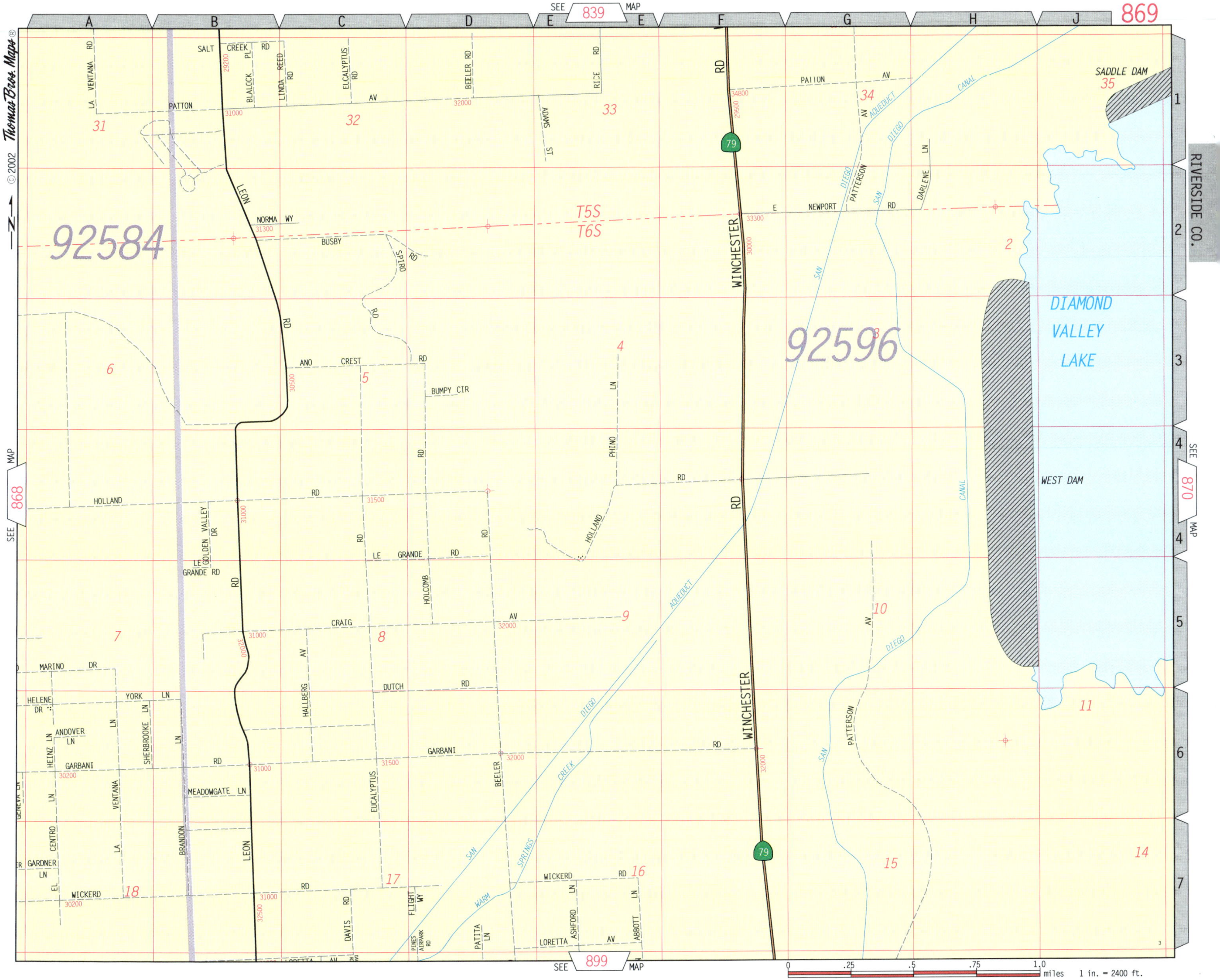
SEE 839 MAP
SEE 868 MAP
SEE 870 MAP
SEE 899 MAP
A
B
C
D
E
F
G
H
J
1
2
3
4
5
6
7
Thomas Bros. Maps ©
© 2002
N
RIVERSIDE CO.
92584
92596
T5S
T6S
DIAMOND VALLEY LAKE
SADDLE DAM
WEST DAM
SALT CREEK RD
PATTON AV
LA VENTANA RD
BLALOCK PL
LINDA REED RD
EUCALYPTUS RD
BEELER RD
RICE RD
ADAMS ST
LEON RD
NORMA WY
BUSBY
SPIRO RD
ANO CREST RD
BUMPY CIR
WINCHESTER RD
PATTERSON AV
DARLENE LN
E NEWPORT RD
SAN DIEGO AQUEDUCT
SAN DIEGO CANAL
PHINO LN
HOLLAND RD
GOLDEN VALLEY DR
LE GRANDE RD
HOLCOMB RD
CRAIG AV
DUTCH RD
HALLBERG AV
MARINO DR
HELENE DR
YORK LN
ANDOVER LN
HEINZ LN
SHERBROOKE LN
GARBANI RD
MEADOWGATE LN
VENTANA
GENEVA LN
CENTRO LN
LA
BRANDON
BEELER
EUCALYPTUS
GARDNER LN
EL
WICKERD RD
DAVIS RD
FLIGHT WY
PINES AIRPARK RD
PATITA LN
ASHFORD LN
LORETTA AV
ABBOTT LN
WARM SPRINGS CREEK
79
29200
31000
32000
34800
29500
31300
33300
30000
30500
31500
30200
32500
31
32
33
34
35
2
4
5
6
7
8
9
10
11
14
15
16
17
18
0 .25 .5 .75 1.0 miles 1 in. = 2400 ft.

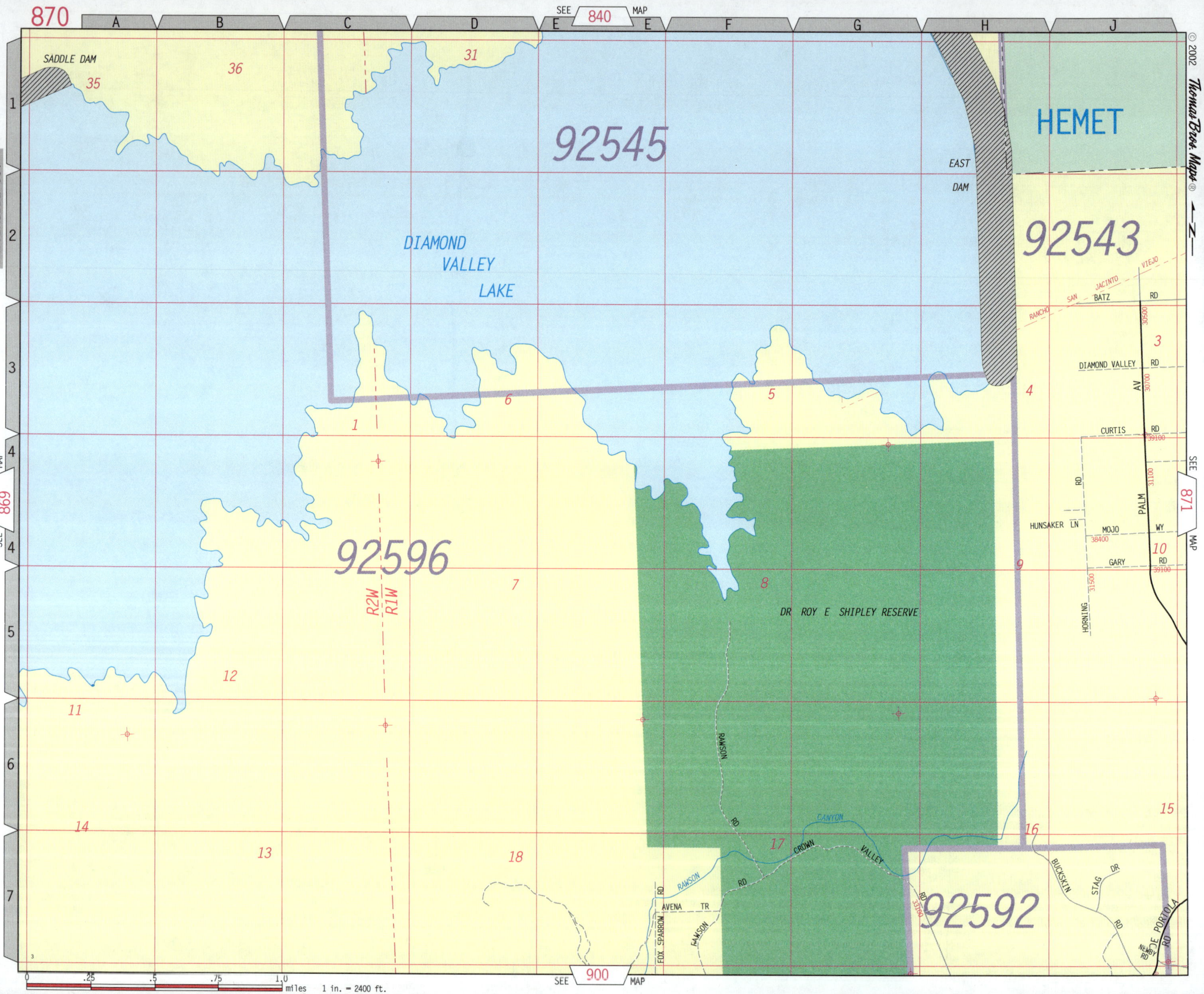
SEE 840 MAP
SADDLE DAM
DIAMOND VALLEY LAKE
92545
HEMET
EAST DAM
92543
RANCHO SAN JACINTO VIEJO
BATZ RD
DIAMOND VALLEY RD
CURTIS RD
PALM AV
HUNSAKER LN
MOJO WY
GARY RD
HORNING RD
92596
R2W R1W
DR ROY E SHIPLEY RESERVE
RAWSON RD
CANYON
CROWN VALLEY RD
AVENA TR
FOX SPARROW RD
BUCKSKIN
STAG DR
DE PORTOLA RD
NEWBY RD
92592
RIVERSIDE CO.
SEE 869 MAP
SEE 871 MAP
SEE 900 MAP
miles 1 in. = 2400 ft.

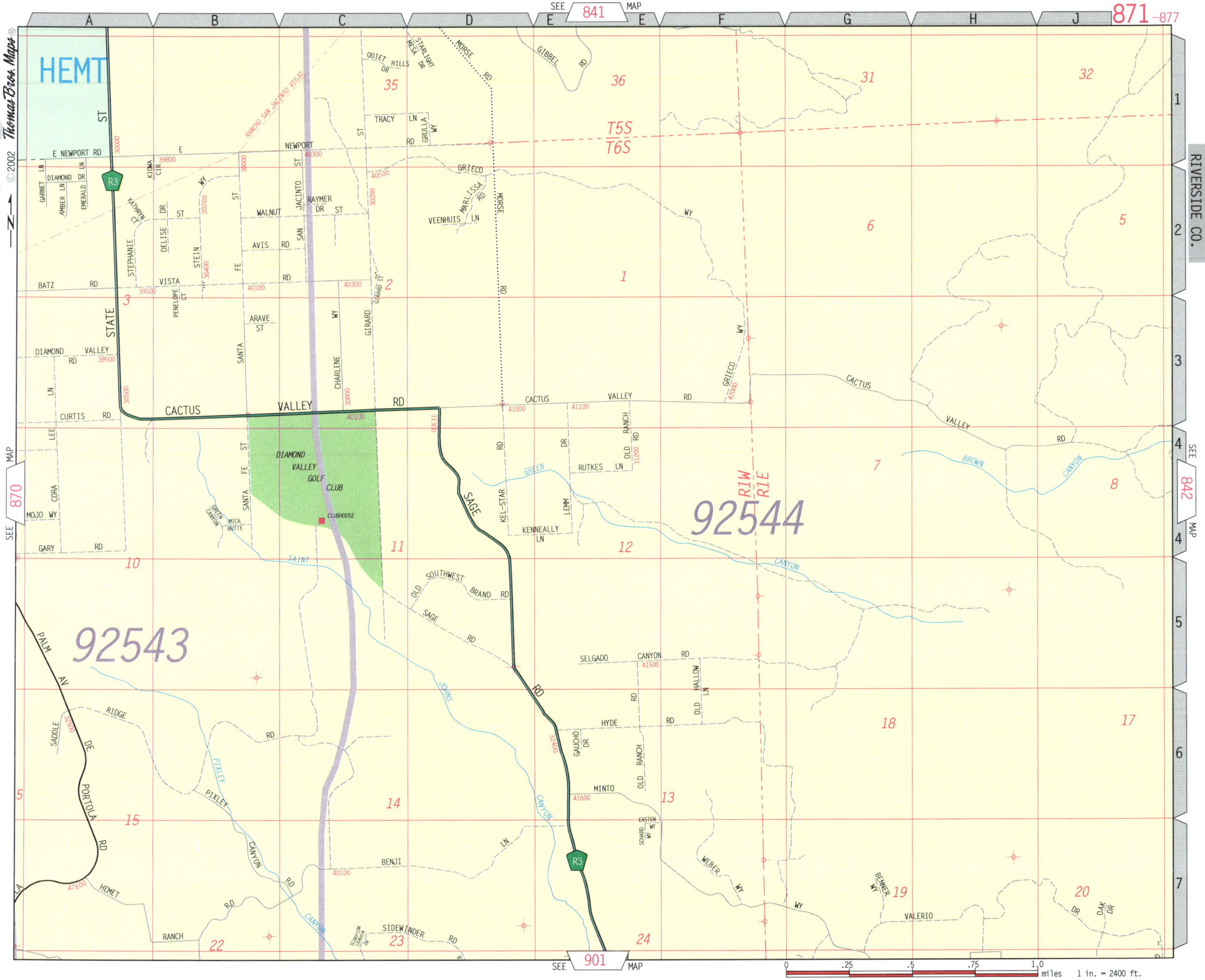
SEE 841 MAP
HEMT
E NEWPORT RD
NEWPORT
CACTUS VALLEY RD
STATE ST
DIAMOND VALLEY GOLF CLUB
CLUBHOUSE
SAGE RD
92544
92543
T5S
T6S
R1W
R1E
RIVERSIDE CO.
SEE 870 MAP
SEE 842 MAP
SEE 901 MAP
PALM AV
DE PORTOLA RD
HEMET RANCH RD
SAINT JOHNS CANYON
PIXLEY CANYON RD
BROWN CANYON
GREEN CANYON
SELGADO CANYON RD
HYDE RD
MINTO
BENJI
SIDEWINDER RD
VALERIO
WEBER WY
GRIECO WY
MORSE RD
GIBBEL RD
SOUTHWEST BRAND RD
OLD SAGE RD
KEL-STAR RD
KENNEALLY LN
RUTKES LN
OLD RANCH RD
OLD HALLOW LN
GAUCHO DR
DIAMOND VALLEY RD
CURTIS RD
MOJO WY
GARY RD
BATZ RD
VISTA RD
AVIS RD
WALNUT ST
RAYMER DR
SAN JACINTO ST
SANTA FE ST
CHARLENE WY
GIRARD ST
ARAVE ST
TRACY LN
GRULLA WY
QUIET HILLS DR
MESA DR
STARLIGHT
VEENHUIS LN
MARLISSA RD
KIOWA CIR
KATHRYN CT
STEPHANIE
DELISE DR
STEIN WY
PENELOPE CT
GARNET LN
AMBER LN
DIAMOND DR
EMERALD LN
CORA
LEE LN
SADDLE RIDGE RD
RANCHO SAN JACINTO VIEJO
MICA BUTTE
GREEN CANYON
SCORPION CANYON DR
BENNER WY
OAK DR
EASTEN WY
SCHARD WY
R3
0 .25 .5 .75 1.0 miles
1 in. = 2400 ft.

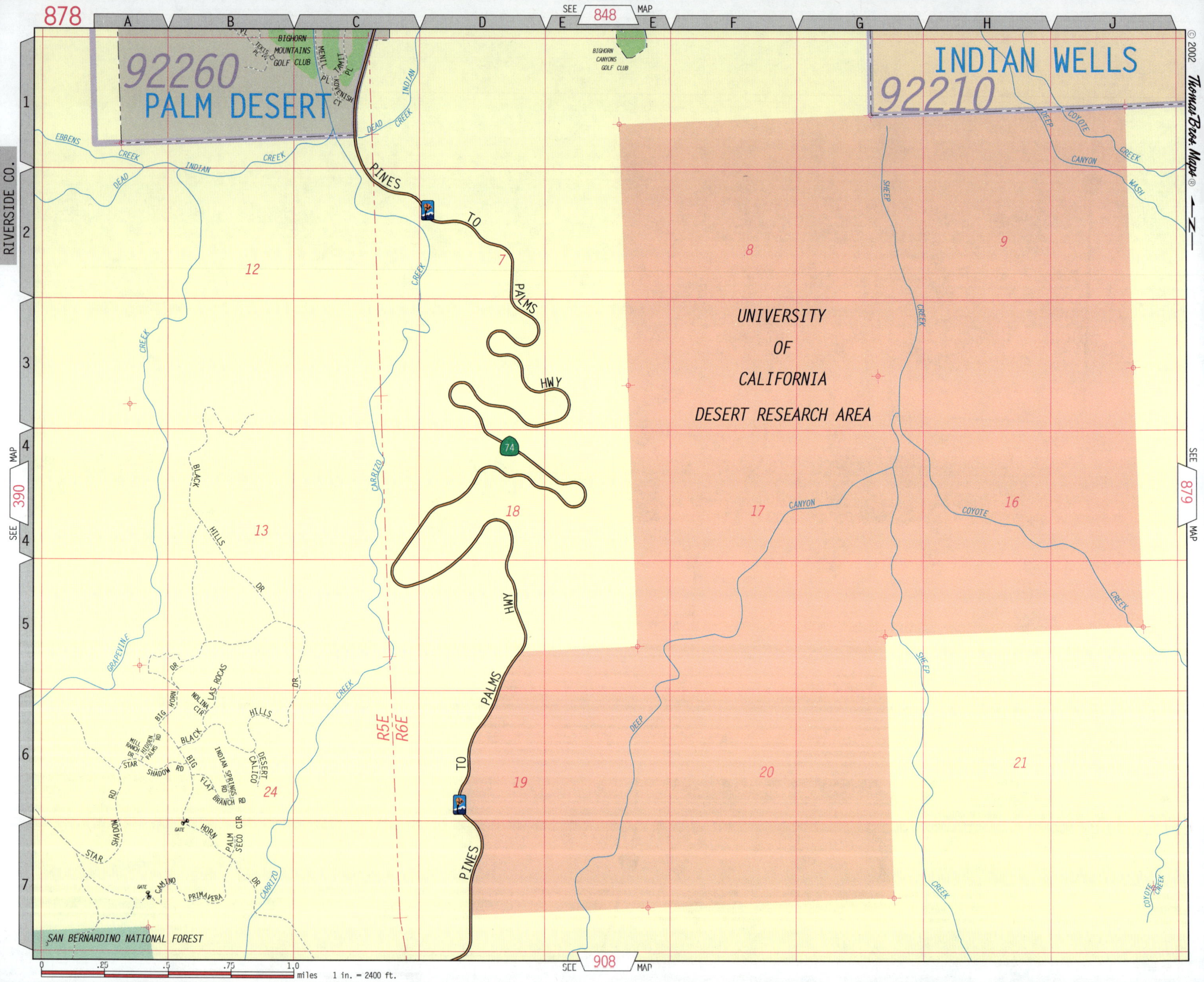
A
B
C
D
E
F
G
H
J
1
2
3
4
5
6
7
SEE 848 MAP
SEE 908 MAP
SEE 390 MAP
SEE 879 MAP
RIVERSIDE CO.
92260
PALM DESERT
INDIAN WELLS
92210
BIGHORN MOUNTAINS GOLF CLUB
BIGHORN CANYONS GOLF CLUB
UNIVERSITY OF CALIFORNIA DESERT RESEARCH AREA
PINES TO PALMS HWY
74
EBBENS CREEK
INDIAN CREEK
DEAD INDIAN CREEK
DEEP CANYON
COYOTE CREEK
COYOTE CANYON
COYOTE CREEK WASH
SHEEP CREEK
CARRIZO CREEK
GRAPEVINE CREEK
BLACK HILLS DR
BIG HORN DR
LAS ROCAS
NOLINA CIR
MILL RANCH DR
HIDDEN PALMS RD
STAR SHADOW RD
INDIAN SPRINGS RD
DESERT CALICO
FLAT BRANCH RD
HORN
PALM SECO CIR
CAMINO PRIMAVERA
GATE
R5E
R6E
SAN BERNARDINO NATIONAL FOREST
7
8
9
12
13
16
17
18
19
20
21
24
0 .25 .5 .75 1.0 miles 1 in. = 2400 ft.

SEE 849 MAP

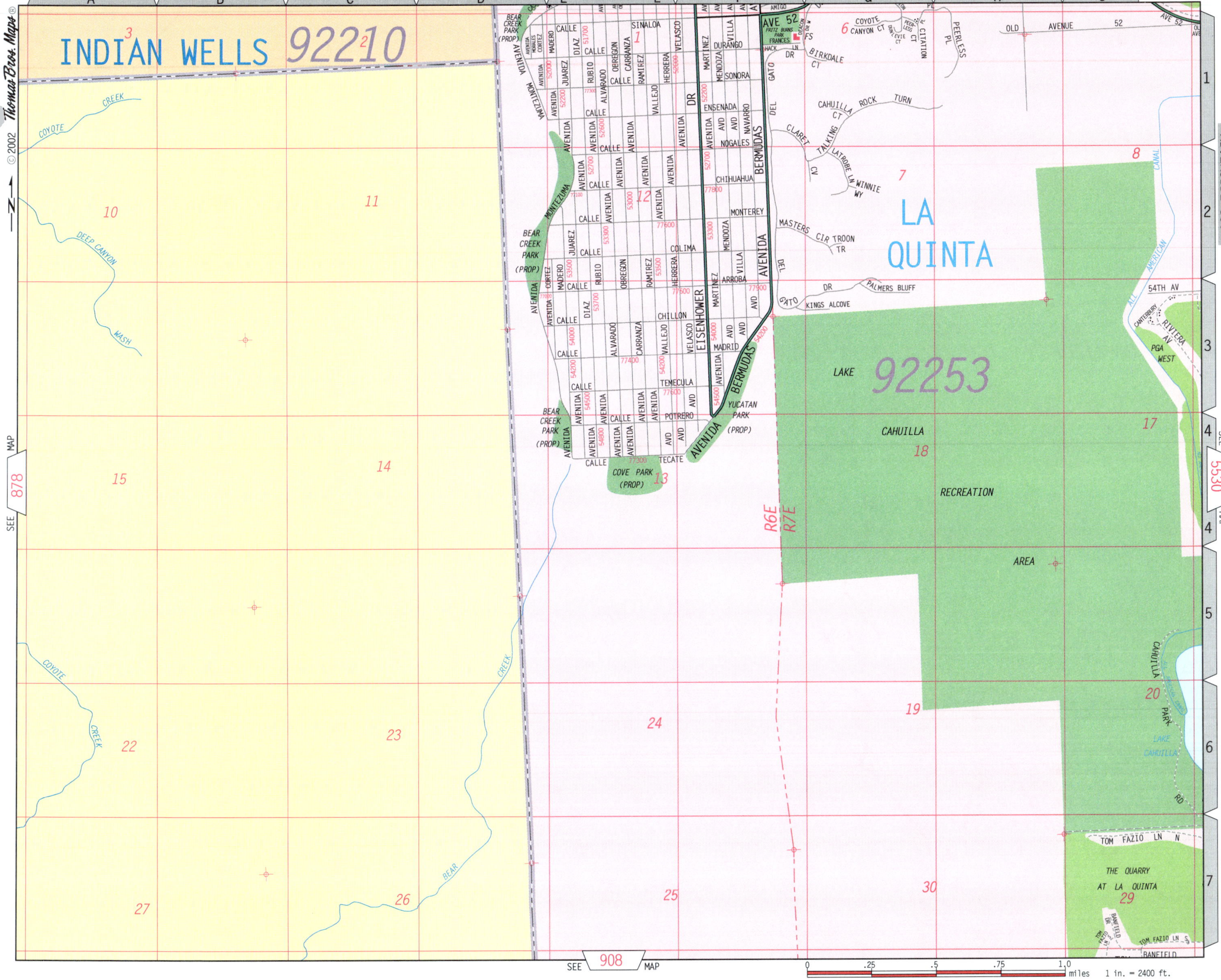

SEE 908 MAP

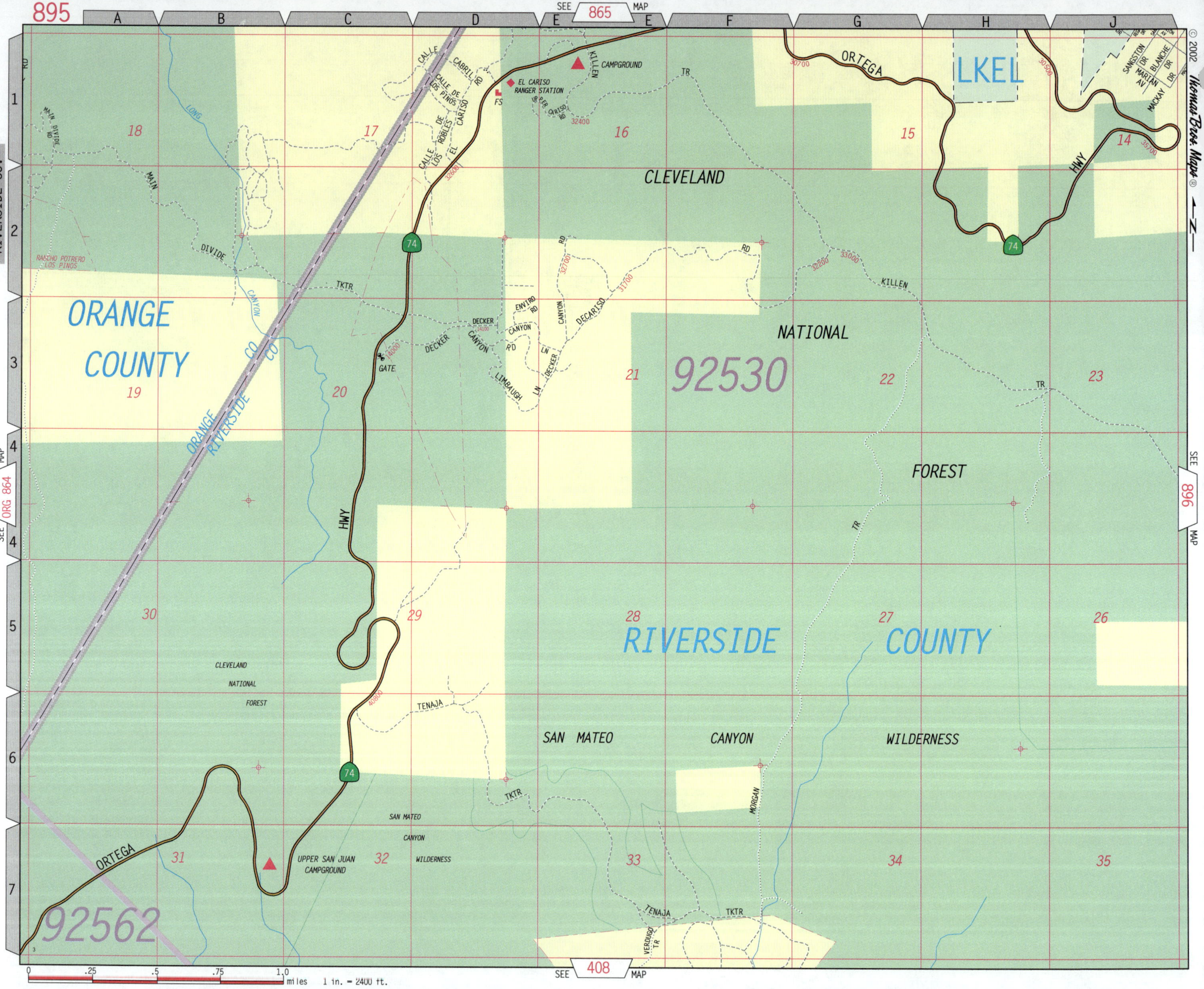
ORANGE COUNTY
RIVERSIDE COUNTY
CLEVELAND NATIONAL FOREST
92530
92562
SAN MATEO CANYON WILDERNESS
HWY 74
ORTEGA
KILLEN CAMPGROUND
EL CARISO RANGER STATION
UPPER SAN JUAN CAMPGROUND
DECKER CANYON RD
DECARISO RD
LIMBAUGH LN
TENAJA TKTR
MORGAN TR
VERDUGO TR
MAIN DIVIDE RD
LONG CANYON
GATE
LKEL
RANCHO POTRERO LOS PINOS
RIVERSIDE CO.
SEE 865 MAP
SEE ORG 864 MAP
SEE 896 MAP
SEE 408 MAP
1 in. = 2400 ft.
© 2002 Thomas Bros. Maps

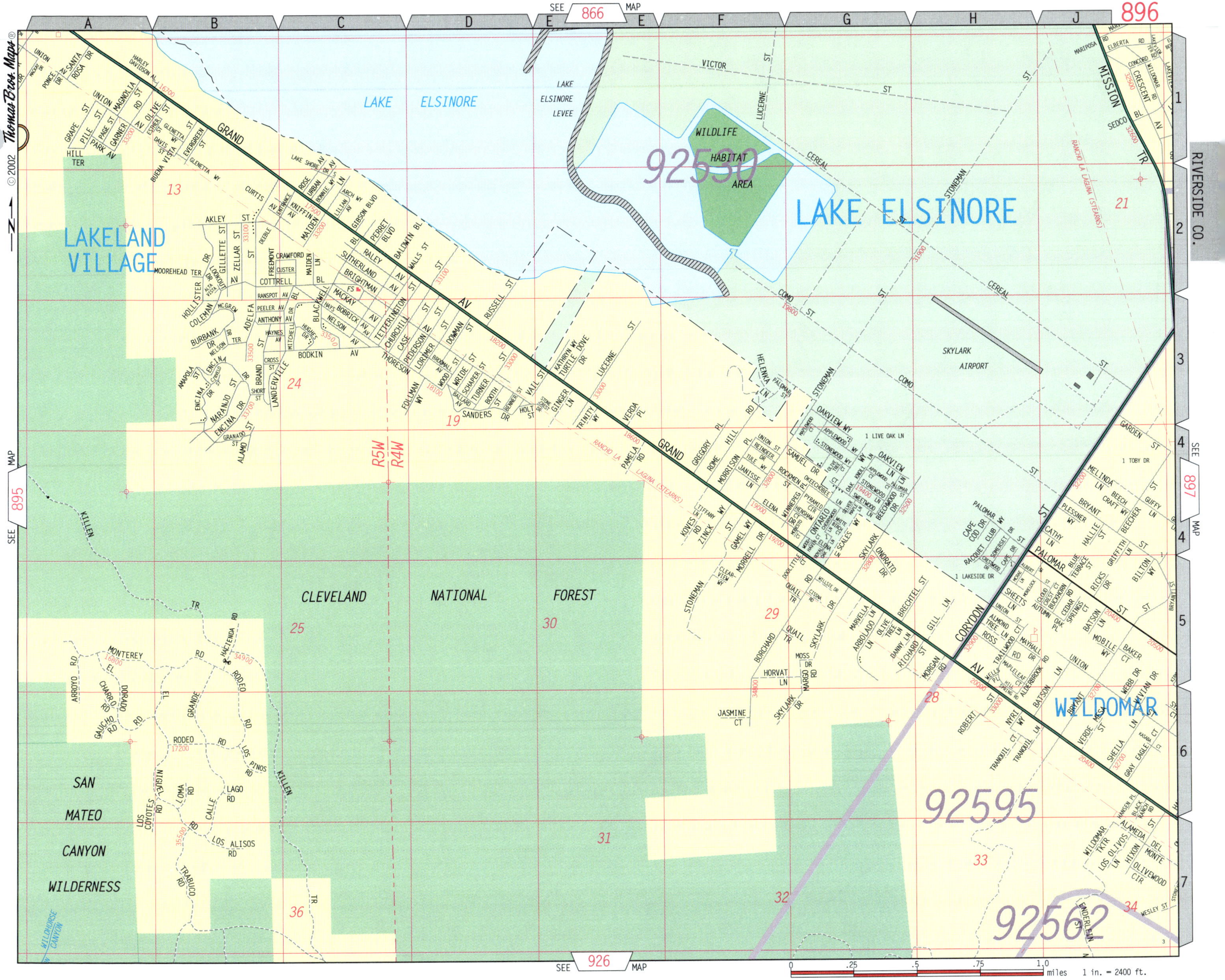
SEE 866 MAP
A
B
C
D
E
F
G
H
J
1
2
3
4
5
6
7
LAKE ELSINORE
LAKE ELSINORE LEVEE
WILDLIFE HABITAT AREA
92530
LAKE ELSINORE
LAKELAND VILLAGE
SKYLARK AIRPORT
GRAND AV
MISSION TR
RIVERSIDE CO.
CLEVELAND NATIONAL FOREST
SAN MATEO CANYON WILDERNESS
R5W
R4W
92595
WILDOMAR
92562
PALOMAR ST
CORYDON ST
RANCHO LA LAGUNA (STEARNS)
KILLEN TR
SEE 895 MAP
SEE 897 MAP
SEE 926 MAP
Thomas Bros. Maps
© 2002
miles
1 in. = 2400 ft.

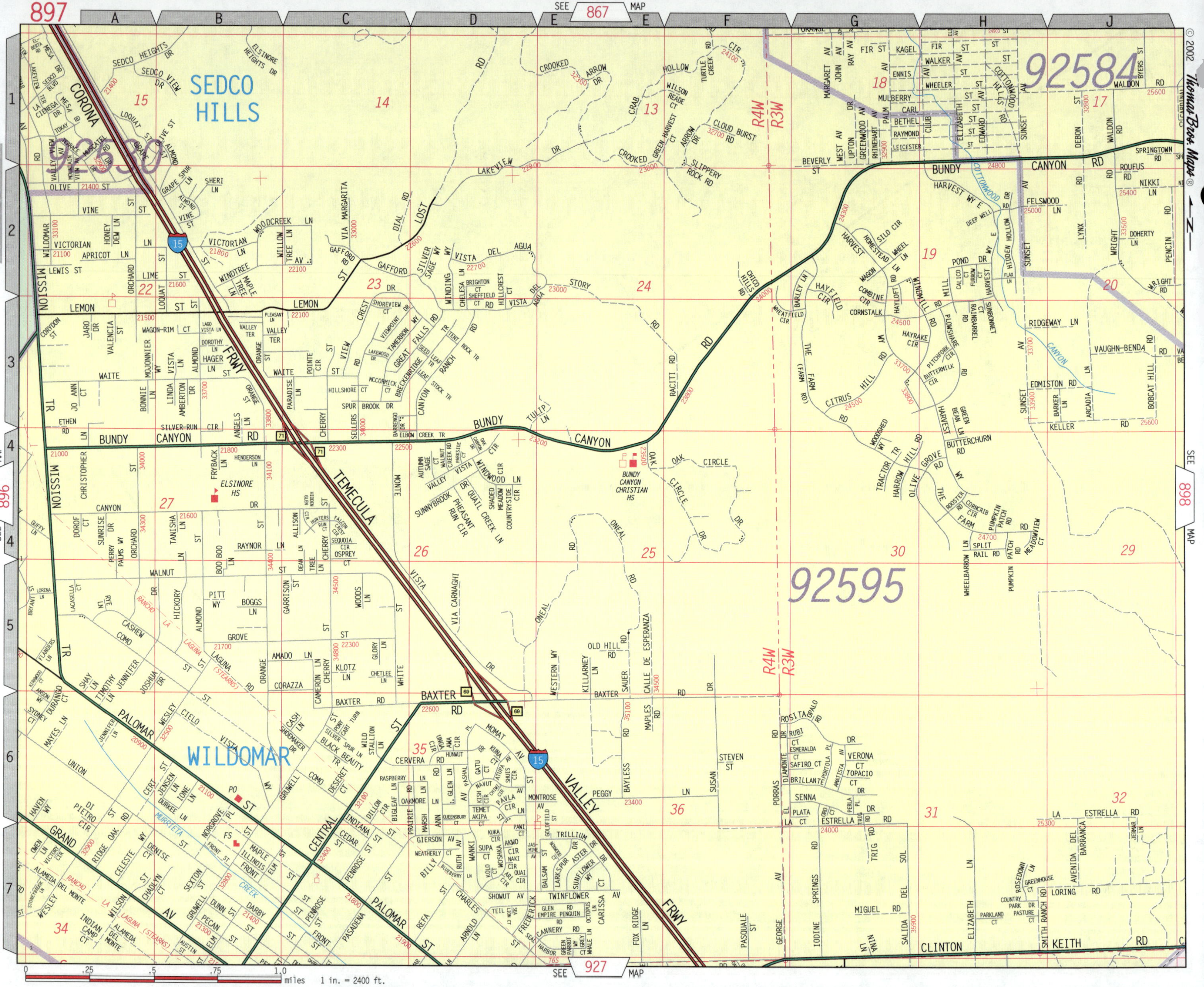
SEE 867 MAP
SEE 927 MAP
SEE 896 MAP
SEE 898 MAP
RIVERSIDE CO.
SEDCO HILLS
WILDOMAR
92530
92584
92595
R4W
R3W
CORONA FRWY
TEMECULA VALLEY FRWY
15
71
69
BUNDY CANYON RD
LEMON ST
MISSION TR
PALOMAR ST
GRAND AV
CENTRAL AV
BAXTER RD
CLINTON KEITH RD
OLIVE ST
LAKE VIEW DR
LOST RD
GAFFORD ST
ELSINORE HS
BUNDY CANYON CHRISTIAN HS
MURRIETA CREEK
LAGUNA (STEARNS)
CORYDON ST
SEDCO HEIGHTS DR
ELSINORE HEIGHTS DR
CROOKED ARROW DR
VISTA DEL AGUA
VIA CARNAGHI
ONEAL RD
CALLE DE ESPERANZA
HARVEST WY E
COTTONWOOD CANYON
SUNSET AV
WALDON RD
SPRINGTOWN RD
WRIGHT RD
1 in. = 2400 ft.
0 .25 .5 .75 1.0 miles
© 2002 Thomas Bros. Maps ®

SEE 868 MAP

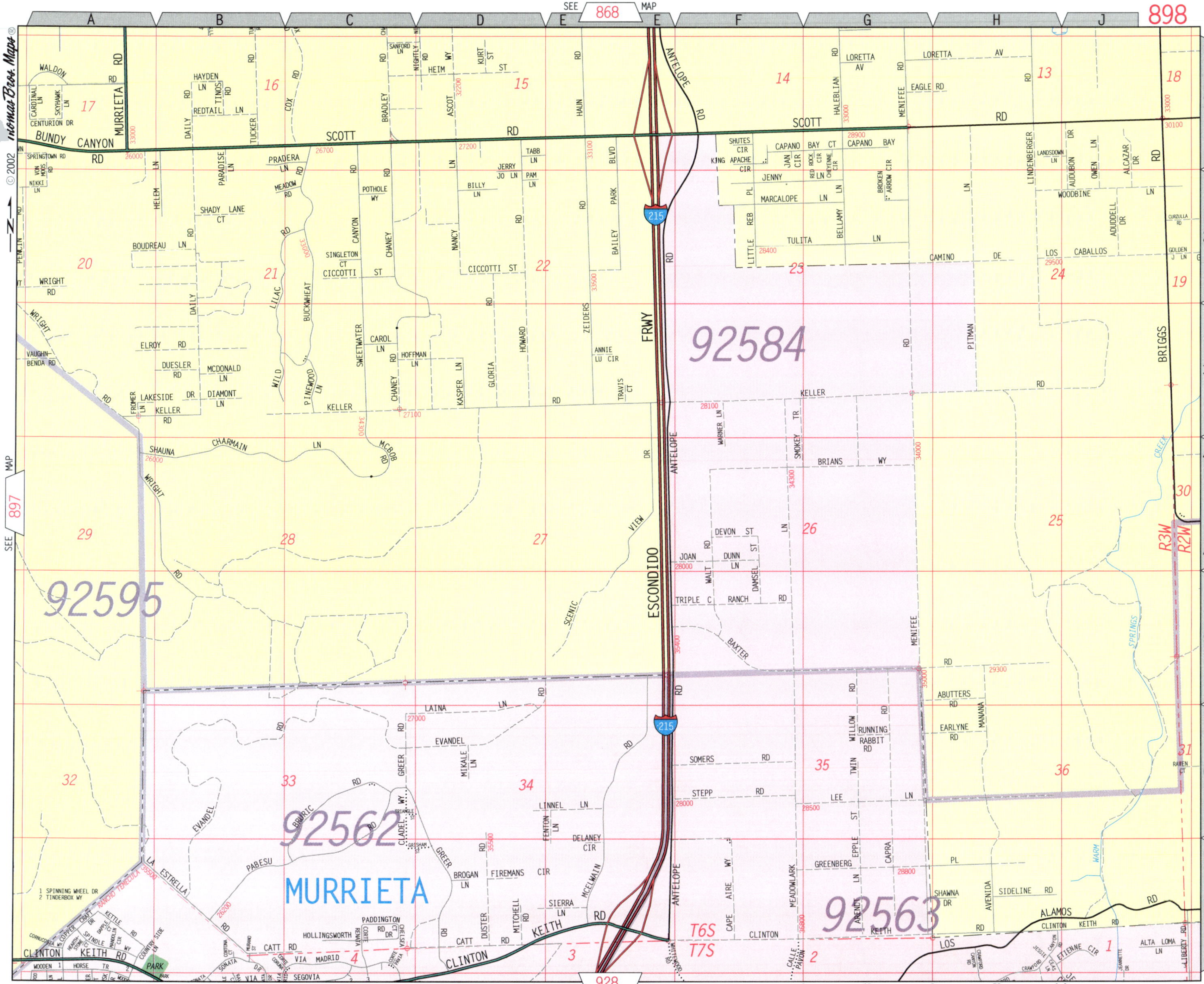

SEE 897 MAP
SEE 899 MAP
SEE 928 MAP

0 .25 .5 .75 1.0 miles 1 in. = 2400 ft.

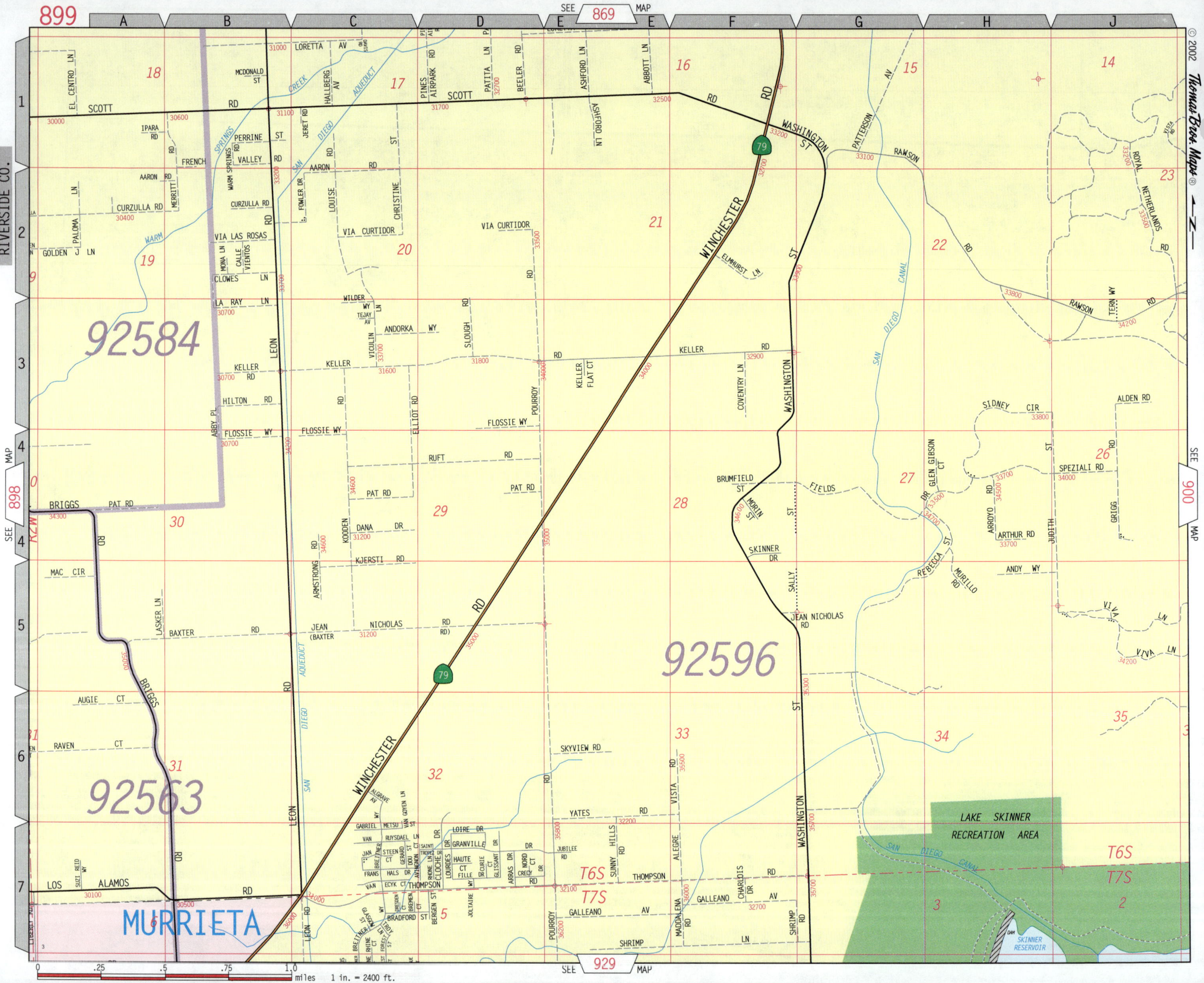
SEE 869 MAP
A
B
C
D
E
F
G
H
J
RIVERSIDE CO.
SEE 898 MAP
SEE 900 MAP
SEE 929 MAP
92584
92596
92563
MURRIETA
LAKE SKINNER RECREATION AREA
SKINNER RESERVOIR
T6S
T7S
R2W
WINCHESTER RD
WASHINGTON ST
SCOTT RD
LEON RD
KELLER RD
BRIGGS RD
RAWSON RD
PATTERSON AV
SAN DIEGO AQUEDUCT
SAN DIEGO CANAL
WARM SPRINGS CREEK
LORETTA AV
MCDONALD ST
PERRINE ST
FRENCH
VALLEY RD
AARON RD
CURZULLA RD
VIA LAS ROSAS
CLOWES LN
LA RAY LN
HILTON RD
FLOSSIE WY
PAT RD
MAC CIR
BAXTER RD
JEAN NICHOLAS RD
AUGIE CT
RAVEN CT
LOS ALAMOS RD
THOMPSON RD
GALLEANO AV
SHRIMP RD
YATES RD
SKYVIEW RD
VIA CURTIDOR
ANDORKA WY
SLOUGH RD
POURROY RD
RUFT RD
DANA DR
KJERSTI RD
ELMHURST LN
COVENTRY LN
BRUMFIELD ST
FIELDS
SKINNER DR
SIDNEY CIR
ALDEN RD
SPEZIALI RD
ARTHUR RD
ANDY WY
VIVA LN
REBECCA ST
MURILLO RD
GLEN GIBSON CT
ROYAL NETHERLANDS RD
TERN WY
1 in. = 2400 ft.
miles
0 .25 .5 .75 1.0

SEE 870 MAP

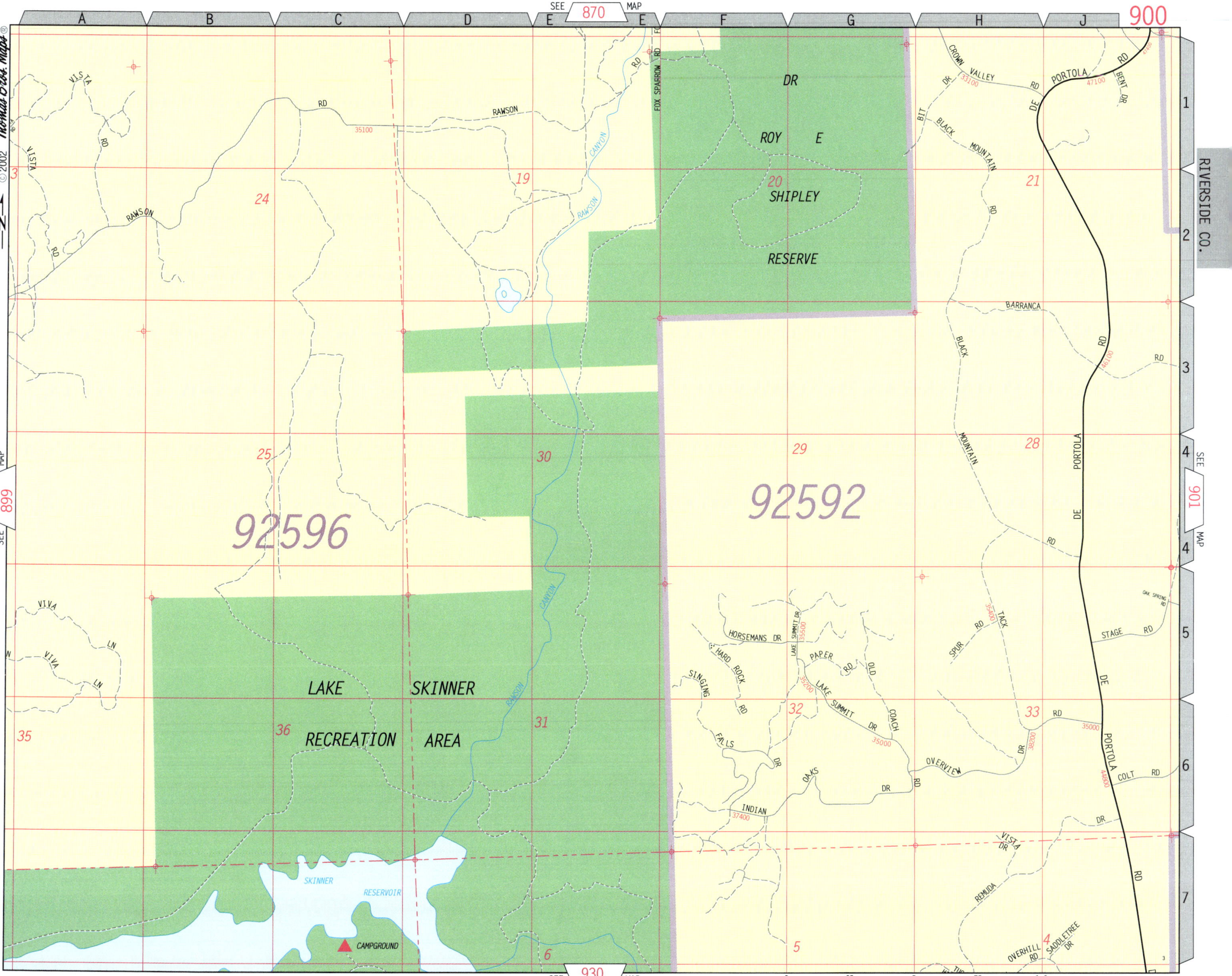

SEE 899 MAP
SEE 901 MAP
SEE 930 MAP

0 .25 .5 .75 1.0 miles 1 in. = 2400 ft.

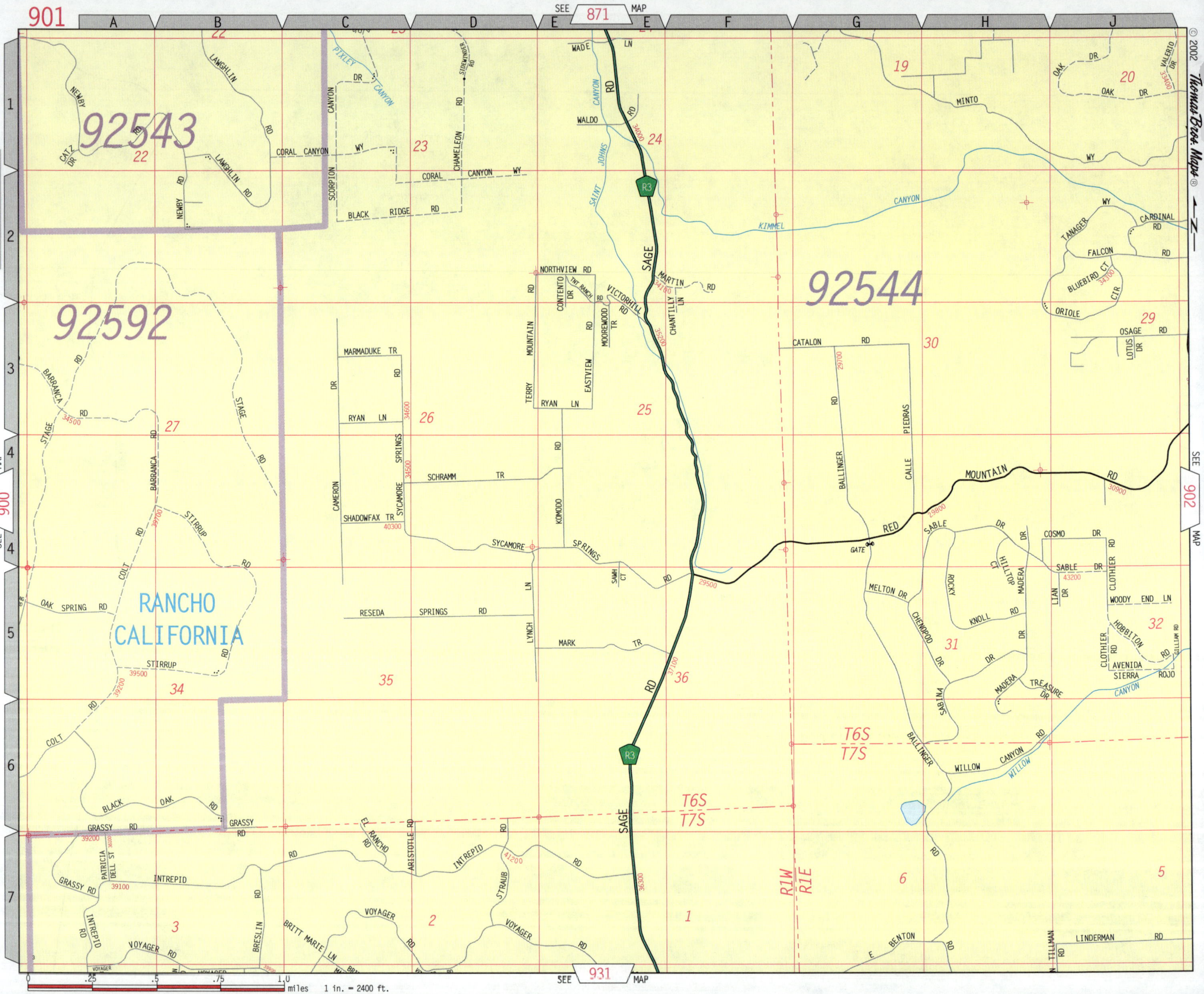
SEE 871 MAP
SEE 931 MAP
SEE 900 MAP
SEE 902 MAP
RIVERSIDE CO.
A
B
C
D
E
F
G
H
J
1
2
3
4
5
6
7
92543
92592
92544
RANCHO CALIFORNIA
NEWBY
LAWGHLIN
CATZ DR
CORAL CANYON WY
PIXLEY CANYON
SCORPION CANYON DR
SIDEWINDER RD
CHAMELEON RD
BLACK RIDGE RD
WADE LN
WALDO RD
SAINT JOHNS CANYON
SAGE RD
R3
KIMMEL CANYON
MINTO WY
OAK DR
VALERIO DR
TANAGER WY
CARDINAL RD
FALCON RD
BLUEBIRD CT
ORIOLE CIR
OSAGE RD
LOTUS DR
NORTHVIEW RD
CONTENTO DR
TNT RANCH RD
VICTORHILL RD
MARTIN RD
CHANTILLY LN
MOOREWOOD TR
TERRY MOUNTAIN RD
EASTVIEW RD
RYAN LN
MARMADUKE TR
CAMERON DR
SYCAMORE SPRINGS
SCHRAMM TR
SHADOWFAX TR
KOMODO RD
SYCAMORE SPRINGS RD
SAWH CT
CATALON RD
BALLINGER RD
CALLE PIEDRAS
RED MOUNTAIN RD
GATE
SABLE DR
COSMO DR
CLOTHIER RD
HILLTOP CT
MADERA DR
ROCKY KNOLL RD
LIAN DR
WOODY END LN
MELTON DR
CHENOPOD DR
HOBBITON RD
GILLIAM RD
AVENIDA SIERRA ROJO
TREASURE DR
SABINA
WILLOW CANYON RD
BARRANCA RD
STAGE RD
STIRRUP RD
COLT RD
OAK SPRING RD
RESEDA SPRINGS RD
LYNCH LN
MARK TR
BLACK OAK RD
GRASSY RD
EL RANCHO RD
ARISTOTLE RD
INTREPID RD
STRAUB RD
PATRICIA DELL ST
BRESLIN RD
VOYAGER RD
BRITT MARIE LN
BENTON
TILLMAN RD
LINDERMAN RD
T6S
T7S
R1W
R1E
19
20
22
23
24
25
26
27
29
30
31
32
34
35
36
1
2
3
5
6
© 2002 Thomas Bros. Maps®
N
0 .25 .5 .75 1.0 miles 1 in. = 2400 ft.

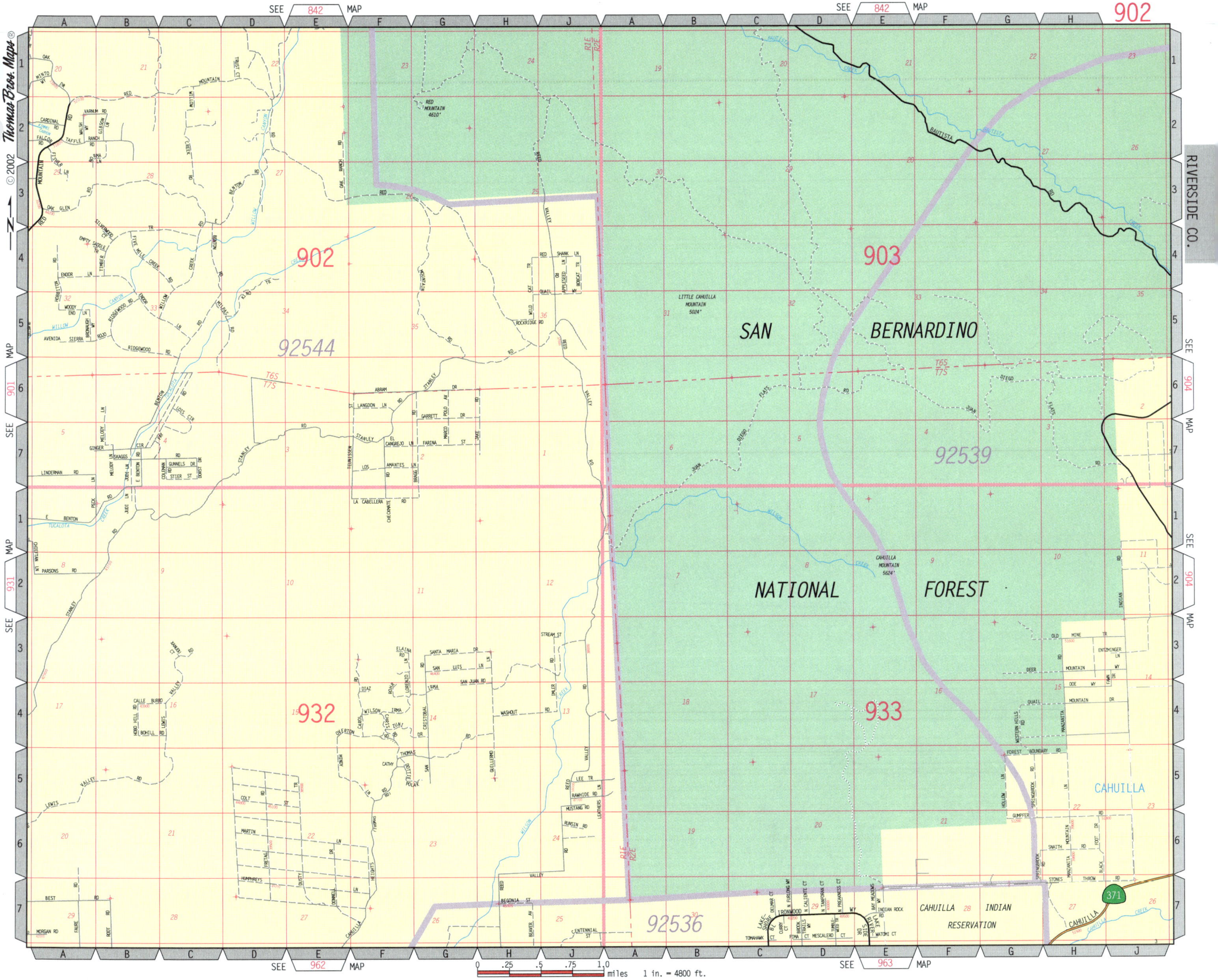
SEE 842 MAP
SEE 842 MAP
SEE 901 MAP
SEE 931 MAP
SEE 904 MAP
SEE 904 MAP
SEE 962 MAP
SEE 963 MAP
RIVERSIDE CO.
902
903
932
933
92544
92539
92536
SAN BERNARDINO NATIONAL FOREST
RED MOUNTAIN 4610'
LITTLE CAHUILLA MOUNTAIN 5024'
CAHUILLA MOUNTAIN 5624'
CAHUILLA
CAHUILLA INDIAN RESERVATION
T6S
T7S
R1E
R2E
371
BAUTISTA
WILSON
0 .25 .5 .75 1.0 miles 1 in. = 4800 ft.
© 2002 Thomas Bros. Maps®

SEE 844 MAP
SEE 844 MAP

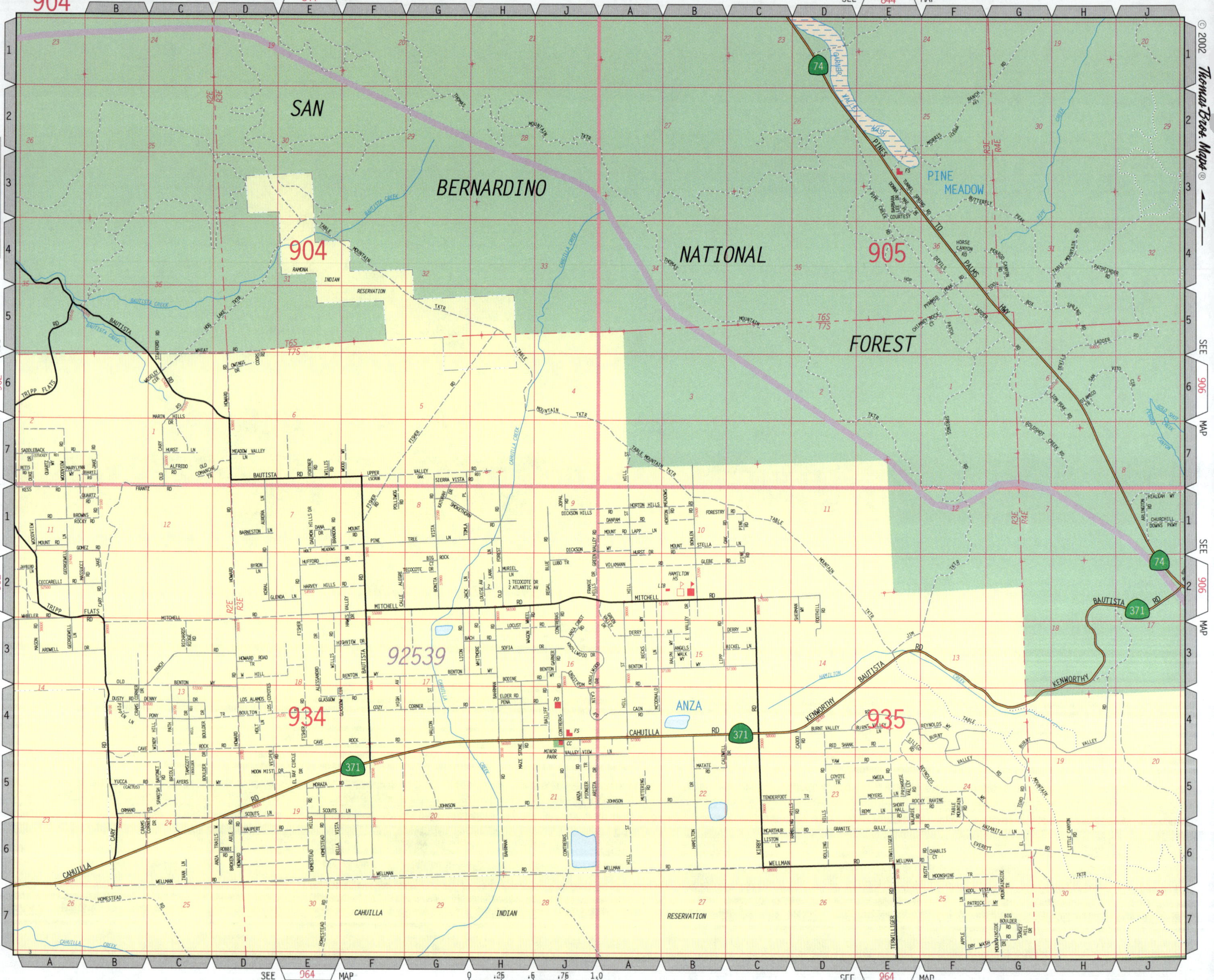

SEE 902 MAP
SEE 902 MAP
SEE 906 MAP
SEE 906 MAP
SEE 964 MAP
SEE 964 MAP

SEE 389 MAP
SEE 390 MAP

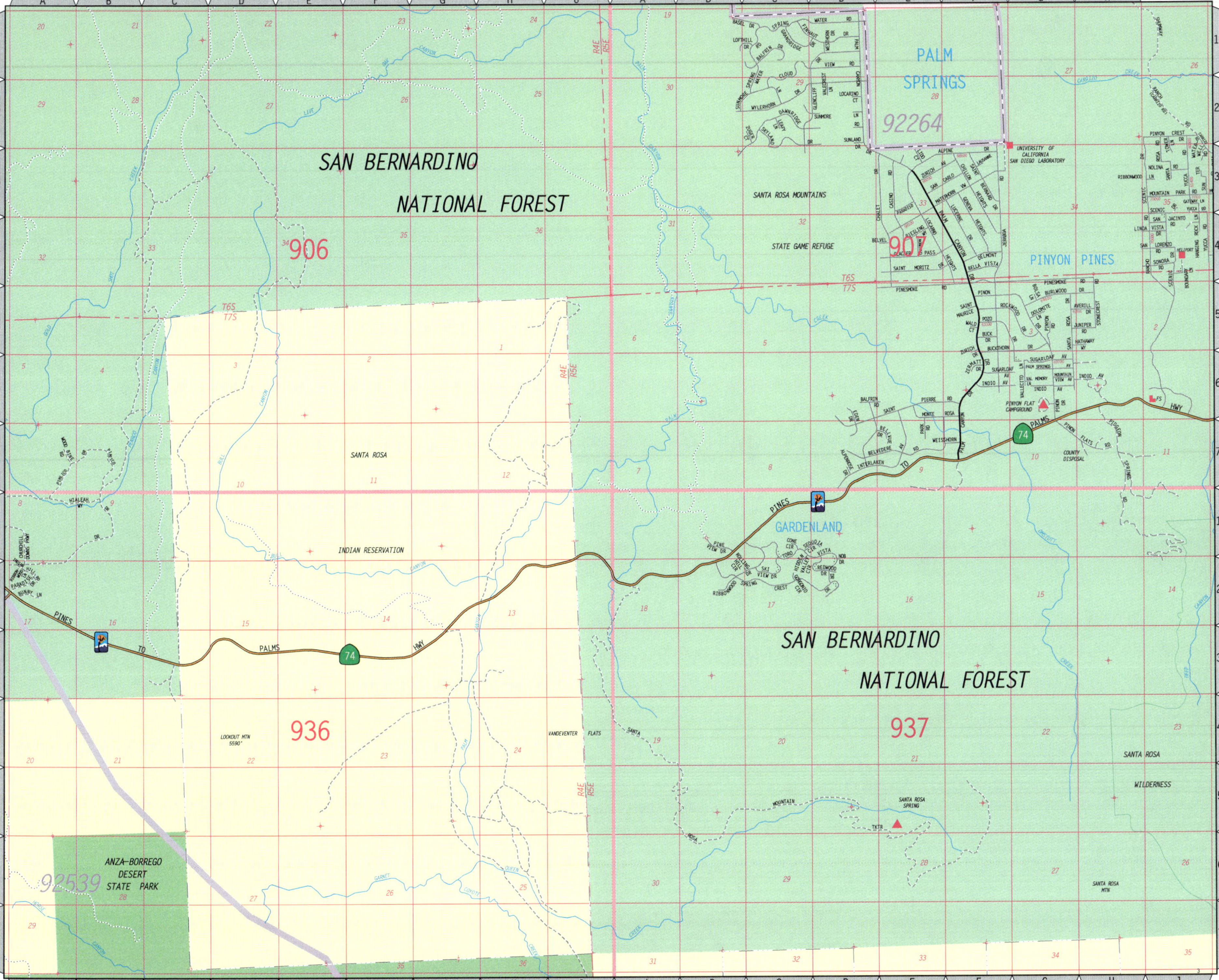

SEE 904 MAP
SEE 908 MAP
SEE 409 MAP
SEE 410 MAP

0 .25 .5 .75 1.0 miles 1 in. = 4800 ft.

SEE 878 MAP
SEE 879 MAP

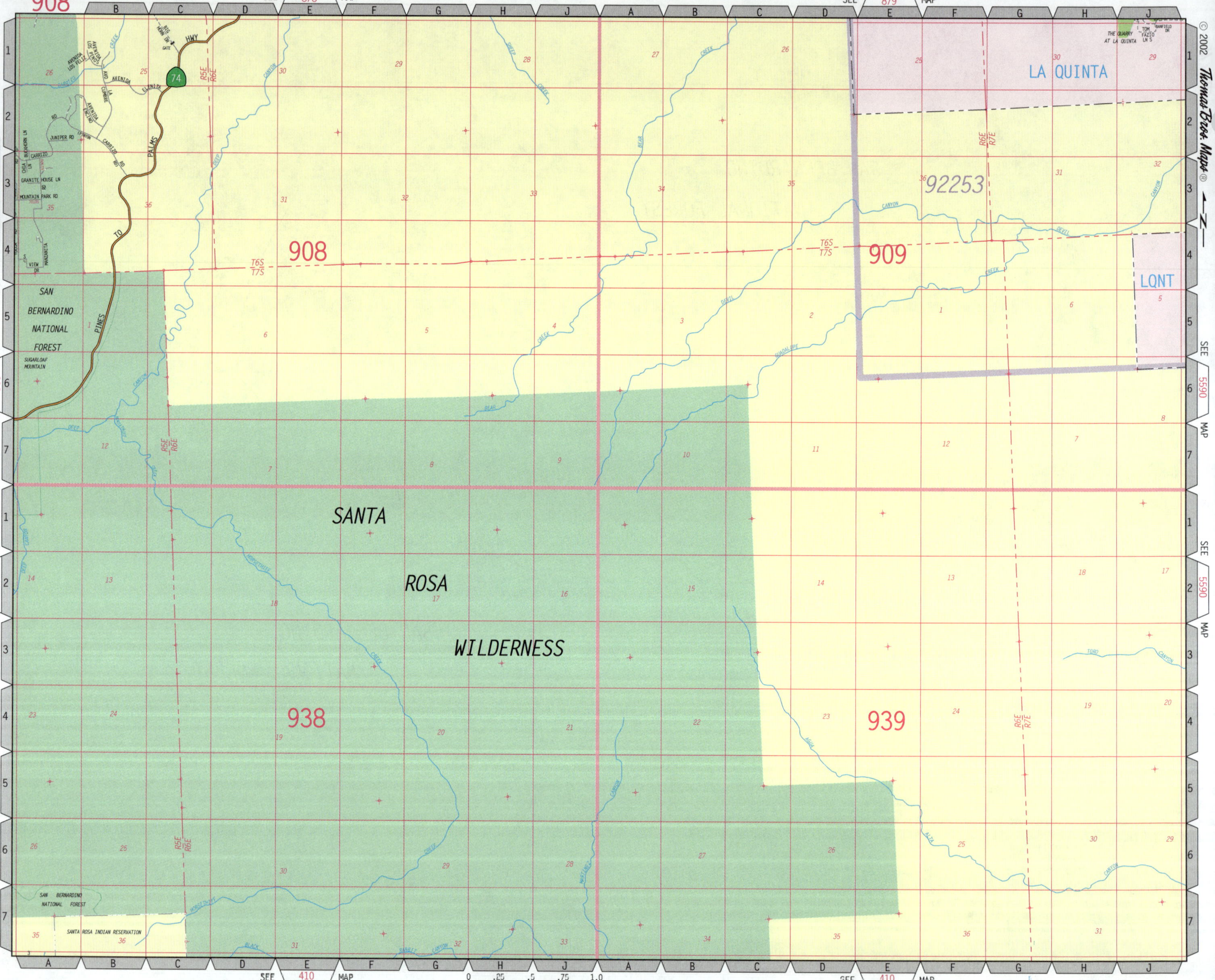

SEE 906 MAP
SEE 906 MAP
SEE 5590 MAP
SEE 5590 MAP
SEE 410 MAP
SEE 410 MAP

0 .25 .5 .75 1.0 miles 1 in. = 4800 ft.

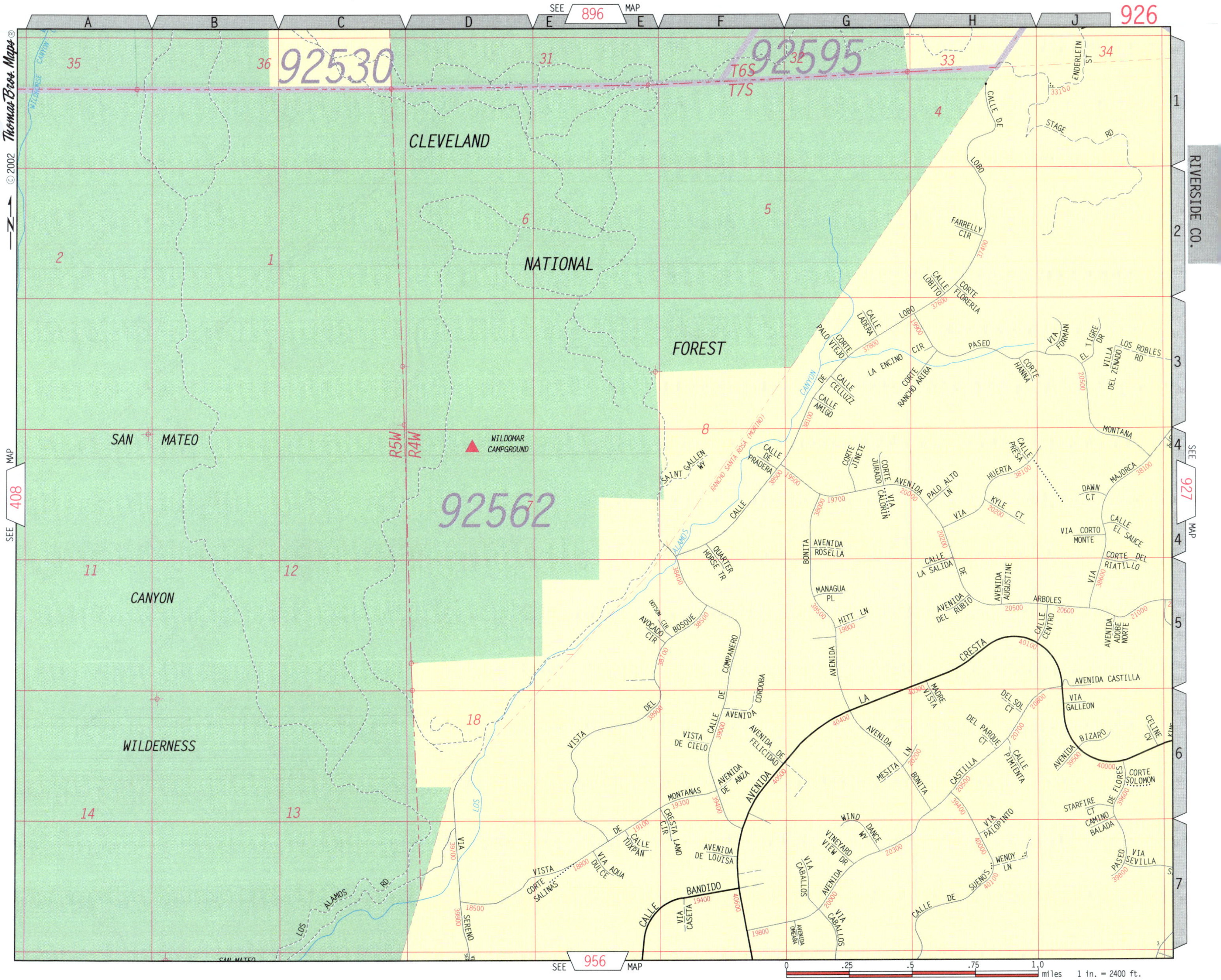
SEE 896 MAP
A
B
C
D
E
F
G
H
J
1
2
3
4
5
6
7
Thomas Bros. Maps®
© 2002
N
92530
92595
92562
T6S
T7S
R5W
R4W
35
36
31
32
33
34
2
1
6
5
4
8
7
11
12
18
14
13
CLEVELAND
NATIONAL
FOREST
SAN MATEO
CANYON
WILDERNESS
WILDOMAR CAMPGROUND
WILDHORSE CANYON
RIVERSIDE CO.
SEE 408 MAP
SEE 927 MAP
SEE 956 MAP
ENDERLEIN ST
33100
STAGE RD
CALLE DE LOBO
FARRELLY CIR
37400
CALLE LOBITO
CORTE FLORERIA
37600
LOBO
CALLE LADERA
37800
19900
CORTE PALO VIEJO
CIR
LA ENCINO
CORTE RANCHO ARIBA
PASEO
CORTE HANNA
VIA FORMAN
EL TIGRE DR
VILLA DEL ZENADO
LOS ROBLES RD
20500
MONTANA
CANYON
DE
CALLE CELLUZZ
CALLE AMIGO
38100
RANCHO SANTA ROSA (MORINO)
CALLE DE PRADERA
SAINT GALLEN WY
CORTE JINETE
CORTE JURADO
VIA CALORIN
AVENIDA
20000
PALO ALTO LN
HUERTA
CALLE PRESA
38100
MAJORCA
38100
DAWN CT
19500
38500
19700
38000
VIA
KYLE CT
20200
CALLE
ALAMOS
QUARTER HORSE TR
BONITA
AVENIDA ROSELLA
20200
CALLE LA SALIDA
DE
VIA CORTO MONTE
CALLE EL SAUCE
CORTE DEL RIATILLO
VIA
38600
38400
MANAGUA PL
AVENIDA AUGUSTINE
ARBOLES
AVENIDA DEL RUBIO
20500
20600
AVENIDA ADOBE NORTE
21000
DOTSON CIR
AVOCADO CIR
BOSQUE
38500
38100
HITT LN
38500
19800
COMPANERO
AVENIDA
CALLE CENTRO
40100
CRESTA
AVENIDA CASTILLA
CORDOBA
DE
AVENIDA
DEL
38900
LA
40300
MADRE VISTA
DEL SOL CT
20800
VIA GALLEON
VISTA
VISTA DE CIELO
CALLE
39000
AVENIDA DE FELICIDAD
40400
AVENIDA
DEL PARQUE CT
20700
CALLE PIMIENTA
BIZARO
CELINE CV
AVENIDA
39500
40000
CORTE SOLOMON
MONTANAS
19300
39400
AVENIDA DE ANZA
AVENIDA
40500
MESITA
LN
20200
BONITA
CASTILLA
20500
39400
STARFIRE CT
DE FLORES
39600
CAMINO BALADA
DE
19100
CALLE TUXPAN
CRESTA CIR
CRESTA LAND
WIND DANCE WY
VIA PALOPINTO
40000
20300
VINEYARD VIEW DR
VIA
39700
VISTA
CORTE SALINAS
18800
VIA AQUA DULCE
AVENIDA DE LOUISA
VIA CABALLOS
AVENIDA
WENDY LN
SUENOS
40100
PASEO
39800
VIA SEVILLA
LOS
LOS ALAMOS RD
18500
39900
SERENO
CALLE
BANDIDO
19400
VIA CASETA
40600
19800
AVENIDA OMEGA
20000
VIA CABALLOS
CALLE DE
SAN MATEO
0 .25 .5 .75 1.0 miles 1 in. = 2400 ft.

SEE 897 MAP

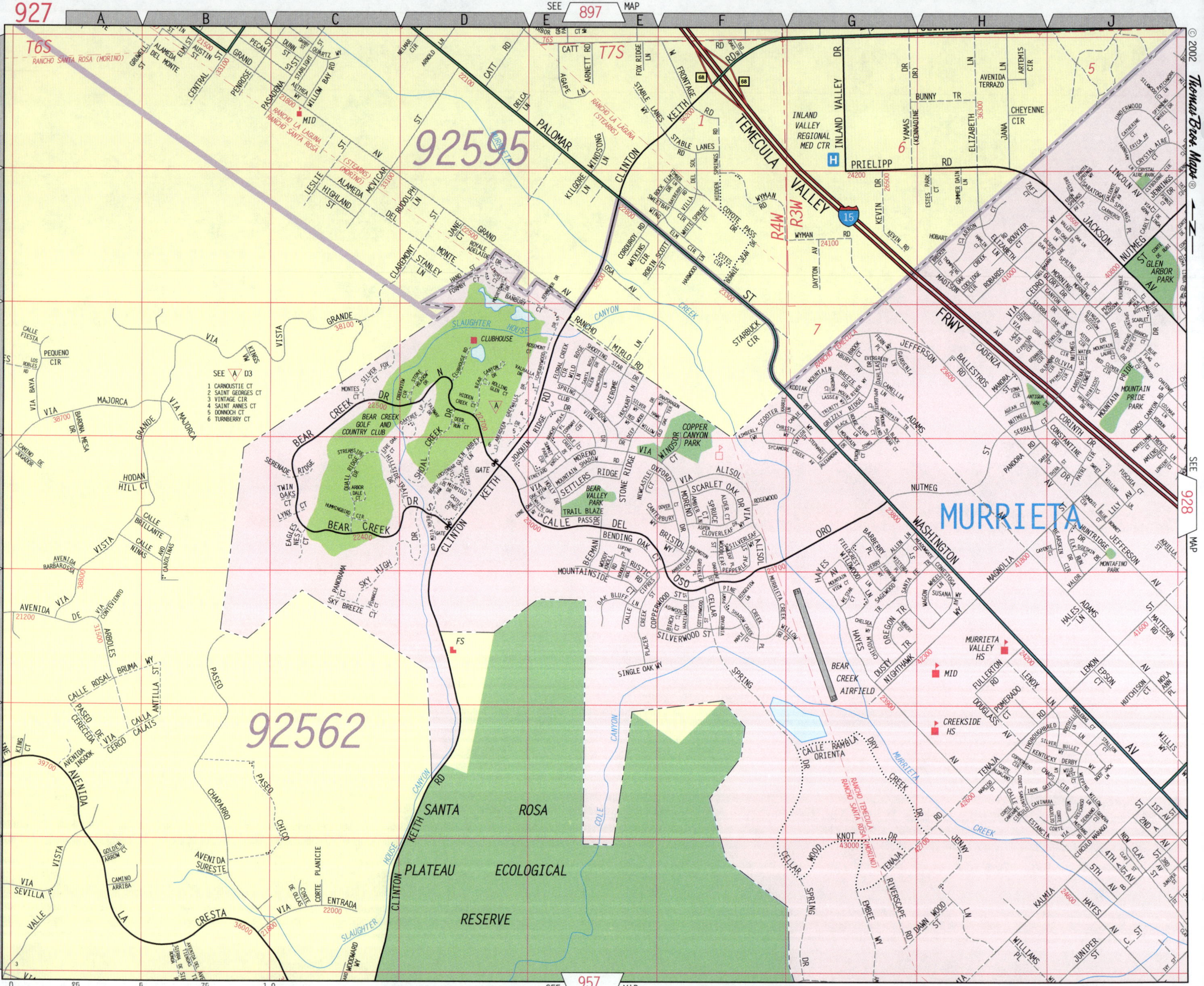

SEE 926 MAP

SEE 928 MAP

SEE 957 MAP

SEE 898 MAP

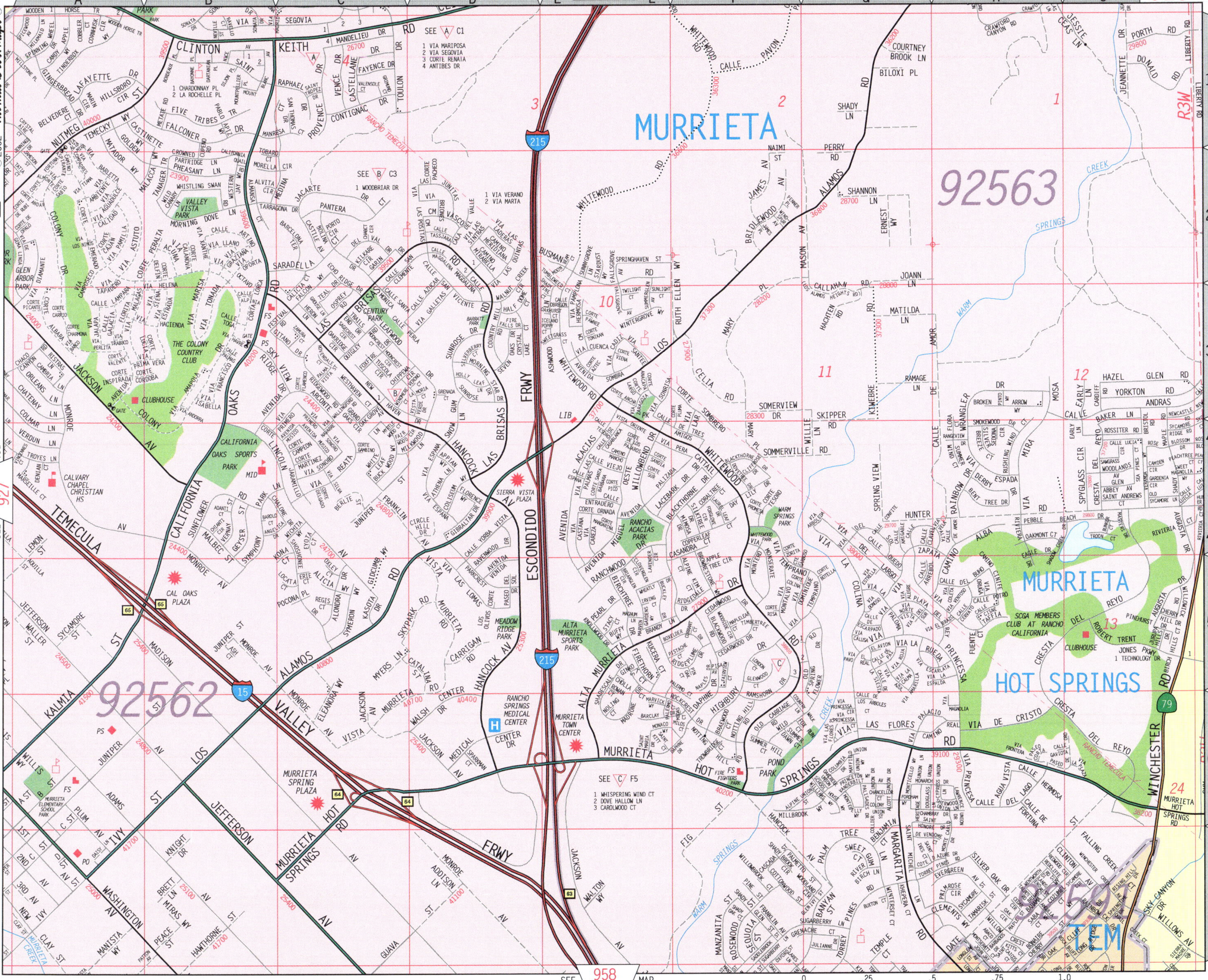

SEE 927 MAP

SEE 929 MAP

SEE 958 MAP

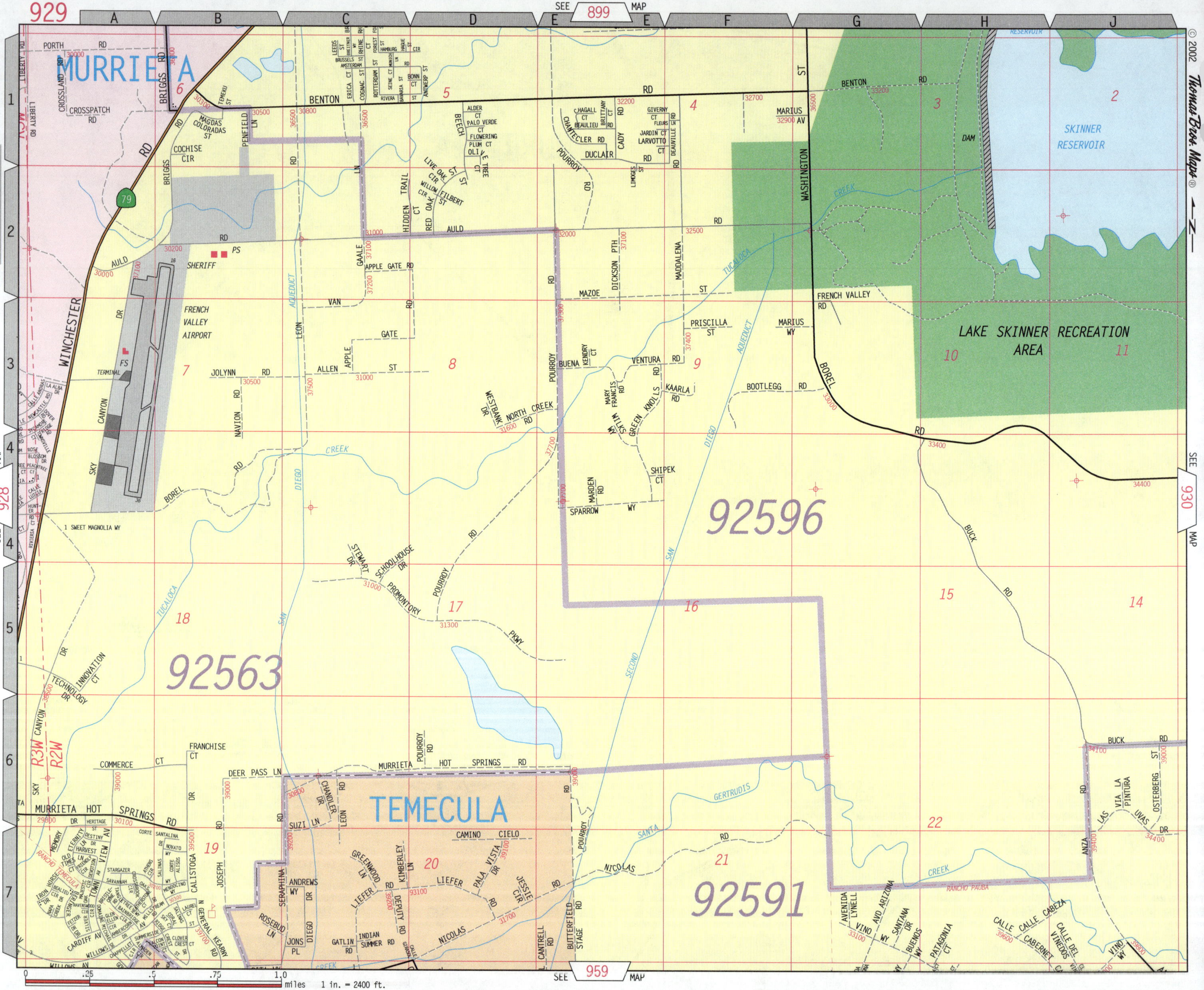

0 .25 .5 .75 1.0 miles 1 in. = 2400 ft.

SEE 900 MAP

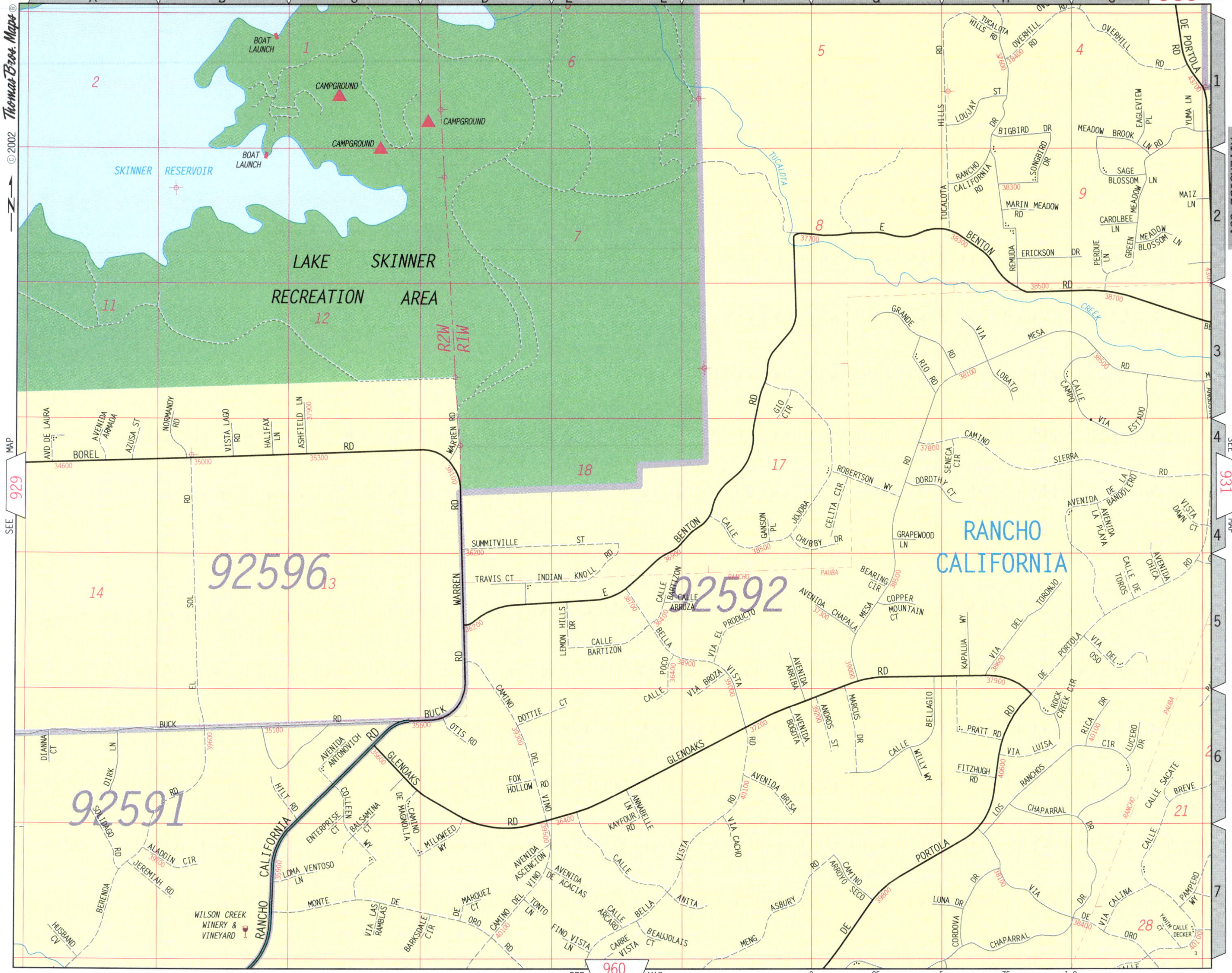

SEE 929 MAP
SEE 931 MAP
SEE 960 MAP

0 .25 .5 .75 1.0 miles 1 in. = 2400 ft.

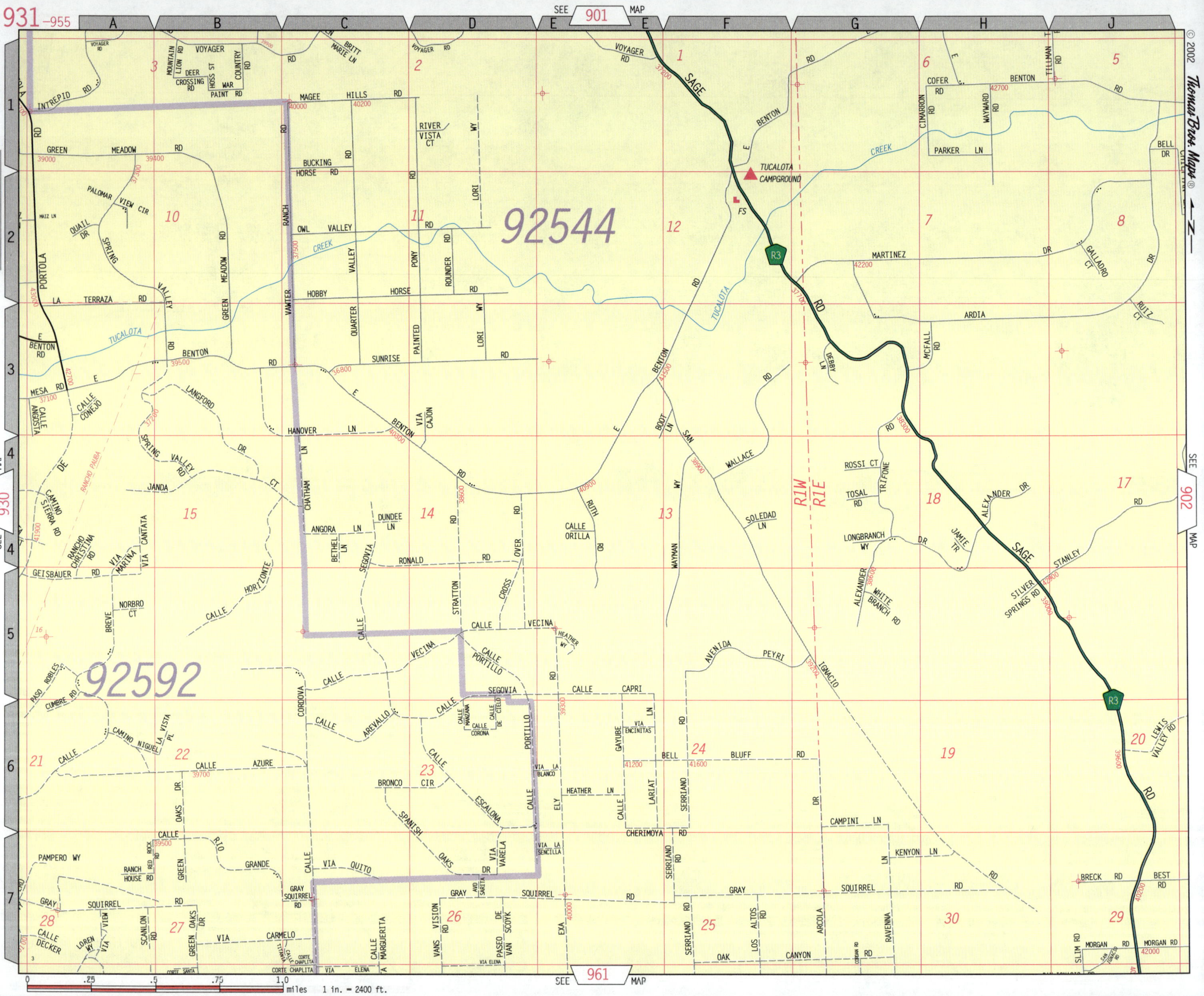
SEE 901 MAP
SEE 930 MAP
SEE 902 MAP
SEE 961 MAP
RIVERSIDE CO.
© 2002 Thomas Bros. Maps ®
92544
92592
R1W R1E
TUCALOTA CAMPGROUND
FS
TUCALOTA CREEK
SAGE RD
R3
BENTON RD
E BENTON RD
VOYAGER RD
INTREPID RD
MAGEE HILLS RD
GREEN MEADOW RD
BUCKING HORSE RD
RIVER VISTA CT
PALOMAR VIEW CIR
QUAIL DR
SPRING VALLEY RD
OWL VALLEY RD
PONY RD
ROUNDER RD
LORI WY
HOBBY HORSE RD
VALLEY QUARTER
PAINTED RD
SUNRISE RD
VANTER RD
RANCH
PORTOLA RD
LA TERRAZA RD
MESA RD
CALLE ANGOSTA
CALLE CONEJO
LANGFORD DR
HANOVER LN
VIA CAJON
JANDA
CHATHAM LN
ANGORA LN
BETHEL LN
DUNDEE LN
RONALD RD
SEGOVIA
STRATTON RD
CROSS
OVER RD
CALLE ORILLA
RUTH RD
BOOT LN
SAN
WALLACE RD
SOLEDAD LN
WAYMAN WY
IGNACIO
AVENIDA PEYRI
MARTINEZ DR
GALLADRO CT
ARDIA
RUIZ CT
MCFALL RD
DEBBY LN
COFER RD
CIMARRON RD
WAYWARD RD
PARKER LN
TILLMAN
BELL DR
ROSSI CT
TRIFONE
TOSAL RD
LONGBRANCH WY
DR
JAMIE TR
ALEXANDER DR
WHITE BRANCH RD
SILVER SPRINGS RD
STANLEY RD
LEWIS VALLEY RD
CAMINO SIERRA RD
RANCHO CHRISTINA RD
VIA MARTINA
VIA CANTATA
GEISBAUER RD
HORIZONTE
CALLE
NORBRO CT
BREVE
PASO ROBLES
CUMBRE RD
CAMINO NIGUEL
LA VISTA PL
CALLE AZURE
CALLE VECINA
CALLE PORTILLO
SEGOVIA
CALLE AREVALLO
CALLE ESCALONA
BRONCO CIR
SPANISH OAKS DR
VIA VARELA
PORTILLO
CALLE CAPRI
GAYUBE LN
VIA ENCINITAS
BELL BLUFF RD
HEATHER LN
ELY
LARIAT
SERRIANO RD
CHERIMOYA RD
CAMPINI LN
KENYON LN
PAMPERO WY
RANCH HOUSE RD
RED ROCK RD
CALLE RIO GRANDE
GRAY SQUIRREL RD
VIA QUITO
CALLE MARGUERITA
VANS VISION RD
PASEO DE VAN SCOYK
EXA
LOS ALTOS RD
ARCOLA
RAVENNA
OAK CANYON RD
BRECK RD
BEST RD
MORGAN RD
SLIM RD
CALLE DECKER
LOREN WY
VIA VIEW
SCANLON RD
GREEN OAKS DR
VIA CARMELO
CORTE CHAPLITA
VIA ELENA
miles 1 in. = 2400 ft.

SEE 926 MAP

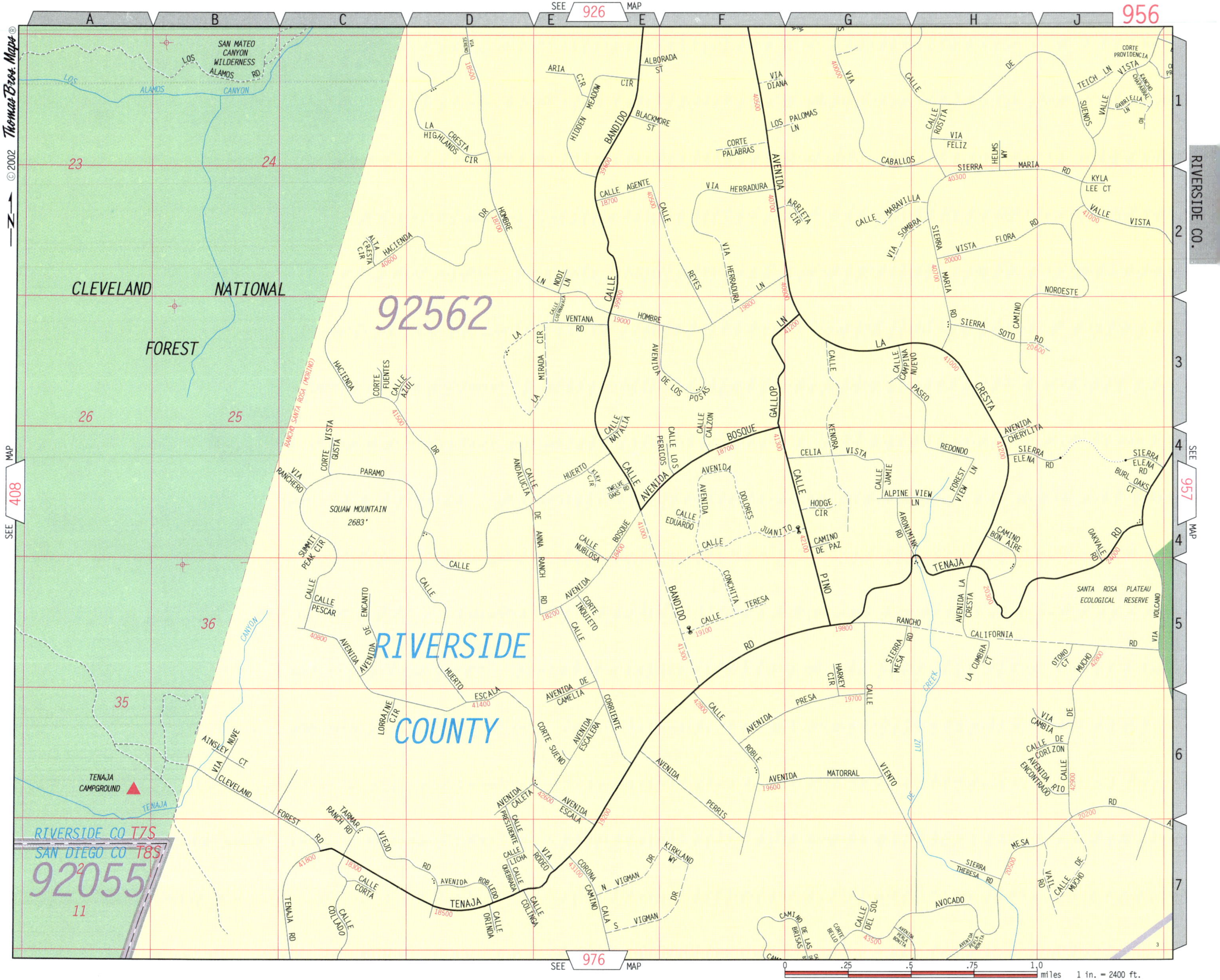

SEE 976 MAP

0 .25 .5 .75 1.0 miles 1 in. = 2400 ft.

SEE 927 MAP

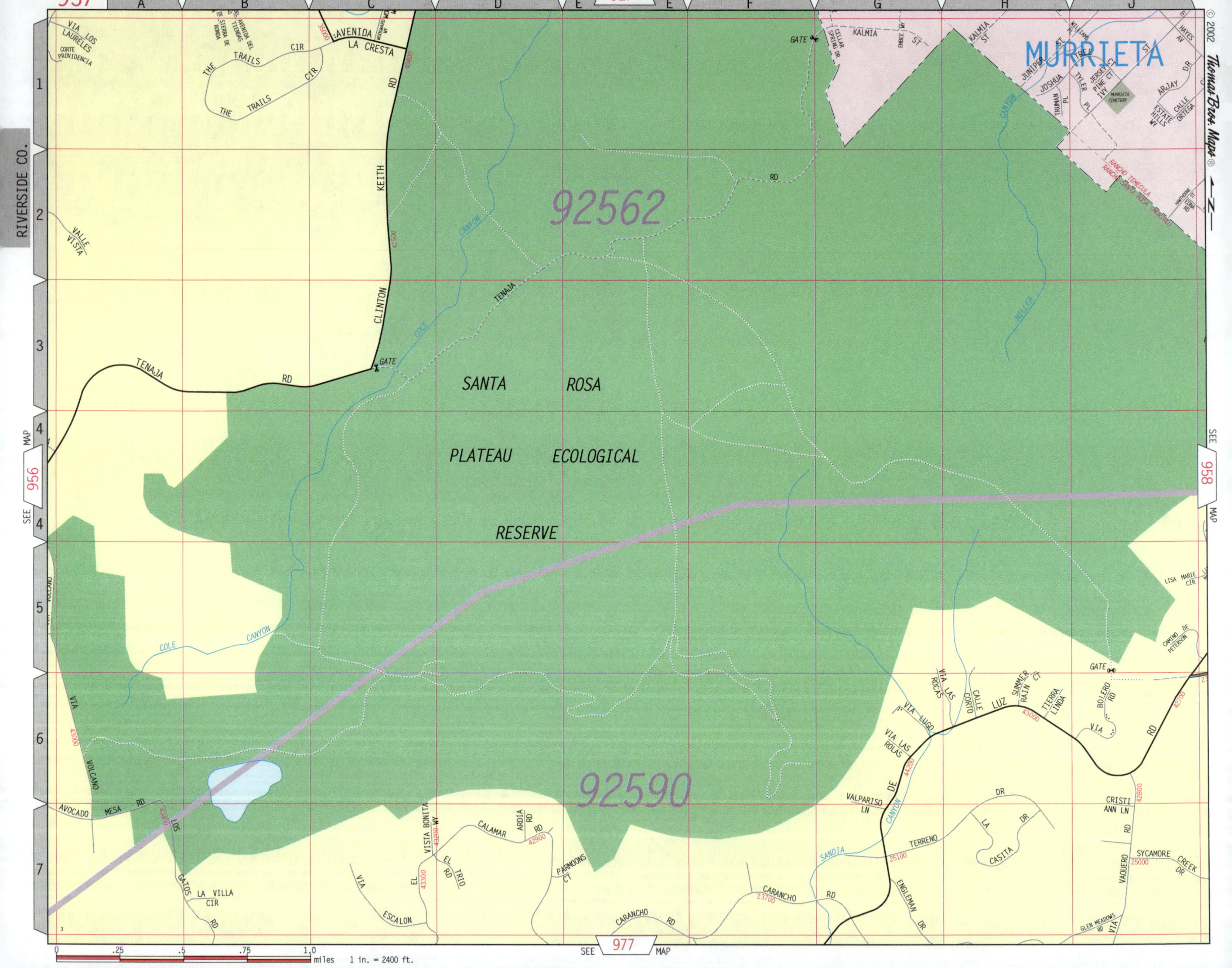

SEE 977 MAP

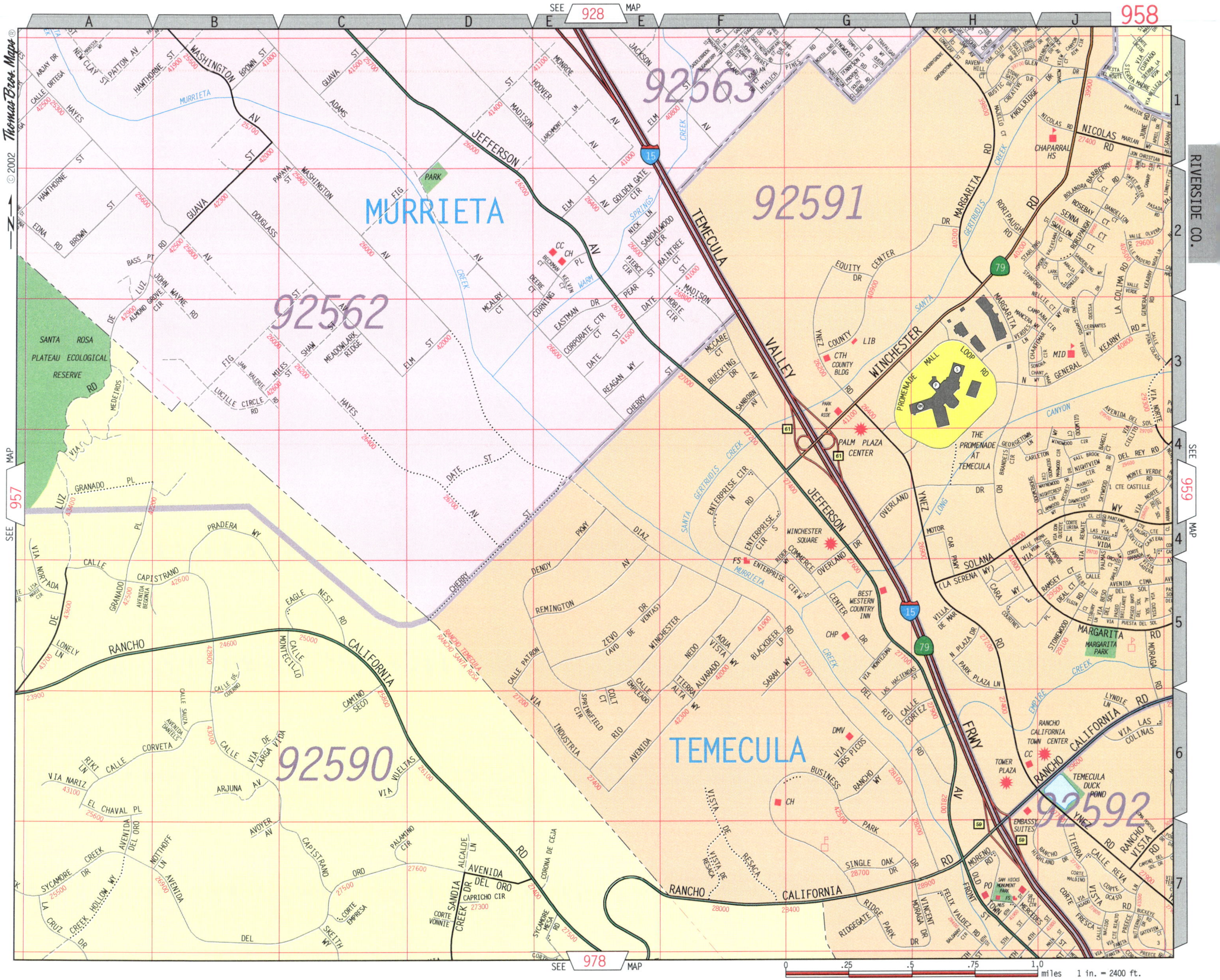
SEE 928 MAP
A
B
C
D
E
F
G
H
J
MURRIETA
TEMECULA
92563
92591
92562
92590
92592
RIVERSIDE CO.
SANTA ROSA PLATEAU ECOLOGICAL RESERVE
CHAPARRAL HS
THE PROMENADE AT TEMECULA
PROMENADE MALL LOOP RD
PALM PLAZA CENTER
WINCHESTER SQUARE
BEST WESTERN COUNTRY INN
RANCHO CALIFORNIA TOWN CENTER
TOWER PLAZA
TEMECULA DUCK POND
EMBASSY SUITES
MARGARITA PARK
SAM HICKS MONUMENT PARK
TEMECULA VALLEY FRWY
JEFFERSON AV
WINCHESTER RD
RANCHO CALIFORNIA RD
MARGARITA RD
YNEZ RD
WASHINGTON AV
CLINTON KEITH RD
SEE 957 MAP
SEE 959 MAP
SEE 978 MAP
miles 1 in. = 2400 ft.
Thomas Bros. Maps
© 2002

SEE 929 MAP

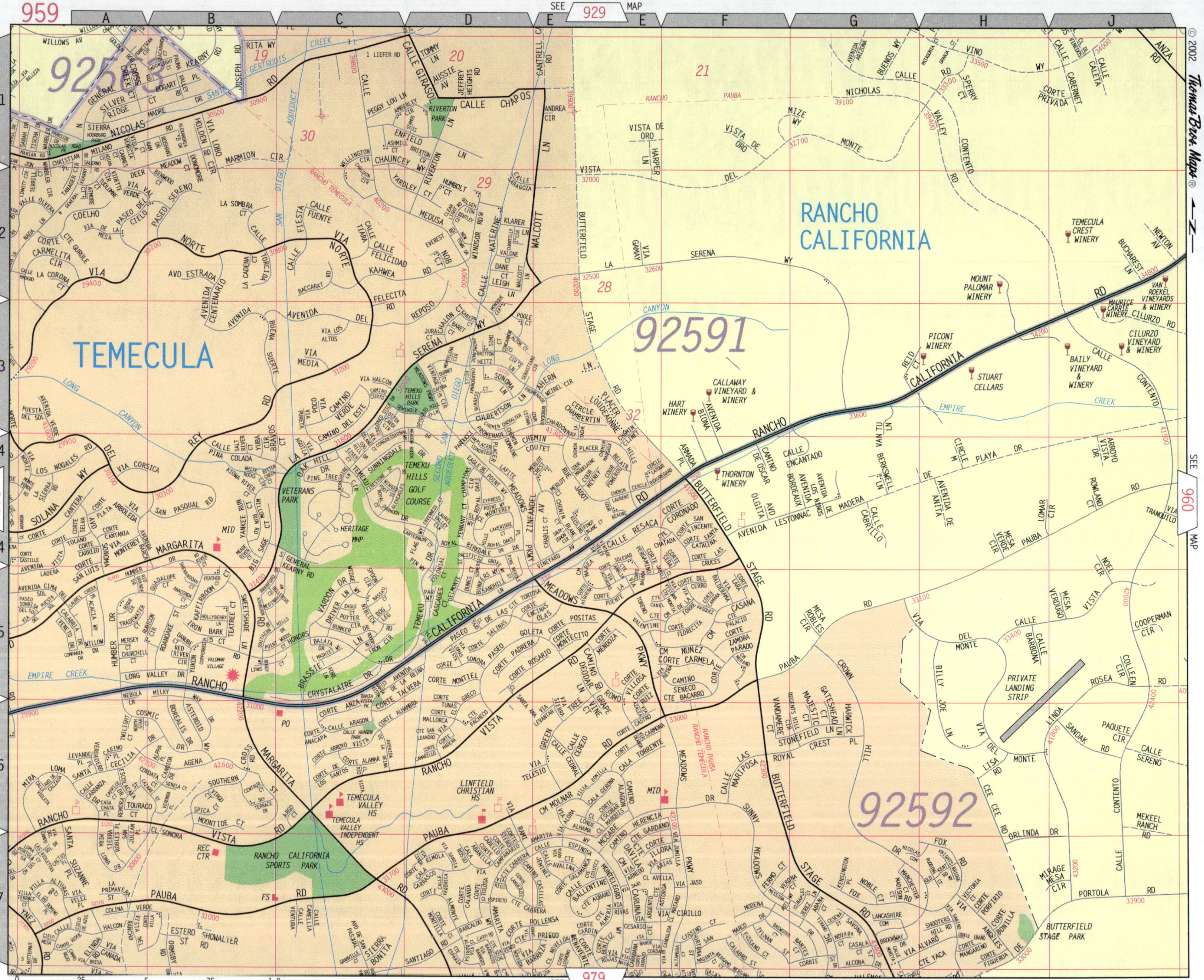

SEE 958 MAP

SEE 960 MAP

0 .25 .5 .75 1.0 miles 1 in. = 2400 ft.

SEE 979 MAP

SEE 930 MAP

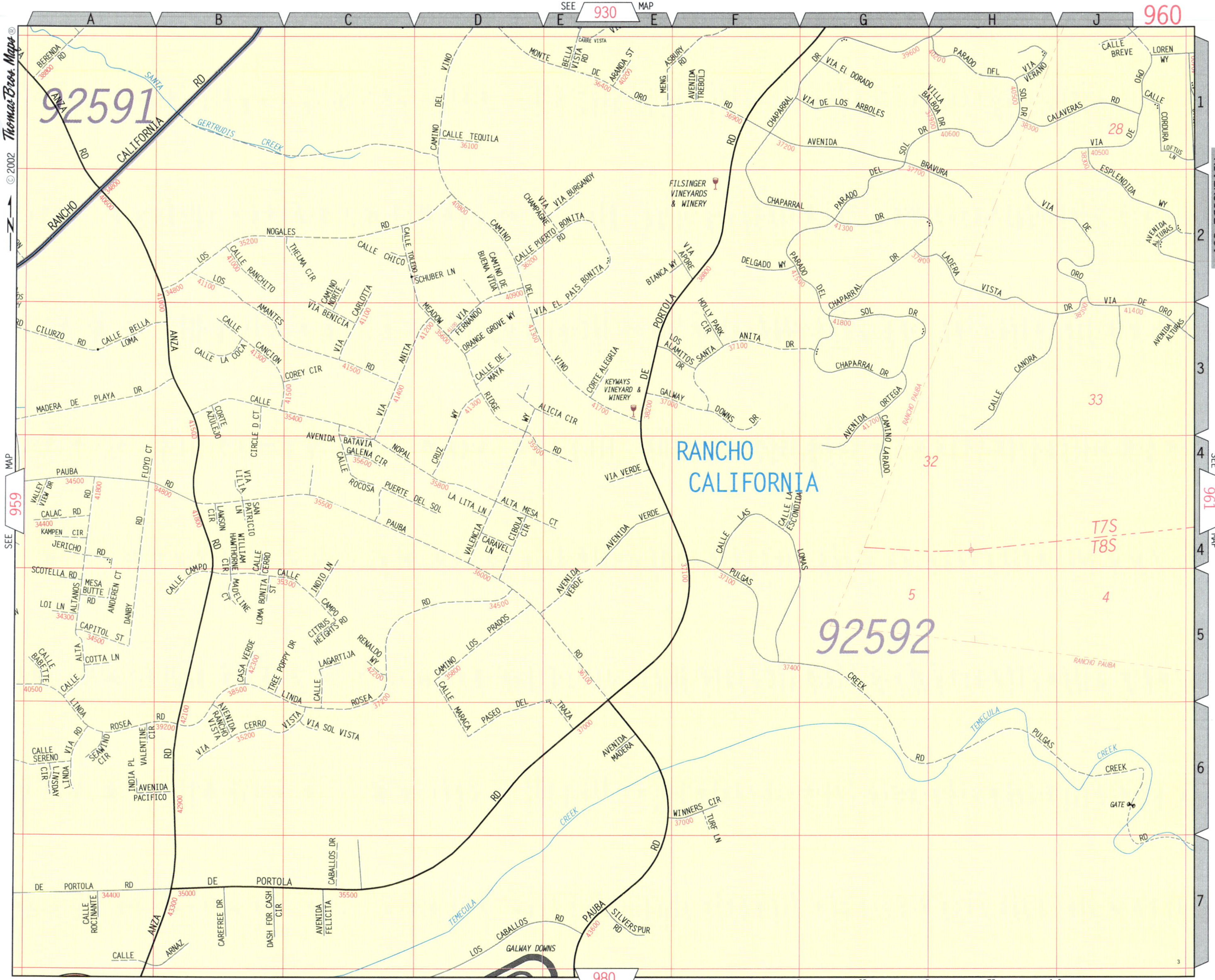

SEE 980 MAP

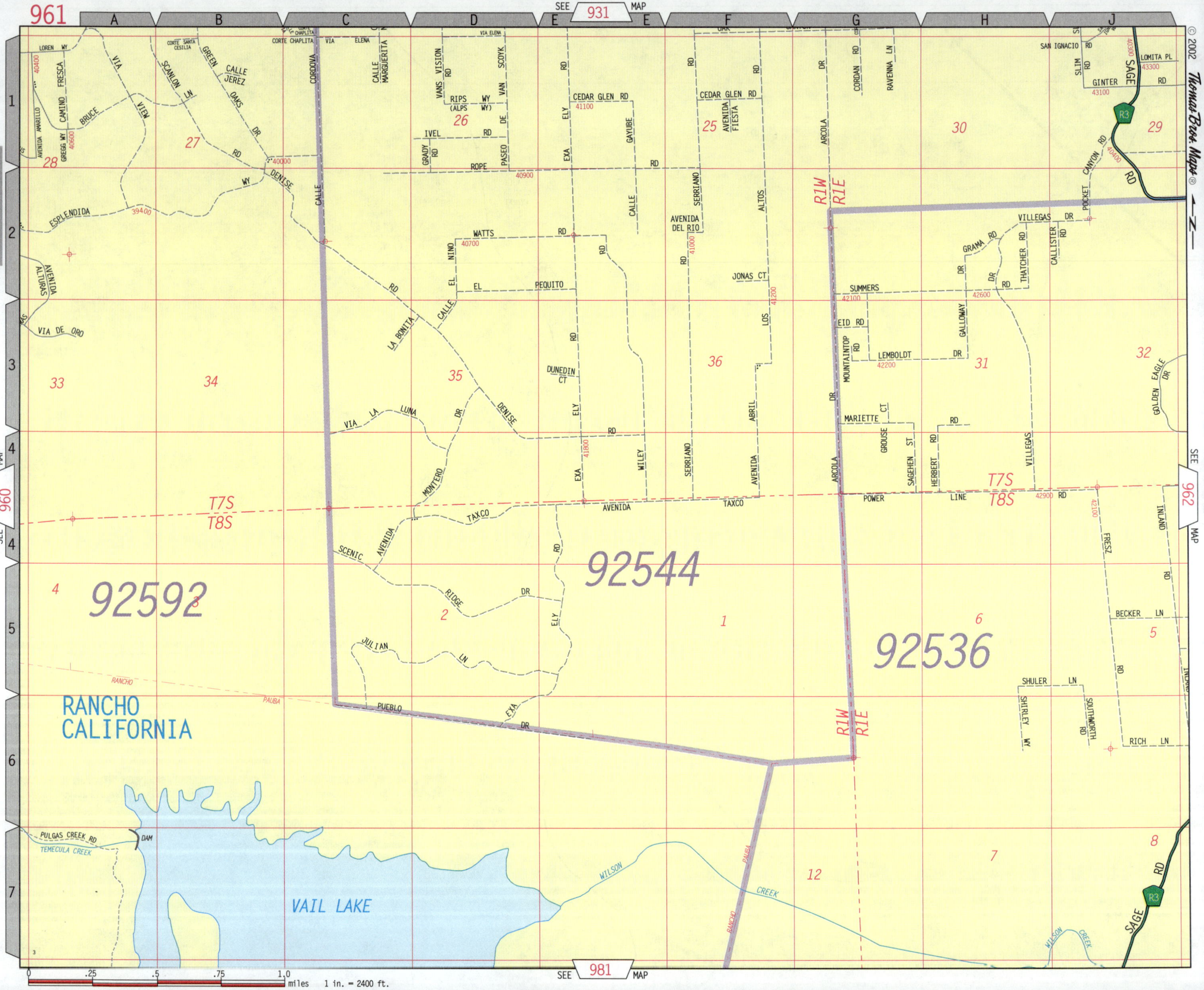
SEE 931 MAP
A
B
C
D
E
F
G
H
J
1
2
3
4
5
6
7
RIVERSIDE CO.
© 2002 Thomas Bros. Maps ®
SEE 960 MAP
SEE 962 MAP
SEE 981 MAP
LOREN WY
CAMINO FRESCA
AVENIDA AMARILLO
GREGG WY
BRUCE
VIA VIEW
SCANLON LN
GREEN OAKS DR
CALLE JEREZ
CORTE SANTA CESILIA
CORTE CHAPLITA
CORDOVA
VIA ELENA
CALLE MARGUERITA
VANS VISION RD
VIA ELENA
SCOYK
VAN DE PASEO
RIPS WY
(ALPS WY)
IVEL RD
GRADY RD
ROPE RD
40900
40000
40400
40600
DENISE WY
ESPLENDIDA
39400
CALLE
EXA
ELY
CEDAR GLEN RD
41100
GAYUBE
CALLE
SERRIANO
AVENIDA DEL RIO
CEDAR GLEN RD
AVENIDA FIESTA
ALTOS
CORDAN RD
RAVENNA LN
ARCOLA DR
SAN IGNACIO RD
SLIM RD
SAGE
LOMITA PL
43300
GINTER RD
43100
40300
R3
POCKET CANYON RD
40400
R1W R1E
VILLEGAS DR
CALLISTER RD
GRAMA RD
THATCHER RD
AVENIDA ALTURAS
WATTS RD
40700
NINO EL
EL PEQUITO
CALLE
LA BONITA
RD
JONAS CT
41000
41200
LOS ABRIL
SUMMERS
42100
42600
DR
GALLOWAY
EID RD
MOUNTAINTOP RD
LEMBOLDT DR
42200
VIA DE ORO
DUNEDIN CT
VIA LA LUNA
DR
DENISE
GOLDEN EAGLE DR
MARIETTE CT
GROUSE
SAGEHEN ST
HERBERT RD
VILLEGAS
MONTERO
41800
WILEY
SERRIANO
AVENIDA
ARCOLA
T7S
T8S
POWER LINE RD
42900
TAXCO
AVENIDA TAXCO
42100
FRESZ
INLAND RD
SCENIC AVENIDA
RIDGE DR
ELY
92544
92592
92536
BECKER LN
JULIAN LN
SHULER LN
SHIRLEY WY
SOUTHWORTH RD
RICH LN
RANCHO PAUBA
PUEBLO EXA DR
RANCHO CALIFORNIA
PULGAS CREEK RD
TEMECULA CREEK
DAM
VAIL LAKE
WILSON CREEK
PAUBA
RANCHO
SAGE RD
R3
WILSON CREEK
1
2
3
4
5
6
7
8
12
25
26
27
28
29
30
31
32
33
34
35
36
0
.25
.5
.75
1.0
miles 1 in. = 2400 ft.

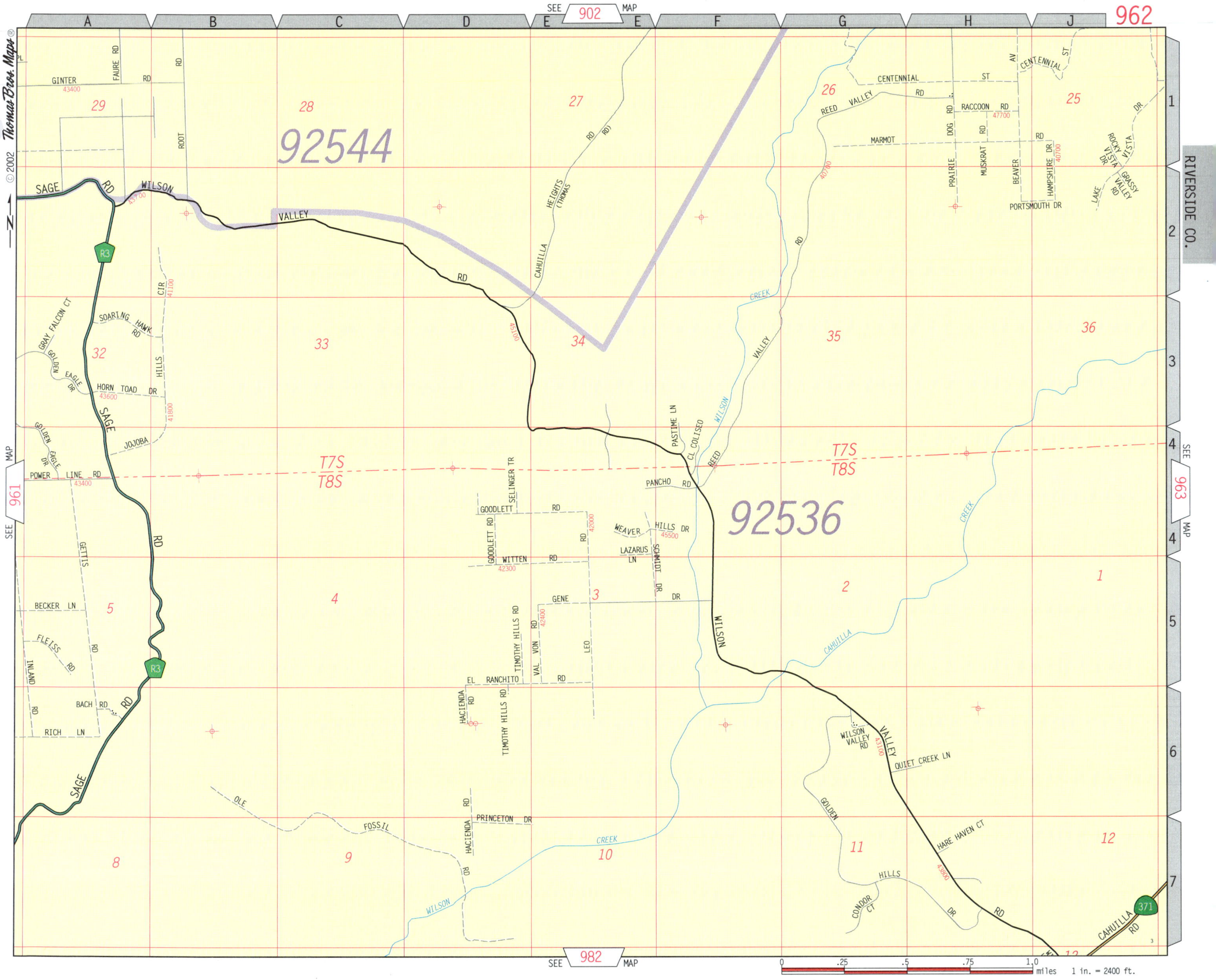
SEE 902 MAP
A
B
C
D
E
F
G
H
J
1
2
3
4
5
6
7
92544
92536
RIVERSIDE CO.
SEE 961 MAP
SEE 963 MAP
SEE 982 MAP
T7S
T8S
SAGE RD
WILSON VALLEY RD
R3
CAHUILLA RD
371
GINTER RD
FAURE RD
ROOT RD
REED VALLEY RD
CENTENNIAL ST
RACCOON RD
MARMOT RD
PRAIRIE DOG RD
MUSKRAT RD
BEAVER RD
HAMPSHIRE DR
PORTSMOUTH DR
ROCKY VISTA DR
GRASSY VALLEY RD
LAKE
CAHUILLA HEIGHTS (THOMAS RD)
WILSON CREEK
CAHUILLA CREEK
SOARING HAWK RD
GRAY FALCON CT
GOLDEN EAGLE DR
HORN TOAD DR
HILLS CIR
JOJOBA
POWER LINE RD
GETTIS RD
BECKER LN
FLEISS RD
INLAND RD
BACH RD
RICH LN
SELINGER TR
GOODLETT RD
WITTEN RD
WEAVER HILLS DR
LAZARUS LN
SCHMIDT DR
PASTIME LN
COLISEO CL
PANCHO RD
GENE DR
TIMOTHY HILLS RD
VAL VON RD
LEO
EL RANCHITO RD
HACIENDA RD
PRINCETON DR
OLE
FOSSIL
QUIET CREEK LN
HARE HAVEN CT
GOLDEN HILLS DR
CONDOR CT
miles
1 in. = 2400 ft.
© 2002 Thomas Bros. Maps®

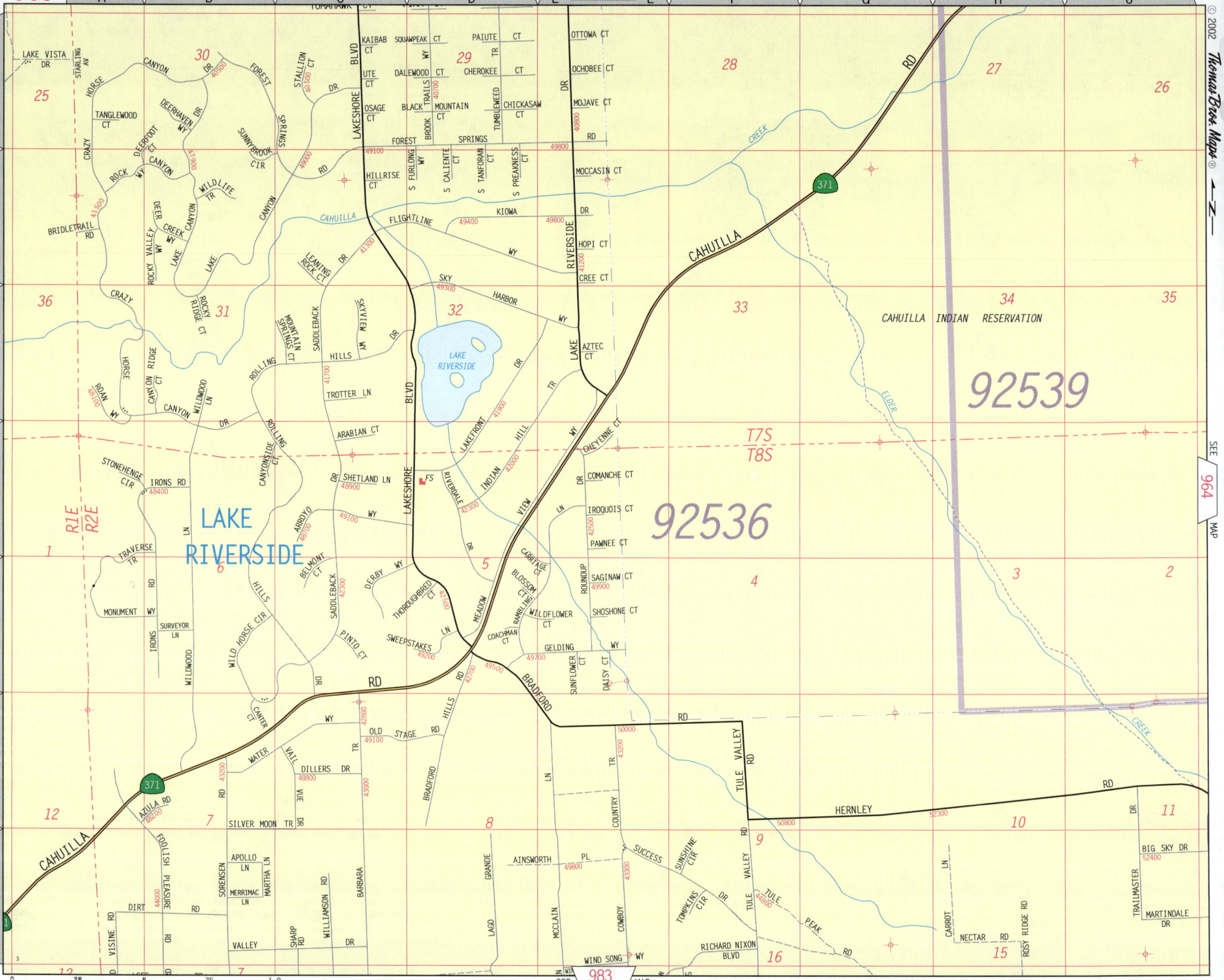
SEE 902 MAP
SEE 962 MAP
SEE 964 MAP
SEE 983 MAP
RIVERSIDE CO.
LAKE RIVERSIDE
92536
92539
CAHUILLA INDIAN RESERVATION
T7S
T8S
R1E
R2E
LAKE RIVERSIDE
CAHUILLA RD
LAKESHORE BLVD
RIVERSIDE DR
BRADFORD RD
TULE VALLEY RD
HERNLEY RD
CAHUILLA CREEK
ELDER CREEK
FS
371
miles 1 in. = 2400 ft.
© 2002 Thomas Bros. Maps®

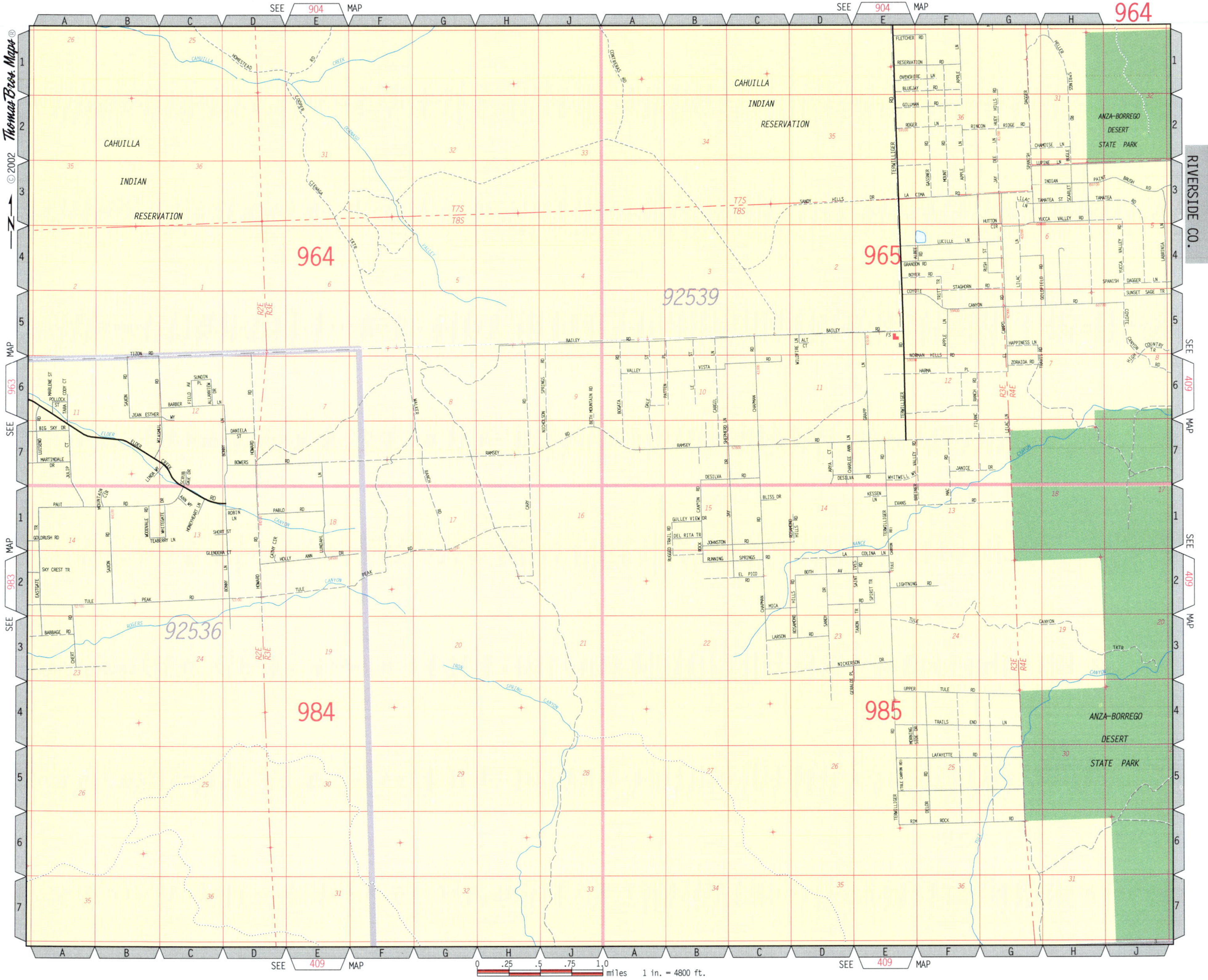
SEE 904 MAP
CAHUILLA INDIAN RESERVATION
964
965
984
985
92539
92536
T7S
T8S
R2E R3E
R3E R4E
ANZA-BORREGO DESERT STATE PARK
RIVERSIDE CO.
SEE 963 MAP
SEE 983 MAP
SEE 409 MAP
CAHUILLA CREEK
HOMESTEAD RD
COOPER
CIENAGA
TERWILLIGER RD
SANDY HILLS DR
LA CIMA RD
BAILEY RD
RAMSEY RD
TULE PEAK RD
TULE CANYON
ELDER CREEK
BIG SKY DR
MARTINDALE DR
GOLDRUSH RD
SKY CREST TR
BABBAGE RD
TIZON RD
JEAN ESTHER WY
BARBER
DANIELA ST
BOWERS
PABLO RD
ROBIN LN
SHORT ST
TEABERRY LN
GLENDORA CT
HOLLY
LUNDAHL
WALKER
RANCH RD
NICHOLSON
SPRINGS
BETH MOUNTAIN RD
BOGATA
DALE
PATTEN
VISTA
VALLEY
CARGIL
SHEPHERD LN
CHAPMAN
WILDFIRE LN
GRAPP
DESILVA RD
BLISS DR
GULLEY VIEW DR
DEL RITA TR
JOHNSTON RD
RUNNING SPRINGS RD
EL PICO RD
COLINA LN
LIGHTNING RD
MICA
LARSON RD
NICKERSON DR
UPPER TULE RD
TRAILS END LN
LAFAYETTE RD
RIM ROCK RD
IRON SPRING CANYON
ROGERS CANYON
NANCE CANYON
WHITWELL
KESSEN LN
EVANS
JANICE DR
FLETCHER RD
RESERVATION RD
BLUEJAY RD
GILLMAN RD
ROGER LN
RINCON RIDGE RD
CHAMOISE LN
LUPINE LN
INDIAN
PAINT BRUSH RD
TAMATEA ST
YUCCA VALLEY RD
LUCILLE LN
GRANDON RD
BOYER RD
STAGHORN RD
CANYON RD
COYOTE CANYON
HAPPINESS LN
ZORAIDA RD
NORMAN HILLS RD
HARMA PL
SUNSET SAGE TR
SPANISH DAGGER LN
COUNTRY TR
SEE 409 MAP
0 .25 .5 .75 1.0 miles 1 in. = 4800 ft.

SEE 956 MAP

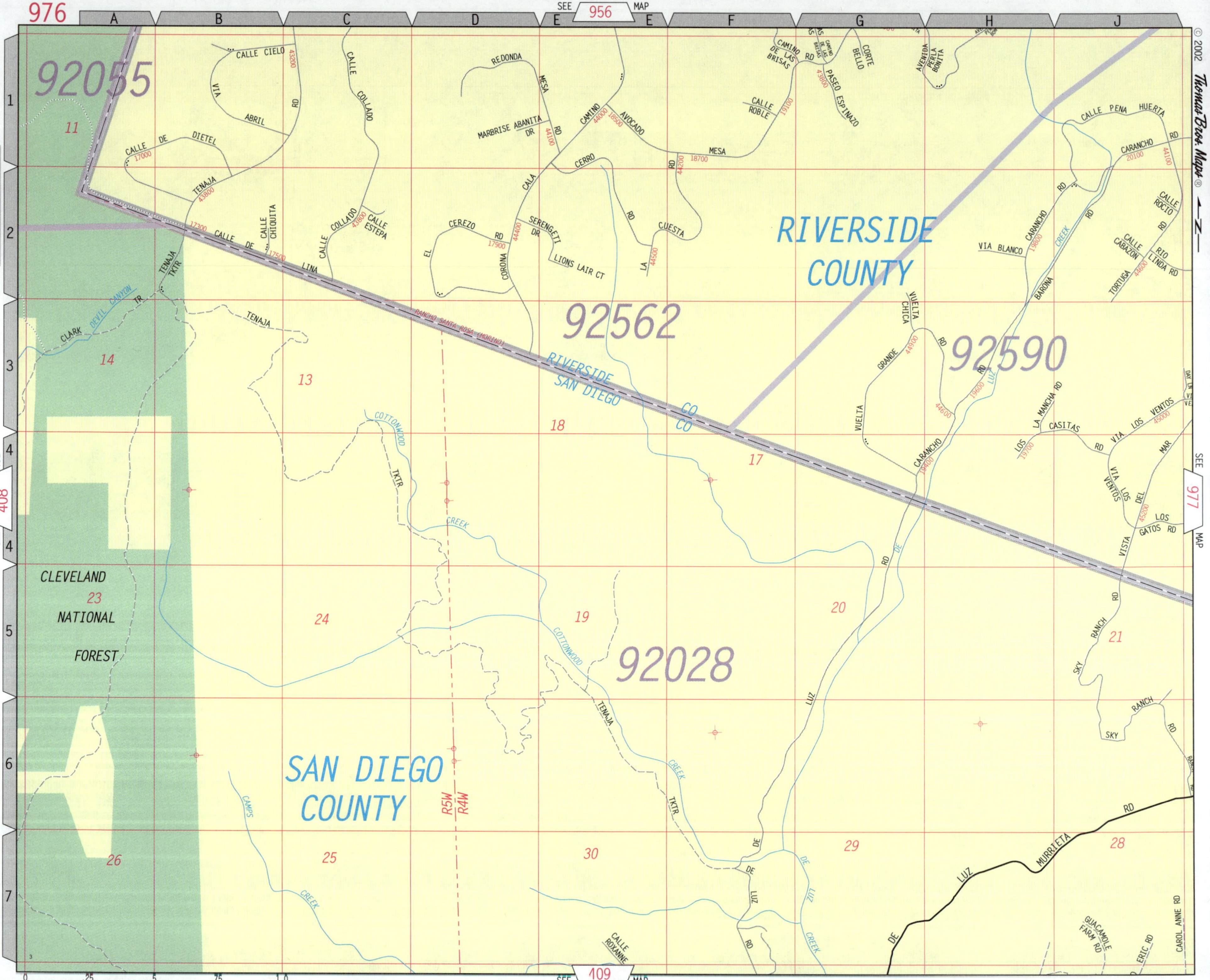

SEE 408 MAP

SEE 977 MAP

SEE 409 MAP

0 .25 .5 .75 1.0 miles 1 in. = 2400 ft.

SEE 957 MAP

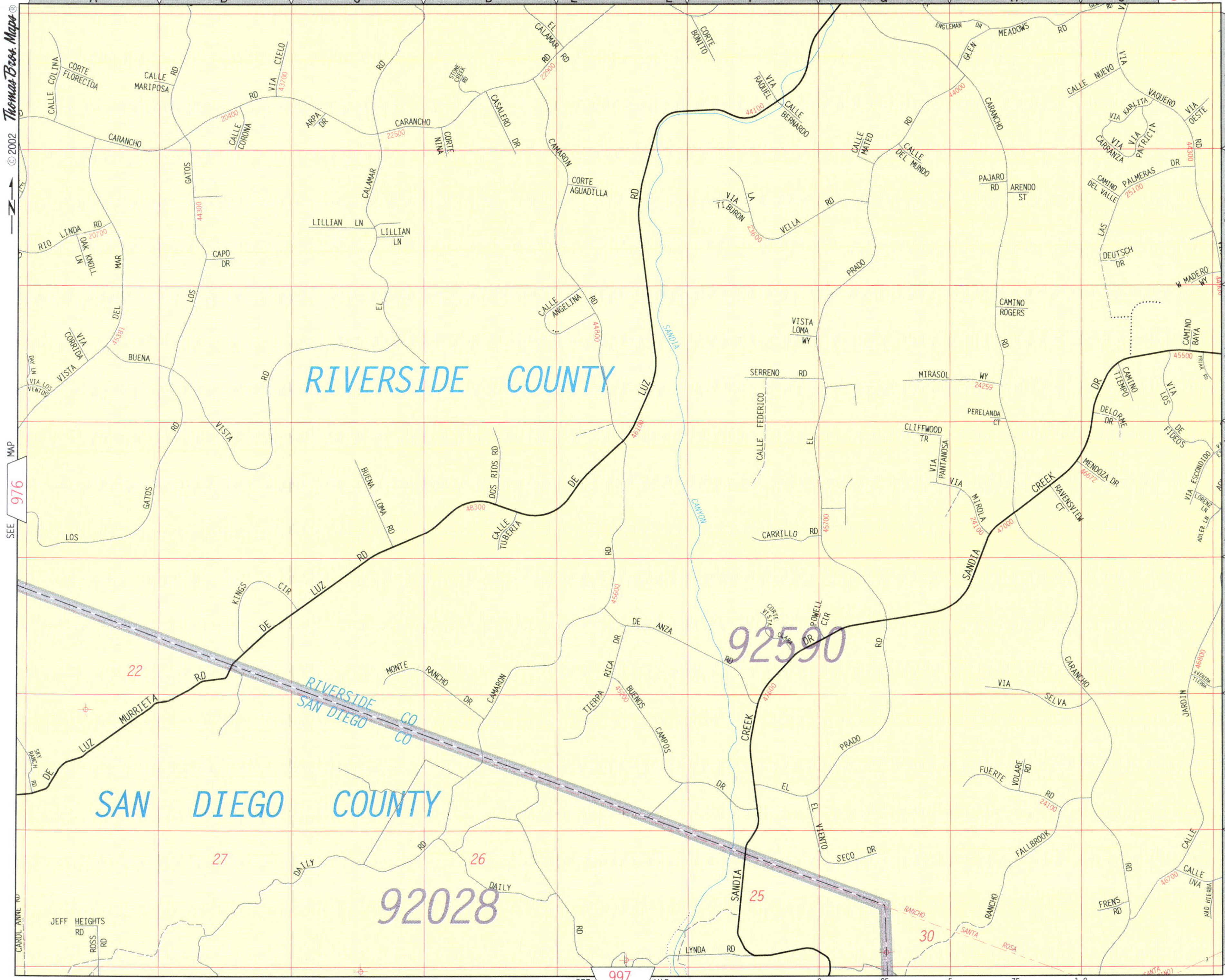

SEE 997 MAP

SEE 958 MAP

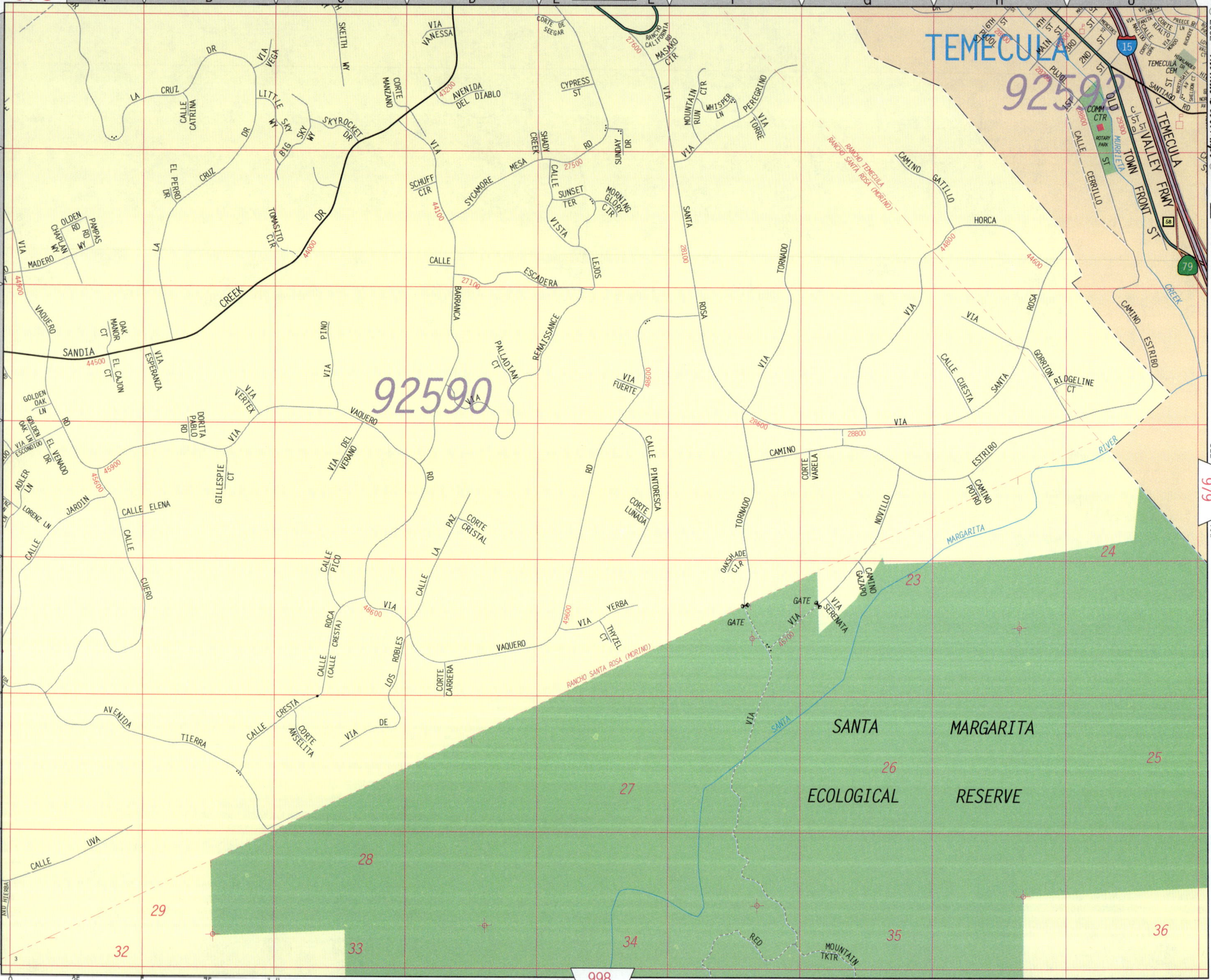

SEE 977 MAP

SEE 979 MAP

SEE 998 MAP

0 .25 .5 .75 1.0 miles 1 in. = 2400 ft.

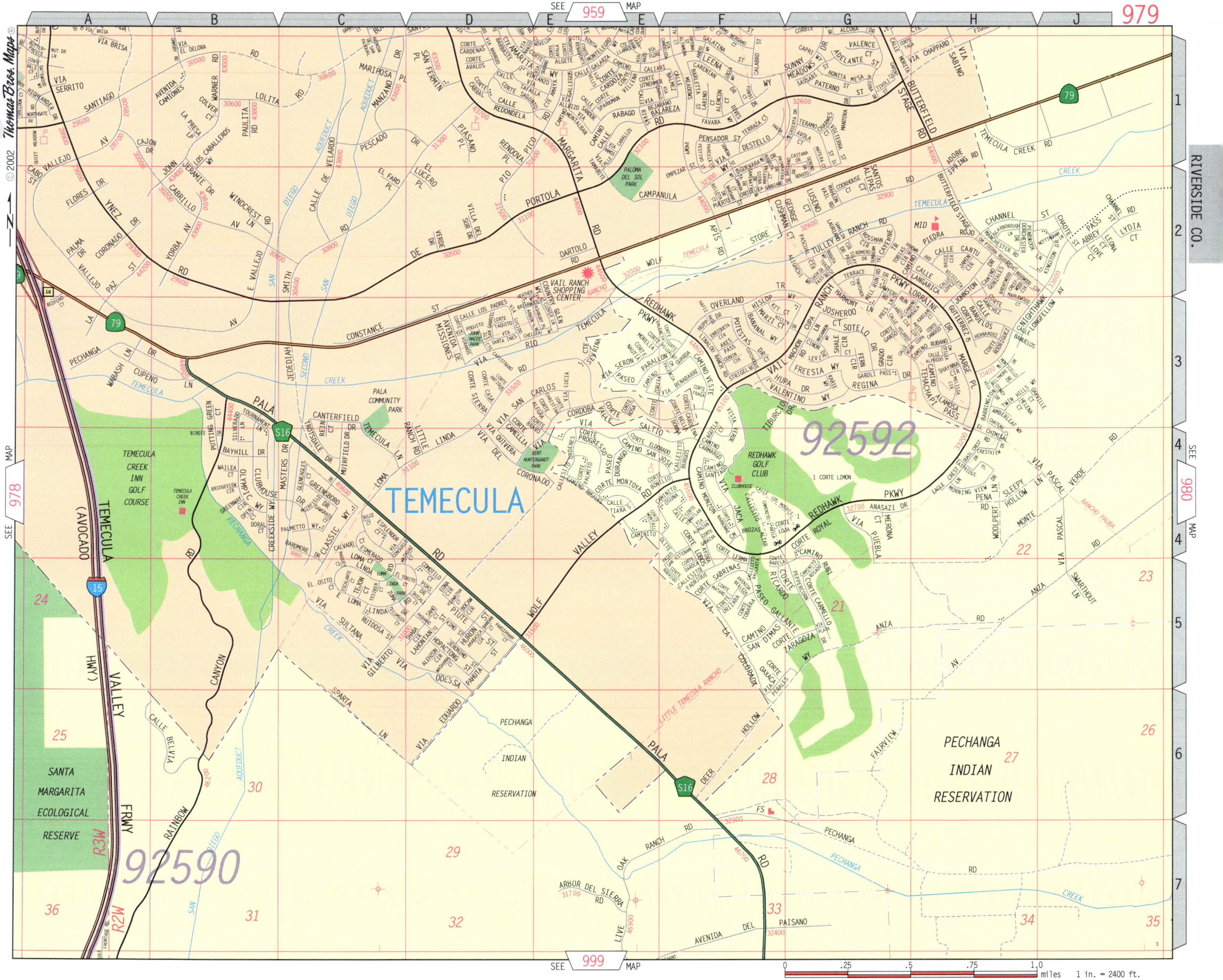
SEE 959 MAP
SEE 999 MAP
SEE 978 MAP
SEE 980 MAP
RIVERSIDE CO.
TEMECULA
92592
92590
TEMECULA CREEK INN GOLF COURSE
REDHAWK GOLF CLUB
PALOMA DEL SOL PARK
PALA COMMUNITY PARK
VAIL RANCH SHOPPING CENTER
SANTA MARGARITA ECOLOGICAL RESERVE
PECHANGA INDIAN RESERVATION
TEMECULA (AVOCADO HWY) VALLEY FRWY
TEMECULA CREEK
PECHANGA CREEK
MARGARITA RD
BUTTERFIELD STAGE RD
REDHAWK PKWY
PALA RD
WOLF VALLEY RD
PECHANGA PKWY
CONSTANCE ST
PORTOLA
RAINBOW CANYON RD
ANZA RD
AVENIDA DEL PAISANO
OAK RANCH RD
DEER HOLLOW
R3W
R2W
0 .25 .5 .75 1.0 miles 1 in. = 2400 ft.

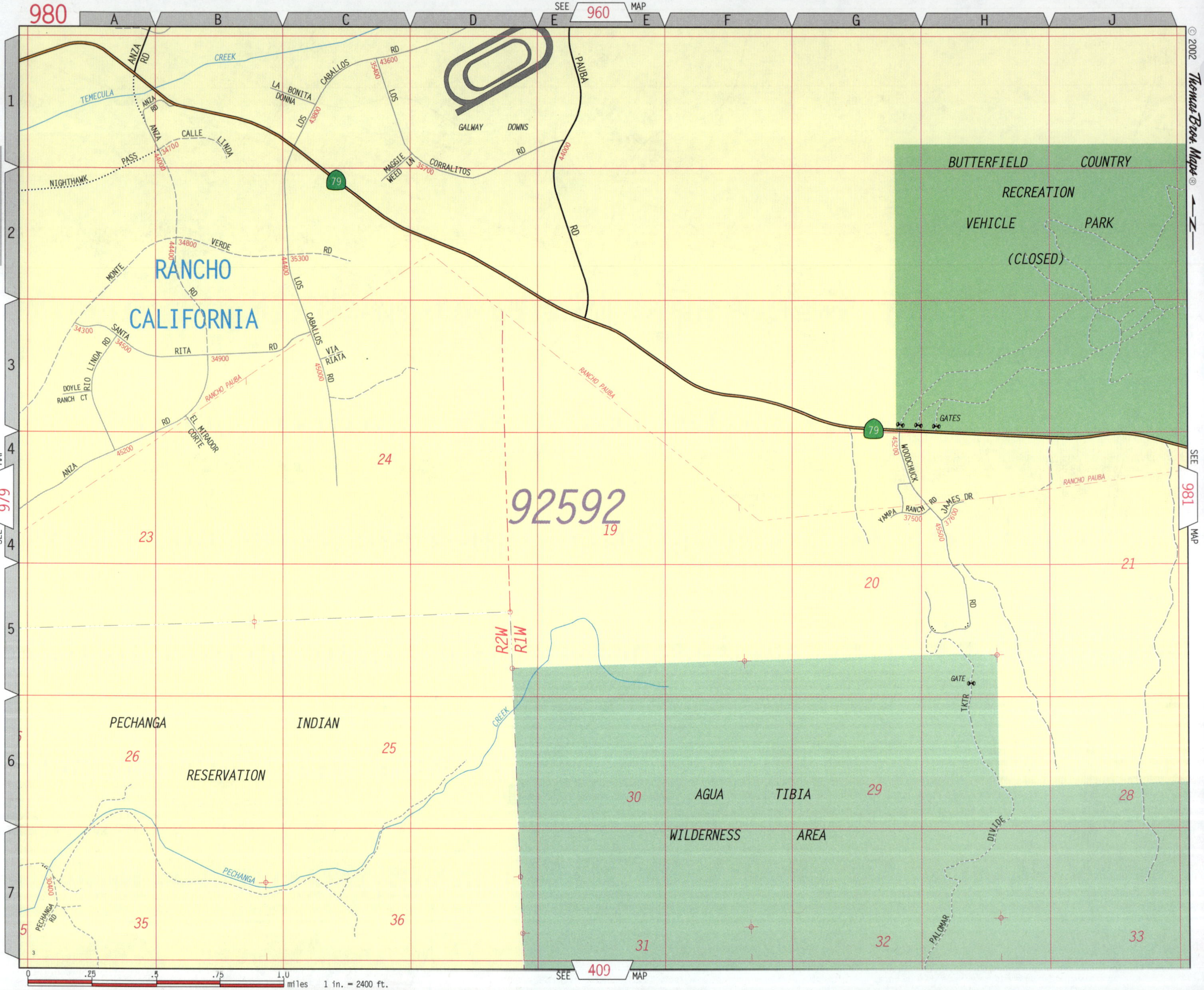
SEE 960 MAP
A
B
C
D
E
F
G
H
J
1
2
3
4
5
6
7
RIVERSIDE CO.
ANZA RD
CREEK
TEMECULA
LA BONITA
DONNA
CABALLOS
RD
43600
35400
LOS
43800
PAUBA
RD
GALWAY DOWNS
CALLE LINDA
34700
44000
PASS
NIGHTHAWK
79
MAGGIE WEED LN
CORRALITOS
35700
BUTTERFIELD COUNTRY
RECREATION
VEHICLE PARK
(CLOSED)
34800 VERDE
35300
44400
RANCHO
CALIFORNIA
MONTE
SANTA
34300
34500
RITA
34900
VIA RIATA
45000
RIO LINDA RD
DOYLE RANCH CT
RANCHO PAUBA
EL MIRADOR CORTE
45200
GATES
WOODCHUCK
24
23
92592
19
YAMPA RANCH RD
37500
JAMES DR
37600
45500
20
21
SEE 979 MAP
SEE 981 MAP
R2W
R1W
GATE
TKTR
PECHANGA INDIAN
RESERVATION
26
25
30
AGUA TIBIA
WILDERNESS AREA
29
28
DIVIDE
PECHANGA
30400
PECHANGA RD
35
36
31
32
PALOMAR
33
SEE 409 MAP
0 .25 .5 .75 1.0 miles 1 in. = 2400 ft.

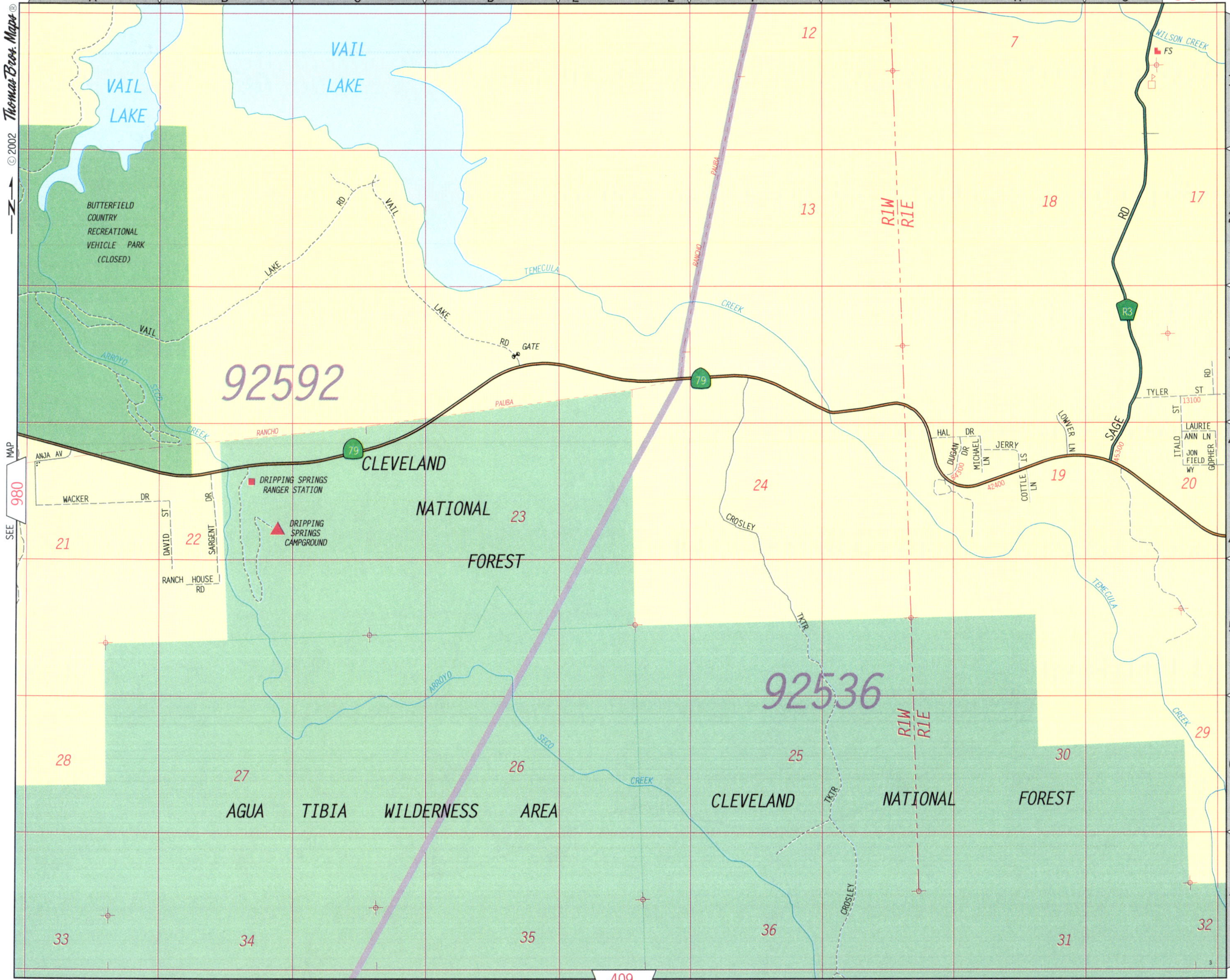

0 .25 .5 .75 1.0 miles 1 in. = 2400 ft.

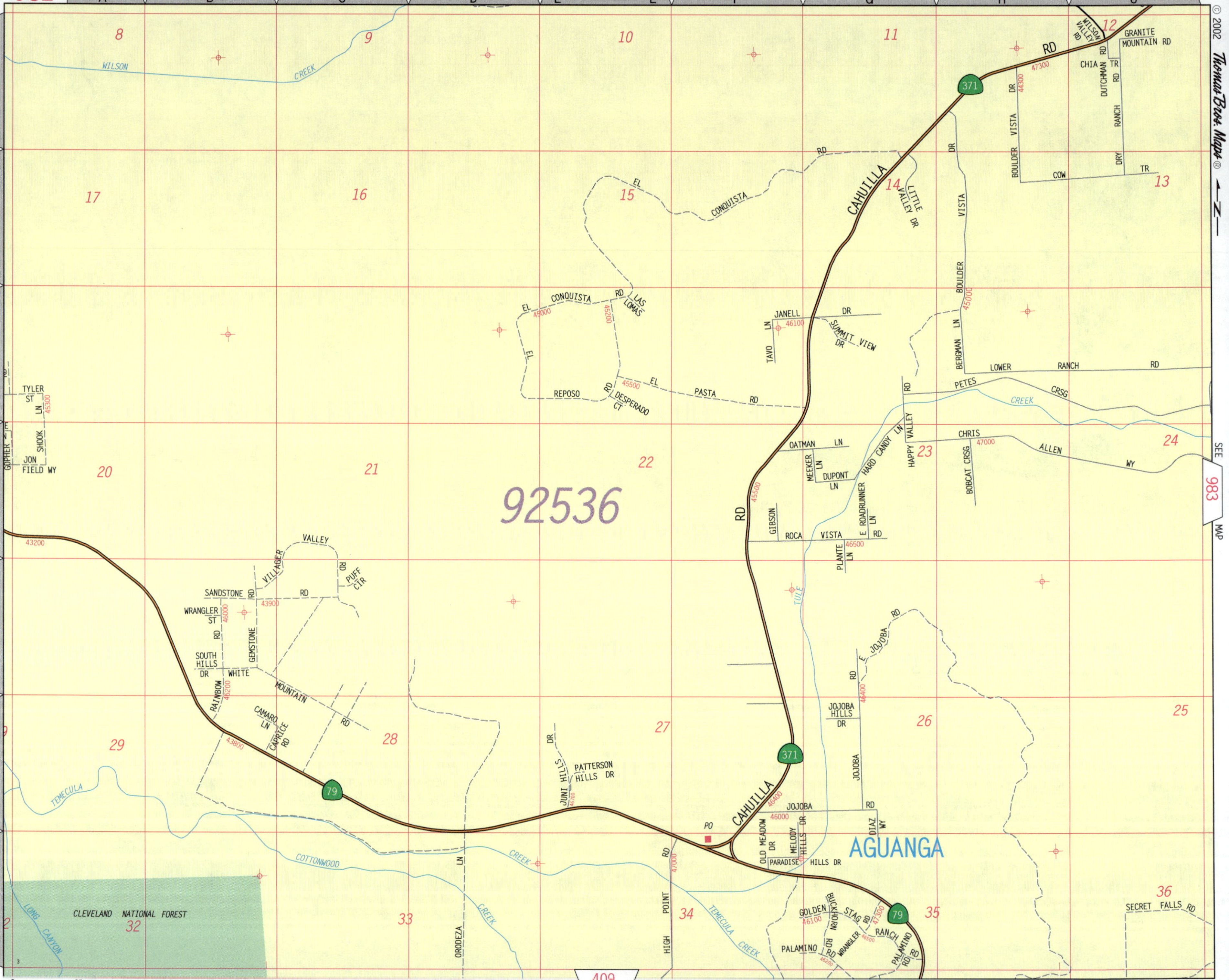

0 .25 .5 .75 1.0 miles 1 in. = 2400 ft.

SEE 963 MAP

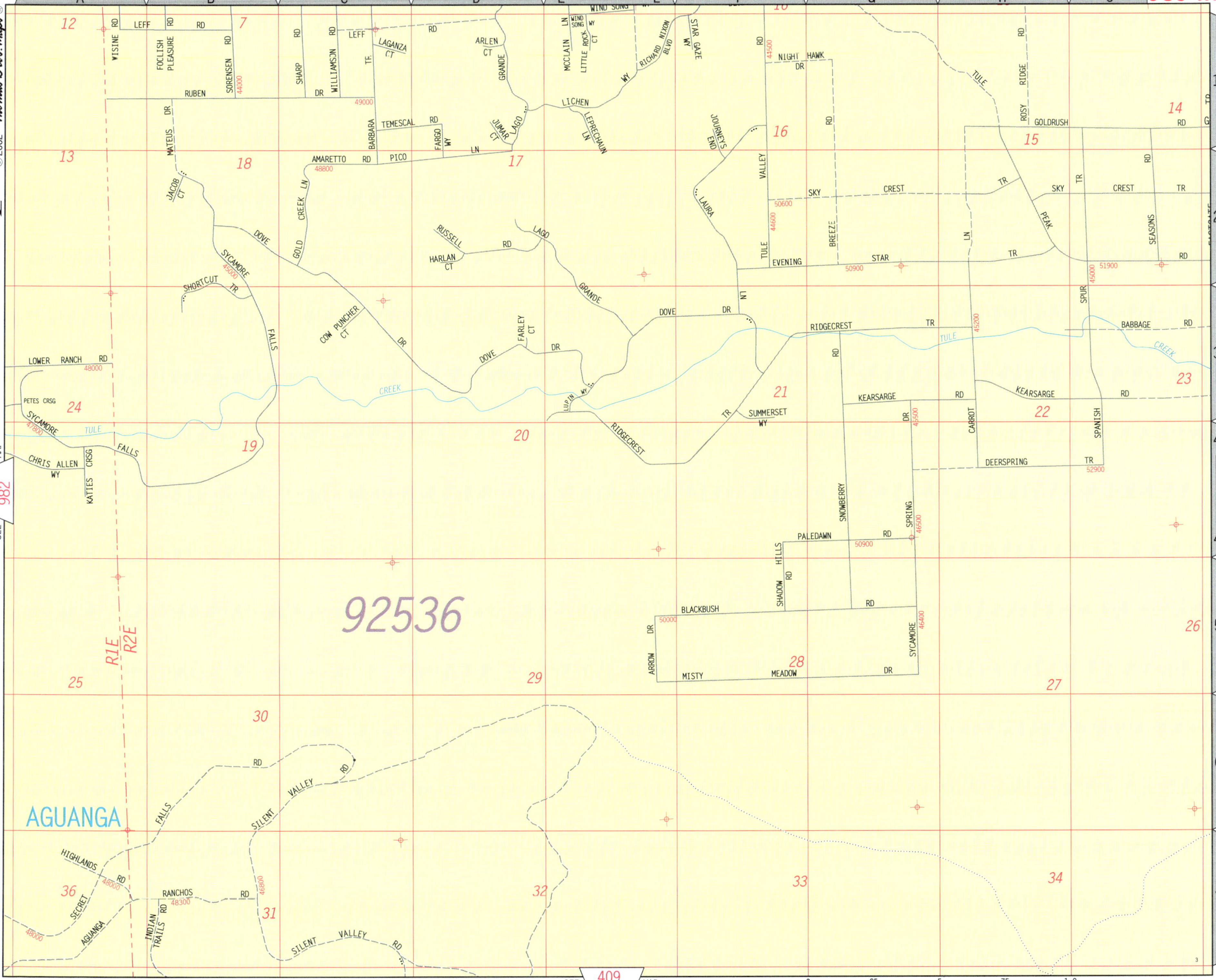

SEE 982 MAP

SEE 964 MAP

SEE 409 MAP

SEE 977 MAP

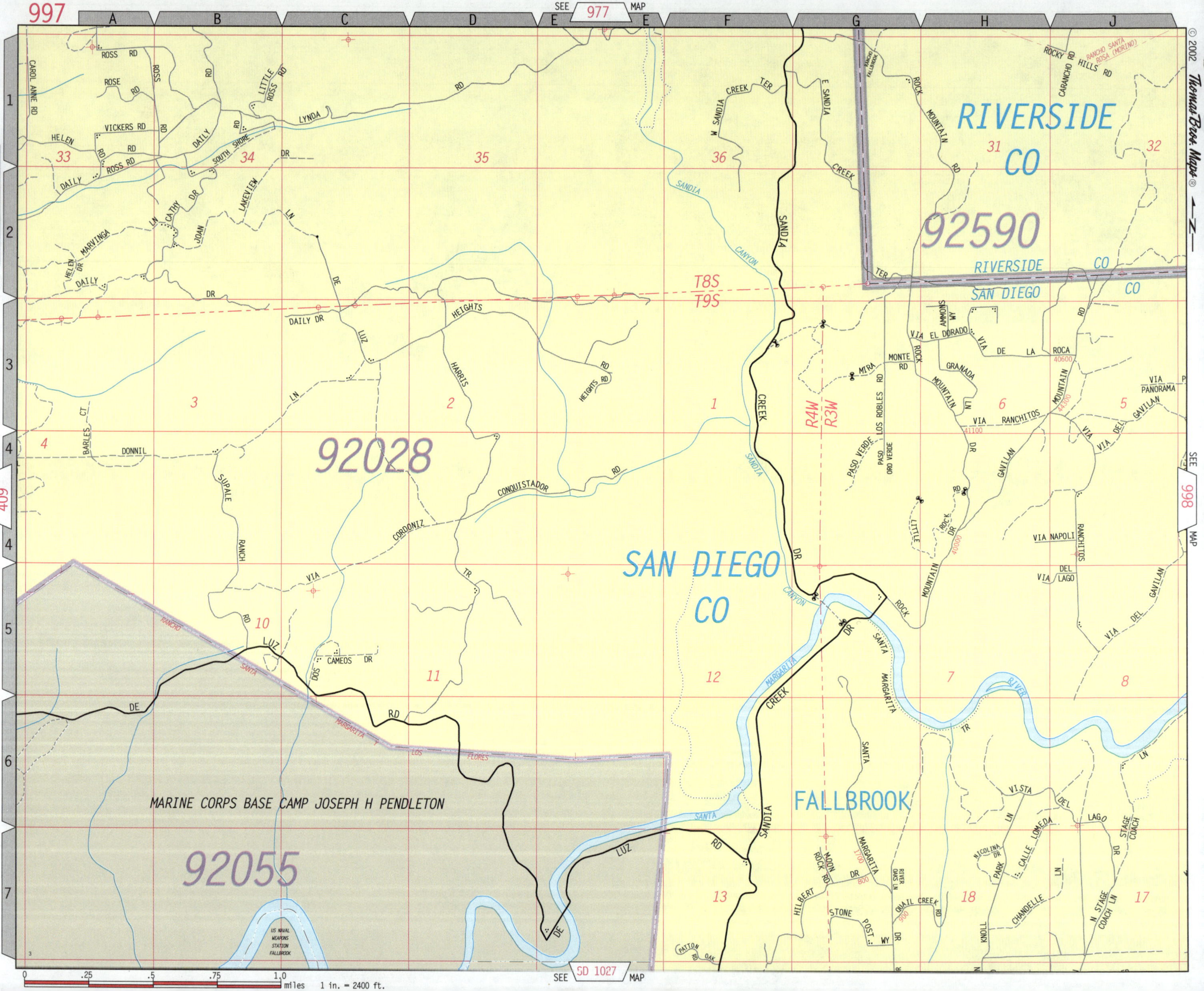

SEE SD 1027 MAP

SEE 978 MAP

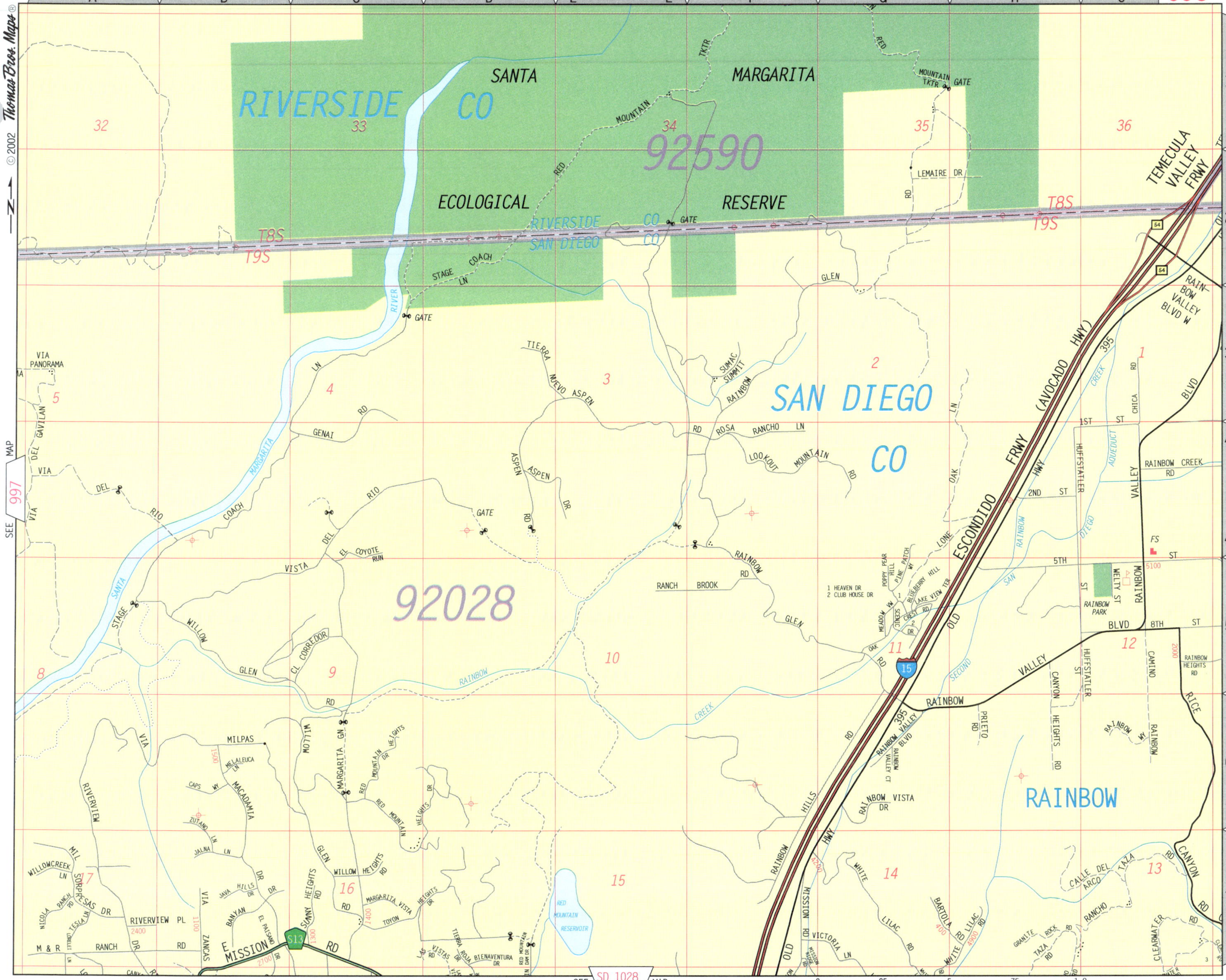

SEE 997 MAP

SEE 999 MAP

SEE SD 1028 MAP

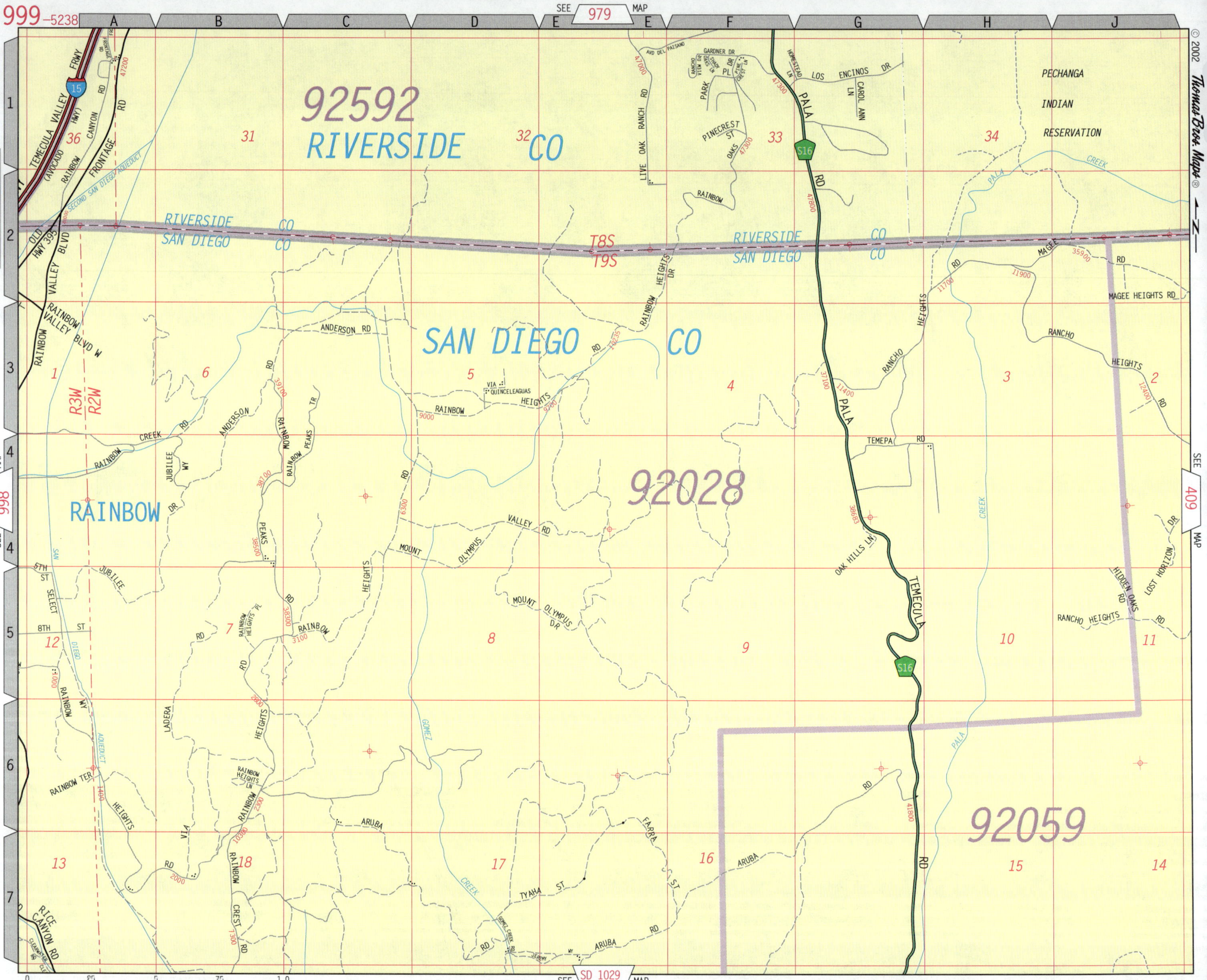

0 .25 .5 .75 1.0 miles 1 in. = 2400 ft.

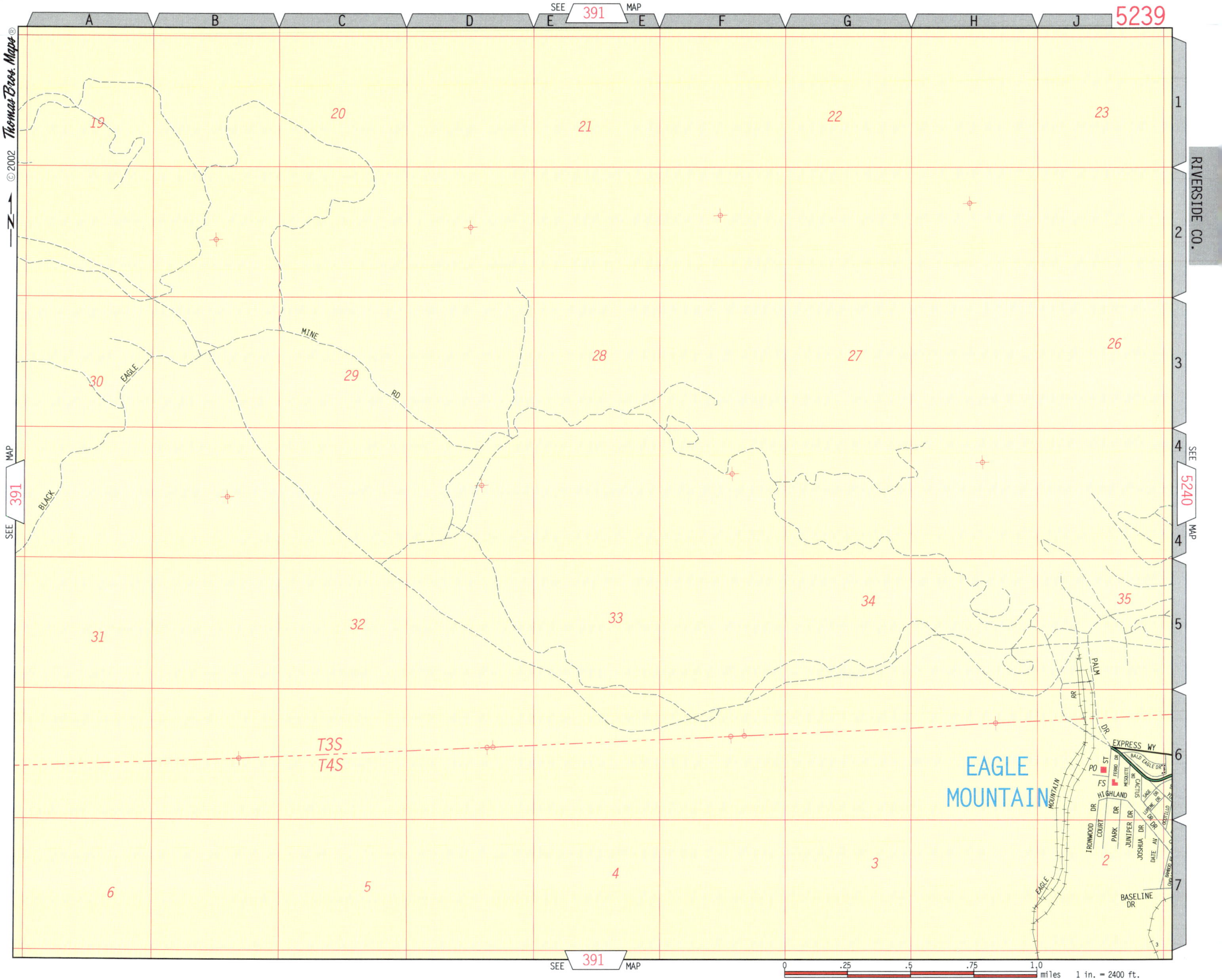

Thomas Bros. Maps®
© 2002
N
A
B
C
D
E
F
G
H
J
1
2
3
4
5
6
7
SEE 391 MAP
SEE 5240 MAP
RIVERSIDE CO.
19
20
21
22
23
30
29
28
27
26
31
32
33
34
35
6
5
4
3
2
MINE
RD
EAGLE
BLACK
T3S
T4S
EAGLE
MOUNTAIN
PALM
RR
DR
EXPRESS WY
BALD EAGLE DR
ST
PO
FS
FERRO DR
MESQUITE
CACTUS
HIGHLAND
SAGE
MOUNTAIN
DR
IRONWOOD
COURT
PARK
DR
JUNIPER DR
JOSHUA DR
DATE AV
OCOTILLO
EAGLE
BASELINE
DR
0
.25
.5
.75
1.0
miles
1 in. = 2400 ft.

SEE 391 MAP

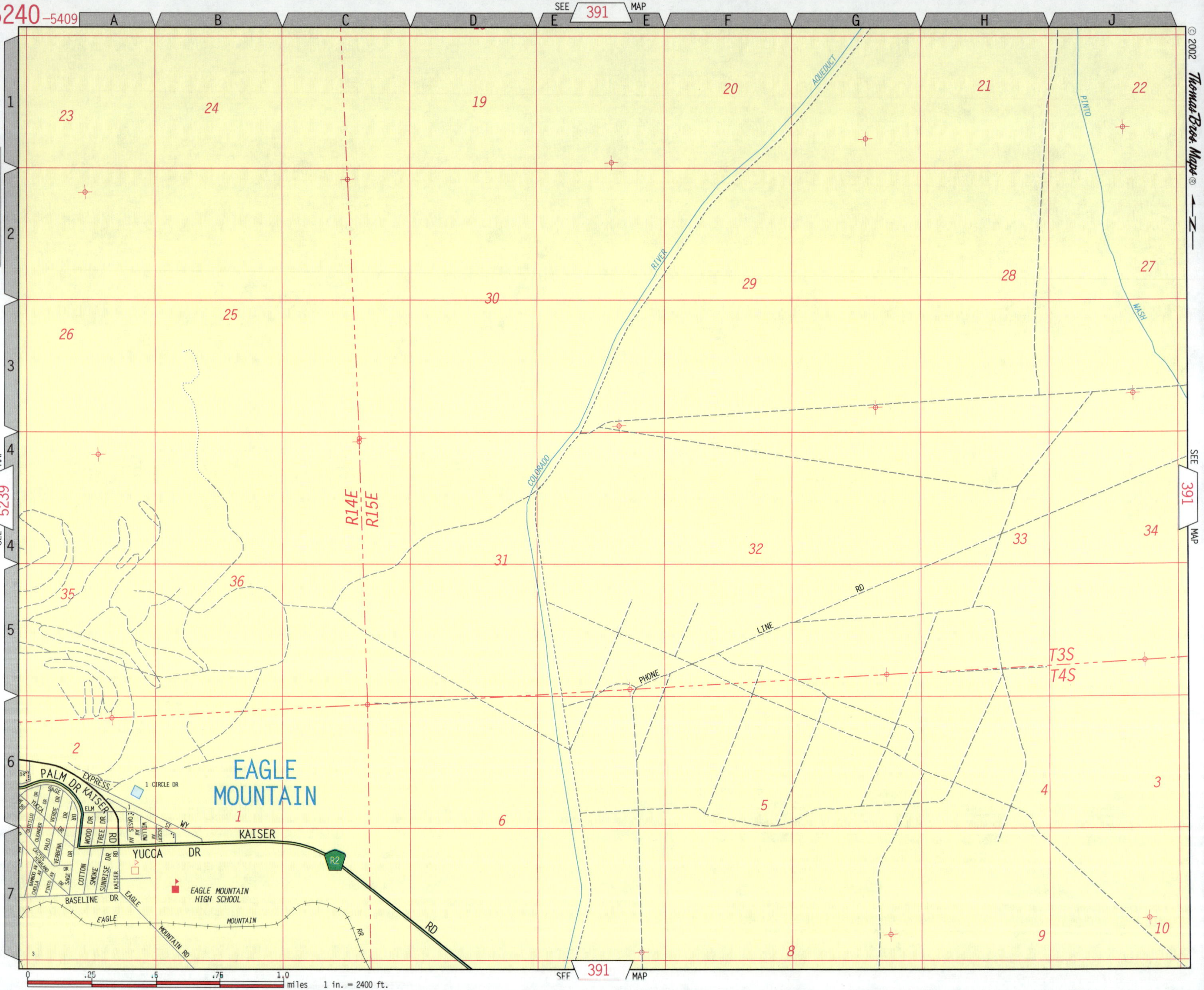

SEE 5239 MAP

SEE 391 MAP

SEE 391 MAP

0 .25 .5 .75 1.0 miles 1 in. = 2400 ft.

SEE 390 MAP
SEE 5470 MAP
SEE 819 MAP
SEE 5411 MAP
A
B
C
D
E
F
G
H
J
1
2
3
4
5
6
7
Thomas Bros. Maps
© 2002
RIVERSIDE CO.
92203
92201
92253
INDIO
BERMUDA DUNES
LA QUINTA
INDIO GOLF CLUB
LANDMARK GOLF CLUB
LANDMARK GOLF PKWY
RANCHO CASABLANCA COUNTRY CLUB
BERMUDA DUNES AIRPORT
INDIO BLVD
FRWY
AVENUE 40
AVENUE 42
AVENUE 44
AVENUE 45
MONROE ST
JACKSON ST
MADISON ST
JEFFERSON ST
BURR ST
CLINTON ST
FRED WARING DR
MILES AV
GOLF CENTER PKWY
INDIO SPRINGS DR
ALL AMERICAN CANAL
SOUTH BAY DR
NORTH SHORE DR
LAKE VIEW DR
LAKE CREST CT
WHITEWATER STORMWATER CHANNEL
COACHELLA VALLEY
NORTH JACKSON PARK
NATIONAL GUARD ARMORY
VILLAGE SQUARE
MILES AVENUE PARK
DOMINGUEZ PARK
HERITAGE PALMS GOLF CLUB
CONT HS
MID
DMV
FS
SEE B J6
1 CL DE PALMA
2 VIA TUCSON
3 ENTRADA DORADA
4 PLACITAS LOS PALMAS
SEE A D7
1 REGENT WY
2 SAINT THOMAS LN
R7E
R8E
0 .25 .5 .75 1.0 miles
1 in. = 2400 ft.

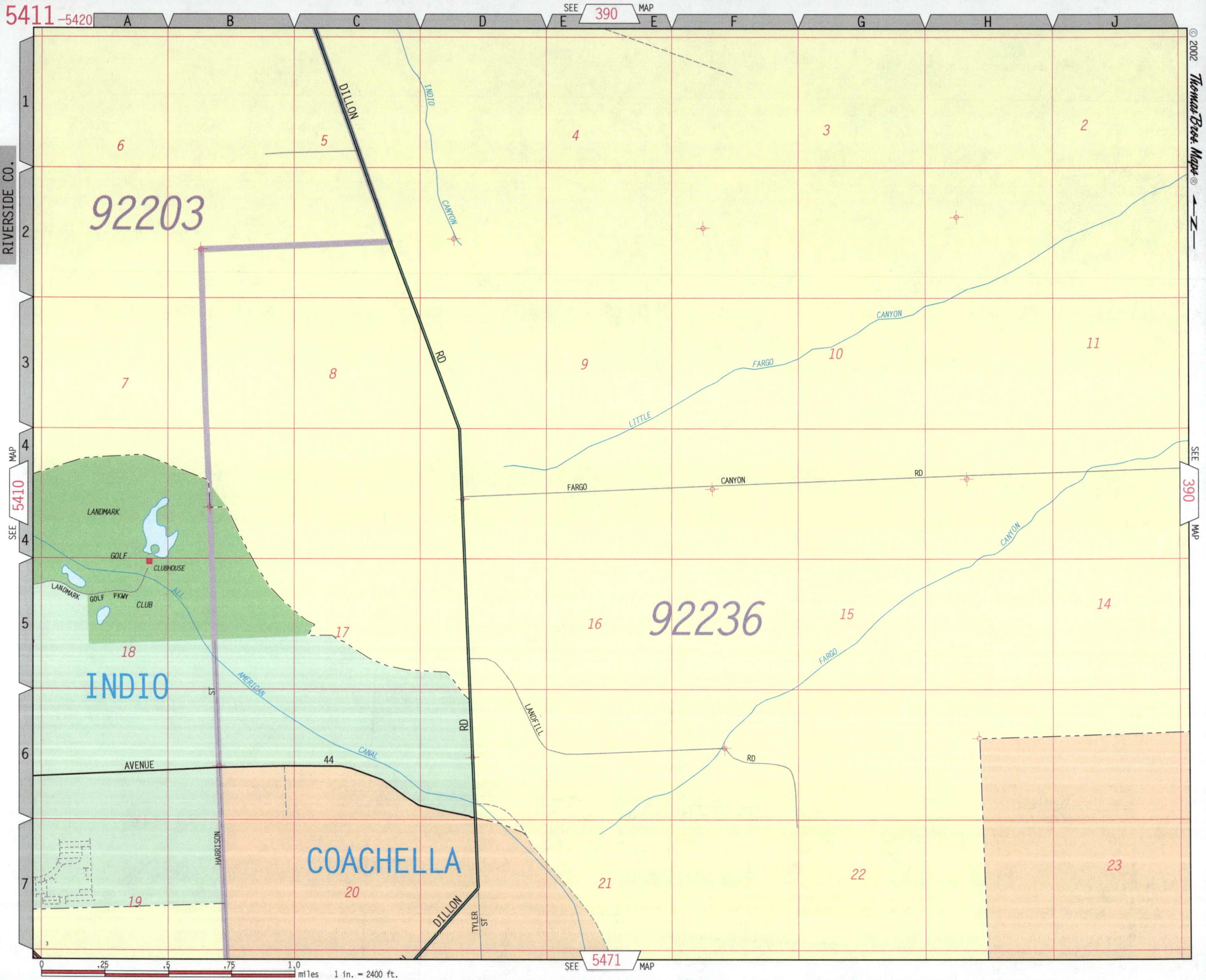
SEE 390 MAP
A
B
C
D
E
F
G
H
J
1
2
3
4
5
6
7
RIVERSIDE CO.
DILLON
INDIO
CANYON
92203
6
5
4
3
2
RD
7
8
9
10
11
LITTLE
FARGO
CANYON
SEE 5410 MAP
SEE 390 MAP
FARGO
CANYON
RD
LANDMARK
GOLF
CLUBHOUSE
LANDMARK
GOLF
PKWY
CLUB
ALL
AMERICAN
CANAL
17
18
16
92236
15
14
INDIO
ST
LANDFILL
RD
AVENUE
44
RD
HARRISON
COACHELLA
19
20
21
22
23
DILLON
TYLER
ST
0
.25
.5
.75
1.0
miles
1 in. = 2400 ft.
SEE 5471 MAP

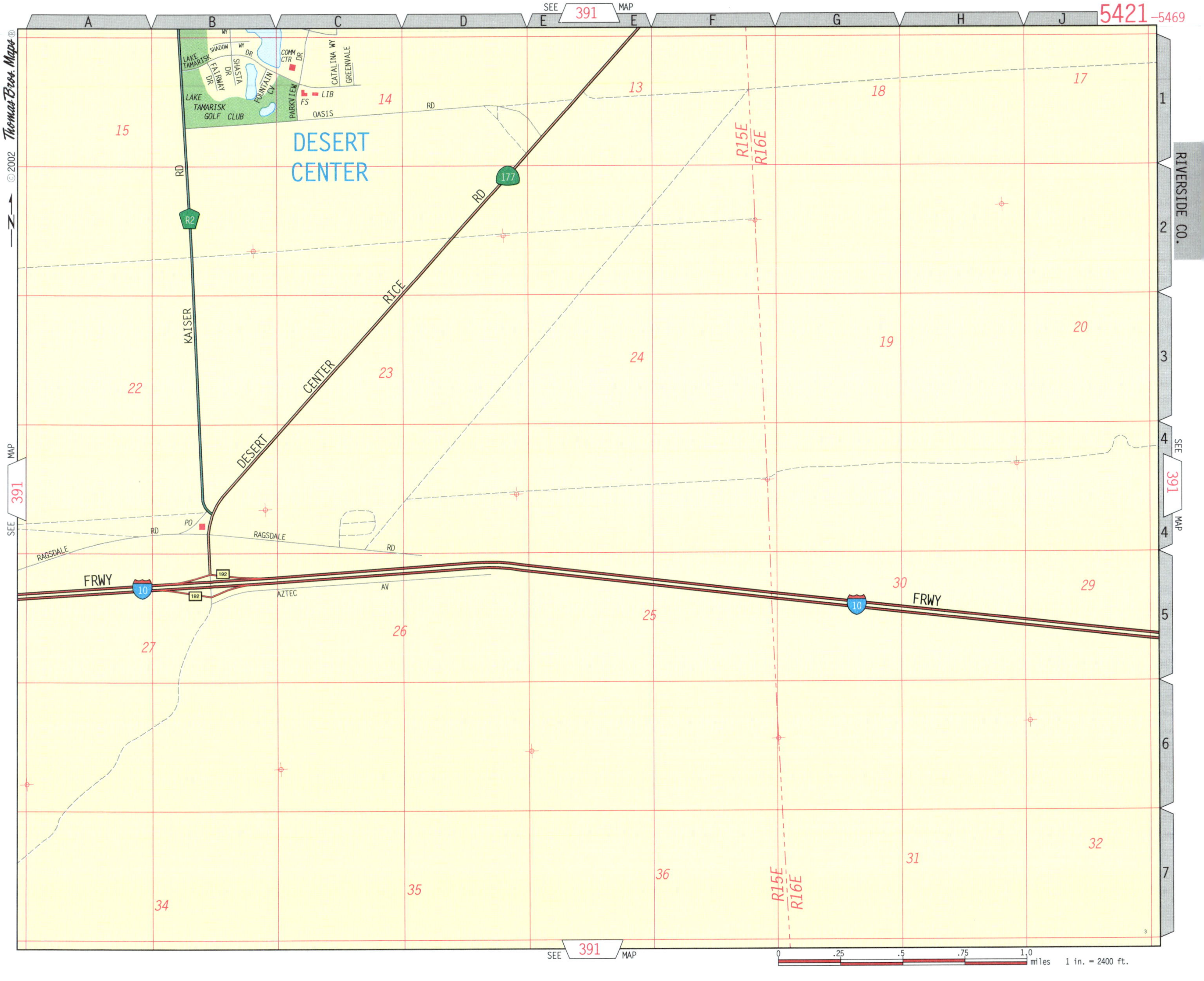

SEE 391 MAP
SEE 391 MAP
SEE 391 MAP

SEE 5410 MAP

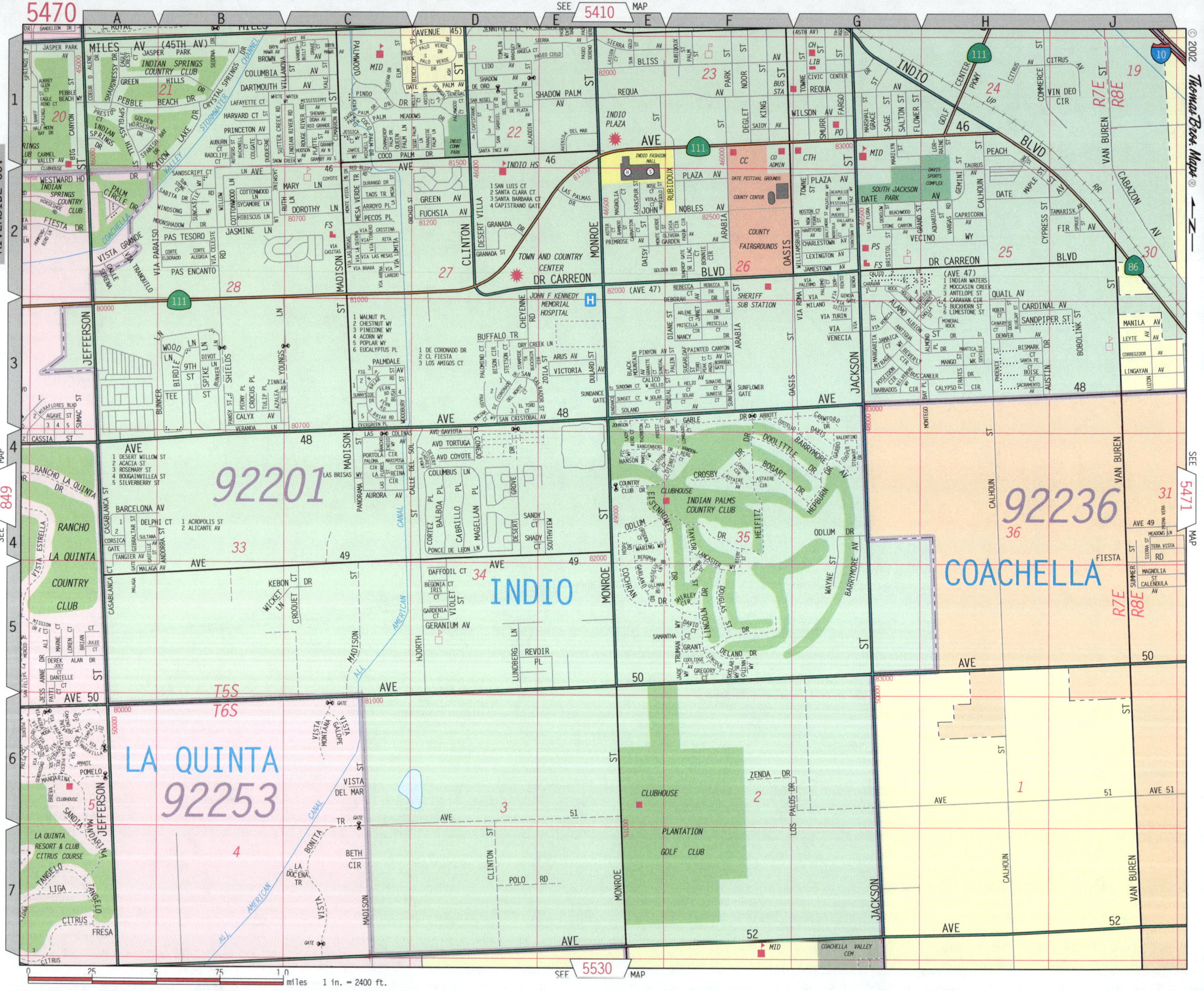
RIVERSIDE CO.
INDIO
92201
COACHELLA
92236
LA QUINTA
92253
T5S
T6S
R7E
R8E
MILES AV (45TH AV)
INDIAN SPRINGS COUNTRY CLUB
INDIAN SPRINGS COUNTRY CLUB
WESTWARD HO
FIESTA DR
PAS TESORO
PAS ENCANTO
JASMINE LN
DOROTHY LN
INDIO HS
TOWN AND COUNTRY CENTER
DR CARREON
JOHN F KENNEDY MEMORIAL HOSPITAL
INDIO PLAZA
INDIO FASHION MALL
REQUA AV
BLISS AV
CIVIC CENTER
COUNTY CENTER
COUNTY FAIRGROUNDS
DATE FESTIVAL GROUNDS
SHERIFF SUB STATION
SOUTH JACKSON DATE PARK
DAVIS SPORTS COMPLEX
INDIO BLVD
VAN BUREN ST
CABAZON
CALHOUN ST
JACKSON ST
MONROE ST
CLINTON ST
MADISON ST
JEFFERSON ST
OASIS ST
ARABIA ST
AVE 47
AVE 48
AVE 49
AVE 50
AVE 51
AVE 52
INDIAN PALMS COUNTRY CLUB
CLUBHOUSE
RANCHO LA QUINTA
LA QUINTA COUNTRY CLUB
LA QUINTA RESORT & CLUB CITRUS COURSE
PLANTATION GOLF CLUB
ALL AMERICAN CANAL
COACHELLA VALLEY CEM
STORMWATER CHANNEL
SEE 5471 MAP
SEE 849 MAP
SEE 5530 MAP
© 2002 Thomas Bros. Maps
0 .25 .5 .75 1.0 miles 1 in. = 2400 ft.

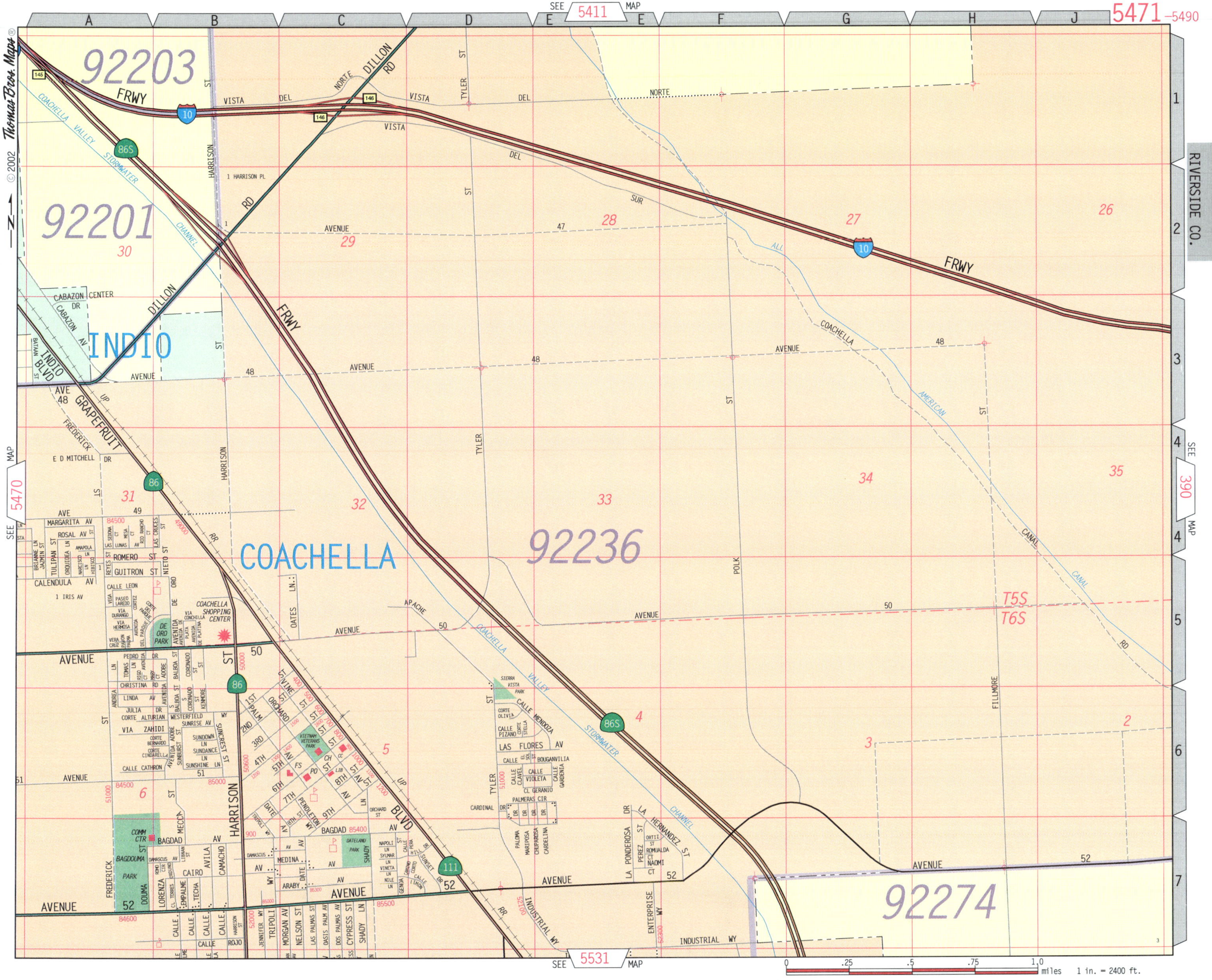

SEE 5411 MAP
A
B
C
D
E
F
G
H
J
1
2
3
4
5
6
7
Thomas Bros. Maps ®
© 2002
92203
92201
92236
92274
INDIO
COACHELLA
RIVERSIDE CO.
SEE 390 MAP
SEE 5470 MAP
SEE 5531 MAP
FRWY
VISTA DEL NORTE
VISTA DEL SUR
DILLON RD
HARRISON ST
TYLER ST
POLK ST
FILLMORE ST
AVENUE 47
AVENUE 48
AVENUE 49
AVENUE 50
AVENUE 51
AVENUE 52
COACHELLA VALLEY STORMWATER CHANNEL
ALL AMERICAN CANAL
COACHELLA CANAL RD
GRAPEFRUIT BLVD
INDIO BLVD
CABAZON CENTER DR
CABAZON AV
1 HARRISON PL
FREDERICK ST
E D MITCHELL DR
MARGARITA AV
ROSAL AV
ROMERO ST
GUITRON ST
CALENDULA AV
1 IRIS AV
CALLE LEON
COACHELLA SHOPPING CENTER
DE ORO PARK
OATES LN
APACHE
SIERRA VISTA PARK
CALLE MENDOZA
LAS FLORES AV
BOUGANVILIA
PALMERAS CIR
CARDINAL DR
LA PONDEROSA DR
PEREZ ST
HERNANDEZ ST
ENTERPRISE WY
INDUSTRIAL WY
VIETNAM VETERANS PARK
DATELAND PARK
BAGDAD AV
BAGDOUMA PARK
COMM CTR
CAIRO
MEDINA
ARABY
PENDLETON
ORCHARD
TRIPOLI
CYPRESS ST
SHADY LN
FRWY
T5S
T6S
10
86
86S
111
146
26
27
28
29
30
31
32
33
34
35
2
3
4
5
6
0 .25 .5 .75 1.0 miles 1 in. = 2400 ft.

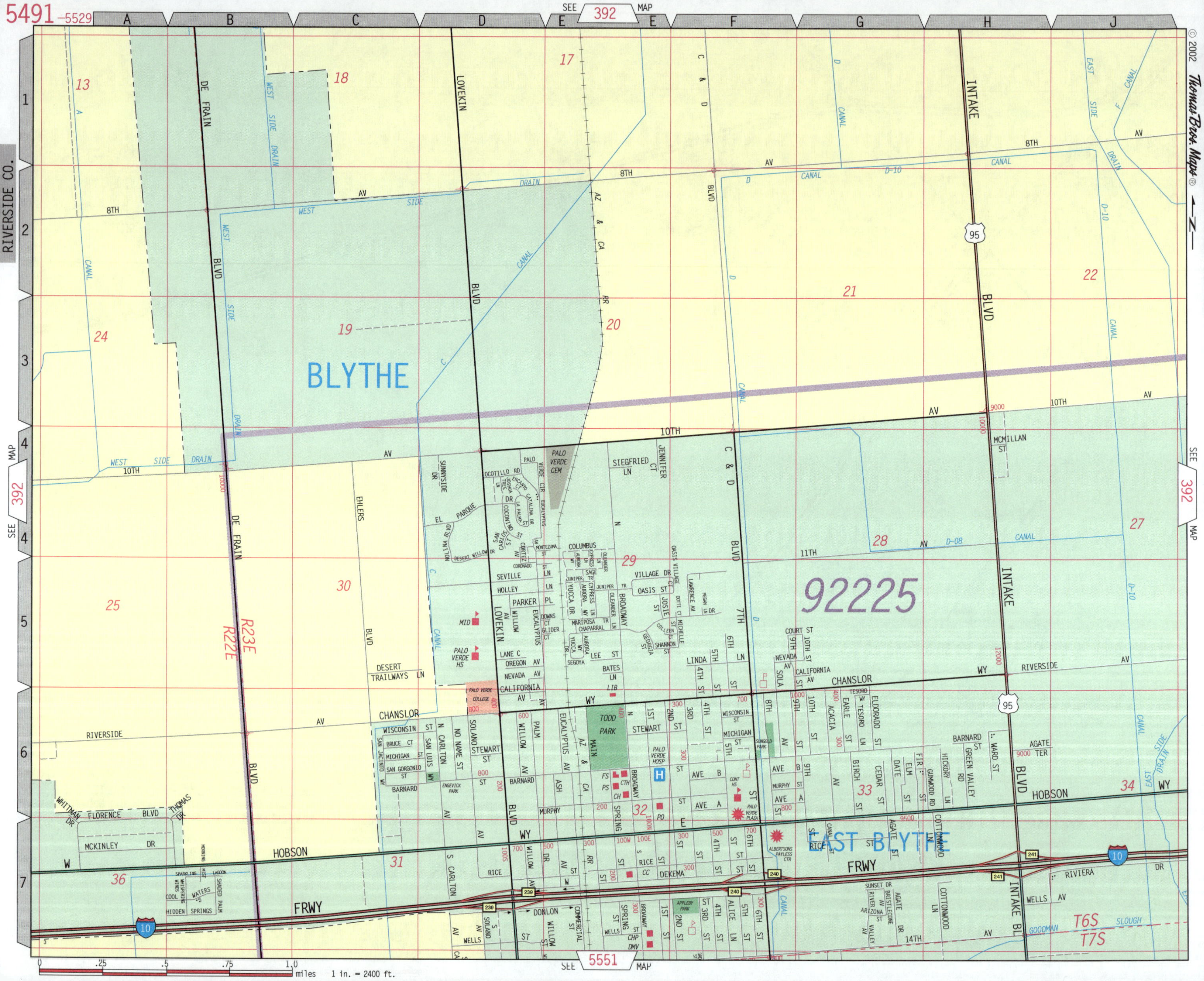
SEE 392 MAP
A
B
C
D
E
F
G
H
J
1
2
3
4
5
6
7
RIVERSIDE CO.
BLYTHE
92225
EAST BLYTHE
DE FRAIN BLVD
LOVEKIN BLVD
INTAKE BLVD
C & D BLVD
8TH AV
10TH AV
11TH
WEST SIDE DRAIN
WEST SIDE CANAL
D CANAL
D-10
D-08
EHLERS BLVD
DESERT TRAILWAYS LN
CHANSLOR WY
RIVERSIDE AV
HOBSON WY
W FRWY
FLORENCE BLVD
THOMAS DR
WHITMAN DR
MCKINLEY DR
RICE
DONLON
DEKEMA
WELLS
RIVIERA DR
GOODMAN
SLOUGH
MCMILLAN ST
SIEGFRIED LN
JENNIFER CT
PALO VERDE CEM
PALO VERDE COLLEGE
PALO VERDE HS
MID
TODD PARK
PALO VERDE HOSP
CONT HS
PALO VERDE PLAZA
ALBERTSONS PAYLESS CTR
APPLEBY PARK
SUNGOLD PARK
ENGEVICK PARK
FS
PS
CTH
CH
LIB
PO
CC
CHP
DMV
BROADWAY
MAIN
SPRING
7TH
AZ & CA RR
R23E
R22E
T6S
T7S
95
10
239
240
241
13
17
18
19
20
21
22
24
25
27
28
29
30
31
32
33
34
36
0 .25 .5 .75 1.0 miles 1 in. = 2400 ft.
SEE 5551 MAP
SEE 392 MAP
© 2002 Thomas Bros. Maps ®

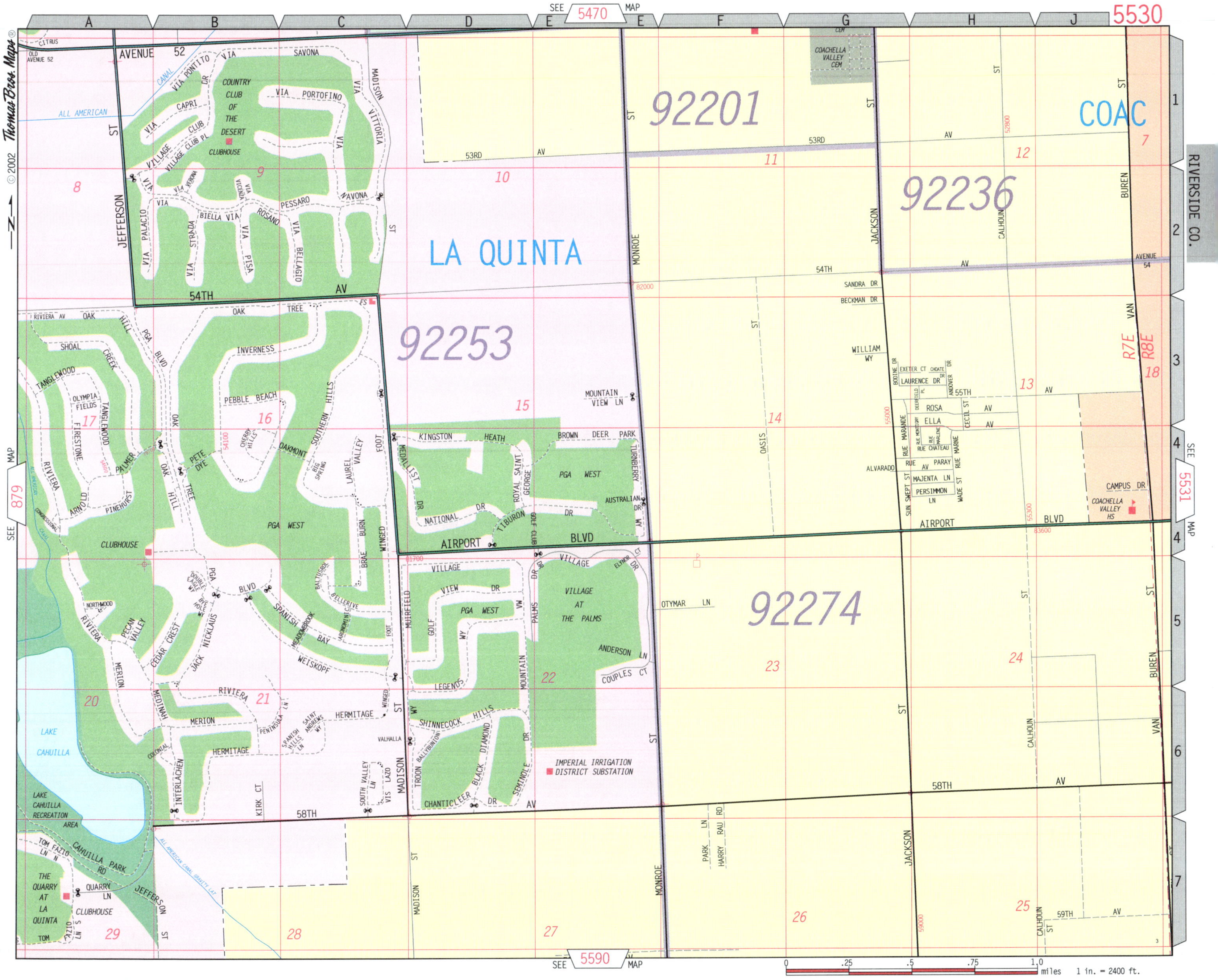
SEE 5470 MAP
SEE 5590 MAP
SEE 5531 MAP
SEE 879 MAP
A
B
C
D
E
F
G
H
J
1
2
3
4
5
6
7
Thomas Bros. Maps
© 2002
RIVERSIDE CO.
LA QUINTA
COAC
92201
92236
92253
92274
R7E
R8E
AVENUE 52
CITRUS
OLD AVENUE 52
ALL AMERICAN CANAL
JEFFERSON ST
COUNTRY CLUB OF THE DESERT
CLUBHOUSE
VIA PORTOFINO
VIA VITTORIA
MADISON ST
SAVONA
CAPRI
VILLAGE CLUB PL
VIA PONTITO
PESSARO
NAVONA
VIA PALACIO
VIA STRADA
BIELLA
ROSANO
VIA BELLAGIO
VIA PISA
54TH AV
53RD AV
MONROE ST
JACKSON ST
CALHOUN ST
VAN BUREN ST
AVENUE 54
SANDRA DR
BECKMAN DR
WILLIAM WY
OASIS ST
EXETER CT
LAURENCE DR
55TH AV
ROSA AV
ELLA AV
ALVARADO
MAJENTA LN
PERSIMMON LN
CAMPUS DR
COACHELLA VALLEY HS
COACHELLA VALLEY CEM
AIRPORT BLVD
OAK TREE
RIVIERA AV
SHOAL CREEK
TANGLEWOOD
OLYMPIA FIELDS
FIRESTONE
INVERNESS
PEBBLE BEACH
PGA BLVD
SOUTHERN HILLS
OAKMONT
PETE DYE
CHERRY HILLS
BIG SPRING
LAUREL VALLEY
FOOT
PALMER
ARNOLD
PINEHURST
CONGRESSIONAL
PGA WEST
BRAE BURN
WINGED
MOUNTAIN VIEW LN
KINGSTON HEATH
BROWN DEER PARK
TURNBERRY
MEDALLIST DR
ROYAL SAINT GEORGE
NATIONAL DR
TIBURON DR
AUSTRALIAN
GOLF CLUB
VILLAGE AT THE PALMS
VILLAGE VIEW DR
MUIRFIELD
GOLF
LEGENDS
ELYNOR CT
ANDERSON LN
COUPLES CT
OTYMAR LN
NORTHWOOD
PECAN VALLEY
CEDAR CREST
JACK NICKLAUS
SPANISH BAY
MEADOWBROOK
WEISKOPF
BALTUSROL
BELLERIVE
MERION
MEDINAH
RIVIERA
PENINSULA
SAINT ANDREWS WY
HERMITAGE
VALHALLA
SHINNECOCK HILLS
BALLYBUNION
TROON
BLACK DIAMOND
SEMINOLE
CHANTICLEER DR
MOUNTAIN
IMPERIAL IRRIGATION DISTRICT SUBSTATION
INTERLACHEN
COLONIAL
KIRK CT
SOUTH VALLEY LN
VIS LAZO
58TH AV
LAKE CAHUILLA
LAKE CAHUILLA RECREATION AREA
TOM FAZIO LN
CAHUILLA PARK RD
THE QUARRY AT LA QUINTA
QUARRY LN
ALL AMERICAN CANAL GRAVITY LAT
PARK LN
HARRY RAU RD
59TH AV
0 .25 .5 .75 1.0 miles 1 in. = 2400 ft.

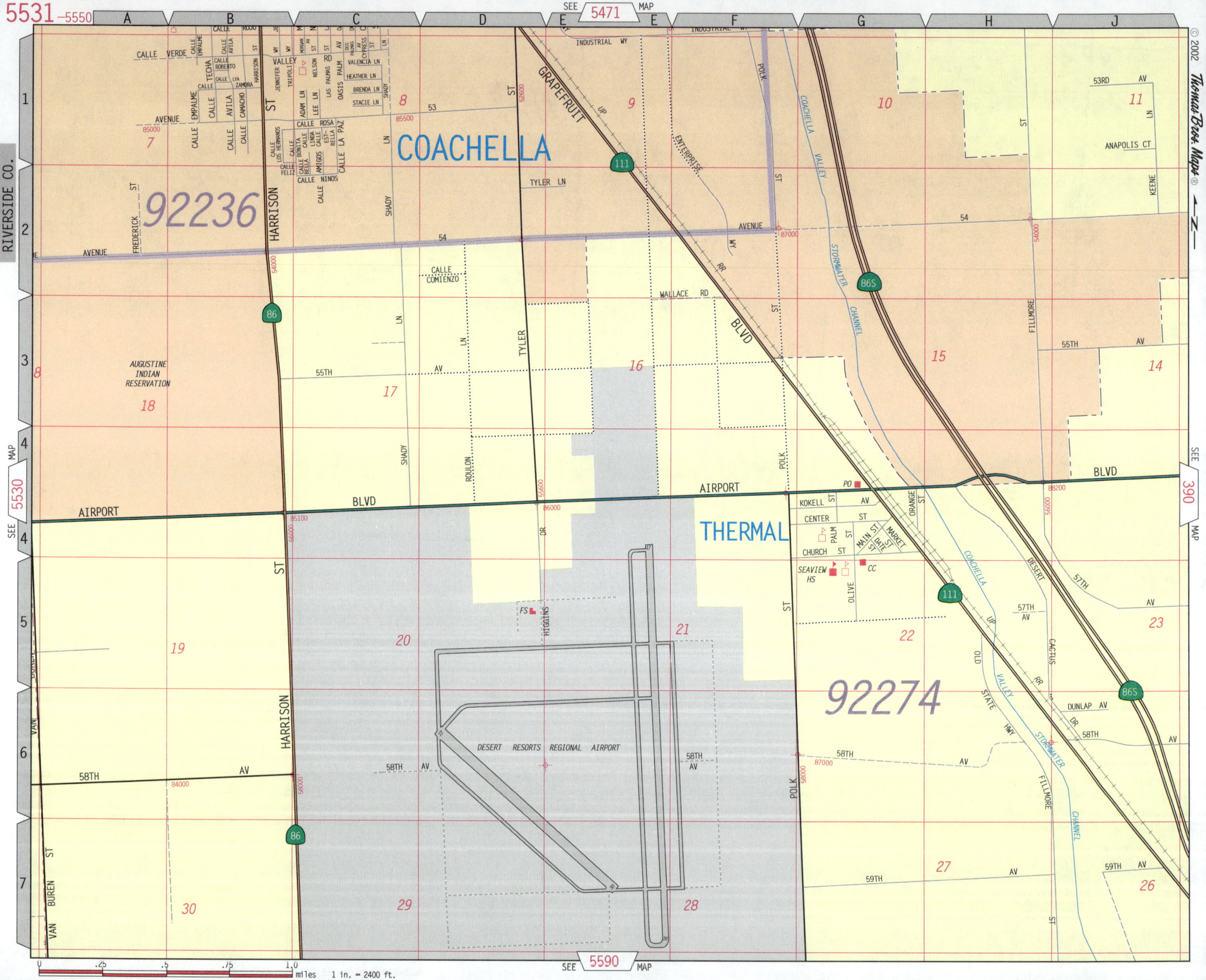

SEE 5471 MAP
SEE 5530 MAP
SEE 390 MAP
SEE 5590 MAP
RIVERSIDE CO.
© 2002 Thomas Bros. Maps ®
COACHELLA
THERMAL
92236
92274
AUGUSTINE INDIAN RESERVATION
DESERT RESORTS REGIONAL AIRPORT
AIRPORT BLVD
HARRISON ST
GRAPEFRUIT BLVD
AVENUE 54
AVENUE 53
55TH AV
57TH AV
58TH AV
59TH AV
TYLER ST
POLK ST
FILLMORE ST
VAN BUREN ST
SHADY LN
ROULON LN
HIGGINS DR
CALLE VERDE
CALLE COMIENZO
WALLACE RD
INDUSTRIAL WY
ENTERPRISE WY
TYLER LN
FREDERICK ST
KEENE LN
ANAPOLIS CT
53RD AV
DUNLAP AV
KOKELL ST
CENTER ST
CHURCH ST
PALM ST
MAIN ST
DATE ST
MARKET ST
ORANGE ST
OLIVE ST
CACTUS ST
OLD STATE HWY
SEAVIEW HS
PO
FS
CC
COACHELLA VALLEY STORMWATER CHANNEL
UP RR
miles 1 in. = 2400 ft.

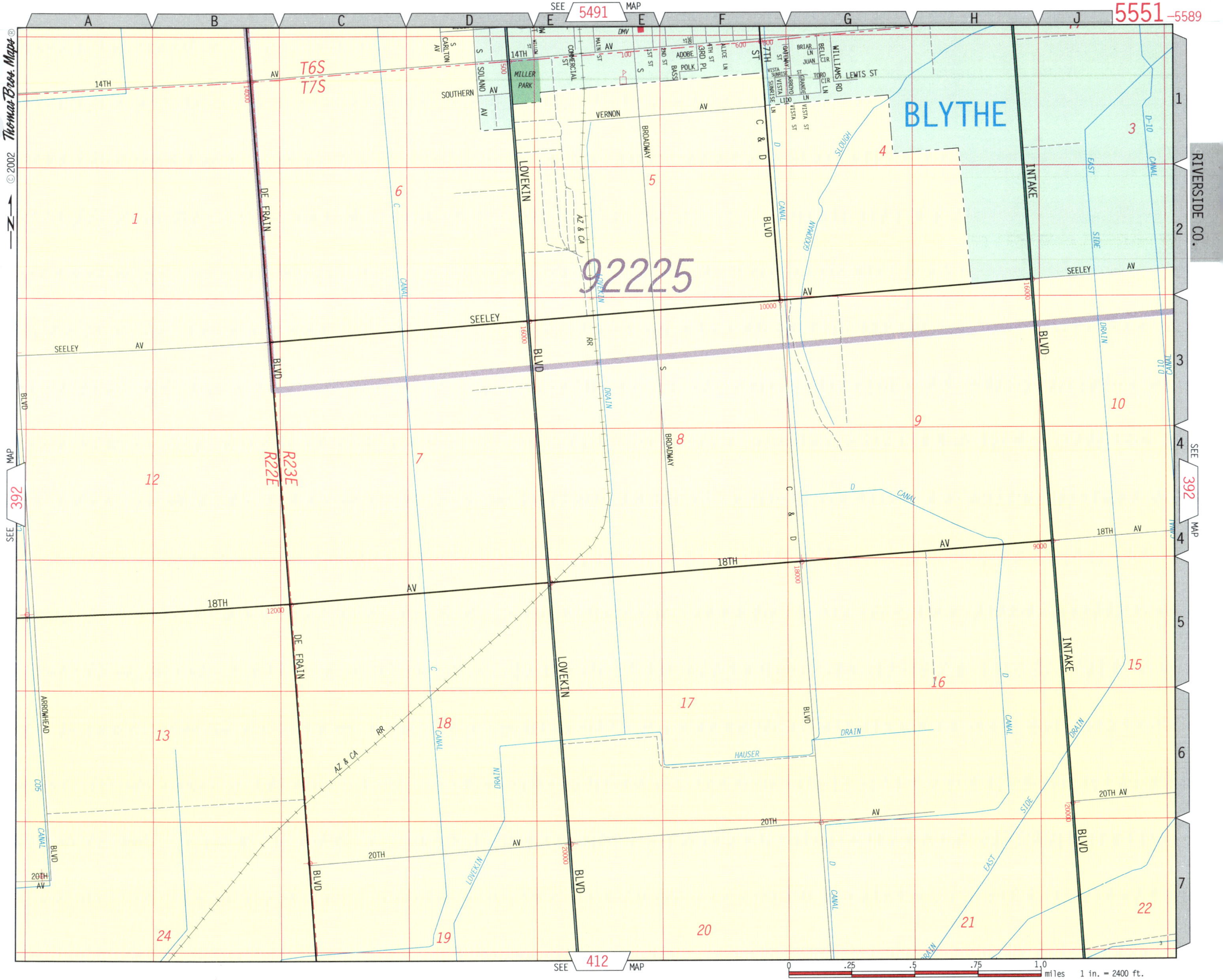
SEE 5491 MAP
A
B
C
D
E
F
G
H
J
1
2
3
4
5
6
7
BLYTHE
92225
RIVERSIDE CO.
T6S
T7S
R23E
R22E
14TH AV
SOUTHERN AV
SOLANO AV
CARLTON AV
MILLER PARK
COMMERCIAL ST
MAIN ST
DMV
ADOBE
POLK
BASS
3RD PL
4TH ST
ALICE LN
7TH ST
GATEWAY ST
VISTA SUNRISE
SUNRISE LN
LIDO
VISTA ST
ARROYO
GRANDE
BRIAR LN
JUAN
BELL CIR
TORO CIR
WILLIAMS RD
LEWIS ST
VERNON AV
BROADWAY
C & D BLVD
SLOUGH
GOODMAN
D CANAL
INTAKE BLVD
EAST SIDE DRAIN
D-10 CANAL
SEELEY AV
DE FRAIN BLVD
LOVEKIN BLVD
AZ & CA RR
C CANAL
LOVEKIN DRAIN
18TH AV
20TH AV
HAUSER DRAIN
ARROWHEAD BLVD
C05 CANAL
EAST SIDE DRAIN
SEE 392 MAP
SEE 392 MAP
SEE 412 MAP
0 .25 .5 .75 1.0 miles
1 in. = 2400 ft.
1
3
4
5
6
7
8
9
10
12
13
15
16
17
18
19
20
21
22
24

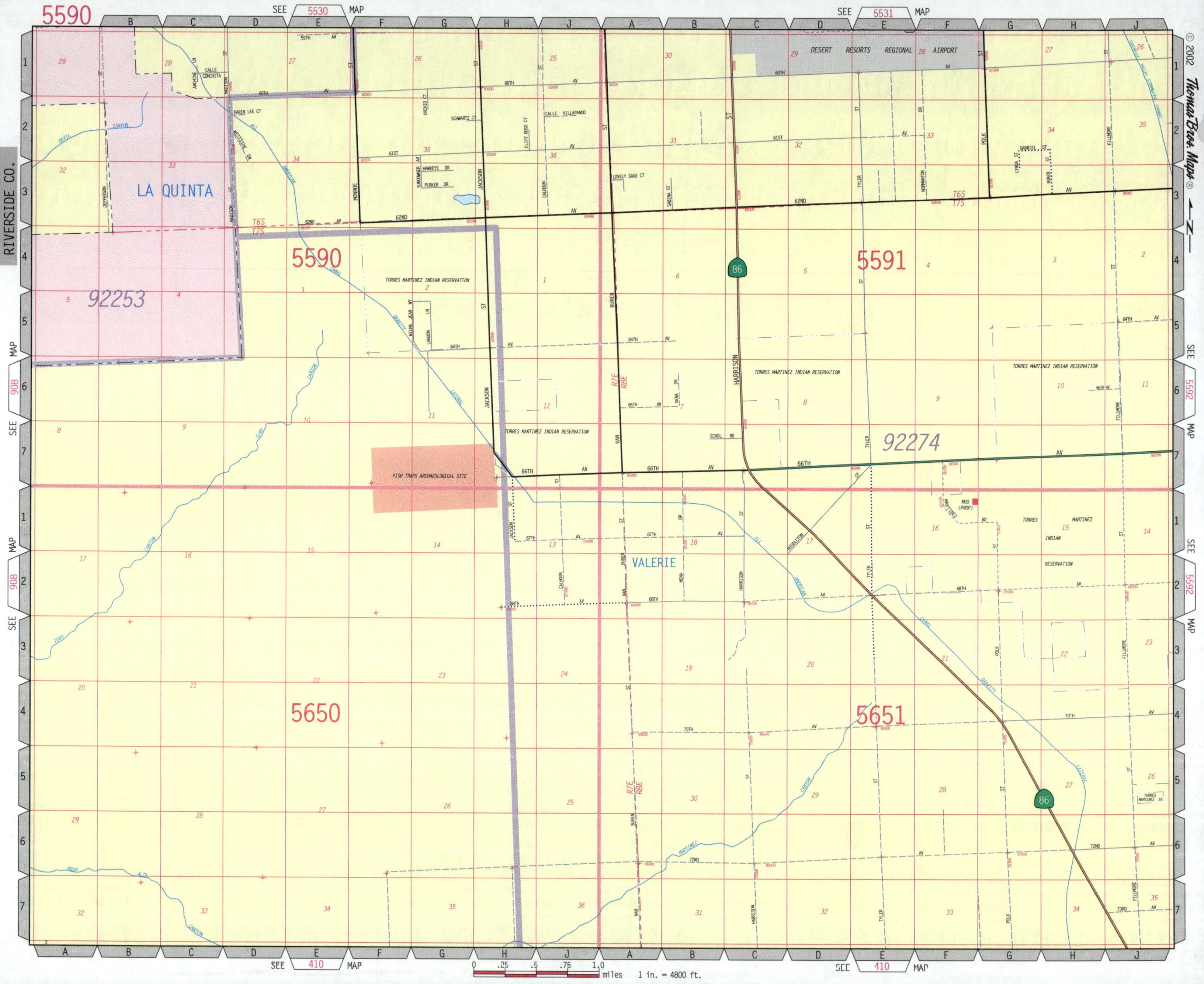
5590
SEE 5530 MAP
SEE 5531 MAP
RIVERSIDE CO.
© 2002 Thomas Bros. Maps ®
LA QUINTA
92253
5590
5591
5650
5651
92274
VALERIE
DESERT RESORTS REGIONAL AIRPORT
TORRES MARTINEZ INDIAN RESERVATION
FISH TRAPS ARCHAEOLOGICAL SITE
MUS (PROP)
T6S
T7S
R7E
R8E
60TH AV
61ST AV
62ND AV
64TH AV
65TH AV
66TH AV
67TH AV
68TH AV
70TH AV
72ND AV
73RD AV
59TH AV
MONROE ST
JACKSON ST
CALHOUN ST
VAN BUREN ST
HARRISON ST
TYLER ST
POLK ST
FILLMORE ST
MADISON ST
JEFFERSON ST
ALL AMERICAN CANAL
GRAVITY LATERAL
DEVIL CANYON
TORO CANYON
MARTINEZ CANYON
AGUA ALTA CANYON
SEE 908 MAP
SEE 5592 MAP
SEE 410 MAP
0 .25 .5 .75 1.0 miles 1 in. = 4800 ft.

SEE 390 MAP
SEE 390 MAP

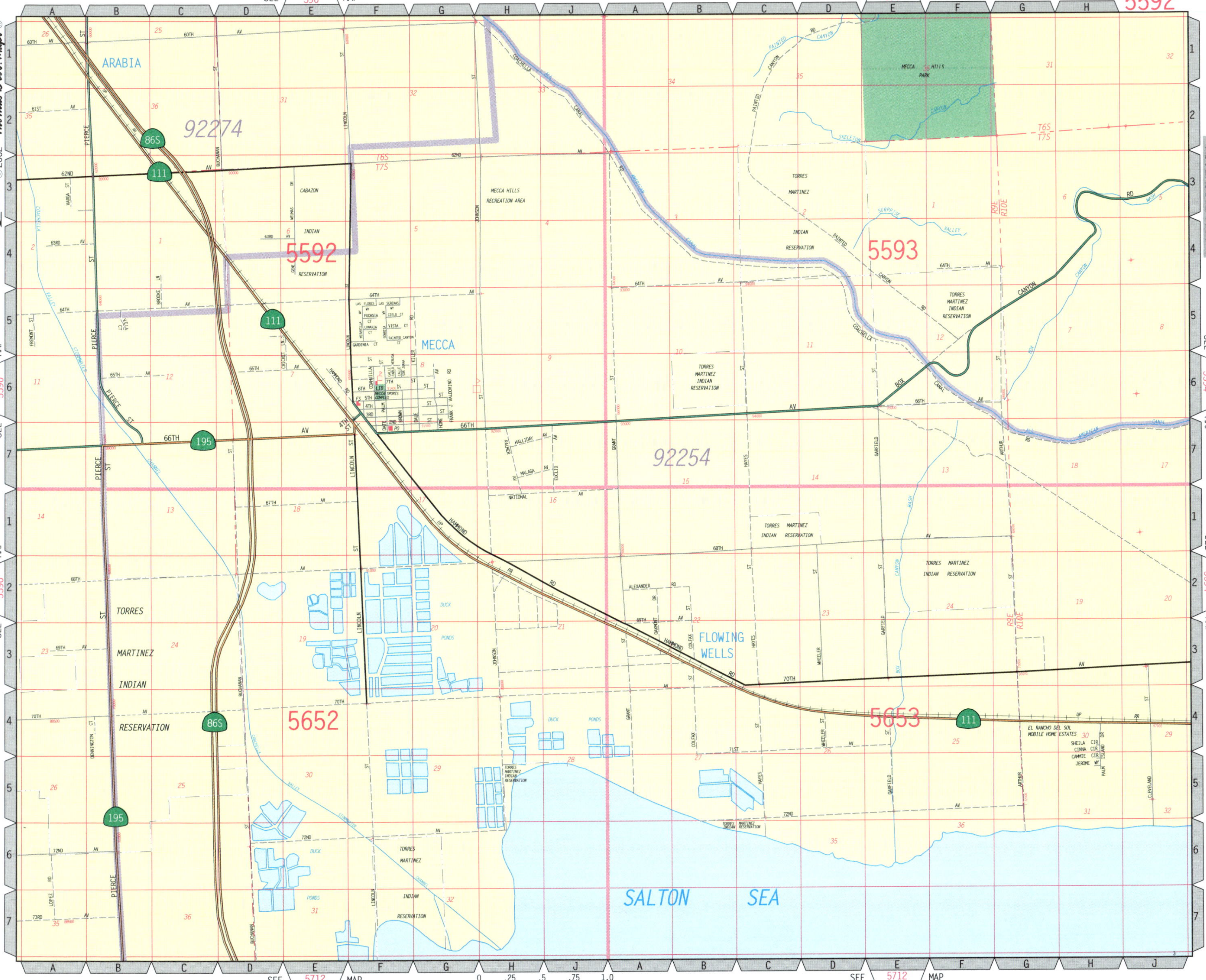

SEE 5590 MAP
SEE 5594 MAP
SEE 5712 MAP
SEE 5712 MAP

0 .25 .5 .75 1.0 miles 1 in. = 4800 ft.

SEE 390 MAP
SEE 410 MAP
SEE 5592 MAP
SEE 5714 MAP
RIVERSIDE CO.
© 2002 Thomas Bros. Maps ®
5594
5595
5654
5655
92254
NORTH SHORE
DESERT BEACH
SALTON SEA
SALTON SEA STATE REC AREA
111
BOX CANYON RD
HIDDEN SPRING CANYON
OROCOPIA CANYON
COACHELLA CANAL
ALL AMERICAN CANAL
CLUB VIEW DR
POWER LINE RD
70TH AV
72ND AV
73RD AV
68TH AV
69TH AV
UP RR
VANDER VEER RD
BAY DR
DESERT BEACH DR
PARKSIDE DR
THE BRADSHAW TR
DOS PALMAS SPRINGS
R10E R11E
T6S T7S
T7S T8S
0 .25 .5 .75 1.0 miles 1 in. = 4800 ft.

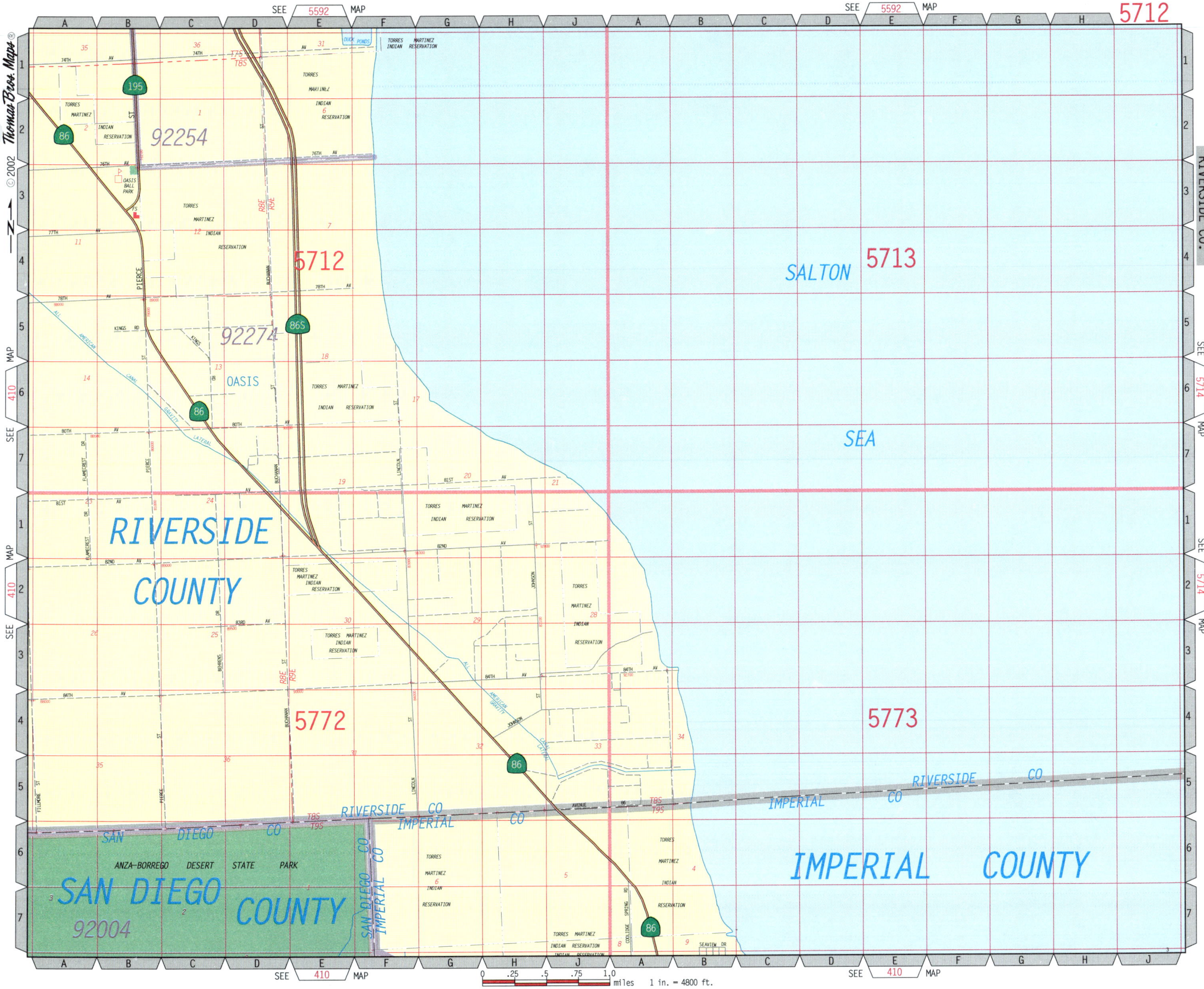
SEE 5592 MAP
SEE 5592 MAP
SEE 410 MAP
SEE 410 MAP
SEE 5714 MAP
SEE 410 MAP
SEE 5714 MAP
RIVERSIDE CO.
5712
5713
5772
5773
SALTON
SEA
RIVERSIDE
COUNTY
IMPERIAL COUNTY
SAN DIEGO COUNTY
SAN DIEGO CO
IMPERIAL CO
RIVERSIDE CO
ANZA-BORREGO DESERT STATE PARK
OASIS
OASIS BALL PARK
92254
92274
92004
TORRES MARTINEZ INDIAN RESERVATION
DUCK PONDS
74TH AV
76TH AV
77TH AV
78TH AV
80TH AV
81ST AV
82ND AV
83RD AV
84TH AV
KINGS RD
PIERCE ST
BUCHANAN ST
LINCOLN ST
JOHNSON ST
FLAMECREST DR
BEHRENS ST
FILLMORE ST
COOLIDGE ST
SPRING RD
SEAVIEW DR
AVENUE 86
ALL AMERICAN CANAL
GRAVITY LATERAL
ALL AMERICAN GRAVITY CANAL LATERAL
195
86
86S
T7S
T8S
T9S
R8E
R9E
0 .25 .5 .75 1.0 miles 1 in. = 4800 ft.

SEE 5594 MAP
SEE 5594 MAP
SEE 5712 MAP
SEE 410 MAP
SEE 410 MAP
SEE 410 MAP
RIVERSIDE CO.
92254
111
SALTON SEA
STATE RECREATION
AREA
CORVINA
BEACH
BOAT
LAUNCH
DESERT AIRE DR
POWER
LINE
RD
R10E
R11E
5714
5715
5774
5775
RIVERSIDE
COUNTY
SALTON
SALTON SEA
STATE REC
AREA
EAGLE MOUNTAIN RD
SALT CREEK RD
SALT CREEK
SALT
CREEK
BEACH
HOT SPRINGS RD
RIVERSIDE CO
IMPERIAL CO
IMPERIAL COUNTY
0 .25 .5 .75 1.0 miles 1 in. = 4800 ft.

LIST OF ABBREVIATIONS

PREFIXES AND SUFFIXES

AL	ALLEY
ARC	ARCADE
AV, AVE	AVENUE
AVCT	AVENUE COURT
AVD	AVENIDA
AVD D LA	AVENIDA DE LA
AVD D LOS	AVENIDA DE LOS
AVD DE	AVENIDA DE
AVD DE LAS	AVENIDA DE LAS
AVD DEL	AVENIDA DEL
AVDR	AVENUE DRIVE
AVEX	AVENUE EXTENSION
AV OF	AVENUE OF
AV OF THE	AVENUE OF THE
AVPL	AVENUE PLACE
BAY	BAY
BEND	BEND
BL, BLVD	BOULEVARD
BLCT	BOULEVARD COURT
BLEX	BOULEVARD EXTENSION
BRCH	BRANCH
BRDG	BRIDGE
BYPS	BYPASS
BYWY	BYWAY
CIDR	CIRCLE DRIVE
CIR	CIRCLE
CL	CALLE
CL DE	CALLE DE
CL DL	CALLE DEL
CL D LA	CALLE DE LA
CL D LAS	CALLE DE LAS
CL D LOS	CALLE DE LOS
CL EL	CALLE EL
CLJ	CALLEJON
CL LA	CALLE LA
CL LAS	CALLE LAS
CL LOS	CALLE LOS
CLTR	CLUSTER
CM	CAMINO
CM D	CAMINO DE
CM DL	CAMINO DEL
CM D LA	CAMINO DE LA
CM D LAS	CAMINO DE LAS
CM D LOS	CAMINO DE LOS
CMTO	CAMINITO
CMTO DEL	CAMINITO DEL
CMTO D LA	CAMINITO DE LA
CMTO D LAS	CAMINITO DE LAS
CMTO D LOS	CAMINITO DE LOS
CNDR	CENTER DRIVE
COM	COMMON
COMS	COMMONS
CORR	CORRIDOR
CRES	CRESCENT
CRLO	CIRCULO
CRSG	CROSSING
CST	CIRCLE STREET
CSWY	CAUSEWAY
CT	COURT
CTAV	COURT AVENUE
CTE	CORTE
CTE D	CORTE DE
CTE DEL	CORTE DEL
CTE D LAS	CORTE DE LAS
CTO	CUT OFF
CTR	CENTER
CTST	COURT STREET
CUR	CURVE
CV	COVE
DE	DE
DIAG	DIAGONAL
DR	DRIVE
DRAV	DRIVE AVENUE
DRCT	DRIVE COURT
DRLP	DRIVE LOOP
DVDR	DIVISION DR
EXAV	EXTENSION AVENUE
EXBL	EXTENSION BOULEVARD
EXRD	EXTENSION ROAD
EXST	EXTENSION STREET
EXT	EXTENSION
EXWY	EXPRESSWAY
FOREST RT	FOREST ROUTE
FRWY	FREEWAY
FRY	FERRY
GDNS	GARDENS
GN, GLN	GLEN
GRN	GREEN
GRV	GROVE
HTS	HEIGHTS
HWY	HIGHWAY
ISL	ISLE
JCT	JUNCTION
LN	LANE
LNCR	LANE CIRCLE
LNDG	LANDING
LNDR	LANE DRIVE
LNLP	LANE LOOP
LP	LOOP
MNR	MANOR
MT	MOUNT
MTWY	MOTORWAY
MWCR	MEWS COURT
MWLN	MEWS LANE
NFD	NAT'L FOREST DEV
NK	NOOK
OH	OUTER HIGHWAY
OVL	OVAL
OVLK	OVERLOOK
OVPS	OVERPASS
PAS	PASEO
PAS DE	PASEO DE
PAS DE LA	PASEO DE LA
PAS DE LAS	PASEO DE LAS
PAS DE LOS	PASEO DE LOS
PAS DL	PASEO DEL
PASG	PASSAGE
PAS LA	PASEO LA
PAS LOS	PASEO LOS
PASS	PASS
PIKE	PIKE
PK	PARK
PKDR	PARK DRIVE
PKWY, PKY	PARKWAY
PL	PLACE
PLWY	PLACE WAY
PLZ, PZ	PLAZA
PT	POINT
PTAV	POINT AVENUE
PTH	PATH
PZ DE	PLAZA DE
PZ DEL	PLAZA DEL
PZ D LA	PLAZA DE LA
PZ D LAS	PLAZA DE LAS
PZWY	PLAZA WAY
RAMP	RAMP
RD	ROAD
RDAV	ROAD AVENUE
RDBP	ROAD BYPASS
RDCT	ROAD COURT
RDEX	ROAD EXTENSION
RDG	RIDGE
RDSP	ROAD SPUR
RDWY	ROAD WAY
RR	RAILROAD
RUE	RUE
RUE D	RUE DE
RW	ROW
RY	RAILWAY
SKWY	SKYWAY
SQ	SQUARE
ST	STREET
STAV	STREET AVENUE
STCT	STREET COURT
STDR	STREET DRIVE
STEX	STREET EXTENSION
STLN	STREET LANE
STLP	STREET LOOP
ST OF	STREET OF
ST OF THE	STREET OF THE
STOV	STREET OVERPASS
STPL	STREET PLACE
STPM	STREET PROMENADE
STWY	STREET WAY
STXP	STREET EXPRESSWAY
TER	TERRACE
TFWY	TRAFFICWAY
THWY	THROUGHWAY
TKTR	TRUCK TRAIL
TPKE	TURNPIKE
TRC	TRACE
TRCT	TERRACE COURT
TR, TRL	TRAIL
TRWY	TRAIL WAY
TTSP	TRUCK TRAIL SPUR
TUN	TUNNEL
UNPS	UNDERPASS
VIA D	VIA DE
VIA DL	VIA DEL
VIA D LA	VIA DE LA
VIA D LAS	VIA DE LAS
VIA D LOS	VIA DE LOS
VIA LA	VIA LA
VW	VIEW
VWY	VIEW WAY
VIS	VISTA
VIS D	VISTA DE
VIS D L	VISTA DE LA
VIS D LAS	VISTA DE LAS
VIS DEL	VISTA DEL
WK	WALK
WY	WAY
WYCR	WAY CIRCLE
WYDR	WAY DRIVE
WYLN	WAY LANE
WYPL	WAY PLACE

DIRECTIONS

E	EAST
KPN	KEY PENINSULA NORTH
KPS	KEY PENINSULA SOUTH
N	NORTH
NE	NORTHEAST
NW	NORTHWEST
S	SOUTH
SE	SOUTHEAST
SW	SOUTHWEST
W	WEST

DEPARTMENT STORES

BD	BLOOMINGDALES
BN	THE BON MARCHE
D	DIAMONDS
DL	DILLARDS
G	GOLDWATERS
GT	GOTTSCHALKS
H	HARRIS
IM	I MAGNIN
MA	MACY'S
ME	MERVYN'S
MF	MEIER & FRANK
N	NORDSTROM
NM	NEIMAN-MARCUS
P	J C PENNEY
RM	ROBINSONS MAY
S	SEARS
SF	SAKS FIFTH AVENUE

BUILDINGS

CC	CHAMBER OF COMMERCE
CH	CITY HALL
CHP	CALIFORNIA HIGHWAY PATROL
COMM CTR	COMMUNITY CENTER
CON CTR	CONVENTION CENTER
CONT HS	CONTINUATION HIGH SCHOOL
CTH	COURT HOUSE
DMV	DEPT OF MOTOR VEHICLES
FAA	FEDERAL AVIATION ADMIN
FS	FIRE STATION
HOSP	HOSPITAL
HS	HIGH SCHOOL
INT	INTERMEDIATE SCHOOL
LIB	LIBRARY
MID	MIDDLE SCHOOL
MUS	MUSEUM
PO	POST OFFICE
PS	POLICE STATION
SR CIT CTR	SENIOR CITIZENS CENTER
STA	STATION
THTR	THEATER
VIS BUR	VISITORS BUREAU

OTHER ABBREVIATIONS

BCH	BEACH
BLDG	BUILDING
CEM	CEMETERY
CK	CREEK
CO	COUNTY
COMM	COMMUNITY
CTR	CENTER
EST	ESTATE
HIST	HISTORIC
HTS	HEIGHTS
LK	LAKE
MDW	MEADOW
MED	MEDICAL
MEM	MEMORIAL
MHP	MOBILE HOME PARK
MT	MOUNT
MTN	MOUNTAIN
NATL	NATIONAL
PKG	PARKING
PLGD	PLAYGROUND
RCH	RANCH
RCHO	RANCHO
REC	RECREATION
RES	RESERVOIR
RIV	RIVER
RR	RAILROAD
SPG	SPRING
STA	SANTA
VLG	VILLAGE
VLY	VALLEY
VW	VIEW

STREET Block City ZIP Pg-Grid

A

A AV
- RivC 92518 717-D7
20000 RivC 92567 778-H4
A RD
22000 CLTN 92313 646-E3
22000 CLTN 92324 646-E3
22000 GTER 92313 646-E3
22000 GTER 92324 646-E3
A ST
- HEMT 92545 840-F2
- PER 92570 777-F7
- RivC 92570 777-F7
100 RivC 92518 747-D1
3600 RivC 91752 644-A6
34400 YCPA 92399 649-H1
39700 HEMT 92543 841-B5
42000 MURR 92562 927-J6
42000 MURR 92562 928-A6
43900 RivC 92544 (812-A6 See Page 782)
68500 CTHC 92234 817-E1
N A ST
100 PER 92570 807-F2
1200 PER 92570 777-F7
21600 RivC 92570 777-F7
S A ST
- PER 92570 807-F3
W A ST
1800 HEMT 92545 840-G2
AARON DR
12000 MORV 92557 717-F2
AARON RD
30500 RivC 92584 899-A2
31100 RivC 92596 899-C2
AARON ALAN DR
25000 PER 92585 837-H2
25000 RivC 92585 837-H2
ABACO CT
- MURR 92563 928-H7
ABALONE WY
- RivC 92203 789-G7
- RivC 92211 789-G7
ABANA CT
- TEM 92592 959-G7
ABAZO DR
15400 MORV 92555 748-A1
ABBEY CT
2200 RIV 92507 686-D3
ABBEY RD
- RivC 92592 979-J2
ABBEY PINES DR
1200 PER 92571 778-A2
ABBEYWOOD DR
13400 RivC 92883 835-C4
ABBOTSFORD DR
3100 RIV 92503 744-G2
ABBOTSWOOD RD
1100 PER 92571 778-A2
ABBOTT
82500 INDO 92201 5470-F3
ABBOTT LN
32500 RivC 92596 869-E7
32700 RivC 92596 899-E1
42000 RivC 92544 841-F2
ABBY CT
76800 PDST 92211 819-C2
ABBY PL
34100 RivC 92596 899-B4
34100 RivC 92584 899-B4
ABBY RD
- RMIR 92270 788-B6
ABDEL CIR
47300 PDST 92260 848-F3
ABEDUL ST
16100 MORV 92551 747-H3
ABEJA CIR
- PMSP 92264 787-B7
ABEL STEARNS AV
6800 RivC 92509 684-J5
6800 RivC 92509 685-A5
ABERDARE ST
11500 LMLN 92354 647-F2
ABERDEEN DR
- COR 92881 773-G2
3500 RIV 92507 686-D5
11400 FONT 92337 644-F3
38200 MURR 92562 927-D4
ABERDEEN LN
- RivC 92585 808-E3
28600 RivC 92567 808-E3
ABERNATHY DR
- RIV 92506 716-F2
5700 RIV 92507 716-F2
ABETO WY
- TEM 92592 979-F1
ABILENE PL
- NRCO 92860 743-F2
ABILENE RD
5600 RIV 92506 715-H2
ABINGTON DR
13500 RivC 92883 835-C5
ABINGTON PL
22600 MORV 92553 717-B5
ABRAHAM AV
2800 RIV 92503 715-A7
ABRAM DR
46000 RivC 92544 902-F6
ABRAMS DR
8500 RIV 92508 746-F2
ABREU DR
21300 RivC 92570 836-J1
21300 RivC 92570 837-A1
ABRIGO RD
1000 PMSP 92262 756-C7
ABRIGO WY
45600 INDW 92210 849-B2
ABRIL DR
27500 CTHC 92234 757-B5
ABRONIA TR
45800 PDST 92260 848-G2
ABURY AV
- MURR 92562 927-G3
ABUTTERS RD
29000 MURR 92584 898-H5
29000 RivC 92584 898-H5
ACACIA
38900 RivC 92223 690-H4
ACACIA AV
400 BLY 92225 5491-G6
400 HEMT 92543 810-J7
1300 HEMT 92544 811-F7
1300 RivC 92544 811-F7
3800 NRCO 92860 713-E3
12800 DHSP 92240 697-D4
18300 RivC 92532 836-D7
34700 YCPA 92399 649-J3
34900 YCPA 92399 650-A3
43800 RivC 92544 (812-A7 See Page 782)
E ACACIA AV
100 HEMT 92543 811-B7
W ACACIA AV
100 HEMT 92543 811-A7
300 HEMT 92543 810-J7
1700 HEMT 92545 810-H7
1700 HEMT 92545 840-E1
ACACIA CT
27300 RivC 92883 835-C5
81500 INDO 92201 5410-D7
ACACIA DR
43600 PDST 92260 818-E7
44400 PDST 92260 848-E1
ACACIA LN
35500 YCPA 92399 650-B3
N ACACIA RD E
2300 PMSP 92262 756-G5
N ACACIA RD W
2200 PMSP 92262 756-G5
ACACIA ST
- LQNT 92253 5470-A4
500 LKEL 92530 866-F6
900 COR 92879 743-E7
4100 RIV 92503 714-H5
11400 LMLN 92354 647-C2
21800 RivC 92570 807-B6
24100 RivC 92584 867-G7
ACACIA WY
- TEM 92591 959-A5
900 HEMT 92543 810-J7
ACACIA GLEN DR
100 RIV 92506 716-D4
ACADEMY AV
6000 RIV 92506 716-A2
ACADEMY DR
41100 RivC 92544 841-D2
ACADIA DR
5100 RIV 92505 714-A6
ACANTO DR
64500 RivC 92264 816-E2
ACAPULCO CIR
1200 COR 92882 773-A2
ACAPULCO DR
- PDST 92260 818-G3
ACAPULCO PL
8200 RIV 92504 715-A3
ACAPULCO ST
- RMIR 92270 787-J6
ACAPULCO TR
33100 RivC 92276 788-F4
ACAPULCO WY
- INDO 92201 5470-G2
ACARO DR
14300 RivC 92570 805-E2
ACCESS RD
99000 RivC 92254 (5654-D5 See Page 5594)
ACE CIR
2300 PMSP 92262 756-E5
ACELA CT
6200 RIV 92506 716-B3
ACHESON WY
11100 RIV 92505 714-E7
11100 RIV 92505 744-E1
ACOFF RD
20100 RivC 92241 727-A5
ACOMA AV
65000 DHSP 92240 696-F4
66700 DHSP 92240 697-A4
ACORN DR
700 SJCT 92583 780-J6
27400 RivC 92883 835-B5
ACORN LN
1000 COR 92880 743-C2
52000 RivC - (813-H5 See Page 782)
S ACORN PL
2400 ONT 91761 643-B5
ACORN ST
5700 RIV 92504 684-H7
6000 RIV 92504 714-H1
ACORN WY
38300 YCPA 92399 650-J5
38300 YCPA 92399 651-A5
81200 INDO 92201 5470-C3
S ACORNGLEN PL
2600 ONT 91761 643-C6
ACRE ST
1700 NRCO 92860 743-D1
ACROPOLIS CIR
39000 RMIR 92270 818-D3
ACROPOLIS DR
11300 YCPA 92399 650-D1
ACROPOLIS ST
48800 INDO 92201 5470-B4
ADA CT
3600 RIV 92505 744-E2
ADAGE WY
2300 RIV 92506 715-H4
ADAIR AV
6500 RIV 92503 714-F1
ADALIN WY
42500 PDST 92211 819-D6
ADAM AV
30400 LKEL 92530 866-C4
ADAM LN
52900 COAC 92236 5531-C1
ADAMS
82100 INDO 92201 5410-E6
ADAMS
67700 CTHC 92234 787-C7
ADAMS AV
100 RivC 92518 747-C1
7000 RivC 92324 647-B6
23600 MURR 92562 927-G3
24500 MURR 92562 928-A6
25100 MURR 92562 958-C1
27600 RivC 92585 808-D7
27800 RivC 92585 838-E1
ADAMS CIR
300 COR 92882 743-B4
1400 SJCT 92583 811-C3
ADAMS CT
11800 YCPA 92399 650-A2
ADAMS DR
54500 RivC - 814-D5
ADAMS LN
35200 YCPA 92399 650-A2
ADAMS ST
- RivC 92203 789-H7
300 BAN 92220 721-H4
1800 RIV 92504 715-A2
1800 RIV 92504 745-E1
3700 LKEL 92530 865-H4
11600 YCPA 92399 650-A2
28000 RivC 92596 839-D5
29500 RivC 92596 869-E1
38100 RivC 92203 819-H2
39000 INDO 92203 819-H2
40700 RivC 92201 819-H4
43300 LQNT 92253 819-H7
44600 LQNT 92253 849-H2
E ADAMS ST
200 CLTN 92324 646-D1
ADANTI CT
- MURR 92562 928-B4
ADDICOTT CIR
3700 COR 92881 773-J5
ADDISON CT
17800 CHLS 91709 712-B6
ADDISON LN
25600 MURR 92562 928-D7
ADDISON ST
11700 YCPA 92399 650-A2
ADELA DR
1700 HEMT 92545 840-H2
ADELAID ST
46900 INDW 92210 849-B3
ADELAIDE CT
2700 RIV 92506 715-G3
ADELANTE ST
- TEM 92592 979-G1
ADELANTO DR
27000 RivC 92883 835-C4
ADELE AV
51800 RivC 92230 723-G6
ADELE CT
11000 MORV 92557 687-B7
ADELE LN
6900 RivC 92509 645-B5
ADELFA ST
33000 RivC 92530 896-B3
ADELINA AV
3100 NRCO 92860 713-E5
ADELINA RD
68800 CTHC 92234 757-E6
ADELINE AV
12800 MORV 92553 717-C4
ADELITO DR
49800 LQNT 92253 849-G5
ADELLA ST
11100 SBdC 92354 647-E1
ADELONY LN
30900 RivC 92567 779-A6
ADEN WY
3900 RIV 92504 715-D2
ADIAN CT
40000 TEM 92591 959-A1
ADIOS ST
13700 MORV 92555 718-D5
ADIRONDACK DR
300 COR 92881 773-D3
ADIRONDACK LN
- RIV 92508 746-E2
ADJER ST
25200 RivC 92584 867-J7
25500 RivC 92584 868-A7
ADLEA VISTA
- CTHC 92234 787-G7
ADLER LN
45500 RivC 92590 978-A4
45600 RivC 92590 977-J4
ADLER PL
6800 RIV 92503 714-F1
ADMIRALTY AV
9100 RIV 92503 714-H4
ADMIRALTY CIR
- RIV 92503 714-J4
ADMIRALTY CT
- RIV 92503 714-H4
44400 RivC 92544 (812-B5 See Page 782)
ADMIRALTY WY
98600 RivC 92254 (5654-D2 See Page 5594)
ADOBE
500 BLY 92225 5551-F1
ADOBE AV
1900 COR 92882 742-H7
1900 COR 92882 772-H1
10200 RIV 92503 714-F6
ADOBE DR
44400 RivC 92544 842-B1
ADOBE RD
82100 INDO 92201 5410-E6
ADOBE ST
300 LKEL 92530 866-F5
ADOBE WY
- MORV 92555 748-C1
1000 PMSP 92262 756-F4
ADOBE SPRING RD
33300 TEM 92592 979-H1
ADOBE SPRINGS DR
73000 RivC 92260 818-E2
ADONIS DR
43800 PDST 92260 818-D7
ADONIS PL
2300 COR 92882 773-B1
ADRIA CIR
- PDST 92211 819-A4
ADRIANA AV
10300 RIV 92505 714-F6
ADRIENNE AV
22500 MORV 92553 717-B5
ADRIENNE DR
1600 COR 92882 742-J7
ADRIENNE WY
26100 RivC 92544 841-E1
ADUDDELL DR
33300 RivC 92584 898-J2
ADWICK ST
100 COR 92881 773-D3
AEGEAN DR
9300 RIV 92503 715-A7
AERIAL CT
6500 RIV 92506 716-A4
AERIE RD
71200 RivC 92260 848-A6
AERO LN
4200 RivC 92509 685-C2
AFFIRMED ST
2400 PER 92571 777-H6
AFORTUNADO DR
66400 DHSP 92240 696-J1
AFTON LN
28800 RivC 92584 868-G7
AFTON WY
24600 MORV 92557 717-F2
AGAPE LN
36200 RivC 92595 927-E1
AGATE CT
46900 INDW 92210 849-B3
AGATE DR
13300 BLY 92225 5491-G7
15500 FONT 92337 644-F3
AGATE LN
11900 CLTN 92324 645-J3
24100 RivC 92548 809-F4
AGATE ST
4100 RivC 92509 644-E7
4300 RivC 92509 684-E2
13100 BLY 92225 5491-G6
AGATE TER
8800 BLY 92225 5491-H6
AGATHA LN
2900 RIV 92507 686-C3
AGAVE LN
73400 PDST 92260 848-F5
AGAVE PL
9200 RIV 92503 715-A7
AGAVE ST
- LQNT 92253 5470-A3
14200 MORV 92553 717-G6
AGEAN CT
41400 MURR 92562 927-H3
AGENA ST
42000 TEM 92592 959-B6
AGILE CT
2500 PER 92571 777-H5
AGNES PL
5400 RIV 92504 715-B1
AGNES ST
500 BEAU 92223 690-J6
1300 COR 92882 743-A4
14500 RivC 92230 723-B5
AGNES WILSON RD
- RivC - 392-D2
AGNEW AV
26000 RivC 92548 839-C1
AGOSTO WY
500 HEMT 92545 810-H6
AGRIPINA LN
32100 RivC 92584 868-G7
AGUA CALIENTE TR
31900 CTHC 92234 787-B3
AGUA CAYENDO RD
12500 DHSP 92240 697-B5
AGUA MANSA RD
1300 RivC 92509 645-F6
19600 SBdC 92509 645-F6
19700 RLTO 92509 645-F6
W AGUA MANSA RD
400 CLTN 92324 646-A1
500 SBdC 92324 646-A1
1600 CLTN 92324 645-H3
1600 CLTN 92316 645-H3
1700 RLTO 92324 645-H3
1700 RLTO 92316 645-H3
2300 RLTO 92509 645-H3
AGUANGA RANCHOS RD
47700 RivC 92536 409-G5
47700 RivC 92536 982-J7
47700 RivC 92536 983-A7
AGUA SAL CIR
- RivC 92254 (5654-D5 See Page 5594)
AGUAVE AV
78600 RivC 92211 819-G1
AGUA VISTA
39000 MURR 92563 928-H6
AGUILA CT
45200 RivC 92592 979-F4
AGUILA PASS
15200 MORV 92555 747-J1
AGUILA ST
1500 BAN 92220 722-D3
AGUILAR ST
9300 RIV 92503 715-A7
AGUSTA DR
24700 MORV 92551 717-G7
AHERN LN
31400 TEM 92591 959-E3
AILANTHUS DR
1500 HEMT 92545 840-G3
AINSDALE WY
5400 RIV 92505 714-A5
AINSLE CT
42000 RivC 92544 841-F2
AINSLEY AV
11300 RIV 92505 714-A2
AINSLEY CT
- RivC 92562 956-B6
AINSWORTH PL
4800 RIV 92504 685-D6
14600 RivC 92530 865-E4
43900 RivC 92536 963-D7
AIR FORBES AV
30500 MORV 92555 718-J7
30500 MORV 92555 719-A7
31000 RivC 92555 719-A7
AIRLANE DR
200 PMSP 92262 786-H2
AIRLIFT ST
1400 SJCT 92582 780-H6
AIRMAN DR
14600 RivC 92518 716-F7
14600 RivC 92518 746-G1
AIROSA PL
23600 MORV 92557 687-D6
AIRPORT BLVD
81000 LQNT 92253 5530-D4
83000 RivC 92274 5530-H4
83500 COAC 92274 5530-H4
83600 COAC 92274 5531-A4
83600 RivC 92274 5531-F4
88000 RivC 92274 390-F11
AIRPORT CIR
300 COR 92880 742-J3
AIRPORT DR
6700 RIV 92504 714-J2
E AIRPORT DR
2700 ONT 91761 643-C1
AIRPORT RD
- PMSP 92262 786-J2
- PMSP 92262 787-A2
AIRPORT WY
- PER 92571 747-D6
AIRPORT CENTRE DR
- PMSP 92262 786-J2
4000 PMSP 92264 786-J3
4000 PMSP 92264 787-B4
AIRSTREAM WY
27100 RivC 92585 838-D3
AJILWOOD CT
28100 RivC 92584 868-F5
AJO LN
73000 PDST 92260 848-E5
AKERS LN
22300 RivC 92570 777-B1
AKES PASS
32400 TEM 92592 979-F3
AKIPA CT
22700 RivC 92595 897-D6
AKLEY ST
17000 RivC 92530 896-B2
AKRON LN
21600 RivC 92567 779-G7
AKRON ST
15500 RivC 92508 746-C3
AKWO CIR
22900 RivC 92595 897-D7
ALABAMA ST
- RDL 92373 647-H1
8800 RIV 92503 684-F7
43200 PDST 92211 819-C6
ALABASTER CT
11800 FONT 92337 644-D4
ALADDIN
- PMSP 92264 786-E5
ALADDIN CIR
39700 RivC 92591 930-A7
ALADDIN ST
45300 INDO 92201 5470-D1
ALAMAR MESA DR
36100 HEMT 92545 840-C6
36100 RivC 92545 840-C6
ALAMEDA AV
10600 SBdC 92316 645-F1
ALAMEDA CT
15200 LKEL 92530 865-H1
35900 RMIR 92270 787-G6
ALAMEDA DR
17100 RivC 92570 776-A7
67800 DHSP 92240 697-C5
ALAMEDA DEL MONTE
10500 RivC 92595 896-J7
20700 RivC 92595 897-A7
21100 RivC 92595 927-B1
ALAMITOS ST
24600 LMLN 92354 647-B1
ALAMO DR
47200 PDST 92260 848-E4
ALAMO LN
2900 HEMT 92545 840-F4
ALAMO ST
- INDO 92201 5470-G3
4300 RIV 92501 645-H7
33600 RivC 92530 896-B4
ALAMONTE CT
48300 PDST 92260 848-E5
ALAMOS DR
22300 RivC 92570 806-A1
ALAN CIR
48300 PDST 92260 848-E4
ALASKA AV
43800 PDST 92211 819-C7
ALASTAIR CIR
- COR 92882 773-B4
ALBA CT
- LQNT 92253 819-G6
1400 RIV 92507 716-G2
ALBA WY
14800 MORV 92553 717-H7
ALBANY CT
1900 SJCT 92582 810-F2
ALBANY DR
26000 RivC 92586 838-A5
ALBANY ST
3400 RIV 92503 714-H7
ALBARIAN WY
16000 RivC 92504 745-G4
ALBATROSS WY
99000 RivC 92254 (5654-D5 See Page 5594)
ALBEE RD
42400 RivC 92539 (965-F4 See Page 964)
ALBEMARLE RD
900 HEMT 92543 810-J5
ALBERT ST
20000 RivC 92595 896-H5
ALBERTA AV
81000 RivC 92201 5410-C7
ALBERTA LN
13300 RivC 92555 719-B4
ALBERTO CIR
3700 PMSP 92262 756-C3
ALBION DR
- INDO 92201 5470-G3
4500 RIV 92503 714-H4
ALBION LN
28000 RivC 92584 868-E4
ALBION WY
11900 MORV 92557 717-C1
ALBORADA ST
19000 RivC 92562 956-E1
ALBRIDGE DR
3500 COR 92881 773-D4
ALCALA CT
11600 FONT 92337 644-E3
ALCALDE LN
- RivC 92590 958-D7
ALCAZAR DR
33000 RivC 92584 898-J1
ALCITA RD
68100 CTHC 92234 787-D1
ALCOA CIR
500 COR 92880 743-B3
ALCOBA DR
- TEM 92592 959-G7
- TEM 92592 979-G1
ALCOLA CIR
100 PDST 92211 818-J3
ALCORN DR
21600 MORV 92557 716-J1
ALCOT CIR
- PDST 92211 819-E3
ALCOTT CT
900 HEMT 92543 841-B3
ALCOTT DR
6500 RIV 92506 716-B4
ALCOTT UNION DR
- MURR 92563 928-G6
ALCOVE PL
21200 RivC 92570 775-E7
24800 MORV 92557 717-F1
ALDEN CIR
78500 LQNT 92253 849-G1
ALDEN RD
5400 RIV 92506 685-E6
34200 RivC 92596 899-J3
ALDER AV
10600 SBdC 92316 645-B2
11200 FONT 92337 645-B3
41000 RivC 92544 811-D7
ALDER CIR
36000 YCPA 92399 650-E6
ALDER CT
- MURR 92562 927-F4
- RivC 92596 929-D1
S ALDER DR
2400 ONT 91761 643-B5
ALDER LN
48100 PDST 92260 848-F4
E ALDER LN
1700 CLTN 92324 646-G1
ALDER ST
800 COR 92879 743-E7
18000 RivC 92570 746-B7
18400 RivC 92570 776-B2
ALDERBROOK RD
32700 RivC 92595 896-H6
S ALDER CREEK DR
2600 ONT 91761 643-B6
ALDER CREEK RD
11500 RivC 92880 742-B5
ALDERGATE DR
- RivC 92584 838-F7
- RivC 92584 868-E1
ALDERIDGE CT
16600 RivC 92503 745-A5
ALDERPOINT CT
6700 RIV 92506 716-D4
ALDERWOOD AV
- RivC 92880 713-A2
200 RIV 92506 716-D5
ALDERWOOD ST
25600 RivC - 814-D6
ALDREN CT
11100 MORV 92555 688-E7
ALDRICH CT
4300 RIV 92503 714-H4
ALEGRE AV
2500 HEMT 92545 810-G5
ALEGRE CT
6200 RIV 92506 716-A3
ALEGRE DR
9200 DHSP 92240 696-H1
ALEGRE VISTA RD
35500 RivC 92596 899-F7
ALEGRIA
80300 INDO 92201 5470-B2
ALEHZON CIR
31000 TEM 92592 979-D5
E ALEJO RD
100 PMSP 92262 786-F1
W ALEJO RD
100 PMSP 92262 786-D1
ALENA CT
28000 RivC 92544 841-G4
ALENCON CT
- TEM 92592 979-F1
ALEPPO WY
25100 MORV 92553 717-G7
ALERICH ST
29500 RivC 92585 808-H4
ALESANDRO RD
- PMSP 92264 786-C2
ALESSANDRO AV
100 SJCT 92583 811-C2
200 RivC 92583 811-C1
1100 RivC 92583 781-C7
ALESSANDRO BLVD
100 RIV 92508 716-B4
500 RIV 92506 716-B4
1500 RivC 92506 716-B4
2300 RIV 92506 715-J1
2500 RivC 92553 716-B4
20900 RivC 92518 716-B4
21900 MORV 92553 716-B4
21900 MORV 92553 717-B6
25900 MORV 92555 717-F6
25900 MORV 92555 718-A5
30700 MORV 92555 719-A5
30800 RivC 92555 719-A5
E ALESSANDRO BLVD
100 RIV 92506 716-E6
100 RIV 92508 716-E6
ALESSANDRO DR
38100 RivC 92539 (934-E4 See Page 904)
73500 PDST 92260 848-F1
ALESSANDRO PL
300 SJCT 92583 811-C3
ALESSANDRO RD
- BAN 92220 722-B2
2000 BAN 92220 692-B7
N ALESSANDRO ST
100 HEMT 92543 811-A6
S ALESSANDRO ST
100 HEMT 92543 811-A7
300 HEMT 92543 841-A1
ALEXA WY
43500 RivC 92544 811-J6
ALEXANDER DR
- CTHC 92234 757-F7
- CTHC 92234 787-F1
42100 RivC 92544 931-H4
ALEXANDER RD
- RivC 92254 (5653-A2 See Page 5592)
ALEXANDER ST
14000 RIV 92506 716-G6
14000 RivC 92508 716-G6
14000 RivC 92506 716-G6
17500 RivC 92570 746-G7
18300 RivC 92570 776-G2
ALEXANDER WY
600 PMSP 92262 756-E5
ALEXANDRA DR
- COR 92881 773-E2
1100 SJCT 92583 811-D3
23800 MURR 92562 927-G4
ALEXANDRIA AV
- RivC 92880 683-D4
ALEXANDRIA CT
- INDO 92201 5410-A7
ALEXANDRIA DR
40000 TEM 92591 959-B1
ALEXANDRIA ST
- RIV 92508 746-E2
ALEXANDRIA VALE
- INDO 92201 5410-A7
ALEXE ST
500 BEAU 92223 690-H6
ALEXIS DR
13000 MORV 92553 717-C4
ALEXIS LN
25300 RivC 92584 867-J7
ALFALFA DR
69700 CTHC 92234 787-G3
ALFALFA RD
19000 RivC 92567 779-A1
ALFALFADALE RD
2000 PER 92571 777-H6
ALFARO DR
- RMIR 92270 818-D6
ALFRED CIR
38900 RivC 92223 690-G3
ALFREDO RD
53600 RivC 92539 904-C7
ALGIERS
- PMSP 92264 786-C6
ALGODONES TR
- PMSP 92264 786-G6
ALGONA AV
100 SJCT 92583 811-C1
ALGONQUIN CIR
45700 INDW 92210 848-J2
ALGONQUIN LN
10400 RIV 92505 744-G1
ALGONQUIN PL
73400 RivC 92276 788-F3
ALGRAVE AV
- RivC 92596 899-C6
ALHAMBRA AV
6200 RIV 92505 714-B3
ALHAMBRA DR
2200 PMSP 92264 786-F7
ALHAMBRA ST
1900 NRCO 92860 713-C4
ALI CT
- LQNT 92253 5470-A5
ALICANTE AV
6000 RivC 92509 645-E4
80000 INDO 92201 5470-B4
ALICANTE DR
25100 RivC 92548 809-A7
25200 RivC 92585 808-G7
30000 RivC 92548 808-H7
ALICE LN
300 BLY 92225 5491-F7
300 BLY 92225 5551-F1
25900 RivC 92544 811-D7
29800 RivC 92567 808-H1
ALICE MARBLE LN
73100 PDST 92260 848-E3
ALICE SPRINGS PL
400 RIV 92508 716-E6
ALICIA CIR
36200 RivC 92592 960-D3
ALICIA CT
- PMSP 92264 787-A5
ALICIA LN
72400 RMIR 92270 818-D5
ALICIA PL
2500 HEMT 92545 810-F5
ALICIA WY
24800 MURR 92562 928-C5
ALICIENTE DR
27500 RivC 92883 835-B5
ALIGHCHI WY
44600 TEM 92592 979-G2
ALISA VIEJO CT
15700 MORV 92555 748-C2
ALISO CT
- RIV 92508 746-E1
ALISO DR
- CTHC 92234 787-C6
- PMSP 92264 787-C6
14500 FONT 92337 644-C1
14500 SBdC 92337 644-C1
ALISO RD
5100 RIV 92505 714-B5
68100 CTHC 92234 787-E2
ALISO ST
700 COR 92879 743-E7
S ALISO CREEK DR
2500 ONT 91761 643-C6
ALISON WY
900 SJCT 92583 811-C3
ALITA DR
16700 RivC 92504 745-H5
ALITE WY
3100 RIV 92503 744-E3
ALL AMERICAN WY
1700 COR 92879 743-H6
ALLAN ST
18600 RivC 92532 866-E1
29400 LKEL 92532 866-D2
ALLANVIEW DR
43300 RivC 92536 964-C6
W ALLEE RANCH RD
1800 CLTN 92324 645-J3
ALLEGHENY AV
700 BEAU 92223 721-C3
ALLEGHENY ST
3500 COR 92881 773-D4
ALLEGRE CIR
700 COR 92879 743-G2
ALLEGRE DR
800 COR 92879 743-G2
ALLEGRO CT
- RivC 92211 819-F2
ALLEGRO DR
78000 RivC 92211 819-F2
ALLEN AV
16700 RivC 92518 746-H5
26300 RivC 92548 839-A2
32000 RivC 92545 839-C2
36500 CTHC 92234 787-F7
37000 CTHC 92234 817-F1
ALLEN DR
800 COR 92879 743-F3
ALLEN LN
74300 RivC 92241 758-G1
ALLEN ST
200 BAN 92220 722-D2
31000 RivC 92563 929-C3
ALLEN WY
25500 LMLN 92354 647-D3
S ALLEN WY
1200 CLTN 92324 646-G2
ALLENBY ST
10400 RIV 92505 714-G7
ALLENDALE DR
5500 RIV 92507 716-F1
ALLENHURST ST
- RIV 92508 746-E1
ALLENTOWN DR
26100 RivC 92586 838-A5
ALLEPPO CT
1100 HEMT 92545 840-H3
ALLERGATE CT
29100 RivC 92584 868-F1
ALLEY E
- PMSP 92264 786-H5
ALLEY WY
- LMLN 92354 647-C1
ALLIES PL
22800 MORV 92553 717-B5
ALLIGATOR POND RD
41400 RivC 92201 819-G4
ALLIN LN
1300 BAN 92220 721-D5
ALLIS PL
4200 RIV 92501 685-F4
ALLIS ST
29700 LKEL 92530 865-J2
ALLISON LN
5200 RivC 92509 684-B3
34300 RivC 92595 897-C4
ALLISS CT
800 COR 92879 743-F1
ALLSPICE ST
25100 RivC 92544 811-J5
25100 RivC 92544 (812-A6 See Page 782)
ALLSTATE DR
- RIV 92501 685-G1
ALL VIEW DR
200 BAN 92220 722-B1
ALL VIEW PL
10 NRCO 92860 713-H2
ALLWOOD DR
11500 RIV 92503 744-E3
ALLWOOD ST
5900 RivC 92509 685-B3
ALLYN DR
13300 MORV 92553 716-J4
ALMA CT
- PMSP 92264 787-A5
ALMA LN
11500 FONT 92337 644-G3
ALMA ST
23000 RivC 92570 807-D6
ALMADEN CIR
- RivC 92563 929-A7
- TEM 92591 929-A7
- TEM 92591 959-A1
ALMADEN LN
27200 RivC 92585 838-C3
ALMANOR CT
16200 MORV 92551 747-J3
ALMANSA CT
39500 MURR 92562 928-B2
ALMAR ST
5100 RIV 92505 714-B5
ALMARIE WY
500 HEMT 92544 811-G6
ALMERIA ST
2100 COR 92879 743-H2
ALMOND AV
10500 SBdC 92337 644-C2
10900 FONT 92337 644-B2
36200 CALI 92320 690-B6
ALMOND CT
11700 LMLN 92354 647-C3
ALMOND DR
1000 COR 92882 742-F5
1400 PER 92571 807-J1
11900 FONT 92337 644-C4
12600 SBdC 92324 647-A5
ALMOND PL
- INDO 92201 5470-H3
ALMOND ST
3800 RivC 92501 685-G4
14000 RivC 92230 723-E6
21600 RivC 92595 897-B1
ALMOND WY
400 BAN 92220 722-C1
ALMOND GROVE CIR
42700 MURR 92562 958-A3
ALMOND TREE LN
20000 RivC 92595 896-H5
ALMOND TREE PTH
18300 RivC 92504 745-J7
18300 RivC 92504 775-J1
ALMOND TREE ST
1800 HEMT 92545 840-H4
ALMONDWOOD DR
27000 RivC 92883 835-C4
ALMSIDE WY
4000 RIV 92505 744-E1
ALNE DR
2500 HEMT 92545 810-F4
ALOE LN
- RivC 92503 744-J7
ALOHA DR
1000 PMSP 92264 786-E6
ALOHA RD
22300 RivC 92570 807-B2
ALOLA ST
- BAN 92220 722-C3
ALOMA DR
49800 RivC 92230 723-B4
ALONA ST
12800 MORV 92553 717-D3
ALONDRA DR
700 HEMT 92545 810-F5
40500 MURR 92562 928-C5
ALONDRA WY
2700 PMSP 92264 786-H4
ALONDRO DR
4400 RivC 92509 684-F1
ALOSTA LN
15300 MORV 92555 747-J1
ALPARAS CIR
25700 MORV 92551 747-H3
ALPENROSE DR
- RivC - (907-D7 See Page 906)
ALPHA CT
400 SJCT 92583 811-C1
ALPHA PL
42400 TEM 92592 959-B6
ALPHA ST
25000 MORV 92557 687-G7
ALPINE CT
15200 LKEL 92530 865-H1
25400 MURR 92562 928-F5
ALPINE DR
500 PER 92570 807-F6
11800 FONT 92337 644-F4
68400 RivC - (907-E3 See Page 906)
ALPINE ST
700 HEMT 92545 840-H2
ALPINE WY
11000 RIV 92505 714-C3
22000 RivC 92262 725-F7
52900 RivC - 814-A6
ALPINE UNION ST
- MURR 92563 928-F6
ALPINE VIEW LN
- RivC 92562 956-G4
ALPS RD
3000 COR 92881 773-D3
ALPS WY
40700 RivC 92544 961-D1
ALSACE CT
1900 SJCT 92583 811-F4
ALSACE LN
44000 RivC 92544 (812-A5 See Page 782)
ALSTON PL
6300 RivC 92509 684-G6
ALT CT
58200 RivC 92539 (965-D5 See Page 964)
ALTA AV
- RivC 92585 838-C3
ALTA DR
13700 MORV 92553 716-J5
35200 YCPA 92399 650-A4
ALTA ST
5700 RivC 92509 685-D1
ALTABRISA WY
1000 MORV 92557 687-A5
ALTA CALLE
- RivC 92571 748-D3
ALTA COLINA WY
45500 INDW 92210 849-A2
ALTA CRESTA CIR
- RivC 92562 956-C2
ALTADENA DR
8900 RIV 92503 714-E1
ALTA LOMA DR
900 COR 92882 743-B6
2900 PMSP 92264 786-H4
ALTA LOMA LN
29700 MURR 92563 898-J7
ALTA LOMA WY
7100 RIV 92503 684-E7
ALTAMAR CIR
13400 RivC 92883 835-C4
ALTA MAR DR
- RivC 92509 684-G2
ALTA MESA CT
35900 RivC 92592 960-D4
ALTA MESA DR
400 RIV 92507 686-E3
ALTAMIRA DR
75600 INDW 92210 849-B2
ALTA MIRA WY
4900 RIV 92505 714-B6

STREET Block City ZIP Pg-Grid

ALTAMURA CT
- TEM 92592 959-F7
- TEM 92592 979-F1
ALTA MURRIETA DR
26400 MURR 92563 928-E6
ALTANOS RD
42100 RivC 92592 960-A5
ALTA VISTA
33300 RivC 92530 896-B2
ALTA VISTA AV
600 COR 92882 743-C7
ALTA VISTA CT
400 SJCT 92583 811-C4
ALTA VISTA DR
- RMIR 92270 817-G3
4100 RIV 92501 685-F5
4100 RIV 92506 685-F5
25000 MORV 92557 687-G6
31300 RDL 92373 649-A5
31500 YCPA 92373 649-A5
ALTA VISTA WY
27400 RivC 92585 838-D5
27700 RivC 92586 838-C5
ALTEJO BELLA
9300 RivC 92223 691-A2
ALTHEA AV
2300 RLTO 92316 645-G1
ALTHEA WY
- RivC 92595 927-C1
3500 RivC 92509 645-A7
ALTO CIR
400 PMSP 92264 786-E7
ALTO DR
43100 RivC 92544 811-H7
ALTO LAGO DR
15500 RivC 92570 805-F1
ALTON CT
100 CALI 92320 650-A7
40800 TEM 92591 959-D3
ALTON ST
6300 RivC 92509 685-A1
ALTON WY
7300 RIV 92506 715-G6
ALTURA CT
3100 COR 92882 742-F6
ALTURA DR
200 PER 92570 807-D2
1000 RIV 92507 686-C3
ALTURA PL
1500 BAN 92220 721-J2
ALTURA ST
10700 SBdC 92337 644-B1
ALTURAS CREEK DR
26400 MORV 92555 717-J4
26400 MORV 92555 718-A4
ALTYRA CT
13400 RivC 92883 835-C4
ALVA CT
68000 CTHC 92234 757-D7
ALVA DR
38500 RivC 92223 690-G3
ALVA PL
14200 RivC 92570 775-D6
ALVA RD
29000 RivC 92567 778-G7
ALVARADO AV
83000 RivC 92274 5530-G4
ALVARADO CIR
3600 COR 92882 742-E6
6000 RivC 92509 684-J5
ALVARADO RD
400 PMSP 92262 756-C4
ALVARADO ST
15000 RivC 92530 865-F4
ALVARES DR
15100 RivC 92570 805-F5
ALVAREZ CT
4600 RIV 92507 685-J6
ALVISO AV
6900 RivC 92509 684-J4
6900 RivC 92509 685-A5
ALVISO RD
22200 RivC 92570 777-B2
ALVITA CIR
39600 MURR 92562 928-B2
ALYSHEBA ST
2400 PER 92571 777-H5
ALYSSUM LN
10700 MORV 92557 687-E6
AMADO LN
22000 RivC 92595 897-B5
E AMADO RD
100 PMSP 92262 786-E1
W AMADO RD
100 PMSP 92262 786-D1
AMADOR CT
15200 LKEL 92530 865-H1
AMALFI DR
- PDST 92211 819-B4
16300 RivC 92570 775-H4
AMANDA AV
26000 RivC 92545 839-F1
AMANDA CT
7300 RIV 92504 715-E4
AMAPOLA LN
84300 COAC 92236 5471-A4
AMAPOLA ST
33600 RivC 92530 896-B3
AMARETTO RD
48800 RivC 92536 983-C2
AMARILLO CT
- RIV 92501 686-A1
AMARILLO ST
4100 RivC 92509 644-E7

AMARILLO WY
2100 PMSP 92264 786-G4
AMARITA WY
- TEM 92592 959-D7
43500 TEM 92592 979-D1
AMARYLLIS WY
- PDST 92260 818-H7
AMATISTA AV
- RivC 92595 897-G6
AMATOL RD
25000 RivC 92548 809-D6
AMBASSADOR AV
19200 RivC 92881 773-J3
AMBASSADOR CIR
- LQNT 92253 819-J7
- LQNT 92253 5410-A7
- RMIR 92270 788-A7
AMBER CIR
3000 COR 92882 742-G5
AMBER DR
600 RivC 91752 683-E4
2700 COR 92882 742-F5
2700 HEMT 92545 810-F4
AMBER LN
- MURR 92562 927-F4
900 LKEL 92530 865-H4
12800 YCPA 92399 650-C5
30100 RivC 92543 871-A2
AMBER ST
8800 RIV 92503 715-A6
72900 PDST 92260 848-E4
AMBER WY
100 PER 92571 777-H7
AMBERCORN DR
30200 RivC 92563 929-A7
AMBERGATE PL
7600 RIV 92504 715-C2
AMBER GLEN ST
1100 COR 92881 773-E4
AMBERHILL AV
- RivC 92880 683-D4
AMBER HILL TR
12000 MORV 92557 717-G2
AMBER HILL WY
17700 CHLS 91709 712-A5
AMBERLEAF CT
- MURR 92562 927-F5
16200 RivC 92504 745-G6
AMBERLEAF WY
- RivC 92592 979-H3
AMBERLEY CIR
39800 TEM 92591 959-C1
AMBERLEY DR
24000 MORV 92553 717-E4
AMBER RIDGE LN
4200 HEMT 92545 840-E4
AMBER SKY ST
600 BAN 92220 721-G4
AMBERSWEET ST
- COR 92881 773-G5
AMBERTON DR
33700 RivC 92595 897-B3
AMBERWOOD CT
3500 LKEL 92530 865-H4
15800 RivC 92504 745-G5
AMBERWOOD DR
1100 HEMT 92543 840-H1
11900 FONT 92337 644-C4
AMBERWOOD PL
34500 YCPA 92399 649-J6
AMBORELLA WY
- RivC 92584 868-F4
AMBRO CT
43100 RivC 92220 691-G4
AMBROSE CIR
3400 COR 92882 773-C4
AMBROSIA ST
72600 PDST 92260 848-D3
AMBROSIO CIR
18500 RivC 92881 773-H2
AMBROSIO DR
10600 DHSP 92240 697-A3
AMBS DR
4200 RIV 92505 744-B1
AMELIA RD
22100 RivC 92570 807-B1
AMELIA WY
1400 PMSP 92262 756-F5
AMERICA CT
- LQNT 92253 819-J7
AMERICAN AV
600 BEAU 92223 721-A3
AMERICAN CIR
300 COR 92880 742-J5
AMERICAN DR
1200 RIV 92501 645-H7
1300 RIV 92501 685-H1
AMERICAN RIVER RD
900 RivC 92880 742-B5
E AMERICAN RIVER RD
3800 ONT 91761 643-D6
AMERSFOOT WY
28500 RivC 92586 838-A7
AMES AV
16400 LKEL 92530 865-J2
AMETHYST DR
1600 PER 92571 777-H7
46200 INDW 92210 849-B2
55700 RivC 92282 724-E2
AMETHYST ST
1300 RIV 92507 686-B3
AMETISTA DR
1600 SJCT 92583 811-C4
AMHERST AV
1000 HEMT 92544 811-F5

AMHERST AV
80700 INDO 92201 5470-B1
AMHERST CT
- RMIR 92270 818-A2
26400 LMLN 92354 647-G3
AMHERST ST
800 COR 92880 742-J1
900 COR 92880 743-A1
AMHURST CT
26600 RivC 92586 838-B5
AMHURST DR
3200 RIV 92503 744-E2
AMIENS CT
41100 MURR 92562 927-J4
AMIGO DR
1700 HEMT 92545 810-H6
AMIGOS PL
8800 RIV 92504 715-B6
AMIR DR
46700 PDST 92260 848-F3
AMITE LN
30000 RivC 92276 788-J2
AMITY CT
10100 RIV 92503 714-G5
AMMONS WY
40700 SDCo 92028 997-H3
AMOROSE ST
14600 RivC 92530 865-E4
15000 LKEL 92530 865-E4
AMSTERDAM DR
3000 RIV 92504 715-B6
AMSTERDAM RD
31200 RivC 92596 929-C1
AMWOOD WY
29600 TEM 92591 958-J4
AMY CIR
30000 CTHC 92234 787-C1
AMY CT
- RIV 92504 715-B5
AMY DR
400 BAN 92220 721-F3
3100 COR 92882 742-E5
AMY LN
26000 RivC 92544 811-C7
26000 RivC 92544 841-D1
AMY WY
2500 RIV 92506 715-H3
ANABEL ST
6200 RivC 92509 685-A5
ANACAPA CIR
49700 LQNT 92253 849-F5
ANACAPA PL
11500 RIV 92505 714-B7
ANACAPA WY
44200 PDST 92260 818-G7
ANACONDA CT
30400 TEM 92591 959-B5
ANAHEIM ST
11200 RIV 92505 714-B4
ANA MARIA PL
1900 PMSP 92264 786-F5
ANA MARIA ST
14200 RivC 92230 723-D5
ANAPOLIS CT
88000 RivC 92274 5531-J1
ANASAZI DR
32600 RivC 92592 979-G4
ANAWOOD PL
26000 RivC 92544 811-J7
26100 RivC 92544 841-J1
ANCASH CT
23600 RivC 92570 807-D4
ANCHOR CIR
69100 RivC 92254 (5654-D2 See Page 5594)
ANCHOR RD
27200 RivC 92584 868-D4
ANCHOR WY
15100 LKEL 92530 865-J7
ANCHORAGE ST
3500 HEMT 92545 810-E6
ANCHOVY RD
78900 RivC 92201 819-G4
ANCHUK RD
10100 MORV 92557 687-E5
ANCLA LN
39300 HEMT 92543 810-J6
39300 HEMT 92543 811-A6
ANCLADERO CT
16400 MORV 92551 747-H3
ANDALUCIA CT
2800 PMSP 92264 816-E1
ANDALUCIA DR
25600 RivC 92544 811-H7
ANDALUSIA AV
6000 RivC 92509 645-E5
ANDALUSIAN DR
- NRCO 92860 743-J1
- NRCO 92860 744-A1
ANDALUZ WY
- COR 92882 773-B3
ANDEE DR
1400 PMSP 92264 786-G5
ANDEREN CT
42100 RivC 92592 960-A5
ANDERSON AV
3300 RIV 92507 686-A4
ANDERSON CT
28700 RivC 92586 838-C7
ANDERSON DR
200 HEMT 92544 811-E6
ANDERSON LN
- LQNT 92253 5530-E5
ANDERSON RD
5600 SDCo 92028 999-C3

ANDERSON RD
20500 RivC 92570 836-H4
20500 RivC 92570 777-A5
ANDERSON ST
10900 LMLN 92354 647-B1
ANDERSON WY
11500 LMLN 92354 647-B2
ANDES WY
300 COR 92881 773-D2
35800 YCPA 92399 650-C4
ANDORKA WY
31400 RivC 92596 899-C3
ANDORRA ST
48600 INDO 92201 5470-B4
ANDORRA WY
300 CTHC 92234 817-G1
ANDOVER CT
5900 RIV 92506 716-B2
ANDOVER DR
- RivC 92274 5530-H3
ANDOVER LN
- RivC 92584 869-A6
ANDOVER ST
3400 RivC 92879 744-A5
ANDRA CIR
43800 RivC 92201 5410-D6
ANDRADE AV
43100 RivC 92544 811-H6
ANDRE CT
25900 MORV 92553 717-J3
ANDREA AV
42200 RivC 92544 841-F1
ANDREA CIR
- TEM 92591 959-E1
ANDREA LN
- COAC 92236 5471-A6
900 COR 92880 743-C3
ANDREAS RD
100 PMSP 92262 786-E2
E ANDREAS RD
1300 PMSP 92262 786-F1
ANDREAS CANYON DR
- PDST 92260 848-D6
ANDREAS CANYON RD
- RivC - 816-E3
ANDREAS HILLS DR
3300 PMSP 92264 816-G2
3300 RivC 92264 816-G2
ANDREAS PALMS DR
1000 PMSP 92264 816-F1
ANDREAS PALMS DR N
1000 PMSP 92264 816-F1
ANDRETTI ST
12500 MORV 92553 717-C3
ANDREW LN
- COR 92881 773-F2
- SBDO 92408 646-J1
ANDREW ST
9100 RIV 92503 715-A6
9200 RIV 92503 714-J6
ANDREWS AV
500 SJCT 92583 811-C2
ANDREWS CIR
17000 RivC 92518 746-J5
70800 RMIR 92270 788-A7
ANDREWS CT
39500 RivC 92203 819-J2
ANDREWS WY
30800 TEM 92591 929-C7
ANDROMEDA LN
16900 RivC 92504 745-F5
ANDROS ST
39500 RivC 92592 930-G6
ANDY WY
33900 RivC 92596 899-H5
ANEMONE CIR
10700 MORV 92557 687-F6
ANGE LN
43500 RivC 92544 811-J5
ANGEL LN
- RIV 92508 746-E1
ANGEL WY
26500 RivC 92544 841-D2
ANGELA AV
5700 RivC 92509 684-D4
ANGELA CT
81600 INDO 92201 5470-D1
ANGELA DR
16000 RivC - 726-G1
ANGELA WY
300 SJCT 92583 811-A1
ANGEL CANYON DR
- RivC 92503 744-B5
ANGEL CANYON TR
- PMSP 92262 755-H2
- RivC 92262 755-H2
ANGELICA CT
- RivC 92503 744-D5
ANGELICA DR
- MURR 92562 928-B4
ANGELLA WY
24500 MORV 92551 747-F4
ANGELO ST
4300 RIV 92507 686-A6
ANGELS LN
33800 RivC 92595 897-B4
ANGELS CAMP RD
74000 PDST 92260 818-G5
ANGELS WALK WY
57000 RivC 92539 (935-B3 See Page 904)
ANGELUS HILL RD
1400 HEMT 92545 840-F4
ANGELUS VISTA
17000 RivC 92240 727-B2

ANGELUS VISTA
17000 RivC 92241 727-B2
ANGEL VIEW TR
17500 RivC 92241 727-J2
ANGIE LN
24300 MORV 92557 687-E7
ANGLEWOOD DR
47000 PDST 92260 848-E3
ANGORA LN
40100 RivC 92544 931-C4
ANGULLA WY
- MURR 92563 928-H7
ANGUS ST
- RivC 92880 683-D7
ANGUS WY
- RIV 92508 716-E7
ANISE ST
25700 MORV 92553 717-H4
ANITA CIR
48100 PDST 92260 848-E4
ANITA DR
28700 RivC 92587 837-F7
ANITA LN
38700 CTHC 92234 817-D3
ANITA PL
6000 RIV 92504 685-A7
ANITA RD
19000 RivC 92258 725-G5
ANITA ST
11100 SBdC 92354 647-E1
ANITA WY
34100 RMIR 92270 787-G5
ANJA AV
45400 RivC 92592 981-A4
ANJOU CT
1800 SJCT 92583 811-F4
ANN CT
1300 PER 92570 807-D2
ANN LN
- RMIR 92270 817-H3
ANN ST
1700 SJCT 92583 781-A5
ANN WY
19300 RivC 92570 806-E1
44000 RivC 92536 (984-C1 See Page 964)
ANNA LN
500 BEAU 92223 690-J6
25400 RivC 92584 867-J5
68300 CTHC 92234 817-D2
ANNA ST
2600 RIV 92506 715-H2
ANNABELLE LN
39400 RivC 92592 930-E6
ANNA LYNN LN
30800 RivC 92548 839-B1
ANNANDALE AV
7800 DHSP 92240 656-F7
7800 RivC 92240 656-F7
ANNANDALE PL
- RivC 92880 683-D4
ANNANDALE RD
29100 RivC 92586 868-B1
ANNAPOLIS CIR
100 SBDO 92408 646-H1
1900 COR 92881 773-H5
ANN ARBOR CT
11800 RIV 92505 714-A5
ANNE CT
20700 RivC 92567 779-A5
ANNELIES CIR
4100 HEMT 92544 811-F4
ANNETTE AV
25800 MORV 92551 747-J1
ANNETTE DR
32800 RivC 92530 866-A7
ANNETTE PL
400 COR 92879 773-D1
ANNETTE ST
38000 RivC 92211 819-C1
ANNIE LU CIR
27800 RivC 92584 898-E3
ANNISA AV
3600 HEMT 92544 811-F5
ANN MARIE CT
14000 MORV 92553 717-E6
ANO CREST RD
30600 RivC 92596 869-C3
ANSELM CIR
11300 FONT 92337 644-G2
ANSELM DR
10600 SBdC 92337 644-G1
ANSON WY
20600 RivC 92595 897-A6
ANTARES DR
2800 RIV 92503 715-A7
ANTELOPE
- DHSP 92240 696-J7
200 HEMT 92543 810-J7
ANTELOPE DR
2400 COR 92882 772-H1
ANTELOPE RD
24300 RivC 92585 808-E4
25600 RivC 92585 838-E1
29200 RivC 92584 868-E1
29400 RivC 92586 868-E1
32000 RivC 92584 898-E1
33200 MURR 92584 898-F4
34900 MURR 92563 898-F7
ANTELOPE ST
83000 INDO 92201 5470-H2
E ANTELOPE WY
3100 ONT 91761 643-C5
E ANTELOPE CREEK DR
3700 ONT 91761 643-C6

ANTENNA DR
14200 RivC 92223 720-G5
ANTHERIUM DR
17700 CHLS 91709 712-A5
ANTHIRIUM AV
600 PER 92571 777-J6
ANTHONY AV
17300 RivC 92530 896-B3
ANTHONY LN
10000 RivC 92223 690-H4
ANTHONY PL
14300 MORV 92555 718-B6
ANTIBES DR
36000 MURR 92562 928-D1
ANTIETAM DR
3100 RIV 92503 744-G2
ANTIGUA CIR
1200 PMSP 92264 786-G4
ANTIGUA CT
2300 HEMT 92545 810-G6
ANTIGUA DR
- INDO 92201 5470-G3
11300 RivC 91752 683-G3
ANTIGUA ST
300 HEMT 92545 810-G6
ANTILLA ST
39300 RivC 92562 927-B6
ANTILLES DR
14500 MORV 92553 717-H7
ANTIOCH AV
6100 RIV 92504 685-B7
6100 RIV 92504 715-B1
ANTIQUE PL
3700 PER 92571 778-A2
ANTLER CT
23700 MORV 92553 717-D4
ANTLER RD
3200 ONT 91761 643-B5
E ANTLER RD
3100 ONT 91761 643-A5
ANTONELL CT
1200 BEAU 92223 721-A1
ANTONIA PL
5800 RivC 92509 685-C1
ANTONIA WY
69600 RMIR 92270 787-G5
ANTONIO CIR
- LMLN 92354 647-F2
ANTWERP ST
- RivC 92596 929-D1
ANZA CT
47600 INDO 92201 5470-F3
69500 CTHC 92234 757-G7
ANZA DR
900 PMSP 92264 786-F6
ANZA RD
3500 PMSP 92262 756-D4
39000 RivC 92591 929-J7
39100 RivC 92539 (934-J5 See Page 904)
39700 RivC 92591 959-J1
39700 RivC 92591 960-A1
40600 RivC 92592 960-B3
43600 RivC 92592 980-A1
45500 RivC 92592 979-G5
ANZA TR
2700 PMSP 92264 786-H5
ANZA CREST RD
38100 RivC 92539 (934-J3 See Page 904)
ANZANITA LN
59700 RivC 92539 (935-F6 See Page 904)
ANZA TRAILS W
39700 RivC 92539 (934-D6 See Page 904)
ANZIS WY
32400 RivC 92548 809-E7
ANZUELO CIR
3000 PMSP 92264 786-H5
APACHE
- COAC 92236 5471-C5
APACHE CIR
1800 PMSP 92264 786-F5
APACHE LN
18000 CHLS 91709 712-B6
APACHE RD
500 PER 92570 807-E3
1000 PMSP 92264 786-F5
45300 INDW 92210 849-B2
APACHE ST
43600 INDO 92203 5410-H6
APACHE TR
700 RIV 92507 686-D6
13400 RivC 92230 723-A3
APALOOSA WY
100 PDST 92211 819-A3
APAPAS LN
1600 SJCT 92583 811-D3
APAWAMIS RD
9500 RivC 92240 696-E1
APELA DR
52300 RivC - (843-J1 See Page 842)
52500 RivC - 844-A1
APEX AV
100 BAN 92220 721-D3
APEX WY
28200 RivC 92570 836-F7
APIS RD
44200 RivC 92592 979-F2
44200 TEM 92592 979-F2
APOLLO LN
48600 RivC 92536 963-B7

APOSTLE LN
1700 RIV 92506 716-A4
APPALOOSA AV
5400 RivC 92509 684-B4
APPALOOSA CT
21500 CYNL 92587 867-A3
APPALOOSA DR
11500 FONT 92337 644-G3
APPALOOSA LN
- PER 92571 778-A2
APPALOOSA ST
- NRCO 92860 713-C6
APPIAN WY
- INDW 92210 849-E1
- MURR 92562 928-D4
- PDST 92211 819-A4
1500 SJCT 92583 811-E3
3100 COR 92881 773-D3
6200 RIV 92506 715-H3
14600 FONT 92337 644-C4
APPLE AV
3000 RivC 92509 645-B7
APPLE DR
11100 CALI 92320 690-C6
APPLE LN
40400 RivC 92539 (935-F7 See Page 904)
41400 RivC 92539 (965-F1 See Page 964)
APPLE WY
21800 RivC 92567 779-H7
APPLE BLOSSOM LN
300 LKEL 92530 865-G1
1000 COR 92881 773-E3
14100 MORV 92553 717-G6
APPLE BLOSSOM WY
1400 HEMT 92545 840-D4
APPLEBY CT
13300 MORV 92553 717-C4
APPLEBY ST
200 COR 92881 773-D4
APPLE CANYON RD
- RivC - 844-J7
- RivC - (845-B5 See Page 844)
56400 RivC - (874-J1 See Page 844)
APPLE CREEK DR
1300 PER 92571 807-J1
1400 PER 92571 777-J7
APPLE CREEK RD
26500 RivC 92586 868-B2
APPLECROSS DR
5500 RIV 92507 716-F1
APPLEGATE CT
- MURR 92562 927-G3
APPLEGATE DR
2000 COR 92882 742-H6
16300 FONT 92337 644-H2
APPLE GATE RD
37200 RivC 92563 929-C2
APPLE ORCHARD LN
2700 RIV 92506 715-H1
APPLESEED LN
35100 RivC 92544 902-J4
APPLETON DR
25500 RivC - (813-H5 See Page 782)
APPLETON ST
5100 RIV 92504 685-B7
APPLE TREE CIR
39600 MURR 92563 928-F5
APPLETREE DR
100 PER 92571 777-H7
APPLE TREE LN
8800 RivC 92223 690-J2
8800 RivC 92223 691-A2
11700 FONT 92337 644-E3
APPLE TREE ST
2500 HEMT 92545 840-G4
APPLEWOOD CT
- LKEL 92530 896-G4
S APPLEWOOD DR
2600 ONT 91761 643-B6
APPLEWOOD ST
43800 RivC 92544 811-J5
43800 RivC 92544 (812-A5 See Page 782)
APPLEWOOD WY
19100 LKEL 92530 896-G4
APRICOT AV
11200 SBdC 92337 644-B2
30000 RivC 92567 778-H6
30800 RivC 92567 779-A6
APRICOT LN
- RivC 92211 819-H2
400 HEMT 92543 841-B1
5400 RIV 92506 715-H1
21300 RivC 92595 897-A2
APRICOT PL
1600 COR 92879 743-J6
APRIL CT
15700 MORV 92551 747-F2
APRIL DR
13100 RivC 92503 744-B5
39300 TEM 92591 958-J1
APRIL LN
800 BAN 92220 721-J4
APRIL SHOWER DR
3500 RivC 92503 744-B4
APTOS ST
19900 RIV 92508 746-F2
20200 RIV 92518 746-F3
AQUA CT
11300 FONT 92337 644-C3

AQUA DR
35100 CTHC 92234 787-F6
AQUAMARINE DR
- INDW 92210 849-B3
34400 YCPA 92399 649-H2
AQUAMARINE LN
900 COR 92882 742-J6
900 COR 92882 743-A5
AQUANETTA CIR
1800 PMSP 92264 786-F5
AQUANETTA DR
1800 PMSP 92264 786-F5
AQUARIUS CIR
2700 RIV 92503 744-G3
AQUARIUS ST
46500 INDO 92201 5470-H2
AQUATIC WY
24900 RivC 92544 811-G5
AQUA VISTA WY
27400 TEM 92590 958-F5
AQUEDUCT LN
- RMIR 92270 817-G2
AQUEDUCT RD
16800 RivC 92241 728-D2
AQUEDUCT RD Rt#-62
- RivC - 391-H1
AQUEDUCT WY
22700 MORV 92553 717-B4
AQUILA CT
25500 RivC 92586 837-J7
AQUILLA ST
24200 MURR 92562 927-J4
24200 MURR 92562 928-A5
AQUINO CIR
1000 COR 92879 743-G2
ARAB LN
5100 RivC 92509 684-B3
ARABASCA CIR
31300 TEM 92592 979-D5
ARABIA ST
43100 INDO 92201 5410-F6
45700 INDO 92201 5470-F2
ARABIAN AV
16500 RivC 92504 745-H4
ARABIAN CT
16000 FONT 92337 644-G3
49000 RivC 92536 963-C4
ARABIAN PL
100 COR 92879 743-H2
ARABIAN WY
2200 COR 92879 743-J2
8700 CALI 92320 690-C1
ARABY
- PMSP 92264 786-E6
ARABY AV
85200 COAC 92236 5471-C7
ARABY CIR
2900 PMSP 92264 786-H5
ARABY DR
1800 PMSP 92264 786-H6
ARAGON DR
17000 RivC 92570 776-A7
ARALIA CT
27500 TEM 92591 958-J2
ARALIA DR
9200 RIV 92503 715-A7
ARALIA WY
1100 HEMT 92545 840-G3
ARANDA ST
40200 RivC 92592 960-E1
ARAPAHO RD
300 PER 92570 807-E3
ARAPAHO ST
- NRCO 92860 713-C6
ARAPAHOE
46500 INDW 92210 849-F2
ARAPAHOE CIR
10500 RivC 92223 691-C4
78600 INDW 92210 849-F2
ARAPAHOE CT
78500 INDW 92210 849-F2
ARAPAHOE LN
78600 INDW 92210 849-F2
ARAPAHOE ST
- PMSP 92264 786-C2
3200 RIV 92503 715-B6
ARAPAHOE TER
78500 INDW 92210 849-F2
ARAPAHOE WY
46700 INDW 92210 849-F2
ARAPAHOE VISTA
77300 INDW 92210 819-E7
ARAUCANA ST
25500 RivC 92544 (812-B6 See Page 782)
ARAVE ST
40000 RivC 92543 871-B3
ARBOLA CIR
79000 LQNT 92253 819-H7
ARBOLADO LN
34100 RivC 92530 896-G5
ARBOLEDA DR
72700 PDST 92260 818-D7
ARBOL REAL AV
30400 RivC 92276 758-D7
30400 RivC 92276 788-D2
ARBOR CIR
200 RivC 91752 683-E5
ARBOR CT
- PMSP 92264 787-A5
ARBOR DR
6800 RIV 92504 715-A2
61500 RivC 92240 695-H5
ARBOR LN
44600 TEM 92592 979-D3

ARBOR PKWY
700 HEMT 92545 840-G2
ARBOR WY
34400 YCPA 92399 649-H2
ARBOR DALE CT
22400 MURR 92562 927-C4
ARBOR DEL SIERRA RD
31700 RivC 92592 979-E7
ARBORETUM CIR
- COR 92881 773-F4
ARBORETUM DR
- COR 92881 773-F4
ARBOR GLEN CT
2000 COR 92879 744-B2
ARBOR GLEN RD
78100 RivC 92211 819-F1
ARBOR RIDGE RD
800 PER 92571 777-J2
800 PER 92571 778-A2
ARBORWOOD CIR
1300 COR 92882 773-A1
ARBUCKLE SCHOOL RD
5500 RivC 92509 685-D2
ARCADIA CT
2800 PMSP 92262 756-C4
ARCADIA LN
33800 RivC 92595 897-J3
47000 PDST 92260 848-G3
ARCADIA ST
8100 RivC 92881 774-A4
11700 YCPA 92399 650-A2
19600 RivC 92881 773-J4
ARCADIAN CT
69100 CTHC 92234 787-F1
S ARCADIAN SHORES AV
- ONT 91761 683-A1
S ARCADIAN SHORES RD
2500 ONT 91761 643-A6
ARCARO ST
13500 MORV 92555 718-D4
ARCATA CT
- PMSP 92264 786-J5
ARCH WY
6100 RIV 92506 685-D7
6300 RIV 92506 715-D1
6600 RIV 92504 715-D1
17500 RivC 92530 896-C2
ARCHDALE ST
2100 RIV 92506 715-J1
2100 RIV 92506 716-A1
ARCHER AV
1500 BAN 92220 721-D5
ARCHER CIR
- COR 92882 773-B3
ARCHER RD
19700 RivC 92570 775-G4
ARCHER ST
6200 RivC 92509 684-E6
ARCHIBALD AV
6100 RivC 92880 388-H3
6200 RivC 92880 683-A7
6200 RivC 92880 713-A3
8200 RivC 92880 712-J5
ARCHIBEK DR
29500 RivC 92567 778-G7
ARCHIE AV
27000 MORV 92555 718-B2
ARCHIE VALLEY CT
900 CALI 92320 649-G7
ARCHINE LN
59000 RivC 92253 5590-C1
ARC LIGHT DR
14500 RivC 92518 716-G7
14800 RivC 92518 746-G1
ARCO RD
27900 RivC 92596 839-G5
ARCOLA DR
39600 RivC 92544 931-G7
40200 RivC 92536 961-G1
40200 RivC 92544 961-G1
ARCULEO RD
- RivC 92570 805-F5
ARDELL LN
13400 MORV 92555 718-C4
ARDEN DR
67800 CTHC 92234 817-C3
ARDIA DR
37100 RivC 92544 931-H3
ARDIA RD
43100 RivC 92590 957-D7
ARDMORE DR
26100 RivC 92544 811-J7
26200 RivC 92544 841-J1
ARDMORE ST
1000 RIV 92507 686-B1
25800 RivC 92584 837-J7
ARDOS ST
12700 MORV 92553 717-H3
ARDSLEY CT
4300 RIV 92505 714-F6
ARDWELL DR
52500 RivC 92539 (934-A3 See Page 904)
ARECA PALM DR
30500 RivC 92548 839-A1
ARENA CT
800 HEMT 92545 810-G5
ARENA BLANCA RD
67700 DHSP 92240 697-B5
ARENAS LN
1600 SJCT 92583 811-D4
ARENAS RD
400 PMSP 92262 786-D2

E ARENAS RD
1700 PMSP 92262 786-F2
ARENDO ST
24400 RivC 92590 977-H2
ARENDT LN
35700 MURR 92563 898-G7
ARENGA PALM DR
30600 RivC 92548 839-A2
ARENISCA VERDE DR
12300 MORV 92557 717-H2
AREZZO
- INDW 92210 819-B5
ARFON WY
3700 RIV 92501 685-F3
ARGENTINA CT
4600 RIV 92507 686-A6
ARGENTINE CT
14600 FONT 92337 644-C2
ARGO CT
43000 TEM 92592 959-C6
ARGO PL
12700 MORV 92553 717-D3
ARGONAUT DR
25500 MORV 92553 717-H6
ARGUELLO DR
11600 RivC 91752 683-G4
ARGUS CT
8600 RIV 92504 715-A4
ARGYLE CIR
2900 COR 92879 744-B2
ARGYLE WY
5300 RIV 92506 716-A1
ARI CIR
22800 RivC 92595 897-D7
ARIA CIR
- RivC 92562 956-E1
ARICAL CT
14400 MORV 92553 717-B6
ARIEL CT
28900 RivC 92586 837-J7
ARIES LN
2700 RIV 92503 744-H2
ARIES WY
11000 RivC 91752 683-H3
ARISTA DR
39200 RivC 92539 (934-J5 See Page 904)
39200 RivC 92539 (935-A5 See Page 904)
ARISTOTLE CT
23200 MORV 92553 717-C5
ARISTOTLE RD
36000 RivC 92544 901-D7
ARIZONA AV
10900 RIV 92503 744-F3
ARIZONA ST
1100 PER 92571 747-D7
1300 BLY 92225 5491-G7
ARJAY DR
42600 MURR 92562 957-J1
42600 MURR 92562 958-A1
ARJUNA AV
26000 RivC 92590 958-B6
ARLEN CT
49500 RivC 92536 983-D1
ARLENE CT
82300 INDO 92201 5470-F3
ARLENE DR
900 PMSP 92264 786-G4
82400 INDO 92201 5470-F3
ARLENE WY
1700 PER 92570 807-F5
ARLINGTON AV
100 NRCO 92860 713-J1
100 RIV 92505 713-J1
2100 RIV 92506 716-A2
2200 RIV 92506 715-G2
4500 RIV 92504 715-B2
6000 RIV 92504 714-H2
6700 RIV 92503 714-E2
10000 RIV 92505 714-A1
ARLINGTON DR
32500 YCPA 92399 649-D5
ARLINGTON RD
- RivC - (935-J1 See Page 904)
ARLINGTON ST
- MURR 92562 927-F4
ARLINGTON WY
700 COR 92879 743-F1
25000 HEMT 92543 810-J6
ARLINGTON MINE RD
- RivC - 391-K7
- RivC - 392-A7
ARLISS CT
11800 GTER 92313 646-F3
ARLISS DR
11900 GTER 92313 646-F3
ARLISS LN
11800 GTER 92313 646-F3
ARLISS ST
600 RivC 92507 646-D6
ARLISS WY
11800 GTER 92313 646-F3
ARLISS DELL
11700 GTER 92313 646-F3
ARMADA PL
41300 RivC 92591 959-F4
ARMAGOSA DR
- RIV 92508 716-C7
- RIV 92508 746-C1
ARMANAC CT
41500 PDST 92260 818-F4
ARMANDO DR
20400 RivC 92567 779-A4

RIVERSIDE CO.

STREET
Block City ZIP Pg-Grid

ARMATA AV
81700 INDO 92201 5410-D7
ARMATA DR
- COR 92881 773-E3
ARMENIA DR
- CTHC 92234 787-E5
ARMINTROUT DR
17000 RivC 92504 745-H5
ARMISTICE ST
4100 RivC 92509 685-E4
ARMOUR WY
75700 PDST 92211 819-A5
ARMSTRONG RD
1100 FONT 92337 645-C4
2000 RivC 92509 645-A6
34600 RivC 92596 899-C5
ARMSTRONGS DR
- COR 92881 773-E3
ARMY RD
- RivC - 411-K3
ARNETT CT
4300 RIV 92503 714-H4
ARNETT RD
36100 RivC 92595 927-E1
ARNICO ST
2000 PMSP 92262 756-J5
ARNOLD AV
- PER 92571 777-F6
16300 LKEL 92530 865-J1
66000 RivC 92240 726-H1
ARNOLD BLVD
14500 RivC 92518 716-J7
14800 RivC 92518 746-J1
15000 RivC 92518 747-A1
ARNOLD DR
16600 RivC 92518 746-J5
ARNOLD LN
32200 RivC 92595 897-D7
32200 RivC 92595 927-D1
ARNOLD PALMER
55300 LQNT 92253 5530-A4
AROBLES CT
15500 MORV 92555 747-J1
ARONIMINK RD
- RivC 92562 956-G4
ARONOMINIC
- LQNT 92253 5530-C5
ARORA ST
3600 RivC 92509 685-D2
AROSA WY
44100 LQNT 92253 819-H7
ARPA DR
44000 RivC 92590 977-C1
ARQUILLA RD
- PMSP 92264 786-F5
N ARQUILLA RD
500 PMSP 92262 786-F1
600 PMSP 92262 756-F7
ARRAS DR
- RivC 92596 899-D7
ARRIBA RD
73500 RivC 92276 758-F6
ARRIETA CIR
- RivC 92562 956-G2
ARRON CT
40900 MURR 92562 927-H2
ARROW DR
46400 RivC 92536 983-E5
ARROW PL
6000 RivC 92509 684-F5
ARROW RD
22500 RivC 92567 809-E1
ARROW TR
48000 PDST 92260 848-F4
ARROW CREEK DR
1400 PER 92571 777-H7
1400 PER 92571 807-H1
ARROWHEAD BLVD
- RivC - 392-B9
- RivC - 412-C2
- RivC - 5551-A6
ARROWHEAD CIR
1800 PER 92570 807-E5
ARROWHEAD DR
200 PDST 92211 819-D4
7500 RivC 92509 684-H3
ARROWHEAD RD
68700 CTHC 92234 787-E4
ARROWHEAD ST
3300 RIV 92503 715-A6
ARROW LEAF
10000 MORV 92557 687-C5
ARROWLEAF CIR
- RivC 92883 804-B4
ARROWPOINT TR
27000 RivC 92883 835-C5
ARROWVIEW DR
30400 RivC 92548 808-J6
30400 RivC 92548 809-A6
ARROWWOOD DR
10900 RIV 92505 714-E7
ARROYO AV
300 COR 92879 743-E5
55400 RivC 92282 724-E1
ARROYO DR
1800 RIV 92506 686-A7
2100 RIV 92506 685-H7
8900 RivC 92324 687-F2
74500 INDW 92210 848-H2
E ARROYO DR
2800 DHSP 92240 696-H4
W ARROYO DR
12500 DHSP 92240 696-H4
ARROYO LN
1300 NRCO 92860 713-F5

ARROYO LN
18000 CHLS 91709 712-B6
ARROYO PL
81000 INDO 92201 5470-C2
ARROYO RD
6000 PMSP 92264 787-C5
34500 RivC 92596 899-H4
34800 RivC 92530 896-A6
ARROYO WY
48700 RivC 92536 963-C4
ARROYO PARK DR
16600 MORV 92551 747-H4
ARROYO VIEJO DR
1500 SJCT 92583 811-D4
ARROYO VISTA DR
900 PMSP 92264 786-J3
41500 RivC 92592 959-J4
ARROYO VISTA ST
600 BLY 92225 5551-G1
ARRUDA CT
20700 RivC 92570 776-G2
ARTEMIS CIR
36100 RivC 92595 927-H1
ARTESIA RD
19500 RivC 92241 727-E5
ARTESIAN ST
3500 RIV 92503 714-G7
E ARTESIAN ST
100 SJCT 92583 811-B1
300 RivC 92583 811-B1
ARTHUR
- CTHC 92234 787-D6
ARTHUR AV
1200 RIV 92501 645-J7
1200 RIV 92501 685-H1
ARTHUR CIR
300 COR 92879 743-H4
ARTHUR RD
33700 RivC 92596 899-H4
ARTHUR ST
- RivC - (5593-G7 See Page 5592)
- RivC - (5653-G5 See Page 5592)
- RivC 92254 (5593-G7 See Page 5592)
- RivC 92254 (5653-G5 See Page 5592)
ARTHUR ASHE LN
72900 PDST 92260 848-E3
ARTHURS CT
81700 INDO 92201 5410-D7
ARTLO AV
100 PER 92570 807-G6
ARTURO WY
7200 COR 92879 743-H7
ARUBA CT
69500 CTHC 92234 787-G7
79200 RivC 92201 819-H4
ARUBA PL
14600 MORV 92553 717-H7
ARUBA RD
- SDCo 92059 999-F7
6400 SDCo 92028 999-C6
ARUS AV
81700 INDO 92201 5470-E3
ARVONNA ST
13300 MORV 92553 716-J4
ARYA CT
44100 RivC 92539 (965-D7 See Page 964)
ARYANA AV
3000 NRCO 92860 713-F5
ASA WY
6400 RivC 92509 685-A3
ASBURY CIR
3600 COR 92882 742-E6
ASBURY ST
32600 RivC 92596 839-F5
ASCALON AV
76800 PDST 92211 819-D5
ASCONA TER
72800 RMIR 92270 818-D2
ASCOT CIR
76700 PDST 92211 819-C2
ASCOT CT
11200 RIV 92503 744-F2
ASCOT ST
2200 COR 92879 743-J2
ASCOT WY
32000 RivC 92584 868-D7
32200 RivC 92584 898-D1
ASH AV
100 BLY 92225 5491-E6
45000 RivC 92201 5410-D7
45000 RivC 92201 5470-D1
ASH CT
- MURR 92562 928-B5
1700 BEAU 92223 690-J5
ASH DR
16700 FONT 92337 644-J1
ASH RD
200 PMSP 92262 786-E2
ASH ST
- RivC 92220 782-D1
600 SJCT 92583 811-A2
2500 COR 92881 773-E2
5300 RivC 92509 684-B4
22700 RivC 92883 804-C3
29000 LKEL 92530 865-G1
ASHBERRY CT
77500 PDST 92211 819-E4
ASHBURN RD
- TEM 92591 959-B5

ASHBURY PL
21800 RivC 92570 805-D1
44600 TEM 92592 979-E3
ASHBURY WY
1400 PER 92571 777-H7
1400 PER 92571 807-H1
ASHBY CIR
- PMSP 92262 756-C4
ASHBY LN
28600 RivC 92567 808-E1
ASHDALE DR
3000 COR 92881 773-F4
ASH DALE WY
29500 RivC 92587 867-E2
ASHER DR
1100 PMSP 92262 756-E7
ASHFIELD LN
37900 RivC 92596 930-C4
ASHFORD CIR
1000 COR 92881 773-F1
22600 MORV 92557 717-B2
ASHFORD LN
32500 RivC 92596 869-E7
32800 RivC 92596 899-E1
E ASHGATE CT
3200 ONT 91761 643-B6
ASHGATE PL
3200 ONT 91761 643-B6
ASHGATE WY
3200 ONT 91761 643-B6
E ASHGATE WY
2700 ONT 91761 643-B6
ASHLAND CIR
1100 COR 92880 743-B1
ASHLAND PL
12600 RivC 92503 744-B4
ASHLAND WY
- YCPA 92399 649-E2
ASHLEAF CT
3700 RIV 92504 715-C3
ASHLEY CT
- RIV 92508 716-E7
700 PER 92570 807-E2
68400 CTHC 92234 787-G5
ASHLEY PL
- LQNT 92253 849-H1
ASHLEY ST
700 HEMT 92545 840-G2
7200 RivC 92324 647-B6
ASHLEY WY
- LQNT 92253 849-H1
ASHMEAD DR
4900 HEMT 92544 811-G5
ASHMILL CT
31200 TEM 92591 959-C1
ASHTON CT
7900 RivC 92509 684-G5
ASHTON PL
1000 PER 92571 778-A2
ASHTREE LN
1800 HEMT 92545 840-G4
E ASH TREE LN
1800 CLTN 92324 646-G1
ASHURST CT
600 PMSP 92262 756-C4
ASHWOOD AV
23500 MORV 92557 687-D7
ASHWOOD CT
- LQNT 92253 849-H1
- MURR 92562 927-F5
3000 RIV 92503 744-E3
ASHWOOD LN
39000 MURR 92563 928-E3
E ASHWOOD LN
1900 CLTN 92324 646-H1
ASHWOOD WY
1100 HEMT 92543 840-H1
ASISTENCIA DR
67100 CTHC 92234 787-B1
ASLAN CT
11900 MORV 92557 717-D1
ASPEL RD
27500 RivC 92585 838-E5
ASPEN AV
25000 LMLN 92354 647-C2
ASPEN CIR
11900 GTER 92313 646-E3
ASPEN CT
- RIV 92508 746-E2
- RivC 92584 868-F5
- SJCT 92583 780-J5
900 COR 92879 743-F7
ASPEN DR
- MURR 92562 927-F4
- SDCo 92028 998-D4
2000 HEMT 92545 840-G3
ASPEN LN
300 PER 92570 807-F5
1000 BAN 92220 721-F2
E ASPEN LN
1900 CLTN 92324 646-H1
ASPEN PL
22900 CYNL 92587 867-D2
ASPEN RD
3400 SDCo 92028 998-E3
ASPEN ST
800 COR 92879 743-F6
43800 INDO 92201 5410-C6
ASPENCLIFF CT
11500 FONT 92337 644-H3
ASPENWOOD CT
25600 MORV 92557 717-H1
ASPENWOOD DR
1100 COR 92881 773-E4

ASPENWOOD WY
28000 RivC 92584 868-E5
ASTAIRE AV
82300 INDO 92201 5470-F4
ASTAIRE CIR
82300 INDO 92201 5470-F4
ASTER CIR
23700 MURR 92562 927-J3
ASTER CT
46500 INDO 92201 5470-E2
ASTER DR
35500 RivC 92595 897-E7
74000 PDST 92260 818-G7
ASTER ST
800 HEMT 92545 840-G2
11400 LMLN 92354 647-B2
ASTER LEAF LN
10600 MORV 92557 687-E6
ASTEROID WY
41700 TEM 92592 959-B6
ASTI CIR
- PDST 92211 819-A4
ASTI WY
- TEM 92592 959-F7
ASTORIA CIR
2800 COR 92879 744-A2
ASTORIA DR
6700 RIV 92503 714-E1
ASTORIA ST
3000 COR 92879 744-A2
ATALLAH DR
- COR 92882 773-B3
ATCHISON CIR
11300 RIV 92503 744-E2
ATCHISON PL
71000 RMIR 92270 788-A6
S ATCHISON ST
800 CLTN 92324 646-H1
ATHENA CT
1000 RIV 92507 686-C3
ATHENA LN
- MURR 92562 928-D4
ATHENON AV
19800 RivC 92570 775-H4
ATHENS CIR
- COR 92882 773-A2
39000 RivC 92563 929-A7
ATHENS DR
11800 MORV 92557 717-A1
ATHENS ST
- RMIR 92270 787-J7
500 RIV 92507 686-D7
9700 RivC 92509 684-B2
ATHERTON CIR
2000 COR 92879 743-H3
ATHOL ST
400 SJCT 92583 811-C2
ATKINS RD
19100 RivC 92258 725-H5
ATLANTA AV
1600 RIV 92507 686-B3
ATLANTIC AV
13000 DHSP 92240 696-G4
15000 RivC 92240 696-G7
15300 RivC - 726-G2
15300 RivC 92240 726-G2
37800 RivC 92539 (934-H2 See Page 904)
ATLANTIC CIR
- COR 92882 773-B3
23000 MORV 92553 717-C3
ATLANTIC DR
- COR 92882 773-B3
ATLAS DR
1900 RIV 92501 685-G1
ATMORE CT
40300 TEM 92591 959-A2
ATRIUM WY
69800 RMIR 92270 817-G2
ATTENBOROUGH PL
2700 RIV 92503 744-G3
ATTENBOROUGH WY
600 SJCT 92583 781-A7
ATTICA DR
- RIV 92508 746-E1
ATUPA AV
35200 RivC 92595 897-D6
ATWATER AV
1100 RIV 92506 716-C3
ATWOOD AV
13000 MORV 92553 717-E4
ATWOOD CIR
600 COR 92879 743-E3
ATWOOD CT
400 RIV 92506 716-E5
ATWOOD DR
300 COR 92879 743-E3
AUBORN CT
- RMIR 92270 818-A3
AUBREY GLEN CT
- INDO 92201 849-J1
- INDO 92201 5470-A1
AUBRY ST
20900 RivC 92570 836-J6
21300 RivC 92570 837-A5
AUBURN AV
- RivC 92583 781-D6
- SJCT 92583 781-D6
11700 YCPA 92399 650-A2
AUBURN CT
1700 PER 92570 807-F5
2800 PMSP 92262 756-C4
6500 RIV 92506 716-B4
11700 YCPA 92399 650-B2
80400 INDO 92201 5470-B1

AUBURN ST
- HEMT 92545 810-F4
AUBURNDALE ST
800 COR 92880 743-B2
AUBURN RIDGE DR
3600 PER 92571 777-J2
3600 PER 92571 778-A2
AUCILLA CT
27500 RivC 92545 839-J4
AUCKLAND CT
28100 RivC 92586 838-A6
AUDELO ST
- LKEL 92530 865-F3
15200 RivC 92530 865-F4
AUDREY AV
9100 RIV 92503 714-H3
AUDREY CIR
42500 PDST 92260 818-H6
AUDUBON DR
33000 RivC 92584 898-J2
AUDUBON PL
3400 RIV 92501 685-J3
AUGIE CT
30100 RivC 92563 899-A6
AUGUST CIR
13000 RivC 92503 744-B5
AUGUSTA AV
64000 RivC 92240 656-D7
64900 DHSP 92240 656-D7
AUGUSTA CT
2000 SJCT 92582 810-F2
AUGUSTA DR
- MURR 92563 928-J4
- RMIR 92270 788-C5
200 PDST 92211 818-J1
26700 RivC 92586 838-C6
30400 CTHC 92234 787-F1
75400 INDW 92210 848-J1
75400 INDW 92210 849-A1
AUGUSTA PZ
1600 PMSP 92264 787-C3
AUGUSTA ST
700 HEMT 92545 840-H2
AUGUSTA WY
- TEM 92592 979-F1
6000 BAN 92220 721-C4
AUGUSTINE RD
- RivC - 411-E3
AULD RD
30000 RivC 92563 929-A2
32100 RivC 92596 929-D2
AULD ST
7200 RIV 92503 684-E7
25200 RivC 92544 811-H6
AURIGA CT
28700 RivC 92586 837-J7
AURORA AV
- INDO 92201 5470-C4
3100 INDO 92201 5410-C7
5700 RivC 91752 683-G5
AURORA CT
11800 FONT 92337 644-D4
AURORA DR
200 PER 92571 777-H6
2100 PMSP 92262 756-F5
27000 RivC 92544 841-D3
AURORA LN
900 COR 92881 773-E4
37000 RivC 92539 904-D7
37000 RivC 92539 (934-D1 See Page 904)
AURORA RD
17300 RivC 92241 728-A2
69900 RivC 92241 727-H2
AURORA ST
- RIV 92508 746-E1
AURORA WY
- BLY 92225 5491-E4
78800 LQNT 92253 819-G6
AURORA VISTA RD
32000 CTHC 92234 787-E3
AUSSIE AV
31300 TEM 92591 959-D1
AUSTENE CIR
14100 MORV 92553 717-F6
AUSTIN CIR
- COR 92881 773-E6
AUSTIN CT
- SJCT 92583 780-J5
100 SJCT 92582 810-H1
7000 RIV 92503 714-E1
11400 FONT 92337 644-D3
AUSTIN DR
47500 INDO 92201 5470-J3
AUSTIN ST
21300 RivC 92595 897-B7
21300 RivC 92595 927-B1
AUSTRALIAN DR
- LQNT 92253 5530-E4
AUTO BLVD
300 HEMT 92545 840-C1
AUTO DR
7900 RIV 92504 715-C5
AUTOBAHN CT
- RIV 92504 715-C5
AUTO CENTER DR
- LQNT 92253 849-H3
200 COR 92880 742-G4
200 COR 92882 742-G4
3100 RIV 92504 715-C5
S AUTO CENTER DR
700 ONT 91761 643-F3
AUTO CENTER WY
- LQNT 92253 849-H3
AUTO MALL DR
12700 MORV 92555 718-D3

AUTO MALL DR
26200 HEMT 92545 840-C2
AUTO MALL PKWY
12500 MORV 92555 718-C2
AUTO PARK RD
36400 CTHC 92234 787-D7
AUTRY CT
17800 CHLS 91709 712-A5
AUTUMN DR
2300 RIV 92507 686-B3
AUTUMN LN
800 COR 92881 773-E2
4600 BAN 92220 721-E3
78500 RivC 92211 789-G7
AUTUMN PL
11700 FONT 92337 644-C3
AUTUMN WY
400 BAN 92220 721-G4
AUTUMN MIST LN
800 SJCT 92582 780-H6
AUTUMN OAK PL
20100 RivC 92595 896-H5
AUTUMN RIDGE PL
- RIV 92506 715-F4
AUTUMN RIDGE RD
3200 ONT 91761 643-B7
AUTUMN SAGE CT
200 RIV 92506 716-E4
34000 RivC 92595 897-D4
AUTUMNWALK DR
12700 RivC 92503 744-B5
AUTUMN WINDS DR
28300 RivC 92585 838-E1
AUTUMNWOOD LN
1100 PER 92571 778-A2
AVALON AV
1300 BEAU 92223 720-H1
11700 YCPA 92399 649-J2
AVALON LN
32000 RivC 92584 868-H7
AVALON ST
1800 RivC 92509 645-E7
2900 RivC 92509 685-D1
AVEIRO RD
11600 FONT 92337 644-E3
AVELLINO CIR
100 PDST 92211 818-J3
AVENA TR
- RivC 92596 870-F7
AVENA WY
34400 YCPA 92399 649-H2
AVENIDA ABRIL
41800 RivC 92544 961-F3
AVENIDA ACACIAS
37600 MURR 92563 928-E4
AVENIDA ADOBE
50600 COAC 92236 5471-B5
AVENIDA ADOBE NORTE
38900 RivC 92562 926-J5
AVENIDA ALICANTE
43700 PDST 92211 819-E6
AVENIDA ALTA LOMA
12000 DHSP 92240 697-C4
AVENIDA ALTURA BELLA
9200 RivC 92223 691-A2
AVENIDA ALTURAS
41400 RivC 92592 960-J2
41400 RivC 92592 961-A2
AVENIDA ALVARADO
41900 TEM 92590 958-F5
51300 LQNT 92253 849-E7
51600 LQNT 92253 879-E1
AVENIDA ALVERA
30000 CTHC 92234 757-E7
30000 CTHC 92234 787-E1
AVENIDA AMARILLO
40400 RivC 92592 961-A1
AVENIDA AMOR
100 PMSP 92264 786-E7
AVENIDA ANDORRA
200 CTHC 92234 817-G1
300 CTHC 92234 787-H7
AVENIDA ANDRA
- PDST 92260 818-G3
AVENIDA ANSELMO
48900 LQNT 92253 849-F5
AVENIDA ANTONOVICH
39100 RivC 92591 930-C6
AVENIDA ARCADA
40700 PDST 92260 818-F4
AVENIDA ARCONTE
24300 MURR 92562 928-C3
AVENIDA ARIZONA
39600 RivC 92591 929-G7
39600 RivC 92591 959-G1
AVENIDA ARMADA
37800 RivC 92596 930-A4
AVENIDA ARRIBA
38900 RivC 92592 930-F5
AVENIDA ARTEAGA
77100 LQNT 92253 849-D5
AVENIDA ASCENCION
36300 RivC 92592 930-D7
AVENIDA ATEZADA
15200 RivC 92240 697-B7
15500 RivC 92240 727-B1
AVENIDA AUGUSTINE
38600 RivC 92562 926-H5
AVENIDA AVILA
13100 RivC 92503 744-F5
AVENIDA BAJA
7300 RivC 92509 684-H1
AVENIDA BARBADOS
3700 RivC 92503 744-F5

AVENIDA BARBAROSSA
21100 RivC 92562 927-A5
AVENIDA BARCA
41300 TEM 92591 959-A4
AVENIDA BARONA
65500 DHSP 92240 696-G1
AVENIDA BATAVIA
35600 RivC 92592 960-C4
AVENIDA BEGONIA
42400 RivC 92590 958-A5
AVENIDA BELLEZA
27500 CTHC 92234 757-C5
46200 RivC 92592 979-F5
AVENIDA BERMUDAS
51200 LQNT 92253 849-F7
51600 LQNT 92253 879-F2
AVENIDA BICICLETA
33200 TEM 92592 979-H2
AVENIDA BIONA
41300 RivC 92591 959-F3
AVENIDA BIZARO
39400 RivC 92562 926-J6
AVENIDA BOGOTA
39500 RivC 92592 930-F6
AVENIDA BONITA
38400 RivC 92562 926-G5
AVENIDA BORDEAUX
- RivC 92592 959-F4
AVENIDA BOSQUE
18200 RivC 92562 956-E4
AVENIDA BRAVURA
37100 RivC 92592 960-G1
AVENIDA BRISA
39800 RivC 92592 930-F6
AVENIDA BUENA SUERTE
30800 TEM 92591 959-B3
AVENIDA BUENA VENTURA
78100 LQNT 92253 849-G7
AVENIDA CABALLEROS
400 PMSP 92262 786-E1
1500 PMSP 92262 756-E3
AVENIDA CADENA
65500 DHSP 92240 696-G1
AVENIDA CALAFIA
40700 PDST 92260 818-E4
AVENIDA CALANDRIA
300 HEMT 92545 810-H6
AVENIDA CALETA
- RivC 92562 956-D6
AVENIDA CAMIONES
43500 TEM 92592 979-B1
AVENIDA CAROLINAS
38700 RivC 92562 927-B4
AVENIDA CARRANZA
51200 LQNT 92253 849-E7
51500 LQNT 92253 879-E1
AVENIDA CASTILLA
19400 RivC 92562 926-J5
AVENIDA CENTENARIO
40600 TEM 92591 959-B3
W AVENIDA CERCA
200 PMSP 92262 756-C3
AVENIDA CERROVISTA
40300 RivC 92223 691-A2
AVENIDA CHAGRES
25200 RivC 92544 811-J6
AVENIDA CHAPALA
37400 RivC 92592 930-G5
AVENIDA CHERYLITA
20100 RivC 92562 956-H4
AVENIDA CHICA
- RivC 92592 930-J5
AVENIDA CIELO
43000 INDO 92203 5410-J6
AVENIDA CIMA DEL SOL
29700 TEM 92591 958-J5
29800 TEM 92591 959-A5
AVENIDA CLUB LA QUINTA
- LQNT 92253 849-F5
AVENIDA CODORNIZ
45400 INDW 92210 849-A1
AVENIDA CONCHITA
41600 RivC 92562 956-F5
AVENIDA CONDESA
28200 CTHC 92234 757-E6
AVENIDA CONTENTO
100 PMSP 92264 786-E7
AVENIDA CORDOBA
19200 RivC 92562 926-F6
AVENIDA CORTEZ
49500 COAC 92236 5471-A5
51700 LQNT 92253 879-D1
AVENIDA COYOTE
81400 INDO 92201 5470-D4
AVENIDA DANIELS
- RivC 92590 958-B6
AVENIDA DE ACACIAS
36200 RivC 92592 930-E7
AVENIDA DE ANITA
- RivC 92592 959-H4
AVENIDA DE ANZA
19300 RivC 92562 926-F6
AVENIDA DE ARBOLES
19500 RivC 92562 926-J5
21600 RivC 92562 927-A5
AVENIDA DE CALMA
- MORV 92555 748-A2
AVENIDA DE CALZADA
29600 TEM 92592 959-A6
AVENIDA DE CAMELIA
- RivC 92562 956-E6

AVENIDA DE CIRCO
15700 MORV 92555 748-A2
AVENIDA DE CORTEZ
29600 RivC 92586 868-D2
AVENIDA DE ENCANTO
- RivC 92562 956-C5
AVENIDA DE FELICIDAD
19400 RivC 92562 926-F6
AVENIDA DE FIESTA
29700 RivC 92586 868-D2
AVENIDA DE LA BANDOLERO
38500 RivC 92592 930-J4
AVENIDA DE LA FAMILIAS
13000 RivC 92240 696-E5
AVENIDA DE LA REINA
41500 TEM 92592 959-D5
AVENIDA DE LAS FLORES
28700 RivC 92587 837-G7
28900 RivC 92587 867-G1
AVENIDA DE LAS MONTANAS
69300 CTHC 92234 787-G6
AVENIDA DE LAURA
37800 RivC 92596 930-A4
AVENIDA DEL BARRANCA
35500 RivC 92595 897-J7
AVENIDA DEL DIABLO
27200 RivC 92590 978-D1
AVENIDA DEL MAR
81800 INDO 92201 5470-E1
AVENIDA DELORES
9500 DHSP 92240 696-G1
AVENIDA DE LORING
16200 MORV 92551 747-H3
AVENIDA DEL ORO
25000 RivC 92590 958-A7
AVENIDA DE LOS NINOS
- RivC 92592 959-G4
AVENIDA DE LOS POSAS
41200 RivC 92562 956-F3
AVENIDA DE LOUISA
19300 RivC 92562 926-F7
AVENIDA DEL PADRE
30000 CTHC 92234 757-E7
30000 CTHC 92234 787-E1
AVENIDA DEL PAISANO
32100 RivC 92592 979-F7
32100 RivC 92592 999-E1
AVENIDA DEL PARQUE
49900 COAC 92236 5471-A5
AVENIDA DEL REPOSO
30700 TEM 92591 959-D3
AVENIDA DEL RIO
300 SJCT 92582 810-J3
41400 RivC 92544 961-F2
AVENIDA DEL RUBIO
38600 RivC 92562 926-H5
AVENIDA DEL SOL
- RMIR 92270 787-H7
200 PDST 92260 818-E4
600 COR 92882 773-C2
29500 TEM 92591 958-J3
36100 CTHC 92234 787-G7
AVENIDA DEL TIENDAS
40400 RivC 92562 927-B7
40400 RivC 92562 957-B1
AVENIDA DEL VISTA
600 COR 92882 742-J6
2300 COR 92882 772-H1
AVENIDA DEL YERMO
30000 CTHC 92234 757-E7
30000 CTHC 92234 787-E1
AVENIDA DE MISIONES
44500 TEM 92592 979-D3
AVENIDA DE ORO
49500 COAC 92236 5471-B5
AVENIDA DE PALMA
6300 RivC 92509 685-A3
AVENIDA DE PLATA
49800 COAC 92236 5471-B5
AVENIDA DE PLATINA
49900 COAC 92236 5471-B5
AVENIDA DE REAL
29500 RivC 92586 868-D2
AVENIDA DE SAN PASQUAL
43200 TEM 92592 959-C7
43200 TEM 92592 979-C1
AVENIDA DESCANSO
15000 RivC 92240 697-A7
15500 RivC 92240 727-A1
15500 DHSP 92240 697-A7
AVENIDA DE VENTAS
29600 RivC 92586 868-D2
41800 TEM 92590 958-E5
AVENIDA DIAZ
51200 LQNT 92253 849-E7
51600 LQNT 92253 879-E1
AVENIDA DIOSA
28300 CTHC 92234 757-E6
AVENIDA DOLORES
41300 RivC 92562 956-F4
AVENIDA DON BENITO
6800 RivC 92509 685-A5
AVENIDA DORADO
65500 DHSP 92240 696-G1

AVENIDA DUQUESA
28300 CTHC 92234 757-E6
AVENIDA ELENITA
- RivC - 908-B2
S AVENIDA ELENORA
200 PMSP 92262 786-G2
AVENIDA EL MUNDO
31000 CTHC 92234 787-D2
AVENIDA EL NIDO
49000 LQNT 92253 849-F5
AVENIDA EL PUEBLO
31000 CTHC 92234 787-D2
AVENIDA EMPRESA
13100 RivC 92503 744-F5
AVENIDA ENCINO
59200 RivC - 908-B2
AVENIDA ENTRADA
69900 CTHC 92234 787-H7
AVENIDA ESCALA
40700 RivC 92562 956-D6
AVENIDA ESCALERA
18500 RivC 92562 956-E6
AVENIDA ESTRADA
2000 HEMT 92545 810-G6
30400 TEM 92591 959-B2
40700 PDST 92260 818-E4
AVENIDA ESTRELLA
28500 RivC 92587 837-G7
AVENIDA EVELITA
400 PMSP 92264 786-J3
800 PMSP 92264 787-A4
AVENIDA FELICITA
43300 RivC 92592 960-C7
AVENIDA FERNANDO
48000 LQNT 92253 849-E5
AVENIDA FEY NORTE
3300 PMSP 92262 756-J6
AVENIDA FIESTA
40400 RivC 92544 961-F1
AVENIDA FLORENCITA
15000 RivC 92240 697-A7
15500 RivC 92240 727-A1
AVENIDA FLORIBUNDA
1200 SJCT 92583 811-D3
AVENIDA FLORITA
40000 MURR 92562 928-A3
AVENIDA FRANCESCA
28200 RivC 92585 838-D6
AVENIDA GARNETTE
1100 SJCT 92583 811-D3
AVENIDA GATO
42900 RivC 92544 811-H7
AVENIDA GAVIOTA
28300 RivC 92587 837-G7
28900 RivC 92587 867-F1
AVENIDA GRACIA
16100 RivC 92240 727-A1
E AVENIDA GRANADA
200 PMSP 92264 786-E7
AVENIDA HACIENDA
20000 RivC 92508 716-F6
20400 RIV 92508 716-G6
AVENIDA HALAGO
27500 RivC 92585 838-D5
AVENIDA HERMOSA
13200 DHSP 92240 697-C5
AVENIDA HERRERA
51000 LQNT 92253 849-E7
51500 LQNT 92253 879-E1
AVENIDA HIERBA
46700 RivC 92590 977-J7
E AVENIDA HOKONA
400 PMSP 92264 786-E5
AVENIDA HORTENSIA
26000 RivC 92544 811-H7
26100 RivC 92544 841-H1
AVENIDA INSOOK
21200 RivC 92562 927-A6
AVENIDA INTERNO
27500 RivC 92585 838-D4
AVENIDA ISABELLA
43200 INDO 92203 5410-J6
AVENIDA JALISCO
66000 DHSP 92240 696-H1
AVENIDA JOAQUIN
25900 RivC 92585 838-A3
AVENIDA JUAREZ
29900 CTHC 92234 757-E7
30000 CTHC 92234 787-E1
51500 LQNT 92253 849-E7
51600 LQNT 92253 879-E1
AVENIDA LA CRESTA
35100 RivC 92562 957-C1
35300 RivC 92562 927-A7
36800 RivC 92562 926-G6
39100 RivC 92562 956-G3
AVENIDA LA CUMBRE
59200 RivC - 908-B2
AVENIDA LADERA
65500 DHSP 92240 696-G2
AVENIDA LA FONDA
78000 LQNT 92253 849-F7
AVENIDA LA GAVIOTA
31000 CTHC 92234 787-D2
AVENIDA LA JARITA
78600 LQNT 92253 849-G7
AVENIDA LALO GUERRERO
68500 CTHC 92234 787-E7
AVENIDA LA PALOMA
31000 CTHC 92234 787-D2
AVENIDA LA PAZ
28000 CTHC 92234 757-D6
29800 CTHC 92234 787-D1

AVENIDA LA PLAYA
38500 RivC 92592 930-J4
AVENIDA LAS PALMAS
- LQNT 92253 849-J2
100 RMIR 92270 818-C6
AVENIDA LA TORRES
78600 LQNT 92253 849-G7
AVENIDA LA VISTA
28100 CTHC 92234 757-E6
AVENIDA LESTONNAC
- RivC 92592 959-F4
AVENIDA LIRIO BLANCO
- RMIR 92270 818-D4
AVENIDA LOS FELIZ
58700 RivC - 908-A1
AVENIDA LOS NINOS
30000 CTHC 92234 757-E7
30000 CTHC 92234 787-E1
AVENIDA LOS PINOS
58800 RivC - 908-B1
AVENIDA LOS RAMBLOS
- RMIR 92270 787-H7
AVENIDA LOS VERDES
48900 LQNT 92253 849-G6
AVENIDA LUNA
14100 RivC 92508 716-G6
AVENIDA LYNELL
39500 RivC 92591 929-G7
AVENIDA MADERA
36900 RivC 92592 960-E6
AVENIDA MADERO
51600 LQNT 92253 849-D7
51600 LQNT 92253 879-E1
AVENIDA MADRID
25100 RivC 92548 808-J6
AVENIDA MADRUGADA
49400 LQNT 92253 849-E6
AVENIDA MANANA
35000 RivC 92584 898-H6
35500 RivC 92563 898-H6
AVENIDA MANZANA
15000 RivC 92240 697-A7
15500 RivC 92240 727-A1
17300 RivC 92241 727-A2
AVENIDA MARAVILLA
27700 CTHC 92234 757-D5
30000 CTHC 92234 787-E1
AVENIDA MARBELLA
28600 RivC 92584 868-F2
AVENIDA MARIPOSA
6400 RivC 92509 685-A3
AVENIDA MARQUESA
28300 CTHC 92234 757-E6
AVENIDA MARTINEZ
51000 LQNT 92253 849-F7
51600 LQNT 92253 879-F1
AVENIDA MATORRAL
19600 RivC 92562 956-G6
AVENIDA MENDOZA
51000 LQNT 92253 849-F7
51600 LQNT 92253 879-F1
AVENIDA MERCED
15200 RivC 92240 697-B7
16000 RivC 92240 727-B1
AVENIDA MICHAELINDA
6600 RivC 92509 685-A3
AVENIDA MIGUEL OESTE
39500 MURR 92563 928-E4
AVENIDA MIRAFLORES
43300 RivC 92544 811-J6
AVENIDA MIRAVELLA
300 HEMT 92545 810-G6
AVENIDA MIRAVILLA
8500 RivC 92223 651-B7
8500 RivC 92223 691-A1
9200 RivC 92223 690-J3
AVENIDA MIROLA
15200 RivC 92240 697-B7
15500 RivC 92240 727-B1
AVENIDA MONTEFLORA
15000 RivC 92240 697-A7
15500 RivC 92240 727-A1
AVENIDA MONTERO
49400 LQNT 92253 849-G5
AVENIDA MONTEZUMA
51300 LQNT 92253 879-D1
77100 LQNT 92253 849-F7
AVENIDA MORAGA
1900 PMSP 92264 786-D6
AVENIDA MORALES
51800 LQNT 92253 879-D1
AVENIDA MUNOZ
14000 RIV 92508 716-G6
AVENIDA MUSICO
24300 MURR 92562 928-C4
AVENIDA NARANJA
78600 LQNT 92253 849-H7
AVENIDA NAVARRO
51100 LQNT 92253 849-F7
51600 LQNT 92253 879-F1
AVENIDA NUESTRA
78000 LQNT 92253 909-G7
AVENIDA OBREGON
51400 LQNT 92253 849-E7
51600 LQNT 92253 879-E1
AVENIDA OBREGON N
49900 LQNT 92253 849-E5
AVENIDA OLANCHA
200 PMSP 92264 786-F4
AVENIDA OLGITA
- RivC 92592 959-F4
AVENIDA OLIVOS
2000 HEMT 92545 810-G6

STREET
Block City ZIP Pg-Grid

N AVENIDA OLIVOS
800 PMSP 92262 756-E7
AVENIDA OMEARA
39100 RivC 92562 926-G7
AVENIDA ORONTES
100 CTHC 92234 787-F7
AVENIDA ORTEGA
200 PMSP 92264 786-E5
41500 RivC 92592 960-G3
AVENIDA PACIFICA
28700 RivC 92584 868-G3
AVENIDA PACIFICO
34800 RivC 92592 960-A6
AVENIDA PALIZADA
39700 MURR 92563 928-E4
N AVENIDA PALMAS
800 PMSP 92262 756-E7
E AVENIDA PALMERA
200 PMSP 92264 786-E4
AVENIDA PALOMA
45400 INDW 92210 849-A1
AVENIDA PALOS VERDES
1200 PMSP 92262 756-E6
N AVENIDA PALOS VERDES
700 PMSP 92262 756-E7
AVENIDA PERLA BONITA
19400 RivC 92562 956-G7
19400 RivC 92562 976-H1
AVENIDA PERRIS
- RivC 92562 956-F6
AVENIDA PESCADOR
13100 RivC 92503 744-F5
AVENIDA PEYRI
41600 RivC 92544 931-F5
AVENIDA PICO
65800 DHSP 92240 696-H1
AVENIDA POSADA
84200 INDO 92203 5410-J6
AVENIDA PRESA
19600 RivC 92562 956-G6
AVENIDA PRIMAVERA
28000 CTHC 92234 757-E6
AVENIDA QUINTANA
27000 CTHC 92234 757-C4
AVENIDA RAMADA
15000 RivC 92240 697-A7
15500 RivC 92240 727-A1
25300 RivC 92548 808-J7
AVENIDA RAMBLA
15200 RivC 92240 697-B7
15500 RivC 92240 727-B1
AVENIDA RAMIREZ
51000 LQNT 92253 849-E7
51500 LQNT 92253 879-E1
AVENIDA RANCHO VISTA
41500 RivC 92592 960-B6
AVENIDA REATA
- PMSP 92264 787-B7
AVENIDA REQUEJO
26200 SBdC 92354 647-F2
AVENIDA RIO ENCONTRADO
21300 RivC 92562 956-J6
AVENIDA ROBLE
28800 RivC 92587 837-F7
29000 RivC 92587 867-F1
AVENIDA ROBLEDO
18000 RivC 92562 956-D7
AVENIDA ROSA MUNDI
1100 SJCT 92583 811-E3
AVENIDA ROSARIO
- PDST 92260 818-F4
AVENIDA ROSELLA
19700 RivC 92562 926-G4
AVENIDA ROUNDELAY
1300 SJCT 92583 811-E3
AVENIDA RUBIO
51200 LQNT 92253 849-E7
51600 LQNT 92253 879-E1
AVENIDA SAN GABRIEL
3200 PMSP 92262 756-F4
AVENIDA SAN PASQUAL NORTE
- PMSP 92264 786-J5
- PMSP 92264 787-A6
AVENIDA SAN SEBASTIAN
1800 PER 92571 777-H7
AVENIDA SAN TIMOTEO
9300 RivC 92223 690-J3
9300 RivC 92223 691-A3
AVENIDA SARITA
- RivC 92544 931-D7
- RivC 92592 931-D7
AVENIDA SERENA
12300 DHSP 92240 697-D4
AVENIDA SEVILLA
- PMSP 92264 816-G2
AVENIDA SIERRA ROJO
43200 RivC 92544 901-J5
43800 RivC 92544 902-A5
AVENIDA SOLANA
- PDST 92260 818-F4
AVENIDA SOMBRA
24800 MURR 92563 928-E3
AVENIDA SONOMA
41800 TEM 92591 959-A4
AVENIDA SONRISA
39600 RivC 92223 690-J3
AVENIDA SUENOS
66100 DHSP 92240 696-H1

AVENIDA SURESTE
21600 RivC 92562 927-B7
AVENIDA TAXCO
40400 RivC 92544 961-D4
AVENIDA TERRAZO
700 COR 92882 773-C2
24800 RivC 92595 927-H1
27400 CTHC 92234 757-C5
AVENIDA TIERRA
46100 RivC 92590 977-J5
46100 RivC 92590 978-B6
AVENIDA TIGRE
42700 RivC 92544 811-G7
AVENIDA TORTUGA
81400 INDO 92201 5470-D4
AVENIDA TREBOLO
40400 RivC 92592 960-F1
AVENIDA TUJUNGA
78500 LQNT 92253 849-G6
AVENIDA ULTIMO
78500 LQNT 92253 849-G6
AVENIDA VALDEZ
30000 CTHC 92234 787-E2
AVENIDA VALENCIA
6600 RivC 92509 685-A3
25000 RivC 92548 808-J6
AVENIDA VALLEJO
51200 LQNT 92253 849-E7
51500 LQNT 92253 879-E1
AVENIDA VELASCO
51100 LQNT 92253 849-F7
51600 LQNT 92253 879-F1
AVENIDA VENIDA
40000 MURR 92562 928-D5
AVENIDA VERACRUZ
3700 RivC 92503 744-F5
AVENIDA VERDE
36600 RivC 92592 960-E4
40000 TEM 92591 959-A3
AVENIDA VILLA
51000 LQNT 92253 849-F7
51700 LQNT 92253 879-F1
AVENIDA VISTA
13000 DHSP 92240 697-D5
AVENIDA VISTA BONITA
49100 LQNT 92253 849-E6
AVENIDA VISTA LADERA
42000 TEM 92591 958-J5
42000 TEM 92591 959-A4
AVENIDA VIZCAYA
25100 RivC 92548 808-J6
AVENIDA XIMINO
29700 CTHC 92234 757-E7
30000 CTHC 92234 787-E1
AVENIR WY
30200 RivC 92584 868-G3
AVENTINE CT
41500 PDST 92260 818-F4
AVENUE A
- RivC - 392-B8
400 BLY 92225 5491-F6
16000 RivC 92518 747-B4
34900 YCPA 92399 649-J3
34900 YCPA 92399 650-B3
AVENUE B
400 BLY 92225 5491-F6
900 CALI 92320 649-H7
18300 RivC 92570 746-D7
34200 YCPA 92399 649-H3
34900 YCPA 92399 650-A3
AVENUE B CT
34500 YCPA 92399 649-J3
AVENUE C
18100 RivC 92570 776-C1
33600 YCPA 92399 649-F3
34900 YCPA 92399 650-A3
AVENUE D
18000 RivC 92570 776-C1
31900 YCPA 92399 649-C3
34900 YCPA 92399 650-B3
AVENUE DEL SOL
17100 FONT 92337 645-A2
AVENUE E
18300 RivC 92570 776-D2
31300 YCPA 92399 649-B4
34900 YCPA 92399 650-A4
AVENUE EYE
33900 YCPA 92399 649-G6
35600 YCPA 92399 650-B6
AVENUE F
15800 RivC 92518 747-A3
AVENUE G
33800 YCPA 92399 649-H6
34900 YCPA 92399 650-A6
AVENUE H
33800 YCPA 92399 649-G6
34900 YCPA 92399 650-C6
AVENUE I
33900 YCPA 92399 649-G6
35600 YCPA 92399 650-B6
AVENUE J
33900 YCPA 92399 649-H7
AVENUE JUAN BAUTISTA
4500 RivC 92509 685-A4
AVENUE JUAN DIAZ
5500 RivC 92509 685-A6
5700 RivC 92509 684-J5
AVENUE K
500 CALI 92320 649-G7
AVENUE L
200 CALI 92320 649-F7
200 CALI 92320 650-A7

AVENUE L
400 CALI 92320 689-G1
E AVENUE L
100 CALI 92320 650-B7
W AVENUE L
100 CALI 92320 650-A7
AVENUE N
31700 RDL 92373 649-B5
AVENUE OF THE STATES
77900 PDST 92211 819-F5
AVENUE 1
300 LKEL 92530 866-F5
AVENUE 2
200 LKEL 92530 866-G5
AVENUE 3
300 LKEL 92530 866-G5
AVENUE 4
300 LKEL 92530 866-G5
AVENUE 5
300 LKEL 92530 866-G5
AVENUE 6
100 LKEL 92530 866-G5
AVENUE 9
300 LKEL 92530 866-G5
AVENUE 10
300 LKEL 92530 866-H6
AVENUE 11
300 LKEL 92530 866-H6
AVENUE 12
300 LKEL 92530 866-H6
AVENUE 37
- INDO 92203 789-J7
- RivC 92203 789-J7
AVENUE 38
39300 RivC 92211 819-E1
40200 RivC 92276 819-E1
78500 RivC 92211 789-G7
78900 RivC 92203 819-J1
79400 INDO 92203 819-J1
79700 INDO 92203 5410-A1
79700 RivC 92203 5410-A1
80200 INDO 92203 390-D8
81000 RivC 92203 390-D8
AVENUE 39
79000 RivC 92203 819-H2
79000 INDO 92203 819-H2
80000 RivC 92203 5410-A2
80000 INDO 92203 5410-A2
AVENUE 40
78500 RivC 92203 819-G3
78500 RivC 92211 819-G3
78500 INDO 92203 819-G3
78500 INDO 92211 819-G3
79900 RivC 92203 5410-D2
80000 INDO 92203 5410-D2
AVENUE 41
78100 PDST 92201 819-H4
78100 RivC 92201 819-H4
AVENUE 42
78000 PDST 92201 819-G5
78000 RivC 92201 819-G5
79500 RivC 92201 5410-A4
79900 INDO 92201 5410-A5
79900 INDO 92203 819-G5
79900 INDO 92203 5410-A4
AVENUE 43
80200 INDO 92201 5410-B5
84000 INDO 92203 5410-J5
AVENUE 44
82000 INDO 92201 5410-E6
83400 INDO 92203 5410-J6
84000 INDO 92203 5411-C6
84000 INDO 92236 5411-C6
84000 COAC 92236 5411-C6
AVENUE 45
82900 INDO 92201 5410-G7
83500 INDO 92201 5470-J1
AVENUE 46
80400 INDO 92201 5470-E1
AVENUE 46 Rt#-111
82000 INDO 92201 5470-H1
AVENUE 47
78500 LQNT 92253 849-H3
85000 COAC 92236 5471-E2
AVENUE 48
78400 LQNT 92253 849-J4
79600 LQNT 92253 5470-C4
80000 INDO 92201 5470-E3
83000 COAC 92236 5470-J3
84000 RivC 92201 5470-J3
84000 RivC 92201 5471-A3
84000 COAC 92236 5471-A3
84200 INDO 92201 5471-A3
84700 RivC 92236 5471-A3
84700 INDO 92236 5471-B3
AVENUE 49
80000 INDO 92201 5470-C4
84000 COAC 92236 5470-J4
84100 COAC 92236 5471-A4
AVENUE 50
77800 LQNT 92253 849-G6
79800 LQNT 92253 5470-E5
80000 INDO 92201 5470-E5
82800 COAC 92236 5470-J5
82800 RivC 92236 5470-J5
83800 COAC 92236 5471-B5
AVENUE 51
81300 INDO 92201 5470-E6
83100 RivC 92236 5470-J6
84100 COAC 92236 5470-J6
84100 COAC 92236 5471-B6
AVENUE 52
51200 LQNT 92253 849-J7
51200 LQNT 92253 879-F1

AVENUE 52
79100 LQNT 92253 5530-B1
81300 INDO 92201 5470-F7
81300 LQNT 92253 5470-F7
81300 RivC 92253 5470-F7
81800 INDO 92236 5470-F7
81800 RivC 92201 5470-F7
81800 RivC 92236 5470-J7
84100 COAC 92236 5470-J7
84100 COAC 92236 5471-A7
87500 RivC 92274 5471-F7
AVENUE 53
84500 COAC 92236 5531-D1
AVENUE 54
79700 LQNT 92253 5530-J2
84100 COAC 92274 5530-J2
84100 COAC 92274 5531-H2
84100 COAC 92236 5530-J2
84100 COAC 92236 5531-D2
85000 RivC 92274 5531-D2
AVENUE 86
- RivC 92274 (5773-A5 See Page 5712)
86000 RivC 92274 (5772-J5 See Page 5712)
AVERILL CT
3800 RIV 92503 744-C2
AVERILL DR
69900 RivC - (907-H5 See Page 906)
AVERY DR
1900 PMSP 92264 786-G4
AVERY CANYON RD
- RivC 92544 841-E6
AVIATION DR
1700 COR 92880 742-H3
AVIATION WY
3200 PMSP 92262 786-H1
AVIDA DR
29500 RivC 92584 868-A2
29600 RivC 92584 867-J2
AVIGNON CT
400 RivC 92501 646-A7
AVILA DR
700 HEMT 92543 840-J2
49300 LQNT 92253 849-G5
AVINGNON CT
- RivC 92596 899-D7
AVIS CT
11000 MORV 92557 687-D7
AVIS RD
40000 RivC 92543 871-B2
AVITA CIR
44700 TEM 92592 979-H3
AVLIS LN
7600 RivC 92509 684-H1
AVOCADO AV
- PER 92571 777-G6
AVOCADO CIR
19200 RivC 92562 926-E5
AVOCADO HWY I-15
- RivC - 979-A4
- RivC - 998-H3
- RivC - 999-A2
- SDCo - 998-H3
- TEM - 979-A4
AVOCADO LN
26500 MORV 92555 718-A1
AVOCADO ST
2100 COR 92882 742-H7
3300 RIV 92507 686-D4
35500 YCPA 92399 650-B1
AVOCADO WY
- RivC 92503 745-A7
1300 HEMT 92545 840-E3
12200 RivC 92503 744-H6
29000 LKEL 92530 865-F1
AVOCADO MESA RD
18700 RivC 92562 976-E1
19700 RivC 92562 957-A7
20000 RivC 92562 956-H7
AVOCET CIR
25000 RivC 92544 (812-B6 See Page 782)
AVOLA CT
- TEM 92592 979-G1
AVON ST
3800 RivC 92509 644-D7
4200 RivC 92509 684-D1
AVONDALE DR
600 COR 92879 743-H3
75800 PDST 92211 819-A2
AVONDALE ST
3700 PER 92571 778-A2
AVONDALE WY
5200 RIV 92506 685-J7
5200 RIV 92506 715-J1
15900 RivC 92530 865-J7
AVOYER AV
26000 RivC 92590 958-B7
AWA CIR
35100 RivC 92595 897-D6
AYERS WY
53000 RivC 92539 (934-C5 See Page 904)
AYERS ROCK RD
- RIV 92508 716-E7
AYLESBURY DR
24000 MORV 92553 717-E4
AYR CT
- RIV 92508 716-F6
AZAELIA DR
53900 RivC - 814-C5
AZAHAR
79400 LQNT 92253 849-J6

AZALEA
- RivC 92503 744-B4
AZALEA CIR
1100 COR 92882 743-B7
AZALEA CIR E
900 PMSP 92264 816-F1
AZALEA CIR W
900 PMSP 92264 816-F1
AZALEA CT
100 RDL 92373 647-J2
16800 RivC 92503 744-J5
AZALEA DR
38100 RivC 92260 818-F1
AZALEA LN
13300 YCPA 92399 650-B6
AZALEA RD
24700 RivC - 814-E4
AZALEA ST
4000 RIV 92503 714-H5
47800 INDO 92201 5470-B3
AZALEA TR
- RivC - 389-J8
- RivC - (783-J7 See Page 782)
- RivC - (813-H1 See Page 782)
- RivC 92220 389-J8
- RivC 92220 (783-J7 See Page 782)
- RivC 92220 (813-H1 See Page 782)
AZALEA WY
800 HEMT 92545 810-G5
AZANIA AV
61000 RivC 92282 695-G4
AZRA CT
2500 PER 92571 777-G5
AZTEC AV
- RivC - 5421-C5
AZTEC CT
41500 RivC 92536 963-E3
AZTEC DR
2800 RivC 92509 645-B6
45000 INDW 92210 849-D1
AZTEC LN
1800 COR 92879 743-H1
AZTEC ST
43500 INDO 92203 5410-H6
AZUL CIR
400 PMSP 92264 786-E6
AZUL CT
5300 RIV 92505 714-B5
AZULA RD
48200 RivC 92536 963-B6
AZUR DR
30900 CTHC 92234 787-G1
AZURE CT
11300 FONT 92337 644-D3
AZURE LN
700 COR 92879 743-J2
AZURE HILLS LN
45900 INDW 92210 848-J3
AZURITE CIR E
74400 PDST 92260 818-H6
AZURITE ST
6000 RivC 92509 684-D5
AZUSA CT
6500 RivC 92509 645-B6
AZUSA ST
37800 RivC 92596 930-A4

B

B AV
20000 RivC 92567 778-H4
B ST
- HEMT 92545 840-F2
100 RivC 92518 747-C1
200 BEAU 92223 720-G3
10400 RivC 91752 644-A5
33600 YCPA 92399 649-G2
41800 MURR 92562 928-A6
41900 MURR 92562 927-J7
44000 RivC 92544 (812-A6 See Page 782)
68500 CTHC 92234 817-E1
S B ST
- PER 92570 807-G4
BABB AV
5100 RIV 92503 714-F3
BABBAGE RD
51700 RivC 92536 983-J3
52000 RivC 92536 (984-A3 See Page 964)
BABBLING BROOK CIR
- RivC 92584 867-H1
BABCOCK AV
43000 RivC 92544 811-H6
BABCOCK DR
13300 RivC 92879 744-A5
BACCARAT RD
30700 TEM 92591 959-C2
BACH RD
43600 RivC 92536 962-A6
55800 RivC 92539 (934-G3 See Page 904)
BACK WY
12400 MORV 92553 717-E2
BADEN CT
44400 PDST 92260 818-H7
BADGER ST
39700 RivC 92211 819-E2
S BADGERGLEN PL
2700 ONT 91761 643-C6

BADGER SPRINGS TR
23900 MORV 92557 687-E7
BAFFIN DR
3200 RIV 92503 744-G2
BAGATELLE ST
13100 MORV 92553 717-C4
BAGDAD AV
84600 COAC 92236 5471-B7
BAGGETT DR
4200 RIV 92505 714-F6
BAHADA RD
2700 PMSP 92262 756-G4
68300 CTHC 92234 817-D2
BAHAMA DR
500 HEMT 92543 840-J3
BAHAMA WY
- MURR 92563 928-H7
BAHIA DR
29800 CYNL 92587 867-F2
BAHIA PL
3400 RIV 92507 686-E4
BAHIA ST
300 PER 92571 807-H2
BAHLER ST
33600 RivC 92567 809-G3
BAHRMAN RD
38100 RivC 92539 (934-H4 See Page 904)
BAILEY RD
56000 RivC 92539 964-J5
56400 RivC 92539 (965-D5 See Page 964)
BAILEY ST
16300 LKEL 92530 865-J2
BAILEY PARK BLVD
33000 RivC 92584 898-E2
BAILIFF RD
38600 RivC 92539 (934-J4 See Page 904)
BAILLY ST
20300 RivC 92570 746-G7
21500 RivC 92570 747-A7
BAIN ST
3800 RivC 91752 644-A7
4300 RivC 91752 684-A1
BAINBRIDGE CIR
- COR 92882 773-B3
39400 RivC 92563 929-A7
BAIRD ST
1400 COR 92882 742-J7
BAIRNDALE DR
24300 MORV 92553 717-E5
BAKAL DR
20700 RIV 92508 746-H1
BAKER AV
7400 RivC 92881 773-H5
7400 COR 92881 773-H5
BAKER CT
- RMIR 92270 817-J1
20400 RivC 92595 896-J5
BAKER LN
- MURR 92563 928-J4
11100 RIV 92505 714-C5
BAKER ST
900 SJCT 92583 781-A7
6200 RivC 92509 684-D6
16500 LKEL 92530 836-A7
16500 LKEL 92530 866-A1
BALACLAVA DR
41300 RivC 92201 819-G4
BALADA CT
49000 LQNT 92253 849-G5
BALANCIN WY
26000 MORV 92555 747-J1
BALATA DR
30900 TEM 92591 959-C5
BALBOA CIR
900 PMSP 92264 786-F6
BALBOA CT
27200 RivC 92544 841-E3
BALBOA DR
100 PMSP 92264 787-A6
600 COR 92879 743-G3
BALBOA LN
13000 MORV 92553 717-B4
BALBOA PL
- INDO 92201 5470-D4
BALBOA ST
50000 COAC 92236 5471-B5
S BALBOA ST
50300 COAC 92236 5471-B6
BALBOA WY
5700 RIV 92504 715-B2
BALDARAY CIR
42200 TEM 92590 958-H7
BALD EAGLE DR
- RivC - 5239-J6
- RivC - 5240-A6
BALD EAGLE LN
11700 MORV 92557 716-J1
73100 PDST 92260 818-E4
BALDI CT
39600 RivC 92223 690-J4
BALDWIN AV
5600 RivC 92509 684-F5
BALDWIN BLVD
33000 RivC 92530 896-C2
BALDWIN DR
1400 COR 92881 773-F4
BALDWIN ST
- COR 92881 773-F5
BALDY CT
24600 RivC 92883 804-E6

BALDY RD
24600 RivC - (813-J3 See Page 782)
BALDY PEAK DR
26000 RivC 92586 868-A1
BALDY VIEW CIR
1300 COR 92882 742-F6
BALESTRIERI RD
24800 RivC 92544 (812-B5 See Page 782)
BALFORE ST
2800 RIV 92506 715-H2
BALFRIN DR
- RivC - (907-C1 See Page 906)
BALFRIN RD
- RivC - (907-D6 See Page 906)
BALI DR
- PMSP 92264 786-E5
BALL RD
24900 RivC 92585 808-D6
BALLAD PL
4000 RIV 92505 744-D1
BALLANTINE PL
10700 RIV 92503 744-F2
BALLARD AV
18100 RivC 92530 896-D3
BALLESTROS RD
23600 MURR 92562 927-H3
BALLEW WY
43300 RivC 92544 811-H5
BALLINGER PL
6300 RIV 92506 716-C3
BALLINGER RD
29800 RivC 92544 901-G4
BALLYBUNION
- LQNT 92253 5530-D6
BALMORAL CT
10200 RIV 92503 744-H1
BALMORE CT
- INDO 92201 5410-B6
BALSA RD
29700 RivC 92584 868-E2
BALSAM DR
12800 RivC 92282 724-E1
BALSAM LN
700 RivC 92882 742-H5
43000 PDST 92260 818-H6
BALSAM ST
35500 RivC 92595 897-E7
BALSAM WY
700 HEMT 92545 840-G2
BALSAMINA CT
39500 RivC 92592 930-C7
BALSAWOOD DR
1800 HEMT 92545 840-F4
BALTIC AV
2600 RIV 92507 686-C3
BALTIC CT
16700 MORV 92551 747-F4
BALTIMORE AV
12200 MORV 92557 717-H2
BALTIMORE ST
46600 INDO 92201 5470-G2
BALTRA DR
16200 RivC 92570 775-H4
BALTRUSTROL DR
25800 RivC 92586 838-A7
BALTUSROL
- LQNT 92253 5530-C5
BALTUSROL CIR
40100 PDST 92211 819-D3
BALZAC CIR
6500 RIV 92506 716-C4
BAMBI CT
13300 MORV 92553 717-D4
BAMBOO AV
- RivC - 5239-J7
- RivC - 5240-A7
BAMBOO CT
- FONT 92337 645-B1
24600 MORV 92553 717-F7
BAMBOO LN
9100 RIV 92503 715-A7
BAMBOO ST
46500 INDO 92201 5470-E2
BAMBOO PALM DR
30600 RivC 92548 839-A1
BANANA AV
10500 SBdC 92337 644-B1
10500 SBdC 92337 644-B2
11200 FONT 92337 644-B4
BANANAL WY
44700 TEM 92592 979-F3
BANANAWOOD CT
11600 FONT 92337 644-B3
BANAS RD
23700 SBdC 92324 646-H3
BANBURY CT
22600 MURR 92562 927-D2
BANBURY DR
900 HEMT 92544 811-F5
3600 RIV 92505 744-G1
3700 RIV 92505 714-F7
BANBURY CROSS RD
19800 RivC 92570 775-J4
BANCROFT ST
4600 RIV 92504 714-J2
25900 LMLN 92354 647-E3
BANCROFT WY
800 LKEL 92530 866-G5
27200 RivC 92544 841-F3
BANDAN CT
31300 TEM 92592 979-D5

BANDANA RD
35200 RivC 92276 788-H5
BANDERA DR
13200 RivC 92883 835-B5
BANDERA ST
61500 RivC 92240 695-H5
BANDINI AV
3400 RIV 92506 685-E6
BANDIT WY
24500 RivC 92883 804-F7
BANDIT BLUFF WY
22200 RivC 92567 779-G7
22200 RivC 92567 809-G1
BANDY CT
15300 MORV 92551 747-F1
BANEBERRY ST
13500 MORV 92553 717-H4
BANFF ST
73000 RivC 92276 788-E3
BANFF WY
32200 CTHC 92234 787-D3
BANFF SPRINGS ST
- INDO 92201 849-J1
- INDO 92201 5470-A1
BANFIELD DR
- LQNT 92253 879-J7
- LQNT 92253 (909-J1 See Page 908)
BANGOR AV
11400 LMLN 92354 647-F2
BANGOR LN
- RIV 92506 716-D6
BANKS DR
4200 RIV 92501 685-G2
BANKSIDE DR
36300 CTHC 92234 787-D7
36900 CTHC 92234 817-D1
BANNER CT
6200 RIV 92504 685-C7
BANNER ST
21400 RivC 92567 778-H6
BANNING CANYON RD
- BAN 92220 651-G7
- RivC 92220 651-G7
9700 BAN 92220 691-G1
BANNING IDLW PAN HWY Rt#-243
- BAN 92220 722-B5
- RivC 92220 722-B5
16900 RivC 92220 389-G7
19900 RivC 92220 (783-B1 See Page 782)
22600 RivC 92220 (813-H1 See Page 782)
23700 RivC - (813-H1 See Page 782)
23800 RivC - 814-A5
BANNOCK DR
- RIV 92507 716-F2
BANTA DR
5500 RivC 91752 683-G4
BANTA PL
26000 MORV 92555 717-J3
BANTAM WY
44600 RivC 92544 (812-B6 See Page 782)
BANTON CIR
- COR 92882 772-J2
BANYAN DR
1300 SDCo 92028 998-B7
BANYAN ST
39000 MURR 92563 928-G7
40500 MURR 92563 958-F1
BANYAN TREE LN
2600 HEMT 92545 840-G4
BANYON PL
6600 RIV 92506 715-G4
BANYON GROVE CT
- RivC 92211 819-F1
BAPTISIA CT
21100 MORV 92557 716-H1
BARACOA DR
42300 RivC 92201 819-H5
BARANDA CT
40500 PDST 92260 818-F4
BARBADOS CIR
- INDO 92201 5470-G3
BARBADOS DR
- MURR 92563 928-H7
BARBADOS ST
1400 HEMT 92543 840-J4
BARBADOS WY
42100 RivC 92201 819-J5
BARBARA AV
13100 YCPA 92399 650-B5
BARBARA CT
3300 RIV 92506 715-F2
BARBARA DR
- PER 92570 807-D2
71200 RMIR 92270 818-C7
BARBARA LN
35500 YCPA 92399 650-B5
BARBARA ST
13200 MORV 92553 717-A4
BARBARA TR
42800 RivC 92536 963-C7
43600 RivC 92536 983-C1
BARBARA WY
900 LKEL 92530 865-H4
BARBARA LEE DR
35000 RivC - (905-E3 See Page 904)
BARBARA STANWYCK RD
- RMIR 92270 817-G4

BARBAZON DR
12700 MORV 92555 717-J3
BARBER CT
5500 BAN 92220 721-D5
BARBER DR
500 HEMT 92543 841-A3
BARBER LN
53500 RivC 92536 964-C6
BARBER ST
30000 LKEL 92530 866-B3
BARBERRY CT
39700 TEM 92591 958-J2
BARBERRY LN
- FONT 92337 645-A2
48900 PDST 92260 848-E4
BARBERRY PL
- MURR 92562 927-G4
BARBET CT
11500 MORV 92557 717-C1
BARBOUR ST
700 BAN 92220 722-A4
1600 BAN 92220 721-J4
E BARBOUR ST
800 BAN 92220 722-C4
BARBURY ST
3400 COR 92881 773-D3
BARCA CREEK DR
400 PER 92571 807-H1
BARCELONA AV
6000 RivC 92509 645-E4
80000 INDO 92201 5470-A4
N BARCELONA CIR
700 PMSP 92262 756-G7
BARCELONA DR
- RMIR 92270 818-C6
27200 RivC 92883 835-C5
32800 RivC 92276 788-F3
BARCELONA LN
100 PDST 92211 818-H2
100 PDST 92211 819-A3
BARCELONA ST
1300 COR 92882 773-A2
BARCELONA TER
39800 MURR 92562 928-C2
BARCELONA WY
6800 RIV 92504 715-C2
BARCLAY DR
11800 MORV 92557 717-A1
25700 MURR 92563 928-E6
BARCLAY ST
9900 RIV 92503 714-H7
BAR D DR
- PDST 92260 848-C6
BARDMOOR AV
6300 BAN 92220 721-C5
BARDMORE DR
30800 TEM 92592 979-C4
BARDWELL AV
5200 RIV 92506 685-J7
5200 RIV 92506 715-J1
BARET CT
- TEM 92591 959-D3
BARGIL CT
41700 TEM 92591 958-J4
BARILOCHE LN
4500 HEMT 92544 811-F6
BARINGTON DR
40000 PDST 92211 819-E3
BARISTO RD
100 PMSP 92262 786-D2
68000 CTHC 92234 787-D2
BARK ST
- FONT 92337 645-A1
BARKDALE LN
6600 RivC 92509 645-C4
BARKER LN
13300 RivC 92879 744-A5
33900 RivC 92595 897-J3
BARKSDALE CIR
40000 RivC 92592 930-C7
BARKSHATT ST
17500 LKEL 92530 866-B3
BARKWOOD RD
6800 RIV 92506 715-G4
BARLES CT
38800 SDCo 92028 997-A4
BARLETTA ST
- TEM 92592 979-F1
BARLEY LN
2400 COR 92881 773-E2
33300 RivC 92595 897-G3
BARLEY RD
24000 MORV 92557 687-E6
BARNABY CT
3400 RIV 92504 715-E3
BARNACLE DR
- RivC 92254 (5654-G6 See Page 5594)
BARNARD CT
- RMIR 92270 818-B3
BARNARD ST
200 BLY 92225 5491-C6
BARNES CT
100 CALI 92320 650-A7
100 CALI 92320 690-A1
12100 MORV 92557 717-G2
64900 RivC 92240 656-E7
BARNES LN
25100 RivC 92584 867-J7
25600 RivC 92584 868-A7
BARNES RD
20200 RivC 92570 776-G5
BARNESTON LN
54000 RivC 92539 (934-D1 See Page 904)

BARNETT DR
24700 RivC 92544 811-J5
BARNETT RD
2600 PER 92570 808-B7
2600 PER 92570 838-B1
14500 PER 92585 838-B1
14500 RivC 92585 838-B3
BARNHART LN
1400 NRCO 92860 713-E4
BARNHILL RD
43000 RivC 92544 841-H1
BARNSLEY WY
600 COR 92879 744-A2
BARNSTABLE
33300 RivC 92530 865-F6
BARNSTABLE PL
7300 RIV 92506 716-D6
BARNSTAPLE CT
37000 HEMT 92545 810-D7
BARNWOOD LN
- RIV 92508 746-D1
BAROLO CT
- MURR 92562 928-B4
BARONA RD
- PMSP 92264 816-F2
1700 PMSP 92264 786-H6
19800 RivC 92590 976-H2
BARONA MESA DR
38400 RivC 92562 927-A3
BARONI RD
25200 RivC 92585 808-D7
BARONS CIR
77500 PDST 92211 819-E3
BARONS CT
22500 MORV 92553 717-B3
BARRA CT
1400 RIV 92507 716-F2
BARRANCA CT
69700 RMIR 92270 787-G6
BARRANCA DR
6200 RIV 92506 716-B3
BARRANCA RD
34400 RivC 92592 900-H3
34400 RivC 92592 901-A3
BARREL CACTUS
61200 RivC 92258 725-H2
61200 RivC 92282 725-H2
BARREL CACTUS RD
67500 RivC 92241 727-B4
BARRENGO DR
22500 RivC 92595 897-C4
BARRET RD
100 RIV 92507 686-E5
BARRETT AV
1600 PER 92571 777-G2
BARRINGTON CT
4700 RIV 92506 685-E5
26000 RivC 92586 838-A7
BARRINGTON DR
- RivC 92592 979-H3
BARRON CT
30400 RivC 92548 809-A6
BARROW ST
300 COR 92881 773-D4
BAR RU LN
1800 RDL 92373 649-A5
BARRY CIR
29600 RivC 92587 867-D2
BARRYMORE AV
48500 INDO 92201 5470-G4
BARRYMORE PL
- PMSP 92262 756-F6
BARRYWOOD LN
- HEMT 92545 840-D4
BARSANTI DR
- TEM 92592 979-F2
BARTEL DR
4400 RIV 92503 714-H5
BARTH ST
700 COR 92879 743-E6
BARTLETT AV
3700 RivC 92501 645-J6
BARTOLA RD
- SDCo 92028 998-G7
BARTON RD
200 CLTN 92324 646-C4
200 GTER 92324 646-C4
200 GTER 92313 646-C4
1300 RDL 92373 647-F1
3100 LMLN 92354 646-C4
3100 LMLN 92354 647-A1
21500 SBdC 92324 646-C4
21600 CLTN 92313 646-C4
26100 SBdC 92354 647-E1
26400 LMLN 92373 647-F1
26600 SBdC 92373 647-F1
E BARTON RD
1600 CLTN 92324 646-J1
3100 CLTN 92354 646-J1
3100 CLTN 92408 646-J1
23300 CLTN 92313 646-G2
23300 GTER 92313 646-G2
BARTON ST
7100 RIV 92506 716-F6
8700 RIV 92508 746-F5
8800 RIV 92518 746-F5
9400 RIV 92508 716-F6
9400 RivC 92508 716-F6
16000 RivC 92508 746-F5
16000 RivC 92518 746-F5
17500 RivC 92570 746-F7
18100 RivC 92570 776-F1
BARTON CREEK CIR
20600 COR 92883 773-J6

STREET	Block	City	ZIP	Pg-Grid
BIG ROCK CT				
	55400	RivC	92539	(934-G2
			See Page	904)
BIG ROCK DR				
	7800	RivC	92509	684-G3
BIG ROCK RD				
	52900	RivC	-	814-A5
BIG SAGE CT				
	41500	TEM	92591	959-B5
BIG SIOUX RD				
	-	RMIR	92270	788-A7
BIG SKY CT				
	13500	YCPA	92399	650-C6
BIG SKY DR				
	52300	RivC	92536	964-A7
	52400	RivC	92536	963-J7
BIG SKY WY				
	43500	RivC	92590	978-C2
BIG SPRING				
	-	LQNT	92253	5530-C4
BIG SPRING CT				
	700	COR	92880	742-H1
BIG SPRING DR				
	300	BAN	92220	721-E4
BIG SPRINGS RD				
	200	RIV	92507	686-E5
BIG SPRINGS RANCH RD				
	27200	RivC	92544	841-C3
BIG SUR ST				
	100	COR	92881	773-D3
BIG TEE DR				
	23000	CYNL	92587	867-D4
	23000	LKEL	92532	867-D4
BIG TIMBER RD				
	22100	RivC	92557	687-A3
BILLIE DR				
	25000	MORV	92553	717-G7
BILLINGS CT				
	-	SJCT	92583	780-J6
BILLOWS CT				
	800	SJCT	92582	780-H6
BILL TILDEN LN				
	73100	PDST	92260	848-E3
BILLY LN				
	27300	RivC	92584	898-D2
BILLY ANN RD				
	35200	RivC	92595	897-D7
BILLY JOE LN				
	41400	RivC	92592	959-H5
BILOXI DR				
	26000	MORV	92555	717-J3
BILOXI PL				
	28800	MURR	92563	928-G1
BILTMORE CIR				
	1200	COR	92882	743-A7
BILTMORE DR				
	-	RivC	92592	979-H3
	1200	COR	92882	743-A7
BILTMORE PL				
	800	PMSP	92264	786-E4
BILTON WY				
	32300	RivC	92595	896-J5
BING PL				
	39900	RivC	92223	691-A4
BING CROSBY DR				
	-	RMIR	92270	817-H3
BINGHAM AV				
	10500	RIV	92505	714-E6
BINGHAM DR				
	-	COR	92882	773-B3
BINNIE ST				
	64300	RivC	92240	696-E6
BION DR				
	24300	MORV	92553	717-F5
BION WY				
	34400	CTHC	92234	787-G5
BIRCH AV				
	10800	SBdC	92316	645-D1
	25200	LMLN	92354	647-C2
BIRCH CIR				
	1300	COR	92879	743-F6
BIRCH CT				
	-	MURR	92562	927-F5
	12300	YCPA	92399	649-J3
BIRCH DR				
	700	SJCT	92583	780-J6
BIRCH LN				
	400	PER	92570	807-F5
	1000	SJCT	92582	810-J2
BIRCH RD				
	68500	DHSP	92240	697-D4
BIRCH ST				
	500	LKEL	92530	866-D3
	1100	COR	92879	743-F7
	5900	RIV	92506	685-E7
	11000	SBdC	92316	645-D1
	11200	FONT	92337	645-D2
	11200	SBdC	92337	645-D2
	12400	YCPA	92399	649-J4
	12600	BLY	92225	5491-G6
	18300	RivC	92570	746-C7
	18500	RivC	92570	776-C2
	45000	RivC	92201	5410-D7
	45000	RivC	92201	5470-D1
BIRCHCREST CIR				
	-	LQNT	92253	849-H1
BIRCH HILLS CT				
	-	MURR	92563	928-J5
BIRCHLEAF DR				
	3400	COR	92881	773-C4
BIRCHLEAF LN				
	4600	HEMT	92545	840-D3
BIRCHTREE DR				
	25400	MURR	92563	928-E5
BIRCHTREE ST				
	-	FONT	92337	645-A2
BIRCHWOOD DR				
	700	BEAU	92223	690-J7
	13300	MORV	92553	717-G4
BIRCHWOOD LN				
	600	COR	92882	773-C2
BIRD LN				
	39800	RMIR	92270	817-H3
BIRD CENTER DR				
	1100	PMSP	92262	756-J7
BIRDIE CIR				
	-	COR	92883	803-G1
BIRDIE DR				
	-	COR	92883	773-G7
	-	COR	92883	803-G1
	1400	BAN	92220	721-D6
	30400	TEM	92592	979-B4
BIRDIE LN				
	-	HEMT	92545	810-D6
	-	INDO	92201	5470-B3
BIRDIE WY				
	1900	PMSP	92264	787-B5
	48200	PDST	92260	848-F4
BIRDS EYE DR				
	16800	RivC	92570	805-J2
	16900	RivC	92570	806-A2
BIRDSONG CT				
	23600	MORV	92557	687-D7
BIRDSONG LN				
	1300	COR	92881	773-G2
BIRDY CT				
	29200	RivC	92567	808-G1
BIRKDALE CIR				
	-	RMIR	92270	788-A5
BIRKDALE CT				
	78000	LQNT	92253	879-G1
BIRKDALE RD				
	26100	RivC	92586	838-A6
BIRKDALE WY				
	11300	RIV	92503	744-E2
BIRMINGHAM AV				
	9400	RivC	92509	684-C2
BIRMINGHAM DR				
	900	COR	92881	773-F1
BISCAYNE AV				
	6700	RIV	92503	714-F1
BISCAYNE DR				
	40900	PDST	92211	819-E4
BISHOP DR				
	1200	HEMT	92545	840-H3
BISHOP PL				
	1400	RIV	92506	715-G7
	76700	PDST	92211	819-C2
BISHOP WY				
	-	COR	92881	773-C3
	-	COR	92882	773-C3
BISKRA RD				
	71300	RMIR	92270	818-A6
N BISKRA RD				
	900	PMSP	92262	756-F4
BISKRA ST				
	44300	INDO	92201	5410-F7
BISMARK CT				
	44300	RivC	92544	(812-B5
			See Page	782)
	83600	INDO	92201	5470-H3
BISNAGA AV				
	2200	PMSP	92264	786-H6
BISON				
	300	HEMT	92543	810-J7
BISON CIR				
	47400	INDO	92201	5470-D3
BISON DR				
	13600	RivC	92883	835-C4
E BISON WY				
	3100	ONT	91761	643-A6
BISSELL PL				
	200	SJCT	92582	810-J2
BIT DR				
	-	RivC	92592	900-H1
	-	RivC	92596	900-H1
BITSY ST				
	16000	MORV	92551	747-H3
BITTER CREEK CT				
	41300	TEM	92591	959-B4
BITTERROOT CT				
	69000	RivC	92241	727-E2
BIXBY DR				
	2800	RivC	92509	645-B6
BLACK BEAR CT				
	-	MURR	92562	927-G3
BLACK BEAUTY TR				
	22200	RivC	92595	897-C6
BLACKBERRY PL				
	6400	RIV	92505	714-B3
BLACKBIRD CIR				
	23700	MORV	92557	687-D5
BLACKBIRD DR				
	26400	RivC	92586	868-B2
BLACKBURN RD				
	12300	RivC	92503	744-H6
	13900	RivC	92503	745-A6
	15300	RivC	92504	745-C6
BLACKBUSH RD				
	14500	MORV	92553	717-J7
	50200	RivC	92536	983-F5
BLACK CANYON DR				
	24300	RivC	92883	804-E6
BLACK DEER DR				
	13200	RivC	92883	835-B4
BLACKDEER LP				
	42100	TEM	92590	958-F5
BLACK DIAMOND				
	-	LQNT	92253	5530-D6
BLACK DUCK DR				
	23500	CYNL	92587	867-E4
BLACK EAGLE DR				
	73500	RivC	92276	788-F2
BLACK EAGLE MINE RD				
	-	RivC	-	390-K7
	-	RivC	-	391-A6
	-	RivC	-	5239-A4
BLACK ELM CT				
	13600	MORV	92553	717-H5
BLACK FOOT DR				
	39600	RivC	92539	(933-H6
			See Page	902)
BLACKFOOT DR				
	77300	INDW	92210	819-E7
BLACKFOOT WY				
	45300	INDW	92210	849-A1
BLACKHAWK CIR				
	3200	RIV	92503	744-H1
BLACKHAWK CT				
	-	RivC	92585	838-D6
BLACKHAWK DR				
	46300	INDW	92210	849-D2
BLACK HAWK LN				
	11600	MORV	92557	716-J1
BLACK HAWK ST				
	-	PMSP	92264	786-C2
BLACKHEATH DR				
	29900	RivC	92584	868-F2
BLACKHILLS DR				
	7400	RivC	92509	684-H2
BLACK HILLS DR				
	56300	RivC	-	878-B4
BLACK HORSE CIR				
	26500	RivC	92883	835-B4
BLACK HORSE DR				
	30900	CYNL	92587	867-E4
E BLACK HORSE DR				
	2700	ONT	91761	683-A1
BLACK HORSE WY				
	39900	RivC	92260	818-F3
BLACK MESA LN				
	39800	RivC	92260	818-F3
BLACKMORE ST				
	18900	RivC	92562	956-E1
BLACK MOUNTAIN AV				
	47500	INDO	92201	5470-E3
BLACK MOUNTAIN CT				
	49000	RivC	92536	963-C1
BLACK MOUNTAIN RD				
	33800	RivC	92592	900-H1
BLACK MOUNTAIN TR				
	-	MURR	92562	927-G3
	-	RivC	-	389-H7
	-	RivC	-	(783-H5
			See Page	782)
	-	RivC	92220	(783-H5
			See Page	782)
	77200	INDW	92210	849-D1
BLACK OAK AV				
	28300	MORV	92555	688-D6
BLACK OAK CIR				
	-	COR	92881	773-D4
BLACK OAK PL				
	2200	RIV	92506	716-A3
BLACK OAK RD				
	39400	RivC	92592	901-A6
BLACK OAK TR				
	36800	YCPA	92399	650-E6
BLACK PINE DR				
	-	PER	92571	778-B2
BLACKPINE DR				
	300	COR	92879	743-D3
BLACKPINE PL				
	2400	ONT	91761	643-B5
BLACK POWDER RD				
	26400	RivC	92532	835-E3
BLACK RABBIT RD				
	46000	PDST	92260	848-G2
	46500	INDW	92210	848-G2
BLACK RANCH RD				
	33000	RivC	92595	896-J6
BLACK RIDGE RD				
	40100	RivC	92544	901-C2
BLACK ROCK RD				
	-	RivC	-	392-A11
BLACK SHADOW DR				
	15100	MORV	92551	747-G1
BLACKSMITH PTH				
	19500	RivC	92881	773-H4
BLACKSMITH WY				
	-	NRCO	92860	743-G2
BLACK STALLION DR				
	-	RivC	92324	647-D7
	-	RivC	92324	687-C1
BLACK STAR CANYON RD				
	9000	RivC	92882	772-F4
	9600	OrCo	-	772-C6
	9600	OrCo	92808	772-F4
BLACK STAR SCE RD				
	-	OrCo	-	772-A6
	-	OrCo	92862	772-A6
BLACKSTONE AV				
	2800	RIV	92504	715-E4
BLACKSTONE CT				
	11300	FONT	92337	644-D3
BLACKTHORNE DR				
	25300	MURR	92563	928-F4
BLACKWALNUT DR				
	700	HEMT	92544	811-E5
BLACK WALNUT ST				
	25500	MORV	92553	717-H5
BLACKWELL BLVD				
	32900	RivC	92530	896-C2
BLACKWOLF DR				
	-	COR	92883	773-H6
BLACKWOLF WY				
	-	COR	92883	773-H6
BLACKWOOD CT				
	-	FONT	92337	645-A1
BLACKWOOD RD				
	25400	MURR	92563	928-F5
BLACKWOOD ST				
	-	FONT	92337	645-A2
	6900	RIV	92506	716-D4
BLAINE ST				
	100	RIV	92507	686-B4
E BLAINE ST				
	200	COR	92879	743-D4
W BLAINE ST				
	200	COR	92880	743-D4
BLAIR RD				
	63000	PMSP	92258	726-B3
	66000	RivC	-	726-H3
	66000	RivC	92240	726-H3
BLAIR ST				
	3600	RivC	92879	743-H5
BLAKE DR				
	25700	MORV	92553	717-H6
BLAKE LN				
	-	CHLS	91709	712-B5
BLALOCK PL				
	28500	RivC	92596	839-C7
	29200	RivC	92596	869-B1
BLANCA ST				
	600	HEMT	92545	810-G6
BLANCHARD PL				
	5000	RIV	92504	715-C1
BLANCHARD ST				
	600	BAN	92220	722-C2
BLANCHE AV				
	49200	RivC	92230	723-B5
BLANCHE DR				
	33000	RivC	92530	866-A7
	33000	RivC	92530	895-J1
	33200	RivC	92530	896-A1
BLANCO ST				
	24300	RivC	92557	687-E3
BLANDO RD				
	2100	PMSP	92262	756-E5
BLANIK AV				
	-	RivC	92585	808-J3
	29000	RivC	92567	808-G3
BLAZE LN				
	-	RivC	92585	838-C3
BLAZEWOOD DR				
	11900	FONT	92337	644-C4
BLAZEWOOD ST				
	1100	RIV	92507	716-C1
	1100	RIV	92507	686-C7
BLAZING STAR CT				
	40800	MURR	92562	927-J3
BLAZING STAR LN				
	47100	PDST	92260	848-E3
BLAZING STAR TR				
	44300	LQNT	92253	819-J7
BLEEKER CT				
	11200	RIV	92505	714-B4
BLEHM ST				
	4800	RIV	92505	714-B7
BLENHEIM ST				
	1900	RIV	92507	686-A2
BLISS AV				
	82000	INDO	92201	5470-E1
BLISS DR				
	58000	RivC	92539	(985-C1
			See Page	964)
BLOCKER DR				
	16600	RivC	92504	745-H5
BLODGETT ST				
	900	SJCT	92583	780-J5
BLOOM WY				
	7500	RIV	92504	715-E5
BLOOMFIELD AV				
	32600	RivC	92276	788-E3
BLOOMFIELD LN				
	2200	COR	92882	742-G6
BLOOMFIELD RD				
	20500	RIV	92508	746-G2
BLOOMING CT				
	78600	RivC	92211	819-G1
BLOOMING MEADOW RD				
	23500	MORV	92557	717-D1
BLOOMSBURY LN				
	30600	CTHC	92234	787-H1
BLOOMWOOD CT				
	4800	HEMT	92545	840-D3
BLOSSOM AV				
	1300	RDL	92373	647-J2
	12700	YCPA	92399	650-B4
BLOSSOM CIR				
	-	RivC	92211	819-G2
BLOSSOM CT				
	43000	RivC	92544	841-H1
	49600	RivC	92536	963-D5
BLOSSOM LN				
	6300	CHLS	91709	712-A5
	39600	PDST	92211	819-A3
BLOSSOM WY				
	3100	RIV	92506	715-F2
BLOSSOMCREEK LN				
	900	COR	92880	743-C3
BLOSSOMFIELD WY				
	-	SJCT	92583	811-E4
BLOSSOM HILL DR				
	900	COR	92880	743-B2
BLOSSOM HILL LN				
	21400	MORV	92557	716-H2
BLOSSOM TIME CT				
	16200	RivC	92503	744-C4
BLOSSOMWOOD CT				
	28000	RivC	92584	868-E5
BLUE CIR				
	38100	RivC	92260	818-F1
BLUEBELL PL				
	-	RIV	92508	746-D1
BLUEBELL ST				
	26000	RivC	92586	838-A4
BLUEBELL WY				
	1000	HEMT	92545	840-G2
BLUEBERRY LN				
	22700	RivC	92595	897-D7
	43800	PDST	92210	819-A7
BLUEBERRY RD				
	14800	MORV	92553	717-F7
BLUEBERRY HILL				
	-	SDCo	92028	998-G5
BLUE BILL CT				
	23700	MORV	92557	687-D5
BLUEBIRD AV				
	36700	RMIR	92270	788-A7
BLUEBIRD CT				
	34100	RivC	92544	901-J2
BLUE BIRD DR				
	22800	CYNL	92587	867-D3
BLUEBIRD LN				
	1700	COR	92882	742-J6
	22700	GTER	92313	646-F5
BLUEBLOSSOM CT				
	-	COR	92881	773-C4
	-	COR	92882	773-C4
BLUE BONNET CT				
	41300	MURR	92562	927-J4
BLUEBONNET RD				
	20600	RivC	92567	779-C4
BLUEBRIAR ST				
	14700	MORV	92553	717-G7
BLUE CANYON RD				
	-	HEMT	92545	810-D6
BLUECHIP CIR				
	15700	MORV	92551	747-H2
BLUE CREST				
	900	COR	92882	743-B6
BLUE DIAMOND LN				
	27600	RivC	92585	808-D7
BLUEFAN DR				
	45500	INDO	92201	5470-C1
BLUE FLAG CT				
	23900	MURR	92562	927-J3
BLUE FLAG RD				
	55300	RivC	92282	724-D1
BLUE FLAG ST				
	9000	RivC	92883	804-C3
S BLUE FOX DR				
	2600	ONT	91761	643-A6
BLUEGRASS CT				
	24300	MORV	92553	717-F7
	27100	RivC	-	844-C2
BLUEGRASS WY				
	69800	CTHC	92234	787-G1
BLUEGUM DR				
	23400	MORV	92553	717-D4
BLUE GUM DR				
	26400	RivC	92532	836-D7
	26600	RivC	92532	866-D1
BLUE HAVEN CT				
	16100	RivC	92503	744-D4
BLUE HERON CIR				
	16000	RivC	92504	775-G1
BLUE HERON CT				
	29800	CYNL	92587	867-D2
BLUEHILL RD				
	17100	RivC	92504	745-J4
BLUE HILLS DR				
	27000	RivC	92586	838-C7
BLUE JAY CT				
	25400	RivC	92584	867-J6
BLUE JAY DR				
	11100	RIV	92505	714-C4
BLUEJAY LN				
	2100	COR	92879	773-E1
BLUE JAY LN				
	11600	FONT	92337	644-F3
	76600	INDW	92210	849-C1
BLUEJAY RD				
	59000	RivC	92539	(965-E1
			See Page	964)
BLUEJAY ST				
	47200	INDO	92201	5470-H3
BLUEJAY WY				
	1500	HEMT	92545	840-E4
BLUE LAGOON CIR				
	30600	RivC	92584	868-F3
BLUE LAKE ST				
	11500	FONT	92337	644-H3
BLUELEAF ST				
	25800	MORV	92553	717-J4
BLUE LUPIN LN				
	11600	MORV	92557	717-C1
BLUE MESA DR				
	27600	RivC	92883	835-C5
BLUE MOUND CT				
	-	PER	92571	778-B2
BLUE MOUNTAIN CT				
	12700	GTER	92313	646-F5
BLUE MOUNTAIN RD				
	3200	PMSP	92262	756-F4
BLUE OAK ST				
	3400	COR	92881	773-F5
BLUE PALM DR				
	-	RivC	92211	789-G6
BLUE RIBBON LN				
	14100	MORV	92555	718-A6
BLUE RIBBON RD				
	22700	RivC	92548	809-C2
	22700	RivC	92567	809-C2
BLUERIDGE CT				
	72300	PDST	92260	848-C5
BLUERIDGE DR				
	4300	RIV	92505	714-D7
BLUE RIDGE LN				
	200	SJCT	92583	781-B5
S BLUE RIDGE LN				
	1100	CLTN	92324	646-G1
BLUE RIDGE PL				
	23700	MORV	92557	687-D6
BLUE RIDGE RD				
	13300	BLY	92225	392-D10
BLUE RIVER DR				
	-	PDST	92211	819-B3
BLUE SKY RD				
	19000	RivC	92570	806-E2
BLUE SKY WY				
	-	LQNT	92253	849-F7
BLUE SPRINGS CIR				
	5400	RivC	92509	685-C3
BLUE SPRUCE CT				
	13600	MORV	92553	717-H5
BLUE SPRUCE DR				
	2600	HEMT	92545	840-F4
BLUE SPRUCE WY				
	-	COR	92881	773-E4
BLUE TEAL DR				
	22600	CYNL	92587	867-C3
BLUE TERRACE ST				
	32300	RivC	92595	896-J5
BLUE VISTA CIR				
	55500	RivC	92282	724-E2
BLUE WATER CT				
	17200	RivC	92503	744-G6
BLUEWOOD DR				
	13900	FONT	92337	644-B4
BLUEWOOD PL				
	11300	MORV	92557	687-E7
BLUFF RD				
	24600	RivC	-	814-A4
S BLUFF RD				
	1200	CLTN	92324	646-F2
BLUFF ST				
	3300	NRCO	92860	713-A6
	4000	BAN	92220	692-A6
	4600	NRCO	92860	712-J7
	5300	NRCO	92860	742-H1
	8500	RivC	92220	651-G7
	8700	BAN	92220	651-G5
	9200	BAN	92220	691-G2
	9200	RivC	92220	691-G2
BLUFFWOOD DR				
	6100	RIV	92506	716-A3
BLUMA AV				
	13500	RivC	92240	696-E6
BLUME CIR				
	-	RivC	92584	868-C3
BLUNTLEAF CT				
	12500	MORV	92553	717-H3
BLUSHING BRANCH CT				
	22800	MORV	92557	687-B4
BLYTHE WY				
	18300	RivC	-	392-A11
BOARDWALK				
	41800	PDST	92211	818-J5
BOARDWALK DR				
	4700	RIV	92503	714-G5
BOAT HAVEN DR				
	30000	CYNL	92587	867-F3
BOATING WY				
	22400	CYNL	92587	867-C2
BOATSWAIN LN				
	1700	PER	92571	777-J7
BOBBITT AV				
	-	COR	92881	773-G5
	17800	RivC	92508	746-B3
BOBBITT ST				
	-	COR	92881	773-J5
	7100	RivC	92881	773-H5
BOBBY JONES WY				
	40700	RivC	92223	691-B5
BOBCAT				
	-	DHSP	92240	696-J7
BOBCAT CRSG				
	45500	RivC	92536	982-H4
BOBCAT DR				
	13400	RivC	92883	835-B4
BOBCAT LN				
	7600	RIV	92508	716-D6
BOBCAT RD				
	42500	RivC	92220	721-F5
BOBCAT TR				
	35100	RivC	92544	902-J4
BOBCAT HILL RD				
	33700	RivC	92595	897-J3
BOB HOPE DR				
	32800	RivC	92270	788-B3
	32800	RMIR	92270	788-B3
	36600	RMIR	92270	818-C2
BOB O LINK DR				
	2000	PMSP	92264	787-B5
BOBOLINK LN				
	11500	MORV	92557	717-C1
BOBOLINK ST				
	47200	INDO	92201	5470-J3
BOBRICK AV				
	17500	RivC	92530	896-C3
BOBWHITE CT				
	18800	SBdC	92316	645-E1
BOB WHITE LN				
	200	RivC	92507	646-E6
BOCA PL				
	11700	RivC	91752	683-F5
BOCA CHICA TR				
	73400	RivC	92276	788-F4
BOCA RATON PL				
	32700	RivC	92276	788-E3
BOCAW CIR				
	45600	TEM	92592	979-D5
BOCA WEST AV				
	1400	BAN	92220	721-D5
BOCCACCIO CT				
	21200	MORV	92557	716-H1
BODEGA CT				
	25000	RivC	92544	(812-A5
			See Page	782)
	26400	MORV	92555	718-A4
BODELL DR				
	18100	RivC	92570	806-C5
BODEWIN CT				
	6900	RIV	92506	715-J5
BODIE PL				
	-	NRCO	92860	743-G1
BODIE RD				
	42100	PDST	92260	818-G5
BODIE ST				
	33300	YCPA	92399	649-F4
BODINE DR				
	-	RivC	92274	5530-G3
BODINE RD				
	56000	RivC	92539	(934-H3
			See Page	904)
BODKIN AV				
	17400	RivC	92530	896-C3
BOEING ST				
	13500	MORV	92553	717-B5
BOGART AV				
	4900	RIV	92505	714-D6
BOGART DR				
	82400	INDO	92201	5470-F4
BOGART PL				
	30300	TEM	92591	959-B1
BOGATA RD				
	43400	RivC	92539	(965-A6
			See Page	964)
BOGERT TR				
	-	PMSP	92264	816-E1
	3100	RivC	92264	816-G2
BOGEY WY				
	42100	TEM	92591	959-B5
BOGGS LN				
	21800	RivC	92595	897-B5
BOGIE CT				
	-	HEMT	92545	810-E6
	5300	RivC	92509	685-D3
BOGOSO LN				
	26200	MORV	92555	747-J1
	26300	MORV	92555	748-A1
BOGUE ST				
	14600	MORV	92553	717-F7
BOGUTA WY				
	44500	TEM	92592	979-G2
BOG WALK CT				
	79100	RivC	92201	819-H6
BOHILL RD				
	43900	RivC	92544	(932-B4
			See Page	902)
BOHLEN RD				
	37100	RivC	92539	(935-B1
			See Page	904)
	37900	RivC	92539	(905-B7
			See Page	904)
BOICE LN				
	1100	RIV	92506	715-H6
BOISE CT				
	-	INDO	92201	5470-H3
BOISE ST				
	4100	RIV	92501	685-H1
S BOISE CREEK PL				
	2800	ONT	91761	643-D6
BOLANDRA CT				
	27400	TEM	92591	958-J2
BOLD FORBES CT				
	-	PER	92571	777-G5
BOLD RULER LN				
	8800	RivC	92509	684-D2
BOLD STYLE AV				
	32000	MORV	92555	719-C6
BOLD VENTURE ST				
	100	PER	92571	777-G5
BOLERO CIR				
	1500	PMSP	92264	786-F6
BOLERO DR				
	400	BAN	92220	721-F2
	7600	RivC	92509	684-G3
	11400	FONT	92337	644-E3
BOLERO RD				
	5800	PMSP	92264	787-C6
BOLINA DR				
	24300	MURR	92562	928-C2
BOLIVAR ST				
	5600	RIV	92505	714-B4
BOLLERO PL				
	800	COR	92882	743-C4
BOLO CT				
	-	RivC	92530	835-D4
	13800	RivC	92223	720-G4
BOLSA LN				
	-	RivC	-	(907-G5
			See Page	906)
BOLSA RD				
	-	CTHC	92234	757-C4
BOLT LN				
	500	HEMT	92544	811-G6
BOLTON AV				
	7600	RIV	92503	714-G5
BOLTON DR				
	38500	RivC	92223	720-G5
BON AIR DR				
	300	PMSP	92262	756-D3
BONAIRE WY				
	-	MURR	92563	928-H7
	-	MURR	92563	958-H1
BONANZA CIR				
	700	COR	92879	743-G3
BONANZA DR				
	16500	RivC	92504	745-G4
	78000	RivC	92211	789-F7
	78000	RivC	92211	819-F1
BONANZA PL				
	29600	CYNL	92587	867-D2
BONANZA RD				
	-	RivC	92262	755-F1
BOND AV				
	12600	CLTN	92324	645-J5
BOND DR				
	300	PER	92570	807-D2
	61100	RivC	92258	725-G3
	61100	RivC	92282	725-G3
BOND ST				
	5900	RIV	92506	716-A2
BONHAM ST				
	20300	RivC	92570	776-G1
	21600	RivC	92570	777-A1
	21700	RivC	92570	747-A7
BONHILL ST				
	6000	RivC	92509	685-B3
BONITA				
	-	RMIR	92270	787-H7
BONITA AV				
	200	SJCT	92583	811-A1
	3400	RIV	92506	715-F1
	10000	RIV	92503	714-F6
	10300	RIV	92505	714-F7
	14200	RivC	92230	723-B4
BONITA CIR				
	2600	PMSP	92264	786-E7
BONITA DR				
	9100	RivC	92223	690-H2
	17100	RivC	92570	776-A7
	35300	YCPA	92399	650-B7
BONITA LN				
	-	PDST	92260	818-G4
	83000	INDO	92201	5410-G6
BONITA HEIGHTS DR				
	-	MORV	92555	748-A2
BONITA MESA ST				
	-	TEM	92592	979-G1
BONITA VERDE CT				
	15700	MORV	92555	748-C2
BONITA VISTA CT				
	26100	RivC	92586	838-A6
BONITA VISTA RD				
	29200	RivC	-	844-G4
	29400	RivC	-	(845-A5
			See Page	844)
	37000	RivC	92539	904-G7
	37000	RivC	92539	(934-G2
			See Page	904)
BONN CT				
	-	RivC	92596	929-C1
BONNER ST				
	10600	RIV	92505	714-E6
BONNET CIR				
	-	RivC	92584	867-H1
BONNEVILLE ST				
	10400	RIV	92505	714-G7
BONNIE CIR				
	300	COR	92880	742-H4
	46600	INDO	92201	5470-F2
BONNIE CT				
	27000	RivC	92544	841-E2
BONNIE DR				
	2300	PER	92570	808-B6
BONNIE LN				
	200	COR	92880	742-H4
	33700	RivC	92595	897-A3
BONNIE WY				
	32900	RivC	92530	896-C2
BONNIE BRAE ST				
	1900	RIV	92506	686-A7
BONNIE JEAN DR				
	32000	RivC	92595	927-F2
BONNIE LEA DR				
	32800	RivC	92530	865-J7
BONNIE VIEW AV				
	11200	MORV	92555	688-D7
BONNIE VIEW DR				
	28200	RivC	92596	839-B6
BONNY LN				
	43400	RivC	92536	964-D7
	44000	RivC	92536	(984-D2
			See Page	964)
BONNYVIEW CIR				
	-	COR	92882	772-J2
BONSAI LN				
	-	FONT	92337	645-A2
BON VIEW AV				
	15700	SBdC	91710	712-E1
BON VIEW DR				
	-	RIV	92508	746-E1
BOO BOO LN				
	34400	RivC	92595	897-B4
BOOM BOOM RD				
	31100	RivC	92548	809-B4
BOON PL				
	900	COR	92881	743-J7
BOONE CT				
	5900	RIV	92506	685-E7
BOOT LN				
	38200	RivC	92544	931-E3
BOOTH ST				
	33200	RivC	92530	896-D3
BOOTHILL CIR				
	-	RMIR	92270	817-J4
BOOTHILL LN				
	42000	MURR	92562	927-J6
BOOTHILL RD				
	-	RMIR	92270	817-J4
BOOT JACK LN				
	42100	MURR	92562	927-J6
BOOTLEGG RD				
	32600	RivC	92596	929-F3
BOQUERON WY				
	79800	RivC	92201	5410-A5
BORCHARD RD				
	19300	RivC	92530	896-F5
BORCO ST				
	26000	RivC	92544	(812-E7
			See Page	782)
BORDEAUX CT				
	12900	MORV	92555	717-J3
BORDEAUX DR				
	2800	RIV	92503	715-A7
BORDEAUX LN				
	3900	HEMT	92544	811-F5
BORDEAUX PL				
	39500	MURR	92562	928-B1
BORDEN LN				
	12100	YCPA	92399	649-E3
BORDER AV				
	1100	COR	92882	743-A6
	1400	COR	92882	742-J7
	2000	COR	92882	772-H1
BOREALIS DR				
	41700	TEM	92592	959-B6
BOREL RD				
	33300	RivC	92596	929-G3
	34400	RivC	92596	930-A4
	37900	RivC	92563	929-B4
BORGES ST				
	-	RivC	92880	683-D7
BORON DR				
	1900	COR	92881	773-G2
BOROS CT				
	64800	RivC	92240	696-F1
BORREGO CIR				
	24600	RivC	92883	804-E6
BORREGO DR				
	74800	PDST	92260	848-H2
BORREGO RD				
	69500	CTHC	92234	757-G7
BORREGO GATE				
	82400	INDO	92201	5470-F3
BORSCH LN				
	23000	MORV	92557	717-C2
BOS CIR				
	43400	RivC	92544	811-J5
BOSLEY LN				
	12500	RivC	92883	835-A4
BOSMA CT				
	18800	RivC	92570	776-C2
S BOSTICK AV				
	200	CLTN	92324	646-C3
	1700	CLTN	92313	646-C4
	12000	GTER	92313	646-C3
	12000	GTER	92324	646-C3
BOSTON CIR				
	3500	RIV	92503	744-E2
BOSTON CT				
	82700	INDO	92201	5470-G2
BOSTON DR				
	1200	COR	92881	773-F4
	27500	RivC	92586	838-A5
BOSTON ST				
	500	HEMT	92545	810-F6
BOSTWICK DR				
	24300	MORV	92553	717-E6
BOSWELL CT				
	5900	RIV	92507	716-F2
BOTANY CT				
	-	LKEL	92532	867-E6
BOTANY DR				
	27100	RivC	92570	837-A5
BOTANY BAY RD				
	7400	RIV	92508	716-E6
BOTTLE BRUSH DR				
	78700	LQNT	92253	849-G5
BOTTLEBRUSH LN				
	27000	RivC	92586	838-B4
BOTTLEBRUSH ST				
	1300	COR	92882	743-A7
BOTTLETREE WY				
	1100	HEMT	92545	840-H3
BOUDREAU LN				
	26000	RivC	92584	898-A2
BOUGAINVILLAEA DR				
	1400	BEAU	92223	690-J7
BOUGAINVILLEA AV				
	12700	RivC	92282	724-E1
BOUGAINVILLEA CIR				
	200	PDST	92260	818-H4
BOUGAINVILLEA DR				
	78500	RivC	92211	789-G7
BOUGAINVILLEA ST				
	-	LQNT	92253	5470-A4
BOUGAINVILLEA WY				
	-	RivC	92503	744-J7
BOUGANVILLIA CIR				
	2300	COR	92879	743-J2
BOULDER AV				
	18600	RivC	92508	746-C5
BOULDER DR				
	1200	COR	92882	742-E6
	26000	RivC	-	814-D7
BOULDER DR				
	38700	RivC	92539	(934-C4
			See Page	904)
	55300	RivC	92282	724 E1
	80800	INDO	92201	5410-C6
BOULDER RD				
	55200	RivC	92282	694-D7
	55300	RivC	92282	724-D1
BOULDER BLUFFS				
	2300	RIV	92506	715-J3
BOULDER CREEK DR				
	38100	RivC	92260	818-E1
BOULDER CREEK LN				
	6800	RIV	92506	716-A5
BOULDER HILL RD				
	38600	RivC	92539	(934-C5
			See Page	904)
BOULDER RIDGE DR				
	26200	MORV	92555	687-J7
	26300	MORV	92555	688-A7
BOULDER VISTA DR				
	31700	LKEL	92532	866-J5
	44300	RivC	92536	982-H2
BOULTON RD				
	54000	RivC	92539	(934-D4
			See Page	904)
BOUNDARY LN				
	2700	RIV	92503	744-H2
	65900	RivC	-	(907-J5
			See Page	906)
BOUNDARY RD				
	1600	PER	92571	778-A7
	1800	PER	92571	777-J6
BOUNTIFUL ST				
	-	RIV	92508	746-D3
BOUNTY AV				
	98500	RivC	92254	(5654-C3
			See Page	5594)
BOUNTY TR				
	7900	RivC	92509	684-G2
BOUNTY WY				
	800	SJCT	92583	780-J6
BOUQUET CIR				
	900	COR	92881	773-E3
BOUQUET RDG				
	38000	MURR	92562	927-E5
BOUQUET CANYON DR				
	100	PDST	92211	818-J3
	100	PDST	92211	819-A3
BOUQUET CANYON PL				
	23700	MORV	92557	687-D6
BOURBON				
	18500	RivC	92532	836-D7
BOURGES ST				
	29700	LKEL	92530	865-G3
BOUVIER CT				
	40900	MURR	92562	927-H2
BOVEE CIR				
	-	RivC	92211	789-F6
BOWDEN DR				
	79300	RivC	92201	819-H4
BOWDOIN ST				
	-	COR	92880	712-J7
	-	COR	92880	742-J1
	1700	COR	92880	743-A1
E BOWEN RD				
	-	PER	92571	807-H1
W BOWEN RD				
	-	PER	92571	807-G1
	600	PER	92570	807-E1
BOWER ST				
	24800	MORV	92553	717-G4
BOWERS RD				
	53900	RivC	92536	964-D7
BOWIE CIR				
	32300	RivC	92276	788-F2
BOWIE CT				
	2600	RIV	92507	685-J5
BOWLING GREEN DR				
	3900	RIV	92501	685-H2
BOWMAN ST				
	3300	RivC	92501	646-A7
	3300	RivC	92501	686-A1
BOX C DR				
	-	PDST	92260	848-C6
BOX CANYON RD				
	-	RivC	-	390-J11
	-	RivC	-	(5593-E6
			See Page	5592)
	-	RivC	-	5594-C4
	-	RivC	92254	(5593-E6
			See Page	5592)
	19100	RivC	92881	773-H3
BOX CANYON TR				
	600	PDST	92211	819-C3
BOXELDER DR				
	25400	MURR	92563	928-E5
BOX ELDER RD				
	31700	RivC	-	(875-J4
			See Page	844)
BOX MOUNTAIN RD				
	45300	INDW	92210	849-E1
BOX RIDGE PL				
	77300	INDW	92210	849-E1
BOX SPRINGS BLVD				
	100	RIV	92507	686-E7
	100	RivC	92507	686-E7
	6000	RIV	92507	716-H2
	11400	RivC	92507	716-G1
BOX SPRINGS RD				
	600	RIV	92507	716-G1
	20700	RivC	92507	716-G1
	20900	MORV	92557	716-H2
	21800	MORV	92557	717-A2

STREET Block City ZIP Pg-Grid

BOX SPRINGS FEEDER
- RIV 92506 716-A7
BOX SPRINGS MOUNTAIN RD
9000 RivC 92557 686-H3
9000 RivC 92557 687-A3
BOXTHORN LN
73100 PDST 92260 848-E5
BOXWOOD CT
23000 RivC 92595 897-E7
BOXWOOD DR
- RivC 92503 744-J7
600 RivC 91752 683-E4
69600 CTHC 92234 787-F3
BOXWOOD PL
5000 RIV 92506 685-G6
BOYD AV
1700 COR 92881 773-G5
1700 RivC 92881 773-H5
BOYD CT
4700 RIV 92507 685-H6
BOYER AV
40700 RivC 92544 841-C1
BOYER RD
59000 RivC 92539 (965-E4 See Page 964)
BOYNTON LN
29500 RivC 92586 868-C2
BOY SCOUT RD
- RivC 92324 688-B3
- RivC 92373 688-B3
BRABHAM ST
23000 MORV 92553 717-C3
BRACEBRIDGE RD
100 RIV 92506 716-D5
BRADCLIFF CT
- YCPA 92399 649-E2
BRADCLIFF DR
- YCPA 92399 649-E2
BRADDOCK RD
26500 RivC 92586 868-B1
BRADEN PL
2500 RIV 92503 744-H3
BRADFORD CIR
1100 COR 92882 743-B4
78400 LQNT 92253 819-G7
BRADFORD CT
900 SJCT 92583 781-A7
BRADFORD RD
49500 RivC 92536 963-D5
BRADFORD ST
- RivC 92596 899-C7
7000 RIV 92503 684-F7
7000 RIV 92503 714-F1
BRADFORD HILLS RD
42700 RivC 92536 963-D6
BRADLEY DR
- BAN 92220 721-C6
BRADLEY RD
1500 PER 92585 808-C5
3000 PER 92571 778-B2
20400 RivC 92571 778-B5
27000 RivC 92586 838-C5
27100 RivC 92584 868-C6
29000 RivC 92586 868-C2
32500 RivC 92584 898-C1
BRADLEY ST
800 RIV 92506 715-G7
1700 RIV 92504 715-F7
BRADLEY WY
45100 INDO 92201 5410-D7
45100 INDO 92201 5470-D1
BRADSHAW CIR
28000 MORV 92555 718-D6
BRADSHAW DR
- RivC 92585 838-A3
BRADSHAW LN E
400 PMSP 92262 786-J3
BRADSHAW LN W
400 PMSP 92262 786-J3
BRADSON WY
8100 RivC 92509 684-F1
BRADY LN
600 HEMT 92544 811-C6
1000 CALI 92320 649-J7
1000 CALI 92320 689-J1
BRAE BURN
- LQNT 92253 5530-C5
BRAE BURN AV
64300 RivC 92240 696-E2
BRAEBURN DR
1800 RivC 92882 742-H6
BRAEMAR CT
- INDO 92201 5410-B6
BRAEMAR DR
- RMIR 92270 817-G2
BRAEMAR LN
3200 COR 92882 742-E5
BRAEMAR PL
4600 RIV 92501 685-F4
BRAEWOOD AV
12600 MORV 92553 717-D3
BRAEWOOD CT
39800 MURR 92563 928-F6
BRAGA RD
15600 FONT 92337 644-F3
BRAGG RD
36000 RivC 92544 902-G7
36600 RivC 92544 (932-G1 See Page 902)
BRAGG ST
2800 RIV 92503 715-B7
BRAHMS LN
28800 MORV 92555 718-E4

BRAMA ST
- RivC 92880 683-D7
BRAMBLE CT
- LKEL 92532 867-E5
BRAMBLE LN
900 COR 92880 743-C2
BRANA RD
20700 RIV 92508 746-G1
S BRANCH DR
1000 CLTN 92324 646-G1
BRANCH ST
24900 MORV 92553 717-G5
BRAND ST
33400 RivC 92530 896-B3
BRANDEIS CIR
- TEM 92591 958-H4
- RMIR 92270 818-A3
BRANDIGO CIR
100 PDST 92211 818-J3
BRANDING IRON LN
- RIV 92508 716-D7
- RIV 92508 746-D1
34500 RivC 92276 788-H5
BRANDING IRON WY
25200 MORV 92553 717-G3
BRANDON CT
7200 RIV 92506 715-J6
BRANDON LN
- FONT 92337 644-E2
31800 RivC 92584 869-B7
32400 RivC 92596 869-B7
BRANDON RD
37400 RivC 92539 (934-E1 See Page 904)
BRANDON WY
200 HEMT 92545 810-F7
1100 SJCT 92582 810-H1
BRANDT DR
13900 MORV 92553 717-F6
BRANDY LN
39700 MURR 92563 928-E5
BRANDYWINE AV
1200 RIV 92507 686-A1
38000 RivC 92211 819-G1
BRANDYWINE CT
26400 RivC 92586 838-B5
BRANDYWINE DR
26000 RivC 92586 838-A5
BRANDYWINE LN
900 COR 92880 743-B2
BRANFORD DR
- TEM 92591 959-B5
BRANIGAN WY
10300 RIV 92505 714-E6
BRANSON LN
25800 RivC 92548 809-B7
25800 RivC 92548 839-B1
BRANSON PL
- YCPA 92399 649-E2
BRASA LN
15300 MORV 92555 747-J1
BRASADO WY
- RIV 92508 716-C7
BRASSIE LN
30800 TEM 92591 959-C5
BRASSIE PL
5900 PMSP 92264 787-C5
BRATTA RD
9400 RivC 92557 686-J3
BRAVO DR
1600 COR 92879 743-G2
BRAVOS CT
41200 TEM 92591 959-C4
BRAY CT
7900 RivC 92509 684-G2
BRAYTON AV
- RivC 92880 712-H4
BRAZIER DR
17800 RivC 92508 746-C7
18400 RivC 92570 776-C1
BRAZOS LN
100 PER 92571 807-H2
BREAKWATER ST
29400 LKEL 92530 865-F3
BRECHTEL ST
32700 RivC 92530 896-G5
BRECK RD
43100 RivC 92544 931-J7
BRECKENRIDGE AV
- BAN 92220 721-C6
BRECKENRIDGE CIR
1800 COR 92879 743-H3
BRECKENRIDGE DR
78800 LQNT 92253 849-H7
BRECKENRIDGE TR
33500 RivC 92595 897-C3
BRECKIN CT
41100 MURR 92562 927-H2
BREE CT
12400 YCPA 92399 650-B3
BREEZE RD
44000 RivC 92536 983-G2
BREEZE WY
37100 RivC 92211 789-G7
38000 RivC 92211 819-G1
BREEZEWOOD ST
100 COR 92879 744-F5
16200 MORV 92551 747-G3
BREEZY CIR
500 BAN 92220 721-H4
BREEZY WY
23300 MORV 92557 717-C1
BREEZY MEADOW CT
23500 MORV 92557 687-C6

BREEZY MEADOW DR
10600 MORV 92557 687-C6
BREEZY PASS RD
40700 PDST 92211 819-F4
BREINER VALLEY RD
44100 RivC 92539 (965-F7 See Page 964)
44100 RivC 92539 (985-F1 See Page 964)
BREITHORN CT
11200 RivC 92503 744-G4
BREITNER WY
- RivC 92596 899-C7
- RivC 92596 929-C1
BREMEN CT
- RivC 92596 899-C7
BREMEN ST
22700 MORV 92553 717-B4
BRENDA LN
- RivC 92506 745-G3
40700 RivC 92544 841-C1
85500 COAC 92236 5531-C1
BRENDA WY
- CTHC 92234 787-C1
BRENDAN CT
43600 RivC 92544 811-J6
BRENER CIR
10900 MORV 92557 687-E6
BRENNAN AV
600 PER 92571 777-F1
4200 PER 92571 747-F7
BRENT LN
33700 RivC 92567 779-G6
BRENTON ST
6600 RivC 92509 645-C4
BRENTRIDGE DR
- COR 92881 773-E4
BRENTSTONE ST
14800 MORV 92553 717-G7
E BRENTSTONE ST
3900 ONT 91761 643-C5
BRENTWOOD AV
4200 RIV 92506 685-E6
25900 LMLN 92354 647-E2
27500 RivC 92586 838-C5
BRENTWOOD CIR
400 HEMT 92543 840-H1
1300 COR 92882 742-J7
BRENTWOOD DR
1400 COR 92882 742-J7
S BRENTWOOD DR
2000 PMSP 92264 787-B5
BRENTWOOD LN
13000 MORV 92553 717-B4
BRENTWOOD PL
26000 RivC 92544 811-J7
44500 TEM 92592 979-H2
BRENTWOOD ST
22500 GTER 92313 646-E3
BRENTWOOD WY
- PDST 92260 818-J2
1200 HEMT 92545 840-F4
BRESLIN RD
36800 RivC 92544 901-B7
36800 RivC 92544 931-B1
BRETT LN
41700 MURR 92562 928-B7
BRETT RD
14200 RivC 92230 723-B5
BRETTON WOODS PL
17300 RivC 92504 745-H7
BREVA
50500 LQNT 92253 5470-A6
BREWER LN
700 PER 92570 807-E2
BREWER ST
21600 RivC 92570 837-B4
BREWSTER CT
- TEM 92592 959-F7
BREWSTER DR
12400 MORV 92555 717-J2
BREWSTER LN
27900 RivC 92584 868-E5
BRIAN CIR
6200 RivC 92509 684-G6
BRIAN CT
- LQNT 92253 5470-A5
- PDST 92260 848-E6
BRIAN ST
500 HEMT 92544 811-C6
BRIAN WY
100 RivC 92507 646-E6
14100 RivC 92503 745-C4
BRIANA ST
14700 MORV 92553 717-E7
BRIANNE LN
49000 COAC 92236 5471-A5
BRIANS WY
28500 MURR 92584 898-G4
BRIAR LN
9800 BLY 92225 5551-G1
BRIAR PL
14100 RivC 92570 805-D1
N BRIAR RD
- INDO 92201 5470-C3
S BRIAR RD
81200 INDO 92201 5470-C3
BRIARCLIFF CT
- RMIR 92270 818-A2
BRIARCLIFFE LN
8700 RIV 92508 746-H2
BRIARGLEN CIR
25400 MURR 92563 928-E5
BRIARHAVEN LN
2700 COR 92882 773-B2

BRIAR KNOLL CT
11000 RIV 92505 714-B2
BRIAR KNOLL PL
11800 MORV 92557 717-D1
BRIARLEA RD
26500 RivC 92584 868-B5
BRIARVALE ST
3400 RivC 92879 744-A5
BRIARWOOD
79300 LQNT 92253 849-J6
BRIARWOOD AV
41800 RivC 92544 811-E7
BRIARWOOD CT
11800 LMLN 92354 647-E3
BRIARWOOD DR
8200 RIV 92504 715-B4
22800 RivC 92883 804-B3
46300 INDW 92210 848-H3
BRIARWOOD LN
800 COR 92879 743-H2
BRIARWOOD PL
31500 TEM 92592 979-D3
BRIARWOOD ST
800 COR 92879 743-E1
BRICE CIR
44600 TEM 92592 979-H2
BRICE WY
17600 RivC 92241 727-E2
E BRICKELL ST
4100 ONT 91761 643-D1
E BRICKELL PRIVADO
4500 ONT 91761 643-E1
BRIDALWOOD LN
- RMIR 92270 818-D5
BRIDGE ST
15800 RivC 92555 749-G3
19000 RivC 92582 779-G1
19000 RivC 92567 779-G1
23000 RivC 92582 749-G7
23000 RivC 92567 749-G7
E BRIDGE ST
2600 CLTN 92324 646-J4
BRIDGEPORT RD
1100 COR 92882 773-A1
BRIDGER ST
25900 MORV 92557 717-J2
26000 MORV 92555 717-J2
BRIDGES ST
40000 RivC 92223 691-A3
BRIDGETTE WY
- LQNT 92253 849-H1
BRIDGEVIEW CIR
30500 TEM 92592 979-B4
BRIDGEWATER DR
15600 FONT 92337 644-E3
BRIDGEWATER LN
19200 RIV 92508 746-D4
28600 RivC 92584 868-F3
BRIDGEWAY DR
- RIV 92505 744-D1
BRIDGEWOOD CIR
12700 RivC 92503 744-B4
BRIDGEWOOD ST
800 COR 92881 773-E2
BRIDLE LN
600 NRCO 92860 713-G5
BRIDLE PTH
38600 RivC 92539 (934-C5 See Page 904)
BRIDLE RD
22000 RivC 92583 781-E6
BRIDLE TR
3000 PMSP 92264 786-H5
BRIDLECREST RD
- NRCO 92860 743-G1
BRIDLE PATH CIR
8300 RivC 92509 684-F2
BRIDLE TRAIL RD
25100 MORV 92553 717-G3
BRIDLETRAIL RD
48300 RivC 92536 963-A2
BRIDLEWOOD AV
- MURR 92563 928-F2
BRIDLEWOOD CIR
1300 COR 92882 773-A1
BRIENER CT
11100 RIV 92505 714-C4
BRIERCLIFF DR
43300 RivC 92544 811-J7
BRIGGS RD
23300 RivC 92585 808-J3
24300 RivC 92548 808-J3
25500 RivC 92548 838-J1
25500 RivC 92585 838-J1
28500 RivC 92584 838-J7
29000 RivC 92584 868-J1
32500 RivC 92584 898-J3
34400 RivC 92584 899-A4
34400 RivC 92563 898-J3
34400 RivC 92563 899-A4
34600 RivC 92596 899-A5
36100 MURR 92596 899-A5
36100 MURR 92596 929-B1
36100 MURR 92563 899-A5
36100 MURR 92563 929-B1
36500 RivC 92563 929-B2
BRIGGS ST
3900 RivC 92509 685-C2
BRIGHT WY
300 PER 92571 777-H6
BRIGHTMAN AV
17600 RivC 92530 896-C2
BRIGHT MORNING CT
16200 RivC 92503 744-D4

BRIGHTON CIR
2000 COR 92881 773-F1
BRIGHTON CT
4400 HEMT 92544 811-F5
22500 MORV 92557 717-B2
22700 RivC 92595 897-D2
BRIGHTON DR
5100 RIV 92506 685-E5
BRIGHTON ST
- MURR 92563 928-H7
42500 PDST 92211 819-E5
BRIGHTRIDGE LN
16400 RivC 92503 744-J4
BRIGHT ROCK DR
40000 PDST 92211 819-B4
BRIGHT STAR TR
11300 MORV 92557 687-F7
BRIGID CT
12800 YCPA 92399 649-G5
BRIGIN PL
- MURR 92562 927-J2
BRILEY CT
14900 RivC 92570 805-E4
BRILL RD
21800 MORV 92553 716-J5
21800 MORV 92553 717-A5
BRILLANTE DR
- RivC 92595 897-G6
BRIM ST
100 COR 92881 773-D2
BRINTON AV
1000 BAN 92220 721-E2
BRINTON ST
400 SJCT 92583 811-A1
BRISA CT
1800 RIV 92506 716-A1
BRISBANE CT
- FONT 92337 645-B1
BRISBANE DR
400 RIV 92508 716-E6
30000 CTHC 92234 787-G1
BRISBANE ST
600 HEMT 92545 810-E6
BRISCOE ST
3600 RIV 92506 685-F7
BRISTLECONE AV
300 BLY 92225 5491-G7
BRISTLECONE RD
30200 RivC 92563 929-A7
BRISTLECONE ST
16400 LKEL 92530 865-J3
BRISTOL AV
25200 MORV 92557 717-G1
BRISTOL CT
1300 SJCT 92583 811-D3
15600 FONT 92337 644-E2
35500 RMIR 92270 788-B6
BRISTOL LN
27000 RivC 92584 868-C5
BRISTOL RD
- MURR 92563 928-J4
BRISTOL ST
11100 RIV 92505 714-C5
46700 INDO 92201 5470-G2
BRISTOL WY
- MURR 92562 927-F4
400 COR 92879 744-A3
BRISTOLWOOD RD
200 HEMT 92543 810-J5
200 HEMT 92543 811-A5
BRITE VIEW DR
25300 RivC 92544 (812-B6 See Page 782)
BRITTANIA CT
12800 MORV 92553 717-B3
BRITTANIA RD
200 HEMT 92543 810-J5
200 HEMT 92543 811-A5
BRITTANY AV
5400 RIV 92506 716-A1
BRITTANY CT
- RivC 92596 929-E1
1600 SJCT 92583 811-E5
69400 CTHC 92234 787-G5
BRITTANY DR
500 COR 92879 744-A2
BRITTLEBUSH CIR
23800 MORV 92557 687-D5
BRITT MARIE LN
40000 RivC 92544 901-C7
40000 RivC 92544 931-C1
BRITTON CIR
31300 TEM 92591 959-D3
BRITTON WY
22400 GTER 92313 646-E4
BRIX ST
42300 RivC 92544 841-G4
BRIXTON CT
12200 MORV 92557 717-A2
BRIXTON CV
40400 TEM 92591 959-D1
BROADACRE PL
7700 RIV 92504 715-F7
BROADBENT RD
200 RIV 92507 686-E5
BROADEN LN
15000 RivC 92508 746-B1
BROADLEAF CIR
3400 COR 92881 773-E4
BROADLEAF LN
12500 MORV 92553 717-H3
BROADMOOR AV
26800 RivC 92586 838-C4
BROADMOOR CIR
32800 RivC 92276 788-F3

BROADMOOR CT
600 RivC 92882 742-G5
BROADMOOR DR
2500 PMSP 92264 787-B5
73000 RivC 92276 788-E3
BROADMOOR ST
3700 RIV 92503 715-A4
BROADSTONE WY
28500 RivC 92584 868-F2
BROADVIEW DR
20600 RivC 92570 775-G5
BROADWAY
200 LKEL 92530 865-G2
14000 RivC 92230 723-D5
N BROADWAY
100 BLY 92225 5491-E5
10800 RivC 92225 5491-E5
S BROADWAY
100 BLY 92225 5491-E7
400 BLY 92225 5551-E1
500 RivC 92225 5551-E1
15900 RivC - 5551-F4
BROADWAY ST
200 LKEL 92530 865-H2
BROCK AV
40600 RivC 92544 841-C1
40800 RivC 92544 811-D7
BROCKTON AV
2700 RIV 92501 685-H3
4600 RIV 92506 685-E7
6200 RIV 92506 715-E1
BROCKTON DR
1300 COR 92882 743-A7
BRODERICK CT
42800 HEMT 92544 811-H6
BRODERICK DR
10700 RIV 92505 714-D6
BRODIAEA AV
14300 MORV 92555 717-H6
15800 MORV 92555 718-A6
23000 MORV 92553 717-C6
BROE RD
8400 RivC 92324 687-G2
BROGAN LN
27200 MURR 92562 898-D7
BROKEN ARROW CIR
28800 RivC 92584 898-G2
BROKEN ARROW LN
67500 RivC 92241 727-B3
BROKEN ARROW ST
2800 NRCO 92860 713-B5
BROKEN ARROW TR
73300 PDST 92260 848-F4
BROKEN ARROW WY
- MURR 92563 928-H3
BROKEN AXLE RD
39600 RivC 92539 (934-D6 See Page 904)
BROKEN BIT CIR
13000 RivC 92883 835-B3
BROKEN BOW CIR
- PER 92571 778-A1
BROKEN BOW DR
19000 RIV 92508 716-D6
BROKEN FEATHER DR
2500 NRCO 92860 713-C4
BROKEN LANCE DR
2500 NRCO 92860 713-C4
BROKEN TOP CT
- INDO 92201 849-J1
BROKEN TWIG DR
3600 NRCO 92860 713-C4
BROKERS TIP CT
- PER 92571 777-G5
BROMLEY AV
22200 LKEL 92530 866-A2
BROMLEY RD
42200 RivC 92544 841-G4
BROMPTON ST
22600 MORV 92553 717-B3
BRONAUGH WY
35500 RivC 92544 902-A5
BRONC CT
22100 CYNL 92587 867-B2
BRONCO CIR
- RivC 92592 931-C6
E BRONCO DR
2900 ONT 91761 643-A7
BRONCO LN
2400 NRCO 92860 713-B5
5800 RivC 92509 685-B3
BRONSON WY
2000 RIV 92506 716-A1
5100 RIV 92506 686-A7
BRONTE RD
- CHLS 91709 712-A5
BRONWYN DR
1100 COR 92882 742-F6
BRONZE LN
11800 FONT 92337 644-D4
BROOK CT
- MURR 92562 927-G3
BROOK DR
23500 CYNL 92587 867-E2
BROOKDALE AV
6200 RivC 92509 685-A2
BROOKDALE DR
1300 COR 92880 743-B1
BROOKE LN
63000 RivC 92274 5592-C5
BROOKFIELD DR
8400 RivC 92509 684-F2
29700 RivC 92586 868-B2
BROOKHAVEN CIR
400 COR 92879 743-H4

BROOKHAVEN DR
1800 COR 92879 743-H3
23200 MORV 92553 717-C3
BROOKHAVEN LN
- RivC 92203 789-F6
BROOKHILL PL
4900 RIV 92507 686-B7
BROOKHILL TER
4800 RivC 92509 684-G1
BROOKHOLLOW CIR
4600 RivC 92509 684-D2
BROOKHOLLOW WY
22900 MORV 92557 687-C3
BROOKLAWN DR
300 BAN 92220 721-D3
BROOKLAWN PL
5000 RIV 92504 715-C1
BROOKLINE AV
9200 RivC 92240 696-E1
BROOKLINE WY
28100 MORV 92555 718-E6
BROOKMEAD DR
10300 MORV 92557 687-B5
BROOKMERE AV
25900 LMLN 92354 647-E3
BROOKMORE CT
- RIV 92505 714-C6
BROOKNOLL AV
6900 RivC 92509 684-J2
6900 RivC 92509 685-A2
BROOKRUN CT
- RIV 92505 744-D1
BROOKS AV
32600 RivC 92555 749-E2
BROOKS LN
- YCPA 92399 649-E5
BROOKS ST
4900 RIV 92506 685-G6
BROOKSHIRE RD
200 HEMT 92543 810-J5
200 HEMT 92543 811-A5
BROOKSIDE AV
1200 RDL 92373 647-H2
36600 CALI 92320 690-D6
36600 BEAU 92223 690-G5
36600 BEAU 92320 690-D6
36600 RivC 92223 690-G5
36600 RivC 92320 690-D6
39800 RivC 92223 691-A5
40000 BEAU 92223 691-A5
41200 RivC 92220 691-C5
41200 BAN 92220 691-C5
E BROOKSIDE CT
2900 ONT 91761 643-A6
BROOKSIDE DR
4200 HEMT 92545 840-D4
5800 BAN 92220 721-D4
BROOKSIDE LN
- BEAU 92223 720-G2
E BROOKSIDE ST
2700 ONT 91761 643-A6
BROOKSIDE WY
19700 RivC 92570 776-F1
BROOKSTONE CT
- RIV 92505 714-C6
BROOKSTONE DR
15200 MORV 92551 747-E1
BROOKSTONE LN
30500 RivC 92530 865-F5
BROOKSVIEW DR
55700 RivC 92282 724-E1
BROOK TRAILS WY
40200 RivC 92536 963-D1
40700 RivC 92536 (933-D7 See Page 902)
BROOKVIEW CT
15500 RivC 92504 745-F5
BROOKVIEW WY
69500 CTHC 92234 787-G1
BROOKVILLE
79300 LQNT 92253 849-J6
BROOKWAY DR
- TEM 92592 959-G7
BROOKWAY PL
10300 RIV 92505 714-F6
BROOKWOOD
25900 RivC 92544 811-E7
BROOKWOOD DR
900 COR 92880 743-B2
BROOKWOOD LN
17600 CHLS 91709 712-B5
BROOMALL AV
18000 RivC 92530 896-D3
BROSSEAU ST
21000 RivC 92567 779-A6
BROTHERTON ST
3600 RivC 92879 743-J5
BROWCA ST
25300 RivC 92544 811-J6
BROWN AV
12200 SBdC 92509 645-G5
12300 RivC 92509 645-G5
31000 RivC 92567 779-A5
80700 INDO 92201 5470-B1
BROWN ST
200 SJCT 92583 811-A2
17600 RivC 92570 746-H7
18300 RivC 92570 776-H1
22200 RivC 92570 806-H2
30600 LKEL 92530 865-J2
41800 MURR 92562 958-B1
65800 RivC 92254 5592-F6
BROWN WY
74800 PDST 92260 818-G5

BROWN BEAR TR
- BEAU 92223 690-J6
- BEAU 92223 691-A6
BROWN DEER PK
- LQNT 92253 5530-E4
BROWN DOVE CIR
24400 MORV 92557 687-F6
BROWNESTONE WY
25400 MURR 92563 928-F4
BROWN HAWK RD
32700 RivC 92567 779-E7
BROWNING CIR
- COR 92880 742-J1
BROWNING CT
12600 GTER 92313 646-E5
BROWNING ST
- RivC 92507 646-E6
12800 GTER 92313 646-E6
BROWNLANDS DR
32900 RivC 92555 749-E3
BROWN RABBIT DR
73300 RivC 92260 818-F2
BROWNS ROCKY RD
52800 RivC 92539 (934-A1 See Page 904)
BROWNSTOWN DR
41500 RivC 92201 819-G5
BROWNYARD DR
400 PER 92570 807-D2
BRUCE AV
8300 RIV 92503 714-F2
BRUCE CT
1300 BLY 92225 5491-C6
BRUCE LN
39100 RivC 92592 961-A1
BRUIN DR
500 RIV 92507 686-D7
2000 COR 92879 773-F1
BRUMA WY
21400 RivC 92562 927-A5
BRUMELIA CT
25700 MORV 92553 717-H3
BRUMFIELD ST
32800 RivC 92596 899-F4
BRUNER RD
- RivC 92585 808-D6
BRUNNER LN
68000 RivC 92240 697-C7
BRUNSTANE CIR
- COR 92882 773-A3
BRUNSTANE LN
- COR 92882 773-A2
BRUNSWICK AV
8200 RIV 92504 715-A2
8500 RIV 92504 714-J3
8700 RIV 92503 714-J3
BRUNSWICK CIR
2900 COR 92879 744-B2
BRURIC RD
26500 MURR 92562 898-C6
BRUSCA PL
6000 RIV 92506 685-G7
S BRUSH CREEK PL
2600 ONT 91761 643-C6
BRUSHWOOD DR
72400 PDST 92260 818-C7
BRUSHY HOLLOW CIR
12500 YCPA 92399 649-F4
BRUSHY HOLLOW DR
33400 YCPA 92399 649-F4
BRUSSELS ST
- RivC 92596 929-C1
BRYAN ST
10300 RIV 92505 714-F6
BRYAN LEE CT
40100 PDST 92211 819-F3
BRYANT RD
15700 RivC 92504 775-G1
BRYANT ST
- BAN 92220 722-B3
900 YCPA 92399 650-A2
900 CALI 92320 650-B7
1000 CALI 92320 690-B1
2000 RivC 92530 896-J4
2000 RivC 92595 896-J4
20300 RivC 92595 897-A5
W BRYANT ST
100 RLTO 92316 645-H1
E BRYCE CT
2500 CLTN 92324 646-J4
BRYCE WY
3500 RIV 92506 715-F2
BRYCE CANYON WY
400 SJCT 92583 781-A6
BRYNHURST DR
3500 RIV 92504 715-C4
BRYN MAWR AV
11300 LMLN 92354 647-E3
80700 INDO 92201 5470-B1
BRYN MAWR LN
2500 RIV 92507 686-B3
BRYN MAWR ST
- RMIR 92270 818-A1
BRYNOR RD
67900 CTHC 92234 817-D2
BUBBLING WELL RD
2600 RIV 92501 685-G2
BUBBLING WELLS RD
14800 DHSP 92240 697-B7
14900 RivC 92240 697-B7
15500 RivC 92240 727-B2
17000 RivC 92241 727-B2
BUCCANEER CT
42400 RivC 92201 819-J5

BUCCANEER DR
- INDO 92201 5470-G3
- RivC 92585 838-C3
BUCHANAN
- CTHC 92234 787-A7
BUCHANAN CT
2500 PER 92571 777-H5
BUCHANAN ST
700 HEMT 92543 810-J5
1100 LKEL 92530 865-H4
3500 RIV 92503 744-B2
4100 COR 92879 744-B2
56000 RivC 92274 390-F11
58000 RivC 92274 5592-D3
66800 RivC 92254 5592-D3
66800 RivC 92254 (5652-D4 See Page 5592)
72500 RivC 92254 5712-D4
76000 RivC 92274 5712-D4
81000 RivC 92274 (5772-D4 See Page 5712)
BUCHAREST LN
40800 RivC 92591 959-J2
BUCHMAN ST
- LKEL 92530 865-J2
BUCK BLVD
- RivC - 392-B9
- RivC - 412-B1
BUCK DR
69200 RivC - (907-F5 See Page 906)
BUCK PL
8300 RIV 92504 715-B3
BUCK RD
34000 RivC 92596 929-H4
34100 RivC 92591 929-J6
34300 RivC 92596 930-B6
34300 RivC 92591 930-B6
36100 RivC 92592 930-D6
BUCKBOARD LN
- NRCO 92860 713-F7
- RIV 92508 746-D1
13600 YCPA 92399 650-E6
67500 RivC 92241 727-B3
BUCKBOARD TR
33800 RivC 92567 809-G1
73300 PDST 92260 848-F4
BUCKBUSH LN
8800 RIV 92508 746-G2
BUCKEYE CIR
800 COR 92881 773-E4
BUCKEYE LN
26500 RivC 92544 842-D1
BUCKEYE PL
5000 RIV 92505 714-C6
BUCKEYE RD
43600 TEM 92592 958-J7
43700 TEM 92592 959-A7
43700 TEM 92592 979-A1
43700 TEM 92592 978-J1
BUCKEYE ST
- COR 92881 773-D4
BUCKHORN LN
- RivC - 908-A3
BUCKHORN RD
32500 RivC 92595 896-J5
47200 RivC 92536 982-G7
BUCKHORN ST
83000 INDO 92201 5470-H3
BUCKHORN TR
49500 RivC 92260 848-C6
BUCKHORN WY
25600 RivC - 814-B6
BUCKING BAY DR
26900 RivC 92883 835-C4
BUCKINGHAM DR
400 SJCT 92583 781-A7
BUCKINGHAM PL
8100 RIV 92504 715-B4
BUCKINGHAM RD
11600 LMLN 92354 647-F3
BUCKINGHAM ST
44500 INDO 92201 5410-D7
BUCKINGHAM WY
- RMIR 92270 788-C6
2700 COR 92879 744-A3
BUCKING HORSE RD
40000 RivC 92544 931-C1
BUCKLAND LN
25500 MORV 92553 717-H5
BUCKLEY DR
25500 MURR 92563 928-E5
BUCKNELL CT
45900 INDO 92201 5470-B1
BUCKNELL ST
300 HEMT 92544 811-D6
BUCKNELL WY
- COR 92881 773-D4
BUCKSKIN CIR
47600 INDO 92201 5470-D3
BUCKSKIN LN
100 NRCO 92860 713-H4
BUCKSKIN PL
2100 RIV 92506 716-A2
BUCKSKIN RD
32900 RivC 92543 870-J7
32900 RivC 92592 870-J7
32900 RivC 92592 900-J1
BUCKSKIN ST
- PER 92571 778-B2
BUCKSKIN TRAIL DR
13600 RivC 92883 835-C5
BUCK SPRINGS DR
73000 RivC 92260 818-E2

BUCK TAIL DR
23400 CYNL 92587 867-E4
BUCKTHORN DR
12000 MORV 92557 717-C2
68600 RivC - (907-F5 See Page 906)
BUCKTHORN PL
- RivC 92584 838-E6
- RivC 92585 838-E6
BUCKTHORN WY
100 COR 92881 773-C3
BUCKWHEAT RD
33000 RivC 92584 898-C3
BUCK WOOD WY
40000 MURR 92562 928-C4
BUD CT
5800 RIV 92506 715-H2
BUDDY LN
20600 RivC 92570 836-H4
BUDDY ROGERS AV
- CTHC 92234 787-F7
- CTHC 92234 817-F1
BUDDY ROGERS DR
36900 CTHC 92234 787-E7
BUECKING DR
- TEM 92590 958-F3
BUENA CIR
43600 PDST 92260 818-G7
BUENA FORTUNA LN
25500 MORV 92551 747-H3
BUENA LOMA RD
45300 RivC 92590 977-C4
BUENA MESA CT
15900 MORV 92555 748-C2
BUENA MESA DR
26200 RivC 92586 838-A6
34900 CALI 92320 689-J2
BUENA TIERRA
1700 PMSP 92262 756-F6
29700 RivC 92586 868-D2
BUENA VENTURA RD
32000 RivC 92563 929-E3
32000 RivC 92596 929-E3
BUENA VILLAGE CT
25600 MORV 92551 747-H3
BUENA VISTA AV
4600 RIV 92501 685-F3
4800 RivC 92501 685-F3
65000 DHSP 92240 696-G4
66700 DHSP 92240 697-A4
N BUENA VISTA AV
100 COR 92882 743-C4
S BUENA VISTA AV
100 COR 92882 743-B7
2100 COR 92882 773-B2
BUENA VISTA CT
- RMIR 92270 817-F3
400 CALI 92320 649-H7
BUENA VISTA DR
11200 FONT 92337 644-B2
11200 SBdC 92337 644-B2
E BUENA VISTA DR
1000 PMSP 92262 756-F7
BUENA VISTA PKWY
500 HEMT 92543 841-A1
BUENA VISTA RD
21500 RivC 92590 977-A3
BUENA VISTA ST
400 HEMT 92543 841-A3
1400 HEMT 92543 841-A3
33000 RivC 92530 896-B2
N BUENA VISTA ST
200 HEMT 92543 811-A5
S BUENA VISTA ST
100 HEMT 92543 811-A7
300 HEMT 92543 841-A2
1200 SJCT 92583 811-A7
1400 SJCT 92543 811-A7
BUENOS WY
33200 RivC 92591 929-G7
33200 RivC 92591 959-G1
BUENOS AIRES DR
42200 RivC 92544 811-F7
BUENOS CAMPOS DR
45200 RivC 92590 977-E5
BUFFALO
300 HEMT 92543 810-H7
BUFFALO DR
11200 RIV 92505 714-A2
BUFFALO RD
3100 ONT 91761 643-A5
S BUFFALO RD
2400 ONT 91761 643-B5
BUFFALO TR
- RivC 92883 835-C5
81800 INDO 92201 5470-D3
BUFFALO MEADOWS RD
28400 RivC 92373 688-D1
BUFF BAY CT
79100 RivC 92201 819-H6
BUFFY WY
39900 MURR 92563 928-E5
BUGGYWHIP CT
24700 CYNL 92587 867-B2
BUICK AV
700 SJCT 92582 810-J3
BULLET SHOT ST
20500 RivC 92518 746-F1
BUMPY CIR
31900 RivC 92596 869-D3
BUNCHBERRY LN
37200 MURR 92562 927-E3
BUNCHE PL
2400 RIV 92507 685-J6

STREET Block City ZIP Pg-Grid

BUNCH GRASS TR
13000 YCPA 92399 650-E5
BUNDY AV
16700 RivC 92518 746-H5
BUNDY WY
600 COR 92882 773-C3
BUNDY CANYON RD
21000 RivC 92595 897-D3
24800 RivC 92584 897-H2
25400 RivC 92584 898-A1
BUNKER CT
- MURR 92563 928-J4
BUNKER DR
30900 TEM 92591 959-C5
BUNKER LN
47800 INDO 92201 5470-B3
BUNKER ST
2900 RIV 92504 715-E4
BUNKER HILL CIR
1400 SJCT 92583 811-D5
BUNKERHILL DR
27200 RivC 92883 835-C5
BUNKER HILL RD
3400 BAN 92220 721-F3
BUNKERS WY
- TEM 92591 959-D5
BUNNY LN
38200 RivC - (936-A2 See Page 906)
BUNNY TR
24500 RivC 92595 927-H1
BUNTIN WY
44500 RivC 92544 (812-B6 See Page 782)
BUNTING DR
- RLTO 92316 645-H2
BURBANK DR
- RivC 92530 896-B3
BURCH ST
20400 RivC 92570 746-G7
21400 RivC 92570 747-A7
BURCHEL RD
72000 RMIR 92270 818-C4
BURD CT
13600 MORV 92553 717-C5
BURDETT PL
26000 RivC 92544 811-C7
26000 RivC 92544 841-C1
BURGANDY CT
34900 YCPA 92399 649-J4
34900 YCPA 92399 650-A4
BURGE AV
3800 RIV 92505 744-E1
3900 RIV 92505 714-E7
BURGESS CT
- TEM 92591 959-D3
BURGESS WY
26400 RivC 92586 838-B6
BURGUNDY AV
4800 RIV 92506 685-D7
BURGUNDY LN
38600 RivC 92211 819-G1
S BURGUNDY PL
1900 ONT 91761 643-E4
BURKE CT
64800 RivC 92240 696-F1
BURKE ST
11300 FONT 92337 644-H2
BURL DR
3400 RivC 92501 646-A7
11300 FONT 92337 644-B2
BURLESON CT
25200 RivC 92548 809-A7
BURLINGAME DR
5700 RIV 92504 685-A7
BURLINGTON CIR
20900 RIV 92508 746-H2
BURLINGTON WY
26200 RivC 92586 838-A6
BURL OAKS CT
20700 RivC 92562 956-J4
BURLWOOD DR
69500 RivC - (907-G5 See Page 906)
BURNEY PASS DR
13200 MORV 92555 717-J5
BURNHAM CT
10000 RIV 92503 714-F5
BURNING TREE DR
800 RivC 92882 742-G6
30700 CYNL 92587 867-D4
S BURNING TREE DR
3500 ONT 91761 683-A1
BURNING WOOD DR
22900 RivC 92883 804-C4
BURNS AV
11800 GTER 92313 646-D3
BURNS LN
23800 SBdC 92324 646-J3
BURNS ST
20500 RivC 92570 776-G2
BURNS AND ALLEN RD
- RMIR 92270 817-G4
BURNSIDE CT
6700 RIV 92504 715-C1
BURNT VALLEY LN
58800 RivC 92539 (935-E4 See Page 904)
BURNT VALLEY RD
58500 RivC 92539 (935-D4 See Page 904)
BURR ST
300 COR 92882 743-B6
38000 INDO 92203 390-D8
38000 INDO 92203 5410-B1
42800 INDO 92201 5410-B6
BURRO LN
16700 RivC 92570 775-J6
BURR OAK CT
- PER 92571 778-B2
BURR OAK RD
73500 RivC 92276 758-F6
BURR OAK WY
1700 HEMT 92545 840-H3
BURROWEED LN
46000 PDST 92260 848-F2
BURRUS CT
77500 PDST 92211 819-E3
BURSERA WY
72600 PDST 92260 848-D3
BURT ST
400 RivC 92583 811-C1
400 SJCT 92583 811-C1
BURTON DR
39500 RMIR 92270 818-D3
BURTON RD
1200 PER 92570 807-D4
23900 RivC 92570 807-D4
BURTON ST
500 LKEL 92530 866-F5
900 HEMT 92545 840-G2
10500 RIV 92505 714-E7
N BURTON WY
200 PMSP 92262 786-G1
BURWOOD CT
600 RIV 92506 716-E4
BURWOOD DR
14500 RivC 92570 805-D1
BUSBY RD
31000 RivC 92596 869-C2
BUSH AV
14100 RivC 92508 716-C7
14100 RIV 92506 716-C7
BUSH CIR
- COR 92881 773-F3
BUSH ST
47500 INDO 92201 5470-C3
BUSHMAN AV
30300 LKEL 92530 866-B4
BUSHNELL AV
5400 RIV 92505 714-D4
BUSHTON PL
20500 RivC 92570 775-G5
BUSHY TAIL TR
1300 SJCT 92583 781-A6
BUSINESS DR
10500 FONT 92337 644-A1
S BUSINESS PKWY
1700 ONT 91761 643-A3
BUSINESS WY
2200 RIV 92501 685-J2
BUSINESS CENTER DR
100 COR 92880 742-J4
22400 MORV 92553 717-B6
BUSINESS PARK DR
- PER 92571 777-G3
41900 TEM 92590 958-G6
BUSMAN RD
- MURR 92563 928-E2
BUTCH DR
32500 CTHC 92234 787-G3
BUTIA PALM AV
30600 RivC 92548 839-A2
BUTLER DR
4900 RIV 92505 714-B6
BUTLER LN
41800 RivC 92544 841-F2
BUTLER RD
28500 RivC 92596 839-B7
BUTLER BAY PL
49500 RivC 92201 819-J4
BUTLER NATIONAL RD
- COR 92883 773-H7
BUTTE DR
6600 RIV 92505 714-E1
S BUTTE CREEK PL
2800 ONT 91761 643-D6
BUTTERCHURN RD
24600 RivC 92595 897-H4
BUTTERCUP CT
17600 CHLS 91709 712-A5
BUTTERCUP DR
800 HEMT 92545 810-G5
23800 MURR 92562 927-J3
BUTTERCUP LN
44300 LQNT 92253 819-J7
BUTTERCUP PL
22600 CYNL 92587 867-C1
BUTTERFIELD DR
1600 COR 92880 742-G3
1600 COR 92880 743-A3
3100 RivC 92880 742-F3
BUTTERFIELD RD
2700 RIV 92503 745-A1
2900 RIV 92503 714-J7
2900 RIV 92503 715-A7
BUTTERFIELD ST
11500 LMLN 92354 647-E2
BUTTERFIELD TR
RivC - 411-G3
BUTTERFIELD RANCH RD
6000 CHLS 91709 712-A4
BUTTERFIELD STAGE RD
39000 RivC 92591 929-E7
39000 TEM 92591 929-E7
39100 RivC 92591 959-E2
39100 TEM 92591 959-E2
41700 RivC 92592 959-F4
41700 TEM 92592 959-F6
43500 TEM 92592 979-G1
44200 RivC 92592 979-H2
BUTTERFLY CT
38000 YCPA 92399 650-J6
BUTTERFLY DR
13600 YCPA 92399 650-H7
39200 RivC 92399 650-G7
BUTTERFLY PALM DR
26000 RivC 92548 839-A1
BUTTERFLY PEAK RD
35200 RivC - (905-F3 See Page 904)
BUTTERMILK CIR
24500 RivC 92595 897-H3
BUTTERNUT DR
43700 TEM 92592 959-A7
43700 TEM 92592 979-A1
43700 TEM 92592 958-J7
43700 TEM 92592 978-J1
BUTTERNUT LN
700 RivC 92882 742-H5
BUTTERNUT ST
1800 COR 92882 743-A7
BUTTERS AV
29900 LKEL 92530 866-B3
BUTTERWOOD DR
- RivC 92584 867-H1
BUTTON DR
41500 RMIR 92270 818-B5
BUTTONBUSH CT
23900 MURR 92562 927-J3
N BUTTONWILLOW CIR
900 PMSP 92262 756-G7
BUTTONWOOD CIR
12600 RivC 92503 744-B4
BUTTONWOOD CT
1100 HEMT 92545 840-G3
BUTTONWOOD DR
43000 PDST 92260 818-G6
BUXTON AV
15100 MORV 92551 747-F1
BUXTON CT
- MURR 92563 928-G7
BUYS LN
31400 RivC 92548 809-C6
BYE HOLE WY
56100 LQNT 92253 5530-B5
BYERLY RD
31000 RivC 92596 839-B7
BYERS RD
27500 RivC 92586 837-J5
BYERS ST
25500 RivC 92584 867-J3
26000 RivC 92570 837-J3
26000 RivC 92585 837-J3
33000 RivC 92584 897-J1
BYHAM LN
9300 RivC 92223 690-G2
BYRD ST
3100 SJCT 92582 780-C6
31900 RivC 92548 839-D1
BYRNE RD
4200 RivC 92509 644-J7
BYRNE ST
18100 SBdC 92316 645-C1
BYRON LN
54000 RivC 92539 (934-D2 See Page 904)
BYRON PL
42600 RivC 92201 819-F5
BYRON ST
3600 RivC 92879 743-J5
18700 RivC 92570 776-H1
21500 RivC 92570 777-A1

C

C AV
20000 RivC 92567 778-G4
20700 RivC 92571 778-G4
C ST
- HEMT 92545 840-G2
1100 COR 92882 743-B5
33500 YCPA 92399 649-F2
41900 MURR 92562 928-A6
41900 TEM 92590 978-J1
41900 TEM 92592 978-J1
42100 MURR 92562 927-J7
43600 RivC 92544 811-J6
43800 RivC 92544 (812-A6 See Page 782)
68500 CTHC 92234 817-E1
N C ST
- PER 92570 807-G2
S C ST
- PER 92570 807-G3
C&D BLVD
- BLY 92225 5491-F4
- BLY 92225 5551-F1
- RivC - 392-C9
- RivC 92225 5551-F1
7400 RivC - 5491-F1
8300 RivC 92225 5491-F4
19400 RivC - 5551-F4
CABALLERO CT
11300 FONT 92337 645-A2
CABALLERO DR
11800 FONT 92337 644-A4
CABALLEROS DR
42600 RivC 92201 819-J5
CABALLEROS RD
2000 NRCO 92860 713-C7
CABALLEROS CANON
21900 RivC 92567 779-F7
CABALLO RD
15200 MORV 92555 747-J1
CABALLOS DR
43000 RivC 92592 960-C7
CABANA CIR
- RivC 92254 (5654-D2 See Page 5594)
CABANA CT
2200 COR 92879 743-H2
40500 PDST 92260 818-F4
CABANA ST
3000 RivC 91752 644-A5
CABAZON AV
84100 INDO 92201 5470-J2
84100 INDO 92201 5471-A3
84100 RivC 92201 5470-J2
84100 RivC 92201 5471-A3
CABAZON LN
100 PER 92571 807-H2
CABAZON ST
14500 RivC 92230 723-D5
CABAZON CENTER DR
84300 INDO 92201 5471-A3
CABAZON PEAK DR
38500 RivC 92260 818-E2
CABERN CT
- TEM 92591 959-D3
CABERNET CT
10000 RivC 92509 644-A4
CABERNET DR
3000 FONT 92337 644-A4
3000 RivC 91752 644-A5
CABILDO CIR
1500 PMSP 92264 786-F6
CABIN CIR
38000 RivC 92260 818-F1
CABIN PL
- RIV 92508 746-D2
CABLE CIR
1800 RIV 92506 716-A3
CABLE LN
18300 RivC 92570 746-F7
18300 RivC 92570 776-F1
CABO ST
44200 TEM 92592 978-J2
44200 TEM 92592 979-A2
CABOT AV
12000 MORV 92557 717-J1
CABOT RD
14000 DHSP 92240 696-G7
16000 DHSP - 726-G1
16000 RivC - 726-G1
CABRILLO AV
30000 TEM 92592 979-B2
44700 PDST 92260 848-G1
CABRILLO CIR
300 COR 92879 743-H4
CABRILLO DR
1200 HEMT 92543 810-H6
9000 RIV 92503 714-E1
27200 RivC 92586 868-D2
CABRILLO LN
78100 INDW 92210 849-F2
CABRILLO LP
- LMLN 92354 647-C1
CABRILLO PL
- INDO 92201 5470-D4
W CABRILLO RD
200 PMSP 92262 756-C5
CABRILLO WY
78000 LQNT 92253 849-H5
CABRINI DR
35300 YCPA 92399 650-B5
CACHANILLA CT
- PDST 92260 818-H7
CACHUMA RD
74900 INDW 92210 818-J7
CACHUMA ST
300 PER 92571 777-H7
CACTUS AV
10800 SBdC 92316 645-F3
10800 RLTO 92316 645-F3
11800 RivC 92509 645-F3
18800 RivC 92508 716-B7
20000 RivC 92518 716-G7
22000 RivC 92553 717-B7
22000 RivC 92518 717-D6
22200 MORV 92553 717-D6
26000 MORV 92555 717-G6
26000 MORV 92555 718-A6
S CACTUS AV
2300 SBdC 92316 645-F1
CACTUS CIR E
14700 RivC 92518 716-F7
14700 RivC 92518 746-G1
CACTUS CIR W
15100 RivC 92518 716-F7
15100 RivC 92518 746-F1
CACTUS CT
11800 FONT 92337 644-A4
55800 RivC 92282 724-F2
72700 PDST 92260 848-D3
CACTUS DR
400 RivC - 5239-J6
400 RivC - 5240-A7
10200 DHSP 92240 696-H2
16000 RivC 92240 726-J1
72400 PDST 92260 818-C7
CACTUS LN
38500 RivC 92260 818-E2
69600 CTHC 92234 787-G3
CACTUS PL
29900 TEM 92592 959-A7
E CACTUS RD
1100 PMSP 92264 786-F4
CACTUS ST
1600 COR 92882 772-J1
43300 INDO 92201 5410-F6
CACTUS TR
36800 YCPA 92399 650-E5
CACTUS APPLE DR
67600 RivC 92241 727-B4
CACTUS FLOWER DR
27700 RivC 92585 838-E5
CACTUS TREE LN
- HEMT 92545 840-E4
CACTUS VALLEY RD
39500 RivC 92543 871-D3
40700 RivC 92544 871-D3
CACTUS VALLEY RD Rt#-R3
39600 RivC 92543 871-B3
40200 RivC 92544 871-B3
CADBURY DR
11200 RIV 92505 714-A2
CADDO AV
4000 RivC 92509 685-D3
CADENA DR
29500 RivC 92585 808-H7
CADENZA DR
23600 MURR 92562 927-H3
CADET ST
2800 RIV 92504 715-F4
CADIZ
1000 COR 92882 773-B2
CADIZ CIR
1900 PMSP 92264 786-G5
CADIZ CT
1700 HEMT 92545 810-H6
5200 RivC 92509 685-A3
CADIZ DR
- RMIR 92270 818-B4
CADOO RD
38400 RivC 92539 (935-D4 See Page 904)
CADWELL CT
1300 RIV 92506 716-B2
CADY RD
36500 RivC 92596 929-E1
CAFERA LN
31200 TEM 92591 959-D3
CAGNEY CT
14500 MORV 92553 717-E7
CAHUILLA AV
65000 DHSP 92240 696-G4
66700 DHSP 92240 697-A4
CAHUILLA CT
- LQNT 92253 879-G1
27600 RivC 92544 841-E4
CAHUILLA DR
- MORV 92555 747-J3
- MORV 92555 748-A3
26700 RivC - (843-J1 See Page 842)
CAHUILLA RD
100 PMSP 92262 786-D2
CAHUILLA RD Rt#-371
41700 RivC 92536 963-F2
43400 RivC 92536 962-J7
43400 RivC 92536 982-G2
43500 RivC 92539 (933-H7 See Page 902)
43500 RivC 92539 963-F2
45400 RivC 92539 (934-A6 See Page 904)
54700 RivC 92539 (935-A4 See Page 904)
N CAHUILLA RD
400 PMSP 92262 786-D1
600 PMSP 92262 756-D7
CAHUILLA ST
6700 RivC 92509 685-A4
E CAHUILLA ST
2000 CLTN 92324 646-H2
S CAHUILLA ST
1200 CLTN 92324 646-H2
CAHUILLA WY
- RivC 92260 848-B6
- PDST 92260 848-C6
CAHUILLA FALLS
- PDST 92260 848-D6
CAHUILLA HEIGHTS RD
38900 RivC 92544 (932-E7 See Page 902)
40200 RivC 92536 962-E2
40200 RivC 92544 962-E2
CAHUILLA HILLS DR
- PMSP 92264 786-E7
CAHUILLA PARK RD
- LQNT 92253 879-J5
- LQNT 92253 5530-A7
CAICOS CT
- MURR 92563 928-H7
- MURR 92563 958-H1
CAIN RD
- RivC 92539 (934-J4 See Page 904)
57000 RivC 92539 (935-A4 See Page 904)
CAIRN CT
- RIV 92508 716-E7
CAIRNHILL RD
25200 RivC - 814-B5
CAIRO
100 PMSP 92264 786-E5
CAIRO AV
84700 COAC 92236 5471-B7
CAJALCO BLVD
17000 RivC 92570 806-A1
CAJALCO EXWY
- PER 92570 777-D2
- PER 92571 777-D2
23000 RivC 92570 777-D2
CAJALCO RD
- COR 92883 773-J6
8000 COR 92883 774-A5
8000 COR 92881 774-A5
8600 RivC 92883 774-A5
8600 RivC 92881 774-E4
8900 RivC 92570 774-E4
12700 RivC 92570 775-F4
16800 RivC 92504 775-F4
16800 RivC 92504 776-B3
16800 RivC 92570 776-B3
21500 RivC 92570 777-A3
CAJON CIR
3100 PMSP 92264 786-J4
CAJON DR
- COR 92882 773-B1
17000 RivC 92570 776-A7
43700 TEM 92592 979-A1
CAJON ST
1700 HEMT 92544 811-C5
CAKES PL
22500 RivC 92570 837-C3
CAL CT
7800 RivC 92509 644-G7
CALABASH AV
10500 SBdC 92337 644-B2
11100 FONT 92337 644-B4
CALABRIA DR
- TEM 92591 959-A5
25500 MORV 92551 747-H3
CALABRO ST
- TEM 92592 959-F7
- TEM 92592 979-F1
CALAC RD
34400 RivC 92592 960-A4
CALA CARRASCO
31200 TEM 92592 959-D7
CALADA DR
13800 MORV 92553 717-E5
CALADA RD
28800 CTHC 92234 757-D6
CALA DEL VALLE
39000 MURR 92562 928-D2
CALA GERONA
32000 TEM 92592 959-E6
CALAIS CT
6700 RIV 92506 716-B4
CALAIS PL
24900 RivC 92544 (812-A5 See Page 782)
CALA ROSSO
42900 TEM 92592 959-D7
CALATHEA RD
1700 HEMT 92545 840-E4
CALA TORRENTE
32100 TEM 92592 959-E6
CALAVERAS RD
38400 RivC 92592 960-H1
CALCUTTA DR
22600 CYNL 92587 867-C4
CALDERA CT
5100 RIV 92507 686-D7
CALDERON LN
- RivC 92532 836-B3
CALDWELL CT
26200 RivC 92570 837-B2
CALDWELL DR
22000 RivC 92241 727-A7
22800 RivC 92241 757-A1
38400 RivC 92539 (935-B5 See Page 904)
CALDY AV
11500 LMLN 92354 647-F2
CALEDONIA DR
19300 RIV 92508 746-E4
CALENDULA AV
49200 COAC 92236 5471-A5
84000 COAC 92236 5470-J5
CALENDULA ST
26900 RivC 92883 835-C5
CALEO BAY
47000 LQNT 92253 849-G3
CALETA WY
1200 PMSP 92262 756-F6
CALF ST
- RivC 92880 683-D6
CALGARY CT
29200 RivC 92586 868-B1
CALHOUN CIR
500 COR 92879 744-A2
CALHOUN CT
1300 HEMT 92544 811-B6
CALHOUN PL
500 HEMT 92543 811-A7
CALHOUN ST
500 COR 92879 744-A2
46000 INDO 92201 5470-H2
48200 COAC 92236 5470-H4
49800 RivC 92236 5470-H7
52800 RivC 92236 5530-H2
54000 RivC 92274 5530-H6
59000 RivC 92274 5590-J3
66000 RivC 92274 (5650-J2 See Page 5590)
CALICIA CT
39800 MURR 92562 928-C3
CALICO AV
55400 RivC 92282 724-E2
82100 INDO 92201 5470-E3
CALICO CIR
7100 COR 92881 773-H4
7100 RivC 92881 773-H4
44000 LQNT 92253 819-J7
CALICO CT
- NRCO 92860 743-J1
33300 RivC 92595 897-H2
CALICO LN
2500 PMSP 92262 756-G5
CALICO RD
70200 RMIR 92270 817-H4
CALICO ST
83000 INDO 92201 5470-G2
CALICO TR
2800 COR 92882 773-B2
CALICO CACTUS LN
47200 PDST 92260 848-E4
N CALIENTE CT
40600 RivC 92536 (933-D7 See Page 902)
S CALIENTE CT
41000 RivC 92536 963-D2
CALIENTE DR
2100 PMSP 92264 786-F7
13000 DHSP 92240 696-J5
CALIENTE PL
30400 CYNL 92587 867-B3
CALIENTE RD
1800 PMSP 92264 786-F5
CALIENTE SPRINGS AV
- MURR 92562 927-J2
CALIFORNIA
33000 RivC 92530 865-G6
CALIFORNIA AV
- GTER 92313 646-D7
- RivC 92507 646-D7
- BEAU 92223 720-H1
100 RivC 92223 720-H5
700 BLY 92225 5491-G5
1700 COR 92881 743-G7
1700 COR 92881 773-G2
3500 NRCO 92860 713-H1
4200 RIV 92503 714-H5
7700 RIV 92504 715-A3
8700 RIV 92503 715-A3
10300 RIV 92505 714-E6
23500 RivC 92545 809-J3
23600 RivC 92545 810-A3
23800 HEMT 92545 809-J5
25000 HEMT 92545 810-A7
25900 HEMT 92545 840-A1
26100 RivC 92545 840-A1
28500 RivC 92596 840-A7
S CALIFORNIA AV
700 PMSP 92264 786-J3
CALIFORNIA DR
76500 PDST 92211 819-E5
CALIFORNIA PL
23700 RivC 92587 837-F7
34900 YCPA 92399 650-A6
CALIFORNIA ST
900 PER 92571 747-D7
900 YCPA 92399 650-A3
900 CALI 92320 650-A7
1000 CALI 92320 690-A1
10900 LMLN 92373 647-F1
10900 SBdC 92373 647-F1
26400 LMLN 92354 647-F1
N CALIFORNIA ST
100 LKEL 92530 865-G2
S CALIFORNIA ST
100 LKEL 92530 865-G2
CALIFORNIA OAKS RD
39000 MURR 92562 928-B4
CALIFORNIA QUAIL RD
24100 MURR 92562 928-B2
CALIFORNIA STAGE RD
- RivC 92320 689-H6
- RivC 92320 690-A7
- RivC 92320 719-J1
- RivC 92320 720-A1
CALIMESA BLVD
8600 CALI 92320 689-H1
9500 CALI 92320 690-A4
11800 CALI 92320 649-G7
13300 YCPA 92399 649-D5
CALISTOGA DR
38900 RivC 92563 929-B7
CALKINS AV
18000 LKEL 92530 866-C3
CALL DR
3300 RIV 92503 715-A6
CALL WY
1400 COR 92882 742-J6
1400 COR 92882 743-A6
CALLA CALAIS
21400 RivC 92562 927-A6
CALLAHAN CT
1100 SJCT 92582 810-H1
CALLAHAN RD
28600 MURR 92563 928-G3
CALLANDER ST
27600 MORV 92555 748-C2
CALLAO CT
2200 HEMT 92545 810-G6
CALLAO ST
300 HEMT 92545 810-G6
CALLAWAY CT
- YCPA 92399 649-E2
43300 PDST 92260 818-G6
CALLAWAY DR
2100 SJCT 92583 811-E4
CALLE ABAJO
- PMSP 92264 787-D6
CALLE ABRONIA
500 PMSP 92264 786-E3
CALLE ACER
27400 RivC 92585 838-D5
CALLE AGENTE
- RivC 92562 956-E2
CALLE AGUA
25700 MORV 92551 747-J3
CALLE AGUILAR
68500 CTHC 92234 787-E6
CALLE AJO
500 PMSP 92264 786-E3
CALLE ALAGON
68500 CTHC 92234 787-E6
CALLE ALCAZAR
68500 CTHC 92234 787-E6
CALLE ALEGRE
37700 RivC 92539 (934-F2 See Page 904)
CALLE ALFREDO
33200 TEM 92592 979-H3
CALLE ALPINIA
- MURR 92562 928-B3
CALLE ALTA
28800 MURR 92563 928-H4
42300 RivC 92592 960-A5
CALLE ALTO
26200 MORV 92555 747-J1
CALLE ALVARADO
100 PMSP 92262 786-E2
N CALLE ALVARADO
200 PMSP 92262 786-E1
CALLE AMAPOLA
12600 DHSP 92240 697-D5
CALLE AMARGOSA
300 HEMT 92545 810-H6
CALLE AMIGABLE
38000 MURR 92563 928-G4
CALLE AMIGO
19500 RivC 92562 926-G3
78000 LQNT 92253 849-F7
CALLE AMIGOS
53300 COAC 92236 5531-C2
S CALLE AMIGOS
100 PMSP 92264 786-F3
CALLE ANDALUCIA
- RivC 92562 956-D4
CALLE ANDRAS
- MURR 92563 929-A3
29300 MURR 92563 928-J3
CALLE ANGELINA
22800 RivC 92590 977-D3
CALLE ANGOSTA
38100 RivC 92592 931-A3
CALLE ANGOSTURA
9700 RIV 92503 744-J1
9700 RIV 92503 745-A1
CALLE ANITA
39500 RivC 92592 930-E7
CALLE ANTILLES
3700 RivC 92503 744-F5
CALLE ARAGON
31000 TEM 92592 959-C6
CALLE ARANDA
41000 TEM 92591 959-A4
CALLE ARANDAS
3100 PMSP 92264 787-D6
CALLE ARBOLEDA
1800 HEMT 92545 810-H6
CALLE ARCARO
36400 RivC 92592 930-E7
CALLE ARDILLA
- RMIR 92270 787-H7
CALLE AREVALLO
40000 RivC 92592 931-C6
CALLE ARNAZ
34500 RivC 92592 960-B7
CALLE ARREBOL
38200 MURR 92563 928-G5
CALLE ARRIBA
100 PMSP 92264 787-D5
CALLE ARROBA
77100 LQNT 92253 879-F3
CALLE ARRUZA
36900 RivC 92592 930-E5
CALLE ARTINO
24000 MURR 92562 928-B2
CALLE AURORA
16300 MORV 92551 747-J3
CALLE AVELLA
41300 TEM 92592 959-E7
CALLE AVILA
34800 CTHC 92234 787-E5
51500 COAC 92236 5471-B7
52300 COAC 92236 5531-B1
CALLE AYORA
45600 RivC 92592 979-F4
CALLE AYRTON
27100 RivC 92586 868-C2
CALLE AZTECA
68000 DHSP 92240 697-C5
CALLE AZUCAR
- MURR 92562 928-D3
CALLE AZUL
- RivC 92562 956-D3
CALLE AZURE
39700 RivC 92592 931-B6
CALLE BABETTE
42300 RivC 92592 960-A5
CALLE BAHIA VISTA
- TEM 92592 959-C5
CALLE BALAREZA
- TEM 92592 979-E1
CALLE BALLENTINE
42900 TEM 92592 959-E7
CALLE BALMEZ
- TEM 92592 979-F1
CALLE BALSERO
27300 RivC 92586 838-D6
CALLE BANDIDO
- PMSP 92264 787-B7
19000 RivC 92562 956-E1
39300 RivC 92562 926-F7
CALLE BANUELOS
- RivC 92592 979-H3
44700 TEM 92592 979-H3
CALLE BARBONA
42200 RivC 92592 959-H5
CALLE BARCALDO
31600 TEM 92592 959-D7
CALLE BARCELONA
68300 CTHC 92234 787-D5
78000 LQNT 92253 849-F7
CALLE BARRANCA
9000 DHSP 92240 696-H1
CALLE BARTIZON
36700 RivC 92592 930-E5
CALLE BEGONIA
400 PMSP 92262 786-H2
CALLE BELCANTO
30000 RivC 92584 868-F3
CALLE BELLA
53300 COAC 92236 5531-C2
CALLE BELLAGIO
39200 RivC 92592 930-G6
CALLE BELLA LOMA
34600 RivC 92592 960-A3
CALLE BELVIA
30200 RivC 92592 979-B6
CALLE BERNARDO
44000 RivC 92590 977-F1
CALLE BISQUE
73700 PDST 92260 818-F4
CALLE BLANCO
68100 DHSP 92240 697-C5
CALLE BOLSA
68000 DHSP 92240 697-C5
CALLE BONITA
53000 COAC 92236 5531-C1
68200 DHSP 92240 697-C4
CALLE BOUGANVILIA
86000 COAC 92236 5471-E6
CALLE BRAVO
100 PMSP 92264 786-E5
CALLE BREVE
38700 RivC 92592 931-A5
39400 RivC 92592 930-J6
40200 RivC 92592 960-J1
CALLE BRILLANTE
21400 RivC 92562 927-A4
CALLE BRISA
- LQNT 92253 849-H5
CALLE BURRO
43900 RivC 92544 (932-B4 See Page 902)
CALLE CABALLOS
- TEM 92592 979-E1
CALLE CABAZON
20100 RivC 92590 976-J2
CALLE CABERNET
39800 RivC 92591 929-H7
39800 RivC 92591 959-J1
CALLE CABEZA
33800 RivC 92591 929-J7
CALLE CABRA
68500 CTHC 92234 787-E6
CALLE CABRIL
- OrCo - 895-D1
- RivC 92530 895-D1
CALLE CABRILLO
- RivC 92592 959-G4
CALLE CADIZ
78000 LQNT 92253 849-F7
CALLE CALETA
40100 RivC 92591 959-J1
CALLE CALMOSO
68200 DHSP 92240 697-C4
CALLE CALZON
- RivC 92562 956-F4
CALLE CAMACHO
51500 COAC 92236 5471-B7
52300 COAC 92236 5531-B1
CALLE CAMELIA
15200 MORV 92555 747-J1
15300 MORV 92555 748-A1
CALLE CAMELLIA
- TEM 92592 959-C7
CALLE CAMPINA NUEVO
40700 RivC 92562 956-G3
CALLE CAMPO
35000 RivC 92592 960-B5
38100 RivC 92592 930-H3
CALLE CANCION
40500 RivC 92592 960-B3
CALLE CANORA
41300 RivC 92592 960-H3
CALLE CANTU
33200 TEM 92592 979-H2
CALLE CAPISTRANO
42100 RivC 92590 958-A5
CALLE CAPRI
40900 RivC 92544 931-E5
CALLE CARABANA
43400 TEM 92592 959-E7
43400 TEM 92592 979-E1
CALLE CARRANZA
30000 TEM 92592 959-A6
CALLE CASABLANCA
39400 MURR 92563 928-E4
CALLE CASERA
28000 RivC 92585 838-D5
CALLE CASITA
16700 RivC 92241 727-E1
CALLE CASTANO
15500 MORV 92555 748-A1
CALLE CATALDO
31700 TEM 92592 959-D7
CALLE CATHRON
84500 COAC 92236 5471-A6
CALLE CATRINA
43500 RivC 92590 978-B1
CALLE CAZADERO
300 HEMT 92545 810-H6
CALLE CEDRAL
41700 TEM 92592 959-E6
CALLE CELLUZZ
19600 RivC 92562 926-G3
CALLE CENTRO
38800 RivC 92562 926-J5
CALLE CEREZO
41800 TEM 92592 959-E6
CALLE CERRILLO
28500 TEM 92590 978-J2
CALLE CERRITO
68000 DHSP 92240 697-C5
CALLE CERRO
41800 RivC 92592 960-B5
CALLE CERVATO
38200 MURR 92563 928-H5
CALLE CHAPALA
2800 PMSP 92264 787-D6
CALLE CHAPOS
31700 TEM 92591 959-D1
CALLE CHIA
600 PMSP 92264 786-E3
CALLE CHICO
35400 RivC 92592 960-C2
CALLE CHIHUAHUA
77200 LQNT 92253 879-F2
CALLE CHILLON
77100 LQNT 92253 879-E3
CALLE CHIQUITA
44000 RivC 92562 976-B2
CALLE CIELO
17400 RivC 92562 976-B1
CALLE CIPRES
- MURR 92562 927-E5
CALLE CISNE
29100 MURR 92563 928-H5
CALLE CLAIRE
- PDST 92260 818-G3
CALLE CLAVEL
38000 MURR 92563 928-G4
51000 COAC 92236 5471-D6
CALLE COLIMA
77000 LQNT 92253 879-E2
CALLE COLINA
- CTHC 92234 757-G7
43600 RivC 92590 977-A1
CALLE COLINGA
- RivC 92562 956-D7
CALLE COLISEO
- RivC 92536 962-F4
CALLE COLLADO
43000 RivC 92562 956-C7
43100 RivC 92562 976-C1
CALLE COMIENZO
85000 RivC 92274 5531-D2
CALLE CONCHITA
80800 RivC 92253 5590-C1
CALLE CONEJARA
2200 PMSP 92262 756-G7
CALLE CONEJO
39200 RivC 92592 931-A3
48000 INDO 92201 5470-D4
CALLE CONFITE
38000 MURR 92563 928-G4
CALLE CONSTANCIA
100 RDL 92373 647-J2
CALLE CONTENTO
39100 RivC 92591 959-H1
40600 RivC 92592 959-J3
CALLE CORDOBA
68300 CTHC 92234 787-D5
CALLE CORDOVA
38900 RivC 92592 931-C6
39900 RivC 92544 931-C6
40100 RivC 92544 961-C1
40100 RivC 92592 961-C1
CALLE CORDURA
40400 RivC 92592 960-J1
CALLE CORONA
40600 RivC 92592 931-D6
44000 RivC 92590 977-B1
CALLE CORREDOR
2100 SDCo 92028 998-C5
CALLE CORRIENTE
41900 RivC 92562 956-E6
CALLE CORTA
- RivC 92562 956-C7
CALLE CORTEZ
28700 TEM 92590 958-G6
CALLE CORTO
42900 RivC 92590 957-H6
CALLE CORVETA
25700 RivC 92590 958-A6
CALLE CRESTA
45700 RivC 92590 978-C5
CALLE CUERNAVACA
41000 RivC 92562 956-E3
CALLE CUERO
45500 RivC 92590 978-A5

STREET Block City ZIP Pg-Grid

CALLE CUESTA
45000 RivC 92590 978-H3
CALLE CURACSO
3700 RivC 92503 744-F5
CALLE DE AMOR
36900 MURR 92563 928-H3
CALLE DE CABALLOS
29000 RivC 92585 808-H7
CALLE DECANSO
68200 DHSP 92240 697-D4
CALLE DE CARLOS
4300 PMSP 92264 787-A3
E CALLE DE CARLOS
3800 PMSP 92264 786-J3
3800 PMSP 92264 787-B4
CALLE DE CIELO
39300 RivC 92592 931-D6
CALLE DECKER
39100 RivC 92592 930-J7
39100 RivC 92592 931-A7
CALLE DE COMPANERO
38300 RivC 92562 926-F5
CALLE DE CORIZON
- RivC 92562 956-J6
CALLE DE CUERNO
26200 RivC 92590 958-B6
CALLE DE DIETEL
17000 RivC 92562 976-B1
CALLE DE ESCARPADO
28700 MURR 92563 928-G5
CALLE DE ESPERANZA
34500 RivC 92595 897-E5
CALLE DE ESTRELLAS
- PMSP 92264 787-A7
CALLE DE FLORA VISTA
800 PMSP 92262 756-F7
CALLE DE FORTUNA
39100 MURR 92563 928-H6
CALLE DE JIMENEZ
11900 MORV 92555 718-A1
CALLE DEL ALBA
200 PER 92571 807-H1
CALLE DE LA PAZ
28700 MURR 92563 928-G5
CALLE DEL ARCO
1400 SDCo 92028 998-J7
CALLE DE LAS FLORES
59700 RivC 92262 725-E7
CALLE DE LA SIESTA
38400 MURR 92563 928-G5
CALLE DE LA SILLA
72800 PDST 92260 848-E5
CALLE DE LAS NUBES
- PMSP 92264 787-A7
CALLE DE LAS ROSAS
- RMIR 92270 818-D3
CALLE DEL BUHO
29000 MURR 92563 928-H5
CALLE DEL CALLADO
100 PMSP 92264 787-D5
CALLE DEL CASA
9500 RIV 92503 745-A1
CALLE DEL CORRAL
17500 RivC 92504 746-A4
CALLE DEL DIOS
9400 DHSP 92240 696-H1
CALLE DE LEON
27600 RivC 92585 808-D5
CALLE DEL ESPACIO
- PMSP 92264 787-A7
CALLE DE LINA
17300 RivC 92562 976-C2
CALLE DEL LAGO
28600 MURR 92563 928-H6
CALLE DEL LIRIO
- RivC 92883 804-A1
CALLE DEL MUNDO
24100 RivC 92590 977-G2
CALLE DEL NORTE
- RMIR 92270 787-J2
200 PER 92570 807-G2
75500 INDW 92210 849-B1
CALLE DE LOBO
37000 RivC 92562 926-H1
CALLE DEL ORO
1600 COR 92882 742-G7
CALLE DE LOS ARBOLES
28600 MURR 92563 928-G6
CALLE DE LOS CAMPESINOS
47300 PDST 92260 848-D4
CALLE DEL OSO ORO
22900 MURR 92562 927-F5
CALLE DE LOS PINOS
- OrCo - 895-D1
- RivC 92530 895-D1
CALLE DE LOS ROBLES
32500 RivC 92530 895-D1
CALLE DE LOS ROMOS
18000 RivC 92258 726-E3
CALLE DE LOS VIENJOS
- PMSP 92264 787-A7
CALLE DEL SOL
- INDO 92201 5470-D4
- PMSP 92264 787-D6
43500 RivC 92562 956-G7
CALLE DEL SUR
75500 INDW 92210 849-A1
CALLE DEL VINEDOS
39800 RivC 92591 929-J7
39800 RivC 92591 959-J1

S CALLE DE MARIA
1000 PMSP 92264 786-F4
CALLE DE MAYA
41200 RivC 92592 960-D3
N CALLE DE MIMOSAS
800 PMSP 92262 756-G7
CALLE DE MUCHO
42800 RivC 92562 956-J5
CALLE DENIA
68700 CTHC 92234 787-E6
CALLE DE ORO
- RMIR 92270 787-J3
CALLE DE PALMA
43600 INDO 92203 5410-H5
N CALLE DE PINOS
800 PMSP 92262 756-G7
CALLE DE PRADERA
19400 RivC 92562 926-F4
CALLE DE RICARDO
4300 PMSP 92264 787-A3
E CALLE DE RICARDO
3800 PMSP 92264 786-J3
3800 PMSP 92264 787-B4
CALLE DE SUENOS
39400 RivC 92562 926-H7
39800 RivC 92562 956-J1
CALLE DE TESORO
25000 MURR 92563 928-E4
CALLE DE TOROS
- RivC 92592 930-J5
CALLE DE TRES AMIGOS
25100 MURR 92563 928-F4
CALLE DE VECINOS
9000 DHSP 92240 696-J1
CALLE DE VELARDO
43600 TEM 92592 979-C1
CALLE DE VERANO
200 PDST 92260 818-F6
CALLE DE VIAJERO
84000 INDO 92203 5410-J6
CALLE DIABLO
1800 HEMT 92545 810-H6
9000 DHSP 92240 696-H1
CALLE DIAZ
23200 MORV 92557 717-C2
CALLE DURANGO
77100 LQNT 92253 879-F1
CALLE EDMUNDO
29600 RivC 92586 868-D2
CALLE EDUARDO
- RivC 92562 956-F4
CALLE ELENA
- RivC 92590 978-B4
CALLE ELENITA
9100 RivC 92223 691-A2
CALLE EL NINO
41000 RivC 92544 961-D2
CALLE EL SAUCE
20900 RivC 92562 926-J4
N CALLE EL SEGUNDO
100 PMSP 92262 786-E1
S CALLE EL SEGUNDO
100 PMSP 92262 786-E2
CALLE EMILIANO
26500 RivC 92585 838-A3
CALLE EMPALME
51800 COAC 92236 5471-B7
52200 COAC 92236 5531-B1
CALLE EMPLEADO
- TEM 92590 958-E5
CALLE ENCANTADO
- RivC 92592 959-G4
N CALLE ENCILIA
100 PMSP 92262 786-E1
S CALLE ENCILIA
100 PMSP 92262 786-E2
500 PMSP 92264 786-E2
CALLE ENCINITAS
- RMIR 92270 818-C6
CALLE ENSENADA
77200 LQNT 92253 879-F1
CALLE ENTRADA
- RMIR 92270 787-G5
CALLE ENTRADERO
25000 MURR 92563 928-E4
CALLE ESCADERA
26800 RivC 92590 978-D2
CALLE ESCALA
- RMIR 92270 787-H7
- RMIR 92270 817-H1
CALLE ESCALONA
39400 RivC 92592 931-D6
CALLE ESCORIAL
9000 DHSP 92240 696-H1
CALLE ESPANA
39700 MURR 92563 928-E4
CALLE ESPEJO
68600 CTHC 92234 787-E6
CALLE ESPERANZA
48600 LQNT 92253 849-F4
CALLE ESPINOSA
31800 TEM 92592 959-E7
CALLE ESPIRITO
31700 TEM 92592 959-D7
CALLE ESPLANADE
9800 RIV 92503 744-J1
CALLE ESPUELA
16900 RivC 92504 745-J5
CALLE ESTADO
78000 LQNT 92253 849-F7
CALLE ESTANCIA
24300 MURR 92562 927-H6
CALLE ESTEPA
17800 RivC 92562 976-C2

CALLE ESTRELLA
49800 LQNT 92253 849-E6
53100 COAC 92236 5531-C1
CALLE FAMILIA
25900 MORV 92551 747-J1
CALLE FEDERICO
45000 RivC 92590 977-F4
E CALLE FELICIA
1900 PMSP 92262 786-G2
CALLE FELICIDAD
31200 TEM 92591 959-C2
CALLE FELIPE
78400 LQNT 92253 849-G6
CALLE FELIZ
53200 COAC 92236 5531-B2
CALLE FIESTA
21100 RivC 92562 927-A3
40300 TEM 92591 959-C2
47700 INDO 92201 5470-D3
CALLE FLORA
49000 LQNT 92253 849-D5
CALLE FLORES
17000 RivC 92504 745-J5
CALLE FLORISTAS
48200 LQNT 92253 849-G4
CALLE FORTUNA
300 HEMT 92545 810-G6
78100 LQNT 92253 849-F7
CALLE FUEGO
25900 MORV 92551 747-J3
40000 TEM 92591 958-J4
CALLE FUENTE
40300 TEM 92591 959-C2
CALLE FUNDADOR
9400 DHSP 92240 696-J1
9400 RivC 92240 696-J1
CALLE GALACIA
40400 MURR 92562 928-A3
CALLE GALARZA
31900 TEM 92592 979-E1
CALLE GANADO
27500 RivC 92585 838-D5
CALLE GARDENIA
- PMSP 92262 786-H2
51000 COAC 92236 5471-E6
CALLE GAVIOTA
28100 RivC 92586 838-D6
29300 MURR 92563 928-H6
CALLE GAYUBE
39300 RivC 92544 931-E6
40400 RivC 92544 961-E1
CALLE GERANIO
86000 COAC 92236 5471-D6
CALLE GIRASOL
31400 TEM 92591 929-C7
31400 TEM 92591 959-D1
CALLE GRANDE
34900 RivC 92530 896-B6
CALLE GRANT
79600 RivC 92201 819-J5
CALLE GREGORIO
26500 RivC 92585 838-A3
CALLE GUATAMALA
51200 LQNT 92253 849-G7
CALLE GUAYMAS
50700 LQNT 92253 849-H6
CALLE HABERIO
27400 RivC 92585 838-D6
CALLE HALCON
30100 TEM 92592 959-A7
CALLE HELENE
30600 RivC 92276 788-E1
CALLE HERMOSA
4800 RivC 92509 685-B4
38900 MURR 92563 928-H6
CALLE HIDALGO
77400 LQNT 92253 849-E7
CALLE HILARIO
44100 TEM 92592 979-G3
CALLE HORIZONTE
38600 RivC 92592 931-B5
CALLE HUENEME
51200 LQNT 92253 849-G7
CALLE HUERTA
78400 LQNT 92253 849-G5
CALLE HUERTO
- RivC 92562 956-E4
CALLE IDAHO DR
38800 RMIR 92270 817-H2
CALLE ILOILO
51200 LQNT 92253 849-G7
CALLE JABILI
- TEM 92592 959-E4
CALLE JACUMBA
51300 LQNT 92253 849-G7
CALLE JAMIE
- RivC 92562 956-G4
CALLE JARDIN
46300 RivC 92590 977-J6
46800 RivC 92590 978-A4
CALLE JAZMIN
100 PMSP 92262 786-H2
CALLE JEMINEZ
42900 TEM 92592 959-E7
CALLE JEREZ
40000 RivC 92592 961-B1
CALLE JESSICA
30100 RivC 92276 758-D7
30100 RivC 92276 788-D1
CALLE JOJOBA
38200 RivC 92592 930-F4
CALLE JUANITO
19100 RivC 92562 956-F4
CALLE KALIMA
51400 LQNT 92253 849-G7

CALLE KATERINE
40500 TEM 92591 959-D2
CALLE KENORA
- RivC 92562 956-G4
CALLE LA COCA
35000 RivC 92592 960-B3
CALLE LA CUESTA
2700 RIV 92503 745-A1
CALLE LADERA
19600 RivC 92562 926-G3
27500 RivC 92585 838-D5
CALLE LA ESCONDIDA
31900 RivC 92592 960-F4
CALLE LAGARTIJA
42200 RivC 92592 960-C5
CALLE LAMPARA
40500 MURR 92562 928-A3
CALLE LANGARICA
33200 TEM 92592 979-H2
CALLE LANTANA
- PDST 92260 818-H7
CALLE LA PAZ
45400 RivC 92590 978-D4
53000 COAC 92236 5531-C1
CALLE LA REINA
- RMIR 92270 818-D4
CALLE LA SALIDA
38800 RivC 92562 926-H5
CALLE LAS BRISAS
20000 RivC 92570 775-G4
CALLE LAS BRISAS N
77500 PDST 92211 819-E6
CALLE LAS BRISAS S
77500 PDST 92211 819-F7
CALLE LAS BRISAS W
43500 PDST 92211 819-E6
CALLE LAS LOMAS
37100 RivC 92592 960-F4
CALLE LAS MARIPOSA
- TEM 92592 959-F6
CALLE LAS PALMAS
34300 CTHC 92234 787-D5
CALLE LAS RAMBLAS
- LQNT 92253 849-G6
CALLE LAS TIENDAS
68000 DHSP 92240 697-C5
CALLE LEANDRO
200 CTHC 92234 787-F7
CALLE LEON
68200 CTHC 92234 787-D5
84500 COAC 92236 5471-A5
CALLE LICHA
- RivC 92562 956-D7
E CALLE LILETA
1800 PMSP 92262 786-G2
CALLE LIMON
85600 COAC 92236 5471-D7
CALLE LINDA
- MORV 92555 748-A2
34700 RivC 92592 980-B1
53100 COAC 92236 5531-C1
CALLE LISTA
- RMIR 92270 787-H7
CALLE LOBITO
19900 RivC 92562 926-H2
CALLE LOMA
200 PER 92570 807-G2
CALLE LOMA ROJA
2700 RIV 92503 744-J1
CALLE LOMA VERDE
2700 RIV 92503 744-J1
CALLE LOMEDA
1400 SDCo 92028 997-H7
CALLE LONDE
42800 TEM 92592 959-E6
CALLE LOPEZ
33200 TEM 92592 979-H2
CALLE LORETO
2700 PMSP 92264 787-D6
N CALLE LORO
900 PMSP 92262 756-G7
CALLE LOS HERMANOS
53100 COAC 92236 5531-B1
CALLE LOS HIBISCOS
- RMIR 92270 818-D3
CALLE LOS MOCHIS
33100 RivC 92592 979-F4
CALLE LOS PADRES
31600 TEM 92592 979-D3
CALLE LOS PERICOS
- RivC 92562 956-E4
CALLE LUCIA
29400 MURR 92563 928-J4
CALLE LUICIA
29800 MURR 92563 928-J4
29800 MURR 92563 929-A4
CALLE LUSTROSOS
28200 RivC 92585 838-D6
CALLE LYA
84800 COAC 92236 5531-B1
CALLE MADERO
40400 TEM 92591 958-J2
40600 TEM 92591 959-A2
CALLE MADRID
77100 LQNT 92253 879-F3
CALLE MADRIGAL
400 CTHC 92234 817-G1
CALLE MAGDALENA
24500 MURR 92562 928-D2
CALLE MANCHA
68600 CTHC 92234 787-E6
CALLE MANZAMITLA
2900 PMSP 92264 787-D6
CALLE MANZANA
39300 RivC 92592 931-D6

CALLE MANZANITA
- RMIR 92270 818-D4
CALLE MARACA
42400 RivC 92592 960-D6
CALLE MARAVILLA
- RivC 92562 956-G2
N CALLE MARCUS
500 PMSP 92262 786-F1
600 PMSP 92262 756-F7
S CALLE MARCUS
1000 PMSP 92264 786-F4
CALLE MARGUERITA
40100 RivC 92544 931-C7
40100 RivC 92544 961-C1
CALLE MARIA
50100 LQNT 92253 849-E6
CALLE MARIPOSA
20200 RivC 92590 977-A1
CALLE MARQUIS
32000 TEM 92592 959-E6
CALLE MARSALA
28600 RivC 92584 868-F3
CALLE MARTOS
35500 CTHC 92234 787-E6
CALLE MATARO
43200 TEM 92592 959-F7
CALLE MATEO
44400 RivC 92590 977-G2
CALLE MAZATLAN
76900 LQNT 92253 849-E6
CALLE MEDUSA
40100 TEM 92591 959-D2
CALLE MENDOZA
50000 COAC 92236 5471-E6
CALLE MERIDA
- RMIR 92270 787-H7
CALLE MIRA COPA
44600 TEM 92592 979-G3
CALLE MONACO
11500 MORV 92557 716-J1
CALLE MONADA
3700 RivC 92503 744-F5
CALLE MONFORTE
68800 CTHC 92234 787-E6
CALLE MONSERATE
- CTHC 92234 787-F6
CALLE MONTECILLO
42800 RivC 92590 958-C5
CALLE MONTEREY
77100 LQNT 92253 879-F2
CALLE MONTIGO
35600 CTHC 92234 787-E6
CALLE MONTORO
68900 CTHC 92234 787-E6
CALLE MORA
34000 CTHC 92234 787-E5
CALLE MORELOS
3100 PMSP 92264 787-D6
CALLE MORITA
43100 TEM 92592 959-G7
43100 TEM 92592 979-G1
CALLE MULA
68800 CTHC 92234 787-E6
CALLE NACIDO
43300 TEM 92592 958-J7
43300 TEM 92592 978-J1
CALLE NATALIA
- RivC 92562 956-E4
CALLE NAVARRO
23300 RivC 92570 837-D1
CALLE NAVARROS
- RMIR 92270 787-H7
- RMIR 92270 817-H1
CALLE NINAS
21300 RivC 92562 927-A4
CALLE NINOS
53300 COAC 92236 5531-C2
CALLE NOGALES
300 HEMT 92545 810-G6
23100 MORV 92557 717-C2
77200 LQNT 92253 879-F1
CALLE NOPAL
35000 RivC 92592 960-C4
CALLE NORTE
78000 LQNT 92253 849-G6
CALLE NOVELDA
31700 TEM 92592 959-D7
31800 TEM 92592 979-E1
CALLE NUBLOSA
18000 RivC 92562 956-E4
CALLE NUEVO
24800 RivC 92590 977-J1
CALLE OAXACA
50000 LQNT 92253 849-E6
CALLE OBISPO
51000 LQNT 92253 849-G7
CALLE OBREGON
24800 MURR 92563 928-E3
CALLE OESTE
36500 CTHC 92234 787-G7
CALLE ORENSE
78400 LQNT 92253 849-G6
CALLE ORILLA
41000 RivC 92544 931-E4
CALLE ORINDA
39300 RivC 92562 956-D7
CALLE ORIZABA
77600 LQNT 92253 849-E6
CALLE ORO
40600 PDST 92260 818-F4
CALLE ORTEGA
42500 MURR 92562 957-J1
42500 MURR 92562 958-A1
CALLE PABLO NERUDA
65500 RivC 92254 5592-F6

CALLE PALMAS
- MURR 92562 928-B3
29700 TEM 92591 958-J5
CALLE PALMETO
- LQNT 92253 819-J7
CALLE PALO
27300 RivC 92586 838-D6
CALLE PALO FIERRO
500 PMSP 92264 786-E3
CALLE PALOMA
50600 LQNT 92253 849-G6
CALLE PANTANO
29700 TEM 92591 958-J4
CALLE PAPAGAYO
2100 PMSP 92262 756-G7
CALLE PARAMO
- RivC 92562 956-C4
CALLE PASITO
1800 HEMT 92545 810-H6
CALLE PATRON
- TEM 92590 958-D5
S CALLE PAUL
800 PMSP 92264 787-A3
CALLE PAVON
- MURR 92563 898-F7
- MURR 92563 928-F1
CALLE PEDREGOSA
200 PER 92570 807-G2
CALLE PENA HUERTA
19800 RivC 92590 976-J1
CALLE PERA
51700 COAC 92236 5471-D7
CALLE PERLA
- MURR 92562 928-C3
CALLE PESCAR
40800 RivC 92562 956-C5
CALLE PETUNIA
600 PMSP 92262 786-H2
CALLE PICO
45600 RivC 92590 978-C5
CALLE PIEDRAS
34400 RivC 92544 901-G3
CALLE PIMIENTA
38500 RivC 92562 926-H6
CALLE PINA COLADA
30500 TEM 92591 959-B4
40800 TEM 92591 958-J3
CALLE PINATA
16700 MORV 92551 747-J4
CALLE PINO
41600 RivC 92562 956-G5
CALLE PINTORESCA
45100 RivC 92590 978-E4
CALLE PIZANO
86000 COAC 92236 5471-D6
CALLE PLACIDO
- LQNT 92253 819-H7
- LQNT 92253 849-H1
CALLE POCO
36300 RivC 92592 930-E5
CALLE POMPEII
30000 RivC 92584 868-G2
CALLE PORTILLO
39000 RivC 92544 931-D5
39000 RivC 92592 931-D6
CALLE POTRERO
54700 LQNT 92253 879-E4
CALLE POTRO
29100 MURR 92563 928-H5
CALLE PRESA
20200 RivC 92562 926-H4
CALLE PRESIDENTE
- RivC 92562 956-D6
CALLE PRIMA
21500 MORV 92557 716-J1
CALLE PRIMA VERA
29700 TEM 92591 958-J4
CALLE PROSPERO
- LQNT 92253 819-J7
CALLE PUERTO BONITA RD
36200 RivC 92592 960-D2
CALLE PUESTA DEL SOL
200 PER 92570 807-G2
CALLE QUEBRADA
- RivC 92562 956-D7
CALLE QUEDO
38000 MURR 92563 928-G5
N CALLE QUETZAL
800 PMSP 92262 756-G7
CALLE QUIETA
84000 INDO 92203 5410-J5
CALLE QUITO
50500 LQNT 92253 849-G6
CALLE RABANO
27400 RivC 92585 838-D6
CALLE RAMBLA ORIENTA
42700 MURR 92562 927-G6
CALLE RANCHITO
41000 RivC 92592 960-B2
CALLE RAPHAEL
- CTHC 92234 787-G6
CALLE REDONDELA
31700 TEM 92592 979-D1
CALLE REGINA
- RMIR 92270 787-H7
CALLE REMO
78400 LQNT 92253 849-G5
CALLE RENFRO
15000 MORV 92551 747-H1
CALLE RESACA
32000 TEM 92592 959-E4

CALLE REVA
43000 TEM 92592 958-J7
CALLE REYES
40500 RivC 92562 956-F2
CALLE RINANNA
- CTHC 92234 787-F7
CALLE RIO GRANDE
39500 RivC 92592 931-B7
CALLE RIO VISTA
- TEM 92592 959-C6
CALLE RIVAS
- TEM 92592 979-E1
CALLE RIVERO
- RMIR 92270 787-H7
CALLE ROBERTO
84800 COAC 92236 5531-B1
CALLE ROBLE
18900 RivC 92562 976-F1
42800 RivC 92562 956-F6
CALLE ROCA
500 PMSP 92264 786-E3
45700 RivC 92590 978-C5
CALLE ROCINANTE
43300 RivC 92592 960-A7
CALLE ROCIO
20200 RivC 92590 976-J2
CALLE ROCOSA
41400 RivC 92592 960-C4
CALLE ROJO
84500 COAC 92236 5471-B7
N CALLE ROLPH
400 PMSP 92262 786-F1
600 PMSP 92262 756-F7
S CALLE ROLPH
1100 PMSP 92264 786-F4
CALLE RONDO
50700 LQNT 92253 849-H7
CALLE ROSA
15400 MORV 92555 748-A1
85100 COAC 92236 5531-C1
CALLE ROSAL
21200 RivC 92562 927-A5
CALLE ROSARITA
50000 LQNT 92253 849-E6
CALLE ROSE
24100 RivC 92570 807-D5
CALLE ROSITA
40400 RivC 92562 956-H1
CALLE ROXANNE
40400 SDCo 92028 976-E7
CALLE SACATE
- RivC 92592 930-J6
CALLE SALISIPUEDES
200 PER 92570 807-G2
CALLE SAMA
34700 CTHC 92234 787-E5
CALLE SAN ANTONIO
3800 PMSP 92264 786-J3
3900 PMSP 92264 787-A3
CALLE SAN CARLOS
68900 CTHC 92234 787-F6
CALLE SAN CLEMENTE
39400 MURR 92562 928-D2
CALLE SANDOR
- TEM 92592 979-E1
CALLE SAN JUAN DE LOS LAGOS
22700 MORV 92553 717-C6
CALLE SAN MARTINE
29700 RivC 92584 868-G2
CALLE SAN RAPHAEL
3800 PMSP 92264 786-J3
3900 PMSP 92264 787-A3
CALLE SAN SABASTIAN
- SJCT 92583 780-J6
CALLE SANTA ANA
42100 TEM 92592 959-D5
CALLE SANTA BARBARA
- LQNT 92253 819-J7
- LQNT 92253 849-J1
CALLE SANTA CRUZ
500 PMSP 92264 787-A3
CALLE SANTA FE
68800 CTHC 92234 787-F6
CALLE SANTA MONICA
24400 MURR 92562 928-C3
CALLE SANTA ROSA
500 PMSP 92264 786-E3
N CALLE SANTA ROSA
400 PMSP 92262 786-E1
CALLE SANTIAGO
35500 CTHC 92234 787-E6
CALLE SANTONA
35200 CTHC 92234 787-E6
CALLE SAN VICENTE
24400 MURR 92562 928-D2
CALLE SARAGOZA
31700 TEM 92591 959-D2
CALLE SAUSALITO
2800 RIV 92503 715-A7
CALLE SAUZA
42900 RivC 92590 958-B6
CALLE SEAMA
78400 LQNT 92253 849-G5
CALLE SEGOVIA
38800 RivC 92544 931-C4
38900 RivC 92592 931-C4
CALLE SERANAS
48100 LQNT 92253 849-G4
CALLE SERENA
16300 MORV 92551 747-J3
46300 LQNT 92253 5470-A2
CALLE SERENO
- RivC 92592 959-J6
- RivC 92592 960-A6

CALLE SESTAO
34700 CTHC 92234 787-E5
CALLE SIERRA
7000 RivC 92882 742-A7
CALLE SINALOA
77100 LQNT 92253 879-E1
CALLESITO ALTAR
44800 RivC 92592 979-F4
CALLESITO BURGOS
45200 RivC 92592 979-F4
CALLESITO FADRIQUE
32100 RivC 92592 979-F5
CALLESITO ORDENES
45400 RivC 92592 979-E4
CALLESITO VALLARTA
45900 RivC 92592 979-F5
CALLE SOLANA
35300 CTHC 92234 787-F6
CALLE SOLANO
- RMIR 92270 787-H7
CALLE SOMBRA
12000 MORV 92557 717-C2
CALLE SONOMA
- CTHC 92234 787-G6
CALLE SONORA
30300 TEM 92592 959-B7
77200 LQNT 92253 879-F1
CALLE SONRISA
- LQNT 92253 849-J1
CALLE SONSECA
35300 CTHC 92234 787-E6
CALLE SOR JUANA
65500 RivC 92254 5592-F6
CALLE TAFALLA
68600 CTHC 92234 787-E5
CALLE TAJO
41400 TEM 92592 959-D5
CALLE TAMAZUCA
51200 LQNT 92253 849-G7
CALLE TAMPICO
- CTHC 92234 757-G7
9400 RIV 92503 715-A7
77800 LQNT 92253 849-G7
CALLE TANQUE VERDE
84200 INDO 92203 5410-J5
CALLE TARGA
84200 INDO 92203 5410-J6
CALLE TASSJARA
24300 MURR 92562 928-D2
CALLE TECATE
77100 LQNT 92253 879-E4
CALLE TECHA
51900 COAC 92236 5471-B7
52300 COAC 92236 5531-B1
CALLE TECUALA
7400 PMSP 92264 787-D6
CALLE TEMECULA
77100 LQNT 92253 879-E3
CALLE TEQUILA
36100 RivC 92592 960-D1
CALLE TERESA
19100 RivC 92562 956-F5
CALLE TIARA
40400 TEM 92591 959-C2
CALLE TIARA S
31900 RivC 92592 979-E4
CALLE TIERRA SANTA
2800 RIV 92503 715-A7
2800 RIV 92503 745-A1
CALLE TITANIA
40100 RivC 92592 931-B7
CALLE TOBARA
34500 CTHC 92234 787-E5
CALLE TOGA
- MURR 92562 928-B3
CALLE TOLEDO
41300 RivC 92592 960-C2
68400 CTHC 92234 787-E5
CALLE TOLOSA
68600 CTHC 92234 787-E5
CALLE TOMAS
700 PMSP 92264 787-A3
29600 RivC 92586 868-D2
36100 CTHC 92234 787-G7
CALLE TORCIDA
40200 TEM 92591 959-B2
CALLE TORRES ORDUNO
51600 COAC 92236 5471-B7
CALLE TORTOSA
68500 CTHC 92234 787-E5
CALLE TOSCA
- RivC 92276 788-J4
- RivC 92276 789-A4
CALLE TRANQUILIDAD
75700 INDW 92210 849-B2
CALLE TRUJILLO
34500 CTHC 92234 787-E5
CALLE TUBERIA
45400 RivC 92590 977-D4
CALLE TUXPAN
39900 RivC 92562 926-E7
CALLE UVA
25800 RivC 92590 977-J7
25800 RivC 92590 978-A7
CALLE VALLARTA
28000 RivC 92585 838-D5
CALLE VECINA
40000 RivC 92592 931-D5
40300 RivC 92544 931-D5
CALLE VEGA
- RMIR 92270 787-H7
- RMIR 92270 817-H1
CALLE VENTURA
- TEM 92592 959-C7

CALLE VERDE
100 PMSP 92264 787-D5
84600 COAC 92236 5531-B1
CALLE VERONICA
43000 TEM 92592 959-D7
CALLE VIEJO
25000 MURR 92563 928-E4
CALLE VIENTO
- RivC 92562 956-G6
CALLE VIENTOS
33500 RivC 92596 899-B2
CALLE VILLAPANDO
83600 RivC 92274 5590-J2
CALLE VIMIANZO
31700 TEM 92592 979-D1
CALLE VIOLETA
29500 TEM 92592 959-A6
86000 COAC 92236 5471-D6
CALLE VISTA
33700 RivC 92592 959-J5
CALLE VISTA DR
14000 RivC 92508 716-F6
CALLE VISTA LEJOS
27900 RivC 92590 978-E2
CALLE VISTA VERDE
- LQNT 92253 819-H7
CALLE YBARRA
- MORV 92555 718-D2
CALLE YORBA VISTA
39900 MURR 92562 928-D4
CALLE YUCATAN
77400 LQNT 92253 849-E7
CALLE ZAFIRO
7600 RivC 92509 684-H2
CALLE ZAMORA
84700 COAC 92236 5531-B1
CALLE ZORITA
35300 CTHC 92234 787-E6
CALLE ZORRO
- PMSP 92264 787-B7
CALLIANDRA ST
72700 PDST 92260 848-E4
CALLIE LN
6400 RivC 92509 684-G6
CALLISTER RD
41000 RivC 92536 961-J2
CALLITA ST
25500 MORV 92551 747-H3
CALLITA BARBARA
73000 RivC 92276 788-E1
CALLITA BELL
73000 RivC 92276 788-E1
CALLITA BONNIE
73000 RivC 92276 788-E1
CALLOWAY LN
- RivC 92203 789-G6
CALLOWAY ST
22300 RivC 92570 807-B1
CALMHILL DR
4200 RIV 92503 714-G5
CALONA PL
2300 SJCT 92583 811-E5
CALUMET CT
15800 RivC 92506 745-H3
CALVADO CT
30800 TEM 92592 979-C4
CALVARY CIR
1600 RDL 92373 647-H1
CALVERT AV
26000 RivC 92545 839-H1
CALVIN CT
6600 RIV 92506 715-D1
CALVIN ST
11600 YCPA 92399 650-B2
CALYPSO CIR
- INDO 92201 5470-H3
CALYPSO RD
77800 PDST 92211 819-E3
CALYX AV
80600 INDO 92201 5470-B3
CAMARILLO
100 PMSP 92264 786-J6
100 PMSP 92264 787-A6
CAMARO LN
44000 RivC 92536 982-B6
CAMARON RD
43800 RivC 92590 977-D1
46600 SDCo 92028 977-D6
CAMAS DR
26100 RivC 92544 841-D1
CAMBERN AV
18600 LKEL 92532 866-D1
18600 RivC 92532 866-E1
CAMBRIA CIR
- MORV 92557 687-C4
CAMBRIA CT
- RIV 92501 686-A1
- SJCT 92583 780-J6
CAMBRIA DR
12300 YCPA 92399 649-E4
CAMBRIA LN
24000 MURR 92562 928-A3
26200 LMLN 92354 647-F2
CAMBRIDGE AV
2700 HEMT 92545 840-F2
41500 RivC 92201 819-J4
CAMBRIDGE CT
900 SJCT 92583 781-A7
22500 MORV 92557 717-A2
71600 RMIR 92270 788-B6
CAMBRIDGE CT N
3200 PMSP 92264 786-H4
CAMBRIDGE CT S
3200 PMSP 92264 786-H4

CAMBRIDGE DR
- RivC 92584 868-G1
300 SJCT 92583 781-A6
CAMBRIDGE RD
11800 LMLN 92354 647-F3
CAMBRIDGE SQ
1100 COR 92882 743-A6
CAMBRIDGE ST
11200 RIV 92503 744-E3
CAMDEN CIR
- MURR 92563 928-J4
CAMDEN CT
300 COR 92879 744-B2
900 HEMT 92545 840-G2
CAMDEN LN
3200 COR 92882 773-B3
CAMDEN RD
200 SJCT 92582 810-F2
CAMDEN ST
1900 RIV 92506 716-A2
CAMDEN WY
27500 RivC 92586 838-B5
CAMEL
- PMSP 92264 786-C6
CAMELBACK CIR
- COR 92883 773-J6
CAMELBACK DR
79400 RivC 92201 819-J5
79600 RivC 92201 5410-A5
CAMELIA DR
700 PER 92571 777-J6
8100 RIV 92504 715-A3
8500 RIV 92504 714-J3
CAMELIA WY
400 SJCT 92583 811-A1
CAMELLIA CT
2800 COR 92882 742-F5
70500 RMIR 92270 787-J7
CAMELLIA DR
900 BEAU 92223 690-J7
13300 YCPA 92399 650-B6
40700 RivC 92544 841-C2
CAMELLIA LN
- MURR 92562 927-G3
CAMELLIA ST
600 PMSP 92262 756-E4
CAMELLO
75200 PDST 92211 818-J4
CAMELOT
- RMIR 92270 817-J2
CAMELOT AV
26100 LMLN 92354 647-E2
CAMELOT DR
1500 COR 92882 742-J6
1500 COR 92882 743-A6
33100 YCPA 92399 649-E4
CAMELOT RD
7900 RIV 92503 714-F5
CAMELOT WY
81900 INDO 92201 5410-E7
CAMEO AV
800 HEMT 92543 840-J3
CAMEO CT
10500 RIV 92505 714-D5
CAMEO DR
600 PMSP 92264 786-D4
13900 SBdC 92337 644-B1
CAMEO WY
600 PMSP 92264 786-F6
CAMEO DUNES PL
78300 LQNT 92253 849-G2
CAMEO PALM DR
46300 LQNT 92253 849-G3
CAMERO DR
47400 RivC 92536 982-G7
CAMERON DR
11100 RIV 92505 714-D7
34200 RivC 92544 901-C4
CAMERON LN
34900 RivC 92595 897-C6
CAMERON ST
900 CLTN 92324 646-H1
35900 CTHC 92234 787-G6
CAMERON WY
7800 RivC 92509 684-G6
CAMERON GLEN RD
3700 PER 92571 777-J2
CAMERYN CT
- MURR 92562 927-G3
CAMIE LN
27500 RivC 92585 808-D7
CAMILLA CIR
32300 RivC 92276 788-F2
CAMILLE DR
21900 RivC 92567 778-H7
CAMINATA DR
- TEM 92592 979-F2
CAMINITO AVILA
44900 RivC 92592 979-F4
CAMINITO DEL LAGO
84000 INDO 92203 5410-J6
CAMINITO DEL SOL NORTE
26000 RivC 92586 868-A1
CAMINITO DEL SOL OESTE
29100 RivC 92586 868-A1
CAMINITO DEL SOL SUR
26000 RivC 92586 868-A1
CAMINITO OLITE
45500 RivC 92592 979-F4
CAMINITO OSUNA
32100 RivC 92592 979-F4

STREET
Block City ZIP Pg-Grid

CAMINITO ROSADO
32500 RivC 92592 979-G5
CAMINO CIR
800 COR 92882 743-C7
CAMINO ALAGON
- TEM 92592 959-E6
CAMINO ALAMOSA
44700 TEM 92592 979-H3
CAMINO ALBA
28800 MURR 92563 928-H4
CAMINO ALCALA
28900 RivC 92584 868-G2
CAMINO ALTURAS
200 PMSP 92264 786-D5
CAMINO AMAPOLA
1300 PMSP 92264 786-F3
CAMINO AMARILLO
79200 LQNT 92253 819-H7
CAMINO ANGUILLA
3700 RivC 92503 744-F5
CAMINO ARRIBA
21400 RivC 92562 927-A7
CAMINO ARROYO N
- PDST 92260 818-F5
CAMINO ARROYO S
- PDST 92260 818-G5
CAMINO ARROYO PL
- PDST 92260 818-F5
CAMINO ARROYO SECO
- RivC 92592 930-G7
CAMINO ASPIRANTE
23600 MURR 92562 928-A2
CAMINO AVENTURA
66000 RivC 92240 726-H1
66500 DHSP 92240 726-J1
66700 RivC 92240 727-A1
CAMINO AZUL
44000 LQNT 92253 819-H7
CAMINO BALADA
20400 RivC 92562 926-J7
CAMINO BARRANCA
2100 PMSP 92264 786-D6
CAMINO BAYA
45100 RivC 92590 977-J3
CAMINO BELLA
27500 RivC 92585 838-D5
CAMINO BELLAGIO
25500 MORV 92551 747-H4
CAMINO BON AIRE
41700 RivC 92562 956-H4
CAMINO BONITA
- CTHC 92234 787-G6
CAMINO BROZAS
32300 RivC 92592 979-F4
CAMINO BUENA VISTA
200 PMSP 92264 786-D6
CAMINO CABALLERO
- RivC 92504 745-E4
CAMINO CALIARI
32000 TEM 92592 979-E1
CAMINO CAMPANERO
66500 DHSP 92240 696-J7
66500 DHSP 92240 697-A7
66500 RivC 92240 697-A7
CAMINO CAMPESINO
65500 DHSP 92240 696-J7
65500 DHSP 92240 697-A7
66800 RivC 92240 697-A7
CAMINO CAMPOS VERDES
- TEM 92591 958-J3
CAMINO CAPISTRANO
9400 DHSP 92240 696-G1
CAMINO CARMARGO
32000 RivC 92592 979-F4
CAMINO CARMELITA
100 PMSP 92264 786-D6
CAMINO CARUNA
- TEM 92592 959-E7
CAMINO CASANA
41800 TEM 92592 959-F5
CAMINO CASILLAS
43100 TEM 92592 959-E7
CAMINO CASTILLO
25500 MORV 92551 747-H4
CAMINO CENTRO
1100 PMSP 92262 756-D6
CAMINO CIELO
31300 TEM 92591 929-D7
75700 INDW 92210 849-B1
CAMINO CINIFE
38200 MURR 92563 928-H5
CAMINO CLARABOYA
27500 RivC 92585 838-D4
N CAMINO CONDOR
800 PMSP 92262 756-G7
CAMINO CORTO
400 SJCT 92582 810-J1
41100 TEM 92591 959-C3
51800 COAC 92236 5471-D7
CAMINO CRISTAL
29600 RivC 92584 868-G2
CAMINO DE BUENA VIDA
35700 RivC 92592 960-D2
CAMINO DE CAPISTRANO
- RivC 92504 745-E4
CAMINO DE DORADO
45400 INDW 92210 849-A1
CAMINO DE ESTRILLA
16000 RivC 92504 745-E4
CAMINO DE GLORIA
20400 RIV 92508 716-G6

CAMINO DE JUGADOR
21100 RivC 92562 927-A4
CAMINO DE LAS BRISAS
- CTHC 92234 787-G6
43500 RivC 92562 956-G7
43500 RivC 92562 976-F1
CAMINO DE LAS COLINAS
43000 INDO 92203 5410-J5
CAMINO DE LA TORRE
41700 TEM 92592 959-F5
CAMINO DEL AURORA
84000 INDO 92203 5410-J5
CAMINO DE LA VISTA DR
11700 MORV 92557 717-G1
CAMINO DEL CERRO
40200 RMIR 92270 817-H3
CAMINO DEL CORTO
1100 PMSP 92262 756-D7
CAMINO DEL ESTE
31100 TEM 92591 959-C3
CAMINO DEL KHAIL
24700 RivC 92532 806-C6
CAMINO DEL MAR
36200 CTHC 92234 787-G7
CAMINO DEL MIRASOL
1100 PMSP 92262 756-D6
CAMINO DEL NINOS
2600 COR 92882 742-F7
CAMINO DEL NORTE
500 LKEL 92532 866-F4
500 RivC 92532 866-F4
600 PMSP 92262 756-C6
CAMINO DEL NORTE AV
8500 RivC 92223 691-B1
CAMINO DE LORENZO
- RivC 92504 745-F4
CAMINO DELORES
29600 RivC 92586 868-C2
CAMINO DEL ORO
14000 RivC 92508 716-G6
79100 LQNT 92253 819-H7
CAMINO DE LOS CABALLOS
29000 MURR 92584 898-J2
29000 RivC 92584 898-J2
CAMINO DEL PIEDRA
18100 RivC 92532 806-C6
CAMINO DEL PLATA CT
2500 COR 92882 742-G7
CAMINO DEL RANCHO
1100 HEMT 92543 840-J2
CAMINO DEL REY
45400 INDW 92210 849-B1
CAMINO DEL SERENAH
24700 RivC 92532 806-C6
CAMINO DEL SOL
200 HEMT 92543 840-J2
1000 PER 92571 807-H1
9300 DHSP 92240 696-G1
20000 RivC 92508 716-G6
20300 RIV 92508 716-G6
40100 RMIR 92270 817-H4
CAMINO DEL SOL DR
30800 TEM 92592 958-J7
30800 TEM 92592 959-A7
CAMINO DEL TAZZRAF
18000 RivC 92532 806-C6
CAMINO DEL VALLE
25000 RivC 92590 977-J2
CAMINO DEL VINO
39100 RivC 92592 930-D6
40100 RivC 92592 960-D1
CAMINO DE MAGNOLIA
39300 RivC 92592 930-C6
CAMINO DE MINAS
800 SJCT 92583 811-D4
CAMINO DE ORO
700 SJCT 92583 811-D4
CAMINO DE ORO WY
24900 MORV 92557 717-G1
CAMINO DE OSCAR
- RivC 92592 959-F4
CAMINO DE PACO
75400 INDW 92210 819-B7
75700 INDW 92210 849-B1
CAMINO DE PAZ
19500 RivC 92562 956-G4
CAMINO DE PETERSON
42400 RivC 92590 957-J5
42400 RivC 92590 958-A5
CAMINO DE PLATA
700 SJCT 92583 811-D3
75500 INDW 92210 849-A1
CAMINO DESCANSO
200 PMSP 92264 786-D6
CAMINO DE WALDO
- RivC 92504 745-E4
CAMINO DONAIRE
27700 RivC 92585 838-D4
CAMINO EL PARDO
1900 PER 92571 777-J6
CAMINO EL PASO
1800 PER 92571 777-J7
CAMINO ENCANTO
100 PMSP 92264 786-E6
CAMINO ESTRIBO
28100 RivC 92590 978-H4
28600 TEM 92590 978-J3
CAMINO FLORES
26000 MORV 92555 747-J1
26200 MORV 92555 748-A1

CAMINO FRESCA
40300 RivC 92592 961-A1
CAMINO GALLEGOS
43500 TEM 92592 979-E1
CAMINO GATILLO
44500 RivC 92590 978-H2
CAMINO GAZAPO
45600 RivC 92590 978-G5
CAMINO GONZALES
44500 TEM 92592 979-H2
CAMINO GRANDE
400 SJCT 92582 810-J1
15400 MORV 92551 747-J1
CAMINO GRANDE HERMOSA
43700 INDO 92203 5410-J6
CAMINO GUARDA
32100 RivC 92592 979-F3
CAMINO HERENCIA
41300 TEM 92592 959-E6
CAMINO HERMOSA
39000 MURR 92563 928-E3
CAMINO HERNANDEZ
33400 TEM 92592 979-H3
CAMINO IDILIO
66000 RivC 92240 726-J1
66700 RivC 92240 727-A1
CAMINO JALAN
68300 CTHC 92234 787-D5
CAMINO JUANITO
16400 MORV 92551 747-H3
CAMINO JUAREZ
25900 RivC 92585 838-A2
CAMINO LA CRESTA
44000 LQNT 92253 819-H7
CAMINO LARGO
26300 MORV 92555 748-A1
CAMINO LAS POSITAS
39200 MURR 92562 928-D2
CAMINO LAVANDA
44000 LQNT 92253 819-H7
CAMINO LORADO
41500 RivC 92592 960-G3
N CAMINO LOS BANOS ST
200 SJCT 92583 781-D7
200 SJCT 92583 811-D1
S CAMINO LOS BANOS ST
100 SJCT 92583 811-D2
CAMINO LOS GALLOS
500 PER 92571 777-J7
CAMINO LOS PRADOS
35800 RivC 92592 960-D5
CAMINO MANCHO
25000 MURR 92563 928-E4
CAMINO MARACA
33000 TEM 92592 979-H3
CAMINO MAREA
31800 TEM 92592 959-E5
CAMINO MARLINA
25500 MORV 92551 747-H4
CAMINO MARTINEZ
17600 RivC 92570 776-B3
CAMINO MERANO
42300 TEM 92592 959-F5
CAMINO MERIDIANA
24500 MURR 92562 928-D2
CAMINO MIRABELLA
24500 MURR 92562 928-D2
CAMINO MIRA MONTE
43000 INDO 92203 5410-J6
CAMINO MIRANDA
1700 SJCT 92583 811-E4
CAMINO MIRASOL DR
16700 RivC 92241 727-F1
CAMINO MOLNAR
31900 TEM 92592 959-E6
CAMINO MONTE
1900 PMSP 92264 786-D6
E CAMINO MONTE VISTA
100 PMSP 92262 756-D6
CAMINO MONTURA
4300 RivC 92509 644-B7
CAMINO MONZON
45300 RivC 92592 979-F4
CAMINO MORENA
500 PER 92571 777-J7
CAMINO NIGUEL
39500 RivC 92592 931-A6
CAMINO NOROESTE
20100 RivC 92562 956-J2
CAMINO NORTE
41000 RivC 92592 960-C3
W CAMINO NORTE
200 PMSP 92262 756-D6
CAMINO NUNEZ
32000 TEM 92592 959-F5
CAMINO OTILIA
44800 TEM 92592 979-H3
CAMINO PACIFICO
- RMIR 92270 787-G5
CAMINO PALENCIA
44800 RivC 92592 979-F3
CAMINO PALOMA
84000 INDO 92203 5410-J6
CAMINO PAROCELA
100 PMSP 92264 786-D3
4600 PMSP 92264 787-B3
E CAMINO PAROCELA
200 PMSP 92264 786-E3
3800 PMSP 92264 787-A3
E CAMINO PELICANA
2300 PMSP 92262 756-G7

CAMINO PEPITA
29700 RivC 92584 868-G2
CAMINO PERLA
27400 RivC 92585 838-D6
CAMINO PIEDRA ROJO
32100 TEM 92592 979-H2
CAMINO POTRO
45400 RivC 92590 978-H4
CAMINO PRIMAVERA
- RivC - 878-B7
CAMINO PRIMROSE
1300 PMSP 92264 786-F3
CAMINO PRINCIPAL
84100 INDO 92203 5410-J6
CAMINO PRIVADO
- LQNT 92253 5470-A6
CAMINO QUINTANA
77200 LQNT 92253 849-E6
CAMINO RABAGO
- TEM 92592 979-E1
CAMINO RAINBOW
1900 SDCo 92028 998-J6
CAMINO REAL
- RMIR 92270 787-H3
- RMIR 92270 818-D4
3900 RivC 92509 644-H6
4300 RivC 92509 684-H1
15600 MORV 92555 748-C2
28800 MURR 92563 928-H6
43600 INDO 92203 5410-J6
N CAMINO REAL
500 PMSP 92262 786-E1
600 PMSP 92262 756-E7
S CAMINO REAL
500 PMSP 92264 786-E3
500 PMSP 92262 786-E3
2500 PMSP 92264 816-F1
CAMINO REAL CIR
600 HEMT 92543 810-H6
CAMINO ROGERS
24300 RivC 92590 977-H3
CAMINO ROJOS
3300 PMSP 92262 756-J6
CAMINO ROMO
42100 TEM 92592 959-E5
CAMINO ROSADA
79100 LQNT 92253 819-H7
CAMINO ROSALEEN
1300 SJCT 92583 811-E3
CAMINO ROSALES
31700 RivC 92592 979-E4
CAMINO RUBANO
32300 TEM 92592 979-H3
CAMINO RUBI
32400 RivC 92592 979-G5
CAMINO SAN BENITO DR
3400 RivC 92503 744-B4
CAMINO SAN DIMAS
32100 RivC 92592 979-F5
CAMINO SAN JOSE
32000 RivC 92592 979-E4
CAMINO SAN MIGUEL
3800 PMSP 92264 786-J3
3900 PMSP 92264 787-A3
CAMINO SAN SIMEON
3700 PMSP 92264 786-J3
3800 PMSP 92264 787-A3
CAMINO SANTIAGO
32300 RivC 92592 979-F4
CAMINO SECO
26700 RivC 92590 958-C6
CAMINO SEDA
5100 RivC 92509 684-G2
CAMINO SENECO
32100 TEM 92592 959-F5
CAMINO SIERRA RD
37700 RivC 92592 930-H4
38900 RivC 92592 931-A4
CAMINO SILVOSO
67200 RivC 92240 727-B1
CAMINO SOBRE VISTA
3700 RivC 92503 744-F5
W CAMINO SUR
200 PMSP 92262 756-D7
CAMINO TIEMPO
45100 RivC 92590 977-J3
CAMINO TOBAGO
3700 RivC 92503 744-F5
CAMINO VACUNA
27400 RivC 92585 838-D6
CAMINO VASCO
24300 MURR 92562 928-D2
CAMINO VERDE
- CTHC 92234 787-F7
31000 TEM 92591 959-C3
CAMINO VESTE
44800 RivC 92592 979-F3
CAMINO VIDA
2300 PMSP 92264 786-G6
CAMINO VIEJO
- RivC 92504 745-F4
CAMINO VISTA
- LQNT 92253 849-J1
CAMINO ZANGRI
69000 RivC 92240 697-G6
69000 RivC 92241 697-G6
CAMISA LN
- PDST 92260 818-F5
CAMMIE CIR
- RivC 92254 (5653-H5 See Page 5592)
CAMON DR
28300 RivC 92570 836-J7

CAMP CT
15300 MORV 92551 747-G1
CAMPANA CIR
- TEM 92591 958-H3
CAMPANA CT
69700 RMIR 92270 787-G6
CAMPANILLA WY
25500 MORV 92551 747-H2
CAMPANULA WY
32200 TEM 92592 979-E2
CAMPBELL AV
5600 RIV 92505 714-B4
8300 RIV 92503 714-F3
28700 MORV 92555 718-E6
CAMPBELL ST
100 LKEL 92530 866-H7
3400 RivC 92509 644-C6
4100 RivC 92509 684-C1
35800 CTHC 92234 787-D7
CAMPEON CIR
1300 PMSP 92262 756-G6
CAMPERO DR
5900 RivC 92509 684-G4
CAMPHOR CT
900 SJCT 92582 810-J2
CAMPHOR WY
1500 LKEL 92530 865-G3
CAMPHORTREE CT
9000 RivC 92883 804-C3
CAMPHORWOOD AV
26000 RivC 92544 811-D7
CAMPINI LN
42100 RivC 92544 931-G6
CAMPO ROJO
43700 TEM 92592 959-A7
CAMPOS RD
21000 RivC 92570 776-H6
CAMPOS ST
21000 RivC 92570 776-G6
CAMPO VERDE
30000 TEM 92592 959-A7
CAMPUS DR
2000 YCPA 92399 649-C2
2400 NRCO 92860 713-D6
4800 RIV 92505 714-B7
4800 RIV 92505 744-B1
83600 COAC 92274 5530-J4
E CAMPUS DR
3800 RIV 92507 686-D5
N CAMPUS DR
400 RIV 92507 686-D5
S CAMPUS DR
400 RIV 92507 686-D6
W CAMPUS DR
3800 RIV 92507 686-D5
CAMPUS LN
- CTHC 92234 787-E4
CAMPUS PKWY
2600 RIV 92507 716-J3
2800 RIV 92507 717-A3
22000 MORV 92553 717-A3
CAMPUS ST
10900 LMLN 92354 647-B1
CAMPUS WY
200 LKEL 92530 866-D4
1000 HEMT 92543 811-C6
1700 HEMT 92544 811-C6
CAMPUS VIEW DR
200 RIV 92507 686-D4
E CAMPUS VIEW DR
100 RIV 92507 686-F4
CAMRA WY
18100 RivC 92508 746-B2
CAMROSE DR
30400 CTHC 92234 787-G1
CANADA CIR
35700 CTHC 92234 787-F6
CANADA WY
9700 RIV 92503 744-J2
CANAL DR
12100 GTER 92313 646-F4
CANAL RD
- SBDO 92408 647-A1
CANAL ST
2800 RivC 92509 645-A7
2900 RivC 92509 685-D1
10300 RivC 92503 744-J4
11600 GTER 92313 646-E3
13000 BLY 92225 5491-G7
20800 RivC 92570 806-H2
CANALETO WY
22500 MORV 92557 687-B4
CANARY CIR
39500 TEM 92591 958-J2
CANARY CT
800 LKEL 92530 865-J4
11900 GTER 92313 646-F4
83500 INDO 92201 5470-H3
E CANARY CT
3200 ONT 91761 643-B5
CANARY DR
11600 FONT 92337 644-F3
CANARY LN
600 COR 92879 743-E7
CANBERRA WY
7500 RIV 92508 716-E6
CANDELARIA LN
29600 RivC 92567 808-G1
CANDELERIA CIR
49700 LQNT 92253 849-F5
CANDICE CT
15100 MORV 92551 747-H1
CANDIDA DR
42500 TEM 92592 959-B6

CANDLEBUSH CT
24500 MORV 92557 687-F6
CANDLELIGHT CIR
1900 COR 92880 713-A7
CANDLE LIGHT DR
6300 RivC 92509 684-H5
CANDLENUT CT
24700 MORV 92557 687-F6
CANDLE SHOE CT
23500 MORV 92557 717-D1
CANDLESTICK WY
2100 PER 92571 777-H6
CANDLEWICK CT
5200 RIV 92506 685-J7
5200 RIV 92506 715-J1
CANDLEWOOD DR
32000 CTHC 92234 787-D3
41800 RivC 92223 691-B5
CANDLEWOOD ST
3400 RivC 92879 744-A5
74100 PDST 92260 848-G2
CANDOR CT
14600 MORV 92553 717-J7
CANDY DR
900 COR 92880 743-B2
CANDY LN
26100 RivC 92544 841-E1
CANDY APPLE WY
39800 MURR 92562 898-A7
39800 MURR 92562 928-A1
CANFIELD CT
4800 RivC 92509 684-F2
CANFIELD WY
11900 SBdC 92316 645-G4
CANMORE CT
5300 RIV 92507 716-F1
CANNERY RD
- RivC 92595 897-E7
CANNES AV
3100 RivC 92501 646-A7
CANNES CT
40000 TEM 92591 959-A1
44300 PDST 92260 818-H7
CANNES DR
1200 COR 92882 743-A7
CANNICH RD
- RIV 92507 716-F2
CANNON DR
27700 RivC 92585 838-D6
CANNON RD
100 RIV 92506 716-C5
CANNONADE CT
2500 PER 92571 777-H5
CANOE CV
16700 MORV 92551 747-G4
CANOE DR
- RivC 92880 683-D4
CANOGA PL
6800 RIV 92504 715-B2
CANON DR
500 PMSP 92264 786-H3
CANTARINI RD
8700 RivC 92557 687-A2
CANTEBURY RD
3800 RIV 92504 715-B3
CANTEEN
35400 RivC 92276 788-H5
CANTER CT
9400 RivC 92509 684-C2
42700 RivC 92536 963-B6
CANTER LN
30500 RivC 92585 808-J3
30500 RivC 92585 809-A3
N CANTERA CIR
500 PMSP 92262 786-G1
CANTERBURY
- LQNT 92253 879-J3
CANTERBURY CIR
600 COR 92879 744-B2
CANTERBURY CT
15600 FONT 92337 644-E3
31400 TEM 92591 959-D4
34900 YCPA 92399 649-J4
34900 YCPA 92399 650-A4
74800 PDST 92260 848-J3
CANTERBURY DR
6600 CHLS 91709 712-B6
CANTERBURY PL
1200 PER 92571 778-A2
CANTERBURY RD
400 HEMT 92545 840-H1
4100 RIV 92504 715-A2
CANTERBURY ST
- RivC 92585 838-D6
600 COR 92879 744-B2
CANTERBURY WY
- MURR 92562 927-E4
CANTERFIELD DR
30700 TEM 92592 979-C3
CANTERRA CIR
79200 LQNT 92253 819-H7
CANTERRA DR
79100 LQNT 92253 819-H7
CANTINA WY
2200 PMSP 92264 786-E6
CANTOR CIR
48300 INDO 92201 5470-F4
CANTRELL RD
39700 TEM 92591 929-E7
39700 TEM 92591 959-E1
CANVASBACK CIR
11600 MORV 92557 717-C1
CANYON CIR
200 PMSP 92264 816-D1
1200 COR 92880 743-B1

CANYON CIR
24400 RivC 92883 804-H6
CANYON CT
- INDW 92210 848-J3
CANYON DR
- PDST 92260 848-D6
1800 RDL 92373 649-A5
11300 SBdC 92399 650-E1
12100 YCPA 92399 650-E4
18000 LKEL 92530 866-C4
21000 RivC 92595 897-A4
21000 LKEL 92532 866-J6
21000 LKEL 92532 867-A6
24500 RivC 92587 837-G6
26600 RivC - 844-A1
S CANYON DR
2100 SBdC 92324 646-H4
2100 CLTN 92324 646-J4
CANYON LN
72300 PDST 92260 848-C5
CANYON PL
10200 RivC 92220 691-D4
10200 RivC 92223 691-D4
11000 BAN 92220 691-C7
W CANYON PL
400 PMSP 92262 756-D7
CANYON RD
25700 LMLN 92354 647-D3
25800 SBdC 92354 647-D3
25800 SBdC 92373 647-G4
CANYON RDG
31800 LKEL 92532 866-J5
31800 LKEL 92532 867-A5
CANYON BREEZE LN
25000 RivC - (813-J5 See Page 782)
CANYON CLUB DR
22400 CYNL 92587 867-C3
CANYON COUNTRY RD
68800 RivC 92240 697-D7
CANYON CREEK
- RMIR 92270 788-A7
CANYON CREEK CIR
16900 RivC 92503 744-G5
CANYON CREEK DR
16900 RIV 92507 716-D1
CANYON CREST
- PDST 92260 848-D5
- RivC 92880 713-B1
CANYON CREST CIR
1600 COR 92882 742-E6
CANYON CREST DR
1200 COR 92882 742-E6
2600 RIV 92507 686-D4
5300 RIV 92507 716-D2
5400 RIV 92506 716-D2
11900 FONT 92337 644-D4
12100 RivC 92509 644-D4
CANYON CREST LN
48900 PDST 92260 848-D5
CANYON CREST RD
700 BEAU 92223 690-J7
13300 YCPA 92399 650-D6
CANYON CREST WY
11900 FONT 92337 644-D4
CANYON ESTATE DR
1500 PMSP 92264 786-G6
CANYON ESTATES CT
6100 RIV 92506 716-C3
CANYON ESTATES DR
23000 RivC 92883 804-C4
31600 LKEL 92532 866-H5
31800 LKEL 92532 867-A6
CANYON HEIGHTS CT
36200 YCPA 92399 650-D6
CANYON HEIGHTS DR
13300 YCPA 92399 650-D6
CANYON HEIGHTS RD
100 PMSP 92264 816-D1
1500 SDCo 92028 998-H5
CANYON HILL DR
1700 RIV 92506 716-A4
CANYON HILLS DR
37400 YCPA 92399 650-G6
CANYON HILLS RD
23000 RivC 92883 804-C4
CANYON HOUSE RD
- RivC 92282 655-F1
49100 RivC - 655-H2
49100 SBdC 92256 655-F1
CANYON LAKE DR N
22300 CYNL 92587 867-C3
CANYON LAKE DR S
22400 CYNL 92587 867-D3
CANYONLANDS CT
17500 RivC 92241 727-E2
CANYON OAK DR
23600 MURR 92562 927-H2
CANYON PARK DR
6000 RIV 92507 716-J3
CANYON PINE RD
1400 BEAU 92223 690-J7
CANYON PINES PL
9000 RivC 92883 804-C4
CANYON PLAZA DR
- CTHC 92234 787-C7
CANYON RANCH RD
9700 MORV 92557 687-F4
33500 RivC 92595 897-D3
CANYON RIDGE CIR
2200 NRCO 92860 713-D3
CANYON RIDGE CT
42100 RivC 92536 963-B3
CANYON RIDGE DR
1700 PER 92571 778-C2

CANYON RIDGE RD
14100 RivC 92503 745-C4
14200 RIV 92503 745-C4
CANYON RIM CIR
39300 TEM 92591 928-J7
39300 TEM 92591 958-J1
CANYON SANDS DR
2400 PMSP 92264 787-A6
CANYON SHADOWS PL
9000 RivC 92883 804-C4
CANYON SHORES DR
68500 CTHC 92234 787-E6
CANYONSIDE CIR
4100 RivC 92509 685-A2
CANYONSIDE CT
42000 RivC 92536 963-B4
CANYON SOUTH DR
2600 PMSP 92264 786-E7
CANYON SPRINGS PKWY
2600 RIV 92507 716-J2
2800 RIV 92507 717-A2
22000 MORV 92553 717-A2
CANYONSTONE DR
15200 MORV 92551 747-E1
CANYON TERRACE DR
7500 RivC 92509 684-H4
36200 YCPA 92399 650-D6
CANYON TRAIL RD
24400 RivC - 814-A3
CANYON VIEW CIR
2700 COR 92882 773-C1
CANYON VIEW DR
- RivC 92883 804-B3
300 CALI 92320 689-J2
13400 YCPA 92399 650-D6
16500 RivC 92504 745-F5
31500 LKEL 92532 866-H5
49500 PDST 92260 848-F6
CANYON VIEW LN
2600 COR 92882 773-C2
S CANYON VIEW LN
1100 CLTN 92324 646-H1
CANYON VIEW PL
- NRCO 92860 743-F2
CANYON VISTA
- RivC 92203 789-H6
CANYON VISTA DR
200 PMSP 92264 786-E7
E CANYON VISTA DR
3000 CLTN 92324 646-J3
3000 CLTN 92324 647-A3
CANYON VISTA RD
10200 MORV 92557 687-E5
32000 CTHC 92234 787-E3
CANYONWIND RD
12400 RivC 92503 744-J5
12600 RivC 92503 745-A5
CANYON WOODS CIR
24000 MORV 92557 687-E6
CANYON WOODS DR
- COR 92881 773-F4
CAPANO BAY
28700 RivC 92584 898-G1
CAPANO BAY CT
28500 RivC 92584 898-F1
CAPARY RD
5300 RivC 92509 685-D3
CAPAY BAY CT
26400 MORV 92555 717-J4
26400 MORV 92555 718-A4
CAPAY BAY DR
13300 MORV 92555 717-J4
CAPE CT
1800 RIV 92506 716-A3
12300 MORV 92557 717-H2
CAPE DR
2700 COR 92882 772-J2
32400 LKEL 92530 896-H5
CAPE LN
- YCPA 92399 649-F4
CAPE AIRE WY
35500 MURR 92563 898-F7
CAPE COD CT
34600 YCPA 92399 649-J5
CAPE COD DR
32400 LKEL 92530 896-H4
CAPE COD ST
24800 MORV 92553 717-F7
CAPE ELIZABETH WY
100 RIV 92506 716-D6
CAPELLA CT
5300 RivC 91752 683-H3
CAPELLA ST
16000 RivC 92504 745-G4
16000 RivC 92506 745-G4
CAPELLO DR
14700 RivC 92570 775-E7
21700 RivC 92570 805-F1
CAPE MENDOCINO CT
26400 MORV 92555 717-J4
26400 MORV 92555 718-A4
CAPET ST
2100 SJCT 92583 811-E5
CAPE VERDE DR
77700 PDST 92211 819-E6
CAPEWEED LN
8700 RIV 92508 746-G2
CAPILAND RD
9300 RivC 92240 696-E1
CAPILANO DR
27100 RivC 92586 838-C7
W CAPISTRANO CT
1000 PMSP 92262 756-C6
CAPISTRANO ST
300 HEMT 92544 811-C6

CAPISTRANO ST
800 COR 92882 743-B7
45600 INDO 92201 5470-D1
CAPISTRANO WY
6400 RIV 92504 715-C1
48500 LQNT 92253 849-G4
CAPISTRANO GATE
81500 INDO 92201 5470-D2
CAPITAL ST
1800 COR 92880 742-J4
CAPITAL PEAK LN
- RIV 92508 746-E3
CAPITOL DR
11600 RIV 92503 744-E3
CAPITOL ST
34500 RivC 92592 960-A5
CAPITOLA LN
25000 RivC 92548 808-J7
25000 RivC 92548 809-A6
CAPITOL REEF PL
69200 RivC 92241 727-E2
CAPO DR
21800 RivC 92590 977-B2
CAPRA RD
35000 MURR 92563 898-G7
35000 MURR 92584 898-G7
E CAPRI
3100 ONT 91761 643-B6
CAPRI CIR
1700 PMSP 92264 786-G4
4400 NRCO 92860 713-F3
CAPRI CT
44300 PDST 92260 818-H7
CAPRI DR
- RivC 92201 819-H5
CAPRI LN
1400 SJCT 92583 811-E3
CAPRI ST
100 RMIR 92270 787-H7
CAPRI WY
- TEM 92592 979-G1
CAPRICE CT
30200 TEM 92592 959-A6
CAPRICE RD
46500 RivC 92536 982-B6
CAPRICE WY
7000 RIV 92504 715-F5
CAPRICHO CIR
27300 RivC 92590 958-D7
CAPRICORN AV
83400 INDO 92201 5470-H2
CAPRICORN CIR
2800 RIV 92503 744-G2
CAPRIOLE RD
3500 RIV 92503 744-C3
CAPS WY
2500 SDCo 92028 998-B6
CAPTAINS WK
- RivC 92254 (5654-D2 See Page 5594)
CAPTIVA CIR
- COR 92882 773-B4
CAPTIVA PL
- CTHC 92234 757-D5
CARA WY
29400 TEM 92591 958-H5
69500 RMIR 92270 787-G5
CARACAS PL
42500 RivC 92201 819-G5
CARAMIA CT
35500 CALI 92320 690-A3
CARANCHO RD
19300 RivC 92590 976-J1
20200 RivC 92590 977-A1
23000 RivC 92590 957-E7
27300 RivC 92590 997-J1
CARAVAN
- PMSP 92264 786-E6
CARAVAN CIR
- INDO 92201 5470-H3
26600 RivC 92883 835-C4
CARAVAN ST
83000 INDO 92201 5470-G2
CARAVEL LN
35900 RivC 92592 960-D4
CARAWAY CT
- SJCT 92582 780-H6
2100 COR 92879 743-H1
CARAWAY LN
19800 RIV 92508 746-E2
CARBIDE DR
1200 COR 92881 773-G2
CARBOB LN
25900 RivC 92544 811-G7
E CARBON CT
2500 CLTN 92324 646-J4
CARDELINA DR
51200 COAC 92236 5471-E7
CARDIFF AV
- RivC 92563 929-A7
CARDIFF CIR
10200 RIV 92503 714-E1
CARDIFF LN
11400 LMLN 92354 647-F2
CARDIFF RD
- MURR 92563 928-J3
CARDIFF ST
500 COR 92879 743-G5
42500 PDST 92211 819-E5
45200 RivC 92544 (812-D7 See Page 782)
CARDILLO AV
2200 PMSP 92262 756-C5
CARDINAL AV
24000 MORV 92551 747-E4

CARDINAL AV
83600 INDO 92201 5470-H3
CARDINAL CT
11800 FONT 92337 644-D4
11800 LMLN 92354 647-G3
22100 GTER 92313 646-D5
CARDINAL DR
86000 COAC 92236 5471-D6
CARDINAL LN
200 RivC 92507 646-E6
32700 RivC 92584 898-A1
CARDINAL RD
43300 RivC 92544 901-J2
43400 RivC 92544 902-A2
CARDINAL ST
22200 GTER 92313 646-E4
CARDINAL FLOWER DR
40900 MURR 92562 927-J3
CARDINUS DR
19000 RivC 92570 776-D2
CARDONA PL
800 HEMT 92543 840-J2
CAREFREE DR
43500 RivC 92592 960-B7
CARE FREE RD
- RivC 92220 389-G7
CAREFREE WY
1900 COR 92880 713-A7
CARENTAN DR
- TEM 92592 979-F1
CAREY RD
67500 CTHC 92234 787-C6
67500 PMSP 92264 787-C6
CARGIL LN
43100 RivC 92539 (965-B6 See Page 964)
CARHART AV
22100 GTER 92313 646-E3
CARIBOU
1100 HEMT 92543 810-H7
CARIBOU CIR
- COR 92881 773-E5
10100 MORV 92557 687-D5
S CARIBOU PL
2500 ONT 91761 643-A5
E CARIBOU CREEK CT
3600 ONT 91761 643-C7
CARILLO CT
29000 MORV 92555 718-F1
29100 MORV 92555 688-F7
CARILLO RD
2100 PMSP 92262 756-F5
CARINA CT
25500 RivC 92586 837-J6
CARINDA CT
77500 PDST 92211 819-E3
CARINI CT
- TEM 92592 979-G1
CARINO PL
42400 TEM 92592 959-A6
CARIOCA LN
6500 RIV 92506 716-B4
CARISSA AV
6400 RIV 92504 715-A1
CARISSA CT
35600 RivC 92595 897-E7
CARL DR
2700 HEMT 92545 810-F7
CARL PL
- SBDO 92408 646-J1
CARL ST
2900 RIV 92507 686-B3
24500 RivC 92584 897-G1
24500 RivC 92595 897-G1
CARL WY
200 HEMT 92545 810-F7
CARLA CT
77600 PDST 92211 819-E3
CARLA LN
- RMIR 92270 817-H3
CARLA JEAN ST
14700 MORV 92553 717-F7
CARL-DENNY DR
1100 CLTN 92324 646-F2
CARLENE CIR
2300 COR 92882 773-A1
CARLENE ST
2300 COR 92882 773-A1
CARLETON CT
1500 COR 92881 773-G4
CARLETON WY
- TEM 92591 958-H4
CARLIE DR
- MURR 92562 927-G3
CARLINGFORD AV
4900 RIV 92504 685-C6
CARLISLE CT
11700 MORV 92557 717-C1
CARLITA CIR
- RivC 92570 806-H3
CARLITA ST
20500 RivC 92570 806-G2
CARLO DR
6000 RIV 92504 685-D7
6300 RIV 92506 715-D1
6300 RIV 92504 715-D1
CARLOS ST
16900 RivC 92240 727-A1
CARLOTA WY
100 RivC 92507 646-F6
CARLOTTA DR
1200 HEMT 92543 810-H6
41000 PDST 92211 819-A5
CARLSBAD CIR
2300 HEMT 92545 840-G1

STREET Block City ZIP Pg-Grid

CARLSBAD CIR
33400 RivC 92276 788-F4
CARLSBAD WY
3400 RIV 92506 715-F1
CARLSON PL
4400 RIV 92503 714-G5
N CARLTON AV
200 BLY 92225 5491-D6
S CARLTON AV
200 BLY 92225 5491-D7
300 RivC 92225 5491-D7
400 RivC 92225 5551-D1
CARLTON PL
2000 RIV 92507 686-A6
2100 RIV 92507 685-J6
CARLY CT
- MURR 92562 927-J2
22300 RivC 92570 806-H2
CARLYLE DR
7900 RivC 92509 684-G5
CARMA CT
2800 RIV 92503 715-B7
N CARMALITA ST
100 HEMT 92543 811-A7
S CARMALITA ST
100 HEMT 92543 811-A7
300 HEMT 92543 841-A1
CARMAN LN
24300 MORV 92551 747-E2
CARMAN PL
44000 LQNT 92253 819-G7
CARMEL CIR
2000 COR 92882 742-H7
43600 PDST 92260 818-F7
CARMEL DR
- PMSP 92264 786-J6
CARMEL RD
28800 RivC 92586 838-B7
29100 RivC 92586 868-B1
CARMEL WY
300 HEMT 92545 840-G1
5300 RIV 92506 715-H1
CARMELA CT
18000 RivC 92532 836-C7
CARMELA DR
27700 CTHC 92234 757-B5
CARMELITA AV
19500 RivC 92881 774-A4
CARMELITA CIR
40300 TEM 92591 959-A2
CARMEL VALLEY AV
- INDO 92201 849-J1
- INDO 92201 5470-A1
CARMEL VERDE LN
15500 MORV 92551 747-H2
CARMEN AV
49000 RivC 92230 723-B5
CARMEN DR
600 SJCT 92583 811-C2
CARMINE ST
11600 RIV 92505 714-B7
CARMODY CT
100 RDL 92373 647-H2
CARMODY ST
100 RDL 92373 647-H2
CARNABY ST
12900 MORV 92553 717-B4
CARNATION AV
2000 HEMT 92545 840-G2
CARNATION CT
8100 RIV 92503 714-G2
46500 INDO 92201 5470-E2
CARNATION DR
- RivC 92883 804-B4
CARNATION LN
12100 MORV 92557 717-G2
CARNATION ST
500 PMSP 92262 756-E4
12600 RivC 92880 683-D6
CARNATION WY
17800 CHLS 91709 712-A5
CARNEGIE AV
42200 RivC 92544 841-F1
S CARNEGIE AV
300 ONT 91761 643-C2
CARNELIAN LN
75600 INDW 92210 849-A3
CARNEROS CT
- MURR 92562 927-J2
CARNES CIR
78600 LQNT 92253 819-G7
CARNES DR
24800 RivC 92548 808-J6
CARNEY CT
4200 RIV 92507 686-E5
CARNOUSIE DR
- BAN 92220 721-B6
CARNOUSTIE AV
28700 MORV 92555 718-E6
CARNOUSTIE CT
22800 MURR 92562 927-B3
CAROB CIR E
- PMSP 92264 786-H5
CAROB CIR S
- PMSP 92264 786-H5
CAROB CIR W
- PMSP 92264 786-H5
CAROB CT
1100 HEMT 92545 840-G3
44000 INDO 92201 5410-D7
72700 PDST 92260 848-D2
CAROB LN
1000 NRCO 92860 713-F3
CAROB ST
30000 LKEL 92530 865-G3

CAROB WY
5100 RIV 92505 714-B6
CAROB TREE DR
- DHSP 92240 696-G4
CAROBWOOD WY
6700 RIV 92506 716-D4
CAROL DR
16000 RivC - 726-G1
CAROL LN
13800 RivC 92570 775-C7
33500 RivC 92584 898-C3
CAROL PL
27400 MORV 92555 718-C2
CAROL RD
38100 RivC 92544 (932-F4
See Page 902)
CAROL WY
- SBDO 92408 646-J1
700 HEMT 92543 841-A2
5300 RivC 92509 685-D3
CAROL ANN LN
47400 RivC 92592 999-G1
CAROL ANNE RD
40000 SDCo 92028 997-J7
40000 SDCo 92028 976-J7
40000 SDCo 92028 977-A7
CAROLBEE LN
- RivC 92592 930-J2
CAROLE DR
27000 RivC 92570 837-C4
CAROLEE AV
24300 MORV 92551 747-F1
CAROLINA AV
15000 MORV 92551 747-J1
19000 MORV 92551 717-J7
CAROLINA CIR
800 COR 92882 773-B3
CAROLINAS LN
- RivC 92880 683-D4
CAROLINE CT
4300 RIV 92506 715-E1
40600 RivC 92544 841-C1
42500 PDST 92211 818-J6
CAROLWOOD CT
25500 MURR 92563 928-E6
CAROLWOOD DR
1600 COR 92882 742-J7
CAROLYN AV
24600 MORV 92553 717-F5
CAROLYN CT
- PER 92570 807-D3
37000 RMIR 92270 787-J7
CARON CT
1400 PER 92571 807-J1
1500 PER 92571 777-J7
CAROUSEL DR
20400 RivC 92570 776-G7
CARRERA CT
- RMIR 92270 818-D3
CARRERA DR
1700 SJCT 92583 781-E7
15500 FONT 92337 644-F4
CARRERA PL
- RMIR 92270 818-D3
CARRE VISTA
40200 RivC 92592 930-E7
40200 RivC 92592 960-E1
CARRIAGE CIR
100 HEMT 92545 840-C1
CARRIAGE CT
49600 RivC 92536 963-D4
CARRIAGE DR
1000 NRCO 92860 713-F3
CARRIAGE LN
1000 COR 92880 712-J7
1000 COR 92880 713-A7
1300 PER 92571 778-A2
1700 PMSP 92262 756-G6
CARRIAGE TR
72800 PDST 92260 848-E5
CARRIAGE HEIGHTS CIR
9500 MORV 92557 687-C4
CARRICK ST
3900 RIV 92505 714-E7
3900 RIV 92505 744-E1
CARRIE LN
- LQNT 92253 849-H1
11400 MORV 92555 688-D7
CARRIE ST
1700 SJCT 92583 781-A5
CARRIGAN RD
40400 MURR 92562 928-D5
CARRILLO RD
23600 RivC 92590 977-F4
CARRIZO CIR
73100 PDST 92260 848-E5
CARRIZO RD
- RivC - (907-J2
See Page 906)
- RivC - 908-B2
CARROL CT
25500 LMLN 92354 647-D2
CARROLL DR
67800 CTHC 92234 817-C3
CARROLL ST
17900 RivC 92570 747-A6
18400 RivC 92570 777-A1
CARROT LN
43300 RivC 92536 963-H7
44300 RivC 92536 983-H4
CARROTWOOD CT
1100 HEMT 92545 840-G3
CARSON AV
16000 LKEL 92530 865-H1

CARSON LN
- NRCO 92860 743-H1
CARSON RD
5500 RIV 92506 715-G1
70100 RMIR 92270 817-H4
CARSON ST
600 HEMT 92543 811-B6
CARSON CITY WY
- NRCO 92860 743-H1
CARTAGENA DR
1000 MORV 92557 687-A5
CARTAGENA WY
- RMIR 92270 818-D5
CARTER AV
3900 RIV 92501 645-H7
CARTER DR
- PER 92570 807-D2
22500 RivC 92570 807-D2
CARTER LN
- COR 92881 773-F3
40400 RivC 92201 819-G3
CARTESIAN WY
27700 MORV 92555 718-C4
CARTHAGE ST
3800 RIV 92501 685-H2
CARTHAY DR
1100 NRCO 92860 713-F2
CARTIER DR
25700 MORV 92557 717-H1
W CARTIER LN
1300 CLTN 92324 646-A2
CARTWHEEL CIR
- COR 92880 712-J7
- COR 92880 713-A7
- COR 92880 743-A1
CARTWRIGHT DR
15700 RivC 92508 746-B3
CARVER CT
9500 RIV 92503 714-J6
CARY RD
37700 RivC 92539 (934-B2
See Page 904)
43000 RivC 92539 964-H5
44000 RivC 92539 (984-H1
See Page 964)
CARY ST
2900 RIV 92504 715-D4
CASA DR
13000 RivC 92240 696-D5
CASA WY E
300 RLTO 92316 645-G2
CASABLANCA CT
48800 INDO 92201 5470-A5
CASA BLANCA ST
7500 RIV 92504 715-D4
11300 YCPA 92399 650-D1
CASABLANCA ST
48800 INDO 92201 5470-A4
CASA BONITA AV
23800 RivC 92587 867-D1
CASA CHATA PL
30100 TEM 92592 959-A6
CASA DE ADOBE DR
500 SJCT 92583 781-A6
CASA DEL RIO
- LQNT 92253 849-H5
CASA DEL SOL
- LQNT 92253 849-D7
- LQNT 92253 879-D1
CASA ENCANTADOR RD
25500 MORV 92551 747-H1
26000 MORV 92555 747-H1
26200 MORV 92555 748-A1
CASA FANTASTICO RD
25800 MORV 92551 747-J1
CASA GRANDE DR
66600 DHSP 92240 696-J1
66800 DHSP 92240 697-A1
CASA GRANDE ST
15200 MORV 92551 747-H1
CASALA CT
- TEM 92592 959-G7
CASALERO DR
43800 RivC 92590 977-D1
CASA LINDA PL
26300 MORV 92555 717-J1
26300 MORV 92555 718-A1
CASA LOMA CT
25800 RivC 92544 811-E7
CASA LOMA DR
14800 MORV 92553 717-G7
CASA LOMA RD
12600 DHSP 92240 697-B5
CASANDRA CT
39600 MURR 92563 928-F5
74700 INDW 92210 848-J2
CASANDRA LN
1000 COR 92879 743-H2
CASAS DE MARIPOSA
- INDW 92210 849-C1
CASA VERDE
42300 RivC 92590 960-B5
E CASA VERDE WY
1100 PMSP 92262 786-F1
CASA VIDA CIR
- LQNT 92253 849-H5
CASBAH WY
42200 PDST 92211 819-C5
CASCABEL WY
2800 RIV 92503 715-B7
CASCADA CIR
- TEM 92592 979-G1
CASCADA CT
11800 FONT 92337 644-F4

CASCADA ST
- MURR 92563 928-F7
CASCADAS CIR
- LQNT 92253 849-J4
CASCADE CT
1600 RDL 92373 647-H2
CASCADE DR
2000 COR 92879 743-H2
22500 CYNL 92587 867-C2
24900 RivC - 814-A5
CASCADE LN
7400 RivC 92509 684-H5
CASCADE ST
100 RDL 92373 647-H2
12900 YCPA 92399 650-B5
CASCADES CIR N
69000 RivC 92241 727-E2
CASCADES CT
42000 TEM 92591 959-D5
69100 CTHC 92234 787-F1
CASCADES DR
64900 DHSP 92240 696-F1
64900 RivC 92240 696-F1
CASCADIA DR
78600 RivC 92201 819-G3
CASCADIAN WY
1800 SJCT 92583 811-D4
CASCO CT
14100 MORV 92553 717-E6
CASCO DR
22300 RivC 92570 806-A1
CASE RD
- PER 92570 807-H4
500 PER 92570 808-A5
2600 PER 92570 838-B1
CASE ST
20100 RivC 92881 773-H5
33000 RivC 92530 896-C3
CASERTA DR
- TEM 92592 979-G1
CASERTA LN
100 PDST 92211 818-J3
CASEY CIR
5000 BAN 92220 721-E2
CASEY CT
24900 MORV 92557 687-F4
CASH LN
31900 RivC 92595 897-C6
CASHEW ST
20500 RivC 92595 897-A5
CASHEW TREE ST
1700 HEMT 92545 840-G4
CASILLA CT
- MORV 92557 687-D4
CASINO DR
31700 LKEL 92530 866-H5
31700 RivC 92530 866-J6
CASINO RD
26000 RivC 92544 811-J7
26100 RivC 92544 841-J1
60400 RivC - (907-E3
See Page 906)
CASITA CT
2100 HEMT 92545 810-G6
CASITAS CIR
1300 COR 92882 743-A7
CASITAS DR
- LQNT 92253 849-J4
CASITAS WY
2200 PMSP 92264 786-G4
CASMALIA CT
- MORV 92557 687-C4
CASPER CT
13500 MORV 92553 717-C5
CASPER LN
900 BAN 92220 721-D4
CASPER ST
- SJCT 92583 780-J5
CASPIAN CT
- RivC 92880 683-D6
CASPIAN WY
13700 MORV 92553 717-D5
CASS ST
10600 RIV 92505 714-E7
CASSALERIA AV
14900 MORV 92555 719-C7
CASSANDRA DR
23500 RivC 92587 837-E7
CASSIA AV
7700 RIV 92504 715-C3
CASSIA DR
44100 INDO 92201 5410-D7
CASSIA PL
48800 PDST 92260 848-F5
CASSIA ST
- LQNT 92253 849-J3
- LQNT 92253 5470-A4
CASSIA WY
44500 INDO 92201 5410-D7
CASSIDY CIR
8200 RivC 92509 684-F1
CASSIDY PL
17800 CHLS 91709 712-A5
CASSINO CT
- TEM 92592 959-F7
CASSLER DR
25800 RivC - 814-E6
CASTAIC ST
3400 RIV 92501 685-J1
CASTANA DR
- TEM 92592 979-G1
CASTAS CT
25500 MORV 92551 747-H2
CASTELAR CT
1100 COR 92882 742-F6

CASTELLANA E
200 PDST 92260 818-F6
CASTELLANA N
200 PDST 92260 818-F6
CASTELLANA S
100 PDST 92260 818-E6
CASTELLANA W
100 PDST 92260 818-E6
CASTELLANE DR
36100 MURR 92562 928-C1
CASTELLANO RD
1200 RivC 92509 645-E5
CASTELLION RD
15500 FONT 92337 644-F3
CASTILE AV
39600 MURR 92562 928-C2
CASTILE WY
5000 RIV 92507 686-C7
CASTILE CANYON RD
43500 RivC 92583 811-H3
43800 RivC 92583 (812-A2
See Page 782)
CASTILLE DR
500 HEMT 92543 810-H6
CASTILLE ST
48700 INDO 92201 5470-A5
CASTINETTE WY
23700 MURR 92562 928-A1
CASTLE CT
200 SJCT 92583 811-C1
76800 PDST 92211 819-C2
CASTLE ST
- RivC 92518 717-D7
CASTLEBROOK AV
24800 MORV 92553 717-G7
CASTLE CRAG DR
22600 CYNL 92587 867-C2
CASTLE CREST DR
600 RivC 91752 683-D4
CASTLEMAN ST
3800 RIV 92503 714-H5
CASTLE OAK DR
3700 RIV 92505 744-E1
CASTLEPEAK DR
- COR 92883 773-H7
CASTLE PEAK DR
- RIV 92508 746-E2
CASTLE PINE CT
4900 RivC 92509 684-G2
CASTLE PINES AV
4800 BAN 92220 721-E5
CASTLE PINES CT
22800 MURR 92562 927-D4
CASTLE PINES DR
- COR 92883 773-G7
78600 LQNT 92253 849-G6
CASTLE PINES WY
- COR 92883 773-J6
CASTLE REAGH PL
3500 RIV 92506 685-F6
CASTLE ROCK CIR
- COR 92880 713-A7
CASTLEROCK TR
- RivC 92570 776-J2
CATALEJO LN
25500 MORV 92551 747-H1
CATALINA DR
6600 RIV 92504 715-D1
10900 BLY 92225 5491-D4
CATALINA ST
25000 MURR 92562 928-D5
CATALINA WY
26500 RivC - 5421-C1
73100 PDST 92260 818-E7
CATALON RD
42000 RivC 92544 901-G3
CATALPA AV
12700 DHSP 92240 697-D4
CATALPA PL
8500 RIV 92504 715-A3
CATALPA TR
- PMSP 92264 786-G6
CATALUNA CIR
27400 RivC 92585 838-D2
CATAMARAN WY
600 PER 92571 777-J7
CATANO RD
29400 RivC 92584 867-J2
29400 RivC 92584 868-A1
CATAWBA AV
10600 FONT 92337 644-G2
10600 SBdC 92337 644-G2
CATAWBA PL
11400 FONT 92337 644-G3
CAT CANYON RD
49100 PDST 92260 848-C6
49100 RivC 92260 848-C6
CAT CANYON WY
71500 RivC 92260 848-B5
CATCHEN RD
3400 BAN 92220 721-F2
CAT CREEK RD
49400 RivC 92260 848-B5
CATERPILLAR CT
2200 RivC 92509 645-E6
CATES WY
24100 RivC 92570 805-F6
CATHCART PL
6000 RIV 92506 716-A2
CATHEDRAL CIR
3700 COR 92880 773-H6
CATHEDRAL ST
- RivC 92584 838-D6
- RivC 92585 838-D6

CATHEDRAL CANYON DR
32000 CTHC 92234 787-E7
35600 PMSP 92264 787-E7
37000 CTHC 92234 817-E1
CATHERINE CIR
1300 COR 92880 713-A7
CATHERINE CT
- MURR 92562 927-J1
CATHY
46200 RivC 92544 (932-F5
See Page 902)
CATHY CIR
100 PMSP 92262 756-G3
44500 RivC 92536 (984-D2
See Page 964)
CATHY DR
39700 SDCo 92028 997-B2
CATHY LN
20000 RivC 92595 896-J4
CATHY PL
6600 RIV 92504 715-B1
CATLIN
72000 RivC 92241 728-C4
CATLIN AV
33000 RivC 92545 839-F2
CATMINT CIR
22700 MORV 92557 717-B1
CATON CT
17500 RivC 92504 746-A4
CATRON RD
36400 YCPA 92399 650-D1
CATS CLAW RD
67500 RivC 92241 727-B2
CATS CLAW TR
11900 SBdC 92399 651-C2
CATS PAW CT
- RMIR 92270 818-D1
CATSPAW DR
6300 RIV 92505 714-B3
CATT RD
23100 RivC 92595 897-D7
23100 RivC 92595 927-D1
26300 MURR 92562 898-B7
CATTAIL DR
800 COR 92882 742-G5
39000 MURR 92563 928-F4
CATTAIL LN
22800 MORV 92557 717-B1
CATTLE CREEK DR
6700 CHLS 91709 712-B6
CATZ DR
39200 RivC 92543 901-A1
CAULFIELD CT
1300 RIV 92506 716-B5
CAVALCADE CT
2400 PER 92571 777-H5
CAVALIER DR
40800 RivC 92544 841-D1
CAVALRY CT
- RivC 92883 835-D5
CAVALRY WY
11500 FONT 92337 644-E3
CAVANDISH LN
13200 MORV 92553 717-E4
CAVENDISH DR
25500 HEMT 92545 810-E7
CAVE ROCK RD
53000 RivC 92539 (934-B4
See Page 904)
CAWSTON AV
100 SJCT 92582 810-E3
300 HEMT 92545 810-E7
700 SJCT 92582 780-E7
1200 HEMT 92545 840-E2
CAYENNE CT
25800 MORV 92553 717-H4
CAYENNE TR
44500 TEM 92592 979-G2
CAYENTE CT
41600 MURR 92562 927-H4
CAYLA CT
25500 RivC 92586 837-J5
CAYMAN AV
25300 MORV 92551 747-H2
CAYMAN CIR
15700 MORV 92551 747-H2
CAYMAN ST
1400 HEMT 92543 840-J4
CAYUGA LN
77000 INDW 92210 849-D1
CAYUGA PL
41100 RivC 92544 841-D3
CAYUSE CT
15200 RivC 92506 745-G1
CECCARELLI RD
52500 RivC 92539 (934-A2
See Page 904)
CECELIA DR
600 SJCT 92583 811-D2
CECIL AV
15500 RivC 92508 746-B2
CECIL CT
43500 RivC 92544 811-J6
CECIL DR
11600 RivC 92282 695-A3
CECIL PL
16700 RivC 92504 745-G5
CECIL ST
55000 RivC 92274 5530-H3
CECILIA CT
4300 RIV 92503 714-J3
CECILIA DR
1100 COR 92881 773-G1

CECINA WY
40700 RivC 92201 819-G4
CEDAR AV
- RivC - (875-J4
See Page 844)
- RivC - (905-F2
See Page 904)
3800 NRCO 92860 713-D4
10700 SBdC 92316 645-E3
32200 RivC 92584 867-G7
34300 YCPA 92399 649-H2
34900 YCPA 92399 650-A2
43000 RivC 92544 811-H5
CEDAR CIR
- MURR 92563 928-H7
CEDAR DR
32800 RivC 92530 865-J7
52600 RivC - (813-J5
See Page 782)
52800 RivC - 814-A5
CEDAR LN
- LKEL 92530 865-G4
34500 YCPA 92399 649-H3
CEDAR PL
500 HEMT 92543 811-A6
CEDAR PT
- PER 92571 778-B2
CEDAR RD
68600 CTHC 92234 787-E4
CEDAR ST
500 SJCT 92583 811-A2
800 COR 92879 743-E6
3000 RIV 92501 685-G4
4900 RivC 92509 684-C2
11700 SBdC 92316 645-E3
12000 RivC 92509 645-E3
12500 BLY 92225 5491-G6
18000 RivC 92570 746-C7
18200 RivC 92570 776-D1
21500 RivC 92595 897-C7
21600 RivC 92570 777-A4
25700 RivC - 814-D6
E CEDAR ST
2700 ONT 91761 643-A4
S CEDAR ST
700 CLTN 92324 646-E1
CEDAR WY
11500 LMLN 92354 647-C2
CEDAR BREAKS WY
1200 SJCT 92583 781-B6
CEDARBROOK AV
12900 MORV 92553 717-H3
CEDAR CREEK RD
- RivC 92880 683-B7
- RivC 92880 713-B1
CEDAR CREEK TER
23600 MORV 92557 687-D6
CEDAR CREST
79900 LQNT 92253 5530-B5
CEDARCREST DR
26300 RivC 92586 838-B6
CEDAR CREST DR
52700 RivC - (813-J4
See Page 782)
52700 RivC - 814-A4
CEDAR GLEN CIR
2100 COR 92879 743-H2
E CEDARGLEN CT
3300 ONT 91761 643-B6
CEDAR GLEN DR
2000 COR 92879 743-H2
25400 RivC - 814-B6
CEDAR GLEN RD
41100 RivC 92544 961-E1
E CEDAR GLEN RD
3400 ONT 91761 643-B6
CEDAR GROVE CT
- RivC 92880 713-A1
CEDARGROVE PTH
18700 RivC 92504 775-J1
CEDARHILL DR
1400 RIV 92507 686-B7
CEDARHILL LN
- LKEL 92532 867-D6
CEDARPINE CT
4200 RIV 92505 714-E7
CEDAR PINES DR
1400 COR 92881 773-F4
CEDAR RIDGE CIR
4200 NRCO 92860 713-D3
CEDAR RIDGE LN
3500 COR 92881 773-E4
41000 RivC 92223 691-C5
S CEDAR RIDGE PL
2600 ONT 91761 643-A6
CEDAR RIVER CT
17500 RivC 92241 727-F2
CEDARSPRING DR
2800 HEMT 92545 840-D4
CEDAR SPRINGS CT
32500 RivC 92595 896-J5
CEDAR TREE DR
10700 MORV 92557 687-D6
CEDAR VIEW DR
700 BEAU 92223 690-J7
CEDARWOOD CIR
12600 RivC 92503 744-B4
CEDARWOOD DR
- RivC 92503 744-B7
39400 MURR 92563 928-F5
CEDARWOOD LN
35100 YCPA 92399 650-A2
CEDROS CIR
49000 LQNT 92253 849-F5

CEE CEE RD
42200 TEM 92592 959-H6
42200 RivC 92592 959-H6
CELADON ST
11300 FONT 92337 644-D2
CELANO CIR
100 PDST 92211 818-J3
CELEBRATION LN
500 PER 92570 807-F5
CELERY LN
1200 COR 92879 743-H1
CELESTE CT
- FONT 92337 644-H2
CELESTE DR
200 RIV 92507 686-D4
CELESTE WY
32700 RivC 92595 897-A7
CELESTIAL CIR
- COR 92882 773-A3
CELESTIAL DR
19000 RivC 92570 806-D2
CELIA RD
27900 MURR 92563 928-F3
CELIA J LN
22000 RivC 92567 778-H7
CELIA VISTA
- RivC 92562 956-G4
CELINE CV
39700 RivC 92562 926-J6
CELITA CIR
38500 RivC 92592 930-G4
CELLA LN
34900 YCPA 92399 649-J4
34900 YCPA 92399 650-A4
CELLAR SPRING DR
- MURR 92562 927-F5
- MURR 92562 957-G1
CELLINI DR
8700 RIV 92503 714-J4
CELTIC CIR
- RivC 92585 838-C2
CELTIC CT
1300 RIV 92507 716-F2
CEMENT PLANT RD
20700 SBdC 92324 646-B1
CENTAUR CT
30700 TEM 92592 959-B6
CENTAUR RD
18400 RivC 92504 775-G1
CENTENNIAL CIR
2600 COR 92882 772-J1
40700 PDST 92260 818-E4
CENTENNIAL LN
200 RMIR 92270 817-H2
CENTENNIAL ST
46900 RivC 92536 962-G1
47600 RivC 92536 (932-J7
See Page 902)
47900 RivC 92536 (933-A7
See Page 902)
CENTENNIAL WY
2400 COR 92882 772-J1
CENTER AV
3400 NRCO 92860 713-G4
CENTER CT
48000 PDST 92260 848-E5
S CENTER DR
1200 CLTN 92324 646-G2
CENTER ST
- PER 92571 808-A2
100 RivC 92507 646-D6
200 LKEL 92530 866-F6
1800 PER 92571 778-A7
1900 RivC 92324 646-H6
1900 RivC 92324 647-A7
4000 RivC 92571 778-A5
4200 PER 92571 748-A7
4200 RivC 92571 748-A7
8400 COR 92883 774-B6
12000 MORV 92557 716-H2
87000 RivC 92274 5531-G4
E CENTER ST
100 RivC 92507 646-F6
500 RivC 92324 646-F6
W CENTER ST
1000 RivC 92507 646-A6
2300 RivC 92501 646-A6
CENTERPOINT DR
22600 MORV 92553 717-B2
CENTINELLA CT
800 HEMT 92544 811-F5
CENTRAL AV
100 RIV 92506 686-E7
100 RIV 92506 716-D1
100 RIV 92507 686-B7
100 RIV 92507 716-D1
100 RIV 92507 686-E7
100 HEMT 92543 841-A1
300 HEMT 92543 840-J1
500 LKEL 92530 866-C2
2300 RIV 92506 715-D1
4600 RIV 92504 715-A1
6200 RIV 92504 714-H1
7400 RIV 92503 714-H1
14200 RivC 92555 749-G3
18400 RivC 92555 389-E7
28600 RivC 92567 808-F1
40200 RivC 92544 841-B1
E CENTRAL AV
100 HEMT 92543 841-A1
CENTRAL ST
31700 RivC 92595 897-C7
32800 RivC 92595 927-B1
CENTRAL OVERLAND RD
- RivC 92223 720-B1

CENTRAL OVERLAND RD
- RivC 92320 689-J6
- RivC 92320 690-A7
- RivC 92320 720-B1
CENTREPOINTE DR
1100 CLTN 92324 646-F1
CENTURIAN ST
12900 RivC 92282 724-A1
CENTURION DR
25700 RivC 92584 898-A1
CENTURION PL
3200 ONT 91761 643-A7
3500 ONT 91761 683-A1
S CENTURION WY
3500 ONT 91761 683-B1
CENTURY AV
1300 RIV 92506 716-A3
1900 RIV 92506 715-J3
CENTURY CT
26200 RivC 92544 841-J1
CENTURY HILL DR
2200 RIV 92506 716-A3
CENTURY PARK DR
69800 CTHC 92234 787-G1
CERCLE BEAUREGARD
32200 TEM 92591 959-E4
CERCLE CHAMBERTIN
41200 TEM 92591 959-E3
CERCLE LATOUR
32300 TEM 92591 959-E4
CEREAL ST
20700 LKEL 92530 896-G1
CEREMONY AV
23500 MORV 92551 747-G2
W CERES RD
900 PMSP 92262 756-C7
CERES WY
11000 RivC 91752 683-H4
CERRITA WY
13400 DHSP 92240 697-B5
CERRITOS DR
- PMSP 92264 786-G3
300 PMSP 92262 786-G1
42800 RivC 92201 819-J5
E CERRITOS DR
500 PMSP 92262 786-G2
N CERRITOS DR
200 PMSP 92262 786-G2
S CERRITOS DR
100 PMSP 92264 786-G2
1400 PMSP 92264 786-G4
W CERRITOS DR
200 PMSP 92262 786-G1
CERRITOS RD
500 PMSP 92262 756-G5
500 PMSP 92262 786-G1
CERRITOS WY
400 CTHC 92234 817-G1
CERRO RD
- RivC 92562 976-E1
CERT ST
32400 RivC 92595 897-A6
CERVANTES CT
2900 PMSP 92264 816-E1
CERVANTES WY
- TEM 92591 958-J3
CERVATI
- LKEL 92532 866-J4
CERVERA RD
22500 RivC 92595 897-C6
CERVEZA CIR
- COR 92881 773-E5
CERVIN CIR
32400 TEM 92592 979-F3
CESENA ST
- TEM 92592 959-G7
CESSNA CIR
300 COR 92880 742-J3
CETRINO
- LQNT 92253 849-J7
- LQNT 92253 5470-A7
CHABELA DR
41900 SJCT 92583 781-F7
41900 RivC 92583 781-F7
CHABLIS AV
3000 RivC 92509 644-B5
S CHABLIS AV
1600 ONT 91761 643-H3
CHABLIS CT
38400 RivC 92539 (935-F6
See Page 904)
41600 TEM 92591 959-E4
CHABOT CIR
39500 MURR 92562 928-C2
CHABOT CT
7100 RIV 92506 715-J5
CHACO CANYON RD
40800 MURR 92562 928-A3
40900 MURR 92562 927-J3
CHAD CT
26500 HEMT 92544 811-F6
26600 RivC 92544 842-D1
CHADBOURNE AV
5600 RIV 92505 714-D2
CHADE LN
31000 RivC 92584 868-C5
CHADLYN CT
32900 RivC 92595 897-A7
CHADWICK PL
4800 RIV 92503 714-J2
CHADWICK RD
11400 RivC 92880 742-A5
CHAGALL CT
- RivC 92596 929-E1
13700 MORV 92553 717-C5

CHALAKA PL
100 PDST 92260 848-C7
CHALDON CIR
31000 TEM 92591 959-C1
CHALET DR
60200 RivC - (907-E4
See Page 906)
CHALGROVE DR
1400 COR 92882 742-J6
CHALLEN AV
4400 RIV 92503 714-F3
CHALLIS CT
23400 MORV 92553 717-D5
CHALON CT
- TEM 92591 959-D3
CHALON RD
19900 RivC 92570 775-H4
CHALONE DR
- MURR 92562 928-B4
CHAMAEROP PALM LN
45700 INDO 92201 5470-C1
CHAMBER ST
9100 RIV 92503 714-H3
CHAMBERS AV
25000 RivC 92586 837-H4
25000 RivC 92585 837-H4
25900 RivC 92586 838-A4
27500 RivC 92585 838-D4
42000 RivC 92544 841-G3
CHAMBERS ST
500 HEMT 92543 840-J4
1300 HEMT 92545 840-J4
39500 HEMT 92543 841-A3
CHAMBRAY DR
- MURR 92563 928-G6
22700 MORV 92557 717-B2
CHAMELEON RD
33000 RivC 92544 901-D1
CHAMISE CT
1100 HEMT 92545 840-G3
CHAMISE ST
- COR 92882 773-B2
CHAMISE WY
2500 HEMT 92545 840-F3
CHAMOISE LN
60000 RivC 92539 (965-G2
See Page 964)
CHAMOMILE CIR
11700 MORV 92557 717-B1
CHAMONIX CT
44100 PDST 92260 818-H7
S CHAMPAGNE AV
1400 ONT 91761 643-H3
CHAMPAGNE CIR
26100 RivC 92544 841-E1
CHAMPAGNE CT
4500 RIV 92505 714-F5
CHAMPAGNE DR
35500 CALI 92320 690-A3
CHAMPAGNE LN
78800 RivC 92211 819-G1
CHAMPION AV
18100 LKEL 92530 866-C4
CHAMPION CT
29300 RivC 92586 868-B1
CHAMPION DR
30500 CYNL 92587 867-D4
CHAMPION WY
- RivC 92880 713-A1
CHAMPIONS CIR
- TEM 92591 959-D4
CHAMPIONS DR
- RivC 92320 690-C7
28300 RivC 92584 868-F2
CHAMPIONSHIP DR
14900 MORV 92555 718-E7
28000 MORV 92555 748-D1
CHAMPLAIN DR
1800 COR 92880 743-B1
1800 COR 92880 713-A7
CHAMPLAIN ST
12000 MORV 92557 717-H2
CHANARAL AV
2200 HEMT 92545 810-G6
CHANARAL WY
300 HEMT 92545 810-G6
CHANCE DR
13800 COR 92882 773-B3
CHANCELLOR CT
- MURR 92563 928-G6
CHANDELLE LN
1500 SDCo 92028 997-H7
CHANDLER AV
35100 CALI 92320 689-J3
CHANDLER DR
39000 TEM 92591 929-C6
CHANDLER LN
- RivC 92509 684-G5
CHANDLER ST
13800 RivC 92880 713-A3
14100 RivC 92880 712-H3
14800 SBdC 91710 712-H3
CHANDLER WY
77800 PDST 92211 819-E3
CHANDRA LN
- RMIR 92270 817-H1
CHANEY RD
33000 RivC 92584 898-C2
CHANEY ST
100 LKEL 92530 866-D3
CHANLIN WY
11600 YCPA 92399 650-D1
CHANNEL CT
- RMIR 92270 788-C6

STREET Block City ZIP Pg-Grid

CHANNEL DR
- LQNT 92253 849-G1
39100 CTHC 92234 817-C3
CHANNEL ST
- RivC 92592 979-H2
CHANNEL RUN RD
71600 RivC 92241 728-A1
CHANNEL WAY DR
30100 CYNL 92587 867-E3
CHANNING DR
11100 RIV 92505 744-E1
CHANNING ST
100 RDL 92373 647-H2
CHANNING WY
400 LKEL 92530 866-G5
41800 RivC 92544 841-F3
CHANSLOR WY
100 BLY 92225 5491-G5
1000 RivC 92225 5491-C6
CHANT ST
- PER 92571 777-H5
CHANTECLER RD
- RivC 92596 929-E1
CHANTEL CT
2400 PER 92570 807-E7
CHANTEL DR
900 COR 92879 743-J1
CHANTEMAR WY
- TEM 92591 958-H3
CHANTICLEER CIR
- COR 92883 773-G6
CHANTICLEER DR
- LQNT 92253 5530-D6
CHANTILLY CIR
3400 RIV 92506 685-F7
40500 TEM 92591 959-D2
CHANTILLY LN
34100 RivC 92544 901-F3
CHANTRY DR
14200 MORV 92553 717-H6
CHANTRY RD
24000 SBdC 92324 646-J5
24000 SBdC 92324 647-A5
E CHANTRY RD
3100 CLTN 92324 647-A5
CHANTRY ST
- FONT 92337 644-H2
CHANUTE AV
- RivC 92518 717-C7
CHAOTE ST
- RivC 92592 979-J2
33200 TEM 92592 979-J2
CHAPALA DR
4900 RIV 92507 686-C7
5200 RIV 92507 716-C1
CHAPARRAL AV
13700 FONT 92337 644-A3
CHAPARRAL CT
36200 YCPA 92399 650-D7
CHAPARRAL DR
100 BLY 92225 5491-E5
100 PDST 92260 818-F5
600 RivC 91752 683-E5
3800 NRCO 92860 713-F4
14300 FONT 92337 644-C3
38400 RivC 92592 930-H6
39500 RivC 92592 960-F1
CHAPARRAL LN
22400 GTER 92313 646-E3
CHAPARRAL RD
- RivC 92503 745-F7
1500 PMSP 92262 756-E6
13100 RivC 92282 724-E2
17300 RivC 92504 745-F6
E CHAPARRAL ST
2700 ONT 91761 683-A1
CHAPARRAL TR
13500 YCPA 92399 650-D6
13700 CALI 92320 650-D7
CHAPARRAL WY
29500 CYNL 92587 867-B2
30500 LKEL 92532 866-J5
CHAPARROSA WY
38500 RivC 92260 818-F2
CHAPEL ST
5900 RIV 92503 714-F3
CHAPEL HILL RD
47600 PDST 92260 848-D4
CHAPELTON DR
43500 RivC 92201 819-H6
CHAPLAN WY
44300 RivC 92590 978-A2
CHAPMAN LN
25000 RivC 92548 808-J6
CHAPMAN PL
3800 RIV 92506 685-F6
CHAPMAN RD
43100 RivC 92539 (965-C6 See Page 964)
44300 RivC 92539 (985-C2 See Page 964)
CHAPMAN ST
11500 LMLN 92354 647-E2
CHAPMAN HEIGHTS RD
33100 YCPA 92399 649-E2
CHAPPAREL WY
500 BAN 92220 721-E3
CHAPPAROSA DR
- RivC 92264 816-F2
CHAPPEL RD
70100 RMIR 92270 817-H1
CHAPPELLET CIR
- RivC 92563 929-A7
- RivC 92563 959-A1

CHAPS CIR
24300 MURR 92562 927-H6
CHAPS LN
15300 FONT 92337 644-E3
CHAR PL
- RMIR 92270 817-H2
CHARA ST
13600 MORV 92553 717-H5
CHARDONEY WY
3000 RivC 91752 643-J4
3000 RivC 91752 644-A5
3300 FONT 92337 643-J4
CHARDONNAY CT
11700 FONT 92337 643-J4
CHARDONNAY PL
700 HEMT 92544 811-F5
39500 MURR 92562 928-B1
CHARDONNAY WY
78800 RivC 92211 819-G1
CHARINA LN
25000 RivC 92548 809-A6
25700 RivC 92548 839-A1
CHARING RD
12900 MORV 92553 716-J4
CHARLEE CT
15100 MORV 92551 747-J1
CHARLEE ANN LN
44100 RivC 92539 (965-D7 See Page 964)
CHARLENE WY
30500 RivC 92544 871-C3
CHARLES AV
6300 RivC 91752 683-H6
CHARLES CT
26600 RivC 92544 841-C2
CHARLES ST
- PMSP 92262 756-G3
- BAN 92220 722-B4
3100 RIV 92501 685-J2
3100 RIV 92501 686-A2
35600 RivC 92595 897-D7
CHARLES GABRIEL CIR
16700 RivC 92518 746-J4
CHARLESTON DR
10400 RIV 92503 744-G2
CHARLESTOWN AV
82700 INDO 92201 5470-G2
CHARLESTOWN DR
27600 RivC 92586 838-B4
CHARLESWORTH DR
38000 CTHC 92234 817-D2
CHARLETTE LN
24300 RivC 92585 808-G5
CHARLEY CT
26800 MORV 92555 688-A7
CHARLOIS DR
36000 RivC 92596 899-F7
CHARLOTTE DR
44200 RivC 92544 842-A1
CHARLOTTE LN
- RivC 92509 684-D4
CHARLOTTE WY
4800 RIV 92504 685-D6
4800 RIV 92506 685-D6
CHARLTON AV
42700 RivC 92544 811-G6
42800 HEMT 92544 811-G6
E CHARLTON AV
4000 HEMT 92544 811-F6
CHARMES CT
- TEM 92592 979-G1
CHARMIN CIR
500 HEMT 92544 811-F6
CHARRO RD
16700 RivC 92530 896-A5
CHARTER OAK LN
9500 RIV 92503 745-A1
CHARTWELL DR
700 RIV 92506 715-J5
CHASE AV
2800 RivC 92567 778-F6
CHASE CIR
- COR 92882 773-A3
CHASE DR
100 COR 92881 773-G3
100 COR 92882 773-C2
100 COR 92879 773-D2
1500 COR 92882 772-J3
CHASE RD
3200 RivC 92501 646-A7
3200 RIV 92501 646-A7
CHASE ST
600 SJCT 92582 780-H7
1000 SJCT 92583 780-J6
S CHASE CANYON LN
1700 CLTN 92324 647-A3
CHASE SCHOOL RD
34400 RivC 92276 788-J6
CHASTITY RD
- RivC 92567 779-G3
- SJCT 92567 779-H3
CHATEAU CIR
74800 INDW 92210 848-H2
CHATEAU CT
- RivC 92592 979-H3
1500 SJCT 92583 811-E5
3600 RIV 92505 744-E2
13500 FONT 92337 644-A3
26000 MORV 92555 717-J1
CHATEAU RIDGE LN
- RIV 92506 716-A5
CHATEAU VIEW DR
700 RIV 92506 715-J5
CHATENAY LN
24000 MURR 92562 927-J3

CHATENAY LN
24000 MURR 92562 928-A3
CHATHAM DR
5400 RIV 92506 715-J1
CHATHAM LN
27600 RivC 92585 838-E5
38400 RivC 92544 931-C4
CHATHAM ST
34800 YCPA 92399 649-J4
CHATHAM WY
- PDST 92260 818-G4
700 SJCT 92583 811-C3
CHATSWORTH CT
26200 RivC 92586 868-B1
CHATTERTON LN
2300 NRCO 92860 713-C7
CHAUCER CIR
9000 RIV 92503 715-A6
CHAUCER LN
71700 RMIR 92270 788-B6
CHAUCER RD
- RivC 92584 838-D6
- RivC 92585 838-D6
CHAUCER ST
11400 MORV 92557 686-H7
11400 MORV 92557 716-H1
CHAUDHURI CIR
26500 RivC 92544 841-G1
CHAUMONT
- RivC - (907-E4 See Page 906)
CHAUMONT ST
15100 LKEL 92530 865-G3
CHAUNCEY WY
40400 TEM 92591 959-C1
CHAUNCY PL
2400 RIV 92506 715-J2
CHAVEZ RD
17000 RivC 92508 746-D5
CHECKERBERRY CT
1100 HEMT 92545 840-G3
CHECKMATE RD
36400 RivC 92544 902-F7
36600 RivC 92544 (932-F1 See Page 902)
CHEETAH LN
3000 COR 92882 773-C2
CHEINIA CT
- RivC 92883 835-C5
CHEKHOV DR
1000 RIV 92506 716-C4
CHELBANA WY
15100 MORV 92551 747-H1
CHELESA LN
33400 RivC 92595 897-D3
CHELSEA AV
1600 RDL 92373 647-H2
CHELSEA CIR
100 PDST 92260 848-D2
CHELSEA CT
- MURR 92562 898-C7
24800 RivC 92544 (812-A4 See Page 782)
CHELSEA PL
900 SJCT 92583 781-A7
CHELSEA ST
22600 MORV 92553 717-B3
CHELSEA WY
- MURR 92562 927-G5
500 COR 92879 744-B2
25800 RivC 92544 811-J7
31500 TEM 92592 979-D3
CHELTENHAM RD
- RivC 92504 745-H7
CHEMIN CHEVALIER
- TEM 92591 959-D3
CHEMIN CLINET
32200 TEM 92591 959-E4
CHEMIN COUTET
- TEM 92591 959-D4
CHEMIN DOMAINE
- TEM 92591 959-D3
CHEMIN LA TACHE
- TEM 92591 959-E4
CHEMIN LAURENT
32200 TEM 92591 959-E4
CHEMIN MARGAUX
41300 TEM 92591 959-E4
CHENIN BLANC CT
41500 TEM 92591 959-E4
CHENOPOD DR
42100 RivC 92544 901-G5
CHEQUERS CT
5100 RIV 92507 686-C7
CHERBOURG AV
3500 LKEL 92530 865-H5
CHERBOURG DR
8800 RIV 92504 715-B6
CHERI WY
25900 MORV 92551 747-J1
CHERIE CT
1300 SJCT 92583 811-D3
CHERIMOYA CIR
11300 FONT 92337 644-G2
CHERIMOYA RD
41200 RivC 92544 931-E7
CHERISH CT
19100 RIV 92508 746-D4
CHEROKEE AV
1700 NRCO 92860 743-C1
CHEROKEE CIR
400 BAN 92220 721-G4
CHEROKEE CT
49500 RivC 92536 963-D1

CHEROKEE PL
2600 NRCO 92860 743-C1
CHEROKEE RD
1400 COR 92881 773-G3
77600 INDW 92210 849-F2
N CHEROKEE RD
- PER 92570 807-E2
S CHEROKEE RD
- PER 92570 807-E3
CHEROKEE ST
- PMSP 92264 786-C2
3200 RIV 92503 744-H1
CHEROKEE WY
2500 PMSP 92264 787-A5
2600 PMSP 92264 786-J6
CHERRY AV
800 BEAU 92223 721-A2
2600 BEAU 92223 691-A7
7800 RivC 92223 691-A4
10500 SBdC 92337 644-C2
10900 FONT 92337 644-C2
21400 RivC 92570 807-A7
CHERRY CV
15800 RivC 92262 725-E7
CHERRY DR
1300 HEMT 92545 840-G3
CHERRY LN
500 BEAU 92223 720-J3
1100 CALI 92320 689-H1
CHERRY ST
- COR 92881 773-D4
- MURR 92562 958-E3
- MURR 92563 928-H7
- MURR 92563 958-H1
- MURR 92590 958-D5
- RivC 92590 958-D5
- TEM 92590 958-E3
- TEM 92591 928-H7
- TEM 92591 958-H1
300 BAN 92220 722-C1
800 RIV 92507 686-D4
11800 RivC 91752 683-F6
33600 RivC 92595 897-C4
CHERRYBARK LN
2700 COR 92881 773-D2
CHERRY BLOSSOM LN
300 LKEL 92530 865-G1
CHERRY CROFT DR
11100 YCPA 92399 650-C1
CHERRY ESTATES CT
38700 RivC 92223 690-G3
CHERRYGROVE CT
- TEM 92591 928-H7
- TEM 92591 958-H1
CHERRY HILL AV
6300 BAN 92220 721-C4
CHERRY HILL DR
- MURR 92563 928-J5
CHERRYHILL DR
4900 RIV 92507 686-B7
CHERRY HILLS
80500 LQNT 92253 5530-B4
CHERRY HILLS BLVD
25600 RivC 92586 837-J6
25600 RivC 92586 838-A6
CHERRY HILLS CT
1000 RivC 92882 742-G5
CHERRY HILLS DR
- RMIR 92270 788-C5
5000 PMSP 92264 787-B5
10500 RivC 92223 691-C5
CHERRY OAK RD
39400 RivC 92223 690-J2
CHERRY OAK CANYON RD
39400 RivC 92223 690-J1
CHERRY PARK DR
39000 RivC 92223 690-H3
CHERRYSTONE AV
38500 RivC 92223 690-G2
CHERRYTREE DR
1800 PER 92571 777-H7
CHERRY TREE LN
34200 YCPA 92399 649-H4
36200 CALI 92320 690-B6
CHERRY TREE RD
39200 RivC 92223 690-H2
CHERRY VALLEY BLVD
10500 RivC 92223 691-A4
36000 CALI 92320 690-C5
36000 RivC 92320 690-C5
37200 RivC 92223 690-C5
CHERRY VALLEY ACRES
500 BEAU 92223 690-H6
CHERRY VISTA DR
400 PER 92571 807-H1
CHERRYWOOD AV
200 RIV 92506 716-D5
CHERRYWOOD CIR
1400 COR 92881 773-F4
CHERRYWOOD DR
12000 FONT 92337 644-B4
25900 RivC 92544 811-D7
36100 YCPA 92399 650-C5
37800 MURR 92562 927-E3
CHERRYWOOD LN
32700 LKEL 92530 896-G4
E CHERRYWOOD LN
1700 CLTN 92324 646-G1
CHERT RD
45300 RivC 92536 (984-A3 See Page 964)
CHERVIL CT
13800 MORV 92553 717-J5

CHERYL DR
29300 RivC 92587 867-F2
CHERYL ST
42800 HEMT 92544 811-H6
CHERYL WY
3500 RIV 92506 715-F1
CHESAPEAKE LN
8700 RIV 92508 746-H2
CHESAPEAKE RD
11900 MORV 92557 717-C1
CHESAPEAKE WY
1800 COR 92880 743-A1
CHESHIRE DR
13400 MORV 92553 717-E5
CHESLEY CT
5200 RIV 92505 714-B5
CHESTER ST
6000 RIV 92504 685-A7
64100 RivC 92240 696-D5
CHESTERFIELD RD
8400 RIV 92508 746-H2
CHESTER MORRISON WY
27000 RivC 92584 868-C3
CHESTNUT AV
400 BEAU 92223 720-J3
CHESTNUT CIR
- COR 92881 773-G3
CHESTNUT DR
1300 SJCT 92583 780-H7
3400 NRCO 92860 713-A6
26300 RivC 92544 841-D1
CHESTNUT LN
1800 COR 92881 773-G1
CHESTNUT ST
2900 RIV 92501 685-G4
8400 COR 92883 774-A6
N CHESTNUT ST
100 LKEL 92530 866-E5
S CHESTNUT ST
100 LKEL 92530 866-E5
CHESTNUT WY
47500 INDO 92201 5470-C3
CHETLEE LN
22400 RivC 92595 897-C5
CHEVIOT CT
77500 PDST 92211 819-E3
CHEVY LN
15100 RivC 92570 805-F6
CHEVY CHASE RD
26200 RivC 92586 838-B7
CHEYENNE CIR
400 BAN 92220 721-G4
24800 RivC 92595 927-H1
33200 RivC 92584 898-G2
CHEYENNE CT
49900 RivC 92536 963-E4
CHEYENNE DR
77300 INDW 92210 819-E7
CHEYENNE RD
800 COR 92880 742-H1
900 COR 92860 742-H1
900 NRCO 92860 742-H1
2900 RIV 92506 715-G2
47000 INDO 92201 5470-D3
CHEYENNE TR
40700 RivC 92223 691-B4
CHEYENNE WY
1500 RDL 92373 647-J2
CHIA CIR
46500 INDO 92201 5470-F2
CHIA DR
47800 PDST 92260 848-E4
CHIA LN
70700 RivC - 908-A3
CHIA PL
67200 CTHC 92234 787-B1
CHIA RD
3600 PMSP 92262 756-J6
E CHIA RD
600 PMSP 92262 756-E6
CHIA TR
28300 RivC 92544 841-G5
47800 RivC 92536 982-J1
CHIANTE CT
13300 MORV 92553 717-D5
CHIANTI
- INDW 92210 819-B6
CHIANTI CIR
- MURR 92562 928-B4
CHICA RD
2500 SDCo 92028 998-J3
CHICAGO AV
1200 RIV 92507 686-B7
4800 RIV 92506 686-B7
5200 RIV 92506 716-B2
5200 RIV 92507 716-B2
7800 RivC 92508 716-B7
10900 RivC 92508 746-B1
16500 RivC 92504 746-B4
24500 RivC 92544 811-J6
24500 RivC 92583 811-J6
CHICAGO ST
600 COR 92882 773-C2
CHICK RD
- RivC 410-L4
CHICKADEE CIR
200 RivC 92507 646-E6
CHICKADEE LN
52500 RivC - (813-J5 See Page 782)
CHICKADEE WY
53700 RivC - 844-B1
CHICKASAW CT
49500 RivC 92536 963-D1

CHICKASAW PASG
10200 RIV 92503 744-H1
CHICKORY DR
18500 RivC 92504 776-A1
CHICO CIR
1500 PMSP 92264 786-F6
67000 RivC 92241 727-A5
CHICO DR
2000 PMSP 92264 786-G6
17000 RivC 92570 806-A1
CHICO HILLS RD
33400 RivC 92595 897-F2
CHICORY AV
1400 COR 92882 742-G6
CHICORY RD
15800 FONT 92337 644-G3
CHICORY ST
74000 PDST 92260 848-G2
CHIEF LN
11200 MORV 92557 687-C7
CHIEF JOSEPH RD
29600 RivC 92586 868-B2
CHIEFTAN LN
37200 RivC 92544 (932-A1 See Page 902)
CHIFNEY LN
8700 RivC 92509 684-E4
CHILLON HTS
60200 RivC - (907-F3 See Page 906)
CHILTERN WY
3400 COR 92881 773-D4
N CHIMAYO DR
67000 CTHC 92234 757-B6
S CHIMAYO DR
67200 CTHC 92234 757-B6
W CHIMAYO DR
67000 CTHC 92234 757-B6
CHIMAYO RD
31000 RivC 92276 788-J2
CHIMNEY FLATS DR
39700 RivC 92260 818-F3
CHIMNEY ROCK CT
- RivC - (905-E5 See Page 904)
CHIMNEY ROCK DR
- PER 92571 778-B2
CHINA DR
- RivC 92585 838-C3
CHINABERRY ST
12100 YCPA 92399 649-A3
CHINCHE ST
15100 RivC 92530 865-F4
E CHINO AV
2700 ONT 91761 683-A1
W CHINO DR
200 PMSP 92262 786-D1
CHINO LN
700 HEMT 92544 811-C5
CHINO RD
47800 RivC 92220 692-H6
CHINO CANYON RD
600 PMSP 92262 756-B6
W CHINO CANYON RD
300 PMSP 92262 756-D6
CHINO CORONA RD
7900 SBdC 92880 712-E3
16300 SBdC 91710 712-E3
CHINOOK CT
- PER 92571 778-C3
CHINOTTO CIR
900 COR 92881 773-E3
CHINOTTO LN
19500 RIV 92508 746-E3
CHINO VALLEY FRWY Rt#-71
- CHLS - 712-A3
- CHNO - 712-A3
- SBdC - 712-A3
CHIP WY
29800 CYNL 92587 867-D4
CHIPMUNK DR
54400 RivC - 814-D5
CHIPMUNK TR
14900 RivC 92220 721-F7
CHIPPENDALE ST
24800 MORV 92553 717-F6
CHIPPEWA CIR
- COR 92881 773-D4
39800 MURR 92562 928-C3
CHIPPEWA DR
75000 INDW 92210 848-J2
CHIPPEWA RD
18600 RivC 92532 836-D6
CHIPPEWA TR
24000 MORV 92557 687-E7
CHIQUITA CIR
5500 RivC 92509 685-A3
N CHIQUITA CIR
500 PMSP 92262 786-G1
CHIRICAHUA DR
31800 RivC 92276 788-F3
CHISHOLM TR
100 RDL 92373 647-J2
10200 RivC 92223 691-C3
CHISHOLM WY
2700 RIV 92506 715-H1
CHISOLM TR
- MURR 92562 927-G5
CHISOLM TRAIL CIR
1700 COR 92882 772-H1
CHITTENDEN CIR
4100 RivC 92509 685-D3
CHIWI CIR
35300 RivC 92595 897-D6

CHOATE DR
- RivC 92274 5530-H3
CHOCOLATE LILLY LN
16500 RivC 92570 805-J3
CHOCOLATE MOUNTAIN RD
77200 INDW 92210 849-E2
CHOCTA CIR
45300 INDW 92210 849-B1
CHOCTAW CT
800 PER 92570 807-E3
CHOCTAW RD
32000 RivC 92276 788-J2
CHOLAME WY
45600 INDW 92210 849-C2
CHOLLA AV
800 RivC - 5240-A7
CHOLLA CT
39600 MURR 92563 928-E5
CHOLLA DR
9500 DHSP 92240 696-G3
10000 RivC 92240 696-G3
14400 MORV 92553 717-G6
72300 PDST 92260 818-C7
CHOLLA LN
- PDST 92260 848-C6
40000 RMIR 92270 818-D4
CHOLLA PL
2900 PMSP 92264 786-H6
CHOLLA RD
13100 RivC 92282 724-F2
49500 RivC 92260 848-A6
CHOLLA ST
- INDO 92201 5470-H3
CHOLLA TR
13000 YCPA 92399 650-E6
CHOLLA WY
71200 RivC 92260 848-B6
CHRIS CIR
28500 RivC 92532 836-E7
CHRIS CT
9000 RivC 92509 684-D1
CHRIS DR
38000 CTHC 92234 817-D2
CHRIS RD
38500 RivC 92544 (932-F4 See Page 902)
CHRIS ALLEN WY
46500 RivC 92536 982-H4
46700 RivC 92536 983-A4
CHRISTA CT
- PDST 92260 818-F4
CHRISTIAN ST
42500 PDST 92260 818-H6
CHRISTIANE CIR
3000 HEMT 92545 810-F5
CHRISTIE DR
1400 RIV 92507 716-G1
CHRISTIE ST
600 BAN 92220 722-A2
CHRISTINA CT
15000 LKEL 92530 865-H3
CHRISTINA RD
- COAC 92236 5471-A5
E CHRISTINA WY
1000 PMSP 92262 756-F6
CHRISTINE AV
7400 RivC 92509 644-H7
7400 RivC 92509 684-H1
CHRISTINE LN
31000 RivC 92567 779-A4
CHRISTINE ST
33100 RivC 92596 899-C2
CHRISTMAS TREE LN
19000 RivC 92570 806-E4
CHRISTO CT
20400 RivC 92570 775-G5
CHRISTOPHER CT
25500 RivC 92544 (812-A6 See Page 782)
43100 RivC 92220 691-G6
CHRISTOPHER LN
- COR 92881 773-G5
33800 RivC 92595 897-A4
CHRISTOPHER PL
8900 RIV 92503 714-J4
CHRISTY DR
5300 BAN 92220 721-D3
CHRISTY WY
- MURR 92562 927-F3
- RivC 92276 788-C2
CHRYSANTHEMUM WY
76600 PDST 92211 819-C2
CHUBBY DR
37400 RivC 92592 930-F4
CHUCKAWALLA TR
19300 RivC 92241 727-C4
CHUCKAWALLA WY
71700 RivC 92260 848-B5
CHUCK WAGON CT
- PER 92571 778-B2
CHUCKWAGON CT
34900 RivC 92276 788-H5
CHUCKWALLA RD
75700 RivC 92276 789-A2
E CHUCKWALLA RD
300 PMSP 92262 756-E6
CHUCKWALLA SPRINGS RD
- RivC - 411-F2
CHUCKWALLA VALLEY RD
- RivC - 391-F10
CHUKAR LN
12300 MORV 92555 718-A2

CHULA VISTA DR
28000 RivC 92586 838-D6
CHULA VISTA WY
10000 RIV 92503 684-E7
E CHUMASH AV
2000 CLTN 92324 646-H2
CHUMASH CT
8800 RivC 92509 684-E1
CHUPAROSA DR
51200 COAC 92236 5471-E7
CHUPEROSA LN
37300 CTHC 92234 817-E2
CHUPEROSA RD
2700 PMSP 92262 756-G4
CHURCH ST
20500 RivC 92570 776-H5
21700 RivC 92570 777-A5
87000 RivC 92274 5531-G4
W CHURCH ST
900 RivC 92507 646-C6
CHURCHILL CT
30200 TEM 92591 959-A5
CHURCHILL DR
11200 RIV 92503 744-E2
CHURCHILL LN
- RMIR 92270 817-J3
- RMIR 92270 818-A3
CHURCHILL ST
33000 LKEL 92530 896-C3
33000 RivC 92530 896-C3
CHURCHILL DOWNS PKWY
- RivC - (935-J1 See Page 904)
- RivC - (936-A1 See Page 906)
CIALEK LN
34200 RivC 92567 809-H1
CIBOLA CIR
36000 RivC 92592 960-D4
N CIBOLA CIR
900 PMSP 92262 756-G7
CICCOTTI ST
26700 RivC 92584 898-C2
CIDRA
- LQNT 92253 849-J7
CIEGA CREEK DR
39000 RivC 92260 818-F2
CIEGO DR
79700 RivC 92201 819-J5
79700 RivC 92201 5410-A5
CIELITO DR
28700 RivC 92530 835-F7
28700 RivC 92530 865-F1
45400 INDW 92210 849-A2
CIELO CT
- RivC 92254 5592-F5
W CIELO DR
1000 PMSP 92262 756-C6
CIELO LN
11500 LMLN 92354 647-D2
CIELO AZUL WY
13400 DHSP 92240 697-B5
CIELO DE AZUL
43300 TEM 92592 959-A7
CIELO MESA
30000 TEM 92592 959-A7
CIELO VISTA
200 CTHC 92234 787-E5
CIELO VISTA RD
32200 CTHC 92234 787-E3
CIELO VISTA WY
21200 RivC 92595 897-B6
CIENEGA DR
32800 YCPA 92399 649-E5
CIENEGA PL
40700 RivC 92201 819-G4
CILURZO RD
34500 RivC 92592 959-J3
34500 RivC 92592 960-A3
CIMARRON CT
69500 CTHC 92234 757-G7
CIMARRON DR
2400 HEMT 92545 840-G2
CIMARRON LN
800 COR 92879 743-H2
CIMARRON PL
900 COR 92879 743-H2
CIMARRON RD
2800 RIV 92506 715-G2
16100 LKEL 92530 865-H2
37100 RivC 92544 931-H1
45500 INDO 92201 5470-C1
69600 CTHC 92234 757-G7
CIMARRON TR
10300 RivC 92223 691-C4
CIMARRON WY
67500 CTHC 92234 757-C7
CIMMARON CANYON
- RivC 92203 789-G6
- RivC 92211 789-G6
S CINDEE LN
1300 CLTN 92324 646-H2
CINDY CIR
1800 COR 92882 743-C7
CINDY CT
- LQNT 92253 849-H1
300 COR 92882 743-C7
CINDY LN
2700 HEMT 92545 810-F7
10500 RIV 92505 714-D3
CINNA CIR
71200 RivC 92254 (5653-H4 See Page 5592)

CINNABAR DR
6300 RivC 92509 645-B7
6300 RivC 92509 685-A1
CINNABAR WY
500 PER 92571 777-J7
CINNAMON DR
14600 FONT 92337 644-D4
CINNAMON LN
1000 COR 92882 742-F5
CINNAMON CREEK CT
23500 MORV 92557 717-D1
CINNAMON TEAL DR
30300 CYNL 92587 867-E3
CINON DR
32700 TEM 92592 979-G3
CIPRESSO CIR
41100 MURR 92562 927-H3
CIRCELI WY
300 HEMT 92545 810-F7
CIRCLE DR
- RivC 92373 689-B4
1500 RivC - 5240-A6
18900 SBdC 92316 645-F3
23600 RivC 92587 837-E6
24800 LMLN 92354 647-B1
43700 INDO 92201 5410-G6
N CIRCLE DR
54200 RivC - 814-D6
S CIRCLE DR
54000 RivC - 814-E6
CIRCLE DR E
43700 INDO 92201 5410-G6
CIRCLE DR W
43600 INDO 92201 5410-G6
CIRCLE LN
1600 RDL 92373 647-J3
CIRCLE TER
32300 RivC 92373 689-C4
CIRCLE WY
52200 RivC - 814-E6
CIRCLE A DR
- PDST 92260 848-C6
CIRCLE B DR
20000 RivC 92241 727-A5
CIRCLE C RD
- BEAU 92223 389-F7
- BEAU 92223 721-C7
- BEAU 92583 389-F7
CIRCLE CITY DR
700 COR 92879 743-E6
CIRCLE D CT
41100 RivC 92592 960-B4
CIRCLE FIVE DR
33600 RivC 92567 809-G4
CIRCLE HILL DR
40100 MURR 92562 928-D4
CIRCLE LAZY J RD
4500 RIV 92501 685-G2
CIRCLE M
41300 RivC 92592 959-H4
CIRCLE OF THE PEPPERS
16800 RivC 92570 775-H4
CIRCLE VIEW DR
5400 RIV 92505 714-A5
25300 RivC - 814-E6
CIRCLING HAWK DR
17000 RivC 92570 806-A2
CIRCULO CAVINARA
42400 MURR 92562 927-H6
CIRCULO MARAGO
42300 MURR 92562 927-J7
CIRCULO SAN SORRENTO
1000 PMSP 92262 756-E3
CIRCUS DR
- RivC 92585 838-C3
CIRRUS WY
900 SJCT 92582 780-H6
4100 RIV 92503 714-G5
CIRVELO ST
17200 RivC 92530 896-B3
S CISCO ST
800 CLTN 92324 646-G1
CISSNA RD
19500 RivC 92530 896-G5
CITA AV
15900 RivC 92504 745-G4
CITADEL
- RMIR 92270 818-B3
CITADEL CT
7900 RIV 92503 714-G4
CITADEL ST
24800 MORV 92551 747-G3
CITATION AV
29000 RivC 92585 808-G7
CITATION CIR
200 COR 92880 742-H4
CITATION CT
52000 LQNT 92253 879-G1
CITATION DR
2400 NRCO 92860 713-F6
CITRICADO LN
- RIV 92508 716-C7
- RIV 92508 746-C1
CITROCADO RANCH ST
- COR 92879 773-D2
CITRON ST
100 COR 92882 743-A7
E CITRON ST
300 COR 92879 743-D7
CITRUS
78800 LQNT 92253 849-H7
79100 LQNT 92253 879-J1
79100 LQNT 92253 5470-A7

CITRUS
79100 LQNT 92253 5530-A1
CITRUS AV
- PER 92571 777-H6
900 PER 92571 778-A6
900 RivC 92507 646-B7
900 RIV 92507 646-B7
10600 FONT 92337 644-G3
10700 SBdC 92337 644-G2
23700 RivC 92570 777-E6
27100 RivC 92571 778-C6
45600 INDO 92201 5470-H1
CITRUS CT
72700 PDST 92260 848-D3
CITRUS DR
4200 RIV 92507 686-D6
CITRUS ST
- RivC 92567 779-B2
600 BEAU 92223 690-J6
13100 RivC 92880 713-B2
14000 RivC 92230 723-D4
CITRUS WY
700 COR 92882 773-C2
CITRUS GLEN CIR
2000 RivC 92503 744-H4
CITRUS GLEN LN
16000 FONT 92337 644-G3
CITRUS GROVE CT
- RivC 92504 745-E3
CITRUS GROVE RD
19500 RIV 92508 746-E3
CITRUS HEIGHTS RD
42100 RivC 92592 960-C5
CITRUS HILL RD
24100 RivC 92595 897-G3
CITRUS PARK CIR
- RivC 92503 745-D3
CITRUS VALLEY AV
- RivC 92880 713-A1
CITRUS VIEW CIR
16000 RivC 92504 745-H3
CITRUS VIEW DR
43700 RivC 92544 842-A4
CITRUS WOOD LN
2000 RivC 92503 744-J4
CITY CENTER CT
22500 GTER 92313 646-E4
CITY COLLEGE DR
3400 RIV 92506 685-G6
CITY VIEW CIR
7000 RIV 92506 716-D5
CIVETTA LN
5300 RIV 92505 714-C5
CIVIC DR
100 PMSP 92262 786-H1
CIVIC DR W
400 PMSP 92262 786-H1
CIVIC CENTER DR
100 INDO 92201 5470-G1
CLADEL WY
35400 MURR 92562 898-C7
CLAIBORNE AV
- BEAU 92223 720-G2
CLAIR CT
100 BAN 92220 721-D3
CLAIRE AV
66000 RivC 92240 726-H1
CLAIRE RD
20900 RivC 92570 837-A7
21100 RivC 92570 836-J7
CLAIRE ST
300 RivC 92501 646-B6
CLANCY LN
72200 RMIR 92270 818-C5
CLANCY LN S
- RMIR 92270 818-C5
CLARA CT
11200 RIV 92505 714-B2
CLARA PL
23500 RivC 92587 837-E7
CLARA VISTA LN
10200 RIV 92503 714-F6
10400 RIV 92505 714-F6
CLARE WY
- HEMT 92545 810-H5
CLAREMONT AV
10600 SBdC 92316 645-F1
20500 RivC 92507 716-G1
CLAREMONT ST
33100 RivC 92595 927-C2
38000 RivC 92562 927-C2
CLARENCE ST
14800 RivC 92240 697-C7
CLARENDON CT
6100 RIV 92506 716-B3
CLARET CV
- LQNT 92253 879-F1
CLARETA DR
35100 CTHC 92234 787-C6
CLARICE ST
25100 RivC 92324 687-G2
CLARIDGE DR
5900 RIV 92506 716-C2
CLARIDGE PL
- PDST 92260 818-G4
CLARION CT
- YCPA 92399 649-E2
CLARISSA RD
19000 RivC 92570 776-D7
19500 RivC 92570 806-F1
CLARK AV
2600 NRCO 92860 713-D6
12900 FONT 92337 643-H3
CLARK DR
40200 RivC 92544 841-C1

STREET	Block	City	ZIP	Pg-Grid
CLARK LN				
	33900	YCPA	92399	649-G4
CLARK PL				
	28300	RivC	92587	837-F6
CLARK RD				
	72400	RivC	92241	728-B3
CLARK ST				
	900	RivC	92501	646-A7
	900	RivC	92501	686-A1
	1000	RIV	92501	686-A1
	5800	ONT	91761	643-H3
	11600	MORV	92557	716-J1
	16000	RivC	92518	746-J4
	17600	RivC	92570	746-J7
	18400	RivC	92570	776-J1
	20800	RIV	92508	746-J4
CLARK TR				
	-	SDCo	92028	976-A3
CLARKE CT				
	-	RivC	92508	716-B7
CLARKE RD				
	2500	PMSP	92262	756-G5
CLARKSDALE DR				
	4400	RIV	92505	714-D7
CLASSIC WY				
	45500	TEM	92592	979-C4
CLASSICO WY				
	1500	COR	92882	742-G7
CLAUBART CT				
	5600	RivC	92509	684-E4
CLAUDETTE DR				
	7900	RivC	92509	684-G6
CLAUDETTE COLBERT RD				
	100	RMIR	92270	817-G4
CLAUDIA ST				
	2300	COR	92882	773-B1
	42500	PDST	92260	818-H5
CLAUDINE ST				
	14700	MORV	92553	717-F7
CLAVEL CT				
	-	PDST	92260	818-H7
CLAY CT				
	72900	PDST	92260	848-E4
CLAY RD				
	52400	RivC	92282	694-D7
	52500	RivC	92282	724-D1
CLAY ST				
	6000	RivC	92509	684-F5
	24700	MURR	92562	927-J7
	24900	MURR	92562	928-A7
CLAY CANYON DR				
	8900	RivC	92883	804-B3
CLAY CANYON RD				
	10300	RivC	92883	804-F3
CLAYCROFT LN				
	11800	RIV	92505	714-A4
CLAYMORE CT				
	1400	RIV	92507	716-F2
CLAYSTONE AV				
	23000	RivC	92883	804-C3
CLAYTON ST				
	400	NRCO	92860	713-G3
	800	PER	92570	807-D4
	800	RivC	92570	807-D4
CLAYVILLE WY				
	-	COR	92882	772-J2
CLEAR CT				
	2600	BAN	92220	721-H4
CLEARBROOK CT				
	28600	RivC	92584	868-F1
CLEARBROOK DR				
	500	COR	92880	743-C3
E CLEAR CREEK LN				
	1500	CLTN	92324	646-G1
CLEAR LAKE RD				
	3100	ONT	91761	643-B5
CLEAR LAKE ST				
	100	PER	92571	777-H7
CLEAR LIGHT RD				
	40400	TEM	92591	959-D2
CLEAR SKY WY				
	38400	RivC	92211	819-G1
CLEAR SPRING WY				
	17300	RivC	92503	744-F5
CLEAR SPRINGS DR				
	700	COR	92879	743-J2
CLEARVIEW CIR				
	-	COR	92882	772-J2
CLEARVIEW DR				
	25800	RivC	92544	811-E7
CLEARVIEW PL				
	8600	RivC	92509	684-E1
CLEARVIEW WY				
	19000	RivC	92530	896-F5
CLEARWATER DR				
	-	COR	92880	742-H3
	600	PER	92571	777-J7
	24600	MORV	92551	747-F3
CLEAR WATER DR				
	29900	CYNL	92587	867-E2
CLEARWATER RD				
	8800	SDCo	92028	998-J7
	8800	SDCo	92028	999-A7
CLEARWATER WY				
	15700	RivC	92262	725-E7
CLEAR WELL RD				
	75600	RivC	92276	788-H5
CLEARWOOD AV				
	200	RIV	92506	716-D5
CLEARY ST				
	-	RivC	92584	868-D3
CLEEK PL				
	6000	PMSP	92264	787-C5
CLEGHORN DR				
	700	COR	92879	743-H3
CLEMENT RD				
	24900	RivC	-	814-A4
CLEMENT ST				
	29600	LKEL	92530	865-J2
CLEMENTE AV				
	25300	RivC	92548	809-A7
CLEMENTE GARDEN LN				
	26000	RivC	92544	811-G7
CLEMENTINE DR				
	-	RivC	92880	713-A2
CLEMENTS WY				
	39600	MURR	92563	928-H7
CLEMSON CT				
	13700	MORV	92555	718-E5
CLEMSON ST				
	-	RMIR	92270	818-A2
CLEMSON WY				
	1300	RIV	92507	686-G1
CLETA DR				
	5500	RIV	92505	714-C4
CLEVELAND				
	-	CTHC	92234	787-A7
CLEVELAND AV				
	-	COR	92881	773-C5
	2500	RIV	92504	715-E6
	5400	ONT	91761	683-C3
	5400	RivC	92880	683-C5
	7000	RivC	92880	713-D2
	8900	RIV	92503	715-C7
	8900	RIV	92503	745-A1
	8900	RIV	92504	745-A1
	9900	RIV	92503	744-G3
	10700	RivC	92503	744-G3
	32400	RivC	92584	867-J7
CLEVELAND CT				
	1100	LKEL	92530	865-H4
CLEVELAND ST				
	96700	RivC	92254	(5653-J5 See Page 5592)
CLEVELAND WY				
	100	COR	92881	773-C5
CLEVELAND FOREST RD				
	17900	RivC	92562	956-B6
CLIFF CT				
	-	RivC	92567	779-B7
	6200	RIV	92506	715-G1
CLIFF ST				
	79000	RivC	92201	819-H4
CLIFFHILL PL				
	100	RivC	92501	646-B6
CLIFFORD ST				
	6600	RIV	92504	715-B1
	42500	PDST	92260	818-J6
CLIFFROSE CT				
	14900	MORV	92553	717-F7
CLIFF ROSE CT				
	60000	RivC	92274	5590-H2
CLIFFROSE DR				
	25500	MURR	92563	928-F4
CLIFFSHIRE AV				
	13100	RivC	92879	744-A5
CLIFFSIDE DR				
	4600	RIV	92506	685-E5
CLIFF TOP CT				
	27800	RivC	92585	838-E6
CLIFF VALLEY CIR				
	5600	RivC	92509	684-D4
CLIFFWOOD CT				
	-	RIV	92505	744-C1
CLIFFWOOD TR				
	24100	RivC	92590	977-G4
CLIFTON BLVD				
	5700	RIV	92504	685-A7
CLIFTON CT				
	25600	MORV	92553	717-H6
CLIFTON ST				
	70500	RivC	92241	727-H3
CLIFTON FORGE ST				
	76500	PDST	92211	819-C6
CLIMBING ROSE DR				
	22400	MORV	92557	717-B1
CLING WY				
	1000	CALI	92320	649-J7
CLINTON AV				
	-	MURR	92563	928-H7
	-	TEM	92591	928-H7
	26000	HEMT	92545	839-G1
	26000	RivC	92545	839-G1
	31800	RivC	92548	839-C1
CLINTON CIR				
	500	COR	92879	743-H3
CLINTON ST				
	43400	INDO	92201	5410-D7
	43500	RivC	92201	5410-D7
	45100	RivC	92201	5470-D2
	45100	INDO	92201	5470-D2
CLINTON KEITH RD				
	24600	MURR	92562	898-D7
	24900	MURR	92562	928-B1
	25600	RivC	92595	897-H7
	25600	RivC	92595	898-A7
	27800	MURR	92563	898-F7
	28900	RivC	92595	927-E2
	29000	RivC	92563	898-H7
	31500	RivC	92562	927-C7
	32300	MURR	92562	927-D4
	38800	RivC	92562	957-C3
CLIO CT				
	4400	RIV	92503	714-J3
CLIPPER CT				
	23200	CYNL	92587	867-E2
CLIVE WY				
	16500	RivC	92570	775-J4
CLOCHE DR				
	-	RivC	92596	899-D7
CLOTHIER RD				
	35000	RivC	92544	901-J5
CLOUDBURST DR				
	13300	RivC	92883	835-B4
CLOUD BURST RD				
	32700	RivC	92595	897-F1
CLOUDBURST TR				
	12400	MORV	92555	718-D2
CLOUD CREST CT				
	32500	RivC	92595	896-J5
CLOUD CREST WY				
	1300	SJCT	92582	780-J6
CLOUDCREST WY				
	2500	RIV	92507	686-D3
CLOUD DANCE CT				
	27700	RivC	92585	838-D5
CLOUD HAVEN DR				
	10800	MORV	92557	687-F6
CLOUDREST WY				
	27200	RivC	92544	841-F3
CLOUD VIEW RD				
	-	RivC	-	(907-C2 See Page 906)
CLOUD VIEW WY				
	78100	LQNT	92253	849-G6
CLOUDY CIR				
	2800	BAN	92220	721-G4
CLOVER AV				
	24100	MORV	92551	747-E1
CLOVER CT				
	-	RIV	92508	746-D3
	1000	HEMT	92545	840-G2
	12800	YCPA	92399	649-E5
CLOVER LN				
	900	COR	92880	743-C2
	3000	ONT	91761	643-B7
	40500	PDST	92260	818-E4
	44700	TEM	92592	979-E3
CLOVER PL				
	3200	ONT	91761	643-B7
	3300	ONT	91761	683-B1
CLOVER ST				
	900	SJCT	92582	810-J2
S CLOVER WY				
	3500	ONT	91761	683-B1
CLOVER CREEK LN				
	-	RivC	92584	867-H1
CLOVER CREST CT				
	-	RivC	92563	929-B7
CLOVERDALE DR				
	14400	FONT	92337	644-C3
CLOVERDALE RD				
	12700	RivC	92880	683-B6
	13700	RivC	92880	388-H5
CLOVERDALE ST				
	1100	RIV	92501	645-H7
CLOVERFIELD RD				
	14700	MORV	92553	717-F7
CLOVERFIELD ST				
	2300	PER	92571	777-J6
CLOVERGLEN CIR				
	25400	MURR	92563	928-E5
CLOVERIDGE WY				
	-	RivC	92203	789-F5
CLOVERLEAF CIR				
	1900	COR	92880	713-A7
CLOVER LEAF PL				
	1300	HEMT	92545	840-E4
CLOVERLEAF WY				
	-	MURR	92562	927-F4
CLOVIS PL				
	6400	RIV	92504	715-C1
CLOWES LN				
	30800	RivC	92584	899-B2
	30800	RivC	92596	899-B2
CLUB AV				
	32500	RivC	92584	897-H1
	32800	RivC	92595	897-H1
	33000	RivC	92584	867-G7
CLUB CIDR				
	-	PMSP	92264	787-C6
CLUB CIR				
	800	CTHC	92234	787-F5
CLUB CT				
	-	RMIR	92270	818-B5
	1100	RIV	92506	716-C2
CLUB DR				
	-	HEMT	92545	810-E7
	21400	RivC	92570	807-A7
	40000	PDST	92211	819-B3
	45300	INDW	92210	849-C2
E CLUB DR				
	400	PMSP	92262	786-E3
W CLUB DR				
	400	PMSP	92262	786-E3
CLUB RD				
	69100	CTHC	92234	787-F6
CLUB CIRCLE DR				
	6000	RivC	92509	684-H5
	12900	DHSP	92240	697-C4
	73700	PDST	92260	848-F2
CLUBHOUSE BLVD				
	8400	RivC	92240	656-E7
	8400	RivC	92240	696-D2
CLUB HOUSE DR				
	-	RivC	-	844-D1
	-	SDCo	92028	998-G5
CLUBHOUSE DR				
	-	NRCO	92860	713-J7
	1900	HEMT	92545	810-G5
	45300	TEM	92592	979-B4
CLUB HOUSE DR				
	67600	RivC	92241	727-B4
CLUB HOUSE RD				
	5700	RivC	92509	684-G4
CLUBHOUSE RD				
	22600	MURR	92562	927-D3
CLUBHOUSE WY				
	40800	PDST	92211	819-C3
CLUB TERRACE DR				
	46200	INDW	92210	849-D2
CLUB VIEW DR				
	-	RivC	92254	(5654-C3 See Page 5594)
	22900	MURR	92562	927-E3
	40000	RMIR	92270	818-A4
CLUB VILLA DR				
	-	INDW	92210	819-B6
CLUNY CIR				
	5100	RIV	92505	714-B6
CLYBOURNE CIR				
	40300	MURR	92562	927-J2
CLYDE WY				
	4500	RivC	92509	684-G1
CLYDESDALE AV				
	9900	RivC	92509	684-B4
CLYDESDALE CT				
	-	NRCO	92860	743-H1
	38600	HEMT	92543	810-H4
E CLYDESDALE ST				
	-	ONT	91761	683-A1
COACH RD				
	500	HEMT	92545	840-H1
COACHELLA DR				
	49000	LQNT	92253	849-F5
COACHELLA CANAL RD				
	-	COAC	92236	390-F11
	-	COAC	92236	5471-G3
	-	RivC	-	410-K2
	-	RivC	-	(5655-D6 See Page 5594)
	-	RivC	92254	5592-H1
	-	RivC	92254	(5593-D5 See Page 5592)
	-	RivC	92254	5594-A7
	-	RivC	92254	(5654-F3 See Page 5594)
	-	RivC	92254	(5655-D6 See Page 5594)
	-	RivC	92274	390-F11
	-	RivC	92274	5592-H1
COACHMAN CIR				
	2100	COR	92881	773-F2
COACHMAN CT				
	49600	RivC	92536	963-D5
COACHMAN LN				
	2000	COR	92881	773-F2
	12100	MORV	92557	717-C2
COAHUILLA ST				
	-	RivC	92254	5592-F6
COAL AV				
	16000	LKEL	92530	835-H7
COAL RD				
	27800	LKEL	92530	835-H6
COALINGA CT				
	29800	RivC	92586	868-B2
COATBRIDGE DR				
	-	RIV	92508	716-E7
COBALT CIR				
	29000	RivC	92584	868-G1
COBALT DR				
	78000	LQNT	92253	819-F7
COBALT WY				
	42000	PDST	92260	818-G5
COBB RD				
	70100	RMIR	92270	817-H1
COBB ST				
	7100	RIV	92503	684-E7
COBBLE DR				
	27100	RivC	92883	835-B5
COBBLE LN				
	1600	HEMT	92543	840-H3
COBBLE CREEK DR				
	-	RivC	92880	713-B1
	22400	MORV	92557	687-B5
COBBLER CT				
	39800	MURR	92562	898-A7
	39800	MURR	92562	928-A1
COBBLESTONE CIR				
	12700	RivC	92503	744-B4
COBBLESTONE LN				
	14700	RivC	92530	865-E4
COBBLESTONE ST				
	29000	RivC	92567	808-G2
COBLE DR				
	-	CTHC	92234	787-E5
COBRA LN				
	15700	MORV	92551	747-G2
COBRE ST				
	15200	RivC	92530	865-F4
COBY CT				
	6300	RIV	92506	715-F1
COCHISE CIR				
	30200	RivC	92563	929-B1
COCHISE DR				
	12100	RIV	92505	744-B2
	12100	RIV	92503	744-B2
COCHISE RD				
	200	PER	92570	807-D3
COCHISE WY				
	45600	INDW	92210	849-B2
COCHITI DR				
	14500	MORV	92553	717-H7
COCHRAN AV				
	10400	RIV	92505	714-E7
	10800	RIV	92505	744-D1
COCHRAN CT				
	64800	RivC	92240	656-F7
COCHRAN DR				
	48900	INDO	92201	5470-E5
COCKATIEL DR				
	23700	MORV	92557	717-D1
COCO CT				
	1200	RIV	92506	715-H5
COCOMO ST				
	-	PMSP	92264	786-C2
COCONINO ST				
	10800	BLY	92225	5491-D4
COCONUT LN				
	26500	MORV	92555	718-A3
COCONUT WY				
	16400	LKEL	92530	865-F1
COCOPAH CIR				
	75500	INDW	92210	849-A2
COCOPAH CT				
	12100	MORV	92557	717-H2
COCOPAH LN				
	4100	RIV	92505	744-C1
COCOPAH TR				
	-	PMSP	92264	786-G6
COCO PALM CT				
	1600	COR	92879	743-J6
COCO PALM DR				
	45700	INDO	92201	5470-C1
COCOPLUM LN				
	32700	CTHC	92234	787-F3
COCOS PALM AV				
	30600	RivC	92548	839-A2
CODORNIZ CIR				
	-	PMSP	92264	787-B7
CODY AV				
	32200	RivC	92276	788-E2
CODY CT				
	2900	RIV	92503	744-G3
COEN LN				
	30300	RivC	92567	778-J5
COEUR D ALENE DR				
	-	INDO	92201	5470-A1
COFER RD				
	42500	RivC	92544	931-H1
COFFEE BERRY CIR				
	23000	RivC	92883	804-B4
E COG HILL CT				
	2900	ONT	91761	643-A6
COG HILL DR				
	-	COR	92883	773-H6
	-	TEM	92591	959-C4
COG HILL RD				
	2100	BAN	92220	721-D6
COGNAC CT				
	1800	SJCT	92583	811-F4
COGNAC LN				
	12700	MORV	92555	717-J3
COGNAC ST				
	-	RivC	92596	929-C1
COLADA CT				
	41500	PDST	92260	818-G4
COLBERN DR				
	1400	COR	92881	773-G3
COLBURN ST				
	28700	RivC	92596	839-F7
COLBY CIR				
	900	COR	92880	743-A1
COLDBROOK LN				
	45000	LQNT	92253	849-G1
COLDBROOK ST				
	16400	MORV	92551	747-G4
S COLD CREEK WY				
	2600	ONT	91761	643-B5
COLD SPRING				
	23600	MORV	92557	687-D7
COLD SPRING CIR				
	17500	RivC	92503	744-G6
COLDSPRINGS LN				
	2600	COR	92882	773-C2
S COLD SPRINGS PL				
	2500	ONT	91761	643-C5
COLD SPRINGS RD				
	24100	RivC	92587	837-F5
COLD SPRINGS WY				
	73100	RivC	92260	818-E2
COLD WATER CT				
	-	COR	92881	773-G3
COLDWATER CT				
	23600	MORV	92557	687-D5
COLE AV				
	900	NRCO	92860	713-F5
	9000	RIV	92508	746-E3
	16700	RivC	92508	746-E6
	18700	RivC	92570	776-E2
COLE ST				
	1200	LKEL	92530	866-G5
	25300	LMLN	92354	647-C1
COLEBRIDGE DR				
	38400	PDST	92211	818-F1
COLE CREEK CT				
	37300	MURR	92562	927-E4
COLEEN ST				
	15400	FONT	92337	644-E2
COLEMAN AV				
	17200	RivC	92530	896-B3
COLEMAN RD				
	46600	RivC	92544	902-C7
COLEMAN ST				
	8100	RIV	92504	715-B4
	11300	MORV	92557	687-G7
COLEVILLE CIR				
	-	COR	92881	773-D4
COLFAX CIR				
	300	COR	92879	743-G4
COLFAX CT				
	6600	RIV	92506	716-B4
COLFAX ST				
	69400	RivC	92254	(5653-B3 See Page 5592)
COLGATE CT				
	26500	RivC	92544	841-E2
	45800	INDO	92201	5470-B1
COLGATE DR				
	-	RMIR	92270	818-B3
COLGATE WY				
	2500	RIV	92507	686-B3
COLIMA LN				
	100	PER	92571	807-H2
COLINA WY				
	5000	RIV	92507	686-C7
COLINA VERDE				
	30300	TEM	92592	959-A7
COLISEUM ST				
	-	PER	92571	807-G1
COLISEUM WY				
	39900	MURR	92562	928-D4
COLLEEN CIR				
	42100	RivC	92592	959-J5
COLLEEN CT				
	300	BLY	92225	5491-E5
	15300	RivC	92508	746-B2
COLLEEN WY				
	39400	RivC	92592	930-C6
COLLEGE AV				
	4900	RIV	92505	714-B5
COLLEGE BLVD				
	20300	RIV	92507	716-F1
	20300	RivC	92507	716-F1
COLLEGE PL				
	4200	RIV	92507	686-D6
E COLLEGE VIEW CIR				
	-	PDST	92211	818-G1
W COLLEGE VIEW CIR				
	-	PDST	92211	818-F1
COLLEGIAN WY				
	41000	RivC	92544	841-D2
COLLEGIATE CIR				
	-	RMIR	92270	818-C4
COLLETT AV				
	300	COR	92879	743-G3
	10700	RIV	92505	714-D7
	11300	RIV	92505	744-C1
COLLIE CT				
	13500	MORV	92555	718-A5
COLLIER AV				
	17500	LKEL	92530	836-A7
	17500	LKEL	92530	866-B1
COLLIER AV Rt#-74				
	18000	LKEL	92530	866-C2
COLLIER UNION DR				
	-	MURR	92563	928-G7
COLLINGSWOOD DR				
	11700	MORV	92557	717-C1
COLLINGWOOD ST				
	2800	RIV	92504	715-E4
COLLINS ST				
	6000	RivC	92509	684-E5
COLMAR LN				
	23900	MURR	92562	927-J3
	23900	MURR	92562	928-A3
COLOGNE DR				
	24800	RivC	92544	(812-A5 See Page 782)
COLOMA WY				
	6500	RivC	92509	645-A7
COLOMBARD CT				
	13500	FONT	92337	644-A4
COLONIAL				
	-	LQNT	92253	5530-A6
COLONIAL AV				
	6300	BAN	92220	721-C5
COLONIAL CIR				
	3700	LKEL	92530	865-H3
COLONIAL CT				
	17600	CHLS	91709	712-A5
	41900	TEM	92591	959-D5
COLONIAL DR				
	-	RMIR	92270	788-B5
	800	RivC	92882	742-G5
	6000	RIV	92506	685-F7
	30400	CTHC	92234	787-G1
	73100	RivC	92276	788-E2
COLONIAL WY				
	1300	SJCT	92583	811-C3
COLONY DR				
	40000	MURR	92562	928-A2
COLONY PL				
	9000	RIV	92503	714-H3
COLONY RD				
	13500	RivC	92240	696-D5
COLONY WY				
	-	COR	92881	773-G3
	-	PMSP	92262	756-F6
COLONY UNION ST				
	-	MURR	92563	928-G6
COLORADO AV				
	8300	RIV	92504	715-A2
	8400	RIV	92504	714-H4
	8700	RIV	92503	714-H4
COLORADO CT				
	71000	RMIR	92270	788-A7
COLORADO DR				
	700	HEMT	92544	811-G5
COLORADO ST				
	13000	YCPA	92399	649-F5
COLORADO RIVER RD				
	3800	ONT	91761	643-C6
	4900	RivC	-	392-D9
COLT AV				
	15400	FONT	92337	644-F2
COLT CT				
	-	TEM	92590	958-E5
COLT DR				
	26500	RivC	92883	835-B4
COLT LN				
	5400	RivC	92509	684-B3
COLT RD				
	35700	RivC	92592	900-J6
	35700	RivC	92592	901-A5
COLT ST				
	18500	RivC	92508	746-C3
	44800	RivC	92544	(932-D5 See Page 902)
E COLT WY				
	2900	ONT	91761	643-A7
COLUMBARD DR				
	2000	PMSP	92264	786-G5
COLUMBIA AV				
	300	RIV	92507	686-B1
	2000	RIV	92501	686-A1
	3400	RIV	92501	685-J1
	3900	RIV	92501	645-H7
	12200	YCPA	92399	649-G4
	28200	RivC	92596	839-F7
	80700	INDO	92201	5470-B1
COLUMBIA CIR				
	3700	COR	92881	773-H5
COLUMBIA CT				
	11800	LMLN	92354	647-G3
COLUMBIA DR				
	-	RMIR	92270	818-A2
COLUMBIA ST				
	25800	RivC	92544	811-D7
	25800	HEMT	92544	811-D7
	26100	RivC	92544	841-D2
N COLUMBIA ST				
	100	HEMT	92544	811-D7
COLUMBIA UNION DR				
	-	MURR	92563	928-G6
COLUMBINE CT				
	300	PER	92570	807-F2
COLUMBINE DR				
	-	PDST	92260	818-H6
COLUMBO ST				
	11700	MORV	92557	716-J1
COLUMBUS				
	-	BLY	92225	5491-E4
COLUMBUS AV				
	6100	RIV	92504	684-J7
	6100	RIV	92504	685-A7
COLUMBUS DR				
	26100	RivC	92586	868-B1
COLUMBUS LN				
	-	INDO	92201	5470-D4
COLUNGA ST				
	2000	CLTN	92324	646-H1
COLUSA CT				
	-	RIV	92504	715-B5
COLVER CT				
	43500	TEM	92592	979-B1
COLVIN RD				
	-	SJCT	92567	780-A6
COMANCHE AV				
	10300	RIV	92503	744-G1
COMANCHE CIR				
	10000	RivC	92223	691-B3
	30400	CYNL	92587	867-F3
COMANCHE CT				
	-	RivC	92223	650-H7
	-	RivC	92399	650-H7
	2300	NRCO	92860	713-D4
	49900	RivC	92536	963-E4
COMANCHE LN				
	76900	INDW	92210	849-D1
COMARAGO CT				
	-	COR	92883	773-H6
COMBERTON ST				
	34900	YCPA	92399	649-J2
	34900	YCPA	92399	650-A2
COMBINE CIR				
	24400	RivC	92595	897-G2
COMBS WY				
	-	COR	92882	773-A2
COMER AV				
	3300	RIV	92507	685-J5
COMET				
	-	PMSP	92264	786-J5
COMET AV				
	-	SBdC	91710	712-F3
	16900	SBdC	92880	712-F3
COMET CT				
	5400	RivC	91752	683-H3
	22300	RivC	92570	806-H2
COMFORT CT				
	24300	MORV	92553	717-F7
COMISKEY CT				
	1200	PER	92571	807-G1
COMMANCHE ST				
	43300	INDO	92203	5410-H6
COMMERCE CT				
	-	LQNT	92253	849-H2
	29800	RivC	92563	929-A6
COMMERCE DR				
	-	PER	92571	777-G3
COMMERCE LN				
	1500	SJCT	92543	811-A4
	1500	SJCT	92583	811-A4
S COMMERCE PKWY				
	300	ONT	91761	643-C2
COMMERCE ST				
	-	RivC	92254	(5654-D5 See Page 5594)
	1500	COR	92880	742-J4
	1500	COR	92880	743-A4
	1700	NRCO	92860	743-D1
	3000	RIV	92507	685-J4
	45100	INDO	92201	5410-H7
	45100	INDO	92201	5470-H1
COMMERCE WY				
	10500	FONT	92337	643-J1
	21900	GTER	92313	646-D4
COMMERCE CENTER DR				
	-	MORV	92553	717-A7
	-	RivC	92553	717-A7
	23000	RivC	92570	777-C1
	27400	TEM	92590	958-G4
COMMERCIAL AV				
	-	RivC	92507	646-C6
COMMERCIAL RD				
	500	PMSP	92262	756-H7
	500	PMSP	92262	786-H1
	68300	CTHC	92234	787-D7
E COMMERCIAL RD				
	300	SBDO	92408	647-A1
COMMERCIAL ST				
	-	PER	92570	807-H4
	100	BLY	92225	5491-E7
	200	BLY	92225	5551-E1
COMMONS VALLEY DR				
	38500	RivC	92260	818-E2
COMMONWEALTH AV				
	100	SJCT	92583	811-B4
	500	HEMT	92543	811-A4
	500	SJCT	92543	811-A4
	37100	HEMT	92545	810-E4
	38500	HEMT	92543	810-E4
COMMONWEALTH PL				
	3400	RIV	92503	744-D3
COMMUNICATIONS CENTER DR				
	100	RIV	92506	716-C5
COMMUNTY COLLEGE DR				
	500	SJCT	92583	781-A6
	700	SJCT	92583	780-J6
COMO CIR				
	-	PDST	92211	819-A4
COMO CT				
	-	LQNT	92253	819-G6
COMO ST				
	18900	LKEL	92530	896-F2
	20500	RivC	92595	897-A5
COMOTILO CT				
	31200	TEM	92592	979-D5
COMPADRE DR				
	1400	PMSP	92264	786-H4
COMPADRE RD				
	300	PMSP	92262	786-H3
	400	PMSP	92264	786-H3
COMPANIA DR				
	-	TEM	92591	959-A5
COMPASS CT				
	2600	LKEL	92530	865-J7
COMPASS DR				
	-	RivC	92254	(5654-F5 See Page 5594)
	22900	CYNL	92587	867-D2
COMPIEGNE DR				
	44100	RivC	92544	(812-A5 See Page 782)
COMPTON AV				
	600	COR	92879	743-G6
	1800	COR	92881	773-G2
COMPUTER WY				
	2600	PMSP	92262	756-H7
COMSTOCK AV				
	6800	RIV	92503	714-E1
COMSTOCK CT				
	28700	RivC	92585	808-F5
COMSTOCK RD				
	3200	BAN	92220	721-F3
	10200	RivC	92883	804-E6
COMWELL ST				
	27100	RivC	92586	838-C4
CONARD AV				
	18600	RivC	92532	866-D1
CONATY PL				
	9300	RIV	92503	715-A7
CONCANNON CT				
	41000	TEM	92591	959-D3
CONCEPCION RD				
	68000	CTHC	92234	757-D7
CONCHA CIR				
	1500	PMSP	92264	786-F6
CONCHA CT				
	-	LQNT	92253	849-F6
CONCHA DR				
	5200	RivC	91752	683-G4
CONCHA LN				
	2600	PMSP	92264	786-H6
CONCHELLA DR				
	70300	RivC	92254	(5654-D4 See Page 5594)
CONCHITA RD				
	75700	RivC	92276	789-A2
CONCHITA WY				
	2200	PMSP	92264	786-G4
CONCHO DR				
	75100	INDW	92210	848-J2
CONCHO LN				
	-	PMSP	92264	786-H6
CONCORD AV				
	8800	RIV	92503	714-H3
	13300	RivC	92879	743-J5
	13300	RivC	92879	744-A5
CONCORD CIR				
	1400	SJCT	92583	811-D5
	3700	LKEL	92530	865-H3
	11300	FONT	92337	644-G2
CONCORD LN				
	-	RivC	92585	838-D5
CONCORD RD				
	32400	RivC	92530	896-J1
CONCORD WY				
	15800	MORV	92551	747-E2
CONCORDIA WY				
	17800	CHLS	91709	712-B6
CONCORDIA RANCH RD				
	14100	RivC	92532	835-D3
CONDIE DR				
	22200	RivC	-	726-J7
CONDIT AV				
	35600	CALI	92320	690-A2
CONDOR CIR				
	2600	COR	92882	772-H2
CONDOR CT				
	12600	GTER	92313	646-F5
	43800	RivC	92536	962-G7
CONDOR CV				
	-	RivC	92211	789-G6
CONDOR DR				
	6500	RivC	92509	685-A1
CONDOR WY				
	1200	SJCT	92583	811-D3
S CONDOR CREEK LN				
	2700	ONT	91761	643-C6
CONE CIR				
	66200	RivC	-	(937-C1 See Page 906)
CONEJO CIR				
	-	PDST	92260	818-F5
CONEJO DR				
	24000	RivC	92587	867-F1
CONEJO ST				
	1900	COR	92882	743-B7
	2000	COR	92882	773-B1
CONEJO TR				
	-	PMSP	92264	786-G5
CONESTOGA				
	74800	RivC	92276	788-J5
CONESTOGA AV				
	-	MURR	92562	927-H4
CONESTOGA CIR				
	1300	COR	92881	773-G2
CONESTOGA CT				
	1500	RDL	92373	647-J2
	26400	RivC	92586	868-B1
CONESTOGA LN				
	5400	RIV	92504	685-B7
	18000	CHLS	91709	712-A6
CONESTOGA RD				
	500	SJCT	92583	781-A6
	17700	RivC	92570	776-B3
CONESTOGA ST				
	1100	COR	92881	773-F2
CONESTOGA WY				
	-	NRCO	92860	743-F2
CONGRESS DR				
	3500	RIV	92503	744-D3
E CONGRESS ST				
	100	CLTN	92324	646-D1
W CONGRESS ST				
	100	CLTN	92324	646-C1
CONGRESS WY				
	1300	SJCT	92583	811-C3
CONGRESSIONAL				
	55700	LQNT	92253	5530-A4
CONGRESSIONAL DR				
	-	TEM	92591	959-C4
CONGRESSIONAL RD				
	9500	RivC	92240	696-E1
CONIFER CIR				
	1600	COR	92879	743-F7
CONIFER CT				
	6800	RIV	92506	716-E4
CONKLIN ST				
	200	LKEL	92530	866-F5
CONLEY CT				
	24700	MORV	92553	717-F6
CONN WY				
	2000	RDL	92373	649-B5
CONNECTICUT DR				
	28200	RivC	92587	837-D6
	28900	RivC	92587	867-E1
CONNECTICUT ST				
	42900	PDST	92211	819-D6
CONNECTOR ST				
	3600	RIV	92501	685-H2
CONNEMARA CT				
	15600	MORV	92555	748-B2
CONNERS LN				
	400	RivC	92507	646-D6
CONNIE CT				
	300	HEMT	92544	811-F6
CONNIE WY				
	25700	RivC	92586	837-J5
CONNING ST				
	3600	RivC	92509	644-B6
	4100	RivC	91752	644-A7
CONQUISTADOR RD				
	3100	SDCo	92028	997-D4
CONRAD WY				
	6300	RIV	92506	716-C3
CONSOLE RD				
	-	RivC	92324	687-H4
CONSTABLE RD				
	16000	RivC	92504	745-E4
CONSTANCE ST				
	30800	TEM	92592	979-C3
CONSTANTINE CIR				
	11800	MORV	92557	717-A1
CONSTANTINE DR				
	23800	MURR	92562	927-J3
CONSTELLATION DR				
	28900	RivC	92586	837-J7
CONSTELLATION PL				
	2900	RIV	92503	715-A7
CONSTELLATION WY				
	24600	MORV	92551	747-F3
CONSTITUTION DR				
	1400	COR	92882	772-J1
CONSUELO DR				
	600	PMSP	92262	786-E1
CONSUL AV				
	18600	RivC	92881	773-J3
CONSUMER CIR				
	1500	COR	92880	743-A4
CONTADORA DR				
	700	COR	92879	743-E5
CONTAINER CIR				
	1900	RivC	92509	645-E6
CONTAY WY				
	5100	RivC	92509	685-D3
CONTENTO DR				
	34100	RivC	92544	901-E3
CONTIGNAC DR				
	26700	MURR	92562	928-C1
CONTINENTAL DR				
	8700	RIV	92504	715-B6
	23100	CYNL	92587	867-E4
CONTOUR AV				
	30900	RivC	92567	779-A6
S CONTOUR RD				
	30000	RivC	92555	749-C3
W CONTOUR RD				
	-	RivC	92555	719-E7
	-	RivC	92555	749-C1
CONTOUR RD W				
	-	RivC	92555	749-C2
CONTRERAS RD				
	38000	RivC	92539	(934-J3 See Page 904)
	40000	RivC	92539	(935-A7 See Page 904)
	40000	RivC	92539	(965-A1 See Page 964)
CONVERSE AV				
	31200	RivC	92567	779-A6
CONVERSE RD				
	800	CTHC	92234	787-E6
CONWAY DR				
	8500	RIV	92504	714-J2
	8700	RIV	92503	714-H3
CONWAY LN				
	31100	RivC	92584	868-E5
COOK AV				
	7800	RIV	92503	714-F5
	9300	RIV	92505	714-E6
COOK CIR				
	1800	COR	92882	743-C7
COOK CT				
	22800	RivC	92570	806-E3
COOK ST				
	1700	COR	92882	743-C7
	35500	RivC	92276	788-J6
	37400	RivC	92211	788-J6
	38000	PDST	92211	818-J3
	38000	PDST	92260	818-J3
	38100	PDST	92211	788-J7
	44000	INDW	92210	818-J7
	44400	INDW	92210	848-J1
	45800	PDST	92260	848-J1
COOKHOUSE CT				
	32700	TEM	92592	979-G2
COOKMAN DR				
	19200	RivC	92220	782-D1
COOKS AV				
	-	SJCT	92583	781-D7
COOL CT				
	12300	MORV	92557	717-H2
COOL BREEZE CT				
	16200	RivC	92503	744-D4
COOL CREEK DR				
	29200	RivC	92586	868-B1
E COOLEY DR				
	1000	CLTN	92324	646-F1
S COOLEY DR				
	700	CLTN	92324	646-F1
E COOLEY LN				
	1600	CLTN	92324	646-H1
COOLIDGE				
	-	CTHC	92234	787-A7
COOLIDGE AV				
	-	INDO	92201	5470-F5
	500	HEMT	92543	810-J5
	6800	RIV	92506	715-E3
	7000	RIV	92504	715-E3
COOLIDGE CIR				
	500	COR	92879	743-G4
	41100	MURR	92562	927-H2
COOLIDGE ST				
	1600	COR	92879	743-H3
COOLIDGE SPRING RD				
	3800	ImCo	92274	(5773-A7 See Page 5712)
COOLWATER CT				
	28500	RivC	92584	868-F1
COOLWATER DR				
	11200	RIV	92505	714-A2
COOLWATER LN				
	16200	FONT	92337	644-H3
COOL WATERS				
	-	BLY	-	5491-A7
COOMBE HILL DR				
	25900	RivC	92586	838-A6
COONEN DR				
	5100	RIV	92503	714-F3

STREET
Block City ZIP Pg-Grid

COOPER
48200 INDO 92201 5470-G4
COOPER DR
- CALI 92320 689-J4
COOPER RD
19400 RivC 92258 725-H5
COOPER ST
1700 HEMT 92545 810-H5
COOPER CIENAGA TKTR
- RivC 92539 964-E2
COOPERMAN CIR
34300 RivC 92592 959-J5
COOPERS AV
900 COR 92879 743-G3
COOPER VIEW DR
23100 RivC 92587 867-D2
COORS RD
36200 RivC 92539 904-D6
COOS RD
20400 LKEL 92570 836-H6
COPE CT
13600 MORV 92553 717-C5
COPENHAGEN RD
3000 RIV 92504 715-B6
COPENHAGEN ST
400 HEMT 92545 810-F6
COPLASA ST
30500 RivC 92530 865-G4
COPLEN CIR
1700 COR 92882 772-J1
COPLEY LN
9000 RIV 92503 715-B7
S COPPER LN
2600 SBDO 92408 647-A1
COPPERBEECH LN
42200 TEM 92591 959-B5
COPPER COVE LN
25600 MORV 92553 717-H6
COPPER CRAFT DR
39400 MURR 92562 898-A7
COPPER CREEK DR
4800 BAN 92220 721-E5
COPPERFIELD AV
5800 RIV 92506 715-H2
COPPERHEAD CIR
24300 MURR 92562 927-H6
COPPER HILL PL
23800 MORV 92557 687-D7
COPPER LANTERN DR
6400 RIV 92503 714-G2
COPPERLEAF CT
25200 MURR 92563 928-F4
COPPERMINE ST
4500 RIV 92501 645-H7
COPPER MOUNTAIN CT
37700 RivC 92592 930-G5
COPPER QUEEN LN
17500 RivC 92570 806-B4
COPPER RIDGE DR
- RivC 92883 804-B3
3500 COR 92882 742-E5
COPPERSTONE CT
37500 RivC 92211 789-G7
COPPERWOOD ST
- MURR 92562 927-E5
COQUINA ST
900 HEMT 92543 840-J3
CORA PL
13400 MORV 92553 717-F4
CORAL AV
800 HEMT 92543 840-J3
CORAL CIR
- COR 92882 773-A3
CORAL CT
- FONT 92337 645-A1
15200 LKEL 92530 865-G3
CORAL DR
42000 RivC 92201 819-G5
CORAL LN
- FONT 92337 645-A2
100 PMSP 92264 786-E5
CORAL ST
2800 COR 92882 773-A2
15800 RivC 92262 725-E7
CORAL BELLS CIR
74500 PDST 92260 818-H6
CORALBERRY DR
2900 RIV 92504 715-C6
CORALBERRY ST
12900 MORV 92553 717-H3
CORAL CANYON WY
40000 RivC 92543 901-B1
40000 RivC 92544 901-D2
CORA LEE LN
30700 RivC 92543 871-A4
CORAL GABLES
74800 INDW 92210 848-J2
CORAL GABLES CIR
1300 COR 92881 773-F3
CORAL GABLES CT
74900 PDST 92260 848-J3
CORAL HILLS RD
200 PER 92570 807-F2
CORAL LEAF LN
6700 RIV 92506 716-D4
CORAL REEF RD
99000 RivC 92254 (5654-D4 See Page 5594)
CORAL RIDGE DR
6100 RIV 92505 714-B3
CORAL SKY CT
39500 RivC 92563 929-B7
CORALTREE CT
25300 MURR 92563 928-F4
CORAL TREE CT
29800 RivC 92584 868-F2
CORAL TREE DR
9100 RIV 92503 715-A7
CORALWOOD CT
- RivC 92880 713-A2
CORAZON AV
100 PMSP 92262 756-C3
CORAZZA
22000 RivC 92595 897-B5
CORBETT LN
23200 RivC 92567 808-G3
CORBIE CT
9400 CALI 92320 690-A2
CORBIE ST
- TEM 92592 959-G7
CORDAN RD
40200 RivC 92544 931-G7
40200 RivC 92544 961-G1
CORDATA CT
- TEM 92592 959-A6
S CORDILLERA AV
2100 CLTN 92324 646-J4
CORDOBA DR
26000 RivC 92545 840-A1
CORDOBA WY
200 PDST 92260 818-E4
CORDON PL
14500 MORV 92553 717-E7
CORDOVA AV
1600 RDL 92373 647-H2
S CORDOVA AV
200 CLTN 92324 646-C3
CORDOVA CT
- PMSP 92264 787-C6
CORDOVA DR
1300 HEMT 92543 810-H6
39900 RivC 92592 930-H7
CORDOZA ST
1900 COR 92882 743-B7
1900 COR 92882 773-B1
CORDUROY RD
32500 RivC 92562 927-E2
COREY CIR
35400 RivC 92592 960-C3
COREY LN
12800 YCPA 92399 649-G5
71900 RivC 92260 848-C5
COREY ST
6200 RivC 92509 684-D6
CORFU CT
44000 PDST 92260 818-H7
CORFU WY
3000 COR 92882 773-A2
CORI DR
500 HEMT 92543 811-A5
CORIANDER CIR
2100 COR 92879 743-H1
CORIANDER CT
25700 MORV 92553 717-H7
CORINA RD
21700 RivC 92570 777-A7
21700 RivC 92570 807-A1
CORINGA PL
8100 RivC 92509 684-G1
CORINTH DR
23800 MURR 92562 927-J3
CORINTHIAN WY
7000 RIV 92506 716-B6
7100 RivC 92508 716-B6
CORINTO CT
2200 HEMT 92545 810-G6
CORINTO WY
300 HEMT 92545 810-G6
CORKILL RD
14500 RivC 92241 697-G6
16000 RivC 92241 727-G2
CORK OAK CIR
23600 MURR 92562 927-H3
CORK SEED WY
10300 MORV 92557 687-D5
CORKWAY CIR
23100 MURR 92562 927-E3
CORLEY CT
24800 MORV 92553 717-F4
CORNCRIB CIR
34300 RivC 92595 897-H4
CORNELL AV
11500 RivC 92507 716-F1
CORNELL CT
11800 YCPA 92399 650-B2
CORNELL DR
- RMIR 92270 818-B3
35300 YCPA 92399 650-A2
CORNELL LN
11700 YCPA 92399 650-B2
CORNELL ST
25800 RivC 92544 811-D7
26100 RivC 92544 841-D2
26400 LMLN 92354 647-F2
N CORNELL ST
100 HEMT 92544 811-D7
CORNERSTONE CIR
- COR 92880 742-J1
CORNERSTONE DR
- RivC 91752 643-E5
CORNERSTONE WY
- COR 92880 742-J1
1000 COR 92880 743-A1
1000 COR 92880 713-A7
CORN FIELD CT
- RivC 92584 867-H1
CORNFLOWER WY
600 PER 92571 777-J6
CORNHUSK CIR
39800 MURR 92562 898-A7
39800 MURR 92562 928-A1
CORNING PL
41600 MURR 92562 958-E3
CORNISH AV
44700 RivC 92544 (812-B6 See Page 782)
CORN SPRINGS RD
- RivC - 391-C11
CORNSTALK RD
24400 RivC 92595 897-G3
CORNUCOPIA CT
4400 BAN 92220 721-E2
CORNUCOPIA WY
23500 MURR 92562 898-A7
CORNWALL AV
5300 RIV 92506 716-A1
CORONA AV
300 COR 92879 743-E3
1300 NRCO 92860 743-E2
1700 NRCO 92860 713-F3
CORONA DR
- CTHC 92234 787-C6
- PMSP 92264 787-C6
CORONA EXWY Rt#-71
17900 CHLS 91709 712-C6
17900 RivC 92880 712-C6
17900 RivC 92880 742-D4
CORONA FRWY I-15
- COR - 743-F6
- COR - 773-H1
- COR - 774-A6
- COR - 804-D4
- LKEL - 835-B2
- LKEL - 836-A5
- LKEL - 866-C1
- RivC - 773-H4
- RivC - 804-D4
- RivC - 835-B2
- RivC - 836-A5
- RivC - 866-C1
- RivC - 867-A7
- RivC - 897-A1
CORONA RD
20000 COR 92881 773-J5
CORONA ST
- SJCT 92583 780-J6
500 HEMT 92545 810-H6
20000 RivC 92881 773-J5
CORONA WY
25600 RivC - 814-D6
CORONA CALA CAMINO
43100 RivC 92562 956-E7
43300 RivC 92562 976-D2
CORONADA DR
26000 MORV 92555 717-J1
CORONA DE CEJA
- RivC 92590 958-E7
CORONADO AV
800 PMSP 92262 756-C6
CORONADO DR
200 COR 92879 773-D1
43800 TEM 92592 979-A2
CORONADO ST
400 BLY 92225 5491-D5
50000 COAC 92236 5471-B5
S CORONADO ST
50200 COAC 92236 5471-B6
CORONADO WY
6800 RIV 92504 715-C2
27100 RivC 92586 838-C6
CORONADOS CIR
49000 LQNT 92253 849-F5
CORONA ELSINORE RD
20500 COR 92883 774-A6
21600 RivC 92883 774-A6
21600 RivC 92883 804-B1
CORONA VALLEY AV
- RivC 92880 713-A1
N CORONET CIR
900 PMSP 92262 756-C7
CORONET DR
1100 RIV 92506 716-C5
CORONITA ST
8000 RivC 92881 774-A4
COROVA CT
- SJCT 92583 811-D4
CORPORATE ST
14200 MORV 92553 717-B6
CORPORATE TER
100 COR 92879 743-G4
CORPORATE WY
41500 PDST 92260 818-H5
72200 RivC 92276 788-C1
CORPORATE CENTER CT
41500 MURR 92562 958-E3
CORPORATE CENTER DR
- LQNT 92253 849-H2
CORPORATE CENTRE PL
5900 RIV 92507 716-J3
CORRAL CIR
4800 BAN 92220 721-E3
CORRAL RD
68400 CTHC 92234 787-E3
CORRAL ST
2000 NRCO 92860 712-J7
9400 RivC 92509 684-C5
CORRAL CANYON LN
- PER 92571 778-B2
CORREGIDOR AV
84000 RivC 92201 5470-J3
84100 RivC 92201 5471-A3
CORREGIDOR DR
34000 CTHC 92234 787-F5
CORRELL ST
6000 RIV 92504 685-C7
CORRIDOR DR
- RivC 91752 643-E5
CORRINNE WY
17400 RivC 92504 745-G6
CORSICA AV
15200 RivC 92506 745-G2
CORSICA CT
- PMSP 92264 816-F2
CORSICA DR
800 COR 92879 743-H2
CORSICA LN
25100 RivC 92585 837-H2
26300 RivC 92585 838-A2
CORSICA GATE
80000 INDO 92201 5470-A4
CORSO ALTO AV
20900 RivC 92567 779-D5
CORSON AV
21300 RivC 92570 746-H6
21600 RivC 92570 747-A6
25100 RivC 92584 867-J5
25600 RivC 92584 868-A5
CORTA RD
68100 CTHC 92234 787-D1
CORTA LORCA
39900 MURR 92562 928-B3
CORTE ABANILLA
42900 TEM 92592 959-D7
CORTE ADELITA
26900 RivC 92585 838-A3
CORTE AGUADILLA
22800 RivC 92590 977-E2
CORTE ALAMAR
31000 TEM 92592 959-C6
CORTE ALBANO
42900 TEM 92592 959-E7
CORTE ALBARA
40300 MURR 92562 928-A3
CORTE ALDALANO
24300 MURR 92562 927-H6
CORTE ALEGRA
45000 TEM 92592 979-E3
CORTE ALEGRIA
38200 RivC 92592 960-E3
CORTE ALGETE
31800 TEM 92592 979-E1
CORTE ALHAMBRA
31200 TEM 92592 959-C6
CORTE ALISOS
- RivC 92563 929-B7
CORTE ALMERIA
43200 TEM 92592 959-E7
CORTE ALMONTE
43000 TEM 92592 959-D7
CORTE ALTURIAN
84400 COAC 92236 5471-A6
CORTE AMALIA
41500 TEM 92592 959-E5
CORTE AMAYA
43600 TEM 92592 979-E1
CORTE ANACAPA
25000 MURR 92563 928-E3
31000 TEM 92592 959-C6
CORTE ANCHA
25000 MURR 92563 928-E3
CORTE ANDAR
23600 MURR 92562 928-A2
CORTE ANSELITA
- RivC 92590 978-C6
CORTE ANTIGUA
44800 TEM 92592 979-D3
CORTE ANZA
31000 TEM 92592 959-C6
CORTE ARGENTO
- TEM 92592 959-E7
CORTE ARROYO VISTA
30900 TEM 92592 959-C6
CORTE ASTORGA
43300 TEM 92592 959-F7
CORTE AVALINA
31900 TEM 92592 959-E7
CORTE AVALOS
31500 TEM 92592 979-D1
CORTE AYALA
- TEM 92592 979-E1
CORTE AZTEC
24900 MURR 92563 928-E3
CORTE AZULEJO
41400 RivC 92562 960-B3
CORTE BACARRO
33000 TEM 92592 959-F5
CORTE BALBOA
41600 TEM 92592 959-E5
CORTE BARBASTE
43500 TEM 92592 959-D7
43500 TEM 92592 979-D1
CORTE BARELA
32400 RivC 92592 979-F5
CORTE BELLA
39800 PDST 92260 818-E3
CORTE BELLA DONNA
45000 TEM 92592 979-F3
CORTE BELLO
19400 RivC 92562 956-G7
19400 RivC 92562 976-G1
CORTE BENAVENTE
43300 TEM 92592 959-E7
43300 TEM 92592 979-E1
CORTE BENISA
43500 TEM 92592 979-E1
CORTE BENITEZ
43300 TEM 92592 959-E7
CORTE BERNARDO
84500 COAC 92236 5471-A6
CORTE BONILIO
32000 RivC 92592 979-E4
CORTE BONILLA
33000 TEM 92592 959-H7
CORTE BONITO
23300 RivC 92590 977-F1
CORTE BOTELLA
25600 MURR 92563 928-G5
CORTE BRAVO
45000 TEM 92592 979-D3
CORTE CABELLO
42900 TEM 92592 959-D7
CORTE CABRAL
43600 TEM 92592 979-D1
CORTE CABRERA
42900 TEM 92592 959-D7
CORTE CAJAN
40200 MURR 92562 928-A2
CORTE CALANDA
43000 TEM 92592 959-D7
CORTE CALANOVA
- MURR 92562 928-B2
CORTE CAMARA
41700 TEM 92592 959-F5
CORTE CAMARILLO
31300 TEM 92592 959-D6
CORTE CAMELLIA
45000 TEM 92592 979-D4
CORTE CAMPEON
40300 MURR 92562 928-C4
CORTE CANARIO
33300 TEM 92592 979-H3
CORTE CANEL
32000 TEM 92592 959-E5
CORTE CANTANIA
30200 TEM 92591 959-A4
CORTE CANTANTE
42500 MURR 92562 927-H6
CORTE CANTERA
29900 TEM 92591 958-J4
29900 TEM 92591 959-A4
CORTE CAPISTRANO
44600 TEM 92592 979-D3
CORTE CAPRI
28600 RivC 92584 868-F3
CORTE CARDENAS
31600 TEM 92592 979-D1
CORTE CARDIN
32100 TEM 92592 959-E7
CORTE CARDOZA
43500 TEM 92592 979-E1
CORTE CARMELA
32000 TEM 92592 959-F5
CORTE CARMELLO
46200 RivC 92592 979-G5
CORTE CARMONA
32100 TEM 92592 959-E6
CORTE CAROLINA
45000 TEM 92592 979-F3
CORTE CARRERA
45900 RivC 92590 978-D5
CORTE CARRIO
23600 MURR 92562 928-A3
CORTE CARRIZO
30100 TEM 92591 959-A4
CORTE CASA
44800 TEM 92592 979-D3
CORTE CASTILLE
29900 TEM 92591 958-J4
29900 TEM 92591 959-A4
CORTE CASTILLO
7700 RivC 92509 684-G2
CORTE CASTRO
31900 TEM 92592 959-E6
CORTE CHAPLITA
39800 RivC 92592 931-C7
39800 RivC 92592 961-C1
CORTE CHARMONA
23700 MURR 92562 928-A3
CORTE CHATADA
32300 TEM 92592 959-E4
CORTE CHRISTINA
45000 TEM 92592 979-E3
CORTE CINDARELLA
84500 COAC 92236 5471-A6
CORTE COELHO
30000 TEM 92591 959-A2
CORTE COLINA
25500 MURR 92563 928-F5
CORTE COLUCCI
42900 TEM 92592 959-E7
CORTE COPA
29500 TEM 92592 978-J1
CORTE CORDOBA
24100 MURR 92563 928-A3
CORTE CORONADO
32300 TEM 92592 959-F4
CORTE CRISTAL
26900 RivC 92590 978-D4
CORTE CRUZADA
29700 RivC 92584 868-G2
CORTE DAROCA
32100 RivC 92592 979-F5
CORTE DAVILA
- TEM 92592 959-E7
CORTE DE FLORES
25000 RivC 92570 807-D7
CORTE DEL CERRO
32100 TEM 92592 959-F5
CORTE DELFIN
40200 MURR 92562 928-B2
CORTE DELGADO
24600 MURR 92562 928-C4
CORTE DE LOS PAJAROS
25100 MURR 92563 928-E4
CORTE DE LOS SANTOS
30900 TEM 92592 959-C6
CORTE DEL PARQUE
84600 COAC 92236 5471-A5
CORTE DEL RIATILLO
20700 RivC 92562 926-J5
CORTE DEL SOL
900 SJCT 92582 810-H3
15800 MORV 92555 748-C2
CORTE DE OLLAS
40300 RivC 92562 927-C7
CORTE DE OPALO
40500 MURR 92562 928-A2
CORTE DE RUBI
40500 MURR 92562 927-J2
40500 MURR 92562 928-A2
CORTE DESCANSO
42300 MURR 92562 927-J6
CORTE DE SEEGAR
27300 RivC 92590 978-E1
CORTE DE SOL
- RMIR 92270 818-D4
CORTE DURAZO
43400 TEM 92592 959-E7
43400 TEM 92592 979-E1
CORTE EBANO
32900 TEM 92592 959-H7
CORTE EL CONDOR
27400 RivC 92544 841-D3
CORTE ELDORADO
32000 RivC 92592 979-E4
CORTE EMPRESA
- RivC 92590 958-C7
CORTE ENCINAS
31600 TEM 92592 959-D5
CORTE ENTRADA
4400 RivC 92509 684-H1
CORTE ESCOBAR
32000 TEM 92592 959-E6
CORTE ESPARZA
- TEM 92592 959-D7
CORTE FALDAS
29800 TEM 92591 958-J4
CORTE FIGUEROA
32900 TEM 92592 959-H7
CORTE FLORADORA
1300 SJCT 92583 811-E3
CORTE FLORECIDA
21000 RivC 92590 977-A1
CORTE FLORECITA
32000 TEM 92592 959-F5
CORTE FLORERIA
20000 RivC 92562 926-H2
CORTE FORTUNA
40200 MURR 92562 928-A2
CORTE FRAGA
44900 RivC 92592 979-F3
CORTE FRESCA
43000 TEM 92592 958-J7
CORTE FUENTES
- RivC 92562 956-C3
CORTE GABAIVA
32200 RivC 92592 979-F4
CORTE GANSO
33100 TEM 92592 979-G3
CORTE GARBOSO
39400 MURR 92563 928-G5
CORTE GARDANO
41300 TEM 92592 959-E7
CORTE GATUN
43300 RivC 92544 811-J6
CORTE GRANADA
1500 SJCT 92583 811-E3
29800 TEM 92591 958-J5
CORTE GURULE
29700 TEM 92591 959-A2
CORTE GUTIERREZ
44700 TEM 92592 979-H3
CORTE HANNA
38000 RivC 92562 926-H3
CORTE HIGUERA
41600 TEM 92592 959-E5
CORTE HILDALGO
44700 RivC 92592 979-F3
CORTE ILLORA
41300 TEM 92592 959-E7
CORTE INQUIETO
- RivC 92562 956-E5
CORTE INSPIRADA
24000 MURR 92562 928-A3
CORTE JARAMILLO
24400 MURR 92562 928-C4
CORTE JINETE
38100 RivC 92562 926-G4
CORTE JURADO
38100 RivC 92562 926-G4
CORTE LANDEROS
43000 TEM 92592 959-D7
CORTE LA PUENTE
31900 TEM 92592 959-E5
CORTE LARA
41700 TEM 92592 959-F5
CORTE LARGO
25000 MURR 92563 928-E3
CORTE LAS CRUCES
32200 TEM 92592 959-F4
CORTE LAS LUNAS
1000 SJCT 92582 810-H3
CORTE LATEUZA
- LKEL 92532 866-J4
- LKEL 92532 867-A4
CORTE LERMA
45700 RivC 92592 979-F5
CORTE LIMON
33200 RivC 92592 979-G4
CORTE LLAMAS
32100 TEM 92592 979-E1
CORTE LOBOS
45600 RivC 92592 979-F4
CORTE LOGRONO
43400 TEM 92592 959-E7
43400 TEM 92592 979-E1
CORTE LOJA
33200 RivC 92592 979-F4
CORTE LUCIA
- CTHC 92234 787-G6
40400 MURR 92562 928-A3
CORTE LUCIDO
- RivC 92563 928-J7
- RivC 92563 958-J1
CORTE LUNADA
27900 RivC 92590 978-F3
CORTE MADERA
- LKEL 92532 866-J4
- LKEL 92532 867-A4
31400 TEM 92592 959-D6
CORTE MAGDALENA
28300 RivC 92586 838-D6
CORTE MALBINO
28200 TEM 92592 958-J7
CORTE MALLORCA
31300 TEM 92592 959-D6
CORTE MANDARINA
25100 MURR 92563 928-E4
CORTE MANGARINO
32900 TEM 92592 959-H7
CORTE MARTINEZ
40300 MURR 92562 928-C4
CORTE MATARO
46100 RivC 92592 979-F5
CORTE MENDOZA
- TEM 92592 959-E5
CORTE MONTECITO
31800 TEM 92592 959-E5
CORTE MONTIA
- TEM 92592 959-F5
CORTE MONTIEL
31400 TEM 92592 959-D5
CORTE MONTILLA
43100 TEM 92592 959-D7
CORTE MONTOYA
31800 RivC 92592 979-E4
CORTE MONTRIL
45600 RivC 92592 978-E4
CORTE MORELIA
44700 RivC 92592 979-E3
CORTE NARBONNE
45400 RivC 92592 979-F4
CORTE NAUTIA
44700 RivC 92592 979-E3
CORTE NINA
- RivC 92590 977-D1
CORTE OAXACA
46000 RivC 92592 979-F5
CORTE OCASO
28300 TEM 92592 958-J7
CORTE OLIVIA
86000 COAC 92236 5471-D6
CORTE ORIZABA
32100 RivC 92592 979-F5
CORTE ORNADA
25000 MURR 92563 928-E4
CORTE PACHECO
31400 TEM 92592 959-D6
39000 MURR 92562 928-D2
CORTE PADRERA
31600 TEM 92592 959-D5
CORTE PALABRAS
19200 RivC 92562 956-F1
CORTE PALACIO
32200 TEM 92592 959-F5
CORTE PALLAZO
- LKEL 92532 866-J4
- LKEL 92532 867-A4
CORTE PALMITO
45100 RivC 92592 979-E4
CORTE PALO VIEJO
19600 RivC 92562 926-G3
CORTE PARADO
32200 TEM 92592 959-F5
CORTE PAWNEE
24900 MURR 92563 928-E3
CORTE PERALTA
40100 MURR 92562 928-B2
CORTE PERGAMINO
41500 TEM 92592 959-E4
CORTE PICANTE
23600 MURR 92562 928-A3
CORTE PICCOLO
- INDW 92210 849-E2
CORTE PICO
39600 MURR 92563 928-E4
CORTE PLANICIE
40300 RivC 92562 927-C7
CORTE PLATA
30100 TEM 92591 959-A4
CORTE PLUMA
39200 MURR 92563 928-F3
CORTE POLLENSA
31700 TEM 92592 959-E7
CORTE PORFIRIO
33000 TEM 92592 959-H7
CORTE PORTOFINO
28400 RivC 92584 868-F3
CORTE POSITAS
31800 TEM 92592 959-E5
CORTE PRIEGO
31800 TEM 92592 959-E7
CORTE PRIVADA
33500 RivC 92591 959-H1
CORTE PROGRESSO
31800 RivC 92592 979-E4
CORTE PROMESA
25500 MURR 92563 928-F4
CORTE PROVIDENCIA
21000 RivC 92562 956-J1
21000 RivC 92562 957-A1
CORTE RAFFINI
- LKEL 92532 866-J4
CORTE RANCHO ARIBA
37800 RivC 92562 926-G3
CORTE RENATA
36000 MURR 92562 898-C7
36000 MURR 92562 928-C1
CORTE RETIRO
28200 RivC 92586 838-D6
CORTE RIALTO
43300 TEM 92592 958-J7
43400 TEM 92592 978-J1
CORTE RICARDO
46100 RivC 92592 979-F5
CORTE RIMOLA
31300 TEM 92592 959-D7
CORTE RISA
25500 MURR 92563 928-F5
CORTE RIVERA
- LKEL 92532 866-J4
CORTE RODRIGO
45700 RivC 92592 979-F5
CORTE RODRIGUEZ
44800 TEM 92592 979-H3
CORTE ROJELIO
24400 MURR 92562 927-J6
CORTE ROSA
45000 TEM 92592 979-E3
CORTE ROSAIRE
1400 SJCT 92583 811-D3
CORTE ROSARIO
31600 TEM 92592 959-E5
CORTE ROSSA
- LKEL 92532 866-J4
CORTE ROYAL
32500 RivC 92592 979-G4
CORTE RUIZ
31900 TEM 92592 959-E6
CORTE SABIO
23700 MURR 92562 928-A2
CORTE SABRINAS
32100 RivC 92592 979-F5
CORTE SAGUNTO
31900 TEM 92592 979-D1
CORTE SALAMANCA
42900 TEM 92592 959-E7
CORTE SALINAS
31400 TEM 92592 959-D5
39900 RivC 92562 926-E7
CORTE SANCHEZ
44500 TEM 92592 979-H3
CORTE SANDIA
25100 MURR 92563 928-E4
CORTE SAN GABRIEL
44600 TEM 92592 979-D3
CORTE SANINO
24300 MURR 92562 927-H6
CORTE SAN LEANDRO
31300 TEM 92592 959-D6
CORTE SAN LUIS
29900 TEM 92591 959-A5
CORTE SAN MARCO
73200 PDST 92260 818-E3
CORTE SAN REMO
28500 RivC 92584 868-F3
CORTE SANTA BARBARA
25000 MURR 92563 928-E4
CORTE SANTA CATALINA
32200 TEM 92592 959-F4
CORTE SANTA CESILIA
39600 RivC 92592 961-B1
CORTE SANTALINA
30400 RivC 92563 929-B7
CORTE SAN VINCENTE
32200 TEM 92592 959-F4
CORTE SEDA
41600 TEM 92592 959-F4
CORTE SELVA
41800 TEM 92591 959-A4
CORTE SERENA
- CTHC 92234 787-G6
CORTE SERIUI
- LKEL 92532 866-J4
CORTE SEVRINA
44800 TEM 92592 979-E3
CORTE SIERO
42900 TEM 92592 959-D7
CORTE SIERRA
44800 TEM 92592 979-D3
CORTE SOLE
73100 PDST 92260 818-E3
CORTE SOLEDAD
31900 TEM 92592 959-E4
CORTE SOLOMON
20800 RivC 92562 926-J6
CORTE SOMBRERO
25100 MURR 92563 928-F3
CORTE SONORA
31300 TEM 92592 959-D5
CORTE SPARKMAN
- TEM 92592 979-E1
CORTE STELLA
86000 COAC 92236 5471-D6
CORTE STRAZA
- LKEL 92532 866-J4
- LKEL 92532 867-A4
CORTE SUENO
- RivC 92562 956-E6
CORTE SUERTE
28800 RivC 92584 868-G2
CORTE SUR
25100 MURR 92563 928-E4
CORTE TALVERA
31100 TEM 92592 959-C5
CORTE TAQUITO
31500 TEM 92592 979-D3
CORTE TECOLOTE
26000 RivC 92544 811-H7
26000 RivC 92544 841-H1
CORTE TESORO
39200 MURR 92563 928-F4
CORTE TOBARRA
32200 RivC 92592 979-F5
CORTE TOLANO
29800 TEM 92591 959-A4
CORTE TOLOSA
43100 TEM 92592 959-D7
CORTE TOMATLAN
32200 RivC 92592 979-F4
CORTE TONIKAN
24900 MURR 92563 928-E3
CORTE TORTOSA
31600 TEM 92592 959-D5
CORTE TUNAS
31300 TEM 92592 959-D6
CORTE URIBA
29600 TEM 92591 958-J4
CORTE UTNEHMER
- TEM 92592 979-E1
CORTE VALENCIA
44700 RivC 92592 979-E3
CORTE VALENTE
24100 MURR 92562 928-A3
CORTE VALENTINE
41800 TEM 92592 959-E5
CORTE VALLE
45100 TEM 92592 979-E3
CORTE VARELA
45200 RivC 92590 978-G4
CORTE VERANOS
44600 TEM 92592 979-D3
CORTE VIENA
24900 MURR 92563 928-E3
CORTE VILLA
43000 TEM 92592 959-B7
CORTE VILLENA
43600 TEM 92592 979-E1
CORTE VILLOSA
42400 TEM 92592 959-E5
CORTE VISTA CLARA
46000 RivC 92590 977-F5
CORTE VISTA GUSTA
- RivC 92562 956-C4
CORTE VONNIE
27200 RivC 92590 958-D7
CORTE YACA
33100 TEM 92592 959-H7
33100 TEM 92592 979-G1
CORTEZ AV
900 BLY 92225 5491-D4
CORTEZ CT
26700 RivC 92544 842-B2
CORTEZ DR
700 HEMT 92545 810-F5
900 COR 92882 773-B1
900 COR 92882 743-B7
CORTEZ LN
78100 INDW 92210 849-F3
79600 LQNT 92253 849-J2
CORTEZ PL
- INDO 92201 5470-D4
W CORTEZ RD
200 PMSP 92262 756-D5
CORTEZ ST
3400 RIV 92504 715-C3
CORTE ZAMORA
32200 TEM 92592 959-F5
CORTE ZARAGOZA
32100 RivC 92592 979-G5
CORTE ZORITA
25500 MURR 92563 928-F4
44900 RivC 92592 979-E3
45000 TEM 92592 979-E3
CORTINA DR
2500 RIV 92504 715-F4
CORTLAND LN
25500 RivC 92548 809-F7
CORTO DR
11500 RivC 91752 683-G3
CORTONA
- INDW 92210 819-A7
CORTONA CT
36000 MURR 92562 898-B7
CORTRITE AV
25100 RivC 92548 809-F6
25600 RivC 92548 839-F1
26100 RivC 92545 839-F1
CORUNA
36000 MURR 92562 898-B7
CORVADO DR
67100 RivC 92241 727-A5
CORVALLIS CT
5800 RIV 92506 716-A2
CORVINA DR
99000 RivC 92254 (5654-D6 See Page 5594)
CORVUS WY
28500 RivC 92586 837-J6
CORWIN LN
4700 RIV 92503 714-G3
CORWIN PL
900 HFMT 92544 811-F4
CORY CT
8500 RIV 92508 746-G2
CORY LN
22800 RivC 92570 747-C7
CORY ANN CT
800 PER 92570 807-E1
CORYDON AV
1200 NRCO 92880 713-A7
1900 COR 92880 713-A7
2300 NRCO 92860 713-B5
CORYDON ST
900 COR 92880 742-J1
900 COR 92880 743-A1
1000 COR 92880 713-A7
31600 LKEL 92530 896-H5
31600 LKEL 92530 897-A3
31600 LKEL 92595 897-A3
31600 RivC 92530 896-H5
31600 RivC 92530 897-A3
31600 RivC 92595 897-A3
32400 LKEL 92595 896-H5
32400 RivC 92595 896-H5
COSGROVE CT
17100 RivC 92504 745-G5
COSMIC DR
42000 TEM 92592 959-A6
COSMO DR
42900 RivC 92544 901-H4
COSTA BRAVA CIR
- COR 92879 743-F3
COSTA MESA DR
200 PMSP 92264 786-J6
68000 RivC 92254 (5654-C2 See Page 5594)
COSTELLO
- INDO 92201 5470-F3
COSTELLO AV
20500 RivC 92570 746-G7
COSTO LN
800 HEMT 92543 841-A2
COTA AV
2300 COR 92882 773-C2
COTA ST
100 COR 92882 743-C4
300 COR 92880 743-C4
900 NRCO 92860 743-D3
COTA WY
45400 INDW 92210 849-E1
COTATI CT
- MORV 92557 687-C4
COTE LN
3400 RIV 92501 685-J1
3400 RIV 92501 686-A1
COTEAU DR
1600 RIV 92504 745-E2
COTE D AZURE DR
39100 MURR 92563 928-G7
COTTA LN
34500 RivC 92592 960-A5
COTTAGE DR
2400 COR 92881 773-G4
COTTAGE LN
46200 PDST 92260 848-F2
COTTAGE ST
2600 RIV 92507 685-H5
COTTLE LN
45500 RivC 92536 981-H4
COTTON CIR
73800 RivC 92260 818-F2
COTTON CT
64900 RivC 92240 696-E1
COTTONCREEK LN
1900 COR 92880 713-A7
COTTONTAIL CT
7400 RivC 92509 684-H2
74700 RivC 92276 788-H4
COTTONTAIL DR
28000 RivC 92587 837-F6
COTTONWOOD AV
- RIV 92507 716-H5
100 RIV 92506 716-D5
2300 SJCT 92582 810-C2
21600 MORV 92553 716-J5
21600 RivC 92553 716-J5
21700 MORV 92553 717-G4
25900 MORV 92555 717-G4
26200 MORV 92555 718-A4
30300 MORV 92555 719-A4
34300 RivC 92567 779-H3
34500 SJCT 92567 779-H3
35400 SJCT 92567 780-A4
W COTTONWOOD AV
700 SJCT 92582 810-H1
700 SJCT 92582 811-A1
COTTONWOOD CIR
- RivC 92880 683-B7
1200 COR 92879 743-F6
COTTONWOOD CT
900 COR 92879 743-F7
E COTTONWOOD CT
2900 ONT 91761 643-A6
COTTONWOOD CV
77800 INDW 92210 849-F3
COTTONWOOD DR
- CALI 92320 650-A7
COTTON WOOD DR
1100 RivC - 5240-A7
COTTONWOOD DR
11200 CALI 92320 690-B6
19100 RivC 92241 727-C4

STREET
Block City ZIP Pg-Grid

E COTTONWOOD DR
1700 CLTN 92324 646-G1
COTTONWOOD LN
13000 BLY 92225 5491-H6
46300 INDO 92201 5470-B2
COTTONWOOD RD
700 BAN 92220 722-A2
900 BAN 92220 721-J2
11600 RivC 92220 692-F7
12700 RivC 92282 724-D1
15900 PMSP - 724-F7
52300 RivC 92282 694-E7
E COTTONWOOD RD
300 PMSP 92262 756-E6
COTTONWOOD ST
- MURR 92562 927-F5
- MURR 92563 928-F7
700 COR 92879 743-E7
24000 RivC 92584 867-F7
33200 RivC 92567 809-F2
35000 RivC 92567 810-A2
COTTONWOOD TR
13600 YCPA 92399 650-E5
E COTTONWOOD TR
2700 ONT 91761 643-A6
COTTONWOOD CANYON
52000 RivC 92282 694-E7
COTTONWOOD CANYON RD
- CYNL 92587 867-C4
- LKEL 92532 867-C4
COTTONWOOD HILLS RD
24100 RivC 92584 867-G7
31000 LKEL 92532 867-D5
31200 RivC 92532 867-G7
31200 RivC 92595 867-G7
32500 RivC 92584 897-H1
COTTONWOOD SPRINGS RD
- RivC - 390-J9
COTTRELL BLVD
17300 RivC 92530 896-B2
COUDURES WY
400 PER 92571 777-H6
COUGAR
- DHSP 92240 696-J7
COUGAR RD
25000 RivC - 814-F4
COUGAR ST
22900 RivC 92570 777-C1
COUGAR WY
400 BEAU 92223 690-H6
900 BEAU 92223 691-A6
1100 RivC 92223 691-A6
COUGAR CANYON DR
23000 MORV 92557 687-C6
COUGAR CANYON RD
3300 HEMT 92545 840-E4
COUGHLIN CT
22400 RivC 92567 779-H7
22400 RivC 92567 809-H1
COULTER DR
25000 RivC - 814-B5
COUNCIL LN
22200 RivC 92570 777-B1
COUNTESS DR
1200 COR 92882 773-A2
COUNT FLEET CT
11400 MORV 92557 716-J1
COUNTRY DR
28200 RivC 92570 836-F7
COUNTRY LN
6500 RIV 92505 714-C2
COUNTRY PL
100 CALI 92320 650-A7
12800 YCPA 92399 649-F5
COUNTRY RD
24300 RivC 92557 687-E3
36900 RivC 92544 931-B1
COUNTRY BLUFFS RD
11000 RIV 92505 714-B1
COUNTRY CANYON RD
24100 MORV 92557 687-E5
COUNTRY CLUB BLVD
300 LKEL 92530 866-F6
COUNTRY CLUB DR
- PDST 92260 848-C6
100 NRCO 92860 713-J7
400 BAN 92220 721-C4
900 RIV 92506 716-B2
1300 SJCT 92583 780-H7
10200 RivC 91752 644-A6
20000 RivC 92583 780-J3
42900 INDO 92201 5410-A4
50600 INDO 92201 819-G3
50600 RivC 92201 819-G3
50600 RivC 92201 5410-A4
53400 RivC - 844-B1
53700 RivC - 814-B7
69200 RivC 92241 727-E1
70000 RMIR 92270 817-J3
70800 RMIR 92270 818-C3
73000 PDST 92260 818-G3
73100 RivC 92260 818-G3
75000 PDST 92211 818-G3
75300 PDST 92211 819-D3
78000 PDST 92201 819-G3
82000 INDO 92201 5470-E4
N COUNTRY CLUB DR
69100 RivC 92241 727-F1
S COUNTRY CLUB DR
69200 RivC 92241 727-F1
COUNTRY CLUB LN
1000 COR 92880 743-A1
12100 GTER 92313 646-F4
COUNTRY CREEK CT
13500 YCPA 92399 650-C6
COUNTRY CREEK DR
35700 YCPA 92399 650-B6
COUNTRY CREST DR
22300 MORV 92557 687-A4
COUNTRYDALE RD
- RIV 92505 714-C7
COUNTRY FAIR DR
- RivC 92584 867-H1
COUNTRY FLOWER LN
11600 MORV 92557 717-C1
COUNTRY GATE RD
22400 MORV 92557 687-A5
COUNTRY GLEN CT
13500 YCPA 92399 650-C6
COUNTRY GLEN WY
44500 TEM 92592 979-E2
COUNTRY GROVE DR
10300 MORV 92557 687-B5
COUNTRY GROVE WY
4600 HEMT 92545 840-D3
COUNTRY HILLS LN
2000 RivC 92503 744-J4
COUNTRY LANE RD
10200 RivC 91752 684-A4
COUNTRY MANOR DR
800 COR 92881 773-E2
COUNTRY MANOR LN
17200 RivC 92508 745-J2
17200 RivC 92508 746-A2
COUNTRY MILL RD
39400 MURR 92562 928-D3
E COUNTRY OAKS LP
3600 ONT 91761 643-C6
S COUNTRY OAKS LP
2900 ONT 91761 643-C7
COUNTRY PARK DR
- RivC 92595 897-H7
COUNTRY PINE RD
18500 RivC 92570 776-C7
COUNTRYRISE LN
- RIV 92505 744-C1
COUNTRY ROSE CT
800 COR 92882 773-C1
COUNTRY ROSE LN
600 COR 92882 773-C2
COUNTRYSIDE CIR
22700 RivC 92595 897-D4
COUNTRYSIDE DR
11300 FONT 92337 644-A3
COUNTRYSIDE LN
3200 COR 92881 773-F4
COUNTRY SIDE LN
39400 MURR 92562 898-A7
COUNTRYSIDE PL
3800 NRCO 92860 713-F4
COUNTRYSIDE ST
900 HEMT 92545 840-G2
COUNTRYSIDE WY
22800 MORV 92557 687-B4
COUNTRY SQUIRE DR
14000 MORV 92555 718-B6
COUNTRY SQUIRE RD
- RivC 92570 806-H2
COUNTRY VIEW LN
6200 RIV 92504 685-B7
COUNTRY VIEW RD
15000 RivC 92282 695-E7
15000 RivC 92282 725-E1
COUNTRY VILLAGE DR
200 SJCT 92583 781-A6
COUNTRY VILLAGE RD
3000 FONT 92337 644-A6
3000 RivC 91752 644-A6
3000 RivC 92509 644-A6
COUNTRY WALK LN
25900 MURR 92563 928-F6
COUNTRYWOOD LN
2600 RIV 92506 715-G4
COUNTRY WOODS LN
26500 RivC - 814-C7
COUNT TURF ST
100 PER 92571 777-H5
COUNTY CENTER DR
40600 TEM 92591 958-G3
COUNTY CIRCLE DR
4000 RIV 92503 714-G6
COUNTY FARM RD
9900 RIV 92503 714-G6
COUNTY LINE LN
500 CALI 92320 649-G7
COUNTY LINE RD
100 CALI 92320 650-C7
100 YCPA 92399 650-A7
200 CALI 92320 649-F7
33400 YCPA 92399 649-H7
38600 RivC 92399 650-J7
38700 RivC 92223 650-H6
38700 RivC 92223 651-A6
E COUNTY LINE RD
4300 ONT 91761 643-H4
4300 RivC 91752 643-H4
11800 FONT 92337 643-H4
11800 ONT 92337 643-H4
13400 FONT 92337 644-A4
COUPLES CT
- LQNT 92253 5530-E5
COUPLES RD
- COR 92883 773-H7
COURAGE ST
13800 MORV 92553 717-B6
COUR BEAUNE
41400 TEM 92591 959-E4
COURBETTE DR
3600 RIV 92503 744-D3
COUR CITRAN
- TEM 92591 959-D3
COUR MAGDELAINE
32100 TEM 92591 959-E4
COUR MEYNEY
32100 TEM 92591 959-E4
COUR POMEROL
32700 TEM 92591 959-E4
COURSEY DR
22800 RivC 92570 807-C7
COURT ST
100 RivC - 5239-J7
1000 BLY 92225 5491-F5
COURT E
- SJCT 92583 780-J5
COURTESY DR
59200 RivC - (905-E3 See Page 904)
COURT F
- SJCT 92583 780-J6
COURTLAND DR
5900 RIV 92506 716-B2
COURTNEY CIR
6100 RivC 92509 684-G5
COURTNEY CT
18300 SBdC 92316 645-D1
COURTNEY LN
- RivC 92570 805-F4
74500 RivC 92241 728-G7
COURTNEY PL
29400 TEM 92591 958-H5
COURTNEY ST
900 HEMT 92543 810-J5
3700 COR 92881 773-G6
COURTNEY BROOK LN
28900 MURR 92563 928-G1
COURTSIDE DR
- PDST 92260 818-F4
COVE
200 PMSP 92264 786-H7
N COVE DR
74800 INDW 92210 848-J1
S COVE DR
74800 INDW 92210 848-J1
COVE LN
68500 CTHC 92234 787-E7
COVE PL
78700 RivC 92201 819-G6
COVE ST
4200 HEMT 92545 840-E5
COVECREST CIR
30500 RivC 92584 868-G3
COVE GATE
75000 INDW 92210 848-J1
COVELL ST
19500 RivC 92508 746-E5
COVELLO ST
6100 RivC 92509 685-A4
COVENTRY CIR
2900 COR 92879 744-A2
76800 PDST 92211 819-C2
COVENTRY DR
5200 RIV 92506 685-J7
5200 RIV 92506 715-J1
COVENTRY LN
15600 FONT 92337 644-F2
34000 RivC 92596 899-F3
COVENTRY ST
2900 COR 92879 744-B2
COVE POINTE CIR
77700 INDW 92210 849-F2
COVER ST
4100 RIV 92506 685-D7
COVERED WAGON CT
- RivC 92399 650-G7
COVERED WAGON TR
46000 PDST 92260 848-G2
COVE VIEW ST
22600 CYNL 92587 867-D3
COVEY RD
24600 MORV 92557 687-F5
COVEY ST
17000 RivC 92258 726-D2
COVEY QUAIL LN
13800 MORV 92553 717-F5
COVINGTON CIR
- COR 92881 773-E2
COVINGTON DR
- PDST 92260 818-H2
COVINGTON LN
52600 RivC - (813-J4 See Page 782)
COVINGTON WY
24500 MORV 92557 717-F1
27800 RivC 92586 838-A5
COW TR
47300 RivC 92536 982-H2
COWAN RD
19300 RivC 92570 776-B3
COWBELL AL
54500 RivC - 844-D1
COWBOY DR
74800 RivC 92276 788-J5
74900 RivC 92276 789-A5
COWBOY COUNTRY TR
43200 RivC 92536 963-E7
COW CANYON RD
12800 RivC 92883 835-A6
COWELL ST
17400 LKEL 92530 866-B3
COWHIDE RD
900 COR 92882 773-B2
COWIE AV
23100 RivC 92570 807-B4
COWPOKE CT
27000 RivC 92883 835-B4
COW PUNCHER CT
48900 RivC 92536 983-C3
COX
1200 LKEL 92530 866-G5
COX RD
32500 RivC 92584 868-C7
32500 RivC 92584 898-C1
COX ST
23200 PER 92570 807-C4
23200 RivC 92570 807-C4
COX WY
- COR 92879 743-E6
COYOTE
- DHSP 92240 696-J7
COYOTE CIR
1500 COR 92882 743-A6
27600 RivC 92587 837-F5
COYOTE DR
100 PMSP 92264 787-C6
1400 COR 92882 743-A6
COYOTE LN
32600 RivC 92584 867-H7
COYOTE RD
48300 RivC - 848-A5
48300 RivC 92260 848-A5
COYOTE ST
6400 CHLS 91709 712-B6
45700 RivC 92220 782-D1
COYOTE TR
43300 RivC 92220 721-G6
58500 RivC 92539 (935-D5 See Page 904)
COYOTE WY
81000 INDO 92201 5470-C2
COYOTE BUSH RD
8600 RIV 92508 746-G2
8800 RIV 92518 746-G3
COYOTE CANYON CT
78300 LQNT 92253 879-G1
COYOTE CANYON RD
43300 RivC 92539 (965-E5 See Page 964)
COYOTE CREEK
79000 LQNT 92253 849-H6
COYOTE CREEK PTH
77200 INDW 92210 849-E1
COYOTE MESA DR
- RivC 92883 835-D5
COYOTE PASS DR
22900 RivC 92595 927-F2
COZUMEL CT
- MURR 92563 928-H7
- RIV 92501 686-A1
COZY CIR
26100 RivC 92544 841-E1
COZY CORNER RD
55000 RivC 92539 (934-F4 See Page 904)
CRAB HOLLOW CIR
23500 RivC 92595 897-E1
CRAFTON AV
11900 SBdC 92374 649-A2
11900 SBdC 92399 649-A2
11900 YCPA 92399 649-A2
CRAFTON HILLS CT
11900 YCPA 92399 649-A3
CRAFTON HILLS DR
31600 SBdC 92374 649-B3
31600 SBdC 92399 649-B3
31600 YCPA 92399 649-B3
CRAFTON HILLS RIDGE TR
10900 SBdC 92399 649-C2
11300 YCPA 92399 649-C2
CRAFTON POINTE DR
11900 YCPA 92399 649-B2
CRAGHILL DR
54500 RivC - 814-D5
CRAGMONT AV
25600 MORV 92557 687-H7
CRAIG AV
25100 RivC 92584 867-J5
25800 RivC 92584 868-A5
31000 RivC 92596 869-C5
CRAIG DR
24100 MORV 92553 717-E6
CRAIG PL
1500 RIV 92507 686-G1
CRAMER ST
60300 RivC 92262 725-F7
CRAMS CORNER DR
38600 RivC 92539 (934-B4 See Page 904)
CRANBERRY LN
1000 COR 92882 742-E5
CRANE CT
11600 MORV 92557 717-D1
CRANE ST
500 LKEL 92530 866-D2
12400 GTER 92313 646-F5
29400 LKEL 92532 866-D2
CRANE TER
15900 RivC 92530 865-J7
CRANFORD AV
3500 RIV 92507 686-B5
CRAPE MYRTLE DR
12500 MORV 92553 717-G5
CRATER DR
28100 RivC 92570 836-F6
CRATER LAKE CT
69000 RivC 92241 727-E2
CRAWFORD
17400 RivC 92530 896-C2
CRAWFORD DR
82700 INDO 92201 5470-G3
CRAWFORD ST
400 COR 92882 743-C5
CRAWFORD CANYON RD
29100 MURR 92563 898-H7
29200 MURR 92563 928-H1
CRAZY HORSE CT
2400 NRCO 92860 713-C4
CRAZY HORSE CANYON DR
40500 RivC 92536 963-A2
CREAG AV
25700 RivC 92548 809-C7
25800 RivC 92548 839-C1
CREATIVE DR
39600 TEM 92591 958-H1
CRECY DR
- RivC 92596 899-D7
CREE CT
49900 RivC 92536 963-E2
CREE LN
25300 RivC - 814-C5
CREE RD
5700 PMSP 92264 787-C6
35200 CTHC 92234 787-C6
35200 RivC 92234 787-C6
CREEK CIR
200 RIV 92507 686-E3
CREEKDALE WY
- RIV 92505 714-C7
CREEK HOLLOW WY
- RivC 92590 958-A7
CREEKRIDGE LN
4700 HEMT 92545 840-D4
CREEKRUN DR
- RIV 92505 714-C7
- RIV 92505 744-C1
CREEKSIDE DR
- RMIR 92270 817-J1
1700 HEMT 92545 840-E4
31500 LKEL 92532 866-J5
E CREEKSIDE DR
3400 ONT 91761 643-B6
CREEKSIDE LN
1100 COR 92880 743-B2
CREEKSIDE RD
16500 RivC 92503 744-F4
CREEKSIDE WY
45600 TEM 92592 979-B4
CREEKSTONE DR
24000 MORV 92551 747-E1
CREEKVIEW CIR
38100 MURR 92562 927-D3
CREEKVIEW TR
- RivC 92506 745-J2
CREEKWOOD CT
1100 PER 92571 807-J1
3500 RivC 92503 744-B4
CREEKWOOD DR
23800 MORV 92557 687-D5
CREIGHTON ST
11800 RIV 92505 714-A6
CRENSHAW CIR
- COR 92883 773-H7
4700 BAN 92220 721-E5
CRENSHAW DR
700 HEMT 92543 841-B3
CREOSOTE TR
15800 RivC 92282 724-F7
CRESCENT
400 LKEL 92530 866-G5
CRESCENT AV
3900 RIV 92501 685-H3
32400 LKEL 92530 896-J1
32400 RivC 92530 896-J1
W CRESCENT CIR
2200 CLTN 92324 646-H4
CRESCENT DR
500 PMSP 92262 786-C1
66700 DHSP 92240 697-A3
CRESCENT BAY CT
- YCPA 92399 649-H5
CRESCENT FALLS
- PDST 92260 848-D6
CRESCENT MOON CT
16200 RivC 92503 744-D3
CRESENT ST
- RivC 92203 789-G6
CRESENT BEND CIR
30500 RivC 92584 868-G3
CRESENT CANYON DR
22700 RivC 92570 806-F3
CREST AV
4600 RIV 92503 714-E1
7100 RIV 92503 684-E7
12100 RivC 92509 645-G4
12100 SBdC 92509 645-G4
82100 INDO 92201 5410-E5
CREST DR
27100 RivC 92544 841-C3
54500 RivC - 814-D7
CREST LN
12900 RivC 92282 724-E1
26600 RivC - 844-A2
CREST RD
9300 RivC 92324 687-F3
32400 RivC 92373 689-C5
CREST ST
61500 RivC 92240 695-H5
CRESTA DR
1800 PMSP 92264 786-F5
CRESTA RD
1200 COR 92879 743-G4
CRESTA DEL NORTE
- RivC 92563 958-J1
CRESTA DEL REYO
37700 MURR 92563 928-J4
CRESTA LAND CIR
39900 RivC 92562 926-F6
CRESTA VERDE DR
- RMIR 92270 817-G3
CRESTBROOK DR
900 RIV 92506 716-C6
10300 MORV 92557 687-B5
CRESTHAVEN CT
26200 LMLN 92354 647-F2
CRESTHAVEN DR
6300 RIV 92506 715-J3
CRESTKNOLL DR
9500 CALI 92320 690-A3
CREST LAKE DR
300 PDST 92211 818-J2
CRESTLAKE LN
17400 RivC 92503 744-G5
CRESTLINE DR
3200 COR 92881 773-D3
18400 RivC 92532 836-D5
29100 RivC 92584 837-J7
29100 RivC 92584 867-J1
29100 RivC 92584 868-A1
CRESTMONT CIR
800 COR 92882 773-B2
26000 RivC 92586 868-A1
CRESTMONT PL
- RIV 92508 746-E1
CRESTMOOR DR
34200 RivC 92567 809-H2
CRESTMORE RD
3400 RivC 92509 685-E3
CRESTON WY
- BEAU 92223 720-G2
CRESTONE DR
26100 RivC 92586 838-A4
CREST PARK CIR
5000 RIV 92507 686-D7
CRESTPOINT CT
- RIV 92505 744-C1
CREST RIDGE DR
- RIV 92507 716-G2
CRESTRIDGE DR
11500 RivC 92880 742-B5
CRESTSPRINGS LN
1100 RIV 92506 716-C5
CRESTVIEW
20000 RivC 92583 780-J3
CRESTVIEW AV
35500 YCPA 92399 650-B2
CRESTVIEW CIR
14500 MORV 92555 718-D6
CREST VIEW CT
6300 RIV 92506 716-B4
CRESTVIEW CT
11900 YCPA 92399 650-B2
43200 RivC 92220 691-G4
CRESTVIEW DR
- RivC 92592 979-H4
100 PMSP 92264 786-D5
3600 NRCO 92860 713-H2
4000 LKEL 92530 865-G4
CREST VIEW DR
8700 RivC 92883 804-B3
CRESTVIEW DR
24900 LMLN 92354 647-C2
26100 RivC - 814-C7
26400 RivC - 844-C1
35600 YCPA 92399 650-B2
48100 PDST 92260 848-D5
69200 RivC 92241 727-F1
CRESTVIEW ST
300 COR 92882 743-B7
E CRESTVIEW ST
100 COR 92879 743-D7
CRESTVIEW TER
78300 LQNT 92253 849-G2
CRESTWOOD CIR
44600 TEM 92592 979-H2
CRESTWOOD DR
19800 LKEL 92530 896-H5
69200 RivC 92241 727-E1
CRESTWOOD PL
2900 RIV 92503 714-J7
2900 RIV 92503 744-J1
26000 RivC 92544 811-J7
CRETE CT
- RIV 92506 716-C3
CREVASSE CT
1500 RIV 92506 715-G7
CREWS HILL DR
27000 RivC 92586 838-C7
CRICKET CT
19300 SBdC 92316 645-F3
CRICKET CV
39900 PDST 92211 819-D3
CRICKET DR
11700 SBdC 92316 645-F3
CRICKET LN
- RivC 92254 5592-E6
CRIDGE ST
2500 RIV 92507 685-H6
3300 RIV 92506 685-H6
CRILLY LN
31400 YCPA 92399 649-A4
CRIMSON CT
22700 RivC 92883 804-B3
CRIMSON DR
78200 LQNT 92253 819-F7
CRIMSON RIDGE CT
- RIV 92518 746-F2
CRINER TER
78300 RivC 92201 819-F4
CRISTEN RD
19400 RivC 92258 725-J5
CRISTI ANN LN
25200 RivC 92590 957-J6
CRISTOBAL AV
2200 HEMT 92545 810-G6
CRISTOL PL
44000 LQNT 92253 819-G7
CROCKER CIR
11300 MORV 92555 688-D7
CROCUS LN
38000 PDST 92211 819-B1
CROCUS PL
47800 INDO 92201 5470-B3
CRODOVA WY
25200 MORV 92557 717-G1
CROFT CT
2200 RIV 92506 715-J1
CROFTBORO RD
14800 MORV 92553 717-G7
CROHAMHURST CT
29000 RivC 92586 868-B1
CROMWELL CT
- RMIR 92270 817-J2
- RMIR 92270 818-A1
CROOKED ARROW DR
32600 RivC 92595 867-E7
32800 RivC 92595 897-E1
CROOKED STICK DR
- TEM 92591 959-C3
CROOKED STICK LN
- COR 92883 773-H7
CROP RD
18800 RivC 92504 775-J2
CROQUET CT
49100 INDO 92201 5470-C5
CROSBY DR
28900 RivC 92586 838-C7
82200 INDO 92201 5470-F4
CROSBY LN
73100 PDST 92260 848-E5
CROSLEY TKTR
- RivC 92536 409-F5
45200 RivC 92536 981-F4
CROSS ST
100 PER 92570 807-G4
2400 RivC 92503 744-G3
2500 RIV 92503 744-G2
17400 RivC 92530 896-B3
CROSSBROOK CIR
39400 RivC 92563 929-A7
CROSS CREEK
- RivC 92570 776-H4
CROSS CREEK CIR
9700 MORV 92557 687-B4
CROSS CREEK CT
39700 TEM 92591 959-A1
CROSS HILL DR
29400 RivC 92587 867-D2
29900 CYNL 92587 867-D3
CROSSING GREEN CIR
10200 MORV 92557 687-B5
CROSSLAND RD
36300 MURR 92563 929-A1
CROSSLEY RD
600 PMSP 92264 787-C4
31800 CTHC 92234 787-C2
CROSSMONT PL
12800 MORV 92553 717-D3
CROSS OVER RD
38800 RivC 92544 931-D5
CROSSPATCH RD
29900 MURR 92563 929-A1
CROSS RAIL LN
- NRCO 92860 713-J7
- NRCO 92860 714-A7
- NRCO 92860 743-J1
CROSS RIVER DR
6200 RivC 92509 684-H5
CROSSWATER ST
- INDO 92201 849-J1
CROSSWINDS CT
17300 LKEL 92530 865-G2
CROW CIR
45300 INDW 92210 849-B1
CROW LN
3900 RivC 92509 685-A1
CROW RD
29000 RivC 92544 841-D6
CROW ST
800 CALI 92320 649-E7
32500 YCPA 92373 649-D7
CROWELL AV
3400 RIV 92504 715-B4
CROWLEY LN
10700 RivC 92507 686-G7
CROWLEY VIEW CIR
5400 RivC 92509 684-C4
CROWN CT
35500 RMIR 92270 788-C6
CROWN DR
5900 RivC 91752 683-G5
CROWN ST
- RivC 92211 789-G6
CROWN WY
81700 INDO 92201 5410-E7
CROWN CREEK CIR
17700 RivC 92503 744-G6
CROWNED PARTRIDGE LN
24000 MURR 92562 928-B2
CROWNE HEIGHTS DR
26100 LMLN 92354 647-E3
CROWN HILL DR
- TEM 92592 959-G5
CROWN POINT CT
29300 RivC 92586 868-C1
CROWN RANCH RD
4100 COR 92881 773-D6
CROWN RIDGE RD
400 PER 92570 807-F2
CROWN VALLEY RD
33000 RivC 92596 870-G7
33100 RivC 92592 870-G7
33100 RivC 92592 900-H1
CROWN VIEW DR
1300 COR 92882 742-J6
CROWNWORTH ST
3400 RivC 92879 744-A5
CROWS NEST PL
39300 HEMT 92543 810-J4
39300 HEMT 92543 811-A4
CROYANCE DR
1400 RIV 92504 745-E3
CRUDEN BAY DR
- BAN 92220 721-D6
CRUISE CIRCLE LN
23500 CYNL 92587 867-F4
CRUMPTON RD
28000 LKEL 92570 836-G7
28000 RivC 92570 836-G7
CRUSADER PL
22200 CYNL 92587 867-B2
CRUZ WY
41200 RivC 92592 960-D4
CRYER DR
18800 RivC 92220 782-C2
CRYSTAL AV
8400 RIV 92504 715-A3
CRYSTAL CIR
2500 RivC 92509 645-A5
CRYSTAL CT
3700 PMSP 92264 786-J4
CRYSTAL DR
300 SJCT 92583 811-C3
CRYSTAL LP
47200 INDW 92210 849-B3
CRYSTAL AIRE CT
40300 MURR 92562 927-J1
40300 MURR 92562 928-A1
CRYSTALAIRE DR
31100 TEM 92591 959-C5
CRYSTAL ANN CT
21800 RivC 92570 806-A1
CRYSTAL BAY CT
- RMIR 92270 818-A2
CRYSTAL CREEK RD
600 PER 92571 807-J1
CRYSTAL DOWNS DR
- COR 92883 773-H6
CRYSTAL DOWNS ST
1500 BAN 92220 721-D5
CRYSTAL HILL RD
11000 MORV 92555 687-J7
CRYSTAL HILL ST
5900 RIV 92504 715-A2
CRYSTAL LAKE CT
3200 ONT 91761 643-B5
39400 MURR 92562 928-D3
E CRYSTAL LAKE RD
3100 ONT 91761 643-A5
CRYSTAL RIDGE CIR
3200 COR 92882 742-E6
CRYSTAL RIDGE CT
1700 RIV 92506 716-A5
CRYSTAL SPRINGS DR
- INDO 92201 5470-B1
13300 RivC 92883 835-B4
15800 RivC 92262 725-E7
S CRYSTAL SPRINGS PL
2600 ONT 91761 643-B5
CRYSTAL SPRINGS RD
22200 RivC 92567 778-J7
22200 RivC 92567 808-J1
CRYSTAL VIEW TER
- RivC 92508 716-B6
CUANDO WY
12500 DHSP 92240 697-B5
22000 RivC 92567 779-C7
22000 RivC 92567 809-C1
CUAUTLA RD
21000 RivC 92570 776-E6
CUCAMONGA AV
15700 SBdC 91710 712-E1
17200 SBdC 92880 712-E3
CUCAMONGA ST
6700 RIV 92505 714-E1
CUDAHY CT
8900 RIV 92503 714-F1
CUDY CIR
39000 RivC 92260 818-G2
CUETA DR
- RMIR 92270 818-D5
CUFF RD
- RivC - 411-C2
CULBERTSON LN
31200 TEM 92591 959-D3
CULEBRA LN
43800 RivC 92201 819-H6
CULLCUMBER DR
1100 COR 92882 742-E6
CULLEN CT
11200 RIV 92505 744-D1
CULVER PL
- PMSP 92262 756-F6
CUMBERLAND CT
- RivC 92203 789-G6
6600 RIV 92506 715-D1
CUMBERLAND ST
600 COR 92882 743-C6
CUMBRE RD
39200 RivC 92592 931-A6
CUMBRES CT
67100 CTHC 92234 757-B6
CUMIN ST
13800 MORV 92553 717-J5
CUMMING AV
25000 RivC 92585 808-G7
25600 RivC 92585 838-G1
CUPA LN
44700 TEM 92592 979-G3
CUPENO LN
30100 TEM 92592 979-A3
CUPENO RD
40000 MURR 92562 928-B2
CURIE CT
- RivC 92596 899-D7
CURRAN DR
4300 RIV 92503 714-G5
CURRANT CT
39500 MURR 92563 928-F5
CURRY CIR
2100 COR 92879 743-H2
CURRY CT
2100 COR 92879 743-H2
40200 RivC 92536 (933-C7 See Page 902)
CURRY ST
14800 MORV 92553 717-J7
CURTIN AV
22400 RivC 92241 728-G7
23400 RivC 92241 758-G1
CURTIS AV
17300 RivC 92530 896-B2
CURTIS CIR
13900 MORV 92555 718-E5
CURTIS DR
1000 NRCO 92860 713-F6
CURTIS RD
38700 RivC 92543 870-J3
38900 RivC 92543 871-A3
CURTIS ST
16500 RivC 92555 749-G4
20700 RivC 92567 779-C6
CURZULLA RD
30200 RivC 92584 898-J2
30200 RivC 92584 899-A2
30800 RivC 92596 899-B2
CUSHENBERRY DR
23800 MORV 92553 717-D4
CUSHING LN
21500 RivC 92570 776-F7
21500 RivC 92570 806-F1
CUSTER
17400 RivC 92530 896-C2
CUSTER CIR
- COR 92881 773-C4
CUSTER ST
11900 YCPA 92399 650-B2
CUTCA VALLEY TKTR
- RivC 92536 409-F5
CUTCHOQUE DR
32500 TEM 92592 979-F3
CUTTER DR
29700 CYNL 92587 867-E2
CUTTER WY
- RivC 92254 (5654-D2 See Page 5594)
CUTTERS RD
52300 RivC 92539 (903-J7 See Page 902)
CUTWOOD LN
6600 RIV 92506 716-E4
CUYAMA LN
19700 RIV 92508 746-E2
CUYAMACA DR
13000 DHSP 92240 696-H5
CYCLAMEN WY
38800 PDST 92211 819-B2
CYNTHIA ST
500 BEAU 92223 690-J5
4400 RIV 92505 714-E6
26300 RivC 92544 841-C1
CYPRESS AV
500 SJCT 92583 811-C1
7400 RIV 92503 714-F3
9900 RIV 92505 714-C3
10500 FONT 92337 644-G3
10900 SBdC 92337 644-H2
16000 CHNO 91710 712-B1
21000 RivC 92570 806-J5
21200 RivC 92570 807-A5
40500 RivC 92583 811-C1
W CYPRESS AV
1500 RDL 92373 647-J3
CYPRESS CT
300 COR 92879 744-B2
CYPRESS DR
- SJCT 92583 780-J6
600 RivC 91752 683-F4
71100 RMIR 92270 818-A4
CYPRESS LN
- BLY 92225 5491-E4
70600 RMIR 92270 787-J7
70800 RMIR 92270 788-A7
CYPRESS PL
23700 RivC 92587 837-E7
CYPRESS RD
2700 PMSP 92262 756-G4
55300 RivC 92282 694-D7
CYPRESS RD
69200 CTHC 92234 787-F1
CYPRESS ST
600 BEAU 92223 690-J6
2400 HEMT 92545 840-F2
12100 YCPA 92399 649-G3
25200 LMLN 92354 647-C2
27400 RivC 92590 978-E1
46500 INDO 92201 5470-H2
52300 COAC 92236 5471-C7
52300 COAC 92236 5531-C1
CYPRESS WY
400 PER 92570 807-F5
CYPRESS GROVE DR
6900 RIV 92506 716-D5
CYPRESS POINT DR
300 PDST 92211 818-J1
800 BAN 92220 721-C4
1900 RivC 92882 742-H5
28800 RivC 92584 868-F2
40900 RivC 92223 691-C5
78700 LQNT 92253 849-H6
S CYPRESS POINT DR
2800 ONT 91761 643-A6
S CYPRESS POINT PL
2600 ONT 91761 643-A6
CYPRESS POINT WY
- TEM 92591 959-D4
CYPRESS SANDS LN
14100 MORV 92553 717-H6
CYPRESS UNION LN
- MURR 92563 928-H6
CYRIL LN
43600 RivC 92544 811-J5
CYRISE LN
400 BEAU 92223 720-H1
CYRUS LN
17300 RivC 92504 746-A6

D

D ST
- HEMT 92545 840-F2
- RivC 91752 644-A5
1100 COR 92882 743-A5
3000 NRCO 92860 713-D5
41900 MURR 92562 928-A7
41900 TEM 92590 978-J1
43800 RivC 92544 811-J7
43800 RivC 92544 (812-A7 See Page 782)
68500 CTHC 92234 817-E1
N D ST
100 PER 92570 807-G2
S D ST
- PER 92570 807-G3
D ST S
14200 BLY 92225 392-D11
14200 RivC - 392-D11
14200 RivC 92225 392-D11
14200 BLY - 392-D11
DABNEY DR
24300 MORV 92553 717-F5
DAEMON HILLS DR
37400 RivC 92539 (934-E1 See Page 904)
DAFFODIL CIR
- RivC 92211 789-H7
DAFFODIL CT
- INDO 92201 5470-D5
6400 RivC 92880 683-D6
42300 RivC 92544 841-G3
DAFFODIL DR
- RivC 92883 804-B4
700 RIV 92507 686-D7
5200 RIV 92507 716-E2
76400 PDST 92211 819-C2
DAFFODIL LN
13300 YCPA 92399 650-B6
DAFFODIL ST
1100 COR 92882 743-B7
DAFFODIL WY
1900 HEMT 92545 810-G5
DAGAY CANYON RD
15500 RivC 92570 775-F4
DAGGET CREEK PTH
27200 PER 92587 837-H4
DAGMAR LN
32900 RivC 92548 809-F6
DAHL DR
13600 MORV 92553 717-F5
DAHLIA CIR
1500 COR 92882 743-A7
76200 PDST 92211 819-B2
DAHLIA CT
900 HEMT 92545 840-H2
27000 RivC 92586 838-B4
DAHLIA DR
- RivC 92883 804-B4
DAHLIA LN
5300 RIV 92507 686-D7
5300 RIV 92507 716-E2
DAHLIA ST
12900 FONT 92337 643-H2
DAHLIA WY
- TEM 92591 958-J5
38500 PDST 92211 819-B2
DAHLIAS WY
- MURR 92562 927-G3
DAILY DR
2300 SDCo 92028 997-A2
DAILY RD
2500 SDCo 92028 997-B1
12400 RivC 92220 692-F7
12400 RivC 92220 722-F1

STREET	Block	City	ZIP	Pg-Grid
DAILY RD				
	32800	RivC	92584	898-B1
	48400	SDCo	92028	977-C7
DAIMLER ST				
	13600	MORV	92553	717-H5
DAIRY RD				
	13000	YCPA	92399	650-E5
DAISEY DR				
	900	BEAU	92223	690-J7
DAISY AV				
	24700	LMLN	92354	647-B2
DAISY CIR				
	1100	COR	92882	743-B7
DAISY CT				
	12800	YCPA	92399	649-E4
	42700	RivC	92536	963-E5
DAISY DR				
	-	RivC	92883	804-B4
DAISY LN				
	-	MURR	92562	928-A7
	-	PDST	92211	818-G1
	-	RIV	92508	746-D1
DAISY ST				
	600	PMSP	92262	756-E4
	46600	INDO	92201	5470-E2
DAISY WY				
	2100	HEMT	92545	810-G5
DAISY FIELD CT				
	-	LKEL	92532	867-D6
DAISY FIELD LN				
	10600	MORV	92557	687-E6
DAKIN DR				
	2400	COR	92882	773-B1
DAKOTA AV				
	3000	RIV	92506	715-G1
DAKOTA CIR				
	10200	RivC	92223	691-B4
DAKOTA DR				
	28100	RivC	92587	837-E6
DAKOTA PL				
	12100	YCPA	92399	649-F3
DAKOTA TR				
	44300	INDW	92210	819-E7
	44600	INDW	92210	849-E1
DAKOTA SPRINGS WY				
	-	MURR	92562	927-J2
DALCROSS CT				
	5500	RIV	92507	716-F1
DALE AV				
	100	BEAU	92223	720-H1
DALE CIR				
	1200	COR	92880	743-B1
DALE CT				
	14500	LKEL	92530	865-E1
	21800	RivC	92567	778-F7
	49300	RivC	92230	723-B5
DALE ST				
	-	PER	92571	807-H2
	800	PER	92571	808-A2
	26400	RivC	92545	839-H2
	43100	RivC	92539	(965-A6 See Page 964)
DALEA AV				
	81700	INDO	92201	5410-D6
DALEA CIR				
	44000	LQNT	92253	819-J7
DALEA LN				
	48800	PDST	92260	848-F5
DALEHURST RD				
	11700	MORV	92555	688-A7
	11700	MORV	92555	718-A1
DALE KILER RD				
	65800	RivC	92254	5592-G6
DALE MESA DR				
	9400	CALI	92320	690-A3
DALES DR				
	2800	NRCO	92860	713-B7
DALES ST				
	6000	RIV	92504	684-J7
	27600	RivC	92585	838-G5
DALEWOOD CT				
	49200	RivC	92536	963-C1
DALGETY ST				
	-	COR	92882	773-A2
DALKE DR				
	17100	RivC	92504	745-F5
DALKE LN				
	17100	RivC	92504	745-F6
DALLA AV				
	16600	RivC	92518	746-H5
DALLAS AV				
	17200	RivC	92508	746-C5
DALLEY WY				
	3900	RivC	92509	644-D7
DALTON CT				
	-	RDL	92373	647-J1
DALTON DR				
	13500	RivC	92883	835-C5
DALY AV				
	3400	RivC	92509	685-E2
DAMASCUS AV				
	73500	RivC	92254	(5654-E7 See Page 5594)
	84600	COAC	92236	5471-A7
DAMASCUS RD				
	14500	MORV	92555	718-B6
DAMASCUS ST				
	13300	YCPA	92399	649-J6
	35700	YCPA	92399	650-C6
DAMASK ROSE CT				
	-	RivC	92211	819-F2
DAMIAN ST				
	23500	MORV	92553	717-D3
DAMON ST				
	6800	RIV	92504	715-D2
DAMSEL ST				
	30700	MURR	92584	898-F5
DAMSON DR				
	44900	RivC	92544	842-C2
DANA AV				
	6300	RivC	91752	683-G7
DANA CT				
	200	SJCT	92583	811-A2
DANA DR				
	31200	RivC	92596	899-C4
	54600	RivC	92539	(934-E1 See Page 904)
DANA LN				
	25000	MORV	92551	747-G2
DANA ST				
	1500	COR	92879	743-D7
	1900	COR	92879	773-D1
DANAVON WY				
	49800	RivC	92260	848-B6
DANBROOK DR				
	6200	RIV	92506	716-B3
DANBURY CT				
	300	COR	92879	744-B2
DANBURY DR				
	28100	RivC	92586	838-A6
DANBURY ST				
	12500	RivC	92282	724-A1
DANBY RD				
	41800	RivC	92592	960-A5
DANCING WATERS RD				
	78500	RivC	92211	789-G7
DANCY CIR				
	9000	RIV	92508	746-E3
DANDELION CT				
	-	RIV	92508	746-D2
	25700	MORV	92553	717-H5
	27400	TEM	92591	958-J2
DANDELION DR				
	-	LQNT	92253	819-J7
	-	LQNT	92253	849-J1
	-	LQNT	92253	5410-A7
DANDELION LN				
	17600	CHLS	91709	712-A5
DANDELION ST				
	12600	RivC	92880	683-D6
DANE CT				
	700	HEMT	92543	810-J5
	31700	TEM	92591	959-D2
DANIEL DR				
	3000	HEMT	92545	810-F5
	4400	RIV	92503	714-G5
DANIEL RD				
	26500	RivC	92584	868-C6
DANIELA ST				
	53900	RivC	92536	964-D7
DANIELLE CIR				
	-	PMSP	92264	787-C4
DANIELLE CT				
	-	LQNT	92253	5470-A5
DANIELLE WY				
	15000	LKEL	92530	865-G4
DANIELSON RD				
	22700	RivC	92570	806-F3
DANIGER AV				
	5900	RIV	92505	714-B4
DANITH PL				
	76800	PDST	92211	819-C6
DANNY LN				
	33000	RivC	92530	896-G5
DANNY KAYE RD				
	100	RMIR	92270	817-J3
DANPAM RD				
	56800	RivC	92539	(934-J1 See Page 904)
	56800	RivC	92539	(935-A1 See Page 904)
DANT ST				
	16600	RivC	92508	746-D4
DANTE CIR				
	6400	RIV	92506	716-C4
DANUBE CT				
	-	RivC	92544	(812-A5 See Page 782)
	30400	TEM	92591	959-B5
DANUBE WY				
	3100	RIV	92503	744-H1
DANVERS DR				
	7300	RIV	92506	716-D6
	7300	RIV	92508	716-D6
DAPHNE CT				
	25700	MORV	92553	717-H3
DAPHNE DR				
	25300	MURR	92563	928-F6
DAPPLE CT				
	39400	MURR	92562	898-A7
DAPPLE LN				
	4600	RivC	92509	684-E2
DARBY RD				
	78900	RivC	92201	819-G6
DARBY ST				
	500	COR	92879	744-B2
	21300	RivC	92595	897-B7
	21700	RivC	92595	927-C1
DARCEE DR				
	6100	RivC	92509	684-H5
DARDANELLE CT				
	26200	MORV	92555	717-J4
DARIEN CT				
	5600	RIV	92505	714-C4
DARIEN DR				
	42700	RivC	92201	819-J5
DARIN DR				
	18400	RivC	92570	777-B1
DARK CANYON RD S				
	2800	CLTN	92324	646-J5
	2900	RivC	92324	646-J5
	12500	SBdC	92324	646-J5
DARKSTAR DR				
	24600	MORV	92557	687-F5
DARKWOOD DR				
	400	RIV	92506	716-E4
DARLA DR				
	69700	CTHC	92234	787-G3
DARLENE DR				
	27400	MORV	92555	718-B2
DARLENE LN				
	6900	RivC	92509	645-B5
	33700	RivC	92596	869-H2
DARNELL DR				
	15000	RivC	92530	865-G6
DARR RD				
	23500	RivC	92567	809-F3
DARRELL DR				
	78600	RivC	92201	819-G5
DARREN CIR				
	9200	RivC	92509	684-D1
DARTANIAN PL				
	39500	MURR	92562	928-B1
DARTMOUTH AV				
	20000	RivC	92507	686-F7
	80600	INDO	92201	5470-B1
DARTMOUTH CIR				
	2900	COR	92879	744-B2
DARTMOUTH DR				
	-	RMIR	92270	818-A1
DARTMOUTH ST				
	2900	COR	92879	744-B2
	25800	RivC	92544	811-E7
	25900	RivC	92544	841-E2
N DARTMOUTH ST				
	100	HEMT	92544	811-E7
DARTOLO RD				
	44000	TEM	92592	979-E2
DARWIN AV				
	12500	GTER	92313	646-E5
DARWIN DR				
	2800	RIV	92504	715-C6
DARYLL RD				
	54900	RivC	-	814-E6
DASH FOR CASH CIR				
	43300	RivC	92592	960-B7
DATE				
	12600	BLY	92225	5491-G6
DATE AV				
	-	RivC	-	5239-J7
	600	BEAU	92223	690-J6
	900	COAC	92236	5471-B6
	34900	YCPA	92399	649-J2
	34900	YCPA	92399	650-A2
	51700	RivC	92230	723-G6
	83000	INDO	92201	5470-G2
DATE CT				
	3200	LKEL	92530	865-G1
DATE ST				
	300	LKEL	92530	865-G1
	500	HEMT	92543	811-A6
	1400	HEMT	92544	811-B6
	2700	RIV	92507	685-H6
	19600	RivC	92567	779-B2
	34700	YCPA	92399	649-J2
	39900	MURR	92563	928-H7
	39900	MURR	92591	928-H7
	39900	TEM	92591	928-H7
	40900	MURR	92563	958-E3
	41200	MURR	92562	958-E3
	41300	TEM	92591	958-E3
	56000	RivC	92274	5531-G4
DATE GARDEN DR				
	31600	RivC	92276	788-C2
DATE PALM AV				
	81200	RivC	92201	5470-C1
DATE PALM CIR				
	-	RivC	92503	744-J7
DATE PALM CT				
	47600	PDST	92260	848-G4
DATE PALM DR				
	26000	CTHC	92234	757-E4
	30000	CTHC	92234	787-F2
	37000	CTHC	92234	817-F1
	49500	LQNT	92253	849-H5
DATE PALM LN				
	69800	CTHC	92234	817-H1
	69800	RMIR	92270	817-H1
DATE PALM ST				
	-	RivC	92254	5592-F7
DATIL DR				
	29500	RivC	92587	867-F2
DATIL WY				
	72400	RivC	92276	788-D2
DAUBY CT				
	17300	RivC	92508	746-F6
DAUCHY AV				
	14600	RIV	92508	716-C7
	14600	RivC	92508	716-C7
	14700	RIV	92508	746-C2
	14700	RivC	92508	746-C2
DAUGHERTY RD				
	900	NRCO	92860	743-F1
DA VALL DR				
	30900	RivC	92270	757-H7
	30900	RivC	92270	787-H2
	30900	RMIR	92270	787-H2
	30900	CTHC	92234	787-H2
	37000	RMIR	92270	817-H1
DA VALL ESTATES DR				
	-	RMIR	92270	817-H1
DAVE AV				
	12000	RivC	92240	696-E5
DAVE CIR				
	3000	HEMT	92545	810-F5
DAVE RD				
	33300	RivC	92567	779-F6
DAVE ST				
	-	RivC	-	392-B10
DAVE KELLEY RD				
	68900	CTHC	92234	787-F4
DAVENPORT PL				
	11100	RIV	92505	714-D7
	11100	RIV	92505	744-D1
DAVENTRY RD				
	2300	RIV	92506	685-J7
DAVID CT				
	-	INDO	92201	5470-F5
DAVID LN				
	23500	MORV	92557	717-D2
DAVID PL				
	12200	MORV	92557	717-D2
DAVID ST				
	2800	RIV	92506	715-F3
	45600	RivC	92592	981-B4
DAVID WY				
	8000	RivC	92509	684-G6
DAVID JONES RD				
	1000	PER	92570	807-D5
	23300	RivC	92570	807-D5
DAVID MOUNTAIN RD				
	14000	RivC	92223	720-F5
DAVIDS RD				
	1000	PER	92571	807-G1
DAVIDSON ST				
	3800	RivC	92879	743-J5
DAVIE DR				
	67900	CTHC	92234	817-C2
DAVIES RD				
	1500	RIV	92501	685-J2
DA VINCI DR				
	1200	SJCT	92583	811-D3
	2200	RIV	92506	715-G5
DAVIS				
	82700	INDO	92201	5470-G3
DAVIS AV				
	16600	RivC	92518	746-G5
DAVIS RD				
	14200	MORV	92555	718-H6
	15000	MORV	92555	748-J1
	15300	RivC	92555	748-J1
	15800	RivC	92555	749-A4
	17400	RivC	92567	749-A7
	17400	RivC	92567	779-A1
	32500	RivC	92596	869-C7
	32500	RivC	92596	899-C1
	72700	PDST	92260	848-E4
DAVIS ST				
	100	RivC	92530	896-B1
	100	LKEL	92530	866-C4
	1600	COR	92882	743-D7
	11000	MORV	92557	687-E7
	11500	MORV	92557	717-E2
DAVIS WY				
	2800	PMSP	92262	756-E4
	25800	LMLN	92354	647-E2
DAVRIL CIR				
	1400	COR	92880	743-A3
DAWES LN				
	2700	COR	92879	744-A2
DAWES ST				
	400	PER	92571	777-E2
	1000	LKEL	92530	866-G6
	3900	RIV	92503	714-G6
	21100	RivC	92570	776-H2
	68900	CTHC	92234	817-F1
E DAWES ST				
	-	PER	92571	777-J2
W DAWES ST				
	-	PER	92571	777-G2
DAWN CT				
	20600	RivC	92562	926-J4
DAWN DR				
	11200	RIV	92505	714-B5
DAWN LN				
	28500	RivC	92596	839-C7
DAWN WY				
	200	BAN	92220	721-D3
DAWNCREST CIR				
	29800	TEM	92591	958-J4
DAWNRIDGE DR				
	1600	COR	92882	742-H6
DAWNRIDGE RD				
	-	RivC	-	(907-C2 See Page 906)
DAWN VIEW CIR				
	10200	MORV	92557	687-F5
DAWNVIEW CT				
	27000	RivC	92883	835-C4
DAWN WOOD ST				
	42900	MURR	92562	927-H7
DAWSON RD				
	22400	RivC	92571	808-D2
	24000	RivC	92585	808-D4
	26000	RivC	92585	838-D3
DAWSON ST				
	20000	RivC	92571	778-D4
DAWSON CANYON RD				
	10600	RivC	92883	804-D4
	11100	RivC	92570	804-G4
	11900	RivC	92570	805-B3
DAY LN				
	45000	RivC	92590	977-A3
DAY ST				
	11900	MORV	92557	717-A2
	11900	RIV	92557	717-A2
	12200	RIV	92553	717-A2
	12200	RIV	92507	717-A2
	12200	MORV	92553	717-A4
	17700	RivC	92570	747-A7
	18400	RivC	92570	777-A2
DAYBREAK CT				
	800	SJCT	92582	780-H6
DAYBREAK DR				
	26700	RivC	92883	835-C4
DAYBREAK LN				
	15300	FONT	92337	644-E3
DAYBREAK ST				
	2300	HEMT	92545	840-G2
DAYBREAK TR				
	11300	MORV	92557	687-E7
	11500	MORV	92557	717-E1
DAYBREAK WY				
	700	BAN	92220	721-G4
E DAY CREEK				
	3100	ONT	91761	643-A6
DAYFLOWER CT				
	2000	PER	92571	777-J6
DAYLILLY ST				
	-	FONT	92337	645-B2
DAYLILY CIR				
	74500	PDST	92260	818-H6
DAY LILY DR				
	25400	MURR	92563	928-F4
DAY STAR CIR				
	-	COR	92881	773-E4
DAYSTAR DR				
	200	PER	92571	777-H6
DAYTON AV				
	36700	RivC	92595	927-G2
DAYTON CT				
	-	SJCT	92583	780-J6
DAYTONA AV				
	9000	RIV	92503	714-F1
	73500	RivC	92254	(5654-E7 See Page 5594)
DBL DIAMOND DR				
	34500	RivC	92276	788-H4
DEACON DR E				
	78500	LQNT	92253	849-G7
DEACON DR W				
	51200	LQNT	92253	849-G7
	51200	LQNT	92253	879-F1
DEACON ST				
	26000	RivC	92570	837-J2
	26000	RivC	92585	837-J2
DEADWOOD CT				
	8200	RivC	92373	688-D1
DEADWOOD DR				
	2800	COR	92882	773-B2
DEADWOOD TR				
	10100	RivC	92223	691-B4
DEAL CT				
	29500	TEM	92591	958-J5
DEAN LN				
	34400	RivC	92595	897-C5
DEAN WY				
	5500	RIV	92504	715-A1
DEANA CT				
	26200	MORV	92555	717-J2
DEANE CIR				
	33100	RivC	92276	788-E3
DE ANNA RANCH RD				
	-	RivC	92562	956-E4
DEANNE CT				
	43500	RivC	92544	811-J7
DE ANZA AV				
	6300	RIV	92506	715-E1
DE ANZA CIR				
	800	COR	92882	743-C4
DE ANZA DR				
	100	SJCT	92583	811-A1
	200	ImCo	92274	(5773-B7 See Page 5712)
	600	SJCT	92582	810-J1
	600	SJCT	92582	811-A1
	900	SJCT	92582	780-F5
DE ANZA RD				
	23000	RivC	92590	977-E5
N DE ANZA RD				
	2600	PMSP	92262	756-D4
DE ANZA WY				
	73600	PDST	92260	848-F1
DEARDORFF DR				
	600	HEMT	92544	811-C5
DEATH VALLEY RD				
	42200	RivC	92220	721-E6
DEAUVILLE RD				
	-	RivC	92596	929-F1
DEAVER DR				
	3100	COR	92882	742-E5
DEBBIE DR				
	-	LQNT	92253	849-H1
DEBBIE LN				
	3200	RivC	92501	646-B6
	30700	RivC	92567	779-A4
N DEBBY DR				
	200	PMSP	92262	786-G2
DEBBY LN				
	38000	RivC	92544	931-G3
	75500	INDW	92210	849-A2
DEBERA DR				
	32100	LKEL	92530	865-H4
DE BERRY ST				
	21500	SBdC	92324	646-D4
	21700	GTER	92313	646-D4
E DE BERRY ST				
	300	CLTN	92324	646-C4
DEBON ST				
	32000	RivC	92584	867-J7
	32800	RivC	92584	897-J1
DEBORAH CT				
	100	RIV	92507	686-E3
	13500	YCPA	92399	650-C6
DEBORAH DR				
	82200	INDO	92201	5470-F3
DEBORAH PL				
	1400	BEAU	92223	690-J7
DEBORAH RD				
	1800	PMSP	92262	756-G5
DEBRA WY				
	11000	MORV	92557	687-D7
DE BRASK AV				
	17200	LKEL	92530	866-A2
DEBRA SUE LN				
	23200	RivC	92570	807-D7
DECADE CT				
	2200	RIV	92506	716-A3
DE CAMP CT				
	5300	RIV	92504	715-B2
DECARISO RD				
	31700	RivC	92530	895-E3
DE CARLO RD				
	15900	RivC	92570	805-G3
DECATUR WY				
	27500	RivC	92586	838-A5
DECEMBER CT				
	12900	RivC	92503	744-B4
E DECEPTION RD				
	22000	RivC	92241	390-C6
DECKER RD				
	17500	RivC	92570	747-B7
	18300	RivC	92570	777-B1
DECKER CANYON LN				
	14000	RivC	92530	895-D3
DECKER CANYON RD				
	13900	RivC	92530	895-D3
DECLARATION CT				
	-	LQNT	92253	819-J7
	-	LQNT	92253	5410-A7
DE CORONADO DR				
	47600	INDO	92201	5470-D3
DEDEAUX LN				
	23800	RivC	92570	807-C4
DEEBLE ENTRANCE				
	33000	RivC	92530	896-B2
DEE BOB CT				
	29300	RivC	92567	808-G1
DEEGAN ST				
	2700	SJCT	92582	780-D7
DEEPAK RD				
	1000	PMSP	92262	756-F6
DEEP CANYON RD				
	10000	MORV	92557	687-D5
	43000	PDST	92260	818-H7
	44400	PDST	92260	848-H2
DEEP CREEK DR				
	48800	PDST	92260	848-D5
DEEP VALLEY TR				
	12200	MORV	92555	718-D2
DEEP WELL RD				
	900	PMSP	92264	786-F5
	24800	RivC	92595	897-H2
DEEPWOOD CIR				
	41800	TEM	92591	958-J4
DEEP WOOD DR				
	37300	MURR	92562	927-E3
DEER RUN				
	1500	COR	92882	743-A6
DEERBERRY DR				
	25800	MORV	92553	717-J3
DEERBROOK CIR				
	-	LQNT	92253	849-H1
	-	RivC	92211	819-F2
DEER BROOK RD				
	35700	YCPA	92399	650-C1
DEER CREEK CIR				
	25800	RivC	92584	838-A7
	26600	RivC	92584	868-A1
DEER CREEK CT				
	13500	RivC	92883	835-C5
DEERCREEK DR				
	-	COR	92881	773-F2
	8600	RIV	92508	746-F2
DEER CREEK LP				
	-	ONT	91761	643-B6
DEERCREEK RD				
	9800	MORV	92557	687-B4
DEER CREEK WY				
	48300	RivC	92536	963-B2
DEER CROSSING RD				
	39600	RivC	92544	931-B1
DEERE CT				
	26300	MURR	92562	958-D2
DEERFERN AV				
	23900	MORV	92553	717-E4
DEERFIELD CIR				
	1800	COR	92882	772-H1
DEERFIELD CT				
	-	RMIR	92270	818-A3
DEERFIELD DR				
	10600	RivC	92223	691-C5
DEERFIELD PL				
	-	RivC	92274	5530-H3
DEERFIELD RD				
	5900	RIV	92504	685-B7
DEERFOOT CT				
	40700	RivC	92536	963-A2
DEER FOOT LN				
	27000	RivC	-	844-A2
DEER GRASS DR				
	72900	PDST	92260	848-E4
DEER HAVEN CIR				
	700	PDST	92211	819-C3
DEERHAVEN WY				
	48300	RivC	92536	963-B1
DEER HILL PL				
	13600	MORV	92553	717-G5
DEERHILL RD				
	400	PER	92570	807-F2
DEER HOLLOW DR				
	-	COR	92882	772-J2
DEER HOLLOW WY				
	-	RivC	92592	979-F6
	-	TEM	92592	979-F6
DEERHORN DR				
	2300	RIV	92506	715-J2
DEERLODGE CIR				
	-	COR	92881	773-D4
DEER MEADOW RD				
	30100	TEM	92591	959-A2
DEER MOUNTAIN WY				
	51000	RivC	92539	(933-G3 See Page 902)
DEERPARK DR				
	13200	MORV	92553	717-E4
DEER PASS LN				
	30500	RivC	92563	929-B6
DEER PATH RD				
	25200	RivC	-	(813-H5 See Page 782)
DEER RUN CT				
	22700	MURR	92562	927-D3
DEERSKIN DR				
	27700	RivC	92585	838-D5
DEER SPRING CT				
	-	PDST	92211	818-J3
DEERSPRING TR				
	51400	RivC	92536	983-H4
DEER SPRING WY				
	-	PDST	92211	818-J4
DEERVIEW DR				
	-	RivC	92324	688-C4
DEERWEED CIR				
	8800	RivC	92883	804-B4
DEERWOOD DR				
	800	SJCT	92583	780-H7
	6700	RIV	92506	716-E4
DEERWOOD LN				
	12000	MORV	92557	717-E2
DEFIANCE WY				
	11600	MORV	92557	717-F1
DE FOREST CIR				
	3100	RivC	91752	643-H5
DE FRAIN BLVD				
	-	RivC	92225	5491-B4
	6800	BLY	-	5491-B1
	8900	BLY	92225	5491-B4
	17000	RivC	-	5551-C5
	17000	RivC	92225	5551-B2
	23100	RivC	-	412-C1
DEGHER CT				
	8300	RIV	92504	715-A3
DEGLET NOOR ST				
	43100	INDO	92201	5410-F6
	45100	INDO	92201	5470-F1
DE GRAZIA RD				
	6600	RIV	92506	715-G5
DEHAVIN CT				
	24000	RivC	92570	807-D5
DEKALB ST				
	21100	RIV	92508	746-H3
DEKAY AV				
	300	RivC	92518	747-C1
W DEKEMA ST				
	-	BLY	92225	5491-E7
DEKENS CT				
	-	BLY	-	392-B9
DE LA LAMA ST				
	30500	RivC	92530	865-F4
DE LA LUZ CIR				
	600	PER	92571	807-J2
DEL AMO ST				
	21500	MORV	92557	716-J1
DELANCY LN				
	1800	COR	92881	773-H5
DELANEY CIR				
	27700	MURR	92562	898-E7
DELANO DR				
	-	INDO	92201	5470-F5
	8700	RIV	92503	714-J3
	26200	RivC	-	814-B7
	26500	RivC	-	844-A2
DELAPP DR				
	3300	HEMT	92545	810-F6
DE LARA LN				
	26000	RivC	92585	838-A2
DE LA VALLE DR				
	15600	MORV	92555	748-C2
DE LA VEGA CT				
	-	MORV	92555	748-C1
DE LA VISTA				
	5700	RivC	92509	685-B2
DELAWARE PL				
	77600	PDST	92211	819-E6
DELAWARE ST				
	7100	RIV	92504	715-D3
	43100	PDST	92211	819-E6
DEL BRIENZA				
	-	LKEL	92532	866-J3
DELCA LN				
	32400	RivC	92595	927-D1
DEL CERRO WY				
	2400	HEMT	92545	840-G1
DEL COPPARO				
	-	LKEL	92532	867-A3
DEL CORONADO DR				
	45700	PDST	92260	848-H2
DELCRESTA DR				
	10000	MORV	92557	687-B5
DEL DIOS CIR				
	44800	INDW	92210	819-A7
DELFBUSH ST				
	14800	MORV	92553	717-G7
DELFERN LN				
	9300	RivC	92509	684-C1
DEL FIORE				
	-	LKEL	92532	867-A3
DEL FLORA DR				
	3000	HEMT	92545	810-F5
DELGADO CT				
	24100	MORV	92553	717-E5
DELGADO DR				
	45400	INDW	92210	849-D1
DELGADO RD				
	1200	PMSP	92262	756-F5
DELGADO WY				
	37100	RivC	92592	960-F2
DEL GATO DR				
	52000	LQNT	92253	879-F1
DEL HAVEN RD				
	21600	RivC	92883	804-C1
DELHI PL				
	42600	RivC	92201	5410-A5
DELIA CT				
	-	RIV	92504	715-B5
DELICIOUS DR				
	-	RivC	92544	811-H6
DELICIOUS LN				
	10800	RivC	92223	691-B5
DELILAH ST				
	1600	COR	92879	743-H4
DE LINES DR				
	700	PER	92570	807-F1
	1300	PER	92570	777-F7
DELISE DR				
	30100	RivC	92543	871-B2
DELL AV				
	3900	RivC	92509	644-J7
DELLA LN				
	11800	SBdC	92324	646-C3
DELLA ST				
	7600	RIV	92503	714-G4
DEL LAGO RD				
	1800	PMSP	92262	756-G5
DELLA ROBBIA LN				
	49000	PDST	92260	848-E5
DELLVALE PL				
	11800	RIV	92505	714-A5
DELLWOOD DR				
	11500	RIV	92503	744-E3
DEL MAR				
	200	PMSP	92264	786-J6
DEL MAR CIR				
	100	RivC	91752	683-E5
DEL MAR CT				
	30000	TEM	92592	959-A7
DELMAR CT				
	40000	RivC	92536	(933-C7 See Page 902)
DEL MAR DR				
	1000	HEMT	92545	810-G5
DEL MAR LN				
	100	RMIR	92270	817-H2
DEL MAR RD				
	2200	NRCO	92860	713-A7
DEL MAR WY				
	1200	PMSP	92262	756-F6
	2200	COR	92882	742-G7
	4900	RIV	92504	715-C1
DEL MESA DR				
	19400	SBdC	92316	645-G3
DEL MESA RD				
	-	HEMT	92545	810-C6
DELMONT				
	68600	RivC	-	(907-F4 See Page 906)
DEL MONTE CT				
	78900	LQNT	92253	849-H6
DEL MONTE DR				
	700	HEMT	92543	841-B3
	28600	RivC	92586	838-B7
	28900	RivC	92586	868-B1
DEL MONTE LN				
	27200	RivC	92586	838-D5
DELMONTE ST				
	-	TEM	92591	959-D5
DEL MONTE ST				
	5300	RIV	92504	715-B2
DEL NORTE CT				
	47600	INDO	92201	5470-D3
DEL NORTE DR				
	1400	COR	92879	743-G3
DEL NORTE WY				
	72500	RivC	92276	788-C1
DEL OBISPO RD				
	15700	FONT	92337	644-F2
DELOR RD				
	46100	RivC	92539	(985-F5 See Page 964)
DELORME DR				
	24900	RivC	92590	977-J3
DE LOSS DR				
	8500	RIV	92508	746-H2
DEL PARQUE CT				
	39200	RivC	92562	926-H6
DEL PASEO CT				
	20100	RivC	92570	776-F1
DEL PASO WY				
	1300	PMSP	92262	756-F5
DELPHI CT				
	10000	RIV	92503	744-H1
	80100	INDO	92201	5470-A4
DELPHINIUM AV				
	22400	MORV	92555	718-A7
	24000	MORV	92553	717-E7
	25900	MORV	92555	717-H7
DELPHINIUM DR				
	2000	PER	92571	777-J6
DELPHINUS DR				
	25400	RivC	92586	837-J6
DEL PIZZOLI				
	-	LKEL	92532	867-A3
DEL RAY CT				
	6000	RIV	92506	685-F7
	9300	DHSP	92240	696-H1
DEL RAY LN				
	9500	DHSP	92240	696-H1
DEL REY				
	-	RMIR	92270	787-H7
DEL REY RD				
	29600	TEM	92591	958-J4
	29600	TEM	92591	959-A4
DEL REY ST				
	45500	INDO	92201	5470-D1
DEL RIO RD				
	27800	TEM	92590	958-G6
DEL RITA TR				
	57100	RivC	92539	(985-B1 See Page 964)
DEL ROSA DR				
	26500	RivC	92544	841-F1
DEL ROSA PL				
	6900	RIV	92504	715-B2
DEL SANTELLO				
	-	LKEL	92532	867-A3
DEL SOL				
	43800	INDO	92203	5410-J6
DEL SOL CT				
	39200	RivC	92562	926-H6
N DEL SOL RD				
	300	PMSP	92262	756-D4
DEL SUR DR				
	11500	RivC	91752	683-G5
DELTA CIR				
	-	COR	92881	773-D4
DELTA DR				
	30400	RivC	92567	778-J6
DELTA ST				
	79000	RivC	92201	819-H4
DELTA WY				
	11200	RIV	92505	714-D7
DEL TORINO				
	-	LKEL	92532	867-A3
DELUCA WY				
	-	TEM	92592	979-F2
DELUX				
	200	LKEL	92530	866-E5
DE LUZ RD				
	800	SDCo	92028	997-A6
	800	SDCo	92055	997-A6
	31700	SDCo	92028	976-F7
	42400	RivC	92590	958-A5
	42500	MURR	92562	958-A3
	42600	RivC	92590	957-G6
	43000	RivC	92562	958-A3
	43800	RivC	92590	977-E4
DE LUZ HEIGHTS RD				
	2500	SDCo	92028	997-C2
DE LUZ MURRIETA RD				
	35900	SDCo	92028	976-G7
	35900	SDCo	92028	977-A6
DEL VAL DR				
	39500	MURR	92562	928-C2
DEL VALLE CT				
	69700	RMIR	92270	787-G6
DEL VISTA CT				
	11800	YCPA	92399	649-J2
DEL WEBB BLVD				
	-	RivC	92203	789-F4
	37000	RivC	92211	789-G7
	38000	RivC	92211	819-F1
DE MARCO RD				
	-	RIV	92508	746-E1
DE MARQUEZ CT				
	39500	RivC	92592	930-D7
DEMETER PL				
	2800	RivC	92509	685-E1
DEMING CT				
	5800	RIV	92506	716-A2
DEMIT ST				
	33300	RivC	92548	809-F5
DEMPSEY AV				
	17200	LKEL	92530	866-A3
DEMPSEY DR				
	75500	PDST	92211	819-A5
DENAIR CT				
	-	RIV	92508	716-E7
DENDY PKWY				
	-	TEM	92590	958-D5
DENIAN CT				
	41100	MURR	92562	928-A4
DENISE CT				
	5500	RIV	92506	715-J1
	21000	RivC	92595	897-A7
DENISE RD				
	40000	RivC	92544	961-D3
	40000	RivC	92592	961-B2
DENISE WY				
	800	COR	92880	743-D2
	34100	RMIR	92270	787-G5
DENIZEN HEIGHTS RD				
	26400	RivC	92544	842-D1
DENNEY PL				
	6100	RIV	92504	684-J7
	6100	RIV	92504	685-A7
DENNINGTON CT				
	-	RivC	92274	(5652-B4 See Page 5592)
DENNIS DR				
	6000	RivC	91752	683-J5
DENNIS WY				
	900	SJCT	92582	780-J7
DENNY DR				
	29700	LKEL	92530	866-B2
	53300	RivC	92539	(934-B4 See Page 904)
DENSLOW ST				
	46500	INDO	92201	5470-G2
DENTON ST				
	2700	RIV	92507	685-H6
DENVER AV				
	83500	INDO	92201	5470-H3
DENVER CT				
	23100	MORV	92553	717-C4
DEODAR AV				
	12500	DHSP	92240	697-D4
DEODAR CT				
	9100	RIV	92503	715-A7
DEODAR LN				
	-	TEM	92592	959-E5
DE ORO AV				
	81500	INDO	92201	5470-D1
DE PALMA RD				
	12700	RivC	92883	388-K10
	12700	RivC	92883	835-A2
DE PASSE WY				
	700	HEMT	92544	841-C2
	700	RivC	92544	841-C2
DE PLATA AV				
	81500	INDO	92201	5470-D1
DE PLATA CT				
	45500	INDO	92201	5470-D1
DE PORTOLA RD				
	30500	TEM	92592	979-D2
	32400	RivC	92543	871-A6
	33000	TEM	92592	959-H7
	33000	RivC	92592	959-H7
	33000	RivC	92592	979-D2
	34200	RivC	92592	960-E3
	39400	RivC	92592	930-J1
	41900	RivC	92592	931-A4
	43800	RivC	92592	900-H1
	47000	RivC	92543	870-J7
	47000	RivC	92592	870-J7
DEPOT DR				
	100	COR	92880	743-D4
DEPOT ST				
	3300	RIV	92504	715-D4
DEPRAD ST				
	21000	RivC	92570	806-J4
	21500	RivC	92570	807-B4
	23000	PER	92570	807-B4
DEPUTY RD				
	39200	TEM	92591	929-C7
DERBY DR				
	-	MURR	92563	928-H4
	9400	RivC	92509	684-C2
DERBY ST				
	800	COR	92882	773-B2
DERBY WY				
	48800	RivC	92536	963-C5
DEREK ALAN DR				
	-	LQNT	92253	5470-A5
DERONDA AV				
	61200	RivC	92282	695-G4
DERRY LN				
	56900	RivC	92539	(935-A3 See Page 904)
DESCANSO CIR				
	29700	CTHC	92234	757-D7
DESCANSO DR				
	13900	RivC	92570	805-C1
	14100	RivC	92570	775-D7
	41200	RivC	92544	841-E4
DESCANSO LN				
	78400	LQNT	92253	849-G4
DESERET CT				
	32000	RivC	92595	897-C6
DESERT AV				
	1700	RivC	-	5240-B6
DESERT DR				
	-	LQNT	92253	849-F4
	71900	RMIR	92270	818-C6
DESERT RDG				
	13600	RivC	92883	835-C6
DESERT TER				
	11500	DHSP	92240	696-E4
DESERT WY				
	500	PMSP	92264	786-J3
DESERT ACACIA LN				
	9200	RivC	92883	804-C3
DESERT AIR CT				
	64800	RivC	92240	656-E7
DESERT AIR DR				
	72000	RMIR	92270	818-C6
DESERT AIR ST				
	45100	LQNT	92253	849-H1
DESERTAIRE DR				
	74300	RivC	92254	(5655-A7 See Page 5594)
	74400	RivC	92254	(5715-A1 See Page 5714)
DESERT ANGEL DR				
	39700	RivC	92260	818-F3
DESERT ARROYO TR				
	-	INDW	92210	848-G6
DESERT BAJADA TR				
	-	INDW	92210	848-G5
DESERT BARRANCA TR				
	-	INDW	92210	848-G5
DESERT BEACH DR				
	-	RivC	92254	(5654-D6 See Page 5594)

RIVERSIDE CO.

STREET
Block City ZIP Pg-Grid

DESERT BLOOM TR
- INDW 92210 848-F5
- PDST 92260 848-F5
DESERT BUTTE TR
49500 INDW 92210 848-H5
DESERT CACTUS DR
56000 RivC 92274 5531-H4
DESERT CALICO
56800 RivC - 878-B6
DESERT CENTER RICE RD
- RivC - 5421-B4
DESERT CENTER RICE RD Rt#-62
- RivC - 391-G2
DESERT CENTER RICE RD Rt#-177
- RivC - 391-E7
- RivC - 5421-E1
DESERT CHARM RD
28900 RivC 92241 390-D8
DESERT CIRCLE DR
72800 PDST 92260 848-F4
DESERT CITY RD
12000 DHSP 92240 695-H4
12000 RivC 92240 695-H4
DESERT CLOUD TR
- INDW 92210 848-H6
DESERT CLUB DR
50800 LQNT 92253 849-F7
DESERT COVE AV
70300 RMIR 92270 817-H3
DESERT CREEK LN
40300 RMIR 92270 818-C4
DESERT CREST AV
16500 RivC 92241 727-F1
DESERT CREST DR
79200 LQNT 92253 849-J1
DESERT EAGLE CT
45200 LQNT 92253 849-J1
DESERT FALL WY
78200 LQNT 92253 849-G6
DESERT FALLS CIR
- PDST 92211 819-A3
DESERT FALLS CT
100 PDST 92211 819-A2
DESERT FALLS DR
- PDST 92211 818-J2
100 PDST 92211 819-A3
DESERT FALLS DR E
100 PDST 92211 819-A2
DESERT FALLS DR N
400 PDST 92211 819-A1
400 PDST 92211 818-J1
DESERT FALLS PKWY
1100 PDST 92211 818-J2
DESERT FERN LN
- PDST 92260 848-C6
DESERT FLOWER DR
48700 PDST 92260 848-D5
S DESERT FOREST AV
2600 ONT 91761 643-A6
DESERT FOX CT
- BEAU 92223 690-J6
DESERT FOX DR
45200 LQNT 92253 849-J1
DESERT GARDEN TR
- PDST 92260 848-G5
DESERT GREENS DR E
38100 RivC 92260 818-F2
DESERT GREENS DR N
73100 RivC 92260 818-E1
DESERT GREENS DR S
39600 RivC 92260 818-F3
DESERT GREENS DR W
38200 RivC 92260 818-E1
DESERT GROVE DR
48100 INDO 92201 5470-D4
DESERT HAVEN RD
18000 RivC 92241 728-C4
DESERT HILLS CT
45200 LQNT 92253 849-J1
DESERT HILLS RD
29000 RivC 92586 838-C7
29100 RivC 92586 868-C1
DESERT HOLLY CIR
400 PMSP 92262 756-D5
DESERT HOLLY DR
100 PDST 92211 819-C3
DESERT HOLLY ST
73100 PDST 92260 848-E3
DESERT HORIZONS DR
44800 INDW 92210 849-A1
53100 INDW 92210 819-A7
DESERT JEWEL DR
29600 RivC 92584 868-H1
DESERT LAKES CIR
400 PMSP 92264 786-J5
DESERT LAKES DR
- PMSP 92264 786-J5
- PMSP 92264 787-A5
100 RMIR 92270 818-D4
DESERT LAWN DR
10500 CALI 92320 690-B5
10700 RivC 92320 690-D7
11300 BEAU 92223 720-E1
11300 RivC 92223 690-D7
11300 RivC 92223 720-E1
DESERT LILY DR
46300 PDST 92260 848-E2
DESERT MALLOW
10100 MORV 92557 687-D5
DESERT MIRAGE DR
38600 PDST 92260 818-H2

DESERT MOON DR
29100 RivC 92276 758-F7
30000 RivC 92276 788-F2
DESERT MOUNTAIN CIR
78200 RivC 92201 819-F5
DESERT OAK LN
- MURR 92562 927-H2
DESERT OASIS TR
- INDW 92210 848-G6
DESERT PALM DR
30000 RivC 92276 758-E7
30000 RivC 92276 788-E1
DESERT PALMS DR
1700 PMSP 92262 786-G1
E DESERT PALMS DR
1900 PMSP 92262 786-G1
DESERT PARK AV
1800 PMSP 92262 756-G5
DESERT PARK DR
30000 RivC 92276 758-E7
30000 RivC 92276 788-E1
75300 INDW 92210 848-J2
75300 INDW 92210 849-A1
DESERT PRINCESS DR
28000 CTHC 92234 757-C6
DESERT ROCK CT
79300 LQNT 92253 849-J1
DESERT ROCK LN
8600 RIV 92508 746-F2
DESERT ROCK RD
31700 RivC 92241 390-D8
DESERT ROSE DR
- CTHC 92234 787-C6
- PMSP 92264 787-C6
73200 PDST 92260 848-E4
DESERT ROSE LN
74100 INDW 92210 848-G3
DESERT SAGE CT
47600 PDST 92260 848-G4
DESERT SAND AV
6700 RIV 92505 714-B2
DESERT SAND CT
45200 LQNT 92253 849-J1
DESERT SAND RD
64000 RivC 92240 696-D5
DESERT SHORES PKWY
- INDO 92201 5470-D4
DESERT SPRINGS CIR
- PDST 92260 818-G4
DESERT SPRINGS DR
39600 PDST 92260 818-H3
DESERT STAR BLVD
74000 PDST 92260 818-G7
DESERT STAR ST
10200 MORV 92557 687-D5
DESERT STREAM DR
79200 LQNT 92253 849-H1
DESERT SUN DR
39500 RMIR 92270 818-B3
DESERT TENAJA TR
- INDW 92210 848-G6
DESERT TERRACE DR
29300 RivC 92584 868-G1
DESERT TRAILWAYS LN
- RivC 92225 5491-C5
DESERT VALLEY LN
45300 INDW 92210 849-A2
DESERT VIEW AV
12900 RivC 92282 724-F1
64700 RivC 92240 696-E4
65000 DHSP 92240 696-G4
66700 DHSP 92240 697-B4
DESERT VIEW CT
45200 LQNT 92253 849-J1
DESERT VIEW DR
500 PMSP 92264 786-J3
72000 PDST 92260 848-D4
DESERT VIEW RD
15000 RivC 92282 695-G7
15300 RivC 92282 725-F1
68100 CTHC 92234 817-D2
DESERT VILLA
46500 INDO 92201 5470-D2
DESERT VISTA
200 CTHC 92234 787-E6
DESERT VISTA CT
73700 PDST 92260 848-G4
DESERT VISTA RD
32000 CTHC 92234 787-E3
DESERT WEST DR
100 RMIR 92270 787-H6
DESERT WILLOW CIR
300 PMSP 92262 756-E5
DESERT WILLOW CT
74000 PDST 92260 818-G2
DESERT WILLOW DR
- BLY 92225 5491-D5
- DHSP 92240 696-G4
25100 MORV 92553 717-G6
39000 PDST 92260 818-H2
78000 RivC 92211 789-F7
DESERT WILLOW LN
1100 COR 92879 743-F7
DESERT WILLOW ST
- LQNT 92253 849-J3
- LQNT 92253 5470-A4
DESERT WIND CT
79200 LQNT 92253 849-J1
DESI DR
77000 INDW 92210 849-D2
DESIERTO DR
45500 INDW 92210 849-A2
DESIERTO VISTA
- PMSP 92264 787-B7

DESILVA RD
57400 RivC 92539 (965-B7
See Page 964)
DE SOL A SOL
- LQNT 92253 5470-A6
DE SOTO DR
500 HEMT 92543 810-J6
DESOTO PL
14800 MORV 92553 717-H7
DE SOTO ST
22200 GTER 92313 646-E4
DESPERADO CT
45500 RivC 92536 982-E3
DESPERADO DR
4700 RivC 92509 684-G2
14000 RivC 92530 835-D4
DESSA CT
700 PER 92570 807-E2
DESSIE WY
43300 RivC 92544 811-J5
DESTINY DR
30100 RivC 92563 929-A7
DETROIT DR
3300 RIV 92504 715-C4
DETROIT ST
1300 NRCO 92860 713-E3
DEUTSCH DR
25000 RivC 92590 977-J2
DE VENDOME CT
39100 MURR 92563 928-G7
DEVENER ST
400 RivC 92507 646-B7
DEVERON CT
5300 RIV 92507 716-F1
DE VICENZO CT
9000 RivC 92240 696-D1
DEVILS CANYON DR
38200 RivC 92260 818-E1
DEVILS GARDEN
5600 RivC 92282 655-J4
DEVILS LADDER RD
59300 RivC - (905-F4
See Page 904)
DEVINE CIR
11200 RivC 92503 744-F3
DE VINNA CT
40500 RivC 92544 841-C3
DEVON CT
- RIV 92508 716-E7
DEVON RD
18800 RivC 92881 773-H2
DEVON ST
- MURR 92584 898-F4
DEVONPORT CT
37000 HEMT 92545 810-D7
DEVONSHIRE AV
3300 HEMT 92545 810-D7
E DEVONSHIRE AV
100 HEMT 92543 811-A6
200 HEMT 92544 811-B6
W DEVONSHIRE AV
100 HEMT 92543 811-A6
300 HEMT 92543 810-H6
1800 HEMT 92545 810-F7
35200 RivC 92545 810-A7
DEVONSHIRE DR
2000 COR 92879 773-F1
DEVONSHIRE RD
2500 RIV 92506 715-H1
DEVONSHIRE ST
42500 PDST 92211 819-E5
DEVOTION AV
39200 RivC 92563 929-A7
DE WAIDE AV
25200 RivC 92544 811-J6
DEWDROP CIR
23200 MORV 92553 717-C3
DEWEY AV
4400 RIV 92506 715-C1
4700 RIV 92504 715-B1
34900 YCPA 92399 649-J2
34900 YCPA 92399 650-A2
DEWEY DR
26700 RivC 92545 839-F3
DEXTER AV
18000 RivC 92532 866-C1
18200 LKEL 92532 866-C1
DEXTER DR
2400 RIV 92501 685-G2
DEXTER PL
18700 LKEL 92532 866-D2
DIA PL
30000 CTHC 92234 787-B1
DIABLO
- PMSP 92264 786-C2
DIABLO CT
2000 HEMT 92545 810-G6
DIABLO RD
12000 DHSP 92240 695-J6
12000 RivC 92240 695-J6
13000 RivC 92258 695-J6
13000 RivC 92258 725-J2
17000 PMSP 92258 725-J2
DIABLO ST
61500 RivC 92240 695-H5
DIADOMITE WY
42000 PDST 92260 818-G5
DIAL RD
33000 RivC 92595 897-C2
DIAL WY
21600 RivC 92883 804-B1
DIAMANTE CT
700 SJCT 92583 811-C4

DI AMICO TR
60800 RivC - (905-H6
See Page 904)
DIAMOND AV
18900 RivC 92241 728-F4
DIAMOND CIR
6400 RivC 92509 684-G6
DIAMOND DR
100 LKEL 92530 866-H6
39200 RivC 92543 871-A2
DIAMOND ST
7300 RIV 92504 715-E4
DIAMOND WY
200 PER 92571 777-H7
DIAMOND BACK RD
11300 RivC 92883 804-H4
DIAMOND DUST LN
25200 RivC 92548 809-B6
DIAMOND E DR
- PDST 92260 848-C6
DIAMOND HEAD WY
10000 RIV 92503 714-E3
DIAMOND POINT DR
13200 YCPA 92399 650-E6
DIAMOND VALLEY RD
39100 RivC 92543 870-J3
39100 RivC 92543 871-A3
DIAMONDVIEW CIR
3000 COR 92882 742-F6
DIAMONDVIEW ST
3100 COR 92882 742-E6
DIAMONT LN
26300 RivC 92584 898-B3
DIANA AV
6900 RIV 92506 715-E3
7000 RIV 92504 715-C4
8800 RIV 92503 715-A6
9800 RIV 92503 714-H7
10100 RIV 92503 744-F1
10300 RIV 92505 744-F1
DIANA CIR
1000 PMSP 92262 756-F6
DIANA LN
500 HEMT 92543 811-B5
12700 MORV 92553 717-F3
N DIANA ST
100 PER 92570 807-D2
S DIANA ST
- PER 92570 807-D3
DIANE DR
- LQNT 92253 849-H1
DIANE LN
67700 CTHC 92234 787-C1
DIANE ST
47100 INDO 92201 5470-F3
DIANE WY
900 LKEL 92530 865-H4
DIANNA CT
39600 RivC 92591 930-A6
39600 RivC 92596 930-A6
DIANNE DR
1500 COR 92881 773-G3
DIAZ
45800 RivC 92544 (932-F4
See Page 902)
DIAZ RD
- MURR 92562 958-E4
27400 TEM 92590 958-E4
DIAZ WY
- RivC 92536 982-G6
DICKENS CT
- RMIR 92270 788-C5
12700 GTER 92313 646-D5
DICKENS DR
- RivC 92584 868-C3
DICKENS ST
- CHLS 91709 712-A5
5900 RIV 92506 715-H2
DICKINSON LN
- COR 92880 742-J1
DICKINSON RD
21100 MORV 92557 716-H1
25400 RivC - 814-E5
DICKSON PTH
37100 RivC 92596 929-E2
DICKSON WY
56800 RivC 92539 (934-J1
See Page 904)
56800 RivC 92539 (935-A1
See Page 904)
DICKSON HILLS RD
56700 RivC 92539 (934-J1
See Page 904)
56700 RivC 92539 (935-A1
See Page 904)
DIEBENKORN CT
18900 RivC 92508 746-D1
DIEGE CT
64300 RivC 92240 696-D1
DIEGO DR
39600 TEM 92591 929-C7
DIEGO WY
27200 RivC 92584 868-D7
DIGBY CT
100 RIV 92506 716-D5
DIGBY DR
800 HEMT 92545 810-G5
DIGGER PINE DR
8700 RIV 92508 746-G3
DIJON CT
28700 RivC 92584 868-G3
DIJON PL
39600 MURR 92562 928-B1
S DIJON ST
29500 LKEL 92530 865-G3

DILBECK DR
13300 MORV 92553 717-E4
DILL CIR
1200 COR 92879 743-H1
DILLERS DR
48800 RivC 92536 963-C6
DILLON AV
83000 INDO 92201 5410-G7
N DILLON AV
100 SJCT 92583 811-A2
500 SJCT 92582 810-J1
500 SJCT 92582 811-A2
S DILLON AV
100 SJCT 92583 811-A2
DILLON CIR
32100 RivC 92595 897-C6
DILLON RD
- BAN 92220 651-E7
- BAN 92220 691-E1
39400 RivC 92236 390-D8
39400 RivC 92236 5411-C1
39400 RivC 92203 390-D8
39400 RivC 92203 5411-C1
43100 INDO 92236 5411-D7
44600 COAC 92236 5411-D7
45000 COAC 92236 5471-C1
60500 RivC 92282 725-F2
61200 RivC 92258 725-G2
61500 PMSP 92258 725-G2
62000 PMSP 92258 726-A2
62500 RivC 92258 726-A2
65000 RivC - 726-F2
66000 RivC 92240 726-F2
66600 RivC 92240 727-F1
68400 RivC 92241 727-F1
71000 RivC 92241 728-B2
75500 RivC 92241 390-D8
85200 RivC 92201 5471-B3
85200 RivC 92236 5471-B3
DILL WEED ST
14900 MORV 92553 717-J7
DIMITRA DR
24100 MORV 92553 717-E6
DINAH SHORE DR
68000 CTHC 92234 787-D4
69500 RMIR 92270 787-F4
70600 RMIR 92270 788-A4
71000 RivC 92270 788-A4
72200 PDST 92211 788-A4
DI PIETRO CIR
20800 RivC 92595 897-A6
DIPLOMAT AV
19000 RivC 92881 773-J3
DIRK LN
39100 RivC 92591 930-A6
39100 RivC 92596 930-A6
DIRT RD
- RivC 92570 775-C6
48300 RivC 92536 963-A7
DISCOVERY DR
700 SJCT 92583 780-H7
DISCOVERY WY
11300 RIV 92503 744-E2
DISCOVERY BAY DR
78400 RivC 92201 819-F5
DISHNER DR
16200 RivC 92504 745-G4
DISNEY DR
48100 INDO 92201 5470-F4
DISTRIBUTION WY
- RivC 91752 683-E1
DITAS DR
- RIV 92508 716-E7
DITTANY ST
25600 MORV 92553 717-H5
DIVES WY
- TEM 92592 979-F1
DIVINA ST
- PMSP 92264 786-C2
DIVISION ST
5600 RIV 92506 715-G2
DIVOT LN
- INDO 92201 5470-B3
2000 PMSP 92264 787-B5
DIX HILL RD
27100 RivC 92585 838-C2
DIXIE DR
40100 HEMT 92543 841-B2
40100 RivC 92543 841-B2
S DIXIE DR
1000 HEMT 92543 841-B2
DIXIE LN
3400 RivC 92503 744-B4
DIXON DR
41100 RivC 92544 811-D7
DIXON WY
2700 COR 92882 773-C2
DIZA ST
23300 MORV 92553 717-D5
DOANE AV
4700 RIV 92505 714-D6
DOCK RD
74400 RivC 92241 728-G7
DOCKERY LN
23500 RivC 92570 807-E4
DOCKSIDE PL
28700 RivC 92584 868-G4
DO DAH LN
10400 RivC 92223 690-G4
DODD ST
4700 RivC 91752 684-A5
11600 YCPA 92399 650-B2
DODGE WY
- NRCO 92860 713-H7
- NRCO 92860 743-H1

DODGE WY
24700 MORV 92553 717-F6
DODGE CITY PL
- NRCO 92860 743-F2
DODSON WY
1200 RIV 92507 686-B1
DOE CT
23900 MORV 92553 717-E4
DOE WY
51600 RivC 92539 (933-H4
See Page 902)
DOE CANYON RD
- RivC - 842-H1
DOESKIN CT
24000 MURR 92562 927-J4
DOE SPRING CIR
3500 COR 92882 742-E5
DOE SPRING RD
3400 COR 92882 742-E5
DOGIE PL
22100 CYNL 92587 867-B1
DOG LEG CIR
39600 TEM 92591 959-C5
DOGWOOD
33000 RivC 92548 809-F4
DOGWOOD CIR
12600 RivC 92503 744-B4
DOGWOOD CIR E
900 PMSP 92264 816-F2
DOGWOOD CIR W
900 PMSP 92264 816-E1
DOGWOOD CT
11300 FONT 92337 644-C2
DOGWOOD DR
3100 COR 92882 742-F5
DOGWOOD RD
55200 RivC - 814-E4
DOGWOOD TR
13600 YCPA 92399 650-E6
DOGWOOD WY
- NRCO 92860 743-G1
2900 HEMT 92545 840-F3
DOHENEY WY
72000 RMIR 92270 818-C3
DOHENY DR
11200 RIV 92505 714-B4
DOHERTY LN
25400 RivC 92584 897-J2
DOHERTY ST
12500 COR 92879 744-B3
12500 RIV 92503 744-B3
DOHNEY CT
- COR 92881 773-D4
DOLAN DR
24200 MORV 92553 717-E5
DOLBEER ST
16400 LKEL 92530 835-J7
16400 LKEL 92530 865-J1
DOLE CT
11300 RIV 92505 714-B4
DOLF CT
8400 RIV 92508 746-G1
DOLLAR RD
26900 RivC 92241 390-D7
DOLLY DR
900 LKEL 92530 865-H4
DOLLY LN
11900 MORV 92555 718-A1
DOLMAR CT
75700 PDST 92211 819-A5
DOLOMITE LN
- RivC - (907-G5
See Page 906)
DOLORES AV
49500 RivC 92230 723-B5
W DOLORES CT
1100 PMSP 92262 756-C6
DOLORES RD
26200 RivC 92570 837-B2
DOLORES ST
3100 RIV 92504 715-E3
DOLPHIN DR
800 PER 92571 807-H1
99400 RivC 92254 (5654-D4
See Page 5594)
DOLPHIN ST
1900 RIV 92506 716-A3
DOMAINE MICHAEL DR
- RivC 92563 929-A7
S DOME LN
- RivC - 844-B1
DOME ST
23400 MORV 92553 717-D5
DOMENIGONI PKWY
100 HEMT 92543 840-G5
100 HEMT 92543 841-A6
100 HEMT 92545 840-G5
33000 RivC 92596 839-F7
33500 RivC 92596 840-B7
35200 RivC 92545 840-B7
DOMENO
- RivC - 410-L4
W DOMINGUEZ RD
300 PMSP 92262 756-D4
DOMINGUEZ RANCH RD
1300 COR 92882 742-C5
DOMINION AV
3100 RIV 92506 715-G2
DON DR
39000 HEMT 92543 810-J5
DONAHUE CT
23100 MORV 92553 717-C3
DON ALBERTO LN
1100 SJCT 92582 810-H2

DONALD AV
3500 RIV 92503 715-A6
3600 RIV 92503 714-J4
DONALD RD
29700 MURR 92563 928-J1
DONALD ST
34800 RivC 92545 839-J1
34800 RivC 92545 840-A1
DONALD CAMP RD
- OrCo 92808 772-A5
- OrCo 92862 772-A5
DONATELLO DR
300 COR 92882 773-B4
DON BUDGE LN
73200 PDST 92260 848-E3
DON CARLOS CT
1100 SJCT 92582 810-H2
DONCASTER DR
23600 MORV 92553 717-D3
DON COYOTE TR
- PMSP 92264 786-G6
DONDER CT
3400 RIV 92507 686-E4
DONEGAL WY
- BAN 92220 691-F2
DON ENGLISH WY
13500 DHSP 92240 697-E5
DON GOODWIN DR
2700 RIV 92507 686-C3
DON JUAN
18200 RivC 92532 866-C1
DON JUAN CIR
26500 RivC 92544 841-F1
DON LARSON LN
72800 PDST 92260 848-E3
DONLON ST
500 BLY 92225 5491-D7
DON LUIS CIR
1100 COR 92879 743-H1
DON MIGUEL CIR
100 PDST 92260 818-E5
DONNA CIR
36600 RMIR 92270 787-J7
DONNA DR
600 BEAU 92223 720-J1
DONNA LN
1000 CALI 92320 650-A7
1000 CALI 92320 690-A1
18400 RivC 92570 747-C7
18400 RivC 92570 777-C1
DONNA WY
500 SJCT 92583 811-E2
8400 RivC 92509 684-F1
DONNA MAE PL
59300 RivC - (905-E3
See Page 904)
DONNELL DR
39500 RivC 92544 (932-E7
See Page 902)
DONNELLY DR
900 RIV 92507 716-D1
DONNER TR
10100 RivC 92223 691-C4
DONNER WY
2800 RivC 92509 645-B7
DONNIL LN
2300 SDCo 92028 997-A4
DONNOCH CT
22800 MURR 92562 927-B3
DONNY CIR
- RivC 92203 789-H6
- RivC 92211 789-H6
DONOMORE CT
40200 TEM 92591 959-B1
DONOVAN CT
2800 RIV 92504 715-C6
DON QUIXOTE DR
- RMIR 92270 818-D5
DOOLEY PL
16800 RivC 92504 745-H3
DOOLITTLE AV
6500 RIV 92503 714-G1
DOOLITTLE CIR
16800 RivC 92518 746-H5
DOOLITTLE CT
33000 RivC 92530 896-F5
DOOLITTLE DR
82500 INDO 92201 5470-F4
DORA CT
5800 RIV 92506 715-H2
DORADO CT
5200 RivC 92509 685-A3
DORADO DR
25500 RivC 92586 837-J7
DORADO ST
2200 COR 92879 743-H2
DORADO VILLAS DR
- INDW 92210 848-J3
DORAL CT
1000 BAN 92220 721-D5
30600 TEM 92592 979-B4
DORAL DR
44800 INDW 92210 818-J7
64200 RivC 92240 696-D1
DORAL ST
50000 LQNT 92253 849-H6
DORAL WY
28600 MORV 92555 718-E7
69200 CTHC 92234 787-F1
DORCAS LN
23000 RivC 92567 809-G3
DORCHESTER CIR
2900 COR 92879 744-B2
DORCHESTER DR
- RivC 92592 979-H2

DORCHESTER DR
2500 RIV 92506 685-H7
DORCHESTER LN
20900 RivC 92570 836-H7
DOREEN DR
27600 RivC 92586 837-J5
DORINDA DR
6400 RIV 92503 714-E1
DORIS DR
5900 RivC 92509 685-B2
DORITA PABLO RD
- RivC 92590 978-B3
DORLEN ST
2800 RIV 92504 715-E4
DORN RD
38000 CTHC 92234 817-E2
DORNER DR
24400 MORV 92553 717-E5
DORNOCH CT
1400 BAN 92220 721-E5
DOROF CT
34300 RivC 92595 897-A4
DOROTHY CT
37700 RivC 92592 930-G4
DOROTHY DR
1900 RIV 92507 686-A2
6000 RIV 92505 714-D3
DOROTHY LN
21700 RivC 92595 897-B3
22200 RivC 92567 779-B7
22200 RivC 92567 809-B1
80700 INDO 92201 5470-C2
DOROTHY ANNA DR
300 BAN 92220 721-E2
DORSET DR
11400 RIV 92503 744-E3
DORSET ST
5900 RivC 92509 685-B3
DORSEY ST
29300 RivC 92586 868-D1
DORST DR
36600 RivC 92544 902-C7
DORUFF AV
43800 RivC 92544 811-J6
43800 RivC 92544 (812-A6
See Page 782)
DORVAL CT
25400 RivC 92584 867-J2
25400 RivC 92584 868-A2
DOS CAMEOS DR
38400 SDCo 92028 997-C5
DOS CASAS PL
8600 RIV 92504 715-B5
DOS PALMAS AV
52200 COAC 92236 5471-C7
52200 COAC 92236 5531-C1
DOS RIOS AV
12100 GTER 92313 646-F4
DOS RIOS RD
45100 RivC 92590 977-D4
DOTSON CIR
38700 RivC 92562 926-E5
DOTTI CT
- BLY 92225 5491-F5
DOTTIE
38900 RivC 92544 (932-F5
See Page 902)
DOTTIE CT
36300 RivC 92592 930-D6
DOUBLE BUTTE
27800 RivC 92585 839-D5
DOUBLE BUTTE ST
3300 HEMT 92545 840-F3
S DOUBLEDAY AV
200 ONT 91761 643-C1
DOUBLE DIBBLE DR
- RivC 92567 779-F6
DOUBLE EAGLE WY
56000 LQNT 92253 5530-B5
DOUBLE TREE DR
2600 RIV 92506 715-G4
25600 RivC - 814-B6
DOUBLE VIEW DR
52300 RivC - (843-H2
See Page 842)
52300 RivC - 844-A2
DOUGHERTY RD
18300 RivC 92570 747-B7
18300 RivC 92570 777-B1
DOUGLAS AV
3500 RIV 92507 686-A5
DOUGLAS CT
800 HEMT 92543 841-A2
DOUGLAS DR
- PMSP 92262 756-G3
9300 RIV 92503 715-A7
DOUGLAS PL
900 YCPA 92399 650-B7
900 CALI 92320 650-B7
DOUGLAS ST
- INDO 92201 5470-F5
900 CALI 92320 650-B7
1000 CALI 92320 690-B1
1000 YCPA 92399 650-B2
DOUGLAS WY
- COR 92882 772-J2
- COR 92882 773-A2
64300 RivC 92240 696-E5
DOUGLAS FIR CIR
- RIV 92518 746-F3
DOUGLASIS CT
21200 MORV 92557 716-H2
DOUGLASS AV
24200 MURR 92562 927-H5
25800 MURR 92562 958-B2

DOUGLASS UNION LN
- MURR 92563 928-G6
DOUMA ST
51500 COAC 92236 5471-A7
DOVE CIR
2100 COR 92882 742-H7
43300 RivC 92220 691-G4
DOVE CT
2000 COR 92882 742-H7
31700 YCPA 92399 649-B2
DOVE DR
600 PER 92570 807-F2
48500 RivC 92536 983-B2
DOVE LN
6700 RIV 92506 715-G4
15700 FONT 92337 644-F3
DOVE RD
46300 INDW 92210 849-E2
DOVE ST
22200 GTER 92313 646-E5
47200 INDO 92201 5470-H3
DOVE CANYON DR
- RivC 92503 745-C5
DOVE HALLOW LN
25500 MURR 92563 928-E6
DOVE HILL CT
1900 BAN 92220 721-E6
DOVEHILL DR
17200 RivC 92503 744-G6
DOVEHURST ST
14900 MORV 92553 717-G7
DOVER CIR
1200 COR 92880 713-B7
1200 COR 92880 743-B1
DOVER CT
- MURR 92562 927-F4
- RMIR 92270 788-B5
400 SJCT 92583 781-A7
5900 RIV 92504 685-C7
DOVER LN
1700 HEMT 92545 840-H1
11500 FONT 92337 644-F3
DOVER RD
- MURR 92563 929-A3
DOVE RUN CIR
41200 PDST 92211 819-C4
DOVERWOOD DR
11100 RIV 92505 714-B6
DOVERWOOD PL
26000 RivC 92544 811-J7
DOVERWOOD ST
1100 COR 92880 743-A1
DOVETREE DR
39100 MURR 92563 928-F4
DOVE VALLEY WY
- RivC 92880 713-B1
DOVING LN
18900 RivC 92508 746-D5
DOW ST
11500 MORV 92555 688-D7
DOWELL LN
18000 RivC 92241 728-E2
DOWLING RD
28100 RivC 92570 837-A7
DOWMAN ST
33000 RivC 92530 896-D3
DOWN ST
1900 RIV 92507 686-A2
DOWNEN AV
100 HEMT 92543 810-J7
DOWNEY ST
6100 RivC 92509 684-D6
DOWNING CT
1400 COR 92882 742-J7
DOWNING ST
22400 MORV 92553 717-B3
DOWNS CT
400 BLY 92225 5491-E5
DOYLE ST
3100 RIV 92504 715-B5
DOYLE RANCH CT
- RivC 92592 980-A3
DRACAEA AV
21500 MORV 92553 716-J4
21500 RivC 92553 716-J4
21700 MORV 92553 717-A4
25900 MORV 92555 717-F4
26200 MORV 92555 718-A4
30100 MORV 92555 719-A4
DRAKE CT
45000 INDO 92201 5470-C1
DRAKE DR
500 RivC 91752 683-E4
DRAKE PL
9600 RIV 92503 744-J1
9600 RIV 92503 745-A1
DRAKE ST
2800 COR 92882 773-A2
DRAPER ST
5100 RIV 92505 714-E4
DRAWBRIDGE AV
81600 INDO 92201 5410-D7
DRAYTON DR
- CHLS 91709 712-A6
DRAYTON PL
4600 RIV 92503 714-F5
DR CARREON BLVD
81500 INDO 92201 5470-D2
DREAM ST
11800 MORV 92557 717-C1
DREAMGLOW LN
19800 RivC 92570 776-E4
DREAMS LN
38500 RivC 92203 819-J1

DREAMSICLES WY
- COR 92879 773-D2
DREE CIR
23300 RivC 92570 777-D2
DRESDEN CT
- RivC 92596 899-C7
DRESDEN PL
5200 RIV 92505 714-B6
DRESSAGE LN
12000 RIV 92503 744-C3
DRESSIN DR
24100 MORV 92553 717-E7
DREW CT
12600 MORV 92553 717-D3
DREXEL AV
4300 RIV 92505 714-D7
DREXEL ST
3300 RIV 92503 744-F2
DREXELL DR
38400 PDST 92211 818-F1
DREYCOTT WY
33100 RivC 92530 865-G6
DRIFTING SANDS CIR
33900 RivC 92276 788-G4
DRIFTWOOD CIR
100 RivC 91752 683-F5
DRIFTWOOD CT
200 LKEL 92530 865-H2
1800 PER 92571 777-J7
2900 NRCO 92860 713-B5
DRIFTWOOD DR
8500 RIV 92504 714-J2
8700 RIV 92503 714-H3
11300 FONT 92337 644-B2
74400 PDST 92260 848-H2
S DRIFTWOOD DR
1000 PMSP 92264 786-F4
DRIFTWOOD LN
3300 LKEL 92530 865-G2
S DRIFTWOOD PL
2400 ONT 91761 643-A5
DRIFTWOOD ST
1000 COR 92880 743-A1
DRISCOL
30200 LKEL 92530 866-C4
DRISCOLL RD
18100 RivC 92241 728-C3
DRISCOLL ST
38400 PDST 92211 818-F1
DRIVER CT
- HEMT 92545 810-D7
DRIVER LN
41800 TEM 92591 959-C5
E DRIVER RD
6000 PMSP 92264 787-C5
DRIVERS WORLD PKWY
- CLTN 92324 646-F1
DRIVING RANGE RD
- COR 92883 773-H7
- COR 92883 803-H1
3800 RivC 92509 685-D3
DROMEDARY CIR
- CTHC 92234 787-F6
DROVER WY
22100 CYNL 92587 867-B1
DRUMMER CIR
1400 SJCT 92583 811-D5
DRUMMOND DR
2200 RIV 92506 685-J7
2200 RIV 92506 715-J1
DRUMMOND ST
25200 RivC 92544 811-J6
DRURY CT
4300 RIV 92505 714-E7
DRURY LN
- RMIR 92270 817-J3
22500 MORV 92557 717-B2
DRURY ST
400 BAN 92220 722-B3
DRY CREEK DR
24000 MURR 92562 927-G6
50100 LQNT 92253 849-H6
DRY CREEK LN
81600 INDO 92201 5470-D3
DRYDEN ST
29200 LKEL 92530 865-H2
DRY FALLS DR
26600 RivC 92883 835-B4
N DRY FALLS RD
600 PMSP 92262 756-C7
600 PMSP 92262 786-C1
DRY GULCH PL
- NRCO 92860 743-G1
- PER 92571 778-B2
DRY GULCH RD
19400 RivC 92881 773-H3
74400 RivC 92241 728-G7
74400 RivC 92241 758-G1
DRY RANCH RD
44300 RivC 92536 982-J2
DRY WASH RD
59000 RivC 92539 (935-F7
See Page 904)
DUANE AV
29500 RivC 92584 868-H6
DUANE RD
2300 PMSP 92262 756-E5
DUB CT
32300 RivC 92584 868-A7
DUBLIN CT
3400 HEMT 92545 810-F6
DUBLIN PL
27000 RivC 92883 835-A4
DUBLIN WY
2400 SBDO 92408 646-J1

STREET
Block City ZIP Pg-Grid

ELMHURST CT
30900 CTHC 92234 787-G1
ELMHURST DR
1000 COR 92880 743-A2
12600 MORV 92555 718-A3
ELMHURST LN
33500 RivC 92596 899-F2
EL MINERAL RD
17000 RivC 92570 806-A4
ELMIRA CT
- RIV 92508 746-E1
EL MIRADOR BLVD
9200 DHSP 92240 696-J1
EL MIRADOR CTE
34800 RivC 92592 980-B3
EL MIRADOR RD
400 PER 92571 777-J7
EL MOLINO AV
4800 RIV 92504 715-B2
EL MOLINO VIEJO
27300 RivC 92584 868-D4
EL MONTE DR
10500 RivC 92223 691-A5
EL MONTE ST
300 SJCT 92583 811-B3
ELMRIDGE CT
- RIV 92506 716-D4
ELMTREE DR
100 PER 92571 777-H7
ELMVIEW DR
12500 RIV 92503 744-C4
12500 RivC 92503 744-C4
ELMWOOD AV
100 HEMT 92543 841-A1
200 HEMT 92543 840-J1
ELMWOOD CIR
300 RivC 91752 683-F5
ELMWOOD CT
3500 RIV 92506 685-E5
13900 MORV 92553 717-H5
ELMWOOD DR
3400 RIV 92506 685-G6
38600 RMIR 92270 817-H2
ELMWOOD ST
21200 RivC 92570 776-H3
21700 RivC 92570 777-A3
ELNA LN
44800 RivC 92544 (812-C6
See Page 782)
ELNA WY
38600 CTHC 92234 817-D3
EL NIDO AV
1600 PER 92571 778-B3
20100 RivC 92571 778-B5
EL NIDO PL
12600 DHSP 92240 697-B4
EL NIDO RD
18000 RivC 92570 806-C4
EL NIGUEL RD
34900 RivC 92530 896-B6
EL NITA LN
1300 HEMT 92544 811-B7
1300 RivC 92544 811-B7
EL NORTE DR
- RivC 92585 809-A3
ELORA CT
4400 RIV 92503 714-J3
E EL ORO WY
1900 PMSP 92262 786-G1
EL OSITO CT
31000 TEM 92592 979-C5
EL PADRO ST
7100 RIV 92504 715-D2
EL PAISANO DR
1000 SDCo 92028 998-B7
EL PALOMINO DR
5600 RivC 92509 684-G5
EL PARAISO DR
25400 RivC 92548 808-J7
EL PARQUE DR
700 BLY 92225 5491-D4
EL PASEO
1700 PMSP 92262 756-G7
72200 PDST 92260 848-D1
EL PASEO AV
82100 INDO 92201 5410-E6
EL PASEO RD
14100 RivC 92508 716-F6
EL PASO DR
- NRCO 92860 743-G1
EL PASO WY
900 HEMT 92545 810-G5
EL PASTA RD
45500 RivC 92536 982-E3
EL PEQUITO
40700 RivC 92544 961-D2
EL PERRO DR
44300 RivC 92590 978-B2
EL PICO LN
27200 RivC 92586 838-C6
EL PICO RD
57700 RivC 92539 (985-C2
See Page 964)
EL PLACER RD
- PMSP 92262 786-J3
500 PMSP 92264 786-J3
EL PLOMO CIR
5900 RivC 92509 684-J4
EL PORTAL
1700 RIV 92506 716-B3
73800 RivC 92276 788-F1
W EL PORTAL
100 PMSP 92264 786-D5
EL POZITO DR
15300 RivC 92570 775-G7

EL PRADO RD
16200 CHNO 91710 712-A1
44100 RivC 92590 977-F4
EL PUEBLO ST
900 HEMT 92545 810-G5
EL PUENTE ST
27100 RivC 92586 838-C6
EL RANCHITO RD
45100 RivC 92536 962-D5
EL RANCHO CIR
2100 HEMT 92545 810-G5
EL RANCHO DR
27000 RivC 92586 868-C1
27100 RivC 92586 838-C7
EL RANCHO RD
36000 RivC 92544 901-C6
EL RAY CIRCLE DR
39300 RivC 92539 (934-E5
See Page 904)
EL REPOSO RD
45100 RivC 92536 982-D3
EL REY CIR
500 PER 92571 807-J2
EL RIO AV
5300 RivC 92509 645-F7
EL RIO LN
9400 DHSP 92240 696-G1
EL RIVINO RD
18800 RivC 92509 645-F4
19400 SBdC 92316 645-F4
19400 SBdC 92509 645-F4
19500 RLTO 92509 645-F4
EL ROBLE
- RMIR 92270 787-H7
EL ROSARIO DR
- PER 92571 777-G4
ELROY RD
26000 RivC 92584 898-A3
ELSA CT
900 COR 92881 743-F7
26600 RivC 92544 841-D2
EL SEGUNDO WY
16400 RivC 92241 727-E1
EL SERAPE TR
18800 RivC 92241 727-B3
EL SERENE LN
200 CALI 92320 649-J7
ELSIE LEE CIR
4600 BAN 92220 721-E2
ELSINORE LN
23700 RivC 92587 837-E6
ELSINORE RD
1800 RIV 92506 686-A7
2100 RIV 92506 685-H7
E ELSINORE WY
3300 ONT 91761 643-C5
ELSINORE HEIGHT
100 LKEL 92530 866-F5
ELSINORE HEIGHTS DR
32400 RivC 92595 867-B7
32700 RivC 92595 897-B1
ELSMERE DR
100 RIV 92506 716-B4
EL SOBRANTE
400 COR 92879 743-F5
EL SOBRANTE RD
12100 RivC 92503 744-H7
12700 RivC 92503 745-B7
14300 RivC 92503 775-E1
16200 RivC 92504 775-E1
16200 RivC 92570 775-E1
EL SOL RD
38000 RivC 92596 930-B5
EL SOL ST
51000 COAC 92236 5471-D6
EL SOL WY
7400 RIV 92504 715-E4
EL SOMBRERO LN
67500 RivC 92241 727-B3
ELSWORTH ST
13000 MORV 92553 717-B6
14500 RivC 92518 717-B6
EL TECOLOTE RD
30500 RivC 92548 839-A1
EL TIGRE DR
37700 RivC 92562 926-J3
ELTON LN
21600 RivC 92567 779-G7
EL TORITO CT
31100 TEM 92592 979-C5
EL TORO CIR
1800 COR 92882 742-J6
2100 HEMT 92545 810-G5
EL TORO CT
81700 INDO 92201 5470-D3
EL TORO DR
- RMIR 92270 818-D6
EL TORO RD
- RivC 92570 805-H6
23500 RivC 92570 805-B5
24200 RivC 92532 806-B6
24900 RivC 92532 836-C1
25500 LKEL 92532 836-D5
28500 RivC 92532 866-C1
28900 LKEL 92530 866-C1
31300 CTHC 92234 787-F2
39400 RivC 92539 (935-G6
See Page 904)
EL TORO CUT OFF RD
28100 LKEL 92532 836-E5
28100 LKEL 92570 836-E5
28100 RivC 92570 836-E7
EL TRIO RD
43300 RivC 92590 957-D7

EL VENADO DR
45300 RivC 92590 978-A4
EL VIENTO SECO DR
46500 RivC 92590 977-F6
ELVIRA DR
29500 RivC 92567 808-G1
ELWOOD AV
- FONT 92337 644-G2
ELWOOD CT
2500 PER 92571 777-H5
ELY DR
14900 MORV 92553 717-H7
ELYCE CT
23800 MORV 92553 717-D4
ELYNOR CT
- LQNT 92253 5530-E5
EMBASSY ST
27200 RivC 92586 838-C4
EMBEE WY
42800 MURR 92562 927-G7
43000 MURR 92562 957-G1
EMELITA ST
20400 RivC 92570 775-F5
EMERADO
40100 MURR 92562 928-A2
EMERALD AV
82900 INDO 92201 5410-G7
EMERALD CT
1200 PMSP 92264 786-J4
35300 YCPA 92399 650-B6
EMERALD CV
- RivC 92201 819-F3
36900 RivC 92203 789-H7
EMERALD DR
- LQNT 92253 819-F7
11600 LMLN 92354 647-F2
12800 RivC 92282 724-D1
EMERALD LN
30000 RivC 92543 871-A2
EMERALD ST
1100 HEMT 92543 840-J3
1300 COR 92882 743-B6
7400 RIV 92504 715-D4
22100 GTER 92313 646-E5
EMERALD WY
1600 PER 92571 777-H7
35300 YCPA 92399 650-B6
EMERALD BAY CT
- YCPA 92399 649-H5
EMERALD CREST DR
78000 RivC 92201 819-F3
EMERALD DESERT DR
76400 PDST 92211 789-A7
76400 PDST 92211 819-B1
EMERALD KEY CT
28800 RivC 92584 868-G1
EMERALD LAKE CT
17200 RivC 92503 744-G6
EMERALDPORT ST
- COR 92881 773-F4
EMERETT LN
26300 RivC 92571 778-A5
EMERGENCY ROOM
ACCESS RD
39500 RMIR 92270 818-C2
EMERICK RD
24800 RivC - 814-B5
EMERSON CT
2400 COR 92882 772-J1
EMERSON DR
2400 COR 92882 772-H1
38400 PDST 92211 818-F1
EMERSON ST
4100 RIV 92506 685-D7
4800 RIV 92504 685-D7
45800 RivC 92544 (812-E7
See Page 782)
EMERY ST
5800 RivC 92509 685-A4
EMIL WY
28900 RivC 92567 808-F2
EMILY CT
3400 RIV 92504 715-B5
EMILY DR
1200 HEMT 92545 810-F4
EMILY LN
700 BEAU 92223 690-J7
EMILY WY
34000 RMIR 92270 787-G5
EMMA LN
15700 MORV 92551 747-F2
EMMA ST
3300 RivC 91752 644-A6
EMMERSON ST
25700 LMLN 92354 647-D3
EMORY CT
27500 RivC 92586 838-A4
EMORY ST
3600 COR 92881 773-D4
EMPALMO RD
68000 CTHC 92234 757-D6
EMPEROR DR
30300 CYNL 92587 867-F3
EMPEROR RD
25800 RivC 92548 808-J7
25800 RivC 92548 838-J1
26000 RivC 92585 838-J3
EMPEZAR ST
- TEM 92592 979-F2
EMPIRE CENTER BLVD
N
10500 FONT 92337 645-A1
EMPIRE CENTER BLVD
S
- FONT 92337 645-A2

EMPIRE PENGUIN RD
- RivC 92595 897-E7
EMPTY SADDLE CT
13000 RivC 92883 835-B4
EMPTY SADDLE TR
44000 RivC 92544 902-A4
ENCANTO CT
10300 BLY 92225 5491-D4
23900 SBdC 92324 646-J2
69500 RMIR 92270 787-G6
ENCANTO DR
1000 SJCT 92582 810-J1
1000 SJCT 92582 780-J7
26000 PER 92585 838-C3
26000 RivC 92585 838-C3
27000 RivC 92586 838-C5
ENCANTO LN
100 PER 92571 807-H2
11600 SBdC 92324 646-J3
11600 CLTN 92324 646-J3
ENCANTO ST
800 COR 92881 773-E2
ENCANTO WY
9800 RIV 92503 714-E1
ENCELIA PL
73400 PDST 92260 848-F5
ENCELIA WY
71700 RivC 92260 848-B5
ENCHANTED DR
64000 RivC 92240 696-D5
ENCHANTED WY
24800 MORV 92557 717-F1
ENCHANTED CANYON DR
1500 PER 92570 777-D7
1500 PER 92570 807-C1
1500 RivC 92570 777-D7
ENCILIA LN
- PMSP 92264 786-J6
ENCINA CT
81500 INDO 92201 5470-D3
ENCINA DR
17200 RivC 92530 896-B3
ENCINAS CT
11300 RIV 92505 714-B5
ENCINAS DR
11300 RIV 92505 714-B5
ENCINITAS RD
68000 CTHC 92234 757-D6
ENCINITAS WY
- MORV 92555 748-A2
ENCINO DR
200 PMSP 92264 787-C6
28100 RivC 92586 838-D6
ENCINO PL
800 COR 92882 742-J6
ENCINO RD
55500 RivC - 814-F4
ENCORE LN
3600 PER 92571 778-A3
ENDERLEIN ST
33100 RivC 92562 896-J7
33100 RivC 92562 926-J1
33100 RivC 92595 896-J7
33800 RivC 92595 926-J1
ENDICOTT DR
10800 RIV 92505 714-D7
ENDOR LN
43800 RivC 92544 902-A4
ENFIELD LN
31200 TEM 92591 959-C1
77500 PDST 92211 819-E2
ENFIELD PL
6000 RIV 92506 716-B3
ENGEL DR
2300 RIV 92506 715-G5
2300 RIV 92504 715-G5
ENGELMANN DR
- COR 92881 773-C3
- COR 92882 773-C3
ENGINEER DR
72100 RivC 92276 788-C1
ENGLEMAN DR
- RivC 92590 957-G7
- RivC 92590 977-G1
ENGLEMANN OAK ST
- MURR 92562 927-H2
ENGLEWOOD ST
27100 MORV 92555 748-B2
ENGLISH DR
3700 HEMT 92544 811-E5
ENGLISH PL
1600 COR 92879 743-J6
ENGSTROM RD
56500 RivC 92539 (934-J3
See Page 904)
56700 RivC 92539 (935-A3
See Page 904)
ENLOE DR
8100 RivC 92509 684-G1
ENNIS ST
24600 RivC 92584 897-G1
ENOCH AV
33800 YCPA 92399 649-G5
ENRIQUETA CIR
32400 TEM 92592 979-F3
ENSENADA DR
- PER 92571 777-G4
700 HEMT 92545 810-G6
ENSENADA LN
- PDST 92260 818-G3
ENSENADA WY
5500 RIV 92504 715-B2
ENSIGN ST
- BAN 92220 722-B1

ENSLEY CT
5200 RIV 92505 714-B5
ENSUENO CT
1000 HEMT 92545 810-G5
ENTERPRISE AV
900 SJCT 92582 810-J2
1800 RIV 92507 686-A5
ENTERPRISE CIR N
41600 TEM 92590 958-F4
ENTERPRISE CIR S
41500 TEM 92590 958-F4
ENTERPRISE CIR W
27400 TEM 92590 958-F5
ENTERPRISE CT
1200 COR 92882 743-A4
39400 RivC 92592 930-C7
ENTERPRISE DR
- RLTO 92316 645-H3
- RLTO 92509 645-H3
ENTERPRISE WY
29400 LKEL 92530 866-C2
52000 COAC 92236 5471-E7
52500 COAC 92236 5531-F1
54000 COAC 92274 5531-F1
ENTRADA CIR
49700 LQNT 92253 849-F5
ENTRADA DEL PARQUE
- LMLN 92354 647-C1
ENTRADA DORADA
43700 INDO 92203 5410-H5
ENTRADA LAS BRISAS
43900 PDST 92211 819-E7
ENTRANZ BLVD
10200 RivC 92373 689-C5
ENTREPRENEUR LN
39600 PDST 92211 819-E3
ENTZMINGER LN
37600 RivC 92539 (933-H3
See Page 902)
ENVIRO RD
33000 RivC 92530 895-D3
ENVOY AV
19000 RivC 92881 773-J3
ENVOY DR
29000 RivC 92567 778-H5
EONA CIR
31200 TEM 92592 979-D5
EPHEDRA LN
46500 PDST 92260 848-E3
EPPLE ST
35600 MURR 92563 898-G7
EPSON CT
24400 MURR 92562 927-J5
EQUESTRIAN DR
9300 RIV 92503 745-C3
EQUESTRIAN LN
- NRCO 92860 713-A7
16400 RivC 92504 775-H2
EQUITY DR
27700 TEM 92591 958-G2
ERIC CIR
- RMIR 92270 818-C3
ERIC LN
5200 RivC 92509 684-B3
ERIC RD
2400 SDCo 92028 976-J7
ERICA AV
- MURR 92562 927-J1
ERICA CT
- RivC 92596 929-C1
7200 RIV 92506 716-D6
ERICA LN
11500 FONT 92337 644-F3
ERICK DR
- COR 92881 773-G2
ERICKSON DR
38400 RivC 92592 930-H2
ERICKSON WY
- RIV 92508 746-D1
- RivC 92508 746-D1
ERICSON DR
25600 MORV 92553 717-H7
ERIDANUS DR
28500 RivC 92586 837-J7
ERIE CT
40600 MURR 92562 928-C5
44000 INDW 92210 818-J7
ERIE DR
3300 RIV 92503 744-G1
ERIN CT
3700 RIV 92501 685-J1
ERIN DR
13600 MORV 92555 717-J5
41500 RivC 92544 841-E1
ERIN ST
74000 PDST 92260 818-G7
ERIN WY
- SBDO 92408 646-J1
ERLINDA CT
39000 RivC 92223 690-H3
ERMA CT
25200 RivC 92544 811-H6
ERMER ST
3600 RivC 91752 644-A6
ERNEST LN
8500 RIV 92508 746-H2
ERNEST WY
28800 MURR 92563 928-G2
ERVIN LN
33300 RivC 92545 839-G2
ERWIN CT
26300 RivC 92544 841-E1
ERWIN ST
500 CALI 92320 649-H7

ESCALA DR
6100 RivC 91752 683-G5
ESCALANTE CT
45300 TEM 92592 979-C5
ESCANABA ST
- PMSP 92264 786-C2
ESCENA CT
13200 YCPA 92399 650-D6
ESCENA DR
36100 YCPA 92399 650-D6
ESCENA ST
36200 YCPA 92399 650-D6
ESCHELMAN LN
16500 SBdC 92337 644-H2
ESCHSCHOLTZIA AV
- RivC 92518 747-A1
ESCOBA DR
2900 PMSP 92264 786-H5
ESCOLACATA DR
42500 TEM 92592 959-A6
ESCONDIDO CT
24800 MORV 92557 717-F1
ESCONDIDO EXWY
I-215
- MORV - 716-H3
- PER - 747-B2
- PER - 777-D2
- PER - 807-G2
- RIV - 716-H3
- RivC - 716-H3
- RivC - 717-A7
- RivC - 747-B2
- RivC - 777-D2
ESCONDIDO FRWY I-15
- RivC - 998-H5
- SDCo - 998-H5
ESCONDIDO FRWY
I-215
- MURR - 898-E5
- MURR - 928-D5
- MURR - 958-E1
- PER - 807-J3
- PER - 808-A4
- PER - 838-C4
- RivC - 808-A4
- RivC - 838-C4
- RivC - 868-E1
- RivC - 898-E5
ESCORIAL CT
10100 MORV 92557 687-A5
ESMERADO CT
45200 TEM 92592 979-C4
ESMERALDA CT
- RivC 92595 897-F6
ESPADA DR
22400 RivC 92567 808-F1
ESPADA RD
68000 CTHC 92234 757-D6
ESPANA DR
7000 RIV 92504 715-F4
ESPARTA AV
61200 RivC 92282 695-G4
ESPERANZA AV
50000 RivC 92230 723-C6
ESPERANZA DR
1100 COR 92879 743-H1
16500 RivC 92570 805-J1
16800 RivC 92570 806-A1
ESPERANZA ST
3000 RIV 92504 715-E4
26200 LMLN 92354 647-F3
ESPINAZO ST
- INDW 92210 849-D1
ESPIRIT CIR
44200 RivC 92544 (812-A6
See Page 782)
ESPLANADE AV
35500 HEMT 92545 810-B4
35500 RivC 92545 810-B4
35500 RivC 92582 810-B4
35500 SJCT 92582 810-B4
E ESPLANADE AV
100 SJCT 92583 811-B3
W ESPLANADE AV
400 SJCT 92583 811-A3
3100 HEMT 92545 810-G3
3100 SJCT 92582 810-G3
38900 HEMT 92543 810-G3
39200 SJCT 92582 811-A3
39200 HEMT 92543 811-A3
ESPLANADE DR
100 RMIR 92270 818-B3
ESPLENDIDA WY
38300 RivC 92592 960-J2
38700 RivC 92592 961-A2
40000 RivC 92544 961-A2
ESPLENDOR CT
45300 TEM 92592 979-C4
ESSEX AV
400 HEMT 92545 810-F6
ESSEX CT
- TEM 92591 959-C4
ESSEX LN
1700 HEMT 92545 840-H1
ESSEX ST
500 COR 92879 744-B2
6000 RIV 92504 685-A7
6200 RIV 92504 715-A1
ESSEX WY
400 BAN 92220 721-E4
ESTANCIA DR
- RivC 92203 789-F4
ESTATE DR
26500 RivC - 844-A1
27000 RivC 92586 838-C7

ESTATE HILLS WY
25100 MURR 92562 957-J1
ESTATES RD
39900 RMIR 92270 817-H3
ESTELLE ST
13400 RivC 92879 743-H5
13400 RivC 92879 744-A4
ESTELLE MOUNTAIN RD
13100 RivC 92570 805-G3
ESTELLITA DR
71300 RMIR 92270 818-A6
ESTELO CT
78500 LQNT 92253 819-G7
ESTERO ST
30500 TEM 92592 959-B7
ESTES CIR
23200 RivC 92595 927-F2
ESTES CT
6300 RIV 92506 715-F1
ESTES PARK CT
36500 RivC 92595 927-H2
ESTHER DR
900 COR 92882 773-B1
ESTHER LN
25700 RivC 92585 837-J4
25700 RivC 92585 838-A4
25700 RivC 92586 837-J4
25700 RivC 92586 838-A4
ESTHER ST
33000 RivC 92530 896-A1
ESTIO CIR
1100 PMSP 92262 756-F5
ESTIO RD
68000 CTHC 92234 757-D6
ESTRADA DR
4100 RivC 92509 685-A1
ESTRADA ST
61500 RivC 92240 695-H5
ESTRADA WY
100 CTHC 92234 787-F7
ESTRADO CIR
2100 COR 92882 743-A7
2100 COR 92882 773-A1
ESTRADO DR
2000 COR 92882 743-A7
ESTRELITA DR
60500 RivC 92282 695-F7
ESTRELLA
- RMIR 92270 818-B3
ESTRELLA AV
66000 DHSP 92240 696-H4
66700 DHSP 92240 697-A4
ESTRELLA CT
4200 HEMT 92544 811-F4
ESTRELLA LN
1000 PER 92570 807-E7
ESTRELLA ST
500 SJCT 92582 810-J1
ESTRELLAS LN
25500 MORV 92551 747-H1
ESTRELLITA ST
9600 RIV 92503 714-H5
ESTUDILLO AV
100 SJCT 92583 811-B2
ETERNAL DR
14400 MORV 92553 717-E6
ETERNITY LN
39100 RivC 92563 929-A7
ETHANAC RD
100 PER 92570 837-H1
600 PER 92570 838-A1
1400 PER 92585 838-A1
21200 RivC 92570 837-A2
25800 RivC 92570 838-A1
26700 RivC 92585 838-C1
ETHAN ALLEN CIR
1400 SJCT 92583 811-D5
ETHAN ALLEN WY
- RivC 92585 838-E5
ETHEN RD
21000 RivC 92595 897-A3
ETHLENE DR
32800 RivC 92530 866-A7
32800 RivC 92530 865-J7
ETIENNE CIR
29600 MURR 92563 898-J7
ETIENNE ST
15300 LKEL 92530 865-G3
ETIWANDA AV
3000 RivC 91752 643-H7
4600 RivC 91752 683-H2
S ETIWANDA AV
100 ONT 91761 643-H3
1500 FONT 92337 643-H3
1800 ONT 92337 643-H3
ETNA CT
43200 RivC 92544 811-H6
ETON DR
22500 GTER 92313 646-F3
ETON LN
11400 RivC 92507 686-F7
11400 RivC 92507 716-F1
EUCALYPTUS
39000 RivC 92223 690-H3
EUCALYPTUS AV
- YCPA 92399 649-J1
300 BLY 92225 5491-D4
1200 COR 92879 743-E6
3300 RIV 92507 685-J4
9700 ONT 91710 683-A4
10500 ONT 91761 683-A4
18000 RivC 92532 836-C7
21500 RivC 92570 807-A7
21600 MORV 92553 716-J4
21800 MORV 92553 717-B3

EUCALYPTUS AV
21800 RIV 92507 716-J4
21800 RIV 92507 717-A4
25900 MORV 92555 717-F3
26300 MORV 92555 718-C2
30500 MORV 92555 719-A3
35300 YCPA 92399 650-A1
EUCALYPTUS CT
- FONT 92337 645-A2
1800 PER 92570 807-G5
6200 RivC 92509 684-E5
15100 RivC 92230 723-F6
19800 RivC 92567 779-A3
EUCLID AV
- RivC 92254 5592-J7
- RivC 92254 (5652-J1
See Page 5592)
100 BEAU 92223 720-H2
EUCLID AV Rt#-83
6500 CHLS 91709 712-B4
6500 CHLS 91710 712-B4
6500 CHNO 91710 712-B4
15700 SBdC 91710 712-B4
EUCLID CT
4100 RIV 92504 715-C2
EUCLID ST
- HEMT 92545 810-F4
EUGENA AV
24800 MORV 92553 717-F5
EUGENE DR
- RivC - 392-A11
EUGENE RD
600 PMSP 92264 787-A3
EUGENE ST
5700 RIV 92506 685-E7
21600 RivC 92570 837-A2
EULER WY
600 HEMT 92544 811-C6
EUPHEMIA RD
19500 RivC 92570 776-E7
EUREKA AV
20600 RivC 92571 778-B5
34100 YCPA 92399 649-G4
35100 YCPA 92399 650-A4
EUREKA DR
6800 RIV 92505 714-E1
6900 RIV 92503 714-E1
EUREKA ST
1800 COR 92882 743-A7
15000 RivC 92530 865-G4
33700 YCPA 92399 649-G4
40200 BEAU 92223 721-A3
EURTON LN
28700 RivC 92584 868-G6
EVA PL
6600 RIV 92504 715-B1
EVANDEL RD
35000 MURR 92563 898-B6
EVANS CT
11300 MORV 92555 688-C7
EVANS LN
16700 RivC 92241 727-J1
EVANS PL
3700 PER 92571 778-A1
EVANS RD
- PER 92571 808-A2
1600 PER 92571 778-A2
2600 PER 92570 808-B7
2600 PER 92570 838-B1
3700 PER 92571 777-J2
20600 RivC 92571 778-A5
26000 RivC 92570 838-B1
26000 RivC 92585 838-B3
29700 RivC 92584 868-B4
30000 RivC 92584 868-B4
48900 RivC 92539 (985-E1
See Page 964)
EVANS ST
200 BAN 92220 722-D2
300 SJCT 92583 811-C3
7100 RIV 92504 715-D4
10800 LMLN 92354 647-B1
22500 RivC 92570 807-C2
EVANSTON CIR
1100 COR 92881 773-G2
EVE CIR
3600 RivC 91752 644-A6
EVELYN DR
5100 BAN 92220 721-D3
EVELYN PL
6600 RIV 92504 715-B1
EVELYN ST
19700 RivC 92881 773-J4
EVELYN WY
900 HEMT 92543 841-B2
27000 RivC 92543 841-B3
EVENING SHADOW CT
24800 MORV 92557 687-F6
EVENINGSIDE LN
5500 RivC 92509 684-F3
EVENINGSIDE RD
37400 RivC 92211 789-G7

EVENING SNOW
23300 MORV 92557 687-C5
EVENING STAR CIR
3400 COR 92881 773-E4
77300 INDW 92210 819-E7
EVENING STAR DR
- RivC 92585 838-D5
- RMIR 92270 817-J4
EVENING STAR LN
800 COR 92881 773-E4
EVENING STAR RD
16700 RivC 92506 745-H2
EVENING STAR TR
49800 RivC 92536 983-F2
EVENINGWIND DR
2100 COR 92879 743-J3
EVEREST AV
3500 RIV 92503 714-J5
EVEREST RD
31400 TEM 92591 959-D2
EVEREST WY
3000 COR 92881 773-D2
EVERETT RD
39800 RivC 92539 (935-F6
See Page 904)
EVERETTS WY
16400 RivC 92504 745-H4
EVER-GLO RANCH RD
17600 RivC 92570 806-A2
EVERGREEN AV
26500 MURR 92563 928-H7
EVERGREEN DR
500 RivC 91752 683-E4
900 SJCT 92583 780-H7
3400 ONT 91761 643-B6
EVERGREEN LN
1400 COR 92879 743-E7
3900 BAN 92220 721-E1
EVERGREEN PL
100 PER 92571 777-H6
81000 INDO 92201 5470-C3
EVERGREEN ST
- MURR 92562 927-G3
800 HEMT 92543 840-J1
33000 RivC 92530 896-B1
EVERGREEN WY
5100 RIV 92507 686-D7
EVERGREEN ASH
400 PDST 92211 818-J1
EVERGREEN PEAR
400 PDST 92211 819-A1
EVERLEE CT
3200 RivC 92509 645-A7
EVERTON PL
1100 RIV 92507 686-B5
EVERWOOD DR
2800 RIV 92503 744-E3
EVONVALE DR
9000 RivC 92883 804-C2
EWARTON RD
78300 RivC 92201 819-G4
EWING CIR
9000 RIV 92508 746-E3
EXA ELY RD
39100 RivC 92544 931-E7
40000 RivC 92544 961-E1
42500 RivC 92592 961-D6
EXCALIBUR CT
- RMIR 92270 788-B5
EXCELSIOR ST
12500 RivC 92282 724-B1
EXCISE AV
- ONT 91761 643-B3
S EXCISE AV
2000 ONT 91761 643-B4
EXECUTIVE DR
2000 PMSP 92262 756-J5
EXETER
- RMIR 92270 817-J2
EXETER AV
13200 RivC 92879 744-A5
EXETER CT
- RivC 92274 5530-G3
1300 SJCT 92583 811-C3
EXETER ST
11200 LMLN 92354 647-C1
EXETER WY
- COR 92882 773-C4
EXMOOR CT
4200 RivC 92509 685-D4
27800 RivC 92586 838-B7
EXPLANADA ST
900 COR 92879 743-H2
EXPRESS WY
- RivC - 5239-J6
- RivC - 5240-A6
EXTRAVAGANZA LN
19400 RivC 92570 776-C3
EYE ST
400 LKEL 92532 866-G4
EYOTA CT
40500 MURR 92562 928-C4
EYOTA DR
13100 MORV 92555 717-J3
EYOTA PL
4200 RIV 92505 744-B1
EYRE CT
12300 MORV 92557 717-H2
EYTEL RD
68900 CTHC 92234 787-F4

F

F ST
- HEMT 92545 840-F2

F ST
100 RivC 92518 747-D1
500 LKEL 92532 866-G4
43900 RivC 92544 (812-A7
See Page 782)
68500 CTHC 92234 817-E1
N F ST
1000 PER 92571 807-H1
S F ST
100 PER 92570 807-H3
FABER CT
76500 PDST 92211 819-C6
FABIAN LN
10700 RivC 92223 690-D5
FAGAN BLVD
5600 RivC 92509 684-E4
FAGIN ST
7300 RivC 92509 684-H5
N FAIR CIR
800 PMSP 92262 756-C7
FAIRBANKS AV
4400 RivC 92509 684-J1
FAIRBANKS ST
500 COR 92879 744-A2
FAIR BANKS WY
3700 COR 92881 773-H5
FAIRBURN CT
8300 RIV 92504 715-A3
FAIRBURN DR
22600 GTER 92313 646-F3
FAIRCHILD AV
- RivC 92518 717-D7
FAIRCHILD DR
- RivC 92880 713-A2
6600 RIV 92506 715-G3
FAIR COVE LN
11300 RIV 92503 744-F3
FAIRCREST CIR
25800 RivC 92544 (812-B7
See Page 782)
FAIRCREST RD
- RivC 92508 746-E1
FAIR DAWN LN
24700 MORV 92557 687-F5
FAIRFAX AV
3600 RIV 92506 685-G6
FAIRFIELD CT
11000 RIV 92505 714-C4
FAIRFIELD DR
13300 RivC 92883 835-B5
FAIRFIELD RD
9700 MORV 92553 717-E5
E FAIRFIELD ST
3000 ONT 91761 643-A5
FAIRGLEN PL
- COR 92881 773-F2
FAIRGROUNDS ST
4000 RIV 92501 685-H1
FAIRGROVE CT
26100 RivC 92544 811-H7
FAIRHAVEN DR
11200 RIV 92505 714-A2
44200 PDST 92260 848-D1
46900 PDST 92260 818-D7
FAIRHILL DR
1400 RIV 92507 686-B7
FAIRHILL PL
- RivC 92509 684-G2
FAIR ISLE CT
- COR 92883 773-F6
FAIR ISLE DR
1300 RIV 92507 716-F1
5600 RIV 92506 716-F1
FAIRLANE CIR
- RivC 91752 683-E5
FAIRLANE DR
5800 RIV 92506 716-A2
26100 RivC 92586 838-A5
FAIRLEIGH WY
26700 RivC 92544 841-E2
FAIRMONT DR
1300 COR 92882 743-A6
FAIRMONT ST
32500 YCPA 92399 649-D5
FAIRMOUNT BLVD
1400 RIV 92501 685-H2
FAIRMOUNT CT
2500 RIV 92501 685-H2
FAIROAK TR
36100 YCPA 92399 650-E6
FAIR OAKS AV
20800 COR 92883 774-B6
FAIR OAKS LN
12500 RivC 92503 744-B4
FAIRPORT CT
8700 RIV 92503 714-J4
8700 RIV 92503 715-A4
FAIR RIDGE CT
16200 RivC 92503 744-D4
FAIRVIEW AV
- RivC 92544 841-J5
1800 RIV 92506 686-B7
1800 RIV 92506 716-A1
2100 RIV 92506 715-J1
25100 RivC 92544 (812-A7
See Page 782)
26100 RivC 92544 842-A3
43500 RivC 92544 811-J5
44500 RivC 92592 979-G6
N FAIRVIEW CIR
900 PMSP 92262 756-C7
FAIRVIEW CT
- MURR 92563 928-F5
FAIRVIEW DR
1600 COR 92880 743-B1

STREET
Block City ZIP Pg-Grid

FAIRVIEW DR
1700 COR 92880 713-A7
10700 RivC 92223 691-A5
33700 YCPA 92399 649-F4
FAIRVIEW RD
60700 RivC 92282 695-F6
FAIRVIEW ST
33100 RivC 92530 865-G7
FAIRWAY
- COR 92883 773-G7
FAIRWAY CIR
1700 PMSP 92264 787-C4
N FAIRWAY CIR E
6000 PMSP 92264 787-C3
N FAIRWAY CIR W
1600 PMSP 92264 787-C3
FAIRWAY DR
- BEAU 92223 690-F7
- RivC - 5421-B1
- YCPA 92399 649-E2
26600 RivC - 844-A2
38200 MURR 92562 927-D3
70800 RMIR 92270 817-J4
70800 RMIR 92270 818-A1
74000 PDST 92260 848-G2
74900 INDW 92210 848-G2
75300 INDW 92210 849-A2
FAIRWAY LN
1100 CALI 92320 689-J1
FAIRWAY RD
69200 RivC 92241 727-F1
FAIRWAY DUNES DR
- PDST 92211 788-E7
- PDST 92211 818-E1
FAIRWAY OAKS AV
1000 BAN 92220 721-D6
W FAIRWAY OAKS AV
4800 BAN 92220 721-E5
FAIR WEATHER DR
23500 CYNL 92587 867-F2
FAIR WOOD CIR
39900 MURR 92562 928-C4
FAITH DR
35100 YCPA 92399 650-A2
FAITH ST
- COR 92882 773-C2
3600 RIV 92504 715-B4
FALCON CIR
2600 COR 92882 772-H2
FALCON CT
1200 SJCT 92583 811-D3
15800 FONT 92337 644-F3
FALCON DR
12000 RivC 92240 695-J4
FALCON LN
12100 MORV 92555 718-A2
FALCON RD
43100 RivC 92544 901-J2
43400 RivC 92544 902-A2
FALCON WY
39800 MURR 92562 928-C3
FALCON CREST CIR
22300 RivC 92595 897-C4
FALCONCREST DR
1400 COR 92879 743-G2
FALCON CREST DR
2100 RIV 92506 716-A2
FALCONER DR
23700 MURR 92562 928-B1
FALCON POINT CT
30300 RivC 92563 929-A7
FALCON VIEW CIR
400 PDST 92211 819-C3
FALCON VIEW LN
32100 RivC 92548 809-D6
FALCONWOOD CT
- RivC 92211 819-G2
FALKIRK AV
5200 RIV 92506 685-J7
5200 RIV 92506 715-J1
FALLBROOK AV
1400 HEMT 92545 840-E4
38400 RivC 92211 819-G1
FALLBROOK CT
13500 RivC 92883 835-C5
FALLBROOK DR
800 COR 92880 743-B2
FALLBROOK CANYON DR
- RivC 92883 804-C4
FALL CREEK CT
28700 RivC 92584 868-F1
FALLENLEAF DR
3100 COR 92882 742-E5
FALLEN LEAF DR
20000 RivC 92570 777-C4
FALLHAM RD
17200 RivC 92258 726-E2
FALLING CREEK CT
27000 TEM 92591 928-J7
FALLING LEAF DR
54600 RivC - 814-D5
FALLING LEAF LN
300 BAN 92220 721-E2
5600 RivC 92509 684-G4
FALLING OAK DR
2400 RIV 92506 715-G4
FALLING ROCK LN
74200 INDW 92210 849-A3
FALLING SPRINGS RD
13300 YCPA 92399 650-G6
FALLING STAR DR
13400 RivC 92883 835-C4
FALLING WATER WY
18400 RivC 92504 775-J1

FALL RIVER RD
23000 MORV 92557 717-C1
FALLS CT
100 PDST 92211 819-A2
FALLS CREEK RD
15800 RivC 92282 724-F7
FALLSGROVE AV
- MURR 92563 928-E2
FALLSVALLE LN
10100 RIV 92503 714-E1
FALMOUTH CT
300 COR 92879 743-H4
FALMOUTH DR
79000 RivC 92201 819-H7
FALSTERBOR DR
26000 RivC 92586 838-A6
FAMILY CIR
27200 RivC 92586 837-J4
FAN LN
27000 RivC 92586 838-C3
FAN BAY PL
1600 COR 92879 743-J6
FANITA CT
24500 MORV 92551 747-F1
FAN PALM DR
2300 COR 92879 744-F5
FAN PALM LN
- RivC 92503 744-J6
- RivC 92503 745-A7
FAN PALM WY
- RivC 92211 789-G6
FANTAIL DR
72300 RivC 92254 (5654-G5
See Page 5594)
FANWOOD CT
3300 RIV 92503 744-E3
FARBO CT
29600 RivC 92584 868-A2
FARGO CIR
2300 COR 92881 773-F2
FARGO RD
- CALI 92320 690-B7
- RivC 92320 690-B7
5400 RIV 92506 715-H1
FARGO ST
27600 RivC 92585 838-F5
45100 INDO 92201 5410-G7
45100 INDO 92201 5470-G1
FARGO WY
44200 RivC 92536 983-D1
FARGO CANYON RD
86000 RivC 92236 5411-E4
FARINA ST
46500 RivC 92544 902-G7
FARLEY AV
20300 RivC 92881 774-G5
FARLEY CT
45100 RivC 92536 983-D3
FARLEY DR
4400 RivC 92509 684-G1
FARM RD
33400 RivC 92595 897-G3
FARMHOUSE LN
- RIV 92508 746-D2
FARMINGTON DR
6500 RIV 92504 715-C1
FARMINGTON RD
25500 RivC 92584 867-J4
25500 RivC 92584 868-A4
FARMSTEAD ST
15700 MORV 92551 747-H2
FARMWOOD DR
14300 MORV 92553 717-H6
FARNHAM LN
40300 MURR 92562 927-J1
FARNHAM PL
3500 RIV 92503 714-J6
FARNSWORTH ST
28500 RivC 92596 839-E7
FAROOQ TR
800 PER 92570 807-F7
FARRA ST
- SDCo 92028 999-E6
FARRAGUT AV
22300 MORV 92553 717-B5
FARRAH CT
22000 RivC 92567 779-F7
FARRAR DR
12600 LMLN 92324 647-B5
FAR REACH PL
- PER 92571 778-B2
FARREL RD
68200 CTHC 92234 817-D1
FARRELL DR
2900 PMSP 92262 786-H1
N FARRELL DR
100 PMSP 92262 786-H1
2400 PMSP 92262 756-G4
S FARRELL DR
100 PMSP 92262 786-H4
500 PMSP 92264 786-H4
FARRELL RD
31200 RivC 92548 809-B5
FARRELL ST
26600 RivC 92586 838-B4
FARRELLY CIR
20100 RivC 92562 926-H2
FARRIER AV
6700 RIV 92503 714-F1
FAR VIEW RD
67700 RivC 92240 697-C7
67700 RivC 92240 727-C1
FASHION PL
5000 RIV 92504 715-C1

FASHION WY
500 BAN 92220 722-A4
FASSANO CT
- TEM 92592 959-F7
FATIMA WY
69700 CTHC 92234 787-G1
FAURE RD
39800 RivC 92544 (932-A7
See Page 902)
40300 RivC 92544 962-A1
FAVARA CIR
100 PDST 92211 818-J3
FAVARA DR
- TEM 92592 979-F1
FAVELA DR
5800 RivC 92509 684-G4
E FAWN CT
3100 ONT 91761 643-A6
FAWN DR
38400 RivC 92539 (933-J4
See Page 902)
FAWN ST
23900 MORV 92553 717-E4
FAWN WY
11300 YCPA 92399 650-C1
FAWN LAKE PL
2300 CYNL 92587 867-D2
FAWNRIDGE CT
27300 RivC 92883 835-B5
FAWNRIDGE DR
22400 RivC 92262 725-F7
22400 RivC 92262 755-F1
FAWN SPRINGS DR
38500 RivC 92260 818-F2
FAY
23600 RivC 92570 777-D6
FAY AV
24500 MORV 92551 747-F1
FAY RD
- RivC 92532 836-B3
36000 RivC 92544 902-C7
FAY ST
300 BAN 92220 722-B3
FAYE ST
43700 INDO 92201 5410-G6
FAYENCE DR
26800 MURR 92562 928-C1
FAYETTE CT
- RIV 92504 715-B5
FEATHER CT
30600 TEM 92591 959-B5
FEATHER TR
73400 PDST 92260 848-F4
FEATHERBROOK CT
22700 MORV 92557 687-B4
FEATHERHILL DR
27000 RivC 92883 835-C4
FEATHER PEAK DR
800 COR 92882 773-B4
FEATHER RIVER RD
4400 RivC 92880 742-B4
FEATHERTOP RD
8700 RIV 92508 746-F2
FEBRUARY DR
13300 RivC 92879 744-A5
FEDERAL DR
4200 RIV 92501 685-H1
FELDMAN AV
30100 LKEL 92530 866-C3
FELECITA RD
31200 TEM 92591 959-C3
FELICIA AV
25600 RivC 92586 837-J4
FELICITY PL
- CTHC 92234 787-F6
FELIPE PL
800 HEMT 92543 840-J2
FELISA CT
3200 RivC 92509 645-B7
FELISA ST
13000 MORV 92553 717-J3
FELIX CT
2800 RIV 92503 715-B7
FELIX VALDEZ RD
28400 TEM 92590 958-H7
FELIZ CT
35500 RMIR 92270 787-G6
FELIZ ST
400 PER 92571 807-H2
FELLOWS WY
23900 RivC 92570 806-G5
FELSPAR ST
4200 RivC 92509 644-D7
4200 RivC 92509 684-D3
FELSWOOD LN
25100 RivC 92584 897-H2
FELT CT
12300 MORV 92557 717-G2
FELTON CT
41000 RivC 92544 841-D2
FENIMORE DR
12100 MORV 92555 718-D1
FENNEL DR
2100 COR 92879 743-H1
FENNER CT
14000 MORV 92553 717-E6
FENSMUIR ST
3400 RIV 92503 744-E2
FENTON LN
35500 MURR 92562 898-E6
FENTON RD
10700 MORV 92557 687-E6
FENWAY LN
1200 PER 92571 807-G1

FENWICK PL
2800 RIV 92504 715-C6
FERBER DR
37100 RMIR 92270 787-H7
37100 RMIR 92270 817-H1
FERDINAND CT
2600 PER 92571 777-H5
FERGUSON AV
16600 RivC 92518 746-G5
FERGUSON CT
4200 RIV 92505 714-D7
FERGUSON DR
42100 RivC 92544 841-F1
FERMI CT
1200 SJCT 92583 811-D3
FERMO CT
- TEM 92592 959-F7
FERN AV
7500 RIV 92504 715-D4
15700 CHNO 91710 712-B1
24900 LMLN 92354 647-C2
31000 RivC 92567 779-A2
W FERN AV
1300 RDL 92373 647-J3
FERN CIR
44800 TEM 92592 979-G3
FERN DR
54700 RivC - 814-D7
FERN LN
23800 SBdC 92324 646-J4
23800 CLTN 92324 646-J4
FERN PL
- MURR 92562 927-G3
500 HEMT 92543 841-B1
FERN RD
- INDO 92201 5470-C3
S FERN RD
- INDO 92201 5470-C3
FERN ST
14000 RivC 92230 723-D4
FERNANDEZ RD
32400 RivC 92567 749-D7
S FERNANDO ST
900 CLTN 92324 646-D1
FERNBUSH ST
25500 MORV 92553 717-H4
FERN CANYON DR
500 PMSP 92264 786-D3
FERNDALE CT
2800 COR 92881 773-E2
FERNDALE DR
1000 COR 92881 773-E2
FERNDELL ST
24600 MORV 92553 717-F7
FERNEDALE CT
26200 MORV 92555 717-J4
FERNGREEN DR
- HEMT 92545 840-D4
FERN HOLLOW DR
3200 COR 92881 773-F4
FERN LAND DR
52700 RivC - (813-J4
See Page 782)
52700 RivC - 814-A4
FERNLEAF DR
10100 MORV 92557 687-D5
25300 RivC - 814-C5
29900 RivC 92584 868-F2
FERNLEAF LN
1100 COR 92881 773-F3
FERN VALLEY RD
24300 RivC - 814-F4
FERNVIEW PL
11100 MORV 92557 687-F7
FERNVIEW WY
- MURR 92562 927-G4
FERNWOOD AV
11300 FONT 92337 644-B3
FERNWOOD CIR
1300 COR 92880 713-A7
FERNWOOD DR
800 SJCT 92583 780-H7
68400 DHSP 92240 697-D4
FERNWOOD WY
12000 FONT 92337 644-B4
FERNWOOD GLEN CT
- RivC 92211 819-G2
FERRARI DR
18000 RivC 92508 716-B7
FERRIDAY PL
4400 RIV 92505 714-D7
FERRINGTON DR
1800 COR 92880 713-A7
FERRO DR
200 RivC - 5239-J6
FESCUE CT
13000 RivC 92883 835-B4
FESTIVAL DR
37000 RivC 92211 789-G7
37900 RivC 92211 819-G1
FESTIVAL RD
- MURR 92562 928-B3
FESTIVAL WY
- INDO 92201 5470-G2
13400 MORV 92553 717-D4
FESTIVO ST
- TEM 92592 979-F1
FESTUS CIR
21600 RivC 92570 837-A2
FETLOCK WY
1100 RIV 92506 716-C6
FETZER DR
- RivC 92563 929-A7
FICKE RD
73600 RivC 92241 728-E3

FICUS CT
25600 MORV 92557 717-H1
FICUS DR
32800 CTHC 92234 787-F4
FICUS ST
15000 LKEL 92530 865-G4
FIDDLELEAF RD
15700 FONT 92337 644-F2
FIDDLENECK LN
73200 PDST 92260 848-E2
FIELD AV
43200 RivC 92536 964-C6
FIELD LN
2500 RIV 92501 685-G2
FIELDCREST CT
13200 MORV 92553 717-D4
FIELDCREST LN
- MURR 92562 927-G4
FIELDING RD
2100 RIV 92506 685-J7
2100 RIV 92506 715-J1
2100 RIV 92506 716-A1
FIELDS DR
32900 RivC 92596 899-G4
FIELDS RD
11700 RivC 92220 692-H7
11900 RivC 92220 722-H2
12500 BAN 92220 722-H2
FIELDSTONE CIR
12600 RivC 92503 744-B4
FIELDSTONE DR
100 PER 92570 837-H1
FIESTA AV
7100 RIV 92504 715-F4
FIESTA CT
11300 FONT 92337 645-A2
FIESTA DR
79700 LQNT 92253 849-J2
79700 LQNT 92253 5470-A2
FIESTA LN
100 PER 92571 807-H2
11300 FONT 92337 644-H2
FIESTA PL
26000 RivC 92544 811-G7
FIESTA RD
84000 COAC 92236 5470-J4
84000 COAC 92236 5471-A4
N FIESTA RD
1400 PMSP 92262 756-E6
FIFE CT
100 RIV 92506 716-D5
FIFTH ST
300 NRCO 92860 713-C5
FIFTIES WY
- INDO 92203 819-G3
- INDO 92211 819-G3
- RivC 92203 819-G3
- RivC 92211 819-G3
FIG CT
3200 LKEL 92530 865-G1
FIG DR
32800 CTHC 92234 787-F3
FIG LN
- FONT 92337 645-A2
FIG PL
81000 INDO 92201 5470-C3
FIG ST
1000 SJCT 92582 810-J2
6700 RIV 92506 715-D1
20700 RivC 92570 836-H3
40000 MURR 92563 928-F7
41000 MURR 92562 958-C2
41000 RivC 92562 958-B3
FIG WY
29000 LKEL 92530 865-F1
FIG TREE CT
1600 HEMT 92545 840-G4
FIGTREE LN
20500 RIV 92508 746-G2
FIGUARO DR
100 PMSP 92264 787-A7
FIGWOOD CT
13900 FONT 92337 644-B3
FIGWOOD DR
14100 FONT 92337 644-B3
FIGWOOD WY
25800 MORV 92553 717-H7
FIJI DR
24300 MORV 92551 747-F2
FILANC RANCH RD
43500 RivC 92539 (965-F7
See Page 964)
FILAREA TR
13000 YCPA 92399 650-E6
FILAREA TR N
36800 YCPA 92399 650-E6
FILAREA TR S
36800 YCPA 92399 650-E6
FILAREE AV
15200 MORV 92551 747-F1
26300 MORV 92555 747-J1
26300 MORV 92555 748-A1
FILBERT ST
- RivC 92596 929-D2
800 COR 92879 743-F6
FILIPPI LN
12900 FONT 92337 643-H2
FILLE DR
- RivC 92596 899-D7
FILLMORE CT
800 HEMT 92543 810-J5
FILLMORE ST
2700 RivC 92503 744-E3
2700 RIV 92503 744-E3
3700 RIV 92505 744-D2

FILLMORE ST
48000 COAC 92236 5471-H6
52000 RivC 92274 5471-H6
52000 RivC 92274 5531-H6
52000 COAC 92274 5531-H3
59000 RivC 92274 (5591-J2
See Page 5590)
66000 RivC 92274 (5651-J3
See Page 5590)
78000 RivC 92274 410-E3
84000 RivC 92274 (5772-A5
See Page 5712)
FILLY CT
26900 RivC 92883 835-B4
FILLY LN
300 NRCO 92860 713-H1
4600 RivC 92509 684-E2
FINCH CT
11600 FONT 92337 644-G3
FINCH DR
- RivC 92399 650-G7
16200 RivC 92570 805-H4
FINCH ST
22700 GTER 92313 646-F4
32700 RivC 92596 839-F6
FINCHER WY
- RMIR 92270 817-J2
- RMIR 92270 818-A3
FINCHLEY AV
10900 RIV 92505 714-D7
FINHAUT DR
- RivC - (907-C1
See Page 906)
FINLEY DR
24100 MORV 92553 717-E6
FINLEY RD
2100 PMSP 92262 756-G4
FINLY CT
3800 RIV 92501 685-J1
FINO VISTA LN
36300 RivC 92592 930-E7
FIR
23600 RivC 92570 777-D6
FIR AV
24000 MORV 92553 717-E3
26000 MORV 92555 717-G3
26300 MORV 92555 718-A3
83800 INDO 92201 5470-J2
FIR LN
- FONT 92337 645-A2
FIR ST
- RivC - (875-J4
See Page 844)
1800 COR 92882 743-A7
12500 BLY 92225 5491-G6
24400 RivC 92584 897-G1
25600 RivC - 814-D5
FIRCREST LN
4100 RivC 92509 644-E7
FIREBIRD LN
8900 RIV 92503 714-F1
FIREBRAND AV
2100 PER 92571 777-H6
FIRECAT RD
35000 RivC 92545 810-A3
E FIRECREST CT
2900 ONT 91761 643-A5
FIRE DANCE LN
76700 PDST 92211 819-C5
FIRE FALLS DR
24700 MURR 92562 928-D3
FIREMANS CIR
35800 MURR 92562 898-D7
FIRENZA
- INDW 92210 819-B7
FIRE RING CIR
15400 RivC 92570 805-F5
FIRESIDE CIR
1400 SJCT 92583 811-D5
FIRESIDE DR
7000 RIV 92504 715-G5
7000 RIV 92506 715-G5
FIRESTONE
55000 LQNT 92253 5530-A3
FIRESTONE CIR
6200 BAN 92220 721-C5
FIRESTONE DR
200 PDST 92211 818-J2
FIRESTONE PZ
1700 PMSP 92264 787-C3
FIRESTONE ST
- TEM 92591 959-C4
FIRETHORN AV
1300 RIV 92504 745-D3
1400 RivC 92504 745-D3
FIRETHORN CT
39600 MURR 92563 928-E5
FIRETHORN RD
15700 FONT 92337 644-F3
FIRETHORNE DR
- RivC 92203 789-G6
- RivC 92211 789-G6
FIRETHORNE PL
- COR 92881 773-G1
FIREWOOD ST
20400 RivC 92570 776-G5
FIRST ST
900 NRCO 92860 743-F1
FIR TREE CT
1800 HEMT 92545 840-G4
FIR TREE DR
3900 RIV 92505 744-E1
FIRWOOD CT
600 RIV 92506 716-E4
36100 YCPA 92399 650-C5

FISCHER RD
6400 RIV 92507 716-H3
FISHER AV
- RivC - 392-B8
FISHER CT
100 CALI 92320 650-A7
FISHER LN
44000 RivC 92544 902-A2
FISHER RD
36100 RivC 92539 904-G7
37000 RivC 92539 (934-F1
See Page 904)
FISHER ST
1100 HEMT 92545 840-D5
1300 PER 92570 807-B4
21400 RivC 92570 806-J4
21900 RivC 92570 807-B4
28200 RivC 92545 840-D5
S FISHER ST
1300 HEMT 92545 840-D4
FISHERMAN CT
29700 CYNL 92587 867-F2
FITZ ST
24200 MORV 92551 747-F2
FITZGERALD PL
- RivC 92584 868-C4
FITZHUGH RD
37800 RivC 92592 930-H6
FIVE MILE CREEK RD
44100 RivC 92544 902-B4
FIVE TRIBES TR
23700 MURR 92562 928-B1
FLAG WY
41700 TEM 92591 959-D4
FLAGLER ST
27000 RivC 92586 838-C4
FLAG PIN DR
- COR 92883 773-G7
FLAG POLE CT
29900 RivC 92567 778-H6
FLAGSTAFF AV
32500 RivC 92276 788-E3
FLAGSTAFF RD
400 LKEL 92530 866-F5
FLAGSTONE AV
8600 RIV 92503 714-F4
FLAGSTONE LN
73900 PDST 92260 848-G2
FLAIR CT
4500 PER 92571 747-G7
FLAME AV
200 PER 92571 777-H6
FLAMECREST DR
80000 RivC 92274 5712-A7
80000 RivC 92274 (5772-A1
See Page 5712)
FLAMENCO
40100 MURR 92562 928 C3
FLAMETREE WY
1800 HEMT 92545 840-G3
FLAMING ARROW DR
13700 MORV 92553 717-G5
FLAMING GORGE LN
1000 COR 92882 742-E5
FLAMINGO DR
- RivC 92254 (5654-D3
See Page 5594)
1300 COR 92879 743-F2
15700 FONT 92337 644-F3
FLAMINGO ST
22100 GTER 92313 646-D5
FLAMINGO BAY LN
14100 MORV 92553 717-H6
FLANAGAN LN
17000 RivC 92504 745-F6
FLANDERS LN
32300 RivC 92595 897-A5
FLANDERS RD
2500 RIV 92507 686-D3
FLANNERY ST
900 LKEL 92530 865-J4
FLASH CT
2200 PER 92571 777-H6
FLAT BRANCH RD
- RivC - 878-B6
FLATIRON CT
- RIV 92508 746-E2
FLAX LN
24800 RivC 92595 897-H2
FLAX PL
9200 RIV 92503 715-A7
FLEETWOOD CIR
72700 PDST 92260 818-D7
FLEETWOOD DR
2000 RivC 92509 645-G7
3100 RIV 92503 744-E3
FLEETWOOD LN
6100 CHLS 91709 712-A5
FLEISS RD
43300 RivC 92536 961-J5
43300 RivC 92536 962-A5
FLEMING WY
82600 INDO 92201 5410-F7
FLEMINGTON RD
1200 RIV 92506 716-B5
FLEMMING ST
3600 RivC 92509 644-D6
FLETCHA ST
12000 YCPA 92399 650-C3
FLETCHER DR
700 COR 92882 773-B4
FLETCHER PL
21500 RivC 92570 776-E7
21600 RivC 92570 806-E1

FLETCHER RD
59000 RivC 92539 (965-E1
See Page 964)
FLEURS LN
- RivC 92596 929-E1
FLICKER WY
200 PER 92571 777-H6
FLIGHT RD
6900 RIV 92504 714-H2
FLIGHT ST
23600 MORV 92553 717-D2
FLIGHT WY
32500 RivC 92596 869-D7
FLIGHTLINE WY
49100 RivC 92536 963-C2
FLIGHTWOOD CIR
4300 HEMT 92544 811-F5
FLINT CT
1300 SJCT 92583 811-C3
FLINT DR
25800 MORV 92553 717-H6
FLINT ST
- COR 92883 773-G7
600 LKEL 92532 866-G4
E FLINT ST
100 LKEL 92530 866-F4
W FLINT ST
100 LKEL 92530 866-D4
S FLINT WY
2600 SBDO 92408 647-A1
FLINTLOCK TR
12000 MORV 92557 717-H2
FLINTRIDGE CT
2100 RIV 92506 685-J7
2100 RIV 92506 686-A7
FLINTRIDGE LN
- RivC 92883 804-B3
FLINTSTONE CT
29000 RivC 92567 808-G2
FLOR CIR
400 PMSP 92264 786-E7
FLORA AV
65500 DHSP 92240 696-G4
66700 DHSP 92240 697-A4
FLORA CT
- MURR 92563 928-H4
FLORAL AV
2900 RIV 92507 686-F3
21000 RivC 92570 806-J5
21200 RivC 92570 807-A5
FLORAL GRV
30100 CTHC 92234 787-H1
30100 CTHC 92234 757-G7
FLORAL CREEK CIR
37100 MURR 92562 927-E3
FLORAL PARK ST
1400 COR 92881 773-F4
FLORA SPIEGEL WY
2600 COR 92881 773-E2
FLORAVISTA CT
2900 RIV 92503 744-H1
FLORA VISTA ST
200 SJCT 92582 810-J1
FLORAWOOD CT
3600 RIV 92505 744-E2
FLORDASON DR
300 CALI 92320 649-J7
FLORENCE BLVD
12300 BLY - 5491-A7
FLORENCE DR
16000 RivC - 726-G1
FLORENCE LN
- PDST 92211 819-A4
11800 FONT 92337 644-F3
FLORENCE ST
1300 COR 92882 773-A2
3700 HEMT 92545 810-E6
6000 RIV 92504 685-A7
19100 RivC 92570 776-H3
38500 RivC 92223 720-G1
38500 BEAU 92223 720-G1
FLORENCE WY
24900 MURR 92562 928-D4
FLORENTINA DR
- RMIR 92270 818-D6
FLORES DR
43900 TEM 92592 979-A2
FLORES ST
1900 HEMT 92545 810-G6
FLOREY ST
1000 PER 92571 807-G1
S FLOREZ ST
900 CLTN 92324 646-D1
FLORIDA AV
76500 PDST 92211 819-C7
FLORIDA AV Rt#-74
100 HEMT 92543 811-C7
1500 HEMT 92544 811-C7
2800 RivC 92544 811-E7
6400 RivC 92545 840-B1
6400 HEMT 92545 840-B1
33500 RivC 92545 839-G1
34000 HEMT 92545 839-G1
43800 RivC 92544 (812-B7
See Page 782)
W FLORIDA AV Rt#-74
100 HEMT 92543 811-A7
300 HEMT 92543 810-H7
1600 HEMT 92545 810-E7
4000 HEMT 92545 840-E1
FLORIDA ST
700 BAN 92220 722-C1
2100 BAN 92220 692-C7
3400 RIV 92507 686-D4
31500 RDL 92373 649-B5

FLORIDA ST
32000 YCPA 92373 649-B5
S FLORIDA ST
200 BAN 92220 722-C4
FLORINE AV
2900 RivC 92509 645-A7
43700 PDST 92260 818-H7
FLORY WY
6600 RIV 92504 715-D1
FLOSSIE WY
30700 RivC 92596 899-D3
FLOWER ST
300 HEMT 92544 811-C6
11300 RIV 92505 714-B6
45700 INDO 92201 5470-G1
FLOWERHILL DR
31000 LKEL 92532 867-E6
FLOWER HILL LN
500 PDST 92260 818-F4
FLOWERING PLUM CT
- RivC 92596 929-D1
FLOWERS ST
6000 CHNO 91710 712-A1
FLOYD AV
25600 RivC 92585 837-J2
25700 RivC 92585 838-A2
FLOYD CT
41600 RivC 92592 960-A4
FLOYD DR
- COR 92883 773-H7
FLYING F DR
- PDST 92260 848-C6
FLYING SEA RD
40900 PDST 92211 819-E4
FLYNN
21200 RivC 92570 746-H6
FLYNN ST
100 RivC 92507 646-D6
FOBES RANCH RD
- RivC - (845-F7
See Page 844)
- RivC - (875-E3
See Page 844)
FOGG RD
- CLTN 92324 646-A1
FOGG ST
300 CLTN 92324 646-E1
E FOGG ST
100 CLTN 92324 646-D1
W FOGG ST
400 CLTN 92324 646-C1
FOLK SPRING DR
3300 COR 92881 773-F4
FOLLANSBEE RD
72100 RMIR 92270 818-C4
FOLLMAN WY
33400 RivC 92530 896-D3
FOLSOM ST
1800 PER 92571 777-H7
FONDI CT
- TEM 92592 979-F1
FONDULAC ST
100 PMSP 92264 786-C2
FONT AV
7100 RivC 92509 684-J4
FONTAINBLEAU DR
12900 MORV 92555 717-J3
FOOLISH PLEASURE RD
42900 RivC 92536 963-B7
43600 RivC 92536 983-B1
FOOTE CT
10700 RIV 92505 714-E7
10900 RIV 92505 744-E1
FOOTHILL AV
4900 RIV 92503 714-F4
21300 RivC 92571 778-C5
22200 RivC 92571 808-C1
FOOTHILL DR
1500 BAN 92220 721-E1
FOOTHILL PK
1500 COR 92881 773-G4
FOOTHILL PKWY
- COR 92882 773-A3
E FOOTHILL PKWY
100 COR 92881 773-D3
100 COR 92882 773-D3
W FOOTHILL PKWY
100 COR 92882 773-C2
FOOTHILL RD
38100 RivC 92539 (935-D2
See Page 904)
47200 RivC 92220 692-F6
67000 CTHC 92234 817-C3
FORBES AV
- RivC 92518 717-C7
FORBES CIR
78500 LQNT 92253 819-G7
FORD AV
300 HEMT 92543 810-J5
16800 RivC 92241 728-B1
FORD DR
- RivC - 392-A11
FORD PL
4200 RIV 92505 714-F6
FORD ST
600 COR 92879 743-E6
FORDHAM CT
- RMIR 92270 818-B3
FORDHAM DR
26400 RivC 92586 838-B6
FORDHAM PL
11800 RIV 92505 714-A6
FORDHAM WY
- MURR 92563 928-G6

FORE DR
25800 RivC 92544 811-J7
FORE LN
42200 TEM 92591 959-C5
FOREMAN AV
12600 MORV 92553 717-G3
FOREST DR
24300 RivC - 814-F4
81300 RivC 92201 5410-D6
S FOREST DR
900 CLTN 92324 646-G1
FOREST LN
28500 RivC 92587 837-F7
35100 YCPA 92399 650-A2
FOREST ST
4400 RIV 92507 685-H6
36200 RivC 92596 899-C7
36200 RivC 92596 929-C1
FOREST VW
16400 LKEL 92530 865-F1
FOREST BOUNDARY RD
22200 RivC 92883 804-C2
51200 RivC 92539 (933-G5
See Page 902)
FORESTDALE DR
2300 RIV 92507 686-G1
FORESTER DR
700 COR 92880 743-C3
FOREST HAVEN DR
54700 RivC - 814-E4
FOREST HIGHLANDS CIR
- COR 92883 773-H6
FOREST HILL DR
54300 RivC - 814-C7
FOREST HILLS DR
300 RMIR 92270 787-J5
300 RMIR 92270 788-A4
FOREST KNOLL DR
54600 RivC - 814-D5
FOREST LAKE DR
53200 RivC - 814-A5
FOREST OAKS AV
4800 BAN 92220 721-E4
FOREST OAKS DR
- COR 92881 773-E3
FOREST OAKS WY
28400 MORV 92555 718-E7
FOREST PARK DR
600 RivC 92501 646-A7
FORESTRY RD
57700 RivC 92539 (935-B1
See Page 904)
FOREST SPRINGS RD
48500 RivC 92536 963-B1
FOREST VIEW DR
- COR 92882 772-J2
FOREST VIEW LN
- RivC 92562 956-H4
FORLORI CIR
- RivC 92570 806-G3
FORMBY CT
22500 MURR 92562 927-D2
FORMBY DR
12200 MORV 92557 717-B2
FORMOSA ST
4100 RivC 92509 644-H7
4400 RivC 92509 684-H1
FORREST DR
22200 RivC 92570 806-J1
22200 RivC 92570 807-A4
FORSYTE ST
24000 MORV 92557 687-E7
FORT DR
3800 RivC 92509 685-D2
FORT FREMONT AL
5400 RivC 92509 685-D2
FORT KENT CT
7200 RIV 92506 716-D6
FORTNER RD
36900 RivC 92539 904-E7
FORTUNA RD
1400 NRCO 92860 713-E5
68700 CTHC 92234 757-E6
FORTUNA WY
- RLTO 92316 645-H2
FORTUNA DEL SUR DR
25500 MORV 92551 747-H2
FORTUNE BAY LN
24600 MORV 92551 747-F4
FORUM WY
1700 COR 92881 743-F7
FOSTER DR
6300 RIV 92506 715-G3
FOSTER RD
8900 RivC 92883 804-B1
FOSTER ST
17800 LKEL 92530 866-B3
FOSTER LAKE RD
25100 RivC - 814-B5
FOSTORIA LN
- RivC 92203 789-F4
FOUCH LN
11800 MORV 92557 717-F1
FOULOIS AV
21000 RivC 92518 746-H4
FOUNTAIN AV
900 RivC 92507 646-C6
FOUNTAIN CV
- RivC - 5421-B1
FOUNTAIN DR
500 RivC 91752 683-E4
FOUNTAIN ST
46000 RivC 92220 722-C5

STREET
Block City ZIP Pg-Grid

HARVEST LN
- RIV 92506 715-F4
30100 RivC 92563 929-A7
HARVEST RD
400 PER 92571 777-J6
24200 MORV 92557 687-E6
HARVEST WY
33200 RivC 92595 897-G2
HARVEST WY E
33100 RivC 92595 897-H2
HARVEST CREST
- COR 92881 773-E2
HARVEST MOON LN
800 BAN 92220 721-H2
HARVEST MOON RD
64000 RivC 92240 696-D6
HARVEST VALLEY AV
- RivC 92880 713-A1
HARVEY AV
200 RivC 92507 646-D6
HARVEY LN
14000 RivC 92503 745-C4
HARVEY PT
- CHLS 91709 712-A6
HARVEY WY
44500 RivC 92544 (812-B6 See Page 782)
HARVEY HILLS RD
54500 RivC 92539 (934-E2 See Page 904)
HARVILL AV
17700 RivC 92570 747-C6
18400 RivC 92570 777-C1
S HARVILL AV
20800 RivC 92570 777-E6
HARVILL LN
3500 RivC 92503 744-B4
E HARWICK DR
100 SBDO 92408 646-J1
W HARWICK DR
100 SBDO 92408 646-H1
100 CLTN 92324 646-H1
HARWICK LN
- TEM 92592 959-G6
HARWOOD CIR
6700 PMSP 92264 787-D6
HARWOOD CT
4800 RivC 92509 684-F2
HARWOOD LN
32300 RivC 92595 927-F2
HARZBURG RD
25700 RivC 92584 868-A2
HASKELL RD
72800 RivC 92276 788-D2
HASKELL ST
8700 RIV 92503 715-B6
HASTINGS BLVD
9000 RivC 92509 644-C7
HASTINGS LN
1600 RIV 92506 715-G6
HASTINGS ST
42500 PDST 92211 819-E5
HATCHET CACTUS DR
67600 RivC 92241 727-B4
HATHAWAY PL
2000 RIV 92506 715-H5
HATHAWAY ST
- BAN 92220 722-D3
S HATHAWAY ST
- BAN 92220 722-D4
1600 RivC 92220 722-D5
HATHAWAY WY
- RivC - (907-H5 See Page 906)
HATHAWAY CANYON RD
11100 RivC 92220 692-C2
HATTIE AV
51800 RivC 92230 723-G7
HATTON PL
55200 RivC 92282 724-D1
HAUN RD
27700 RivC 92586 868-D2
30000 RivC 92584 868-E4
32500 RivC 92584 898-E1
HAUPERT RD
54000 RivC 92539 (934-D6 See Page 904)
HAUSTEEN CT
14000 MORV 92553 717-E6
HAUTE CT
- RivC 92596 899-D7
HAVASU CT
74900 INDW 92210 848-J1
HAVASU ST
1800 PER 92571 777-H7
HAVEN AV
12900 ONT 91761 643-B7
12900 ONT 91761 683-B2
14100 ONT 91710 683-B3
N HAVEN AV
100 ONT 91761 643-B2
S HAVEN AV
100 ONT 91761 643-B5
HAVEN ST
- LKEL 92530 865-F4
HAVEN WY
32900 RivC 92595 897-A6
HAVENCREST ST
100 PER 92571 777-G2
HAVENHURST AV
4000 RIV 92507 686-F5
HAVENHURST DR
20600 RivC 92567 779-C4
HAVENRIDGE DR
- COR 92883 773-H7

HAVEN ROCK CT
13100 RivC 92883 835-B5
HAVEN TREE LN
1300 COR 92881 773-F4
HAVEN VIEW DR
6400 RivC 92509 684-G5
HAVENWOOD CT
700 COR 92882 742-J5
HAVENWOOD RD
16300 MORV 92551 747-G3
HAVENWOOD ST
23500 MORV 92557 717-D1
HAVERFORD AV
4000 RIV 92507 686-F5
HAVERHILL CT
3000 RIV 92506 715-G2
HAVILLAND LN
5900 RIV 92504 715-A1
HAVSTAD DR
11300 LMLN 92354 647-E2
HAWAII CIR
76500 PDST 92211 819-C6
HAWARDEN DR
5800 RIV 92506 715-H2
HAWES VALLEY DR
39800 RivC 92539 (934-F3 See Page 904)
HAWK CIR
2600 COR 92882 772-H2
HAWK DR
1000 SJCT 92583 811-E3
3900 RivC 92509 685-A1
HAWKCREST AV
1400 COR 92879 743-G2
HAWKEYE DR
82500 RivC 92274 5590-G3
HAWKEYE RD
23300 RivC 92570 805-H4
HAWK HILL TR
76700 PDST 92211 819-C4
HAWKINS CT
33100 RivC 92567 809-F2
HAWKLEY DR
6500 RIV 92506 716-B4
HAWKWOOD TR
25300 MORV 92557 717-G1
HAWTHORNE AV
9100 RIV 92503 714-H5
21500 RivC 92570 746-J6
21500 RivC 92570 747-A6
HAWTHORNE DR
3400 COR 92881 773-D4
HAWTHORNE ST
31100 RivC 92584 867-J5
41700 MURR 92562 928-B7
41800 MURR 92562 958-A1
42800 MURR 92562 957-J2
HAYDEN AV
1700 RivC 92881 773-G5
1700 COR 92881 773-G5
HAYDEN CT
- LKEL 92530 865-G3
8600 RIV 92504 715-A4
HAYDEN LN
26200 RivC 92584 898-B1
HAYES
- CTHC 92234 787-D6
HAYES AV
24100 MURR 92562 927-G5
24800 MURR 92562 957-J1
24900 MURR 92562 958-A1
HAYES CIR
500 COR 92879 743-G4
HAYES ST
9400 RIV 92503 714-H6
22300 RivC 92570 807-B2
66400 RivC 92254 (5593-C7 See Page 5592)
66400 RivC 92254 (5653-C3 See Page 5592)
HAYFIELD CIR
33400 RivC 92595 897-G2
HAYFIELD RD
- RivC - 390-L10
HAYGEN ST
17800 RivC 92508 746-B4
HAYGOOD WY
28400 RivC 92532 836-E7
HAYLOFT PL
- RIV 92508 746-D2
HAYLOFT RD
33400 RivC 92595 897-G3
HAYMARKET DR
10700 RIV 92503 744-G2
HAYNES AV
17400 RivC 92530 896-B3
HAYNES DR
3900 RivC 92509 685-B2
HAYRAKE CIR
24500 RivC 92595 897-G3
HAYS AV
17500 RivC 92530 896-C3
HAYS ST
- BAN 92220 722-A3
800 BAN 92220 721-H3
E HAYS ST
- BAN 92220 722-B3
HAYSTACK DR
27000 RivC 92883 835-B4
HAYSTACK RD
72600 PDST 92260 848-E4
HAYSTACK MOUNTAIN DR
73300 RivC 92260 818-E1

HAYWORTH CT
22200 RivC 92883 804-C2
HAZEL CANYON LN
44300 PDST 92260 818-H7
HAZELCREST CT
26500 MORV 92555 718-A3
HAZELDELL DR
11700 RIV 92505 714-B7
HAZEL GLEN RD
- MURR 92563 928-J3
- MURR 92563 929-A3
HAZELNUT CT
22700 RivC 92883 804-B3
HAZELTINE PZ
6000 PMSP 92264 787-C3
E HAZELTINE ST
2900 ONT 91761 643-A6
HAZELTINE WY
- COR 92883 773-F7
14500 MORV 92555 718-E6
HAZELWOOD CIR
25000 RivC 92544 (812-B6 See Page 782)
HAZELWOOD CT
16300 MORV 92551 747-G3
HAZELWOOD DR
400 RivC 91752 683-E4
10800 MORV 92557 687-D6
HAZELWOOD ST
- MURR 92562 927-F5
HAZY WY
2600 BAN 92220 721-H4
HEACOCK ST
10000 MORV 92557 687-E5
11400 MORV 92557 717-E2
12200 MORV 92553 717-E5
14500 RivC 92518 717-E7
15000 MORV 92551 717-E7
15000 MORV 92551 747-E2
15000 RivC 92518 747-E2
HEAD CIR
29900 LKEL 92530 866-B3
HEADLY RD
21000 RivC 92570 776-G6
HEALD AV
17900 LKEL 92530 866-C4
E HEALD AV
100 LKEL 92530 866-F5
W HEALD AV
100 LKEL 92530 866-D4
HEALY PL
1700 RIV 92506 716-B3
HEARST WY
600 COR 92882 773-B4
HEARTHSIDE DR
1300 COR 92882 773-A1
HEARTHSTONE CT
39600 MURR 92562 898-A7
HEARTLAND WY
- COR 92881 773-G4
68800 RivC 92240 697-E6
HEARTLEAF ST
12500 MORV 92553 717-H3
HEARTWOOD DR
19900 RivC 92570 776-F1
HEATH CT
4900 HEMT 92544 811-G6
24600 MORV 92551 747-F1
HEATHCLIFF DR
11200 RIV 92505 714-A3
HEATHER CIR
1200 COR 92880 743-B2
HEATHER CT
- PDST 92260 848-E6
HEATHER GN
50000 LQNT 92253 849-J6
HEATHER LN
- RivC 92544 931-E6
1400 RIV 92504 745-E2
1600 RDL 92373 647-J3
15000 LKEL 92530 865-H4
32200 RivC 92584 868-H7
85300 COAC 92236 5531-C1
HEATHER WY
41100 RivC 92544 931-E5
44600 TEM 92592 979-D3
69500 RMIR 92270 787-G5
HEATHERBROOK CIR
3300 COR 92881 773-G4
HEATHERBROOK DR
3200 COR 92881 773-G4
HEATHERGLEN RD
16300 MORV 92551 747-H3
HEATHERSTONE CT
39500 RivC 92563 929-A7
HEATHERTON LN
5100 RIV 92505 714-B6
HEATHERWOOD DR
- PDST 92211 818-F1
6200 RivC 92509 684-G6
HEATHERWOOD WY
31000 LKEL 92532 867-D6
HEATHROW DR
11200 RIV 92503 744-F3
HEATON LN
29000 RivC 92584 868-G5
HEAVEN DR
- SDCo 92028 998-G5
HEAVENLY WY
2400 COR 92881 773-G3
HEBRON CT
- RIV 92508 746-E2
HECHT RD
23000 RivC 92587 867-D2

HEDGEHOG ST
72500 PDST 92260 848-D2
HEDGES DR
800 COR 92880 742-J1
800 COR 92880 743-A1
HEDRICK AV
4600 RIV 92505 714-E5
8200 RIV 92503 714-E4
HEIDI RD
3900 RIV 92504 715-A3
HEIDI LISA LN
18000 RivC 92532 866-C1
HEIFITZ DR
48000 INDO 92201 5470-F4
HEIGHTS RD
- SDCo 92028 997-E3
HEIL DR
24800 MORV 92553 717-F6
HEIM AV
17900 LKEL 92530 866-C4
HEIM ST
27000 RivC 92584 898-D1
HEINZ LN
RivC 92584 869-A6
HEIRLOOM AV
1400 PER 92571 807-H1
1400 PER 92571 777-H7
HEITZ CT
43300 PDST 92260 818-F6
HEITZ LN
31200 TEM 92591 959-D3
HEIZER DR
15400 RivC 92570 775-G5
HELEM LN
33200 RivC 92584 898-B2
HELEN AV
51500 RivC 92230 723-G6
81100 RivC 92201 5410-C7
HELEN DR
39700 SDCo 92028 997-A2
HELEN RD
2300 SDCo 92028 997-A1
HELENA AV
7900 RIV 92504 715-B4
HELENA CIR
200 PMSP 92262 786-H1
HELENA CT
- RivC 92592 979-H3
HELENA ST
- RivC 92373 689-C5
900 CLTN 92324 646-H1
HELENE DR
26300 MORV 92555 717-J2
26300 MORV 92555 718-A2
30000 RivC 92584 868-J6
30000 RivC 92584 869-A6
HELENE WY
27200 RivC 92585 838-C3
HELENKA LN
18800 LKEL 92530 896-F3
HELEN MOODY LN
73000 PDST 92260 848-E3
HELGA LN
11800 MORV 92555 718-A1
HELICOPTER CIR
300 COR 92880 742-J3
E HELIO CT
82200 INDO 92201 5470-F3
W HELIO CT
82100 INDO 92201 5470-E3
HELIOS RD
15700 RivC 92503 775-G1
15700 RivC 92504 775-G1
HELIOTROPE DR
47100 PDST 92260 848-F4
HELIOTROPE WY
23700 MORV 92557 687-D5
HELIX ST
5600 RivC 92509 685-C3
HELLER DR
2700 RivC 92509 645-B6
HELLER SPRINGS RD
40900 RivC 92539 (965-H1 See Page 964)
HELLMAN AV
16300 SBdC 91710 712-H3
16800 RivC 92880 712-H3
16800 SBdC 92880 712-H3
HELM CIR
- RivC 92254 (5654-G5 See Page 5594)
HELMCREST DR
5900 RivC 92509 684-H5
HELMS RD
73300 RivC 92241 728-D2
HELMS WY
40000 RivC 92562 956-H1
HELMSDALE ST
13200 MORV 92553 717-E4
HEMET ST
100 HEMT 92544 811-F6
700 RivC 92544 811-F7
1100 SJCT 92583 811-F6
10300 RIV 92505 714-G7
24400 RivC 92583 811-F6
26000 RivC 92544 841-F1
HEMET LAKE RD
55900 RivC - (874-F2 See Page 844)
HEMET RANCH RD
- RivC 92543 871-A7
- RivC 92544 871-A7
HEMINGS WY
- LQNT 92253 819-J7
- LQNT 92253 5410-A7

HEMINGWAY CT
- RivC 92584 868-C3
41900 PDST 92211 819-A5
HEMINGWAY DR
- COR 92880 712-J7
- COR 92880 742-J1
6500 RIV 92506 716-C4
HEMLOCK AV
10500 FONT 92337 644-E2
23000 MORV 92557 717-C2
26200 MORV 92555 718-A2
HEMLOCK CIR
1600 COR 92879 743-E7
HEMLOCK ST
23500 LKEL 92532 867-G6
23500 LKEL 92595 867-E7
23500 RivC 92595 867-E7
23900 RivC 92532 867-G6
24100 RivC 92584 867-G6
HEMPLE ST
32100 RivC 92595 867-A7
HEMPSTEAD CT
26400 RivC 92586 838-B5
HEMPSTEAD LN
- RIV 92508 746-E1
HEMSTREET PL
25900 RivC - 814-E6
HENDERSON LN
21800 RivC 92595 897-B4
HENDERSON RD
69000 RivC 92240 697-E7
69000 RivC 92241 697-E7
HENDRICKS CIR
300 COR 92879 744-A3
HENDRY AV
9100 RIV 92503 714-J5
9100 RIV 92503 715-A5
HENNESY ST
1800 PER 92571 777-H7
HENRY RD
19900 RivC 92241 728-G6
23300 RivC 92241 758-G1
HENRY TER
18400 RivC 92570 747-A7
18400 RivC 92570 777-A1
HENSHAW CT
19200 RivC 92530 896-G4
HENSLER AV
21000 RivC 92570 806-H3
HEPBURN DR
48500 INDO 92201 5470-G4
HERBERT AV
- LKEL 92530 866-G6
HERBERT RD
41900 RivC 92536 961-H4
HERBERT ST
22000 RivC 92570 837-B3
29600 LKEL 92530 866-A2
HERBORN ST
15000 LKEL 92530 865-H3
HERCULES WY
11000 RivC 91752 683-H4
HEREFORD DR
8600 SBdC 91710 712-G2
HEREFORD WY
33300 RivC 92530 865-F6
HERITAGE CIR
2200 COR 92882 773-A1
HERITAGE CT
69400 CTHC 92234 787-F1
HERITAGE DR
2300 COR 92882 772-J1
2300 COR 92882 773-A1
12000 MORV 92557 717-B2
S HERITAGE LN
2400 SBDO 92408 646-J1
HERITAGE ST
30100 RivC 92563 929-A6
HERITAGE WY
- PDST 92211 819-A1
12600 MORV 92553 717-B3
37400 RivC 92211 789-G7
HERITAGE GROVE RD
14900 RivC 92504 745-E3
N HERITAGE PALMS DR
- INDO 92201 5410-A6
S HERITAGE PALMS DR
44000 INDO 92201 5410-B7
HERITAGE RANCH RD
1300 SJCT 92583 780-J6
HERITAGE UNION LN
- MURR 92563 928-G6
HERMAN DR
11900 RIV 92505 744-B1
HERMANO WY
13200 DHSP 92240 697-C5
HERMINIA CT
11200 MORV 92555 688-E7
HERMITAGE
- LQNT 92253 5530-B6
HERMITAGE DR
41500 RivC 92201 819-H5
HERMITAGE LN
9500 RIV 92503 715-A7
9500 RIV 92503 745-A1
HERMITAGE WY
28000 RivC 92586 838-A6
HERMOSA AV
1000 BAN 92220 722-C1
S HERMOSA AV
400 BAN 92220 722-C4
HERMOSA DR
700 PMSP 92264 786-F3
1200 RIV 92504 745-E1
1300 COR 92879 743-G3

HERMOSA DR
16000 RIV 92506 745-G1
N HERMOSA DR
100 PMSP 92262 786-F2
600 PMSP 92262 756-F4
S HERMOSA DR
100 PMSP 92262 786-F2
HERMOSA LN
44200 PDST 92260 818-G7
HERMOSA PL
800 BAN 92220 722-C2
W HERMOSA PL
100 PMSP 92262 756-D7
HERMOSA ST
400 HEMT 92543 840-J1
18700 RivC 92508 746-C2
S HERMOSA ST
1300 BAN 92220 722-C5
HERMOSILLO LN
- PDST 92260 818-G3
HERMOSILLO RD
68000 CTHC 92234 757-D7
HERNANDEZ CT
2100 CLTN 92324 646-H1
HERNANDEZ RD
24300 RivC 92570 807-C5
HERNE CT
15300 MORV 92551 747-F1
HERNLEY RD
51600 RivC 92536 963-G6
HERON DR
900 COR 92879 743-G2
HERON LN
100 RivC 92507 646-E6
24300 MURR 92562 928-C3
HERRERA CT
5300 RIV 92505 714-B5
HERSCHEL LN
13100 MORV 92555 718-H4
HERSEY CT
28600 RivC 92586 838-A7
HERSHEY CT
1900 SJCT 92582 810-F2
HERSHEY WY
10000 RIV 92503 684-E7
S HERT ST
900 CLTN 92324 646-C1
HESHMET ST
28000 HEMT 92543 841-B5
HESS LN
21900 RivC 92567 778-J7
HESSE RD
37700 RivC 92223 690-E5
HESTER DR
100 CTHC 92234 787-E5
HEWITT AV
400 SJCT 92583 811-C3
HEWITT ST
1100 SJCT 92583 811-C4
2100 HEMT 92544 811-C4
2100 SJCT 92544 811-C4
3400 RIV 92501 685-H3
HEXAMER DR
28500 RivC 92567 808-H4
HIALEAH CIR
2300 NRCO 92860 713-B7
HIALEAH LN
- RMIR 92270 817-G2
HIALEAH WY
- RivC - (935-J1 See Page 904)
- RivC - (936-A1 See Page 906)
HIAWATHA CT
31200 TEM 92592 979-D5
HIAWATHA LN
13300 MORV 92553 717-G4
HIAWATHA PL
3400 RIV 92501 685-H3
HIAWATHA ST
100 PMSP 92264 786-C2
HIBBARD VW
12800 RivC 92503 745-A4
HIBISCO ST
49200 COAC 92236 5471-A5
HIBISCUS AV
18000 RivC 92508 746-B3
HIBISCUS CT
1200 BAN 92220 722-A1
41100 MURR 92562 927-J3
HIBISCUS DR
69500 CTHC 92234 787-G3
HIBISCUS LN
80600 INDO 92201 5470-B2
HIBISCUS RD
3700 PER 92571 778-A2
HIBISCUS ST
1100 COR 92882 743-A7
HIBLER AV
- RivC - 392-B10
HICHORY TREE LN
- BEAU 92223 720-G2
HICKENLOOPER CT
11800 MORV 92555 718-F1
HICKOCK WY
3000 RIV 92506 715-G1
HICKORY AV
900 SJCT 92583 780-H7
HICKORY DR
1300 HEMT 92545 840-G3
HICKORY LN
8500 RIV 92504 715-A4
12500 BLY 92225 5491-H6
34400 RivC 92595 897-B5

HICKORY TREE LN
18000 RivC 92504 746-A7
HICKORY WOOD DR
- HEMT 92545 840-D4
HICKS LN
- RivC 92282 724-F7
HICKS ST
21000 RivC 92570 776-H2
HIDALGO DR
17100 RivC 92570 806-A1
HIDALGO PL
3800 RIV 92501 685-G4
HIDALGO ST
12500 DHSP 92240 697-C5
HIDALGO WY
1900 PMSP 92262 756-F6
HIDATSA ST
4100 RivC 92509 685-D4
HIDDEN LN
3800 RIV 92504 715-B3
HIDDEN CANYON DR
- LQNT 92253 849-F4
HIDDEN CANYON RD
30500 LKEL 92532 866-J5
HIDDEN COVE CT
2000 CLTN 92324 646-J4
2000 SBdC 92324 646-J4
HIDDEN COVE DR
- YCPA 92399 649-H5
12500 RivC 92503 744-C4
HIDDEN COVE RD
75200 INDW 92210 849-A4
HIDDEN CREEK CT
22700 MURR 92562 927-D3
HIDDEN CREEK DR
27400 RivC 92883 835-A5
HIDDEN CREEK ST
1100 COR 92881 773-E2
HIDDEN GLEN CIR
34300 RivC 92595 897-C4
HIDDEN HEIGHTS DR
- RivC 92399 650-H7
HIDDEN HILLS CIR
2900 COR 92882 742-F6
HIDDEN HILLS WY
2800 COR 92882 742-F6
HIDDEN HOLLOW DR
33100 RivC 92595 897-H2
HIDDEN LAKE DR
29000 RivC 92584 838-G7
29000 RivC 92584 868-G1
HIDDEN MEADOW CIR
- RivC 92562 956-E1
HIDDEN OAK DR
11500 RivC 92880 742-B5
HIDDEN OAKS RD
- SDCo 92028 999-J5
- SDCo 92059 999-J5
HIDDEN PALMS DR
44000 PDST 92260 818-H7
78500 RivC 92211 789-G7
HIDDEN PALMS RD
- RivC - 878-A6
HIDDEN RIVER
- RivC 92880 713-B1
HIDDEN RIVER RD
78200 PDST 92201 819-F6
78200 RivC 92201 819-F6
HIDDEN SPRINGS
- BLY - 5491-B7
HIDDEN SPRINGS DR
4500 COR 92881 773-E6
4500 COR 92883 773-E6
9400 MORV 92557 687-B4
10400 RivC 92557 687-B4
HIDDEN SPRINGS RD
35400 RivC 92545 810-A5
36300 RivC 92595 927-F2
HIDDEN STAR CT
- RivC 92883 835-D5
HIDDEN TRAIL CT
- RivC 92596 929-C2
HIDDEN TRAILS DR
2600 NRCO 92860 713-E6
HIDDEN VALLEY CIR
- RivC - (937-C2 See Page 906)
HIDDEN VALLEY DR
- NRCO 92860 743-J1
1900 NRCO 92860 713-J7
E HIDDEN VALLEY LN
3000 CLTN 92324 646-J3
HIDDEN VALLEY PKWY
100 COR 92860 743-E2
100 NRCO 92860 743-E2
100 COR 92879 743-E2
1600 NRCO 92879 743-E2
HIDDEN VALLEY RD
16600 RivC 92570 805-J4
16900 RivC 92570 806-A4
HIDDEN VALLEY TR
- INDW 92210 848-H5
HIDDEN VALLEY TR S
- INDW 92210 848-H6
HIDDEN WATER PL
39000 RivC 92260 818-F2
HIDE A LN
26600 RivC - 844-C1
HIDEAWAY LN
11500 FONT 92337 644-H3
HIDEOUT LN
3000 COR 92882 773-B3
HIDEWAY PL
1900 COR 92881 773-G1

HIDING BASS PL
22700 CYNL 92587 867-D3
HIERS AV
4700 RIV 92505 714-D6
HIGDON DR
26900 RivC 92324 688-A5
HIGGINS DR
56800 RivC 92274 5531-E5
HIGGINS RD
37400 RivC 92539 (933-J1 See Page 902)
HIGH AV
38600 RivC 92539 (934-F4 See Page 904)
HIGH PL
10200 RivC 92223 690-J4
N HIGH RD
600 PMSP 92262 756-C7
600 PMSP 92262 786-C1
HIGH ST
200 LKEL 92530 866-F6
1400 BAN 92220 722-B1
4500 RIV 92507 685-J6
21500 RivC 92570 776-J5
21500 RivC 92570 777-A5
39600 RivC 92223 690-J4
39800 RivC 92223 691-A4
HIGH BLUFF CT
16300 RivC 92503 744-E4
HIGHBURY DR
39500 MURR 92563 928-F6
HIGHCLIFF CIR
1200 COR 92882 742-F6
HIGHCLIFF RD
3200 RIV 92506 685-G7
3200 RIV 92506 715-G1
13200 RivC 92570 805-C6
HIGH COUNTRY CIR
17000 RivC 92570 806-A3
HIGH COUNTRY DR
- RivC 92324 687-J3
- RivC 92324 688-A3
HIGH COUNTRY TR
61000 RivC 92539 (965-J6 See Page 964)
HIGH CREST DR
31800 LKEL 92532 866-J5
HIGHGROVE
53100 RivC - 814-A4
HIGHGROVE PL
1300 RivC 92507 646-B6
HIGHGROVE ST
600 COR 92882 773-B2
HIGHGROVE PASS RD
1200 RivC 92324 646-H7
1200 RivC 92324 686-J1
HIGH HILL RD
36500 RivC 92539 (903-J7 See Page 902)
36900 RivC 92539 (933-J1 See Page 902)
HIGH KNOLL CIR
7300 RivC 92881 773-H3
HIGHLAND AV
- RivC 92507 646-C6
12000 DHSP 92240 697-C4
32200 SBdC 92374 649-A1
36000 YCPA 92399 650-C1
HIGHLAND BLVD
29000 MORV 92555 688-F7
29200 MORV 92555 718-G1
HIGHLAND DR
- RivC - 5239-J6
- RivC - 5240-A7
S HIGHLAND DR
500 PMSP 92264 786-J3
HIGHLAND PL
4500 RIV 92506 685-E5
HIGHLAND ST
22000 RivC 92595 927-C2
HIGHLANDER DR
300 RIV 92507 686-D3
43900 TEM 92592 978-J1
43900 TEM 92592 979-A1
HIGHLAND HOME RD
- BAN 92220 721-E2
1100 BAN 92220 691-E7
14400 RivC 92220 721-E5
HIGHLAND MESA LN
24200 MORV 92557 687-E5
HIGHLAND OAKS DR
13500 YCPA 92399 650-J6
13600 RivC 92399 650-J6
HIGHLAND PALMS DR
26000 RivC 92548 839-A1
46700 LQNT 92253 849-G2
HIGHLANDS RD
500 LKEL 92530 865-H4
47900 RivC 92536 983-A7
HIGHLAND SPRINGS AV
- BAN 92220 721-C2
200 BEAU 92223 721-C2
1900 BEAU 92223 691-C7
10600 RivC 92220 691-C5
10600 RivC 92223 691-C5
11200 BAN 92220 691-C5
HIGHLAND SPRINGS DR
73100 RivC 92260 818-E2
HIGHLAND VIEW DR
600 COR 92882 742-E5
HIGHLAND VISTA WY
400 PER 92570 807-F2
HIGH MEADOW DR
10800 MORV 92557 687-D6

HIGH NOON CT
14100 MORV 92553 717-H6
HIGH PEAK DR
800 RIV 92506 716-D5
HIGH PINE RD
18000 RivC 92570 776-C2
HIGH PLAINS WY
- PER 92571 778-B3
HIGHPOINT AV
28500 MORV 92555 718-E6
HIGHPOINT DR
500 COR 92879 743-J3
6000 RIV 92505 714-E3
HIGH POINT RD
47000 RivC 92536 982-E7
HIGH POINT TKTR
- RivC 92536 409-G5
- RivC 92536 982-F7
HIGH POST RD
23300 RivC 92567 809-H3
HIGH PRAIRIE TR
7600 RivC 92509 684-H5
HIGH RANCH CIR
10100 RivC 92220 691-G3
HIGH RES WY
13400 RivC 92570 775-B6
HIGHRIDGE DR
2100 COR 92879 743-H3
HIGHRIDGE ST
800 RIV 92506 745-G1
1400 RIV 92506 715-G7
HIGHVIEW CT
17100 RivC 92503 744-F4
HIGH VIEW DR
800 RIV 92506 716-D5
HIGHVIEW DR
12700 RDL 92373 649-A5
54700 RivC 92539 (934-E3 See Page 904)
HIGHVIEW LN
22700 RivC 92557 687-B3
HIGH WATER WY
19300 RivC 92881 773-H3
HIGHWAY Rt#-62
- DHSP 92282 655-J7
- DHSP 92282 695-H1
- RivC 92282 695-H4
- RivC 92282 725-G1
61600 RivC 92282 655-J4
HIGHWAY Rt#-74
- LKEL 92530 866-D2
- LKEL 92532 836-E7
- LKEL 92532 866-D1
- LKEL 92570 836-F6
- PER 92570 807-F3
- RivC 92532 836-E7
- RivC 92532 866-E1
- RivC 92570 807-E4
- RivC 92570 836-J3
- RivC 92570 837-B1
HIGHWAY Rt#-78
- RivC - 412-A2
HIGHWAY Rt#-79
- RivC 92536 409-G5
- TEM 92590 979-A2
- TEM 92592 979-H1
24600 RivC 92536 982-A4
28900 TEM 92590 978-J2
33500 RivC 92592 979-J1
33500 RivC 92592 980-A1
42500 RivC 92536 981-F3
42500 RivC 92592 981-D3
HIGHWAY Rt#-86
- ImCo 92274 (5772-J5 See Page 5712)
- ImCo 92274 (5773-A6 See Page 5712)
66900 RivC 92274 (5591-C7 See Page 5590)
66900 RivC 92274 (5651-C1 See Page 5590)
73000 RivC 92274 410-E3
74000 RivC 92274 5712-A1
81000 RivC 92274 (5772-D1 See Page 5712)
HIGHWAY Rt#-86S
- COAC 92236 5471-D5
- COAC 92274 5471-G7
- COAC 92274 5531-G1
- RivC 92254 5592-D5
- RivC 92254 (5652-D1 See Page 5592)
- RivC 92254 5712-D1
- RivC 92274 390-F11
- RivC 92274 5471-F7
- RivC 92274 5531-H4
- RivC 92274 5712-E2
- RivC 92274 (5772-E1 See Page 5712)
62000 RivC 92274 5592-A1
HIGHWAY Rt#-111
- ImCo - (5775-H4 See Page 5714)
- PMSP 92262 725-A5
- PMSP 92282 724-G3
- PMSP 92282 725-A4
- RivC - (5715-B6 See Page 5714)
- RivC - (5775-E1 See Page 5714)
- RivC 92254 (5652-F1 See Page 5592)
- RivC 92254 5714-G1
- RivC 92254 (5715-A4 See Page 5714)

HIGHWAY Rt#-111
- RivC 92282 724-F3
56000 RivC 92274 5531-G4
58900 RivC 92274 390-F11
58900 RivC 92274 5592-A1
63300 RivC 92254 5592-D4
72100 RMIR 92270 818-C7
72100 PDST 92260 818-C7
72700 PDST 92260 848-D1
73600 RivC 92254 (5654-A4 See Page 5594)
74800 INDW 92210 848-J1
75000 INDW 92210 849-C1
78300 LQNT 92253 849-F1
79500 LQNT 92253 5470-A3
80200 INDO 92201 5470-E1
96400 RivC 92254 (5653-A3 See Page 5592)
HIGHWAY U.S.-95
- RivC - 392-D1
HIGHWOOD ST
24700 MORV 92551 747-G3
HILBERT DR
500 SDCo 92028 997-G7
HILDA CT
24300 MORV 92551 747-F2
HILDEGARDE ST
13400 MORV 92553 717-A5
HILDY LN
2100 PMSP 92262 756-G4
HILGARD ST
3700 COR 92882 773-B4
W HILL
54000 RivC 92539 (934-D3 See Page 904)
HILL AV
30200 LKEL 92530 866-C4
HILL CT
9000 RivC 92557 687-F3
S HILL CT
2100 CLTN 92324 646-H4
HILL DR
9400 RivC 92223 690-G2
11000 LMLN 92354 647-B1
85600 COAC 92236 5471-D7
HILL PL
5000 RivC 92509 684-D2
HILL ST
2500 RIV 92504 715-F5
25800 RivC - 814-E6
33000 RivC 92530 865-H6
37400 RivC 92539 (935-A2 See Page 904)
37900 RivC 92539 (905-A7 See Page 904)
HILL TER
16500 RivC 92530 896-A1
HILLANDALE CT
200 RIV 92507 686-F5
HILLANDALE RD
22700 MORV 92557 687-B7
HILLARY CT
6100 RIV 92506 685-G7
HILLCREST
40000 RivC 92223 691-A4
HILLCREST AV
1500 RIV 92501 685-J2
1500 RIV 92501 686-A1
HILLCREST CT
1000 CALI 92320 690-B1
33400 RivC 92595 897-D3
HILLCREST DR
- PDST 92260 818-H2
11900 FONT 92337 644-A4
HILLCREST LN
44200 RivC 92544 (812-B7 See Page 782)
HILLCREST RD
68300 CTHC 92234 817-D1
HILLCREST ST
900 HEMT 92545 840-G2
1100 COR 92880 743-B1
11200 LMLN 92354 647-C1
HILLGATE ST
23900 MORV 92557 687-E7
HILL GRASS DR
10500 MORV 92557 687-F6
HILLHURST CT
26400 RivC 92586 868-B2
HILLHURST DR
7600 RIV 92508 716-E6
9500 MORV 92557 687-F4
HILLIGOSS DR
100 CTHC 92234 787-E5
HILLKIRK AV
1300 NRCO 92860 743-E2
HILLMAN CT
25600 RivC 92586 837-J4
HILLMER CT
21200 MORV 92557 686-H7
HILLMER DR
25000 HEMT 92543 810-J6
HILLPOINTE DR
27700 RivC 92585 838-D5
HILLRISE CT
49000 RivC 92536 963-C2
HILLRISE LN
1300 NRCO 92860 713-E7
HILLRISE RD
42900 RivC 92220 691-F3
HILLSBORO CIR
- MURR 92562 928-A1
HILLSBOROUGH LN
10000 RIV 92503 714-E1

STREET
Block City ZIP Pg-Grid

HILLSBOROUGH WY
400 COR 92879 744-A2
HILLSDALE AV
28200 MORV 92555 718-D6
HILLSDALE RD
20800 RIV 92508 746-H2
HILLSDALE ST
55300 RivC - 814-E6
HILLSHORE CT
22300 RivC 92595 897-C3
HILLSIDE AV
1500 NRCO 92860 743-F1
1800 NRCO 92860 713-G3
6100 RIV 92504 685-B7
6300 RIV 92504 715-A2
HILLSIDE DR
4000 BAN 92220 691-E7
4000 BAN 92220 721-E1
11800 FONT 92337 644-E3
23800 RivC 92587 837-F7
HILLSIDE LN
- LKEL 92530 865-F4
800 NRCO 92860 713-G6
900 NRCO 92860 743-F1
HILLSIDE PL
10400 RivC 92220 691-D5
10600 BAN 92220 691-D7
HILLSIDE ST
7500 RivC 92881 773-J3
HILLSIDE TRAIL DR
38300 MURR 92562 927-C4
HILLSON CIR
43300 RivC 92544 811-H5
HILL SPRING RD
20100 RivC 92595 896-H5
HILLS RANCH RD
22500 RivC 92567 808-H2
HILLTOP CIR
1800 COR 92882 742-H6
HILLTOP CT
34900 RivC 92544 901-H4
HILL TOP DR
- RivC 92532 835-H2
HILLTOP DR
1700 RDL 92373 649-A4
HILL TOP DR
20600 RivC 92507 686-G6
HILLTOP DR
43000 RivC 92220 721-F6
E HILLTOP DR
1600 CLTN 92324 646-G2
HILLTOP LN
1400 NRCO 92860 743-E1
68300 CTHC 92234 817-D2
HILL TOP RD
- RivC 92570 805-J7
- RivC 92570 806-A5
HILLTOP RD
60800 RivC 92282 695-F7
73400 RivC 92241 390-B5
HILLVIEW CV
1400 PMSP 92264 816-G2
1400 RivC 92264 816-G2
HILLVIEW DR
300 HEMT 92544 811-C6
3400 RivC 92503 744-B4
22300 RivC 92570 807-B2
HILL VIEW LN
13600 YCPA 92399 650-C7
HILLWARD CT
9100 RIV 92508 746-D3
HILO AV
27100 RivC 92584 868-C6
HILO LN
800 PMSP 92264 786-E5
HILT RD
39200 RivC 92591 930-B6
HILTON DR
24600 MORV 92557 717-F1
HILTON RD
30700 RivC 92596 899-B3
HILTON HEAD DR
- RMIR 92270 788-B5
1100 BAN 92220 721-D5
HIMALAYA DR
300 COR 92881 773-D3
HINCKLEY ST
25700 LMLN 92354 647-D2
HINES AV
4100 RIV 92505 714-E7
HINSON ST
12000 MORV 92555 718-D2
HIS WY
4200 RivC 92509 644-B7
HISLOP WY
32500 TEM 92592 979-F3
HITCHING POST PL
- RIV 92508 746-D1
HITCHING RAIL CT
13100 RivC 92883 835-B4
HITT LN
19800 RivC 92562 926-G5
HIXON ST
33000 RivC 92595 896-J7
HJORTH ST
48100 INDO 92201 5470-D5
HOAG AV
- COR 92881 773-G4
HOANZL RD
15800 RivC 92504 745-G6
HOBART CIR
300 COR 92879 743-G4
HOBART CT
23400 MURR 92562 927-H2

HOBART DR
9000 RIV 92503 714-E1
HOBBITON RD
35000 RivC 92544 902-A5
43100 RivC 92544 901-J5
HOBBS WY
28000 MORV 92555 688-D7
HOBBY HORSE RD
40000 RivC 92544 931-C2
HOBIE CIR
26800 MURR 92562 958-F3
HOBO HILL RD
38500 RivC 92544 (932-B4
See Page 902)
E HOBSON WY
200 BLY 92225 5491-H6
1900 BLY 92225 392-D10
W HOBSON WY
- RivC - 392-B10
100 BLY 92225 5491-B7
1500 RivC 92225 5491-B7
1900 RivC - 5491-B7
1900 BLY - 5491-B7
9200 BLY - 392-B10
HODAN HILL CT
21300 RivC 92562 927-A4
HODGE CIR
19500 RivC 92562 956-G4
HOEGER RD
23900 RivC 92883 804-C6
HOEHN
20900 RivC 92570 776-H5
HOFF AV
16000 LKEL 92530 865-H1
HOFFA LN
16500 RivC 92504 745-H3
HOFFER ST
- BAN 92220 722-A2
1000 BAN 92220 721-D2
E HOFFER ST
200 BAN 92220 722-B2
HOFFMAN AV
8600 RIV 92504 715-B5
HOFFMAN CT
11300 FONT 92337 645-A2
HOFFMAN LN
27000 RivC 92584 898-C3
HOFFMAN TR
52600 RivC - (813-J4
See Page 782)
HOGAN AV
800 BAN 92220 721-D4
HOGAN DR
28900 RivC 92586 838-B7
41500 PDST 92211 819-B5
HOGAN LN
- RIV 92508 716-E7
HOG LAKE TKTR
53600 RivC 92539 904-C5
HOHOKAM CT
26200 RivC 92586 868-B2
HOLBECK CT
13300 MORV 92553 717-E4
HOLBOROW AV
16800 LKEL 92530 865-J2
16800 LKEL 92530 866-A2
HOLBROOK WY
6800 RIV 92504 715-B2
HOLCOMB RD
30600 RivC 92596 869-D5
HOLCOMB WY
16300 RivC 92504 745-G4
HOLCOMB CREEK PL
200 ONT 91761 643-C7
HOLDEN CIR
40000 TEM 92591 959-B1
HOLDEN DR
17500 RivC 92570 776-B4
HOLDER AV
43500 RivC 92544 811-J5
HOLDING ST
3200 RIV 92501 685-J2
HOLE AV
10000 RIV 92503 714-E6
10200 RIV 92505 714-E6
HOLE IN ONE CT
- HEMT 92545 810-E6
HOLIDAY CT
1100 COR 92879 743-F6
HOLIDAY LN
25300 RivC 92544 (812-B6
See Page 782)
HOLLADAY ST
8800 RivC 92509 684-E5
HOLLAND RD
25000 LKEL 92532 867-F6
25000 RivC 92584 867-J4
25600 RivC 92584 868-A4
30700 RivC 92584 869-A4
30800 RivC 92596 869-E4
HOLLENBECK DR
10700 RIV 92505 714-E7
HOLLEY LN
400 BLY 92225 5491-D5
HOLLIE DR
- RivC 92324 687-J4
- RivC 92324 688-A3
HOLLINGSWORTH DR
- MURR 92562 898-C7
HOLLIS CT
11800 LMLN 92354 647-G3
HOLLIS LN
20800 RivC 92570 775-B6
HOLLISTER DR
- RivC 92203 789-F4

HOLLISTER DR
33200 RivC 92530 896-B3
38400 PDST 92211 818-F1
HOLLOW LN
39100 RivC - (933-G5
See Page 902)
39100 RivC 92539 (933-G5
See Page 902)
HOLLOWBROOK WY
- RivC 92880 713-B1
HOLLOW HILL LN
23700 SBdC 92324 646-H4
HOLLOWOOD CT
1400 PER 92571 807-J1
3400 RivC 92503 744-B4
HOLLY CIR
1100 COR 92882 743-B7
HOLLY CT
800 BAN 92220 721-F2
9100 RivC 92324 687-G3
11900 GTER 92313 646-F3
45500 INDO 92201 5470-D1
HOLLY DR
- MURR 92562 927-E4
600 HEMT 92543 840-J1
60200 RivC 92262 725-F7
HOLLY LN
1100 CALI 92320 689-H1
8500 RIV 92504 714-J3
8800 RIV 92503 714-H3
HOLLY ST
11700 GTER 92313 646-E3
12200 SBdC 92509 645-H4
12600 RivC 92509 645-H6
HOLLY ANN DR
54000 RivC 92536 (984-D2
See Page 964)
HOLLYBERRY LN
25800 MORV 92553 717-J3
30600 TEM 92591 959-B5
HOLLYBROOK ST
25600 MORV 92553 717-H3
HOLLYCREEK WY
- COR 92881 773-E4
HOLLYGLEN CIR
12600 RivC 92503 744-B4
HOLLY GLEN DR
400 RivC 91752 683-F5
HOLLYHOCK DR
16700 MORV 92551 747-H4
76300 PDST 92211 819-C3
HOLLYHOCK LN
4900 RIV 92505 714-C6
HOLLYHOCK ST
43300 INDO 92201 5410-D6
HOLLYHOCK WY
- LKEL 92532 867-D6
HOLLYLEAF LN
8600 RIV 92508 746-G2
HOLLY LEAF LN
24700 MURR 92562 928-D3
HOLLYLEAF WY
100 COR 92881 773-C4
HOLLY OAK CIR
1100 PMSP 92264 786-G4
HOLLY OAK DR
- FONT 92337 644-D3
HOLLY OAK LN
41000 MURR 92562 927-J3
HOLLY PARK CIR
41100 RivC 92592 960-F3
HOLLYRIDGE DR
6400 RIV 92504 715-A1
HOLLY SPRINGS DR
3800 COR 92881 773-C5
HOLLYVALE LN
4200 HEMT 92545 840-E3
HOLMAN WY
22500 RivC 92241 390-C7
22500 RivC 92276 390-C7
HOLMES AV
10700 RivC 91752 683-J6
HOLMES ST
1000 CALI 92320 650-C7
11600 YCPA 92399 650-C2
HOLMES WY
900 CALI 92320 650-C7
HOLSTEIN ST
5100 RivC 92509 685-D4
HOLSTER ST
2000 COR 92880 742-H1
HOLT LN
38700 RivC 92539 (934-D4
See Page 904)
HOLT ST
3400 RIV 92504 715-D2
33100 RivC 92530 896-D3
HOLT MEADOWS DR
54500 RivC 92539 (934-E2
See Page 904)
HOLYOKE PL
4600 RIV 92507 686-B6
HOMBRE LN
18500 RivC 92562 956-D2
HOMBRE RD
900 COR 92880 742-J1
HOMBRIA DR
27100 CTHC 92234 757-C5
HOME AV
- RivC 92254 5592-G7
HOMELAND AV
25900 RivC 92548 839-C1
HOMER CIR
3000 RivC 91752 644-A4
HOMES AV
23500 RivC 92567 809-F3

HOMESTEAD DR
- RivC 92570 806-F1
14100 MORV 92553 717-F6
HOMESTEAD LN
33200 RivC 92595 897-G2
47300 RivC 92592 999-F1
HOMESTEAD PL
5100 RIV 92504 715-C1
HOMESTEAD RD
900 COR 92880 742-H1
39600 RivC 92539 (934-E6
See Page 904)
40000 RivC 92539 964-D1
72600 PDST 92260 848-D4
HOMESTEAD ST
6000 RivC 92509 684-C5
HOMESTEAD HILLS RD
39400 RivC 92539 (934-E6
See Page 904)
HOMEWOOD CT
4100 RIV 92506 685-F5
HOMEWOOD DR
11300 FONT 92337 644-B2
HOMEWOOD PL
11400 FONT 92337 644-B3
HOMME AV
- PDST 92260 818-G4
HONDO CIR
900 COR 92882 773-B2
HONDO BARRANCA
25500 MORV 92551 747-H2
HONDURAS PL
42600 RivC 92201 819-G5
HONEY AV
28200 RivC 92596 839-E6
HONEY CIR
10300 RivC 91752 644-A5
HONEY LN
18100 RivC 92532 836-C7
E HONEYBROOK WY
3400 ONT 91761 643-B6
HONEY DEW LN
33100 RivC 92595 897-A2
E HONEYGLEN WY
3600 ONT 91761 643-C6
HONEY GROVE WY
800 COR 92880 743-C3
HONEYHEART LN
44100 RivC 92536 (984-C1
See Page 964)
HONEY HILL CT
11800 GTER 92313 646-G3
HONEY HILL DR
11800 GTER 92313 646-G4
HONEY HOLLOW
11500 MORV 92557 687-C7
11500 MORV 92557 717-C1
HONEYRUN RD
24900 RivC 92584 867-H1
HONEYSUCKLE CIR
2600 COR 92881 773-G3
HONEYSUCKLE CT
- LKEL 92532 867-D6
12000 MORV 92557 717-F2
HONEYSUCKLE DR
1400 BEAU 92223 691-A7
76300 PDST 92211 819-B3
HONEYSUCKLE ST
4000 RIV 92501 685-H1
HONEYSUCKLE WY
2300 HEMT 92545 840-G2
HONEYWOOD DR
1000 COR 92882 742-E5
HONOR CT
200 PER 92571 807-H1
HONORS DR
31100 TEM 92591 959-C5
HONORS LN
- COR 92883 773-G6
HOOFBEAT WY
22000 CYNL 92587 867-B1
HOOFPRINT TR
- RivC 92276 788-J5
HOOK LN
31900 RivC 92584 868-G7
HOOP WY
1700 HEMT 92545 840-H3
HOOPER DR
2000 SJCT 92583 811-F4
HOOVER
- CTHC 92234 787-A7
HOOVER AV
26100 MURR 92562 958-E1
HOOVER ST
44000 INDO 92201 5410-D6
HOOVER VIEW DR
16200 RivC 92504 745-G3
HOP ST
600 PER 92570 807-F3
HOPACTONG ST
45500 TEM 92592 979-D5
HOPE AV
8900 RIV 92503 714-J4
HOPE CIR
26300 MORV 92555 717-J2
26300 MORV 92555 718-A2
HOPE DR
28900 RivC 92586 838-B7
48900 INDO 92201 5470-E4
HOPE LN
74400 RivC 92241 728-G7
HOPE SQ
39000 RMIR 92270 818-C3

HOPE ST
70700 RMIR 92270 787-J7
HOPE BAY RD
78300 RivC 92201 819-F5
HOPEWELL AV
41500 RivC 92201 819-H4
HOPI AV
83500 INDO 92203 5410-H6
HOPI CIR
32300 RivC 92276 788-F2
HOPI CT
41200 RivC 92536 963-E2
HOPI RD
45500 INDW 92210 849-D2
HOPI SPRINGS CT
27500 RivC 92883 835-C5
HOPKINS DR
54200 RivC - 844-C1
W HOPKINS RD
1700 CLTN 92324 645-J3
HOPKINS ST
10900 RivC 91752 643-H5
HOP PATCH SPRINGS RD
- RivC - (935-F1
See Page 904)
59300 RivC - (905-E4
See Page 904)
HOPPER RD
27200 RivC 92241 390-D7
HOPSEED CIR
8600 RIV 92508 746-F2
HORACE DR
22300 RivC 92567 809-C1
HORACE ST
2400 RIV 92506 715-G2
HORADO LN
25500 MORV 92551 747-H2
HORATIO AV
900 COR 92882 773-B1
HORIZON CT
800 SJCT 92582 780-J6
HORIZON DR
12100 RivC 92240 695-H4
HORIZON LN
- PDST 92260 848-D5
6100 RivC 92509 685-B3
HORIZON RD
28000 CTHC 92234 757-E6
HORIZON ST
- COR 92881 773-G5
HORIZON WY
26200 MORV 92555 687-J7
75000 INDW 92210 818-J7
HORIZON PALMS CIR
43900 LQNT 92253 819-H7
HORNBEAM CT
1100 HEMT 92545 840-G3
HORNING RD
31000 RivC 92543 870-J5
HORN TOAD DR
43600 RivC 92536 962-A3
HORSE CANYON RD
5800 RivC 92509 684-D5
59900 RivC - (905-F4
See Page 904)
HORSELESS CARRIAGE DR
3100 NRCO 92860 713-D5
HORSEMANS DR
- RivC 92592 900-F5
HORSESHOE LN
4700 RivC 92509 684-F1
HORSESHOE RD
79900 LQNT 92253 849-J2
79900 LQNT 92253 5470-A2
HORSESHOE TR
21600 RivC 92567 779-G6
22200 RivC 92567 809-F1
HORSETHIEF CANYON RD
26000 RivC 92883 835-B3
HORTON CT
24100 MORV 92553 717-E5
HORTON HILLS RD
57000 RivC 92539 (935-A1
See Page 904)
HORTON MEADOWS RD
37400 RivC 92539 (935-B1
See Page 904)
HORVAT LN
19600 RivC 92530 896-F5
HOSKINS LN
21500 RivC 92570 776-E7
HOSPITAL WY
- RivC 92518 717-D7
HOSPITALITY DR
600 RMIR 92270 787-H5
HOSS ST
37000 RivC 92544 931-B1
HOSTETTLER RD
- RivC 92883 835-D4
15600 RivC 92530 835-D4
HOTCHKISS ST
14200 MORV 92555 718-F6
HOTEI LN
52700 RivC - (813-J5
See Page 782)
52800 RivC - 814-A5
HOTSPRING DR
- COR 92880 743-C3
HOT SPRINGS AV
41900 RivC 92583 781-E6
41900 SJCT 92583 781-E6
72400 RivC 92241 720-C3

HOT SPRINGS RD
- ImCo - (5775-H4
See Page 5714)
- RivC - (5775-H4
See Page 5714)
9300 RivC 92883 804-C4
21200 RivC 92241 728-H7
23500 RivC 92241 758-H1
HOT WELL RD
22800 RivC 92241 390-D7
HOUGHTON AV
3800 RIV 92501 685-G2
HOUSER PL
1200 RIV 92506 715-H7
HOUSTON DR
14200 MORV 92553 717-J6
HOUSTON WY
31600 RDL 92373 649-A5
HOVLEY CT
- PDST 92260 818-E4
HOVLEY LN
- RMIR 92270 818-D4
HOVLEY LN E
74800 PDST 92260 818-G5
75000 PDST 92211 818-G5
75300 PDST 92211 819-E5
75700 INDW 92211 819-A5
HOVLEY LN W
73000 PDST 92260 818-E4
HOWARD AV
4000 RIV 92507 685-H5
HOWARD CIR
3700 PMSP 92262 756-C3
HOWARD DR
24700 RivC 92544 811-J6
HOWARD MNR
- RivC 92544 841-E2
HOWARD RD
30700 RivC 92539 (934-D2
See Page 904)
32200 RivC 92584 868-D7
33100 RivC 92584 898-D3
36200 RivC 92539 904-D6
43000 RivC 92536 964-D7
44000 RivC 92536 (984-D2
See Page 964)
HOWARD ST
100 COR 92879 743-D5
26900 RivC 92586 838-B3
HOWARD ROAD TR
54000 RivC 92539 (934-D3
See Page 904)
HOWE AV
1800 RIV 92506 716-A1
HOWE PL
14200 RivC 92223 720-G5
HOWE ST
3500 COR 92881 773-G5
HOWLAND RD
55400 RivC - 814-F4
HOWLETT
17800 LKEL 92530 866-B3
HOYA PL
3000 RIV 92503 715-A6
HOYLAKE CT
28600 RivC 92586 838-A7
HOYLAKE DR
- INDO 92201 5410-A6
HOYLAKE RD
9500 RivC 92240 696-F1
HOYT ST
3500 RIV 92504 715-C3
H SPIEGEL WY
1400 COR 92881 773-F4
HUB CIR
28200 RivC 92585 838-E6
HUB RD
28200 RivC 92585 838-D6
HUBBARD ST
11000 MORV 92557 687-F7
11500 MORV 92557 717-F1
HUBERT WY
22500 RivC 92567 809-E2
HUCKABY LN
37200 MURR 92562 927-E3
37200 RivC 92562 927-E3
HUCKLEBERRY DR
500 PER 92571 777-J6
3000 COR 92882 742-F5
HUDDEN ST
4200 RIV 92505 744-B1
HUDSON AV
2700 COR 92881 773-E2
80800 INDO 92201 5470-C1
S HUDSON AV
1400 ONT 91761 643-F3
HUDSON CT
- PDST 92211 818-J4
25800 LMLN 92354 647-E2
HUDSON RD
2200 PMSP 92262 756-G5
HUDSON ST
5700 RivC 92509 684-D5
HUDSON BAY DR
16700 MORV 92551 747-F4
HUERTA CT
69500 RMIR 92270 787-G6
HUERTA WY
2800 NRCO 92860 713-G6
HUEY HILLS RD
41200 RivC 92539 (965-G2
See Page 964)
HUFFORD RD
54600 RivC 92539 (934-E2
See Page 904)

HUFFSTATLER ST
1900 SDCo 92028 998-H4
HUGHES AL
3300 RIV 92503 714-G7
3300 RIV 92503 744-H1
HUGHES DR
33400 RivC 92530 896-C3
HUGO RD
15400 MORV 92551 747-J1
HUGULEY DR
4900 RIV 92505 714-C6
HULA LN
- PMSP 92264 786-E5
HULEN PL
2800 RIV 92507 686-A3
HULL ST
2600 PER 92570 808-A7
2600 PER 92570 838-A1
26000 RivC 92570 838-A1
26000 RivC 92585 838-A3
HUMBER DR
11300 RivC 91752 683-G3
41700 TEM 92591 959-A5
HUMBER RD
55400 RivC - 814-E5
HUMBLE ST
6000 RivC 92509 685-B1
HUMBOLDT CT
5000 RIV 92507 686-E7
HUMBOLDT LN
- COR 92881 773-E5
HUMBOLT CT
31000 TEM 92591 959-D2
HUMMINGBIRD CIR
22300 MURR 92562 927-C4
HUMMINGBIRD CT
- RivC 92399 650-G7
26400 LMLN 92354 647-F3
HUMMINGBIRD DR
74800 INDW 92210 848-J2
HUMMINGBIRD LN
1500 RivC 92882 742-H6
79800 LQNT 92253 5470-A2
HUMMINGBIRD PL
11600 MORV 92557 717-C1
HUMMINGBIRD WY
1300 HEMT 92545 840-D4
17600 CHLS 91709 712-B5
HUMPHREYS LN
44800 RivC 92544 (932-D7
See Page 902)
HUNCO WY
- LKEL 92530 866-C2
HUNGARIAN ST
- RivC 92880 683-D6
HUNGRY HORSE DR
- PER 92571 778-C3
HUNSAKER LN
38300 RivC 92543 870-H4
HUNT AV
7000 RivC 92509 644-J7
16700 LKEL 92530 865-J2
16700 LKEL 92530 866-A2
HUNT CIR
1100 COR 92882 743-A6
HUNT CT
6700 RIV 92506 715-G4
HUNT RD
9100 RivC 92883 804-C5
HUNTER BLVD
2500 RivC - 392-C9
HUNTER RD
28800 MURR 92563 928-G4
38700 MURR 92563 929-A4
HUNTER ST
3700 RivC 92509 644-C6
20100 RivC 92570 776-F3
HUNTER HILL DR
6000 CHLS 91709 712-A4
HUNTER POINT RD
78000 RivC 92211 819-F1
HUNTERS CT
22800 RivC 92883 804-B3
HUNTERS RUN CT
22100 RivC 92595 897-C4
HUNTINGTON ST
1700 RIV 92504 715-F6
1700 RIV 92506 715-F6
HUNTINGTON WY
800 PER 92571 778-A2
HUNTLEY DR
600 COR 92882 773-C3
24600 MORV 92557 687-F7
HUNTRIDGE DR
24000 MURR 92562 927-J4
S HUNTS LN
800 CLTN 92324 646-H1
1000 CLTN 92408 646-H1
HUNTSMAN ST
6500 RivC 92509 685-A2
HUNWUT DR
22600 RivC 92595 897-D6
HUPA DR
32700 TEM 92592 979-F3
HUPA PL
4100 RIV 92505 744-B1
HUPP DR
32400 TEM 92592 979-F3
HURON CIR
- COR 92881 773-E5
HURON DR
75100 INDW 92210 848-J1
HURON ST
24900 LMLN 92354 647-C2
31200 TEM 92592 979-D5

HURSH ST
29800 LKEL 92530 865-J2
HURST DR
57100 RivC 92539 (935-A2
See Page 904)
HURST LN
53600 RivC 92539 904-C7
HURSTLAND AV
- BEAU 92223 720-G2
HUSAIN RD
- COR 92881 773-E6
HUSBAND CV
34500 RivC 92591 930-A7
HUSHABYE LN
1000 COR 92880 743-C2
HUSTON DR
700 RIV 92507 686-D3
45600 RivC 92220 782-C1
HUTCHISON CT
41800 MURR 92562 927-J5
HUTH WY
74200 RivC 92241 728-G6
HUTTON CIR
59700 RivC 92539 (965-G3
See Page 964)
HUTTON CT
23800 MORV 92553 717-D4
HUTTON LN
31700 YCPA 92399 649-B3
HUXLEY DR
26000 MORV 92555 717-J5
HUXLEY ST
- YCPA 92399 650-B2
HYACINTH DR
23800 MURR 92562 927-J3
HYACINTH LN
10500 MORV 92557 687-F6
12800 RivC 92282 724-D1
HYANNIS CT
- RIV 92506 716-E6
HYATT AV
100 HEMT 92545 810-B7
100 HEMT 92545 840-B1
25100 RivC 92545 810-B7
HYATT RD
20900 RivC 92570 836-J6
21200 RivC 92570 837-A6
HYDE RD
32200 RivC 92544 871-E6
HYDE PARK CIR
2900 RIV 92506 715-H2
HYDE PARK LN
- COR 92881 773-E2
HY FINERMAN DR
1700 PMSP 92262 786-F3
HYTHE ST
12300 MORV 92557 717-B2

I

I ST
- HEMT 92545 840-F2
400 LKEL 92532 866-G4
IBERIA CT
69500 RMIR 92270 787-G6
IBERIA ST
10900 RivC 91752 643-H6
IBEX ST
14300 MORV 92553 717-G6
ICEFIELD CT
10200 RivC 92883 804-E6
ICE HOUSE DR
- PER 92571 778-C3
ICELANDIC ST
- RivC 92880 683-D7
ICELAND POPPY CT
25300 MURR 92563 928-E3
IDA
27200 RivC 92544 841-E3
IDA AV
51300 RivC 92230 723-G6
IDA ST
200 COR 92882 743-A5
IDAHO PL
23300 RivC 92587 837-D7
IDAHO ST
3300 RIV 92507 686-D4
42100 PDST 92211 819-E5
IDALEONA DR
15200 RivC 92570 805-F1
IDALEONA RD
16500 RivC 92570 805-J1
16900 RivC 92570 806-A1
IDE AV
26400 RivC 92545 839-F2
IDYLLBROOK DR
53100 RivC - 844-A1
53300 RivC - 814-B7
IDYLLMONT RD
52500 RivC - (843-J2
See Page 842)
52800 RivC - 844-A1
IDYLLWILD DR
100 SJCT 92583 811-B1
300 SJCT 92583 781-A7
700 SJCT 92582 780-J6
700 SJCT 92582 781-A7
IDYLLWILD LN
7000 RIV 92503 714-E1
7100 RIV 92503 684-E7
IDYLLWILD RD
Rt#-243
25600 RivC - 814-C5
26600 RivC - 844-C2

IDYLLWILD NATIONAL FOREST HWY
45200 RivC 92544 (812-D7
See Page 782)
45900 RivC - (812-D7
See Page 782)
46500 RivC - 842-G1
47600 RivC - (843-B2
See Page 842)
51800 RivC - 844-A5
IEMEZ CIR
5000 RivC 92509 685-D4
IKES PL
- CTHC 92234 787-D7
ILA LN
20500 RivC 92570 776-G1
ILEX CT
4200 RIV 92503 714-G5
ILLINOIS AV
600 BEAU 92223 721-A3
1400 PER 92585 838-C1
1600 RivC 92585 838-C1
43200 PDST 92211 819-D6
ILLINOIS ST
1800 RIV 92507 686-A6
21200 RivC 92595 897-B7
29900 LKEL 92530 866-A3
IMAGE DR
3700 PER 92571 778-B2
IMLER RD
38000 RivC 92544 (932-J4
See Page 902)
IMPATIENS CIR
76000 PDST 92211 819-B2
IMPERIA DR
1800 COR 92882 743-A7
IMPERIAL ST
2800 RIV 92504 715-F4
IMPERIAL WY
25000 HEMT 92543 810-J6
IMPRESIVO DR
1700 COR 92879 743-G2
INAJA ST
12600 DHSP 92240 697-C5
INCA CIR
1500 PMSP 92264 786-H4
INCA CT
43300 INDO 92203 5410-H6
INCA DR
76800 INDW 92210 849-D1
INCA PL
4100 RIV 92505 744-B2
INCOME AV
33300 RivC 92555 749-G3
INDEPENDENCE AV
300 SJCT 92583 811-B3
INDEPENDENCE CIR
2600 COR 92882 772-J2
70600 RMIR 92270 787-J7
INDEPENDENCE CT
11700 RIV 92503 744-D3
INDEPENDENCE WY
- LQNT 92253 819-J7
- LQNT 92253 5410-A7
2400 COR 92882 772-J1
INDIA PL
42800 RivC 92592 960-A6
INDIAN AV
2000 PER 92571 777-F3
4300 PER 92571 747-F7
4600 PER 92551 747-F7
12000 RivC 92240 696-D6
14000 RivC 92258 696-D6
14000 RivC 92258 726-D2
N INDIAN AV
- RivC - 655-J5
6000 DHSP 92240 656-B6
6000 RivC - 656-B6
6000 RivC 92240 656-B6
9000 DHSP 92240 696-D2
9000 RivC 92240 696-D2
18000 RivC 92258 726-D3
61900 RivC 92282 655-J5
INDIAN CIR
500 PER 92570 807-E3
INDIAN CV
- PDST 92260 848-E7
INDIAN RD
37400 RivC 92539 (933-J2
See Page 902)
INDIAN ST
11000 MORV 92557 687-F7
11400 MORV 92557 717-F2
12200 MORV 92553 717-F4
15200 MORV 92553 747-F2
16100 MORV 92551 717-F7
INDIAN TKTR
- RivC - 388-K10
- RivC 92883 388-K10
S INDIAN TR
500 PMSP 92264 786-E3
INDIANA AV
6600 RIV 92506 715-E3
7000 RIV 92504 715-E3
8700 RIV 92503 715-A6
9200 RIV 92503 714-H7
10000 RIV 92503 744-H1
12500 RivC 92503 744-A5
13200 RivC 92879 744-A5
13500 RivC 92879 743-J6
13700 COR 92879 743-J6
77100 PDST 92211 819-D6
INDIANA ST
21500 RivC 92595 897-C6

INDIAN BOW CIR
13300 RivC 92883 835-B5
INDIAN CAMP CT
21000 RivC 92595 897-A7
INDIAN CAMP RD
6200 RivC 92509 684-H5
50000 LQNT 92253 849-J6
INDIAN CANYON DR
- BAN 92220 721-B6
N INDIAN CANYON DR
- RivC 92258 726-D7
100 PMSP 92262 786-D1
600 PMSP 92262 756-D2
20000 PMSP 92258 726-D7
20100 PMSP - 726-D7
21700 PMSP - 756-D2
S INDIAN CANYON DR
100 PMSP 92262 786-E3
500 PMSP 92264 786-E3
INDIAN CANYON LN
44200 PDST 92260 818-H7
INDIAN CANYON RD
45700 INDW 92210 849-E2
INDIAN CREEK DR
26900 RivC 92883 835-C4
INDIAN CREEK RD
- RivC - 782-G7
- RivC - (812-B5
See Page 782)
- RivC 92583 782-G7
- RivC 92583 (812-F2
See Page 782)
INDIAN CREEK TR
15700 RivC 92506 745-J3
16000 RivC 92504 745-J3
INDIAN CREEK WY
73300 RivC 92260 818-E1
INDIAN HILL RD
4600 RIV 92501 685-F3
61700 RivC - (936-A2
See Page 906)
INDIAN HILL TR
41600 RivC 92536 963-D4
INDIAN HILLS WY
72500 PDST 92260 848-D5
INDIAN HORSE DR
2000 NRCO 92860 713-C7
INDIAN KNOLL RD
36500 RivC 92592 930-D5
INDIAN KNOLLS CIR
8300 RivC 92509 684-F4
INDIAN OAKS DR
37400 RivC 92592 900-F6
INDIAN PAINT BRUSH LN
61400 RivC 92539 (965-J3
See Page 964)
INDIAN PAINT BRUSH RD
60700 RivC 92539 (965-H3
See Page 964)
INDIAN PALMS DR
5500 RivC 92509 684-F4
12000 RivC 92240 696-D4
INDIAN PAW ST
100 PMSP 92264 786-C2
INDIAN RIDGE DR
39700 PDST 92211 819-C3
INDIAN RIVER RD
45500 INDO 92201 5470-C1
INDIAN ROCK RD
24900 RivC - 814-E5
49900 RivC 92536 (933-E7
See Page 902)
INDIAN SCHOOL LN
500 BAN 92220 722-A1
E INDIAN SCHOOL LN
- BAN 92220 722-B1
INDIAN SPRING RD
31800 LKEL 92532 866-J5
31800 LKEL 92532 867-A5
INDIAN SPRINGS DR
- INDO 92201 5470-A1
INDIAN SPRINGS RD
- PMSP 92264 787-B3
- RivC - 878-B6
INDIAN SUMMER RD
31200 TEM 92591 929-C7
INDIAN TRAIL RD
42900 RMIR 92270 818-A6
INDIAN TRAILS RD
48300 RivC 92536 983-B7
INDIAN TREE DR
40200 RivC 92544 841-C3
INDIAN WATERS
83000 INDO 92201 5410-H2
INDIAN WELLS LN
45300 INDW 92210 849-C1
INDIAN WELLS RD
400 BAN 92220 721-D4
INDIAN WOOD CT
78900 LQNT 92253 849-H6
INDICA RD
1500 HEMT 92545 840-E4
INDIGO DR
78100 LQNT 92253 819-F7
INDIGO LN
68300 CTHC 92234 817-D2
INDIGO HILLS DR
2200 COR 92879 743-J2
INDIO AV
69600 RivC - (907-F6
See Page 906)
INDIO BLVD
79500 INDO 92203 819-J4

STREET Block City ZIP Pg-Grid

INDIO BLVD
79500 INDO 92203 5410-A4
79900 INDO 92201 5410-A4
83000 INDO 92201 5470-G1
INDIO BLVD Rt#-86
83500 INDO 92201 5470-H1
84000 INDO 92201 5471-A3
INDIO CT
11600 YCPA 92399 649-J2
INDIO LN
41800 RivC 92592 960-C5
INDIO SPRINGS DR
84200 INDO 92203 5410-J7
INDIO SPRINGS PKWY
- INDO 92203 5410-J6
INDIO TERRACE PK
83700 INDO 92203 5410-H6
INDUS ST
29000 RivC 92584 837-H7
29000 RivC 92586 837-H7
INDUS WY
4100 RIV 92503 744-C2
INDUSTRIAL AV
1600 NRCO 92860 743-D1
6100 RIV 92504 684-J6
6100 RIV 92504 685-A6
37000 HEMT 92545 840-E2
S INDUSTRIAL DR
2800 RLTO 92316 645-H2
INDUSTRIAL PL
600 PMSP 92264 786-E3
81500 INDO 92201 5410-D6
INDUSTRIAL WY
100 COR 92882 743-A4
900 SJCT 92582 810-J2
86000 COAC 92236 5471-D7
86000 COAC 92236 5531-E1
INDUSTRY AV
11700 FONT 92337 643-H4
INEZ CT
10000 RIV 92503 714-H7
INEZ ST
800 HEMT 92543 841-A2
N INEZ ST
100 HEMT 92543 811-A7
S INEZ ST
100 HEMT 92543 811-A7
300 HEMT 92543 841-A1
INGALL CIR
16500 LKEL 92530 865-J1
16500 LKEL 92530 866-A1
INGLENOOK AV
2100 SJCT 92583 811-D5
INGLEWOOD AV
9200 RivC 92240 696-F1
INGLEWOOD CT
11500 RIV 92503 744-E3
INGRAM DR
4900 RivC 92880 742-B5
INLAND AV
10800 RivC 91752 643-G5
INLAND RD
42100 RivC 92536 961-J4
42800 RivC 92536 962-A5
INLAND VALLEY DR
36400 RivC 92595 897-G7
36400 RivC 92595 927-G1
INNER CIRCLE DR
5500 RIV 92506 716-C1
INNISBROOK LN
40500 PDST 92211 819-D4
INN KEEPER LN
900 COR 92881 743-F7
INNKEEPER LN
70000 RMIR 92270 817-G1
INNOVATION CT
38500 RivC 92563 929-A5
INSLEY DR
22000 RivC 92240 726-J7
22000 RivC 92241 726-J7
22600 RivC 92241 756-J1
INSPIRATION DR
5400 RIV 92506 715-J1
INSPIRATION LN
52900 RivC - 844-A1
INSPIRATION PT
22500 CYNL 92587 867-C1
INSPIRATION LAKE DR
28100 RivC 92584 868-E3
INTAKE BLVD
14200 BLY 92225 5491-H7
14200 BLY 92225 5551-H2
16000 RivC - 5551-J5
16000 RivC 92225 5551-H2
21000 RivC - 412-C1
INTAKE BLVD U.S.-95
- RivC 92225 5491-H1
100 BLY 92225 5491-H5
5000 RivC - 392-C9
7000 RivC - 5491-H1
INTERCHANGE ST
3100 RIV 92501 686-A1
INTERLACHEN
- LQNT 92253 5530-B6
INTERLACHEN LN
40900 PDST 92211 819-D4
INTERLAKEN AV
- RivC - (907-D7 See Page 906)
INTERLECHEN DR
25800 RivC 92586 838-A7
INTERNATIONAL BLVD
- RMIR 92270 787-H6
INTERNATIONAL PARK RD
- RivC 92223 691-A3
INTERVALE DR
5400 RIV 92506 716-B2
INTREPID RD
39100 RivC 92544 901-A7
39100 RivC 92544 931-A1
39100 RivC 92592 931-A1
INVAREY ST
26700 RivC 92586 838-C4
INVERNESS
54000 LQNT 92253 5530-B3
INVERNESS CIR
10700 RivC 92223 691-C5
INVERNESS CT
- INDO 92201 5410-A6
- TEM 92591 959-D4
28300 RivC 92584 868-F2
INVERNESS DR
- COR 92881 773-H6
- COR 92883 773-H6
- CTHC 92234 757-F7
- CTHC 92234 787-G1
- RMIR 92270 788-A6
100 RMIR 92270 787-J5
5900 BAN 92220 721-C5
75000 INDW 92210 848-J1
INVERNESS ST
3300 RIV 92507 686-E4
INVERNESS WY
40600 PDST 92211 819-D4
INVESTOR PL
1000 SJCT 92582 810-J2
INVESTORS PL
26200 RivC 92544 841-C1
INVIERNO DR
1300 PMSP 92264 786-F4
INVITATION DR
- RivC 92585 838-B3
INWOOD CT
28400 RivC 92586 838-B6
INWOOD DR
11500 RIV 92503 744-E3
INYO DR
12100 RivC 92240 695-H4
INYO RD
33000 RivC 92548 809-F4
IODINE SPRINGS RD
35800 RivC 92595 897-G7
35800 RivC 92595 927-G1
IONA CIR
41400 MURR 92562 927-H3
IONE LN
32400 RivC 92595 897-B6
IOWA AV
- RivC 92501 646-B7
- RivC 92507 646-B7
600 RIV 92507 646-B7
800 RIV 92507 686-B1
S IOWA AV
2400 CLTN 92324 646-C6
2700 RivC 92507 646-C6
2700 RivC 92501 646-C6
IOWA ST
- RDL 92373 647-H1
17200 LKEL 92530 866-A3
42600 PDST 92211 819-D5
IPARA RD
30500 RivC 92584 899-A1
IRA CT
8400 RIV 92508 746-H1
IRENE ST
5800 RivC 92509 685-C1
50400 RivC 92230 723-D5
IRIDE CIR
2600 MURR 92562 927-H3
IRIS AV
- RivC 92518 747-E2
11300 LMLN 92354 647-B2
16800 RivC 92504 745-H3
17300 RivC 92504 746-A3
17700 RivC 92508 746-A3
24000 MORV 92551 747-E2
26100 MORV 92555 747-J2
26200 MORV 92555 748-B1
84400 COAC 92236 5471-A5
IRIS CIR
1100 COR 92882 743-B7
IRIS CT
- INDO 92201 5470-D5
6300 RivC 92880 683-D6
16800 RivC 92503 744-H5
79700 LQNT 92253 819-J7
IRIS DR
1200 BEAU 92223 691-A7
IRIS LN
100 RMIR 92270 818-A1
34800 YCPA 92399 649-J3
IRIS RD
55000 RivC - 814-E6
IRIS ST
2700 RIV 92507 685-H6
IRIS WY
2000 HEMT 92545 810-G5
IRIS GROVE CIR
1400 COR 92881 773-F4
IRIS GROVE DR
1500 COR 92881 773-F4
IRMA
38400 RivC 92544 (932-F4 See Page 902)
IRMA ST
27100 RivC 92570 836-J5
IRON CIR
39600 TEM 92591 959-C5
IRON BARK CT
30400 TEM 92591 959-B5
IRON BARK DR
- RivC 92203 789-G6
IRON BARK RD
100 COR 92879 744-F5
IRONBARK RD
24000 MORV 92557 687-E6
IRON GATE LN
42200 MURR 92562 927-H6
IRON HILLS WY
2800 RIV 92506 715-H1
IRON HORSE DR
- RivC 92563 929-A7
IRON HORSE RD
20200 RivC 92567 779-A4
IRONS RD
42100 RivC 92536 963-B4
IRONSIDES CIR
2500 COR 92882 772-J1
IRONSTONE DR
7700 RivC 92509 684-H3
IRONTREE DR
73100 PDST 92260 848-E5
IRONWOOD
70700 RMIR 92270 787-J7
70800 RMIR 92270 788-A7
IRONWOOD AV
22000 MORV 92557 717-E1
26000 MORV 92555 717-E1
26300 MORV 92555 718-A1
30000 RivC 92555 688-J7
30000 RivC 92555 689-A7
30000 RivC 92555 718-H1
IRONWOOD DR
- RivC - 5239-J7
- RivC 92399 650-G6
6800 RIV 92506 716-E5
37200 YCPA 92399 650-G6
65500 DHSP 92240 696-G5
66700 DHSP 92240 697-A5
IRONWOOD PL
1600 COR 92879 743-J6
IRONWOOD ST
500 HEMT 92543 840-J1
15100 LKEL 92530 865-G3
73000 PDST 92260 848-E2
IRONWOOD TR
13100 YCPA 92399 650-E5
IRONWOOD WY
49100 RivC 92536 (933-C7 See Page 902)
IROQUOIS CT
49900 RivC 92536 963-E4
IROQUOIS DR
76700 INDW 92210 849-C2
IROQUOIS RD
500 PER 92570 807-E3
IROQUOIS ST
68500 CTHC 92234 817-E1
IRVINE LN
26600 RivC 92586 868-B2
IRVING CT
39800 MURR 92563 928-E5
IRVING ST
1200 RIV 92504 745-C1
2300 RIV 92504 715-B7
2500 RIV 92503 715-B6
IRWIN CIR
78700 LQNT 92253 819-G7
IRWIN ST
1000 SJCT 92583 811-B3
ISAACS PL
24000 HEMT 92543 810-H4
ISABELLA ST
4300 RIV 92501 685-F4
ISAIC LN
8500 RIV 92508 746-G2
ISERAL LN
28000 RivC 92585 838-E5
ISHBELL CT
200 RivC 92507 646-D6
ISLA MARIA CIR
16200 MORV 92551 747-J3
ISLAND CIR
70100 RivC 92254 (5654-D3 See Page 5594)
ISLAND DR
38800 RMIR 92270 818-B2
ISLETA CT
28700 CTHC 92234 757-C6
ISLETA LN
15500 MORV 92551 747-H2
ITALO ST
45300 RivC 92536 981-J4
IVAN LN
39800 RivC 92539 (934-C6 See Page 904)
IVANHOE AV
5000 RIV 92503 714-F3
IVANPAH PL
4100 RIV 92505 744-B2
IVEL RD
40600 RivC 92544 961-D1
IVERNESS AV
- RivC 92203 789-F5
IVERSON PL
1300 RIV 92506 716-B2
IVES PL
5700 RIV 92506 716-A2
IVORY AV
25300 MORV 92551 747-H3
IVORY PALM DR
26000 RivC 92548 839-B1
IVY CIR
1300 COR 92879 743-F7
IVY CT
3200 LKEL 92530 865-G1
IVY LN
11700 MORV 92557 717-G1
IVY ST
900 HEMT 92545 840-G2
2800 RIV 92506 685-H7
41600 MURR 92562 928-A7
42100 MURR 92562 927-J7
42200 MURR 92562 957-J1
IVY GLEN DR
300 RivC 91752 683-E4
IVY SPRINGS CT
10000 MORV 92557 687-B5
IVYWOOD CT
- RivC 92880 713-A2

J

J ST
- HEMT 92545 840-F2
400 LKEL 92532 866-G4
5000 RivC 92509 684-C3
68500 CTHC 92234 817-E1
JACARA LN
15500 MORV 92551 747-H2
JACARANDA CIR
11300 FONT 92337 644-G2
JACARANDA CT
39700 TEM 92591 959-B1
46300 INDW 92210 848-H3
JACARANDA RD
2600 PMSP 92264 786-H6
JACARANDA ST
800 COR 92879 743-J6
3100 RIV 92504 715-E3
JACARANDA WY
- RivC 92503 744-J7
2700 HEMT 92545 840-F3
55200 RivC 92282 724-E1
JACARTE DR
24300 MURR 92562 928-C2
JACCARD CIR
700 BAN 92220 722-A4
JACINTO DR
22300 RivC 92570 806-A1
JACINTO ST
31500 RivC 92567 779-C7
JACINTO VIEW RD
800 BAN 92220 722-A3
1100 BAN 92220 721-F3
E JACINTO VIEW RD
1400 BAN 92220 722-D3
JACK CIR
30400 RivC 92567 778-J3
JACK LN
37700 RivC 92539 (934-G2 See Page 904)
JACKAL DR
77000 RivC 92211 819-E2
JACKASS RD
11300 RivC 92220 691-G5
JACK B CLARKE WY
- RIV 92507 685-H4
JACK BENNY RD
- RMIR 92270 817-G4
JACK FROST CT
3600 RivC 92503 744-A5
JACKIE DR
26600 RivC 92544 841-C2
JACK IVEY DR
- RivC 92276 788-H5
JACK KRAMER LN
72700 PDST 92260 848-D3
JACK NICKLAUS
- LQNT 92253 5530-B5
JACK RABBIT TR
- BEAU 92223 720-A4
15300 RivC 92223 719-H6
15300 RivC 92223 720-A4
15300 RivC 92223 749-G1
15300 RivC 92223 749-H1
79100 LQNT 92253 849-H6
JACKSON AV
- TEM 92591 958-E1
23400 MURR 92562 927-J2
23900 MURR 92562 928-A3
26300 MURR 92563 958-E1
27600 RivC 92585 838-D1
28900 MURR 92563 928-E7
JACKSON CIR
1400 SJCT 92583 811-D5
JACKSON ST
1700 RIV 92504 745-B1
2200 RIV 92503 745-B1
2800 RIV 92503 715-A5
3800 RIV 92503 714-H3
40200 INDO 92203 5410-G3
42800 INDO 92201 5410-G6
45200 INDO 92201 5470-G1
48000 COAC 92236 5470-G3
50300 RivC 92236 5470-G3
51700 INDO 92236 5470-G7
52100 RivC 92236 5530-G2
53000 RivC 92201 5530-G2
53000 RivC 92274 5530-G2
58000 RivC 92274 5590-H3
61900 RivC - 5590-H6
66000 RivC 92274 (5650-H1 See Page 5590)
JACKSON WY
300 HEMT 92543 811-B6
2500 RIV 92503 715-B7
2500 RIV 92503 745-B1
JACLYN AV
25000 MORV 92557 687-G7
JACOB CT
44600 RivC 92536 983-B2
JACOB DR
8500 RIV 92508 746-G2
JACOBS CIR
16100 RivC 92504 745-G5
JACOBS ST
900 CLTN 92324 646-H1
JACQUELINE CIR
42600 PDST 92260 818-H6
JACQUES RD
1800 PMSP 92262 756-E6
JACQUETTA AV
15000 MORV 92551 717-H7
15000 MORV 92551 747-J1
JADE AV
1600 PER 92571 777-H7
JADE CT
46600 INDW 92210 849-A2
JADE DR
300 HEMT 92543 841-A3
500 HEMT 92543 840-J3
JADE LN
500 PMSP 92264 786-D4
JADE ST
6300 RivC 92509 685-A2
JADE WY
- INDO 92201 5470-F5
JADESTONE DR
38900 RivC 92211 819-G2
JADESTONE LN
900 COR 92882 742-J5
1000 COR 92882 743-A6
JADIDA AV
47300 PDST 92260 848-F4
JAELENE ST
26600 RivC 92586 838-B4
JAFFA CT
77000 PDST 92211 819-C5
JAGO ST
14500 RivC 92230 723-D5
JAGUAR DR
6200 RIV 92506 716-A3
JAGUAR WY
49900 RivC 92260 848-B6
JAKE RD
36000 RivC 92544 902-H7
36800 RivC 92539 904-B7
36900 RivC 92539 (934-B2 See Page 904)
JALANIE LN
15700 MORV 92551 747-F2
JALKUT WY
- RMIR 92270 818-C6
JALNA LN
2600 SDCo 92028 998-B7
JALOUSIE DR
78000 RivC 92211 819-F1
JAM ST
- HEMT 92544 811-H6
JAMAICA CIR
10100 RIV 92503 714-E1
JAMAICA CT
- INDO 92201 5470-G3
JAMAICA LN
41100 RivC 92544 841-D1
JAMAICA SANDS DR
41300 RivC 92201 819-J4
JAMAICA SANDS LN
25900 MORV 92553 717-J6
JAMARA CT
- TEM 92592 979-F2
JAMAWAG RD
25100 RivC 92548 809-B7
JAMES AV
- MURR 92563 928-F2
JAMES CT
16400 RivC 92504 745-H4
JAMES DR
37600 RivC 92592 980-H4
JAMES PL
- MURR 92563 928-F2
JAMES ST
2800 COR 92881 773-F3
JAMES WY
1700 HEMT 92544 811-C5
JAMES BIRCH RD
36400 YCPA 92399 650-D1
JAMES KENNY RD
17800 RivC 92508 746-D7
JAMESON CT
1400 RIV 92507 716-G1
JAMESON DR
54200 RivC - 814-D5
JAMESON RD
2300 RivC 92883 804-B4
73800 PDST 92211 818-F1
JAMESON ST
- MURR 92562 928-A2
3900 NRCO 92880 743-B1
JAMESTOWN AV
- RivC 92880 683-D4
12400 RivC 92240 695-H4
82700 INDO 92201 5470-G2
JAMESTOWN DR
2900 RIV 92504 715-C6
26400 RivC 92586 838-B5
JAMIE TR
38700 RivC 92544 931-H4
JAMIE WY
41700 RMIR 92270 818-D5
81000 INDO 92201 5470-C1
JAMIESON ST
33000 RivC 92530 865-G7
JAMIN CIR
33300 TEM 92592 979-H2
JAN AV
32400 RivC 92584 867-G7
JAN CIR
3000 PMSP 92262 756-G4
33200 RivC 92584 898-F1
JANA LN
36100 RivC 92595 897-H7
36100 RivC 92595 927-H1
JANAE WY
2800 HEMT 92545 810-F6
JANAN CT
100 BAN 92220 721-D3
JANDA CT
39400 RivC 92592 931-A4
39900 RivC 92544 931-A4
JANE CT
33100 RivC 92595 927-D2
JANE LN
67800 CTHC 92234 787-C1
JANE ST
2700 RIV 92506 715-F2
6000 RivC 92509 684-H5
JANELL DR
46100 RivC 92536 982-F3
JANESSA CT
1200 SJCT 92583 811-D3
JANET AV
7700 RIV 92503 714-F3
47000 INDO 92201 5470-F3
JANET CIR
800 PMSP 92262 756-E4
JANET ST
5800 RivC 92509 685-B2
JANET KAY DR
24300 MORV 92553 717-E7
JANEVA CT
400 HEMT 92543 841-B1
JANICE DR
59400 RivC 92539 (965-F7 See Page 964)
JANIE CT
14200 MORV 92553 717-J6
JANIE ST
7300 RivC 92509 684-H5
N JANIS DR
2300 PMSP 92262 756-C5
JANIS LN
31400 RivC 92567 779-B7
JANIS ST
8100 RIV 92504 715-B3
JANSSE LN
18900 RivC 92530 896-F4
JANNEY DR
26100 RivC 92586 868-A2
JAN ROY LN
- RivC 92570 777-F7
JANSEN RD
20500 RivC 92570 775-J6
JAN STEEN CT
- RivC 92596 899-C7
JANTAR LN
22800 RivC 92570 807-C1
JANUARY CT
13300 RivC 92879 744-A5
JAN VALERIE RD
26000 MURR 92562 958-B3
JAQUELINE TR
17100 RivC 92504 745-J3
17100 RivC 92506 745-J3
JARANA RD
68500 CTHC 92234 757-E6
JARDIN CT
- RivC 92596 929-E1
- RMIR 92270 787-G6
JARED CIR
6200 RivC 92509 685-A3
JARED LN
43500 RivC 92544 811-J7
JARO DR
33500 RivC 92595 897-A3
JARRELL CT
29200 RivC 92567 778-G7
JARVIS ST
4600 RIV 92506 685-D7
21200 RivC 92570 837-A5
E JARVIS ST
- PER 92571 807-H2
JASMINE AV
16700 RivC 92503 744-H5
23000 RivC 92595 897-D7
JASMINE CIR
1300 COR 92880 713-A7
2800 HEMT 92545 840-G3
JASMINE CT
1800 SJCT 92583 811-E4
19200 RivC 92530 896-F6
24500 MORV 92557 687-F6
35500 YCPA 92399 650-B6
JASMINE DR
1200 BEAU 92223 691-A7
12400 RivC 92240 695-H4
JASMINE LN
36500 RMIR 92270 787-J7
36600 RMIR 92270 788-A7
46000 INDO 92201 5470-B2
JASMINE PL
11800 FONT 92337 644-C4
73600 PDST 92260 848-F5
JASMINE ST
900 FONT 92337 643-J1
5800 RIV 92504 684-J7
JASMINE WY
- INDW 92210 818-H7
1100 HEMT 92545 840-F3
JASON CT
- PER 92571 747-H7
200 COR 92879 744-B3
2000 PMSP 92262 756-J5
43000 RivC 92544 841-H1
JASON PL
25600 MORV 92557 717-H1
JASPER LN
5300 RIV 92506 716-B1
JASPER WY
21900 RivC 92570 777-F7
JASPER PARK AV
- INDO 92201 849-J1
- INDO 92201 5470-A1
JAVA ST
15400 MORV 92551 747-F2
JAVA HILLS DR
1400 SDCo 92028 998-B7
JAVELINA CT
6900 RivC 92509 684-J1
6900 RivC 92509 685-A1
JAVIER PL
25600 MORV 92557 717-H1
JAY CIR
24000 MORV 92553 717-E3
JAY CT
8500 RIV 92508 746-G2
JAY DR
44100 RivC 92539 (965-C7 See Page 964)
44400 RivC 92539 (985-C1 See Page 964)
JAYBIRD LN
52000 RivC 92539 (933-J2 See Page 902)
52300 RivC 92539 (934-A2 See Page 904)
JAY DEE LN
41700 RivC 92539 (965-G3 See Page 964)
JAYHAWK DR
7600 RivC 92509 684-H2
JAYME JOY WY
- COR 92879 773-D2
JAYNE ST
64300 RivC 92240 696-E5
JAZMIN ST
49000 COAC 92236 5471-A5
JAZZ LN
- PER 92570 807-F3
JC RD
11600 FONT 92337 645-B4
JEAN ST
20700 RivC 92570 776-J1
21600 RivC 92570 777-A1
JEAN ESTHER WY
53000 RivC 92536 964-B6
JEAN MARIE WY
2100 PER 92571 777-J6
JEANNETTE DR
36200 MURR 92563 898-J7
36200 MURR 92563 928-J1
JEAN NICHOLAS RD
31000 RivC 92596 899-C5
JEANNIE ST
5000 RivC 91752 684-A3
JEDEDIAH SMITH RD
30200 TEM 92592 979-C3
JEFF CT
1400 RIV 92501 685-J1
JEFFERSON AV
23600 MURR 92562 927-G3
24200 MURR 92562 928-A5
25300 MURR 92562 958-D1
27200 TEM 92590 958-G4
27800 RivC 92585 808-D7
27800 RivC 92585 838-E1
JEFFERSON CIR
- COR 92881 773-F3
S JEFFERSON LN
900 CLTN 92324 646-D1
JEFFERSON RD
17000 RivC 92240 727-B2
17000 RivC 92241 727-B2
JEFFERSON ST
1100 LKEL 92530 865-H4
1600 RIV 92504 745-F2
1700 RIV 92504 715-C3
2000 BAN 92220 721-G4
13200 YCPA 92399 650-C6
20000 RivC 92570 746-F6
38100 RivC 92203 5410-A2
39000 INDO 92203 5410-A3
41000 INDO 92203 819-J3
42000 INDO 92201 5410-A6
42500 LQNT 92201 5410-A6
44000 LQNT 92253 5410-A6
44400 INDO 92201 5470-A3
44400 LQNT 92253 5470-A7
46000 LQNT 92253 5530-A2
58100 LQNT 92253 5590-B3
80000 RivC 92253 5590-B3
JEFFERY CIR
2500 HEMT 92545 810-G4
JEFFERY DR
- RivC 92324 688-A3
JEFFERY PINE RD
53400 RivC - 814-B6
JEFF HEIGHTS RD
- SDCo 92028 977-A7
JEFFREY PL
2500 RivC 92509 644-D6
JEFFREY HEIGHTS RD
39900 TEM 92591 959-D1
JELANIE LN
34800 RivC 92545 809-J4
JELLY WY
- HEMT 92544 811-H6
JENKINS DR
24500 MORV 92553 717-F6
JENKS CIR
400 COR 92880 743-A3
JENKS DR
1500 COR 92880 742-J3
1500 COR 92880 743-A3
JENNA CIR
1900 COR 92881 773-F1
JENNIE ST
3400 RivC 92509 685-C1
JENNIFER AV
41700 RivC 92544 841-F3
JENNIFER CT
10000 BLY 92225 5491-E4
10000 RivC 92225 5491-E4
35500 RMIR 92270 788-B6
81600 INDO 92201 5410-D7
JENNIFER DR
34500 RivC 92595 897-A5
JENNIFER LN
- YCPA 92399 650-C6
6100 RivC 92509 684-G5
32400 RivC 92595 897-A6
JENNIFER ST
- RDL 92373 647-J2
JENNIFER WY
200 BAN 92220 722-A1
52200 COAC 92236 5471-B7
52200 COAC 92236 5531-B1
JENNI LISA CT
9800 RivC 92223 690-G3
JENNINGS DR
- MURR 92562 927-J2
- MURR 92562 928-A2
JENNINGS ST
- RIV 92508 746-E1
JENNY LN
24500 MURR 92562 927-H7
28200 RivC 92584 898-F2
JENSEN CIR
1700 RIV 92506 716-B3
JENSEN CT
22900 GTER 92313 646-G4
JENSEN LN
32500 RivC 92595 897-B6
JENSEN RANCH RD
5600 RivC 92509 685-B3
JEPSON CT
26300 RivC 92544 841-E1
JERABOA RD
60000 RivC - (907-F4 See Page 906)
JERAMIE DR
44000 TEM 92592 979-B2
JERANELLA CT
13900 MORV 92555 718-E5
JEREMIAH CT
4500 RIV 92503 714-H4
JEREMIAH DR
19700 LKEL 92532 836-F7
JEREMIAH RD
39600 RivC 92591 930-A7
JEREMY WY
36000 SDCo 92028 999-D7
JERET RD
33000 RivC 92596 899-C1
JEREZ LN
- TEM 92592 959-G7
JERI DR
10700 RIV 92505 714-E6
JERICHO RD
34300 RivC 92592 960-A4
JERMAR LN
35500 RivC 92595 897-J7
JERNIGAN ST
29700 LKEL 92530 865-H2
JEROME LN
37000 RivC 92562 927-E3
37100 MURR 92562 927-E3
JEROME ST
6700 RIV 92504 715-B1
JEROME WY
- RivC 92254 (5653-H5 See Page 5592)
JERONIMO ST
45600 TEM 92592 979-D5
JERRY CT
10700 RivC 91752 683-J5
JERRY LN
25100 RivC 92544 (812-A6 See Page 782)
JERRY ST
- RivC 92536 981-H4
31000 RivC 92555 719-A4
JERRY ALLEN LN
- MURR 92562 927-G4
JERRY JO LN
27400 RivC 92584 898-D1
JERSEY DR
9100 RIV 92503 714-H4
JERSEY ST
- RivC 92880 683-D6
JERSEY PINE CT
42800 MURR 92562 957-J1
JESSAMYN CT
1500 RIV 92506 715-G7
JESS ANNE DR
- LQNT 92253 5470-A6
JESSE LN
19200 RIV 92508 716-D7
19200 RIV 92508 746-D1
JESSICA CT
45800 INDO 92201 5470-C1
JESSICA LN
- COR 92882 773-C3
JESSICA RD
2500 RIV 92506 715-F4
JESSICA ST
200 LKEL 92530 865-H2
JESSICA WY
700 SJCT 92583 811-C3
81000 INDO 92201 5470-C1
JESSIE CIR
39300 TEM 92591 929-D7
JESSIE CEAS LN
36200 MURR 92563 898-H7
36200 MURR 92563 928-J1
JESSIE FAY DR
200 HEMT 92544 811-E6
JET WY
- PER 92571 747-D6
JEWEL
44100 INDO 92201 5410-H6
JEWEL CT
17800 RivC 92241 727-E2
JEWEL ST
6500 RivC 92509 645-A7
6500 RivC 92509 685-A1
JFK TR
49200 PDST 92260 848-E6
JIB CIR
- RivC 92254 (5654-D2 See Page 5594)
JILL AV
900 HEMT 92545 840-F2
N JILL CIR
200 PMSP 92262 786-H2
JILL CT
7500 RIV 92508 716-E6
JILL TER
- RMIR 92270 788-B7
JILLIAN ASHLEY WY
1500 COR 92881 773-D2
JIM DR
25800 MORV 92553 717-J4
JIM TKTR
58300 RivC 92539 (935-E3 See Page 904)
58400 RivC - (935-E3 See Page 904)
JIMINEZ CIR
3700 PMSP 92262 756-C3
JIMMY TAYLOR DR
2400 PER 92570 807-E7
2400 PER 92570 837-E1
JIMSON CIR
27500 TEM 92591 958-J2
JIMSON PL
24100 MORV 92553 717-E7
JJ LN
- RivC 92570 775-C6
JOAN AV
7400 RivC 92509 644-H7
JOAN LN
2700 SDCo 92028 997-B2
JOAN DUNN LN
28000 MURR 92563 898-F4
JO ANN CT
33700 RivC 92595 897-A3
JOANN LN
28900 MURR 92563 928-G2
JO ANN ST
13400 MORV 92553 717-F4
JO ANN WY
17900 RivC 92570 746-G7
JOANNE DR
25900 RivC 92544 (812-B7 See Page 782)
JOAQUINE CT
68500 CTHC 92234 787-E1
JOAQUINE WY
68400 CTHC 92234 787-D1
JOAQUIN RIDGE DR
22900 MURR 92562 927-D4
JOCELYN SHELBY WY
1300 COR 92881 773-D2
JODEN RD
9400 RivC 92557 687-E3
JODI AV
900 HEMT 92545 840-F2
JODI CT
26000 MORV 92555 687-J7
JODIE LN
6000 RivC 92509 685-A4
JODY CT
6900 RIV 92506 715-G4
JOEL DR
3200 RivC 92509 645-C7
3200 RivC 92509 685-C1
26200 RivC 92545 839-J1
JO ERIN LN
23400 RivC 92570 807-D4
JOETTA PL
76800 PDST 92211 819-D5
JOEY CT
- LQNT 92253 5470-A5
20700 RivC 92570 746-H6
JOHN AV
33000 RivC 92584 867-G7
33000 RivC 92584 897-G1
JOHN DR
6800 RivC 92509 685-A4
6900 RivC 92509 684-J4
JOHN ST
- BAN 92220 722-B3
2000 RIV 92503 745-A3
2100 RIV 92503 744-J2
21400 RivC 92570 837-A4
JOHN ADAMS ST
- MURR 92563 958-F1
JOHNAR BLVD
- RMIR 92270 818-A2
- RMIR 92270 817-J2
JOHN F KENNEDY DR
- RivC 92518 717-H7
- RivC 92518 747-A1
18000 RivC 92508 746-B1
18200 RIV 92508 746-E1
24000 MORV 92553 717-G7
24000 MORV 92551 717-G7
26000 MORV 92555 717-G7
26000 MORV 92555 718-A7
JOHN JAY AV
- MURR 92563 928-H7
- MURR 92563 958-H1
- TEM 92591 958-H1
JOHN LENNON LN
27400 RivC 92584 868-D4
E JOHN MATICH DR
2100 CLTN 92324 646-H4
JOHN MUIR RD
55000 RivC - 814-E5
JOHN NOBLES AV
82100 INDO 92201 5470-E2
JOHNNY CASH DR
- COR 92881 773-E3
JOHN PAUL AV
34000 RivC 92567 809-H2
JOHNS RD
1000 PER 92571 807-G1
JOHNS ST
21000 RivC 92570 776-J7
21800 RivC 92570 777-A7
JOHN SINN RD
39400 RMIR 92270 818-C3
JOHNSON
- CTHC 92234 787-D7
JOHNSON AV
16400 LKEL 92530 835-J7
16400 LKEL 92530 865-J1
16400 SBdC 91710 712-D3
21300 RivC 92570 776-J2
JOHNSON CIR
- COR 92881 773-F3
JOHNSON CT
9100 RivC 92509 684-D1
JOHNSON DR
82000 INDO 92201 5470-E3
JOHNSON LN
- COR 92881 773-F3
13000 RivC 92220 722-H2
13100 RivC 92230 722-H2
23500 RivC 92587 837-E6
JOHNSON RD
16300 RivC 92241 697-G7
16300 RivC 92241 727-G2
25700 RivC - 814-C6
55200 RivC 92539 (934-G5 See Page 904)
56700 RivC 92539 (935-A5 See Page 904)
JOHNSON ST
- RivC 92254 (5652-H3 See Page 5592)
2400 PER 92571 777-H1
4200 PER 92571 747-H7
12800 RivC 92282 724-C1
60000 RivC 92254 5592-H3
60000 RivC 92274 5592-H3
81500 RivC 92274 5712-H7
81500 RivC 92274 (5772-H2 See Page 5712)
JOHNSTON AV
100 HEMT 92543 841-D2
300 HEMT 92543 840-J2
1700 HEMT 92545 840-F2
40200 RivC 92544 841-D2
E JOHNSTON AV
100 HEMT 92543 841-A2
700 RIV 92543 841-A2
JOHNSTON DR
44500 TEM 92592 979-H3
JOHNSTON RD
57400 RivC 92539 (985-B1 See Page 964)
JOHN WARNER RD
43000 TEM 92592 979-B2
JOHN WAYNE RD
- MURR 92562 958-B2
JOJO WY
8900 RIV 92503 714-F2
JOJOBA
30600 RivC 92567 779-A4
JOJOBA RD
46000 RivC 92536 982-F6
E JOJOBA RD
45900 RivC 92536 982-G5
JOJOBA HILLS CIR
41100 RivC 92536 962-A4
JOJOBA HILLS DR
- RivC 92536 982-G6
JOLA DR
7400 RIV 92506 715-H6

STREET Block City ZIP Pg-Grid

JOLIET WY
27500 RivC 92586 838-B4
JOLLY DR
22800 RivC 92241 727-A7
22800 RivC 92241 757-A1
JOLLY WY
4200 RivC 92509 644-G7
JOLORA AV
19700 RivC 92881 774-A4
JOLTAIRE WY
- RivC 92596 899-D7
JOLYNN RD
30400 RivC 92563 929-B3
JOMAR ST
11600 YCPA 92399 650-D1
JONAH DR
1100 COR 92882 742-E5
JONAS CT
41600 RivC 92544 961-F2
JONATHAN AV
9900 RivC 92223 691-A4
JON CHRISTIAN PL
27400 TEM 92591 958-J1
28200 TEM 92591 959-A1
JONES AV
3800 RIV 92505 714-D1
3800 RIV 92505 744-F1
JONES CT
9000 RivC 92240 696-D1
28300 RivC 92586 838-C6
JONES DR
41900 PDST 92211 819-A5
JONES RD
67500 CTHC 92234 787-C6
JONES ST
1300 HEMT 92543 841-B3
JONESBOROUGH CT
25900 MORV 92553 717-J6
JONESTOWN DR
25500 MORV 92553 717-H6
JON FIELD WY
43100 RivC 92536 981-J4
43100 RivC 92536 982-A4
JON GILBERT LN
1600 BEAU 92223 690-J6
JONI DR
74800 PDST 92260 818-H5
JONNA LN
24400 MORV 92553 717-F6
JONQUIL AV
81400 INDO 92201 5410-D6
JONQUIL CIR
24000 MURR 92562 927-J4
JONQUIL PL
9200 RIV 92503 715-A7
JONQUIL ST
600 HEMT 92545 840-G2
JONS PL
30800 TEM 92591 929-C7
JOPAL RD
37000 RivC 92539 (934-J1
See Page 904)
JOPPE AV
26700 RivC 92545 839-D2
JORDAN AV
100 SJCT 92583 811-B2
N JORDAN AV
100 SJCT 92583 811-B1
JORDAN DR
10300 RIV 92505 714-F6
26900 RivC 92324 687-J4
26900 RivC 92324 688-A4
JORDAN PL
11300 FONT 92337 644-F2
JOSEPH DR
900 HEMT 92545 810-F5
JOSEPH RD
39300 RivC 92563 929-B7
39300 RivC 92563 959-B1
39300 TEM 92591 929-B7
39300 TEM 92591 959-B1
JOSEPH ST
- RIV 92508 746-E1
JOSEPH WY
65500 DHSP 92240 696-J5
JOSEPH CANYON TR
- COR 92881 773-E7
- COR 92883 773-E7
- RivC - 773-E7
JOSEPHINE CT
15100 MORV 92551 747-H1
JOSHEROO CT
32800 TEM 92592 979-G3
JOSHUA AV
25100 MORV 92553 717-G6
JOSHUA CT
- FONT 92337 645-A2
47900 PDST 92260 848-G4
JOSHUA DR
- RivC - 5239-J7
32100 RivC 92595 897-A5
JOSHUA RD
13100 RivC 92282 724-F2
43100 RMIR 92270 818-D7
43400 PDST 92260 818-D7
JOSHUA WY
- HEMT 92545 810-F4
JOSHUA TREE AV
14600 MORV 92553 717-E7
JOSHUA TREE CT
42700 MURR 92562 957-H1
JOSHUA TREE LN
900 COR 92882 742-F5
1100 BLY 92225 5491-D4

JOSHUA TREE PL
1900 PMSP 92264 786-F5
JOSHUA TREE RD
2900 RIV 92503 715-A7
JOSHUA TREE ST
- ONT 91761 643-A7
72700 PDST 92260 848-E2
E JOSHUA TREE ST
2800 ONT 91761 643-A7
JOSIE ST
700 BLY 92225 5491-E5
JOSLIN CT
4300 RIV 92505 714-E7
JOURNEYS END
44200 RivC 92536 983-F1
JOY ST
15100 LKEL 92530 865-J3
16700 LKEL 92530 866-A4
N JOY ST
100 COR 92879 743-E4
S JOY ST
200 COR 92879 743-D5
JOYA DR
- PDST 92260 818-F5
JOYCE DR
1700 PMSP 92262 756-G4
JT EISLEY DR
1400 COR 92881 773-F4
JUAN CIR
- PMSP 92262 756-C3
100 PDST 92260 818-E6
9800 BLY 92225 5551-G1
39200 CTHC 92234 817-D3
JUAN CARLOS DR
- RMIR 92270 818-E5
JUAN DIEGO FLATS RD
48000 RivC - (903-B7
See Page 902)
48000 RivC - (933-B1
See Page 902)
48000 RivC 92544 (933-A1
See Page 902)
49400 RivC 92539 (903-F6
See Page 902)
JUANITA AV
25100 MORV 92551 747-G1
JUANITA CIR
- PMSP 92262 756-C3
JUANITA DR
24100 RivC 92587 867-F1
N JUANITA RD
300 PMSP 92262 786-H1
500 PMSP 92262 756-H7
JUANITA ST
100 HEMT 92543 811-A7
300 HEMT 92543 841-A2
1500 SJCT 92543 811-A4
1500 SJCT 92583 811-A4
3100 RIV 92504 715-E3
11000 LMLN 92354 647-D1
25900 SBdC 92354 647-E1
N JUANITA ST
500 HEMT 92543 811-A6
S JUANITA ST
400 HEMT 92543 841-A1
JUANRO WY
6100 RIV 92504 685-B7
6400 RIV 92504 715-B1
JUAREZ ST
500 BAN 92220 722-C4
JUARO CIR
38100 RivC 92260 818-F1
JUBILEE CIR
38500 RivC 92211 819-G1
JUBILEE DR
5600 SDCo 92028 999-A5
JUBILEE RD
- RivC 92596 899-E7
JUBILEE WY
38900 SDCo 92028 999-B4
JUDD TER
- RMIR 92270 788-B7
JUDGE WARD CT
23500 MORV 92557 717-D2
JUDI LN
36500 RivC 92544 902-B7
36800 RivC 92544 (932-B1
See Page 902)
JUDITH CIR
2300 COR 92882 773-A1
JUDITH PL
25300 MORV 92553 717-G3
JUDITH ST
34200 RivC 92596 899-J4
JUDY CT
10000 RIV 92503 714-H7
JUDY LN
34000 CTHC 92234 787-F5
JUDY ANN DR
14000 RivC 92503 745-C4
JUEL LN
300 HEMT 92544 811-G6
JULEE CT
- LQNT 92253 5470-A5
JULES RD
- RivC 92567 809-E2
JULIA DR
- COAC 92236 5471-A6
JULIA ST
10900 RivC 91752 643-H6
JULIA WY
- RivC 92276 788-C2
JULIAN DR
10000 RIV 92503 684-E7
13000 DHSP 92240 696-H5

JULIAN LN
40300 RivC 92544 961-C5
40300 RivC 92592 961-C5
E JULIAN RD
2600 PMSP 92262 786-H1
JULIANNE DR
40100 MURR 92563 928-G7
JULIE AV
15300 MORV 92551 747-G1
JULIE LN
13300 YCPA 92399 650-D6
26300 RivC 92548 839-B2
26400 RivC 92585 839-B2
JULIE WY
200 HEMT 92545 810-G7
JULIETTE CIR
- COR 92881 773-E5
JULIP CT
43600 RivC 92536 964-A7
44000 RivC 92536 (984-A1
See Page 964)
JULLIAN CIR
1300 COR 92881 773-F3
JULY DR
3400 RivC 92503 744-B5
JUMANO DR
25700 MORV 92551 747-H1
JUMAR CT
49500 RivC 92536 983-D1
JUNE CT
3400 RivC 92503 744-B5
15700 MORV 92551 747-F2
20200 RIV 92508 746-F2
39600 TEM 92591 958-J2
JUNE DR
700 COR 92879 743-H2
JUNE LN
34700 YCPA 92399 649-J5
JUNE RD
16000 RivC 92240 697-D7
16000 RivC 92240 727-D2
17000 RivC 92241 727-D2
39300 TEM 92591 958-J1
JUNE ST
- MURR 92563 928-J5
20200 RivC 92570 836-G3
JUNE WY
26500 RivC 92544 841-D2
JUNEBERRY AV
2200 HEMT 92545 840-G2
JUNEBERRY CIR
100 COR 92881 773-C4
JUNEBERRY CT
12600 MORV 92553 717-H3
JUNE BUG CT
12800 RivC 92503 744-B4
JUNELLE AV
3600 RIV 92506 685-F7
JUNI HILLS DR
46400 RivC 92536 982-E6
JUNIPER AV
10600 FONT 92337 644-J2
10900 SBdC 92337 644-J2
11300 MORV 92555 688-C7
18700 MORV 92555 718-C1
JUNIPER CIR
45700 PDST 92260 848-F2
JUNIPER CT
300 SJCT 92582 810-J2
JUNIPER DR
- RivC - 5239-J7
100 PMSP 92264 787-C6
2800 COR 92882 742-F5
68500 DHSP 92240 697-D4
JUNIPER PL
1000 BAN 92220 721-F2
JUNIPER RD
- RivC - 908-A2
19600 RivC 92570 776-D5
21700 RivC 92570 806-D2
69900 RivC - (907-H5
See Page 906)
JUNIPER ST
700 HEMT 92545 840-G2
21500 RivC 92570 776-A7
21500 RivC 92570 806-A1
40000 MURR 92562 928-C4
42200 MURR 92562 927-J7
42600 MURR 92562 957-H1
42700 RivC 92562 957-H1
73200 PDST 92260 848-F2
JUNIPER TR
100 BLY 92225 5491-E5
JUNIPER FLATS RD
- RivC - 390-D4
21700 RivC 92567 779-E6
22200 RivC 92567 809-F1
23200 RivC 92548 809-B6
25800 RivC 92548 839-B1
JUNIPERHILL LN
100 RIV 92506 716-D4
JUNIPER HILLS RD
24000 RivC 92548 809-F4
JUNIPERO AV
2100 PMSP 92262 756-C5
JUNIPERO DR
82400 INDO 92201 5410-F6
JUNIPERO RD
24400 RivC 92585 808-F5
25700 RivC 92585 838-F1
JUNIPER SPRINGS RD
24000 RivC 92548 809-F5
25300 RivC 92545 809-G7
25300 RivC 92545 839-G1
JUNO ST
25200 RivC 92586 837-J7

JUPITER
- PMSP 92264 786-H7
JUPITER DR
4400 RIV 92505 714-F6
6000 RivC 91752 683-H5
JUPITER HILLS CT
41600 PDST 92211 819-D4
JUPITER HILLS RD
- COR 92883 803-H1
JURA CT
- TEM 92591 959-D3
29600 RivC 92584 868-A2
JURUPA AV
100 RLTO 92316 645-F2
100 SBdC 92316 645-D2
3400 RIV 92506 685-E7
4800 RIV 92504 685-B7
6100 RIV 92504 684-H7
7200 RIV 92503 714-E1
7200 RIV 92504 714-F1
10100 RIV 92503 684-D7
10200 RIV 92505 684-D7
10300 RIV 92505 714-A1
10300 RIV 92505 684-B7
10800 NRCO 92860 683-J7
10800 RivC 92505 683-J7
10800 RIV 92505 713-J1
11400 RIV 92505 713-J1
12900 FONT 92337 643-J2
13100 FONT 92337 644-A2
13700 SBdC 92337 644-G2
16900 FONT 92337 645-A2
17200 FONT 92316 645-A2
17200 SBdC 92337 645-A2
JURUPA RD
6800 RivC 92509 645-A7
6900 RivC 92509 644-J7
6900 RivC 92509 684-G1
10100 RivC 91752 684-A3
10500 RivC 91752 683-G3
E JURUPA ST
2700 ONT 91761 643-B2
JURUPA HILLS DR
- MURR 92563 928-J5
JUSTICE AV
300 SJCT 92583 811-C3
JUSTICE MILL RD
19900 RivC 92570 806-F4
JUSTIN CT
77500 PDST 92211 819-E4
JUSTIN PL
14600 MORV 92553 717-F7
JUST RIGHT WY
- COR 92879 773-D2
JUTLAND DR
25000 RivC 92544 (812-A5
See Page 782)

K

K ST
- HEMT 92545 840-F2
- RivC 92518 747-D1
400 LKEL 92532 866-G4
KAARLA RD
32500 RivC 92596 929-F3
KABIAN CT
33300 TEM 92592 979-H3
KABIAN PK
23900 PER 92570 837-F5
23900 RivC 92587 837-F5
KACHINA CIR
75500 INDW 92210 849-A2
KACHINA CT
27600 RivC 92883 835-C6
KACHINA DR
5400 RivC 92509 684-G3
KADEV AV
9700 RivC 92223 690-H3
KAELAN CT
40300 MURR 92563 958-F1
KAFFIRBOOM CT
41800 TEM 92591 959-B5
KAFTAN WY
26900 MORV 92555 718-B1
KAGEL ST
24500 RivC 92584 897-G1
KAHWEA RD
30700 TEM 92591 959-C2
KAIBAB CT
49100 RivC 92536 963-C1
KAISER RD
1400 RivC - 5240-A6
KAISER RD Rt#-R2
- RivC - 391-C7
- RivC - 5240-B7
- RivC - 5421-B3
KAISON CIR
17300 RivC 92508 746-F6
KALAHARI CT
13900 MORV 92553 717-C5
KALAHARI DESERT DR
76100 PDST 92211 789-A7
76100 PDST 92211 819-A1
KALE ST
15400 MORV 92551 747-G2
KALINA AV
29300 LKEL 92530 865-J2
KALMIA AV
11400 MORV 92555 687-J7
11400 MORV 92555 688-A7
24700 MORV 92557 687-F7
KALMIA ST
- RivC 92562 957-G1
41200 MURR 92562 928-A6

KALMIA ST
41900 MURR 92562 927-H7
42800 MURR 92562 957-G1
KALSMAN DR
13200 RivC 92282 724-B2
KALUS AV
800 COR 92880 743-C3
KAMBER DR
900 HEMT 92543 841-B2
KAMPEN CIR
- RivC 92592 960-A4
KANAN RD
26400 RivC 92586 868-B2
KANDIS CT
41700 RivC 92544 841-F2
KANE ST
3300 RIV 92501 685-H5
KANGNAM RD
- RIV 92508 716-D7
- RivC 92508 716-D7
KANN RD
67300 RivC 92241 727-A2
KANSAS AV
2600 RIV 92507 686-A5
KANSAS ST
- RDL 92373 647-J1
30700 LKEL 92530 866-A3
41400 PDST 92211 819-D5
KAPALUA WY
39200 RivC 92592 930-H5
KAPALUA BAY AV
6200 BAN 92220 721-C5
KAPALUA BAY LN
- COR 92881 773-H6
- COR 92883 773-H6
KAPLAN CREEK DR
24500 PER 92587 837-F4
27500 RivC 92587 837-F4
KARA CIR
9000 RIV 92508 746-E3
KARA CT
- LQNT 92253 849-H1
KAREE DR
4300 HEMT 92544 811-F4
KAREN AV
11100 DHSP 92240 696-B4
12000 RivC 92240 696-B6
16000 RivC 92258 726-B2
17000 PMSP 92258 726-B2
KAREN CT
1700 HEMT 92545 810-H5
KAREN DR
11000 RivC 92223 691-A6
KAREN LN
- PMSP 92262 756-G4
700 COR 92880 743-C2
6200 RivC 92509 645-B5
KAREN ST
39000 CTHC 92234 817-D3
KAREN WY
34300 RMIR 92270 787-G5
KARENDALE CIR
2200 RIV 92506 715-G4
KAREN LYNN DR
13700 MORV 92553 717-D5
KARIANNE LN
6100 RivC 92509 684-H5
KARIE WY
44900 TEM 92592 979-G3
KARIN LEE CT
81000 RivC 92274 5590-D2
KARISA CIR
25700 MORV 92551 747-J2
KARLA ST
32000 RivC 92596 839-D6
KARLISA CV
- PMSP 92264 787-A3
KARRIE LN
- MURR 92562 927-F3
KARRY CT
24300 MORV 92551 747-F1
KASABA CT
20500 RivC 92595 896-J6
KASBA CIR
11500 MORV 92557 717-E1
KASBAH DR
47000 PDST 92260 848-G3
KASEN ST
23800 RivC 92570 777-B6
KASOTA CT
12300 MORV 92557 717-H2
KASOTA DR
40500 MURR 92562 928-C5
KASPER LN
33800 RivC 92584 898-D3
KATHARIN ST
26300 RivC 92544 841-D1
KATHI ST
- RDL 92373 647-J2
KATHLEEN ST
2700 RIV 92506 715-G3
KATHRYN CIR
73600 RivC 92260 818-F2
KATHRYN CT
30200 RivC 92543 871-A2
KATHRYN WY
32800 RivC 92530 896-E3
KATHY AV
4100 RivC 92509 644-H7
KATHY DR
38000 CTHC 92234 817-D2
KATHY LN
26200 RivC 92544 841-E1
36400 YCPA 92399 650-D1

KATIE DR
16700 RivC 92504 745-H5
KATIE LN
9100 RIV 92508 746-D3
KATIES CRSG
45600 RivC 92536 983-A4
KATRINA AV
24300 MORV 92551 747-F1
KATRINA CT
10700 RIV 92505 714-E6
KATRINA LN
1200 SJCT 92583 811-D3
KATURAH DR
37000 RivC 92539 904-G7
37000 RivC 92539 (934-G1
See Page 904)
KATY WY
19600 RivC 92881 773-J4
KATYDID AV
19300 SBdC 92316 645-F3
KAVENISH
75100 INDW 92210 848-J2
KAVENISH WY
- RMIR 92270 818-B2
KAVENISH WY E
200 RMIR 92270 818-C2
KAVENISH WY N
200 RMIR 92270 818-C1
KAVENISH WY S
200 RMIR 92270 818-C2
KAVENISH WY W
200 RMIR 92270 818-C1
KAWEA WY
45500 INDW 92210 849-C1
N KAWEAH RD
1400 PMSP 92262 756-D6
KAY DR
13300 RivC 92879 744-A5
KAY RD
13000 RivC 92240 696-E5
KAYAL AV
11500 MORV 92557 687-H7
11500 MORV 92557 717-H1
KAYE CT
- LQNT 92253 849-H1
KAYFOUR RD
36700 RivC 92592 930-E7
KAYJAY ST
2500 RIV 92503 744-G3
KAYNE ST
20000 RivC 92881 773-H5
KEARNEY ST
1200 RIV 92501 685-J1
KEARSARGE PL
10700 RIV 92503 744-G2
KEARSARGE RD
50900 RivC 92536 983-G3
KEATING DR
6900 RIV 92503 714-F1
KEATS DR
1900 RIV 92501 685-H1
KEBON DR
80700 INDO 92201 5470-B5
KEDGWICK CT
5100 RIV 92505 714-A6
KEE AV
17500 LKEL 92530 866-B2
KEEGAN CT
10100 RIV 92503 714-G5
KEEL DR
32800 LKEL 92530 865-G5
KEEN RD
24000 RivC 92548 809-E4
KEENAN DR
39600 RMIR 92270 818-A3
KEEN CAMP RD
54200 RivC - 844-D6
KEENE LN
53000 RivC 92274 5531-J2
KEEPSAKE LN
200 PER 92571 807-H1
1200 PER 92571 777-H7
KEHL CANYON RD
9500 RivC 92223 690-E3
KEIL RD
69200 RivC 92241 727-F5
KEIM BLVD
- RivC - 412-B3
19300 RivC - 392-B10
KEISSEL RD
8100 RivC 92324 687-F1
8100 RivC 92324 647-F7
KEITH AV
30300 CTHC 92234 787-C1
33600 RivC 92545 839-G1
KEITH ST
1700 COR 92881 773-G6
1800 RIV 92507 686-A4
17000 RivC 92258 726-D2
KELISA LN
- RIV 92504 715-B6
KELLAM AV
100 SJCT 92583 811-A2
KELLEN CT
15100 RivC 92506 745-H1
KELLER AV
9700 RIV 92503 714-E4
10300 RIV 92505 714-D4
KELLER RD
23900 RivC 92584 898-B3
25000 RivC 92595 897-J3
28000 MURR 92584 898-G3
30900 RivC 92584 899-B3
30900 RivC 92596 899-B3

KELLER FLAT CT
34100 RivC 92596 899-E3
KELLEY AV
1200 COR 92882 743-C6
KELLEY LN
26400 RivC 92548 839-C2
26400 RivC 92585 839-C2
38800 RMIR 92270 817-H3
KELLI RD
22700 RivC 92570 805-H3
KELLIE WY
500 HEMT 92543 811-A5
KELLOGG AV
1300 COR 92879 743-E7
1900 COR 92879 773-E1
2300 COR 92881 773-E2
KELLOGG DR
600 BAN 92220 721-F2
KELLOGG RD
19000 RivC 92282 725-F5
19400 RivC 92262 725-F5
KELLOGG ST
- PER 92571 777-G2
11700 LMLN 92354 647-D2
N KELLOGG ST
100 LKEL 92530 866-D5
S KELLOGG ST
100 LKEL 92530 866-D5
KELLY LN
20700 RivC 92570 776-G4
32900 YCPA 92399 649-D4
KELLY RD
6900 DHSP 92282 655-H7
6900 RivC 92282 655-H7
KELSEY CIR
43700 PDST 92210 818-J7
43700 PDST 92210 819-A7
KELSEY CT
- PDST 92210 818-J7
KELSEY PL
6500 RivC 92509 684-E6
KELSEY WY
17400 CHLS 91709 712-A4
KEL-STAR RD
31000 RivC 92544 871-D4
KELTON CT
54300 RivC 92282 724-C2
KELTY DR
- RIV 92508 716-E6
KELVIN CT
26500 MURR 92562 958-E2
KEMP LN
24300 LMLN 92354 647-A1
KEMP ST
600 RIV 92501 646-A7
KEMPE CIR
29600 RivC 92584 868-J6
KEMPER
11700 RIV 92505 714-B7
KEMPER CT
69100 CTHC 92234 787-F1
KEMPER RD
- CTHC 92234 787-F1
KEMPTON AV
71200 RMIR 92270 818-A3
KENBORNE CT
6600 RIV 92506 716-B4
KENDAL RD
- RivC 92220 691-F1
KENDALL DR
19400 RivC 92220 782-D1
KENDALL ST
5100 RIV 92506 685-E6
E KENDALL ST
100 COR 92879 743-D6
W KENDALL ST
100 COR 92882 743-B6
KENDALL WY
12700 RDL 92373 649-A5
KENDRA WY
100 RivC 92507 646-E6
KENDRICK DR
5800 RIV 92507 716-G2
KENDRY CT
37200 RivC 92596 929-E3
KENMIL ST
3400 RIV 92504 715-E3
KENMORE ST
10900 RivC 91752 643-H6
50000 COAC 92236 5471-B6
KENNADINE DR
36100 RivC 92595 897-G7
36100 RivC 92595 927-H1
KENNEALLY LN
41000 RivC 92544 871-D4
KENNEBEC CT
14700 MORV 92553 717-E7
KENNEDY
- CTHC 92234 787-A7
KENNEDY DR
2400 COR 92879 744-A3
KENNEDY LN
23500 RivC 92587 837-E7
KENNEDY ST
8600 RivC 92509 684-D6
KENNEDY HILLS RD
- RivC 92555 389-E7
KENNEMER DR
33100 MURR 92562 927-E2
33100 RivC 92595 927-E2
KENNER AV
82100 INDO 92201 5410-E6
KENNETH CT
38900 RivC 92223 690-G4

KENNETH ST
3800 RivC 92509 644-D7
KENNY WY
4600 HEMT 92544 811-F6
KENOAK PL
20800 RivC 92570 775-H6
KENOSHA CT
24300 RivC 92883 804-E6
KEN ROSEWALL LN
72900 PDST 92260 848-E3
KENSINGTON AV
- RivC 92203 789-F6
- RivC 92211 789-F6
KENSINGTON CIR
25400 MORV 92551 747-H3
KENSINGTON CT
25100 RivC 92544 (812-B5
See Page 782)
KENSINGTON DR
1800 COR 92880 713-A7
1900 SJCT 92583 811-F4
13500 RivC 92883 835-C5
39600 RMIR 92270 818-A3
KENSINGTON PL
- TEM 92592 959-G7
16300 MORV 92551 747-H3
KENSINGTON WY
5000 RIV 92507 686-D7
KENT AV
5200 RIV 92503 714-F3
KENT LN
11700 YCPA 92399 649-J2
KENT PL
- CTHC 92234 787-G1
KENT RD
1700 HEMT 92545 840-H1
54100 RivC - 844-C1
KENTFIELD ST
22200 GTER 92313 646-E5
KENTFIELD WY
- COR 92882 773-A3
KENTIA PALM DR
- RivC 92203 789-G6
- RivC 92211 789-G6
26000 RivC 92548 839-A1
KENTLAND LN
12900 MORV 92553 717-H4
KENTON LN
19900 RivC 92570 777-D3
KENTUCKY AV
76700 PDST 92211 819-C6
KENTUCKY LN
- COR 92882 773-B3
KENTUCKY ST
3300 RIV 92507 686-D4
32100 YCPA 92399 649-C4
KENTUCKY DERBY WY
24300 MURR 92562 927-H6
KENTVILLE ST
8600 RIV 92508 746-F2
KENTWOOD DR
2200 RIV 92507 686-D3
KENWOOD CT
33300 RivC 92530 865-G6
KENWOOD DR
11900 FONT 92337 644-C4
30100 CTHC 92234 757-G7
30100 CTHC 92234 787-G1
KENWOOD PL
5700 RivC 92509 645-D7
5700 RivC 92509 685-D1
KENWORTH CT
- YCPA 92399 649-E2
KENWORTHY BAUTISTA RD Rt#-371
57200 RivC 92539 (935-H3
See Page 904)
58400 RivC - (935-H3
See Page 904)
58400 RivC - (936-A2
See Page 906)
KENYA DR
43100 INDO 92201 5410-B6
KENYON CT
10300 RIV 92505 714-F6
KENYON LN
42400 RivC 92544 931-G7
KEOWN CT
500 RivC 92507 646-D7
KEPLER ST
- RivC 92584 868-C3
KERBER CT
9400 RivC 92509 684-D6
KERIE KAY LN
28000 RivC 92585 838-E5
KERILYN LN
500 HEMT 92544 811-C6
KERN DR
6800 RivC 92509 685-A5
6900 RivC 92509 684-J5
KERN PL
11200 RIV 92505 714-C6
KERNWOOD DR
24000 MORV 92557 717-E1
KERRI PL
4400 RivC 92509 684-G1
KERRIA CT
73400 PDST 92260 848-F6
KERRIA DR
1400 BEAU 92223 691-A7
KERRY LN
6600 RivC 92509 645-B5
KERSTEN RD
39300 RMIR 92270 818-B3

KERTE LN
16000 FONT 92337 644-G3
KESHA CT
600 SJCT 92583 811-C3
KESS RD
52100 RivC 92539 (933-J1
See Page 902)
52300 RivC 92539 (934-A1
See Page 904)
KESSEN LN
58700 RivC 92539 (985-E1
See Page 964)
KESTRAL DR
13300 RivC 92883 835-B4
KESTREL CIR
- COR 92881 773-E5
KESWICK AV
2000 RIV 92506 716-A2
KETCH DR
29700 CYNL 92587 867-F2
KETTENBURG LN
16700 MORV 92551 747-G4
KETTERING CT
11700 MORV 92557 717-C1
S KETTERING DR
100 ONT 91761 643-F2
KETTLE RD
39400 MURR 92562 898-A7
KEUSDER WY
2300 RivC 92503 744-G3
KEVIN CIR
800 COR 92880 743-B2
KEVIN CT
2600 RIV 92506 715-G3
KEVIN DR
26500 RivC 92595 927-G2
KEVIN PL
32800 LKEL 92530 865-J6
KEVIN RD
13400 RivC 92555 719-B4
26700 RivC 92595 927-G2
38000 INDO 92203 5410-B1
KEVIN ST
11900 MORV 92557 717-E1
KEVIN LEE LN
- RMIR 92270 787-H7
- RMIR 92270 817-H1
KEY ST
20300 CLTN 92324 645-J6
KEY WY
67600 DHSP 92240 697-B5
KEY LARGO AV
34000 RMIR 92270 788-D6
KEYS CT
11200 RIV 92503 744-F3
KEYSTONE CIR
- COR 92882 773-C2
KEYSTONE CT
- BAN 92220 721-D6
- RIV 92518 746-F2
KEYSTONE DR
25800 RivC 92570 837-C1
26300 PER 92570 837-C1
KEYS VIEW RD
- RivC - 390-E5
KEYWEST DR
800 COR 92882 773-A3
KEY WEST DR
7600 RIV 92503 714-G4
KHEPERA CT
- MURR 92563 928-G7
KHOURY CT
17500 RivC 92241 727-D2
KICKING HORSE DR
26600 RivC 92883 835-B4
KIDD ST
10200 RIV 92503 714-G6
KIELEY RD
68300 CTHC 92234 787-D7
KIITOS CIR
400 HEMT 92544 811-C6
KIKY CIR
- RivC 92562 956-E4
KILBOURNE AV
6100 RIV 92504 684-J7
KILGORE LN
32500 RivC 92595 927-E2
KILGORE ST
11900 MORV 92557 717-F2
KILIMANJARO CT
300 COR 92881 773-D3
39000 PDST 92211 819-A2
KILIMANJARO DR
38800 PDST 92211 819-A2
KILKARE CIR
39600 MURR 92562 928-C2
KILKENNY DR
3100 RIV 92503 744-G2
KILLARNEY DR
10400 RIV 92503 744-G1
KILLARNEY LN
34800 RivC 92595 897-E5
KILLEN TR
32200 RivC 92530 895-E1
34900 RivC 92530 896-A4
34900 RivC 92530 926-C1
KILLIAN WY
- RMIR 92270 788-B5
KILLINGTON DR
29700 RivC 92586 868-B2
KILMARNOCK WY
8000 RIV 92508 716-E6
KILWORTH DR
- COR 92882 773-C3

KIM CT
25500 MURR 92563 928-F5
KIM LN
8400 RivC 92509 684-E3
KIM RD
26300 RivC 92548 839-A2
26300 RivC 92585 839-A2
KIM WY
7400 RivC 92881 773-H2
KIMBALL
100 LKEL 92530 866-F6
E KIMBALL AV
100 HEMT 92543 811-A7
W KIMBALL AV
100 HEMT 92543 811-A7
300 HEMT 92543 810-J7
KIMBERLEY LN
- TEM 92591 929-C7
KIMBERLY AV
24200 MORV 92557 717-E1
28700 MORV 92555 718-E5
KIMBERLY CT
- SBDO 92408 646-J1
- RMIR 92270 817-J2
31600 LKEL 92532 866-H5
KIMBERLY LN
35000 YCPA 92399 650-A2
75900 PDST 92211 819-A1
KIMBERLY WY
- MURR 92562 927-F3
800 COR 92880 743-C2
KIMBERLY SUE CT
18000 RivC 92532 866-C1
KIMDALE DR
14700 RivC 92570 775-E5
51700 RivC 92230 723-G2
53500 RivC 92282 723-G2
53500 RivC 92282 724-C1
KIMES RD
21000 RivC 92570 836-J3
21000 RivC 92570 837-A3
KIMLIN AV
60600 RivC 92282 725-F2
KIMO ST
45600 TEM 92592 979-D5
KING AV
16000 RivC 92504 745-H4
KING CT
400 HEMT 92543 841-A3
39700 RivC 92562 927-A6
KING RD
19100 RivC 92258 725-H5
KING ST
- BAN 92220 722-A2
1000 BAN 92220 721-D2
5200 RIV 92506 686-A7
43600 INDO 92201 5410-F6
45100 INDO 92201 5470-F1
E KING ST
500 BAN 92220 722-C2
KING APACHE CIR
28200 RivC 92584 898-F1
KING ARTHURS CT
2600 RIV 92506 715-H3
KING EDWARD CT
35500 RMIR 92270 788-B6
KING EDWARD DR
26200 LMLN 92354 647-F3
KINGFISHER CT
700 COR 92879 773-E1
KINGFISHER RD
12600 GTER 92313 646-F5
KINGHORN CT
- INDO 92201 5410-A7
KINGMAN DR
800 NRCO 92860 713-G6
KINGMAN ST
2400 PER 92571 777-H6
KING PALM DR
- INDO 92201 5470-C1
KINGS CIR
- RivC 92590 977-B5
KINGS HWY
16000 LKEL 92530 865-H1
KINGS RD
68300 CTHC 92234 817-E1
78000 RivC 92274 5712-B5
KINGS RD E
2600 PMSP 92264 786-F7
KINGS RD W
2600 PMSP 92264 786-F7
KINGS VW
38400 RivC 92562 927-B3
KINGS ALCOVE
- LQNT 92253 879-G3
KINGSBRIDGE LN
4600 RivC 92509 684-B2
KINGSBURY AV
2700 HEMT 92545 840-F2
KINGSBURY PL
4100 RIV 92503 714-H4
KINGS CANYON LN
44200 PDST 92260 818-H7
KINGS CROSS LN
1700 HEMT 92545 840-H1
KINGSDALE DR
1200 COR 92880 743-B2
KINGSFORD DR
1800 COR 92880 713-A7
1800 COR 92880 743-A1
KINGSGATE DR
800 COR 92882 773-B3
KINGSLEY WY
7400 RIV 92504 715-D2

STREET
Block City ZIP Pg-Grid

KINGSMILL AV
4800 BAN 92220 721-E5
KINGSPORT DR
1600 RIV 92506 715-G6
KINGS RANCH RD
5800 RIV 92505 714-C3
S KINGS RIVER LN
2800 ONT 91761 643-C6
KINGSTON CT
- INDO 92201 5410-A6
29600 RivC 92584 868-F2
KINGSTON DR
- RivC 92592 979-J2
2600 COR 92881 773-E2
79500 RivC 92201 819-J6
79700 RivC 92201 5410-A6
80000 LQNT 92201 5410-A6
KINGSTON LN
21100 RIV 92508 746-H2
KINGSTON RD
3400 BAN 92220 721-F3
KINGSTON ST
11700 GTER 92313 646-F3
KINGSTON HEATH
- LQNT 92253 5530-D4
KINGS WAY CT
- RMIR 92270 817-J3
KINGSWAY CT
14100 MORV 92553 717-F6
KINGSWAY DR
15100 RivC 92530 865-G6
KINGSWELL AV
600 BAN 92220 721-D2
KINGWOOD RD
- MURR 92563 928-G7
- MURR 92563 958-G1
KININGHAM DR
19400 SBdC 92316 645-G4
19500 SBdC 92509 645-G4
KINNEY ST
21200 RivC 92570 776-H2
22000 RivC 92570 777-A2
KINNOW LN
19400 RIV 92508 746-E3
KINNY DR
11600 MORV 92557 717-F1
KINO TR
45000 RivC 92544 902-D5
KINROSS LN
22400 MORV 92557 717-B2
KINSMITH RD
73200 RivC 92241 728-E2
KIOWA CIR
30100 RivC 92543 871-A2
KIOWA CT
22800 MORV 92553 717-B4
KIOWA DR
13000 MORV 92553 717-B4
49600 RivC 92536 963-D2
75100 INDW 92210 848-J2
KIOWA RIVER CT
30800 TEM 92591 959-B4
KIP PL
6100 RivC 92509 685-A5
KIPLING CT
11200 RIV 92505 714-B4
KIPS KORNER RD
2300 COR 92880 743-B1
2300 NRCO 92860 743-B1
2300 NRCO 92860 713-B7
KIRBY DR
4500 RivC 92509 684-H1
KIRBY RD
37000 RivC 92539 (935-C6
See Page 904)
KIRBY ST
100 SJCT 92582 810-G3
600 HEMT 92545 810-G5
600 HEMT 92545 840-G2
N KIRBY ST
100 SJCT 92582 780-G7
100 SJCT 92582 810-G5
100 HEMT 92545 810-G5
100 HEMT 92545 840-G1
KIRK CT
57000 LQNT 92253 5530-B6
KIRK ST
6100 RIV 92506 716-A3
E KIRK ST
400 CLTN 92324 646-D1
KIRKBY CIR
22600 MORV 92557 717-B2
KIRKLAND WY
- RivC 92562 956-F7
KIRKLEE LN
- RIV 92504 715-B5
KIRKMICHAEL CIR
1100 RIV 92507 716-F1
KIRKPATRICK RD
19700 RivC 92570 775-H4
KIRKWOOD
2400 PMSP 92264 787-D6
KIRKWOOD AV
3800 RIV 92501 685-J1
KIRKWOOD CIR
2300 PMSP 92264 787-D6
KIRKWOOD CT
8900 RivC 92240 696-E1
32400 RivC 92595 897-A5
39600 RMIR 92270 818-A3
KIRKWOOD DR
1200 COR 92882 742-H6
KISH CIR
35300 RivC 92595 897-D6

KISMET CIR
24200 MORV 92553 717-E7
KISTLER WY
- RivC 92203 789-F6
KIT AV
500 HEMT 92543 811-A6
KIT CT
44700 TEM 92592 979-F3
KITCHENER ST
1800 RIV 92504 715-F6
1800 RIV 92506 715-F6
KITCHING ST
3400 PER 92571 777-J3
11100 MORV 92557 687-H7
11600 MORV 92557 717-H1
12600 MORV 92553 717-H4
15000 MORV 92551 717-H7
15000 MORV 92551 747-H2
KIT FOX RD
49500 RivC 92260 848-B6
KITT ANSET DR
26100 RivC 92586 838-A7
KITTYHAWK DR
2600 PMSP 92262 756-E5
KITTY HAWK DR
5900 RIV 92504 715-A1
KIVA CT
- PDST 92260 848-C7
KIVA DR
200 PDST 92260 848-C7
KIWEBRE RD
37000 MURR 92563 928-G3
KIWI CIR
2100 COR 92879 773-E1
KIWI CT
- HEMT 92545 840-H4
11500 MORV 92557 717-C1
KIWI WY
16400 LKEL 92530 865-F1
KJERSTI RD
31100 RivC 92596 899-C5
KLAMATH CT
2600 RIV 92503 744-J1
22900 CYNL 92587 867-D2
KLAMATH PL
- PDST 92260 818-G5
KLAMATH RIVER DR
3900 ONT 91761 643-D6
KLARER LN
31700 TEM 92591 959-D2
KLEIN WY
- RivC 92567 779-E6
KLOIBER CT
10700 RIV 92505 714-F7
KLOIBER ST
10800 RIV 92505 744-E1
10800 RIV 92505 714-F7
KLOTZ LN
22200 RivC 92595 897-C5
KLUG CIR
300 COR 92880 742-H3
KLUK LN
3200 RivC 92501 646-B6
KLYNE ST
20100 RivC 92881 773-H5
KNABE RD
21600 RivC 92883 804-B1
KNARR RD
34700 YCPA 92399 649-J5
KNICKERBOCKER LN
4600 RIV 92501 685-E5
KNIFFIN AV
17300 RivC 92530 896-C2
KNIGHT CT
43600 RivC 92544 811-J6
KNIGHT DR
41600 MURR 92562 928-B7
KNIGHTSBRIDGE PL
11700 LMLN 92354 647-F3
KNIGHTS BRIDGE WY
- TEM 92592 959-H7
KNIGHTSWOOD CT
- INDO 92201 5410-A7
KNIGHTSWOOD RD
80300 INDO 92201 5410-B7
KNOB PL
20700 RivC 92570 775-H6
KNOB HILL
25000 RivC - 814-B4
KNOB HILL DR
2200 RIV 92506 715-J2
KNOCH RD
15900 RivC 92555 749-H3
KNOEFLER DR
11900 RIV 92505 744-B1
KNOEFLER PL
4400 RIV 92505 744-B1
12000 RIV 92503 744-B1
KNOLL CT
29200 RivC 92586 868-B1
KNOLL DR
1500 RDL 92373 649-A4
12500 RivC 92240 695-H4
KNOLL RD
35700 YCPA 92399 650-C2
KNOLL WY
3100 RIV 92501 686-A2
KNOLLBROOK PL
17100 RivC 92503 744-F4
KNOLL CREST DR
11100 FONT 92337 644-H2
KNOLL PARK LN
800 SDCo 92028 997-H7
KNOLLRIDGE DR
39600 TEM 92591 958-H1

KNOLLVIEW CIR
38900 CTHC 92234 817-D3
KNOLL VISTA ST
11400 MORV 92555 688-C7
11600 MORV 92555 718-D1
KNOLLWOOD DR
800 RivC 92882 742-G5
13200 RivC 92883 835-B5
29400 MURR 92563 928-E5
56700 RivC 92539 (934-J3
See Page 904)
56700 RivC 92539 (935-A3
See Page 904)
KNOLLWOOD PL
5800 RIV 92506 685-E7
KNOLLWOOD ST
15100 LKEL 92530 865-G4
KNOX CIR
1600 COR 92879 743-G4
KNOX CT
100 RivC 92596 840-A6
200 RIV 92507 686-E5
S KNOX CT
2500 SBDO 92408 646-H1
KNOX ST
17300 MORV 92551 747-F5
KOALA CT
19000 RIV 92508 716-E6
KOCHI DR
13000 MORV 92553 717-C4
KODIAK CT
- MURR 92562 927-G3
- PER 92571 778-B3
KOEPFER RD
- RivC 92570 805-J7
- RivC 92570 806-A6
KOHLBERRY CT
1500 RIV 92507 716-G2
KOHLER CT
- RIV 92506 715-G7
KOKELL AV
87000 RivC 92274 5531-G4
KOLBE RD
61000 RivC 92282 655-H5
KOLO CT
35600 RivC 92595 897-D7
KOMODO RD
34500 RivC 92544 901-E4
KONA CT
40600 MURR 92562 928-C4
KONA LN
400 PMSP 92264 786-E5
KONA PL
4100 RIV 92505 744-B2
KONIC CT
5100 RivC 92509 685-D4
KOODEN RD
34000 RivC 92596 899-C4
KOOL VISTA TR
59700 RivC 92539 (935-F7
See Page 904)
KORAL RD
37500 RivC 92539 (934-D2
See Page 904)
KORDYS LN
24100 RivC 92324 647-D7
KORI CT
6300 RivC 92509 645-B6
KO RIVER CT
30500 TEM 92591 959-B4
KOSCIOLEK RD
12800 MORV 92555 718-C4
KOSLOW CT
78300 RivC 92201 819-G5
KOUMA ST
40300 RivC 92544 841-C3
KOVENISH CT
- PDST 92260 878-C1
KOVES RD
34500 RivC 92530 896-F4
KRAEMER DR
1100 COR 92882 742-F6
KRAFT LN
10200 SBdC 92337 644-J2
KRAMER DR
- RivC 92203 789-H6
KRAMER WY
17300 RivC 92570 776-A3
KRAMERIA AV
16600 RivC 92504 745-G4
17500 RivC 92504 746-B4
17700 RivC 92508 746-B4
19000 RIV 92508 746-B4
24200 MORV 92551 747-F3
KRAMERIA ST
24000 MORV 92551 747-E3
26100 MORV 92555 747-E3
26100 MORV 92555 748-A3
KRANSHIRE RD
64700 RivC 92240 696-E5
KRATKA RIDGE LN
29800 RivC 92586 868-A2
KRESS CT
800 COR 92879 743-E5
KRIS AV
17900 RivC 92241 728-C4
KRISTEN CT
- LQNT 92253 849-H1
12000 MORV 92557 717-D2
KRISTIN CT
45500 INDO 92201 5470-D1
KRISTIN LN
800 HEMT 92545 810-H5
KRISTINA CT
13600 MORV 92553 717-C5

KRISTY LN
26600 RivC 92544 841-F2
KRONEN CT
2600 RIV 92506 715-H2
KRONHOLM CT
9600 CALI 92320 690-A3
KROONEN DR
1300 COR 92882 743-A7
1300 COR 92882 742-J7
KROSS RD
17500 RivC 92508 746-A1
KRUBSACK RD
32000 RivC 92584 868-C7
KRUG AV
73700 PDST 92260 818-F7
KRUSE ST
- PER 92570 807-E3
KUCERA CT
39500 MURR 92563 928-E5
KUDER AV
21600 RivC 92570 746-J6
21600 RivC 92570 747-A6
KUFFEL RD
25300 RivC 92585 837-J1
25800 RivC 92585 838-A1
KUHNS DR
- SJCT 92583 811-A3
KUKA CIR
22700 RivC 92595 897-D7
KUNA CT
22800 RivC 92595 897-D6
KUPFER DR
200 HEMT 92544 811-F7
KURE CT
25700 RivC 92584 868-A2
KURT CT
24200 MORV 92551 747-F1
KURT ST
32000 RivC 92584 868-D7
32500 RivC 92584 898-D1
KWEEA
58600 RivC 92539 (935-E5
See Page 904)
KYBAR RD
76600 PDST 92211 819-C6
KYLA LEE CT
- RivC 92562 956-J2
KYLE CT
1500 RIV 92507 716-G2
20500 RivC 92562 926-H4
KYLE RD
68000 CTHC 92234 787-D7
KYLIE CT
6000 CHLS 91709 712-A4

L

L ST
- HEMT 92545 840-F2
- RivC 92518 747-D2
9700 RivC 92509 684-B5
LA ALBA DR
- MURR 92563 929-A3
LA BARCA RD
15700 MORV 92551 747-J2
LA BARCA WY
24500 MORV 92551 747-F1
LA BARRANCA RD
23900 RivC 92570 806-D5
LA BELLE LN
- RivC 92570 805-F4
LA BERTHA LN
23300 RivC 92587 837-D7
LABETA CIR
44600 TEM 92592 979-G3
LA BONITA
41400 RivC 92544 961-C3
LA BONITA AV
- PER 92571 807-H2
LA BONITA ST
4000 RivC 92509 644-F7
LA BONITA DONNA
34900 RivC 92592 980-B1
LABRADOR CIR
1400 COR 92882 772-J2
LABRADOR PL
10700 RIV 92503 744-G2
LA BREA AV
2600 HEMT 92545 810-G5
S LA BREA RD
1500 PMSP 92264 786-H4
LABRINIA LN
42000 RivC 92539 (965-J4
See Page 964)
LA BRISA CIR
11300 FONT 92337 645-A2
LA BRISAS WY
14700 MORV 92553 717-G7
LA CABELLERA RD
45900 RivC 92544 (932-F1
See Page 902)
LA CADENA CT
- PMSP 92264 816-D1
40500 TEM 92591 959-B2
LA CADENA DR
1900 RIV 92507 686-A3
2200 RIV 92507 685-J3
S LA CADENA DR
600 CLTN 92324 646-C5
1300 SBdC 92324 646-C5
11600 GTER 92313 646-C5
11600 GTER 92324 646-C5
11900 SBdC 92313 646-C5
LA CADENA DR E
100 RivC 92507 646-B7

LA CADENA DR E
100 RIV 92501 646-B7
400 RIV 92507 646-B7
400 RIV 92501 646-B7
900 RIV 92507 686-A1
900 RIV 92501 686-A1
LA CADENA DR W
100 RivC 92501 646-B6
700 RIV 92501 646-B7
1000 RIV 92501 686-A1
2800 CLTN 92324 646-B6
LA CADENA LN
- COR 92879 743-F3
LA CAMPANA WY
3300 PMSP 92262 756-J6
LA CANADA DR
5800 RivC 92509 685-C1
6000 RivC 92509 645-B7
LA CANADA WY
72600 RivC 92276 788-D2
LA CARMELA DR
43700 PDST 92211 818-J7
LA CASA DR
- MORV 92555 748-C1
LA CASA WY
1000 HEMT 92545 810-G5
98800 RivC 92254 (5654-D2
See Page 5594)
LA CASA PACIFICA
84000 INDO 92203 5410-J5
LACASELLA CT
34500 RivC 92595 897-A5
LA CASITA DR
24900 RivC 92590 957-H7
LACE CIR
41200 MURR 92562 927-H3
LACEBARK DR
25400 MURR 92563 928-E4
LACEBARK ST
- FONT 92337 645-A2
LA CERRA CIR
- RMIR 92270 818-B3
LA CERRA DR
- RMIR 92270 818-B4
S LA CERRA DR
- RMIR 92270 818-B4
W LA CERRA DR
- RMIR 92270 818-A4
LACEY OAK DR
600 COR 92881 773-E2
LA CIENEGA DR
21100 RivC 92530 897-A1
LA CIMA RD
2700 COR 92879 744-A2
59000 RivC 92539 (965-E3
See Page 964)
LA CIOTAT WY
3500 RivC 92501 646-A6
LA CITA
73800 RivC 92276 758-F7
LA COLIMA RD
40600 TEM 92591 958-J3
LA COLINA LN
58500 RivC 92539 (985-D2
See Page 964)
LA CONDESA DR
2500 PMSP 92264 786-E7
LA CORONA CT
29800 TEM 92591 959-A2
LA COSTA CIR E
40600 PDST 92211 819-D3
LA COSTA CIR W
40700 PDST 92211 819-D3
LA COSTA CT
- YCPA 92399 649-E2
64800 RivC 92240 656-E7
LA COSTA DR
- RMIR 92270 788-B5
400 BAN 92220 721-C4
800 COR 92879 743-E5
LA COSTA ALTA DR
- MORV 92555 748-C2
LACOVIA DR
43200 RivC 92201 819-H6
LA CRESTA
15500 MORV 92551 747-J1
LA CRESTA DR
500 HEMT 92543 810-H6
29500 RivC 92587 867-F2
75200 PDST 92211 818-J7
LA CRESTA
HIGHLANDS CIR
40300 RivC 92562 956-D1
LA CROSSE AV
11900 GTER 92313 646-D4
12100 CLTN 92313 646-D4
12100 CLTN 92324 646-D4
LA CROSSE WY
- RIV 92508 716-E7
- RIV 92508 746-E1
LA CRUZ CIR
2100 COR 92879 743-H2
LA CRUZ DR
43700 RivC 92590 978-A1
44000 RivC 92590 958-A7
LA CUESTA RD
44200 RivC 92562 976-E2
LA CUMBRA CT
- RivC 92562 956-H5
LA CUMBRE AV
5200 RIV 92505 714-C5
LA CUMBRE CT
500 SJCT 92583 781-A6
LA CUMBRE ST
600 COR 92879 744-A2

LADD AV
11400 MORV 92555 688-D7
LADD CT
41300 RivC 92544 841-D1
LADERA AV
40600 PDST 92260 818-F4
LADERA CIR
1300 PMSP 92262 756-C6
2600 COR 92879 744-A2
LADERA DR
- LQNT 92253 819-H7
79000 LQNT 92253 849-H1
LADERA LN
4600 RIV 92501 685-F3
LADERA ST
- RDL 92373 647-G1
22100 GTER 92313 646-D6
LADERA VISTA DR
37900 RivC 92592 960-H2
LA DOCENA LN
- COR 92879 743-F3
LA DOCENA TR
80700 LQNT 92253 5470-C7
LADOGA PL
7800 RivC 92509 684-G1
LADY BIRD CT
48000 INDO 92201 5470-E4
LA ENCINA DR
200 PMSP 92264 787-C6
LA ENCINO CIR
37800 RivC 92562 926-G3
LA ENTRADA
- SJCT 92583 811-B4
LA ENTRADA AV
26600 RivC - 844-B1
LA ENTRADA CT
- COR 92879 743-F3
LA ENTRADA DR
15500 MORV 92551 747-J2
LA ESTRELLA RD
24000 RivC 92595 897-J6
35500 MURR 92562 898-A7
LAFAYETTE CIR
1300 COR 92882 773-A2
LAFAYETTE CT
80600 INDO 92201 5470-B1
LAFAYETTE DR
- RMIR 92270 818-B3
39900 MURR 92562 928-A1
LAFAYETTE RD
58900 RivC 92539 (985-F5
See Page 964)
LAFAYETTE ST
3900 RIV 92503 714-J4
LA FIESTA DR
3000 HEMT 92545 810-F5
LAFLER DR
1900 RIV 92501 685-H1
LA FLOR LN
- LQNT 92253 849-J1
LA FLORA DR
35200 YCPA 92399 650-A6
LA FORTUNA LN
16100 MORV 92551 747-H3
LAGANZA CT
49100 RivC 92536 983-C1
S LAGARTO WY
- PMSP 92264 786-E6
LA GATITA
72600 RivC 92241 728-C3
LA GLORIA ST
8000 RivC 92881 774-A5
8000 COR 92881 774-A5
LAGO
3200 ONT 91761 643-B6
LAGO DR
78000 LQNT 92253 849-F6
LAGO RD
17300 RivC 92530 896-B6
LAGO DE PALMAS
- PDST 92260 818-G4
LAGO GRANDE
43200 RivC 92536 963-D7
43200 RivC 92536 983-D1
LAGOON CT
2000 HEMT 92545 840-E5
LAGOS WY
67500 CTHC 92234 757-C7
LAGO VISTA LN
21700 RivC 92595 897-B3
LAGUNA AV
300 HEMT 92543 810-J6
15100 RivC 92530 865-G6
15600 LKEL 92530 865-G6
LAGUNA CT
3300 RIV 92506 715-F2
LAGUNA DR
- PMSP 92264 787-A6
500 COR 92879 743-E4
22600 MORV 92553 717-B4
N LAGUNA DR
67300 CTHC 92234 757-B7
S LAGUNA DR
67500 CTHC 92234 757-C7
LAGUNA PL
67300 CTHC 92234 787-B2
LAGUNA RD
20800 RivC 92595 897-B5
LAGUNA HONDA RD
25000 RivC 92544 811-H6
LAGUNA SECA CT
900 BAN 92220 721-D5
LAGUNITA CT
29900 RivC 92584 868-F2
LA HABRA AV
2900 HEMT 92545 810-F5

LA HERNANDEZ ST
86400 COAC 92236 5471-E6
LAHONTAN ST
31100 TEM 92592 979-D5
LA HUERTA RD
25100 RivC 92548 809-E6
LAINA LN
27400 MURR 92562 898-D6
LAIR RD
57100 RivC 92539 (935-B1
See Page 904)
LAIRD RD
39000 BEAU 92223 721-A5
39000 RivC 92223 720-H5
LAIRD ST
43700 RivC 92220 721-E6
LAISTER RD
28100 RivC 92570 836-G6
LA JOLLA AV
700 HEMT 92543 810-J6
LA JOLLA CIR
22500 MORV 92553 717-B4
LA JOLLA DR
- PDST 92260 818-G3
6700 RIV 92504 715-B2
LA JOLLA RD
900 PMSP 92264 786-E5
LAKAREN LN
6100 RivC 92509 684-H5
LAKE DR
23500 RivC 92587 837-E6
32400 RivC 92373 689-C4
LAKE LN
- SJCT 92583 811-B4
LAKE ST
100 HEMT 92544 811-G5
400 RivC 92544 811-G7
500 LKEL 92530 866-F6
6400 RIV 92503 714-G2
15700 RivC 92555 749-D2
24500 RivC 92583 811-G5
26000 RivC 92544 841-G1
26300 LKEL 92532 835-F3
26700 LKEL 92530 835-F4
28300 LKEL 92530 865-G1
LAKE BREEZE CIR
30000 LKEL 92530 865-G3
LAKEBREEZE LN
15000 LKEL 92530 865-F2
LAKE BUENA VISTA WY
5700 BAN 92220 721-C5
LAKE CANYON DR
47500 RivC 92536 963-B2
LAKE CHIMES DR
30400 RivC 92584 868-F3
LAKE CLUB DR
79000 RivC 92201 819-H4
LAKE CREST CT
- INDO 92203 5410-H3
LAKE CREST DR
1100 LKEL 92530 865-H4
17900 RivC 92503 744-H6
LAKECREST LN
200 PDST 92260 818-F4
LAKEFALL CT
- RIV 92505 744-C1
LAKE FOREST DR
29000 RivC 92586 838-C7
29000 RivC 92586 868-C1
LAKE FORK DR
28900 RivC 92584 868-G1
LAKEFRONT DR
41600 RivC 92536 963-D4
LAKEHILL CIR
4500 RIV 92501 685-G3
LAKEHILL PL
3200 RIV 92501 685-G2
LAKE KNOLL PKWY
16400 RivC 92503 744-F5
LAKE KNOLL RD
29100 LKEL 92532 866-F1
LAKELAND DR
67800 CTHC 92234 787-D5
LAKE LA QUINTA DR
78500 LQNT 92253 849-G3
LAKE MATHEWS DR
13800 RivC 92570 805-E1
16700 RivC 92570 806-A2
20500 RivC 92570 775-D5
LAKE MEADOW CT
900 LKEL 92530 865-H4
LAKEMOUNT CT
20700 RivC 92570 775-F6
LAKE MOUNTAIN DR
24200 RivC 92570 805-E6
LAKEN LN
- PDST 92211 819-A4
LAKE PARK DR
800 SJCT 92583 811-E2
LAKE PARK ST
- LKEL 92530 866-G7
LAKE PERRIS DR
- MORV 92555 748-A7
- RivC 92571 748-A7
- RivC 92571 778-A1
LAKEPOINTE DR
30400 RivC 92584 868-F3
LAKE POINTE DR
16900 RivC 92503 744-G7
LAKE POINTE DR
30500 RivC 92584 868-F3
LAKEPOINTE DR E
2700 RivC 92503 744-C4
3400 RIV 92503 744-C4
LAKEPOINTE DR N
16800 RivC 92503 744-G5

LAKEPORT DR
- RIV 92505 714-C7
13300 MORV 92555 717-J4
LAKEPORT LN
- COR 92881 773-F4
LAKERIDGE CT
- TEM 92591 959-D4
LAKERIDGE DR
19900 RivC 92570 775-E5
LAKE RIDGE RD
15600 LKEL 92530 865-H7
LAKE RIVERSIDE DR
40200 RivC 92536 (933-E7
See Page 902)
40300 RivC 92536 963-E3
LAKESHORE BLVD
40100 RivC 92536 (933-C7
See Page 902)
40300 RivC 92536 963-C1
LAKE SHORE DR
- RivC 92373 689-B4
- RMIR 92270 818-D4
LAKESHORE DR
100 LKEL 92530 865-H2
100 LKEL 92530 866-A3
W LAKESHORE DR
200 LKEL 92530 866-D5
LAKE SHORE DR S
17400 RivC 92530 896-C1
LAKESIDE AV
- RDL 92373 647-J2
LAKESIDE CT
16700 RivC 92241 727-F1
LAKESIDE DR
7300 RivC 92509 684-H3
19900 LKEL 92530 896-H5
19900 LKEL 92595 896-H5
22900 MORV 92557 687-B5
26000 RivC 92584 898-A3
44000 INDW 92210 818-J7
44200 INDW 92210 848-J1
E LAKESIDE DR
5100 PMSP 92264 787-B5
LAKESIDE PL
2200 COR 92879 743-J3
LAKE SUMMIT DR
10100 MORV 92557 687-D5
35200 RivC 92592 900-G5
LAKE TAMARISK DR
- RivC - 5421-B1
LAKE TERRACE DR
15200 RivC 92530 865-G6
15600 LKEL 92530 865-H6
LAKE TRAIL CIR
30000 LKEL 92530 865-G3
LAKE VALLEY DR
10900 MORV 92557 687-C6
LAKE VICTORIA DR
16700 MORV 92551 747-G4
LAKEVIEW AV
8400 RivC 92509 684-E6
15200 LKEL 92530 866-A3
LAKE VIEW AV
15200 RivC 92530 865-G6
LAKEVIEW AV
28100 RivC 92567 778-H6
30000 RivC 92567 779-A3
LAKEVIEW AV E
30900 RivC 92567 779-B2
LAKEVIEW CIR
- PMSP 92264 787-A5
LAKE VIEW CIR
200 RivC 91752 683-F5
LAKEVIEW CT
- RivC 92223 690-H2
LAKE VIEW DR
- INDO 92203 5410-H3
LAKEVIEW DR
- PMSP 92264 787-A5
900 COR 92880 743-C2
2900 PER 92571 777-H4
10100 RMIR 92270 788-A6
22700 RivC 92595 897-D2
25100 RivC - 814-A5
31700 LKEL 92532 866-J7
31900 RivC 92595 866-J7
40000 SDCo 92028 997-B2
40000 INDO 92203 5410-J7
LAKE VIEW TER
- SDCo 92028 998-G5
LAKEVIEW TER
32100 RivC 92530 866-J7
32300 RivC 92530 896-J1
32400 RivC 92530 897-A1
LAKE VIEW TR
36700 YCPA 92399 650-E5
LAKE VISTA
- PDST 92260 848-D5
LAKE VISTA DR
1100 LKEL 92530 865-H5
40500 RivC 92536 962-J2
40500 RivC 92536 963-A1
LAKE VISTA RD
23800 MORV 92557 687-C5
LAKEWATCH CT
30400 RivC 92584 868-F3
LAKEWOOD DR
500 RIV 92506 716-E4
22400 RivC 92595 897-C3
LAKEWOOD LN
300 PDST 92260 818-F4
LAKOTA ST
13000 MORV 92553 717-B4
LA LADERA RD
27200 RivC 92585 837-H4

LA LADERA RD
27500 RivC 92586 837-H4
29000 RivC 92584 867-H2
LA LITA LN
35800 RivC 92592 960-D4
W LA LOMA AV
100 CLTN 92324 646-C5
100 SBdC 92324 646-C5
LA LOMA LN
700 COR 92879 744-A2
LA LOMA PL
2800 RIV 92503 744-H2
LA LUNA CIR
11300 FONT 92337 645-A2
LA MANCHA CT
11300 FONT 92337 645-A2
LA MANCHA PL
600 HEMT 92543 840-J1
LA MANCHA RD
45100 RivC 92590 976-H3
LAMAR CT
18700 RivC 92508 746-C2
LA MAR RD
25000 LMLN 92354 647-C1
LA MARILLO CIR
1900 COR 92879 743-H2
LA MART DR
5000 RIV 92507 686-D7
LAMAYO AV
25100 MORV 92557 687-G7
LAMB CANYON RD
Rt#-79
- BEAU 92223 389-E7
- BEAU 92583 389-E7
- RivC 92223 389-E7
- RivC 92555 389-E7
- RivC 92555 780-F1
- RivC 92583 389-E7
14200 RivC 92223 720-G7
LAMBERT DR
11300 RivC 92503 744-F3
LAMBERT PL
39900 RivC 92223 691-A4
LAMBETH CT
19400 RIV 92508 746-E3
LAMBETH ST
12700 MORV 92553 717-B3
LAMBOURNE CT
23000 MORV 92557 717-C1
LAMDIN AV
30200 RivC 92584 868-C3
LAMEL
- RivC 92241 390-C6
LA MERCED
1000 PMSP 92264 786-C6
LA MESA CT
2000 HEMT 92545 810-G6
LA MESA DR
13000 DHSP 92240 696-J5
LA MESA LN
23200 MORV 92553 717-C4
LA MESA ST
46100 INDO 92201 5470-C2
LA MESITA CT
1200 RIV 92507 686-C7
LA MINA LN
17000 RivC 92570 806-A5
LA MIRA DR
- HEMT 92545 810-C6
LA MIRADA CIR
- RivC 92562 956-E3
LA MIRADA DR
500 HEMT 92543 810-H6
S LA MIRADA RD
500 PMSP 92264 786-C3
LA MIRADA WY
6200 RIV 92504 715-C1
LA MISION WY
41400 RivC 92544 841-E3
LAMONT DR
24300 MORV 92553 717-E6
LA MORE RD
22500 PER 92570 807-D2
22500 RivC 92570 807-D2
LA MORENA DR
700 HEMT 92545 810-F5
LA MORIA CT
39800 MURR 92562 928-D3
LAMOS PL
12200 MORV 92557 717-F2
LAMP LIGHTER AV
- PER 92571 807-H2
LAMPLIGHTER CT
15100 LKEL 92530 865-G3
LAMPTON ST
1700 NRCO 92860 713-D6
LANA WY
400 BEAU 92223 720-G2
15300 RivC 92508 746-A2
LANAI CT
4600 RIV 92505 714-D6
LANCASHIRE COM
- TEM 92592 959-G7
LANCASHIRE DR
15000 RivC 92530 865-F5
LANCASTER CIR
2800 COR 92882 773-A2
LANCASTER DR
25700 RivC 92586 838-A5
LANCASTER LN
2600 COR 92882 773-A2
13000 MORV 92553 716-J4
LANCASTER RD
- BAN 92220 722-B1

LANCASTER WY
82200 INDO 92201 5470-F4
LANCE DR
- RIV 92507 716-G4
LANCE LN
37700 RivC 92223 690-E4
LANCELOT CT
1400 HEMT 92545 840-E3
6300 RIV 92506 715-H3
76700 PDST 92211 819-C2
LANCER LN
600 COR 92879 743-E6
LANCER WY
81900 INDO 92201 5410-E7
LANCER GATE
44900 INDO 92201 5410-E7
LANCEWOOD DR
11700 MORV 92557 717-E1
LANCIA ST
25800 MORV 92553 717-J5
LANDAU BLVD
27000 CTHC 92234 757-C4
29500 CTHC 92234 787-D2
LANDERVILLE BLVD
33100 RivC 92530 896-B3
LANDFAIR LN
6600 RivC 92509 645-B5
LANDFILL RD
86000 RivC 92236 5411-D6
LANDFORD ST
- YCPA 92399 649-F2
LANDIN LN
19500 RivC 92508 746-E6
LANDMARK CT
3100 RIV 92503 744-H1
LANDMARK GOLF PKWY
- INDO 92203 5410-J5
- INDO 92203 5411-A5
LANDON CT
16300 RivC 92504 745-G4
LANDON LN
- RivC - 5590-G5
LANDS END
21200 MORV 92557 716-H1
LANDSDALE
1000 PMSP 92264 786-H6
LANDSDOWN LN
29500 RivC 92584 898-H1
LANDSDOWN RD
11700 LMLN 92354 647-F3
LANDS END PL
- CYNL 92587 867-D3
LANDS END ST
- MURR 92563 928-H7
LANDS END WY
26300 RivC 92586 868-B2
LANDY LN
34200 RMIR 92270 788-C5
LANE ST
21600 RivC 92570 776-J1
21600 RivC 92570 777-A1
LANE C
600 BLY 92225 5491-D5
LANE NUMBER 1
- RivC 92373 689-C4
LANE NUMBER 2
- RivC 92373 689-C5
LANE NUMBER 3
- RivC 92373 689-C5
LANG CT
6600 RIV 92506 716-B5
LANGDON LN
46000 RivC 92544 902-F6
LANGFORD DR
39400 RivC 92592 931-B3
LANGHOLM WY
- RIV 92508 716-E6
LANGLEY RD
17500 RivC 92241 728-A2
LANGLOIS RD
16000 RivC 92241 697-H7
16000 RivC 92241 727-H1
N LANGSTAFF ST
100 LKEL 92530 866-E4
S LANGSTAFF ST
100 LKEL 92530 866-E5
LANGSTON PL
4300 RIV 92507 685-J5
LANGTRY CIR
12100 MORV 92557 717-H2
LANIER ST
500 HEMT 92543 841-B1
LANK LN
37600 RivC 92539 (934-H2
See Page 904)
LANSFORD ST
10800 RivC 91752 643-H6
LANSING DR
6200 RivC 92509 684-G6
LANTANA AV
12700 YCPA 92399 650-B5
45000 PDST 92260 848-G1
LANTANA DR
- RivC 92883 804-C3
22200 RivC 92570 837-B2
LANTANA ST
5300 RIV 92504 685-B7
LANTANA VW
- PDST 92260 848-D6
LANTERN HILL LN
29000 LKEL 92530 865-F1
LANTERN LIGHT LN
- PER 92571 778-B2
LANTZ LN
12000 MORV 92555 718-B2

RIVERSIDE CO.

STREET
Block City ZIP Pg-Grid

LA PAIX ST
22200 GTER 92313 646-E4
LA PALMA CIR
900 COR 92879 743-H2
LA PALMA DR
78700 LQNT 92253 819-G7
LA PALMA ST
1100 BLY 92225 5491-D4
LA PALMA WY
- MORV 92555 748-C1
LA PALOMA
1800 PMSP 92264 786-F5
LA PALOMA AV
300 SJCT 92582 810-J1
LA PALOMA DR
- CTHC 92234 757-G7
25300 RivC 92548 808-J7
LA PALOMA LN
9900 DHSP 92240 697-A1
LA PALOMA ST
700 HEMT 92545 810-F6
LA PAZ AV
2500 HEMT 92545 810-F5
LA PAZ CIR
800 COR 92879 743-E1
LA PAZ CT
13400 YCPA 92399 650-B6
LA PAZ DR
- PDST 92260 818-G3
LA PAZ LN
3100 PER 92571 777-G4
4600 RIV 92501 685-G2
LA PAZ RD
70800 RMIR 92270 818-A1
LA PAZ ST
44300 TEM 92592 979-A3
LA PAZ WY
- INDO 92201 5470-G2
200 PDST 92260 818-E4
2100 PMSP 92264 786-F6
LA PIEDRA RD
26000 RivC 92584 868-A3
LA PINA DR
29500 RivC 92587 867-E1
LAPIS CT
9600 RivC 92883 804-C3
LA PONDEROSA DR
51300 COAC 92236 5471-E7
LA POSADA
- RMIR 92270 787-H3
LAPP LN
57100 RivC 92539 (935-A1
See Page 904)
LA PRADA WY
27200 RivC 92586 838-C6
LA PRESA LP
43500 TEM 92592 979-B1
LA PRIMAVERA ST
30000 TEM 92592 959-A7
LA PUEBLA ST
15300 MORV 92551 747-H1
LA PUERTA DR
30100 RivC 92548 808-J7
LA PUERTA DEL SOL
2800 PMSP 92262 756-D4
LA QUINTA DR
- HEMT 92545 810-C6
- LQNT 92253 849-H3
500 BAN 92220 721-C4
LA QUINTA WY
700 NRCO 92860 713-G6
LARABY RD
22900 RivC 92567 808-H2
LARADO LN
1900 NRCO 92860 713-C7
1900 NRCO 92860 743-C1
LARAINE DR
400 BEAU 92223 720-H1
LARAITE RD
- RivC 92262 755-F1
LARAMIE CIR
2300 COR 92881 773-F2
LARAMIE RD
2500 RIV 92506 715-H1
LARAMORE LN
2600 RivC 92509 645-B6
LA RAY LN
30700 RivC 92584 899-B3
30700 RivC 92596 899-B3
LA RAYE DR
34300 YCPA 92399 649-H6
LARBROOK DR
78000 RivC 92211 819-F1
LARCH AV
10600 SBdC 92316 645-E2
LARCHMONT DR
11600 RivC 92880 742-B5
LARCHMONT LN
41000 MURR 92562 958-E1
LARCHWOOD DR
3600 COR 92881 773-E5
11300 FONT 92337 644-C2
LARCHWOOD PL
3500 RIV 92506 685-F6
LARCHWOOD ST
31000 RivC 92584 868-E5
LAREDO CIR
33100 RivC 92276 788-E3
LAREDO CT
- LQNT 92253 849-F6
LAREDO DR
200 PMSP 92264 787-C6
LAREDO LN
- PDST 92211 818-J4
LAREDO RD
5600 RIV 92506 715-G2
LAREDO TR
40800 RivC 92223 691-B4
LA REGAL DR
700 HEMT 92545 810-G5
LA REINA CIR
- INDO 92201 5470-C4
LA REINA CT
- LQNT 92253 849-J1
LA REINA WY
1400 PMSP 92264 786-G5
LARES LN
20400 MURR 92563 928-F7
20400 MURR 92563 958-F1
LA RETA WY
9200 RivC 92509 644-D7
LARGO
400 PDST 92211 819-A4
6500 PDST 92211 818-J4
LARGO CIR
1300 PMSP 92262 756-F5
LARGO CT
11600 LMLN 92354 647-E2
LARGO PL
26100 RivC 92544 841-D1
LARIAT DR
17900 CHLS 91709 712-B6
LARIAT LN
12700 RivC 92240 695-J5
39200 RivC 92544 931-E6
LARI MARK ST
20600 RivC 92570 836-J5
LARINO CT
- TEM 92592 979-F1
LARK CT
11600 FONT 92337 644-F3
27400 TEM 92591 958-J2
LARK DR
76700 INDW 92210 849-C2
LARK LN
1500 COR 92882 742-J7
76600 INDW 92210 849-C2
LARK ST
22100 GTER 92313 646-E5
W LARK ST
200 CLTN 92324 646-B5
LARKDALE CIR
- RivC 91752 683-E5
LARKHALL CT
80700 INDO 92201 5410-B7
LARKHAVEN DR
13000 MORV 92553 717-D4
LARKHILL DR
17600 MORV 92551 747-G6
LARKIN CT
2500 PER 92571 777-G5
8600 RIV 92504 715-A4
8700 RIV 92503 715-A4
LARKMEAD CT
27100 MORV 92555 718-B5
LARKSONG ST
26500 RivC 92544 841-E1
LARKSPUR DR
35600 RivC 92595 897-E7
LARKSPUR LN
45000 PDST 92260 848-F2
LARKSPUR RD
4300 RIV 92504 715-A3
4400 RIV 92504 714-J3
LARKSPUR ST
26400 RivC 92544 841-F1
46300 INDO 92201 5470-E2
LA ROCHELLE PL
23900 MURR 92562 928-B1
LA RONDA DR
- RMIR 92270 818-B3
LA ROSA CT
33500 YCPA 92399 649-F4
LARREA ST
44000 INDO 92201 5410-D7
73800 PDST 92260 848-F2
LARRY WY
8300 RIV 92503 714-G3
LARSEY RD
22500 RivC 92567 808-H1
LARSON AV
26700 RivC 92530 835-E4
LARSON DR
100 CTHC 92234 787-E5
LARSON LN
22300 RivC 92241 390-C7
LARSON RD
15000 LKEL 92530 865-G4
58000 RivC 92539 (985-C3
See Page 964)
LA RUE ST
3100 RivC 92509 645-C7
3100 RivC 92509 685-C1
LARVOTTO CT
- RivC 92596 929-E1
LA SALIDA
69500 CTHC 92234 787-G7
LA SALINA PL
25700 MORV 92551 747-J3
LA SALLE CIR
900 COR 92879 743-H2
LA SALLE RD
13000 DHSP 92240 697-B5
63000 RivC 92240 696-B4
LA SALLE ST
5200 RIV 92505 714-C5
E LA SALLE ST
3500 ONT 91761 643-B2
LAS BARANCAS
2500 COR 92882 773-A1
LAS BEGONIAS
36300 CTHC 92234 787-G7
LAS BRISAS RD
24300 MURR 92562 928-C3
LAS BRISAS WY
- INDO 92201 5470-C4
2500 HEMT 92545 810-F5
LAS CAMELIAS
69400 CTHC 92234 787-G7
LAS CASAS CT
11300 FONT 92337 644-J2
LAS CASCADAS CT
47300 INDW 92210 849-A3
LAS COLINAS
- LQNT 92253 849-J2
LAS COLINAS AV
- INDO 92201 5470-C4
1400 BAN 92220 721-B6
LAS COLINAS CIR
1900 COR 92879 743-H2
LAS CRUCES LN
- PDST 92260 818-G3
LAS CRUCES ST
- COAC 92236 5471-B4
LA SERENA WY
29600 TEM 92591 958-H5
31400 TEM 92591 959-C4
32500 RivC 92591 959-E2
LAS FLORAS WY
30100 RivC 92276 758-D7
30100 RivC 92276 788-E2
LAS FLORES AV
2800 RIV 92503 744-J2
86000 COAC 92236 5471-D6
LAS FLORES DR
- PMSP 92264 787-A7
100 HEMT 92544 811-E7
24300 RivC 92587 867-G1
S LAS FLORES LN
44600 PDST 92260 848-F1
LAS FLORES ST
- INDO 92201 5470-C4
LAS FLORES WY
- RivC 92254 5592-F5
LAS GARDENIAS
69300 CTHC 92234 787-G7
LASH ST
16300 LKEL 92530 865-J2
17800 LKEL 92530 866-A3
LAS HACIENDAS ST
28600 TEM 92590 958-G6
LA SHELL ST
29400 LKEL 92530 866-A2
LA SIERRA AV
2000 RivC 92503 744-H4
2500 RIV 92503 744-E1
3500 RIV 92505 744-E1
4000 RIV 92505 714-B3
10800 RivC 92503 774-G4
15400 RivC 92881 774-G4
16500 RivC 92570 774-G4
LA SIERRA DR
75200 PDST 92211 818-J7
LA SIERRA RD
41300 TEM 92591 959-A4
LASKER LN
34800 RivC 92596 899-A5
LASKEY DR
71800 RivC 92241 728-B4
LAS LINDAS WY
5000 RIV 92505 714-B6
LAS LOMAS
100 PDST 92260 818-E4
45500 RivC 92536 982-E3
LAS LUNAS AV
- COAC 92236 5471-A4
LAS LUNAS ST
100 HEMT 92543 810-J7
LAS LUNITAS AV
- COR 92879 743-F3
LAS MERCEDES CIR
2600 COR 92879 744-A2
LAS MERCEDES LN
2400 COR 92879 743-J2
2400 COR 92879 744-A2
LAS NARANJAS RD
- RivC 92548 809-F7
- RivC 92548 839-F1
LA SOMBRA CT
30600 TEM 92591 959-B2
LAS PALMAS AV
44600 PDST 92260 848-F1
LAS PALMAS CT
2900 RIV 92506 715-G1
22200 RivC 92583 781-F7
LAS PALMAS DR
15800 DHSP 92240 696-J7
15900 DHSP 92240 726-J1
81800 INDO 92201 5470-E2
LAS PALMAS ST
52200 COAC 92236 5471-C7
52200 COAC 92236 5531-C1
LAS PALMERAS DR
24900 RivC 92590 977-J2
LAS PALOMAS DR
25200 MORV 92557 717-G2
LAS PAMPAS WY
3500 PMSP 92264 786-J4
LAS PERAS LN
32500 RivC 92548 809-E6
LAS POSAS DR
15600 MORV 92551 747-J2
LAS POSAS RD
2000 RivC 92882 742-H6
LAS ROCAS
56100 RivC - 878-B6
LAS ROSAS AV
15200 MORV 92551 747-J1
LAS ROSAS DR
1000 SJCT 92583 811-D3
LASSA WY
500 PER 92571 777-H6
LASSALETTE CT
2300 RivC 92503 744-G3
LASSELLE ST
11000 MORV 92555 687-J7
11000 MORV 92557 687-J7
11400 MORV 92555 717-J2
11400 MORV 92557 717-J1
12700 MORV 92553 717-J4
15000 MORV 92555 747-J2
15000 MORV 92551 717-J7
15000 MORV 92551 747-J6
LASSEN CT
6500 RIV 92506 715-F1
45200 INDO 92201 5470-E1
LASSEN DR
- CYNL 92587 867-D2
700 COR 92879 743-H3
2100 SJCT 92583 811-E4
LASSEN WY
500 HEMT 92543 840-H1
LAS SERENAS WY
- RivC 92254 5592-F5
LASSITER RD
6600 RivC 92509 645-B6
LASSO CIR
27000 RivC 92883 835-B4
LASSO CT
6100 RivC 92509 684-C5
LASSO LN
2500 NRCO 92860 713-B6
LASSO WY
- RivC 92883 835-D5
LA STRADA
- LKEL 92532 866-J3
- LKEL 92532 867-A3
LAS TUNAS DR
4700 RIV 92504 715-D1
LAS TUNAS WY
68500 CTHC 92234 817-E2
LA SUBIDA CT
1100 RIV 92507 686-C7
LAS UVAS DR
34100 RivC 92591 929-J6
34400 RivC 92591 930-A7
LAS VEGAS RD
200 PMSP 92262 756-C3
LAS VENTANAS WY
- RIV 92508 716-C7
LAS VIOLETTAS CT
42800 TEM 92592 959-A7
LAS VISTAS DR
44000 LQNT 92253 819-G7
LAS VISTAS RD
900 SDCo 92028 998-C7
LATEEN DR
12700 MORV 92553 717-D3
LA TERRAZA CIR
1000 COR 92879 743-H2
LA TERRAZA RD
39100 RivC 92592 931-A3
E LATHAM AV
100 HEMT 92543 811-B7
W LATHAM AV
100 HEMT 92543 811-A7
300 HEMT 92543 810-H7
1600 HEMT 92545 810-G7
LATHAM ST
4100 RIV 92501 685-G1
LA TIERRA CIR
17100 FONT 92337 645-A2
LA TIERRA ST
600 COR 92879 743-E5
LATIGO CIR
79300 LQNT 92253 819-H7
LATIGO LN
900 COR 92882 773-B2
LATIMER LN
10800 RIV 92503 744-G3
LATISHA LN
42800 PDST 92211 819-E6
LATLEY CIR
44000 RivC 92544 (812-A6
See Page 782)
LATOUR LN
10400 RivC 91752 644-A4
10400 RivC 91752 643-J4
LA TREMOLINA CIR
- COR 92879 743-F2
LA TREMOLINA LN
- COR 92879 743-F2
LATROBE LN
- LQNT 92253 879-G2
LATTA AV
29800 LKEL 92530 866-B3
LAUDER CT
5500 RIV 92507 716-G1
LAUO RD
22100 RivC 92570 807-C1
LAURA DR
33100 RivC 92276 788-F3
LAURA LN
3400 RIV 92506 715-F1
44300 RivC 92536 983-F2
LAURA WY
34300 RMIR 92270 787-G5
LAURA LAKE CT
- LKEL 92530 865-G2
LAURA LAKE DR
300 LKEL 92530 865-G2
LAUREEN CT
11300 FONT 92337 644-F2
LAUREL AV
1200 RIV 92507 686-A2
1500 RDL 92373 647-J3
10500 SBdC 92316 645-C2
11500 LMLN 92354 647-F2
LAUREL CIR
400 PMSP 92262 756-E4
LAUREL CT
27400 MORV 92555 748-C2
30300 RivC 92563 929-B7
LAUREL DR
400 RivC 91752 683-E4
3000 RivC 92509 645-C7
3100 RivC 92509 685-C1
14000 RivC 92503 745-C4
25100 RivC - (813-J5
See Page 782)
LAUREL LN
200 HEMT 92544 811-B7
15000 LKEL 92530 865-H3
LAUREL ST
22300 RivC 92570 806-A1
44100 INDO 92201 5410-D7
LAUREL TR
52300 RivC - (813-J5
See Page 782)
LAURELBROOK DR
6700 RIV 92506 716-D4
LAUREL CANYON CIR
7200 COR 92879 743-H7
LAUREL CANYON WY
- COR 92879 743-H7
- COR 92879 773-H1
- COR 92881 773-H1
LAUREL CREEK DR
- TEM 92591 959-A5
LAUREL CREST DR
55400 RivC 92282 724-E1
LAUREL GATE
81500 INDO 92201 5410-D7
LAUREL LEAF DR
39100 MURR 92563 928-F4
LAURELLEAF PL
1000 COR 92879 743-J6
LAUREL PARK CIR
- RivC 92509 684-F2
LAURELTON LN
6600 CHLS 91709 712-B5
S LAURELTREE DR
2800 ONT 91761 643-B6
LAUREL VALLEY
55500 LQNT 92253 5530-C4
LAUREL VALLEY AV
6200 BAN 92220 721-C5
LAUREL VALLEY CIR
- TEM 92591 959-D4
LAURELWOOD AV
- RivC 92880 713-A2
S LAURELWOOD AV
1500 CLTN 92324 646-H2
LAURELWOOD CIR
1500 COR 92882 742-G6
LAURELWOOD CT
200 LKEL 92530 865-H2
LAURELWOOD DR
5000 RIV 92505 714-C6
LAURELWOOD LN
200 LKEL 92530 865-H2
LAURELWOOD PL
25600 MORV 92557 717-H1
LAUREN CT
200 LKEL 92530 865-H2
LAUREN LN
6800 RivC 92509 645-B4
LAURENA ST
31100 RivC 92567 779-B4
LAURENCE DR
- RivC 92274 5530-G3
LAURENE LN
12700 RivC 92555 719-C3
LAURENRAE ST
19100 RIV 92508 746-D3
LAURESA LN
500 HEMT 92544 811-G6
LAURIANO DR
44500 TEM 92592 979-G2
LAURIE CT
- LQNT 92253 849-H1
LAURIE DR
7300 RIV 92506 715-G6
LAURIE LN
41700 RivC 92544 841-F3
LAURIE ST
25700 MORV 92557 717-H1
LAURIE ANN LN
43100 RivC 92536 981-J4
LAURSEN ST
100 HEMT 92543 811-B7
LAURY LN
12600 MORV 92553 717-H3
LAUSANNE
- RivC - (907-F3
See Page 906)
LAUSANNE ST
28700 LKEL 92530 865-G3
LAVA WY
22800 RivC 92567 808-G2
LA VAUGHN CIR
- COR 92881 773-F3
LA VELLA RD
23500 RivC 92590 977-F2
LAVENDER CIR
- RivC 92211 819-G2
25400 MURR 92563 928-E5
LAVENDER LN
14700 MORV 92553 717-E7
LAVENDER ST
- RivC 92585 838-C3
6300 RivC 92880 683-D6
LAVENDER WY
43500 PDST 92260 818-H6
LA VENTANA CIR
2500 COR 92879 744-A2
LA VENTANA DR
2600 COR 92879 744-A2
LA VENTANA LN
31800 RivC 92584 869-A7
LA VENTANA RD
18600 RivC 92562 956-D3
28500 RivC 92584 839-A7
29000 RivC 92584 869-A1
LAVERDA LN
15100 MORV 92551 747-G1
LA VERNE DR
11300 RIV 92505 714-B6
LA VERNE WY
1600 PMSP 92264 786-F6
LA VESU RD
17100 FONT 92337 645-A2
LA VIDA CT
17000 FONT 92337 644-J3
17000 FONT 92337 645-A3
LA VIDA DR
15800 RivC 92262 725-E7
LA VILLA CIR
21600 RivC 92590 957-B7
LA VINA CT
500 HEMT 92544 811-C6
LA VISTA AV
2800 COR 92879 744-A2
LA VISTA CT
21600 RivC 92570 775-D7
21600 RivC 92570 805-D1
67600 CTHC 92234 757-C6
LA VISTA PL
39400 RivC 92592 931-B6
LAWGHLIN RD
33000 RivC 92543 871-B7
33000 RivC 92543 901-B1
LAWLESS RD
23000 MORV 92557 687-C4
LAWNDALE AV
5000 RIV 92504 715-C1
LAWRENCE AV
- BLY 92225 5491-F5
LAWRENCE CIR
3700 PMSP 92262 756-C3
LAWRENCE CT
26800 RivC 92545 840-A3
LAWRENCE DR
65500 DHSP 92240 696-G4
LAWRENCE ST
2100 PMSP 92264 787-D5
LAWRENCE WY
30100 LKEL 92530 866-B4
LAWRENCE UNION DR
- MURR 92563 928-H6
LAWS RD
11700 RivC 92220 692-G7
11800 RivC 92220 722-G1
LAWSON CIR
41800 RivC 92592 960-B4
LAWSON DR
23700 RivC 92883 804-D5
LAWSON RD
23200 RivC 92883 804-C5
LAWSON WY
6000 RIV 92506 685-F7
LAWTON AV
24300 LMLN 92354 647-B2
LAWTON BLVD
18300 RivC 92570 806-C5
LAWTON CT
11400 LMLN 92354 647-B2
26000 RivC 92544 811-C7
26000 RivC 92544 841-C1
LAWTON WY
24800 LMLN 92354 647-B2
LAXFORD
- SJCT 92583 781-A7
LAXFORD RD
600 SJCT 92583 781-A7
LAYTON CT
3200 RIV 92503 744-E3
LAYTON ST
19800 RivC 92881 773-H5
LAZARE ST
30500 TEM 92592 959-A6
LAZARUS LN
45500 RivC 92536 962-E4
LAZY B DR
- PDST 92260 848-C6
LAZY BROOK DR
13300 RivC 92883 835-B4
LAZY CANYON
22900 RivC 92241 728-F7
LAZY C RANCH RD
- RivC 92262 755-F1
22600 RivC 92262 725-F7
LAZY CREEK RD
25800 RivC 92584 868-A2
26000 RivC 92586 868-A2
LAZY LAGOON LN
15700 RivC 92504 745-G7
LAZY LAKE DR
- LQNT 92253 849-F4
LE ST
43100 RivC 92539 (965-B6
See Page 964)
LEAFHILL PL
4900 RIV 92507 686-B7
LEAF STOCK TR
22500 RivC 92595 897-D3
LEAFWOOD CT
200 RIV 92506 716-D4
LEAFWOOD DR
6400 RivC 92509 645-B6
13400 RivC 92883 835-C5
24300 MURR 92562 928-C3
26200 MORV 92555 717-J2
LEAFWOOD RD
12200 RivC 92503 744-H6
LEAFY LN
- RivC - (907-C2
See Page 906)
LEAH LN
25600 RivC 92586 837-J5
35900 YCPA 92399 650-C6
LEAHY DR
12100 MORV 92557 717-F2
LEANING ROCK CT
48800 RivC 92536 963-C2
LEANN CT
25200 MORV 92553 717-G3
LEANOR ST
26500 RivC 92586 838-B4
LEATHERLEAF RD
11500 FONT 92337 644-F3
LEATHERS LN
39100 RivC 92544 (932-J6
See Page 902)
LEATHERWOOD CT
2700 RIV 92504 715-C6
LE BLAN WY
6500 RIV 92506 716-B4
LECIL ST
2900 RIV 92507 686-B3
LE CONTE DR
900 RIV 92507 686-B7
LEDFORD
74100 RivC 92241 728-F7
LEDO CIR
1900 PMSP 92264 786-F5
LEE LN
- MURR 92584 898-G6
- RivC 92563 898-G6
- RivC 92584 898-G6
28500 MURR 92563 898-G6
52900 COAC 92236 5531-C1
LEE RD
20200 RivC 92570 776-J5
LEE ST
200 BLY 92225 5491-E5
12800 MORV 92553 717-F3
LEE TR
47600 RivC 92544 (932-J5
See Page 902)
47900 RivC 92544 (933-A5
See Page 902)
LEEAN DR
500 HEMT 92544 811-B6
LEEANNE LN
29100 RivC 92584 868-H6
LEEDS ST
- RivC 92596 929-C1
2100 RIV 92506 716-A1
LEENA WY
32000 TEM 92592 979-F1
LEESON LN
1600 COR 92879 743-H6
1600 RivC 92879 743-H6
LEESON WY
3900 RivC 92879 743-J5
LEEWARD DR
- RivC 92254 (5654-G6
See Page 5594)
LEEWARD WY
33100 LKEL 92530 865-J7
LEFF RD
48100 RivC 92536 983-A1
LEGACY CT
26200 RivC 92544 841-J1
LEGACY WY
33700 RMIR 92270 787-J4
LE GAYE ST
15000 LKEL 92530 865-H3
LEGEND LN
27200 RivC 92544 841-C3
LEGENDARY DR
15200 MORV 92555 718-C7
15200 MORV 92555 748-C1
LEGENDS WY
- LQNT 92253 5530-D6
LEGG DR
17500 RivC 92570 776-B4
LEGHORN ST
25500 RivC 92544 (812-B6
See Page 782)
LEGION WY
2900 RIV 92501 685-F2
LE GRAND LN
11000 MORV 92557 687-D6
LE GRANDE DR
2100 HEMT 92544 811-C6
LE GRANDE RD
30800 RivC 92596 869-C4
LE HARVE AV
500 LKEL 92530 865-H4
LE HAVRE LN
1900 SJCT 92583 811-F3
LEHIGH CIR
3400 COR 92881 773-F4
LEHIGH CT
- RMIR 92270 818-B3
LEHIGH LN
11400 RivC 92507 686-F7
11400 RivC 92507 716-F1
LEHR DR
16800 LKEL 92530 866-A3
28300 LKEL 92530 865-J3
LEI DR
200 PMSP 92264 786-E5
LEIANA CT
- RivC 92503 744-D5
LEICESTER ST
24500 RivC 92595 897-G1
24800 RivC 92584 897-G1
LEIF ERICSON DR
12000 MORV 92557 717-H1
LEIGH LN
31600 TEM 92591 959-D2
LEIGH ST
3800 RivC 92509 685-C2
LEILA DR
25900 RivC 92548 839-D1
LEISURE LN
71900 RMIR 92270 818-B5
LEISURE WY
11500 MORV 92557 687-D7
11500 MORV 92557 717-E1
W LEISURE WY
600 PMSP 92262 756-C7
LEITH AV
64900 RivC 92240 696-F1
64900 DHSP 92240 696-F1
LEITH WY
12900 YCPA 92399 650-A5
LELA MAY AV
40600 RivC 92544 841-C1
LELAND AV
6800 RIV 92506 715-F3
LEMA CT
64400 RivC 92240 696-E1
LEMAIRE DR
- RivC 92590 998-G2
LE MANS DR
26100 MORV 92555 717-J3
LEMAY DR
21100 RivC 92518 746-H4
LE MAY WY
500 HEMT 92543 840-J1
LEMBOLDT DR
42100 RivC 92536 961-G3
LEMM DR
31100 RivC 92544 871-E4
LEMON AV
- FONT 92337 644-H2
- PER 92571 777-G6
23700 RivC 92570 777-E6
27000 RivC 92571 778-C6
LEMON ST
1200 COR 92879 743-E6
2900 RIV 92501 685-H3
14900 RivC 92230 723-H6
21000 RivC 92595 897-A3
41300 MURR 92562 927-J5
41300 MURR 92562 928-A4
LEMON GROVE AV
6500 RivC 92509 685-A2
LEMONGROVE AV
82000 INDO 92201 5410-E6
LEMON GROVE LN
1300 COR 92881 773-F5
LEMON GUM LN
1100 HEMT 92545 840-G3
LEMON HEIGHTS RD
24500 RivC 92570 805-C7
LEMON HILLS DR
38600 RivC 92592 930-E5
LEMON VALLEY AV
- RivC 92880 713-A1
LEMONWOOD CIR
10900 MORV 92557 687-E6
LEMONWOOD CT
11600 FONT 92337 644-B3
LEMONWOOD DR
- RivC 92883 804-B3
27900 RivC 92584 868-E2
LENA ST
23200 MORV 92553 717-C4
LENBROOK CIR
8400 RivC 92509 684-F2
LENEL CT
16000 RivC 92504 745-H3
LENISHA LN
- RIV 92508 746-E2
LENITA CIR
2100 COR 92882 743-A7
2100 COR 92882 773-A1
LENNON PL
74700 PDST 92260 818-H5
LENNOX ST
11600 YCPA 92399 650-B2
LENOX AV
7100 RIV 92504 715-F5
7100 RIV 92506 715-F5
LENOX LN
24200 MURR 92562 927-H5
LENWOOD RD
21900 RivC 92570 837-B2
LENZEN ST
27000 MORV 92555 718-B5
LEO CIR
2700 RIV 92503 744-H2
LEO RD
42000 RivC 92536 962-E5
LEO ST
4500 RivC 92509 684-F1
LEON CT
5100 RIV 92505 714-B6
LEON RD
25000 RivC 92548 809-B7
25700 RivC 92548 839-B2
26400 RivC 92585 839-B2
28000 RivC 92596 839-B6
28900 RivC 92596 869-B2
32500 RivC 92596 899-B3
36000 RivC 92596 929-C3
36500 RivC 92563 929-C3
39000 TEM 92591 929-C6
LEON WY
- RMIR 92270 818-D5
LEONA CT
- RivC 92592 979-J2
LEONA DR
28200 RivC 92532 836-D6
LEONARD CT
64900 RivC 92240 696-E1
LEONARD LN
900 SJCT 92582 780-J7
LEONARD RD
- OrCo - 772-C5
- OrCo 92808 772-C5
N LEONARD RD
1800 PMSP 92262 756-C5
LEONARD WY
- COR 92883 773-H7
LEONARDO DR
66500 DHSP 92240 696-G4
LEOPARD LN
900 PER 92571 807-J1
LEOPARD ST
39300 RivC 92211 819-E2
LEOPOLDVILLE CT
38000 PDST 92211 819-A2
LEOTA CT
13400 MORV 92553 717-F4
LEOTA LN
10800 RIV 92503 744-G3
LEPRECHAUN LN
44200 RivC 92536 983-E1
LEROY RD
- RivC 92883 804-C1
LEROY WY
82500 INDO 92201 5410-F7
LES RD
33500 RivC 92276 788-F4
LESCOE CT
5300 RIV 92506 716-A1
LESLIE AV
74500 PDST 92260 818-H6
N LESLIE CIR
200 PMSP 92262 786-H2
LESLIE CT
100 BAN 92220 721-D3
LESLIE DR
1000 HEMT 92543 841-B1
LESLIE ST
32100 RivC 92595 927-C2
LESSER LN
24700 PER 92587 837-G5
24700 RivC 92587 837-G5
LESSIE LN
6600 RIV 92503 714-F2
LESTER AV
4100 COR 92881 773-F6
LESTER CIR
26100 RivC 92883 835-C3
LESTER ST
3900 RIV 92504 715-C3
LETA DR
37700 CALI 92320 690-D1
LETTY LN
30900 RivC 92596 839-B6
LEUCADIA CIR
- COR 92879 743-F3
LEUCADIA LN
10000 RIV 92503 714-E1
LEVANDE PL
30000 TEM 92592 959-A6
LEVI CT
32800 TEM 92592 979-G3
42000 RivC 92544 841-F1
LEW ALLEN CIR
16600 RivC 92518 746-H4
LEWAY DR
- RIV 92508 716-D7
LEWIN PL
11000 RivC 92883 804-G4
LEWIS AV
5400 RIV 92503 714-E4
LEWIS CT
100 COR 92882 743-B4
38900 RivC 92223 690-G4
LEWIS ST
14200 BLY 92225 5551-G1
21000 RivC 92595 897-A2
N LEWIS ST
100 LKEL 92530 866-D4
S LEWIS ST
100 LKEL 92530 866-D5
LEWISIA AV
11700 MORV 92557 716-H1
LEWIS VALLEY RD
44600 RivC 92544 931-J6
44600 RivC 92544 (932-C1
See Page 902)
LEXINGTON AV
82700 INDO 92201 5470-G2
LEXINGTON CT
27900 RivC 92586 838-A5
42100 RivC 92544 841-F3
LEXINGTON DR
1800 COR 92880 713-A7
LEXINGTON PL
2700 RIV 92506 715-H3
LEXINGTON ST
700 HEMT 92545 840-F2
LEYBURN PL
6300 RivC 92509 685-A2
LEYENDA DR
600 COR 92879 743-G3
LEYTE AV
84000 RivC 92201 5470-J3
LIAN DR
35100 RivC 92544 901-J5
LIAN LN
34400 RivC 92567 779-H7
LIANA CT
11900 YCPA 92399 649-B3
LIATRIS LN
16700 MORV 92551 747-H4
LIBBY DR
700 RIV 92507 686-D3
LIBERIA PL
80500 INDO 92201 5410-B6
LIBERTY AV
- LQNT 92253 5410-A7
1700 COR 92881 773-G4
3000 RivC 92881 773-J4
8000 COR 92881 774-A4
8000 RivC 92881 774-A4
LIBERTY CT
2500 SBDO 92408 646-H1
LIBERTY DR
- COR 92881 773-G4
26200 RivC 92544 841-F1
LIBERTY LN
1100 NRCO 92860 713-F4
18800 RivC 92532 836-E7
LIBERTY RD
33700 YCPA 92399 649-G5
36000 MURR 92563 898-J7
36000 RivC 92563 898-J7
36100 MURR 92563 928-J1
36300 MURR 92563 929-A1
LIBNAN ST
51500 COAC 92236 5471-B7
LIBRA DR
2700 RIV 92503 744-H2
LIBRARY ST
100 LKEL 92530 866-E5
LICHEN WY
49700 RivC 92536 983-E1
LICON RD
38000 RivC 92539 (934-G3
See Page 904)
LIDO AV
81500 INDO 92201 5470-D1
LIDO CT
- RivC - (907-E3
See Page 906)
9500 RivC 92240 696-E1
LIDO DR
4200 RIV 92503 714-J4
LIDO LN
800 BLY 92225 5551-F1
LIEFER RD
39000 TEM 92591 929-C7
39400 TEM 92591 959-C1
LIEGE DR
25000 RivC 92544 (812-A5
See Page 782)
LIGA
79200 LQNT 92253 849-J7
79700 LQNT 92253 5470-A7
LIGHTFOOT DR
26800 RivC 92883 835-B4
LIGHTHOUSE DR
- CYNL 92587 867-C3
15100 LKEL 92530 865-J7
15100 RivC 92530 865-J7
LIGHTHOUSE RD
68700 RivC 92254 (5654-D2
See Page 5594)
LIGHTNING RD
59300 RivC 92539 (985-E2
See Page 964)
LIGHTNING FLASH WY
- PER 92571 778-B2
LILA ST
3400 RIV 92504 715-C4
LILAC AV
11200 SBdC 92316 645-G2
S LILAC AV
2200 RLTO 92316 645-G1
2700 SBdC 92316 645-G1
LILAC CIR
- INDW 92210 848-H1
LILAC CT
6400 RivC 92880 683-D6
16800 RivC 92503 744-H5
46700 INDO 92201 5470-F2
LILAC DR
25900 RivC - 814-E6
36200 YCPA 92399 650-D6
LILAC LN
9100 RivC 92223 691-A2
35500 YCPA 92399 650-B6
42200 RivC 92539 (965-G3
See Page 964)

STREET
Block City ZIP Pg-Grid

LILAC ST
- FONT 92337 645-A1
900 HEMT 92545 840-H2
1600 COR 92882 743-B7
LILAC RIDGE DR
1100 PER 92571 778-A2
LILIAN AV
32900 RivC 92530 896-C2
LILIUM CT
21300 MORV 92557 716-H1
LILLIAN LN
100 CTHC 92234 787-F5
21100 RivC 92590 977-C2
LILLIAN ST
3500 RIV 92504 715-C3
LILLIANA DR
100 PMSP 92264 786-D6
LILLIE CIR
39000 CTHC 92234 817-D3
LILY AV
41300 MURR 92562 927-J4
LILY CT
2300 COR 92879 744-F5
25600 MORV 92557 687-H7
81400 INDO 92201 5410-D6
LILY ST
600 PMSP 92262 756-E4
LILY WY
800 HEMT 92545 810-H5
25000 RivC - 814-F4
LIMA
78800 LQNT 92253 849-H7
LIMA HALL RD
41000 RivC 92201 819-G5
LIMBAUGH LN
14000 RivC 92530 895-D3
LIME RD
55300 RivC 92282 694-D7
LIME ST
1200 COR 92879 743-E6
2600 RIV 92501 685-J3
15000 RivC 92230 723-H6
21500 RivC 92595 897-A2
33000 RivC 92530 865-H6
LIMECREST DR
9000 RIV 92508 746-E3
LIMEKLIN DR
37200 YCPA 92399 650-F5
LIMELITE WY
800 COR 92880 743-C3
LIME ORCHARD LN
11400 FONT 92337 644-G3
LIMEROCK AV
4700 HEMT 92544 811-F6
LIMESTONE DR
8400 RIV 92504 715-C6
LIMESTONE ST
83000 INDO 92201 5470-H3
LIMITED ST
200 LKEL 92530 866-D5
W LIMITED ST
100 LKEL 92530 866-E5
LIMOGES ST
- RivC 92596 929-E2
LIMONITE AV
5800 RivC 92509 685-A3
6600 RivC 92509 684-B5
9600 RivC 91752 684-B5
10200 RivC 91752 683-E5
LIMONITE CT
8600 RivC 92509 684-E5
LIMONITE ST
1300 HEMT 92543 840-H3
LIMONITE FRONTAGE RD
6100 RivC 92509 685-A4
LINALOU RANCH RD
44800 TEM 92592 979-F3
LINARES AV
7200 RivC 92509 684-J5
LINCOLN AV
- CTHC 92234 787-D7
1000 COR 92882 773-B3
5900 RIV 92506 715-H2
7000 RIV 92504 715-E4
8900 RIV 92503 715-B7
9500 RIV 92503 745-A1
9600 RIV 92503 744-J1
23600 MURR 92562 927-J2
24400 MURR 92562 928-B4
25200 RivC 92544 (812-B6
See Page 782)
28200 RivC 92596 839-F6
42700 HEMT 92544 811-G6
43000 RivC 92544 811-G6
E LINCOLN AV
4000 HEMT 92544 811-F6
N LINCOLN AV
100 COR 92882 743-B3
400 COR 92880 743-B3
S LINCOLN AV
100 COR 92882 743-B6
2000 COR 92882 773-B2
LINCOLN DR
- INDO 92201 5470-F5
33800 YCPA 92399 649-G3
LINCOLN PL
40900 RivC 92223 691-B5
41200 BAN 92220 691-C5
41200 RivC 92220 691-C5
LINCOLN PL E
- RMIR 92270 787-H7
LINCOLN PL W
- RMIR 92270 787-H7

LINCOLN ST
- RivC - (5652-F7
See Page 5592)
- RivC 92254 (5652-F3
See Page 5592)
600 BAN 92220 722-A4
1300 BAN 92220 721-F4
3400 RivC 92503 744-B4
15100 LKEL 92530 865-E1
39400 RivC 92223 690-J5
39600 RivC 92223 691-A5
61900 RivC 92274 5592-F2
63300 RivC 92254 5592-F5
78000 RivC 92274 5712-F7
81000 RivC 92274 (5772-F5
See Page 5712)
LINCOLN ST Rt#-195
- RivC 92254 5592-F7
LINCOLN ST Rt#-243
1000 BAN 92220 722-B4
E LINCOLN ST
800 BAN 92220 722-B4
S LINCOLN ST
1100 CLTN 92324 646-D1
LINCOLN DOWNS LN
100 RMIR 92270 817-G2
LINCRONA AV
1000 COR 92882 743-B6
LIND TER
1700 COR 92882 742-J7
LINDA AV
- COAC 92236 5471-A6
LINDA CIR
73300 RivC 92260 818-E2
W LINDA CT
100 CLTN 92324 646-C4
LINDA LN
200 HEMT 92544 811-C7
500 BLY 92225 5491-F5
35600 YCPA 92399 650-B2
LINDA WY
34000 CTHC 92234 787-F5
53100 RivC 92536 964-B7
LINDA FLORA
46500 INDO 92201 5470-G2
LINDA LADERA
31900 YCPA 92399 649-B3
LINDA LEE DR
31500 RivC 92584 868-D6
LINDA LOU LN
3000 RIV 92503 744-J1
LINDA REED RD
29200 RivC 92596 869-C1
LINDA ROSEA RD
33000 RivC 92592 959-J6
34000 RivC 92592 960-C5
LINDA VIA RD
42600 RivC 92592 960-A6
LINDA VISTA AV
18700 RivC 92567 749-D7
18700 RivC 92567 779-D1
LINDA VISTA CT
41300 RivC 92544 841-D2
LINDA VISTA DR
500 PMSP 92262 786-C3
800 BAN 92220 722-B2
70000 RivC - (907-H4
See Page 906)
LINDA VISTA LN
33600 RivC 92595 897-B3
LINDA VISTA RD
1200 PMSP 92262 756-F7
LINDA VISTA ST
1500 RDL 92373 647-J3
LINDBERGH CIR
30200 LKEL 92530 866-C4
LINDBERGH DR
7900 RIV 92508 716-D7
LINDBURG PL
- RivC 92571 778-C7
LINDELL RD
18000 RivC 92532 806-B7
18000 RivC 92570 806-C7
25100 RivC 92532 836-B1
LINDEN AV
2500 HEMT 92545 840-G2
10700 SBdC 92316 645-D3
LINDEN CIR
600 COR 92879 743-H3
S LINDEN DR
2200 PMSP 92264 787-A5
LINDEN ST
100 RIV 92507 686-A4
11700 SBdC 92316 645-D3
12100 YCPA 92399 649-G3
LINDENBERGER RD
28000 RivC 92585 838-H6
28600 RivC 92584 838-H7
29100 RivC 92584 868-H2
32500 RivC 92584 898-H2
LINDENHURST ST
- RIV 92508 746-E1
LINDER WY
- HEMT 92545 810-F4
LINDERA CT
35900 RMIR 92270 787-G6
LINDERMAN RD
43000 RivC 92544 901-J7
43000 RivC 92544 902-A7
LINDINA DR
15800 RivC 92504 745-G5
LINDLEY LN
11300 MORV 92555 688-C7
LINDO CIR
1300 PMSP 92262 756-F5

LINDRICK CT
22600 MURR 92562 927-D2
LINDSAY ST
3500 RivC 92509 644-B6
4100 RivC 92509 684-B1
N LINDSAY ST
100 LKEL 92530 866-E5
S LINDSAY ST
100 LKEL 92530 866-D5
LINDSEY CT
1300 SJCT 92583 811-D3
LINDSEY DR
300 PMSP 92262 756-E4
LINDSEY LN
- COR 92882 772-J2
LINDY CT
- RivC 92532 836-E6
LINE ST
300 LKEL 92530 866-E6
LINEBACKER RD
14500 RivC 92518 716-G7
LINE CANYON LN
73800 RivC 92260 818-F2
LINGAYAN AV
84000 RivC 92201 5470-J3
84100 RivC 92201 5471-A3
LINGER LN
54000 RivC - 844-C1
LINGO LN
44300 PDST 92260 818-G7
LINKS AV
4900 BAN 92220 721-E4
LINKS CT
31500 TEM 92591 959-B5
LINKS DR
300 PDST 92211 818-J1
39000 RivC 92211 819-F1
LIN MAR CT
73400 RivC 92241 728-E3
LINN DR
4800 RIV 92505 714-B7
LINN ST
12800 YCPA 92399 650-B5
LINNEA CT
24200 MORV 92553 717-E6
LINNEL LN
27600 MURR 92562 898-D6
LINNET DR
3500 LKEL 92530 865-J4
14100 MORV 92553 717-F6
LINNITT CIR
39500 TEM 92591 959-A2
LINNY CT
22900 RivC 92595 867-D7
LINSDAY CIR
- RivC 92592 960-A6
LINWOOD PL
3700 RIV 92506 685-E6
LINWOOD TER
31200 YCPA 92399 649-A4
LIOLIOS DR
42200 PDST 92211 819-C6
LIOLIOS WY
24400 MORV 92551 747-F2
LIONHEAD AV
4200 RIV 92503 714-H5
LION PEAK RD
36600 RivC - (905-G6
See Page 904)
LIONS LAIR CT
18300 RivC 92562 976-E2
LIPARI DR
15600 MORV 92551 747-F2
LIPP RD
38000 RivC 92539 (935-B3
See Page 904)
LIPPERT LN
21900 RivC 92567 779-B7
LIPPITT LN
16000 RivC 92258 726-E2
LIPPIZAN DR
7300 RivC 92509 684-H3
LISA CIR
33500 RivC 92276 788-F4
LISA LN
13400 RivC 92555 719-B4
18700 RivC 92570 777-C1
26100 RivC 92544 841-F1
LISA RD
- RivC 92592 959-H6
LISA MARIE CIR
25200 RivC 92590 957-J5
25200 RivC 92590 958-A5
LISBON DR
3600 RIV 92503 714-H7
LISBON ST
500 PER 92571 777-H5
LISBON WY
43700 PDST 92211 819-E6
LISHA DR
500 HEMT 92543 840-J1
LISMORE CT
900 HEMT 92543 810-J5
LISTON CT
26800 RivC 92530 835-D4
LISTON LN
58000 RivC 92539 (935-C6
See Page 904)
LITCH LN
18000 RivC 92504 745-G7
LITCHFIELD CT
- BAN 92220 721-B6
LITCHFIELD DR
2700 RIV 92503 744-J1

LITTLE CT
16000 RivC 92508 746-B3
64900 RivC 92240 696-E1
LITTLE WY
38500 RivC 92260 818-E2
LITTLE BEND TR
73400 PDST 92260 848-F4
LITTLE BIGHORN CIR
49800 RivC 92260 848-B6
LITTLE BROOK TR
6400 RivC 92509 684-H5
LITTLE CANYON RD
39500 RivC 92539 (935-H6
See Page 904)
LITTLE CREEK
- CYNL 92587 867-E2
LITTLE DIPPER ST
11000 RivC 91752 683-H5
LITTLE EAGLE CT
- LQNT 92253 849-F4
LITTLE FOX CT
- RivC 92584 868-G1
LITTLE HARBOR DR
- CYNL 92587 867-F3
LITTLE JOHN LN
81700 INDO 92201 5410-D7
LITTLEJOHN WY
33100 RivC 92530 865-F6
LITTLE JULIES WY
11200 RivC 92507 686-F7
13000 RivC 92507 716-F1
LITTLE LAKE RD
42100 RivC 92544 841-F2
LITTLE MORONGO RD
9000 DHSP 92240 656-F7
9000 DHSP 92240 696-F3
12200 RivC 92240 696-F7
15000 RivC 92240 726-F2
15000 RivC 92258 726-F2
LITTLE MOUNTAIN RD
23100 RivC 92567 809-F3
LITTLE PONY DR
- CYNL 92587 867-B3
LITTLER AV
1400 BAN 92220 721-D5
LITTLER CT
13600 MORV 92553 717-B5
LITTLER LN
- COR 92883 773-H7
LITTLE RANCH RD
45800 TEM 92592 979-D4
LITTLE REB PL
33000 RivC 92584 898-F2
LITTLE ROCK CIR
4000 COR 92881 773-D5
LITTLE ROCK CT
43800 RivC 92536 963-E7
43800 RivC 92536 983-E1
LITTLEROCK LN
1200 PER 92570 807-E1
LITTLE ROCK RD
4000 SDCo 92028 997-G4
LITTLE ROSS RD
40300 SDCo 92028 997-B1
LITTLE SKY WY
43500 RivC 92590 978-B1
LITTLESTONE LN
17300 RivC 92504 745-J4
17300 RivC 92504 746-A4
LITTLE VALLEY DR
44500 RivC 92536 982-G2
LITTLE VALLEY RD
20600 RivC 92570 836-H7
W LITTON AV
100 CLTN 92313 646-B3
100 CLTN 92324 646-B3
100 GTER 92313 646-B3
200 SBdC 92324 646-B3
LITTON PL
8700 RIV 92503 715-A4
LIVELY ST
4000 RIV 92505 714-F6
LIVE OAK AV
10000 RivC 92223 690-J4
10500 FONT 92337 644-D2
LIVE OAK CIR
- RivC 92596 929-D1
LIVE OAK CT
38600 MURR 92562 927-C4
LIVE OAK DR
400 RivC 91752 683-F5
7400 RivC 92509 684-G3
LIVE OAK LN
- BEAU 92223 720-G2
19400 LKEL 92530 896-G4
26600 RivC - 844-A2
LIVE OAK PL
800 COR 92882 742-J5
LIVE OAK ST
- INDW 92210 818-H7
1800 HEMT 92545 840-F4
54200 RivC - 844-C1
LIVE OAK CANYON RD
28200 RivC 92373 688-D1
28600 RivC 92373 389-C4
31100 RDL 92373 649-A7
31700 YCPA 92373 649-A7
E LIVE OAK CREEK WY
3700 ONT 91761 643-C5
LIVE OAK RANCH RD
46600 RivC 92592 979-E7
46900 RivC 92592 999-E2
LIVERPOOL LN
1000 SJCT 92583 781-A7
11100 RIV 92503 744-F3

LIVERPOOL LN
11700 MORV 92557 717-C1
LIVERPOOL ST
600 HEMT 92545 810-E6
LIVINGSTON ST
- BAN 92220 722-B3
1900 RIV 92506 716-A2
E LIVINGSTON ST
- BAN 92220 722-C3
S LIVINGSTON ST
- BAN 92220 722-A3
LIVMORE AV
2600 PMSP 92262 786-H1
LIVORNO
- INDW 92210 819-A5
LIZARD ROCK RD
26700 RivC 92570 837-A3
LLOYD ST
44000 RivC 92544 (812-A6
See Page 782)
LLOYD WY
1100 PER 92571 747-D6
LOBELIA CIR
38700 PDST 92211 819-B2
LOBO WY
1400 PMSP 92264 786-F6
LOCARINO CT
- RivC - (907-D2
See Page 906)
LOCARNO HTS
60400 RivC - (907-E4
See Page 906)
LOCATA CT
40600 MURR 92562 928-C5
LOCHABER CT
1300 RIV 92507 716-F1
LOCHINVAR CT
38500 MURR 92562 927-D4
LOCH LOMOND CT
- RMIR 92270 787-J3
LOCH LOMOND DR
- CYNL 92587 867-B4
LOCH LOMOND RD
70500 RMIR 92270 787-H3
70500 RMIR 92270 788-A4
LOCHMOOR DR
5300 RIV 92507 716-G2
5300 RIV 92506 716-F1
LOCH NESS CIR
2100 COR 92881 773-F2
LOCH RAE CT
24400 RivC 92570 807-B6
LOCKERTON LN
- RIV 92506 716-F1
- RIV 92507 716-F1
LOCKEY AV
4100 RIV 92505 714-E7
LOCKFORD CT
20800 RivC 92570 775-F6
LOCKHART LN
40300 RivC 92544 841-C2
LOCKHAVEN LN
4000 RIV 92505 744-D1
4200 RIV 92505 714-D7
LOCKHAVEN RD
- RivC 92584 868-G1
LOCKLAN CT
5400 RIV 92507 716-F1
LOCKWOOD AV
- RivC 92504 745-E7
17900 RivC 92503 745-E7
17900 RivC 92503 775-E1
LOCKWOOD CIR
2000 COR 92881 773-F1
LOCKWOOD DR
34700 YCPA 92399 649-J2
LOCKWOOD LN
1900 COR 92881 773-F1
LOCKWOOD WY
1400 SJCT 92583 811-E4
LOCOVIA CT
79100 RivC 92201 819-H4
LOCUST
17000 LKEL 92530 866-A3
LOCUST AV
10700 SBdC 92316 645-C3
11300 FONT 92337 645-C3
27500 MORV 92555 688-C7
LOCUST RD
56000 RivC 92539 (934-H3
See Page 904)
LOCUST ST
600 COR 92879 743-E7
2600 RIV 92501 685-G4
24000 RivC 92584 867-G7
LODGE DR
23500 RivC 92587 837-E7
LODGE RD
25200 RivC - 814-E5
LODGEPOLE CT
26100 RivC 92544 841-D1
LODGE POLE DR
- PER 92571 778-B2
LODGEPOLE DR
1200 HEMT 92545 840-H3
LODGEPOLE LN
- RIV 92508 746-D2
LODI PL
4100 RIV 92505 744-C1
LOFTHILL DR
- RivC - (907-B1
See Page 906)
LOFTON PL
3700 RIV 92501 685-H1

LOFTUS LN
38900 RivC 92592 960-J1
38900 RivC 92592 961-A1
LOFTY LN
9200 RivC 92223 690-G2
LOGAN CT
6400 RIV 92503 714-F2
LOGAN DR
44300 RivC 92544 (812-B7
See Page 782)
LOGANBERRY CT
25300 MORV 92551 747-G3
LOGAN CREEK RD
24600 RivC - 814-A4
LOGENITA ST
100 PMSP 92264 786-G3
LOI LN
34400 RivC 92592 960-A5
LOIRE DR
- RivC 92596 899-D7
LOIRE VALLEY LN
28700 RivC 92584 868-G3
LOIS AV
51800 RivC 92230 723-G6
LOIS CIR
40800 RivC 92544 902-C6
LOIS CT
40800 RivC 92544 841-D2
LOIS LN
500 BEAU 92223 690-H6
16400 RivC 92504 745-H4
LOLA CT
25600 RivC 92586 837-J5
LOLITA RD
30600 TEM 92592 979-B1
LOMA RD
35000 RivC 92530 896-B6
LOMA BONITA ST
1800 PER 92570 807-F5
41900 RivC 92592 960-B5
LOMA LINDA DR
11300 LMLN 92354 647-D2
LOMA LINDA RD
30700 TEM 92592 979-C4
E LOMA LINDA RD
30600 TEM 92592 979-C5
LOMA PORTOLA DR
42600 TEM 92592 958-J6
42600 TEM 92592 959-A7
LOMAR CIR
41100 RivC 92592 959-H4
W LOMA ROJA DR
100 CLTN 92324 646-C3
LOMAS ST
41500 RivC 92544 841-E2
LOMA SOLA
14100 RivC 92508 716-F6
LOMA VENTOSO LN
35200 RivC 92592 930-C7
W LOMA VERDE DR
100 CLTN 92324 646-C3
LOMA VISTA
77200 LQNT 92253 849-E5
E LOMA VISTA CIR
3100 PMSP 92264 786-J4
LOMA VISTA CT
17000 FONT 92337 644-J3
17000 FONT 92337 645-A2
LOMA VISTA DR
11300 LMLN 92354 647-B2
LOMA VISTA LN
73100 PDST 92260 848-E4
LOMA VISTA RD
67500 DHSP 92240 697-B5
LOMA VISTA ST
1800 RIV 92507 686-A4
12600 YCPA 92399 649-D4
LOMBARD CT
25300 HEMT 92544 811-H6
48000 INDO 92201 5470-F4
LOMBARD LN
11800 YCPA 92399 649-J2
LOMBARDY LN
- COR 92881 773-C3
- COR 92882 773-C3
- BAN 92220 722-B1
11300 MORV 92557 687-G7
LOMITA CIR
1300 PMSP 92264 786-F6
LOMITA DR
200 PER 92570 807-G2
LOMITA PL
43300 RivC 92544 961-J1
43300 RivC 92544 962-A1
LOMITA ST
6700 RIV 92504 714-J2
LOMOND DR
- RIV 92508 716-E7
LONDA LN
16000 RivC 92504 745-H3
LONDON CT
25700 MURR 92563 928-F5
76800 PDST 92211 819-C2
LONDON ST
3400 HEMT 92545 810-E6
LONDON WY
2000 COR 92882 743-A7
LONDONDERRY DR
5900 RIV 92504 685-C7
LONDOS
17500 LKEL 92530 866-B3
LONE TR
4300 RivC 92509 684-F1
LONELY LN
- RivC 92590 958-A5

LONE MESA TR
25400 MORV 92557 717-H2
LONE MOUNTAIN LN
73100 RivC 92260 818-E1
LONE OAK LN
- SDCo 92028 998-G4
LONE OAK WY
- MURR 92562 927-D4
LONE PINE DR
- PER 92571 778-B2
23700 MORV 92557 687-D6
LONE PINE LN
11800 SBdC 92399 651-F2
LONE PINE ST
- RivC 92584 867-H1
LONE RANGER TR
17800 CHLS 91709 712-A5
LONE STALLION LN
13100 RivC 92883 835-B4
LONE STAR CT
1200 CALI 92320 689-J1
LONESTAR DR
2200 NRCO 92860 713-C7
LONE STAR RD
11000 MORV 92557 687-C7
LONE TREE CT
11500 FONT 92337 644-H3
LONE TREE ST
2000 COR 92880 742-J1
LONG ST
- RivC 92585 808-E4
28800 RivC 92567 808-F4
39200 HEMT 92543 810-J6
LONG BRANCH WY
19700 RivC 92881 773-H4
LONGBRANCH WY
41900 RivC 92544 931-G4
LONG CANYON LN
67500 RivC 92241 727-B3
LONG CANYON RD
10500 RivC - 697-E5
10500 RivC 92241 697-E5
13900 RivC 92240 697-E7
16000 RivC 92240 727-E2
16500 RivC 92241 727-E2
LONG COVE CIR
- COR 92883 773-H6
LONG COVE DR
5000 BAN 92220 721-D5
LONGFELLOW AV
- RivC 92592 979-H3
LONGFELLOW ST
28100 RivC 92596 839-E6
LONGHILL ST
6300 RIV 92504 685-A7
6300 RIV 92504 715-A1
LONGHORN DR
29900 CYNL 92587 867-B2
LONGHORN LN
6600 CHLS 91709 712-B6
LONGHORN RD
42200 RivC 92220 721-F7
E LONGHORN ST
2800 ONT 91761 643-A7
LONGHORN WY
- NRCO 92860 743-H1
LONGLEAF ST
- TEM 92591 928-H7
- TEM 92591 958-H1
LONGMONT ST
1900 RIV 92506 716-A2
LONG POINT DR
- CYNL 92587 867-E4
LONGPORT WY
- COR 92881 773-F4
LONG RIDGE DR
39500 TEM 92591 928-J7
39500 TEM 92591 958-H1
LONG SKY DR
- PER 92571 778-B2
LONGS PEAK DR
7600 RivC 92509 684-G2
LONGVALE CT
29800 TEM 92592 978-J1
29800 TEM 92592 979-A1
LONG VALLEY DR
30200 TEM 92591 959-A5
LONGVIEW DR
1700 COR 92882 742-J7
LONG VIEW DR
14000 FONT 92337 644-B4
LONGVIEW LN
24200 RivC 92585 808-H5
LONG VIEW PL
31800 LKEL 92532 866-J5
LONGVUE RD
21000 RivC 92241 728-H7
23300 RivC 92241 758-H1
LONGWOOD PINES LN
1300 COR 92881 773-F4
LOOKING GLASS CIR
700 COR 92882 742-E5
LOOKOUT CIR
20000 RivC 92570 836-G5
LOOKOUT DR
- PDST 92211 819-A3
33100 RivC 92530 896-B2
99100 RivC 92254 (5654-D3
See Page 5594)
LOOKOUT LN
23800 RivC 92883 804-D5
27000 RivC - 844-A1
LOOKOUT PT
2500 NRCO 92860 712-J6

LOOKOUT RD
24700 RivC - 814-D7
LOOKOUT ST
300 LKEL 92530 866-F4
LOOKOUT TER
6600 RIV 92505 714-B2
LOOKOUT WY
14500 MORV 92555 718-E6
LOOKOUT MOUNTAIN RD
2400 SDCo 92028 998-F4
LOOP RD
- RivC - 390-E4
LOPEZ AV
6700 RivC 92509 645-B6
LOPEZ RD
72000 RivC 92274 (5652-A7
See Page 5592)
LOPEZ ST
21600 RivC 92570 807-A3
LOPEZ WY
5600 BAN 92220 721-D5
LOQUAT DR
9200 RIV 92508 746-E4
LOQUAT ST
21300 RivC 92595 897-A1
LORAINE TER
12400 MORV 92553 717-E2
LORCA DR
- RMIR 92270 818-B4
LORD MURPHY CT
21000 MORV 92557 716-H1
LORE HEIGHTS CT
26400 RivC 92544 841-F1
LORELEI LN
2000 SDCo 92028 998-A7
LOREN CT
- LQNT 92253 5470-A5
LOREN LN
21000 RivC 92567 778-J5
LOREN WY
25500 MORV 92553 717-H4
28800 RivC 92592 960-J1
28800 RivC 92592 961-A1
39000 RivC 92592 931-A7
LORENA AV
6300 RivC 91752 683-H6
LORENA LN
20500 RivC 92595 897-A5
LORENA WY
1400 PMSP 92262 756-F5
LORENE LN
1000 SJCT 92582 810-C3
LORENZ LN
25000 RivC 92590 977-J4
25000 RivC 92590 978-A4
LORENZA
51700 COAC 92236 5471-B7
LORENZO DR
11200 RIV 92505 714-B4
LORENZO LN
38200 RivC 92544 (932-F4
See Page 902)
LORETTA AV
28800 RivC 92584 898-G1
31100 RivC 92596 899-C1
32000 RivC 92596 869-E7
LORETTA WY
200 CALI 92320 650-B7
LOREZ DR
12300 MORV 92557 717-G2
LORI CT
1000 NRCO 92860 713-F6
LORI LN
41500 RivC 92544 841-E1
LORI WY
- BAN 92220 721-D3
900 LKEL 92530 865-H4
37100 RivC 92544 931-D2
LORI ANN ST
100 SJCT 92582 810-H2
LORIENT CT
41100 MURR 92562 927-J4
LORIMER ST
33000 RivC 92530 896-D3
LORING DR
3800 RIV 92501 685-F3
LORING RD
25200 RivC 92595 897-J7
LORING RANCH RD
4200 RivC 92509 685-D4
LORISA WY
- RIV 92504 715-B5
LORITA ST
4000 RivC 92509 644-B7
LORNA DR
24800 MORV 92553 717-F6
LORNA ST
800 COR 92882 743-B7
LORRAINE CIR
- RivC 92562 956-C6
LORRAINE DR
1600 COR 92882 743-C7
6500 RIV 92506 715-G3
44600 TEM 92592 979-H2
LORRAINE LN
700 HEMT 92543 841-A2
LORRAINE ST
46000 INDO 92201 5470-H1
LOS ALAMITOS DR
37000 RivC 92592 960-F3
LOS ALAMOS
54000 RivC 92539 (934-D4
See Page 904)
LOS ALAMOS DR
- RMIR 92270 818-A1

LOS ALAMOS RD
- RivC 92270 788-A3
- RivC 92562 926-C7
- RivC 92562 956-B1
2000 PMSP 92262 756-H6
29200 MURR 92563 898-H7
29200 RivC 92563 898-H7
29400 MURR 92563 928-E3
30200 RivC 92563 899-A7
30500 RivC 92596 899-A7
36000 RMIR 92270 788-A3
39200 MURR 92562 928-B6
LOS ALAMOS HEIGHTS RD
28600 MURR 92563 928-G2
LOS ALISOS RD
17200 RivC 92530 896-B7
LOS ALTOS CIR
2300 HEMT 92545 840-G1
LOS ALTOS CT
1000 RIV 92507 686-C7
71000 RMIR 92270 788-A7
LOS ALTOS RD
40000 RivC 92544 931-F7
40200 RivC 92544 961-F3
LOS AMANTES LN
46000 RivC 92544 902-F7
LOS AMANTES RD
47600 RivC 92592 960-B2
LOS AMIGOS CT
47800 INDO 92201 5470-D3
LOS AONE AV
1300 SJCT 92582 810-H2
LOS ARBOLES
77500 LQNT 92253 849-E6
LOS ARBOLES PL
7800 RIV 92504 715-C4
LOS ARROLLOS RD
- RivC 92570 806-A5
LOS CABALLEROS WY
43600 TEM 92592 979-B1
LOS CABALLOS RD
43300 RivC 92592 960-D7
43300 RivC 92592 980-C1
LOS CABOS DR
25500 MORV 92551 747-H2
LOS CAMPOS VERDE
41800 TEM 92591 958-J4
LOS CARRIZOS RD
31500 RivC 92584 868-J6
LOS CASITAS RD
19700 RivC 92590 976-H4
LOS CIELOS DR
28200 RivC 92586 838-C6
LOS COCOS E
37600 RMIR 92270 817-H1
LOS COCOS W
37600 RMIR 92270 817-H1
LOS CORRALITOS RD
38800 RivC 92592 980-C1
LOS COYOTES
38700 RivC 92539 (934-D4
See Page 904)
LOS COYOTES DR
2200 PMSP 92264 787-C5
LOS COYOTES RD
35400 RivC 92530 896-A6
LOS ENCINOS DR
32600 RivC 92592 999-G1
LOS ESTADOS ST
15200 MORV 92551 747-J1
N LOS FELICES CIR E
500 PMSP 92262 756-C4
N LOS FELICES CIR N
600 PMSP 92262 756-C4
N LOS FELICES CIR W
700 PMSP 92262 756-C4
LOS FELICES RD
2700 PMSP 92262 756-C4
LOS FELIZ CT
3600 RIV 92504 715-C3
LOS FLORES
- RMIR 92270 787-H7
LOS GATOS CIR
2300 HEMT 92545 840-G1
LOS GATOS RD
43400 RivC 92562 957-A7
43400 RivC 92590 957-A7
43700 RivC 92590 977-B3
45000 RivC 92590 976-J4
68300 CTHC 92234 757-E6
LOS LIMONES LN
32600 RivC 92545 839-E1
32600 RivC 92548 839-E1
LOS MANOS DR
44700 LQNT 92253 819-H7
44800 LQNT 92253 849-H1
LOS MOLINOS WY
11400 RIV 92505 714-B6
N LOS NIETOS RD
500 PMSP 92262 786-E1
LOS NOGALES RD
29800 TEM 92591 959-A4
34800 RivC 92592 960-B2
LOS OLIVOS DR
11000 MORV 92557 687-G7
LOS OLIVOS LN
33200 RivC 92595 896-J7
LOS OLIVOS WY
5000 RIV 92505 714-B6
LOS OLIVOS CORTE
40100 MURR 92562 928-D5
LOS PALOMAS LN
39400 RivC 92562 956-F1

LOS PALOS DR
50700 INDO 92201 5470-G7
LOS PATOS DR
2400 PMSP 92264 787-C5
LOS PINOS DR
200 PMSP 92264 787-C6
LOS PINOS RD
35100 RivC 92530 896-B6
E LOS POSAS CIR
2900 PMSP 92264 786-H4
LOS PUEBLOS WY
70400 RMIR 92270 787-J7
LOS RANCHERIAS RD
24400 RivC 92545 810-A6
N LOS RANCHERIAS RD
100 HEMT 92545 810-A7
100 HEMT 92545 840-A1
LOS RANCHOS CIR
40800 RivC 92592 930-H6
LOS REYES DR
36700 RMIR 92270 788-A7
37100 RMIR 92270 818-A1
LOS ROBLES DR
1100 PMSP 92262 756-C7
LOS ROBLES RD
21900 RivC 92562 926-J3
21900 RivC 92562 927-A3
40500 SDCo 92028 997-G3
LOS SANTOS
5800 PMSP 92264 787-C5
LOST RD
22600 RivC 92595 897-D2
29000 RivC 92595 867-D7
33000 LKEL 92532 867-E6
33000 LKEL 92595 867-D7
LOST ELK TR
- LQNT 92253 849-F3
LOST HORIZON DR
- SDCo 92059 999-J5
LOS TILOS RD
600 HEMT 92543 841-B1
LOST RIVER DR
- PDST 92211 818-J4
LOST TRAIL CT
13200 RivC 92883 835-B3
LOTKER LN
17000 RivC 92258 725-H3
LOT LINE RD
43000 RivC 92220 691-G4
LOTUS AV
33100 YCPA 92399 649-E5
LOTUS CIR
29200 RivC 92586 868-B1
LOTUS CT
72600 PDST 92260 848-D4
LOTUS DR
34300 RivC 92544 901-J3
LOTUS ST
5700 RivC 92509 645-D7
LOU CIR
46200 INDW 92210 849-D2
LOU ANN CT
21500 RivC 92567 779-D6
LOU ELLA LN
3500 RIV 92507 686-A5
LOUELLA RD
200 PMSP 92262 786-H2
N LOUELLA RD
100 PMSP 92262 786-H2
LOUIS RD
30000 RivC 92548 808-J6
LOUISA LN
25600 RivC 92585 808-G7
25600 RivC 92585 838-G1
LOUISAN RD
68000 RivC 92240 697-C7
LOUISE AV
37800 RivC 92539 (934-H2
See Page 904)
LOUISE DR
600 PMSP 92262 756-E6
LOUISE RD
33100 RivC 92596 899-C2
LOUISE ST
17000 RivC 92258 726-E2
22200 RivC 92570 807-B5
LOUISIANA PL
2900 RIV 92506 715-F4
LOUISIANA ST
43600 PDST 92211 819-D7
LOUIS PASTEUR DR
14800 RivC 92508 746-B1
LOUISVILLE ST
- HEMT 92545 810-E6
LOUJAY ST
38100 RivC 92592 930-H1
LOUNELL DR
22600 RivC 92570 777-C7
LOUNSBERRY RD
20000 RivC 92570 775-H5
LOURDES DR
- RivC 92596 899-D7
LOVAS CT
11400 DHSP 92240 696-C3
LOVAT CT
1400 RIV 92507 716-F2
LOVE CT
- RivC 92592 979-J2
24100 MORV 92553 717-E7
LOVE LN
200 RivC 92532 835-D3
24200 RivC 92570 835-D3
LOVEBIRD LN
16100 RivC 92504 745-F4

STREET
Block City ZIP Pg-Grid

LOVEKIN BLVD
- RivC - 392-C9
100 BLY 92225 5491-D5
400 BLY 92225 5551-D2
600 RivC 92225 5551-D2
6900 RivC - 5491-D1
8900 BLY - 5491-D1
15500 RivC - 5551-E5
21900 RivC - 412-C2
LOVELAND DR
2100 RivC 92509 645-C5
LOVELL ST
800 BAN 92220 721-J5
LOVELY SAGE CT
84000 RivC 92274 (5591-A3 See Page 5590)
LOW CIR
43400 RivC 92544 811-J5
LOWE DR
78600 LQNT 92253 819-G7
E LOWELL ST
2700 ONT 91761 643-A2
N LOWELL ST
100 LKEL 92530 866-D4
S LOWELL ST
100 LKEL 92530 866-D5
LOWER RD
- RivC 92571 748-D4
LOWER ALISO CANYON TR
- CHLS - 742-A4
- RivC 92880 742-A4
LOWER PINE CREST AV
53500 RivC - 814-B7
LOWER RANCH RD
47600 RivC 92536 982-H3
47600 RivC 92536 983-A3
LOWER RV
- RivC 92571 748-D4
LOWER TENT I
- RivC 92571 748-C5
LOWER TENT II
- RivC 92571 748-C4
LOWREY LN
29800 RivC 92584 868-J6
LOWVER LN
45300 RivC 92536 981-H3
LOYOLA CT
300 HEMT 92544 811-D6
LOYOLA ST
2700 RIV 92503 744-J1
2700 RIV 92503 745-A1
LOZANO CT
68800 CTHC 92234 757-E7
LOZANO PL
11600 LMLN 92354 647-D2
LUANE TR
7100 RivC 92324 647-A6
LUANNA POINT DR
41400 RivC 92201 819-G4
LUBO TR
56400 RivC 92539 (934-J2 See Page 904)
LUCAS DR
23600 RivC 92587 837-E6
LUCAS PL
900 COR 92881 743-J7
LUCAS ST
8400 RIV 92504 715-C5
LUCAS CLUB DR
8900 CALI 92320 689-J2
LUCCA
- INDW 92210 819-B6
LUCCA WY
- TEM 92592 979-F1
LUCE CT
82200 INDO 92201 5410-E7
LUCENA AV
11700 FONT 92337 644-F3
LUCERNE DR
- PDST 92260 818-H2
900 HEMT 92543 841-B2
1300 HEMT 92544 841-B2
1300 RivC 92544 841-B2
68500 RivC - (907-F3 See Page 906)
LUCERNE PL
2900 RIV 92506 715-G2
LUCERNE ST
100 LKEL 92530 866-F7
100 LKEL 92530 896-F1
32500 RivC 92530 896-E3
LUCERO DR
40200 RivC 92592 930-J6
LUCHS RD
20200 RivC 92570 775-G5
LUCIA LN
10900 MORV 92551 747-J2
LUCIANA LN
- RivC 92567 779-C7
LUCILLE CT
500 BEAU 92223 690-J6
LUCILLE LN
59000 RivC 92539 (965-F4 See Page 964)
LUCILLE CIRCLE RD
26100 MURR 92562 958-B3
LUCK LN
19400 RivC 92508 746-F7
LUCKY G DR
- PDST 92260 848-B4
LUCKY SPUR LN
13100 RivC 92883 835-B5
LUCRETIA AV
5200 RivC 91752 683-H4

LUCY WY
22000 RivC 92570 747-A7
LUDY BLVD
- RivC - 412-A2
LUGO DR
- RMIR 92270 818-B4
LUGO RD
200 PMSP 92262 786-D2
11400 RivC 92220 692-H6
LUGONIA ST
700 LKEL 92532 866-F4
LUIS DR
13500 DHSP 92240 697-A5
LUISANA
52400 RivC - (843-J1 See Page 842)
LUISENO RD
43300 RivC 92536 964-A7
N LUJO CIR
500 PMSP 92262 786-G1
LUKENS LN
21700 PER 92570 777-C7
21700 PER 92570 807-C2
21700 RivC 92570 777-C7
21700 RivC 92570 807-C2
LUKEWOOD PL
24800 MORV 92553 717-F4
LULLABY LN
1000 COR 92880 743-C2
LUNA CIR
- PMSP 92262 756-F4
LUNA CT
17800 RivC 92504 745-G7
LUNA DR
37800 RivC 92592 930-G7
LUNA LN
31100 RivC 92548 809-B4
LUNA WY
900 SJCT 92583 811-D4
1300 PMSP 92262 756-F4
LUNAR LN
800 BAN 92220 721-H2
LUNARIA CT
- RivC 92254 5592-F5
LUND PL
39900 RivC 92223 651-A7
39900 RivC 92223 691-A1
LUNDAHL LN
44000 RivC 92536 964-E7
44000 RivC 92536 (984-E1 See Page 964)
LUNDBERG LN
49500 INDO 92201 5470-D5
LUNDBORG LN
17000 RivC 92504 775-J2
17000 RivC 92504 776-A2
LUPIN PL
29100 CYNL 92587 867-C1
LUPIN WY
49900 RivC 92536 983-E3
LUPINE AV
83000 INDO 92201 5410-G7
LUPINE CIR
1500 COR 92881 773-G4
LUPINE CT
12900 YCPA 92399 650-E5
LUPINE DR
500 RivC - 5239-J6
500 RivC - 5240-A6
LUPINE LN
25400 MORV 92551 747-H4
45400 PDST 92260 848-F2
60000 RivC 92539 (965-G3 See Page 964)
LUPINE PL
23200 MURR 92562 927-E4
LUPINE TR
36700 YCPA 92399 650-E5
LURIN AV
18000 RivC 92508 746-C4
25300 MORV 92551 747-H4
N LURING DR
100 PMSP 92262 786-G2
LUSENO CT
44300 TEM 92592 979-G2
LUTHER ST
4100 RIV 92506 715-E2
4500 RIV 92504 715-E2
LUTON CT
13200 MORV 92553 717-E4
LUTTRELL LN
20100 RivC 92570 776-F1
LUXOR RD
29400 RivC 92584 868-A1
LUXURY ST
25000 MORV 92557 687-G7
LUZ CIR
1300 PMSP 92264 786-F5
LUZ DEL SOL
41400 TEM 92591 958-J4
LUZON AV
47500 RivC 92201 5470-J3
E LYANS DR
100 RLTO 92316 645-H1
LYDIA AV
7200 RIV 92504 715-E4
LYDIA CT
- PMSP 92264 786-J5
- RivC 92592 979-J2
LYDIA LN
- COR 92882 773-C3
LYDIA JANE RD
- RivC 92548 809-E4
LYKINS LN
33200 RivC 92596 839-G5

LYLE AV
19100 RivC 92881 773-J3
LYLE ST
78900 LQNT 92253 819-H6
LYMAN ST
1900 RIV 92507 686-A3
2100 RIV 92507 685-J3
LYME CT
17400 RivC 92503 744-G6
LYN AV
34800 RivC 92545 839-J1
34800 RivC 92545 840-A1
N LYN CIR
200 PMSP 92262 786-H2
LYNAE WY
2800 HEMT 92545 810-F6
LYNCH LN
11300 RIV 92503 744-F3
35000 RivC 92544 901-D5
LYNCH RD
- RivC 92570 805-G3
LYND CT
12900 YCPA 92399 650-B5
LYNDA RD
2500 SDCo 92028 997-C1
2500 SDCo 92028 977-F7
LYNDA ST
60000 RivC 92274 (5591-G3 See Page 5590)
LYNDEE DR
1100 NRCO 92860 713-F3
LYNDHURST DR
1100 RIV 92507 686-C7
1100 RIV 92507 716-C1
LYNDIE LN
42100 TEM 92591 958-J6
LYNETTE LN
- PMSP 92262 756-G4
20600 RivC 92570 775-B6
LYNFALL ST
35500 YCPA 92399 650-B5
LYNFORD WY
1400 COR 92879 743-F3
LYNN CIR
25700 RivC 92544 811-J7
N LYNN CIR
10300 RivC 91752 644-A5
S LYNN CIR
10300 RivC 91752 644-A6
LYNN WY
7500 RivC 92509 684-H5
LYNNLEE LN
14500 MORV 92555 718-B7
LYNRIDGE CT
1300 RIV 92506 716-B3
LYNWOOD CIR
1900 COR 92881 773-F1
LYNWOOD DR
1000 HEMT 92543 811-B5
LYNX CT
22100 MURR 92562 927-C4
LYNX RD
33000 RivC 92584 897-J2
LYNX ST
45600 RivC 92220 782-D1
LYON AV
200 HEMT 92545 810-H4
300 HEMT 92543 810-H4
300 HEMT 92545 840-H3
300 HEMT 92543 840-H2
700 SJCT 92582 810-H1
700 SJCT 92582 780-H7
1900 RivC 92503 744-F3
3800 RIV 92505 744-E1
4400 RIV 92505 714-D7
LYONS BLVD
72500 RivC 92241 728-C1
LYRA AV
11200 RivC 91752 683-H4
LYRA CT
28500 RivC 92586 837-J6
LYREBIRD CT
11600 MORV 92557 717-D1
LYTELL
30500 LKEL 92530 866-A3
LYTLE LN
68700 CTHC 92234 817-D2
LYTLE CREEK LP
100 ONT 91761 643-C6

M

M ST
- HEMT 92545 840-F2
1100 RIV 92518 747-C1
M & R RANCH RD
2200 SDCo 92028 998-A7
MABELLE
100 LKEL 92530 866-E5
MABEY CANYON RD
1700 COR 92882 772-H2
2100 RivC 92882 772-G2
MABLE CIR
43700 RivC 92544 811-J5
MABREY RD
100 PMSP 92264 786-E5
MAC CIR
30500 RivC 92563 899-A5
MAC RD
44100 RivC 92539 (965-F7 See Page 964)
44400 RivC 92539 (985-F1 See Page 964)
MACADAMIA DR
1300 SDCo 92028 998-B6

MACARTHUR DR
21100 RivC 92567 779-A6
MACARTHUR RD
4000 RIV 92503 714-H5
MACBETH AV
2300 COR 92882 773-B1
MACBETH CT
- RMIR 92270 788-B6
MACBETH PL
2100 RIV 92507 685-J6
2100 RIV 92507 686-A6
MACDILL ST
- RivC 92518 717-C7
MACHA LN
28900 RivC 92567 808-F2
MACHADO ST
29900 LKEL 92530 865-J2
32400 RivC 92530 865-G5
MACHEKA DR
28800 RivC 92567 808-F2
MACHON RD
44800 TEM 92592 979-G3
MACIAS ST
15100 RivC 92530 865-F5
MACINTOSH DR
5500 RIV 92507 716-G1
MACK ST
20300 RivC 92570 776-H5
21500 RivC 92570 777-A5
MACKAY AV
17600 RivC 92530 896-C2
MACKAY DR
33200 RivC 92530 895-J1
33200 RivC 92530 896-A1
MACLEAN RANCH RD
22800 RivC 92548 809-B2
22800 RivC 92567 809-B2
MACY CT
7200 RIV 92503 684-E7
MACY ST
32800 LKEL 92530 865-H6
32900 RivC 92530 865-H7
MADAGASCAR DR
1400 COR 92882 772-J1
MADALENA CIR
15500 FONT 92337 644-F4
MADALENA DR
4500 RivC 91752 683-G1
MADDALENA RD
36000 RivC 92596 899-F7
36500 RivC 92596 929-F2
MADDEN ST
700 HEMT 92543 841-B1
MADDY CT
32300 RivC 92584 868-A7
MADELINE CT
41900 RivC 92592 960-B5
MADELINE PL
4900 RIV 92504 685-C7
MADERA CIR
1800 COR 92879 743-G2
MADERA DR
34900 RivC 92544 901-H5
MADERA ST
700 HEMT 92543 840-J2
MADERA WY
4100 RIV 92503 744-B2
MADERA DE PLAYA DR
33100 RivC 92592 959-G4
34200 RivC 92592 960-A3
MADERO CIR
1300 PMSP 92262 756-F5
MADERO WY
25500 RivC 92590 978-A2
W MADERO WY
45100 RivC 92590 977-J3
45100 RivC 92590 978-A2
MADISON AV
23400 MURR 92562 927-H2
23400 RivC 92595 927-H2
25300 MURR 92562 928-B5
25800 MURR 92562 958-D1
27200 TEM 92590 958-F2
MADISON CT
- TEM 92592 959-G7
MADISON LN
- COR 92881 773-F3
MADISON ST
2200 RIV 92504 715-C2
3700 LKEL 92530 865-H4
11600 YCPA 92399 650-B2
38000 INDO 92203 5410-C2
43200 INDO 92201 5410-C6
45000 INDO 92201 5470-C2
50000 LQNT 92253 5470-C7
52000 LQNT 92253 5530-C1
58000 RivC 92253 5530-D7
58000 RivC 92253 5590-D1
60000 LQNT 92274 5590-D1
60000 RivC 92274 5590-D1
60000 LQNT 92253 5590-D3
MADOLE DR
24000 MORV 92557 717-E1
MADONNA CT
25400 MORV 92557 687-H7
MADRE LN
12800 RivC 92240 695-J5
MADRE VISTA
39100 RivC 92562 926-H6
MADRID AV
100 PDST 92260 818-E6
N MADRID CIR
700 PMSP 92262 756-G7
MADRID CT
2000 RIV 92506 716-A3

MADRID RD
- CTHC 92234 757-C5
MADRID ST
100 RMIR 92270 787-H7
300 HEMT 92545 810-E7
S MAD RIVER LN
2900 ONT 91761 643-C6
MADRONA CIR
2200 PMSP 92264 786-F7
S MADRONA DR
1300 PMSP 92264 786-F6
MADRONA RD
3800 RIV 92504 715-A3
MADRONE DR
25200 MURR 92563 928-E6
MADRONE ST
- FONT 92337 645-A1
MADRONO CT
30600 RivC 92567 779-A4
MAE CT
1300 PER 92570 807-D2
MAES ST
29300 LKEL 92530 865-J2
MAGDALENA
- RMIR 92270 818-B3
MAGDALENA CIR
200 COR 92882 743-B5
MAGDALENO CT
32800 RivC 92530 865-G5
MAGDAS COLORADAS ST
30300 RivC 92563 929-B1
MAGEE RD
35900 SDCo 92028 999-H2
35900 SDCo 92059 999-H2
MAGEE HEIGHTS RD
- SDCo 92059 999-J2
MAGEE HILLS RD
40000 RivC 92544 931-C1
MAGELLAN CIR
- COR 92882 773-A2
MAGELLAN DR
14900 MORV 92553 717-H7
MAGELLAN PL
- INDO 92201 5470-D4
MAGENTA CT
- TEM 92592 959-F7
14500 MORV 92553 717-F7
MAGENTA DR
- LQNT 92253 819-G7
MAGGIE WEED LN
44100 RivC 92592 980-C2
MAGIA CIR
1700 COR 92879 743-G2
MAGNA VISTA DR
13800 RivC 92570 775-C7
MAGNESIA FALLS DR
71600 RMIR 92270 818-C6
73900 PDST 92260 818-E6
MAGNOLIA AV
- COR 92882 773-D1
500 COR 92879 773-D1
500 BEAU 92223 720-J2
800 COR 92879 743-G6
900 COR 92881 743-G6
1200 RDL 92373 647-J2
1300 RivC 92879 743-J5
4500 RIV 92501 685-F7
4500 RIV 92506 685-F7
6100 RivC 92879 744-C3
6200 RIV 92506 715-E1
7000 RIV 92504 715-B4
7700 RivC 92503 744-C3
8600 RIV 92503 715-B4
8800 RIV 92503 714-F7
10300 RIV 92505 714-F7
10600 RIV 92505 744-C3
11500 RIV 92503 744-C3
12700 COR 92879 744-C3
19500 RivC 92567 779-B4
MAGNOLIA CIR
300 HEMT 92543 841-A2
MAGNOLIA CT
46200 INDO 92201 5470-E2
MAGNOLIA DR
48900 SBdC 92256 655-G1
MAGNOLIA RD
1900 PMSP 92262 756-G5
MAGNOLIA ST
- LKEL 92530 865-F4
14200 RivC 92230 723-B5
21600 RivC 92567 779-B6
24000 RivC 92584 867-F7
33000 RivC 92530 896-A1
41300 MURR 92562 927-H5
84000 COAC 92236 5470-J5
84000 COAC 92236 5471-A5
MAGNOLIA WY
11200 CALI 92320 690-C6
MAGNOLIA GLEN DR
200 RIV 92506 716-D4
MAGNUM LN
25400 MURR 92563 928-E5
MAGUEY CT
30300 TEM 92592 979-C4
MAGUGLIN WY
21400 RivC 92570 807-A7
MAHAFFEY ST
900 HEMT 92543 841-B3
MAHER LN
25800 RivC 92570 837-B2
MAHLON VAIL RD
44200 TEM 92592 979-G2
MAHOGANY DR
- FONT 92337 645-A1

MAHOGANY LN
700 PER 92571 807-J1
28000 RivC 92585 808-E5
MAHOGANY ST
300 SJCT 92582 810-J2
1300 COR 92882 743-A7
MAHOGANY WY
15100 LKEL 92530 865-G4
MAIDEN LN
32800 RivC 92530 896-C2
MAIDSTONE CIR
- COR 92883 773-F7
MAIDSTONE ST
400 BAN 92220 721-D4
MAILE LN
16900 MORV 92551 747-H4
MAIN ST
100 RivC 92507 646-C6
100 BLY 92225 5491-E6
200 RivC 92501 645-J7
300 GTER 92313 646-C6
300 RIV 92501 645-J7
400 BLY 92225 5551-E1
1000 RIV 92501 685-J2
3000 PER 92571 778-C4
8800 RivC 92509 684-E5
11300 SBdC 92354 647-A1
15300 RivC 92555 719-E7
15300 RivC 92555 749-E2
16400 LKEL 92530 835-J7
16400 LKEL 92530 865-J1
20400 RivC 92571 778-C4
24200 RivC 92570 807-A6
28900 MORV 92555 718-F6
41800 TEM 92590 958-J7
41800 TEM 92590 978-H1
43500 INDO 92201 5410-F6
49000 RivC 92230 723-B4
87000 RivC 92274 5531-G4
E MAIN ST
100 SJCT 92583 811-C2
N MAIN ST
- COR 92882 743-D3
- LKEL 92532 866-E5
- COR 92879 743-D3
- COR 92880 743-D3
100 LKEL 92530 866-E5
1000 NRCO 92860 743-D3
S MAIN ST
100 COR 92879 743-D6
100 COR 92882 743-D6
100 LKEL 92530 866-E5
1900 COR 92882 773-D1
3700 COR 92881 773-C3
20500 RivC 92882 773-C5
W MAIN ST
100 SJCT 92583 811-A2
MAIN DIVIDE RD
- OrCo - 772-E6
- OrCo - 803-C6
- OrCo - 895-A1
- OrCo 92808 772-B2
- RivC - 388-K10
- RivC - 803-C6
- RivC 92882 772-D2
- RivC 92882 803-A3
N MAIN DIVIDE RD
- OrCo - 865-A6
- RivC 92530 865-D7
- RivC 92530 895-E1
MAIN DIVIDE TKTR
- OrCo - 895-A2
- RivC 92530 895-A2
MAINE ST
77500 PDST 92211 819-E7
MAINSAIL LN
600 PER 92571 777-J7
MAIRFIELD CT
6000 BAN 92220 721-C4
MAITRI RD
10400 RivC 92883 804-E7
MAIZ LN
38900 RivC 92592 930-J2
38900 RivC 92592 931-A2
MAJELA LN
800 HEMT 92543 841-A2
MAJELLO CT
27100 TEM 92591 958-H1
MAJENTA LN
57300 RivC 92274 5530-H4
MAJESTIC CIR
39300 RivC 92563 929-A7
MAJESTIC CT
- TEM 92592 959-G5
5500 RIV 92506 715-J1
MAJESTIC DR
1700 COR 92880 742-J1
1700 COR 92880 743-A1
MAJESTIC PRINCE CT
2400 PER 92571 777-H5
MAJESTIC PRINCE WY
16700 MORV 92551 747-G4
MAJOR DR
26600 RivC 92544 841-D2
N MAJORCA CIR
600 PMSP 92262 756-G6
MAJORCA DR
- RMIR 92270 818-B5
MAJORIE ST
1000 LKEL 92530 866-G6
MAKO LN
1000 PER 92571 807-J1
MALABATA DR
73500 PDST 92260 848-F3

MALACCA WY
23700 MURR 92562 928-B2
MALACHITE ST
1500 HEMT 92543 840-H3
MALAGA AV
- RivC 92254 5592-H7
80100 INDO 92201 5470-A5
MALAGA CIR
1300 PMSP 92264 786-F6
MALAGA CT
- LQNT 92253 849-F6
MALAGA DR
- SJCT 92583 780-J6
- RMIR 92270 818-B4
1200 RivC 92509 645-E5
MALAGA PL
800 HEMT 92543 840-J2
S MALAGA PL
600 ONT 91761 643-G1
MALAGA RD
20800 RivC 92530 866-J7
20900 LKEL 92530 866-H7
20900 RivC 92595 866-J7
21000 RivC 92595 867-A7
24200 RivC 92585 808-H5
25700 RivC 92585 838-H1
MALAGA ST
3700 COR 92882 773-B4
MALAGA GATE
48900 INDO 92201 5470-A5
MALAGON DR
11700 FONT 92337 644-F3
MALBEC ST
- MURR 92562 928-B4
MALBERT ST
100 PER 92570 807-G5
MALIA CIR
44900 LQNT 92253 849-H1
MALIBAR AV
40600 RivC 92544 841-C1
MALIBU
100 PMSP 92264 787-A6
MALIBU CT
13100 MORV 92553 717-B4
E MALIBU CT
2500 CLTN 92324 646-J4
MALIBU DR
6800 RIV 92504 715-B2
MALIBU ST
700 HEMT 92543 810-J6
MALIGNE WY
68000 CTHC 92234 787-D3
MALLARD RD
6700 RIV 92503 714-F1
MALLORCA LN
77200 INDW 92210 849-E1
MALLORCA WY
10600 MORV 92557 687-D6
MALLORIE WY
8700 RIV 92503 714-H3
MALLOW DR
10100 MORV 92557 687-D5
MALLOY CT
1900 COR 92880 743-C3
MALONE AV
24000 RivC 92567 808-H5
24000 RivC 92585 808-H5
25600 RivC 92585 838-H1
MALONE CIR
77500 PDST 92211 819-E3
MALONE ST
8600 RIV 92508 746-H2
MALTA CIR
43600 PDST 92211 819-E6
MALTA PL
3100 RIV 92507 685-J3
14200 RivC 92570 775-E7
MALTBY AV
28700 MORV 92555 718-E5
MALVERN WY
5400 RIV 92506 716-A1
MAMIE WY
48300 INDO 92201 5470-E4
MAMMOTH LN
2000 COR 92879 743-H3
MAMMOTH PL
29200 CYNL 92587 867-D1
MANAGUA PL
19800 RivC 92562 926-G5
MANASSAS DR
- HEMT 92545 840-E3
MANCERA WY
- TEM 92591 958-H3
MANCERO CIR
- COR 92879 743-F2
MANCHESTER AV
42000 RivC 92544 841-F3
MANCHESTER CIR
2900 COR 92879 744-B2
MANCHESTER CT
- TEM 92592 959-G7
1900 SJCT 92582 810-F2
MANCHESTER DR
26700 RivC 92586 838-B5
MANCHESTER LN
- SBDO 92408 646-J1
MANCHESTER PL
3900 RIV 92503 714-J4
3900 RIV 92503 715-A4
MANCHESTER RD
- RivC 92592 979-H2
MANDALAY CT
9800 RIV 92503 714-E1
MANDAN CT
5200 RivC 92509 685-D3

MANDARIN CT
25400 LMLN 92354 647-D2
MANDARIN DR
43800 RivC 92544 841-J4
43800 RivC 92544 842-A4
MANDARIN LN
9000 RIV 92508 746-E3
MANDARIN PL
1200 PER 92571 778-A2
MANDARIN WY
- RivC 92507 746-E6
MANDARINA
50800 LQNT 92253 5470-A6
79000 LQNT 92253 849-J6
MANDAVILLE WY
33100 RivC 92530 865-F6
MANDELIEU DR
26600 MURR 92562 928-C1
MANDEVILLA WY
- COR 92879 743-E3
MANDEVILLE CT
- RivC 92880 713-A2
MANDEVILLE PL
20800 RivC 92570 775-E6
MANDEVILLE RD
79400 RivC 92201 819-J6
MANDOLIN CIR
39400 MURR 92562 898-A7
MANDRA ST
41400 MURR 92562 927-H3
MANECITA CIR
600 PER 92571 807-J2
MANFIELD ST
100 RIV 92507 686-F5
MANGANESE RD
27800 RivC 92587 837-F4
MANGO
50500 LQNT 92253 849-J7
MANGO CT
6700 RIV 92504 714-J2
29000 LKEL 92530 865-F1
MANGO LN
- RivC 92503 744-J7
MANGO ST
29200 LKEL 92530 865-F2
MANGO WK
- INDO 92201 5470-H3
MANGO WY
1700 HEMT 92545 840-H3
16400 LKEL 92530 865-F1
MANGOWOOD DR
13700 MORV 92553 717-H5
MANGROVE CIR
- COR 92881 773-E3
4200 HEMT 92544 811-F5
MANGROVE CT
11900 FONT 92337 644-C4
MANGROVE WY
2600 RIV 92506 715-G4
MANGULAR AV
2100 COR 92882 772-J1
MANHART CIR
4200 RivC 92509 685-D3
MANHASSET ST
- RIV 92508 746-E1
MANHATTAN DR
6900 RIV 92506 715-F3
6900 RIV 92504 715-F3
MANHATTAN WY
- COR 92881 773-D4
MANILA AV
84000 RivC 92201 5470-J3
MANILA CT
16800 FONT 92337 644-J1
MANILA ST
500 RLTO 92316 645-G1
15300 FONT 92337 644-E1
18200 SBdC 92316 645-D1
MANISTA WY
42100 MURR 92562 928-A7
42100 MURR 92562 958-A1
MANITOBA CIR
1700 COR 92882 742-H6
MANITOBA PL
9600 RIV 92503 714-E1
MANITOU DR
45000 INDW 92210 849-D2
MANITOU ST
18600 RivC 92881 773-J2
MANLINE DR
5400 RivC 91752 683-G4
MANN AV
6200 RivC 91752 683-J6
MANNING ST
- YCPA 92399 649-E2
30300 LKEL 92530 866-A3
MANNLE DR
71600 RivC 92260 848-B5
MAN OF WAR LN
25600 RivC 92585 838-G1
MANOR DR
3500 RivC 92509 645-A7
MANOR LN
76800 PDST 92211 819-C3
MANOR WY
- COR 92882 742-D5
MANORGATE RD
- RivC 92211 819-F2
MAN-O-WAR DR
1100 NRCO 92860 713-F5
MANRESA CT
24000 MURR 92562 928-B1
MANSFIELD LN
23000 MORV 92557 717-C1

MANSFIELD WY
30100 CTHC 92234 757-G7
MANTEE PL
24500 MORV 92553 717-F5
MANTICA CT
- INDO 92201 5470-H3
MANTLE DR
- RivC 92585 838-A3
MANTON RD
24800 RivC 92324 687-F2
MANTOVA DR
- TEM 92592 979-G1
MANUEL AV
- LMLN 92354 647-F2
MANUEL RD
8500 RIV 92508 746-G1
MANUFACTURING RD
72100 RivC 92276 788-C2
MANX CT
4200 RIV 92503 714-G5
MANZANA DR
29500 RivC 92587 867-E2
MANZANAR CT
68100 CTHC 92234 757-D6
MANZANILLO ST
14500 RivC 92230 723-E5
MANZANITA AV
24000 MORV 92557 687-E6
28000 MORV 92555 688-D6
83500 INDO 92203 5410-H6
S MANZANITA AV
1000 PMSP 92264 786-F4
MANZANITA CT
100 SJCT 92582 810-J1
69500 CTHC 92234 757-G7
73700 PDST 92260 848-G4
MANZANITA DR
22500 RivC - 814-A4
28400 RivC 92532 836-C7
39200 RivC 92260 818-C8
72400 PDST 92260 818-C7
MANZANITA LN
- LQNT 92253 849-H4
MANZANITA RD
1800 COR 92882 772-H1
2000 COR 92882 742-H7
24600 RivC 92548 809-F6
38200 RivC 92539 (933-H4 See Page 902)
60100 RivC - 908-A4
MANZANITA ST
- INDW 92210 818-H7
- MURR 92563 928-F7
- MURR 92563 958-F1
24100 RivC 92584 867-G7
36400 YCPA 92399 650-D1
MANZANITA WY
2700 HEMT 92545 840-F3
MANZANITA MOUNTAIN LN
39100 RivC 92539 (933-H6 See Page 902)
MANZANITA PARK RD
14000 RivC 92223 720-J5
14000 BEAU 92223 720-J5
14500 RivC 92223 721-A5
14500 BEAU 92223 721-A5
MANZANO
26800 RivC 92590 978-C1
MANZANO DR
43300 TEM 92592 979-C1
MANZO RD
45500 INDW 92210 849-A2
MAPES RD
100 PER 92570 807-H6
1400 PER 92570 808-B6
1600 PER 92585 808-C6
14200 RivC 92585 808-E6
22200 RivC 92570 807-B7
30000 RivC 92548 808-H6
30000 RivC 92548 809-A6
W MAPES RD
800 PER 92570 807-E6
MAPLE AV
100 BEAU 92223 720-J1
10700 SBdC 92316 645-D2
11100 SBdC 92337 645-D2
11800 CLTN 92324 646-C3
11800 GTER 92313 646-C3
21400 RivC 92570 807-A7
26400 LMLN 92354 647-F2
MAPLE CT
- MURR 92562 927-F5
200 SJCT 92582 810-J2
12600 YCPA 92399 649-C4
MAPLE DR
2500 HEMT 92545 840-G4
33100 CTHC 92234 787-F4
MAPLE LN
36100 CALI 92320 690-B6
MAPLE RD
65300 RivC - 726-G1
MAPLE ST
- MURR 92563 928-H7
300 NRCO 92860 713-H4
21200 RivC 92595 897-B7
46200 INDO 92201 5470-H2
N MAPLE ST
100 COR 92880 742-J4
1500 COR 92880 743-A3
S MAPLE ST
100 COR 92880 742-J5
1800 COR 92882 742-J5
MAPLEBROOK LN
- COR 92881 773-F5

MAPLE GLEN DR
- RivC 92880 713-A1
MAPLEGROVE CT
16500 RivC 92503 745-A4
MAPLELEAF CT
20100 RivC 92595 896-H5
39600 MURR 92563 928-F5
MAPLELEAF DR
3400 RivC 92503 744-B4
MAPLE LEAF LN
11900 FONT 92337 644-D4
MAPLERIDGE WY
26500 MORV 92555 718-A3
MAPLES RD
35000 RivC 92595 897-E6
MAPLETON CIR
4300 RivC 92509 684-C1
MAPLE TREE LN
33400 RivC 92595 897-B2
MAPLEWOOD CT
32400 LKEL 92530 896-G4
33500 TEM 92592 979-H2
MAPLEWOOD DR
- RivC 92584 868-F5
- YCPA 92399 650-C5
MAPLEWOOD PL
3900 RIV 92506 685-E6
MARABELLA DR
- RMIR 92270 818-C6
MARABELLA LN
2100 PMSP 92264 786-H6
MARACAIBO CIR E
38500 RivC 92264 816-G2
MARACAIBO CIR W
38500 RivC 92264 816-F2
38800 PMSP 92264 816-F2
MARACAS CT
78700 LQNT 92253 849-G5
MARACAY PL
42500 RivC 92201 819-G5
MARANATHA DR
54100 RivC - 814-C6
MARATHON PL
4600 RIV 92505 714-D6
MARAVILLA DR
200 RIV 92507 686-E4
MARBELLA AV
500 HEMT 92543 840-J2
MARBELLA LN
- PDST 92260 818-G4
MARBER DR
36900 RMIR 92270 787-H7
36900 RMIR 92270 817-H1
MARBETH PL
12100 YCPA 92399 649-A3
MARBETH RD
31400 YCPA 92399 649-A3
MARBLE CT
1200 HEMT 92543 840-H3
MARBLE DR
- RivC 92399 650-G7
55500 RivC 92282 694-E7
55500 RivC 92282 724-E1
MARBLE LN
300 PMSP 92264 786-D4
MARBLEHEAD CIR
23400 CYNL 92587 867-E3
MARBRISE ABANITA DR
18300 RivC 92562 976-D1
MARBRISSA DR
43300 PDST 92260 818-D7
43300 RMIR 92270 818-D7
MARCALOPE LN
28200 MURR 92584 898-F2
28200 RivC 92584 898-F2
MARCELLA LN
40100 RivC 92543 841-B2
MARCH WY
13100 RivC 92879 744-A6
MARCHETA PL
20500 RivC 92570 775-J5
MARCIA CT
900 LKEL 92530 865-H4
6100 RivC 92509 684-G5
MARCIA RD
34300 CTHC 92234 787-F5
MARCOLESCO LN
15000 RivC 92530 865-G4
MARCO POLO AV
36000 RivC 92544 902-G7
MARCUCHIO RD
31300 RivC 92567 779-B7
MARCUS DR
39200 RivC 92592 930-G6
MARCUS LN
28000 RivC 92596 839-B5
MARCUS RD
20400 RIV 92508 746-G1
MARCY WY
900 SJCT 92582 780-J7
900 SJCT 92582 810-J1
MARDEN RD
37700 RivC 92596 929-E4
MARE CIR
8900 RivC 92509 684-D2
MAR-EL ST
11400 MORV 92555 687-J7
MARENGO CT
5200 RIV 92505 714-B5
MARESH CT
76800 PDST 92211 819-C5
MARFA ST
11300 FONT 92337 644-F2
MARGARET AV
700 HEMT 92543 841-B2

RIVERSIDE CO.

STREET
Block City ZIP Pg-Grid

MARGARET AV
25300 MORV 92551 747-H1
33000 RivC 92584 867-G7
33000 RivC 92504 897-G1
MARGARET LN
- YCPA 92399 650-C6
28400 RivC 92544 841-F5
MARGARITA AV
84300 COAC 92236 5471-A4
MARGARITA DR
800 COR 92879 743-E5
MARGARITA GN
1300 SDCo 92028 998-C6
MARGARITA LN
- LMLN 92354 647-F2
MARGARITA RD
- PDST 92260 818-G4
28800 RivC 92532 836-D7
28800 RivC 92532 866-D1
30700 TEM 92591 959-B4
40000 MURR 92563 928-G7
40300 MURR 92591 928-G7
40300 TEM 92591 928-G7
40300 TEM 92591 958-H2
42200 TEM 92592 959-B6
43400 TEM 92592 979-E1
MARGARITA ST
- INDO 92201 5470-G3
700 SJCT 92583 811-D3
25700 MORV 92553 717-H5
MARGARITA VISTA
3000 SDCo 92028 998-C7
MARGARTH ST
21300 RivC 92570 836-J1
21300 RivC 92570 837-A1
MARGATE WY
1200 SJCT 92583 811-C3
30000 CTHC 92234 757-G7
MARGE PL
44800 TEM 92592 979-H3
MARGEAUX LN
2200 SJCT 92583 811-F4
MARGIE WY
4000 RivC 92509 684-J2
MARGO RD
34500 RivC 92530 896-G5
MARGUERITA AV
6500 RIV 92506 715-F3
7000 RIV 92504 715-F3
MARGUERITE CIR
23600 MORV 92557 687-D5
MARGUERITE PL
31600 RivC 92584 868-C6
MARGUERITE ST
2100 PMSP 92264 787-D5
MARGURITE CT
44500 LQNT 92253 819-J7
MARHILL CIR
29700 TEM 92591 958-J4
MARI DR
3600 LKEL 92530 865-H4
MARIA
200 PMSP 92262 786-E1
W MARIA CT
100 CLTN 92324 646-C4
100 SBdC 92324 646-C4
MARIA DR
7700 RivC 92509 684-G5
MARIA RD
35000 CTHC 92234 787-G6
MARIAH CIR
- COR 92879 743-G4
MARIAN AV
16000 RivC 92530 895-J1
MARIAN RD
13900 MORV 92555 718-C5
28800 TEM 92591 959-A1
MARIAN ST
- LKEL 92530 866-G6
MARIAN WY
800 BAN 92220 691-D7
800 BAN 92220 721-D2
27400 TEM 92591 958-J1
28000 TEM 92591 959-A1
MARIAN VIEW DR
54100 RivC - 814-C7
54100 RivC - 844-C1
W MARIAN VIEW DR
53000 RivC - 844-A1
53800 RivC - 814-C7
MARICOPA DR
1400 PMSP 92264 786-F5
3200 RIV 92507 686-F4
MARICOPA ST
- NRCO 92860 713-C7
MARIE DR
2800 RivC 92509 645-E7
2800 RivC 92509 685-E1
32800 RivC 92530 866-A7
32800 RivC 92530 865-J7
MARIE RD
21500 RivC 92570 776-J7
21500 RivC 92570 777-A7
57100 RivC 92539 (935-A2
See Page 904)
MARIE ST
1500 COR 92879 743-D7
8100 RIV 92504 715-B3
24000 RivC 92570 807-C6
25100 RivC 92570 837-C1
MARIELLA ST
3600 RIV 92504 715-D2
MARIETTA CIR
39200 CTHC 92234 817-D3

MARIETTE RD
42100 RivC 92536 961-G3
42100 RivC 92544 961-G3
MARIGOLD AV
12000 MORV 92557 717-F2
MARIGOLD CIR
2600 COR 92881 773-G3
3100 PMSP 92264 816-E1
MARIGOLD DR
43600 PDST 92260 818-G7
MARIGOLD LN
44200 LQNT 92253 819-J7
MARIGOLD PL
9200 RIV 92503 715-A7
MARIGOLD ST
6300 RivC 92880 683-D6
46200 INDO 92201 5470-E2
MARIGOLD WY
2200 HEMT 92545 810-G5
2500 COR 92881 773-G3
MARILEE CT
2800 HEMT 92545 810-F4
MARILYN CIR
67800 CTHC 92234 787-C1
MARILYN DR
7200 RivC 92881 773-J4
MARILYN ST
24400 MORV 92553 717-F4
46000 INDO 92201 5470-G1
MARIMBA DR
49000 LQNT 92253 849-H5
MARIN CIR
23500 MURR 92562 928-A1
MARIN CT
1600 SJCT 92583 811-E4
6600 RIV 92506 716-B4
MARINA DR
- RivC 92254 (5654-D6
See Page 5594)
MARINA RD
1200 COR 92880 743-B2
68000 CTHC 92234 757-D7
MARINE DR
41700 RivC 92544 811-E7
MARINER CIR
2000 COR 92879 773-F1
MARINER DR
600 PER 92571 777-J7
29600 CYNL 92587 867-D2
MARINERS WY
28200 RivC 92584 868-F3
29500 LKEL 92530 865-G3
MARIN HILLS DR
53600 RivC 92539 904-C6
MARINI CT
2000 PMSP 92262 756-J5
MARIN MEADOW RD
38300 RivC 92592 930-H2
MARINO DR
30300 RivC 92584 868-J5
30300 RivC 92584 869-A5
MARINO ST
14600 RivC 92230 723-D5
MARION AV
600 HEMT 92543 841-B2
15100 RivC 92282 695-F7
16000 RivC 92282 725-F2
40700 RivC 92544 841-C2
MARION CT
8900 RIV 92503 715-B7
MARION WY
900 PMSP 92264 786-F5
68000 RivC 92240 697-C7
MARION MOUNTAIN TR
- RivC - (783-J7
See Page 782)
- RivC - (813-J1
See Page 782)
MARION RIDGE DR
24700 RivC - 814-A4
25000 RivC - (813-J7
See Page 782)
25700 RivC - (843-H1
See Page 842)
MARIPOSA AV
- MORV 92551 747-H4
4100 RIV 92503 714-G6
16000 RivC 92504 745-H5
17300 RivC 92504 746-B5
17800 RivC 92508 746-B5
MARIPOSA CIR
- INDO 92201 5470-C4
MARIPOSA CT
2100 SJCT 92583 811-E5
44000 LQNT 92253 819-J7
MARIPOSA DR
400 PMSP 92264 786-E6
500 HEMT 92543 810-H6
1400 COR 92879 743-G3
31800 LKEL 92532 866-J5
48200 PDST 92260 848-F5
51200 COAC 92236 5471-D7
MARIPOSA PL
31400 TEM 92592 979-C1
MARIPOSA RD
21000 RivC 92530 866-J7
21000 RivC 92530 896-J1
MARIPOSA ST
25700 LMLN 92354 647-D2
33900 YCPA 92399 649-G4
MARIPOSA TR
100 BLY 92225 5491-E5
MARISA CT
2800 RIV 92503 715-A7

W MARISCAL RD
300 PMSP 92262 756-D6
MARISMA WY
200 CTHC 92234 787-F7
MARISOL RD
19000 RivC 92570 776-D5
MARITIME CIR
- LKEL 92530 865-F3
MARIUS AV
32900 RivC 92596 929-F1
MARIUS WY
32000 RivC 92596 929-F3
MARJORIE AV
700 HEMT 92543 841-B2
MARJORIE LN
1700 SJCT 92583 781-A5
MARK AV
15700 LKEL 92530 865-J6
MARK CT
4400 RivC 92509 685-A2
MARK DR
13500 DHSP 92240 697-A5
MARK RD
28600 MORV 92555 688-E7
MARK TER
- RMIR 92270 788-B7
MARK TR
41000 RivC 92544 901-E5
MARKET CT
82200 INDO 92201 5410-F6
MARKET DR
400 BAN 92220 721-F2
MARKET PL
- RivC 92211 819-F2
74800 PDST 92260 818-H3
MARKET ST
- PER 92571 777-G2
1600 COR 92880 742-J4
1700 NRCO 92860 713-D6
1800 RivC 92509 645-F6
1900 RIV 92501 685-G1
1900 RivC 92501 645-F6
1900 RivC 92501 685-G1
56000 RivC 92274 5531-G4
82100 INDO 92201 5410-F7
MARKETPLACE WY
34000 PDST 92211 788-D4
34000 RMIR 92270 788-D4
MARKHAM LN
18500 RivC 92570 777-C1
MARKHAM ST
200 PER 92571 747-F7
800 PER 92571 777-A1
800 PER 92571 748-A7
1000 PER 92571 748-A7
16300 RivC 92504 745-H7
17100 RivC 92508 745-H7
17300 RivC 92504 746-A7
17300 RivC 92508 746-A7
17900 RivC 92570 746-A7
19000 RivC 92508 776-G1
19000 RivC 92570 776-G1
21500 RivC 92570 777-A1
22000 RivC 92570 747-C7
E MARKHAM ST
100 PER 92571 747-G7
MARK LESLIE DR
1900 PMSP 92264 786-G4
MARK TWAIN
23600 MORV 92557 687-D7
MARK TWAIN CT
- RivC 92880 683-D4
MARLATT ST
4700 RivC 91752 684-A4
MARLAY AV
5100 ONT 91761 643-G3
11500 FONT 92337 644-A3
12900 FONT 92337 643-H3
MARLBORO WY
300 BAN 92220 721-E2
MARLBOROUGH AV
700 RIV 92507 686-A2
MARLENE ST
8600 RIV 92504 715-B6
8700 RIV 92503 715-B6
43300 RivC 92536 964-A6
43300 RivC 92544 811-J5
MARLEY CIR
24100 RivC 92585 808-F5
MARLEY DR
2600 RIV 92506 715-H2
MARLISSA RD
30100 RivC 92544 871-D2
MARLO CT
26000 RivC 92544 (812-C7
See Page 782)
MARLO WY
6500 RIV 92506 715-G4
MARLOWE CT
75500 PDST 92211 819-E3
E MARLOWE WY
3300 CLTN 92324 647-A5
3300 SBdC 92324 647-A5
MARLYCE LN
900 HEMT 92543 841-B2
900 RivC 92543 841-B2
MARMADUKE TR
40100 RivC 92544 901-C3
MARMALADE CT
19100 RivC 92508 746-D3
MARMALADE LN
- HEMT 92544 811-G6
MARMIAN WY
4500 RIV 92506 715-D1

MARMION CIR
30900 TEM 92591 959-B1
MARMONT PL
12300 MORV 92557 717-G2
MARMOT RD
46800 RivC 92536 962-G1
MARNE CT
- LQNT 92253 5470-A5
24800 RivC 92544 (812-A5
See Page 782)
MARNE WY
30100 RivC 92584 868-G3
MARONDI DR
37000 CALI 92320 690-D1
MAROON PEAK WY
- RIV 92508 746-E2
MAROON TOWN DR
41500 RivC 92201 819-H4
MARQUESA CT
600 HEMT 92543 840-J1
MARQUETTE CT
12300 MORV 92557 717-J2
MARQUEZ RD
22300 RivC 92570 777-B2
MARRAKESH DR
47000 PDST 92260 848-F3
MARRELLI RD
20300 LKEL 92532 866-H1
28500 RivC 92570 836-J7
MARRICOPA CT
- PDST 92211 819-E6
MARRIOTT CIR
1200 COR 92882 743-A7
MARRIOTT LN
72000 RMIR 92270 818-C5
MARS
- PMSP 92264 786-J6
MARS CT
24600 MORV 92553 717-F7
MARS PL
- PMSP 92264 786-J5
11000 RivC 91752 683-H5
MARS ST
- RivC 92881 773-H5
MARSEILLE CT
41100 MURR 92562 928-A4
MARSEL RANCH RD
25200 MORV 92553 717-G3
MARSH LN
35300 RivC 92595 897-D7
MARSH WY
1400 RIV 92501 686-A2
MARSHA CT
2400 RIV 92506 715-G4
40400 RivC 92544 841-C2
MARSHALL AV
16500 LKEL 92530 865-J1
25800 RivC 92544 (812-D7
See Page 782)
25900 RivC 92544 842-D1
MARSHALL LN
1500 COR 92879 743-E7
MARSHALL RD
21200 RivC 92241 728-H7
MARSHALL ST
3500 RIV 92504 715-D3
22900 RivC 92570 807-A4
45700 INDO 92201 5470-G1
E MARSHALL WY
1000 PMSP 92262 756-E7
MARSHALL CANYON RD
10000 RivC 92223 691-B4
MARSHELL RD
16000 RivC 92570 805-H3
MARSTON CT
21300 MORV 92557 716-H1
MARTA CT
25500 RivC 92544 811-J6
MARTE CIR
15100 MORV 92551 747-H1
MARTHA LN
42400 RivC 92536 963-B7
MARTHA ST
- PMSP 92264 787-C5
MARTHA WY
9300 RIV 92503 714-J6
MARTHA CRAWFORD ST
13500 MORV 92555 718-B5
MARTIN LN
10700 RivC 92223 690-J5
44800 RivC 92544 (932-D6
See Page 902)
MARTIN PL
14000 RivC 92503 745-C4
MARTIN RD
41700 RivC 92544 901-E2
48200 BAN 92220 722-H2
48200 RivC 92220 722-H2
48500 RivC 92220 723-A2
MARTIN ST
- BAN 92220 722-B1
4700 RivC 91752 683-J3
11700 LMLN 92354 647-D3
19600 RivC 92570 776-F2
21400 RivC 92570 777-B2
29000 RivC 92571 778-G2
MARTINA CT
- TEM 92592 979-F2
MARTINDALE DR
52200 RivC 92536 963-J7
52200 RivC 92536 964-A7
MARTINEZ AV
6000 RivC 92509 684-J5
MARTINEZ DR
42000 RivC 92544 931-G2

MARTINEZ LN
2600 RIV 92503 744-J1
2600 RIV 92503 745-A1
MARTINEZ RD
66900 RivC 92274 (5591-F7
See Page 5590)
66900 RivC 92274 (5651-F1
See Page 5590)
MARTINGALE DR
4900 RivC 92509 684-F2
MARTINI CT
43300 PDST 92260 818-F6
MARTINIQUE CIR
1200 PMSP 92264 786-G4
MARTINIQUE DR
1400 HEMT 92543 840-J4
78700 RivC 92201 819-G5
MARTINIQUE PL
14100 MORV 92553 717-H6
MARTIN LUTHER KING BLVD
800 RIV 92507 686-A6
2100 RIV 92507 685-J6
MARTOS RD
11600 FONT 92337 644-F3
MARTYNIA CT
21100 MORV 92557 716-H1
MARVALE AV
13100 RivC 92879 744-A5
MARVELLA LN
19600 RivC 92530 896-G5
MARVEN GARDENS WY
25400 MURR 92563 928-E5
MARVICK WY
25700 MURR 92563 928-E6
MARVIEW CT
3700 RIV 92505 744-E1
MARVIN RD
30400 RivC 92567 778-J1
30400 RivC 92567 779-A1
34000 RivC 92582 779-G1
MARVINGA LN
2700 SDCo 92028 997-A2
MARVIN HULL RD
34700 RivC 92545 839-J5
34700 RivC 92545 840-A4
MAR VISTA CT
- PMSP 92264 786-J5
8100 RIV 92504 715-D6
MARWOOD CIR
41800 TEM 92591 958-J4
MARX RD
37100 RMIR 92270 817-J1
MARY CT
- COAC 92236 5471-B5
MARY LN
100 HEMT 92543 841-A1
100 HEMT 92543 840-J1
39900 RivC 92223 691-A6
75500 INDW 92210 849-A2
80800 INDO 92201 5470-B2
MARY PL
28000 MURR 92563 928-F3
MARY ST
2300 RIV 92506 715-F3
20800 RivC 92570 776-H1
21500 RivC 92570 777-A1
MARYBETH LN
14700 RivC 92508 746-B1
MARY ELLEN DR
2900 RivC 92509 645-C7
3100 RivC 92509 685-C1
MARY ELLEN TR
28000 RivC 92585 838-E6
28400 RivC 92584 838-E6
MARY FLEMING CIR
- PMSP 92262 756-F6
MARY FRANCIS RD
37500 RivC 92596 929-E3
MARYHELEN ST
2300 COR 92879 743-J2
W MARYKNOLL DR
100 CLTN 92324 646-B5
MARYLAND AV
- RivC 92880 683-C4
MARY LEE WY
12100 MORV 92555 718-B2
MARYLYNN WY
52700 RivC 92539 904-A7
MARYMOUNT ST
1200 RIV 92501 645-H7
1400 RIV 92501 685-H1
MARYN CT
41900 PDST 92211 819-A5
MARYVALE LN
1700 HEMT 92544 811-C7
MARZI CT
44700 TEM 92592 979-F3
MASAKO CIR
28000 RivC 92590 978-E1
MASHIE DR
71200 RMIR 92270 818-A3
MASHIE RD
6100 PMSP 92264 787-C5
MASHIE WY
30900 TEM 92591 959-C5
MASKUAZ CT
42300 TEM 92592 979-C5
MASON AV
17700 RivC 92508 746-D7
28400 MURR 92563 928-G2
MASON PL
1800 COR 92881 743-F7

MASON RD
38000 RivC 92539 (934-A3
See Page 904)
MASON ST
9500 RIV 92503 714-H6
MASONCREST DR
20100 RivC 92570 776-F6
MASONIC DR
42800 RivC 92544 811-G5
MASSACHUSETTS AV
100 RIV 92507 686-A3
400 BEAU 92223 721-A3
1000 BEAU 92223 720-J1
MASSACHUSETTS CT
42800 PDST 92211 819-D6
N MASSACHUSETTS ST
100 LKEL 92530 865-G2
S MASSACHUSETTS ST
100 LKEL 92530 865-G2
MASSON ST
73800 PDST 92260 818-F7
MASSUCCI RD
37500 RivC 92539 (934-B2
See Page 904)
MASTERS AV
4100 RIV 92507 686-F5
MASTERS CIR
- LQNT 92253 879-F2
MASTERS DR
- COR 92881 773-F5
- MURR 92563 928-J4
1600 BAN 92220 721-D5
20600 COR 92883 773-H6
45500 TEM 92592 979-C4
MATADOR WY
23700 MURR 92562 928-A1
MATARO LN
1100 COR 92882 742-F6
MATATE RD
57500 RivC 92539 (935-B5
See Page 904)
MATEO DR
21400 RivC 92570 776-A7
MATERA CT
- TEM 92592 979-G1
MATERHORN VW
60200 RivC - (907-E3
See Page 906)
MATEROS RD
26000 RivC 92585 838-H4
MATEUS DR
44100 RivC 92536 983-B1
MATHESON DR
5800 RIV 92507 716-F2
MATHEWS PL
900 COR 92881 743-J7
MATHEWS RD
11500 MORV 92557 687-G7
11500 MORV 92557 717-G1
11800 RivC 92220 692-J7
12100 RivC 92220 722-J2
MATHEWS ST
1700 RIV 92507 686-A2
MATHILDA LN
- RIV 92508 716-E7
MATHUR LN
- RivC 92567 779-C7
MATICH ST
100 LKEL 92530 866-C4
MATILDA LN
28800 MURR 92563 928-G3
MATILIJA DR
14000 RivC 92282 695-G6
15200 RivC 92282 725-G1
MATILIZA CT
- RMIR 92270 787-G6
MATISSE CIR
3400 COR 92882 773-C4
MATTERHORN DR
300 COR 92881 773-D3
1300 RIV 92506 715-H6
MATTESON RD
24100 MURR 92562 927-J5
MATTHEW DR
4100 PMSP 92264 787-A6
MATTHEW LN
1700 HEMT 92545 810-H5
MATTHEWS RD
26400 RivC 92585 838-F2
27600 RivC 92585 839-A4
MATTHEWS RD Rt#-74
2300 PER 92570 808-C7
2400 PER 92585 808-C7
14800 RivC 92570 808-C7
14800 RivC 92585 808-C7
25600 RivC 92585 838-D1
MATTIE PL
3800 RIV 92504 715-B4
MATTOLE RD
25000 RivC 92544 (812-A6
See Page 782)
MATTUS WY
24800 MORV 92551 747-G1
MAUDE
26200 RivC 92544 841-B1
MAUDE ST
2600 RIV 92506 715-G2
MAUI LN
700 PMSP 92264 786-E5
MAUI WY
12500 DHSP 92240 697-B5
MAULDIN LN
16000 RivC 92504 745-D4
MAUMEE LN
48900 RivC 92230 723-A2

MAUNALOA PL
1800 NRCO 92860 713-D3
MAUNA LOA RD
16100 RivC - 726-H1
MAUREEN DR
11000 RivC 92223 691-B6
MAURICE ST
32000 RivC 92567 779-C6
MAURICIO ST
19800 LKEL 92570 836-G6
20000 RivC 92570 836-H6
21000 RivC 92570 837-A6
MAVERICK CT
1200 CALI 92320 689-J1
MAVERICK LN
5800 RivC 92509 685-A4
MAVIS ST
22100 GTER 92313 646-D4
MAWR CT
29200 RivC 92586 868-B1
MAXIMO WY
- PDST 92260 818-F5
MAXINE AV
51900 RivC 92230 723-G6
MAXINE CIR
2700 COR 92882 773-C2
MAXINE CT
14000 MORV 92553 717-E6
MAXINE LN
29800 RivC 92584 868-J6
MAXON AV
15700 LKEL 92530 865-J6
MAXWELL CT
4600 RIV 92501 685-E5
MAXWELL LN
900 COR 92881 743-F7
MAXY DR
25200 MORV 92551 747-H3
MAY AV
100 LKEL 92530 866-F5
MAY CT
3300 RivC 92503 744-B5
N MAY DR
1100 PMSP 92262 756-E7
MAY LN
14500 MORV 92553 717-G7
MAYBELLE ST
5900 RIV 92504 715-A1
MAYBERRY AV
200 HEMT 92543 841-A1
300 HEMT 92543 840-J1
40200 RivC 92544 841-C1
43600 RivC 92544 842-A1
44400 RivC 92544 (812-B7
See Page 782)
E MAYBERRY AV
100 HEMT 92543 841-A1
MAYBERRY CIR
200 RivC 91752 683-E5
MAYBERRY ST
26100 SBdC 92354 647-E1
26100 LMLN 92354 647-F1
MAYBROOK CIR
5800 RIV 92506 715-H2
MAYBROOK WY
9500 MORV 92557 687-B4
MAYES LN
32600 RivC 92595 897-A6
MAYFAIR AV
3100 RivC 92509 685-C2
MAYFAIR CIR
- RivC 91752 683-E5
MAYFAIR DR
- RMIR 92270 817-J2
1200 COR 92882 743-A7
42000 PDST 92211 818-J5
MAYFAIR LN
3100 RIV 92506 715-F2
MAYFIELD DR
21400 RivC 92570 746-J6
MAYFIELD UNION WY
- MURR 92563 928-G6
MAYFLOWER CT
12800 RivC 92503 744-B5
MAYFLOWER DR
29800 CYNL 92587 867-E2
MAYFLOWER PL
1900 HEMT 92544 811-C6
N MAYFLOWER ST
100 HEMT 92544 811-C7
S MAYFLOWER ST
100 HEMT 92544 811-C7
MAYHALL DR
20100 RivC 92595 896-H5
MAYHEW LN
31500 RivC 92584 868-C6
MAYHEW RD
24400 RivC 92883 804-F6
MAYNARD DR
25200 MORV 92553 717-G3
MAYNARD LN
8400 RIV 92508 746-H1
MAYOR CT
900 COR 92881 743-J6
MAY PEN RD
42100 RivC 92201 819-G5
MAY RANCH PKWY
1000 PER 92571 778-A2
MAYTEN TREE CT
1100 HEMT 92545 840-G3
MAY VALLEY TKTR
12500 DHSP 92240 697-B5
MAYWOOD CIR
1900 COR 92881 773-F1

MAYWOOD ST
17500 SBdC 92316 645-B1
W MAYWOOD ST
400 SBdC 92316 645-G2
MAZANA DR
700 HEMT 92543 810-H5
MAZATLAN WY
- INDO 92201 5470-G2
MAZE ROCK RD
27500 RivC 92545 840-A4
MAZE STONE CT
24100 RivC 92545 810-B4
MAZE STONE RD
39100 RivC 92539 (934-H5
See Page 904)
MAZIE AV
21300 RivC 92570 837-A4
21900 RivC 92570 836-J4
MAZOE ST
32000 RivC 92563 929-E2
32000 RivC 92596 929-E2
MCABEE AV
28700 MORV 92555 718-F4
MCALBY CT
- MURR 92562 958-D3
MCALLISTER DR
2300 NRCO 92860 713-C6
MCALLISTER ST
2000 RIV 92503 744-H2
2000 RIV 92503 744-J3
16000 RivC 92503 745-A4
MCALPINE LN
- RIV 92508 746-F2
MCARTHUR RD
58000 RivC 92539 (935-C6
See Page 904)
MCBOB RD
34000 RivC 92584 898-C4
MCBRIDE AV
17000 LKEL 92530 866-A2
MCBRIDE PL
23600 MORV 92553 717-D5
MCBURNEY AV
30000 LKEL 92530 866-C3
MCCABE CT
41300 TEM 92590 958-F3
MCCABE DR
- TEM 92592 959-E7
MCCALL BLVD
25600 RivC 92586 837-J5
25600 RivC 92586 838-A5
27100 RivC 92585 838-D5
28000 RivC 92596 839-B6
MCCALL CIR
- COR 92881 773-D5
MCCALL CT
26900 RivC 92586 838-C7
26900 RivC 92586 868-C1
MCCALL DR
- COR 92881 773-E5
MCCALLISTER RD
20500 RivC 92583 780-J4
MCCALL PARK RD
27800 RivC - 844-B4
MCCALLUM WY
68200 CTHC 92234 787-D1
MCCANNA RANCH RD
1200 PER 92571 778-B2
MCCARGER RD
13100 DHSP 92240 697-D6
13100 RivC 92240 697-D6
MCCANN RD
2500 PMSP 92262 756-E5
MCCARTHY RD
3700 PMSP 92262 756-D4
MCCARTY DR
2500 CLTN 92324 647-A4
MCCARTY RD
- SBdC 91710 712-F5
8300 RivC 92880 712-E6
8300 SBdC 92880 712-F5
MCCAUGHEY DR
26000 RivC - 814-E6
MCCLAIN LN
42800 RivC 92536 963-E7
43700 RivC 92536 983-E1
MCCLARREN ST
22100 GTER 92313 646-E3
MCCLINTOCK DR
14000 MORV 92555 717-J6
MCCLOUD DR
14300 MORV 92555 718-D6
S MCCLOUD RIVER RD
2800 ONT 91761 643-D6
MCCLURE CT
26000 RivC 92571 778-B4
MCCONNEL CT
- YCPA 92399 649-E2
MCCONNELL AV
21200 RivC 92518 746-J5
MCCORMICK AV
700 ONT 91761 643-F2
MCCORMICK CT
22500 RivC 92595 897-C3
MCCORMICK DR
47500 PDST 92260 848-C4
MCCORMICK RD
500 HEMT 92543 811-A5
MCCRAY ST
3700 RIV 92506 715-E2
MCCULLY CT
11500 MORV 92557 717-D1
MCCULLY DR
11600 MORV 92557 717-E1

MCDERMOTT RD
43800 RivC 92583 811-H4
43800 RivC 92583 (812-A4
See Page 782)
MCDONALD LN
- COR 92882 773-C3
26300 RivC 92584 898-B3
38300 RivC 92539 (935-A4
See Page 904)
MCDONALD RD
1100 SJCT 92582 810-H1
MCDONALD ST
30900 RivC 92596 899-B1
MCDONNELL ST
13700 MORV 92553 717-B5
MCDOWELL RD
18600 RivC 92508 746-C5
MCDOWELL ST
41000 RivC 92544 841-D1
MCELWAIN RD
3500 MURR 92562 898-E7
MCEWAN LN
16100 RivC 92570 775-H4
MCFADDEN ST
26400 MORV 92555 717-J5
26400 MORV 92555 718-A5
MCFALL RD
37900 RivC 92544 931-H3
MCFARLAND ST
4600 RIV 92506 685-D7
MCFIE RD
24200 RivC 92548 809-D5
MCGALLIARD RD
29500 RivC 92586 868-A2
MCGEE CREEK LN
3900 ONT 91761 643-D6
MCGEHEE DR
13000 RivC 92555 719-B4
MCGILL DR
- RMIR 92270 818-A3
MCGOVERN AV
300 BAN 92220 721-G3
MCGOVERN RD
25600 RivC - (813-J4
See Page 782)
52700 RivC - 814-A4
MCGRATH DR
- COR 92880 743-C4
MCGRAW ST
8500 RIV 92508 746-H2
MCGREW DR
33400 RivC 92530 896-B3
MCGUIRE CIR
400 COR 92880 742-J3
MCGUIRE RD
19100 RivC 92570 776-B2
MCHARG RD
3000 RIV 92503 744-E3
MCINTYRE RD
30500 RivC 92585 808-J2
30500 RivC 92585 809-A3
MCKENZIE LN
- RivC - 844-A5
MCKENZIE ST
3500 RIV 92503 714-H5
MCKIM CT
26700 RivC 92544 841-F2
MCKIMBALL RD
- RivC 92570 777-F7
800 PER 92570 807-F1
1100 PER 92570 777-F7
3000 PER 92571 777-F4
MCKINLEY
- CTHC 92234 787-A7
- PMSP 92264 787-A7
MCKINLEY DR
12300 BLY - 5491-A7
MCKINLEY RD
26000 RivC 92585 838-G4
MCKINLEY ST
100 COR 92879 743-J3
1100 LKEL 92530 865-H4
1500 COR 92879 744-A4
2500 RivC 92879 744-A4
2800 RIV 92506 715-E2
3400 RivC 92503 744-A4
MCKINNEY LN
53000 RivC - 844-A1
MCLACHLIN CIR
75600 PDST 92211 819-A2
MCLANE ST
19000 PMSP 92258 726-C4
MCLAREN LN
6800 RivC 92509 645-B4
MCLAUGHLIN RD
25000 RivC 92585 837-H2
25800 RivC 92585 838-A2
26800 PER 92585 838-C2
30200 RivC 92585 839-A2
30200 RivC 92548 838-G2
30200 RivC 92548 839-A2
MCLEAN AV
33100 RivC 92545 839-F3
MCMACKIN DR
- COR 92881 773-F2
MCMAHON RD
26800 RivC - 844-A2
MCMAHON ST
5700 RIV 92506 715-G2
E MCMANUS DR
2000 PMSP 92262 786-G1
MCMILLAN ST
- BLY 92225 5491-H4
10900 RIV 92503 744-F2

E MCNAMARA ST
4800 ONT 91761 643-F2
MCNEIL CIR
2200 COR 92882 742-J7
2200 COR 92882 772-J1
MCNICHOLL DR
9800 RIV 92503 744-E3
MCPHERSON AV
16300 LKEL 92530 865-J2
MCPHERSON RD
1500 PER 92570 807-E6
22100 RivC 92570 837-B2
23300 RivC 92570 807-E6
26000 PER 92570 837-E1
MCRAE LN
32500 RivC 92595 896-H5
MCVICAR ST
32500 RivC 92595 927-C2
MCWADE AV
31300 RivC 92548 839-C1
MEAD CT
6200 RIV 92504 685-C7
12800 MORV 92553 717-E3
MEAD ST
200 SJCT 92583 811-B1
18700 RivC 92570 776-H2
MEADBURY DR
12600 MORV 92553 717-C3
MEADE RIVER CT
30800 TEM 92591 959-B4
MEADOW CT
13700 FONT 92337 644-A4
MEADOW DR
53200 RivC - 844-A1
MEADOW LN
- RIV 92508 746-D4
900 COR 92882 773-B2
23500 RivC 92570 806-J4
40500 PDST 92260 818-E4
S MEADOW LN
1000 CLTN 92324 646-G2
MEADOW RD
26500 RivC 92584 898-B2
52400 RivC - (813-J5
See Page 782)
MEADOW RDG
- RivC 92880 713-B1
MEADOW ST
13500 YCPA 92399 649-H7
MEADOW VW
- SDCo 92028 998-G5
MEADOW WY
600 BAN 92220 721-E2
MEADOW BLOSSOM LN
38700 RivC 92592 930-J2
MEADOW BLOSSOM RD
31200 RivC 92567 779-B4
MEADOW BREEZE DR
14900 MORV 92553 717-E7
MEADOWBROOK
- LQNT 92253 5530-C5
MEADOWBROOK AV
20800 RivC 92570 836-J4
MEADOWBROOK LN
5800 RIV 92504 685-D7
5900 RIV 92506 685-D7
6000 CHLS 91709 712-A4
MEADOW BROOK LN
38600 RivC 92592 930-J1
MEADOW BROOK WY
- TEM 92591 959-D3
MEADOW CREEK DR
10400 MORV 92557 687-A5
MEADOW CREST CT
10800 RIV 92505 714-C1
MEADOW CREST DR
- MORV 92557 687-G7
MEADOWGATE CIR
12500 MORV 92553 717-C3
MEADOWGATE CT
- MURR 92562 927-G4
MEADOWGATE LN
30700 RivC 92596 869-B6
MEADOW GLEN DR
26600 RivC - 844-B1
MEADOW GRASS WY
24500 MORV 92557 687-F6
MEADOW GROVE ST
44300 RivC 92544 (812-B5
See Page 782)
MEADOW LAKE DR
- INDO 92201 5470-A2
- LQNT 92253 5470-A2
MEADOW LAKE LN
300 BAN 92220 721-D4
MEADOW LAND DR
4700 RivC 92509 684-F2
MEADOWLANDS DR
14100 RivC 92503 745-C4
MEADOWLARK CIR
- COR 92881 773-G4
MEADOWLARK DR
30300 CYNL 92587 867-D4
MEADOWLARK LN
- SBdC 92316 645-F2
MEADOW LARK LN
200 BAN 92220 692-B7
MEADOWLARK LN
400 PER 92570 807-F1
3400 MURR 92584 898-F7
35400 MURR 92563 898-F7
MEADOWLARK RD
27100 RivC - 844-C2
MEADOWLARK RDG
42300 MURR 92562 958-C3

STREET	Block	City	ZIP	Pg-Grid
MEADOWLEAF PL				
	-	HEMT	92545	840-E4
MEADOW MIST CT				
	17700	RivC	92503	744-G7
MEADOWOOD ST				
	700	COR	92882	742-J5
MEADOW RIDGE RD				
	35500	RivC	92592	960-D3
MEADOW ROCK DR				
	17300	RivC	92503	744-H6
MEADOW RUN PL				
	30400	RivC	92584	868-G3
MEADOWS LN				
	84000	COAC	92236	5470-J4
	84100	COAC	92236	5471-A4
MEADOWS PKWY				
	41000	TEM	92591	959-D3
	42000	TEM	92592	959-E5
	42600	TEM	92592	979-F1
MEADOW VALLEY LN				
	54000	RivC	92539	904-D7
MEADOWVIEW CT				
	34400	RivC	92595	897-H4
MEADOW VIEW DR				
	-	RivC	92584	868-F6
MEADOWVIEW DR				
	3400	RivC	92503	744-B4
MEADOW VIEW LN				
	-	RivC	92223	650-G7
	13700	RivC	92399	650-G7
MEADOWVIEW ST				
	1000	COR	92880	743-A1
MEADOW VIEW WY				
	49200	RivC	92536	963-D5
MEADOW WOOD LN				
	31000	LKEL	92532	867-D5
MEADOW WOOD WY				
	11800	MORV	92557	717-D1
MEAGAN LN				
	11200	RIV	92505	714-A2
MEANDER CT				
	24200	MORV	92557	687-E5
MEARS AV				
	3600	RivC	92509	644-J7
	3600	RivC	92509	645-A6
MECCA				
	-	PMSP	92264	786-C6
MECCA AV				
	73600	RivC	92254	(5654-E7 See Page 5594)
MECCA DR				
	-	CTHC	92234	787-F6
MECCA ST				
	51000	COAC	92236	5471-B7
MECCA DALE RD				
	-	RivC	-	390-L4
MECHANICS WY				
	10900	RivC	91752	683-H4
MEDALLION CT				
	1500	PER	92571	807-H1
MEDALLION PL				
	10100	RIV	92503	714-E1
MEDALLIST DR				
	-	LQNT	92253	5530-C4
MEDANO RD				
	67100	CTHC	92234	757-B5
MEDFORD ST				
	8700	RIV	92508	746-H2
MEDFORD WY				
	27600	RivC	92586	838-B5
MEDHI AV				
	39500	HEMT	92543	841-A5
MEDICAL CENTER DR				
	2000	PER	92571	777-H6
	25400	MURR	92562	928-D6
MEDICINE BOW CIR				
	77300	INDW	92210	849-E2
MEDINA AV				
	85200	COAC	92236	5471-C7
MEDINA CT				
	-	PMSP	92264	816-D1
	39300	MURR	92562	928-C2
MEDINA DR E				
	47400	PDST	92260	848-G3
MEDINA DR W				
	47400	PDST	92260	848-F4
MEDINA WY				
	-	RMIR	92270	818-D6
	1700	RIV	92506	716-B2
MEDINAH				
	-	LQNT	92253	5530-B6
MEDINAH DR				
	-	INDO	92201	5410-B6
MEDINAH WY				
	-	TEM	92591	959-B5
	14500	MORV	92555	718-D6
MEDIO DR				
	35500	RMIR	92270	787-G6
MEDITERRANEAN				
	75000	PDST	92211	818-J5
MEDITERRANEAN DR				
	16700	MORV	92551	747-G4
MEDLAR ST				
	12700	YCPA	92399	650-C5
MEDLEY DR				
	11700	MORV	92557	717-B1
MEDOC CIR				
	1900	SJCT	92583	811-F3
MEEKER LN				
	45500	RivC	92536	982-G4
MEERS DR				
	100	SJCT	92582	810-H1
MEGA ST				
	3800	PER	92571	777-G2
MEGAN LN				
	-	BLY	92225	5491-F5
	-	MORV	92551	747-F2
MEGGINSON LN				
	3800	RIV	92503	714-G6
MEGIN AV				
	-	RivC	-	392-A10
MEHAFFEY ST				
	26300	RivC	92586	838-B4
MEHLHORN CIR				
	1400	BAN	92220	721-E6
MEIER ST				
	200	HEMT	92543	811-A6
MEKEEL RANCH RD				
	33900	RivC	92592	959-J6
E MEL AV				
	300	PMSP	92262	756-E6
MEL LN				
	26300	RivC	92544	841-D1
MELALEUCA LN				
	2700	SDCo	92028	998-B6
MELANIE AV				
	3100	NRCO	92860	713-E5
MELANIE PL				
	42500	PDST	92211	818-J6
MELANITA DR				
	27100	CTHC	92234	757-C5
MELBA				
	2000	COR	92879	773-D1
MELBA AV				
	25500	RivC	92548	809-D7
	25700	RivC	92548	839-D1
	26400	RivC	92585	839-D2
MELBA CT				
	11300	FONT	92337	644-F2
MELBOURNE CIR				
	1800	BAN	92220	721-D6
MELBOURNE CT				
	400	HEMT	92545	810-E6
MELBOURNE PL				
	-	RIV	92508	716-E7
MELBOURNE ST				
	5000	RivC	92509	684-C2
MELBY DR				
	29100	RivC	92532	866-E1
MEL CHRIST LN				
	3500	HEMT	92544	811-E6
MELIDO ST				
	25800	RivC	92584	868-A7
MELINDA CT				
	23100	MORV	92553	717-C4
MELINDA LN				
	-	SBDO	92408	646-J1
	20100	RivC	92530	896-J4
	20100	RivC	92595	896-J4
MELISSA CIR				
	9200	RivC	92509	684-D1
	44900	TEM	92592	979-H3
MELISSA CT				
	-	COR	92879	743-G5
	700	BEAU	92223	690-J7
MELISSA LN				
	17000	PMSP	92258	726-A2
MELISSA ST				
	1600	COR	92879	743-G5
MELISSA WY				
	-	SBDO	92408	646-J1
MELITTA RD				
	29600	RivC	92584	868-A2
MELLISA DR				
	900	HEMT	92543	811-A5
MELLOR ST				
	-	COR	92879	773-D2
MELLOW LN				
	100	BEAU	92223	720-H4
	900	BEAU	92223	721-A4
	38700	RivC	92223	720-H4
MELMORE LN				
	31100	RivC	92584	868-H5
MELODY				
	5000	RIV	92505	714-C6
MELODY CIR				
	1600	COR	92882	743-C7
MELODY LN				
	3800	RIV	92504	715-A4
	10300	RivC	92223	690-J4
	11300	DHSP	92240	696-J3
	11900	MORV	92557	717-F1
	26100	RivC	92544	841-F1
	36400	RivC	92544	902-B7
	78100	RivC	92211	819-F2
MELODY HILLS DR				
	46900	RivC	92536	982-F7
MELON LN				
	1200	PER	92571	778-A6
MELOSA WY				
	-	RIV	92504	715-B6
MELROSE AV				
	40300	RivC	92544	811-C7
MELROSE DR				
	1600	COR	92880	743-A1
	36900	CTHC	92234	787-D7
	36900	CTHC	92234	817-E1
MELROSE ST				
	4000	RIV	92504	715-C2
MELTON DR				
	42300	RivC	92544	901-G5
MELVERE PL				
	25800	RivC	92544	811-C7
MELVILLE DR				
	1300	RIV	92506	716-C4
MELVIN ST				
	30900	RivC	92584	868-A5
MELVIN WY				
	-	RivC	92570	746-F7
MEMORIAL PL				
	-	LQNT	92253	5410-A7
MEMORIAL WY				
	12600	MORV	92553	717-A3
MEMORY DR				
	39100	RivC	92563	929-A7
MEMORY LN				
	-	HEMT	92544	811-F6
	11800	SBdC	92399	651-D2
	21400	RivC	92570	746-J7
	28600	RivC	92596	839-B7
	54500	RivC	-	844-D1
MEMORY GLEN PL				
	11600	SBdC	92316	645-F3
MEMPHIS CT				
	-	HEMT	92545	810-E6
MENDIMEN RANCH RD				
	-	RivC	92882	742-A7
MENDOCINO DR				
	6800	RIV	92503	714-E1
MENDOCINO WY				
	30300	RivC	92563	929-B7
MENDOZA DR				
	24800	RivC	92590	977-J4
MENDOZA RD				
	10800	MORV	92557	687-D6
MENDOZA WY				
	3100	RIV	92504	715-E3
MENG ASBURY RD				
	40400	RivC	92592	930-F7
	40400	RivC	92592	960-E1
MENIFEE RD				
	22000	RivC	92567	778-F7
	22000	RivC	92567	808-F4
	23700	RivC	92585	808-G7
	25500	RivC	92585	838-G4
	28500	RivC	92584	838-G7
	29000	RivC	92584	868-G1
	32600	RivC	92584	898-G1
	33500	MURR	92584	898-G5
	35300	MURR	92563	898-G5
MENIFEE LAKES DR				
	29700	RivC	92584	868-G2
MENIFEE SPRINGS CT				
	28700	RivC	92584	868-G3
MENIL PL				
	100	PDST	92260	848-C7
	100	PDST	92260	878-C1
MENLO AV				
	500	HEMT	92543	811-A5
	900	SJCT	92583	811-C5
	1100	HEMT	92543	810-G6
	1400	HEMT	92544	811-C5
	2200	HEMT	92545	810-D6
MENLO CIR				
	5200	PMSP	92264	787-B5
MENNES AV				
	3800	RivC	92509	685-D3
MENOMINEE CT				
	25200	MORV	92553	717-G7
MENTONE PL				
	8800	RIV	92503	715-B6
MENTZELIA CT				
	11700	MORV	92557	716-H1
MERCADANTE LN				
	24700	RivC	92324	687-F2
MERCED DR				
	3700	RIV	92503	744-D2
MERCED RD				
	44100	RivC	92544	(812-A5 See Page 782)
MERCED WY				
	900	HEMT	92545	840-G2
MERCEDES ST				
	28300	TEM	92590	958-H7
	28600	TEM	92590	978-J1
E MERCED RIVER RD				
	3900	ONT	91761	643-D6
MERCER AV				
	10700	RIV	92505	714-F7
	10700	RIV	92505	744-F1
MERCER LN				
	24700	RivC	92584	867-H7
	26800	RivC	92585	838-D3
MERCHANT LN				
	14100	MORV	92555	718-E6
MERCURY				
	100	PMSP	92264	786-H7
MERCURY CIR				
	29000	RivC	92584	868-G2
MERCURY CIR E				
	74200	PDST	92260	818-G5
MERCURY CIR W				
	74000	PDST	92260	818-G6
MERCURY CT				
	4200	RIV	92505	714-F6
	11200	RivC	91752	683-H5
MEREDITH ST				
	4500	RIV	92505	714-E5
MERGANSER CIR				
	1400	COR	92882	772-J1
MERGANZER TR				
	19000	RivC	92241	727-F4
MERIDA CT				
	-	PMSP	92264	816-D1
MERIDA PL				
	11700	RIV	92505	714-B7
MERIDIA AV				
	-	RivC	92203	789-G5
MERIDIAN AV				
	28400	LKEL	92530	835-J7
MERIDIAN CIR				
	700	COR	92882	742-E5
MERIDIAN LN				
	800	COR	92882	742-E5
MERIDIAN ST				
	600	HEMT	92544	811-F5
	1800	SJCT	92583	811-E4
	25800	RivC	92544	811-F7
	26100	RivC	92544	841-F2
N MERIDIAN ST				
	100	HEMT	92544	811-F6
MERIDIAN WY				
	6700	RIV	92505	714-A2
	43700	LQNT	92253	819-G7
MERILL DR				
	-	PDST	92260	818-H2
MERION				
	56600	LQNT	92253	5530-A5
MERION CT				
	6000	BAN	92220	721-C4
MERION DR				
	32300	RivC	92276	788-E2
E MERION ST				
	2800	ONT	91761	643-A6
MERION WY				
	28000	MORV	92555	718-D7
MERIT CT				
	24700	MORV	92553	717-F6
MERIT PKWY				
	900	CTHC	92234	787-F5
W MERITO PL				
	100	PMSP	92262	756-D7
	400	PMSP	92262	786-D1
MERJANIAN RD				
	28700	RivC	92584	868-G7
MERLE CT				
	22900	GTER	92313	646-G3
MERLE DR				
	74500	PDST	92260	818-H5
	75000	PDST	92211	818-H5
MERLIN CT				
	42000	RivC	92544	841-F2
MERLIN DR				
	6300	RIV	92506	715-H3
	44600	INDO	92201	5410-E7
MERLIN LN				
	-	COR	92881	773-E4
MERLOT CT				
	32000	TEM	92591	959-E4
MERLOT CREST				
	32000	TEM	92591	959-E4
MERLYN ST				
	4900	HEMT	92544	811-G6
MERMACK AV				
	18400	RivC	92532	836-D6
	18900	RivC	92570	836-E6
MERONA CT				
	45900	RivC	92592	979-G4
MERRELL AV				
	29600	RivC	92567	778-H7
MERRICK ST				
	8600	RIV	92508	746-H2
MERRIL PL				
	26100	LMLN	92354	647-E2
MERRILL AV				
	3500	RIV	92506	715-D1
	5100	RIV	92504	715-C1
	16400	LKEL	92530	835-J7
	16400	LKEL	92530	865-J1
MERRILL CIR				
	-	HEMT	92545	810-H5
MERRILL LN				
	1700	PER	92571	777-H7
MERRILL ST				
	1500	COR	92882	743-C7
N MERRILL ST				
	100	COR	92882	743-C4
	300	COR	92880	743-C4
S MERRILL ST				
	200	COR	92882	743-C6
MERRILY WY				
	500	HEMT	92544	811-F6
MERRIMAC CT				
	4400	RIV	92503	714-H4
MERRIMAC LN				
	48600	RivC	92536	963-B7
MERRIMENT WY				
	600	PER	92570	807-F3
MERRITT RD				
	33000	RivC	92584	899-B2
MERRIWOOD DR				
	41200	RivC	92544	841-D1
MERRY LN				
	200	BEAU	92223	720-H2
W MERRYFIELDS AV				
	200	CLTN	92324	646-B4
MERRYGROVE CIR				
	23200	MORV	92553	717-C3
MERRY HILL DR				
	11500	RivC	92880	742-B5
MERRYVALE WY				
	72300	PDST	92260	848-C5
MERRYWOOD CIR				
	200	RivC	91752	683-E5
MERRYWOOD LN				
	1700	COR	92882	742-J7
MERSEY CT				
	30200	TEM	92591	959-A5
MERVYN DR				
	65500	DHSP	92240	696-G4
MERWIN ST				
	13600	MORV	92555	718-F6
MESA CT				
	-	COAC	92236	5471-A4
MESA CV				
	45300	INDW	92210	848-H1
MESA DR				
	-	RivC	-	412-A3
	500	COR	92879	743-E3
	1500	RDL	92373	649-A5
	1700	PMSP	92264	786-E5
	8300	COR	92883	774-A6
	14000	RivC	-	392-A11
	32300	RivC	92530	866-J7
	32300	RivC	92530	867-A7
	32400	RivC	92530	897-A1
S MESA DR				
	1800	CLTN	92324	647-A3
MESA PL				
	32500	RivC	92276	788-E3
MESA RD				
	-	CALI	92320	689-H3
	35900	RivC	92592	931-A3
	36000	RivC	92592	930-H3
MESA ST				
	4100	RIV	92507	686-A5
	43200	RivC	92220	691-G5
MESA TR				
	71300	RivC	92260	848-B5
MESA ALTA CIR				
	-	COR	92879	743-F2
MESA BUTTE RD				
	34400	RivC	92592	960-A5
MESA CREST DR				
	13300	YCPA	92399	650-D6
MESA EDGE DR				
	36400	YCPA	92399	650-D6
MESA GRANDE DR				
	12900	YCPA	92399	650-D5
	13700	CALI	92320	650-C7
	35000	CALI	92320	689-J2
	41000	PDST	92211	819-B4
	41500	RivC	92544	841-E5
MESA OAK DR				
	8500	RIV	92508	746-G2
MESA RIDGE LN				
	24300	MORV	92557	687-E5
MESA ROBLES CIR				
	41100	RivC	92592	959-G5
MESA SOL DR				
	13500	YCPA	92399	650-G6
MESA SPRINGS WY				
	22800	MORV	92557	687-B5
MESA TERRACE DR				
	13400	YCPA	92399	650-D6
MESA TOP TR				
	28100	MORV	92555	718-D2
MESA VERDE AV				
	900	COR	92880	743-D3
MESA VERDE CIR				
	41100	RivC	92592	959-H4
MESA VERDE DR				
	-	MORV	92555	748-A2
	13500	YCPA	92399	650-G6
MESA VERDE TR				
	46000	INDO	92201	5470-C2
MESA VERDUGO				
	41900	RivC	92592	959-J5
MESA VIEW DR				
	-	RivC	92584	868-F6
	-	CTHC	92234	787-F5
	72500	PDST	92260	848-E5
MESA VIEW ST				
	24000	HEMT	92543	810-J4
MESA VISTA LN				
	-	RMIR	92270	817-F3
MESA VISTA PL				
	36200	YCPA	92399	650-D6
MESCAL LN				
	48700	PDST	92260	848-F5
MESCALE RD				
	3900	RIV	92504	715-A3
MESCALERO CT				
	49500	RivC	92536	(933-D7 See Page 902)
MESCALITA LN				
	900	NRCO	92860	713-F4
MESITA LN				
	19800	RivC	92562	926-G6
MESQUITE AV				
	100	PMSP	92264	786-J3
	3700	PMSP	92264	787-A4
	9700	DHSP	92240	697-A2
	10100	DHSP	92240	696-J2
	43600	INDO	92203	5410-H6
	68000	CTHC	92234	787-C4
MESQUITE CT				
	72700	PDST	92260	848-D3
	73600	PDST	92260	848-F4
MESQUITE DR				
	-	INDW	92210	818-J7
	-	INDW	92210	848-H1
	300	RivC	-	5239-J6
	2900	RIV	92503	715-A7
	13700	FONT	92337	644-A4
MESQUITE LN				
	2300	COR	92882	772-J1
MESQUITE PL				
	-	PER	92571	778-B2
MESQUITE RD				
	13200	RivC	92282	724-F2
MESQUITE CANYON RD				
	20200	RIV	92508	746-F2
MESQUITE HILLS				
	-	PDST	-	848-C7
	-	PDST	92260	848-C7
MESQUITE RIDGE LN				
	-	RMIR	92270	818-D7
MESQUITE TREE DR				
	34400	RivC	92276	788-J4
MESQUITE VISTA				
	-	BEAU	92223	690-J6
MESSENIA LN				
	18500	RivC	92570	777-D1
MESSINA CT				
	-	LQNT	92253	819-G6
MESSINA DR				
	1700	SJCT	92583	781-E7
MESSINA ST				
	-	TEM	92592	959-F7
METATE PL				
	71100	PDST	92260	848-B6
METATE RD				
	39900	MURR	92562	928-B1
METCALF LN				
	11200	RIV	92505	714-C5
METRIC DR				
	24700	MORV	92557	717-F1
METROPLEX DR				
	73000	RivC	92276	788-C1
METROWAY				
	-	ONT	91761	643-B3
METZ RD				
	22800	RivC	92570	807-C2
W METZ RD				
	100	PER	92571	807-G1
	300	PER	92570	807-F1
MEW CIR				
	13000	RivC	92883	835-B4
MEXICALI ROSE				
	74600	RivC	92276	788-H5
MEXICO WY				
	35400	RivC	92276	788-H5
MEYER CIR				
	300	COR	92879	743-F4
MEYER DR				
	-	RivC	92518	717-D7
	-	RivC	92518	747-C1
MEYERS LN				
	58700	RivC	92539	(935-E5 See Page 904)
MIA AV				
	6600	RIV	92503	714-F1
MIA PL				
	67200	CTHC	92234	787-B1
MIAMI AV				
	10800	SBdC	92316	645-D1
MIAMI CIR				
	45300	INDW	92210	849-B1
MIAMI ST				
	7000	RIV	92506	715-F3
MIAS CANYON RD				
	9100	RivC	92220	651-H7
	9100	RivC	92220	691-H2
	9700	BAN	92220	691-J2
	9700	RivC	92220	692-A4
	11000	BAN	92220	692-A7
MICA DR				
	3200	PMSP	92262	756-F4
MICA RD				
	31200	RivC	92548	809-B4
	58000	RivC	92539	(985-C2 See Page 964)
MICA BUTTE				
	-	RivC	92543	871-B4
MICHAEL DR				
	2200	PMSP	92262	756-B5
MICHAEL LN				
	34900	YCPA	92399	649-J3
	34900	YCPA	92399	650-A3
	45300	RivC	92536	981-H4
MICHAEL RD				
	21400	RivC	92570	776-J6
	21700	RivC	92570	777-A6
MICHAEL ST				
	4200	RIV	92507	686-A6
MICHAEL WY				
	9900	MORV	92557	687-F4
MICHAELS PL				
	900	COR	92881	743-J7
MICHEL RD				
	3500	SJCT	92567	780-B6
	3500	SJCT	92582	780-B6
MICHELE DR				
	32100	LKEL	92530	865-G4
MICHELIN DR				
	11200	RIV	92505	714-C5
MICHELL LN				
	45700	INDO	92201	5470-C1
E MICHELLE DR				
	3000	CLTN	92324	647-A5
MICHELLE LN				
	400	HEMT	92544	811-F6
MICHELLE RD				
	1400	NRCO	92860	713-E5
N MICHELLE RD				
	200	PMSP	92262	786-G2
MICHELLE ST				
	600	BLY	92225	5491-F5
MICHENER DR				
	-	RivC	92584	868-C3
MICHIGAN AV				
	-	BEAU	92223	720-J2
	-	GTER	92313	646-D5
	-	RivC	92507	646-D7
	500	RIV	92507	646-D7
	500	RIV	92507	686-D1
	1300	BEAU	92223	690-J7
MICHIGAN CT				
	44300	INDW	92210	848-J1
MICHIGAN DR				
	77200	PDST	92211	819-D5
MICHIGAN ST				
	600	BLY	92225	5491-C6
MICRO DR				
	-	RivC	91752	683-E1
	-	SBdC	91761	683-E1
MICRO PL				
	22000	PMSP	-	726-H7
	22000	PMSP	-	756-J1
MIDAS CT				
	-	MURR	92563	928-F6
MIDDLE RD				
	-	PMSP	92264	786-G6
MIDDLEBOROUGH RD				
	-	RivC	92503	744-F3
	10900	RIV	92503	744-F3
MIDDLEBROOK WY				
	25100	MORV	92551	747-G3
MIDDLEBURG PL				
	3700	COR	92881	773-H5
MIDDLEBURY WY				
	28600	RivC	92586	838-A6
MIDDLECOFF CT				
	9700	RivC	92240	696-E1
MIDDLE CREEK RD				
	1800	RIV	92506	716-A4
MIDDLEFIELD DR				
	9000	RIV	92508	746-E4
MIDDLE FORK ST				
	-	PER	92571	778-C2
MIDDLE RIDGE DR				
	52700	RivC	-	(843-J1 See Page 842)
	52800	RivC	-	844-A1
MIDDLETON PL				
	3900	RIV	92505	744-E1
MIDDLETON ST				
	34000	RivC	92555	749-G5
	85000	RivC	92274	(5651-D1 See Page 5590)
	86000	RivC	92274	(5591-E7 See Page 5590)
MIDLAND RD				
	-	RivC	-	391-K2
	-	RivC	-	392-A6
	4000	RIV	92505	744-D1
MIDORI LN				
	300	CALI	92320	689-J1
MIDPARK DR				
	69200	RivC	92241	727-E1
MIDSUMMER LN				
	-	RivC	92584	868-F4
MIDVALE DR				
	5600	RIV	92506	715-J2
MIDWAY ST				
	-	RivC	92518	747-D1
	100	PER	92570	807-G4
E MIDWAY ST				
	100	SJCT	92583	811-B5
MIDWAY SUMMIT RD				
	-	RivC	92584	838-F7
	29100	RivC	92584	868-F1
MIGHT CIR				
	9000	RivC	92509	684-D2
MIGUEL RD				
	24300	RivC	92595	897-G7
MIGUEL ST				
	2800	RIV	92506	715-F3
MIHAYLO RD				
	21300	RivC	-	726-H6
	22000	RivC	92240	726-H6
	22500	RivC	92241	726-H6
	22600	RivC	92241	727-A7
	22700	RivC	92241	757-A1
MIKALE LN				
	35100	MURR	92562	898-D6
MIKE LN				
	20300	RivC	92567	779-C4
MIKE REED RD				
	-	SJCT	92567	779-J3
	-	SJCT	92567	780-A5
MIKE TODD LN				
	12800	GTER	92313	646-F5
MIKLICH DR				
	40200	MURR	92563	958-F1
MILAGO DR				
	44300	LQNT	92253	819-H7
MILAN CT				
	-	LQNT	92253	819-F6
	4300	RIV	92505	714-E7
MILAN RD				
	33000	RivC	92545	839-F4
MILANO				
	2700	ONT	91761	643-B6
MILANO CIR				
	-	PDST	92211	819-A4
MILANO RD				
	30000	TEM	92591	959-A1
MILBEN CIR				
	2100	PMSP	92262	756-E5
MILBURN AV				
	1300	RDL	92373	647-J1
MILDRED CT				
	10000	RIV	92503	714-H7
MILDRED ST				
	-	PER	92571	807-H1
MILE HIGH RD				
	-	SBdC	92223	651-C5
MILE HIGH RANCH RD				
	12700	SBdC	92223	651-B6
MILES AV				
	77300	INDW	92210	849-F1
	78900	LQNT	92253	849-F1
	78900	INDO	92201	849-F1
	78900	LQNT	92253	5470-A1
	78900	INDO	92201	5470-A1
	80800	INDO	92201	5410-B7
	81000	RivC	92201	5410-B7
MILES CIR				
	700	COR	92879	743-E7
S MILES CT				
	2100	CLTN	92324	646-C4
MILES ST				
	42500	MURR	92562	958-B3
MILESTONE AV				
	1000	PER	92571	778-A2
MILFORD RD				
	4900	RIV	92504	685-D6
MILFORD HAVEN RD				
	11500	LMLN	92354	647-F2
MILHOLLAND DR				
	42000	RivC	92544	841-F4
MILICE CT				
	5300	RIV	92506	716-B1
MILKMAID LN				
	39800	MURR	92562	898-A7
	39800	MURR	92562	928-A1
MILKWEED WY				
	23500	MORV	92557	687-C6
	39500	RivC	92592	930-D7
MILKWOOD DR				
	23700	MORV	92557	687-D6
MILKWOOD LN				
	39900	MURR	92562	928-C4
MILKY ST				
	-	RivC	92260	818-F2
MILKY WY				
	28500	RivC	92586	837-J7
MILKY WAY DR				
	11000	RivC	91752	683-H5
	30300	TEM	92592	959-B5
MILL ST				
	600	LKEL	92530	866-F5
MILLARD DR				
	11300	RIV	92503	744-E3
MILLARD PASS				
	12900	RivC	92220	723-A2
	12900	RivC	92230	723-A2
	13400	RivC	92230	722-J3
MILLARD CANYON RD				
	-	RivC	92220	389-H5
	11500	RivC	92220	692-J7
MILLBRAE DR				
	1200	RIV	92506	716-C4
MILLBRAE TER				
	3800	PER	92571	778-A2
MILL BRIDGE DR				
	28700	RivC	92584	868-G3
MILLBROOK AV				
	4700	RivC	92509	684-B2
MILLBROOK RD				
	1100	COR	92882	773-A1
MILLBROOK ST				
	21000	RIV	92508	746-H2
MILLBROOK WY				
	-	MURR	92563	928-F6
MILLBURY CT				
	11500	RivC	92880	742-B5
MILL CREEK				
	2800	ONT	91761	643-C6
MILL CREEK DR				
	-	RivC	92584	868-G6
MILLCREEK PL				
	500	COR	92879	743-J3
MILL CREEK ST				
	4200	RivC	92509	685-C2
MILLER CIR				
	1100	COR	92882	743-A6
MILLER RD				
	-	RivC	92570	805-F5
	800	BAN	92220	721-D4
MILLER ST				
	400	PER	92571	777-F2
	9000	RIV	92503	714-J5
	30100	LKEL	92530	866-C3
MILLER WY				
	44500	RivC	92544	(812-B6 See Page 782)
MILLIE DR				
	900	HEMT	92545	810-F5
MILLIGAN DR				
	7900	RIV	92506	715-H7
	7900	RIV	92506	745-H1
S MILLIKEN AV				
	100	ONT	91761	643-D2
	2500	RivC	91752	643-D5
MILL IRON WY				
	900	SJCT	92583	811-D3
MILL POND DR				
	33200	RivC	92595	897-H2
MILLPOND PL				
	-	RIV	92508	746-D2
MILLPOND RD				
	11500	FONT	92337	644-H3
MILL RANCH DR				
	-	RivC	-	878-A6
MILL RUN RD				
	44700	TEM	92592	979-G3
MILLS AV				
	1200	RDL	92373	647-J2
MILLS RD				
	20000	RivC	92570	776-B4
MILLSAP DR				
	24200	MORV	92553	717-E5
MILLSTONE PL				
	23500	MURR	92562	927-J1
	23500	MURR	92562	928-A1
MILLSTREAM LN				
	1100	COR	92880	743-B2
MILLSTREAM RD				
	39500	RivC	92563	929-A7
MILLSWEET PL				
	2600	RIV	92503	744-G3
MILLWOOD RD				
	1300	RIV	92506	716-B4
N MILO DR				
	2200	PMSP	92262	756-C5
MILO RD				
	21100	RivC	92570	836-J5
MILOS CT				
	25300	MURR	92563	928-F6
MILPAS RD				
	35400	RivC	92544	902-C5
MILPITAS WASH RD				
	-	RivC	-	411-K4
MIL SORPRESAS DR				
	1900	SDCo	92028	998-A7
MILTON CT				
	22800	RivC	92324	647-B6
MILTON PL				
	-	RMIR	92270	818-D5
MILTON ST				
	1700	RIV	92507	686-A2
MIMOSA AV				
	2300	HEMT	92545	840-G2
MIMOSA CT				
	29700	RivC	92584	868-E2
MIMOSA DR				
	15100	LKEL	92530	865-G3
	39100	MURR	92563	928-F4
	72800	PDST	92260	818-D7
	78800	RivC	92211	819-G1
MIMOSA LN				
	-	RivC	92503	744-J7
MIMOSA ST				
	3600	RIV	92504	715-C3
MIMOSA HILL CT				
	10700	RIV	92505	714-E6
MIMOSA TREE CT				
	8400	RIV	92504	715-C6
MIMULUS WY				
	40100	TEM	92591	958-J2
MINARET ST				
	200	COR	92881	773-D4
MINARET WY				
	76600	PDST	92211	819-C6
MINAS CT				
	19300	RivC	92570	777-C2
MINDORA DR				
	11400	MORV	92557	716-J1
MINDY LN				
	45400	RivC	92544	(932-E5 See Page 902)
MINE RD				
	-	RivC	-	391-C11
MINERAL ROCK				
	-	INDO	92201	5470-H3
MINERS RD				
	23200	RivC	92570	806-B3
MINERS TR				
	11000	MORV	92557	687-E7
MINERVA CT				
	1000	RIV	92507	686-C3
MINERVA RD				
	68600	CTHC	92234	757-E7
MINHOE RD				
	79600	RivC	92201	819-J6
MINI LN				
	1900	HEMT	92544	811-C6
MINNEHAHA ST				
	200	PMSP	92264	786-F3
MINNESOTA AV				
	77100	PDST	92211	819-D5
MINNESOTA RD				
	8200	RivC	92881	774-A3
	16900	RivC	92881	773-J4
MINNESOTA ST				
	1800	RIV	92507	686-A4
MINNESOTA WY				
	20300	RivC	92507	686-F7
MINNETONKA CT				
	25200	MORV	92553	717-G6
MINNIER AV				
	4600	RIV	92505	714-D6
MINNI LU RD				
	9500	CALI	92320	690-D2
MINONA CT				
	11900	GTER	92313	646-F3
MINONA DR				
	22500	GTER	92313	646-F3
MINOR ST				
	700	SJCT	92583	811-C3
MINORCA ST				
	25500	RivC	92544	(812-C6 See Page 782)
MINT DR				
	55500	RivC	92282	694-E7
	55500	RivC	92282	724-E1
MINT ST				
	3300	COR	92881	773-F4
MINTAGE LN				
	1700	COR	92881	743-F7
MINTERN ST				
	3600	RivC	92509	685-D2
MINTHORN ST				
	100	LKEL	92530	866-D3
MINTHORN ST S				
	600	LKEL	92532	866-F4
MINTO WY				
	41600	RivC	92544	871-E6
	42400	RivC	92544	901-H1
	42900	RivC	92544	902-A1
MINTON RD				
	23800	RivC	92548	809-E6
MINTZER ST				
	2100	CLTN	92324	646-H1
MINUTEMAN DR				
	11700	RIV	92503	744-D3
MINZAH WY				
	73500	PDST	92260	848-F3
MIRA ST				
	32100	RivC	92584	868-J7
MIRACANTO WY				
	10100	MORV	92557	687-B5
MIRACLE HILL RD				
	12000	DHSP	92240	697-B5
MIRADA CIR				
	-	RMIR	92270	817-F2
MIRADA DR				
	1000	PER	92571	778-A2
MIRADERO CT				
	72000	PDST	92260	848-C5
MIRADO AV				
	12200	GTER	92313	646-E4
MIRADOR CT				
	48300	PDST	92260	848-E5
MIRAFLORES BLVD				
	-	LQNT	92253	849-J3
	-	LQNT	92253	5470-A3
MIRAFLORES DR				
	900	COR	92882	773-B3
MIRAGE CIR				
	-	RivC	92211	819-G2
MIRAGE CT				
	800	SJCT	92582	780-H6
	26000	MORV	92555	717-J1
	47700	PDST	92260	848-G4
MIRAGE DR				
	-	CTHC	92234	787-F6
MIRAGE RD				
	42100	RMIR	92270	818-A5
MIRAGE ST				
	900	PER	92571	778-A2
MIRAGE WY				
	-	INDO	92201	5470-G3
	2000	COR	92882	742-H7
MIRAGE COVE DR				
	-	RMIR	92270	817-G3
MIRAGE MESA CIR				
	33400	RivC	92592	959-H7
MIRA LAGO DR				
	21800	RivC	92570	805-G1
E MIRALESTE CT				
	500	PMSP	92262	756-E6
MIRA LOMA DR				
	29500	TEM	92592	959-A6
N MIRA LOMA WY				
	1800	PMSP	92262	756-D6
MIRAMAR				
	200	LKEL	92530	866-F5
MIRAMAR AV				
	700	SJCT	92583	811-D3
MIRAMAR CIR				
	8200	RivC	92509	684-F2
MIRAMAR DR				
	70100	RivC	92254	(5654-D4 See Page 5594)
MIRAMAR PZ				
	1600	PMSP	92264	787-C3
MIRAMAR ST				
	1800	PER	92571	777-H7
MIRA MESA DR				
	12400	YCPA	92399	649-F4
MIRA MONTE CIR E				
	2200	PMSP	92264	787-A5
MIRA MONTE CIR W				
	2300	PMSP	92264	787-A5
MIRAMONTE PL				
	4200	RIV	92501	685-F4
MIRA MONTE RD				
	4100	SDCo	92028	997-G3
MIRA MONTE ST				
	2200	COR	92879	743-H2
MIRANDA DR				
	28200	RivC	92584	868-F3
MIRAS WY				
	-	MURR	92562	928-B7
MIRASOL CIR				
	29700	RivC	92584	868-F2
MIRASOL CT				
	48000	PDST	92260	848-E4
MIRASOL LN				
	-	COR	92879	743-F2
MIRASOL WY				
	24200	RivC	92590	977-G3
MIRA VALLE ST				
	-	COR	92879	743-F2
MIRAVILLA WY				
	-	RivC	92254	5592-F5
MIRA VISTA CT				
	-	COR	92881	773-E3
MIRA VISTA WY				
	2000	PMSP	92262	756-D5
	2900	COR	92881	773-E3
MIRIAM WY				
	22500	GTER	92313	646-F4
	33900	PDST	92211	788-D4
	34000	RMIR	92270	788-D4
MIRILESTE DR				
	22500	RivC	92567	808-F2
MIRR ST				
	20900	RivC	92570	806-H2
MISCHIEF AV				
	32000	RivC	92545	839-D2
	32000	RivC	92548	839-D2
MISSION BLVD				
	-	RivC	92501	685-D2
	2700	ONT	91761	643-A3
	3700	RivC	92509	644-B7
	3700	RivC	91752	644-B7
	5100	RivC	92509	685-B1
	6500	RivC	92509	645-A7
	11300	RivC	91752	643-E5
E MISSION BLVD				
	2800	ONT	91761	643-A3

STREET Block City ZIP Pg-Grid

MISSION CT
- RMIR 92270 787-H6
100 COR 92882 743-C7
100 COR 92882 773-C1
67200 CTHC 92234 787-B2
MISSION DR
- RivC 92584 868-F5
400 CTHC 92234 787-B2
400 PMSP 92262 787-B2
12700 YCPA 92399 649-F5
MISSION DR E
- LQNT 92253 849-J5
- LQNT 92253 5470-A5
MISSION DR W
48400 LQNT 92253 849-H4
E MISSION PL
400 COR 92879 773-D1
MISSION RD
- SDCo 92028 998-F7
11400 RivC 92220 692-H5
25800 LMLN 92354 647-E1
25800 LMLN 92373 647-E1
E MISSION RD
100 COR 92879 773-D1
100 COR 92882 773-D1
E MISSION RD Rt#-S13
2500 SDCo 92028 998-B7
N MISSION RD
700 PMSP 92262 756-D7
W MISSION RD
300 COR 92882 743-C7
300 COR 92882 773-C1
MISSION ST
14500 RivC 92230 723-E5
MISSION TR
100 LKEL 92530 866-J6
10800 RivC 92530 866-J6
27400 RivC 92530 896-J1
27400 LKEL 92530 896-J1
32800 RivC 92595 896-J1
32800 RivC 92595 897-A2
32800 LKEL 92530 897-A2
32800 LKEL 92595 897-A2
MISSION WY
34600 YCPA 92399 649-J4
MISSION BELLS ST
22700 RivC 92883 804-C3
MISSION CREEK DR
76500 PDST 92211 819-C4
MISSION CREEK RD
10000 DHSP 92240 696-C2
10800 DHSP 92240 695-J1
39700 DHSP 92282 695-J1
60500 RivC 92282 655-D5
61000 DHSP 92282 655-H7
MISSION GROVE PKWY N
200 RIV 92506 716-D4
6500 RIV 92508 716-D4
MISSION GROVE PKWY S
7400 RIV 92508 716-D7
MISSION HILLS DR
5000 BAN 92220 721-D5
MISSION HILLS DR E
34900 RMIR 92270 787-H6
MISSION HILLS DR N
10200 RMIR 92270 787-H5
MISSION INDIAN TR
68200 CTHC 92234 787-D3
MISSION INN AV
2300 RIV 92507 685-J4
3200 RIV 92501 685-G3
MISSION LAKES BLVD
63500 DHSP 92240 696-C2
63600 RivC 92240 696-D2
66700 DHSP 92240 697-A2
66900 RivC 92240 697-A2
MISSION PALMS E
- RMIR 92270 787-H7
MISSION PALMS W
- RMIR 92270 787-H7
MISSION PALMS DR
- RMIR 92270 787-H6
MISSION RIDGE RD
200 SDCo 92028 998-F7
MISSION ROCK WY
5000 RivC 92509 685-D3
MISSION VILLAGE DR
400 RIV 92508 716-D6
MISSISSIPPI AV
80800 INDO 92201 5470-C1
MISSOURI DR
77300 PDST 92211 819-E5
MISSOURI ST
1800 RIV 92507 686-A4
MISSOURI TR
28000 RivC 92570 836-H6
N MISTLETOE AV
100 SJCT 92583 811-C1
S MISTLETOE AV
100 SJCT 92583 811-C2
MISTLETOE DR
100 COR 92879 744-F5
MISTY LN
18400 RivC 92570 746-F7
18400 RivC 92570 776-F1
MISTY WY
42200 RivC 92544 811-F7
MISTY GLADE CT
23600 MORV 92557 687-D7
MISTYMEADOW
- RivC 92880 713-B1
MISTY MEADOW CIR
1000 COR 92881 773-E3
MISTY MEADOW DR
38600 RivC 92399 650-G7
50200 RivC 92536 983-F5
MISTY MOUNTAIN DR
2500 COR 92882 772-H2
MISTY RIDGE DR
6700 RIV 92505 714-C2
MISTY RIDGE LN
1600 COR 92882 742-F7
MISTY STREAM WY
1300 COR 92881 773-G3
MISTY VIEW PL
- RIV 92506 715-J6
- RIV 92506 716-A6
MITCHELL AV
4700 RIV 92505 714-C2
MITCHELL CIR
16800 RivC 92518 746-H4
MITCHELL DR
17400 RivC 92530 896-C3
MITCHELL RD
35600 MURR 92562 898-D7
53000 RivC 92539 (934-F2 See Page 904)
56700 RivC 92539 (935-A2 See Page 904)
MIZAR WY
5100 RivC 91752 683-H3
MIZE WY
32800 RivC 92591 959-G1
MOBIL LN
- RivC 92532 836-D7
MOBILE DR
64000 RivC 92240 696-D5
MOBILE WY
20300 RivC 92595 896-J5
MOBLEY AV
3900 RIV 92505 714-E5
MOCCASIN CIR
- CYNL 92587 867-E4
MOCCASIN CT
49900 RivC 92536 963-E2
MOCCASIN CREEK
47000 INDO 92201 5470-H2
MOCCASIN TRAIL CIR
1700 COR 92882 772-H1
MOCHA DR
200 PER 92570 807-E3
MOCKINGBIRD LN
2700 COR 92881 773-E2
3000 HEMT 92544 811-D7
4500 BAN 92220 691-E7
MOCKINGBIRD TR
74000 INDW 92210 848-G3
74000 PDST 92260 848-G3
MOCKINGBIRD CANYON RD
15700 RivC 92504 745-E5
18200 RivC 92504 775-H2
MOCKINGBIRD HILL CIR
17500 RivC 92504 745-G6
MODALO RD
68100 CTHC 92234 787-D1
MODENA DR
- TEM 92592 959-F7
MODESTO CT
32900 RivC 92530 896-G4
MODESTO DR
7900 RIV 92503 714-G5
MODOC CT
23100 RivC 92570 806-A3
MOHAVE CT
10600 MORV 92557 687-C6
44000 INDW 92210 818-J7
S MOHAVE DR
1100 CLTN 92324 646-H2
MOHAWK
- PMSP 92264 786-F3
10100 MORV 92557 687-D5
MOHAWK CIR
41000 RivC 92223 691-C4
45600 INDW 92210 849-B2
MOHAWK PL
- PER 92570 807-E3
MOHAWK RD
3000 BAN 92220 721-G4
MOHAWK TR
3200 RIV 92503 744-H1
MOHAWK MESA TR
25300 MORV 92557 717-G1
MOHICAN CIR
45500 INDW 92210 849-B1
MOHICAN DR
13000 MORV 92555 717-J3
MOHR ST
100 LKEL 92530 866-D4
MOJAVE CT
49900 RivC 92536 963-E1
MOJAVE DR
11400 RivC 91752 683-G3
48800 RivC 92230 722-J3
48800 RivC 92230 723-A3
MOJAVE RD
65700 RivC - 726-H1
MOJAVE SAGE ST
36600 RivC 92211 789-F7
MOJAVE VIEW CIR
1700 COR 92882 772-H1
MOJESKA RD
24200 RivC 92883 804-E6
MOJO WY
38700 RivC 92543 870-J4
MOJO WY
39100 RivC 92543 871-A4
MOJONNIER WY
33600 RivC 92595 897-A3
MOLINA LN
100 PER 92571 807-H2
MOLINO RD
300 PMSP 92262 756-E4
MOLINO WY
5500 RivC 92509 685-D2
MOLINOS CT
68000 CTHC 92234 757-D6
MOLLIES AV
10900 DHSP 92240 696-B3
MOLLY DR
- SBDO 92408 646-J1
MOLLY ST
2700 RIV 92506 715-G3
MOMAT AV
35000 RivC 92595 897-D6
MOMBO WY
21900 RivC 92567 779-B7
MOMENTO AV
200 PER 92571 777-H7
MONA LN
33500 RivC 92596 899-B2
MONA BELL CT
5900 RIV 92504 685-C7
MONACO CIR
1800 PMSP 92264 786-F5
44600 PDST 92260 848-H1
MONACO WY
25300 MURR 92563 928-E6
MONARCH DR
- MURR 92563 928-G6
800 COR 92879 773-E1
900 COR 92881 773-E1
3600 PER 92571 778-A2
MONARCH PASS
- RivC 92211 789-F6
MONARCH ST
900 HEMT 92543 841-B2
MONARCH WY
- RivC 92203 789-F5
MONDALE ST
400 COR 92879 744-A3
MONDAVI CT
43300 PDST 92260 818-F6
MONDAVI ST
2500 SJCT 92583 811-D5
MONDELA ST
11300 FONT 92337 644-F2
MONEAQUE RD
41700 RivC 92201 819-G4
MONET WY
23600 RivC 92585 808-H4
MONEY LN
23300 RivC 92570 777-D4
MONICA WY
25600 RivC 92586 837-J5
MONICO DR
22000 MORV 92557 717-A1
MONIF CIR
1500 COR 92881 773-H3
MONIKA CT
500 BEAU 92223 690-H6
MONIQUE CIR
31800 TEM 92591 959-D3
MONIQUE CT
- RIV 92508 746-E2
MONITER CT
4400 RIV 92503 714-H4
MONK ST
27100 RivC 92586 838-B4
MONO DR
3300 RIV 92506 685-F7
3300 RIV 92506 715-F1
S MONO CREEK WY
2700 ONT 91761 643-C6
MONROE AV
24100 MURR 92562 928-A3
25500 MURR 92562 958-E1
27500 RivC 92585 808-D7
27600 RivC 92585 838-D1
MONROE CIR
1400 COR 92882 772-J1
1400 SJCT 92583 811-D6
E MONROE CT
100 SBDO 92408 646-J1
MONROE LN
26300 RivC 92548 839-C2
26300 RivC 92548 839-C2
MONROE ST
1100 LKEL 92530 865-H4
1400 RIV 92504 745-D1
1900 RIV 92504 715-A4
2000 BAN 92220 721-H4
3100 RIV 92503 715-A4
4200 RIV 92503 714-J2
4200 RIV 92504 714-J2
38100 RivC 92203 390-D8
38100 RivC 92203 5410-D1
38900 INDO 92203 5410-E4
42800 INDO 92201 5410-E6
45000 INDO 92201 5470-E2
52000 RivC 92201 5470-F7
52000 RivC 92201 5530-E2
52000 RivC 92253 5470-F7
52000 RivC 92253 5530-F7
53000 RivC 92274 5530-E2
53000 LQNT 92253 5530-E2
58000 RivC 92274 5590-F3
58000 RivC 92253 5590-F3
MONSERAT CT
- COR 92881 773-G3
MONSERAT CT
74600 INDW 92210 848-H3
MONSIGNOR THOMPSON CIR
600 COR 92882 743-C5
MONTAGUE CIR
900 COR 92879 743-G2
MONTAGUE DR
700 COR 92879 743-G2
MONTALVO RD
- MORV 92557 687-C4
MONTALVO WY
1100 PMSP 92262 756-J7
MONTANA AV
2400 RivC 92509 645-D7
3800 RivC 92509 685-D1
MONTANA ST
3300 RIV 92507 686-A4
23000 RivC 92587 837-D6
MONTANA WY
49100 LQNT 92253 849-H5
MONTANA RANCH RD
1400 COR 92882 742-F7
MONTANA VISTA DR
700 PDST 92211 818-J2
MONTANOSO LN
1200 PER 92570 807-G4
MONTAUK CIR
16900 RivC 92503 744-G6
MONT BLANC DR
11200 RivC 92503 744-G4
MONTCLAIR DR
800 BAN 92220 722-A2
6600 RIV 92504 715-C1
26600 RivC 92544 841-E2
MONTEBELLO PL
600 HEMT 92543 841-A2
MONTEBELLY WY
- MURR 92563 928-G6
MONTE CARLO CT
5000 RIV 92507 686-C7
MONTE CARLO DR
29200 MURR 92563 928-H7
MONTE CARLO ST
100 RMIR 92270 787-H6
MONTECELLO DR
12900 MORV 92555 717-J3
MONTECITO AV
500 HEMT 92543 841-A2
MONTECITO CIR
5900 PMSP 92264 787-C5
MONTECITO DR
- RivC 92567 779-E7
- RivC 92567 809-D1
5900 PMSP 92264 787-C5
75300 INDW 92210 848-J1
75300 INDW 92210 849-A1
MONTECITO LN
27500 RivC 92586 838-C5
MONTE DE ORO RD
35100 RivC 92592 930-C7
36000 RivC 92592 960-D1
MONTEEL PL
8400 RIV 92504 715-A3
MONTEGO CIR
78400 RivC 92201 819-G5
MONTEGO CT
- RivC 92201 819-H6
MONTEGO DR
- PMSP 92264 786-G4
MONTEGO WY
500 ONT 91761 643-B6
MONTEGO BAY DR
14100 MORV 92553 717-J6
78900 RivC 92201 819-H5
MONTEGO BAY PL
- INDO 92201 5470-H3
MONTEJO DR
9800 MORV 92557 687-A4
MONTELEGRO WY
43400 TEM 92592 959-E7
43400 TEM 92592 979-E1
MONTELENA CIR
41000 TEM 92591 959-D3
MONTELIMAR CT
41100 MURR 92562 927-J4
MONTENA
30500 LKEL 92532 866-J4
MONTE RANCHO DR
22500 RivC 92590 977-C5
MONTEREY AV
- RivC 92211 788-E3
100 RMIR 92270 818-E2
100 PDST 92260 818-E7
32000 RivC 92276 788-E3
34000 PDST 92211 788-E3
36200 RMIR 92211 788-E7
36200 RMIR 92211 818-E2
36200 RMIR 92270 788-E7
38500 RivC 92260 818-E2
43900 PDST 92260 848-E1
MONTEREY CIR
100 RivC 91752 683-F5
MONTEREY DR
- SJCT 92583 780-J5
12900 YCPA 92399 650-B5
MONTEREY PL
- TEM 92591 959-D4
500 HEMT 92543 841-A2
MONTEREY RD
200 COR 92879 743-D7
300 COR 92879 773-D1
5100 RIV 92506 685-G7
5200 RIV 92506 715-G1
13400 DHSP 92240 697-B5
MONTEREY RD
16700 RivC 92530 896-A5
E MONTEREY RD
500 COR 92879 743-E7
N MONTEREY RD
200 PMSP 92262 786-H1
500 PMSP 92262 756-H7
W MONTEREY RD
300 COR 92882 743-C7
MONTEREY ST
16400 LKEL 92530 865-J3
MONTEREY WY
2300 SJCT 92583 811-E5
MONTEREY PENINSULA DR
2200 RivC 92882 742-G5
MONTERICO RD
67900 DHSP 92240 697-C4
MONTERO DR
41700 RivC 92544 961-D4
MONTERO RD
5400 RivC 92509 685-A3
MONTE ROSA
68600 RivC - (907-E6 See Page 906)
MONTERRA AV
11600 FONT 92337 644-B3
MONTERRA CIR
48200 PDST 92260 848-E4
MONTES CT
22400 MURR 92562 927-C3
MONTE SERENO CIR
78100 INDW 92210 849-F2
MONTE SERENO DR
46100 INDW 92210 849-F2
MONTE VERDE
74500 PDST 92260 848-H2
MONTE VERDE RD
29600 TEM 92591 958-J4
29600 TEM 92591 959-A4
33100 RivC 92592 979-H4
33600 RivC 92592 980-A2
MONTE VERDE ST
46500 INDO 92201 5470-E2
MONTE VIDEO WY
64800 RivC 92264 816-F2
MONTE VISTA AV
200 SJCT 92583 811-B1
300 HEMT 92543 811-A5
MONTE VISTA DR
300 PMSP 92262 786-D3
700 RIV 92507 686-C7
33500 RivC 92595 897-C4
46000 INDO 92201 5470-C2
MONTE VISTA RD
32000 CTHC 92234 787-E3
MONTE VISTA WY
200 HEMT 92544 811-C7
30000 RivC 92276 758-D7
30000 RivC 92276 788-D2
MONTEZUMA DR
1500 COR 92879 743-G2
MONTEZUMA ST
400 BLY 92225 5491-D4
MONTGOMERY
54700 RivC - 814-D6
MONTGOMERY AV
30700 RivC 92567 779-B6
MONTGOMERY LN
44100 PDST 92260 818-F7
MONTGOMERY ST
4500 RIV 92503 714-G3
MONTICA
200 LKEL 92530 866-F5
MONTICELLO AV
- LQNT 92253 5410-A7
- LQNT 92253 5470-A1
4200 RIV 92503 714-J4
4200 RIV 92503 715-A4
MONTICELLO DR
3300 COR 92881 773-D3
MONTICELLO WY
- MURR 92563 928-G6
- RivC 92592 979-H3
MONTLAKE DR
11100 RIV 92505 744-E2
MONT MARTRE AV
200 RivC 92501 646-B6
MONTOYA DR
600 COR 92882 773-B1
MONTPELIER CT
2000 SJCT 92582 810-F2
MONTREAL ST
3300 HEMT 92545 810-F6
MONTROSE AV
100 SJCT 92583 811-C2
200 RivC 92583 811-C1
500 HEMT 92543 840-H1
1600 HEMT 92543 841-A1
3100 RivC 92583 781-B6
21500 SJCT 92583 781-B6
23000 RivC 92595 897-D6
MONTSERATT CT
- MURR 92563 928-H7
- MURR 92563 958-H1
MONTY CT
15000 RivC 92530 865-F3
MONTY HALL DR
36900 CTHC 92234 787-E7
37000 CTHC 92234 817-E1
MONUMENT DR
2800 RIV 92506 715-F4
21600 RivC 92570 776-A7
21800 RivC 92570 806-A1
MONUMENT WY
48300 RivC 92536 963-E5
MOODY DR
5300 BAN 92220 721-D4
MOODY ST
3800 RivC 92879 743-H5
MOON LN
47800 PDST 92260 848-F4
MOON PL
6100 RivC 91752 683-H5
MOONBEAM CIR
26200 RivC 92586 868-A1
MOON BEAM CT
- MURR 92563 928-E2
MOONBEAM DR
2000 BAN 92220 721-H2
MOON BEAM LN
12100 RivC 92503 744-C4
MOON BOW CT
16200 RivC 92503 744-D4
MOONCREST CIR
24400 MURR 92562 928-C3
MOONCREST CT
24400 MURR 92562 928-C3
MOON CREST DR
11400 RivC 92880 742-B4
MOONDANCE WY
29800 RivC 92586 868-B2
MOONFLOWER CT
40300 PDST 92260 818-E3
MOONGOLD RD
78200 RivC 92211 789-F7
MOONLIGHT CT
700 BAN 92220 721-G4
30300 TEM 92591 959-B1
MOONLIGHT DR
24500 MORV 92551 747-F3
68300 CTHC 92234 817-D2
MOONLIGHT LN
3400 COR 92881 773-E4
MOONLIGHTING DR
43900 RivC 92544 (812-A6 See Page 782)
MOON MIST DR
54200 RivC 92539 (934-D5 See Page 904)
MOONRAKER LN
24200 MORV 92557 717-E1
MOON RANCH RD
69200 RivC 92241 727-D6
MOONRIDGE CIR
2300 COR 92879 743-J2
MOONRIDGE DR
5800 RivC 92509 684-G4
10000 RivC 92503 745-C5
14000 RivC 92585 838-D5
27700 RivC 92585 838-D5
MOONRIDGE LN
72500 PDST 92260 848-B3
MOON ROCK RD
1600 SDCo 92028 997-G7
MOONSEED ST
25700 MORV 92553 717-H4
MOON SHADOW CT
- HEMT 92545 810-G5
MOONSHADOW DR
24600 MORV 92557 687-F5
MOON SHADOW DR
28000 RivC 92276 758-F6
28500 RivC 92584 868-F3
MOONSHADOW DR
80200 INDO 92201 5470-A2
MOONSHINE TR
59700 RivC 92539 (935-F6 See Page 904)
MOONSTONE CIR
7000 RIV 92504 715-F5
7000 RIV 92506 715-F5
MOONSTONE LN
- RivC 92203 789-G6
MOONSTONE ST
1200 HEMT 92543 840-J3
MOONSTONE WY
26300 RivC 92586 868-B2
MOON TERRACE LN
48600 PDST 92260 848-D5
MOONTIDE CT
30600 TEM 92592 959-B6
MOONTIDE LN
24700 MORV 92557 687-F7
MOOR CT
1400 RIV 92507 716-G2
MOORBROOK RD
- RivC 92203 789-F5
MOORE CIR
1400 COR 92882 743-A6
78800 RivC 92201 819-H6
MOORE ST
11300 BAN 92220 691-H7
20500 RivC 92570 776-G2
MOOREHEAD TER
17200 RivC 92530 896-B2
MOORE PARK DR
13000 MORV 92553 717-E4
MOOREWOOD TR
44200 RivC 92544 901-E3
MOORGATE PL
2700 RIV 92506 715-H3
MOORLAND RD
25300 MORV 92551 747-H3
MOORTOWN DR
33100 MURR 92562 927-D2
MOOSE
200 HEMT 92543 810-H7
S MOOSE CREEK LN
2700 ONT 91761 643-C6
S MOOSEDEER DR
2500 ONT 91761 643-A5
MOQUI WY
- RivC 92883 835-C5
MORAB ST
- RivC 92880 683-D7
MORAB WY
- NRCO 92860 743-J1
MORADA CT
2000 HEMT 92545 810-G6
MORAGA AV
6000 RivC 92509 684-J5
MORAGA RD
42000 TEM 92591 958-J5
MORALES WY
- COR 92881 773-H6
- COR 92883 773-H6
MORALIA DR
22600 MORV 92557 687-B4
MORAY CT
- RIV 92508 716-E7
MORAZA RD
54500 RivC 92539 (934-E5 See Page 904)
MORELAND RD
28400 RivC 92585 808-E7
MORELLA CIR
24000 MURR 92562 928-B2
MORELOCK WY
32500 RivC 92595 896-H5
MORENA CIR
25600 MORV 92551 747-H3
MORENO AV
1700 COR 92879 743-E7
1700 COR 92879 773-E1
MORENO DR
33000 CTHC 92234 787-E4
41900 TEM 92590 958-H7
MORENO WY
13200 MORV 92553 717-F4
MORENO BEACH DR
11300 MORV 92555 688-C7
11500 MORV 92555 718-C2
15100 MORV 92555 748-C2
MORENO ROSE PL
13900 MORV 92553 717-H5
MORENO VALLEY FRWY I-215
- MORV - 716-G2
- RIV - 685-J2
- RIV - 686-C4
- RIV - 716-G2
- RivC - 686-C4
- RivC - 716-G2
MORENO VALLEY FRWY Rt#-60
- BEAU - 720-B2
- MORV - 716-H2
- MORV - 717-A2
- MORV - 718-B2
- RIV - 685-J2
- RIV - 716-H2
- RIV - 717-A2
- RivC - 718-G2
- RivC - 719-A2
- RivC - 720-B2
MORENO VISTA ST
25300 MORV 92557 687-G7
MOREY WY
6000 RivC 92509 685-B1
MORFONTAINE ST
- COR 92883 773-H6
MORGAN AV
5500 RivC 92509 684-H3
52200 COAC 92236 5471-C7
52200 COAC 92236 5531-C1
MORGAN DR
2200 NRCO 92860 713-B7
MORGAN LN
15800 FONT 92337 644-G3
MORGAN PL
700 COR 92879 743-F1
MORGAN RD
33000 RivC 92530 896-H5
43000 RivC 92544 931-J7
43400 RivC 92544 (932-A7 See Page 902)
MORGAN ST
100 PER 92571 777-J2
100 PER 92571 778-A2
E MORGAN ST
- PER 92571 777-H2
W MORGAN ST
- PER 92571 777-F2
MORGAN HILL RD
1300 HEMT 92545 840-F4
MORGANTOWN WY
25800 RivC 92586 838-A7
MORICLAIR RD
34100 RivC 92567 809-H3
MORIN ST
32800 RivC 92596 899-F4
MORITA DR
700 COR 92879 744-A2
MORLEY
17000 RivC 92241 728-A1
MORNING DEW DR
10400 MORV 92557 687-F5
MORNING DOVE LN
23800 MURR 92562 928-B2
MORNING DOVE WY
25100 MORV 92551 747-G3
MORNING GLORY CIR
28000 RivC 92590 978-E2
MORNING GLORY CT
- LQNT 92253 819-J7
11300 RivC 92503 744-G4
MORNING GLORY DR
40700 MURR 92562 927-J2
MORNING GLORY ST
24500 MORV 92553 717-F7
MORNING GLORY WY
- COR 92881 773-F5
MORNING HILLS DR
- RIV 92518 746-F3
MORNINGLIGHT CIR
8600 RIV 92508 746-G2
MORNING MIST
1900 BLY - 5491-B7
MORNING MIST CT
- HEMT 92545 810-G5
MORNING MIST DR
24600 MORV 92557 687-F5
MORNING RIDGE DR
10300 MORV 92557 687-F5
MORNING ROCK CIR
16900 RivC 92503 744-G7
MORNINGSIDE AV
6800 RIV 92504 715-A2
MORNINGSIDE CT
41500 RMIR 92270 818-B5
42500 HEMT 92543 841-A2
42500 RivC 92544 841-G3
MORNINGSIDE DR
- RivC 92399 650-H6
300 BAN 92220 721-G3
600 COR 92879 743-H3
13500 YCPA 92399 650-H6
38500 RMIR 92270 818-A3
MORNING SIDE DR
46300 RivC 92539 (985-E4 See Page 964)
MORNINGSIDE DR
8300 RivC 92883 774-A7
69400 RivC 92241 727-F1
MORNING SKY DR
200 PER 92571 777-H6
MORNINGSPRINGS RD
71000 RMIR 92270 818-A3
MORNING STAR
- RivC 92203 789-G6
- RivC 92211 789-G6
MORNING STAR CT
- LQNT 92253 819-G6
MORNING STAR DR
2800 COR 92881 773-G3
24600 MURR 92562 928-D3
75300 INDW 92210 849-A2
MORNING STAR LN
2200 NRCO 92860 713-C4
11300 MORV 92557 687-F7
MORNING STAR RD
40400 RMIR 92270 818-C4
MORNING STAR WY
- LQNT 92253 819-G6
MORNING SUN CT
17600 RivC 92503 744-G7
MORNING SUN LN
3400 COR 92881 773-E4
MORNING VIEW CT
10800 RIV 92505 714-C2
MORNING VIEW DR
- RivC 92592 979-H4
MORNINGVIEW DR
16600 RivC 92504 745-F5
E MORNINGWOOD CT
3300 ONT 91761 643-B6
MOROC CIR
47400 PDST 92260 848-G3
MOROCCO
100 PMSP 92264 786-E5
MOROCCO RD
76600 PDST 92211 819-C5
MORONGA CANYON DR
38900 RivC 92260 818-F3
MORONGO AV
- BAN 92220 721-G3
MORONGO CT
15400 MORV 92551 747-H1
MORONGO LN
100 PER 92571 807-H2
MORONGO RD
100 PMSP 92264 786-E4
12100 RivC 92220 692-E7
12200 RivC 92220 722-D2
12300 BAN 92220 722-D2
68600 CTHC 92234 787-E4
E MORONGO TR
2500 PMSP 92264 786-H5
MORONGO WY
75700 INDW 92210 849-B1
MORONI AV
200 LKEL 92530 866-F5
MORRACO AV
- RivC 92254 (5654-F7 See Page 5594)
MORRELL DR
33200 RivC 92530 896-F5
MORREY LN
27800 MORV 92555 688-C7
MORRIS AV
- LQNT 92253 819-J7
- LQNT 92253 5410-A7
MORRIS ST
400 PER 92571 777-F2
7300 RIV 92503 714-G1
7300 RIV 92504 714-G1
MORRISON PL
32700 RivC 92530 896-F4
MORRISON ST
12000 MORV 92555 718-A2
15100 MORV 92555 748-A1
MORRIS RANCH RD
- RivC - (875-H7 See Page 844)
- RivC - (905-F2 See Page 904)
MORRISTOWN DR
4300 RIV 92505 714-D7
MORRO CT
5100 RivC 91752 683-G3
MORRO WY
1400 LKEL 92530 865-J7
MORRO HILL RD
3300 HEMT 92545 840-F3
MORROPE DESERT DR
76200 PDST 92211 819-A1
MORROW MEADOW DR
16900 RivC 92570 805-J3
16900 RivC 92570 806-A3
MORSE RD
16300 RivC 92241 728-A1
29000 RivC 92544 841-C6
29500 RivC 92544 871-D1
MORSUN CIR
200 PMSP 92262 786-H1
MORTON
1100 HEMT 92543 810-H7
MORTON AV
- LKEL 92530 866-C4
6200 RivC 92509 684-E5
MORTON PL
900 HEMT 92543 811-B7
MORTON RD
11200 MORV 92557 686-H7
11200 MORV 92557 716-H1
MOSER RD
8300 RivC 92883 774-A7
MOSPORT ST
100 HEMT 92544 811-G7
MOSS DR
- HEMT 92545 840-D4
19900 RivC 92530 896-G5
MOSS RD
18600 RivC 92508 716-C6
18800 RIV 92508 716-C6
MOSS CREEK LN
1700 COR 92882 772-H1
MOSS ROSE DR
74500 PDST 92260 818-H7
MOSSWOOD CIR
21200 RivC 92570 806-J4
MOTOR WY
12600 MORV 92555 718-C3
MOTOR CAR PKWY
41900 TEM 92591 958-H4
MOTOR CIRCLE DR
3100 RIV 92504 715-C5
MOTORFAIR DR
- RIV 92506 716-H5
- RIV 92507 716-H5
MOTTLE CIR
70300 RMIR 92270 817-H1
MOULTON DR
- RivC 92570 807-D4
2800 RivC 92503 744-F3
MOUND ST
900 RivC 92507 646-C6
24900 LMLN 92354 647-B1
MOUNT RD
41100 RivC 92539 (965-F3 See Page 964)
52500 RivC 92539 (934-A1 See Page 904)
56800 RivC 92539 (935-A1 See Page 904)
MOUNT ABBOTT ST
4800 RivC 92509 684-H2
MOUNTAIN AV
- PER 92570 807-E5
800 BAN 92220 721-F2
1300 NRCO 92860 743-D1
1400 SJCT 92583 811-E3
1900 NRCO 92860 713-D7
2100 RivC 92583 811-G4
2600 BAN 92220 691-F7
3900 RivC 92220 691-F7
11100 RIV 92505 714-C6
15700 CHNO 91710 712-A1
20100 RivC 92570 836-G3
21100 RivC 92570 806-J6
21300 RivC 92570 807-A6
24200 RivC 92544 811-G4
24700 HEMT 92544 811-G4
28000 RivC 92585 808-E5
MOUNTAIN CIR
43900 RivC 92536 (984-B1 See Page 964)
MOUNTAIN CT
17500 RivC 92503 744-G7
E MOUNTAIN CT
2200 CLTN 92324 646-H4
MOUNTAIN LN
22200 RivC 92570 806-J2
MOUNTAIN RD
12800 RivC 92883 835-B4
MOUNTAIN RDG
- PDST - 848-E7
MOUNTAIN ST
16000 LKEL 92530 865-F1
MOUNTAIN VW
- LQNT 92253 5530-D6
42900 PDST 92211 819-E6
MOUNTAIN ASH CIR
9000 RivC 92883 804-C3
MOUNTAIN BREEZE DR
- MURR 92562 927-G3
MOUNTAIN CLIFF DR
25300 MORV 92557 687-G7
MOUNTAIN COVE DR
46400 INDW 92210 849-F2
MOUNTAIN CREST DR
11100 MORV 92557 687-G7
MOUNTAIN GATE DR
3700 COR 92882 773-B3
MOUNTAIN GROVE LN
1000 COR 92881 773-F2
MOUNTAIN HIGH DR
13900 FONT 92337 644-B4
MOUNTAIN HIGH RD
6600 RIV 92505 714-B2
MOUNTAIN LAUREL CT
23800 MURR 92562 927-J3
MOUNTAIN LION RD
36800 RivC 92544 931-B1
MOUNTAIN MIST ST
16200 RivC 92503 744-D4
MOUNTAIN PARK DR
30500 RivC 92584 868-A4
MOUNTAIN PARK RD
70100 RivC - (907-J3 See Page 906)
70100 RivC - 908-A3
MOUNTAIN PASS DR
- COR 92882 773-B3
MOUNTAIN PRIDE DR
40700 MURR 92562 927-J3
MOUNTAIN RANCH RD
26100 MORV 92555 717-J1
MOUNTAIN RUN CIR
44000 RivC 92590 978-F1
MOUNTAIN SHADOW DR
3100 PMSP 92262 756-F4
7400 RivC 92509 684-H5
MOUNTAIN SHADOW RD
- MURR 92562 927-E4
MOUNTAIN SHADOWS DR
2600 COR 92881 773-E2
MOUNTAIN SHADOWS RD
50100 LQNT 92253 849-H6
MOUNTAINSIDE CT
23000 MURR 92562 927-E5
MOUNTAINSIDE DR
1400 COR 92882 742-E6
40600 RivC 92539 (935-G7 See Page 904)
40700 RivC 92539 (965-G1 See Page 964)
MOUNTAINSIDE RD
24100 MORV 92557 687-E5
MOUNTAINSIDE TR
40400 RivC 92539 (935-G7 See Page 904)
MOUNTAIN SONG LP
- MURR 92562 927-G3
MOUNTAIN SPRING CT
7900 RivC 92324 647-B7
MOUNTAIN SPRINGS
- PDST 92260 848-D6
MOUNTAIN SPRINGS CT
41300 RivC 92536 963-C3
MOUNTAINTOP RD
41500 RivC 92536 961-G3
MOUNTAIN VIEW AV
100 LKEL 92530 866-E6
5100 RIV 92504 685-A7
6100 RIV 92504 684-J7
8700 RivC 92223 690-H2
10900 LMLN 92354 647-D2
15300 RivC 92530 865-G6
33000 RivC 92530 897-A2
45600 PDST 92260 848-G2
49100 RivC 92230 723-C5
69700 RivC - (907-G6 See Page 906)
82000 INDO 92201 5410-E6
MOUNTAIN VIEW CIR
- RivC 91752 683-F5
- RMIR 92270 817-J4
MOUNTAIN VIEW CT
- MURR 92562 927-G5
13200 RivC 92883 835-B5
MOUNTAIN VIEW DR
500 PMSP 92264 786-J3
900 HEMT 92545 810-G5
2100 RivC 92882 742-H5
52900 RivC - 814-A4
MOUNTAIN VIEW LN
30500 RivC 92567 779-A3
35500 YCPA 92399 650-B4
81000 LQNT 92253 5530-E3
S MOUNTAIN VIEW LN
1100 CLTN 92324 646-G1
MOUNTAIN VIEW PL
300 PMSP 92262 756-D7
25500 RivC 92587 837-E7
W MOUNTAIN VIEW PL
200 PMSP 92262 756-D7
MOUNTAIN VIEW RD
200 ImCo 92274 (5773-B7 See Page 5712)
12500 DHSP 92240 697-C7
13600 RivC 92240 697-C7
16000 RivC 92240 727-C3
17000 RivC 92241 727-C3
19900 CTHC 92234 727-C6
22800 MORV 92557 687-A5
22900 RivC 92557 687-A5

STREET Block City ZIP Pg-Grid

MOUNTAIN VIEW ST
35100 YCPA 92399 650-A5
W MOUNTAIN VIEW ST
30100 LKEL 92530 866-C3
MOUNTAIN VISTA DR
- COR 92881 773-G3
73400 PDST 92260 848-F6
74400 INDW 92210 848-H3
MOUNT ARARAT DR
- CTHC 92234 787-E5
MOUNT ASHLAND CT
- MURR 92562 927-G3
MOUNT BACHELOR WY
29500 RivC 92586 868-A1
MOUNT BALDY CT
4100 NRCO 92860 713-J3
MOUNT BALDY DR
2100 RIV 92506 716-H5
MOUNT BALDY ST
1200 PER 92570 807-D3
MOUNT BLANC AV
23900 MURR 92562 928-B1
MOUNT BLANC CT
4100 NRCO 92860 713-J3
MOUNT CANTARA CIR
4100 COR 92882 742-D5
MOUNT DIABLO AV
6500 RIV 92506 715-F2
MOUNT DIABLO ST
1300 PER 92570 807-D3
MOUNT EDEN DR
500 HEMT 92543 840-H1
MOUNT EDNA RD
- RivC 92220 389-G7
MOUNT ELENA CIR
3900 COR 92882 742-D6
MOUNT HOLYOKE
- RMIR 92270 818-A3
MOUNT HOOD DR
500 HEMT 92543 840-H1
MOUNT HOOD RD
8300 RIV 92504 715-A3
MOUNT HUMPHRIES CIR
2300 COR 92879 743-J2
MOUNT HUMPHRIES ST
2200 COR 92879 743-J2
MOUNT INGALLS CT
4000 NRCO 92860 713-J3
MOUNT LASSEN WY
- MURR 92562 927-G3
MOUNT MCKINLEY PL
200 SJCT 92583 781-A6
MOUNT NIGUEL CIR
2800 COR 92882 742-F7
MOUNT OLYMPUS DR
6900 SDCo 92028 999-E5
MOUNT OLYMPUS VALLEY RD
9900 SDCo 92028 999-D4
MOUNT PALMAS CIR
3900 COR 92882 742-D6
MOUNT PALOMAR ST
1200 PER 92570 807-D3
MOUNTPELLIER PL
39700 MURR 92562 928-B1
MOUNT PLEASANT WY
3000 COR 92881 773-D3
MOUNT RAINIER ST
100 PER 92570 807-D3
4800 RivC 92509 684-H2
MOUNT RUBIDOUX DR
3500 RIV 92501 685-F3
MOUNT RUDOLF RD
- RivC 92567 779-F4
MOUNT RUSHMORE DR
- NRCO 92860 713-J3
MOUNT RUSHMORE PL
1100 SJCT 92583 781-B6
MOUNT RUSSELL DR
24000 MORV 92553 717-E6
MOUNT SERENATA CIR
4000 COR 92882 742-D5
MOUNT SHADOWS LN
37800 CTHC 92234 817-D1
MOUNT SHASTA DR
100 NRCO 92860 713-J3
MOUNT SHASTA ST
1300 PER 92570 807-D3
MOUNT SIERRA ST
1200 PER 92570 807-D3
MOUNT SOPRAS CT
- RivC 92508 746-E2
MOUNT TESORO CIR
3900 COR 92882 742-D6
MOUNT THOMPSON CIR
700 COR 92879 743-H2
MOUNT TOBIN CT
4000 NRCO 92860 713-J3
MOUNT VERDE DR
4000 NRCO 92860 713-J3
MOUNT VERNON AV
- RivC 92507 646-F7
700 RivC 92507 686-E1
700 RIV 92507 646-F7
700 RIV 92507 686-E1
11600 GTER 92313 646-E3
S MOUNT VERNON AV
700 CLTN 92324 646-F1
1400 GTER 92313 646-F2
1400 GTER 92324 646-F2
MOUNT VERNON PL
23700 RivC 92587 837-E6
MOUNT VERNON ST
7100 RIV 92504 715-E2

MOUNT VERNON WY
300 COR 92881 773-D3
MOUNT VIEW AV
- BAN 92220 721-H3
MOUNT VIEW RD
68100 CTHC 92234 817-D2
MOUNT WASATCH DR
- RIV 92508 746-E2
MOUNT WHITNEY AV
6600 RIV 92506 715-F2
MOUNT WHITNEY CIR
700 COR 92879 743-H3
MOUTON DR
1400 SJCT 92583 811-E5
MOYANO CIR
800 COR 92882 773-B2
MOYANO ST
800 COR 92882 773-C1
MOZAMBIQUE DR
38200 PDST 92211 819-A1
MOZART LN
- RMIR 92270 818-D4
MOZART WY
13000 MORV 92555 718-E4
MUELLER LN
17500 MORV 92551 747-F6
26800 RivC 92584 868-C6
MUIR ST
3600 RIV 92503 714-H6
MUIRFIELD CT
75000 INDW 92210 848-J1
MUIRFIELD DR
300 PDST 92211 818-J1
11000 RMIR 92270 788-A5
22700 MURR 92562 927-D4
44800 TEM 92592 979-C4
80700 INDO 92201 5410-B7
MUIRFIELD RD
1500 RIV 92506 715-G6
MUIRFIELD ST
14500 MORV 92555 718-D7
MUIRFIELD WY
- CTHC 92234 757-F7
- CTHC 92234 787-F1
- LQNT 92253 849-H6
MUIRFIELD VILLAGE
- LQNT 92253 5530-D5
MULBERRY AV
10500 FONT 92337 644-A4
10500 SBdC 92337 644-A4
MULBERRY CIR
13500 YCPA 92399 650-D6
MULBERRY DR
40500 RivC 92544 841-C2
MULBERRY LN
1100 CALI 92320 689-H1
1200 COR 92879 743-E6
1300 NRCO 92860 713-E4
MULBERRY ST
1200 RIV 92501 686-A2
2300 RIV 92501 685-J3
3700 RIV 92507 685-H4
24500 RivC 92584 897-G1
MULESHOE CT
4300 HEMT 92544 811-F5
MULL AV
10200 RIV 92503 714-E5
10300 RIV 92505 714-E5
MULTIVIEW DR
14800 RivC 92570 775-F6
16900 RivC 92570 776-A5
MUMFORD AV
3000 RIV 92503 744-F3
MUNDO AV
21200 RivC 92570 806-J3
21200 RivC 92570 807-A3
MUNDO DR
1700 HEMT 92545 810-H6
MUNICH LN
- RivC 92596 929-C1
MUNN CIR
73900 RivC 92260 818-G3
MURAL CT
24400 MORV 92553 717-F6
MURAL ST
20000 RivC 92570 776-G3
MURANO ST
36000 MURR 92562 898-B7
MURDOCK CIR
23000 RivC 92587 867-D2
MURDOCK CT
1400 RIV 92507 716-F2
MURIEL DR
3000 RivC 92509 685-C1
14300 MORV 92553 717-H6
MURIEL LN
56100 RivC 92539 (934-H2 See Page 904)
MURILLO RD
33500 RivC 92596 899-H5
MURKESON ST
22500 RivC 92570 805-H2
MURPHY AV
300 RivC 92507 646-E7
MURPHY LN
31000 RivC 92584 868-C5
MURPHY ST
100 BLY 92225 5491-D6
11500 LMLN 92354 647-C2
MURRAY ST
- BAN 92220 692-B7
- RivC 92220 692-B7
100 BAN 92220 722-B1
6800 RIV 92504 714-J2

MURRAY CANYON DR
400 PMSP 92264 816-E1
800 PMSP 92264 786-F7
MURRAY HILL WY
3300 HEMT 92545 840-F4
MURRAY HILLS RD
36500 RivC 92539 (903-J7 See Page 902)
36900 RivC 92539 (933-J1 See Page 902)
MURRIETA RD
- PER 92571 807-J2
800 PER 92570 807-J4
1200 PER 92571 777-J1
1900 PER 92570 808-A7
2600 PER 92570 838-A1
4200 PER 92571 747-J7
25700 RivC 92584 868-A2
26100 RivC 92570 838-A1
26100 RivC 92585 838-A1
27100 RivC 92586 838-A5
28900 RivC 92584 838-A5
29000 RivC 92584 868-A2
32500 RivC 92584 898-A1
MURRIETA CREEK DR
- MURR 92562 927-F5
MURRIETA HOT SPRINGS RD
29700 RivC 92563 928-J6
29700 RivC 92563 929-A6
30800 TEM 92591 929-C6
38200 MURR 92563 928-E6
38300 MURR 92562 928-C7
MUSCATEL RD
21300 RivC 92530 897-A1
MUSEUM DR
100 PMSP 92262 786-D2
MUSICK RD
26000 RivC 92584 868-A5
MUSKEG WY
10800 MORV 92557 687-F6
MUSKET WY
11700 RIV 92503 744-D3
MUSKRAT RD
40500 RivC 92536 962-H2
MUSSELBURGH DR
25800 RivC 92586 838-A7
MUSTANG CT
15600 RivC 92570 775-G5
22100 CYNL 92587 867-B2
MUSTANG DR
34000 RivC 92276 788-J4
34000 RivC 92276 789-A4
S MUSTANG DR
3500 ONT 91761 683-A1
MUSTANG LN
2600 NRCO 92860 713-C7
5900 RivC 92509 685-B1
MUSTANG RD
39400 RivC 92544 (932-J5 See Page 902)
MUSTANG ST
- RivC 92880 683-D7
MUSTARD SEED DR
- RivC 92399 650-G7
MUTH WY
4500 RivC 92509 684-C1
MUTTERING RD
39300 RivC 92539 (935-A5 See Page 904)
MWB PRIVATE RD
- RivC 92241 390-B5
MY WY
- RivC 92570 837-B1
MYER RD
33000 RivC 92567 779-F7
MYERS AV
24000 MORV 92553 717-E3
MYERS LN
40600 MURR 92562 928-C5
MYERS ST
100 HEMT 92545 810-D4
100 HEMT 92545 840-D1
2000 RIV 92503 745-A1
2700 RIV 92503 744-J1
2900 RIV 92503 714-H6
N MYERS ST
300 HEMT 92545 810-D7
MYKONOS LN
- RIV 92506 716-C3
MYRL DR
300 RivC 92223 720-H1
300 BEAU 92223 720-H1
MYRL PL
300 HEMT 92545 810-F6
MYRNA ST
24600 MORV 92553 717-F4
MYRON ST
20000 RivC 92570 776-F3
MYRSINE AV
74300 PDST 92260 818-G6
MYRTLE AV
600 PER 92571 777-J6
15200 LKEL 92530 865-H1
22200 GTER 92313 646-E5
MYRTLE CT
2600 RIV 92506 685-H7
MYRTLE DR
33100 CTHC 92234 787-F4
MYRTLE LN
- FONT 92337 645-B2
MYRTLE ST
1700 COR 92880 742-J1
1800 COR 92880 743-A1
30000 LKEL 92530 865-G3
MYRTLE BEACH DR
- BAN 92220 721-C5

S MYRTLEWOOD AV
1800 CLTN 92324 646-H3
MYRTLE WOOD CT
40000 MURR 92562 928-C4
MYRTLEWOOD DR
500 CALI 92320 689-H1
900 CALI 92320 690-A1
MYSTIC CT
23600 MORV 92553 717-D3
MYSTICAL SPRINGS DR
27200 RivC 92883 835-B5
MYSTIC CANYON DR
6100 CHLS 91709 712-A5

N

N ST
- HEMT 92545 840-F2
- RivC 92518 747-D1
NABIL CIR
1600 COR 92881 773-H3
NACOMAS CT
19300 RivC 92570 777-C3
NADA LN
41000 TEM 92591 959-A2
41000 TEM 92591 958-J2
NADEAU LN
6600 RivC 92509 645-C5
NADIA ST
15600 MORV 92551 747-E2
NADINE CT
20700 RivC 92570 776-G5
NAGAI DR
13500 MORV 92553 717-C5
NAHUM DR
13500 DHSP 92240 697-A5
NAIBARA WY
19900 RivC 92241 727-G4
NAIMI ST
- MURR 92563 928-F2
NAIRN AV
4800 BAN 92220 721-E5
NAIROBI DR
43000 INDO 92201 5410-B6
NAKI CIR
22900 RivC 92595 897-D7
NAKOMA DR
48900 RivC 92230 723-A2
NAMIB DESERT DR
76300 PDST 92211 819-A1
NAN AV
15800 MORV 92551 747-G2
NANCE ST
100 PER 92571 747-D7
20300 RivC 92570 746-G7
21400 RivC 92570 747-A7
E NANCE ST
100 PER 92571 747-H7
NANCI LN
1700 SJCT 92583 781-A5
NANCY AV
9800 RivC 92223 690-G3
NANCY CT
36700 RMIR 92270 787-J7
45800 INDW 92210 849-A2
NANCY DR
16400 RivC - 726-H1
82200 INDO 92201 5470-F3
NANCY LN
33000 RivC 92584 898-D2
30700 RMIR 92270 787-J7
NANCY WY
5200 RIV 92503 714-F4
NANDINA AV
1300 PER 92571 747-C6
1300 RivC 92518 747-A6
17300 RivC 92504 745-J6
17300 RivC 92504 746-B6
17300 RivC 92508 745-J6
17300 RivC 92508 746-B6
20000 RivC 92570 746-G6
20000 RivC 92518 746-G6
21600 RivC 92570 747-A6
24300 MORV 92551 747-E5
NANDINA CT
- COR 92881 773-G3
46300 INDW 92210 848-H3
NANDINA ST
22900 GTER 92313 646-F3
NANTES CT
- TEM 92592 959-G7
NANTUCKET PL
2700 RIV 92506 715-G3
NANWOOD DR
23800 MORV 92553 717-D5
NAOMI CT
86400 COAC 92236 5471-E7
NAOMI DR
26200 RivC 92544 841-F1
NAPA CT
1500 SJCT 92583 811-E5
15200 LKEL 92530 865-H1
22200 GTER 92313 646-E5
NAPA LN
4200 RIV 92505 744-B1
NAPA PL
48700 RivC 92230 723-A2
NAPA CREEK DR
- RivC 92563 929-A7
NAPA VALLEY CT
13000 MORV 92555 718-A4
NAPLES CT
- TEM 92592 959-G7
NAPLES DR
900 COR 92882 773-B3

NAPLES RD
22100 MORV 92557 717-A1
39600 MURR 92563 928-F5
78300 LQNT 92253 819-G7
NAPOLEON ST
10200 RivC 92223 691-A4
NAPOLI CIR
11900 FONT 92337 644-F4
NAPOLI CT
2000 COR 92881 773-G1
NAPOLI LN
85500 COAC 92236 5471-C7
NAPOLI WY
1500 SJCT 92583 811-E3
NARANJA DR
29500 RivC 92587 867-E2
78800 RivC 92211 819-G1
NARANJA ST
22500 MORV 92557 717-B1
NARANJO ST
33600 RivC 92530 896-B3
NARBONNE CT
3700 RIV 92503 714-H6
NARCISCO LN
49300 COAC 92236 5471-A5
NARCISO CT
42500 MURR 92562 927-H6
NARCISSUS CIR
23600 MORV 92557 687-D5
NARCISSUS DR
- RivC 92211 819-G2
NARCISSUS LN
- LKEL 92532 867-D6
6200 CHLS 91709 712-A5
NARCISSUS WY
39200 PDST 92211 819-B3
NARNIA DR
9300 RIV 92503 715-A6
NASH ST
3400 RIV 92501 686-A6
3500 RIV 92501 646-A7
NASHLAND AV
3500 LKEL 92530 865-J4
NASHVILLE CT
- HEMT 92545 810-E6
NASON ST
11200 MORV 92555 688-B7
11800 MORV 92555 718-B2
15100 MORV 92555 748-B1
NASSAU CT
- RivC 92880 683-C4
39600 TEM 92591 959-C5
NASSAU PL
79900 RivC 92201 5410-A5
NASSAU ST
- RIV 92508 746-E1
NASTURTIUM WY
38200 PDST 92211 819-C2
NATALIE LN
1800 RIV 92506 716-A4
NATALIE RD
5900 CHLS 91709 712-A4
NATALIE JOY ST
28100 HEMT 92543 841-B5
NATCHEZ RD
5900 RivC 92509 684-D5
NATHAN DR
20600 RIV 92508 746-G1
43600 RivC 92544 811-J6
43700 RivC 92544 (812-A6 See Page 782)
NATHENE LN
6600 RivC 92509 645-B5
NATIONAL AV
- RivC 92254 (5653-A1 See Page 5592)
92400 RivC 92254 (5652-H1 See Page 5592)
NATIONAL DR
- LQNT 92253 5530-D4
11700 RIV 92503 744-D3
NATIVE DR
300 BAN 92220 721-F3
NATIVE ST
- PER 92571 777-G2
NATIVE DANCER WY
1000 NRCO 92860 713-F5
NATIVITY LN
28000 RivC 92585 808-E6
N NATOMA DR
67500 CTHC 92234 757-B6
W NATOMA DR
28400 CTHC 92234 757-B6
NATWAR LN
5200 PER 92571 747-C5
NAUMANN AV
26000 RivC 92548 839-B2
NAUTICAL CT
29700 CYNL 92587 867-C2
NAVAJA CIR
15600 MORV 92551 747-J2
NAVAJO CIR
1800 PMSP 92264 786-F5
NAVAJO CT
43300 INDO 92203 5410-H6
NAVAJO DR
500 BAN 92220 721-G4
700 RIV 92507 686-D7
1800 PMSP 92264 786-F5
45500 INDW 92210 849-C1
NAVAJO RD
100 PER 92570 807-D3
NAVAJO ST
43500 INDO 92203 5410-H6
61800 RivC 92240 695-J5

NAVAJO TR
32000 CTHC 92234 787-D4
NAVAJO SPRINGS RD
32400 RivC 92595 867-D7
NAVANO ST
900 CLTN 92324 646-H1
NAVARRE CT
41500 PDST 92260 818-F4
NAVARRE DR
1100 HEMT 92543 810-H5
NAVARRO DR
700 COR 92879 743-G3
NAVEL CT
- RivC 92503 744-J7
6600 RIV 92506 715-E1
29000 LKEL 92530 865-F1
NAVEL WY
15000 LKEL 92530 865-F1
NAVION RD
37500 RivC 92563 929-B4
NAVTEM PL
- PDST 92260 848-B7
NAVUT AV
22700 RivC 92595 897-D6
NAVY CANYON DR
- HEMT 92545 810-D6
NEAL WY
700 HEMT 92543 811-A5
NEARFALL DR
700 COR 92880 743-C3
NEATHERLY CIR
1100 COR 92880 743-B1
NEBRASKA AV
10800 RIV 92505 714-D6
NEBRASKA LN
33900 YCPA 92399 649-G5
NEBRASKA ST
30700 LKEL 92530 866-A3
33500 YCPA 92399 649-G5
N NEBRASKA ST
100 LKEL 92530 865-G2
S NEBRASKA ST
100 LKEL 92530 865-G2
NEBRASKA WY
13100 YCPA 92399 649-G6
NEBULA LN
30200 TEM 92592 959-A5
NEBULAE WY
- RMIR 92270 817-G3
NECTAR AV
- HEMT 92544 811-H6
- RivC 92544 811-H6
E NECTAR CT
3400 ONT 91761 643-B6
NECTAR RD
51100 RivC 92536 963-H7
NECTAREO
- LQNT 92253 849-H7
NECTARINE AV
2700 RIV 92506 715-H1
NECTARINE CT
29000 LKEL 92530 865-F1
NECTARINE DR
- RivC 92211 819-G2
NECTARINE WY
16400 LKEL 92530 865-F1
NEECE ST
3600 RivC 92879 743-H5
3600 COR 92879 743-H5
NEEDLES CT
2400 PER 92571 777-H3
NEELANS LN
18900 SBdC 92316 645-E1
NEELY LN
15800 RivC 92508 746-B3
NEER ST
31100 RivC 92548 839-B1
NEIGHBORS BLVD
- RivC - 392-B10
NEIGHBOURS BLVD
- RivC - 412-B2
12500 BLY - 392-B10
12500 RivC - 392-B10
NEIGHBOURS BLVD Rt#-78
13800 RivC - 392-B11
20800 RivC - 412-B1
NEIL RD
19700 RivC 92570 836-F7
NEIL ST
6800 RIV 92504 714-J2
22500 RivC 92570 807-B2
NEITZEAL RD
23800 RivC 92570 807-D4
NELLIE CT
- TEM 92591 958-H2
NELLIE ST
4400 RIV 92503 714-H4
NELMAR CIR
32500 RivC 92595 897-D7
32500 RivC 92595 927-D1
NELS CIR
13300 MORV 92555 717-J4
NELSON AV
100 SJCT 92582 810-D1
700 SJCT 92582 780-D7
17600 RivC 92530 896-C3
NELSON DR
1100 BAN 92220 721-D5
NELSON LN
75700 PDST 92211 819-A5
NELSON ST
3500 COR 92881 773-G5
3500 RIV 92506 715-E1
11500 LMLN 92354 647-E2

NELSON ST
52400 COAC 92236 5471-C7
52400 COAC 92236 5531-C1
NELSON TER
17200 RivC 92530 896-B3
NEMAHA CIR
10100 RIV 92503 744-H1
NENA DR
64000 RivC 92274 (5591-B6 See Page 5590)
66000 RivC 92274 (5651-B2 See Page 5590)
NEOTOMAS TR
- PMSP 92264 786-G6
NEPTUNE
- PMSP 92264 786-H7
NEPTUNE DR
- RivC 92254 (5654-D4 See Page 5594)
1800 PER 92571 777-J7
3100 RIV 92503 744-G1
NESSEL ST
4100 RIV 92503 714-J4
NESTWA TR
25100 RivC - (813-J5 See Page 782)
NETAS CT
- PDST 92260 848-B7
NETAS DR
- PDST 92260 848-B7
NETTIE ST
10200 RivC 91752 644-A6
NETTLE CT
1000 COR 92880 743-C2
73400 PDST 92260 848-F5
NETTLETON CT
1300 RIV 92506 716-B3
NEUMA DR
31500 CTHC 92234 787-F2
NEVA PL
6300 RIV 92506 715-F1
NEVADA AV
500 BLY 92225 5491-D5
3700 PER 92571 777-D1
4400 PER 92571 747-E7
NEVADA CIR E
74400 PDST 92260 818-H6
NEVADA CIR W
73900 PDST 92260 818-G6
NEVADA DR
28600 RivC 92587 837-E7
NEVADA ST
- RDL 92373 647-G1
NEVADA WY
2800 RIV 92506 715-H1
NEVILLE DR
77000 INDW 92210 849-D2
NEVILLE ST
36000 MURR 92562 928-B1
NEVIN PL
24700 MORV 92557 717-F2
NEVIS PL
41500 RivC 92201 819-J4
NEW LN
35100 YCPA 92399 650-A6
NEW ARROWHEAD DR
29100 RivC 92584 868-G1
NEW BEDFORD RD
26400 RivC 92586 838-B6
NEWBERRY ST
38700 RivC 92223 690-G3
NEWBURGH ST
- RIV 92508 746-E1
NEWBURY CIR
25800 RivC 92584 867-J1
25800 RivC 92584 868-A1
NEWBURY CT
4700 RIV 92507 686-A6
NEWBURY ST
- YCPA 92399 649-E2
NEWBY DR
4300 RIV 92505 714-E6
NEWBY RD
32700 RivC 92543 870-J7
32700 RivC 92543 871-A7
32700 RivC 92543 901-A1
32700 RivC 92592 870-J7
NEW CANAAN CT
15900 RivC 92504 745-G5
NEWCASTLE CT
- MURR 92562 927-E4
NEWCASTLE DR
39400 PDST 92211 819-C3
NEWCASTLE RD
- MURR 92563 928-J3
- MURR 92563 929-A3
NEWCASTLE ST
4800 RivC 92509 684-C3
NEWCASTLE WY
2800 COR 92879 744-A2
NEW CHICAGO AV
25500 RivC 92544 811-H7
26200 RivC 92544 841-J1
NEW CLAY ST
24600 MURR 92562 927-J6
24900 MURR 92562 928-A7
25100 MURR 92562 958-A1
NEWELL DR
200 RIV 92507 686-E3
NEW ENGLAND DR
1200 COR 92881 773-F3
23500 MORV 92553 717-D5
NEWFIELD CIR
1100 COR 92880 743-B1

NEWGARDEN ST
24800 MORV 92551 747-G3
NEWGATE CT
2900 RIV 92506 715-H2
NEWHALL DR
400 COR 92879 743-E3
NEWHALL ST
19000 PMSP 92258 726-D4
NEW HAMPSHIRE DR
3000 COR 92881 773-F4
NEW HARMONY CT
- RivC 92584 868-G1
NEW HAVEN DR
3800 RIV 92505 744-E1
13500 MORV 92553 717-D5
24400 MURR 92562 928-C3
NEWHOPE ST
14000 MORV 92553 717-B6
NEW HORIZON CT
24700 PER 92587 837-G5
24700 RivC 92587 837-G5
NEW HUB DR
29700 RivC 92586 868-D2
NEW JERSEY ST
3500 SBdC 92373 647-G2
6100 LMLN 92373 647-G2
NEW KIRK DR
2800 RIV 92507 686-C3
NEW LAREDO DR
500 SJCT 92583 781-A6
NEW LONDON PL
1200 RIV 92506 716-C5
NEW LOOK AV
25000 RivC 92545 809-J4
25000 RivC 92545 810-A4
NEWMAN AV
18400 RivC 92508 746-B6
28500 LKEL 92530 835-J7
43000 RivC 92544 811-H5
NEWMARKET DR
11200 RIV 92503 744-F3
NEW MEXICO DR
6900 RIV 92504 715-F4
6900 RIV 92506 715-F4
NEWPORT AV
20000 GTER 92313 646-D3
26100 LMLN 92354 647-F2
NEWPORT CT
- COR 92881 773-D4
NEWPORT DR
- SJCT 92583 780-J5
100 PMSP 92264 786-J6
100 PMSP 92264 787-A6
23500 RivC 92587 837-E7
NEWPORT LN
4800 RIV 92504 685-D6
NEWPORT RD
- LKEL 92532 866-J5
- LKEL 92532 867-A5
16700 RivC 92241 728-A2
23900 CYNL 92587 867-F2
25200 RivC 92596 867-G2
25400 RivC 92587 867-F2
25800 RivC 92584 868-G2
26000 RivC 92586 868-A2
E NEWPORT RD
33000 RivC 92596 869-G2
39200 HEMT 92543 871-A1
39200 RivC 92543 871-C1
40200 RivC 92544 871-C1
NEW PUBLIC ST
- CLTN 92324 646-G1
NEW RIDGE DR
6600 RIV 92506 716-C4
NEWSOME AV
19000 RivC 92508 746-D5
NEW STAR CIR
1000 RIV 92506 716-C5
NEWTON AV
40800 RivC 92591 959-J2
NEWTON DR
1800 COR 92882 742-J7
1800 COR 92882 772-J1
NEWTON LP
- CHLS 91709 712-A5
NEWTON PL
8600 RIV 92508 746-H2
NEWTON ST
3700 COR 92881 773-H5
5600 RivC 92509 645-E7
20000 RivC 92881 773-H5
NEW TOWN DR
40400 TEM 92591 959-D2
NEWVILLE PL
4600 RivC 92509 684-G2
NEW WINDSOR ST
- RIV 92508 746-E2
NEW YORK AV
- RivC 92583 781-C6
- SJCT 92583 781-C6
76500 PDST 92211 819-C6
NEW YORK DR
- COR 92882 773-B3
6900 RIV 92506 715-F4
NEW YORK ST
46600 INDO 92201 5470-G2
NEZ PERCE CIR
41100 RivC 92223 691-C4
NEZ PERCE CT
73600 PDST 92260 848-G4
NEZ PERCE TR
3100 RIV 92503 744-G1
NIAGARA CT
8900 RIV 92508 746-G3
27900 RivC 92586 838-A5

NIAGARA DR
11500 RivC 91752 683-G5
NIBLICK RD
6200 PMSP 92264 787-C5
41800 TEM 92591 959-C5
NICE AV
23900 MURR 92562 928-B1
NICE CT
1500 SJCT 92583 780-J6
44200 PDST 92260 818-H7
NICE DR
1800 COR 92882 743-A7
NICHOLAS PL
800 COR 92882 742-D5
NICHOLAS RD
400 BEAU 92223 720-F3
NICHOLAS VALLEY RD
39100 RivC 92591 959-G1
NICHOLS CT
5300 RIV 92503 714-E4
NICHOLS RD
18000 LKEL 92532 836-A7
18000 RivC 92532 836-A7
29400 LKEL 92530 835-J7
29400 LKEL 92530 836-A7
NICHOLS ST
29600 LKEL 92530 866-A2
NICHOLSON SPRINGS RD
43000 RivC 92539 964-J7
NICK LN
41100 MURR 92562 958-E2
NICK ST
4100 RIV 92501 685-H1
NICKELAUS CT
9400 RivC 92883 804-C3
NICKERSON DR
58500 RivC 92539 (985-D3 See Page 964)
NICKLAUS DR
5400 BAN 92220 721-D5
NICKLAUS ST
1200 HEMT 92543 841-B3
NICKS AV
25400 LMLN 92354 647-D2
NICLYN DR
32600 TEM 92592 979-F3
NICOLA DR
1200 RIV 92506 716-C2
E NICOLA RD N
1900 PMSP 92262 756-G5
W NICOLA RD N
1800 PMSP 92262 756-F5
NICOLA RANCH RD
2100 SDCo 92028 998-A7
NICOLAS COM
- TEM 92592 959-G7
NICOLAS RD
30000 TEM 92591 958-J1
30200 TEM 92591 959-A1
31400 RivC 92591 929-E7
31400 RivC 92596 929-E7
32500 RivC 92563 959-A1
35600 TEM 92591 929-D7
NICOLE CT
24300 MORV 92551 747-F1
26700 RivC 92544 841-D3
NICOLE WY
11300 FONT 92337 644-F2
NICOLET ST
- BAN 92220 722-A3
1000 BAN 92220 721-G3
E NICOLET ST
- BAN 92220 722-C3
NICOLINA DR
1300 SDCo 92028 997-H7
NICOLLET ST
6600 RivC 92504 715-D1
NICOYA CT
12400 YCPA 92399 650-B4
NIDEVER AV
6400 RIV 92504 715-C1
NIDO AV
12400 YCPA 92399 649-G4
NIELSON RD
38700 RMIR 92270 817-H2
NIETO ST
49500 COAC 92236 5471-B5
NIGHTCREST CIR
1100 COR 92881 773-E4
29500 TEM 92591 958-J4
NIGHTFALL WY
24700 MORV 92557 687-F7
NIGHT HAWK CIR
1000 COR 92881 773-F2
NIGHT HAWK DR
50600 RivC 92536 983-F1
NIGHTHAWK PASS
33400 TEM 92592 979-H3
33400 RivC 92592 979-H3
33700 RivC 92592 980-A2
NIGHTHAWK WY
42000 MURR 92562 927-G5
NIGHTINGALE RD
68500 CTHC 92234 817-E2
NIGHTINGALE WY
12400 GTER 92313 646-F5
NIGHTLY RD
32500 RivC 92584 868-D7
32500 RivC 92584 898-D1
NIGHT SHADE ST
25800 RivC 92584 868-A1
NIGHT SHADOW DR
11000 MORV 92555 688-E7

NIGHT SKY DR
- PER 92571 778-B2
NIGHTVIEW CIR
29800 TEM 92591 958-J4
NIGHTWIND CIR
- COR 92882 773-A2
NIGUEL ST
800 COR 92879 743-E1
NIKI WY
3400 RIV 92507 686-B4
NIKKI LN
25500 RivC 92584 897-J2
25500 RivC 92584 898-A2
NILDA DR
69100 CTHC 92234 787-F6
NILE
- PMSP 92264 786-E6
NILE LN
85300 COAC 92236 5471-C7
NIMBUS RD
22100 RivC 92570 807-C1
NIMROD CIR
1100 COR 92880 743-B1
NINA CIR
500 PER 92571 807-J2
NINA CT
5900 RivC 92509 684-G5
NINA LN
- COR 92882 773-A2
35900 RivC 92595 897-G7
NINEBARK ST
12500 MORV 92553 717-H3
NINO WY
11600 RivC 91752 683-F1
NINYA AV
15700 MORV 92551 747-G2
NIPOMA CT
19800 RIV 92508 746-E2
NIPPET LN
16000 MORV 92551 747-H3
NIRO RD
19200 RivC 92570 806-D1
NISBET WY
200 RIV 92507 686-E4
NISPERO
79000 LQNT 92253 849-H6
NITA CIR
43300 RivC 92544 811-H5
NITA DR
12100 MORV 92557 717-F2
NIVIA WY
25600 RivC 92548 809-E7
NIXON DR
6900 RIV 92506 715-E3
7000 RIV 92504 715-E3
NIXON RD
28700 RivC 92530 835-G7
28700 RivC 92530 865-G1
NOAH CIR
1600 COR 92880 742-J1
1600 COR 92880 743-A1
NOAH DR
1700 COR 92880 742-J1
NOB CT
40500 TEM 92591 959-D2
NOB DR
- RivC - (937-D1 See Page 906)
NOBEL CT
3500 RivC 91752 643-J6
NOB HILL RD
8300 RivC 92883 774-B7
8300 RivC 92883 804-B1
NOBLE CT
- TEM 92592 959-G7
NOBLE ST
4800 RIV 92503 714-F3
10000 RivC 92223 690-J4
NOBLE WY
- COR 92882 772-J2
NOBLE CANYON DR
38000 RivC 92260 818-E2
NOBLEWOOD RD
10800 MORV 92557 687-E6
NODI LN
- RivC 92562 956-E2
NOEL CIR
41800 RivC 92592 959-J4
NOGA AV
100 SJCT 92582 810-H2
NOGAL ST
24800 MORV 92553 717-F6
NOGALES ST
6000 RIV 92506 685-E7
NOGALES WY
1900 PMSP 92262 756-F6
NOGUES RD
29700 RivC 92585 808-H3
NOLA ST
43300 RivC 92544 811-J6
NOLA ANN PL
41700 MURR 92562 927-J5
NOLAN AV
400 HEMT 92543 841-A2
NOLAN CIR
78700 LQNT 92253 849-G1
NOLAN LN
17300 RivC 92504 745-E6
NOLAN WY
700 COR 92880 743-C2
NOLETTE AV
1400 HEMT 92545 840-E4
NOLINA BLVD
- BLY 92225 5491-D4

STREET
Block City ZIP Pg-Grid

NOLINA CIR
70200 RivC - 878-B6
NOLINA CT
40100 PDST 92260 818-E4
NOLINA DR
25800 RivC 92584 838-A7
NOLINA RD
- RivC - (907-J3
See Page 906)
NOLINE LN
48800 PDST 92260 848-F5
NOLING CT
25200 MURR 92563 928-E6
NOLZE PL
13800 MORV 92553 717-A5
NONA CT
41100 RivC 92544 841-D3
NO NAME ST
- BLY 92225 5491-D6
NONIE CT
8700 RivC 92223 691-A2
NOOR DR
300 NRCO 92860 713-H2
NOPAL PL
9100 RIV 92503 715-A6
11800 FONT 92337 644-B4
NORBERT ST
22500 RivC 92570 805-J3
NORBRO CT
39500 RivC 92592 931-A5
NORCO DR
1800 NRCO 92860 713-C4
NORCO HILLS RD
900 NRCO 92860 743-H1
900 COR 92879 743-G2
1200 NRCO 92860 713-J7
NORCONIAN DR
3400 NRCO 92860 713-D4
NORCREST ST
1100 COR 92880 743-B1
NORD CT
- RivC 92596 899-D7
NORDAL AV
41600 RivC 92544 841-E1
NORDEN DR
30400 RivC 92548 808-J5
30400 RivC 92548 809-A6
NOREEN LN
33700 YCPA 92399 649-F4
NORELLE DR
3000 RivC 91752 643-J5
3100 RivC 91752 644-A5
NORFOLK CT
46600 INDO 92201 5470-G2
NORFOLK DR
3200 RIV 92503 744-F2
NORFOLK ST
1400 COR 92880 743-B2
NORGATE CIR
- RivC 92880 742-B5
NORGROVE PL
32500 RivC 92595 897-B7
NORLOTI ST
2000 PMSP 92262 756-J5
NORMA DR
23400 RivC 92587 837-E7
NORMA LN
31100 RivC 92544 902-A2
NORMA ST
22200 RivC 92570 807-C7
NORMA WY
31300 RivC 92596 869-B2
NORMAN AV
66000 RivC 92240 726-H1
NORMAN RD
19500 RivC 92241 728-D3
21000 RivC 92567 778-J5
40600 BEAU 92223 691-B6
40600 RivC 92223 691-B6
NORMAN WY
5500 RIV 92504 715-A1
NORMANDIE PL
5800 RIV 92504 685-D7
5800 RIV 92506 685-D7
NORMANDO CT
15300 MORV 92551 747-J1
NORMANDY CT
1700 SJCT 92583 811-E5
2000 PMSP 92264 786-G5
NORMANDY LN
11600 LMLN 92354 647-E2
NORMANDY RD
37800 RivC 92596 930-B4
NORMANDY TER
1000 COR 92880 743-C2
S NORMANDY TER
1300 COR 92882 743-B6
NORMANDY WY
- RMIR 92270 788-B6
NORMAN HILLS RD
59200 RivC 92539 (965-E6
See Page 964)
NORMANTON DR
60000 RivC 92274 (5591-F3
See Page 5590)
NORRIS CIR
23500 MORV 92557 717-D2
NORRIS LN
22400 RivC 92567 808-F1
NORRIS ST
- RivC 92555 749-F5
NORRISGROVE DR
23100 RivC 92570 777-C4
NORTADA DR
27000 CTHC 92234 757-B5

NORTH AV
- RivC 92518 717-D7
NORTH BLVD
200 PER 92570 807-G4
NORTH DR
100 NRCO 92860 713-H1
21000 RivC 92567 778-J6
NORTH ST
8400 COR 92883 774-B5
22800 RivC 92583 811-B1
NORTH WY
- ONT 91761 643-A1
NORTHAM CT
37000 HEMT 92545 810-D7
NORTHAMPTON AV
69600 CTHC 92234 757-G7
NORTHBEND ST
2200 RIV 92501 685-H2
NORTH CREEK RD
31600 RivC 92563 929-D3
NORTHCROFT RD
4300 RivC 92509 644-C7
4300 RivC 92509 684-C1
NORTH END RD
- MURR 92563 958-G1
NORTHERN DANCER DR
24600 MORV 92551 747-F4
NORTH FORK DR
- RivC 92260 818-E1
NORTHGATE AV
43800 TEM 92592 978-J1
44000 TEM 92592 979-A1
NORTHGATE ST
700 RIV 92507 646-C7
700 RIV 92507 686-D2
NORTHHAMPTON DR
1500 RIV 92506 715-G6
NORTH LAKE DR
15100 LKEL 92530 865-F3
15100 RivC 92530 865-F3
NORTHLAKE ST
17300 RivC 92503 744-G5
NORTHMOOR DR
2500 RivC 92882 742-G5
40700 RivC 92223 691-B4
NORTHPARK DR
- RIV 92508 716-E7
- RIV 92508 746-E1
NORTHPOINTE ST
29200 LKEL 92530 865-G3
NORTH POLE LN
3600 RivC 92503 744-A4
NORTH PORT LN
28500 RivC 92584 868-F3
NORTH RIDGE DR
53900 RivC - 814-C5
NORTHRIDGE RD
6700 RIV 92506 716-C4
NORTHROP DR
7400 RIV 92506 716-E6
7400 RIV 92508 716-E6
NORTH SHORE DR
- INDO 92203 5410-G2
- RivC 92254 (5654-D4
See Page 5594)
NORTHSHORE DR
200 LKEL 92530 865-G2
NORTH SHORE DR
300 RivC 91752 683-E5
NORTHSHORE DR
26100 MORV 92555 687-J7
26200 MORV 92555 717-J1
NORTH SHORE DR
54200 RivC - 814-C7
S NORTH SHORE DR
2800 ONT 91761 643-A6
3500 ONT 91761 683-A1
S NORTH SHORE PL
2400 ONT 91761 643-A5
NORTH SHORE ST
- RivC 92276 788-C1
NORTH STAR AV
11000 RivC 91752 683-H4
NORTHSTAR AV
18000 RivC 92508 746-F7
NORTHSTAR CIR
- COR 92882 773-C2
NORTH STAR CT
42700 TEM 92592 959-A6
NORTHSTAR DR
8600 RIV 92508 746-E2
NORTHVIEW DR
34100 YCPA 92399 649-G4
NORTH VIEW DR
48600 PDST 92260 848-E5
NORTHVIEW LN
33600 YCPA 92399 649-F4
NORTHVIEW PL
5700 RIV 92506 685-D6
NORTHVIEW RD
41000 RivC 92544 901-E2
NORTH WINDS DR
25700 RivC 92585 838-E1
NORTHWOOD
79600 LQNT 92253 5530-A5
NORTHWOOD AV
- BAN 92220 721-D4
NORTHWOOD DR
5600 RivC 92509 684-F4
28000 RivC 92586 838-B6
NORTHWOOD RD
30100 RivC 92241 390-D8
NORTON LN
15100 MORV 92551 747-F1
15200 MORV 92551 717-F7

NORTON PL
4600 RIV 92506 685-F5
NORWALK CT
5600 RIV 92505 714-C4
NORWEGIAN ST
- RivC 92880 683-D7
NORWICH CT
12700 MORV 92553 717-B3
29300 RivC 92586 868-B1
NORWICH DR
- RIV 92508 746-E2
NORWICH WY
900 COR 92882 743-A6
NORWOOD AV
6400 RIV 92505 714-D2
NORWOOD DR
25100 RivC - (813-H5
See Page 782)
NOTNIL CT
11700 MORV 92557 717-E1
NOTNIL WY
15000 LKEL 92530 865-F1
NOTRE DAME CIR
2500 COR 92881 773-G3
NOTRE DAME CT
26100 RivC 92544 811-G7
26100 RivC 92544 841-G1
NOTRE DAME WY
2400 COR 92881 773-G3
NOTTHOFF LN
- RivC 92590 958-B7
NOTTINGHAM AV
81600 INDO 92201 5410-D7
NOTTINGHAM DR
- CTHC 92234 787-G1
800 COR 92880 743-B2
5200 RIV 92506 685-J7
5200 RIV 92506 715-J1
26200 LMLN 92354 647-F3
NOTTINGHAM LN
- RivC 92592 979-J2
NOTTINGHAM ST
15000 RivC 92530 865-F5
27300 RivC 92544 841-F3
NOTTING HILL RD
39700 MURR 92563 928-F6
NOVA LN
11000 RivC 91752 683-H4
25600 RivC 92585 837-J3
25700 RivC 92585 838-A3
NOVAK ST
3400 RivC 92509 645-A6
NOVARA CT
- TEM 92592 959-G7
NOVARO LN
100 PER 92571 807-H2
NOVA SCOTIA DR
2900 RIV 92506 715-F3
NOVATO TER
- RMIR 92270 818-D6
NOVATO WY
10300 RIV 92505 714-E2
30400 RivC 92563 929-B7
NOVELLA CT
11000 MORV 92557 687-H7
NOVEMBER DR
3500 RivC 92503 744-B4
NOVIO CT
35900 RMIR 92270 787-G6
NOYER LN
4200 RivC 92509 685-C2
NUBLADO CIR
26000 MORV 92551 747-J3
NUBS CT
29900 RivC 92584 868-A2
NUCKOLLS CT
43100 RivC 92544 841-H2
NUECESS CT
15500 MORV 92551 747-J2
S NUEVA VISTA DR
800 PMSP 92264 786-J3
800 PMSP 92264 787-A4
NUEVO CIR
- FONT 92337 644-J2
NUEVO DR
10700 FONT 92337 644-J1
79300 LQNT 92253 819-H7
NUEVO RD
1100 PER 92571 778-E7
22800 RivC 92570 807-C1
23000 RivC 92570 777-F7
25200 RivC 92571 778-E7
28700 RivC 92567 778-E7
30500 RivC 92567 779-A7
E NUEVO RD
100 PER 92571 777-H7
900 PER 92571 778-A7
W NUEVO RD
100 PER 92571 777-G7
300 PER 92570 777-F7
21400 RivC 92570 777-F7
24000 PER 92570 807-E1
24000 RivC 92570 807-E1
NUEVO ST
600 HEMT 92545 810-G6
NUEVO VALLEY DR
28600 RivC 92567 808-F3
NUGGET CT
1200 CALI 92320 689-J1
NUTMEG CIR
3400 RIV 92503 744-E2
NUTMEG DR
3100 COR 92882 742-F5
NUTMEG ST
13200 MORV 92553 717-H4

NUTMEG ST
39500 MURR 92562 928-A1
40300 MURR 92562 927-J2
NUTMEY LN
1400 HEMT 92545 840-D4
NUT TREE LN
3700 RIV 92501 685-J1
NUTWOOD CIR
1900 COR 92881 773-F1
NUTWOOD CT
11700 FONT 92337 644-C3
NYASA DR
38600 PDST 92211 819-A2
NYE AV
3600 RIV 92505 714-F7
3600 RIV 92505 744-F1
NYRI WY
33000 RivC 92595 896-H6

O

O ST
- HEMT 92545 840-F2
- RivC 92518 717-C7
- RivC 92518 747-C1
OAHU LN
900 PMSP 92264 786-C6
OAK
- RivC 92220 782-D1
OAK AV
2100 HEMT 92545 840-G2
2400 COR 92882 773-A2
OAK CIR
- MURR 92563 928-H7
OAK CT
12500 YCPA 92399 649-D4
25700 MORV 92557 717-H1
OAK DR
11200 CALI 92320 690-B6
32900 RivC 92544 871-J7
32900 RivC 92544 901-J1
33500 RivC 92544 902-A1
OAK GN
52700 RivC - (813-J4
See Page 782)
52700 RivC - 814-A4
OAK LN
11600 YCPA 92399 649-J2
39000 SBdC 92399 651-B1
OAK PL
14200 DHSP 92240 697-B6
OAK RD
37200 RivC 92539 (935-C1
See Page 904)
OAK ST
11300 SBdC 92316 645-E3
20200 RivC 92570 836-H6
21400 RivC 92570 776-A7
21800 RivC 92570 806-A1
46100 INDO 92201 5470-H1
OAKADO LN
75500 RivC 92276 789-A2
OAK BARK LN
10200 RivC 91752 644-A4
OAK BENCH RD
11700 SBdC 92399 651-D2
OAK BLUFF LN
- MURR 92562 927-E5
OAKBRIDGE DR
29500 RivC 92586 868-B2
OAKBROOK DR
2900 RIV 92503 744-E3
OAKBURL CIR
1300 COR 92882 773-A1
OAK CANYON DR
34000 RivC 92595 897-D4
OAK CANYON RD
41500 RivC 92544 931-F7
OAK CIRCLE DR
23500 RivC 92595 897-E4
OAK CLIFF DR
39200 TEM 92591 928-H7
39600 TEM 92591 958-H1
OAK CREEK DR
- YCPA 92399 650-B7
3500 ONT 91761 643-C6
OAK CREEK RD
8900 RivC 92223 690-H2
40900 MURR 92562 927-H2
OAKCREEK UNION
- MURR 92563 928-G6
OAKCREST CIR
100 RivC 91752 683-F5
OAK CREST DR
2100 RIV 92506 716-A2
2100 RIV 92506 715-J2
2200 PMSP 92264 786-G4
12900 YCPA 92399 651-A5
12900 YCPA 92399 650-J5
OAK CREST DR E
2300 PMSP 92264 786-H4
OAK CREST DR S
1100 PMSP 92264 786-G4
OAK CREST DR W
1100 PMSP 92264 786-G4
OAKCREST LN
1200 COR 92882 742-F6
OAK CREST RD
- SDCo 92028 998-G5
OAKDALE DR
14000 RivC 92570 775-D7
OAKDALE LN
21100 RIV 92508 746-H2
OAKDALE RD
29000 RivC 92584 838-A7

OAKDALE RD
29000 RivC 92584 868-A1
OAKDALE ST
900 COR 92880 743-B2
12600 RivC 92880 683-D6
OAK DELL ST
13000 MORV 92553 717-C4
OAK FIELD RD
23800 MORV 92557 687-D6
OAK FLATS DR
73500 RivC 92260 818-F1
S OAK GLEN LN
900 CLTN 92324 646-H1
OAK GLEN RD
8300 RivC 92223 651-A6
8300 RivC 92223 691-A1
8900 RivC 92223 690-H3
11400 SBdC 92399 651-C1
11800 YCPA 92399 649-J1
12900 YCPA 92399 651-A6
13100 YCPA 92399 650-A1
32400 YCPA 92373 649-D5
43500 RivC 92544 902-A3
OAK GROVE AV
40000 MURR 92562 928-C4
OAK GROVE CIR
1100 COR 92881 773-E4
OAK GROVE DR
- RivC 92373 688-H1
OAK GROVE RD
37000 YCPA 92399 650-F5
OAKHAM CT
15200 MORV 92551 747-F1
OAK HAVEN WY
1300 HEMT 92545 840-D3
OAK HILL
54000 LQNT 92253 5530-A3
OAKHILL CT
13500 YCPA 92399 650-G6
OAK HILL DR
- TEM 92591 959-C4
E OAK HILL DR
2800 ONT 91761 643-A5
S OAK HILL DR
2400 ONT 91761 643-A5
OAK HILL LN
11300 YCPA 92399 650-C1
OAK HILL PL
- RivC - 844-C1
OAK HILLS LN
- SDCo 92028 999-G5
OAKHURST AV
4900 BAN 92220 721-E4
OAKHURST CT
25300 MURR 92563 928-E3
OAKHURST DR
300 SJCT 92583 811-C3
OAKHURST PL
8200 RIV 92504 715-C4
OAK KNOLL CT
11500 FONT 92337 644-C3
OAK KNOLL DR
11300 FONT 92337 644-C3
23700 MORV 92557 687-D6
OAK KNOLL LN
- LKEL 92530 896-G4
44600 RivC 92590 977-A2
OAK KNOLL RD
52700 RivC - (813-J5
See Page 782)
OAKLAND AV
2200 HEMT 92545 810-G6
11700 YCPA 92399 649-J2
14600 HEMT 92543 810-H6
33200 HEMT 92543 811-A6
E OAKLAND AV
100 HEMT 92543 811-C6
1200 HEMT 92544 811-C6
OAKLAND WY
1100 COR 92882 743-A6
OAKLAND HILLS DR
800 BAN 92220 721-D4
1900 RivC 92882 742-H5
OAKLAND HILLS ST
32000 RivC 92276 788-E2
OAK LEAF CIR
- RivC 92880 683-B7
E OAKLEAF CT
3400 ONT 91761 643-B6
OAK LEAF DR
12800 RivC 92282 724-D1
S OAKLEAF DR
900 CLTN 92324 646-G1
OAK LEAF LN
25100 RivC - (813-H5
See Page 782)
E OAKLEAF RD
3300 ONT 91761 643-B6
OAKLEAF ST
- MURR 92562 927-F4
OAK LEAF WY
10200 RivC 91752 644-A4
OAKLEY AV
3600 RIV 92501 685-J2
OAKLEY DR
14100 RivC 92503 745-C4
OAKLINGTON RD
- MURR 92563 928-F7
- MURR 92563 958-F1
OAKMAN LN
33000 RivC 92545 839-E2
OAK MANOR CT
44600 RivC 92590 978-A3
OAK MEADOW DR
6500 RIV 92506 716-D4

OAK MESA DR
13300 YCPA 92399 650-F6
OAKMONT
- LQNT 92253 5530-C4
OAKMONT AV
26800 RivC 92586 838-C5
OAKMONT CT
- MURR 92563 928-H4
700 RivC 92882 742-G5
OAKMONT DR
- RivC 92254 (5653-A3
See Page 5592)
- RMIR 92270 788-A6
300 PDST 92211 818-J1
5700 BAN 92220 721-D4
26600 RivC 92586 838-B7
E OAKMONT ST
2800 ONT 91761 643-A6
OAKMORE LN
22500 RivC 92595 897-C6
OAKMOUNT BLVD
8600 RivC 92240 656-F7
8700 RivC 92240 696-F2
OAK MOUNTAIN DR
13400 YCPA 92399 650-F6
OAK PARK DR
18300 RivC 92504 776-A1
OAK RANCH RD
34200 RivC 92544 902-E3
OAK RIDGE CIR
3900 NRCO 92860 713-D4
OAKRIDGE CIR
24300 MURR 92562 928-C3
OAKRIDGE CT
- RIV 92518 746-G3
OAKRIDGE DR
- COR 92882 742-D6
OAK RIDGE DR
36300 YCPA 92399 650-D5
OAK RUN CIR
10900 MORV 92557 687-E6
OAKSHADE CIR
- RivC 92590 978-F5
OAK SPRING RD
39100 RivC 92592 900-J5
39100 RivC 92592 901-A5
OAK SPRINGS DR
13800 RivC 92260 818-F3
S OAK SPRINGS PL
2500 ONT 91761 643-C5
OAK SPUR RD
37100 YCPA 92399 650-F5
OAKSTONE CT
25200 MORV 92553 717-G6
OAKTHORN CIR
8600 RIV 92508 746-G2
OAK TREE
54100 LQNT 92253 5530-B3
OAK TREE AV
6300 BAN 92220 721-C4
OAK TREE CIR
19500 RivC 92509 684-B4
OAK TREE DR
- RMIR 92270 788-B5
OAKTREE DR
100 PER 92571 777-G6
OAK TREE LN
11700 YCPA 92399 649-J2
OAKTREE LN
19500 RivC 92508 746-E5
24900 RivC 92584 867-H7
OAKTREE LP
38200 MURR 92562 927-D3
OAKTREE WY
4200 HEMT 92545 840-D4
OAKVALE RD
- RivC 92562 956-J4
OAK VALLEY DR
31100 RivC 92548 809-B7
OAK VIEW DR
- BEAU 92223 690-F7
- BEAU 92223 720-F1
- RivC 92223 690-F7
OAKVIEW LN
19400 LKEL 92530 896-G4
OAK VIEW LN
39200 RivC 92223 690-H2
OAK VIEW PL
- MURR 92562 927-E4
OAKVIEW PL
20700 RivC 92570 775-H6
OAK VIEW RD
36800 YCPA 92399 650-F5
OAKVIEW WY
19000 LKEL 92530 896-G3
OAKVILLE CT
- RivC 92592 979-H3
OAKWOOD CIR
31800 YCPA 92399 649-B3
OAKWOOD CT
300 COR 92879 744-B3
900 CALI 92320 650-A7
OAKWOOD DR
11100 LMLN 92354 647-A1
11100 CLTN 92324 647-A1
11300 FONT 92337 644-B2
OAKWOOD PL
3500 RIV 92506 685-E6
OAKWOOD ST
500 SJCT 92543 811-A4
500 SJCT 92583 811-A4
500 HEMT 92543 811-A4
500 HEMT 92583 811-A4
21100 RivC 92570 776-H3
21400 RivC 92570 777-A3

OAKWOOD ST
25600 RivC - 814-D6
OAKWOOD WY
48500 PDST 92260 848-D5
OASIS
100 PMSP 92264 786-E5
OASIS AV
1500 RivC - 5240-A6
OASIS CT
47800 PDST 92260 848-G4
OASIS DR N
- CTHC 92234 787-F6
OASIS DR S
- CTHC 92234 787-F6
OASIS PL
- CTHC 92234 787-F6
OASIS RD
- RivC - 5421-C1
100 PMSP 92262 756-D4
OASIS ST
100 BLY 92225 5491-E5
43600 INDO 92201 5410-F6
45000 INDO 92201 5470-F2
54000 RivC 92274 5530-F4
OASIS TR
71200 RivC 92260 848-B5
71300 RivC - 848-B5
OASIS CLUB DR
41000 PDST 92211 819-D4
OASIS PALM AV
52200 COAC 92236 5471-C7
52200 COAC 92236 5531-C1
OASIS SPRING DR
- RivC 92211 819-G2
OASIS VIEW CIR
28200 RivC 92584 838-F7
OASIS VILLAGE CT
800 BLY 92225 5491-F4
OATES LN
24900 RivC - 814-A4
49400 COAC 92236 5471-C5
OATMAN LN
46100 RivC 92536 982-F4
OBAN CIR
24700 MORV 92551 747-F1
OBISPO DR
12200 MORV 92557 717-F2
OBLIQUE
45900 RivC 92220 782-D1
OBREGON CT
68500 CTHC 92234 757-E7
OBSERVATION DR
12100 GTER 92313 646-F5
OBSIDIAN CT
29100 RivC 92567 808-G2
OBSIDIAN DR
16800 RivC 92508 746-C6
OCALA CIR
- COR 92881 773-E5
OCALA CT
11500 MORV 92557 717-E1
OCAMPO ST
10200 RIV 92503 714-F5
OCANA CT
15700 FONT 92337 644-F3
OCANA LN
15500 MORV 92551 747-J1
OCASA DR
5600 RivC 91752 683-G5
OCASEY CT
21200 MORV 92557 716-H1
OCCIDENTAL CIR
2500 RIV 92507 686-B3
OCEAN AV
400 PER 92571 807-H1
OCEAN CT
5200 RIV 92505 714-E4
OCEANDER ST
14300 RivC 92282 695-G6
OCEAN DUNES ST
27100 MORV 92555 748-B2
OCELOT CIR
3000 COR 92882 773-C3
OCHEE CIR
700 COR 92879 743-G3
OCHOBEE CT
49900 RivC 92536 963-E1
OCONTO CT
25200 MORV 92553 717-G7
OCOTILLO AV
100 PMSP 92264 786-E4
25000 MORV 92553 717-G6
82200 INDO 92201 5410-E6
OCOTILLO DR
600 RivC - 5240-A7
6900 RIV 92506 715-H5
11300 FONT 92337 644-D2
33700 RivC 92548 809-G4
42300 RMIR 92270 818-B6
44000 LQNT 92253 819-H7
45300 PDST 92260 848-E2
OCOTILLO LN
- PDST 92260 848-C6
OCOTILLO RD
600 BLY 92225 5491-D4
10500 DHSP 92240 696-J3
13200 RivC 92282 724-F2
13900 DHSP 92240 697-A5
15500 RivC 92240 725-E1
68600 CTHC 92234 787-E4
OCOTILLO TR
19800 RivC 92241 727-C4
OCTILLO CT
73800 PDST 92260 848-G4

OCTOBER CT
3400 RivC 92503 744-B5
OCTOPUS LN
- RivC 92595 897-E7
ODELL AV
100 SJCT 92582 810-D1
700 SJCT 92582 780-D6
ODELL ST
5200 RivC 92509 685-E2
ODEN WY
- RivC - 392-B10
ODESSA CT
20800 RIV 92508 746-H2
ODESSA DR
- TEM 92591 958-J3
12100 MORV 92557 717-G2
ODLUM DR
82100 INDO 92201 5470-E4
OES QUEST LN
12200 RivC 92503 744-H7
O FERRALL DR
21000 RivC 92570 777-A6
OFFICER DAVID
VASQUEZ RD
300 CTHC 92234 787-E7
OGDEN WY
3800 RIV 92501 685-H2
OHIO CT
12200 YCPA 92399 649-B3
77300 PDST 92211 819-D7
OHIO PL
23300 RivC 92587 837-D6
OHIO ST
200 LKEL 92530 865-G2
1800 RIV 92507 686-A6
24500 MORV 92557 717-F1
OILNUT CT
13100 MORV 92553 717-H4
OISE DR
30200 RivC 92584 868-G3
OJAI CIR
6000 BAN 92220 721-C4
OJAI PL
73400 RivC 92276 788-F2
OKEECHOBEE LN
19200 LKEL 92530 896-G4
19200 RivC 92530 896-G4
OKLAHOMA AV
76700 PDST 92211 819-C6
OKUMA RD
26000 RivC 92584 868-A7
OLANCHA RD
68700 CTHC 92234 787-E4
OLD RD
23300 RivC 92570 806-J4
OLD 215 FRONTAGE RD
13000 MORV 92553 716-J4
13000 RivC 92553 716-J4
13700 MORV 92553 717-A6
13700 RivC 92553 717-A6
OLD AGENCY RD
26400 RivC 92544 841-H1
S OLD ARCHIBALD
RANCH RD
3200 ONT 91761 643-A7
3300 ONT 91761 683-A1
OLD AVENUE 52
- LQNT 92253 879-H1
- LQNT 92253 5530-A1
OLD BANNING
IDYLLWILD RD
15000 BAN 92220 721-H7
15000 BAN 92220 722-A6
15000 RivC 92220 721-H7
15000 RivC 92220 722-A6
15200 RivC 92220 389-F7
24300 RivC - (813-H3
See Page 782)
OLD BLYTHE VIDAL RD
- RivC - 392-C2
OLD BRIDGE CT
11500 FONT 92337 644-H3
OLD BRIDGE RD
1700 RIV 92506 716-A4
OLD CARRIAGE RD
39800 MURR 92563 928-F6
OLD CARY RD
36500 RivC 92539 904-C7
36900 RivC 92539 (934-C1
See Page 904)
OLD CASTLE RD
15400 FONT 92337 644-F3
OLD COACH RD
35000 RivC 92592 900-G5
OLD COMANCHE TR
53800 RivC 92539 904-C7
OLD CONTROL RD
51700 RivC - (813-H7
See Page 782)
51700 RivC - (843-H1
See Page 842)
OLD COUNTRY RD
24000 MORV 92557 687-E6
OLD DALE RD
- RivC - 390-K6
OLD ELSINORE RD
20000 RivC 92570 776-J4
20100 RivC 92570 777-A6
22000 RivC 92570 807-B1
OLDEN RD
25400 RivC 92590 978-A2
OLDENBURG LN
- NRCO 92860 743-J1
- NRCO 92860 744-A1

OLDENBURG ST
4100 RivC 92509 685-D3
OLD FARM ST
25100 MORV 92553 717-G5
OLD FASHION WY
11100 RivC 92503 744-G4
OLD FIELD AV
11500 FONT 92337 644-B3
OLD FOREST RD
37000 RivC 92539 904-H7
37000 RivC 92539 (934-H2
See Page 904)
OLD GROVE RD
- RivC 92504 745-E3
OLD HALLOW LN
- RivC 92544 871-F6
OLDHAM LN
18700 RivC 92570 776-G2
OLD HAMNER RD
3900 NRCO 92860 713-E3
OLD HARBOR DR
43300 RivC 92201 819-J6
OLD HICKORY RD
1100 COR 92882 773-A1
OLD HILL RD
23300 RivC 92595 897-E5
OLD HWY 395
- SDCo 92028 998-H5
47900 RivC 92592 999-A2
47900 SDCo 92028 999-A2
OLD KENT RD
- TEM 92592 959-H7
OLD LAKE DR
23000 MORV 92557 687-C6
OLD LIMONITE AV
10400 RivC 91752 684-A5
OLD LIVE OAK AV
11600 FONT 92337 644-D3
OLD MEADOW DR
47100 RivC 92536 982-F7
OLD MILL RD
5200 RIV 92504 685-C7
24800 RivC - (813-J4
See Page 782)
E OLD MILL RD
100 COR 92879 743-D7
W OLD MILL RD
100 COR 92882 743-C7
OLD MINE TR
51300 RivC 92539 (933-H3
See Page 902)
OLD MOUNTAIN AV
1200 SJCT 92583 811-E3
OLD NUEVO RD
500 PER 92571 777-G7
OLD OAK CT
7900 RIV 92506 715-G7
OLD OAK TER
37300 MURR 92562 927-F3
OLD OAKS DR
36000 RivC 92595 927-F1
OLD PAINT WY
22100 CYNL 92587 867-B1
OLD PERRIS BLVD
- MORV 92557 687-G7
OLD PROSPECTOR TR
74000 PDST 92260 848-G2
OLD QUARRY RD
2100 RIV 92506 716-A1
OLD RANCH RD
1300 COR 92882 772-J1
1300 COR 92882 773-A1
5600 RIV 92504 685-C6
29200 RivC 92532 866-F2
31200 RivC 92544 871-E4
53100 RivC 92539 (934-B3
See Page 904)
E OLD RANCH RD
1500 CLTN 92324 646-G1
OLD ROUTE 79
20300 RivC 92583 780-J3
OLD SECOND ST
500 SJCT 92583 811-C3
OLD SETTLERS LN
6500 RIV 92504 715-C1
OLD SOUTHWEST
BRAND RD
40700 RivC 92544 871-D5
OLD SPRING RD
11500 FONT 92337 644-H2
39600 MURR 92563 928-G5
OLD STAGE RD
500 SJCT 92583 781-A6
49100 RivC 92536 963-C6
OLD STATE HWY
33000 RivC 92545 839-F2
57000 RivC 92274 5531-H5
OLD SYCAMORE LN
- MURR 92563 928-J4
OLD TEMESCAL RD
700 COR 92879 773-E1
900 COR 92881 773-F1
1600 RivC 92881 773-H1
OLD TIMES CT
30000 RivC 92563 929-A7
OLD TOWN FRONT ST
28300 TEM 92590 958-H7
28700 TEM 92590 978-J1
OLD TRAIL DR
1300 COR 92882 772-J2
1300 COR 92882 773-A2
OLD TROON CT
- INDO 92201 5410-B6
OLD VALLEY DR
23200 MORV 92553 717-C3

OLD WARSON CIR
- COR 92883 773-H6
OLD WAVERLY CIR
- COR 92883 773-H6
OLD WINDMILL RD
30500 RivC 92584 868-D4
OLD WRANGLER RD
22100 CYNL 92587 867-B1
OLE LN
- RivC 92585 838-C3
OLEA AV
81700 INDO 92201 5410-D7
OLEA LN
18500 RivC 92570 746-C7
OLEANDER
1100 LKEL 92530 866-D4
OLEANDER AV
100 MORV 92551 747-H6
1100 PER 92571 747-D7
1100 RivC 92518 747-D7
10500 FONT 92337 644-H2
10900 SBdC 92337 644-H2
12200 RivC 92503 744-H6
18300 RivC 92532 866-D1
20100 RivC 92570 746-F7
21400 RivC 92570 747-C6
24000 PER 92551 747-H6
26200 MORV 92555 747-H6
26200 MORV 92555 748-A6
26200 PER 92571 748-A6
26200 RivC 92571 748-A6
81700 INDO 92201 5410-D6
OLEANDER CIR
1300 COR 92880 713-A7
OLEANDER CT
6700 RIV 92506 715-H5
OLEANDER DR
300 SJCT 92582 810-J2
700 RivC - 5240-A7
32000 CTHC 92234 787-G3
32800 RivC 92530 865-J7
55700 RivC 92282 724-E1
60800 DHSP 92282 695-F6
60900 RivC 92282 695-F6
OLEANDER LN
700 BLY 92225 5491-E4
OLEANDER RD
500 PMSP 92264 787-A3
OLEANDER ST
700 HEMT 92543 840-J1
OLEANDRO CIR
41100 MURR 92562 927-H3
OLE FOSSIL RD
44000 RivC 92536 962-B6
OLENA RD
4100 HEMT 92545 840-E4
OLEO RANCH RD
20600 RivC 92570 777-B5
OLGA WY
1400 PMSP 92262 756-F5
OLINDA DR
- PMSP 92264 787-A7
OLINDA ST
- COR 92879 743-F2
OLIVA CT
2000 CLTN 92324 646-H1
OLIVAS AV
22000 RivC 92567 778-G7
22200 RivC 92567 808-G1
OLIVE
100 LKEL 92530 866-E5
OLIVE AV
200 BEAU 92223 720-G2
1200 RivC 92223 720-H5
15800 RivC 92555 749-F3
16000 RivC 92504 745-J3
21000 RivC 92570 806-J6
21300 RivC 92570 807-A6
29000 RivC 92584 838-G7
30200 RivC 92584 839-A7
30500 RivC 92596 839-C7
33700 RivC 92596 840-A7
43200 RivC 92544 811-J6
43800 RivC 92544 (812-A6
See Page 782)
W OLIVE AV
1200 RDL 92373 647-J2
OLIVE CIR
- FONT 92337 644-J2
OLIVE CT
7600 RivC 92509 644-H7
73800 PDST 92260 818-G7
OLIVE DR
26300 RivC 92544 841-C1
OLIVE ST
6300 RivC 92509 685-A2
10800 SBdC 92316 645-E1
14000 RivC 92230 723-F4
15400 RivC 92530 865-H7
21100 RivC 92530 897-A2
21100 RivC 92530 896-A1
21300 RivC 92595 897-B1
21500 RivC 92570 776-A7
21700 RivC 92570 806-A2
24000 RivC 92584 867-F7
32900 LKEL 92530 896-A1
56000 RivC 92274 5531-G5
E OLIVE ST
200 COR 92879 743-D5
W OLIVE ST
100 COR 92882 743-C6
E OLIVE WY
1000 PMSP 92262 756-E7
OLIVE CREEK DR
500 PER 92571 807-J1

STREET Block City ZIP Pg-Grid

OLIVECREST WY
1400 PER 92571 807-J1
OLIVEDALE DR
12000 FONT 92337 644-C4
OLIVE GROVE RD
34100 RivC 92595 897-G4
OLIVE GROVE ST
- LKEL 92530 865-F4
OLIVE LAKE BLVD
11400 BLY 92225 392-D11
OLIVER ST
11900 MORV 92555 718-C2
15100 MORV 92555 748-C1
OLIVERA AV
82200 INDO 92201 5470-F2
OLIVE TREE CT
- RivC 92596 929-D1
32500 LKEL 92530 896-G4
OLIVETREE DR
100 PER 92571 777-H7
OLIVE TREE LN
- RivC 92532 835-J4
1100 HEMT 92543 841-B1
33000 RivC 92530 896-G5
OLIVEWOOD AV
4400 RIV 92501 685-G7
4600 RIV 92506 685-G7
OLIVEWOOD CIR
- COR 92882 773-C2
20600 RivC 92595 896-J7
OLIVE WOOD PLAZA DR
23200 MORV 92553 717-C2
OLIVIA WY
7900 RivC 92509 684-G1
OLLA RD
40200 RivC 92544 841-C4
OLLIE WY
24700 HEMT 92543 810-J5
OLMSTEAD ST
21800 RivC 92583 781-C6
OLSEN VIEW CT
44200 RivC 92544 (812-A7 See Page 782)
44200 RivC 92544 842-A1
OLSON AV
26000 RivC 92548 839-D2
26300 RivC 92585 839-D2
OLYMPIA AV
21000 RivC 92570 806-J6
21500 RivC 92570 807-A6
OLYMPIA DR
6700 RIV 92503 714-E1
OLYMPIA PL
73200 RivC 92276 788-E2
OLYMPIA WY
300 HEMT 92543 840-H1
28600 RivC 92586 838-C7
OLYMPIA FIELDS
79700 LQNT 92253 5530-A3
OLYMPIA FIELDS DR
- COR 92883 773-H6
OLYMPIC AV
800 BAN 92220 721-D4
OLYMPIC CT
44900 INDW 92210 848-J1
OLYMPIC DR
1200 COR 92881 743-G7
48500 PDST 92260 848-D5
OLYMPIC WY
45500 TEM 92592 979-B4
77200 PDST 92211 819-D3
OLYMPUS CT
26300 MORV 92555 717-J2
26300 MORV 92555 718-A2
OMAHA CT
1500 RIV 92507 686-B2
OMAHA DR
25100 MORV 92551 747-G4
OMAR PL
42100 PDST 92211 819-C5
OMAR ST
- BAN 92220 721-E2
10000 RIV 92503 714-H7
OMEGA ST
6200 RIV 92506 716-C3
OMNI DR
25100 RivC 92544 811-J5
ONAKNOLL DR
20500 RivC 92570 775-E5
21200 RivC 92570 805-E1
ONATE DR
25600 MORV 92557 717-H2
ONDA CIR
16200 MORV 92551 747-J3
ONEAL RD
23000 RivC 92595 897-E4
ONE HORSE WY
39100 RivC 92260 818-F2
ONEIDA ST
24400 MORV 92553 717-F4
ONEIL
40100 RivC 92223 691-A5
ONLY CT
26300 RivC 92544 841-D1
ONORATO DR
19600 RivC 92530 896-G4
ONOTA AV
2300 RIV 92504 715-F5
ONTARIO AV
1300 COR 92882 773-H3
1400 COR 92882 772-J1
1600 COR 92881 773-H3
1600 COR 92882 742-H7
2000 RivC 92882 742-H7
19100 RivC 92508 746-D7
ONTARIO AV
19300 RivC 92881 773-H3
E ONTARIO AV
100 COR 92879 773-E1
100 COR 92882 773-B1
500 COR 92881 773-E1
W ONTARIO AV
100 COR 92882 773-A1
ONTARIO CT
44200 INDW 92210 848-J1
ONTARIO FRWY I-15
- COR - 743-E3
- NRCO - 713-E6
- NRCO - 743-E3
- ONT - 643-E5
- RivC - 643-E5
- RivC - 683-F6
- RivC - 713-E2
ONTARIO ST
10000 RIV 92503 684-E7
10000 RIV 92503 714-E1
ONTARIO WY
19000 LKEL 92530 896-G4
19000 RivC 92530 896-G4
ONTINA RD
67100 CTHC 92234 757-B5
ONTIVEROS CT
- INDW 92210 849-D1
ONYX AV
600 HEMT 92543 840-J3
ONYX CT
46200 INDW 92210 849-C2
ONYX DR
400 PMSP 92264 786-D4
ONYX PL
12200 MORV 92557 717-G2
OPAL AV
600 HEMT 92543 840-J3
OPAL DR
1700 PER 92571 777-H7
48200 PDST 92260 848-D5
OPAL ST
1300 COR 92882 743-B6
3400 RivC 92509 645-B7
3600 RivC 92509 685-B1
OPAL BURT RD
- SJCT 92567 780-A6
OPALO DR
- PMSP 92264 816-E2
OPALO RD
- RivC 92595 897-G6
OPEN CT
30600 TEM 92592 979-B4
OPINE LN
25100 RivC 92548 809-A6
OPORTO DR
24700 MORV 92557 717-F2
OPPERMAN RD
68500 RivC 92240 697-D7
N OPUNTIA RD
1400 PMSP 92262 756-E6
ORADON WY
2800 HEMT 92545 810-F6
ORAN CT
44000 PDST 92260 818-H7
ORAN DR
18100 RivC 92570 746-C7
ORANGCREST RD
38400 RivC 92211 819-G1
ORANGE AV
- PER 92571 777-H5
100 BEAU 92223 720-J2
800 PER 92571 778-A5
1200 RDL 92373 647-G1
1300 BEAU 92223 690-J7
20800 RivC 92570 776-H6
21900 RivC 92570 777-D5
26200 RivC 92571 778-A5
26400 LMLN 92373 647-G1
26400 SBdC 92373 647-G1
30900 RivC 92567 779-A5
S ORANGE AV
700 PMSP 92264 786-J3
W ORANGE AV
- PER 92571 777-F5
ORANGE PL
41100 RivC 92544 811-D7
ORANGE ST
- RIV 92501 646-A7
- RivC 92501 646-A7
1000 RIV 92501 686-A1
1100 RIV 92501 685-J2
1200 COR 92879 743-E6
13200 RivC 92880 713-C1
14000 RivC 92230 723-C5
15400 RivC 92530 865-H7
19700 RivC 92567 779-B2
20100 RivC 92881 773-J5
21900 RivC 92583 781-E6
24000 RivC 92584 867-G7
24900 RivC 92570 807-A7
30600 LKEL 92530 866-A3
33500 RivC 92595 897-B3
56000 RivC 92274 5531-G4
ORANGE BLOSSOM CIR
14300 RivC 92503 745-D3
16000 FONT 92337 644-G3
ORANGE BLOSSOM CT
17900 RivC 92570 746-H7
28700 LKEL 92530 865-H2
ORANGE BLOSSOM LN
- RivC 92503 744-J7
75600 PDST 92210 819-A7
ORANGE BLOSSOM WY
15100 LKEL 92530 865-F1
ORANGECREEK CIR
24000 MORV 92557 687-E6
ORANGE CREEK RD
400 PER 92571 777-H7
ORANGECREST CT
16800 RivC 92504 745-G5
ORANGECREST ST
3700 COR 92881 773-E5
ORANGECREST WY
25400 LMLN 92354 647-D2
ORANGE GROVE AV
- HEMT 92544 811-G7
4500 RIV 92501 685-G5
ORANGEGROVE AV
500 BLY 92225 5491-D5
28000 RivC 92584 868-E2
82000 INDO 92201 5410-E5
ORANGEGROVE CIR
1200 COR 92879 743-G3
ORANGE GROVE CIR
11800 MORV 92555 718-G1
ORANGE GROVE ST
11400 LMLN 92354 647-B2
ORANGE GROVE WY
- MURR 92562 927-G5
15200 LKEL 92530 865-G1
41200 RivC 92592 960-D3
ORANGEHAVEN LN
16400 RivC 92503 745-A4
16500 RivC 92503 744-J4
ORANGE HEIGHTS LN
- COR 92881 773-B4
100 COR 92882 773-B4
ORANGE HILLS DR
700 COR 92881 773-E2
ORANGEMONT LN
12100 RivC 92503 744-H4
ORANGEMONT WY
27100 RivC 92544 841-F3
ORANGE TERRACE PKWY
8600 RIV 92508 746-E2
8900 RivC 92518 746-E2
ORANGETREE DR
100 PER 92571 777-G7
ORANGE TREE LN
- RivC 92507 646-F6
ORANGETREE LN
32000 CTHC 92234 787-F3
ORANGE TREE ST
- BAN 92220 721-D5
ORANGE VALE LN
2500 RIV 92503 744-G3
ORANGE VIEW CIR
2100 RivC 92503 744-H4
ORANGE VISTA WY
4600 RIV 92506 715-D1
ORANGEWIND LN
16300 RivC 92503 744-J4
ORANGEWOOD CT
22900 GTER 92313 646-G4
ORANGEWOOD DR
2800 RLTO 92316 645-G2
7900 RIV 92504 684-G7
ORANGEWOOD LN
- RivC 92503 744-J7
25500 RivC 92544 811-J6
ORANGEWOOD SQ
1300 COR 92882 743-A6
ORBIT CT
25300 MORV 92551 747-H3
ORCA AV
400 PER 92571 807-J1
ORCABESSA DR
78400 RivC 92201 819-G5
ORCHARD AV
- HEMT 92544 811-H6
400 COAC 92236 5471-B6
ORCHARD CIR
2200 COR 92882 773-A1
ORCHARD DR
1900 PER 92571 777-G6
ORCHARD LN
600 BAN 92220 722-B4
2300 COR 92882 773-A1
50000 LQNT 92253 849-J6
S ORCHARD LN
900 CLTN 92324 646-G1
ORCHARD PL
40400 RivC 92223 691-B3
ORCHARD ST
1400 COAC 92236 5471-C6
7100 RIV 92504 715-C3
33000 RivC 92530 897-A2
33000 RivC 92595 897-A2
38000 RivC 92223 690-H3
ORCHARD CREST LN
2600 COR 92881 773-E2
ORCHARD GROVE WY
6100 RIV 92505 714-B3
ORCHARD HEIGHTS AV
11000 BEAU 92223 691-B7
11800 BEAU 92223 721-B1
ORCHARD PARK CT
1800 SJCT 92583 811-D4
ORCHARD PARK DR
8400 RIV 92508 746-H2
ORCHARD VIEW LN
10400 RivC 92503 744-H4
ORCHID CT
- TEM 92591 958-J5
25400 MORV 92553 717-H5
60000 RivC 92274 5590-G2
ORCHID LN
12100 MORV 92557 717-F2
ORCHID ST
1000 HEMT 92545 840-G2
13000 YCPA 92399 650-A5
ORCHID ST
46400 INDO 92201 5470-D2
ORCHIDTREE CT
40200 PDST 92260 818-E3
N ORCHID TREE LN
200 PMSP 92262 786-G1
ORCO PKWY
9400 RivC 92509 684-C1
ORDWAY ST
5800 RIV 92504 684-J7
OREANA WY
15700 RivC 92262 725-E7
OREGON AV
500 BLY 92225 5491-D5
OREGON CIR
43500 PDST 92211 819-C6
OREGON PL
28000 RivC 92587 837-E6
OREGON ST
1100 PER 92571 747-D7
33000 RivC 92530 865-G6
OREGON TR
- MURR 92562 927-G5
100 RivC 92262 755-F1
300 BAN 92220 721-F2
40800 RivC 92223 691-B4
O REILLY CT
70800 RMIR 92270 787-J7
E ORELLA CIR
2900 PMSP 92264 786-H4
ORIOLE AV
12200 GTER 92313 646-F4
12800 RivC 92507 646-F6
ORIOLE CIR
34100 RivC 92544 901-J3
ORIOLE CT
3600 LKEL 92530 865-J4
73300 PDST 92260 848-F5
ORIOLE DR
11100 RIV 92505 714-C4
ORIOLE LN
500 COR 92879 773-E1
ORION CT
25500 RivC 92586 837-J7
43800 LQNT 92253 819-H7
ORION ST
11400 RIV 92505 714-B5
ORION WY
16400 MORV 92551 747-F4
43000 LQNT 92253 819-H6
ORIS DR
67300 DHSP 92240 697-B5
ORLAND RD
19200 RivC 92570 776-E6
ORLANDO DR
7900 RIV 92503 714-G4
ORLEANS CIR
3100 COR 92882 773-B3
ORLEANS DR
12800 MORV 92555 717-J3
ORLEANS LN
24000 MURR 92562 928-A3
ORLEANS WY
3000 COR 92882 773-B3
ORLINDA DR
33500 RivC 92592 959-H7
ORLY PL
4600 RIV 92507 685-J6
ORMAND DR
53000 RivC 92539 (934-B5 See Page 904)
ORMA VISTA DR
63000 RivC 92240 696-B5
ORMISTA DR
24600 MORV 92553 717-F5
ORMSBY RD
43400 TEM 92592 959-B7
43400 TEM 92592 979-B1
ORO CT
- RivC 92595 897-G6
2000 HEMT 92545 810-G6
9300 DHSP 92240 696-H1
OROCOPIA RD
- PMSP 92264 786-G6
ORODEZA LN
47000 RivC 92536 982-D7
47000 RivC 92536 409-G5
ORO GLEN DR
15800 MORV 92551 747-H2
ORO GRANDE CIR
44800 INDW 92210 819-A7
ORO LOMO ST
67500 DHSP 92240 697-B4
ORONTES WY
100 CTHC 92234 787-F7
ORO PRADO
100 PMSP 92264 786-E6
OROVILLE RD
70600 RMIR 92270 817-J4
OROZCO DR
6900 RivC 92506 715-H6
ORPINGTON AV
44700 RivC 92544 (812-B6 See Page 782)
ORQUIDEA LN
49200 COAC 92236 5471-A5
ORR WY
63700 PMSP 92258 726-C4
ORRICK RD
18900 RivC 92508 746-D2
ORTEGA CT
2000 HEMT 92545 810-G6
ORTEGA DR
67500 DHSP 92240 697-B5
ORTEGA HWY Rt#-74
30700 LKEL 92530 865-H7
32300 RivC 92530 865-F7
32300 RivC 92530 895-G1
32300 RivC 92530 896-A1
34100 RivC 92562 408-J3
34100 RivC 92562 895-G1
ORTEGA RD
68200 CTHC 92234 787-E4
ORTIZ RD
32400 RivC 92548 809-E6
ORTIZ ST
86400 COAC 92236 5471-E7
ORTONA ST
- TEM 92592 959-F7
- TEM 92592 979-F1
ORVIETO
- INDW 92210 819-C6
ORVILLE WRIGHT DR
16700 RivC 92518 746-J4
OSA AV
22900 RivC 92562 927-E2
OSAGE AV
4000 RivC 92509 685-E3
OSAGE CT
45400 INDW 92210 849-B1
49100 RivC 92536 963-C1
OSAGE RD
800 PER 92570 807-E3
43300 RivC 92544 901-J3
43400 RivC 92544 902-A3
OSAGE TR
75700 INDW 92210 849-B1
OSBORNE LN
26300 RivC 92548 839-C2
26300 RivC 92585 839-C2
OSBOURNE AV
17600 CHLS 91709 712-A5
OSBURN PL
5400 RIV 92506 685-F7
OSHUA DR
26000 MORV 92555 717-J4
OSLO CT
400 HEMT 92545 810-E6
OSO DR
1100 COR 92879 743-F3
OSPREY CT
22300 RivC 92595 897-C4
OSPREY LN
21700 MORV 92557 716-J1
OSPREY RD
39800 MURR 92562 928-C3
OSPREY ST
1100 SJCT 92583 811-D3
OSSIPEE ST
43800 RivC 92544 811-J6
OSTERBERG ST
39000 RivC 92591 929-J6
OSULLIVAN RD
28100 RivC 92585 838-E4
OSUMA RD
11600 FONT 92337 644-F3
OSUNA CT
5100 RivC 91752 683-G3
OSWEGO CIR
5200 PMSP 92264 787-B5
OSWEGO DR
6100 RIV 92506 716-B3
OSWEGO LN
45600 INDW 92210 849-D1
OTHELLO CT
- RMIR 92270 788-B6
OTHELLO LN
900 COR 92882 773-B1
OTIS DR
24800 MORV 92553 717-G6
OTIS RD
39100 RivC 92592 930-D6
OTONO CT
- RivC 92562 956-J5
OTONO DR
1200 PMSP 92264 786-F4
OTT ST
200 COR 92882 743-B4
OTTAWA AV
3500 RIV 92507 686-A5
OTTAWA ST
35800 CTHC 92234 787-F6
OTTER CREEK CIR
- TEM 92591 959-C3
OTTOWA CT
49900 RivC 92536 963-E1
OTYMAR LN
82000 RivC 92274 5530-F5
OUIDA DR
8600 RIV 92504 715-A4
8700 RIV 92503 715-A4
OUR WY
24800 PER 92587 837-H4
OUR GANG CIR
- CTHC 92234 787-H3
OUTER HWY S
25300 LMLN 92354 647-C2
31100 YCPA 92373 649-B4
31200 RDL 92373 649-B4
OUTLAW CIR
13100 RivC 92883 835-B4
OUTLAW WY
11000 MORV 92557 687-C7
OUTLAW MINE RD
- RivC - 391-A4
OUTPOST DR
1700 COR 92882 742-H7
OUTRIGGER DR
- CYNL 92587 867-F2
OUTRIGGER DR
- RivC 92254 (5654-F6 See Page 5594)
OUTRIGGER ST
29100 LKEL 92530 865-G3
OVANTE RD
67100 CTHC 92234 757-B5
OVAR CT
15400 FONT 92337 644-F3
OVENSHIRE LN
59000 RivC 92539 (965-E1 See Page 964)
OVERCREST DR
12100 YCPA 92399 649-A3
31100 SBdC 92374 649-A3
OVERHILL RD
14500 RivC 92282 695-F7
38400 RivC 92592 900-H7
38400 RivC 92592 930-H1
OVERLAND CT
- PDST 92260 818-H2
12000 FONT 92337 644-B4
OVERLAND DR
- TEM 92591 958-G5
11500 FONT 92337 644-A3
41700 TEM 92590 958-G5
OVERLAND ST
3800 RIV 92503 715-A4
4000 RIV 92503 714-J4
E OVERLAND ST
1700 CLTN 92324 646-G1
OVERLAND TR
10200 RivC 92223 691-C4
32300 TEM 92592 979-F3
OVERLOOK DR
52600 RivC - (813-J5 See Page 782)
52700 RivC - 814-A5
OVERLOOK GN
200 PMSP 92264 786-D5
OVERLOOK PKWY
600 RIV 92506 715-H5
1000 RIV 92506 716-B5
OVERLOOK RD
200 PMSP 92264 786-D5
OVERTON AV
10000 RIV 92503 714-E4
OVERTON RD
45400 RivC 92544 (932-E4 See Page 902)
OVERTURE DR
60100 RivC 92262 725-F7
OVERVIEW CT
- RivC 92399 650-H7
OVERVIEW DR
38200 RivC 92592 900-H6
OWARI LN
9000 RIV 92508 746-D3
OWEN LN
33000 RivC 92584 898-J2
33000 RivC 92595 897-A7
S OWENS RIVER LN
2600 ONT 91761 643-C6
OWETZAL LN
100 RivC 92507 646-E6
OWINGS DR
54000 RivC 92539 904-D6
OWL CT
6500 RivC 92509 685-A1
OWL DR
500 PER 92570 807-F2
OWL LN
48800 PDST 92260 848-F5
OWL TREE RD
16600 RivC 92504 745-H7
17300 RivC 92504 746-A7
OWL VALLEY RD
40000 RivC 92544 931-C2
OXBOW DR
27700 RivC 92545 839-G5
OX BOW LN
11000 RivC 92881 774-G5
OXFORD CIR
1300 COR 92880 713-A7
OXFORD CT
- RMIR 92270 818-A3
26700 RivC 92544 841-E2
OXFORD DR
- MURR 92562 927-E4
1200 COR 92880 713-A7
OXFORD LN
1000 SJCT 92583 781-A7
OXFORD ST
- MURR 92563 928-F7
- MURR 92563 958-F1
1600 RIV 92507 686-B1
OXLEY CT
24800 MURR 92562 928-C5
OXNARD ST
26400 RivC 92586 868-B2

P

P ST
- HEMT 92545 840-F2
PABESU RD
2600 MURR 92562 898-B7
PABLO DR
300 PMSP 92262 786-D3
PABLO LN
1500 SJCT 92583 811-D4
PABLO RD
13700 MORV 92555 718-E5
54000 RivC 92536 (984-D1 See Page 904)
PABLO ST
28900 RivC 92567 808-F2
PABLO APIZ WY
39900 MURR 92562 928-B1
PACATO RD
25500 MORV 92551 747-H2
PACE CT
1400 RIV 92501 645-H7
PACE DR
24500 MORV 92557 717-F2
PACE LN
30600 RivC 92241 390-D8
PACER DR
2200 NRCO 92860 713-B6
PACER WY
8300 RivC 92509 684-F5
PACHAPPA DR
6000 RIV 92506 685-G7
6000 RIV 92506 715-G1
PACHAPPA HILL
3200 RIV 92506 685-G7
PACHEA TR
27200 RivC 92544 841-B4
27600 RivC 92543 841-B4
PACHECO CT
5800 RivC 92509 684-J4
6900 RivC 92509 685-A5
PACHETA SQ N
73600 RivC 92276 788-F2
PACHETA SQ S
73600 RivC 92276 788-F2
PACIFIC AV
100 RivC 92507 646-C6
500 COR 92881 773-D3
1400 NRCO 92860 743-C1
1900 NRCO 92860 713-C7
3400 RivC 92509 645-B7
3500 RivC 92509 685-B1
11300 FONT 92337 643-J4
16000 RivC - 726-G1
43800 RivC 92201 5410-D6
PACIFIC RD
700 COR 92881 773-D3
PACIFIC ST
83000 INDO 92201 5410-G7
PACIFICA CT
27200 RivC 92544 841-E3
PACIFICA LN
- PDST 92260 818-G3
PACIFICA WY
25700 HEMT 92545 809-J7
25700 HEMT 92545 839-J1
PACIFICA SUR
83800 INDO 92203 5410-H6
PACIFIC CHANNEL WY
29800 RivC 92586 868-B2
PACIFIC GREEN CT
42700 HEMT 92544 811-G6
PACIFIC GROVE WY
- TEM 92591 959-D4
PACIFIC PRIVADO
- ONT 91761 643-D2
PACKARD CIR
1600 COR 92881 773-G4
PACKARD ST
3600 RivC 92509 685-D2
27500 RivC 92585 838-G5
PACKER DR
68500 RivC 92241 727-D2
PACOIMA CT
26200 RivC 92586 868-B2
PACOS RDG
- RivC 92883 835-C5
PACTFIELD PL
- YCPA 92399 649-E2
PADDINGTON CT
- MURR 92563 958-G1
PADDINGTON DR
8900 RIV 92503 715-A6
PADDINGTON RD
- MURR 92562 898-C7
PADDOCK LN
2100 NRCO 92860 713-D7
PADEN ST
4100 RIV 92504 715-B3
PADRE CT
10500 RIV 92505 714-D2
15800 MORV 92551 747-H2
PADRE WY
2800 COR 92882 773-B2
PADRON WY
- RMIR 92270 818-D5
PADUA CIR
46500 INDO 92201 5470-F2
PADUA WY
1000 PMSP 92262 756-F5
PAGE CIR
1200 COR 92882 742-J6
PAGE ST
32800 RivC 92530 896-A1
PAGEANT PL
40400 RivC 92544 841-C3
PAHUTA ST
31300 TEM 92592 979-D5
PAHUTE DR
22700 MORV 92553 717-B4
PAIGE AV
15000 MORV 92551 717-E7
15000 MORV 92551 747-E1
PAIGE CIR
- RivC 92585 838-C3
PAINE DR
3400 RIV 92503 744-E2
PAINTBRUSH TR
18000 RivC 92241 727-C3
PAINTED CV
- LQNT 92253 849-H6
PAINTED CANYON AV
82300 INDO 92201 5470-F3
PAINTED CANYON CT
- RivC 92254 5592-F5
PAINTED CANYON RD
- RivC - 390-G11
- RivC - (5593-C2 See Page 5592)
48800 RivC 92260 848-B5
69400 RivC - 848-B5
PAINTED CANYON ST
3800 PER 92571 777-H2
PAINTED DESERT CT
42500 RivC 92544 841-G3
PAINTED DESERT DR
29400 RivC 92584 868-H1
45400 INDW 92210 849-B1
75200 INDW 92210 848-J3
PAINTED HILLS DR
60400 RivC 92282 695-F7
PAINTED HILLS RD
13000 RivC 92282 695-F7
59200 RivC 92282 725-D2
PAINTED MOUNTAIN DR
- PDST 92211 788-E7
PAINTED PONY RD
37500 RivC 92544 931-D3
PAINTED ROCK CIR
32100 RivC 92276 788-F2
PAINTERS PTH
72000 PDST 92260 818-C7
72100 PDST 92260 848-C1
PAISANO RD
48800 RivC 92260 848-C6
PAISANO WY
7800 RivC 92509 684-G3
PAISLEY AV
400 HEMT 92543 840-J1
400 HEMT 92543 841-A1
PAISLEY CT
5700 RIV 92507 716-F2
PAIUTE CIR
10100 RivC 92223 691-C4
PAIUTE CT
49500 RivC 92536 963-D1
PAJARO RD
1000 PMSP 92262 756-E5
24300 RivC 92590 977-H2
PAJERO DR
1300 COR 92882 743-A7
1300 COR 92882 742-J7
PALA CIR
44300 LQNT 92253 819-H7
PALA PL
11000 RivC 91752 683-H3
PALA RD Rt#-S16
45000 TEM 92592 979-B3
46000 RivC 92592 979-E6
47000 RivC 92592 999-G1
47800 SDCo 92028 999-G1
PALACE DR
38900 PDST 92211 819-C2
PALACIO DEL MAR
- CTHC 92234 787-G7
PALADORA LN
6900 RivC 92509 645-B4
PALA FOXIA PL
21000 MORV 92557 716-H1
PALA LOMA CT
27500 MORV 92555 748-C2
PALA MESA DR
- COR 92879 743-F2
PALAMINA CIR
4300 RivC 92509 685-D4
PALAMINO CIR
- RivC 92590 958-C7
PALAMINO PL
16700 RivC 92504 745-H3
PALAMINO RD
46100 RivC 92536 982-F7
PALA PALMS DR
76400 INDW 92210 849-C1
PALA TEMECULA RD Rt#-S16
37100 SDCo 92028 999-G3
38600 SDCo 92059 999-G3
PALATIUM CIR
19000 RivC 92570 777-C2
PALA VISTA DR
39400 TEM 92591 929-D7
PALEDAWN RD
50600 RivC 92536 983-F4
PALEN ST
47500 INDO 92201 5470-F3
PALENCIA CT
- LQNT 92253 849-F6
PALENCIA DR
5800 RivC 92509 684-G4
PALERMO CT
25300 MURR 92563 928-F5
43500 LQNT 92253 819-G6
47000 INDO 92201 5470-G2
N PALERMO DR
2200 PMSP 92262 756-C5
PALERMO LN
- COR 92879 743-F2
PALETERO RD
67600 CTHC 92234 757-C5
PALI DR
100 PMSP 92264 786-E6
1800 NRCO 92860 713-D3
PALISADE CIR
5100 RIV 92506 685-H7
PALISADE PL
13100 MORV 92553 717-B4
PALISADES DR
- MURR 92563 928-G6
500 PMSP 92262 786-D2
2700 COR 92882 742-E4
2700 RivC 92882 742-E4
2900 COR 92880 742-E4
PALISADES ST
1200 PER 92570 807-G4
PALLADIAN CT
- RivC 92590 978-D3
PALM AV
- BEAU 92223 720-J2
100 SJCT 92582 810-J4
100 HEMT 92543 810-J4
300 COAC 92236 5471-B6
300 SJCT 92582 780-J7
400 HEMT 92543 840-J2
1100 COR 92879 743-D6
1300 BEAU 92223 690-J6
4700 RIV 92506 685-E6
4700 RIV 92501 685-E6
6200 RIV 92506 715-E1
21500 GTER 92313 646-C4
21500 SBdC 92313 646-C4
21500 SBdC 92324 646-C4
30500 RivC 92543 870-J4
30900 RivC 92567 779-A2
31400 RivC 92543 871-A5
32400 RivC 92584 867-G7
32500 RivC 92584 897-G1
32800 RivC 92595 897-G1
43500 RivC 92544 811-J6
43800 RivC 92544 (812-A6 See Page 782)
E PALM AV
73600 RivC 92254 (5654-E7 See Page 5594)
S PALM AV
700 PMSP 92264 786-J3
W PALM AV
200 CLTN 92313 646-C4
200 CLTN 92324 646-C4
200 GTER 92313 646-C4
73600 RivC 92254 (5654-E7 See Page 5594)
PALM BLVD
32000 CTHC 92234 787-G3
PALM CIR
- RivC 91752 683-F5
PALM CT
6800 RIV 92504 715-E2
6800 RIV 92506 715-E2
12100 GTER 92313 646-F4
36700 RMIR 92270 787-H7
PALM DR
- RivC - 5239-J5
100 BLY 92225 5491-D6
200 ImCo 92274 (5773-B7 See Page 5712)
1000 RivC - 5240-A6
9300 DHSP 92240 696-J1
14500 RivC 92240 696-J7
15500 DHSP 92240 726-J2
16000 RivC 92240 726-J2
18000 LKEL 92530 866-C4
22300 PMSP 92241 756-J1
22300 RivC 92240 756-J1
22300 PMSP - 756-J1
28300 RivC 92587 837-F6
33700 YCPA 92399 649-G3
PALM LN
12000 MORV 92555 718-A1
19100 RivC 92241 728-D4
PALM RDG
- PDST 92260 848-D6
PALM ST
17300 RivC 92503 745-E7
18000 RivC 92503 775-E1
24000 RivC 92570 807-A6
44300 INDO 92201 5410-F7
45100 INDO 92201 5470-F1
50200 RivC 92230 723-D4
56000 RivC 92274 5531-G4
PALM VW
29000 LKEL 92530 865-G1
PALMA DR
- RMIR 92270 818-A4
44000 TEM 92592 979-A2
PALMA VISTA ST
40000 MURR 92562 928-C3
W PALM CANYON
- PMSP 92264 786-E5
PALM CANYON DR
9100 RivC 92883 804-C4
38000 RivC 92264 816-F6
38000 RivC - 816-F6
60000 RivC - (907-D1 See Page 906)
PALM CANYON DR Rt#-111
- PMSP 92262 725-E6
- RivC 92262 725-E6
- RivC 92262 755-G1
E PALM CANYON DR
- RivC 92234 787-B6
1800 PMSP 92264 786-E5
4100 PMSP 92264 787-A6
67400 CTHC 92234 787-B6
68600 CTHC 92234 817-E1
E PALM CANYON DR Rt#-111
4700 PMSP 92264 787-A6
N PALM CANYON DR
100 PMSP 92262 786-D2
600 PMSP 92262 756-D7
N PALM CANYON DR Rt#-111
- PMSP 92262 755-J2
1700 PMSP 92262 756-B3
S PALM CANYON DR
100 PMSP 92262 786-E4
500 PMSP 92264 786-E4
2600 PMSP 92264 816-E1
3100 RivC - 816-E1
3100 RivC 92264 816-E1
PALM CIRCLE DR
80000 LQNT 92253 5470-A2
PALM CREST DR
72000 RMIR 92270 818-C4
PALMDALE AV
81100 INDO 92201 5470-C3
PALMDALE CIR
2300 HEMT 92545 840-G1
PALMDALE RD
36600 RMIR 92270 787-H7
36600 RMIR 92270 817-H1
PALM DESERT DR N
73000 PDST 92260 848-E1
PALM DESERT DR S
73000 PDST 92260 848-E1
PALMEA DR
14200 MORV 92553 717-G6
PALMENTO DR
10300 RIV 92505 714-F6
PALMER AV
- RivC 92254 5592-H7
- RivC 92254 (5652-H1 See Page 5592)
PALMER DR
500 HEMT 92543 841-A3
5200 BAN 92220 721-D4
PALMER ST
1200 RivC 92507 646-B6
PALMERAS CIR
86000 COAC 92236 5471-D6
PALMERS BLUFF
- LQNT 92253 879-G3
PALMETTO AV
10500 FONT 92337 645-A1
PALMETTO CT
- RivC 92503 744-J7
PALMETTO LN
- COR 92881 773-E3
41500 PDST 92211 819-E4
PALMETTO ST
- MURR 92563 928-F7
PALMETTO WY
45600 TEM 92592 979-C4
PALMETTO PALM AV
30600 RivC 92548 839-B1
PALM GARDEN PL
78300 LQNT 92253 849-G2
PALM GREENS PKWY
73000 RivC 92260 818-E2
PALM HAVEN DR
72000 RMIR 92270 818-C4
PALM HILLS DR
- PMSP 92264 787-B6
PALMILLA CIR
43400 PDST 92260 818-H7
PALM ISLAND DR
70000 RivC 92254 (5653-H5 See Page 5592)
PALM LAKE
- PDST 92211 818-J6
PALM LAKE CIR
33800 RivC 92276 788-F4
PALM LANE ST
21500 RivC 92570 776-J4
21500 RivC 92570 777-A4
PALM LEAF CT
72700 RivC 92276 788-C2
PALM MEADOWS CT
25600 MORV 92557 717-H1
PALM MEADOWS DR
45700 INDO 92201 5470-C1
PALM OASIS
2600 PMSP 92264 787-C6
3300 CTHC 92234 787-C6
PALM OASIS AV
59700 RivC 92262 725-E7
PALM ROYALE DR
43900 LQNT 92253 819-F7
PALMS DR
- LQNT 92253 5530-E5
PALM SECO CIR
57400 RivC - 878-B7
PALM SHADOW DR
75200 INDW 92210 848-J1
75200 INDW 92210 849-A1
PALM SHADOWS DR
25600 MORV 92557 717-H1
PALM SPRINGS AV
63700 RivC - (907-G6 See Page 906)
PALM SPRINGS STATION RD
63700 PMSP - 726-D5
PALM TERRACE LN
11100 RIV 92505 714-B4
PALM TREE AV
78200 RivC 92211 819-G2
PALM TREE DR
1400 PMSP 92264 786-F5
PALM TREE LN
- RivC 92532 835-H3
26300 MURR 92563 928-G7

STREET Block City ZIP Pg-Grid

PEBBLE BEACH DR
6100 BAN 92220 721-C4
28000 RivC 92586 838-B5
28900 RivC 92586 868-B1
S PEBBLE BEACH DR
2000 PMSP 92264 787-B5
PEBBLE BEACH WY
- INDO 92201 5470-A1
PEBBLE BROOK DR
9500 MORV 92557 687-B4
PEBBLECREEK LN
400 PDST 92260 818-F4
PEBBLE CREEK WY
25000 MORV 92551 747-G4
PEBBLESTONE DR
22700 RivC 92567 808-F2
PECAN AV
11100 CALI 92320 690-B6
32100 YCPA 92399 649-C4
PECAN CIR
1800 COR 92882 743-A7
PECAN PL
11200 RIV 92505 714-B4
13600 MORV 92553 717-F5
PECAN ST
14000 RivC 92230 723-C4
21300 RivC 92595 897-B7
21400 RivC 92595 927-B1
33400 YCPA 92399 649-F4
PECAN WY
11500 LMLN 92354 647-C3
PECAN TREE ST
2100 HEMT 92545 840-G4
PECAN VALLEY
79800 LQNT 92253 5530-A5
PECHANGA DR
29900 TEM 92592 979-A3
PECHANGA RD
29900 RivC 92592 979-G7
30200 RivC 92592 980-A7
PECK LN
36600 RivC 92544 902-B7
36600 RivC 92544 (932-A1
See Page 902)
E PECK ST
200 LKEL 92530 866-E5
W PECK ST
100 LKEL 92530 866-E5
PECOS PL
22200 CYNL 92587 867-B1
81000 INDO 92201 5470-C2
PECOS RD
70200 RMIR 92270 817-H4
PECOS ST
2300 COR 92881 773-F2
PECOS WY
2900 RIV 92506 715-H1
PEDERSON ST
33100 RivC 92530 896-D3
PEDLEY AV
3400 NRCO 92860 713-H4
PEDLEY RD
3700 RivC 92509 644-E7
4200 RivC 92509 684-E4
PEDLEY SUBSTATION RD
4800 NRCO 92860 713-J1
4800 RIV 92505 713-J1
PEDRO DR
- COAC 92236 5471-A5
PEDRO BUFF DR
41300 RivC 92201 819-G4
PEELER AV
17400 RivC 92530 896-B3
PEELER ST
1800 COR 92882 742-J7
PEERLESS PL
78500 LQNT 92253 879-G1
78700 LQNT 92253 849-G7
PEGASUS CT
- RivC 92276 789-A5
PEGASUS DR
6100 RIV 92503 714-H2
PEGASUS RD
25400 RivC 92586 837-J7
PEGGY AV
7400 RivC 92509 644-H7
PEGGY LN
10500 RIV 92505 714-D4
23400 RivC 92595 897-E6
PEGGY WY
- CTHC 92234 787-C1
6400 RivC 92509 684-E6
PEGGY LOU LN
31000 TEM 92591 959-C1
PEINETA RD
67100 CTHC 92234 757-B5
PELADORA RD
68000 CTHC 92234 757-D6
PELHAM PL
1500 RIV 92506 716-B2
PELICAN DR
300 RivC 92507 646-E6
PELICAN LN
900 COR 92879 743-G2
PELICAN HILL CT
- INDO 92201 849-J1
PELION RD
25500 RivC 92584 867-J2
25600 RivC 92584 868-A2
PELL
1100 LKEL 92530 866-G5
S PELLISIER RD
- RivC 92501 646-A6
2100 CLTN 92501 646-A6
2800 CLTN 92324 646-A6
12800 RIV 92501 646-A6
PEMBE LN
75800 PDST 92211 819-A3
PEMBERTON PL
19100 RIV 92508 716-D6
PEMBRIDGE DR
12700 MORV 92553 717-B3
PEMBROKE AV
2900 HEMT 92545 840-F2
8700 RIV 92503 714-H3
PEMBROKE CIR
2900 COR 92879 744-B2
PEMBROKE ST
11400 LMLN 92354 647-E2
PEMBROOK PL
- YCPA 92399 649-F2
PENA RD
43300 RivC 92592 979-H4
56000 RivC 92539 (934-H4
See Page 904)
PENA WY
11300 RivC 91752 683-G3
PENASCO CIR
22600 RivC 92567 808-F2
PENASCO GRANDE
1900 PER 92570 807-F5
PENBROOK LN
- RivC 92592 979-H2
22700 RivC 92567 809-E2
PENCIN RD
33100 RivC 92584 897-J2
PENDLETON AV
11300 YCPA 92399 650-C1
PENDLETON RD
- BAN 92220 722-A1
PENDLETON ST
10300 RIV 92505 714-F7
PENDLETON WY
1000 COAC 92236 5471-C6
PENELOPE CT
30600 RivC 92543 871-B3
PENELOPE LN
- COR 92882 773-C3
PENFIELD LN
36500 RivC 92596 929-B1
36500 RivC 92563 929-B1
PENFIELD PL
2300 RIV 92507 686-G1
PENINSULA LN
- LQNT 92253 5530-B6
PENLAND RD
53100 RivC 92282 723-J1
53100 RivC 92282 724-A1
PENNANT CT
- TEM 92591 959-D4
PENNER PL
- MURR 92563 928-F2
PENNINGTON PL
15700 RivC 92504 745-F5
PENNSYLVANIA AV
- BEAU 92223 721-A3
1300 BEAU 92223 691-A7
2300 RIV 92507 685-J6
N PENNSYLVANIA ST
100 LKEL 92530 865-H2
S PENNSYLVANIA ST
100 LKEL 92530 865-H2
PENNY DR
8300 RIV 92503 714-F2
13300 YCPA 92399 649-J6
PENNY LN
800 SJCT 92583 781-A7
13100 YCPA 92399 650-A5
21000 RivC 92241 728-J5
32300 RivC 92545 839-E2
PENNY PL
28200 RivC 92570 837-A7
PENNYROYAL DR
4500 RivC 92880 742-B5
PENROD DR
4000 RIV 92505 714-E7
4000 RIV 92505 744-E1
PENROD CANYON RD
35300 RivC - (905-G4
See Page 904)
PENROSE DR
400 COR 92880 743-D3
PENROSE LN
35500 YCPA 92399 650-B6
PENROSE ST
32100 RivC 92595 897-C7
32800 RivC 92595 927-B1
PENSADOR ST
- TEM 92592 979-F1
PENSKE ST
12500 MORV 92553 717-C3
PENUNURI PL
21000 MORV 92557 686-H7
PENWOOD LN
7400 RivC 92509 684-H5
PEONY PL
- INDO 92201 5470-B3
PEORIA LN
8700 RivC 92557 687-A3
PEPITA CT
- RIV 92508 746-C1
PEPPER
200 LKEL 92530 866-G6
PEPPER AV
81500 INDO 92201 5410-D7
S PEPPER AV
10500 SBdC 92324 646-A1
10900 CLTN 92324 646-A1
PEPPER CT
15000 MORV 92551 717-E7
15000 MORV 92551 747-E1
23100 MORV 92553 717-E7
PEPPER DR
21400 RivC 92570 807-A6
32800 RivC 92530 865-J7
PEPPER ST
- FONT 92337 644-J2
- HEMT 92545 810-F4
11300 SBdC 92316 645-E3
15200 MORV 92553 717-A6
PEPPERBUSH DR
13000 MORV 92553 717-H4
PEPPERCORN DR
- RivC 92592 979-G5
PEPPERGRASS ST
74100 PDST 92260 848-G2
PEPPERGRASS WY
10400 MORV 92557 687-D6
PEPPER HILL DR
14900 RivC 92570 805-E6
PEPPERLEAF ST
- MURR 92562 927-F5
PEPPERMILL DR
24300 MORV 92557 687-E6
PEPPER RIDGE LN
10500 MORV 92557 687-D6
PEPPERTREE DR
100 PER 92571 777-G7
PEPPER TREE DR
1300 HEMT 92545 840-G3
PEPPERTREE DR
74600 PDST 92260 848-H2
PEPPERTREE LN
1200 COR 92879 743-D6
PEPPER TREE LN
1700 CLTN 92324 646-G1
PEPPERTREE LN
2200 RIV 92506 715-G5
PEPPER TREE LN
23700 SBdC 92324 646-H3
67800 RivC 92241 727-C4
PEPPER TREE WY
100 SJCT 92583 811-C1
PEPPERWOOD CIR
200 RivC 91752 683-E5
PEPPERWOOD DR
75100 INDW 92210 848-J2
75100 INDW 92210 849-A2
PEPPERWOOD LN
2400 COR 92882 742-G7
PEPPERWOOD ST
100 SJCT 92582 810-H2
PEQUENA DR
67700 DHSP 92240 697-B5
PEQUENA LN
- LQNT 92253 849-E6
PEQUENA ENTRADA
18300 RivC 92570 747-B7
18300 RivC 92570 777-A1
PEQUENO CIR
21200 RivC 92562 927-A3
S PEQUENO CIR
2500 PMSP 92264 786-F7
PEQUENO CORTE
900 SJCT 92582 810-H3
PERA ST
1300 COR 92882 743-C7
PERALTA PL
6600 RivC 92509 685-A4
6700 RivC 92509 684-J4
PERCHERON AV
7300 RivC 92509 684-J3
PERCIVAL DR
6300 RIV 92506 715-G3
PERDIDO DR
- PMSP 92264 816-E1
PERDIDO BAY WY
5800 BAN 92220 721-D5
PERDUE LN
37500 RivC 92592 930-J2
PEREGRIN DR
3600 COR 92881 773-E5
PEREGRINE WY
22900 RivC 92570 747-C7
PERELANDA CT
24300 RivC 92590 977-H3
PEREZ RD
68300 CTHC 92234 787-D7
PEREZ ST
51500 COAC 92236 5471-E7
PERHAM CT
14100 MORV 92553 717-E6
PERHAM DR
14300 MORV 92553 717-E7
PERIA DR
- PMSP 92264 816-E2
PERIDOT AV
900 HEMT 92543 840-J3
PERIDOT CIR
29100 RivC 92584 868-G2
PERIGEE ST
31600 RivC 92567 779-C7
PERIWINKLE CT
23700 MURR 92562 927-J2
40300 PDST 92260 818-E4
PERIWINKLE DR
69400 CTHC 92234 787-F2
PERIWINKLE LN
600 PER 92571 777-J5
PERKINS DR
14000 RivC 92503 745-C3
PERLA CT
800 SJCT 92583 811-D4
PERLA PL
- RivC 92595 897-G6
PERLITA CIR
100 PMSP 92264 786-E7
PERLITA PL
11800 FONT 92337 644-C4
PERLITA RD
68100 CTHC 92234 787-D1
PERNELL PL
38900 RivC 92223 690-G2
PEROU ST
100 PER 92570 807-G4
PERRAS AV
- RivC 92276 788-J5
PERRET BLVD
32900 RivC 92530 896-C2
PERRIER DR
26100 MORV 92555 717-J3
PERRINE ST
30800 RivC 92596 899-B1
PERRIS BLVD
10000 MORV 92557 687-F5
11500 MORV 92557 717-G2
12400 MORV 92553 717-G4
15000 MORV 92551 717-G7
15000 MORV 92551 747-G2
N PERRIS BLVD
- PER 92570 807-G1
200 PER 92571 807-G1
900 PER 92571 777-G2
4100 PER 92571 747-G7
4600 PER 92551 747-G7
4600 MORV 92551 747-G7
S PERRIS BLVD
- PER 92570 807-G3
PERRISITO ST
1000 PER 92570 807-F4
PERRY RD
28500 MURR 92563 928-G2
30700 RivC 92530 865-F5
PERRY ST
900 RivC 92571 778-A1
900 PER 92571 777-J1
900 PER 92571 778-A1
20500 RivC 92570 776-G1
21500 RivC 92570 777-A1
W PERRY ST
100 PER 92571 777-E1
PERRY HEIGHTS DR
16200 RIV 92504 745-G3
16200 RivC 92504 745-G3
PERRY PALMS WY
34400 RivC 92595 897-A4
PERSHING DR
4400 RIV 92503 714-H4
PERSIMMON AV
34900 YCPA 92399 649-J2
34900 YCPA 92399 650-A2
PERSIMMON LN
83100 RivC 92274 5530-H4
PERSIMMON PL
2700 RIV 92506 715-H1
PERSIMMON RD
13500 MORV 92553 717-G5
PERSIMMON ST
1600 COR 92879 743-J6
35500 YCPA 92399 650-B2
PERSIMMONS LN
43600 RivC 92544 811-J6
PERTH LN
500 RIV 92508 716-E6
PERTHSHIRE PL
- RIV 92507 716-F2
PESCADERO CIR
700 COR 92879 743-G3
PESCADO DR
31000 TEM 92592 979-C1
PETALUMA AV
26400 MORV 92555 718-A4
PETE DYE
- LQNT 92253 5530-B4
PETE DYE ST
14800 MORV 92555 718-D7
PETE LEHR DR
16700 LKEL 92530 866-H7
PETER CHRISTIAN CIR
- COR 92881 773-F3
PETER D MCINTYRE AV
8700 RivC - 412-C1
PETERS LN
32000 RivC 92567 779-C6
PETERS ST
7300 RIV 92504 715-D4
PETERSFIELD RD
41700 RivC 92201 819-G5
PETERSON RD
38900 RMIR 92270 817-H3
PETER WILKS CT
- RivC 92880 683-D4
PETES CRSG
47700 RivC 92536 982-H3
47700 RivC 92536 983-A3
PETITE CT
5900 RIV 92504 715-A1
PETTEGREW RD
10700 RivC 92507 686-G7
PETTIT ST
10800 MORV 92555 688-D7
10800 RivC 92555 688-D6
11400 MORV 92555 718-D2
PETUNIA CT
27000 RivC 92586 838-B4
PETUNIA WY
3000 COR 92881 773-F4
72000 RMIR 92270 818-C6
PEYTON PL
41200 RivC 92544 841-D2
PFEIFER WY
16800 RivC 92570 775-J4
17200 RivC 92570 776-A4
PGA BLVD
55400 LQNT 92253 5530-A3
PHEASANT DR
22900 CYNL 92587 867-D3
PHEASANT ST
800 COR 92881 773-E2
PHEASANT WY
- RivC 92880 713-B1
PHEASANT HILL PL
42800 RivC 92544 841-G4
PHEASANT KNOLL LN
13800 MORV 92553 717-F5
PHEASANT KNOLL RD
- RivC 92880 713-B1
PHEASANT RUN CIR
6700 RivC 92509 685-A1
6800 RivC 92509 684-J1
34200 RivC 92595 897-D4
PHEASANT RUN RD
7400 RivC 92509 684-H5
PHILADELPHIA CT
3500 RIV 92503 744-D3
PHILADELPHIA ST
4300 ONT 91761 643-F4
4300 RivC 91752 643-F4
9500 RivC 92509 644-A4
10000 FONT 92337 644-A4
11800 FONT 92337 643-J4
11800 ONT 92337 643-J4
E PHILADELPHIA ST
2700 ONT 91761 643-A4
PHILBIN AV
7400 RIV 92503 714-F3
PHILIPS WY
70000 RMIR 92270 817-H2
PHILLIP AV
8500 RIV 92503 714-F2
PHILLIP RD
30500 RivC 92567 779-A3
PHILLIPS AV
200 BAN 92220 722-C2
N PHILLIPS RD
500 PMSP 92262 786-E1
700 PMSP 92262 756-E7
PHILLIPS ST
1700 RivC 92570 807-D6
25200 RivC 92570 837-D1
PHILO ST
14300 MORV 92553 717-F7
PHINO LN
30900 RivC 92596 869-E4
PHLOX PL
48800 PDST 92260 848-F5
PHOEBE CT
73200 PDST 92260 848-F5
PHOEBE RD
30500 RivC 92584 868-A4
PHOENIX AV
6400 RIV 92504 715-B2
PHOENIX ST
47500 INDO 92201 5470-H3
PHOENIX WY
25500 RivC 92586 837-J7
28800 RivC 92584 837-J7
PHOENIX PALM DR
26000 RivC 92548 839-A1
PHONE LINE RD
- RivC - 391-D6
- RivC - 5240-E5
PHYLLIS AV
13600 MORV 92553 717-A5
PHYLLIS JACKSON LN
74800 PDST 92260 818-H7
PIAFFE PL
3600 RIV 92503 744-D3
PIASANO PL
43600 TEM 92592 979-D1
PIC WY
48200 INDO 92201 5470-E4
PICACHO DR
4300 RIV 92507 686-E6
PICADILLY WY
2000 COR 92882 743-A7
PICARD CT
64600 RivC 92240 696-E1
PICAROY PL
26200 MORV 92555 717-J3
PICASSO CT
25300 MORV 92553 717-G7
PICCADILLY SQ
700 HEMT 92544 811-F5
PICCADILLY ST
100 RMIR 92270 787-H7
6600 RIV 92506 715-F2
PICK PL
16400 RivC 92504 745-F3
PICKER ST
5400 RIV 92503 714-G4
PICKFAIR ST
36600 CTHC 92234 787-E7
PICKFORD WY
11300 MORV 92557 687-D7
PICKWICK ST
3400 RIV 92503 744-E2
PICO AV
100 SJCT 92583 811-B2
7100 RivC 92509 684-J5
20100 RivC 92571 778-E3
22200 RivC 92567 778-E3
22200 RivC 92567 808-E2
23600 RivC 92585 808-E4
PICO LN
49100 RivC 92536 983-C2
PICO RD
400 PMSP 92262 756-C4
PICO ST
- COR 92881 773-G1
21700 GTER 92313 646-D5
PICO VISTA WY
25000 MORV 92557 687-G7
25300 RivC 92557 687-G7
PICTON ST
26100 LMLN 92354 647-F2
PIDGEON SPRINGS RD
- RivC - (907-H7
See Page 906)
- RivC - (937-H1
See Page 906)
PIEDMONT DR
2400 RIV 92506 715-J2
PIEDMONT WY
27400 RivC 92544 841-F3
PIEDRAS RD
22100 RivC 92570 806-C3
PIEDRA VISTA
- SJCT 92567 810-A1
500 SJCT 92567 780-A7
PIERCE AV
16800 LKEL 92530 865-J2
PIERCE CIR
26600 MURR 92562 958-E2
PIERCE CT
500 HEMT 92543 810-J5
PIERCE ST
3500 RIV 92503 744-C1
5000 RIV 92505 744-C1
7800 RIV 92505 714-B7
28200 LKEL 92530 835-J7
28200 LKEL 92530 836-A7
28700 LKEL 92530 865-J1
52000 RivC 92274 390-F11
59000 RivC 92274 5592-B2
64000 RivC 92254 5592-B6
78500 RivC 92274 5712-B7
80000 RivC 92274 (5772-C5
See Page 5712)
PIERCE ST Rt#-86
77000 RivC 92274 5712-B4
PIERCE ST Rt#-195
66000 RivC 92254 5592-B7
66000 RivC 92254 (5652-B7
See Page 5592)
66000 RivC 92274 (5652-B7
See Page 5592)
66000 RivC 92274 5592-B7
73000 RivC 92254 5712-B4
73000 RivC 92274 5712-B4
PIER POINTE CIR
30600 RivC 92584 868-G4
PIERROTT AV
16800 LKEL 92530 866-A2
PIERSON BLVD
61000 DHSP 92282 695-G4
61000 RivC 92282 695-G4
61300 DHSP 92240 695-H4
61300 RivC 92240 695-H4
62000 DHSP 92240 696-A4
63500 RivC 92240 696-A4
66700 DHSP 92240 697-A4
PIERSON RD
25100 RivC 92548 809-A7
25700 RivC 92548 839-A1
PIGEON CT
18800 SBdC 92316 645-E1
PIGEON PASS RD
- MORV 92553 717-C2
100 RivC 92507 646-F7
500 RivC 92324 646-F7
1200 RivC 92324 686-H1
1200 RivC 92507 686-H1
1900 RivC 92557 686-H1
1900 RivC 92557 687-A2
9400 MORV 92557 687-C5
11400 MORV 92557 717-C2
PIGEON SPRINGS DR
38100 RivC 92260 818-E1
PIKE DR
300 COR 92879 743-E3
700 HEMT 92544 811-G5
PIKE ST
11900 RIV 92505 744-B1
16500 LKEL 92530 866-A1
PIKES CT
5000 RivC 92509 684-G2
PIKES PEAK DR
4000 NRCO 92860 713-J3
PIKES PEAK RD
- RivC 92320 689-H6
PIKES PEAK WY
- MORV 92555 718-E7
PILE ST
32700 RivC 92530 896-A1
PILGRIM RD
1500 RDL 92373 647-H5
1500 SBdC 92373 647-F5
PILKINGTON RD
66500 RivC 92240 726-J7
66500 RivC 92240 756-J1
66600 RivC 92241 756-J1
66700 RivC 92241 757-A1
PILLAR RD
28400 LKEL 92532 836-F7
PILOT DR
- RivC 92254 (5654-F5
See Page 5594)
PIMA CT
10400 RIV 92503 744-G1
49200 RivC 92536 (933-D7
See Page 902)
PIMA RD
45500 INDW 92210 849-D2
PIMLICO DR
61300 RivC - (936-A1
See Page 906)
62800 RivC - 906-A7
PIMLICO LN
200 RMIR 92270 817-H2
PIMLICO WY
11600 MORV 92557 716-J1
PIMPERNEL DR
600 COR 92881 773-E2
PIN WY
31300 TEM 92591 959-D4
PINA
- LQNT 92253 849-H7
PINACATE RD
27500 RivC 92585 838-D1
PINACATE RD Rt#-74
26100 RivC 92545 839-D1
28100 RivC 92585 838-F1
30000 RivC 92548 838-F1
30200 RivC 92548 839-A1
PINA VISTA DR
53000 RivC - 814-A4
PINCHOT WY
- COR 92882 773-C3
PINCKNEY WY
26900 RivC 92586 868-C1
PINDO DR
81100 INDO 92201 5470-C1
PINE
26600 RivC - 814-C7
PINE AV
- RivC 92880 712-E1
800 SJCT 92582 810-H4
1100 RDL 92373 647-J1
6100 CHLS 91709 712-B2
6100 CHNO 91710 712-B2
6700 SBdC 91710 712-E1
24000 HEMT 92543 810-H4
26400 RivC - 814-D7
26500 RivC - 844-D1
32400 RivC 92584 867-F7
32400 RivC 92532 867-F7
32400 RivC 92595 867-F7
PINE CT
14500 RivC 92504 745-D3
PINE DR
38600 RivC 92223 690-G3
PINE LN
16500 FONT 92337 644-H1
PINE PL
68100 CTHC 92234 787-D5
PINE RD
37500 RivC 92539 (935-C1
See Page 904)
53000 RivC - 814-A4
PINE ST
- MURR 92563 928-F7
- RivC - (875-J4
See Page 844)
100 SJCT 92582 810-H2
800 COR 92879 743-E6
3000 RIV 92501 685-F4
11400 SBdC 92399 651-B1
11900 SBdC 92316 645-E4
12000 RivC 92509 645-E4
14500 RivC 92230 723-C5
21400 RivC 92570 807-A7
30600 LKEL 92530 866-A3
S PINE ST
700 CLTN 92324 646-D1
PINE BENCH RD
39700 SBdC 92399 651-D1
PINEBROOK CT
12800 MORV 92553 717-H3
PINECONE CT
29200 RivC 92584 868-A1
PINECONE DR
800 COR 92880 743-C3
1500 RIV 92507 686-B3
PINE CONE LN
11900 MORV 92557 716-J2
PINECONE LN
18700 RivC 92504 776-B1
PINECONE WY
47500 INDO 92201 5470-C3
S PINECONE WY
2500 ONT 91761 643-B5
PINE COVE RD
52400 RivC - (813-J4
See Page 782)
52800 RivC - 814-A5
PINE CREEK PL
- MURR 92562 927-F5
PINE CREST AV
53700 RivC - 814-D5
PINE CREST DR
1900 RivC 92882 742-H5
PINECREST DR
7800 RIV 92506 715-H7
PINE CREST LN
47200 RivC 92592 999-F1
PINECREST ST
32200 RivC 92592 999-F1
PINE FALLS TR
6300 RivC 92509 604-H5
PINE FIELD DR
23900 MORV 92557 687-D6
PINEGLEN CIR
- HEMT 92545 840-D4
PINEHURST
55600 LQNT 92253 5530-A4
PINEHURST CIR
200 RivC 91752 683-E5
64400 RivC 92240 696-E1
PINEHURST DR
- COR 92881 773-E3
- MURR 92563 928-J5
400 BAN 92220 721-D4
700 HEMT 92545 840-G2
800 LKEL 92530 865-H3
5300 RIV 92504 685-D5
5300 RIV 92506 685-D5
PINEHURST LN
700 PDST 92260 818-H4
PINEHURST PZ
1700 PMSP 92264 787-C3
PINEHURST RD
26900 RivC 92586 868-C1
PINEKNOLL AV
- RivC 92211 789-G7
- RivC 92211 819-G1
PINELANE CIR
8700 RIV 92508 746-G2
PINE MESA CT
13600 YCPA 92399 650-F6
PINE NEEDLE ST
- TEM 92591 959-D4
PINE NEEDLES CT
- RIV 92518 746-F3
PINE NEEDLES LN
25100 RivC - (813-J4
See Page 782)
PINENUT PTH
- RivC 92880 683-B7
PINE PATCH WY
- SDCo 92028 998-G5
PINE RIDGE CT
7800 RivC 92509 684-G4
PINERIDGE CT
13500 YCPA 92399 650-G6
PINE RIDGE RD
52200 RivC - (813-J5
See Page 782)
PINES AIRPARK RD
32800 RivC 92596 869-D7
32800 RivC 92596 899-D1
PINE SMOKE PL
23800 MORV 92557 687-D6
PINESMOKE RD
67700 RivC - (907-E5
See Page 906)
PINES TO PALMS HWY Rt#-74
- PDST 92260 848-E2
28800 RivC - 844-D6
30000 RivC - (874-E1
See Page 844)
51900 PDST - 848-C7
51900 PDST - 878-C2
51900 RivC - 878-C2
51900 RivC 92260 878-C2
51900 PDST 92260 878-C2
54500 RivC - 908-B5
56900 RivC - (875-A4
See Page 844)
58100 RivC - (905-E2
See Page 904)
60500 RivC - (907-H6
See Page 906)
60600 RivC - (935-J1
See Page 904)
61400 RivC - (936-A2
See Page 906)
64200 RivC - (937-C1
See Page 906)
PINE TREE CIR
- TEM 92591 959-C4
PINETREE DR
100 PER 92571 777-H6
PINE TREE LN
55000 RivC 92539 (934-F1
See Page 904)
PINE TREE WY
100 RIV 92506 716-D4
PINE VALLEY DR
- RMIR 92270 788-B5
73200 RivC 92276 788-E2
PINE VALLEY RD
500 BAN 92220 721-C4
26000 RivC 92586 838-A5
PINE VALLEY WY
20600 COR 92883 773-J6
PINE VIEW DR
- RivC - (937-B1
See Page 906)
13700 RivC 92399 650-G7
13700 YCPA 92399 650-G7
PINEWOOD CIR
- RMIR 92270 788-A6
PINEWOOD CT
- CALI 92320 650-A7
- RivC 92880 713-A1
PINEWOOD DR
- COR 92881 773-F5
PINEWOOD LN
12900 YCPA 92399 650-D5
33800 RivC 92584 898-C3
PINEWOOD ST
19900 RivC 92570 776-H3
21700 RivC 92570 777-A3
PININA CT
15600 MORV 92555 748-B2
PINKERTON PL
2800 RIV 92506 715-H1
PINK MOSS CT
9000 RivC 92883 804-C3
PINK STAR ST
2400 PER 92571 777-H5
PINNACLE CIR
2500 COR 92879 743-J2
2500 COR 92879 744-A2
PINNACLE CT
39100 MURR 92562 927-C5
PINNACLE DR
- CTHC 92234 787-F1
PINNACLE ST
4800 RivC 92509 684-H2
PINNACLE CREST
- PDST - 848-E7
- PDST 92260 848-E7
PINNACLE RIDGE RD
- RIV 92506 715-J6
- RIV 92506 716-A6
PINNELL ST
16800 LKEL 92530 866-A2
PINNIE CT
- MURR 92562 927-J2
PINO DR
75300 PDST 92211 818-J4
PIN OAK CT
39700 MURR 92563 928-F5
PINON CT
11900 YCPA 92399 649-B3
73700 PDST 92260 848-G4
PINON DR
17000 RivC 92570 776-A7
62000 RivC - (907-F5
See Page 906)
PINON FLATS RD
- RivC - (907-G7
See Page 906)
PINOT BLANC CT
32000 TEM 92591 959-E4
PINTAIL CT
11600 MORV 92557 717-C1
PIN TAIL DR
22300 CYNL 92587 867-C3
PINTO AV
900 RivC - 5240-A7
PINTO CT
48900 RivC 92536 963-C5
PINTO DR
29300 CYNL 92587 867-C1
PINTO LN
2400 NRCO 92860 713-F7
PINTO PL
3500 PER 92571 778-C2
5000 NRCO 92860 713-H1
S PINTO PL
3600 ONT 91761 683-A1
PINTO RD
- RivC - 390-K10
- PMSP 92264 786-F4
PINTO ST
4500 RivC 92509 685-A3
PINTO WY
- MURR 92563 928-H3
6700 DHSP 92240 696-J2
PINTO BASIN RD
- RivC - 390-J8
PINTO CREEK CIR
44000 INDW 92210 819-E7
PINTO PALM WY
36700 RMIR 92270 787-J7
PINYON AV
82100 INDO 92201 5470-E3
PINYON CIR
1700 COR 92882 743-C7
PINYON CT
- FONT 92337 644-H2
1800 HEMT 92545 840-G4
PINYON RD
- RivC - 908-A2
62900 RivC - (907-G5
See Page 906)
PINYON ST
16400 LKEL 92530 865-J3
73200 PDST 92260 848-F2
PINYON CREST DR
70300 RivC - (907-J2
See Page 906)
PINYON FLAT CIR
1500 HEMT 92545 840-F4
PINZON CT
26000 MORV 92555 717-J2
PIONEER AV
16600 CHNO 91710 712-B3
43600 RivC 92544 841-J1
43700 RivC 92544 811-J7
43700 RivC 92544 (812-A7
See Page 782)
43700 RivC 92544 842-A1
PIONEER DR
3500 RivC 92509 685-D2
PIONEER RD
55000 RivC - 814-E4
72600 RivC 92241 728-C3
PIONEER TR
100 RivC 92262 755-F1
39200 RivC 92539 (934-J5
See Page 904)
PIONEER CAMP WY
- PER 92571 778-B3
PIONEER RIDGE RD
11000 MORV 92557 687-C7
PIO PICO RD
31500 TEM 92592 979-D2
PIPE CREEK RD
35000 RivC - (905-E3
See Page 904)
PIPELINE RD
60600 RivC 92282 725-F4
60800 RivC 92258 725-H4
PIPELINE TKTR
- ANA 92808 742-A7
- RivC 92882 742-A7
PIPER PL
2900 RIV 92503 744-J1
PIPER RD
34000 RivC 92567 809-H1
PIPESTONE CT
17500 RivC 92241 727-E2
PIPING ROCK RD
28500 RivC 92586 838-C7
29100 RivC 92586 868-D1
PIPPEN LN
38700 RivC 92539 (934-B4
See Page 904)
PIPPIN WY
40400 RivC 92223 691-B5
PIRATES ST
- INDO 92201 5470-H3
PIRKER DR
82500 RivC 92274 5590-G3
PIRU DR
5600 RivC 91752 683-G4
PISA
- INDW 92210 819-B5
PISA AV
25300 MURR 92563 928-F5
PISCES CIR
2700 RIV 92503 744-G2
PISCES CT
- LQNT 92253 819-H6
PISCES WY
- LQNT 92253 819-H6
PISGAH PEAK RD
11600 SBdC 92399 650-J2
12400 YCPA 92399 650-F6
28800 SBdC 92399 651-A1
PISGAH PEAK-OAK GLEN RD
38000 SBdC 92399 650-J2
38200 SBdC 92399 651-A3
PISTACHE CT
25400 MURR 92563 928-F5
PITAHAYA ST
72600 PDST 92260 848-D2
PITCHFORK CIR
24600 RivC 92595 897-H3
PITMAN LN
31700 RivC 92584 868-H6
33000 RivC 92584 898-H3
33500 MURR 92584 898-H3
PITT WY
21700 RivC 92595 897-B5
PIUTE ST
45400 TEM 92592 979-D5
PIUTE CREEK DR
7200 RivC 92881 773-H3
PIXIE
40600 RivC 92544 841-C2
PIXLEY CANYON RD
- RivC 92543 871-B6
PIZZARO CT
25800 MORV 92557 717-H1
PLACENTIA AV
- PER 92571 777-H4
900 PER 92571 778-A4
26200 RivC 92571 777-H4
26200 RivC 92571 778-A4
W PLACENTIA AV
100 PER 92571 777-F4
PLACENTIA LN
3600 RIV 92501 646-A6
3700 RivC 92501 645-J6
3700 RIV 92501 645-J6
PLACENTIA ST
600 PER 92571 777-D4
16000 RivC 92570 775-H5
23400 RivC 92570 777-D4
PLACER BELAIR
32100 TEM 92591 959-E4
PLACER CONDRIEU
- TEM 92591 959-D4
PLACER CREEK ST
- MURR 92562 927-E5
PLACER HILLS CT
23500 RivC 92570 806-B4
PLACER LAFITE
- RivC 92591 959-D4
- TEM 92591 959-D4
PLACER LOUDEAONNE
41300 TEM 92591 959-E3
PLACERVILLE RD
70300 RMIR 92270 817-J4
PLACID CT
11500 SBdC 92324 646-J2
PLACID DR
1000 COR 92880 743-C1
PLACID LN
23800 SBdC 92324 646-J2
23800 CLTN 92324 646-J2
PLACID PL
- CTHC 92234 787-F6
PLACID HILL DR
13200 RivC 92883 835-B5
PLACITA DE ALEGRIA
84000 INDO 92203 5410-J6

STREET
Block City ZIP Pg-Grid

RED MOUNTAIN DAM DR
3300 SDCo 92028 998-D7
RED MOUNTAIN HEIGHTS DR
2800 SDCo 92028 998-C6
RED OAK DR
5100 RivC 92509 684-H2
RED OAK LN
- MURR 92562 927-J2
RED OAK ST
- RivC 92596 929-D2
RED OAK WY
1700 HEMT 92545 840-H3
REDONDA MESA RD
43600 RivC 92562 976-D1
REDONDO LN
600 COR 92882 773-C3
REDONDO ST
3900 RIV 92505 714-E7
REDONDO WY
900 HEMT 92543 840-H2
RED PINE PL
300 PER 92570 807-G5
S REDPINE PL
2600 ONT 91761 643-B6
RED PONY LN
16000 RivC 92504 775-H1
RED POPPY LN
20400 RIV 92508 746-G3
20400 RIV 92518 746-G3
REDPORT DR
- COR 92881 773-F4
RED RIVER CIR
30400 TEM 92591 959-B5
RED RIVER RD
300 PDST 92211 819-A3
11300 MORV 92557 687-F7
REDRIVER WY
800 COR 92882 773-B3
RED ROCK AV
4900 RIV 92503 714-G4
RED ROCK CIR
33200 RivC 92584 898-G2
73000 RivC 92260 818-E2
REDROCK CT
11900 FONT 92337 644-C4
REDROCK DR
2300 COR 92882 742-G6
RED ROCK RD
39800 RivC 92592 931-A7
RED ROCK WY
- NRCO 92860 713-J7
RED SETTER PL
29900 CYNL 92587 867-E3
RED SHANK LN
47300 RivC 92544 902-J4
RED SHANK RD
58500 RivC 92539 (935-D4 See Page 904)
RED SKY CT
16300 RivC 92503 744-E4
RED SPRUCE PL
300 PER 92570 807-G5
REDSTAR CT
4200 RIV 92505 714-D7
4200 RIV 92505 744-D1
RED STONE CIR
12500 YCPA 92399 649-F4
REDTAIL DR
900 COR 92879 743-F2
REDTAIL LN
26300 RivC 92584 898-B1
RED WILLOW WY
23300 MURR 92562 927-E3
REDWING CIR
300 COR 92882 773-C2
25500 RivC 92544 811-J6
REDWING DR
400 COR 92882 773-C2
14200 MORV 92553 717-H6
REDWOOD AV
10500 FONT 92337 644-D2
10600 SBdC 92337 644-D2
REDWOOD CIR
- MURR 92563 928-H7
REDWOOD CT
900 COR 92879 743-F7
11300 FONT 92337 644-D3
REDWOOD DR
- RivC - (937-D2 See Page 906)
2100 HEMT 92545 840-G3
2800 RIV 92501 685-G2
11900 FONT 92337 644-D4
22700 RivC 92570 747-B7
29700 CYNL 92587 867-C2
REDWOOD DR N
3000 PMSP 92262 756-E4
REDWOOD DR S
2800 PMSP 92262 756-E4
REDWOOD LN
12900 YCPA 92399 650-D5
34800 CALI 92320 689-H2
REDWOOD ST
1100 COR 92879 743-F6
REDWOOD TR
12900 YCPA 92399 650-E5
REED AV
12200 GTER 92313 646-E4
REED CIR
300 COR 92879 743-E4
67800 CTHC 92234 787-C1
REED CT
- RMIR 92270 818-B3

REEDER
16500 RivC 92570 805-J4
16500 RivC 92570 806-A4
REED VALLEY RD
34300 RivC - 902-H2
34600 RivC 92544 902-J5
38100 RivC 92544 (932-J5 See Page 902)
38100 RivC 92544 (933-A1 See Page 902)
40000 RivC 92536 (932-H7 See Page 902)
40100 RivC 92536 962-G1
REEDY WOODS LN
33600 YCPA 92399 649-F3
REES ST
4100 RIV 92504 715-B3
REEVES WY
25400 RivC - (813-J5 See Page 782)
REFA ST
32200 RivC 92595 897-D7
REGAL CT
1500 RIV 92506 716-B2
REGAL DR
600 PMSP 92262 756-C7
REGAL BLUE RD
37700 RivC 92539 (934-J2 See Page 904)
REGAL OAKS PL
3600 PER 92571 778-B2
REGAL VISTA CT
21200 RivC 92570 775-D6
REGATEO DR
700 HEMT 92543 810-J5
REGATTA DR
- RivC 92254 (5654-D1 See Page 5594)
16000 RivC 92530 865-J7
REGATTA WY
14800 LKEL 92530 865-F1
REGENCY CIR
17200 RivC 92503 744-F6
REGENCY DR
- RMIR 92270 817-J3
3000 PMSP 92264 787-D6
REGENCY RD
24000 RivC 92548 809-F4
REGENCY ST
800 PER 92571 777-J2
800 PER 92571 778-A2
REGENCY WY
39100 PDST 92211 819-C3
REGENCY RANCH RD
16000 RivC 92504 745-E4
REGENT CIR
1200 COR 92882 743-A7
REGENT CT
26000 RivC 92544 811-H7
REGENT DR
1200 COR 92882 743-A7
REGENT PL
2500 RIV 92507 685-J6
REGENT WY
44900 INDO 92201 5410-C7
REGENTS HILL CIR
- TEM 92592 959-F5
REGINA DR
32900 TEM 92592 979-G3
REGINA WY
- COR 92882 773-B3
REGIS CT
24900 MURR 92562 928-C5
REGIS DR
13600 MORV 92555 717-J5
REGULUS DR
1200 RIV 92506 716-C4
REID CT
11300 RIV 92505 714-B4
40800 RivC 92591 959-G3
REID ST
29700 LKEL 92530 866-B2
REIHER DR
42400 RivC 92544 841-G4
REIMS CIR
5900 RIV 92505 714-B4
REIMS CT
24800 RivC 92544 (812-A5 See Page 782)
REIN CT
44800 TEM 92592 979-C4
REINA CT
45400 INDW 92210 849-C1
REINDEER CT
13100 RivC 92503 744-A4
REINDEER DR
19000 RivC 92530 896-F4
S REINDEER LN
2400 ONT 91761 643-A5
REINDEER ST
13300 MORV 92553 717-D4
REINER CIR
16000 RivC 92504 745-G4
REINHARD WY
24900 RivC 92883 804-C7
REINHART ST
900 SJCT 92583 811-D4
REINS RD
74800 RivC 92276 788-J5
REISS RD
24000 RivC 92570 806-E6
RELAY DR
38500 RivC 92223 720-G5
RELIANCE DR
11200 RIV 92505 744-D1

REMBRANDT CIR
- COR 92882 773-B3
REMBRANDT DR
300 COR 92882 773-C3
14700 MORV 92553 717-G7
REMEMBRANCE DR
1400 PER 92571 807-H1
1500 PER 92571 777-H7
REMINGTON AV
- TEM 92590 958-E5
REMINGTON DR
600 BAN 92220 721-F2
7600 RIV 92503 714-G4
REMINGTON RD
27400 RivC 92545 839-H5
REMINGTON ST
1400 COR 92879 743-F3
REMORA ST
42500 TEM 92592 959-A6
REMUDA DR
36500 RivC 92592 900-H7
36900 RivC 92592 930-H2
REMY LN
58700 RivC 92539 (935-E5 See Page 904)
RENA CT
13700 MORV 92553 717-C5
RENA WY
900 BEAU 92223 720-G2
2900 RIV 92507 686-E3
RENALDO WY
42200 RivC 92592 960-C5
RENCHER CT
15100 MORV 92551 747-H1
RENDOVA PL
43800 TEM 92592 979-D1
RENE DR
26200 RivC 92544 841-C1
RENE LN
22000 GTER 92313 646-D4
RENEE AV
4000 RivC 92509 685-C2
RENEE CIR
1900 PMSP 92264 786-G4
RENFREW WY
- RIV 92508 716-E6
RENNER ST
10600 RIV 92505 714-F7
RENOIR AV
25200 MORV 92553 717-H7
RENTAL CAR RD
10500 ONT 91761 643-A1
RENTON PL
26100 RivC 92544 841-D1
REPOSE PL
- CTHC 92234 787-F6
REPOSO ST
300 SJCT 92582 810-J1
REPOSO WY
12500 DHSP 92240 697-B4
REPPLIER RD
- BAN 92220 722-B1
W REPPLIER RD
- BAN 92220 722-B1
REPUBLIC ST
5800 RIV 92504 684-J7
REQUA AV
82000 INDO 92201 5470-E1
RESEARCH DR
800 PMSP 92262 756-H7
2600 COR 92880 742-G4
2600 COR 92882 742-G4
RESEARCH PARK DR
- RIV 92507 686-D2
RESEDA DR
12100 YCPA 92399 649-A3
RESEDA SPRINGS RD
40400 RivC 92544 901-C5
RESERVATION RD
59000 RivC 92539 (965-E1 See Page 964)
RESERVE DR
- INDW 92210 848-G6
- PDST 92260 848-G5
- RivC 92276 788-C1
RESERVOIR AV
28000 RivC 92567 778-J4
30300 RivC 92567 779-A2
RESERVOIR DR
2100 NRCO 92860 713-F6
RESERVOIR RD
9400 RivC 92509 644-C6
RESERVOIR CANAL RD
700 SBdC 92374 649-A1
RESORTER BLVD
41300 PDST 92211 819-D3
RESOURCE DR
- RLTO 92316 645-G3
RESOURCE WY
22700 MORV 92553 717-B6
REVENA AV
11800 RIV 92505 744-C1
REVERE AV
40300 RivC 92544 811-C7
REVERE PL
24000 MORV 92551 747-E2
REVERE RD
3400 RIV 92503 744-E3
REVIERE DR
28800 RivC 92584 868-G3
REVOIR PL
81600 INDO 92201 5470-D5
REX RD
32600 RivC 92567 809-E2

REX ST
15200 MORV 92551 747-F1
REX WY
9200 RIV 92508 746-E3
REXFORD DR
3600 HEMT 92545 840-E4
6400 RIV 92504 715-B1
S REXFORD DR
1500 HEMT 92545 840-E4
REXFORD LN
21900 RivC 92567 779-C7
REXFORD WY
3200 COR 92882 773-C3
REYES ST
49400 COAC 92236 5471-A5
REYNARD AV
8500 RIV 92503 714-F4
REYNOLDS RD
3800 RIV 92503 714-G6
27000 RivC 92585 837-H5
27500 RivC 92586 837-H5
REYNOLDS ST
25900 LMLN 92354 647-E2
REYNOLDS WY
58900 RivC 92539 (935-F4 See Page 904)
RHEA DR
23400 MORV 92557 717-D1
RHEA LN
21700 RivC 92567 778-H6
RHEINGANS CT
42300 RivC 92544 841-G5
RHIANNON WY
44700 TEM 92592 979-G3
RHINE CT
- RivC 92596 899-C7
- RivC 92596 929-C1
RHINEHART AV
32800 RivC 92595 897-G1
RHINELANDER DR
9900 RIV 92503 714-H7
9900 RIV 92503 744-H1
RHODA ST
1100 LKEL 92530 866-G6
RHODE ISLAND CT
77300 PDST 92211 819-D5
RHODES AV
23800 RivC 92570 777-E7
RHODES LN
- RIV 92506 716-C3
RHONDA
- PMSP 92262 756-G4
RHONDA LN
- RivC 92567 778-G7
RHONDA RD
6100 RIV 92504 685-B7
6400 RIV 92504 715-B1
RHONDA LEE RD
- RivC 92504 775-G1
RHONE LN
- RivC 92596 899-D7
RIATA TR
73300 PDST 92260 848-F4
RIBBONWOOD CT
1100 HEMT 92545 840-F3
73200 PDST 92260 848-E5
RIBBONWOOD DR
67100 RivC - (937-B2 See Page 906)
RIBBONWOOD LN
38000 RivC - (936-A2 See Page 906)
70000 RivC - (907-H3 See Page 906)
RICA DR
39800 RivC 92592 930-J6
RICARDO AV
66500 DHSP 92240 696-G4
RICCA ST
7700 RIV 92504 715-D4
RICE RD
3900 RIV 92506 685-F5
28000 RivC 92596 839-E6
32400 RivC 92596 869-E1
RICE ST
100 BLY 92225 5491-D7
RICE CANYON RD
1200 SDCo 92028 998-J6
1200 SDCo 92028 999-A7
RICH LN
43100 RivC 92536 961-J6
43100 RivC 92536 962-A6
RICHARD
13700 DHSP 92240 696-J5
RICHARD ST
17400 LKEL 92530 866-B2
21300 RivC 92570 837-A3
34100 RivC 92530 896-G5
RICHARD M NIXON CT
18300 RivC 92508 746-C1
RICHARD NIXON BLVD
50200 RivC 92536 983-E1
50400 RivC 92536 963-F7
RICHARDS AV
28700 MORV 92555 718-E6
RICHARDS RD
700 PER 92571 807-G1
RICHARDSON DR
22500 RivC - 726-J7
22500 RivC - 756-J1
22500 RivC 92240 756-J1
RICHARDSON ST
11200 LMLN 92354 647-C1

RICHARDS RIDGE RD
38000 RivC 92539 (934-C3 See Page 904)
RICHBROUGH RD
42200 RivC 92544 841-F2
RICHEY CIR
300 COR 92879 744-A3
RICHEY DR
13700 RivC 92570 775-C6
RICHEY ST
300 COR 92879 744-A3
300 COR 92879 743-J3
RICHIE CIR
11100 LMLN 92354 647-C1
RICHLAND LN
25800 RivC 92570 837-C2
RICHLAND ST
10800 RIV 92503 744-F2
RICHMAN DR
10900 LMLN 92354 647-A1
S RICHMOND CT
2600 SBDO 92408 646-J1
RICHMOND RD
26400 RivC 92545 839-G2
RICHMOND ST
11600 RIV 92505 714-B6
RICHMONT RD
11000 LMLN 92354 647-C1
RICH SPRINGS WY
13000 RivC 92883 835-B3
RICKENBACKER AV
5800 RIV 92504 684-G7
RICKENBACKER CIR
16700 RivC 92518 746-H4
RICKS DR
32300 RivC 92595 896-J5
RICO CT
- RivC 92880 683-D7
RIDER RD
19900 RivC 92570 776-E3
RIDER ST
1300 PER 92571 778-D3
1700 RivC 92571 778-D3
17300 RivC 92570 776-B4
21500 RivC 92570 777-A4
E RIDER ST
- PER 92571 777-H3
700 PER 92571 778-A3
W RIDER ST
200 PER 92571 777-F3
RIDER WY
41700 TEM 92590 958-F5
RIDGE CIR
73000 RivC 92260 818-E1
RIDGE RD
200 LKEL 92530 866-F5
300 PMSP 92264 786-D5
3800 RIV 92501 685-H2
RIDGE ST
100 LKEL 92530 866-E5
RIDGE CANYON DR
16900 RivC 92506 745-J2
RIDGE CREST
26400 RivC - 814-D7
RIDGECREST AV
2500 NRCO 92860 713-F6
RIDGECREST CIR
3400 COR 92881 773-D4
RIDGECREST DR
100 COR 92881 773-D4
11600 RIV 92505 714-A5
12100 YCPA 92399 649-A3
15300 FONT 92337 644-E3
31700 LKEL 92532 866-H5
RIDGECREST LN
11500 MORV 92557 687-F7
11500 MORV 92557 717-F1
72300 PDST 92260 848-D5
RIDGE CREST ST
39500 RivC 92563 929-B7
39600 RivC 92563 959-B1
RIDGECREST TR
49800 RivC 92536 983-G3
RIDGEDALE DR
21000 RivC 92570 775-D7
21400 RivC 92570 805-D1
39600 MURR 92563 928-F5
RIDGEFIELD TER
10600 MORV 92557 687-C6
RIDGEGATE
42200 TEM 92590 958-G7
RIDGELINE CT
28500 RivC 92590 978-H3
RIDGELINE DR
1400 RIV 92506 715-H7
2600 COR 92882 742-E5
7100 RivC 92509 684-J3
RIDGEMONT DR
11300 MORV 92557 687-H7
RIDGEMONT WY
1400 COR 92882 743-A5
RIDGEMOOR RD
25400 RivC 92584 837-J7
25700 RivC 92584 838-A7
26000 RivC 92586 838-B7
RIDGEMORE DR
1600 PMSP 92264 816-G2
RIDGE OAK RD
32700 RivC 92595 897-A7
RIDGE PARK DR
43500 TEM 92590 958-G7
RIDGEPLUME DR
25200 MURR 92563 928-F5
RIDGE POINT CT
23800 MORV 92557 687-D5

RIDGESIDE DR
6600 RIV 92506 716-C4
RIDGESTONE DR
29100 RivC 92504 868-F1
RIDGE TOP AV
34100 RivC 92567 809-H2
RIDGETOP DR
6900 RIV 92506 716-D5
RIDGEVIEW AV
5400 RivC 91752 683-J5
RIDGEVIEW CIR N
3500 PMSP 92264 786-J5
RIDGEVIEW CIR S
3500 PMSP 92264 786-J5
RIDGEVIEW CIR W
1700 PMSP 92264 786-J5
RIDGE VIEW DR
31800 LKEL 92532 866-J5
31800 LKEL 92532 867-A5
RIDGEVIEW DR
54300 RivC - 814-C6
S RIDGE VIEW DR
1700 CLTN 92324 647-A3
RIDGEVIEW LN
- MURR 92562 927-F5
RIDGEVIEW PL
36300 YCPA 92399 650-D7
RIDGEVIEW TER
2000 RivC 92882 742-H5
RIDGEWATER WY
22400 MORV 92557 687-A4
RIDGEWAY AV
15600 RivC 92508 746-B3
68600 CTHC 92234 787-G1
RIDGEWAY LN
25000 RivC 92595 897-H3
RIDGEWOOD CT
14200 FONT 92337 644-B3
RIDGEWOOD DR
900 COR 92881 773-F1
4200 RivC 92509 685-A2
11400 FONT 92337 644-B3
RIDGEWOOD RD
24300 MURR 92562 928-C3
44100 RivC 92544 902-B5
RIDING RING RD
2600 NRCO 92860 713-C7
RIESLING CT
41500 TEM 92591 959-E4
RIESLING WY
68200 RivC - (907-E4 See Page 906)
RIFLE RIDGE TR
25300 MORV 92557 717-G2
RIGEL
100 PMSP 92264 786-H7
RIGEL WY
4800 RivC 91752 683-H3
RIGGS RD
12000 MORV 92557 716-J2
RIGO CT
- COAC 92236 5471-A5
RIKI LN
42600 RivC 92590 958-A6
RILEY CIR
43400 RivC 92544 811-J5
N RILEY ST
100 LKEL 92530 866-E5
RILEY WY
6200 RivC 92509 685-A3
RIM DR
72300 PDST 92260 848-D5
RIM RD
2100 PMSP 92264 786-J6
26300 RivC 92544 842-C1
RIM CANYON RD
22300 RivC 92570 804-H3
RIM CREST DR
4200 NRCO 92860 713-D3
RIMCREST LN
24300 MORV 92557 687-E5
RIMPAU AV
400 COR 92879 743-F6
1500 COR 92881 743-F7
1500 COR 92881 773-F2
RIMROAD
1300 RIV 92506 715-H6
RIMROCK CIR
800 COR 92882 773-B2
RIMROCK DR
900 PER 92570 807-E1
RIM ROCK PL
29900 CYNL 92587 867-E3
RIMROCK RD
25000 RivC - 814-E5
RIM ROCK RD
58900 RivC 92539 (985-E6 See Page 964)
RIMVIEW CT
5900 RIV 92506 716-C2
12300 YCPA 92399 649-G6
RIMVIEW RD
24100 MORV 92557 687-E6
RINCON AV
1900 RIV 92506 686-A7
RINCON CT
100 PER 92571 807-H2
RINCON RD
41000 RMIR 92270 817-H4
RINCON ST
10900 LMLN 92354 647-A1
E RINCON ST
100 COR 92879 743-D4
W RINCON ST
300 COR 92880 743-A2

W RINCON ST
600 COR 92880 742-J1
RINCON RIDGE RD
59600 RivC 92539 (965-F2 See Page 964)
RINGBIT CT
15300 RivC 92506 745-G2
RING RANCH RD
- BEAU 92223 720-G2
RIO RD
5500 RivC 92509 685-B4
37900 RivC 92592 930-G3
RIO ST
- RMIR 92270 787-J7
RIO ARAPAHO RD
- CTHC 92234 757-C4
RIO ARBOLITOS RD
- CTHC 92234 757-C4
RIO ARENOSO
- LQNT 92253 849-H5
RIO BLANCO
- PMSP 92264 787-B3
RIO BRAVO DR
4800 BAN 92220 721-D6
RIO BRAVO RD
- CTHC 92234 757-C4
14100 MORV 92553 717-H6
RIO CAMINO CT
11300 FONT 92337 645-A2
RIO COLORADO RD
- CTHC 92234 757-C4
RIO DEL SOL RD
27500 RivC 92276 758-B5
27500 RivC 92276 788-C1
43300 RMIR 92270 818-C7
RIO DULCE RD
- CTHC 92234 757-C4
RIO FELICIA RD
- CTHC 92234 757-B4
RIO GRANDE AV
80800 INDO 92201 5470-C1
RIO GRANDE DR
14600 MORV 92553 717-H7
14900 MORV 92551 717-H7
14900 MORV 92551 747-H1
41800 TEM 92591 959-A5
RIO GUADALUPE RD
- CTHC 92234 757-B4
RIO HONDO DR
14500 MORV 92553 717-H7
RIOLANI PL
4300 NRCO 92860 713-D3
RIO LARGO RD
- CTHC 92234 757-B4
RIO LINDA RD
20900 RivC 92590 976-J2
20900 RivC 92590 977-A2
45000 RivC 92592 980-A3
RIO MADRE DR
- CTHC 92234 757-B4
RIO NEDO
41900 TEM 92590 958-E6
RIO OSO RD
- CTHC 92234 757-B4
RIO PECOS DR
- CTHC 92234 757-C4
RIO RANCH RD
3500 COR 92882 742-E6
RIO RANCHO CT
- COAC 92236 5471-A4
RIO RANCHO WY
5500 RIV 92504 685-B7
RIO ROSALIA DR
- CTHC 92234 757-B4
RIOS AV
22800 RivC 92570 777-C2
RIOS RD
700 HEMT 92545 810-G5
RIO SECO
- LQNT 92253 849-H5
RIO SECO DR
- PMSP 92264 816-E2
- RivC 92264 816-E2
RIO SILVERADO
- CTHC 92234 757-C4
RIO TIERRA
25900 MORV 92555 747-J4
RIO VISTA
5000 RivC 92882 742-A7
RIO VISTA DR
- CTHC 92234 757-B4
400 PMSP 92262 786-E1
26200 RivC 92544 (812-B7 See Page 782)
26200 RivC 92544 842-B1
27000 RivC 92586 868-C1
RIPARIAN WY
12000 MORV 92557 717-B2
RIPCHAK RD
1400 COR 92879 743-G4
RIPLEY WY
1400 BAN 92220 722-B1
RIPPLE CREEK DR
9700 MORV 92557 687-B4
S RIPPLING BROOK PL
2700 ONT 91761 643-A6
RISING GLEN RD
55300 RivC - 814-F6
RISING HILL DR
39100 TEM 92591 928-J7
RISING SUN RD
19000 RivC 92881 773-J3
RISTRAS LN
24000 MURR 92562 928-A3

RISUENO RD
68000 CTHC 92234 757-D7
RITA CT
8800 RIV 92503 714-J4
RITA WY
30500 TEM 92591 959-B1
RITAS LN
24200 RivC 92570 805-F6
RITTENWOOD CT
11200 RivC 92503 744-G4
RITTER AV
25700 RivC 92548 839-C1
RITTER CIR
42400 PDST 92211 818-J5
RITTER PTH
6100 CHLS 91709 712-A5
RIVARD RD
24800 MORV 92551 747-F5
RIVA RIDGE ST
2600 PER 92571 777-H5
RIVENDEL DR
- COR 92883 773-G7
RIVENDELL TER
25300 MORV 92553 717-G3
RIVER DR
500 NRCO 92860 713-E2
54500 RivC - 814-D6
RIVER RD
100 COR 92880 743-B1
1500 COR 92880 713-A7
1600 PER 92570 807-F7
2000 NRCO 92880 713-A7
2000 NRCO 92860 713-A7
2700 NRCO 92880 712-J5
2700 NRCO 92860 712-J5
9000 RivC 92880 712-H5
21300 RivC 92570 836-J3
21300 RivC 92570 837-A4
27200 PER 92570 837-F1
RIVER RUN
- RIV 92507 716-G4
RIVER ST
1700 SJCT 92583 811-F4
RIVERA AV
1400 BAN 92220 721-E5
RIVERA ST
500 RIV 92501 645-H6
1500 RIV 92501 685-G1
31300 RivC 92596 929-C1
RIVERBAY WY
- RIV 92505 714-C7
RIVERBEND CIR
- COR 92881 773-F2
RIVERBEND LN
4300 RivC 92509 685-B3
RIVER BIRCH LN
39800 MURR 92563 928-G7
RIVER CREST DR
5800 RIV 92507 716-H2
RIVERDALE DR
42000 RivC 92536 963-D4
RIVERDALE PL
6800 RivC 92509 684-E6
RIVER GLEN CT
28500 RivC 92584 868-F3
RIVERGLEN DR
- RIV 92505 744-C1
RIVER GLEN DR
- RivC 92509 684-H1
RIVERHILL PL
11900 RIV 92503 744-D3
RIVERLANE DR
81300 RivC 92201 5410-C6
RIVER OAKS LN
- SDCo 92028 997-G7
RIVER RIDGE DR
- RIV 92507 716-F3
1900 NRCO 92860 713-D4
RIVER ROCK RD
- COR 92881 774-C4
- RivC 92881 774-C4
78900 LQNT 92253 849-H6
RIVER RUN CT
10300 MORV 92557 687-B5
RIVERSCAPE RD
24300 MURR 92562 927-G7
RIVERSIDE AV
- BLY 92225 392-D10
- BLY 92225 5491-H5
4700 RIV 92506 685-G6
6100 RIV 92506 715-F2
11900 CLTN 92324 645-H3
11900 CLTN 92501 645-H3
11900 RLTO 92316 645-H3
11900 RLTO 92324 645-H3
11900 RLTO 92501 645-H3
12500 RivC - 5491-A6
12500 RivC 92225 5491-A6
12800 RivC 92501 645-H3
14400 BLY - 392-B10
14400 RivC - 392-B10
17000 RivC 92508 746-B6
S RIVERSIDE AV
2300 RLTO 92316 645-H2
RIVERSIDE DR
- RivC 92518 717-D7
- RivC 92518 747-D2
3100 ONT 91761 643-F7
11300 RivC 91752 643-F7
29100 LKEL 92530 866-C1
33000 RivC 92530 865-G6
RIVERSIDE DR Rt#-74
29200 LKEL 92530 866-B2
31100 LKEL 92530 865-H5

E RIVERSIDE DR
2700 ONT 91761 643-B7
N RIVERSIDE DR
600 PMSP 92264 786-F3
S RIVERSIDE DR
700 PMSP 92264 786-F4
RIVERSIDE FRWY I-215
- CLTN - 646-E3
- GTER - 646-E3
- RIV - 646-E3
- RIV - 685-J2
- RIV - 686-A2
- RivC - 646-E3
RIVERSIDE FRWY Rt#-91
- ANA - 742-C5
- COR - 742-C5
- COR - 743-B4
- COR - 744-B2
- RIV - 685-H5
- RIV - 686-A2
- RIV - 714-H7
- RIV - 715-B5
- RIV - 744-B2
- RivC - 742-C5
RIVERSIDE PL
700 PMSP 92264 786-E3
RIVERSIDE ST
20000 LKEL 92532 836-H6
20000 LKEL 92570 836-H6
20000 RivC 92570 836-H6
21000 RivC 92570 837-A6
RIVERSIDE COUNTY PLAYGROUND RD
25600 RivC - 814-B7
RIVERSTONE ST
- COR 92881 773-H6
- COR 92883 773-H6
RIVERTON LN
30900 TEM 92591 959-D2
RIVER VALLEY AV
300 BLY 92225 5491-G7
RIVERVIEW CIR
- COR 92881 773-F2
RIVERVIEW DR
1000 SDCo 92028 998-A6
3500 RivC 92509 685-B2
22100 RivC 92570 837-B4
RIVERVIEW PL
2400 SDCo 92028 998-A7
RIVER VISTA CT
37600 RivC 92544 931-D1
RIVERWALK PKWY
- RIV 92505 714-C7
- RIV 92505 744-C2
RIVERWOOD WY
12600 RivC 92503 744-B4
RIVIERA
55300 LQNT 92253 5530-A4
RIVIERA AV
1200 BAN 92220 721-D4
54200 LQNT 92253 879-J3
54200 LQNT 92253 5530-A3
RIVIERA BLVD
26800 RivC 92586 838-C5
RIVIERA CT
11400 MORV 92557 687-G7
RIVIERA DR
- BLY 92225 392-D10
- BLY 92225 5491-J7
- COR 92883 773-G6
- MURR 92563 928-H4
1000 PDST 92260 818-J4
25500 RivC 92544 811-H6
75300 INDW 92210 848-J1
75300 INDW 92210 849-A1
RIVIERA LN
15500 FONT 92337 644-F4
RIVIERA RD
- CTHC 92234 757-D5
RIVIERIA CT
- MURR 92563 928-J4
- MURR 92563 929-A4
RIZA AV
51500 RivC 92230 723-G6
ROADRUNNER
- DHSP 92240 696-J7
ROADRUNNER CT
73600 PDST 92260 848-G4
ROADRUNNER DR
- COR 92881 773-F5
76700 INDW 92210 849-C1
ROADRUNNER LN
- INDO 92201 849-J2
46000 LQNT 92253 849-J2
E ROADRUNNER LN
- RivC 92536 982-G4
ROADRUNNER RD
3100 SJCT 92582 810-C3
ROAD RUNNER RDG
12700 RivC 92503 744-J5
12700 RivC 92503 745-A5
ROADRUNNER TR
15000 RivC 92220 721-G7
17000 RivC 92504 745-H5
ROADRUNNER WY
600 PER 92570 807-F2
ROADS END DR
20200 RivC 92570 776-G6
ROAN CIR
13100 RivC 92883 835-B5
ROAN CT
2000 NRCO 92860 713-C7

E ROAN ST
2800 ONT 91761 643-A7
ROAN WY
48100 RivC 92536 963-A3
ROANOAK PL
6700 RIV 92506 716-C4
ROANOAKE ST
42000 TEM 92591 959-B5
ROANOKE RD
25600 RivC 92586 837-J6
25600 RivC 92586 838-A6
ROANOKE ST
1900 SJCT 92582 810-F2
ROAN RANCH RD
28300 RivC 92585 808-E3
ROBARDS WY
40800 MURR 92562 927-H2
ROBB RD
15300 LKEL 92530 865-G1
ROBBI RD
53800 RivC 92539 (934-D6 See Page 904)
ROBBY RD
64200 RivC 92240 696-D6
ROBERGE AV
- BAN 92220 721-H3
ROBERT CIR
39000 CTHC 92234 817-D3
ROBERT CT
- MURR 92562 927-G5
ROBERT DR
700 HEMT 92543 841-A2
ROBERT RD
31400 RivC 92276 788-D2
ROBERT ST
21800 RivC 92570 837-A2
33000 RivC 92595 896-H6
ROBERT WY
9400 RivC 92509 644-C7
ROBERTA DR
27500 RivC 92586 837-J5
ROBERTA ST
2000 RIV 92507 686-A3
ROBERTO DR
2100 PMSP 92262 756-E5
ROBERTS AV
10200 RivC 92320 690-B5
10200 CALI 92320 690-B5
ROBERTS CT
300 CALI 92320 649-J7
ROBERTS LN
16700 RivC 92241 727-J1
ROBERTS RD
200 RDL 92373 647-J2
10400 CALI 92320 689-J4
10400 CALI 92320 690-A4
13000 RivC 92240 696-D5
13300 YCPA 92399 650-B6
17700 RivC 92508 746-B1
18500 RivC 92241 727-J3
ROBERTSON ST
17200 LKEL 92530 866-A2
31100 RivC 92548 839-B1
ROBERTSON WY
37500 RivC 92592 930-G4
ROBERT TRENT JONES PKWY
29500 MURR 92563 928-J5
ROBIE CT
24300 MORV 92551 747-F2
ROBIN CT
600 COR 92879 773-E1
13300 YCPA 92399 649-H6
26400 LMLN 92354 647-F2
83500 INDO 92201 5470-H3
ROBIN DR
700 LKEL 92530 865-J4
11600 FONT 92337 644-F3
26800 RivC - 844-B1
76700 INDW 92210 849-C1
ROBIN LN
24800 MORV 92557 687-F7
53800 RivC 92536 (984-D1 See Page 964)
76600 INDW 92210 849-C1
ROBIN RD
2900 RIV 92506 685-G7
2900 RIV 92506 715-H1
21500 RivC 92567 779-F6
77600 PDST 92211 819-E6
ROBIN WY
22500 GTER 92313 646-F6
ROBINBROOK CT
- RivC 92880 713-B1
ROBINBROOK PL
1300 HEMT 92545 840-D3
ROBIN NEST CT
13800 MORV 92553 717-F5
ROBIN SCOTT ST
32500 RivC 92562 927-E2
ROBINSON AV
5800 RIV 92503 714-E3
9100 RIV 92505 714-D3
ROBINSON ST
19300 RivC 92570 777-A2
ROBINWOOD DR
24300 MORV 92557 687-E6
ROBLE DR
24700 RivC - 814-F4
ROBLES LN
23100 RivC 92570 837-D1
ROBLES PL
800 COR 92882 742-J5
ROBLYNN ST
3800 RIV 92504 715-A4

RIVERSIDE CO.

STREET Block	City	ZIP	Pg-Grid
ROBUSTA DR			
-	RivC	92503	745-A7
ROBYN CT			
15000	RivC	92530	865-F3
ROCA CIR			
2600	COR	92879	744-A2
ROCA VISTA RD			
-	RivC	92536	982-F4
ROCHE LN			
29000	RivC	92584	868-G6
ROCHELLE CT			
6100	RivC	92509	684-G5
ROCHELLE LN			
-	COR	92882	773-C3
ROCHELLE RD			
100	PMSP	92262	756-D5
67300	DHSP	92240	697-B5
ROCHESTER AV			
-	ONT	91761	643-E4
S ROCHESTER AV			
100	ONT	91761	643-E1
ROCHESTER CIR			
2900	COR	92879	744-B2
ROCHESTER RD			
69600	CTHC	92234	787-G1
ROCHESTER ST			
5000	RIV	92504	715-B1
ROCK CIR			
2300	PMSP	92262	756-E5
38100	RivC	92260	818-F1
ROCK CT			
4900	RivC	91752	683-H3
ROCK PL			
17800	RivC	92503	745-C5
ROCK 1			
-	PMSP	92264	786-G5
ROCK 2			
-	PMSP	92264	786-G5
ROCK 3			
-	PMSP	92264	786-G5
ROCK 4			
-	PMSP	92264	786-G6
ROCK 5			
-	PMSP	92264	786-G6
ROCK 6			
-	PMSP	92264	786-G6
ROCK 7			
-	PMSP	92264	786-G6
ROCK 8			
-	PMSP	92264	786-G6
ROCK 9			
-	PMSP	92264	786-G6
ROCK 10			
-	PMSP	92264	786-G6
ROCK 11			
-	PMSP	92264	786-G6
ROCK 12			
-	PMSP	92264	786-G6
ROCK 13			
-	PMSP	92264	786-G6
ROCK 14			
-	PMSP	92264	786-G6
ROCK 15			
-	PMSP	92264	786-G6
ROCK 16			
-	PMSP	92264	786-G6
ROCK 17			
-	PMSP	92264	786-G6
ROCKBERRY CT			
-	LQNT	92253	849-G1
ROCK BLUFF AV			
27000	TEM	92591	928-H7
27000	TEM	92591	958-J1
ROCK CANYON RD			
44400	RivC	92539	(965-B7 See Page 964)
44400	RivC	92539	(985-B1 See Page 964)
ROCK CANYON WY			
48300	RivC	92536	963-A2
ROCK CREEK CIR			
38300	RivC	92592	930-H6
ROCKCRESS ST			
9000	RivC	92883	804-C3
ROCKCREST DR			
1700	COR	92880	742-J1
1700	COR	92880	743-A1
13500	MORV	92553	717-E5
25200	MURR	92563	928-F6
ROCKDALE DR			
54000	RivC	-	814-C5
S ROCKEFELLER AV			
100	ONT	91761	643-E2
ROCK ELM DR			
32000	RivC	92595	927-F2
ROCKER RD			
-	HEMT	92545	810-D6
ROCKFORD CIR			
7900	RivC	92509	684-G4
ROCKFORD ST			
25300	RivC	92544	811-H6
ROCK HARBOR CT			
28900	RivC	92584	868-G1
ROCK HILL			
10000	MORV	92557	687-D5
ROCKHILL WY			
2900	RIV	92506	685-G7
ROCK HOLLOW ST			
-	INDO	92201	5470-G2
ROCKHURST CT			
5000	RIV	92503	714-F4
ROCKINGHAM PL			
3800	RIV	92504	715-B3
ROCKING HORSE CIR			
8500	RivC	92509	684-E4
ROCKING HORSE CT			
-	LKEL	92530	865-F3
-	RivC	92530	865-F3
ROCKING HORSE TR			
33600	RivC	92567	779-G6
ROCKING RM LN			
3200	NRCO	92860	743-B1
ROCKING RT LN			
-	NRCO	92860	743-E1
ROCKLEDGE DR			
4900	RIV	92506	685-G7
ROCKLEDGE LN			
400	PER	92570	807-F2
ROCKMEN ST			
19000	RivC	92530	896-F4
ROCKMERE DR			
52900	RivC	-	814-A4
ROCK MINE RD			
15000	DHSP	92282	695-C7
15000	RivC	92282	695-C7
15000	RivC	92282	725-C1
ROCK MOUNTAIN DR			
-	RivC	92590	997-G3
40000	SDCo	92028	997-G3
40500	SDCo	92028	977-G7
ROCK MOUNTAIN RD			
-	RivC	92590	997-G1
ROCK PILE LN			
21900	RivC	92567	779-F7
ROCKPORT CT			
13800	MORV	92553	717-D5
ROCKPORT DR			
-	MORV	92555	718-A4
ROCKRIDGE CIR			
30500	LKEL	92532	866-J5
ROCK RIDGE CT			
700	COR	92880	742-H1
ROCKRIDGE DR			
11900	FONT	92337	644-D4
ROCKRIDGE LN			
11300	FONT	92337	644-D2
14800	FONT	92337	644-D4
ROCK RIDGE RD			
900	COR	92880	742-H1
ROCKRIDGE RD			
7200	RivC	92509	684-J3
30500	RivC	92530	865-E5
47100	RivC	92544	902-H5
ROCKROSE CT			
-	PDST	92210	818-J7
ROCK ROSE CT			
-	RivC	92880	713-A1
ROCK ROSE PL			
10700	MORV	92557	687-F6
ROCK SPRINGS AV			
-	NRCO	92860	743-F1
S ROCK SPRINGS PL			
2500	ONT	91761	643-B5
ROCK SPRINGS TR			
24800	MORV	92557	687-F7
ROCKSPUR CT			
11500	MORV	92555	688-A7
ROCK VIEW DR			
42000	RivC	92544	841-F4
ROCKVIEW DR			
55300	RivC	92282	724-E1
ROCK VISTA DR			
-	RivC	92584	867-H1
600	COR	92879	744-A2
ROCKWELL RD			
2200	RIV	92506	715-G5
19900	RivC	92881	773-H5
ROCKWOOD CIR			
6700	PMSP	92264	787-D6
ROCKWOOD DR			
2700	RIV	92503	744-E4
69200	RivC	-	(907-F5 See Page 906)
ROCKWOOD ST			
27000	RivC	92586	838-A4
ROCKY LN			
-	RMIR	92270	788-B7
3200	ONT	91761	643-B7
S ROCKY PL			
3500	ONT	91761	683-B1
ROCKY TR			
-	RivC	92260	848-B5
ROCKY WY			
3200	ONT	91761	643-B7
25600	RivC	-	814-B6
ROCKY BLUFF RD			
16000	RivC	92570	805-H3
16800	RivC	92570	806-A3
ROCKY CREEK			
-	PDST	92260	848-E7
ROCKY CREEK DR			
16600	RivC	92503	744-F5
ROCKY GLEN RD			
16200	RivC	92570	805-J4
16500	RivC	92570	806-A4
ROCKY HILLS RD			
22100	RivC	92570	807-B1
25700	RivC	92590	997-H1
ROCKY KNOLL RD			
34900	RivC	92544	901-H5
ROCKY MOUNTAIN WY			
-	MORV	92555	718-E7
ROCKY PEAK RD			
24500	RivC	92585	808-F6
ROCKY POINT DR			
-	RivC	92254	(5654-F5 See Page 5594)
ROCKY POINT RD			
24500	RivC	-	814-A3
ROCKY RAVINE RD			
59100	RivC	92539	(935-E5 See Page 904)
ROCKY RIDGE CT			
41400	RivC	92536	963-B3
ROCKY RIDGE RD			
11000	MORV	92557	687-D7
ROCKY TOP RD			
21000	RivC	92570	806-H2
ROCKY VALLEY WY			
41000	RivC	92536	963-B2
ROCKY VIEW DR			
3900	NRCO	92860	713-D4
ROCKY VISTA CT			
17400	RivC	92503	744-G6
ROCKY VISTA DR			
40700	RivC	92536	962-J1
RODEO DR			
5800	RivC	92509	685-C1
5800	RivC	92509	645-C7
S RODEO PL			
3100	ONT	91761	643-A7
RODEO RD			
4900	RIV	92504	685-E5
17300	RivC	92530	896-B5
35500	YCPA	92399	650-B2
68200	CTHC	92234	817-D1
N RODEO RD			
1400	PMSP	92262	756-E6
RODEO WY			
72300	RMIR	92270	818-C3
RODGERS LN			
36400	YCPA	92399	650-D1
ROD LAVER LN			
73100	PDST	92260	848-E3
RODNEY AV			
19100	RivC	92508	746-D7
RODRIGUEZ AV			
5500	BAN	92220	721-D5
ROGER LN			
59100	RivC	92539	(965-E2 See Page 964)
ROGER ST			
27100	RivC	92544	841-F3
ROGERS LN			
300	CALI	92320	649-J7
ROGERS RD			
2100	PMSP	92262	756-G4
21400	RivC	92570	776-J6
ROGERS ST			
11100	RIV	92505	714-C6
ROGUE CIR			
30200	TEM	92591	959-A5
ROHR			
38500	RivC	92544	(932-F4 See Page 902)
ROJA ST			
11800	MORV	92557	717-A1
ROJO AV			
8600	CALI	92320	690-D1
ROJO CIR			
1500	PMSP	92264	786-F5
ROLAND DR			
-	MURR	92563	958-F1
ROLAND LN			
21300	RivC	92241	728-J6
ROLANDA DR			
23400	MORV	92553	717-D5
ROLAND HILLS DR			
-	RivC	92544	(812-B7 See Page 782)
-	RivC	92544	842-B1
ROLANDO RD			
28700	LKEL	92530	835-F7
28700	LKEL	92530	865-F1
ROLLF PL			
27000	HEMT	92545	840-B3
ROLLING GLEN CT			
38000	MURR	92562	927-D3
ROLLING HILL CIR			
-	RivC	-	(937-B1 See Page 906)
ROLLING HILLS AV			
5000	BAN	92220	721-D4
ROLLINGHILLS DR			
1000	COR	92880	743-B2
ROLLING HILLS DR			
6700	RIV	92505	714-B1
8500	RivC	92883	804-B3
25600	RivC	92584	867-J6
25700	RivC	92584	868-A6
41000	RivC	92536	963-B3
ROLLING HILLS RD			
38400	RivC	92539	(935-D6 See Page 904)
ROLLING KNOLL DR			
72300	PDST	92260	848-D5
ROLLING MEADOW CT			
1700	SJCT	92583	781-A5
ROLLING MEADOWS DR			
22500	RivC	92570	805-J5
ROLLING RIDGE RD			
2400	RIV	92506	715-H3
ROLLINS CT			
11100	MORV	92555	687-J6
11100	MORV	92557	687-J6
ROMA CT			
1200	SJCT	92583	811-E3
7000	RIV	92506	716-D5
ROMA ST			
-	RMIR	92270	787-J7
ROMAIN CT			
400	HEMT	92544	811-C6
ROME DR			
-	LQNT	92253	819-F7
ROME BEAUTY WY			
40300	RivC	92223	691-B5
ROME HILL RD			
32400	LKEL	92530	896-F4
32600	RivC	92530	896-F4
ROMELIA WY			
700	SJCT	92583	811-C3
ROMERO DR			
32900	TEM	92592	979-G2
ROMERO RD			
26600	SBdC	92373	647-G2
ROMERO ST			
-	COAC	92236	5471-A5
ROMFORD CT			
12200	MORV	92557	717-B2
ROMO CIR			
51600	COAC	92236	5471-B7
ROMONA PL			
31000	LKEL	92532	867-A6
ROMUALDA CT			
86400	COAC	92236	5471-E7
RON CIR			
1000	HEMT	92545	810-F5
RONALD CT			
37800	CTHC	92234	817-D1
RONALD RD			
21700	RivC	92567	779-H6
40200	RivC	92544	931-C4
RONALD ST			
2800	RIV	92506	715-F3
44600	RivC	92201	5410-C7
RONCADOR PL			
2800	RIV	92503	715-B7
RONDA CT			
500	CALI	92320	650-C7
RONDA DR			
-	RMIR	92270	818-D6
RONDA ST			
600	HEMT	92543	810-H6
RONELL RD			
15600	RivC	92570	775-G4
ROOSEVELT			
-	CTHC	92234	787-A7
ROOSEVELT AV			
500	COR	92879	743-H4
ROOSEVELT CIR			
500	COR	92879	743-H4
ROOSEVELT DR			
1100	LKEL	92530	865-H4
ROOSEVELT RD			
300	BAN	92220	722-A1
ROOSEVELT ST			
3700	RIV	92503	714-H6
16700	RivC	92504	746-B6
16700	RivC	92508	746-B6
ROOSTER RD			
24600	RivC	92595	897-H4
ROOT RD			
40200	RivC	92544	(932-B7 See Page 902)
40200	RivC	92544	962-B1
40400	RivC	92536	962-B1
ROPE RD			
40500	RivC	92544	961-D2
ROPEWALK LN			
6000	RIV	92505	714-D3
RORIMER DR			
2000	RivC	92509	645-B5
RORIPAUGH RD			
27500	TEM	92591	958-H2
ROSA AV			
83000	RivC	92274	5530-H3
W ROSA CT			
100	CLTN	92324	646-C4
100	SBdC	92324	646-C4
ROSA WY			
25000	RivC	-	814-B5
ROSAL AV			
84300	COAC	92236	5471-A4
ROSAL RD			
3900	RivC	92509	685-B1
ROSALIA AV			
900	HEMT	92543	810-H6
ROSALIE AV			
40600	RivC	92544	841-C1
ROSALINE RD			
25400	RivC	-	(813-J5 See Page 782)
ROSAMOND HILLS RD			
44700	RivC	92539	(985-D1 See Page 964)
ROSA RANCHO LN			
4200	SDCo	92028	998-F4
ROSARIO AV			
600	SJCT	92583	811-C2
ROSARITA DR			
11100	LMLN	92354	647-A1
ROSARITO WY			
1200	PMSP	92262	756-F5
ROSARY AV			
21800	RivC	92567	778-H7
21900	RivC	92567	808-H1
ROSAS CT			
-	COR	92879	743-J2
ROSE AV			
700	PMSP	92262	756-C7
700	PMSP	92262	786-C1
2100	HEMT	92545	840-G2
4900	RIV	92505	714-C5
13800	SBdC	92337	644-F1
15400	RivC	92530	896-C2
17400	LKEL	92530	866-A3
19000	SBdC	92316	645-F1
19300	RLTO	92316	645-F1
ROSE CIR			
1100	COR	92882	743-B7
ROSE CT			
900	NRCO	92860	713-F3
82200	INDO	92201	5470-E2
ROSE LN			
18100	SBdC	92316	645-C1
ROSE RD			
2300	SDCo	92028	997-A1
36000	HEMT	92545	810-C6
ROSE ST			
15500	RivC	92530	865-H7
ROSEBAY CT			
8700	RIV	92508	746-F2
25600	MORV	92553	717-H3
27400	TEM	92591	958-J2
ROSE BLOSSOM DR			
-	MURR	92563	928-J4
-	MURR	92563	929-A4
ROSEBRIAR DR			
12200	YCPA	92399	649-D3
ROSEBRUGH LN			
24700	RivC	92544	811-H5
ROSEBUD CIR			
-	COR	92882	773-C2
ROSEBUD DR			
400	RivC	91752	683-E4
ROSEBUD LN			
30500	TEM	92591	929-B7
ROSECLIFF CIR			
-	RivC	92880	683-D4
S ROSEDALE AV			
1800	CLTN	92313	646-C4
1800	CLTN	92324	646-C4
1800	GTER	92313	646-C4
2100	GTER	92324	646-C4
2100	SBdC	92324	646-C4
ROSEDALE DR			
9600	CALI	92320	690-A3
20900	RIV	92508	746-H3
ROSEDOWN LN			
-	RivC	92595	897-H7
ROSE GARDEN DR			
300	HEMT	92544	811-C6
ROSEGLEN WY			
1000	COR	92882	743-A6
ROSE HAVEN WY			
4900	HEMT	92545	840-D4
ROSEHILL DR			
1200	RIV	92507	686-B7
ROSE HILL DR			
11900	FONT	92337	644-C4
ROSE ISLE CT			
28800	RivC	92584	868-G3
ROSELEAF PL			
24000	MORV	92557	687-E7
ROSELLE PL			
3600	RivC	92509	685-B1
ROSE MARIE LN			
16200	RivC	92504	745-F4
ROSEMARY AV			
14600	MORV	92553	717-J7
ROSEMARY CIR			
1100	COR	92879	743-H1
ROSEMARY CT			
2000	HEMT	92545	840-G1
81500	INDO	92201	5410-D7
ROSEMARY DR			
8400	RIV	92508	746-G2
ROSEMARY LN			
31700	RivC	92276	788-D2
ROSEMARY ST			
-	LQNT	92253	5470-A4
ROSEMEADOW CT			
23500	MORV	92557	687-C6
ROSEMOND ST			
33300	YCPA	92399	649-E4
ROSEMONT AV			
15500	RivC	92240	697-D7
ROSEMONT CIR			
1800	SJCT	92583	811-D4
ROSEMONT CT			
22800	MURR	92562	927-E3
ROSEMONT DR			
-	RivC	92203	789-F5
34200	YCPA	92399	649-H6
ROSEMONT WY			
27200	RivC	92544	841-F3
ROSEMOUNT RD			
69100	CTHC	92234	787-F1
ROSENA CIR			
-	FONT	92337	644-J2
ROSE QUARTZ DR			
23500	RivC	92570	806-C4
ROSERIDGE CT			
-	COR	92883	773-G6
ROSE RIDGE DR			
-	PDST	92211	818-E1
ROSE SAGE CT			
47100	PDST	92260	848-F3
ROSE VIEW LN			
30500	RivC	92276	788-D1
ROSEWOOD			
-	MURR	92562	927-F4
ROSEWOOD CIR			
300	RivC	91752	683-F5
33500	TEM	92592	979-H2
ROSEWOOD CT			
73300	PDST	92260	848-F5
ROSEWOOD DR			
100	CALI	92320	650-A7
ROSEWOOD PL			
900	HEMT	92543	840-J1
1400	COR	92880	743-B2
3500	RIV	92506	685-F6
ROSEWOOD ST			
-	MURR	92563	928-F7
ROSHANI DR			
40000	TEM	92591	959-B1
ROSILLA CT			
8900	RivC	92883	804-B3
ROSITA AV			
19700	RivC	92881	774-A4
ROSITA DR			
-	RivC	92595	897-F6
ROSLYN ST			
3400	RIV	92504	715-C4
ROSS LN			
35100	YCPA	92399	650-A6
ROSS PL			
12300	YCPA	92399	649-B4
ROSS RD			
2600	SDCo	92028	997-A1
20000	RivC	92595	896-H5
40300	SDCo	92028	977-A7
ROSS ST			
3400	RIV	92503	714-G7
12800	MORV	92553	717-F3
ROSSBO AV			
10600	RIV	92505	714-E6
ROSSI CT			
41900	RivC	92544	931-G4
ROSSINI CT			
8900	RIV	92503	684-F7
ROSSITER RD			
-	MURR	92563	928-J4
ROSSMAN CIR			
32900	TEM	92592	979-G2
ROSSMUIR ST			
3600	RIV	92504	715-D2
ROSTRATA AV			
28200	RivC	92532	836-D7
28500	RivC	92532	866-D1
ROSY RIDGE RD			
43800	RivC	92536	963-H7
43800	RivC	92536	983-H1
ROSY SKY CIR			
17200	RivC	92503	744-G6
ROTH RD			
19000	RivC	92570	776-E6
ROTHBURY DR			
24000	MORV	92553	717-E4
ROTTERDAM ST			
-	RIV	92508	746-E1
36400	RivC	92596	929-C1
ROUDEL LN			
46300	LQNT	92253	849-J2
ROUFUS RD			
25400	RivC	92584	897-J2
ROUGE RIVER LN			
-	MURR	92562	927-G3
ROUGE RIVER RD			
45500	INDO	92201	5470-C1
ROUGH WY			
42100	TEM	92591	959-C5
ROULON LN			
54000	RivC	92274	5531-D4
ROUNDER RD			
37500	RivC	92544	931-D2
ROUND HILL CT			
41100	RivC	92223	691-C5
ROUND ROBIN DR			
52000	RivC	92220	(813-H1 See Page 782)
ROUNDTABLE CIR			
9000	RivC	92509	684-D2
ROUND TABLE DR			
-	RIV	92507	686-B3
ROUND TABLE ST			
44600	INDO	92201	5410-D7
ROUND TREE CT			
11500	RivC	91752	683-G4
ROUNDTREE CT			
24400	PER	92587	837-G4
ROUNDUP DR			
41900	RivC	92536	963-E5
67700	RivC	92241	727-B3
ROUNDUP RD			
2400	NRCO	92860	712-J7
2400	NRCO	92860	713-A7
4400	NRCO	92860	742-J1
19100	RivC	92570	806-D1
68300	CTHC	92234	787-D3
ROUNER DR			
6000	RivC	92509	645-E4
ROUSE RD			
25000	RivC	92585	837-H3
25800	RivC	92585	838-A3
26000	RivC	92586	838-A3
ROUSELLE DR			
10200	RivC	91752	644-A5
10500	RivC	91752	643-J5
ROVATO ST			
-	TEM	92592	979-G2
ROVENDALE CT			
24400	MURR	92562	928-C3
ROWAN CT			
39500	MURR	92563	928-E5
ROWAN DR			
1500	RIV	92507	716-G2
ROWE DR			
23700	MORV	92557	717-D1
ROWENA DR			
3100	COR	92882	773-B3
21700	MORV	92557	716-J1
ROWLAND CT			
41100	RivC	92592	959-J4
ROWLEY LN			
31300	RivC	92567	779-B7
ROXANNE LN			
-	COR	92882	773-C3
ROXANNE RD			
13800	MORV	92555	718-E5
22300	RivC	92324	647-A6
ROXBURY AV			
10800	SBdC	92316	645-D1
ROXBURY DR			
600	PMSP	92264	786-H3
800	COR	92882	742-F5
3800	HEMT	92545	840-E3
72300	RMIR	92270	818-C3
ROXBURY PL			
5700	RIV	92506	716-A2
ROY CT			
500	BEAU	92223	690-J6
ROYAL AV			
12700	GTER	92313	646-D5
ROYAL CIR			
400	COR	92879	743-E3
40300	RivC	92544	841-C2
ROYAL ST			
-	RMIR	92270	787-H4
ROYAL ABERDEEN DR			
-	INDO	92201	5410-B6
ROYAL ANNE CT			
39000	RivC	92223	690-H4
ROYAL BIRKDALE DR			
-	TEM	92591	959-D4
80100	INDO	92201	5410-A7
ROYAL CANYON LN			
74300	PDST	92260	818-G7
ROYAL CREST PL			
-	TEM	92592	959-F6
ROYAL DORNOCH CT			
-	TEM	92591	959-C4
ROYAL DORNOCH DR			
80300	INDO	92201	5410-B7
ROYAL DUKE CT			
9900	RivC	92223	690-H3
ROYALE DR			
26200	LMLN	92354	647-F3
ROYALE PL			
5800	RIV	92506	715-J2
ROYALE ST			
24100	MORV	92557	687-E7
ROYALE ADELAIDE DR			
22600	MURR	92562	927-D2
22600	RivC	92595	927-D2
ROYAL HILL DR			
2100	RIV	92506	716-A2
4000	RIV	92506	715-J1
ROYAL HUNT RIDGE DR			
6900	RIV	92506	715-H5
ROYAL LYTHAM DR			
80700	INDO	92201	5410-B7
ROYAL NETHERLANDS RD			
33200	RivC	92596	899-J1
ROYAL OAK DR			
22500	RivC	92570	806-E2
ROYAL OAK LN			
32800	LKEL	92530	896-G4
ROYAL OAKS CIR			
1000	COR	92882	773-B2
ROYAL OAKS CT			
33300	YCPA	92399	649-F4
ROYAL OAKS DR			
-	TEM	92591	959-D4
ROYAL OWL RD			
1400	NRCO	92860	713-E4
ROYAL PALM BLVD			
11100	RIV	92505	744-E2
ROYAL PALM DR			
41500	RivC	92544	841-E1
73200	PDST	92260	848-E1
ROYAL PALM LN			
-	RivC	92503	744-J6
-	RivC	92503	745-A6
ROYAL PALMS DR			
68800	CTHC	92234	787-E5
ROYAL PINE CIR			
4300	RivC	92509	644-D7
4300	RivC	92509	684-D1
ROYAL RIDGE DR			
5600	RIV	92506	715-J1
5600	RIV	92506	716-A1
ROYAL SAGE CT			
-	RivC	92203	789-F6
-	RivC	92211	789-F6
ROYAL SAINT GEORGE			
-	LQNT	92253	5530-D4
ROYAL SAINT GEORGE DR			
-	INDO	92201	5410-B6
ROYAL SUMMIT CIR			
-	COR	92881	773-D5
ROYAL TROON CT			
-	BAN	92220	721-D6
ROYAL TROON DR			
80200	INDO	92201	5410-A7
ROYALTY RD			
4000	RivC	92509	685-A1
ROYAL VISTA CIR			
-	COR	92881	773-D5
ROYAL VISTA WY			
-	RivC	92203	789-H6
ROYALWOODS CIR			
300	RivC	91752	683-E5
ROYA RIDGE LN			
1100	COR	92881	773-E4
ROYCE ST			
3900	RIV	92503	715-A4
4000	RIV	92503	714-J4
ROY EMERSON LN			
72800	PDST	92260	848-E3
ROYLENE DR			
25600	RivC	92586	837-J5
RUBEN DR			
48000	RivC	92536	983-B1
RUBEN ST			
60000	RivC	92274	(5591-H3 See Page 5590)
RUBER LN			
-	RivC	92548	809-F5
RUBI CT			
-	RivC	92595	897-F6
800	SJCT	92583	811-D4
RUBICON CIR			
42000	TEM	92591	959-B5
RUBIDOUX AV			
5100	RIV	92504	685-C6
5300	RIV	92506	685-D6
RUBIDOUX BLVD			
1000	RivC	92509	645-E4
2900	RivC	92509	685-D1
RUBIDOUX ST			
44700	INDO	92201	5410-F7
45000	INDO	92201	5470-F1
RUBY AV			
100	HEMT	92543	841-A3
400	HEMT	92543	840-J3
83000	INDO	92201	5410-G7
RUBY CT			
12800	MORV	92553	717-E3
RUBY DR			
500	PER	92571	807-H2
1300	PER	92571	777-H7
63000	RivC	92240	696-B5
RUBY LN			
-	RMIR	92270	817-H3
1200	CALI	92320	689-J1
12300	YCPA	92399	649-C4
RUBY ST			
1200	RivC	92507	646-B6
RUBY RED CT			
9300	RIV	92508	746-E4
RUCKER LN			
4100	RIV	92504	715-A3
RUDBECKIA CIR			
11800	MORV	92557	716-J1
RUDDEROW			
22400	RivC	92241	390-C7
RUDELL RD			
7400	RivC	92881	773-H4
RUDICILL ST			
9600	RIV	92503	714-J7
RUDOLPH LN			
33100	RivC	92595	927-D2
RUDY CT			
76500	PDST	92211	819-C6
RUE CHABLIS			
1800	SJCT	92583	811-F4
RUE CHATEAU			
83000	RivC	92274	5530-H4
RUE CHENIN BLANC			
1800	SJCT	92583	811-F4
RUE DE LA SHARMIE			
27100	RivC	92544	841-D3
RUE JADOT			
41300	TEM	92591	959-E4
RUE MARANDE			
55000	RivC	92274	5530-G4
RUE MARLENE			
83100	RivC	92274	5530-H4
RUE MARNE			
55200	RivC	92274	5530-H4
RUE MERLOT			
1800	SJCT	92583	811-F4
RUE MONTIGNY			
55000	RivC	92274	5530-H4
RUE PARAY			
83200	RivC	92274	5530-H4
RUE PINOT BLANC			
1800	SJCT	92583	811-F4
RUFFIAN RD			
25000	RivC	92585	837-H2
RUFT RD			
31800	RivC	92596	899-D4
RUGBY CT			
-	COR	92881	773-C4
-	COR	92882	773-C4
RUGBY LN			
24600	MORV	92551	747-F1
RUGGED TRAIL RD			
44800	RivC	92539	(985-B2 See Page 964)
RUGGIE RD			
27700	RivC	92585	838-C3
RUGGIERI LN			
4700	HEMT	92544	811-G5
RUIDOSA ST			
31100	TEM	92592	979-C5
RUIS CT			
4000	RivC	92509	685-E3
RUIZ CT			
43100	RivC	92544	931-J3
RUIZ RD			
12400	RivC	92220	722-J2
RUMSEY DR			
2700	RIV	92506	685-H7
2700	RIV	92506	715-H1
RUNAWAY BAY DR			
78300	RivC	92201	819-G5
RUNDELL DR			
13500	MORV	92553	717-D5
RUNNING BEAR CIR			
-	CYNL	92587	867-E4
RUNNING BEAR WY			
-	PER	92571	778-A2
RUNNING DEER RD			
13000	MORV	92553	717-D4
15100	LKEL	92530	865-F1
15100	RivC	92530	865-F1
RUNNING GAIT LN			
8400	RivC	92509	684-E4
RUNNING GUN LN			
8900	RivC	92557	686-J2
RUNNING H DR			
-	PDST	92260	848-B4
RUNNING HORSE DR			
13400	MORV	92553	717-E4
RUNNING HORSE RD			
71500	RivC	92241	728-A2
RUNNING RABBIT CT			
-	CYNL	92587	867-D3
RUNNING RABBIT RD			
35300	MURR	92563	898-G6
RUNNING SPRINGS CT			
1200	COR	92882	742-E6
RUNNING SPRINGS DR			
100	PDST	92211	818-J4
100	PDST	92211	819-A4
RUNNING SPRINGS RD			
57400	RivC	92539	(985-B2 See Page 964)
RUNSIN RD			
47500	RivC	92544	(932-J6 See Page 902)
RUPARD			
400	LKEL	92530	866-F5
RUPLEY PL			
4000	RIV	92505	714-F7
RUPPERT ST			
19000	PMSP	92258	726-C4
RUSH ST			
-	PMSP	92264	787-C4
42500	RivC	92539	(965-G4 See Page 964)
S RUSH CREEK WY			
2500	ONT	91761	643-C5
RUSHING WIND CT			
-	MURR	92563	928-H4
RUSHMORE AV			
12700	RivC	92282	694-B7
12700	RivC	92282	724-B1
RUSHMORE CT			
-	HEMT	92545	840-E3
RUSHMORE DR			
400	COR	92879	743-E3
RUSSELL AV			
24000	RivC	92508	746-C2
RUSSELL DR			
2100	COR	92879	743-H3
RUSSELL LN			
44200	PDST	92260	818-F7
49100	INDO	92201	5470-E5
RUSSELL RD			
-	RivC	92536	983-D2
RUSSELL ST			
-	MORV	92555	718-F5
3300	RIV	92501	685-J2
32800	RivC	92530	896-D3
RUSSELL WY			
300	PER	92571	777-H4
RUSSIAN RIVER LN			
2800	ONT	91761	643-D6
RUSSO RD			
-	RivC	92571	778-A5
RUSTIC DR			
11900	FONT	92337	644-C4
RUSTIC LN			
6200	RivC	92509	685-A1
RUSTIC PL			
11700	FONT	92337	644-C3
RUSTIC RD			
23300	MURR	92562	927-E4
RUSTIC GLEN DR			
39500	TEM	92591	958-H1
RUSTIC ROCK			
-	PDST	92260	848-B4
RUSTIN AV			
1600	RIV	92507	686-C2
RUSTLER WY			
900	COR	92882	773-B2
RUSTON CIR			
13800	COR	92879	743-J6
RUSTRIDGE PL			
1800	COR	92881	773-G1
RUSTY RD			
14700	RivC	92508	716-B7
39500	RivC	92539	(935-F6 See Page 904)
RUTGERS CT			
-	RMIR	92270	818-B3
RUTGERS ST			
300	HEMT	92544	811-D6
45800	INDO	92201	5470-B1
RUTH AV			
35500	RivC	92595	897-D7
RUTH LN			
12400	YCPA	92399	649-E4
31500	RivC	92548	809-C4
80700	INDO	92201	5470-C2
RUTH RD			
38600	RivC	92544	931-E4
RUTH WY			
7900	RIV	92506	715-G7
7900	RIV	92506	745-G1
RUTHANN DR			
3300	RivC	92509	645-C7
3300	RivC	92509	685-C1
RUTH ELLEN WY			
37100	MURR	92563	928-F3
RUTILE ST			
4500	RivC	92509	684-B1
RUTKES LN			
41200	RivC	92544	871-E4
RUTLAND AV			
5200	RIV	92503	714-F2
7000	RIV	92503	684-F7
RUTLAND DR			
700	COR	92882	742-E5
RUTLEDGE AV			
43300	PDST	92260	818-G6
RUTLEDGE WY			
43400	PDST	92260	818-G6
RV WY			
-	INDO	92203	5410-G5
RV CENTER DR			
1200	CLTN	92324	646-E2
RYAN AV			
17200	LKEL	92530	866-A3
RYAN CT			
1100	SJCT	92582	810-H1
RYAN LN			
17900	LKEL	92530	866-C3
40100	RivC	92544	901-C3
RYAN ST			
16800	RivC	92518	746-H5
RYAN WY			
11300	MORV	92557	687-C7
79700	RivC	92201	819-J5
79700	RivC	92201	5410-A5
RYANS WY			
37000	RivC	92211	819-F1
RYCREST DR			
41700	TEM	92591	958-J4
RYCROFT DR			
6500	RIV	92506	716-B4
RYDER WY			
14900	MORV	92555	718-E7
RYE LN			
34600	RivC	92595	897-A5
RYWAY PL			
46400	PDST	92260	848-F3
S			
SAAR ST			
44000	RivC	92544	(812-A5 See Page 782)
SABA CT			
-	MURR	92563	928-H7
SABADO CT			
500	HEMT	92545	810-G6
SABINA CT			
16400	MORV	92551	747-H3
SABINA DR			
42300	RivC	92544	901-H6
SABINA ST			
61000	RivC	92274	(5591-B3 See Page 5590)
SABINA PEAK CIR			
300	COR	92881	773-D3
SABITA DR			
80300	INDO	92201	5470-B2
SABITA WY			
1400	PMSP	92262	756-F5
SABLE DR			
33700	RivC	92544	901-H4
SABRINA CT			
79700	RivC	92203	819-J3
SACATAN CIR			
46100	INDW	92210	849-D2
SACKETT CT			
20100	RivC	92881	773-H5
SACRAMENTO AV			
-	INDO	92201	5470-H3
SACRAMENTO ST			
4400	RIV	92504	715-A3
SADDLE CT			
-	CYNL	92587	867-B2
SADDLE DR			
26500	RivC	-	844-A2
SADDLE WY			
700	NRCO	92860	713-G5
SADDLEBACK DR			
2000	COR	92879	743-H2
41200	RivC	92536	963-C3
SADDLEBACK LN			
31000	RivC	92584	868-D5
SADDLEBACK RD			
15500	RivC	92506	745-G3
52000	RivC	92539	(903-J7 See Page 902)
52300	RivC	92539	904-A7
SADDLEBAG CT			
24300	MURR	92562	927-J6
SADDLEBRED CT			
-	RivC	92880	683-D7
SADDLEBROOK LN			
16300	MORV	92551	747-H4
SADDLEBROOK ST			
-	MURR	92563	928-F7
-	MURR	92563	958-F1
SADDLE CREEK DR			
8200	RivC	92509	684-E2
SADDLE CREST PL			
16100	RivC	92506	745-G2
SADDLEHORN DR			
-	RivC	92276	789-A4
SADDLEHORN TR			
300	PDST	92211	819-A4
SADDLE RIDGE DR			
31700	LKEL	92532	866-H5

STREET Block City ZIP Pg-Grid

SADDLE RIDGE RD
11000 MORV 92557 687-C7
32400 RivC 92543 871-A6
SADDLETREE DR
- RivC 92592 900-J7
SADIE ST
25300 RivC 92570 807-B7
25300 RivC 92570 837-B1
SAFARI
- PMSP 92264 786-E5
SAFARI BLUM DR
22600 RivC 92241 728-G7
22700 RivC 92241 758-G1
SAFARI PARK DR
100 PMSP 92264 786-J6
SAFFRON CIR
1100 COR 92879 743-H1
SAFFRON CT
9300 RIV 92503 714-H5
44500 LQNT 92253 819-J7
SAFIRO CT
- RivC 92595 897-G6
11800 FONT 92337 644-C4
SAGE
- BLY 92225 5491-E5
SAGE AV
100 SJCT 92582 810-J2
1900 COR 92882 742-H7
1900 COR 92882 772-H1
9100 RIV 92503 714-H5
11300 FONT 92337 644-C2
17000 RivC 92504 745-J3
17300 RivC 92504 746-A3
SAGE CT
12000 YCPA 92399 649-B3
72700 PDST 92260 848-D2
SAGE DR
- INDW 92210 818-H7
- CTHC 92234 787-C6
- PMSP 92264 787-C6
400 RivC - 5239-J6
400 PMSP 92262 786-E3
400 RivC - 5240-A6
11100 LMLN 92354 647-A2
SAGE LN
45000 PDST 92260 848-E2
69600 CTHC 92234 787-G3
SAGE PL
- CYNL 92587 867-E3
SAGE RD
- RivC 92544 871-D5
SAGE RD Rt#-R3
31300 RivC 92544 871-D4
32600 RivC 92544 901-E2
36300 RivC 92544 931-F1
40200 RivC 92544 961-J1
40700 RivC 92544 962-A2
40700 RivC 92536 961-J7
40700 RivC 92536 962-A3
43100 RivC 92536 981-J4
SAGE ST
20500 RivC 92570 746-G7
45700 INDO 92201 5470-G1
SAGE BLOSSOM LN
37500 RivC 92592 930-J2
SAGEBRUSH
61200 RivC 92258 725-H1
61200 RivC 92282 725-H1
SAGEBRUSH AV
55600 RivC 92282 724-E2
78500 LQNT 92253 849-G5
SAGEBRUSH DR
74500 PDST 92260 848-H1
SAGEBRUSH RD
- RivC 92585 838-D6
S SAGEBRUSH RD
1000 PMSP 92264 786-F4
SAGEBRUSH ST
43200 INDO 92201 5410-E6
SAGEBRUSH TR
18300 RivC 92241 727-B3
SAGEBUSH LN
900 NRCO 92860 713-F4
SAGECREST CIR
24300 MURR 92562 928-C3
SAGECREST DR
- SJCT 92583 780-J5
- SJCT 92583 781-A5
10400 MORV 92557 687-F5
31500 LKEL 92532 866-H5
SAGEFLOWER LN
48700 PDST 92260 848-D5
SAGE GROUSE LN
12300 MORV 92555 718-A2
SAGEHEN ST
41900 RivC 92536 961-G4
SAGE TREE LN
2600 NRCO 92860 713-A6
SAGEWOOD CT
15800 RivC 92504 745-G5
SAGEWOOD DR
40000 PDST 92260 818-E3
SAGEWOOD LN
3100 COR 92882 742-F5
4700 HEMT 92545 840-D4
SAGEWOOD PL
11300 MORV 92557 687-E7
SAGEWOOD ST
- MURR 92562 927-G5
SAGINAW CT
49900 RivC 92536 963-E5
SAGINAW PL
1500 RIV 92506 716-B2
SAGITTARIUS DR
10600 RIV 92503 744-G2

SAGO PALM CIR
- INDO 92201 5470-C1
SAGO PALM DR
26000 RivC 92548 839-B1
SAGUARO CT
36500 RMIR 92270 787-J7
SAGUARO DR
300 PMSP 92264 787-C6
78600 LQNT 92253 849-G5
SAGUARO LN
- INDW 92210 818-H7
SAGUARO RD
9100 RIV 92503 715-A6
SAGUARO ST
5900 RivC 92509 684-C5
43600 INDO 92201 5410-E6
SAGUARO WY
11900 FONT 92337 644-B4
SAGUARO GATE
43800 INDO 92201 5410-E6
SAHALEE CT
- YCPA 92399 649-E2
SAHARA
- PMSP 92264 786-E5
SAHARA RD
2000 PMSP 92262 756-G6
71300 RMIR 92270 818-B5
SAHARA DESERT DR
76600 PDST 92211 819-A1
SAHO CT
31100 TEM 92592 979-D5
SAIDY AV
82600 INDO 92201 5470-F1
SAIL CIR
- RivC 92254 (5654-D2
See Page 5594)
SAILFISH PT
22800 MURR 92562 927-D4
SAINT ALBANS LN
11700 LMLN 92354 647-F3
SAINT ALBERTS DR
32500 CTHC 92234 787-D3
SAINT ANDREWS
12100 RMIR 92270 788-A6
SAINT ANDREWS CT
700 RivC 92882 742-G5
29600 MURR 92563 928-J4
75200 INDW 92210 848-J1
75300 INDW 92210 849-A1
SAINT ANDREWS DR
- INDO 92201 5410-A6
- RIV 92508 716-F6
26600 RivC 92586 838-B7
29800 RivC 92584 868-F2
32300 RivC 92276 788-E3
E SAINT ANDREWS DR
2900 ONT 91761 643-A6
SAINT ANDREWS PL
11800 LMLN 92354 647-E3
80200 INDO 92201 5410-A7
SAINT ANDREWS PZ
6100 PMSP 92264 787-C3
SAINT ANDREWS RD
- CTHC 92234 757-F7
E SAINT ANDREWS ST
2700 ONT 91761 643-A6
SAINT ANDREWS WY
- LQNT 92253 5530-C6
6000 BAN 92220 721-C4
SAINT ANNES CT
22800 MURR 92562 927-B3
SAINT ANNES BAY DR
41500 RivC 92201 819-G5
SAINT ANTON CIR
11200 RIV 92505 714-B5
SAINT AUGUSTINE DR
6000 RIV 92506 716-B3
77700 PDST 92211 819-F6
SAINT BARTHELEMY DR
800 HEMT 92543 840-J3
SAINT BERNARD DR
60300 RivC - (907-F3
See Page 906)
SAINT BIMINI CIR N
900 PMSP 92264 786-G4
SAINT CHARLES PL
16700 LKEL 92530 865-J3
75100 PDST 92211 818-J5
SAINT CHRISTOPHER LN
25000 MORV 92553 717-G5
SAINT CLAIR AV
15100 LKEL 92530 865-G2
SAINT CLAIR RD
31200 RivC 92548 809-B5
SAINT CROIX DR
1400 HEMT 92543 840-J3
77700 PDST 92211 819-F7
SAINT CROIX ST
15800 MORV 92551 747-F2
SAINT CROIX WY
4600 BAN 92220 721-E5
SAINT DAVID ST
- LMLN 92354 647-F2
SAINT ELMOS CT
300 PER 92571 777-H6
SAINT EMILION LN
2000 SJCT 92583 811-F4
SAINT FRANCIS DR
19900 RIV 92508 746-F2
SAINT GALLEN WY
19200 RivC 92562 926-F4
SAINT GEORGE CIR
1000 PMSP 92264 786-G4

SAINT GEORGE CIR N
900 PMSP 92264 786-G4
SAINT GEORGE DR
42200 RivC 92201 819-G5
SAINT GEORGE PL
4000 RIV 92504 715-B2
SAINT GEORGE WY
16700 MORV 92551 747-G4
SAINT GEORGES CT
22800 MURR 92562 927-B3
SAINT HELENA CT
44900 INDW 92210 849-A1
SAINT HELENA DR
700 COR 92879 743-H3
SAINT HONORE DR
39100 MURR 92563 928-G6
SAINT IVES CT
29200 MURR 92563 928-G7
SAINT IVES RD
45100 RivC 92539 (985-E2
See Page 964)
SAINT JAMES CT
6700 RIV 92504 715-C2
SAINT JAMES DR
- COR 92882 773-B3
14300 MORV 92553 717-E6
SAINT JAMES PL
42200 PDST 92211 818-J5
SAINT JOHN PL
500 HEMT 92543 811-A7
SAINT JOHN WY
- LKEL 92530 866-C4
SAINT JOHNS CT
100 RMIR 92270 818-A2
SAINT KITT CT
25300 MURR 92563 928-E6
SAINT KITTS CT
- MURR 92563 928-H7
43500 PDST 92211 819-F6
SAINT LAWRENCE ST
1600 RIV 92504 745-E1
2100 RIV 92504 715-D5
SAINT LUCIA CIR
1000 PMSP 92264 786-G4
SAINT LUCIA CT
79200 RivC 92201 819-J4
SAINT MARGARETS BAY
79500 RivC 92201 819-J5
SAINT MARIA DR
25300 MURR 92563 928-E6
SAINT MARYS CT
100 RMIR 92270 818-A2
SAINT MARYS ST
26100 RivC 92586 838-A6
SAINT MAURICE
- RivC - (907-F5
See Page 906)
SAINT MICHAEL PL
39600 PDST 92211 819-C3
SAINT MICHEL LN
29100 MURR 92563 928-G7
SAINT MICHELE PL
2100 SJCT 92583 811-E5
SAINT MINA CT
1500 RivC 92324 646-J6
SAINT MORITZ DR
15600 RivC - (907-E4
See Page 906)
SAINT PAUL PL
4000 RIV 92504 715-B2
SAINT PIERRE LN
31700 LKEL 92530 865-H3
SAINT PIERRE RD
68000 RivC - (907-E6
See Page 906)
SAINT RAPHAEL DR
23600 MURR 92562 928-B1
SAINT THOMAS AV
24300 MORV 92551 747-F2
SAINT THOMAS CIR
1000 PMSP 92264 786-G4
SAINT THOMAS DR
25600 RivC 92544 811-H7
78700 RivC 92201 819-G5
SAINT THOMAS LN
45000 INDO 92201 5410-C7
SAINT TROPEZ CT
14100 MORV 92553 717-J6
SAINT TROPEZ DR
- RivC 92596 899-D7
26600 MURR 92562 928-C1
S SAINT TROPEZ DR
2800 ONT 91761 643-B6
SALADIN DR
76600 PDST 92211 819-C6
SALAM PL
600 SJCT 92583 811-D2
SALDANA CT
15500 FONT 92337 644-G4
SALDINA CIR
2200 COR 92879 743-H2
SALEM CIR
4800 BAN 92220 721-E4
SALEM CT
28000 RivC 92586 838-A5
S SALEM CT
2600 SBDO 92408 646-H1
SALEM DR
1000 COR 92881 773-E3
SALEM RD
69300 CTHC 92234 787-F1
SALEM WY
6200 RIV 92506 715-G3
SALERNO CT
- LQNT 92253 819-G6

SALERNO DR
4300 RIV 92503 714-J3
SALERNO RD
30000 TEM 92591 959-A1
SALIDA DEL SOL
35600 RivC 92595 897-G7
SALINAS DR
39200 RivC 92563 929-B7
39700 RivC 92563 959-B1
SALISBURY DR
10500 RIV 92503 744-G1
SALISBURY ST
- BAN 92220 691-E1
SALIX AV
21400 MORV 92557 716-H1
SALLY LN
16100 RivC 92504 745-E4
SALLY ST
24800 RivC 92596 899-F5
SALLY ANNE CIR
8900 RivC 92509 684-D2
SALMON RIVER RD
1100 RIV 92501 645-G7
SALMON RIVER WY
3800 ONT 91761 643-C6
SALPAT PL
40500 RivC 92544 841-C1
SALTBUSH CT
10400 MORV 92557 687-F5
SALT CEDAR ST
73100 PDST 92260 848-F3
SALTCOATS DR
- RIV 92508 716-E6
SALT CREEK RD
- RivC - 410-K3
- RivC - (5715-J7
See Page 5714)
31000 RivC 92596 869-B1
SALT CREEK WY
3900 ONT 91761 643-C6
SALTER RD
20500 RivC 92570 776-G7
21800 RivC 92570 806-G1
SALTON ST
45700 INDO 92201 5470-G1
SALTON VW
6900 RivC 92282 655-H6
SALTON VIEW DR
70300 RivC 92254 (5654-E4
See Page 5594)
SALTON VIEW RD
12000 RivC 92282 695-G7
SALT RIVER CT
41300 TEM 92591 959-B4
SALVADORI CIR
1400 COR 92882 772-J2
SALVIA RD
66500 PMSP 92241 756-J1
SAMANIEGO RD
17800 RivC 92508 746-A1
SAMANTHA CT
- INDO 92201 5470-E5
SAMANTHA DR
- ONT 91761 643-D7
- RivC 91752 643-D7
- SBdC 91761 643-D7
SAMANTHA PL
5800 RivC 92509 685-C1
SAMAR CT
900 COR 92880 743-C2
SAMAR RD
25600 RivC 92584 867-J2
SAMILIN CIR
44500 TEM 92592 979-G2
SAMPLE CT
12800 MORV 92555 717-J3
SAMPSON AV
1700 COR 92879 743-H5
2200 COR 92879 744-A4
12500 RIV 92503 744-A4
SAMPSON CT
43100 RivC 92544 811-H6
SAMS CTO
27600 RivC 92883 835-C6
SAMSARA CT
300 PER 92570 807-F2
SAMUEL DR
19100 RivC 92530 896-G4
19200 LKEL 92530 896-G4
SAMUEL LN
22700 MORV 92557 687-B7
SAMUEL ST
3100 RIV 92504 715-D4
SANALAMAR DR
40500 RivC 92544 841-C1
SAN ALMADA RD
1400 COR 92882 742-D5
SAN ALVARADO CIR
1700 COR 92882 742-D6
SAN ANDREAS AV
4500 RIV 92501 685-E5
SAN ANDREAS RD
400 BAN 92220 722-B1
SAN ANDREAS ST
67500 DHSP 92240 697-B6
SAN ANDRES DR
1700 HEMT 92545 840-H2
SAN ANGELO RD
2600 PMSP 92262 756-H5
SAN ANSELMO AV
44000 PDST 92260 818-E7
44300 PDST 92260 848-E1
SAN ANSELMO ST
400 HEMT 92545 810-G6

SAN ANTONIO AV
15700 CHNO 91710 712-B1
SAN ANTONIO CIR
44600 PDST 92260 848-E1
SAN ANTONIO DR
2000 COR 92882 742-G7
30000 CTHC 92234 787-B2
SAN ANTONIO RD
1800 PMSP 92262 756-H6
SAN ANTONIO ST
25500 MORV 92557 687-H7
67500 RivC 92240 697-B7
SAN ARDO AV
31000 CTHC 92234 787-F2
SAN ARDO RD
66700 DHSP 92240 696-J2
66700 DHSP 92240 697-A2
SAN ARTURO AV
2100 HEMT 92545 810-G6
SAN BAHIA ST
400 HEMT 92545 810-G6
SAN BENITO CIR
44600 PDST 92260 848-E1
SAN BENITO DR
1700 HEMT 92545 840-H2
SAN BENITO LN
700 COR 92879 743-H3
SAN BERNARDO AV
2100 HEMT 92545 810-G6
SANBORN AV
- TEM 92590 958-F3
SANBORN ST
17000 RivC 92258 726-D2
SANBORN WY
1100 PMSP 92262 756-C5
SAN BRUNO RD
66700 DHSP 92240 696-J2
66700 DHSP 92240 697-A2
SANBURG CT
12700 GTER 92313 646-D5
SANBURG WY
12600 GTER 92313 646-D5
SAN CARLO
68500 RivC - (907-E3
See Page 906)
SAN CARLOS AV
44400 PDST 92260 818-F7
44400 PDST 92260 848-F1
SAN CARLOS CIR
800 COR 92879 743-H2
SAN CARLOS DR
100 HEMT 92543 840-J2
73200 RivC 92276 788-E3
SAN CARLOS RD
66800 DHSP 92240 697-A2
W SAN CARLOS RD
100 PMSP 92262 756-D4
SAN CARLOS ST
10600 BLY 92225 5491-D4
34900 YCPA 92399 649-J7
34900 YCPA 92399 650-A7
SAN CLEMENTE CIR
1400 COR 92882 742-E6
44600 PDST 92260 848-E1
SAN CLEMENTE LN
1500 COR 92882 742-D6
SAN CLEMENTE RD
1900 PMSP 92262 756-H6
SAN CLEMENTE ST
500 HEMT 92545 810-G6
SAN CRISTOBAL AV
81600 INDO 92201 5470-D3
SAN CRISTOBAL DR
1200 RIV 92506 716-C2
SAN CRISTOBAL RD
38100 RivC 92544 (932-G5
See Page 902)
SAN CRISTOBAL BAY DR
14200 MORV 92553 717-H6
SAN CRISTOVAL CIR
74700 PDST 92260 818-H7
SANDAK RD
42300 RivC 92592 959-J6
SANDALWOOD CIR
41100 MURR 92562 958-E2
SANDALWOOD CT
600 RIV 92507 686-D3
SANDALWOOD DR
300 CALI 92320 689-H1
1700 PMSP 92262 756-G6
SANDALWOOD PL
- RivC 92211 819-G1
SANDBERG PL
15100 RivC 92570 805-F6
SANDBERG ST
2800 RIV 92506 715-H2
SANDBOW ST
24000 MORV 92557 687-E7
SAND CANYON CIR
23200 RivC 92883 804-C4
SAND CANYON RD
11200 SBdC 92374 649-A1
11300 SBdC 92399 649-A1
12000 YCPA 92399 649-B2
SANDCASTLE CT
14200 MORV 92553 717-H6
SANDCASTLE DR
1800 PER 92571 777-J7
32900 LKEL 92530 865-G5
SANDCASTLE LN
75700 PDST 92211 819-A4
SANDCLIFF RD
1800 PMSP 92264 786-G5

SAND CREEK TR
25400 MORV 92557 717-H2
SAND CREST
10100 MORV 92557 687-C5
SAND DUNE DR
42100 PDST 92211 819-C5
SAND DUNE RD
40500 RMIR 92270 818-B4
SANDEE WY
25500 RivC 92585 837-J2
SANDERLING CT
9200 RivC 92240 696-E1
SANDERLING WY
27500 TEM 92591 958-J2
SANDERS DR
18100 RivC 92530 896-D3
SANDERS RD
74800 RivC 92276 788-J2
SANDERSON AV
100 SJCT 92582 810-F2
700 SJCT 92582 780-F3
2100 RivC 92555 780-F3
2100 RivC 92582 780-F3
2100 RivC 92583 780-F3
24000 HEMT 92545 810-F2
N SANDERSON AV
100 HEMT 92545 810-F7
S SANDERSON AV
100 HEMT 92545 810-F7
200 HEMT 92545 840-F2
SANDERSONS PASS
18300 RivC 92532 836-C6
SAND FLOWER PL
78300 LQNT 92253 849-G2
SAND HILL
- DHSP 92240 696-J7
- DHSP 92240 697-A7
- RivC 92240 697-A7
SANDHILL DR
8500 RIV 92508 746-G2
SANDHILL LN
- TEM 92591 959-D5
SANDI LN
26900 MORV 92555 718-B1
SANDIA
- LQNT 92253 5470-A6
SANDIA CT
12000 MORV 92557 717-B2
68400 CTHC 92234 757-D6
SANDIA RD
2800 PMSP 92262 756-H5
SANDIA ST
1300 COR 92882 743-C7
SANDIA CREEK DR
38200 SDCo 92028 977-F7
38200 SDCo 92028 997-F2
43000 RivC 92590 958-D7
43600 RivC 92590 978-A3
44700 RivC 92590 977-H5
E SANDIA CREEK TER
4000 RivC 92590 997-G1
4000 SDCo 92028 997-G1
W SANDIA CREEK TER
3600 SDCo 92028 997-F1
SAN DIEGO AV
6300 RIV 92506 715-F1
44600 PDST 92260 848-E1
SAN DIEGO DR
1500 COR 92882 742-G7
30100 CTHC 92234 787-B1
66500 DHSP 92240 696-J2
SAN DIMAS ST
400 HEMT 92545 810-G6
48500 LQNT 92253 849-F4
SAND ISLAND WY
28500 RivC 92584 868-F3
SANDLEWOOD DR
1100 HEMT 92543 840-H1
SANDLEWOOD PL
1400 COR 92880 743-B2
SAN DOMINGO DR
300 PMSP 92264 787-C6
SANDOVAL AV
5900 RivC 92509 684-J5
6200 RivC 92509 685-A5
SANDPIPER
1700 PDST 92260 848-D1
SANDPIPER CT
- CYNL 92587 867-D2
11500 MORV 92557 687-D7
11500 MORV 92557 717-E1
SANDPIPER CT W
- PDST 92260 818-F4
SANDPIPER DR
3000 COR 92881 773-F4
4000 RivC 92509 685-A1
14700 LKEL 92530 865-F2
76700 INDW 92210 849-D1
SANDPIPER LN
1300 COR 92881 773-G3
SANDPIPER ST
- BAN 92220 721-D4
83600 INDO 92201 5470-H3
SANDPIPER WY
1800 PER 92571 777-J7
SANDPOINT LN
100 RIV 92506 716-D5
SANDRA CT
- LMLN 92354 647-F3
SANDRA DR
2100 RivC 92509 645-B5
11000 RivC 92223 691-B6
82900 RivC 92274 5530-G2
SANDRA LN
18000 RivC 92570 806-C3

SANDRA RD
1800 PMSP 92262 756-G5
SANDRA DEE WY
17000 RivC 92570 806-A1
SANDRIA AV
12200 MORV 92555 718-A2
SAND ROCK RD
35200 RivC 92276 788-H5
SANDS AV
8600 RIV 92504 715-A4
SAND SAGE CT
47100 PDST 92260 848-F3
SANDSAL CIR
36400 RMIR 92270 787-J7
SANDSCRIPT CT
80300 INDO 92201 5470-B2
SANDSCRIPT WY
46100 INDO 92201 5470-B2
SAND SPRING DR
3200 PMSP 92262 756-F4
SANDSTONE LN
12500 RivC 92503 744-C4
72400 PDST 92260 848-D4
SANDSTONE PL
11300 MORV 92557 687-E7
SANDSTONE RD
43700 RivC 92536 982-B5
SANDSU CIR
36400 RMIR 92270 787-J7
SANDTRACK RD
6900 RIV 92506 716-B4
SANDTRAP DR
- COR 92883 803-G1
27600 RivC 92586 838-B4
SANDTRAP PL
- HEMT 92545 810-D7
SANDWAGON CIR
800 HEMT 92544 811-F5
SANDWOOD ST
27000 RivC 92586 838-A3
SANDY CT
- INDO 92201 5470-D4
29700 CTHC 92234 757-C7
43100 RivC 92544 811-H6
SANDY DR
39300 RivC 92211 819-G2
45100 RivC 92539 (985-D3
See Page 964)
SANDY LN
6500 RIV 92505 714-C2
SANDY TER
17500 RivC 92504 746-A3
SANDY BAY RD
42800 RivC 92201 819-G5
SANDY CREEK DR
12200 RivC 92503 744-C4
SANDY GALE LN
40700 PDST 92211 819-F3
SANDY GLADE AV
24000 MORV 92557 687-E7
SANDY HILLS DR
57800 RivC 92539 (965-D3
See Page 964)
SANDY LODGE RD
25600 RivC 92586 837-J5
25700 RivC 92586 838-A6
SAN ELJAY AV
30100 CTHC 92234 757-F7
30200 CTHC 92234 787-F1
SAN FELIPE AV
7500 RIV 92504 715-C3
SAN FELIPE DR
- PER 92571 777-G4
25800 RivC 92544 811-H7
SAN FELIPE RD
- PMSP 92264 786-G6
9600 DHSP 92240 696-J1
9600 DHSP 92240 697-A2
68500 CTHC 92234 757-E6
SAN FERMIN PL
43400 TEM 92592 979-D1
SAN FERNANDO DR
1500 COR 92882 742-G7
SAN FERNANDO ST
11300 MORV 92557 687-H7
SAN FIDEL WY
67300 DHSP 92240 697-B4
SANFORD LN
27000 RivC 92584 898-C1
SAN FRANCISCO DR
800 HEMT 92543 840-J2
SAN GABRIEL CIR E
30600 CTHC 92234 787-B1
SAN GABRIEL CIR W
30600 CTHC 92234 787-B1
SAN GABRIEL ST
45500 INDO 92201 5470-D1
SAN GABRIEL WY
2400 COR 92882 742-G7
SAN GORGONIO AV
- BAN 92220 722-B2
1500 BAN 92220 692-B7
SAN GORGONIO AV Rt#-243
400 BAN 92220 722-B5
S SAN GORGONIO AV Rt#-243
1300 BAN 92220 722-B4
SAN GORGONIO DR
300 COR 92879 743-E4
7200 RIV 92506 716-H6
SAN GORGONIO LN
65000 DHSP 92240 696-F6
SAN GORGONIO RD
1800 PMSP 92262 756-H6

SAN GORGONIO RD
71300 RMIR 92270 818-A5
SAN GORGONIO ST
1300 BLY 92225 5491-C6
67500 DHSP 92240 697-B6
SAN GORGONIO TR
- PMSP 92264 786-G6
SAN GORGONIO WY
900 HEMT 92543 840-H2
73100 PDST 92260 848-E1
SANGSTON DR
33000 RivC 92530 865-J7
33000 RivC 92530 866-A7
33100 RivC 92530 895-J1
SAN HELENA AV
69000 CTHC 92234 787-F2
SAN HELICE CT
2300 HEMT 92545 810-G6
SAN HUERTA ST
600 HEMT 92545 810-G6
SAN IGNACIO DR
700 HEMT 92543 840-J2
SAN IGNACIO RD
38100 RivC 92544 931-F4
42600 RivC 92544 961-H1
SAN ISIDRO ST
48600 LQNT 92253 849-F4
SANITA DR
78500 LQNT 92253 819-G7
SANITARIUM DR
24800 LMLN 92354 647-B1
SAN JACINTO AV
- PER 92570 807-C3
1100 SJCT 92583 781-B6
1100 RivC 92583 781-B6
20600 RivC 92570 806-H3
21300 RivC 92570 807-A3
26600 RivC 92571 808-E2
26600 RivC 92585 808-E2
28000 RivC 92567 808-G2
44700 PDST 92260 848-G1
82000 INDO 92201 5410-E7
E SAN JACINTO AV
200 PER 92571 807-J2
200 PER 92570 807-H2
500 PER 92571 808-A2
N SAN JACINTO AV
100 SJCT 92583 811-B1
200 RivC 92583 781-B7
200 RivC 92583 811-B1
200 SJCT 92583 781-B7
S SAN JACINTO AV
100 SJCT 92583 811-B1
S SAN JACINTO AV Rt#-79
400 SJCT 92583 811-B3
W SAN JACINTO AV
- PER 92570 807-F2
1500 RivC 92570 807-D3
SAN JACINTO CIR
500 COR 92879 743-E4
SAN JACINTO DR
- MORV 92555 718-D7
200 PMSP 92262 786-D2
700 COR 92879 743-E4
42100 RMIR 92270 818-A5
SAN JACINTO LN
65000 DHSP 92240 696-F6
SAN JACINTO RD
14800 RivC 92282 695-F7
23500 RivC 92587 837-E6
26600 RivC 92585 838-E3
54900 RivC - 814-E5
68300 CTHC 92234 817-E1
71200 RivC - (907-J4
See Page 906)
SAN JACINTO ST
900 HEMT 92543 841-B2
900 RivC 92543 841-B2
900 RivC 92544 841-B2
26500 HEMT 92544 841-B2
30100 RivC 92543 871-C2
67500 RivC 92240 697-B7
N SAN JACINTO ST Rt#-79
100 HEMT 92544 811-B7
100 HEMT 92543 811-B7
S SAN JACINTO ST
100 HEMT 92543 811-B7
100 HEMT 92544 811-B7
18500 HEMT 92544 841-B1
18500 RivC 92544 841-B1
18500 HEMT 92543 841-B1
S SAN JACINTO ST Rt#-79
1800 SJCT 92583 811-B5
SAN JACINTO TR
- PMSP 92264 786-G6
SAN JACINTO WY
300 BLY 92225 5491-C6
E SAN JACINTO WY
1000 PMSP 92262 756-F7
SAN JACINTO RIDGE TKTR
- RivC - (812-G1
See Page 782)
- RivC - (813-A4
See Page 782)
SAN JACINTO RIVER RD
200 LKEL 92530 866-H6
SAN JOAQUIN DR
1200 PMSP 92264 786-H4
30200 CTHC 92234 787-B2

SAN JOAQUIN DR E
- CYNL 92587 867-C1
SAN JOAQUIN DR W
- CYNL 92587 867-C1
SAN JOAQUIN WY
6700 RIV 92503 714-E1
SAN JOSE AV
44200 PDST 92260 818-G7
44200 PDST 92260 848-G1
SAN JOSE DR
600 HEMT 92543 840-J2
42000 RivC 92583 781-F7
67000 CTHC 92234 787-B1
SAN JOSE RD
200 PMSP 92264 786-E6
66000 DHSP 92240 696-H2
SAN JUAN AV
7500 RIV 92504 715-C3
13300 YCPA 92399 650-A6
44500 PDST 92260 818-F7
44500 PDST 92260 848-F1
SAN JUAN DR
- RMIR 92270 788-B6
600 HEMT 92543 840-H2
1600 HEMT 92545 840-H2
11300 LMLN 92354 647-B2
30000 RivC 92548 808-J6
72700 PDST 92260 818-D7
SAN JUAN RD
2600 PMSP 92262 756-H6
46600 RivC 92544 (932-G4
See Page 902)
66000 DHSP 92240 696-H2
SAN JUAN ST
600 COR 92879 743-E5
11000 LMLN 92354 647-A1
SAN JULIAN PL
42600 TEM 92592 959-A7
SAN LAZARO CT
900 HEMT 92543 840-H2
SAN LEANDRO AV
13500 YCPA 92399 650-A6
SAN LEANDRO CT
- RMIR 92270 788-A6
25900 RivC 92544 811-H7
SAN LEANDRO DR
1700 HEMT 92545 840-H2
SAN LORENZO DR
1700 HEMT 92545 840-H2
11000 DHSP 92240 697-A3
SAN LORENZO LN
1100 COR 92882 742-F6
SAN LORENZO RD
500 PMSP 92264 786-E4
62500 RivC - (907-J4
See Page 906)
SAN LORENZO RIVER RD
3600 ONT 91761 643-C6
E SAN LORENZO RIVER RD
3500 ONT 91761 643-C6
SAN LUCAS DR
1100 LMLN 92354 647-B1
13400 YCPA 92399 650-B7
SAN LUCAS RD
1000 PMSP 92264 786-F3
10200 DHSP 92240 696-J2
SAN LUCAS ST
48600 LQNT 92253 849-F4
SAN LUCAS TR
33300 RivC 92276 788-E4
SAN LUIS CT
81500 INDO 92201 5470-D2
SAN LUIS DR
100 PER 92571 777-G4
800 HEMT 92543 840-J1
44000 PDST 92260 818-D7
SAN LUIS LN
46400 RivC 92544 (932-G3
See Page 902)
SAN LUIS RD
66300 DHSP 92240 696-H2
SAN LUIS WY
300 BLY 92225 5491-D6
SAN LUIS REY AV
44500 PDST 92260 818-G7
44500 PDST 92260 848-F1
SAN LUIS REY DR
500 PMSP 92264 787-B3
30000 CTHC 92234 787-B1
31800 PMSP 92262 787-B2
SAN LUPE AV
25500 MORV 92551 717-H7
25500 MORV 92551 747-H1
SAN MARCO DR
- TEM 92592 959-F7
SAN MARCO WY
100 PMSP 92262 756-C4
SAN MARCOS AV
3800 RIV 92504 715-C2
44600 PDST 92260 848-E1
SAN MARCOS DR
- RMIR 92270 788-B6
500 HEMT 92543 840-H2
1700 HEMT 92545 840-H2
24500 LMLN 92354 647-A1
SAN MARCOS PL
600 SJCT 92583 811-B2
43000 RivC 92544 811-H7
SAN MARCUS RD
66300 DHSP 92240 696-J2
SAN MARINO CIR
- RMIR 92270 787-J7
- RMIR 92270 788-A6

SAN MARINO CIR
74000 PDST 92260 848-G1
SAN MARINO CT
- LQNT 92253 819-G6
1100 COR 92881 773-G1
SAN MARINO LN
25800 RivC 92544 811-H7
SAN MARINO RD
2800 PMSP 92262 756-H5
SAN MARINO ST
600 HEMT 92545 810-G6
SAN MARINO WY
74100 PDST 92260 848-G1
SAN MARTIN CIR
3100 PMSP 92264 786-J4
SAN MATEO
- RDL 92373 647-J1
SAN MATEO AV
3800 RIV 92504 715-C2
44500 PDST 92260 848-E1
SAN MATEO CIR
100 HEMT 92543 840-H2
2500 PMSP 92264 786-H4
3600 COR 92882 742-D5
SAN MATEO DR
1300 PMSP 92264 786-H4
11100 LMLN 92354 647-A1
67000 CTHC 92234 787-B1
N SAN MATEO ST
- RDL 92373 647-J1
SAN MATEO WY
43100 RivC 92544 811-H7
SAN MICHELE RD
24200 MORV 92551 747-F5
SAN MIGUEL DR
500 COR 92879 743-E4
1300 BEAU 92223 690-H7
1300 BEAU 92223 720-H1
SAN MIGUEL RD
10400 DHSP 92240 696-J3
SAN MIGUEL WY
43100 RivC 92544 811-H7
SAN MIGUELITO DR
31000 RivC 92276 788-E2
SANNELLE ST
16800 LKEL 92530 866-A2
SAN NICHOLAS AV
73200 PDST 92260 818-E7
SAN NICOLAS CT
1100 COR 92882 742-F6
SAN NICOLAS ST
1000 HEMT 92543 840-H2
SAN NIGEL AV
81500 INDO 92201 5470-D1
SAN ONOFRE AV
44500 PDST 92260 848-H1
SAN PABLO AV
1200 RDL 92373 647-J2
43000 PDST 92260 818-F7
44400 PDST 92260 848-F1
SAN PABLO DR
800 HEMT 92543 840-J2
35200 YCPA 92399 650-A6
SAN PABLO RD
10500 DHSP 92240 696-H2
SAN PADRE AV
2100 HEMT 92545 810-G6
SAN PADRE CT
2400 HEMT 92545 810-G6
SAN PASCUAL AV
43400 PDST 92260 818-F7
44300 PDST 92260 848-F1
SAN PASQUAL RD
30500 TEM 92591 959-B4
SAN PASQUEL ST
500 HEMT 92545 810-G6
SAN PATRICIO LN
41700 RivC 92592 960-B4
SAN PEDRO AV
2300 HEMT 92545 810-G6
SAN PEDRO PL
10300 RIV 92505 714-E2
SAN PEDRO ST
48500 LQNT 92253 849-F5
SAN PIERRE RD
55400 RivC 92282 724-E1
SAN PONTE RD
1300 COR 92882 742-D6
SAN QUINTIN AV
26000 RivC 92584 868-A3
SAN RAFAEL AV
44400 PDST 92260 818-F7
44400 PDST 92260 848-F1
SAN RAFAEL DR
800 HEMT 92543 840-J2
1500 COR 92882 742-H7
9500 DHSP 92240 696-J1
E SAN RAFAEL DR
100 PMSP 92262 756-D4
SAN RAFAEL RD
66600 DHSP 92240 696-J2
66700 DHSP 92240 697-A2
W SAN RAFAEL RD
100 PMSP 92262 756-C4
SAN RAFAEL WY
3700 RIV 92504 715-D3
SAN RAMON DR
800 HEMT 92543 840-J2
4000 COR 92882 742-D6
SAN REMO
100 PDST 92260 818-F4
SAN REMO DR
1800 COR 92882 743-A7
SAN REMO RD
66600 DHSP 92240 696-J2

RIVERSIDE CO.

STREET
Block City ZIP Pg-Grid

SAN REMO RD
66700 DHSP 92240 697-A2
SAN REMO WY
3200 RivC 92501 646-B6
SAN RIBAS RD
11700 FONT 92337 644-F3
SAN RICARDO AV
11300 MORV 92557 687-H7
SANRIVE AV
- GTER 92313 646-D6
- RivC 92507 646-D6
SAN ROGELIO ST
500 HEMT 92545 810-G6
SAN ROQUE RD
15600 FONT 92337 644-F3
SAN ROSEN CT
34900 YCPA 92399 649-J7
34900 YCPA 92399 650-A7
SAN SALVADOR ST
47500 INDO 92201 5470-D3
SAN SEBASTIAN CIR
4200 COR 92882 742-C6
SAN SEBASTIAN CT
- CTHC 92234 757-D5
SAN SEBASTIAN DR
- RMIR 92270 818-D6
SAN SEVAINE WY
4000 RivC 91752 644-A7
6600 RivC 91752 643-J7
SAN SIMEON
- PMSP 92264 786-J6
SAN SIMEON CT
- RMIR 92270 788-B7
SAN SIMEON DR
1500 COR 92882 742-G7
1700 HEMT 92545 840-H2
9600 DHSP 92240 696-J1
9600 DHSP 92240 697-A1
74900 PDST 92260 818-J7
SAN SIMEON PL
- RMIR 92270 788-B7
SAN SIMEON WY
3600 RIV 92506 715-E1
SANSOME ST
25000 RivC 92544 811-G6
SAN SUSANNA AV
69000 CTHC 92234 787-F2
SANTA ANA
- PMSP 92264 786-J6
- PMSP 92264 787-A6
SANTA ANA AV
5900 RIV 92505 714-B3
12900 FONT 92337 643-H1
13300 FONT 92337 644-E1
13700 SBdC 92337 644-A1
16900 FONT 92337 645-A1
17300 FONT 92316 645-A1
17500 SBdC 92316 645-E1
E SANTA ANA AV
100 RLTO 92316 645-H1
W SANTA ANA AV
100 RLTO 92316 645-G1
500 SBdC 92316 645-G1
SANTA ANA ST
5100 ONT 91761 643-F1
E SANTA ANA ST
3800 ONT 91761 643-C1
SANTA ANA RIVER TR
- CHLS - 742-A5
5000 RivC 92880 742-B4
5000 RivC 92882 742-A5
SANTA ANITA AV
44700 PDST 92260 848-G1
SANTA ANITA DR
37000 RivC 92592 960-F3
SANTA ANITA LN
- RMIR 92270 817-H2
SANTA ANITA RD
2100 NRCO 92860 713-A7
2100 NRCO 92860 743-B1
SANTA ANITA ST
8000 RivC 92881 774-A3
SANTA BARBARA CIR
200 PDST 92260 818-E5
SANTA BARBARA CT
81500 INDO 92201 5470-D2
SANTA BARBARA DR
30800 CTHC 92234 787-B2
SANTA BARBARA ST
2000 COR 92882 743-B7
2000 COR 92882 773-B1
25400 MORV 92557 687-H7
W SANTA CATALINA RD
100 PMSP 92262 756-C4
SANTA CECILIA DR
30000 TEM 92592 959-A6
SANTA CLARA CIR
400 HEMT 92543 840-H2
3600 COR 92882 742-D5
SANTA CLARA CT
81500 INDO 92201 5470-D2
SANTA CLARA DR
- RMIR 92270 788-A6
SANTA CLARA WY
100 PMSP 92262 756-D4
SANTA CLARITA CORTE
- RivC 92570 806-B2
SANTA CRUZ DR
3200 RIV 92507 686-E4
SANTA CRUZ RD
9000 DHSP 92240 696-H2
SANTA CRUZ ST
800 COR 92882 773-B1
SANTA DOMINGO WY
1700 HEMT 92545 840-H2

SANTA ELENA CIR
3600 COR 92882 742-D5
W SANTA ELENA RD
300 PMSP 92262 756-D6
SANTA ELENA WY
900 HEMT 92545 840-H2
SANTA FE AV
100 SJCT 92583 811-B3
3700 RIV 92507 685-H5
SANTA FE CT
600 PER 92570 807-F1
13500 RivC 92883 835-C5
83600 INDO 92201 5470-H3
SANTA FE CV
45400 INDW 92210 848-J1
S SANTA FE LN
800 CLTN 92324 646-G1
SANTA FE ST
700 SJCT 92583 811-B5
700 HEMT 92543 811-B5
1700 SJCT 92543 811-B5
27300 RivC 92543 841-B3
30100 RivC 92543 871-B3
N SANTA FE ST
100 HEMT 92543 811-B6
S SANTA FE ST
100 HEMT 92543 811-B7
300 HEMT 92543 841-B2
1100 RivC 92543 841-B2
SANTA FE TR
- MURR 92562 927-G5
75100 PDST 92211 818-J7
SANTA FE WY
- NRCO 92860 743-F2
SANTA INEZ AV
81500 INDO 92201 5470-D1
SANTA INEZ ST
2000 COR 92882 743-C7
2000 COR 92882 773-C1
SANTA LUCIA DR
100 HEMT 92543 840-H2
SANTA MARGARITA AV
44600 PDST 92260 848-H1
SANTA MARGARITA DR
1100 SDCo 92028 997-G6
SANTA MARIA
- PMSP 92264 786-J6
- PMSP 92264 787-A6
SANTA MARIA DR
- CYNL 92587 867-F2
900 HEMT 92543 840-J2
46400 RivC 92544 (932-G3
See Page 902)
SANTA MARIA ST
35200 YCPA 92399 650-A6
SANTA MONICA
- PMSP 92264 786-J6
- PMSP 92264 787-A6
SANTA MONICA DR
1700 HEMT 92545 840-H2
SANTANA CT
- CYNL 92587 867-D2
SANTANA DR
39500 RivC 92591 929-G7
SANTANA WY
- COR 92879 773-E1
500 COR 92881 773-E1
SANTA PAULA
- PMSP 92264 786-J6
- PMSP 92264 787-A6
SANTA PAULA DR
200 HEMT 92543 840-H2
SANTA PAULA ST
600 COR 92882 773-C1
SANTA RITA PL
- BAN 92220 722-B1
SANTA RITA RD
34300 RivC 92592 980-A3
SANTA RITA ST
8000 RivC 92881 773-J4
8000 RivC 92881 774-A4
SANTA ROSA AV
82100 INDO 92201 5410-E7
SANTA ROSA CIR
3500 COR 92882 742-E6
74000 PDST 92260 818-G7
SANTA ROSA CT
44800 INDW 92210 819-A7
SANTA ROSA DR
- MORV 92555 748-A2
700 HEMT 92543 840-H2
33000 RivC 92530 896-A1
34700 YCPA 92399 649-J6
35200 YCPA 92399 650-A6
44800 INDW 92210 819-A7
63100 RivC - (907-G5
See Page 906)
W SANTA ROSA DR
400 PMSP 92262 786-D3
SANTA ROSA RD
27000 RivC 92571 808-C3
27000 RivC 92585 808-C3
28100 RivC 92567 808-E3
66000 DHSP 92240 696-H2
70200 RivC - (907-J3
See Page 906)
SANTA ROSA ST
400 SJCT 92583 811-A1
29500 CTHC 92234 757-G7
SANTA ROSA WY
7400 RIV 92504 715-E4
73100 PDST 92260 818-E7
SANTA ROSA GLEN DR
37200 MURR 92562 927-E3

SANTA ROSALE
28400 RivC 92567 808-F4
28400 RivC 92585 808-F4
SANTA ROSALIA DR
30000 RivC 92584 868-B2
SANTA ROSALIA RD
26200 RivC 92584 868-B5
SANTA ROSA MINE RD
17300 RivC 92570 806-B2
SANTA ROSA MOUNTAIN TKTR
- RivC - (936-J2
See Page 906)
- RivC - (937-A4
See Page 906)
SANTA SUSANA DR
1500 HEMT 92543 840-H2
SANTA SUZANNE PL
42700 TEM 92592 959-A6
SANTA TERESA WY
700 HEMT 92545 840-H2
SANTA URSULA ST
48800 LQNT 92253 849-F4
SANTA VICTORIA ST
900 HEMT 92543 840-H2
SANTA YNEZ
- RMIR 92270 787-J6
SANTA YNEZ AV
44500 PDST 92260 848-G1
SANTA YNEZ CT
25000 RivC 92544 (812-A6
See Page 782)
SANTA YNEZ WY
2300 PMSP 92264 786-H4
SANTA YSABEL DR
13000 DHSP 92240 696-H6
SANTEE CT
42200 RivC 92544 811-F7
SANTEE PL
4300 RIV 92504 714-J3
SANTELMO RD
68000 CTHC 92234 757-D6
SAN THOMAS
25600 MORV 92557 687-H7
SAN THOMAS DR
24000 MURR 92562 928-C1
SANTIAGO CIR
8200 RivC 92509 684-F1
SANTIAGO DR
24500 MORV 92551 747-F2
42200 RivC 92544 811-G7
SANTIAGO PL
42700 RivC 92201 5410-A5
SANTIAGO RD
- CTHC 92234 757-D5
12000 RivC 92220 692-G7
12000 RivC 92220 722-G1
29100 TEM 92590 978-J1
29200 TEM 92592 978-J1
29300 TEM 92592 979-A1
31100 TEM 92592 959-D7
SANTIAGO WY
300 PMSP 92264 786-E7
1700 HEMT 92545 840-H2
E SANTIAGO CREEK WY
3700 ONT 91761 643-C6
SANTILINDE DR
24700 RivC 92545 839-J4
SAN TIMOTEO ST
78200 LQNT 92253 849-F5
SAN TIMOTEO CANYON RD
- CALI 92320 689-F5
- RivC 92223 689-F5
- RivC 92223 719-J1
- RivC 92223 720-B1
- RivC 92320 689-F5
- RivC 92373 389-C4
- RivC 92555 689-F5
- RDL 92373 647-H2
- SBdC 92373 647-G2
28400 RivC 92373 688-E2
31600 RivC 92373 689-A3
37600 BEAU 92223 720-B1
SANTO DR
300 SJCT 92583 811-C2
E SANTO ANTONIO DR
1100 CLTN 92324 646-F1
S SANTO ANTONIO DR
1000 CLTN 92324 646-E2
SANTO DOMINGO DR
- RMIR 92270 788-B7
SANTOLINA CT
- SJCT 92582 780-H6
SANTOLINA DR
43300 PDST 92260 818-G6
SAN TOMAS ST
67500 RivC 92240 697-B7
SANTORINI RD
- RIV 92506 716-C3
SANTORO DR
29500 CTHC 92234 757-G7
30000 CTHC 92234 787-G2
SANTOS ALIPAS CT
44300 TEM 92592 979-G2
SANTO THOMAS CIR
3500 COR 92882 742-E6
SANTO TOMAS AV
2900 PER 92571 777-G4
SANTO TOMAS DR
700 HEMT 92545 840-H2
SAN TROPEZ DR
4300 RivC 92509 644-D7
4300 RivC 92509 684-D1

SAN VICENTE AV
8200 RIV 92504 715-A2
8400 RIV 92504 714-J3
8700 RIV 92503 714-J3
31000 CTHC 92234 787-F2
SAN VICENTE DR
1500 HEMT 92543 810-H6
SAN VICENTE ST
48300 LQNT 92253 849-G4
SAN VINCENTE CIR
200 PDST 92260 818-E5
SAN VISCAYA CIR
4200 COR 92882 742-C5
SAN VITO CIR
- RivC - (905-H6
See Page 904)
SANWOOD RD
23100 RivC 92567 809-F2
SAN YNEZ DR
800 HEMT 92543 840-J2
SAN YSIDRO AV
31000 CTHC 92234 787-F2
SAN YSIDRO CIR
43800 PDST 92260 818-J7
SAPHIRE DR
1600 PER 92571 777-H7
SAPPHIRE LN
800 COR 92882 742-J6
SAPPHIRE PL
1100 HEMT 92543 841-A3
SAPPHIRE ST
12800 RivC 92282 724-E1
SAQUARO CT
73900 PDST 92260 848-G4
SARA CT
6100 RivC 92509 684-G5
9500 RIV 92503 714-J6
SARA LN
17300 CHLS 91709 712-A4
SARABIA ST
30600 RivC 92530 865-F5
SARADELLA CT
24100 MURR 92562 928-C2
SARAGOSSA DR
64800 RivC 92264 816-F2
SARAH CT
- COR 92879 743-E6
11300 FONT 92337 644-F2
SARAH DR
23400 RivC 92570 837-A3
39300 TEM 92591 959-A1
SARAH PL
1300 ONT 91761 643-F2
SARAH ST
13600 YCPA 92399 650-C7
13900 MORV 92553 717-G5
67300 CTHC 92234 787-C2
SARAH WY
42100 TEM 92590 958-F5
SARANAC PL
8700 RIV 92508 746-H2
SARASOTA PL
32800 RivC 92276 788-E3
SARATOGA CIR
2300 NRCO 92860 713-B7
SARATOGA DR
- RivC 92585 838-C3
SARATOGA LN
200 RMIR 92270 817-H2
SARATOGA ST
3100 RIV 92503 744-H1
SARATOGA SPRINGS PL
- MURR 92562 927-J2
SARAZEN ST
900 HEMT 92543 841-B3
SARAZEN WY
76800 PDST 92211 819-A5
SARDIS LN
21700 RivC 92567 779-G7
SARGENT DR
45500 RivC 92592 981-B4
SARI CT
42300 PDST 92211 819-C5
SARI RD
69500 RivC 92241 727-F4
SARIA CT
41400 MURR 92562 927-H4
SARITA DR
13500 DHSP 92240 696-J5
SARONA CIR
100 PDST 92211 818-J3
SARONA CT
1400 SJCT 92583 780-J6
SARSAPARILLA DR
7200 RivC 92881 773-H4
SASKIA PASS
32700 TEM 92592 979-G2
SASSARI ST
- TEM 92592 979-G1
SASSY LN
29000 RivC 92532 866-E1
SATELLITE DR
15900 RivC 92570 805-H5
SATIN BELL DR
11500 RivC 92880 742-B5
SATINLOAF DR
33300 CTHC 92234 787-F4
SATINWOOD CT
1400 RIV 92501 685-J1
N SATURMINO DR
100 PMSP 92262 786-G1
S SATURMINO DR
100 PMSP 92262 786-G2
SATURMINO RD
PMSP 92264 786-G6

SATURN
100 PMSP 92264 786-J5
SATURN CIR
- RMIR 92270 817-H3
4800 RIV 92503 714-F4
SATURN LN
6000 RivC 91752 683-H5
SATURN WY
26500 RivC 92544 841-D2
SATURNIA
- INDW 92210 819-B5
E SATURNINO RD
200 PMSP 92262 786-E2
SAUBEL RD
12000 RivC 92220 692-G7
12000 RivC 92220 722-G1
SAUCON VALLEY ST
32100 RivC 92276 788-E2
SAUER RD
34600 RivC 92595 897-E5
SAUNDERS ST
4500 RIV 92501 685-G5
4600 RIV 92506 685-G6
SAUNDERS MEADOW DR
26100 RivC - 844-A2
SAUNDERS MEADOW RD
26200 RivC - 844-D1
26400 RivC - 814-C7
SAUVIGNON CIR
31900 TEM 92591 959-E4
SAVAGE DR
100 CTHC 92234 787-E5
SAVANNAH
- RivC 92503 744-A4
SAVANNAH DR
4400 RIV 92505 714-D7
5000 BAN 92220 721-D5
SAVANNAH PL
- RivC 92880 683-C4
SAVANNAH OAKS DR
30100 RivC 92563 929-A7
SAVANNA LA MAR DR
78700 RivC 92201 819-G4
SAVONA DR
1200 COR 92882 743-A7
11800 FONT 92337 644-F4
SAVONA ST
- TEM 92592 959-G7
8800 RIV 92508 746-H2
SAVORY LN
- SJCT 92582 780-H6
SAVOY ST
9000 RIV 92503 714-H4
SAWGLASS DR
- BAN 92220 721-C5
SAWGO RD
20500 RivC 92570 776-G7
SAWGRASS CIR
29500 MURR 92563 928-J4
77400 PDST 92211 819-D3
SAWGRASS CT
30900 TEM 92592 979-C4
SAWGRASS RD
30100 CTHC 92234 757-F7
30100 CTHC 92234 787-F1
SAWGRASS CREEK LN
20600 COR 92883 773-H6
SAWH CT
35000 RivC 92544 901-E5
SAWLEAF PL
- MURR 92562 927-F4
SAW MILL RD
7100 COR 92881 773-H3
7100 RivC 92881 773-H3
SAWMILL CANYON WY
73600 RivC 92260 818-F1
SAWTOOTH CIR
3700 COR 92881 773-D5
SAWTOOTH CT
24300 RivC 92883 804-E6
SAWYERS RUN RD
44600 TEM 92592 979-G2
SAXON CT
4600 RivC 92509 685-B3
SAXON RD
43000 RivC 92536 964-B6
43000 RivC 92539 964-B6
44100 RivC 92536 (984-B2
See Page 964)
SAYAN PL
14300 MORV 92553 717-F6
SAYWARD CIR
- RIV 92503 744-D3
SCALES WY
32700 LKEL 92530 896-G4
32700 RivC 92530 896-G4
SCANLON RD
40100 RivC 92592 931-A7
40100 RivC 92592 961-B1
SCARAMELLA CIR
26500 HEMT 92545 840-E2
SCARBOROUGH CIR
400 COR 92879 744-B2
SCARBOROUGH LN
- RivC 92592 979-H2
SCARBOROUGH PL
2700 RIV 92503 744-G3
SCARBOROUGH WY
33500 RMIR 92270 788-B6
SCARLET CT
40800 MURR 92562 927-J3
78200 LQNT 92253 819-F7
SCARLET DR
68800 CTHC 92234 787-F4

SCARLET BUGLE
41700 RivC 92539 (965-H3
See Page 964)
SCARLET OAK DR
- MURR 92562 927-F4
SCARLET SAGE WY
22200 MORV 92557 717-A1
SCARSDALE ST
- RIV 92508 746-E2
SCENIC DR
- SDCo 92028 998-G5
400 LKEL 92530 866-G5
3500 RivC 92509 644-J6
3500 RivC 92509 645-A6
25200 RivC - 814-E6
60500 RivC - (907-J3
See Page 906)
60500 RivC 92282 695-F7
63000 DHSP 92240 696-B3
68900 CTHC 92234 787-E5
SCENIC LN
9200 RivC 92557 687-F3
SCENIC TER
- RivC 92373 689-B4
SCENIC VW
700 PMSP 92264 786-D4
SCENIC CREST DR
13500 YCPA 92399 650-J6
13500 YCPA 92399 651-A6
20400 LKEL 92570 836-H7
20400 RivC 92570 836-H7
SCENIC CREST LN
2700 COR 92881 773-E2
SCENIC RIDGE DR
17400 RivC 92503 744-H6
31500 LKEL 92532 866-J5
40300 RivC 92544 961-C4
SCENIC VIEW DR
25200 RivC - 814-A5
34000 RivC 92584 898-E5
SCENIC VIEW RD
14100 RivC 92570 775-D6
SCHAD LN
35300 YCPA 92399 650-A3
SCHAEFER AV
9500 ONT 91761 683-A2
SCHAFER PL
40600 PDST 92211 819-E4
SCHAFFER RD
24600 RivC - 814-A4
SCHAPER ST
33200 RivC 92530 896-D3
SCHARD WY
32600 RivC 92544 871-E7
SCHAYLEEN CT
13700 MORV 92553 717-D5
SCHEELITE ST
5900 RivC 92509 684-D5
SCHEESLEY ST
20900 RivC 92570 806-H3
SCHIDELL RD
32000 RivC 92276 788-J2
SCHIRMER DR
23000 RivC 92587 867-D2
SCHLEISMAN RD
- SBdC 91710 712-H1
12500 RivC 91752 683-D7
12600 RivC 92880 683-D7
13000 RivC 92880 713-A1
14100 RivC 92880 712-H1
SCHLUNDT ST
- RivC 92571 808-C1
25200 RivC 92571 778-C7
SCHMIDT DR
42000 RivC 92536 962-E4
SCHOLAR CT
41200 RivC 92544 841-D2
SCHOLES ST
4000 RivC 92509 644-F7
SCHOOL CIR
6600 RIV 92506 715-E1
SCHOOL ST
100 COR 92882 743-C4
SCHOOLHOUSE DR
38100 RivC 92563 929-C5
SCHOOLHOUSE LN
- RIV 92508 746-D1
- RivC 92508 746-D1
SCHOOL HOUSE WY
- MURR 92563 928-G6
SCHOOL PARK DR
27000 RivC 92584 868-C3
SCHOONER DR
- CYNL 92587 867-E2
SCHOONER LN
29300 LKEL 92530 865-G3
SCHOONER WY
- RivC 92254 (5654-D2
See Page 5594)
SCHRAMM TR
40400 RivC 92544 901-D4
SCHRODER RD
19900 RivC 92567 779-B3
SCHUBER LN
35500 RivC 92592 960-D2
SCHUFF CIR
26900 RivC 92590 978-D2
SCHULTZ RD
25900 RivC 92544 (812-D7
See Page 782)
SCHULTZ WY
900 SJCT 92582 810-J3
SCHUYLER AV
11100 RIV 92505 714-D7

SCHWARTZ CT
82000 RivC 92274 5590-G2
SCIMITAR WY
76900 PDST 92211 819-D5
SCIOTO CT
1500 BAN 92220 721-D5
SCIROCCO RD
42900 PDST 92211 819-C5
SCOOTER WY
- MURR 92562 927-F3
SCORPIO CIR
2700 RIV 92503 744-G2
SCORPION CANYON DR
33400 RivC 92544 871-C7
33400 RivC 92544 901-C2
SCOT LN
26300 RivC 92544 841-D1
SCOTCH LN
3200 LMLN 92324 647-A5
3200 SBdC 92324 647-A5
SCOTELLA RD
34400 RivC 92592 960-A5
SCOTIA LN
1700 PMSP 92262 756-H6
22700 MORV 92557 717-B2
SCOTT AV
5300 RIV 92504 715-B1
SCOTT LN
26600 MORV 92555 718-A2
SCOTT RD
26000 RivC 92584 898-C1
28000 MURR 92584 898-F1
30600 RivC 92584 899-A1
30600 RivC 92596 899-D1
73600 RivC 92241 728-E3
SCOTT ST
600 BAN 92220 722-E4
2300 SJCT 92582 810-C1
22700 RivC 92324 647-B6
SCOTT WY
22200 RivC 92570 747-B7
SCOTTS LN
500 NRCO 92860 713-G2
SCOTTSDALE DR
16800 RivC 92504 775-J2
SCOTTSDALE RD
16700 RivC 92504 775-J2
17400 RivC 92504 776-A2
SCOTT VICTOR CIR
26000 MORV 92555 717-J1
SCOTTY LN
13100 MORV 92553 717-E4
SCOTTY WY
9400 RivC 92883 804-C3
SCOUT CT
- CYNL 92587 867-B1
E SCOUT CT
2900 ONT 91761 683-A1
SCOUT LN
4700 RIV 92501 685-F3
SCOUT PT
- PER 92571 778-B2
SCOUTS LN
53800 RivC 92539 (934-D5
See Page 904)
SCOVELL AV
100 SJCT 92583 811-A2
400 SJCT 92582 810-J2
400 SJCT 92582 811-A2
SCRIBNER DR
22800 MORV 92553 717-B4
N SCRIVNER ST
100 LKEL 92530 866-D4
S SCRIVNER ST
100 LKEL 92530 866-D5
SCRUB OAK DR
44000 RivC 92536 964-C7
SCRUB OAK RD
55000 RivC 92539 904-F7
SCRUB OAK TR
12900 YCPA 92399 650-E5
SCULLY WY
6600 RivC 92509 645-B6
SEA BISCUIT ST
28000 MORV 92555 718-D5
SEABREEZE CT
- SBdC 92316 645-E2
SEA BREEZE DR
- RivC 92254 (5654-J7
See Page 5594)
- RivC 92254 (5655-A7
See Page 5594)
SEABRIGHT PL
22500 RivC 92567 809-E1
SEABROOK LN
23000 MORV 92557 717-C1
SEACREST CIR
- RivC 92254 (5654-D2
See Page 5594)
SEAFARER WY
23300 MORV 92557 717-C1
SEAFORTHIA PALM DR
26000 RivC 92548 839-A1
S SEAGULL AV
2500 ONT 91761 643-A5
SEA GULL DR
70300 RivC 92254 (5654-E4
See Page 5594)
SEA HORSE CIR
- CYNL 92587 867-E3
SEA HORSE CT
9600 RivC 92509 684-C4
SEAHORSE WY
- RivC 92254 (5654-F5
See Page 5594)

SEA ISLAND CT
- TEM 92591 959-C3
SEA ISLAND LN
40900 PDST 92211 819-D4
SEAL HARBOR CT
- RivC 92595 897-D7
SEA LION CT
- RivC 92595 897-D7
SEAL ROCK CT
800 RivC 92544 811-G5
SEAN CT
10600 RivC 92555 688-D6
SEA PINE DR
29300 RivC 92584 868-G1
SEAPINES CT
1400 BAN 92220 721-E5
SEA PINES CT
37700 MURR 92563 928-J4
SEAPORT CIR
11500 MORV 92557 687-E7
11500 MORV 92557 717-E1
SEARS CT
1100 NRCO 92860 713-F4
SEARSON DR
13500 MORV 92553 717-F5
SEASCAPE AV
98500 RivC 92254 (5654-C3
See Page 5594)
SEASONS RD
44300 RivC 92536 983-J2
SEASONS WY
50800 LQNT 92253 849-G7
SEATON AV
18400 RivC 92570 747-C7
18400 RivC 92570 777-C2
SEATON PL
24100 MORV 92557 717-E1
SEATTLE LN
- RivC 92548 809-G4
- RivC 92567 809-G4
SEATTLE ST
600 HEMT 92545 810-E6
SEATTLE SLEW DR
16500 MORV 92551 747-G4
SEAVIEW DR
200 ImCo 92274 (5773-B7
See Page 5712)
SEA VIEW DR
99200 RivC 92254 (5654-D6
See Page 5594)
SEA VIEW RD
25000 RivC 92548 809-C7
SEA VIEW WY
70100 RivC 92254 (5654-E5
See Page 5594)
SEA VISTA DR
7700 RIV 92508 716-D7
SEAWIND CIR
42600 RivC 92592 960-A6
SEBASTIAN AV
7100 RivC 92509 684-H4
SEBASTIANI CIR
31500 TEM 92591 959-D3
SEBASTIANI WY
43500 PDST 92260 818-G7
SEBRING DR
5200 RivC 92509 684-H3
SECOND ST
900 NRCO 92860 713-E7
900 NRCO 92860 743-B1
3300 COR 92880 743-B1
SECORY ST
39300 HEMT 92543 810-J6
SECRETARIAT CIR
16700 MORV 92551 747-G4
SECRETARIAT DR
16700 MORV 92551 747-G4
SECRET FALLS RD
47700 RivC 92536 982-J7
47700 RivC 92536 983-A7
SECURITY AV
12600 CLTN 92324 645-J5
SECURITY CIR
3000 RivC 91752 643-G5
SEDALIA PL
1500 RIV 92506 716-B2
SEDA VERDE LN
- LQNT 92253 849-J4
SEDCO BLVD
21000 RivC 92530 896-J1
21000 RivC 92530 897-A1
SEDCO HEIGHTS DR
21400 RivC 92595 897-A1
21600 RivC 92595 867-B7
SEDCO VIEW DR
32500 RivC 92595 897-A1
SEDGEWICK AV
3800 RIV 92507 685-J5
5000 RIV 92506 685-J7
SEDLOCK DR
- COR 92881 773-D4
SEDONA CIR
- MURR 92563 928-H4
SEDONA CT
- COAC 92236 5471-A4
- PDST 92211 819-F6
SEDONA DR
- INDO 92201 5410-B7
- INDO 92201 5470-B1
- RIV 92518 746-F3
6800 RivC 92509 645-A7
6800 RivC 92509 685-A1
6900 RivC 92509 684-J1
SEDONA LN
- NRCO 92860 743-E2

SEED LEAF TR
22500 RivC 92595 897-D3
SEELEY AV
8700 RivC 92225 392-B11
8700 RivC 92225 5551-D3
8700 BLY 92225 392-B11
8700 BLY 92225 5551-J2
12200 RivC - 392-B11
12200 RivC - 5551-A3
SEELEY CT
100 RivC 92507 646-E6
SEELEY DR
44700 LQNT 92253 819-G7
44800 LQNT 92253 849-G1
SEELEY ST
15000 RivC 92282 695-G7
15200 RivC 92282 725-G2
SEGA LN
- FONT 92337 645-A2
SEGNER DR
42300 RivC 92544 841-G4
SEGO LN
75000 PDST 92211 818-J5
SEGO PALM LN
45700 INDO 92201 5470-D1
SEGOYA
- BLY 92225 5491-E5
SEGURA CT
73100 PDST 92260 848-E4
SEINE CT
- RivC 92544 811-J5
- RivC 92596 929-C1
SEISER CT
6900 RIV 92506 716-C5
SELBY AV
7600 RivC 92880 712-J2
SELBY CIR
42000 TEM 92591 958-J5
SELDON WY
- CHLS 91709 712-A6
SELECT WY
- SDCo 92028 999-A5
SELGADO CANYON RD
41200 RivC 92544 871-E5
SELINGER TR
42100 RivC 92536 962-D4
SELKIRK AV
10200 RIV 92503 714-F6
SELKIRK DR
200 COR 92881 773-D4
SELLERS RD
33500 RivC 92595 897-C4
SELMA AV
4000 RIV 92503 714-G6
SELROCCO DR
36600 CALI 92320 650-B7
36600 CALI 92320 690-C1
SEMENA ST
- TEM 92592 979-F1
SEMINOLE CT
400 BAN 92220 721-D4
30400 CTHC 92234 787-F1
SEMINOLE DR
- LQNT 92253 5530-D6
48200 BAN 92220 722-J2
48200 RivC 92220 722-J2
48300 RivC 92230 722-J2
48700 RivC 92230 723-A3
SEMINOLE PASG
10300 RIV 92503 744-H1
SEMINOLE RD
4100 PMSP 92264 787-A6
77700 INDW 92210 849-F2
SEMINOLE ST
- TEM 92591 959-C3
300 PMSP 92264 786-F3
SENA CT
- RivC 92276 788-C2
SENA ST
2400 COR 92882 773-B2
SENATOR WY
1300 SJCT 92583 811-C3
SENDERO DEL CHARRO
16700 RivC 92504 746-A4
SENECA CIR
24500 MORV 92553 717-F6
38300 RivC 92592 930-H4
SENECA DR
25400 RivC - 814-E5
SENECA LN
77000 INDW 92210 849-D1
SENECA PASS
10100 RIV 92503 744-H1
SENEGAL CT
81300 INDO 92201 5470-D1
SENEGAL PL
45500 INDO 92201 5470-D1
SENELA CT
30300 TEM 92592 959-B6
SENNA CIR
36100 YCPA 92399 650-E6
SENNA CT
27400 TEM 92591 958-J2
SENNA DR
- RivC 92595 897-G6
SENNA LN
8700 RIV 92508 746-G2
SENOLA AV
21100 RivC 92570 836-J4
21300 RivC 92570 837-A4
SENORA RD
68500 CTHC 92234 757-E7
SEPTEMBER WY
13100 RivC 92503 744-B5

W SEPULVEDA RD
300 PMSP 92262 756-D4
SEPULVEDA WY
5500 RivC 92509 684-J6
5500 RivC 92509 685-A6
SEQUOIA AV
- ONT 91761 643-C5
SEQUOIA CIR
- RivC - (937-C1
See Page 906)
1200 HEMT 92545 840-G3
22300 RivC 92595 897-C4
SEQUOIA DR
1500 BEAU 92223 690-J7
2200 HEMT 92545 840-G3
SEQUOIA DR N
3000 PMSP 92262 756-E4
SEQUOIA DR S
2800 PMSP 92262 756-E4
SEQUOIA LN
41200 RivC 92544 841-D1
SEQUOIA PL
- PMSP 92264 786-F7
SEQUOIA ST
- MURR 92563 928-F7
800 COR 92879 743-E7
4000 RIV 92503 714-H5
SERANO RD
12200 RivC 92220 692-F7
SERAPE CT
13100 YCPA 92399 650-D5
SERAPE DR
36100 YCPA 92399 650-D6
SERAPHINA RD
39200 TEM 92591 929-C7
39200 RivC 92563 929-C7
39800 TEM 92591 959-C1
SERENA CIR
1200 PMSP 92262 756-F6
SERENA CT
- RMIR 92270 817-F3
SERENA DR
200 PDST 92260 818-E5
1000 SJCT 92583 780-J6
SERENA ST
1300 BAN 92220 722-C1
22200 RivC 92570 807-B7
SERENA WY
32800 LKEL 92530 865-H6
SERENADE
35000 RivC 92276 788-H5
SERENADE RDG
22100 MURR 92562 927-B4
SERENADE ST
3600 PER 92571 778-A2
SERENATA CT
49000 LQNT 92253 849-G5
SERENDIPITY RD
5300 RivC 92509 684-B4
12000 DHSP 92240 696-B6
12000 RivC 92240 696-B6
SERENE DR
1000 COR 92880 743-C2
SERENGETI DR
18300 RivC 92562 976-D2
SERENITY LN
15100 RivC 92530 865-G6
SERENITY RD
- CTHC 92234 787-F6
SERENO DR
- TEM 92592 979-G1
SERFAS CLUB DR
300 RivC 92882 742-G6
600 COR 92882 742-F6
600 COR 92880 742-G6
600 RivC 92880 742-G6
SERI CT
5000 RivC 92509 685-D4
SERLET CT
27800 RivC 92584 868-E6
SERPENS CT
25500 RivC 92586 837-J7
SERPENTINE DR
100 RIV 92507 686-F1
900 RivC 92507 686-F1
SERRA DR
25800 MORV 92557 717-H2
SERRAI CT
41200 MURR 92562 927-H3
SERRANA RD
400 PER 92570 807-F1
SERRANO DR
900 COR 92879 743-E3
SERRANO LN
44100 INDO 92201 5410-G7
SERRANO PL
4800 RIV 92504 685-D6
41600 RivC 92544 841-E2
SERRANO ST
12500 YCPA 92399 649-C4
SERRANO WY
- RMIR 92270 818-D2
SERRENO RD
23400 RivC 92590 977-F3
SERRIANO RD
39200 RivC 92544 931-F6
40200 RivC 92544 961-F2
SERVICE CT
1800 RIV 92507 686-A3
SERVICE RD
38500 RMIR 92270 817-J2
SESAME ST
27100 RivC 92544 841-C3
SETON CT
- RMIR 92270 818-B2

STREET Block	City	ZIP	Pg-Grid
SETTING SUN CIR			
16100	RivC	92503	744-C4
SETTING SUN TR			
74000	PDST	92260	848 G2
SETTLERS RDG			
-	MURR	92562	927-E4
SETTLES DR			
200	CTHC	92234	787-E5
SEVEN HILLS DR			
1100	HEMT	92545	840-G3
14100	RivC	92503	745-C4
SEVEN LAKES DR			
4100	PMSP	92264	786-J5
4200	PMSP	92264	787-A5
SEVEN OAKS DR			
39400	MURR	92562	928-D3
67900	CTHC	92234	787-D5
SEVEN OAKS PL			
68000	CTHC	92234	787-D5
SEVENOAKS ST			
6100	CHLS	91709	712-A5
SEVEN OAKS TR			
12900	YCPA	92399	650-E5
SEVEN SPRINGS DR			
73800	RivC	92260	818-F2
SEVEN SPRINGS WY			
16700	RivC	92504	775-J1
17100	RivC	92504	776-A1
SEVENTH ST			
100	NRCO	92860	713-E3
SEVERN WY			
12100	RIV	92503	744-B2
SEVILLE CIR			
100	PDST	92260	818-E6
N SEVILLE CIR			
700	PMSP	92262	756-G7
SEVILLE CT			
-	CTHC	92234	757-D5
SEVILLE DR			
-	RMIR	92270	818-B4
600	HEMT	92543	810-H6
SEVILLE LN			
400	BLY	92225	5491-D5
SEVILLE ST			
-	INDO	92201	5470-H3
W SEVILLE ST			
200	CLTN	92313	646-C3
200	CLTN	92324	646-C3
SEVILLE WY			
7000	RIV	92504	715-F4
SEWELL ST			
-	FONT	92337	644-J2
SEXTON LN			
5600	RivC	92509	685-C3
SEXTON ST			
32700	RivC	92595	897-B7
SEYMOUR ST			
4000	RIV	92505	714-E7
SHABA CIR			
30900	TEM	92592	979-D5
SHADDOCK CIR			
9100	RIV	92508	746-E3
SHADED MEADOW CIR			
22700	RivC	92595	897-D4
SHADED PALM			
-	BLY	-	5491-B7
SHADEL RD			
27000	RivC	92585	838-F5
27000	RivC	92586	838-C5
SHADESCALE DR			
25200	MURR	92563	928-E6
SHADE TREE LN			
3000	RIV	92503	714-J7
3000	RIV	92503	744-J1
SHADE TREE WY			
800	COR	92880	743-C3
E SHADID DR			
3000	CLTN	92324	647-A4
3100	CLTN	92324	646-J4
SHADOW AV			
81700	INDO	92201	5470-D1
SHADOW DR			
11500	FONT	92337	644-A3
SHADOW LN			
42100	RivC	92544	811-F7
SHADOW WY			
43900	RivC	-	5421-B1
SHADOWBROOK ST			
12600	MORV	92553	717-H3
SHADOW CANYON CIR			
2700	NRCO	92860	713-B4
SHADOW CANYON CT			
2700	NRCO	92860	713-B5
SHADOW CREEK			
-	MURR	92562	927-F5
SHADOW CREEK DR			
-	MURR	92563	928-H5
E SHADOW CREEK WY			
3500	ONT	91761	643-C6
SHADOW CREST CIR			
1000	COR	92881	773-E3
SHADOW CREST DR			
27000	CTHC	92234	757-B5
SHADOWFAX TR			
40100	RivC	92544	901-C4
SHADOWGLEN WY			
1300	COR	92882	743-A5
SHADOW GROVE CT			
7400	RivC	92881	773-H3
SHADOW HILL DR			
2200	RIV	92506	715-J1
SHADOW HILLS RD			
46100	RivC	92536	983-F5
74500	PDST	92260	848-H1
SHADOW LAKE DR			
73700	PDST	92260	848-F2
SHADOWMARK LN			
12000	MORV	92555	718-A2
SHADOW MOUNTAIN DR			
45600	PDST	92260	848-E2
SHADOW MOUNTAIN LN			
15400	RivC	92530	865-H6
15600	LKEL	92530	865-H6
30000	RivC	92276	789-A2
SHADOW MOUNTAIN WY			
41200	RivC	92544	841-E3
SHADOW OAKS CIR			
400	COR	92879	743-G4
SHADOW OAKS DR			
25600	RivC	-	(813-H6 See Page 782)
SHADOWOOD ST			
6900	RIV	92506	716-D5
SHADOW PALM AV			
81800	INDO	92201	5470-E1
SHADOW PALM WY			
41200	RivC	92544	841-E3
SHADOW RIDGE LN			
22700	MORV	92557	687-B5
SHADOW RIDGE RD			
-	PDST	92211	788-E7
SHADOW SPRINGS DR			
9500	MORV	92557	687-B4
SHADOW VALLEY DR			
18300	RivC	92881	773-H1
SHADOW VALLEY LN			
38400	RivC	92399	650-F7
SHADOW VALLEY RD			
-	RivC	92276	788-J5
-	RivC	92276	789-A5
SHADOW VIEW CT			
39500	TEM	92591	958-J1
SHADOW VISTA			
-	PDST	92260	848-E5
SHADWELL CIR			
-	LQNT	92253	819-J7
-	LQNT	92253	5410-A7
SHADY CIR			
19100	RIV	92508	746-D3
SHADY CT			
-	INDO	92201	5470-D4
38300	RivC	92399	650-F7
SHADY LN			
28500	MURR	92563	928-G1
28700	RivC	92596	839-C7
41800	RivC	92544	841-E1
51000	COAC	92236	5471-C7
52300	COAC	92236	5531-C1
54000	RivC	92274	5531-C4
SHADYBEND DR			
12500	MORV	92553	717-C3
SHADY BROOK CIR			
-	MURR	92563	928-F7
SHADY BROOK DR			
28600	RivC	92584	868-F1
SHADYBROOK LN			
600	COR	92879	743-J3
SHADY BROOK RD			
-	CALI	92320	689-H2
SHADY CREEK			
-	RivC	92590	978-E1
SHADYDALE LN			
5000	RivC	92880	742-B5
SHADY GLADE RD			
10900	MORV	92557	687-D6
SHADY GLEN CT			
23300	MORV	92557	717-D1
SHADY GLEN LN			
2400	SBDO	92408	646-J1
SHADY GLEN ST			
-	MURR	92563	928-F7
SHADY GROVE DR			
100	RIV	92507	686-E4
SHADY LANE CT			
26300	RivC	92584	898-B2
SHADY MAPLE RD			
-	MURR	92563	928-J4
SHADY MILL RD			
1100	COR	92882	773-A1
SHADY OAK CT			
-	MURR	92563	928-F7
SHADY OAK DR			
400	COR	92882	773-C2
SHADY OAKS DR			
1400	PER	92571	807-J1
1500	PER	92571	777-J7
SHADY OAKS LN			
47200	RivC	92592	999-F1
SHADY PALMS CIR			
33800	RivC	92276	788-F4
SHADY PINE CT			
25300	MURR	92563	928-E2
SHADY RIDGE CIR			
24100	MORV	92557	687-E5
SHADY ROCK DR			
-	RivC	92503	744-D5
SHADY SIDE LN			
18000	RivC	92504	745-J7
SHADY VIEW DR			
17800	CHLS	91709	712-B6
25800	RivC	-	814-F6
48600	PDST	92260	848-E5
SHADY VIEW ST			
10000	RIV	92503	744-H1
SHADYWOOD ST			
26000	RivC	92586	838-A4
SHAFFER CT			
12700	MORV	92553	717-D3
SHAFFER ST			
800	COR	92879	743-F3
SHAGBARK RD			
10900	MORV	92557	687-F6
SHAIN CIR			
3000	COR	92881	773-D3
SHAKER DR			
5800	RIV	92506	716-B2
SHAKESPEARE CT			
-	RMIR	92270	818-D5
21300	MORV	92557	716-H1
SHAKESPEARE DR			
1200	RIV	92506	716-C4
SHALE CIR			
200	COR	92882	743-B4
44800	TEM	92592	979-G3
SHALER ST			
43100	RivC	92544	811-H6
SHALIMAR PL			
2800	RIV	92504	715-C6
SHALU AV			
25600	MORV	92557	717-H1
SHAMBLIN CT			
2600	RIV	92504	715-F4
6700	RIV	92506	715-F4
SHAMEL CT			
5100	RIV	92505	714-C6
SHAMEL ASH DR			
25200	MORV	92551	747-H2
SHAMOUTI DR			
9200	RIV	92508	746-E4
SHAMROCK			
37700	RivC	92539	(934-G2 See Page 904)
SHAMROCK AV			
3800	RIV	92501	685-H1
SHAMROCK ST			
1000	COR	92880	743-B2
SHAMROCK WY			
4100	HEMT	92544	811-F6
E SHAMROCK VIEW DR			
24100	RivC	92548	809-G4
W SHAMROCK VIEW DR			
33500	RivC	92548	809-G5
SHANA CT			
800	PER	92570	807-F1
SHANA PL			
900	SJCT	92583	811-D3
SHANDWICK CIR			
-	COR	92882	773-A3
S SHANE DR			
2600	CLTN	92324	647-A5
SHANE LN			
35500	CALI	92320	690-A3
SHANGRI LN			
34700	YCPA	92399	649-J2
SHANNON CIR			
25600	RivC	92544	(812-A7 See Page 782)
SHANNON DR			
34900	RivC	92545	840-A1
SHANNON LN			
28800	MURR	92563	928-G2
SHANNON RD			
6400	RIV	92504	715-A1
SHANNON ST			
200	BLY	92225	5491-E5
3500	COR	92881	773-G5
SHANNON WY			
-	PMSP	92262	756-F5
SHAQUILE ST			
-	COR	92882	773-B2
SHARK ST			
400	PER	92571	807-J1
SHARON AV			
9600	RIV	92503	714-G5
SHARON RD			
1800	PMSP	92262	756-G6
SHARON ST			
19700	RivC	92570	836-F7
19700	LKEL	92532	836-F7
SHARON WY			
5700	RivC	92509	684-J4
9400	CALI	92320	690-A3
29800	RivC	92584	868-J7
SHARON ANN LN			
20300	RivC	92570	777-E4
SHARONDALE RD			
9400	CALI	92320	690-A3
SHARONKNOLL CT			
35600	CALI	92320	690-A3
SHAROSE DR			
40400	RivC	92544	841-C2
SHARP DR			
25600	RivC	92544	811-H6
SHARP RD			
21600	RivC	92570	807-A7
43700	RivC	92536	963-C7
43700	RivC	92536	983-C1
SHARP ST			
-	RivC	91752	643-E7
SHARPLESS RD			
68300	CTHC	92234	817-E2
SHARRON WY			
36000	YCPA	92399	650-C6
SHASTA CIR			
-	COR	92881	773-D4
SHASTA DR			
-	COR	92881	773-D4
44100	RivC	-	5421-B1
SHASTA LN			
-	COR	92881	773-D4
77000	INDW	92210	849-D1
SHASTA PL			
2300	SJCT	92583	811-E5
12300	MORV	92557	717-H2
32200	RivC	92276	788-E2
SHASTA ST			
34800	YCPA	92399	649-J2
34900	YCPA	92399	650-A2
SHASTA WY			
500	HEMT	92543	840-H1
600	BEAU	92223	690-J7
3600	RIV	92506	715-F1
SHATTO PL			
4400	RIV	92506	715-E1
SHAUGNESSY DR			
-	INDO	92201	5470-A1
SHAUNA CHARMAIN LN			
26000	RivC	92584	898-A4
26000	RivC	92595	898-A4
SHAVER ST			
200	SJCT	92583	811-B3
SHAW CT			
22700	RivC	92570	837-C3
SHAW ST			
-	MURR	92562	958-C3
SHAWNA DR			
29000	MURR	92563	898-H7
29000	RivC	92563	898-H7
SHAWNEE AV			
8800	RIV	92503	715-B6
SHAWNEE CIR			
76100	INDW	92210	849-B1
SHAWNEE CT			
69300	CTHC	92234	787-F1
SHAWNEE DR			
3300	NRCO	92860	713-B6
SHAWNEE RD			
300	PER	92570	807-D3
SHAY LN			
32400	RivC	92595	897-A5
SHAYNNA CIR			
33300	TEM	92592	979-H3
SHEARER LN			
15300	RivC	92504	745-E6
SHEBA WY			
76500	PDST	92211	819-C6
SHEEHAN CIR			
1800	BAN	92220	721-D6
SHEEHAN DR			
43300	RivC	92201	819-G6
SHEETS LN			
20000	RivC	92595	896-H5
SHEFFIELD AV			
5500	RIV	92506	716-A2
SHEFFIELD CT			
22700	RivC	92595	897-D2
76900	PDST	92211	819-C2
SHEFFIELD DR			
12100	MORV	92557	717-B2
SHEFFIELD RD			
11400	FONT	92337	644-F3
SHEFFIELD ST			
27300	RivC	92544	841-F3
SHEILA CIR			
-	RivC	92254	(5653-H4 See Page 5592)
SHEILA LN			
32700	RivC	92595	896-J6
SHEILA ST			
15300	MORV	92551	747-G1
SHELBURNE LN			
1600	RIV	92506	716-B4
SHELBY DR			
3800	RIV	92504	715-A3
SHELDON CT			
44000	TEM	92592	978-J1
SHELL DR			
72400	RivC	92254	(5654-G5 See Page 5594)
SHELLEY CIR			
-	COR	92880	742-J1
SHELLEY ST			
35600	YCPA	92399	650-B6
SHELLEY WY			
3500	RIV	92503	714-J6
SHELLICIA CIR			
4200	RivC	92509	685-A2
SHELLIE LN			
40600	RivC	92544	841-C2
SHELLY CT			
16800	FONT	92337	644-J1
SHELLY LN			
700	HEMT	92543	841-B2
SHELTER DR			
31700	RivC	92276	788-C2
SHELTON DR			
15100	RivC	92570	775-F4
SHENANDOAH AV			
80800	INDO	92201	5470-C1
SHENANDOAH CT			
30400	TEM	92591	959-B4
SHENANDOAH DR			
-	HEMT	92545	840-E3
SHENANDOAH RD			
1800	COR	92879	743-H3
2700	RIV	92506	715-H2
SHENANDOAH WY			
7500	RivC	92509	684-H5
SHEPARD DR			
100	CTHC	92234	787-E5
SHEPARD CREST DR			
800	COR	92882	773-B4
SHEPARDSON DR			
24600	LMLN	92354	647-B1
SHEPHERD LN			
-	PDST	92211	818-G1
43800	RivC	92539	(965-B7 See Page 964)
SHEPPARD ST			
6000	RIV	92504	685-A7
SHERBORN ST			
17600	COR	92879	743-H6
SHERBROOKE LN			
31800	RivC	92584	869-A6
SHERI LN			
21800	RivC	92595	897-B2
SHERIDAN CIR			
1600	COR	92882	743-C7
SHERIDAN CT			
-	YCPA	92399	649-E2
6200	RIV	92504	685-C7
SHERIDAN RD			
26900	RivC	92241	390-D7
N SHERIDAN ST			
100	COR	92882	743-D4
100	COR	92880	743-D4
S SHERIDAN ST			
200	COR	92882	743-C6
SHERIE CT			
400	BEAU	92223	720-H1
N SHERIFF AV			
100	SJCT	92583	811-B1
S SHERIFF AV			
100	SJCT	92583	811-B2
SHERMAN AV			
22000	MORV	92553	717-A5
N SHERMAN AV			
100	COR	92882	743-A4
S SHERMAN AV			
100	COR	92882	743-A5
SHERMAN DR			
3900	RIV	92503	714-J4
3900	RIV	92503	715-A5
53200	RivC	-	814-A5
SHERMAN RD			
1500	PER	92585	808-D6
2800	PER	92585	838-D1
3000	PER	92571	778-C4
20400	RivC	92571	778-C4
24000	RivC	92585	808-D4
25600	RivC	92585	838-D3
27500	RivC	92586	838-D5
30000	RivC	92584	868-D4
SHERMAN WY			
38100	RivC	92539	(935-D2 See Page 904)
64200	RivC	92240	696-D5
SHERRY CIR			
39000	CTHC	92234	817-D3
SHERRY DR			
2900	HEMT	92545	810-F5
SHERRY LN			
7800	RivC	92509	684-G1
34700	YCPA	92399	649-J6
SHERWIN CT			
13600	MORV	92555	718-B4
S SHERWIN CREEK PL			
2600	ONT	91761	643-C7
SHERWOOD CIR			
26300	MORV	92555	717-J2
26300	MORV	92555	718-A2
SHERWOOD CT			
11300	FONT	92337	644-D2
SHERWOOD DR			
33100	RivC	92530	865-G6
44700	INDO	92201	5410-E7
SHERWOOD PL			
8100	RIV	92504	715-B4
SHERWOOD RD			
-	RMIR	92270	788-B5
SHERWOOD UNION LN			
-	MURR	92563	928-H6
SHERYL AV			
74800	PDST	92260	818-H6
74900	PDST	92211	818-H6
SHERYL LN			
15700	MORV	92551	747-F2
SHETLAND CIR			
-	NRCO	92860	713-H7
SHETLAND LN			
4400	RivC	92509	684-E1
48900	RivC	92536	963-C4
SHICALI CT			
31100	TEM	92592	979-D5
SHIDAY CT			
23100	MORV	92553	717-C4
SHIELD LN			
22400	RivC	92567	779-H7
22400	RivC	92567	809-J1
SHIELDS RD			
46000	INDO	92201	5470-B3
SHIELLS AV			
2700	RivC	92509	645-B6
SHIFTING SANDS TR			
32000	CTHC	92234	787-D4
SHILOH DR			
-	RivC	92567	808-H2
SHINING STAR LN			
3200	COR	92881	773-E4
SHINNECOCK DR			
600	BAN	92220	721-C4
SHINNECOCK HILLS			
-	LQNT	92253	5530-D6
SHIPEK CT			
-	RivC	92596	929-E4
SHIRAY RANCH RD			
12600	MORV	92553	717-G3
SHIRE LN			
5100	RivC	92509	684-B3
SHIRE PL			
-	NRCO	92860	743-J1
SHIREBOURN RD			
13000	MORV	92553	717-G4
SHIRLEE RD			
67600	CTHC	92234	787-C6
SHIRLEON DR			
42200	RivC	92220	721-F7
SHIRLEY CIR			
-	INDO	92201	5470-F5
W SHIRLEY CT			
100	CLTN	92324	646-C4
SHIRLEY DR			
-	LKEL	92530	865-H3
1600	COR	92882	743-C7
SHIRLEY LN			
300	NRCO	92860	713-H3
SHIRLEY ST			
9900	RIV	92503	714-G7
SHIRLEY WY			
42500	RivC	92536	961-H6
SHOAL DR			
-	RivC	92254	(5654-G5 See Page 5594)
SHOAL CREEK			
79600	LQNT	92253	5530-A3
SHOALCREEK DR			
-	COR	92883	773-H7
SHOAL CREEK DR			
38200	MURR	92562	927-D4
SHOAL CREEK ST			
400	BAN	92220	721-D4
SHOEMAKER DR			
21200	RivC	92595	897-C6
SHOEMAKER RD			
1700	RIV	92506	716-A1
SHOOK LN			
45300	RivC	92536	982-A4
SHOOTERS HILL RD			
-	TEM	92592	959-H7
SHOOTING STAR DR			
23000	MURR	92562	927-E3
SHOOTING STAR LN			
-	COR	92882	773-A3
SHOPPERS LN			
-	RMIR	92270	788-D4
74400	PDST	92211	788-D4
SHORB ST			
15500	RivC	92508	746-C2
E SHORE LN			
35500	CTHC	92234	787-E6
N SHORE LN			
68500	CTHC	92234	787-E6
S SHORE LN			
68500	CTHC	92234	787-E6
SHORECLIFF CT			
14800	LKEL	92530	865-F2
SHORECLIFF DR			
29300	LKEL	92530	865-F2
SHORE CREST TER			
10200	MORV	92557	687-D5
SHOREHAM AV			
24700	MORV	92553	717-F7
SHORELINE DR			
1400	LKEL	92530	865-J7
30100	RivC	92584	868-F2
SHOREPINE CT			
3000	RIV	92504	715-C5
SHORE RIDGE DR			
30600	RivC	92584	868-G4
SHOREVIEW CT			
22300	RivC	92595	897-C3
SHOREVIEW DR			
2200	COR	92879	743-J3
SHOREWOOD CT			
41800	TEM	92591	958-H4
SHORT ST			
-	RivC	92518	747-D1
1100	PER	92570	807-G4
2300	RIV	92503	744-H3
2300	RivC	92503	744-H3
16500	RivC	92555	749-G3
17200	RivC	92530	896-B3
53600	RivC	92536	(984-C1 See Page 964)
SHORTCUT TR			
48300	RivC	92536	983-B3
SHORT HALL RD			
58800	RivC	92539	(935-E5 See Page 904)
SHORTRIDGE AV			
21200	RivC	92570	776-J2
SHORTY WY			
3000	PMSP	92262	786-H1
SHOSHONE AV			
3100	RIV	92503	744-H2
SHOSHONE CT			
49900	RivC	92536	963-E5
SHOSHONE DR			
76300	INDW	92210	849-B1
SHOSHONEAN TR			
-	PMSP	92264	786-G6
SHOSHONEE DR			
24700	MURR	92562	928-C4
SHOTGUN TRAIL RD			
13300	RivC	92883	835-B3
SHOWALTER RD			
43000	TEM	92592	959-B7
SHOWCASE PKWY			
-	INDO	92203	5410-F5
SHOWDOWN LN			
11200	MORV	92557	687-C7
SHOWUT AV			
22800	RivC	92595	897-D7
SHREEDER PL			
23500	RivC	92587	837-E7
SHRIER DR			
17000	LKEL	92530	866-A3
SHRIMP LN			
32800	RivC	92596	899-F7
SHRIMP RD			
36100	RivC	92596	899-F7
SHUBERT ST			
-	MORV	92555	718-F3
SHUGART WY			
2700	RivC	92503	744-F3
SHUIS CIR			
35200	RivC	92595	897-D6
SHULER LN			
42800	RivC	92536	961-H5
SHUMWAY RANCH RD			
-	RivC	-	(907-J1 See Page 906)
SHUTES CIR			
28200	RivC	92584	898-F1
SIAMESE PL			
6400	RIV	92505	714-B3
SIDANA RD			
13300	YCPA	92399	650-A6
SIDELINE RD			
29300	RivC	92563	898-H7
SIDEWINDER RD			
40200	RivC	92544	871-C7
40200	RivC	92544	901-D1
SIDMOUTH CT			
37000	HEMT	92545	810-D7
SIDNEY CIR			
33600	RivC	92596	899-H3
SIDNEY ST			
1800	BAN	92220	722-B1
3400	RIV	92503	715-A6
3500	RIV	92503	714-J6
SIECK RD			
500	RIV	92501	646-A6
SIEGAL AV			
20200	RIV	92508	746-E1
SIEGFRIED LN			
10200	BLY	92225	5491-E4
SIENA			
-	INDW	92210	819-A6
SIENA CT			
-	LQNT	92253	819-G7
69500	CTHC	92234	787-G6
SIENA DR			
-	RivC	92201	819-H5
-	TEM	92592	979-F2
44400	PDST	92260	818-H7
44400	PDST	92260	848-H1
SIERRA AV			
2400	RivC	92509	645-A4
2400	NRCO	92860	713-E4
10700	FONT	92337	644-J3
10900	SBdC	92337	644-J3
11500	FONT	92337	645-A4
81700	INDO	92201	5470-D1
SIERRA BLVD			
12000	DHSP	92282	695-G6
12200	RivC	92282	695-G6
SIERRA CT			
35600	YCPA	92399	650-B2
SIERRA DR			
1300	SJCT	92583	780-J6
22400	RivC	92262	725-F7
23800	RivC	92587	837-F7
SIERRA LN			
27500	MURR	92562	898-E7
35600	YCPA	92399	650-B2
SIERRA ST			
4500	RIV	92504	715-B2
4500	RIV	92506	715-C2
49000	COAC	92236	5470-J4
SIERRA TR			
23000	CYNL	92587	867-D1
SIERRA VW			
-	PDST	92260	848-E5
SIERRA WY			
900	PMSP	92264	786-E6
SIERRA BELLO CT			
25500	MORV	92551	747-H4
SIERRA BONITA			
31200	TEM	92592	959-C7
SIERRA BRAVO CT			
25500	MORV	92551	747-H4
SIERRA CADIZ CT			
25500	MORV	92551	747-H4
SIERRA CALMO CT			
25500	MORV	92551	747-H4
SIERRA CROSS WY			
5100	RivC	92509	685-D3
SIERRA DEL LEON			
2600	COR	92882	742-F7
SIERRA DEL SOL			
27000	RivC	92276	758-E6
30000	RivC	92276	788-E2
SIERRA DE RONDA			
1400	PMSP	92264	786-F6
40400	RivC	92562	927-B7
40400	RivC	92562	957-B1
SIERRA ELENA RD			
20200	RivC	92562	956-H4
SIERRA ESPADAN RD			
1800	PER	92571	777-J7
SIERRA GLEN DR			
11800	RIV	92505	714-A5
SIERRA LA VIDA			
-	RivC	92563	958-J1
SIERRA LEONE CT			
25500	MORV	92551	747-H3
SIERRA LINDA ST			
31300	YCPA	92399	649-A4
SIERRA MADRE N			
-	PDST	92260	818-F4
SIERRA MADRE S			
300	PDST	92260	818-F5
SIERRA MADRE DR			
2300	PMSP	92264	786-E7
2700	PMSP	92264	816-E1
30100	TEM	92591	959-A1
39100	RivC	92563	928-J7
39100	RivC	92563	958-J1
SIERRA MADRE WY			
-	RMIR	92270	818-B3
200	COR	92881	773-D3
SIERRA MARIA RD			
40200	RivC	92562	956-H2
SIERRA MESA CIR			
13800	MORV	92553	717-A5
SIERRA MESA RD			
40200	RivC	92562	956-G5
SIERRA OAK DR			
23600	MURR	92562	927-H3
SIERRA RIDGE DR			
-	RIV	92507	716-G3
SIERRA SENECA DR			
1200	SJCT	92583	781-A6
SIERRA SOTO RD			
20100	RivC	92562	956-H3
SIERRA THERESA RD			
-	RivC	92562	956-H7
SIERRA TREE LN			
10900	RIV	92505	714-C4
SIERRA VERDE RD			
23200	RivC	92548	809-B3
SIERRA VISTA			
-	LQNT	92253	849-J1
SIERRA VISTA AV			
-	RIV	92505	714-C7
SIERRA VISTA DR			
11200	LMLN	92354	647-A2
72700	PDST	92260	818-D7
72800	PDST	92260	848-E1
SIERRA VISTA LN			
13300	MORV	92553	716-J4
SIERRA VISTA RD			
35300	YCPA	92399	650-A5
55700	RivC	92539	904-G7
SIERRA VISTA ST			
400	COR	92882	743-B5
4900	RIV	92505	714-B5
SIESTA CT			
39300	HEMT	92543	810-J5
SIESTA LN			
11400	RivC	92883	804-G5
SIESTA TR			
-	PMSP	92264	787-B7
73400	PDST	92260	848-F4
SIEVERT WY			
12900	YCPA	92399	649-F5
SIGNAL CT			
37900	RivC	92211	819-G1
SIGNATURE DR			
-	COR	92883	773-G7
-	COR	92883	803-H1
SIGNATURE ST			
9200	RivC	92509	644-D7
SILAS PHELPS DR			
-	RivC	92880	683-D4
SILENT CIR			
1000	COR	92880	743-C2
SILENT CREEK RD			
25100	MORV	92553	717-G5
SILENT VALLEY RD			
46600	RivC	92536	983-B6
SILICA CT			
1200	HEMT	92543	840-H3
SILICO RD			
58800	RivC	92539	(935-E4 See Page 904)
SILK ST			
-	FONT	92337	645-A1
SILK OAK DR			
8600	RIV	92508	746-E2
SILKTASSEL RD			
20300	RIV	92508	746-G2
SILKTREE CT			
40000	PDST	92260	818-E3
SILK TREE DR			
-	FONT	92337	644-D3
SILKTREE DR			
39100	MURR	92563	928-F4
SILK TREE LN			
43100	PDST	92260	818-H6
SILKTREE PL			
1100	COR	92879	743-J6
SILKWOOD CT			
23400	MURR	92562	927-J1
SILKWOOD DR			
900	COR	92882	742-F5
SILKY PASS			
44600	TEM	92592	979-G2
SILO CIR			
24400	RivC	92595	897-G2
SILO ST			
-	RIV	92508	746-D2
-	RivC	92508	746-D2
SILVER CIR			
-	RMIR	92270	787-H7
SILVER CT			
27300	RivC	92584	868-D4
SILVER LN			
13300	MORV	92553	717-H4
47900	PDST	92260	848-F4
SILVER RUN			
11000	MORV	92557	687-D7
SILVER ST			
100	LKEL	92530	866-D4
SILVERADO AV			
4700	BAN	92220	721-E5
SILVERADO CIR			
2100	PMSP	92264	786-F6
SILVERADO CT			
13200	RivC	92883	835-B5
SILVERADO LN			
45400	TEM	92592	979-B4
SILVERADO MTWY			
-	OrCo	-	803-B7
SILVERADO PL			
7900	RIV	92503	714-G4
S SILVERADO CREEK PL			
2600	ONT	91761	643-C6
SILVER ARROW DR			
25100	MORV	92553	717-G5
SILVERBERRY CT			
24600	MURR	92562	928-D3
SILVERBERRY ST			
-	LQNT	92253	5470-A4
SILVERBIRCH RD			
16300	MORV	92551	747-G3
SILVER BREEZE CT			
-	MURR	92563	928-H4
SILVER BULLET WY			
24300	MURR	92562	927-H6
SILVER CANYON LN			
44200	PDST	92260	818-G7
SILVER CLOUD CIR			
3600	NRCO	92860	713-C4
SILVER CLOUD CT			
27500	RivC	92883	835-C5
SILVER CLOUD DR			
3400	NRCO	92860	713-C4
SILVER CREEK CIR			
44000	INDW	92210	819-E7
SILVERCREEK RD			
900	COR	92882	773-B2
SILVERCREST LN			
19700	RIV	92508	746-E2
SILVER DEW DR			
28900	HEMT	92543	841-B6
28900	RivC	92543	841-B6
SILVER DOLLAR ST			
22400	RivC	92883	804-C2
SILVER EAGLE CIR			
1100	COR	92881	773-E4
SILVER FALLS DR			
29000	RivC	92584	838-G7
SILVERFERN LN			
900	COR	92880	743-B2
SILVER FIR DR			
53400	RivC	-	814-B6
SILVER FOX CT			
38000	MURR	92562	927-C3
SILVER HAWK WY			
23300	MURR	92562	927-E3
SILVER HILLS DR			
7800	RIV	92506	715-H7
SILVER LAKE TER			
-	RivC	92203	789-G7
-	RivC	92211	789-G7
SILVER LAKES AV			
400	BAN	92220	721-D4
SILVERLEAF CIR			
400	COR	92882	773-C2
10500	MORV	92557	687-E6
SILVERLEAF CT			
-	RivC	92211	789-F6
73100	PDST	92260	848-E5
SILVERLEAF LN			
6800	RIV	92506	716-D5
26600	RivC	92544	841-H2
SILVERLEAF WY			
-	MURR	92562	927-F4
SILVER MAPLE LN			
32600	LKEL	92530	896-G4
SILVER MOON TR			
17000	RivC	92241	727-F2
48600	RivC	92536	963-B6
73400	PDST	92260	848-F4
SILVER OAK CIR			
-	RivC	92563	929-A7
2300	COR	92882	773-A1
2300	PMSP	92264	786-G4
SILVER OAK DR			
-	MURR	92563	928-H7
2200	COR	92882	773-A1
SILVER OAK PL			
6700	RIV	92506	716-D4
SILVER OAK WY			
1800	HEMT	92545	840-G3
SILVER PALM DR			
30800	RivC	92548	839-B1
SILVER RIDGE CT			
30100	TEM	92591	959-A1
SILVER ROCK RD			
-	HEMT	92545	810-D6
SILVER-RUN CIR			
21700	RivC	92595	897-B4
SILVER SADDLE CT			
30000	CYNL	92587	867-B3
E SILVER SADDLE ST			
2800	ONT	91761	643-A7
SILVER SAGE DR			
78000	RivC	92211	789-F7
SILVER SAGE WY			
33200	RivC	92595	897-D2
SILVER SANDS CIR			
30500	RivC	92584	868-F3
SILVER SANDS PKWY			
74000	PDST	92260	818-G4
SILVER SPRINGS LN			
-	NRCO	92860	713-H7
-	NRCO	92860	743-H1
SILVER SPRINGS PL			
-	NRCO	92860	713-J7
SILVER SPRINGS RD			
42800	RivC	92544	931-H5
SILVER SPUR AV			
11400	FONT	92337	644-F3
SILVER SPUR LN			
21300	RivC	92595	897-C6
72300	RMIR	92270	818-D4
SILVER SPUR RD			
-	PDST	92260	848-C6
15600	RivC	92504	745-F4
SILVERSPUR RD			
36500	RivC	92592	960-E7
SILVER SPUR TR			
47700	PDST	92260	848-F4
SILVER SPUR WY			
-	NRCO	92860	743-G1
SILVER STAR CT			
16700	RivC	92506	745-H2
SILVER STAR DR			
2000	BAN	92220	721-H2
SILVER STIRRUP DR			
27600	RivC	92883	835-B6
SILVER STONE RD			
3500	PER	92571	778-C2
SILVER STRIKE DR			
23400	CYNL	92587	867-E3
SILVER TIP LN			
55400	RivC	-	814-F5
SILVERTON CT			
10900	RivC	92881	774-G4
SILVERTREE RD			
14800	MORV	92553	717-F7
SILVERWOOD CIR			
1900	COR	92881	773-F1
SILVERWOOD CT			
44000	RivC	92544	902-B3
SILVERWOOD DR			
-	RivC	92880	713-A1
43800	RivC	92201	5410-C6
SILVERWOOD LN			
24100	MORV	92553	717-E7
SILVERWOOD ST			
-	MURR	92562	927-F5
SILVESTRE CT			
700	COR	92879	743-F1
SIMI CT			
41000	TEM	92591	959-D3
SIMMEI ST			
2100	RivC	92570	777-B6
SIMMONS AV			
3800	RIV	92505	744-D2
SIMMONS WY			
26500	RivC	92544	841-D2
SIMMS RD			
100	PMSP	92262	756-D4
SIMON DR			
78600	LQNT	92253	849-G2
SIMON WY			
32500	RivC	92548	809-E5
SIMPKINS RD			
21600	RivC	92570	807-A7
SIMPSON AV			
400	HEMT	92543	840-J1
SIMPSON RD			
29000	RivC	92585	838-H6
29200	RivC	92584	838-H6
30200	RivC	92584	839-A6
30200	RivC	92585	839-A6
30500	RivC	92596	839-G6
33600	RivC	92545	839-G6
34500	RivC	92596	840-A6
34500	RivC	92545	840-A6
39500	HEMT	92543	841-A5
SIMS ST			
200	BAN	92220	721-J2
SINAI CIR			
200	COR	92881	773-D3
SINALOA ST			
24500	MORV	92557	717-F2
SINCLAIR AV			
5800	RIV	92505	714-E3
SINCLAIR PL			
28500	RivC	92544	841-E5
SINCLAIR ST			
-	PER	92571	777-G3
600	PER	92571	778-A3
11700	MORV	92555	718-G2
SING RD			
-	RivC	92220	651-F7
SINGER ST			
24600	MORV	92557	717-F2
SINGINGBIRD LN			
17000	RivC	92504	775-J1
17000	RivC	92504	776-A1
SINGING FALLS DR			
35700	RivC	92592	900-F5
SINGING HILLS DR			
4800	BAN	92220	721-D6
SINGING PALMS DR			
78500	LQNT	92253	849-G2
SINGING WOOD DR			
2900	COR	92882	773-B2
SINGING WOOD LN			
29500	RivC	92586	868-B2
SINGLE OAK DR			
28700	TEM	92590	958-G7
SINGLE OAK WY			
-	MURR	92562	927-E5

STREET Block City ZIP Pg-Grid

SINGLETON CT
26800 RivC 92584 898-C2
SINGLETON DR
- RLTO 92316 645-H3
SINGLETON RD
35000 CALI 92320 689-J3
35300 CALI 92320 690-A3
SINGLETON WY
10000 RIV 92503 714-F5
SINGLETREE LN
16300 RivC 92506 745-H2
SINSONTE CIR
1200 COR 92882 773-A2
SIOUX CIR
400 BAN 92220 721-G4
10100 RIV 92503 744-H1
SIOUX DR
500 PER 92570 807-E3
77300 INDW 92210 849-E2
SIR BARTON WY
16500 MORV 92551 747-G4
SIR BEDIVERE DR
1500 RIV 92507 686-G1
SIR DAMAS DR
2400 RIV 92507 686-B3
SIRE CIR
4600 RivC 92509 684-D1
SIR GALAHAD DR
1400 RIV 92507 686-B3
SIR GAWAIN DR
1500 RIV 92507 686-G1
SIRIUS WY
11200 RivC 91752 683-H4
SIROCCO AV
81200 RivC 92201 5410-C7
81500 INDO 92201 5410-D7
SIR TRISTAM DR
1400 RIV 92507 686-B3
SISKEN CT
23000 GTER 92313 646-G3
SISKIYOU CIR
3400 RivC 92503 744-B4
SISKIYOU LN
2000 COR 92879 743-H3
SITTON PEAK TKTR
- RivC 92562 408-K2
SIVAT DR
- PDST 92260 848-B7
SIWANOY DR
9600 RivC 92240 696-E1
SIXTH ST
- NRCO 92860 713-G3
SKAGGS RD
36400 RivC 92544 902-B7
SKEEN CT
28200 RivC 92585 838-E6
SKEITH WY
43300 RivC 92590 958-C7
43300 RivC 92590 978-C1
SKINNER DR
32800 RivC 92596 899-F4
SKIPJACK DR
30000 CYNL 92587 867-G3
SKIPPER RD
27300 MURR 92563 928-G3
SKIPPERS WAY DR
30000 CYNL 92587 867-F3
SKI VIEW DR
67200 RivC - (937-C2 See Page 906)
SKOFSTAD ST
3800 RIV 92505 744-E1
SKOKIE CT
28500 RivC 92586 838-A6
SKOV ST
39000 HEMT 92543 810-J5
SKUNK ST
25400 RivC 92548 809-C7
SKY DR
21900 RivC 92567 778-H7
22200 RivC 92567 808-H1
SKY LN
10000 RivC 92223 690-G4
SKY WY
68300 CTHC 92234 817-D2
SKYBIRD LN
23800 RivC 92883 804-G5
SKY BLUE WATER TR
31000 CTHC 92234 787-D3
SKY BREEZE CT
22300 MURR 92562 927-C5
SKYBROOK ST
25500 MORV 92553 717-H3
SKY CANYON DR
37100 RivC 92563 929-A4
39200 RivC 92563 928-J7
SKY COUNTRY DR
11000 RivC 91752 683-H5
SKYCREST DR
16700 RivC 92504 745-H3
SKYCREST RD
- RivC 92211 789-H7
SKY CREST TR
50600 RivC 92536 983-G2
52200 RivC 92536 (984-A2 See Page 964)
SKYE DR
2100 RIV 92506 715-G5
SKY HARBOR WY
49300 RivC 92536 963-D2
SKYHAWK LN
32700 RivC 92584 898-A1
SKYHAWK PL
7000 RIV 92506 716-B5

SKY HIGH DR
38800 MURR 92562 927-C5
SKYHILL PL
21600 RivC 92570 775-C7
21600 RivC 92570 805-D1
SKYLAND DR
- RivC - (907-C2 See Page 906)
24600 MORV 92557 687-F7
SKYLANE DR
3400 RivC 92509 645-A7
SKYLAR WY
- INDO 92201 5470-F5
SKYLARK CIR
2100 COR 92882 773-C1
SKYLARK DR
3600 RIV 92505 744-E1
11900 FONT 92337 644-C4
32400 LKEL 92530 896-G4
32400 RivC 92530 896-G4
SKYLARK TR
75200 INDW 92210 848-J2
75200 INDW 92210 849-A2
SKY LIGHT DR
37400 RivC 92211 789-F7
SKYLINE CIR
14000 RivC 92570 805-C1
SKYLINE DR
- RivC 92882 772-G3
- RivC 92882 773-A4
3200 COR 92882 772-J3
3200 COR 92882 773-A3
12000 DHSP 92240 697-D3
17000 LKEL 92530 866-A3
74400 RivC 92241 728-G3
SKYLINE RD
11200 RivC 92883 804-G3
SKYLINE TER
4800 RivC 92509 684-G2
SKYLINE WY
25300 RivC - 814-A5
SKYLINK DR
22700 CYNL 92587 867-D4
SKYLINKS DR
6600 RivC 92509 685-A2
SKYLOFT DR
5400 RivC 92509 684-J3
SKY MEADOW ST
5700 RivC 92509 685-C2
SKY MESA LN
77200 INDW 92210 849-E1
SKY MESA RD
23000 RivC 92548 809-B2
SKYPARK RD
40500 MURR 92562 928-C5
SKY POINT DR E
4900 PMSP 92264 787-B3
SKY POINT DR N
500 PMSP 92264 787-B3
SKY POINT DR W
4700 PMSP 92264 787-B3
SKY RANCH RD
40000 SDCo 92028 976-J5
40500 SDCo 92028 977-A6
SKYRIDGE DR
- RivC 92503 744-D5
SKY RIDGE DR
600 COR 92882 773-C3
SKY RIDGE RD
20100 RivC 92241 728-F7
SKYROCK DR
24500 MORV 92557 687-F7
SKYROCKET DR
26600 RivC 92590 978-C1
SKYSAIL DR
- RMIR 92270 817-J5
SKY TERRACE DR
30600 TEM 92592 959-B6
SKY VALLEY RD
20700 RivC 92241 728-J5
SKYVIEW CIR
- BAN 92220 721-E4
SKYVIEW DR
- RivC 92203 789-H6
1700 HEMT 92545 810-G5
SKY VIEW DR
2300 PMSP 92264 786-E6
22000 RivC 92262 725-E7
E SKYVIEW DR
1800 CLTN 92324 646-H2
SKYVIEW LN
800 SJCT 92582 780-H6
3200 COR 92882 742-E5
SKYVIEW RD
6800 RivC 92509 685-A4
6900 RivC 92509 684-H5
32000 RivC 92596 899-E6
SKYVIEW WY
41200 RivC 92536 963-C3
SKY VIEW RIDGE DR
24400 MURR 92562 928-B3
SKYWARD WY
43700 LQNT 92253 819-H7
72700 PDST 92260 848-E4
SKYWOOD DR
41800 TEM 92591 958-J4
SKYWOOD ST
16200 MORV 92551 747-G3
SLACK PL
200 CALI 92320 689-J1
SLANCH
- RivC 92220 782-D1
SLATE AV
1300 HEMT 92543 840-J3

SLATE WY
25000 RivC - 814-A5
SLATE CREEK DR
25000 MORV 92551 747-G4
SLATER CIR
- ONT 91761 643-D2
SLAWSON AV
11500 MORV 92557 687-H7
11500 MORV 92557 717-H1
SLEEPING DEER PT
- PER 92571 778-B3
SLEEPY HOLLOW LN
45500 RivC 92592 979-H4
SLEEPY HOLLOW RD
- BAN 92220 721-D6
SLEGERS ST
34600 RivC 92555 389-E7
34600 RivC 92555 749-J6
SLEW OF GOLD CT
2400 PER 92571 777-H5
SLICE WY
- TEM 92591 959-D4
SLIM RD
39900 RivC 92544 931-J7
39900 RivC 92544 961-J1
SLIPPERY ROCK RD
32900 RivC 92595 897-F1
SLOAN CT
24700 MORV 92553 717-F6
SLOAN DR
400 COR 92879 744-A3
SLOOP DR
29700 CYNL 92587 867-E2
SLOPE DR
9600 RivC 92223 690-G3
SLOUGH RD
33700 RivC 92596 899-D3
SLUMPSTONE ST
29000 RivC 92567 808-G2
SLY FOX RD
24300 MORV 92557 687-E6
SMALL ST
4500 RIV 92504 714-J3
4500 RIV 92504 715-A3
SMALL CANYON LN
- RivC 92506 745-J2
SMALL CREEK LN
- RivC 92506 745-J2
SMERBER RD
7300 RivC 92881 773-H2
SMILEY BLVD
- RivC 92324 688-A2
27000 RivC 92555 688-B4
SMILEY HEIGHTS DR
1500 RDL 92373 647-J3
SMILEY HEIGHTS RD
1100 RDL 92373 647-J4
SMITH AV
6300 RivC 91752 683-G7
16600 LKEL 92530 865-J2
N SMITH AV
100 COR 92882 743-A4
100 COR 92880 743-A4
S SMITH AV
100 COR 92882 743-A5
100 COR 92880 743-A5
SMITH CT
64800 RivC 92240 696-F1
SMITH LN
22700 RivC 92570 806-B3
SMITH RD
700 HEMT 92544 811-G5
19700 RivC 92570 776-B4
20300 RivC 92241 728-J5
27500 RivC 92545 839-J4
28300 RivC 92532 836-D7
SMITH ST
3600 RivC 92509 685-C2
SMITH RANCH RD
35800 RivC 92595 897-J7
SMITTY WY
400 COR 92879 743-G5
SMOKERIDGE TR
300 CALI 92320 689-J1
SMOKETHORN RD
55400 RivC 92539 (934-G1 See Page 904)
SMOKETHORN ST
100 COR 92881 773-C4
SMOKETREE
61200 RivC 92258 725-H1
61200 RivC 92282 725-H1
SMOKE TREE AV
43100 INDO 92201 5410-F6
SMOKETREE CT
73800 PDST 92260 848-G4
SMOKETREE DR
1000 COR 92882 742-F5
SMOKE TREE DR
1200 RivC - 5240-A7
SMOKE TREE LN
1800 PMSP 92264 786-G5
SMOKETREE LN
15700 FONT 92337 644-F3
40700 RMIR 92270 817-H4
SMOKE TREE PL
16100 MORV 92551 747-F3
SMOKETREE ST
21500 RivC 92570 776-J4
21500 RivC 92570 777-A4
SMOKE TREE ST
43100 INDO 92201 5410-F5
SMOKEWOOD AV
2200 PMSP 92264 786-H6

SMOKEWOOD CIR
10500 DHSP 92240 697-A2
SMOKEWOOD DR
- MURR 92563 928-H4
1500 NRCO 92860 713-E6
SMOKEY TR
34000 MURR 92584 898-F4
SMOKEY HILL LN
6100 CHLS 91709 712-A5
SMUGGLERS POINT DR
29700 CYNL 92587 867-E2
SMURR ST
43600 INDO 92201 5410-G6
45000 INDO 92201 5470-G1
SNAITH RD
51400 RivC 92539 (933-H6 See Page 902)
SNAKE RD
- RivC 92532 836-B2
SNAKE RIVER RD
4500 RIV 92501 645-H7
SNAPDRAGON CIR
- PMSP 92264 816-E1
SNAPDRAGON CT
1000 COR 92880 743-C1
2200 HEMT 92545 840-G1
SNAPDRAGON LN
11600 MORV 92557 717-B1
SNAPDRAGON WY
23300 MURR 92562 927-F3
SNEAD DR
500 HEMT 92543 841-A3
28700 RivC 92586 838-C7
28700 RivC 92586 868-C1
SNEAD ST
1300 BAN 92220 721-D5
SNIPE CIR
10000 MORV 92557 687-D5
SNOWBERRY RD
45200 RivC 92536 983-G4
SNOWBERRY ST
4200 RIV 92504 715-A3
SNOWBIRD LN
- COR 92882 773-C2
SNOW CREEK DR
26000 RivC 92586 868-A2
S SNOW CREEK LN
2900 ONT 91761 643-C6
SNOW CREEK RD
14200 RivC 92282 724-G6
15700 PMSP - 724-F7
SNOW CREEK TR
13000 YCPA 92399 650-E5
SNOW CREEK WY
80700 INDO 92201 5470-B1
SNOW CREEK CANYON
41000 PDST 92211 819-B5
SNOWDAN RD
15600 FONT 92337 644-E3
SNOWDRIFT DR
3600 RivC 92503 744-A4
SNOWGRASS TR
5800 RivC 92509 684-D5
SNOW GUM LN
39800 MURR 92562 928-D4
SNOW LINE CIR
39100 SBdC 92399 651-B1
SNOWMASS PEAK WY
- RIV 92508 746-E2
SNOW VIEW CT
11300 YCPA 92399 650-B1
SNOW VIEW DR
21500 RivC 92262 725-E7
SNOW WATER PL
22500 CYNL 92587 867-C1
SNYDER AV
32100 RivC 92548 809-D7
SOAP ROOT TR
13000 YCPA 92399 650-E6
SOARING HAWK RD
43600 RivC 92536 962-A3
SOBOBA AV
500 SJCT 92583 811-C2
E SOBOBA CTO
24000 RivC 92583 811-H4
24500 RivC 92544 811-H4
SOBOBA DR
400 BAN 92220 721-G4
SOBOBA RD
- RivC 92583 811-G2
- SJCT 92583 811-F1
20500 RivC 92583 780-J4
20500 RivC 92583 781-C5
21900 SJCT 92583 781-A4
N SOBOBA RD
600 SJCT 92583 781-F7
600 SJCT 92583 811-F1
900 RivC 92583 781-E6
SOBOBA ST
- SJCT 92583 811-G4
25800 RivC 92544 811-G7
26100 RivC 92544 841-G2
N SOBOBA ST
100 HEMT 92544 811-G6
700 RivC 92544 811-G6
SOBRANTE DR
22300 RivC 92570 806-B1
E SODA SPRINGS CT
3500 ONT 91761 643-C6
SOFIA DR
56000 RivC 92539 (934-H3 See Page 904)
SOFTWIND DR
12600 MORV 92553 717-D3

SOL CT
26800 RivC 92544 841-F2
SOLA AV
300 BLY 92225 5491-F5
SOLA ST
43400 INDO 92201 5410-F6
SOLAMA WY
- BAN 92220 721-C5
SOLANA TR
- PMSP 92264 787-B7
SOLANA WY
29600 TEM 92591 958-H5
29600 TEM 92591 959-A4
SOLANO AV
100 BLY 92225 5491-D6
82000 INDO 92201 5470-E3
S SOLANO AV
300 BLY 92225 5491-D7
300 RivC 92225 5491-D7
400 BLY 92225 5551-D1
400 RivC 92225 5551-D1
SOLANO CT
15200 LKEL 92530 865-H1
SOLANO DR
500 HEMT 92545 810-H6
6600 RivC 92509 645-B7
SOLANO LN
100 PER 92571 807-H2
SOLANO PL
- CTHC 92234 757-D5
SOLANO ST
900 COR 92882 773-B1
SOLAR CIR
- COR 92882 773-B3
E SOLAR CT
82200 INDO 92201 5470-F3
W SOLAR CT
82200 INDO 92201 5470-E3
SOLAR DR
17000 RivC 92570 776-A7
SOLAR PASS
22700 RivC 92570 806-F3
SOLEDAD DR
6100 RIV 92504 685-A7
6100 RIV 92504 715-A1
SOLEDAD LN
41800 RivC 92544 931-F4
SOLERA WY
1200 PER 92571 807-H1
SOLIDAGO RD
39300 RivC 92591 930-A6
SOLITARE CIR
23800 MORV 92557 687-D5
SOLVANG PL
7700 RIV 92503 714-G4
SOL VISTA DR
30100 RivC 92584 868-A3
SOMBRA WY
1000 SJCT 92582 810-J1
SOMBRERO CT
78200 RivC 92201 819-F5
SOMERA RD
72700 PDST 92260 848-D4
SOMERDALE ST
3200 RivC 92879 744-A5
SOMERS RD
28000 MURR 92563 898-F6
SOMERSET
32400 LKEL 92532 866-J5
SOMERSET CIR
400 COR 92879 744-A3
SOMERSET CT
700 HEMT 92545 810-H5
15400 FONT 92337 644-F3
SOMERSET DR
4800 RIV 92507 685-H7
32400 LKEL 92530 896-H4
SOMERSET RD
- YCPA 92399 649-F2
SOMERSET WY
42700 RivC 92201 819-G5
SOMERSET HILLS
- TEM 92591 959-D5
SOMERVIEW DR
28300 MURR 92563 928-F3
SOMIA CT
46900 PDST 92260 848-F3
SOMIS DR
3300 RIV 92507 686-E4
SOMMA DR
20300 RivC 92570 775-D5
SOMME CT
28800 RivC 92584 868-G2
SOMMERSET DR
72200 PDST 92260 848-C5
SOMMERVILLE RD
28600 MURR 92563 928-F4
SONATA CT
40700 PDST 92260 818-G4
SONATA DR
23700 MURR 92562 928-B1
23800 MURR 92562 898-B7
SONDGROTH CT
48000 RivC 92260 848-A5
SONESTA WY
78800 LQNT 92253 819-H7
SONGBIRD DR
38300 RivC 92592 930-H2
SONNET DR
23000 MORV 92557 687-C7
SONNET HILL LN
1300 COR 92881 773-F4
SONNY LN
15100 RivC 92508 746-B2

SONOMA CIR
32300 RivC 92276 788-F2
SONOMA DR
2300 SJCT 92583 811-E5
2800 RIV 92504 715-C6
SONOMA LN
31400 TEM 92591 959-D3
SONOMA OAKS AV
3600 PER 92571 778-A2
SONORA AV
83000 INDO 92201 5410-G7
SONORA CIR
- TEM 92591 958-H3
SONORA CT
3700 PMSP 92264 786-J4
SONORA DR
1300 COR 92882 743-A7
1500 HEMT 92543 810-H6
9700 DHSP 92240 696-G2
72700 PDST 92260 818-D7
SONORA LP
- LMLN 92354 647-D1
SONORA PL
2800 RIV 92504 715-E4
SONORA RD
200 PMSP 92264 786-E4
70000 RivC - (907-J4 See Page 906)
70100 RMIR 92270 817-H4
SONRISA DR
2900 COR 92881 773-D3
SONRISA ST
700 HEMT 92543 810-J6
SONRISA WY
- RivC 92254 5592-F5
SONY WY
23600 RivC 92570 807-A4
SOPHIE ST
24200 RivC 92570 807-D7
25000 RivC 92570 837-D1
SOPWITH DR
44000 RivC 92544 (812-A5 See Page 782)
SORENSEN RD
43200 RivC 92536 963-B7
43700 RivC 92536 983-B1
SORIA CT
15700 FONT 92337 644-G4
SORREL DR
1200 HEMT 92545 840-H3
SORREL LN
30700 CYNL 92587 867-F4
SORRENTO CT
44400 PDST 92260 848-H1
SORRENTO DR
8700 RIV 92503 714-J4
SORRENTO LN
1400 SJCT 92583 811-E3
SORRENTO WY
- RMIR 92270 788-A6
SOTELO DR
32900 TEM 92592 979-G3
SOTELO RD
24800 PER 92587 837-G4
SOTO AV
4000 RivC 92509 644-J7
SOTO DR
25500 RivC 92570 837-C1
SOTO ST
- RivC 92509 684-J1
SOTOGRANDE CIR
- COR 92883 773-G7
SOUDER ST
20200 RivC 92570 776-G3
SOUNDVIEW CIR
1300 COR 92881 773-F4
SOUTH BLVD
200 PER 92570 807-G4
SOUTH ST
- RIV 92507 686-B7
SOUTH TR
17900 CHLS 91709 712-B5
SOUTHAMPTON CT
4800 RIV 92503 714-J2
SOUTH BAY DR
- INDO 92203 5410-G3
SOUTH BEND RD
- MURR 92563 958-G1
SOUTH BORDER
35100 RivC 92276 788-H5
SOUTHCLIFF RD
72000 PDST 92260 848-C4
SOUTHERN AV
900 BLY 92225 5551-D1
SOUTHERN CROSS RD
30500 TEM 92592 959-B6
SOUTHERN HILLS
- LQNT 92253 5530-C4
SOUTHERN HILLS AV
32500 RivC 92276 788-E3
SOUTHERN HILLS DR
- TEM 92591 959-B5
1000 BAN 92220 721-D5
SOUTH FORK DR
3400 NRCO 92860 713-H4
30400 CYNL 92587 867-F3
SOUTH FOUR WHEEL DR
1900 NRCO 92860 713-D7
1900 NRCO 92860 743-D1
SOUTHGATE ST
12700 MORV 92553 717-B3
SOUTHHAMPTON CT
4100 HEMT 92544 811-F5
SOUTH HILLS DR
43700 RivC 92536 982-B5

SOUTHPORT DR
1600 RIV 92506 715-G6
SOUTHRIDGE CIR
2000 PMSP 92264 786-J6
SOUTHRIDGE DR
2000 PMSP 92264 786-J6
6900 RIV 92506 716-C5
SOUTHRIDGE LN
11800 FONT 92337 644-A4
SOUTHSHORE DR
200 LKEL 92530 865-H2
SOUTH SHORE RD
40000 SDCo 92028 997-B1
SOUTH VALLEY LN
57000 LQNT 92253 5530-C6
SOUTHVIEW
- INDO 92201 5470-E4
SOUTHWALK ST
22400 MORV 92553 717-B3
SOUTHWIND WY
- YCPA 92399 649-E2
SOUTHWOOD DR
14100 FONT 92337 644-B3
SOUTHWORTH RD
42500 RivC 92536 961-J6
SOVANA
- INDW 92210 819-B5
SOVEREIGN WY
2600 RIV 92506 715-H3
SOZA RD
5600 RivC 92282 655-J4
SPAATZ CIR
16800 RivC 92518 746-H5
SPACE DR
16100 MORV 92551 747-H3
SPACE CENTER CT
3200 RivC 91752 643-H6
SPAIN LN
17400 RivC 92504 746-A5
SPALDING AV
19000 RivC 92508 746-D6
SPALDING DR
79300 RivC 92201 819-H4
SPANIEL LN
26300 RivC 92586 838-B3
SPANISH BAY
- LQNT 92253 5530-B5
SPANISH BAY DR
- INDO 92201 5470-A1
SPANISH BAYONET RD
39200 RivC 92539 (934-C5 See Page 904)
SPANISH DAGGER
40900 RivC 92539 (965-G3 See Page 964)
SPANISH DAGGER LN
61800 RivC 92539 (965-J4 See Page 964)
SPANISH HILLS DR
11000 RivC 92883 804-G5
SPANISH HILLS LN
- LQNT 92253 5530-C6
SPANISH OAKS DR
- RivC 92592 931-C6
SPANISH SPUR TR
44300 RivC 92536 983-J4
SPANISH TRAIL CV
5900 BAN 92220 721-C5
SPANKY DR
32500 CTHC 92234 787-H3
SPAR CIR
72300 RivC 92254 (5654-F6 See Page 5594)
SPARACIO RD
28100 RivC 92585 808-E6
SPARKEY WY
41000 RivC 92201 819-F4
SPARKLE DR
30200 CYNL 92587 867-C3
SPARKLING DR
29100 RivC 92584 868-F1
SPARKLING LAGOON
- BLY - 5491-B7
SPARKMAN CT
25400 MURR 92562 928-D6
SPARKY WY
42600 RivC 92201 819-F5
SPARROW CIR
3400 RIV 92503 744-E2
SPARROW DR
11600 FONT 92337 644-G3
SPARROW WY
32000 RivC 92563 929-E4
32000 RivC 92596 929-E4
SPARROW HAWK DR
30500 CYNL 92587 867-E4
SPARTA LN
45400 TEM 92592 979-C6
46000 RivC 92592 979-C6
SPARTON RD
10800 RIV 92505 714-C5
SPAULDING DR
11100 RIV 92505 714-D7
11100 RIV 92505 744-D1
SPECTACULAR BID ST
2400 PER 92571 777-H5
SPEER CT
26000 RivC 92544 (812-E7 See Page 782)
SPENCER DR
700 PMSP 92262 756-E5
1500 NRCO 92860 713-E6
SPERRY CT
39500 RivC 92591 959-H1

SPEYSIDE RD
- RIV 92507 716-F2
SPEZIALI RD
34000 RivC 92596 899-J4
SPICA CT
30400 TEM 92592 959-B6
SPICEWOOD AV
39800 MURR 92562 898-A7
39800 MURR 92562 928-A1
SPICEWOOD CIR
- RivC 92880 683-B7
SPICEWOOD LN
2700 RIV 92504 715-C6
SPIETH WY
100 RIV 92507 686-E4
SPIKE LN
- INDO 92201 5470-B3
SPINDLE WY
23500 MURR 92562 898-A7
SPINDLETOP DR
7300 RivC 92881 773-H3
SPINDLEWOOD DR
- RivC 92880 713-B1
SPINDRIFT CIR
29200 LKEL 92530 865-G2
SPINDRIFT CT
30800 RivC 92584 868-G4
SPINNAKER DR
600 PER 92571 777-J6
15900 LKEL 92530 865-J7
15900 RivC 92530 865-J7
SPINNAKER LN
14700 MORV 92553 717-E7
SPINNAKER WY
68100 RivC 92254 (5654-D2 See Page 5594)
SPINNING WHEEL DR
39700 MURR 92562 898-A7
39700 MURR 92562 928-A1
40100 MURR 92562 927-J1
SPIRIT CT
4500 RIV 92501 645-H7
SPIRIT TR
45300 RivC 92539 (985-E2 See Page 964)
SPIRIT KNOLL CT
- NRCO 92860 713-F3
SPIRO RD
30000 RivC 92596 869-C2
SPLENDOR WY
11300 MORV 92557 687-G7
SPLIT RAIL RD
24600 RivC 92595 897-H4
SPOKANE ST
2700 PER 92571 777-H4
SPOON CIR
41900 TEM 92591 959-C5
SPOON RD
5900 PMSP 92264 787-C6
SPOTTED PONY DR
26600 RivC 92883 835-B4
SPRADLIN LN
26400 RivC 92548 839-B2
SPRAY DR
29900 CYNL 92587 867-E3
SPRING CT
4400 BAN 92220 721-E3
SPRING LN
1700 COR 92882 742-J7
SPRING PL
2600 BAN 92220 721-H4
SPRING RD
8900 RivC 92324 687-F2
15800 DHSP 92240 696-J7
15900 DHSP 92240 726-J1
SPRING ST
- BAN 92220 651-E7
100 BLY 92225 5491-E6
24200 RivC 92570 807-A7
25100 RivC 92570 837-A1
26700 RivC 92570 836-H4
E SPRING ST
200 RivC 92507 646-F7
N SPRING ST
100 LKEL 92530 866-E4
S SPRING ST
100 LKEL 92530 866-E5
W SPRING ST
100 RivC 92507 646-B7
1100 RIV 92507 646-B7
SPRING VW
37600 MURR 92563 928-G4
SPRING BRANCH CT
23800 MURR 92562 927-J3
SPRINGBROOK CT
- LQNT 92253 849-H1
- RIV 92508 746-D3
SPRINGBROOK RD
39100 RivC 92539 (933-G5 See Page 902)
SPRINGBROOK ST
1100 COR 92880 743-B1
SPRING CREEK RD
13500 RivC 92503 744-B5
SPRING CREST DR
67100 RivC - (937-B2 See Page 906)
SPRINGCREST RD
11800 MORV 92557 717-A1
21700 MORV 92557 716-J1
SPRINGDALE DR
22500 MORV 92557 687-B5
SPRING DEEP TER
30500 RivC 92584 868-F3

SPRINGER DR
4900 HEMT 92544 811-G5
SPRINGFIELD CIR
- TEM 92590 958-E6
SPRINGFIELD LN
77500 PDST 92211 819-E3
SPRINGFIELD ST
11100 RIV 92505 714-B2
SPRING GARDEN ST
1800 RIV 92507 686-A1
3100 RIV 92501 686-A1
SPRINGHAVEN ST
- MURR 92563 928-E2
SPRINGHILL DR
2700 COR 92882 773-C2
SPRING HILL WY
17900 RivC 92503 744-H7
SPRING LAKE WY
30500 RivC 92584 868-F3
SPRING MEADOW CT
27700 RivC 92585 838-E5
SPRING MEADOW DR
- COR 92881 773-G4
22900 MURR 92562 927-E3
SPRING MIST CT
900 SJCT 92582 780-J6
SPRINGOAK CT
11500 FONT 92337 644-C3
SPRINGOAK LN
11300 FONT 92337 644-C2
SPRING OAK PL
- MURR 92562 927-J2
SPRING PARK PL
17900 RivC 92503 744-H7
SPRINGROCK LN
11500 FONT 92337 644-G3
SPRINGSIDE DR
29400 RivC 92584 868-F1
SPRINGSMIST DR
22600 MORV 92557 687-B5
SPRINGTIME DR
39200 TEM 92591 928-J7
SPRINGTIME WY
78100 LQNT 92253 849-F7
SPRINGTOWN RD
25500 RivC 92584 897-J1
25500 RivC 92584 898-A1
SPRINGTREE DR
1800 PER 92571 777-G7
SPRINGTREE WY
22900 MORV 92557 687-C3
SPRING VALLEY RD
37300 RivC 92592 931-A2
SPRING VIEW CT
17900 RivC 92503 744-H7
SPRING VIEW DR
4600 BAN 92220 721-E3
SPRING VIEW LN
17900 RivC 92503 744-H7
SPRING VIEW PL
5200 BAN 92220 721-D3
SPRING WATER RD
- PMSP 92264 (907-C1 See Page 906)
- RivC - (907-C1 See Page 906)
SPRINGWAY CT
- RIV 92505 714-C6
SPRING WINDS DR
28100 RivC 92585 838-E1
SPRINGWOOD CIR
44500 RivC 92544 (812-B6 See Page 782)
SPRINGWOOD CT
- RIV 92505 744-D1
SPRINGWOOD LN
18800 RivC 92570 776-F2
SPRINGWOOD ST
700 COR 92882 742-J5
SPRINT CT
1200 RIV 92506 716-C6
SPRUCE
- HEMT 92545 840-G2
26600 RivC - 814-D7
SPRUCE AV
10700 SBdC 92316 645-F3
28900 MORV 92555 718-E2
32400 RivC 92584 867-G7
SPRUCE CT
- MURR 92562 927-F4
700 BEAU 92223 690-J7
SPRUCE ST
300 LKEL 92530 865-G2
300 RIV 92507 686-A3
1000 COR 92879 743-E6
2100 RIV 92507 685-J2
2200 RIV 92501 685-H2
12200 DHSP 92240 697-D4
46500 INDO 92201 5470-J2
E SPRUCE ST
2800 ONT 91761 643-A4
SPRUCE GROVE CT
- RivC 92880 713-A1
SPRUCEWOOD PL
25600 MORV 92557 717-H1
SPRUCEWOOD ST
32000 LKEL 92532 867-D5
SPRUCEWOOD WY
- LKEL 92532 867-D5
SPRUNGLE CIR
23200 RivC 92587 867-D2
SPUR DR
- NRCO 92860 713-H3
SPUR PL
79800 RivC 92201 819-J5

SPUR RD
- RivC 92592 900-H5
SPUR ST
5900 RivC 92509 684-C5
SPUR BRANCH CIR
13200 RivC 92883 835-B4
SPUR BROOK DR
22300 RivC 92595 897-C3
SPYGLASS AV
6200 BAN 92220 721-C5
64200 RivC 92240 696-D1
SPYGLASS CIR
11500 MORV 92557 687-E7
11500 MORV 92557 717-E1
37700 MURR 92563 928-J4
SPYGLASS DR
- COR 92883 773-G7
15300 LKEL 92530 865-F2
75000 INDW 92210 818-J7
75100 INDW 92210 819-A7
SPYGLASS LN
72600 PDST 92260 848-D5
SPYGLASS PZ
1500 PMSP 92264 787-C3
SPY GLASS WY
30600 CYNL 92587 867-C4
SPYGLASS HILL DR
- LQNT 92253 849-H6
SPYGLASS HILL LN
- TEM 92591 959-D3
SPYGLASS HILL ST
- INDO 92201 5470-A1
SQUAB RD
11200 MORV 92557 687-B7
SQUAW MOUNTAIN RD
9800 RivC 92883 804-D6
SQUAWPEAK CT
49300 RivC 92536 963-C1
SQUAW VALLEY DR
29500 RivC 92586 868-A2
SQUIRE PL
200 COR 92879 743-D7
SQUIRREL LN
26700 RivC 92544 842-D2
STABLE LANES RD
36300 RivC 92595 927-F1
STABLE LANES WY
- RivC 92595 927-E1
STACEY AV
24200 MORV 92551 747-F1
STACEY PL
26300 RivC 92548 839-A2
26300 RivC 92585 839-A2
STACIE LN
85500 COAC 92236 5531-C1
STACY CT
1100 RIV 92507 686-B1
39900 MURR 92563 928-E5
STACY WY
1300 SJCT 92583 811-D3
STACY LYNN DR
13500 MORV 92555 717-J5
STADIUM AV
4500 RIV 92501 685-G5
STAFFORD PL
69600 CTHC 92234 787-G1
STAFFORD RD
36200 RivC 92539 904-C6
STAFFORD ST
- RivC 92880 683-D4
23400 RivC 92570 807-E5
STAG DR
- RivC 92592 870-J7
STAGE DR
34500 RivC 92276 788-J5
STAGE RD
- RivC 92562 926-J1
34000 RivC 92592 901-B3
34600 RivC 92592 900-J5
STAGECOACH DR
1800 COR 92880 742-J1
1800 NRCO 92860 742-J1
1800 COR 92860 742-J1
1800 RivC 92860 742-J1
1900 NRCO 92880 712-H7
1900 NRCO 92880 742-J1
1900 RivC 92880 712-H7
1900 RivC 92880 742-J1
STAGECOACH LN
- RIV 92508 746-D1
STAGE COACH LN
1600 SDCo 92028 997-J6
2000 SDCo 92028 998-D2
N STAGE COACH LN
1100 SDCo 92028 997-J7
STAGE COACH RD
100 RivC 92262 755-F1
STAGECOACH RD
2700 PMSP 92264 786-H6
31500 RivC 92567 779-F7
STAGECOACH TR
31800 RivC 92567 779-D7
STAGE LINE DR
74500 RivC 92276 788-H5
STAGELINE ST
10200 RivC 92883 804-E6
STAGE STOP RD
- PMSP 92262 755-E2
- RivC 92262 755-E2
STAGEWOOD ST
27000 RivC 92586 838-A4
STAGHORN CIR
23900 MORV 92557 687-E5
STAGHORN CT
- RivC 92399 650-G7

STREET
Block City ZIP Pg-Grid

SUNFLOWER GATE
82400 INDO 92201 5470-F3
SUNGATE DR
600 COR 92879 743-J3
SUNGATE WY
- CTHC 92234 817-F1
SUNGLOW DR
2100 BAN 92220 721-G2
11100 MORV 92557 687-F7
SUNGOLD AV
- RivC 92880 713-A2
SUN GOLD ST
44300 INDO 92201 5410-E7
45000 INDO 92201 5470-E1
SUNGROVE CIR
10300 RIV 92503 744-J4
SUNHARBOR CT
14700 LKEL 92530 865-F1
SUNHAVEN WY
11200 RIV 92505 714-B3
SUNJOY DR
600 HEMT 92543 811-A5
SUNKIST CIR
1200 COR 92882 742-J6
SUNKIST DR
600 BAN 92220 721-G2
SUN LAKE TER
17200 RivC 92503 744-G6
SUN LAKES BLVD
4800 BAN 92220 721-C4
SUN LAKES VILLAGE DR
200 BAN 92220 721-C4
SUNLAND DR
- RivC - (907-D2
See Page 906)
SUNLAND PL
5900 RIV 92504 685-B7
SUNLAND RD
68000 RivC 92240 727-C1
SUNLIGHT CIR
1000 RIV 92506 716-C5
SUNLIGHT CT
- MURR 92563 928-E3
SUNLIGHT DR
34300 YCPA 92399 649-H5
35300 YCPA 92399 650-B5
SUNLINE DR
23500 MORV 92553 717-D4
SUNLIT CT
13000 MORV 92553 717-D4
SUNMEADOW CIR
- COR 92881 773-F5
SUNMEADOW ST
- COR 92881 773-F5
SUNMIST CIR
17000 RivC 92504 745-H5
SUNMORE LN
- RivC - (907-D2
See Page 906)
SUNNINGDALE DR
- TEM 92591 959-C4
300 RMIR 92270 788-A4
3300 RMIR 92270 787-J5
SUNNINGDALE ST
1800 BAN 92220 721-E6
SUNNY AV
26400 RivC 92548 839-B2
SUNNY CIR
5800 RivC 91752 683-H5
SUNNY CV
1600 COR 92882 742-J6
SUNNY LN
69700 CTHC 92234 787-J7
70000 RMIR 92270 787-J7
70800 RMIR 92270 788-A7
SUNNY TR
73400 PDST 92260 848-F4
SUNNYBANK DR
- HEMT 92545 840-E4
SUNNYBROOK CIR
48500 RivC 92536 963-B1
SUNNYBROOK DR
2000 BAN 92220 721-H2
9600 MORV 92557 687-A4
22600 RivC 92595 897-D4
77800 PDST 92211 819-E3
SUNNY CANYON ST
23100 RivC 92570 777-D4
SUNNY DALE PZ
1700 PMSP 92264 787-C3
SUNNY DAYS DR
38000 RivC 92211 819-F1
SUNNY DUNES PL
300 PMSP 92264 786-E3
SUNNY DUNES RD
300 PMSP 92264 786-D3
3900 PMSP 92264 787-A3
SUNNYGLEN DR
12800 MORV 92553 717-D3
SUNNYGROVE LN
- MURR 92563 928-E2
SUNNY HALO CT
100 PER 92571 777-H5
SUNNY HEIGHTS RD
1300 SDCo 92028 998-C7
SUNNYHILL DR
4000 RivC 92509 644-G7
SUNNY HILLS DR
2600 NRCO 92860 713-B6
SUNNY HILLS RD
35800 RivC 92596 899-E7
SUNNYMEAD BLVD
23000 MORV 92553 717-G2
SUNNY MEADOW LN
6000 CHLS 91709 712-A4
SUNNYMEADOWS DR
12500 MORV 92553 717-C3
SUNNY MEADOWS DR
43400 TEM 92592 959-F6
43500 TEM 92592 979-G1
SUNNYMEAD RANCH PKWY
23000 MORV 92557 687-C5
SUNNY RIDGE DR
24500 MORV 92557 687-F7
SUNNY ROCK RD
31300 RivC 92236 390-D7
31300 RivC 92241 390-D8
SUNNYSAGE DR
4000 RivC 92509 685-A1
SUNNYSANDS DR
2100 PER 92570 807-E6
SUNNYSIDE AV
400 RDL 92373 647-J3
SUNNYSIDE DR
2100 BAN 92220 721-H2
3300 RIV 92506 685-F7
3300 RIV 92506 715-D1
4000 BAN 92220 721-G1
5300 RIV 92504 715-B1
10200 BLY 92225 5491-D4
11000 YCPA 92399 650-A1
81000 INDO 92201 5470-C3
SUNNYSLOPE AV
10800 RIV 92505 714-D6
11100 RivC 92223 691-A6
11200 BEAU 92223 691-A6
17200 LKEL 92530 866-A3
SUNNYSLOPE LN
22100 RivC 92262 725-F7
SUNNYSLOPE RD
29900 RivC 92241 390-D8
SUNNY SUMMIT LN
48900 PDST 92260 848-D5
SUNNYVALE CT
25600 RivC 92584 837-J7
25700 RivC 92584 838-A7
SUNNYVALLE DR
6700 RIV 92505 714-B2
SUNNY VIEW DR
2800 PMSP 92262 756-E4
SUNNYWOOD ST
26000 RivC 92586 838-A3
SUNPARK DR
2100 PER 92570 807-E6
SUN RAY CT
11900 SBdC 92256 655-G1
SUNRAY CT
13600 MORV 92553 717-E5
SUN RAY CT
13600 RivC 92503 744-D4
SUN RIDGE CIR
- RMIR 92270 818-A1
SUNRIDGE CIR
2100 RivC 92503 744-H4
SUNRIDGE DR
9100 RIV 92508 746-D4
SUNRISE AV
- BAN 92220 721-H2
15000 RivC 92230 723-G6
15800 DHSP 92240 696-J7
15900 DHSP 92240 726-J1
84700 COAC 92236 5471-B6
SUNRISE CIR
- RivC 91752 683-E5
32200 CTHC 92234 787-G3
SUNRISE CT
2400 BAN 92220 721-H3
41400 RMIR 92270 818-B5
82300 INDO 92201 5470-F3
SUNRISE DR
- RMIR 92270 818-B4
1300 RivC - 5240-A7
6200 BAN 92220 721-C5
25500 RivC - 814-A6
31800 LKEL 92532 866-J6
34300 RivC 92595 897-A4
60000 RivC 92282 725-E1
69300 CTHC 92234 787-F3
SUNRISE LN
45400 PDST 92260 848-H1
SUNRISE PL
2400 RIV 92506 715-J1
SUNRISE RD
400 PER 92570 807-F2
16700 RivC 92241 727-F1
36800 RivC 92544 931-C3
SUNRISE ST
900 HEMT 92545 840-G2
SUNRISE WY
1600 COR 92882 742-J6
25700 LMLN 92354 647-D2
32900 RivC 92530 865-J7
32900 RivC 92530 866-A7
N SUNRISE WY
100 PMSP 92262 786-F1
600 PMSP 92262 756-F3
3200 PMSP - 756-F3
S SUNRISE WY
100 PMSP 92262 786-G4
500 PMSP 92264 786-G4
SUNRISE CANYON AV
- RivC 92203 789-F6
78100 RivC 92211 789-F6
SUNRISE HILL DR
14800 RivC 92508 716-B7
14800 RivC 92508 746-B1
SUNRISE MOUNTAIN VW
78100 RivC 92211 789-F7
SUNRISE MOUNTAIN VW
78600 RivC 92203 789-H7
N SUNRISE RIDGE DR
79400 LQNT 92253 819-J7
S SUNRISE RIDGE DR
79400 LQNT 92253 819-J7
SUNROSE DR
4200 RIV 92505 714-D7
24800 MURR 92562 928-D3
SUNROSE LN
49200 PDST 92260 848-E6
SUNROSE ST
22600 RivC 92883 804-B4
SUNSCAPE LN
- CTHC 92234 817-F1
SUNSEEKER PL
- CTHC 92234 817-F1
SUNSET AV
- SJCT 92583 781-B7
- BAN 92220 721-G1
800 RivC 92220 721-G7
1000 PER 92571 778-A7
2500 RIV 92506 715-J2
4000 RivC 92220 691-G6
4000 BAN 92220 691-G6
10500 DHSP 92240 696-J3
15500 LKEL 92530 865-F2
23700 RivC 92570 777-E7
24900 RivC 92584 867-H7
27200 RivC 92571 778-C7
30900 RivC 92567 779-A6
32500 RivC 92584 897-H1
33000 RivC 92595 897-H3
S SUNSET AV
- BAN 92220 721-G3
SUNSET CIR
6600 RIV 92505 714-B2
SUNSET CT
2700 NRCO 92860 713-B4
82000 INDO 92201 5470-E3
E SUNSET CT
2100 CLTN 92324 646-H4
SUNSET DR
1200 BLY 92225 5491-G7
2300 RIV 92506 715-J1
25100 RivC - (813-J5
See Page 782)
32000 CTHC 92234 787-F2
32900 RivC 92530 865-J7
51800 COAC 92236 5471-D7
SUNSET LN
1700 COR 92882 742-H7
13100 MORV 92553 717-G4
23100 RivC 92567 809-G2
41000 RivC 92544 841-D2
45200 PDST 92260 848-H1
SUNSET RD
8100 COR 92883 774-A6
SUNSET TER
44300 RivC 92590 978-E2
SUNSET TR
16100 RivC 92506 745-G2
SUNSET WY
11500 DHSP 92240 696-B4
N SUNSET WY
100 PMSP 92262 786-G1
SUNSET HILL DR
40600 RivC 92539 (935-G7
See Page 904)
SUNSET KNOLL WY
43300 BAN 92220 691-G6
SUNSET LAKE CIR
30800 RivC 92584 868-G4
SUNSET MEADOW DR
10900 RIV 92505 714-B1
SUNSET RANCH DR
6000 RIV 92506 716-A2
SUNSET RANCH RD
5800 RIV 92506 716-A2
N SUNSET RIDGE DR
79200 LQNT 92253 819-H7
S SUNSET RIDGE DR
79200 LQNT 92253 819-H7
SUNSET RIDGE RD
- RivC 92503 745-C5
SUNSET SAGE TR
61100 RivC 92539 (965-J5
See Page 964)
SUNSET VIEW CT
72800 RMIR 92270 818-D3
SUNSET VIEW DR
17400 RivC 92504 745-A5
25800 RivC - 814-E6
SUNSHINE
35100 RivC 92276 788-H5
SUNSHINE CIR
- COR 92881 773-F5
43300 RivC 92536 963-F7
SUNSHINE CIR E
2200 PMSP 92264 786-H3
SUNSHINE CIR N
500 PMSP 92264 786-G3
SUNSHINE CIR S
2100 PMSP 92264 786-G3
SUNSHINE CIR W
500 PMSP 92264 786-G3
SUNSHINE CT
43300 RivC 92544 811-J7
SUNSHINE DR
600 BAN 92220 721-G2
SUNSHINE DR W
500 PMSP 92264 786-G3
SUNSHINE LN
- RIV 92508 746-D1
84700 COAC 92236 5471-B6
SUNSHINE ST
600 BAN 92220 721-G4
SUNSHINE TER
- RivC 92211 789-F6
SUNSHINE WY
2100 PMSP 92264 786-G3
69700 CTHC 92234 787-G3
SUNSHINE HILLS RD
52000 RivC 92539 (933-J1
See Page 902)
SUNSTONE AV
900 HEMT 92543 840-H3
SUNSTONE CT
80400 INDO 92201 5470-B2
SUN STREAM CIR
24800 MORV 92557 687-F6
SUNSTREAM DR
- COR 92879 743-H3
- RivC 92584 868-F2
SUN SUMMIT DR
16100 RivC 92503 744-D4
SUNSWEPT CT
13400 MORV 92553 717-D4
SUNSWEPT DR
1300 SJCT 92582 780-H6
15100 LKEL 92530 865-F2
SUN SWEPT ST
55500 RivC 92274 5530-H4
SUNTAN LN
1000 PMSP 92264 786-F5
SUNUP CIR
1600 RIV 92501 685-H1
SUN VALLEY DR
70100 RMIR 92270 817-H1
SUN VALLEY LN
600 COR 92879 743-J3
72500 PDST 92260 848-D4
SUN VALLEY RD
24000 MORV 92553 717-E3
W SUNVIEW AV
200 PMSP 92262 756-C3
SUNVIEW CIR
17300 RivC 92504 745-F6
SUNWAY DR
11000 RivC 92883 804-G4
SUNWEST DR N
900 HEMT 92545 810-G5
SUN WEST RD
- RIV 92508 716-E7
SUNWOOD PL
28000 RivC 92584 868-E5
SUPA CT
22800 RivC 92595 897-D7
SUPAI ST
35000 SJCT 92567 810-A1
35100 RivC 92567 809-J1
35100 RivC 92567 810-A1
SUPALE RANCH RD
38600 SDCo 92028 997-B4
SUPERIOR AV
24500 MORV 92551 747-F4
SUPERIOR CT
100 PER 92571 777-H6
44000 INDW 92210 818-J7
SUPERIOR ST
4300 RIV 92505 714-E6
SURFSIDE AV
98500 RivC 92254 (5654-C3
See Page 5594)
SURFSIDE CT
23500 RivC 92587 837-E6
SURREY CIR
400 COR 92879 744-B2
SURREY CT
- RMIR 92270 817-J2
- RMIR 92270 818-A2
15500 RivC 92506 745-H2
SURREY WY
34800 RivC 92276 788-H5
E SURREY WY
2800 ONT 91761 643-A7
SURRY RD
25900 RivC 92584 868-A4
SURTEES CT
23100 MORV 92553 717-C3
SURVEYOR LN
48400 RivC 92536 963-B5
SUSAN AV
- PMSP 92262 756-G4
SUSAN CT
42600 PDST 92260 818-H6
SUSAN DR
30500 CTHC 92234 787-E1
34800 RivC 92595 897-F6
SUSAN LN
100 HEMT 92543 841-A1
2800 PER 92571 777-F5
SUSAN ST
- YCPA 92399 650-C6
1500 BEAU 92223 690-J7
3500 RIV 92504 715-C4
SUSAN WY
13600 DHSP 92240 696-J6
SUSANA CT
14400 MORV 92553 717-E6
SUSANA WY
- MURR 92562 927-H5
SUSAN LEE CT
200 CALI 92320 689-J1
SUSANNE ST
600 COR 92882 743-C7
SUSSEX CT
- RMIR 92270 817-J2
- RMIR 92270 818-A2
SUSSEX RD
700 SJCT 92583 781-B7
18600 RivC 92504 775-H1
SUSSEX ST
42500 PDST 92211 819-E5
SUTHERLAND AV
17500 RivC 92530 896-C2
SUTHERLAND DR
1300 RIV 92507 716-F2
SUTRO CT
25200 HEMT 92544 811-H6
SUTTER AV
11700 YCPA 92399 650-B2
SUTTER CT
35600 YCPA 92399 650-B2
SUTTER LN
1600 COR 92879 743-E7
SUTTER WY
1400 RIV 92501 685-J1
SUTTER CREEK RD
45900 INDO 92201 5470-B1
SUTTERS PL
1300 HEMT 92545 840-E3
SUTTERS MILL RD
42000 PDST 92260 818-G6
SUTTLES DR
15900 RivC 92504 745-H4
15900 RivC 92506 745-H4
SUTTON PL
- RivC - 392-D1
4400 NRCO 92860 713-F2
SUTTON PL E
- PDST 92211 818-J4
SUTTON PL S
- PDST 92211 818-J4
SUTTON PL W
- PDST 92211 818-J4
SUUWAT WY
- PDST 92260 848-B7
SUWANEE ST
4500 RIV 92501 645-G7
SUZAN ST
20800 RivC 92570 836-J5
SUZANNE DR
11900 FONT 92337 644-D4
SUZI LN
30800 TEM 92591 929-C7
SUZI REID WY
35800 RivC 92563 899-A7
SWAIN CT
4100 RIV 92507 686-F5
SWALLOW CT
27400 TEM 92591 958-J2
SWALLOW LN
5100 RIV 92505 714-C5
SWALLOW HILL CIR
20000 RivC 92570 777-D4
SWAN AV
29200 LKEL 92530 865-J2
SWAN LN
1300 COR 92879 743-F2
SWAN RD
15700 FONT 92337 644-F3
SWAN ST
23300 MORV 92557 717-C1
SWAN POINT DR
30000 CYNL 92587 867-F3
SWAPS ST
13500 MORV 92555 718-D5
SWARENS CT
15300 MORV 92551 747-G1
SWARTHMORE CT
- RMIR 92270 818-B2
SWARTHOUT LN
45800 RivC 92592 979-J5
SWAYZEE CT
500 RivC 92507 646-D7
SWEDLOW TR
39700 SBdC 92399 651-D2
SWEENEY DR
23200 MORV 92553 717-C5
SWEEPSTAKES LN
49200 RivC 92536 963-C5
SWEETBAY CIR
22900 RivC 92595 927-E2
SWEETBAY RD
20000 RIV 92508 746-F2
SWEET BRIER CIR
39800 TEM 92591 958-J2
SWEETBUSH LN
44000 LQNT 92253 819-J7
SWEET BUSH LN
72900 PDST 92260 848-D4
SWEET CLOVER CIR
23500 MORV 92557 687-C6
SWEET CLOVER CT
- RivC 92880 683-B7
SWEETFERN ST
13000 MORV 92553 717-H4
SWEETGRASS CT
25300 MURR 92563 928-E3
SWEET GRASS DR
25100 MORV 92553 717-G5
SWEET GUM CT
- MURR 92563 928-G7
SWEETLEAF ST
25800 MORV 92553 717-H3
SWEET MAGNOLIA WY
- MURR 92563 928-J4
- MURR 92563 929-A4
SWEET MEADOW ST
- PER 92571 778-B2
SWEETPEA CIR
22700 MORV 92557 717-B1
SWEET PEA CT
40800 MURR 92562 927-J3
SWEETPEA ST
800 HEMT 92545 840-G2
SWEET PEA WY
76200 PDST 92211 819-B2
SWEET PETUNIA LN
15400 RivC 92508 746-A2
SWEET RAIN WY
2400 COR 92881 773-F3
SWEETS RD
17700 RivC 92241 727-J2
SWEETSER DR
600 RivC 92507 646-D7
SWEETSHADE LN
42000 TEM 92591 959-B5
SWEETSPICE ST
13100 MORV 92553 717-H4
SWEETWATER CIR
3400 COR 92882 742-E5
SWEETWATER DR
3200 ONT 91761 643-B7
11200 RIV 92505 714-A2
38300 PDST 92211 819-A2
SWEET WATER LN
31900 RivC 92548 839-D1
SWEETWATER CANYON RD
33500 RivC 92584 898-C3
SWEET WELL RD
74500 RivC 92276 788-H6
SWEET WILLIAM LN
23900 MURR 92562 927-J4
SWEETWOOD CT
100 RIV 92506 716-D5
19300 LKEL 92530 896-G4
SWEETWOOD LN
19400 LKEL 92530 896-G4
SWEGLES LN
12000 MORV 92557 717-D2
SWENSON ST
11200 RIV 92505 714-A2
SWIFT ST
- RivC 92584 868-C2
SWING DR
5400 RivC 92509 684-F4
SWINGLE ST
44500 RivC 92201 5410-C7
SWISS CT
- RivC 92880 683-D7
SWITCHBACK LN
2700 COR 92882 773-B2
N SYBIL RD
200 PMSP 92262 786-H1
SYCAMORE AV
7800 RIV 92504 715-B3
20200 COR 92883 774-B6
SYCAMORE CIR
- MURR 92563 928-J7
500 PMSP 92262 756-E4
SYCAMORE DR
11200 CALI 92320 690-B6
SYCAMORE LN
1000 COR 92879 743-F6
1000 SJCT 92582 810-J2
12900 YCPA 92399 650-D5
80400 INDO 92201 5470-B2
SYCAMORE RD
65700 RivC - 726-G2
SYCAMORE ST
900 COR 92879 743-H4
1600 PER 92570 807-G5
12000 SBdC 92316 645-E4
39600 MURR 92563 928-H7
41300 MURR 92562 928-A5
SYCAMORE TR
12900 YCPA 92399 650-E6
SYCAMORE CANYON BLVD
- RIV 92506 716-H4
600 RIV 92507 686-D6
5400 RIV 92507 716-G2
11600 RivC 92507 716-G2
SYCAMORE CANYON CT
2000 RIV 92507 716-G2
SYCAMORE CANYON RD
9600 MORV 92557 687-B4
SYCAMORE CREEK AV
- MURR 92562 927-F4
SYCAMORE CREEK DR
25200 RivC 92590 957-J7
25200 RivC 92590 958-A7
SYCAMORE FALLS
44700 RivC 92536 983-B2
SYCAMORE HILL DR
- RIV 92506 716-A3
SYCAMORE MESA RD
27400 RivC 92590 978-D2
28200 RivC 92590 958-E7
SYCAMORE RIDGE RD
- MURR 92563 928-J4
- MURR 92563 929-A4
SYCAMORE SPRING DR
45500 RivC 92536 983-G5
SYCAMORE SPRINGS RD
34400 RivC 92544 901-C4
SYDNEY CT
20600 RivC 92595 896-J6
20600 RivC 92595 897-A6
SYDNEY ST
3300 HEMT 92545 810-E6
SYDNEY BLUE CIR
- RivC 92883 804-C3
SYDNEY HARBOUR DR
- RIV 92508 716-E7
SYKES DR
24300 MORV 92553 717-E4
SYLLMAR CIR
200 CALI 92320 650-B7
SYLMAR DR
13500 MORV 92553 717-D5
SYLMAR LN
7200 RivC 92881 773-H5
85500 COAC 92236 5471-C7
SYLVAN AV
500 BAN 92220 721-G3
SYLVAN DR
8300 RIV 92503 714-F2
SYLVAN WY
52200 RivC - (813-H5
See Page 782)
SYLVANA LN
8500 RivC 92223 650-H7
8500 RivC 92223 690-H1
SYLVESTER CT
14400 MORV 92553 717-J6
SYLVESTER DR
14500 MORV 92553 717-J7
SYLVESTER RD
20800 RivC 92530 866-J7
SYLVIA AV
27500 RivC 92585 838-D3
SYMERON CT
1000 PER 92570 807-F1
SYMERON WY
40500 MURR 92562 928-C5
SYMPHONY PARK LN
- MURR 92562 928-B5
SYPUS CT
27200 RivC 92587 867-G1
SYRACUSE CT
26600 RivC 92544 841-E2
SYRACUSE ST
- RIV 92508 746-E2

T

T ST
- RivC 92518 747-C1
TABB LN
27500 RivC 92584 898-D1
TABBY CT
11200 RIV 92505 714-B3
TABER ST
900 COR 92881 773-F2
TABITHA WY
1100 COR 92882 773-A1
TABLA CT
900 HEMT 92545 810-G5
TABLE MOUNTAIN RD
59300 RivC 92539 (935-F5
See Page 904)
60400 RivC - (905-H4
See Page 904)
TABLE MOUNTAIN TKTR
54600 RivC 92539 904-E4
56100 RivC 92539 (905-A7
See Page 904)
59700 RivC 92539 (935-C1
See Page 904)
TABOR DR
11900 MORV 92557 717-E1
TABOR HILL CT
1500 SJCT 92583 811-E4
TACAYNE RD
16000 RivC 92570 775-H5
TACHEVAH DR
3300 PMSP 92262 756-J7
68000 CTHC 92234 757-D7
E TACHEVAH DR
100 PMSP 92262 756-F7
TACK RD
38200 RivC 92592 900-H5
TACO WY
66700 DHSP 92240 696-J2
TACOMA
13100 MORV 92553 717-G4
TACOMA CT
- CTHC 92234 787-F1
TAEGE RD
- RivC 92399 650-J7
TAEGE RANCH RD
7200 RivC 92324 647-A6
TAFFLE RANCH RD
43600 RivC 92544 902-A2
TAFT
- CTHC 92234 787-A7
TAFT AV
300 HEMT 92543 810-J5
TAFT CIR
- COR 92881 773-F3
TAFT CT
40800 MURR 92562 927-H2
TAFT LN
- COR 92881 773-F3
TAFT ST
1700 NRCO 92860 713-E3
3700 RIV 92503 714-H6
16500 RivC 92508 746-C6
TAHITIAN PL
33500 YCPA 92399 649-F4
TAHOE CIR
2300 HEMT 92545 840-G1
44100 INDW 92210 818-J7
44100 INDW 92210 848-J1
TAHOE CT
3700 RIV 92506 715-E1
S TAHOE DR
2500 ONT 91761 643-B5
TAHOE ST
100 PER 92571 777-H7
TAHOMA PL
5800 RIV 92505 714-C3
TAHQUITZ AV
100 SJCT 92583 811-A1
300 HEMT 92543 840-J1
82000 INDO 92201 5410-E7
N TAHQUITZ AV
100 HEMT 92543 810-J7
TAHQUITZ DR
100 PMSP 92262 786-D2
25300 RivC - 814-D6
TAHQUITZ RD
25100 RivC - 814-E5
68300 CTHC 92234 817-D1
E TAHQUITZ CANYON WY
100 PMSP 92262 786-F2
W TAHQUITZ CANYON WY
100 PMSP 92262 786-D2
TAHQUITZ VIEW DR
54200 RivC - 814-D7
TAKAJIMA RD
20000 RivC 92567 779-B3
TAKOTA LN
45600 INDW 92210 849-D2
TALBERT
1200 LKEL 92530 866-G5
TALBERT DR
36800 CTHC 92234 787-G7
TALBOT CIR
2300 COR 92882 773-A1
TALBOT CT
24600 MORV 92551 747-F1
TALBOT RD
- MURR 92563 928-H7
TALCEY TER
800 RIV 92506 715-H6
TALKING ROCK TURN
- LQNT 92253 879-G2
TALLANDSIA CT
25600 MORV 92553 717-H5
TALLEY CT
4800 RIV 92503 714-H2
TALLOWOOD DR
- RivC 92211 789-G6
TALL PINES RD
52600 RivC - (813-J3
See Page 782)
TALLY RD
28400 RivC 92584 838-D7
TALLY HO LN
1300 NRCO 92860 743-E1
TALSHIRE LN
1900 COR 92881 773-F1
TALUS LN
- RivC 92203 789-G5
TAMALA AV
69100 CTHC 92234 787-E6
TAMAR DR
12000 DHSP 92240 697-A5
TAMARA DR
12800 MORV 92553 717-G3
TAMARA RD
67100 CTHC 92234 757-B5
TAMARACK DR
- COR 92881 773-C3
- COR 92882 773-C3
TAMARACK LN
1800 HEMT 92545 840-G4
TAMARACK RD
54200 RivC 92282 724-C2
TAMARACK ST
25100 LMLN 92354 647-C2
TAMARACK WY
3000 RivC 91752 644-A5
TAMARIND AV
10600 FONT 92316 645-B2
10600 SBdC 92316 645-B2
TAMARIND DR
2000 PER 92571 777-J6
TAMARIND LN
8200 RivC 92509 684-F5
TAMARINE POD CT
- RivC 92203 789-G7
- RivC 92211 789-G7
TAMARISK AV
83800 INDO 92201 5470-J2
TAMARISK CIR
36100 YCPA 92399 650-E6
TAMARISK DR
- BAN 92220 721-B6
200 ImCo 92274 (5773-B7
See Page 5712)
25900 RivC 92544 811-D7
TAMARISK LN
- COR 92881 773-G4
700 PMSP 92262 756-E7
16500 RivC 92240 726-J1
70400 RMIR 92270 787-J7
70800 RMIR 92270 788-A7
TAMARISK PL
9200 RIV 92503 715-A7
E TAMARISK RD
100 PMSP 92262 756-F7
TAMARISK ST
39500 MURR 92563 928-H7
72700 PDST 92260 848-D3
TAMARISK FLOWER DR
- RivC 92211 789-G7
TAMARISK ROW DR
37900 PDST 92211 819-D2
72200 PDST 92211 788-F4
TAMARISK ROW DR
72200 RivC 92211 788-E4
TAMARISK WEST DR
1000 RMIR 92270 817-H1
TAMARIX PL
23800 RivC 92587 837-F7
TAMATEA RD
60300 RivC 92539 (965-H3
See Page 964)
TAMATEA ST
60300 RivC 92539 (965-G3
See Page 964)
TAMERRON WY
33500 RivC 92595 897-C3
TAMIT PL
100 PDST 92260 848-C7
100 PDST 92260 878-C1
TAMMERLANE WY
18000 RivC 92504 746-A7
TAMMY CT
10400 RivC 92220 691-H4
TAMMY LN
8700 RivC 92509 684-E1
E TAM O SHANTER CT
2700 ONT 91761 643-A6
TAM OSHANTER PZ
1600 PMSP 92264 787-C3
TAMPICO CIR
- COR 92879 743-F3
TAMPICO DR
72700 PDST 92260 848-D1
TAMRA LN
16400 RivC 92504 745-H4
TAMSCOTT DR
38600 RivC 92539 (934-C5
See Page 904)
TANAGER CIR
40200 TEM 92591 959-A2
TANAGER CT
26400 LMLN 92354 647-F3
TANAGER ST
21900 GTER 92313 646-D5
TANAGER TR
23800 MURR 92562 928-B2
TANAGER WY
33700 RivC 92544 901-J2
TANBARK WY
1700 HEMT 92545 840-H3
TANBERRY LN
28100 MORV 92555 718-D6
TANDIKA TR N
38100 PDST 92211 819-A1
TANDIKA TR S
39300 PDST 92211 819-B3
N TANFORAN CT
40000 RivC 92536 (933-D7
See Page 902)
S TANFORAN CT
40800 RivC 92536 963-D2
TANFORAN DR
10100 RIV 92503 714-E1
TANFORAN LN
100 RMIR 92270 817-H2
TANFORD LN
1000 COR 92881 773-F1
TANGARINE CT
- RivC 92211 789-G7
TANGELO
51200 LQNT 92253 5470-A7
TANGELO AV
27700 RivC 92544 841-J4
27700 RivC 92544 842-A4
TANGELO DR
19400 RIV 92508 746-E3
TANGERINE ST
800 COR 92879 743-F7
TANGERINE WY
- RivC 92503 744-J7
3100 RIV 92506 715-F2
29000 LKEL 92530 865-F2
TANGIER AV
80000 INDO 92201 5470-A4
TANGIER RD
47400 PDST 92260 848-G3
71500 RMIR 92270 818-B6
TANGIERS
100 PMSP 92264 786-C6
TANGLETREE WY
30200 RivC 92563 929-A7
TANGLEWOOD
54300 LQNT 92253 5530-A3
TANGLEWOOD CT
48300 RivC 92536 963-A1
TANGLEWOOD DR
1300 COR 92882 742-G6
26400 RivC 92586 838-B7
TANGLEWOOD LN
300 RMIR 92270 818-C5
54500 RivC - 814-D7
54500 RivC - 844-D1
TANGLEWOOD TR
100 PDST 92211 819-A3
TANGO CT
49000 LQNT 92253 849-G5
TANGO BAR CIR
23700 RivC 92567 808-H4
TANISHA LN
34300 RivC 92595 897-B4
TANNER CIR
400 RivC 92507 646-E7
TANNER ST
39300 HEMT 92543 810-J4
TANYA AV
3300 HEMT 92545 840-F2
TAOS CT
28400 CTHC 92234 757-C6
TAOS CV
45300 INDW 92210 848-J1
TAOS DR
2900 RivC 92509 685-D1
26000 RivC 92586 868-A2
TAOS RD
48800 RivC 92230 723-H3
TAOS TR
81000 INDO 92201 5470-C2
TAP CIR
- PER 92570 807-F3
TAPATIA RD
23500 RivC 92548 809-C3
TAPIA WY
2700 RivC 92509 645-B6
TARA CIR
9200 RivC 92509 684-D1
TARA DR
36200 CALI 92320 690-B6
TARA LN
1800 NRCO 92860 713-D5
34700 YCPA 92399 649-J6
TARA CODY CT
43200 RivC 92536 964-A6
TARANO LN
16700 MORV 92551 747-G4
TARARA DR
23500 MORV 92557 687-D6
S TARA RIDGE CT
1700 CLTN 92324 647-A3
TARBUTTON RD
14800 DHSP 92240 697-B7
14900 RivC 92240 697-B7
TAREYTON DR
1300 RIV 92506 716-B3
TARMAR RANCH RD
- RivC 92562 956-C6
TAROCCO DR
3000 COR 92881 773-E3
TAROCCO LN
19500 RIV 92508 746-E4
TARON TR
45400 RivC 92539 (985-E3
See Page 964)
TARR RD
38000 INDO 92203 5410-A1
38000 RivC 92203 5410-A1
TARRAGON WY
14700 MORV 92553 717-J7
TARRAGONA DR
6000 RivC 92509 645-E4
24000 MURR 92562 928-B2
TARRYTON CT
31200 YCPA 92399 649-A3
TARTAN WY
- BEAU 92223 720-G2
TARTARIAN DR
9900 RivC 92223 690-H4
TASCHNER DR
25000 HEMT 92543 810-J6
TASMAN ST
26100 MORV 92555 717-J2
TATE CT
5400 RIV 92505 714-C5
TATE RD
27400 RivC 92584 838-D6
TATIA CT
- MURR 92562 927-J2
- MURR 92562 928-A2
TATUM CT
6700 RivC 92509 685-A2
TAUPE AV
25300 MORV 92553 717-H7
TAURUS AV
83400 INDO 92201 5470-H1
TAURUS CIR
2800 RIV 92503 744-G2
TAURUS CT
- LQNT 92253 819-H6
TAVA LN
200 PDST 92211 818-J4
200 PDST 92211 819-A4
16000 RivC 92504 745-H3
41000 RivC 92544 841-D1
TAVO LN
45000 RivC 92536 982-F3
TAYLOR
13200 MORV 92553 717-E4
TAYLOR AV
- PDST 92260 818-H2
1300 COR 92882 743-C7
2000 COR 92882 773-C1
TAYLOR CT
1100 LKEL 92530 865-H4
11100 LMLN 92354 647-B1
TAYLOR DR
- BEAU 92223 690-F6
10100 RivC 92223 690-F4
TAYLOR LN
29300 RivC 92567 808-G1
TAYLOR PL
40000 RivC 92203 819-J3
TAYLOR RD
- RivC 92570 837-B1
TAYLOR ST
- MURR 92562 927-G4
100 HEMT 92543 811-B7
300 HEMT 92543 841-B1
1400 LKEL 92530 866-G6
11800 RIV 92503 744-C3
12700 GTER 92313 646-C6
24800 LMLN 92354 647-B1
32700 RivC 92596 939-E6

STREET / Block City ZIP Pg-Grid

TOUCHE DR
700 SBdC 92316 645-F2
TOULON CT
3400 RivC 92501 646-A6
TOULON DR
1800 COR 92882 743-A7
36000 MURR 92562 928-C1
TOUMEY LN
2700 COR 92881 773-E2
TOUPLO LN
16100 MORV 92551 747-F3
TOURACO CT
- TEM 92592 959-A6
TOURAINE CT
15700 MORV 92555 748-C2
TOURMALINE AV
83000 INDO 92201 5410-G6
E TOURMALINE AV
83300 INDO 92201 5410-H6
TOURMALINE CT
8600 RivC 92509 684-E1
TOURMALINE DR
12900 RivC 92282 724-E1
TOURNAMENT DR
6300 RivC 92509 685-A1
TOURNAMENT LN
45300 TEM 92592 979-B3
TOURNAMENT WY
81900 INDO 92201 5410-E7
TOURS ST
29700 LKEL 92530 865-G3
TOWER LN
60500 RivC - (907-J3 See Page 906)
TOWER RD
3200 PMSP 92262 786-J1
5100 RIV 92506 685-D6
TOWER ST
23600 MORV 92553 717-D2
TOWERGROVE DR
500 COR 92879 743-H3
TOWER VIEW CT
28100 RivC 92585 808-E6
TOWLE CIR
100 PDST 92211 818-J3
TOWN CIR
22200 MORV 92553 717-A2
TOWN AND COUNTRY DR
1800 NRCO 92860 713-D5
11200 RIV 92505 744-E2
TOWN CENTER WY
44400 PDST 92260 818-D7
44400 PDST 92260 848-D1
TOWNE ST
43100 INDO 92201 5410-G6
45100 INDO 92201 5470-G1
TOWNGATE BLVD
22300 MORV 92553 717-B3
TOWNSEND DR
7800 RivC 92509 684-G5
23200 GTER 92313 646-G3
TOWNSEND ST
100 LKEL 92530 866-C4
TOWNSENDIA AV
21200 MORV 92557 716-H1
TOWNSVILLE CT
- MURR 92563 929-A4
TOWN VIEW AV
39000 RivC 92563 929-A7
TOYON PL
700 COR 92882 742-J5
TOYON RD
4300 RIV 92504 714-J2
4300 RIV 92504 715-A3
TOYON HEIGHTS DR
3100 SDCo 92028 998-C7
TRABERT CIR
400 RivC 92507 646-D6
TRABUCO CT
200 PER 92571 807-H2
TRABUCO DR
22300 RivC 92570 806-A1
33100 LKEL 92530 865-H7
TRABUCO RD
35500 RivC 92530 896-B7
TRACI ST
700 HEMT 92543 810-J5
TRACTOR TR
34100 RivC 92595 897-G4
TRACY CIR
43800 RivC 92201 5410-D6
TRACY LN
28400 RivC 92373 688-E1
40500 RivC 92544 871-C1
TRACY PL
- RMIR 92270 818-A4
TRADE AV
12600 CLTN 92324 645-J5
TRADE CENTER DR
3200 RIV 92507 686-B4
TRADER PL
43100 INDO 92201 5410-D6
TRADEWATER CT
30300 TEM 92591 959-A5
TRADEWIND PL
600 COR 92879 743-J3
TRADEWINDS CIR
29300 LKEL 92530 865-F2
TRADE WINDS DR
24000 RivC 92585 808-E6
25800 RivC 92585 838-E1
TRADITION ST
200 PER 92571 807-H1
TRADITION TR
51500 LQNT 92253 849-G7
51700 LQNT 92253 879-G1
TRAFAGLAR SQ
- RMIR 92270 788-C5
TRAFALGAR AV
2000 RIV 92506 716-A3
2200 RIV 92506 715-J3
TRAFALGAR RD
15800 FONT 92337 644-G2
TRAFALGAR SQ
- RMIR 92270 788-C6
TRAFALGAR WY
- MURR 92563 928-G7
- MURR 92563 958-G1
TRAIL CIR
2300 PMSP 92262 756-E5
73200 RivC 92260 818-E2
E TRAIL CT
2200 CLTN 92324 646-J4
TRAIL ST
4200 NRCO 92860 713-A7
4500 NRCO 92860 712-J7
5300 NRCO 92860 742-J1
TRAIL BLAZE PASS
- MURR 92562 927-E4
TRAILBLAZER RD
13800 RivC 92570 775-C7
TRAIL CANYON DR
5100 RivC 91752 683-H4
TRAILER LN
- PDST 92260 848-B4
TRAILHEAD CT
27600 RivC 92883 835-C5
TRAILHEAD PT
9200 RivC 92509 684-D4
TRAILHILL CT
- RIV 92505 714-C6
TRAILMASTER DR
43100 RivC 92536 963-J7
TRAILMORE CT
- RIV 92505 714-C6
TRAILS END
10100 RIV 92503 745-A3
54600 RivC - 844-D1
TRAILS END DR
24300 MURR 92562 928-C3
TRAILS END LN
58900 RivC 92539 (985-F4 See Page 964)
TRAILSIDE CIR
- COR 92881 773-F2
TRAILVIEW LN
800 COR 92881 773-F2
TRAILWINDS DR
16100 FONT 92337 644-G3
TRAILWOOD CT
32600 RivC 92595 896-H5
TRAIL WOOD RD
24000 RivC 92545 810-B4
TRAMVIEW RD
200 PMSP 92262 756-C3
TRAM VIEW RD
1300 RivC 92240 696-F6
TRAMWAY RD
- PMSP 92262 755-H6
- PMSP 92262 756-A5
TRAN CT
- RivC 92585 838-C3
TRANCAS CT
26400 RivC 92586 868-B2
E TRANCAS DR
29300 CTHC 92234 757-C7
S TRANCAS DR
67800 CTHC 92234 757-C7
W TRANCAS DR
29700 CTHC 92234 757-C7
TRANQUIL CT
- RivC 92595 896-H6
TRANQUIL LN
1000 COR 92880 743-C2
33000 RivC 92595 896-H6
TRANQUIL PL
- CTHC 92234 787-F6
TRANQUIL WY
24700 MORV 92557 717-F1
TRANQUILLO PL
42100 RivC 92201 819-J5
TRANSIT AV
- GTER 92313 646-C7
- RivC 92507 646-C7
TRANSITION RD
- RivC 92571 748-C5
TRAUTWEIN RD
8100 RIV 92508 716-D7
8100 RIV 92508 746-D1
14300 RIV 92506 716-D7
TRAVAS RD
15800 FONT 92337 644-G2
TRAVELODGE LN
38200 RMIR 92270 817-H3
TRAVERS CT
14300 MORV 92553 717-E6
TRAVERS DR
14000 MORV 92553 717-E6
TRAVERSE TR
48300 RivC 92536 963-A5
TRAVIS AV
- RivC 92518 717-C7
- RivC 92518 747-D1
30000 CTHC 92234 787-D1
TRAVIS CT
100 SJCT 92582 810-J1
33800 RivC 92584 898-E3
36300 RivC 92592 930-D5
TRAVIS RD
43300 RivC 92539 (965-H6 See Page 964)
TRAVIS ST
1300 RivC 92543 841-B3
1300 HEMT 92543 841-B3
TRAXLER LN
- RivC 92570 746-G6
TREASURE DR
24500 MORV 92557 717-F1
42800 RivC 92544 901-H5
TREASURE ST
200 PER 92571 807-H1
TREASURE TR
68300 CTHC 92234 817-D2
TREASURE ISLAND DR
22100 CYNL 92587 867-B3
TREBOR RD
4600 RIV 92503 714-H3
TREE LN
34400 RivC 92595 897-C5
TREE BARK LN
- PER 92571 778-C3
TREE FARM LN
- RIV 92518 746-F3
TREEHAVEN PL
1500 RIV 92507 686-G1
TREEHILL PL
5000 RIV 92507 686-B7
TREEHOUSE LN
500 COR 92879 743-J3
TREELINE DR
500 COR 92879 743-J3
TREEMONT PL
2200 COR 92879 743-J2
TREE POPPY DR
42400 RivC 92592 960-B5
TREETOP LN
16600 RivC 92503 744-J5
TREEVIEW LN
1400 RIV 92506 715-H5
TRELANEY RD
16300 FONT 92337 644-H2
TRELEVEN AV
18200 LKEL 92530 866-C3
TRELLIS LN
28300 RivC 92570 836-F7
28300 LKEL 92570 836-F7
TRENMAR LN
- SBdC 92316 645-F1
TRENT DR
23200 RivC 92587 867-F1
TRENTO CIR
100 PDST 92211 818-J3
TRENTON AV
1000 COR 92880 713-A7
1000 COR 92880 743-A1
TRENTON CIR
1300 SJCT 92583 811-D5
TRENTON DR
1400 RIV 92506 716-B2
TRENTON WY
- RivC 92264 816-F3
9600 RivC 92240 696-E1
28100 RivC 92586 838-B5
TRES CERRITOS AV
35000 HEMT 92545 810-A6
35000 RivC 92545 810-A6
TRESSEN TR
- COR 92881 773-E4
TREVINO WY
5400 BAN 92220 721-D5
TREVOR LN
1000 COR 92881 773-F1
3900 HEMT 92544 811-F7
TREY AV
7800 RIV 92503 714-F3
TRIADOR ST
2100 COR 92879 743-H2
TRIANGLE ST
27000 MURR 92562 898-C6
TRIBECCA ST
77200 INDW 92210 849-D1
TRIBUTARY DR
10300 MORV 92557 687-B5
TRICIA LN
76900 PDST 92211 819-C2
TRIDENT CIR
20800 RivC 92570 806-H1
TRIESAN WY
5300 RivC 92509 685-D4
TRIFONE RD
38200 RivC 92544 931-G4
TRIG RD
35500 RivC 92595 897-G6
TRIGGER DR
22000 CYNL 92587 867-B2
TRILLIUM DR
23000 RivC 92595 897-E7
TRIMERO CIR
67000 RivC 92241 727-A5
TRIMPOT LN
- RIV 92504 715-B5
TRINETTE DR
1500 BEAU 92223 690-J7
TRINIDAD CIR
38700 RivC 92264 816-F3
TRINIDAD DR
79700 RivC 92201 819-J5
79700 RivC 92201 5410-A5
TRINIDAD ST
1400 HEMT 92543 840-J4
TRINITY
- RMIR 92270 817-J2
TRINITY CIR
- COR 92881 773-D4
41500 RivC 92201 819-J4
TRINITY CT
3400 RIV 92506 685-F7
TRINITY LN
- COR 92881 773-D4
TRINITY WY
2300 SJCT 92583 811-E5
33000 RivC 92530 896-E3
TRINITY BAY CT
16700 MORV 92551 747-F4
TRINITY RIVER WY
- MURR 92562 927-G3
TRIOLO TR
36000 RivC 92545 840-C6
TRIPEPI ST
64000 RivC 92258 726-D3
TRIPLE C RANCH RD
28000 MURR 92584 898-F5
TRIPLE CROWN CIR
3100 NRCO 92860 713-F5
TRIPLE CROWN RD
28900 RivC 92585 838-F1
30500 RivC 92548 809-A7
TRIPOLI DR
99500 RivC 92254 (5654-E7 See Page 5594)
TRIPOLI ST
1100 RIV 92507 686-C4
TRIPOLI WY
1000 COAC 92236 5471-B6
51800 COAC 92236 5531-B1
TRIPP FLATS RD
35600 RivC 92539 (903-J6 See Page 902)
35600 RivC 92539 904-A6
36900 RivC 92539 (933-J1 See Page 902)
37000 RivC 92539 (934-A2 See Page 904)
TRISHA WY
16400 RivC 92504 745-H4
TRISTAN LN
- PDST 92211 819-A4
TRITT TR
42700 RivC 92539 (965-F4 See Page 964)
TRIUMPH LN
11300 MORV 92557 687-E7
11400 MORV 92557 717-E1
TROFEO CIR
1100 PMSP 92262 756-G7
TROJAN CT
- RMIR 92270 818-A2
5000 RIV 92507 686-D7
TRONTI WY
17600 RivC 92504 745-F7
TROON CIR
12000 RMIR 92270 788-A5
TROON CT
- MURR 92563 928-J4
- RIV 92508 716-E7
9600 RivC 92240 696-E1
28600 RivC 92586 838-A7
TROON TR
- LQNT 92253 879-G2
TROON WY
- LQNT 92253 5530-D6
TROPIC CT
11400 MORV 92557 687-G7
TROPICAL PARK LN
200 RMIR 92270 817-H2
TROPICANA DR
2700 RIV 92504 715-B7
26900 RivC 92585 838-C3
W TROPICA RANCHO RD
600 CLTN 92324 646-B2
19600 SBdC 92324 646-B2
TROQUATO LN
17600 RivC 92504 746-A3
TROTH ST
4700 RivC 91752 683-J3
TROTMAN AV
2900 NRCO 92860 713-F5
TROTSDALE DR
44900 TEM 92592 979-C3
TROTTER LN
- FONT 92337 644-E3
49000 RivC 92536 963-C3
TROTTER TR
1900 NRCO 92860 713-B7
1900 NRCO 92860 743-B1
TROUBLE CT
10700 RivC 92223 690-D5
TROVARE WY
- RMIR 92270 788-A6
TROVITA CIR
9200 RIV 92508 746-E4
TROVITA DR
900 COR 92881 773-E3
TROWBRIDGE CT
39900 MURR 92563 928-F6
TROY LN
- RivC 92585 838-A3
9300 RIV 92508 746-E4
13600 RivC 92585 837-J3
36200 RivC 92596 899-C7
TROYES LN
23900 MURR 92562 927-J4
24000 MURR 92562 928-A4
S TRUCKEE RIVER LN
2900 ONT 91761 643-D6
TRUDY ST
23700 RivC 92570 805-J5
TRUE COUNTRY CT
78300 RivC 92201 819-F4
TRUELSON AV
25900 RivC 92545 839-G1
TRUFFAUT DR
21600 RivC 92567 779-E6
TRUJILLO WY
6100 RivC 92509 684-J5
TRUMAN
- CTHC 92234 787-A7
TRUMAN CT
800 HEMT 92543 810-J5
TRUMAN PL
24800 MURR 92562 957-H1
TRUMAN ST
3700 RivC 92879 743-J5
3700 RivC 92879 744-A5
TRUMAN WY
- INDO 92201 5470-F5
TRUMBLE RD
1500 PER 92585 808-C7
25000 RivC 92585 808-C7
25600 RivC 92585 838-C3
25600 PER 92585 838-C1
TRUMP ST
- PER 92571 777-G2
TRUMPETS CT
8900 RivC 92883 804-B3
TRUST CT
33700 RivC 92544 902-D1
TRUST WY
11400 MORV 92555 688-C7
TRYON AV
30500 RivC 92555 749-F4
TUBAC TR
33200 RivC 92276 788-E3
TUCALOTA HILLS RD
36900 RivC 92592 900-H7
36900 RivC 92592 930-H1
TUCKAWAY AV
6200 BAN 92220 721-C5
TUCKER RD
32700 RivC 92584 868-B7
32700 RivC 92584 898-B1
TUCSON AV
- NRCO 92860 743-F2
TUCSON CIR
43100 PDST 92211 819-E6
TUCSON CT
- SJCT 92583 780-J5
5900 RIV 92504 685-B7
TUCSON PL
32600 RivC 92276 788-E3
TUDOR CIR
- COR 92882 772-J2
TUDOR CT
2000 RIV 92506 716-A2
TUDOR DR
1900 SJCT 92583 811-F4
TUDOR LN
76900 PDST 92211 819-D3
TUDOR WY
16900 FONT 92337 644-J3
TUFTS CIR
900 COR 92880 743-A1
TULANE AV
11400 RivC 92507 716-F1
TULANE CT
- RMIR 92270 818-A2
25000 RivC 92544 (812-A5 See Page 782)
TULARE DR
800 COR 92882 773-A3
2000 PMSP 92264 786-F6
TULARE ST
600 RivC 92507 646-D6
TULE WY
18900 RivC 92530 896-F4
TULE CANYON RD
44100 RivC 92539 (965-E7 See Page 964)
44400 RivC 92539 (985-E2 See Page 964)
TULE CANYON TRUCK TKTR
58900 RivC 92539 (985-E3 See Page 964)
TULE PEAK RD
43500 RivC 92536 963-F7
43800 RivC 92536 983-H1
52200 RivC 92536 (984-A2 See Page 964)
54500 RivC 92539 (984-E2 See Page 964)
TULE VALLEY RD
42900 RivC 92536 963-F6
43700 RivC 92536 983-F2
TULIP AV
24700 LMLN 92354 647-B2
TULIP CT
- RivC 92883 804-B4
2000 RIV 92507 686-A6
2400 HEMT 92545 840-G2
31000 LKEL 92532 867-D5
TULIP LN
33800 RivC 92595 897-D3
TULIP PL
47800 INDO 92201 5470-B3
TULIP ST
1100 COR 92882 743-A7
TULIPAN ST
49300 COAC 92236 5471-A5
TULIPTREE CIR
12200 RivC 92503 744-H5
TULITA LN
28500 RivC 92584 898-F2
TULLEY RANCH RD
32700 TEM 92592 979-G2
TULSA AV
4900 RIV 92505 714-C6
TULSA CT
- HEMT 92545 810-E6
TUMACACORI DR
73500 RivC 92276 788-F2
TUMBLEWEED CIR
1900 COR 92882 742-H7
TUMBLEWEED CT
25300 MURR 92563 928-E2
TUMBLEWEED DR
22100 CYNL 92587 867-B2
TUMBLEWEED LN
73100 PDST 92260 848-E2
TUMBLEWEED ST
5800 RivC 92509 684-C5
E TUMBLEWEED ST
2700 ONT 91761 683-A1
TUMBLEWEED TR
19100 RivC 92241 727-C4
40200 RivC 92536 963-D1
40300 RivC 92536 (933-D7 See Page 902)
TUNDAR CIR
2600 COR 92879 744-A2
TUNDAR LN
2600 COR 92879 743-J2
2600 COR 92879 744-A2
S TUNGSTEN CT
2600 SBDO 92408 646-J1
TUNGSTEN PL
42500 PDST 92260 818-G6
TUNIS
200 PMSP 92264 786-C6
TUNIS RD
71600 RMIR 92270 818-B6
TUNITAS RD
67600 DHSP 92240 697-B4
TUNNEL SPRING RD
- RivC - (905-E3 See Page 904)
TUOLOMNE CT
40200 TEM 92591 959-A2
S TUOLUMNE PL
2800 ONT 91761 643-C6
TUOMINEN WY
26400 RivC 92544 841-D1
TUPELO CT
- RivC 92584 868-F6
TUPELO RD
27000 RivC 92584 868-C6
TURCKEL LN
28300 RivC 92596 839-B6
TURENDOT ST
76900 PDST 92211 819-C5
TURF LN
43000 RivC 92592 960-F6
TURF PARADISE LN
200 RMIR 92270 817-H2
TURFWOOD ST
- RivC 92586 838-A4
TURK CT
24700 RivC 92544 811-G5
TURLEY ST
1200 RIV 92501 685-J1
TURLOCK DR
8500 RIV 92504 715-C6
TURMERIC WY
25600 MORV 92553 717-H4
TURNBERRY CT
- CTHC 92234 787-F1
- INDO 92201 5410-B6
38300 MURR 92562 927-B3
TURNBERRY DR
- BAN 92220 721-C5
11000 RMIR 92270 788-A6
TURNBERRY LN
1900 COR 92881 773-F1
44800 INDW 92210 819-A7
TURNBERRY ST
15600 MORV 92555 748-B2
TURNBERRY WY
- LQNT 92253 5530-E4
TURNBERRY ISLE DR
- RivC 92203 789-H7
- RivC 92211 789-H7
- RivC 92211 819-H1
TURNBULL AV
17200 LKEL 92530 866-A2
TURNBULL RD
4400 RIV 92503 714-H4
TURNER AV
1700 COR 92881 773-G5
13700 ONT 91761 683-A2
S TURNER AV
1400 ONT 91761 643-A3
3400 ONT 91761 683-A1
TURNER LN
34600 YCPA 92399 649-J7
TURNER ST
33000 RivC 92530 896-D3
TURNESA CT
6800 RivC 92240 696-E1
TURNINGBEND WY
11300 RIV 92505 714-B4
S TURNSTONE AV
2600 ONT 91761 643-A5
TURQUERIES AV
42000 PDST 92211 819-D6
TURQUESA DR
1500 SJCT 92583 811-D3
TURQUOISE DR
100 PER 92571 777-H7
1300 COR 92882 743-A7
12900 RivC 92282 724-E1
TURQUOISE ST
1100 HEMT 92543 840-J3
2700 RIV 92507 686-B3
TURRELL CT
18900 RivC 92508 716-D7
TURRELL WY
- RIV 92508 716-D7
- RivC 92508 716-D7
TURTLE DR
- BAN 92220 721-C6
TURTLECREEK CT
22700 MORV 92557 687-B4
TURTLE CREEK RD
32900 RivC 92595 867-F7
32900 RivC 92595 897-F1
TURTLE DOVE DR
32800 RivC 92530 896-E3
TURTLE DOVE LN
14500 RivC 92220 721-H6
TURTLE ROCK RD
34100 RivC 92555 749-G3
TURTON LN
12100 MORV 92557 717-B2
N TUSCAN RD
600 PMSP 92262 756-C5
TUSCARORA CIR
24500 MORV 92553 717-F6
TUSCOLA CIR
24400 MURR 92562 928-C3
TUSCOLA PL
4100 RIV 92505 744-B2
TUSCOLA ST
11800 MORV 92557 717-H2
TUSTIN CT
- SJCT 92583 780-J5
N TUXEDO CIR
900 PMSP 92262 756-C7
TWAIN CIR
6500 RIV 92506 716-C4
TWEED WY
- RIV 92508 716-F6
TWELVE OAKS RD
- RivC 92562 956-E4
TWENTY GRAND ST
2500 PER 92571 777-G5
TWENTYNINE PALMS HWY Rt#-62
- RivC - 391-C1
- RivC - 655-G1
- RivC 92282 655-G1
49100 SBdC 92256 655-G1
TWILIGHT CIR
16200 RivC 92503 744-C4
TWILIGHT CT
- MURR 92563 928-E3
42700 TEM 92592 959-A6
TWILIGHT WY
11000 MORV 92555 688-E7
TWIN ARROW CIR
29100 RivC 92584 868-G2
TWIN CANYON DR
21700 RivC 92567 779-H6
23200 GTER 92313 646-G3
TWIN CREEK LN
24500 RivC 92570 805-E6
TWINFLOWER AV
23000 RivC 92595 897-E7
TWINFLOWER CT
13100 MORV 92553 717-J4
TWIN HILLS DR
5000 BAN 92220 721-D4
TWIN HILLS WY
- RivC 92592 979-H3
TWINING AV
21000 RivC 92518 746-J5
TWINING ST
3800 RivC 92509 685-D3
TWIN KNOLLS DR
6100 CHLS 91709 712-A5
TWIN LAKES DR
17700 RivC 92508 746-B2
TWINLEAF LN
2600 COR 92881 773-D2
TWIN OAKS CT
22100 MURR 92562 927-C4
TWIN PALMS DR
200 PMSP 92264 786-E5
TWIN PINES RD
48600 RivC - 389-G7
48600 RivC 92220 389-G7
TWIN SPRINGS RD
40300 RivC 92544 841-C4
TWIN STAR RD
1400 PMSP 92262 756-F4
TWIN WILLOW RD
35200 MURR 92563 898-G6
35200 MURR 92584 898-G6
TWO BUNCH PALMS TR
65000 DHSP 92240 696-F6
66600 DHSP 92240 697-A5
TWO TREES RD
300 RIV 92507 686-F3
300 RivC 92507 686-F3
TWYLA JANE LN
17200 RivC 92504 776-A2
TYAHA ST
- SDCo 92028 999-D7
TYANN CT
24400 MORV 92551 747-F1
TYLER AV
27400 RivC 92585 838-D1
TYLER CT
25600 RivC 92586 837-J5
TYLER LN
86000 COAC 92236 5531-D2
TYLER PL
24800 MURR 92562 957-J1
TYLER RD
- RivC 92570 777-A3
TYLER ST
2700 RIV 92503 744-H2
3400 RIV 92505 744-H2
3400 RIV 92505 714-E1
3400 RIV 92503 714-E4
7200 RIV 92503 684-D7
7200 RIV 92505 684-D7
42900 RivC 92536 981-J3
43200 RivC 92536 982-A3
45500 COAC 92236 5411-D7
45500 COAC 92236 5471-D1
52000 COAC 92236 5531-D3
53900 COAC 92274 5531-D3
53900 RivC 92274 5531-D3
60000 RivC 92274 (5591-E3 See Page 5590)
66000 RivC 92274 (5651-E2 See Page 5590)
72000 RivC 92274 410-E3
TYLMAN ST
- TEM 92592 959-F7
TYROL DR
15900 SBdC 92337 644-G1
15900 FONT 92337 644-G1
TYROLITE ST
4200 RivC 92509 644-G7
4200 RivC 92509 684-G1
TYSON CT
6600 RIV 92506 716-B4
TYSON RD
20900 RivC 92570 836-J6
21100 RivC 92570 837-A6

U

U ST
- RivC 92518 747-C1
ULLA LN
3700 LKEL 92530 865-G5
ULLER LN
29200 RivC 92567 808-G1
ULLMAN RD
82100 INDO 92201 5470-E5
ULMER ST
16800 LKEL 92530 866-A2
24500 LKEL 92530 865-J2
ULYSSES ST
- MORV 92555 718-J5
UMPQUA WY
17800 RivC 92241 727-E2
UNA ST
18500 RivC 92570 776-G1
UNDERWOOD CIR
23500 MURR 92562 927-J1
UNDERWOOD DR
- FONT 92316 645-A1
- FONT 92337 645-A1
UNGA CIR
35100 RivC 92595 897-D6
UNION AV
9800 RivC 91752 644-A7
9800 RivC 92509 644-A7
9800 RivC 92509 684-B1
13000 FONT 92337 643-J4
16000 RivC 92530 865-J7
16000 RivC 92530 895-J1
16100 RivC 92530 896-A1
UNION ST
10200 RivC 92223 690-F5
11000 BEAU 92223 690-F5
18900 RivC 92530 896-F4
20000 RivC 92595 896-H5
20500 RivC 92595 897-A6
UNION HILL DR
27200 RivC 92586 837-J4
UNITAS CT
- RivC 92585 838-A3
UNITED RD
12000 RivC 92240 696-F6
UNITY CT
14300 MORV 92553 717-E7
UNIVERSE DR
3200 RivC 91752 643-F5
UNIVERSITY AV
900 RIV 92507 686-B5
2100 RIV 92507 685-J5
3300 RIV 92501 685-G4
24300 LMLN 92354 647-A1
UNIVERSITY CIR
- RMIR 92270 818-C4
UNIVERSITY CT
24700 LMLN 92354 647-B1
UNIVERSITY DR
26600 RivC 92544 841-D2
UNIVERSITY DR N
700 RIV 92507 686-D6
UNIVERSITY DR S
700 RIV 92507 686-D6
UNIVERSITY PL
700 RIV 92507 686-D6
UPLAND WY
11700 DHSP 92240 697-A3
11900 DHSP 92240 696-J3
UPPER DR
100 COR 92882 773-B4
400 COR 92881 773-E4
UPPER RD
- RivC 92571 748-D3
UPPER CARISO RD
14200 RivC 92530 895-D1
UPPER CREST CT
27200 RivC 92586 837-J4
UPPERHILL DR
5100 RIV 92507 686-C7
UPPER RIM ROCK RD
24500 RivC - 814-E4
UPPER RV
- RivC 92571 748-D4
UPPER TENT I
- RivC 92571 748-D4
UPPER TENT II
- RivC 92571 748-D4
UPPER TERRACE DR
3600 RIV 92505 744-E2
UPPER TULE RD
58900 RivC 92539 (985-E4 See Page 964)
UPPER VALLEY RD
55000 RivC 92539 904-F7
UPPER WAY WEST DR
72400 PDST 92260 848-C4
UPTON CT
2700 RivC 92509 645-B6
UPTON DR
32700 RivC 92584 897-G1
32700 RivC 92595 897-G1
URBAN AV
32900 RivC 92530 896-C2
URBAN ST
6800 RIV 92504 715-A2
URBANA AV
3500 RivC 91752 643-H6
UTAH CIR
77000 PDST 92211 819-D6
UTAH ST
700 RIV 92507 686-D4
23300 RivC 92587 837-E6
UTE CT
49100 RivC 92536 963-C1
UTE DR
26000 MORV 92555 717-J4
UTE PL
4200 RIV 92505 744-C1
UTE TR
41100 RivC 92223 691-C4
UTICA ST
7000 RIV 92506 716-D5
UTILITY ACCESS RD
2500 CLTN 92324 646-J2
UTILITY ACCESS RD N
200 CLTN 92324 646-B2
UTILITY ACCESS RD S
100 CLTN 92324 646-B3
UTILITY ACCESS RD W
1400 CLTN 92324 646-A3
1700 CLTN 92501 646-A4
UZZANO
- INDW 92210 819-B6

V

VACATION DR
22000 CYNL 92587 867-B1
VAIL RD
43500 RivC 92562 956-J7
VAIL ST
33000 RivC 92530 896-D3
VAIL WY
5000 RivC 91752 683-G3
VAIL BROOK DR
29600 TEM 92591 958-J4
VAIL LAKE RD
39200 RivC 92592 981-C2
VAIL RANCH PKWY
32400 TEM 92592 979-F3
44900 RivC 92592 979-F3
VAIL VUE DR
42900 RivC 92536 963-C6
VAILWOOD DR
4900 HEMT 92544 811-G5
VALARIE CIR
70800 RMIR 92270 788-A7
VALARIE RD
39600 RivC 92539 (935-E6 See Page 904)
VAL DEANE WY
27000 RivC 92544 841-E2
VALDEZ AV
5000 RivC 92509 684-J4
5000 RivC 92509 685-A4
VALDIVIA WY
1100 PMSP 92262 756-J7
VALDOSTA CIR
700 COR 92879 743-G3
VALE CREST
- PDST 92260 848-D6
VALECREST DR
24800 MORV 92557 717-F1
VALECREST LN
- RivC - (907-D2 See Page 906)
VALENCE CT
- TEM 92592 979-G1
VALENCIA AV
1100 HEMT 92543 810-H6
82100 INDO 92201 5410-E7
VALENCIA CIR
- MORV 92555 748-A2
VALENCIA CT
- LQNT 92253 849-F6
VALENCIA DR
- RMIR 92270 818-B4
9000 DHSP 92240 697-A1
9000 DHSP 92240 696-J1
VALENCIA LN
85400 COAC 92236 5531-C1
VALENCIA RD
500 COR 92881 773-D4
2600 PMSP 92262 756-H5
VALENCIA ST
500 PER 92571 777-H5
6800 RIV 92504 715-D2
27800 CTHC 92234 757-D5
33500 RivC 92595 897-A3
VALENCIA WY
15000 LKEL 92530 865-F1
41200 RivC 92592 960-D4
75200 PDST 92211 818-J4
VALENCIA HILL DR
2800 RIV 92507 686-E4
VALENSOLE CT
26800 MURR 92562 928-C1
VALENTINE CIR
42900 RivC 92592 960-A6
VALENTINE LN
4300 HEMT 92544 811-F6
VALENTINO
82900 INDO 92201 5470-G4
VALENTINO WY
32600 TEM 92592 979-F3
VALERIANA CT
40100 TEM 92591 958-J2
VALERIE CT
12200 MORV 92555 717-J2
VALERIO DR
33200 RivC 92544 871-G7
33400 RivC 92544 901-J1
VALET WY
600 BAN 92220 722-A4
VALE VISTA DR
11300 FONT 92337 644-B2
VALGIO DR
37500 CALI 92320 690-D1
VALHALLA
- LQNT 92253 5530-C6
VALHALLA DR
22800 MURR 92562 927-D3
VALIANT ST
11600 RIV 92505 714-A5
N VALLARTA CIR
600 PMSP 92262 756-G7
VALLAT RD
23700 RMIR 92270 818-C3
VALLECITO AV
700 BEAU 92223 721-B3
VALLECITO LN
63700 RivC - (907-G6 See Page 906)
VALLE DE COSTA
- CTHC 92234 787-G7
VALLE HEIGHTS RD
26400 RivC 92544 842-D1
VALLEJO AV
28500 TEM 92592 979-A2
VALLEJO DR
900 HEMT 92543 840-J2
1300 COR 92882 742-J6
E VALLEJO RD
44000 TEM 92592 979-B2
VALLEJO ST
3100 RIV 92503 744-F2
VALLE LINDO
11700 MORV 92555 688-C7
11700 MORV 92555 718-C1
VALLE OLVERA
29600 TEM 92591 958-J2
29600 TEM 92591 959-A2
VALLE PACIFICO DR
17900 RivC 92570 806-C5
VALLE VERDE
29700 TEM 92591 958-J2
VALLE VISTA
21600 RivC 92562 927-A7
40000 RivC 92562 926-J7
40000 RivC 92562 956-J1
41000 RivC 92562 957-A2
75600 INDW 92210 849-A1
VALLE VISTA WY
16100 RivC 92506 745-G2
VALLEY BLVD
25600 RivC 92586 837-J5
25700 RivC 92585 837-H3
28800 RivC 92584 837-J6
29000 RivC 92584 867-J1
29200 RivC 92584 868-A1
VALLEY DR
100 PMSP 92264 786-D4
1400 BAN 92220 722-B1
6400 RIV 92505 714-C1
48600 RivC 92536 963-B7
E VALLEY DR
38000 RivC 92539 (935-B3 See Page 904)
VALLEY RD
21700 RivC 92567 779-D7
85000 COAC 92236 5531-B1
VALLEY ST
22600 RivC 92570 805-H3
VALLEY TER
21800 RivC 92595 897-B3
VALLEY WY
3400 RivC 92509 645-A7
5400 RivC 92509 644-J7
5400 RivC 92509 684-J1

RIVERSIDE CO.

STREET Block City ZIP Pg-Grid

VALLEY CREST CIR
10400 MORV 92557 687-A6
VALLEY CREST LN
72300 PDST 92260 848-C5
VALLEY FORGE DR
4600 RivC 92509 684-B1
VALLEY GLEN CIR
24100 MORV 92557 687-E5
VALLEY GLEN DR
4700 RivC 92880 742-B5
VALLEY MEADOW AV
- RivC 92880 713-A2
VALLEY MEADOWS DR
12600 MORV 92553 717-D3
VALLEY OAK LN
- MURR 92562 927-J2
VALLEY RANCH DR
23300 MORV 92553 717-C3
VALLEY RANCH RD
24700 MORV 92557 687-F4
VALLEY RANCHO TR
200 SJCT 92583 781-B5
VALLEY SPRINGS DR
12900 MORV 92553 717-C3
S VALLEY SPRINGS LN
1100 CLTN 92324 646-G1
VALLEY SPRINGS PKWY
6100 RIV 92507 716-J3
6400 MORV 92553 716-J3
21300 RivC 92553 716-J3
VALLEYVALE DR
16100 FONT 92337 644-G2
VALLEY VIEW AV
1400 NRCO 92860 743-E2
1600 NRCO 92860 713-F5
32300 RivC 92530 866-J7
32800 RivC 92530 897-A2
VALLEY VIEW DR
300 RivC 92223 720-G1
16000 RivC 92258 725-H2
22000 RivC 92567 778-H7
24400 LMLN 92354 647-A2
41700 RivC 92592 960-A4
48500 PDST 92260 848-D5
54200 RivC - 814-D7
69500 RivC 92241 727-F1
N VALLEY VIEW DR
100 HEMT 92543 810-H7
VALLEY VIEW LN
- RivC 92539 (935-A5 See Page 904)
25400 MORV 92557 717-G1
56500 RivC 92539 (934-J5 See Page 904)
VALLEY VIEW ST
12600 YCPA 92399 649-H4
VALLEY VISTA AV
- RivC 92203 789-G5
VALLEY VISTA CIR
22600 RivC 92595 897-D4
VALLEY VISTA DR
67700 CTHC 92234 817-C2
VALLEY VISTA LN
23200 RivC 92567 808-F4
56800 RivC 92539 (965-A6 See Page 964)
VALLEYWOOD CT
25200 MORV 92553 717-G6
VAL MEMORY LN
69400 RivC - (907-G6 See Page 906)
VAL MONTE DR
200 HEMT 92543 841-A2
VAL MONTE ST
- BAN 92220 722-C3
E VALMONTE NORTE
300 PMSP 92262 786-E1
E VALMONTE SUR
300 PMSP 92262 786-E1
VALMY LN
2400 PMSP 92262 756-H5
VALOMBROSA DR
28200 RivC 92584 868-F2
VALONE CT
31700 TEM 92591 959-D2
VALOR CIR
2100 COR 92882 742-J7
2100 COR 92882 772-J1
VALOR DR
2000 COR 92882 742-J7
2000 COR 92882 743-A7
41500 MURR 92562 927-J5
VALPARAISO DR
9600 DHSP 92240 696-J2
9600 DHSP 92240 697-A1
VALPARISO LN
23900 RivC 92590 957-G6
VALVERDA AV
11600 RIV 92505 714-B7
VAL VERDE
23300 PER 92571 777-D1
VAL VERDE DR
400 HEMT 92543 841-A2
VALVIEW AV
21400 RivC 92570 777-E6
VAL VIEW ST
12500 MORV 92553 717-F3
VAL VISTA PL
5800 RIV 92504 685-C7
VAL VON RD
42400 RivC 92536 962-E5
VALYERMO TR
28000 CTHC 92234 757-D6
VAN WY
600 PER 92570 807-F1

VANADIUM PL
42500 PDST 92260 818-G6
VAN BUREN AV
27600 RivC 92585 838-D1
VAN BUREN BLVD
3300 RIV 92503 714-G1
4100 RIV 92503 715-A7
4400 RivC 91752 643-H7
4400 RivC 91752 644-A7
4400 RivC 91752 684-A1
4500 RivC 92509 684-E6
5600 RIV 92503 745-A1
6700 RIV 92503 684-E6
7000 RivC 92503 684-E6
10900 RIV 92504 745-C3
13500 RivC 92503 745-C3
13500 RivC 92504 745-F4
17300 RivC 92504 746-B3
17700 RivC 92508 746-B3
18500 RIV 92508 746-B3
20000 RIV 92518 746-F3
20000 RivC 92518 746-F3
21500 RivC 92518 747-A3
VAN BUREN CIR
1300 SJCT 92583 811-D5
VAN BUREN ST
21900 GTER 92313 646-D5
45300 INDO 92201 5470-J1
47000 RivC 92201 5470-J4
48600 COAC 92236 5470-J4
50300 RivC 92236 5470-J7
52000 COAC 92236 5530-J3
52000 RivC 92236 5530-J3
54000 COAC 92274 5530-J3
54000 RivC 92274 5530-J3
57500 RivC 92274 5531-A7
59000 RivC 92274 (5591-A7 See Page 5590)
66000 RivC 92274 (5651-A2 See Page 5590)
W VAN BUREN ST
200 CLTN 92324 646-B5
VANCE ST
3100 RIV 92504 715-B5
VANCHELLE CT
41700 RivC 92544 841-E1
VANDA CIR
43500 PDST 92260 818-G7
VANDAGRIFF WY
- COR 92883 773-F7
VANDAMERE CT
- TEM 92592 959-F6
VAN DELL RD
2100 RivC 92509 645-E6
VANDENBERG AV
21200 RivC 92518 746-H5
VANDENBERG CT
82300 INDO 92201 5470-F4
VANDENBERG DR
24500 MORV 92551 747-F1
82100 INDO 92201 5470-E4
VANDER ST
100 COR 92880 742-J4
VANDERBEKEN DR
21500 RivC - 726-H7
VANDERBILT AV
- MURR 92563 928-G6
VANDERBILT CIR
3400 COR 92881 773-F4
VANDERBILT CT
26100 RivC 92544 811-G7
26100 RivC 92544 841-G1
45000 INDO 92201 5470-C1
VANDERBILT DR
3500 COR 92881 773-F4
VANDERBILT ST
- ONT 91761 643-B3
E VANDERBILT ST
4800 ONT 91761 643-F3
VANDERHILL CIR
23200 RivC 92570 806-A4
VANDER VEER RD
68300 RivC 92254 (5654-D2 See Page 5594)
VAN ECYK CT
- RivC 92596 899-C7
VANESSA CT
25100 MORV 92553 717-G7
VANESSA LN
1000 SJCT 92583 811-D3
VANESSA ST
6000 RIV 92504 685-A7
VAN FLEET AV
37100 CTHC 92234 817-E1
VAN FLEET DR
1800 SJCT 92583 811-D4
VAN GAALE LN
36500 RivC 92596 929-C3
36500 RivC 92563 929-C3
VAN GOGH AV
14700 MORV 92553 717-G7
VAN GOYEN LN
- RivC 92596 899-C7
VANGUARD WY
8700 RIV 92503 714-F1
VAN LINDEN CT
41700 RivC 92544 841-E1
VAN RUYSDAEL LN
- RivC 92596 899-C7
VANS VISION RD
40000 RivC 92544 931-D7
40000 RivC 92544 961-D1
VAN TU LN
41000 RivC 92592 959-G4

VAQUERO CT
16200 RivC 92504 745-H4
VAQUERO DR
13800 FONT 92337 644 A4
VAQUERO RD
34000 CTHC 92234 787-F5
N VAQUERO RD
1400 PMSP 92262 756-E6
VAQUERO WY
- COR 92879 744-A2
VARDON CT
64500 RivC 92240 696-E1
VARDON DR
41800 TEM 92591 959-C5
VARDON WY
77000 PDST 92211 819-B5
VARELA LN
29000 RivC 92585 838-G1
30500 RivC 92548 839-A1
VARGA ST
62300 RivC 92274 5592-A3
VARGAS RD
46500 INDO 92201 5470-H2
VARNER RD
27200 CTHC 92234 757-E2
27200 RivC 92276 757-H5
28000 RivC 92276 758-A7
52400 CTHC 92234 727-B7
52400 RivC 92241 727-B7
52400 RivC 92241 757-E2
65400 RivC - 726-H6
66100 RivC 92240 726-H6
66500 RivC 92241 726-H6
71900 RivC 92276 788-C2
74500 RivC 92276 789-A7
74500 RivC 92276 819-D2
74900 RivC 92211 819-D2
78300 RivC 92203 819-H3
78300 INDO 92203 819-H3
78300 INDO 92211 819-H3
VARNUM RD
33900 RivC 92544 902-A2
VASILI LN
500 BEAU 92223 690-J6
VASQUEZ LN
18300 RivC 92532 866-D1
VASQUEZ PL
2200 RIV 92507 685-J6
2200 RIV 92507 686-A6
VASSAR DR
1700 RIV 92507 686-A6
VASSAR ST
26500 RivC 92544 841-E2
VAUGHAN ST
600 NRCO 92860 713-G5
VAUGHN RD
- RivC - 410-L4
VAUGHN-BENDA RD
25300 RivC 92595 897-J3
25500 RivC 92584 898-A3
25500 RivC 92595 898-A3
VAWTER RANCH RD
37300 RivC 92544 931-C3
VECINO WY
83300 INDO 92201 5470-G2
VEE BEE ST
17500 RivC 92241 728-D4
VEENHUIS LN
40700 RivC 92544 871-D2
VEGA
100 PMSP 92264 786-H7
49500 COAC 92236 5471-A5
VEGA AV
7200 RivC 92509 684-J5
VEGA RD
67800 CTHC 92234 787-D1
VELA CT
- RivC 92254 5592-B5
- RivC 92274 5592-B5
VELARDO DR
35100 YCPA 92399 650-A4
74000 PDST 92260 818-G7
E VELDT
42300 RMIR 92270 818-B6
VELERIA CT
800 PER 92570 807-E4
800 RivC 92570 807-E4
VELIE DR
74900 PDST 92260 818-H5
VELLA RD
500 PMSP 92264 787-A3
VELLANTO WY
13600 MORV 92553 717-F5
VELO CT
5300 RIV 92506 716-B1
VELVET CT
- RIV 92503 714-H3
VELVETLEAF ST
12800 MORV 92553 717-H3
VENCE DR
36000 MURR 92562 928-C1
VENETIA RD
2700 PMSP 92262 756-H5
VENETIAN DR
11800 MORV 92557 717-G1
VENETO DR
- TEM 92591 959-A5
VENICE CT
44000 PDST 92260 818-H7
VENICE DR
43800 LQNT 92253 819-G7
VENORA WY
17400 RivC 92508 746-E6
VENTAN ST
27300 RivC 92586 838-C4

VENTANA CIR
1500 BAN 92220 721-D5
VENTANA CT
40700 PDST 92260 818-E4
VENTURA AV
500 COR 92879 743-G4
VENTURA DR
27000 CTHC 92234 757-B5
VENTURA RD
2600 PMSP 92262 756-H5
VENTURE DR
11000 RivC 91752 643-G5
VENTURI DR
5200 BAN 92220 721-D4
VENUS
- PMSP 92264 786-H7
VENUS CT
11000 RivC 91752 683-H5
VENUS DR
- RMIR 92270 817-G3
31500 RivC 92567 809-C1
VERA CT
40600 RivC 92544 811-C7
VERA DR
69100 CTHC 92234 787-F5
VERA LN
24200 MORV 92557 687-E7
VERA ST
6000 RIV 92504 685-A7
VERA CRUZ
2700 COR 92882 773-A2
84500 COAC 92236 5471-A5
VERA CRUZ RD
2900 PMSP 92264 786-H4
VERAMAR CT
1100 COR 92882 742-F6
VERANDA LN
- RIV 92508 746-D1
2800 COR 92882 773-A2
80400 INDO 92201 5470-B4
VERANDA WY
- MURR 92563 928-J4
VERANO DR
1300 PMSP 92264 786-F4
VERANO RD
68100 CTHC 92234 787-D1
VERANO WY
12900 YCPA 92399 649-F5
W VERBA SANTA DR
45500 PDST 92260 848-E2
VERBENA AV
15500 RivC 92282 725-F1
82100 INDO 92201 5410-E6
VERBENA CT
- INDW 92210 818-H7
1700 SJCT 92583 781-A5
48600 RivC 92260 848-B5
VERBENA DR
- LQNT 92253 849-J1
900 RivC - 5240-A7
8000 RIV 92504 715-A3
8500 RIV 92504 714-J3
9900 DHSP 92240 697-A2
9900 RivC 92240 697-A2
44500 LQNT 92253 819-J7
66700 DHSP 92240 696-J1
E VERBENA DR
1200 PMSP 92262 756-F7
VERBENA LN
83000 INDO 92201 5410-G7
VERBENA RD
68800 RivC 92240 697-E7
VERBENIA AV
13000 RivC 92282 724-E2
VERBENIA RD
72500 RMIR 92270 818-D4
VERBOOM ST
28000 RivC 92596 839-B6
VERDA PL
32900 RivC 92530 896-E3
VERDADERO PL
42500 TEM 92592 959-A6
VERDE DR
43500 TEM 92592 979-D2
VERDE ST
3500 RIV 92504 715-D3
VERDE WY
- PDST 92260 818-G4
VERDE GRANDE CT
26100 RivC 92586 838-A6
VERDE MESA ST
32800 RivC 92595 896-J6
VERDES LN
- TEM 92591 958-H3
VERDE VISTA LN
- RMIR 92270 817-F3
VERDI CT
1300 SJCT 92583 811-E3
VERDUGO
100 RIV 92507 716-D2
VERDUGO DR
1500 COR 92879 743-G3
VERDUGO PL
- PMSP 92262 756-F6
VERDUGO RD
46900 RivC 92220 692-E6
VERDUN LN
23900 MURR 92562 927-J3
23900 MURR 92562 928-A4
W VEREDA NORTE
100 PMSP 92262 756-D6
VEREDA REAL
15100 RivC 92570 805-F5
E VEREDA SUR
600 PMSP 92262 756-E7

W VEREDA SUR
100 PMSP 92262 756-D7
VERMILLION DR
64000 RivC 92250 726-D1
VERMONT AV
2200 RIV 92507 685-J5
2200 RIV 92507 686-A6
VERMONT DR
3000 COR 92881 773-F4
VERMONT ST
41700 RivC 92544 841-E4
VERNA CT
- PMSP 92262 756-G7
VERNAL ST
2300 SJCT 92582 810-C1
VERNAY ST
- MURR 92562 928-B4
VERNOLA WY
2600 RivC 92509 645-B6
VERNON AV
3900 RivC 92509 644-F7
4200 RivC 92509 684-F1
10300 RivC 92225 5551-E1
N VERNON AV
100 SJCT 92583 811-C2
S VERNON AV
400 SJCT 92583 811-C2
VERNON RD
15000 RivC 92282 695-F7
15400 RivC 92282 725-F1
VERONA AV
700 SJCT 92583 781-E7
VERONA CT
- LQNT 92253 819-G6
- RivC 92595 897-G6
- TEM 92592 959-F7
VERONA DR
11800 FONT 92337 644-F4
VERONA LN
33400 RivC 92548 809-F5
VERONA RD
2600 PMSP 92262 756-H5
67000 CTHC 92234 757-B5
VERONA ST
6900 RIV 92503 714-E1
11600 YCPA 92399 650-B2
VERONDA PL
30300 TEM 92592 959-B6
VERONICA AV
31500 RivC 92584 868-B6
VERONICA CT
- LMLN 92354 647-F3
VERONO CT
39800 MURR 92562 928-D3
VERSAILLES CIR
1200 RIV 92506 716-C4
VERSAILLES CT
15600 MORV 92555 748-C2
VERSAILLES DR
1400 PMSP 92264 786-G4
VERSAILLES PL
200 RivC 92501 646-A6
VERSAILLES ST
2100 SJCT 92583 811-F5
15200 LKEL 92530 865-G3
VERTA ST
20000 RivC 92570 776-G4
VESPER CIR
2200 COR 92879 773-D1
VESPER RD
39100 RivC 92539 (934-D5 See Page 904)
VESPUCCI AV
25600 MORV 92557 717-H2
VETERANS MEMORIAL ST
1800 NRCO 92860 713-D4
VIA ABEJA
36500 CTHC 92234 787-H7
VIA ABRIL
17300 RivC 92562 976-B1
E VIA ACAPULCO
1900 PMSP 92262 756-G7
VIA ACAPULCO N
600 PMSP 92262 756-G6
VIA ACUNA
40200 MURR 92562 928-B2
VIA AGUADULCE
39900 MURR 92562 928-A2
VIA AGUILA
1800 PMSP 92264 786-F5
41200 TEM 92591 959-C4
VIA ALBA CT
1200 COR 92881 773-G1
VIA ALBERCA
5300 RIV 92507 716-E2
VIA ALCORISA
43400 TEM 92592 959-D7
VIA ALDEA
- CTHC 92234 787-G6
- LQNT 92253 5470-A6
VIA ALEGRE
38200 MURR 92563 928-G5
VIA ALGERIA
16600 MORV 92551 747-H4
VIA ALHAMA
42800 TEM 92592 959-E6
VIA ALICIA DR
15200 MORV 92551 747-H1
VIA ALISO
- LQNT 92253 849-J2
VIA ALISOL
23700 MURR 92562 927-F4
VIA ALLEGRE
75700 INDW 92210 849-B1

VIA ALLEGRO
- CTHC 92234 787-C7
VIA ALLRIZO
31900 TEM 92592 979-E1
VIA ALMAZAN
32200 RivC 92592 979-F4
VIA ALMONTE
23600 MURR 92562 928-A2
VIA ALONDRA
- LQNT 92253 819-F7
VIA ALORA
- TEM 92592 959-E6
VIA ALTA MIRA
- MURR 92562 928-A1
200 PMSP 92262 756-E7
VIA ALTAMIRA
33700 CTHC 92234 787-E4
VIA ALVARO
33100 TEM 92592 959-G7
VIA AMADOR
23300 MORV 92557 687-C5
VIA AMALFI
- CTHC 92234 787-C7
VIA AMANTE
- LQNT 92253 5470-A6
30100 RivC 92584 868-F2
64300 RivC 92264 816-E2
VIA AMAPOLA
40300 MURR 92562 928-B3
VIA AMARILLA
38500 MURR 92563 928-G6
VIA AMBIENTE
39900 MURR 92562 928-A2
VIA AMISTAD
48500 LQNT 92253 849-F4
VIA ANDORRA
- MURR 92562 928-B3
VIA ANGELES
4300 TEM 92592 959-H7
VIA ANITA
41300 RivC 92592 960-C3
VIA ANTIBES
- LQNT 92253 849-H3
3700 RivC 92503 744-F5
VIA ANTONIO
700 RivC 92882 742-H5
VIA APOLINA
10100 MORV 92557 687-C5
VIA APORE
41000 RivC 92592 960-F2
S VIA APPIA
1000 CLTN 92324 646-D1
VIA AQUA DULCE
39900 RivC 92562 926-E7
VIA ARBOL
23200 MORV 92557 687-C5
VIA ARBOLEDA
28600 MURR 92563 928-G4
30100 TEM 92591 959-A4
VIA ARENA
46800 INDO 92201 5470-C2
VIA ARIAS
41300 TEM 92592 959-F7
VIA ARNEDO
- TEM 92592 959-E7
VIA ARUBA
3700 RivC 92503 744-F5
VIA ASADO
- TEM 92592 958-J7
VIA ASTURIAS
- TEM 92592 959-E5
VIA ASTUTO
23900 MURR 92562 928-A2
VIA AVANTE
- LQNT 92253 849-H3
VIA AZALEA
42300 TEM 92592 959-E6
VIA AZUL
38500 MURR 92563 928-G5
VIA BADALONA
43600 PDST 92211 819-E6
VIA BALDERAMA
41800 TEM 92592 959-F5
VIA BANCO
40500 MURR 92562 928-A3
VIA BANDE
32100 TEM 92592 959-E7
VIA BANDITA
28200 RivC 92585 838-D6
VIA BARBATO
73000 PDST 92260 818-D3
VIA BARCELONA
3900 HEMT 92545 810-E6
VIA BARCELONA RD
12700 YCPA 92399 649-H5
VIA BARLETTA
23800 MURR 92562 928-A2
VIA BARRANCA
15400 RivC 92570 775-G6
44300 RivC 92590 978-D3
VIA BARRAZA
31800 TEM 92592 959-D7
VIA BARROZO
43400 TEM 92592 959-D7
43400 TEM 92592 979-D1
VIA BAYA
38000 RivC 92562 927-A3
VIA BEJARANO
- TEM 92592 979-E1
VIA BELLA
- RMIR 92270 787-J3
- RMIR 92270 788-A3
VIA BELLAGIO
- LQNT 92253 5530-C2

VIA BELLEZA
- RivC 92563 958-J1
- RivC 92563 959-A1
VIA BENABARRE
32000 RivC 92592 979-F3
VIA BENICIA
1200 CTHC 92234 787-F3
41100 RivC 92592 960-C3
VIA BENITO
23600 RivC 92548 809-C4
VIA BERNARDO
600 COR 92882 742-J5
600 RivC 92882 742-J5
VIA BESO DEL SOL
42100 TEM 92591 958-J5
VIA BIELLA
- LQNT 92253 5530-B2
VIA BLAIRO
- COR 92879 743-F3
VIA BLAIRO CIR
- COR 92879 743-F2
VIA BLANCO
19600 RivC 92590 976-H2
VIA BOLERO
49200 LQNT 92253 849-G5
VIA BOLERO RD
42600 RivC 92590 957-J6
VIA BONITA
- RMIR 92270 787-J3
16900 FONT 92337 644-J3
16900 FONT 92337 645-A3
VIA BRAVA
81000 INDO 92201 5470-C2
VIA BRIONES
24300 MURR 92562 928-D2
VIA BRISA
30300 TEM 92592 959-A7
30300 TEM 92592 979-A1
45000 INDW 92210 849-B1
VIA BROZA
36900 RivC 92592 930-F5
VIA BUENA DR
34200 YCPA 92399 649-H5
VIA BUENA VISTA
40100 RMIR 92270 817-H3
VIA BURGANDY
36300 RivC 92592 960-E2
VIA CABALLO
- PDST 92211 819-A4
VIA CABALLOS
39600 RivC 92562 926-G7
39700 RivC 92562 956-G1
VIA CABANA
26200 RivC 92584 868-B3
VIA CACHO
39600 RivC 92592 930-F7
VIA CADIZ
39000 MURR 92563 928-E3
VIA CAJON
38200 RivC 92544 931-D3
VIA CALI
31700 TEM 92592 959-D7
VIA CALIDAD
39900 MURR 92562 928-A2
VIA CALIENTE
78300 LQNT 92253 819-G7
VIA CALINA
39900 RivC 92592 930-J7
VIA CALLISTO
5600 RIV 92506 716-D2
VIA CALORIN
- RivC 92562 926-G4
6500 RivC 92509 685-A2
VIA CALUSA
28700 MURR 92563 928-G5
VIA CAMBIA
- RivC 92562 956-H6
VIA CAMPANARIO
31700 TEM 92592 959-D7
VIA CAMPECHE
4900 RIV 92507 686-C7
VIA CAMPO
- RMIR 92270 787-H3
VIA CAMPOSECO
- MURR 92562 928-A3
VIA CANADA
30300 TEM 92592 959-A7
VIA CANDELEDA
42300 TEM 92592 959-F7
43500 TEM 92592 979-F1
VIA CANTATA
38700 RivC 92592 931-A4
VIA CAPRI
- CTHC 92234 787-D7
- LQNT 92253 5530-B1
300 COR 92879 744-B3
300 HEMT 92545 810-E7
11400 LMLN 92354 647-E2
VIA CAREZA
39700 MURR 92563 928-E4
VIA CARISMA
100 PMSP 92264 786-E6
VIA CARLOS CT
25500 MORV 92551 747-H1
VIA CARLOTTA
41100 RivC 92592 960-C3
VIA CARMEL
- LQNT 92253 849-H4
VIA CARMELO
39600 RivC 92592 931-B7
VIA CARNAGHI
34500 RivC 92595 897-D5
VIA CARO
- TEM 92592 959-E7

VIA CARRANZA
44300 RivC 92590 977-J1
VIA CARTAGO
900 RIV 92507 716-D1
VIA CASCADITA
28200 RivC 92585 838-D6
VIA CASETA
39600 RivC 92562 926-F7
VIA CASITAS
17800 CHLS 91709 712-B5
81000 INDO 92201 5470-C2
VIA CASITAS DR
700 HEMT 92545 810-F5
VIA CASTANA
- PDST 92211 818-J5
39700 MURR 92563 928-E4
VIA CATALINA
44700 LQNT 92253 819-G7
44700 LQNT 92253 849-G1
VIA CAVALO
- TEM 92592 979-E1
VIA CEDRO
- PDST 92211 818-J5
- PDST 92211 819-A5
40900 MURR 92562 927-H2
VIA CELESTE
46500 INDO 92201 5470-B2
VIA CERCO
21300 RivC 92562 927-A6
VIA CERDA
43000 TEM 92592 959-D7
VIA CEREZO
5600 RIV 92506 716-D2
VIA CERRO
2200 RivC 92509 645-F6
VIA CERRO VISTA
35200 RivC 92592 960-B6
VIA CERVANTES
5700 RIV 92506 716-D2
VIA CESARIO
41300 TEM 92592 959-E7
VIA CHAMPAGNE
40700 RivC 92592 960-D2
VIA CHAPPARO
33100 TEM 92592 979-H1
VIA CHEPO
5300 RIV 92507 716-D1
VIA CHICA
500 PMSP 92262 786-E1
600 PMSP 92262 756-E7
VIA CICADA
36600 CTHC 92234 787-H7
VIA CIELITO
41100 TEM 92591 958-J4
VIA CIELO
43700 RivC 92590 977-B1
VIA CIELO DR
2700 COR 92882 742-G6
VIA CIELO AZUL
- PDST 92260 818-H7
VIA CINTA
- PDST 92211 818-J4
VIA CIRILLO
41300 TEM 92592 959-F7
VIA COIBA
1300 RIV 92506 716-C2
VIA COLETA
38200 MURR 92563 928-H5
VIA COLINA
11700 MORV 92555 718-C1
VIA COLUSA
68900 CTHC 92234 787-E3
E VIA COLUSA
300 PMSP 92262 786-E1
VIA COMA CT
1100 COR 92881 773-G1
S VIA COMO DEL LAGO
1000 CLTN 92324 646-E2
VIA COMPADRES
- MURR 92562 928-A2
VIA CONCEPCION
700 RIV 92506 716-D1
VIA CONCHILLA
84700 COAC 92236 5471-B5
VIA CONDOTTI
39900 RMIR 92270 817-J3
VIA CONEJO
5700 RIV 92506 716-B2
VIA CONQUISTADOR
49000 LQNT 92253 849-J5
VIA CONSUELO
42300 TEM 92592 979-C4
VIA CONTENTA
27900 MORV 92555 688-D7
VIA CONTEVIENTO
38800 RivC 92562 927-A5
VIA CORAZON
30000 RivC 92584 868-F2
VIA CORAZON DR
2600 COR 92882 742-G6
VIA CORDARO
32200 TEM 92592 959-E7
VIA CORDOBA
31500 TEM 92592 979-E3
32200 RivC 92592 979-E3
VIA CORDONIZ
2500 SDCo 92028 997-C4
VIA CORDOVA
31700 LKEL 92530 865-H4
47300 LQNT 92253 849-H3
VIA CORONA
45300 INDW 92210 849-B1
VIA CORONADO
44300 LQNT 92253 819-G7

VIA CORRIDA
44900 RivC 92590 977-A3
VIA CORRIDO
78500 LQNT 92253 849-G5
VIA CORSICA
300 HEMT 92545 810-E7
30100 TEM 92591 959-A4
VIA CORTA
- LQNT 92253 849-H5
500 PMSP 92262 786-E1
600 PMSP 92262 756-E7
VIA CORTE
23500 RivC 92548 809-B4
VIA CORTEZ
15200 MORV 92551 747-J1
VIA CORTO E
16000 DHSP 92240 726-J1
16000 RivC 92240 726-J1
VIA CORTO W
16000 DHSP 92240 726-J1
16000 RivC 92240 726-J1
VIA CORTO MONTE
20600 RivC 92562 926-J4
VIA COSTA BRAVA
99000 RivC 92254 (5654-D4 See Page 5594)
VIA COTA
28800 RivC 92584 868-G2
VIA CRISTINA
81000 INDO 92201 5470-C2
VIA CUENCA
24800 MURR 92563 928-E3
VIA CUESTA
5700 RIV 92506 716-B2
VIA CUESTA AL SOL
42000 TEM 92591 958-J5
VIA CUMBRE
40300 RMIR 92270 817-H4
VIA CURTIDOR
31200 RivC 92596 899-C2
VIA CURVA
4300 RivC 92509 685-A2
VIA CURVADO
- RivC 92563 958-J1
VIA DE AGUILA
21000 RivC 92570 775-G6
VIA DEANDA
- TEM 92592 959-E6
VIA DE ANZA
200 CTHC 92234 787-E4
17000 FONT 92337 644-J3
17000 FONT 92337 645-A2
VIA DE AZULEJOS
100 PMSP 92264 787-C5
VIA DEBRA
27100 RivC 92586 868-D2
VIA DE CRISTO
37600 MURR 92563 928-H6
VIA DE GEMA LINDA
23800 MURR 92562 927-J2
23800 MURR 92562 928-A2
VIA DE LA LUNA
15000 LKEL 92532 867-B5
VIA DE LA MANCHA
1000 PMSP 92262 786-F1
VIA DE LA MESA
30100 TEM 92591 959-A2
VIA DE LA REAL
- MORV 92555 718-C7
- MORV 92555 748-D1
VIA DE LARGA VIDA
26400 RivC 92590 958-B6
VIA DE LA ROCA
40600 SDCo 92028 997-J3
VIA DE LA VALLE
15000 LKEL 92532 867-B4
VIA DE LA ZANJA
1200 CLTN 92324 646-G2
1200 SBdC 92313 646-G2
VIA DEL CAMPO
42700 TEM 92592 959-A7
VIA DEL CHRISTO
43000 PDST 92211 818-J7
VIA DEL CIELO
40100 RMIR 92270 817-H4
VIA DEL CORONADO
31400 TEM 92592 979-D4
VIA DEL ECO
1100 HEMT 92543 841-B2
VIA DEL FIERRO
30000 RivC 92584 868-F3
S VIA DEL FONTANA
1000 CLTN 92324 646-F1
VIA DEL GAVILAN
41700 SDCo 92028 997-J3
41900 SDCo 92028 998-A4
VIA DEL LAGO
1700 SDCo 92028 997-J5
15000 LKEL 92532 867-B5
15600 MORV 92555 748-C1
15700 RivC 92571 748-D3
S VIA DEL LAGO
1000 CLTN 92324 646-E1
VIA DEL LARGO
38000 MURR 92563 928-G5
VIA DEL MESA
1100 HEMT 92543 840-J2
VIA DEL MONTE
- TEM 92592 959-H5
41500 RivC 92592 959-H5
44500 LQNT 92253 819-F7
VIA DEL NORTE
- MORV 92557 687-C4
36500 CTHC 92234 787-H7

VIA DEL ORO
40100 RMIR 92270 817-H3
VIA DE LOS ARBOLES
37500 RivC 92592 960-G1
VIA DE LOS FIDEOS
42200 RivC 92590 977-J4
42200 RivC 92590 978-A4
VIA DEL OSO
38700 RivC 92592 930-J5
VIA DE LOS ROBLES
45800 RivC 92590 978-C5
VIA DEL PRADO
6400 CHLS 91709 712-B5
VIA DEL RANCHO
6300 CHLS 91709 712-B5
VIA DEL RANCHO VISTA
22900 RivC 92570 807-C5
VIA DEL RIO
1300 COR 92882 743-A6
1400 COR 92882 742-J6
1700 RivC 92882 742-J6
43200 SDCo 92028 998-A4
VIA DEL SENOR
31500 RivC 92548 809-C2
E VIA DEL SIENA
900 CLTN 92324 646-D1
S VIA DEL SIENA
1000 CLTN 92324 646-E1
VIA DEL SOL
- LQNT 92253 819-F7
24400 MORV 92553 717-F5
28600 MURR 92563 928-G4
VIA DEL SUR
36600 CTHC 92234 787-H7
38300 MURR 92563 928-G5
VIA DEL TECOLOTE
5300 RIV 92507 716-D1
VIA DEL TORONJO
38600 RivC 92592 930-H5
VIA DE LUNA
700 COR 92882 743-A5
VIA DE LUZ
700 COR 92882 743-A5
VIA DEL VERANO
- RivC 92590 978-C4
VIA DE MODA
- LQNT 92253 849-J6
- LQNT 92253 5470-A6
VIA DENZO
- TEM 92592 959-D7
VIA DE ORO
37900 RivC 92592 930-J7
38900 RivC 92592 960-J1
41300 RivC 92592 961-A3
VIA DE PALMAS DR
12100 MORV 92555 717-J2
VIA DESTELLO
- TEM 92592 979-F1
VIA DIABLO
62500 DHSP 92240 696-B3
VIA DIAMANTE
40500 MURR 92562 928-A2
VIA DIANA
19500 RivC 92562 956-F1
VIA DIJON
78300 LQNT 92253 819-G7
VIA DOMADOR
28100 RivC 92585 838-D6
VIA DOMINGO
68000 DHSP 92240 697-C5
75300 PDST 92211 818-J5
VIA DOMINIQUE
39500 MURR 92563 928-G5
VIA DON BENITO
300 CTHC 92234 817-G1
N VIA DONNA
1200 PMSP 92262 756-F6
VIA DONOSO
5300 RIV 92507 716-C1
28600 MURR 92563 928-G5
VIA DON QUIXOTE
40000 TEM 92591 958-J4
VIA DOROTHEA
- RivC 92532 836-D7
VIA DOS CAMINOS
5700 RIV 92504 685-D6
VIA DOS CERROS
5500 RIV 92507 716-D1
VIA DOS PICOS
43000 TEM 92590 958-G6
VIA DULCINEA
- PDST 92260 818-H7
VIA DURANGO
84500 COAC 92236 5471-A5
VIA ECHO
200 CTHC 92234 787-E4
VIA EDUARDO
31100 TEM 92592 979-D6
32000 RivC 92276 788-J2
VIA EL BRAZO
29100 MURR 92563 928-H5
VIA EL DELORA
30600 TEM 92592 979-B1
VIA EL DORADO
4200 SDCo 92028 997-H3
37500 RivC 92592 960-G1
VIA ELEGANTE
70000 RMIR 92270 787-H7
VIA ELENA
40300 RivC 92544 961-C1
40600 RivC 92544 931-D7
VIA EL GRECO
41700 TEM 92592 959-D6

STREET Block	City	ZIP	Pg-Grid
VIA EL MIRADOR			
-	PMSP	92262	756-F6
VIA EL PAIS BONITA			
36200	RivC	92592	960-E3
VIA EL PAVO REAL			
28600	MURR	92563	928-G5
VIA EL PRODUCTO			
38800	RivC	92592	930-F5
VIA EL RANCHO			
16000	DHSP	92240	726-J1
16000	RivC	92240	726-J1
VIA ENCANTO			
48500	LQNT	92253	849-F4
VIA ENCINITAS			
41200	RivC	92544	931-E6
VIA ENSENADA			
400	PMSP	92264	786-E6
VIA ENTRADA			
6500	CHLS	91709	712-B5
21800	RivC	92562	927-C7
27700	RivC	92585	838-D5
84000	INDO	92203	5410-J5
S VIA ENTRADA			
1500	PMSP	92264	786-E5
VIA ESCALANTE			
5300	RivC	92509	684-J4
VIA ESCALON			
43500	RivC	92590	957-C7
VIA ESCARLATA			
38400	MURR	92563	928-G5
VIA ESCONDIDO			
25000	RivC	92590	977-J4
25000	RivC	92590	978-A4
E VIA ESCUELA			
300	PMSP	92262	756-E5
W VIA ESCUELA			
100	PMSP	92262	756-D5
VIA ESPADA			
-	MURR	92563	928-H4
VIA ESPANA			
-	MURR	92562	928-D4
3700	RivC	92503	744-F5
VIA ESPERANZA			
44800	RivC	92590	978-B3
VIA ESTADO			
38100	RivC	92592	930-J4
VIA ESTANCIA			
45000	INDW	92210	849-A1
VIA ESTRADA			
100	CTHC	92234	787-F7
40200	MURR	92562	928-B3
VIA ESTRELLA			
28700	MURR	92563	928-G5
E VIA ESTRELLA			
1200	PMSP	92264	786-F7
VIA ESTRELLADA			
1000	SDCo	92028	997-H7
VIA EYTEL			
400	PMSP	92262	756-E7
VIA FANITA			
-	TEM	92592	958-J7
-	TEM	92592	978-J1
VIA FELIPE			
700	RivC	92882	742-J5
VIA FELIZ			
1100	CTHC	92234	787-F3
20000	RivC	92562	956-H1
VIA FERMATO			
38500	RivC	92264	816-F2
VIA FERNANDO			
39900	RivC	92592	960-D3
VIA FINALDI WY			
-	COR	92881	773-G4
VIA FIRENZE			
-	LQNT	92253	849-G4
VIA FIRENZE WY			
1700	COR	92881	773-G4
VIA FLORA			
6500	CHLS	91709	712-B5
VIA FLORE			
32200	TEM	92592	979-E1
VIA FLORENCE			
78500	LQNT	92253	849-H3
VIA FLORENCIA			
6500	RivC	92509	685-A3
72100	RMIR	92270	788-D5
VIA FLORENCIO			
39100	RMIR	92270	817-H3
VIA FONDA			
73500	PDST	92260	818-F4
VIA FORMAN			
37700	RivC	92562	926-J3
VIA FORTUNA			
38000	RivC	92264	816-E2
VIA FRANCISCO			
40200	MURR	92562	928-B3
VIA FRESNO			
1100	CTHC	92234	787-F3
VIA FRONTERA			
17900	CHLS	91709	712-B5
29200	MURR	92563	928-H6
VIA FRONTERAS			
17300	RivC	92504	745-G6
VIA FUERTE			
27700	RivC	92590	978-E3
VIA GALLEON			
20900	RivC	92562	926-J6
VIA GALLETAS			
-	MURR	92562	928-D3
VIA GAMAY			
40400	RivC	92591	959-E2
VIA GANDIA			
42800	TEM	92592	959-D7
VIA GENOA			
47000	INDO	92201	5470-G3
VIA GIBRALTAR			
77800	PDST	92211	819-F7
VIA GILBERTO			
30900	TEM	92592	979-C5
VIA GOLONDRINA			
84100	INDO	92203	5410-J6
VIA GORRION			
44900	RivC	92590	978-H3
VIA GRANADA			
43900	PDST	92211	819-E7
VIA GRANDE			
100	PMSP	92264	787-D6
1000	CTHC	92234	787-F3
VIA GRAZIANA			
40100	MURR	92562	928-B2
VIA GRAZIANNA			
-	LQNT	92253	849-H3
VIA GUERRO			
-	TEM	92592	979-E1
VIA HACIENDA			
24000	MURR	92562	928-B3
VIA HALCON			
41000	TEM	92591	959-C3
VIA HAMACA AV			
25700	MORV	92551	747-J4
VIA HAVRE			
24300	MURR	92562	928-B3
VIA HELENA			
24000	MURR	92562	928-B3
VIA HERMOSA			
48100	LQNT	92253	849-G4
84500	COAC	92236	5471-A5
VIA HERRADURA			
40500	RivC	92562	956-F2
VIA HORCA			
44600	RivC	92590	978-H2
VIA HUERTA			
38100	RivC	92562	926-H4
77100	LQNT	92253	849-E6
VIA HUERTO			
100	PMSP	92264	786-E6
VIA IMPRESSO			
16300	MORV	92551	747-J3
VIA INDIGO			
10000	MORV	92557	687-C5
VIA INDUSTRIA			
-	TEM	92590	958-E6
VIA ISABELLA			
24300	MURR	92562	928-B3
VIA ISLA			
1400	PMSP	92264	786-F5
VIA IXTAPA			
1200	COR	92882	773-A2
VIA JACA			
45500	RivC	92592	979-F4
VIA JACARA CT			
25800	MORV	92551	747-J4
VIA JALAPA			
40300	MURR	92562	928-A3
VIA JARDIN			
-	LQNT	92253	849-H4
VIA JASO			
41400	TEM	92592	959-F7
VIA JOSEFA			
600	RivC	92882	742-H5
VIA JOSEFINA			
34200	RMIR	92270	788-D5
VIA JUMILLA			
42800	TEM	92592	959-F7
VIA JUNIPERO SIERRA			
5600	RIV	92506	716-D2
VIA KANNELA			
25700	MORV	92551	747-J3
VIA KARLITA			
25000	RivC	92590	977-J1
VIA KATALINA			
-	LQNT	92253	849-J6
VIA KORON			
47200	LQNT	92253	849-H3
VIAL CIR			
22700	RivC	92557	687-B2
VIA LA BLANCO			
40800	RivC	92544	931-E6
40800	RivC	92592	931-E6
VIA LA BRISA LN			
1000	COR	92882	742-F6
VIA LA CALMA			
28800	MURR	92563	928-G5
VIA LA COLINA			
38000	MURR	92563	928-G5
VIA LA COLORADA			
45900	RivC	92592	979-F5
VIA LA CRESTA			
17800	CHLS	91709	712-A5
VIA LADERA RD			
1400	SDCo	92028	999-B6
VIA LA ESPALDA			
28900	MURR	92563	928-H5
VIA LAGO			
74900	INDW	92210	848-J2
VIA LAGOS			
11400	LMLN	92354	647-E2
VIA LA LUNA			
40300	RivC	92544	961-C3
VIA LANTANA			
-	PDST	92260	818-H4
VIA LA PALOMA			
500	RIV	92507	716-D1
38200	MURR	92563	928-G5
VIA LA PINTURA			
39100	RivC	92591	929-J6
VIA LA PLAZA			
29400	MURR	92563	928-J6
VIA LA QUINTA			
26600	RivC	92544	841-E2
VIA LA QUINTA			
46700	INDO	92201	5470-C2
VIA LAR			
39200	MURR	92563	928-F4
VIA LAREDO			
81100	INDO	92201	5470-C2
VIA LARGA			
11300	FONT	92337	645-A2
11300	FONT	92337	644-J2
VIA LA RUEDA			
28800	MURR	92563	928-G5
VIA LAS CHACRAS			
29700	TEM	92591	958-J4
VIA LAS COLINAS			
29400	TEM	92592	958-J6
VIA LA SENCILLA			
40800	RivC	92544	931-E7
40800	RivC	92592	931-E7
VIA LAS FLORES			
-	RMIR	92270	787-H3
28500	MURR	92563	928-G6
VIA LAS FLORES PL			
38700	MURR	92563	928-G6
VIA LAS JUNITAS			
24300	MURR	92562	928-D2
VIA LAS LADERAS			
24500	MURR	92562	928-D2
VIA LAS LOMAS			
25000	MURR	92562	928-D5
VIA LAS MESAS			
81000	INDO	92201	5470-C2
VIA LAS NUBES			
5600	RIV	92506	716-D2
VIA LAS PALMAS			
100	PMSP	92262	756-C6
30000	RivC	92276	758-F7
30500	RivC	92276	788-F1
39700	MURR	92563	928-E4
N VIA LAS PALMAS			
100	PMSP	92262	756-D6
S VIA LAS PALMAS			
200	PMSP	92262	756-D7
VIA LAS QUINTAS			
39000	MURR	92562	928-D2
VIA LAS RAMBLAS			
40000	RivC	92592	930-C7
VIA LAS ROCAS			
43000	RivC	92590	957-H6
VIA LAS ROLAS			
43100	RivC	92590	957-G6
VIA LAS ROSAS			
30700	RivC	92584	899-B2
30700	RivC	92596	899-B2
46700	INDO	92201	5470-C2
VIA LAS SINTRAS			
39000	MURR	92562	928-D2
S VIA LATA			
800	CLTN	92324	646-F1
VIA LA VIDA			
38000	TEM	92591	958-J4
S VIA LAZO			
2300	PMSP	92264	786-E6
VIA LEON			
32000	RivC	92276	789-A2
VIA LEVANTAR			
31800	TEM	92592	959-E6
VIALE VENETO			
39800	RMIR	92270	817-J3
VIA LIAGO			
20800	RivC	92570	775-G6
21300	RivC	92570	805-G1
VIA LIDO			
11400	LMLN	92354	647-E2
VIA LILIA			
41600	RivC	92592	960-B4
VIA LIMA			
-	PDST	92211	819-A4
VIA LINDA			
48700	LQNT	92253	849-E5
VIA LINDA CT			
12700	YCPA	92399	649-H4
VIA LINDA DR			
700	HEMT	92545	810-F5
W VIA LIVORNO			
900	PMSP	92262	756-C5
VIA LLANO			
24000	MURR	92562	928-B2
VIA LOBATO			
37700	RivC	92592	930-H3
VIA LOBO			
40000	TEM	92591	959-B1
W VIA LOLA			
100	PMSP	92262	756-D7
VIA LOMA			
5800	RIV	92506	716-C2
VIA LOMAS VISTA			
41700	TEM	92592	959-D5
VIA LOMITA			
46700	INDO	92201	5470-C2
VIA LORCA			
-	LQNT	92253	849-G3
VIA LORCA DR			
15400	MORV	92551	747-H1
VIA LORETO AV			
12000	DHSP	92240	696-G4
VIA LOS ALTOS			
40100	RMIR	92270	817-H4
40800	TEM	92591	959-C3
VIA LOS CABALLEROS			
16900	RivC	92504	745-J5
VIA LOS LAURELES			
21000	RivC	92562	956-J1
21000	RivC	92562	957-A1
VIA LOS NINOS			
23800	MURR	92562	928-A2
VIA LOS NINOS			
27700	RivC	92532	836-D5
VIA LOS VENTOS			
45100	RivC	92590	977-A3
45200	RivC	92590	976-J3
VIA LUCIA			
44900	TEM	92592	979-E3
VIA LUCIDO			
44600	TEM	92592	979-D3
VIA LUGANO			
300	COR	92879	744-B3
VIA LUGO			
43000	RivC	92590	957-G6
VIA LUISA			
-	RivC	92592	930-H6
VIA LUNADO			
16700	MORV	92551	747-H4
VIA LUSSO			
38100	RivC	92264	816-F2
VIA MADRID			
23700	MURR	92562	898-C7
23700	MURR	92562	928-C1
VIA MAGELLAN			
43500	PDST	92211	819-F6
VIA MAGNOLIA			
28900	MURR	92563	928-H6
VIA MAJORCA			
37200	RivC	92562	927-A3
38500	RivC	92562	926-J4
43500	PDST	92211	819-E6
VIA MALAGAS			
40300	MURR	92562	928-A3
VIA MANZANO			
75200	PDST	92211	818-J4
VIA MARAVILLA			
-	LQNT	92253	5470-A6
VIA MARCOS			
700	RivC	92882	742-J5
VIA MARENGO			
-	CTHC	92234	787-F7
VIA MARGARITA			
33000	RivC	92595	897-C2
VIA MARGUERITA			
18800	RivC	92570	777-B2
VIA MARIA DR			
26000	RivC	92544	(812-C7 See Page 782)
VIA MARIA BUENA			
5600	RIV	92506	716-C2
VIA MARIE CIR			
34200	YCPA	92399	649-H5
VIA MARINA			
38600	RivC	92592	931-A5
VIA MARIPOSA			
36000	MURR	92562	928-D1
76000	INDW	92210	849-B1
VIA MARISA			
-	MURR	92562	928-B3
VIA MARSALA			
28900	RivC	92584	868-G2
VIA MARTA			
-	MURR	92562	928-D2
72100	RMIR	92270	788-C6
VIA MAZATLAN			
2100	PMSP	92264	786-E6
2700	COR	92882	773-A2
VIA MEDEIROS			
43000	RivC	92562	958-A3
VIA MEDIA			
16000	RivC	92530	866-A7
40900	TEM	92591	959-C3
VIA MELODIA			
78500	LQNT	92253	849-G5
VIA MENSABE			
5600	RIV	92506	716-C2
VIA MERCED			
1100	CTHC	92234	787-F3
VIA MESA VERDE			
800	RIV	92507	716-D1
VIA MILANO			
2900	COR	92879	744-B3
82700	INDO	92201	5470-G3
VIA MILPAS			
2500	SDCo	92028	998-B6
VIA MINDI			
800	RIV	92506	716-D2
VIA MINORCA			
-	CTHC	92234	787-F7
VIA MIRAGE			
74000	RivC	92254	(5654-J7 See Page 5594)
N VIA MIRALESTE			
500	PMSP	92262	786-E1
700	PMSP	92262	756-E5
VIA MIRA MOSA			
37400	MURR	92563	928-H4
VIA MIROLA			
24100	RivC	92590	977-H4
VIA MODENA DR			
-	COR	92881	773-G5
VIA MONDO			
29600	TEM	92592	978-J1
VIA MONSERATE			
39300	MURR	92563	928-F4
VIA MONTALBAN			
-	TEM	92592	979-E1
VIA MONTALVO			
39400	MURR	92563	928-F5
VIA MONTANA			
-	LQNT	92253	849-G3
11600	FONT	92337	645-A3
15000	RivC	92240	697-A7
15500	RivC	92240	727-A1
VIA MONTARA			
-	MORV	92557	687-C4
VIA MONTE			
-	RMIR	92270	818-E4
11400	FONT	92337	644-J2
VIA MONTEGO			
10400	MORV	92557	687-C5
43600	PDST	92211	819-F6
VIA MONTEREY			
30100	TEM	92591	959-A4
VIA MONTERO			
39300	MURR	92563	928-F5
VIA MONTESSA			
-	LQNT	92253	849-H3
VIA MONTE VISTA			
500	PMSP	92262	786-C1
500	PMSP	92262	756-C5
VIA MONTEZUMA			
28500	TEM	92590	958-G5
VIA MONTIGO			
-	LQNT	92253	849-H3
VIA MORENO			
22900	MURR	92562	927-E4
VIA NANZO			
43500	TEM	92592	979-D1
VIA NAPOI			
13100	RivC	92503	744-F5
VIA NAPOLI			
1500	SDCo	92028	997-H4
VIA NARAVILLA			
29600	RivC	92586	868-C2
VIA NARIZ			
43100	RivC	92590	958-A6
VIA NAVARRE			
-	MURR	92562	928-C4
VIA NAVONA			
-	LQNT	92253	5530-C2
VIA NAYA			
32000	TEM	92592	959-E7
VIA NEGOCIA			
1700	PMSP	92262	756-F6
VIA NICE			
-	LQNT	92253	849-G4
VIA NORTADA			
42200	RivC	92590	958-A5
VIA NORTE			
11400	LMLN	92354	647-E2
16000	RivC	92530	865-J7
28800	TEM	92591	958-J3
28900	TEM	92591	959-B2
N VIA NORTE			
1500	PMSP	92262	756-D6
VIA NORTE DR			
8300	RIV	92503	714-F1
VIA NORTE VISTA			
28800	MURR	92563	928-G5
VIA NOVILLO			
45400	RivC	92590	978-G4
VIA NUEVO			
1000	RIV	92507	716-C1
VIA NUVE			
-	RivC	92562	956-B6
VIA OCOTILLO			
74000	RivC	92254	(5655-A7 See Page 5594)
VIA OCTAVO			
24000	MURR	92562	928-B2
VIA ODESSA			
45300	TEM	92592	979-D5
VIA OESTE			
25300	RivC	92590	977-J1
33000	RivC	92530	865-J7
VIA OJOS DEL CIELO			
36700	HEMT	92545	810-D5
VIA OLIVA			
9900	RIV	92503	714-H7
W VIA OLIVERA			
100	PMSP	92262	756-D5
VIA OLIVIA			
23600	MURR	92562	927-J3
VIA OLVERA			
68900	CTHC	92234	787-E3
VIA OPERA			
-	LQNT	92253	849-H4
VIA OPORTA			
-	MURR	92562	928-B2
VIA ORIZABA			
700	RIV	92506	716-D2
VIA ORO			
25900	LMLN	92354	647-E2
VIA ORSORNO			
200	PDST	92260	818-G6
VIA ORUGA			
38200	MURR	92563	928-H5
VIA ORVIETO			
-	LQNT	92253	849-G3
VIA PACIFICA			
1200	COR	92882	743-A7
2100	COR	92882	773-A1
VIA PADOVA WY			
-	COR	92881	773-G5
VIA PAJARO			
10400	MORV	92557	687-C5
VIA PALACIO			
-	LQNT	92253	5530-A2
28600	MURR	92563	928-G6
VIA PALERMO			
30000	RivC	92584	868-F2
82700	INDO	92201	5470-G2
VIA PALMA			
43700	PDST	92211	819-E7
VIA PALMERA			
31400	RivC	92548	809-C3
VIA PALMILLA			
-	LQNT	92253	5470-A6
VIA PALMIRA			
-	PDST	92260	818-H7
VIA PALOMA			
29600	RivC	92567	778-H7
VIA PALOMINO			
44600	LQNT	92253	819-G7
44700	LQNT	92253	849-G1
VIA PALOPINTO			
20400	RivC	92562	926-H7
VIA PAMILLA			
40000	MURR	92562	928-A2
VIA PAMPLONA			
16600	MORV	92551	747-H4
39000	MURR	92563	928-E3
VIA PANORAMA			
800	BAN	92220	721-J2
40500	SDCo	92028	997-J3
40500	SDCo	92028	998-A3
VIA PANTANOSA			
45300	RivC	92590	977-G4
VIA PARAISO			
46500	INDO	92201	5470-B2
N VIA PARAISO			
1200	PMSP	92262	756-C7
VIA PARAISO CIR			
600	COR	92882	773-C2
VIA PARDAL			
1000	RIV	92506	716-C2
VIA PARED			
31500	RivC	92276	788-D1
VIA PARQUE LOMA			
3700	HEMT	92544	811-E6
VIA PASCAL			
45200	RivC	92592	979-J4
VIA PASTOREL			
10300	MORV	92557	687-C5
VIA PATRICIA			
44200	RivC	92590	977-J2
VIA PAVION			
44500	LQNT	92253	819-F7
44700	LQNT	92253	849-G1
VIA PAVON			
1200	COR	92882	773-A2
10100	MORV	92557	687-C5
VIA PERA			
25100	MURR	92563	928-F4
VIA PERALES			
32100	RivC	92592	979-F6
VIA PEREGRINO			
28000	RivC	92590	978-F1
VIA PERLITA			
23900	MURR	92562	928-A3
VIA PESCADERO			
10000	MORV	92557	687-C5
VIA PESSARO			
-	LQNT	92253	5530-C2
VIA PIANOSA			
3600	RIV	92503	714-H7
VIA PINO			
44800	RivC	92590	978-C3
VIA PINTADA			
1000	RIV	92507	716-C1
VIA PISA			
-	LQNT	92253	5530-B2
VIA PLATA			
32300	RivC	92592	979-G5
VIA PLAYA DEL REY			
28600	MURR	92563	928-G5
VIA POCO			
41100	TEM	92591	959-C3
VIA POMPA			
49400	LQNT	92253	849-G5
VIA PONTE DE ORO			
800	RIV	92507	716-E2
VIA PONTITO			
-	LQNT	92253	5530-B1
VIA POQUITO			
31400	TEM	92592	979-D3
VIA PORTO			
10000	MORV	92557	687-C5
VIA PORTOFINO			
-	LQNT	92253	5530-C1
VIA PRADO			
24100	RivC	92570	805-G5
VIA PRIMA VERA			
24100	MURR	92562	928-A3
VIA PRIMERO			
24300	MURR	92562	928-C3
VIA PRINCESA			
28100	MURR	92563	928-H6
VIA PRINCESSA			
28100	MURR	92563	928-H5
VIA PRINCESSA CIR			
28400	MURR	92563	928-G6
VIA PRINCESSA CT			
28300	MURR	92563	928-G6
VIA PUCON			
200	PDST	92260	818-G6
VIA PUEBLA			
45800	RivC	92592	979-G4
VIA PUEBLO			
600	RIV	92507	686-D7
VIA PUENTE			
-	LQNT	92253	849-J6
VIA PUENTE CT			
-	LQNT	92253	849-J6
VIA PUESTA DEL SOL			
-	LQNT	92253	5470-A6
29700	TEM	92591	958-J5
29800	TEM	92591	959-A5
VIA PURETA			
41100	TEM	92591	959-C3
VIA QUEDO			
15000	RivC	92240	697-A7
15500	RivC	92240	727-A1
VIA QUINCELEAGUAS			
39100	SDCo	92028	999-D3
VIA QUINTO ST			
25800	MORV	92551	747-J4
VIA QUITO			
40000	RivC	92592	931-C7
VIA QUIVERA			
45100	TEM	92592	979-D4
VIA RAMI			
-	TEM	92592	959-D6
VIA RAMOS			
-	TEM	92592	979-E1
VIA RANCHERO			
-	RivC	92562	956-C4
VIA RANCHITOS			
39900	SDCo	92028	997-H3
VIA RANCHO			
16200	RivC	92506	745-G3
VIA RAQUEL			
43800	RivC	92590	977-F1
VIA RAVENNA			
47200	LQNT	92253	849-G3
VIA RAYA			
-	TEM	92592	959-E7
VIA RAZO			
43500	TEM	92592	979-E1
VIA REAL			
9300	DHSP	92240	696-H1
27500	RivC	92585	838-D5
VIA REATA			
40100	MURR	92562	928-C4
VIA REFUGIO			
22800	RivC	92570	806-C3
VIA REINA			
-	TEM	92592	959-F5
VIA RENAISSANCE			
-	RivC	92590	978-E3
VIA RENATE			
41900	TEM	92591	958-J4
VIA RENECA			
200	PDST	92260	818-G6
VIA RENGO			
200	PDST	92260	818-G6
VIA RIATA			
17000	FONT	92337	645-A3
35400	RivC	92592	980-C3
VIA RICARDO			
5300	RivC	92509	645-G6
VIA RICCI			
-	TEM	92592	959-D7
VIA RIO			
11400	LMLN	92354	647-E2
VIA RIO TEMECULA			
2900	RivC	92592	979-D3
2900	TEM	92592	979-D3
VIA RISSO			
64300	RivC	92264	816-F2
VIA RITA			
81000	INDO	92201	5470-C2
VIA RIVAS			
32200	TEM	92592	959-E7
VIA ROBERTA			
38000	RivC	92264	816-F2
VIA ROBERTO MIGUEL			
1400	PMSP	92262	756-J6
VIA RODEO			
-	RivC	92562	956-E7
VIA ROJA			
28700	MURR	92563	928-G5
VIA ROJAS			
32200	TEM	92592	959-E7
VIA ROMA			
-	CTHC	92234	787-D7
47000	INDO	92201	5470-G3
VIA ROMA CIR			
-	COR	92881	773-G5
VIA ROSANO			
-	LQNT	92253	5530-B2
VIA ROYALE			
74800	INDW	92210	848-J2
VIA RYAN DR			
1500	COR	92879	743-G3
VIA SABINO			
43400	TEM	92592	959-H7
43400	TEM	92592	979-H1
VIA SAJO			
-	TEM	92592	959-E7
VIA SALERNO			
30000	RivC	92584	868-F2
VIA SALERNO CT			
25800	MORV	92551	747-J4
VIA SALIDA			
1400	PMSP	92264	786-E4
VIA SALTIO			
31700	RivC	92592	979-E4
31700	TEM	92592	979-E4
VIA SALVIA			
13100	RivC	92503	744-F5
VIA SAN CARLOS			
31400	TEM	92592	979-D3
VIA SAN CLARA			
-	LQNT	92253	849-H4
VIA SAN DIMAS			
1000	PMSP	92262	756-E3
VIA SAN JACINTO			
5300	RIV	92506	716-B1
VIA SAN JOSE			
3900	RIV	92504	715-B2
VIA SAN LUIS			
4000	RIV	92504	715-B2
VIA SAN MICHAEL			
1000	PMSP	92262	756-E4
VIA SAN NICOLO			
39700	PDST	92260	818-E3
VIA SAN REMO			
-	CTHC	92234	787-C7
VIA SANTA INES			
31500	TEM	92592	979-D3
VIA SANTANA			
22600	RivC	92567	808-F2
VIA SANTA ROSA			
27600	RivC	92590	978-F2
VIA SANTEE			
25000	MURR	92563	928-E3
VIA SANTIAGO			
1100	COR	92882	743-A6
1400	COR	92882	742-J5
1500	RivC	92882	742-J5
VIA SAUSALITO			
23300	MORV	92557	687-C5
VIA SAVONA			
-	LQNT	92253	5530-C1
9900	RIV	92503	714-H7
VIA SCENA			
39800	PDST	92260	818-E3
VIA SCENICA			
-	LKEL	92532	867-A4
VIA SEGOVIA			
-	LQNT	92253	849-G1
23600	MURR	92562	928-C1
23900	MURR	92562	898-C7
VIA SELVA			
24000	RivC	92590	977-H6
VIA SENDERO			
26800	RivC	92544	842-B2
VIA SERENA			
75600	INDW	92210	849-A2
VIA SERENATA			
45600	RivC	92590	978-G5
VIA SERENIDAD			
-	LQNT	92253	5470-A6
VIA SERENO			
39500	RivC	92562	926-D7
39800	RivC	92562	956-D1
VIA SERON			
31800	RivC	92592	979-E3
VIA SERRANO			
42300	MURR	92562	927-J6
VIA SERRITO			
29900	TEM	92592	979-A1
VIA SEVILLA			
21100	RivC	92562	926-J7
21100	RivC	92562	927-A7
29800	TEM	92591	958-J4
78200	LQNT	92253	819-G7
VIA SEVILLE			
1200	CTHC	92234	787-F3
VIA SICILY			
82900	INDO	92201	5470-G3
VIA SIENA			
40300	MURR	92562	928-B3
VIA SIERRA			
41700	TEM	92592	959-E6
48600	LQNT	92253	849-E5
VIA SIERRA HERMOSA			
11100	RivC	92883	804-G5
VIA SIERRA NEVADA			
600	RIV	92507	716-D1
VIA SILVA			
-	MURR	92562	928-C4
VIA SIMPATICO			
-	LQNT	92253	5470-A6
VIA SIN CUIDADO			
-	LQNT	92253	849-J6
-	LQNT	92253	5470-A6
VIA SIN CUIDADO CT			
-	LQNT	92253	849-J6
-	LQNT	92253	5470-A6
VIA SIN PRISA			
-	LQNT	92253	849-J6
VIA SOCIO			
23100	RivC	92548	809-C2
W VIA SOL			
200	PMSP	92262	756-D6
VIA SOLA			
16000	RivC	92530	865-J7
VIA SOLANA			
-	RMIR	92270	787-H3
48000	LQNT	92253	849-G4
VIA SOL ARRIVA			
-	MORV	92555	748-C2
VIA SOLEDAD			
1400	PMSP	92264	786-E4
84000	INDO	92203	5410-J6
VIA SOL VISTA			
35400	RivC	92592	960-C6
VIA SOMBRA			
-	RivC	92562	956-G2
11600	FONT	92337	645-A3
VIA SONATA			
78500	LQNT	92253	849-G5
VIA SONOMA			
2400	PMSP	92264	786-G5
VIA SONORO			
40200	MURR	92562	928-C4
VIA SONRISA			
39100	MURR	92563	928-E3
VIA SONROSEO			
29600	RivC	92586	868-C2
VIA SORRENTO			
-	CTHC	92234	787-D7
47000	INDO	92201	5470-G2
S VIA SORRENTO			
1000	CLTN	92324	646-E1
VIA SOTELO DR			
5700	RIV	92506	716-C1
VIA STRADA			
-	LQNT	92253	5530-B2
VIA SULTANA			
45100	TEM	92592	979-C5
VIA SUSANA			
900	RIV	92506	716-C2
VIA TAFALLA			
31800	TEM	92592	979-D1
VIA TAFFIA			
38100	MURR	92563	928-H5
VIA TAMARITE			
-	TEM	92592	979-E1
VIA TAPADERO			
-	MURR	92562	928-A3
VIA TEJON AV			
25800	MORV	92551	747-J4
VIA TELESIO			
31700	TEM	92592	959-D6
VIA TEMPRANO			
39300	MURR	92563	928-F5
VIA TENIS			
1100	PMSP	92262	756-G6
VIA TERRENO			
5600	RIV	92506	716-D2
VIA TIAMA			
-	MURR	92562	928-A2
VIA TIBURON			
-	RivC	92590	977-F2
VIA TIOGA			
1500	RIV	92506	716-B2
VIA TONADA			
-	MURR	92562	928-B3
VIA TORENO			
-	TEM	92592	959-E5
VIA TORERO			
46700	INDO	92201	5470-C2
VIA TORINO			
-	CTHC	92234	787-D7
VIA TORNADO			
44800	RivC	92590	978-F2
VIA TORRE			
27500	RivC	92590	978-F1
VIA TORTOLA			
3700	RivC	92503	744-F5
VIA TOSCANA			
-	INDW	92210	819-B5
-	INDW	92211	819-B5
2900	COR	92879	744-B3
VIA TRABUCO			
-	MURR	92562	928-A3
VIA TRAMONTO			
39700	PDST	92260	818-E3
VIA TRANQUILO			
-	LQNT	92253	5470-A2
-	RivC	92592	959-J4
VIA TREVI			
-	CTHC	92234	787-C7
VIA TRIESTE			
-	LQNT	92253	849-H4
-	CTHC	92234	787-C7
VIA TRINIDAD			
1900	RivC	92882	742-H5
VIA TUCSON			
84200	INDO	92203	5410-H5
VIA TURIN			
82800	INDO	92201	5470-G3
VIA ULTIMO			
16200	MORV	92551	747-J3
W VIA VADERA			
700	PMSP	92262	756-C7
VIA VAIL			
72000	RMIR	92270	788-C4
VIA VALDEZ			
26800	RivC	92585	838-A3
31700	LKEL	92530	865-J3
VIA VALENCIA			
40100	RMIR	92270	817-H3
VIA VALEROSA			
27100	RivC	92586	868-C2
VIA VALLARTA			
-	LQNT	92253	849-J4
1100	RIV	92506	716-C1
VIA VALLE			
15100	LKEL	92530	865-H3
VIA VALVERDE			
-	CTHC	92234	787-F7
VIA VAL VERDE			
30200	TEM	92591	959-A2
VIA VANESSA			
27000	RivC	92590	978-D1
VIA VAQUERO RD			
42800	RivC	92590	957-J7
43600	RivC	92590	977-J1
44600	RivC	92590	978-A3
E VIA VAQUERO RD			
2700	PMSP	92262	786-H2
VIA VARELA			
-	RivC	92592	931-D7
VIA VARGAS DR			
24100	MORV	92553	717-E5
VIA VASQUEZ			
41800	TEM	92592	959-F5
VIA VEGA			
43300	RivC	92590	978-B1
VIA VELA			
38000	MURR	92563	928-H4
VIA VELEZ PL			
30000	TEM	92592	959-A7
VIA VELIS			
43500	TEM	92592	979-E1
VIA VENECIA			
82800	INDO	92201	5470-G3
VIA VENETO			
-	CTHC	92234	787-C7
S VIA VENETO			
1000	CLTN	92324	646-E1
VIA VENITO			
-	INDW	92210	849-E2
VIA VENTANA			
31500	RivC	92276	788-D1
78700	LQNT	92253	849-H5
VIA VENTOSO			
38300	MURR	92563	928-H5
VIA VERANO			
-	MURR	92562	928-D2
40100	RivC	92592	960-H1
VIA VERBENA			
74500	RivC	92254	(5655-A7 See Page 5594)
VIA VERDE			
-	RMIR	92270	787-J3
1000	CTHC	92234	787-F3
31700	LKEL	92530	865-H3
41000	RivC	92592	960-E4
VIA VERONA			
-	LQNT	92253	5530-B2
-	CTHC	92234	787-C7
VIA VERTEX			
44900	RivC	92590	978-B3
VIA VICENZA			
-	LQNT	92253	5530-B2
VIA VIEJO			
100	CTHC	92234	787-F7
1100	RIV	92507	716-C1
VIA VIENTECITO			
26700	RivC	92544	842-C2
VIA VIENTO			
29700	RivC	92584	868-G2
VIA VIENTO LN			
1000	COR	92882	742-G6
VIA VIEW			
40000	RivC	92592	931-A7
40500	RivC	92592	961-A1
E VIA VILLAGGIO			
-	INDW	92210	849-F2
N VIA VILLAGGIO			
-	INDW	92210	849-E1
W VIA VILLAGGIO			
-	INDW	92210	849-E2
VIA VILLANUEVA			
2500	PMSP	92264	787-A5
VIA VISTA			
15000	RivC	92240	697-A7
15500	RivC	92240	727-A1
VIA VISTA DR			
1100	RIV	92506	716-B4
VIA VISTA GRANDE			
38400	MURR	92562	927-C3
38400	RivC	92562	927-C3
VIA VISTANA			
-	TEM	92592	959-F5
VIA VITTORIA			
-	LQNT	92253	5530-C1
VIA VOLCANO			
43000	RivC	92562	956-J5
43000	RivC	92562	957-A6
VIA VON BATSCH			
25000	MORV	92557	717-G1
VIA VUELTAS			
26700	RivC	92590	958-C6
VIA WANDA PL			
25700	MORV	92551	747-H4
VIA XANTHE			
40100	MURR	92562	928-B2
VIA XAVIER LN			
25900	MORV	92551	747-J4
VIA YERBA			
27700	RivC	92590	978-E5
VIA YOLO			
1200	CTHC	92234	787-F3
VIA ZAHIDI			
84400	COAC	92236	5471-A6
VIA ZANCAS			
1000	SDCo	92028	998-B7
VIA ZAPATA			
500	RIV	92507	716-D1
28800	MURR	92563	928-G4
VIA ZARAGOZA			
39200	MURR	92563	928-E3
VIA ZURICH			
-	LQNT	92253	849-H4
VIA ZURITA CT			
25900	MORV	92551	747-J4
VICCHIO			
-	INDW	92210	819-A5
VICENTIA AV			
2400	COR	92882	773-C2
N VICENTIA AV			
100	COR	92882	743-C4
900	COR	92880	743-D3
S VICENTIA AV			
100	COR	92882	743-C6
1900	COR	92882	773-C1
VICEROY AV			
4900	NRCO	92860	713-H1
VICKERS DR			
6400	RIV	92504	715-A1
VICKERS RD			
2400	SDCo	92028	997-A1
VICKEY ST			
34900	YCPA	92399	649-J6
34900	YCPA	92399	650-A6
VICKI LN			
38000	CTHC	92234	817-D2
VICKSBURG CT			
-	HEMT	92545	840-E3
4200	RIV	92505	714-D7
VICKY LN			
41400	RivC	92544	841-E2
VICTOR DR			
14200	MORV	92553	717-F7
31300	CTHC	92234	787-F2

STREET Block City ZIP Pg-Grid

VICTOR ST
200 BAN 92220 722-A1
20800 LKEL 92530 896-F1
VICTORHILL RD
41400 RivC 92544 901-E2
VICTOR HUGO DR
18400 RivC 92508 746-C1
VICTORIA AV
100 COR 92879 743-D5
3800 RIV 92507 685-J5
4900 RIV 92506 685-H7
5300 RIV 92506 715-H1
7000 RIV 92504 715-B7
8900 RIV 92503 715-B7
9100 RIV 92503 745-A1
9700 RIV 92503 744-G3
11000 RivC 92503 744-G3
81800 INDO 92201 5470-E3
N VICTORIA AV
100 SJCT 92583 811-A2
S VICTORIA AV
100 SJCT 92583 811-A2
VICTORIA CT
- TEM 92592 959-H7
VICTORIA DR
- LQNT 92253 849-H1
67700 CTHC 92234 787-E5
69600 RMIR 92270 787-F5
VICTORIA LN
100 CALI 92320 650-A7
100 PDST 92211 818-H2
4200 SDCo 92028 998-F7
26200 LMLN 92354 647-F3
VICTORIA RD
1900 PMSP 92262 756-G5
VICTORIA ST
22200 GTER 92313 646-E3
VICTORIA BROOKE LN
33000 RivC 92530 865-G5
VICTORIA DESERT DR
76500 PDST 92211 789-A7
76500 PDST 92211 819-A1
VICTORIA FALLS DR
35600 RMIR 92270 788-B6
VICTORIA HILL DR
5000 RIV 92506 685-H7
VICTORIAN DR
42800 RivC 92544 811-H5
VICTORIAN LN
21000 RivC 92595 897-A2
VICTORIA PARK DR
2600 RIV 92506 715-H2
VICTORY AV
400 BAN 92220 722-B5
1800 BAN 92220 721-H5
VICTORY CIR
33000 RivC 92595 897-A7
VICTORY DR
72000 RMIR 92270 788-C5
VICULIN LN
33700 RivC 92596 899-C3
VIDA CT
23300 MORV 92553 717-C4
VIDEO RD
3600 PMSP 92262 756-C3
VIDETTE CIR
40200 TEM 92591 959-A2
VIEJO DR
44900 RivC 92544 842-C1
VIEJO RD
39300 RivC 92562 956-C7
VIELE AV
- BEAU 92223 720-G3
VIENNA WY
8400 RIV 92508 746-H1
VIENTO CT
- RIV 92508 716-C7
VIENTO DR
1100 HEMT 92543 810-H5
VIEW CIR
800 COR 92881 773-E4
VIEW DR
34700 YCPA 92399 649-J3
37700 RivC 92399 650-F7
38400 RivC 92223 690-F4
63500 DHSP 92240 696-C2
S VIEW DR
70700 RivC - (907-J4 See Page 906)
70700 RivC - 908-A4
VIEW LN
700 COR 92881 773-D4
7500 RivC 92881 773-J2
11000 RivC 92883 804-G5
25800 RivC 92544 (812-D7 See Page 782)
VIEW RD
39900 RMIR 92270 817-H3
VIEWCREST CT
1200 COR 92882 742-E6
VIEW CREST DR
14500 RivC 92504 745-D5
33300 RivC 92595 897-C3
VIEWCREST LN
2900 RIV 92503 744-G3
VIEW PARK CT
6800 RIV 92503 714-G1
VIEWPOINT CT
34200 YCPA 92399 649-H5
VIEWPOINT DR
33300 RivC 92595 897-C3
VIEWPOINT RD
15800 RivC 92504 745-G4
VIEWPOINTE CIR
600 COR 92881 773-D4
VIEWPOINTE LN
700 COR 92881 773-D4
VIEWTOP CIR
800 COR 92881 773-E4
VIEWTOP LN
500 COR 92881 773-D4
N VIGMAN DR
- RivC 92562 956-E7
S VIGMAN DR
- RivC 92562 956-E7
VIGO CT
44000 PDST 92260 818-H7
VIKING CT
6900 RIV 92506 715-F4
VILLA CT
100 PDST 92211 819-A2
500 PMSP 92262 756-C4
28500 RivC 92585 808-F4
VILLA DR
25200 LMLN 92354 647-C2
VILLA LN
11400 LMLN 92354 647-C2
VILLA RD
77700 PDST 92211 819-E4
VILLA ST
900 RivC 92507 646-B7
1000 RIV 92507 646-C7
VILLA ALTURAS DR
29800 TEM 92592 959-A7
VILLABA RD
15300 FONT 92337 644-E3
VILLA BALBOA DR
37600 RivC 92592 960-H1
VILLA BONILLA
32000 TEM 92592 959-E6
VILLA CALIMESA LN
1100 CALI 92320 689-G1
VILLA CHAPARRAL RD
600 SJCT 92583 781-A6
VILLA DEL RIO RD
15500 FONT 92337 644-F3
VILLA DEL SOL
36400 RivC 92595 927-F2
VILLA DEL SUR DR
43700 TEM 92592 979-D2
VILLA DEL ZENADO
37700 RivC 92562 926-J3
VILLA DE MAR
29400 TEM 92591 958-H5
VILLA FRANCA ST
2500 RIV 92503 744-G3
VILLAGE CT
- PDST 92260 848-H1
13600 YCPA 92399 650-D7
VILLAGE DR
- LQNT 92253 5530-E5
100 BLY 92225 5491-E5
14500 FONT 92337 644-C3
68000 CTHC 92234 787-D5
VILLAGE RD
300 HEMT 92544 811-C6
10400 MORV 92557 687-D6
13300 YCPA 92399 650-C6
VILLAGE SQ E
400 PMSP 92262 786-E3
VILLAGE SQ N
800 PMSP 92262 786-E3
VILLAGE SQ S
800 PMSP 92262 786-E3
VILLAGE SQ W
400 PMSP 92262 786-E3
VILLAGE WY
- RIV 92508 746-D3
VILLAGE CENTER DR
54200 RivC - 814-D6
74800 INDW 92210 848-H1
74800 PDST 92260 848-H1
VILLAGE CLUB DR
- LQNT 92253 5530-A1
VILLAGE CLUB PL
- LQNT 92253 5530-B2
VILLAGE LOOP DR
1300 COR 92879 743-G3
VILLAGER VALLEY RD
43900 RivC 92536 982-B5
VILLAGE VIEW DR
54300 RivC - 814-D7
VILLAGE WAY DR
22000 CYNL 92587 867-B3
VILLAGE WEST DR
16400 RivC 92518 746-J5
VILLAGGIO PL
- RMIR 92270 818-A2
VILLA GROVE DR
16700 RivC 92504 745-D5
VILLA HERMOSA
11800 MORV 92557 717-G1
VILLA KNOLL DR
20800 RivC 92570 775-H5
VILLA LINKS LN
- PDST 92260 818-J4
VILLA MILANO
- LKEL 92532 867-A3
VILLA MONTES CIR
700 COR 92879 743-G2
VILLANOVA PL
1200 RIV 92506 716-C4
VILLANOVA ST
45000 INDO 92201 5470-C1
VILLANUEVA ST
15700 FONT 92337 644-F2
VILLA PIAZZA
- LKEL 92532 867-A3
VILLA RAVENA
- LKEL 92532 867-A3
VILLA REAL
- LKEL 92532 867-A3
VILLA ROMA
- LKEL 92532 867-A3
VILLA SCENCERO
- LKEL 92532 867-A3
VILLA TERRACE CT
42800 TEM 92592 959-A7
VILLA TRIZZA
- LKEL 92532 867-A3
VILLA VALTELENA
- LKEL 92532 867-A3
VILLA VENECIA
40000 TEM 92591 959-A1
VILLA VISTA AV
6500 RivC 92509 685-A2
VILLA WOODS DR
4600 RivC 92509 684-F1
VILLEGAS DR
41700 RivC 92536 961-H2
VILLELA CT
5400 RivC 92509 685-A3
VILLENA WY
300 PDST 92260 818-F4
VILLETA DR
44400 LQNT 92253 819-G7
VILLINES AV
1200 SJCT 92583 811-E4
VIMINAL RD
1700 PMSP 92262 756-H5
VINCENNES CT
41100 MURR 92562 927-J4
41100 MURR 92562 928-A4
VINCENT AV
26200 RivC 92545 839-E2
VINCENTE DR
14200 MORV 92553 717-E6
VINCENTIA RD
2600 PMSP 92262 756-H5
VINCENT MORAGA DR
28300 TEM 92590 958-H7
VIN DEO CIR
83800 INDO 92201 5470-J1
VINE AV
400 COAC 92236 5471-C5
1400 PMSP 92262 756-D6
N VINE AV
1400 PMSP 92262 786-D1
VINE ST
2400 NRCO 92860 713-A6
3000 RIV 92507 685-J3
8400 COR 92883 774-B5
21100 RivC 92595 897-A2
21900 RivC 92583 781-E6
22000 SJCT 92583 781-E6
27500 RivC 92585 838-F5
VINEHILL ST
14800 MORV 92553 717-G7
14900 MORV 92551 717-G7
VINELAND PL
39700 RivC 92223 690-J4
VINELAND ST
37900 RivC 92223 690-F4
VINELL AV
27600 RivC 92570 836-J5
VINETA LN
25300 RivC 92548 809-D7
85500 COAC 92236 5471-C7
VINEWOOD DR
- RivC 92203 789-F5
VINEWOOD PL
27000 MORV 92555 718-B4
VINEYARD AV
11000 CALI 92320 690-B6
31700 TEM 92591 959-E4
VINEYARD PKWY
- MURR 92562 927-F5
VINEYARD ST
35200 YCPA 92399 650-A4
VINEYARD WY
3100 RIV 92503 744-H1
VINEYARD KNOLL DR
37400 MURR 92562 927-E4
VINEYARD VIEW DR
39600 RivC 92562 926-G7
VINO WY
33000 RivC 92591 929-G7
33200 RivC 92591 959-H1
S VINTAGE AV
900 ONT 91761 643-G2
VINTAGE CIR
- BAN 92220 721-D6
1100 COR 92881 773-E4
37200 MURR 92562 927-B3
41000 TEM 92591 959-D3
VINTAGE DR
12000 FONT 92337 644-A4
45900 INDW 92210 848-J2
VINTAGE DR E
45800 INDW 92210 848-J2
46000 INDW 92210 849-A3
VINTAGE DR W
73900 INDW 92210 848-G3
73900 PDST 92260 848-G3
VINTAGE PL
- FONT 92337 644-A5
- RivC 92509 644-A5
VINTAGE HILLS DR
- TEM 92592 959-E4
VINTAGE WOODS DR
19000 RIV 92508 716-D7
VINTON PL
41000 RivC 92544 841-D2
VIOLA CT
82200 INDO 92201 5470-E2
VIOLA DR
3200 RivC 92501 646-B6
VIOLA ST
26500 RivC 92544 841-E1
VIOLA TER
6300 CHLS 91709 712-A5
VIOLET CIR
38700 PDST 92211 819-B1
VIOLET CT
- LQNT 92253 849-H1
VIOLET ST
- INDO 92201 5470-D5
200 COR 92882 743-C4
1000 HEMT 92545 840-G2
VIOLETA DR
600 PMSP 92262 786-E1
VIPER RD
9100 RivC 92373 688-G3
VIRAGO RD
31800 RivC 92567 809-C1
VIRGIE CT
- RIV 92508 716-E7
VIRGINIA AV
42400 PDST 92211 819-C6
VIRGINIA DR
300 SJCT 92583 811-A1
VIRGINIA LN
10500 RivC 92223 690-G5
24200 MORV 92557 717-E1
VIRGINIA PL
5800 RIV 92506 685-E7
VIRGINIA RD
3000 PMSP 92262 756-D4
VIRGINIA ST
13200 MORV 92555 719-A5
15200 MORV 92555 749-A1
15200 RivC 92555 749-A1
15200 RivC 92555 719-A7
VIRGINIA LEE CT
900 SJCT 92583 811-D4
VIRGO CIR
2700 RIV 92503 744-H2
VIRGO CT
42900 TEM 92592 959-B6
VIRGO RD
15600 RivC 92241 390-B5
16000 RivC 92241 728-B1
VIRTUE VISTA DR
7900 RivC 92509 684-G3
VISALIA WY
25800 RivC 92544 (812-D7 See Page 782)
VISCAY CT
5200 RivC 92509 685-A3
VISINE RD
43600 RivC 92536 963-A7
43600 RivC 92536 983-A1
VISTA AV
3500 RIV 92501 685-J2
26400 LKEL 92570 836-G4
26400 RivC 92570 836-G4
31800 RivC 92548 839-C1
S VISTA AV
2700 RLTO 92316 645-G2
2700 SBdC 92316 645-G2
VISTA CT
- NRCO 92860 712-J7
- RivC 92254 5592-F5
VISTA DR
- RivC 92592 900-H7
1800 PMSP 92262 756-C5
12500 LMLN 92324 647-B5
38000 CTHC 92234 817-D2
VISTA LN
100 CALI 92320 650-A7
11600 YCPA 92399 650-B4
VISTA PL
26000 RivC 92545 839-G1
66700 DHSP 92240 697-A3
VISTA RD
1600 PER 92585 808-C5
27700 RivC 92585 808-D5
34400 RivC 92596 900-A1
34400 RivC 92596 899-J1
39500 RivC 92543 871-B2
40000 RivC 92544 871-B2
VISTA VW
15000 LKEL 92530 865-F1
37200 RivC 92399 650-G7
37200 YCPA 92399 650-G7
VISTA WY
- RivC - 844-A4
2700 HEMT 92544 811-E6
11800 YCPA 92399 649-J2
23100 RivC 92587 867-D2
VISTA BONITA CT
3400 RivC 92509 685-B1
VISTA BONITA TR
52700 LQNT 92253 5470-C7
VISTA BONITA WY
43200 RivC 92590 957-C7
VISTA CABALLERO
21300 RivC 92570 746-J6
VISTA CALICO
- LQNT 92253 849-J4
VISTA CERRO DR
16400 RivC 92241 727-F1
VISTA CHINO
3700 PMSP 92262 756-J6
3800 CTHC 92234 757-C6
3800 PMSP 92262 757-C6
72000 RivC 92276 758-D5
E VISTA CHINO
Rt#-111
100 PMSP 92262 756-H6
W VISTA CHINO
100 PMSP 92262 756-D6
VISTA CIELO
17100 FONT 92337 645-A3
48100 LQNT 92253 849-G4
VISTA COLINA CIR
1000 COR 92882 742-G6
VISTA CONEJO DR
16400 MORV 92551 747-J3
VISTA CORONA
75200 PDST 92211 818-J4
VISTA DAWN CT
38900 RivC 92592 930-J4
38900 RivC 92592 931-A4
VISTA DE CERROS DR
11900 MORV 92555 717-J1
VISTA DE CIELO
19100 RivC 92562 926-F6
VISTA DEL AGUA
- RMIR 92270 787-G5
22700 RivC 92595 897-D2
VISTA DEL AGUILA
6000 RivC 92509 684-J5
VISTA DE LA MONTANA
100 PMSP 92264 787-D5
VISTA DEL BOSQUE
38500 RivC 92562 926-F5
VISTA DEL CABALLERO
5700 RivC 92509 685-A4
VISTA DEL CAZADOR
6000 RivC 92509 684-J5
VISTA DEL CERRO DR
1000 COR 92879 743-H2
VISTA DEL FUENTE
78500 INDW 92210 849-F2
VISTA DEL LADERO
- RMIR 92270 787-H5
VISTA DEL LAGO
19900 RivC 92570 777-C3
VISTA DEL LAGO DR
1500 SDCo 92028 997-J6
17800 RivC 92503 745-D6
VISTA DEL LUNA
- RMIR 92270 787-G5
VISTA DEL MAR
44300 RivC 92590 977-A2
45100 RivC 92590 976-J4
45600 SDCo 92028 976-J4
80900 LQNT 92253 5470-C6
VISTA DEL MAR ST
- MORV 92555 748-A2
VISTA DEL MONTE
- RMIR 92270 787-H5
600 HEMT 92543 841-B3
VISTA DEL MONTE RD
32200 RivC 92591 959-G1
VISTA DEL MONTE WY
2800 COR 92882 773-C2
VISTA DEL NORTE
85000 COAC 92236 5471-C1
VISTA DEL OESTE
100 PMSP 92264 787-D5
VISTA DE LOMA
600 HEMT 92543 841-B2
VISTA DEL ORO
43000 INDO 92203 5410-J5
VISTA DEL PALO
71000 RivC 92260 848-B5
VISTA DEL RANCHO
30200 TEM 92592 959-A7
VISTA DEL REY
75500 INDW 92210 849-B1
VISTA DEL RIO
2900 SDCo 92028 998-C4
71800 RMIR 92270 818-C4
VISTA DEL SOL
16200 RivC 92241 727-F1
20300 RivC 92570 775-G5
30000 RivC 92276 758-F7
30500 RivC 92276 788-F1
39900 RMIR 92270 818-D2
47900 PDST 92260 848-G4
78500 INDW 92210 849-F2
VISTA DEL SUR
85500 COAC 92236 5471-E2
VISTA DEL VALLE
9200 DHSP 92240 696-J1
27600 RivC 92544 841-F4
68000 CTHC 92234 817-D2
VISTA DEL VERDE
6900 RivC 92509 684-J4
6900 RivC 92509 685-A4
VISTA DE MONTANAS
19200 RivC 92562 926-F6
VISTA DE NOPAL
48300 LQNT 92253 849-G4
VISTA DE ORO
5700 RivC 92509 685-B2
30000 RivC 92276 758-G7
30500 RivC 92276 788-G1
32800 RivC 92591 959-E1
VISTA DE RESACA
43700 TEM 92590 958-F7
VISTA DORADO DR
44900 INDW 92210 849-B2
VISTA DUNES RD
38000 RMIR 92270 818-D2
VISTA ENCANTADA
- RMIR 92270 787-J3
VISTA ESTRELLA
- LQNT 92253 849-J4
- LQNT 92253 5470-A4
VISTA FAMOSO DR
25500 MORV 92551 747-H1
VISTA FLORA
- LQNT 92253 849-E6
VISTA FLORA RD
20000 RivC 92562 956-H2
VISTA GALOPE
50100 LQNT 92253 5470-C6
VISTA GRANDE
80000 LQNT 92253 5470-A2
VISTA GRANDE AV
2100 PMSP 92262 756-C5
VISTA GRANDE DR
900 HEMT 92543 840-J2
14000 RIV 92506 716-F6
14000 RIV 92508 716-F6
14000 RivC 92508 716-F6
14200 RivC 92518 716-F6
67000 RivC 92241 727-A5
VISTA GRANDE WY E
22700 GTER 92313 646-F2
VISTA GROVE CIR
1700 RivC 92503 744-J4
VISTA HAYA
- PDST 92211 819-A4
VISTA HERMOSA
- RMIR 92270 787-G5
VISTA HERMOSA DR
12200 MORV 92557 717-G2
VISTA HUERTO
75200 PDST 92211 818-J5
VISTA LAGO DR
- PDST 92211 818-J2
VISTA LAGO RD
37800 RivC 92596 930-B4
VISTA LAGUNA
- LQNT 92253 849-G4
VISTA LAZO
81600 LQNT 92253 5530-C6
VISTA LOMA DR
- RMIR 92270 817-G3
VISTA LOMA WY
23500 RivC 92590 977-F3
VISTA LOMAS LN
1000 COR 92882 742-G6
VISTA LORETA
- LKEL 92532 866-J3
VISTA LUNA
- LQNT 92253 849-J5
VISTA MIRASOL
- LQNT 92253 849-J5
VISTA MONTANA
1000 SJCT 92582 810-J3
41500 RivC 92544 841-E4
50000 LQNT 92253 5470-C6
VISTA MONTE
100 PDST 92260 848-D2
VISTA MOREE CT
27700 RivC 92544 841-H4
VISTA MURRIETA RD
25100 MURR 92562 928-D5
VISTA NORTE
15800 RivC 92570 775-G5
VISTA OESTE
66900 DHSP 92240 697-A1
VISTA ORIENTE
25100 MURR 92563 928-E4
VISTA ORO
- PDST 92260 848-D2
500 PMSP 92264 786-E3
VISTA PALERMO
- LKEL 92532 866-J3
- LKEL 92532 867-A3
VISTA PALOMINO
- LQNT 92253 849-J4
VISTA PASEO
- PDST 92260 848-D3
VISTARA DR
- RMIR 92270 818-D7
VISTA REAL
- RMIR 92270 787-H5
VISTA REAL ST
700 COR 92879 743-H2
VISTA RIDGE CIR
2200 NRCO 92860 713-D3
VISTA RIO DR
- HEMT 92545 810-C6
VISTA RIPALTI
- LKEL 92532 866-J3
VISTA ROSA
77400 LQNT 92253 849-E5
VISTA ROYALE
- PDST 92260 848-D2
VISTA ROYALE CIR E
200 PDST 92211 818-J2
VISTA ROYALE CIR W
200 PDST 92211 818-J2
VISTA ROYALE DR
200 PDST 92211 818-J1
VISTA SADDLE BACK DR
22600 RivC 92570 805-J2
VISTA SANTA ROSA
- RMIR 92270 818-D5
45200 INDW 92210 849-F2
VISTA SERENA AV
1200 BAN 92220 722-C1
VISTA SUELTO RD
27000 RivC 92555 688-C6
VISTA SUNRISE LN
600 BLY 92225 5551-F1
VISTA SUNRISE ST
800 BLY 92225 5551-F1
VISTA TIERRA
48600 LQNT 92253 849-F4
VISTA TOSCANA
- LKEL 92532 866-J3
VISTA VALLE
- PDST 92260 848-D3
VISTA VENTURA
49200 LQNT 92253 849-E5
VISTA VERDE
15700 RivC 92570 775-G5
45300 RivC 92592 979-F4
VISTA VERDE DR
24600 MURR 92562 928-D3
N VISTA VESPERO
1100 PMSP 92262 756-C7
VISTA VIEJO DR
48600 PDST 92260 848-D5
VISTA VIEW TER
1700 RIV 92506 716-A5
VITA LN
13000 YCPA 92399 650-C5
VIVA LN
- RivC 92596 900-A5
34200 RivC 92596 899-J5
VIVIAN CIR
2300 COR 92882 773-A1
3500 PMSP 92262 756-J6
VIVIAN DR
32600 RivC 92595 896-J6
VIVIAN LN
100 HEMT 92543 841-A1
VIVIAN WY
6700 RIV 92506 715-F3
VIVIENDA AV
11900 GTER 92313 646-C3
VIVIENDA CT
22000 GTER 92313 646-D3
VIXEN TRAIL CIR
1700 COR 92882 772-H1
VOGE LN
- RivC 91752 684-A4
VOLANTE CT
- FONT 92337 645-A2
VOLANTE DR
11300 FONT 92337 645-A2
VOLARE RD
46900 RivC 92590 977-H6
VOLKMANN RD
57100 RivC 92539 (935-A2 See Page 904)
VOLTA WY
- TEM 92592 979-F2
VOLTAIRE DR
1100 RIV 92506 716-C4
VOLTAIRE VISTA
- SJCT 92567 779-J6
34000 RivC 92567 779-H6
VOLTERRA
- INDW 92210 819-B6
VOLTERRA ST
- TEM 92592 979-G1
VOLTURNO RD
1700 PMSP 92262 756-H5
VON DEHN RD
- RMIR 92270 818-B2
VON EUW DR
28100 RivC 92596 839-C5
VONITA CIR
2600 COR 92879 744-A2
VON JANGO RD
- RivC 92570 776-C6
VON MOOS RD
33000 RivC 92584 898-A2
VONNIE CT
6300 RIV 92504 685-A7
6300 RIV 92504 715-A1
VOSBURG CT
1800 SJCT 92583 811-D4
VOUGHT ST
22500 MORV 92553 717-B5
VOYAGER RD
39400 RivC 92544 901-A7
39400 RivC 92544 931-A1
VUELTA CHICA
44700 RivC 92590 976-G2
VUELTA GRANDE RD
44600 RivC 92590 976-G3
VULCAN CT
17400 RivC 92504 746-A5

W

W ST
200 RivC 92518 747-D1
WABASH CT
4500 RIV 92501 645-H7
WABASH DR
3800 RivC 91752 644-A7
WABASH LN
44700 TEM 92592 979-A3
WACKER DR
3800 RivC 91752 643-J7
39100 RivC 92592 981-A4
WACK WACK PZ
1700 PMSP 92264 787-C3
WADE AV
4400 PER 92571 747-D7
4400 PER 92571 777-D1
WADE LN
41000 RivC 92544 901-E1
WADE ST
55500 RivC 92274 5530-H4
WADE WY
- COR 92881 773-H6
WAGER LN
17900 RivC 92570 746-G7
WAGNER ST
- RivC 92570 807-B1
WAGNER WY
10300 RIV 92505 714-F6
25000 RivC 92544 811-H6
WAGON RD W
10000 RivC 92883 804-E6
WAGON WY
10200 RivC 91752 644-A5
WAGON CREEK LN
- RivC 92584 867-H2
WAGONER LN
3500 RivC 92879 744-A5
3600 RivC 92879 743-J5
WAGON-RIM CT
21600 RivC 92595 897-A3
WAGON TRAIN LN
10800 RivC 91752 683-J5
WAGON TRAIN ST
2300 COR 92880 742-H1
WAGON WHEEL DR
- PER 92571 778-B3
16400 RivC 92506 745-H2
WAGON WHEEL LN
- MURR 92562 927-H5
24400 RivC 92595 897-G2
WAGON WHEEL RD
200 PDST 92211 818-J4
200 PDST 92211 819-A4
2400 NRCO 92860 713-A6
38000 RivC 92539 (934-H3 See Page 904)
WAHL ST
39000 HEMT 92543 810-J5
WAILEA CT
30500 TEM 92592 979-B4
WAILEA DR
- BAN 92220 721-C5
WAINWRIGHT CT
5200 RIV 92507 686-C7
5200 RIV 92507 716-C1
WAITE AV
2700 RivC 92503 744-F3
WAITE ST
3100 RIV 92507 685-J3
21100 RivC 92595 897-A3
WAKE CT
29900 CYNL 92587 867-C3
WAKEBRIDGE DR
4000 RIV 92505 744-D1
4200 RIV 92505 714-D7
WAKEFIELD AV
800 COR 92882 743-B6
31000 RivC 92548 839-C1
WAKEFIELD CIR
- LQNT 92253 849-H1
WAKEFIELD RD
69800 CTHC 92234 787-G1
WAKE FOREST CT
- RMIR 92270 818-B3
WAKEHAM PL
40500 PDST 92211 819-F3
WALCOTT LN
40000 TEM 92591 959-D2
WALD CT
69000 RivC - (907-F5 See Page 906)
WALDEN LN
1700 HEMT 92545 810-H5
WALDEN WY
30900 CTHC 92234 787-G2
43500 RivC 92544 811-J7
WALDO RD
33400 RivC 92544 901-E1
WALDON RD
25400 RivC 92584 897-J1
25600 RivC 92584 898-A1
WALDON WEAVER RD
43200 HEMT 92545 840-D2
WALDORF DR
1700 COR 92882 743-A7
2900 RIV 92507 686-E3
WALES CT
300 SJCT 92583 781-A7
WALFRED WY
27300 MORV 92555 718-B1
WALHAM PL
33300 LKEL 92530 865-H7
S WALIN ST
1200 CLTN 92324 646-G2
WALKENRIDGE DR
3300 COR 92881 773-F4
WALKER AV
- PER 92570 807-H4
100 RivC 92507 646-D6
WALKER DR
21100 RivC 92567 778-J5
WALKER ST
24500 RivC 92584 897-H1
68300 CTHC 92234 787-D1
WALKER CANYON RD
- LKEL 92532 835-G4
- RivC 92532 835-G4
WALKER PASS DR
26400 MORV 92555 717-J4
26400 MORV 92555 718-A4
WALKER RANCH RD
43000 RivC 92539 964-G6
44000 RivC 92539 (984-G1 See Page 964)
WALL CIR
1400 COR 92882 743-A4
WALL RD
19000 RivC 92258 725-H4
WALL ST
43100 RivC 92544 811-H6
E WALL ST
4500 ONT 91761 643-E2
WALLABY LN
- RIV 92508 716-E7
WALLACE AV
20900 RivC 92570 836-J5
21200 RivC 92570 837-A5
WALLACE RD
17500 RivC 92241 728-A2
41700 RivC 92544 931-F4
54400 RivC 92274 5531-E2
WALLACE ST
1700 COR 92881 773-G6
2800 RivC 92509 685-E2
WALLACE WY
26000 RivC - 814-D6
WALLACK PL
26100 LMLN 92354 647-E2
WALLCREST DR
25400 RivC 92548 809-C7
WALLER ST
24400 MURR 92562 928-A5
WALLER WY
400 PER 92571 777-H6
WALLINGFORD RD
40000 MURR 92562 928-C3
WALLINGHAM DR
3200 RIV 92503 744-E3
WALLIS RD
22500 RivC 92567 809-D2
WALLOWA CIR
- COR 92881 773-D4
WALLS ST
33000 RivC 92530 896-D2
WALMAC PL
14200 FONT 92337 644-B4
WALNUT
1100 LKEL 92530 866-D4
WALNUT AV
300 BEAU 92223 720-H3
1400 PER 92571 778-B4
2000 RivC 92571 778-B4
18300 RivC 92532 836-D7
21400 RivC 92570 807-A7
21600 CLTN 92324 646-C3
21600 GTER 92313 646-C3
21700 CLTN 92313 646-C3
36100 CALI 92320 690-B6
WALNUT CIR
- COR 92881 773-D4
WALNUT CT
13900 MORV 92555 718-E5
WALNUT DR
600 LKEL 92530 865-J3
WALNUT LN
- COR 92881 773-D4
WALNUT PL
- INDO 92201 5470-C3
WALNUT ST
- RivC 92570 836-G5
- PER 92571 777-F4
400 HEMT 92543 840-J1
4900 RIV 92505 714-B6
11000 SBdC 92316 645-F2
13000 RivC 92880 713-C1
21000 RivC 92595 897-A5
23100 RivC 92570 777-D4
40200 RivC 92543 871-B2
40300 RivC 92544 871-B2
E WALNUT ST
2700 ONT 91761 643-A6
S WALNUT ST
600 CLTN 92324 646-C1
WALNUT CREEK CIR
24600 MURR 92562 928-D3
WALNUT CREEK RD
34000 RivC 92595 897-D4
WALNUT GROVE AV
- RivC 92880 713-A2
9900 RIV 92503 744-H1
WALNUT PARK WY
3700 HEMT 92544 811-F7
WALSH LN
31500 RivC 92584 868-C5
WALSH RD
18200 RivC 92532 836-B3
WALSH WY
34100 RivC 92544 902-A2
WALSH CENTER DR
- MURR 92562 928-D6
WALT RD
30500 MURR 92584 898-F5
S WALTER CT
1600 CLTN 92324 646-H3
WALTER ST
5300 RIV 92504 715-A1
WALTER WY
2400 HEMT 92545 840-G1
WALTERS DR
53000 RivC - 814-A4
WALTERS ST
14600 RivC 92880 712-H2
14800 SBdC 91710 712-H2
WALTHER AV
28100 RivC 92555 688-D6
WALTON CIR
33500 RivC 92276 788-F4
WALTON ST
3500 RIV 92503 744-D3
WALTON WY
41000 MURR 92563 928-E7
WALTZ RD
500 PER 92570 807-F3
S WANAMAKER AV
100 ONT 91761 643-E2
WANDA CIR
4400 HEMT 92544 811-F6
WANDA LN
25100 RivC 92544 (812-A6 See Page 782)
WANDA WY
3400 RIV 92506 715-F1
53100 RivC - 814-A5
WANDERLUST DR
26000 RivC 92544 811-F7
26000 RivC 92544 841-F1
WANISH PL
- PDST 92260 848-B7
- PDST 92260 878-B1
WANKI AV
35300 RivC 92595 897-D7
WAR ADMIRAL ST
28000 MORV 92555 718-D4
WARBLER AV
12200 GTER 92313 646-E4
WARBLER CIR
39500 TEM 92591 959-A1
WARBLER DR
39300 TEM 92591 959-A1
WARBLER WY
11600 MORV 92557 717-D1
WAR BONNET CIR
46400 INDW 92210 849-D2
WARBONNET DR
900 PER 92570 807-E3
WARBONNET WY
7600 RivC 92880 712-H2
7600 SBdC 91710 712-H2
WAR CLOUD DR
16500 MORV 92551 747-G4
WARD DR
41800 PDST 92211 819-A5
WARD LN
100 CALI 92320 650-A7
100 CALI 92320 690-A1
WARD ST
12600 BLY 92225 5491-H6
WARDELL LN
26500 RivC 92584 868-C6
WARDLOW CIR
2200 COR 92880 742-H5
WARDLOW RD
2200 COR 92880 742-G4
2300 COR 92882 742-G4
WARING AV
200 RivC 92507 646-D6
WARING CT
74800 PDST 92260 818-H7
WARING WY
82200 INDO 92201 5470-E4
WARM CREEK WY
29300 RivC 92584 868-F1
WARMINGTON ST
11200 RivC 92503 744-F4
WARM SANDS DR
500 PMSP 92262 786-F3
500 PMSP 92264 786-F3
WARM SANDS PL
- PMSP 92264 786-E3
E WARM SPRINGS CT
3500 ONT 91761 643-C6
WARM SPRINGS DR
39300 RivC 92260 818-F3
WARM SPRINGS RD
24000 RivC 92883 804-C6
33200 RivC 92596 899-B2
WARNER LN
- MURR 92584 898-F4
WARNER RD
17400 RivC 92555 749-G5
WARNER TR
42200 PDST 92211 819-E6
44000 INDW 92210 819-E7
44000 PDST 92210 819-E7
44500 INDW 92210 849-E1
WAR PAINT RD
39700 RivC 92544 931-B1
WARREN RD
100 SJCT 92582 810-C2
700 SJCT 92582 780-B6
18500 RivC 92508 746-C6
20000 RivC 92570 746-F6
24000 HEMT 92545 810-B6
25500 HEMT 92545 840-C2
28000 RivC 92545 840-C6
35100 RivC 92596 840-C6
37900 RivC 92596 930-D4
38000 RivC 92592 930-D4
N WARREN RD
100 HEMT 92545 810-C7
100 HEMT 92545 840-C1
WARREN ST
4400 RIV 92503 714-G3
21000 RivC 92567 779-D6
44000 INDO 92201 5410-G6
WARWICK CT
4200 HEMT 92544 811-F5
4700 RIV 92503 714-H3
WARWICK DR
8400 RivC 92240 696-E1
WARWICK RD
25600 RivC 92586 837-J6
25600 RivC 92586 838-A6
WARWICK ST
1900 SJCT 92582 810-F2
WARWICK HILLS CT
- YCPA 92399 649-E2

STREET Block City ZIP Pg-Grid

WARWICK HILLS RD
- YCPA 92399 649-E2
WARWICK HILLS WY
5900 BAN 92220 721-C5
WASATCH CT
24600 RivC 92883 804-E6
WASATCH DR
- COR 92881 773-E5
WASHANA CT
31100 TEM 92592 979-D5
WASHATONIA DR
32800 CTHC 92234 787-F3
WASHBURN AV
100 COR 92882 743-D6
100 SJCT 92583 811-B1
WASHBURN CIR
100 COR 92880 743-D4
100 COR 92882 743-D4
WASHBURN RD
18000 RivC 92532 836-B5
N WASHINGTON
- CTHC 92234 787-A7
WASHINGTON AV
- CTHC 92234 787-A7
600 SJCT 92544 811-C4
600 SJCT 92583 811-C4
1900 HEMT 92544 811-F4
2200 RivC 92544 811-F4
2200 RivC 92583 811-F4
15100 LKEL 92530 865-G3
23400 MURR 92562 927-H4
23400 RivC 92595 927-H4
23400 RivC 92562 927-H4
24500 MURR 92562 928-A7
25300 MURR 92562 958-B1
27500 RivC 92545 839-F4
27800 RivC 92585 808-E7
28000 RivC 92596 839-F5
WASHINGTON CT
16700 RivC 92506 745-H3
WASHINGTON DR
33200 YCPA 92399 649-F4
WASHINGTON ST
- RivC 92203 789-F5
- RivC 92276 789-E2
900 PER 92571 747-D7
1100 RIV 92506 745-G1
1300 RIV 92506 715-G7
2200 RIV 92504 715-E2
15100 RivC 92506 745-J4
15400 RivC 92530 865-H7
15600 RivC 92504 745-J6
17500 RivC 92508 745-J6
18300 RivC 92504 775-J1
19800 RivC 92881 773-J5
20000 COR 92881 773-J5
32900 RivC 92596 899-F1
35700 RivC 92596 929-G2
38000 RivC 92211 789-F5
38000 RivC 92211 819-F1
39700 RivC 92201 819-F5
40100 PDST 92201 819-F1
40100 PDST 92211 819-F1
43000 LQNT 92253 819-F5
43000 PDST 92253 819-F5
43400 INDW 92210 819-F7
43400 PDST 92210 819-F7
44600 LQNT 92253 849-G3
44600 INDW 92210 849-G3
E WASHINGTON ST
200 CLTN 92324 646-D2
2200 CLTN 92404 646-J1
WASHOUT RD
46900 RivC 92544 (932-H4
See Page 902)
WASSON CANYON RD
19000 LKEL 92532 866-E2
19000 RivC 92532 866-E2
19400 LKEL 92532 836-G7
27800 RivC 92570 836-H7
28000 LKEL 92570 836-H7
N WATEKA ST
200 SJCT 92583 811-A1
S WATEKA ST
100 SJCT 92583 811-A1
WATER AV
300 PER 92571 777-H5
23500 RivC 92570 777-E5
26300 RivC 92571 778-A5
31000 RivC 92567 779-A5
W WATER AV
400 PER 92571 777-F5
WATER WY
2400 COR 92882 773-B1
48600 RivC 92536 963-B6
WATERBURY CT
4300 RIV 92501 645-H7
WATER
CANYON-PISGAH PEAK
36900 SBdC 92399 650-F2
WATERCRESS CIR
10400 MORV 92557 687-F5
WATERFALL CIR
9800 MORV 92557 687-B4
WATERFALL DR
78500 RivC 92211 789-G7
WATERFALL LN
2200 COR 92882 773-B2
WATERFORD CIR
100 RMIR 92270 818-A1
WATERFORD CT
2400 SBDO 92408 646-J1
WATERFORD LN
- RivC 92548 809-F6
78900 RivC 92211 819-G1

WATERHOLE CANYON DR
28500 RivC 92584 868-F1
WATERLEAF CIR
23700 MORV 92557 687-D6
WATERLILY CIR
- PDST 92260 818-H6
WATERLILY CT
- RivC 92880 683-B7
WATER LILY DR
41000 MURR 92562 927-J3
WATERLOO CT
- RMIR 92270 788-B5
1300 RIV 92506 716-B3
S WATERMAN AV
2500 SBDO 92408 646-J1
2600 CLTN 92408 646-J1
11000 CLTN 92324 646-J1
WATERMAN CANYON WY
9000 RivC 92883 804-C4
WATERMILL LN
30600 RivC 92584 868-F4
WATERSTONE DR
- RIV 92505 714-C7
WATERVIEW CT
- RIV 92505 714-C6
WATER VIEW DR
22800 CYNL 92587 867-D3
WATERWALL CT
- RIV 92505 744-D1
WATERWELL RD
- RivC - (907-J3
See Page 906)
WATERWHEEL DR
13000 RivC 92883 835-B3
WATKINS CIR
32500 RivC 92562 927-E2
WATKINS DR
300 RivC 92507 686-F6
2300 RIV 92507 686-C3
WATKINS GLEN RD
21100 RIV 92508 746-H1
WATOMI CT
49800 RivC 92536 (933-E7
See Page 902)
WATSON RD
100 PER 92570 807-F7
26000 PER 92570 808-A7
27000 RivC 92585 808-C7
30000 RivC 92548 808-H7
30200 RivC 92548 809-A7
WATSON ST
5400 BAN 92220 721-D5
WATSON WY
25100 MORV 92553 717-G4
WATT AV
3800 RIV 92503 744-C2
WATTS LN
4100 HEMT 92545 810-E7
WATTS RD
40700 RivC 92544 961-D2
WAUGH RANCH RD
12300 RivC 92503 744-H6
WAVE CREST CIR
30600 RivC 92584 868-G4
WAVECREST DR
15100 LKEL 92530 865-G5
WAVERLY AV
13100 RivC 92879 744-A5
WAVERLY DR
4600 PMSP 92264 787-B6
29000 RivC 92586 838-A7
29000 RivC 92586 868-A1
WAVERLY RD
38300 RivC 92211 819-F1
WAWONA RD
1500 PMSP 92262 756-D6
WAYCROSS DR
30200 RivC 92548 808-J6
30200 RivC 92548 809-A6
WAYFARER CT
15000 LKEL 92530 865-F3
WAYFARER LN
29300 LKEL 92530 865-F3
WAYFIELD RD
11100 RIV 92505 744-D1
WAYMAN RD
23000 RivC 92548 809-B3
WAYMAN ST
5400 RIV 92504 715-B2
WAYMAN WY
38400 RivC 92544 931-F4
WAYNE CT
3800 RIV 92504 715-A3
WAYNE DR
25800 RivC - 814-E6
WAYNE LN
27800 RivC 92585 808-D5
WAYNE RD
2100 PMSP 92262 756-G4
WAYNE ST
3600 COR 92881 773-G5
49000 INDO 92201 5470-G5
WAYNEWOOD DR
29500 TEM 92591 958-J4
WAYWARD RD
37100 RivC 92544 931-H1
WEATHER WY
400 BAN 92220 721-H4
WEATHERBY DR
3000 RIV 92503 744-F3
WEATHERFIELD LN
1600 RIV 92506 716-B4
WEATHERLY CT
22600 RivC 92595 897-D7

WEATHERVANE PL
- RIV 92508 746-D4
WEATHERWOOD RD
2300 COR 92879 744-F5
WEAVER LN
900 SJCT 92583 811-D4
WEAVER ST
1100 BAN 92220 722-C2
6800 RIV 92504 714-J2
WEAVER HILLS DR
45500 RivC 92536 962-E4
WEB CT
13100 YCPA 92399 649-G5
WEBB CIR
1200 COR 92879 743-F5
WEBB DR
32600 RivC 92595 896-J6
WEBB ST
9600 RivC 92509 684-C2
12100 MORV 92557 717-D2
WEBER AV
11200 MORV 92555 688-D7
WEBER WY
700 LKEL 92532 866-G4
32600 RivC 92544 871-F7
WEBSTER AV
100 SJCT 92582 810-C1
3000 PER 92571 777-E2
4200 PER 92571 747-E7
4700 PER 92551 747-E7
21100 RivC 92570 777-E7
21900 RivC 92570 807-E1
24100 MORV 92553 717-E3
WEBSTER RD
- RIV 92508 716-E7
WECKSLER LN
24000 RivC 92548 809-G5
WEDGE LN
- HEMT 92545 810-D6
WEDGE WY
31100 TEM 92591 959-C5
WEDGEWOOD CIR
200 CALI 92320 689-J1
200 CALI 92320 690-A1
WEDGEWOOD DR
27100 RivC 92544 841-F3
WEDMORE DR
25400 MORV 92553 717-H3
WEDOW DR
15800 MORV 92551 747-G2
WEE BURN WY
28500 RivC 92586 838-A7
WEEPING WILLOW CT
- RivC 92880 713-B1
WEEPING WILLOW DR
16500 RivC 92503 744-J5
16500 RivC 92503 745-A5
WEEPING WILLOW LN
11900 FONT 92337 644-B4
24400 MURR 92562 927-J6
WEEPING WILLOW WY
11200 CALI 92320 690-C6
WEGMAN DR
6900 RivC 92509 645-B5
WEIBEL CIR
31400 TEM 92591 959-E3
WEIKAMP LN
- RivC 92506 745-H1
WEILL CT
24300 MORV 92553 717-E4
WEINHART CT
11300 MORV 92557 687-D7
WEIRICK RD
7700 COR 92883 774-B7
7700 RivC 92883 774-A7
8100 RivC 92883 804-A1
10500 COR 92883 804-A1
WEISKOPF
- LQNT 92253 5530-C5
WEISSHORN
- RivC - (907-E7
See Page 906)
WELBY PL
11900 MORV 92557 717-F1
WELCH DR
18800 RivC 92532 866-E1
WELCH ST
7400 RivC 92509 684-H3
WELCHES CT
42200 RivC 92544 841-F2
WELCOME LN
11600 DHSP 92240 696-J3
WELEBIR ST
11500 LMLN 92354 647-D2
WELFORD PL
33400 LKEL 92530 865-H7
WELLER DR
9700 CALI 92320 690-A3
WELLER PL
11800 MORV 92557 717-F2
WELLES PL
23800 RivC 92587 837-F7
WELLESLEY AV
11700 LMLN 92354 647-G2
11800 SBdC 92373 647-G2
WELLESLEY DR
200 COR 92879 743-H4
WELLESLEY WY
4600 RIV 92507 686-A6
WELLINGTON CIR
500 COR 92879 744-A3
30900 TEM 92591 959-C1
WELLINGTON WY
8000 RIV 92504 715-C3

WELLMAN RD
53000 RivC 92539 (934-C6
See Page 904)
57000 RivC 92539 (935-A6
See Page 904)
WELLS AV
- BLY 92225 5491-H7
7400 RIV 92503 714-E5
10300 RIV 92505 714-D6
16900 LKEL 92530 866-A2
WELLS PL
32900 RivC 92595 896-H5
WELLS RD
3900 BLY - 392-B9
WELLS ST
200 BLY 92225 5491-E7
900 BLY 92225 5491-D7
20700 RivC 92570 776-G3
WELLS FARGO DR
28100 RivC 92532 836-D6
32000 RivC 92276 788-F2
WELLWOOD AV
400 BEAU 92223 720-H1
WELMAR RD
29800 RivC 92584 868-A2
WELSH DR
3400 NRCO 92860 713-B7
WELSH LN
5100 RivC 92509 684-B3
WELTY ST
2200 SDCo 92028 998-J5
WEMBLEY DR
22200 MORV 92557 717-A2
WEMBLEY LN
2000 COR 92881 773-F1
WENATCHEE WY
5100 RivC 92509 685-D3
WENDELL DR
24800 RivC 92544 811-H5
WENDELL WY
3100 RIV 92507 686-D3
WENDELL PARK DR
14700 RivC 92570 775-E5
WENDLANDT RD
21200 RivC 92570 806-J3
WENDOVER DR
7900 RivC 92509 684-G5
WENDOVER RD
28000 RivC 92585 808-E5
WENDY CIR
- RivC 92570 805-F5
WENDY CT
5400 BAN 92220 721-D2
WENDY LN
20400 RivC 92562 926-H7
WENDY RD
- PMSP 92282 724-H3
WENDY WY
25100 MORV 92551 747-G1
WENTE CT
2100 SJCT 92583 811-D4
WENTWORTH DR
3000 HEMT 92545 840-E2
5500 RIV 92505 714-A5
27000 RivC 92586 838-C6
WENTWORTH ST
- MURR 92563 928-H7
WESCOTT CT
28100 RivC 92596 839-F5
WESELEY CIR
53500 RivC 92539 904-C6
WESLEY PL
500 HEMT 92543 841-A1
1500 HEMT 92543 840-H1
WESLEY ST
400 BAN 92220 722-B5
32000 RivC 92595 897-B6
32700 RivC 92596 839-F6
33300 RivC 92595 896-J7
WESLEYAN CT
- RMIR 92270 818-B2
WESPA DR
27500 RivC 92586 837-J5
WEST AV
- RivC - 412-A3
32900 RivC 92595 897-G1
WEST DR
- BEAU 92223 720-G4
9000 DHSP 92240 696-H2
10500 RivC 92240 696-H7
13500 RivC 92223 720-G4
15000 RivC - 696-H7
15000 RivC - 726-H2
16000 RivC 92240 726-H2
28200 RivC 92587 837-E6
WEST RD
- PMSP 92264 786-G6
WEST ST
20800 COR 92883 774-B6
WEST WY
24700 LMLN 92354 647-B2
32900 RivC 92530 865-J7
WESTAR CT
- MURR 92562 927-G5
WESTBANK DR
37500 RivC 92563 929-D3
WESTBOROUGH LN
- RIV 92506 716-A6
WESTBROOK CT
77500 PDST 92211 819-E3
WESTBROOK DR
1200 RIV 92506 715-H7
30100 RivC 92567 778-J7
WESTBROOK ST
1000 COR 92880 743-A1

WESTBURY DR
12900 MORV 92553 717-H3
WESTBURY RD
21100 RIV 92508 746-H1
WESTCHESTER DR
2900 RIV 92503 714-J7
2900 RIV 92503 744-J1
2900 RIV 92503 745-A1
32000 RivC 92276 788-E2
WESTCHESTER WY
- RivC 92880 683-D4
WESTCOURT WY
3300 HEMT 92545 810-F6
WESTERFIELD ST
5100 RivC 92509 685-D3
WESTERFIELD WY
84500 COAC 92236 5471-B6
WESTERLY DR
8600 RIV 92508 746-E2
WESTERLY TR
12100 MORV 92557 717-G2
WESTERLY WY
- RivC 92880 713-B1
16300 MORV 92551 747-G3
WESTERN AV
100 HEMT 92543 810-J7
1800 NRCO 92860 713-B5
1900 NRCO 92860 713-C5
6400 RIV 92505 714-B2
10000 DHSP 92240 696-C4
12000 RivC 92240 696-C6
23000 RivC 92241 390-C7
74800 RivC 92276 788-J5
74900 RivC 92276 789-A5
WESTERN DR
1300 SJCT 92583 780-J6
WESTERN WY
5000 PER 92571 747-D6
34800 RivC 92595 897-E6
WESTERN CREST DR
23100 RivC 92570 806-A3
WESTERN HILLS DR
11100 RIV 92505 714-B2
WESTERN HILLS RD
38700 RivC 92539 (933-G4
See Page 902)
WESTERN JAY WY
39700 MURR 92562 928-B2
WESTERN KNOLLS AV
1100 BEAU 92223 720-E2
WESTERN RIDGE RD
23000 MORV 92557 687-C7
WESTERN VIEW DR
30800 RivC 92548 839-B1
WESTERN VILLAGE DR
1200 SJCT 92583 781-B6
WESTFALL LN
11200 RIV 92505 714-B5
WESTFIELD DR
3000 RIV 92503 744-F3
WESTFORD CT
5100 RIV 92505 714-B6
WEST FOUR WHEEL DR
1900 NRCO 92860 713-D7
WESTGATE CT
7900 RIV 92506 715-H7
WESTHAVEN CT
24400 MURR 92562 928-C3
WESTHORN DR
- RivC - (907-D1
See Page 906)
WESTLAKE CIR
- PMSP 92264 787-A5
WESTLAKE DR
- PMSP 92264 786-J5
- PMSP 92264 787-A5
22500 MORV 92553 717-B4
30100 RivC 92584 868-F3
WESTLAKE TER
300 PMSP 92264 786-J5
300 PMSP 92264 787-A5
WESTLAND RD
23300 RivC 92567 809-H3
23500 RivC 92548 809-H4
WESTLINK DR
29800 RivC 92584 868-F2
WESTLONG
33100 RivC 92530 865-G6
WESTLYNN DR
15100 RivC 92530 865-G6
WESTMINSTER CT
11800 LMLN 92354 647-F3
WESTMINSTER DR
300 SJCT 92583 781-A7
2000 RIV 92506 715-H5
WESTMINSTER PL
400 HEMT 92545 810-F6
WESTMONT AV
600 HEMT 92543 840-H1
1600 HEMT 92543 841-A1
WESTMONT ST
500 RIV 92507 686-D7
WESTON PL
300 HEMT 92543 811-B6
300 HEMT 92543 841-B1
WESTON RD
1300 PER 92570 807-C2
22900 RivC 92570 807-C2
WESTON WY
1500 RIV 92506 715-G6
WESTOVER CIR
21200 RivC 92518 746-J4
WESTOVER WY
28200 RivC 92586 838-B6

WESTPARK DR
7600 RIV 92506 715-H7
WESTPARK LN
1000 COR 92882 743-B7
WEST POINT DR
20000 RivC 92507 716-F1
20100 RivC 92507 686-F7
WESTPORT CIR
- RivC 92880 683-D4
WESTPORT LN
22700 RivC 92567 808-F2
WESTPORT ST
7100 RIV 92506 716-D5
WESTRIDGE AV
26000 RivC 92586 868-A1
37100 RivC 92211 789-F7
37600 RivC 92211 819-F1
WESTRIDGE RD
2700 RIV 92506 715-G2
WEST RIDGE RD
53400 RivC - 844-B1
WEST RIM CIR
5600 RivC 92509 684-C4
WEST SIDE DR
60000 RivC 92282 725-E1
WESTSIDE DR
81000 RivC 92274 5590-D2
WESTVIEW DR
6300 RIV 92506 716-B4
WESTWARD AV
100 BAN 92220 722-A4
600 BEAU 92223 720-F4
1200 BAN 92220 721-F4
2600 RivC 92220 721-F4
38300 RivC 92223 720-F4
E WESTWARD AV
100 BAN 92220 722-C4
WESTWARD DR
13700 FONT 92337 644-A2
WESTWARD ST
47000 BAN 92220 722-F4
47000 RivC 92220 722-F4
WESTWARD HO DR
79300 LQNT 92253 849-H2
79600 LQNT 92253 5470-A2
79600 INDO 92201 849-H2
79600 INDO 92201 5470-A2
WESTWIND DR
14700 LKEL 92530 865-F1
WESTWIND WY
11200 RIV 92505 714-B5
WEST WINDS DR
25800 RivC 92585 838-E1
WESTWOOD CIR
6700 PMSP 92264 787-D6
WESTWOOD CT
69200 RivC 92241 727-E1
WESTWOOD DR
3800 RIV 92504 715-D2
WESTWOOD LN
12000 GTER 92313 646-G3
WESTWOOD PL
1500 HEMT 92543 840-H1
WESTWOOD ST
23100 GTER 92313 646-G3
23400 CLTN 92324 646-J3
23700 SBdC 92324 646-J3
E WESTWOOD ST
2100 CLTN 92324 646-H3
2200 SBdC 92324 646-H3
WETHERLY ST
800 HEMT 92545 840-F2
WETHERLY WY
1900 RIV 92506 716-A2
WEYER ST
4000 RIV 92501 645-H7
4000 RIV 92501 685-H1
WEYMOUTH CT
2800 HEMT 92545 840-F2
WHARTON CT
26600 RivC 92544 841-E2
WHATTA RD
3000 RivC 92509 645-A7
WHEAT RD
53400 RivC 92539 904-C5
WHEAT ST
26000 RivC 92570 837-H2
26000 RivC 92585 837-H2
WHEATFIELD CIR
24000 RivC 92595 897-F3
WHEATLY DR
39700 MURR 92563 928-E5
WHEATON DR
900 COR 92880 743-A1
WHEATON WY
1300 RIV 92507 686-G1
WHEATSTONE DR
28700 RivC 92530 835-F7
28700 RivC 92530 865-F1
WHEEL RD
43500 INDO 92201 5410-D6
WHEELBARROW LN
34400 RivC 92595 897-H5
WHEELER CIR
500 COR 92879 743-H3
WHEELER DR
40500 RivC 92544 841-C2
WHEELER PL
36000 YCPA 92399 650-C2
WHEELER RD
52000 RivC 92539 (933-J3
See Page 902)
52200 RivC 92539 (934-A3
See Page 904)

WHEELER ST
3800 RIV 92503 714-J4
24500 RivC 92584 897-H1
68900 RivC 92254 (5653-D3
See Page 5592)
WHICHA WY
300 HEMT 92544 811-D6
WHIPPLE RD
4600 RIV 92506 685-D6
65900 RivC - 726-H7
66300 RivC - 756-J1
66300 RivC 92240 756-J1
WHIPPORWILL DR
300 RivC 92507 646-E7
WHIRLAWAY CIR
16600 MORV 92551 747-G4
WHIRLAWAY CT
22200 CYNL 92587 867-C2
WHIRLAWAY ST
- PER 92571 777-G5
WHIRLING WIND DR
40900 PDST 92211 819-F4
WHIRLWIND CIR
2900 BAN 92220 721-G4
WHISKEY CREEK
7200 RivC 92881 773-H4
WHISPER LN
28100 RivC 92590 978-F1
WHISPER RDG
41700 RivC 92544 841-E4
WHISPERING BROOK WY
17000 RivC 92503 744-G5
WHISPERING PALMS TR
29800 CTHC 92234 757-D7
29900 CTHC 92234 787-D2
WHISPERING PINES RD
8900 RivC 92223 691-A2
WHISPERING SPUR DR
16100 RivC 92504 745-F4
WHISPERING TREE DR
8200 RivC 92509 684-F4
WHISPERING TREE LN
1200 COR 92882 742-E6
WHISPERING WIND CT
25900 MURR 92563 928-E6
WHISPERING WIND LN
1300 COR 92881 773-G3
WHISPERING WINDS
- BLY - 5491-B7
WHISPERING WINDS WY
23500 MORV 92557 717-D1
WHISPERING WOOD LN
900 PER 92571 778-A2
WHISTLER CT
- INDO 92201 849-J1
WHISTLER ST
12300 GTER 92313 646-F4
WHISTLER WY
2300 RIV 92506 715-H4
WHISTLING SWAN RD
23900 MURR 92562 928-B2
WHITAKER LN
28000 RivC 92596 839-E5
WHITE AV
26200 RivC 92545 839-D1
WHITE CT
- RivC 92585 838-C2
WHITE DR
72800 PDST 92260 848-E5
WHITE ST
17400 RivC 92508 746-D6
21100 RivC 92518 746-H4
34500 RivC 92595 897-C5
WHITE BIRCH CT
19400 LKEL 92530 896-G4
WHITE BIRCH LN
25200 MORV 92553 717-G5
WHITE BLOSSOM CIR
16400 RivC 92503 744-J4
16400 RivC 92503 745-A4
WHITE BRANCH RD
41900 RivC 92544 931-G5
WHITE CANYON DR
29100 RivC 92584 838-F7
29100 RivC 92584 868-F1
39400 RivC 92260 818-F3
WHITECLIFF WY
900 COR 92882 743-A5
WHITE CLOUD PL
- PER 92571 778-B2
WHITE COVE CT
30200 CYNL 92587 867-F3
WHITECROWN CIR
10200 RivC 92883 804-E6
WHITE DOVE LN
19100 RivC 92508 746-D7
WHITE FEATHER DR
15900 RivC 92504 745-G5
WHITE FOX CT
- LQNT 92253 849-F4
WHITEGATE AV
7300 RIV 92506 715-G7
WHITEGATE DR
44100 RivC 92536 (984-C1
See Page 964)
WHITE GOLD CT
15800 RivC 92504 745-G4
WHITEHALL CT
- RMIR 92270 818-A3
- RMIR 92270 817-J3
WHITEHALL ST
12900 MORV 92553 717-B4
WHITEHAVEN LN
7300 RIV 92506 715-G6

WHITE HOLLY DR
1400 COR 92881 773-F4
WHITE HORSE LN
1900 NRCO 92860 713-C7
1900 NRCO 92860 743-C1
WHITE HORSE TR
76000 PDST 92211 819-B3
WHITE LEAF LN
40000 MURR 92562 928-C4
WHITE LILAC RD
4200 SDCo 92028 998-G7
WHITE LILY CIR
22600 MORV 92557 717-B1
WHITE MOUNTAIN CIR
- COR 92881 773-D5
WHITE MOUNTAIN RD
44000 RivC 92536 982-B5
WHITE MOUNTAIN WY
- MORV 92555 718-E7
WHITE OAK DR
3500 BAN 92220 721-F2
10500 RIV 92505 744-F1
25500 RivC 92544 811-J6
WHITE OAK LN
- MURR 92562 927-E4
1400 COR 92882 742-G6
WHITE OAK RD
200 LKEL 92530 865-H2
WHITE OWL CT
- RivC 92880 713-B1
WHITEOWL CT
23600 MORV 92553 717-D4
WHITE PALMS WY
- RivC 92211 789-F6
WHITE PINE CT
11600 FONT 92337 644-C3
WHITE RIVER LN
100 COR 92881 773-C4
100 COR 92882 773-C4
WHITEROCK LN
- HEMT 92545 840-E4
20000 RIV 92508 746-F2
WHITE ROCKS CIR
30800 TEM 92591 959-B4
WHITE SAGE CT
3300 COR 92881 773-F5
22400 RivC 92883 804-C3
WHITESAGE TR
19100 RivC 92241 727-C4
WHITE SAIL PL
29800 CYNL 92587 867-D2
WHITE SAILS CT
29000 LKEL 92530 865-F2
WHITE SAND TR
28100 MORV 92555 718-D2
WHITE SANDS DR
73700 RivC 92276 788-F4
WHITE SPRUCE CT
32000 RivC 92595 927-F2
E WHITESTAG RD
3100 ONT 91761 643-A5
WHITESTONE DR
2100 RIV 92506 716-A3
WHITE STONE LN
73800 PDST 92260 848-F2
WHITE SUN WY
- RMIR 92270 818-D6
WHITE TIP LN
900 PER 92571 807-J1
WHITE WAKE DR
29900 CYNL 92587 867-F3
WHITEWATER
- DHSP 92240 696-J7
WHITEWATER CTO
- PMSP 92282 725-A3
15000 RivC 92282 725-B2
WHITEWATER PL
71600 RMIR 92270 818-B5
WHITEWATER RD
9700 MORV 92557 687-B4
WHITEWATER WY
71700 RMIR 92270 818-B5
WHITE WATER WY
80700 INDO 92201 5470-B1
WHITEWATER CANYON
RD
10500 RivC 92282 694-J1
10500 RivC 92282 695-A3
12600 RivC 92282 725-B1
WHITEWATER CLUB DR
1700 PMSP 92262 756-H4
WHITE WOOD CIR
25700 MORV 92553 717-H7
WHITEWOOD CT
1600 COR 92882 742-J5
WHITEWOOD RD
36000 MURR 92563 898-E7
36000 MURR 92563 928-F1
WHITFORD AV
11000 RIV 92505 714-D6
WHITING RD
- RivC - (783-J4
See Page 782)
WHITING WY
9200 RIV 92508 746-D4
WHITMAN CT
6500 RIV 92506 716-C4
WHITMAN DR
2000 SJCT 92583 811-B1
12700 BLY - 5491-A6
WHITMAN RD
25800 RivC 92586 838-A5
71900 PDST 92260 848-C5
71900 RivC 92260 848-C5

WHITMAN WY
- COR 92880 712-J7
- COR 92880 742-J1
WHITMORE RD
38000 RivC 92539 (934-H3
See Page 904)
WHITNEY DR
400 HEMT 92543 840-H1
7400 RivC 92509 684-G2
WHITTIER AV
100 HEMT 92543 841-C1
300 HEMT 92543 840-H1
1700 HEMT 92545 840-H1
11300 LMLN 92354 647-F3
11300 SBdC 92354 647-F3
11800 LMLN 92373 647-F3
11900 SBdC 92373 647-F3
26800 RivC 92545 839-F3
27700 RivC 92596 839-F5
40200 RivC 92544 841-C1
40200 HEMT 92544 841-C1
44000 RivC 92544 842-A1
E WHITTIER AV
100 HEMT 92543 841-A1
W WHITTIER AV
35000 HEMT 92545 840-C2
WHITTIER CT
- RMIR 92270 818-B2
WHITTIER PL
3800 RIV 92501 685-G4
WHITTIER ST
22600 RivC 92324 647-B6
WHITWELL WY
58800 RivC 92539 (965-E7
See Page 964)
WIASMUL RD
43400 RivC 92536 964-C7
43400 RivC 92539 964-C7
WICHITA DR
9500 RIV 92503 714-J7
9600 RIV 92503 744-J1
WICHITA WY
13100 MORV 92555 717-J3
40500 MURR 92562 928-C4
WICKER WY
17200 RivC 92504 745-F6
WICKERD RD
25300 RivC 92584 867-J7
25300 RivC 92584 868-A7
30000 RivC 92584 869-E7
30600 RivC 92596 869-E7
WICKET LN
- INDO 92201 5470-B5
WICKFORD PL
- YCPA 92399 649-F2
WICKHAM DR
3000 RIV 92503 744-F2
WICKLOW DR
3000 RIV 92503 744-F3
WIDE CANYON RD
16400 RivC 92241 728-D2
WIDGEON PL
23000 CYNL 92587 867-D3
WIEHE AV
6000 RIV 92506 685-D7
E WIER RD
200 SBDO 92408 646-J1
300 SBDO 92408 647-A1
S WIER RD
2600 CLTN 92408 646-J1
2600 SBDO 92408 646-J1
WIGEON DR
- COR 92882 773-A2
1400 COR 92882 772-J2
WIGWAM DR
500 PER 92570 807-E3
WIGWAM ST
300 PMSP 92264 786-C2
WIKETMAL PL
- PDST 92260 848-B7
WIKIL CT
- PDST 92260 848-C7
WIKIL PL
- PDST 92260 848-C7
WILBUR CT
4200 HEMT 92544 811-F5
WILBUR ST
3500 RIV 92503 715-A6
3600 RIV 92503 714-J5
WILCOX SQUARE AL
5400 RivC 92509 685-D2
WILD BURRO TR
22500 RivC 92557 687-A3
WILD CALLA DR
24500 MORV 92557 687-F6
WILD CANARY LN
39800 MURR 92562 928-B2
S WILD CANYON DR
2100 CLTN 92324 646-H4
WILDCAT DR
77000 RivC 92211 819-E2
WILDCAT LN
4300 RivC 92503 744-G3
WILD CAT TR
35100 RivC 92544 902-H5
WILD DUNES CIR
- COR 92883 773-H6
WILDER WY
31200 RivC 92596 899-C3
WILDERNESS AV
5800 RIV 92504 684-H7
6100 RIV 92504 714-H1
WILDERNESS CIR
2900 COR 92882 742-F7

WILDERNESS DR
3000 COR 92882 742-F6
WILD FIRE CIR
30500 RivC 92567 779-A4
WILD FIRE CT
27500 RivC 92883 835-C5
WILDFIRE LN
43100 RivC 92539 (965-D6
See Page 964)
WILD FLAX LN
11700 MORV 92557 717-D1
WILD FLECKEN RD
22100 RivC 92557 687-A3
WILDFLOWER AV
2100 HEMT 92545 840-G2
WILDFLOWER CT
2100 COR 92879 743-H3
49600 RivC 92536 963-D5
WILD FLOWER DR
39600 MURR 92563 928-F6
WILDFLOWER LN
- PDST 92210 819-A7
12500 RivC 92503 744-J4
12600 RivC 92503 745-A4
33300 YCPA 92399 649-F4
38500 RivC 92399 650-G7
WILDFLOWER PL
17600 CHLS 91709 712-A5
WILDFLOWER WY
18800 RivC 92504 775-J2
WILD GERANIUM LN
22600 MORV 92557 717-B1
WILD HORSE CIR
42600 RivC 92536 963-B5
WILD HORSE CT
- PER 92571 778-B3
WILDHORSE CT
24600 RivC 92883 804-E6
WILD HORSE DR
100 PDST 92211 819-A3
WILDING PL
6600 RIV 92506 716-B4
WILDLIFE RD
7400 RivC 92881 773-J2
WILDLIFE TR
40500 RivC 92536 963-B2
WILD LILAC CT
- RivC 92880 713-A1
WILD LILAC LN
12900 YCPA 92399 650-E6
WILD LILAC RD
33300 RivC 92584 898-B3
WILD MUSTANG RD
24300 MURR 92562 927-J6
WILD OAK CIR
- HEMT 92545 840-E4
WILD OAK WY
2200 COR 92879 743-J3
WILDOMAR RD
32300 RivC 92530 866-J7
32400 RivC 92530 896-J1
32700 RivC 92530 897-A2
33000 RivC 92595 897-A2
WILDOMAR TKTR
33200 RivC 92595 896-J7
WILD ONION RD
15400 RivC 92570 805-G4
WILD PONY DR
8400 RivC 92509 644-E7
8400 RivC 92509 684-F1
WILD POPPY LN
38300 YCPA 92399 650-J6
WILD RICE DR
23100 CYNL 92587 867-D3
WILD ROSE LN
37200 MURR 92562 927-E3
WILD ROSE ST
43200 INDO 92201 5410-C6
WILD ROSE WY
1500 RIV 92507 686-G1
WILD SAGE CT
27800 RivC 92585 838-E5
WILDSPUR TR
53800 RivC - 844-C1
WILD STALLION LN
21500 RivC 92595 897-C6
WILD TURKEY CIR
1800 COR 92880 742-J4
WILD WEST CT
24400 MURR 92562 927-J6
WILDWOOD CIR
6700 PMSP 92264 787-D6
WILDWOOD DR
600 HEMT 92543 840-J1
54500 RivC - 814-D7
WILDWOOD LN
- MURR 92562 927-G4
400 PER 92571 777-J6
23100 RivC 92570 777-D4
42100 RivC 92536 963-B3
48900 PDST 92260 848-D5
WILDWOOD PL
3800 COR 92879 744-F5
WILDWOOD ST
15900 MORV 92551 747-F2
WILDWOOD WY
4600 RIV 92503 714-J3
WILDWOOD CANYON RD
33400 YCPA 92399 649-H5
34900 YCPA 92399 650-A5
WILDWOOD VIEW DR
37200 YCPA 92399 650-F6
WILEY RD
41000 RivC 92544 961-E4

RIVERSIDE CO.

STREET Block City ZIP Pg-Grid

60TH ST
10500 RivC 91752 683-J5
61ST AV
82000 RivC 92274 5590-F2
83600 RivC 92274 (5591-C2 See Page 5590)
88000 RivC 92274 5592-A2
61ST ST
9000 RivC 92509 684-C5
62ND AV
- RivC 92254 5592-G3
- RivC 92254 (5593-A3 See Page 5592)
81600 RivC 92274 5590-E3
83500 RivC 92274 (5591-D3 See Page 5590)
88000 RivC 92274 5592-A3
63RD AV
8300 RivC 92509 684-E5
88000 RivC 92274 5592-A4
63RD ST
8800 RivC 92509 684-D5
11000 RivC 91752 683-G6
64TH AV
- RivC - (5593-F4 See Page 5592)
- RivC 92254 5592-F5
- RivC 92254 (5593-A4 See Page 5592)
82700 RivC - 5590-G5
83000 RivC 92274 5590-G5
83000 RivC 92274 (5591-A5 See Page 5590)
88000 RivC 92274 5592-A5
64TH ST
8800 RivC 92509 684-D6
11300 RivC 91752 683-G6
65TH AV
- RivC 92254 5592-B6
84900 RivC 92274 (5591-A6 See Page 5590)
65TH ST
8900 RivC 92509 684-D6
11500 RivC 91752 683-G6
12900 RivC 92880 683-D6
66TH AV
- RivC - (5593-E6 See Page 5592)
- RivC 92254 5592-G7
- RivC 92254 (5593-E6 See Page 5592)
83000 RivC - 5590-H7
83000 RivC 92274 5590-H7
83500 RivC 92274 (5591-A7 See Page 5590)
88000 RivC 92274 5592-G7
66TH AV Rt#-195
- RivC 92254 5592-C7
66TH ST
11000 RivC 91752 683-H6
67TH AV
- RivC 92254 (5652-D1 See Page 5592)
83000 RivC 92274 (5650-H1 See Page 5590)
83500 RivC 92274 (5651-A1 See Page 5590)
68TH AV
- RivC 92254 (5652-A2 See Page 5592)
- RivC 92254 (5653-B1 See Page 5592)
83000 RivC - (5650-H2 See Page 5590)
83000 RivC 92274 (5650-H2 See Page 5590)
83500 RivC 92274 (5651-A2 See Page 5590)
88000 RivC 92274 (5652-A2 See Page 5592)
98600 RivC 92254 (5654-C1 See Page 5594)
68TH ST
- RivC 92880 683-C7
11400 RivC 91752 683-E7
69TH AV
- RivC 92254 (5653-A3 See Page 5592)
88500 RivC 92274 (5652-A3 See Page 5592)
98700 RivC 92254 (5654-C2 See Page 5594)
70TH AV
- RivC 92254 (5652-E4 See Page 5592)
69900 RivC 92274 (5651-B4 See Page 5590)
88100 RivC 92274 (5652-A4 See Page 5592)
93800 RivC 92254 (5653-C3 See Page 5592)
97200 RivC 92254 (5654-A3 See Page 5594)
71ST AV
- RivC 92254 (5653-B4 See Page 5592)
72ND AV
- RivC - (5653-C5 See Page 5592)
- RivC 92254 (5652-E6 See Page 5592)
- RivC 92254 (5653-C5 See Page 5592)
84000 RivC 92274 (5651-B6 See Page 5590)
72ND AV
88400 RivC 92274 (5652-A6 See Page 5592)
99000 RivC 92254 (5654-E5 See Page 5594)
73RD AV
- RivC 92254 (5654-F6 See Page 5594)
87900 RivC 92274 (5651-J7 See Page 5590)
88100 RivC 92274 (5652-A7 See Page 5592)
74TH AV
- RivC 92254 5712-C1
88000 RivC 92274 410-E3
88000 RivC 92274 5712-A1
76TH AV
87000 RivC 92274 410-E3
87800 RivC 92274 5712-B3
89000 RivC 92254 5712-E2
77TH AV
87000 RivC 92274 410-E3
88000 RivC 92274 5712-A4
78TH AV
87000 RivC 92274 410-E3
88000 RivC 92274 5712-E4
80TH AV
58300 RivC 92539 (985-D2 See Page 964)
87000 RivC 92274 410-E3
88000 RivC 92274 5712-D6
81ST AV
88000 RivC 92274 (5772-A1 See Page 5712)
89500 RivC 92274 5712-G7
82ND AV
88000 RivC 92274 (5772-G1 See Page 5712)
83RD AV
89000 RivC 92274 (5772-D3 See Page 5712)
84TH AV
88000 RivC 92274 (5772-H3 See Page 5712)
92000 RivC 92274 (5773-A3 See Page 5712)
85TH AV
- RivC 92274 (5772-J4 See Page 5712)
- RivC 92274 (5773-A4 See Page 5712)
I-10 FRWY
- BAN - 721-C3
- BAN - 722-H2
- BEAU - 690-C6
- BEAU - 720-E1
- BEAU - 721-A3
- BLY - 5491-B7
- CALI - 649-G7
- CALI - 689-G1
- CALI - 690-A4
- COAC - 5471-C1
- CTHC - 757-C3
- INDO - 819-G3
- INDO - 5410-A4
- INDO - 5470-J1
- PMSP - 724-G3
- PMSP - 725-B2
- PMSP - 726-A4
- PMSP - 756-J1
- PMSP - 757-A1
- RivC - 690-B5
- RivC - 720-E1
- RivC - 722-H2
- RivC - 723-J3
- RivC - 724-A3
- RivC - 725-B2
- RivC - 726-D5
- RivC - 756-J1
- RivC - 757-A1
- RivC - 758-A7
- RivC - 787-J1
- RivC - 788-A1
- RivC - 789-A7
- RivC - 819-B1
- RivC - 5410-J7
- RivC - 5421-D5
- RivC - 5470-J1
- RivC - 5471-A1
- YCPA - 649-A4
I-15 AVOCADO HWY
- RivC - 979-A4
- RivC - 998-H3
- RivC - 999-A2
- SDCo - 998-H3
- TEM - 979-A4
I-15 CORONA FRWY
- COR - 743-F6
- COR - 773-H1
- COR - 774-A6
- COR - 804-D4
- LKEL - 835-B2
- LKEL - 836-A5
- LKEL - 866-C1
- RivC - 773-H4
- RivC - 804-D4
- RivC - 835-B2
- RivC - 836-A5
- RivC - 866-C1
- RivC - 867-A7
- RivC - 897-A1
I-15 ESCONDIDO FRWY
- RivC - 998-H5
- SDCo - 998-H5
I-15 ONTARIO FRWY
- COR - 743-E3
- NRCO - 713-E6
- NRCO - 743-E3
- ONT - 643-E5
- RivC - 643-E5
- RivC - 683-F6
- RivC - 713-E2
I-15 TEMECULA VALLEY FRWY
- MURR - 927-F1
- MURR - 928-A4
- MURR - 958-F2
- RivC - 897-C4
- RivC - 927-F1
- RivC - 979-A4
- RivC - 998-J2
- RivC - 999-A1
- TEM - 958-F2
- TEM - 978-J1
- TEM - 979-A4
I-215 ESCONDIDO EXWY
- MORV - 716-H3
- PER - 747-B2
- PER - 777-D2
- PER - 807-G2
- RIV - 716-H3
- RivC - 716-H3
- RivC - 717-A7
- RivC - 747-B2
- RivC - 777-D2
I-215 ESCONDIDO FRWY
- MURR - 898-E5
- MURR - 928-D5
- MURR - 958-E1
- PER - 807-J3
- PER - 808-A4
- PER - 838-C4
- RivC - 808-A4
- RivC - 838-C4
- RivC - 868-E1
- RivC - 898-E5
I-215 MORENO VALLEY FRWY
- MORV - 716-G2
- RIV - 685-J2
- RIV - 686-C4
- RIV - 716-G2
- RivC - 686-C4
- RivC - 716-G2
I-215 RIVERSIDE FRWY
- CLTN - 646-E3
- GTER - 646-E3
- RIV - 646-E3
- RIV - 685-J2
- RIV - 686-A2
- RivC - 646-E3
Rt#-R2 KAISER RD
- RivC - 5240-B7
- RivC - 5421-B3
Rt#-R2 YUCCA DR
- RivC - 5240-A7
Rt#-R3 CACTUS VALLEY RD
39600 RivC 92543 871-B3
40200 RivC 92544 871-B3
Rt#-R3 SAGE RD
31300 RivC 92544 871-D4
32600 RivC 92544 901-E2
36300 RivC 92544 931-F1
40200 RivC 92544 961-J1
40700 RivC 92544 962-A2
40700 RivC 92536 961-J7
40700 RivC 92536 962-A3
43100 RivC 92536 981-J4
Rt#-R3 STATE ST
100 HEMT 92543 811-A7
200 HEMT 92543 841-A6
29000 HEMT 92543 871-A1
29000 RivC 92543 841-A6
29000 RivC 92543 871-A3
Rt#-R3 S STATE ST
500 HEMT 92543 841-A1
Rt#-S13 E MISSION RD
2500 SDCo 92028 998-B7
Rt#-S16 PALA RD
45000 TEM 92592 979-B3
46000 RivC 92592 979-E6
47000 RivC 92592 999-G1
47800 SDCo 92028 999-G1
Rt#-S16 PALA TEMECULA RD
37100 SDCo 92028 999-G3
38600 SDCo 92059 999-G3
Rt#-60 FRWY
- RIV - 685-F1
- RivC - 643-D6
- RivC - 644-A6
- RivC - 645-A7
- RivC - 685-B1
Rt#-60 MORENO VALLEY FRWY
- BEAU - 720-B2
- MORV - 716-H2
- MORV - 717-A2
- MORV - 718-B2
- RIV - 685-J2
- RIV - 716-H2
- RIV - 717-A2
- RivC - 718-G2
- RivC - 719-A2
Rt#-60 MORENO VALLEY FRWY
- RivC - 720-B2
Rt#-60 POMONA FRWY
- ONT - 643-A5
- RIV - 685-H2
- RivC - 643-A5
Rt#-62 HIGHWAY
- DHSP 92282 655-J7
- DHSP 92282 695-H1
- RivC 92282 695-H4
- RivC 92282 725-G1
61600 RivC 92282 655-J4
Rt#-62 TWENTYNINE PALMS HWY
- RivC - 391-C1
- RivC 92282 655-G1
49100 SBdC 92256 655-G1
Rt#-71 CHINO VALLEY FRWY
- CHLS - 712-A3
- CHNO - 712-A3
- SBdC - 712-A3
Rt#-71 CORONA EXWY
17900 CHLS 91709 712-C6
17900 RivC 92880 712-C6
17900 RivC 92880 742-D4
Rt#-74 E 4TH ST
100 PER 92570 807-H3
Rt#-74 W 4TH ST
100 PER 92570 807-G3
Rt#-74 COLLIER AV
18000 LKEL 92530 866-C2
Rt#-74 FLORIDA AV
100 HEMT 92543 811-C7
1500 HEMT 92544 811-C7
2800 RivC 92544 811-E7
6400 RivC 92545 840-B1
6400 HEMT 92545 840-B1
33500 RivC 92545 839-G1
34000 HEMT 92545 839-G1
43800 RivC 92544 (812-B7 See Page 782)
Rt#-74 W FLORIDA AV
100 HEMT 92543 811-A7
300 HEMT 92543 810-H7
1600 HEMT 92545 810-E7
4000 HEMT 92545 840-E1
Rt#-74 GRAND AV
15300 LKEL 92530 865-H6
15400 RivC 92530 865-H6
Rt#-74 HIGHWAY
- LKEL 92530 866-D2
- LKEL 92532 836-E7
- LKEL 92532 866-D1
- LKEL 92570 836-F6
- PER 92570 807-F3
- RivC 92532 836-E7
- RivC 92532 866-E1
- RivC 92570 807-E4
- RivC 92570 836-J3
- RivC 92570 837-B1
Rt#-74 IDYLLWILD NAT FRST HWY
45200 RivC 92544 (812-D7 See Page 782)
45900 RivC - (812-D7 See Page 782)
46500 RivC - 842-G1
47600 RivC - (843-B2 See Page 842)
51800 RivC - 844-A5
Rt#-74 MATTHEWS RD
2300 PER 92570 808-C7
2400 PER 92585 808-C7
14800 RivC 92570 808-C7
14800 RivC 92585 808-C7
25600 RivC 92585 838-D1
Rt#-74 ORTEGA HWY
30700 LKEL 92530 865-H7
32300 RivC 92530 865-F7
32300 RivC 92530 895-G1
32300 RivC 92530 896-A1
34100 RivC 92562 408-J3
34100 RivC 92562 895-G1
Rt#-74 PINACATE RD
26100 RivC 92545 839-D1
28100 RivC 92585 838-F1
30000 RivC 92548 838-F1
30200 RivC 92548 839-A1
Rt#-74 PINES TO PALMS HWY
- PDST 92260 848-E2
28800 RivC - 844-D6
30000 RivC - (874-E1 See Page 844)
51900 PDST - 848-C7
51900 PDST - 878-C2
51900 RivC 92260 878-C2
51900 PDST 92260 878-C2
54500 RivC - 908-B5
56900 RivC - (875-A4 See Page 844)
58100 RivC - (905-E2 See Page 904)
60500 RivC - (907-H6 See Page 906)
60600 RivC - (935-J1 See Page 904)
61400 RivC - (936-A2 See Page 906)
64200 RivC - (937-C1 See Page 906)
Rt#-74 REDLANDS AV
500 PER 92570 807-J3
Rt#-74 RIVERSIDE DR
29200 LKEL 92530 866-B2
31100 LKEL 92530 865-H5
Rt# 78 28TH AV
14400 RivC - 412-B1
Rt#-78 32ND AV
- RivC - 412-B2
Rt#-78 HIGHWAY
- RivC - 412-A2
Rt#-78 NEIGHBOURS BLVD
13800 RivC - 392-B11
20800 RivC - 412-B1
Rt#-78 RANNELS BLVD
- RivC - 412-B2
Rt#-79 BEAUMONT AV
100 BEAU 92223 720-H4
Rt#-79 GILMAN SPRINGS RD
- RivC 92555 780-G2
19600 RivC 92583 780-G2
Rt#-79 HIGHWAY
- RivC 92536 409-G5
- TEM 92590 979-A2
- TEM 92592 979-H1
24600 RivC 92536 982-A4
28900 TEM 92590 978-J2
33500 RivC 92592 979-J1
33500 RivC 92592 980-A1
42500 RivC 92536 981-F3
42500 RivC 92592 981-D3
Rt#-79 LAMB CANYON RD
- BEAU 92223 389-E7
- BEAU 92583 389-E7
- RivC 92223 389-E7
- RivC 92555 389-E7
- RivC 92555 780-F1
- RivC 92583 389-E7
14200 RivC 92223 720-G7
Rt#-79 N RAMONA BLVD
200 SJCT 92583 811-A1
600 SJCT 92583 781-A7
Rt#-79 S SAN JACINTO AV
400 SJCT 92583 811-B3
Rt#-79 N SAN JACINTO ST
100 HEMT 92544 811-B7
100 HEMT 92543 811-B7
Rt#-79 S SAN JACINTO ST
1800 SJCT 92583 811-B5
Rt#-79 STATE ST
20400 RivC 92583 780-J4
21000 SJCT 92583 780-J4
21200 SJCT 92583 781-A5
21200 RivC 92583 781-A5
Rt#-79 N STATE ST
400 SJCT 92582 781-A6
400 SJCT 92583 781-A6
Rt#-79 WINCHESTER RD
26200 RivC 92545 839-G4
27800 RivC 92596 839-F7
29300 RivC 92596 869-F2
32700 RivC 92596 899-F2
36000 RivC 92596 929-A3
36000 MURR 92596 899-C6
36000 MURR 92596 929-A3
36500 RivC 92563 929-A3
36500 MURR 92563 929-A3
37900 RivC 92563 928-J6
37900 MURR 92563 928-J6
39000 TEM 92591 928-J6
39200 TEM 92591 958-G3
41200 TEM 92590 958-G3
Rt#-83 EUCLID AV
6500 CHLS 91709 712-B4
6500 CHLS 91710 712-B4
6500 CHNO 91710 712-B4
15700 SBdC 91710 712-B4
Rt#-86 GRAPEFRUIT BLVD
84500 COAC 92236 5471-A3
Rt#-86 HARRISON ST
49500 COAC 92236 5471-B7
52200 COAC 92236 5531-B2
54000 RivC 92274 5531-B6
54000 COAC 92274 5531-B2
58900 RivC 92274 (5591-C6 See Page 5590)
Rt#-86 HIGHWAY
- ImCo 92274 (5772-J5 See Page 5712)
- ImCo 92274 (5773-A6 See Page 5712)
66900 RivC 92274 (5591-C7 See Page 5590)
66900 RivC 92274 (5651-C1 See Page 5590)
73000 RivC 92274 410-E3
74000 RivC 92274 5712-A1
81000 RivC 92274 (5772-D1 See Page 5712)
Rt#-86 INDIO BLVD
83500 INDO 92201 5470-H1
84000 INDO 92201 5471-A3
Rt#-86 PIERCE ST
77000 RivC 92274 5712-B4
Rt#-86S FRWY
- COAC - 5471-B2
- RivC - 5470-J1
- RivC - 5471-A1
Rt#-86S HIGHWAY
- COAC 92236 5471-D5
- COAC 92274 5471-G7
- COAC 92274 5531-G1
- RivC 92254 5592-D5
- RivC 92254 (5652-D1 See Page 5592)
- RivC 92254 5712-D1
- RivC 92274 390-F11
- RivC 92274 5471-F7
- RivC 92274 5531-H4
- RivC 92274 5712-E2
- RivC 92274 (5772-E1 See Page 5712)
62000 RivC 92274 5592-A1
Rt#-91 RIVERSIDE FRWY
- ANA - 742-C5
- COR - 742-C5
- COR - 743-B4
- COR - 744-B2
- RIV - 685-H5
- RIV - 686-A2
- RIV - 714-H7
- RIV - 715-B5
- RIV - 744-B2
- RivC - 742-C5
Rt#-111 AVENUE 46
82000 INDO 92201 5470-H1
Rt#-111 GENE AUTRY TR
600 PMSP 92262 787-A1
700 PMSP 92262 756-J6
700 PMSP 92262 786-J1
900 PMSP 92264 787-B4
Rt#-111 GOLF CENTER PKWY
44400 INDO 92203 5410-H7
44400 INDO 92201 5410-H7
45000 INDO 92201 5470-H1
Rt#-111 GRAPEFRUIT BLVD
100 COAC 92236 5471-B5
54000 COAC 92274 5531-D1
54000 RivC 92274 5531-D1
87000 COAC 92236 5531-D1
Rt#-111 HIGHWAY
- ImCo - (5775-H4 See Page 5714)
- PMSP 92262 725-A5
- PMSP 92282 724-G3
- PMSP 92282 725-A4
- RivC - (5715-B6 See Page 5714)
- RivC - (5775-E1 See Page 5714)
- RivC 92254 (5652-F1 See Page 5592)
- RivC 92254 5714-G1
- RivC 92254 (5715-A4 See Page 5714)
- RivC 92282 724-F3
56000 RivC 92274 5531-G4
58900 RivC 92274 390-F11
58900 RivC 92274 5592-A1
63300 RivC 92254 5592-D4
72100 RMIR 92270 818-C7
72100 PDST 92260 818-C7
72700 PDST 92260 848-D1
73600 RivC 92254 (5654-A4 See Page 5594)
74800 INDW 92210 848-J1
75000 INDW 92210 849-C1
78300 LQNT 92253 849-F1
79500 LQNT 92253 5470-A3
80200 INDO 92201 5470-E1
96400 RivC 92254 (5653-A3 See Page 5592)
Rt#-111 PALM CANYON DR
- PMSP 92262 725-E6
- RivC 92262 725-E6
- RivC 92262 755-G1
Rt#-111 E PALM CANYON DR
4700 PMSP 92264 787-A6
Rt#-111 N PALM CANYON DR
- PMSP 92262 755-J2
1700 PMSP 92262 756-B3
Rt#-111 E VISTA CHINO
100 PMSP 92262 756-H6
Rt#-177 DESERT CENTER RICE RD
- RivC - 391-E7
- RivC - 5421-E1
Rt#-195 66TH AV
- RivC 92254 5592-C7
Rt#-195 LINCOLN ST
- RivC 92254 5592-F7
Rt#-195 PIERCE ST
66000 RivC 92254 5592-B7
66000 RivC 92254 (5652-B7 See Page 5592)
66000 RivC 92274 (5652-B7 See Page 5592)
66000 RivC 92274 5592-B7
73000 RivC 92254 5712-B4
73000 RivC 92274 5712-B4
Rt#-243 S 8TH ST
- BAN 92220 722-A4
Rt#-243 BANNING IDLW PAN HWY
- BAN 92220 722-B5
Rt#-243 BANNING IDLW PAN HWY
- RivC 92220 722-B5
16900 RivC 92220 389-G7
19900 RivC 92220 (783-B1 See Page 782)
22600 RivC 92220 (813-H1 See Page 782)
23700 RivC - (813-H1 See Page 782)
23800 RivC - 814-A5
Rt#-243 IDYLLWILD RD
25600 RivC - 814-C5
26600 RivC - 844-C2
Rt#-243 LINCOLN ST
1000 BAN 92220 722-B4
Rt#-243 SAN GORGONIO AV
400 BAN 92220 722-B5
Rt#-243 S SAN GORGONIO AV
1300 BAN 92220 722-B4
Rt#-371 CAHUILLA RD
41700 RivC 92536 963-F2
43400 RivC 92536 962-J7
43400 RivC 92536 982-G2
43500 RivC 92539 (933-H7 See Page 902)
43500 RivC 92539 963-F2
45400 RivC 92539 (934-A6 See Page 904)
54700 RivC 92539 (935-A4 See Page 904)
Rt#-371 KENWORTHY BAUTISTA RD
57200 RivC 92539 (935-H3 See Page 904)
58400 RivC - (935-H3 See Page 904)
58400 RivC - (936-A2 See Page 906)
U.S.-95 HIGHWAY
- RivC - 392-D1
U.S.-95 INTAKE BLVD
- RivC 92225 5491-H1
100 BLY 92225 5491-H5
5000 RivC - 392-C9
7000 RivC - 5491-H1

RIVERSIDE POINTS OF INTEREST

AIRPORTS

FEATURE NAME / Address City, ZIP Code	PAGE-GRID
AJO-CORONA MUNICIPAL BUTTERFIELD DR & AVIATION DR, COR, 92880	742 - H2
BANNING MUNICIPAL 200 HATHAWAY ST, BAN, 92220	722 - E3
BEAR CREEK AIRFIELD NIGHTHAWK WY & HAYES AV, MURR, 92562	927 - G5
BERMUDA DUNES 79880 AVE 42, RivC, 92201	5410 - A4
BLYTHE OFF I-10, RivC	392 - A10
DESERT CENTER OFF HWY 177, RivC	391 - E8
DESERT RESORTS REGL 56850 HIGGINS DR, RivC, 92274	5531 - D6
FLABOB 4130 MENNES AV, RivC, 92509	685 - C3
FRENCH VALLEY SKY CANYON DR, RivC, 92563	929 - B3
HELIPORT (SEE PAGE 906) SCENIC DR & SONORA RD, RivC	907 - J4
HEMET-RYAN WARREN RD & STETSON AV, HEMT, 92545	840 - D2
ONTARIO INTL 2900 E AIRPORT DR, ONT, 91761	643 - B1
PALM SPRINGS INTL 3400 E TAHQUITZ CANYON WY, PMSP, 92262	786 - J1
PERRIS VLY AND PARACHUTING CTR 2091 GOETZ RD, PER, 92570	807 - H5
RIVERSIDE MUNICIPAL 6951 FLIGHT RD, RIV, 92504	714 - H1
SKYLARK 20701 CEREAL ST, LKEL, 92530	896 - H3

BEACHES, HARBORS & WATER REC

FEATURE NAME / Address City, ZIP Code	PAGE-GRID
HEMET RESERVOIR (SEE PAGE 844) HWY 74 NEAR IDYLLWILD, RivC	874 - F3
LAKE CAHUILLA CAHUILLA PARK RD, LQNT, 92253	5530 - A6
LAKE PERRIS 17801 LAKE PERRIS DR, RivC, 92571	748 - D6
MORENO BEACH VIA DEL LAGO & LAKE PERRIS STA, RivC, 92571	748 - D5
PERRIS BEACH VIA DEL LAGO & LAKE PERRIS STA, RivC, 92571	748 - C6

BUILDINGS

FEATURE NAME / Address City, ZIP Code	PAGE-GRID
ANNENBURG CTR FOR HEALTH-SCIENCES 39000 BOB HOPE DR, RMIR, 92270	818 - C2
BOYS CLUB 450 S SUNRISE WY, PMSP, 92262	786 - G2
JURUPA COMM CTR 4810 PEDLEY RD, RivC, 92509	684 - E1
LOUIS RUBIDOUX NATURE CTR 5370 RIVERVIEW DR, RivC, 92509	685 - A5
MIRA LOMA SPACE CTR 3401 ETIWANDA AV, RivC, 91752	643 - H6
NORCO COMM CTR 3900 ACACIA ST, NRCO, 92860	713 - E3
PALM SPRINGS UNIFIED DIST 980 E TAHQUITZ CANYON WY, PMSP, 92262	786 - E2
RAINCROSS SQUARE 3443 ORANGE ST, RIV, 92501	685 - H3
STATE FORESTRY DEPARTMENT 210 W SAN JACINTO AV, PER, 92570	807 - G2
UPS DISTRIBUTION CTR 3480 E JURUPA ST, ONT, 91761	643 - B3

BUILDINGS - GOVERNMENTAL

FEATURE NAME / Address City, ZIP Code	PAGE-GRID
CALIFORNIA INST FOR WOMEN 16756 CHINO CORONA RD, SBdC, 91710	712 - E2
CALIFORNIA NARCOTICS REHAB CTR WESTERN AV & 5TH ST, NRCO, 92860	713 - C5
COUNTY ADMINISTRATIVE CTR 46209 OASIS ST, INDO, 92201	5470 - F1
COUNTY BLDG 41002 COUNTY CENTER DR, TEM, 92591	958 - G3
COUNTY COURT HOUSE 227 N D ST, PER, 92570	807 - G2
COURTHOUSE 505 S BUENA VISTA AV, COR, 92882	743 - C5
PALM SPRINGS MUNICIPAL COURT 3255 E TAHQUITZ CANYON WY, PMSP, 92262	786 - J2
RIVERSIDE COUNTY ADMIN 4080 LEMON ST, RIV, 92501	685 - H4
RIVERSIDE COUNTY ADMIN 3939 13TH ST, RIV, 92501	685 - G4
RIVERSIDE CO ECONOMIC DEV-AGENCY 3525 14TH ST, RIV, 92501	685 - G5
RIVERSIDE COURTHOUSE 4050 MAIN ST, RIV, 92501	685 - G4
SUPERIOR COURT 46200 OASIS ST, INDO, 92201	5470 - G1
SUPERIOR COURTHOUSE 265 N BROADWAY, BLY, 92225	5491 - E6
TEMECULA COURT HOUSE 41002 COUNTY CENTER DR, TEM, 92591	958 - G3

CEMETERIES

FEATURE NAME / Address City, ZIP Code	PAGE-GRID
AGUA MANSA MEM CEM 2001 W AGUA MANSA RD, CLTN, 92316	645 - H3
COACHELLA VALLEY CEM 82925 AVE 52, RivC, 92201	5470 - G7
CORONA CEM RIMPAU AV & MAGNOLIA AV, COR, 92879	743 - F6
CRESTLAWN MEM PK 11500 ARLINGTON AV, RIV, 92505	713 - J2
DESERT LAWN MEM PK 11251 DESERT LAWN DR, CALI, 92320	690 - C6
DESERT MEM PK CEM 69920 RAMON RD, CTHC, 92234	787 - G2
ELSINORE VALLEY CEM 18170 COLLIER AV, LKEL, 92530	866 - C2
EVERGREEN CEM 4414 14TH ST, RIV, 92501	685 - F4
GREEN ACRES MEM GARDENS 11715 CEDAR AV, SBdC, 92316	645 - F3
MONTECITO MEM PK 24145 BARTON RD, CLTN, 92324	646 - J2
MOUNTAIN VIEW CEM 1315 EDGAR AV, BEAU, 92223	720 - H1
MURRIETA CEM IVY ST, MURR, 92562	957 - J1
OLIVEWOOD CEM 3300 CENTRAL AV, RIV, 92506	715 - G1
PALO VERDE CEM 10700 10TH AV, BLY, 92225	5491 - E4
PERRIS VALLEY CEM 915 N PERRIS BLVD, PER, 92571	807 - G1
RIVERSIDE NATL CEM 22495 VAN BUREN BLVD, RivC, 92518	747 - B5
SAN GORGONIO MEM PK 2201 SAN GORGONIO AV, BAN, 92220	692 - A7
SAN JACINTO VALLEY CEM 24900 SANTA FE ST, SJCT, 92583	811 - B5
STEWART SUNNYSLOPE CEM 1ST ST & PENNSYLVANIA AV, BEAU, 92223	721 - A4
TEMECULA CEM C ST, TEM, 92592	978 - J1

CHAMBERS OF COMMERCE

FEATURE NAME / Address City, ZIP Code	PAGE-GRID
ANZA VALLEY (SEE PAGE 904) 56481 CAHUILLA RD HWY 371, RivC, 92539	934 - J4
BANNING 123 E RAMSEY ST, BAN, 92220	722 - B3
BEAUMONT 450 E 4TH ST, BEAU, 92223	720 - J3
BLYTHE 201 S BROADWAY, BLY, 92225	5491 - E7
CALIMESA 528 MYRTLEWOOD DR, CALI, 92320	689 - H1
CANYON LAKE 31640 RAILROAD CANYON RD, CYNL, 92587	867 - E4
CATHEDRAL CITY 68845 PEREZ RD SUITE 6, CTHC, 92234	787 - F7
COACHELLA 1648 6TH ST, COAC, 92236	5471 - C6
CORONA 904 E 6TH ST, COR, 92879	743 - E5
DESERT HOT SPRINGS 11711 WEST DR, DHSP, 92240	696 - H3
GRAND TERRACE 12139 MOUNT VERNON AV, GTER, 92313	646 - E4
HEMET/SAN JACINTO 395 E LATHAM AV, HEMT, 92543	811 - A7
IDYLLWILD 54295 VILLAGE CENTER DR, RivC	814 - D6
INDIO 82503 HWY 111, INDO, 92201	5470 - F1
JURUPA 7920 LIMONITE AV, RivC, 92509	684 - G5
LAKE ELSINORE 132 W GRAHAM AV, LKEL, 92530	866 - E5
LA QUINTA 78371 HWY 111, LQNT, 92253	849 - G2
LOMA LINDA 25541 BARTON RD, LMLN, 92354	647 - D1
MIRA LOMA 5506 TROTH ST, RivC, 91752	683 - J3
MORENO VALLEY 22500 TOWN CIR, MORV, 92553	717 - B3
MURRIETA 26370 BECKMAN CT, MURR, 92562	958 - E2
NORCO 2816 HAMNER AV, NRCO, 92860	713 - E6
PALM DESERT 73710 FRED WARING DR, PDST, 92260	818 - F7
PALM SPRINGS 190 W AMADO RD, PMSP, 92262	786 - D1
PALM SPRGS DSRT RSRTS CONV &-VIS BUR 69930 HWY 111, RMIR, 92270	817 - G2
PERRIS VALLEY 155 E 4TH ST, PER, 92570	807 - G3
RANCHO MIRAGE 42464 RANCHO MIRAGE LN, RMIR, 92270	818 - B6
RIVERSIDE 3985 UNIVERSITY AV, RIV, 92501	685 - G4
RIVERSIDE VSTRS & CONV BUR 3443 ORANGE ST, RIV, 92501	685 - H4
SKY VALLEY 20905 HOT SPRINGS RD, RivC, 92241	728 - H4
SUN CITY 26878 CHERRY HILLS BLVD, RivC, 92586	838 - C6
TEMECULA VALLEY 27450 YNEZ RD, TEM, 92591	958 - H6
THERMAL 87229 CHURCH ST, RivC, 92274	5531 - G5
THOUSAND PALMS 72715 LA CANADA WY, RivC, 92276	788 - D2
YUCAIPA VALLEY 35139 YUCAIPA BLVD, YCPA, 92399	650 - A3

CITY HALLS

FEATURE NAME / Address City, ZIP Code	PAGE-GRID
BANNING 99 E RAMSEY ST, BAN, 92220	722 - B3
BEAUMONT 550 E 6TH ST, BEAU, 92223	720 - J3
BLYTHE 235 N BROADWAY, BLY, 92225	5491 - E6
CALIMESA 908 PARK AV, CALI, 92320	649 - H7
CANYON LAKE 31532 RAILROAD CANYON RD, CYNL, 92587	867 - E4
CATHEDRAL CITY 68700 AVD LALO GUERRERO, CTHC, 92234	787 - E7
COACHELLA 1515 6TH ST, COAC, 92236	5471 - C6
CORONA 815 W 6TH ST, COR, 92882	743 - C5
DESERT HOT SPRINGS 65950 PIERSON BLVD, DHSP, 92240	696 - H3
GRAND TERRACE 22795 BARTON RD, GTER, 92313	646 - F3
HEMET 450 E LATHAM AV, HEMT, 92543	811 - A7
INDIAN WELLS 44950 EL DORADO DR, INDW, 92210	849 - B1
INDIO 100 CIVIC CENTER DR, INDO, 92201	5470 - G1
LAKE ELSINORE 130 S MAIN ST, LKEL, 92530	866 - E5
LA QUINTA 78495 CL TAMPICO, LQNT, 92253	849 - G7
LOMA LINDA 25541 BARTON RD, LMLN, 92354	647 - D1
MORENO VALLEY 14177 FREDERICK ST, MORV, 92553	717 - C6
MURRIETA 26442 BECKMAN CT, MURR, 92562	958 - E2
NORCO 2870 CLARK AV, NRCO, 92860	713 - D6
PALM DESERT 73510 FRED WARING DR, PDST, 92260	818 - F7
PALM SPRINGS 3200 E TAHQUITZ CANYON WY, PMSP, 92262	786 - H2
PERRIS 101 N D ST, PER, 92570	807 - G2
RANCHO MIRAGE 69825 HWY 111, RMIR, 92270	817 - G1
RIVERSIDE 3900 MAIN ST, RIV, 92501	685 - H4
SAN JACINTO 201 E MAIN ST, SJCT, 92583	811 - B2
TEMECULA 43200 BUSINESS PARK DR, TEM, 92590	958 - F6

COLLEGES & UNIVERSITIES

FEATURE NAME / Address City, ZIP Code	PAGE-GRID
CALIFORNIA BAPTIST UNIV 8432 MAGNOLIA AV, RIV, 92504	715 - B4
COLLEGE OF THE DESERT 43500 MONTEREY AV, PDST, 92260	818 - E6
CRAFTON HILLS COLLEGE 11711 SAND CANYON RD, YCPA, 92399	649 - C2
LA SIERRA UNIV 4700 PIERCE ST, RIV, 92505	714 - C7
LOMA LINDA UNIV ANDERSON ST & BARTON RD, LMLN, 92354	647 - C1
MOUNT SAN JACINTO COLLEGE 1499 N STATE ST, SJCT, 92583	781 - A6
MOUNT SAN JACINTO COLLEGE --MENIFEE VLY 28237 LA PIEDRA RD, RivC, 92584	868 - E4
PALO VERDE COLLEGE 811 W CHANSLOR WY, BLY, 92225	5491 - D6
RIVERSIDE COMM COLLEGE 4800 MAGNOLIA AV, RIV, 92506	685 - G5
RIV COMM COLLEGE MORENO VLY-CAMPUS 16130 LASSELLE ST, MORV, 92555	748 - A3
RIVERSIDE COMM COLLEGE NORCO 2001 3RD ST, NRCO, 92860	713 - C6
UNIV OF CALIFORNIA RIVERSIDE 900 UNIVERSITY AV, RIV, 92507	686 - C5
UC RIVERSIDE MORENO FLD STA JOHN F KENNEDY DR, MORV, 92555	718 - A7

DEPARTMENT OF MOTOR VEHICLES

FEATURE NAME / Address City, ZIP Code	PAGE-GRID
BANNING 1034 W RAMSEY ST, BAN, 92220	722 - A3
BLYTHE 430 S BROADWAY, BLY, 92225	5491 - E7
HEMET 1200 S STATE ST, HEMT, 92543	841 - A3
INDIO 44480 JACKSON ST, INDO, 92201	5410 - G7
NORCO 3201 HORSELESS CARRIAGE RD, NRCO, 92860	713 - D5
PALM SPRINGS 950 N FARRELL DR, PMSP, 92262	756 - H7
RIVERSIDE 6280 BROCKTON AV, RIV, 92506	685 - E7
RIVERSIDE 6235 RIVER CREST DR, RIV, 92507	716 - H3
TEMECULA 27851 DIAZ RD, TEM, 92590	958 - G6

ENTERTAINMENT & SPORTS

FEATURE NAME / Address City, ZIP Code	PAGE-GRID
CASTLE AMUSEMENT PARK 3500 POLK ST, RIV, 92505	744 - F1
CONVENTION CENTER 277 N AVD CABALLEROS, PMSP, 92262	786 - E1
COUNTY CENTER 82675 HWY 111, INDO, 92201	5470 - F2
COUNTY FAIRGROUNDS DR CARREON BLVD & ARABIA ST, INDO, 92201	5470 - F2
DATE FESTIVAL GROUNDS 46350 ARABIA ST, INDO, 92201	5470 - F2
GALWAY DOWNS PAUBA RD & LOS CABALLOS RD, RivC, 92592	980 - D1
INDIAN WELLS TENNIS GARDEN WASHINGTON ST & FRED WARING DR, INDW, 92210	819 - E7
LAKE ELSINORE DIAMOND 500 DIAMOND DR, LKEL, 92530	866 - H7
LAKE PERRIS FAIRGROUNDS 18700 LAKE PERRIS DR, RivC, 92571	748 - A7
OASIS WATER PARK 1500 GENE AUTRY TR, PMSP, 92264	787 - B4
PALM SPRINGS STADIUM SUNRISE WY, PMSP, 92262	786 - G2
TENNIS STADIUM HWY 111, INDW, 92210	849 - C1
UNIV OF CAL RIV STADIUM CANYON CREST DR & LINDEN ST, RIV, 92507	686 - D4

GOLF COURSES

FEATURE NAME / Address City, ZIP Code	PAGE-GRID
ARROYO FAIRWAYS MBLE HOME CLUB 42751 FLORIDA AV, RivC, 92544	811 - H7
AVONDALE CC 75800 AVONDALE DR, PDST, 92211	819 - A2
BEAR CREEK GOLF AND CC 22640 BEAR CREEK DR N, MURR, 92562	927 - C3
BERMUDA DUNES CC 42360 ADAMS ST, RivC, 92201	819 - H5
BIGHORN CANYONS GC CANYON DR & PINES TO PALMS HWY, PDST, 92260	848 - D6
BIGHORN GC 255 PALOWET DR, PDST, 92260	848 - B7
BIGHORN MOUNTAINS GC 255 PALOWET DR, PDST, 92260	878 - B1
CALIMESA GOLF & CC 1300 3RD ST, CALI, 92320	689 - H2
CANYON CC 1100 MURRAY CANYON DR, PMSP, 92264	786 - F7
CANYON CREST CC 975 COUNTRY CLUB DR, RIV, 92506	716 - C1
CANYON ESTATES GC 2323 MADRONA DR, PMSP, 92264	786 - F6
CANYON LAKE CC 32001 RAILROAD CANYON RD, CYNL, 92587	867 - C4
CANYON SOUTH GC 1097 MURRAY CANYON DR, PMSP, 92264	816 - F1
CATHEDRAL CANYON CC 68311 PAS REAL, CTHC, 92234	787 - D5
CHAPARRAL CC 100 CHAPARRAL DR, PDST, 92260	818 - F5
CHERRY HILLS GC 26583 CHERRY HILLS BLVD, RivC, 92586	838 - A6
CLUB AT MORNINGSIDE, THE 39033 MORNINGSIDE DR, RMIR, 92270	817 - J3
COLONIAL CC 25115 KIRBY ST, HEMT, 92545	810 - F6
COLONY CC, THE 40603 COLONY DR, MURR, 92562	928 - B3
COTTONWOOD GC 13671 FREDERICK ST, MORV, 92553	717 - B5
COUNTRY CLUB OF THE DESERT JEFFERSON ST & AVE 52, LQNT, 92253	5530 - B1
COUNTRY VILLAGE GC 10301 COUNTRY CLUB DR, RivC, 91752	644 - A5
CREEKSIDE GC 3151 E RIVERSIDE DR, ONT, 91761	643 - B6
CRESTA VERDE GC 1295 CRESTA RD, COR, 92879	743 - F4
DATE PALM CC 36200 DATE PALM DR, CTHC, 92234	787 - G7
DESERT CREST CC 69400 S COUNTRY CLUB DR, RivC, 92241	727 - F1
DESERT DUNES GC 19300 PALM DR, RivC, 92241	727 - A4
DESERT FALLS CC 1111 DESERT FALLS PKWY, PDST, 92211	818 - J2
DESERT HORIZONS CC 44900 DESERT HORIZONS DR, INDW, 92210	819 - A7
DESERT ISLAND CC 71777 FRANK SINATRA DR, RMIR, 92270	818 - B1
DESERT PRINCESS CC 28555 LANDAU BLVD, CTHC, 92234	757 - B6
DESERT WILLOW GOLF RESORT 38500 PORTOLA AV, PDST, 92260	818 - G1
DIAMOND VALLEY GC 40188 SAGE RD, RivC, 92543	871 - C4
EAGLE GLEN GC 1800 EAGLE GLEN PKWY, COR, 92883	773 - G7
ECHO HILLS GC 545 E THORNTON AV, HEMT, 92543	841 - B3
ELDORADO CC 46000 FAIRWAY DR, INDW, 92210	849 - B2
EL PRADO GC 6555 PINE AV, CHNO, 91710	712 - A2
EL RIVINO CC 5530 EL RIVINO RD, SBdC, 92316	645 - F3
EMERALD DESERT CC 76000 FRANK SINATRA DR, PDST, 92211	819 - A1
FAIRMOUNT PK GC 2681 DEXTER DR, RIV, 92501	685 - G1
GENERAL OLD GC 6104 VILLAGE WEST DR, RivC, 92518	747 - A4
GOLDEN ERA GC 19781 HWY 79, RivC, 92583	780 - H3
GOLF CENTER AT PALM DESERT 74945 SHERYL AV, PDST, 92260	818 - H6
GOLF RESORT AT INDIAN WELLS,-THE 44500 INDIAN WELLS LN, INDW, 92210	819 - C7
GOOSE CREEK GC 11418 68TH ST, RivC, 91752	683 - H7
GREEN RIVER GC 5215 GREEN RIVER RD, RivC, 92880	742 - A5
HERITAGE PALMS GC 44291 S HERITAGE PALMS DR, INDO, 92201	5410 - A7
HIDDEN SPRINGS CC 15500 BUBBLING WELLS RD, RivC, 92240	697 - B7
HIDDEN VALLEY GC 10 CLUBHOUSE DR, NRCO, 92860	713 - J6
HIGHLAND SPRINGS CC 10890 DEERFIELD DR, RivC, 92220	691 - B5
HIGHLAND SPRINGS VILLAGE GC 10370 CHISHOLM TR, RivC, 92223	691 - C4
INDIAN HILLS CC 5700 CLUB HOUSE DR, RivC, 92509	684 - G4
INDIAN PALMS CC 48630 MONROE ST, INDO, 92201	5470 - F4
INDIAN RIDGE CC 76375 COUNTRY CLUB DR, PDST, 92211	819 - B4
INDIAN SPRINGS CC 46080 JEFFERSON ST, LQNT, 92253	5470 - A2
INDIAN WELLS CC 46000 CLUB DR, INDW, 92210	849 - C2
INDIO GC 83040 AVE 42, INDO, 92203	5410 - G4
IRONWOOD CC 49200 MARIPOSA DR, RivC	848 - G6
IVEY RANCH CC 74580 VARNER RD, RivC, 92276	788 - H5
JURUPA HILLS CC 6161 MORAGA AV, RivC, 92509	684 - J5
LAKES CC, THE 75375 COUNTRY CLUB DR, PDST, 92211	819 - A3
LAKE TAMARISK GC 26251 PARKVIEW DR, RivC	5421 - B1
LANDMARK GC 42010 GOLF CENTER PKWY, INDO, 92203	5410 - J4
LA QUINTA CC 77750 AVE 50, LQNT, 92253	849 - G5
LA QUINTA RESORT & CLUB CITRUS-COURSE 50503 JEFFERSON ST, LQNT, 92253	5470 - A7
LA QUINTA RESORT & CLUB MTN-COURSE 50200 AVD VISTA BONITA, LQNT, 92253	849 - E6
LA QUINTA RESORT AND CLUB-DUNES COURSE WASHINGTON ST & AVENUE 50, LQNT, 92253	849 - H6
MARINE MEM GC GOLF COURSE RD, SDCo, 92055	409 - A8
MARRAKESH CC 47000 MARRAKESH DR, PDST, 92260	848 - F3
MARRIOTT DESERT SPRINGS RESORT 74855 COUNTRY CLUB DR, PDST, 92260	818 - G4
MARRIOTTS RANCHO LAS PALMAS-RESORT 42000 BOB HOPE DR, RMIR, 92270	818 - D5
MENIFEE LAKES CC 29875 MENIFEE LAKES DR, RivC, 92584	868 - F1
MESQUITE CC 2700 E MESQUITE AV, PMSP, 92264	786 - G3
MISSION HILLS CC 34600 MISSION HILLS DR, RMIR, 92270	787 - H3
MISSION HILLS NORTH GC 70705 RAMON RD, RMIR, 92270	787 - H2
MISSION LAKES CC 8484 CLUBHOUSE BLVD, RivC, 92240	696 - D1
MONTEREY CC 41500 MONTEREY AV, PDST, 92260	818 - E5
MORENO VALLEY RANCH GC 28095 JOHN F KENNEDY DR, MORV, 92555	718 - E6
MOUNTAIN VIEW CC 2121 MOUNTAIN VIEW DR, RivC, 92882	742 - G5
MOUNTAIN VISTA GC 38180 DEL WEBB BLVD, RivC, 92211	789 - F7
NORTH GC 26660 MCCALL BLVD, RivC, 92586	838 - B5
OAK VALLEY GC 37600 14TH ST, BEAU, 92223	690 - E7
OASIS CC, THE 42300 CASBAH WY, PDST, 92211	819 - C5
ODONNELL GC 301 N BELARDO RD, PMSP, 92262	786 - D1
OUTDOOR RESORT AND CC 69411 RAMON RD, CTHC, 92234	787 - G3
PALM DESERT CC 77200 CALIFORNIA DR, PDST, 92211	819 - D6
PALM DESERT GREENS CC 73750 COUNTRY CLUB DR, RivC, 92260	818 - E1
PALM DESERT RESORT CC 77333 COUNTRY CLUB DR, PDST, 92211	819 - D4
PALM ROYALE CC 78259 INDIGO DR, LQNT, 92253	819 - F7
PALM SPRINGS CC 2500 WHITEWATER CLUB DR, PMSP, 92262	756 - G4
PALM VALLEY CC 76200 COUNTRY CLUB DR, PDST, 92211	819 - B2
PANORAMA VILLAGE GC 1401 TEAKWOOD PL, HEMT, 92543	840 - H1
PARADISE KNOLLS GC 9330 LIMONITE AV, RivC, 92509	684 - C6
PGA WEST 56150 PGA BLVD, LQNT, 92253	5530 - B4
PLANTATION GC 50991 MONROE ST, INDO, 92201	5470 - F7
PORTOLA CC 42500 PORTOLA AV, PDST, 92260	818 - G5
QUAIL RANCH GC 15960 GILMAN SPRINGS RD, RivC, 92555	719 - F7
QUARRY AT LA QUINTA, THE 79700 QUARRY LN, LQNT, 92253	5530 - A7
RANCHO CASABLANCA CC 84136 AVE 44, INDO, 92203	5410 - J5
RANCHO LA QUINTA CC 79250 AVE 50, LQNT, 92253	849 - J4
RANCHO MIRAGE CC 38500 BOB HOPE DR, RMIR, 92270	818 - C2
REDHAWK GC 45100 REDHAWK PKWY, RivC, 92592	979 - F4
RIVERSIDE GC 1011 ORANGE ST, RIV, 92501	645 - J7
SANDS RV CC 16400 BUBBLING WELLS RD, RivC, 92240	727 - B1

GOLF COURSES

FEATURE NAME	Address City, ZIP Code	PAGE-GRID
SANTA ROSA CC	38105 PORTOLA AV, PDST, 92260	818 - F1
SCGA MEMBERS CLUB AT RANCHO-CALIFORNIA	38275 MURRIETA HOT SPRINGS RD, MURR, 92563	928 - H5
SEVEN HILLS GC	1537 S LYON AV, HEMT, 92545	840 - G3
SEVEN LAKES CC	4100 SEVEN LAKES DR, PMSP, 92264	787 - A5
SHADOW MTN GC	73800 IRONWOOD ST, PDST, 92260	848 - F2
SKYLINKS GC RIVERSIDE	6720 VAN BUREN BLVD, RIV, 92503	714 - G1
SOBOBA SPRINGS ROYAL VISTA GC	1020 SOBOBA RD, SJCT, 92583	781 - E7
SPRINGS CLUB, THE	1 DUKE DR, RMIR, 92270	818 - A3
SUNCREST CC	73450 COUNTRY CLUB DR, RivC, 92260	818 - E2
SUN LAKES CC & GOLF	850 S COUNTRY CLUB DR, BAN, 92220	721 - D5
SUNRISE CC	71601 COUNTRY CLUB DR, RMIR, 92270	818 - B4
TAHQUITZ CREEK PALM SPRINGS	1885 GOLF CLUB DR, PMSP, 92264	787 - B5
TAMARISK CC	70240 FRANK SINATRA DR, RMIR, 92270	787 - J7
TEMECULA CREEK INN GC	44501 RAINBOW CANYON RD, TEM, 92592	979 - A4
TEMEKU HILLS GC	31346 RANCHO CALIFORNIA RD, TEM, 92591	959 - D4
THUNDERBIRD CC	70612 HWY 111, RMIR, 92270	818 - A3
TOMMY JACOBS BEL AIR GREENS	1001 S EL CIELO RD, PMSP, 92264	786 - H4
TOSCANA CC	FRED WARING DR & EL DORADO DR, INDW, 92210	819 - A6
TRI PALM ESTATES CC	32610 DESERT MOON DR, RivC, 92276	788 - E3
VICTORIA CC	2521 ARROYO DR, RIV, 92506	685 - J7
VILLAGE AT THE PALMS	VILLAGE DR & PALMS DR, LQNT, 92253	5530 - E5
VINTAGE CLUB, THE	75001 VINTAGE DR, INDW, 92210	848 - J3
WESTIN MISSION HILLS RESORT	71501 DINAH SHORE DR, RMIR, 92270	788 - A5
WOODHAVEN CC	41555 WOODHAVEN DR E, PDST, 92211	819 - E4
YUCIAPA VALLEY GC	33725 CHAPMAN HEIGHTS RD, YCPA, 92399	649 - G2

HOSPITALS

FEATURE NAME	Address City, ZIP Code	PAGE-GRID
CORONA REGL MED CTR	800 S MAIN ST, COR, 92882	743 - D5
DESERT REGL MED CTR	1150 N INDIAN CANYON DR, PMSP, 92262	756 - E7
EISENHOWER MEM	39000 BOB HOPE DR, RMIR, 92270	818 - C2
HEMET VALLEY MED CTR	1117 E DEVONSHIRE AV, HEMT, 92543	811 - B6
INLAND VALLEY REGL MED CTR	36485 INLAND VALLEY DR, RivC, 92595	927 - G1
KAISER FOUNDATION HOSP-RIVERSIDE	10800 MAGNOLIA AV, RIV, 92505	744 - F1
KENNEDY, JOHN F MEM HOSP	47111 MONROE ST, INDO, 92201	5470 - E3
LOMA LINDA UNIV CHILDRENS	11234 ANDERSON ST, LMLN, 92354	647 - B1
LOMA LINDA UNIV COMM MED	25333 BARTON RD, LMLN, 92354	647 - D2
LOMA LINDA UNIV MED CTR	11234 ANDERSON ST, LMLN, 92354	647 - B1
MENIFEE VALLEY MED CTR	28400 MCCALL BLVD, RivC, 92585	838 - E5
MORENO VALLEY COMM	27300 IRIS AV, MORV, 92555	748 - C1
PALO VERDE	250 N 1ST ST, BLY, 92225	5491 - E6
PARKVIEW COMM HOSP MED CTR	3865 JACKSON ST, RIV, 92503	714 - J5
PETTIS MEM VETERANS MED CTR	11201 BENTON ST, LMLN, 92354	647 - C1
RANCHO SPRINGS MED CTR	25500 MEDICAL CENTER DR, MURR, 92562	928 - D6
REDLANDS COMM	350 TERRACINA BLVD, RDL, 92373	647 - J3
RIVERSIDE COMM	4445 MAGNOLIA AV, RIV, 92501	685 - G5
RIVERSIDE CO REGL MED CTR	26520 CACTUS AV, MORV, 92555	718 - A6
SAN GORGONIO MEM	600 HIGHLAND SPRINGS AV, BAN, 92220	721 - C2
VALLEY PLAZA DOCTORS	2224 MEDICAL CENTER DR, PER, 92571	777 - G6

HOTELS

FEATURE NAME	Address City, ZIP Code	PAGE-GRID
BEST WESTERN COUNTRY INN	27706 JEFFERSON AV, TEM, 92590	958 - G5
BEST WESTERN DATE TREE MOTEL	81909 INDIO BLVD, INDO, 92201	5410 - C6
BEST WESTERN EL RANCHO	550 BEAUMONT AV, BEAU, 92223	720 - H3
BEST WESTERN HEMET	2625 W FLORIDA AV, HEMT, 92545	810 - G7
BEST WESTERN IMAGE SUITES	24840 ELDER AV, MORV, 92557	717 - F2
BEST WESTERN KINGS INN	1084 POMONA RD, COR, 92882	743 - B4
BEST WESTERN LAKE PERRIS	480 S REDLANDS AV, PER, 92570	807 - H3
BEST WESTERN LAS BRISAS HOTEL	222 S INDIAN CANYON DR, PMSP, 92262	786 - E2
BEST WESTERN RIVERSIDE	10518 MAGNOLIA AV, RIV, 92505	714 - F7
BEST WESTERN SAHARA	825 W HOBSON WY, BLY, 92225	5491 - D7
COMFORT INN	903 W HOBSON WY, BLY, 92225	5491 - D7
COUNTRY SIDE INN	2260 GRIFFIN WY, COR, 92879	744 - A3
COURTYARD BY MARRIOTT	1300 TAHQUITZ CANYON WY, PMSP, 92262	786 - F2
COURTYARD BY MARRIOTT	1510 UNIVERSITY AV, RIV, 92507	686 - B5
DAYS INN SUITES	69151 E PALM CANYON DR, CTHC, 92234	817 - F1
DOUBLETREE RESORT	67967 VIS CHINO, CTHC, 92234	757 - C6
DYNASTY SUITES CORONA	1805 W 6TH ST, COR, 92882	742 - J5
DYNASTY SUITES RIVERSIDE	3735 IOWA AV, RIV, 92507	686 - B5
EMBASSY SUITES	29345 RANCHO CALIFORNIA RD, TEM, 92592	958 - H7
EMBASSY SUITES HOTEL	74700 HWY 111, PDST, 92260	848 - H1
GLEN IVY HOT SPRINGS RESORT	25000 GLEN IVY RD, RivC, 92883	804 - C7
GRIFFINS, MERV RESORT HOTEL	4200 E PALM CANYON DR, PMSP, 92264	787 - A5
HAMPTON INN	1590 UNIVERSITY AV, RIV, 92507	686 - B5
HAMPTON INN	2000 N PALM CANYON DR, PMSP, 92262	756 - D5
HOLIDAY INN EXPRESS	11043 MAGNOLIA AV, RIV, 92505	744 - E1
HOLIDAY INN EXPRESS	74675 HWY 111, PDST, 92260	848 - H1
HOLIDAY INN PALM MTN RESORT	155 S BELARDO RD, PMSP, 92262	786 - D2
HOLIDAY INN RIVERSIDE	3400 MARKET ST, RIV, 92501	685 - H3
HYATT GRAND CHAMPIONS RESORT	HWY 111, INDW, 92210	849 - C1
HYATT REGENCY SUITES	285 N PALM CANYON DR, PMSP, 92262	786 - D1
INDIAN WELLS RESORT HOTEL	76661 HWY 111, INDW, 92210	849 - C1
LA QUINTA HOTEL GOLF & TENNIS-RESORT	49499 EISENHOWER DR, LQNT, 92253	849 - E5
MARRIOTT DSRT SPGS RESORT & SPA	74855 COUNTRY CLUB DR, PDST, 92260	818 - H3
MARRIOTT RANCHO LAS PALMAS RES	41000 BOB HOPE DR, RMIR, 92270	818 - C5
MIRAMONTE RESORT	76477 HWY 111, INDW, 92210	849 - B1
MISSION INN	3649 MISSION INN AV, RIV, 92501	685 - H4
PALM DESERT RESORT	77333 COUNTRY CLUB DR, PDST, 92211	819 - D4
PALM SPRINGS HILTON RESORT	400 E TAHQUITZ CANYON WY, PMSP, 92262	786 - E2
PALM SPRINGS MARQUIS HOTEL &-VILLAS	150 S INDIAN CANYON DR, PMSP, 92262	786 - E2
QUALITY INN	1269 E PALM CANYON DR, PMSP, 92264	786 - F5
RACQUET CLUB RESORT HOTEL	2743 N INDIAN CANYON DR, PMSP, 92262	756 - D4
RAMADA HOTEL RESORT	1800 E PALM CANYON DR, PMSP, 92264	786 - G5
RAMADA INN	3885 W FLORIDA AV, HEMT, 92545	810 - E7
RENAISSANCE ESMERALDA RESORT	HWY 111, INDW, 92210	849 - C1
RITZ CARLTON RANCHO MIRAGE, THE	68900 FRANK SINATRA DR, RMIR, 92270	817 - F2
RIVIERA RESORT & RACQUET CLUB	1600 N INDIAN CANYON DR, PMSP, 92262	756 - E6
ROADSIDE INN	23330 SUNNYMEAD BLVD, MORV, 92553	717 - C2
ROYAL PLAZA INN	82347 HWY 111, INDO, 92201	5470 - F1
SHADOW MTN RESORT & RACQUET-CLUB	45750 SAN LUIS REY AV, PDST, 92260	848 - F2
SHILO INN	1875 N PALM CANYON DR, PMSP, 92262	756 - D5
SPA HOTEL & MINERAL SPRINGS	100 N INDIAN CANYON DR, PMSP, 92262	786 - E2
TEMECULA CREEK INN	44501 RAINBOW CANYON RD, TEM, 92592	979 - B4
TRAVELERS INN	72322 HWY 111, PDST, 92260	818 - D7
TRAVELODGE PALM SPRINGS	333 E PALM CANYON DR, PMSP, 92264	786 - E5
VACATION INN	74715 HWY 111, PDST, 92260	848 - H1
VAGABOND INN	1699 S PALM CANYON DR, PMSP, 92264	786 - E5
WESTIN MISSION HILLS RESORT	71333 DINAH SHORE DR, RMIR, 92270	788 - A4
WYNDHAM PALM SPRINGS HOTEL	888 E TAHQUITZ CANYON WY, PMSP, 92262	786 - E2

LIBRARIES

FEATURE NAME	Address City, ZIP Code	PAGE-GRID
ANZA BRANCH (SEE PAGE 904)	57430 MITCHELL RD, RivC, 92539	935 - B2
ARLINGTON BRANCH	9556 MAGNOLIA AV, RIV, 92503	714 - J6
BANNING	21 W NICOLET ST, BAN, 92220	722 - B3
BEAUMONT CITY	125 E 8TH ST, BEAU, 92223	720 - H3
CALIMESA BRANCH	908 PARK AV, CALI, 92320	649 - H7
CANYON LAKE BRANCH	31508 RAILROAD CANYON RD, CYNL, 92587	867 - E4
CASA BLANCA BRANCH	2985 MADISON ST, RIV, 92504	715 - E4
CATHEDRAL CITY BRANCH	33520 DATE PALM DR, CTHC, 92234	787 - F4
COACHELLA BRANCH	1538 7TH ST, COAC, 92236	5471 - C6
CORONA	650 S MAIN ST, COR, 92882	743 - D5
DESERT HOT SPRINGS BRANCH LIB	11691 WEST DR, DHSP, 92240	696 - H3
GLEN AVON BRANCH	9244 GALENA ST, RivC, 92509	684 - D1
GRAND TERRACE BRANCH	22795 BARTON RD, GTER, 92313	646 - F3
HEMET	510 FLORIDA AV, HEMT, 92543	811 - A7
HIGHGROVE BRANCH	690 CENTER ST, RivC, 92507	646 - D6
IDYLLWILD BRANCH	54185 PINE CREST AV, RivC	814 - C6
INDIO BRANCH	200 CIVIC CENTER DR, INDO, 92201	5470 - G1
KAISER BRANCH	11155 ALMOND AV, FONT, 92337	644 - C2
LAKE ELSINORE BRANCH	400 W GRAHAM AV, LKEL, 92530	866 - E5
LAKE TAMARISK BRANCH	43880 LAKE TAMARISK DR, RivC	5421 - C1
LA QUINTA BRANCH	78080 CL ESTADO, LQNT, 92253	849 - F7
LA SIERRA BRANCH	4600 LA SIERRA AV, RIV, 92505	714 - D6
LOMA LINDA BRANCH	25581 BARTON RD, LMLN, 92354	647 - D1
MARCY BRANCH	3711 CENTRAL AV, RIV, 92506	715 - E1
MECCA-NORTH SHORE BRANCH	65250 COAHUILLA ST, RivC, 92254	5592 - F6
MORENO VALLEY	25480 ALESSANDRO BLVD, MORV, 92553	717 - H5
MURRIETA	39589 LOS ALAMOS RD, MURR, 92563	928 - E3
NORCO BRANCH	3954 OLD HAMNER RD, NRCO, 92860	713 - E4
NUEVO BRANCH	29990 LAKEVIEW AV, RivC, 92567	778 - J4
PALM DESERT BRANCH	73300 FRED WARING DR, PDST, 92260	818 - E7
PALM SPRINGS	300 S SUNRISE WY, PMSP, 92262	786 - G2
PALO VERDE VALLEY DIST	125 W CHANSLOR WY, BLY, 92225	5491 - E6
PERRIS BRANCH	163 E SAN JACINTO AV, PER, 92570	807 - G2
RANCHO MIRAGE	42520 BOB HOPE DR, RMIR, 92270	818 - C6
RIVERSIDE CENTRAL	3581 MISSION INN AV, RIV, 92501	685 - H4
RUBIDOUX BRANCH	5763 TILTON AV, RivC, 92509	685 - C2
SAN JACINTO BRANCH	165 W 7TH ST, SJCT, 92583	811 - B2
SUN CITY BRANCH	26982 CHERRY HILLS BLVD, RivC, 92586	838 - C6
TEMECULA BRANCH	41000 COUNTY CENTER DR, TEM, 92591	958 - G3
THOUSAND PALMS BRANCH	72715 LA CANADA WY, RivC, 92276	788 - D2
VALLE VISTA BRANCH-(SEE PAGE 782)	43975 E FLORIDA AV, RivC, 92544	812 - A7
YUCAIPA BRANCH	12040 5TH ST, YCPA, 92399	649 - H3

MILITARY INSTALLATIONS

FEATURE NAME	Address City, ZIP Code	PAGE-GRID
CHOCOLATE MTN NAVAL RES AERIAL-GUNNERY	THE BRADSHAW TR, RivC	410 - K3
MARCH AIR RESERVE BASE	RIVERSIDE DR & CACTUS AV, RivC, 92518	717 - D7
USMC BASE CAMP JOSEPH H-PENDLETON	SAN DIEGO FRWY & BASILONE RD, SDCo, 92055	997 - B6
NATL GUARD ARMORY	E 6TH ST & RIMPAU AV, COR, 92879	743 - E5
NATL GUARD ARMORY	NICOLET ST & 20TH ST, BAN, 92220	721 - H3
US NAVAL WEAPONS CENTER	4TH ST, NRCO, 92860	713 - D5
US NAVAL WEAPONS STA FALLBROOK	FALLBROOK RD, SDCo, 92055	997 - B7

MUSEUMS

FEATURE NAME	Address City, ZIP Code	PAGE-GRID
AGUA CALIENTE CULTURAL MUS	219 S PALM CANYON DR, PMSP, 92262	786 - D2
AGUA MANSA CEM MUS	2001 W AGUA MANSA RD, CLTN, 92316	645 - H3
COACHELLA VALLEY MUS &-CULTURAL CTR	82616 MILES AV, INDO, 92201	5410 - F7
DEAN, EDWARD MUS	9401 OAK GLEN RD, RivC, 92223	690 - J2
LAKE PERRIS REGL INDIAN MUS	17801 LAKE PERRIS DR, RivC, 92571	748 - A5
MALKI MUS	11795 FIELDS RD, RivC, 92220	692 - H6
MARCH AFB FIELD MUS	VAN BUREN BLVD & ESCONDIDO EXW, RivC, 92518	747 - B3
MISSION INN MUS	3696 MAIN ST, RIV, 92501	685 - H4
MOUSLEY MUS OF NATURAL HIST	35308 PANORAMA DR, YCPA, 92399	650 - A1
ORANGE EMPIRE RAILWAY MUS	2201 S A ST, PER, 92570	807 - G6
PALM SPRINGS AIR MUS	745 GENE AUTRY TR, PMSP, 92262	756 - J7
PALM SPRINGS DESERT MUS	101 MUSEUM DR, PMSP, 92262	786 - D2
RIVERSIDE ART MUS	3425 MISSION INN AV, RIV, 92501	685 - H4
RIVERSIDE MUNICIPAL MUS	3720 N ORANGE ST, RIV, 92501	685 - H4
SAN JACINTO VALLEY MUS	181 E MAIN ST, SJCT, 92583	811 - B2
SWEENEY ART GALLERY	3701 CANYON CREST DR, RIV, 92507	686 - D4
TEMECULA VALLEY MUS	28314 MERCEDES ST, TEM, 92590	958 - H7
UCR CALIFORNIA MUS OF-PHOTOGRAPHY	3824 MAIN ST, RIV, 92501	685 - H4
VAGLE, MARY MUS AND NATURE CTR	11501 CYPRESS AV, FONT, 92337	644 - H3

OPEN SPACE PRESERVES

FEATURE NAME	Address City, ZIP Code	PAGE-GRID
AGUA TIBIA WILDERNESS AREA	RivC, 92592	981 - B6
BIGHORN SHEEP PRESERVE	FRANK SINATRA DR & HWY 111, RMIR, 92270	817 - E4
BIG MORONGO CANYON PRESERVE	TWENTYNINE PALMS HWY, RivC	655 - J2
BOX SPRINGS MOUNTAIN RESERVE	9699 BOX SPRINGS MOUNTAIN RD, RivC, 92557	686 - G3
COACHELLA VALLEY PRESERVE	THOUSAND PALMS CANYON RD, RivC, 92276	788 - J3
EL DORADO OPEN SPACE	WARREN ST, RIV, 92503	714 - G4
HARFORD SPRINGS RESERVE	GAVILAN RD, RivC, 92570	776 - B7
LAKE MATHEWS ESTELLE MTN-RESERVE	13225 CAJALCO RD, RivC, 92570	805 - B4
LIVING DESERT NATURE PRESERVE,-THE	47900 PORTOLA AV, INDW, 92210	848 - H4
MAGNESIA CANYON ECOLOGICAL-RESERVE	SOUTH OF STATE HWY 111, RMIR, 92270	817 - H7
MOUNT SAN JACINTO STATE-WILDERNESS	BANNING IDYLLWILD RD, RivC	814 - C1
QUAIL RUN OPEN SPACE	5020 QUAIL RUN RD, RIV, 92507	686 - E7
SAN JACINTO WILDERNESS AREA	BANNING IDYLLWILD RD, RivC	814 - G3
SAN MATEO CANYON WILDERNESS	ORTEGA HWY, RivC, 92562	926 - A4
SANTA ANA RIVER WILDLIFE AREA	5500 RIVERVIEW DR, RivC, 92509	685 - A5
SANTA MARGARITA ECOLOGICAL-RESERVE	RED MOUNTAIN TKTR, RivC, 92590	998 - D1
SANTA ROSA PLATEAU ECOLOGICAL-RESERVE	22115 TENAJA RD, RivC, 92562	958 - A3
SANTA ROSA WILDERNESS-(SEE PAGE 908)	PINES TO PALMS HWY, RivC	938 - F1
SHIPLEY, DR ROY E RESERVE	CROWN VALLEY RD, RivC, 92596	900 - F2
SYCAMORE CANYON WILDERNESS PK	CENTRAL AV, RIV, 92506	716 - D3
WILDLIFE HABITAT AREA	CEREAL ST & LUCERNE ST, LKEL, 92530	896 - F1
YOUNGLOVE, NORTON RESERVE	IRONWOOD AV, RivC, 92555	719 - D1

PARK & RIDE

FEATURE NAME	Address City, ZIP Code	PAGE-GRID
CORONA	N MAIN ST & E GRAND BLVD, COR, 92879	743 - D4
CORONA COMM CHURCH	VIA DEL RIO & AVD DEL VISTA, COR, 92882	742 - J6
COUNTRY VILLAGE	10180 GRANITE HILL DR, RivC, 92509	644 - A6
GRAND AV	15887 GRAND AV, LKEL, 92530	865 - J7
LAKE ELSINORE	CORONA FRWY & HWY 74, LKEL, 92532	866 - D2
LA SIERRA	PIERCE ST & RALEY DR, RIV, 92505	744 - B1
METROLINK EAST ONTARIO STA	3330 E FRANCIS ST, ONT, 91761	643 - B4
MIRA LOMA	12105 LIMONITE AV, RivC, 91752	683 - F5
MIRA LOMA	MISSION BLVD & 60 FRWY, RivC, 91752	643 - H6
MORENO VALLEY	12321 PIGEON PASS RD, MORV, 92557	717 - B2
NORCO	3945 OLD HAMNER RD, NRCO, 92860	713 - E4
RANCHO CALIFORNIA	41327 WINCHESTER RD, TEM, 92591	958 - G3
RIVERSIDE	1899 FOUR WHEEL DR, NRCO, 92860	743 - D1
RIVERSIDE	ROUTE 60 FRWY & ORANGE ST, RIV, 92501	685 - J2
TOWNGATE	22500 TOWN CIR, MORV, 92553	717 - B3
TYLER MALL	TYLER ST & RIVERSIDE FRWY, RIV, 92503	744 - G1
YUCAIPA	31341 HAMPTON RD, YCPA, 92399	649 - A4

PARKS & RECREATION

FEATURE NAME	PAGE-GRID
7TH STREET PK, YCPA	649 - G4
ADAMS PK, LQNT	819 - H7
AGATE PK, RivC	684 - E2
AGRICULTURAL PK, RIV	684 - E7
AGUA CALIENTE PK, CTHC	787 - B1
ALTA MURRIETA SPORTS PK, MURR	928 - E5
ANTIGUA PK, MURR	927 - H3
ANZA-BORREGO DSRT ST PK, RivC	409 - L4
APPLEBY PK, BLY	5491 - F7
ARLINGTON PK, RIV	714 - H6
ARROYO PK, DHSP	696 - H4
AVALON PK, RivC	645 - E6
BAGDOUMA PK, COAC	5471 - A7
BAHIA VISTA PK, TEM	959 - C5
BAILEY, LEONARD PK, LMLN	647 - F2
BANTA BEATTY PK, PER	807 - G2
BARISTO PK, PMSP	786 - E2
BARRATT PK, MURR	928 - D3
BAYSIDE PK, MORV	717 - F5
BEAR VALLEY PK, MURR	927 - E4
BERGAMONT PK, RIV	746 - E3
BETHUME PK, MORV	747 - H4
BOGART COUNTY PK, RivC	691 - B2
BONDS, BOBBY PARK & SPORTS-COMPLEX, RIV	686 - A5
BORDER PK, COR	772 - H1
BORDWELL PK, RIV	686 - A6
BRENTWOOD PK, COR	742 - J7
BROOKSIDE PK, RDL	647 - H2
BROOKS, TED PK, NRCO	713 - A6
BROWN, AB SPORTS COMPLEX, RIV	646 - A6
BRYANT, JOHN PK, RIV	714 - G3
BURNS, FRITZ PK, LQNT	879 - F1
BUTTERFIELD COUNTRY REC-VEHICLE, RivC	981 - A2
BUTTERFIELD PK, CHLS	712 - A5
BUTTERFIELD STAGE PK, TEM	959 - J7
BUTTERFIELD STAGE TRAIL PK, -COR	743 - A3
CAHUILLA HILLS PK, PDST	848 - D2
CALIFORNIA AQUEDUCT PK, MORV	747 - H3
CALIFORNIA OAKS SPORTS PK, -MURR	928 - B4
CALIMESA PK, YCPA	649 - H6
CALLE ARAGON PK, TEM	959 - C6
CARLSON PK, RIV	685 - F3
CARPENTER HAMILTON PK, BAN	722 - B3
CASTLEVIEW PK, RIV	716 - B3
CATAWBA PK, FONT	644 - F2
CENTENNIAL SPORTS PK, RivC	684 - H1
CENTURY PK, CTHC	787 - H1
CENTURY PK, MURR	928 - C3
CHAPARRAL PK, FONT	644 - B3
CHINO HILLS STATE PK, CHLS	742 - A5
CITRUS COMM PK, COR	773 - F3
CITY PK, LKEL	866 - E5
CITY PK, COR	743 - E5
CIVIC CTR PK, PDST	818 - F6
CLARK MEM PK, NRCO	713 - E3
CLAY PK, RivC	684 - G6
CLEVELAND NATL FOREST, RivC	772 - E3
COLLETT PK, RIV	714 - E7
COMMUNITY PK, RivC	788 - C1
CONTRERAS PK, COR	743 - C4
COOK SPORTS COMPLEX, PDST	818 - H6
COPPER CANYON PK, MURR	927 - F3
COPPER CREEK PK, PER	777 - H6
CORSINI COYOTE PK, DHSP	697 - D5
CREEKSIDE PK, CALI	649 - G7
CRESTA VERDE PK, COR	743 - H3
CROOKS, HULDA PK, LMLN	647 - D3
CRYSTAL AIRE PK, MURR	927 - J2
DARIO VASQUEZ PK, RIV	685 - J5
DATELAND PK, COAC	5471 - C7
DAUER, RICH PK, CLTN	646 - G1
DAVIS SPORTS COMPLEX, INDO	5470 - H2
DEMUTH PK, PMSP	787 - A4
DE ORO PK, COAC	5471 - B5
DERR, DON PK, RIV	715 - B6
DESERT HIGHLAND PK, PMSP	756 - C3
DOMINGUEZ PK, INDO	5410 - E7
DOUBLE BUTTE PK, RivC	839 - C4
DRUDIN PK, SJCT	811 - B2
EAGLE GLEN COMM PK, COR	773 - H6
EDGAR CANYON NATURE PK, RivC	690 - J4
ELM GROVE REC AREA, LKEL	866 - D5
EL POTRERO PK, MORV	747 - J4
ENGEVICK PK, BLY	5491 - D6
EVANS, SAMUEL SPORTS COMPLEX, -RIV	685 - F5
FAIRMOUNT PK, RIV	685 - G2
FAIRVIEW PK, COR	743 - B1
FAIRWAY PK, MORV	718 - C7
FIRE FIGHTERS PK, MURR	928 - F6
FLAG HILL PK, YCPA	650 - B3
FOSS FIELD PK, PER	807 - G2
GATEWAY PK, MORV	687 - D6
GIBBEL PK, HEMT	810 - G7
GLEN ARBOR PK, MURR	927 - J2
GRIFFIN PK, COR	744 - B3
HACK, FRANCES PK, LQNT	849 - F7
HARDY, RUTH PK, PMSP	756 - E7
HARRISON PK, RIV	744 - J1
HENLEY, MARY PK, HEMT	840 - G2
HICKS, SAM MONUMENT PK, TEM	958 - H7
HIDDEN SPRINGS COMM PK, MORV	687 - A4
HIGHLAND PK, RIV	686 - D3
HOT SPRINGS PK, DHSP	696 - J2

FEATURE NAME Address City, ZIP Code	PAGE-GRID
HUMBER PK, RivC	814 - F3
HUNTERGARDT, KENT PK, TEM	979 - D4
HUNTER PK, RIV	686 - B1
HUNTERS HILL PK, CHLS	712 - A4
HUNT PK, RIV	714 - J4
HUSTED PK, COR	743 - C6
IDYLLWILD PK AND NATURE CTR, - RivC	814 - B6
INGALLS PK, NRCO	713 - J4
IRONWOOD PK, PDST	848 - E4
ISLANDER PK, RIV	686 - F4
JFK VETERANS MEM PK, MORV	747 - F1
JONES, DON PK, RIV	715 - C3
JOSHUA TREE NATL PK, RivC	697 - G2
JOY STREET PK, COR	743 - D6
JURUPA CULTURAL CTR, RivC	644 - H6
KABIAN COUNTY PK, PER	837 - E4
KELLOGG PK, COR	743 - E7
KIPS KORNER PK, NRCO	713 - B7
KNOWLES PK, RivC	684 - C2
LAKE CAHUILLA REC AREA, LQNT	5530 - A6
LAKE ELSINORE REC AREA, LKEL	865 - J4
LAKE PERRIS STATE REC AREA, - RivC	748 - F2
LAKEPOINT PK, LKEL	866 - E6
LAKE SKINNER REC AREA, RivC	930 - C2
LA QUINTA SPORTS COMPLEX, - LQNT	849 - H5
LARAMORE PK, RivC	683 - H5
LA SIERRA PK, RIV	714 - C5
LINCOLN PK, RIV	685 - H5
LINCOLN PK, COR	743 - B7
LINN, MYRA PK, RIV	714 - E6
LIONS PK, BAN	722 - C4
LOMA LINDA PK, TEM	979 - C5
LONG, BOB MEM BALLPARK, PER	807 - J2
LORENZI, DON SPORTS COMPLEX, - RIV	714 - J4
LORING PK, RIV	685 - F3
LOW PK, RIV	715 - E2
MACEE, JOHN PK, TEM	979 - D3
MACHADO PK, LKEL	865 - H3
MANGULAR PK, COR	772 - J1
MARCH FIELD PK, RivC	747 - D1
MARGARITA PK, TEM	958 - J5
MAZE STONE PK, RivC	809 - J2
MCCALL MEM PK, RivC	844 - A4
MCLEAN, MARTHA ANZA NARROWS- PK, RIV	685 - B6
MCVICKER PK, LKEL	865 - F3
MEADOW RIDGE PK, MURR	928 - D5
MEADOWS PK, CHLS	712 - A4
MECCA HILLS PK, RivC- (SEE PAGE 5592)	5593 - E1
MECCA SPORTS COMPLEX, RivC	5592 - F6
MEM PK, RivC	685 - B2
MERRILL PK, COR	743 - C6
METZ PK, PER	807 - G2
MILES AVENUE PK, INDO	5410 - F7
MILLER PK, BLY	5551 - D1
MINOR PK, RivC- (SEE PAGE 904)	934 - J4
MISSION SPRINGS PK, DHSP	696 - J6
MISTLETOE PK, SJCT	811 - C2
MITCHELL, ADRIENNE MEM PK, - MORV	717 - B5
MONTAFINO PK, MURR	927 - J4
MORENO VALLEY COMM PK, MORV	717 - C4
MORRISON PK, MORV	718 - A4
MOUNT RUBIDOUX PK, RIV	685 - F3
MOUNT SAN JACINTO STATE PK, - RivC	814 - A1
MOUNTAIN GATE COMM PK, COR	773 - C3
MOUNTAIN GATE GREEN BELT, COR	773 - B3
MOUNTAIN PRIDE PK, MURR	927 - J3
MOUNTAIN VIEW PK, RIV	685 - D7
MURRIETA PK, MURR	928 - A6
MYSTIC CANYON PK, CHLS	712 - A5
NEWMAN PK, RIV	685 - G5
NICHOLS PK, RIV	715 - B1
NICOLAS ROAD PK, TEM	959 - A1
NOBLE CREEK PK, RivC	690 - G7
NORCO COMM CTR PK, NRCO	713 - D3
NORTH JACKSON PK, INDO	5410 - G5
NORTH PK, RIV	685 - H4
OAK PK, FONT	644 - B4
OAK TREE PK, LKEL	865 - F2
OASIS BALL PK, RivC	5712 - B3
ONTARIO PK, COR	773 - A1
ORANCO BOWMEN ARCHERY RANGE, - CHNO	712 - B4
PACER PK, NRCO	713 - B6
PALA COMM PK, TEM	979 - C3
PALM DESERT COMM PK, PDST	818 - G6
PALM DESERT CC PK, PDST	819 - E5
PALM DESERT SOCCER PK, PDST	818 - H5
PALOMA DEL SOL PK, TEM	979 - E2
PANORAMA PK, CTHC	757 - D6
PARAGON PK, PER	777 - H4
PARKVIEW PARK, COR	743 - H2
PARMENTER PK, NRCO	713 - F6
PARQUE AMISTAD, MORV	747 - J1
PASS VALLEY PK, BAN	722 - C2
PATTERSON, E T PK, RIV	686 - A4
PEDRORENA PK, MORV	747 - H2
PEOPLES PK, DHSP	696 - J2
PICO PK, GTER	646 - D5
PINE COVE PK, RivC	814 - A3
POND PK, MURR	928 - F6
PRADO AIR PK, SBdC	712 - E5
PRADO BASIN PK, RivC	712 - H6
PRADO FLOOD CONTROL BASIN, - COR	743 - A2
PRADO PARKS STABLES, SBdC	712 - D2

FEATURE NAME Address City, ZIP Code	PAGE-GRID
PRADO REC DOG TRAINING- FACILITY, SBdC	712 - B5
PRADO REGL PK, CHNO	712 - B3
PRADO TIRO SHOOTING RANGE REC- AREA, CHNO	712 - B4
PROMENADE COMM PK, COR	744 - A3
RANCHO PK, SJCT	811 - D3
RANCHO ACACIAS PK, MURR	928 - E4
RANCHO CALIFORNIA SPORTS PK, - TEM	959 - B7
RANCHO LOMA PK, RIV	744 - D1
RANCHO MIRA LOMA, RivC	644 - A5
RANGEL PK, BEAU	720 - G3
REID PK, RIV	646 - A7
REPPLIER PK, BAN	722 - B2
RICE VALLEY OFF HWY VEH AREA, - RivC	391 - L2
RIDGE CREST PK, MORV	718 - E7
RIDGELINE PK, COR	742 - F6
RIVER ROAD PK, COR	743 - C2
RIVERSIDE SPORT CTR, RIV	686 - C4
RIVERTON PK, TEM	959 - D1
RIVERTRAILS PK, NRCO	713 - G1
ROCK VISTA PK, COR	743 - J2
ROTARY PK, TEM	978 - J1
RUTLAND PK, RIV	714 - F1
SALLEE PK, SJCT	811 - B1
SALTON SEA STATE REC AREA, - RivC (SEE PAGE 5594)	5654 - G7
SAN BERNARDINO NATL FOREST, - RivC	814 - H7
SAN JACINTO PK, CYNL	867 - D2
SAN JACINTO RIVER PK, RivC	781 - A4
SANTA ANA RIVER REGL PK, RivC	713 - B3
SANTANA REGL PK, COR	773 - E1
SEARLES SPORTS PK, HEMT	811 - A4
SERFAS CLUB PK, COR	742 - G6
SHADOW PK, FONT	644 - C3
SHAMEL, A D PK, RIV	715 - E2
SHERIDAN PK, COR	743 - C5
SIERRA PK, CYNL	867 - D1
SIERRA VISTA PK, COAC	5471 - D5
SIMPSON PK, RivC	841 - G6
SNIPES, NEIL PK, NRCO	713 - D4
SOUTH JACKSON PK, INDO	5470 - G2
SOUTHRIDGE PK, FONT	644 - D3
SPYGLASS PK, COR	773 - G7
STEWART PK, BEAU	720 - J2
STEWART, RUSSELL MEM PK, PER	807 - G3
STREETER PK, RIV	715 - C1
SUMMERHILL PK, LKEL	866 - J5
SUMMER LAKE PK, LKEL	865 - G2
SUNDANCE PK, NRCO	713 - A6
SUNGOLD PK, BLY	5491 - F6
SUNNYMEAD PK, MORV	717 - F3
SUNRISE PK, PMSP	786 - G3
SWANSON PK, RIV	716 - A2
SWICK & MATICH PK, LKEL	866 - E5
SYLVAN PK, BAN	721 - G2
TAFT PK, RIV	716 - D4
TEHACHAPI PK, COR	743 - H3
TEMECULA DUCK POND, TEM	958 - J6
TEMEKU HILLS PK, TEM	959 - D3
TERRACE HILLS COMM PK, GTER	646 - F4
THUNDERSKY PK, RIV	746 - G2
TODD PK, BLY	5491 - E6
TOWNGATE MEM PK, MORV	717 - B4
TOWN SQUARE PK, CTHC	787 - E7
TUDAR, MARTIN JURUPA HILLS- REGL PK, FONT	644 - J3
TUSCANY HILLS COMM PK, LKEL	867 - A3
UCR BOTANIC GARDENS, RIV	686 - E5
VALLEY VISTA PK, MURR	928 - B2
VALLEY WIDE REGL PK, SJCT	810 - J3
VETERANS PK, TEM	959 - C4
VICTORIANO PK, MORV	747 - H2
VICTORIA PK, COR	743 - D6
VICTORIA PK, PMSP	756 - E5
VIETNAM VETERANS PK, COAC	5471 - C6
VILLAGE PK, FONT	644 - F3
VILLAGE PK, COR	743 - G3
VILLEGAS PK, RIV	715 - E4
VOORBURG PK, TEM	959 - A1
WARDMAN PK, DHSP	696 - H2
WARM SPRINGS PK, MURR	928 - F4
WASHINGTON PK, RIV	715 - F4
WAYNE MAKIN/SHEARER SPORTS- COMPLEX, NRCO	713 - B5
WELCH MEM PK, HEMT	811 - A7
WESTBLUFF PK, MORV	687 - C6
WESTON PK, MORV	717 - J4
WESTON PK, HEMT	811 - B7
WHITE PK, RIV	685 - G4
WHITEWATER PK, RMIR	818 - B5
WHITEWOOD PK, MURR	928 - F4
WHITTIER, JG PK, WHIT	388 - C5
WINEVILLE PK, RivC	683 - G4
WOLFSON PK, RMIR	817 - H1
WOODLAND PK, MORV	717 - H7
YOST PK, RivC	644 - H6
YUCAIPA REGL PK, YCPA	649 - H1
YUCCA PK, INDO	5410 - E6

PERFORMING ARTS

MUNICIPAL AUDITORIUM 3485 MISSION INN AV, RIV, 92501	685 - H4
RAMONA BOWL RAMONA BOWL RD, RivC, 92544	841 - D4

POINTS OF INTEREST

FEATURE NAME Address City, ZIP Code	PAGE-GRID
BIG LEAGUE DREAMS SPORTS PK DATE PALM DR, CTHC, 92234	787 - F4
CHERRY VALLEY GRANGE HALL 10468 N BEAUMONT AV, RivC, 92223	690 - H4
CLARK, BEN PUB SAFETY TRAINING- CTR BARTON ST & NANDINA AV, RivC, 92518	746 - G5
HOPE, BOB CULTURAL CTR 73000 FRED WARING DR, PDST, 92260	818 - E7
INDIAN CANYONS PALM CANYON & ANDREAS CANYON, RivC	816 - F3
LUISENO KIOSK OFF VIA DEL LAGO, RivC, 92571	748 - C5
MOORTEN BOTANICAL GARDEN 1701 S PALM CANYON DR, PMSP, 92264	786 - E5
MORENO KIOSK VIA DL LAGO, RivC, 92571	748 - D3
MORENO VALLEY EQUESTRIAN CTR REDLANDS BL & LOCUST AV, MORV, 92555	688 - F6
PALM SPRINGS AERIAL TRAMWAY TRAMWAY RD, PMSP, 92262	755 - F7
PERRIS KIOSK LAKE PERRIS DR, RivC, 92571	748 - A6
PRADO TIRO SHOOTING RANGE 17501 POMONA RINCON RD, CHNO, 91710	712 - B4
RANCHO MIRAGE RACQUET CLUB 70707 FRANK SINATRA DR, RMIR, 92270	817 - H2
RUBIDOUX GRANGE HALL 3865 RIVERVIEW DR, RivC, 92509	685 - C2
TAHQUITZ FALLS WEST OF PALM CYN DR, PMSP, 92264	786 - C5

POINTS OF INTEREST - HISTORIC

CABOTS OLD INDIAN PUEBLO 67616 DESERT VIEW AV, DHSP, 92240	697 - B4
CALIFORNIA CITRUS STATE HIST PK 1879 JACKSON ST, RIV, 92503	745 - B2
FISH TRAPS ARCHAEOLOGICAL SITE JACKSON ST & 66TH AV, RivC	5590 - F7
GILMAN HIST RANCH WILSON ST, BAN, 92220	721 - H1
IDYLLWILD TREE MONUMENT VILLAGE CENTER DR, RivC	814 - D6
INDIAN RELIC ARCHAEOLOGICAL- SITE PINE CREST AV, RivC	814 - D4
JENSEN-ALVARADO HIST RANCH AND- MUS 4307 BRIGGS ST, RivC, 92509	685 - B2
MARCH FIELD HIST DIST GRAEBER ST & MEYER DR, RivC, 92518	747 - C1
MOCKINGBIRD CANYON- ARCHAEOLOGICAL SITE MOCKINGBIRD CANYON RD & HARLEY, RivC, 92504	775 - H1
RINCON RANCHO YORBA-SLAUGHTER- ADOBE 17127 POMONA RINCON RD, CHNO, 91710	712 - A3
SAN BERNARDINO RANCHO- ASISTENCIA 26930 BARTON RD, RDL, 92373	647 - G1
TRUJILLO ADOBE HIST AREA S PELLISIER RD, RivC, 92501	646 - A6
WHITEWATER ADOBE I-10 & HWY 111, PMSP, 92282	724 - H3
YUCAIPA ADOBE 32183 KENTUCKY ST, YCPA, 92399	649 - C5

SCHOOLS - PRIVATE ELEMENTARY

ADVOCATE S 9994 COUNTY FARM RD, RIV, 92503	714 - G6
AGAPE CHRISTIAN 8775 MAGNOLIA AV, RIV, 92503	715 - A5
AZURE HILLS ADVENTIST 22577 CITY CENTER CT, GTER, 92313	646 - F4
BAPTIST CHRISTIAN 26089 GIRARD ST, RivC, 92544	811 - C7
BETHEL CHRISTIAN 2425 VAN BUREN BLVD, RIV, 92503	745 - A1
BUNDY CANYON CHRISTIAN 23411 BUNDY CANYON RD, RivC, 92595	897 - E4
CALVARY BIBLE CHRISTIAN 68550 DINAH SHORE DR, CTHC, 92234	787 - E4
CALVARY CHRISTIAN 1325 MOUNTAIN AV, BAN, 92220	721 - F2
CALVARY CHAPEL CHRISTIAN 11960 PETTIT ST, MORV, 92555	718 - D1
CHERRY VALLEY BRETHREN BEAUMONT AV & VINELAND ST, RivC, 92223	690 - H4
CHRISTIAN CTR ACADEMY 1401 S MOUNT VERNON AV, CLTN, 92324	646 - F2
CHRISTIAN HERITAGE 1450 W 6TH ST, COR, 92882	743 - A5
CHRISTIAN OF THE DESERT 40700 YUCCA LN, RivC, 92201	819 - F3
COMM CHRISTIAN 41762 STETSON AV, RivC, 92544	841 - F2
CORONA CHRISTIAN 1901 W ONTARIO AV, COR, 92882	742 - H7
CROSSROADS CHRISTIAN 1400 FULLERTON AV, COR, 92879	743 - E7
DESERT CHAPEL CHRISTIAN 630 S SUNRISE WY, PMSP, 92264	786 - G3
GRACE CHRISTIAN 8223 CALIFORNIA AV, RIV, 92504	715 - B3
GRACE LUTHERAN CHRISTIAN 1811 S LINCOLN AV, COR, 92882	743 - B7
HARVEST CHRISTIAN 6115 ARLINGTON AV, RIV, 92504	715 - A2
HAWARDEN HILLS ACADEMY 6696 VIA VISTA DR, RIV, 92506	716 - B4
HEMET CHRISTIAN 825 GILBERT ST, HEMT, 92543	840 - J2
HILLCREST 29275 SANTIAGO RD, TEM, 92592	978 - J1
IMMANUEL BAPTIST 45 MICHIGAN AV, RivC, 92507	646 - D6
IMMANUEL LUTHERAN 5545 ALESSANDRO BLVD, RIV, 92506	715 - J1
ISLAMIC ACADEMY OF RIVERSIDE 1038 W LINDEN ST, RIV, 92507	686 - C4
KIDS WORLD 41956 3RD ST, TEM, 92590	978 - J1
LA SIERRA ACADEMY 4900 GOLDEN AV, RIV, 92505	714 - C6
LINFIELD CHRISTIAN 31950 PAUBA RD, TEM, 92592	959 - D6
MARYWOOD COUNTRY DAY 72850 CLANCY LN, RMIR, 92270	818 - D5
MESA GRANDE ACADEMY 975 FREMONT ST, CALI, 92320	650 - C7
MONTESSORI IN REDLANDS 1890 ORANGE AV, RDL, 92373	647 - G1
MONTESSORI OF CORONA 937 COTA ST, COR, 92880	743 - D3
MORENO CHRISTIAN 26755 ALESSANDRO BLVD, MORV, 92555	718 - A5
MORENO VALLEY BAPTIST 25560 ALESSANDRO BLVD, MORV, 92553	717 - H5
OUR LADY OF PERPETUAL HELP 82470 BLISS AV, INDO, 92201	5470 - F1
OUR LADY OF PERPETUAL HELP 6686 STREETER AV, RIV, 92504	715 - C1
OUR LADY OF VICTORY 601 E PALMER ST, COMP, 90221	388 - A7
PALM DESERT LEARNING TREE CTR 42675 WASHINGTON ST, PDST, 92211	819 - F5
PALM VALLEY 35525 DA VALL DR, RMIR, 92270	787 - H6
PRECIOUS BLOOD 117 W NICOLET ST, BAN, 92220	722 - B2
QUEEN OF ANGELS 4824 JONES AV, RIV, 92505	714 - E5
RIVERSIDE BAPTIST 9015 MAGNOLIA AV, RIV, 92503	714 - J5
RIVERSIDE CHRISTIAN DAY 3612 ARLINGTON AV, RIV, 92506	715 - E2
RIVERSIDE CHRISTIAN 3532 MONROE ST, RIV, 92503	715 - A5
RIVERSIDE GARDEN 1085 W LINDEN ST, RIV, 92507	686 - C4
SACRED HEART 43775 DEEP CANYON RD, PDST, 92260	818 - H7
SAINT CATHERINE OF ALEXANDRIA 3728 ARLINGTON AV, RIV, 92506	715 - F2
SAINT EDWARD 500 S MERRILL ST, COR, 92882	743 - C5
SAINT FRANCIS DE SALES 4205 MULBERRY ST, RIV, 92501	685 - H5
SAINT HYACINTH ACADEMY 275 S VICTORIA AV, SJCT, 92583	811 - B2
SAINT JAMES 250 W 3RD ST, PER, 92570	807 - G3
SAINT JEANNE DE LESTONNAC 32650 AVD LESTONNAC, RivC, 92592	959 - F4
SAINT JOHNS 26410 COLUMBIA ST, RivC, 92544	841 - D1
SAINT MEL 4160 CORONA AV, NRCO, 92860	713 - F3
SAINT THERESA 455 S COMPADRE RD, PMSP, 92262	786 - H3
SAINT THOMAS 9136 MAGNOLIA AV, RIV, 92503	714 - J5
SON SHINE CHRISTIAN 5430 RIDGEVIEW AV, RivC, 91752	683 - J3
TEMECULA CHRISTIAN 29825 SANTIAGO RD, TEM, 92592	979 - A1
TEMECULA VALLEY CHRISTIAN CTR 43300 BUSINESS PARK DR, TEM, 92590	958 - G7
TEMPLE CHRISTIAN 745 N PERRIS BLVD, PER, 92571	807 - G1
VALLE VISTA CHRISTIAN- (SEE PAGE 782) 45252 FLORIDA AV, RivC, 92544	812 - C6
YUCAIPA CHRISTIAN 34784 YUCAIPA BLVD, YCPA, 92399	649 - J3
ZION LUTHERAN 721 E CHANSLOR WY, BLY, 92225	5491 - F5

SCHOOLS - PRIVATE HIGH

ADVOCATE 11980 MOUNT VERNON AV, GTER, 92313	646 - E3
ARROWHEAD CHRISTIAN ACADEMY 105 TENNESSEE ST, RDL, 92373	647 - J1
BAPTIST CHRISTIAN 26089 GIRARD ST, RivC, 92544	811 - C7
BETHEL CHRISTIAN 2425 VAN BUREN BLVD, RIV, 92503	745 - B1
BUNDY CANYON CHRISTIAN 23411 BUNDY CANYON RD, RivC, 92595	897 - E4
CALVARY BIBLE CHRISTIAN 68550 DINAH SHORE DR, CTHC, 92234	787 - E4
CALVARY CHAPEL CHRISTIAN 24225 MONROE AV, MURR, 92562	928 - A4
CALVARY CHRISTIAN 1325 MOUNTAIN AV, BAN, 92220	721 - F2
CHRISTIAN CTR ACADEMY 1401 S MOUNT VERNON AV, CLTN, 92324	646 - F2
CHRISTIAN HERITAGE 1450 W 6TH ST, COR, 92882	743 - A5
CHRISTIAN OF THE DESERT 40700 YUCCA LN, RivC, 92201	819 - F3
CORONA CHRISTIAN 1901 W ONTARIO AV, COR, 92882	742 - H7
IDYLLWILD ARTS ACADEMY- (SEE PAGE 842) 52500 TEMECULA RD, RivC	843 - J1
LA SIERRA ACADEMY 4900 GOLDEN AV, RIV, 92505	714 - C6
LINFIELD CHRISTIAN 31950 PAUBA RD, TEM, 92592	959 - D6
MESA GRANDE ACADEMY 975 FREMONT ST, CALI, 92320	650 - C7
MORENO CHRISTIAN 26755 ALESSANDRO BLVD, MORV, 92555	718 - A5
MORENO VALLEY BAPTIST 25560 ALESSANDRO BLVD, MORV, 92553	717 - H5
NOTRE DAME 7085 BROCKTON AV, RIV, 92506	715 - E2
PALM VALLEY 35525 DA VALL DR, RMIR, 92270	787 - H6
PANORAMA CHRISTIAN 33981 YUCAIPA BLVD, YCPA, 92399	649 - G3
RIVERSIDE CHRISTIAN 3532 MONROE ST, RIV, 92503	715 - A5
TEMPLE CHRISTIAN 745 N PERRIS BLVD, PER, 92571	807 - H1
WOODCREST CHRISTIAN 18401 VAN BUREN BLVD, RivC, 92508	746 - C3

SCHOOLS - PUBLIC ELEMENTARY

ADAMS 2350 BORDER AV, COR, 92882	772 - H1
ADAMS 8362 COLORADO AV, RIV, 92504	715 - A2
ADAMS, JOHN 50800 DESERT CLUB DR, LQNT, 92253	849 - F6
AGUA CALIENTE 30800 SAN LUIS REY DR, CTHC, 92234	787 - B1
ALCOTT 2433 CENTRAL AV, RIV, 92506	715 - J1
ALTA MURRIETA 39475 WHITEWOOD RD, MURR, 92563	928 - F5
ANTHONY, SUSAN B 2665 GILBERT AV, COR, 92881	773 - F3
APPLEBY, FELIX J 401 3RD ST, BLY, 92225	5491 - F7
ARBUCKLE, INA 3600 PACKARD, RivC, 92509	685 - D2
ARLANZA 5891 RUTLAND AV, RIV, 92503	714 - F3
ARMADA 25201 JOHN F KENNEDY DR, MORV, 92551	717 - G7
ARNOLD HEIGHTS 15801 HARMON ST, RivC, 92518	747 - A2
AVAXAT 24300 LAS BRISAS RD, MURR, 92562	928 - C2
BAUTISTA CREEK 441 LAKE ST, HEMT, 92544	811 - G6
BEAR VALLEY 26125 FIR AV, MORV, 92555	717 - J3
BETHUNE, MARY MCLEOD 25390 KRAMERIA ST, MORV, 92551	747 - H4
BOX SPRINGS 11900 ATHENS DR, MORV, 92557	717 - A1
BROWN, RUTH 241 N 7TH ST, BLY, 92225	5491 - F6
BRYANT 4324 3RD ST, RIV, 92501	685 - G3
BRYN MAWR 11680 WHITTIER AV, LMLN, 92354	647 - F2
BUBBLING WELLS 67501 CM CAMPANERO, RivC, 92240	697 - B7
BUCHANAN, DANIEL N 40121 TORREY PINES RD, MURR, 92563	928 - G7
BUTTERFIELD 13400 KITCHING ST, MORV, 92553	717 - H4
BUTTERFIELD 16275 GRAND AV, RivC, 92530	866 - A7
BUTTERFIELD RANCH 6350 MYSTIC CANYON DR, CHLS, 91709	712 - A6
CABAZON 50126 RAMONA ST, RivC, 92230	723 - C4
CAHUILLA 677 E TACHEVAH DR, PMSP, 92262	756 - E7
CAHUILLA 833 MESQUITE AV, PMSP, 92264	786 - E4
CA SCHOOL FOR THE DEAF 3044 HORACE ST, RIV, 92506	715 - G2
CALIMESA 13523 2ND ST, YCPA, 92399	650 - A6
CAMINO REAL 4655 CM REAL, RivC, 92509	684 - H1
CANYON CREST 11851 CHERRY AV, FONT, 92337	644 - C4
CARTER, JAMES EARL 74251 HOVLEY LN E, PDST, 92260	818 - G5
CASTLE VIEW 6201 SHAKER DR, RIV, 92506	716 - B3
CATHEDRAL CITY 68752 BUDDY ROGERS DR, CTHC, 92234	787 - F6
CENTRAL 295 N SAN GORGONIO AV, BAN, 92220	722 - B3
CHAPPARAL HILLS 24850 DELPHINIUM AV, MORV, 92553	717 - F7
CHAVEZ 1730 CHERRY AV, BEAU, 92223	691 - A6
CHAVEZ, CESAR 1150 PAS GRANDE, COR, 92882	742 - H6
CHAVEZ, CESAR 49601 AVD DE ORO, COAC, 92236	5471 - B5
CIELO VISTA 650 S PAS DOROTEA, PMSP, 92264	787 - A3
CLOVERDALE 12050 KITCHING ST, MORV, 92557	717 - H1
COLE CANYON 23750 VIA ALISOL, MURR, 92562	927 - F4
COLLETT 10850 COLLETT AV, RIV, 92505	714 - E7
COLLIER, WILLIAM 20150 MAYHALL DR, RivC, 92595	896 - H5
COOLEY RANCH 1000 S COOLEY DR, CLTN, 92324	646 - H1

FEATURE NAME	Address City, ZIP Code	PAGE-GRID
CORONITA	1757 VIA DL RIO, COR, 92882	742 - J6
CORSINI, JULIUS	68750 HACIENDA AV, DHSP, 92240	697 - E5
COTTONWOOD	44260 SAGE RD, RivC, 92536	981 - J1
CREEKSIDE	13563 HEACOCK ST, MORV, 92553	717 - E5
CREEK VIEW	3742 LYTLE CREEK LP, ONT, 91761	643 - C6
CRESTMORE	18870 JURUPA AV, SBdC, 92316	645 - E2
CURRAN, E HALE	40855 CHACO CANYON RD, MURR, 92562	928 - A3
DARCY, MICHAEL	11645 ELM AV, FONT, 92337	644 - F3
DE ANZA	1089 DE ANZA DR, SJCT, 92582	780 - J7
DUKE, BOBBY	85358 BAGDAD AV, COAC, 92236	5471 - C7
DUNLAP	32870 AVE E, YCPA, 92399	649 - D4
EAGLE MTN	1434 KAISER RD, RivC	5240 - A7
EDGEMONT	21790 EUCALYPTUS AV, MORV, 92553	716 - J4
EISENHOWER, DWIGHT D.	83391 DILLON AV, INDO, 92201	5410 - H7
EL CERRITO	7581 RUDELL RD, RivC, 92881	773 - J4
EL POTRERO	16820 VIA PAMPLONIA DR, MORV, 92551	747 - H4
ELSINORE	512 W SUMNER ST, LKEL, 92530	866 - E4
EMERSON	4660 OTTAWA AV, RIV, 92507	686 - A6
FINCHY, KATHERINE	777 E TACHEVAH DR, PMSP, 92262	756 - E7
FOOTHILL	2601 S BUENA VISTA AV, COR, 92882	773 - B2
FOOTHILL	8230 WELLS AV, RIV, 92503	714 - G4
FORD, GERALD R	44210 WARNER TR, INDW, 92210	819 - E7
FRANKLIN	19661 ORANGE TERRACE PKWY, RIV, 92508	746 - E2
FRANKLIN	2650 OAK AV, COR, 92882	773 - A2
FREMONT	1925 ORANGE ST, RIV, 92501	685 - J2
FRUITVALE	2800 W FRUITVALE AV, HEMT, 92545	810 - F5
GARRETSON	1650 GARRETSON AV, COR, 92879	743 - D7
GLEN AVON	4352 PYRITE ST, RivC, 92509	684 - F1
GLEN VIEW	21200 OLEANDER AV, RivC, 92570	746 - J7
GOOD HOPE	24050 THEDA ST, RivC, 92570	807 - B5
GRAHAM, DONALD	35450 FREDERICK ST, RivC, 92595	897 - E6
GRAND TERRACE	12066 VIVIENDA AV, GTER, 92313	646 - D4
GRANITE HILL	9371 GRANITE HILL DR, RivC, 92509	644 - C6
GRANT	4011 14TH ST, RIV, 92501	685 - G4
HAMILTON (SEE PAGE 904)	57550 MITCHELL RD, RivC, 92539	935 - B2
HARRISON	2901 HARRISON ST, RIV, 92503	744 - J1
HARVEST VALLEY	29955 WATSON RD, RivC, 92585	808 - J7
HAWTHORNE	9174 INDIANA AV, RIV, 92503	715 - A6
HAYMAN, JEAN	21440 LEMON ST, RivC, 92595	897 - A3
HEMET	633 E KIMBALL AV, HEMT, 92543	811 - B7
HEMMERLING	1928 W NICOLET ST, BAN, 92220	721 - J3
HENDRICK RANCH	25570 BRODIAEA AV, MORV, 92553	717 - H6
HIDDEN SPRINGS	9801 HIDDEN SPRINGS DR, MORV, 92557	687 - B4
HIGHGROVE	690 CENTER ST, RivC, 92507	646 - D6
HIGHLAND	2301 ALHAMBRA ST, NRCO, 92860	713 - D3
HIGHLAND	700 HIGHLANDER DR, RIV, 92507	686 - D3
HOFFER	1115 E HOFFER ST, BAN, 92220	722 - C2
HOME GARDENS	13550 TOLTON AV, RivC, 92879	743 - J5
HONEY HOLLOW	11765 HONEY HOLLOW, MORV, 92557	717 - C1
HOOVER, HERBERT	44300 MONROE ST, INDO, 92201	5410 - E7
HYATT	4466 MOUNT VERNON AV, RIV, 92507	686 - F6
HYATT, EDWARD	400 E SHAVER ST, SJCT, 92583	811 - B3
IDYLLWILD	STATE HWY 243, RivC	814 - C7
INDIAN HILLS	7750 LINARES AV, RivC, 92509	684 - H5
JACKSON	4585 JACKSON ST, RIV, 92503	714 - H3
JACKSON, ANDREW	82850 KENNER ST, INDO, 92201	5410 - G6
JEFFERSON	1040 S VICENTIA AV, COR, 92882	743 - C6
JEFFERSON	4285 JEFFERSON ST, RIV, 92504	715 - B2
JOHNSON	44640 CLINTON ST, INDO, 92201	5410 - D7
JURUPA HILLS	10755 OLEANDER AV, FONT, 92337	644 - H1
JURUPA VISTA	15920 VILLAGE DR E, FONT, 92337	644 - G3
KELLEY, JOHN	87163 CENTER ST, RivC, 92274	5531 - G4
KENNEDY, JOHN F	45100 CLINTON ST, INDO, 92201	5470 - D1
KENNEDY, ROSEMARY	6411 MITCHELL ST, RIV, 92505	714 - C2
KIRKPATRICK, CALLIE	28800 REVIERE DR, RivC, 92584	868 - G3
LA GRANADA	10346 KELLER AV, RIV, 92505	714 - E4
LANDAU	30310 LANDAU BLVD, CTHC, 92234	787 - D1
LIBERTY	9631 HAYES ST, RIV, 92503	714 - H6
LINCOLN, ABRAHAM	74100 RUTLEDGE WY, PDST, 92260	818 - G6
LINCOLN ALTERNATIVE	1041 FULLERTON AV, COR, 92879	743 - E6
LINDLEY, DELLA S	31495 ROBERT RD, RivC, 92276	788 - D2
LINN , MYRA	10435 BRANIGAN WY, RIV, 92505	714 - F6
LITTLE LAKE	26091 S MERIDIAN ST, RivC, 92544	811 - F7
LONGFELLOW	3610 EUCALYPTUS AV, RIV, 92507	685 - J5
LUISENO	13500 MOUNTAIN RD, RivC, 92883	835 - C5
MACHADO	15150 JOY ST, LKEL, 92530	865 - J3
MADISON	3635 MADISON ST, RIV, 92504	715 - D3
MADISON, JAMES	80845 AVE 46, INDO, 92201	5470 - C2
MAGNOLIA	3975 MAPLEWOOD PL, RIV, 92506	685 - F7
MARTINEZ, SAUL	65705 JOHNSON ST, RivC, 92254	5592 - H6
MCAULIFFE, CHRISTA	4100 GOLDEN AV, RIV, 92505	744 - D1
MCKINLEY, WILLIAM	2050 AZTEC LN, COR, 92879	743 - H1
MEAD VALLEY	21100 OLEANDER AV, RivC, 92570	746 - H7
MECCA	65250 COAHUILLA ST, RivC, 92254	5592 - F6
MENIFEE	26301 GARBANI RD, RivC, 92584	868 - B6
MIDLAND	11440 DAVIS ST, MORV, 92557	687 - E7
MISSION BELL	4020 CONNING ST, RivC, 92509	644 - B7
MONROE	8535 GARFIELD ST, RIV, 92504	715 - A4
MONROE, JAMES	42100 YUCCA LN, RivC, 92201	819 - F5
MORENO	26700 COTTONWOOD AV, MORV, 92555	718 - A4
MORRISON, CHESTER W	30250 BRADLEY RD, RivC, 92584	868 - C3
MOUNTAIN VIEW	6180 STREETER AV, RIV, 92504	685 - C7
MOUNTAIN VISTA	49750 HJORTH ST, INDO, 92201	5470 - D5
MURRIETA	24725 ADAMS AV, MURR, 92562	928 - A6
NICOLAS VALLEY	39600 N GENERAL KEARNEY RD, RivC, 92563	929 - B7
NORCO	1700 TEMESCAL AV, NRCO, 92860	743 - F1
NORTH RIDGE	25101 KALMIA AV, MORV, 92557	687 - G7
NUVIEW UNION	29680 LAKEVIEW AV, RivC, 92567	778 - J4
OAK PARK	14200 LIVE OAK AV, FONT, 92337	644 - B4
OASIS	88775 76TH AV, RivC, 92274	5712 - B3
ORRENMAA	3350 FILLMORE ST, RIV, 92503	744 - E3
PACHAPPA	6200 RIVERSIDE AV, RIV, 92506	715 - F1
PACIFIC AVENUE	6110 45TH ST, RivC, 92509	685 - B3
PALM	751 PALM AV, BEAU, 92223	720 - J3
PALMS	255 E JARVIS ST, PER, 92571	807 - H2
PALM SPRINGS INDEPENDENT-STUDIES	1281 GENE AUTRY TR, PMSP, 92262	756 - J6
PALM VIEW	1390 7TH ST, COAC, 92236	5471 - C6
PALOMA	42940 VIA RAMI, TEM, 92592	959 - D6
PARK AVENUE	445 S PARK AV, PER, 92570	807 - F3
PARK HILL	1157 E COMMONWEALTH AV, SJCT, 92583	811 - D4
PARKRIDGE FOR THE ARTS	750 CORONA AV, COR, 92879	743 - D3
PAUBA VALLEY	33125 REGINA DR, TEM, 92592	979 - H3
PEDLEY	5871 HUDSON ST, RivC, 92509	684 - D4
PENDLETON, PETER	84750 CL ROJO, COAC, 92236	5471 - B7
PERALTA	6450 PERALTA PL, RivC, 92509	685 - A5
PERRIS	500 S A ST, PER, 92570	807 - F3
PRADO VIEW	2800 RIDGELINE DR, COR, 92882	742 - F6
PROMENADE	550 HAMILTON DR, COR, 92879	744 - A2
RAIL RANCH	25030 VIA SANTEE, MURR, 92563	928 - E3
RAILROAD CANYON	1300 MILL ST, LKEL, 92530	866 - G6
RAINBOW RIDGE	15950 INDIAN AV, MORV, 92551	747 - F2
RAMONA	24801 BAY AV, MORV, 92553	717 - F5
RAMONA	41051 WHITTIER AV, RivC, 92544	841 - D1
RANCHO	31530 LA SERENA WY, TEM, 92591	959 - C3
RANCHO MIRAGE	42985 INDIAN TRAIL RD, RMIR, 92270	818 - A5
RANCH VIEW	3300 OLD ARCHIBALD RD, ONT, 91761	643 - A7
REAL, MANUEL	21705 MARTIN ST, RivC, 92570	776 - J2
RECHE CANYON	3101 E CANYON VISTA DR, CLTN, 92324	647 - A3
REDHAWK	32045 CM SAN JOSE, RivC, 92592	979 - E4
REET , A	755 N A ST, PER, 92570	807 - F2
RIDGE CREST	28500 JOHN F KENNEDY DR, MORV, 92555	718 - E7
RIDGEMOOR	25455 RIDGEMOOR RD, RivC, 92584	837 - J7
RIVERA, TOMAS	20440 RED POPPY LN, RIV, 92518	746 - G3
RIVERVIEW	4600 PEDLEY AV, NRCO, 92860	713 - G2
ROMOLAND	25890 ANTELOPE RD, RivC, 92585	838 - E1
ROOSEVELT, THEODORE	83200 DR CARREON BLVD, INDO, 92201	5470 - G2
RUSTIC LANE	6420 RUSTIC LN, RivC, 92509	685 - A1
SANDERS, NAN	1461 N A ST, PER, 92570	807 - F1
SAN JACINTO	136 N RAMONA BLVD, SJCT, 92583	811 - B1
SEAVIEW	87225 CHURCH ST, RivC, 92274	5531 - G5
SENECA	11615 WORDSWORTH RD, MORV, 92557	716 - H1
SERRANO	24100 DELPHINIUM AV, MORV, 92553	717 - E7
SHADOW HILLS	14300 SHADOW DR, FONT, 92337	644 - C3
SIERRA VISTA	3560 CORONA AV, NRCO, 92860	713 - F4
SKY COUNTY	5520 LUCRETIA AV, RivC, 91752	683 - H4
SPARKMAN, JOAN F	32225 PIO PICO RD, TEM, 92592	979 - E1
STALLINGS	1980 FULLERTON AV, COR, 92879	773 - F1
STONE AVENUE	5111 STONE AV, RivC, 92509	684 - F3
SUGARHILL	24455 OLD COUNTRY RD, MORV, 92557	687 - E6
SUMMIT	650 MAGNOLIA AV, BEAU, 92223	720 - J3
SUNNYMEAD	12875 HEACOCK ST, MORV, 92553	717 - E3
SUNNYMEADOWS	23200 EUCALYPTUS AV, MORV, 92553	717 - C3
SUNNY SANDS	69310 MCCALLUM WY, CTHC, 92234	787 - F1
SUNNYSLOPE	7050 38TH ST, RivC, 92509	644 - J7
TAFT, WILLIAM HOWARD	959 MISSION GROVE PKWY N, RIV, 92506	716 - D4
TEMECULA	41951 MORAGA RD, TEM, 92591	958 - J5
TEMECULA PREP	43750 MARGARITA RD, TEM, 92592	979 - D1
TERRACE	6601 RUTLAND AV, RIV, 92503	714 - F2
TERRACE VIEW	22731 GRAND TERRACE RD, GTER, 92313	646 - F3
TOVASHAL	23801 SAINT RAPHAEL DR, MURR, 92562	928 - B1
TROTH STREET	5565 TROTH ST, RivC, 91752	683 - J4
TRUMAN, HARRY S	78870 AVE 50, LQNT, 92253	849 - H5
TUSCANY HILLS	23 PONTE RUSSO, LKEL, 92532	867 - A2
TWINHILL	11000 CAMPBELL AV, RIV, 92505	714 - C4
TWO BUNCH PALMS	14250 WEST DR, DHSP, 92240	696 - H6
VAIL	29915 MIRA LOMA DR, TEM, 92592	959 - A6
VALLECITOS	5211 5TH ST, SDCo, 92028	998 - J5
VALLE VISTA	43900 MAYBERRY AV, RivC, 92544	842 - A1
VALLEY	12333 8TH ST, YCPA, 92399	649 - F3
VALLEY VIEW	11750 GRAMERCY PL, RIV, 92505	714 - B6
VALLEY VIEW	21220 MAURICE ST, RivC, 92567	779 - C6
VALLEY VIEW	85270 VALLEY RD, COAC, 92236	5531 - C1
VAL VERDE	2656 INDIAN AV, PER, 92571	777 - F5
VAN BUREN	9501 JURUPA RD, RivC, 92509	684 - C2
VAN BUREN, MARTIN	47733 VAN BUREN ST, INDO, 92201	5470 - J3
VICENTIA	2005 S VICENTIA AV, COR, 92882	743 - C7
VICTORIA	2910 ARLINGTON AV, RIV, 92506	715 - H2
VICTORIANO	25650 LOS CABOS DR, MORV, 92551	747 - H2
VINTAGE HILLS	42240 CM ROMO, TEM, 92592	959 - E5
VISTA DEL MONTE	2744 N VIA MIRALESTE, PMSP, 92262	756 - E4
WASHINGTON	1220 PARKRIDGE AV, COR, 92880	743 - C1
WASHINGTON	2760 JANE ST, RIV, 92506	715 - G4
WASHINGTON, GEORGE	45768 PORTOLA AV, PDST, 92260	848 - G2
WELLWOOD	715 WELLWOOD AV, BEAU, 92223	720 - H2
WENZLOFF, EDWARD L	11625 WEST DR, DHSP, 92240	696 - H3
WEST RIVERSIDE	3972 RIVERVIEW DR, RivC, 92509	685 - C2
WESTSIDE	82225 AIRPORT BLVD, RivC, 92274	5530 - F5
WHITE, MARGARET	610 S BROADWAY, BLY, 92225	5551 - E1
WHITTIER	400 W WHITTIER AV, HEMT, 92543	841 - A1
WILDOMAR	21575 PALOMAR ST, RivC, 92595	897 - C7
WILDWOOD	35972 SUSAN ST, YCPA, 92399	650 - C6
WILSON, WOODROW	750 S 8TH ST, CLTN, 92324	646 - D1
WINCHESTER	28751 WINCHESTER RD, RivC, 92596	839 - F6
WITHROW	30100 AUDELO ST, RivC, 92530	865 - F3
WOODCREST	16940 KRAMERIA AV, RivC, 92504	745 - J4
WOODROW WILSON	1750 SPYGLASS DR, COR, 92883	773 - G7
YUCAIPA	12375 CALIFORNIA ST, YCPA, 92399	650 - A3
ZIMMERMAN, WALTER	11050 LINDEN ST, SBdC, 92316	645 - D1

SCHOOLS - PUBLIC HIGH

FEATURE NAME	Address City, ZIP Code	PAGE-GRID
ALESSANDRO	26866 SAN JACINTO ST, RivC, 92544	841 - B2
ALVORD	3606 PIERCE ST, RIV, 92503	744 - D3
AMISTAD	44801 GOLF CENTER PKWY, INDO, 92201	5410 - H7
ARLINGTON	2951 JACKSON ST, RIV, 92503	715 - B6
BANNING	100 W WESTWARD AV, BAN, 92220	722 - B4
BAYSIDE COMM	13911 PERRIS BLVD, MORV, 92553	717 - G5
BEAUMONT	1591 CHERRY AV, BEAU, 92223	691 - A6
BLOOMINGTON	10750 LAUREL AV, SBdC, 92316	645 - B1
BUENA VISTA	300 S BUENA VISTA AV, COR, 92882	743 - B5
CA SCHOOL FOR THE DEAF	3044 HORACE ST, RIV, 92506	715 - G2
CANYON SPRINGS	23100 COUGAR CANYON DR, MORV, 92557	687 - C6
CATHEDRAL CITY	69250 DINAH SHORE DR, CTHC, 92234	787 - F4
CENTENNIAL	1820 RIMPAU AV, COR, 92881	743 - F7
CHAPARRAL	27215 NICOLAS RD, TEM, 92591	958 - J1
COACHELLA VALLEY	83800 AIRPORT BLVD, COAC, 92274	5530 - J4
CORONA	1150 W 10TH ST, COR, 92882	743 - A6
CREEKSIDE	24150 HAYES AV, MURR, 92562	927 - H6
DESERT HOT SPRINGS	PIERSON BLVD & CHOLLA DR, DHSP, 92240	696 - G3
DISTRICT COMM DAY	515 E 7TH ST, PER, 92570	807 - H4
EAGLE MOUNTAIN	KAISER RD & EAGLE MOUNTAIN RD, RivC	5240 - B7
ELSINORE	21800 CANYON DR, RivC, 92595	897 - B4
GREEN VALLEY	35912 AVE H, YCPA, 92399	650 - C6
HAMILTON (SEE PAGE 904)	57550 MITCHELL RD, RivC, 92539	935 - B2
HEMET	41701 STETSON AV, RivC, 92544	841 - E3
HORIZON	13031 ORANGE ST, RivC, 92880	713 - C1
INDIO	81750 AVE 46, INDO, 92201	5470 - D2
JURUPA VALLEY	10551 BELLEGRAVE AV, RivC, 91752	683 - J2
KAISER	11155 ALMOND AV, FONT, 92337	644 - C2
KING, MARTIN LUTHER	9301 WOOD RD, RIV, 92508	746 - C3
LA QUINTA	79255 WESTWARD HO DR, LQNT, 92253	849 - J2
LA SIERRA	4145 LA SIERRA AV, RIV, 92505	714 - E7
LINCOLN, ABRAHAM	4341 VICTORIA AV, RIV, 92507	685 - J5
MARCH MOUNTAIN	24551 DRACAEA AV, MORV, 92553	717 - F4
MORENO VALLEY	23300 COTTONWOOD AV, MORV, 92553	717 - C4
MOUNTAIN VIEW	699 YOUNG ST, SJCT, 92582	780 - J7
MT SAN JACINTO CONTINUATION	30800 LANDAU BLVD, CTHC, 92234	787 - D1
MURRIETA VALLEY	24105 WASHINGTON AV, MURR, 92562	927 - H5
NORCO	2065 TEMESCAL AV, NRCO, 92860	713 - F7
NORTE VISTA	6585 CREST AV, RIV, 92503	714 - E2
NORTH, JOHN W	1550 3RD ST, RIV, 92507	686 - B4
NUEVA VISTA	6836 34TH ST, RivC, 92509	645 - A7
ORTEGA	265 SAN JACINTO RIVER RD, LKEL, 92530	866 - H6
PALM DESERT	43570 PHYLLIS JACKSON LN, PDST, 92260	818 - H7
PALM SPRINGS	2401 E BARISTO RD, PMSP, 92262	786 - G2
PALM SPRINGS INDEPENDENT-STUDIES	1281 GENE AUTRY TR, PMSP, 92262	756 - J6
PALOMA VALLEY	31375 BRADLEY RD, RivC, 92584	868 - C5
PALO VERDE	667 N LOVEKIN BLVD, BLY, 92225	5491 - D5
PERRIS	175 E NUEVO RD, PER, 92571	807 - H1
PERRIS LAKE	418 W ELLIS AV, PER, 92570	807 - G4
POLYTECHNIC	5450 VICTORIA AV, RIV, 92506	715 - H1
RAINCROSS	6401 LINCOLN AV, RIV, 92506	715 - G3
RAMONA	7675 MAGNOLIA AV, RIV, 92504	715 - C3
RANCHO VERDE	17750 LASSELLE ST, MORV, 92555	747 - J6
RUBIDOUX	4250 OPAL ST, RivC, 92509	685 - B2
SAN JACINTO	500 IDYLLWILD DR, SJCT, 92583	781 - A7
SANTIAGO	1395 E FOOTHILL PKWY, COR, 92881	773 - F4
SEAVIEW PUB	87225 CHURCH ST, RivC, 92274	5531 - G5
SHERMAN INDIAN	9010 MAGNOLIA AV, RIV, 92503	715 - A5
TEMECULA VALLEY	31555 RANCHO VISTA RD, TEM, 92592	959 - C6
TEMECULA VALLEY INDEPENDENT	31340 RANCHO VISTA RD, TEM, 92592	959 - C6
TEMESCAL CANYON	28755 EL TORO RD, RivC, 92532	836 - B7
TWIN PALMS	190 N 5TH ST, BLY, 92225	5491 - F6
VALLEY VIEW	13135 NASON ST, MORV, 92555	718 - B3
VAL VERDE	2935 INDIAN AV, PER, 92571	777 - F4
WEST VALLEY	3401 W HARRISON AV, HEMT, 92545	840 - F4
YUCAIPA	33000 YUCAIPA BLVD, YCPA, 92399	649 - D3

SCHOOLS - PUBLIC INTERMEDIATE

FEATURE NAME	Address City, ZIP Code	PAGE-GRID
ARIZONA	11045 ARIZONA AV, RIV, 92503	744 - F3
AUBURNDALE	1255 RIVER RD, COR, 92880	743 - C1
CITRUS HILL	3211 S MAIN ST, COR, 92881	773 - D3
CORONA FUNDAMENTAL	1230 S MAIN ST, COR, 92882	743 - D6
LOMA VISTA	11050 ARLINGTON AV, RIV, 92505	714 - B3
NORCO	2711 TEMESCAL AV, NRCO, 92860	713 - F6
RANEY, LETHA	1010 W CITRON ST, COR, 92882	743 - B7
WELLS	10000 WELLS AV, RIV, 92503	714 - F4

SCHOOLS - PUBLIC JUNIOR HIGH

FEATURE NAME	Address City, ZIP Code	PAGE-GRID
MOUNTAIN VIEW	1575 CHERRY AV, BEAU, 92223	691 - A7
YUCAIPA	12358 6TH ST, YCPA, 92399	649 - G4

SCHOOLS - PUBLIC MIDDLE

FEATURE NAME	Address City, ZIP Code	PAGE-GRID
ACACIA	1200 E ACACIA AV, HEMT, 92543	811 - B7
ALESSANDRO	23301 DRACAEA AV, MORV, 92553	717 - C4
BADGER SPRINGS	24750 DELPHINIUM AV, MORV, 92553	717 - F7
BLYTHE	825 N LOVEKIN BLVD, BLY, 92225	5491 - D5
BROWN, DAVID A	21861 GRAND AV, RivC, 92595	927 - C1

SCHOOLS - PUBLIC MIDDLE

FEATURE NAME / Address City, ZIP Code	PAGE-GRID
CAHUILLA DESERT ACADEMY 82489 AVE 52, RivC, 92201	5470 - F7
CENTRAL 4795 MAGNOLIA AV, RIV, 92506	685 - F5
CHEMAWA 8830 MAGNOLIA AV, RIV, 92503	715 - A5
COFFMAN, NELLIE N 34603 PLUMLEY RD, CTHC, 92234	787 - G5
COOMBS, SUSAN B 1151 W WILSON ST, BAN, 92220	722 - A2
CREE, RAYMOND 1011 E VISTA CHINO, PMSP, 92262	756 - E6
DARTMOUTH 41535 MAYBERRY AV, RivC, 92544	841 - E1
DAY, JAMES GEN KEARNY & CM CAMPOS VERDE, TEM, 92591	958 - J3
DESERT SPRINGS 66755 TWO BUNCH PALMS TR, DHSP, 92240	697 - A6
EARHART, AMELIA 20202 APTOS ST, RIV, 92518	746 - F2
ELSINORE 1203 W GRAHAM AV, LKEL, 92530	866 - D5
GAGE, MATTHEW 6400 LINCOLN AV, RIV, 92506	715 - G3
HARRIS, RUTH 11150 ALDER AV, SBdC, 92316	645 - B1
INDIO 81195 MILES AV, INDO, 92201	5470 - C1
JEFFERSON, THOMAS 83089 HWY 111, INDO, 92201	5470 - G1
JURUPA 8700 GALENA ST, RivC, 92509	684 - E1
LANDMARK 15261 LEGENDARY DR, MORV, 92555	748 - C1
LA QUINTA 78900 AVE 50, LQNT, 92253	849 - H6
MARGARITA 30600 MARGARITA RD, TEM, 92591	959 - B4
MENIFEE VALLEY 26255 GARBANI RD, RivC, 92584	868 - B6
MIRA LOMA 5051 STEVE ST, RivC, 92509	684 - B2
MISSION 5961 MUSTANG LN, RivC, 92509	685 - C1
MONTE VISTA 181 N RAMONA BLVD, SJCT, 92583	811 - B1
MOUNTAIN SHADOWS 30401 RESERVOIR AV, RivC, 92567	778 - J3
MOUNTAIN VIEW 13130 MORRISON ST, MORV, 92555	718 - A4
NICOLET 101 E NICOLET ST, BAN, 92220	722 - B2
NORTH MOUNTAIN 1202 E 7TH ST, SJCT, 92583	811 - D2
PALM 11900 SLAWSON AV, MORV, 92557	717 - H1
PALM DESERT 74200 RUTLEDGE WY, PDST, 92260	818 - G6
PINACATE 1990 S A ST, PER, 92570	807 - F5
RIVERA, TOMAS 21675 MARTIN ST, RivC, 92570	776 - J2
SANTA FE 831 E DEVONSHIRE AV, HEMT, 92543	811 - B6
SHIVELA 24515 LINCOLN AV, MURR, 92562	928 - B4
SIERRA 4950 CENTRAL AV, RIV, 92504	715 - C1
SOUTHRIDGE 14500 LIVE OAK AV, FONT, 92337	644 - C3
SUNNYMEAD 23996 EUCALYPTUS AV, MORV, 92553	717 - E3
TEMECULA 42075 MEADOWS PKWY, TEM, 92592	959 - F6
TERRACE HILLS 22579 DE BERRY ST, GTER, 92313	646 - F4
TERRA COTTA 29291 LAKE ST, LKEL, 92530	865 - G2
THOMPSON 42400 NIGHTHAWK WY, MURR, 92562	927 - H5
UNIVERSITY HEIGHTS 1155 MASSACHUSETTS AV, RIV, 92507	686 - C3
VAIL RANCH 33340 CAMINO PIEDRA ROJO, TEM, 92592	979 - H2
VISTA HEIGHTS 23049 OLD LAKE DR, MORV, 92557	687 - C6
VISTA VERDE 25777 KRAMERIA ST, MORV, 92551	747 - J3
WILSON, WOODROW 83501 DILLON AV, INDO, 92201	5410 - H7
WORKMAN, JAMES 69300 30TH AV, CTHC, 92234	757 - F7
YOKLEY, GRACE 2947 S TURNER AV, ONT, 91761	643 - A6

SHOPPING - COMMUNITY

FEATURE NAME / Address City, ZIP Code	PAGE-GRID
ALBERTSONS PAYLESS CTR 7TH ST & HOBSON WY, BLY, 92225	5491 - F7
ALESSANDRO PLAZA 23750 ALESSANDRO RD, MORV, 92553	717 - E5
AMADO CTR 333 N PALM CANYON DR, PMSP, 92262	786 - D1
ARLINGTON PLAZA VAN BUREN BLVD & ARLINGTON AV, RIV, 92503	714 - G2
ARLINGTON SQUARE ARLINGTON AV & MADISON ST, RIV, 92504	715 - C2
BEAR VALLEY SHOPPING CTR ALESSANDRO BLVD & PERRIS BLVD, MORV, 92553	717 - G5
BROCKTON ARCADE BROCKTON AV & NELSON ST, RIV, 92506	715 - E1
BROOKSIDE PLAZA ALABAMA ST & BARTON RD, RDL, 92373	647 - H1
BUTTERFIELD STAGE SQUARE PARKRIDGE AV & N MAIN ST, COR, 92880	743 - D3
BUTTERFIELD VALLEY VILLAGE SUNNYMEAD BLVD & PERRIS BLVD, MORV, 92553	717 - G3
CALIMESA PLAZA COUNTY LINE RD & CALIMESA BL, CALI, 92320	649 - G7
CAL OAKS PLAZA CALIFORNIA OAKS RD, MURR, 92562	928 - B5
CANYON CREST TOWNE CTR CENTRAL AV & CANYON CREST DR, RIV, 92507	686 - D7
CANYON PLAZA SOUTH 67555 CANYON DR, CTHC, 92234	787 - C7
CANYON SPRINGS PLAZA 12125 DAY ST, MORV, 92557	717 - A2
CATHEDRAL CITY MARKETPLACE DATE PALM DR & DINAH SHORE DR, CTHC, 92234	787 - E5
CATHEDRAL CITY SHOPPING PLAZA E PALM CANYON DR & MELROSE DR, CTHC, 92234	787 - E7
CATHEDRAL PLAZA DATE PALM DR & E PALM CANYON, CTHC, 92234	817 - F1
CATHEDRAL VILLAGE DATE PALM DR & RAMON RD, CTHC, 92234	787 - F3
CENTRE POINTE AT COLTON E SANTO ANTONIO DR & S MT VERN, CLTN, 92324	646 - F1
COACHELLA SHOPPING CTR HWY 86 & AVE 50, COAC, 92236	5471 - B5
CORONA HILLS MARKETPLACE MCKINLEY ST & PROMENADE AV, COR, 92879	743 - J3
CORONA HILLS PLAZA RIVERSIDE FRWY & MCKINLEY ST, COR, 92879	743 - J4
CORONA MAIN STREET PLAZA 380 N MAIN ST, COR, 92880	743 - D4
CORONA PLAZA E 6TH ST & S MAIN ST, COR, 92879	743 - D5
CORONA TOWNE CTR S LINCOLN AV & 91 FRWY, COR, 92882	743 - B5
CORONA VILLAGE ONTARIO AV & MAGNOLIA AV, COR, 92879	773 - D1
COURTYARD, THE E WASHINGTON ST & I-215, CLTN, 92324	646 - F2
DE ANZA PLAZA LIMONITE AV & CAMINO REAL, RivC, 92509	684 - G5
DESERT CROSSING FRED WARING DR & HWY 111, PDST, 92260	818 - C7
DESERT HILLS PREMIUM OUTLETS 48400 SEMINOLE DR, RivC, 92230	722 - J2
DESERT HOT SPRINGS TOWN CTR PALM DR & TWO BUNCH PALMS TRAI, DHSP, 92240	696 - J6
DIAMOND VALLEY CTR W STETSON AV & S STATE ST, HEMT, 92543	841 - A3
EL PASEO WALK HWY 111 & SAN PABLO AV, PDST, 92260	848 - F1
FARMERS CORNER S SAN JACINTO ST & MENLO AV, SJCT, 92583	811 - B5
FESTIVAL AT MORENO VALLEY, THE HEMLOCK AV & NITA DR, MORV, 92557	717 - E2
FIVE POINTS CTR PIERCE ST & LA SIERRA AV, RIV, 92505	714 - D6
FOOD FOR LESS CTR MAGNOLIA AV & MCKINLEY ST, COR, 92879	744 - A4
GARDENS ON EL PASEO EL PASEO AV & SAN PABLO AV, PDST, 92260	848 - F2
GATEWAY TOWN CTR HAMNER AV & MOUNTAIN AV, NRCO, 92860	743 - D2
GOLDEN MILE CTR RAMON RD & DATE PALM DR, CTHC, 92234	787 - E2
HARDMAN CTR 5188 ARLINGTON AV, RIV, 92504	715 - C2
HEMET PLAZA FLORIDA AV & S YALE ST, HEMT, 92544	811 - C7
HEMET VALLEY CTR W FLORIDA AV & SANDERSON AV, HEMT, 92545	810 - E7
INDIO PLAZA 82128 HWY 111, INDO, 92201	5470 - E1
JENSENS CTR EL PASEO & LARKSPUR LN, PDST, 92260	848 - F1
JURUPA GRAND CTR JURUPA AV & GRAND AV, RIV, 92504	685 - C7
JURUPA VALLEY SPECTRUM LIMONITE AV & EL PALOMINO DR, RivC, 92509	684 - G5
LAKE ELSINORE CITY CTR 31500 GRAPE ST, LKEL, 92532	866 - J6
LAKE ELSINORE OUTLET CTR 17600 COLLIER AV, LKEL, 92530	866 - B1
LAKE ELSINORE TOWN CTR MISSION TR & CAMPBELL ST, LKEL, 92530	866 - J7
LAKESHORE VILLAGE MARKETPLACE OLD LAKE DR & SUNNYMEAD RANCH, MORV, 92557	687 - C5
LANDAU PLAZA RAMON RD & LANDAU BLVD, CTHC, 92234	787 - D2
LA QUINTA PLAZA CTR 78401 HWY 111, LQNT, 92253	849 - G2
LA QUINTA VILLAGE CALLE TAMPICO & WASHINGTON ST, LQNT, 92253	849 - G6
LA SIERRA PLAZA LA SIERRA & MAGNOLIA AV, RIV, 92505	744 - E1
LINCOLN ARCADE CTR 1111 S STATE ST, HEMT, 92543	841 - A2
LINCOLN PLAZA 2975 VAN BUREN BLVD, RIV, 92503	715 - A7
LOEHMANNS PLAZA RACQUET CLUB RD & PALM CANYON, PMSP, 92262	756 - D5
LOMA LINDA PLAZA MOUNTAIN VIEW AV & BARTON RD, LMLN, 92354	647 - E1
MAGNOLIA TOWN CTR 6085 MAGNOLIA AV, RIV, 92506	685 - E7
MARSHALLS RIVERSIDE PROMENADE TYLER ST & MAGNOLIA AV, RIV, 92503	714 - G7
MENIFEE TOWN CTR NEWPORT RD & ESCONDIDO FRWY, RivC, 92584	868 - E2
MISSION GROVE PLAZA ALESSANDRO BL & TRAUTWEIN RD, RIV, 92508	716 - D6
MISSION TRAIL PLAZA RAILROAD CYN RD & MISSION TR, LKEL, 92530	866 - H6
MONTEREY SHORE PLAZA MONTEREY AV & DINAH SHORE DR, PDST, 92211	788 - D4
MORENO VALLEY CTR 12252 PERRIS BLVD, MORV, 92557	717 - G2
MORENO VALLEY PLAZA HEACOCK ST & SUNNYMEAD BLVD, MORV, 92553	717 - D3
MURRIETA SPRING PLAZA I-15 & MURRIETA HOT SPRINGS RD, MURR, 92562	928 - C6
MURRIETA TOWN CTR 40485 MURRIETA HOT SPRINGS RD, MURR, 92563	928 - E6
NEWPORT PLAZA NEWPORT RD & BRADLEY RD, RivC, 92586	868 - C2
NEXUS TOWN CTR LA SIERRA AV & RIVERSIDE FRWY, RIV, 92503	744 - E2
ONE ELEVEN LA QUINTA WASHINGTON ST & HWY 111, LQNT, 92253	849 - G2
ORANGECREST PLAZA TRAUTWEIN RD & VAN BUREN BLVD, RIV, 92508	746 - E3
PALM PLAZA CTR I-15 FRWY & WINCHESTER RD, TEM, 92591	958 - G4
PALM SPRINGS MARKETPLACE N SUNRISE WY & E VISTA CHINO, PMSP, 92262	756 - G6
PALMS TO PINES CTR EL PASEO & LARKSPUR LN, PDST, 92260	848 - F1
PALMS TO PINES WEST HWY 111 & EL PASEO, PDST, 92260	848 - D1
PALOMAR VILLAGE RANCHO CALIFORNIA & MARGARITA, TEM, 92591	959 - B5
PALO VERDE PLAZA HOBSON WY & 7TH ST, BLY, 92225	5491 - F6
PEDLEY SQUARE LIMONITE AV & VAN BUREN BLVD, RivC, 92509	684 - E5
PERRIS PLAZA N PERRIS BLVD & NUEVO RD, PER, 92571	777 - G7
PERRIS TOWNE CTR N PERRIS BLVD & NUEVO RD, PER, 92571	807 - G1
PERRIS VALLEY SPECTRUM N PERRIS BLVD & W ORANGE AV, PER, 92571	777 - G5
PIGEON PASS PLAZA 11875 PIGEON PASS RD, MORV, 92557	717 - C1
PLAZA AT SUNRISE 555 S SUNRISE WY, PMSP, 92262	786 - F2
PLAZA DE MONTEREY COUNTRY CLUB DR & MONTEREY AV, PDST, 92260	818 - E3
POINT HAPPY WASHINGTON ST & HWY 111, LQNT, 92253	849 - G1
RAMONA PLAZA FLORIDA AV & N SAN JACINTO ST, HEMT, 92544	811 - B7
RANCHO CALIFORNIA TOWN CTR RANCHO CALIFORNIA RD & YNEZ RD, TEM, 92591	958 - J6
RANCHO LAS PALMAS BOB HOPE DR & HWY 111, RMIR, 92270	818 - C6
RIMROCK SHOPPING CTR E PALM CYN DR & GENE AUTRY TR, PMSP, 92264	787 - A6
SIERRA DEL ORO TOWNE CTR 2621 GREEN RIVER RD, COR, 92882	742 - F6
SIERRA VISTA PLAZA 25030 HANCOCK AV, MURR, 92562	928 - D4
SMOKE TREE VILLAGE CTR 1775 E PALM CANYON DR, PMSP, 92264	786 - G5
SOUTHRIDGE PLAZA CHERRY AV & LIVE OAK AV, FONT, 92337	644 - D3
STANFORD CTR FLORIDA AV & STANFORD ST, RivC, 92544	811 - F7
STATER PLAZA E STETSON AV & S STATE ST, HEMT, 92543	841 - A2
SUN CITY CTR 26870 CHERRY HILLS BLVD, RivC, 92586	838 - C6
SUN LAKES VILLAGE HIGHLAND SPRINGS AV & I-10, BAN, 92220	721 - C3
SUNNYMEAD PLAZA SUNNYMEAD BLVD & PERRIS BLVD, MORV, 92553	717 - F3
SUNNYMEAD TOWNE CENTRE ALESSANDRO BLVD & PERRIS BLVD, MORV, 92553	717 - G6
SUNNYMEAD VILLAGE 24685 ALESSANDRO BLVD, MORV, 92553	717 - F6
SUNRISE MARKET PLACE N SUNRISE WY & E VISTA CHINO, PMSP, 92262	756 - F6
SUNRISE SQUARE N SUNRISE WY & E VISTA CHINO, PMSP, 92262	756 - F6
TEMESCAL VILLAGE PLAZA 1181 MAGNOLIA AV, COR, 92879	743 - G7
TOWER PLAZA YNEZ RD & RANCHO CALIFORNIA RD, TEM, 92591	958 - H6
TOWN & COUNTRY CTR HWY 111 & DR CARREON BLVD, INDO, 92201	5470 - D2
TOWN CTR PLAZA FRED WARING DR & TOWN CTR WY, PDST, 92260	818 - D7
TOWNGATE COMM SHOPPING CTR MORENO VLY FRWY & FREDERICK ST, MORV, 92553	717 - B3
TOWN SQUARE UNIVERSITY AV & CHICAGO AV, RIV, 92507	686 - A5
TYLER VILLAGE 10200 INDIANA AV, RIV, 92503	744 - H1
UNIVERSITY CTR BLAINE ST & WATKINS DR, RIV, 92507	686 - D4
UNIVERSITY TOWN CTR UNIVERSITY AV & IOWA AV, RIV, 92507	686 - C5
VAIL RANCH SHOPPING CTR HWY 79 & REDHAWK PKWY, TEM, 92592	979 - E2
VAN BUREN PLAZA VAN BUREN BLVD & PHILBIN AV, RIV, 92503	714 - G3
VILLAGE AT INDIAN WELLS, THE HWY 111 & COOK ST, INDW, 92210	848 - H1
VILLAGE SQUARE JACKSON ST & AVENUE 44, INDO, 92201	5410 - G6
VILLAGE WEST SHOPPING CTR W FLORIDA AV & SANDERSON AV, HEMT, 92545	810 - F7
VINEYARD, THE S PALM CANYON DR & BARISTO RD, PMSP, 92262	786 - D2
WARING PLAZA HWY 111 & PARK VIEW DR, PDST, 92260	818 - C7
WESTGATE PLAZA LA SIERRA & MAGNOLIA AV, RIV, 92505	744 - E1
WIEST PLAZA TYLER ST & MAGNOLIA AV, RIV, 92503	714 - F7
WINCHESTER SQUARE JEFFERSON AV & OVERLAND DR, TEM, 92590	958 - G4
WOODCREST PLAZA WASHINGTON ST & VAN BUREN BLVD, RivC, 92504	745 - J4
YUCAIPA SQUARE YUCAIPA BL & 5TH ST, YCPA, 92399	649 - H3

SHOPPING - REGIONAL

FEATURE NAME / Address City, ZIP Code	PAGE-GRID
GALLERIA AT TYLER 3570 TYLER ST, RIV, 92503	714 - G7
HEMET VALLEY MALL 2200 W FLORIDA AV, HEMT, 92545	810 - G7
INDIO FASHION MALL 82227 HWY 111, INDO, 92201	5470 - E1
MORENO VALLEY MALL AT TOWNGATE 22500 TOWN CIR, MORV, 92553	717 - A2
PALM SPRINGS MALL 191 S FARRELL DR, PMSP, 92262	786 - G2
PALM SPRINGS PROMENADE 123 N PALM CANYON DR, PMSP, 92262	786 - D2
PROMENADE AT TEMECULA, THE WINCHESTER RD & YNEZ RD, TEM, 92591	958 - H4
RIVERSIDE PLAZA 3621 RIVERSIDE PZ, RIV, 92506	715 - F1
WESTFIELD SHOPPINGTOWN PALM-DESERT 72840 HWY 111, PDST, 92260	848 - D1

TRANSPORTATION

FEATURE NAME / Address City, ZIP Code	PAGE-GRID
AMTRAK PALM SPRINGS STA 6001 PALM SPRINGS STATION RD, PMSP	726 - D5
GREYHOUND BUS STA 311 N INDIAN CANYON DR, PMSP, 92262	786 - D1
GREYHOUND BUS STA 3911 UNIVERSITY AV, RIV, 92501	685 - G4
GREYHOUND BUS STA 412 E 4TH ST, PER, 92570	807 - H3
GREYHOUND BUS STA 45524 OASIS ST, INDO, 92201	5470 - G1
METROLINK EAST ONTARIO STA 3330 E FRANCIS ST, ONT, 91761	643 - B4
METROLINK PEDLEY STA 6001 PEDLEY RD, RivC, 92509	684 - E5
METROLINK RIV-DOWNTOWN STA 4066 VINE ST, RIV, 92507	685 - H5
METROLINK RIV-LA SIERRA STA 10901 INDIANA AV, RIV, 92503	744 - F2
METROLINK WEST CORONA STA 155 S AUTO CENTER DR, COR, 92880	742 - G4

WINERIES

FEATURE NAME / Address City, ZIP Code	PAGE-GRID
BAILY VINEYARD 33833 RANCHO CALIFORNIA RD, RivC, 92592	959 - J3
CALLAWAY VINEYARD 32720 RANCHO CALIFORNIA RD, RivC, 92591	959 - F3
CILURZO VINEYARD 41220 CL CONTENTO, RivC, 92592	959 - J3
FILSINGER VINEYARDS 39050 DE PORTOLA RD, RivC, 92592	960 - F2
GALLEANO 4231 WINEVILLE RD, RivC, 91752	643 - G7
HART 41300 AVD BIONA, RivC, 92591	959 - F3
KEYWAYS VINEYARD 37338 DE PORTOLA RD, RivC, 92592	960 - E3
MAURICE CARRIE 34225 RANCHO CALIFORNIA RD, RivC, 92592	959 - J3
MOUNT PALOMAR 33820 RANCHO CALIF RD, RivC, 92591	959 - H2
PICONI 33410 RANCHO CALIFORNIA RD, RivC, 92591	959 - H3
SAN ANTONIO 2802 S MILLIKEN AV, ONT, 91761	643 - D6
STUART CELLARS 33515 RANCHO CALIFORNIA RD, RivC, 92592	959 - H3
TEMECULA CREST 40620 CL CONTENTO, RivC, 92591	959 - J2
THORNTON 32575 RANCHO CALIFORNIA RD, RivC, 92592	959 - F4
VAN ROEKEL VINEYARDS 34567 RANCHO CALIFORNIA RD, RivC, 92592	959 - J2
WILSON CREEK VINEYARD 35960 RANCHO CALIFORNIA RD, RivC, 92591	930 - B7

RAND McNALLY

Thank you for purchasing The Thomas Guide®!
Our goal is to provide you with the information you need.

Please complete the information below so we will be able to serve you better in the future. We value your comments and suggestions for improvements, and feedback on corrections. This information can also be e-mailed to: **consumeraffairs@randmcnally.com**. *(This information is for internal use ONLY and will not be distributed or sold to any external third party.)*

The Thomas Guide® Title:

ISBN# **Edition Year:**

2ND FOLD LINE

Today's Date: ______

1. Your Name: ______ Title: ______
2. Address ☐ Business ☐ Personal: ______
3. City/State/Zip: ______
4. Phone Number: ______ E-mail address: ______
5. Age Group: ☐ 18 – 24 ☐ 25-31 ☐ 32-40 ☐ 41- 50 ☐ 51+
6. Company name: ______
7. Type of business: ______
8. Where did you purchase this Thomas Guide? (store name & location) ______
9. How often do you purchase an updated Thomas Guide? ☐ Annually ☐ Every 2 Years ☐ Other ______
10. How often do you use it? ☐ Daily ☐ Weekly ☐ Monthly ☐ Other ______
11. What do you use your Thomas Guide for?
    ☐ Find Address ☐ Find Unincorporated Areas ☐ Navigation ☐ Identifying Routes ☐ Other ______
12. Do you use it for: ☐ Business ☐ Personal ☐ Both

1st FOLD LINE

13. If you have used the Digital Edition software:
    What features do you use? ______
    How often do you use it? ☐ Daily ☐ Weekly ☐ Monthly ☐ Other ______
14. What information would you add/correct in this Thomas Guide to better meet your needs?
    Map Page # ______ Grid # ______ Index Page # ______
    ☐ Street Name Missing ☐ Street Name Misspelled ☐ Street Information Incorrect
    ☐ Incorrect Location for Point of Interest ☐ Index Error ☐ Other
15. Please provide any additional comments and suggestions you have: ______
16. Would you like to receive information about updated editions and special offers from Rand McNally? ☐ Yes ☐ No

CUT ALONG DOTTED LINE

CUT ALONG DOTTED LINE

TG-LTri